THE INTERPRETER'S DICTIONARY OF THE BIBLE

An Illustrated Encyclopedia

IDENTIFYING AND EXPLAINING ALL PROPER NAMES AND
SIGNIFICANT TERMS AND SUBJECTS IN
THE HOLY SCRIPTURES, INCLUDING THE APOCRYPHA
With Attention to Archaeological Discoveries and
Researches into the Life and Faith of Ancient Times

מלאה הארץ דעה את־יהוה

The earth shall be full of the knowledge of the Lord—ISAIAH 11:9c

NASHVILLE   *Abingdon Press*   NEW YORK

ISBN 0-687-19273-0
Library of Congress Catalog Card Number: 62-9387

I
MANUFACTURED BY THE PARTHENON PRESS, AT
NASHVILLE, TENNESSEE, UNITED STATES OF AMERICA

ABBREVIATIONS

א — Codex Sinaiticus
A — Codex Alexandrinus
AA — *Alttestamentliche Abhandlungen*
AAA — *Annals of Archaeology and Anthropology*
AASOR — *Annual of the American Schools of Oriental Research*
Ab. — Aboth
Add. Esth. — Additions to Esther
AFO — *Archiv für Orientforschung*
AJA — *American Journal of Archaeology*
AJSL — *American Journal of Semitic Languages and Literatures*
AJT — *American Journal of Theology*
Akkad. — Akkadian
Amer. Trans. — *The Complete Bible, an American Translation* (Smith and Goodspeed)
ANEP — J. B. Pritchard, ed., *The Ancient Near East in Pictures*
ANET — J. B. Pritchard, ed., *Ancient Near Eastern Texts*
AO — *Der alte Orient*
APAW — *Abhandlungen der Preussichen Akademie der Wissenschaften*
Apoc. — Apocrypha
Apocal. Bar. — Apocalypse of Baruch
Aq. — Aquila
'Ar. — 'Aruk
ARAB — D. D. Luckenbill, *Ancient Records of Assyria and Babylonia*
Arab. — Arabic
'Arak. — 'Arakin
Aram. — Aramaic
ARE — J. H. Breasted, *Ancient Records of Egypt*
ARN — Aboth d'Rabbi Nathan
art. — article
ARW — *Archiv für Religionswissenschaft*
ASAE — *Annales du service des antiquités de l'Égypte*
Asmp. Moses — Assumption of Moses
ASV — American Standard Version (1901)

AT — *Altes* or *Ancien Testament*
ATR — *Anglican Theological Review*
'A.Z. — 'Abodah Zarah

B — Codex Vaticanus
BA — *Biblical Archaeologist*
Bar. — Baruch
Barn. — The Epistle of Barnabas
BASOR — *Bulletin of the American Schools of Oriental Research*
B.B. — Baba Bathra
Bek. — Bekereth
Bel — Bel and the Dragon
Ber. — Berakoth
Bez. — Bezah
B.K. — Baba Ḳamma
bk. — book
B.M. — Baba Meziʻa
Bibl. — *Biblica*
Bibl. Stud. — *Biblische Studien*
Bik. — Bikkurim
BS — *Bibliotheca Sacra*
BW — *Biblical World*
BWANT — *Beiträge zur Wissenschaft vom Alten und Neuen Testament*
BWAT — *Beiträge zur Wissenschaft vom Alten Testament*
BZ — *Biblische Zeitschrift*
BZAW — *Beihefte zur Zeitschrift für die alttestamentliche Wissenschaft*
BZF — *Biblische Zeitfragen*

C — Codex Ephraemi Syri
ca. — *circa* (about)
CDC — Cairo Genizah Document of the Damascus Covenanters (The Zadokite Documents)
cf. — *confer* (compare)
ch. — chapter
Chr. — Chronicles
Clem. — Clement (I and II)
Clem. Misc. — Clement of Alexandria *Miscellanies*
Col. — Colossians
col. — column
Cor. — Corinthians
CSEL — *Corpus Scriptorum Ecclesiasticorum Latinorum*

D — Codex Bezae; Codex Claromontanus; Deuteronomist source
Dan. — Daniel
Dem. — Demai
Deut. — Deuteronomy
Did. — The Didache
div. — division
DSS — Dead Sea Scrolls

E — east; Elohist source
EB — Early Bronze Age
EB — *Études bibliques*
Eccl. — Ecclesiastes
Ecclus. — Ecclesiasticus
ed. — edited, edition, editor
e.g. — *exempli gratia* (for example)
Egyp. — Egyptian
EH — *Exegetisches Handbuch zum Alten Testament*
EI — Early Iron Age
Eph. — Ephesians
'Er. — 'Erubin
ERV — English Revised Version (1881-85)
Esd. — Esdras
esp. — especially
Esth. — Esther
ET — *Expository Times*
Ethio. — Ethiopian
Euseb. Hist. — Eusebius *History of the Christian Church*
Euseb. Onom. — Eusebius *Onomasticon*
Exod. — Exodus
Exp. — *The Expositor*
Ezek. — Ezekiel

fem. — feminine
fig. — figure (illustration)
FRLANT — *Forschungen zur Religion und Literatur des Alten und Neuen Testaments*

G — Greek
Gal. — Galatians
Gen. — Genesis
Giṭ. — Giṭṭin
Gordon — C. H. Gordon, *Ugaritic Manual*
Gr. — Greek
GSAI — *Giornale della società asiatica italiana*

v

GTT — *Gereformeerd theologisch Tijdschrift*

H — Hebrew; Holiness Code
Hab. — Habakkuk
Hag. — Haggai
Ḥag. — Ḥagigah
Ḥal. — Ḥallah
HAT — *Handbuch zum Alten Testament*
HDB — James Hastings, ed., *A Dictionary of the Bible*
Heb. — Hebrew; the Letter to the Hebrews
HERE — James Hastings, ed., *Encyclopedia of Religion and Ethics*
Herm. Mand. — The Shepherd of Hermas, Mandates
Herm. Sim. — The Shepherd of Hermas, Similitudes
Herm. Vis. — The Shepherd of Hermas, Visions
Hitt. — Hittite
HKAT — *Handkommentar zum Alten Testament*
Hor. — Horayoth
Hos. — Hosea
HS — *Die heilige Schrift des Alten Testaments*
HTR — *Harvard Theological Review*
HUCA — *Hebrew Union College Annual*

ICC — International Critical Commentary
i.e. — *id est* (that is)
IEJ — *Israel Exploration Journal*
Ign. Eph. — The Epistle of Ignatius to the Ephesians
Ign. Magn. — The Epistle of Ignatius to the Magnesians
Ign. Phila. — The Epistle of Ignatius to the Philadelphians
Ign. Polyc. — The Epistle of Ignatius to Polycarp
Ign. Rom. — The Epistle of Ignatius to the Romans
Ign. Smyr. — The Epistle of Ignatius to the Smyrnaeans
Ign. Trall. — The Epistle of Ignatius to the Trallians
intro. — introduction
Iren. Her. — Irenaeus *Against Heresies*
Iron — Iron Age
Isa. — Isaiah

J — Yahwist source
JA — *Journal asiatique*
JAOS — *Journal of the American Oriental Society*
Jas. — James
JBL — *Journal of Biblical Literature and Exegesis*
JBR — *Journal of Bible and Religion*

JEA — *Journal of Egyptian Archaeology*
Jer. — Jeremiah
JJGL — *Jahrbuch für jüdische Geschichte und Literatur*
JNES — *Journal of Near Eastern Studies*
Jos. Antiq. — Josephus *The Antiquities of the Jews*
Jos. Apion — Josephus *Against Apion*
Jos. Life — Josephus *Life*
Jos. War — Josephus *The Jewish War*
Josh. — Joshua
JPOS — *Journal of the Palestine Oriental Society*
JQR — *Jewish Quarterly Review*
JR — *Journal of Religion*
JRAS — *Journal of the Royal Asiatic Society*
JSOR — *Journal of the Society of Oriental Research*
J.T. — Jerusalem Talmud
Jth. — Judith
JTS — *Journal of Theological Studies*
Jub. — Jubilees
Judg. — Judges
Just. Apol. — Justin Martyr *Apology*
Just. Dial. — Justin Martyr *Dialogue with Trypho*

KAT — *Kommentar zum Alten Testament*
Kel. — Kelim
Ker. — Kerithoth
Keth. — Kethuboth
KHC — *Kurzer Hand-Kommentar zum Alten Testament*
Ḳid. — Ḳiddushin
Ḳil. — Ḳil'ayim
KJV — King James Version
KUB — *Keilschrifturkunden aus Boghazköi*

L — Lukan source
Lam. — Lamentations
Lat. — Latin
LB — Late Bronze Age
Lev. — Leviticus
LXX — Septuagint

M — Matthean source
M. — Mishna
Ma'as. — Ma'asroth
Ma'as Sh. — Ma'aser Sheni
Macc. — Maccabees
Mak. — Makkoth
Maksh. — Makshirin
Mal. — Malachi
Mart. Polyc. — *The Martyrdom of Polycarp*
masc. — masculine
Matt. — Matthew
MB — Middle Bronze Age
Meg. — Megillah

Me'il. — Me'ilah
Mek. — Mekilta
Men. — Menaḥoth
mg. — margin
MGWJ — *Monatsschrift für Geschichte und Wissenschaft des Judentums*
Mic. — Micah
Miḳ. — Miḳwa'oth
M.Ḳ. — Mo'ed Ḳaṭan
MS, MSS — manuscript, manuscripts
MT — Masoretic Text
MVAG — *Mitteilungen der vorderasiatisch-aegyptischen Gesellschaft*

N — north
n. — note
Nah. — Nahum
Naz. — Nazir
NE — northeast
Ned. — Nedarim
Neg. — Nega'im
Neh. — Nehemiah
NF — Neue Folge
Nid. — Niddah
NKZ — *Neue kirchliche Zeitschrift*
NS — Nova series
NT — New Testament
NTS — *New Testament Studies*
NTSt — *Nieuwe theologische Studien*
NTT — *Nieuw theologisch Tijdschrift*
Num. — Numbers
NW — northwest

Obad. — Obadiah
Ohol. — Oholoth
OL — Old Latin
OLZ — *Orientalistische Literaturzeitung*
'Or. — 'Orlah
OT — Old Testament

P — Priestly source
p., pp. — page, pages
Par. — Parah
PEQ — *Palestine Exploration Quarterly (Palestine Exploration Quarterly Fund)*
Pers. — Persian
Pes. — Pesaḥim
Pesiḳ. dRK — Pesiḳta di Rab Kahana
Pesiḳ. R. — Pesiḳtha Rabbathi
Pet. — Peter
Phil. — Philippians
Philem. — Philemon
Phoen. — Phoenicia
Pir. R. El. — Pirke di Rabbi Eliezer
PJ — *Palästina Jahrbuch*
pl. — plate (herein, color illustration)
Pliny Nat. Hist. — Pliny *Natural History*

Polyc. Phil. — The Epistle of Polycarp to the Philippians

Prayer Man. — The Prayer of Manasseh

Prov. — Proverbs

Ps., Pss. — Psalm, Psalms

PSBA — Proceedings of the Society of Biblical Archaeology

Pseudep. — Pseudepigrapha

Pss. Sol. — Psalms of Solomon

pt. — part

PTR — Princeton Theological Review

Q — Quelle ("Sayings" source in the gospels)

1QH — Thanksgiving Hymns

1QIsᵃ — Isaiah Scroll (published by the American Schools of Oriental Research)

1QIsᵇ — Isaiah Scroll (published by E. L. Sukenik, Hebrew University, Jerusalem, Israel)

1QM — War Scroll

1QpHab — Habakkuk Commentary

1QS — Manual of Discipline

1QSa — Rule of the Congregation

RB — Revue biblique

REJ — Revue des études juives

Rev. — Revelation

rev. — revised, revision, reviser

R. H. — Rosh Hashanah

RHPR — Revue d'histoire et de philosophie religieuses

RHR — Revue de l'histoire des religions

Rom. — Romans

RR — Ricerche religiose

RS — Revue sémitique

RSR — Recherches de science religieuse

RSV — Revised Standard Version (1946-52)

RTP — Revue de théologie et de philosophie

S — south

Sam. — Samuel

Samar. — Samaritan recension

Sanh. — Sanhedrin

SE — southeast

sec. — section

Shab. — Shabbath

Sheb. — Shebi'ith

Shebu. — Shebu'oth

Shek. — Shekalim

SL — Series Latina

Song of S. — Song of Songs

Song Thr. Ch. — Song of the Three Children (or Young Men)

Soṭ. — Soṭah

SPAW — Sitzungsberichte der Preussischen Akademie der Wissenschaften

STZ — Schweizerische theologische Zeitschrift

Suk. — Sukkah

Sumer. — Sumerian

Sus. — Susanna

SW — southwest

SWP — Survey of Western Palestine

Symm. — Symmachus

Syr. — Syriac

Ta'an. — Ta'anith

Tac. Ann. — Tacitus Annals

Tac. Hist. — Tacitus Histories

Tam. — Tamid

Tanḥ. — Tanḥuma

Targ. — Targum

T.B. — Babylonian Talmud

TdbK. — Tanna debe Eliyahu

Tem. — Temurah

Ter. — Terumoth

Tert. Apol. — Tertullian Apology

Tert. Marcion — Tertullian Against Marcion

Tert. Presc. Her. — Tertullian Prescriptions Against the Heretics

Test. Asher — Testament of Asher

Test. Benj. — Testament of Benjamin

Test. Dan — Testament of Dan

Test. Gad — Testament of Gad

Test. Iss. — Testament of Issachar

Test. Joseph — Testament of Joseph

Test. Judah — Testament of Judah

Test. Levi — Testament of Levi

Test. Naph. — Testament of Naphtali

Test. Reuben — Testament of Reuben

Test. Simeon — Testament of Simeon

Test. Zeb. — Testament of Zebulun

Theod. — Theodotion

Theol. — Theology

Theol. Rundschau — Theologische Rundschau

Thess. — Thessalonians

Tim. — Timothy

Tit. — Titus

TLZ — Theologische Literaturzeitung

Tob. — Tobit

Toh. — Tohoroth

Tosaf. — Tosafoth

Tosef. — Tosefta

TQ — Theologische Quartalschrift

trans. — translated, translation, translator

Tristram NHB — H. B. Tristram, The Natural History of the Bible

TSBA — Transactions of the Society of Biblical Archaeology

TSK — Theologische Studien und Kritiken

TT — Theologisch Tijdschrift

TU — Texte und Untersuchungen zur Geschichte der altchristlichen Literatur

TWNT — Theologisches Wörterbuch zum Neuen Testament

Ṭ.Y. — Ṭebul Yom

Ugar. — Ugaritic

'Uḳ. — 'Uḳzin

vol. — volume

vs., vss. — verse, verses

VT — Vetus Testamentum

Vulg. — Vulgate

W — west

WC — Westminster Commentaries

Wisd. Sol. — Wisdom of Solomon

WZKM — Wiener Zeitschrift für die Kunde des Morgenlandes

Y — Yahweh

Yeb. — Yebamoth

Yom. — Yoma

ZA — Zeitschrift für Assyriologie und verwandte Gebiete

Zab. — Zabin

ZAW — Zeitschrift für die alttestamentliche Wissenschaft

ZDMG — Zeitschrift der deutschen morgenländischen Gesellschaft

ZDPV — Zeitschrift des deutschen Palästina-Vereins

Zeb. — Zebaḥim

Zech. — Zechariah

Zeph. — Zephaniah

ZNW — Zeitschrift für die neutestamentliche Wissenschaft und die Kunde der älteren Kirche

ZS — Zeitschrift für Semitistik

ZST — Zeitschrift für systematische Theologie

ZThK — Zeitschrift für Theologie und Kirche

RA rä. Alternately: RE rä. The Egyptian sun-god, whose chief cult center was Thebes. *See* EGYPT.

RAAMAH rā′ə mə [רעמה]. Alternately: RAAMA [לעמא] (I Chr. 1:9). A son of Cush, and the father of Sheba and Dedan, hence the name of an Arabian locality (Gen. 10:7; I Chr. 1:9). The traders of Sheba and Dedan are reported to have brought the best of spices, all sorts of precious stones, and gold to Tyre in exchange for the latter's wares (Ezek. 27:22). Since the LXX renders the word by "Regma" ('Ρεγμὰ), many have identified Raamah with a city of that name mentioned by Ptolemy and located on the Persian Gulf. A better identification is with the city of Raamah near Ma'in in SW Arabia, which is mentioned in a Minean inscription as being the scene of an attack on one of their caravans by raiders from Sheba and Haulan.   S. COHEN

RAAMIAH. Alternate form of REELAIAH.

RAAMSES. Alternate form of RAMESES (CITY).

***RABBAH** răb′ə [רבה, great *or* capital city] (Josh. 13:25; II Sam. 11:1; 12:27, 29; I Chr. 20:1; Jer. 49:3; Ezek. 25:5; Amos 1:4). Alternately: RABBAH OF THE AMMONITES ăm′ə nīts [רבת בני עמון, great *or* capital city of the sons of Ammon] (Deut. 3:11; II Sam. 12:26; 17:27; Jer. 49:2; Ezek. 21:20—H 21:25); KJV RABBAH (RABBATH) OF THE CHILDREN OF AMMON —əth, ăm′ən. The capital city of Ammon.

1. General situation.* The name, location, and nature of the site of modern Amman leave no doubt of its identity with the ancient capital of the Ammonite kingdom, Rabbah. Situated some twenty-three miles E of the Jordan River in the valley which forms the course of the upper Jabbok (Wadi ez-Zerqa, or modern Wadi Amman), Rabbah is the only city in Transjordan which biblical tradition clearly designates as Ammonite. The Iron Age settlement seems to have been divided into at least two parts: the "royal city" (II Sam. 12:26), probably composed of the principal fortress or royal citadel, and situated on top of the lofty triangular plateau (acropolis) that rises precipitously N of the Wadi

Amman; and the "city of waters" (vs. 27), apparently referring to some kind of fortification guarding a large source of water for the city in the valley of the Jabbok. Following the destruction of the Ammonite kingdom in the sixth century, Rabbah was not rebuilt until Hellenistic times, when the city was renamed Philadelphia (*see* § 3 *below*). This name prevailed throughout the Greek and Roman period, but disappeared after the Arab conquest of the land, when it reverted to a part of its ancient and now contemporary name, Amman. By far the vast majority of the beautiful and important ruins which are still visible at Amman stem from the Greek and Roman city.* The rude stone monuments (dolmens, cromlechs, and menhirs) that have been surveyed in the vicinity of Amman appear to come from the prehistoric period, and thus are not specifically Ammonite. Figs. RAB 1, 2.

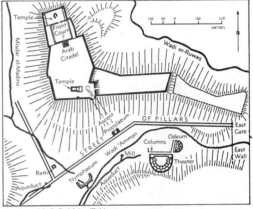

Courtesy of J. C. B. Mohr, Tübingen

1. Rabbah (Philadelphia, modern Amman)

2. Modern Amman (Rabbath-Ammon, Philadelphia) viewed from Roman theater

2. Archaeological history and remains. The earliest Ammonite occupation of Rabbah does not antedate the Late Bronze Age (*ca.* 1550-1200). Archaeological excavation at Amman by the Italians (1927-29) uncovered the remains of an ancient surrounding wall resting on natural rock on the lowest terrace of the E part of the acropolis. Unfortunately, few aids for dating were discovered, so that the fifteenth-century date assigned to the wall cannot be proved. However, more recent excavation near the

Amman airport has disclosed a Late Bronze Age shrine, constructed with large blocks of unhewn stone, and revealing remarkable quantities of weapons, seals, scarabs, jewelry, and pottery. Among the latter have been found for the first time in Transjordan the remains of over a hundred Mycenean vases of various forms, which clearly fix the Late Bronze date. The curious isolation of the small shrine in the open country 2½ miles E of Amman would seem to suggest its use by seminomadic peoples and caravan traders of the early Ammonite kingdom. The ancient commercial highway between Damascus and Arabia ran directly through Rabbah.

Several Iron Age tombs have been cleared at Amman whose main contents point to a Late Iron II date (*ca.* 700-600). Outside these tombs, however, there are no architectural remains which can be dated with any certainty to the early Ammonite kingdom. What is left of the old city walls seems to stem from the time of the Ptolemies. From an architectural standpoint, the most important period at Amman was the age of the Antonines (second century A.D.), from which comes the great bulk of Roman remains. These include the el-Kal'ah, or citadel, situated on the main acropolis N of the Wadi Amman, and on which are the ruins of two temples (one dedicated to Zeus Ammon) and a cultic complex. Two other acropolises are without ruins, although some scholars consider the second eminence to have been the site of the Early Iron Age capital. Among the splendid constructions in the valley of the Wadi Amman S of the main acropolis is a long street of pillars, which branch out to the NW in a transverse valley. Along this avenue, from W to E, are arranged an aqueduct, a bath, the so-called Nymphaeum, the already-mentioned propylaeum, the famous amphitheater (largest in Syria, seating some six thousand spectators), the so-called Odeum, and an E gate and wall, the latter apparently constituting the only blockade against easy entrance to the city by marauding Bedouin. This magnificent array of Roman remains shows the extent to which the city participated in the prosperity of E Palestine during the second-third centuries A.D.

3. Political history. On the basis of evidence from archaeological explorations, ancient Rabbah would seem to have been established as early as the thirteenth century. There are only two references to the city in biblical literature going back to a time before the tenth century. The first is a tradition preserved by the Deuteronomist (Deut. 3:11) that the bed of the Bashanite king OG was kept in Rabbah (*see* ZAMZUMMIM). The second reference occurs in a geographical explanation of the location of Aroer, which, according to Josh. 13:25, was "east of Rabbah."

The most extensive biblical references to Rabbah are in connection with David's siege of the Ammonite capital in the early tenth century B.C. (II Sam. 11-12; *see* AMMON § 3d). For the first time in the history of Ammon, the capital was besieged and captured, after a bitter struggle (II Sam. 11:1, 22-24; 12:26; I Chr. 20:1). It would appear, from the parallel accounts describing this event (II Sam. 12:26-31; I Chr. 20:1-3), that Joab only directed the initial phase of the siege, capturing the "royal city" (עיר המלוכה; lit., "the city of the kingdom"; *see* § 1 *above*)

and the "city of waters" (עיר המים; *see* § 1 *above*); while David, upon being summoned from Jerusalem, led forth the reserve troops and administered the decisive blow that overwhelmed the entire city (II Sam. 12:28-29). Subsequently, David pillaged the Ammonite capital, and before returning to Jerusalem, organized the citizens of Rabbah, as well as others from neighboring Ammonite settlements, into a labor *corvée* (vss. 30-31). Throughout the remaining years of the United Monarchy, Rabbah continued under Israelite suzerainty. But sometime during the first half of the ninth century, the Ammonites regained their independence, earning a scathing condemnation from Amos, who prophesied the destruction of Rabbah (Amos 1:14).

No further mention of the Ammonite capital occurs in biblical literature until near the end of the seventh century B.C. Jeremiah acknowledges the last important expansive movement of the Ammonites at this time, and foresees the eventual military demise and destruction of Rabbah at the hands of Israel (Jer. 49:2-3). Finally, Ezekiel envisions God commissioning him to mark a way for the sword of the king of Babylon (Nebuchadrezzar) to come to Rabbah (Ezek. 21:20), and thus punish the rebellious Ammonites. The ultimate destruction of the Ammonite capital by the invading Arab hordes *ca.* 580 B.C. is vividly described by Ezekiel in his oracle against the Ammonites (Ezek. 25:5).

The name of Rabbah is nowhere mentioned in the OT in connection with Jewish history of the postexilic period. We next hear of it after its capture by Ptolemy Philadelphus (285-247), in whose honor the city was renamed Philadelphia. In 259, however, the governor Zenon still called the city by its indigenous name, which (in the form Rabbatamana, τὰ ῾Ραβ-βατάμμανα) was retained by Polybius and Stephen of Byzantium. According to Polybius (V.71), the city was captured from Ptolemy Philopator by Antiochus III the Great in 218 B.C., after a severe and protracted siege, which was broken only through the help of a captive, who revealed the existence of a subterranean passage by which the citadel garrison obtained its water supply. A nineteenth-century survey of the site revealed the remains of a reservoir and aqueduct which possibly belong to this subterranean passage described by Polybius. In 199 B.C., Philadelphia passed under the Lagides after Antiochus' victory at Panion. In the time of Hyrcanus (135-107), so Josephus (Antiq. XIII.viii.1; xv.3) informs us, a Zeno Cotylas was tyrant over the city. In 63 B.C., Philadelphia became a city of the Decapolis, held by the Arabs (Jos. War I.vi.3), who were in open hostility to the Jews in the years 66 and 44 (Antiq. XX.i.1; War II.xviii.1) until finally defeated by Herod in 30 B.C. (War I.xix.5-6). Philadelphia did not belong to the province of Arabia until the time of Trajan (A.D. 106). In the middle of the fourth century A.D., Ammianus Marcellinus listed it as one of the great fortified cities of Coele-Syria. It later became the seat of a Christian bishop, forming one of the nineteen sees of *Palaestina tertia*. In 635 Philadelphia succumbed to the Arab conquest under Yezid. In the tenth century the Arab geographer Mukaddasi described it as the capital of the Belqa district lying on the border of the desert, where it has continued as an important city to this day. Unfortunately the installation of Circassians there in 1878 has been prejudicial to the preservation of some of the ancient buildings.

Bibliography. C. Conder, *Survey of Eastern Palestine* (1889), pp. 19-64. D. Mackenzie, "Megalithic Monuments of Rabbath Ammon," *Annual of PEF* (1911), pp. 1-40. H. C. Butler, *Ancient Architecture in Syria: Southern Syria, Ammonitis (Publication of the Princeton University Archaeological Expedition to Syria,* II, A, 1; 1919), pp. 34-35. R. Bartoccini, "Scavi ad Amman della Missione Archaeologica italiana," *Bolletino, Associazione Internationale degli Studi Mediterranei,* vol. I (1930), no. 3, pp. 15-17; vol. III (1932), no. 2, pp. 16-23; vol. IV (1933-34), nos. 4-5, pp. 10-15. K. Galling, *Biblisches Reallexikon* (1937), pp. 432-35. F.-M. Abel, *Géographie de la Palestine* (1938), II, 424-25. R. Bartoccini, "La Rocca Sacra degli Ammoniti," *Atti del IV Congresso Nazionale di Studi Romani* (1938), p. 308. D. Mackenzie, *RB,* 64 (1957), 218-20.   G. M. LANDES

***RABBAH (OF JUDAH).** A village of Judah in the highland district of Jerusalem (Josh. 15:60; it probably also appeared in the Benjaminite list after Kiriath-jearim in Josh. 18:28, but was accidentally omitted).

Rabbah may be the Rubutu of the Amarna Letters (cf. *ANET* 488-89, nos. 287, 289-90), which seems to lie in the immediate vicinity of Jerusalem, as does Rabbah, whose present location remains unknown.

V. R. GOLD

RABBI, RABBONI răb′ī, rə bō′nī [ῥαββί or ῥαββεί =רִבִּי, my master, *from* רב, master (*cf.* רבב, be great); ῥαββουνί or ῥαββουνεί=רבּונִי, my master, *from* רב, a *heightened form of* רב]. Alternately: MASTER. One learned in the Mosaic law; hence a teacher of the law. In modern Judaism the rabbinate is an ordained office. Formerly, however, it was simply a title of respect, addressed to learned laymen, sometimes indicating a master as contrasted with servants, but more often a teacher as contrasted with his pupils. It could even be used of Yahweh as teacher of Moses (Ab. 1.6). In the Talmudic era *rab* was used chiefly of Babylonian teachers and *rabbi* of Palestinian ones. Rabbi Yehudah Hannasî, who edited the Mishna, came to be known pre-eminently by the title "Rabbi" without the need to give his name. *See* TALMUD.

In the NT, "rabbi" is simply an honorific title with no overtones of official appointment. It is applied to teachers of the law in general (Matt. 23:7-8), and even to John the Baptist by John's disciples (John 3:26). In all other cases, both "rabbi" and "rabboni" mean Jesus, and are used in direct address to him. This occurs twice in Matthew and four or five times in Mark—the textual evidence for Mark 10:51 is conflicting. Supremely it is the Fourth Gospel which has Jesus honored in this way. It is done by inquirers (John 1:49; 6:25) and even a Pharisee (3:2), as well as by Jesus' own followers (4:31; 9:2; 11:8). As John 1:38; 20:16 say, however, "rabbi" and "rabboni" have the same import (though they have not the same literal meaning) as "teacher," and the latter occurs frequently in the Synoptics.

See also DISCIPLE; TEACHER.   PIERSON PARKER

RABBITH răb′īth [רבּית]. A border town in Issachar (Josh. 19:20). "Rabbith" is an error for "DABERATH," a Levitical town in Issachar (Josh. 21:28; I Chr. 6: 72—H 6:57), not otherwise mentioned in Josh. 19:

17-23. This view is strongly supported by LXX B, which reads "Daberoth" in place of "Rabbith" in Josh. 19:20.   G. W. VAN BEEK

RABBONI. *See* RABBI.

RAB-MAG răb′măg [רב־מג, *see below*] (Jer. 39:3, 13). The designation of a court official of the Babylonian king; probably derived from Akkadian *rab mugi* (also *mugu* and *munga*), which, however, appears only in Assyrian texts. The meaning of the word is unknown in Akkadian.

Bibliography. E. Klauber, *Assyrisches Beamtentum* (1910), p. 52, note 2.   A. L. OPPENHEIM

RABSACES. KJV Apoc. form of RAB-SHAKEH.

RAB-SARIS răb′sə rīs [רב־סרים; Akkad. *ša-rēši,* attendant—*lit.,* he who stands by (the king)] (II Kings 18:17; Jer. 39:3, 13). Chief eunuch. This is an Assyrian loan word in Hebrew and other Semitic languages, a euphemistic designation for the eunuchs at the Assyrian court. The role and function of these eunuchs has been recently elucidated by a series of Middle Assyrian texts that set forth instructions for the personnel of the royal harem, etc.

Bibliography. E. F. Weidner, "Hof- und Harems-Erlässe assyrischer Könige aus dem 2. Jahrtausend v. Chr.," *AFO,* 17 (1954-55), 257 ff.   A. L. OPPENHEIM

RAB-SHAKEH răb′shə kə [רב־שקה, Assyrian *loan word*] (II Kings 18:17, etc.); KJV Apoc. RABSACES răb′sə sēz. The designation of the chief cupbearer of the king. This Assyrian and Babylonian court official was of high rank and often in charge of administrative duties.   A. L. OPPENHEIM

RACA rä′kä [ῥακά, ῥαχά; Aram. ריקא, ריקה, *see below*]. A term of reproach or insult, indicating a person who is contemptible in some way. Jesus is quoted as saying in Matt. 5:22 that anyone who uses this expression to a brother (RSV translates "insults his brother") will be "liable to the council." Since the word is used nowhere else in the NT, and rarely elsewhere, its precise meaning is difficult to determine.

"Raca" has usually been taken as a transliteration of the Aramaic *rêqâ,* meaning an inferior or stupid person; related to *rêqān,* "empty" or, figuratively, "ignorant." In Ber. 32*a* Baraita a commander greets a pious man praying. When the man continues his prayer without answering, the commander demands why he does not reply to the greeting, calling him *rêqâ.* In Ber. 75*a* Rabbi Jochanan addresses a pupil who laughed at one of his lectures as *rêqâ.* In Midrash Qoh. 9:15 (44*b*) Noah says to his contemporaries: "Woe to you *rêqayyâ!* Tomorrow the flood will come; repent." In Midrash Ps. 137:5 an ex-wife of a king calls her second husband *rêqâ,* probably referring to his inferior status.

On the other hand, discovery of a Greek papyrus letter, dated Feb. 6 (or 9), 257 B.C., in which ῥαχᾶν is used ('Αντίοχον τòν ῥαχᾶν) has suggested to some scholars that the word is a Greek term of abuse of uncertain meaning. The spelling ῥαχά in Matt. 5:22 has better MS support than ῥακά (א D W and most

OL as against B—the passage being mutilated in A C and p⁴⁵), and Tertullian and Cyprian also support ῥαχά.

Bibliography. H. L. Strack and P. Billerbeck, *Kommentar zum NT aus Talmud und Midrash*, I (1922), 276 ff; E. C. Colwell, "Has 'Ραϰά a Parallel in the Papyri?" *JBL*, LIII (1934), 351-54; E. J. Goodspeed, *Problems of NT Translation* (1945); M. Smith, "Notes on Goodspeed's *Problems*, etc.," *JBL*, LXIV (1945), 501 ff.   T. S. KEPLER

RACAL rā'kăl [רכל, trade, commerce]; KJV RACHAL rā'kăl. A village in S Judah, presently unidentified, to which David sent some booty taken from the Amalekites (I Sam. 30:29). LXX B reads "CARMEL," which is probably the original reading.
     V. R. GOLD

RACE, RACE COURSE. *See* GAMES; MAN, ETHNIC DIVISIONS OF.

RACHAB. KJV form of RAHAB (PERSON) in Matt. 1:5.

RACHAL. KJV form of RACAL.

RACHEL rā'chəl [רחל, ewe; 'Ραχήλ]. The younger daughter of Laban; Jacob's second wife; and the mother of Joseph and Benjamin.

Like Rebekah, her aunt and mother-in-law, Rachel first appears in the OT narrative at a well (Gen. 29:1-14). The well was located near Haran in Mesopotamia, whither, according to the early JE tradition, Jacob had fled from his brother, Esau. Having arrived at the well, he encountered this beautiful shepherdess, the daughter of his uncle Laban. Jacob was immediately attracted to his cousin and agreed to work seven years under Laban in return for her hand (vss. 15-30). The seven years "seemed to him but a few days because of the love he had for her" (vs. 20). At the end of the stipulated time, however, the crafty Laban surreptitiously substituted Leah, his older and less attractive daughter, for Rachel in the wedding ceremony. When Jacob discovered the deception, his commitment to the elder sister was legally consummated, and he was powerless to escape the contract. In order to gain Rachel, he was forced to spend seven more years in the service of Laban. Once he received her for his wife, Jacob's love for Rachel was greater than his love for Leah.

Rachel was not immediately fruitful after her marriage, and she was both impatient and jealous when Leah gave birth to Reuben, Simeon, Levi, and Judah (Gen. 29:31-35). Her only recourse was to give Jacob her handmaid, Bilhah, for children—a custom paralleled in the Nuzi Tablets (*see* NUZI). The children of this union, Dan and Naphtali, were named by Rachel, indicating her claim to them (30:1-8). Rachel's burning desire for fruitfulness can be seen in her request for Reuben's mandrakes, which she believed would bring fertility (vss. 14-16). It was not until after Zilpah, Leah's handmaid, had borne Gad and Asher (vss. 9-12), and Leah had given birth to Issachar, Zebulun, and Dinah (vss. 17-21), that God at last remembered Rachel. To her was born Joseph (vss. 22-24), who was to become the father of Ephraim and Manasseh (41:50-52).

When Jacob determined to return to his homeland, both Rachel and Leah concurred in his decision (Gen. 31:1-16). As they fled, Rachel stole her father's household gods (*see* TERAPHIM), which would ensure both success and the family inheritance (vss. 17-35). Laban's concern in pursuing them was not so much for his lost daughters as for his lost gods. His search was in vain, since Rachel had hidden them in the saddle of her camel and sat upon them. Her explanation to her father was that she could not rise because the "way of women" was upon her (vs. 35).

Jacob's favoritism for Rachel and Joseph is reflected by their position in the processional which he formed when they were returning to Palestine and about to meet Esau. They were placed last, where they would be safest in case of violence (Gen. 33:1-2).

The death of Rachel came with the birth of her second child, as the company was moving S between Bethel and Ephrath (Gen. 35:16-21; cf. 48:7). When she learned that it was a son, she called his name Ben-oni ("son of my sorrow"), but Jacob named him Benjamin ("son of my right hand"). She was buried near Ephrath in the territory of Benjamin, and Jacob erected a pillar to mark her tomb. *See* RACHEL'S TOMB.

In only two passages outside Genesis does the OT mention Rachel. Ruth 4:11 refers to Rachel and Leah as those who founded the house of Israel, and Jeremiah 31:15 depicts her as weeping at the fate of her children (the N kingdom represented by Ephraim, Joseph's son) who had been exiled by Assyria.

The Hebrew idea of corporate personality would suggest that the Rachel traditions have another level of significance in addition to being stories of important individuals. They reflect tribal relations and history. The exact nature of this history is not easily discerned, but certain tentative conclusions can be advanced.

Some of those who see no evidence of real personal history in the Rachel stories think it is possible that there was originally a Rachel tribe or clan. Its totem could have been the ewe (רחל), which would suggest a nomadic group.

More certain is the historical situation of the tribes of Israel, reflected by the family of which Rachel was a member. The sons of Jacob-Israel by Rachel, Leah, Bilhah, and Zilpah represent the twelve-tribe amphictyony which flourished during the period of the judges. Thus the sons of Rachel, Joseph and Benjamin, were prominent members of this Israelite confederation of tribes which were united by their common worship of Yahweh.

That Joseph was born to Rachel in the region of Haran reveals the memory of an Aramean origin of the "house of Joseph." Since Rachel's second son, Benjamin, was not born until she went to Palestine, it might be surmised that this tribe was formed only on that soil, perhaps as the result of a split of Ephraim. On the other hand, it could indicate that Benjamin was the first tribe to enter Palestine, and thus was already there when the other tribes arrived.

The entry of the Joseph tribes into Palestine after the other tribes is possibly reflected in the order of the births of Jacob's children. But since Rachel's son

Joseph, and particularly Joseph's son Ephraim, became pre-eminent in the N where these traditions were formed, they present Rachel and Joseph as favored by Jacob.

The geographical propinquity of Ephraim and Benjamin after the Conquest would seem best to explain the fact that Joseph and Benjamin were full brothers. If there is significance in the fact that Dan and Naphtali are the sons of Rachel's handmaid, Bilhah, it is not immediately obvious. Only Bilhah's son Dan was ever geographically contiguous to Ephraim and Benjamin. This tradition might reflect a preconquest relation.

In the NT there is a single reference to Rachel. The passage concerning Rachel's weeping for her children in Jer. 31:15 is used by the author of Matthew in connection with the slaying of the infants by Herod (Matt. 2:16-18).

Bibliography. M. Noth, *Das System der Zwölf Stämme Israels* (1930); J. Bright, *Early Israel in Recent History Writing* (1956); M. Noth, *The History of Israel* (1958).   M. NEWMAN

*RACHEL'S TOMB. The burial place of Rachel, Jacob's wife. The traditional location, *ca.* a mile N of Bethlehem on the W side of the Jerusalem road, was indicated very early by a gloss on Gen. 35:19; 48:7, and accepted by early Christian writers. At least as early as the fourth century A.D. there was a monument there, later described as a pyramid of twelve stones representing the twelve sons of Jacob. The present building consists of a domed room *ca.* twenty-four feet square, erected by the Crusaders, and an adjoining square vestibule containing a mihrab (Muslim place of prayer), added by Sir M. Montefiore when he purchased the monument for the Jews in 1841.

Gen. 35:16-19 tells that Rachel died on the way from Bethel to Ephrath "when they were still some distance from Ephrath" (vs. 16) and that she was buried there. The gloss: "that is, Bethlehem," erroneously identifies this Ephrath with the district of EPHRATHAH, in which Bethlehem was situated (Ruth 4:11; Mic. 5:2—H 5:1). However, both I Sam. 10:2 ("Rachel's tomb in the territory of Benjamin") and Jer. 31:15:

> A voice is heard in Ramah,
> lamentation and bitter weeping.
> Rachel is weeping for her children,

assume a situation N of Jerusalem for her grave. A passage in Midrash Rabbah shows that the two con-

3. Though erected by Crusaders in the twelfth century of the Christian era, this tomb has played an interesting traditional role.

tradictory traditions caused difficulty for rabbinic exegetes in the early Christian period. Matthew's quotation of Jer. 31:15 with reference to the slaughter of infants around Bethlehem (Matt. 2:16-18) would indicate that he accepted the traditional view.

Fig. RAC 3.

Bibliography. B. Meistermann, *A New Guide to the Holy Land* (1923), pp. 299-301.   S. V. FAWCETT

RADDAI răd'ī [רדי] (I Chr. 2:14). The fifth son of Jesse the Bethlehemite, and, consequently, an elder brother of David.

RAFT [דברות, towed objects, *from* Aram. דבר, lead, guide; רפסדות]. A floating collection of logs, timber, etc., fastened together, for their own conveyance or for a support.

Both words cited above refer to the method which Hiram of Tyre used to transport cedar and cypress logs by sea from Lebanon to Joppa. The rafts were presumably towed by boats. It is possible that rafts were used as ferries at the more important fords of the Jordan, for the transportation of objects too heavy for the backs of animals. Such rafts may have had their buoyancy increased by the use of inflated animal hides. It is instructive that in postbiblical Jewish Aramaic the word מעברא, *ma'bᵉrâ*, used for "FORD" in the OT (Josh. 2:7, etc.), also has the meaning "ferry."   W. S. McCULLOUGH

RAFTERS [קורות (*with* LXX; *in* I Kings 6:15-16, MT-KJV קירות, WALLS; *in* I Kings 7:7, MT-KJV קרקע, FLOOR); רהיט (Song of S. 1:17; *Kethibh* רחיט)]. Beams supporting the roof of a building.

RAGAE, RAGAU. See RAGES; *also* REU.

RAGES rā'jēz ['Ράγοι, 'Ράγαια, 'Ραγαί; Old Pers. *Râgâ*]; *in* Jth. 1:5, 15 RAGAE rā'jē ['Ραγαῦ; *see below*]; KJV RAGAU rā'gô. An important, strategically located, and well-fortified city in NE Media of the Persian Empire, situated *ca.* five miles SE of its modern counterpart, the Persian capital of Teheran, and generally identified with the present extensive and imposing ruins of Ray (Rai, Rhay, Rhey, etc.). It is mentioned six times in Tobit: 1:14; 4:1, 20; 5:5; 6:12; 9:2. In Jth. 1:5, 15 Ragae refers to the general region, as in Diodorus Siculus (19.2) and in one of two references in the Behistun Inscription. Cf. Strabo (XI.9.1; 13.6); the *Avesta* (Vendidad 1.15; Yasna 19.18); Ptolemy *Geography* VI.5.4; etc., and various Pahlavi texts.

Located just S of the high mountain range of Alborz, bordering the Caspian Sea in an area which controls the "Caspian Gates," the city played an important part in the wars of Media and of Alexander the Great and his successors. It is one of the oldest centers of civilization in Iran, modern excavation (*see bibliography*) indicating occupation from *ca.* 5000 B.C. and, except for interruptions occasioned by earthquakes and several invasions (Parthians, Arabs, Afghans, Mongols), down to the end of the fourteenth century. It was long an important center of Zoroastrianism and between the seventh and early thirteenth centuries it flourished as a large Mohammedan metropolis.

Bibliography. A. V. Jackson, "A Historical Sketch of Ragha, the Supposed Home of Zoroaster's Mother," *Spiegel Memorial Volume* (1908), pp. 237-45. The main accounts of excavations in 1934-36 under the direction of E. F. Schmidt. *University of Pennsylvania Bulletin*, vol. V, no. 5 (1935), pp. 41-49; vol. VI, no. 3 (1936), pp. 79-87; vol. VI, no. 4 (1936), pp. 133-36. A. T. Olmstead, *History of the Persian Empire* (1948), pp. 30, 111, 114-15. A. WIKGREN

RAGUEL răg'yoō əl, rə gū'əl [רְעוּאֵל; LXX 'Pαγουηλ]. **1.** A member of the tribe of Naphtali living in Ecbatana; the husband of Edna, and the father of Sarah, Tobias' wife (Tob. 3:7, etc.). *See* TOBIT, BOOK OF; TOBIAS 1.

2. An (arch)angel (Enoch 20:4; cf. 23:4).

3. KJV form of REUEL in Num. 10:29, etc.

L. HICKS

RAHAB rā'hăb [רחב, wide, broad; NT 'Pαάβ, 'Pαχάβ *in* Matt. 1:5]; KJV RACHAB —kăb *in* Matt. 1:5. The harlot who sheltered the men sent by Joshua to spy out Jericho.

1. In the OT. According to the narrative (Josh. 2:1-21), which was preserved because Rahab was still living at the time of its composition (cf. 6:25), Joshua sent two men in secret to assess the strength of Canaan, especially Jericho. They lodged in the house of Rahab the harlot. Naturally the news soon reached the king, and he sent messengers to Rahab commanding her to produce her lodgers. Although she had actually hidden the spies in stalks of flax on the roof of her house, she told the messengers that she had seen the men but that they had left the city a short time before. Following this false lead, the agents of the king pursued them as far as the fords of the Jordan. Thereupon Rahab visited the men on the roof and told them that she and the people of Jericho had heard of the mighty deeds of Yahweh, and that she knew Yahweh to be "God in heaven." On this basis she asked the spies to swear that she and her clan would be spared from the coming destruction. The men agreed, and Rahab let them down by a rope through the window—her house was built in the city wall. For purposes of identification she tied a scarlet thread in her window. After the conquest of Jericho, Joshua told the spies to bring out Rahab and her clan; then the city was burned (Josh. 6:17, 22-25).

There is no further mention of Rahab in the OT, but according to rabbinic tradition she was one of the four most beautiful women in the world and an ancestress of eight prophets (including Jeremiah) and a prophetess (Huldah; Meg. 14*b*, 15*a*).

2. In the NT. According to Matthew's genealogy of Jesus, Rahab was the wife of Salmon and the mother of Boaz (Matt. 1:5). The early church fathers took for granted the identification of this Rahab with the Rahab of JOSHUA, but this was later doubted. The unique spelling 'Pαχάβ may indicate that Matthew distinguished the two. Elsewhere in the NT, Rahab is cited as an example of justification by works in Jas. 2:25, but in Heb. 11:31 as one who because of her faith did not perish.

See also PROSTITUTION; JERICHO 1. J. F. ROSS

RAHAB (DRAGON) [רהב, *see below*]. One of the names of the mythological dragon vanquished by Yahweh in a primordial combat. On this myth, its significance and its parallels, *see* COSMOGONY.

The name Rahab is found only in poetic passages of the OT (viz., Job 9:13; 26:12; Ps. 89:10; Isa. 30:7; 51:9-10), and all these occur in books written after the seventh century B.C. Its meaning is uncertain. According to one view, the name derives from רהב, "be proud, arrogant"; according to another, it is to be connected with Akkadian *ra'ābu*, "rage" or "be agitated." With the latter may be compared the Egyptian *hmhm.t*, "the roaring, turbulent one," as a name of the mythological dragon 'Apep.

The LXX renders ὑπερήφανος ("overweening") in Ps. 89:10; κῆτος ("sea monster") in Job 9:13; 26:12. In Ps. 87:4, it merely transliterates (ρααβ); in Isa. 30:7 it does not recognize a proper name; and in Isa. 51:9 it omits the word altogether.

The Vulg. usually renders *superbus* (*Superbia* in Isa. 30:7). In Job 9:13, however, it identifies the "helpers of Rahab" (with whom we may compare the helpers of Tiamat in the Babylonian creation myth, Enuma Eliš, I.105-7) with submarine creatures who support the world (*qui portant orbem*). The notion of such creatures is widespread in world folklore.

In Ps. 87:4; Isa. 30:9 the ancient mythological name is used figuratively to designate Egypt, the former passage likening that foreign power to the proud monster who was eventually reduced to impotence (for MT שבת הם, read המשבת, "who was stilled"). T. H. GASTER

RAHAM rā'hăm [רחם, mercy, love] (I Chr. 2:44). A descendant of Judah; son of Shema, and the father of Jorkeam.

RAHEL rā'hĕl. KJV form of RACHEL in Jer. 31:15.

RAIMENT. *See* DRESS AND ORNAMENTS.

RAIN [מטר=NT ὑετός, falling of rain, the rain which falls; גשם=NT βροχή, downpour of rain; זרם (Job 24:8; KJV SHOWERS; *elsewhere* STORM; TEMPEST); ὄμβρος, rainstorm with wind (Luke 12: 54)]. Most of the annual rainfall in Palestine occurs in the three months early December to early March. This is preceded by the EARLY RAIN and followed by the "latter rain" (*see* SPRING RAIN). The summer months are almost rainless.

See also PALESTINE, CLIMATE OF; DROUGHT; SEASONS. R. B. Y. SCOTT

*****RAINBOW** [ἶρις (Rev. 4:3; 10:1); τόξον (Ecclus. 43:11)]; BOW IN THE CLOUD [קשת] (Gen. 9:13). The reflection and refraction of sunlight by a curtain of falling rain, producing a bow or arc of the prismatic colors visible to an observer facing away from the sun. Frequently it has as background the cloud mass of a retreating thunderstorm, so that it appears as a "bow in the cloud," an appropriate symbol of a storm that is past. It is the bow which Yahweh has set aside after shooting the arrows of his lightning (Lam. 2:4; Hab. 3:9-11), and becomes the sign of Yahweh's covenant that "the waters shall never again become a flood to destroy all flesh" (Gen. 9:8-17). Regarded with awe and admiration for its beauty (Ecclus. 43:11), the rainbow became a feature of

scenes laid in heaven (Ezek. 1:28; Rev. 4:3; 10:1).
                                    R. B. Y. SCOTT

RAISIN-CAKES [אשישות] (Isa. 16:7). Alternately: CAKES OF RAISINS (II Sam. 6:19; Hos. 3:1); KJV FLAGONS OF WINE. Food prepared by the pressing of dried grapes. Because it is virtually imperishable, such food is suitable for travel and for military provisions (II Sam. 6:19; 16:1; cf. I Sam. 25:18; 30:12; I Chr. 12:40). A festive food (Isa. 16:7), it was apparently also used in the cult of the fertility goddesses (Song of S. 2:5; Hos. 3:1; cf. Jer. 7:18; 44: 19). *See* BAAL 1; FERTILITY CULTS; HOSEA.

   Bibliography. B. Duhm, *Das Buch Jesaia* (1914), on Isa. 16:7; K. Galling, *Biblisches Reallexikon* (1937), p. 84.
                                    J. A. WHARTON

RAISINS [צמוקים]. Raisins often appear in lists of provisions (I Sam. 25:18; 30:12; II Sam. 16:1; I Chr. 12:40—H 12:41). They were prepared by soaking bunches of grapes in oil and water and spreading them in the sun to dry. RAISIN-CAKES are mentioned both as a common food and as offerings in pagan cults.   J. F. ROSS

RAKEM rā'kĕm [רקם] (I Chr. 7:16). A grandson of Manasseh. In Hebrew this name is the pausal form of the name Rekem.

RAKKATH răk'ĭth [רקת] (Josh. 19:35). A fortified town in Naphtali. It is perhaps located at Tell Eqlatiyeh, a small site with EB, MB, and some LB remains near the Sea of Chinneroth, *ca.* 1½ miles N of Tiberias. The Israelite town may have been situated at the foot of Tell Eqlatiyeh near the perennial spring 'Ain el-Fuliyeh. If this is not the site, it is possible that Rakkath is located beneath modern Tiberias, as suggested by the Talmud.

   Bibliography. W. F. Albright, "The Jordan Valley in the Bronze Age," *AASOR*, 6 (1926), 26.   G. W. VAN BEEK

RAKKON răk'ŏn [רקון, shore(?), narrow place(?)] (Josh. 19:46). A village of Dan; presumably on or near the Nahr el-'Auja (River Jarkon), not far from the Mediterranean, according to the context. Since the Greek text omits it, some suggest that it is a doublet of the preceding Me-jarkon. Others propose identification with Tell er-Reqqeit, *ca.* 1⅔ miles N of the mouth of the Nahr el-'Auja.

   Bibliography. F.-M. Abel, *Géographie de la Palestine*, II (1938), 433; M. Noth, *Das Buch Josua* (1953), pp. 120 ff; G. E. Wright and F. Filson, *Westminster Historical Atlas to the Bible* (rev. ed., 1956), p. 126.   V. R. GOLD

RAM răm [רם; Ἀράμ]; KJV NT ARAM âr'əm. **1.** An ancestor of King David (Ruth 4:19; I Chr. 2:9); and an ancestor of Jesus, according to Matt. 1:3-4 (called Arni in Luke 3:33). It is to be noted, in view of 2 *below,* that this Ram is named as a brother of Jerahmeel in I Chr. 2:9.

   2. The first-born son of Jerahmeel of Judah (I Chr. 2:25, 27).

   3. Head of the family of Elihu, one of the friends of Job (Job 32:2).   E. R. ACHTEMEIER

RAM (ANIMAL) [איל]. The mature male of the sheep. The ram was a possible sacrificial offering in a number of ritual situations, including the peace offering (e.g., Lev. 1:10) and the guilt offering (5:15; 6:6). The ram was used for meat (Gen. 31:38); rams' skins were employed with other materials as coverings for the tabernacle (Exod. 26:14) and presumably other shelters; and the horns of the ram were commonly used in early times for trumpets (see Josh. 6:4-13).

The ram gains certain prestige in the OT as a central element in several passages of special force or significance. It is the ram, caught by his horns in the thicket, that provides the climax and denouement of the powerful story of the near-sacrifice of Isaac in Gen. 22 (see vs. 13). The early declaration of the prophetic temper placed on the lips of Samuel is another case in point:

Has Yahweh as great delight in burnt offerings and sacrifices,
   as in obeying the voice of Yahweh?
Behold, to obey is better than sacrifice,
   and to hearken than the fat of rams (I Sam. 15:22).

Isaiah puts it in even more intense language, and employs the ram along with other animals of sacrifice to make his point:

   What to me is the multitude of your sacrifices?
      says Yahweh;
   I have had enough of burnt offerings of rams
      and the fat of fed beasts;
   I do not delight in the blood of bulls,
      or of lambs, or of he-goats (Isa. 1:11).

Yet again in prophetism, as an introduction to the familiar so-called prophetic summary of Mic. 6:8, the ram figures:

   Will Yahweh be pleased with thousands of rams,
      with ten thousands of rivers of oil?
   Shall I give my first-born for my transgression,
      the fruit of my body for the sin of my soul?
   He has showed you, O man, what is good;
      and what does Yahweh require of you
   but to do justly, and to love kindness [חסד],
      and to walk humbly with your God?
                                    (Mic. 6:7-8).

See also SHEEP; SHEPHERD; LAMB.   B. D. NAPIER

RAM, BATTERING. *See* BATTERING RAM.

RAMAH rā'mə [רמה, הרמה, height, the height; Ῥαμά, *see* 3 *below*]. **1.** A border town in Asher (הרמה; Josh. 19:29). The biblical context clearly indicates that Ramah was situated in the N part of Asher, and probably in the vicinity of Tyre, but the exact location of the ancient town is unknown. The identification accepted by most scholars is Ramia, a village located in the hill country approximately eleven miles E of Ras en-Naqura, at the E foot of Khirbet Belat. A number of sarcophagi and rock-cut tombs have been found in the immediate vicinity. It has also been suggested that Ramah in Asher may be the same as Ramah in Naphtali, which is probably to be identified with er-Rameh. If this suggestion is correct, the appearance of Ramah in both territorial lists is to be explained by the fact that the town was located on the common territorial border and was presumably settled by both tribes.

   Bibliography. A. Alt, "Die Reise," *PJB*, 23 (1927), 46; R. Dussaud, *Topographie historique de la Syrie antique et Médiévale* (1927), p. 11.

2. A fortified town in Naphtali (הרמה; Josh. 19:
36). It is probably to be identified with er-Rameh, a
village located approximately fifteen miles W of
modern Safed on the route to Acco. The ancient site
is perhaps located beneath the highest point of the
modern village.

Bibliography. J. Ben Zevi, "A Third Century Aramaic Inscription in er-Rāma," *JPOS*, 13 (1933), 94.

G. W. VAN BEEK

3. A town in the inheritance of Benjamin, near
the frontier between the kingdoms of Israel and
Judah (רמה; Josh. 18:25; KJV RAMA in Matt. 2:18,
CIRAMA sĭ rā'mə in I Esd. 5:20).

Baasha, king of Israel, fortified it in an attempt to
enforce a blockade of Judah from the N. Subsequently, when Baasha's energies and attention were
diverted to the defense of his N border against Damascus, Asa of Judah dismantled Ramah and used
its stones and timbers to fortify nearby Geba and
Mizpah (I Kings 15:17, 21-22; II Chr. 16:1, 5-6). In
587 B.C., Ramah seems to have been a gathering
point from which the captain of Nebuchadrezzar's
guard conducted the amassed captives of Jerusalem
and Judah into Babylonian exile. Here Jeremiah
was released from his bonds and permitted the freedom either of accompanying the captives or of remaining with the remnant in Judah (Jer. 40:1, 4). At
the close of the Captivity, Ramah was one of the
villages reoccupied by returning Benjaminites (Ezra
2:26; Neh. 7:30; 11:33). Near this town was the traditional site of the tomb of Rachel (I Sam. 10:2; Jer.
31:15; Matt. 2:18).

Ramah is found in frequent association with certain well-known towns to the N of Jerusalem. In
Josh. 18:25 it is listed between Gibeon and Beeroth;
the palm tree of Deborah is located between Ramah
and Bethel (Judg. 4:5); a Levite journeying northward past Jerusalem came at nightfall to Gibeah, not
yet having reached Ramah (Judg. 19:13-14); the Assyrian army is envisioned by Isaiah as making a
southward march on Jerusalem, passing in succession
through Geba, Ramah, and Gibeah (Isa. 10:29);
Hosea mentions Ramah in close association with
Gibeah (Hos. 5:8); and in the lists of those who returned from Exile, the sons of Ramah and Geba are
enumerated as but a single contingent (Ezra 2:26;
Neh. 7:30; I Esd. 5:20).

The references cited above so circumscribe the ancient site as to make practically certain its identity
with modern er-Ram, *ca.* five miles N of Jerusalem,
two miles N of Gibeah, three miles E of Gibeon, and
two miles W of Geba. With such an identification
both Eusebius (*Onomasticon*) and Josephus (Antiq.
VIII.xii.3) would agree.

Bibliography. G. A. Smith, *Historical Geography of the Holy
Land* (11th ed., 1904), pp. 247-56; E. G. Kraeling, *Bible Atlas*
(1956), pp. 271-72; L. H. Grollenberg, *Atlas of the Bible*
(1959), p. 160.

4. A town in the hill country of Ephraim (רמה).
Alternately: RAMATHAIM-ZOPHIM răm'ə thā'-
əm zō'fĭm (רמתים צופים; the first word means "the two
heights," and צופים is probably an error for צופי, "a
Zuphite," the ם having been inadvertently written
twice; I Sam. 1:1). It was the native home, official
residence, and burial place of Samuel (I Sam. 1:19;
2:11; 7:17; 8:4; 25:1; 28:3).

In the introductory reference to the site, to specify
which of several Ramahs is intended, it is called
Ramathaim-Zophim (I Sam. 1:1; cf. 1:19). This
designation is grammatically unsound and, following
the LXX, the second element of it should probably
be emended (*see above*) to read "a Zuphite"—i.e., an
inhabitant of a district called Zuph. It is suggestive
in this regard that Zuph appears both in the ancestry
of Samuel (I Sam. 1:1) and as the name of the district in which his residence was located (9:5-6, 18).
The aforementioned reference may, therefore, be
read: "There was a certain man of Ramathaim [i.e.,
the Ramath with the two heights], a Zuphite of the
hill country of Ephraim." In subsequent references
to the site, Ramah, the customary short form of the
name, is employed (I Sam. 1:19; 2:11; 7:17; etc.).

From their home in Ramah, the parents of Samuel were accustomed to make an annual pilgrimage
to the religious center of Shiloh to worship and sacrifice (I Sam. 1:3, 19). At Ramah, his official residence, Samuel built an altar; here also he administered justice to Israel; and from this point he went
on annual circuit, exercising a similar ministry in
Bethel, Gilgal, and Mizpah (7:16-17). It was at
Ramah that the elders of Israel assembled to Samuel
to ask for the appointment of a king (8:4); here it
was that Saul, the one to be anointed, first encountered the prophet of God (9:5-10:8); and to here
Samuel returned following his final separation from
the rejected king of Israel (15:34-35). Having
anointed David successor to Saul, Samuel arose and
returned to his home (16:13). David fled to him there
from the jealous wrath of Saul, and the two of them
took refuge at Naioth in Ramah (19:18-19). Seeking
to capture David there, both Saul and his messengers
prophesied before the prophets (19:19-24); from there
David fled, soon to become leader of a refugee band
(20:1; 22:1-2). In Ramah Samuel died and was
buried in his house (25:1; 28:3).

In 145 B.C., as head of a toparchy called Rathamin,
the site and its surroundings were detached from
Samaria and assigned instead to the province of
Judah (I Macc. 11:34). Eusebius (*Onomasticon*) identifies the site with the Arimathea of the NT (Matt.
27:57; John 19:38) and locates it in the vicinity of
Diospolis (Lydda); Jerome further specifies the
nearby district of Timnah. The same two writers
identify the town with Remphis—the modern Rentis,
which is located *ca.* nine miles NE of Lydda on the
W slope of the hill country of Ephraim. Whereas
many present-day scholars have followed the authority of the *Onomasticon* in the matter, some have
preferred Beit-Rima, a hill village some five miles
farther E and twelve miles NW of Bethel.

Bibliography. G. A. Smith, *The Historical Geography of the
Holy Land* (11th ed., 1904), p. 254, note 7; S. R. Driver,
*Notes on the Hebrew Text and the Topography of the Books of
Samuel* (1913), pp. 1-4; F.-M. Abel, *Géographie de la Palestine*,
II (1938), 428-29; E. G. Kraeling, *Bible Atlas* (1956), p. 177;
M. Noth, *The History of Israel* (1958), p. 376.

W. H. MORTON

5. A town of Simeon in the Negeb of Judah. In
Josh. 19:8 it is called "Ramah of the Negeb" (ראמת
נגב; KJV "RAMATH rā'măth of the south"); in
I Sam. 30:27, "RAMOTH rā'mŏth of the Negeb"
(רמות נגב; KJV "south Ramoth"). In Josh. 19:8 it is

made equivalent to BAALATH-BEER. It was one of the cities to which David made presents from the booty he gained from the Amalekites (I Sam. 30:27). The site is unknown. Both passages should perhaps be read "Ramah of the South" (so Josh. 19:8 LXX).

S. COHEN

6. Same as RAMOTH-GILEAD (II Kings 8:29; II Chr. 22:6).

RAMATH OF THE SOUTH. KJV form of Ramah of the Negeb. *See* RAMAH 5.

RAMATHAIM-ZOPHIM. *See* RAMAH 4.

RAMATHEM răm'ə thĕm. KJV Apoc. form of RATHAMIN (I Macc. 11:34).

RAMATHITE rā'mə thīt [רמתי]. A native of Ramah. The term is used in I Chr. 27:27 to designate the chief husbandman of David's vineyards. Which of several towns of this name is here referred to is unknown.

RAMATH-LEHI rā'mīth lē'hī [רמת לחי, hill of the jawbone]. The place where Samson routed a group of Philistines with the jawbone of an ass for a weapon (Judg. 15:17). *See* LEHI.

RAMATH-MIZPEH rā'mīth mīz'pə [רמת המצפה] (Josh. 13:26). A town assigned to the tribe of Gad in the settlement of Palestine; sometimes identified with Mizpeh of Gilead. *See* MIZPAH 1.

RAMESES (CITY) răm'ə sēz [רעמסס; Egyp. *(pr)-r'-ms-sw*, (the house of king) Ramses; LXX *and* Apoc. Ῥαμεσση]. Alternately: RAAMSES rā ăm'sēz. The royal residence city in the Egyptian Delta, under the Nineteenth and Twentieth Dynasties, *ca.* 1300-1100 B.C.

When the Children of Israel began the sojourn in Egypt, they settled in the land of Goshen, alternatively the land of Rameses (Gen. 47:11). Under the Oppression they were forced to help build the store cities of Pithom and Raamses (Exod. 1:11). The city of Rameses was the starting point of the Exodus, distant from the desert by two days' marches (Exod. 12:37; Num. 33:3-6).

Egyptian sources show that Ramses II (*see* RAMSES) was the namer and thus the founder of the city. Thebes remained a S and seasonal capital, while Rameses was the N capital and chief residence of the pharaohs for nearly two centuries. Although the Egyptian texts which praise the town are overeffusive, it was clearly an active city. It was located in the E desert and had harbors for seagoing vessels, and its ships also sailed S to other towns within Egypt. The poetical praise of the city tells of abundant fruits and nearby marshlands and fishing regions. Its frontier character is emphasized by the statement that it lies "between Djahi [the Syrian-Palestinian seacoast] and Egypt" and that it is "the south front of every foreign country, the north front of Egypt." These texts speak for a location close to the Sinai Desert but in a region having vineyards and olive groves, marshes and fisheries, and accessible by ship

from the Nile and the Sea. The N half of the E Delta best fits all these factors.

Unfortunately, scholars do not agree upon the precise location of Rameses. The pharaohs named Ramses, particularly Ramses II, were generous in naming towns after themselves. Further, references to this city have been excavated in Delta towns which can make no serious claim to being the location. Formerly, when the land of GOSHEN was thought to be coterminous with the modern Wadi Tumilat, the SE extension of the Delta, excavators sought Rameses in that valley. But a site in that valley, although suitable for the Israelites' herds, would not conform to the Egyptian texts, and Jth. 1:9-10 is probably correct in understanding Goshen to be simply the E Delta. Few scholars now push the claims of two Ramesside sites in the Wadi Tumilat, Tell el-Maskhutah or Tell er-Retaba, as the site of Rameses, although the former of these may have been PITHOM.

In 1918 the British scholar Alan Gardiner examined all the evidence and came to the tentative conclusion that Rameses had been located at the extreme NE, at Pelusium. However, after excavations had been undertaken at Tanis (*see* ZOAN), Gardiner decided that Rameses was to be found at Tanis, modern San el-Hagar. Certainly this was an important site for much of Egyptian history, and the excavations have shown that it flourished under the pharaohs named Ramses. As an important and well-located city, it is a strong candidate for the capital at that time. Increasingly scholars are thinking of an exodus which began across the N part of Sinai.

Recently another claimant has appeared at modern Qantir, fifteen miles S of Tanis. Here there were a Ramesside palace and a military post, and the place seems to be a center for inscriptions commemorating the worship of Ramses II as a god. One text lists Tanis and (Per-)Rameses separately, and some of the material excavated at Tanis is derivative from other places, so that there is no guarantee that inscriptions bearing the name Rameses were originally at home there. Fortunately for the understanding of the geography of the Exodus, Tanis and Qantir are very close together.

Bibliography. A. H. Gardiner, *JEA,* V (1918), 127-38, 179-200, 242-71; XIX (1933), 122-28; *Ancient Egyptian Onomastica,* II (1947), 171*-75*, 278*-79*. L. Habachi, *Annales du Service des Antiquités de l'Égypte,* LII (1954), 443-562.

J. A. WILSON

RAMIAH rə mī'ə [רמיה, Yahu is exalted; Apoc. Ἱερμάς]; KJV Apoc. HIERMAS hī ûr'məs (Ezra 10:25; I Esd. 9:26). One of those listed as having married foreign wives in the time of Ezra.

Bibliography. M. Noth, *Die israelitischen Personennamen* (1928), pp. 35, 145.

B. T. DAHLBERG

RAMOTH (PERSON). KJV form of JEREMOTH.

RAMOTH rā'mŏth [ראמות]. A Levitical town in the territory of Issachar (I Chr. 6:73—H 6:58). It is the same as JARMUTH (Josh. 21:29), which occupies an identical position in the Levitical town list of Josh. 21:29, and probably the same as REMETH in Josh. 19:21. In all probability, the form "Ramoth" is more original than "Jarmuth," since the former is supported by readings in LXX A and B. A number of identifications have been proposed, but none is satisfactory. One of the sites mentioned in this connection is Kokab el-Hawa, the Crusading Belvoir, located *ca.* seven miles N of Beth-shan. Its situation on a plateau 999 feet above sea level in a region of springs is attractive; however, the identification must be regarded as uncertain.

Bibliography. C. R. Conder and H. H. Kitchener, *SWP,* II (1882), 77, 85, 117-19; W. F. Albright, "The Topography of the Tribe of Issachar," *ZAW,* N.F. 3 (1926), p. 231.

                        G. W. Van Beek

***RAMOTH-GILEAD** rā′məth gĭl′ĭ əd [רמת גלעד, רמת בגלעד, ראמות בגלעד, ראמת בגלעד, רמות גלעד]. An important fortress in Gilead situated in the E part of the territory of Gad. It is often called simply Ramah.

1. History. Ramoth-gilead was one of the three cities of refuge in E Palestine and a Levitical city; it was the residence of the prefect of Solomon's sixth region, which included Havvoth-jair and the Argob (Deut. 4:43; Josh. 21:38; I Kings 4:13). After the division of the kingdom of Israel (*ca.* 935 B.C.) the region became exposed to attacks from Syria and apparently was annexed to the latter country, either in the wars of Ben-hadad I against Baasha (I Kings 15:20) or as a result of the appeasement policy of Omri. This loss apparently rankled in the hearts of Israel, but it was not until after the Battle of Qarqar (853 B.C.) that Ahab made an effort to recover the place; it has been suggested that Ramoth-gilead had been promised him by Ben-hadad II as the price of his help against the Assyrians, and that the king of Syria failed to keep his promise. Ahab summoned Jehoshaphat of Judah as his ally, and went to fight with the encouragement of all the prophets except Micaiah the son of Imlah. The battle that ensued was indecisive; but Ahab was fatally wounded by a random arrow, and the army of Israel retired without accomplishing its purpose (I Kings 22).

Ca. ten years later Joram the son of Ahab had greater success. He captured the city and placed a garrison there under the charge of Jehu. He was wounded in the fighting that resulted when the Syrians made a counterattack; and while he was recuperating at Jezreel, a disciple of Elisha came to Ramoth-gilead and anointed Jehu as king. After this choice had been ratified by the army, Jehu set out for Jezreel, taking precautions that no one should leave the city and betray his plans; driving furiously, he surprised Joram, killed him, and seized the throne (II Kings 8:28–9:28).

Ramoth-gilead is not mentioned again in the Bible, but it must have shared the fate of the Gilead region, which was overrun by Hazael, who fought against Jehu and his weak successors; it was recovered by Jeroboam II, only to fall in the eighth century to the might of the Assyrians.

2. Location. The site of Ramoth-gilead is to be sought in a place which has a strong natural position in N Gilead, near the Syrian border, close to a plain where chariots could maneuver, and which was in existence during the Israelite period. The place that fulfils all these requirements is Tell er-Ramith on the Wadi Shomer, a three-knolled hill which rises commandingly over the nearby plain. Its name also is a natural derivative from Ramoth.

Bibliography. N. Glueck, "Explorations in Eastern Palestine IV," *AASOR,* vols. XXV-XXVIII (1951), pt. I, pp. 95-100.
                        S. Cohen

RAMPART [חל, חיל, encirclement]. The outer fortification encircling a city, consisting of a broad embankment usually made of earth.

It is not always clear whether the Hebrew word refers to the rampart or to the moat between the rampart and the wall. Cities in Palestine said to have such defenses were Abel of Beth-maacah (II Sam. 20:15); Jezreel (I Kings 21:23; RSV "bounds," reading חלק for חל with some Hebrew MSS and versions; KJV "wall"), and Jerusalem (Pss. 48:13—H 48:14; 122:7 KJV [RSV WALLS]; Lam. 2:8), though in the last case only the N side was thus fortified (*see* JERUSALEM); it seems likely, however, that they were usual for most fortified cities. The term "rampart" is sometimes used of fortifications in general, as in the case of Thebes, whose rampart was a sea (Nah. 3:8), or Tyre (Zech. 9:3).

See also FORTIFICATION.   J. W. Wevers

RAM'S HORN (SHOPHAR). *See* MUSICAL INSTRUMENTS.

RAMSES răm′sēz [Egyp. *rʿ-ms-sw,* (the sun-god) Ra is the one who begot him; Akkad. *Riamashshi;* Ῥαμέσσης]. The name carried by eleven pharaohs of the Nineteenth and Twentieth Dynasties in Egypt.

Ramses I (1303-1302 B.C.) founded the Nineteenth Dynasty. The preceding dynasty had won Egypt's Asiatic empire, but had been stained by the heresy of AKH-EN-ATON. Ramses was first a military man and then a vizier, who apparently seized the throne in a time of dynastic weakness. The Eighteenth Dynasty had arisen in the S of Egypt. The Nineteenth

From *Atlas of the Bible* (Thomas Nelson & Sons Limited)

4. On the helmet of Ramses II (1290-1224 B.C.) is the serpent Uraeus, and in his hand is a scepter, both symbols of his regal authority; probably from Karnak

had a N devotion to the sun-god Ra of On (Heliopolis) and to Seth, god of deserts, mountain thunder, and foreign countries. The dynasty moved its capital to the NE Delta; and the successor of Ramses I, Seti I, took energetic steps to try to regain the Asiatic empire, which had been lost in the reign of Akhen-Aton.

The long reign of Ramses II (1290-1224) left an indelible mark upon Egypt.* He built extensively, and he attached his name to monuments of his predecessors. His reign began in war against the Hittites and achieved a dignified peace. The sheer fact of long stability under a single ruler made him a model for the emulation of his successors. In point of fact, he does not seem to have had the energy, vision, or taste of his father, Seti I; and after the death of Ramses II, Egypt's external and internal problems came to rapid crises. Since he founded in the Delta the royal residence city, Per-Rameses, which is the biblical store city RAMESES, he is the traditional Pharaoh of the Oppression. Ramses II completed the great hypostyle hall in the temple of Karnak, built the Rameseum at Thebes as his mortuary temple, executed the great cliff temple of Abu Simbel in Nubia, and erected colossi at Memphis and numerous other monuments in Egypt, Nubia, and Asia. Fig. RAM 4.

At the beginning of his reign Ramses II inherited a serious political problem. At the time of Egypt's military weakness under Akh-en-Aton, the Hittites of Anatolia had spread their power and had come to dominate N Syria, taking lands which had once been part of the Egyptian Empire. At the same time there was a great migration of the "Sea Peoples" into the E Mediterranean and its coasts. Among these Sea Peoples there were elements which were later to become essential components of the Greeks and the Romans, such as Achaeans, Dardanians, Mysians, Sardinians, and also the Philistines. These people were raiders by land and sea, and they endangered Egypt's lucrative trade from Asia. In the first instance, many of them combined with the Hittites against the Egyptians. Then within a century they overran and overturned the Hittite state.

In Ramses II's fifth year he marched N to fight against the Hittites and their Anatolian and Sea People allies in Syria. Through brash stupidity Ramses walked into a Hittite ambush at Kadesh on the Orontes. His personal courage and the timely arrival of reinforcements released him from disgraceful defeat. He was able to retire to Egypt in good order and there carved acres of wall space with a boastful claim of victory over the Hittites. However, his subsequent campaigning in Asia was chiefly in Palestine, carried out against such towns as Ashkelon, Eltekeh, and Merom.

The Hittites themselves found the Sea Peoples a constant threat and were perhaps affected by the slowly growing power of Assyria. In Ramses II's twenty-first year hostilities between Egypt and the Hittites were ended by a solemn treaty of peace and mutual assistance against an outside aggressor. In the pharaoh's thirty-fourth year the alliance was cemented by his marriage to the daughter of the Hittite king. For nearly forty years there was peace and prosperity. Ramses II lived on, to sire a tremendous family, build extensively, and celebrate at least eleven jubilees of rule.

The cult of Ramses II as a god was active in his own lifetime. His real and fictional exploits were used to build him into a legendary hero for the next millennium, with an analogy to the later figures of Alexander and Caesar. It is entirely possible that some, at least, of the Children of Israel were employed as slave labor on the building enterprises of Ramses II, such as the cities of Pithom and Rameses. Practically all those who ultimately came to form the Hebrew nation had some tradition of Egyptian domination, either as slaves in Egypt or as Palestinian vassals under the Egyptian Empire. This common experience could be unified and personalized by making the Egyptian oppressor a single figure, Ramses II, under whom some of them had been in bondage. There is more than poetic justice in seeing him as the Pharaoh of the Oppression.

Ramses II was succeeded by his son MER-NE-PTAH. Wars against foreign invaders and the internal weakness of the state brought the Nineteenth Dynasty into disorder, and ca. 1200 B.C. there was even a brief interlude in which an Asiatic usurper ruled Egypt. From this disorder the Twentieth Dynasty redeemed the land.

Ramses III (1195-1164)* did his best to model his reign upon that of his famed namesake, going so far as to copy whole scenes and inscriptions from Ramses II. The internal politics of the reign of Ramses III are clouded with obscurity; his foreign problems are specifically stated. The movements of the Sea Peoples came to a climax, and the older populations along the E Mediterranean coast were being dislodged. Twice Ramses III had to defend his W frontier against Libyan invasions. In his eighth year

Courtesy of the University Museum of the University of Pennsylvania

5. Limestone statue of Ramses III (1195-1164 B.C.)

he met a major crisis, the attack by a swarm of Sea Peoples, among whom the Philistines were a chief factor. They had overwhelmed the Hittites and established a camp in Syria as base for their proposed invasion of the Egyptian Delta. On land Ramses fought them along the seacoast of Syria-Palestine, but their fleet had to be met within the mouths of the Nile. He was victorious in both the land and the naval battle. Temporarily the S movement of the Sea Peoples had been checked. Yet within thirty-five years Egypt withdrew from her Asiatic empire and abandoned her copper mines in Sinai, while the Philistines settled along the Palestinian coast. In its total force, the immigration of the Sea Peoples finished both the Hittite and the Egyptian empires, deposited the Philistines in the land of Canaan, permitted the Children of Israel to become a nation, produced those difficult adjustments of new peoples which led to the siege of Troy, and was the first chapter in the history of Greece and Rome. Fig. RAM 5.

The later years of Ramses III were marked by internal disorders, with strikes by the unpaid government laborers and a palace conspiracy which probably took the life of the pharaoh. The long period of Egyptian domination of the E Mediterranean world was drawing to a close, and she was becoming that futilely intriguing force which she was in the days of Isaiah.

Ramses III left a political-religious will, in which he confirmed the temples of Egypt in the estates which they possessed at his death. The data are not clear enough for precision, but they do demonstrate that in the twelfth century B.C. the Egyptian temples owned an extraordinary proportion of the "free" and slave peoples in Egypt, of the agricultural land, and of movable property, and enjoyed huge annual incomes. In an awesome way the document illustrates the secular power of the Egyptian priesthood.

The age of the later Ramessides may be summarized briefly. A bronze base for a small statue of Ramses VI found at Megiddo need not necessarily mean Egyptian occupation of that Canaanite town *ca.* 1150 B.C., as this type of object was sometimes a royal gift to a friendly prince. With the coming of the Iron Age, Egypt, which had no iron, suffered a crippling economic inflation, and there was widespread distress and lawlessness. Mercenary soldiers, deprived of their chance for foreign booty, roamed through Egypt and pillaged defenseless towns. An era of open corruption began, with bold and unchecked robbery of the treasures in the royal and noble tombs at Thebes.

By 1100 B.C. the pharaoh had become a feeble palace figure, and there was a contest for power among the vizier, the army commander, and the high priest of Amon at Thebes. In the end the military man won out and founded the Twenty-first Dynasty *ca.* 1090. However, it was a victory of compromise, and the rule of Egypt was divided between merchant princes of Tanis (Zoan) in the Delta and the generals who also held the priesthood at Thebes.

Just before 1100 an Egyptian commissioner went to Byblos (Gebal) in Phoenicia, to purchase cedar for the temple of Amon at Karnak. His misfortunes at the hands of some of the Sea Peoples settled along the coast of Palestine and the brusque treatment

which he received from the prince of Byblos vividly illustrate the low esteem which the once mighty power of Egypt was now accorded in that part of Asia where she had once been dominant.

Bibliography. J. H. Breasted, *Cambridge Ancient History,* II (1924), 131-95; J. A. Wilson, *The Burden of Egypt* (1951), pp. 239-92; G. Steindorff and K. C. Seele, *When Egypt Ruled the East* (2nd ed., 1957), pp. 248-70.   J. A. WILSON

RANSOM [כפר, cover, bribe, appeasement, obliteration, reparation, *cf.* Akkad. *kapāru,* wipe off; פדיון, redemption, *cf.* Akkad. *padū,* liberate, ransom; Arab. *fidan,* release price; λύτρον, means of release, price of ransoming]. Something given which "covers" or cancels an incurred claim over a person or a group; the price of deliverance from an incurred status (cf. Exod. 21:30; I Sam. 14:45; Job 33:24; 36:18-19; Ps. 49:7-9; Prov. 6:35 KJV [RSV COMPENSATION]; Isa. 43:3; Jer. 31:11 in vss. 7-14). The life Jesus lived and his death are the means of release from the powers of law, sin, and death (Matt. 20:28; Mark 10:45; I Tim. 2:6; cf. Isa. 52:13–53:12).

See also ATONEMENT; PROPITIATION; REDEEM; SALVATION.

Bibliography. J. Pedersen, *Israel: Its Life and Culture,* I-II (1946), 399.   T. M. MAUCH

RAPE. *See* CRIMES AND PUNISHMENTS § C3.

RAPHA rā′fə [רפא, he (God) has healed, *probably shortened form of* Raphael (*cf. also* בית רפא *and* רפוא); LXX Ραφη; KJV רפה (RSV RAPHAH); *confusion exists between* רפא *and* רפה *when used as a common noun,* GIANT(S)]. The fifth son of Benjamin, according to I Chr. 8:2; but he is not mentioned in the list of Benjamin's sons in Gen. 46:21, where Naaman is fifth.

See also GIANT.   L. HICKS

RAPHAEL răf′ĭ əl, rā′fĭ— [רפאל; Ραφαήλ]. The angel of healing, who was sent to remove the white films from the eyes of Tobit and to bind Asmodeus, the evil demon, so that Sarah, daughter of Raguel, might marry Tobias son of Tobit (for the whole story, *see* TOBIT).

The names of specific angels are rarely mentioned in the Bible, and only in the later books. The Talmud records that the names were derived from Babylon—i.e., they are ascribed to Parthian influence (*see* ANGEL). Raphael's name is not found in the canonical books. In Enoch 20:3 he is recognized as second in the order of angels. He is also described as binding Azazel hand and foot and throwing him into a pit (Enoch 10:4).

In many ways Raphael may be compared to MICHAEL. The appearance of these angels in the later literature is evidence of the growing importance in popular belief of angelic intervention in human affairs.

See the bibliography under TOBIT.

    S. B. HOENIG

RAPHAH rā′fə [רפה] (I Chr. 8:37); KJV RAPHA. Alternately: REPHAIAH rĭ fā′yə [רפיה] (I Chr. 9:43). A descendant of Saul of Benjamin; son of Binea, and the father of Eleasah.

RAPHAIM răf'ĭ əm ['Ραφαίν; Vulg. *Raphaïm*] (Jth. 8:1). Ancestor of Judith; listed in her genealogy as son of Ahitub, and the father of Gideon.

J. C. SWAIM

RAPHIA rə fī'ə ['Ραφία, 'Ράφεια]. A city *ca.* fifteen miles SW of Gaza. Although not mentioned in the Bible, it existed from OT times. Modern Rafah is on the site of Raphia, which ancient sources describe as halfway between Rhinocolura and Gaza (Strabo XVI.ii.31; Polybius V.80). It was important as the last city of Palestine on the great military highway from Asia to Egypt, and was regarded as the first city of Syria (Jos. War IV.xi.5). The territory of Raphia extended as far as the Egyptian border.

The strategic position of the city made it a military outpost and fated it to be the site of many battles between Egypt and the nearest ruling power of Asia. Here Sargon II of Assyria defeated the Egyptians in 720 B.C. It was largely Jewish until late in the fourth century B.C., when it fell under the Ptolemies of Egypt and became predominantly Greek. Raphia was the site of the famous battle in which Ptolemy Philopator severely defeated Antiochus the Great in 217 B.C. (III Macc. 1:2; Polybius V.80). Captured by Alexander Janneus *ca.* 97 B.C., it was again restored as a Hellenistic city by Gabinius in 55 B.C. (Jos. Antiq. XIII.xiii.3; XIV.v.3).

Bibliography. W. O. E. Oesterley and T. H. Robinson, *A History of Israel* (1932), I, 379; II, 179, 204, 291. F.-M. Abel, *Géographie de la Palestine,* I (1933), 310; II (1938), 147, 172, 431-32.   D. C. PELLETT

RAPHON rā'fŏn [Ραφών]. A city near Carnaim (Karnaim) where Judas Maccabeus defeated the Syrian general Timothy (I Macc. 5:37-43). It may be the same as Anrapha in the list of Thutmose III. Since Carnaim is the same as ASHTEROTH-KARNAIM, the modern Sheikh Sa'ad, Raphon is probably the village of er-Rafeh on the right bank of the Nahr el-Ehreir, about eight miles NE of that site.

S. COHEN

RAPHU rā'fū [רפוא, healed] (Num. 13:9). The father of Palti, who was sent from the tribe of Benjamin to spy out the land of Canaan.

Bibliography. M. Noth, *Die israelitischen Personennamen* (1928), p. 179.

RAS SHAMRA räs shäm'rə. The name of a Syrian mound, meaning "fennel mound." Here was located ancient UGARIT.

RASSIS răs'ĭs ['Ρασσίς]; KJV RASSES răs'ēz (Jth. 2:23). A place, apparently near Cilicia, the people of which were devastated by the army of Holofernes. Some have thought the name to be a corruption of "Tarsus," as the Vulg. suggests. Others relate it to a Rossos mentioned by the ancient geographers Strabo (*Geography* XIV.5.19; XVI.2.8) and Ptolemy (*Geography* V.14), which Stummer believes is the modern Arsus, a Grecianized form of the Semitic *Ras(s)ûs.* Since the momentous Battle of Issus was fought near Jebel Arsus, the writer may have had this event in mind in mentioning this otherwise obscure spot.

Bibliography. F. Stummer, *Geographie des Buches Judith* (1947), pp. 24-25.   E. W. SAUNDERS

RATHAMIN răth'ə mĭn [Ραθαμιν]; KJV RAMATHEM răm'ə thĕm [Ραμαθεμ]; ASV RAMATHAIM răm'ə thā'əm [Ραμαθαιμ]. One of the three toparchies which Demetrius Nicator of Syria (*ca.* 150 B.C.) took from Samaria and gave to Jonathan Maccabeus (I Macc. 11:34). Since the other two toparchies were Apherima (Ephraim) and Lydda, this must have been in the same region of Palestine as they were. However, no such place is known to have existed; furthermore Josephus, who used I Maccabees as a source, gives the name as "Ramatha" in a parallel passage (Antiq. XIII.iv.9). Hence it is probable that "Rathamin," although attested by the oldest MSS, is an early corruption from "Ramathem" or "Ramathaim," due to the fact that the succession of the consonants "r-th-m" was more agreeable to the Greek ear than "r-m-th." This toparchy would then be the district around the well-known home of the prophet Samuel.

See also RAMAH 4.   S. COHEN

RATHUMUS. KJV Apoc. form of REHUM 2.

RATTLES-SISTRUM. *See* MUSICAL INSTRUMENTS.

RAVEN [ערב, *'ôrēbh, possibly onomatopoeic; cf.* Akkad. *āribu, ēribu;* Arab. *ghariba,* be black; *ghurāb,* crow, raven; κόραξ (Luke 12:24); *cf.* Lat. *cornix,* crow; *corvus,* raven]. The largest of the passerine birds, a member of the Corvidae family, which includes also the crows, rooks, jackdaws, magpies, jays, and choughs. The ravens, like the rooks, are conspicuous by their black plumage (cf. Song of S. 5:11), but the other genera are less soberly colored. The raven is essentially a scavenger, but it will attack any weak or defenseless young living animal (cf. Prov. 30:17; on crows' picking out the eyes of their prey, see Aristophanes *Birds* 582-83).

Among the unclean birds we find "every raven according to its kind" (Lev. 11:15; cf. Deut. 14:14); this phrase suggests a group of birds resembling the common raven (*Corvus corax*), and it is therefore probable that ערב is a general term for the whole family. Tristram found no fewer than eight species of this group in Palestine in his day—viz., three ravens, two jackdaws, one crow, one rook, and one chough (*NHB* 200). That ravens are able to obtain the necessary food, both for themselves and for their young, is cited in both the OT and the NT as illustrative of the providential care of God for his creation (Job 38:41; Ps. 147:9; Luke 12:24; cf. "birds of the air" in Matt. 6:26). Two of the most familiar raven references are in the flood story (Gen. 8:7) and the account of Elijah's being fed by the ravens (I Kings 17).

W. S. McCULLOUGH

RAZIS rā'zĭs ['Ραζείς (A), Ραζίς (V*ᵛⁱᵈ)] (II Macc. 14:37-46). One of the elders of Jerusalem whose kindness earned him the name "father of the Jews." He was sought out by Nicanor as an object of contempt against the Jews; but to escape such ignominy, he committed suicide, the account of which is rather gory.   C. T. FRITSCH

RAZOR [תַעַר, LXX ξυρόν; מוֹרָה, LXX σίδηρος, any instrument of iron]. A cutting instrument used in SHAVING or cutting the hair (forbidden to the NAZARITE). The razor may have been a simple knife, probably elongated with rounded end, or an elaborate instrument, sometimes decorated. Ezekiel symbolically employs his sword as a barber's razor (Ezek.

Courtesy of the University Museum of the University of Pennsylvania

6. Egyptian bronze razor with handle, blade partly broken; from Buhen, Nubia (1550-1090 B.C.)

Courtesy of the University Museum of the University of Pennsylvania

7. Egyptian bronze razor blade, from the Eighteenth Dynasty (1550-1350 B.C.)

5:1). תַעַר in Jer. 36:23 is probably a PENKNIFE (so RSV). Figs. RAZ 6-7.

Bibliography. For some of the suggested archaeological examples, see: R. A. S. Macalister, *Gezer*, II (1912), 267-68, 271; III (1912), pls. CXCVIII (especially nos. 5-10), CXCIX (note nos. 10-11). W. M. F. Petrie, *Tools and Weapons* (1917), pp. 49-50, pls. LX-LXI; *Ancient Gaza*, vol. I (1931), pl. XXI:117; vol. II (1932), pl. XV:81; vol. III (1938), pl. XXIV:136. W. F. Albright, *Tell Beit Mirsim*, vol. III, *AASOR*, XXI-XXII (1941-43), 78, pl. 61:17.　　　　　R. W. FUNK

RE rā. Alternately: RA rä. The Egyptian sun-god, whose chief cult center was Thebes. *See* EGYPT.

REAIAH rē ā′yə [רְאָיָה, Y has seen]; KJV REAIA in I Chr. 5:5; AIRUS ā i′rəs [ʼΙαῖρος] in I Esd. 5:31.
1. A Judahite; son of Shobal and father of Jahath (I Chr. 4:2); called Haroeh in I Chr. 2:52.
2. A Reubenite; son of Micah and father of Baal (I Chr. 5:5).
3. Head of a family of temple servants, or Nethinim, who returned from the Exile with Zerubbabel (Ezra 2:47=Neh. 7:50; I Esd. 5:31).

E. R. ACHTEMEIER

REAPING. The harvesting of grain by hand. The worker grasps a few stalks and cuts them off with a small sickle made of flints set in a wooden or bone haft or, especially after the tenth century B.C., a small curved blade. *See* AGRICULTURE.

REBA rē′bə [רֶבַע] (Num. 31:8; Josh. 13:21). One of the five Midianite kings killed in battle by the Israelites under Moses. In Num. 31 the battle is apparently

to be set against the background of the religious apostasy into which Israel had fallen under Midianite enticements (ch. 25). In Josh. 13, however, the five Midianite leaders, called princes of Sihon, are said to have fallen in the same battle in which Moses defeated Sihon the Amorite king.　　　　R. F. JOHNSON

REBEKAH rĭ bĕk′ə [רִבְקָה, *probably* cow]; NT REBECCA [ʼΡεβέκκα, *after* LXX *of* OT *form*] (Rom. 9: 10). Daughter of Bethuel, sister of Laban, wife of Isaac, and mother of Esau and Jacob.

Older etymologies derive this name from the root רבק, "to tie fast," with reference to Rebekah's "binding" beauty. But it more probably comes by metathesis from the feminine of the word בָּקָר, "cattle," analogously to other names in the patriarch narratives, such as Rachel ("ewe") and perhaps Leah ("cow") and Zilpah ("short-nosed animal").

Rebekah is introduced in the Genesis narrative in ch. 24, which recounts her betrothal and marriage to ISAAC. The virgin daughter of the Aramean Bethuel, Abraham's nephew (22:23; 25:20), she was renowned for her beauty (24:15-16). Her hospitality in drawing water for Abraham's servant according to his special prayer was taken by him as a token that she was to be Isaac's wife (24:10-27). After negotiations with her family (vss. 28-60), she was conducted to Isaac for their wedding (vss. 66-67).

After twenty years of barrenness (Gen. 25:21, 26), Rebekah conceived twins as a result of Isaac's prayer. Alarmed at their struggling inside her, she obtained an oracle concerning their perpetual hostility (vss. 22-23). After Esau and Jacob were born (vss. 24-26), the latter became her favorite (vs. 28).

In Gen. 26, Rebekah and Isaac are represented as repeating the roles of Sarah and Abraham in ch. 20, passing themselves off as sister and brother out of fear of the Philistines, in whose territory they were dwelling. When, however, the king Abimelech discerned their true relationship, he sternly reprimanded them for giving his people an occasion for sin (26: 6-11).

Rebekah and Isaac joined in disapproving Esau's marriage with two Hittite women (Gen. 26:34-35), but favoritism brought family strife when Rebekah plotted with Jacob to cheat Esau out of the blessing Isaac intended for him (27:5-17). As a result she had to urge Jacob to flee to Paddan-aram to escape Esau's revenge (vss. 42-46). Apparently Jacob never saw his mother again. Her death is not mentioned, but Gen. 49:31 reports that she was buried in the cave of Mach-pelah.

The only NT mention of Rebekah is in Rom. 9: 10-12, where the oracle of Gen. 25:23 is cited as a demonstration of divine elective purpose.

Bibliography. H. Bauer, "Was bedeutet Rebekka?" *ZDMG*, LXVII (1913), 344; "Die hebräischen Eigennamen als sprachliche Erkenntnisquelle," *ZAW*, XLVIII (1930), 78.

S. J. DE VRIES

RECAH rē′kə [רֵכָה]; KJV RECHAH. An unknown place in Judah (I Chr. 4:12). Perhaps one should read "Rechab" with the LXX B (cf. 2:55).

RECHAB rē′kăb [רֵכָב, *rēkhābh, probably* rider, *from* to mount, ride, *or possibly a contraction of* רִכְבְּאֵל (*the* god of Barrakab); LXX 'Ρηχάβ]; RECHABITES rĕk'ə bīts. 1. A son of Rimmon, a Benjaminite from Beeroth. He and his brother Baanah were captains of raiding bands under Saul's son Ishbosheth. They murdered their master and brought his head to David, who, instead of rewarding them as they had hoped, ordered them executed, their hands and feet severed, and their bodies hanged beside the pool at Hebron (II Sam. 4).

* 2. Father or ancestor of J(eh)onadab, the zealous supporter of Jehu in the extermination of the house of Ahab and the violent suppression of Baal-worship (II Kings 10:15-27; see JONADAB 2). The name Rechab became the patronymic designating a group of devotees of the nomadic way of life, the "house of the Rechabites." All our direct information about these Rechabites comes from Jer. 35, where we learn that during Nebuchadrezzar's attack on Judah and siege of Jerusalem, the Rechabites took refuge in the city (vs. 11). They had apparently been living a seminomadic life in the Judean wilderness. They could not have been very numerous, for Jeremiah brought the entire group, the "whole house of the Rechabites," into a single chamber of the temple. He set pitchers of wine and cups before them and bade them drink, but they refused and cited the commands of Jonadab the son of Rechab, their father: "You shall not drink wine, neither you nor your sons for ever; you shall not build a house; you shall not sow seed; you shall not plant or have a vineyard; but you shall live in tents all your days, that you may live many days in the land where you sojourn" (vss. 6-7). These commands, they claimed, they had obeyed. Jeremiah commended their loyalty and contrasted their example with the rest of the inhabitants of Judah and Jerusalem who had been disobedient to the persistent commands of the Lord. The prophet, accordingly, pronounced doom on the unfaithful Judeans, but for the house of the Rechabites he prophesied that Jonadab the son of Rechab would never lack a man to stand before the Lord (vss. 18-19).

The origins of the Rechabites are obscure. The expression "Jonadab the son of Rechab, our father" (Jer. 35:6), is ambiguous; from this alone we could not be sure whether Jonadab or Rechab was considered the founder of the group. It is made clear, however, by vs. 19 that it was Jonadab, rather than Rechab, who was reckoned as the father of the order. Why then were they called Rechabites? We have no knowledge of J(eh)onadab's father, and it may be that the Rechab who is commemorated in the name of the order was a more distant ancestor. An item of the Chronicler's genealogical notes (I Chr. 2:55) is generally taken as a clue to Rechabite origins: the text mentions three families of scribes who dwelt at Jabez, the Tirathites, the Shimeathites, and the Sucathites, and adds (vs. 55b): "These are the Kenites who came from Hammath, the father of the house of Rechab." This enigmatic statement identifies Hammath as the "father of the house of Rechab" (אבי בית רכב). The view that Hammath was the father of Rechab and the grandfather of J(eh)onadab is unlikely. Now Hammath is otherwise unknown as a personal name and occurs elsewhere only as the name of a town in the territory of Napthali (Josh. 19:35). The genealogies of I Chr. 1-9 contain other personifications of place names, and it may be that the intent of this note was to give the Rechabites local connections, but the wording of the text is strange. Most interesting is the implication that the house of Rechab is of Kenite extraction. The Kenites and Midianites (see MIDIAN) were seminomadic tribes on the S borders of Canaan. Many scholars think that the Kenites were the original worshipers of Yahweh and that Moses' Kenite or Midianite father-in-law introduced him to the worship of this god. Groups of Kenites entered Canaan with the Israelites and dwelt among them mostly on the S borders of Judah (Judg. 1:15; I Sam. 15:6; 27:10; 30:29), and one group under Heber pitched tent near Kedesh in Naphtali in the same general region as Hammath, in the time of Deborah (Judg. 4:11, 17). It was the wife of this nomad Kenite chief who struck a crowning blow in an early clash of the Israelites with the Canaanites (4:18-22; 5:24-27). Jehonadab the son of Rechab and his followers may have been descendants of Kenite nomads such as Heber. In Jehu's time these proto-Rechabites were probably a nomad clan who pastured their flocks in marginal areas of the N kingdom, perhaps centering around the town of Hammath in Naphtali. However, the connection between the followers of Jehonadab the son of Rechab and the later house of the Rechabites who took refuge in Jerusalem in Jeremiah's time is not clear; perhaps some of Jehonadab's partisans or descendants migrated to Judah. At any rate, the later Judean Rechabites regarded Jehonadab as their founder.

The rule imposed by Jehonadab is the essence of nomadism. Conflict and antipathy between followers of the nomadic, pastoral mode of life and those of the sedentary, agricultural way is intrinsic and universal. This conflict appears already in Sumerian myths where the farmer is favored over the shepherd. Conversely, in the OT story of Cain and Abel the divine predilection is in favor of the shepherd, and this bias is evident throughout the OT. It was the lawless Cain who first built a city (Gen. 4:17). The patriarchal sagas point up the classic simplicity and ideal purity of the nomad life. The prophetic opposition to the Canaanite way of life drew inspiration from the idealization of the pre-Canaanite past when Israel was a beloved child innocent of Canaanite practices. The law was represented as having been given in this period before Israel was thoroughly contaminated. Elijah in his bitter struggle against Baal-worship gained renewed strength and resolution through a pilgrimage to the desert abode of his god. Amos, Hosea, and Jeremiah contrast Israel's purity in the wilderness with her defilement in Canaan. There were, of course, varieties and degrees of opposition to Canaanite culture. The S tribes were slower to conform than the N tribes, and this was doubtless due in large measure to their closer connections with nomad traditions and ideals. The Rechabites struck at the root of the evil, the tendency to assimilate, by making the nomad mode of life a religious obligation and by rejecting virtually everything Canaanite—except the language.

The Rechabite regulations are the normal ways of nomads. The tent is the nomad abode, and the word continued as an appellative for "dwelling" long after the Israelites had accommodated themselves to houses. The tent peg with which Jael slew Sisera is a fitting symbol of nomad opposition to sedentary culture. The prohibition of agriculture expresses the nomad disdain of such pursuits as unmanly and degrading. The total abstinence from wine is not so much a reaction to the drunken orgies of the Canaanite fertility rites as an attempt to preserve the conditions of nomad life, in which wine was unknown. (The prohibition of wine is reminiscent of the vow of the NAZIRITE, and it may be that the Rechabites influenced the development of this institution.) While the Rechabites were apparently zealous Yahwists like Jehonadab—all the Rechabite names attested contain the element *yeho-* or *-yah:* Jehonadab, Jaazaniah, Habbaziniah, Jeremiah, Malchijah—still their orders are nomadic rather than Yahwistic. Almost identical prohibitions are reported by Diodorus Siculus (XIX. 94) among the Nabateans, their purpose being to remain poor and thus free from fear of subjection by covetous neighbors.

The evidence that the Rechabites as a group survived the Babylonian exile is rather tenuous. There is reference to one Malchijah the son of Rechab, ruler of the district of Beth-haccherem ("house of the vineyard"!) who was given the honor of repairing the Dung Gate in Nehemiah's restoration of Jerusalem (Neh. 3:14); but this is, of itself, evidence that he no longer adhered strictly to the Rechabite rules. The pressure of circumstances must have forced many Rechabites to change their mode of life. In late postexilic times there dwelt at Jabez three families of scribes of Rechabite lineage (I Chr. 2:55). The Talmud (B.B. 91*b*) understood the "potters" mentioned in I Chr. 4:23 to be descendants of Jonadab the son of Rechab. The prophecy of Jeremiah (35: 19) would naturally tend to keep the name and the traditions of the Rechabites alive. The expression "stand before the LORD" (*see* WORSHIP IN THE OT) usually connotes sacerdotal service in the temple (Targ. so interprets this passage), and Jewish tradition has it that the Rechabites entered the temple service by the marriage of their daughters to priests. The LXX superscription of Ps. 71—H 70, missing in the Hebrew, connects the psalm with the sons of Jonadab and the first exiles, and this has been taken as evidence that the Rechabites were among the Levite singers. According to the Talmud (Ta'an. 26*a*), the Rechabites had a special day, the seventh of Ab, for participation in the wood festival of the priests and the people. Hegesippus (Euseb. Hist. II. 23) relates that at the martyrdom of James "one of the priests of the sons of Rechab, of the Rechabites who are mentioned by Jeremiah the prophet," protested the crime. This statement, however, is suspect, since Epiphanius (*Heresy* LXXVIII.14) substitutes "Symeon the brother of James" for "the Rechabite."

Travelers have found "Rechabites" in various places. Benjamin of Tudela (twelfth century) reported that he found near El Jubar in Arabia a community of 100,000 Jews who abstained from wine and meat, gave tithes to teachers, and devoted themselves to study and to weeping for Jerusalem. In the nineteenth century Joseph Wolff thought to have found them in Mesopotamia and in Yemen, and Pierotti reported that he had met a tribe calling

themselves Rechabites near the Dead Sea. The name Rechabites was adopted by a short-lived fraternal order, founded in New England in the middle of the nineteenth century, devoted to total abstinence from alcoholic beverages.

See also ESSENES; KENITES; NOMADISM; POVERTY; WINE AND STRONG DRINK.

Bibliography. K. Budde, *Das nomadische Ideal im AT* (1896); *Die Religion des Volkes Israel* (1899), pp. 112-14. E. Meyer, *Die Israeliten und ihre Nachbarstämme* (1906), pp. 88-89, 129-41. I. Friedlaender, "The Jews of Arabia and the Rechabites," *JQR*, 1 (1910), 253-57. K. Kohler, "The Essenes and the Apocalyptic Literature," *JQR*, 11 (1920-21), 145-68. J. W. Flight, "The Nomadic Idea and Ideal in the OT," *JBL*, 42 (1923), 158-226. P. Humbert, "La logique de la perspective nomade chez Osée et l'unité d'Osée," *Marti Festschrift* (1925), pp. 158-66. L. Gautier, *A propos des Rékabites, Études sur la religion d'Israël* (1927), pp. 104-29. H. Schmökel, "Yahweh and the Kenites," *JBL*, 52 (1933), 212-29. S. Nyström, *Beduinentum und Jahvismus* (1946).   M. H. POPE

RECHAH. KJV form of RECAH.

*RECONCILIATION, RECONCILE. The coming to agreement of two or more persons after misunderstanding or estrangement. There are many instances of this in the Bible, but the dominant theme is the reconciliation of man to God. Man's condition is diagnosed as one of alienation from God his Maker. But the Bible affirms that God has taken steps to overcome this alienation, and has in Christ provided the means of reconciliation.

This is one aspect of the biblical doctrine of redemption. It is in strong contrast to secular thought, which can speak only of man's being reconciled to himself, his fellow man, or his environment. The Bible recognizes the need of reconciliation on these levels, but these relationships are derivative from the common dependence of all on God, and the basic need is to be in right standing with him.

1. In the OT. Basically, sin (*see* SIN, SINNER) in the OT is the breaking of COVENANT obligation. It is variously regarded as missing the mark (חטא); as unconscious wandering from the right path (שׁללה); as deliberate turning aside from the right way (עון)— here the will is involved; as rebellion (פשׁע)—here the thought is of a personal God who is disobeyed; as guilt before a judge—a more forensic idea (רשׁע). The sacrificial system was designed to "atone" for these sins, full account being taken of the fact that most of them are not deliberate transgressions (Lev. 4:1-5; 16:16-17). For wilful sins (Num. 15:30-31) no sacrifice availed, but restitution was required, in some cases the death of the offender. In all cases penitence was presupposed. This was insisted on by the prophets, and found classic expression in Ps. 51; Ezek. 18.

The essential meaning of the regular verb for "atone" (כפר) is uncertain. It may derive from a Babylonian root signifying "wash away," implying the notion of sin as physical impurity; or from an Arabic root signifying "cover," in which case the original conception is perhaps more personal, of sin as a barrier causing estrangement between God and man. The subject of the verb is sometimes the priest, sometimes God. It is to be noted that in Hebrew usage God is never the object of this verb: "atonement" in the OT means expiation of sin, never the placation of God. God provides atonement for man, but does not need to have his own attitude changed.

Other Hebrew terms to be considered are סלח ("forgive"), used with both sin and the sinner as object; פדה ("ransom")—e.g., in Ps. 130:8; גאל ("redeem"), especially in Isa. 43; 44:22-28; 49:7-26.

In the Hebrew we have to consider the terminology of sin and atonement, and the total OT assessment of the problem of man's estrangement from his Maker. This is focused in the classic narrative of Gen. 3, where man and woman, after exposure to temptation, feel unfit to face God. They are aware that God's command has not been obeyed; simultaneous with knowledge of right is consciousness of having done wrong. How is this gulf to be bridged? Man's only hope is the fact that God continues to feel concern for his creature, even though the immediate expression of this concern is punishment. *See* ATONEMENT; MEDIATOR.

2. In the NT. The Greek terms to be considered are mainly the Greek verb καταλλάσσω, its compound ἀποκαταλλάσσω (three times), and its cognate noun καταλαγή. Behind them lie OT ideas of atonement (Lev. 8:15; etc.).

The meaning of these terms is restoration of harmony between man and God. Apart from the reconciling power which God exerts, man is alienated from God; he is ἄθεος, "without God," living on his own resources, and deprived of hope (Eph. 2:12). Another way of describing this alienation is to view it as due to sin; on this view it is the expiation of the sin which effects reconciliation. Sin, as Paul understands it, is an objective state in which man finds himself, even apart from his own choice. *See* SIN.

The main sense is the reconciliation of man to God. Subordinate senses are reconciliation of man with his fellows (Matt. 5:24; I Cor. 7:11) and reconciliation of Jew and Gentile (Rom. 11:7-32; Eph. 2-3).

Four passages demand consideration:

a) Rom. 5:8-11. Here the estrangement between man and God is described as enmity (cf. Rom. 11:28; Col. 1:21). It is misplaced ingenuity to argue, with some commentators, whether this implies that God hates sinners or only that sinful men hate God—or whether this hatred is mutual. The reference is rather to the objective condition; the broken relationship is a gulf needing to be bridged. The enmity mentioned in Jas. 4:4 is less objective, for here the possibility of opposing God by deliberate choice is envisaged. Paul's thought is at a deeper level, where the question of human will is not primarily in view (but cf. Rom. 8:7). The notion of hostility has an OT root in Exod. 23:22; Isa. 1:24; and the frequent references in the Psalms to "enemies." The concept of the divine wrath is in Paul's mind—i.e., the reaction of holy love to sin and the secular attitude (*see* WRATH OF GOD). But it is the divine love (Rom. 5:8) which is at work in this situation making a new harmony possible. Only God could do this; man as sinner is helpless (vs. 6). It is not God's attitude which needs to be changed, but man's. God may be said to hate sin, but at the same time he loves the sinner (vss. 6-8). The expression of God's love was Christ and his self-sacrifice.

How this could become effective for reconciliation Paul does not elucidate. We must assume that he conceived Christ's death to have the efficacy attributed to the blood of sacrificial victims—viz., of releasing new potencies which took the place of the sin of the participators in sacrificial worship (so Rom. 3:25; 8:3); or of inaugurating a covenant (Mark 14:24; I Cor. 11:25). Alternatively we may suppose that in some way Christ exhausted the power of sin (II Cor. 5:21; Gal. 3:13), or overcame the demonic forces which cause sin and misery (I Cor. 2:6, 8; Col. 2:15). *See* MEDIATOR.

b) Col. 1:20-22 (perhaps the maturest thought of Paul). Here the reconciliation is extended to beings other than man (vs. 20*b*), and the moral perfection which is its ultimate outcome is emphasized (vs. 22*b*). Christ's death is again underlined as the means.

c) II Cor. 5:14-21. As a Christian preacher and church organizer, Paul has a message about reconciliation which God has already effected for mankind which was not truly living, but spiritually dead —i.e., because of sin (vss. 19, 21). Entirely new possibilities have been created, and are available when one is "in Christ"—i.e., has made the full response of faith (vs. 17). Christ entered the sinful human environment (vs. 21) and accepted its consequences, even to the point of actually dying (vs. 15). Insofar as God was active in him, this created a new situation, with benefits for all men (vs. 15) and the world (vs. 19). The participle in vs. 19, "reconciling," does not imply that this is a process not yet complete; it indicates the continuous activity of God during Christ's earthly ministry. But the benefits have been secured, and only await appropriation by successive generations of mankind to whom the appeal of Christian preaching is to be made (vs. 20).

d) Eph. 2:12-17. This passage has in view the fact of Christian experience that the apparently insoluble antipathy of Jew and non-Jew can be overcome. Christ has removed the barrier (vs. 14) and "slain" the hostility (vs. 16; the RSV misses the subtle point here: it is not really Christ who is slain on the cross, but the hostility which separates men from one another and from God). Gentiles as well as Jews find their true life and spiritual home in the divinely indwelt society which Christ inaugurated (vss. 18:22; *see also* PEACE IN THE NT). This is evidence of divine operation, since the gulf between Gentile and Jew was regarded in the ancient Roman Empire as more unbridgeable than the modern disparity between East and West, Communist and non-Communist.

Summarizing, we note: (*a*) It is God who effects reconciliation. He is the subject, mankind the object. God takes the initiative; only he can act in this situation of estrangement. (*b*) Reconciliation is not a process, but a completed act. "We have now received our reconciliation" through Christ (Rom. 5:11). (*c*) Christ is the agent of reconciliation; more particularly, his atoning death (Rom. 5:6-9).

Bibliography. J. Denney, *The Christian Doctrine of Reconciliation* (1917), is still worth consulting; also his *Death of Christ* (1902). Outstanding among recent work is V. Taylor, *Forgiveness and Reconciliation* (1941), especially pp. 83-129.

E. C. BLACKMAN

RECORDER [מַזְכִּיר, *from* זכר (*Hiph'îl*), cause to remember; בעלמעם (I Esd. 2:17; KJV STORYWRITER)]. An official of high rank in the royal court of Israel. Perhaps originally he kept in mind the decrees and the judgments of the king, and possibly the customs (mores) of the people. He is closer to the CHANCELLOR or cupbearer than to the scribes. He advised the king and probably was in charge of royal chronicles and annals. Jehoshaphat served as recorder for both David and Solomon (II Sam. 8:16; I Kings 4:3; I Chr. 18:15). Joah son of Asaph represented Hezekiah in negotiations with the Assyrian Rabshakeh (II Kings 18:18, 37; Isa. 36:3, 22). He was also involved in the payment of laborers in the repairs to the temple made under Josiah (II Chr. 34:8, where he seems to outrank or at least parallel the governor of the city).   C. U. WOLF

RED. Pigment of varying intensities of red was obtained from insects, vegetables, and minerals in ancient times (*see* COLORS; CRIMSON; SCARLET; VERMILION). However, where the word "red" has been selected to translate Hebrew or Greek terms in the Bible, the reference is primarily to the color of natural objects.

In the OT, the most characteristic of these words is אדם or אדום and its derivatives. The ruddy, healthy appearance of the newborn Esau is expressed by אדמוני in Gen. 25:25, and rendered by πυρράκης in the LXX (*see* EDOM for the connection between Edomites and the color red). Elsewhere אדם as the color of pottage (Gen. 25:30), wine (Prov. 23:31), the sacrificial heifer (Num. 19:2), and horses (Zech. 1:8; 6:2) is also translated "red." The word אדמדם designates the "reddish" hue appearing in garments (Lev. 13:49), or on body spots (Lev. 13:19, 24, etc.) where LEPROSY is suspected.

The use of derivatives of אדם to describe rams' skins (Exod. 25:5, etc.) and war shields (Nah. 2:3) suggests the artificial production of "red" color. In Isa. 63:1-2 a play upon words is implied in the similarity between Edom (אדום) and the red (אדם) apparel which the eschatological conqueror wears.

Through popular etymology a relationship between אדמים ("red") and דם ("blood") is indicated in the allusion to water appearing as "red as blood" (II Kings 3:22). The significance of the color red as a symbol of sin is apparent in Isa. 1:18.

Other Hebrew words have also been interpreted as referring to natural red color. A red (חמר) face follows weeping (Job 16:16), and eyes are red (חכלילי) or dull from wine (Gen. 49:12). In Ps. 75:8, "foaming" (RSV) is a more precise translation of חמר than "red" (KJV); likewise "porphyry" (RSV) is a more accurate rendering of בהט than "red" (KJV) in Esth. 1:6. The word חמר is translated "red" in Isa. 27:2 KJV; however חמד "pleasant" (RSV), was probably the original reading.

In the NT, the Greek verb πυρράζω, "to be fiery red," is used to describe the color of the sky (Matt. 16:2-3); and πυρρός identifies the color of the apocalyptic horse (Rev. 6:4) and dragon (12:3).
                                            C. L. WICKWIRE

RED HEIFER [פרה אדמה, *lit.* a red cow (Num. 19:2, 5-6, 8-10); δάμαλις, heifer (Heb. 9:13)]. The animal whose ashes were the principal ingredient of the "water for impurity" used to counteract uncleanness caused by contact with death. *See* CLEAN AND UNCLEAN §§ 3*a*, 4; DEATH; WATER FOR IMPURITY.

The ritual of the red heifer is described in the OT only in Num. 19, where it comes as a direct command of Yahweh to Moses and Aaron, and is referred to in the Mishna, tractates Ohaloth and Parah. A red heifer which had never been put to profane or common use, and which was unmarred by lameness, blindness, or the like (and, hence, was acceptable as a sacrifice [Lev. 22:20-25; Deut. 17:1]), was brought to the priest, taken outside the camp, and slaughtered (Num. 19:2-3). The officiating priest sprinkled some of the blood seven times toward the front of the tent of meeting (vs. 4), making the animal sacred to Yahweh. It was not, however, a true sacrifice, since the carcass was burned outside the camp, not at the altar. Probably the subsequent use of the ash to remove uncleanness made the animal offensive to the holiness of Yahweh, and prevented its being brought into the sanctuary. The entire animal was burned, including the blood and dung: this was a unique case in OT rituals, where the blood was normally drained off and sprinkled at the altar. The priest threw cedar wood, hyssop, and scarlet thread on the burning carcass, so that all were reduced to ash together (vs. 6). The same three substances were used in the purification of cured lepers (*see* LEPROSY), but in this case the hyssop and cedar wood, bound together with the scarlet thread, were used to apply the cleansing agent to the leper (Lev. 14:6-7). The cleansing and healing power of HYSSOP, the tough durability of the CEDAR, and the red color of the thread, suggestive of blood, have powerful symbolic value in such rituals, but they are clearly components of secondary importance to the ashes of the heifer (Num. 19:10, 17; Heb. 9:13). A clean person gathered the composite ash and stored it "outside the camp in a clean place" (Num. 19:9) until it was needed to treat a case of uncleanness caused by death (i.e., a person who had touched a dead body, a human bone, or a grave, or who had been in a dwelling where a dead body lay; vss. 14, 16, 18).

When such a case arose, some of the ash was added to spring water in a vessel, and the resultant mixture, called the WATER FOR IMPURITY (מי נדה—i.e., the "water for the removal of impurity"), was sprinkled from a bunch of hyssop over an infected person and over the interior and exterior of a contaminated house. Contact with the dead produced a seven-day uncleanness, and the "water for impurity" had to be applied on the third and seventh days under penalty of expulsion from Israel (vss. 13, 18-19).

The officiating priest (vs. 7), the one who burned the heifer (vs. 8), the one who gathered the ash (vs. 10), and the one who sprinkled the water (vs. 19) became "unclean until evening." Most commentators ascribe this uncleanness to contact with a sacred object, on the analogy of the later rabbinic doctrine that touching the sacred books "defiled the hands." Since, however, priests were not made unclean by handling sacred objects in their normal duties, it seems better to appeal to the ancient principle of association. The heifer, which was to remove uncleanness, became unclean in advance of its use, just as an unused coffin or an empty gallows causes revulsion to some because of the associations of the use to which it will be put.

The ordinary word for "cow" (פרה), not the specific term for "heifer" (עגלה), is used in Num. 19. The translation "heifer" is a deduction from the further description of the animal (vs. 2), which implies that it is young, and is supported by a passage in the Canaanite Baal Epic, where the Ugaritic equivalents of the Hebrew "cow" and "heifer" are used in parallelism in reference to the same animal (Baal V.1.18). The red color suggests blood, the most powerful of all OT cleansing agents; but, since the Hebrew terminology of color is not exact, it may also refer to the reddish-brown color of the earth (*see* COLORS), and reflect a pre-Israelite stage of the ritual in which it was a sacrifice to placate the spirits of the dead which dwell beneath the earth. *See* DEAD, ABODE OF.

The heifer (עגלה) was a sacrificial animal in Israel from earliest times (Gen. 15:9; I Sam. 16:2), and female lambs and goats were preferred as sin offerings (חטאת; Lev. 4:28; 5:6; 14:10, 13; Num. 6:14), a term applied to the red heifer (Num. 19:17). A heifer, killed in an uncultivated valley beside a running stream, was used to purge the land of the blood-guilt incurred in an unsolved murder. The elders of the village nearest the scene of the crime were made to declare their ignorance of the murder and to wash their hands over the body of the slain animal (Deut. 21:1-9). The heifer became a symbol of beauty (Jer. 46:20), sexuality (50:11), and stubbornness (Hos. 4:16).

The law of the red heifer is one of those rituals which, like the release of the scapegoat (Lev. 16) and the ordeal of jealousy (Num. 5:11-31; *see* AZAZEL; WATER OF BITTERNESS), came into Israelite practice from pagan sources, probably through the mediation of the Canaanites. The dead are universally objects of dread, and societies as far removed from one another as the Aztecs of Mexico and the Greeks of the classical period saw in them a potent source of uncleanness. The spirits of the dead could injure the community of the living unless the prescribed ritual precautions were taken. These frequently involved bovine animals. In India the urine of the ox is used in purification from the dead, and some hill tribes sacrifice water buffalo to the shades of their ancestors at the annual Guar.

The cults of death and of fertility were interrelated in ancient thought on the principle that such mighty opposites as life and death somehow belong together. The Baal Epic relates that the dead fertility-god, imprisoned in the underworld, had intercourse with a heifer, the deity thus revitalizing himself in the realm of the dead (Baal I.5.17-22). The practice of spreading the ashes of sacrifice on the fields to increase their productivity is attested from antiquity.

Since the fertility cults and the cult of the dead were prohibited in Israel, the ritual of the red heifer had to be modified and reinterpreted in Israelite cult practice. The stain of uncleanness is an offense against Yahweh's holiness and a violation of his will for Israel. As long as it remains, it jeopardizes Israel's relationship to her God. Uncleanness in priestly thought was, therefore, equivalent to sin (*see* CLEAN AND UNCLEAN § 5b; SIN; HOLINESS), and the red heifer was interpreted as a sin offering (חטאת; Num. 19:9, 17). It was not, however, a sacrifice in the strict sense, because it was not burned upon the altar (*see* SACRIFICE AND OFFERINGS). It was a sin offering only in the sense of "something that removes sin."

While water is the most common cleansing agent employed in OT priestly law, it serves in this case merely to carry the ashes of the heifer, which are the real cleansing agent. The writer of Hebrews recognized this when he compared the "ashes of a heifer," which purified the flesh, with the blood of Christ, which purified the "conscience from *dead* works" (Heb. 9:13-14). In this ritual spring water (מים חיים; lit., "living water") is specified as being a more potent symbol of life and cleansing than the standing water of a cistern. Semimagical liquids, like the "water for impurity," were widely used in purification rituals, and two close analogies are found in the OT: the "water of bitterness" (Num. 5:11-31) for the detection of a suspected adulteress, and the "water of expiation" (8:7) for the purification of the Levites.

Bibliography. W. R. Smith, *The Religion of the Semites* (1889), pp. 140-388. G. B. Gray, *Numbers*, ICC (1903), pp. 241-56.
L. E. TOOMBS

RED SEA [ים סוף, *lit.*, Sea of Reeds *or* Rushes]; THE SEA [הים]; THE TONGUE OF THE SEA OF EGYPT [לשון ים מצרים] (Isa. 11:15). The term "Red Sea," which is the literal rendition of the Greek Ἐρυθρὰ θάλασσα (cf. Vulg. *Mare Rubrum, Mare Erythraem*), is of unknown origin. Various suggestions for the origin of the name have been made. The classical writers explained it as coming from Erythras, a king who ruled in Erythrae, one of the Ionian cities in Asia Minor. Others have suggested that the name is derived from the red corals which line its shores and cover the floor of the sea. And still others imply that its name comes from the color of the Edomite and Arabian mountains which border on its E shores, and from the glow of the sky reflected in its waters.

The name *Yam Sûph*, "Sea of Reeds [or Rushes]," appears to have been originally applied only to the area bordering on the S extension of Lake Menzaleh, near Baal-zephon. According to an Egyptian text, there were in antiquity two bodies of water near Rameses: (*a*) the "water of Horus" (Shihor; Isa. 23:3; Jer. 2:18); and (*b*) "Papyrus Lake," which in the Egyptian is called by the same word as in Hebrew, *Sûph*. Later *Yam Sûph* came to be applied to the Gulf of Aqabah, and perhaps to the Gulf of Suez (Num. 33:10-11 is the only clear reference to this gulf in the OT; however, its validity depends upon the verification of the location of Elim on the traditional route to Sinai; Exod. 16:1 knows of no camping by *Yam Sûph* after they left Elim), and eventually to the entire body of water known as the Red Sea.

In antiquity the Red or the Erythrean Sea included both the Indian Ocean and the Persian Gulf. Today, however, it is limited only to the arm of the sea which separates Africa from Arabia, and which extends from the Gulf of Aden (Straits of Bab el-Mandeb) in the latitude 20° 40′ N to the head of the

Gulf of Suez, latitude 30° N, and which is now joined to the Mediterranean by the Suez Canal. Its total length is *ca.* 1,200 miles, and its width varies from *ca.* 250 miles in the S half to *ca.* 130 miles at Ras Mohammed in the latitude 27° 45' N, where the sea is divided into two gulfs forming a V shape and enclosing between them the Sinai Peninsula, with the Gulf of Suez to the W and the Gulf of Aqabah (also referred to as Aelanitic) to the E. The Gulf of Suez has a length of approximately 130 miles and is *ca.* 18 miles wide, while the Gulf of Aqabah is *ca.* 90 miles long and *ca.* 15 miles wide.

The Red Sea is a part of a great rift-valley system which probably was formed in the Tertiary Age. It forms one of the most marked features of the earth's crust. The rift valley of the Jordan and the Dead Sea continues southward to the Wadi el-'Arabah, and its submerged section forms the Gulf of Aqabah. Another rift valley forming the Gulf of Suez and running southward meets it, and together they form the main basin of the Red Sea, the depth of which is over 7,200 feet.

The Red Sea presents a number of peculiarities. There are no large rivers draining into it. The climate, being hot and dry, causes a large degree of evaporation, resulting in the greater salinity of its waters than in the open ocean. Its level is maintained by a surface current which flows in from the Indian Ocean, while a current of very salty water flows outward at a depth of 300-6,000 feet below the surface. The water is clear and almost green, and it is one of the warmest bodies of water of the earth. The mean temperature of the surface water is 77° in the N, 80° near the middle, and 84° in the S. Below the surface at a depth of 1,200 feet, there is a uniform temperature in all parts of the sea. This high temperature of the water, along with its purity, makes it very favorable for all kinds of marine life, which exists in abundance.

Biblical connections with the Red Sea are limited to two phases of Israel's history: (*a*) the story of the Exodus, the most important event in which—the crossing of the sea—took place in the area between the Mediterranean and the Gulf of Suez; and (*b*) the Judean control of the seaport EZION-GEBER-ELATH on the Gulf of Aqabah. Here Solomon, in partnership with Hiram king of Tyre, built and operated a commercial fleet and carried on a profitable trade with OPHIR and other E countries (I Kings 9:26-27; 10:11, 22). Here, too, Solomon operated extensive copper mines and refineries which produced enough copper for domestic consumption and for the export trade. Archaeological excavations in this area have found the largest copper smelting and refinery plant ever uncovered in the Near East. After Solomon, the exploitation of the copper mines of the Arabah and the use of the seaport Ezion-geber languished. King Jehoshaphat attempted to revive the overseas trade by building a fleet of ships "to go to Ophir for gold; but they did not go, for the ships were wrecked at Ezion-geber" (I Kings 22:48). His son Jehoram lost the region to the Edomites, who successfully revolted against his rule (II Kings 3:20). It was recovered by Amaziah and Uzziah through a reconquest (II Kings 14:22), and finally lost permanently by Ahaz, when Edom (so RSV, with *Qere*; KJV "Syria"—i.e., Aram —with *Kethibh*) became its possessor (II Kings 16:6).

The equating of *Yam Sûph* with the Red Sea presents a problem. There are no reeds in either gulf. Reeds or rushes thrive only in the sweet-water marshes, and these are found only in the marshes N of the Gulf of Suez. In the account of the crossing of the sea and the drowning of the Egyptian pursuers in its waters (Exod. 13:18; 14:21-29; 15:4, 21; and other passages where the allusion to this event is made) the translators of the English Bible have either assumed that the expression *Yam Sûph* or "the sea" invariably refers to the Red Sea, or use the traditional translation "Red Sea" even though the reference may not be to the same waters referred to elsewhere (as in Num. 21:4; Deut. 2:1; I Kings 9:26; etc., where the Gulf of Aqabah is meant). However, a glance at the map of the region where the Israelites found themselves at the time of the crossing of the sea, and the geographical location of the most northerly extremity of the Gulf of Suez, will show immediately that both expressions, *Yam Sûph* and "the sea," in the above passages cannot refer to the Red Sea or even to the Gulf of Suez. In order to have reached even the most northerly tip of the Gulf of Suez, the Israelites would first have had to cross a long tract of the desert to reach it; this feat would have been impossible for them to accomplish before the pursuing Egyptian chariot army would have been upon them. Both terms must then refer in this account, not to the body of water properly known as the Red Sea, but to the marshy area N of the Gulf of Suez, in the region of the S extension of Lake Menzaleh. The Israelites, not being a maritime people, made no distinction in their vocabulary between a body of water such as a lake and the sea. Both are referred to as "sea." The confusion of *Yam Sûph* with the Red Sea probably goes back to the Greek translators of the LXX, who equated *Yam Sûph* with *Erythra Thalassa*, the "Red Sea." This rendition passed into English translations by way of the Vulg. On the other hand, Luther, who relied on the Hebrew, rendered *Yam Sûph* correctly by calling it *Schilfmeer*, "Sea of Reeds."

On the basis of the findings of the recent archaeological explorations in both the Suez and the Aqabah area, the prevalent view that in antiquity both gulfs extended farther N has been completely disproved. No appreciable change in geographical extension has taken place in the last 3,500 years.

Where, then, was the crossing of *Yam Sûph?* Among the various theories, each of which has some point in its favor, the following have been suggested:

a) The traditional S route. The Hebrews started their itinerary from Rameses (Josephus claims that they started from Letopolis, now Old Cairo), which was located, according to this theory, at Qantir, and went to Succoth and from there to "Etham, on the edge of the wilderness." Finding their way blocked by border fortifications, they journeyed southward on the W side of the Bitter Lakes, and crossed into the wilderness at their S extremity. Migdol and Baal-zephon were, according to this theory, located somewhere in the vicinity of the lower end of the Bitter Lakes, which at the time of the Exodus were linked to the Gulf of Suez. The expression "Sea of Reeds" could have been applied either to the Gulf of Suez or to the part of the sea which connected it to the Bitter Lakes.

b) The central crossing. According to this theory, the Hebrews left Rameses (which might have been located either at San el-Hagar or at Qantir) and, after crossing the Pelusiac arm of the Nile, proceeded to Succoth (Tell el-Mashkhuta). Thence they went to the Lake Timsah, which they crossed either on the N end at Ismailieh, or on the S end. It is quite possible that the name *Yam Sûph* was originally applied to the lakes of the isthmus.

Assuming that the archaeological identification of Rameses with Tanis is correct, and that the "Papyrus Lake" was in its vicinity, the Hebrews, after leaving Rameses, headed first southward to Succoth (Tell el-Mashkhuta), where they hoped to escape into the wilderness of Etham by way of the Wadi Tumilat in the area of Lake Timsah. Finding their way blocked, they turned northeastward, and camped before "Pi-ha-hiroth, between Migdol and the sea, in front of Baal-zephon" (Exod. 14:1-2). According to a Phoenician letter, a temple of god Baal-zephon was located near Tell Defneh. It was at this point that the Israelites crossed the *Yam Sûph,* which was perhaps located at the S extension of the present Lake Menzaleh.

c) The N crossing. This theory identifies *Yam Sûph* with Lake Sirbonis, which is located between Pelusium and Raphia and is now called Lake Bardawil. It suggests that the escape of the Israelites was by a N route, by way of the narrow strip of land which separates the lake from the Mediterranean Sea. This theory involves giving up the identification of Succoth with Tell el-Mashkhuta, and identifying it with a place at or near Mohammediyeh. Migdol is then connected with Tell el-Her, and Baal-zephon with Zeus Kasios (Greek designation for Baal-zephon), who had a sanctuary on a knoll on the shores of Lake Sirbonis. Moreover, around this lake there are large areas of reeds, which would make the name *Yam Sûph* quite appropriate. According to this theory, the Israelites first made the march from Rameses to Etham; then, using military strategy, they turned northward toward the sea, thus giving the pursuing Egyptians the appearance that they were confused and lost. The Israelites, fleeing across the narrow, sandy strip, succeeded in crossing it, before the Egyptians could overtake them. The disaster which destroyed the Egyptians was probably due to a break-through of the narrow sandy strip by a strong E wind, and thus caused the water of the sea to pour into the lake basin.

Bibliography. O. Eissfeldt, *Baal Zaphon, Zeus Kasios und der Durchzug der Israeliten durchs Meer* (1932); N. Glueck, "Exploration in Eastern Palestine," *AASOR*, XV (1934-35), 1 ff; W. F. Albright, *BASOR*, no. 109 (Feb., 1948), pp. 15 ff; J. Neumann, "Evaporation from the Red Sea," *IEJ*, vol. II (1952), no. 1, pp. 153 ff; G. E. Wright, *Biblical Archaeology* (1957), pp. 60 ff.   J. L. MIHELIC

REDEEM, REDEEMER, REDEMPTION.

The legal process of redemption provides the biblical writers with one of their basic images for describing God's saving activity toward man. Originally a secular concept, it became of great theological importance in the OT—especially in Deuteronomy, Psalms, and Second Isaiah—and to a lesser degree in the NT. Its central position in the vocabulary of modern Christian theology, where the terms have a currency quite disproportionate to the relative infrequency of their appearance in the NT, seems to be due to the influence of Luther.

1. The legal concept of redemption in the OT
   a. The root פדה (*pādhâ*)
   b. The root גאל (*gā'al*)
   c. The word כפר (*kôpher*)
2. The theological concept of redemption in the OT
   a. The redemption of Israel
   b. The redemption of individuals
3. The use of the concept in the NT
Bibliography

1. The legal concept of redemption in the OT. The words "redeem," "redeemer," and "redemption" are used to translate derivatives of two Hebrew roots, פדה and גאל, which, like their English equivalents, designate a process by which something alienated, or at least subject to alienation, may, in some circumstances, be recovered for its original owner by the payment of a sum of money. The thing alienated may be either real property or an animal or the legal freedom of a person. The term may also be applied to the saving of a life which has become legally forfeit.

a. The root פדה *(pādhâ).* This is the more general of the two terms and has cognates of related meaning in other Semitic languages; in the OT it is never used except with regard to the redemption of persons or other living beings. Thus the owner of an ox, known to be dangerous, which has killed a person may be allowed to save his own life by payment of a redemption price (*pidhyôn;* Exod. 21:30). A woman who has been legally betrothed may be redeemed if she proves unsatisfactory to her prospective husband (Exod. 21:8). By Hebrew law, all the first-born are to be sacrificed to God, but provision is made for redeeming the first-born of men and unclean animals by the payment of a fixed amount (Num. 18:15-16). An advance beyond the idea of money payment provides for the redemption of first-born children by the consecration of the Levites to God's service (Num. 3:45); even here, however, the surplus children, over and above the number of the Levites, must be redeemed by a payment of money (Num. 3:46-51). The term פדה designates objectively the act of redemption and (unlike גאל) implies nothing with respect to the status of the person who performs it, or his obligation to do so.

b. The root גאל *(gā'al).* This is a purely Hebrew word, belonging to the realm of family law, which denotes primarily the action of the next of kin to recover the forfeited property of a kinsman or to purchase his freedom if he has fallen into slavery. It is closely bound up with the conception of the solidarity of the family group. Thus Lev. 25:25 provides that if a man is forced to sell some portion of his property because he has fallen into debt, his next of kin, if he has the means, is under obligation to repurchase it for him. Ruth 4:4-6; Jer. 32:6-12 are good illustrations of how the law operated in practice. Lev. 25:47-49 allows the near kinsman the privilege of redeeming a poor relative who may have sold himself into slavery because of debt. So intimate is the relationship between the root גאל and the family that the participial form gô'ēl (unlike the corresponding form of פדה) can be translated, not only "redeemer," but also "nearest kin" or "next of kin," as in Ruth 2:20; 4:1. Since the nearest of kin also has the duty of avenging a murder, the word gô'ēl in the phrase gô'ēl haddām can be translated "the avenger" of blood (Num. 35:19). *See* AVENGER OF BLOOD.

In addition to the primary technical sense just described, גאל can also be used in a quite general way to mean simply "redeem" or "deliver," especially when the reference is to the redemption of inanimate property (as in Lev. 27:15, 19-20).

c. The word כפר *(kōpher).* While the verbal root כפר (probably meaning "to cover") has a purely religious sense in Hebrew and its different forms are usually translated by some variation of the phrase "to make atonement" (*see* ATONEMENT), the noun kōpher has a secular meaning and is translated either by something like "bribe" (Amos 5:12) or, in the context of a redemptive action, by "ransom," as in Exod. 21:30; Ps. 49:7-8, where "ransom" (kōpher) is associated with "redemption" (pidhyôn, a derivative of פדה).

2. The theological concept of redemption in the OT. Since the essential purpose of a redemptive act is to deliver a person or thing from captivity or loss, it becomes an appropriate image for God's saving actions among men. Against the background of Hebrew law, the image had a vividness which can hardly be realized by men of different background and culture.

a. The redemption of Israel. The term is widely used with reference to Yahweh's deliverance of his people from Egypt (Exod. 6:6; 15:13 [גאל]; Deut. 7:8; 9:26 [פדה]; Ps. 106:10 KJV [גאל]); the terms גאל and פדה are used without difference of meaning and without pressing the metaphor to include the thought of God's having paid a redemptive price.

In the days of the Babylonian exile, it was inevitable that the image should be used to describe Israel's similar deliverance from her second period of captivity. Redemption is one of the basic concepts of Second Isaiah (Isa. 43:1; 44:22-23; 52:9; etc.), who overwhelmingly prefer the root גאל because of its connotations of intimate relationship and personal responsibility. The word "Redeemer" (gô'ēl) is one of the prophet's favorite names for God (44:24; 47:4; etc.), pointing, as it does, not merely to the fact that Yahweh delivers his people, but that he has an obligation to do so because of having adopted them for his own. He is their "Next of Kin." The thought of a redemption price, however, is specifically excluded in Isa. 45:13; 52:3 and appears only half seriously in 43:3.

By a natural extension, the term "redemption" could also be used for God's deliverance of his people out of any trouble at all (Ps. 25:22; Hos. 13:14 [פדה and גאל]). The concept of redemption from sin appears nowhere except possibly in Ps. 130:8.

b. The redemption of individuals. The concept of redemption could also be applied quite naturally to God's deliverance of individuals from troubles of various kinds. It is occasionally found in this sense in the older literature (e.g., Gen. 48:16; II Sam. 4:9) and is frequent in the Psalms (e.g., 26:11; 49:15; 69:

18 [גאל and פדה]; 103:4). The most striking instance is Job's conviction that God is his personal redeemer (gô'ēl) and must therefore ultimately vindicate his integrity (Job 19:25).

3. The use of the concept in the NT. In contrast to the frequency with which these words occur in the OT, their use in the NT is relatively limited, probably because of the difference in cultural background which made other images such as ATONEMENT; SACRIFICE; and JUSTIFICATION more intelligible and appealing. The word "ransom" (λύτρον and ἀντίλυτρον) occurs only three times (Matt. 20:28 = Mark 10:45; I Tim. 2:6), but its occurrence in the first two of these passages is nevertheless of fundamental importance for understanding Jesus' own conception of his death as a redemptive act. He gives a new depth to the concept of redemption by associating with it the idea—derived from Isa. 53:5-6, 10—of a substitutionary sacrifice.

The derived verb "to redeem or ransom" (λυτρόω) occurs in connection with the death of Christ only in Tit. 2:14 (reflecting Ps. 130:8); I Pet. 1:18-19, which introduces the idea that the blood of Christ is the ransom price. The other two occurrences of the verbal idea (the first in a different form; Luke 1:68; 24:21) merely express the OT idea of redemption as the deliverance of Israel from oppression.

In the Pauline letters the noun "redemption" (ἀπολύτρωσις) occurs rarely and ordinarily only in the general sense of "deliverance" (Rom. 3:24; 8:23; I Cor. 1:30; Eph. 1:14 KJV; 4:30), although in Eph. 1:14 KJV the image of the Hebrew legal process may be in the author's mind. Only in Eph. 1:7 does the idea of the blood of Christ as a redemption price appear (the similar phrase in Col. 1:14 KJV is textually dubious and is omitted in the RSV). In Heb. 9:15 the term is also used in a quite general way as a synonym of "atonement" or "forgiveness." The use of the concept "redemption" in the NT in its proper Christian theological sense always implies deliverance from sin and its effects, rather than merely from death or trouble.

The concept of God's saving work among men as a process of redemption from possession or control by an alien power is, in spite of its infrequent use in the NT, one of the fundamental concepts of the Bible. The interpreter must, however, beware of pressing the metaphor too far—of asking, e.g., to whom the ransom price was paid. The biblical emphasis is on the fact of deliverance, not on the details of a legal process.

Bibliography. J. Stamm, *Erlösen und Vergebung im AT* (1940); A. Kirchgässner, *Erlösung und Sünde im NT* (1950); A. R. Johnson, "The Primary Meaning of √גאל," *Supplements to Vetus Testamentum*, I (1953), 67-77; E. Osterloh and H. Engelland, eds., *Biblisches-Theologisches Wörterbuch zur Lutherbibel* (1954), pp. 117-20. R. C. DENTAN

REED [קנה, qānê, Akkad. qanū, Ugar. qn(m); אבה, 'ēbhê; אגמון, 'agmôn; אחו, 'āḥû (Egyp. *loan word*), Ugar. aḫ; גמא, gōmê; סוף, sûph (Egyp. *loan word*); κάλαμος]. The flowering stalk of any of several species of tall aquatic grasses, and more generally any object of similar shape. Qānê seems to have been the generic word similar to the English word "reed," for its use is quite broad. Several Hebrew words refer to reedlike plants. The RSV translates five of them with "reed," but not consistently; the KJV, only two, primarily *qānê*.

1. *Qānê*. This plant is referred to in I Kings 14:15: the prophet Ahijah predicted the Lord would smite Israel "as a reed shaken in the water." It also occurs in the description of the Servant who will not break a "bruised reed" (Isa. 42:3; cf. Matt. 12:20), and in an obscure allusion to "beasts that dwell among the reeds" in Ps. 68:30—H 68:31 (cf. KJV "company of spearmen").

The largest of the reed grasses, *Arundo donax* L., the "giant reed," provides a sturdy, bamboolike stalk, sometimes as much as ten feet long, useful for many purposes. The smaller reed, *Phragmites communis* Trin., is more common, however, and thus considered by some scholars the more likely one (*see* FLORA § A11). It is used metaphorically, to describe Egypt as a "staff of reed" that broke when Israel relied upon it (Ezek. 29:6) and as "that broken reed of a staff" (II Kings 18:21). In Ezek. 40:5 is a "measuring reed" (*qānê*) "six long cubits" in length (*ca.* ten feet, four inches) with which the measurements of the ideal temple of the future are given (40:5-7; 41:8; 42:16-19; cf. Rev. 11:1; 21:15-16; *see* WEIGHTS AND MEASURES). Apparently it might designate the beam of a balance, and so come to mean "scales." (The English word "canon," referring particularly to spiritual authority, probably stems ultimately from this word, through the Greek and the Latin.) *Qānê* is used also of the "shaft" and "branches" of the sacred lampstand (Exod. 25:31-32; 37:17-18). In Job 31:22 ("shoulder blade") it designates the humeral bone of the upper arm (cf. Ugar. references in Gordon 62:4; 67:VI:20). *See also* CALAMUS; CANE; SWEET CANE.

2. *'Ēbhê*. The strange expression *'aniyyôth 'ēbhê*, "skiffs of reed," in Job 9:26 (KJV "swift ships") is now generally recognized to refer to the papyrus-reed boats (=אמג ילכ in Isa. 18:2) which moved swiftly over the Nile in ancient times ("skiffs of reed"). The phrase is in a figure depicting Job's assurance of his swift-approaching death. *See* SKIFF.

3. *'Agmôn*. Zohary identifies this reed with the genus Scirpus, a sedge grass (*see* FLORA § A11*d*), while others prefer the genus Juncus or rush, both of which are common to swampy areas. The word is twice used metaphorically in Isaiah along with palm branches: once in a figure of God's punishment of Israel (9:14—H 9:13), and again in an oracle against Egypt (19:15); the KJV uses "rush." The identification is based on the noun *'agam*, meaning a "pool" (cf. Akkadian *agammu*, "swamp," and Arabic *'ajam*, "pool of reeds"). In Jer. 51:32 *'agammîm* may refer to the swamp reeds which are burned (so KJV), but many scholars prefer to follow the LXX (cf. RSV "bulwark"). In Job 41:2—H 40:26 *'agmôn* may refer to a "rope" (KJV "hook") made from the rush, while in 41:20—H 41:12 it probably refers to burning "rushes" (KJV "caldron"). The drooping, flowering panicles of the rush are a figure for criticism of fasting in Isa. 58:5 (RSV "rush"; KJV "bulrush"). *See* RUSH.

4. *'Āḥû*. appears in Gen. 41:2, 18; Job 8:11, and clearly refers to the reed grass (KJV "meadow," "flag"). Twice in a Ugaritic fragment (Gordon 76:

II:9, 12) *aḥ* appears in a context which has been interpreted to refer to Lake Semachonitis (Lake Huleh in Galilee), implying marsh grass. In Hos. 13:15 the puzzling "among brothers" (so KJV; *ben 'āḥîm*) is now considered by many to be an error for "as the reed plant" (so RSV; reading *ka'aḥāwîm*), for a flora reference best fits the context. *See* FLAG.

5. *Gômê*. This is the papyrus reed. It is translated "rush" in Isa. 35:7, "BULRUSH" in Exod. 2:3. In Job 8:11; Isa. 18:2 it is translated "PAPYRUS" (KJV "rushes," "bulrushes").

6. *Sûph*. This reed is identified by Zohary (*see* FLORA § A11*c*) as the cattail, *Typha angusta* Bery et Choub. The RSV translates "reed" only in Exod. 2: 3, 5 (KJV FLAG), in the familiar story of Moses in the papyrus-reed basket which was placed among the reeds by the Nile. In Jonah 2:5—H 2:6 it is translated "weeds." *Yam-sûph* occurs twenty-four times in the OT and is given the meaning "RED SEA," although it literally means "Sea of Reeds." Several water bodies are given this designation in the OT. In Deut. 1:1 a place by the name of SUPH (KJV "Red sea") is mentioned, but its location is unknown.

7. Κάλαμος. In the NT the common Greek word κάλαμος is used for a reed (Matt. 11:7; Luke 7:24; etc.), a staff (Matt. 27:29, etc.), a measuring rod (Rev. 11:1, etc.), and a reed pen (III John 13). A reed was given in mockery to Jesus as a royal staff by the soldiers before his crucifixion (Matt. 27:29-30; Mark 15:19). In John 19:29 vinegar is offered to Jesus on the cross, with HYSSOP (in the parallels in Matt. 27:48; Mark 15:36, a "reed"). The RSV shifts to "rod" for the passages in Revelation (11:1; 21:15-16), which reflect Ezekiel's "reed" for measuring the future temple.

See also HYSSOP; KANAH; MUSIC AND MUSICAL INSTRUMENTS.

Bibliography. H. N. and A. L. Moldenke, *Plants of the Bible* (1952), pp. 50-51, 120-21, 172-73, 222-23.   J. C. TREVER

REELAIAH rē'ə lī'ə [רעליה] (Ezra 2:2). Alternately: RAAMIAH rā'ə mī'ə [רעמיה] (Neh. 7:7); Apoc. RESAIAH rĭ sā'yə ['Ρησαίας] (I Esd. 5:8), KJV REESAIAS rē'ə sā'yəs; Apoc. inserts also REELIAH rē'ə lī'ə, KJV REELIUS —əs ['Ρεελίας (A), Βοροελείας (B)], perhaps a copyist's attempt to correct marginally the preceding form. One of those whose names head the list of exiles returned from Babylon. Which MT variant of the name is correct is uncertain.   B. T. DAHLBERG

*REFINING [זקק, צרף; πυροῦσθαι]. Reducing to a fine state; metaphorically, cleansing, purifying.

The two Hebrew terms refer to two different processes. The first (זקק; lit., "to filter or strain," and used also of distilling rain [Job 36:27] and refining wine [Isa. 25:6]) has reference to melting, the physical process of changing metal from a solid to a liquid and rendering the metal purer by removal of dross (I Chr. 28:18; 29:4; Job 28:1; Ps. 12:6). The second term (צרף, specifically meaning "smelt," Akkadian *ṣarpu*) has reference to the extraction by fire supplemented by chemical reactions from ores found in nature (Isa. 1:25; 48:10; Jer. 6:29; 9:7—H 9:6; used of refining by smelting in II Sam. 22:31; Pss. 12:6—H 12:7; 17:3; etc.).

Melting, or cupellation, required a heated crucible or "fining pot" of well-fired POTTERY (*see also* FURNACE). The earliest smelting (*see* BRONZE) was by bonfires, ore heaped on fuel. Later the shaft furnace, fed from the top, with the end product withdrawn from the bottom, was developed. Still later, with higher temperatures required for iron-ore smelting (e.g., Solomonic EZION-GEBER), came a furnace with natural forced draft.* Refineries fully operating with fire by night and smoke by day made vivid symbols of purification (Isa. 1:25-26; Zech. 13:9; Mal. 3:3) and judgment (Isa. 1:22; Jer. 6:27-30; Ezek. 22:17-22). Fig. EZI 41.

Techniques of refining were adapted to the metal ore. GOLD and TIN required simple melting. Crucibles retaining melted COPPER were found near two blast furnaces (Philistine?) at Tell Qasile.* The most extensive refinery excavated in Palestine is at Ezion-geber; the copper and iron ore came from Solomon's Arabah mines. The process of silver-lead refining (*see* SILVER; LEAD) is reflected in Jer. 6:27-30. Ezek.

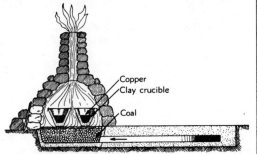

Copper
Clay crucible
Coal

Courtesy of the Israel Exploration Society

8. Drawing of a reconstructed copper-smelting furnace, from Tell Qasile

22:20-22 pictures a jeweler melting scraps to recover silver (cf. Ps. 12:6; Prov. 17:3; 25:4; 27:21; Zech. 13:9). Three IRON refineries at Tell Jemmeh are dated by the excavator to the twelfth century B.C. These are smaller in size but of the same design as those in Solomon's "Pittsburgh." Fig. REF 8.

Lacking local ores, the Bible peoples probably did only the final refining of metals. In copper and iron production, however, at least in Solomon's time, Israelite smelters and refineries excelled.

Bibliography. F. Petrie, *Gerar* (1928); N. Glueck, *The Other Side of the Jordan* (1940), chs. 3-4; R. J. Forbes, *Metallurgy in Antiquity* (1950), pp. 9-10, 34, 97-98, 300; B. Maisler, *The Excavations at Tell Qasile* (1951); C. Singer *et al.*, eds., *A History of Technology*, I (1954), 564-65, 574, 579, 581, 585-90, 633.
P. L. GARBER

REFUGE [מָעוֹז, stronghold; מִשְׂגָּב, secure height; מָנוֹס, place of escape; מַחְסֶה, place of refuge]. The idea of "refuge" in the OT may be traced back to the language of warfare—the "secure height" and the "strong rock," etc., describe both natural and artificial protection afforded by the rocky landscape of Canaan's mountain regions (cf. Judg. 6:2; I Sam. 13:6; Isa. 2:19).

"Refuge" as an epithet of Yahweh is one of many synonymous expressions describing him as the protector of men (cf. "rock," "fortress," etc., in Ps. 18:1-2), a concept which is predominantly found in the book of Psalms and other psalm literature in the OT (e.g., Deut. 32:3 ff; Jer. 16:19; 17:12-18; Nah. 1:2-8).

The pious "take refuge" in the "shadow of his wings" (Ruth 2:12; Pss. 17:8; 36:7; *see* WINGS; SHADOW); this may mean the temple in Jerusalem in some instances (cf. Pss. 57:1; 61:4; 63:7). Also, they take refuge "in him" (Pss. 2:12; 5:11; 16:1; Prov. 30:5; Nah. 1:7; cf. Isa. 57:13).

See CITY OF REFUGE for this technical use of the term.

Bibliography. M. Tsevat, *A Study of the Language of the Biblical Psalms* (1955), in the *JBL* Monograph Series, IX, 4-5, 14-20, 39, 48-52.
J. A. WHARTON

REFUGE, CITY OF. *See* CITY OF REFUGE.

REGEM rē'gəm [רֶגֶם, friend] (I Chr. 2:47). One of the sons of Jahdai, a Calebite.

REGEM-MELECH rē'gəm mĕl'ĭk [רֶגֶם מֶלֶךְ, *but perhaps to be read with* Syr. רַב מַג מֶלֶךְ, chief officer of the king] (Zech. 7:2). One of the deputies sent by the people of Bethel to inquire of the temple priests regarding fasting, in the time of Zechariah. The use of such a title here may be due to a scribal gloss. *See* bibliography.

Bibliography. D. W. Thomas, Exegesis of Zechariah, *IB*, VI (1956), 1082; M. Noth, *Die israelitischen Personennamen* (1928), Index no. 1245.
B. T. DAHLBERG

REGENERATION [ἀναγεννᾶν; παλιγγενεσία; γεννᾶν ἄνωθεν, *see below*]. Transcendence beyond mortal life by encounter with Christ through the kerygma, whereby at death one is granted eschatological life, to which one repeatedly arises already during this life. Thus union with Christ is the continuing Christian experience of selfhood.

Ἀναγεννᾶν (lit., "rebeget" or "rebear") occurs only in I Pet. 1:3, 23 (ἀρτιγέννητος, in I Pet. 2:2, means "recently born"). Παλιγγενεσία (lit., a "becoming again"), occurs as "regeneration" only in Tit. 3:5. Γεννᾶν ἄνωθεν in John 3:3, 7, probably means "beget from above," since ἄνωθεν always has this meaning elsewhere in John (3:31; 19:11, 23), and the other Johannine modifiers of γεννᾶν are in harmony with this meaning: "from God" (1:13); "of (water and) the Spirit" (3:5-6, 8), rather than "of the flesh" (3:6; cf. 1:13). Furthermore, the Johannine explanation of regeneration in the Prologue and in ch. 3 is in terms of "him who came from heaven" (3:13; cf. 6:32-58), and here again ἄνωθεν is used (3:31; in 8:23 ἐκ τῶν ἄνω = ἄνωθεν). The term is then introduced into the saying of Jesus (which Just. Apol. I.61.4 cites using ἀναγεννᾶν; cf. Mark 10:15 and parallels), to exclude the objection (John 3:4; Just. Apol. 61.5) of an impossible second natural birth, which would be from below (cf. already Job 1:21; Ps. 139:13-15; eschatologically Isa. 26:19 and bBer. 15b on Prov. 30:15-16), and to bring the saying of Jesus into the framework of Johannine theology (cf. 3:36).

The nearest parallel to this usage is the Naassene interpretation of the Eleusinian mystery (Hippolytus *Ref.* V.3), where "the generation [γένεσις] that is spiritual, heavenly, from above [ἄνω]," is explained: "We who are spiritual come flowing down from above [ἄνωθεν], from Adam." Similarly in the Gospel of Truth 22:3-4: "If a person has the gnose, he is a being from on high."

The translation "beget again" is linguistically possible (though not in the case of the Aramaic מליעילא), and certainly the begetting from above is understood as a begetting again. To this extent Nicodemus' restatement (John 3:4), though crude, is accurate: δεύτερον . . . γεννηθαι, lit., "be born . . . a second time" (in contrast to "once born"; cf. Just. Apol. I.61.5). The general propriety of translating different though similar Greek terms with the same English term is strengthened when one observes, e.g., Justin associating (Dial. 138.2) πάλιν . . . γένεσθαι of Jesus with ἀναγεννᾶν of the believer, and citing (Apol. I.61.4) the same saying as John 3:3 with ἀναγεννᾶν instead of γεννᾶν ἄνωθεν (cf. Hesychius' definition of παλιγγενεσία: τὸ ἐκ δευτέρου ἀναγεννηθῆναι, ἢ ἀνακαινισθῆναι).

The lateness and the rarity of "regeneration" in the NT are partly due to the absence of any equivalent term in Hebrew, Aramaic, and the LXX (πάλιν γένωμαι in Job 14:14 refers to a questionable afterlife; the variant ἀναγεννηθείς, in the Ecclesiasticus Prologue, is a scribal error). The variation in terminology when the idea is finally introduced not only reflects the availability of the various expressions in the Hellenistic world (see § A below), but also indicates that the development of the idea and experience within primitive Christianity had already advanced to the stage where the appropriation of the various terms could take place spontaneously and independently at different points in the NT. An analysis of the idea of regeneration where the term occurs (see § B1 below) will make it possible to trace the development even prior to the introduction of the term (see § B2 below).

A. In the Hellenistic world
B. In the NT
  1. The usage of the term
    a. At baptism
    b. Through a divine seed
    c. In union with Christ
    d. The original eschatological setting
  2. The development of the regeneration experience
    a. Jesus
    b. Jas. 1:18
    c. Paul
Bibliography

A. IN THE HELLENISTIC WORLD. "Regeneration" (παλιγγενεσία) was used by the Stoics to designate the cosmic restoration following upon the world conflagration (Philo On the Eternity of the World 8 also uses [πάλιν] ἀναγέννωσις of this Stoic view). The popularized form of this usage was appropriated to designate the RESTORATION after the Flood (Philo On Moses II.65; I Clem. 9:4), after the Exile (Jos. Antiq. XI.iii.9), and after the final destruction of the present evil aeon (Matt. 19:28). The Pythagoreans used the term individualistically to designate the transmigration of souls, and the term became current for various kinds of individual restoration, such as Cicero's return from exile (Letters to Atticus VI.6). Plutarch designates the divinity's restoration to life

after dismemberment in the myths of Dionysus (the E at Delphi 9) and Osiris (Isis and Osiris 35) as "regeneration." As the fertility cults developed into mystery religions with an increasingly personal and individual goal, "regeneration" was appropriated to designate the salvation attained for the believer by means of initiation.

For Apuleius (Metamorphoses XI) this usage is still somewhat unusual (quodam modo renatus), and occurs in contexts where initiation is most nearly a literal return to life: in Lucius' restoration from animal to human form (XI.16), and in restoration from the threshold of death (XI.21). Apuleius' regeneration takes place by means of a cultic voyage through the cosmos imitating death and restoration to life (XI.21.23), and achieves deliverance from fate —a more happy and glorious life, a blessed afterlife, and, if obedient, an extension of this life beyond the limit set by fate (XI.6, 15, 21, 25). The rite was climaxed by a presentation of the initiate dressed in the form of the solar divinity (XI.24), which suggests deification. Some such usage had already been attested indirectly by Philo (Questions and Answers on Exodus II.46), when he presented Moses' ascent of Sinai as a "second birth [δευτέρα γένεσις] better than the first," for it is not "mixed with a body" or of "corruptible parents," but is the pure mind, with God as father and no mother; it is "divine birth," "deification" by ascension "above the heavens" (II.40; cf. II.29).

The so-called "Mithras liturgy" in the great Paris magic papyrus explains how "regeneration" (μεταγεννᾶν; πάλιν γένεσθαι) is effected by means of a cultically experienced ascension (see ASCENSION § 1) through the various gates of heaven, during which one beholds "with immortal spirit" (by inhalation) the "immortal origin," the elements—i.e., one's heavenly "perfect body"—and the "immortal Aeon and Ruler of the flaming diadem," the sun-god and Mithra. During the vision one is free from the "perishable nature of mortals," and although one then returns from ecstasy to earthly existence, the cultic "transfer to immortal birth" from "mortal birth" has provided assurance of "immortality"— i.e., one's ascension at death.

An inscription from Rome dated A.D. 376 (CIL VI.510) refers to a person's having been "reborn for eternity [renatus in aeternum] by taurobolium and criobolium," although other inscriptions suggest that after twenty years one needed to repeat this Phrygian rite (which consisted in placing the initiate in a pit beneath the sacrifice, to be drenched in its blood). The spring festival of this cult, imitating Attis' emasculation so as to be united with Cybele, is interpreted philosophically by Sallust (On the Gods and the World 4) as "cutting off the further process of generation"; then follow a milk diet "as though we were being born again [ὥσπερ ἀναγεννωμένων]," and festivities representing, "as it were, a return up to the gods."

Tractate XIII of the Corpus Hermeticum is a secret discourse of Hermes Trismegistus to his son Tat, explaining and thereby mediating "regeneration" (παλιγγενεσία; ἀναγεννᾶν occurs only as a conjectural emendation): "Stop the working of your bodily senses, and then will deity be born in you" (XIII.7). The ten "powers" (virtues) of God dispel the twelve "punishments" (vices), and themselves enter the initiate to constitute the "Logos"—i.e., the new man as one's divine self: "The intellectual birth has been put together . . . and we have been deified by birth" (XIII.10). One has "passed forth out of oneself into an immortal body" (XIII.3): "I am in heaven and in earth, in water and in air; I am in beasts and plants . . . everywhere" (XIII.11). Immortality (i.e., ascension at death) is assured. This intellectually mediated regeneration developed historically out of a more typical sacramental regeneration, as is apparent in IV.4, where the same enlightenment comes by baptism in a great basin filled with mind.

This survey indicates a rather consistent usage of "regeneration" to designate a sacramental anticipation of victory over death, transforming one's nature and giving assurance of immortality; such experiences were both more common and more ancient than the surviving instances of the term. As Tertullian (On Baptism 5) noted, this usage of the term is also that of the NT (except for Matt. 19:28), although the NT understanding of the experience cannot be determined by a preconceived definition, but only by an analysis of the NT material.

B. IN THE NT. 1. The usage of the term "regeneration." From the passages where the terms for "regeneration" occur, certain common traits can be established, which will both provide the basis for locating the experience before the term occurs, and serve to draw attention to the distinctive features in the various passages on the topic.

a. At baptism. Tit. 3:5 refers to the "washing of regeneration," where the term "washing" (λουτρόν) is the technical Hellenistic term for ceremonial washing (Just. Apol. I.62.1), which in the case of the NT church can only mean baptism (cf. especially Acts 22:16; Eph. 5:26; Heb. 10:22). John 3:5 explains regeneration as birth "of water and the Spirit," where a customary association of regeneration with baptism is probably reflected, even though John (like Corpus Hermeticum IV) may here, as in 4:14; 7:38-39, wish to transcend the literal element; the saying was probably already in a baptismal setting in Mark 10:15, as in Just. Apol. I.61.4. Such a baptismal context is confirmed by the discussion of baptism (John 3:22-30; 4:1-2) within the regeneration passage (cf. I John 5:6-8). In I Peter the baptismal passage 3:20-21 is so similar to the context of regeneration in 1:3, 23 ("through the resurrection of Jesus Christ" [3:21; 1:3]; the setting within the kerygma [3:18, 22; 1:23-25]; the initial ethical commitment [3:21; 2:1-2]), and the material of 1:3-4:11 is so similar to baptismal motifs in the early church, that one generally concedes the setting of regeneration in I Peter to be baptismal, just as Justin (Dial. 138) sees regeneration in the baptismal material included in I Pet. 3:20-21. Justin's own decription of regeneration (Apol. I.61.3) is conclusive for the association of baptism and regeneration: "Then they are brought by us where there is water, and with the manner of regeneration with which we ourselves were regenerated, they are regenerated: For in the name of God, the Father and Lord of the universe, and of our Savior Jesus Christ, and of the Holy Spirit, they then perform the washing in water."

b. Through a divine seed, contrasted to human seed. I Pet. 1:23-25 speaks of being born anew "not of perishable seed but of imperishable, through the living and abiding word of God" (cf. Mark 4:13-20 and parallels; Jas. 1:18, 21), which is contrasted to all flesh, which withers and falls. Quite similarly, John 1:13 speaks of being born "not of blood nor of the will of the flesh nor of the will of man, but of God" (cf. Jas. 1:15, 18), and John 3:6 contrasts "that which is born of the flesh" with "that which is born of the Spirit." From I John 3:9 it is clear that being begotten of God rather than of the devil means receiving God's "seed," the word of God (John 5:38; 15:7; I John 1:10). The Valentinians (Tert. On the Flesh of Christ 19) saw in John 1:13 an allusion to the "mysterious seed of the elect and spiritual"; their Gospel of Truth (43.10-14) says that the children of God "are in that true and eternal life and speak of the perfect Light filled with the seed of the Father." Corpus Hermeticum XIII.1-2 is also similar to John: "I know not . . . from what womb a man can be born again, nor of what seed. —Oh son, [the womb] is intellectual wisdom in Silence, and the seed is the true Good. —Who is the begetter? . . . —The will of God." Just. Apol. I.61.10 contrasts the first birth "of liquid seed" (in Dial. 125.5; 140.2 "fleshly seed") with regeneration; believers have within them "seed from God" (32.8), here specifically identified with the Word. Somewhat similarly, the "Mithras liturgy" contrasts the "perishable nature of mortals" with rebirth by God's imperishable right hand (cf. I Pet. 1: 23): "Begotten of the mortal womb of X and of seed-filled fluid, and, today regenerated by thee, . . . made immortal."

On the other hand, Tit. 3:5 is on this point an exception, for here the Pauline contrast of man's works and God's grace provides the context of rebirth, while the divine presence is given the traditional baptismal and Pauline designation "Holy Spirit" (cf. John 3:5-6, 8; Just. Apol. I.61.3, 13). Even where in the NT the concept of seed does occur, the prominence of faith, correlative to the tendency to understand the seed as the word, tends to maintain the existential understanding of regeneration.

c. In union with Christ. I Pet. 1:3 says that rebirth is "through the resurrection of Jesus Christ from the dead" (see also 3:21b), while 1:23 says it is "through the living and abiding word of God," the gospel (1: 25; cf. I Cor. 4:15; Eph. 1:13; Col. 1:5; I Thess. 2:13), which accompanies baptism (I Pet. 3:18-22; cf. Eph. 5:26). Since the content of I Peter's gospel is Christ's suffering and glory (1:11; 2:21 ff; 3:18, 22; 4:1, 13; 5:1, 9-10)—i.e., his resurrection from the dead (1:21)—the word of God and the resurrection coincide, and the person thereby regenerated is "in Christ" (3:16; 5:10, 14). Similarly, in Tit. 3:4-5 the salvation at the appearance of Christ coincides with our regeneration. A somewhat similar sentiment seems to be at the base of the choice of the rather unusual designation for regeneration in John. The answer to Nicodemus' question: "How can this be?" (John 3:9) consists in the parallel between regeneration and the Johannine kergyma of Christ's descent and ascent (3:13, etc.): Birth "from above" (3:3, 7) —i.e., "from God" (1:13)—is possible because Christ is "from above" (3:31; 8:23)—i.e., "from God" (8:42; cf. 3:2, 16-17, 34; etc.). Regeneration means union with the incarnation: "To all who received him, who believed in his name, he gave power to become children of God" (1:12); "he who believes in the Son has eternal life" (3:36).

Regeneration as union with Christ has been somewhat formalized by Justin in Apol. I.61, where baptism presupposes acceptance of Christian doctrine and takes place in the name of the Trinity. But Justin reveals in Dial. 138 what is still implied in such formal statements, when he sees in the eight persons on the ark (symbolizing baptism) a hint of the resurrection date, and adds: "For Christ, being the first-born of every creature, became again [πάλιν . . . γένεσθαι] the beginning of another race regenerated [ἀναγεννᾶν] by Himself through water and faith and wood, containing the mystery of the cross." Here christological and regeneration terminology tend to coincide, as is also the case in I John 5:18, where "He who was born of God" keeps "any one born of God." Thus some of the development toward the term "regeneration" may be reflected in or derive from the designation of Jesus as "first-born of the dead" (Col. 1:18; Rev. 1:5; cf. Rom. 8:29), and in the concept of Jesus' being "begotten" at his baptism (Luke 3:22 D; cf. Mark 1:11 and parallels) or resurrection (Acts 13:33; Heb. 1:5; 5:5; cf. Acts 2:24; Rom. 1:4; Heb. 7:28), in which the believer shares at his regeneration (*see also* NEW MAN). On the other hand, a preference for the traditional language of the kerygma in describing one's own experience may partially account for the delay in introducing the term "regeneration"—e.g., in the case of Paul.

d. The original eschatological setting. In I Pet. 1:3-7 the significance of "regeneration" is expressed in terms of the eschatological message of primitive Christianity: One is born again to a "living hope . . . and to an inheritance which is imperishable, undefiled, and unfading, kept in heaven for you, who by God's power are guarded through faith for a salvation ready to be revealed in the last time, . . . at the revelation of Jesus Christ." Thus one is reborn into eschatological existence (1:20), so that in Christ one's relation to the old regime is that of suffering, and to the consummation that of joy. It is a life of faith, not sight (1:8); of ethical responsibility, not presumption (1:17). Similarly, the "sure saying" in which "regeneration" occurs in Titus conforms to the "then . . . now" pattern, with the appearance of Christ as the turning point to which regeneration unites us, so that we "become heirs in hope of eternal life." Yet here the relation to the Parousia has disappeared, and the emphasis falls upon salvation already attained through the divine epiphany. This development is even more apparent in the Johannine literature, where regeneration achieves eternal life now. Yet in John 3:3, 5, the earlier language of seeing or entering the kingdom of God occurs, and it is apparent that this saying on regeneration has developed out of the original eschatological message of Jesus (Mark 10:15 and parallels). Apart from this saying, Justin likewise neglects the original eschatological context for interpreting regeneration, and yet reveals this context by his return to earlier baptismal categories (cf. John the Baptist and Acts), in

viewing regeneration in terms of repentance and the remission of sins (Apol. I.61.2, 10; 66:1), which in Dial. 138.3 is given its original significance: "escape from the impending judgment of God."

2. The development of the regeneration experience. a. Jesus. The baptismal and eschatological settings into which the term "regeneration" was introduced, as well as the specific recurrence of language from the eschatological preaching of John the Baptist and Jesus, indicate that the initial meaning of the regeneration experience was in terms of Jesus' basic pattern: "Repent, for the kingdom of God is near." The imminence of the kingdom of God called forth a complete break with the old and a radically new beginning. One way to convey this message was to pronounce the blessing of eschatological existence upon those who in one way or the other represented existence outside the present regime: the poor and hungry (Luke 6:20-23 and parallel), the tax collectors and harlots (Matt. 21:31-32 and parallel), the afflicted (Matt. 10:7-8 and parallel; 11:4-6 and parallel; Luke 4:18-19; 14:21), the demoniacs (Matt. 12:28 and parallel), and the children: "Unless you turn and become like children, you will never enter the kingdom of heaven" (Matt. 18:3 and parallels). "Turn and become" may reflect a Semitic idiom meaning "become again" (cf. the form of the saying in Clement of Alexandria, *Exhortation* IX.82.4: ἢν γὰρ μὴ αὖθις ὡς τὰ παιδία γένησθε καὶ ἀναγεννηθῆτε). Yet the legitimacy for the subsequent use of this saying to introduce the term "regeneration" (John 3:3, 5; Just. Apol. I.61.4) lies in the radicality of the eschatological repentance for which it and the other illustrations called, not in the assumption of a specific theological interpretation of repentance in terms of rebirth by Jesus.

b. Jas. 1:18. The Jewish direction for developing theologically such an illustration as Jesus provided is evident in the somewhat similar rabbinic comparison of the new proselyte with a newborn child (from Rabbi Jose ben Halaphta, mid–second century A.D., on). The comparison is not between conversion and birth, but, as the use of the saying indicates, between a child who has no past and a proselyte radically separated from his past—both have a completely new existence. The Jewish idea of creation and eschatological re-creation provided the theological context for conversion, as in the similar saying of Rabbi Jose ben Zimra (third century), that he who converts a Gentile "is as if he had created him." This is true even where the idea of birth is employed: "I make you a new creature, like a woman who is pregnant and gives birth" (Rabbi Judah bar Simon, fourth century, using Exod. 2:2 to interpret Exod. 4:12). Here we have a formal analogy to Jas. 1:18, where the somewhat difficult expression: "He brought us forth" (ἀποκύειν), perhaps suggested from 1:15, is explained: "that we should be a kind of first fruits of his creatures"; for God's fatherhood is that of Creator (vs. 17). Thus this verb of birth, in spite of similarities in its context to NT regeneration passages, has not yet produced a doctrine specifically of "regeneration," or of the mystical traits usually accompanying it; such a development of the term does take place in Clement of Alexandria *Instructor* I.6.42, 45, where the concept of birth dominates the presentation and ἀποκύειν = ἀναγεννᾶν.

In the Epistle of Barnabas 6:11-19; 16:8 one finds the same preference for Jewish terms of creation in describing regeneration as in James, although the terminology and understanding have moved noticeably nearer to that of Paul and I Peter. "Since then he made us new [ἀνακαινίζειν] by the remission of sins he made us another type, that we should have the soul of children, as though he were creating us afresh [ἀναπλάσσειν]." As in I Pet. 2:2, comparison is made (6:17) to the child's diet of milk (prophesied in Exod. 33:3), which is the "word," "his word of faith" (16:9), as in Jas. 1:18, 21; I Pet. 1:23-25, by which "God truly dwells in us" (16:8-10; cf. 6:15). The nearest terminological approach to "regeneration" is in 16:8: "When we received the remission of sins, and put our hope on the Name, we became new, being created again from the beginning [ἐγενόμεθα καινοί, πάλιν ἐξ ἀρχῆς κτιζόμενοι]."

c. Paul. Paul also uses the Jewish concept of creation rather than that of birth to designate regeneration, when he describes it as "new creation" (II Cor. 5:17; Gal. 6:15; cf. Eph. 2:10, 15; 4:24; Col. 3:10), and here too the eschatological radicality of primitive Christianity is apparent: "The old has passed away, behold, the new has come" (II Cor. 5:17). But when in Gal. 6:14 this is expressed in terms of Jesus' cross, "by which the world has been crucified to me, and I to the world," it is apparent that union with Christ has become a new category for describing regeneration. This is effected at baptism (Rom. 6:3-11; Gal. 3:27; Col. 2:11-13): "Baptism into Christ Jesus" means "baptism into his death," "crucifixion of our old self with him so that the sinful body might be destroyed," "burial with him"; to this "putting off the body of flesh in the circumcision of Christ" there corresponds "putting on Christ"—"being raised [or made alive together] with him," so as to be "alive to God in Christ Jesus" and "walk in newness of life" (cf. Tit. 3:5). The resulting regenerate life can be described mystically as "Christ living in me" (Rom. 8:10; II Cor. 13:3, 5; Gal. 2:20; Phil. 1:21; Col. 1:27; 3:4, 11; cf. Eph. 3:17), or, somewhat similarly, as bearing already the eschatological Spirit (I Cor. 12: 13, etc.), or glory (II Cor. 3:18), or inner man (II Cor. 4:16). Paul can in a mixed metaphor speak of his birth pangs until Christ is formed in the believers (Gal. 4:19; cf. Rom. 8:22), and of his "begetting" (γεννᾶν) his converts (I Cor. 4:14-15; Philem. 10; cf. II Cor. 6:13; I Thess. 2:11); and in an allegory on Sarah and Hagar he contrasts the Jerusalem above as our "mother" with Mount Sinai "bearing children for slavery" (Gal. 4:24-26). In this context Paul can say (vs. 29): "As at that time he who was born according to the flesh persecuted him who was born according to the Spirit, so it is now." Yet he explains sonship to God only in terms of adult "adoption" to eschatological "heirs" (Rom. 8:14-23; Gal. 3:26-4:7; cf. Tit. 3:7; I Pet. 1:4). The mystic experience itself is described as "transformation" (II Cor. 3:18), by which the final resurrection "form" of Christ (Rom. 8:29) can, in view of the inbreaking new age (Rom. 12:2), be received now (Gal. 4:19). This concept is parallel to that of regeneration in Hellenistic literature, as is also evident, e.g., in the Euchologion of Serapion 19.3: "Form all those who are being regenerated (with) thy divine and inexpressible

form"; in Rom. 12:2 "transformation" is synonymous with "renewal," which is then in Tit. 3:5 identified as "regeneration." *See* NEW BIRTH.

Thus Paul attains in his concept of "transformation" the basic ingredients of the NT concept of "regeneration": the movement from Jewish terms into the more mystic categories characteristic of Hellenistic religiosity, and the persistence within these categories of the basically eschatological understanding of Christian existence. According to this understanding, regenerate life is lived out of the future—i.e., is transcendent—and thus is characterized by hiddenness (Col. 3:3-4; cf. I Pet. 1:4-5) rather than worldly demonstrability (I Cor. 12-14); by the continuing paradox of life in death to the present evil aeon, rather than in worldly success (contrast, e.g., I Cor. 4:11-13; II Cor. 1:8-9; 4:8-12; 6:8-10, with I Cor. 4:8-10); and by the ethical commitment to "be what you are" in Christ (Rom. 6:11-13; 12:1-2; 13:12-14; Gal. 5:24-25; Col. 3:1-17; etc.), rather than by any presuming upon an acquired status (I Cor. 10:1-12). The same is true in I John, where the triumphant indicative that those who are "begotten of God" do not, cannot, sin (3:9; 5:18), but do "overcome the world" (5:4), can be expressed inversely: it is those who do righteousness (2:29), love (4:7), and believe that Jesus is the Christ (5:1), who are "begotten of God"; both forms of expression are used for exhortation, and are parallel to the confession and forgiveness of sin (1:7-2:3).

Bibliography. P. Gennrich, *Die Lehre von der Wiedergeburt, die christliche Zentrallehre in dogmengeschichtlicher und religionsgeschichtlicher Beleuchtung* (1907). A. von Harnack, "Die Terminologie der Wiedergeburt und verwandter Erlebnisse in der ältesten Kirche," *TU*, XLII:3 (1918), 97-143. A. Dieterich, *Eine Mithrasliturgie* (3rd ed., 1923), especially pp. 157-79. R. Reitzenstein, *Die hellenistischen Mysterienreligionen* (3rd ed., 1927). M.-J. Lagrange, "La regeneration et la filiation divine dans les mystères d'Eleusis," *RB*, XXXVIII (1929), 63-81, 201-14. H. R. Willoughby, *Pagan Regeneration* (1929). J. Pascher, Η ΒΑΣΙΛΙΚΗ ΟΔΟΣ. *Der Königsweg zu Wiedergeburt und Vergottung bei Philon von Alexandreia (Studien zur Geschichte und Kultur des Altertums*, XVII:3-4; 1931). F. Büchsel, "γεννάω," "ἀναγεννάω," and "παλιγγενεσία," *TWNT*, I (1933), 663-74, 685-88. H. Jonas, "Erlosung," *Gnosis und spätantiker Geist*, I (1933), 199-210. A. D. Nock, *Conversion* (1933); also *JBL*, LII (1933), 132-33. V. Jacono, "La παλιγγενεσία in S. Paolo e nel ambiente pagano," *Bibl.*, XV (1934), 369-98. J. Dey, ΠΑΛΙΓΓΕΝΕΣΙΑ. *Ein Beitrag zur Klärung der religionsgeschichtlichen Bedeutung von Tit 3,5 (Neutestamentliche Abhandlungen* XVII:5; 1937). G. van der Leeuw, *Religion in Essence and Manifestation* (1938), chs. 22, 49, 79; *Religion in Geschichte und Gegenwart* (2nd ed., 1931), V, 1910 ff. W. L. Knox, *Some Hellenistic Elements in Primitive Christianity* (1944), pp. 90-94. E. Sjöberg, "Wiedergeburt und Neuschöpfung im palästinischen Judentum," *Studia Theologica*, IV (1951), 44-85. R. Bultmann, *Das Evangelium des Johannes* (1952), pp. 93 ff.

The *Eranos-Jahrbuch* (1939) consists of *Vorträge über die Symbolik der Wiedergeburt in der religiösen Vorstellung der Zeiten und Völker* (e.g., in primitive Christianity by E. Buonaiuti). See also the *excursi* in *HNT* to I Pet. 2:2; I John 3:9 (H. Windisch and H. Preisker); John 3:3 (W. Bauer); Tit. 3:5 (M. Dibelius and H. Conzelmann); Rom. 6:4 (H. Lietzmann).

On individual problems: J. Louw, "De Vraag naar de Beteekenis van ἄνωθεν, Johannes 3:3," *NTSt*, XXIII (1940), 53-56. R. Perdelwitz, *Die Mysterienreligion und das Problem des I. Petrusbriefes (Religionsgeschichtliche Versuche und Vorarbeiten* XI:3; 1911); see also E. G. Selwyn, *The First Epistle of St. Peter* (1946), pp. 306-9. C.-M. Edsman, "Schöpferwille und

Geburt Jac 1 18," *ZNW*, XXXVIII (1939), 11-44; see also M. Dibelius and H. Greeven, *Der Brief des Jakobus* (1956), especially *Ergänzungsheft*, p. 13; L. E. Elliott-Binns, "James 1.18: Creation or Redemption?" *NTSt*, III (1957), 148-61.

J. M. Robinson

REGISTER. The formal inscribing of the names of the heads of houses and militarily fit men in lists prepared for military or civil Census, or Genealogy. Such registration lists were of extreme importance for the genealogical interests of later Judaism.

J. A. Wharton

REHABIAH rē'ə bī'ə [רחביהו, רחביה, Yahu has made wide] (I Chr. 23:17; 24:21; 26:25). Son of Eliezer, and grandson of Moses. He was chief of one of the family groupings of Levites set aside for temple duties.

Bibliography. M. Noth, *Die israelitischen Personennamen* (1928), p. 193.   R. F. Johnson

REHOB rē'hŏb [רחב, רחוב, spacious area, market].
1. The father of Hadadezer, king of Zobah (II Sam. 8:3, 12).
2. A signatory of the covenant made in the days of Nehemiah (Neh. 10:11).   E. R. Achtemeier
3. *See* Beth-rehob.
4. A border town in Asher (Josh. 19:28, 30), assigned to the Levites (Josh. 21:31; I Chr. 6:75—H 6: 60), whose Canaanite inhabitants Asher was unable to drive out (Judg. 1:31). It is perhaps to be identified with Tell el-Gharbi (or Berweh), located *ca.* seven miles E-SE of Acco in the plain. The site, which dominates an important road to the interior, was occupied in the Middle Bronze, Late Bronze II, Iron I, and Hellenistic-Roman periods.

Bibliography. W. F. Albright, "Contributions to the Historical Geography of Palestine," *AASOR*, II-III (1923), 27-28; J. Garstang, *Joshua, Judges (The Foundations of Bible History;* 1931), pp. 98, 241, 397-98.   G. W. Van Beek

REHOBOAM rē'ə bō'əm [רחבעם, may the people expand; NT Ροβοάμ]; KJV NT ROBOAM rō-bō'əm. King of Judah *ca.* 922-915 B.C.; son and successor of Solomon; first king of the S after the disruption of the kingdom at Solomon's death.

In the LXX the name appears as Ροβοάμ, presumably on the basis of the contemporary "Jeroboam" of the N; hence the English "Rehoboam." It is equally possible, however, that "Rehoboam" provided the model for "Jeroboam," and that both are throne names. The emphasis on the power of the people as against that of the king may be deliberately intended by the use of the names. The verbal element is רחב, "to be widened" or "to expand"; or it may be an Arabic root meaning "to be generous." The element עם means "people"; or it may refer to the god Amm, or "the (divine) kinsman, or protector, or uncle." The latter meaning is unlikely.

Rehoboam became king at the age of forty-one and reigned seventeen years (I Kings 14:21; II Chr. 12:13). The Chronicler adds that he "was young and irresolute and could not withstand" Jeroboam and his followers at the time of the Disruption (II Chr. 13:7). Doubtless this refers to the "young men" (I Kings 12:8; II Chr. 10:8), whose advice Rehoboam

followed. The problem of chronology is exceedingly complicated (*see* Chronology of the OT). In the light of the available evidence, both biblical and extrabiblical, a date *ca.* 922 seems most reasonable for Solomon's death and Rehoboam's accession. If this date is correct, it appears likely that Rehoboam reigned only some eight years. His mother was Naamah the Ammonitess.

He came to the throne at a very difficult time. Solomon had ruled as a despot, and as a result had roused bitter resentment, especially among the N tribes. The forced-labor system (the hated *corvée*) in particular ran counter to the spirit of the freedom-loving Israelites. Closely allied to this was Solomon's attempt to break the old tribal spirit by dividing the land (with the exception of Judah, which seems to have received preferential treatment in this regard) into twelve roughly equal administrative districts. It is possible that Judah had already been divided up into administrative districts by David. This scheme was, no doubt, devised in order to facilitate the collection of taxes. In many ways it disregarded completely the old tribal boundaries. Solomon seems to have been able to keep the people in subjection; at least they refrained from open rebellion during his lifetime. A smoldering resentment, however, was burning, and it came to a head at Solomon's death. Presumably Rehoboam had already been crowned king at Jerusalem (I Kings 12:6, 12*b*-13, 15). But this did not satisfy the N part of the country. "All Israel" (I Kings 12:1; II Chr. 10:1)—the reference must be only to the N tribes—gathered together at Shechem, the cultic center of the old N amphictyony, to make Rehoboam king, and there he came in person. Before he was accepted, however, the people demanded a lightening of the crushing load imposed upon them by Solomon. Rehoboam consulted with his father's old advisers. The key word in their reply was the word "serve" (I Kings 12:7). A leadership of service of this kind, however, had no appeal for Rehoboam, who then took counsel with the young men, his intimates and associates, who said: "Thus shall you speak to this people . . . , 'My father chastised you with whips, but I will chastise you with scorpions'" (I Kings 12:9-11; II Chr. 10:9-11). This advice Rehoboam chose to follow and his harsh answer meant the revolt of the N. The once proud empire of David and Solomon was no more.

Rehoboam's reaction to the assertion of independence revealed a high degree of irresponsibility. He sent Adoram (I Kings 12:18) or Hadoram (II Chr. 10:18) or Adoniram (I Kings 4:6), "taskmaster over the forced labor," to head off the incipient revolt. The people stoned him to death. In fear for his life, the king mounted his chariot and fled to Jerusalem, where he gathered together "all the house of Judah, and the tribe of Benjamin, a hundred and eighty thousand chosen warriors [the figures cannot be accepted as reliable], to fight against the house of Israel, to restore the kingdom to Rehoboam the son of Solomon" (I Kings 12:21; II Chr. 11:1). The planned campaign did not materialize, for, through the intervention of Shemaiah (I Kings 12:24; II Chr. 11:4), the men of Judah and Benjamin returned home.

Jeroboam probably appealed for help to the

Pharaoh Shishak of Egypt, whose protégé he had been for many years (I Kings 11:40), and Rehoboam's army apparently disbanded because of an unmistakable warning from Egypt that reprisals would follow the contemplated attack. Yet, "there was war between Rehoboam and Jeroboam continually" (I Kings 14:30; II Chr. 12:15). The reference here is in all probability to border warfare. It would appear that the territory of Benjamin was included in the S kingdom, while the former Danite territory was divided between the two kingdoms.

The Chronicler records that Rehoboam began to build cities for defense in Judah (II Chr. 11:5-12). Of the fifteen cities mentioned, none was in the territory of Benjamin (cf. vss. 10, 12b). The section interrupts the connection between vss. 1-4 and 13-17, and it cannot be assumed from its present position that the events described took place near the beginning of Rehoboam's reign. The Chronicler noted the fortress building prior to Shishak's invasion because he considered the loss of the fortresses as one of the punishments for Rehoboam's disloyalty to Yahweh (II Chr. 12:4). There are strong grounds, however, for the view that the building of the fortresses took place after the Egyptian invasion, as a direct result of it.

The list of towns named is interesting in view of their locations. The first four were to the E of Judah, the next four to the SW, the next three to the S, the next three to the NW, with Hebron by itself. No mention is made of fortress building to the N, apart from Aijalon. But perhaps this was not possible because of continuous border warfare. Does this list of cities represent the limits of Judah at this time? This is possible, especially if the time was after the Egyptian invasion. Noteworthy is the fact that such a boundary line would exclude the territory of Simeon, and might explain the later reference to this territory in the reign of Asa as being outside Judah (II Chr. 15:9). The more probable view, however, is that this list represents only the fortresses built by Rehoboam. There were also other fortresses which belonged to the time of Solomon. It is further to be noted that though the fortresses are said to have been very strong, there is no mention of horses and chariots.

The biblical account (I Kings 14:25-26; II Chr. 12:2-9) gives but meager information in regard to the invasion of SHISHAK. Fortunately, however, he himself has preserved details on the walls of the great Karnak temple in Upper Egypt. These indicate both the extent and the ferocity of the invasion. Not only was Judah involved, as Kings and Chronicles seem to imply, but also Philistia, the N kingdom as far N as Megiddo, Transjordan, and even Edom as far S as Ezion-geber, which seems to have been destroyed at this time. The suggestion that the list should be read boustrophedon (the alternation of lines from left to right and right to left) may be expected to produce interesting results and provide further details of the campaign. It seems clear from the available evidence that a strong and united Israel stood in the way of Egypt's revived dream of empire, and even before Solomon's death Shishak may have begun to plot against him. This would explain his receiving at his court the exiles Hadad the Edomite and Jeroboam the son of Nebat (I Kings 11:14-40). Shishak himself had been a Libyan noble, and his army was composed of barbarian troops from Libya and Ethiopia (II Chr. 12:2 ff). They wrought widespread devastation everywhere. One hundred and fifty places are named on the great Karnak Inscription as having been taken. This picture has been confirmed by archaeology. Such towns as Debir and Ezion-geber were destroyed at this time. A fragment of a stele bearing the king's name was found at Megiddo. The great fortifications at Sharuhen, SE of Gaza, may indicate that Egypt used this place as a base of operations for the invasion. Jerusalem itself was not captured, but a very heavy tribute was imposed on the land.

As a result of this experience Rehoboam set about fortifying his kingdom. Most of the fortresses named commanded approaches from the S and the W. It seems clear that further attacks from Egypt were expected, but with Shishak's death (ca. 914) these did not materialize. It is possible that remains of Rehoboam's fortifications have been found at LACHISH and at AZEKAH.

The Chronicler records that Judah was strengthened considerably by the arrival of the priests and Levites from the N, who had been deprived by Jeroboam of their means of livelihood (II Chr. 11:13-17). They were accompanied by "those who had set their hearts to seek the Lord God of Israel." For three years, under their influence, Judah prospered. Then Rehoboam forsook the law of the Lord, and punishment came upon him in the form of an Egyptian invasion of the land. This took place in Rehoboam's fifth year, ca. 918 (I Kings 14:25; II Chr. 12:2). The Chronicler's picture is clearly dependent upon his viewpoint. Shishak's invasion occurred in the fifth year of the king. This must have come as the result of disloyalty to Yahweh. Such disloyalty belonged therefore to the fourth year of his reign. For his first three years he was loyal. The picture which the Deuteronomist presents is very different (I Kings 14:22-24). It is clear that the pagan influences for which Solomon was largely responsible continued during Rehoboam's reign. These affected worship both in the temple and throughout the land. In this connection it is to be noted that the king's mother was an Ammonitess. Specific mention is made of the construction of high places, pillars, and Asherim. In addition, there were male cult prostitutes in the land. Rehoboam's reign was characterized by religious perversions (cf. II Chr. 12:14).

The section dealing with Rehoboam's family (II Chr. 11:18-22) has no parallel in Kings, and raises a difficult problem. Of the king's eighteen wives only two are named—Mahalath and Maacah the daughter of a certain Absalom (probably not David's son; II Sam. 14:27; 18:18). He preferred the latter, and intended to make her eldest son, Abijah, king in his stead. The Chronicler gives the name of Abijah's mother as Micaiah the daughter of Uriel of Gibeah (II Chr. 13:2). The two statements are often harmonized by changing "Micaiah" to "Maacah" on the evidence of some of the versions, and assuming that Uriel of Gibeah was Tamar's husband. The problem is complicated still further by the evidence of Kings, which makes Maacah the daughter of Abishalom the mother of both Abijah and Asa (I Kings 15:2b, 10b), and yet claims Asa as Abijah's son (vs. 8*b*). It seems best to consider Micaiah the daughter of Uriel of Gibeah as the mother of Abijah, and Maacah the daughter of Absalom (or Abishalom) as the mother of Asa, and to regard the section II Chr. 11:18-23 as coming from another source which was later inserted in Chronicles. It is difficult to account satisfactorily for these verses in their present context. The same judgment of another source is true also for II Chr. 12:13-14, which runs counter to the Chronicler's representation of Rehoboam as a young man (13:7).

As his source the Chronicler names the "chronicles of Shemaiah the prophet and of Iddo the seer" (II Chr. 12:15). Of such a prophetic work—others of similar nature are mentioned later—nothing is known.

Bibliography. J. H. Breasted, *Ancient Records of Egypt*, no. 4 (1906-7), paragraphs 709 ff. W. F. Albright, "The Amorite Form of the Name Hammurabi," *AJSL*, XXXVIII (1922), 140-41. N. Glueck, "The Second Campaign at Tell el-Kheleifeh (Ezion-geber:Elath)," *BASOR*, 75 (1939), 8-22. R. S. Lamon and G. M. Shipton, *Megiddo*, I (1939), 60-61. W. F. Albright, "The Excavation of Tell Beit Mirsim," III, *AASOR*, XXI-XXII (1943), 38 (note 14), 67; "The Chronology of the Divided Monarchy of Israel," *BASOR*, 100 (1945), 16-22. J. B. Pritchard, ed., *ANET* (2nd ed., 1955), pp. 242-43. M. B. Rowton, "The Date of the Founding of Solomon's Temple," *BASOR*, 119 (1950), 20 ff. J. A. Montgomery, *The Book of Kings*, ICC (1951), pp. 244-70. E. R. Thiele, *The Mysterious Numbers of the Hebrew Kings* (1951), pp. 55 ff. W. F. Albright, "New Light from Egypt on the Chronology and History of Israel and Judah," *BASOR*, 130 (1953), 4-8. A. Alt, *Kleine Schriften zur Geschichte des Volkes Israel*, II (1953), 306-15. W. Rudolph, *Chronikbücher* (1955), pp. 227-35. G. E. Wright, *Biblical Archaeology* (1957), pp. 146 ff.

H. B. MacLean

REHOBOTH rĭ hō′bŏth [רחבות, broad places].
1. *See* Rehoboth-ir.

2. The name of one of the wells dug by Isaac and his men in the Valley of Gerar (Gen. 26:17-22). After the Philistines had appropriated for themselves the first two wells, the third one resulted in no quarrel, so the name Rehoboth, signifying enough room for all, was given to it. There are several large wells, or cisterns, at Ruheibeh, ancient Rehoboth, *ca.* nineteen miles SW of Beer-sheba. Though these date from the Byzantine period, the patriarchs, using even more rudimentary tools, undoubtedly dug similar cisterns in the rock in their day.

3. An Edomite city, home of King Shaul (Gen. 36: 37; I Chr. 1:48). The RSV translation, "on the Euphrates," for the more literal "on the river" is confusing, since the reference here is to a place, not in Mesopotamia, but probably somewhere in N Edom, as yet unidentified.

Bibliography. N. Glueck, *Explorations in Eastern Palestine*, vol. II, *AASOR*, 15 (1934-35), 100-10; F.-M. Abel, *Géographie de la Palestine*, II (1938), 435. V. R. Gold

REHOBOTH-IR rĭ hō′bŏth ĭr′ [רחבת עיר] (Gen. 10:11); KJV THE CITY OF REHOBOTH. A city in Assyria between Nineveh and Calah, built by Asshur. No such city name is known from the cuneiform sources. Since *reḥōbhōth* means "open space" and *'îr* means "city," the term has been compared with the cognate Assyrian *rêbît ali*, "open spaces in a city," "square," "unbuilt area"; and specifically with *rêbît Ninua*, by which the Assyrians designated unbuilt

areas on the periphery of Nineveh. It is conceivable that instead of Rehoboth-Ir, "the city 'Open Spaces,' " the text of Gen. 10:11 originally read "the open spaces of the city" and referred to peripheral sections of the city of Nineveh, which is mentioned immediately before. T. Jacobsen

REHUM rē′əm [רחום, *hypocoristic for* (the Deity) has been merciful; Apoc. 'Ράθυμος (I Esd. 2:16-30; *perhaps erroneously for* 'Ράουμος), 'Ροῖμος (I Esd. 5:8)]; KJV Apoc. RATHUMUS rə thōō′məs (I Esd. 2:16-30), ROIMUS rō′ĭ məs (I Esd. 5:8). **1.** One of those whose names head the list of exiles returned from Babylon with Zerubbabel (Ezra 2:2; I Esd. 5:8). In Neh. 7:7 the name is Nehum (נחום), probably a scribal error.

2. An official in the Persian government for the province "Beyond the River" (Trans-Euphratia), which included Palestine. With one Shimshai the scribe, he cosponsored a letter to King Artaxerxes opposing the rebuilding of Jerusalem by the Jews after the Exile (Ezra 4:8-16). With a supporting reply from the royal court, he and Shimshai, with their associates, forced the work to a halt (vss. 17-24; cf. I Esd. 2:16-30).

Bibliography. R. A. Bowman, Exegesis of Ezra, *IB*, III (1954), 599-600.

3. A Levite, son of Bani; one of those who aided Nehemiah with the repair of the Jerusalem wall (Neh. 3:17).

4. One of the chiefs of the people, signatory to the covenant of Ezra (Neh. 10:25); possibly related to 1 *above*.

5. A corruption of Harim 1 (Neh. 12:3).

Bibliography. M. Noth, *Die israelitischen Personennamen* (1928), pp. 38, 187. B. T. Dahlberg

REI rē, rē′ī [רעי, friendly(?)] (I Kings 1:8). A Judean officer who sided with Solomon in the struggle for David's throne. Variants in the ancient versions include "his [Shimei's] friends" and "David's friend" (i.e., Shimei); but the MT is preferable.

J. M. Ward

REINS. *See* Kidneys; Bit.

REJOICE. *See* Joy.

REKEM rē′kəm [רקם, friendship]. **1.** One of the five kings of Midian who were slain by Moses and the people of Israel in obedience to the command of Yahweh (Num. 31:8; Josh. 13:21). According to the narrative, the war was one of Yahweh's vengeance upon Midian because the Midianites had beguiled the Israelites into worshiping Baal-peor and because Zimri of the tribe of Simeon had taken as a wife Cozbi, the daughter of a Midianite prince (cf. Num. 25)—both acts of apostasy. However, as it stands in the Priestly Code, the narrative serves primarily to furnish a precedent for the law regulating the distribution of booty.

2. A descendant of Caleb; a son of Hebron; and the father of Shammai (I Chr. 2:43-44).

3. A city within the territory allotted by Joshua to the tribe of Benjamin. Its location still remains uncertain (Josh. 18:27). E. R. Achtemeier

RELEASE, YEAR OF. A name mistakenly applied in practically all English versions of the Bible to the SABBATICAL YEAR, based upon an incorrect translation, which originated with the LXX, of the Hebrew verb שׁמט and its derivative noun, שׁמטה in Deut. 15: 1-3, 9; 31:10. The Vulg. renders שׁמטה more justifiably as "remission." Far more correct would be the designation, not of the Sabbatical Year, but rather of the Jubilee Year (see JUBILEE, YEAR OF) as the Year of Release, based upon its function as the year of the proclamation of דרור, "liberty throughout the land to all its inhabitants" (Lev. 25:10), and the specific name, שׁנת הדרור, the "Year of Liberty" (Ezek. 46:17) and its function as the year of liberty or release of Jews enslaved to fellow Jews, and also of release or restoration of property held in temporary possession by one Jew to its original Jewish owner or his family.   J. MORGENSTERN

RELIGION [θρησκεία (alternately WORSHIP); θεοσέβεια (KJV GODLINESS); εὐσέβεια (alternately PIETY; GODLINESS; GODLY LIFE; KJV GODLINESS; HOLINESS); 'Ιουδαϊσμός (Gal. 1:13-14 KJV; RSV JUDAISM)]. The words translated "religion" are used almost exclusively in the later, more Hellenistic NT writings, to refer (a) to the practice of the (proper) religious observances or patterns of worship—i.e., to correct cultic behavior; (b) to a recognized structure of religious-ethical behavior, covering all man's duties to God and man; and (c) especially in the Pastorals, to obedience to the Christian faith conceived as a deposit and a discipline.

The infrequent use of "religion" in the Bible is due to the fact that the concept of "religion" is itself alien to the core of biblical thought. The basic meaning of faith to the Hebrew is the concrete response of the whole man to God's call and obedience to his command, not intellectual acceptance of a body of truth or even correct observance of special cultic acts. Primary for faith is man's relation to God, not his relation to faith structure or cult practice.

The introduction of the general concept of "religion" into the late NT writings meant the weakening, if not the abandonment, of the revelation character of Christianity. "Religion," now meaning the Christian religion, becomes a system of doctrine, an organization, an approved pattern of behavior and form of worship.

Thus the primary importance of the term "religion" in the NT is in its pointing to the shift which was taking place in the Hellenistic churches, from the Hebrew understanding of faith as concrete obedience of the whole man to God, to faith as an ecclesiastically approved system of doctrine, worship, and behavior.

Bibliography. J. H. Ropes, *St. James* (1916), pp. 181-82; J. G. Tasker, "Religion," *Dictionary of the Apostolic Church*, II (1918), 315; M. Dibelius, Note on I Tim. 2:1-2, *Die Pastoral Briefe* (2nd ed., 1931), pp. 24-25; B. S. Easton, *The Pastoral Epistles* (1947), p. 218; C. Spicq, *Les Épitres Pastorales* (1947), pp. 125-34; R. Bultmann, *Theology of the NT*, II (1955), 213.
                    F. D. GEALY

REMALIAH rĕm'ə lī'ə [רמליהו]. The father of the Israelite usurper Pekah (II Kings 15:25, etc.).

REMEMBRANCE. See MEMORIAL.

REMETH rē'mĭth [רמת]. A border town in the territory allotted to Issachar (Josh. 19:21). It is probably the same as RAMOTH in I Chr. 6:73—H 6:58 and JARMUTH in Josh. 21:29, which are variants of the name of a Levitical town in this territory.
                    G. W. VAN BEEK

REMISSION. See FORGIVENESS.

REMMON. KJV alternate form of RIMMON 3-4.

REMMON-METHOAR rĕm'ən mĕth'ō är. KJV translation of רמון המתאר (Josh. 19:13). See RIMMON 4.

***REMNANT** [שׁאר, שׁארית, *and other words derived from the roots* פלט, שׁרד, *and* יתר; λεῖμμα, ὑπόλειμμα]. The portion of a community which is left, in the case of a devastating calamity; the portion upon which the possible future existence of the community depends.

In the secular realm, passages such as Josh. 10:40; II Chr. 20:23-24; Jer. 50:26 illustrate the principle of total destruction in which there is to be no remnant (see BAN); and Gen. 32:7-8—H 32:8-9; Judg. 21:16-17, the meaning of "remnant" as bearer of the further existence of a community. The theological use of the term develops where there is mention of the judgment of the holy God on everything sinful and ungodly; where one is also aware, however, of the compassionate mercy of God, who remains faithful to his work of salvation and permits a remnant to escape from the judgment. The concept "remnant" includes, accordingly, not only a destructive but also a constructive meaning. It refers to the judgment passed but at the same time to its merciful limitation by God's free grace. The accent can be placed differently, according to the circumstances: Isa. 17:6 shows an ironic use of the term "remnant" as a threat; Mic. 5:7-8—H 5:6-7, its paradoxically exaggerated promissory character in the proclamation of salvation.

In the history of the biblical concept of a remnant is mirrored a long trail of faith in salvation, from the early narrators through the prophets and apocalyptic writers, down to Paul in Rom. 9:11. Even the author of the J document speaks of the merciful deliverance of a remnant of the bearers of the promise from the destructive divine judgment: Noah in the Flood (Gen. 6:5-8; 7:1, 23); Lot in the destruction of Sodom (18:17-33; 19:1-29; cf. 45:7). The story of Elijah reveals the belief in the existence of a remnant of seven thousand who are true to Yahweh in Israel (I Kings 19:17-18).

Amos seems to assume on the part of his opponents a popular remnant idea bearing the stamp of eschatological salvation, when, in the face of their objections, he treats with irony or bitterly attacks every self-confident remnant hope (Amos 3:12; 5:3; 6:9; 9:1). Israel cannot simply equate itself with the remnant. Nevertheless, there remains also in his thinking for those who seek Yahweh and the good, the possibility that they may survive the judgment as a remnant (5:4, 6, 14-15). To be sure, all self-assurance is qualified by the "may be" (5:15), which makes salvation ultimately depend on God's free grace.

While the idea of a remnant is not found in Hosea, it plays a significant role in the case of Isaiah (7:3)

and his disciples (4:2 ff; 10:20-22; 11:10-16; 28:5; 37:32). As in the case of Amos, it belongs first of all in the proclamation of judgment (10:19; 17:5-6; 30:17; cf. 1:8). However, the name Shear-jashub, "A remnant shall repent" (7:3; see SHEAR-JASHUB; REMNANT SHALL RETURN, A), which was given to the eldest son of the prophet, proclaims and guarantees that a remnant will return to God. Prerequisite for this return are conversion and faith (7:9):

> If you will not believe,
>> surely you shall not be established.

But it is God alone who permits the remnant (1:9). Nowhere does Isaiah say with sufficient clarity who will belong to the remnant. One may probably reckon among them him (6:7), his children and disciples (8:18), and the "afflicted of his people" who find refuge in Zion (14:32).

A fully developed remnant expectation is found in Zephaniah. He identifies the remnant with the poor and humble, both in his admonition (2:3):

> Seek the LORD, all you humble of the land,
>> who do his commands;
> seek righteousness, seek humility;
>> perhaps you may be hidden
>> on the day of the wrath of the LORD;

and in the promise (3:12-13):

> For I will leave in the midst of you
>> a people humble and lowly.
> They shall seek refuge in the name of the LORD,
>> those who are left in Israel.

As in Isaiah, it is God's act which creates the remnant; with it, justice is re-established (Zeph. 3:13). The remnant, as a spiritual Israel, is clearly differentiated from the political Israel.

Jeremiah and Ezekiel both give up any claim to the traditional remnant concept in their proclamation of a total judgment (Jer. 8:3; 15:1-3; Ezek. 5:1-2; 15:7). In the vision of the two baskets of figs (Jer. 24) Jeremiah proclaims the final judgment upon "Zedekiah the king of Judah, his princes, the remnant of Jerusalem who remain in this land, and those who dwell in the land of Egypt" (vs. 8), while the "exiles from Judah" (vs. 5) are to be replanted and built up anew. It is significant that the term "remnant," which still expresses too strongly the continuity in the history of the people, is not expressly used for these people, though the ideas related to it are—ideas which, to be sure, find their fulfilment only after the national death. In the case of Ezekiel, who himself suffers severely under the ruthless proclamation of judgment (Ezek. 9:8; 11:13), the escapees from the catastrophe of Jerusalem will be the only proof of the suitability of the judgment (14:21-23). Like Jeremiah, he anticipates the function of the remnant of the exiles (11:14-20), but without applying the term "remnant" to them, as is done in Isa. 46:3.

The postexilic community can call itself the remnant which was left (Hag. 1:12-14; 2:2; Zech. 8:6, 11-12; Ezra 9:8, 14-15; Neh. 1:2-3). Moreover, the remnant continues as a future greatness in numerous promises of salvation from the period after the catastrophe of Jerusalem, promises which cannot be more accurately dated (Supplements to Isaiah: 4:2; 10:20-22; 11:11-16; 28:5-6; 37:32; to Jeremiah: 23:3; 31:

7b γ; to Obadiah: vs. 17; to Micah: 2:12-13; 5:7-8—H 5:6-7; 7:18; to Zephaniah: 2:7, 9). In Zech. 9:7; 14:16 the promise also applies to heathen nations or their remnant.

On the topic of the continuation of the idea of the remnant in the late Jewish apocalyptic writings, cf., e.g., Enoch 83:8; II Esd. 12:34; 13:48; II Bar. 40:2; Sibylline Oracles 5:384. In the NT the idea plays an important role in Paul's discussion of the course of God's salvation in Rom. 9-11 (see 9:27; 11:5). *See also* CHURCH, IDEA OF; ISRAEL, NAME AND ASSOCIATIONS OF; PEOPLE OF GOD.

Bibliography. R. de Vaux, "Le reste d'Israël," *RB*, XLII (1933), 526-39; R. Volz, *Die Eschatologie der jüdischen Gemeinde im neutestamentlichen Zeitalter* (1934), pp. 352-53; W. E. Müller, *Die Vorstellung vom Rest im AT* (1939); O. Schilling, *"Rest" in der Prophetie des AT* (1942); S. Garofalo, *La nozione del Resto d'Israele* (1944); J. C. Campbell, "God's People and the Remnant," *Scottish Journal of Theology*, III (1950), 78-85; V. Maag, *Text, Wortschatz und Begriffswelt des Buches Amos* (1951), pp. 199-200, 246-52; E. W. Heaton, *JTS*, N.S. III (1952), 27-39, on the root שאר and the doctrine of the remnant; L. Köhler, "שאר ישוב und der nackte Relativsatz," *Vetus Testamentum*, III (1953), 84-85; F. Dreyfus, "La doctrine du reste d'Israël chez le prophète Isaïe," *Revue des Sciences Philosophiques et Théologiques*, XXXIX (1955), 361-86; J. W. Miller, *Das Verhältnis Jeremias und Hesekiels sprachlich und theologisch untersucht* (1955), pp. 165-68.   E. JENNI

REMPHAN. KJV form of REPHAN.

RENDING OF GARMENTS. *See* MOURNING.

*REPENTANCE. The translation of several words expressing a variety of ideas, ranging from (*a*) a change of mind, (*b*) the feeling of regret or remorse, to (*c*) repentance in the ethico-religious sense, turning away from sin and back to God. The last of the three is most prominent and most significant in the Bible. The emphasis may rest on the negative side, of turning away from SIN, disobedience, or rebellion; it may also fall on the positive side, the turning back to God, the beginning of a new religious or moral life.

1. Terminology. The commonest term for "repentance" in the OT is שׁוּב, "turn back" (Jer. 8:4; Ezek. 33:19), which occurs frequently in the Prophets. Less common is נחם, "to be sorry, repent" (Exod. 13:17; Ps. 106:45). The LXX translates שׁוּב by ἐπιστρέφων, "turn about," and ἀποστρέφω, "turn back." נחם is translated by μεταμέλομαι, "to change one's mind," and by μετανοέω, "repent." The NT does not follow the practice of the LXX, but uses μετανοέω to render the thought-content of שׁוּב; this usage has support in other Greek translations of the Hebrew Bible and in Hellenistic Judaism.

In the NT the verb μετανοέω, "repent," occurs thirty-two times (Matt. 3:2; 4:17; 11:20; etc.); the noun μετάνοια, "repentance," twenty-two times (Matt. 3:8; Mark 1:4; Luke 3:3; etc.); the verb μεταμέλομαι, "to change one's mind, repent," six times. The verb ἐπιστρέφω is used sixteen times in the sense "turn back, be converted" (Matt. 13:15; Luke 22:32; Acts 15:19; I Pet. 2:25); and the noun ἐπιστροφή, "turning back, CONVERSION," occurs in Acts 15:3.

2. In the OT. Israel owes obedience to God, falls under judgment when it strays, and can only recover his favor by renouncing sin and turning back to him. Defeat in warfare or failure of harvest is understood as a manifestation of the divine wrath and becomes an occasion for repentance. There are days of national repentance, such as that described in Neh. 9. An individual may also experience judgment and turn back to God, as Ahab does after Elijah denounces him (I Kings 21). There is a ritual of repentance: the rending of one's clothing, fasting, putting on sackcloth, sitting in ashes. There are liturgies of repentance; notable examples are preserved in Isa. 63:7–64:12; Dan. 9:4-19; Hos. 6; 14.

The prophets emphasize that man's relation to God is personal, and that sin roots in a wrong relationship to God. Repentance also is personal: it is a reorientation of the entire person and a return to Yahweh. Genuine repentance leads to obedience, unqualified trust in God, rejection of all idols, and refusal to lean upon human help. The growth of the personal understanding of sin and repentance is accompanied by criticism of religious formalism (Hos. 6:6; Amos 5:21-24). Repentance is renewal of life; it demands a new heart and spirit (Ezek. 18:31). It is a human possibility because it is the result of the divine redemption (Isa. 44:22; Jer. 31:33; Ezek. 11:19; 36:26).

3. In the NT. John the Baptist continues the prophetic demand for repentance: "Bear fruit that befits repentance . . . . Every tree . . . that does not bear good fruit is cut down and thrown into the fire" (Matt. 3:8, 10). A new development is his relating of repentance to the imminent kingdom of God and to a BAPTISM granting FORGIVENESS of sins.

The preaching of Jesus resembles that of John the Baptist. Repentance is necessary for life under the kingly rule of God (Mark 1:15; Luke 13:1-3). It involves the total person: "The tree is known by its fruit" (Matt. 12:33); "Cleanse the inside of the cup and of the plate, that the outside also may be clean" (Matt. 23:26; cf. Mark 7:15). But he deepens the prophetic demand in his interpretation of the inwardness of sin (Matt. 5:28); by his insistence on the second mile (vs. 41) and love to enemies (vs. 44); and by the radical rejection of everything that hinders return to God (Matt. 5:29; 6:19; 7:13; Mark 3:31-35; 10:21): "Whoever of you does not renounce all that he has cannot be my disciple" (Luke 14:33). Repentance means becoming another person: "Unless you turn and become like children, you will never enter the kingdom of heaven" (Matt. 18:3). Entrance to the kingdom is for the poor in spirit, the receptive, the small and helpless. He offends the Pharisees by his associations with tax collectors and sinners and even more by his theological justification of his conduct: "I have not come to call the righteous, but sinners to repentance" (Luke 5:32).

The new element in Jesus' preaching of repentance appears at this point. The prophets know that God must give the sinner a new heart and spirit. Repentance in the deepest sense is beyond human powers. They look forward to the time when God will perform the miracle of raising men from the valley of dry bones (Ezek. 37). Jesus announces that the time has come: "The time is fulfilled, and the kingdom of God is at hand; repent, and believe in the gospel" (Mark 1:15). Repentance is no longer only

demand; it has become possibility, for what is impossible with men is possible with God (10:27). Repentance is completed by FAITH. Return to God is now no longer response to law but to a person; it is discipleship. Jesus points to himself with magisterial confidence as the fulfilment of the Law and the Prophets. Repentance and faith are two sides of the same coin. There can be no genuine repentance which is not also the acceptance of the divine promise spoken in Jesus of Nazareth.

In the preaching of the apostolic church repentance is basic (Acts 3:19; 5:31; 8:22; II Cor. 7:9; Heb. 6:1; Rev. 2:21). It is connected with baptism as the beginning of the life in Christ (Acts 2:38; 13:24; 19:4). It is related to faith (Acts 20:21; 26:18; Heb. 6:1), and to forgiveness (Luke 24:47; Acts 3:19; 8:22). It is a turning away from evil (Acts 3:26; 8:22; II Cor. 12:21; Heb. 6:1; Rev. 2:22; 9:20), and a return to God (Acts 20:21; 26:20; I Pet. 2:25; Rev. 16:9), based on the work of Christ (Acts 3:19; 5:31; 17:30). Repentance is at once man's responsibility (Acts 2:38; 3:19; 8:22; 17:30; 26:20) and a gift of God (Acts 3:26; 5:31; 11:18; Rom. 2:4; II Cor. 7:9; II Tim. 2:25; Rev. 2:21) through the Spirit (Acts 10:45; 11:15).

The term "repentance" occurs infrequently in the writings of Paul and not at all in the Fourth Gospel or the Johannine letters. This indicates no depreciation of the place of repentance in the Christian life, but rather points to the development of specialized theological vocabularies which emphasize the element of newness in the Christian life. For both Paul and John repentance is included in faith. Paul speaks of faith as union with Christ, the death of the old nature, the putting on of the new humanity, resurrection to newness of life, and new creation. The Johannine literature presents the life in Christ as rebirth; movement from death to life and from darkness to light; or as the triumph of truth over falsehood, love over hatred, God over the world.

Bibliography. E. D. Burton in H. R. Willoughby, ed., *NT Word Studies* (1927); A. H. Dirksen, *The NT Concept of Metanoia* (1932); W. Eichrodt, *Theologie des ATs,* III (1939), 118-41; O. Michel, μεταμέλομαι, *TWNT,* IV (1942), 630-33. E. Würthwein, μετάνοια, *TWNT,* IV (1942), 972-1004. A. Richardson, *An Introduction to the Theology of the NT* (1958), pp. 31-34.   W. A. QUANBECK

REPHAEL rĕf'ĭ əl [רפאל] (I Chr. 26:7). The second son of Shemaiah; a gatekeeper, an "able man," who served in the temple at Jerusalem. According to tradition, he was set apart for service by David.

REPHAH rē'fə [רפח, rich(?)] (I Chr. 7:25). An Ephraimite. His parentage is obscured by the present Hebrew text, which gives no father's name. The intention may have been to name Sheerah, builder of Beth-horon, as his mother.

Bibliography. M. Noth, *Die israelitischen Personennamen* (1928), p. 231.   R. F. JOHNSON

REPHAIAH rĭ fā'yə [רפיה]. Alternately RAPHAH rā fə [רפה] (I Chr. 8:37 = 4 *below*); KJV RAPHA.
1. A descendant of David and Solomon of Judah; the son of Jeshaiah and the father of Arnan (I Chr. 3:21).
2. A Simeonite, and one among the five hundred

men of that tribe who made their home in the vicinity of Mount Seir, after having destroyed the Amalekites dwelling there (I Chr. 4:42).

3. A member of the tribe of Issachar, and a son of Tola (I Chr. 7:2). He is reported to have been a mighty warrior.

4. A descendant of Saul of Benjamin; son of Binea, and the father of Eleasah (I Chr. 9:43).

5. Son of Hur, and one of those who helped to rebuild the wall of Jerusalem in the days of Nehemiah (Neh. 3:9). He had charge of half of one of the five governmental districts into which postexilic Judah was divided (the Jerusalem district formed the middle area). It can therefore be assumed that he belonged to a family which had remained in Judah after the downfall of the southern kingdom in 586 B.C.   E. R. ACHTEMEIER

*REPHAIM rĕf'ĭ əm [רפאים, רפא, רפה (*the last two always with the article*); Ugar. *rpi, rpum, etc.;* Phoen. רפאם]. **1.** The shades, the dead, inhabitants of SHEOL. They are the weak, shadowy continuations of the living who have now lost their vitality and strength. This suggests an etymological association with the verb רפה, "to sink down, relax," in the sense of sinking down to the underworld, Sheol, and being powerless. A more likely derivation is from the Hebrew verb רפא, "to heal" (Arabic *rafa'a,* "to mend, stitch together"), so that we may think of the dead as a community bound together in a common existence in Sheol. The Rephaim are not extinct souls, but their life has little substance. Except in one instance (Isa. 26:19), their case is hopeless; they cannot praise God (Ps. 88:10—H 88:11); they have no wisdom or understanding (Prov. 9:18; 21:16). Yet they may be thought to tremble in fear (Job 26:5), to be guests at a feast (Prov. 9:18), and to greet those who come to join their company (Isa. 14:9); and there is also a suggestion that they are the aristocracy of the dead (Isa. 14:9; 26:14).

The Sidonian kings Tabnith and Eshmunazar (*ca.* 300 B.C.) in the inscriptions on their sarcophagi express the curse that any tomb-robber who molests or disturbs them may have no resting place among the Rephaim.

The most numerous references to the Rephaim, and the earliest, are to be found in the Ras Shamra Texts. A verbal form is used once in the sense "to become a shade." The nominal form used with more than one meaning (*see 2 below*) is frequent. In the legend of Keret, this just king bemoans the loss of his whole family, who have become Rephaim, inhabitants of the nether world. Another group of texts, commonly associated with the legend of Aqhat, may be classed together under the general heading "Rephaim." These texts, though fragmentary, seem to describe how El, the supreme god of the Canaanite pantheon, summons the Rephaim ("shades") and the chthonian deities to his palace. They engage in a week of feasting, seemingly in honor of victorious Baal. The interesting feature in these texts is the probable identification of the Rephaim as chthonian deities. This may well be the origin of the Hebrew term, which, appearing in late biblical texts, indicates the persistence among the Hebrews of Canaanite thought-forms.

2. An ethnic term designating the pre-Israelite people of Palestine. It is frequently translated in the KJV and once in the RSV (I Chr. 20:4) as "GIANTS." A form in the singular, always with the definite article, הרפה, occurs in II Sam. 21:16, 18, 20, 22, and in a slightly variant form in the parallel passages in Chronicles (הרפא in I Chr. 20:6, 8; הרפאים in vs. 4); in all these cases the RSV translates "giants" and the KJV "giant."

Israelite popular tradition ascribed gigantic stature to the Rephaim. Og, king of Bashan, their last survivor, was the possessor of a massive iron bedstead, nine cubits long and four cubits broad, according to Deut. 3:11. They are described (Deut. 2:11, 20) as being tall as the Anakim (*see* ANAK). The references from II Samuel and I Chronicles noted above mention the unusually large weapons and the great stature of the Rephaim. This tradition of the aboriginal giants, probably a product of Hebrew folklore, was, no doubt, partially inspired by the megalithic structures of the Neolithic period found in the Transjordan region, the area with which the Rephaim are most commonly, though not exclusively, associated. They were known by various names; thus the Moabites called them EMIM, the Ammonites called them ZAMZUMMIM, and they were identified with the Anakim (Deut. 2:11, 20).

"Rephaim" as an ethnic term may also be found in the Ugaritic literature. In the legend of Aqhat, Danel is regularly described by the epithet "Rephaite" or "Rapha-man," and this is frequently a parallel to "hero." The champion of Baal is called "Repubaal." These usages lead one to think of manly vigor and vitality rather than of the shadowy inhabitants of the nether world, and may indicate the source of the Hebrew tradition which identifies the Rephaim with the giants.

The relation between the two usages of "Rephaim" is obscure. Perhaps it is to be found in the sense of "community"—on the one hand, the general group of pre-Israelite inhabitants of Palestine, and on the other hand, the community of those who lead a common life in Sheol.

Bibliography. G. E. Wright, "Troglodytes and Giants," *JBL,* LVII (1938), 305-9; J. Gray, "The Rephaim," *PEQ,* 84 (1949), 127-39; G. R. Driver, *Canaanite Myths and Legends,* OT Studies, no. 3 (1956), pp. 9-10, 67-71, 155.
                                                R. F. SCHNELL

REPHAIM, VALLEY OF [עמק רפאים]; KJV alternately VALLEY OF THE GIANTS (Josh. 15:8; 18:16). A broad valley, or rather a hollow plain, near Jerusalem, named for the early inhabitants of Palestine, to whom popular traditions ascribed a gigantic stature (*see* ANAK; NEPHILIM; REPHAIM 2). Consequently the Valley of Rephaim was interpreted κοιλὰς τῶν Γιγάντων, τῶν Τιτάνων, by the LXX and by Josephus (Antiq. VII.iv.1); cf. the KJV rendering "valley of the giants" in Josh. 15:8; 18:16.

The Valley of Rephaim is mentioned in the description of the common boundary of the tribes of Judah and Benjamin (Josh. 15:8; 18:16); from E to W, the boundary went up along the Valley of Hinnom (*see* HINNOM, VALLEY OF THE SON OF), passed by the N end of the Valley of Rephaim, and reached the Waters of NEPHTOAH, securely identified with the springs at Lifta, NW of Jerusalem. These data point to the plain of the Baqa' in the SW suburbs of Jerusalem, from which it is easy to gain access to the Valley of Deir el-Musallabeh (the Greek monastery of the Holy Cross), and from there to the heights of Romema. The Valley of Rephaim is mentioned in several episodes of the flight of David against Philistine invaders who ascended from the lowlands up the Wadi Serar, and deployed in the Valley of Rephaim, from which they were in easy reach of both Jerusalem and Bethlehem (II Sam. 5: 18, 22; 23:13; I Chr. 11:15; 14:9). The identification of BAAL-PERAZIM with the Ras en-Nadir is in accordance with the presumed location of the Valley of Rephaim (II Sam. 5:20; I Chr. 14:11). The Valley of Rephaim is described as rich in grain (Isa. 17:5). *See* map "Jerusalem in OT Times" under JERUSALEM.

Bibliography. H. Vincent, *Jérusalem Antique* (1912), pp. 118-24; G. Dalman, *Jerusalem und sein Gelände* (1930), p. 212; F.-M. Abel, *Géographie de la Palestine*, I (1933), 402.

G. A. BARROIS

REPHAN rē'făn ['Ρεφάν, Ρεμφαν (Textus Receptus, whence KJV; *cf.* Vulg. *Rempham*), Ρεμφα, Ρομφα, Ρομφαν, Ρεμφαμ; LXX *also* Ραιφαν]; KJV REMPHAN rĕm'făn. The LXX rendering, cited in Acts 7:43, of the name of a god which is given in the MT as כיון (*see* KAIWAN). The erroneous Greek form appears to have resulted from the mistaking of כ for ר, and the transliteration of ו, properly taken as consonantal, by φ. Rephan or Kaiwan, clearly an astral deity, is the Babylonian name for Saturn.

F. W. BEARE

REPHIDIM rĕf'ə dĭm [רפידים] (Exod. 17:1; 19:2; Num. 33:14-15). A stopping place of the Israelites between the Wilderness of Sin and the Wilderness of Sinai. In Num. 33:14-15 two additional encampments, Dophkah and Alush between Sin and Rephidim (vss. 12-14), are given.

Three events are connected with this name: (*a*) In this vicinity, the people found fault with Moses because of his inability to provide water for their thirst and put the Lord to the proof; hence the place came to be known as MASSAH AND MERIBAH (Exod. 17: 1-7). (*b*) The defeat of Amalek took place here, and was commemorated by the erection of an altar which was called YAHWEH-NISSI (Exod. 17:8-16). (*c*) The visit of Jethro, Moses' father-in-law, who counseled Moses about appointing judges (Exod. 18), may be inferred from its position in the narrative and from Exod. 18:5 to have been thought to have taken place in this vicinity, though most scholars today believe that its locale must rather have been Mount Sinai itself.

The location of Rephidim depends on the location of Mount Sinai. Various sites have been proposed for the mount of law-giving—i.e., the S tip of Sinai Peninsula, Kadesh-barnea, and Midian.

In view of the fact that the traditional location of Mount Sinai has persisted for nearly fifteen centuries and the further fact that the geographical locations of some of the stopping places mentioned in Num. 33 appear as reasonable, though none have been identified with absolute certainty, the traditional location which places the mountain of God near the apex of the peninsula, is still preferable to either Kadesh-barnea or Midian. Both the latter localities present more problems than they solve. The difficulties which are encountered in accepting the traditional site can be eliminated by the assumption that the account of Exodus and the wilderness wandering consists of a number of separate strands of tradition, which have been fused together in the course of time.

In view of this, Rephidim must be located somewhere in the S tip of the peninsula in the proximate area of the modern Jebel Musa, either Wadi Feiran or more probably Wadi Refayid.

Bibliography. E. H. Palmer, *The Desert of the Exodus* (1872), pp. 21-22; W. M. Flinders Petrie, *Researches in Sinai* (1906), p. 249; G. Beer, "Exodus," *HAT* (1939), pp. 25-26; E. G. Kraeling, *Bible Atlas* (1956), pp. 107-9; W. F. Albright, *From Stone Age to Christianity* (2nd ed., 1957), p. 262; E. G. Wright, *Biblical Archaeology* (1957), p. 64. J. L. MIHELIC

REPTILE [רמש; ἑρπετόν]. Any of a class of cold-blooded, air-breathing, vertebrate animals, crawling on the belly or creeping on short legs. *See* CREEPING THINGS; SERPENT.

RESAIAH. Apoc. alternate form of REELAIAH.

RESEN rē'zən [רסן] (Gen. 10:12). A city in Assyria mentioned as a great city built by Asshur between Nineveh and Calah. No major city thus located is known from Assyrian sources. Identification with an Assyrian village Rēsh-êni, mentioned by Sennacherib in connection with his work to supply Nineveh with water, and situated NE of Nineveh, has been proposed but cannot be considered very plausible.

T. JACOBSEN

RESERVOIR [מקוה, *from* קוה, collect]. A storage place. Reservoirs for the storage of rain water were common in biblical times, and traces of many can still be seen. Isa. 22:11 refers to the reservoir (KJV "ditch") between the two walls for the water of the Old Pool. It was presumably made by Hezekiah. For discussion, *see* JERUSALEM § 6*c*.

See also CISTERN; POOL; WATER WORKS § 4.

W. L. REED

RESH rĕsh (Heb. rāsh) [ר, *r* (*Rêsh*)]. The twentieth letter of the Hebrew ALPHABET as it is placed in the KJV at the head of the twentieth section of the acrostic psalm, Ps. 119, where each verse of this section of the psalm begins with this letter.

RESHEPH rē'shĕf [רשף, flame, firebolt]. 1. A member of the great N tribe of Ephraim; son of Rephah, and the father of Telah (I Chr. 7:25).

E. R. ACHTEMEIER

2. A proper name, translated as a common noun in Deut. 32:24; Pss. 76:4; 78:48; Job 5:7; Song of S. 8:6.

Resheph is well attested as a Canaanite deity in offering lists and theophoric names from Ras Shamra, in the Egyptian Papyrus Harris (late Nineteenth Dynasty), and in Aramaic inscriptions from Syria (eighth century B.C.). In the Keret epic of Ras Shamra he is the god of plague or mass destruction. In Egyptian sculpture he is portrayed with a helmet garnished with gazelle horns; this suggests that he

From H. Gressmann, *Altorientalische Texte und Bilder zum Alten Testament* (Berlin: Walter de Gruyter & Co.)

9. The god Resheph, from Horbet in the Nile Delta, Nineteenth Dynasty (*ca.* 1310-1200 B.C.)

was the deity named Mekal, so depicted on a stele from the fourteenth century at Beth-shan, the title meaning possibly "he who consumes" (from כלה). Apart from Beth-shan, another cult center of Resheph was probably Arsuf (later Apollonia) on the coast of Jaffa. There is probably a reminiscence of this plague-deity in Hab. 3:5, where "plague" (דבר) and "pestilence" (רשף) are the attendants of Yahweh.

Fig. RES 9.

Bibliography. G. A. Cooke, *A Textbook of North Semitic Inscriptions* (1903), pp. 55-57, 159-71 (Aramaic inscriptions from Syria); S. A. Cook, *The Religion of Ancient Palestine in the Light of Archaeology* (1930), pp. 112-16; J. Leibovitch, "Un nouveau dieu égypto-cananéen," *Annales du Service des Antiquités de l'Egypte*, LXVIII (1948), 435-47.   J. GRAY

RESPECT OF PERSONS. Recognition of the strength, merit, and significance of another (הדר, lit., "to pay honor to"): Lev. 19:32; Lam. 5:12; cf. Mark 12:6; 15:43; Rom. 13:7; I Thess. 4:12; 5:12; I Tim. 3:4; I Pet. 2:18).

The OT and the NT set forth instances in which respect of persons is invalid. Laws concerning holiness of behavior state that judgment is to be made without respect of persons: when one judges, it is prohibited "to lift up the face" (נשא פנים), "to defer" (הדר)—i.e., in both cases, "to show partiality" (Lev. 19:15). The phrase נשא פנים appears in the Hebraistic λαμβάνειν πρόσωπον, "to receive the face of," "to accept the person of"—i.e., "to favor specially"; the two words form words like προσωπολήμπτης, "a special favorer," "a respecter of persons," "one who shows partiality." It was said to Jesus: "You speak and teach rightly, and show no partiality" (Luke 20: 21). God shows no partiality; he is no respecter of persons (Acts 10:34; cf. Rom. 2:11; Gal. 2:6; Eph. 6:9; Col. 3:25). Jas. 2:1 advises: "My brethren, show no partiality." *See also* ACCEPTANCE.

T. M. MAUCH

REST. The translation of a number of biblical words with the connotation "repose." For the word in another sense, *see* REMNANT.

1. In the OT. In the OT the words used for "rest" are: (*a*) נוח, "rest," "settle down," "remain" (Gen. 8:4; Exod. 33:14; Deut. 3:20; Josh. 1:13-15; 23:1; Ruth 1:9; 3:1; II Sam. 7:1, 11; I Kings 5:4; I Chr. 22:9; Job 3:17-19), "repose" (Isa. 23:12); (*b*) רגע (Job 21:13), which refers specifically to the "peace" of Sheol (cf. also Jer. 6:16); and (*c*) שבת (Exod. 20: 10; 23:12; 31:15-17), "rest," "cease," or "desist."

Usually the rest is purely physical (cf., e.g., Gen. 8:4: "The ark came to rest upon the mountains of Ararat"). Even when it is men who rest—or, more often, are given rest by God—the rest is bodily rather than spiritual. This physical or bodily rest is of many kinds. The first to be mentioned in the OT is that which consists in the possession by the people of God of a secure dwelling place in the Promised Land; thus the assurance which God gave to Moses: "My presence shall go with thee, and I will give thee rest" (Exod. 33:14 KJV), means: "I myself will go, and will settle you [my people Israel, rather than Moses individually] in the land which I have promised you" (cf. especially Deut. 3:20; Josh. 1:13-15). It also means freedom from war (Josh. 23:1; II Sam. 7:1, 11; I Kings 5:4; etc.). Solomon is called a "man of rest" (so KJV) or a "man of peace" (so RSV; I Chr. 22:9), not because of his quiet and peaceable disposition, but because God will give him "peace from all his enemies round about" and "peace and quiet to Israel in his days." The rest which Naomi desired for her widowed daughters-in-law is simply the security and comfort of a good marriage (Ruth 1:9; 3:1; RSV "home"). The rest of the SABBATH (שבת) is simply freedom from ordinary work; it is enjoyed, not only by the pious Israelite, but also by his servants, by aliens living in his land, and by his cattle (Exod. 20:10). Its purpose is refreshment (23:12); God himself "was refreshed" after the work of creation by resting on the seventh day (31:15-17). The only significant reference to the rest of death is in the book of Job (3:17-19); this rest is complete inactivity, scarcely distinguishable from sheer nonexistence—yet, even so, preferable to a life of continual sorrow. The same idea is found in Ecclesiasticus (22:11; 30:17, where the condition of the dead is called "eternal rest").

There does not appear to be any certain instance in the OT of "rest" in the sense of "inward peace," "tranquillity of mind." In Jer. 6:16, which is sometimes cited as an instance, the rest which the people are bidden to find by walking in the good way is, as the context plainly indicates, political and social security and well-being, and "for your souls" means only "for yourselves." In Ps. 37:7, "Rest in the LORD" (KJV) is a mistranslation; the meaning is given correctly in the RSV: "Be still before the LORD" (cf. KJV mg.).

2. In the NT. In the NT explicit references to rest are few, and most of them are of little or no religious or theological significance. In the first three gospels and in Revelation the Greek words used are the verb ἀναπαύειν and the verbal noun ἀνάπαυσις. It has been asserted that the compound ἀνα-παυειν expresses a temporary, and the simple παύειν a final, cessation of some kind; but, though this is usually true, there are exceptions—e.g., Rev. 14:13, where the compound is used of what is clearly a final cessation; Luke 8:24, where the simple form is used of what is no less clearly a temporary cessation. But ἀναπαύειν and ἀνάπαυσις do often denote a temporary rest, and so come to mean simply "refreshment" of any kind. In all four instances of the verb in the Pauline letters (I Cor. 16:18; II Cor. 7:13; Philem. 7, 20), this is the meaning (similarly, Ignatius repeatedly speaks of having been refreshed by fellow Christians "in every way"). The simplest understanding of the gracious promise of Matt. 11:28-29 is, therefore, that Jesus offers to "all who labor and are heavy-laden" refreshment, relief from their weariness, which will enable them to carry on their labor, but under his easy yoke, which makes their burden light (cf. Vulg., *reficiam vos* and Luther's translation, *will euch er-quicken;* both mean "I will refresh you"). But ancient interpreters (e.g., Origen, Chrysostom) took the burden from which Christ releases men to be the burden of their sins, and most recent commentators take it to be the burden of the Jewish law as interpreted by the scribes and Pharisees (cf. Matt. 23:4); in either case the relief promised must be final, not temporary.

The only NT writer who has much to say about rest is the author of the Letter to the Hebrews (Heb. 3:7–4:11). For him the consummation of the Christian gospel is that those who truly believe it will enter into God's rest, the rest which God himself has enjoyed ever since, his works of creation finished, he rested on the seventh day (Gen. 2:2). The argument starts from the words ascribed to God in Ps. 95: "They [i.e., the disobedient and rebellious generation of the wilderness wanderings] shall never enter my rest." Here "my rest" means simply the land of Canaan. But the author of Hebrews gives the phrase (LXX κατάπαυσιςμον) a wider and deeper meaning, interpreting it in the light of Gen. 2:2 (where κατέπαυσεν is the word used in the LXX) as God's own rest, which it was his gracious purpose that his people should share. That purpose is not frustrated by the failure of those to whom the promise was first made; "because of unbelief" (Heb. 3:19) they were not able to enter God's rest, but this means that it remains for others to enter it (4:6). The good news of this possibility has now been proclaimed to us; and having believed it, we shall certainly enter that rest (4:1-3; here εἰσερχόμεθα is a futuristic present; cf. Vulg. *ingrediemur*). Yet only if we hold our first confident belief firm to the end (3:4); we must therefore exert ourselves to enter it, for we too may fail by disobedience (here, as often, hardly to be distinguished from unbelief), as the people under Moses did. When we do attain that rest, exertion is at an end, for it is a "sabbath rest" (σαββατισμός—a word found only here in the Greek Bible, and possibly one coined by the writer); "whoever enters God's rest also ceases [κατέπαυσεν] from his labors [ἔργων] as

God did from his" (4:9-10). Nothing more is said about the nature of the rest, but it cannot be supposed to be a state of complete inactivity, like the rest of the wicked, the weary, the prisoners, in Job (3:17-19). In the similar passage in Revelation (14:13) the blessed dead are said to rest from their "labors" (κόπος), so then it may be possible to distinguish between work which is toilsome and wearisome and work which is done easily and gladly. But this distinction cannot be made when God's own works are in question. Probably the language of Hebrews has been determined by the naïve anthropomorphism of the Genesis passage, and does not adequately express the writer's conception of the blessedness of the redeemed in heaven—or of the blessedness of God himself.

None of the other references to rest in the NT is of any religious significance. But it may be noted that the Greek word ἄνεσις, which means "loosening," "relaxation," "remission" (cf. Acts 24:23; II Cor. 8:13), is rendered, in the three other places in which it occurs, by "rest," both in the KJV and in the RSV, in the contexts quite correctly (II Cor. 2: 13; 7:5; II Thess. 1:7).　　J. Y. CAMPBELL

RESTITUTION. See CRIMES AND PUNISHMENTS § C7.

RESTORATION [השיב; ἀποκαθιστάναι, -άνειν; ἀποκατάστασις]. The destiny of the cosmos seen as the attainment of its original purpose and the preservation of its historical achievement.

The concept of cosmic "restoration" is rooted in the instinct of primitive cultures to experience the reality of temporal occurrence only as re-enactment of primeval archetypes. Babylonian astronomy (Berossos) developed the concept of an endless series of "great years" or aeons of astronomically determined duration, with alternating (Iranian) world conflagration (cf. Zephaniah) and (Babylonian) flood. This view was elevated to philosophical status especially by the Stoics, who taught a periodic conflagration followed by a "restoration" (*Stoicorum Veterum Fragmenta* II.190.19-20) or "regeneration" (*Marc Aurelius* XI.1; in the NT, Matt. 19:28), in which the same events recur in each cycle: "How many Chrysippuses, how many Socrateses, how many Epictetuses has the aeon already consumed!" (*Marc Aurelius* VII.19). This cyclic concept was in principle superseded in Persian eschatology by the view of a final transfiguration in which all would be saved. This linear or single-cycle view (minus universal salvation) became determinative for Hebrew-Christian thought, in its effort to understand historical events whose unique significance transcended the cyclic archetypal pattern. Thus the subjection of historical occurrence to nonhistorical categories gave way to a view in which distinctive historical occurrence could itself become determinative for the construction of the meaningful pattern of history. This meant, to be sure, that the concept of restoration must accept a secondary role in the understanding of history. Yet it continued to supply eschatology with archetypal material drawn both from the concept of creation and from the decisive occurrences of Hebrew and Christian history.

The verb "restore" became in the OT a technical term for the political restoration of Israel by God (Ps. 16:5 LXX; Jer. 15:19; 16:15; 23:8 LXX; 24:6; Ezek. 16:55 LXX; Hos. 11:11). This concept is attached to Elijah in Mal. 4:6, where he is prophesied as returning to "restore [LXX ἀποκαθιστάναι; RSV 'turn'] the hearts of fathers to their children and the hearts of children to their fathers, lest I come and smite the land with a curse." In Ecclus. 48:10 he "restore[s] [καθιστάναι] the tribes of Jacob." The problem of reconciling John the Baptist with this Elijah role of "restoring all things" (ἀποκαθιστάνειν πάντα) finds expression in Matt. 17:11; Mark 9:11-13. Luke instead places this Jewish concept of "restoring [ἀποκαθιστάνειν] the kingdom to Israel" on the lips of the disciples at the Resurrection (Acts 1: 6), as an occasion for correcting the view of the nearness of the kingdom and of its limitation to Israel. The expression "restoration of all things" (ἀποκατάστασις πάντων) occurs in Acts 3:21, and other allusions to the Elijah tradition in the context suggest some such connection in the source material employed by Luke; yet in its Lukan form the passage seems to say no more than that Jesus waits in heaven "until the time for establishing all that God spoke by the mouth of his holy prophets from of old." Origen made a technical term of the expression ἀποκατάστασις πάντων in connection with his doctrine, based upon Neoplatonism, that souls (and even demons) could in the afterlife be purified, and thus ultimately all would be saved—a view rejected especially by the Fifth Ecumenical Synod at Constantinople in A.D. 553. In the NT the view of the completeness of Christ's victory (John 1:29; 4:42; 12:32; Rom. 5:18; 8:19 ff; 11:32; I Cor. 15:22-28; II Cor. 5:19; Phil. 2:10; I Tim. 2:4; I John 2:2; 4:14) does not eliminate the Jewish idea of a realistic judgment, but rather serves as the positive basis for the call to radical decision.

Bibliography. H. Meyer, "Die Lehre von der ewigen Wiederkunft aller Dinge," *Beiträge zur Geschichte des christlichen Altertums und der Byzantinischen Literatur, Festgabe für A. Ehrhard* (1922), pp. 359-80; W. Bousset and H. Gressmann, *Die Religion des Judentums im späthellenistischen Zeitalter* (1926), especially pp. 232, 278-79, 283-84, 502 ff; H. L. Strack and P. Billerbeck, "Das Wirken des wiederkehrenden Elias in der messianischen Zukunft," *Kommentar zum NT aus Talmud und Midrasch,* IV (1928), 779-98; M. Eliade, *The Myth of the Eternal Return* (1949); C. Lenz, "Apokatastasis," *RAC,* I (1950), 510-16; W. Michaelis, *Versöhnung des Alls. Die frohe Botschaft von der Gnade Gottes* (1950); G. van der Leeuw, "Urzeit und Endzeit," *Eranos-Jahrbuch* 1949, XVII (1950), 11-51.

For the debate as to the meaning of the OT idiom שׁוּב שְׁבוּת: E. Preuschen, *ZAW,* XV (1895), 1 ff; E. L. Dietrich, *Beiheft* 40 of *ZAW* (1925); O. Procksch, "Wiederkehr und Wiedergeburt," *Das Erbe Martin Luthers und die gegenwärtige theologische Forschung* (Ihmels *Festschrift;* 1928), pp. 1-18; E. Baumann, *ZAW,* XLVII (1929), 17-44; L. Köhler and W. Baumgartner, *Lexicon in VT Libros* (1953), p. 940.

J. M. ROBINSON

RESURRECTION. The raising of the dead.

1. Forms of the doctrine
2. Resurrection in the OT
3. Foreign influences and parallels
4. Resurrection in the Apoc. and the Pseudep.
5. Attitude of Jewish sects
   a. In the Dead Sea Scrolls
   b. Essenes
   c. Sadducees
   d. Pharisees
   e. Samaritans
6. Folklore of resurrection
Bibliography

1. Forms of the doctrine. "Resurrection" is a blanket term covering three different, but related, beliefs:

a) That the essential self (or "soul") of an individual is awakened from the sleep of death shortly after the latter occurs, or after the dissolution of the body;

b) That the bodies of the dead will eventually be resuscitated, at the end of the present world;

c) That the righteous among the dead will be raised collectively, after a Last Judgment, either to a rarefied, eternal existence on some other plane, or to rebirth in a world which will succeed this one.

Resurrection is thus conceived either as an individual experience or as a common, eschatological event; either as an awakening from the body or as an awakening in it; either as universal or as selective; either as an inevitable continuance in eternity or as a privileged birth in a new creation.

This diversity of view is due to the fact that the doctrine was evolved in different philosophies to resolve different problems. Thus, where death was regarded as a sleep—a concept ubiquitous in primitive and ancient thought—resurrection was the inevitable waking, a natural and normal sequel. Where time was regarded as a cyclic, rather than a linear, process (*see* COSMOGONY), resurrection supplied an answer to the question of what would happen to the selves ("souls") of the deceased when the present cycle ended and a new world was brought into being. Lastly, during periods of religious persecution and martyrdom, it provided a necessary assurance to the faithful that they would indeed be rewarded hereafter, and the reprobate duly punished.

There are differences also in the symbols by which the doctrine is expressed. The prevailing image—from which, indeed, the term itself is derived—is that of waking from sleep (e.g., Dan. 12:2). But the analogy of the vegetable world, with its incessant rhythm of decay and revival, suggests also the alternative picture of reflorescence (e.g., Ecclus. 46:12).

2. Resurrection in the OT. Although it is today a cardinal tenet of both Judaism and Christianity, the doctrine of resurrection was not evolved in Israel until the Hellenistic period. The only positive reference to it in the OT occurs in the very late book of Daniel (168 B.C.), where it is said (12:1-2) that, at the end of the present world, following the appearance of Michael, the peculiar angel of Israel, "many of those who sleep in the dust of the earth shall awake, some to everlasting life, and some to shame and everlasting contempt." Written during the oppressive reign of Antiochus IV Epiphanes, this passage does not represent a natural development of previous Hebrew thinking, but is simply a clever exploitation of popular "pagan" notions, designed, on the one hand, to reassure the devout, and, on the other, to hoist the infidels with the petard of their own apostatic beliefs. For it is not difficult to recognize in the figure of Michael a thinly disguised version of the Iranian Saoshyant, the savior who will come at the end of the present era to vindicate the righteous, discomfit the wicked, and resurrect the dead; while the condemnation of the faithless to everlasting shame echoes the fate assigned to them in Mazdean and Zoroastrian teaching (e.g., Zend Avesta, Yasht 16; Bundahesh 11.6; etc.).

To be sure, attempts have been made to trace a doctrine of resurrection in earlier portions of the OT, but none of the evidence adduced stands up under closer scrutiny.

Thus, in the parade passage, Isa. 26:19 ("Thy dead shall live, their dead bodies shall rise," etc.), the language is purely hyperbolic; the desired regeneration of a spiritually inert and virtually "dead" community of Israel is likened metaphorically and poetically to the quickening of languishing soil under the influence of even a slight morning drizzle (טל). What has seemed to all the world like a barren "ghost land" will yet yield a belated harvest (וארץ רפאים תפיל [where תפיל=תאפיל; cf. Exod. 9:32]).

Similarly, the famous words of Job 19:25-27 ("I know [rather, 'If only I knew'] that my Vindicator lives," etc.) express a desperate hope for the impossible—a *cri de coeur*—rather than a confidence in the inevitable. The inmost yearning which consumes me, says the tortured man of Uz, is that I could but leave some permanent, written record of my case; that I could be sure that someone, be he even the last man on earth, would someday arise to constitute a live champion of my cause (ואני ידעתי גאלי חי ואחרון על־עפר יקום); that even beyond these torments of the flesh, I might see before me a benign God, and not, as now, mere coldhearted opponents! All this voices no definite belief in the raising of the dead.

Again, Ps. 17:15 ("When I awake, I shall be satisfied with beholding thy form") does not, in fact, refer to waking from the sleep of death, but simply voices the prayer, or expectation, of one who has sought refuge in a sanctuary that he will, indeed, be safe overnight and wake to see his divine "host" in the morning! In other words, the passage is to be interpreted in the context of asylum and *epopteia* (*see* bibliography), rather than of resurrection.

Other passages that have been quoted (e.g., Deut. 32:39; I Sam. 2:6; Pss. 16:10-11; 49:15; 73:24) really allude only to rescue from imminent death, not to resuscitation after it; while the assertion in Ps. 1:5 that "the wicked will not stand in the judgment" refers merely to their inevitable collapse when duly arraigned, not to any doctrine of trial and resurrection at Doomsday.

3. Foreign influences and parallels. It is often asserted that, even if not expressly articulated in their earlier scriptures, a belief in resurrection can scarcely have failed to penetrate to the Israelites, because it is well attested among their neighbors. This assertion is completely erroneous. It is based on (*a*) the frequent designation of Mesopotamian gods as "bringing the dead to life" (*muballiṭ mîti*) or even as retrieving them from the nether world, and (*b*) the widespread diffusion of myths and rituals revolving around so-called "dying and reviving gods"—e.g., the Babylonian TAMMUZ and the Ugaritic BAAL. The fact is, however, that the designation in question refers only to preserving in life one who is at the point of death, not to actual resuscitation of the dead; while the Tammuz-type god is, in the final analysis, simply a personification of the rhythm of nature, so that the portrayal of him as alternately dying and reviving has no bearing whatsoever on the doctrine of a general human resurrection. Besides, it should be observed that, at least in some cases, such gods, though indeed mourned as if dead, are not, in fact, said to have died and been resurrected, but only, like Persephone, to have been trapped alive (e.g., "bound" [Akkadian *kamû*]) in the nether world and subsequently retrieved, or to have withdrawn from the earth in high dudgeon and been subsequently appeased (e.g., in certain versions of the Hittite Telipinu myth; cf. Hos. 5:6).

Nor can any doctrine of a general resurrection be deduced from the fact that in the Mesopotamian poem of the Descent of Ishtar to the Nether World (*ANET* 106 ff) the dead are said to rise along with Tammuz and "savour the incense"—i.e., partake of a ritual meal. For this poem was evidently designed for an annual festival, and the reference is simply to the widespread belief that on such occasions the ancestral dead temporarily rejoin their living kinsmen.

The plain truth is that there is no evidence in ancient Mesopotamian literature of any real doctrine of resurrection; while the Egyptians asserted only that after the demise of the body, the dead came into untrammeled possession of his essential self (*ka*) and attained a state of rarefied beatitude (*'aḫ*). In accordance with what Edward Tylor (*Primitive Culture*) characterized as the "continuance theory," the dead was regarded as defunct, but not deceased, and the problem was not how he could attain immortality, but how he could fail to do so. The prevalent attitude is evident both from the designation of the dead as the "weary," inert" (Egyptian *nny, wrḏ 'ib;* Ugaritic, Phoenician, *r-p-'-m*, if derived from *r-ph-y*, "be slack, flaccid"; cf. οἱ καμόντες, and see *Odyssey* IX.474-75), and from descriptions of their shadowy existence. The latter is represented ambivalently as a consummation of essential being and as a cheerless attenuation of it, the body being variously regarded as a temporary encumbrance or as a necessary complement. On the one hand, e.g., the departed are said, in the Egyptian Book of the Dead (*ANET* 9), to inhabit the "silent land," where sexual pleasure is replaced by beatific detachment (*'aḫ*), and gourmanderie by spiritual repose; while, on the other, in the Mesopotamian poem of Ishtar's Descent to the Nether World (*ANET* 107), they are portrayed as dwelling in darkness and squalor, feeding on dust and mud.

Broadly speaking, it was this conception that obtained in Israel before the Hellenistic period. The dead are likewise described in the OT as "weary" (Job 3:17) and "without vigor" (Ps. 88:4), dwelling in silence (דומה; Pss. 94:17; 115:17), whence they can never return (Ps. 88:11; Prov. 21:16; Isa. 26:14). *See* DEAD, ABODE OF THE.

On the other hand, while the formal doctrine of

resurrection cannot be traced to ancient Near Eastern sources, certain specific ideas which later became woven into the Judeo-Christian concept do indeed appear, in less dogmatic form, in Semitic and Egyptian myth and legend, and may therefore have been incorporated from time-honored popular lore current also in the Holy Land.

Thus (a) the idea of the resurrection of the body is foreshadowed in the belief that certain heroic characters who met their deaths through dismemberment were subsequently restored to life by the miraculous reassemblage of their limbs. This notion, which is indeed a commonplace of world folk tale (e.g., the resuscitation of Lemminkäinen in the Finnish *Kalevala;* the tale of Cola Marcione in Basile's *Pentamerone*), is familiar, of course, from the Egyptian myth of Osiris. It occurs also in the Ugaritic Poem of Baal, where the dismembered Mot (cf. I AB, ii.30-37), god of aridity and death, is eventually resuscitated, to fight another day. Moreover, it is virtually certain that the Ugaritic Poem of Aqhat ended with a similar resuscitation of the slain youth after vultures had devoured his flesh and bone. In all these cases, however, what is involved is something unusual and extraordinary, not the normal and inevitably destiny of all the dead. Besides, in the case of Mot, and in at least some representations of the myth of Osiris, this trait of the story simply dramatizes and symbolizes the process of sowing and reaping, rather than a real resuscitation of the human dead.

Again (b), the element of a last judgment, though articulated mainly on the pattern of Iranian teachings, may be recognized as at least partially a projection into a common, eschatological event of what had, in fact, long been believed to be the destiny of the individual dead. For such inquisition in the afterworld is not only abundantly attested in Egypt (e.g., Book of the Dead; *ANET* 34-35), but there are also sporadic traces of it in Mesopotamian belief, as when the constellation Libra is described as the "scales of the dead," and it seems also to be mentioned on sundry Babylonian funeral inscriptions found in the Elamite city of Susa. It should not be overlooked, however, that similar ideas always obtained among the Greeks (cf. *Iliad* III.278-79; XIX.259; Aeschylus *Eumenides* 267 ff; *Supplices* 414 ff; Democritus, fragments 199, 297; Plato *Phaedrus* 248 F; *Gorgias* 523; *Laws* IX.870; *Phaedo* 112 E) and might thus have reached the Jews of the Hellenistic period from other than purely oriental sources.

4. Resurrection in the Apoc. and the Pseudep. In most of the intertestamental scriptures, the doctrine of resurrection is fused with that of rewards and punishments, and, as a matter of fact, it developed alongside an increased insistence on fidelity to the covenant. The most common form of the belief is that all souls will be summoned to judgment at the last day, but that only the righteous will be resurrected—i.e., restored from the attenuated state imposed by bodily demise (Pss. Sol. 3:16; 14:7; 15:15; Enoch 91-104; Test. Simeon 6; Test. Levi 18; Test. Judah 25; Test. Zeb. 10; II Bar. 30; Adam and Eve 13; cf. also Jos. Antiq. XVIII.i.3; War II.viii.14; T.B. Ta'an. 7a; Keth. 111b), the wicked being then consigned to final perdition or "second death" (Pss. Sol.

13:9; II Bar. 50:1 ff; Jerusalem Targ. Deut. 33:6; Targ. Isa. 14:19; 22:14; 65:5, 15, 19; Jer. 51:39).

There is no decisive evidence that resurrection was ever conceived during this period as universal. The only passages which might possibly be construed in this sense are II Esd. 7:32, 37, for the references in Test. Judah 25; Test. Benj. 10 are certainly Christian interpolations. Such a construction, however, depends, in the last analysis, upon the ambiguity of the term "resurrection"; for what is envisaged is simply a general awakening of the dead to judgment, but not of all of them to ultimate revival. The Tosefta, on the other hand, does take up the problem (Sanh. 13.2), and it is laid down that pious Gentiles, too, and not only Israelites, were eligible for a portion in the world to come. By and large, however, there was a marked tendency to regard Israelites as especially qualified for the privilege (Enoch 1-36; 37-50 [Similitudes]; 83-90 [Dream-Visions]; II Macc. 7, *passim;* 12:43-44; II Bar. 50-51:6; M. Sanh. 10.1), by virtue especially of the covenant which God had made with them (Enoch 60:6). This covenant, however, was operative only so long as Israel observed its terms. Hence, certain exceptions were specified. Those, e.g., who denied the authority of the Torah were excluded (Mishna, *loc. cit.;* T.B. Keth. 111b), as were also those who shamed their fellow men in public (B.M. 59a) and, according to Akiba, those who "read outside books"—i.e., accepted as scripture what had been pronounced heretical (Sanh., *loc. cit.*).

There was likewise a divergence of view about whether the dead would be resurrected to live a life of immortality or actually to populate the newly created world. The former was originally termed "eternal life" (חיי עולם [Dan. 12:2]; Aramaic חיי עלמא [Targ. Onqelos, Lev. 18:5; Deut. 33:6; Targ. I Sam. 2:6; Ezek. 20:11-12, 21; Hos. 14:10]; Syriac עלמא דלא מאית, "immortal world" [Apoc. Bar. 51:3]; עלמא דסוף לית לה, "the unending world" [II Bar. 15:7; 44:15]; also חיי עולמים, "eternal years" [M. Tamid vii.4]; ζωὴ αἰώνιος [Pss. Sol. 3:16; II Macc. 7:9, 36; cf. Enoch 37:4; 40:9; II Enoch 50:2; 65:10; IV Macc. 15:3]); and the latter, the "world to come" (העולם הבא [M. Ab. 2.7; T.B. Kid. 40b; Keth. 111a; Sot. 7b (baraitha); P.T. Keth. 35a; Shek. 47c]; Aramaic עלמא דאתי [Jerusalem Targ. I, Deut. 13:10; Targ. Ruth 2.18; T.B. Sanh. 98a]), and the dead were said in each case to "inherit" or "acquire" it. In the course of time, however, the distinction was obscured, and the two terms came to be used as synonyms, to denote the hereafter in general.

There was likewise some difference of opinion as to whether resurrection was spiritual or corporeal. This divergence comes out especially in the book of Enoch, which is really a corpus of scriptures attributed to that ancient sage. In chs. 1-36, in 62:14, and again in the dream-visions of chs. 83-90, what is envisaged is resurrection of the body, whereas in chs. 91-94 it is resurrection of the soul. The former is likewise the view of II Bar. 50-51:6, while the declarations of the martyred brothers in II Macc. 7 presuppose a resurrection of the flesh and even a reassemblage of dismembered limbs (cf. also 12:43-44). A later (Pharisaic?) interpolation in Ecclus. 46:12—completely out of harmony with the general Sadducean outlook of that book—also speaks of bones' rising "from where they lie."

Attempts have been made to stratify these various views chronologically, but since the precise dates of many intertestamental writings are still in doubt, and since they emanate from different schools of thought and different environments, such attempts are at present precarious.

5. Attitude of Jewish sects. There was no consensus concerning resurrection among the various Jewish sects which flourished in the days of the Second Commonwealth.

a. In the Dead Sea Scrolls. The attitude of the Qumran sectaries is ambiguous. In the Manual of Discipline (II.25) and frequently in the Book of Hymns (III.19-23; VII.29-31; XI.10-14; XVIII.26-30) there is reference to the belief that the faithful share a common estate with the angels ("holy ones") and stand forever in the presence of God. It remains doubtful, however, whether this is to be translated in the future tense and understood as an assurance of eventual resurrection, or whether it refers simply, in the common language of mysticism, to the inclusion of the earthly devout in the wider "communion of the saints" (cf. Eph. 2:19).

Furthermore, a fragmentary passage in the War Scroll (XII.5) has been interpreted as an allusion to "those that shall rise from the earth" at the time of the final battle of God against the forces of Belial. More probably, however, the Hebrew words (קמי ארץ) refer to "upstarts on earth" who will then be discomfited.

Lastly, in 1QH VI.34 ff, allusion is made, in an eschatological context, to a "raising of the flag" by them "that lie in the dust" and to a "lifting of the banner" by "this worm which is man." This passage has been construed as a reference to resurrection, but it is equally possible that it refers rather to an impious insurrection of earth-born reprobates, whom God will subdue.

b. Essenes. The views expressed in the Scrolls accord in general with those attributed by Josephus (Antiq. XVIII.i.5; War II.viii.11) to the ESSENES, with whom, indeed, the Qumran sectaries may be identical (*see* DEAD SEA SCROLLS). They held that although bodies were perishable, souls endured and mounted upward, the good to a realm of bliss, the evil to be consigned to a place of torment. This view is expressed also in Wisd. Sol. 3:1 ff; 5:16; Jub. 25; while something of the same kind—though without the reference to ultimate judgment—appears in Eccl. 12:7 ("The dust returns to the earth as it was, and the spirit returns to God who gave it"). The latter statement, it may be added, reproduces to a nicety the Iranian doctrine in the funeral inscription of Antiochus I of Commagene, to the effect that the body will rest in the tomb "through immeasurable time," after the soul, "beloved of God, has been sent to the heavenly throne of Zeus Oromasdês."

c. Sadducees. The Sadducees denied resurrection altogether (Acts 23:8; 26:8; Jos. Antiq. XVIII.i.4; War II.viii.14; T.B. Sanh. 90b), and it is their attitude that is reflected especially in Ecclesiasticus (7:17; 10:11; 17:27-28, 30, 32; 28:6), which even supports it by quoting a well-known Greek saying (Epicharmus; see Euripides *Supplices* 531-36; *Orestes*

1086-88; *Chrisippus* fragment 839; cf. Lucretius *De rerum natura* II.998) to the effect that "all things that are of the earth turn to the earth again, and all things that are of the waters return to the sea."

d. Pharisees. The Pharisees, on the contrary, accepted the doctrine, excluding only certain specific categories of apostates from the privilege of resurrection (cf. M. Ab. 4.22; Soṭ. 9.15; Sanh. 10.1). It is their attitude that became normative in Judaism. It finds expression especially in the second of the Eighteen Benedictions recited in every Jewish service ("Thou, O Lord, art mighty for ever, Who quickenest the dead in abundant mercy . . . and keepest faith with those who sleep in the dust")—a benediction cited already in the Mishna (R.H. 4.5) and probably inserted in the Standing Prayer in deliberate rebuttal of the claims of the Sadducees. It is likewise expressed in the ancient form of the doxology (Kaddish) now recited at the burial service ("Magnified and hallowed be His great name, Who will hereafter renew the world, quicken the dead and raise them to life everlasting"); and again in the blessing intoned on visiting a graveyard (T.B., Ber. 58b [baraitha]; Tosef. Ber. 6.9: "Blessed art Thou, O Lord, . . . who formed you in judgment . . . and put you to death in judgment . . . and will hereafter restore and quicken you in judgment"). Furthermore, a profession of belief in the immortality of the soul and the resurrection of the dead occurs at the beginning of the daily morning service (cf. T.B. Ber. 60a).

e. Samaritans. It is commonly asserted that the Samaritans had no belief in resurrection. This view, however, must be received with caution, for the fact is that a fairly detailed description of that eschatological event is given by the fourth-century writer Marqeh (*see bibliography*) in his exposition of Deut. 32 and is repeated and elaborated in several later treatises. It must be observed, however, that our present text of Marqeh is by no means free of later Islamizing additions, and Islamic influence is, of course, all too evident in the medieval writings of the sect. The question is, therefore, whether Marqeh's statements represent a genuine Samaritan view later adopted by Islam or whether the borrowing was the other way about. At present there seems no way of deciding the issue.

6. Folklore of resurrection. Finally, a number of folkloristic ideas later associated with the doctrine of resurrection may here claim a brief comment.

a) The eschatological resurrection will be accomplished through Elijah (M. Soṭ. 9.15). This doctrine is derived from Mal. 4:5—H 3:23. The prophet, however, is here but a Judaized version of the Iranian Saoshyant, to whom the same mission is ascribed (Yasht 16; Bundahesh 11.6; cf. also Ganj-i-Shakiyan, 133, ed. Sanjana; Dinkart, ed. Sanjana, V, 332). There is added point in this adaptation inasmuch as the prophet is identified by Malachi (3:1) with the "messenger of the covenant," and, as we have seen (§ 4 *above*), it is precisely the covenant that assures the faithful in Israel of their eventual revival. In Enoch 39:6; 45:3; 51:5; 61:8, the place of Elijah is taken by "the Elect One."

b) The righteous will shine like stars (Dan. 12:3; II Esd. 7:97, 125; Enoch 104:2). If the reference is, indeed, to the righteous dead, it is pertinent to point out that the location of the dead in the stars was a common idea in Greco-Roman paganism. Hadrian, e.g., held that the soul of his friend Antinoüs had become a star (Dio Cassius LXIX.ii.14). It is likewise abundantly attested in classical Greek and Roman sources and may be traced even further back to the Egyptian Book of the Dead and the Pyramid texts.

c) The righteous will be clad in special, pure garments (Enoch 62:15-16; 108:12; II Esd. 2:39, 45; 1QS 4.8 [cf. also Rev. 3:4-5, 18; 4:4; 6:11; 7:9, 13-14; Hermas *Similitudes* 8:2]). This idea recurs also in Iranian teaching (Yasht 55.2; Bundahesh 30.28). It is closely associated with the further notion that:

d) The righteous will emit a special fragrance (II Bar. 29:7; Asmp. Moses 29; 38; 40). This, too, is derived by one scholar from Iranian sources. The aforementioned Samaritan treatise by Marqeh has an interesting passage anent this concept: "When the good and the evil are (at last) foregathered, what a difference will appear between them! The good will give forth an acceptable fragrance, and their garments will be new, even as it is said, 'Thy garment hath waxed not old upon thee' [Deut. 8:4]. . . . But, over against them, the wicked will emit an evil, mephitic smell, redolent of dust and fire, and their garments will be tattered."

See also Resurrection in the NT.

Bibliography. J. D. Davis, "The Future Life During the Pre-Persian Period," *Protestant Theological Review*, VI (1908), 246-68; R. H. Charles, *A Critical History of the Doctrine of a Future Life in Israel, in Judaism, and in Christianity* (2nd ed., 1913); F. Nötscher, *Altorientalischer und alttestamentlicher Auferstehungsglauben* (1926); R. M. Grant, "The Resurrection of the Body," *JR*, XXVIII (1948), 120-30, 188-208; H. Birkeland, "The Belief in the Resurrection of the Dead in the OT," *Studia Theologia*, I (1950), 60 ff; C. Larcher, "La doctrine de la résurrection dans l'AT," *Lumen Vitae*, III (1952), 11-34; H. H. Rowley, *The Faith of Israel* (1956), ch. 6, pp. 150-76.

On *epopteia*, see: F. Nötscher, *"Das Angesicht Gottes schauen" nach babylonischer und alttestamentlicher Auffassung* (1924).

On the later Jewish views, see: D. Castelli, *JQR*, I (1888-89), 314-52; A. Marmorstein, *AJT*, XIV (1915), 577 ff; J.-B. Frey, *Bibl.*, XIII (1932), 129 ff.

For Marqeh's exposition of Deut. 32, see: M. Heidenheim, ed., *Memar Marqah* (1896), pp. 91-93. Cf. M. Gaster, *Samaritan Eschatology* (1932). T. H. Gaster

*RESURRECTION IN THE NT. Though the event itself is nowhere described, the resurrection of Jesus Christ represents the watershed of NT history and the central point of its faith. On the historical plane it marks the division between the earthly life of Jesus and the apostolic age; but it is seen also as nothing less than a new act of creation, signalizing the divide between the old world and the new and inaugurating that resurrection order of life which is one day to be the only one. It has connections backward with the promise of Resurrection already held out in the OT and the Apoc., and forward with the general resurrection at the last day (*see* Eschatology of the NT). But its center is that invisible point on the "third day," where faith and history meet in a relationship which remains as problematic as it is indissoluble.

A. *THE RESURRECTION OF CHRIST AND RESURRECTION IN GENERAL.* It is necessary to emphasize from the start that, from the NT point of view, the resurrection of Christ is not, and cannot be, understood as a typical instance of resurrection in general. It is a unique event, and not one of a class in relation either to the expectation of other individuals or to other raisings from the dead in the biblical narrative. It is by definition the resurrection of the Messiah.

1. The Resurrection and the resurrection hope. Nowhere in the NT is the resurrection hope deduced from the resurrection of Christ, as if his survival of death were the supreme instance that proved or guaranteed eternal life for others. "In Christ," indeed, and in his resurrection, others, and potentially all men, are included (I Cor. 15:22). And for Christians the resurrection hope is reinforced and redefined (cf. I Pet. 1:3) as a sharing in the risen life and body of Christ, both in the present and in the future (*see* §§ D1*c*, 2*a*, *below*). But nowhere is the prospect or even the certainty of life after death derived from the resurrection of Christ as its one sure example. For Jesus, the assurance of a general resurrection rests upon something independent of and prior to the event of the Resurrection—namely, the conviction that God "is not God of the dead, but of the living" (Mark 12:26-27). Even for Paul, who insists so strongly on the corporate character of the resurrection of Christ, the Resurrection is not the ground for accepting belief in resurrection in general —a hope that he already entertained as a Pharisee (Acts 23:6). He does not say, If Christ had not been raised, there would be no resurrection, but, "If there is no resurrection of the dead, then Christ has not been raised" (I Cor. 15:13). You cannot, he argues to the Corinthians, deny the resurrection of all men while accepting the resurrection of one man. But this is not to say that belief in the resurrection of all men depends upon accepting the resurrection of one. Moreover, Paul does not draw general conclusions from the resurrection appearances of Christ. Neither in his writings nor in the gospels is there any suggestion that the appearances prove, or even confirm, survival of death. The resurrection hope is never argued from them.

Nor is it argued that in the resurrection body of

the Lord we see the type or pledge of our own. Even when Paul goes on in the second half of I Cor. 15 to speak of the resurrection body of Christians, he draws no inference or analogy from his earlier record of the resurrection appearances of Christ, which are listed simply for their evidential value. He does not say that our resurrection body will be like his, only that its character will be determined entirely by the gift of God, "as he has chosen" (I Cor. 15:38). The resurrection of Christ is a unique event. He rises the "first-born among many brethren" (Rom. 8:29); but in this he is "pre-eminent" (Col. 1:18) rather than typical. (On the connection between Christ's resurrection and the future resurrection of those who belong to him, *see* § D2*a below.*)

2. The Resurrection and other raisings from the dead. Jesus is not the only one to be raised from the dead in the NT; but again, his resurrection is not simply one of a class. In fact, the noun ἀνάστασις ("resurrection") is never used of these other raisings. Even in the Lazarus story it is reserved by Martha for the general resurrection at the last day (John 11:24), and by Jesus for himself (11:25). This raising is, indeed, unique in being viewed consciously and deliberately as an anticipatory sign, both of the general resurrection and of the resurrection of Jesus. In the Synoptic stories (Mark 5:21-43 and parallels; Luke 7:11-17) and in Acts (9:36-42; 20:7-12) there is no such specific reference, though in Matt. 11:5 = Luke 7:22 the raising of the dead is part of the evidence given to John the Baptist for answering his question whether Jesus is the one "who is to come." But though the raisings, like the healings, are signs of the End (cf. Matt. 10:7-8), anticipations within this age of the eschatological deliverance of the body (*see* MIRACLE), all other men apart from Jesus are restored to life only to die again. Their death is merely postponed. Indeed, it is often debatable how far over the boundary of death they have passed. This is not to. say that by medical standards they would not have been certified as dead. Of this there can be no question in the case of Lazarus (John 11:39) or even of the widow's son (Luke 7:12-14) or Dorcas (Acts 9:37); though the accounts of Jairus' daughter (Mark 5:39 and parallels) and Eutychus (Acts 20:10) could be read to imply that nothing more than resuscitation was required. What the language indicates is, rather, that for the Hebrew mind there was no absolute division between life and death. Death was, from one point of view, a weak form of life. At death the soul or spirit left the body but could be called back into it, if not too far gone (cf. II Kings 4:32-35; *see* DEATH; SOUL; SPIRIT). This is what Paul means by saying of Eutychus that "his life [lit., soul] is in him" (Acts 20:10), or Luke of Jairus' daughter that "her spirit returned" (Luke 8:55). Of the latter, Jesus says she "is not dead but sleeping" (Mark 5:39 and parallels), and even of Lazarus: "I go to awake him out of sleep" (John 11:11). They are indeed dead; but in all these cases the dead person is simply called back to life, and this is indicated by the corpse's opening its eyes and sitting up (Acts 9:40) or sitting up and beginning to speak (Luke 7:15). Raising the dead is the continuation of healing beyond a certain point. The restorative power is of God, but the

agents of it, as in the classic case of Elisha and the son of the Shunammite woman (II Kings 4:32-37), may be purely human. Indeed, raising the dead is included as part of the regular mission program laid upon the Twelve (Matt. 10:8).

But the resurrection of Jesus is quite different. There is no suggestion of mere resuscitation; he has passed right over the border into the realm of the departed spirits (*see* SHEOL); he is not brought back simply to this life, destined to die again, but raised forever to the right hand of God; this is effected, not through any human agency, but by God alone; and only of his raising does the NT use the term "the resurrection." This last point introduces the most decisive distinction of all between the resurrection of Jesus and any other: his is the resurrection of the Messiah.

3. The resurrection of the Messiah. For the earliest Christian preaching it is the Resurrection that designates Jesus as the Christ, the Son of God (Acts 2:36; 13:33; Rom. 1:4). This is the point at which his reign as Messiah begins, when, so far from returning to the confines of the present age, he enters upon and inaugurates the age of GLORY. At the hour when Jesus is glorified (Luke 24:26; John 12:23; Acts 3:13; Rom. 6:4; I Pet. 1:21; etc.), God's messianic act is complete, and the age to come has begun to supersede this one. And, conversely, it is because in it Jesus is declared unequivocally to be the Messiah that the raising of Jesus can be spoken of as "the resurrection"—as the beginning, i.e., of the general resurrection, the inauguration of the last day (*see* § D1*d below*). For prior to the "third day," the term "the resurrection" could have no reference except to the "last day." "In the resurrection" meant for Jesus' contemporaries and for Jesus himself "when they rise from the dead" (Mark 12:23, 25; cf. John 11:24). It was what happened "on the third day," and the eschatological significance attached to it, that alone could make men think of applying the term ἡ ἀνάστασις, "*the* resurrection," to a point within history.

B. *THE PROSPECT OF THE RESURRECTION.* It follows from what has just been said that the Resurrection would have appeared quite different in prospect from what it came to be seen in retrospect. But the question must be raised whether Jesus had any prospect of the Resurrection, and, if so, whether any evidence of his prospect is afforded by our existing documents. These were written to set forth the postresurrection faith of the apostolic church: they were not written as documentaries to put on record how Jesus himself saw the event beforehand. Nevertheless, they do record as an integral part of their gospel the fact that Jesus himself spoke unwaveringly of the coming vindication by God of his person and cause. And sometimes this vindication is expressed quite specifically in terms of resurrection out of death.

There can be little doubt that these predictions, which sound like a knell through the second half of Mark's Gospel (8:31; 9:31; 10:33-34; and parallels), have been touched up in the light of events. This applies particularly to the details of the last prediction, with its reference to Jesus' being delivered to the chief priests and the scribes, who will condemn him and deliver him to the Gentiles, who will mock, spit upon, and scourge him. But there is a growing tendency of scholars to recognize in the basic predictions something that may well have its origin with Jesus himself. Apart from details read back from the passion narrative, the language can be shown to take its color from Isa. 52–53, and in the Hebrew rather than the LXX version. This, indeed, cannot be said of the final, and for us crucial, clause that "after three days" the Son of man "will rise again." But neither can this clause be derived with any exactitude from subsequent events. For it was not strictly "after three days" that Jesus rose, but "on the third day," as Matthew and Luke recognize by their corrections at this point. Moreover, the whole clause evidently reflects the words of Hos. 6:2:

> After two days he will revive us;
> on the third day he will raise us up,
> that we may live before him;

And it is by no means improbable that Jesus should likewise have seen his vindication as Son of man, representing the whole people of God, in terms of resurrection—a pattern for the restoration of Israel long since made classic by Ezek. 37. In any case, it has been argued, the very use of the term "SON OF MAN" implies the idea of vindication out of suffering (cf. Dan. 7:13-27), and no prophecy in which this was the central figure could end simply on the note of humiliation.

That Jesus foresaw some such vindication by God as the end of his ministry of humiliation and death is made more probable by the recurrence of this theme in other forms in his teaching. These other expressions of it also help to clarify how he understood it.

The saying most closely similar to the passion predictions is that of Luke 13:32-33: "Go and tell that fox, 'Behold, I cast out demons and perform cures today and tomorrow, and the third day I finish my course [lit., I am perfected]. Nevertheless I must go on my way today and tomorrow and the day following; for it cannot be that a prophet should perish away from Jerusalem.'" The "perfecting" of Jesus is in some mysterious way linked with his death in Jerusalem, with the "accomplishment" (it is the same root in Greek) of that "baptism" by which hitherto he has been constricted (Luke 12:50) and which, with the "cup," is the gateway to his "glory" (Mark 10:35-40). These convictions of a coming glory, when the sovereignty of God, "until now" subject to the despite of its enemies (Matt. 11:12), shall be vindicated in power (Mark 9:1; cf. Luke 22: 15-18), reach their climax in the assertion that, as Son of man, Jesus is to come in glory to the Father and be seated in victory at his right hand (Mark 14: 62 and parallels). Such, at any rate, is one well-supported interpretation of the trial saying. As in Dan. 7:13-27, the Son of man, representing the "saints of the Most High," comes to the throne of God to be given judgment in the face of his oppressors and to receive the kingdom, the power, and the glory. On this showing, Jesus' predictions of his rising again out of death and of his exaltation in glory from the hour of the Passion (cf. Matt. 26:64; Luke 22:69: "from now on") refer to the same act of God, which is to vindicate him as Christ and Son

of man. Both have an eschatological reference, to the final messianic act of God, which only the events of the third day were to prove to be located in the midst of history.

The objection, therefore, that Jesus could not have spoken to his disciples of his rising after three days, or they would not have been so surprised by it, loses much of its force. When the disciples, who are regularly represented as baffled by this saying (Mark 9:32 and parallels; Luke 18:34), questioned among themselves what the rising (of the Son of man) from the dead might mean (Mark 9:9-10), they could have given to it no other reference than the general resurrection at the last day. Hence their subsequent question about Elijah (9:11-13): for was not he to come first, "before the great and terrible day of the LORD" (Mal. 4:5)? It was only the evidence of the event itself that could open their eyes, "for as yet they did not know [i.e., understand] the scripture, that he must rise from the dead" (John 20:9). The initial effect of the event was to shatter the expectations which later it was found to confirm. The coming vindication of the Son of man of which Jesus had spoken so often to deaf ears—and so plainly (Mark 8:32)—was fulfilled in a way they could never have guessed, by a rising, not at the end of history, however imminently that might have been expected, but within history. And yet this was not simply one more temporary anticipation of the final resurrection; it was the beginning of "the resurrection," of the new world, itself. For it was the resurrection of the Son of man, of the Christ.

C. *THE FACT OF THE RESURRECTION.*
1. The empty tomb. The earliest records do not speak specifically of the empty tomb, and this has in consequence been held to be a subsequent embellishment or materialization of a tradition that originally knew nothing of it. It is, however, often overlooked how insistently they speak of the full tomb. Both in the primitive Pauline summary (I Cor. 15:4) and in the Acts preaching (13:29), Jesus' BURIAL is specifically mentioned (cf. Rom. 6:4). And against the natural presumption that under Roman law the body of Jesus as a condemned criminal would have been thrown into a lime pit or left to rot, or permitted interment by the Jews in a common grave, the tradition that he was given burial in a tomb, with its circumstantial explanation in all the gospel accounts (Matt. 27:57-61; Mark 15:42-47; Luke 23:50-56; John 19:38-42), must be accepted as one of the most firmly grounded facts of Jesus' life. (This must also be set against the counterargument that naturally the body could not have been produced to refute the resurrection story, since it would already have disintegrated beyond recognition.)

The empty tomb may not receive specific mention in the most primitive evidence—though in contrast, e.g., with the Virgin Birth, it is an integral part of the earliest gospel account. But even in the pregospel tradition, insofar as this can be reconstructed from the Pauline letters and the Acts speeches (*see* PREACHING), it is almost certainly implicit. The statements: "that he was buried, that he was raised on the third day" (I Cor. 15:4), that "they took him down from the tree, and laid him in a tomb. But God raised him from the dead" (Acts 13:29-30), and that "he was not abandoned to Hades, nor did his flesh see corruption" (Acts 2:31), all imply belief in a bodily resurrection. Indeed, it would have been inconceivable for a Jew to think of resurrection except in bodily terms. As I Cor. 15:35 indicates, the issue involved in the question: "How are the dead raised?" was, not whether it would be with a body, but: "With what kind of body do they come?" A bodiless resurrection, or the notion that a man might be "spiritually" raised while his body lay on in the tomb, would have seemed to the Jew an absurdity. In whatever form the Resurrection was first proclaimed by the apostles, it must have implied an empty sepulchre. The stories about it may, indeed, be secondary—they must be judged on their own merits—but the idea that they represent a materialization of an originally "spiritual" understanding of the resurrection event betrays a purely modern viewpoint. This, of course, says nothing as to whether the resurrection of Jesus *was* a bodily event, only that from the beginning it must have been believed and preached as such.

When we turn to the gospels, their evidence on the empty tomb is in substance unanimous. There are, indeed, differences of detail which at times have been given an exaggerated prominence (*see bibliography*). Thus, there are the variations in the names and number of the women who visited the tomb. Matthew (28:1) speaks of "Mary Magdalene and the other Mary" (i.e., from 27:56: "Mary the mother of James and Joseph"); Mark (16:1) of "Mary Magdalene, and Mary the mother of James [and of Joses (15:40, 47)], and Salome"; Luke (24:10) of "Mary Magdalene and Jo-anna and Mary the mother of James and the other women with them"; John (20:1) of "Mary Magdalene" only (though the "We do know where they have laid him" of the next verse implies the presence of others). There are divergent accounts of the exact degree of darkness when they arrived (Mark 16:2 and parallels; John 20:1) and of the motives from which they came (Mark and Luke: to anoint the body; Matthew: to see the grave; John: unspecified [cf. 11:31; 20:11]).

Again, the description of the figure or figures at the tomb varies. According to Mark 16:5, the women, on entering the tomb, "saw a young man sitting on the right side, dressed in a white robe." In Matt. 28: 2-3, in what is part of an obvious embellishment, "an angel of the Lord descended from heaven and came and rolled back the stone, and sat upon it. His appearance was like lightning, and his raiment white as snow." According to Luke 24:3-4: "When they [the women] went in they did not find the body. While they were perplexed about this, behold, two men stood by them in dazzling apparel" (cf. 24:23: "a vision of angels"). In John, while the two disciples had seen nothing in the tomb but the graveclothes, Mary subsequently "stooped to look into the tomb; and she saw two angels in white, sitting where the body of Jesus had lain, one at the head and one at the feet" (20:11-12). Furthermore, there is some divergence about what these figures said (Matt. 28:5-7; Mark 16:6-7; Luke 24:5-7, vss. 6b-7 being clearly editorial; John 20:13) and how the women responded (Matt. 28:8; Mark 16:8; Luke 24:8-9; John 20:13-14 [but cf. 20:2, 18]).

None of these, however, is the kind of difference that impugns the authenticity of the narrative. Indeed, they are all precisely what one would look for in genuine accounts of so confused and confusing a scene. The very absence of uniformity or harmonization tells against any subsequent fabrication or agreed story, and the reserve and relatively minor legendary accretions, even in Matthew, contrast greatly with the highly colorful accounts—e.g., in the Gospel of Peter 6-12 and in the Gospel According to the Hebrews (according to Jerome *Of Illustrious Men* 2, 16).

But, details of description apart, the basic witness is extraordinarily unanimous. It is that through the good offices of Joseph of Arimathea the body of Jesus, swathed in linen, was given hurried burial outside Jerusalem on the Friday night in a rock tomb which was subsequently closed by a large stone. After the rest imposed by the sabbath, the women came at dawn on Sunday, to find the stone rolled away from the tomb and the body gone. The natural supposition was that the grave had been disturbed by human agents: "*They* have taken the Lord out of the tomb, and we do not know where they have laid him" (John 20:2). According to the Synoptists, however, the figure or figures at the tomb insist that Jesus has risen (in John this communication comes from Jesus himself, and in Matthew from both sources), and the women are charged to tell the disciples; "but these words seemed to them an idle tale, and they did not believe them" (Luke 24:11).

There is nothing in the records to suggest that the turn of events was anything but utterly unexpected, and no suggestion, except in John 20:8, where it is said the Beloved Disciple "saw and believed," that the empty tomb by itself was anything but bewildering and perplexing (cf. Luke 24:3-4). To say that it was the product of wishful thinking is to ignore the fact that it was the last thing that the women or the disciples could have wished. And when they found the tomb empty, their sole desire was to recover the body: "Sir, if you have carried him away, tell me where you have laid him, and I will take him away" (John 20:15). The theory that the disciples had themselves stolen the body, recorded by Matthew as put out by the Jews (28:13-15), implies that the whole subsequent preaching of the Resurrection was based on a conscious fraud; and this is as psychologically improbable as the supposed original action. The currency of this theory is testimony only to the fact that those who had most interest in doing so could neither deny the tomb was empty nor produce the body. Nor does it solve anything to postulate some entirely unidentified and unidentifiable robbers who vanished with the body as mysteriously as they came. The only alternative explanations—that the women visited the wrong grave, or that Jesus merely swooned on the cross and subsequently extricated himself from the linen bands and the tomb—have failed to command any serious measure of support. And all these explanations are bound to write off the detailed description of the graveclothes in John 20:6-7, which has none of the marks of incipient legend, such as characterize the story of the watch in Matt. 27:62–28:15.

Recent scholars have, therefore, tended to abandon

the attempt to give rationalistic explanations of the narrative as it stands. The whole story is seen rather as the inevitable representation in "mythological" terms of what began as the purely spiritual acknowledgment of the cross of Christ, not as a defeat, but as the victory of God. This acknowledgment, it is said, is what the Resurrection originally meant (and what it essentially means), and it was this conviction, and not any empty tomb, that dawned upon the disciples on the third day. This view embodies the modern existentialist presumption that "authentic" events take place in the realm of decision rather than of physical change.

The only issue relevant here, however, is whether or not this interpretation does justice to the scriptural evidence. It cannot, as we have seen, seriously claim to be supported by any evidence prior to the gospel records themselves; for there is no hint of any earlier preaching except of a bodily resurrection. Moreover, if the whole story of the empty tomb were a subsequent construction—and either the women found the body as they expected, or they did not go at all, or there was no tomb in the first place—it is difficult to believe that the resultant tradition would have shown either the agreements or the disagreements which it now does. Many, in fact, will continue to find it easier to believe that the empty tomb produced the disciples' faith than that the disciples' faith produced the empty tomb.

Nevertheless, there is no suggestion in the NT that to believe in the Resurrection means to believe in the empty tomb. For the empty tomb is not itself the Resurrection, any more than the shell of the chrysalis is the butterfly. Moreover, however objective it may appear, it can never be decisive. On the face of it, it looks the most public and solid piece of evidence: either it was empty or it was not. Yet the fact that the body was not produced will never prove that it could not have been produced. And, even if the tomb could be certified empty with complete assurance, what would it establish? Precisely, as the women realized with dismay, that "he is not here."

2. The appearances. According to all our accounts, it was the appearances, not the tomb, that were decisive for the disciples' faith. And there can be no doubt that they were an essential part of the earliest witness. Paul gives a detailed list of them in I Cor. 15:5-7 as forming part of the original tradition that he had himself received; and he adds that most of the witnesses were still alive. There are further accounts in all the gospels. The evidence of Mark 16:9-20 must be discounted, as clearly not belonging to the original text; but the majority of scholars would agree that it replaces an ending, now lost, which included an appearance to the disciples (cf. 16:7). *See* MARK, GOSPEL OF.

While some of the equations must remain uncertain, there appear to be records of at least eleven different appearances, apart from that to Paul (I Cor. 15:8; cf. Acts 9:3-8; 22:6-11; 26:12-18), which he himself claimed as one of the series:

1. To the women (Matt. 28:9-10)
2. To Mary Magdalene (John 20:11-18)
3. To Peter (I Cor. 15:5; Luke 24:34; cf. Mark 16:7?)
4. To two disciples on the road to Emmaus (Luke 24:13-31)

5-8. To the Eleven and other disciples
5. Luke 24:36-49; John 20:19-23 (=I Cor. 15:5?)
6. John 20:24-29
7. Matt. 28:16-20 (cf. Mark 16:7?)
8. Acts 1:6-9 (= Luke 24:50-51? =I Cor. 15:7?)
9. To seven disciples (John 21:1-14)
10. To more than five hundred brethren (I Cor. 15:6)
11. To James (I Cor. 15:7)

Three aspects of these appearances call for comment: (*a*) their recipients; (*b*) their location; (*c*) their form.

a) The common feature in all the appearances is that they were granted to those who were already followers of Christ. The consistent record of the NT is that the visions of Jesus after the Resurrection did not lie within the natural power of any who might wish to see him. He had not returned, like Lazarus, to public inspection (cf. John 12:9). The primitive account was that "God . . . made him manifest," and that "not to all the people but to us who were chosen by God as witnesses" (Acts 10:40-41); and the later descriptions all emphasize that the initiative lay with Christ in making himself visible: "he appeared" (Luke 24:34; Acts 1:3; 9:17; 13:31; I Cor. 15:5-8); "he revealed himself" (John 21:1, 14); "he presented himself alive" (Acts 1:3). The appearances were assurances given to those who had previously accepted him, not proof to compel faith or confound doubt (cf. John 14:19-23). It is only with the apocryphal Gospel of Peter (ch. 9) that the Resurrection itself is described as a public event and the rising Jesus is seen by unbelievers.

b) There is no similarly uniform tradition as regards the place of the appearances. Those that are localized (and none of the ones recorded in I Cor. 15 is) divide into two groups: in Jerusalem or its environs (1-6, 8); and in Galilee (7, 9). Mark 16:7 seems to presuppose a Galilee tradition, which Matthew confirms (though he also records a fleeting appearance to the women at the tomb); Luke has an exclusively Jerusalem tradition, as has John except in his Epilogue (ch. 21). There is no way of harmonizing these variant traditions, but equally no insuperable difficulty in supposing that appearances took place in both areas. It has been suggested that the appearances, first in Jerusalem, then in Galilee, and finally again in Jerusalem, correspond with where the disciples would naturally have been during, between, and again during, the festivals of Passover and Pentecost. Others have detected doctrinal interests of the different evangelists in Galilee and Jerusalem respectively and have seen the divergence as theological.

c) It is widely stated that there are divergences also in the form of the appearances, and that while Paul witnesses to purely spiritual visions, they are represented as progressively more materialistic as the gospel tradition develops. The only real evidence for this thesis, which reflects the same presupposition observed in relation to the empty tomb—namely, that a purely spiritual resurrection is more probable and therefore more primitive—is that Paul regarded all the other appearances as conforming to the pattern of his own vision on the Damascus Road. But there is little basis for such a deduction. So far from regarding his own vision as normative, he marvels at his right to include it in the series at all. Paul, in fact, says nothing about the manner of the appearances, nor does he equate even his own seeing of the Lord (I Cor. 9:1) with his other "visions and revelations" (II Cor. 12:1-7). In the gospel records it is arbitrary to arrange the appearances in order of increasing materialization. There is none in Mark, and there are no details in Matthew except that the women "took hold of his feet" (28:9), an action expressly forbidden to Mary Magdalene in John 20:17. All the appearances, in fact, depict the same phenomenon, of a body identical yet changed, transcending the limitations of the flesh yet capable of manifesting itself within the order of the flesh. We may describe this as a "spiritual" (I Cor. 15:44) or "glorified" (cf. I Cor. 15:43; Phil. 3:21) body (though Paul himself does not apply such language to the resurrection appearances), so long as we do not import into these phrases any opposition to the physical as such. It is, indeed, the two evangelists who most insist upon the physical character of the manifestations (Luke 24:39-43; John 20:20, 27) who state most specifically that Jesus had already, by the time of the appearances, "enter[ed] into his glory" (Luke 24:26) and been "glorified" (John 13:31, etc.; cf. 20:22 with 7:39).

The impression that Paul witnesses to apparitions of the glorified Christ, whereas the gospels stress the continuity with his earthly form, is only partially valid. The gospels do stress the identity between the risen Lord and the Jesus whom the disciples knew and remembered. But the theological purpose of the resurrection stories is just as much to present this Jesus as exalted in the Father's glory. Indeed, there is no ultimate distinction between what might be called resurrection and ascension appearances. Though the emphasis may differ as the first shock of recognition passes, they are all demonstrations of Jesus as not only alive but sovereign. Thus Matthew, perhaps like Mark before him, closes upon a vision of the exalted Christ (Matt. 28:16-20) which in its language echoes that of the Son of man in Dan. 7:14, to whom

> was given dominion
> and glory and kingdom,
> that all peoples, nations, and languages
> should serve him;
> his dominion is an everlasting dominion,
> which shall not pass away,
> and his kingdom one
> that shall not be destroyed.

Even Acts 1:1-11, which equates the Ascension with the termination of the appearances (contrast Luke 9:51; 22:69; 24:26, where Christ's "taking up" to the power and glory of the Father is associated with the Passion and the Resurrection), treats this moment as one of adieu rather than of glorification. The moment of glory has already occurred, and the appearances are regarded as lying the other side of Jesus' enthronement as Lord and Christ. The primitive witness was that Jesus was "designated Son of God in power" (the essential message of the ASCENSION) "by [or from] his resurrection from the dead" (Rom. 1:4); and this would point to a manifestation of Jesus in glory at the time of the Resurrection declaring him to be Son of God, such as is anticipated in the transfiguration vision (Mark 9:2-8 and parallels), whose meaning was to be revealed only when "the Son of man should have risen from the dead" (Mark 9:9).

It was the appearances which, according to our evidence, transformed the apostles. If we do not accept that the appearances produced the belief, then we have to postulate that the belief produced the appearances. They then become, if not pure hallucinations, at any rate the projections, objectivizations, of an already formed conviction that Jesus was alive and sovereign: the disciples believed themselves into seeing. But this still leaves unexplained where they derived the idea that he could be alive—nothing, on the face of it, seems to have been further from their minds. Moreover, the accounts of the appearances betray no trace of mass suggestion, but (except in the case of the five hundred brethren at once) speak of separate manifestations to persons and groups who show no other signs of suggestibility or hysteria; in fact, doubt and incredulity mix in their minds in equal proportion with frightened joy.

In contrast with the empty tomb, the resurrection appearances look far less tangible as evidence. It can never be proved that they were seen except by those who were previously prepared to believe. Yet we are here at one of the turning points of world history: no belief in the Resurrection, no Christian church. And, without those experiences in some form that was not illusory, is it possible to account for that belief and for the radical and permanent transformation of the disciples that followed? Yet, once more, what do the appearances by themselves prove? They provide, for those interested in physical research, a reasonably well-documented case of temporary survival; but nothing in themselves of any religious significance. They spelled resurrection only to those who had already begun to recognize in Jesus the Christ, the Son of God. And this introduces the third and apparently most intangible set of evidence.

3. The experience of the living Christ. If the appearances had been merely psychic phenomena, one would expect the sense that Jesus was alive to have grown progressively less vivid once the disciples ceased to be "in touch," and those who had not seen the evidence to be as skeptical as third parties usually are to such supposed communications from the dead—let alone to reports of miraculously empty graves. But, in fact, the conviction became only the more settled once the appearances had ceased, and those who had not seen were won to just as living a faith as those who had. Moreover, the ground of appeal even for those who had shared in the appearances was not the past experiences so much as the present experience. Paul may have appealed to his vision of the risen Lord for his authority as an apostle (I Cor. 9:1; 15:8-9) and for explaining his changed manner of life (Acts 22:1-21; 26:1-23); but he never reverts to it as the ground of his present faith. The basis for this is the abiding experience of the "Christ who lives in me" (Gal. 2:20) and the continuing knowledge of the "power of his resurrection" (Phil. 3:10). Similarly, it was to the signs of the living Christ, to "this which you see and hear" (Acts 2:33), to the powers now at work in his name (Acts 3:15-16; 4:30; etc.), that the first apostles appealed, as much as to the events they witnessed, for "their testimony to the resurrection of the Lord Jesus" (Acts 4:33).

This abiding and transforming experience, grounded, not on the reports of others, but on the firsthand awareness of the living Christ, is what made and sustained the Christian church. And the very existence of the church, not merely as the historical consequence of past phenomena but as the embodiment of a present faith, is itself a major part of the evidence of the Resurrection. Indeed, it was this present conviction, which thrills through the letters, that alone caused the other evidence to be preserved. The NT evidence for the Resurrection is to be seen not merely in the closing chapters of the gospels; it is to be seen above all in the faith which prompted the very composition of the gospels.

Moreover, though the present experience of the living Christ may look the weakest evidence of all—for it is less public even than the appearances, and quite intangible—yet the continuing existence of the Christian church which lives by this experience is the fact of history that is least open to doubt. No one can deny its existence, however skeptical he may be of the empty tomb or the appearances. And, finally, this knowledge of the living, victorious Christ is the only real evidence for affirming that he is risen, that he lives with God, as distinct from saying that he is not in his grave or that he survived as a ghost for a few weeks. As the NT writers were well aware, to assert that Jesus is alive now is to make a claim that only his continued presence and activity, and not simply past facts, however well authenticated, can sustain and confirm.

And yet the Resurrection remains for the NT, not primarily an experience, but an event. It uses the phrase "witnesses of the Resurrection," not of all who can testify to its power, but only of those who were eyewitnesses of the event—or rather of the identity between the risen Christ whom they had seen and the man with whom they had companied "during all the time that the Lord Jesus went in and out among us, beginning from the baptism of John until the day when he was taken up from us" (Acts 1:21-22; cf. 10:41; 13:31). The Resurrection is not simply the risen Christ, an abiding presence with which every generation is contemporaneous, but an act of God in history of which only those can be witnesses who were there to see. "Those who have not seen" may be equally "blessed" (John 20:29); but they are dependent, nevertheless, for their belief upon the "word" of those who have (John 17:20). The continuing presence of the living Christ can never detach the Christian faith in the Resurrection from history. Each generation is not equidistant from it: every successive generation has to go back to the apostolic witness. The "many proofs" (Acts 1:3) of

the Resurrection which the NT sets down are recorded, not simply as historical explanations of the apostles' own faith, but as the acts of God to which all subsequent faith must remain the response. Yet neither are the historical facts by themselves the witness: "We are witnesses to these things, and so is the Holy Spirit whom God has given to those who obey him" (Acts 5:32). The signs of the Resurrection in the life of the believer and the church are the indispensable internal testimony, without which Jesus might have been "raised" but could not have been preached as "risen."

D. *THE MEANING OF THE RESURRECTION.* 1. For the present time. *a. The identity of the risen one.* "It is the Lord!" (John 21:7): such for the disciples was the first instinctive reaction to the Resurrection. That he was "alive" (Luke 24:23), "risen indeed" (Luke 24:34), and that it was really he, was the great and staggering marvel. "I have seen the Lord," says Mary Magdalene to the disciples (John 20:18); "We have seen the Lord," say the disciples to Thomas (John 20:25). Was it really possible? Incredulity and doubt run right through the narratives (Matt. 28:17; Luke 24:11, 38, 41; John 20:25, 27; 21:4; and even 21:12). The emphasis laid upon physical aspects of the Lord's risen body is not in the interest of materialization for its own sake but of placing beyond dispute his identity: "See my hands and my feet, that it is I myself [ἐγώ εἰμι αὐτός]; handle me, and see" (Luke 24:39); "he showed them his hands and his side. Then the disciples were glad when they saw the Lord" (John 20:20; cf. vss. 25, 27). Every appearance has at its heart a recognition scene, in which Jesus either says something (Matt. 28:9; John 20:16, 19, 26; cf. Acts 9:5 and parallels) or does something (Luke 24:30-31, 39-43; John 20:20, 27; 21:6, 13) which establishes his identity.

The actions by which this recognition is achieved are not fortuitous. They fall into two groups: (*a*) displaying the marks of the Passion (Luke 24:39; John 20:20, 27); and (*b*) sharing food (Luke 24:30, 35, 41-43; John 21:12-13; Acts 1:4 RSV mg.; 10:41; cf. Mark 16:14). The latter action recalls the Jesus, not only of the Last Supper, with his promise of eating and drinking new in the kingdom of God (Matt. 26:29; Mark 14:25; Luke 22:16-22), but also of that other messianic meal with bread and fish (Mark 6:30-44 and parallels; John 6:1-15) after which prematurely they sought to make him king (cf. especially John 21: 13 with 6:11). The lines are redrawn between the Passion and the glory. Only those who have continued with him in his trials can eat with him at his table in his kingdom (Luke 22:28-30), and only those who have shared the suffering of the Son of man can recognize that same figure in power (Matt. 28:18); for thus it was necessary for the Christ to enter into his glory (Luke 24:26; cf. Mark 10:37-38). The sole recipients of the resurrection appearances can be those able to recognize, not simply the physical scars—others could have vouched for his identity at this level—but the spiritual continuity: those, in other words, who, in a more than literal sense, "came up with him from Galilee to Jerusalem" (Acts 13:31; cf. Mark 10:32-34).

For this reason the identity of Jesus through death and life is not confined to the first moments of recognition. It is one of the abiding marks of the NT witness that it should be "this Jesus" (Acts 1:11; 2:23) that was dead who is risen and ascended and shall come again. The returning Lord cannot appear without the marks of the nails (John 20:25), the Lamb victorious is the Lamb standing, "as though it had been slain" (Rev. 5:6), and the "living one" is by definition the one "who died" (Rev. 1:18; 2:8). This note of continuity is preserved throughout the apostolic preaching, from the first crude antithesis: "The God of our fathers raised Jesus whom you killed by hanging him on a tree. God exalted him at his right hand as Leader and Savior" (Acts 5:30-31), to the final climax of Paul's most mature writing: "It is Christ Jesus, who died, yes, who was raised from the dead, who is at the right hand of God, who indeed intercedes for us" (Rom. 8:34 RSV mg.). "We see Jesus, . . . crowned with glory and honor because of the suffering of death" (Heb. 2:9): this unexpungeable relationship of the risen glory with suffering and death is what ties the apostolic faith to history. The experience of the living Christ is not the awareness of the ever-present lordship of God in Christ, which was temporarily darkened by the Cross; it is the knowledge of a victory inaugurated only through the once-and-for-all act of the Cross. The tense of the Resurrection is the perfect, and not simply the aorist or the present.

b. The vindication of God in Christ. If the first reaction of the disciples was that Jesus was alive, the second was the realization that he had been raised by and to the right hand of God. He not only lived but also reigned. All that men had done had been overturned by the vindicating action of God: "The stone which was rejected by you builders . . . has become the head of the corner" (Acts 4:11); "this Jesus . . . you crucified and killed by the hands of lawless men. But God raised him up" (Acts 2:23-24). The constant NT emphasis is not simply that Christ has risen, but that God has raised him or that he has been raised (by God; Acts 2:32; 3:15; 4:10; 5:30; etc.; Rom. 4:24-25; 6:4; 8:11; I Cor. 15:4; II Cor. 4:14; Gal. 1:1; Eph. 1:20; Heb. 13:20; etc.). This action is associated with the Spirit (Rom. 1:4; 8:11; I Tim. 3:16; I Pet. 3:18), the power (II Cor. 13:4), and the glory of God (Rom. 6:4). Indeed, that God "raised him from the dead" and that he "gave him glory" (I Pet. 1:21) are virtually synonymous. For the consistent witness is that God raised Jesus, not from the underworld back to earth, but up to heaven.

By virtue of the Resurrection, Jesus "has gone into heaven and is at the right hand of God, with angels, authorities, and powers subject to him" (I Pet. 3:21-22). It is impossible in the Greek to distinguish between his being raised "by" the right hand of God and "to" the right hand of God (Acts 2:33; 5:31). The various phrases are all descriptions of the single act by which "God has highly exalted him and bestowed on him the name which is above every name" (Phil. 2:9). Hence it is no coincidence that in the earliest preaching the Resurrection is associated with Jesus' designation by God as the "man of his right hand" (equated in Ps. 80:17 with the "son of man")

—namely, as Lord and Christ (Acts 2:36), Son (Acts 13:33; Rom. 1:4), Savior (Acts 5:31), and Judge (Acts 10:42; 17:31). This is the moment when God's seal is placed unmistakably upon all that Jesus was and did—and has still to do. For to him he has also "subjected the world to come" (Heb. 2:5; cf. Eph. 1:21). As the "living one," Jesus has the "keys of Death and Hades" (Rev. 1:18), and in his triumph the principalities and powers have already been disarmed and exposed (Col. 2:15). They have yet, indeed, finally to be "destroyed," but even now he reigns and must reign "until he has put all his enemies under his feet" (I Cor. 15:24-28).

c. Union with the life of Christ. Resurrection is always seen by the NT, not simply as the moment when Jesus himself was "crowned with glory and honor" (Heb. 2:9) and "passed through the heavens" (Heb. 4:14), but as the moment also when he "opened the kingdom of heaven to all believers" and inaugurated the "new and living way" (Heb. 10:20) between man and God. This is the point when the constriction that had hitherto confined the work of Jesus (Luke 12:50) is broken. The powers of the kingdom were at work in him (Matt. 12:28 = Luke 11:20), but, in his own words: "Unless a grain of wheat falls into the earth and dies, it remains alone; but if it dies, it bears much fruit" (John 12:24). The Resurrection is the point of release, when the "life" that Jesus came to bring (John 10:10) is poured forth in power and let loose in all the world.

This finds expression in a number of different ways. First, and most obviously, the Resurrection means that Jesus is restored to his friends, never again to be parted from them (cf. John 16:22). The reunion of Jesus with his disciples is a powerful motif in the gospel narratives, especially in the Fourth Gospel: "I will not leave you desolate; I will come to you" (John 14:18). The "you will see me" of John 14:19 corresponds to the promise given to the disciples in Mark 16:7. And this restoration is not a mere human reunion but a permanent divine indwelling (John 14:23): "Lo, I am with you always, to the close of the age" (Matt. 28:20).

The restoration of Jesus to his disciples is closely paralleled by the promised outpouring of the HOLY SPIRIT. In Luke-Acts the gift of the Spirit, like the Ascension, is separated temporally from the moment of the Resurrection, but theologically they are all part of a single complex, as is evident in Acts 2:32-33: "This Jesus God raised up, and of that we all are witnesses. Being therefore exalted at the right hand of God, and having received from the Father the promise of the Holy Spirit, he has poured out this which you see and hear." This connection between the exaltation of Christ to the Father and his gift of the Spirit recurs in Eph. 4:8-10. In the Fourth Gospel the gift of the Spirit is clearly understood as contingent upon the glorification of Jesus (John 7:39). The Counselor cannot come unless Jesus goes (16:7); and the inbreathing of the Spirit is the direct gift of the risen Christ (20:22), with whose presence, indeed, he is equated (cf., e.g., 14:28; 16:7). He, like Jesus, is promised to the disciples "to be with you for ever" (14:16).

If the Resurrection means that Jesus through the

Spirit is to be with the disciples, it means equally that the disciples are to be with Jesus, to share his risen life: "Because I live, you will live also . . . you in me, and I in you" (John 14:19-20); "when I go and prepare a place for you, I will come again and will take you to myself, that where I am you may be also" (14:3; cf. II Cor. 4:14). That God "made us alive together with Christ . . . and raised us up with him, and made us sit with him in the heavenly places" (Eph. 2:5-6), is one of the fundamental convictions of the NT (cf. Col. 2:12; 3:1). This conviction is equally expressed in the future tense: "God raised the Lord and will also raise us up by his power" (I Cor. 6:14; *see* § D2 *below*). But there is no contradiction here. Paul immediately follows his statement in Rom. 6:8 that "if we have died with Christ, we believe that we shall also live with him," by reminding his readers that they are "men who have been brought from death to life" (6:13; cf. vs. 11). The message that God sent his Son into the world that we might "live through him" (I John 4:9), and that "life" (which is essentially the "life of Jesus" [II Cor. 4:10-11]) is a present possession of the Christian, requires no emphasis. "If Christ has not been raised, . . . you are still in your sins" (I Cor. 15: 17), "dead through the trespasses and sins in which you once walked" (Eph. 2:1-2, 5). It is the Resurrection through which the new life, with its forgiveness of sins, is offered (Acts 5:30-31; 13:37-38); for he was "raised for our justification" (Rom. 4:25). This new life is mediated through faith (Gal. 2:20), which is essentially faith in the God who "gives life to the dead" (Rom. 4:17; cf. II Cor. 1:9) and "raised [Jesus] from the dead" (Rom. 10:9-10); and through Baptism, which is the act whereby the death and resurrection of Christ are reproduced in us (Rom. 6:3-5; Col. 2:12; I Pet. 3:21).

d. The beginning of the new age. To say that the Resurrection designates Jesus as the Christ is but another way of stating that it inaugurates the messianic age, the new creation. "In Jesus" the apostles are able to proclaim the "resurrection from the dead" (Acts 4:2). "By being the first to rise from the dead" (Acts 26:23), "he is the beginning" (Col. 1:18): in him "the resurrection," which belongs to the age to come (Luke 20:34-36), has already set in. In his person it is no longer reserved for the "last day"; he is even now the "resurrection and the life" (John 11: 24-25).

Yet once again the new age is not confined to his person. He is but the "first-born from the dead" (Col. 1:18; Rev. 1:5; cf. Rom. 8:29), the "first fruits" of the new order (I Cor. 15:20, 23). In one sense he remains unique. Even the resurrection of those who "belong to Christ" still waits upon "his coming" (I Cor. 15:23), though Matthew, as an anticipatory portent, associates the exhumation of "many bodies of the saints" with the Resurrection itself (Matt. 27: 52-53). Even those raised from the dead by Jesus and the apostles have still to die again. Only he is exempt from this (Acts 13:34; Rom. 6:9); for the rest of mankind the "last enemy" remains (I Cor. 15:26). Yet at the same time Jesus promises that "he who believes in me, though he die, yet shall he live, and whoever lives and believes in me shall never die" (John 11:25-26). "If any one is in Christ, he is a new

creation [or, there is the new creation]; the old has passed away, behold, the new has come" (II Cor. 5:17). Those "born anew . . . through the resurrection of Jesus Christ from the dead" (I Pet. 1:3) can be said already to have been "glorified" (Rom. 8:30), or, more exactly, to be "partaker[s] in the glory that is to be revealed" (I Pet. 5:1); they have "tasted . . . the powers of the age to come" (Heb. 6:5) and "passed from death to life" (John 5:24; I John 3:14).

Nevertheless, all this language is proleptic and is constantly balanced by other language which puts beyond doubt that that to which the Christian has been born anew is essentially "living hope," an "inheritance" (I Pet. 1:3-4), of which in the "Holy Spirit of promise" (KJV) we have but the "guarantee . . . until we acquire possession of it" (Eph. 1:14; cf. Rom. 8:23; II Cor. 1:22; 5:5). Those who teach a completely realized eschatology, "that the resurrection is past already," are uncompromisingly condemned (II Tim. 2:18).

2. For the future. *a. The resurrection hope.* According to Acts 23:6, it was for the "hope and the resurrection of the dead" that Paul felt himself to be on trial. This may appear a curious statement, seeing that it was clearly as a Christian that Paul was being charged and that he explicitly affirms of his accusers that it was a "hope . . . which these themselves accept" (24:15). There are, indeed, tactical motives behind his line of defense at this point (23:6-9). Nevertheless, there is a sense in which Paul sees the whole Christian gospel as involved in this hope —negatively, because if it is "incredible . . . that God raises the dead" (26:8), then "our preaching is in vain. . . . We are even found to be misrepresenting God, because we testified of God that he raised Christ, whom he did not raise if it is true that the dead are not raised" (I Cor. 15:14-15); and positively, because "in fact Christ has been raised from the dead" (I Cor. 15:20) and in this the resurrection hope is included, for "Christ" is a representative figure. That "in Christ shall all be made alive" (I Cor. 15:22) is but another way of stating the Christian gospel of Christ as the new Adam, of all humanity restored in him (cf. Rom. 5:15-21; I Cor. 15:45-49).

The connection between Christ's resurrection and the future resurrection of those who are in him is emphasized as strongly as the conviction that those who are "in Christ Jesus" are already "alive to God" (Rom. 6:11): "If we have been united with him in a death like his, we shall certainly be united with him in a resurrection like his" (Rom. 6:5); "God raised the Lord and will also raise us up by his power" (I Cor. 6:14); "If the Spirit of him who raised Christ Jesus from the dead dwells in you, he who raised Christ Jesus from the dead will give life to your mortal bodies also through his Spirit which dwells in you" (Rom. 8:11).

This last passage again draws attention to the Holy Spirit as the vital link, not only between Christ's resurrection and ours, but also between our present and our future state. That "what is mortal" will be "swallowed up by life" is even now guaranteed by the gift of the Spirit (II Cor. 5:4-5). For the Spirit is the anticipation of the End in the present, and the events at the "last trumpet" when "we shall all be changed" (I Cor. 15:51-52) are but the climax to that transformation wrought by the Spirit by which already "we . . . are being changed into his likeness from one degree of glory to another" (II Cor. 3:18). For Christ "will change our lowly body to be like his glorious body, by the power which enables him to subject all things to himself" (Phil. 3:21); and this power is the Spirit, through whom even now "our inner nature is being renewed every day" (II Cor. 4:16). The process by which we are "transformed," ultimately to be "conformed" to the body of his glory (Phil. 3:21; cf. Rom. 8:29), is but the same process by which Christ himself is "formed" in us (Gal. 4:19). And this begins at baptism, where, by incorporation into the body of Christ, we come to "belong to another, to him who has been raised from the dead" (Rom. 7:4). By such language Paul relates the risen life at present known in Christ to the resurrection yet to come. The agent of this continuity through change is, from the divine side, the Spirit; its vehicle, from the human side, is the BODY.

b. The resurrection body. "Flesh and blood cannot inherit the kingdom of God, nor does the perishable inherit the imperishable" (I Cor. 15:50). This is fundamental, and neither Paul nor any other NT writer speaks or could speak of the "resurrection of the flesh [σάρξ]." But he does speak of the resurrection of the body (σῶμα). The "physical body" (I Cor. 15:44) is indeed "perishable" (vs. 42) and "mortal" (Rom. 6:12; 8:11). Nevertheless, "this perishable nature must put on the imperishable, and this mortal nature must put on immortality" (I Cor. 15:33). This process, as we have seen, is closely connected, for Paul, with "putting on Christ" (Rom. 13:14; Gal. 3: 27); for this is to "put on the new nature" (KJV "the new man"; Eph. 4:24; Col. 3:10). The new man is Christ (Eph. 2:15; 4:13; cf. Col. 3:11), the "last" or "second" Adam (I Cor. 15:45-47), and the resurrection body is, in the first instance, the body of Christ, in union with which and as members of which our own bodies are quickened and glorified (cf. I Cor. 6:14-15). To be raised is to "bear the image of the man of heaven" (I Cor. 15:49). Paul does not, in fact, discuss the resurrection body of any but those who "belong to Christ" (I Cor. 15:23), since it is solely in the context of their resurrection and the doubting of it by the Thessalonians (I Thess. 4:13) and the Corinthians (I Cor. 15:12) that he writes.

As regards the nature of the resurrection body, Paul's sole point is to stress that, for all the identity of person, there is a radical discontinuity of form. "What you sow does not come to life unless it dies. And what you sow is not the body which is to be. . . . But God gives it a body as he has chosen" (I Cor. 15:36-38). The Corinthians were questioning whether the dead could be raised, because they had no physical body (I Cor. 15:35), and whether the living needed to be, precisely because they had. Both, Paul insists, are in exactly the same position: "We shall not all sleep, but we shall all be changed" (I Cor. 15:51); and those that are alive will have no advantage over those that have fallen asleep (I Thess. 4:15; cf. II Cor. 4:14).

c. The resurrection and the Parousia. Those that are alive are those "who are left until the coming of the Lord," and Paul at first includes himself among

them: "The dead in Christ will rise first; then we who are alive" (I Thess. 4:16-17); "the dead will be raised imperishable, and we shall be changed" (I Cor. 15:52). His confidence seems to have waned in II Cor. 4:12-14, where he says: "Death is at work in us, but life in you," and expresses the faith that "he who raised the Lord Jesus will raise us also with Jesus and bring us with you into his presence." And he may later have viewed the prospect of death rather differently. In II Cor. 5:4 his preference is clearly for living on, that "what is mortal may be swallowed up by life" without his having first to be "unclothed." But in Phil. 1:23 his "desire is to depart and be with Christ, for that is far better." Nevertheless, even here he says: "I know that I shall remain" (vs. 25)—though this need not mean until the "day of Christ" (vss. 6, 10); and the aspiration of 3:11 "that if possible I may attain the resurrection from the dead" probably implies that he is now reckoning himself among those who must go through the process of death. But it remains true that Paul is always writing to a situation in which only a minority of Christians will need to be raised "from among the dead."

The focus of hope is always the PAROUSIA, the coming of Christ, rather than the raising of the dead. Nor is there any question of the dead being raised prior to this or independently of it (II Cor. 5:1 cannot with any consistency be interpreted of the moment of death. "We have a building from God" is probably best referred to the present anticipation in the body of Christ of the "heavenly dwelling" for which we long). Indeed, even at the Parousia it is only "those who belong to Christ" who are raised (I Cor. 15:23; I Thess. 4:16). Paul never brings this resurrection into relation with his belief in the general resurrection "of both the just and the unjust" (Acts 24:15), though this latter is presumably associated in I Cor. 15:24 with τέλος (the "end," or possibly the "rest"—i.e., of the dead). The author of Revelation alone specifies two resurrections, for Christians and for the "rest of the dead," separated by a thousand years (Rev. 20:4-5). Other writers appear to envisage a single resurrection for believers and nonbelievers at the "last day" (e.g., John 5:28-29; 6:39-40, 44, 54; 11:24; Luke 14:14).

But for Paul the important point is the theological unity between the resurrection of Christians and the parousia of Christ. It is not merely that they occur together (cf. Phil. 3:20-21); the dead are raised precisely in order to participate in the messianic victory. For when Christ comes, it is "to be glorified in his saints" (II Thess. 1:10; cf. Rom. 8:17). The Parousia is to be a corporate appearing (Col. 3:4), the "coming of our Lord Jesus Christ and our assembling to meet him" (II Thess. 2:1). And from this the dead in Christ—as risen men—cannot be excluded. "For since we believe that Jesus died and rose again, even so, through Jesus, God will bring with him those who have fallen asleep" (I Thess. 4:14; cf. II Cor. 4:14). And it is in relation to their "coming" (i.e., at the Parousia) that Paul raises the question of their resurrection body (I Cor. 15:35). Just as the resurrection of Christ was not simply restoration to life but exaltation to victory, so it is with the resurrection of those that are in him. The purpose of their "coming to life again" is that they may "reign with

Christ" (Rev. 20:4). The resurrection of Christians and the parousia of Christ are essentially one. The trumpet that marks the one (I Cor. 15:52) marks the other (Matt. 24:31; I Thess. 4:16). And it is the trumpet of the victory of God in Christ, the purpose of whose death and resurrection was that "whether we wake or sleep we might live with him" (I Thess. 5:10), or, in the more resounding phrase of Rom. 5: 17, "reign in life through the one man Jesus Christ."

Bibliography. There are extensive articles in *Encyclopaedia Biblica* (1903; P. W. Schmiedel gives the best presentation of the radical critical position, where the "contradictions" of the gospel narratives are ruthlessly exposed); *HDB* (1908; W. J. Sparrow-Simpson—conservative and summary); *Dictionary of the Apostolic Church* (1918; J. M. Shaw—much the most comprehensive). Each of these has a full bibliography to date of publication.

Representative expositions of the older conservative case: H. Latham, *The Risen Master* (1901); J. Orr, *The Resurrection of Jesus* (1908).

Representative expositions of the liberal case: K. Lake, *The Historical Evidence for the Resurrection of Jesus Christ* (1907); C. R. Bowen, *The Resurrection in the NT* (1911); S. V. McCasland, *The Resurrection of Jesus* (1932).

More recent studies: P. Gardner-Smith, *The Narratives of the Resurrection* (1926); F. Morison, *Who Moved the Stone?* (1930); M. Goguel, *La foi à la résurrection de Jésus* (1933); J. Baillie, *And the Life Everlasting* (1934), pp. 137-56; R. H. Lightfoot, *Locality and Doctrine in the Gospels* (1938); P. Althaus, *Die Wahrheit des christlichen Osterglaubens* (1940); W. Michaelis, *Die Erscheinungen des Auferstandenen* (1944); A. M. Ramsey, *The Resurrection of Christ* (1945); H. von Campenhausen, *Der Ablauf der Osterereignisse und das leere Grab* (1952); C. H. Dodd, "The Appearances of the Risen Christ: An Essay in Form-Criticism of the Gospels," in D. E. Nineham, ed., *Studies in the Gospels* (1955); O. Cullmann, *Immortality of the Soul or Resurrection of the Dead?* (1958).

On the issues concerning the Resurrection raised by R. Bultmann's essay "NT and Mythology," in H. W. Bartsch, ed., *Kerygma and Myth* (English trans., 1953), pp. 1-44, see: G. Stählin, "On the Third Day," *Interpretation*, X (1956), 282-99; R. R. Niebuhr, *Resurrection and Historical Reason* (1957); J. Knox, *The Death of Christ* (1958), pp. 175-82.

J. A. T. ROBINSON

RESURRECTION OF CHRIST, BOOK OF, BY BARTHOLOMEW THE APOSTLE. *See* BARTHOLOMEW THE APOSTLE, BOOK OF THE RESURRECTION OF CHRIST BY.

REU rōō, rē'ū [רְעוּ, friend, companion, *probably shortened form of* REUEL; *cf.* Akkad. *personal name Ra'ū and* Aram. [רְעוּיה; 'Ραγαύ]; in Luke 3:35 KJV RAGAU rā'gô. A Shemite; the son of Peleg, and the father of Serug (Gen. 11:18-21; I Chr. 1:25; Luke 3:35). If the name is cognate with Akkadian Ra'ilu, an island in the Euphrates just below 'Anat, it may identify both a Mesopotamian site and a tribe.

L. HICKS

REUBEN rōō'bən [רְאוּבֵן, *perhaps meaning* substitute (*for another child*), *from* Arab. *r'b*, to restore, *ending -en*]; REUBENITE —bə nīt [רְאוּבֵנִי]. The first-born son of Jacob, and the *heros eponymos* of the tribe of Reuben. Because Reuben, born of Leah (Gen. 29:32; folk etymology), was Jacob's first-born son, he was always first in the list of the descendants of Jacob (Gen. 35:23; 46:8-9; Exod. 1:2; I Chr. 2:1). In the story of Joseph his role as a leader is bound up with this fact (Gen. 37:21-22, 29; 42:22, 37; 48:5). Reuben found the mandrakes which brought Jacob back to his mother in the etiological legend which explains the name of Issachar (30:14). Tribal history is hidden in the tradition that Reuben lay with his father's concubine Bilhah (35:22).

The tribe of Reuben must at one time have been an important tribe. There is no other way to explain its position of priority in the twelve-tribe system. Its history obviously began in the land W of the Jordan. This is indicated by the fact that the description of the border between Judah and Benjamin, which in its origins dates from the time before statehood, knows a landmark, on the last slope of the Judean highland toward the Valley of the Jordan, named for a Reubenite (the stone of Bohan the son of Reuben; Josh. 15:6; 18:17). It is also evident from the fact that the tradition of Reuben's crime against Bilhah is localized in the region of Migdal-eder (RSV "tower of Eder"; Gen. 5:21-22) in the hill country of Judah in the neighborhood of Bethlehem, to judge from Mic. 4:8 when compared with 5:2—H 5:1 (RSV "tower of the flock" is Hebrew "Migdal-eder"). Reuben's relations to Judah and to the Leah group in general, like those of Gad, date from the early period of the Israelite occupation of the land. The tribe then declined, presumably in connection with the events which lie behind Gen. 35:22. The first statement in the Blessing of Jacob also alludes to this:

> Reuben, you are my first-born,
> . . . .
> pre-eminent in pride and pre-eminent in power.
> Unstable as water [lit., "You boiled over
> like water"], you shall not have pre-eminence
> because you went up to your father's bed
> (Gen. 49:3-4).

The Blessing of Moses expresses Reuben's precarious situation even more clearly:

> Let Reuben live, and not die,

and attaches to it the wish that his men might nevertheless still continue to be a respectable number (Deut. 33:6).

Whether the two statements have in mind Reuben's situation in the land E of the Jordan cannot be determined. It could be that Reuben had already completed the crossing at the time of the Battle of Deborah. For, unlike the tribe of Judah, which S of the crossbar of Canaanite city-territories, was forced into its separate development, Reuben could maintain connections with the Israelite amphictyony. For this reason, Reuben is rebuked in the Song of Deborah for not having taken part in the battle (Judg. 5:15 ff). Like Gilead (Gad), which is named immediately after it, Reuben could easily have found the way across the Jordan. Probably the remnants of the tribe moved over into the land E of the Jordan either along with the Gadites or soon after them. The second alternative is supported by the fact that, according to the lists of towns in Num. 32; Josh. 13, the Reubenites settled in a relatively confined area in the middle of the larger Gadite territory, and perhaps also by the fact that for this very reason they could, unlike the Gadites, keep their blood pure. How the events in the tradition of the rebellion of the

Reubenites Dathan and Abiram (Num. 16:1; Deut. 11:6), which was already known to the Yahwist, fit into the history up to that time, remains an open question. In the period of the kings, Reuben, as a consequence of its insignificance, played no further role. Its fate was interwoven with the history of Gad.

The later literature makes note of Reuben almost exclusively in statistical connections or in schematic presentations which group "Reuben, Gad, and the half-tribe of Manasseh" together. To the latter belong numerous passages of the Deuteronomic historical work which have as their content the premature apportioning of the land E of the Jordan and the resulting obligation to assist in the conquest of the land W of the Jordan. Even the Chronicler, with the exception of the usual genealogy (I Chr. 5:1, 3) which has been expanded as over against the sources in Gen. 46; Num. 26, is able to report on only two individual Reubenites, beyond schematic remarks concerning Reuben, Gad, and the half-tribe of Manasseh (I Chr. 5:18, 26; 26:32). One of these two as the leader of thirty men (11:42) outshoots the list of the Thirty in II Sam. 23, while the other as chieftain of the Reubenites is said to have been led away into exile by Tiglath-pileser (I Chr. 5:6). In the lists Reuben's position of honor is generally respected, though there are significant exceptions, all of them in favor of Judah. In Deut. 27:13, Reuben occupies the first place only in the list of those who are to utter the curse. In the Priestly Code, Reuben has the first position in the list of the heads of tribes (Num. 1:5), of the first muster (1:20-21), of the scouts (13:4), and in the genealogical order (26:5, 7; see also Exod. 6: 14). In the order for encampment and marching (Num. 2:10, 16), in the list of the offerings of the leaders (7:30), and in the sequence for breaking camp (10:18), Reuben has to give precedence to Judah, but ranks at the beginning of the second group of three who camp on the S side of the sanctuary. In the apportionment commission for the land W of the Jordan, Reuben is naturally excluded, and instead named first in the traditional group, Reuben, Gad, and the half-tribe of Manasseh (34:14). Reuben appears associated only with Gad in connection with a P narrative which deals with the bestowal and the division of the land E of the Jordan (ch. 32, mixed with JE). In the lists of the Levite cities Reuben has likewise yielded precedence to Judah and is classified along with Gad and Zebulun in the last group (Josh. 21:7, 36; I Chr. 6:63, 78—H 6:48, 63). The Chronicler's own lists give precedence to Reuben in the series of twelve (I Chr. 27:16) and in the supplement concerning the E Jordanians (12:37—H 12: 38). In the general plan of I Chr. 1-9, Reuben is relegated to the third place in favor of Judah (and Simeon). In Ezek. 48:6, Reuben receives the strip to the N of Judah, but the first of the gates of Jerusalem is immediately named for Reuben (vs. 31). A geographical point of view might have been decisive in the insertion of Reuben to the N of Judah, while Gad receives the most southerly strip, since Reuben's old settlement area in the E lay a bit farther N than that of Gad, which once reached to the Arnon. The author of Ezek. 48 is, therefore, of another and historically more correct opinion than

the one who divided up the list of towns in Josh. 13 so that the S fell to Reuben and the N to Gad.

In the NT, Reuben is mentioned only in Rev. 7:5, as the second tribe after Judah.

For the territory of Reuben, *see* TRIBES, TERRITORIES OF, § D8*b*. *See* the bibliography under ASHER.

K. ELLIGER

REUEL roo'əl [רְעוּאֵל, friend, companion, of God; *cf.* Aram. (Elephantine) *proper names* רעויה *and* רעיא, *and* Palmyrene רעי; רעייא; LXX 'Ραγουήλ]; KJV RAGUEL rə gū'əl in Num. 10:29. **1.** Son of Esau and Basemath the daughter of Ishmael (Gen. 36:4, 10; I Chr. 1:35); the father of the Edomite clan chiefs (אַלּוּפִים) Nahath, Zerah, Shammah, and Mizzah (Gen. 36:13, 17; I Chr. 1:37). This genealogy points to a close relationship existing very early among Israelite, Edomite, and Arabian tribes.

2. The father-in-law(?) of Moses (Exod. 2:18 [J]; Num. 10:29 [JE]). The traditions are not unanimous concerning either the name or the tribal affiliation of the father of Moses' wife. Elsewhere J calls him Hobab; E uniformly names him Jethro. He is identified with the Midianites in Exod. 2:16; 3:1 (cf. 4:18-20) and with the Kenites in Judg. 1:16; 4:11. Some solutions offered are: (*a*) All three names may refer to the same person; (*b*) Reuel may be a tribal rather than personal appellation; (*c*) Hobab may be Moses' brother-in-law; (*d*) Hobab and Jethro may designate the father-in-law, with Reuel as Hobab's father (and being a gloss at Exod. 2:18). The last is widely accepted.

3. The father of Gadite leader Eliasaph (Num. 2: 14; same as DEUEL).

4. A Benjaminite, grandfather of Meshullam (I Chr. 9:8).

Bibliography. M. Noth, *Die israelitischen Personennamen* (1928), pp. 153-54.   L. HICKS

REUMAH roo'mə [רְאוּמָה] (Gen. 22:24). Nahor's concubine, whose four sons were eponymous ancestors of Aramean tribes generally located N of Damascus and related secondarily to the Israelites.

*REVELATION. In the Bible, primarily a matter of God's initiative rather than of man's search and discovery. Its realm is even more prominently history and the world of human affairs than the world of nature; and God is described as revealing himself—his actions, his designs, his character—rather than as communicating propositions. Supremely, he has revealed himself in Christ; and the gospel is a summary of this revelation. Scripture, as the record of this revelation, accordingly ranks also as a medium of revelation.

God's revelation can be received only by the humble and receptive; from the proud and opinionated it is kept concealed (*see* MYSTERY). But among such as are humble and obedient, it is for all, without distinction. Within this general sphere, revelation of particular kinds is granted to chosen prophets and seers. *See* DIVINATION; INSPIRATION AND REVELATION; PROPHET, PROPHETISM; VISION.

Finally, in the future there is yet to come a decisive exposure of what is spurious, and a full disclosure of the glory of God. *See* APOCALYPTICISM; PAROUSIA.

1. Terminology. The chief words in use are גלה ("remove" or "uncover") and ἀποκαλύπτω, ἀποκάλυψις ("uncover," "uncovering"). There is no noun in Hebrew corresponding to ἀποκάλυψις (in this sense), although of course there are words denoting "vision," etc., which are partly equivalent. Hebrew not only uses גלה as "disclose," but also the phrase גלה אזן ("uncover the ear") as "communicate a secret" (I Sam. 9:15; Job 33:16; etc.; though in Ruth 4:4 it merely means "tell"). Cf. also the *pi'el* of the verb in the phrase ויגל יהוה את־עיני בלעם, "The LORD opened [lit., 'uncovered'] the eyes of Balaam" (Num. 22:31; and see Num. 24:4, 16; Ps. 119:18). In Greek there are, besides ἀποκαλύπτω and ἀποκάλυψις, such words as ἐπιφάνεια ("appearing"), δηλόω ("disclose," "indicate"), σημαίνω ("show," "make known"), φανερόω ("[make] manifest"), χρηματίζω ("reveal [as by a divine oracle]"), which, in some contexts at least, are relevant to this theme.

2. The meaning of "revealed religion." The Hebrew and Christian religions are both described as "revealed religions," in the sense that they both claim that they are what they are because God has himself taken the initiative and revealed himself, rather than because man, by his own searching, has discovered the truth. Revelation is, therefore, in such a connection, to be distinguished from discovery, and the Bible lays far more stress on the former than on the latter. In the Areopagus speech in Acts 17, Paul says, admittedly, that God has so constituted mankind that they "feel after him"— i.e., grope for him as a discoverer feels for the truth; but even here the culmination of the thought is not the theme of discovery but rather of God's self-manifestation in the Incarnation: he "has fixed a day on which he will judge the world in righteousness by a man whom he has appointed, and of this he has given assurance to all men by raising him from the dead." Thus, it is God who takes the initiative: he is a "revealer of mysteries" (Dan. 2:47); he declares the past and the future and "reveals the tracks of hidden things" (Ecclus. 42:19).

3. The nature of biblical revelation. *a. Historical.* The particular words under review are not actually applied to manifestations of God in nature. This is not to say that the Bible does not describe "theophanies" in terms of natural phenomena: Pss. 19:1-6; 29 are—to go no further—splendid examples of this, the one in terms of astronomy, the other in terms of a majestic thunderstorm. Even more explicitly, in Rom. 1:19-20 the heathen are blamed for failing to recognize a clear revelation of God in nature ("Ever since the creation of the world his invisible nature, namely, his eternal power and deity, has been clearly perceived in the things that have been made"); and the fact that they were not granted a more specific type of revelation is regarded as no excuse for their idolatry. Again, allusions are made in two of the Pauline speeches in the Acts (14:15-17; 17:24 ff) to the revelation of God through his created world. But this conception of God in nature is far less characteristic of the Bible than the idea that God reveals himself chiefly in his design for and in his dealings with men—i.e., in history. The now familiar distinction between "general" and "special" revelation is not explicitly made by the biblical writers, and its discussion does not belong here. It is enough to say simply that God is represented in the Bible as revealing himself in his actions and in his designs, and, most decisively of all, in Jesus Christ. Amos 3:7 declares that God does nothing without revealing his secret to his servants the prophets; Dan. 2 is full of the ability of the inspired seer to unfold the designs of God by interpreting dreams about what is soon to become history (cf. Dan. 10:1). It is in history—whether the history of Israel or of the surrounding nations—that God's design is mostly to be perceived, and this is how he chooses to reveal himself; and it is through Israel, and most of all through their Messiah, that the other nations receive the revelation (Luke 2:32).

b. Personal rather than propositional. It is further to be noted—though not all ages and branches of Christendom lay equal stress on this—that, in the Bible, God's self-revelation is personal rather than propositional (*cf.* GOD, NT, § 4). That is to say, ultimately revelation is in relationship, "confrontation," communion, rather than by the communication of facts: it is himself that God reveals, or his actions, his RIGHTEOUSNESS, his WRATH, rather than statements about himself.

Even when revelation can be reduced to a statement, it is, for the biblical writers, a statement of God's will and purpose—something, i.e., closely concerned with his person, and involving an obedient response (*see* KNOWLEDGE)—rather than the mere communication of information. Thus, in Gen. 35:7 allusion is made in terms of revelation ("there God had revealed himself to him") to Jacob's dream of the ladder (Gen. 28); and it is true that the dream included a specific promise about Jacob's posterity. Yet in essence the vision was concerned with God's purpose and his character as strength and protection to a man in need. So again, although there are accounts of soothsaying, yet the great prophets are more concerned with morals. Samuel can, indeed, tell Saul what has become of his father's asses (I Sam. 9:6); but he is far more intent upon God's plan for the leadership of Israel, and all that this will involve for Saul by way of response (vs. 20). Indeed, it was the divine revelation of a drastic moral judgment that began Samuel's prophetic career as a small child (I Sam. 3, where note the remarkable phrases in vss. 1, 21; Samuel's ministry marked a revival of revelation).

Similarly, Elisha uses divination by music, but he uses it in the interests of the wars of the Lord (II

Kings 3:15). And the great writing prophets from the eighth century B.C. onward, to whom God "revealed his secret" (Amos 3:7), are almost wholly occupied, so far as their words survive, with politics, morals, and, (cf. I Pet. 1:12) the relation of these to the future. This is not to say that mere curiosity about the future is satisfied by revelation: God's revelation is essentially the practical manifestation of his will—his TORAH—for "the secret things belong to the LORD our God; but the things that are revealed belong to us and to our children for ever, that we may do all the words of this law" (Deut. 29:29). Of the future vindication of God's ways among his people it may be said (II Sam. 7:27) that God has revealed his plan for the house of David; or (Isa. 40:5) that "the glory of the LORD shall be revealed" (*see* GLORY; and cf. Isa. 53:1; 56:1). But such revelation is a matter of the general destiny of the people of God, and of the triumph of right over wrong; it is not the divulging of curious details.

4. Revelation in the NT. So it is also, and even more evidently, in the NT. It is true that particulars may on occasion be revealed: it is revealed to Simeon by a divine oracle (χρηματίζω) that he shall not die before seeing the Messiah (Luke 2:26); Paul may have divine admonitions to go somewhere or to refrain from going somewhere else (Acts 16:6 ff; Gal. 2:2), or may be forewarned about details of the shipwreck (Acts 27:23-26); even the choice of the twelfth apostle, to take the place of Judas, is divinely revealed—and that by the casting of lots (Acts 1:24-26; and *see* LOTS § 2); but the characteristic meaning of revelation is, once more, essentially the personal revelation of God himself, and supremely in Christ. Thus Paul writes: God "was pleased to reveal his Son to me" (Gal. 1:16); and in John 1:18 "the only Son, who is in the bosom of the Father, he has made him known" (ἐξηγήσατο); so John 17:6: "I have manifested thy name" (*see* NAME, PROPER). In the same way, when Peter makes his confession of Jesus as Son of God, it is described as due to a divine revelation (Matt. 16:17); and the parables and miracles of Jesus become, to those who have ears and eyes, manifestations that God is uniquely present in the ministry of Jesus (see Mark 4:11; Luke 11:20; John 14:11). Jesus, as the Word of God (John 1:1), gathers up all the previous piecemeal utterances of God's self-revelation (Heb. 1:1); he is "vocal to those who can perceive," to adapt a phrase from Pindar (*Olympian Odes* II.85).

Another way of saying the same thing is that, in the NT, it is the gospel which is the contents of revelation. It must be added that this gospel includes what is called the WRATH OF GOD (*see also* GOD, NT, § 5b) as well as his mercy; and that it is the moral judgments of God that are stressed by Paul when he is speaking to the heathen about revelation and the gospel (Rom. 1:17-18: "In it [the gospel] the righteousness of God is revealed through faith for faith; . . . the wrath of God is revealed"; cf. Acts 17:31; 24:25; also Rev. 15:4). But, be that as it may, the gospel is the contents of revelation (Rom. 3:21: "The righteousness of God has been manifested"— i.e., God's way of righteousness; Gal. 1:11-12: "The gospel which was preached by me . . . came through a revelation of Jesus Christ"—and even if this repre-

sents Paul's particular divine commission to preach *to the Gentiles,* it still illustrates the main point; cf. 3:23, of the revealing of "faith," which, in this context, means the good news of salvation through faith). And since the gospel is for all Christians as such, there is no exclusiveness in this revelation. It is not for some inner circle of the specially instructed, but for all Christians, to receive this revelation and progressively to learn the will of God (Eph. 1:17; Phil. 3:15).

It will be seen that such a conception of revelation corresponds closely with the characteristically biblical meaning of MYSTERY—namely, God's design, concealed for a time or from those who are not receptive, in order now (in the NT era) to be revealed when the time is ripe, and to the recipients who are ready (see Rom. 16:25-26; Gal. 1:12; Eph. 3:3). It is a striking paradox that "mystery" is so often associated in the NT with words of revelation—ἀποκαλύπτω and ἀποκάλυψις ("reveal," "revelation"); γινώσκω, γνωρίζω ("know," "make known"); φανερόω ("disclose"); λαλέω, λέγω ("speak"). But the mystery is divulged only to those who are humble and obedient, and the idea correlative to the revealing of the mystery is that of concealing. From the unreceptive, the proud, the opinionated, it is held back, as is indicated in such diverse passages as the following: "Thou hast hidden these things from the wise and understanding and revealed them to babes" (Matt. 11:25); "Though he had done so many signs before them, yet they did not believe in him; it was that the word spoken by the prophet Isaiah might be fulfilled:

'Lord, who has believed our report,
and to whom has the arm of the Lord been revealed?' "
(John 12:37-38; cf. 17:6 ff);

"None of the rulers of this age understood this; for if they had, they would not have crucified the Lord of glory" (I Cor. 2:8); "Their minds were hardened; for to this day, when they read the old covenant, that same veil remains unlifted, because only through Christ is it taken away" (II Cor. 3:14).

Indeed, the gospels may be viewed as written round the twin themes of veiling and unveiling. Broadly speaking, whereas the Synoptic gospels portray the hidden Messiah—Jesus carefully concealing his identity except from those who are ready to understand him—the Fourth Gospel portrays men veiling their own eyes from him, and obdurately refusing to recognize who he is. Thus, for the Synoptists, Jesus himself is "veiled," while for the Fourth Gospel it is the Jews who wear the veil (as in II Cor. 3:14). But in both cases alike, there is a revelation of the "mystery"—through parables, deeds, and character—to those who are receptive; and although in John the actual word "reveal" occurs only once, and then only in the Isaianic phrase cited above (John 12:38), the theme of revelation is clear enough through the use of such a word as "signs" (*see* SIGNS AND WONDERS) for the miracles, and the use of φανερόω ("manifest") and GLORY. Moreover, it is noticeable that, in this gospel, the Baptist has to have the concealed Jesus divinely indicated to him (John 1:33) and then proceeds to indicate him to others (vss. 29 ff). This, it seems, is in keeping with certain phases of Jewish messianic expectation, according to which there was to be a *Messias absconditus* who has in due course to become *revelatus* (see Enoch 62:7; II Esd. 7:28-29; 12:32; 13:26, 52, though there are perhaps Christian interpolations here; see also Just. Dial. 8, 110).

5. **The mode of revelation.** The Bible provides ample illustrations of DIVINATION—by casting LOTS, by the use of omens, by intepreting dreams, etc. But, in keeping with the tenor of what has already been said, it is characteristic of the Bible that the ideal in the OT is on a higher level than these techniques, and that in the NT this ideal is claimed as intended to be entered upon by all Christians alike. The OT ideal is expressed in the noble words relating to God's special relations with Moses: "And [the LORD] said, 'Hear my words: If there is a prophet among you, I the LORD make myself known to him in a vision, I speak with him in a dream. Not so with my servant Moses; he is entrusted with all my house. With him I speak mouth to mouth, clearly, and not in dark speech; and he beholds the form of the LORD' " (Num. 12:6-8).

Now, it is true that in I Cor. 13:12 this language is clearly echoed (especially when the Greek is compared with the LXX of Numbers) in Paul's description, not of present conditions, but of the future fruition of God's promises; but from elsewhere it is evident, nonetheless, that for the ordinary Christian even here and now is claimed an intercourse with God, through Christ, which is already comparable with that Mosaic ideal. And perhaps the most significant passage for the NT conception of how revelation takes place is I Cor. 2. Here Paul speaks of that which cannot be found by discovery (in the sense defined in § 2 *above*):

" 'What no eye has seen, nor ear heard,
   nor the heart of man conceived,
   what God has prepared for those who love him'
      [phrases from Isa. 64–65],

God has revealed to us through the Spirit" (vss. 9-10). And then he goes on to draw a daring analogy between the human self-consciousness and the divine. As man's thoughts, he says, are known only by the "spirit of the man which is in him" (or, as we might say, by a man's self-consciousness), so it is only the Spirit of God that can comprehend the thoughts of God (vs. 11). But if a man will admit into himself this Spirit of God, then he receives an understanding of what God himself can give, beyond the power of unaided human consciousness: "Now we have received not the spirit of the world, but the Spirit which is from God, that we might understand the gifts bestowed on us by God" (vs. 12). And thus to receive the Spirit of God is to have the mind of Christ (vs. 16). The same thought—that revelation is a gift of the Spirit of God through Christ—seems to underlie Eph. 1:17: "that the God of our Lord Jesus Christ, the Father of glory, may give you a spirit of wisdom and of revelation in the knowledge of him" (cf. Wisd. Sol. 9:17-18).

This tallies remarkably well with the famous passage in Matt. 11:25 ff; Luke 10:21 ff, where Christ himself is the means of revelation: "No one knows the Father except the Son and any one to whom the Son chooses to reveal him." And it is the "babes" who are chosen; it is those who are humble enough to obey who find out the will of God (John 7:17); cf. Ecclus. 1:6 ff; 3:18 (some MSS only; cf. vs. 20, and *see* MYSTERY § 2); 4:18; 51:23. Thus, by the Spirit we receive the mind of Christ, and Christ is the revealer of the mind of God (cf. I John 2:23). This is the typically Christian account of revelation; to receive the Spirit of God's Son is to be enabled to cry "Abba! Father!" (see Rom. 8:14-17; Gal. 4:6; *see also* GOD, NT, § 5*b*). The subject of man's response may be pursued further by reference to the pregnant biblical word "KNOWLEDGE."

But while this is the essence of Christian revelation, and is for all Christians as such—all who respond with obedience and are ready to "know" God in this sense—there is also, within the sphere of this commonly shared gift, the more specialized gift of "prophecy." This means a heightened sensitiveness to the guidance of God in given situations, by which a prophet is enabled to read, and pass on to others, the will of God (I Cor. 14:1, 6, 26). But even this, be it noted, is under the control of the ordinary discrimination of the assembled congregation, the *communis sensus fidelium* (I Cor. 14:29); and it is tested by its usefulness for the building up of the community (I Cor. 14:1-5, 26, 30-33). It must be added that in II Cor. 12:1 ff, reference is made to some special revelation granted to Paul, the contents of which cannot be passed on. For the meaning of this, see the commentaries.

6. **Revelation through scripture.** If the gospel, culminating in Jesus, is supremely God's self-revelation, then scripture, as the record of this mighty act of God in history, with its preparation and its accomplishment, necessarily also ranks as a medium of revelation. This is a theme which, naturally, is not systematically developed within scripture itself. But Dan. 9:2 appears to allude to the use of the writings of Jeremiah as a divine oracle; the Dead Sea Scrolls exemplify a Jewish treatment of written prophecy as a medium of revelation, or of confirmation that God is at work in the affairs of the moment; and the NT is full of the idea that the Scriptures, fulfilled in Jesus, provide a divine confirmation of his unique mission. Moreover, the recognition of scripture as a medium through which the Spirit of God speaks is explicit in Hebrews (see 3:7 and *passim*; cf. John 10:34-35; II Tim. 3:15-16; II Pet. 1:19-21). *See* SCRIPTURE, AUTHORITY OF; INSPIRATION AND REVELATION.

7. **Revelation and the future: apocalyptic.** The ultimate revelation of God's purposes is cast still into the future by the NT, which is orientated toward the day when Christ will be fully and finally revealed in all the glory of God (Luke 17:30; Rom. 8:18; I Cor. 1:7; Col. 3:4; II Thess. 1:7; I Pet. 1:5, 7, 13; 4:13; 5:1; I John 3:2); and thus God's judgments will be manifest (Rom. 2:5), and reality will be uncovered (Matt. 10:26: "Nothing is covered that will not be revealed"; cf. Mark 4:22; Luke 12:2; I Cor. 3:13; 4:5: "the Lord . . . , who will bring to light the things now hidden in darkness and will disclose the purposes of the heart"). Insight into the meaning of present woes and their ultimate outcome

in the triumph of God can thus be styled apocalypse, "revelation" (Dan. 10:1; Rev. 1:1), and the term has given its name to a whole genre of writing (apocalyptic), both Jewish and Christian. Besides the Apocalypse of John (*see* REVELATION, BOOK OF), there are other NT examples of this sort of writing, notably Mark 13 and the parallels in Matthew and Luke. In II Thess. 2:3 ff a kind of apocalypse of Satan—a parody of the PAROUSIA of the Messiah—is described as imminent. For interpretations of what was here intended, see the commentaries.

The degree to which this type of literature (*see* APOCALYPSES, APOCRYPHAL; APOCALYPTICISM) is genuinely in the "prophetic" line may be measured by its degree of loyalty to the general tenor of the Bible, which (as already noted) finds revelation rather in the character and purposes of God himself than in specific and detailed propositions, or in the communicating of mere information, or in the satisfying of mere curiosity about the future. Just as "the testimony of Jesus is the spirit of prophecy" (Rev. 19:10), so the test of authenticity in Christian revelation is whether the will of God in Christ is involved and is obeyed (cf. II Cor. 12:7-10). In Rom. 8:19 it is the true sonship—filial obedience to God—that is to be revealed. *See* PROPHET, PROPHETISM, and note Deut. 18:21-22; I Kings 22, as throwing light on true and false revelation.

Bibliography. H. W. Robinson, ed., *Record and Revelation* (1938), pp. 303 ff; E. G. Selwyn, *I Peter* (1946), pp. 250 ff; J. Dupont, *Gnosis* (1949), pp. 194-97; R. Bultmann, "Gnosis," *JTS,* N.S. iii.I (1952), pp. 10 ff; J. Baillie, *The Idea of Revelation in Recent Thought* (1956). See also books on theology of the NT (e.g., F. C. Grant, R. Bultmann, E. Stauffer, P. Feine, A. Richardson).   C. F. D. MOULE

*REVELATION, BOOK OF ('Αποκάλυψις 'Ιωάννου, *see* REVELATION). The last book in the NT canon, written originally to the "seven churches that are in Asia" (i.e., the Roman province of that name in W Asia Minor) by John, an early Christian seer (*see* § B *below*). This is the only complete example in the NT scriptures of a type of literature—apocalypse—which had a great vogue among both Jews and Christians *ca.* the beginning of the Christian era (*see* APOCALYPTICISM). John's apocalypse far transcends all others of its class in the endeavor to present a theodicy or theology of history, to portray both "what is and what is to take place" (1:19) in the perspective of God's eternal purpose relative to man and his salvation. It is a dramatization of the gospel message sent forth in letter form and intended to be read aloud in the churches (1:3). As befits such a bold undertaking to set forth the mind and purpose of God as seen in redemptive history (*Heilsgeschichte*), John attributes his knowledge of it to "revelation" which came to him from God through Jesus Christ, or alternatively through "his angel" (1:1-2, 19; 4:1; 19:10; 22:8).

A. General character
  1. Literary types: Letter and drama
  2. Literary affinity: Prophecy and apocalyptic
  3. Style and diction
B. Authorship
C. Date
D. Methods of interpretation

E. Contents
  1. Structure as determining interpretation
    a. The sevenfold drama pattern
    b. Stage props for the drama
    c. The cosmic stage of John's drama
    d. Prologue and epilogue
  2. Outline
  3. Symbolism and thought-frames
    a. Origins
    b. Teaching content
  4. Message: theology of history
F. Canonicity
  1. Europe
  2. North Africa
  3. Egypt
  4. The East
G. Text
Bibliography

A. *GENERAL CHARACTER.* Of no other book of the NT is it so true that an understanding of its contents and message depends to a degree upon an examination of certain features which appear to characterize it. These are of a literary sort and may be examined conveniently under three heads, as follows:

1. Literary types: Letter and drama. All apocalyptic literature is dramatic in character, its varied scenes being reported as "visions" by the seer, who regales his readers with an account of his insights into the meaning of human history, age by age, or of his travels on earth, in heaven or hell, and the like. This is true both of pagan apocalypses, like Vergil's

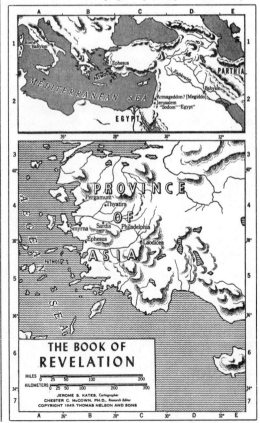

THE BOOK OF
REVELATION

MILES 0 25 50 100 200
KILOMETERS 0 50 100 200 300

JEROME S. KATES, Cartographer
CHESTER C. McCOWN, PH.D., Research Editor
COPYRIGHT 1949, THOMAS NELSON AND SONS

Aeneid, and of Jewish and Christian examples, such as those circulated under the names of Enoch, Baruch, Esdras, the canonical Daniel, and portions of Ezekiel. John's book is no exception in this respect. Indeed, the dramatic form appears to be carried through in this work with a relentlessness not elsewhere to be found (*see* § E1 *below*). John alone, however, among apocalyptic writers has superimposed upon the dramatic structure of his book another structure—that of a letter. Failure to discern this dual literary character of John's work has led to much misunderstanding on the part of his interpreters. To disentangle the one form (drama) from the other (letter) is fortunately an easy task. The marks of the letter form appear only in an opening salutation (1:4-6) and a closing benediction (22:21). All that lies between is drama.

Paul appears to have been the first Christian writer to present the gospel (particularly its theological expression and ethical implications) in letter form. Indeed, his first extant letter (I Thessalonians) may represent the earliest endeavor to give any sort of literary expression to the gospel message (*ca.* 51). John follows Paul's characteristic formulas closely, giving us in his apocalypse the fourfold pattern: (*a*) salutation proper ("John to the seven churches that are in Asia" [1:4*a*]); (*b*) opening benediction ("Grace to you . . . on earth" [4*b*-5*a*]); (*c*) prayer, or as here doxology ("To him who loves us . . . Amen" [5*b*-6]); and (*d*) closing benediction ("The grace of the Lord Jesus be with all the saints" [22:21]).

It has been suggested that the letter should be considered to embrace only ch. 1 or, at most, chs. 1-3. But such an analysis of the contents of the book destroys at once its literary structure and its doctrinal unity. As it now stands, the letter ends, not at 1:20 nor yet at 3:22, as some have proposed, but at 22:21 with the closing benediction, thus embracing the entire book. Moreover, the drama is said by John to concern itself with both "what is" and "what is to take place hereafter" (1:19). Accordingly, the drama, as well as the letter, must include the contents of chs. 2-3 (i.e., the present condition of the church, at least in John's time—briefly, "what is"), as well as the elaborate setting in 1:7-20, against which as background the condition of the church is portrayed. To conclude the letter at the end of either ch. 1 or ch. 3 would result in our having a letter prefixed to a drama—and that a truncated one—a hybrid otherwise unknown to literature! It would seem far more likely that John first wrote his drama (1:7–22:20), and that thereafter, with a view to bringing it to the church's attention, he superimposed the letter form upon it. Indeed, what other course was open to him? He could neither have wished to have his drama enacted upon the Greco-Roman stage of his day, in view of its debased character, nor have achieved its showing had he desired it. John's drama was from the first intended as a "parlor" drama—to be read in private or at public assembly of a local church.

In John's day all books were brought out in the form of scrolls (*see* WRITING AND WRITING MATERIALS), and the title was appended on a small piece of papyrus or parchment attached at one end of the scroll. Such a title appears in Rev. 1:1-3, be-

ginning: "The revelation of Jesus Christ, which God gave him to show to his servants. . . ." (The title appearing in the RSV—"The Revelation to John"—is a late addition to the book.) When the Apocalypse was added to the other books of the NT canon and the whole was published in codex form like our modern books, this title would have been transferred to the inside of the book, thus further complicating its structure.

2. Literary affinity: Prophecy and apocalyptic. John terms his book an apocalypse (the Anglicized form of the Greek word meaning "revelation"; cf. 1:1), and such it is in its literary form. But unlike all other Jewish and Christian apocalyptists, John claims for his work a close affinity in spirit and content with the writings of the Hebrew prophets as well. Thus, against his one reference to the book as being an apocalypse, John speaks of it as prophecy in six places (1:3; 19:10; 22:7, 10, 18-19); he places himself in the category of the "prophets" (22:9); he says his function is that of prophesying (10:11); and, like the prophets before him, he claims to hear God's Word directed to himself (1:2, 9). Among the noncanonical apocalypses only II Baruch appears ever to make such a claim for its author (10:1). Moreover, whereas in that entire literature such an inclusive term as "the prophets" occurs only twice (I Enoch 108:6; Sibylline Oracles 3:781), in John's book alone it is found seven times (10:7; 11:18; 16:6; 18: 20, 24; 22:6, 9), thus exhibiting his deep attachment to the works of the Hebrew prophets. And as final confirmation of this attachment it is to be noted that he quotes directly phrases and clauses from their writings in some 150 passages, as reference to a modern Greek text such as Nestlé's serves to indicate. The conclusion appears irresistible, therefore, that, while in its literary form John's work is to be classed with the apocalypses of his day, its teaching purports to be far closer to that of the Hebrew prophetic scriptures than is that of these contemporaries. John's book is to a degree saturated with the Hebrew prophetic thought-frames and symbolism (*see* § E3 *below*), and it may well be that it was for this reason his book was included within the canon of the NT, whereas others not so characterized were rejected.

3. Style and diction. The Commentaries (*see bibliography*) should be consulted for a detailed statement on this subject. Here but two phenomena may be noted: (*a*) so many solecisms—probably of both a conscious and an unconscious nature—appear in this apocalypse as to have given rise to the suggestion that for John's work a "grammar of ungrammar" must needs be written; (*b*) of no other NT writer perhaps may it be so truly said that he "thinks in Aramaic and writes in Greek." It is just possible that these two characteristics of John's book should be considered one, or, at any rate, that the second is the cause of the first. And if this proves to be the case, then this phenomenon will accord well with what has been said above relative to John's close affinity in doctrinal matters with the Hebrew prophets and will be said below about his employing the Semitic thought-frames and symbolism. *See* § E3 *below.*

B. AUTHORSHIP. As already noted (*see* § A2 *above*), John the seer who wrote the Revelation was consciously imbued with the prophetic spirit and fire. He was a theist who shared the passionate belief of an Amos and a Paul in God's universal concern for mankind and for its salvation (7:9 ff; cf. Amos 9:7; Rom. 5:18; Gal. 3:28). John believed in God's omniscience—his universal insight into the needs of his creation (4:6; 5:6); his providential care of his people (7:2 ff); his universal saving purpose through the Lamb that was slain (5:6, 13); his redemptive activity through the incarnate life of Jesus (12:4-6) and in the history of the church (12:13-17). This author was, moreover, perhaps the church's first scholar to attempt the construction of a philosophy (or, better perhaps, a theology) of history (*see* § E4 *below*), and perhaps the first possessed of the literary ability to present the gospel in the form of drama. This John was the pastor of at least the "seven churches" of Asia, and he wrote to them out of a shepherd's concern for his flock, while temporarily exiled from them in the penal colony of Patmos,* "on account of the word of God and the testimony of Jesus" (1:9), which had formed the subject of his preaching. Fig. PAT 23.

Little more can be said of this author, as he tells us no more than this about himself. But from the beginning of the church's history much speculation has been rife about him. It was the almost universal belief of the ancient church from the middle of the second century that the author was the apostle John. Justin and Hippolytus at Rome, Tertullian in North Africa, Clement and Origen of Alexandria, Irenaeus of Lyons, all spoke of this John as one of the Lord's apostles (or disciples). Modern scholarship, however, has remained unconvinced, preferring to identify the John of Revelation rather with John Mark, John the Elder (*see* JOHN, LETTERS OF), an otherwise unknown John, or a pseudonymous writer claiming for his work the prestige attaching to the name of the apostle. Further, theories of redaction or of editing (with possibly Jewish or pagan antecedents) have been seriously entertained by scholars of the stature of Julius Wellhausen, Adolf Jülicher, and R. H. Charles.

The arguments advanced for the modern theories are not all equally cogent, either as telling against the apostolic authorship or as establishing the identity of the author otherwise. E.g., to suggest that the John who wrote: "He who conquers, I will grant him to sit with me on my throne" (Rev. 3:21), cannot have heard Jesus saying to him: "To sit at my right hand or at my left is not mine to grant" (Mark 10:40), is to overlook the fact that in the one instance it is the risen Christ, in the other the historic Jesus, who speaks. Moreover, there is good evidence that even the latter had told his disciples that they would "sit on thrones judging the twelve tribes of Israel" (Luke 22:30*b;* cf. Matt. 19:28*b*, Q). It ought to be obvious that the Revelation and Q passages have to do with a fact in the moral order, whereas the Markan saying is dealing with a crass misunderstanding of Jesus' kingdom teaching, one which he can correct only with a reply at the kindergarten level thus far attained by the sons of Zebedee. Statements of this nature at two levels of understanding do not clash; they are like "ships which pass in the night" and are without logical relation to one another.

Again, arguments based on the linguistic phenomena of respectively the Fourth Gospel and the Revelation are unconvincing. These two works not only share a dramatic flare that is unmistakable, but the underlying thought-frames of both are Semitic. The argument, too, based on the supposed early date of the apostle John's death—while, no doubt, telling against the authorship by *this* John (unless the Apocalypse of John be dated early in the first century)—does not invalidate the possibility that some other John wrote both the Fourth Gospel and the Revelation. It is suggestive that Lohmeyer has found it possible to attribute both works to a single author—John the Elder.

Nonetheless, it cannot be said that John the seer of Revelation has been identified with any known John in the first century of the church's life. There must have been many Christians of this name in those early days, and there is no internal proof that the church's tradition identifying the seer with the apostle of the same name is correct. We know the John of Revelation only as the seer or prophet and shepherd that he claims to be.

C. DATE. The date of writing of Revelation is nearly as uncertain as its authorship. In any case it is impossible to argue—as some have done—either from date to authorship or the reverse; for neither datum has been established to the general satisfaction of scholars who have studied the problems involved. As regards the church's tradition in the matter, the following facts are known: (*a*) A diversity of dates was suggested for the book by late writers, including the reigns of Claudius (41-54), Nero (54-68), and Trajan (98-117). Certainly it does not commend these dates that they were proposed only by late writers like Epiphanius, Jerome, and others of the fourth and later centuries and on inconclusive evidence or none. The two earlier emperors were, no doubt, suggested on the basis of a literal interpretation of such passages as Rev. 6:9; 11:1 ff, to the effect that the Herodian temple was still standing in the author's lifetime. 12: 1-6 also has been interpreted as referring to the church's flight from Jerusalem to Pella across the Jordan during the First Jewish War (66-70). Such so-called internal evidence depends, as is obvious, upon a literal or historical type of interpretation which is, to say the least, questionable (*see* § D *below*). (*b*) The earlier church writers converged on a date in the reign of Domitian (81-96); such appears to be the united testimony of Melito of Sardis, Irenaeus, Clement of Alexandria, Origen, Victorinus, and Eusebius—church fathers ranging from the second to the fourth century. Jerome, too, knows of this tradition.

A number of modern scholars, rejecting both sets of early tradition, have attempted to establish a date in the reign of Vespasian (69-79), on the basis of the three passages above mentioned—as they would refer equally to this reign as to that of Nero—and additionally on Rev. 17:10; 18:4. But the same criticism applies to the interpretation of 18:4 as to that of the three others, while 17:10 is of such an enigmatical nature that no endeavor to reckon which seven emperors of Rome John has in mind has proved generally acceptable. It would be more in character with the generally symbolic nature of the book to suppose that "seven" here stands for the total list of Roman emperors. This list was not yet complete when John wrote, for the reason that the Roman Empire had not yet come to an end. It would also accord well with John's practice to speak of the reigning monarch—whoever he might be—as the "sixth" and to identify him further with the "eighth," each figure standing in its way for the Antichrist (the true Messiah Jesus' number being 888). *See* Six Hundred and Sixty-six.

On the whole, the Domitianic date appears to accord best with the thesis of Revelation and with the contemporary condition of the church as represented in it. While it is not impossible that churches other than those mentioned in either the Acts or the Pauline letters existed in the province of Asia as early as the reign of Nero or of Vespasian, it is unlikely that the church had by such an early period reached the low moral and spiritual ebb reflected in Rev. 2–3 (cf. particularly the condition of the churches at Ephesus, Pergamum, Thyatira, Sardis, and Laodicea). Then, too, the attitude of the church toward the Empire had undergone great change from the earlier one reflected in Mark 12:17; Rom. 13:1; and even in I Pet. 2:13-17. Domitian strenuously insisted on the recognition of the divinity of the imperial line and by his day emperor-worship was the one universal cultus in Asia Minor, the one sort of pagan worship which is portrayed in Revelation as intolerable (cf. 13:11-18). Moreover, the Nero Redivivus theory in the developed form in which this figure is seen "combining in his own person the characteristics of Beliar and the Antichrist" (Charles) is found in Revelation (17:8-11; cf. 13:1 ff)—a fact which argues for a late date and most likely the reign of Domitian. Finally, a late date is suggested for the book if—as seems likely—John employed a number of the other NT books in searching for materials for his own (e.g., Matthew, Luke, I and II Corinthians, Galatians, Ephesians, Colossians, I Thessalonians, I Peter, and James).

D. *METHODS OF INTERPRETATION.* It is perhaps not surprising that a variety of methods of interpretation should have been tried with reference to Revelation. Not only does the book seem an enigma in itself in view of its visionary pattern, its curious figures (beasts, dragon, horsemen, hordes of demons, angels, and the rest), and its cosmic catastrophes; but it has much to say as well of the eschatological time—a subject about which the church has never made up its collective mind satisfactorily. Accordingly, Christian scholars have always approached a study of John's book with minds biased on the subjects with which it deals, and the net result has been chaotic. A cursory summary of the types of interpretation applied to the book includes:

Historico-eschatological interpretations—taking their clue from passages like Rev. 1:1, 19; 20:5-10, the author has been thought to be dealing with a chronological scheme that is either (*a*) contemporary, so that the whole sweep of his visionary program is limited to his own times (whether these be found in the reigns of Nero, Vespasian, Domitian, or another); (*b*) futuristic—i.e., limited entirely to the eschatological time at the end of history, a time identified on this view with the period immediately preceding, contemporary with, and following upon the "thousand years" literally interpreted (20:1-10); or (*c*) generally historical, either in the sense that the seer as a philosopher of history endeavors to present the whole panorama of history from the divine standpoint, as was done by other apocalyptists, or that he predicts specific events as about to happen throughout the span of world history, or that he has in mind certain characteristic types of the divine redemptive activity which find repeated expression throughout history and likewise characteristic human attempts to resist and thwart the divine will.

Literary-analytical approaches—some have seen the book as the end product of a series of editors or redactors who have worked over and assembled materials derived from many sources (Jewish, Babylonian, Egyptian, and the like); this method generally sees in the book strata of varying dates and origin, dislocations of particular passages, editorial or redactional misunderstanding of the original author's intent.

Allegorical methods—the Alexandrian school of biblical interpretation (dating from the second century) treated this book, along with the rest of scripture, with its allegorical method of exegesis, a method undoubtedly more readily justified here than in many other portions of the Bible, as the book is throughout an allegory of a sort by the author's own expressed intent (cf. 1:20; 11:8; 12:1, 9), but a method failing to serve any useful purpose when the bounds set by John's ideological scheme are transgressed.

Dramatic interpretations—that John's book is highly dramatic in style has long been recognized, and various interpretations based on this fact have been proposed. This last method is here favored. It is suggested that the book readily divides itself into seven Acts, each Act having in turn seven Scenes, and that so to divide it is to follow out the original intent of its author. Act I of this schema, then, gives us the picture of the church contemporary with the author—i.e., "what is" in his terminology (1:19)—and Acts II–VII similarly present us with "what is to take place hereafter"—i.e., the church and the world in the eschatological time. *See* §§ E1-2, 4, *below.*

The several methods of interpretation, it should be noted, are not all mutually exclusive. It is possible, e.g., to combine the dramatic method with several of the others (with the generally historical and literary-analytical approach), and this seems to be required by John's original intention.

E. *CONTENTS.* It has already been observed that the seer of the NT apocalypse was a martyr suffering for his evangelistic activity (1:9; *see* §B *above*). We may well believe, then, that it was the same evangelistic zeal that prompted him to obey the command to write down the content of the visions contained in his book (cf. 1:19), and that he was well aware, moreover, that the dramatic character of his writing served to provide a new medium for the setting forth of the gospel message—a medium not previously employed by the church in her evangelistic effort. Other evangelists and writers had invented or, at any rate, adopted the literary media known as "gospel," "letter," even history (Acts), and had used them effectively in the church's missionary enterprise. It remained for John to employ the dramatic potentialities of the apocalypse to the same end.

1. Structure as determining interpretation. Considerations arising from the contents of the book suggest that the key to its proper interpretation lies in the discovery of its dramatic structure as intended by its author and some appreciation of the cultural background motivating his choice of this particular evangelistic medium. John was clearly heir to two cultural traditions—the Hebrew-Christian and the Greco-Roman—upon both of which he unhesitatingly drew in the composition of his work, or, if one prefer, both of which were interwoven into the matrix of his "visions." His method of combining these traditions—whether through the subconscious channels of the genuine mystic's visions or through the intentioned devices of the literary artist matters little in the end—may be exhibited under the following heads:

a. The sevenfold drama pattern. As is well known, from ancient times the number seven symbolized completeness or finality to the Semitic mind. And it has been obvious to all of John's interpreters that he adopted this symbolism. The seven seals, seven spirits of God, seven trumpets, seven bowls, and the like are clear examples of this fact. As Lohmeyer has remarked, the number seven is the "formative principle of the work" and appears in its every part, whether small or large. It would seem obvious, then, that we should look for an all-embracing sevenfold pattern as forming the framework of a book built on this formative principle. Further, inasmuch as some of the larger portions of the drama are subdivided into seven smaller parts, it seems reasonable to look for all the portions to be so divided.

This would give us seven major divisions with seven minor ones each, or—to employ the language of dramatic art—seven Acts, each with seven Scenes. Acts I (the seven letters; 2:1-3:22), II (the seven seals; 6:1-8:1); III (the seven trumpets; 8:7-11:18), and V (the seven bowls; 16:2-21) present us with no difficulty at this point: each divides itself on the author's own showing into seven subdivisions or Scenes as indicated by the groups of sevens employed. Only Acts IV, VI, and VII, accordingly, afford us any problem for solution in this matter. But there are several considerations that suggest clues for the resolution of this problem, as follows: first, there is a parallelism of structure between Acts III and V which is patent and which has long been noted by commentators (*see* § E2 *below*). Lying between these two Acts, then, are the contents of 11: 19-15:4; and the contents of ch. 14 are of such a nature as to suggest that John intended them to represent in some sense the climax of his theme—the salvation of the church and the triumph of the Lamb—toward which all that precedes builds up and from which all that is subsequent falls away. It appears that 14:1-5 suggests itself rather clearly as the exact middle of the drama and that this passage, accordingly, should be labeled "Act IV, Scene 4." We have, then, a point from which to proceed in both directions.

Secondly, on either side of this middle point (or, more accurately, 11:19-15:4; 17:1-20:10) we appear

to have two sets of materials which are as clearly parallel to each other in both message and structure as we have just observed Acts III and V to be. Thus, there are in these parallel sections two women (12: 1 ff; 17:3 ff), two beasts (13:1 ff; 17:6 ff); again, "another beast which rose out of the earth" (13:11 ff) and which from its description is readily identified with the emperor-worship cultus, and opposite its description in the other section the "final cosmic oratorio" which declares in terms of a Christian worship service the doom of the world culture (18:1-19:10). Further, the Lamb and the martyrs (14:1-5) opposite the Word of God and his retinue (19:11 ff) —rather obvious complements of each other. Similarly, the angel with an eternal gospel (14:6 ff) opposite the angel standing in the sun (19:17-18), the judgment scene at 14:14-20 and the judgment by battle at 19:19-21, and finally, the hymn of salvation in 15:2-4 as opposed to the final judgment of Satan in 20:1-2. The complementary nature of these opposite sets of passages is altogether too obvious to have been accidental.

Thirdly, a remarkably confirmatory check on the parallelism arrived at above is supplied by the discovery that John signalizes each change of scene in what may now be termed Acts IV and VI (and further, in Act VII as well) with the use of an introductory word meaning to "see" or "show" (εἶδον, ὤφθη, δείξω σοι, and/or ἔδειξεν μοι). In Acts I, II, III, and V the change of scene was, of course, sufficiently well indicated by the announcement of the successive items in each group of seven objects (letters, seals, trumpets, bowls) concerned with the action. It appears to have escaped the notice of students of Revelation (with the single exception of Austen Farrer, who independently made the same discovery) that in the remaining three Acts John employs εἶδον (13:1-2, 11; 14:1, 6, 14; 15:2; 17:3, 6; 18:1; 19:11, 17, 19; 20:1, 4, 11-12; 21:1-2, 22), ὤφθη (11:19; 12:1, 3), and δείξω σοι (17:1; 21:9) and/or ἔδειξεν μοι (21:10; 22:1) to accomplish the like end. (Outside what is now to be known as Acts IV, VI, and VII, it should be noted that εἶδον is employed indiscriminately by the seer, ὤφθη and ἔδειξεν μοι not at all, and δείξω σοι only at 4:1—i.e., at John's introduction to the heavenly scene!) That is to say, in Acts IV, VI, and VII the simple device of changing scenes by the employment of one or other of these introductory words is accomplished with absolute precision, and the same holds for indicating a shift of stage props. Except for such changes, moreover, the words indicated are never employed in these Acts, though in 12:1, 3; 21:9-10, a certain redundancy occurs. I.e., at 12:1, 3, at the opening of Scene 1 of Act IV, ὤφθη for rather obvious reasons occurs twice rather than once only as everywhere else in the three Acts indicated. But comparison of this Scene with its opposite number in Act VI, together with the general considerations already advanced above which indicate the complementary nature of the Scenes in Acts IV and VI, makes it apparent that here John has slipped into the use of two ὤφθη's as, so to speak, the equivalent of one εἶδον employed elsewhere. The second redundant use of words occurs at 21:9-10, where both δείξω σοι and ἔδειξεν μοι occur at the opening of Scene 5 in Act VII—surely an excusable blunder, if such it be. The three considerations just advanced serve to furnish us, then, with Acts IV, VI, and VII, and these further subdivided into seven Scenes each. The sevenfold character of the drama is thus complete.

b. Stage props for the drama. If the seven-times-sevenfold structure of the drama found in Revelation follows the Semitic pattern, it seems equally certain that in several respects John borrows from the known setup of the Greco-Roman stage. The first of these concerns the stage settings which precede each of the seven Acts as now determined. These include the seven golden lampstands (1:9-20); the throne of God and the four creatures, the twenty-four elders, the slain Lamb and the mighty host of all created beings, together with the articles of furniture in the heavenly throne room (chs. 4-5); the altars of sacrifice and of incense (8:2-6); the ark of the covenant (11:19); the sanctuary or "tent of witness" (15: 1, 5-8; 16:1; 17:1-2); and the church enthroned with Christ (20:4-6). Some of John's interpreters have so far misunderstood his purpose in these sections as to imagine them to represent independent visions or main divisions of the book. But some of them are obviously so short and pointless in themselves as to render such an interpretation untenable. On the other hand, the two longer passages involved (1:9-20; chs. 4-5) are found at the two strategic points in the drama requiring considerable change of scenery —viz., respectively for Act I, which gives us a picture of the historic church with all its weaknesses and strengths, and for Act II, wherein against the background of the heavenly throne room we are to discern God's entire purpose in history.

It is to be expected that these Acts, which, so to speak, set the stage for all that transpires throughout the book, will require considerable elaboration of their settings as compared with the Acts which follow. Further, it is to be noted that such action as takes place in the passages here under discussion (e.g., in 1:9-20, where the Son of man is seen walking about in the midst of his church; and in chs. 4-5, with their episode of the scroll with the seven seals and the hymns sung by all creation in praise of God and the Lamb) is what might well be termed background action and constitutes a part of the stage setting for John's presentation of his theme. Such activity is not part of the dramatic action which goes into the production of the Scenes. The picture of the Son of man in his activity among the churches is a necessary backdrop for describing his lordly sway over the church universal as portrayed in the seven Scenes which follow in Act I. Similarly, the picture of God upon his throne surrounded by all the creatures of earth and heaven, together with the church as represented by the twenty-four elders, constitutes a necessary foil to the elaboration of God's purpose in history and his method of accomplishing it through the Lamb as this is set forth in the seven Scenes of Act II.

It is instructive to note in this connection that the hymns of both creatures and elders in 4:8-11 are indicated as proceeding eternally—a neat way of suggesting that this is stage-prop material (or alternatively, the music corresponding to that of the Greek chorus) and not part of the scenic activity carrying forward the theme of the drama. In like fashion it seems clear that the "new song" and the acclamations in honor of the Lamb in 5:8-14 are merely anticipatory of the dramatic action which is to follow with the opening of the seven seals—i.e., the background functioning of the chorus. While all these stage props are taken bodily from the furnishings of the Jewish temple (seven lampstands, ark of the covenant, altars, etc.) or else serve to give expression to the Christian ideology (Lamb, elders, content of the hymns, and the like) and to concepts shared by both church and synagogue (the four creatures representing all God's animate creation, the angels of the Presence and of God's wrath), at the same time, however, their very use as stage settings is suggestive of the Greco-Roman stage, and, as we shall see particularly in connection with Act VII, no other locus can account for the peculiar succession of the events.

c. The cosmic stage of John's drama. Not only the stage furnishings, but also the over-all contours or larger dimensions of the scenery on John's cosmic stage, are suggestive at once of the arrangement of the Jewish temple and of the Greco-Roman stage. It is to be recalled that long before the first century A.D. this stage had attained a high degree of development with a recognized and rather definitely standardized plan. The theater at Ephesus, e.g., which may well have been in John's mind—both his subconscious as he "saw" his visions and the conscious as he wrote down what he saw—was, like the generality of theaters of the day, semicircular in shape and had a capacity of some twenty-five thousand people. Long before the first century A.D. the circular floor arranged to accommodate the chorus and orchestra had assumed this semicircular shape and was backed by an elevated stage upon which was erected a *skene* (σκηνή, whence our "scene") or building—formerly of wood or boughs, but now of stone—which formed a sort of backdrop for all the action as well as a convenient dressing room for the actors. On either side of this *skene* were erected two wings or *paraskenia* (i.e., side scenes), and before it a *prothyron* or porch which could conveniently represent the front of a palace or the façade of a temple. In the Hellenistic period a *proskenion*, or stage before the *skene* with its *prothyron* and between the *paraskenia*, was devised. This was continued into the Roman period and was found in the theater at Ephesus.

Much more of a more doubtful kind might be said at this point, but it is needful to recall merely those details which may with reasonable certainty be said to have characterized the theater from the third century B.C. forward. For it is here suggested that John conceived of the cosmic stage on which was to be enacted the drama of the Christian theology of history (or the gospel drama) as assuming in general the aspect with which his readers would long have been familiar. If we replace respectively the *skene, prothyron,* and *proskenion* with the sanctuary (or Holy Place and Holy of Holies); the *paraskenia* with the great white throne and the twenty-four thrones of the twenty-four elders arranged in semicircular fashion on either side of it (their seats being placed on the emerald rainbow which John says thrust out from the throne of God on either side; 4:3-4); the customary pagan altar, which stood in the foreground on the level of the orchestra with the altar of sacrifice; and then, as occasion requires, conceive of the other furnishings mentioned (lampstands, altar of incense, sea of glass and of fire, etc.) as introduced onto this cosmic stage, we appear to have in these simple substitutions for the furnishings of the Greco-Roman stage as known to John's readers the proper arrangements for his cosmic drama as he saw it.

d. Prologue and epilogue. There appears to be but one touch left to make complete the picture of an unmistakable similarity between the Greco-Roman drama and its theatrical accouterments and the NT apocalypse. This concerns the matter of the prologue and the epilogue, which were regular features of such drama. And it is now proposed that Rev. 1:7-8—verses which to the casual reader appear to serve no useful purpose and which have always proved a stumbling block to translators and commentators as not being related in any way to their context—take on great significance when viewed as a prologue and as containing the accustomed announcements by the "herald" or interpreter of the theme of the play and by the *deus ex machina.* Aeschylus' *Agamemnon* begins with a soliloquy by a "watchman"; similarly, Euripides' *Hippolytus* has a prologue in which the cosmic significance of the story is represented. In the Roman drama also from the time of Plautus and Terence, and so long before John's day, prologues had been employed for one purpose and another. And, although the pagan god (the so-called *deus ex machina*) was ordinarily brought onto the stage only after man had so tragically involved his affairs that a god was required to disentangle the snarl made in the skein of life, in the Greek new comedy the gods were at times introduced in the prologue with a view to giving needed instruction about the dramatic situation. It is here suggested, therefore, that John's prologue contains an announcement by a herald of the "star" of his drama—namely, Jesus Christ (vs. 7)—and the imprimatur of the living God as "sponsor" of its action throughout (vs. 8). The epilogue (22:6-20), similarly, contains the imprimatur of the Lord himself, his Spirit, and the author of the drama, John, as its prophetic medium, upon the truth which the drama sets forth—a technique which once again appears in the Greek drama.

2. Outline. In conformity with what has been said above about the literary form of Revelation (letter and drama in one; *cf.* §§ A1, E1, *above*), a new outline of the book is herewith proposed. In the light of the preceding discussion, this outline should prove self-explanatory as far as its form is concerned. Its content will be discussed below (*see* §§ E3-4).

I. The title of the apocalypse, 1:1-3
II. Salutation to the seven churches, 1:4-6
III. Prologue: Two voices (herald and Lord God), 1:7-8
IV. Act I: The church on earth, 1:9–3:22
   A. Setting: The seven golden lampstands, 1:9-20
   B. The letters to the seven churches, chs. 2–3
      Scene 1: The passionless church (Ephesus), 2:1-7
      Scene 2: The persecuted church (Smyrna), 2:8-11

      Scene 3: The tolerant church (Pergamum), 2:12-17
      Scene 4: The compromising church (Thyatira), 2:18-29
      Scene 5: The dead church (Sardis), 3:1-6
      Scene 6: The missionary church (Philadelphia), 3:7-13
      Scene 7: The arrogant church (Laodicea), 3:14-22
V. Act II: God's purpose in history, 4:1–8:1
   A. Setting: The throne of God, 4:1-8*a;* odes of creatures and elders, 4:8*b*-11; the sealed book and the Lamb, 5:1-7; hymns, 5:8-14
   B. The opening of the seven seals, 6:1–8:1
      Scene 1: The rider on the white horse, 6:1-2
      Scene 2: The rider on the red horse, 6:3-4
      Scene 3: The rider on the black horse, 6:5-6
      Scene 4: The rider on the yellow horse, 6:7-8
      Scene 5: Prayer of the martyrs, 6:9-11
      Scene 6: The eschatological events, 6:12–7:17 (cosmic catastrophes, 6:12-17; sealing of the martyrs, 7:1-8; the martyrs in heaven, 7:9-17)
      Scene 7: Silence in heaven, 8:1
VI. Act III: The church in tribulation, 8:2–11:18
   A. Setting: The altars, prayers of the saints, 8:2-6
   B. The sounding of the seven trumpets, 8:7–11:18
      Scene 1: Hail and fire fall, 8:7
      Scene 2: A mountain cast into the sea, 8:8-9
      Scene 3: A star falls on rivers and springs, 8:10-11
      Scene 4: Heavenly bodies darkened, 8:12; an eagle announces three woes, 8:13
      Scene 5 (woe 1): Pit of the abyss; locusts, 9:1-12
      Scene 6 (woe 2): Four angels released, 9:13-15; two hundred million horsemen, 9:16-21; angel with the little book, ch. 10; times of the Gentiles, two prophets, the evil city, 11:1-14
      Scene 7 (woe 3): Worship in heaven, 11:15-18
VII. Act IV: The salvation of the church, 11:19–15:4
   A. Setting: The ark of the covenant, 11:19
   B. The showing of the seven pageants, 12:1–15:4
      Scene 1: The woman and the dragon, ch. 12
      Scene 2: The beast arising from the sea, 13:1-10
      Scene 3: The beast arising from the land, 13:11-18

Scene 4: The Lamb with the 144,000 martyrs, 14:1-5

Scene 5: Announcement of doom to Babylon, 14:6-13

Scene 6: The son of man on a white cloud and the winepress of God's wrath, 14:14-20

Scene 7: Hymn of the Lamb chanted by the saved, 15:1-4

VIII. Act V: The world in agony, 15:5–16:21

A. Setting: The tent of witness, 15:5–16:1

B. The pouring out of the seven bowls, 16:2-21

Scene 1: Plague to the earth (boils on men), 16:2

Scene 2: Plague to the sea (blood), 16:3

Scene 3: Plague to rivers and springs (blood), 16:4-7

Scene 4: Plague to the sun (burning heat), 16:8-9

Scene 5: Plague to the beast's throne (darkness), 16:10-11

Scene 6: Plague to the Euphrates (Armageddon), 16:12-16

Scene 7: Plague to the air (devastation), 16:17-21

IX. Act VI: The judgment of the world, 17:1–20:3

A. Setting: An angel issuing from the sanctuary, 17:1-2

B. The unfolding of the seven plagues, 17:3–20:3

Scene 1: The woman on the scarlet beast, 17:3-5

Scene 2: The beast at war with the woman, 17:6-18

Scene 3: The final cosmic oratorio, 18:1–19:10

Scene 4: The Word of God on the white horse, 19:11-16

Scene 5: The angel standing in the sun, 19:17-18

Scene 6: The Battle of Armageddon, 19:19-21

Scene 7: Satan cast into the abyss, 20:1-3

X. Act VII: The church in the Millennium, 20:4–22:5

A. Setting: The church enthroned with Christ, 20:4-6; Satan's limited authority and defeat, 20:7-10

B. The fulfilling of God's sevenfold plan, 20:11–22:5

Scene 1: The old heaven and old earth, 20:11

Scene 2: The Last Judgment, 20:12-15

Scene 3: The new heaven and new earth, 21:1

Scene 4: The new Jerusalem, 21:2-8

Scene 5: Measuring of the city, 21:9-21

Scene 6: The city's illumination, 21:22-27

Scene 7: The city's source of life, 22:1-5

XI. Epilogue: Imprimaturs on the book, 22:6-20

XII. Closing benediction, 22:21

By way of comparison with this outline, the following synopses of representative outlines of others working in this field are given. Those of Lohmeyer and Rissi have been chosen because these writers have observed a sevenfold pattern of sorts as dominating the seer's purpose; those of Charles and Lund as examples of the type of scholarship which, to advance its critical theories, resorts to considerable rearrangement of the materials found in Revelation. In this respect, Lund gives John's book far more drastic treatment than Charles, who, like the other two scholars mentioned, also finds the book capable of a sevenfold treatment, though one quite different in detail from either of theirs or from that proposed here. *See* Table 1.

3. Symbolism and thought-frames. These are the stuff or fabric out of which an author fashions his message. They may be considered from the standpoint of their origins and from that of their essential content or teaching.

a. Origins. Much research has been expended on the possible background and origin of John's thought and imagery. Babylonian, Zoroastrian, Egyptian, and other pagan sources have been claimed for his reference to the "seven spirits" (1:4), and for his cosmological views relative to creation, heaven, hell, and the sea (4:1 ff; 20:14), to the "woman clothed with the sun" (12:1), to the "great red dragon" (12:3), and to numerous other items. It is also claimed by some that these pagan sources have been mediated to John either through the current Gnosticism or by means of Jewish apocryphal or apocalyptic writings. Among the Dead Sea Scrolls, that dealing with the "War of the Sons of Light with the Sons of Darkness" affords interesting parallels with John's "war . . . in heaven, Michael and his angels fighting against the dragon" (12:7-12); while there appear to be frequent ideological and linguistic coincidences with the cosmological and resurrection narratives recovered by Sumerologists. Pseudepigraphical writings such as I and II Enoch, II Esdras, the Testaments of the Twelve Patriarchs, and II Baruch also afford unnumbered parallels. Probably the significance to be attributed to source criticism of this sort involves the recognition of the existence of a certain "stock in trade" common to all Jewish and Christian apocalyptists. But the mediating agencies of most, if not all, of these materials, from whatever source, are the OT scriptures, on the one hand, and the common Christian tradition, on the other. *See* § A2 *above.*

b. Teaching content. John's thought-frames—whatever be their ultimate origin and mediation—are generally those of the Hebrew prophets, supplemented by the Christian additions common to all the NT writings. These include the ideas of the sovereignty of God, his holiness and righteousness, justice, truth, eternity, and love; a chosen people of God as contrasted with the generality of mankind; the Lord of the church envisioned as "one like a son of man"; a witnessing and martyred people; the elders of the congregation ruling with God or alternatively with Christ; the efficacy of prayer and the worship of God built around the same (18:1–19:8). Emblematic prophecy typical of prophets like Hosea, Ezekiel, and Jeremiah is to be seen in the portrayal of the Son of man's Lordship over and redemptive

Table 1
Synopsis of Representative Outlines of Revelation

LOHMEYER[1]	RISSI[2]	CHARLES[3]	LUND[4]
I. *Proömium*, 1:1-3	I. A. *Proömium*, 1:1-8	Prologue, 1:1-3	I. Prologue, 1:1-20 A. Angel, 1:1-3
II. *Prolog*, 1:4-8		I. Introduction A. Greeting, 1:4-8	B. Jesus, 1:4-8
III. **Ermahnender Teil*, 1:9–3:22	B. *Eingangsvision*, 1:9-20 C. **2:1–3:22*	B. John's call, 1:9-20 II. *Seven letters, 2:1–3:22	C. Commission of the church, 1:9-20 II. *Seven epistles, 2:1–3:22
IV. **Apokalyptischer Teil*, 4:1–21:4 *Einleitung*, 4:1–5:14	II. D. 1. *V. von Gott*, 4:1-11 2. *Vision vom Lamm*, 5:1-14	III. Vision of God and seven-sealed book, 4:1–5:14	III. *Seven seals, 4:1–8:5 A. Salvation, 4:1–5:14
A. **Sieben Siegel-visionen*, 6:1–8:1	*3. *Sieben Siegel*, 6:1–8:1	IV. Judgments, 6:1–20:3 A. First 6 seals, 6:1-17 B. Judgment stayed, 7:1-8	B. Judgment, 6:1-17; 8:1, 3-5 C. Salvation, 7:1-17
B. **Sieben Posaunen-visionen*, 8:2–11:15	*4. *Sieben Posaunen*, 8:2–11:19	C. Proleptic vision, 7:9-17 D. Seventh seal, 8:1, 3-5, 2, 6, 13 E. Demonic woes, 9:1-11, 14a F. Proleptic digression, 10:1–11:13 G. Demonic woe, 11:14b-19	IV. *Seven trumpets, 8:2, 6-12; 8:13; 9:1-21; 11:14-19 A. Judgment, 8:2, 6-12 B. Eagle, 8:13 C. Judgment, 9:1-21; 11:14-18 D. Sanctuary, 11:19 V. Church's testimony in Empire, 10:1-11 A. Angel, 10:1 B. Sea, earth, 10:2, 5, 8 C. Seven thunders, 10:3-4
C. **Reich des Drachen*, 11:15–13:18		H. Demonic woe, cont'd., 12:1–13:18	VI. Church's testimony in Judaism, 11:1-13
	*5. *Schilderung des Endgeschehens*, 12:1–14:20		VI'. Church persecuted by Judaism, 12:1-17
D. **Menschensohn*, 14:1-20		I. Proleptic vision, 14:1-7 J. Proleptic vision, 14:8-11, 14, 18-20	V'. Church persecuted by Empire, 13:1-18
E. **Sieben Schalen-visionen*, 15:1–16:21	*6. *Sieben letzte Plagen*, 15:1–16:21		IV'. *Seven bowls, 15:1, 5-8; 16:1-21
		K. Martyred host, 15:2-4 L. *Seven bowls, 15:5–16:21	A. Sanctuary, 15:1, 5, 8 B. 3 bowls, 16:1-4 C. Angel and altar, 16:5-7 D. 4 bowls, 16:8-21 III'. *Seven angels, 14:1-20; 15:2-4 A. Salvation, 14:1-5 B. Judgment, 14:6-20 C. Salvation, 15:2-4

[1] E. Lohmeyer, *Handbuch zum NT* (Tübingen, Germany: J. C. B. Mohr).
[2] M. Rissi, *Zeit und Geschichte in der Offenbarung des Johannes* (Zürich, Switzerland: Zwingli Verlag).
[3] R. H. Charles, *Revelation*, ICC (Edinburgh: T. & T. Clark; New York: Charles Scribner's Sons).
[4] N. W. Lund, *Chiasmus in the NT: A Study in Formgeschichte* (Chapel Hill, N. C.: University of North Carolina Press).

LOHMEYER	RISSI	CHARLES	LUND
F. *Fall Babylons, 17:1–19:10	7. Babylon und Tier, 17:1–19:10	M. Successive judgments, 17:1–20:3	II'. *Seven angels, 17:1–22:5
G. *Vollendung, 19:11–21:4	III. E. *Parusie, 19:11–22:5		
		V. Millennial kingdom, 21:9–22:2, 14-15, 17; 20:4-6, 7-10	
		VI. Great white throne, 20:11-15	
		VII. Everlasting kingdom, 21:5a, 4d, 5b, 1-42bc; 22:3-5	
V. Verheissender Teil, 21:5–22:7			
A. Verheissung Gottes, 21:5-8			
B. Verheissung des Engels, 21:9–22:5			
C. Verheissung Christi, 22:6-7			
VI. Epilog, 22:8-19	F. Epilog, 22:6-21	Epilogue, 21:5c, 6b-8; 22:6-7, 18a, 16, 13, 12, 10; 22:8-9, 20-21	I'. Epilogue, 22:6-21
A. Worte des Engels, 22:8-9			A. The angel, 22:6-9
B. Worte Christi, 22:10-16			B. The coming Jesus, 22:10-15
C. Worte des Sehers, 22:17-19			C. John's commission to the church, 22:16-21
VII. Schluss, 22:20-21			

Note: An asterisk (*) indicates seven subdivisions, either those suggested by John himself—the letters, seals, trumpets, bowls—or others discovered by the scholar indicated.

activity for his church in the opening vision (1:12-20), in the action of the angel in heaving the "stone like a great millstone" into the sea (18:21-24), and the like. John presents these prophetic teachings after the usual apocalyptic fashion through the medium of a characteristic and striking symbolism, which is partly obscure but for the most part intelligible even to moderns who stand at a distance culturally and chronologically from his day. Thus, God's sovereignty as in all apocalypses is expressed by the vision of the divine throne room (chs. 4–5); his unapproachable holiness by that of the "sea of glass mingled with fire" (15:2; cf. 4:6; see SEA OF GLASS); his grace by a rainbow (4:3; cf. Gen. 9:12-13); his omniscience by the "seven spirits of God sent out into all the earth" (5:6); his judgment upon all his creation by the fact that "from his presence earth and sky fled away" (20:11). Similarly, the kingdom of evil is symbolized by the dragon and his angels (12:7 ff; 20:2-3; see DRAGON); and the corporate sin of the race, together with the secular might which incarnates it, is represented by a swarm of locusts (9:3 ff) and "troops of cavalry" (9:13-19). The evil messiah of this kingdom finds expression under the form of the "beast rising out of the sea" (13:1), and the cultic priesthood which gives it a religious sanction under that of "another beast which rose out of the earth" (13:11). See BEAST 4.

Further, the archangel Michael stands for Christ in his victorious battling with the forces of unrighteousness (12:7-10); "seven lampstands" for the church universal (1:20; see SEVEN CHURCHES); "seven stars" for the "angels" (variously interpreted to mean bishops, messengers, heavenly counterparts, or the spiritual core; see ANGELS OF THE SEVEN CHURCHES) of the seven churches (1:20); "Sodom and Egypt," or alternatively "Babylon" and the city or world of mankind "where their Lord was crucified," for the contemporary world culture (11:8; 18:2); the "new Jerusalem" for the church or people of God (21:2; see NEW JERUSALEM); the "woman clothed with the sun" for the community of God's people out of which his messiah comes (12:1); the "great harlot who is seated upon many waters" for the evil community of the beast (17:1); finally, the "river of the water of life" (22:1) and the "tree of life" (22:2) for the final salvation which God affords his people. In addition, as already indicated above (see § E1), the background and stage setting for all John's "visions" are supplied from the various paraphernalia of tabernacle and temple, such as the lampstands (1:12), golden bowls full of incense (5:8), the altar of sacrifice (6:9), the golden altar of incense (8:3), the sanctuary with its ark of the covenant (11:19); and all these retain their usual significance as found in the OT scriptures.

The symbol creating the most difficulty for students of John's Apocalypse is the number of the beast (SIX HUNDRED AND SIXTY-SIX [13:18]). Most of the tyrants of history, from Nero to Kaiser Wilhelm and Hitler, as well as the pope of the Roman Catholic Church, have at one time and another been said both to answer to the description of the beast and to furnish in the numerical values attaching to their names in Hebrew or Greek the amount of the sum indicated. Almost as much difficulty has attended the decoding of the meaning of the famous four horsemen at 6:1-8. Perhaps the best suggestion proposed is that the parallelism to be found between this passage and those at Matt. 24:6 ff; Mark 13:7 ff; Luke 21:9 ff offers an intelligible solution to the problem. In the event that this suggestion is adopted, the four figures on horseback represent, respectively, war or conquest, international or civil strife, famine, and death. In any case, the riders on the white horses at 6:2; 19:11 ff have nothing in common, the latter being clearly defined as "the Word of God." *See further* DEATH, SECOND; ARMAGEDDON.

4. Message: theology of history. Employing, as we have seen, the drama with its Greek stage and stage props, and the symbolism and thought-frames of both apocalypse and Hebrew prophecy, John endeavors in his book to set forth the divine philosophy (or theology) of history. This, to all intents, is the gospel—i.e., an account of God's redemptive activity—and this is carried through in the context of both man's general futility and the church's ineffectiveness. The seer is concerned to comfort a persecuted church and to exhort it to exercise a stronger faith and hope in the sovereign Lord of history (2:10, 13; 3:11-12; 6:11; 12:6). But his purpose far exceeds the mere wish to console and to focus the church's attention upon its own tribulations—however great these may appear to be. His earnest desire—subtly expressed at times, no doubt—is to place the church's dire extremity (Act III) in the context of the world's equally great need (Act V), on the one hand, and of God's redemptive purpose, on the other. For the church is at once the company of the saved (3:5; 15: 2-4) and the redemptive agency by which God will both save (11:1-14) and rule (2:26 ff; 3:21; 20:4-6) the world. Accordingly, it is a mistake to see in the book merely consolation for Christians experiencing persecution. John's intention, it is true, includes this note, but it far transcends the wish to make the church more introspective than it already is. Nor is there here (any more than in the teaching of Jesus himself) a morbid attitude toward martyrdom such as appears, e.g., in the church of the second century (e.g., in the case of Ignatius of Antioch). There is, it is true, in the gospel as John dramatizes it what for the moment can only be called "bitter," as this gospel's full demand upon the church's powers is set forth (10:10; 11:1-14); and in his view there can be no escape from the necessity of carrying through to this bitter end (10:11). But the focus of attention throughout the book is neither upon the church's sufferings nor upon her exclusive salvation, but rather upon God's ultimate saving purpose and upon the church's part in its achievement.

Revelation opens with a vision of the Son of man walking in the midst of his church as its Lord (1: 12-16), and holding in his right hand its spiritual core (the "angels of the seven churches" [1:20]) as its Savior. John says that, being "in the Spirit on the Lord's day" (1:10—the first reference to Sunday, if it be such, employing this phrase, in Christian literature; otherwise, perhaps a reference to the eschatological time, the phrase then being the equivalent of Amos' "day of the LORD"), he heard behind him a loud voice, and that, turning round, he saw, not im-

mediately the voice's owner, but rather a seven-branched lampstand or seven separate lampstands symbolizing the church, and only thereafter the church's Lord in its midst (1:12 ff). This is a good example of John's symbolic method—if one would see Jesus, he means to say, let him look at the church, for it is here that he is to be found!

The church is realistically portrayed in Act I as it was in John's day. If one thinks of the seven-branched lampstand of the temple as standing erect on Patmos with a strong light behind it to the SW, then its arms will cast their shadow upon the land in such a way as severally to connect the two wayward churches of Ephesus and Laodicea (the outermost branch), the two faithful churches of Smyrna* and Philadelphia (the middle branch), and the churches of Pergamum and Sardis (the innermost branch), which with that of Thyatira at the apex between them, stand respectively for tolerance of the evil courtship of emperor-worship, compromise with the pagan deification of the state for which it is sponsor, and death of the spirit of true worship in which it must issue. Such is—we are constrained to believe—a true picture of the church at the end of the first century as the seer sees it and as he portrays it for that church's admonition. Figs. SMY 70-71; REV 10.

But if in Act I we see the church as it is on earth, equally in Act II we are transported into the heavenly regions that we may view the historical scene in the perspective of God's eternal purpose.* The seven-sealed book (5:1-7) contains, as the following seven Scenes clearly indicate, a synopsis of God's plan for man in history. Scenes 1-4 present us with a picture of the rise and fall of empires and of the cyclic futility of man's life when he is left to himself (6:1-8). John never again mentions the four horsemen, because it is not his wish to dwell on man's futility, but rather to develop the theme of God's contrasting providence and grace. In the midst of this futility, the church—for which as a whole we believe the "martyrs" to stand (cf. 7:3-4, 13-14; Luke 14:27)—can only pray for deliverance and vindication (6:9-11; Scene 5), and for the moment its prayer is answered with the gift of the court dress of the heavenly throne room. Scene 6 then follows with a brief synopsis of the eschatological events which are to be portrayed in far greater detail in Acts III and V. Finally, Scene 7 gives us a picture of all the creatures of God's universe "frozen" on the stage, that we may for a brief "half an hour" meditate upon the divine purpose as disclosed in this comprehensive act (8:1). Fig. REV 11.

Acts III and V are complementary, as their successive scenes clearly indicate, and together they elaborate the eschatological events already narrated in 6:12-7:17. Act III portrays for us the church in the tribulation of the last times, even as Act V in like manner sets forth the effect on the secular world of the same distressing events. The more drastic effect of the cosmic catastrophes upon the world, as compared with their effect upon the church, is apparent as Scenes 1-4 of the two Acts are compared. This is John's parabolic way of saying that cosmic calamities cannot really touch God's people (cf. 16: 2; 9:4). The same lesson appears in the fact that, on

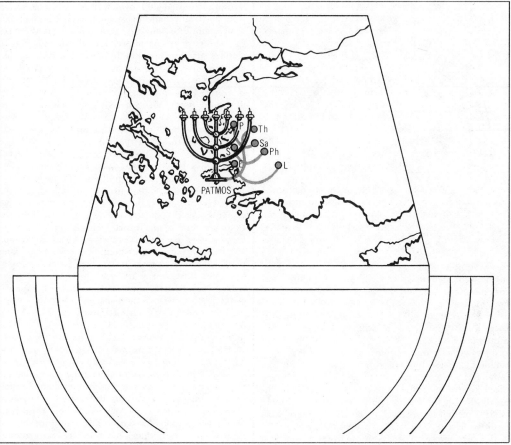

John W. Bowman

10. Stage setting (based on an approximate location of the places depicted) for Act I of Revelation: Ephesus (E) and Laodicea (L), two "bad" churches, are connected by the lowest arm of the lampstand; Smyrna (S) and Philadelphia (Ph), two "good" churches, similarly are at either end of the middle arm; and Pergamum (P), Thyatira (Th), and Sardis (Sa) represent a progression from *tolerance*, through *compromise*, to *death* in dealing with sin.

the one hand, the prayers of the saints are indicated as bringing forth God's effective action within history (8:2-6; 11:15-18), while, on the other hand, the world cannot even approach his sanctuary during the tribulation of these times (15:8; cf. 16:21). During the eschatological time man is surrounded and harassed by corporate sin (9:1-12) and the secular power implementing it (9:16-21); these are respectively set forth in terms of a swarm of creatures like locusts and a horde of demonic cavalrymen, the imagery in both cases being derived from the book of Joel. At the same time, however, the church's evangelism proceeds apace in the city of Vanity Fair (called Sodom, Egypt, Jerusalem, Babylon [11:8; 16:19]—hence, any city and any land of like character); and, though martyred, the church rises and ascends like its Lord into heaven (11:1-14). From the co-ordination of this passage with its opposite number in 16:12-16, it becomes clear that the so-called Battle of Armageddon is one of ideologies (gospel versus *badspel*), not of guns and bombs (cf. 19:11-16, 21).

Similarly, Acts IV and VI are complementary, the one presenting the *modus operandi* of God's salvation of his people during the eschatological tribulation,

the other that of his judgment on the secular culture opposed to his will. And here the chronological scheme with which John is working becomes clear. For in 12:5 the entire incarnate life of our Lord is indicated (from Incarnation to Ascension)! It should be clear, accordingly, that for John the eschatological time embraces the whole period of the church's history from Incarnation to the end of time, as both of these Acts end in their closing Scenes with the final judgment of Satan and his hosts (14:14-20; 20:1-2).

In Act VII we have the "play within the play." The church is now seen to be seated with Christ and reigning with him throughout the Millennium (20:4-6)—a period to be reckoned according to God's time, not man's, and hence the equivalent of the "day of the Lord" (cf. II Pet. 3:8-10) or the entire sweep of the eschatological period. The seer makes this time span clear from his remark that this is the period of the "first resurrection"—i.e., of the moral one experienced by man within history (cf. Rom. 6:1-11; Eph. 2:1-10). To say as John does that the church reigning with Christ is privileged to observe the successive pageants presented in the seven Scenes of this Act, is simply to credit it alone with the spiritual in-

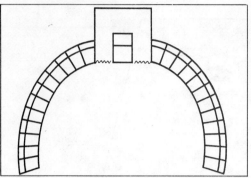

John W. Bowman

11. Stage setting for Acts II-VII of Revelation: The "sanctuary" of the heavenly temple (taking the place of the theater's *skene*) stands open, showing the "throne" and ark of the covenant; the twenty-four thrones for the elders correspond to the theater's *paraskeneia*.

sight required to foresee the eternal purposes of God in their completeness. Accordingly, throughout history the church is led by the Spirit to see that all creation is in God's sight judged as unworthy (Scene 1; 20:11), that he will judge all men in like manner (Scene 2; 20:12-15), that he will create a new cosmos after his own liking (Scene 3; 21:1), and that he is progressively bringing ever nearer the "new Jerusalem," Christ's church and bride (Scenes 4-7). The judgment in Scene 2 here presents the final stumbling block to every endeavor to interpret this book literally, for on the basis of such interpretation there is no place left for it to occur. For the interpretation outlined herein, however, no difficulty presents itself —this Scene, like all others of the drama, occurs on the stage, of course!

F. *CANONICITY.* At an early date Revelation was employed as authoritative by church fathers throughout the church.

1. **Europe.** Hermas (95-100), himself an apocalyptic writer at Rome, used its imagery (e.g., a woman to represent the church and a beast to stand for its enemy); while Justin Martyr, who lived and wrote in Rome a half century later, both employed the book and mentioned its author by name. The so-called Muratorian Canon, a second-century list of the books of the NT, remarks of it: "And John in the Apocalypse, although he writes to seven churches, yet speaks to all." Irenaeus, bishop of Lyons (175), also used the work, and it is quoted in the contemporary letter of the churches of Vienne and Lyons with the introductory formula indicating it as scripture. The OL MSS g and m (eighth or ninth century), representing a translation of about the same period, contained the book. Finally, under the influence of Jerome, it found a place in the Vulg. (391-404).

2. **North Africa.** The OL MS h (sixth or seventh century), containing a translation of the African type which goes back presumably to the second century, has fragments of Revelation along with the other NT writings. Tertullian (*ca.* 200) and Cyprian (*ca.* 235-58) both wrote in Latin; and the former possibly, the latter assuredly, employed the African Latin translation of the NT, including that of Revelation. Tertullian specifically speaks of it as by "John the apostle." The Council of Carthage (397) in this area, under the influence of Athanasius, adopted a canon including all the books of the NT accepted by the church universal ever since.

3. **Egypt.** Clement of Alexandria (212) is our first authority here to quote the book, and this he does under the name of the apostle John. He is followed by Origen (*ca.* 235), who gives Revelation a place among the "generally accepted" books of the NT canon. The contemporary Chester Beatty Papyrus (P[47]), emanating from this area, is the earliest Greek exemplar of John's work; the Sahidic version (second to fourth century) also contains fragments of it. Dionysius of Alexandria (third century) challenged the Johannine authorship of the book, though he accepted it as canonical. It is found as well in the Bohairic version (of uncertain date). Finally, in his Festal Letter of 367, Athanasius included Revelation in his canon—a matter of great moment for the latter tradition of the church.

4. **The East.** In the area for which John wrote his book, Papias, bishop of Hierapolis (early second century), appears to have been the first on record to have employed it as authoritative; he was followed by Melito of Sardis (160-90), who wrote a commentary upon it. During the same period Apollonius is said to have used it, as did also Methodius, bishop of Olympus—both of Asia Minor. In addition, there are possible traces of its having been known to and used by the Valentinian Gnostics of the same area. In N Syria, Revelation experienced perhaps its most checkered career. Bishop Theophilus of Syrian Antioch (*ca.* 181) used and quoted from the book according to Eusebius, and Lucian (*ca.* 312) —the probable creator of the Byzantine text of the NT—incorporated it into that version, which became the standard Greek text of the Eastern Empire. But Bishop Rabbula of Edessa (411-35) omitted Revelation, along with the minor Catholic letters, from the Peshitta Version of the Syr., and it was not incorporated into this translation until 508 at the behest of Bishop Philoxenus of the Syrian Hierapolis. This is perhaps as satisfactory a history generally as could be expected of the only extensive bit of apocalyptic writing to be included in the NT scriptures.

G. *TEXT.* The witnesses for the text of Revelation divide themselves into three groups constituted respectively of: (*a*) P[18,47]ℵ ACP 0207; (*b*) 046 and about forty cursives (incl. 1); and (*c*) the bulk of the cursives containing the Byzantine text. The Chester Beatty Papyrus (P[47]) of the third century exhibits the most striking originality of all these witnesses, while agreeing on the whole with the group indicated. (For the versions and fathers, *see* § F *above.*) On the whole, the text of Revelation is fairly certain. A majority of the variants appear to deal with the curious solecisms in which the book abounds (*see* § A3 *above*); scribes from time to time endeavored particularly to correct the author's grammar in the matter of gender, number, and case of noun and adjective, and in that of mood and tense of the verb.

The most striking variants concern the number of the beast at 13:18 (*see* SIX HUNDRED AND SIXTY-SIX), and the spelling of "Armageddon" (*see* HAR-MAGEDON). Other important readings about which some doubt exists include: 1:5—λύσαντι or λούσαντι; 4:3—ἴρις or ἱερεῖς; 10:3-4—the number of the "thunders" ("seven" or indeterminate); 15:3—the "King of the nations" or the "King of the ages"; 19:9—retention of "of the marriage" with "feast . . . of the Lamb"; 19:13—the participle to accompany ἱμάτιον; and 20:9—the addition of ἀπὸ τοῦ θεοῦ after πῦρ. Interesting variants of an interpretive type include: Βασιλεῖς καὶ ἱερεῖς for Βασιλείαν, ἱερεῖς (1:6; 5:10); πρωτότοκος for πρῶτος (1:17; 2:8); ἐβάπτισας for ἐβάστασας (2:3); ἀπὸ τοῦ ξύλου for τοῦ μάννα (2:17); τὸ θηρίον τὸ τέταρτον for τὸ θηρίον (11:7); and omission of "This is the second death, the lake of fire," in 20:14.

There is little or no evidence for dislocation of text on an extensive scale in Revelation. The only likely exceptions occur at 15:1, which should possibly follow after vss. 2-4, and at 20:7-10, which might well follow immediately after vs. 3.

Bibliography. Commentaries: H. B. Swete (1906). R. H. Charles, ICC (2 vols.; 1920), by far the most extensive in English. E. B. Allo, *Saint Jean L'Apocalypse* (1921). T. Zahn (2 vols.; 3rd ed., 1924). E. Lohmeyer, *Handbuch zum NT* (2nd ed., 1933). M. Rist, Introduction and Exegesis of Revelation, *IB*, XII (1957), 347-551. M. Kiddle, Moffatt NT Commentary.

Introductions to literature of the NT by: Jülicher, Moffatt, Goodspeed, Scott, Clogg, etc.

Important special studies relating to the background of the Greco-Roman stage: M. Beiber, *The History of the Greek and Roman Theater* (1939). W. Beare, *The Roman Stage* (1950). H. D. F. Kitto, *Greek Tragedy: A Literary Study* (2nd ed., 1950).

Important special studies relating to the structure of Revelation: R. G. Moulton in *The Modern Reader's Bible* (1907). N. W. Lund, *Chiasmus in the NT: A Study in Formgeschichte* (1942). A. Farrer, *A Re-birth of Images* (1949). M. Rissi, *Zeit und Geschichte in der Offenbarung des Johannes* (1952). J. W. Bowman, *The Drama of the Book of Revelation* (1955); "The Revelation to John: Its Dramatic Structure and Message," *Interpretation*, IX (1955), 436-53, upon which this article has largely drawn.   J. W. BOWMAN

REVENGE, REVENGER. *See* AVENGER OF BLOOD.

REVERENCE. There is no typical word in the original languages of the Bible corresponding to the English "reverence" (cf. εὐλάβεια, "godly fear," "reverence," only in Heb. 12:28; cf. 5:7). "Reverence" is sometimes used (cf. "revere," "reverent") for the Hebrew יראה, FEAR, "awe," when deep respect other than that owed to God is implied (Lev. 19:3, 30; 26:2; Judg. 6:10; I Kings 18:3, 12; in a different idiom: Ps. 119:48). The KJV uses the word "reverence" (RSV "obeisance") for השתחוה, "to bow down," where one bows in homage to a man (II Sam. 9:6; I Kings 1:31; Esth. 3:2, 5).

The expression φόβος Χριστοῦ (Eph. 5:21), "fear of Christ" (RSV "reverence for Christ"), challenges the adequacy of the time-honored phrase "fear of the Lord" (Acts 9:31; Rom. 3:18; II Cor. 5:11; cf. 7:1) to contain the full dimension of man's response to God's fearful righteousness expressed in love. In the light of this passage and other NT exhortations to mutual subjection "in the Lord" (Eph. 6:1; Col. 3:18; cf. Eph. 6:9; Col. 4:1), the term "reverent" in I Pet. 3:2 (KJV "fear") is a fitting translation (cf.

Eph. 5:33, where the KJV has "reverence," the RSV "respect," for φοβεῖσθαι, "to fear"; cf. Deut. 32:51; I Pet. 3:15). The RSV uses "respect" for ἐντρέπεσθαι, "to shame oneself before another"—i.e., to respect him (KJV "reverence") in Matt. 21:37; Mark 12:6; Luke 20:13; Heb. 12:9.   J. A. WHARTON

REVILE. *See* SCOFFER.

REWARD. The English word "reward" may have a neutral meaning of "recompense for good or evil," but most often it suggests a benefit or favorable compensation. In the RSV, with few exceptions (cf. Luke 23:41; Acts 1:18), "reward" means some positive outcome or return. Yet one must take account of the larger complex of thought, where good and evil are rewarded and punished, and man's responsibility and accountability are involved in the ethical scene. Related terms come into the picture, such as "wages," "hire," "recompense," "requital."

The operation of this reward ranges from the natural compensation man to man to God's recognition of obedience and service, from a happy outcome in this life to a gracious recompense in the life to come.

It is to be noted that the words used in Hebrew and Greek suggest the idea of the wholeness of an action, the completion of the deed. Just as work is completed for a man in the payment of his wages, so it is assumed that action naturally carries an entail in its outcome, whether of reward or of punishment. The overtones of a commercial transaction are not absent, as when reward is referred to as "wages." The Hebrew terms most often used are גמל, "to deal with, to benefit, to reward" (גמול, "act, benefit, recompense"); עקב, "end, reward, wages," sometimes used as a preposition, "in reward of"; פעלה, "labor, wages"; שוב, "to return, to do a second time, to reward"; שכר, "hire, reward" (משכרת, "wages, reward"); שלם, "to be whole, to complete, to restore, to requite."

The Greek terms give the sense of a wage return and an equivalent compensation. The word μισθόω, with its cognates μισθός, μίσθιος, μισθωτός, has a first meaning of "payment for services." The word ἀνταποδίδωμι, with its cognates ἀνταπόδομα and ἀνταπόδοσις, suggests an equal return; the prefixes ἀντί and ἀπό reinforce the idea of corresponding repayment. The Letter to the Hebrews uses a late Greek word, μισθαποδοσία.

  1. In the OT
  2. In the Apoc.
  3. In the teaching of Jesus
  4. In the letters of Paul
  5. In the rest of the NT
  Bibliography

1. In the OT. This article is concerned with reward in its ethical and religious dimensions. The covenant of God with Israel was the evidence of God's loving favor; it promised good things to Israel on condition of their obedience to the command of God. Disobedience was a violation of the covenant and would bring disaster and death. Israel was to observe what was right and good in the sight of the

Lord that they might prosper and come into possession of the land. In the period of the wanderings failure to obey, on the part of leaders and people, brought suffering and death. The history of the judges and the kings was written in terms of reward for faithfulness and punishment for sin and idolatry. Earthly victory and welfare depended on obedience (Josh. 1:7-9; Judg. 2).

In the Psalms and the wisdom literature this "neat doctrine of rewards and punishments" was applied to the individual life. The good life was assured on the basis of obedience and discipline, and wisdom came to be identified with the good life. The first psalm illustrates the fortunes of the wise, pious man and the ungodly fool. Elsewhere in the Psalms this neat mechanical pattern breaks down when the psalmist prays for forgiveness and says:

> He does not deal with us according to our sins,
> nor requite us according to our iniquities
> (Ps. 103:10).

Proverbs follows the orthodox doctrine, but the writer or writers of Ecclesiastes found that life did not work out so neatly and the doctrine of retribution did not always apply in the span of the individual life. They sound a cynical note as they see the righteous suffer and the wicked prosper, or as they observe a common fate for all.

In the book of Job the friends take the position that righteousness is rewarded by welfare and long life, while sickness and poverty are the recompense for sin. In his suffering Job acknowledges that he has sinned, and yet he observes around him the wicked prospering. Job maintains his integrity before God, and for him the answer lies beyond the pattern of strict reward for righteousness and punishment for evil.

2. In the Apoc. Tobit illustrates a mechanical righteousness done with a view to reward. He tithes, gives alms, buries the dead, makes pilgrimage. Yet he suffers blindness and affliction in captivity. His piety appears to go unrewarded, and his wife complains: "Where are your charities and your righteous deeds?" (Tob. 2:14). The theme of the book is that good deeds register with God, and finally Tobit is vindicated with good success for him and his family. "Give alms. . . . So you will be laying up a good treasure for yourself against the day of necessity. For charity delivers from death . . ." (4:7, 9-10).

In the book of Judith one theme is basic: If the Israelites sin, they are vulnerable to the enemy; but if there is no transgression, God will protect the nation from attack.

In Ecclesiasticus we see the individual application of rewards and punishments. Here piety is identified with wisdom (15:1), and the reward is more wisdom (6:18). "Do no evil, and evil will never befall you" (7:1). The freedom of man to choose good or evil is in his own hands, and he is held accountable for his choice.

> Do your work before the appointed time,
> and in God's time he will give you your reward
> (51:30).

The author is aware of a certain skepticism concerning God's accounting, as though man might hope to

escape punishment (5:1-7), but he warns that suddenly God's wrath will go forth.

Mattathias in I Maccabees exhorts his sons to be zealous for the law and the covenant, and he recalls how the great leaders of the past, Abraham, Joseph, Joshua, David, had been rewarded for their faithfulness to God's commandment (2:51-60).

II Maccabees enlarges the range of reward and punishment with the idea of resurrection. The arrogance of the heathen will receive just punishment in the judgment of God and no resurrection to life, while the faithful martyr can look beyond death to his vindication at the hand of God (7:9, 29, 35-37).

Full reward in life after death is clearly stated in the Wisdom of Solomon:

> The righteous live for ever,
> and their reward is with the Lord;
> the Most High takes care of them.
> Therefore they will receive a glorious crown
> and a beautiful diadem from the hand of the Lord
> (5:15-16).

Even in this world the life of wisdom leads to security, honor, and prosperity.

3. In the teaching of Jesus. In the Judaism in which Jesus lived, God punished sin and rewarded righteousness. The Jewish teachers would say that "good deeds deserved the favor of God and the reward he promised" (G. F. Moore [*see bibliography*]). "Judaism has no hesitation about recognizing the merit of good works, or in exhorting men to acquire it and to accumulate a store of merit laid up for the hereafter." II Esdras and Tobit refer to the treasure of good works laid up. As the commandments of the law were multiplied, so the number of rewards for those who kept the commandments was to be multiplied in the afterlife. The lawyer in Luke 10:25 ff, with his question: "What shall I do to inherit eternal life?" provides an example of good works with a view to reward from God; Jesus' reply is in the same pattern: "Do this, and you will live" (10:28). It should be noted that the development of Jewish apocalyptic speculation concerning the Age to Come opened up a great prospect of reversal and reward.

Reward is an almost constant feature of Jesus' teaching (cf. the Beatitudes). Occasionally the outcome is in the sequence of this life, as is probably meant in Matt. 7:1-3, but more often it is in the spiritual relation with God (Matt. 6:4, 6, 18) or in the Next Age (Matt. 6:20; Mark 10:21: treasure in heaven). At other times Jesus calls for service without reference to reward (Luke 9:57-62; 14:25-33).

The reward motive is sharply curbed in the parable of the laborers (Matt. 20:1-16), where the payment of one denarius is for all, or in the parable of the servant from the field, whose hard labor created no merit: "We are unworthy servants; we have only done what was our duty" (Luke 17:7-10). In the judgment scene of Matt. 25 the righteous are rewarded with a place in the kingdom, but their service to the thirsty, hungry, naked, was so far from being done for a reward that the righteous were unaware of what they had done. In Mark 10:29-31, Jesus promises to the faithful disciples hundredfold restitution plus eternal life. But this can be understood as suggesting no consciously chosen reward. Only suffering and privation in this life, but a reversal in the life to come. Incidentally, the reader of the Greek Testament should not always insist on the purposive aim in all the ἵνα clauses, for very often the writers made no clear distinction between purpose and result, confusing purpose with common sequence. Similarly when Jesus said: "If any one would be first, he must be last of all and servant of all" (Mark 9:35), he was not offering the first place as the consciously chosen goal to be achieved by humility—such self-centered humility would not be humility at all. How far Jesus' teaching was from self-seeking reward appears in the paradox: "Whoever would save his life will lose it; and whoever loses his life for my sake and the gospel's will save it" (Mark 8:35). Other goals and causes come first: "Seek first his kingdom and his righteousness, and all these things shall be yours as well" (Matt. 6:33).

Discussion of Jesus' reward ethics should include the following considerations: (a) the reward is of the same character as the principle, action, or service enjoined; (b) the reward can be understood as the necessary consequence of the way of life Jesus taught; life moves on to these outcomes and results, and God can be counted on to preserve the moral and spiritual order; (c) the rewards are included in the salvation offered as the gift of God to all men who will respond in faith; (d) the goal to which Jesus directed men is not self-aggrandizement, but self-forgetful service in God's kingdom, which is ours, not by merit, but by the grace of God.

In the consideration of rewards we can see the sharpest difference between the Synoptic gospels and the Fourth Gospel. Eternal life in the Fourth Gospel rests on belief, but this life is not a reward of the future after death—death for the believer is no more —eternal life is a present possession which the Son communicates. Faith and its outcome have been telescoped in this eternal life, which the believer now enjoys. Relics of the older eschatological scheme persist in reference to the judgment and the resurrection. Jesus says he goes to prepare a place for his disciples; the Counselor will come as compensation for Jesus' departure. But the future reward becomes a present possession in fellowship with the Father and the Son.

4. In the letters of Paul. Paul's great theme is that God in Christ freely justifies the believer and that he thereupon enters into the privileges of the new life in Christ. In this new state the believer enjoys the gifts of the Spirit in reward and victory in the moral struggle. Ideally the man in Christ has ceased from sin, and the law of commandments has no more power over him.

However, Paul just as persistently asserts man's responsibility for his actions and his accountability before the judgment seat of God or Christ: "We shall all stand before the judgment seat of God" (Rom. 14:10; cf. II Cor. 5:10). This judgment is individualized and particularized in Rom. 2:6-8: "He will render to every man according to his works: to those who by patience in well-doing seek for glory and honor and immortality, he will give eternal life; but for those who are factious and do not obey the truth, but obey wickedness, there will be wrath and fury"

(see also Gal. 6:7-8). In this judgment there will be gradations of punishment (Col. 3:25) or rewards (II Cor. 5:10; Eph. 6:8). Paul warns his readers that a so-called believer could be rejected (I Cor. 6:9-11).

At a few points Paul refers to reward in this life (II Cor. 9:6 ff; Eph. 6:2 ff; Phil. 4:17-19). But in general he finds that in this life there are only pain and hardship, and he projects the rewards for the Christian into the future at the Judgment or in the coming kingdom. The great reward will be the possession of eternal life (Gal. 6:8), which is also considered as participation in the kingdom of God. (The figure of the athletic contest, with its prize, is a familiar one in Paul's letters—e.g., I Cor. 9:23-27; Phil. 3:13 ff.) In the kingdom each individual will receive his award in proportion to his record on earth.

This apparent contradiction between justification by faith and the recompense principle has been much discussed. Both doctrines are clearly represented in Paul's thinking, and he does not seem to be aware of a contradiction. A certain adjustment of thinking does appear in Rom. 6:23: "The wages of sin is death, but the *free gift* of God is eternal life in Christ Jesus our Lord." But Paul as a Jew would naturally think in terms of human accountability before God, with the consequent rewards and punishments. The fact is that the teaching of justification by faith is properly set against the background of God's judgment of man, and it derives its meaning from that judgment. Human accountability is basic to the order of life for all men, but Paul sees the Christian entering on a new order of life in the Spirit where victory over sin is assured and where judgment will not bring the wrath of God but final vindication.

In the Pastoral letters that have been credited to Paul, there are frequent references to good works and their rewards (I Tim. 6:18-19; II Tim. 4:6-8). Eternal life is a prize to be won.

5. In the rest of the NT. In the Letter to the Hebrews we hear of the promise of rest (4:1), into which men should strive to enter. God is aware of the good deeds of the believer, who should seek through faith and patient endurance to inherit the promises (6:10-12). Christ has offered the perfect sacrifice for the sin of man, and yet the believer could fall away and finally face the fearful prospect of judgment and fire (3:12; 10:26-31). For the believer who confidently endures, there will be a reward (10:35; μισθαποδοσία). The author of Hebrews cites as an example Moses, who looked to a reward (11:26). Even Jesus "for the joy that was set before him endured the cross" (12:2).

The Letter of James deals vigorously with the idea of man's accountability before the whole law on the basis of his deeds. "Faith by itself, if it has no works, is dead" (2:17). The doer of righteousness will be blessed in this life (1:25), and his endurance of trial will be rewarded by the possession of strong, complete character. But all men face the imminence of judgment. The crown of life is promised to the man of tested faith, but evil men can anticipate only misery in the life to come (5:1-6).

The author of I Peter confidently looks forward to the Christian hope at the revelation of Jesus Christ. Faithful men suffer trial now, but then they will enter their inheritance and receive the crown of glory.

Instead of underscoring reward, he says in 1:9: "As the outcome [τέλος] of your faith you obtain the salvation of your souls." For all men there is the prospect of judgment, with a dire end for those who disobey the gospel of God. Yet there are many exhortations and injunctions without any reference to reward. For the slave in his suffering it is enough to have the approval of God.

The book of Revelation was written for the vindication of those who suffer now but who will have a share in the heavenly Jerusalem. In the seven letters at the beginning the portion of the faithful is described as the tree of life, the crown of life, the hidden manna, etc. The series of seven seals, trumpets, and bowls deal with the disasters coming upon the wicked, and part of the reward for the saints seems to be to gloat over the wicked in their suffering (18:20). The judgment of God brings wrath upon the wicked, but to the saints there will be exemption from hunger, thirst, sorrow, and suffering. God will reward them with rest, "for their deeds follow them" (14:13). And they will reign with Christ.

Bibliography. G. F. Moore, *Judaism* (1927); M. S. Enslin, *The Ethics of Paul* (1930); F. V. Filson, *St. Paul's Conception of Recompense* (1931); K. E. Kirk, *The Vision of God* (1931); J. Weiss, *The History of Primitive Christianity* (1914; English trans., 1937); E. F. Scott, *The Nature of the Early Church* (1941); M. Burrows, *An Outline of Biblical Theology* (1946); P. Ramsey, *Basic Christian Ethics* (1952). P. E. DAVIES

REZEPH rē'zĕf [רֶצֶף; Assyrian-Babylonian *Raṣappa*]. A town mentioned with Gozan (Assyrian Guzana, modern Ras-el-'Ain) and Harran in the message of Sennacherib's commander to Hezekiah (II Kings 19: 12; Isa. 37:12) as an example of cities long ago captured by the Assyrians and not delivered by their own local gods. Reseph was located near the W end of Jebel Singar and had in 701 B.C., when Sennacherib's commander referred to it, been in Assyrian hands for a century or so, for it is known to have been an Assyrian provincial capital at least since Adad-nirari III (810-782). Most probably it was incorporated as an integral part of Assyria by Shalmaneser III after his campaign in that region in 838. Harran and Gozan, mentioned with it, seem to have been incorporated under Adad-nirari III.

Bibliography. E. Forrer, *Die Provinzeinteilung des Assyrischen Reiches* (1920), p. 16. T. JACOBSEN

REZIA. KJV form of RIZIA.

REZIN rē'zĭn [רְצִין; LXX B 'Ρασειν *in* Isa. 7; Aq., Symm., Theod., 'Ραειν *in* Isa. 8; MT *doubtless has vocalized improperly the* Canaanite *expression of the name* (rasyôn); *cf.* LXX 'Ραασσών *in* II Kings; *cf.* Syr. *rāṣân*; Aram. רְעִין *for* ra'yân, pleasant, agreeable, *indicated by* Akkad. *ra-ḫi-a-nu*]; DAISAN dā'sən (I Esd. 5: 31). King of Damascus (died 732 B.C.). Born at Bit-Hadara near Damascus, he became the "head of Damascus" (Isa. 7:8). In 738 B.C., like Menahem of Israel (II Kings 15:19-20) and other kings of Syria, he paid tribute to the Assyrian king, Tiglath-pileser III.

During the reign of King Ahaz of Judah, apparently because he was frustrated in an attempt to persuade Ahaz to join an alliance against Assyria, Rezin joined King Pekah of Israel in an attack on Judah with the intention of placing an Aramean on the throne of Judah (II Kings 16:5-6; Isa. 7:1, 6). Although the Arameans of Damascus extended their influence southward E of the Jordan, the assertion that Rezin displaced the Jews of Elath and colonized the place with Arameans (II Kings 16:6) may be unhistorical, resting on a confusion in spelling between "Aram" (ארם) and "Edom" (אדם), since the Edomites usually dominated that region. Rezin's attack on Jerusalem failed, but King Ahaz was terrified (Isa. 7:1-2). Despite the prophet Isaiah's advice to remain calm and trust in God because the power of the "two smoldering stumps of firebrands" was about spent (vss. 4, 7-9, 16), Ahaz sent treasures of his temple and palace as a rich bribe to persuade the Assyrian king to help Judah against Rezin and his ally Pekah (II Kings 16:7-8).

When Tiglath-pîleser III attacked in 733 B.C., Pekah of Israel was assassinated, and Hoshea, the nominee of the Assyrian king, was installed as king of Israel (II Kings 15:29-30). Rezin briefly resisted, then fled "like an antelope" to Damascus, where he was besieged like a "caged bird," according to the Assyrian annals. Unable to take Damascus at once, the Assyrian turned against the Arabs, Tyrians, and Philistines who had been the allies of Damascus and might be expected to send assistance against the Assyrians. The gardens and parks that surrounded Damascus were destroyed; and 591 towns near the city, including Rezin's birthplace, Bit-Hadara, were laid waste. In 732 B.C., Damascus was captured, and many of its inhabitants were exiled. Rezin was executed (II Kings 16:9). Schrader claims that Rawlinson found an Akkadian record of the slaying of Rezin but that the slab was left in Asia and subsequently disappeared. After the fall of the city, the kingdom of Damascus lost its independence entirely and was made into an Assyrian province.

The name Rezin appears again in the postexilic period in the listing of the "sons of Rezin" among the temple servants (*see* NETHINIM) that formed part of the postexilic community (Ezra 2:48; Neh. 7:50).

Rezin is not to be confused with an earlier Aramean, REZON (רְזוֹן), who was contemporary with Solomon (I Kings 11:23-25).

Bibliography. E. Schrader, *Cuneiform Inscriptions and the OT* (1885-88), I, 257; E. G. Kraeling, *Aram and Israel* (1918); M. Thilo, *In welchem Jahre geschah die sogenannte syrisch-efraemitische Invasion* (1918); B. Landsberger, *Sam'al* (1948), pp. 66-67, note 169; J. B. Pritchard, ed., *ANET* (2nd ed., 1955), p. 283; M. F. Unger, *Israel and the Aramaeans of Damascus* (1957), pp. 95-101, 175-78. R. A. BOWMAN

REZON rē'zən [רְזוֹן, prince] (I Kings 11:23). An Aramean leader who was an adversary of Solomon. Rezon began his career in the service of Hadadezer, but left him, probably after the defeat of the Aramean coalition by David, to become the captain of an independent company of marauders. When Israelite control over Damascus weakened during the reign of Solomon, Rezon seized the city and made it the center of a new and powerful Aramean state. Probably he is to be identified with Hezion, grandfather of Ben-hadad I (I Kings 15:18).

Bibliography. M. F. Unger, *Israel and the Arameans of Damascus* (1957), pp. 54-58.   R. W. CORNEY

RHEGIUM rē'jĭ əm [τὸ 'Ρήγιον] (Acts 28:13). A town in S Italy where Paul stopped on the way to Rome; the modern Reggio or Reggio Calabria.

Rhegium is on the Strait of Messina, which here separates Italy and Sicily by a width of *ca.* seven miles. It appeared to the ancients that Sicily had been "rent" (from ῥήγνυμι) from the continent by earthquake; hence this town was called Rhegium. This was the explanation given by Aeschylus (Fragment 230); but others preferred to derive the name from *regium,* the Latin word for "royal" (Strabo VI.258).

According to Strabo (VI.257), Rhegium was first settled by Chalcidians, together with some Messenians from the Peloponnesus, the latter being the people who settled Messina across the strait. The foundation of Rhegium probably took place in the latter part of the eighth century B.C. *Ca.* 494 B.C., contemporary with Gelon of SYRACUSE, Anaxilas was tyrant of the city (Herodotus VI.23; VII.165).

In 427 B.C., Athenian forces undertook to seize Sicily, and Rhegium provided them a base and contributed ships (Diodorus XII.54). In 415 B.C., however, when the Athenians were moving against Syracuse, where they were soon to suffer disaster, Rhegium held back from active alliance (Diodorus XIII.3). Soon afterward, the city resisted the rise of Dionysius the Elder in Syracuse, and warfare ensued, the result of which was the demolition of Rhegium by Dionysius in 387 B.C. (Strabo VI.258). Dionysius the Younger, who ruled Syracuse 367-343 B.C., rebuilt Rhegium and called it Phoebia, in honor of Phoebus (Apollo), whose son he claimed to be.

In 280 B.C., Pyrrhus, king of Epirus, invaded Italy, and Rhegium, fearing both him and also the Carthaginians, who dominated the sea, requested a garrison from the Romans. Four thousand men were placed in the city under command of Decius, but after a time the protectors, seeing the favorable situation and great wealth of the city, massacred or expelled the citizens and took it for themselves. In 271 B.C. the evildoers were punished and Rhegium restored to its own citizens (Polybius I.7).

In the Punic Wars, Rhegium was almost taken by Hannibal (Polybius IX.7), but maintained its independence and remained loyal to Rome (Livy XXIII.xxx.9). After the earthquake of 91 B.C., Rhegium was in want of population, but Augustus Caesar settled some of the men of his expeditionary forces there, and at the beginning of the first century A.D. the city was fairly populous (Strabo VI.258-59). Under Augustus it took the name of Rhegium Julium (Ptolemy Geography III.1).

Bibliography. Philipp, "Regium," *Pauly-Wissowa,* Zweite Reihe, I (1914), cols. 487-502.   J. FINEGAN

RHEIMS VERSION rēmz. A term applied to the NT section of the official Roman Catholic English Bible, the DOUAY VERSION. Cardinal William Allen encouraged the professors of canon law at Douay in 1578 to prepare the version, and Gregory Martin carried the translation through to its completion (1582). It was begun at the English College at Douay, France, but because of political upheavals the work was moved to Rheims, where the NT was completed; hence the term "Rheims Version." It was based on the "authenticall Latin"—i.e., the Vulg.

See also VERSIONS, ENGLISH, § 6.   J. R. BRANTON

RHESA rē'sə ['Ρησά] (Luke 3:27). An ancestor of Jesus.

RHETORIC AND ORATORY. In English these two terms are clearly distinguished: rhetoric is the art of composition by which language, whether written or spoken, becomes descriptive, interpretative, or persuasive; while oratory is the art of effective public speech. The latter term may even describe the contents of the speech as well as its manner. Both rhetoric and oratory presuppose grammar, whose rules are fundamental to both composition and delivery, and indispensable for a proper understanding of both the written and the spoken word.

In both Greek and Latin, however, the terms were identical: ῥητορικὴ τέχνη (Latin *ars rhetorica*) meant the art of the orator or public speaker, a fact which reminds us that "oral" literature long preceded written, and that the art of public speaking antedated the writing of books. The origins of Greek rhetoric (from which Latin was derived) go back at least to Homer, for his heroes are constantly engaged in public speaking and debate. Like all Greek art, poetry, music, architecture, sculpture, and painting, like Greek history and Greek religion, Greek rhetoric was a natural expression of the Hellenic spirit. Those who engaged readily in public debate obviously desired to win either public approval or a case in court. The keen dialogue so common in the tragedies and in Aristophanes was more than clever banter—as so often in Shakespeare. The debaters meant to score.

1. Teachers of rhetoric. The earliest teachers of the art of rhetoric were two Sicilians, Corax and his pupil Tisias, who came to Athens in the fifth century B.C. and opened a school. Tisias became in turn the teacher of the Sophist Gorgias and the orators Isocrates and Lysias. The main object of the teaching was to train orators for effective pleading in the law courts. Hence they studied not only the principles of delivery ("elocution") but also those of logic and persuasion, and also the details of traditional Greek law. They cultivated the art of plausibility—many of the cases defended by the orators depended upon purely circumstantial evidence and "probability" (τὸ εἰκός). Gorgias, who is forever pictured in Plato's *Dialogues,* introduced the emphasis on emotional appeal, thus producing a type of oratory (the decorative, ceremonial, or "epideictic") quite distinct from the forensic or legal type, hitherto in use. Later experts, like Thrasymachus, Protagoras, and Theodorus of Byzantium, developed the rules by which rhetorical effects could be gained and prose made as captivating as poetry—which to a Greek was irresistible. The criticisms which Plato leveled against the Sophists as a group and against all "sophistic" in argumentation, logic, and presuppositions, especially the absence of fixed moral principles, resulted in the meaning which ever since has been attached to "sophistry." These men cared nothing for either moral presuppositions or moral consequences, but only for winning cases in court, or for political advantage in the struggles for social control in the disturbed Hellenic and international world of their time. The tragic case of Andocides (see his *On the Mysteries*) illustrates the attitude. He had grown up in Athens, an idle, irresponsible young man about town; now, years later, he finds himself on trial for his life as a desecrator of the Eleusinian rites and of the sacred household stones, the *hermae*. His behavior and his arguments reflect the shallowness of his Sophistic education.

Isocrates was an exception: he viewed rhetoric as a kind of philosophy, a training for the good life, and a means of sharing in the privileges and responsibilities of citizenship. But the older view—viz., that rhetoric was a conjurer's bag of tricks for amazing the hearers or persuading the court (often including a jury of five hundred)—prevailed, and in time came to be looked upon as the crown and climax of education, and the proof of both its value and its validity. When the younger Pliny visited his old school, his first question was, "How are the lads doing in oratory? And how are they doing in the courts, after they get out?" Success was the test, then as now. The first teacher of all, Corax, agreed that Tisias was to pay his fee only if he won his first case in court— and had, eventually, to bring suit against his pupil. It was the first case Tisias had ever defended. Corax insisted, "If I win the case, I will receive payment by the verdict; if I lose, I claim payment under our contract." "No," replied the pupil, "if I win, I will not have to pay; if I lose, I won't pay." The court dismissed the case, with the remark, "A bad crow [κόραξ] lays bad eggs."

2. Criticism by philosophers. The criticism of Plato and the constructive work of Isocrates, Aristotle, and Theophrastus led to a higher conception of the orator and his art, which, though neglected by the ordinary lawyer and politician, was influential with the great orators and literary critics of antiquity. No one ever made a more careful study of his art than Demosthenes or Cicero. Yet even the teaching of rhetoric failed to maintain the highest level, and the fourth century saw the beginning of a florid, highly emotional, even sensuous style known as "Asianic" (Hegesias of Magnesia was the chief proponent). It resulted in the practice of the writing and delivery of "declamations" in the schools, all based upon strict rules and following artificial examples, not the works of the great orators, but flowery "models of eloquence" written by the teachers. The so-called *Progymnasmata*, or preparatory exercises, of the first century B.C. provided a drill in various kinds of writing—fables, histories, elegies, pleas—but not political speeches, as these were not encouraged under the Hellenistic monarchies or, later, under the Roman Empire. This artificial kind of rhetoric continued to receive the criticism of philosophers and those literary men who stood for the classical tradition in education (the "Atticists" of 50 B.C. and later). The high standards of the past were recalled, and the sober influence of Roman political thought and speech had a good and growing influence. The so-called "canon" or standard list of the Attic orators was drawn up, Demosthenes heading the list. The Roman Cicero, who studied in Greek schools (Athens and Rhodes) and seriously cultivated the art all his life, is probably the best example of the fusion of Greek and Latin oratory.

3. Influence on the NT. It is not surprising that attempts have been made to trace the influence of classical standards of rhetoric and oratory in the NT. (The OT and the Apoc. are exempt from this influence, as basically Semitic literature, though traces of Greek style have been found in II Maccabees and elsewhere.) The best example is the Letter to the Hebrews, which Hermann Von Soden outlined as an example of Greek oratory. It has a *proemium* (1:1-4: 13), designed to win good will; a *diēgēsis*, or statement of the case (4:14-6:20), designed to win favor; an *apodeixis*, or demonstration (7:1-10:18), designed to complete the persuasion of the hearers; and an epilogue (10:19-13:21). But the author's development of the theme is far more direct and his cumulative logic far more powerful: (*a*) Christ is superior to angels (1:1-2:18); (*b*) he is superior to Moses (3:1-4:13); (*c*) he is the supreme High Priest, superior to Aaron, like Melchizedek; and his ministry is in the heavenly, not the earthly, sanctuary, where his offering of himself is final and forever effective (4:14-10:18). The rest of the homily or "epistle" is hortatory and practical (10:19-13:25). The most one can say is that the work is the finest example of Greek prose in the NT, and that Greek rhetorical standards (not rules or models) have influenced the writer, who was certainly a man of superior education.

Other examples that have been chosen to illustrate classical influence include Paul's speech before the Areopagus (Acts 17:22-31), which begins with an attempt to win favor (the usual *captatio benevolentiae*) and continues with a proclamation of the gospel of revelation and coming judgment; obviously Paul's speech (the account in Acts is barely an outline) was not modeled on the Greek orators, but ended like a Hebrew prophet's grave warning of doom. Another is the speech of Stephen in Acts 7; but this is like dozens of other brief surveys of Hebrew-Jewish history, of which we have examples in the Bible and elsewhere, even in the "historical" psalms. There is nothing "Greek" or "oratorical" about it. On the other hand, the forensic speeches in Acts, Paul's defense on the steps of the Castle of Antonia (Acts 22: 1-21; it was interrupted in vs. 22 and never finished), or the one before the Sanhedrin (23:1-9; scarcely a speech, for it had only begun when it ended in a wrangle); or Tertullus' professional opening of the prosecution (24:2-8) and Paul's reply (vss. 10-21); or the climactic speech before Festus, Agrippa, and Bernice (26:1-23)—these speeches all reflect the skill of the author of Acts, but do not show any of the explicit organization or composition which was typical of Greek and Latin oratory. Any educated man on trial for his life would follow this procedure, trying to make contact with his judge or judges, to establish common ground, and to show that his words and actions had been reasonable and right. Paul was no Greek rhetorician reciting a speech carefully memorized in advance. His style was far more like that of the popular Cynic-Stoic "diatribe," the speech in the market place which these street preachers of ethical and political philosophy used in their efforts to improve mankind. He positively rejected the artful literary and rhetorical devices of the "wise in this age" (see his defense in I Cor. 1-4; II Cor. 10-13). The same is true of other parts of the NT—e.g., the discourses of Jesus in Matthew and John, or the logic of Romans or Galatians, the dramatic denouement of Revelation, or the gnomic "wisdom" sayings of James. There are echoes of oratory and of orators here and there, but no studied imitation. The early Christians were not, for the most part, taken from the learned or the politically dominant class; and their religion, their sacred scriptures, their worship, their very vocabulary, were Semitic, biblical, Greco-Jewish. Their "models," so far as they had any, for scripture exposition or exhortation were not Greek or Roman, but biblical—i.e., they were taken from or inspired by the LXX, the earliest Bible of the early Christians. It was in a later period, in the second century and afterward, that the artificial and florid popular rhetoric of the time began to influence Christian preaching and writing, especially sermons.

See also EDUCATION IN THE NT.

Bibliography. See the editions of the Greek and Roman orators in the Loeb Classical Library, where the original text and an English translation are on opposite pages, with good introductions and notes. Also Aristotle *Rhetoric;* Demetrius *On Style;* Longinus; and Quintilian, in the Loeb series.

See also: L. von Spengel, *Rhetores Graeci* (1853-56); R. C. Jebb, *The Attic Orators* (1876); F. Blass, *Die Attische Beredsamkeit* (1887-98); G. A. Saintsbury, *History of Criticism* (1900); E. Norden, *Die Antike Kunstprosa* (1909); R. Bultmann, *Der Stil der Paulinischer Predigt und die Kynisch-Stoische Diatribe* (1910); P. Wendland, *Die Hellenistisch-römische Kultur in ihren Beziehungen zu Judentum und Christentum* (1912); J. F. Dobson, *The Greek Orators* (1919); C. S. Baldwin, *Ancient Rhetoric and Poetic* (1924); R. W. Livingstone, *The Mission of Greece* (1928); E. Hatch, *The Influence of Greek Ideas on Christianity* (new ed., 1957). F. C. GRANT

RHODA rō'də ['Ρόδη, rose] (Acts 12:13). Apparently a slave in the house of Mary, the mother of John Mark; it is possible, however, that she was simply a member of the household or one of the company assembled and praying. She joyfully recognized Peter's voice outside the door, after his release from imprisonment. She was probably a Christian.

Tradition claims this house as the place where the Last Supper was held, and it was perhaps the headquarters of the Jerusalem church.

B. H. THROCKMORTON, JR.

RHODES rōdz ['Ρόδος]. A Greek island and city in the SE of the Aegean Sea (Ezek. 27:15; Acts 21:1). Rhodes is the largest island in the Aegean after Crete, measuring some forty-two by seventeen miles, and separated from Asia Minor by a channel *ca.* ten miles wide. Its central part is mountainous, its coasts have good harbors, and in summertime it has safe anchorage on the E side. As the natural station for Aegean traffic en route to the Orient, Rhodes early developed into a prosperous trade center.

The earliest inhabitants were of unknown Bronze Age origins. Minoan merchants founded a colony on the NW coast near Ialysos and were followed by Greek settlers who lived in Mycenean sites all over the island. Later colonization was by Dorian Greeks, who developed the cities of Ialysos, Lindos, and Kameiros into leading trade centers. Colonies were sent abroad, and oriental trade went especially through the port of Lindos.

Liberated from the Persians, Rhodes became part of the Delian League (477 B.C.). In 408 the three old cities united in the foundation of a new capital, the city of Rhodes on the NE point of the island near the sanctuary of the sun-god Helios.

The new Rhodian state became a leading power in the Greek world. Its capital was designed along modern lines of town-planning, following the system of Hippodamus of Miletus. Its opportunities increased in Hellenistic times, when the trade to Alexandria,

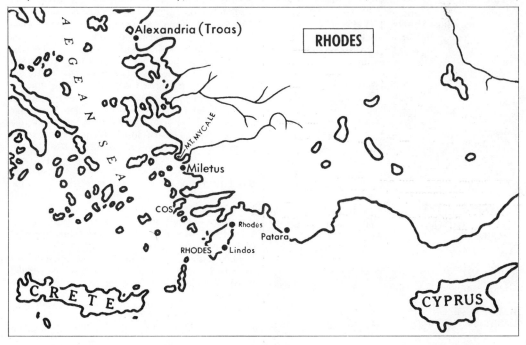

to Cyprus, and to Phoenicia was going through the port of Rhodes. The famous siege by Demetrius in 305-304 B.C., successfully withstood, led to the erection of the Colossus of Rhodes, a bronze statue of Helios 105 feet high at the entrance to the harbor. This statue, one of the seven wonders of the world, was demolished by an earthquake *ca.* 227 B.C. The general earthquake damage was soon repaired, but the Colossus was left lying near its base.

Rhodes with its large fleet was a supporter of the Roman cause and a protector of Greek shipping against the Mediterranean pirates. Its fortunes turned in 167 B.C., when the Romans declared Delos a free port and reduced the Rhodian possessions.

The city of Rhodes afterward was of greater cultural than commercial importance. The philosopher Panetius (*ca.* 185-109 B.C.), head of the Stoa, came from Rhodes (Lindos). Posidonius (135-50 B.C.), although a Syrian, made Rhodes his home and founded a school there which was attended by many Romans.

A disaster befell Rhodes in 43 B.C., when Cassius mercilessly stripped the city of its material wealth. All gold and silver was collected from private and public resources. Many Rhodian works of art were transported to Rome on this occasion.

In imperial times Rhodes was a favorite resort for the Romans, whether travelers or exiles. Tiberius spent eight years on the island. In the first century A.D. the city, its monuments, and its artistic wealth were still a source of admiration to visitors (cf. Strabo XIV.652; Pliny Nat. Hist. XXXIV.36).

The archaeology of the ancient city of Rhodes is insufficiently known because of the extensive rebuilding of the town. Its most famous monuments date from the period when the Knights of Saint John founded a state on the island (1309-1522). Lindos and Kameiros are better preserved, as are the cemeteries of Ialysos.

Paul's ship on its way from Miletus and Cos to Patara stopped at Rhodes in accordance with ancient navigational routine (Acts 21:1). The LXX reading of "Rhodians" in Gen. 10:4; I Chr. 1:7 for "Dodanim" seems a late substitution based on familiarity with Rhodian sea power. "Rhodes" in Ezek. 27:15 (based on the LXX) is historically possible as a reference to Rhodian trade with Tyre.

Bibliography. D. Magie, *Roman Rule in Asia Minor* (1950), pp. 71-73; R. Matton, *Rhodes* (1954).　　M. J. MELLINK

RHODOCUS rŏd′ə kəs ['Ρόδοκος] (II Macc. 13:21). A traitor of the Jewish army of Judas Maccabeus. He communicated secret information about Beth-zur, the citadel which Judas had strengthened. He was discovered, found guilty, and imprisoned.

RIBAI rī′bī [רִיבַי] (II Sam. 23:29; I Chr. 11:31). The father of Ittai, who was a member of the company of the Davidic Mighty Men known as the "Thirty" and was from Gibeah of the Benjaminites.

RIBBAND. Archaic form of "ribbon," used by the KJV to translate פְּתִיל (RSV CORD) in Num. 15:38.

RIBLAH rĭb′lə [רִבְלָה; Arab. *Ribla*]; KJV DIB-LATH dĭb′lăth in Ezek. 6:14. An ancient Syrian

town situated S of the Lake of Hums in the vicinity of KADESH ON THE ORONTES. Its geographical position is where, in ancient times, the military highways to Egypt and Mesopotamia crossed.

Riblah is known from the time when the kingdom of Judah had to fight its uneven contest for its life, first against the Egyptians and then against the Babylonians. After the death of King Josiah in the battle at Megiddo against Pharaoh Neco in 609 B.C., his younger son Jehoahaz was made king—his eldest son Eliakim, being pro-Egyptian, had lost the confidence of the people. Neco did not approve the election of Jehoahaz. According to II Kings 23:33, Neco imprisoned him at Riblah and made his brother Eliakim king, and as Jehoiakim the latter ascended the throne. He was more or less an Egyptian vassal and had to pay tribute to Neco.

After the defeat of Neco at Carchemish in 606, Nebuchadrezzar of Babylon took over the hegemony in the Near East (cf. II Kings 24:7: "The king of Egypt did not come again out of his land"); so Jehoiakim became tributary to him. After a few years, however, he refused to pay the tribute; and because of this, Nebuchadrezzar pushed into Palestine with his armies. Jehoiakim died suddenly, and his son Jehoiachin (Jeconiah), eighteen years of age, became king after him. His foreign policy was along the same line his father had followed. This led to the capture of Jerusalem in 597. In the shadow of the Babylonian, the last king of Jerusalem, Mattaniah —or Zedekiah, as he called himself as king—ruled over the country until 586, when Nebuchadrezzar put an end to the Jerusalemite kingdom.

At first Jeremiah the prophet seems to have been successful in persuading the king not to undertake anything which might annoy Nebuchadrezzar. But after the death of Neco, Zedekiah was unable to master the situation, and the war party predominated. Because of this development, Nebuchadrezzar immediately came to the scene and encamped at Riblah; so the town was the place from which Nebuchadrezzar determined the fate of the last king of Jerusalem, when he destroyed the city. Zedekiah tried to escape, but at Jericho he was overtaken and then brought before the king of Babylon to Riblah: "[They] passed sentence upon him. They slew the sons of Zedekiah before his eyes, and put out the eyes of Zedekiah, and bound him in fetters, and took him to Babylon" (II Kings 25:5-7; cf. Jer. 52).

In one of his inscriptions, found at Wadi Brissa, Nebuchadrezzar alludes to his stay at Riblah.

A. HALDAR

RICHES. *See* WEALTH.

*RIDDLE [חִידָה; *verb* חוּד, to propound a riddle; Aram. אֲחִידָה (Dan. 5:12)]. A literary form involving a matching of wits: the challenger hints at a concealed meaning which the contestant is to discover.

The classic biblical example of the riddle is Samson's in Judg. 14, and the setting may be typical. At his wedding feast, as a game with stakes Samson proposes his riddle (vs. 14):

> Out of the eater came something to eat.
> Out of the strong came something sweet.

Within the Samson narrative the riddle alludes to the honey which Samson had found in the carcass of the lion. So exceptional was his finding of honey thus, that his guests were at a disadvantage and had to be told. It was Samson's wife who gave them the answer (vs. 18*a*):

> What is sweeter than honey?
> What is stronger than a lion?

Samson surmised their source and accused them, and in his accusation used the riddle style (vs. 18*b*):

> If you had not plowed with my heifer,
> you would not have found out my riddle.

Now it is quite possible that both the riddle and what here passes for its answer are really older than the Samson narrative and themselves prompted the story of the slain lion and the swarm of bees, rather than the reverse. Actually the answer, in question form, is itself a riddle the solution of which is not hard to find: it is love which is "sweeter than honey" and "stronger than a lion." If this is correct, then Samson's riddle must have had another answer, and this, too, can be found out. One may eat too much at a celebration and overly indulge in sweet wine, and the results may be drastic, so that from the eater his food may come forth and from even the strong the sweet. This not uncommon experience may have been the original solution to Samson's riddle, and both riddles may well have been old folk sayings before they were woven into the Samson narrative, sayings quite appropriate at a wedding feast.

The propounder of a riddle is sly. He has observed an amusing analogy, and he is both revealing and keeping it for himself as one who peeps at a treasure held between cupped hands. The riddle is a form of humor and akin to the figures: fable, allegory, parable, simile. The numerical proverb, which has a Canaanite (Ugaritic) ancestry, may be a derivative of the still more ancient riddle form.

But the riddle was not merely a game. It was a test of wisdom. Solomon's renown rested largely on his skill at solving riddles: "When the queen of Sheba heard of the fame of Solomon . . . , she came to test him with hard questions [lit., 'riddles']. . . . And Solomon answered all her questions." And the queen of Sheba saw "all the wisdom of Solomon" (I Kings 10:1-5; II Chr. 9:1-4). Another great king, who shall arise "at the latter end of the indignation," is characterized as a "king of bold countenance, one who understands riddles" (Dan. 8:19, 23). It is the wise who deal in riddles, and skill in understanding them is wisdom (Prov. 1:5-6; cf. Ps. 49:1-4—H 49:2-5). Riddles were, moreover, a deposit of tradition and lore, "dark sayings from of old, . . . that our fathers have told us. . . . The glorious deeds of the Lord" (Ps. 78:1-4). And the riddle was a literary form employed for communication even by the prophets. Ezekiel called his song of eagles and a cedar tree a "riddle and . . . an allegory" (17:2; cf. 20:49—H 21:5). Many prophetic utterances which are not thus specifically designated riddles have the same form and probably developed from the riddle type of literary expression. Isaiah's "song of the vineyard" is a good example—the riddle propounded in detail in 5:1-6 is solved in vs. 7:

> For the vineyard of the Lord of hosts
> is the house of Israel.

(Cf. also Ezek. 15.)

In fact, the riddle was one of the media by which God was thought to reveal himself. Of Daniel it was said: "An excellent spirit,.knowledge, and understanding to interpret dreams, explain riddles, and solve problems were found in this Daniel" (5:12), and so endowed, he interpreted the cryptic revelation written on the wall. Tradition distinguished Moses as one prophet with whom God communicated directly, "mouth to mouth, clearly, and not in dark speech" (חידות; Num. 12:8; cf. Jer. 23:28). That this was Moses' distinctiveness implies the normality of divine communication through "dark speech." There was probably more to the riddle than appears on the surface. It seems to be a heritage from the age of mythology, when men sought to get power over gods and nature by uncovering their carefully guarded secrets.

Bibliography. H. Torczyner, "The Riddle in the Bible," *HUCA,* I (1924), 125-49; A. Bentzen, *Introduction to the OT,* I (1952), 177-78.   S. H. Blank

RIDGE OF JUDEA jōō dē′ə [ὁ πρίων τῆς Ἰουδαίας] (Jth. 3:9). A geographical term of obscure meaning. It has been suggested that πρίων ("saw") was a translation of משׂור ("saw"), which was misread for מישׁור ("plain"). But the Plain of Esdraelon is called עֵמֶק, not מישׁור. The OL took the genitive πρίονος for a proper name. The words are lacking in the Vulg.   P. Winter

RIE. KJV translation of כסמת in Exod. 9:32; Isa. 28:25 (KJV FITCHES in Ezek. 4:9). This is now believed to be SPELT (so RSV) or possibly emmer (*see* FLORA § A1*b*), both of which are kinds of wheat. Rye, *Secale cereale* L., was not indigenous to Bible lands, but is a grain common to cold climates.   J. C. Trever

RIGHT HAND. The side or direction, as well as the hand itself; often used in a figurative sense (ימין; δεξιός; "right, right hand," with or without the corresponding words for Hand; cf. Josh. 1:7; Judg. 5:26; II Sam. 2:21; Matt. 5:30; Luke 1:11). For ימין, "south," *see* BENJAMIN 1; TEMAN.

In common with most cultures, the OT and the NT assign special significance to the right hand as the hand of strength (Job 40:14; Ps. 45:4; cf. Luke 6:6; Acts 3:7), the hand of blessing and unique capacity (Gen. 48:14; Exod. 29:20; Ezek. 21:22; cf. Matt. 25:33; 27:29; Rev. 1:16-17); while the left hand is unusually deceptive and deadly (Judg. 3:15, 21; 20:16; II Sam. 20:9-10). As the symbol of total strength, the right hand is the side on which a man is threatened (Job 30:12; Ps. 91:7) or accused (Zech. 3:1), and where his deliverer must stand to protect him (Pss. 16:8; 109:31; 121:5; cf. Acts 2:25). The place at one's right is the seat of dignity and honor (I Kings 2:19; Ps. 45:9).

The "right hand of God" is the OT metaphor of his mighty power by which he creates (Isa. 48:13), wages war, and delivers his people (Deut. 33:2; Ps. 89:13; cf. Exod. 15:6-12; Pss. 17:7; 18:35; 139:10). Its withdrawal means judgment and ill fortune (Ps.

74:11; cf. 77:10; Lam. 2:3), and he may even use it against his own people (Lam. 2:4; but cf. Isa. 62:8).

Ps. 110:1 is the normative passage for the "right hand of God" in the NT. Originally it may have alluded quite concretely to the enthronement of Israel's king in the throne room immediately south (ימין) of the temple—i.e., at the "right hand" (the place of ultimate honor) of Yahweh conceived as present in the sanctuary. This psalm is quoted or echoed many times in the NT as a virtually constant element of the apostolic witness to the exalted Christ, reigning in honor and power at the right hand of God (Mark 12:36; Acts 2:34-35; Heb. 1:13; cf. Acts 5:31; Rom. 8:34; Eph. 1:20; Col. 3:1; Heb. 8:1; 10:12; 12:2; I Pet. 3:22). For Matt. 22:41 ff, *see bibliography.*

Bibliography. S. Johnson, Exegesis of Matthew, *IB,* VII (1951), 526-27; H. G. Liddell and R. Scott, *Greek-English Lexicon* (9th ed., 1951), pp. 240, 740; C. H. Dodd, *According to the Scriptures* (1952), pp. 34-35, 108, 120.   J. A. WHARTON

RIGHTEOUSNESS IN THE OT. Righteousness as it is understood in the OT is a thoroughly Hebraic concept, foreign to the Western mind and at variance with the common understanding of the term. The failure to comprehend its meaning is perhaps most responsible for the view of OT religion as "legalistic" and as far removed from the graciousness of the NT. However, within the past one hundred years, thanks largely to the efforts of German scholars (*see bibliography*), this important motif of biblical faith has been clarified.

The concept deserves some negative definitions. In the OT it is not behavior in accordance with an ethical, legal, psychological, religious, or spiritual norm. It is not conduct which is dictated by either human or divine nature, no matter how undefiled. It is not an action appropriate to the attainment of a specific goal. It is not an impartial ministry to one's fellow men. It is not equivalent to giving every man his just due.

Rather, righteousness is in the OT the fulfilment of the demands of a relationship, whether that relationship be with men or with God. Each man is set within a multitude of relationships: king with people, judge with complainants, priests with worshipers, common man with family, tribesman with community, community with resident alien and poor, all with God. And each of these relationships brings with it specific demands, the fulfilment of which constitutes righteousness. The demands may differ from relationship to relationship; righteousness in one situation may be unrighteousness in another. Further, there is no norm of righteousness outside the relationship itself. When God or man fulfils the conditions imposed upon him by a relationship, he is, in OT terms, righteous.

1. Terminology of righteousness. *a. In the OT.* The terms for righteousness are consistently צדק (masculine) and צדקה (feminine), there being no significant difference in the employment of the masculine and feminine nouns. The verb is צדק, "to be righteous," "to be just," "to be in the right," with the *hiph'il* form הצדיק translated "to justify," "to declare righteous." צדיק is the adjective "just," "righteous."

b. In the LXX. The LXX most frequently translates צדיק with δίκαιος (without exception in the Psalms); צדק (verb) with δικαιοῦν; צדק (noun) with δικαιοσύνη (less frequently with δίκαιος); and צדקה with δικαιοσύνη. Thus the LXX usage little illumines the meaning of צדק. Exceptions to this are formed by the use of ἄμεμπτος, "blameless," "faultless" (Job 22:3), and καθαρός εἶναι, "to be clean, pure" (Job 4:17), for צדק (verb); ἀληθής, "true" (Isa. 41:26), πιστός, "faithful,"."true" (Job 17:9), and εὐσεβής, "reverent," "pious," "religious" (Prov. 12:12; Isa. 24:16; 26:7), for צדיק; ἐλεημοσύνη, "pity," "compassion" (Ps. 35:24—G 34:24), and κρίσις, "judgment," "decision" (Isa. 11:4; 51:7), for צדק (noun); ἐλεημοσύνη (Deut. 24:5—G 23:5; Isa. 1:27; etc.), ἔλεος, "pity," "mercy," "compassion" (Isa. 56:1; Ezek. 18: 19, 21), εὐφροσύνη, "joy," "gladness" (Isa. 61:10), and κρίμα, "judgment," "sentence," "lawsuit" (Isa. 9: 6), for צדקה. However, from the LXX usage we learn little about the basic meaning of צדק.

c. Etymology of צדק. The etymology of צדק also little illumines its meaning. Using the Arabic, most lexicons and commentators have defined the basic meaning of the root צדק as "straightness," "hardness," "firmness"; and discussion of the subject has centered around the question of which meaning is to be preferred—"straightness" usually is favored. However, it has been increasingly recognized that none of these meanings can explain the variety of ways in which the stem is employed. E.g., the RSV translates (צדק(ה sometimes with "vindication" (Ps. 103:6; Jer. 51:10), "deliverance" (Isa. 46:12; Mic. 7:9), "saving deeds" (I Sam. 12:7), "saving help" (Ps. 40:10), "righteous help" (Ps. 71:24), or "salvation" (Job 33:26), sometimes with "equity" (II Sam. 8:15) or "right" (Isa. 5:23), sometimes with "uprightness" (Jer. 4:2) or "truth" (Ps. 52:3), sometimes with "triumph" (Judg. 5:11) or "victory" (Ps. 48:10; Isa. 41:2), even with "prosperity" (Prov. 8:18). How can the basic meaning of "straightness" help to explain such a variety of usage? Obviously the only course is to examine the use of צדק in each of its contexts, to note its synonyms and antonyms, and to try to find a common factor governing its use. When this is done, it becomes clear that צדק is a concept of relationship and that he who is righteous has fulfilled the demands laid upon him by the relationship in which he stands.

2. Righteousness in social relations. There were demands in Israel which were imposed by the family relationship. Thus Tamar, who had played the harlot, was more righteous than Judah because she fulfilled these demands, while Judah did not (Gen. 38: 26). Again, David was righteous because he refused to slay Saul, with whom he stood in a covenant relation (I Sam. 24:17; 26:23), and he condemned those who murdered Ish-bosheth, Saul's son (II Sam. 4:11). But after the downfall of Saul's house, Mephibosheth had no right to expect kindness from the new king (II Sam. 19:28). The demands of righteousness changed with the relationship.

Generally, the righteous man in Israel was the man who preserved the peace and wholeness of the community, because it was he who fulfilled the demands of communal living. Like Job, he was a blessing to his contemporaries, and thus צדק is sometimes correlated with "mercy" (Hos. 2:19). He cared for the poor, the fatherless, the widow (Job 29:12-15; 31:16-19; cf. Deut. 24:13; Prov. 29:7), even defending their cause in the law court (Job 29:16; 31:21; cf. Prov. 31:9). He gave liberally (Ps. 37:21, 25-26; Prov. 21:26), providing also for the wayfarer and guest (Job 31:31-32), counting righteousness better than any wealth (Job 31:24-25; Ps. 37:16; Prov. 16: 8). He was a good steward of his land (Job 31:38-40) and work animals (Prov. 12:10), and his servants were treated humanely (Job 31:13). He lived at peace with his neighbors (Job 31:1-12), wishing them only good (Job 31:29-30; cf. 29:24). When he was in authority, his people rejoiced (Prov. 29:2), and he exalted the nation (Prov. 14:34). He was a joy to his family (Prov. 23:24), his path was like the dawn (Prov. 4:18), and his very memory itself was a blessing (Prov. 10:7). When it went well with him, the whole city rejoiced over his welfare (Prov. 11:10). He was an immovable factor for good (Prov. 10:25, 30; 12:3, 12), who knew blessing (Prov. 10:6; Isa. 3:10) and long life (Ps. 92:12; Prov. 10:16; 11:19; 12:28), posterity (Ps. 37:37-38) and prosperity (Prov. 13:21, 22, 25; 15:6), the fulfilment of his desires (Prov. 10: 24, 28; 11:23), and deliverance from trouble (Prov. 11:8; 12:21; 24:16). He lived in peace and prosperity, because he upheld the peace and prosperity—in short, the physical and psychical wholeness—of his community by fulfilling the demands of the communal and covenant relationship (cf. Ps. 15:2-5; Isa. 33:15). For this reason צדק sometimes stands parallel with שלם (Isa. 48:18; 60:17; cf. Pss. 72:3, 7; 85:10; *see* PEACE). For this reason it can be translated "prosperity" (Prov. 8:18). And for this reason, too, its meaning can be "truth" (Ps. 52:3; cf. Prov. 12:17), for right speech upholds the covenant relationships existing within a community (Ps. 15:2-4; Prov. 8:8; 10:11, 20, 31; 16:13; Isa. 59:4; cf. 45:19); it is righteousness.

It is understandable then that in most of the passages listed above and in most others the OT sets over against the צדיק the רשע, the evildoer, the wicked, not because the latter violates a norm of ethical action existing within the community, but because he destroys the community itself by failing to fulfil the demands of the community relationship. The רשע is he who exercises force and falsehood, who ignores the duties which kinship and covenant lay upon him, who tramples the rights of others under foot. His sin is not murder, theft, falsehood, evil in itself, but evil which is committed against one

with whom he stands in relationship. Murder of one outside the covenant may be considered righteous (Judg. 5:11 [see vs. 26]; II Kings 10:9); murder of a covenant partner is always unrighteous.

3. Righteousness as a forensic concept. These facts help to explain the forensic use of צדק. The term is often used as a correlate to שפט, "to judge," or משפט, "judgment" (Deut. 25:1; I Kings 8:32; Pss. 9:4; 33:5; 143:2; Prov. 1:3; Isa. 1:21; Jer. 11:20; Amos 5:7; etc.), and the verb appears almost exclusively in a forensic context (e.g., Job 33:32; Isa. 43: 9). (Some hold that its use is only forensic.) Thus one might conclude that righteousness is a legal concept.

In one sense this is true. He who is righteous is he who is judged to be in the right (Exod. 23:7; Deut. 25:1). But again, the demands of communal relationship are determinative. That which is right in a legal sense is that which fulfils the demands of the community relationship, and the sole function of the judge is to maintain the community, to restore right to those from whom it has been taken (II Sam. 15:4; Ps. 82:3). Thus righteousness as a forensic concept is not an impartial decision between two parties, based on a legal norm, such as is known in Western law, but protecting, restoring, helping righteousness, which helps those who have had their right taken from them in the communal relationship to regain it. Righteousness is the fulfilment of the communal demands, and righteous judgments are those which restore community (Exod. 23:7-8; Deut. 1:16; 16:18, 20; Ps. 82:3; Prov. 17:15; 18:5; 24: 24). Thus the constant plea of the prophets is for righteousness in the gate, for a restoration of the foundations of the communal life (Isa. 5:23; 29:21; 59:4; 14; Jer. 22:3, 15; Amos 5:12; Hab. 1:4; cf. Ps. 72:2; Prov. 31:9). In such contexts there is no difference between ethical and legal standards. They are one, both equivalent to the demands of community.

Not only was it the function of the judge to uphold the community in Israel, however. This was one of the main duties of the king. He, too, was responsible for protecting and restoring the right (cf. Hos. 13: 10). This was his covenant duty, to preserve righteousness, and in so doing, he himself was righteous (II Sam. 8:15 = I Chr. 18:14; I Kings 10:9 = II Chr. 9:8; Ps. 45:6-7; Prov. 16:12; cf. II Sam. 23:3-4; Isa. 16:5). Thus in Ps. 72 we have a picture of the peace and prosperity wrought by a king who judges righteously, and Jeremiah's appeal to the despotic Jehoiakim is for justice and righteousness (Jer. 22:3, 15). Further, when the Messiah comes, his kingdom will prosper through righteous judgments (Isa. 9:7; 11:3*b*-5; Jer. 23:5-6; 33:14-16; cf. Isa. 16:5) which will defend the people against all evil (Isa. 32:1-8).

The צדיק then in Israel was he who fulfilled the demands of the relationships in which he stood, and thus צדק often stands parallel with זכה, "to be clean" (Job 15:14); with תם, "blameless" (Job 9:20); or with נקי, "innocent" (Exod. 23:7). The צדיק did right, as right was defined by the relationship.

4. Righteousness as a covenant concept. Because Israel stood in a covenant relationship with Yahweh, righteousness was also a religious concept. To be righteous, Israel had to fulfil the demands of her relationship with Yahweh, and this included obedience to the law of the Lord (Ps. 1). But here we must avoid two misunderstandings:

First, not all righteousness had a religious basis. E.g., in Gen. 38:26 there is really no thought of the religious relation to Yahweh. An act on the social plane is not righteous because it at the same time satisfies a demand of the law, though this of course often happened. It is righteous because it fulfils the demands of a social relationship. The relationship is always the determinative factor.

Secondly, we must observe that Israel's relationship to Yahweh was not dependent on her righteousness. Israel's righteousness consisted in the fulfilment of the demands of her relationship with Yahweh, but righteous or unrighteous, she still stood in relationship. The covenant relation was prior to all law and all demands. Yahweh had chosen Israel. That was the basic fact of her existence. All else followed after. (This is very important in view of § 9 *below*.)

Further, Yahweh's station within the covenant relationship was that of Lord. He was Lord of the covenant, its initiator, its defender, its preserver. He and he alone upheld it. Only he could break it. Israel could reject her God and thereby bring his wrath upon her, but she could not escape her relationship with God. The relationship might be one of wrath, which led to Israel's destruction, but nevertheless it was a relationship. God initiated the covenant. He alone could nullify it (cf. Ps. 89:28-37).

Thus in the OT there is nothing legalistic about the relation of Israel with her God. It is a relation based, not on law, but on grace, on Yahweh's loving choice of a few oppressed Semitic tribes in Egypt to be his people, his peculiar treasure (Exod. 19:4-5). And because this is true, it is a relationship received primarily with joy and thanksgiving by the people Israel. Celebration, joyfulness, praise—these are the primary notes of Hebrew faith, as the Psalter attests.

Within this relationship of grace the law is given as a guide by God to his covenant people. Its purpose is to make Israel holy as Yahweh is holy (Lev. 19), and the revelation of the law to Israel is also an act of God's grace, for of all the people of the earth, Yahweh chooses to guide Israel. Thus Israel loves the law (Ps. 40:8); it is her meditation day and night (Ps. 1:2), a gift more to be desired than gold and sweeter than honey (Ps. 19:10).

But the law is meaningless outside the relationship, outside the covenant. He who receives Yahweh's election in faith, who places his life under Yahweh's lordship, also follows the law, for the law is God's guidance within the covenantal relationship. For him who lacks such faith, for him who stands outside the relationship, the law is worthless. The context of the law is the holiness, the lordship, of Yahweh. The law protects this lordship. It provides for the sole worship of Yahweh (Exod. 20:3-7; Lev. 20:8; Deut. 6:13-15); it forbids sin, because sin dishonors God (Lev. 18:1-5; 19:2; 22:2, 32; Deut. 7:6; etc.). He who does not in faith accept the context of the law, the lordship of Yahweh, cannot be righteous before Yahweh, though he fulfil all other precepts of the law. Faith is the presupposition of the law, and works without such faith are useless. Obedience to the law does not make a man righteous.

The relationship to Yahweh, the relationship of faith, is primary.

This is evidenced in the law itself. Were righteousness to depend solely on the fulfilment of the law, any sin would shut off the sinner from God's grace. But such is not the case. The law itself provides for a day of atonement for Israel's sins (Lev. 16), and there is constant provision for restoration of right relationship with God and with the community. One thing, however, is unpardonable: the rejection of God's law "with a high hand" (Num. 15:30), rebellion against his lordship, lack of repentance— in short, faithlessness. The failure to acknowledge Yahweh's lordship in humility and repentance, the failure to accept in faith his provisions for restoration to communion with him, the failure to acknowledge in his law his gracious leading of his people—these are unforgivable, the OT equivalents of the sin against the Holy Spirit, for they constitute a faithless rejection of Yahweh's grace, and the law without faith is useless. The fulfilment of the law does not constitute righteousness, but he who is righteous fulfils the law because he accepts it in faith as God's gracious guidance of him. Neither works nor works accompanied by faith make for righteousness, but rather only faith, which is manifested in works. Faith is the fulfilment of the relationship to Yahweh and is thereby righteousness (Gen. 15:6; Hab. 2:4). *See* § 8 *below*.

5. **Yahweh as righteous.** Throughout the OT it is proclaimed that Yahweh is righteous (II Chr. 12:6; Neh. 9:8; Pss. 7:9; 103:17; 111:3; 116:5; Jer. 9: 24; Dan. 9:14; Zeph. 3:5; Zech. 8:8; etc.), and not once, not even in the book of Job, is he held to be unrighteous. Indeed, righteousness is one of the major motifs in the witness to God's person, as he reveals himself in his actions. But Yahweh's righteousness consists, not in action consonant with his inner nature, certainly not in works which conform to some norm or standard of right outside and above him. Nor is Yahweh's righteousness, as it is commonly thought, a distributive justice which rewards the good and punishes the evil, as good and evil are defined in the law. Yahweh's righteousness is his fulfilment of the demands of the relationship which exists between him and his people Israel, his fulfilment of the covenant which he has made with his chosen nation. We might therefore note that only he who stood within the covenant could speak of Yahweh as righteous.

Now in the OT the righteousness of Yahweh is most often portrayed in forensic terms, and it is usually in his function as judge of the earth that he is pictured as righteous (Pss. 9:4, 8; 50:6; 96:13; 99:4; Isa. 5:16; 58:2; Jer. 11:20). So as with the human judge, he upholds the right. He helps those who have had their right taken from them to regain it. He does this on behalf of Israel. He protects and restores her right. This is Yahweh's righteousness. This is his fulfilment of his relationship with her. The purpose of his judgment is the preservation of community, of his covenant with Israel (Pss. 89; 94; *cf.* § 3 *above*).

Thus Israel constantly appeals to Yahweh's righteousness for deliverance from trouble (Pss. 31:1; 88 [note vs. 12]; 143:11), from enemies (Pss. 5:8; 143:1), from the wicked (Pss. 36; 71:2); for vindication of her cause before her foes (Ps. 35:24). Yahweh is righteous insofar as he heeds these pleas. His righteousness consists in his intervention for his people, in his deliverance of Zion (Ps. 48; צדק is here translated "victory" [vs. 10]), in his salvation of his chosen nation (I Sam. 12:7-12; צדקה is here translated "saving deeds" [vs. 7]). So Jeremiah waits confidently for Yahweh's righteous vengeance on his enemies (Jer. 11:20; cf. Ps. 71:24). So exiled Israel hears the promise of victory over her oppressors (Isa. 54:14-17). So her people should call on their God in the day of trouble (Ps. 50:15). For Yahweh maintains the cause of the afflicted and needy (Ps. 140:12). His decision is for his people over against all other peoples of the world (Isa. 43:1-7; 54:11-17).

In short, Yahweh's righteous judgments are *saving* judgments (Ps. 36:6), and Deutero-Isaiah can therefore speak of Yahweh as a "righteous God and a Savior" (Isa. 45:21). Yahweh's salvation of Israel is his righteousness, his fulfilment of his covenant with her. This is confirmed by the fact that צדק is often translated "saving deeds" (I Sam. 12:7), "deliverance" (Pss. 22:31; 51:14; 65:5; Isa. 46:12-13; 51:1, 5-6, 8), or "vindication" (Isa. 62:1-2), and that it is often placed in parallelism with "salvation" (Ps. 40:10; 51:14; Isa. 61:10). As judge of the earth, Yahweh decides for his people, delivering and saving them. This is his righteousness. And this is Israel's "triumph" (Judg. 5:11; Isa. 45:25), God's "victory" (Ps. 48:10).

6. The afflicted as righteous. God's saving judgments on behalf of his covenant people bring us to a second definition of the צדיק in the OT. Not only is he righteous who fulfils the demands of a relationship, but also he who has had his right taken away from him within such a relationship. This view forms part of the backdrop of § 5 *above*, and of course again the thinking is largely forensic. The judge intervenes to restore the right to him who has been deprived of it. He decides in favor of the deprived one, of him who is needy. He declares the oppressed or afflicted one to be צדיק, to be in the right.

Thus from the time of the enslavement in Egypt, Israel has been in the right over against her enemies (Ps. 103:6), and God has been her champion, putting down her foes (Ps. 68). Over against her enemies Israel is always righteous. Her righteousness consists in the fact that she is oppressed and deprived of her right (cf. Isa. 54:14; but *see* §§ 7-8 *below*).

However, the same is true within the community of Israel itself. Those who are righteous are those who are victims of oppressors (Ps. 14:5), of enemies (Ps. 69:28), of wicked rulers (Ps. 94:21), of violent men (Ps. 140:13). And their hope is the Lord, for he it is who restores their right, who saves those who are bowed down (Pss. 116:6; 146:8). His judgments are always favorable (Ps. 146:7-9) for the oppressed and the hungry, the prisoner and the blind, the widow and the fatherless, the alien and the poor (Amos 2:6). We thus see why the words for the poor and needy, דל, רש, עני, אביון, are placed parallel with צדיק. They are righteous before God. Yahweh restores their right. Thus again Yahweh's righteous judgments are saving judgments.

7. Righteousness and sinfulness. These facts seem strange, however, when we consider that often in the OT he who is called צדיק is at the same time sinful. Indeed, the OT has no hesitation in portraying Israel's persistent sin before her God, and the confession of the psalmist is that "no man living is righteous before thee" (Ps. 143:2). Yet this same psalmist appeals to Yahweh's righteousness, to Yahweh's saving judgments (vss. 1, 11) for deliverance from his adversaries (vss. 3, 9, 12). He is not alone in this appeal (cf. Ps. 51:14), and other psalmists witness to God's salvation of them despite their sinfulness (Pss. 40:10 [cf. vs. 12]; 65:5 [cf. vs. 3]; 103:17 [cf. vss. 3, 10-12]). They unhesitatingly number themselves among the righteous (Pss. 32:11 [cf. vss. 1-5]; 69:28 [cf. vs. 5]). Indeed, Yahweh's righteousness is sometimes the source of forgiveness (Pss. 51:14; 103:11-12, 17).

Despite such facts, we need not dwell too long on the point that throughout the OT Yahweh condemns evil. His righteous judgments restore the right to those from whom it has been taken, but they also put down the wicked. Those judgments which bring salvation for Israel at the same time bring destruction upon her foes (Ps. 58:10-11; Isa. 11:4; 61:1-2; Hab. 3:12-13; Mal. 4; cf. Hag. 2:22-23; Zeph. 2:8 ff; Zech. 14). The Lord has a day of vengeance on behalf of his people (Isa. 34:8), and his righteousness and vengeance go hand in hand (Isa. 59:16-19; cf. Pss. 7:11-13; 129:4; Isa. 45:25; Jer. 11:20). When Yahweh saves, he also recompenses (Isa. 35:4; 40:10; 62:11). And the same is true within Israel. In his work of restoring the right, Yahweh punishes the sinner (Exod. 23:7; I Kings 8:32 = II Chr. 6:23; Ps. 51:4; Lam. 1:18). There are two sides to his righteousness: salvation and condemnation; deliverance and punishment.

However—and this is an important point—Yahweh's righteousness is never solely an act of condemnation or punishment. There is no verse in the OT in which Yahweh's righteousness is equated with his vengeance on the sinner, and not even Isa. 5:16 or 10:22 should be understood in such a manner. Because his righteousness is his restoration of the right to him from whom it has been taken, it at the same time includes punishment of the evildoer; but the punishment is an integral part of the restoration. Only because Yahweh saves does he condemn. His righteousness is first and foremost saving. He is a "righteous God and a Savior."

It seems clear, however, that that which gives the oppressed Israel or the afflicted person within Israel his ground for hope in Yahweh's deliverance is not his sinlessness. His righteousness consists not in ethical or moral blamelessness. He often openly confesses his transgressions. Further, though he is righteous over against his enemy, his righteousness consists not solely in this fact. One cannot simply identify the poor and oppressed with the צדיקים in the OT. Yahweh, who punishes the wicked, does not overlook the sin of the afflicted because the latter is bowed down. No, the poor and oppressed have a further righteousness which is all-important before Yahweh, and this righteousness is their faith, their fulfilment of their relationship with Yahweh.

8. Righteousness and faith. Wherever you find an appeal to Yahweh's righteousness or salvation or deliverance in the OT, you find the attitude of faith. It takes many forms, but it is characterized primarily by a complete dependence on God. Those who are faithful are those who wait for him (Isa. 33:2; Mic. 7:7-9), who hope in him (Pss. 69:6; 71:5, 14; 146:5), who seek after him (Ps. 69:6, 32), who trust in him (Pss. 71:5; 143:8); cf. Ps. 33. They are those who know Yahweh (Ps. 36:10), who fear him (Ps. 103:11, 13, 17), who love his name (Ps. 69:36). He is their fortress. In a world in which they are oppressed and needy, the Lord is their sole refuge (Pss. 5:7-12; 14:6; 31; 36:7; 52:6-7; 71:1-3; 94:22; 118:8-9; 143:9). Thus, as opposed to those who trample them underfoot, as over against those who trust in riches (Ps. 52:7), they trust in Yahweh, crying to him in their distress (Pss. 35; 88: 116; 140), bowing before his judgments (Pss. 94:12; 118:18), acknowledging their sin (Pss. 32; 51), offering to him a broken spirit and a contrite heart (Ps. 51:17). Yahweh is their only hope and sure salvation. They turn to him in faith.

Such faith is the righteousness of the afflicted, Israel's fulfilment of her relationship with Yahweh. Not because she is oppressed does Yahweh forgive Israel's sin, not because she is needy does he deliver his sinful nation, but because she repents of her sin and throws herself on his mercy. Israel's religion is her righteousness over against all the peoples of the earth. Thus Isaiah writes:

> Zion shall be redeemed by justice,
>> and those in her who repent, by righteousness.
> But rebels and sinners shall be destroyed together,
>> and those who forsake the Lord shall be consumed
>>> (1:27-28).

Righteousness here is the saving judgment of Yahweh which intervenes on behalf of the repentant. It is a thought similar to that set forth by the psalmist:

> The salvation of the righteous is from the Lord;
>> he is their refuge in the time of trouble.
> The Lord helps them and delivers them;
>> he delivers them from the wicked, and saves them,
>> *because they take refuge in him* (37:39-40).

This is Israel's righteousness, that she repents and takes refuge in her God, that she trusts in him, that she is faithful. Her faith is the fulfilment of her relationship with Yahweh (*cf.* § 4b above).

In this sense Israel calls *herself* righteous (Ps. 37: 39), not because she is ethically or morally blameless (Pss. 32:11; 69:28), not because she thinks she merits God's salvation, but because she believes, because God is her refuge (Pss. 5:12; 14:5; 31:18; 33:1; 36:10; 52:6; 94:15, 21; 118:15, 20). She knows her faith to be her one sure foundation:

> Love the Lord, all you his saints!
>> The Lord preserves the faithful,
>> but abundantly requites him who acts haughtily.
> Be strong, and let your heart take courage,
>> all you who wait for the Lord!
>>> (Ps. 31:23-24).

9. Justification and the covenant. Israel's confidence that her faith in Yahweh will lead to her salvation rests, however, on one further fact: God's choice of her and his covenant with her. As has

been pointed out (*see* § 5 *above*), Yahweh's righteousness consists in his salvation of his chosen people. By preserving his people, Yahweh fulfils the demands of the covenant relation. And the covenant relation is prior to Israel's righteousness. Righteous or unrighteous, believing or unbelieving, she stands in a covenant relationship with her God, a relationship which can be nullified by Yahweh alone. Until Yahweh rejects her (cf. Hosea), Israel stands under the shadow of Yahweh's saving arm (Isa. 40:10-11; 52:10).

This is the message primarily of Deutero-Isaiah, and here we are brought to a third meaning of righteousness in the OT. Not only is he צדיק who fulfils the demands of the relationship in which he stands, and not only is he righteous who has been deprived of his right within such relationship. He also is righteous who has righteousness imputed to him. In this sense, righteousness is justification by God, a "being-declared-righteous" by the Lord of the covenant (cf. Isa. 60:21).

The gift of such righteousness is announced in the great eschatological witness of Deutero-Isaiah. Israel is a sinful folk, sunk in idolatry (Isa. 44:9-20; 50:11), full of transgressions (53:5-6, 8, 11), who is unable to confess her God rightly (48:1), who has burdened him with her evil (43:24), who has refused to call upon her savior (43:22). For this reason Yahweh has given her into the hand of her captors (42:24-25; 47:6) to suffer double punishment for her sins (40:1), to drink the full measure of the wrath of the Lord (51:17-20), to be refined in the furnace of affliction (48:9-11), to be bruised (53:10) and forsaken (54:7-8). And in the middle of her exile Israel thinks herself to be lost, her way hidden from the Lord (40:27), her people rejected forever (49:14; 50:1). In short, Israel has forgotten the covenant. She has forgotten her relationship to Yahweh, because Yahweh is wrathful toward her for her sin.

Deutero-Isaiah's glad message is that the covenant still stands. Yahweh cannot forget his child (49:15), or, in another figure, he has not divorced his wife Israel (50:1; cf. 54:5-6). His relationship with his people endures. His word, his promise, his agreement, stands forever (40:8; 55:11). This is Israel's hope, that the covenant is yet good. If she seeks deliverance, let her look to the rock from which she was hewn, to the promise to Abraham and the covenant with the fathers (51:1-8). There is Israel's hope. For the word of the Lord stands forever.

Without such word, Israel has no hope, for she has no righteousness of her own. She does not do the right (48:18-19; *cf.* §§ 2-4 *above*), and for this she has been punished. True, because she is oppressed by her captors, she can plead God's saving help. She is righteous in that her right has been taken from her (*cf.* § 6 *above;* 41:17-20; 42:14-22; 43:14; 45:14; 46:1-2; 47 [note vs. 6]; 48:14; 49:23-26; 51: 13-14, 21-23; 54:14-17). But even this Israel does not do. She does not call on Yahweh (43:22), because she does not believe. It is as if she were blind and deaf (42:18-20; 43:8). She is stubborn of heart (46: 12) and stiff-necked (48:4), rebelling against God from her birth (48:8). She will not trust him or rely upon him (50:10), for she thinks he has no power to deliver (50:2). She has no faith and therefore ultimately no righteousness of her own.

Deutero-Isaiah's exhortation to such a people is to believe, to cast themselves on the Lord: "Have you not known? Have you not heard?" he cries (40: 28), ". . . they who wait for the LORD shall renew their strength" (40:31), and his entire witness to God's power and majesty is intended to inspire trust in the saving help of Israel's God (e.g., 40:12-31). Yahweh will save Israel, for Yahweh has chosen her (41:8-10; 43:1-7; 44:1-5, 22; 46:3-4; cf. 49:8-13). His covenant stands, despite Israel's unrighteousness. God intervenes for the cause of his afflicted folk before all the peoples of the earth (51:22). He will deliver her from exile (43:14); he will forgive her sin (43:25; 44:22; cf. 54:9); he will care for her as a shepherd cares for his flock (40:11).

In short, Yahweh will fulfil the demands of the covenant relationship. He will maintain his righteousness. He will do so by justifying Israel, by imputing righteousness to her who has no righteousness, by delivering her who has no right to be delivered (46:12-13). And this will be Israel's righteousness before all the world, that God helps her (50:9; cf. 52:13–53:12). In God's righteousness, Israel will be established (54:14); in his salvation of her, she shall be declared צדיק (45:24-25). Despite her failure to do the right, despite her lack of faith, Yahweh, the creator, the king, the judge of all the earth, will decide in her favor. Deutero-Isaiah's plea is that Israel but faithfully accept such deliverance. It is no wonder that the tone of the Second Isaiah is one of joy and celebration (cf. 52:7-10).

Righteousness in the OT, then, is the fulfilment of the demands of a relationship, whether with men or with God. And though man's righteousness fails, God's endures. He intervenes on behalf of his own, saving them from bondage, forgiving their sin, declaring them to be in the right before himself and all the world. The connection with the NT message of salvation in Jesus Christ seems obvious, for "while we were yet sinners Christ died for us" (Rom. 5:8). *See* RIGHTEOUSNESS IN THE NT.

Bibliography. H. Schultz, "Die Lehre von der Gerechtigkeit aus dem Glauben im alten und neuen Bunde," *Jahrbücher für Deutsche Theologie*, 70 (1862), 510-72. E. Kautzsch, *Ueber die Derivate des Stammes* צדק *im alttestamentlichen Sprachgebrauch* (1881). H. Schultz, *AT Theologie* (1889), pp. 420-24, 540-43. H. Cremer, *Die paulinische Rechtfertigungslehre im Zusammenhange ihrer geschichtlichen Voraussetzungen* (1899); *Biblischtheologisches Wörterbuch des NT Griechisch* (11th ed., 1923). J. Pedersen, *Israel, Its Life and Culture* (4 vols.; 1926). K. H. Fahlgren, *Sedaka, nahestehende und entgegengesetzte Begriffe im AT* (1932). W. Eichrodt, *Theologie des ATs*, Teil I (4th ed., 1950). G. von Rad, " 'Gerechtigkeit' und 'Leben' in der Kultsprache der Psalmen," *Festschrift Alfred Bertholet zum 80. Geburtstag* (1950), pp. 418-37; "Die Anrechnung des Glaubens zur Gerechtigkeit," *TLZ*, Nummer 3, 76. Jahrgang (1951), pp. 130-31; *Theologie des ATs*, I (1957), 368-80.

E. R. ACHTEMEIER

RIGHTEOUSNESS IN JEWISH LITERATURE, 200 B.C.-A.D. 100 [צדק, צדקה; δικαιοσύνη; Lat. *justitia*].

The Jewish literature of the period 200 B.C.-A.D. 100 comprises the canonical books Ecclesiastes, Daniel, and Esther in the OT, the apocryphal and pseudepigraphic books of the OT, the writings of Philo and Josephus, and, perhaps, also the recently discovered DEAD SEA SCROLLS. Of frequent occurrence in the translations of this literature are the English words "righteous," "righteously," and "righteousness," and their equivalents in other languages. These terms are generic for all forms of approved conduct. Naturally they are also terms of ardent commendation. Commendation, as distinguished from any clear reference, seems to be, at times, their only function (Wisd. Sol. 1:15; Ecclus. 26:28; Enoch 81:4, 7; 94:3).

1. The qualities constituting righteousness
   a. The positive side of righteousness
   b. The negative side of righteousness
   c. Righteousness in occupations
   d. Righteousness and prayer
   e. Unique meanings of "righteousness"
   f. Righteousness and severity
2. Benign aspects of the divine implications of righteousness
   a. Divine attributes of righteousness
   b. God's righteousness toward Israel
   c. God's bestowal of righteousness upon man
   d. The righteousness of God's commands
   e. God's favors to righteous people
   f. Material benefits
   g. Spiritual benefits
   h. Remission of sin
   i. The righteous at the last judgment
   j. The righteous at the resurrection
   k. The righteous at the time of the Messiah
   l. The righteous in Paradise
3. Austere aspects of the divine implications of righteousness
   a. Israel's sins and punishments
   b. Punishments of the high and mighty
   c. The last judgment
   d. Hell
4. The righteousness of man
   a. Man's lack of righteousness
   b. Man's righteousness
   c. Righteous individuals
   d. Righteous Israel
   e. Partisan sense of "righteous"
   f. Righteousness taught
   g. The troubles of the righteous
   h. The triumphs of the righteous
5. Nonconformist views
   a. The naturalistic approach
   b. Sharp distinction between righteousness and unrighteousness
   c. Doubts
Bibliography

1. The qualities constituting righteousness. This literature, of course, leaves us in no doubt regarding the nature of righteousness. Righteousness is understood to consist in the possession of certain qualities and in the absence of certain other qualities.

a. The positive side of righteousness. Righteousness is identified or closely associated with such traits as mercy (II Esd. 8:36; Tob. 3:2; Ecclus. 44:10; II Macc. 1:24; Enoch 39:5; 71:3; Slavonic Enoch 42: 11); beneficence (II Macc. 1:24; Sibylline Oracles III.234); benevolence (Tob. 1:3; 14:11; Ecclus. 7:10;

40:24); goodness of heart (Tob. 14:11; Wisd. Sol. 1:1); love of neighbor (Jub. 7:20; 20:2); compassion for the poor and weak (Asmp. Moses 11:17; Test. Benj. 4:4); gentleness (Slavonic Enoch 42:11); the capacity for giving joy (Enoch 104:12); innocence (Sus. 53); forbearance (Slavonic Enoch 9:1; Syriac Apocal. Bar. 24:2; Manual of Discipline); humility (IV Ezra 8:49); compunction about one's short-comings (Pss. Sol. 3:7; 13:5); cultivation of one's soul (Philo *On Husbandry* V); truthfulness (Tob. 1:3; 3:2; 4:6; Wisd. Sol. 5:6; I Macc. 7:18; IV Ezra 7:114; Aristeas 306; Enoch 10:16; 62:3; Slavonic Enoch 42:11; Pss. Sol. 3:6; Test. Dan 1:3; Apocal. Abraham 27:18; Thanksgiving Hymns II.2-19; IV.40); justice (Aristeas 147; Jub. 7:34), especially toward the needy, as in Isa. 11:5 (Formulary of Blessings), and including fairness even toward the ill-behaved (Ecclus. 42:2); chastity (II Esd. 6:32; Aristeas 152; Enoch 69:11; Jub. 7:20; 20:23; 25:1); honoring of parents (Jub. 7:20); kindness toward all one's kindred (Jub. 31:3); concord among kindred (Jub. 7:26); fidelity (Enoch 108:13; IV Ezra 7:114; Formulary of Blessings; War Scroll, referring to Isa. 11:5); integrity (1QS VIII.20–IX.6); constancy (Jub. 1:25); courage (IV Macc. 1:18); manliness (IV Macc. 1:18; 2:23); mastery over one's impulses (Aristeas 215; IV Macc. 3:1; 5:24; 7:22); poise (IV Macc. 5:24); steadfastness amid poverty and illness (Pss. Sol. 16:14 [or 15]); moderation (IV Macc. 1:18; Aristobulus 2:66); temperance (Wisd. Sol. 8:7; Aristeas 278); sobriety (Aristeas 209); appreciation of virtues in others (Test. Benj. 4:4); thoughtfulness (IV Macc. 1:18; 2:23); intelligence (IV Macc. 1:18); wisdom (Wisd. Sol. 10:13; Syriac Apocal. Bar. 66:2; Enoch 32:3; 48:1; 99:10; Sibylline Oracles III.218; 1QH II.2-19); wise discrimination (Aristeas 151). The question is raised by Philo whether righteousness and ignorance are compatible (*Questions on Genesis* on Gen. 20:4). The righteous keep their hearts open to knowledge (Manual of Discipline; 1QH II.2-19), including knowledge of God's judgments (1QS II.25–III.12) and of the things that belong to eternity (1QM XVI.11–XVII.15). They recognize the righteousness of God (Pss. Sol. 3:5). According to Philo (*Allegory of the Jewish Law* 24.78): "The righteous man, exploring the nature of exist-ences, makes the surprising find that all things are a grace of God." The righteous praise God (Pss. Sol. 15:5; Tob. 13:6, 8). They deem it a small matter to be divinely afflicted (Pss. Sol. 3:4), esteeming God's judgments as righteous even when those judg-ments are adverse to themselves (Pss. Sol. 3:3-4). They "can endure the narrow things because they hope for the wide" (IV Ezra 7:18).

b. *The negative side of righteousness.* The right-eous person is free of such traits or doings as avarice (Sibylline Oracles III.234), bloodshed (Jub. 7:23), destructiveness (Jub. 7:26), violence (Enoch 91:18-19; 102:10; Aristeas 147; Jub. 35:13), injuring others (Aristeas 168, 232), peculation (Jub. 23:21), removal of landmarks (Sibylline Oracles III.630), envy (Jub. 7:26; Test. Benj. 4:4), oppression (Sibylline Oracles III.630), and tyrannizing (Aristeas 147-48).

c. *Righteousness in occupations.* Judges, to be righteous, must practice equity (Wisd. Sol. 9:3).

Especially must they observe scruple in their dealings with widows and orphans (Slavonic Enoch 42:7, 9). They must eschew bribery (Aristeas 209; Jub. 21:4; Asmp. Moses 5:3), partiality (Jub. 21:4; Slavonic Enoch 9:1), and venality (Asmp. Moses 5:3). Simi-larly employers. In reply to his question: "How could he build in such a way that his structures would endure after him?" King Ptolemy is coun-seled: "If he never dismissed any of those who wrought such works and never compelled others to minister to his needs without wages . . . for it is the deeds that are wrought in righteousness that abide continually" (Aristeas 258-59). To the king's query: "Whom ought we to appoint as officers over the forces?" the reply is: "Those who excel in courage and righteousness and those who are more anxious about the safety of their men than to gain a victory by risking their lives through rashness" (Aristeas 281). Also involved in righteous conduct is the ob-servance of the RELEASE every fifth year (Jub. 7:37) —not, as in Deut. 15, every seventh year. *See* OCCUPATIONS.

d. *Righteousness and prayer.* Characteristic of the righteous is recourse to prayer (Enoch 47:2; 97:3, 5; 99:3). At the last judgment, the righteous, imitat-ing such as Abraham, Moses, and David, who prayed for others, will intercede for the ungodly (II Esd. 7:41; IV Ezra 7:102, 111). The righteous suppli-cate also in heaven (Enoch 39:5). Every day they beseech the Almighty in behalf of the damned in hell (Apocal. Sophonias 17:5). One of these writings alleges that the righteous in heaven had to be placed far from the underworld in order to be kept from hearing the groans of the wicked and imploring God's mercy upon them (Elijah 9:2). *See* PRAYER.

e. *Unique meanings of "righteousness."* Seldom is the word "righteousness" associated with matters of ritual conformity (Jub. 20:2) such as burnt offer-ings (Ecclus. 7:31; cf. Deut. 33:19), tithes and pil-grimages (Tob. 1:6-7), and the avoidance of for-bidden foods (Tob. 1:10-12) and of idolatry (Bar. 6:73). Sometimes Hebrew idiom permits the word "righeousness" to mean "credit for *being* righteous" (Bar. 2:17). Sometimes it means "good fortune" (Ecclus. 44:10), and sometimes "divine punishment" (Ecclus. 16:22). But the most frequent of these spe-cial usages lies in the application of the term to the practice of almsgiving (Tob. 1:3; 12:8; 14:11; Ecclus. 40:24; Slavonic Enoch 9:1; IV Ezra 7:35). Such is the sense of the word "righteousness" in Dan. 4:24, where it is thus translated by the LXX. Similarly the Greek text of Ecclesiasticus says ἐλεημοσύνη ("alms-giving"), wherever the GENIZAH Hebrew says צדקה ("righteousness"). Later, in the rabbinic writings, the Hebrew word for "charity" is always the same as the Hebrew word for "righteousness"; just as, in English, "morality," while it signifies commendable conduct of all kinds, carries also the special mean-ing of probity in matters sexual. Such is, in the litera-ture we are considering, the identification of right-eousness with the giving of alms.

f. *Righteousness and severity.* Yet righteousness is, at the same time, compatible with harshness. Com-mended as an act of righteousness is the practice of burning the harlot (Jub. 20:4). We are told that the brothers Levi and Simeon wrought righteousness when they slew the Shechemites (Jub. 30:18, 23; *see* SHECHEM). God is praised as a righteous judge because Jews, who had worn amulets dedicated to a certain idol, were among those who fell in battle (II Macc. 12:41). Philo believes in righteous anger (*On Flight and Finding* 17.90; *On Dreams* I.15.91; II.1.7).

According to this literature, the righteous will praise God's justice when they will have the gratification of beholding the extermination of their foes (Pss. Sol. 4:8). Especially is this boon to occur at the last judgment (Enoch 5:6; 62:12; 95:3; 96:1; 98:12; 99:3, 6; Apocal. Elijah 41:4) and in the days of the Messiah (Jub. 23:30). The righteous are assured:

> Fear not the sinners, ye righteous;
> For again will the Lord deliver them into your hands,
> That ye may execute judgment upon them according
> to your desires (Enoch 95:3).

The sinners are told: "Know that ye shall be delivered into the hands of the righteous, and they shall cut off your necks and slay you, and have no mercy upon you" (Enoch 98:12). The righteous will remember the sins which the sinners have committed (Enoch 99:16). In order to curse the sinners, they will ascertain the names of the sinners (Enoch 5:6). Then they will have the angels place the sins of the sinners before the Most High, thus keeping God reminded (Enoch 99:3).

2. Benign aspects of the divine implications of righteousness. In various ways righteousness is associated with God. The ancient predication that God is righteous occurs in this literature countless times, often with striking turn of phrase: God is the light of righteousness (Test. Zeb. 9:8), righteous beyond reckoning (Enoch 63:3); his righteousness is unending (Manual of Discipline) and eternal (Tob. 3:2). *See* GOD, OT VIEW OF.

a. Divine attributes of righteousness. Among God's righteous attributes are his mercy (II Esd. 8:36; Jub. 31:25; IV Ezra 8:12) and compassion (Asmp. Moses 11:17; Apocal. Esd. 1:12) and the abatement of his anger (Dan. 9:16). His compassion extends even to such as have no wealth of good works (II Esd. 8:36; IV Ezra 8:32). It enfolds, in its healing, also the Gentiles (Test. Zeb. 9:8). For all "who lift not the hand against" God's judgments, there is pardon and salvation (Zadokite Fragment 9:52-53).

b. God's righteousness toward Israel. Righteous are God's works (Dan. 9:14; 1QH I.5-39; IV.40). These include God's choice and consecration of Israel (II Macc. 1:25), his covenant with Israel (Jub. 22:15), and his care for Israel (Bar. 5:9; Pss. Sol. 8:32). God will give Israel salvation when, amid the heathen, they turn to him (Jub. 1:15-16). He will save them and gather them from among the Gentiles (Test. Naph. 8:3). He will plant them in their land as a plant of righteousness that will never be uprooted (Jub. 36:6). His sanctuary will be restored in their midst (Jub. 1:17). He will disclose to them abounding peace (Jub. 1:16).

c. God's bestowal of righteousness upon man. Included in God's righteous works are his bestowal of righteousness upon human beings (Bar. 5:2, 9; Wisd. Sol. 12:16; Aristeas 280; Jub. 1:16; Manual of Dis-

cipline; 1QH II.2-19; IV.5-40; XIV.1-27; XVI.1-19) and his transformation of people's character from evil to good (Manual of Discipline). Human righteousness has God as its source (Bar. 5:9; Jub. 16:26). Man turns his thoughts to God and is thus imbued with righteousness (Wisd. Sol. 15:3; Jub. 1:20). Until the God of righteousness appears, wars will have no end (Test. Judah 22:2).

d. The righteousness of God's commands. Similarly righteous are God's commands (Ecclus. 17:14; Pss. Sol. 14:1-2; Sibylline Oracles III.630; Apocal. Abraham 31:5) and precepts (Syriac Apocal. Bar. 61:6; 1QS II.25–III.12). Consummately righteous is God's law (IV Macc. 13:24; Aristeas 131; Sibylline Oracles III.580; Aristobulus 2:66; Pseudo-Philo 11:15; Zadokite Document I.1–II.12). The minutiae of the law are, according to Aristeas, not trivial; their purport is that of fostering righteousness. God gave statutes to Moses, not apropos creeping things (Aristeas 168-69) or mice and weasels, but in order to inculcate righteousness (Aristeas 144). The birds forbidden for food are "wild and carnivorous, . . . preying upon the tame birds, seizing lambs and kids, pouncing upon human beings, alive or dead" (Aristeas 145, 147). The prohibition of such creatures "thus teaches that those for whom those laws were ordained must practice righteousness in their hearts." Similarly the Jewish practice of ritual hand washing is a token that the person has done no evil (Aristeas 306); it is a symbol of righteousness and truth. Referring to the phylacteries, one of the translators remarks: "Upon our hands a symbol is fastened showing we ought to perform every act in righteousness" (Aristeas 159).

e. God's favors to righteous people. The phrase that God is the God of the righteous (Prayer Man. 8; Joseph and Asenath 12:1) becomes meaningful in the light of the innumerable favors that God lavishes upon righteous people (Enoch 41:8; 45:6; 49:3; 58:2, 4; 94:4; Pss. Sol. 3:4). To God, the righteous are acceptable (Ecclus. 35:6; Enoch 94:1; 1QS VIII.20–IX.6). Their prayers, a delightful offering to him (Zadokite Fragment 14:1; cf. Prov. 15:8), will bring that for which they petition (Apocal. Elijah 42:1). God rejoices in the righteous (Ecclus. 35:6; Enoch 94:1; 1QS VIII.20–IX.6); blesses the righteous (Enoch 99:10; Pss. Sol. 3:14; 9:7); he is faithful to the righteous (Pss. Sol. 13:12; 14:1-2; 16:14-15), gracious to the righteous (Pss. Sol. 3:14; 13:12; Enoch 92:4), loves the righteous (Aristeas 209; Jub. 1:25), has compassion on the righteous (Pss. Sol. 2:35) and mercy on the sons of the righteous (Tob. 13:9). He rewards the righteous (Wisd. Sol. 10:17; IV Ezra 8:33), compensating them as one pays a laborer (Wisd. Sol. 2:22; Enoch 104:13; Apocal. Esd. 1:14). The angels maintain a strict record of each person's deeds (Pss. Sol. 9:6; Apocal. Sophonias 3:5; 1QH XVI.1-19). The person who sows the seed of righteousness shall reap sevenfold (Slavonic Enoch 42:11). God confers upon the righteous joy and ecstasy (Test. Adam 2:11). For the righteous, he renews the world (Apocal. Abraham 17:13).

f. Material benefits. The righteous and their works are in God's hands (Eccl. 9:1; Wisd. Sol. 3:1). God preserves their lot (Enoch 48:7). He makes plain their way (Pss. Sol. 10:3). He brings their efforts to success (Aristeas 18). They shall inherit good things (IV Ezra 7:17). They shall be happy and prosperous (Tob. 14:11; Enoch 1:8; 94:4; Sibylline Oracles III. 580). They shall acquire houses (Enoch 91:13). Tilled in righteousness, the earth will yield abundance (Enoch 10:18). Especially rewarded with good crops shall be those who, in righteousness, grant release every fifth year (Jub. 7:37). Also envisioned is success at arms. At the time of Sennacherib's invasion, King Hezekiah's righteousness was King Hezekiah's hope (Syriac Apocal. Bar. 63:3). *See* REWARD.

g. Spiritual benefits. But the gains are not exclusively material. Some are spiritual. In the name of his righteousness, God strengthens the spirit of righteous people (Enoch 41:8). He will put faithfulness in their habitation (Enoch 108:13). His wisdom, which has marvelously guided them (Wisd. Sol. 10:17), will be revealed to them (Enoch 48:7; 91:10; 104:12). To the righteous and the elect will be disclosed the mysteries of creation (Enoch 93:10; 104:12-13). In the book of Enoch, this linkage of the righteous and the elect occurs constantly. Frequent also is the nexus of the righteous and the holy. *See* REWARD.

h. Remission of sin. Not all authors agree with those among them who hold that the righteous are guilty of no sins for which to repent (Pss. Sol. 9:7) or for which to be reproved (Apocal. Shadrach 15:2). The righteous do, at times, sin; but, among the manifestations of the divine righteousness, is God's forbearance—toward righteous and wicked alike (Syriac Apocal. Bar. 24:2). God exonerates the righteous who, like Shadrach (Apocal. Shadrach 12: 5), thoroughly expiate their sins with chastisement and fasting (Pss. Sol. 3:8). The faithful shall have pardon (Zadokite Fragment 9:52-54); God's wrath abates toward such as have piety in their souls (Sibylline Oracles IV.169). Though the righteous stumble, they nonetheless recognize the righteousness of God and look for divine help (Pss. Sol. 3:5). God, in fact, warns the righteous and reproves him like a dear son (Pss. Sol. 13:8-9). This reproof is feeble by comparison with the doom in store for sinners (Pss. Sol. 13:6-7). The chastisement of the righteous is not destructive (Pss. Sol. 10:3; cf. Ps. 118:18). Lest sinners gloat at seeing the righteous punished, the punishment of the righteous is mild (Pss. Sol. 13:7). The belief is expressed that the worship of idols or the partaking of forbidden food under compulsion entails no divine penalty (IV Macc. 8:22). In brief, God, who is righteous, liquidates the sins of the righteous (Pss. Sol. 13:9). *See* FORGIVENESS.

i. The righteous at the last judgment. The present world is unable to furnish the righteous with all they have been promised; it is a world full of impotence and sin (IV Ezra 4:27). The righteousness of God requires, accordingly, that the righteous be favored at the last judgment (Enoch 38:1; 62:8; 99:10; IV Ezra 9:13). God will appoint, for the righteous, angelic guardians until he puts an end to every wickedness (Enoch 100:5). A fragrant tree will be available to the righteous, at the last judgment, with food for the elect (Enoch 25:4). The Son of Man will be a staff to the righteous that they fall not (Enoch 48:4). Hunger, sword, and death shall avoid

the righteous (Pss. Sol. 15:7). They shall escape the upheavals of those turbulent times and shall beget thousands of children (Enoch 10:17). *See* ESCHATOLOGY OF THE APOC. AND PSEUDEP.

j. The righteous at the resurrection. For the righteous there will be RESURRECTION from the grave (Enoch 62:15). God will not suffer the bodies of the righteous to be handed over to AZAZEL (Apocal. Abraham 13:11). Though they sleep the long sleep, they can look forward without fear (Enoch 100:5; 102:4; Syriac Apocal. Bar. 11:4; 14:12). They shall arise from that sleep (Enoch 91:10; 92:3). From the treasuries in which souls are preserved (IV Ezra 4: 39), they shall, at the resurrection, come forth in radiance (Syriac Apocal. Bar. 30:2; 51:1). For them is prepared all goodness, gladness, and glory (Enoch 51:5).

k. The righteous at the time of the Messiah. Then there is the messianic age when the righteous shall have, upon their faces, the brightness of God (Enoch 38:4). They shall bask in the light of the sun (Enoch 58:2-3). The light of the sun will, in fact, not be needed (Pseudo-Philo 26:13); for upon the righteous shall glow the light of eternal life (Enoch 58:2-3). Clothed in garments of joy (Enoch 62:15; II Esd. 7: 17:99), they shall live; they shall be established (Apocal. Abraham 29:18). *See* MESSIAH (JEWISH).

l. The righteous in Paradise. According to Enoch, there exists for the righteous a garden located in the third part of the fourth quarter of the earth (60:23; 77:3). Yet the chief guerdon for the righteous is a PARADISE beyond earth (II Esd. 7:17; 1QM XVI.11-XVII.15). At times it is difficult to distinguish between the glories of this Paradise and the mundane glories of the messianic age. E.g., speaking of the last days, Slavonic Enoch 65:8 foretells the great epoch when all the righteous shall be assembled and time shall be no more. "There will be neither years nor months nor days nor hours." In all events, there gleams for the righteous the world on high (Greek Bar. 10:5). Just as our present world was created for the righteous (IV Ezra 9:13), so also was the next world created for the righteous (Syriac Apocal. Bar. 15:7). Men were intended to be righteous and deathless in a Paradise on earth (Enoch 69:11; Pss. Sol. 13:9, 11; 14:3). This was not achieved in the earthly Paradise, but it is to be achieved in the Paradise supernal (Wisd. Sol. 5:15). Ezra saw in hell lions, dogs, and flames, but the righteous strode through them all into heaven (Vision of Esd. 58). As a slave obtains his freedom if he does well by his master, so do the righteous enter the kingdom celestial (Vision of Esd. 66).

The souls of the righteous are in the hands of God (Wisd. Sol. 3:1). Dwelling with him, they have peace, refreshment, and rest (Enoch 39:4-5; 71:14; Apocal. Esd. 1:12; Apocal. Shadrach 16:5). They are destined for gladness and glory (Enoch 25:7; 103:1, 3). They shall be resplendent (Enoch 108:14). They shall be strong as fiery lights (Enoch 39:7). Ezra saw thousands of such, and their abodes were sumptuous (Vision of Esd. 59).

We are told that the spirits of the righteous abide in a compartment near a bright spring of water (Enoch 22:9). There is no darkness (Apocal. Sophonias 2:2). And these glories shall endure forever. In the book of Enoch such words as "forever" and "eternal" are favorites.

In that supernal world reside Enoch, the patriarchs, Moses, Elijah, and the angels (Apocal. Esd. 5:22). The role of the angels is frequent and varied (Greek Bar. 12:3; Enoch 39:5; 60:2; 61:2-3; 70:3). The "secrets of the righteous" are mentioned several times. By these are meant felicities too profound for comprehension (Enoch 38:3; 49:2; 71:3). One who dies in righteousness is indeed blessed (Enoch 81:4). Considering the rest in store for them (Pseudo-Philo 28:10), the righteous do well to leave this transient and evil world (Enoch 81:9).

3. Austere aspects of the divine implications of righteousness. Divine righteousness, however, consists not only of graciousness but also of austerity. Retribution for the sinner is stressed repeatedly (Wisd. Sol. 1:8; 12:13; 17:2; Aristeas 131; Enoch 91:12; 97:1; Jub. 21:4; VI Esd. 15:7; III Macc. 2:3; Pss. Sol. 2:34-35; 3:14; 17:21). Life's adversities are punishments divinely and deservedly inflicted upon individuals and upon nations (Ecclus. 10:8; Pss. Sol. 2:10; 9:10; 1QH I.5-39; XII). The unrighteous are objects of God's hatred (Slavonic Enoch 66:1); God's Righteousness personified scolds Unrighteousness personified (VI Esd. 16:51). And the divine judgment brooks no escape (Ecclus. 26:28; Add. Esth. 5:4 [or 16:4]). Judas Maccabeus invokes God's righteousness when he wreaks bloody vengeance upon Joppa for the atrocities committed by that city upon its Jewish inhabitants (II Macc. 12:6). Sometimes the manner of the punishment is the manner of the sin (Wisd. Sol. 12:23; Enoch 100:7). Cain, e.g., who killed Abel with a stone, was himself killed by a falling stone (Jub. 4:31). "Innocent blood cries up unto me," says God (VI Esd. 15:8). *See* GOD, OT VIEW OF.

a. Israel's sins and punishments. Israel's misfortunes, such as the dispersion (Pss. Sol. 9:2; IV Ezra 14:32) or the persecutions waged by Antiochus (IV Macc. 4:21) or the entry of Pompey into Jerusalem (Pss. Sol. 8:17, 26), were but manifestations of divine righteousness (Tob. 3:2, 5; 13:9; Add. Esth. 3:12 [or 14:1]; 3:18 [or 14:7]; 5:21 [or 16:21]; Bar. 1:15; 2:6, 9, 12; Song Thr. Ch. 4 [or 27]; 5 [or 28]; Jub. 1:16; Pseudo-Philo 35:4). The righteousness of God's judgments should be acclaimed even by those who are stricken (Add. Esth. 3:18 [or 14:7]; Song Thr. Ch. 5; Jub. 1:6; Enoch 108:13; Pss. Sol. 5:1; 8:24, 40; 9:3-4; 14:1; 18:8; Zadokite Fragment 9:52-53). Philo teaches that divine punishment is something which the conscience-stricken would do well to seek (*That the Worse Is Wont to Attack the Better* XL).

b. Punishments of the high and mighty. Particular attention is called to God's judgments on the wealthy and powerful (Enoch 63:9; 96:4; 99:16). God's righteousness was manifest when Ptolemy Philometer, profanely intruding into the Jewish temple, was stricken with paralysis (III Macc. 2:21-22). Similarly was the intruder Apollonius felled, not by human power but by heavenly power (IV Macc. 4:13).

c. The last judgment. At the last judgment the wicked will be overwhelmed (Enoch 27:3; 38:1; 60:6; 96:1; 97:3; 98:13-14: Pss. Sol. 9:5; 13:11; Apocal.

Elijah 41:5). The Prince of Wickedness will be humbled (1QM XVII). Everyone will receive according to his deserts; there will be no substitutions of one person for another (IV Ezra 7:106). The godless will be smitten by hunger, sword, and death (Enoch 50:4; Pss. Sol. 15:8). Their seed will be uprooted (Wisd. Sol. 3:16). The righteous themselves will not escape unless they have previously repented of their shortcomings (Syriac Bar. 85:12; Vision of Esd. 65). *See* ESCHATOLOGY OF THE APOC. AND PSEUDEP.

d. Hell. Counterbalancing the heaven of the righteous, a HELL awaits sinners (Pss. Sol. 14:4-7). By divine righteousness, King Antiochus, e.g., is headed for those torments (IV Macc. 9:9; 11:3; 12:12). The righteous tortures suffered by the damned are seen by Sophonias (Apocal. Sophonias 2:5). To the agonies of those condemned ones is added the misery of their beholding, from the fires of hell, the felicities of the righteous with the angels in heaven (Enoch 108:14; Apocal. Esd. 1:9).

4. The righteousness of man (*see* MAN, NATURE OF, OT). *a. Man's lack of righteousness.* Some authors are persuaded that God alone possesses righteousness (Ecclus. 18:2; 1QH I; IV), and that man is devoid of righteousness (Dan. 9:18; Ecclus. 5:8; IV Ezra 8:32; Zadokite Document VII; cf. Deut. 9:5); man is enthralled in wrongdoing and deceit (1QH I), uncleanness, defilement, and contempt (Jub. 21:21). Some writers, while expounding no doctrine of total depravity, refer to their own age (Syriac Apocal. Bar. 85:3) or to some bygone age (Bar. 4:13; Wisd. Sol. 5:6; Pss. Sol. 17:19 [or 21]) or to some coming age (Jub. 23:21; IV Ezra 5:11) as utterly lacking in righteousness. Reference to the shortcomings of the Maccabees is seen in Pss. Sol. 1:3. Familiar are the plaintive words of Eccl. 3:16: "I saw . . . in the place of justice, even there was wickedness, and in the place of righteousness, even there was wickedness." One author puts it that the very laws which are tokens of righteousness are evidences of unrighteousness; without these laws, men would constantly transgress (Heraclitus of Ephesus VII.10.5).

b. Man's righteousness. Other stretches of this literature are less disheartened. Many are the passages which affirm or assume that the world does contain, has contained, or will contain some righteous people (Ecclus. 27:8; Song Thr. Ch. 63-64 [or 86]; Slavonic Enoch 35:1; Apocal. Abraham 27:6; 1QH XVI; 1QM XIII). Philo contends that, in man, righteousness and unrighteousness are commingled (*Questions on Genesis* on Gen. 18:23); this is not far from the view in Eccl. 7:20: "There is not a righteous man on earth who does good and never sins." Philo declares that, while every vice loves the body, righteousness loves the soul (*Who Is the Heir of Divine Things* 50), and man does have a soul. Philo maintains likewise that some sins are involuntary, and sins of this type he regards as halfway between sin and righteousness (*Questions on Genesis* on Gen. 20:4). One author observes that, if the righteous are few, it must be remembered that the more precious a metal, the rarer its deposits (II Esd. 7:51 ff).

The allurements of Satan need not always hold sway (Jub. 1:20). In Syriac Apocal. Bar. 61:6 righteousness is asserted to have been widely prevalent in the time of David, and in 85:1 at certain other times. The righteous were exalted by King Josiah (66:2). And righteousness will again prevail at some epoch in the future (Enoch 10:16, 21; 107:1; Jub. 23: 26). When the Messiah comes, thirty thousand righteous will attend him (Elijah 6:1). In fact, a certain number of the righteous must have entered the world before it will be possible for the Messiah to appear (Enoch 47:4; IV Ezra 4:35). In the messianic age, righteousness will be universal (Enoch 10:21; 39:6; 71:16; 81:7; 107:1; Slavonic Enoch 65:8; Pss. Sol. 17:26-27, 29, 32) and everlasting (Dan. 9:24). The godless will vanish (Enoch 91:14; IV Ezra 5 [or 7]:114). Sin will become extinct (Pss. Sol. 17:27, 32; VI Esd. 13:53).

c. Righteous individuals. Certain individuals have been outstanding for righteousness: Enoch (Test. Benj. 9:1; Apocal. Esd. 5:22; Apocal. Sophonias 14: 3), Noah (Ecclus. 44:17), Abraham (Prayer Man. 8; Jub. 14:6; 20:9; 23:10; Enoch 93:5; Syriac Apocal. Bar. 58:1; Apocal. Esd. 5:22; Apocal. Sophonias 14: 3), Isaac (Prayer Man. 8; Jub. 31:23; 36:6; Syriac Apocal. Bar. 58:1; Apocal. Esd. 5:22; Apocal. Sophonias 14:3), Jacob (Prayer Man. 8; Wisd. Sol. 10:10; Apocal Esd. 5:22; Syriac Apocal. Bar. 58:1; Apocal. Sophonias 14:3), Simeon (Jub. 30:23), Levi (Jub. 30:19, 23), Joseph (Wisd. Sol. 10:13), Job (Aristeas Fragment 11), Moses (Apocal. Esd. 5:22; Pseudo-Philo 24:6), David (Apocal. Sophonias 14:3; Pseudo-Philo 62:9), Solomon (Pss. Sol. 1:2), Elijah (Apocal. Esd. 5:22; Apocal. Sophonias 14:3), Hezekiah (Syriac Apocal. Bar. 63:3), Ezra (II Esd. 6:32), the translators of the Pentateuch (Aristeas 43), and one of the authors of the Book of Hymns (1QH XVI). According to passages, some of which are regarded by modern scholars as Christian interpolations, supreme righteousness imbues the Messiah (Enoch 38:2; 62:8; Pss. Sol. 18:8; Elijah 6:1), the Elect One (Enoch 39:6; 51:2; 53:6; 62:2), the Son of Man (Enoch 46:3; 48:4; 71:14), the Son of David (Pss. Sol. 17:26-27).

d. Righteous Israel. Often the Jews are spoken of as a righteous nation or race or people or seed (Add. Esth. 1:6 [or 11:7]; 1:8 [or 11:9]; Wisd. Sol. 10:15, 20; 16:23; 18:7; Prayer Man. 1; Enoch 10:16; 65:12; 93:2; Jub. 16:26; 20:9; 25:3; 36:6; Sibylline Oracles III.218, 234, 580; Test. Naph. 8:3; 1QpHab 2 on Hab. 2:4). At least Israel, when restored, is to be worthy of this designation (Jub. 1:17). "Peace of righteousness" is to be the name of Jerusalem (Bar. 5:4). A double garment of righteousness is to be donned by Jerusalem; the righteousness of Jerusalem is to be like a diadem set upon the head (Bar. 5:2). *See* Israel, History of.

e. Partisan sense of "righteous." Sometimes it is obvious that the appellative "righteous" labels a given party, political or religious (Enoch 93:6; 103:9; Pss. Sol. 17:22; 1QH VII.6-25; 1QM III.1-11), opposed to some other party identifiable as the "ungodly" or the "wicked" (Wisd. Sol. 2:12; Dead Sea Scrolls Commentary on Ps. 37:32-33). According to Charles, the "righteous" in Enoch 108:14 are the Essenes. It is surmised that the unrighteous kings and mighty ones in Enoch 38:5 may be either some heathen or some opposing party of Jews.

f. Righteousness taught. Much is said about the teaching of righteousness and teachers of righteousness. Noted for teaching or exhorting or adjuring or training others for righteousness are such personages as Enoch (Enoch 13:10; 14:1; 91:3-4, 18-19; 94:1, 3-4), Noah (Jub. 7:20, 26), Abraham (Jub. 20: 2), Levi (Jub. 31:15; Test. Levi 13:5), Judah (Jub. 31:15), Benjamin (Test. Benj. 9:1), Solomon (Wisd. Sol. 1:1), Ben Sirach (Ecclus. 7:1), Tobit (Tob. 4:5; 13:6), the mother of the seven martyred brothers (IV Macc. 17:5), the Sibyl (Sibylline Oracles III. 630), and the translators of the Pentateuch (Aristeas 215, 267).

As a specific personality, a "Teacher of Righteousness" is mentioned in the Zadokite Fragment, known since 1910 (1:7; 4:7; 8:10; 9:29, 39, 50, 53), and also in the Dead Sea Scrolls, more recently discovered (1QH II.2-19; I; Commentary on Ps. 37). Here, however, this Teacher of Righteousness and the Messiah are not identical.

Also envisioned is the winning of converts to righteousness by those who have themselves exemplified righteousness (Dan. 12:3; Ecclus. 32:16; The Dead Sea Scrolls [The Zadokite Document, VIII]). Akin to teaching righteousness is the act of blessing righteous people. Such blessings are spoken by various notables (Enoch 82:4; 99:10; Slavonic Enoch 42:11; Jub. 36:16). Enoch supplicates that the righteous community might be enabled to endure forever (Enoch 84:6).

g. The troubles of the righteous. Contrary to much that we have noted already, the lot of the righteous on earth is often described as a sad one (Wisd. Sol. 3:1-2; IV Ezra 4:27). The righteous are constantly subject to the abuse and the persecutions of the wicked (Wisd. Sol. 2:10; Sus. 33; Syriac Apocal. Bar. 64:2; Apocal. Elijah 38:3; Enoch 81:9; 95:7; 96:8; 100:7, 10; 101:3; 104:10; Slavonic Enoch 9:1; Zadokite Fragment 1:15). A victim of such mistreatment is, among others, the righteous Son of God (Wisd. Sol. 2:18-19). Sometimes the victim is the entire Jewish nation (Add. Esth. 1:6 [or 11:7]; Wisd. Sol. 10:15; 17:2; IV Ezra 10:22). The righteous are, by word and deed, a reproof to the ungodly, and this the ungodly resent (Wisd. Sol. 2:1-21).

h. The triumphs of the righteous. But, upon the arrival of the Messiah, God will bring retribution and deliverance (Pss. Sol. 2:34; Enoch 47:1-2; 103:9; VI Esd. 15:8). Then will the righteous have rest from oppression (Enoch 53:7). Then will the tables be turned. The righteous will then wield dominion (Wisd. Sol. 3:8; Enoch 50:2; 65:12; Syriac Apocal. Bar. 52:5). Kings and other persons of might will be given into their hands (Enoch 38:5). The foes of the righteous shall vanish like straw in fire, shall sink like lead in water (Enoch 48:9).

Armed with God's breastplate, sixty chosen of the righteous will hasten to Jerusalem and combat "the shameless one"—whoever, in the political commotions of those days, this may have been (Apocal. Elijah 37:5). The Son of David is to shatter the unrighteous ruler (Pss. Sol. 17:22). He is to drive away sinners (Enoch 91:12; Pss. Sol. 17:23) and to rule with righteousness and energy (Pss. Sol. 17:42). Also in the celestial hereafter will the righteous judge the godless; righteous youth will sit in judgment over the aged wicked (Wisd. Sol. 4:16). The righteous will confront his oppressor, and the wicked shall realize how the righteous brim with power (Wisd. Sol. 5:6).

5. Nonconformist views. This literature is not without breaks in its dominant orthodoxy.

a. The naturalistic approach. Here and there reference to the supernatural subsides, and righteousness is seen in a context of natural, observable occurrences. This obtains particularly in the Letter of Aristeas. King Ptolemy wishes to know how he can live amicably with different races. The translator to whom this question is addressed replies: "By acting the proper part toward each and taking righteousness as your guide" (Aristeas 267). With these we might range the words of Ecclus. 10:8: "Because of unrighteous dealings, injuries, and riches got by deceit, the kingdom is translated from one people to another." Similarly naturalistic is the admonition of Enoch 91:4:

> Love uprightness, . . .
> Walk in righteousness. . . .
> And it shall guide you in good paths,
> And righteousness shall be your companion.

From passages such as these, reference to the supernatural is absent.

b. Sharp distinction between righteousness and unrighteousness. Yet, on the whole, this literature allows scant leeway for skepticism. Though it deals extensively with social conflict, it understands such conflict only as a warfare between the "righteous" and the "wicked" (1QM III.1-11). It applauds the "righteous" for doing what it condemns the "wicked" for doing. Though, to its thinking, "God created both righteous and sinners as he created day and night" (Apocal. Esd. 2:9); though the righteous, as well as the wicked, contribute to the world's confusion (Apocal. Abraham 17:13); and though unrighteousness can even have a defender (II Esd. 16:51); these writings harbor not the least surmise that ethical standards can vary from group to group, one group branding as sinful what another lauds as meritorious, while both groups can be similarly conscientious and sincere.

c. Doubts. There is reference—to be sure, dissenting reference—to the Sadducean denial that the dead will be resurrected: "As we die, so die the righteous; what benefit do they reap of their deeds?" (Enoch 102:6). There is dissenting reference to the observation that the righteous are carried off while the impious prosper (Syriac Apocal. Bar. 15:3). Some uncertainty is divulged as to what will befall the righteous at the destruction of Jerusalem (Syriac Apocal. Bar. 67:4). Yet the only outright abandonment of the belief in supernatural reward and punishment appears in the book of Ecclesiastes, the oldest of these writings. The words are familiar: "There is a righteous man who perishes in his righteousness" (Eccl. 7:15). "There are righteous men to whom it happens according to the deeds of the wicked, and there are wicked men to whom it happens according to the deeds of the righteous" (Eccl. 8:14). "One fate comes to all, to the righteous and the wicked" (Eccl. 9:2). "Be not righteous over-

much" (Eccl. 7:16). Curiously, the nonconformist book of Ecclesiastes attained canonization while many of the conformist works remained apocryphal and pseudepigraphic, including even such conformist writings as the Wisdom of Solomon and the Psalms of Solomon attributed, like Ecclesiastes, to the illustrious king. Accounting for this phenomenon might yield a fascinating chapter in the history of this literature.

Bibliography. E. Kautzsch, *Die Apokryphen und Pseudepigraphen des Alten Testaments* (1900); H. L. Strack, *Die Sprüche Jesu, des Sohnes Sirachs, der jüngst gefundene hebräische Text* (1903); H. M. Hughes, *The Ethics of Jewish Apocryphal Literature* (1909); B. Violet, *Die Esra-Apokalypse* (1910); R. H. Charles, *The Apoc. and Pseudep. of the OT* (1913); P. Riessler, *Altjüdisches Schrifttum ausserhalb der Bibel* (1928); *Philo* in the Loeb Classical Library (1949); T. H. Gaster, *The Dead Sea Scriptures in English Translation* (1956).

ABRAHAM CRONBACH

*RIGHTEOUSNESS IN THE NT. The use of the concept "righteousness" in the NT presumes a covenant relationship, which, for its preservation, needs the active participation of both covenant partners. Thus, the one who upholds, and therefore participates in, this covenant relationship is designated "righteous"; and, as in the OT (*see* RIGHTEOUSNESS IN THE OT), those acts which preserve a covenant relationship, either between God and man, or between man and man, are righteous, while those acts which break this relationship are unrighteous. Although an act which upholds the covenant relationship may also be of an ethicomoral nature, it is nevertheless not designated a "righteous" act because it conforms to some ethical norm, either divine or human. Rather, the act is righteous because the covenant relationship has, for its preservation, required such an act from that party to the relationship.

In the prevailing NT use of this concept, God's righteousness is most clearly demonstrated in his saving acts on behalf of man, whereby God, in Christ, upholds, and thus restores, the covenant relationship with sinful man. Man's righteousness, on the other hand, consists of, and depends upon, his trusting acceptance of God's saving act in Christ, whereby man accepts the restored covenant relationship with God.

1. Terminology
2. Righteousness as a relational concept
   a. As relationship to God
   b. As relationship between men
   c. As meeting the demands of a relationship
3. God as the sole source (through Christ) of righteousness
4. Reliance on God alone (through faith in Christ) for righteousness
5. Righteousness and personal benefit
6. Other uses of the concept of righteousness
   a. As a forensic term
   b. As retributive justice
7. Righteousness and conformity to a norm
Bibliography

1. Terminology. The noun δικαιοσύνη is most commonly translated "righteousness" (Matt. 3:15; etc.; in the KJV virtually without exception where this word appeared in their MSS). Depending on context, however, δικαιοσύνη may be translated "piety" (Matt. 6:1), "justice" (Acts 24:25), "justification" (Gal. 2:21), "right" (I John 2:29), or "what is right" (Eph. 5:9). The phrase εἰς δικαιοσύνην is also translated either "(may) be justified" (Rom. 10:4), or "is justified" (Rom. 10:10), the context again being determinative. Δίκαιος, the adjective, in addition to the two most common translations, "righteous" (Matt. 9:13) and "just" (Matt. 5:45), is also translated, again depending on the context, "right" (Luke 12:57), "innocent" (Matt. 27:4), "sincere" (Luke 20:20), "upright" (Tit. 1:8), and, in one instance, "justly" (Col. 4:1). The verb δικαιόω has the sense of "showing to be righteous" (Matt. 11:19), or "declaring" or "pronouncing righteous" (Luke 7:29), but its most common English translation is "to justify" (Rom. 3:30; *see* JUSTIFICATION). The remaining NT words which belong to this conceptual framework appear much less frequently than those listed above. The noun δικαίωμα signifies a concrete expression of righteousness, either in act or in command. Thus it can be translated "just requirement" (Rom. 8:4; cf. 1:32), or "righteous deed" (Rev. 19:8). But it can also be translated simply as "righteousness" where the context warrants (Rom. 5:18; this translation is preferred in the KJV, where it predominates over all other translations of this word), and in some instances simply as "precepts" (Rom. 2:26), where the righteous aspect of those precepts is made clear by the context. Δικαίωσις, signifying the act of pronouncing righteous, occurs only twice in the NT, and is translated "justification" (Rom. 4:25), or "acquittal" (Rom. 5:18). The adverb δικαίως, "righteously" (I Pet. 2:23 KJV), or "justly" (Luke 23:41), can also, as the context demands, be translated by such a word as "upright" (Tit. 2:12), or, in a phrase, "come to your right mind" (I Cor. 15:34). Two nouns, each occurring only once in the NT, round out the terminology of righteousness: εὐθύτης, which occurs in Heb. 1:8 ("righteous"), and δικαιοκρισία, which is used in Rom. 2:5 ("righteous judgment").

In addition to what can be learned from the words which designate the positive aspect of righteousness, much can be learned from a study of those words which describe the negative aspect of this concept: unrighteousness. Such words as ἀδικία, a noun translated "unrighteousness" (I John 1:9), or "injustice" (Rom. 9:14), or "iniquity" (II Tim. 2:19), or "wickedness" (Rom. 1:18); or the adjective ἄδικος, meaning "unrighteous" (Luke 16:11; cf. Matt. 5:45, where it is used in direct contrast to δίκαιος), or "unjust" (Rom. 3:5*b*)—such words will often throw no little light on the positive meaning of the term "righteousness." These two words, along with the verb ἀδικέω ("to do harm or injury"; "to act unjustly"; cf. Acts 25:11), the noun ἀδίκημα ("an unrighteous or unjust act"; cf. Rev. 18:5), and the adverb ἀδίκως ("unjustly"; I Pet. 2:19), need to be considered in any examination of the total meaning of the concept "righteousness" in the NT.

2. Righteousness as a relational concept. The great majority of instances (*but see* § 6 *below*) where the concept "righteousness" occurs in the NT require, to explain the various contexts within which this concept is found, an underlying thought-pattern, which may be formulated in this way: God, who in his grace desires fellowship with men, chose the peo-

ple of Israel with whom to establish a covenant (Exod. 24; Deut. 7:7 ff). God promised to be their God (and therefore save them), and Israel promised to be his people (and therefore obey him). Through human rebellion and sin, this covenant was broken, and, since only the innocent party (in this case, God) can re-establish a broken covenant, man cannot restore the covenant fellowship with God. Though the Jews held that the law embodied the demands which the covenant relationship with God laid upon man, once that covenant relationship is abrogated through sin, the law is powerless to restore man to fellowship with God. Therefore, meeting the demands of the law ("righteousness based on law"), though in men's eyes righteous because fulfilling the demands of the covenant relationship, cannot be considered righteous by God, since this covenant relationship has been broken by man.

But through Christ, God has now re-established the covenant relationship, thus making it possible for man to have fellowship with God. This restored relationship lays a twofold demand on men: that they admit their failure, through sin, to uphold the covenant with God (repentance), and accept the restored covenant relationship as an act based, not on their merit, but on God's grace (faith). In addition to accepting this fellowship with God, man must accept, and uphold, fellowship within the community that God's covenant act calls into being.

Thus, the NT sees righteousness on two levels: accepting the covenant relationship with God (by repentance, faith, and obedience), and with the covenant community (acting unselfishly). In both instances, however, righteousness depends ultimately on God's act of restoring the covenant with sinful men through Christ; and therefore there can be no true righteousness apart from a relationship of fellowship with God. Only as God forgives sin and re-establishes the relationship by his saving act in Christ, can man stand within that fellowship, and therefore be righteous before God.

a. As relationship to God. That the NT uses the concept "righteousness" to designate a relationship between man and God is shown in a variety of passages. Cornelius, a centurion, is called a "righteous" man, not because he acts in accordance with some moral norm, but because he is a "God-fearing" man —i.e., one whose attitude toward God is the attitude which the relationship to God requires (Acts 10:22; cf. vs. 35). Elymas the magician is an "enemy of all righteousness" because, as a "son of the devil," he makes "crooked the straight paths of the Lord"—i.e., he destroys the relationship with God by obscuring the requirements of this relationship (Acts 13:10). Simon is in the "bond of unrighteousness" because he proves by his desire to buy the "gift of God" that he is outside a positive relationship to God (Acts 8:20, 23). Jesus calls a judge "unrighteous" (Luke 18:6), not because the judge refused to heed the pleas of the woman (he does resolve to vindicate her), nor because his judgments were perverted. He is called unrighteous apparently because he "neither feared God nor regarded man" (Luke 18:2); i.e., the judge met the demands neither of the relationship to God nor of that to man. Satan's servants, bent on destroying the relationship between God and man, nevertheless, in order to gain an advantage, pose as "servants of righteousness"—i.e., as those who would uphold the relationship rather than destroy it (II Cor. 11:15). Jesus is called "righteous" because, by his act of sacrifice, he brings men to God (I Pet. 3:18). Those who trust in themselves for their righteousness are told that they are less righteous than a confessed sinner who knows righteousness depends on his relationship to God (Luke 18:9 ff), but those who "hunger and thirst for righteousness" are assured that this longing will be satisfied by God (Matt. 5:6; the passive χορτασθήσονται to be understood as Semitic periphrasis to avoid use of the divine name).

John the Baptist, who preached repentance and a new relationship to God about to come (Matt. 3:2), is acknowledged a "righteous" man even by his executor (Mark 6:20). For Paul, the righteous are those who stand in a positive relationship of trust in God; because of their faith, the Corinthians stand in a positive relationship to God, and are not to be "mismated" with the unrighteous, who stand outside that relationship (II Cor. 6:14). Only the man who has yielded himself to God and thus accepted the divine-human relationship can yield his "members" as "instruments of righteousness" (Rom. 6:13; cf. vs. 19). Indeed, righteousness is so closely bound up with the relationship to God that once he has pronounced the verdict of "righteous," no one can disagree (Rom. 8:33), and Jesus' righteousness will be proved at the end of his earthly life by the fact that he goes to the Father, thus making evident the relationship between himself and God (John 16:8, 10).

The difficult use of the word "righteousness" in the report of Jesus' baptism (Matt. 3:15) is also best understood in relational terms. John's baptism constituted part of his call to repentance in preparation for the coming kingdom of God. As such, it was a demand that all men, including the Jews, admit by repentance and baptism that a radically new relationship to God was necessary. Thus, by his submission to John's baptism, Jesus also recognizes the necessity of this new covenant relationship, which God will bring about by the establishment of his kingdom. Jesus "fulfils all righteousness" through submitting to John's baptism, because by it he points to man's need for repentance, thus validating John's announcement of a new relationship to God. To recognize the baptism by participating in it is to welcome the new relationship that the baptism announces, and thus to "fulfil all righteousness." God's kingdom, in turn, is also inseparably related to God's "righteousness," because in his kingdom he re-establishes and upholds the covenant relationship which sinful men have broken. For this reason, God's kingdom and his righteousness are closely identified in the message of Jesus (Matt. 6:33; 13:43; cf. Matt. 5:10; Rom. 14:17; I Cor. 6:9), and the consummation of that kingdom is described as the place where "righteousness dwells" —i.e., where the divine-human relationship will be permanent (II Pet. 3:13; cf. Heb. 12:23, where those in heaven are termed "just men made perfect").

b. As relationship between men. The words "righteous" and "unrighteous" are often used to describe the preserving or breaking of a relationship between men. Thus, in Jesus' discussion of the steward who used his position to his own advantage (Luke 16:1 ff),

the antithesis is between a faithful steward and an unrighteous one—i.e., between one who is faithful to his relationship with his master, and one who is not (vs. 10). The steward mentioned here is "unrighteous" (vs. 8; RSV "dishonest") precisely because he has broken the relationship of trust with his master (vs. 2). Similarly, in the parable of the laborers in the vineyard, the owner is not unrighteous, although he pays the same wage for different labor. In paying the one denarius to all, the owner in no way breaks the relationship with the laborers by rejecting the requirements of this relationship: both parties had agreed to one denarius when the relationship was established (Matt. 20:2). Therefore, the action cannot be called "unrighteous" (vs. 13). In describing the type of action necessary for the "righteous" man (Matt. 5:20), Jesus uses several examples of actions which, because they are not motivated by compassion, will break a relationship. To hate a man as surely breaks the relationship of compassion with him as to kill him (vss. 21 ff); to desire a woman lustfully as surely breaks the relationship of compassion as to fulfil the deed (vss. 27 ff); to hate an enemy destroys any possibility of coming into a positive relationship with him (vss. 43 ff). Such actions, because they render the relationship of compassion impossible, are unrighteous.

Again, in order to gain information on the basis of which to try to convict Jesus, the Jews must enter the inner circle around him. To do this, they send spies who pretend to be "righteous"—i.e., who pretend to be in a positive relationship with him—in order to gain the desired information (Luke 20:20; RSV "sincere"). The money paid to Judas is called the "reward of his unrighteousness" (Acts 1:18; RSV "wickedness"), because by his act of betrayal he decisively broke the relationship of trust between himself and Jesus. The author of II Peter tells his readers it is a "righteous thing" for him to arouse them by way of reminder—i.e., this act is consonant with the relationship existing between them (II Pet. 1:13). It is also a "righteous thing" for children to obey their parents, because in this way the relationship between them is upheld (Eph. 6:1).

Paul tells the Philippians that it is a "righteous thing" for him to feel as he does about them, because this feeling strengthens, rather than weakens, the relationship between them (Phil. 1:7). Even Paul's ironic plea to the Corinthians for forgiveness for an "unrighteousness" (II Cor. 12:13; RSV "wrong") is based on the fact that they were "less favored" than the other churches in not being allowed to support him. To the extent that the Corinthians were unable to do this, and thus were not enabled to establish as close a relationship to Paul as the other churches, to that extent Paul was "unrighteous" toward them!

c. As meeting the demands of a relationship. When a covenant relationship is established, both partners of the agreement assume certain responsibilities for upholding it. To meet these responsibilities is to uphold the relationship, and therefore such acts are called "righteous." Thus, Elizabeth and Zechariah are "righteous before God," because they obey fully all the "commandments and ordinances of the Lord," and therefore, by their act of obedience, they fulfil the demands of the covenant relationship (Luke 1:6).

These demands may vary with individual situations. Noah is an "heir of righteousness" because at a time when it seemed ill advised, he built an ark at the command of the God he trusted, thus meeting the demands which his relationship to God laid upon him (Heb. 11:7; cf. II Pet. 2:5). Abraham was "pronounced righteous" (ἐδικαιώθη) when, in trustful obedience to God, he was willing to offer his son Isaac on the altar, thus fulfilling the demand which the covenant relationship to God laid upon him at that point (Jas. 2:21 ff). Hence, the two elements necessary to uphold the covenant are trust in God and obedience to his will. Thus James affirms that a man is called righteous "by works and not by faith alone" (2:24), though both are necessary (vs. 23). Seen in this light, Paul has a similar position. For Paul, sin and righteousness are mutually exclusive, denoting the absence or presence of the covenant relationship (Rom. 6:20). Either one does not trust and obey God, thus failing to meet the demands of the relationship (trust in, and obedience to, God), and thus is sinful (unrighteous), or one does trust and obey God, thus meeting the demands, and then one is righteous (vss. 18-19). Because, for Paul, the demands of the covenant relationship with God are filled by "obedience," he uses this word in a strange manner (see especially vs. 16): to "yield to obedience," or even "obey obedience," means simply to uphold the covenant relationship with God by meeting its demand of obedience to God. To become "enslaved to obedience" thus means to perform all acts within the context of upholding the divine-human relationship. What Paul understands as the demands of this covenant relationship he makes clear in his ethical admonitions: these are the acts required of those who stand within, and mean to uphold, the covenant relationship (within which they stand as a sheer gift of grace, through Christ; *see* § 3 *below*). These same demands James calls "works" (2:21 ff); in both cases, the demands of the divine-human covenant relationship are met by trusting obedience to God.

3. God as the sole source (through Christ) of righteousness. Man, through his disobedience, rejected the demands which the covenant relationship with God laid upon him, thus breaking this relationship. Since the covenant relationship is broken by man, God is released from his covenant promise to save man. If God fulfils this promise, the covenant relationship will be upheld *despite* man's act, and man, by participating in it, may still be righteous; if God allows the covenant relationship to remain broken *because* of man's act, no man can be righteous. Thus, whether or not the covenant relationship is upheld depends solely on God's act. Therefore, since God, by his act in Christ, did uphold the relationship by meeting its demand (salvation for man), God is the sole source of righteousness.

No man has fulfilled the demands of that covenant relationship with God, and therefore no man is righteous (Rom. 3:10). The Gentiles (1:18 ff) have not acknowledged God in the way their relationship to him required (vs. 21). The Jews have also rejected the demands which the covenant relationship laid upon them (2:17 ff). Thus, all men have broken their relationship to God, are sinners (3:9), and are devoid of righteousness (vss. 10-18). Nor will the plea that

they have kept the demands of the law enable the Jews to claim righteousness—i.e., that they still uphold the covenant relationship with God. That law cannot be the basis of anyone's claim to righteousness, because of its close relationship to sin (vs. 20). To keep the law would be to meet the demands of the covenant relationship, and thus those acts would be righteous, were it not for the fact that the relationship to God has been broken by man's disobedience. Therefore, although to do the works of the law is to fulfil the demands of a relationship, they are not righteous in God's eyes, because the covenant whose demands the law represents has been broken. Only in those who participate in the restored relationship can the righteousness of the law be fulfilled (τὸ δικαίωμα τοῦ νόμου; Rom. 8:4); and only God, as the "innocent party," can decide whether or not to uphold his relationship with man, and thus restore man's relationship to him. Therefore God alone decides the fate of the covenant relationship, and therefore God alone is the source of righteousness. It is God who "pronounces righteous"; there is no other (8:33).

It is acknowledgment of this fact that underlies the activity of John the Baptist. The people who accepted John's baptism of repentance have, by this act, pronounced God righteous; i.e., they admit by sharing in John's baptism of repentance that God alone is the source of their relationship with him, and therefore that God alone is the source of righteousness (Luke 7:29). The Pharisees and the lawyers, on the other hand, rejected this baptism, and thus they rejected God's purpose for themselves (vs. 30)—i.e., that they too admit that righteousness alone is from God. By this rejection these men do not, by clear implication, "pronounce God righteous" by admitting that their relationship to God depends on God alone. They want their own righteousness, and thus deny themselves all righteousness (cf. Luke 16:15).

Thus, it is the witness of the NT that God has elected to uphold the covenant relationship with sinful man. God has decided to be merciful toward man's unrighteousness; he has decided not to "remember their sins" (Heb. 8:12; cf. Jer. 31:34). Despite man's perfidy and unrighteousness, God upholds the covenant relationship, thereby proving his righteousness. This righteousness has characterized God's dealings with Israel. Despite Israel's continued perfidy and unrighteousness by breaking the covenant agreement, God nevertheless remained faithful to the requirements of that covenant. In this faithfulness, God's righteousness is demonstrated (Rom. 3:2-3; in this context, "faithfulness" in vs. 3 and "righteousness" [RSV "justice"] in vs. 5 point to the same thing: God upholds the covenant relationship).

This same righteousness comes most clearly to light in Christ. In him, the twofold aspect of God's righteousness is shown, especially in Christ's sacrifice on the cross. On the one hand, God, by this sacrifice, enables man to be saved, thus upholding the covenant relationship with man by fulfilling his promise made within that relationship: the salvation of man. In thus fulfilling the demand and upholding the relationship, God proves himself righteous (Rom. 3:26a). On the other hand, because Christ's sacrifice on the cross is a supreme act of obedience to God's will, Christ thereby fulfils the demand of the covenant relationship upon man: obedience to God. Thus, the relationship is restored for man; and man, by participating in this relationship, can be righteous (vs. 26b). But, because man's righteousness depends on God's act in Christ, God is still the source of righteousness (cf. John 17:25, where the context indicates that God is called "righteous" because he has sent Christ as an evidence of his love for man, thus restoring, by this act, the broken relationship). But more, Christ has now become both the proof of God's righteousness, and the hope of man's righteousness (vss. 25-26). Therefore, for the NT, righteousness is centered in Christ.

It is Christ's act of obedience, in his death on the cross, that nullifies the disobedience of man whereby man broke the covenant relationship with God. This act of obedience restores the relationship of man with God by fulfilling the demand that the relationship had laid upon man: obedience to God. Therefore, by Christ's act of obedience the covenant relationship is restored, and man, by participating in it, may be righteous (Rom. 5:19). Because this is man's only chance for righteousness (participation in the covenant relationship with God), there can no longer be any question of "righteousness through the law" (9:31; cf. 10:3). If the relationship between God and man could be upheld by man's ability to preserve the relationship by meeting its demands (the law), then Christ need not have died in obedience to God, thus fulfilling for man the demand of the relationship, and thus upholding the relationship. But such was not the case; righteousness is possible for man only through the death of Christ, by whom the relationship is restored and upheld (Gal. 2:21; cf. I Pet. 2: 24). Christ alone upholds the relationship; his "act of righteousness" in restoring the covenant relationship leads to a "living righteousness" through participation in this relationship for all men (Rom. 5:18; RSV "acquittal and life"). Thus, because of Christ, a man, despite his sin in failing to obey God and thus meet the demands of the relationship, can nevertheless share in the relationship, and thus be righteous (cf. 8:10).

Because this is so central, the NT witness never tires of formulating and reformulating statements in which Christ is designated the source of man's righteousness (especially in Paul), or in which Christ is identified with righteousness or is specifically called "the Righteous."

Because Christ alone has met the demand for obedience which the covenant relationship laid upon man, Paul can say that God made him "our righteousness" (I Cor. 1:30), or can affirm that we are now pronounced righteous "by his blood" (Rom. 5: 9a), referring to the act of obedience on the cross. A man's righteousness comes "in the name of the Lord Jesus Christ" (I Cor. 6:11); and this righteousness, because it depends, not on what man did, but on what Christ did for him, can only be regarded as a gracious gift (Rom. 3:24; cf. Tit. 3:5). Because Christ's act of obedience fulfilled the demands of the relationship for all men, Christ the righteous one died for man the unrighteous, thereby bringing men to God by restoring the divine-human relationship for

man (I Pet. 3:18). Christ's sacrificial act of obedience means that the sin of rebellion is placed upon Christ and overcome by him, thus making it possible for man to become, through Christ, the "righteousness of God" (II Cor. 5:21). The results of the relationship with God (the "fruits of righteousness") are inseparably linked to Christ, by whose act the relationship is restored (Phil. 1:11). It is through Christ that men receive the "free gift of righteousness"— i.e., their participation in the restored covenant relationship is based on Christ's act and thus is a free gift, not on their merit and thus a reward (Rom. 5:17).

All of this means that Christ is the proof that God has decided to preserve the relationship, thus restoring for man the chance of participating in it. It is in this act of Christ, whereby God makes known this decision, therefore, that a man becomes righteous— i.e., he enters again into a positive relationship with God. But since this relationship to God is the sole criterion for man's righteousness, a man is righteous only when he enters again into this relationship. Thus, when the NT says that God "reckons a man righteous" or "pronounces him righteous" (the RSV regularly translates this verb, δικαιόω, as "justify"), it means simply that God, through the act of Christ's obedience, has upheld, and thus, for man, restored, the relationship. Therefore, the problem of whether a man is really righteous, or only treated by God "as if" he were righteous, rests on a misunderstanding of the nature of righteousness. Righteousness is a matter of man's relationship to God, not an ethical state. When man is in a positive relationship to God, through God's act in Christ, that man is truly "righteous," because he is, by God's act, reintroduced into a positive relationship to God. God does not treat man "as if" man were righteous; God, through Christ, restores the covenant relationship, and therefore the man who, by God's gracious decision, participates in this relationship is in fact "righteous" (cf. Rom. 8:33).

Because Christ's act of obedience fulfils the covenant demand and therefore is, par excellence, the righteous act, the NT frequently identifies Christ with righteousness by applying the title "Righteous" to him. Peter accuses the Jews of having rejected the "Holy and Righteous One" (Acts 3:14). Stephen, in his defense, accuses the Jews of having killed the prophets who announced the coming of "the Righteous One" (7:52). Ananias tells Paul that it was God's will for Paul to be converted by seeing the "Righteous One" (22:14; RSV "Just One"). The author of I John bases his exhortations on the apparently accepted fact that Christ is righteous, and that therefore man's righteousness is linked to Christ's (I John 2:29; cf. 2:1; 3:7).

4. Reliance on God (through faith in Christ) for righteousness. Since, therefore, God, through Christ, is the sole source of righteousness, man must rely on him (by faith) for his own righteousness. This necessity of reliance on God carries with it the necessity of admitting that man is incapable of his own righteousness—i.e., is incapable of restoring or upholding the covenant relationship. To admit this, however, is to allow God to show his righteousness by forgiving sins and restoring righteousness—i.e., relationship to himself—to men (I John 1:9). Because John the Baptist leveled the same demand, he came in the "way of righteousness"; i.e., both John's personal austerity and his message of repentance displayed his complete reliance on God to fulfil the demands of the divine-human relationship. All a man could offer to such a relationship was repentance—i.e., admission of failure to meet the demands of the relationship (Matt. 21:32). Because the Pharisees refused repentance, thereby refusing to admit their failure in regard to the covenant relationship, they are looked upon as the chief examples of unrighteousness. They are the ones who "justify themselves"; but this act is an "abomination in the sight of God" (Luke 16:15; cf. 18:9). By this act, they refuse to rely on God for their righteousness. For this reason, the poor sinner who could only plead for mercy (Luke 18:13), thus relying on God to uphold the relationship, did participate in that relationship, whereas the Pharisee, boasting before God of his own righteousness (vss. 11-12), was denied this participation. He was not "pronounced righteous" by God (vs. 14). Although outwardly the Pharisees, with their legal minutiae, gave the impression of fulfilling the demands of the relationship, in reality these acts effectively blocked their sharing in it (Matt. 23:28). Unless, therefore, a man's righteousness is greater than that of the Pharisees, he will never see the consummation of the covenant relationship: the kingdom of heaven (Matt. 5:20). Man's only hope of participating in the relationship which God alone upholds is to admit this fact; to rely on his own "righteousness"—i.e., his own ability to uphold the relationship with God—is to deny himself participation in this relationship. Thus, Simeon is righteous because, in looking for the "consolation of Israel" which God alone can provide, he acknowledges that God alone can fulfil the demands of the broken covenant relationship. For his expectant waiting, rather than relying on his own works (and for recognizing God's true righteousness! cf. Luke 2: 27 ff), Simeon is "righteous" (vs. 25).

That man must rely on God to uphold the covenant relationship, and thus must rely on God for his righteousness, is the particular emphasis of Paul. Such reliance on God, Paul called FAITH. This alone was the basis for any righteousness, any participation in the covenant relationship. Only on the basis of faith does God pronounce a man righteous by accepting him into a positive relationship to himself (Rom. 5:1); and since the "fulness of time" (Gal. 4:4; cf. Rom. 5:6, where κατὰ καιρόν apparently has this sense), only on the basis of faith in Jesus Christ (Rom. 3:26).

To emphasize the meaning of faith, upon which righteousness depends, Paul contrasts the righteousness of faith with that of the law. Paul was convinced that the demands of the law could be met—i.e., that there was a "righteousness under the law"; he had, in fact, achieved it (Phil. 3:6b). But it was of no avail; this "righteousness" did nothing toward restoring, and thus upholding, the relationship with God. There was a "righteousness" of the law, but it could not aid a living relationship with God (Rom. 9:31). Discovering this after his conversion, Paul renounced such a "righteousness" of "his own"—i.e., based on his own efforts to uphold the covenant relationship by works of the law (Phil. 3:9). True righteousness is not from the law; it is from reliance on God alone—i.e., through faith that God in Christ has restored and upholds the covenant relationship (Gal. 2:16). Therefore, the Jews who do not rely on God's righteousness, but who seek, by works of the law, to establish their own righteousness—i.e., seek to uphold the covenant relationship by fulfilling its demands—have no righteousness at all (Rom. 10:3). Whether for Jew or for Gentile, righteousness must come from God alone, and in reliance on God alone (Rom. 3: 30); true righteousness is based solely on faith, not on works of the law (vs. 28).

But God gave the law to the Jews. If it was not meant to lead to righteousness—i.e., to show man how to uphold the divine-human relationship by meeting its demands—how is the law to be understood? What is the relationship of law to righteousness by faith? To understand this, one must understand Paul's conception of the history of the covenant relationship between God and man.

For Paul, God's original covenant with man laid upon man the demand of obedience. This covenant was broken by the first man, Adam, through his act of disobedience (Rom. 5:19; cf. Gen. 3:3 ff). Therefore, even the law points, not to an original covenant, but to a restored covenant, restored on the basis of, and thus dependent on, God's grace, not man's works. Thus, no man can be righteous—i.e., preserve the covenant relationship—by works of the law, since even the law was introduced into a situation where the relationship was upheld only by God's righteousness—namely, his faithfulness to his covenant promise. Thus, even possessing the law, man can remain in covenant relationship to God, and thus be righteous, only by admitting that participation in this relationship depends on God's grace, not man's acts. But this, thinks Paul, was misunderstood by the Jews, who thought that by keeping the law, they thus fulfilled the demands of the covenant relationship, and that thus they could have their own righteousness (could remain in the covenant relationship on the strength of their fulfilment of its demands) without being dependent on God for their participation in the relationship. In short, they relied, not on God (faith), but on themselves (works) to meet the demands of, and thus uphold, the covenant relationship. Because of this misunderstanding, the Jews pursued the righteousness of the law as though it depended on works, not on faith (Rom. 9:32). But the necessity of relying on God alone to uphold the relationship, to which the law pointed, was then most clearly displayed in Christ's self-sacrificing act of obedience. Thus Christ becomes the end and consummation (τέλος) of the law, because he makes unavoidably clear that reliance on God alone makes man righteous—i.e., allows him to participate in the covenant relationship (Rom. 10:4).

Therefore, says Paul, from the beginning, only faith "is reckoned as" righteousness (as upholding the covenant relationship), and he shows what this means in a discussion of Abraham, the father of the Jews (Rom. 4). God promised that he would do what Abraham could not: give Abraham an heir (vss. 18-19; cf. Gen. 15:1 ff). Abraham believed this promise; he trusted that God would do what he said (Rom. 4:20-21). This act of trust on Abraham's part accepted the conditions of that covenant relationship (cf. Gen. 15:18): it depended totally on God's act to initiate and uphold it (Rom. 4:18). Therefore, this act of trust in God, because it accepted the relationship with God by relying on him and not on man to uphold it, is a righteous act (vs. 22). Because the law and circumcision came *after* this act of trusting acceptance of the covenant relationship (Rom. 4:11; Gal. 3:17), they cannot be the basis of Abraham's relationship to God (Rom. 4:13).

Therefore, this act of trust is the means whereby Abraham accepted the relationship with God in the only way it can be accepted: relying on God alone to uphold it; and thus this act is "reckoned as righteous." Abraham accepted God's promise because he trusted God, and thus he entered into the covenant relationship which God offered him. Therefore, this trust (faith) is reckoned as righteousness—i.e., as accepting the covenant relationship with God.

This was not, however, limited to Abraham. It is true of all men (Rom. 4:23-24). To trust that God will uphold the covenant relationship with man, though man has broken it; to rely on God (in Christ) to do this, not on oneself (by works), is to accept the relationship, and thus be righteous (Phil. 3:7-9). Therefore, this act of acceptance (faith), whereby man admits that God has done what man could not —restored the covenant relationship in Christ—this act is a righteous act, because only by such an admission can a man accept the covenant relationship with God. So long as man refuses to trust that God (in Christ) has restored the covenant relationship, and tries to uphold it himself by meeting its demands (works of the law), which he cannot do, so long man remains outside a positive relationship to God (Gal. 5:4). To trust that God in Christ has restored the covenant relationship is the only way man can live in this relationship, and thus be righteous (Rom. 1:17; cf. Gal. 3:11; Heb. 10:38). Therefore, faith is not another work—it is the admission that works are of no avail in preserving the covenant relationship between God and man. The admission that a man can contribute nothing is the only thing a man can contribute to the relationship with God, and therefore this admission alone (faith) is a righteous act.

Therefore, for Paul, to be "counted righteous by faith" means to accept the fact that one is righteous (i.e., participates in the covenant relationship with God), not by one's own act, but by God's act in Christ, whereby God upheld, by grace, this relationship. Thus, the terms "righteous by faith" (Rom. 5:1), "righteous by grace" (Rom. 3:24), and "righteous by Christ's blood" (Rom. 5:9; RSV "justified" in each of these instances) all mean the same for Paul: the covenant relationship with God exists because, through Christ's act of sacrificial obedience, God alone upholds it. Therefore, because "righteousness," like "salvation," is a gift of God's grace in Christ, the two are often closely linked (Rom. 3:24; 10:10; I Cor. 1:30; cf. Matt. 13:49; 25:46; Tit. 3:7; for the negative aspect, cf. II Thess. 2:10, 12). Indeed, to participate in the covenant relationship (righteousness) is to participate in God's fulfilment of this covenant (salvation, or eternal life); the two cannot be separated. Man must rely for both on God alone.

5. Righteousness and personal benefit. The covenant relationship between God and man, which God by his act in Christ restored and upholds, places a demand, as do all relationships, on man. This demand is faith (*see* § 4 *above*): the acknowledgment that man can contribute nothing to the establishment or upholding of this covenant relationship, and trust that God, despite this, can and will allow the relationship to remain intact. But the restored (new) relationship also includes the creation of a new community among men. Therefore, those who share in the new divine-human relationship also share in the new community, and thus, the covenant relationship places a demand on man over against his fellow man. The nature of this demand is determined by the nature of the covenant. Because the act whereby man can participate again in the covenant relationship is the obedient self-sacrifice of Christ, who thus acted, not for his own benefit, but for the benefit of sinful man, those who participate in the covenant relationship are also expected to act for the benefit, not of themselves, but of others. Thus, men are expected to glorify God and boast in him, not in themselves (Rom. 4:2; I Cor. 1:30-31; Gal. 6:14), and they are to serve, not themselves, but their fellow men (Matt. 22:36 ff). Thus, the demand which the new covenant relationship lays upon man in relation to God is faith; and in relation to man, the demand is that one's action be to the benefit of others, not oneself. To act for the benefit of others is thus to uphold the relationship by meeting its demand, and therefore it is righteous; by the same token, to act for one's own benefit, to the neglect of others, is unrighteous.

Thus, Jesus is righteous because he acted for the benefit of others. He does not seek his own will, but the will of God, and therefore his "judgment" is righteous: it also serves God's will, not his own (John 5:30). There is no unrighteousness in Jesus, because he seeks, not his own glory, but the glory of the One who sent him (7:18). This activity of Jesus on behalf of others did not end with his obedient self-sacrifice on the cross; it continues to the present time. He is still an "advocate with the Father" (παράκλητος ... πρὸς τὸν πατέρα) for sinful men, and therefore is termed the "righteous one" (I John 2:1). Thus, the relation of man and man is determined by the relation of God and man; God's acts are acts of mercy, independent of the worth of the recipient (cf. Matt. 5:45-48); so must man's be.

Thus, the "righteous" are those who have met the demands toward their fellow men which are laid on them by their participation in the covenant relationship. They have fed the hungry, given drink to the thirsty, and performed other acts of mercy (Matt. 25:34 ff). And because the nature of the relationship between men is determined by the nature of the relationship between God and man, fulfilment of the demands of the former is also fulfilment of the demands of the latter (Matt. 25:37 ff, especially vs. 40). Again, those who have invited the poor and the lame to the feast will be deemed righteous in the Last Judgment, because their actions have been solely for the benefit of the recipients. Those guests cannot "repay" the righteous (Luke 14:14). Paul assures the Corinthians that he has done nothing unrighteous (οὐδένα ἠδικήσαμεν), because he has not taken advantage of them—i.e., used them for his own gain (II Cor. 7:2). In the same sense, those who go to great lengths to avoid acting for personal benefit to the detriment of the relationship with their fellow men are considered by the NT as especially righteous. Men who act in this way are said to "suffer for righteousness' sake" (I Pet. 3:14). Such men will suffer discomfort and even death rather than, by resisting, act to their own benefit and thus break the relationship (Matt. 5:10-11; I Cor. 6:7; cf. Jas. 5:6, where the righteous man avoids resistance even to death). In this sense Jesus' admonition to avoid resistance must be understood: it concerns refusal to act for personal benefit, whatever the cost, but it is not a demand to avoid all forceful action, where this action would benefit another or bring glory to God (Matt. 5:38 ff; cf. 21: 12 ff; John 2:15).

On the other hand, those who do act for personal benefit are called "unrighteous" in the NT. They do not meet the demands toward their fellow man which the covenant relationship places upon them. Thus, Jesus warns men not to perform their acts of righteousness (δικαιοσύνη; RSV "piety") for the purpose of being admired by men (Matt. 6:1). Such acts do not uphold the relationship. For the same reason, Jesus was unrelenting in his condemnation of the Pharisees: they performed the outward semblance of righteousness, but they acted from selfish motives. Therefore, the charge of hypocrisy is leveled against them (Matt. 23:13, 25, 28, etc.); they do what they do, not for the benefit of their fellow men, but for their own benefit ("to be seen by men"; vss. 5 ff). As God acted in love, thus fulfilling the relationship with man, and upholding it, so man must act in love toward his fellow man, thus fulfilling the demands toward his fellow man which the covenant relationship lays on him (I John 3:10).

A lack of unity within a group is also termed "unrighteousness" when it is based on a factious spirit that seeks to uphold its own view to the disregard of others (Rom. 2:8; cf. Jas. 3:16 ff). For this reason, Paul is so deeply concerned about the manifestations of disunity in Corinth (I Cor. 1:10 ff). If the demand of the covenant relationship—seeking the good of others—is upheld, unity is the result. Thus Christian unity and righteousness go hand in hand.

6. Other uses of the concept of righteousness. Although the great majority of cases where the terminology of righteousness is employed in the NT are best understood in a relational sense, these words are also used in other contexts, where this meaning is less apparent, if it exists at all.

a. As a forensic term. Although it can be argued that part, at least, of the terminology of "righteousness" is forensic in origin (*see* JUSTIFICATION), the instances where this is clearly the case are somewhat limited in the NT. In this sense, that is "just" which corresponds to the facts (cf. Luke 12:57; Acts 4:19). If an accusation distorts the facts, it is unjust; the man falsely accused, on the other hand, is just because the facts favor him and refute the accusation. Thus, the centurion beneath the cross exclaims that Jesus must surely have been "just" (Luke 23:47; RSV "innocent"; cf. Matt. 27:4, where the witness of some MSS to ἀθῷον, "innocent," and others to δίκαιον, "just," indicates an early overlapping in their

meanings) because various natural phenomena, as well as his manner of death, suggest that the allegations against him were untrue (Luke 23:44 ff). In the same sense, Pilate's wife warns her husband to have nothing to do with "that righteous man"; the context of the trial makes it clear that she regards the accusations against him to be untrue (Matt. 27:19). Jesus refutes the charge that he is a "glutton and a drunkard" with the statement that "wisdom is justified by her deeds," indicating that the facts will vindicate him of such charges (Matt. 11:19). The lawyer who asks Jesus about the central element of the law seeks to "justify himself" by asking who his neighbor is. He wants to clear himself of Jesus' implied accusation that he has not kept the command to "love his neighbor" (Luke 10:29). Jesus tells his listeners to decide for themselves what is right (Luke 12:57); the preceding context indicates that he is speaking of a correct interpretation of the facts (Luke 12:54 ff; cf. John 7:24, where a "just" judgment is contrasted with one based only on appearances).

The forensic nature of part of the vocabulary of "righteousness" is also indicated when it is employed to describe legal proceedings. This is especially true in Acts, where this vocabulary is consistently employed in describing Paul's experiences with Roman judicial proceedings. Gallio says that Paul is not charged with any serious injustice (ἀδίκημα; Acts 18:14), and Paul himself affirms the same thing before Felix (Acts 24:20; cf. 24:25; 25:10-11). The same general use of the terms is evident when the NT describes the Last Judgment; in this context, the legal simile of judgment extends to the use of forensic terminology in describing God's (or Jesus') action on that last day (Acts 17:31; II Tim. 4:8; etc.).

b. As retributive justice. There are also some instances in the NT where the words under study seem to mean "justice" in the retributive sense. Thus, God is called just (δίκαιος) in his judgments because he has "given blood to drink" to those who shed the blood of saints and prophets. God is just because he gave them "their due" (Rev. 16:5-6; vs. 7 is probably also to be understood in this sense). Again, because God has avenged the murder of his servants by judging and thus destroying Babylon, his judgments are just: they give Babylon due measure for what she gave (Rev. 19:2; cf. 15:4; 19:11). God considers it "just" to repay with suffering those who cause Christians to suffer (II Thess. 1:6)—again clearly a retributive statement. Christians are assured that God is not so unjust that he will not reward the acts of love which Christians show in serving their fellow saints (Heb. 6:10). In these and a few other instances, the element of retribution is clearly included in the vocabulary of "righteousness."

Yet it must be noted that this use does not contradict the use in a relational sense. The retributive punishment of God is against those who harm the covenant people (cf. II Thess. 1:6; Rev. 16:5 ff; 19:2), whereas the just rewards are given to those who act on behalf of their fellow men, thus upholding their relationship (Heb. 6:10). Therefore, though not on the surface, the relational understanding of "righteousness" seems to underlie the retributive sense.

7. Righteousness and conformity to a norm. If, as has been stated, righteousness is to be understood basically as a relational term, then it is also true that it cannot mean basically "conformity to a (moral) norm." This is not to say that morality and righteousness are unrelated in the NT, but it is to say that righteousness is fundamentally more concerned with the covenant relationship with God, and more particularly with man's broken and restored relationship to God, than it is with man's moral shortcomings and ethical ideals. Aside from the fact that righteousness as meaning conformity to a moral norm would mean that God too conforms to this norm, since God is called "righteous" (an idea incompatible with the NT view of God's sovereignty), such an understanding makes it difficult to explain how the term "righteousness" can so often be applied to God's saving act on behalf of those who are supremely unrighteous and thus morally delinquent (Rom. 5:8, among others). That believing God is "reckoned as righteousness" (Gal. 3:6), particularly when illustrated by Abraham, indicates that action in conformity to some ethical norm is not what is counted as righteous. In this case, righteousness clearly denotes a trusting relationship to God (Gal. 3:8; Heb. 10:38). If righteousness is a moral state, then to reckon those as righteous who are not morally pure is either to be blind to the facts or simply to disregard them. To say that God reckons men as righteous now on the basis of what they will one day (perhaps) become is not justified by the NT; there is no evidence for such a proleptic justification.

The clear statement of Paul that no man is counted righteous before God on the basis of works should be enough to eliminate moral conformity from consideration (Gal. 3:11, etc.). The affirmation that none is righteous (Rom. 3:10 ff) means that none has remained within the covenant relationship with God (Rom. 1:18–3:9), not that no moral action has ever been performed. The fact that Paul can use the blanket term "unrighteous" to describe those outside the Christian fellowship at Corinth (I Cor. 6:1) means it can hardly refer to a moral state; Paul himself acknowledges that the moral state of some within the fellowship is lower than that of most outside it (I Cor. 5:1-2). Jesus' condemnation of those who thought righteousness consisted only in conformity to a norm (the Pharisees), and his association with those whose morals were of the lowest type in his world (harlots, tax collectors, "sinners"), indicates that Jesus was not interested primarily in moral purity but in a relationship of repentance and trust in God (cf. Luke 18:9 ff). And Jesus himself is called "righteous," not because his acts conform to a moral norm (quite the contrary; cf. Luke 7:34), but because by his obedient, sacrificial death, he brings men into a new relationship to God (Luke 19:10; I Pet. 3:18), and thus Jesus, not man's moral acts, is man's "righteousness" (I Cor. 1:30).

Bibliography. H. Cremer in J. Koegel, ed., *Biblisch-theologisches Woerterbuch* (10th ed., 1915), under appropriate Greek words; E. Vischer, "Rechtfertigung im NT," *Die Religion in Geschichte und Gegenwart* (2nd ed., 1930), vol. IV, cols. 1,745-48; A. Nygren, *Commentary on Romans* (trans. C. C. Rasmussen; 1949), pp. 9 ff and *passim;* R. Bultmann, *Theology of the NT* (trans. K. Grobel; 1951), vol. I, sections 28-31; G. Quell and G. Schrenck, *Righteousness,* vol. IV of *Bible Key Words from Kittel* (trans. and notes by J. R. Coates; 1951); E. De W.

Burton, *Galatians* (1952), pp. 460-74; P. Althaus, *Der Brief an die Römer,* vol. VI of *Das NT Deutsch* (1954), pp. 12 ff; E. Schweizer, "Gerechtigkeit Gottes im NT," *Die Religion in Geschichte und Gegenwart* (3rd ed., 1958), vol. II, cols. 1,406-7.

P. J. ACHTEMEIER

RIMMON rĭm'ən [רמון, pomegranate(?), *or* the thunderer(?); *cf.* Akkad. *ramanu,* to roar]. **1.** A Beerothite; the father of Baanah and Rechab, the men who killed Ish-bosheth (II Sam. 4:2, 5, 9).

E. R. DALGLISH

2. The deity whom Naaman the Syrian and the king of Syria worshiped in his temple, probably at Damascus (II Kings 5:18). The god was known to the Assyrians as Ramanu, a title of Hadad, the god of storm, rain, and thunder, called in Syria "Baal"— i.e., the lord par excellence. The identity of Rimmon with Hadad and his significance in the religion of the Syrians of Damascus is confirmed by the fact that "Hadad" occurs as an element in the theophoric name Ben-hadad, borne by several kings of Syria, and Tabrimmon, the father of Ben-hadad the contemporary of Asa of Judah (I Kings 15:18).

On the particular features of this god and his cult, *see* BAAL (DEITY); HADADRIMMON.

Bibliography. M. Jastrow, *The Religion of Babylonia and Assyria* (1898), pp. 156-61; A. S. Kapelrud, *Baal in the Ras Shamra Texts* (1952), pp. 31-37. For further bibliography, *see* BAAL (DEITY).   J. GRAY

3. A town in S Judah whose full name is Ain Rimmon (EN-RIMMON; Josh. 15:32, where "Ain" and "Rimmon" are separated by "and" but almost certainly belong together). First assigned to Simeon (Josh. 19:7; I Chr. 4:32), it became a part of Judah's Negeb district of Beer-sheba (Josh. 15:32). Returnees from the Exile settled in En-rimmon (Neh. 11:29). In the final chapter of Zechariah, the whole Judean hill country as far S as Rimmon is envisioned as becoming a plain, with Jerusalem towering above it (Zech. 14:10).

Eusebius speaks of Erimmon (En-rimmon) as a very large Jewish village *ca.* sixteen (Roman) miles S of Eleutheropolis, in the middle of the Darome (i.e., the S part of Judea). En-rimmon in S Judah is usually identified with Khirbet er-Ramamin, nine miles N-NE of Beer-sheba.

4. A town in central Zebulun (Josh. 19:13) on the S edge of the Plain of Asochis (Sahl el-Battof), identified with modern Rummaneh, a village six miles N-NE of Nazareth. "Remmon-Methoar" (Josh. 19: 13 KJV) is a nonexistent place. "Methoar" is properly corrected to read "it bends toward" in the RSV.

It became a Levitical city (I Chr. 6:77, where Rimmono=Rimmon; cf. LXX Remmon). "Dimnah" (Josh. 21:35), otherwise unknown, almost certainly should be read "Rimmon," with initial *r* (ר) misread as *d* (ד). The OL text, which depends heavily on the B text, reads "Remmon" here, a good support for the proposed corrected reading.

During the period of the Crusades the town was known as Romeneh.

5. The rock of Rimmon, near Gibeah; the place to which the remnant of the Benjaminites fled to escape from the victorious Israelites who had determined to punish Gibeah and Benjamin for the atrocity perpetrated by the men of Gibeah against a Levite and his concubine (Judg. 20:45-47). Later, an embassage from the congregation of Israel invited the six hundred escaped Benjaminites to return from their hiding place and provided them with wives from Jabesh-gilead and Shiloh (Judg. 21:13 ff). The place was probably the limestone outcropping *ca.* four miles E of Bethel on which the modern village of Rammun now stands. Ravines protect it from approach from the N, S, and W; in it are many caves in which the Benjaminites could have taken refuge.

If the suggested reading of Isa. 10:27 is correct in the RSV, Rimmon was one of the places on the route to Jerusalem taken by the Assyrian conqueror.

Bibliography. A. Saarisalo, "Topographical Researches in Galilee," *JPOS,* 9 (1929), 27-40; F.-M. Abel, *Géographie de la Palestine,* II (1938), 437 and *passim;* W. F. Albright, "The List of Levitic Cities," *Louis Ginzberg Jubilee Volume* (1945), English section, pp. 49-73. V. R. GOLD

RIMMONO rĭ mō'nō. Alternate form of RIMMON 4 in I Chr. 6:77—H 6:62 (cf. Josh. 19:13; 21:35).

RIMMON-PEREZ rĭm'ən pĭr'ĭz [רמן פרץ, pomegranate of the pass (breach)—*i.e.,* the pomegranate pass(?)] (Num. 33:19-20); KJV RIMMON-PAREZ —pâr'ĭz. One of the stopping places of the Israelites between Rithmah and Libnah.

RING. The translation of the following words:

a) טבעת (alternately "signet ring"). A term applied to a number of different kinds of rings. There was a finger ring which was a sign of authority—i.e., signet ring (Gen. 41:42; Esth. 3:10, 12; 8:2, 8, 10). Taken in war as booty, it was then presented as an offering to the Lord (Num. 31:50). In Isa. 3:21 it is an article of luxury. *See* SIGNET.

This term applies also to rings for staves and curtains of the tabernacle (Exod. 26:29; 27:4, 7) and the ark (Exod. 25:12, 14-15, etc.), for breastpiece and ephod (Exod. 28:23-24, etc.), for the incense altar (Exod. 30:4; 37:27), and for the altar of burnt offering (Exod. 38:5, 7).

b) גליל ("cylinder"). A ring for holding drapery cords (Esth. 1:6). The KJV translates this word "gold ring" (RSV "rounded gold") in Song of S. 5:14, where it refers figuratively to arms.

c) נום. A nose ring, earring, or ring in general. *See* NOSE RING; EARRING 1.

d) חותם. A seal ring. *See* DRESS AND ORNAMENTS § A6.

e) Δακτύλιος (Luke 15:22). A symbol of dignity.

f) Σφραγίς. A seal ring. *See* DRESS AND ORNAMENTS § A6.

g) Χρυσοδακτύλιος (Jas. 2:2). A gold ring signifying wealth and position.

The KJV translates גב "ring" in Ezek. 1:18 (RSV "rim" [of a wheel]). J. M. MYERS

RINNAH rĭn'ə [רנה, ringing cry] (I Chr. 4:20). A son of Shimon; one of the members of the S tribe of Judah.

RIPHATH rī'făth [ריפת]. Son of Gomer and grandson of Japheth (Gen. 10:3). Riphath is non-Semitic and probably Anatolian, together with his brothers,

Ashkenaz and Togarmah, as well as their father, Gomer. In I Chr. 1:6 "Diphath" (דיפת) occurs instead of "Riphath," but about thirty Hebrew MSS, the LXX, and the Vulg. read "Riphath" also there, supporting "Riphath" as the correct form.

C. H. GORDON

RISSAH rĭs'ə [רסה, dew drop(?), rain(?), *or* ruin(?)] (Num. 33:21-22). A stopping place of the Israelites in the wilderness between Libnah and Kehelathah. The location is unknown.

RITHMAH rĭth'mə [רתמה, broom plant] (Num. 33: 18-19). The stopping place of the Israelites in the wilderness after Hazeroth. The location is unknown.

RITUAL. *See* WORSHIP IN THE OT; WORSHIP IN NT TIMES, JEWISH; WORSHIP IN NT TIMES, CHRISTIAN.

RIVER. The translation of several terms in the Bible. *See also* BROOK; FLOOD; VALLEY.

The four terms usually translated "river" are: (*a*) נהר (Gen. 2:10; Num. 24:6), used more than 120 times, frequently for the Euphrates (Gen. 15:18; Deut. 1:7); (*b*) נחל (Lev. 11:9; Deut. 2:37; the RSV frequently translates "valley" where the context requires it—e.g., Gen. 26:19; Deut. 2:36); (*c*) יאר, יאור, frequently designating the NILE (Gen. 41:1; Exod. 1:22), but also the Nile tributaries or canals (Exod. 7:19; II Kings 19:24), and in one passage, the Tigris (Dan. 12:5-7); (*d*) ποταμός, used in the LXX for the preceding terms, and also in the NT (Mark 1:5 [the Jordan]; John 7:38; Rev. 8:10).

Other words translated less frequently "river" are: יובל (Jer. 17:8 KJV [RSV "stream"]); אפיקים (Ezek. 6:3 KJV [RSV "ravines"]; Joel 1:20 KJV [RSV "brooks"]); פלגים (Job 29:6 KJV; Ps. 1:3 KJV; RSV "streams"). As indicated above, the most descriptive English word in translating is sometimes difficult to select. In Ps. 93:3; Hab. 3:8, where the feminine and masculine plural of נהר occur (KJV-RSV "floods," "rivers"), the symbolism is that of the primordial waters, paralleling the primordial sea.

Biblical rivers mentioned by name, in addition to those above, are: ABANAH; AHAVA; CHEBAR; GIHON; GOZAN; HIDDEKEL; JABBOK; KISHON; PHARPAR; PISHON; RIVER OF EGYPT; ULAI.

Rivers are frequently referred to in indicating geographical boundaries (Josh. 1:4; Judg. 4:13; I Kings 4:21). They were used in irrigation (*see* AGRICULTURE); bathing (Exod. 2:5); as means of transportation (Isa. 18:2); in defense (Nah. 3:8); for drinking (Exod. 7:18), fishing (Lev. 11:9), and healing (II Kings 5:10); as places of theophany (Gen. 32:22-23), baptism (Matt. 3:6), and prayer (Acts 16:13).

Rivers are mentioned in a figurative sense to suggest the prosperity of a region (Num. 24:6; Ps. 65:9; Isa. 66:12) over which God's power extends; the drying up of the rivers was a symbol of tragedy (Job 14:11; Isa. 19:5). Righteousness is compared to a perennial stream (נחל איתם; Amos 5:24), and God's blessing to a "river of the water of life" (Rev. 22:1). Of special note are the pictures of a river which

flowed from Eden (Gen. 2:10 ff) and the river or
rivers to flow from the temple in the new age (Ezek.
47:1-12; Zech. 14:8; Rev. 22:1-2; cf. John 7:38;
Rev. 12:15).   W. L. REED

RIVER OF EGYPT. *See* EGYPT, BROOK OF; EGYPT,
RIVER OF.

RIVER OF THE WILDERNESS. KJV translation
of "brook of the Arabah." *See* ARABAH, BROOK OF.

RIZIA rĭ zī'ə [רִצְיָא] (I Chr. 7:39); KJV REZIA. A
chief in the tribe of Asher, and a mighty warrior.

RIZPAH rĭz'pə [רִצְפָּה, glowing coal, heated stone,
bread baked in ashes]. Daughter of Aiah, and a
concubine of Saul. After the death of Saul, Abner
took Rizpah as his wife (II Sam. 3:7). This act
amounted to a claim to the throne (cf. I Kings 2:22);
and Ishbaal, Saul's son, and now king in name only,
challenged Abner's loyalty. Abner then made good
his claim to the actual leadership of the kingdom by
beginning his negotiation to make David king in
Israel (II Sam. 3:7-21). Later, when a famine was
regarded as due to Saul's guilt in slaying Gibeonites,
David made expiation by handing over seven of the
sons of Saul, two sons of Rizpah and five of Merab,
to be hanged (21:1-9). Then Rizpah began a heroic
vigil by the bodies, keeping off the birds and beasts
of prey, from the beginning of the barley harvest until the rain finally came. Then at last the burial could
be made, and "after that God heeded supplications
for the land" (21:10-14).   D. HARVEY

ROAD. A frequent translation of דֶּרֶךְ (Gen. 38:14,
16; Num. 22:23, 34; Deut. 2:8, 27; etc.; alternately
WAY, as commonly in the KJV wherever "road" in
the ordinary sense is intended), and an occasional
translation of נְתִיבוֹת (Isa. 59:8; Jer. 6:16; 18:15),
מְסִלָּה (I Chr. 26:16, 18), and ὁδός (Matt. 21:8; Mark
10:32; 11:8; Luke 9:57; 10:4, 31; 19:36; 24:32, 35;
Acts 8:26, 36; 9:17, 27).

Roads and trade routes figured prominently in the
geography and history of Palestine, which served as
the land bridge among the empires of the ancient
Near East. Many of the trade routes were strategically important in commerce and military activities,
and as sacred ways for pilgrims traveling to religious
shrines. Understandably, such great religious centers
as Jerusalem and Damascus also became commercial
centers.

The importance of roads and travel is evident in
biblical history. The roads which crossed Palestine
led to many countries. Caravansaries along these
routes realized tremendous profits from charges for
services and from tolls. Fortresses located at crucial
points along these routes allowed for control both of
military and of commercial movements.

The major route from Palestine to Egypt lay along
the coast. The exiles to Babylon in 586 probably
went around the Fertile Crescent and down the
Euphrates to Babylon, though there were caravan
routes eastward across the Syrian Desert from
Damascus, Amman, etc. According to Neh. 7:66-69,
a group of returning exiles brought horses, mules,

camels, and asses with them; food and water for such
a caravan could have been provided far more easily
along the Fertile Crescent than across the Syrian
Desert.

The most famous road system in biblical lands was
the Great West Road, or the Road to the Sea; this
system had many branches. One joined Damascus
and Dothan, crossing the Jordan between Merom
and Galilee. Another branch went W from Safed to
Acre through the valley between Upper and Lower
Galilee. A branch also went through Capernaum and
down the Plain of Gennesaret, joining the W branch
at Ramah. A much-traveled section went from Capernaum through the Plain of Esdraelon, probably S of
Mount Tabor, to Megiddo and down the coastal
plain to Egypt. A shorter branch connected Capernaum with the Plain of Esdraelon by way of Tiberias
and Beth-shan. The route to Acco connected with a
caravan route which ran from the region of Mount
Carmel to Antioch. Main roads also joined Galilee
and the Plain of Esdraelon with Jerusalem, Hebron,
and Beer-sheba. There was a road in very ancient
times from Jericho up to a point N of Jerusalem (Ai)
and on down to the region of Joppa.

A major N-S route joined Asia Minor with the
spice routes from Arabia; this route ran S from
Damascus and down the plateau on the E side of
the Jordan. It has served as a pilgrimage road to
Mecca into modern times. Branches off this road led
into Palestine at several points (see, e.g., Gen. 37:
25; *see also* KING'S HIGHWAY).* A major road ran
westward from Petra to Gaza and would seem to
have joined routes from Arabia, thus allowing goods
from Arabia and the E to be carried up the coastal
plain from Gaza. Many of the great cities in the
Syrian and Jordanian deserts (e.g., Palmyra in the
eleventh century B.C.; and the Nabatean cities, including Petra, in the second century A.D.) were essentially caravan cities and military outposts. Fig.
KIN 7.

Hittites, Babylonians, Assyrians, and Persians, all
built roads for commercial and military purposes in
the Near East. The Romans built numerous roads in
the area in efforts to consolidate and maintain the
political and military interests of their empire and to

Courtesy of Denis Baly

12. Roman road from Amman to Yajuz and then to
Jerash, showing fallen milestones beside the road

From *Atlas of the Bible* (Thomas Nelson & Sons Limited)

13. Roman road between Aleppo and Antioch on the Orontes

strengthen the Pax Romana generally. Many of their roads, which were built and maintained at great expense, are still visible, especially in Jordan. Figs. ROA 12-13.

Jesus of Nazareth seems to have shown a preference for byways. His native town was near several major caravan routes and Roman roads. Nazareth was connected by road with the Mediterranean, Megiddo, Jerusalem, and the Sea of Galilee. At nearby Sepphoris a great road led to the Phoenician coastal towns; eastward a road ran across the Valley of Jezreel, S of Beth-shan, and across the Jordan. A road system joined the populous towns around the W side of the Sea of Galilee. After going down the E side of the Jordan, Jesus probably took the ancient road from Jericho through Wadi Qelt (the Jericho road) to Jerusalem. Paul frequently traveled the great highways of Palestine, Asia Minor, and parts of Europe. He entered Rome on the Appian Way, which may still be traveled between Brindisi and Rome.

See also Trade and Commerce; Travel and Communication.   H. F. Beck

ROADS AND TRAVEL. *See* Travel and Communication.

ROBBER, ROBBERY. *See* Crimes and Punishments § C7c.

ROBE. The translation of the following words:

a) מעיל (alternately "coat"; "garment"). A coat without sleeves. *See* Dress and Ornaments § A2.

b) כתנת (alternately "coat"). A long shirtlike tunic, a symbol of official status (II Sam. 15:32; Isa. 22:21), and worn by priests (Exod. 28:4; 29:5, 8; etc.). On כתנת פסים ("long robe with sleeves"; KJV "coat of many colors"), *see* Cloth § 6.

c) אדרת (alternately Mantle 1). A cape or loose coat; a robe of state (Jonah 3:6; cf. Mic. 2:8).

d) בגד. Any kind of garment. This term is used of the robe of kings in I Kings 22:10, 30; II Chr. 18:9, 29.

e) פתיגיל (a loan word; "rich robe"; KJV "stomacher"). Apparently a garment of fine material (Isa. 3:24).

f) Χλαμύς. A short mantle or cloak, generally a military cape. This term is used to designate the scarlet robe placed on Jesus by Roman soldiers (Matt. 27:28, 31).

g) Στολή. A garment, especially a long, flowing robe or dress (Mark 12:38; 16:5; Rev. 22:14). This term is used for the robe of the prodigal son (Luke 15:22) and of scribes (Luke 20:46) and for the white garments of martyrs (Rev. 6:11) and the redeemed (7:9, 13-14).

h) Ἐσθής (Acts 1:10; 12:21; "apparel" in Luke 23:11). Clothes, raiment.

i) Ἱμάτιον. An outer garb worn over the χιτών (Matt. 26:65; I Pet. 3:3; Rev. 19:13, 16). This term is used to designate the purple robe of Jesus (John 19:2, 5). *See* Dress and Ornaments § A1.

j) Ποδήρης (Rev. 1:13). A garment extending to the feet.   J. M. Myers

ROBOAM. KJV NT form of Rehoboam.

ROCK. *See* Palestine, Geology of.

ROCK BADGER [שפן; *see bibliography*]; KJV CONEY. Alternately: BADGER (Ps. 104:18; Prov. 30:26). Any of a family of small ungulate mammals, the hyraxes, of which *ca.* fourteen species are known. The only variety found outside Africa is the Syrian hyrax (*procavia syriaca*). Except for its inconspicuous ears, the appearance of the hyrax is like that of the rabbit, which it also resembles in size. Unlike the rabbit, it does not burrow but lives in rocky regions. To use the term "badger" for this animal is without any justification; Bodenheimer prefers the term "coney." *See* Fauna § A2d.

The propensity of this animal for rocks is alluded to in Ps. 104:18; Prov. 30:26. In Lev. 11:5; Deut. 14:7 it is placed among the unclean animals, though the statement that it is a ruminant is unfounded. Tristram observes (*NHB* 76) that the "constant motion of the little creature's jaws" may have suggested that it was chewing its cud.

Bibliography. For שפן as a personal name in a Sinai inscription, see *BASOR,* no. 110 (1948), p. 21.
     W. S. McCullough

ROD [שבט; מקל, מטה, חטר; ῥάβδος]. Alternately: STAFF; POLE. A stick cut from the stem or branch of a tree and used for numerous purposes. Straight staffs, thicker at one end than at the other and of varying lengths, were the protection and support of shepherds and travelers on foot. They might also serve as poles for carrying burdens, as shafts for arrows or spears, and as instruments for inflicting punishment. A shorter staff with a knobbed end, often studded with nails or bits of flint, served the soldier and the shepherd as a weapon. Artificial rods, resembling the natural sticks, could be described by the same words—e.g., "rod of iron" (Ps. 2:9; Rev.

19:15). Two of the words (מטה, שבט) may also mean "TRIBE."

The translation "rod" (more frequent in the KJV than in the RSV) is preferred for each of these words in certain contexts. Thus, while מטה may mean the stem of a growing plant (Ezek. 19:11-14), a soldier's weapon (I Sam. 14:27, 43; "staff"), or a king's SCEPTER (Ps. 110:2), it is translated "rod" chiefly when it refers to the wonder-working rods of Moses and Aaron, which began as simple shepherds' staffs, but were endowed by Yahweh with supernatural powers and figured prominently in the miracles in Egypt and in the wilderness (Exod. 4; 7-8; Num. 17).

Similarly, שבט may refer to the stick used for threshing cummin (Isa. 28:27); to the staff of authority, especially the king's scepter (Ps. 125:3); to the staff with which the shepherd marshals and counts his sheep (Lev. 27:32; Mic. 7:14); or to the club with which he defends his flock (Ps. 23:4); but, when translated "rod," it usually means a scourge, the instrument of punishment, either human or divine (e.g., a "rod for the back of fools" [Prov. 26:3]; Assyria as the rod of the Lord's anger [Isa. 10:5; the parallel term מטה is here rendered "staff"]).

חטר is also a scourge (Prov. 14:3), and מקל refers principally to the pealed sticks cut from a variety of trees, by means of which Jacob influenced the breeding of Laban's flocks and herds (Gen. 30:37-41). This word appears in Jeremiah's vision in the "rod of almond" (Jer. 1:11); it is frequently translated "staff."

In the NT ῥάβδος reflects OT usage, referring to an instrument of punishment (I Cor. 4:21), to a measuring stick (Rev. 11:1), or to Aaron's rod (Heb. 9:4).   L. E. TOOMBS

RODANIM rō'də nĭm [רודנים] (I Chr. 1:7). Rhodians. *See* RHODES.

Though Gen. 10:4 has "Dodanim" (דדנים; so, too, some Hebrew MSS in I Chr. 1:7), the LXX again has 'Ρόδιοι, "Rhodians." The *d* (ד) and the *r* (ר) are similar in the Hebrew script, and since Dodanim/Rodanim are included among the Greeks (especially the islanders), "Rhodians" fits in quite well. On the other hand, "Dodanim," being the *lectio difficilior* (i.e., the more problematic reading), deserves careful consideration precisely because it is obscure; for no scribe would change the clear "Rhodians" into the obscure "Dodanim," though the opposite could easily happen, and perhaps did.   C. H. GORDON

ROE, ROEBUCK [יחמור] (Deut. 14:5; I Kings 4:23 —H 5:3; KJV FALLOW DEER); KJV צבי (Deut. 12:15, *etc.*), צביה (Song of S. 4:5, *etc.*), RSV GAZELLE; יעלה (Prov. 5:19), RSV DOE]. The roe DEER (*Capreolus capreolus*), a very graceful animal. It is one of the smallest members of the deer family, the adult male standing *ca.* twenty-six inches in shoulder height. Its antlers rise almost vertically from the head, becoming forked only near their summit. Bodenheimer (*see* FAUNA § A2eiv) claims that there is no word for this kind of deer in the OT.   W. S. McCULLOUGH

ROGELIM rō'gə lĭm [רגלים, (place of) fullers]. A city in E Gilead; the home of Barzillai, who befriended David when he arrived in Mahanaim in flight from Absalom (II Sam. 17:27-29; 19:31—H 19:32). It was apparently located on the Jabbok, in the hills E of Mahanaim. Abel suggested a possible site in Tell Barsina, from the similarity of the name to Barzillai, but Glueck (*see bibliography*) found no evidence of a settlement there before the Roman period, and suggested instead the nearby Zaharet Soq'ah, a strong IA fortress dominating the neighborhood.

Bibliography. N. Glueck, *AASOR*, XXV-XXVIII (1951), 176-77.   S. COHEN

ROHGAH rō'gə [רוהגה] (I Chr. 7:34). A member of the tribe of Asher; the first-born son of Shemer.

ROIMUS. KJV Apoc. form of REHUM.

ROLL [מגלה; KJV ספריא (Ezra 6:1; RSV ARCHIVES; *see also* BOOK); KJV גליון (Isa. 8:1; RSV TABLET); κεφαλίς (Heb. 10:7; KJV "volume")]. A leather or papyrus scroll. *See* WRITING AND WRITING MATERIALS § C.

ROMAMTI-EZER rō măm'tĭ ē'zər [רממתי עזר] (I Chr. 25:4, 31). One of the musicians, sons of Heman, appointed by David to serve in the sanctuary. But the names in vs. 4 appear to form a liturgical prayer and may not refer to real persons.

See also GIDDALTI.   B. T. DAHLBERG

ROMAN EMPIRE rō'mən. The complex of political, military, social, and cultural forces which controlled the Mediterranean world and Western Europe from *ca.* 30 B.C. to the fifth century A.D. Christianity arose within the Empire and developed primarily within its confines, being recognized as the religion of the state in the fourth century.

1. Expansion; acquisition of provinces
2. Population and social structure
3. Agriculture, industry, trade, and communications
4. Money and banking
5. Taxes and government finance
6. Social conditions
7. Roman law
8. Astrology, magic, religion, and philosophy
9. Scientific knowledge and research
10. Literature
11. Rome and Christianity
12. Christian views of the Empire
Bibliography

1. Expansion; acquisition of provinces. The Roman Empire came into existence through a long process of development in which the little city-state of Rome (traditionally founded by Romulus and Remus in 753 B.C.) extended its power at first under kings, some of whom were Etruscan, and after 508 under a republican form of government headed by two magistrates elected annually. For two centuries, however, Rome was rent by class struggles which accompanied, and were lessened by, a series of treaties and wars with the nearby Latin League. By 275 Rome had gained control of all Italy and was ready to enter the struggle for world power with the divided successors of Alexander the Great. In 264, when the Carthaginians from North Africa, rivals of Rome in the contest for Mediterranean trade, occupied part of Sicily, Rome attacked them, and with the aid of a newly constructed navy finally drove them out in 241. Between 237 and 219 the Carthaginians occupied Spain, and in 218 their General Hannibal crossed the Alps to invade N Italy, whence he moved S, severely defeated the Roman armies, and was able to remain until 203. By that time the Romans had worn out his army, had driven the Carthaginians out of Spain, and had landed an army in Africa. In 201 Carthage became a dependent ally of Rome. Fifty years later, attacked by the king of Numidia but not supported by the Romans, Carthage took up arms against him, only to be attacked in turn by Roman forces, which finally took the city and destroyed it (146).

Meanwhile, Rome had been intervening in Eastern affairs, aiding Pergamum against Macedonia (an ally of Carthage for a time) and finally making Greece a Roman dependency; Macedonia was annexed as a province in 148, and Corinth was destroyed two years later. Similarly the Romans intervened in Asia Minor, though after smashing the army of Antiochus III in 189 they withdrew their troops. In 133, however, Rome was forced to exercise permanent authority in Asia; the king of Pergamum bequeathed his kingdom to the Roman people. Still farther E, a Roman legate prevented an expedition against Egypt, threatened by Antiochus IV, but neither Syria nor Egypt was regarded as subject to Roman rule.

Because of the contacts with Greece made in these ventures, Greek teachers came to Rome and there strongly influenced important circles of the nobility, though many Romans still preferred old-fashioned ways. It was impossible, however, to retain the primitive (and partly imaginary) simplicity of the past, in view of Rome's growing responsibilities in world affairs. Moreover, internal conflicts began to occupy attention. In the last century of the Republic, from 135 to 30, the class struggle became acute. Two slave wars in Sicily (135-132 and 103-101), as well as that later led by Spartacus in Italy (73-71), were symptomatic, but there were also sharp conflicts between the Senate and the other classes. A popular dictatorship under Marius (107-100) was followed by a conservative reaction under Sulla (88-79), combined with further foreign military ventures. After Sulla's death the Republic was rent by conflicts between various generals and the Senate, and by incessant intrigues on the part of all. The orator and consul (63) Cicero hoped for the creation of a moderate central party, but the Senate could not bring itself to co-operate with him. The state came to be controlled by three politically minded generals, the first "triumvirate" of Pompey, CAESAR, and Crassus, a millionaire real-estate speculator. After Crassus' death, Caesar ultimately broke with Pompey, and, after a civil war, achieved supreme power, only to be murdered in 44. Another struggle for power followed; it was won by AUGUSTUS, the real founder of the Roman Empire. For details of the reigns of his successors, see TIBERIUS CAESAR; CA-

LIGULA; CLAUDIUS; NERO; VESPASIAN; TITUS; DOMITIAN. See also EMPEROR; EMPEROR-WORSHIP.

The expansion of Roman power from Italy throughout the Mediterranean world was thus a gradual, and partly an involuntary or at least unpremeditated, process. Sicily, Sardinia, and Corsica were annexed in 241 and 238, at the end of the first Carthaginian war, and Spain in 197, after the second. During and after the third Carthaginian war, Macedonia (148), Africa—including Carthage (146)—and Achaea (146) were taken over. Thirteen years later Pergamum was received by the king's will. The next half-century saw the occupation of Transalpine and Cisalpine Gaul, as well as Cilicia in E Asia Minor; and between 74 and 58 the Romans acquired Cyrene and Bithynia by the wills of the local kings, as well as Crete (68), Syria (63), Cyprus (58), and the rest of Gaul by direct military action.

After Augustus' rise to power, his defeat of Antonius and Cleopatra made Egypt a Roman province (31), and before his death the provinces of Illyricum (27), Galatia (25), Raetia, Noricum (after 16 B.C.), Judea (A.D. 6), and Pannonia (9) were added to the Empire. Under Tiberius, Cappadocia became a province (17); under Claudius, Mauretania (42), Britain (43), Moesia (44), and Thrace (46). All these areas had previously been either occupied by Roman troops or governed by pro-Roman rulers. In later times only a few provinces were acquired, and, especially in the East, they were held only temporarily.

At its height the Empire thus included the whole Mediterranean world and extended from Britain S to Morocco, thence E to Arabia, N to Turkey and Rumania, and W along the Danube to the Rhine. Britain was defended by a fortified wall, and in Germany and to the E there were rough forts and legionary camps. During the first century of the Christian era there were between twenty-five and twenty-eight legions constantly under arms. At full strength each legion was composed of six thousand officers and men, in addition to an equal number of native auxiliary troops.

2. Population and social structure. The population of the Empire has been given widely varying estimates; the figure generally accepted is approximately 54,000,000, of which about 1,000,000 lived in the city of Rome. In the year 47 ca. 6,000,000 persons, including women and children, were carried on the census rolls of Romans in Italy. In the total population there may have been as many as 5,000,000 Jews. With these figures may be contrasted the 6,000 Pharisees mentioned by Josephus and the 5,000 Christians found in Acts 4:4.

The social structure of the Empire resembled a pyramid. At the top were the 600 members of the SENATE and their families. Below them were the knights or equestrians, 1,800 in the late Republic but increased in number by Augustus. While senators had to possess the equivalent of 1,000,000 sesterces, knights needed to have only 400,000. The vast majority of Roman citizens belonged to neither order and were sometimes called plebeians. In addition there were many freedmen, ex-slaves who usually did not become citizens. Finally there were the slaves, who perhaps constituted a third of the population.

Related to this structure was that of the state, beginning with the EMPEROR and proceeding downward through his council to the heads of government departments (see PROCURATOR), the administrators of Rome and the provinces (prefects and proconsuls [see PROCONSUL]), and other officials. In the imperial period it was customary for a member of the two upper classes to pass through a regular sequence of offices (cursus honorum) in order to have a career in government service.

3. Agriculture, industry, trade, and communications. The most important crops of the Empire were wheat (especially in Egypt, which supplied the city of Rome), grapes, olives (for oil), and vegetables. Papyrus also came from Egypt. Mining, both open-cut and underground, was carried on for gold, silver, lead, tin, copper, and iron. Most of the mines belonged to the state and were worked by slaves. Marble was quarried chiefly in Greece, though some use was also made of the Italian stone. Manufacturing in pottery, textiles, leather, metals, and glass was the work chiefly of slaves and freedmen, sometimes associated in syndicates which provided capital and banking facilities for the various branches of the business. Agricultural and manufactured goods were transported either overland on the excellent Roman road system (stone and concrete) or through the Mediterranean and other seas by ship. Highwaymen continued to present difficulties, but at sea the pirates had been exterminated, and Roman patrol vessels safeguarded both the Mediterranean and the W coast of Europe. In the early Empire 120 vessels a year sailed to India, exporting linen, coral, glass, and metals, and importing perfumes, spices, gems, ivory, pearls, and Chinese silk. The government had a courier service for official mail, though other mail had to be sent by private messengers.

4. Money and banking. One of the most important factors in the unity of the Roman Empire was the uniform system of imperial coinage. Under the Republic both foreign and domestic conflicts were almost invariably followed by a sharp reduction in the value of currency. Under the Empire, however, for nearly two centuries the basic silver coin, the denarius, retained most of its value and circulated at par with the various local drachmas of the East. During this period there was only a gradual decline in the weight (20 per cent) and silver content (40 per cent) of the denarius, though the way was prepared for the critical devaluation and price inflation of the third century, once more by the cost of wars.

The Roman currency was a medium not only of exchange but also of propaganda. In 44 B.C. the Senate ordered the first portrait of a living ruler placed on the coins; this new precedent was followed by Caesar's assassins, by his successors in the Triumvirate, and by the later emperors. Religious, military, and political symbols were placed on the reverse sides of various issues; they informed the Roman people of the emperor's health, his long reign, the births of his children, his choice of an heir, his various military campaigns, and the posthumous deification of himself and members of his family. The occasional repetition of symbols called attention to important anniversaries. In other words, Roman coins had a function resembling one of the functions of modern postage stamps.

Commerce and investment were facilitated by private banks and moneylenders, and a system of clearances made currency shipments unnecessary. In 51 B.C. the Senate set the maximum interest rate at 12 per cent, though loans in kind and on crops and cargoes were exempted because of the risks involved. Endowments and large estates generally earned a return between 5 and 6 per cent.

5. Taxes and government finance. Roman taxes included customs duties levied at various transit points, as well as such levies as 1 per cent on sales and 5 per cent on emancipations of slaves and inheritances of Roman citizens. Other sources of revenue included bequests, fines, booty acquired in war, and the proceeds from the state-owned mines and the imperial estates. A direct tax called tributum was levied outside Italy on land and personal property; the rate is not known. Rights to collect provincial taxes, including tithes on agricultural produce, were usually sold to publicani (hence "publicans"), who formed companies which had shareholders at Rome and elsewhere. These companies were supervised by procurators, but abuses were fairly common. Under the Republic most taxes were paid into a treasury controlled by the Senate, but under the Empire this treasury, though continuing to function, became much less important than the fiscus, theoretically the private property of the emperor and his heirs.

In Augustus' day the annual income of the treasury was apparently around 400,000,000 sesterces (100,-000,000 denarii), but by the time of Vespasian imperial revenues may well have approached 2,500,-000,000. He is said to have stated that after the civil wars 40,000,000,000 sesterces were needed to make the Empire solvent; perhaps he had a capital sum in mind. In any event, taxes were almost constantly increased.

State policy was not guided by economic considerations. E.g., in A.D. 33 Tiberius suddenly enforced an old law requiring capitalists to invest in Italian land. The not unnatural result was a financial panic, which the emperor mitigated by advancing 100,000,-000 sesterces to private banks for real-estate loans.

6. Social conditions. It is even more difficult to generalize about family life in the Roman Empire than it is to generalize about it today. From antiquity we have few usable statistics, and much of our information about Rome, if it can be called information, comes from satirists, who necessarily described extreme cases. It is fairly plain, however, that the political chaos of the first century B.C. and the influx of a great deal of new money to Rome were reflected in the family life, not only of the wealthy, but also of other classes. The size of families sharply diminished, and emancipated Roman women often scandalized moralists. Under Augustus legislation was enacted to make divorce more difficult, to discourage adultery, and to encourage larger families, especially in the upper classes. This legislation was confirmed and strengthened by nearly all Augustus' successors, though this very fact suggests that legislation was not a panacea. In the early Empire neither abortion nor the abandonment of infants was forbidden. A law of the late Republic, enforced by Domitian, provided a fine of 10,000 sesterces for male homosexual acts.

In spite of legislation, and the complaints of moralists like Musonius Rufus and Seneca, the allusions in Martial's epigrams and the wall scribblings at Pompeii reflect a way of life against which both Jews and Christians vigorously protested. Paul's letters written to CORINTH show how in his opinion Christians had to keep separate from the world.

It should not be forgotten, however, that there were innumerable families in which such erosion had not taken place. We do not often hear of them (any more than in modern newspapers), but their existence is occasionally indicated by papyrus letters, funerary inscriptions, and such writers as the younger Pliny and Plutarch. Juvenal's picture of Roman matrons in his sixth satire owes a good deal to his own misogyny.

The influx of wealth at Rome also resulted in a remarkable increase in legacy-hunting, and played its part in the rise of professional informers during the first century. Parasites surrounded the unmarried rich, and were often rewarded by legacies. Augustus endeavored to check this practice by forbidding bequests to unmarried adults and by reducing the amount which could be left to childless married persons. Some of the later emperors forbade bequests to themselves, though such bequests were regarded as a form of insurance for the residue of the estate. And because of the vagueness of the laws against treason it was possible for informers to attack the rich and receive bounties. Many emperors tried to prevent this abuse, and false witnesses were often severely punished.

7. Roman law. The Empire was governed not only by men but also by law. In the last century of the Republic, Roman law had become highly developed, and the emperors, as chief magistrates of the state, rendered decisions which themselves had the force of law. Jurists were members of the imperial council, and their decisions too were binding.

The law was concerned not only with protecting the state, the citizen, and private property, but also with social conditions related to all three (*see* § 6 *above*). In imperial times greater stress came to be laid upon equity than upon the observance of exact legal forms. And long before the triumph of Christianity there was an improvement in the legal status of women and of slaves, partly under the influence of the STOICS. Slaves could possess property, even though in theory it belonged to their masters, and they could use it to buy their freedom. They were also protected by law against mistreatment.

It should not, however, be supposed that the Romans shared the modern notion of punishment as aimed at the correction of the offender. The penalties for private offenses were chiefly intended to redress the wrong done; penalties for public offenses were essentially vindictive, and are exemplified in Roman condemnations of Christians to be crucified, beheaded, burned alive, drowned, and delivered to wild animals.

8. Astrology, magic, religion, and philosophy. In the Roman world of the first century both astrology and magic played a significant role, and astrologers, while occasionally expelled from Italy, exercised strong influence over most of the emperors. Arising in the Orient, astrology was closely related to astronomical theory and to philosophical doctrines of fate, especially among Stoics. Magic was forbidden by Roman law when it resulted in damage to persons or their property, but its abiding popularity is attested by the NT and the church fathers, as well as by classical writers and the extant magical papyri. *See* SIMON MAGUS.

Magic was often associated with the foreign cults and prophecies which flourished in the Empire as in the late Republic. These cults, often called "mystery religions," came chiefly from the Orient and in general were modifications of ancient local or national religions. While the traditional civic cults of Greece and Italy continued to exist and were supported by local governments, to some extent they were overshadowed by the new expressions of the ancient Eastern religions, and a fair number of Romans, especially of the middle class, were initiated into their rites. The oriental gods could provide "salvation" or escape from fate, and sometimes from death. The most important of them were the Egyptian Isis, the Great Mother from Asia Minor, and the Persian Mithras, though it should not be forgotten that the Greek mysteries of Demeter at Eleusis continued to be very prominent; several Roman emperors were initiated there, and the Eleusinian mysteries seem to have influenced the forms assumed by their oriental competitors.

The worship of Isis, occasionally repressed at Rome under the late Republic and even in the early Empire, gradually spread throughout the Roman world. Her public rites, together with testimonies to her miraculous powers, made her cultus attractive. Similarly the Great Mother was publicly advertised. Both Isis and the Mother had begging priests who went everywhere. Mithraism, on the other hand, was private and had no special priestly class in the Roman Empire. It was often spread by soldiers, and its worship took place in Mithraeums, which were usually underground. It does not seem to have been an important rival to Christianity until the end of the second century.

As far as we can tell from early Christian literature, Christians found stronger competition among philosophers than among oriental priests. One reason for this is obvious: Christianity felt itself to be closer to philosophy than to other religions, with the partial exception of Judaism. The writings of the second-century apologists reflect the Christian effort to come to terms with philosophy, especially religious-minded Middle Platonism. The process must have begun much earlier, however. The story of Paul at Athens (Acts 17) looks programmatic, even if we cannot be sure that his speech was correctly reported (*see* ACTS OF THE APOSTLES). In the Greco-Roman world there were not only teachers who instructed classes in their own (or their teachers') philosophical doctrines, but also street preachers, especially Cynics and Stoics, who delivered "diatribes" on moral and even on theological topics. The form of address they used is sometimes reflected in the Pauline letters and in James.

Philosophers generally advocated monotheism, and the tendency in this direction was also reflected in the innumerable popular or scholarly identifications of one god or goddess with others. Isis, e.g., was known as the "countless-named," because she was such a central point for equations, while Jews and Christians were conspicuous because of their denial that their God was known by nonbiblical names. It should be added that as far as we know, the adherents of nonbiblical religions never had any difficulties in coming to terms with EMPEROR-WORSHIP; they might advocate monotheism, but it was not an exclusive monotheism.

Philosophers felt free to reinterpret the old Roman official religion and to distinguish "philosophical theology" from "civil theology." Civil theology consisted of their analysis of the twelve gods officially recognized by the state and served by a college of sixteen pontiffs, chief of whom was the Pontifex Maximus, after 12 B.C. the emperor himself. This body presided over the official rites regularly performed at Rome. There were other colleges, such as that of the augurs, who discovered whether the gods approved or opposed official actions. The arrangements at Rome were imitated in the provinces and in the colonies. But as has been noted, Rome tolerated other religions, at least as long as they were not regarded as threatening either the established religion or traditional morality.

9. Scientific knowledge and research. The state of natural science in the early Empire was marked by some optimism about the future of discovery (expressed, e.g., by Philo, Seneca, and Pliny the Elder), along with a great deal of traditionalism in most areas of investigation. Little fresh investigation was carried on, and in medicine the influence of philosophical systems overshadowed and often prevented clinical observation. Surgical instruments, however, continued to be improved, and the gynecology of Soranus includes a good deal of common sense. The study of various peoples (ethnology) continued, though often under the influence of a romantic primitivism, and the study of geography was advanced by the successes of the Roman legions. Geographical theory, however, was simply borrowed from earlier Greek writers, and after Hipparchus (*ca.* 120 B.C.) astronomy was largely a matter of systematization and of correlation with astrology. The gulf between theory and technology may be illustrated by Roman failure to employ the equivalent of the machine gun, invented by Greeks but not used by the legions. It is, of course, a question whether this failure was a fortunate or an unfortunate one.

Pliny (Nat. Hist. II.118) claims that science is not advancing because of contemporary materialism, but this claim explains little. It might better be said that science was held in check by idealistic philosophies and inadequate technical work, and by a failure to maintain mathematics in a fruitful relation to the data of experience. The existence of slavery made unnecessary a quest for labor-saving devices.

10. Literature. The beginning of the Empire was heralded by a group of semiofficial poets and historians who were in part supported by the circle around AUGUSTUS. The most important of these poets was Vergil, whose *Aeneid* traced the history of Rome back to the Trojan War and laid emphasis on the "manifest destiny" of the Empire. Other poets included Horace and Ovid. The historian Livy traced Roman history from its beginnings to 9 B.C. and tried to create an interpretation which would be useful for administrators. Related to the group was the adviser and historian of Herod the Great, Nicholas of Damascus, whose universal history was used by Josephus. An admirer of the new empire, Strabo, wrote a geography in this period; around the same time PHILO JUDEUS tried to construct a Jewish-Greek philosophical system.

From the middle of the first century we have the tutor of Nero and would-be philosopher and dramatist, Seneca; the moral philosopher Musonius Rufus; and the antiquarian and encyclopedist Pliny the Elder, who suffocated when he remained too close to the erupting Vesuvius.

From the end of the first century and the beginning of the second come the histories and apologetic works of JOSEPHUS; the Histories and Annals of Tacitus; and the Lives of the Twelve Caesars by Suetonius. The *Institutes of Oratory* of the famous rhetorician Quintilian was published *ca.* 95. Among the poets should be mentioned Martial, whose twelve books of epigrams appeared at intervals between 86 and 101; and Juvenal, whose satires were published early in the second century. Both writers are important for our understanding of Roman social life; both undoubtedly exaggerate its weaknesses (*see* § 6 *above*). Greek moralists and philosophers include Dio Chrysostom, Plutarch, and Epictetus.

In addition to these major writers there were also the less important writers of romances, forerunners of the second-century apocryphal Acts. *See* ACTS, APOCRYPHAL.

Apart from this writing, more or less creative, there was also the development and use of anthologies in schoolteaching; from the early imperial period come anthologies of poetry and collections of philosophical opinions (doxographical writings) arranged according to subjects. Such anthologies and collections were used by Jewish and Christian apologists. Literary criticism also flourished, chiefly as a part of rhetorical education. The student would learn to analyze grammar, composition, and style; he would also be trained to judge the authenticity of documents and of narratives regarded as historical. Such judgments are later reflected in early Christian and anti-Christian criticism of the Bible.

11. Rome and Christianity. The Roman attitude toward the early church cannot be viewed in isolation from the Roman attitude toward other foreign religions. Pliny, Tacitus, and Suetonius regard Christianity as "superstition"; by this they mean that it is a novel foreign religion brought to Rome by unenlightened members of the lower classes. Just as the Jews believed that idolatry led to adultery, so Romans believed that foreign superstitions led inevitably to sexual promiscuity or cannibalism, or to both. The belief is reflected in Livy's account of the suppression of the Bacchanalia in 186 B.C. (*From the Founding of the City* XXXIX–XL), an account which was written, not for purely historical reasons, but to serve as a statement of the Augustan attitude (cf. Dio Cassius LII.36); and something like it seems to have been in Pliny's mind as he described the activities of Christians (Epistle X.96). Similarly the Druids of Gaul were regarded as inhumanly barbarous, since human sacrifice was said to be a part of their rites; and both Augustus and Claudius took action against them. The religion of Isis was foreign, and under Tiberius a flagrant instance of immorality resulted in prosecution (from the Roman viewpoint) or persecution (from that of Isiacs). But since this case was exceptional, Rome did not carry on continuous warfare against the cult.

In Roman eyes Christianity was a superstition since it was obviously foreign; it had arisen in Judea. It was a superstition because it involved the worship of a criminal condemned by a Roman governor, and its adherents were (therefore?) suspected of immorality. Its missionary zeal, its eschatological emphasis, and its unwillingness to relate itself either to Judaism (a religion tolerated in the Empire) or to the state cults meant that it could only be regarded as at least potentially subversive.

The earliest report about Christianity to come to Roman attention must have been that sent by Pontius Pilate to the emperor, but it was never made public, and so-called Acts of Pilate are forgeries. At a later date, under CLAUDIUS, there were Jewish riots at Rome in which the name Chrestus was involved. The picture in the book of Acts, according to which Roman officials either protected or ignored Christians, seems to be correct; in Palestine it was only when the Roman procurator was absent that James the Lord's brother was put to death (62). Yet there was considerable antipathy toward Christians, or toward some Christians, and after the fire at Rome under NERO, Christians were put to death. It remains a question whether any legislation specifically anti-Christian was introduced. Under DOMITIAN, Christians seem to have been investigated in relation to problems arising out of Judaism. In the letter of Pliny to Trajan (Epistle X.96) it looks as if suspicions of clandestine immorality, including cannibalism, were reflected.

12. Christian views of the Empire. Within the NT itself different views of the Empire are expressed. Jesus' opponents claimed that he was obstructing tax payments (Luke 23:2), but when he was asked for a judgment on the payment of tribute to "Caesar," he replied that what belongs to Caesar should be paid him (Mark 12:17 and parallels). According to the Fourth Gospel, he told Pilate that Roman jurisdiction was given "from above" (John 19:11). Writing early in Nero's reign, Paul told Roman Christians that they owed obedience, loyalty, and tax payments to the state (Rom. 13:1-7; cf. Iren. Her. V.24). Similar views are expressed in Tit. 3:1 (cf. I Tim. 2:2); I Pet. 2:13-17.

On the other hand, just as in Judaism (where Philo and Josephus were pro-imperial and apocalyptic writers were not), there were also apocalyptic writings which, under the threat of persecution by self-deifying emperors, did not hesitate to proclaim the imminent destruction of the Empire by God (II Thess. 2:7; *see* REVELATION). The apologist Justin did not hesitate to threaten the Antonine emperors (mid–second century) with perpetual punishment; his pupil Tatian denounced the Empire as wicked.

To a considerable extent these writers shared in a widespread attitude of hostility toward the Empire, found especially in frontier provinces which did not appreciate the benefits of the "wasteland" situation which the Romans called "peace" (cf. Tac. *Agricola* XXX). This attitude is reflected in the innumerable rebellions against the Empire during the first and second centuries, and in the fairly frequent mutinies of Roman troops in the provinces. The accuracy of Roman historians is confirmed by their descriptions of the hostility of subject peoples. Somehow these nations preferred liberty to the blessings both of Roman rule and of Greco-Roman culture. The Romans were equally hostile toward many of their subjects, perhaps especially the "superstitious" Egyptians and the "immoral" Syrians.

There were influential Christians who in spite of persecution expressed their loyalty to the state. Athenagoras stated that the rule of Marcus Aurelius and his son was given them by God, and Melito held that Christianity, which had grown up with the Empire, and had been persecuted only by bad emperors, should be its state religion. This hope, realized in the fourth century, was at least in part a natural outgrowth of the ecumenical mission of the church. The Roman Empire became, officially at any rate, Christian.

Bibliography. Reference works: Pauly-Wissowa, *Realenzyklopädie der klassischen Altertumswissenschaft* (1894—). *Oxford Classical Dictionary* (1949).

On expansion and social structure: E. Gibbon, *The History of the Decline and Fall of the Roman Empire* (ed. J. B. Bury; 1896, vol. I. M. Rostovtzeff, *A History of the Ancient World*, vol. II (1927). A. E. R. Boak, *A History of Rome to A.D. 565* (2nd ed., 1929). M. Cary, *A History of Rome Down to the Reign of Constantine* (1935). *Cambridge Ancient History*, vols. X–XII (1934-39). M. Cary and T. J. Haarhoff, *Life and Thought in the Greek and Roman World* (1940). N. Lewis and M. Reinhold, *Roman Civilization*, vol. II: *The Empire* (1955)—invaluable collection of translations.

On agriculture, industry, trade, and communications: M. P. Charlesworth, *Trade-Routes and Commerce of the Roman Empire* (2nd ed., 1926). M. Rostovtzeff, *The Social and Economic History of the Roman Empire* (1st ed., 1926). M. Wheeler, *Rome Beyond the Imperial Frontiers* (1954).

On money and financial matters: W. S. Davis, *The Influence of Wealth in Imperial Rome* (1910). H. Mattingly, *Roman Coins* (1928). T. Frank, *An Economic Survey of Ancient Rome* (5 vols.; 1933-40). M. Grant, *Roman Imperial Money* (1953).

On social conditions: J. Carcopino, *Daily Life in Ancient Rome* (1940).

On Roman law: A. Berger, "Law and Procedure, Roman," *Oxford Classical Dictionary* (1949), pp. 484-91. *Encyclopedic Dictionary of Roman Law* (1953).

On astrology, magic, religion, and philosophy: F. Cumont, *Astrology and Religion Among the Greeks and Romans* (1912); *Oriental Religions in Roman Paganism* (1911; 4th French ed., with full notes, 1929). A. D. Nock, *Conversion* (1933). R. E. Witt, *Albinus and the History of Middle Platonism* (1937). M. P. Nilsson, *Greek Piety* (1948). F. Cumont, *Lux Perpetua* (1949). H. I. Bell, *Cults and Creeds in Graeco-Roman Egypt* (1953). F. H. Cramer, *Astrology in Roman Law and Politics* (1954).

On scientific knowledge and research: H. Diels, *Antike*

Technik (2nd ed., 1920). A. Reymond, *History of the Sciences in Graeco-Roman Antiquity* (1927). J. O. Thomson, *History of Ancient Geography* (1948). R. M. Grant, *Miracle and Natural Law in Graeco-Roman and Early Christian Thought* (1952).

On literature: H. Diels, *Doxographi Graeci* (1879; reprinted 1929). M. L. Clarke, *Rhetoric at Rome* (1953). J. W. and A. M. Duff, *A Literary History of Rome in the Silver Age from Tiberius to Hadrian* (1953).

On Christianity in the Roman Empire: H. Grégoire, *Les persécutions dans l'empire romain* (1951). R. M. Grant, *The Sword and the Cross* (1955). E. Stauffer, *Christ and the Caesars* (English trans. R. G. Smith; 1955).

On Christian views of the Empire: C. J. Cadoux, *The Early Church and the World* (1925). H. Fuchs, *Der geistige Widerstand gegen Rom in der antiken Welt* (1938). C. N. Cochrane, *Christianity and Classical Culture* (1944).

R. M. GRANT

ROMAN RELIGION.

1. Prehistoric origin
2. Early Roman religion
3. The religion of Numa
4. The state religion
5. Syncretism
Bibliography

1. Prehistoric origin. The origin of Roman religion was prehistoric. It consisted mainly of ancient, really "primitive," rites and practices, observed and perpetuated with no attempt at explanation, with no reference to any divine revelation or command, but solely because they belonged to ancestral custom (the *mos maiorum*). These rites had been found to work, or—more often—their neglect had been found to be disastrous; hence it was everywhere assumed that they must be observed with meticulous care. Although the rite was usually some form of sacrifice, there were many other kinds: supplications, lustrations, lectisterniums (banquets set before the gods), circumambulations, processions, and other symbolic acts. Roman religion was essentially a system of ritual, without a theology, or an authorized set of religious beliefs, or any organized system of religious instruction. Cicero defined religion as the "cult of the gods" (*On the Nature of the Gods* II.8); this term meant more than worship and included care, devotion, and constant attention to their needs and demands.

Hence Roman religion was legalistic, with specific requirements which men must meet if they hoped for specific responses on the part of the higher powers. A Roman did not hesitate to accompany his prayer with the formula: "I give so that you may —or will—give." He also made it clear that his gift was meant for one particular god or group of gods and no other, and if he was not sure of the identity or sex of the god, he said so: *sive mas sive femina.* And he explicitly stated and reiterated just what his offering was: cakes, a fat sow, a lamb or goat. The language is as specific and explicit as a lawyer's formulation of a deed, a transfer, or a claim. At the same time additional requirements or demands on the part of the higher powers were often set forth, and also special divine guidance in severe crises, through oracles (especially the Sibylline books, which were nevertheless obscure and needed interpretation) or the art of divination (especially the "reading" of

the markings observed on the liver of the sacrificial animal). Both the Sibylline Oracles and the art of divination were an inheritance from the Etruscans, though the origin of divination was very ancient and probably must be traced to Babylonia.

In brief, the general character of ancient Roman religion was "primitive"—i.e., prehistoric—with many surviving features of animism, magic, and polydaemonism. Certain "sacred" places or things possessed supernatural power, which was conceived of more or less as the Polynesians conceived of *mana;* or were indwelt by supernatural beings, though one could not be sure just how personal they were, what their names or functions, or whether they were friendly or unfriendly to their neighbors. In dealing with the supernatural, it was of paramount importance that the correct formula be used. Any mistake, such as omission, repetition, or transposition of words, was unlucky and invalidated the whole procedure: one must begin the rite and the accompanying formula or formulas all over again. Most of the rites were so old that there was no explanation of either their origin or their meaning; some scholars have argued that they originated at a predeistic stage in religious development, when only semi-personal local powers were addressed, not gods— personal gods came later, under Greek influence. But it is not certain that any such "predeistic" state of religion ever existed in Italy. Nor can we ascribe all this to "primitive" religion, about which we know very little—we do not know even the conditions of life among really primitive men. What we find in Roman religion, in historical times, is the survival, modification, and eventual submergence of prehistoric rites which were shared in some measure with other Italian peoples but were preserved and recorded only at Rome or under Roman influence.

The oldest inhabitants of Italy were, as far as archaeology can trace them, a presumably indigenous group of people among whom were settled various invading or immigrant nations, chiefly one branch of the Indo-European family (early Latin reflects this migration), but also including such other groups as the Greeks in S Italy (Magna Graecia) and Sicily, and the Etruscans (probably coming from SW Asia Minor) who occupied NW Italy, W and N of the Tiber and along the coast as far as the latitude of Pisa and Florence, and in the NE even farther. Other groups were the Ligurians along the coast N and W of the Etruscans, and the recurrently invading Celts in the lower ranges of the Alps, the Dolomites, and the Po Valley.

2. Early Roman religion. The traditional date of the founding of Rome was 753 B.C., when a group of shepherds, farmers, and traders established a stronghold upon two of the seven hills, the Palatine and the Capitol, and set up their market on the bank of the Tiber, far enough inland to escape the pirates and raiders who infested most of the Mediterranean in that era. The description of the Arcadian Evander's humble city on the Palatine, in Vergil's *Aeneid,* book VIII, is improbable archaeologically and historically, but it conveys the deep feeling of the "numinosity" of the Palatine, which was the real center of Roman religion throughout its long history. During the era of the Etruscan kings, when the great temple to Jupiter, Juno, and Minerva was erected on the Capitol, there was a tendency to transform Roman religion into a spectacular state cult; but even centuries later, when Augustus dedicated his chapel to Apollo, it was on the Palatine, the hill below which lay the Sacred Way and where lived the Vestal Virgins in their holy house, and where also were the home of the Flamen Dialis and the temple of Vesta. It was the oldest street in Rome, and beside it were preserved the oldest and most sacred monuments of Roman religion and government. Officially the Capitol was the religious center of the Roman Empire; in reality the Palatine was the sacred hill which enshrined the deepest religious loyalties.

3. **The religion of Numa.** The traditional founder and codifier of religious law and lore was the second Etruscan king, Numa Pompilius; hence the oldest elements in Roman religion were often referred to as the "religion of Numa." In reality, the rites were far older than Numa, and reflect the period of slow social, political, and economic development which long antedated the founding of Rome and which also in the rural districts long survived the founding, the period of the Etruscan kings, and even the five centuries of the Republic (509-27 B.C.)

Since there is no contemporary record—the later historians and poets were no better off than we are —the most authentic clues to the early religion of Rome are the festivals recorded in the pre-Julian calendars, fragments of more than twenty of which still survive, though usually with added notes (in smaller letters) from a far later period. The "primitive" year began in the spring (January and February were ignored). March was the first month, the time for the spring sowing, the trimming of the vines, and other agricultural activities; but it was also the month for polishing (or lustrating) the war trumpets, exercising and drilling the cavalry horses, and invoking Mars, the god or numen of war. The armed dance of the Salii, another expression of the war spirit, also took place; for war was an annual, seasonal occupation, and began each year in this month. April followed with its Fordicidia on the fifteenth, the sacrifice of a pregnant sow for the purpose of ensuring or increasing fertility, the Cerealia on the nineteenth and the Parilia or Palilia on the twenty-first, the Vinalia on the twenty-third in honor of the numina of grain, fruit, and wine (or vines) respectively, and the Robigalia on the twenty-fifth, designed to ward off rust from the growing crops. These are obviously ancient agricultural festivals, each with its appropriate rites.

The ritual can be learned from the ancient antiquarians (e.g., from Varro, the fragments of whose famous work on *Antiquities Human and Divine* are to be found as quotations in Augustine's *City of God*, or from Dionysius of Halicarnassus, Plutarch, Macrobius, Athenaeus, or Johannes Lydus) or from the poets (e.g., Ovid, whose *Fasti* covers the first half of the year—i.e., from January to June; it was written in the time of Augustus, and never finished, as Ovid was banished). Often the descriptions of the ancient rites are exact, but their interpretation

is overlaid with much later Greek identification and explanation, together with the writer's own fanciful guesses—a feature especially pronounced in Ovid. However, we can make out the essential character of most of the "primitive" rites. E.g., the Ambarvalia, or lustration of the fields, consisted in a circumambulation of the farm by its owner and his *familia* (which included the slaves), all dressed in white, and leading a group of animals for the sacrifice—viz., a sow, a sheep, and a young bull (the *suovetaurilia*); Tibullus says (II.1) that the last named was originally a male lamb. Another rustic rite was the annual sacrifice at the landmark, where the borders of farms adjoined; it was a ritual sacred to Terminus, and was accordingly named the Terminalia. Other rites were concerned with the sowing, harvesting, and garnering of the crops, and the making of wine or the preserving and storing up of seed for the coming year.

One of the strangest rites was that of the "October Horse," when the off-horse in the team which won the chariot race was sacrificed to Mars; its head and tail were cut off and taken by a runner to the Regia, where once the king had been entrusted with these powerful instruments of magic, and hung up so that the blood could drip on the hearth. Later a contest was held, and the winning group carried off the head to their own quarter in the lower town. All this had nothing to do with Mars as the god of war, but as giver of the harvest: so powerful was he that all good things were his gift, including both victory in war and an ample food supply. The strange chant and solemn procession (or dance, with its peculiar "three step") of the Arval Brethren was also addressed to Mars and invoked a blessing on the crops; originally, perhaps, it was thought to produce or to ensure such a blessing. It was because of later Greek influence and the identification of the Roman gods with the Greek that men came to think of Mars chiefly as the war god (Ares) and little more.

Still another "primitive" rite was the Lupercalia (February 15), somehow associated with the protection of small domestic animals from the wolves (*lupus* = "wolf"), but more specifically connected with fertility. At the SW corner of the Palatine mount, near an ancient cavern, a dog and some goats were sacrificed. Young men were smeared with the blood, which was then wiped off with wool (a lucky material) dipped in milk; then they ran about the Palatine settlement with strips of the fresh goatskins, striking with them everyone they met. These blows were especially welcome to women, for it was thought that they averted barrenness and ensured fertility. Other ideas were connected with the ritual, as is often the case with ancient rites; but the prevailing or most widely accepted interpretation seems to have been that of fertility magic.

It was this early agricultural religion which formed the fundamental and most permanent stratum of Roman religion. With the Etruscans and the Greeks had come temples, statues of gods (conceived now as personal beings, human in form), divination, and mythology. These new emphases had a transforming effect upon the religion of the city dwellers, though the old rituals survived in the rural districts. The offering of a young lamb to the spirit resident in a spring; a few beans or flowers offered to a tree nymph or to the family ghosts; the pious observance of ancestral customs, such as the ritual of the communal Lar or Lares, the family Genius, or the Penates (guardians) of the household storeroom—all these are described by the Augustan poets, Vergil, Horace, Tibullus, Ovid. But they were in reality survivals from an age long past, and were now to be found chiefly on the farms and in the country towns.

4. The state religion. On the other hand, the public religion of the Roman state (especially as observed in Rome itself) was thoroughly organized. At its head was the pontifical college, which included the several pontiffs (originally three, later increased to six, nine, fifteen, or sixteen); the fifteen flamens, including the three leading ones, the *flamen Dialis* (priest of Jupiter) and those of Mars and Quirinus; the Vestal Virgins, in charge of the rites of Vesta and the sacred undying fire on her hearth; and the Rex sacrorum (king of rites, who inherited the ancient priestly functions of the early kings). The presiding officer of the college was the Pontifex Maximus, and next to him the Rex sacrorum. It was the duty of this college to oversee all public rites and religious ceremonies, to ascertain the will of the gods either through divination (by augurs) or through consultation and interpretation of the Sibylline books. But in time the whole system fell into disrepute, especially when, under the later Republic, commanders and magistrates did not hesitate to manipulate the auspices or the calendar or the interpretation of signs or portents in furtherance of their own purposes.

Originally a simple "primitive" religion (i.e., prehistoric), thoroughly legalistic and eudaemonistic in conception and aim, the "religion of Numa" might perhaps have developed into a noble code of morals and worship, somewhat comparable to the Hebrew. But the Roman religion was not permitted to develop in this way; foreign influences, especially mythological and artistic, and the absence of any group or order comparable to the prophets of Israel, doomed it to sterility and eventual extinction. It was chiefly the Greek influence, unfortunately, which brought to bear, not only an alien mythology, but also a skeptical philosophy, at a time when internal crisis and decay already threatened to destroy the religion of Rome.

5. Syncretism. It was the age of syncretism. As Rome had grown in political importance, conquering the entire Italian peninsula and Sicily, driving its rival Carthage from the Mediterranean and finally destroying it, and conquering eventually the whole of Southern and Western Europe, North Africa, Asia Minor, Egypt, and the Near East, new tendencies had steadily arisen, in consequence of this vast international expansion—tendencies which were destined to alter the whole character of Rome. The gods of the conquered had flocked into the city, brought there by the *invocatio* or the invitation or the vows of conquering generals and by their now enslaved votaries. In the great crisis following the Battle of Cannae (211 B.C.), an embassy was sent, at the direction of a Sibylline oracle as interpreted by the decemvirs, to Pessinus in Phrygia; and the sacred stone of Cybele, the Great Mother of the Gods, was brought to Rome, enshrined in the temple of Victory until her own *aedes* or shrine could be completed, and her worship entrusted to authentic Phrygian priests. Similarly the rites of Dionysus (identified with Bacchus, and thus in turn with Pater Liber) were introduced, though with severe restrictions, especially after the scandal caused by the "orgies" or drunken worship of the Bacchants in 168 B.C., when the Senate issued a decree forbidding Romans to take part in them. But the precedent had already been set, and the steady influx of foreign gods and their cults continued, in later centuries with increasing popularity and finally with irresistible consequences for the ancestral cultus and its round of associated ideas.

In the NT period, from *ca.* 50 to 150, the tide of "orientalism," which included new superstitions, new kinds of magic, astrology, "mystery" cults, and occultism in general, was still held somewhat in check; but after Marcus Aurelius, the "last of the Romans" (died 180), the floodgates were opened, and under the third-century Severi the Eastern cults swept westward without hindrance. It is quite improbable that the early Christians were influenced by the mystery cults; the period of popularity of these cults, in the West, came later. Nor was the early church inclined to adopt or adapt ancient Roman religious customs —the whole religious outlook of the church was too Hebraic, too biblical, to find values in primitive pagan rites; above all, the hope of redemption through Christ and the eschatological expectation of the coming kingdom of God found little contact or support in Roman religion—save only where, as in Vergil, Roman religious thought had already been influenced by similar ideas: Vergil's *Fourth Eclogue* seems to echo the messianic hope, especially as set forth in Isaiah. Indeed, the church of the first century met the greatest threat to its existence when it confronted the imperial cultus (the worship of *Roma* and the emperor; see the Revelation to John, especially chs. 13; 17–18). Emperor-worship was one more importation from the East, and not an original element in Roman religion; its spirit was essentially political and even commercial, not religious, though it celebrated the establishment of world peace under Augustus, and was meant to be a "religion of all good men." But Christians were not able to participate, any more than Jews were (the Jews, fortunately, were exempt from this requirement). The result, for the church, was long decades of martyrdom during the repeated persecutions which broke out from the first century to the fourth.

The real impact of Roman religion upon Christianity was seen long after the persecutions had ended, when the political ideas and ideals of responsible world government, of the universal maintenance of law and order, and of a hierarchical organization of society came to expression and fulfilment in Latin Catholicism. After the third century the language of the Western church was Latin; its conception of sainthood was tinged with the ancient ideal of sobriety, seriousness, even solemnity (*gravitas*), which had been characteristic of the earliest type of religious feeling in Italy. Its conception of worship and devotion was formed on the ancient Roman appreciation of piety (*pietas*), with its strong attachment to family and especially filial duties; its great virtues of humility (*humilitas*), as contrasted with pride or arrogance (*superbia*)—Augustine insisted upon this as firmly as Vergil had done (q. I Pet. 5:5)— and of loyalty (*fiducia*), which came to include the church's theology as well as its ethics, so that men spoke of the duty of belief and of unquestioning acceptance of theological definitions and of ecclesiastical authority—all these basic characteristics of Latin Catholicism, which placed a stamp on the whole of Western Christianity for many centuries (including that of modern times), were a legacy from the best elements in the ancient Roman character, now combined, sweetened, and inspired by the ethics of the gospel, but also modified by new circumstances and conditions. These are factors of far greater importance than the more overt and obvious emphasis on such matters as correct ritual, often noted by church historians and others. It is only the earliest beginning of this religious and cultural process that can be traced in the NT; but it is indubitably present, and its later development is foreshadowed in more than one passage—e.g., in Mark, the gospel of the martyr church at Rome; in Luke-Acts, where the gospel is exonerated and approved, if not accepted, by Roman officials; and in the Letter to the Romans, where the duty of loyalty and obedience to the representatives of the great world state is clearly expressed (ch. 13). Only Revelation takes a wholly negative attitude toward Rome and its cultus—a fact fraught with dire consequences for more than one group of early Christian enthusiasts and nonconformists who saw nothing good but only evil in the pagan world and its religions.

Bibliography. J. B. Carter, *The Religion of Numa* (1906); T. R. Glover, *The Conflict of Religions Under the Early Roman Empire* (1909); W. W. Fowler, *The Religious Experience of the Roman People* (1911); P. Wendland, *Hellenistisch-römische Kultur* (2nd ed., 1912); G. Wissowa, *Religion und Kultus der Römer* (2nd ed., 1912); F. Cumont, *Les religions orientales dans le paganisme romain* (4th ed., 1929; English trans. of 1st ed., 1901); F. Altheim, *A History of Roman Religion* (English trans.; 1938); *Cambridge Ancient History* (1923-39), especially vols. VII-VIII, X; N. Turchi, *La Religione di Roma Antica* (1939); H. J. Rose, *Ancient Roman Religion* (1948); F. C. Grant, *Hellenistic Religions* (1953); R. M. Grant, *The Sword and the Cross* (1955); F. C. Grant, *Ancient Roman Religion* (1957).

F. C. GRANT

*ROMANS, LETTER TO THE. A letter written by the apostle Paul to "all God's beloved in Rome," and now found as the sixth book of the NT canon and the first in order of the letters. It is the longest of all Paul's letters and offers the most comprehensive account of his understanding of the gospel of Christ as the effectual divine remedy for the plight of man, the universal sinfulness and guilt which no human effort can remove. Though it retains some elements of the true letter, a personal communication prepared for a particular group of readers rather than a literary construction employing the form of the letter, it approaches more nearly than any other of the apostle's writings to the formal theological treatise; certainly it must be said that the exposition of the theology is not developed in immediate relation to particular problems or errors of the Roman church.

The general importance of this letter in the history of Christian theology cannot be overestimated, and it remains indispensable to the understanding of most of the fundamental doctrines of the Christian faith and the potentialities of the Christian life.

1. Authenticity and integrity
2. Destination
3. Occasion and purpose
4. Outline of contents
5. The argument
   a. The main theme
   b. The plight of man
   c. The theme restated
   d. Key terms
   e. The Christian life
   f. Subsidiary theme (excursus)
Bibliography

1. Authenticity and integrity. The authenticity of the letter is not seriously questioned and is not, in fact, open to question. The rejection of Romans involves the rejection of all the Pauline letters, for there is no other letter with any greater claim to authenticity which could serve as a standard of comparison. There are clear evidences of its use by other Christian writers before the end of the first century and in the first half of the second century—in other NT writings and in the Apostolic Fathers; and before the end of the second century it is listed and cited under Paul's name. Every list of the Christian scriptures which has come down to us includes Romans among the letters of Paul. The external evidence of authenticity could not be stronger, and the internal evidence fully supports the tradition. The letter belongs to the first generation of the church, and there is much in it which could not reasonably be related to any later situation; the language includes scores of words and phrases which are characteristic of the vocabulary of Paul; and there is nothing to suggest the mind or training of a writer who could not be identified with the apostle on the ground of what we know of him from other sources. The author of Romans is certainly the author of Galatians and of I and II Corinthians also, and there is overwhelming evidence that these letters are the work of the man whose name they bear.

The question of integrity is raised chiefly in connection with the ending of the letter. First, the Doxology (16:25-27) is probably a later addition; secondly, the remainder of ch. 16 is regarded by many as a separate letter, which is more likely to have been addressed to Ephesus than to Rome; and thirdly, there is a good deal of evidence to show that in early times there were copies of the letter in circulation which ended with ch. 14.

The style and vocabulary of the great Doxology are not Pauline, and practically all commentators are agreed that it is not from his hand. As there are indications that the earliest collections of the Pauline letters ended with Romans, it has been suggested that the Doxology may have been composed as a fitting conclusion to the whole body of Paul's correspondence. In phraseology and temper, it recalls the Pastoral letters. Doubts of its authenticity are confirmed by the variations in the position which it holds in different MSS. A few MSS omit it altogether; the vast majority of them place it at the end of ch. 14; a relatively small number, but those of the highest quality, have it at the end of ch. 16, where it is found in English versions; a few include it in both these places; and in one, but that the oldest of all, the Chester Beatty Papyrus P[46], it is put at the end of ch. 15, and the scribe has put a line under it before the beginning of ch. 16, as if to emphasize that in his view the letter ended at this point.

The presence of the Doxology at the end of ch. 14 must go back to some copy or copies in which the letter ended at this point. None of our extant MSS, however, fail to include chs. 15–16. The evidence that some early copies ended with ch. 14 is confirmed by Origen of Alexandria (early third century), who tells us that Marcion cut away from this letter all that follows 14:23; and adds that some codices "which have not been rashly handled by Marcion" insert the Doxology at this point. This would suggest that the shortening of the letter was independent of Marcion, and that he simply happened to have it in the abbreviated form in which it was already circulating. Some early Latin lists of chapter headings, found in such great codices of the Vulg. as Amiatinus and Fuldensis, pass directly from 14:23 to the doxology, even though the codices themselves contain chs. 15–16.

There is, nevertheless, no reason for suspecting that ch. 15, at least, did not form part of the original letter. Certainly the first part of the chapter (vss. 1-6) follows upon the thought of ch. 14 without any break, completing the discussion of how to deal with the "man who is weak in faith" (14:1); and there is not a line in the remainder of the chapter that does not reflect the mind and breathe the spirit of Paul, and at the same time throw light upon his conception of his apostolic task and his purpose in writing the letter.

Ch. 16 is another matter. The letter comes to a natural ending with ch. 15, and even has a brief blessing to close it (vs. 33). The commendation of Phoebe the deaconess, with which ch. 16 begins, would more naturally. be addressed by Paul to a church which already knew him than to a church to which he was a stranger. But a greater difficulty is occasioned by the long list of greetings to friends of Paul. It would be surprising, in the first instance, to find that Paul has so many Christian friends in a city which he has never visited, that he should know the houses in which they meet for worship and the groups which are associated together in one capacity or another (vss. 11, 14-15). But when we find that the list includes Aquila and Prisca, who had been expelled from Rome by the Emperor Claudius, had given Paul a home at Corinth, and had later been associated with him at Ephesus (Acts 18:2-3, 18-19, 26); and immediately after them mentions Epaenetus, who is described as the "first convert in Asia for Christ"; and when we observe the closeness of the relations between the apostle and many of the others

whom he names here ("kinsmen and . . . fellow prisoners; . . . my beloved in the Lord; . . . our fellow worker in Christ; . . . the beloved Persis," etc.), we are almost forced to the conclusion that this chapter was addressed to the church at Ephesus, the capital of the Roman province of Asia, where Paul had worked for several years. The warning against troublemakers (vss. 17 ff) also accords better with a church for which Paul has pastoral responsibility than with a church which he knows only through the reports of others, and which he addresses with a measure of diffidence (15:14-15) and with every effort to avoid even the appearance of criticism. There is, in fact, a wide measure of agreement among scholars that this chapter is a letter, or part of a letter, addressed by Paul to the church at Ephesus, which somehow became attached to the Letter to the Romans when the letters were collected into a corpus.

This conclusion is challenged by a number of scholars, who feel that the hypothesis of an Ephesian address for the chapter raises more difficulties than it solves. Some feel that a letter consisting almost entirely of personal greetings is inconceivable. This type of objection need not be taken too seriously. Obviously, the primary purpose of the letter is to commend the visiting deaconess, to make sure that she is welcomed in a strange city. With a whole sheet of papyrus available, why should not the apostle use the rest of it for greetings to his friends and for a word of warning against troublemakers? Nor does it seem at all unnatural that he should include in the greetings a few personal tributes to old and valued friends.

To the demand that the proponents of this hypothesis explain how the salutation of this letter came to disappear, it is sufficient to reply that II Cor. 10-13 is widely regarded as a separate letter, and that no difficulty is felt about the absence of a separate salutation.

There is also the question of just how this Ephesian note became attached to the Roman letter. One would be justified in pressing this question only if we could otherwise picture with the utmost clarity the methods of the collector of the Pauline letters and the whole editorial process through which the collection passed. The question of how this letter became attached to the letter to the Romans is trifling in comparison with that of the composition of II Corinthians, and still more trifling in comparison with that of the reception of the Pastorals into the corpus. It has been suggested that the chapter is possibly a pseudonymous addition, which may have been introduced at the same time as the Pastorals. Once it is realized that the objections to the Ephesian hypothesis carry very little weight, it becomes unnecessary to resort to the hypothesis that the chapter is not from the hand of Paul at all.

The conclusion here, then, is that the letter to the Romans consisted originally of chs. 1–15, and that ch. 16 is part of a letter originally addressed to the church at Ephesus. It may be added that the interpretation of the letter as a whole is not significantly affected by the critical conclusion that may be reached about the origin of ch. 16.

2. Destination. The earliest MSS set above the opening words of the letter the brief title πρὸς Ῥωμαίους, "To Romans." This phrase could, of course, be employed only in relation to a collection, and is to be ascribed to an early editor; in later MSS it is elaborated into such designations as "The epistle of the blessed apostle Paul to the Romans." The text of the letter itself mentions the Christians of Rome in the Salutation: "Paul . . . to all God's beloved in Rome, who are called to be saints" (1:1, 7; cf. vs. 15).

It has been suggested, however, that the Roman address is secondary, and that the letter was composed in the first instance as a general letter. This conjecture was inspired by the observation that there is testimony to the existence in early times and in widely scattered areas of the church of copies which omitted the words ἐν Ῥώμῃ ("in Rome") in 1:7 and τοῖς ἐν Ῥώμῃ in 1:15. The nature of the evidence does not allow us to ascribe the omission to mere scribal inadvertence. It is perhaps best explained as liturgically motivated. At all events, it is clear that entire paragraphs at the beginning and end of the letter (1:8-15; 15:14-33) are addressed, not to the church in general, but to a particular local church; and there can be no shadow of doubt that this is the church at Rome.

Nothing is known of the founding of the Roman church. When Paul wrote his letter, this church was well established and already known and esteemed throughout the Christian world (1:8; 15:23-29). It was composed mainly of Gentiles, with a certain number of Jewish members, and was certainly a Greek-speaking community, which means that its membership was drawn chiefly from the Levantine population of the city. This Greek character continued until the later years of the second century, for it is not until then that we find the earliest Latin documents of the Roman church. It must have been founded before A.D. 50, for the conflicts which its coming occasioned within the Jewish community led to an edict of the Emperor Claudius by which the Jews were expelled from Rome (Suetonius *Life of Claudius* 25; Acts 18:2); but there is no indication that it had any distinguished leadership before the arrival of Paul and subsequently of Peter, who came to be revered as the joint founders of the church in the capital. *See* ROME (CHURCH).

3. Occasion and purpose. Paul himself indicates with unusual clearness the circumstances which impelled him to write this letter. He had long hoped and prayed that he might be able to visit the Roman church, but had hitherto been prevented from doing so, no doubt by the insistent demands of other work (1:9-13). Now at last he sees some prospect of making the journey to the capital. He has completed the tasks which he set for himself in the Eastern provinces and is looking forward to a mission in Spain; and he hopes to visit the Romans in passing and to secure their support for his projected mission (15: 17-24). First, however, he must make a trip to Jerusalem with a contribution which his Gentile churches of Greece and Macedonia have raised for the poor of the Jerusalem church, a material return for the spiritual blessings which they have received from their Jewish brethren in the faith (15:25-27); as soon

as he has completed this task, he will be passing through Rome on his way to Spain (vss. 28-29). He is doubtful about the kind of reception which may be awaiting him in Jerusalem, and he asks for his readers' prayers (vss. 30-32).

The letter is written primarily to pave the way for his intended visit. As the Apostle to the Gentiles, he is conscious of a responsibility to Romans as to the men of all nations (1:5-6, 13-15), and he is eager to discharge it. In part, he feels that he has some contribution to make toward the strengthening of their faith, and he is quick to add that he counts on receiving, as well as conferring, a blessing (1:11-12). He disavows any desire to suggest that their own faith and knowledge are deficient (15:14), and almost apologizes for his boldness in writing to remind them of what they already know (15:15). It is clear, however, that he has more ambitious ends in view than this. Although he does not state it in so many words, he is manifestly bent on removing misunderstandings of his gospel which he fears may have been formed at Rome (3:7-8; 6:1; 9:1-2; etc.). If he invites their support of his mission in Spain, he feels that they have a right first to know from his own testimony the substance of his teaching, to be assured that they can support him wholeheartedly.

Yet we are inclined to feel that a broader, perhaps only partly conscious, purpose lies behind the letter. After all, it goes far beyond the scope of the brief statement of faith which would suffice to give proof of his soundness as a Christian teacher. This careful and wide-ranging exposition of the significance of the gospel seems to come close to a formal, definitive account of the apostle's mature understanding of the Christian faith. Can it be that he half-divines the central place which the church of the capital is destined to attain in Christendom, and chooses it as the initial recipient, that it may also be the lasting guardian, of his greatest theological legacy? In the mother church of Jerusalem he cannot have too great confidence; as he goes up on his last visit, he must fear, not only the dangers that may beset him at the hands of unbelievers, but mistrust and suspicion on the part of the Christian believers themselves (15:31). A strategic insight seems to have guided him in the establishment of his key churches throughout his missionary career; may not the same strategic insight have enabled him to perceive that the chief city of the world must shortly become the capital of the growing empire of Christ? In some degree, then, the Letter to the Romans would partake of the nature of an encyclical, addressed *urbi et orbi,* giving permanent expression to Paul's clear understanding of the nature of the gospel, of its relation to the OT and to the Judaism of the law, and of its power to bring the whole of man's life into new relationship with God and into new powers and glories.

As the letter was written when Paul was on the point of leaving for Jerusalem with the great collection which his Gentile churches had gathered (15: 25 ff), it was probably dispatched from Corinth shortly before he set sail with his companions, representatives of the churches which had shared in making the collection (Acts 20:3-4). The date cannot be determined with certainty, but will fall between 54 and 57 (*see* CHRONOLOGY OF THE NT; PAUL). The long and painful conflict reflected in the Corinthian letters will have ended, with the complete victory of the apostle, and he will have had the leisure and the freedom from intense anxiety which would permit him to undertake so massive a work of theological construction as the Letter to the Romans.

4. Outline of contents. With the omission of ch. 16, the letter falls into three main divisions (II-IV in the following outlines), with an introduction and a conclusion.

5. The argument. *a. The main theme.* The Salutation (1:1-7), much more extended than in any of the other letters, conveys in brief Paul's conception of his commission and of the high glory of the Christ whom he preaches, and intimates that the breadth of his apostolate is such as to include the Romans, to whom he extends the apostolic greeting of grace and peace. The thanksgiving to God, which follows (vss. 8-15), begins in accordance with common Greek practice, but is extended far beyond the conventional into a warm expression of Paul's eagerness to visit Rome, and of his sense of responsibility to communicate to men of every race and condition the gospel which has been entrusted to him.

He now announces the central theme of his apostolic preaching (1:16-17). The gospel of God, for which he has been "set apart," is defined as the "power of God [put forth to bring] salvation to every one who has faith," and as the "righteousness of God revealed through faith for faith." The two expressions are substantially parallel in meaning, for the "righteousness" of God is here used, not in the abstract Greek sense of moral uprightness, but in the active Hebrew sense of that which vindicates the right, that which brings the victory of right over wrong, the power which is put forth to overthrow evil and make truth and goodness triumphant. God's "righteousness" *is* his salvation, his saving power making itself effectual (cf. Isa. 51:4-8 KJV, with its refrain: "My salvation shall be for ever, and my righteousness [RSV 'deliverance'] shall not be abolished"). Again, the repeated insistence on faith, with the appeal to the words of Habakkuk which promise life to the man who is "righteous through faith," introduces one of the fundamental tenets of the apostle's teaching, which is related to the universalism of the gospel ("to the Jew first and also to the Greek"), and will be shown to be the correlative of grace (cf. 4:16 KJV: "Therefore it is of faith, that it might be by grace") and the antithesis of legalism, of a doctrine that makes salvation depend upon human moral achievement.

b. The plight of man. The universal need of salvation is now demonstrated by an analysis of the condition of mankind (1:18-3:20). The state of the world is here defined in terms of religion and morals in the narrowest sense; there is no trace of concern for social injustice, economic distress, or military and political despotism. All the evil of the world is seen as deriving ultimately from man's wilful rejection of the truth of God, which is manifested in the works of nature in such wise as to leave man with no excuse for his failure to give God the honor that is his due. This primal repudiation of responsibility to God has clouded the human mind and led to the immense folly of idolatry; and the worship of false gods has issued in an increasing corruption of mind and action and a dreadful harvest of vice and debauchery (1:18-32).

Up to this point, Paul has spoken chiefly of the moral corruption of Gentile society. With the beginning of the second chapter, he turns his attention to the stern critic of these vices, and accuses him of being himself guilty of the crimes which he is rebuking in others. With vs. 17, he tells us explicitly that the censor whom he has in mind is the Jew, with his complacent feeling of superiority over the Gentile, who boasts that he has the "embodiment of knowledge and truth" in the law, but who by breaking the law is dishonoring God. Paul insists that God shows no partiality; evil will be punished and goodness rewarded to Jew and Gentile alike. The good Gentile will put to shame the Jewish transgressor. The Jew has, indeed, had many advantages (3:1 ff) but these do not mitigate his guilt.

The apostle has now shown that "all men, both Jew and Greeks [i.e., Gentiles], are under the power of sin"; the Scriptures themselves, addressed primarily to "those who are under the law," support the massive indictment of evil and godlessness and show that the whole world is guilty before God. And the law can do nothing to clear men of the charge; it can bring only the knowledge of sin (3:9-20).

c. The theme restated. Paul is now prepared to restate his main theme in greater fulness, in the light of his analysis of the plight of mankind. This wider statement (3:21-26), let us note, is placed in its entirety under the rubric: "Now . . . apart from law" (νυνὶ δὲ χωρὶς νόμου); it is most unfortunate that our translations generally fail to reflect the weight which this phrase carries by virtue of its position at the beginning of the paragraph. Paul blazons abroad in his headline that in the manifesting of his righteousness God is now (i.e., in the gospel) acting "apart from law." He is not dealing with men as a judge deals with culprits on the basis of violations of the law. This rubric governs the interpretation of all that follows, and forbids us to insist on purely "forensic" interpretations of the verb "justify" (vss. 24, 26), despite the all but unanimous authority of Protestant commentators. Paul's first words have put us on notice that he is not using the language of the law courts to describe God's gracious dealings with sinful men.

This fuller statement of the theme takes up again the language of 1:17, interpreting the gospel in terms of God's "righteousness," manifested through faith—now defined as "faith in Jesus Christ"—and for faith, "for all who believe." Again, the thought is not simply that God is revealing himself as righteous in his own person, but that he is acting with power to make right triumphant over wrong, good over evil. All men are in the same condition before God—sinful, guilty, and unable of themselves to put things right; and God has provided the means for all alike of annulling guilt, of expiating sin, of breaking man's bondage. "There is no distinction; since all have sinned and fall short of the glory of God, they are justified by his grace as a gift, through the redemption which is in Christ Jesus, whom God put forward as an expiation by his blood, to be received by faith" (vss. 22b-25a). The three key words here are "Justi-fication," "redemption" (*see* Redeem), and "Ex-piation"; and each of them requires careful attention.

d. Key terms. The noun "righteousness" (of God), the verb "justify," and the adjective "just" (or "righteous"), which all occur in this passage, are renderings of three words which in Greek are cognate (δικαιο-σύνη, δικαιόω, δίκαιος). The verb and the adjective must therefore be interpreted in harmony with the sense of "righteousness" which has been indicated above. The usual sense of the verb in Greek is to "declare righteous," or "pronounce not guilty"—the verdict of the judge, the antithesis of "find guilty," or "condemn." This is the "forensic" interpretation of the word, which has been all but unanimously upheld by Protestant theologians from Luther down. Despite this weight of authority, this interpretation is far from satisfactory here. It leaves us with the monstrous notion, which is not adequately defended by resort to the magic word "paradox," that God "pronounces men righteous" who are in fact guilty of sinning against him! It would be easier to defend the rendering "make righteous" (Goodspeed), which has at least the sanction of practically all pre-Reformation interpreters; indeed, if God's word does not go forth void, his pronouncement itself makes a man righteous; he speaks, and it is done. Justification is not to be regarded as a legal fiction. But in this context, the meaning of "justified" is substantially "forgiven" (cf. 4:6-8), with the addition of the positive factor that man is brought into a right relationship with God. Guilt is annulled and sins forgiven; but more than that, the believer is "put in the right" before God. And the greatest emphasis is laid upon the fact that this is wholly God's doing; we are "justified by his grace as a gift," not in any sense or degree as a compensation for merit.

The second key term is "redemption" (ἀπολύτρωσις). The basic thought here is of deliverance. In common Greek usage it would suggest the emancipation of a slave or of a captive upon the payment of a ransom (λύτρον), and this is the initial meaning here: the slave of sin is set free (the thought of the price paid for his redemption is not introduced here). But in a well-known OT usage, the word is employed figuratively to signify the deliverance of Israel from Egypt. God "redeemed" his people when he brought them forth out of the land of Egypt, out of the house of bondage. This was the redemption with which the life of the people of God began and on which it continued to be based. Again, in later time, the promised return of Israel from captivity in Babylon was described under the same figure of redemption; the exodus from Egypt became a type of the new exodus, the restoration of the exiles. Now in the gospel, the "redemption which is in Christ Jesus" brings an infinitely greater deliverance, not of Israel but of all mankind, not from a temporal captivity but from the bondage of the spirit.

The third of our key words is "expiation." The Greek word ἱλαστήριον, which Paul uses here, is related to a verb ἱλάσκομαι, which commonly means "propitiate," and in ordinary usage would convey the thought of appeasing an angry deity, assuaging his wrath, rendering him propitious. Ancient Greek paganism knew many rites which were intended to serve this very end. But the Jewish scholars who translated the OT into Greek used the same verb in a quite different sense. To them it was unthinkable that the righteous anger of God should be averted by any rites of sacrifice. They used the verb ἱλάσκομαι to translate the Hebrew כפר ("cover"), to signify the "covering" or purging of sins, not the propitiating of God. This is the sense in which Paul uses the noun here. The death of Christ is conceived as a sacrifice by which the sins of men are purged. His "blood"—i.e., the offering of his life—is represented as having the mystical power to expiate the sins of man and thus to remove the evil infection which debars him from communion with a holy God. So far is God from requiring to be propitiated that it is he himself who provides this sacrifice of expiation —he has put Christ forward "as an expiation by his blood, to be received by faith." It is not a matter of

divine anger to be appeased by sacrifice, but of divine love that removes the stain of sin which makes communion with him impossible.

Throughout this restatement, Paul has brought out insistently the thought that this triumph over sin is wholly God's doing. Guilty, enslaved, defiled, man has nothing to contribute. He can only make the response of faith, trusting himself to God, believing that God is able and willing to do for him what he can by no means do for himself—to remove the burden of his guilt, break his bondage to sin, blot out his sins with all their defilements. In all this there is no place for boasting; faith can only receive God's bounty.

In ch. 4, Paul undertakes to show that the gospel of grace, of justification by faith, is in essential harmony with the OT revelation. Though it is "apart from law," nevertheless "the law and the prophets bear witness to it" (3:21). He appeals for illustration to the story of Abraham and to the testimony of the Psalms. Even Abraham was not justified by "works," but by his faith in God; and the psalmist proclaims the blessedness, not of the man who can claim a personal virtue, but of the man who has been forgiven. The Abraham story also witnesses to the universalism of the gospel, for it shows that Abraham's faith was reckoned to him for righteousness before he was circumcised; and thus the promises made to Abraham are not limited to the people of the circumcision but are extended to all who share his faith, faith in the God who raises the dead; and so to all who share the Christian faith in the God who raised Christ from the dead.

e. The Christian life. Paul now begins to recount the spiritual blessings that belong to the new standing before God to which the Christian believer has been admitted, and invites his readers to enjoy them (5:1-11). He speaks of peace with God, the hope of sharing his glory, joy that is only intensified through suffering, divine love that is poured into our hearts through his Holy Spirit. The love of God, unconditioned and unmerited, is set in high relief against our complete unworthiness as "helpless, . . . ungodly, . . . sinners, . . . enemies." Here is the assurance of final salvation. If God could so manifest his love toward us while we were his enemies, how much more will he continue to love us and to complete his work of salvation for us, now that we have been reconciled to him through the death of his Son?

The following paragraph (vss. 12-21) brings the thought back full circle to the analysis of the state of mankind with which Paul began (1:18-3:20), and sets forth in glowing words the all-embracing triumph of grace over universal sin. In his opening analysis, Paul had been concerned chiefly to show that sin involved all mankind in guilt; here he speaks of sin as bringing death upon all. A universal condition is met by a universal remedy. Taking the story of the Fall (Gen. 3) as the basis of his imagery, he sets Adam and Christ in contrast as type and antitype—the one through disobedience bringing sin and death into the corporate life of humanity, the other through obedience bringing righteousness and life eternal. Christ has inaugurated a new humanity in which grace reigns "through righteousness to eternal life," whereas, apart from him, "sin reigned in death" (vs. 21).

The next step in the argument is to deal with possible misunderstandings and wilful misinterpretations, such as Paul must have encountered many times in his missionary career. First, there is the antinomian perversion of his doctrine (*see* ANTINOMIANISM). If it be true that "where sin increased, grace abounded all the more" (5:20), then why not go on sinning? "What shall we say then? Are we to continue in sin that grace may abound?" (6:1). And secondly, there is the objection of the man who has been brought up, like Paul himself, to revere the law: Paul's language would almost lead one to say that law is itself an evil, to equate the law with sin! (7:7). These are the difficulties with which the apostle deals in the sixth and seventh chapters.

Paul begins his rebuttal of the antinomian error by bidding his readers have in mind all that is involved in Christian baptism. The immersion in the water was a kind of burial, a participation in the death of Christ, a radical parting from the old life of sin. It is unthinkable that after having thus "died to sin" (6:2), we should any longer live in it. He thinks of baptism as a sacrament which effectively accomplishes that which it represents—our participation in Christ's death, our participation also in his risen life. "For if we have been united with him [σύμφυτοι, lit., 'grown together,' of *organic* unity] in a death like his, we shall certainly be united with him in a resurrection like his" (6:5). He bids us therefore think of ourselves as we are in truth—"dead to sin and alive to God in Christ Jesus" (vs. 11).

In a second approach, he takes up the thought of the old life as a form of slavery—slavery to sin. The slave of sin has been emancipated, and has become a "slave of righteousness" (vs. 18). He is summoned to give the same wholehearted service to his new master as he once gave to sin. Paul admits that the figure is not adequate (vs. 19); later in the letter he makes it clear that God does not call men into a new bondage, but into the freedom of a son in his father's house (8:15; cf. John 8:34-36). And he concludes with a magnificent statement of the illimitable difference in the issue: all the difference between death and eternal life. "For the wages of sin is death, but the free gift of God is eternal life in Christ Jesus our Lord" (vs. 23).

Paul now turns to the more difficult question of the relation of the Christian life to the law (*see* LAW IN THE NT). Here is the central point of conflict between Christianity and the Pharisaic Judaism in which Paul had been reared; for he was, he tells us (Phil. 3:5-6), "a Hebrew born of Hebrews; as to the law a Pharisee, . . . as to righteousness under the law blameless." Now he takes the radical position that the Christian, as he has died to sin, has also died to the law; the regime of law is applicable only within the sphere of that old life which the Christian has renounced, which came to an end for him in his baptism. Here Paul uses the figure of the marriage relationship. As long as the husband is living, the wife is bound to him by law and cannot contract a new relationship without adultery; but the death of her husband releases her from her obligations under this law. So now Christians "have died to the law through the body of Christ, so that [they] may belong to another" (7:4)—i.e., to Christ himself. The figure is again unsatisfactory, since it leads into the thought that the partner who has died is thereby free to contract a new marriage; but Paul is content with the basic thought that through death the Christian has entered into a new union with Christ in which the relationships and obligations of the old life no longer apply. "Now we are discharged from the law, dead to that which held us captive" (vs. 6); and we serve God no longer in terms of an external law, but "in the new life of the Spirit."

Paul now finds it necessary to go more deeply into the whole question of the nature and effect of the law. If baptism into Christ's death means dying to the law, as it means dying to sin; if emancipation from sin means also emancipation from the law, are we not saying that the law is sin? (7:7). From such a conclusion Paul's whole being recoils in horror. "By no means!" (KJV "God forbid.") It is the law which has made sin known. The law is indeed God's law, and is in itself holy and just and good. The evil is not in the law, but in the nature of man. "We know that the law is spiritual; but I am carnal [σαρκινός, 'fleshly'], sold under sin" (vs. 14). Deep down in man, below the level of the rational mind and will, there is a predisposition to evil too powerful to be overcome by the conscious mind's approval of the good and hatred of the evil. (*See* FLESH IN THE NT.) To a being so constituted, the law, even in its inherent goodness, acts as a provocation to the sinful impulses and brings, not life, but death. Man is at war with himself, and his moral perception is overcome by the irrational drive of evil within. "I delight in the law of God, in my inmost self, but I see in my members another law at war with the law of my mind and making me captive to the law of sin which dwells in my members" (vss. 22-23). In this conflict of the mind with the flesh, victory can be gained only through Jesus Christ our Lord.

The secret of this victory is the theme of ch. 8: it is the Spirit of God (*see* HOLY SPIRIT) dwelling within. "The law of the Spirit of life in Christ Jesus has set me free from the law of sin and death" (vs. 2). Here is the mightier power that comes in to help our weakness, enabling us to fulfil the "just requirement of the law" (vs. 4), and bringing to us life and peace (vs. 6). This is the Spirit of sonship, which enables us to call God "Father," and to know ourselves as his sons, destined to share the glories of his Son Jesus Christ (vss. 14 ff). And in this new life of our spirits, transformed by the divine Spirit which is the Spirit of Christ himself, lies the hope and pledge of a renewal of the whole creation. "The creation itself will be set free from its bondage to decay and obtain the glorious liberty of the children of God" (vs. 21). The Spirit aids us in our prayers and intercedes for us according to God's will. Thus we see how God brings us to the destiny which his foreknowledge and predestination have prepared for us, that we should "be conformed to the image of his Son, in order that he might be the firstborn among many brethren" (vs 29); calling us into his service, forgiving our sins and putting us right with him, and finally imparting to us something of the divine glory. And Paul ends his exposition of his great theme with a tremendous assurance of the triumphant love of God in Christ, from which no power can ever separate us.

This exposition of the gospel, now completed, is to be made the ground of an exhortation to live a life in accordance with the will of the God who has so freely showered upon us the riches of his grace. But this exhortation is to be deferred for some time, while the apostle enters upon a lengthy discussion of the great theological problem which has been raised for him by the success of the Gentile mission and the repudiation of the gospel by the mass of the Jewish people. This is the theme of the next three chapters.

f. Subsidiary theme (excursus). Chs. 9–11 constitute a relatively self-contained section within the letter, neither depending upon the preceding argument nor required as further ground for the exhortations which are to follow (12:1-2). Commentators have been sharply divided in their judgments of its relationship to the letter as a whole and to the main theme. To some, it has seemed to be in no sense subsidiary, but an integral part of the main argument, a necessary complement to chs. 6–7. There Paul had refuted criticisms of his gospel based on the charge that it led to the negation of all morality and the denigration of law itself; here he deals with the objection that it nullifies God's promises to Israel and so represents God himself as unfaithful. Some have even gone so far as to hold that this section is the very heart of the letter, and that all the preceding argument has been but a preparation. Yet to others the passage has seemed to be so complete in itself, so loosely related to the general structure of the letter, that it can be regarded as a prior composition, perhaps a stock "sermon" on this topic, which the apostle had used before and had constructed independently, without any thought of addressing it to the Roman church.

Against this it must be said that the argument of the section is by no means so coherent as one would expect in an independent construction with which the writer was wholly satisfied. It conveys much more the immediate struggle with recalcitrant thoughts which cannot be brought wholly within an ordered compass. It strongly suggests a man thinking on his feet and shaping his words as his amanuensis sets them down on the MS. The thought is constantly interrupted by tentative suggestions of one kind and another as the apostle seems to grasp eagerly at anything that may soften in some degree the stark predestinarianism (*see* PREDESTINATION) by which he feels himself bound. There are, moreover, some few but distinct points of contact with things on which the apostle has touched in the earlier chapters, sufficient to indicate that the section was composed in the immediate context of the letter. The problem itself has been adumbrated in 3:1-8; and the exalted contemplation of the divine blessings set forth in ch. 8 leads naturally enough to the apostle's distress at the recollection that his own kindred are excluded from the enjoyment of the promises fulfilled in Christ.

At the same time, the section can hardly be regarded as integral to the main argument. If these three chapters had disappeared from the earliest copies and were no longer extant, it would never occur to any reader that there was anything missing between the end of the eighth chapter and the beginning of the twelfth. They are not needed to complete the apostle's exposition of the meaning of the gospel, nor to enrich his description of the life in the Spirit. The problem which is here attacked is not, in fact, raised by the doctrine of justification in itself, but by the concrete historical development which has been witnessed in the preceding decade of the apostle's career—the hardening of the Jewish people in opposition to the church and the gospel, and the concomitant success of the mission to the Gentiles. It seems necessary, therefore, to regard the section, not as an integral part of the main argument, but as an excursus upon a collateral theological problem.

The section begins abruptly, with nothing to prepare the transition from the rhapsodies of assurance which sound forth so magnificently at the close of ch. 8 to the passionate outburst with which the apostle voices his concern for the salvation of Israel and rehearses the glorious privileges that have been accorded to his "kinsmen by race" (9:1-5). His vehemence leads us to infer that he is reacting to the unfair charge, which must often have been laid against him, that in his concern for carrying the gospel to the Gentiles he has become a renegade to his own people and that he no longer sets much store by the heritage of religion to which he was born. In his repudiation of any such thought of neglectfulness, he will even go so far as to affirm that his mission to the Gentiles is intended "to make [his] fellow Jews jealous, and thus save some of them" (11:14).

But the main problem to which Paul now turns is that which is presented to a Christian Jew by the spectacle of the general rejection of the gospel by the Jews and the readiness with which it is being accepted by the Gentiles of the Roman provinces. The people to whom the promises of God were given in the first instance, renewed in successive generations, and sealed by covenant, are not sharing in the fulfilment of these promises in Christ. Is God then untrue to his own promises to the patriarchs? Or, as he will put the question later: "Has God rejected his people?" For Israel's rejection of the gospel must, in the last analysis, be attributed to the will of God; the apostle never doubts that God has foreordained both the "hardening" of Israel (11:25) and the calling of the Gentiles into the church.

The problem is not at first clearly stated; rather, the answer is in part anticipated. "It is not as though the word of God had failed" (9:6). The Israel of the promises is not to be identified with the Israel of natural descent. (Unfortunately, Paul does not keep this simple distinction clearly in mind throughout, and his failure to do so leads to a lack of clarity.) From the days of the patriarchs, it is clearly shown in scripture that the promises are limited in their application to an elect number within the elect race; and Paul insists that the divine election does not rest on merit but solely on God's "call" (9:6-13).

Here Paul turns aside for a moment to deal with an objection. If God exercises his will in so arbitrary a manner, if his purpose of election takes no account of merit, then the challenge is raised: "Is there injustice on God's part?" (vs. 14). The answer takes the form of an uncompromising reaffirmation of the absolute sovereignty of God: "He has mercy upon whomever he wills, and he hardens the heart of whomever he wills" (vs. 18). It must be said that this answer is not addressed to the objection at all: the question of justice or injustice in the exercise of the divine will is completely disregarded. And when it is further objected that on this basis no place is left for human moral responsibility (vs. 19), Paul flatly replies that man is presumptuous if he asks God for his reasons (vss. 20-21). The apostle is still refusing to deal with the objection itself—once again he is falling back on the infinite transcendence of God, which makes unthinkable any attempt to justify his ways or ask his reasons. Yet he cannot really content himself with the erection of such a stone wall. He goes on to suggest, now somewhat tentatively, afterward (ch. 11) with increasing assurance, that under this appearance of arbitrary will there is a divine purpose of all-embracing mercy (vss. 22-24). And he cites the prophetic scriptures to show that God has revealed his purpose, both of calling the Gentiles into his family of love (vss. 25-26; in Hosea, the words promise the restoration to favor of a chastened Israel, not the calling of Gentiles), and of preserving only a remnant of Israel from destruction (vss. 27-29).

It is impossible to feel that Paul has dealt at all successfully with the difficulties which are raised by his unqualified assertion of the arbitrariness of the divine will. The absolute will of God cannot be thus affirmed except in the context of an equally firm insistence on the infinite wisdom and infinite love which that will expresses. Without this wisdom and love, the absolute will cannot but take on the appearance of a monstrous tyranny. Paul is, of course, fully persuaded that the will of God is exercised in perfect wisdom and love; but he has caused himself and his readers needless difficulty by disregarding everything except the divine will for the purposes of this argument. At the same time, we must realize the profound truth of Paul's central principle, that man is not the measure of all things, that man cannot without intolerable presumption call God to account! He must trust, and through faith seek understanding (*fides quaerens intellectum*).

Returning to his theme (vss. 30-31), Paul at last gives explicit statement to the concrete historical fact which has occasioned his problem: Israel, with all its prior advantages, has failed to attain the righteousness (justification) which it had sought through the discipline of law; while Gentiles, without any such striving, have attained justification through faith. But Paul now seeks the cause of Israel's failure, not in the mysterious and unchallengeable divine decree of reprobation, but in the misguided zeal of the nation itself, which has persistently failed to understand and follow the way of righteousness through faith ("God's righteousness"), and failed to understand that Christ is the end of the law (9:30–10:4). And the righteousness which is based on law and is a matter of human achievement ("their own" righteousness [vs. 3]) is to be clearly distinguished from the "righteousness based on faith," which is the gift of God in the gospel of Christ (10:5-12). Faith is awakened in men by the preaching of the gospel, and Israel has not lacked opportunity to hear the word; nevertheless, she has failed to understand and to respond (vss. 14-21).

Yet it would not be true to say that God has rejected his ancient people of Israel. Paul himself is a living proof to the contrary. Amid the general apostasy, as in the day of Elijah, "there is a remnant, chosen by grace." It must nonetheless be recognized that the nation as a whole is hardened against the gospel (11:1-10). But this apostasy is not the end of the story. Even now it has issued in the extension of salvation to the Gentiles; the fall of Israel has enriched the world; and Paul envisages an incalculably greater conversion of Israel. His own mission to the Gentiles, he avers, has in view the winning of his fellow Jews, if only through provoking them to jealousy of the benefits which the gospel is bringing to the Gentiles (vss. 11-16).

Paul now interjects a warning to the Gentiles against despising the Jews as rejected of God. He holds that there is something unnatural about the admission of Gentiles to the holy community, as if a shoot of wild olive had been grafted into a cultivated stock in place of the natural branches which had been cut off; but this should cause the grafted shoot to fear for itself, rather than to be vain. The fable is awkwardly developed, especially when it is suggested that the grafted shoot may in turn be cut off and the natural branches grafted again into their old place—surely the weirdest horticulture! And Paul appears to be quite unconscious that "the Gentiles" are an entity only to a Jew; there was no sense of unity, merely as non-Jews, among the heterogeneous peoples of the city and the Roman provinces. The lasting interest of the passage lies chiefly in its reflection of Paul's view of the church as the true continuation of the historic community of Israel, branching from the one ancient root. For all his radical critique of Judaism, he never ceases to hold the Christian faith firmly in unity with its OT inheritance; and the continuity is not solely or even primarily in the realm of thought—it is the organic continuity of a living community (vss. 17-24).

The "mystery" of the final salvation of all Israel is now unveiled. Alienated though they now are through disobedience, God still purposes to show them mercy, "for the gifts and the call of God are irrevocable." Here the apostle seems to abandon his fundamental distinction between the spiritual Israel and the Israel of natural descent (9:6-7), and the whole conception of an elect remnant (11:5-7). He reverts again to the notion that God has given his promise to all Israelites without distinction: "As regards election they are beloved for the sake of their forefathers." Despite this inconsistency, there remains the great thought that even in unbelief and hostility they are still in God's hands, and his purpose of mercy will in the end triumph over their present disobedience (vss. 25-32). And in this confidence that even the severity of God issues at last in the manifestation of his mercy, Paul bursts into a noble prayer of adoration and wonder (vss. 33-36).

6. Ethical instruction. In his other letters, the ethical instructions and exhortations of Paul appear to arise directly out of disorders or problems that have actually come to light in the life of the particular church to which he is writing. This is most obvious in I Corinthians (see especially 1:10-12; 5:1; 7:1; 11:17), but it is almost as evident in Philippians, Galatians, Colossians, and the Thessalonian letters. In the case of Romans, it is not at all certain that the apostle has any specific knowledge of the moral and spiritual condition of his readers or of any problems that may be causing them concern. At the most, he may possibly have heard that there were divisions, and even some acrimony and censoriousness, in the Roman church over the scruples of some members in matters of foods and of the observance of holy days; for he makes this the subject of a long and earnest discussion (14:1–15:13). Yet even here, it seems likely that he is writing out of his wealth of experience with other Gentile churches, in the knowledge that Rome will need much the same kind of instruction as was required by Corinth. The ethical section of Romans (12:1–15:13), like the great doctrinal exposition of the previous chapters, thus takes on something of the nature of a general treatise. Paul here sets forth the main lines of his ethical teaching, not at all in the manner of an essay on moral philosophy, but in the form of an appeal to Christian believers to live in accordance with the gospel of the grace of God.

The first two verses of the section (12:1-2) form the rubric under which the whole body of instruction and exhortation stands. Paul is giving us an ethic of redemption, not a system of morals applicable to mankind in general. He has made it abundantly clear that man in his natural state is not capable of moral achievement: those who are in the flesh cannot please God (8:9). He is addressing his appeal to those who are in the Spirit, in whom the Spirit of God dwells. The moral appeal thus rests upon the experience of redemption, the "mercies of God"; it requires, first of all, the offering of the whole being in sacrifice to God, the rejection of the pressures of conformity to the "world" or "age" in which we live, and the complete inward transformation "by the renewal of the mind," which issues in practical obedience to the will of God. The moral life of the Christian, that is to say, is not determined by his own nature as man or by his environment, but by his relationship to God in Christ.

Further, this is an ethic of the church, of participation in the corporate life of the Christian community. For Paul, the Christian is not envisaged as a practitioner of private virtue, but as a member of the body of Christ, living in a nexus of mutual responsibilities and benefits. He is formed for the life of the church, as Aristotle's man was held to be formed for the life of the city. He is therefore under obligation to use the gifts of grace (χαρίσματα; vs. 6) which God had bestowed upon him for the benefit of the whole society of faith. This passage (vss. 3-13) reads like a summary of the longer discussion of the same theme in I Cor. 12.

But the church lives in the midst of a pagan society, under a pagan government, and the apostle must show how the Christian is to behave toward his pagan neighbors and governors. He is called to return good for evil, without taking vengeance into his own hands, to "overcome evil with good" (vss. 4-21). The powers of government derive ultimately from God, and are a terror to wrongdoers; the Christian must obey his rulers, not out of mere dread of the punishment which attends disobedience, but "for the sake of conscience," recognizing that they are servants of God and exercise their functions under his authority (13:1-7). Paul is far from conceiving Christianity as a proletarian revolution against the tyrannies of a master class! This positive view of the state as an organ of the divine government of the world has had a profound influence upon the relations of the church with the state throughout history; but it must, of course, be recognized that it does not provide in itself an immediate answer to all the problems, especially in the new form which they take in the presence of totalitarian governments. It remains true that civic responsibilities fall within the realm of religious duties for a Christian, whatever tensions may be occasioned by a conflict of loyalties.

The whole duty of the Christian may be summed up under the one commandment, which embraces all the moral obligations of man: "You shall love your neighbor as yourself" (vss. 8-10; see LOVE IN THE NT). The nearness of the great day of salvation should spur us to the complete renunciation of evil and complete dedication to Christ (vss. 11-14).

A particular problem of moral theology, arising out of the ramifications of the sacrificial system of ancient paganism, gives the apostle occasion to teach great lessons of tolerance, humility, respect for the opinions and even for the scruples of others, and consideration for the weak (14:1–15:13). The problem itself—whether Christians are free to eat meat which has been offered for sale after a rite of sacrifice to local deities—no longer exists for us; but the apostle's teaching carries us beyond the limits of the particular problem to the underlying principles which are to govern the Christian approach. Nothing is more characteristic of Paul than this habit of penetrating—and leading his readers to penetrate—beneath a particular or local problem to the fundamental principles of Christian truth which determine the Christian's answer. So here he leads us to see that we must look upon the brother whose scruples we do not share, or who does not share our scruples, not as a morally inferior person, but as one whom God has accepted. How then shall we presume to pass judgment on him? We must be concerned rather with the account which we must give of ourselves to God (14:1-12). What is indifferent to you may be more than a needless scruple on the part of your brother; it may be a stumbling block to him. Then you must set his welfare above your own liberty, for "if your brother is being injured by what you eat, you are no longer walking in love. Do not let what you eat cause the ruin of one for whom Christ died" (vs. 15). Our regard for our brother must be measured by the infinite value that Christ has set on him, and for the sake of his conscience we must limit our freedom (vss. 13-23). And the apostle supports his teaching by the example of Christ himself (15:1-2).

7. Text. The major problems of the transmission of the text of the letter have been dealt with in §§ 1-2 *above*. As with all the NT books, the textual tradition is excellent, immeasurably superior to that of any other ancient literature. The greater part of the text of chs. 5-16 is included in the Chester Beatty Papyrus Codex of the Pauline letters (P^{46}), written not much later than A.D. 200, probably at Alexandria. It provides confirmation of the substantial accuracy of the general MS tradition, which begins with the great fourth-century codices Vaticanus (B) and Sinaiticus (ℵ) and continues with hundreds of additional Greek MSS; early versions in Coptic, Latin, and Syriac; and innumerable citations in the works of the early fathers. Such a mass of evidence inevitably presents us with thousands of variant readings; but it is surprising to find how seldom there is real reason for dispute over the reading to be preferred. A few examples of particular interest may be noted.

5:1: The reading ἔχωμεν (subjunctive; "Let us have [peace with God]") against ἔχομεν (indicative; "we have") is supported by an overwhelming weight of MS evidence. In this instance, some good commentators feel obliged to set aside the evidence of the MSS and read the indicative. One scholar holds the subjunctive to be an error and suggests that this error goes back to the autograph—the scribe took the word down wrong from the lips of Paul! But it must be said that the difficulty of interpreting the subjunctive is not so great as to justify the rejection of the MS evidence.

10:9: Here Codex B, with some Egyptian support, has the striking reading: "If you confess the word with your mouth, 'Jesus is Lord'" (ἐὰν ὁμολογήσῃς τὸ ῥῆμα ἐν τῷ στόματί σου ὅτι κύριος Ἰησους), while virtually all other MSS omit "the word" (τὸ ῥῆμα) and have the accusative κύριον Ἰησοῦν in place of the direct quotation ὅτι Κύριος Ἰησοῦς. In this instance, the reading of B cannot be explained as a scribal corruption. It adds great vigor to the phrase, lifting it out of the commonplace, summing up "the word of faith which we preach" (vs. 8) as the proclamation that "Jesus is Lord." Despite the lack of supporting attestation, we are almost forced to conclude that Codex B has preserved the legitimate text.

13:1: Here the Beatty Papyrus lends unexpected support to the Western reading, which would be rendered: "Be subject to all governing authorities."

16:24: The Beatty Papyrus agrees with the great Alexandrian witnesses in omitting this verse, which is included in virtually all the minuscules and in some important witnesses to the Western text.

Bibliography. Commentaries: W. Sanday and A. C. Headlam (1895; subsequent editions unaltered) is still the only full-scale commentary in English. M. J. Lagrange (1931) in Roman Catholic scholarship of the highest quality. C. H. Dodd, Moffatt NT Commentary (1932). K. Barth, *Römerbrief* (1926; 1st ed., 1918), trans. E. C. Hoskyns (1933), is more important for its impact on contemporary theology than for any elucidation of Paul's thought. H. Lietzmann, *Handbuch zum NT* (4th ed.), 1933). K. E. Kirk, Clarendon Commentary (1937). A. Nygren, *Romarbrevet* (1944), trans. C. C. Rasmussen (1949), is a major contribution from the great Lutheran theologian. J. Knox, *IB*, vol. IX (1954). O. Michel, *Kritisch-*

Exegetischer Kommentar über das NT begründet von H. A. W. Meyer (10th ed., 1954-55); C. K. Barrett (1957).

F. W. BEARE

ROME (CHURCH) rōm. This is an attempt to put together all that we can learn about the Christian community of Rome in the NT period from the meager and fragmentary materials available to us. These consist of: (*a*) a few references, some of them doubtful, in classical writers (Suetonius, Tacitus); (*b*) inferences that may be drawn from Christian writings addressed to the Roman church (letters of Paul and of Ignatius, and possibly Hebrews), or emanating from it (I Clement; probably Paul's Imprisonment letters—Colossians and Philemon, more doubtfully Philippians, and Ephesians if it is regarded as Pauline; probably also Mark, and perhaps I Peter); (*c*) occasional references elsewhere in the NT (Acts; the Pastorals); (*d*) fragments of tradition preserved in later Christian writings, where a few grains of fact may be winnowed from the heaps of legend; and (*e*) a modicum of archaeological evidence, extremely difficult to evaluate.

1. Origins. It is probable that Christianity came to Rome very early in the apostolic age, but nothing is known about the founding of the church there. According to Acts 2:10, there were "visitors from Rome, both Jews and proselytes," among the crowds who heard Peter's first sermon on the day of Pentecost, and it has been suggested that these would surely carry the gospel to their fellow citizens. Apart from the difficulty of taking the Pentecost story as a baldly factual narrative, it must be noted that "every nation under heaven" (Acts 2:5) could equally well be supposed to have received the gospel early, through the representatives who were present at Pentecost. One tradition, preserved in the pseudo-Clementines, attributes the first preaching of the gospel in Rome to Barnabas; another, more widely held and almost official, reports that Peter came there as early as A.D. 42. None of this can be taken seriously.

The first trace of Christian activity in the capital is probably to be found in the words of Suetonius (*Life of Claudius* 25), who tells us that Claudius "expelled the Jews from Rome because they were continually rioting at the instigation of Chrestus." Even this reference is doubtful, for Chrestus may be the name of a Jewish agitator; but it seems likely that "Christus" is meant, and that Suetonius is giving us a garbled reference to disturbances in the Jewish community over the propagation of the gospel, perhaps at the time of its first introduction. Aquila and Priscilla, Paul's associates at Corinth, were expelled from Rome under this edict (Acts 18:2), and as there is no intimation that they were converted by Paul, it would seem that they had been members of a Christian group in Rome. There is reason to hold, therefore, that Christianity came to Rome sometime before the year 50, and that it drew its first members from the ranks of the synagogue, as happened so frequently elsewhere.

2. Character. Paul's Letter to the Romans, written no later than 58 and perhaps as early as 53, throws no great light upon the character of the Roman community or upon the conditions prevailing within it. Paul had not yet been to Rome himself, and was dependent upon the reports of others for such knowledge as he possessed. His words are based upon the assumption that he is writing to a predominantly Gentile community (see, e.g., Rom. 1:13: "I have often intended to come to you . . . in order that I may reap some harvest among you as well as among the rest of the Gentiles"); he even feels that he must warn them not to despise the Jews, the natural branches of the olive tree into which they have been grafted, that they may share its richness (Rom. 11:17-19). At the same time, he knows that some of his readers will be Jews (2:1-3:20), and he can speak of Abraham as "our forefather according to the flesh" (4:1). And, indeed, the whole argument against the possibility of justification by the works of the law presupposes that the community has had some indoctrination in the Jewish insistence on the "righteousness which is based on the law" (10:5), and needs to be schooled further in the meaning of the "righteousness that comes from God" (10:3)—the "righteousness of God through faith in Jesus Christ for all who believe" (3:22).

The question will always arise of how far his exposition is based on the particular character and needs of the Roman community, and how far it reflects simply his own experience of the problems and needs of any Gentile church of the time. Yet some confirmation of the supposition that the church at Rome had a Jewish cast is afforded by a passage from the fourth-century Latin commentator known as Ambrosiaster, who claims that "it is generally admitted [*constat*] that in the time of the apostles there were Jews . . . living in Rome; those among them who had become believers delivered to the Romans the tradition that while professing Christ they should keep the law." He holds that they should be praised rather than blamed, for "without seeing any miracles . . . or any of the apostles, they accepted faith in Christ, though according to a Jewish rite." But is this properly regarded as a confirmation from an independent tradition, or is it an inference drawn by Ambrosiaster from the letter itself? Is he explaining how it came that the great Roman church needed to be taught that we "have died to the law through the body of Christ, . . . dead to that which held us captive, so that we serve not under the old written code but in the new life of the Spirit" (Rom. 7:4, 6)?

3. Literary sources. The tradition that Philippians, Colossians, Philemon, and Ephesians were written from Rome has been challenged by many modern scholars in favor of the hypothesis that they were written from Caesarea, or earlier still, from Ephesus. Ephesians tells us nothing of the church from which it is written. Colossians and Philemon tell us something of Paul's companions, and of his conversion of the fugitive slave Onesimus; in Col. 4:11, it is intimated that Paul was not being supported by Christian Jews, except for Aristarchus, Mark, and Jesus Justus: "These are the only men of the circumcision among my fellow workers . . . , and they have been a comfort to me." Philippians likewise mentions division in the community over the attitude toward Paul: "Most of the brethren have been made confident in the Lord because of my imprisonment, and are much more bold to speak the word of God without fear"; but there are some who "preach Christ from envy and rivalry, . . . out of partisanship, not sincerely but thinking to afflict me in my imprisonment" (Phil. 1:14-17). In the same letter greetings are sent from "those of Caesar's household" (4:22); and we are told that "it has become known throughout the whole praetorian guard . . . that my imprisonment is for Christ" (1:13). If this letter was written from Ephesus or from Caesarea, the words need mean no more than that there are Christians in the imperial civil service ("Caesar's household") and in the governor's headquarters (the praetorium, not "praetorian guard"); but if the tradition of a Roman origin can be maintained, they will suggest that the gospel has made its way into the imperial court itself and into the emperor's bodyguard, and that the Roman church has ceased to be —if it ever was—entirely proletarian.

The personal references in the Pastorals can be adduced only with the greatest reserve; few critics now regard these letters as authentic, and even if it is held that they embody some genuine Pauline fragments, no one can tell with certainty when or where they may have been written. Two passages in II Timothy deserve particular attention; if we can persuade ourselves that Paul wrote them, and wrote them from Rome, they will throw some light on the conditions of his imprisonment and his relations with the Roman church. In II Tim. 1:15-18, the writer speaks of a general alienation from him of Asian Christians, naming two of the leaders; and he speaks with feeling of Onesiphorus, "for he often refreshed me; he was not ashamed of my chains, but when he arrived in Rome he searched for me eagerly and found me." This suggests that the Roman church so far turned against Paul in his imprisonment that none of its members could even tell Onesiphorus where he was to be found; Onesiphorus was obliged to make his own search. The second passage (II Tim. 4:9-17) likewise suggests that Paul was deserted by many of his closest friends, and that he was given no support at his first appearance in court (vs. 16). But we must hesitate to form judgments on the basis of materials supplied by a pseudonymous writing.

Tacitus (Ann. XV. 44) and Suetonius (*Life of Nero* 16) tell of the mass persecutions which the Roman church suffered under Nero, but give no useful information about the nature of the community, except that it was very large: Tacitus speaks of a "mighty multitude" which perished amid the most horrible tortures. Both these Latin writers hold that the punishment was justified; the Christians were detested for their evil practices, for their hatred of the human race (Tacitus); they were a "race of men given to a new and deadly superstition" (Suetonius). This is, of course, no more than a retailing of popular calumnies. According to the tradition, Paul and Peter were both put to death in this persecution, which began in 64.

Mark, the earliest gospel, probably made at Rome within the decade following the Neronian persecution, may be regarded as the deposit of the tradition concerning Jesus in the scope and form wherein it was known and prized by the Roman church at this time. Its central emphasis on the way of the cross is not, indeed, peculiarly Roman; it is entirely in keeping with the emphasis of early Christian preaching and piety as reflected in the Pauline letters (the "preaching of the cross"; "Christ crucified"; "crucified with Christ"; "baptized into his death"; etc.). Yet it derives an added poignancy from the experience of martyrdom through which the church had been passing; and the Christ of Mark is under one aspect the great exemplar of martyrdom, the heroic "pioneer and perfecter of our faith, who for the joy that was set before him endured the cross, despising the shame" (Heb. 12:2). As one of the principal sources of Matthew and Luke, as well as in itself, this gospel must be acknowledged to be the first of the great and enduring contributions made by the church of Rome to catholic Christianity. Negatively, it must be said that Mark does not confirm the suggestion that the Roman church had an important Jewish element; it is distinctly a document of Gentile Christianity.

The Emperor Domitian (81-96) toward the end of his reign sentenced many Romans of noble family to death or banishment. Among those executed were his own cousin the consul Flavius Clemens, and a former consul, M. Acilius Glabrio; Domitilla, the wife of Flavius, was banished. It is often affirmed—with more confidence than the evidence permits—that these three suffered as Christians. The catacomb of Domitilla and that of Priscilla, who may have been the wife of Glabrio, are among the earliest Christian cemeteries at Rome, but there appears to be no evidence for their use by Christians as early as the first century. The letter sent to the Corinthian church by the Roman church, known to us as I Clement, which was probably composed toward the end of the first century, begins with a reference to a succession of calamities which had recently burst suddenly upon the Roman community, but gives no indication of their nature.

It is held by some critics that Hebrews was addressed to the Roman church at about this time, and was an appeal to it to assume the responsibility incumbent upon it of teaching other churches; it found a quick response in I Clement, addressed to Corinth, and in I Peter, addressed to the provinces of Asia Minor. The date and destination of Hebrews are as much in doubt as the name of the author; but it will be agreed that about this time the Roman church began to acquire a position of leadership among the churches. It intervened at Corinth, through I Clement, to deal with an internal dispute, a challenge to the established authorities within the Corinthian church; and less than twenty years later, Ignatius of Antioch addresses it in terms of marked respect, and employs phrases which suggest the recognition of some kind of primacy ("presides in the chief place of the Roman territory"; "presiding [προκαθημένη] in love"). The significance of these phrases is much disputed. It is perhaps more important that neither Clement nor Ignatius makes any reference to a Roman bishop; in both letters it is the Roman church that is in view, and there is no indication that it was monarchically governed. This is especially remarkable in the case of Ignatius, who is concerned above all things to exalt the authority of the episcopate. I Peter, addressed to the churches of the Asiatic

provinces at this period, is generally held to have been written from Rome, but it throws no light upon the life of the Roman community, unless we can give credit to a recent theory that it is a liturgical document issued by Rome for the guidance of other communities (a "Paschal liturgy" [F. L. Cross]; *ein urchristliches Gottesdienst* [H. Preisker]). *See* PETER, FIRST LETTER OF.

All the documents addressed to the Roman church or issuing from it during this period, and until the end of the second century, are in Greek. The Roman Christians of apostolic and postapostolic times were Greek-speaking, drawn mainly from the great Levantine population of the city. Latin Christianity did not begin in Rome, but in North Africa.

Bibliography. Major commentaries on Romans, especially O. Michel (1955). Also: A. von Harnack, *Analecta zur ältesten Geschichte des Christentums in Rom* (1905); M. Dibelius, "Rom und die Christen im ersten Jahrhundert," in Heidelberg *Sitzungsberichte* (1924), pp. 18-29; E. J. Goodspeed, *History of Early Christian Literature* (1942).   F. W. BEARE

*ROME, CITY OF. Capital of the Roman Republic and Empire and of modern Italy; halfway down the W coast of Italy and about ten miles up the Tiber River from the port of Ostia.

1. Description
2. Administrative divisions
3. Buildings of the early Empire
4. Living conditions
5. Police and fire fighting; crime
6. Foreigners in Rome
7. Jews and Christians
    a. Location of groups
    b. Peter and Paul
    c. Catacombs
    d. Early churches
Bibliography

1. Description. The city is described in the Natural History (III.66-67) of the elder Pliny: "In the principate and censorship of Vespasian and Titus, in the 826th year after the city's foundation (A.D. 73), the walls of Rome, embracing the seven hills, measured 13.2 miles in circumference. The city is divided into 14 districts, and has 265 intersections with guardian *Lares,* or titular deities. A measurement running from the milestone set up at the head of the Roman Forum to each of the city gates—which today

1) Circus of Gaius and Nero
2) Baths of Nero
3) Baths of Agrippa
4) Campus Agrippae
5) Saepta Julia
6) Circus Flaminius
7) Forum of Augustus
8) Forum of Caesar
9) Forum of Peace
10) Mamertine Prison
11) Temple of Vestal Virgins
12) Arch of Titus
13) House of Tiberius
14) House of Augustus
15) Flavian Amphitheater
16) Circus Maximus
17) Praetorian Camp

From E. G. Kraeling, *Bible Atlas*, copyright by Rand McNally & Co.

number 37 if the Twelve Gates are counted as one and the seven of the old gates that no longer exist are omitted—gives a total of 20.765 miles in a straight line. But the measurement of all the thoroughfares block by block, from the same milestone to the outermost edge of the buildings including the Praetorian Camp, totals a little more than 60 miles. And if one should consider in addition the height of the buildings, he would assuredly form a fitting appraisal and would admit that no city has existed in the whole world that could be compared with Rome in size. On the east it is enclosed by the Rampart of Tarquin the Proud, a work among the leading wonders of the world, for he raised it as high as the walls where the

Courtesy of the Italian State Tourist Office, New York

15. The ruins of the Temple of Mars in the Roman Forum

approach was level and the city most exposed. On the other sides it was protected by lofty walls or steep hills, but the increasing spread of buildings has added many suburbs." (Orig. tr.)

Like modern cities, Rome had expanded from a central core. The seven hills (Capitol, Palatine, Aventine, Caelian, Esquiline, Viminal, Quirinal) rising to the E of the Tiber Valley were surrounded (except for the Esquiline) by the Wall of Servius, built in 378 B.C., and the areas between them were drained into the Tiber. The Forum Romanum,* center of civic activities, was bounded by four hills; on the nearby Capitol were temples,* the greatest being that of Jupiter (rebuilt by Augustus); on the Palatine were the great houses and palaces of the rich and the emperors; the Caelian was dominated by the great temple of the deified Claudius; and to the NE, on the edge of the Quirinal, were the newer forums of Caesar and Augustus. Figs. ROM 14-15.

2. Administrative divisions. Under Augustus the city was divided into the fourteen districts mentioned by Pliny; they were governed by magistrates annually selected by lot. Beginning in the SE and running in a rough circle counterclockwise, they were as follows: (*a*) Porta Capena, (*b*) Caelimontium, (*c*) Isis and Serapis, (*d*) Templum Pacis, (*e*) Esquiliae, (*f*) Alta Semita, (*g*) Via Lata, (*h*) Forum Romanum, (*i*) Circus Flaminius, (*j*) Palatium, (*k*) Circus Maximus, (*l*) Piscina Publica, and (*m*) Aventinus. Across the river was (*n*) Trans Tiberim. Tacitus tells us (Ann. XV. 40.4) that the fire in Nero's reign left only four districts untouched, while three were completely leveled.

3. Buildings of the early Empire. During the last century of the Republic much building activity had been going on at Rome. We need note only Sulla's temple of Jupiter Capitolinus and his Tabularium, Pompey's great theater decorated with countless statues removed from Greece, and Caesar's temple of Venus Genetrix. Caesar's murder prevented his rebuilding the center of the city, and his plan, modified, was carried out only by Augustus.

After Augustus' victory at Actium (31 B.C.) he proceeded to make Rome a city of marble rather than of brick—though the marble was a veneer over the structural brick or concrete. A new Senate house

Courtesy of the Italian State Tourist Office, New York

14. The Forum at Rome

Courtesy of the Italian State Tourist Office, New York

16. The Pantheon at Rome

Courtesy of the Italian State Tourist Office, New York

18. The Arch of Titus, with the Colosseum in the background

and the mausoleum of the Julian family were erected in 29, and in the same year the temple of Caesar was completed and dedicated. In 28 the Senate authorized Augustus to rebuild or restore eighty-two temples which were in need of repair, and he also built a great temple of Apollo near his own house on the Palatine. The next year his counselor Agrippa erected the Pantheon* on the W side of the Campus Martius. Rebuilt by later emperors, it still bears the inscription "M. Agrippa L. F. Cos. Tertium Fecit." The most important of several altars erected by Augustus was the Ara Pacis Augustae, consecrated in 9 B.C. Other important building operations included the Basilica Julia in the Forum, the Theater of Marcellus, various edifices in the Circus Maximus and the Campus Martius, and three aqueducts. Fig. ROM 16.

Under Tiberius less building activity went on, but he began the temple of the deified Augustus (finished by Caligula) and erected a palace on the Palatine (Domus Tiberiana) and a camp for the praetorian guard. Caligula began a circus W of the Tiber (finished by Nero) and added a wing to the palace of Tiberius. The more practical-minded Claudius devoted his attention to the water supply, building aqueducts (in part still standing) from Subiaco to Rome.

Nero finished the circus near the Vatican and, taking advantage of the land clearance provided by the fire in 64, proceeded to erect his Golden House in a large park, with an elaborate approach from the Forum. A colossal statue of Nero stood in this approach, which consisted of porticoes and colonnades. His successors continued the building program.

Courtesy of the Italian State Tourist Office, New York

17. Air view of the Colosseum and the Arch of Constantine

Vespasian built the Colosseum (finished by Titus);* Titus and Domitian erected baths. Vespasian also began the triumphal Arch of Titus* to commemorate the victories in Palestine. All the Flavians also erected temples and palaces in the center of the city. Figs. ROM 17-18.

4. Living conditions. The public buildings of Rome were magnificent, more than worthy of the emperors who erected them. The houses of the rich, usually on the various hills of the city, were sumptuous. But most Romans lived in tenements (*insulae*), often three or four stories high, and subject like their modern equivalents to collapse or burning. The *insulae* were surrounded by narrow, dirty, dangerous, and noisy streets with an incessant flow of traffic, day and night. On the other hand, the people generally were provided with "bread and circuses" by the state. Since 58 B.C. the majority of them had received a free distribution of wheat; water was also free, and wine was ordinarily very cheap. Admission to the games was also free, and such games, including chariot racing, gladiatorial contests, and theatrical performances, attracted huge crowds. The Circus Maximus could hold 150,000 people; the theater of Pompey, 40,000. By the time of Nero, even slaves were admitted.

5. Police and fire fighting; crime. Under Augustus a kind of police force had been created, consisting of three "urban cohorts" whose prefect was to maintain order in the city. He also established seven cohorts of *vigiles* for fighting fires; each cohort was responsible for two of the fourteen districts of the city. Under ancient Roman law severe penalties for incendiarism had already been provided. No statistics are available for the prevalence of murder, or other crimes against persons or property. Prostitution was not outlawed but regulated; prostitutes, often foreigners, had to be registered with the magistrates, pay a tax, and wear distinctive clothing.

6. Foreigners in Rome. During NT times there was a great influx of foreigners into Rome, especially from the East. Like every great city, Rome was a magnet for the ambitious, the adventurous, and the lazy. Romans constantly complained that Rome was no longer Roman. The foreigners tended to remain in rather isolated groups. They brought their own traditions, cultural and religious, and often formed societies, professional and other, for mutual aid, especially in providing for funerals. They were gradually Romanized and urbanized, but in the process they modified the meaning of Rome.

Two examples of religious groups originally foreign may be given. In the first place, under the Republic conservative magistrates viewed the worship of Isis with great disfavor, while others, in search of popular support, tended to allow the construction of Isiac shrines. Even in the reign of Augustus one of the city districts (*see* § 2 *above*) was apparently named for the Egyptian deities, though it was not until the second or third century that temples of Isis could be described as "everywhere" (*Scriptores Historiae Augustae Caracalla* 9). Archaeology suggests that the goddess had a large number of private chapels even earlier. In the second place, the spread of the worship of the Persian Mithra, at the end of the first century and afterward, led to the construction of many places of worship in Rome, though not, apparently, on the Palatine or Capitoline hills. Excavations reveal the existence, at various times, of about forty-five Mithraea; it has been conjectured that there may have been a hundred of them.

7. Jews and Christians. a. Location of groups. The principal Jewish quarters of the city were in the Trastevere region, in the Subura, on the edge of the Campus Martius, and near the Porta Capena—in other words, in the W, central, NW, and SW sections. Presumably the first Christians lived or met in the same quarters. There were at least thirteen Jewish synagogues at Rome, though not all of them may have existed in the first century. They were those of (*a*) the Augustesians (dedicated to Augustus), (*b*) the Agrippesians (to Agrippa), (*c*) the Volumnesians (to Volumnius, perhaps Roman governor of Syria), (*d*) the Herodians (to Herod?), (*e*) the Campesians (Campus Martius), (*f*) the Siburesians (Subura district), (*g*) the Vernaculi (Jewish slaves born in Rome), (*h*) the Calcarensians (lime-kiln workers), (*i*) the Tripolitans (from Tripolis in Africa), (*j*) the Elaians (from Elaia, in Mysia?), (*k*) the Hebrews (old conservative traditionalists?), (*l*) the Sekeni (?), and (*m*) the Calabrians (?). The names thus come from the persons to whom the synagogues were dedicated (*a-d*), from districts in which they were located (*e-f*), or from the origins or trades of the members (*g-j*). The meaning of the last four is not entirely solved.

b. Peter and Paul. During Nero's reign some Christians were martyred in the Gardens of Agrippina, W of the Tiber in the Campus Vaticanus and near Nero's new Circus. Were Peter and Paul among them? Our earliest evidence for their martyrdom at Rome is given in I Clement, written there *ca.* 96.

Clement seems to refer to both Peter and Paul as martyrs at Rome, and he goes on to speak of the tortures of Christian women in a way that recalls the mythological plays given by Nero. Ignatius of Antioch is another witness; he first speaks of his own impending death and then refers to the apostles Peter and Paul, who gave commands to the Roman church (Ign. Rom. IV.2-3). While neither of these witnesses provides absolute proof that Peter and Paul were martyred at Rome, neither of them disagrees with the statement of Gaius of Rome (*ca.*190): "I can point out the trophies of the apostles. For if you are willing to go to the Vatican or to the Ostian Way you will find the trophies of those who founded this church" (Euseb. Hist. II.25.7). The word "trophies" is difficult to translate. It can refer to monuments or memorials; it is also used by Christian writers to refer to relics of the martyrs. Probably, though not certainly, Gaius believed that Peter had been buried on the Vatican and Paul on the Ostian Way. The probability would be increased if we could be certain that he was arguing against Montanists, who believed that John lay buried at Ephesus. On the other hand, graffiti in the catacombs under St. Sebastian, on the Appian Way, clearly suggest that at a later time there were Christians who believed that Peter and Paul were buried there. A translation of relics to St. Sebastian may have taken place at the time of the persecution under Valerian in 257, around the time when Pope Xystus and his deacons were arrested in the catacombs. And the relics may have remained there until Constantine built the basilicas of St. Peter and St. Paul. Alternatively, the St. Sebastian graffiti may reflect only a cult rival to the Vatican's.

How early was there concern for the relics of martyrs? Interest in such matters was widespread in paganism, but the earliest evidence for Christian concern is provided in the Martyrdom of Polycarp (156 or 167): "We took his bones, more precious than jewels and finer than gold, and put them in a suitable place" (XVIII.2). At an earlier time, Ignatius wrote the Romans that he hoped that the wild beasts would become his tomb and would leave no trace of his body (Ign. Rom. IV.2), and, indeed, there is no trace of the preservation of his relics. Is it likely that in Nero's time Christians would have been allowed to bury the bodies of those condemned for arson? At Lyons in 177 the bodies of martyrs were thrown into the Rhone. It is impossible to tell whether Peter and Paul were buried by Christians or not.

Some light on the belief at Rome around the time of Polycarp is cast by excavations under St. Peter's. In 1939 the pavement of the basilica built by Constantine was found, along with pagan graves and sarcophagi beneath it. Constantine's church had been built on a steep slope on the Vatican hill, and in the midst of a pagan cemetery. These difficulties had been faced so that a little monument, part of a wall built between 160 and 170, could occupy a central position in front of the apse of the church. This monument very probably marks the spot where second-century Christians believed Peter had been martyred, if not buried; but there are no certain traces of a grave beneath it, even though some bones were found.

The probable conclusion to be drawn from the literary and archaeological evidence is that both Peter and Paul were martyred at Rome in the time of Nero, and that in the second century memorials were erected to mark the traditional locations of their martyrdoms, on the Vatican and the Ostian Way (Gaius). In view of the difficulties presented by the cult at St. Sebastian, it is not possible to say with any certainty that they were buried at these locations.

c. Catacombs. Both Jews and Christians had catacombs at Rome; these were subterranean rooms and passageways used, not for meetings, but for the burial of the dead. Six Jewish catacombs have been discovered, and many more Christian ones; among the latter, those of Domitilla, Priscilla, and Callixtus are the earliest, though they are no earlier than the latter half of the second century. They were often richly decorated with wall paintings of religious themes, most of which come from the fourth century (there are a few second- and third-century examples). The figure most commonly portrayed is the good shepherd with his sheep on his shoulder; other examples include Jonah, Noah, Abraham and Isaac, Daniel in the lions' den, the three "children" in the fiery furnace, Susanna and the elders, and the raising of Lazarus. Christian artists obviously owed much to their Jewish predecessors. Since not only Christians but also Gnostics had to bury their dead, there are also catacombs with themes at least probably Gnostic on their walls.

d. Early churches. Questions about Christian ownership of meeting places arose in the third century, and we know that early in the fourth there were at least forty churches at Rome. The most prominent among them were three great basilicas built by Constantine: St. Peter's, St. Paul's outside the walls, and St. John Lateran. St. Maria Maggiore was also a fourth-century foundation. Thus the church at Rome "emerged from the catacombs" to enjoy the warmth and light of imperial favor.

Bibliography. H. Leclerq in *Dictionnaire d'archéologie chrétienne et de liturgie,* vol. II (1910), cols. 2376-2450; G. La Piana, "Foreign Groups at Rome," *HTR,* XX (1927), 183-403; S. B. Platner and T. Ashby, *A Topographical Dictionary of Ancient Rome* (1929); C. R. Morey, *Early Christian Art* (1942); H. Leclerq in *Dictionnaire d'archéologie chrétienne et de liturgie,* vol. XIV (1948), cols. 2783-2816; M. J. Vermaseren, *De Mithrasdienst in Rome* (1951); E. R. Goodenough, *Jewish Symbols in the Greco-Roman Period,* vol. II (1953); M. J. Vermaseren, *Corpus Inscriptionum et Monumentorum Religionis Mithriacae,* vol. I (1956); J. W. Perkins, *The Shrine of St. Peter and the Vatican Excavations* (1957).   R. M. GRANT

ROOF [גג, קורה; στέγη]. In ancient Middle Eastern houses the flat roof, covered with clay, was easy of access and a place where members of the family spent a good amount of time (cf. Josh. 2:6; I Sam. 9:25; II Sam. 11:2; Mark 2:4; Acts 10:9). *See* ARCHITECTURE; HOUSE; UPPER ROOM.   O. R. SELLERS

ROOF CHAMBER. *See* CHAMBER.

ROOM. Words translated "room" have other primary meanings—e.g.: מקום and τόπος, "place"; מרחב, "broad place"; קן, "nest." *See* ARCHITECTURE; CHAMBER; HOUSE; UPPER ROOM.

ROOT [שׁרשׁ; ῥίζα]. A word used almost exclusively in figures of speech—e.g., "the root of the matter" (Job 19:28; cf. Job 28:9; 36:30; I Tim. 6:10; fôr Job 30:4, *see* BROOM).

The root of a man is the resource and security of his life (Jer. 12:2; 17:7-8 [cf. Ps. 1:1-3]; Col. 2:7). Similarly, the roots of a family (Deut. 29:18; cf. Heb. 12:15), a dynasty (Isa. 14:29), or a nation (Ezek. 31:7) represent its anchorage in the past and its present security, the foliage and fruits describing the extent and quality of its posterity (Deut. 29:18; Isa. 37:31; Ezek. 31:5-9). "Uprooting" may then signify judgment and destruction (I Kings 14:15; Pss. 9:6; 52:5; Jer. 24:6; Matt. 15:13; cf. different figures in Isa. 14:30; Amos 2:9; Matt. 3:10).

Israel is often described as a plant under the aspect of Yahweh's election (Ps. 80:15; Rom. 11:16-18), judgment (Isa. 5:24; cf. Matt. 3:10), and restoration (Isa. 27:6; Hos. 14:5-6; Amos 9:15).

The expectation of a coming great ruler from the Davidic dynasty produced the figures "root of Jesse" (Isa. 11:10; cf. vs. 1; Rom. 15:12) and "root of David" (Rev. 5:5; 22:16; *see* BRANCH; MESSIAH [JEWISH]—i.e., the dynasty or the successor in whom the dynasty is epitomized and brought to perfection. Isa. 53:2 probably reflects the language of Akkadian TAMMUZ mythology, used to describe the threatened existence of the "servant."

Bibliography. J. Muilenburg, Exegesis of Isaiah, *IB,* V (1956), 618-20.   J. A. WHARTON

ROPE [חבל, עבת; σχοινίον]. A thick cord formed of twisted strands of leather, sinews, vines, or plant fibers, used for many agricultural, military, nautical, and domestic purposes.

Neither Hebrew nor Greek distinguished between rope and cord, and which word is used in translation depends on the context. The RSV renders "rope" more often than the KJV. The art of rope making is older than either spinning or weaving, and Egyptian and Mesopotamian art shows rope in use for a wide variety of purposes, from towing barges to binding captives. Rope was so cheap in Israel that to wear it as part of the garments was a sign of poverty (Isa. 3:24) or submission (I Kings 20:31). While the Bible gives no details of how ropes were made, it testifies to their numerous uses—for harnessing or leading animals (Job 41:2; Isa. 5:18), for fashioning snares and traps (Job 18:10), for tying prisoners (Judg. 15:13; 16:11-12; cf. Pss. 2:3; 129:4; Ezek. 3:25), for hauling stones and tearing down fortifications (II Sam. 17:13), for ship's tackle (lit., "ropes"; Isa. 33:23), for holding a tent ("cords"; Isa. 33:20), as a measuring line or cord (II Sam. 8:2; Zech. 2:1—H 2:5), and for raising or lowering weights (Josh. 2:15; Jer. 38:11). The only NT use of rope is for the tackling of a ship (Acts 27:32, 40).

See also CORD; TACKLE.   L. E. TOOMBS

ROSE [חבצלת, *ḥabhaṣṣéleth;* ῥόδον]. The true rose (genus *Rosa*) is not mentioned in the Bible, except for its use in the Greek name Rhoda (Acts 12:13); but there are several references to it in apocryphal literature. The KJV in Song of S. 2:1 translates *ḥabhaṣṣéleth* "rose of Sharon," and in Isa. 35:1: "The desert shall rejoice, and blossom as the rose." The RSV preserves "rose" in Song of S. 2:1, but indicates in the margin that the Hebrew means "crocus," with which it translates the word in Isa. 35:1. It is clear that the Hebrew does not mean "rose," but the identification is disputed. *See* CROCUS.

That the true rose was known in ancient Palestine, at least since Greco-Roman times, is no longer disputed. Apparently the expression in II Esd. 2:19: "seven mighty mountains on which roses and lilies grow," refers to the *Rosa phoenicia* Boiss, well known in mountainous regions of Lebanon and Syria. Wisd. Sol. 2:8 ("Let us crown ourselves with rosebuds") may refer to the same flower. Other references in apocryphal literature to ῥόδον seem more likely to imply the oleander (*Nerium oleander* L.), however, which grows profusely along streams even today. Ecclus. 39:13: "like a rose growing by a stream" (some MSS read: "like a cedar"), and Ecclus. 24: 14: "like rose plants in Jericho," clearly fit such an identification. Ecclus. 50:8; Enoch 82:6; 106:2, 10; III Macc. 7:17, other occurrences of ῥόδον, are more difficult to identify; but the oleander might be meant. The Phoenician rose would not fit these contexts.

The so-called "rose of Jericho" sold in Jericho today is not a rose at all but the dried tumbleweed, *Anastatica hierochuntica* L., which opens like a rose when put in water.

See also FLORA § A10.

Bibliography. I. Löw, *Die Flora der Juden,* III (1924), 193-211; H. N. and A. L. Moldenke, *Plants of the Bible* (1952), pp. 205-6. J. C. TREVER

ROSETTA STONE rō zĕt′ə. A partly broken copy of a decree honoring Ptolemy V Epiphanes in 196 B.C. The Rosetta Stone was discovered in August, 1799, near the village of Rosetta in the W Delta of Egypt by Captain Bouchard of the French Army, then campaigning in Egypt under the command of Napoleon. The original inscription contained a complete copy of this decree in hieroglyphic Egyptian, Demotic, and Greek. The chance finding of this trilingual text furnished European scholars the necessary key with which to decipher the hieroglyphic and Demotic scripts, a task which was undertaken shortly thereafter with accumulative success by such pioneers as the Swedish diplomat Akerblad, the English physicist Thomas Young, and the brilliant young French scholar J.-F. Champollion. Fig. ROS 19.

Bibliography. J. Friedrich, *Extinct Languages* (1957), pp. 16-26. T. O. LAMBDIN

ROSH rŏsh [ראש, head, chief] (Gen. 46:21). Seventh son of Benjamin. However, the LXX here names him as son of Bela and thus as Benjamin's grandson. Also, Rosh does not appear among the Benjaminite tribal families in Num. 26:38-39; I Chr. 8: 1-5. Perhaps "Ehi, Rosh, Muppim," in Gen. 46:21 is a corruption of אחירם שפופם in Num. 26:38-39. L. HICKS

ROSIN. KJV Apoc. alternate form of NAPHTHA.

RUBEN rōō′bən. Douay Version form of REUBEN.

RUBY. KJV translation of פנינים (RSV PEARL in Job 28:18; "jewel" in Prov. 3:15; 8:11; 20:15; 31:10;

CORAL in Lam. 4:7). The real ruby, a crystallized variety of corundum of the same chemical constituency as sapphire but differing in color, is not found in excavated sites of the ancient Near East. The best rubies come from Burma, Ceylon, and Siam.

See also JEWELS AND PRECIOUS STONES.
W. E. STAPLES

RUDDER [πηδάλιον, *from* πηδός, oar] (Acts 27:40; Jas. 3:4); KJV alternately HELM (Jas. 3:4). Early in the history of boating it must have become apparent that a dugout or canoe could be steered only from the stern paddle, and this principle was subsequently applied to the management of larger vessels. Egyptian sailing boats *ca.* 2500 B.C. display two paddles at the stern for steering. While shortly after this it was found that one steering oar, controlled by a tiller, would suffice to guide a boat (cf. Herodotus II.96), two paddles were more commonly used in Egypt. Greek ships generally had two steering oars, although Odysseus' sailing craft had only one (*Odyssey* V.255). The use of two paddle-rudders continued into the Roman period, as we know from Acts 27:40 and many other sources. It is probable that such steering oars were operated independently.

See also SHIPS AND SAILING.

Bibliography. A. Neuburger, *The Technical Arts and Sciences of the Ancients* (trans. H. L. Brose; 1930), pp. 490-91.
W. S. McCULLOUGH

RUDDY. The translation of various forms of אדם, "to be red," describing an attribute of male comeliness. While the later passages (Song of S. 5:10; Lam. 4:7) refer to the ruddy complexion of vigorous health, the earlier passages (I Sam. 16:12; 17:42) may possibly refer to red hair (cf. Gen. 25:25).
J. A. WHARTON

RUDIMENT. KJV translation of στοιχεῖον (RSV "elemental spirit") in Col. 2:8, 20. *See* ELEMENT.

RUE [πήγανον]. A strong-smelling perennial shrub with gray-green leaves and lemon-yellow clusters of flowers, *Ruta graveolens* L. (or possibly *Ruta chalepensis* var. *latifolia* [Salisb.] Fiori). It was widely used as a condiment, in medicines, and as a charm. Jesus thus criticized the Pharisees: "You tithe the mint and rue and every herb, and neglect justice and the love of God" (Luke 11:42). The parallel passage (Matt. 23:23) has "dill." The facts that Papyrus 45 (third century) in Luke 11:42 reads "dill," and that rue was not subject to the tithe (M. Sheb. IX.1), indicate that "dill" was probably the original word in the saying.

See also DILL; SPICES.

Bibliography. I. Löw, *Die Flora der Juden,* III (1924), 317-21; H. N. and A. L. Moldenke, *Plants of the Bible* (1952), p. 208; W. F. Arndt and F. W. Gingrich, *A Greek-English Lexicon* (1957), p. 661. J. C. TREVER

RUFUS rōō′fəs [Ῥοῦφος; Lat. *Rufus,* red-haired]. 1. Son of Simon of Cyrene (Mark 15:21), and brother of Alexander. Though Simon is mentioned in all three Synoptic gospels, his sons are referred to only by Mark. They must have been well known in the community to which the Gospel of Mark was ad-

19. Rosetta Stone

dressed, which is usually believed to have been Rome.

2. The recipient of a greeting in Rom. 16:13; called an outstanding Christian. His mother is included in the greeting, and Paul adds that she acted the part of a mother to him as well.

If Rom. 16 is an integral part of Romans, there is a strong probability that Rufus 1 and Rufus 2 are identical. But the increasing tendency to regard this chapter as a separate letter, addressed to Eph-

esus, would make such an identification of these two men considerably less likely.

F. W. GINGRICH

RUG [שְׂמִיכָה]; KJV MANTLE. The covering which Jael put over Sisera (Judg. 4:18) when he entered her tent in flight from Barak. It may have been a rug, a tent curtain, or perhaps a heavy cloak. The versions generally use words denoting heavy wraps used for cold weather and for sleeping, though the

LXX, with δέρρις, implies one of the curtains used to partition the tent.   E. M. GOOD

RUHAMAH rōō hā′mə. KJV translation of רחמה ("pitied"; RSV "She has obtained pity"), a new name to be given Israel in the day of redemption, denoting the change in God's attitude from anger to mercy (Hos. 2:1; cf. vs. 23).

RULER OF SYNAGOGUE [ראש הכנסת; ἀρχισυν-άγωγος]. The leader or president of a SYNAGOGUE; a kind of chargé d'affaires whose particular duty was to care for the physical arrangements of the synagogue services. Several men serving in this capacity are named or mentioned in the NT:

a) Jairus, the father of a twelve-year-old girl whom Jesus raised from death (Mark 5:22-43). However, Matt. 9:18 calls him merely "a ruler."

b) An unnamed man who became indignant when Jesus healed on the sabbath (Luke 13:10-17).

c) Those who permitted Paul and his companions to speak in the synagogue at Pisidian Antioch (Acts 13:14 ff).

d) Crispus, a convert to Christianity at Corinth (Acts 18:8). This is probably the Crispus whom Paul baptized at Corinth (I Cor. 1:14).

e) Sosthenes, also ruler of a Corinthian synagogue at the time of Paul's first missionary journey (Acts 18:17). He was beaten in the presence of the proconsul Gallio, though Acts does not say why. Many have identified him with the Sosthenes of I Cor. 1:1, whom Paul calls "brother" and who was evidently known to the Corinthian church. In that case he had gone to Ephesus, at least for a time, after his conversion. *See* CORINTHIANS, FIRST LETTER TO THE.
                    PIERSON PARKER

RULERS OF THE CITY. *See* CITY AUTHORITIES.

RUMAH rōō′mə [רומה]. The town of Zebidah, the mother of Jehoiakim, and/or her father, Pedaiah (II Kings 23:36). Josephus takes Rumah as the home of Jehoiakim's mother, but he does not locate the place (Antiq. X.v.2). It may perhaps be located at Khirbet Rumeh, near Rimmon in Galilee.

A place called Ruma was the home of two brave Galileans who attacked the Tenth Roman Legion (Jos. War III.vii.21).

It has also been suggested that Rumah is to be identified with ARUMAH.

Presuming that Jehoiakim's immediate ancestors would be expected to come from Judah, a location in Judah has been sought, and "DUMAH" (דומה), in the vicinity of Shechem, in Josh. 15:52 has been taken as a scribal error for "Rumah." Neither this nor the Dumah in Isa. 21:11 (in Edom) is our Rumah.
                    W. L. REED

RUNNEL [רהט, runnel, watering trough] (Gen. 30: 38, 41); KJV GUTTER. Alternately: TROUGH (Exod. 2:16). A watering trough where flocks cared for by Jacob came to drink. In Gen. 30:38, "that is, the watering troughs," has plausibly been taken as an explanatory gloss.

RUNNER. *See* GUARD.

RUSH, RUSHES [*primarily* אגמן]. A reedlike plant, usually associated with river banks and marshes, of the Juncaceae family, particularly those of the genus *Juncus*, and less correctly those of the genus *Scirpus*. The term is used loosely in all English Bibles, to translate several Hebrew words.

See also FLORA § A11; HOOK; PAPYRUS; REED.
                    J. C. TREVER

RUST [חלאה, disease; ἰός, consumer, devourer; βρῶσις, poison]. The biblical terms for rust are associated with various metals and apparently mean "corrosion" generally, something like disease, possibly connected with rust of CEREALS. The rust (KJV "scum") of a "pot" or caldron is a symbol of Jerusalem's "filthy lewdness"; even with repeated intense heatings, the "thick rust does not go out" (Ezek. 24: 1-13). A corrosion term in modern metallurgy is "copper disease"; the oxide of copper is green or gray-green, the color of death. The Letter of Jeremiah 6:12, 24, in ridicule mentions rust (βρῶσις) on gold and silver ornaments of IDOLS. The NT references to rust are: in Matt. 6:19-20, where the word is βρῶσις and precious metals are implied; and in Jas. 5:3, perhaps reflecting Jesus' saying, where the word is ἰός and the metals subject to corrosion are gold and silver.

Bibliography. J. L. Kelso, "Ezekiel's Parable of the Corroded Copper Cauldron," *JBL,* LXIV (1945), 391-93.
                    P. L. GARBER

*RUTH, BOOK OF rōōth [רות, *see below*]. The story of Ruth and Naomi, a tale of human kindness and devotion transcending the limits of national- or self-interest. It is the book of the OT which has long been cited as a perfect example of the art of telling a story.

The name Ruth (רות) is traditionally associated with רעות, "friend, companion," as indicated by the Syriac spelling רעות (cf. Akkadian *ru'u,* "friend, companion"). A derivation which accounts better for the Hebrew spelling of the name is from the root רוה, "be satisfied" (with water), "water abundantly," "refresh" (cf. B.B. 14*b*).

The biblical Ruth was a Moabite woman who had married a Hebrew, a native of Bethlehem in Judah, who was living in Moab. On the death of her husband, she chose to accompany her Hebrew mother-in-law, Naomi, to Bethlehem, instead of returning to her own people. Here she became the wife of Boaz, a kinsman of her husband. Their son was Obed, the father of Jesse, the father of David. Ruth appears, then, as ancestress of David, and so of Jesus, in the genealogy of Jesus Christ (Matt. 1:5).

1. Content
2. Date
3. Purpose
4. Place in the canon
   Bibliography

1. Content. A family from Bethlehem in Judah— Elimelech, his wife Naomi, and their two sons— sought refuge in Moab in a time of famine. The two sons took Moabite wives, Orpah and Ruth. When the death of the men of the family left the three women widows, Naomi resolved to return to her

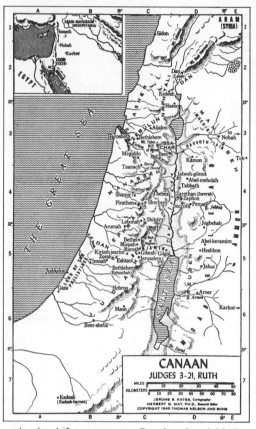

CANAAN
JUDGES 3-21, RUTH

MILES 0   10   20   30   40   50
KILOMETERS 0 10 20 30 40 50 60 70 80

JEROME S. KATES, Cartographer
HERBERT G. MAY, PH.D., Research Editor
COPYRIGHT 1949. THOMAS NELSON AND SONS

former times in Israel" (4:7). The genealogy of David (4:18-22) is like genealogies of the postexilic period in both content and language. In content it seems too brief to cover accurately the whole period from Perez to David. It does not appear in the early accounts of David's ancestry in Samuel, but is the same as that given in I Chr. 2:4-13. The same form of the verb "to beget" appears in the genealogies in Ruth, P, and Chronicles (הוליד in I Chr. 2:4-15, etc.), while a different form appears in earlier writings (ילד in Gen. 10:15, etc.). There are other instances where the language of the book suggests the later period. The word for taking a wife (נשא [1:4]) occurs elsewhere in Ezra, Nehemiah, and Chronicles, while a different verb appears in earlier sources (לקח in Gen. 24:4, etc.). Other words are typical of Aramaic or postexilic usage (שבר [1:13]; עגן; להן; מרא [1:20]; קים [4:7]). The content of the book as a whole, with its story of a foreign woman who became a member of Israel's most respected family, suits the special concern of the postexilic period, with the problem of particularism (cf. Ezra 9-10; Neh. 13) and universalism (cf. Isa. 66:18-23; Jonah). In the Hebrew canon Ruth is found in the *Kethubhim* or Writings, the third and last section of the Bible to be canonized. The combined evidence of the author's view of the past, the language of the book, its content, and its place in the canon, points clearly to a postexilic date. It seems probable, therefore, that the author used deliberately an archaic style suitable for the kind of story he was telling, and that the book may be dated in the postexilic period.

It seems unlikely, however, that the writer of the present book of Ruth created a fictional story to serve his purpose. The argument of the commentators as to whether the main purpose of the book is to enter the controversy over Israel's relation to foreigners, or to tell an idyll of a story with no polemic stress, is an indication of the diversity of materials within the book. The present climax of the story, with the triumphant naming of the child and statement that Obed "was the father of Jesse, the father of David" (4:17), presents certain difficulties in relation to its context. The name Obed is not suggested by the explanatory saying "A son has been born to Naomi," and the connection with David may well have been an addition to the story. The book as it now stands seems to depend upon at least some earlier materials.

There is no indication, however, that the author of Ruth made use of written sources. The tradition that Ruth was once part of the written book of Judges does not seem probable in the light of the difference in content and feeling between the two books. There is no indication that the genealogy of David goes back to any accurate written source. The author's interpretation of the law of levirate marriage and property redemption is not entirely consistent with the law of Deut. 25:5-10. On the other hand, the perfection of story form which the book shows suggests the possibility of a long oral tradition in the course of which the tale was polished and repolished. The use of exactly the right amount of detail is part of the art of the story—Boaz himself passing Ruth food at the noon break, or Ruth saving the remains

native land. In contrast to Orpah, who yielded to the urging of Naomi and returned to her own people, Ruth declared her complete devotion to her mother-in-law (Ruth 1:16-17), and went with her to Bethlehem. Here, at the time of the barley harvest, Ruth received permission to glean in the fields of Boaz, a kinsman of Elimelech. At the end of the harvest, Naomi sent Ruth to ask protection from Boaz, as next of kin. After one nearer kinsman had legally waived his prior right to buy the family property and provide an heir for Elimelech, Boaz took Ruth as his wife. The son born of this marriage was then celebrated as a son "born to Naomi." The family line was thus preserved through the efforts of Ruth and Naomi, and preserved for the greatest distinction, since this child was to be the ancestor of David.

2. Date. According to the tradition of the Talmud (B.B. 14*b*), Samuel was the author of Judges and Ruth, as well as of the book that bears his name. The story of Ruth has its setting in the period of the judges. The excellent classical style of the book, and the use of a number of archaic verbal forms, are entirely appropriate to this earliest period of Hebrew literature. In its present form, however, the book of Ruth shows considerable evidence of a postexilic date—i.e., sometime between 450 and 250 B.C.

The book begins with the characteristic folk-tale description of a time long past: "In the days when the judges ruled" (1:1). It goes on to explain, as if it were obsolete, a custom still known in the time of the writing of Deut. 25:9: "Now this was the custom in of her lunch to take home to Naomi. The growing suspense is carried through perfectly from the time when Ruth "happened to come to the part of the field belonging to Boaz" to the final threat to the whole scheme when the nearer kinsman announced that he would redeem the property. These sound like elements in a folk tale that have been found successful through many tellings. If this is true, the focus of the tale may have shifted from time to time, and the recovery of the original form of the story is probably impossible. The basis may have been the account of an actual friendship. It may even have been an ancient cultic myth of Bethlehem, in which the harvest ritual, the lamenting woman, and the birth of a new child were all connected (cf. W. E. Staples [see bibliography] for a further, and highly conjectural, discussion of cultic elements which may have contributed to the details of the story). Either of these is possible. But whatever the origin, or the date of the original materials, the result is a tale which is a work of art. It is the tale as it now stands, as it has emerged from any process of retelling, which must be considered in the attempt to evaluate the purpose and significance of the present book of Ruth.

3. Purpose. In the opinion of many commentators the achievement of such perfect artistry is a sufficient purpose for the book. Richard Moulton describes the tale as "so delicate in its transparent simplicity that the worst service one can do the story is to comment on it." Judged on the basis of artistry alone, Ruth is clearly an outstanding example of Hebrew literature. It is a delightful short story, beautifully told. The idyllic scene is presented with obvious enjoyment and skill. There is no villain in the story. No reprehensible act is done by any character. But the author has used detail and contrast to such good effect that the difference between ordinary and exceptional goodness stands out clearly against the background of details of common life. Orpah is in no way lacking in dutiful devotion. She is ready to accompany her mother-in-law to a new country, and yields only to a second urging of Naomi to go back to her own people (1:8-14). The nearer kinsman is prepared to accept his responsibility and redeem the property, and yields only when he finds that a marriage is involved which may conflict with his duty to his own inheritance (4:4-6). It is against this background that the unusual magnanimity of Ruth and Boaz is seen in its true perspective. Naomi's final success in bringing about a restoration of the family line is given its proper importance in contrast to her own realistic evaluation of the odds against its likelihood (1:11-13). The only proper conclusion for this tale of heroic perseverance and human kindness is a conclusion of the kind that is given, the greatest reward that a family could receive—its place in the ancestry of David. The story makes an artistic whole. Each detail plays its part, and the conclusion reached after just the right amount of suspense is clearly the right conclusion. In the light of this obvious artistic success, it may well seem an unnecessary perversity to look for any other purpose.

It is true, however, that Ruth, like any good short story, has a theme. A theme mentioned frequently

above is that of human kindness over and above conventional duty. One rabbinic commentator, noting that Ruth does not deal with ritual or legal matters, states positively that it was written to teach "how great is the reward that accrues to those who perform kindly deeds" (Midrash Rabbah, Ruth II.14). Much of the popular appreciation of the book has been in response to this theme, especially as seen in the unselfish devotion of Ruth to Naomi. Ruth's reply to Naomi, beginning with the words: "Entreat me not to leave you or to return from following you; for where you go I will go" (1:16-17), has long been taken as a symbol of true friendship between women, parallel to the famous example of the friendship of David and Jonathan. Here is not simply the loyal devotion to a husband which might be expected from a wife, but devotion to a woman who was both a foreigner and a mother-in-law, beyond any reasonable requirement of duty.

The emphasis of the book, however, is not so much on Ruth's devotion to her mother-in-law, as on the fact that Ruth was accepted in Israel in spite of her foreignness. The point stressed most frequently in the text is that Ruth was a foreigner (1:4, 22; 2:2, 6, 10-13, 21; 4:5, 10). Ruth mentions this twice emphatically when she speaks of Boaz' favor to her (2:10, 13). The adjective "Moabitess" appears at least twice in connection with Ruth where the plot does not demand the title (2:2, 21). Human kindness and devotion are certainly an important theme of the book, but the stress seems to be on the fact that this kindness was not limited by any of the usual prejudices, on the part either of Ruth or of Boaz. Israel Bettan brings out this dual aspect when he describes the theme of the book as the "law of kindness which transcends national boundaries and makes all men kin." It is this double theme, with the emphasis more on a universalism that goes beyond national barriers than on the simple friendship of Ruth for Naomi, that goes through the book as a whole. That "Ruth the Moabitess" could then be the great-grandmother of David is the fitting climax for this theme, and a climax which has caused traditional-minded commentators considerable difficulty (cf. the struggles of Midrash Rabbah to reconcile the exclusion of Moabites required by Deut. 23:3 with Ruth 2:5-6; 4:17).

The concern of postexilic Judaism with this problem of particularism and universalism, and the emphasis of Ruth on the acceptance of the foreigner and on her goodness, is one argument for the date of the book (see § 2 above). In the second half of the fifth century B.C., Nehemiah attempted to put an end to all marriages of Jews with non-Jews on the ground of preserving the original commandment of God (Neh. 10-13; cf. Ezra 9:1-3). Many scholars have taken the book of Ruth as a response to this specific attempt to enforce the separation of Israel from other peoples (see G. A. Cooke, The Book of Ruth, p. xiii, for a summary of this position) and have considered the designation of Moab as Ruth's country of origin as the deliberate choice of a nation excluded by the law Nehemiah attempted to enforce (Deut. 23:3), and yet possible historically because of the fact that David turned to Moab as a place of sanctuary for his parents (I Sam. 22:3-4). Others have seen in Ruth an

expression of liberal feeling protesting the later attitude of exclusiveness over the question of accepting
proselytes to Judaism. A rabbinic comment on Ruth's
going with Naomi (Ruth 1:18) invites the reader to
"come and see how precious in the eyes of the Omnipresent are converts" (Midrash Rabbah, Ruth III.5;
cf. Ruth 2:12 for the treatment of this issue).

It is difficult, however, to find evidence of specific
protest in the book of Ruth. The attitude of the book
is certainly incompatible with racial or religious exclusiveness. But there is no obvious polemic or invective. The choice of Moab could be explained on
historical, as well as ideological, grounds (I Sam. 22:
3-4). It seems impossible, therefore, to limit the purpose of Ruth to an attack against any specific set of
wrongs. The book has, rather, a positive purpose: the
statement in story form of the possibility of good will
and respect for another human being, without any
regard for national or religious intolerance. It is precisely this lack of polemic which makes the book of
Ruth a positive and lasting witness on the side of
universalism in any human situation.

4. Place in the canon. It is certainly partly this
theme of universalism that is responsible for the existence of Ruth as a written book of the Bible. Good
stories were obviously enjoyed in ancient Israel (cf.
Gen. 12:10-20), but for a story to be written down,
and then to be included in the Bible, some further
purpose was required (cf. discussion of this point in
IB, II, 831). The statement of universalism was, no
doubt, one reason for the acceptance of Ruth, as it
was for Jonah. Another, and probably more compelling, reason for the inclusion of Ruth in the canon
was the fact that it deals with the ancestry of David.

In the Hebrew Bible, Ruth is found in the
Kethubhim or Writings, the third section of the canon.
The Talmud puts Ruth first, before the Psalms and
Job, in its listing of the Writings (B.B. 14*b*). In all re-
cent Jewish tradition, however, Ruth belongs with the
Song of Solomon, Lamentations, Ecclesiastes, and
Esther, as one of the five Megilloth, or Scrolls, which
are read on special occasions during the year. The
Song of Solomon is read at Passover, Ruth at
Shabuoth or Weeks, Lamentations on the Ninth of

Ab, Ecclesiastes at Sukkoth or Tabernacles, and
Esther at Purim. In Hebrew Bibles the Megilloth
usually appear in this order, following the order of
the festivals, although in some MSS Ruth comes first,
immediately before the Song of Solomon (*see* CANON
OF THE OT). The LXX did not preserve the division
between the Prophets and the Writings, but put Ruth
after Judges, and Lamentations after Jeremiah, probably because the books deal with the same periods of
history. The Latin translation follows the order of
the LXX. Josephus apparently went further and regarded Ruth as an appendix to the book of Judges.
The Talmudic statement that Samuel was the author
of both Judges and Ruth (B.B. 14*b*) seems to represent an acceptance of this opinion. In the English
translations of the Bible, as in modern versions generally, the tradition of the LXX is maintained, and
Ruth follows Judges.

The place of Ruth in the Hebrew canon, as the
scroll to be read on the Feast of Shabuoth, gives
some indication of the significance of the book in
Jewish tradition. Shabuoth is the biblical festival
celebrating the close of the weeks of the grain
harvest, and Ruth, with its harvest setting, is associated with this festival. The tradition connects
Shabuoth also with the commemoration of the giving of the law, and it is because of this connection
that the holiday has achieved its present importance
for Judaism. It is of interest, therefore, that some
modern commentators have seen the giving of the
law as an act of universal significance, intended as a
gift for all mankind, and Ruth as the book appropriate to the universalism of this festival (cf. Israel
Bettan [*see bibliography*], p. 54).

Bibliography. G. A. Cooke, *The Book of Ruth* (1918); D. B.
MacDonald, *The Hebrew Literary Genius* (1933), pp. 121-23;
R. G. Moulton, *The Modern Reader's Bible* (1937), pp. 1375-
76; W. E. Staples, "The Book of Ruth," *AJSL*, LIII (1937),
145-57; J. R. Slotki, "Ruth," in A. Cohen, ed., *The Five
Megilloth* (1946); H. H. Rowley, "The Marriage of Ruth,"
HTR, XL (1949), 77-99; I. Bettan, *The Five Scrolls* (1950), pp.
49-72; L. P. Smith, Introduction and Exegesis of Ruth, *IB*,
II (1953), 829-52.   D. HARVEY

RYE. *See* SPELT.

S. Symbol sometimes used for SINAITICUS.

SABA, QUEEN OF sā'bə. Douay Version form of SHEBA, QUEEN OF.

SABACHTHANI. *See* ELI, ELI, LAMA SABACHTHANI.

SABAOTH săb'ĭ ŏth [צבאות, *plural of* צבא, army host; σαβαώθ]. *See* HOST OF HEAVEN; GOD, NAMES OF, § C3.

SABAT. KJV Apoc. form of Shebat. *See* CALENDAR.

SABATEAS. KJV Apoc. alternate form of SHABBETHAI.

SABATUS. KJV Apoc. form of ZABAD.

SABBAIAS. Apoc. alternate form of SHEMAIAH.

SABBAN săb'ən. KJV Apoc. form of BINNUI.

***SABBATH** săb'əth [שבת, cessation, desistance]. In origin, the closing day of a seven-day week. The noun is derived from the verb שבת, "to cease, to abstain, to desist from, to terminate, to be at an end." Only secondarily does this verb connote "to be inactive, to rest" (Exod. 21:19; Lev. 26:34-35; II Chr. 36:21). Accordingly, despite the testimony of Josephus (Antiq. I.i.1; Apion II.ii), the connotation "rest" for the noun is at the best questionable and under any circumstances postbiblical.

In the initial stages of its evolution the sabbath was observed as a day upon which all physical labor was taboo, probably because it was regarded as an unlucky, an evil, day, under the control of gods or spirits hostile to mankind. Ultimately it became a day of positive worship of the Deity, characterized not only by complete abstention from all ordinary occupations and activities but also by assemblage in temple or synagogue and sacrifice or prayer and ritual observance there. In this, its major and only persistent aspect, the sabbath is essentially of Jewish origin. Conforming to ancient tradition, Judaism has always observed the sabbath upon the seventh day of the week, Saturday. This was the practice likewise of the early Jewish Christians. Gentile Christianity, however, motivated perhaps by the suggestion of Paul (Col. 2:16-23; cf. I Cor. 16:2; Gal. 4:9-11), gradually shifted its sabbath to Sunday, the first day of the week. In so doing it was influenced in large measure by the considerations that according to biblical tradition light was created upon the first day (Gen. 1:3-5) and that Jesus, the Light of the world, rose from the nether world upon Sunday (Barn. 13.9-10).

1. Origin. In ancient Babylonia a particular day of distinctive character was known as *šabattū* (*šapattū*), a name plainly identical with the Hebrew שבת. It was designated specifically as the "day of quieting of the heart." The precise meaning of this expression is uncertain, but at least the concept of relaxation is implicit therein. Furthermore, the seventh, fourteenth, twenty-first, and twenty-eighth days of certain months, and not improbably of every month, and likewise the nineteenth day—i.e., the forty-ninth, the seven times seventh, day from the first day of the preceding month—were regarded as "evil days." Upon these days the physician, the oracular priest, and, above all, the king might not function in any official or professional capacity whatsoever. While there is no definitive evidence that these successive seventh days were identical with the *šabattū*, it is a reasonable inference that such was actually the case. On the basis of this evidence certain scholars have maintained that the biblical sabbath was of Babylonian origin. Such, however, is not at all the case.

Certainly the conditions of nomadic life out in the Arabian Desert, their original home, where animal husbandry was the primary source of human livelihood, would not have permitted the Hebrew clans or tribes to desist even briefly from ordinary, daily, pastoral activities and observe a weekly sabbath, a day of abstention from all labor. All available evidence indicates unmistakably that the sabbath can have originated only in an agricultural environment. Actually the Hebrews became acquainted with the sabbath only after they had established themselves in Palestine and had settled down there alongside their Canaanite predecessors in the land, whom in some measure they displaced, and had borrowed from them the techniques of tilling the soil, and with this various institutions of agricultural civilization, of which the sabbath was one.

Actually the sabbath had its origin in a unique and rather primitive calendar, distinctly agricultural in character, which was current among the various West Semitic peoples until approximately 1000 B.C. —i.e., until some three centuries, more or less, after the settlement of the Hebrews in Palestine and the adjustment of the majority of their tribes, particularly those dwelling in the more fertile central and N sections of the country, where farming was naturally the dominant occupation, to Canaanite agricultural civilization. This calendar was based upon and recorded the successive stages in the planting, ripening, harvesting, and use of the annual crop. It was one of the institutions of Canaanite culture which these Hebrew newcomers borrowed. It had been current likewise among the Eastern Semites in earlier times, and it was undoubtedly from this calendar that the Babylonian *šabattū* was derived. Accordingly, instead of the Hebrew sabbath's being the outgrowth of the Babylonian *šabattū*, both institutions, the Babylonian *šabattū* and the Hebrew sabbath, sprang from a common source.

This calendar has been aptly designated as the pentecontad calendar because of the significant role which the number 50 played in it. Its basic unit of time-reckoning was the week of seven days. Its secondary time unit was the period of fifty days, consisting of seven weeks—i.e., seven times seven days—plus one additional day, a day which stood outside the week and which was known and celebrated as an עצרה, a festival of conclusion or termination—termination, of course, of the pentecontad or fifty-day period. The year of this calendar consisted of seven pentecontads plus two festival periods, each of seven days or one week, plus one additional day of supremely sacred character, 365 days in all. One of these two seven-day festival periods came immediately after the fourth pentecontad of the year, and the other immediately after the seventh and final pentecontad. Obviously this second seven-day festival was celebrated upon the last seven days of the year and in some respects partook of the nature of a festival of conclusion. The extra day, of supremely sacred character, followed immediately upon this second seven-day festival—i.e., then immediately after the close of the old year. It marked, therefore, the beginning of the new year and so was celebrated as the New Year's Day. It too, like the seven עצרות, the festivals at the close of the seven yearly pentecontads, stood outside the week and had its distinctive name. Upon this day the first sheaf of the crop of the new year was cut, with appropriate ceremonial, and was offered as a sacrifice for the redemption of the remainder of the crop from the possession or control of the Deity and its free and unrestricted use by the people for their daily needs. The seven-day festival coming immediately after the fourth pentecontad—i.e., early in October—was known and observed as the חג האסיף, the Feast of Ingathering (*see* BOOTHS, FEAST OF)—the ingathering, of course, of the annual crop at the close of the harvest season. The second seven-day festival, following immediately upon the seventh pentecontad and coming upon the final seven days of the year and shortly before the vernal equinox, was known as the חג המצות, the Feast of Unleavened Bread (*see* PASSOVER). During the course of this festival and in manifest preparation for the harvesting of the crop of the new year, everything which remained of the old crop, that of the year just ending, was eaten in the form of מצות, "cakes of unleavened bread," and whatever could not be so consumed had to be burned; for, in conformity with a principle and a practice quite common among primitive agricultural peoples, the old crop had to be disposed of completely before even the cutting of the new crop could commence. Under no condition might the crops of two successive years be mingled or be allowed to contact each other in any way, for the result would be disastrous for the community. These various considerations and procedures evidence unmistakably the distinctively agricultural character of this pentecontad calendar.

Table 1 sets forth concisely and graphically the form of this early—in fact, this oldest—calendar current among the various Semitic peoples.

Table 1	
New Year's Day	1 day
1st "Fifty" (Grain Harvest)	49 days
עצרת (Festival of First Fruits)	1 day
2nd "Fifty"	49 days
עצרת	1 day
3rd "Fifty"	49 days
עצרת	1 day
4th "Fifty"	49 days
עצרת	1 day
Festival of Ingathering (אסיף)	7 days
5th "Fifty"	49 days
עצרת	1 day
6th "Fifty"	49 days
עצרת	1 day
7th "Fifty"	49 days
עצרת	1 day
מצות Festival	7 days

Quite plainly the number 7 was basic to this primitive system of time-reckoning. This is evidenced, not only by the institutions already noted—viz., the seven-day week, the pentecontad (i.e., the fifty-day, seven weeks plus one day, time unit), and the year, consisting of seven pentecontads plus two major festival periods, each of seven days' duration, plus one additional day—but also by the added facts that each period of seven years constituted a further and a larger time unit, with the seventh and final year thereof known as the SABBATICAL YEAR, while seven such seven-year periods plus one additional year, known as the Jubilee Year, fifty years in all, constituted the largest, the ultimate, unit of time-reckoning of this calendar. *See* JUBILEE, YEAR OF.

There is abundant evidence that among the early Semites, and even persisting in certain circles down to the present day, the number 7 was regarded as evil, unlucky, a potential source of ill fortune, and therefore to be strictly avoided. Thus, e.g., among the native peasantry of Palestine still today, in counting or measuring, the number 7 is never pronounced, for 7 is the number of the evil spirits, and the mere utterance of their number might well have the effect of summoning them to work their mischief. Among the ancient Babylonians the evil spirits were likewise seven in number; and while they were spoken of freely as a group of seven, no more than six were ever mentioned together by name. Similarly the two groups of beneficent deities, the Igigi and the Anunnaki, consisted each of seven gods. In fact, the common ideogram of the Igigi specifically designated them as "the Seven." But despite this they were generally spoken of as eight in number, while the Anunnaki were regarded as nine. Likewise the various lists of the group of deities known as *Sĭbĭttĭšūnū*, "the Seven," or, more precisely, "They Are Seven," always enumerated eight divine beings. A similar belief or superstition existed among the Phoenicians and no doubt among the closely related Canaanites likewise. Quite similarly in the Bible the seven pre-Israelite peoples of Palestine are frequently referred to and mentioned by name, but, with the exception of three passages (Deut. 7:1; Josh. 3:10; 24:11), the names of no more than six are ever cited together.

All this suggests quite compellingly that this seventh and final day of the week was regarded quite generally by those ancient Semitic peoples which had attained the agricultural stage of civilization as an evil day, a day controlled by evil spirits, a day therefore upon which human labor would certainly not prosper, and which might even incense these evil spirits and induce them to work mischief, not only to him who carried on such labor, but also to his entire community. Accordingly it was, as its name, in both Babylonian and Hebrew, indicates, essentially a day of total abstention from labor, labor of all kinds. There can accordingly be little question that this institution, the seventh-day sabbath, was strictly observed already by the Canaanites and was borrowed from them, as an integral element of their agricultural way of life and practice, by the Israelite newcomers in the land. As a Canaanite religious institution it was entirely negative in character, an evil day, a day of total abstention from labor, but nothing more. It was Israel which, even while retaining this primary manner of celebrating the day, gradually transformed it into a day of gladness of spirit and of positive and joyous worship of the Deity.

2. History. The fundamental role of the sabbath in the religious belief and practice of Israel is demonstrated convincingly by the fact that its strict observance is enjoined in all four biblical decalogues, those concise statements, each summed up in ten short words or commandments, which, voicing what was regarded at the time as the all-essential principles of Israel's religion, constituted the basis of a solemn reaffirmation of the covenant relationship between Yahweh, Israel's God, and his people. *See* TEN COMMANDMENTS.

Exod. 34:21a, the oldest of these decalogic statements with regard to the sabbath, dating from 899 B.C. and formulated in the S kingdom under King Asa, commands abstention from all agricultural labor upon the seventh day. Apparently the commandment contemplates no more than this and does not prohibit other essential forms of work, such as the preparation of food; for the verb עָבַד, here employed, means primarily "to perform agricultural labor, to till the soil" (Gen. 2:5; 3:23; 4:2; Deut. 28:39; II Sam. 9:10; Prov. 12:11; Zech. 13:5). This interpretation of this commandment, as it is worded here, finds strong confirmation in what seems to be an editorial expansion of the commandment (vs. 21b), which, probably added relatively early, admonishes the people emphatically that even during the plowing and harvesting seasons, naturally the two busiest and also most critical periods of the agricultural year, when every moment was precious, the seventh day must be observed strictly by abstention from all labor. It is significant also that here the day is designated only as "the seventh day" and is not called specifically "the sabbath." Moreover, in this commandment the verb שׁבת is used strictly in its primary connotation, "to cease, to desist (from labor)." Equally significant is the fact that while this earliest decalogue enjoins additional ritual practices and is on the whole predominantly ritualistic in

character, it seems to have placed this commandment for the seventh day first upon its list of positive ritual injunctions, quite as if abstention from all farm labor upon the seventh day was regarded as the fundamental ritual institution of the religious practice of even the by no means primarily agricultural S kingdom.

The second decalogue in chronological sequence (Exod. 20:23-24a; 23:10-19 [minus certain passages of late, editorial, supplementary character]) was patterned closely in form and content after the earlier decalogue and emanated from the N kingdom in 841 B.C., at the beginning of the reign of Jehu. There is cogent reason for believing that the prophet Elisha was the chief protagonist in its formulation and promulgation. Under the dynasty of Omri the N kingdom had become relatively prosperous through cultivation, in close association with Tyre, of an active commercial program upon an international scale. Urban life was expanding, and the merchants in particular were growing wealthy. Accordingly in this second decalogue the commandment for the strict observance of the seventh day by abstention from labor (Exod. 23:12a), while closely resembling in form and language the corresponding commandment in the older decalogue, and while specifically continuing to designate this day only as the seventh day and not as the sabbath, and using the verb שׁבת only with the connotation "to desist," provides that the people were to desist, not merely or even primarily from agricultural labor, but rather from work of all types, manifestly from commercial as well as agricultural pursuits. Whether the wording of this commandment, "from all thy labors," contemplates likewise the prohibition of essential, daily tasks in the home is not clear; but, inasmuch as this wording plainly represents an expansion, in terms of the contemporary economic situation of the N kingdom, of the sabbath commandment of the earlier decalogue, it seems more probable that it enjoined complete desistance upon the seventh day only from all occupational activities, but no more. Moreover, in close association with this commandment for the seventh day —in fact, in the commandment immediately adjoining it—this decalogue prescribes the observance of every seventh year by noncultivation of the fields, by allowing them to lie fallow—in other words, by complete desistance from agricultural labors and observance of the SABBATICAL YEAR. And again, still following the pattern set by the older decalogue, the commandment for the observance of the seventh day apparently stood first in the list of ritual prescriptions, quite as if it were regarded in the N kingdom also as the ritual procedure of primary importance. It should be noted likewise that Exod. 23:12b is a postexilic, editorial addition to the original, concisely stated commandment, and that accordingly in this second decalogue also, just as in the first, the seventh day is primarily a day of desistance from all occupational labor rather than a day of conscious and socially motivated rest.

The third decalogue in the order of chronological sequence, the so-called Deuteronomic decalogue, served as the basis of the religious reformation and of the attendant renewal of the covenant with Yahweh in the reign of Hezekiah (II Kings 18:3-7) and again of the parallel action in the reign of Josiah (II Kings 22:3–23:25). This decalogue is recorded in two versions, in Exod. 20:2-17; Deut. 5:6-18. In its original form this decalogue, like its two predecessors, was couched in the form of ten direct and concise commandments, each expressing what had come, under the influence of evolving prophetism, to be regarded as a fundamental principle of the life which Yahweh demanded that his people live in fulfilment of its covenant obligation to him. As is to be expected, the two versions of this decalogue, in their original, concise, unexpanded formulation, are practically identical. But five of the ten commandments have been amplified more or less extensively by postexilic editors. And particularly in this amplification of the sabbath commandment (Exod. 20:8, 10b-11; Deut. 5:12, 14b-15) the two versions differ extensively and significantly.

The original, concise formulation of the sabbath commandment in this third decalogue (Exod. 20:9-10a; Deut. 5:13-14a) seems to have been patterned upon the versions of the corresponding commandment in each of the two older decalogues, for it specifically commends agricultural labor and likewise all other types of work upon the first six days of the week, but strictly forbids all such activities upon the seventh day by the positive declaration that the seventh day is a שבת belonging to, or in honor of, Yahweh. Moreover, by the substitution of כל־מלאכתך, "all thy work," for מעשיך, "thy labors," of the sabbath commandment of the second decalogue, this commandment of this third decalogue apparently prohibits, not only all occupational activities, but also all forms of work, household duties and all other comparable activities included. In other words, it would seem that with this reformation the seventh day has at last become for Israel a day of complete desistance from all types of labor on the part of every person.

Furthermore, in this commandment, as it was worded in its original, concise form, שבת is plainly the formal name or title of the day. But equally plainly its essential connotation here is still "desistance, abstention"—i.e., of course, from all labor—rather than "rest." This consideration suggests very cogently that as late as the religious reformation under Josiah in 621 B.C. the sabbath, in the S as well as in the N kingdom, was still observed primarily in its negative rather than its positive aspect, as a day upon which all labor was strictly taboo, rather than as a day of purposed rest and relaxation from toil. But, very significantly, even in its negative aspect it has now become definitely a day sacred to Yahweh, Israel's God, rather than to the evil spirits. In fact, the inclusion of the provision for sabbath observance in the two older decalogues suggests that already by the beginning of the ninth century B.C. the sabbath had lost in Israel much of its original character as an evil day, closely linked with evil spirits, and had become integrated, though still chiefly in its negative aspect, as a day of desistance from all labor, with the cult of Yahweh.

One further matter of significance is apparent in this third decalogue. Whereas the two earlier decalogues included in their formulations of the essential principles of Israel's covenant relationship with Yah-

weh various cultic institutions and practices, even though they apparently accorded to the sabbath priority therein, in this third decalogue the sabbath is the only cultic institution the observance of which, by prescribed action or conduct, is specifically enjoined. Manifestly the sabbath is here well on its way to becoming the primary cultic institution of Israel's religion.

In the fourth decalogue, that of the Holiness Code, associated with the reaffirmation of Israel's covenant relationship with Yahweh in connection with the dedication of the second temple in 516 B.C., the sabbath commandment (Lev. 19:3aβ) reads, with utmost conciseness: "and you shall keep my sabbaths." The very brevity and directness of this statement, without any definition, as in the sabbath commandment of each of the three earlier decalogues, of precisely wherein sabbath observance consists, suggests very strongly that by the final quarter of the sixth century the approved manner of sabbath observance had become firmly established and even conventional. And plainly too this was, just as the sabbath commandment of the third decalogue had prescribed, complete desistance by all persons from every form of labor.

Moreover, this sabbath commandment is here, within the compass of a single verse, linked closely with the commandment of reverence for parents. This indicates unmistakably that, at least to some degree, this fourth decalogue was patterned directly after the third decalogue, for there too, just as here, these two commandments stand in immediate juxtaposition, although in reverse order. And here too, just as there, the sabbath is represented as belonging definitely and entirely to Yahweh, as being a, or even the, fundamental institution of the approved ritual worship of him. But, quite significantly, this commandment to keep Yahweh's sabbaths is also linked very closely with another commandment, "and [you shall] reverence my sanctuary" (Lev. 19:30). This suggests forcibly that by 516 the sabbath had come to be regarded by the Jewish community of Judea, not only, in its negative aspect, as a day of prescribed desistance from all labor, but also, in a very positive aspect, as a day of rest from toil, which, in turn, made possible assemblage at Yahweh's sanctuary and active worship of him there. Apparently now, at the very commencement of the postexilic era, and specifically with the dedication of the second temple, the sabbath was beginning to acquire an altogether new character and import. It was no longer merely a day of mechanical desistance from all labor, largely because of the persistence of the old and antiquated idea that work performed upon that day would certainly not prosper and might even displease Yahweh and incur his wrath, since the day had now come to be generally regarded as his day. Instead, it had now become a day of rest in a very real sense in honor of Yahweh and also of active worship of him at his restored sanctuary. Very definitely the sabbath had at last become in Israel a ritual institution altogether positive in character.

This record of the history of the sabbath in Israelite religious practice in the pre-exilic period is fully confirmed by other, extra-Pentateuchal references to it. Throughout the entire period of Israel's history covered by the biblical writings the sabbath seems to have been closely linked with the day of the new moon. The latter was apparently also a day upon which human labor was strictly taboo; though why this should have been is far from clear, since very little is known of the import of the new-moon day in the culture and religious practice of Israel prior to the adoption of the lunar calendar in the final quarter of the fifth century B.C. But be that as it may, both New Moon and sabbath were days of complete desistance from labor. Accordingly during the pre-exilic period upon these days certain unusual activities, such as consultation of a prophet or diviner, even when this involved journeying to a considerable distance and attendant labor of servants or slaves (II Kings 4:22-23), seem to have been permissible. The royal bodyguard seems to have been changed regularly upon the sabbath (II Kings 11:5-9; II Chr. 23:4-8). Upon both New Moon and sabbath all shops were closed and all buying and selling, even of such essentials as food, ceased completely, to the dissatisfaction of the shopkeepers eager for profit (Amos 8:5). This situation reflects, no doubt, the prevailing attitude of a certain, and probably a not inconsiderable, section of the urban population of Israel toward the sabbath ca. the middle of the eighth century B.C. But at the same time it illustrates graphically the strong and persistent hold which the taboo of all labor upon the sabbath then had upon all classes of society. On the other hand, the opportunity to desist from labor upon sabbaths, New Moons, and festival days was to the rural population of the country apparently a source of satisfaction and even of general group merriment (Hos. 2:13). Isa. 1:13 suggests that already in the eighth century New Moons and sabbaths, like other festal occasions, were celebrated by certain ritual acts and even perhaps by some specific sacrifice. But if so, this was unquestionably incidental to the primary character of these days as taboo days. Also from this evidence it is plain that already by the middle of the eighth century, and quite probably even somewhat earlier, the word שבת, even though still retaining much of its primary connotation, "desistance, cessation," had come to be used as a proper name, the regular designation for the seventh and final day of the week.

Already in the early postexilic period, as has been noted, and perhaps beginning even during the Exile, a transition of the character of the sabbath set in, from its primary and altogether negative aspect, as a day upon which all labor was strictly interdicted, to one more positive. In all likelihood the role of the SYNAGOGUE, steadily expanding during this period, as a basic institution of Jewish religious life contributed materially to this significant transformation. The original prohibition of all forms of labor upon this day was not qualified in any degree. If anything, it was intensified in some measure; for desistance from labor upon this day now lost in large measure its primary, negative character, as a safeguard against mishap at the hands of supernatural agencies hostile to mankind, and became instead an act of positive homage to Yahweh, Israel's God. As such the sabbath became quite naturally a day of purposed rest and relaxation from the rigorous tasks and obligations of daily life, a day therefore, in some measure

at least, of ease, comfort, and pleasure, a day of high, divinely instituted privilege for Israel, but a privilege also which would ultimately be extended to all mankind (Isa. 66:23 [a very late interpolation between vss. 22 and 24]).

Moreover, this complete freedom from all the activities and responsibilities of daily life upon the sabbath, and this too in the name of Yahweh, made the day quite naturally convenient and appropriate for assemblage in local synagogues and for communal worship there, under approved leadership, of the Deity, to whom, in a very positive sense, the day was now sacred.

Accordingly in the biblical writings of this period the sabbath is represented as the sign of God's sanctification of Israel as his people and of his eternal covenant with it (Exod. 31:13, 16; Ezek. 20:12 [plainly a late interpolation into this extremely composite chapter]; likewise in the writings of the Qumran sectaries [see bibliography]). A somewhat later form of this doctrine told (Jub. 2:17-32) that God chose Israel alone from all the nations to observe the sabbath in his honor, along with and in the very same manner as the highest angels. Exod. 23:12b; Deut. 5:14b (both secondary Deuteronomic amplifications of the original, simple and concise sabbath commandment of the third decalogue and dating from the early postexilic period) state explicitly that the distinct purpose of the sabbath was that servants and domestic animals and likewise the stranger (or perhaps the proselyte to Judaism) sojourning at the time within the household might rest and relax upon the sabbath even as did the master. Moreover, during this period, 516-485, while the second temple was standing and while there was an active program of proselytism of foreigners to Judaism, strict sabbath observance by at least complete abstention from labor was one of the ritual practices imposed upon these converts (Isa. 56:4, 6). Under these circumstances the sabbath tended more and more during this period to lose its original, negative character as an evil day and to become instead distinctly a day of communal rest, assemblage for public worship and even for social activities on a communal plane, a day of general gladness of spirit and of public rejoicing.

The coming of Ezra to Jerusalem in 458 B.C., coupled with his erection, with the permission of Artaxerxes I and even with Persian material assistance, of the third temple; his restoration of the Zadokite priests, who had returned with him from Babylonia, to major priestly office and authority in the new sanctuary; and the inauguration and rigid enforcement of his program of intensive Jewish separatism and ritualism, all of which was reinforced by Nehemiah some twenty-five years later, and which culminated in the formulation of the Priestly Code (see PENTATEUCH) as the official expression of Jewish belief and practice, revived in no small measure something of the original, austere character of the sabbath as a day when all labor and even all undue physical activity were strictly prohibited (Neh. 10:32; 13:15-22; Jer. 17:19-27 [a non-Jeremianic passage, manifestly dating from this middle postexilic period]; Ezek. 22:8, 26; 23:38 [all late interpolations]).

The origin of the sabbath and its character as a

sacred day, a day of abstention from all labor, now came to be explained by the tradition that God had created the world in six days and had himself desisted from all labor and had rested upon the seventh day; therefore he sanctified it and bade Israel rest thereon, even as he had rested (Gen. 1:1–2:3; Exod. 20:11; 31:17). Correspondingly God sent down the manna from heaven for six days, with a double portion, sufficient for two days, upon the sixth day, but let none fall upon the seventh day, impliedly because he was resting upon this day. Accordingly he bade Israel gather its necessary supply of manna daily, but upon the sixth day to gather a two-days' supply, so that it too might observe the sabbath in prescribed manner (Exod. 16:4–36). Accordingly labor of any kind upon the sabbath, even acts so essential as kindling a fire in the home (Exod. 35:3) or moving about unduly from place to place (Exod. 16:29), were forbidden absolutely. The spirit of the post-Ezranic age and the stress which it laid upon the most rigorous sabbath observance are evidenced by the fact that a new term, of definitely technical character and found only in the Priestly Code, was coined, a derivative of the root שבת in its primary connotation, "to cease"—שבתון, "total cessation" (from all manner of activity; Lev. 25:5). Accordingly the compound term שבת שבתון, oft recurring in the P stratum of the Hexateuch, designates the day as a "sabbath of total cessation (from labor)."

In fact, so fundamental did sabbath observance become in the ritual expression of Judaism formulated and supervised by the Zadokite or Aaronite priests of the third temple from the close of the fifth century B.C. onward that the most extreme penalties were prescribed for its violation, at first excommunication from the sacred community of Israel (Exod. 31:14bβ), but ultimately death itself (Exod. 31:14bα; 35:2b; Num. 15:32–36). Whether these extreme penalties were ever actually enforced, and, if so, to what extent, is uncertain, although Jub. 2:25, 27; 50:8, 13, probably voicing an extreme, sectarian point of view, reaffirm this death penalty. But be this as it may, prior to the Maccabean wars, in the second quarter of the second century B.C., pious Jews would not bear arms upon the sabbath, even in self-defense (I Macc. 2:32–38), nor yet, if actually engaged in warfare, would they negotiate for peace upon this day (Jos. War IV.ii.3). Mattathias, the father of the Maccabees, however, instituted the rule that Jews might, and even should, defend themselves actively against national enemies upon the sabbath (I Macc. 2:39–41; Jos. Antiq. XII.vi.2; cf. XIII.i.3; XVIII.ix.2; War I.vii.3). This evidence establishes clearly the fundamental role which sabbath observance in its primary aspect, total abstention from labor, played in Jewish practice from ca. the middle of the fifth century B.C. onward.

However, as might well be imagined, in the course of time differences of opinion with regard to specific activities which might or might not be performed upon the sabbath manifested themselves in various Jewish circles. Of all Jewish groups or sects the Essenes were the most extreme in their principle and procedures of sabbath desistance from labor (Jos. War II.viii.9). Apparently equally extreme in this respect were the sectaries of Qumran (Zadokite

Document XIII.1–27). In fact, the detail and rigidities of their rules for sabbath observance lend strong support to the assumption that these Qumran sectaries were actually Essenes. Furthermore, between the disciples of Hillel and Shammai, the leading rabbinic authorities of the first century B.C., significant differences existed with regard to activities permitted or prohibited upon the sabbath, with the former as a rule the more liberal in their decisions (M. Shab. I.5–8). In the period immediately preceding the destruction of the third temple by the Romans, in A.D. 70, the established penalty for violation of this primary principle of sabbath observance was reduced to the sacrifice of a sin offering (M. Shab. VII.1–4). And ultimately Rabbi Akiba, the foremost rabbinic authority of the first half of the second century A.D., formulated the principle that any labor or physical activity essential to normal existence which could be performed before the sabbath began might under no condition be performed upon the sabbath; but, were this impossible, then its performance upon the sabbath was permitted (M. Shab. XIX.1). Moreover, as this rabbinic dictum implies and as is borne out by abundant evidence, and as is in fact clearly implicit already in the motif of the relatively late biblical (late fifth or early fourth century) narrative of the double portion of manna from heaven upon the sixth day, Friday, as the day preceding the sabbath, and particularly the afternoon thereof, acquired the character and apparently, at least in certain circles, the formal title, of the Day of Preparation (Jub. 2:29; 50:9; Jos. War II.viii.9; Mark 15:42; Luke 23:54; John 19:31, 42)—preparation, of course, for strict sabbath observance by the performance in advance of all tasks, even the most essential, such as the cooking of food, which would otherwise have to be performed upon the sabbath.

In the temple ritual from the middle of the fifth century B.C. onward the sabbath was celebrated in positive manner by special sacrifices (Lev. 23:38; Num. 28:9-10; II Chr. 2:3; 8:13; 31:3; Neh. 10:34; cf. Ezek. 46:4-5 [a passage dating from the period in question]) and by the changing of the BREAD OF THE PRESENCE (Lev. 24:8). The formal commencement of the sacred day, and therefore the precise moment when upon it all labor was to cease, was heralded by a trumpet blast, blown by a priest within the temple precincts; and in the same manner the official termination of the day and, with this, permission to resume labor were announced (Jos. War IV.ix.12; M. Suk. V.5). In private life Jews were forbidden not only all forms of physical labor but also to travel to a distance of more than two thousand cubits from their homes (Zadokite Document X.14–XI.18; Jos. Antiq. XIII.viii.4; Acts 1:12; M. Soṭ. V.3). But, despite the innumerable restrictions which encompassed it, the sabbath was to be, above all else, a joyous day for its celebrants, joyous in appreciation of the privilege of worshiping God upon it (Isa. 58:13). Accordingly fasting upon the sabbath was prohibited (Jub. 50:12; Jth. 8:6; Zadokite Document XIII.13).

But distinguishing the sabbath from the other six days of the week more than all else were, from the sixth century B.C. onward, the weekly assemblies in the local synagogues for communal worship by means of an established and steadily expanding ritual, in which the reading of the Pentateuch and selected passages from the Prophets and the expounding thereof by recognized authorities played a central role (Jos. Antiq. XVI.ii.3; Matt. 4:23; Mark 1:21-22; 6:2; Luke 4:16-21, 31-33; Acts 13:27; 15:21; 17:1-2; 18:4). Quite probably the singing or chanting of selected psalms also constituted an important part of the early synagogal sabbath ritual (cf. Ps. 92:1). There is ample ground for the assumption that prior to the destruction of the third temple by the Romans in A.D. 70 such synagogal worship was in considerable measure sectarian in character. But following this momentous event sabbath worship in the synagogue became, and has been ever since, the primary institution of Jewish ritual. The Sunday-sabbath and ritual worship thereon in the church are quite obviously a part of Christianity's heritage from Judaism.

Bibliography. J. Benziger, *Hebräische Archäologie* (1894), pp. 201-2, 465-66. H. Zimmern, in Winckler and Zimmern, *Die Keilinschriften und das AT* (3rd ed., 1903), pp. 592-94. H. Meinhold, *Sabbat und Sonntag* (1909), pp. 5-76. A. Bertholet, *Biblische Theologie des AT* (1911), pp. 44-46. E. König, *Geschichte des AT Religion* (1912), pp. 235-40. The Zadokite Document, in R. H. Charles, *The Apoc. and Pseudep. of the OT* (1913), II, 785-834. H. Webster, *Rest Days* (1916). J. Morgenstern, "The Origin of Maṣṣoth and the Maṣṣoth Festival," *AJT*, XXI (1917), 275-93. M. P. Nilsson, *Primitive Time Reckoning* (1920), pp. 329-36. G. F. Moore, *Judaism* (1927), II, 21-39. J. Morgenstern, "The Oldest Document of the Hexateuch," *HUCA*, IV (1927), 1-138. W. A. Heidel, *The Day of Yahweh* (1929), pp. 397-441. A. Lods, *Israel* (1932), pp. 437-40. W. O. E. Oesterley, in Oesterley and Robinson, *A History of Israel* (1932), pp. 135-36. S. Langdon, *Babylonian Menologies* (Schweich Lectures; 1933), pp. 89-92. J. Morgenstern, "Amos Studies, III," *HUCA*, XV (1940), 59-304. J. and H. Lewy, "The Origin of the Week and the Oldest West Asiatic Calendar," *HUCA*, XVII (1942-43), 1-152. On the Qumran sectaries' representation of the sabbath as God's eternal covenant with Israel, see "The Oration of Moses" in D. Barthélemy and J. T. Milik, *Qumran Cave I* (1955), pl. 18, 1. 8. J. Morgenstern, "The Decalogue of the Holiness Code," *HUCA*, XXVI (1955), 1-28; "The Calendar of the Book of Jubilees, Its Origin and Its Character," *Vetus Testamentum*, V (1955), 35-76; "The Origin of the Synagogue," *Studi Orientalistici in onore di Giorgio Levi della Vida* (1956), II, 192-201. T. H. Gaster, *The Dead Sea Scriptures* (1956), pp. 69, 77-79, 229, 233.

J. MORGENSTERN

SABBATH DAY'S JOURNEY [σαββάτου ὁδόν]. The distance scribal legislation allowed one to travel on the sabbath.

In Acts 1:12, Mount Olivet is described as a "sabbath day's journey" from Jerusalem. Josephus refers to the distance as 5 furlongs (Antiq. XX.viii.6), and as 6 furlongs (War V.ii.3), thus a distance of 3,031 or 3,637 feet (as measured by the Alexandrine stadion or furlong, which amounts to 606 feet, 2 inches). The phrase, not used elsewhere in the Bible, is derived from Josh. 3:4, where the ark is indicated as 2,000 cubits ahead of the people. From this idea arose the notion that 2,000 cubits constituted the greatest distance from the tabernacle to the outside of the Israelite camp. This thus became the basis of the law that on the sabbath a person could travel no more than 2,000 cubits, the farthest distance one would be from the center of worship. As Exod. 16:29 stated: "Let no man go out of his place on the seventh day," Num. 35:5 further defined the sub-

urbs of the cities of the Levites as measured 2,000 cubits in every direction from the city walls. Rabbinical interpretation defined this as a sabbath day's journey.

The command in Exod. 16:29: "Let no man go out of his place on the seventh day," is interpreted in a Jerusalem Targ.: "Let no man go walking from this place beyond 2,000 cubits on the seventh day." A Targ. based on Ruth 1:16 has Naomi say to Ruth: "We are commanded to keep sabbaths and festivals, and not to walk beyond 2,000 cubits." In the Zadokite Documents there are the two laws for the sabbath day's journey: "Let him not walk about outside his town above 1,000 cubits" (page 10, line 20); and "Let no man go after a beast (on the sabbath) to pasture it outside his town more than 2,000 cubits" (page 11, line 28), thus indicating a different length of journey on the sabbath for different purposes.

Various estimates have been made as to what linear distance constituted 2,000 cubits: a cubit (or ell) by the Hellenistic system of measures was 1 foot, 6 inches, the distance from the elbow to the end of the middle finger; though the Roman system of measure determined this distance as 1 foot, 9 inches. Hence the 2,000 cubits would be 3,000 feet by Hellenistic measure, or 3,600 feet by Roman measure. Egyptian measure viewed a "sabbath day's journey" as 1,000 double-steps. Jerome (*Epistle to Algasiam* X) estimated a "sabbath day's journey" as 2,000 feet: "They are accustomed to say, 'Barachibas and Simeon and Hillel, our masters, have handed down to us that we should walk 2,000 feet on the sabbath.' " Rabbi Nachman ('Er. 42a) said: "If one is on a journey, where the sabbath boundary is not known, take 2,000 medium steps." Scribes were able, however, to figure how a person might go 4,000 cubits on the sabbath: Preceding the sabbath a person could establish his "home" 2,000 cubits away by carrying food for two meals to a given place, one meal to be eaten and the other buried; to mark one's presence at a given spot could establish one's "home"; a person could eye a tree or a wall 2,000 cubits from his residence, and call this his legal "home" on the sabbath; or a person could send out another person to mark the spot for his sabbath "home." Hence, from any of these places an individual could travel 2,000 cubits farther on the sabbath, and thus legally travel 4,000 cubits.

Bibliography. H. L. Strack and P. Billerbeck, *Kommentar zum NT aus Talmud und Midrash*, II (1924), 590 ff. C. Rabin, *The Zadokite Documents*, I: The Admonition; II: The Laws (1954).

T. S. KEPLER

SABBATHEUS. KJV Apoc. alternate form of SHABBETHAI.

***SABBATICAL YEAR.** The final year in a cycle of seven years; an institution of ancient Israelite time-reckoning and religious, social, and economic practice. Originally designated simply as the "seventh year" (Exod. 23:11; Neh. 10:31), it came to be called by Deuteronomic writers the "year of dropping" or "of cancellation [of debts]" (שנת השמטה; Deut. 15:9), and also, by a late redactor of the Priestly Code, the "year of sabbatical desistance [from agricultural activities]" (שנת שבתון; Lev. 25:5). It had its origin in the so-called pentecontad calendar, the earliest calendar current among the ancient Semitic peoples, a calendar of strictly agricultural character, which, as an integral element of the then prevailing Canaanite agricultural civilization of Palestine, the invading nomadic or seminomadic Israelite clans and tribes adopted when they conquered and established permanent residence in the land. In this calendar the seventh or sabbatical year bore to the other years precisely the same relationship as the SABBATH bore to the other days. Just as in this calendar seven days constituted a basic and convenient unit of time-reckoning (see WEEK), with the seventh and final day therein, the sabbath, observed as a taboo day, one upon which agricultural labor was rigorously prohibited, so, correspondingly, seven years constituted another, larger unit of time-reckoning, with the seventh and final year therein observed as a taboo year, in which, for its entire duration, all agricultural labor was "dropped" (the primary connotation of שמט, the root of שממה; cf. II Sam. 6:6; II Kings 9:33; I Chr. 13:9) or interrupted. Whether, like the sabbath day, this seventh year was originally regarded as being controlled by evil spirits is uncertain, but this seems altogether probable.

It is not surprising that the oldest Decalogue in the Bible, the so-called Kenite Code (Exod. 34:17-26), formulated in 899 B.C. in the Southern Kingdom, where, because of the general poverty of the soil, agriculture was normally not a primary source of livelihood, makes no mention of the sabbatical year, even though it does stress the strict observance of the sabbath day. However, the Decalogue next in chronological sequence, that of the so-called Book of the Covenant (Exod. 20:23-24aα; 23:10-19), formulated in 841 B.C. in the Northern Kingdom, where agriculture was always the dominant occupation, does provide, just as might be expected, for the observance of the seventh year (Exod. 23:10-11) as the year in which the land was to be "dropped"—i.e., to remain uncultivated. Moreover, the spontaneous, untilled fruitage of field, orchard, or vineyard could not be retained by the owner thereof for use by himself and his family alone, but might be eaten freely by the poor of the land, those who were not property owners; and what they did not eat was left for consumption by animals, both domestic and wild. Under no condition might the crop of this seventh year be harvested and stored.

A secondary but fairly early stratum of the Book of the Covenant provides for the automatic release of Hebrew male slaves in the seventh year (Exod. 21:2-6). However, this legislation contemplates no more than that the normal period of servitude for a Hebrew, in bondage to a fellow Hebrew, should be six years, reckoned from the moment of entrance into this social state. But this automatic manumission of Hebrew slaves has no connection whatever with the sabbatical year, either in this legislation or in its Deuteronomic reformulation (Deut. 15:12-18) some two centuries later. This conclusion is confirmed by the historic incident recorded in Jer. 34:8-22. The reference there to the legislation in Deut. 15:12-18 is readily apparent. But once again there is no reason whatever to connect this legislation or the procedure on this specific occasion with the sabbatical year.

On the other hand, the legislation in Deut. 15:1-4a definitely links the nationalized institution of the cancellation of debts owed by one Israelite to another with the sabbatical year. In fact this legislation designates the cancellation of debts specifically by the ancient, technical term שממה, "dropping," and so, by clear implication, connects this institution with the שנת השממה, the "year of dropping" or "cancellation," as, in this connection, the Hebrew name may very well be interpreted.

Quite significantly, however, the Deuteronomic Code does not, in any of its primary strata, make any provision whatever for the ancient agricultural institution of leaving the fields lie fallow during the sabbatical year. But what is unquestionably a secondary, postexilic piece of Deuteronomic legislation (Deut. 31:10-13) does make incidental reference to the sabbatical year, and this too under its traditional name, the "year of dropping," by commanding that every seventh year, when the people would assemble at the single, central sanctuary, the temple in Jerusalem, for the celebration of the festival which, still in the early postexilic period, inaugurated the new year, the Torah, or Law, should be read to them (see LAW IN THE OT). Unquestionably it was in conformity with this command that Ezra read the Law to the people, assembled in Jerusalem in order to celebrate the Festival of Ingathering (see BOOTHS, FEAST OF) during the final seven days of the old year, and also upon the eighth day, immediately ensuing, the tenth of the seventh month, the New Year's Day (see NEW YEAR). From this it follows with practical certainty that this new year, inaugurated in just this manner by Ezra and his followers, was a sabbatical year.

Following the overthrow of the Southern Kingdom by the Babylonians and the destruction by them of Jerusalem and other walled cities and the exile of the upper social strata of the nation, the economy of the section of the Jewish people left resident in the land became, of necessity, predominantly agricultural. Accordingly it is not at all surprising that the Holiness Code (see PENTATEUCH), the product in its entirety of the postexilic period, and the primary stratum of which must be correlated with the erection and dedication of the second temple (see TEMPLE, JERUSALEM) in 516 B.C., revived the strict observance of the sabbatical year in the ancient manner, by noncultivation of fields and vineyards (Lev. 25:1-7). On the other hand, as might well be expected of legislation evolving out of the then prevailing, strictly agricultural economy, this code made no provision whatever for the cancellation of debts in the sabbatical year. Instead, the lending of money on interest by one Jew to another was forbidden absolutely and in its stead generous, brotherly provision for needy fellow Jews was earnestly commended (vss. 35-38). And that the Deuteronomic institution of debt-cancellation in the seventh year was generally disregarded, and even practically invalidated, throughout the postexilic period is convincingly evidenced by the economic situation existing within the Jewish community of Palestine of the third quarter of the fifth century B.C. (Neh. 5:1-13). Moreover, in the Holiness Code the automatic release of fellow Israelites, held as slaves, in the seventh year, after six years of servitude, was transferred to the Jubilee

Year (*see* JUBILEE, YEAR OF). From this varied legislation it is readily apparent that in the postexilic period the sabbatical year reverted, at least in large measure, to what it had been originally, a year of complete "dropping" or "interruption" of agricultural labor and of consequent noncultivation of fields, orchards, and vineyards—in other words, a year of strictly sabbatical character in the primary connotation of this term.

Quite significantly, the Priestly Code, formulated during the final quarter of the fifth century B.C. as the constitution of the official Judaism of the next five centuries, makes not the slightest mention of or reference to the sabbatical year and apparently disregarded the ancient institution completely. The reason for this is easily determined. This official Judaism centered in the temple in Jerusalem, the one single, officially legitimized sanctuary for the entire Jewish people. There the well-organized and formally sanctioned ritual worship of Yahweh was closely supervised and administered by the Zadokite or Aaronite priests. Furthermore, as one result of the administrative and civic reforms of Nehemiah in the course of the third quarter of the fifth century B.C., and particularly of his enforced repopulation of Jerusalem and other cities of Judea (Neh. 11), a clear-cut distinction speedily evolved between the urban and the rural sections of the Jewish community of Palestine. The former, and especially the population of Jerusalem, largely tradespeople by occupation and living in immediate contact with the temple, naturally conformed strictly to its official cult, as this was set forth in the Priestly Code. For these townspeople the sabbatical year, in its primary character, as a purely agricultural institution, could have little concrete meaning and appeal. And even more, for them as tradesmen, in their then somewhat precarious economic situation, its observance in its secondary, Deuteronomic phase, as the year of cancellation of debts, would have been practically impossible. However, despite these considerations it would seem that an effort was made, in strict conformity with the now traditional and reversed Mosaic law, to impose upon them the observance of the sabbatical year in both its phases—leaving the fields lie fallow and cancellation of debts (Neh. 10:32*b*). But there is good reason to believe that this program proved to these Jewish city dwellers altogether impracticable and unacceptable. This circumstance will account adequately for the complete silence of the primary stratum of the Priestly Code with regard to the sabbatical year.

Moreover, the rural sections of the Palestinian Jewish community of the end of the fifth century B.C. and thereafter, dwelling in small, open villages at varying distances from the temple, and therefore in their religious beliefs and practices but little amenable to priestly supervision and control, and, moreover, largely shepherds or farmers by occupation, and as such naturally conservative, and even more or less reactionary, in thought, belief, and practice, zealously adhered to many ancient religious institutions; among these, in response to their current way of life, was the old, agricultural pentecontad calendar, and with this the sabbatical year, in its primary aspect of leaving the fields lie fallow, and apparently also, to some extent at least, in its secondary aspect of cancellation of debts. That these Jewish country people continued to observe the sabbatical year by at least leaving the fields lie fallow is evidenced abundantly. Thus, quite significantly, in the original Holiness Code legislation for the sabbatical year (Lev. 25:1-7) two manifestly late, priestly redactorial interpolations can be detected (vss. 4aα [middle], 5*b*), which not only reaffirm the original H legislation for the sabbatical year but even coin for this year the new and decidedly descriptive title שנת שבתון, the "year of sabbatical desistance." There is cogent reason for believing that these particular redactors represented a Jewish sectarian movement of the late fourth or early third century B.C., recruited very largely from the rural sections of the Jewish community of Palestine, and which, at least for its own sectarian purposes, employed a calendar which differed radically from the then official Jewish calendar and which approximated the ancient pentecontad calendar rather closely.

Likewise demonstrating the dominant practice of the Jewish farmers of Palestine of the first half of the second century B.C., I Macc. 6:49, 53-54, tells that Beth-zur fell to Antiochus IV because the food supply of the garrison, necessarily scanty in a sabbatical year, was quickly exhausted (cf. Jos. Antiq. XIV. xvi.2; XV.i.2). Josephus tells likewise that under John Hyrcanus (135-104 B.C.) the Jewish nation refrained from aggressive warfare during the sabbatical year (Antiq. XIII.viii.1; War I.ii.4) and also that Julius Caesar remitted the annual tribute of the Jewish people in the sabbatical year, since in it they neither tilled their fields nor gathered the fruit of their trees (Antiq. XIV.x.6; cf. XI.viii.5-6). Furthermore, just as might be expected, various Jewish sectarian groups, recruited largely—so abundant evidence indicates—from rural, agricultural, and more or less peripheral sections of the Jewish community, stressed the observance of the sabbatical year in its primary aspect, by leaving the fields lie fallow, and also as a convenient unit of time-reckoning. Josephus (Antiq. XI.viii.6) reports that the Samaritans kept the sabbatical year in this manner. And Jubilees, certainly a Jewish sectarian writing, tells (4:18; cf. 50:1-3) that Enoch "recounted the sabbaths of the years" —i.e., unquestionably the sabbatical cycles of seven years, with the seventh and final year of each cycle a sabbatical year, undoubtedly strictly observed by the members of this sect. And, of equal significance, the Qumran sectaries of the final two centuries B.C. and the first two centuries A.D., likewise observed the sabbatical year, and this too in a manner conforming closely, both in content and in terminology, to the biblical prescription, as the "year of dropping," the year of both noncultivation of the soil and cancellation of debts. *See bibliography*.

Quite similarly, rabbinic Judaism, evolving rapidly in the period following the final destruction of the temple, that by the Romans in A.D. 70, sought, in conformity with its fundamental principle of strict adherence to the Mosaic law as this is recorded in the Pentateuch, to observe the sabbatical year in both its phases, letting the fields lie fallow and cancellation of debts. However, steadily changing conditions of Jewish life in Palestine and also the rapidly expanding migration, both voluntary and compulsory, of Jews from Palestine to other lands necessitated all manner of modification, with rabbinic sanction and guidance, of the manner of observance of the sabbatical year. The record of all this is in the Mishna Tractate *Shebi'ith*. And, as might well be anticipated, the ancient institution finally fell into complete desuetude. This is evidenced rather graphically by the fact that the Babylonian Talmud contains in its Tractate *Shebi'ith,* merely the Mishnaic text but no record whatever of discussion thereof and action thereupon by post-Mishnaic rabbinic authorities. The Palestinian Jewish community rapidly became too small and unimportant for its practice with regard to the sabbatical year to have any further significance. And, quite naturally, for Jews dwelling outside Palestine, in foreign lands and among strange peoples with widely divergent cultures, the observance of the sabbatical year in either of its two phases became both meaningless and impracticable. Thus this ancient institution eventually became completely obsolete.

Bibliography. G. Dallman, *Arbeit und Sitte in Palästina,* III (1933), 183-85; J. Morgenstern, "The Oldest Document of the Hexateuch," *HUCA,* IV (1927), 1-138; "The Decalogue of the Holiness Code," *HUCA,* XXVI (1955), 1-28; "The Calendar of the Book of Jubilees, Its Origin and Its Character," *Vetus Testamentum,* V (1955), 35-76.

For references to the Qumran observation of the sabbatical year, see: 1QS X.7-8 in M. Burrows, *The Dead Sea Scrolls of St. Mark's Monastery* (1951), vol. II, fasc. 2; The Oration of Moses 1-7 in D. Barthélemy and J. T. Milik, *Qumran Cave I* (1955), plate XVIII, col. 3; 1QM II.6 in E. L. Sukenik, *Osar Hamegilloth Hagenusoth* (1955), II, 6.   J. MORGENSTERN

SABBEUS. KJV form of Apoc. Sabbaias. *See* SHEMAIAH.

SABEANS sə bēʹənz [סבאא ,שׁבאַ ,שׁבאִי; KJV סבא (Ezek. 23:42; RSV "drunkards")]; SEBA sēʹbə [סבא]; SHEBA shēʹbə [שׁבא]. A Semitic people who dwelt in the SW corner of the Arabian Peninsula, and who traded in spices, gold, and precious stones. Seba is perhaps the name of a Sabean colony in Africa (*see below*); "Sheba" is the Hebrew spelling of "Saba," the S Arabic name of the Sabean state.

The Sabeans occupied that part of SW Arabia

From Bowen and Albright, *Archaeological Discoveries in South Arabia* (Baltimore: The Johns Hopkins Press)

1. Exit of S sluices as seen from the E, showing irrigation in ancient Qataban (Beihan)

which roughly corresponds to modern Yemen; their sphere of influence and the boundaries of their state expanded and contracted at different times with the shifting political scene. This region is one of the most fertile parts of ARABIA, and its productivity was augmented in antiquity through Sabean development of enormous irrigation works, such as the dam and sluices at Marib. Located as they were on the periphery of the ancient Near East at a safe distance from the great empires to the N, the Sabeans enjoyed comparative peace and security throughout all but the last centuries of their history, and they were able to develop their state and culture relatively free from forced foreign influence. Fig. SAB 1.

This location also enabled the Sabeans to play an important role in the economic life of the ancient Near East. On land, they dominated the major caravan route to the N, over which passed frankincense from Dhofar and myrrh from neighboring states. It is in connection with their caravan activities and traffic in incense, precious stones, and gold that the Sabeans were known to biblical writers (Job 6:19; Ps. 72:10, 15; Isa. 60:6; Jer. 6:20; Ezek. 27:22-23; 38: 13). At various times the Sabeans controlled the ports of Muza (near modern Mocha), Ocelis (near Bab el-Mandeb), and probably Eudaemon Arabia (Aden), where cargoes from India and the Far East were exchanged for commodities of the Mediterranean world, and where frankincense and myrrh from N Somaliland and other products from Africa joined the stream of international trade. From these ports sailed Sabean ships to trade with East Africa, Socotra, and probably India. As a result of such economic activities, great wealth flowed into Saba, and it was described by classical writers as *Arabia Felix,* "Happy Arabia."

The recovery of the Sabean civilization began in 1762 with the explorations of a Danish expedition led by Carsten Niebuhr. The Danes were followed by several individual explorers, notably U. E. Seetzen (1810), T. Arnaud (1843), J. Halévy (1869), E. Glaser (four journeys, 1882-94), and A. Fakhry (1947), who copied thousands of S Arabic inscriptions and described numerous ancient sites and remains. The first excavations (1928) were undertaken by C. Rathjens and H. von Wissmann at Huqqa, a site *ca.* fourteen miles N of San'a, where they cleared a small temple. More extensive and productive excavations were carried out at a temple—the so-called Haram Bilqis—near Marib, the ancient Sabean capital, by F. P. Albright for the American Foundation for the Study of Man in 1951-52.

The origins of the Sabeans are shrouded in mystery, though new information is beginning to come to light. Genesis, the earliest known literary source, preserves tantalizing, though somewhat baffling, bits of information. In Gen. 10:7 (=I Chr. 1:9) Sheba, together with Seba, is listed as a descendant of Ham through Cush, and was therefore considered by the author to be related to W and NW peoples. It is clear from this reference and from Ps. 72:10 that Seba and Sheba were not identical, though both names probably go back to S Arabic Saba. Since Seba is directly descended from Cush (Nubia), and since it is clearly associated with Nubia and Egypt in Isa. 43:3, it is probable that Seba was located in

Africa. Furthermore, the similarity of the names Seba and Saba suggests that Seba was a Sabean colony. But according to Gen. 10:28 (=I Chr. 1:22), Sheba and several other S Arabian tribes are descended from Shem through the lineage Arpachshad, Shelah, Eber, and Joktan; here Sheba was believed to be closely related to N and NE peoples. Moreover, Gen. 25:3 (=I Chr. 1:32) lists Sheba as a descendant of Jokshan, the son of Abraham by Keturah, making Sheba and Israel closely related. Taken together, these genealogical references indicate that the Israelites thought that the Sabeans were related to the peoples of the Fertile Crescent—including themselves—on the one hand, and to the peoples of Africa on the other. Such extensive relationships are not surprising, in view of the fact that the Sabeans were engaged in trade and commerce from early times.

For a number of years, scholars disputed the position of Saba in the chronological framework of S Arabian history. Some argued that Ma'in, Qataban, and Hadhramaut chronologically preceded Saba, and that as late as the end of the eighth century B.C., Saba was a nomadic tribe centered in N Arabia. Others held that Saba preceded these states, which they dated as late as the fifth century B.C., and that it was located in S Arabia from early times. Excavations at Hajar Kohlan (ancient Timna', capital of Qataban) brought to light evidence which conclusively proved that the latter view was correct; Saba chronologically preceded the other S Arabian states.

A number of lines of evidence—linguistic and archaeological—suggest that S Arabia was settled by Semites who migrated southward from central or W Arabia in the middle centuries of the second millennium B.C. Whether the founders of Saba were among this group or were part of a later wave of migrants is as yet unknown. In any case, by *ca.* the twelfth century B.C., when travel across stretches of desert became possible as a result of the effective domestication of the camel, the Sabeans seem to have initiated caravan trade with the N. By the tenth century B.C., Saba was so well established that a queen could journey to Palestine—a distance of *ca.* fifteen hundred miles—with a richly laden caravan. Her visit to Solomon (I Kings 10:1-10, 13; II Chr. 9:1-9, 12) must have been concerned with trade, at least partly for the purpose of acquiring an agreement covering the distribution of incense and other commodities in the N that would be beneficial to both Saba and Israel. Presumably her mission was part of a general Sabean commercial expansion in this period, which may have included the colonization of Ethiopia to the W and the development of a trading hegemony over S and W Arabia.

From not later than the ninth to the middle of the fifth century B.C., Saba was governed by rulers who assumed the title *mukarrib* (*MKRB*), a word which probably means "priest (king)." This situation is presumably similar to that which existed in Assyria before the fourteenth century B.C.; there the god was called "king," while his earthly agent—the actual king—was called *shangu,* or "priest." The known *mukarribs* of Saba, numbering over twenty, may be arranged in three groups on the basis of paleography and genealogy. The first group ruled from the ninth century to *ca.* 675 B.C. and included two rulers who

are mentioned in Assyrian inscriptions; Yithi''amara (Assyrian spelling, Iti'amra) by Sargon II, and Karib'il (Assyrian spelling, Karibi'ilu) by Sennacherib. To this period belongs the construction of the S tombs at Marib, though the builders are unknown. The rulers of the second group (*ca.* 675-525 B.C.) are known to have been extremely active in building. The first member of this group—Yadi''il Dhirriḥ, son of Sumuhu'alay—built temples to the moon-god at Sirwah, Marib, and el-Mesajid. Two other *mukarribs* of this period, Sumuhu'alay Yanaf and Yithi''amara Bayyin, cut sluices through solid rock at the S end of the great dam at Marib. The third group ruled *ca.* 525-450 B.C., but little is known of their activities. Throughout the *mukarrib* period, Sabean art and architecture were strongly influenced by the cultures of Mesopotamia and Syro-Palestine.

Ca. 450 B.C., Karib'il Watar, the last *mukarrib,* assumed the title "king of Saba"; the change in title was probably a concession to the times, without any administrative meaning. Karib'il Watar was an ex-

From Bowen and Albright, *Archaeological Discoveries in South Arabia* (Baltimore: The Johns Hopkins Press)

2. Excavations at Marib in Yemen, showing entrance hall and outer structures

From Bowen and Albright, *Archaeological Discoveries in South Arabia* (Baltimore: The Johns Hopkins Press)

3. Bronze statue of Ma'adkarib, found in the Marib excavations

ceedingly energetic ruler. He conquered the kingdom of Ausan in the S with the aid of Qataban and Hadhramaut, which were then vassal states, and captured the cities of Nejran to the N. He is also responsible for many constructions in Saba, as well as in the newly acquired territories. His successors carried out extensive building operations at Marib, including especially the completion of the oval wall and the construction of the entrance hall of the temple of the moon-god; they also extended the great dam at Marib. During the third and second centuries B.C., Saba became increasingly weak, while Qataban and Ma'in emerged as the dominant S Arabian states. In 24 B.C., Augustus Caesar, seeking to share in the lucrative incense trade, dispatched Aelius Gallus on a campaign to conquer this area, according to Strabo. After a disastrous march during which many legionaries were lost, Aelius Gallus laid siege to Marib; however, Marib was spared when, six days later, he lifted the siege, because of lack of water, and returned northward. Figs. SAB 2-3.

Contact with the Greco-Roman world was made early in this period and increased greatly during the first century B.C. and the first century A.D. Objects of Hellenistic art were imported or were made locally from imported molds for wealthy Sabeans. Arretine (Italian *sigillata*) and other imported pottery has also been found at a number of S Arabian sites. Descriptions of S Arabia by a number of writers, including Theophrastus, Eratosthenes, Artemidorus, Diodorus Siculus, and Strabo, appeared during this period.

The period of the Kings of Saba and Dhu-Raidan began *ca.* the middle of the first century A.D. The early years were marked by a struggle for ascendancy and for possession of Qatabanian territory, then held by Hadhramaut. Saba emerged victorious from this struggle. In view of the prominence of tribal names in inscriptions of this period, it seems probable that a decentralization of power occurred in Saba at this time. There was some minor building during this period, especially repairs and additions to Awwam temple at Marib by Karib'il Watar Yuhan'im, his son Halak'amar, and others. Increased contact with the Mediterranean world is reflected by the more accurate descriptions of the region by the author of the *Periplus of the Erythraean Sea,* by Pliny the Elder, and by Claudius Ptolemy.

Ca. A.D. 325, King Shamar Yuhar'ish adopted the title "King of Saba, Dhu-Raidan, Hadhramaut, and Yamanat," following his conquests throughout S Arabia. He is also responsible for the construction of the present N sluices of the Marib dam. Following his reign, Saba and the W part of S Arabia were occupied by the Abyssinians for a generation or more (*ca.* 335-70); and during this period (341-46) Theophilus converted the Sabean ruler to Christianity, no doubt with the support of the Christian ruler of Abyssinia. Toward the end of the fourth century one of his sons, Abkarib As'ad, conquered much of W and central Arabia—and assumed the title "King of Saba, and Dhu-Raidan, and Hadhramaut, and Yamanat, and their Arabs of the highlands and on the coastal plain." Legend holds that Abkarib As'ad journeyed to Medinah, where he adopted Judaism and thereafter made it the state religion of Saba. In the early sixth century the Jewish king, Yusuf As'ar

(Dhu-Nuwas), persecuted the Christians of Nejran, according to Syriac and Greek tradition. When word of this persecution spread, the Christian Abyssinians once again crossed the Red Sea, and in A.D. 525 killed Dhu-Nuwas and his followers. This Abyssinian occupation of Saba covered several decades, perhaps lasting until *ca.* 575. The last Sabean ruler, the Abyssinian viceroy Abraha, made extensive repairs to the Marib dam and undertook an unsuccessful campaign against Mecca, the center of paganism. The Persian occupation of Saba began *ca.* 575 and continued until 628, when Saba surrendered to the forces of Islam.

Bibliography. H. St. J. B. Philby, *The Background of Islam* (1947), chs. 17-21 (earlier chapters are mostly obsolete). W. F. Albright, "The Chronology of Ancient South Arabia in the Light of the First Campaign of Excavation in Qataban," *BASOR,* 119 (1950), 5-15. J. Ryckmans, *L'institution monarchique en Arabie Méridionale avant l'Islam* (Ma'în et Saba; 1951). W. F. Albright, "The Chaldaean Inscriptions in Proto-Arabic Script," *BASOR,* 128 (1952), especially 44-45. G. W. Van Beek, "Recovering the Ancient Civilization of Arabia," *BA,* 15 (1952), especially 2-6. W. F. Albright, review of J. Ryckmans, *L'institution monarchique en Arabie Méridionale avant l'Islam, JAOS,* 73 (1953), 36-40. W. Phillips, *Qataban and Sheba* (1955): a popular account of the first American excavations in S Arabia. B. Segall, "The Sculpture of Arabia Felix: The Hellenistic Period," *AJA,* 59 (1955), 207-14; "Problems of Copy and Adaptation in the Second Quarter of the First Millennium B.C.," *AJA,* 60 (1956), 165-70. W. F. Albright, "A Note on Early Sabean Chronology," *BASOR,* 143 (1956), 9-10. F. P. Albright, R. LeB. Bowen, *et al., Archaeological Discoveries in South Arabia* (1958): contains an excellent study of the history and operation of the Marib dam, and a description of the temple of the moon-god (the Ḥaram Bilqîs) at Marib, based on excavations. G. W. Van Beek, "Frankincense and Myrrh in Ancient South Arabia," *JAOS* (1958); "South Arabian History and Archaeology," *The Biblical World* (studies presented to W. F. Albright): a summary of progress made in South Arabian studies in the past thirty years or so.

G. W. VAN BEEK

SABI sā'bī [Σαβειή (B); Σαβιή (A)]. KJV Apoc. form included in the latter part of the name POCHERETH-HAZZEBAIM.

SABTAH săb'tə [סבתה]. Alternately: SABTA [סבתא] (I Chr. 1:9). A son of Cush, and hence the name of a place in Arabia (Gen. 10:7). It has usually been identified with Sabota in Hadramaut, a noted emporium for salt and incense, but the fact that this name is written as שבות in Sabean inscriptions militates against this view. Another possibility is the Saptha mentioned by Ptolemy, an inland town situated not far from the Persian Gulf.

S. COHEN

SABTECA săb'tə kə [סבתכא]; KJV SABTECHA (Gen. 10:7); SABTECHAH [סבתכה] (I Chr. 1:9). A son of Cush, and hence the name of an Arabian locality. It has not been identified.

SACHAR sā'kär [שכר]; KJV SACAR. 1. A Hararite; the father of Ahiam, who was one of the Mighty Men of David known as the "Thirty" (I Chr. 11:35). In the parallel catalogue his name is given as Sharar the Hararite (II Sam. 23:33). While it is not possible to determine the original proper name, the gentilic "Hararite" is undoubtedly the true reading.

2. A Korahite who is included among the sons of Obed-edom, the eponymous ancestor of one of the families of gatekeepers (I Chr. 26:4; cf. vs. 15).

E. R. DALGLISH

SACHIA sə kī′ə [שכיה] (I Chr. 8:10); KJV SHACHIA shə—. A Benjaminite.

SACK [שׂק, (also SACKCLOTH), Egyp. sag, Coptic sok, Assyrian sakku, Gr. σάκκος; אמתחת, from מתח, spread out; כלי, a vessel or instrument (I Sam. 9:7; KJV VESSEL); צקלון (II Kings 4:42; KJV HUSKS), cf. Vulg., perhaps emend to קלעת, bread bag]. In most references, a container for grain or food. Sacks were perhaps often made of coarse (goat's hair) cloth.

H. F. BECK

SACKBUT. See MUSICAL INSTRUMENTS.

SACKCLOTH [שׂק; σάκκος]. A garment of goat's hair or camel's hair, often worn as a symbol of mourning and by some prophets and captives. See also ASHES; CLOTH; MOURNING.

The "sack" of "sackcloth" is derived from the Hebrew שׂק via the Latin saccus and the Greek σάκκος (cf. Akkadian šaqqu, Aramaic סקא). Authorities do not agree as to the shape of the garment. Some hold that it was a rectangular piece of cloth sewn on the sides and one end, leaving space for head and arms but having the shape of a grain bag. In support of this view may be cited the grain bags (שׂק) carried to Egypt by Joseph's brothers (Gen. 42:25, 27, 35), and the worn-out sacks used by the Gibeonites in their deception of Joshua (Josh. 9:4; cf. Lev. 11:32, where the שׂק is a common household object). Another view is that the sackcloth was a smaller garment such as a loincloth. Representations of Asiatic captives in ancient Near Eastern art often picture them wearing such a garment. In favor of this view may be cited the Hebrew practice of girding (חגר) the loins with sackcloth (II Sam. 3:31; Isa. 15:3; 22:12; Jer. 4:8; etc.), and putting it on the loins (Gen. 37:34; I Kings 20:31; Jer. 48:37; etc.). The fact that the person could be covered or clothed in sackcloth (II Kings 19:1-2; I Chr. 21:16; Esth. 4:2; Ps. 69:11; Isa. 37:1-2; etc.) may indicate that the garment was larger than a loincloth; doubtless its shape changed during the centuries and differed for men and women.

Sackcloth was dark in color, as can be judged by the phrase:

> I clothe the heavens with blackness,
> and make sackcloth their covering

(Isa. 50:3; cf. Rev. 6:12: "The sun became black as sackcloth").

The origin of sackcloth is unknown, although it probably goes back to prehistoric times when it was the only garment worn. There is no indication that the coarseness of the cloth produced physical discomfort when worn, or that it was used for the purpose of self-punishment, but it was put on as a sign of mental anguish at times of personal loss (II Sam. 3:31) and national calamity (II Sam. 3:31; II Kings 6:30; Neh. 9:1).

The use of sackcloth continued over many centuries. Jacob wore it to mourn for Joseph (Gen. 37:

34); Ahab "put sackcloth upon his flesh, and fasted and lay in sackcloth" (I Kings 21:27) in despair at his defeat by Elijah; the elders of Zion put on sackcloth in mourning for Jerusalem (Lam. 2:10); entire families with their cattle, laborers, and slaves girded themselves with sackcloth in time of national crisis (Jth. 4:10; cf. vs. 11, where the sackcloth was spread before the Lord, probably indicating that it was so designated even when not in the form of a garment; cf. Jonah 3:8 for a similar reference to the use of sackcloth with cattle); Mattathias and his sons put on sackcloth when in distress (I Macc. 2:14; 3:47); in the NT it is mentioned as a symbol of repentance (Matt. 11:21; cf. Luke 10:13).

Sackcloth is not mentioned in the Law; its general use seems to have been approved without question. Priests, like others, wore sackcloth (Joel 1:13) at a time of mourning, as did a virgin lamenting for the bridegroom (Joel 1:8). Although Isaiah wore sackcloth on one occasion (Isa. 20:2), it was probably not a normal prophetic garment—the mantle of hair worn by Elijah (II Kings 1:8; cf. Zech. 13:4) and the garment of camel's hair worn by John the Baptist (Matt. 3:4; cf. Mark 1:6) were more substantial robes.

W. L. REED

SACRED STONE [διοπετής; lit., fallen from Zeus] (Acts 19:35). Probably a meteorite which, having fallen from the sky and thus believed to be of supernatural origin, was considered a symbol of Artemis.

B. H. THROCKMORTON, JR.

*SACRIFICES AND OFFERINGS, OT. From the earliest times until the destruction of the second temple in A.D. 70, a dominant element of Hebrew religion was a series of rites and ceremonies, both public and private, in which beasts were dispatched and victuals presented to, or consumed in the presence of, the deity. These are commonly styled sacrifices and offerings, the formal distinction being that a sacrifice does involve the slaughter or burning of an animal, while an offering does not.

The practices in question were diverse and varied not only in form but also in motivation and significance. Some of them were conceived as the presentation of gifts designed to propitiate the god on an outright basis of do ut des ("I give that you may give"). Some were payments of tribute due to him as landlord, king, and lifegiver. Some, again, were designed to provide the fare for a common meal by which god and worshiper might recement their ties; and others had as their object the sustenance of the god while he was on earth, or the purging of sin and the regeneration of the sinner by sanctified blood. Accordingly, they cannot be derived from any one single principle, and, in respect of them, all monogenetic theories of the origin of sacrifice may be safely discountenanced from the start.

From the practical as well as the theoretical point of view, Hebrew sacrifices and offerings are best classified according to their respective motivations. On this basis, four classes may be recognized: (a) gifts and tributes; (b) media of alimentation; (c) media of communion; and (d) media of expiation. Each class is, of course, susceptible of further subdivision. Thus, media of alimentation will include the sustenance of the god on the one hand and of the priests on the other. Similarly, media of expiation will embrace both substitutes, or surrogates, for individual "sinners" and vehicles for eliminating impurity from the community as a whole—i.e., "scapegoats"—while media of communion will cover rites designed to forge or consolidate bonds between men, and also those the purpose of which was to unite the deity with his worshipers.

In elucidating the several particular sacrifices and offerings, we need no longer confine ourselves to the scriptural text. Parallels both in terminology and in practice may now be found in some profusion in other ancient Semitic sources, particularly in ritual texts from Mesopotamia, Ugarit (Ras Shamra), and South Arabia. In addition, there are interesting points of resemblance in Hittite documents, while the resources of modern anthropological studies may also be recruited for purposes of general illustration.

A. Typology
  1. Gifts and tributes
    a. Propitiatory
    b. Tributary (first fruits and tithes)
    c. Votive
    d. Thanksgiving
    e. Freewill offerings
  2. Alimentary
    a. Blood and fat
    b. Daily fare of God
      i. The continual offering
      ii. Schedule of offerings
      iii. The "bread of the Presence"
  3. Covenant and communion (blood sprinkling)
  4. Expiatory
    a. "Sin offering"
    b. "Guilt offering"
    c. Surrogates and scapegoats
B. Special occasions of sacrifices
  1. Public
  2. Private
  3. Sacrifices to the dead
  4. Human sacrifice
  5. Foundation sacrifice
C. Sacrificial procedure
  1. Introductory
  2. Classification of sacrifices
  3. Reserved portions
  4. Priestly portions
  5. Concessions to the poor
D. Material of sacrifices and offerings
E. The condition of purity
  1. Prohibition against breaking bones
  2. Ritual nudity
  3. Apotropaic measures
    a. Salt
    b. Blowing of the ram's horn
    c. Circumambulation of the altar
F. Attitude of the prophets
G. Later developments
  1. Rabbinical Judaism
  2. Sectarian attitudes
Bibliography

A. TYPOLOGY. 1. Gifts and tributes. Whatever their several motivations may have been, all sacrifices and offerings actually involved the presentation of something to or before the deity. Hence they might readily come to be regarded as gifts, and the most generic Hebrew names for them—viz., מתנה (Lev. 23:38; Deut. 16:17; Ezek. 20:26, 31, 39), מנחה (Exod. 29:41; 40:29; Lev. 2:1; etc. [cf. Arabic *manaḥa*, "donate, give use of"]); and קרבן (Lev. 2:1, 4, 7, 12; Num. 31:50; Neh. 10:35; etc.; cf. Mark 7:11), in fact possess that meaning.

These terms were by no means confined to the Israelitic system. The equivalent of מתנה occurs as the name of an offering in a sacrificial tariff from Ras Shamra–Ugarit (Ras Shamra 1939, 1.2), while *mnḥt* likewise denotes an oblation in various Phoenician texts (e.g., Marseilles Tariff, 14; Carthage Tariff, 10; *Corpus Inscriptionum Semiticarum* I, 145). As for קרבן, the corresponding verb is used in the same technical sense in Ugaritic (Ras Shamra 1929, ii.18) and, later, in Palmyrene (*North Semitic Inscriptions,* no. 133). Similarly, in Mesopotamian usage, sacrifices and offerings are sometimes designated by words meaning "gift" (e.g., *qištu, igisu*); while a common term, alike in Ugaritic (Ras Shamra 1929, i.1; ii.15-16; etc.), South Arabic (Glaser, 1150.3; Halévy, 185.5), and in inscriptions from Serabit, in Sinai (cf. W. F. Albright, *BASOR*, 110 [1948], 15), is *t'*, of the same meaning (cf. Arabic *t-w-'*, "donate").

a. Propitiatory. As gifts, sacrifices and offerings would be considered primarily as of the same order as those which had to be presented to a king or other superior when one sought favors from him (Judg. 3:17; I Sam. 10:27; Mal. 1:8; cf. Plato *Republic* 390C: "Gifts persuade both gods and noble kings"). In other words, they would be propitiatory.

This may be further illustrated by the fact that the verb from which קרבן is derived is actually used in Akkadian with the specific connotation of "advancing a plea."

b. Tributary (first fruits and tithes). A gift made to a superior might easily assume the complexion of a tribute, and it is significant in this respect that the terms מתנה and מנחה are, indeed, employed also in the OT of payments made by subjects to overlords (מתנה in Ps. 68:18—H 68:19; מנחה ;לקחת מתנות באדם in Judg. 3:18; II Sam. 8:6; II Kings 20:12; Isa. 39:1; etc.); while the expression "proffer מנחה" is used in Amos 5:25 of bringing an oblation to God, but in I Kings 4:21—H 5:1 of paying tribute to a king.

This use of מתנה finds a parallel in the cognate Akkadian *mandattu* (cf. מדה in Neh. 5:4); while in Akkadian documents from Ugarit, *manḥatu* designates a token of homage rendered to an overlord (cf. W. F. Albright, *BASOR,* 146 [1957], 35), and in a poetic text from the same site (III AB, B 35-36), *mnḥ* is what other gods bring to Baal in recognition of his sovereignty. The association of ideas is further illustrated by the fact that the term *kbd*, which, in the ritual tariffs from Ugarit (Ras Shamra 1929, i.2; ix.13), designates a type of sacrifice, is employed also, in Akkadian texts from that site (cf. *Mission de Ras Shamra,* IV/iii [1955], p. 221, under *kabâdu*), and in South Arabic inscriptions (e.g., Glaser, 150.2; 1083.4; cf. M. Lidzbarski, *Ephemeris,* II, 98), in reference to gifts of homage presented to rulers.

The idea that sacrifices and offerings are tributes rests not only on the general conception of the god as a king, but also, more particularly, on the Near Eastern principle—attested especially in Arabic law —that he who "quickens" the soil, or activates anything, is entitled to a share of the produce. As sender of rainfall, etc., the god claims such due. It is, so to speak, the dividend on his investment, and to withhold it from him is an act not only of impiety but also of embezzlement. Indeed, on the same principle, a portion of the spoils of war was made over to the god who led (or inspired) a victorious army (I Sam. 22:10; II Kings 11:10).

The latter practice is attested also in Mesopotamian sources (e.g., Shalmaneser III = Luckenbill, *Ancient Records of Assyria and Babylonia,* I, §§ 616-17); while in the Ugaritic Poem of Aqhat it is enjoined (I, v.37-38) that the first "bag" (*pr'*) of a successful hunt must likewise be dedicated to the gods.

As such tribute, the god claimed the male FIRST-BORN (בכור, פטר רחם) of all living creatures; though in the case of human beings, as also of unclean animals, provision was made for ransom by monetary or other equivalents (Exod. 13:11-16; 34:19-20; Lev. 27:26; Num. 18:15-17; Deut. 14:23; 15:19). To the god belonged also the FIRST FRUITS of the field (Exod. 22: 29; 23:19; 34:26) and the prime portion (ראשית) of all grain, must, oil, and new-shorn wool (Lev. 23:10; Num. 18:12-14; Deut. 18:4; cf. Neh. 10:37) and of all coarse meal (Num. 15:20-21).

Analogous offerings (*rešêti*) are attested in Mesopotamia, in Phoenician sacrificial tariffs (קדמת; Marseilles, 12; Carthage, 8; *Corpus Inscriptionum Semiticarum* I, 166.3) and in South Arabic inscriptions (*pr'*: Glaser, 1936.3; Halévy, 51.18; 476.3). There are likewise references to them in Hittite sources (e.g., *Keilschrifturkunden aus Boghazköi,* XII 4, iv. 3-4); while among the Greeks first fruits of barley and wheat were presented to Demeter and Korê at Eleusis (Isocrates *Panegyricus* 6 ff; cf. Dittenberger, *Syllogê* [3rd ed.], iv.83); and among the Romans, the first ears of corn were offered to Ceres (Ovid *Fasti* II.520; *Festus,* p. 423 [Lindsay]).

The specification of first fruits and firstlings as tributary offerings was probably influenced by the widespread primitive notion that there is a special "virtue" in new things, which renders them inviolate (cf. Lev. 19:23-25) and by reason of which they must be set apart for the gods or other holy beings. Moreover, it is commonly believed that the surrender of a prime part will protect the rest from hurt and blight.

Originally of undetermined quality, these first fruits were later stabilized as a tenth part, or TITHE (מעשר; Lev. 27:30-32; cf. II Chr. 31:5-6, 12; Neh. 10:38; 12:44; 13:5, 12; Amos 4:4; Mal. 3:8, 10), the identity of the two things—at least in the Deuteronomic system—being evident from a comparison of the parallel passages, Deut. 14:22 ff; 26:2 ff, where the terms "firstlings" and "tithes" are used interchangeably.

Such tithes are mentioned also in texts from Ugarit (cf. *Mission de Ras Shamra,* IV, Index, under *mašaru, mešertu;* Ras Shamra 1929, v.2: '*šr* '*šr*).

c. Votive. Besides being propitiatory or tributary, gifts could also be votive—i.e., consequent upon a VOW or promise to make a concrete payment to a god for fulfilling the wish, or otherwise prospering the interests, of his suppliants. Offerings of this kind

(נדר; Lev. 7:16-17; 22:21; 27; Num. 6:21; 15:3 ff; 30: 11; Deut. 29:21 ff; Jonah 1:16; etc.) could be presented either on making the vow or later, when the request had been granted. Moreover, the vows themselves could be envisaged either as purely speculative, or as formally contractual.

The basic meaning of נדר would seem to be "to set apart"—i.e., to segregate for the god or for sacred use. This meaning is contained also in the expressions פלא נדר (Lev. 22:2; Num. 15:3) and הפליא נדר (Lev. 27:2), for the primary sense of the verb פלא is "to segregate, render special." The corresponding noun (*pl'*) occurs in Ugaritic (III Keret, iii.23) with the signification "vow."

The verb נדר is not infrequent in Phoenician votive stelae (e.g., *Corpus Inscriptionum Semiticarum* I, 92 [Idalion, 354 B.C.] and in Neo-Punic and Nabatean inscriptions (e.g., North Semitic Inscriptions, no. 59, c. 2 [Maktar]; p. 245, n. 1 [El-Qanawat in Jebel Hauran]).

d. Thanksgiving. Where the votive offering is made in acknowledgment of favors received, it naturally tends to merge into the thank offering (תודה; cf. Lev. 7:12-13, 15; 22:29; II Chr. 33:16; Pss. 50:14, 23; 107:22; 116:17; Jer. 17:26; Amos 4:5; etc.), although the two things are, of course, formally distinct, inasmuch as the latter does not imply any previous promise or contract. Moreover, in Lev. 7:15 ff, the offering of thanksgiving is put into the category of a meal consumed by the offrants, and may therefore well have originated—at least in certain cases—in the festive banquet which celebrated the successful issue of anything, and only later have come to be associated with the idea of acknowledging divine favors.

A sacrifice in acknowledgment of the favor (*dbḥ n' mt*) of the sun-goddess (*Špš*) in bringing vines to blossom is mentioned in the Ugaritic text, "Shahar and Shalim," 27; while a common formula in South Arabic sacrificial inscriptions (e.g., *Corpus Inscriptionum Semiticarum* IV, 28.5; 163.17; 180.8; 181.6; 197.12) combines references to votive and thanksgiving offerings in the words: "For past and future favors [*ldt n' mt wtn'm*]."

e. Freewill offerings. Lastly, to the category of gifts belonged the voluntary, or freewill, offering (נדבה; Exod. 35:27-29; 36:3; Lev. 7:16; Num. 15:3; Deut. 12:17; 16:10; 23:23; II Chr. 22:21; 31:14; 35:8; Ezek. 46:12), prompted solely by the impulse of the donor. Since it therefore involved no statutory commandment, and was neither a means for establishing sacramental communion with the god, nor a payment made in respect of a contract with him, the regulations governing it were less stringent than in other cases: the animal offered did not have to be spotless (Lev. 22:23).

2. Alimentary. *a. Blood and fat.* It was a belief of the Semites, as of other ancient peoples, that the immortal and supramundane quality of gods was sustained by their eating special food or imbibing special drink in heaven. Such celestial "food of life" (*akâl balaṭi*) and "water of life" (*mê balaṭi*) play a significant role in the Mesopotamian myth of Adapa (B, 60-62; *ANET* 102). The belief is attested among the Hebrews by Pss. 78:25; 105:40; Wisd. Sol. 16:20. Analogous, of course, are the Vedic soma and amrita, and the Greek nectar and ambrosia.

Accordingly, when the gods came down to earth and sojourned among men, they were temporarily deprived of that substance, and therefore stood in need of constant refreshment by more mundane life-giving substances. Such were, above all, the blood and suet of earthly creatures, for these were considered the primary seats of vitality and energy.

The notion was widespread in antiquity. For the vital quality of blood, cf., among the Hebrews, Gen. 9:4; Lev. 17:11; Deut. 12:23; and for analogous ideas among other peoples, see: Pythagoras, quoted by Diogenes Laertius VIII.30; Servius on Vergil *Aeneid* III.79.

Hence, another of the primary purposes of sacrifice was to supply the gods, while on earth, with blood and suet; and this survived atavistically in the Hebrew system by reserving to Yahweh just those elements of the offertory victims (cf. Exod. 24:5 ff; Lev. 3:14; Deut. 32:37-38; I Sam. 2:15).

b. Daily fare of God. Moreover, when a god took up residence in an earthly habitation in order to render himself more accessible to men and, as it were, to hold rendezvous (יעד) with them, he was treated in the same way as a mortal king, being roused in the morning, washed, dressed, coiffured, fed, and put to bed at night. It was, in fact, this constant ministration to his creature comforts rather than mere acts of adoration, that formed the essence of the statutory sacred offices, and the Hebrew term עבודה, commonly rendered "worship," really implies such service in the widest sense. Similarly, in the Babylonian Epic of Creation (Enuma Eliš, VI.5-8), the primary purpose of man's creation is said to be the provision of a robot who might perform menial chores (*dullu*) for the gods. In this context, sacrifices and offerings provided the daily victuals of the deity.

i. The continual offering. In the Hebrew system, the daily sustenance of God on earth was provided principally by the so-called "continual offering" (תמיד), which consisted of an immolated beast offered whole (עלה), together with a meal or cereal offering (מנחה) and a libation (נסך); cf. Exod. 29:38-42; Lev. 6:13; 24:3-4, 8; Num. 28:3, 6; I Kings 18:29-36; II Kings 25:29-30; II Chr. 2:3; 24:14; Ezra 3:5; 9:4; Ezek. 39:14; 46:13-15; Dan. 9:21; 11:31; 12:11. The rules concerning it seem, however, to have varied at different periods. In I Kings 18:19-36 and again later, in Ezra 9:4; Dan. 9:21, the immolation takes place in the morning, and the cereals are offered in the late afternoon. On the other hand, in Exod. 29:38; Num. 28:1-8; Dan. 8:11-14, both are presented alike in the morning and in the evening.

This last is paralleled in Babylonian practice, for a ritual calendar from Uruk (*ANET* 342-45) prescribes a "heavy meal" (*naptanu rabu*) and a "light meal" (*naptanu quṭṭinu*) alike in the morning and in the evening.

On sabbaths, New Moons, seasonal festivals, and holy days, supplementary offerings (מוסף) were added.

ii. Schedule of offerings. The schedule is given in detail in Num. 28-29. This prescribes a daily whole offering of two yearling he-lambs, one in the morning, the other in the evening. On the sabbath, two further yearling he-lambs are to be sacrificed; while at the New Moon and on the festivals of Un-

leavened Bread and First Fruits, the extra offering is to consist of two young bullocks, one ram, and seven yearling he-lambs without blemish. On the first day of the seventh month—called the "Day of the Blowing of the Trumpet"—and likewise on the tenth day (i.e., the Day of Atonement), the supplementary offering is to comprise one young bullock, one ram, and seven yearling he-lambs without blemish. In the former case, this is to be superogatory to the ordinary New Moon sacrifice. At the Feast of Ingathering, thirteen additional young bullocks are to be offered on the first day, and one less on each of the succeeding six days, together with two rams and fourteen yearling he-lambs without blemish. Finally, on the Feast of 'Aṣereth, immediately after Ingathering, one bullock, one ram, and seven unblemished he-lambs are to be added. Furthermore, on all the aforementioned occasions, except the sabbath, a he-goat is to be offered as a חטאת, or medium of purgation (*see* § A4a *below*); on the Day of Atonement this is to be superogatory to that used in the major purification ceremony (Lev. 16:9).

A fixed scale determines the accompanying meal offerings. Every day one tenth of an ephah (0.105 American bushel) of fine flour is to be presented, soaked in one quarter of a *hîn* (0.40 gallon) of oil, and with each of the two he-lambs is to go a libation of one quarter of a *hîn* of strong drink. Otherwise the rule is that for each young bullock there must be an accompanying offering of three tenths of an ephah of fine flour, and for each he-lamb one tenth. Furthermore, with each young bullock there is to be offered half a *hîn* of wine; with each ram, one third of a *hîn;* and with each he-lamb, one quarter of a *hîn.*

A different schedule, however, is laid down by the prophet Ezekiel (574 B.C.) in his blueprint of the restored temple of the future (45:18-46:15). The daily offering is to consist of one yearling bullock, offered in the morning, along with one sixth of an ephah (0.175 American bushel) of fine flour, and one third of a *hîn* (0.54 gallon) of oil. On sabbaths, six unblemished he-lambs and one unblemished ram are to be presented, plus one ephah of fine flour with the latter, and an optional amount with the former. Each ephah is to be moistened with one *hîn* of oil. On New Moon the quota is to be the same, except for the addition of one young bullock. Moreover, it is as an accompaniment to that beast that the ephah of cereal is to be presented, the amount going with the other animals being optional. During the festivals of Unleavened Bread and Ingathering, the president (נשיא) of the community is to present on its behalf seven young bullocks and seven unblemished rams, together with one ephah of cereal and one *hîn* of oil for each. (No provision is made for the Feast of First Fruits, though it is possible that words relative to this occasion have dropped out of the text of 45:21.)

A young bullock is to be offered as a חטאת at the Feast of the Passover, and a he-goat on each day of the ensuing Festival of Unleavened Bread and of the Feast of Ingathering. Furthermore, on the first day of the first month, and again on the first of the seventh month (so LXX; MT "on the seventh day of the first month"), a bullock is to be offered for the decontamination (חטא) of the sanctuary; drops of its blood are sprinkled on the four corners of the altar fence and at other crucial parts of the building.

Analogous Babylonian sacrificial schedules—though on a more lavish scale—may be found on the famous tablet from Uruk (*ANET* 343-45). The Ugaritic sacrificial tariffs contain but few indications of the calendar dates to which they apply. One of them (Ras Shamra 1929, iii), however, prescribes offerings for each of seven consecutive days, but whether this refers to a seven-day festival or to the seven days of the week we cannot tell. The same document also prescribes "two sheep on the day of the new moon" (line 48: *bym ḥdt ṯn šm*), and elsewhere (ix.10-11) there is an allusion to the king's performing some kind of purificatory ceremony (*mlk brr*) "in the month of Teshrit"—possibly analogous to the Hebrew atonement rites.

iii. The "bread of the Presence." Besides such daily quotas of meat, meal, and drink offerings, Yahweh received also, as statutory fare, the so-called BREAD OF THE PRESENCE (לחם הפנים; Exod. 25:30; I Sam. 21:6; I Kings 7:48; II Chr. 4:19; cf. Exod. 39: 38; Num. 4:7), later known as showbread (לחם המערכת; I Chr. 9:32; 23:29; 28:16; II Chr. 2:4; 13: 11; 29:18; Neh. 10:33; cf. Matt. 12:4; Mark 2:26; Luke 6:4; Heb. 9:2). Alternative names for it were: "bread of God" (לחם אלהים; Lev. 21:6, 8) and "holy bread" (לחם קדש; I Sam. 21:4—H 21:5). According to the prescription in Lev. 24:5-6, it consisted of twelve loaves of fine flour, set upon the altar in two rows of six, and topped with pure frankincense (and, according to the LXX, also with salt). The loaves were changed every sabbath, those that were removed being then eaten by the priests.

There are arresting parallels in Mesopotamian cultus. There too the regular offertory bread is sometimes termed "food of the presence" (*akâl pâni;* V R 24, 18 *c-d*), and it is sometimes said to consist of twelve loaves—a number likewise favored in Hittite sacrificial usage. Moreover, although the fact is nowhere stated in the OT, postbiblical sources (Jos. Antiq. III.vi.6; x.7; M. Men. 5.1) assert that the bread was unleavened, and in Mesopotamian sources it is similarly described (*mutqu*).

3. Covenant and communion (blood sprinkling). In some cases sacrifices and offerings were simply a translation to the cultic sphere of regular social practices. One of the most prominent of these was the custom—attested by our own word "com-pani-on" (cf. אנשי לחם [Obad. 7]; אוכלי לחם [Ps. 41:9—H 41: 10]; בעלי לחם [Ecclus. 9:16])—of forging or reaffirming ties of kinship and alliance by "breaking bread" together. Abram, e.g., thus cemented alliance with Melchizedek, king of Salem (Gen. 14:18-20), and Isaac with Abimelech (26:30); while the Israelites were tied to the Gibeonites through having partaken of food in common (Josh. 9:14). Such usages survive among modern Bedouins. Herodotus relates (IV.172) of the Nasamoneans that they made covenants by drinking out of one another's hands.

Accordingly, it has been suggested by one scholar that the primary and original purpose of sacrifice among the Semites was to forge or cement relations with a god by sharing a meal with him. In support of this view, it is pointed out that in Israelitic thought the relationship between God and his people was in-

deed conceived as that of a COVENANT, and that the OT itself bears witness to the belief that the god participated in communal feasts, and especially in those held to cement alliances. In Deut. 12:7, e.g., the Israelites are commanded that, after the occupation of Canaan, they are to perform sacrifices and offerings and "eat in the presence of Yahweh your God" at his appointed place; while in Exod. 18:12 we are told that when Moses and Jethro concluded an alliance, "Aaron came with all the elders of Israel to eat bread with Moses' father-in-law in the presence of [RSV 'before'] God." Similarly, in the Ugaritic Poem of Aqhat (I, iv.57-58), when Yaṭpan welcomes the maiden Paghat to his tent and offers her his protection, the pledge is sealed by a drink in which the god "who owns the fields" participates (*tqḥ ks bdh, qbʻt bymnh, wyʻn Yṭpn mhr št: byn yšt iln š . . . il dyqny ždm;* cf. Vergil *Aeneid* VIII.274-75: *pocula porgite dextris, Communemque vocate deum, et date vina volentes!*).

To be sure, the generalizing inferences drawn from these evidences have long since been invalidated by the increased information (from Mesopotamian and Ugaritic sources) which was unavailable until recently. Nevertheless, the importance of commensality as one of the elements of Hebrew sacrifices and offerings must indeed be recognized. It should be observed also that the theories regarding the purpose of sacrifice as covenant and communion were formerly based very largely on a description of Saracen sacrificial practices given by Nilus in the fourth century, but it has since been shown that this account is quite unreliable and that the usages in question do not really represent survivals from primitive Semitic antiquity.

It has been suggested also that the Hebrew word אשה, commonly rendered "fire offering" (as if from אש, "FIRE"), is really to be derived from a root אנש, "be sociable," and that the sacrifice thus designated is hence to be regarded as having been designed primarily to effect communion, or social rapport, between god and men. This, however, is doubtful.

In outward recognition of the covenantal bond, it was anciently the custom to sprinkle drops of the sacrificial blood on the persons or dwellings of the participants. In Israelitic sacrificial usage, this survived in the ritual of the PASSOVER, where such blood was dashed on doorpost and lintel, thereby signifying that the occupants of the house were, so to speak, duly registered "kinsmen" of Yahweh and therefore ensured of his protection against hurtful demons (Exod. 12:7, 13, 22-23).

4. Expiatory. a. Sin offering. Any contact with impurity, either physical or moral (and the two were not rigorously differentiated), any infringement of traditional taboos, and any violation of cultic laws, was regarded by the Hebrews as entailing an impairment of the offender's essential "self" (נפש). Out of harmony with the prescribed order of things, he was, until regenerated, in the category of "damaged goods." The Hebrew term for this was חטא, usually rendered "sin." Such a rendering, however, tells but half the story. The primary meaning of the word is "to miss, fall short of," and the reference was not so much to the actual commitment of the offense as to the consequent state of the offender's self. The corresponding Akkadian *ḫaṭû* often possesses the connotation of "unlucky," and the nouns *ḫîṭu* and *ḫiṭîtu* mean "(concrete) damage, loss, or defect" (e.g., Code of Hammurabi, sections 235.18; 267.84; *Archives Royales de Mari,* III, 12.14). The range of meaning is approximately that of the Italian *disgrazia. See* SIN, SINNERS.

To purge this condition, recourse was had to the sacrificial rite known as חטאת (LXX ἁμαρτία; Vulg. *peccatum*), usually rendered "sin offering" (cf. Exod. 29:14, 36; Lev. 4, *passim;* 5:9, 11-12; 6:18, 23; 8:10-14; 10:1-13; 14, *passim;* 16:6, 11, 25, 27; Num. 19:9, 17; 28:22-38; 32:23; II Chr. 29:23-24; Ezek. 40:39; 42:13; 43:21-25; 45:19-22; 46:20; etc.). The rite was performed not only in respect of such moral misdeeds as refusing to testify, but also in order to remove the "contagion" of childbirth and leprosy; while at the major festivals, and likewise at the consecration of priests (Exod. 29:9-34; Lev. 8:10-14), it served to cancel latent pollution. In South Arabic (Sabean) inscriptions, the corresponding term *ḫ-ṭ-'* denotes the performance of a rite designed to rehabilitate a person who has violated sexual taboos—e.g., a woman who has had intercourse during menstruation, or visited a sanctuary at that time.

The rite was two-sided: on the one hand, it removed the contagion; on the other, it regenerated the "infected" individual(s). The former end was usually (though not always) accomplished by having the offrant or priest lay his hand (סמך) on the victim's head (Exod. 29:10, 19; Lev. 1:4; 3:2, 8, 13; 4:4, 24, 29, 33; 16:21; 24:14; Num. 27:18), thereby indicating a transference of the taint. Similarly, among the Toradjas of the Celebes, when a man returns from a long voyage, he has to lay hands upon a dog, in order to transfer to it all malign influences with which he may be charged, before entering his house.

The latter end was served by having the priest apply drops of the sacrificial blood to the right ear, thumb, and big toe of the offrant (Exod. 29:20; Lev. 4, *passim;* 8:23-24; 14:14, 25). Since this blood had been previously "consecrated" by being sprinkled on, or brought into contact with, the altar, the purpose of the procedure was evidently to regenerate the impaired "self" (נפש) of the offender by transferring to him something of the *élan vital* of that holy substance. Not impossibly, the choice of the ear and the right hand and foot effected, or symbolized, the regeneration of the senses on the one hand and the limbs on the other.

Nor was it only human beings who could be thus reconditioned. The altar too could be purged of taint and made over anew into the category of the supramundane (קדוש) by being aspersed with blood of a חטאת. Thus, at the installation of Aaron and his sons —a mere historicization, of course, of practices attending the induction of priests—Moses is said to have slaughtered a bullock as a חטאת and to have applied drops of its blood to the horns (i.e., corner projections) of the altar, pouring out the remainder at the base (Lev. 8:15; cf. Exod. 29:12). Thereby, we are told, he not only "cleared it of taint [ויחטא]," but also "made it holy by purging it [ויקדשהו לכפר עליו]."

b. Guilt offering. Utterly distinct from the חטאת, though often confused with it by modern scholars, was the so-called guilt offering (אשם; LXX πλημ-

μέλεια; KJV "trespass offering"; Lev. 5:16, 19; 7:1-7; 14, *passim;* Num. 5:7-8; 6:12; 18:9; II Kings 12:17; Ezra 10:19). Far from being a vehicle of rehabilitation, this was primarily a fine imposed upon one who had caused material damage to another—e.g., by concealing evidence, swearing rashly, misappropriating property (Lev. 6:1-26), or ravishing a betrothed handmaid (19:20). Originally a purely civic institution, it was later extended to cases of damage or loss occasioned to the deity by fraud (מעל) in respect of sacred things (5:16-17) or by such ritual impurity— e.g., through leprosy (14:12-13) or violation of the Nazirite state (Num. 6:12)—as disqualified a man from rendering his normal service. Indeed, at the return from the Babylonian exile, it was imposed also on those priests who had married Gentile women (Ezra 10:19).

The incorporation of the אשם into the sacrificial system first appears in the Priestly Code (P), which dates from the fifth century B.C. The institution itself, however, was certainly known at an earlier date, for the author (J) of Gen. 26:10 has Abimelech chide Isaac for exposing the Philistines to possible payment of an אשם (for ravishment) by passing off his wife, Rebekah, as his sister; while in I Sam. 6:3-17, the plague-ridden Philistines, anxious to placate Yahweh, are advised by their priests to accompany the return of the captured ark by payment of an אשם.

On the other hand, the oft-repeated statement that the אשם is mentioned in the Ras Shamra Texts is false, for the word (*'aṯm*) so identified is, in fact, Hurrian and occurs only in Hurrian documents (viz., Ras Shamra 1929, vii.6-8; xxxiv.11).

The אשם was not an indemnification, but simply a mulct. Indeed, it had to be paid over and above the actual restitution of the damage (Lev. 5:14-16). Its purpose was punitive, not compensatory, and it corresponded, more or less, to the modern concept of a "debt to society," which implies far more of retaliatory privation than of material restitution. In the popular mind, however, a fine paid to an abstract God in respect of material damage inflicted upon him will readily merge into an act of restitution, and it is therefore not surprising that the payment of it is sometimes described in the OT by the verb "restore, give back" (השיב; Num. 5:7-8; I Sam. 6:3-4, 8, 17).

The basic idea of the אשם may perhaps best be apprehended from two poetic passages in which the point depends on the original meaning of the term. (*a*) In Isa. 53:10 (where no emendation of the text is necessary!), it is said of the Suffering Servant, who undergoes tribulation on behalf of his people, that "if he let his own person serve as an אשם [lit., if his own person render אם תשים אשם נפשו; אשם], then, though Yahweh has chosen [at present] to crush him with sickness, he shall yet see progeny, enjoy long life" (orig. tr.). (*b*) In Joel 1:18, the sorry condition of flocks and herds which lack pasture in a time of famine and divine displeasure, is described in the arresting words: "Even the flocks of sheep are being made to pay their guilt offering" (נאשמו; LXX ἠφανίσθησαν; Vulg. *disperierunt;* RSV "are dismayed"; KJV "are made desolate" [i.e., נשמו]).

c. Surrogates and scapegoats. A common view of expiatory offerings is that they were designed primarily to provide surrogates, or substitutes, for the lives of human offenders, which the god might otherwise claim in retribution. This, e.g., seems, by and large, to have been the view of the ancient rabbis (cf. Zeb. 6a), and modern scholars have resorted to it especially to account for the familiar rite of the scapegoat on the Day of Atonement (Lev. 16; see ATONEMENT, DAY OF). In support of it, reference is made to the frequent use of such substitutes (takpirtu, puḫu) in Babylonian magical ceremonies and Hittite rituals (ANET 346-47), as well as to the virtual ubiquity of the animal ransom (fedu) in modern Arabic popular custom. This view, however, is thoroughly mistaken, for such animals are not in fact substitutes for capital punishment, but merely vehicles for transferring and thereby removing taint and contagion, either actual or prospective. If the animal is eventually put to death, this is purely incidental; the main thing is simply to dispatch it from the community, so that the miasma may be borne away with it. This, e.g., was the function of the human scapegoats (φαρμακοὶ) dispatched from the city at various ancient Greek festivals, as it is also of "the Death" and similar figures in modern folk customs; while the biblical ritual itself prescribes that the beast be dispatched "to a solitary land" (Lev. 16:22)—the Mishna's description (Yom. 6.6) of how it was then pushed over a cliff represents only a later elaboration.

Such disposal of residual miasma was obviously necessary before complete clearance from impurities like leprosy could be effected (cf. Lev. 14). In the case of the scapegoat, however, two further elements enter the picture. First, the scapegoat was not, as modern parlance would suggest, something to which one shifted the blame for one's own transgressions and which was made to pay the price of them. On the contrary, it was a means of removing from the community the taint of sins which had first to be fully and openly confessed (16:21). What it removed, therefore, was miasma, not responsibility. Second, the expulsion of the scapegoat was, among the Hebrews as elsewhere, essentially a public ceremony, and in their case (as again in many parallel instances) it took place just before the opening of the agricultural year, when the community was about to enter upon a new lease of life. Its primary purpose, therefore, was to rid society as a whole of any latent miasma, responsibility for which could not, for one reason or another, be assigned precisely to particular individuals. In such circumstances the only possible means of riddance was by pronouncing a collective, blanket confession of sins and then saddling the collective taint upon some one deputed being. In other words, the scapegoat was representative, not substitutional, and the real and sole purpose of the institution was to do that which had to be done for the public benefit but which could not be done by individuals.

A close parallel to the biblical ritual is afforded by the ceremony called kuppuru (cf. Hebrew kippûrîm, "purgation, atonement"), which took place on the fifth day of the Babylonian festival of Akîtu, celebrated at the beginning of the year. The temple was aspersed and fumigated (cf. Lev. 16:11-16). Then a sheep was beheaded, and the walls of the chapel of Nabu were rubbed with its carcass. This done, head and carcass were tossed into the river, while the slaughterer and the officiating priest were sent out of the city, to observe a quarantine until the end of the festival (cf. vs. 26; see *Keilschrifttexte aus Assur Verschiedenen Inhalts*, p. 120, ii.22-38).

B. SPECIAL OCCASIONS OF SACRIFICE.
1. Public. In addition to those which formed part of the statutory cult, sacrifices were performed publicly on occasions when it was thought necessary to purge the community of the taint of collective misdeed (Lev. 4:13 ff; Num. 15:24-26) or of a plague (II Sam. 24:21-25; I Chr. 21:23), or when an offense committed by the priest might entail grievous consequences for the people (Lev. 4:3 ff; cf. 14; 16:11, 14). The consecration of a temple or altar also required appropriate sacrifices (8:14 ff), and so too did the consecration of priests (Exod. 28; Lev. 8) and the installation of kings (I Sam. 10:8; 11:15). In all these cases, what was involved was the removal of impurity on the one hand and the replenishment of "holiness" on the other.

Sacrifices were offered also before battle (I Sam. 7:9; 13:9). It is not sufficient, however, to say simply that these were propitiatory, for they may equally well have been designed (at least originally) as a means of absorbing "divine" vigor in a moment of crisis.

2. Private. Private sacrifices comprised not only the אשם but also offerings made after childbirth (Lev. 12:6-7) and weaning (I Sam. 1:24) and on concluding personal pacts (Gen. 26:26-30; 31:46-54). Periodic family pilgrimages seem also to have been made to local sanctuaries for the purpose of offering sacrifice (I Sam. 1:3-4), doubtless as a means of recementing ties with the deity.

Sacrifices offered by families and religious guilds are expressly distinguished in the Phoenician tariff from Marseilles (line 16) from those presented by individuals (אדמם). Such a guild was called a mrzḥ (מרזח)—a term derived from the root רזח, "shout," and thus akin to the familiar Greek θίασος, as it is, indeed, rendered by the LXX in Jer. 16:5 (cf. also the Palmyrene inscription, *North Semitic Inscriptions*, no. 140, A 2 [A.D. 132]; Sifre, 47b [ed. Friedmann]). The institution was ancient, for the mrzḥ (marzeʾu) of a god named Šatran is mentioned in Akkadian texts from Ras Shamra–Ugarit. A further reference to "clan offerings" has been tentatively recognized (ANET 155) in the obscure expression dbḥ dgtt in the Ugaritic Poem of Aqhat, C 187-88, 192-93.

3. Sacrifices to the dead. Such sacrifices are seemingly mentioned in Ps. 106:28. Here again, however, caution is in order, for the Hebrew text speaks only of "sacrifices *of* the dead" (זבחי מתים), not *to* them, and all that may really be meant is the common practice of sharing meals with ancestral spirits, who are believed to visit their kinsmen at seasonal festivals. It is to be noted, in fact, that the people themselves are said expressly to have partaken of the fare!

4. Human sacrifice. That human sacrifice was current in early Palestinian religion is abundantly attested by the biblical denunciations of this practice (Lev. 20:2; Deut. 12:30-31; II Kings 16:3; 17:31; 23:10; Ps. 106:37-38; Jer. 7:30-32; 19:3-5; Ezek. 16:20-21; cf. Wisd. Sol. 12:4-6). Moreover, in North Mesopotamian texts of the tenth-seventh centuries B.C.

we hear, indeed, of the cremation of male children in honor of Hadad.

Here too belong the several references in the OT to the passing of children through fire to Molech (Lev. 18:21; II Kings 23:10; Jer. 32:35). What is implied is a matter of debate among scholars. According to the traditional view, Molech is a pagan god (i.e., "the King"), and a deity of this name is certainly mentioned in tablets of the eighteenth century B.C. from Mari and of the Third Dynasty of Ur. Moreover, Diodorus tells us explicitly (XX.14) that children were set before the statue of the Tyrian god Melqarth at Carthage and then passed into a furnace. On the other hand, O. Eissfeldt has argued, from the occurrence of *molch* in Punic votive inscriptions, that the term means simply "votive offering." It is possible also that the Israelite writers have confused with human sacrifice a more innocuous practice, widely attested, of passing children rapidly through a flame as a means of absorbing immortality or giving them extra strength. The practice is most familiar from the classical tales of Demeter and Demophoon (Homeric Hymn to Demeter 237 ff; Apollodorus *Bibliotheca* I.v.1; Ovid *Fasti* IV, 487), Thetis and Achilles (Apollonius *Rhodius Argonautica* IV.869; Apollodorus III.xiii.6), Medea and her children (Pausanias II.iii.1). It is related also concerning Isis and the infant son of the king of Byblos (Plutarch *De Isis et Osiris* XVI), and is reported as current in Timorlaut.

The archaeological evidence for the sacrifice of children is ambiguous. Skeletons of children have been found together at Gezer, Ta'anach, and Megiddo, but it is questionable whether these are anything more than normal interments. Figs. MEG 28; SAC 4.

Jephthah's sacrifice of his daughter (Judg. 11:30-40) is simply a Hebrew version of a widespread folk tale, and the whole point of the story depends on its being something unusual and extraordinary. Accordingly, it cannot be construed as evidence of normative practice.

Courtesy of the Oriental Institute, the University of Chicago

4. Burial jar for infant, found at Megiddo (*ca.* seventeenth-eighteenth century)

5. Foundation sacrifice. To the category of human sacrifice pertains also the practice to which allusion is made in Josh. 6:26; I Kings 16:34, of slaying persons at the foundation of a city or building. This practice, designed to "handsel" the new structure against evil powers, is widespread in world folklore. Often the human victim is walled up alive, or the rite is attenuated to the slaughter of an animal, whose blood is poured over the foundation stone.

C. *SACRIFICIAL PROCEDURE*. 1. Introductory. The most comprehensive term for "sacrifice" in biblical Hebrew is זבח, a word which means primarily "slaughtering" (cf. Arabic *ḏabaḥa*, "slit the throat"). It has therefore been assumed that the original method of dispatching sacral animals was by immolation, and that burning came in later. In further support of this view, it is contended that such an odd expression as "a zebah of oil" (זבח שמן), found in Phoenician sacrificial tariffs (Marseilles, 12; Carthage, 8), can be explained only on the assumption that זבח, "slaughter," was originally the only form of sacrifice known, so that the word was already standardized by the time cereal and other types of offering were introduced.

This inference is quite unwarranted, for the fact is that other terms which had originally denoted particular types of offering came likewise, in the course of time, to be used in an extended (and, strictly speaking, inappropriate) sense. The Arabic *nusk*, e.g., which is indeed used of immolations, is derived from a root meaning primarily "pour out" (cf. נסך), and the same is true of the term *n-q-'*, similarly employed in Akkadian, Amurritic (Mari), Ugaritic, and Syriac (cf. Akkadian *naqû*, "pour"), and of the Hittite *sipant-* (cf. σπένδω). By the same logic, therefore, one could just as well conclude that the earliest form of offering was the libation!

2. Classification of sacrifices. In developed Israelitic usage, sacrifices were divided into the two major categories of (*a*) עלה, "burnt offering," or כליל, burned whole on the altar; and (*b*) זבח or שלם, in which certain parts only were consigned to the altar, the rest being consumed by the offerer(s) or the priest(s). The term עלה is usually explained from the *Hiph'il* of the verb עלה, "cause to ascend," used specifically in reference to sacrifice (I Sam. 7:9-10; 13:9; cf. Ugaritic *š'ly*). It is thought to refer either to the placing of the victim on the altar or to the rising of the smoke in a burnt offering. An alternative view, however, connects the word rather with Arabic *ġ-l-y*, "boil." An equivalent, *'lt*, is recognized by Albright in four inscriptions from Serabit, in Sinai. Otherwise, no cognate of the term has yet been found in any Semitic language, except as a direct borrowing from Hebrew. The כליל (LXX ὁλοκάταυμα; Vulg. *holocaustum;* Targ. Onqelos גמר) recurs in the Phoenician sacrificial tariffs from Marseilles and Carthage, where it is defined as a form of שלם. However, it is there not burned entire on the altar; part of the flesh is assigned to the priests. The term שלם recurs in Ugaritic (Ras Shamra 1929, i.4; iii.17,52; v.7; vi.6; ix.7,15; xvii.18) and Phoenician (Marseilles and Carthage tariffs); while a seemingly related *mšlm* appears in South Arabic altar inscriptions. The meaning is disputed. The versions connect it with

שלום, "peace" (LXX θυσία εἰρηνίκη)—i.e., "peace offering"—designed to effect amicable relations with the deity. In support of this may be cited Akkadian *salimu* in the specific sense of "pact, agreement," and Ugaritic *šlm*, "Danegeld" (Krt,ʼ A 130-31). On the other hand, some scholars would connect the term rather with *šillem* (cf. Arabic *salama*), "pay"—i.e., simply, "payment."

3. Reserved portions. The reserved portions usually consisted of the blood, the omentum, the kidneys with the fat on them, the *lobus caudatus* (יותרת הכבד, "appendage of the liver"; Lev. 8:16), and, in the case of sheep, also the fat tail (אליה; LXX ὀσφύς; Exod. 29:22; Lev. 3:9; 7:3; 8:25; 9:19), these being deemed the seats of vitality (*see* § A2a *above*).

4. Priestly portions. Provision was made for the priests to receive a meed of the sacrifices and offerings for their sustenance. In the case of the חטאת and אשם, everything except the blood and the reserved fat fell to them (Lev. 5:13; 6:18, 22-23; 7:6-7; Num. 18:9-10, 18; Ezek. 44:29; cf. Jos. Antiq. III.ix.3). Of the ordinary זבח, if the vicitim were a sheep or goat, the priests received the leg, jowls, and maw (Deut. 18:1-5); while in the case of an עלה, they also received the skin (Lev. 7:8; cf. Jos. Antiq III.ix.1; Zeb. XII.2-4). Theirs too were the right shank and the breast of every שלם (Lev. 7:30-34), everything "devoted" to the deity (חרם)—e.g., out of the spoils of war (Num. 18:14; Ezek. 44:29)—and the prime portion (ראשית) of corn, must, oil, and new-shorn wool (Num. 18:12; Deut. 18:3-5). They were likewise entitled to the major portions of cereal offerings (Lev. 2:10; 6:9-11; 7:9-10, 14; 10:12-13; Num. 18:10; Ezek. 44:29), after a representative specimen (אזכרה) had been removed (Lev. 2:9, 16; 5:12; 6:8; Num. 5: 26; cf. Ecclus. 35:7; 38:11; 45:16).

The precise meaning of אזכרה is obscure. It is usually derived from זכר, "remember," and rendered, somewhat vaguely, "memorial portion" (cf. LXX μνημόσυνον; Vulg. *memoriale*). An alternative suggestion is, however, that the word is connected with a homonymous זכר, "be fragrant," although the latter is none too well authenticated.

In addition, they received the bread of the Presence, once it had been replaced by a fresh supply (Lev. 24:5-9; cf. Matt. 12:4; Mark 2:26; Luke 6:4; Jos. Antiq. III.ix.4; Suk. V.7-8).

Similar provisions appear elsewhere in the ancient world. Thus, a sacrificial tariff from the Babylonian city of Sippar prescribes that the priests are to receive the skin, loins, ribs, sinews, maw, chitterling, and knuckles of the sacrificial victim; while in the Phoenician tariffs from Marseilles and Carthage, comparable—though not identical—allocations are made, and in the Ugaritic texts (Ras Shamra 1929, i.21; iii.40; ix.8), provision is made for a special gift of fowl (or, a brace of fowl [ʼṣrm; Akkadian *iṣṣuru*]) to "the man of the gods [ʼanš ilm]." In Greek sacrifices the hide went to the priests.

5. Concessions to the poor. Although the amounts of sacrifices and offerings were, in general, precisely defined, concessions were made for the benefit of the poor. Thus, according to the (late?) law of Lev. 4: 23-32, a commoner need bring only a female goat or sheep as a חטאת, whereas a chieftain (נשיא) had

to bring a he-goat, and the anointed priest a bullock. Furthermore, in cases of indigence, two turtledoves might be substituted for the sheep, and, if even these could not be afforded, one tenth of an ephah of fine flour (3:7, 11). Similarly, a poor woman might substitute two turtledoves for the statutory sheep prescribed for purification after childbirth (Lev. 12:8; Luke 2:24), and a poor leper (or victim of vitiligo) might bring one tenth of an ephah of fine flour soaked in oil, together with one *lôg* of oil, in lieu of the normative offering of lambs, fine flour, and oil combined (Lev. 14:21); while in the paschal rite two households could club together, if the provision of the lamb exceeded the resources of either (Exod. 12:4).

Similarly, a Babylonian ritual text prescribes a dove for a nobleman (*rubû*), but only the intestines(?) of a sheep for one of lower degree (*muškenu*); while in the Phoenician tariffs from Marseilles and Carthage it is stated expressly that, if the offerer be a poor man, the priests are to forgo their usual share. The Hittite "Yuzgat Tablet" (Goetze, *Verstreute Boghazköi Texte,* no. 58) prescribes analogously that, while the normal offering to the sun-god in return for favors is to be nine sheep, a poor man need offer only one.

D. *MATERIAL OF SACRIFICES AND OFFER-INGS.* By and large, any clean beast was acceptable as an עלה (Lev. 1:2), but, if it was a quadruped, it had to be male and without blemish (22:22-25).

The sacrifice for an אשם was usually a ram (Lev. 5:15; cf. Ezra 10:19), though in some apparently late laws (Lev. 5:6; 14:12, 22; Num. 6:12) a lamb (כבש) was permitted, and there were even further concessions in cases of poverty (Lev. 5:7, 11).

The beast offered for a חטאת varied with different cases. In that of a private ceremony, a she-goat was prescribed (Num. 15:27); but for the communal חטאת on the Day of Atonement the statutory animals were he-goats, though for the expiation of the priests on the same occasion a bullock was required.

At the release of a Nazirite from his term, a yearling female lamb had to be brought as a חטאת, a yearling he-lamb as an עלה, and a ram as a שלם (Num. 6:13-21). The paschal ceremony required a lamb (Exod. 12:3, 21). The formal prescriptions of the legal codes are well illustrated by the historical narratives, where the following sacrificial animals are mentioned:

a) Bovines. Cattle (בקר; II Sam. 24:22-25); ox (שור; I Sam. 14:34; II Sam. 6:13; I Kings 1:19-25); bull (פר; Judg. 6:26; I Sam. 1:24); cow (פרה; I Sam. 6:14); heifer (עגלה; Gen. 15:9; I Sam. 16:2); young of the herd (בן בקר; I Sam. 14:32); fatling (מריא; II Sam. 6:13; I Kings 1:19, 25).

b) Ovines. Sheep (שה; Gen. 22:7; I Sam. 14:34); ram (איל; Gen. 22:13; I Sam. 15:22); suckling lamb (טלה חלב; I Sam. 7:9).

c) Caprines. Kid (גדי; Judg. 13:15, 19; I Sam. 10:3).

In the Ugaritic texts mention is made of: large cattle (*gdlt;* Ras Shamra 1929, i.3, 5, 8, 13-15, 19, 21; iii.12, 17); small cattle (*dqt;* i.3-4, 18; iii.13, 28, 32); oxen (*ʼalp;* i.5; v.6; ix.8); sheep (*ṣun;* v.1; xxiii.5; *ṣun nqd;* xxii.5; *s;* i.2, 5-7, 10-11, 19; iii.5-6;

ix.2); rams (*dkrm;* v.19; *il;* iii.5); doves (*ynt;* i.2, but uncertain).

A holocaust offered at the obsequies of the god Baal (I AB, i. 19-31) includes seventy buffaloes (*rumm*), seventy oxen (*'alpm*), seventy sheep (*ṣin*), seventy harts (*'aylm*), seventy mountain goats (*y'lm*), and seventy asses (*ḥmrm*). This, however, is offered by the goddess 'Anat, and therefore need not reflect common practice among mortals, but may be a deliberate exaggeration.

In the Phoenician sacrificial tariff from Marseilles (third-second century B.C.; North Semitic Inscriptions, no. 42), the animals specified are: ox, calf, ram, goat, lamb, kid, young of the hart, domestic(?) bird (צפר אגנן), wild fowl, and "game" (צד).

In many cases, the rule is laid down that sacrificial animals are to be not more than one year old (cf. Exod. 12:5; 29:38; Lev. 9:3; 12:6; 14:10; 23:18-19; Num. 6:12, 14-15; 7, *passim;* Ezek. 46:13; etc.); while once (Gen. 15:9) we hear of three-year-olds (cf. also I Sam. 1:24 LXX). A late law (Lev. 22:27) prescribes that they must be at least eight days old.

One-year-old sacrificial animals (*apal/mârat šatti*) are likewise mentioned in Mesopotamian sources; while in the Ugaritic Poem of Baal (II AB, vi.43), the gods are regaled on "one-year-old calves" (*'glm dt šnt*).

With the three-year-old ram, goat, and bullock, cf. the three-year-old heifer of Isa. 15:5; Jer. 48:34 (S. Bochart, *Hierozoicon* [1692], I, 258; E. A. Speiser, *BASOR,* 72 [1938], 15-17). Note also that in Theocritus (XXIX.17) a "three-year friend" (τριέτης φίλος) is a mature friend.

Vegetable offerings consisted in a tithe of the produce (Deut. 14:22) and in the first fruits of the crops (Exod. 23:16; Deut. 26:2). There is also mention of bread (I Sam. 10:3-4), parched ears of corn (Lev. 2:14-16), and oil. Oil was used especially in the preparation of sacrificial cakes (Exod. 29:2, 40; cf. Ezek. 46:14), but is also mentioned as an independent offering (Lev. 14:10-11; cf. Gen. 28:18; 35:14; Mic. 6:7).

Libations of wine usually accompanied the sacrifice of animals (Hos. 9:4; cf. Gen. 35:14; II Kings 16:13) or of bread (Jer. 7:18).

Babylonian sacrificial texts mention, in addition to animals: wine (*karanu*), must (*kurunnu*), date wine (*šikaru*), honey (*dišpu*), cream (*ḥimētu*), and garlic (*šummu*). In the Ugaritic ritual tariffs reference is made to: oil (*šmn;* Ras Shamra 1929, iii.44; *šmn rqm;* iii.21), wine (*yn;* iii.23), spelt (*kśm;* i.19 [cf. Hebrew *kussemeth?*]), and "greenstuff[?]" (*dtt;* i.19); and in the Phoenician tariff from Marseilles the meal offering is said to be soaked (בלל; cf. Exod. 29:2; Lev. 2:4; etc.) in oil or milk.

Leavened food—because leavening necessarily implies fermentation, and fermentation implies putrefaction—was, in general, forbidden in offerings (Exod. 23:18), and was presented only by apostates (Amos 4:5). The taboo was explicit in connection with the Passover and the Feast of Unleavened Bread (Exod. 13:6-7) but, according to Judg. 6:19-21, the bread of God also was unleavened. Such leaven as was necessarily involved in first fruits was given only to the priests, but not set on the altar (Lev. 23:17, 20). Cakes of unleavened bread (רקיקים)

are mentioned in Exod. 29:23; Lev. 8:26; Num. 6:19.

E. THE CONDITION OF PURITY. All sacrifices and offerings involved contact with divinity, and were therefore in the category of the "holy," or supramundane (cf. קדשים as a generic term for them, in Exod. 28:38; Lev. 21:22; 23:6-7, 12; Num. 18:19; II Kings 12:19; II Chr. 29:33; 35:13; Neh. 10:34). Moreover, since, in many cases, the essence of the sacrificial ceremony was to provide a means whereby that quality might be absorbed, care had to be taken to ensure that it be kept free of contamination. Sacrificial animals had therefore to be whole and without blemish (Lev. 1, *passim;* 22:19-20; Deut. 15:21; 17:1; cf. Mal. 1:7, 13); while in the case of cereals, all leavened (i.e., putrefied) food was forbidden in offerings made by fire to the deity (Lev. 2:11; cf. Exod. 23:18; Judg. 6:19-20; Amos 4:5), being permitted only when the sacrificial fare was to be eaten by men (Lev. 7:13; 23:17), and even then, not in the paschal ceremony (Exod. 13:6-7). Furthermore, to ensure absolute purity, the fat of sacred animals, which was consigned to the god, was not allowed to remain on the altar overnight (Exod. 23:18).

The priests and all other participants in a sacrificial ceremony had likewise to be in a state of purity; maimed, deformed, and diseased persons were excluded (Lev. 21:17-23). Precautions had also to be taken to ensure that the portions allotted to the priests be eaten in a place deemed "holy" (Lev. 24:9; Ezek. 42:13; 46:20).

Such regulations reflect standard practice in antiquity. The Babylonians too insisted that sacrificial animals be perfect (*šalmu*), and the Hittites that female beasts presented at the altar be such as had never been covered. Similarly, a common epithet of priests both in Mesopotamia and in Egypt was "the pure one" (*ellu; w'b*); while rigid rules for priestly cleanliness are prescribed also in Hittite texts (e.g., *ANET* 207-10). Lastly, the same insistence that the sacred precincts be kept unsullied obtained both among the Hittites and among the Greeks.

1. Prohibition against breaking bones. The basic requirement that *materia sacra* must be whole and unimpaired finds expression also in the rule, imposed in connection with the paschal sacrifice, that the bones of the victim be not broken (Exod. 12:46; Num. 9:12; cf. John 19:36). Bone, like blood, represents the essential self (cf. עצם, גרם, "self"), so that what is implied is that the life used in a sacramental meal must be unimpaired.

2. Ritual nudity. On the other hand, the supervening prejudices of the Israelites seem to have imposed the discontinuance of another ancient practice originally designed to the same end—namely, that of approaching the altar *in puris naturalibus*, lest clothes convey impurity (cf. Exod. 20:26). At the same time, what was really an attenuation of this usage—viz., the custom of removing one's shoes at a holy place—was indeed retained (cf. Exod. 3:5). Both usages are well attested elsewhere. Ritual nudity is evidenced for early Mesopotamian cultus by plaques from Lagash, Ur, and Nippur, a vase from Uruk, clay figurines from Khafaje. It likewise characterized the pre-Islamic rite of the *ṭawâf*, or ritual circumambulation of the altar, and survived sporadically in Arabic liturgical procedure. Indeed, to this day, Palestinian Arab women sometimes remove their clothes when invoking *welis*.

A seal from Lagash shows a worshiper standing unshod before his god; while Herodian says explicitly (V.6.10) that the Phoenicians removed their linen stockings when entering on holy ground.

3. Apotropaic measures. Closely associated with the foregoing provisions for purity was the necessity of averting noxious and untoward influence (e.g., demons) from sacrifices and offerings. The latter were therefore accompanied by various apotropaic practices.

a. Salt. Every offering had to be accompanied by salt (Lev. 2:13; cf. Ezek. 43:24). According to the LXX (Lev. 24:7), this applied also to the bread of the Presence. In the Levitical prescription, this is associated with the well-known custom of sealing covenants by sharing bread and salt (Num. 18:19), being thus taken to symbolize the covenant thereby established between the god and his human "kinsmen." In that case, the purpose of the salt would have been simply to prevent premature putrefaction of the covenantal fare. It is not improbable, however, that the real purpose—at least originally—was to avert demons, for the belief that salt, being an incorruptible substance, is immune to such corrosive influences and can impart this immunity to any who consume or hold it, is widespread in folklore, surviving even in the Catholic rite of baptism (cf. T.B. Ber. 40a).

The sacrificial use of salt finds parallels in Babylonian, as also in Greek and Roman usage (cf. Theocritus XXIV.97; Tibullus III.4.15).

b. Blowing of the ram's horn. At New Moon, seasonal festivals, and other ceremonial occasions, the ram's horn (שופר) was blown over sacrifices (Num. 10:10). This is explained as a "memorial before Yahweh your God," and in Lev. 23:24 the first day of the seventh month is described as a "day of memorial of the trump" (orig. tr. cf. Num. 29:1; Ps. 81:3—H 81:4). The meaning of this expression is, however, quite obscure, and it seems likely that the original purpose of the trumpet-blowing was to scare away those demons and noxious spirits which are universally believed to be rampant "at the dark o' the moon" and on other crucial calendar dates; for this is standard practice in many parts of the world.

The basic principle would be reflected also in the custom of attaching bells to the robe of the high priest to prevent his meeting death when he entered the holy of holies (Exod. 28:33-35), for bells likewise avert demons.

c. Circumambulation of the altar. To the same order of apotropaic precautions belongs also the practice, mentioned in Ps. 26:6, of circumambulating the altar, for this procedure, likewise widespread in religious usage, is usually designed to keep out demons. Such circuits are mentioned in later sources (e.g., M. Suk. IV.5) as part of the ritual of the Feast of Booths, and they find their counterpart in the circular dance around the altar in early Arabic ritual. Indeed, in South Arabic, the altar was actually called "place of circuit" (*qyf, mqf*). For a classical parallel, cf. Ovid *Metamorphoses* VII.258.

F. *ATTITUDE OF THE PROPHETS.* Once the real nature and function of sacrifice are made clear,

the statements of the prophets about the current observance of it (e.g., Isa. 1:11-14; Amos 5:21-23; Mic. 6:6-9) can be better appreciated. Contrary to a widespread impression that there was a fundamental antithesis on this subject between the religion of the law and that of the prophets, the truth is that the latter were not against sacrifice per se, but simply against the abuse of it; and, as a matter of fact, Isaiah (1:15) inveighed equally against hypocritical prayer. Their protest was directed primarily against the attribution to sacrifice of properties and virtues which in fact it did not, and could not, possess; especially against the view that it expressed of itself the spiritual bond between worshiper and God, that God could thereby be persuaded or compelled, and that a man could be spiritually shriven by being ritually cleansed. Nowhere, however, in all the prophetic literature of the OT, is there any denial of the premise that, within its prescribed limits, sacrifice was indeed an effective religious vehicle; the advance beyond this assumption is entirely postbiblical.

G. *LATER DEVELOPMENTS.* A detailed account of sacrificial usage in the second temple is furnished in the fifth section ("order") of the Mishna, entitled *Qôdhāšîm*, "hallowed things." This includes, besides others, special treatises on: immolations (*Zebhāḥîm*), cereal offerings (*Menāḥôth*), firstlings (*Bekhôrôth*), substitutions (*Temûrah*), sacrilege (*Meˁîlah*), the continual offering (*Tāmîdh*), and offerings of fowl permitted as a concession to the poor (*Qinnîm*).

Sacrifices and offerings were divided broadly into the two categories of (*a*) "sacred in the highest degree" (קדש קדשים) and (*b*) "sacred in lower degree" (קדשים קלים). The former comprised: the whole burnt offering (עולה), the regular cereal offering (מנחה), the clearance ("sin") offering (חטאת), and the mulct (אשם); while the latter covered those offerings of which the presenter also partook (i.e., the שלמים), including the thank offering (תודה), the votive offering (נדר), the freewill offering (נדבה), and the paschal sacrifice (פסח).

In accordance with the rules laid down in the Pentateuch, an animal sacrifice was held to consist in six consecutive acts: (*a*) the imposition of hands on the victim (סמיכה); (*b*) the slaughtering (שחיטה); (*c*) the gathering up of the blood (קבלה); (*d*) the conveyance of the blood to the altar (הולכה); (*e*) the aspersion of the blood (זריקה); and (*f*) the burning of the dedicated portion (הקטרה). If the offering were one of fowl, the three essential acts were: (*a*) the "pinching off" of the head (מליקה; cf. Lev. 1:15; 5:8); (*b*) the squeezing out of the blood against the side of the altar (מצוי); and (*c*) the burning of the dedicated portions (הקטרה).

1. Rabbinical Judaism. There was a difference of opinion as to whether one hand, or both hands, should be used in the act of imposition (סמיכה). The Jerusalem Talmud prescribes the former, but the Babylonian (Men. 95a) the latter. Note, in this connection, that in Num. 27:18 the MT enjoins that Moses is to impose but one hand upon Joshua when ordaining him, yet in vs. 23 it is said that he in fact imposed two hands. The LXX has the plural in both cases, while Samar. and Peshitta read the singular also in the latter verse.

The act was performed by the offerer, but was

omitted when the latter was deaf, blind, mentally defective, a slave, or a woman. It was omitted also at all communal sacrifices, except that offered as a collective אשם (cf. Lev. 4:13) and in the rite of the scapegoat on the Day of Atonement. Furthermore, according to Rabbi Simeon (Men. 92*a*), in the case of a sacrifice offered in expiation of public idolatry, the act was to be performed by the elders, as indicated in Lev. 4:15.

The only wine libations permitted were of red wine; this restriction was based on Ps. 75:8—H 75:9, which was understood to mean: "In Yahweh's hand is a cup of *red* wine." Actually, this is a misinterpretation, for the word rendered "red," חמר, derives from חמר I, "be foaming" (cf. Ugaritic Poem of "Shahar and Shalim" 6: *ḫmr yn*), not from חמר II, "be red."

In treating of the practical efficacy of sacrifices and offerings, the rabbis were careful to distinguish between expiation and atonement. The former implied simply the removal of the taint of sin and the restoration of the damaged psyche (נפש). The latter, however, meant actual reconciliation with God, the re-establishment of an impaired relationship. The one, as Rabbi Judah put it (J. T. Yom. 8.7), could be effected automatically by the very procedure of sacrifice; the other, however, depended entirely on spiritual posture and inward effort—above all, on repentance and amendment (תשובה; J. T. Yom. 8.3; Tosef. Yôm Kippurîm 5.9; cf. Ecclus. 34:12–35; Philo *De plantatione Noë* III.10). All sacrifices except שלמים possessed inherently the power of expiation, and in certain circumstances this applied also to the חטאת and אשם (Yom. 8.5-6; T. B. Yom. 86*a;* J. T. Yom. 45*b;* cf. Mek., Jethrô, 7). That power lay in the blood (B. T. Zeb. 6*a;* Yom. 5*a*), as implied in Lev. 17:11. But the total regeneration of the sinner involved both expiation and atonement together; neither was complete without the other.

Following the destruction of the temple in A.D. 70, prayer was held to be the legitimate substitute for sacrifice (T. B. Ber. 15*a-b,* 33*a;* Suk. 45*a;* Ta'an. 26*a-27b;* Meg. 31*a*), the services of the synagogue being named for the statutory daily oblations—viz., שחרית, "morning service"; מנחה, "afternoon service"; and ערבית, "evening service," with a supplementary מוסף, or "additional service," on New Moons, sabbaths, and holy days.

A foregleam of this concept may be seen in the development of the Hebrew word עתר from the meaning of "sacrifice" (cf. עתר, "fume," in Ezek. 8: 11; Arabic *'athara*), "to entreat." The precentor in the synagogue was held to substitute for the sacrificing priest (T. B. Ber. 8*b*).

In the synagogal services for New Moon and holy days, the appropriate sacrificial regulations are read, from a second scroll, as an additional lesson from the Law; and on the Day of Atonement an account of the sacrificial ritual in the temple (עבודה), based on the Mishna, forms a high light of the additional service (*Mūsāf*).

2. Sectarian attitudes. The attitude of the Dead Sea Covenanters toward sacrifice is a matter of debate among scholars. Some forty careful deposits of animal bones, discovered in 1955 in the Qumran compound, have been explained by R. de Vaux as the remains of offerings; but it is difficult to see how a community so firmly committed to the traditional law could ever have countenanced sacrifice outside the "chosen place" in Jerusalem. Moreover, the quantity of the bones is too small to represent a continuous practice. The literary evidence, too, is ambiguous. In one passage of the so-called Zadokite Document (XI.18) there is, indeed, a provision concerning the dispatch of offerings to the altar. Elsewhere, however (e.g., 1QM II.5-6), reference to sacrifice seems to be made only in prescriptions for the future dispensation of Israel; while in a hymn appended to the Manual of Discipline (col. X) statutory prayers are said to serve as the equivalent of the daily and seasonal oblations ordained in the Law.

This last seems also to have represented the attitude of the ESSENES, for Josephus says of them (War I.iii.5) that they did not make offerings at Jerusalem but "offered sacrifices *within themselves.*" The meaning of these crucial words, however, is disputed. Another interpretation is that they signify rather, *"among* themselves," and thus indicate the existence of an independent sacrificial system.

The view that prayer took the place of sacrifice became normative also, of course, in Christianity (Did. 14).

Bibliography. General: W. R. Smith, *The Religion of the Semites* (3rd ed., 1927); E. O. James, *The Origins of Sacrifice* (1933); A. Bertholet, *Der Sinn des kultischen Opfers* (1942).

On sacrifice in the OT: G. B. Gray, *Sacrifice in the OT* (1924); A. Medebielle, "De sacrificii israelitici origine et natura," *Verbum Domini,* VII (1926), 214-19, 238-44; A. Wendel, *Das Opfer in der altisraelitischen Religion* (1927); A. Bertholet, "Zum Verständniss der ATlichen Opfergedanken," *JBL,* XLIX (1930), 218-33; W. O. E. Oesterley, *Sacrifices in Ancient Israel* (1938); H. H. Rowley, "The Meaning of Sacrifice in the OT," *Bulletin of the John Rylands Library,* XXXIII (1950), 74-110; R. de Vaux, *Les institutions de l'AT,* II (1960), 291-362.

For comparative material: G. Furlani, "Il sacrificio nella religione dei semiti di Babylonia e Assiria," *Atti della Accademia nazionale dei Lincei,* IV (1932), 103 ff; F. X. Kortleiner, *Formae cultus Mosaici cum ceteris religionibus Orientis antiqui comparatae* (3rd ed., 1933); F. Blome, *Die Opfermaterie in Babylonien und Israel* (1934); R. Dussaud, *Les origines cananéennes du sacrifice israélite* (2nd ed., 1948); R. K. Yerkes, *Sacrifice in Greek and Roman Religion and in Early Judaism* (1952); A. Guglielmo, "Sacrifice in the Ugaritic Texts," *Catholic Biblical Quarterly,* XVII (1955), 196-216.

On later developments: O. Schmitz, *Die Opferschauung des späteren Judentums und die Opferaussagen des NTs* (1910).

On commensality: L. R. Farnell, "Sacrificial Communion in Greek Religion," *The Hibbert Journal* (1904); W. T. McCree, "The Covenantal Meal in the OT," *JBL,* XLV (1926), 120-28; F. Bammel, *Das heilige Mahl im Glauben der Voelker* (1950).

On expiatory offerings: W. Schrank, *Babylonische Sühnriten* (1908); A. Medebielle, "Le symbolisme du sacrifice expiatoire en Israel," *Bibl.,* II (1921), 146-69, 273-302; C. F. Jean, *Le péché chez les Babyloniens et les Assyriens* (1925); R. Pettazzoni, *La confessione dei peccati* (1926); P. Scötz, *Schuld-und Sündopfer im AT* (1930); F. Sole, "Concetto di sacrificio di peccato e di espiazione presso il popolo ebraico," *La Scuola Cattolica,* LX (1932), 25-41; L. Moraldi, *Espiazione sacrificale e riti espiatori nell' ambiente biblico* (1956).

On first fruits and tithes: O. Eissfeldt, *Erstlinge und Zehnte im AT* (1917).

On human sacrifice (offerings to Molech): E. Mader, *Die Menschenopfer der alten Hebräer und der benachbarten Völker*

(1919); O. Eissfeldt, *Molk als Opferbegriff im Punischen und Hebräischen und das Ende des Gottes Moloch* (1935); A. Bea, "Kinderopfer für Moloch oder für Jahveh?" *Bibl.*, XVIII (1937), 95-107; W. Kornfeld, "Der Moloch," *Wiener Zeitschrift für die Kunde des Morgenlandes* (1952), 287-313 (against Eissfeldt); H. Dronkert, *De Molochdienst in het OT* (1953; against Eissfeldt).

On incense: M. Löhr, *Das Räuchopfer im AT* (1927); M. Haran, "The Censer Incense and Tamid Incense," *Tarbiz*, XXVI (1956), 115-25 (Hebrew).　　T. H. GASTER

SACRIFICE IN THE NT. *See* ATONEMENT.

SACRILEGE [βδέλυγμα]. Something repulsive, loathsome, disgusting; the filching or the befouling of the sacred. In Mark 13:14 and the parallel in Matt. 24:15, the RSV translates the word "sacrilege" (KJV "abomination of desolation"), but in Luke 16:15; Rev. 17:4-5; 21:27, where it also appears, the RSV uses "abomination." *See* ABOMINATION THAT MAKES DESOLATE.

Matt. 24:15; Mark 13:14 have exactly the same expression as is found in the LXX of Dan. 12:11, and with slight differences in Dan. 9:27; 11:31. In the Daniel passages the "abomination that makes desolate" (שקוץ שמם) refers to the small Greek altar which the Seleucid tyrant Antiochus IV Epiphanes had erected on the altar of burnt offering in the Jewish temple in Jerusalem, and on which swine were offered in December of 168 B.C. This "abomination" is the profanation of the temple, which makes it desolate. Jews could not worship Yahweh in a temple having a pagan altar (cf. I Macc. 1:54).

In Mark 13:14 and the Matthean parallel the reference is not to the second-century profanation of the temple under Antiochus Epiphanes. What, then, is the "desolating sacrilege" in the gospels? The most important interpretations are the following:

a) It has frequently been held that the "desolating sacrilege" refers to a statue of the Roman emperor Caligula which he decided to place in the temple in Jerusalem in A.D. 40. It has been argued, therefore, that Mark 13:14*a* was incorporated in the gospel in 40, when many Christians linked Caligula's threat with the Danielic prophecy and believed that the end prophesied by Jesus had really come. This interpretation has much to commend it, but it has some difficulties as well:

The mad Caligula was murdered in January, A.D. 41, and his statue was never installed. The fulfillment of the Danielic prophecy was thus a threat to the church for only about a year. How, then, did Caligula's intention become so permanently embedded in the gospel record?

The Greek for "sacrilege" is neuter, but the participle translated "set up" is masculine, suggesting that a person was being referred to and not a statue.

The consequences described which are to ensue from the setting up of the sacrilege (vss. 14*b* ff) are hard to harmonize with the setting up of a statue in the temple. They are to occur too suddenly and appear to be conceived as having a supernatural cause.

b) A second interpretation is that the reference is to the Antichrist, or man of sin, or lawless one—i.e., to a supernatural figure such as is expected in II

Thess. 2:3-10; Rev. 12; 19-20. Three questions arise concerning this interpretation:

If an individual is referred to in vs. 14*a*, how is he related to the "false Christs and false prophets" of vs. 22? Is he supernatural, while they are not?

If vss. 14*b*-27 are to be interpreted as describing the situation to exist at the coming of the Antichrist, then can we accept any of these words as authentic words of Jesus?

Is the phrase "set up where it ought not to be" easily taken as describing the Antichrist? Who "sets up" the Antichrist, and where *ought* he to be?

c) A third view is that the reference is to the Roman army at the time of the war in 66-73, when it ravaged Judea and destroyed the temple. Vss. 14*b* ff seem to describe wartime conditions; and, furthermore, this is Luke's interpretation (21:20-24). But there are factors weighing against this view also:

The expression "set up where it ought not to be" does not describe a war.

Do vss. 14*b* ff really describe wartime conditions? Surely vss. 24-27 do not; but do vss. 15-18? Do not all these verses describe a supernatural event, which will not be accomplished by an army (at least by a first-century army) and which will not last for seven years? Luke apparently had another source besides Mark, and it may be older than Mark.

d) A fourth view is that Mark did not intend any particular thing, or person, or event, in 13:14*a*, but that he referred only to some unknown but horrible desecration of the temple, which must take place before the end.

e) Finally, it is possible that the words "desolating sacrilege set up where it ought not to be" were not originally a part of the context at all, and that the context, therefore, does not shed any light on their meaning, which may have to remain a mystery for the present.　　B. H. THROCKMORTON, JR.

SADAMIAS săd′ə mī′əs. KJV Apoc. form of SHALLUM 9.

SADAS sā′dəs. KJV Apoc. form of AZGAD.

SADDEUS. KJV Apoc. form of IDDO.

SADDLE [מרכב, *from* רכב, to ride]. A cloth or leather seat for a rider, strapped to the back of an animal.

In the biblical world asses were the oldest riding animals, and a piece of cloth or leather, fastened by a girth, served as the saddle. Doubtless the wisdom of doubling the cloth, or padding it, must have been recognized, but anything approaching a saddle in the modern sense was unfamiliar to the OT, and appears to have emerged only in Scythia in the fourth century B.C. Thence it came into the Mediterranean area, but it was not fully developed until the Christian era.

The noun "saddle" is found in the Bible only in Lev. 15:9. The verb "to saddle" (חבש, lit., "bind," "bind on"), found only in the OT, is always used of saddling asses (Gen. 22:3; Num. 22:21; II Sam. 17:23; etc.).　　W. S. McCULLOUGH

SADDLECLOTHS [בגדי חפש, cloths *or* clothes of *ḥōphesh; cf.* Akkad. *ḥipšu*, a kind of cloth] (Ezek. 27:

20); KJV PRECIOUS CLOTHES. Ornamental cloths used with saddles "for riding" (לרכבה; KJV "for chariots"). They were a trade item of Tyre from Dedan in Arabia. H. G. May

SADDUC. KJV Apoc. form of ZADOK THE PRIEST.

SADDUCEES săj'ə sēz [צדוקים; Σαδδουκαίοι, *from* ZADOK]. The priestly, aristocratic party in Judaism, whose interests centered in the temple, and whose views and practices opposed those of the PHARISEES. Arising following the Maccabean Rebellion, the Sadducees supported the Hasmonean development of the Jewish state. The Romans attempted to dominate the priesthood by controlling the high priests, but with little success. The Sadducees suffered heavily in the revolt against Rome that culminated in the fall of Jerusalem, and they were no longer influential in Judaism after A.D. 70.

1. Derivation and use of the name
2. History
   a. Origin
   b. The Hasmonean period
   c. Under the Romans
3. Characteristics
4. Views and doctrines
Bibliography

1. Derivation and use of the name. The name Sadducee was probably derived from the Zadok who was, together with Abiathar, priest under David, and was appointed (chief) priest, displacing Abiathar, by Solomon (I Kings 2:26 ff, 35; cf. 1:8; 5:7). Church fathers (e.g., Epiphanius *Heresies* I.14; Jerome *Commentary* on Matt. 22:13), and formerly some scholars, thought that the name was derived from the adjective צדיק (*zadik*), "righteous." However, the vowel change from "i" to "u" is inexplicable. While the name is probably derived from the personal name Zadok, the question has been disputed as to which Zadok. A ninth-century rabbinic legend (ARN 5) names Zadok, a disciple of Antigonus Soko, as the father of the Sadducees. Antigonus, according to the legend, taught that one ought to serve God without expectation of reward. This teaching has been interpreted as a denial of a future life, similar to that noted among the Sadducees. However, the legend is too late to be of historical value. Moreover, it erroneously mentions the Boethusians as a party originating at the same time as the Sadducees. The term "Boethusians" has been shown to be a popular, derisive synonym for Sadducees, originating during Roman times (Jos. Antiq. XIX.vi.2). A conjecture that the Sadducees derived their name from a hypothetical Zadok, perhaps contemporary with Jonathan the Hasmonean, has little to commend it.

It is now commonly accepted that the name Sadducee was derived from Solomon's priest Zadok, who became the father of the Jerusalem priesthood. The reforms of Josiah (621 B.C.), patterned upon the Deuteronomic Code (*see* DEUTERONOMY), left Jerusalem the sole sanctuary in Judah. But while the Code allowed provincial priests to officiate in Jerusalem (Deut. 12; 18:6-8), in practice the provincial priests were prevented from sacrificing there (II Kings 23: 9). It seems possible that it was at this time that the Jerusalem priesthood advanced their claim of descent from Zadok as the test of legitimacy. In Ezekiel's ideal theocracy only the "sons of Zadok" were permitted to "come near to the LORD to minister to him" (Ezek. 40:45-46; 43:19; 44:15; 48:11). It is possible, however, that the requirements of Ezekiel were liberalized or not strictly followed, so that other "Levites" obtained a place among the priests through the expediency of circumventing Zadok in tracing their family line back to Aaron (cf. Lev. 10: 1 ff). The Hebrew text of Ecclesiasticus preserves a special blessing for the priests: "Give thanks unto him that chose the sons of Zadok to be the priests" (51:12), which brings the tradition of the Zadokite origin of the priesthood down to approximately the beginning of the second century B.C. In the NT the high priests and their party are called the Sadducees (Acts 4:1-5; 5:17). In Josephus, Sadducees are identified with the priestly, aristocratic families (Antiq. XVIII.i.4; XX.ix.1; etc.). It seems likely, therefore, that a party, gravitating about the priesthood, that traditionally traced its origin to Solomon's priest Zadok, was known as the Sadducees.

2. History. While the Sadducees derived their name and lineage from the father of the Jerusalem priesthood, it appears that they emerged as a party in Judaism during Maccabean times (*see* MACCABEES; HASMONEAN). Following the ill-conceived attempt to re-establish the monarchy under ZERUBBABEL, leadership among the Jews centered about the priesthood. It was not, however, until recognized divisions, or schools of thought and practice, arose in Judaism that the Sadducees became known as a party.

a. Origin. The Jewish priesthood is traditionally said to have descended from Aaron. Some scholars trace the origin of the Sadducees (as well as that of their name) to Zadok the father of the Jerusalem priests, or to Joshua the priest of the return from Babylon. It is more probable that the Sadducees arose as a party subsequent to the Maccabean Rebellion. The first mention of Sadducees in the days of John Hyrcanus (135-104 B.C.; Jos. Antiq. XIII.x. 5-6) is frequently cited as indicative of the time of their origin. This story in Josephus is problematical, but there are other indications that the Sadducees became recognized as a party subsequent to the Maccabean Rebellion. It appears that the old priestly line, Hellenized in the days of Antiochus IV Epiphanes (175-163), was disrupted by the rebellion (I Macc. 2:44-48; 7:5 ff; cf. 10:14). This necessitated the creation of a new high-priestly line: Simon Maccabeus (142-135) and his successors (I Macc. 14:41; cf. 4:42-46; I Chr. 24:7; possibly Ps. 110). Thus the priestly party of the Sadducees must have grown about the loyal priesthood and centered in the new Hasmonean high priests. Also, at this time the Hasidim, thought to be the forerunners of the Pharisees, were first mentioned (I Macc. 2:42; 7:5-23). About the same time the doctrine of resurrection, a bone of contention between Sadducees and Pharisees, was promulgated in Judaism (Dan. 12:2; *see* DANIEL). Thus, the reorganization of the priesthood and the appearance of factors of differentiation between sectarian parties in Judaism about the time of the Maccabean Rebellion suggests that the Sadducees came to be recognized as a party not long after the reorganization of Judaism under Maccabean leadership.

b. The Hasmonean period. The Hasmoneans continued as high priests until the Roman period, usually with the support of the temple priesthood. Early in the dynasty monarchical aspirations appeared with attempts to re-establish the borders of the Davidic kingdom under John Hyrcanus (135-104 B.C.) and his sons. The Hasmonean break with the Pharisees, possibly under Hyrcanus, was probably over the spectacle of the high priest's engaging in military exploits (cf. I Chr. 28:3, according to which David was prevented from building the temple because he had shed blood). With Aristobulus (104-103), the Hasmoneans adopted the royal title. But when Salome Alexandra (76-67) succeeded her husband, Alexander Janneus (103-76), to the throne, she appointed her elder son, Hyrcanus II, high priest without civil authority. Turning from the priestly (Sadducean) influence, she became greatly influenced by the Pharisees (Simon ben Shetach, a famous Pharisee, was her brother). For the first time the Pharisees became influential in the government (Jos. War I.iv-v; Antiq. XIII.xvi.1-6). Apparently fearing the control of government would be lost by the indolent Hyrcanus, Aristobulus II (67-63), a younger but more vigorous son of Janneus, began an insurrection in which, after his mother's death, he displaced Hyrcanus as high priest and resumed the royal title his father had borne. However, when Hyrcanus was induced by Antipater (the father of Herod the Great) to seek to regain his crown, there followed a struggle between the brothers that was concluded only by the intervention of Rome in 63 B.C. In this struggle the priests supported whichever faction appeared likely to gain control (Jos. War I.vi.1; cf. Antiq. XIV.ii.1). But when the brothers appealed to Pompey, the nation, according to Josephus, was against both of them, complaining that the brothers, though descendants from the priests, were trying to change the form of government from a rule of the priests to a monarchy (Antiq. XIV.iii.2); and when the temple fell before Pompey, the priests, no longer wavering, fanatically continued the temple service in the face of death (Jos. War I.vii.4; Antiq. XIV.iv.3). Pompey appointed Hyrcanus II high priest, in return for his support during the siege, and placed the land under Roman jurisdiction (Jos. War I.vii.6-7; Antiq. XIV.iv.4-5).

c. Under the Romans. As during the Hasmonean period, knowledge of the Sadducees under the Romans is primarily to be derived from Josephus' accounts of the high priesthood. The attempts of Aristobulus II and his son Alexander to unseat Hyrcanus II and restore the Hasmonean monarchy reflect no priestly concern. The rise of Herod, however, did represent a usurpation of power that the priests considered rightfully theirs. Hence, it was possibly Sadducean pressure that stirred Hyrcanus II to bring Herod to trial for the execution of a brigand chief and his followers (Jos. War I.xii.5; Antiq. XIV.xii.2). Likewise, Antigonus, son of Aristobulus II, probably received Sadducean support when he drove out the now pro-Herod Hyrcanus II, and became king and high priest for three years (40-37). For such partisanship the Sadducees suffered in Herod's revenge when he took Jerusalem in 37 B.C. (Jos. War I.xviii.4;

Antiq. XV.i.1). Becoming king (37-4), he adopted the policy of appointing and removing puppet high priests at will. His appointment of Aristobulus III (35-34), a Hasmonean, to quiet family pressures, nearly brought an insurrection to remove Herod in favor of Aristobulus. Shortly thereafter, Herod had him drowned (Jos. War I.xxii.2; Antiq. XV.ii.5-iii.3).

The procession of high priests under Herod's son, Archelaus (4 B.C.–A.D. 6), Herod Agrippa (A.D. 41-44), and the procurators (A.D. 6-41, 44-66), was patently the result of the unsuccessful attempts of the Roman authorities to find high priests who would long continue quietly subservient. The high priesthood of Joazar illustrates the prevailing conditions: Herod appointed Joazar high priest when the high priest Matthias became implicated in the attempt to remove a golden eagle from above the great gate of the temple (Jos. Antiq. XVII.vi.2-4; War I.xxxiii.2-3). Upon Herod's death, the populace demanded unsuccessfully that Joazar be removed in favor of a more fitting high priest (Jos. War II.i.2-3; Antiq. XVII.ix.1-3). However, when Archelaus returned from having his rule confirmed in Rome, he removed Joazar on suspicion that he had participated in the insurrections during his absence (Jos. Antiq. XVII. xviii.1). This apparently was not without cause, since, when Archelaus was exiled to Vienna, the people conferred the high priesthood on Joazar! The prefect of Syria soon removed him in favor of a safe incumbent (Jos. Antiq. XVIII.ii.1). Josephus numbers twenty-eight high priests from the days of Herod until the fall of Jerusalem (Antiq. XX.x.1). Another evidence of the Romans' attempt to control the high priesthood is seen in their insistence on custody of the vestments of the high priest during the periods of the procurators.

Josephus was anxious to show that the leading Jews, the high priests, and the chief Pharisees desired to avert the disastrous revolution of 66-70 (War II.xv.2-4; xvi.2; xvii.2). But this does not hide the fact that Eleazar, the governor of the temple and son of Ananias the high priest, initiated the decisive act of revolt in refusing to accept temple sacrifices for foreigners, thus preventing the daily sacrifices for the Roman emperor. The temple priesthood evidently supported Eleazar, since he was able to enforce the restriction (Jos. War II.xvii.2). This suggests an alignment of a preponderance of the priesthood with Eleazar against the Romans and their puppet high priest; this preponderance of the priesthood certainly was the Sadducees. When Ananias was murdered, Eleazar made a bid against Menahem for leadership of the revolt; he was supported by the Sadducees (Jos. War II.xvii.9). Josephus himself was of an aristocratic, priestly family (Jos. Life I)—a Sadducee, though he later became a Pharisee. It was his Sadducean status that secured for him a command in Galilee early in the war (Jos. War II.xx.4).

Following the destruction of Jerusalem and the temple in A.D. 70, the Sadducees no longer played an important role in Judaism. The reorganization of Judaism at Jamnia (*ca.* 90) was along Pharisaic lines. The loss of Sadducean influence cannot be accounted for simply by the destruction of the temple; the Jews anticipated the rebuilding of the temple. Probably the Sadducees, concentrated about Jerusalem, and being implicated in the war, suffered heavily with the fall of the city. Thus diminished, their influence was overweighed by the preponderance of Pharisees in the postwar period.

3. Characteristics. Scholarly opinion usually has characterized the Sadducees as the high-priestly party that supported Hellenization under Antiochus IV Epiphanes, and revived these interests in support of the Hasmonean dynasty. In Roman times, being at home in the wider world of Hellenistic culture, and with their interests essentially political, they supported the status quo. In contrast, the Pharisees are described as Jews, loyal to the law and repulsing the inroads of Hellenistic influence. In consequence, the Sadducees are regarded as easy collaborationists with the Romans, or, as Josephus suggests (Antiq. XVIII. i.4), without influence on the populace, forced to follow Pharisaic directions. This position, however, embodies serious problems. It is doubtful that influence by Hellenized elements of the priesthood survived the Maccabean Rebellion. Moreover, it has been shown that the Pharisees were influenced by Hellenism to such a degree as to make Hellenism among the Sadducees no longer a remarkable differentiation. Hellenization among both parties, and in Judaism in general, after the Maccabean Rebellion must have been largely incidental and unconscious. Josephus' histories do not support the assertion that the Sadducees were willing tools of the Romans. They at times were obliged to serve as magistrates; but, according to Josephus, they did so reluctantly (Antiq. XVIII.i.4). Moreover, it has been shown that Josephus, in his *Antiquities,* has rewritten the history to exaggerate the importance of the Pharisees and make the Sadducees appear subservient to them. His purpose, apparently, was to suggest that the Romans should support the Pharisees, if they hoped to succeed in their dealings with the Jews. In reality, however, Sadducean influence was eclipsed only after A.D. 70.

Another characterization depicts the Sadducean-Pharisaic distinction as one between economic classes: the aristocratic priesthood against the urban shopkeeper. The Sadducees, slow to shed their inheritance from provincial surroundings, maintained the violence and crudity of the rustic; loud and crude manners maintained aristocratic authority over subordinates. The Pharisees, on the other hand, were mild mannered, as is needful for market-place merchants to induce customers to buy. Again, the Sadducee-Pharisee opposition has been described as a conflict between two theories on the nature of Judaism: the Sadducees were devoted to the politico-secular interests of Judaism as a state; the Pharisees viewed Judaism as a spiritual religion independent of ties to nationalism and politics. Another hypothesis suggests that the Sadducees represented the interests of the temple and its priesthood as compared with the Pharisees, who represented the interests of the synagogue and its teachers. But such sharp demarcations do not seem to have existed between the Sadducees and the Pharisees.

The Sadducees are more readily understood as defenders of their priestly prerogatives. These included their religious interests (the performance of the tem-

ple service and the priestly interpretation of the law) and their political interests (Israel was viewed as a theocratic state properly organized under the leadership of the high priest). The Sadducees learned from the proscription of Judaism by Antiochus IV Epiphanes (I Macc. 14:25-65), and the threat of the Roman emperor Gaius to desecrate the temple (Jos. Antiq. XVIII.viii), that foreign domination was more than a matter of politics; it represented a constant threat to the one important thing, the uninterrupted temple service. And foreign domination abrogated the high priest's right to rule. Likewise, the controversy with the Pharisees over the oral law probably arose from the priestly prerogative to interpret the law. The oral law probably did not arise in opposition to the priestly interpretation of the law. But, since the priesthood was concentrated in Jerusalem, authoritative priestly interpretation of the law was available only at Jerusalem. It may be that the oral law had its origin in lay transmission of priestly interpretation of the law to remote areas of Judaism. This oral commentary on the law was developed and came to be regarded as authoritative by laymen, since they had not the priestly right of immediate interpretation of the law. But the laymen recognized no antagonism against the priesthood in preserving this tradition. However, any tradition of interpretation tended to restrict the priestly prerogative of immediate interpretation of the law. Therefore, the Sadducees rejected the authority of the Pharisaic oral law (Jos. Antiq. XIII.x.6; XVIII.i.4), and consequently were free to agree or to differ with it. The Sadducean student need not regard the teacher as authoritative; it was a virtue to discuss and dispute with him (Jos. Antiq. XVIII.i.4; War II.viii.14). It probably is a mistake to suppose that the Sadducees rejected the Prophets and the Writings, as some Christian fathers suggest (Hippolytus, *Refutation of Heresies* 9:29; Epiphanius, *l. c.* I.14; *see* CANON OF THE OT). But the Sadducees did not receive even these as authoritative commentaries on the law. The law stood alone, unencumbered, subject to immediate interpretation; any tradition of interpretation could be challenged.

4. Views and doctrines. The NT (Matt. 22:23; Mark 12:18; Luke 20:27; Acts 4:1-2; 23:8) and Josephus (Antiq. XVIII.i.3-4; War II.viii.14) agree that the Sadducees denied the doctrine of the resurrection of the body; Josephus adds that they denied all future punishments and rewards, holding that the soul perishes with the body (cf. Hippolytus *Refutation of Heresies* 9:29). According to Acts (23:8), they also denied the existence of angels and spirits. Josephus tells us that they also denied fate (War II.viii.14; Antiq. XIII.v.9). The reason for these denials probably was that the foregoing doctrines were not found in the law.

All our information concerning the Sadducees is from their opponents and must, consequently, be regarded with caution. This is especially so when tendency or bias is noticed in the materials, such as Josephus' treatment of the Sadducees in his *Antiquities*. The rabbinic materials seem frequently to continue this tendency to disparage the Sadducees. This is certainly the case in the later rabbinic literature from the period of the Amoraim, when historical memory of the Sadducees had passed and the name

Zadduki simply signified "heretic." The Tannaitic period may preserve some historical information concerning the Sadducees. However, here, also, a depreciatory tendency is observable. Talmudic sources concur with Josephus' apologetic that in the later days public opinion forced the Sadducees to yield to Pharisaic pressures (Yom. 19*b;* Nid. 33*b;* cf. Jos. Antiq. XVIII.i.4). But this is simply reading the post-seventy situation back into earlier times. Likewise, it is doubtful that the Pharisees had any significant influence upon the priestly functions of the conduct of the temple service and festivals while the temple stood. The rabbinic material certainly is mistaken in depicting Alexander Janneus as deliberately breaking the temple ceremony at the Sukkoth feast to irritate the Pharisees; nor do priestly regulations for this feast constitute opposition to it (Suk. 43*b;* 48*b;* Tosef. Suk. 3.16; cf. Jos. Antiq. XIII.xiii.5). Similarly, the controversies between Sadducees and Pharisees over the fixing of the day of Pentecost (Meg. Ta'an. 1; Men. 65*a*), or the burden of expense for the daily burnt offerings (Meg. Ta'an. 1.1; Men. 65*b;* Shek. 3.1.3), or the disposition of the meal offering (Meg. Ta'an. 8; Men. 6.2), or the degree of purity required of those who officiated at the preparation of the ashes of the Red Heifer (Par. 3.7; Tosef. Par. 3.1-8), or the place of kindling the fire in the incense vessel carried by the high priest on the Day of Atonement (Sifra, Ahare Mot. 3; Yom. 19*b;* 53*a-b;* J. Yom. 1.39*a-b*), can have little historical relevance; these matters fell under priestly jurisdiction while the temple stood. The rabbinic assertion of the literal interpretation of the *lex talionis* (Exod. 21:23; Deut. 19:21) by the Sadducees (Meg. Ta'an. 4; B.K. 84*a*) has been shown to be too late to have historical value.

Whether discussions on matters not so evidently of priestly jurisdiction are more reliable is problematical. The Sadducees appear more lenient than the Pharisees in the treatment of false witnesses in cases of capital punishment; the Sadducees would not inflict the death penalty unless the testimony of the false witness had been decisive in the execution of the accused (Mak. 1.8; Tosef. Sanh. 6.6). Sadducees held the owner responsible for damage done by a slave as by a beast; the Pharisees distinguished between reasonable and unreasonable beings (Yad. 4.7). The Sadducees extended the power of contamination to indirect contact (Yad. 4.7), but rejected the Pharisees' assertion that the scrolls of scripture rendered the hands unclean (Yad. 4.6). They opposed the Pharisaic teaching of '*Eurib*, the merging of several private properties into one to permit the carrying of food and vessels from one house to another on the Sabbath ('Er. 6.2). The Sadducees are said to have interpreted Deut. 21:17; 25:9, regarding inheritance rights and levirate marriage literally, while the Pharisaic teachers were inclined to interpret the words figuratively (Meg. Ta'an. 4; cf. Sifre, Deut. 237; Keth. 46; Yeb. 12.6). In dating civil documents the Sadducees used the phrase "After the high priest of the Most High," and opposed the formula "According to the law of Moses and Israel," introduced by the Pharisees into divorce documents (Meg. Ta'an. 7; Yad. 4.8). It may be that some indication of the nature of Sadduceeism may be preserved in

such descriptions. However, for the most part, even in the period of the Tannaim, the concerns are of a scholastic nature. It would appear that the real issues dividing Sadducees and Pharisees were forgotten.

Bibliography. S. Schechter and C. Taylor, *The Wisdom of Ben Sira* (1899); I. Abrahams, *Studies in Pharisaism and the Gospels,* vols. I-II (1917-24); R. T. Herford, *The Pharisees* (1924); J. W. Lightley, *Jewish Sects and Parties in the Time of Christ* (1925); D. W. Riddle, *Jesus and the Pharisees* (1928); L. Ginzberg, "The Religion of the Pharisees," *Students, Scholars and Saints* (1928), pp. 88-108; E. R. Bevan, *Jewish Parties and the Law, CAH* (1932), pp. 406-16; A. Bentsen, *Zur Geschichte der Zadokiden, ZAW,* vol. 51 (1933), pp. 173-76; L. Baeck, *Die Pharisäer* (1934); B. Z. Bokser, *Pharisaic Judaism in Transition* (1935); J. Jeremias, *Jerusalem zum Zeit Jesu* (1937); L. Finkelstein, *The Pharisees* (1938); S. Zeitlin, "The Pharisees and the Gospels," in I. Davidson, ed., *Essays and Studies in Memory of L. R. Miller* (1938), pp. 235-86; T. W. Manson, "Sadducees and Pharisees—the Origin and Significance of the Names," *Bulletin of the J. Rylands Library,* no. 22 (1938), pp. 144-59; S. Lieberman, *Greek in Jewish Palestine* (1942); S. Zeitlin, *Religious and Secular Leadership* (1943); E. R. Goodenough, *Jewish Symbols in the Greco-Roman Period,* vols. I-IV (1953); M. Smith, "Palestinian Judaism in the First Century," in M. Davis, ed., *Israel: Its Role in Civilization* (1956), pp. 67-81; M. Smith, "The Image of God," *Bulletin of the J. Rylands Library,* no. 40 (1958), pp. 473-512.

A. C. SUNDBERG

SADOC. KJV Apoc. and NT form of ZADOK.

SAFFRON [כרכם, *karkōm*]. A plant and its product used in cooking and medicines. In Song of S. 4:14 the bride is described as a park (cf. Amer. Trans.) in which the choicest of trees and plants appear, and *karkōm* is listed along with imported fragrant spices which are highly prized. Saffron is extracted from the aromatic style and stigma of certain crocuses, particularly the *Crocus sativus* L. The LXX translates it κρόκος. The Arabic equivalent, *kŭrkŭm,* is defined by *za'farān,* from which the English word derives.

See also CROCUS; FLORA § A6*g;* ROSE; FOOD.

Bibliography. I. Löw, *Die Flora der Juden,* II (1924), 7-25; H. N. and A. L. Moldenke, *Plants of the Bible* (1952), p. 87.

J. C. TREVER

SAHIDIC VERSION sə hǐd'ǐk. One of the oldest and textually most important of the ancient translations of the Bible into the several dialects of Coptic. *See* VERSIONS, ANCIENT, § 5.

SAIL [נס (Isa. 33:23; ENSIGN *in* Ezek. 27:7), *cf.* Akkad. *nasāsu,* move to and fro; מפרש (Ezek. 27:7; KJV THAT WHICH THOU SPREADEST FORTH), *from* פרש, spread out]; FORESAIL [ἀρτέμων, *from* ἀρτάω, fasten to] (Acts 27:40; KJV MAINSAIL). A sheet of strong material, usually textile, which is extended on a mast to catch enough wind to propel a vessel through water.

Boats on the Sea of Galilee were fitted with a small sail, as well as with oars (Luke 8:22-23).

Mediterranean ships of the biblical period would have one or two sails, both being square or rectangular; the uncommon word ἀρτέμων in Acts 27:40 probably means "foresail," indicating a two-masted ship. Later a triangular topsail is found set above the mainsail. While ships usually ran before the wind, a skilful captain could travel windward, but this would be uncommon. The importance of the wind is reflected in Acts 27:4, 7, 15.

See also SHIPS AND SAILING.   W. S. McCULLOUGH

SAILOR [ναύτης] (Acts 27:27, 30; Rev. 18:17). As the ship on which Paul was taken to Rome neared Malta, the sailors lowered the dinghy; but the soldiers cut its ropes. Acts says that the sailors were attempting to escape from the ship (why, one would not know); but without the dinghy the ship's passengers could not make shore without running the ship aground.

Revelation records John's vision of the mourning of shipmasters and sailors over the destruction of Rome, for "all who had ships at sea grew rich by her wealth" (Rev. 18:19). *See* SHIPS AND SAILING.

     B. H. THROCKMORTON, JR.

SAINT. A translation of חסיד, קדוש, and ἅγιος, meaning "holy" or "set apart" for God's use.

1. In the OT. As the covenant people, Israel is a holy nation, being consecrated as the peculiar possession of God, who is uniquely holy and the source of HOLINESS. This relationship to God is summed up in the "code of holiness": "You shall be holy; for I the LORD your God am holy" (Lev. 19:2).

The more general term "holy one(s)" (קדש) is applied to those who are specially dedicated to God and consecrated to his service. The attendant angels of the Lord, or the company of the heavenly host or court, are so described in the "blessing of Moses":

> The LORD came from Sinai,
> . . . .
> he came from the ten thousands of holy ones
>   [KJV·"saints"] (Deut. 33:2).

> Let the heavens praise thy wonders, O LORD,
>   thy faithfulness in the assembly of the holy ones!

says the writer of Ps. 89:5 (KJV "saints" instead of "holy ones"). God is depicted "in the council of the holy ones" (Ps. 89:7; KJV "saints"); and the "holy ones" (KJV "saints") are to accompany the Lord in his self-manifestation in the last days (Zech. 14:5). The same conception of the appearance of the angels as ministers of the final judgment is found in the NT in a citation from Enoch 1:9: "Behold, the Lord came with his holy myriads [KJV 'ten thousands of his saints'], to execute judgment on all" (Jude 14). Daniel, in his vision, hears a "holy one"—speaking to another (8:13).

More commonly, the term is used of Israel as God's people. "You are a people holy to the LORD your God; the LORD your God has chosen you to be a people for his own possession, out of all the peoples that are on the face of the earth" (Deut. 7:6); hence, because God "loved his people," "all those consecrated to him [KJV 'saints'] were in his hand" (Deut. 33:3). "Saints" or "holy ones" is a general description of God's people, found in many passages such as:

> Gather to me my faithful ones [ERV-ASV "saints"],
>   who made a covenant with me by sacrifice!
>   (Ps. 50:5).

Holiness is the special quality of the faithful remnant of Israel (cf. Isa. 4:3), and it is with reference to

the loyal nucleus of God's people, especially those who remained steadfast in the persecution under Antiochus, that the word ḥasid ("pious") is used. In a more general sense, this term describes the pious and God-fearing Israelite (II Sam. 22:26; Pss. 12:1; 85:9).

> Love the LORD, all you his saints!
>   The LORD preserves the faithful
>   (Ps. 31:23);

> The LORD loves justice;
>   he will not forsake his saints
>   (Ps. 37:28).

This occurrence of the term in certain psalms raises the difficult question whether or not some or all of the psalms which speak of ḥasidim may be of Maccabean date and allude to the loyalists of that time. On the whole, it is unlikely that the instances mentioned above are Maccabean, but the possibility is somewhat greater in the case of Ps. 79:2, where the "saints" have been slaughtered; Ps. 97:10, which speaks of God's delivering them from the hand of the wicked; and Ps. 149:5, 9 (ḥasidim; RSV "faithful" and "faithful ones"; ERV-ASV "saints"), in the context of the vengeance to be taken by God's people upon their foreign oppressors.

Certainly in Daniel the term denotes the faithful to whom the kingdom will be given in the approaching day of judgment and vindication, who are represented in Daniel's vision by "one like a son of man" (Dan. 7:18, 21-22; cf. vs. 13). These "saints of the Most High" are the pious upholders of the law who as a definite party formed a fanatically loyal body of support for the Maccabean rising so long as the movement retained its character as a holy war for the law and the rightful high priesthood (I Macc. 2:42; 7:13; II Macc. 14:6).

The word is also used in a restricted sense of the priesthood (II Chr. 6:41; Ps. 132:9, 16).

2. In the NT. The faithful of pre-Christian times are called "saints" in Matt. 27:52. Generally, the term describes the Christian community as those who have inherited the covenant privileges as the holy people of a holy God (cf. I Pet. 1:15-16; 2:9). Christians are "saints" by virtue of being "in Christ Jesus" (Phil. 1:1), Christ as Son of man being preeminently the "Holy One of God" (Mark 1:24; Luke 4:34; cf. Luke 1:35; Acts 3:14). Their holiness is in respect of God's calling; they have a vocation as a consecrated people. Hence Paul addresses those who are "called to be saints" (Rom. 1:7). The Corinthian church consists of those "sanctified in Christ Jesus, called to be saints" (I Cor. 1:2). The "saints," as the covenant people, now include Gentiles, who have been made "fellow citizens with the saints" (Eph. 2:19); and as the faithful people they are to fulfil the part of Daniel's "son of man" in the last day: there will be a manifestation of those who are in Christ when Christ is manifested in glory, the "coming of our Lord Jesus with all his saints" (I Thess. 3:13; cf. Col. 3:4), when he will "be glorified in his saints" (II Thess. 1:10). Thus the saints will be associated with Christ in the final judgment of the world, including the angels (I Cor. 6:2-3).

"Saints" naturally becomes a common term for the

members of the church, and the Pauline letters are addressed to the various local communities under this title (Rom. 1:7; I Cor. 1:2; II Cor. 1:1; Eph. 1:1; Phil. 1:1; Col. 1:2). He sends personal greetings to the saints in particular households (Rom. 16:15), and from his own companions or the members of the church where he is staying to Christians elsewhere: "All the saints greet you" (II Cor. 13:13). The same use of "saints" as equivalent to "Christians" is found in Acts (9:13, 32, 41; 26:10); Hebrews (13:24); and Revelation (5:8); and especially of the Christian martyrs in Rev. 16:6; 17:6; 18:24. The "saints" are the object of the pastoral care of the church's ministry (Eph. 4:12), and the future heirs of God's promises (Eph. 1:18; Col. 1:12). Their calling implies a high ethical standard (Eph. 5:3), and the term "saints" is particularly associated with the love shown by Christians to one another, demonstrated in practical service (Rom. 12:13; 16:2; Eph. 1:15; Col. 1:4; I Tim. 5:10; Heb. 6:10). The great example of this is Paul's collection for the Jerusalem church, for the "relief of the saints" (II Cor. 8:4; cf. Rom. 15:25-26; I Cor. 16:1; II Cor. 9:1). Despite the association in late Judaism of poverty with sanctity, we need not suppose that the Jerusalem saints are so called by virtue of their material poverty. They are a church of God's people, like any other group, but of special importance in relation to the Gentile mission.

Jude 3 suggests a tendency to distinguish as "saints" the earliest generation of Christians, to whom the faith was first delivered; but this was not typical of NT thought.

Bibliography. H. F. Hamilton, *The People of God* (1912). R. Asting, *Die Heiligkeit im Urchristentum* (1930). J. Hänel, *Die Religion der Heiligkeit* (1931). R. N. Flew, *The Idea of Perfection in Christian Theology* (1934); *Jesus and His Church* (2nd ed., 1943).   G. W. H. LAMPE

SAKKUTH AND KAIWAN săk'əth, kī'wən [סכות, כיון; *see below*] (Amos 5:26); KJV TABERNACLE, CHIUN kī'ən. Names referring to Israelite apostasy.

These words are patient of two interpretations. "Sakkuth" might be a corruption of *succath* ("tabernacle"), and "Kaiwan" might mean "pedestal." The names, however, probably denote two deities; the mention of the divine star in the sequel in Amos 5:26 suggests that astral deities are denoted, and such are known from Mesopotamian sources as Saccuth (SAK-KUT being the ideogram of Ninib) and Kaiwanu, both being names of the Babylonian Saturn. In both cases the vowels of the original have been replaced by those of שקוץ (*shiqqûs*), "ABOMINATION," as regularly in Hebrew references to pagan deities.

Bibliography. W. Muss-Arnolt, *A Concise Dictionary of the Assyrian Language* (1902), pp. 693-95; W. R. Harper, *Commentary on Amos*, ICC (1936), pp. 137-44.   J. GRAY

SALA, SALAH. KJV forms of SHELAH 1.

SALAMIEL sə lā'mĭ əl [Σαλαμιηλ, God is friendly(?)] (Jth. 8:1); KJV SAMAEL săm'ī əl. An ancestor of Judith; son of Sarasadai. The name is identical with the LXX form of SHELUMIEL and refers presumably to the same person.

SALAMIS săl'ə mĭs [Σαλαμίς, *possibly from* שלם, peace]. A principal city of Cyprus, situated on a shallow inlet on the E coast opposite Syria. The name appears in a variety of spellings; Christian and Byzantine writers usually refer to it as Σαλαμίνη. The received spelling appears first in the Homeric *Hymn to Aphrodite* X.4. Ancient writers recognized the confusion with the island and city of the same name in the Saronian Gulf between Attica and the Peloponnesus (cf. Herodotus IV.162).

From the sixth century B.C. the city was governed by a succession of Greek rulers, perhaps interrupted for a time by Phoenician rule under Hiram III (Σίρωμος). It was at its zenith in the fifth century B.C. under the rule of its city king Enagoras, who repulsed a Persian siege. In the period of the Diadochi the city lost its self-rule and became the residence of the Egyptian governor of Cyprus. In NT times under Roman rule Salamis lost to PAPHOS its distinction as the seat of the island's government. The influential Jewish colony which Paul and Barnabas visited (Acts 13:5) may have been founded before the Roman period, during the dispersion under the Ptolemies. According to an early Christian

Courtesy of the Zion Research Library

5. Marble forum at Salamis

tradition Barnabas was martyred here by a Jewish mob goaded on by visiting Syrian Jews (Acts of Barnabas 22-23). In A.D. 116-17 the Jewish community led the island in a violent rebellion, which resulted in the destruction of the city by Trajan, the ruthless slaughter of the Greek population, and the expulsion of the Jews from Cyprus (Sibylline Oracles V.450 ff; Dio Cassius LXVIII.32.2).

Fig. SAL 5.

Bibliography. Pauly-Wissowa, *Real-Enzyklopädie*, Zweite Reihe, vol. IA (1920), cols. 1832-44; A. H. S. Megaw, "Archaeology in Cyprus, 1954," *Journal of Hellenic Studies*, vol. LXXV (1955), Supplement on Archaeology, pp. 28-34.   E. W. SAUNDERS

SALASADAI. KJV form of SARASADAI.

SALATHIEL. KJV alternate form of SHEALTIEL.

SALECAH săl'ə kə [סלכה]; KJV SALCHAH săl'kə (Deut. 3:10), SALCAH (Josh. 12:5; 13:11; I Chr. 5:11). A city of Gad in the extreme E part of Bashan, and possibly also a district of the same name (Josh. 12:5). It was a part of the kingdom of Og and indicated the limit of his realm toward the NE; it fell to

Courtesy of Denis Baly

6. Salecah (modern Salkhad)

the Israelites when they conquered Bashan. It plays no important part in the Bible.

The site and name have been preserved in the town of Salkhad, the strongest point in the Jebel el-Druze, not far from Qanawat, the biblical Kenath, also called Havvoth-jair. The city is built on a circular hill of basalt, the solidified lava "plug" of an old volcano, which rises more than three hundred feet above the surrounding plain. Nabatean inscriptions found there indicate that it was captured by their king Malik in A.D. 17, and for a time bore the name Tzalhad. Numerous inscriptions from Roman times have also been found.

Fig. SAL 6.

Bibliography. J. L. Porter, *Five Years in Damascus* (1855), II, 172-88; *Giant Cities of Bashan* (1876), pp. 76-77.

S. COHEN

SALEM sā'ləm [שָׁלֵם]. Originally the name of a locality of which Melchizedek was the king (Gen. 14: 18), and which was at times identified with JERUSALEM. This identification appears clearly in Ps. 76:2, where Salem is mentioned in parallelism with Zion, as the abode of God on earth. The same Jewish tradition is cause that the Valley of Shaveh or King's Valley (*see* SHAVEH, VALLEY OF; Gen. 14:17) was tentatively identified with the Kidron. It must be emphasized, however, that the name Salem is not properly another toponym for Jerusalem, nor an abbreviation of the name of the city, the pre-Israelite (pagan) origin of which is certain, but a poetic and religious appellation, in spite of the fancy explanations of Josephus (Antiq. I.x.2) and of medieval commentators.

The identity of Salem and Jerusalem in Gen. 14: 18 has been variously challenged in non-Jewish circles. Jerome, who had accepted it at first (*Hebrew Questions on Gen. 33.18*), gave it up (*Letters* 73.2), and finally came back to it (*Letters* 108.9). The Greek text of Eusebius' *Onomasticon* refers, under the caption "Salem" (no. 152), to Salumias, a village of the Jordan Valley, S of Scythopolis (*see* BETH-SHAN). It is this opinion which Jerome had favored for a time. If accepted, it might lead to the identification of the Salem of Genesis with SALIM (Σαλειμ) near which John baptized (John 3:23), tentatively localized at Umm el-'Amdan. *See* AENON.

According to another tradition, based on the Greek, Latin, and Syriac rendering of Gen. 33:18

reproduced in the KJV, "Shalem, a city of Shechem," Salem might tentatively be identified with the village of Salim, some four or five miles E of Balata-Shechem. *See* SHALEM 2.

Christian speculations of the late Middle Ages sought to localize the meeting of Abraham and Melchizedek on Mount Tabor.

Bibliography. F.-M. Abel, *Géographie de la Palestine*, II (1938), 441-42; H. Vincent, *Jérusalem de l'AT*, II (1956), 612-13.   G. A. BARROIS

SALIM sā'lĭm [Σαλίμ, Σαλείμ] (John 3:23). A place of uncertain location near AENON, where John was baptizing "because there was much water there."

The traditional site is that identified by Eusebius (*ca.* A.D. 335), who is quoted by Jerome (*ca.* A.D. 400; *De Situ et Nom. Hebr.* 165), as eight Roman miles S of Scythopolis (Beth-shan). Nearby are numerous springs. A site favored by some modern scholars is a place called Salim, which is *ca.* four miles E of Shechem (cf. Epiphanius *Heresies* LV.2). *Ca.* three miles away are the copious springs of the Wadi Far'ah. The only likely Judean site is a Wadi Saleim, *ca.* six miles NE of Jerusalem, near which are the springs of another Wadi Far'ah.

Bibliography. F.-M. Abel, "Exploration de la Vallée du Jourdain," *RB*, XXII (1913), 221-24. W. F. Albright, "Some Observations Favoring the Palestinian Origin of the Gospel of John," *HTR*, XVII (1924), 189-95.   D. C. PELLETT

SALLAI săl'ī [סְלָי, *possibly* (God) has restored; *cf.* Arab. *sala'a, but see below and bibliography*]. **1.** A Benjaminite, resident in Jerusalem in the postexilic period, according to Neh. 11:8. But the text of this verse is corrupt, and the name is absent in the parallel I Chr. 9:9. On possible emendations, *see* bibliography.

2. A Levitical house in the postexilic period, according to Neh. 12:20. But vs. 7, as well as some ancient versions, support the reading "Sallu" (סַלּוּ). *See* SALLU 2.

Bibliography. L. W. Batten, *Ezra and Nehemiah*, ICC (1913), pp. 268-69; M. Noth, *Die israelitischen Personennamen* (1928), pp. 39, 174; R. A. Bowman, Exegesis of Nehemiah, *IB*, III (1954), 773.   B. T. DAHLBERG

SALLU săl'oō [סַלּוּא (I Chr. 9:7, סַלָּא (Neh. 11:7), סַלּוּ (Neh. 12:7), *hypocoristic forms for* (God) has restored]. **1.** A Benjaminite among the returned exiles; son of Meshullam (I Chr. 9:7; Neh. 11:7).

2. A Levite or Levitical house among the returned exiles (Neh. 12:7), referred to in vs. 20 as Sallai (סְלָי). The form "Sallu" is better attested in the versions.

Bibliography. M. Noth, *Die israelitischen Personennamen* (1928), p. 174.   B. T. DAHLBERG

SALLUMUS. KJV Apoc. form of SHALLUM 10.

SALMA. Alternate form of SALMON.

SALMON săl'mən [שַׂלְמוֹן (Ruth 4:21); שַׂלְמָה (Ruth 4:20); Σαλμών]. Alternately: SALA sā'lə (Luke 3:32); SALMA săl'mə [שַׂלְמָא] (I Chr. 2:11, 51, 54). **1.** Son of Nahshon; the father of Boaz of the family of Chelubai (Caleb; I Chr. 2:11; Ruth 4:20-21; Matt.

1:4-5; Luke 3:32). As an ancestor of David he is included in the genealogy of our Lord, which in the Matthean account is annotated with the notice that Salmon begat Boaz of Rahab.

2. A Calebite whose father, Hur, was the son of Caleb and Ephrath(ah), or "the Ephrathitess" (I Chr. 2:19, 50-51). Salmon is described as the "father of Bethelehem" (progenitor of Bethlehemite residents) as well as the ancestor of the residents of Atroth-beth-joab, the Netophathites, and the non-Zorite half of the Manahathites; and, finally, the Siphrite families dwelling in Jabez: the Tirathites, Shimeathites, and Sucathites (vss. 54-55; *see bibliography*).

Bibliography. W. Rudolph, *Chronikbücher* (1955).

E. R. DALGLISH

SALMONE săl mōʹnĭ [Σαλμώνη] (Acts 27:7). An E point of Crete; probably the modern Cape Sidero. The Egyptian ship in which Paul and his companions were en route to Rome sailed by this promontory, seeking shelter from adverse Aegean winds by skirting the S coast of the island. The ship had approached the Carian city of Cnidus with great difficulty, perhaps because of unusually strong westerly winds. Rather than risking the danger of the N coast of Crete, the captain chose to follow a familiar course by running before the Aegean winds to the E and S coasts of Crete, thence slowly working westward under the shelter of the island.

Bibliography. J. Smith, *The Voyage and Shipwreck of St. Paul* (4th ed., 1880); Pauly-Wissowa, *Real-Enzyklopädie*, Zweite Reihe, vol. IA (1920), cols. 1986-89. E. W. SAUNDERS

SALOM. KJV Apoc. form of SHALLUM 11.

SALOME sə lōʹmĭ [Σαλώμη = שׁלוֹם, peace, well-being]. 1. A Galilean follower of Jesus; probably the wife of Zebedee, and the mother of James and John.

In Mark 15:40-41 several Galilean women are mentioned as present at the Crucifixion, among them Salome, who later joined in bringing spices for anointing Jesus' body (16:1). Matt. 27:56 quite clearly identifies Salome as the "mother of the sons of Zebedee." In John 19:25 "his mother's sister" probably is to be distinguished from "Mary the wife of Clopas," and Salome may thus be meant. This would make Salome and Zebedee aunt and uncle, and James and John cousins, of Jesus.

It is argued by some scholars that Jesus' committal of his mother to the Beloved Disciple (believed by them to be John) at the Cross (John 19:26-27) thus becomes plausible, as does the ready response of the sons of Zebedee to Jesus' call (Mark 1:19-20).

The above construction of the data, though attractive, rests on supposition built on supposition and cannot be held as more than a possibility.

The transfer of the blame for the request for special preferment in the kingdom from James and John to their mother (cf. Mark 10:35 with Matt. 20:20) is perhaps to be explained as an attempt by Matthew or his source to protect the reputation of these apostles.

2. The daughter of Herodias; unnamed in the gospels (Matt. 14:6; Mark 6:22) but called Salome in Josephus (Antiq. XVIII.v.4). She is said to have danced for Herod Antipas and his guests.

Bibliography. B. F. Westcott, *The Gospel According to St. John*, II (1908), 312-13; H. Windisch, "Kleine Beiträge zur evangelischen Überlieferung," *ZNW*, 18 (1917-18), 73-81; G. Dalman, *"Zum Tanz der Tochter des Herodias," PJ*, XIV (1918), 44-46; P. Ketter, *Christ and Womankind* (English trans., 1937), pp. 305-9; A. E. J. Rawlinson, *St. Mark* (7th ed., 1949), pp. 80-82. E. P. BLAIR

SALT [Heb.-Aram. מלח; ἅλας, ἅλς (Mark 9:49)]. Salt was a necessity of life in biblical times (Ecclus. 39:26). Thus Job asks: "Can that which is tasteless be eaten without salt?" (6:6). In addition to its use as a condiment, it was strewn on sacrifices, both the CEREAL OFFERING (Lev. 2:13) and the BURNT OFFERING (Ezek. 43:24). INCENSE was also to be "seasoned with salt" (Exod. 30:35; KJV "tempered together"). Thus salt appears in a list of provisions for the temple (Ezra 6:9). The practice may be derived from Mesopotamian religion; more probably it reflects the natural association of salt with food.

The custom of rubbing a newborn child with salt (Ezek. 16:4; *see* BIRTH) may have been for medicinal purposes. Possibly, however, it had religious significance, such as to safeguard against demonic influences.

In biblical times salt was generally procured from the area of the DEAD SEA. Zephaniah (2:9) refers to the salt pits of SODOM and GOMORRAH, and Ezekiel hears that although the Dead Sea is to be freshened in the new age, its swamps and marshes are to be left for salt (47:9, 11). The famous story of the transformation of Lot's wife into a pillar of salt (Gen. 19:26) is probably an etiological legend explaining a natural rock-salt formation in the area of Sodom and Gomorrah. *See* LOT. Figs. LOT 37; SOD 73.

The terms "salt," "saltness," and "salty" are often used as images for BARRENNESS or desolation. This usage is derived from the practice of sowing a vanquished city or land with salt (Judg. 9:45), and it has parallels in Assyrian military history. Thus the disobedient land is described as "brimstone and salt, and a burnt-out waste, unsown, and growing nothing" (Deut. 29:23—H 29:22; cf. Job 39:6; Ps. 107:34; Jer. 17:6; Zeph. 2:9). Conversely, however, the life-giving and preservative qualities of salt are often mentioned. Elisha purifies the spring at JERICHO with salt so that "neither death nor miscarriage shall come from it" (II Kings 2:19-22). The expression "covenant of salt" (Num. 18:19; II Chr. 13:5; *see* COVENANT) means a "permanent covenant," since eating salt with someone means to be bound to him in loyalty (cf. Ezra 4:14).

These uses of the term "salt" are also to be found in the NT. Jesus' command: "Have salt in yourselves" (Mark 9:50; cf. Col. 4:6), enjoins the mutual loyalty of the covenant relationship; his description of the disciples as the "salt of the earth" (Matt. 5:13) is probably connected with the above-mentioned life-giving qualities of salt. The prediction: "Every one will be salted with fire" (Mark 9:49), refers to the sacrifice involved in the coming judgment. *See* SALT, CITY OF; SALT, VALLEY OF.

Bibliography. S. A. Cook in W. R. Smith, *Lectures on the Religion of the Semites* (3rd ed., 1927), pp. 594-95; R. J. Forbes, *Studies in Ancient Technology*, III (1955), 157-74. See also the commentaries on Matt. 5:13; Mark 9:49-50. J. F. ROSS

SALT, CITY OF [עִיר הַמֶּלַח]. A city of Judah in the "wilderness" district (Josh. 15:62), to be identified with modern Khirbet Qumran. Remains of Iron II (900-600) buildings have been found but cannot be reconstructed. They are almost certainly those of another fortress comparable to those of MIDDIN; SECACAH; and NIBSHAN. Large numbers of Iron II sherds compare favorably with those found at the Buqe'ah fortresses. A road leading down the Wadi Qumran may actually have been first constructed

Courtesy of Herbert G. May

7. Round cistern at back center in its earlier use goes back to the time when Khirbet Qumran was the City of Salt, period of the Hebrew monarchy (*ca.* eighth-seventh century B.C.).

during the Iron II period to connect the City of Salt with the fortress cities in the Valley of Achor (el-Buqe'ah), just a few miles to the W and the S.

Fig. SAL 7.

Bibliography. M. Noth, "Der alttestamentliche Name der Siedlung auf *chirbet ḳumrān*," *ZDPV,* 71 (1955), 111-23; F. M. Cross and J. T. Milik, "Explorations in the Judaean Buqe'ah," *BASOR,* 142 (1956), 5-17.   V. R. GOLD

SALT, VALLEY OF [גֵּיא מֶלַח, גֵּיא הַמֶּלַח]. A valley in the neighborhood of the Dead Sea, the scene of victories of the Israelites over the Edomites. The first of these was in the time of David, who for the first time conquered Edom (II Sam. 8:13, where the correct reading must be "Edomites" with RSV, as against RSV mg. and KJV "Syrians"). Elsewhere this victory is credited to Abishai (I Chr. 18:12) or, less probably, to Joab (Ps. 60, title—H 60:2). *Ca.* two centuries later, Amaziah again defeated the Edomites, who had won their independence after the death of Jehoshaphat, in the same place, and as a result was able to reconquer a large part of Edom (II Kings 14:7).

Opinions are divided as to the exact location of the Valley of Salt. The Wadi el-Milh, E of Beer-sheba, is a tempting suggestion, because of the similarity of the names; but since in each case the Israelites were the aggressors, the site is more apt to have been in Edomite territory. The most likely place is es-Sebkha, a barren saline stretch S of the Dead Sea.
                                                          S. COHEN

SALT SEA [יָם הַמֶּלַח]. The name applied, in the Pentateuch and in Joshua (Gen. 14:3; Num. 34:3,

12; Deut. 3:17; Josh. 3:16; 12:3; 15:2, 5; 18:19), to the lake now customarily called the DEAD SEA. This designation is derived from the lake's excessive salti-ness—its twenty-five-per-cent solids make it the world's densest in this regard.   W. H. MORTON

SALU sā'loō [סַלּוּא, restored] (Num. 25:14). A Simeonite; the father of Zimri, who was slain when he married Cozbi, a Midianite woman. The marriage of Zimri, the head of a Simeonite family, occurred while Israel was lamenting its earlier apostasy to a Moabite Baal and evoked the wrath of the Israelite leaders.

Bibliography. M. Noth, *Die israelitischen Personennamen* (1928), pp. 174-75.   R. F. JOHNSON

SALUM. KJV Apoc. form of SHALLUM 12.

SALUTATION [ἀσπασμός]. Alternately: GREET-ING. A greeting on meeting. The custom of bidding "peace" to persons greeted developed from OT times (cf. I Sam. 1:17; 25:6; Mark 5:34; Luke 10:5-6). The Greek greeting, "Hail," is χαῖρε, or χαίρετε (Matt. 26:49; 28:9; Luke 1:28). Both the Hebrew and the Greek term are reflected in the salutations of NT letters. *See* LETTER.

For embracing, kissing, cf. Gen. 29:13; Luke 15: 20; Rom. 16:16.   O. J. F. SEITZ

SALVATION, SAVIOR. Salvation may truly be said to be in some sense the ultimate concern of all religion, even of those religions which do not en-visage the need of a savior apart from man himself. Salvation is conceived of in different religions in very different ways, but every religion may be described as in some sense a way of salvation. We need not here inquire whether biblical faith is properly described as "religion," but it should be noted that the Bible would have failed to meet the deepest need of man's being if it did not answer his question about salvation.

Biblical faith, however, is not at all concerned with asking in what salvation consists or in recom-mending techniques, whether mystical or ethical, by which salvation may be attained. It is concerned rather with the proclamation of the fact of salvation, and thus it differs from all "religions" by being kerygmatic in character. The Bible is concerned with the fact that God actually has in concrete historical fact saved his people from destruction; and it pro-claims that the historical salvation thus attested is but the foreshadowing or "type" of the salvation that is to come. This is the theme both of the OT and of the NT. God is a God of salvation: this is the gos-pel of both Jewish and Christian faith. He has saved his people and will save them; in the Bible salvation is both a historical and an eschatological reality. God is often called "Savior," and "Salvation" is in some parts of the Bible a name for God. It is therefore wholly appropriate that the Son of God, by whom the divine purpose of salvation was achieved, should have been called Jesus, which means "savior." Thus, salvation is the central theme of the whole Bible and as such is related to every other biblical theme. Among the other themes, *see* especially ATONEMENT;

Deliverer; Reconciliation; Redeem; Justification.

1. Terminology of salvation in the Bible
    a. In biblical Hebrew
    b. In LXX Greek
    c. In NT Greek
2. Salvation in the OT
    a. Nontheological usage and "salvation history"
    b. Salvation as historical deliverance
    c. Salvation as an eschatological conception
    d. The expectation of a Savior
3. Salvation in the Apoc. and the Pseudep.
4. Salvation in Hellenistic religion
    a. Gnostic tendencies
    b. The imperial cult
5. Salvation in the NT
    a. The ministry and teaching of Jesus
    b. Salvation as historical deliverance
    c. Salvation as an eschatological reality
Bibliography

1. Terminology of salvation in the Bible. "Salvation," "save," and "savior" are words of frequent occurrence throughout the Bible, especially the verb "to save." They range in meaning from the most ordinary, everyday or secular sense to the most profoundly theological and religious; the context alone enables us to determine the sense, as in so many biblical instances of everyday words and phrases which have come into technical theological usage.

a. In biblical Hebrew. In the OT "salvation" is used to translate different Hebrew words, of which the most important are ישועה and ישע from the stem ישע, which is found only in *niph'al* and *hiph'il,* the *hiph'il* having the sense of "to deliver." The root ישע has the fundamental meaning "to be broad," "to become spacious," "to enlarge," and it thus carries the sense of "deliverance," just as conversely "compression," "confinement," and "constraint" carry the sense of being oppressed and in need of deliverance (cf. Luke 12:50). The most significant proper name derived from this root is יהושוע (LXX 'Ιησοῦς; Acts 7:45; cf. Matt. 1:21, 25). "Savior" is the translation of the *hiph'il* participle of ישע—namely, מושיע, as, e.g., in Judg. 3:9, 15; Isa. 19:20; 43:11 (the first two instances RSV translates inconsistently by "deliverer"; possibly the translators wished to retain "savior" for the divine Savior). Other Hebrew words are often used to express the idea of saving or salvation (e.g., at Gen. 19:19; 45:7; 50:20; Exod. 1:17-18; Num. 22:33; Deut. 20:16; Judg. 8:19; I Sam. 12:21; 19:11; II Sam. 19:9; Job 2:6; 20:20; Jer. 51:6, 45; Ezek. 3:18; 18:27). But the word to which attention should chiefly be called is גאל (*gâ'al*), "to redeem"— i.e., to recover property which had fallen into alien hands, to purchase back (e.g., from slavery), etc. The sense of a payment of money falls out of sight, and the word is used as a synonym for "deliver," "save," especially in the Prophets and the Psalter, where it bears particular reference to the saving activity of God. *See* Redeem; Ransom.

Redemption is conceived as deliverance from adversity, oppression, death, and captivity (Egyptian, Babylonian); it is unusual in the OT to come across redemption from sin (but see Ps. 130:8). It is especially in Deutero-Isaiah that Yahweh himself is represented as Israel's *gō'ēl* (Isa. 41:14; 43:14; 44:6, 24; etc.; in all some thirteen times; outside Isaiah, God is called *gō'ēl* only five times).

b. In LXX Greek. The LXX renders the different Hebrew verbs for "save," "save alive," etc., by σώζειν, and hence any distinctions implied in the Hebrew are lost in the Greek. "Salvation" is either σωτηρία or τὸ σωτήριον from the adjective σωτήριος, "saving"; in classical Greek the neuter plural τὰ σωτήρια can mean "deliverance," "safety," or else an offering made in return for safe deliverance; ἡ σωτηρία is the usual classical Greek word for "deliverance," "safety" (Latin *salus*). The meaning of σωτηρία in Hellenistic religion is discussed in § *4a below*. In the LXX "savior" is rendered by σωτήρ (e.g., Judg. 3:9, 15; Isa. 45:15, 21); "redeemer" is λυτρωτής (e.g., Ps. 19:14—G 18:15), ὁ λυτρούμενος (e.g., Isa. 41:14; 43:14; 44:24), or ὁ ῥυσάμενος (e.g., Isa. 44:6; 48:17); and cf. ὁ ῥυόμενος (Isa. 59:20, cited in Rom. 11:26).

c. In NT Greek. When we turn to the NT, we find that σώζειν occurs more than one hundred times; about half these occurrences are found in the gospels. Some fourteen of the gospel instances refer to deliverance from disease or from demon-possession, whereas in the LXX σώζειν never relates specifically to healing. Some twenty other gospel uses refer to rescue from physical peril or from death (e.g., Matt. 8:25; 14:30; Mark 3:4; 15:30-31; Luke 23:39), and the rest, another twenty uses, refer to salvation in the technical theological or specifically religious sense (e.g., Matt. 1:21; 10:22; 19:25).

"Salvation" is rendered by σωτηρία, which is found forty-six times in the NT; τὸ σωτήριον occurs only four times (Luke 2:30; 3:6; Acts 28:28; Eph. 6:17). The adjective σωτήριος occurs only once—in Tit. 2:11: ἡ χάρις σωτήριος, "saving grace." "Savior" is represented by σωτήρ, a word which appears in the gospels only at Luke 1:47; 2:11; John 4:42; and in Acts only at 5:31; 13:23. In the Paulines it occurs twice: Eph. 5:23; Phil. 3:20. It is found ten times in the Pastorals (out of twenty-four appearances in the NT in all), but no fewer than six of these instances refer to "God our Savior." Apart from these six references, only two other passages speak of God as σωτήρ (Luke 1:47; Jude 25); all the remaining sixteen instances refer to Christ as σωτήρ. Instances in II Pet. 1:1; I John 4:14, together with four more in II Peter, complete the tally of uses of σωτήρ in the NT.

It will be noted that the great majority of uses occur in those parts of the NT which probably belong to the period after the death of Paul, but it is not obvious whether any inferences should be drawn from this fact—such as that it was not until toward the end of the first century that, perhaps under the influence of Gnosticism, the title σωτήρ began to be commonly used of Christ.

2. Salvation in the OT. Biblical faith is essentially faith in God as Savior. Its development may be traced in the OT, since it arose in the first place out of the conviction of the Hebrew people that God had saved them from destruction and was fulfilling his purpose of salvation. So far as we can tell, it was the actual historical experience of God's deliverance of

Israel from Egyptian bondage at the Red Sea which formed the basis of the belief that God was the Savior of Israel; we may leave it to the specialists in OT study to discuss whether the Hebrews had any experience of a historical salvation before the days of Moses. There can be no doubt that it was upon the historical experiences of the deliverance from Egypt and the establishment in Canaan that the fundamental certainty of all biblical faith was based:

> Blessed be the Lord,
>> who daily bears us up;
>> God is our salvation.
> Our God is a God of salvation;
>> and to GOD, the Lord, belongs escape from death
>>   (Ps. 68:19-20).

But it is uniquely the genius of the Bible that the historical is transmuted by the eschatological, so that the action of God in the past becomes the type or foreshadowing of his action in the future. The salvation accomplished in history is the promise and warrant of the salvation that shall be in the end time. This is the contribution of the great prophets of Israel, who understand the forthcoming salvation at the end of history as a new act of creation-redemption whereby a new people of God and, indeed, new heavens and a new earth are to be brought into being. It is the claim of the NT that this prophetic expectation has already been fulfilled in its first stages by the coming of Jesus Christ and his church: the new creation is already in existence, though it is visible in this present age only to the eyes of faith. The redeemed still await the final salvation, the passing away of the old order at the great act of creation-salvation by which the new heavens and new earth shall appear.

a. Nontheological usage and "salvation history." It is, of course, natural that "save" and its cognates should be used in the Bible, especially in narrative passages, in quite nontechnical, everyday senses (e.g., Gen. 47:25; Exod. 1:17-18; Josh. 6:25; I Sam. 23:5; II Sam. 19:5). A tribe or nation which is surrounded by hostile tribes or imperial powers is inevitably preoccupied with the problem of its preservation or deliverance from its enemies, and it is not at all surprising that we read very frequently indeed about being saved from one's enemies. Yet the secular or nontechnical use of the "save" words passes over almost imperceptibly into the technical religious use, so that again and again one must hesitate before deciding that this or that usage is completely nontechnical. E.g., we may say that the escape or deliverance of the young Amalekite from the rout of Saul's army on Mount Gilboa (II Sam. 1:3) is a purely nontechnical instance of being saved; but on the other hand, the various escapes of David from the wrath of King Saul (I Sam. 19:10, 18), though they are apparently quite "secular" occasions, are undoubtedly thought of by the narrator of the stories as deliverances for which Yahweh, as David's Savior-God, was responsible. When Israel is said to have been saved from her enemies, the implication is always that it is God who has wrought the deliverance.

It is God who sends "saviors" (Gen. 45:7; Judg.

3:9, 15; II Kings 13:5; Neh. 9:27) and who empowers these human saviors to perform their mighty deeds of deliverance (Judg. 6:15-16); and, indeed, he keeps his ceaseless, unsleeping watch over Israel to preserve her and save her from all evil (Ps. 121). Thus, every deliverance which is experienced by Israel, or by one of those representative individuals (such as David) with whom the fortunes of Israel are bound up, is in reality an instance of the fatherly care of God over Israel his children (Ps. 103:4, 13); and therefore it is rash to say that any use of such words as "save," "deliver," "preserve," "escape," at least in connection with Israel, is entirely nontechnical or secular.

A good illustration of the possible double meaning of deliverance stories is to be found in II Kings 7, where the four starving lepers enter the camp of the besieging Syrian army and find it deserted after the Syrians have fled in fear. When they have eaten and drunk their fill, the lepers bethink themselves of their duty to the starving inhabitants of the besieged city, and they say to one another: "We are not doing right. This day is a day of good news [LXX ἡμέρα εὐαγγελίας], [and] we are silent" (7:9). Have we here merely a secular story of deliverance, or are there not at least undertones of the biblical theme of a historical deliverance as being a day of good tidings, a day of salvation? Every deliverance comes from God, and the biblical point of view would be that there is no salvation—of any kind, secular as well as religious, individual as well as national—except it come from the Lord. "Deliverance belongs to Yahweh" (Ps. 3:8; Jonah 2:9); he is the "rock of our salvation" (Ps. 95:1), the "God of our salvation" (Ps. 79:9; 85:4). All safety, safe dwelling, or security is dependent solely upon God, who throughout the Psalms is called by such titles as Rock (see also Deut. 32:4, 18, 30-31; especially 32:15: "Rock of . . . salvation"; and note Ps. 19:14: "my rock and my redeemer"; Ps. 62:6: "my rock and my salvation"), Strength, Fortress, Shield, etc. (Ps. 18:1-2). National and personal well-being are gifts of God alone, and they must be sought from no other source than the hand of the Lord. It becomes axiomatic with the biblical writers that Israel's security is the God of Israel, not alliances with powerful states like Egypt, and that he alone, and not material possessions or any other natural asset, is the giver of a man's prosperity.

If, then, we are unable always to distinguish between instances of ordinary, everyday contingent deliverances from peril and those deliverances of which the author is God himself, this is because we cannot properly distinguish between the secular and sacred elements in Israel's history. There is a sense in which all Israel's history is *Heilsgeschichte* or "salvation history," so that it is true to say that in this sense there is no secular history in the Bible. Many sections of the biblical history are very similar to portions of the history of other peoples, yet it is the biblical narrative alone which is "salvation history." E.g., the stories of the escapades and escapes of David, the young courtier and adventurer, who made bold raids upon the overbearing Philistines and slew their champion Goliath in single combat, have their counterpart in the national sagas of many nations; they are not unlike the stories of Robin Hood and his Merry Men, beloved of children from generation to generation. Yet the David cycle is sacred history and the Robin Hood cycle is not. This is not because the stories about David are more edifying, more moral, than those about Robin Hood; indeed, in the matter of edification there is little choice between the two cycles. The crucial difference between them is that the David stories belong to the line of salvation history—i.e., the line of God's action in the events of world history, which leads to the achievement of his purpose of the salvation of mankind. It was by a particular series of historical events, through a particular national history, that God's saving purpose in Jesus Christ was fulfilled. It is because salvation is in the name of Jesus Christ, and no other (Acts 4:12), that the biblical history is "salvation history"; and it is for this reason that the salvation story is the story of Abraham, Isaac, Jacob, Moses, Joshua, Rahab the harlot, Gideon, Barak, Samson, Jephthah, David, Samuel, and the prophets (Heb. 11), not the story of Buddha, Confucius, Socrates, Plato, Aristotle, Marcus Aurelius, Plotinus, Mohammed, Rousseau, Marx, Gandhi, Bertrand Russell.

Salvation history is the story of the divine action for our salvation in and through the lives and persons of real flesh-and-blood historical characters, as sensual and as fallible as men usually are, and yet who were, through no virtue of their own, made the instruments of the divine plan for the salvation of the world. Small wonder that in the Bible it is often difficult to distinguish between the ordinary, everyday use of words like "save" and their tremendous theological technical usage, when the everyday stuff of national history has been transmuted into the sacred mystery of salvation history.

The OT shows that the Hebrews were uniquely conscious of their being "encompassed with deliverance" (Ps. 32:7). They knew themselves to be elected by God for his purposes of salvation and were constantly aware of their standing under his perpetual protection and providence:

> The eternal God is your dwelling place,
>   and underneath are the everlasting arms.
> And he thrust out the enemy before you,
>   and said, Destroy.
> So Israel dwelt in safety.
> . . . .
> Happy are you, O Israel! Who is like you,
>   a people saved by Yahweh!
>   (Deut. 33:27-29).

The Psalter contains the most vivid and vigorous "songs of deliverance," which attest the nation's consciousness of God's continuing salvation (e.g., Pss. 18; 30–31; 34; 46; 48; 68; 91; 95–99; 105–107; 116; 118; 136; 145). When Israel suffered adversity, the prophets were ever ready to remind their countrymen that this was not because Yahweh was faithless to his covenant and promise, or because he was too weak to save them, but because by their sin they had rejected the salvation which he was always offering to them and which was theirs upon condition of repentance:

> "Return, O faithless sons,
>   I will heal your faithlessness."
> "Behold, we come to thee;
>   for thou art Yahweh our God.
> Truly the [Baal rites on the] hills are a delusion,
>   the orgies on the mountains.
> Truly in Yahweh our God
>   is the salvation of Israel" (Jer. 3:22-23;
>   cf. also Lam. 3:26 in its context).

b. Salvation as historical deliverance. This conviction of Israel's, that God was their special Savior for all eternity (Isa. 45:17), was based upon the actual experience of deliverance in history. Doubtless there were many occasions, such as those commemorated in certain of the psalms (e.g., 46; 118), when Israel experienced a national deliverance, but the evidence of the OT leaves no room at all for doubt that the determinative experience of Yahweh's salvation was the deliverance from Egyptian bondage, the miracle of the Red Sea and the subsequent experience of God's fatherly care in the wilderness.

It is quite impossible for us today to reconstruct the course of "what happened" at the Exodus, nor does it matter greatly for our present purpose that we cannot do so; the accounts as we now have them in the book of Exodus were written down several centuries after the period of the events which they recount. It is sufficient to note that, whatever their actual experience may have been, the Israelites emerged from the wilderness into Canaan, no longer a welter of tribes, but a people conscious of national identity and bound together by a sense of their common mission and destiny. No doubt, much consolidation was necessary after the settlement in Canaan, as the records make plain; but there can be little doubt that the Israelites had at the coming out of Egypt undergone a profound and transforming experience which had convinced them that they had been the beneficiaries of a supernatural deliverance through the power of Yahweh, to whom forever afterward they were bound by an everlasting covenant. The Lord had worked salvation for Israel at the Red Sea (Exod. 14:13, 30-31; 15:1-2, 13).

This experience of deliverance left its mark upon the whole of Israel's subsequent existence and upon every part of the OT; it was sung in psalmody, recounted in story, and re-enacted in Passover ritual.

> We have heard with our ears, O God,
>   our fathers have told us,
> what deeds thou didst perform in their days,
>   in the days of old (Ps. 44:1; cf. Pss. 78;
>   105–6; 114; 135–36; Exod. 12:1-20;
>   Deut. 6:20-24).

Indeed, it is not too much to say that the making of Israel as a people, and the continuance in later centuries down to the present day of the Jews as a race, bear testimony to the greatness of the event that happened to the tribes that came out of Egypt. Something of a very remarkable kind must have happened to this people, so that alone of all the peoples of the ancient world they have retained, despite the vicissitudes of their checkered history, a self-conscious awareness of their national destiny and distinctiveness. It is upon Israel's experience of salvation in history that the biblical conception of salvation is based. That is to say, the biblical doctrine of salvation is not a theory or a set of ideas about God; it is not a logical deduction from a theistic philosophy; nor yet is it based upon any technique of mystical absorption into the divine. Biblical theology is essentially recital—the recitation of the great things which God has done in history for his people; the biblical doctrine of salvation is an assertion of something which has actually happened. "You shall say to your son, 'We were Pharaoh's slaves in Egypt; and Yahweh brought us out of Egypt with a mighty hand; and Yahweh showed signs and wonders, great and grievous, against Egypt and against Pharaoh and all his household, before our eyes; and he brought us out from there, that he might bring us in and give us the land which he swore to give to our fathers" (Deut. 6:21-23).

The Bible is thus concerned, not with the philosophy of religion, but with proclamation (kerygma), gospel (evangel), the recital of a creed whose clauses consist of historical statements rather than of philosophical or theological propositions. God's character cannot be known in itself or apart from God's own revelation of it in action. The view that God is love is not a conclusion reached philosophically after a long process of reflection upon the being and attributes of God; it is the consequence of his self-revelation through his saving action in history: "It is because Yahweh loves you, and is keeping the oath which he swore to your fathers, that Yahweh has brought you out with a mighty hand, and redeemed you from the house of bondage, from the hand of Pharaoh king of Egypt. Know therefore that Yahweh your God is God, the faithful God who keeps covenant and steadfast love with those who love him and keep his commandments" (Deut. 7:8-9). Salvation, that is to say, is not something that is deduced from the character of God as this has been philosophically discerned; it is the fact from which the people of God deduce his character of love. We do not believe in our ultimate salvation because we first believe that God is love: we believe that God is love because of our experience of salvation.

This is what is implied when we speak of biblical religion as being historical religion, and this also is what differentiates biblical religion from all "religion" —which is why many theologians today doubt the propriety of speaking of biblical "religion" at all. Biblical faith is distinct from all "religion" precisely in respect of its character as historical recital: "[God] has visited and redeemed his people" (Luke 1:68). The worship of God includes the recitation of the historical creed, the proclamation of what God has done. Here, e.g., is the rubric concerning the offering of the first fruits: "You shall take some of the first of all the fruit . . . and . . . put it in a basket, . . . and . . . the priest shall take the basket from your hand, and set it down before the altar of Yahweh your God. And you shall make response before Yahweh your God, 'A wandering Aramean was my father; and he went down into Egypt. . . . And Yahweh heard our voice, and saw our affliction, our toil, and our oppression; and Yahweh brought us out of Egypt with a mighty hand and an outstretched arm . . . ; and he brought us into this place and gave us

this land, a land flowing with milk and honey. And behold, now I bring the first of the fruit of the ground. . . .' And you shall set it down before Yahweh your God, and worship before Yahweh your God" (Deut. 26:2-10). So, too, at the Eucharist in the Christian church solemn recitation was always made of the facts of the historical redemption ("that the Lord Jesus on the night when he was betrayed took bread . . ." [I Cor. 11:23]); so, too, the Christian church in her worship recites the Apostles' and the Nicene Creeds—creeds which are not philosophical statements of our beliefs about God but proclamation of what God himself has actually done in history "for us men and for our salvation."

An important aspect of historical salvation is brought out by the frequent occurrence of the first person plural in the recitation of the events of the deliverance. Though the event may have happened weeks or years or centuries ago, it happened to *us,* who are members of the people for whom the redemption was wrought. In some way the event is part of *our* existence; it is not something dead and gone, something that happened to people who lived a long time ago and has nothing to do with us. "A wandering Aramean was my father; and he went down into Egypt. . . . And Yahweh heard our voice, and saw our affliction . . . ; and Yahweh brought us out of Egypt." "That which was from the beginning, which we have heard, which we have seen with our eyes, which we have looked upon and touched with our hands . . . that which we have seen and heard we proclaim also to you" (I John 1:1-3). The saving event is re-enacted, is made contemporary, in the dramatic anamnesis of the Passover meal or the Lord's Supper: "This day shall be for you a memorial day. . . . You shall observe this rite as an ordinance for you and for your sons for ever. . . . It was a night of watching by Yahweh, to bring them out of the land of Egypt; so this same night is a night of watching kept to Yahweh by all the people of Israel throughout their generations" (Exod. 12:14, 24, 42). "As often as you eat this bread and drink the cup, you proclaim the Lord's death until he comes" (I Cor. 11:26). The act of deliverance, so to speak, remains active and potent throughout the continuing history of the people for whom it was wrought; in the biblical view it is not a mere event of the past, but something that is ever and again made present and real in the lives of those who celebrate it in word and sacrament; the salvation that was once-for-all wrought for the whole people is appropriated by each family or each individual as the family or the individual makes response in worship and thanksgiving (Exod. 12:26-27; Deut. 6:20-25; 26:1-11; John 6:53-58; I Cor. 10:16-17; 11:23-26).

c. Salvation as an eschatological conception. By speaking of salvation as an eschatological event we mean much more than that it is a future event or a future reality. An eschatological reality is one which is even now real, present, and active, and at the same time is not yet realized, made visible (except to faith), or consummated. In the Bible, in both the OT and the NT, salvation is real, achieved, and active, but it is not yet wholly realized, made visible to all, or finally consummated. We live in an intermediate state, "between the times," when by faith we know already the salvation which is ours, although we have not fully appropriated or finally apprehended it. In the OT the salvation of Israel is already assured, for it was achieved at the exodus from Egypt and ratified by the everlasting covenant which God made with Moses on Mount Sinai. According to the teaching of the prophets, God's act of salvation at the Red Sea was active in the history of Israel; it was a continuing redemption, delivering God's people from Assyrian invasion or Babylonian exile; and it would be consummated in the final redemption of God's people at the end of the age, the day of the creation of new heavens and a new earth. It is especially in the prophecy of the Deutero-Isaiah that this doctrine is most fully developed and clearly expressed. There is no divorce or contradiction between the historical and the eschatological, because the former, by becoming active in the present and no mere past-and-gone event, is the matrix and type of the latter; the eschatological salvation, even now active in the present, is the final realization beyond history of that which the historical redemption foreshadowed and promised. Past, present, and future constitute, not three deliverances, but one deliverance. To speak of the biblical view of time as linear is misleading if it obscures this truth.

There is a close connection in biblical thought between salvation and righteousness; indeed, the terms become virtually synonymous, for they both denote the same outgoing quality of the divine character. God saves Israel because he is righteous; it is the worst sin of pride on Israel's part to imagine that God saves her because she is righteous. "Do not say in your heart, after Yahweh your God has thrust them [the Canaanites] out before you, 'It is because of my righteousness that Yahweh has brought me in to possess this land' " (Deut. 9:4-6). It is not because of Israel's worthiness that God delivered her and cleansed her; he has done it "for the sake of [his] holy name" (Ezek. 36:22-32). That is to say, God cannot deny his own nature and break his covenant; though Israel has been faithless to her vow and promise, God will remain faithful; because he is righteous, he will not abandon his people but will find a means of "covering" their sins and justifying them, so that they may stand in his presence as righteous.

> You have burdened me with your sins,
>   you have wearied me with your iniquities.
> [But] I am He
>   who blots out your transgressions for my own sake,
>   and I will not remember your sins.
> Put me in remembrance [of the covenant], let us argue
>   [as in a law court] together;
>   set forth your case, that you may be proved right
>   [i.e., justified] (Isa. 43:24-26).

Thus, it is not because of any righteousness of her own that Israel is saved; she is saved by the righteousness of God; this is what is meant by the assertion that Yahweh is a "righteous God and a Savior" (Isa. 45:21). Righteousness and salvation are inseparable elements of the divine character; there could not be one without the other. Israel's justification is by faith alone; Deutero-Isaiah had long ago enunciated the biblical truth concerning salvation, which later Paul had to recover from beneath the rabbinic doctrine of merit by which it had been obscured, just as, centuries later still, Luther had to recover it once more from beneath the medieval doctrine of salvation by works. Though Paul's exegesis of Hab. 2:4 ("The righteous shall live by his faith"; cf. Rom. 1: 17; Gal. 3:11) may be technically defective, he was not wrong in implying that the prophets had taught a doctrine of justification by faith which had been repudiated by rabbinic Judaism. It is often overlooked how remarkably Paul's doctrine of justification is adumbrated by the OT prophets. The forensic metaphor of justification is based upon the picture of Yahweh as engaged in a lawsuit in a court of justice with his rebellious people (Isa. 1:18; 43:26; Hos. 4:1; 12:2; Mic. 6:2; etc.); and the prophets speak of God's verdict of acquittal, vindication, or justification of Israel (Isa. 43:26; 45:21-23). Indeed, Paul's use of δικαιοῦν is taken over from the LXX, and he employs it to reassert the profound OT conviction that "no man living is righteous before [God]" (Ps. 143:2; cf. I Kings 8:46; Job 9:2-3; 15:14-16; 25: 4; Pss. 51:4; 130:3-4; Eccl. 7:20; Isa. 64:6). His doctrine of justification is already stated in Isa. 59, except that whereas the latter passage looks forward in hope to the coming of a redeemer to Zion, wearing a breastplate of righteousness and a helmet of salvation, Paul proclaims a gospel which is even now the power of God unto salvation—namely, that the righteousness of God has been revealed in Christ (Rom. 1:16-17; 3:25-26), in whom the promised salvation is come. Thus, for Paul as for the Isaianic school, "righteousness" and "salvation" are virtually synonymous terms; or, to put it another way, Paul expresses his doctrine of salvation in terms of his teaching about justification by faith. Salvation is justification, and it is the corollary of the righteousness of God.

In the prophetic view salvation is also virtually synonymous with creation; the saving act is necessarily an act of new creation. It is not an accident that Deutero-Isaiah should have given the clearest expression to be found in the OT both of the doctrine of God as sovereign creator and also of the doctrine of God as redeemer. Much distortion has been caused in Christian theology through a putting asunder of the doctrines of creation and redemption, or through emphasizing one to the neglect of the other. Deutero-Isaiah sees clearly that redemption involves a new creation—another point taken up by Paul in his exposition of the redemptive work of Christ (II Cor. 5:17-18).

The prophets of Israel are not afraid to make use of the old Semitic mythology to convey their profoundest spiritual teaching, so completely have they transcended the old conceptions of the king as God and demythologized the Baal-worship of the surrounding peoples. They represent God's original act of the creation of the 'world as a mighty deed of salvation, in which according to the ancient world picture God defeated the Dragon of the Deep (Tiamat, etc.) and brought order out of the chaos of the waters. The picture of God as King above the waterfloods and Lord of the power of the sea arises out of this ancient myth, which is used by the prophets to represent poetically the omnipotence of the Creator God (e.g., Pss. 93; 95:5; 96; 98). It is worth noting how the picture of God as King above the raging floods is combined with the prophecy of his coming to judge the world in righteousness and how this righteousness is identified with the coming salvation (e.g., Pss. 96:11-13; 97; 98:7-9). The picture of Yahweh as slaying the Dragon of the Sea and thus effecting salvation has survived most vividly in Ps. 74:12-14:

> God my King is from of old,
> > working salvation in the midst of the earth.
> Thou didst divide the sea by thy might;
> > thou didst break the heads of the dragons on the waters.
> Thou didst crush the heads of Leviathan.

It is noteworthy that this picture is embedded in a heartfelt appeal to God to come in righteousness and save his people (by an act of new creation or salvation) from their oppressors.

Deutero-Isaiah thinks of the creation of the world as an act of divine salvation which was the type of the redemption of Israel from Egypt and also of the deliverance of God's people from the Babylonian captivity in his own day. The Creator-Savior, who defeated chaos and established the world, by a new act of creation redeemed Israel from Egypt at the miracle of the Red Sea (cf. Exod. 15:1-12; Pss. 77: 11-20; 114; etc.); now Yahweh was redeeming them again by a new act of creation-salvation, so that the ransomed of Yahweh should return (from Babylon) and come with singing to Zion.

> Awake, awake, put on strength,
> > O arm of Yahweh;
> awake, as in days of old,
> > the generations of long ago.
> Was it not thou that didst cut Rahab in pieces,
> > that didst pierce the dragon?
> Was it not thou that didst dry up the sea,
> > the waters of the great deep;
> that didst make the depths of the sea a way
> > for the redeemed to pass over?
> And the ransomed of Yahweh shall return,
> > and come with singing to Zion (Isa. 51:9-11).

> Thus says Yahweh,
> > your Redeemer, the Holy One of Israel:
> "For your sake I will send to Babylon
> and break down all the [prison] bars.
> . . . .
> I am Yahweh, your Holy One,
> . . . .
> > who makes a way in the sea,
> > a path in the mighty waters"
> > > (Isa. 43:14-16).

The idea of redemption as an act of new creation thenceforward passes into the thought of Judaism; thus in Wisd. Sol. 19:6-8 we read:

> The whole creation in its nature was fashioned anew,
> . . . .
> dry land emerging where water had stood before,
> an unhindered way out of the Red Sea,
> . . . .
> where those protected by thy hand passed through as
> > one nation,
> after gazing on marvelous wonders.

Thus, according to prophetic thought, creation is renewed in redemption, and salvation may be thought of as new creation. When God brought Israel out of Egypt or out of Babylon, he created Israel anew. The idea of a new Israel is implicit in the thought of Yahweh's salvation, and hence it is that with the growth of the expectation of a coming great salvation there appears also the clear hope of a new world. This hope takes different forms, whether (as perhaps in the First Isaiah) it is that of a renewal of the natural order, a paradisal existence as in the beginning of the world (Isa. 9:2-7; 11:1-9), or (as perhaps in the optimistic days of the Deutero-Isaiah, Haggai, and Zechariah) that of a new political world order, with all the nations bringing their tribute and honor into Jerusalem, so that Israel should be the light of the Gentiles and the salvation of the ends of the earth (Isa. 49:5-13; Hag. 2:4-9; Zech. 2:7-13), or (as in the age of disillusionment of the later Isaianic school, when the aspirations of the builders of the second temple had failed of realization) that of new heavens and a new earth which should come into being when the former heavens and earth had passed away (Isa. 65:17; 66:22). With the disappointment of the hope of a renewed Israel and of a more just international and social order in the years after the return from Exile, it was natural that prophetic thought about salvation should become more and more transcendentally eschatological; because God was a God of salvation, he *must* create a new world in which his purpose would be fulfilled and his people would find their rest.

> Behold, I create new heavens
> > and a new earth;
> . . . .
> I create Jerusalem a rejoicing,
> > and her people a joy.

It is in the new Jerusalem of the transcendental order that the paradisal state of innocence shall be restored, when the wolf and the lamb shall feed together and the lion shall eat straw like the ox (Isa. 65:17-25).

So certain was the prophetic expectation that the outgoing, self-realizing righteousness of Yahweh must issue in his people's salvation and justification that they dared to transfer to new heavens and a new earth those aspirations of whose realization they despaired in this world. By the time that the work of the OT prophets is done, the concept of salvation has become thoroughly eschatological; salvation is that which will be established for all the earth on the day of new creation, the great Day of Yahweh; in that day "all flesh" shall come and worship before him (Isa. 66:22-23). The assurance of this salvation is given in the historical acts of redemption which God has already wrought for his people; the knowledge of salvation is possessed by the community which itself has undergone the experience of redemption in its own history, and this knowledge is sustained by the recitation of the mighty acts of God and by obedience to his command to keep the Passover as his anamnesis, a memorial of the deliverance that has taken place and a foretaste of that which is to come. The knowledge of salvation in the Bible is articulated and communicated by the ministry of word and sacrament.

d. The expectation of a Savior. Salvation, of course, implies the existence of a savior, but does not necessarily imply the existence of a savior other than Yahweh himself. The OT, for the most part, speaks of no other savior than Yahweh. As we have seen, Yahweh may send human saviors in certain crises of Israel's history, but the main emphasis of the OT is that it is God himself who saves and that there is no other savior.

> I, I am Yahweh,
> and besides me there is no savior
> (Isa. 43:11; cf. 45:21; Hos. 13:4).

"Vain is the help of man!" (Pss. 60:11; 108:12). In the canonical OT the Messiah is never called "savior"; on the contrary, it is Yahweh who is the "saving refuge of his Anointed" (Ps. 28:8). But the figure of the Messiah in the OT is somewhat unformed and shadowy; insofar as he is only the projection of the King, who was par excellence Yahweh's Anointed (e.g., II Sam. 1:14, 16), it is clear that he will stand in need of God's deliverance (cf. Ps. 144:9-10:

> I will sing a new song to thee, O God;
>
> . . . .
>
> who givest victory to kings,
> who rescuest David thy servant).

Insofar as he is a prophet like Moses, whom God raised up to be his instrument in saving Israel (cf. Deut. 18:15, 18), he may be called "deliverer" or "redeemer" (as, indeed, Stephen calls Moses in Acts 7:35), but in reality he is only the agent of God in the divine work of salvation, for it was God himself who came down to deliver Israel (Exod. 3:8; Acts 7:34).

Deutero-Isaiah portrays a new deliverer of the type of Moses, whose special title was the "Servant of Yahweh" (Exod. 14:31; Deut. 34:5; Josh. 1:1, 13, 15, etc.; II Chr. 1:3; 24:6, 9, etc.); he is God's agent in the work of redemption in the crisis of the return from exile. Who precisely is intended by the figure of the Servant in Deutero-Isaiah is, of course, one of the most vexed questions of OT scholarship. The Isaianic Servant suffers, as Moses did, for the sins of his people and bears their iniquity (Isa. 52:13–53:12), but by his tribulations and obedience ("knowledge") the righteous Servant makes many to be accounted righteous (53:11). One thing only may be said with certainty about the figure of the Isaianic Servant: he is the Moses, the Servant of Yahweh, of the deliverance from the Exile, and he plays in relation to that deliverance the same role Moses played in the deliverance from Egypt. Though he is not the Messiah in the sense in which this term was understood in later Judaism, he is anointed by Yahweh with his Spirit (Isa. 42:1; 48:16; cf. 11:2; 61:1) for the task of proclaiming and securing release for the captives.

It is with this figure of the Spirit-anointed Moses of the new act of redemption that Jesus in the gospels identifies himself (e.g., Luke 4:18-19): knowing nothing of more than one "Isaiah," Jesus and his church understood the prophetic figure whose linea-

ments are sketched in Isa. 9; 11; 40–55; 61; etc., to be a prophecy of Christ himself, anointed with Holy Spirit in his baptism for the new and final work of redemption, which was to take place at the end of the age, the day of new creation. But this is to anticipate the development of the biblical theology.

After the profound theological insights of the Isaianic school had been achieved, the prophetic vision faded, and the great concept of salvation by the divine righteousness alone was obscured in the doctrines of later Judaism, especially those which implied salvation by works of human merit. According to the teaching of the rabbis, the salvation of the individual was to be achieved by the meticulous observance of the detailed commandments of the Torah (law of Moses), and it was possible by a straightforward system of bookkeeping to ascertain a man's prospects of salvation by noting whether his merits exceeded his transgressions. Different schools of rabbis awarded higher or lower points for this work of merit or that transgression, but all observed the same fundamental rules of the game. Moreover, it was generally agreed that a pious Jew who had tried, but had barely succeeded, might draw upon the bank of the superabundant merits of the fathers (Abraham, Isaac, and Jacob) and of the Maccabean heroes. Salvation thus became largely a matter of human achievement assessed by the method of the balance sheet.

Such was the nature of official (rabbinic) Judaism at the end of the OT period and until A.D. 70; but, if we may judge from the evidence of the Qumran literature, the sect type of piety was little better. A fanatical legalism, which ordered a withdrawal from every kind of worldly contact, aimed at the salvation of a small community of the puritanically elect; the salvation which it envisaged was as far removed as possible from that which was proclaimed by Jesus to be available for publicans and sinners. Later Judaism knew only of salvation for the righteous and nothing of the salvation of sinners. It was Jesus and his followers, notably Paul, who undertook a reformation which consisted fundamentally in the rediscovery and assertion of the prophetic doctrine of salvation by the righteousness of God.

3. Salvation in the Apoc. and the Pseudep. The canonical OT says little about a coming savior other than God himself, and its expectation of a saving Messiah is, at best, shadowy (*see* MESSIAH). The position is quite otherwise in the apocryphal and pseudepigraphical literature. The continued frustration of the national aspirations of the Jews under Seleucid or Roman domination gave rise to wishful dreaming about a coming national salvation; and different forms of expectation concerning a deliverer who should be raised up by God are encountered in the literature of the period. There is little agreement concerning the deliverer's origin or nature. This literature thinks, not only of national salvation, but also of individual salvation, and it introduces a doctrine of resurrection which envisages a distribution of rewards and punishments after the individual's death. In some of the literature of the period the expected salvation will take place on this earth, and Jerusalem will be the prosperous center of the messianic kingdom (e.g., Enoch 1–36, with its rather gross and materialistic portrayal of the delights of the age to come). In the Psalms of Solomon, Jerusalem will be purged by a righteous Davidic king, free from sin, ruling over a mighty messianic kingdom (Pss. Sol. 17). But the most striking developments of the period are found in those books (e.g., Enoch 37 ff; Apocalypse of Baruch; Assumption of Moses) in which the scene of the expected salvation is laid beyond this world of time and history in a transcendental future, and in which salvation has become entirely otherworldly. It is new heavens, rather than a new earth, which these apocalyptists think of, and the redeemed community will live in the new heavens, transformed into the likeness of the righteous Messiah (Enoch 82–90).

In the Similitudes (Enoch 37–71) the Messiah is a wholly supernatural being, the Son of man, with whom in a transformed heaven the elect live forever as angelic existences enjoying the closest communion with their messianic redeemer (62:14; *see* ENOCH, BOOK OF; SON OF MAN). The conception of the Isaianic Servant of Yahweh may have influenced the Enochian conception of the heavenly Son of man, who is also called "the Elect One" and "the Righteous One"; as in Deutero-Isaiah, those in Israel who stand in a special relation to God (which is the meaning of "the elect" or "chosen" in the OT) are called "the elect" (Isa. 43:20; 45:4), and the Son of man is righteous because he makes the elect ones righteous, which means that he saves them. "Righteousness shall prevail in his days, and the righteous and elect shall be without number before him forever and ever" (Enoch 39:6-7). God prepared this savior before the creation of the world, and his existence is the guarantee that the oppressed righteous, elect ones shall be delivered at his future epiphany in glory. Though there is much in this conception that is reminiscent of Deutero-Isaiah, especially the connection that is made between righteousness and salvation, it is also true that the deepest insights of that prophet are lacking. There is no conception of the redemption of the elect through the vicarious suffering of the Son of man. He will slay sinners with the word of his mouth, and it is the righteous whom he saves, not the transgressors.

The Targums identify the Isaianic Servant of Yahweh with the Messiah, but they rewrite Isa. 53 in such a way as to make him a national, even a tionalistic, political hero; the latter secures the exaltation of the remnant of Israel and the destruction of her enemies, who submit to the Messiah like a lamb that is led to the slaughter!

It is neither apocalyptic Judaism, as represented by Enoch and other works of its genre, nor rabbinic Judaism, as represented by the Targums, nor yet sectarian Judaism, as represented by the Qumran literature, which recovers the deep insight of OT prophecy, but Jesus and the church. Nor is it the thinking of the apocalyptists which has contributed much to the basic theology of Jesus and his followers beyond certain conventional imagery and phraseology. The theology of the NT is basically a reinterpretation of the OT prophetic plan of salvation, not a hotchpotch of Jewish apocalyptic and Hellenistic

Gnostic fantasies. The NT teaching concerning salvation owes little to any noncanonical work of the intertestamental period that is known to us; there is small connection between the Son of man of Enoch and the Son of man of the gospels. There is no evidence that Jesus was familiar with the Enoch literature (much of which may have first seen the light after his crucifixion), but there is plenty of evidence that he had reflected deeply upon the Isaianic prophecy of salvation, which he recovers and claims to fulfil. "Son of man" as used by Jesus as a self-designation means the "Servant of Yahweh" in Isaiah's sense, not the "Elect One" of the Enochian fantasy. The intertestamental literature is valuable in adding to our background knowledge of the prevalent ideologies of NT times, but it is the canonical OT which is the clue to the understanding of the NT doctrine of salvation. If the Scriptures are those writings which make us "wise unto salvation," then the reformers rightly understood the matter who declared that the apocryphal books "the Church doth read for example of life and instruction of manners; but yet doth it not apply them to establish any doctrine" (Articles of Religion, VI, appended to the Book of Common Prayer; the title of the Article runs: "Of the Sufficiency of the Holy Scriptures for Salvation").

The most significant development in the concept of salvation during the intertestamental period is the transference of the locus of salvation from this world, where the OT firmly grounds it, to the world to come. In the OT, with scarcely an exception (the exceptions are Isa. 26:19; Dan. 12:2), salvation is in this world order, and even the restored paradisal righteousness of Isa. 11:1-9 will belong to this age. Such a passage points, however, toward the conception of a MILLENNIUM or long period of Utopian bliss upon the earth after the intervention in history of God or his Messiah—a doctrine which may be studied, e.g., in II Esdras, where it is taught that when the messianic kingdom has fulfilled its time, the Messiah himself will die (7:29); in II Esd. 7:30-98 also may be studied a characteristic apocalyptic view of the general resurrection and the Judgment. But it would be a mistake to suppose that it was only the apocalyptists who believed in the resurrection of the dead; Jews of entirely different points of view had also come to accept this doctrine before NT times (e.g., Wisd. Sol. 3:1-9); and by the time of Christ all sections of Jewish opinion, save only the conservative Sadducean minority, had come to believe in the RESURRECTION of the dead. Obviously such a doctrine will considerably enlarge the concept of salvation, and we should expect to find significant developments in the doctrine of salvation between the OT and NT.

4. Salvation in Hellenistic religion. Since attempts have been made to explain NT theology in terms of the religious ideas of the Hellenistic world, it is necessary to examine the concept of salvation which is said to have been current in NT times.

a. Gnostic tendencies. In the second and third centuries A.D. the Hermetic literature bears evidence of a widespread myth (often today called the "Gnostic myth"), which certain modern scholars have declared to underlie the NT conception of

Christ as redeemer, especially in Colossians-Ephesians and the Fourth Gospel. These scholars claim that in the first century this myth would have been familiar throughout the Hellenistic world, especially to "intellectuals"; as a religious philosophy it was widely accepted. It is the myth of the Anthropos, or Heavenly Man. Of oriental origin, it comes down from a distant antiquity. A celestial light-being was cast down from heaven, having been vanquished in combat or else because of his folly (cf. the Fall); he fell down to earth, where his personality was shattered into countless atomic units, which in fact are our human selves. These fragments—i.e., mankind—are now imprisoned in evil matter—i.e., our bodies. They are subjected to the demonic rulers of this age, and they have forgotten their real nature and origin. The Gnostic redeemer, however, comes down from heaven to save them; he is the "Heavenly Man" and is sometimes described as the "son" or "image" of the Most High God in heaven. He saves by imparting knowledge (gnosis) of man's real nature and by communicating the passwords by which the soul at death can escape the planetary guardians of the heavenly spheres and so ascend to the world of light: salvation consists in the re-creation of the fallen man into the heavenly person which he was before he fell, the New Man. The heavenly redeemer, while he is on earth, disguises himself in many human forms, so that he may escape the attention of the demonic rulers of the world (cf. I Cor. 2:8).

The myth is incorporated syncretistically into many of the mystery cults of the Hellenistic world, and it is suggested that it has likewise been incorporated into Hellenistic Christianity, notably that of Paul and John. Thus, Paul's "second man . . . from heaven" or "heavenly man" (I Cor. 15:47-48), the "new man" of Col. 3:10, the "perfect man" of Eph. 4:13, and the Son of man in the Fourth Gospel who descends from and ascends into heaven (John 3:13; 6:62; etc.)—all these and similar conceptions show how Hellenistic Christianity reinterpreted the original kerygma of the Aramaic-speaking church, so that it became a kind of Christianized Gnosticism which would be intelligible and congenial to the "higher paganism" of the Greco-Roman world. The whole conception of a gathering into one of a fragmented humanity in the "body" or person of the Son of man from heaven, it is argued, is a Christianized version of the Gnostic myth.

Compelling though this theory seems to be at first sight, it is nevertheless open to serious criticism. In the first place, there is no evidence at all for the existence of the Gnostic myth in the first century, apart from the NT itself; all the evidence is found in literature which cannot be earlier than the later second century: in other words, this literature itself may be the Gnosticizing of biblical-Christian conceptions. Moreover, it is a circular argument to say that, e.g., Colossians-Ephesians embodies the widespread Gnostic myth and then to prove the existence of the myth by citing, not evidence from outside the NT, but Colossians-Ephesians! And, lastly, all the characteristic terms and concepts of salvation which are found in the NT can be elucidated satisfactorily by reference to the OT, the prophetic theology of which is the basis of the NT scheme of salvation. As we shall see, the NT plan of salvation is a rediscovery of the OT prophetic kerygma in the light of the ministry, death, and resurrection of Jesus Christ. There is no need to look for an explanation of the NT doctrine of salvation in a hypothetical myth, which one must assume to have existed, when there is in existence a substantial literature—namely, the canonical OT—in which the NT doctrine of salvation is already set forth in adumbration.

b. The imperial cult. The concept of salvation through political power, an illusion of mankind in every age, expressed itself mythologically in the first century in the cult of emperor-worship. The myth of the divine king, who was the benefactor and savior of his people, was, of course, oriental in origin, and it is probable that it lies behind concepts of the King-Messiah such as are found in Jewish apocalyptic literature. The book of Revelation is a profound study of the rival mythologies of Caesar-worship and Christ-worship, in which the former is shown to be a kind of diabolical perversion or caricature of the worship of the true King of kings and Lord of lords. Julius Caesar was accorded divine honors after his death; but temples were erected in Asia Minor in honor of *divus Augustus* during his lifetime. Augustus and Tiberius kept the cult within reasonable limits, and Claudius was skeptical of his own divinity. But the egocentric Gaius (Caligula) and the paranoiac Nero took their divine status seriously; and so did Domitian at the end of the century. In Asia Minor especially, the divine emperors were worshiped in temples built in their honor and at the imperial games, where the adulation of the crowds was expressed in hymns which ascribed salvation and honor and glory and worship to Caesar as God and Savior of his people. Domitian was hailed as *Dominus et Deus noster,* and throughout Asia the titles of Εὐεργέτης (cf. Luke 22:25) and Σωτήρ were accorded to the emperors. It is against this background that the three ascriptions of σωτηρία to God and Christ found in Revelation (7:10; 12:10; 19:1) are to be understood. The word σωτήρ does not occur in Revelation. If (as was pointed out in § 1c *above*) this word occurs most frequently in the later portions of the NT, the reason may perhaps be, not the influence of a shadowy Gnosticism, but the pressure of an arrogant and persecuting political religion which demanded the worship of the brute force of imperial Rome ("the beast" [Rev. 13]), and which asserted that salvation would be found in submission to the imperial will. *See also* EMPEROR-WORSHIP.

5. Salvation in the NT. The NT in every part claims that the salvation adumbrated in the scriptures of Israel has been fulfilled in the coming of Jesus Christ. Salvation still fundamentally means, as it did in the OT, God's saving action in history, by which he rescues his people from destruction and by which he assures them of the greater salvation that is to come. The whole NT is concerned, therefore, with the proclamation of a gospel, which is the "power of God for salvation" (Rom. 1:16).

a. The ministry and teaching of Jesus. The Synoptic gospels represent the ministry of Jesus as concerned with the work of salvation: "The Son of man came to seek and to save the lost" (Luke 19:10). They represent Jesus himself as teaching that his mission concerns the lost, or the lost sheep of Israel (e.g., Matt. 10:6; 15:24; 18:12-14; Luke 15:3-10; etc.). The distinctive and, indeed, unique feature of his doctrine of salvation is that it is offered to sinners; in this respect there is no parallel to the teaching of Jesus in rabbinic Judaism, apocalyptic, or sectarian Judaism. "Those who are well have no need of a physician, but those who are sick; I came not to call the righteous, but sinners" (Mark 2:17). For this very reason the conventionally religious people and their leaders, the Pharisaic rabbis, were scandalized at him (Matt. 11:19; Mark 2:16; etc.). The issue was whether salvation was by the righteousness of God or by men's own righteousness; it is stated by Jesus with devastating lucidity in the parable of the Pharisee and the publican (Luke 18:10-14). The man who acknowledged that he was a sinner in need of God's mercy went down to his house justified, rather than the man who boasted of his genuinely good works. It was sinners, who knew that they had need of God's forgiveness, who responded to the gospel of Jesus, not the law-observing Pharisees: "The tax collectors and the harlots go into the kingdom of God before you" (Matt. 21:31). At the messianic banquet the guests would be the poor and maimed and blind and lame, gathered together from the highways and hedges (Luke 14:16-24).

All these were justified by their faith, not by their works. "Your faith has saved you"—these words are spoken by Jesus to sinners like the woman who anointed his feet in the house of Simon the Pharisee (Luke 7:50), and they are clearly synonymous with "Your sins are forgiven" (vs. 48). Salvation means the forgiveness of sins, reconciliation with God, and the peace which flows from it: "Your faith has saved you; go in peace" (vs. 50). Repentance and amendment are the conditions of salvation and reconciliation in this sense, as the story of Zacchaeus illustrates: "Today salvation has come to this house" (Luke 19:9). God cannot forgive unless the sinner is in a state of willingness to be forgiven (Luke 15:11-32); Jesus can do nothing for the proud who have no need of the physician (Mark 2:17).

Hence the mission of Jesus, whose object is salvation, is closely bound up with the forgiveness of sins. This is most clearly brought out in the miracle stories of healings, in which the forgiveness of the person healed is emphasized. The formula "Your faith has saved you" is applied to the sick who have been healed (Mark 5:34; 10:52; Luke 17:19), and we are thus reminded that the Greek word σώζειν means "to save" and also "to heal or make whole" —a double meaning essential to the purpose of the miracle stories of healing, but one which is not easy to express in an English translation (the RSV completely misses the point with "Your faith has made you well" [contrast Luke 7:50: "Your faith has saved you"—the same phrase in the Greek, ἡ πίστις σου σέσωκέ σε]). The miracle stories of healing are parables of salvation; they are signs (see SIGNS IN THE NT; MIRACLES) of who Jesus is, at least to those who have eyes to see—i.e., those who have faith in him (cf. "Your *faith* has saved you"). This truth is especially brought out in the story of the paralytic (Mark 2:1-12), where the declaration that the sufferer's sins are forgiven is authenticated by the causing of the paralyzed man to rise and walk. To heal implies the power to forgive sins (both senses of σώζειν). As the Pharisees rightly perceive, healing and forgiveness ("saving") are divine prerogatives (Mark 2:7; cf. John 9:33); the fact that Jesus healed the sick is evidence to the eyes of faith that Jesus is the Messiah. This is true, even though the superstition be rejected that all sickness and suffering are divine punishments for sin—a view which Jesus himself would seem to have denied, although it was the common belief of his day (Luke 13:1-5; John 9:2-3).

The fact is that the healing signs were an integral part of the total picture of the Servant-Son of man which Jesus had discerned in the prophecy of Isaiah and which he applied to himself. In the days of the coming salvation the blind would see, the deaf hear, the lame walk, the dumb sing (Isa. 32:3-4; 35:5-6; 42:7); and it is precisely these Isaianic signs which are fulfilled in the gospel miracle stories of Jesus' healings—as Jesus himself points out to John the Baptist (Matt. 11:4-5; Luke 7:22). The gospel stories are parables of the saving power of Christ; e.g., the leper who is cleansed at Christ's touch in Mark 1:40-45 is a symbol of those who, being sinners, were unable to fulfil God's law but who now, through the compassionate touch of Christ, are able to stand confidently and to offer the things which Moses commanded.

The healings of the demon-possessed (exorcisms) are also parables of Christ's saving mission; they make their point, however, in rather a different way from the stories of the healing of disease. Demon-possession in the popular view, unlike disease, is not punishment for sin; it is quite fortuitous, and might happen to anyone, good or bad. The exorcisms are not connected with forgiveness. They depict Christ as Savior in an altogether different connection. The demons are the emissaries and agents of Satan, who has invaded God's good creation and subjected it to his evil dominion (Luke 4:6; 22:53; John 12:31; I John 5:19; Rev. 13:2). The exorcisms are signs that the house of the "strong man" (i.e., Satan) has been entered and is being spoiled: Satan's kingdom is at an end (Mark 3:26-27). Christ is the conqueror of Satan; his victory is a cosmic victory, involving the liberation of the whole creation from subjection to the evil "powers" which have enslaved it. This important NT theme, graphically set forth in the stories of exorcisms in the gospels, proclaims Christ as liberator, for he has not only loosed us from our sins (Rev. 1:5) but also set us free from bondage to the hostile world powers.

According to Luke, Jesus saw his own mission in terms of the Isaianic Servant's liberating work:

> He has sent me to proclaim release to the captives,
> . . . .
> to set at liberty those who are oppressed
> (Luke 4:18; cf. Isa. 61:1).

The same conception is expressed under the redemption metaphor of Mark 10:45: "The Son of man also came . . . to give his life as a ransom for many." This verse is an echoing of Isa. 53:10-12 and is further testimony to the fact that Jesus conceived of his mission as that of the Servant of the Lord, whom Isaiah had foretold, who would atone for the sins of the world by bearing them and who by his sufferings would effect the release of those who were in bondage to a tyranny more terrible than that of Egypt or Babylon.

Further evidence that Jesus thought of himself and his work in this way is found in the NT accounts of his teaching-sign with the bread and wine, at the Last Supper, whereby he set himself forth as the new sacrificial offering in whose blood a new covenant was ratified between God and a newly redeemed Israel (Matt. 26:26-29; Mark 14:22-25; Luke 22:17-20; I Cor. 11:23-25; cf. Exod. 24:8; Jer. 31:31). The original Moses of the redemption from Egypt had offered to give his life for the forgiveness and salvation of his people (Exod. 32:32); Deutero-Isaiah had foretold a new Moses who would give his life for his people's redemption; and Jesus understood his own death as effecting the salvation of the world through the establishment of a new covenant between God and man. It was Jesus himself who first taught that he was the Savior foretold by the prophet in the words which are quoted by Paul:

"The Deliverer [ὁ ῥυόμενος] will come from Zion,
he will banish ungodliness from Jacob";
"and this will be my covenant with them
when I take away their sins"
(Rom. 11:26-27; Isa. 59:20-21).

The Servant of the Lord, according to the Isaianic prophecy, would establish a new covenant with God's people and enlighten all the nations of the world; he would open the blind eyes and bring out the prisoners from the dungeon (Isa. 42:6-7). It was in this sense that both Jesus and the apostolic church understood his work of salvation.

b. Salvation as historical deliverance. In the NT, as in the OT, salvation is understood to be accomplished by an act of God in human history. Man is not saved by wisdom or right knowledge (Gnosticism), nor by merit or right actions (Judaism), nor yet by mystical absorption into deity (Hellenistic mysticism), but by the act of God in the birth, life, death, resurrection, and ascension of Jesus Christ. Accordingly the Christian message is not a philosophy (σοφία), nor an ethical code, nor yet a technique of mystical practice: it is kerygma, preaching, evangel in the Isaianic sense of proclaiming the fact of liberation (Isa. 40:9; 52:7; 61:1-2). The title Savior (σωτήρ), which in the OT is a name for God, is applied to Christ in the NT (Luke 2:11; John 4:42; Acts 5:31; 13:23; Eph. 5:23; Phil. 3:20; II Tim. 1:10; Tit. 1:4; 2:13; 3:6; II Pet. 1:1, 11; 2:20; 3:2, 18; I John 4:14).

His work of salvation is presented under a considerable variety of images or metaphors, and it is the character of these metaphors which determines whether it is said that we are saved by Christ's death or by his life. Salvation is not exclusively connected with his death, for it is the whole Christ event, including the Resurrection, which is regarded as the saving act of God (Rom. 4:25; 5:10; II Cor. 4:10-11;

etc.). Our salvation depended, not only on the fact that Christ was willing to die, but even more upon the fact that he was willing to be born (II Cor. 8:9; Phil. 2:6-7); the incarnation of the Son of God is itself the act of atonement whereby God and man are brought together in the new humanity of Jesus Christ, and thus the very purpose of Christ's coming into the world was to save sinners (John 3:17; Rom. 8:3; I Tim. 1:15; I John 4:9-10, 14). It is the life of Christ which saves us; but it is natural that, in the metaphors of salvation which are based upon Jewish sacrificial ideas and practices, it should be said that we are saved by his death. The "blood" of Christ is frequently said to be the means of our salvation (Acts 20:28; Rom. 3:25; 5:9; Eph. 1:7; Col. 1:20; Heb. 9:12; 12:24; 13:12; I John 1:7; Rev. 1:5; 5:9; etc.), and in these contexts "blood" is synonymous with "death"; it is a graphic image of the kind of death he died. Christ is represented as the sacrificial victim by whose death communion with God and the forgiveness of sins were obtained, for in the OT all sacrifice is thought of as a means of communion with God; but it is nowhere taught in the NT that God could not have forgiven sins if Christ had not died. The death of Jesus occurred at Passover time, and it is hardly surprising that the metaphors of the Passover and of the paschal lamb should be prominent in NT theology. Jesus is the Christian Passover lamb (Mark 14:22; John 6:51; 19:36; I Cor. 5:7; probably also John 1:29, 36), and the Eucharist in the church became the weekly paschal festival (Easter), the commemoration of the historical deliverance wrought by Jesus and thanksgiving for the covenant of salvation which he had made.

The NT says almost nothing about the Eucharist and its meaning, probably because it was considered improper to commit the most sacred truths of the inmost mystery of the faith to writing and perhaps thus to expose them to profane inspection; but it provides sufficient evidence to show that in the church of the first century, as in that of later centuries, the Eucharist was considered to be par excellence the means by which the Christian community drew upon the life of God and appropriated to itself the benefits of Christ's salvation (John 6:53-56; I Cor. 10:16-21; perhaps Heb. 13:10). Just as the Passover continued and kept alive in Jewish life the tradition of God's deliverance from Egypt, so in the church the Eucharist was the liturgical ἀνάμνησις of the historical sacrifice of Christ and of the deliverance which God wrought through it; the recitation of the events of the Last Supper and of the Passion was from the earliest days an integral part of the Eucharistic rite.

Thus, the death of Christ is set forth in the NT and celebrated in the church as the means of our salvation, but the death was always regarded as a moment in the whole act of deliverance. It is noteworthy that it is the Letter to the Hebrews, with its tremendous emphasis upon the once-only efficacious death of Christ, that stresses most powerfully the significance of Christ's ascension in the work of salvation (Heb. 9:24-26; cf. Eph. 4:8). Other metaphors, like that of reconciliation, stress the fact that it is God himself who is providing for sinners the means of forgiveness and therefore of fellowship with himself (Rom. 5:1-11; II Cor. 5:18-19); it was God who reconciled us to himself through Christ, not Christ who reconciled God to us. God himself is the originator of our salvation, and he is several times called "Savior" in the NT (e.g., Luke 1:47; I Tim. 4:10; Jude 25).

It should be noted too that this act of salvation or reconciliation, which God has accomplished through Christ, is not limited to the human race; salvation in the NT is a cosmic conception. Through Christ, God reconciled all things to himself, whether things upon earth or things in the heavens (Eph. 1:10; Col. 1:20). It is nothing less than the new creation, foretold by the prophets, that has now appeared in Christ, the creation of the new heavens and new earth (II Cor. 5:17). In this age the new creation is discernible only by the eye of faith, and it constitutes the sphere of church; for the church is the new Israel of God, the people of the new act of creation-redemption, who are the first fruits of the consummation that shall be. In this sense it may be said that in the NT there is no salvation outside the church. The church consists of the redeemed, those who are σωζόμενοι, those who are now in the sphere or process of salvation (I Cor. 1:18; II Cor. 2:15). The historical salvation has already taken place, and the existence and preaching of the church provide the evidence of it. The day of salvation heralded by the prophet has dawned for men with faith (Isa. 49:8; II Cor. 6:2; Heb. 3:7–4:13); today, the era of the preaching of salvation, is a day of opportunity and decision: "How shall we escape if we neglect such a great salvation?" (Heb. 2:3). Sometimes it seems to be suggested that the moment of baptism into the church is the time of the individual Christian's salvation (especially at Tit. 3:5: "He saved us . . . by the washing of regeneration and renewal in the Holy Spirit"; cf. Acts 2:47). "By grace you have been saved through faith" (Eph. 2:8; cf. 2:5). The perfect tense shows that, as far as the salvation of the individual Christian is concerned, it is an event which has taken place at a particular and definite moment in his past history. The view would accord with the theological outlook of the apostolic church that, whereas the death of Christ upon Calvary represents the baptism of humanity as a whole into the sphere of salvation, the moment of the death to sin, or resurrection to salvation, of the individual believer is his baptism into Christ's church.

c. Salvation as an eschatological reality. The tension between the historical "even now" and the eschatological "not yet," which we saw was present in the OT conception of salvation, is even more strongly marked in the NT. The saving righteousness of God has been revealed in the historical Christ, but it has been revealed only to faith; and the gospel of Christ, which is the power of God for salvation, is communicated in this age "through faith for faith" (Rom. 1:16-17). But the historical event is only the guarantee of the mighty salvation that is yet to be revealed; it is the means by which salvation is brought to us even now by faith in the midst of history, so that we are saved by the revelation of the righteousness of God.

It is Paul who, alone among the NT writers, explicitly revives the Isaianic conception of the divine righteousness which works salvation, the conception which (as we have noted) underlies Jesus' own understanding of his mission to sinners. Paul uses δικαιοσύνη more than all the other NT writers together; whereas they generally use the word in the normal, rabbinic sense of conduct pleasing to God, Paul uses it in the deeper, Isaianic sense of the outgoing, energizing power of God which works salvation for men. The divine righteousness has appeared in history, working salvation (Rom. 1:16), and it is communicated to us through faith (Phil. 3:9); God has demonstrated his righteousness (i.e., his faithfulness to his covenant promise that he would save his people) by setting forth Christ as an expiation for their sins: the death of Christ has proved that God is righteous and that he justifies—as Isaiah promised that he would—those who have faith in Jesus (Rom. 3:25-26). Our present knowledge of salvation (cf. Luke 1:77), brought to us by Christ, is only an earnest or foretaste of the salvation that we shall know at the parousia of Christ. Our present experience of salvation in the church of Jesus Christ is, as it were, the shadow cast before by the reality of the salvation that is coming; in this sense it is true to say that even the historical salvation that we have known is itself eschatological, the prerevelation of the salvation that is to come. The conception of salvation in the NT is through and through eschatological. Salvation is essentially a future reality which we enjoy even now through faith. It cannot be known apart from faith, because faith is the form of knowing in the age of history. When we say that God has saved us (e.g., Tit. 3:5), we are speaking in characteristically biblical-Hebraic idiom, according to which past and future are identified: to say that God has saved us means that he will save us. The paradox of the "even now" and the "not yet" of salvation means that we are saved or σωζόμενοι by reason of God's coming salvation, which was realized in history in the life, death, and resurrection of Jesus Christ.

Thus, Paul can write: "Salvation is nearer to us now than when we first believed" (Rom. 13:11), or again: "By hope were we saved" (Rom. 8:24 ERV). Salvation in its full and final sense is accomplished in the "day of the Lord Jesus" (I Cor. 5:5); the day of the Lord (i.e., the Parousia) is the "day of salvation" and also the "day of wrath." Both the salvation and the wrath of God have already been revealed in history through Jesus Christ (Rom. 1:17-18), and it is through faith in God's righteousness that we shall be reconciled to God: "We shall be saved from the wrath of God through him" (Rom. 5:9 ERV)—i.e., from the destruction that will overtake the wicked in the day of judgment. Living in the hope of salvation, Christians wait for a Savior from heaven (Phil. 3:20; cf. Tit. 2:13). They are those "who by God's power are guarded through faith for a salvation ready to be revealed in the last time" (I Pet. 1:5; cf. vs. 9), which is to be understood in connection with the promise contained in the preceding verse of an "inheritance which is imperishable, undefiled, and unfading, kept in heaven for you." Christians are "those who are to obtain salvation" (Heb. 1:14), the σωτηρία αἰώνιος (i.e., salvation in the aeon to come) of which Christ is the source (Heb. 5:9). The general attitude of the NT as a whole is that of Heb. 9:28: "Christ, having been offered once to bear the sins of many, will appear a second time, not to deal with sin but to save those who are eagerly waiting for him."

Although the fundamental historical-eschatological pattern of the conception of salvation remains the same in the NT as in the OT, there is nevertheless a significant extension and enrichment of the meaning of salvation in the NT. This is because of the general acceptance in the intertestamental period of the idea of life after death. Salvation now in the NT concerns, not only this life, but also the life of the age to come. Indeed, salvation and the "life of the age to come" are synonymous terms; the Fourth Gospel, e.g., uses σωτηρία only once (John 4:22: "Salvation is from the Jews"), but the conception is identical with that of ζωή, or ζωὴ αἰώνιος, which in biblical Greek does not mean "eternal life" in any Platonic sense, or even "everlasting life" (as if the emphasis were upon duration), but the life of the Aeon—i.e., the age to come. Jesus came that men might have life (John 10:10); he brings to them the waters of salvation or "living water" (John 4:14), which in Johannine language means the life-giving Spirit (John 7:37-39). The Johannine conception of "life" largely replaces the Synoptic "kingdom of God," with which it is synonymous; to enter into the kingdom of God and to enter into life are identical expressions, and both have reference to an eschatological salvation, as a study of Mark 9:43-48 will make clear. To be saved is to enter even now by faith into the life of the age to come and even now to possess it eschatologically; nevertheless, we do not yet possess salvation or "life" in the full and final sense in which it will be ours hereafter; it is only he who endures to the end who will be saved (Mark 13:13).

Not even Jesus himself knows when this end will come (Mark 13:32), and Christians can but exercise steadfast, patient endurance amid the tribulations which will precede it (cf. Heb. 10:25). They must work out their salvation with fear and trembling (Phil. 2:12), not presuming to boast of their condition (I Cor. 10:12). The trials which will precede the end will be unparalleled since the creation of the world, and had not God shortened the days of the tribulation, no flesh could have been saved (Mark 13:19-20).

The final salvation is described by Jesus in pictures drawn from the traditional Jewish imagery of the messianic banquet—a sitting down with Abraham, Isaac, and Jacob in the kingdom of God (Matt. 8:11; Luke 13:28-29). This "sitting at table in the kingdom of God" is anticipated in the church's Eucharist, the banquet of the elect with the Messiah, for whom it is appointed that they shall "eat and drink at [his] table in [his] kingdom" (Luke 22:29-30). The Eucharist is the showing forth of Christ's saving death until he comes (I Cor. 11:26). It proclaims also that salvation is a social reality; there is no individualism in the NT conception of it. All the metaphors of the state of salvation are corporate in character—the Israel of God, the elect, the body of Christ, the communion of saints, the fellowship of the Holy Spirit, the messianic banquet, the kingdom of God, the church, the new man, the new creation. So great is this salvation that the earth cannot contain it; indeed, the whole created order itself is awaiting the day of liberation from its bondage to decay (Rom. 8:19-23).

The scene of the final salvation must be beyond earth and beyond history in the world to come, beyond time, decay, and death; the scene must be laid in the new heavens and new earth of Isaianic prediction, the scene which in his vision the author of Revelation has glimpsed again—the city of God, new Jerusalem, whose temple is the Lord God the Almighty and the Lamb, and where no light of lamp or sun is needed, for the Lord God will be its light forever and ever (Rev. 21:1–22:5). Of course, this is pictorial language, and the poetry is spoiled if it is treated as literal prose; but all our speaking about our ultimate salvation must be in pictures, for we have no other means of communication. This is because we are attempting to speak of a realm which utterly transcends our experience and therefore have no words which can describe it; yet through the gift of the Spirit we can speak of it, since it has been revealed to us. "As it is written,

> 'What no eye has seen, nor ear heard,
> nor the heart of man conceived, .
> what God has prepared for those who love him,'

God has revealed to us through the Spirit" (I Cor. 2:9-10, citing Isa. 64:4; cf. Isa. 65:17).

Bibliography. The books dealing with the biblical theme of salvation are far too numerous to be listed, since all works dealing with biblical theology are relevant. See, e.g., C. F. Burney, *Outlines of OT Theology* (1899). A. B. Davidson; *Theology of the OT* (1904). R. H. Charles, *Religious Development Between the Old and the New Testaments* (1914). G. F. Moore, *Judaism in the First Centuries of the Christian Era*, vols. I–II (1927). W. O. E. Oesterley and T. H. Robinson, *Hebrew Religion* (1930). G. Aulén, *Christos Victor* (1931). O. Eissfeldt, *Einleitung in das AT* (1934). W. Eichrodt, *Theologie des AT*, vols. I–III (1936-39). N. H. Snaith, *Distinctive Ideas of the OT* (1944), pp. 79-93. C. H. Dodd, *Interpretation of the Fourth Gospel* (1953). U. E. Simon, *A Theology of Salvation* (1953). R. Leivestad, *Christ the Conqueror* (1954). H. H. Rowley, *Biblical Doctrine of Election* (1954). A. Bentzen, *King and Messiah* (1955). R. Bultmann, *Theology of the NT*, vol. I (1952); vol. II (1955). E. Stauffer, *NT Theology* (1955). W. D. Davies and D. Daube, eds., *Background of the NT and Its Eschatology* (1956). G. W. H. Lampe, *Reconciliation in Christ* (1956). S. Mowinckel, *He That Cometh* (1956). L. Newbigin, *Sin and Salvation* (1956). A. Richardson, *Introduction to the Theology of the NT* (1958).   ALAN RICHARDSON

SALVE [κολλούριον, κολλύριον, *diminutive of* κολλύρα, a cake] (Rev. 3:18); KJV EYESALVE. A medical compound used for aiding the eyes (cf. Epictetus *Dissertations* II.21.20; III.21.21; Horace *Satires* I.5.30). It is sometimes referred to as "Phrygian powder" and a prescription used at the cult of Asclepius, but such assertions are somewhat tenuous.   T. S. KEPLER

SAMAEL. KJV form of Apoc. SALAMIEL. *See* SHELUMIEL.

SAMAIAS. KJV Apoc. form of SHEMAIAH 17.

*SAMARIA sə mâr′ĭ ə [שֹׁמְרוֹן; Aram. שָׁמְרִין; Σαμάρεια]. The capital city of the N kingdom, Israel.

1. Location
2. History
   a. Israelite
   b. Assyrian
   c. Babylonian
   d. Persian
   e. Hellenistic
   f. Roman
Bibliography

1. Location. Samaria occupies a hill in the central range of Palestine, approximately forty-two miles N of Jerusalem and *ca.* twenty-five miles E of the Mediterranean Sea. It is surrounded on three sides by fertile valleys and slopes, and overlooks the main N-S road connecting Jerusalem with the Plain of Esdraelon and the N. The hill itself is a long E-W ridge which terminates in a summit on the W and is joined to the hills on the E by a long, narrow saddle. The site is easily defensible—a factor which, no doubt, figured in Omri's decision to build his capital there (*see* § *2a below*). On the extreme E end of the ridge is located a modern village whose name, Sebastiyeh, preserves the Herodian name, Sebaste. Fig. SAM 8.

From *Atlas of the Bible* (Thomas Nelson & Sons Limited)
   8. The hill of Samaria, with the modern village of Sebastiyeh on the right

(1909-10), with C. S. Fisher as architect. The second expedition, which was jointly sponsored by Harvard University, Hebrew University (Jerusalem), the Palestine Exploration Fund, the British Academy, and

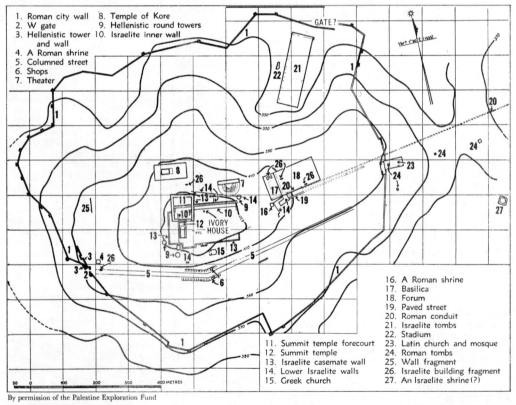

By permission of the Palestine Exploration Fund
   9. Plan of Samaria (Sebaste)

1. Roman city wall
2. W gate
3. Hellenistic tower and wall
4. A Roman shrine
5. Columned street
6. Shops
7. Theater
8. Temple of Kore
9. Hellenistic round towers
10. Israelite inner wall
11. Summit temple forecourt
12. Summit temple
13. Israelite casemate wall
14. Lower Israelite walls
15. Greek church
16. A Roman shrine
17. Basilica
18. Forum
19. Paved street
20. Roman conduit
21. Israelite tombs
22. Stadium
23. Latin church and mosque
24. Roman tombs
25. Wall fragment
26. Israelite building fragment
27. An Israelite shrine(?)

The site has been partially excavated by two different expeditions. From 1908-10, Harvard University sponsored a series of campaigns under the direction of G. Schumacher (1908) and G. A. Reisner the British School of Archaeology (Jerusalem) from 1931-33, and by the above-mentioned British institutions only in 1935, was directed by J. W. Crowfoot with the assistance of E. L. Sukenik, Kathleen Kenyon, and a number of archaeologists and architects. These expeditions cleared a considerable portion of the summit and the ridge to the E and excavated a number of smaller areas on the terraces and slopes; as a result, the history and material culture of the site can be described in some detail. Fig. SAM 9.

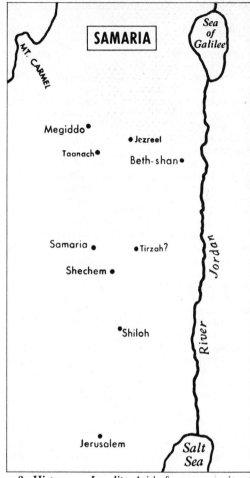

Courtesy of Chester C. McCown

10. Example of Israelite masonry at Samaria

By permission of the Palestine Exploration Fund

11. Retaining walls supporting forecourt of temple to the divine Augustus in Herodian Samaria. At the lower level are the remains of casemate walls, which surrounded the citadel of the period of the Israelite kings.

2. History. *a. Israelite.* Aside from a quantity of EB material found in cuttings in bedrock, the hill was first occupied early in Iron II (*ca.* 870 B.C.), when Omri purchased it from Shemer for two talents of silver and built a city on it, which he named Samaria (I Kings 16:24). Abandoning Tirzah, Omri made Samaria the capital of Israel, a position which it held until the downfall of the N kingdom.

Remains of the Omri-Ahab city (Periods I-II of the Joint Excavations) have been found on the summit, terraces, and slopes of the hill. This city is attributed to both Omri and Ahab, because the constructions of this period are too numerous to have been completed during the remaining six years of Omri's rule, and much must have been finished by his son. Although later construction and quarrying destroyed most of this occupation, the few surviving wall fragments and foundation trenches show that Samaria was a beautifully designed and magnificently constructed city; some of its walls are among the finest ever built in Palestine in any period. The style of masonry used

in them also appears slightly earlier at Megiddo, Taanach, and Beth-shan; it was probably introduced into Palestine by Phoenician masons during the reign of Solomon (I Kings 5:17-18), and was revived in this period, when Phoenician influence was again strong. Figs. SAM 10-11.

The royal quarter, which consisted of a number of buildings and courtyards, occupied the summit. The palace itself must have contained at least two stories, in view of representations of roughly contemporary buildings of this type elsewhere in the Near East, and of II Kings 1:2, which states that Ahaziah, Ahab's son, was fatally injured as a result of falling through the window of an upper room of the palace. On the N side of the courtyard a large, shallow, rectangular pool was discovered, which may have been the "pool of Samaria," where Ahab's blood was washed from his chariot following his death in battle at Ramoth-gilead (I Kings 22:38). Presumably in the royal quarter were also located the temple and the altar, which Ahab built and dedicated to Baal (16:32), but no traces of these structures survive.

The most noteworthy find in this area was a group of more than five hundred fragments of ivory, most of which are inlays* from wooden wall paneling and furniture, although some are from small boxes and toilet articles. It is almost certainly in the sense of inlaid wall panels and inlaid furniture that the references to Ahab's house of ivory (I Kings 22:39) and to beds of ivory (Amos 6:4) must be understood. Some of the fragments are carved in the round, but most are in relief; many are inset with colored glass or paste. In general, their style suggests that they were carved by Syro-Phoenician artisans using Egyptian models. In view of the close relations between Israel and Phoenicia in this period—note that Ahab's wife, Jezebel, was a Phoenician princess (I Kings 16:31) and a strong protagonist of Phoenician culture in Israel (18:4, 19)—the discovery in Israel of ivories from N workshops is not surprising. *See* IVORY. Figs. INL 8; IVO 22.

The royal quarter was surrounded by an enclosure wall, the lower courses of which were laid against a rock scarp. Later—probably during the reign of Ahab —a second enclosure wall was built just outside the earlier one. It varied in thickness from *ca.* twelve feet on the S to more than thirty-two feet on the N and was constructed on the casemate principle—i.e., two parallel walls were joined at intervals by cross walls, and the compartments formed by this design were usually filled with rubble. The topography of the site suggests that the palace area was entered from the E, and in this area six proto-Ionic pilaster capitals, similar to several discovered at MEGIDDO, were found which may have decorated the walls of a monumental entrance. Traces of walls which probably formed another ring of fortifications have been found on the middle terrace below the summit, and on the E side the remains of what may have been a gateway have been discovered. It was probably in this gateway—or in the entrance to the royal quarter— that Ahab and Jehoshaphat sat on thrones and heard Micaiah the prophet speak of impending doom at Ramoth-gilead (I Kings 22:10; II Chr. 18:9). Here, also, business transactions took place in the time of Elisha (II Kings 7:1), and probably through the life of Israelite Samaria. A third defensive system, consisting of a wall and towers, possibly encircled the lower slopes of the hill; walls of impressive buildings belonging to this period were found on these slopes, and it is unlikely that they would have been left defenseless. So strong was this system of fortifications that the city successfully withstood all attempts to take it (e.g., I Kings 20; II Kings 6:24) until the long Assyrian siege (*see* § 2b *below*).

Samaria witnessed the full fury of the revolution, inspired by Elijah and Elisha and carried through by Jehu (*ca.* 842-815 B.C.), which destroyed the Dynasty of Omri. Here, according to II Kings 10:1-

7, the elders of Samaria beheaded seventy sons of Ahab rather than risk warfare with Jehu. Here also Jehu killed the remaining descendants of Ahab, slaughtered Baal-worshipers, and destroyed the temple of Baal which Ahab had built (II Kings 10: 12-28). From the excavations it is clear that the first transformation of the city took place at this time (Period III). There is evidence of destruction to parts of the Omri-Ahab royal quarter on the summit, but whether this destruction resulted from a natural catastrophe—such as an earthquake—or from Jehu's zeal is not known. In any case, much rebuilding and new construction were probably carried on in this period. In view of the fact that Israel's relations with Phoenicia were strained or broken as a result of Jehu's purge, and since Jehu was under tribute to Shalmaneser III of Assyria, according to the Obelisk of Shalmaneser, Samaria's prosperity must have declined significantly at this time.

Little is known of Samaria during the reigns of Jehoahaz (*ca.* 815-801) and Joash (*ca.* 801-786) except that the latter is said to have brought to Samaria treasures from the temple and palace in Jerusalem, after defeating Amaziah of Judah at Beth-shemesh and sacking Jerusalem (II Kings 14:8-14; II Chr. 25: 17-24). Under Jeroboam II (*ca.* 786-746), Samaria enjoyed its greatest period of prosperity. Wealth flowed into the city following Jeroboam's expansion into Syria, Transjordan, and possibly Judah (II Kings 14:23-28), and as a result of his friendly relations with Phoenicia, whose commercial empire in the Mediterranean was at its peak. In the city itself, numerous repairs to fortifications and at least three building phases (Periods IV-VI) attest to increased building activity. But nowhere was the fine construction characteristic of the Omri-Ahab city used in this period; walls were roughly built of stones varying in size and were finished with a coat of plaster. The most important find of this period was a group of sixty-three ostraca (inscribed potsherds)*—containing receipts and orders for various commodities such as oil, wine, and barley—which were discovered in a building just W of the Omri-Ahab palace. All of them apparently belong to the eighth century B.C., and a number date *ca.* 778-770, in the reign of Jeroboam. These ostraca are significant, not because of their contents, but because of the light they shed on Hebrew paleography and on the study of personal names, religion, and state administration of this period. Fig. SAM 12.

12. Ostracon from Samaria (eighth century)

The stability and prosperity enjoyed by Samaria under Jeroboam ended soon after his death. During the next twenty-four years leading to the fall of Samaria, six kings occupied the throne; and of the six, four were assassinated, two of them in Samaria (II Kings 15:8-31). Meanwhile Assyrian power was growing under the leadership of a series of strong rulers, who applied increasing pressure on the small states in Syro-Palestine. According to II Kings 15: 19-20 and the annals of Tiglath-pileser, Menahem (*ca.* 745-738) was forced to pay heavy tribute to Pul (Tiglath-pileser III, *ca.* 745-727) of Assyria to save Samaria—spelled "Samerina" in the Assyrian texts— from siege. Again during the reign of Pekah (*ca.* 737- 732), Tiglath-pileser invaded Israel—this time at the request of Ahaz of Judah (II Kings 16:7-9)—and occupied a large portion of the area N of the Plain of Esdraelon and Gilead (II Kings 15:29). After Pekah was murdered, Tiglath-pileser placed Hoshea on the throne and imposed tribute on him, according to Assyrian inscriptions. With Tiglath-pileser's death, Hoshea rebelled against the new Assyrian king, Shalmaneser V (727-722), who placed him in prison and laid siege to Samaria. The city held out for three years against the most powerful army of the time, but finally capitulated in 722-721 to Sargon II, who meanwhile had succeeded to the Assyrian throne. Part, if not all, of the city was burned, as shown by a burned layer which sealed the remains of this period on the summit. Before and immediately after this catastrophe, Isaiah and Micah repeatedly warned Judah of the consequences of following Israel's footsteps, and on several occasions used the fate of Samaria as an object lesson to Jerusalem (e.g., Isa. 8:4; 10:9-11; Mic. 1:1-7).

b. Assyrian. The events surrounding the fall of Samaria are recorded in the Bible (II Kings 17:1-6, 24) and in Assyrian texts (the annals of Sargon and the so-called "Display Inscription"). After conquering Samaria, Sargon deported 27,290 Israelites, resettling them at various places in the Empire, from Gozen to Media. In turn, he repopulated the city with people from other conquered lands. Samaria was rebuilt—Sargon boasts that it was better than before—and became the headquarters of an administrative district of the Assyrian Empire. Of the buildings of the city itself (Periods VII and VIIa), little is known. The summit was occupied, but only foundation trenches and a few isolated fragments of walls survive. Noteworthy objects attesting to Assyrian domination include: a fragment of an Assyrian stele, a broken cylinder and fragments of clay tablets written in cuneiform, and sherds of Assyrian pottery.

c. Babylonian. With the fall of Nineveh to the Medes and Babylonians in 612 B.C., and the subsequent division of the Assyrian Empire by the victors, Samaria became a Babylonian possession and functioned as a provincial administrative center. Little is known of the city during this period. According to Jer. 41:5, there were still some Yahweh-worshipers in the city, in spite of the earlier Assyrian deportation; and Samaria's unfaithfulness and punishment had not been forgotten (Ezek. 16:44-55; 23). Few building remains of this occupation (Period VIII) have been found at the site. To the E of the earlier Omri-Ahab palace, a part of the summit was leveled

By permission of the Palestine Exploration Fund

13. Rich brown soil layer in the excavations at Samaria, probably of a Babylonian-period garden

and capped with a thick layer of rich brown soil, which probably marks the location of a large garden, a not uncommon feature of Babylonian cities. Fig. SAM 13.

d. Persian. Following the Persian conquest of Babylon in 539 B.C., Samaria became the administrative center of a Persian province, which included Jerusalem and N Judah. In the late sixth and fifth centuries, many of the exiles returned to Judah, and conflicts of interest soon developed between them and the officials of Samaria, centering especially around efforts of the returnees to rebuild Jerusalem (Ezra 4:8-24; Neh. 2:9-20; 4:1-9; 6:1-14). During the late fifth century, Samaria is also mentioned incidentally in the Elephantine Papyri. Fragmentary building remains, coins, Persian seal impressions, and pottery—particularly Attic black- and red-figured ware—witness to the occupation of the site in this period (Period IX).

e. Hellenistic. This period, beginning with the conquest of Palestine by Alexander (332 B.C.) and ending with the Roman occupation under Pompey (63), was one of turmoil and warfare at Samaria. In little more than 250 years, it successively belonged to the Macedonian, Ptolemaic, and Seleucid empires, and finally to the Jewish kingdom. It is therefore not surprising that the most prominent remains of this period are two systems of fortifications. The earliest of these is a series of round towers—each measuring from forty-two to forty-eight feet in diameter—which were built to strengthen the old Israelite wall on the middle terrace. When these towers first came to light during Reisner's excavations, they were tentatively assigned to the time of Jeroboam II, but subsequent discoveries have shown that they must be dated *ca.* 300 B.C. They have been described as the "finest monuments of the Hellenistic age in Palestine." Fig. SAM 14.

The second defense system replaced the Israelite casemate wall around the summit. It consisted of a wall *ca.* thirteen feet thick, constructed of blocks of various shapes and sizes and built with offsets and towers. Portions of a similarly built city wall were also found on the lower slopes near the W gate. These walls were probably constructed *ca.* the middle

14. Hellenistic round tower at Samaria, after the clearance in 1935

of the second century B.C. to protect the Seleucid city from the Maccabees. But between 111 and 107, John Hyrcanus besieged Samaria, and he took it a year later, after which he broke down sections of the walls (Jos. Antiq. XIII.x.2-3). The city remained part of the Jewish kingdom until 63 B.C.

Most of the site was occupied during this period, but only traces of buildings have come to light in the excavations, because later construction destroyed these remains. In spite of unsettled conditions, Samaria was a prosperous city in the Hellenistic age, as shown by the discovery of fragments of sculpture and inscriptions, many coins, and much imported pottery, including Megarian bowls and more than two thousand Rhodian and other stamped jar handles.

f. Roman. This period is divided into three phases. The first phase covers the period from the Roman conquest of Palestine to the First Jewish Revolt (A.D. 66-70). Following the capture of Jerusalem, most of Palestine—including Samaria—was incorporated into the province of Syria; Samaria itself was returned to its own inhabitants (Jos. Antiq. XIV.iv.4). It remained an unwalled city until Gabinius, the provincial governor (57-55 B.C.), gave orders to rebuild the walls (Jos. Antiq. XIV.v.3). In gratitude, the inhabitants renamed the city in honor of Gabinius and remained loyal to Rome. Fragmentary remains of this occupation—found under Herod's temple complex on the summit—show that the city was well planned, with houses and shops arranged in blocks bounded by streets. To this period probably belongs the layout of the forum and possibly the Doric stadium, though the latter may be Herodian.

Samaria regained much of its earlier prominence during Herod's reign, because the city supported him in his struggle with Antigonus (Jos. Antiq. XIV.xv.3). Here Herod left his mother and children for safety (XIV.xv.4); here he married Mariamne (XIV.xv.14); here he entertained Agrippa (XVI.ii.1); and here he had his sons put to death (XVI.xi.7). In 30 B.C., Herod undertook a great program of construction at Samaria (Jos. War I.xxi.2) and renamed the newly built city Sebaste (Σεβαστός, Greek translation of "Augustus") in honor of the emperor. The most noteworthy structure of this period was a large temple,* consisting of a portico and a cella, which stood on a platform *ca.* fourteen feet high. On the N a monu-

mental staircase gave access to the platform from a long forecourt at a lower level.* A large altar stood in the courtyard directly in front of the staircase, and in the debris E of the altar was found a large fragment of a marble statue of an emperor, probably Augustus. To the W of the temple enclosure was a large atrium house; to the S, an apsidal building of unknown purpose; and to the E, buildings which probably served as dwellings for temple priests and servants.* Herod also enclosed Sebaste with a new city wall, which was more than two miles in circumference, and was strengthened at numerous points throughout its length by towers. Entrance to the city

15. Altar and monumental stair of Herodian temple at Samaria

was gained through a gate on the W side—the only one excavated to date—another on the E, and possibly one on the N and another on the S. Figs. SAM 11, 15, 16.

This was the Samaria of Jesus' time. Here Philip preached with much success, and following his mission, Peter and John prayed that the newly baptized converts might receive the Holy Spirit (Acts 8:5-17).

The second phase of the Roman period extends from the end of the First Jewish Revolt to the reign of Constantine (A.D. 274-337). Early in the Jewish Revolt, Sebaste was captured and burned by the rebels. After the revolt was put down, the temple was repaired, and to this reconstruction probably belong the subterranean corridors of the temple complex, a large tower at the NE corner of the forecourt platform, and a fragment of an inscription of Vespasian (A.D. 69-79). But until the late second century A.D., Sebaste received little attention, judging from the scanty remains of this period.

Between *ca.* 180 and 230, Sebaste enjoyed another period of prosperity. During the reign of Severus (193-211), it became a colony known as Lucia Septimia Sebaste, having supported Septimus Severus against Pescennius Niger in a struggle for the Empire. Its new prosperity is reflected by the results of a great building program undertaken during the reign of Severus; it is primarily the remains of this period that survive above ground level. All these new constructions were built of similar stone and in much the same style. The summit temple and the temple of Kore on the terrace N of the summit were thoroughly rebuilt. A small theater* with an external

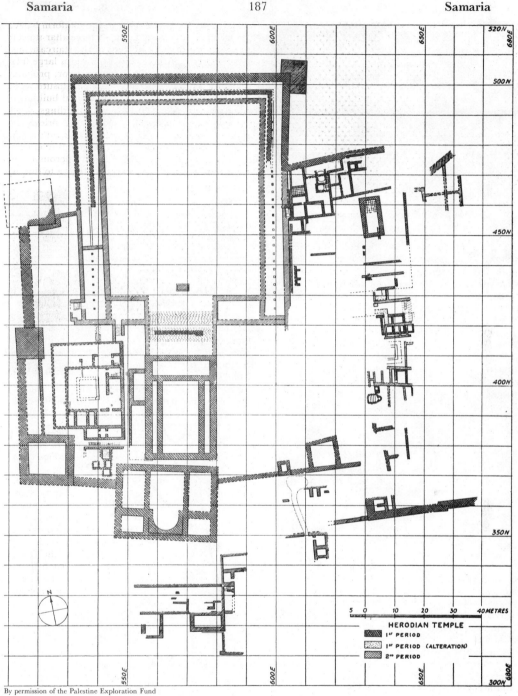

16. Plan of Herodian temple at Sebaste (Samaria) built by Herod the Great

diameter of *ca.* 210 feet was erected on the N slopes of the summit, midway between the summit temple and the forum. The latter, also reconstructed in this period, was rectangular in plan and enclosed by porticoes on all sides. Adjacent to the W side of the forum was a large basilica* which consisted of a central hall with open colonnades on three sides and a semicircular tribunal on the N. N of the forum and just inside the city wall, a large rectangular stadium (for foot racing), with a peristyle supported by 160 columns, was constructed over the remains of the earlier and smaller Doric stadium. The W gate was again rebuilt, and a long columned street was constructed, which connected the W and E gates and ran just S of the summit and forum area. The street averaged *ca.* forty feet in width and was flanked by colonnaded sidewalks, along each of which was a row of shops. Other interesting constructions of this

17. Theater of the late second century A.D. at Samaria, during excavation

18. Basilica cleared by excavations to the floor, showing the semicircular tribunal. The hills of Samaria lie in the background.

period include an aqueduct *ca.* 2¾ miles long, which brought water to the forum from a spring SE of the hill, and several magnificent mausoleums. Figs. SAM 17-18.

The third phase covers the period from Constantine to the Arab conquest (634). With the establishment of Christianity as the religion of the Roman Empire, Sebaste became an episcopal see—bishops of Sebaste attended the councils of Nicea, Constantinople, Chalcedon, and the Synod of Jerusalem—though paganism remained strong in the city during the early part of the period and culminated in anti-Christian riots during the reign of Julian (361-63). Numerous changes took place in the city during this period. Structures particularly associated with paganism were destroyed or reused. The temple of Augustus became a quarry except for the E and W corridors, which were used for a factory and a stable respectively. The basilica was completely rebuilt,

with two apses at the N end, and converted into a cathedral. The summit was occupied by large houses floored with mosaics and complete with baths. A glass factory was located SE of the forum. During this period Sebaste was widely known as the site of the burial of John the Baptist, and two shrines were revered. One was his alleged tomb at the E end of the city under the present mosque; the other marks the traditional place where his head was hidden by Herodias. On this spot, S of the summit, a basilica with three aisles and an apse at the E end was erected, perhaps in the fifth century A.D.

In 634, the city surrendered to 'Amr ibn al 'As, and the Arab occupation of the site began.

Bibliography. G. A. Reisner, C. S. Fisher, and D. G. Lyon, *Harvard Excavations at Samaria* (1924); J. W. and G. M. Crowfoot, *Early Ivories from Samaria* (1938); J. W. Crowfoot, K. M. Kenyon, and E. L. Sukenik, *The Buildings at Samaria* (1942); J. B. Pritchard, ed., *ANET* (2nd ed., 1955), pp. 283-86, 292, 321, 492. J. W. and G. M. Crowfoot and K. M. Kenyon, *The Objects from Samaria* (1957).   G. W. Van Beek

SAMARIA, TERRITORY OF. A region in the hill country of Palestine, named after the capital city of Israel. The boundaries of this territory changed during the centuries, and they cannot be precisely fixed for every period with the scanty information available. In general, however, they corresponded to the combined tribal allotments of Ephraim and W Manasseh, and included the region bounded on the S by a line from Jericho to the Valley of Ajalon, on the W by the coastal plain, on the N by the S edge of the Valley of Jezreel, and on the E by the Jordan

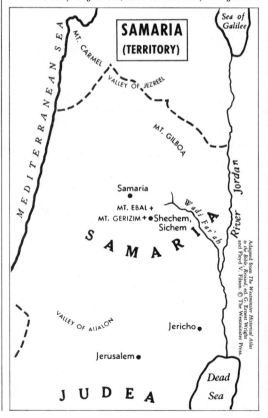

Courtesy of Harriet-Louise H. Patterson

19. The hills of Samaria

River. The territory enclosed by these boundaries measures approximately forty miles from N to S and *ca*. thirty-five miles from E to W. Fig. SAM 19.

The S, or Ephraimite, portion of this region has a relatively high elevation. On both the E and the W side, precipitous valleys lead down to the Jordan Valley and the coastal plain. Access by means of these valleys was difficult but possible, and as a result, this region was somewhat isolated from the outside world. The combination of rich terra-rossa soil and sufficient rainfall made the land fertile and productive.

The N portion consists of a central basin enclosed on the S by the hills of Ephraim; on the E by the central ridge of Palestine, which swings to the NE in this region; on the N by the mountains of Gilboa; and on the W by the Carmel foothills. The topography of this basin is obscured by a number of hills which rise out of its floor. Of these, Mount Ebal (3,100 feet) and Mount Gerizim (2,910 feet)*—located in the center of the basin—are the most notable examples. Agriculturally this region is extremely productive; grain is grown in the alluvium-covered plain; olives and vines thrive on the slopes of the hills (cf. Jer. 31:5). Access to this basin from both the coastal plain on the W and the Jordan Valley on the E was gained with little difficulty by means of several valleys which cut through the surrounding ridges, including principally Wadi esh-Sha'ir on the W and wadies Far'ah and el-Khashneh on the E. Similarly, movement within the basin was easy through a number of broad passes which connect the various plains. The accessibility of this region facilitated the movement of trade, which brought great prosperity to the area. It also exposed the land to influence from other cultures, particularly the Phoenician and Aramean cultures of the N, and it was against the religious and moral aspects of these cultures that the prophets Elijah, Elisha, Amos, and Hosea fought bitterly (e.g., Hos. 7:1; 8:5-7; Amos 4:1). Further, the richness and openness of the territory attracted invaders who, in the course of centuries, overran the land with comparative ease. Figs. GER 24; EBA 2.

This region, of course, did not become known as the territory of Samaria until after the division of the kingdom and the founding of Samaria as the capital of the N kingdom. Thus the reference in I Kings 13:32, belonging to the time of Jeroboam I, is an obvious interpolation. Following the fall of Israel in 722/721 B.C. and the deportation of Israelites, the

Assyrians settled captives from Babylon, Cuthah, Ava, Hamath, and Sepharvaim in the cities of Samaria (II Kings 17:24-26). The Assyrians incorporated the territory in their empire as the province *Samerena,* and ruled the region until the late seventh century, when their control weakened. It was then that Josiah of Judah (*ca.* 640-609) was able to destroy the high places in the cities of Samaria (II Kings 23:19). With the end of the Assyrian Empire in 612, the territory became a Babylonian province.

After the fall of Jerusalem in 587, the N hill country of Judah, including Jerusalem, was added to the province of Samaria. In 539 the Persians conquered Babylon, and the territory became a province or satrapy in the Persian Empire. With the return of the exiles, the governors of this province sought to hinder the returnees who were attempting to rebuild Jerusalem (Ezra 4:8-24; Neh. 2:9-20; 4:1-9; 6:1-14). But with the coming of Nehemiah, the hill country of N Judah was made a separate province, and the S border of the territory of Samaria was established approximately in its pre-Babylonian location. This region became the center of the Samaritans, following the Jewish-Samaritan schism, which took place in the days of Ezra and Nehemiah, and it has remained so. After the fall of the Persian Empire to Alexander the Great, the territory of Samaria was successively ruled by Macedonian, Ptolemaic, and Seleucid rulers. Between 111 and 107 it was incorporated in the new Jewish state, after the capture of Shechem and Samaria, and the destruction of the Samaritan temple on Mount Gerizim by the Maccabean leader John Hyrcanus.

From *Atlas of the Bible* (Thomas Nelson & Sons Limited)

20. The high hills of Samaria, with the temple of Herod in the foreground

In 63 B.C., Pompey assumed control of the territory for the Romans, and it was placed under the supervision of the province of Syria. This region was given to Herod the Great* by Augustus in 30, and Herod bequeathed it to his son Archelaus, who ruled until A.D. 6, when he was deposed by Augustus. It was then placed under the control of appointed Roman procurators, among whom was Pontius Pilate, until A.D. 41. From 41 to 44, the territory was ruled by Herod Agrippa I, but upon his death it was again governed by procurators. The ministry of Jesus and the work of the apostles took place in this period, although the territory of Samaria is rarely mentioned in connection with their activities. Jesus and his disciples generally seem to have followed the Jewish custom of skirting the borders of Samaria in journeying to Judea (e.g., Matt. 19:1; Luke 17:11), but on one occasion they are reported to have traveled through Samaria (John 4:4-9). Following the Resurrection, the disciples obeyed Jesus' command to bear witness in Samaria, among other places (Acts 1:8); and the preaching of Philip, Peter, and John resulted in the formation of churches in this region (Acts 8: 1-25; 9:31; 15:3). Fig. SAM 20.

Bibliography. G. A. Smith, *The Historical Geography of the Holy Land* (1894), pp. 323-41; D. Baly, *The Geography of the Bible* (1957), *passim.* G. W. VAN BEEK

SAMARITAN, THE GOOD sə măr′ə tən. This narrative parable (Luke 10:30-36) contrasts two answers to the question: Who is my neighbor? Two representatives of Jewish law dared not aid a wounded Jew and risk possible contamination through contact with his corpselike figure. Not even traditional hostility between Jews and Samaritans, however, prevented the Samaritan from responding to the Jew's needs. L. MOWRY

*SAMARITAN PENTATEUCH. It is acknowledged that the SAMARITANS accepted as canonical only the Pentateuch, and when in 1616 the first copy of their recension of it became available for study, it was hailed as the earliest source for the Pentateuch text. In 1815 Gesenius demonstrated the fallibility of the assessment, but in 1915 Kahle (*see bibliography*) modified this view by establishing that the evidence of the version, along with the LXX and with some non-

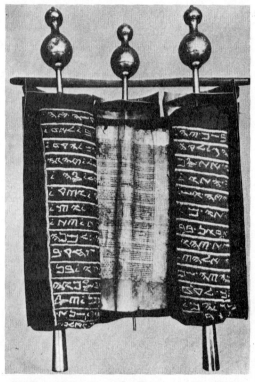

21. Copy of the Samaritan Pentateuch (the Abisha Scroll) at Nablus

LXX NT passages, forms part of the case for his *Vulgärtexte* (*see* TEXT, OT) hypothesis. Two recent discoveries further modify our assessment of the recension:

a) The Qumran MS 4QExᵃ, which Skehan (*see bibliography*) has described (*see* TEXT, OT, § A1a) as obviously related to the Samar., proves its antiquity and constancy of transmission, without priority for its text over the MT.

b) Two independent examinations of photographs of the Abisha Scroll in Nablus (*see bibliography*), which have resulted in favor of the great antiquity of the text. The authenticity of the Abisha Scroll has been generally questioned since Gesenius' time, and Kahle has described it as a mixed MS, partly ancient and partly fourteenth-century.

MSS of the recension have recently become available from before the twelfth century, but in the Paris and Walton Polyglots the text of seventh-century MSS is given, and the critical edition of Von Gall (1914-18) is eclectic, based on medieval MSS.

The recension is estimated to have around six thousand variants from the MT, mainly orthographic; and the numerous textual changes and transpositions—e.g., Gen. 2:2; 5; 11:10-32; Deut. 27:4—reflect Samaritan religious tendencies, as well as genuine variants.

For Aramaic renderings, *see* TARGUM; VERSIONS, ANCIENT. Fig. SAM 21.

Bibliography. G. Gerleman, *Synoptic Studies in the OT* (1948); P. Castro, "El Sefer Abisha," *Sefarad* (1953), pp. 119-29; P. W. Skehan, "Exodus in the Samar. Recension from Qumran," *JBL*, LXXIV (1955), 182-87; R. E. Moody, "Samaritan Material at Boston University: The Boston Collection and the 'Abisha Scroll,' " *Boston University Graduate Journal*, X (1957), 158-60; F. G. Kenyon, *Our Bible and the Ancient MSS* (1958); P. Kahle, *Cairo Geniza* (1959). B. J. ROBERTS

*SAMARITANS sə măr′ə tənz [שמרני; Σαμαρείτης]. Originally, the inhabitants of SAMARIA in general; the term "Samaritans" is now restricted to a particular religious community, or sect, living in that area. The community is of significance for biblical and allied studies for three main reasons: (*a*) it claims to be the remnant of the kingdom of Israel, more specifically of the two half-tribes of Ephraim and Manasseh; (*b*) it possesses an ancient recension of the Pentateuch which differs at several points from the standard (Masoretic) Jewish text and sometimes corroborates readings of the Greek LXX; (*c*) certain of its characteristic doctrines reappear in the Pseudep. of the OT and in the Dead Sea Scrolls, and may therefore help to reconstruct the religious background of those writings and to recover traditions lost to, or abandoned by, "normative" rabbinic Judaism. In addition, the sect is especially familiar to readers of scripture from the parable of the Good Samaritan in the NT (Luke 10:25-37).

Unfortunately, although much has been written on the subject, our knowledge of the Samaritans is very imperfect. Early references to them are scant and confused, while the bulk of their own literature is of late date and extant only in MSS still unpublished. Moreover, since they were for many centuries under Muslim rule and influence, and since most of their writings date from that period, it is often difficult to determine, in cases where Samaritan and Muslim ideas or expressions coincide, whether they both ascend to a common ancient tradition, or whether the Samaritans have simply borrowed and adapted from Islam. This article will be concerned exclusively with those elements of Samaritan history and teaching which bear upon the Bible and the intertestamental period, and it will confine itself mainly to the older sources—e.g., the writings of the fourth-century theologian Marqeh (Mark). Since, however, it will be necessary to draw also upon the later, post-Islamic literature, the reservation just made must be kept firmly in mind. It should be emphasized, in fact, that any comprehensive account of the Samaritans can, at present, be only tentative and provisional, subject in large measure to the better insight of the morrow.

A. ORIGINS. 1. The Jewish view. This view identifies the Samaritans as the descendants of the colonists whom Shalmaneser, king of Assyria, is said to have brought from Cutha, Babylon, Hamath, and other foreign parts after he had conquered Samaria in 722 B.C. and deported the native population (II Kings 17). These colonists, it is added, were later supplemented by others, introduced by Shalmaneser's successors, Esarhaddon and Ashurbanipal, alias "Osnappar" (Ezra 4:2, 10). Whatever knowledge of Judaism they possess is dismissed as purely superficial. The first settlers, runs the story, were beset by an invasion of lions. Thereupon they appealed to the authorities to repatriate one of the priests of Yahweh, that they might learn from him the proper procedure (משפט) of the traditional local cult. The result, however, was a grotesque syncretism; Yahwism served only as a thin veneer spread, for convenience, over an essential and deep-seated heathenism. It was for this basic reason, in fact, that the Samaritans obstructed the efforts of Ezra and Nehemiah to rebuild Jerusalem and re-establish the sanctuary of Yahweh (cf. Ezra 4:2 ff; Neh. 2:19; 4:2 ff).

In accordance with this view, the Jews dub the Samaritans contemptuously "men of Cutha" (כותים), or—in slightly more charitable vein—speak of them as "lion converts" (גרי אריות; Ḳid. 75a-76a), regarding them, at best, as one degree nearer than Gentiles, but still not as full-fledged members of the house of Israel.

2. The Samaritan view. The Samaritans, for their part, dismiss this story as a vile Jewish canard. The deportation in 722, they say, was neither total nor final; the exiles were, in fact, repatriated after fifty-five years! It is the descendants of these native Israelites that they claim to be. According to their version, the breach with the Judeans goes back to the time of Eli, who took it upon himself to set up an apostatic sanctuary of Yahweh at Shiloh, whereas the true "chosen place" prescribed in the law of Moses was Mount Gerizim.* This infamy was later reinforced by the "accursed Ezra," who falsified the sacred text and thereby seduced the people, on their return from the Babylonian exile, to erect the second temple beside the Judean capital. Admittedly, pagan colonists were introduced by the Assyrian monarchs; but these must not be confused with the true, native Israelites. Fig. GER 24.

In harmony with this view, the Samaritans prefer to style themselves Shâmērîm (שמרים)—i.e., "the observant"—rather than Shômerônîm (שמרונים)—i.e., "the inhabitants of Samaria."

3. Critical appraisal. There is something to be said for each of these views, and the truth probably lies between the two extremes.

The biblical story of successive exchange of population, following the fall of Samaria in 722, is confirmed, in its broader outlines, by the Assyrian records.

It is plain from these documents, however, that the Hebrew historian has confused and "telescoped" his data. In the first place, it was not Shalmaneser, but his successor Sargon (who, in fact, completed the siege), that effected the exchange in question. Secondly, it seems more probable that the colonization mentioned in II Kings 17:24 actually took place over several years and under successive monarchs. Thus, the Hamathites were probably transported to Samaria only after Sargon had quelled a revolt in that city in 721 (*Annals* 23 ff)—a revolt in which the Samaritans indeed participated; while the deportation of the Israelites to Media would seem to have counterbalanced one of the Medians to Samaria, following a successful campaign against them in 714 (cf. *Annals* 94 ff). Similarly, the introduction of Babylonians and Cutheans is more plausibly assigned to Ashurbanipal than to Shalmaneser, for it may well have been an act of retribution for their share in the civil war raised by the former's rival, Shamashshum-ukin.

Such confirmation of the biblical account does not prove, however, that the Jews are right in regarding the Samaritans as the mere offspring of the colonists rather than the true scions of Israel; and there is, in fact, much to support the Samaritan claim.

In the first place, Sargon himself says distinctly (*Annals* 11-17; *Prunkinschrift* 23-24) that he deported only 27,290 persons, whereas a computation based on a contemporary record in II Kings 15:19 shows that wealthy landowners alone then numbered 60,000! Furthermore, in II Chr. 34:9, we indeed hear of a "remnant of Israel" still resident in Ephraim and Manasseh about a century later, in the days of Josiah; and the analogy of what happened at the fall of the Southern Kingdom (II Kings 24:14) would suggest that, while more influential citizens may, indeed, have been driven into exile, the proletariat were left where they were. Lastly, it should be pointed out that there is, in fact, nothing in subsequent Samaritan doctrine which betrays any indebtedness to Assyrian ideas, and that the attitude of the Samaritans toward the Jews is wholly and most naturally explicable as a continuance of the inveterate hostility between Israel and Judah.

The most plausible conclusion is, then, that after the fall of Samaria in 722, the local population consisted of two distinct elements living side by side— viz., (a) the remnant of the native Israelites; and (b) the foreign colonists. For tendentious reasons, however, the Jewish version ignores the former; the Samaritan version, the latter.

B. HISTORY. 1. Opposition to Ezra and Nehemiah. On this hypothesis, the story told in Ezra–Nehemiah concerning the attitude of the "Samaritans" at the restoration from the Babylonian exile becomes readily intelligible. The author is writing from a chauvinistically Jewish viewpoint; his reference, therefore, is to the foreign colonists rather than to the native Israelites. These colonists were animated by a twofold fear: First, they feared that what Nehemiah was undertaking in Jerusalem might lead to such a recrudescence of Judean power as would be dangerous to their own several nations. Second, they were scared lest this Jewish attempt to create an *imperium in imperio* might evoke from the Persian government repercussions which would eventuate in the suppression of all minorities, and hence a reduction of their own status. In addition, it is not impossible that the question of the demarcation of boundaries between Samaria and Judah was also involved. Accordingly, it would have been but natural for these foreign colonists to have aligned themselves with the designs of their governor, Sanballat, who had, of course, his own personal reasons for seeking to arrest the growing power of his Judean confrere.

Of a somewhat different complexion is the earlier offer of co-operation with Zerubbabel in 536 B.C. (Ezra 4:2); for although this is usually taken to refer to the Samaritans, the text actually speaks only of "adversaries of Judah and Benjamin" who had been deported (whither is not stated) by Esarhaddon. Accordingly, the passage may allude equally well to general "Gentile Zionists" from other parts. Their offer would very intelligibly have been rejected by a Jewish leader who saw in his movement the spearhead of an essentially national revival, and who did not wish to compromise this main objective by any concessions to a vaguer, ecumenical universalism.

All this, however, does not exclude the possibility that the native Israelites of Samaria offered, for their part, a parallel opposition to Ezra and Nehemiah on more religious grounds. It is true that the Bible has nothing directly to say on this point, but that concurrent attempts were being made to erect the temple on Israelite soil is perhaps indicated by the fact, long since observed by modern scholars, that Ezekiel's blueprint of that edifice seems, in its original form, to have envisaged a location in the Northern kingdom (40:2). Moreover, the famous words of Isa. 66:1:

> Heaven is my throne
>   and the earth is my footstool;
> what is the house which you would build for me?

then acquire added significance as an attempt to put an end to this corroding rivalry by (literally) "calling a plague upon *both* their houses."

2. The Samaritan temple. However it may have begun, the rivalry between the Samaritans and the Jews reached its culmination in the erection by the former of their own distinctive temple on Mount Gerizim.

Unfortunately, we do not know when this took place. Our main reference to the event is furnished by Josephus (Antiq. XI.viii.4), who places it in the reign of Darius Codommanus (335-330 B.C.), the last king of Persia. A Jerusalemitan priest named Manasseh, he tells us, had been expelled for marrying Nicaso, daughter of Sanballat, the governor of Samaria, and then refusing to divorce her. Sanballat, to reward him, obtained permission from the king to have a Samaritan temple built on Gerizim, but the promise was fulfilled only by Alexander the Great.

Scholars have long suspected the authenticity of this story. In the first place, the tale of the irregular marriage seems to be a mere elaboration of a very similar incident, one hundred years earlier, to which allusion is made by Nehemiah (13:28). Secondly, unless Alexander's permission was granted straightway in 332, immediately after the completion of his conquest of the Near East, it is unlikely that it was granted at all, for we know that in the following year he was none too friendly to the Samaritans in consequence of their assassination of Andromachus, the governor of Coele-Syria (cf. Eusebius *Chronicle* II.114 [Schoene]), and also that he exacted savage punishment upon them for revolt (Quintus Curtius *History* IV.5.8). It may be suggested, in fact, that Josephus grotesquely patched his story together by fusing a Jewish and a Samaritan tradition. The Jews, for their part, had tried to pour obloquy on the Samaritan temple by associating it with the familiar incident of the "unfrocked" priest; while the Samaritans had sought to give it equal status with that of the edifice in Jerusalem by inventing a firman on the part of Alexander to match that which the Jews boasted from Cyrus!

Whenever it may have been founded, the Samaritan temple on Gerizim was razed by John Hyrcanus in 129/128 B.C. (Jos. Antiq. XIII.ix.1; War I.ii.6). According to Josephus, this was done in exasperation over their prolonged apostasy and treachery. Already in the days of Antiochus Epiphanes, they are said to have avoided association with the Jews by declaring themselves to be Sidonians and by requesting that their temple be dedicated to Zeus Hellenios (Jos. Antiq. XII.v.5). Such stories, however, must be received with caution; they could very well be mere calumny.

The Samaritans designate as the "era of favor" (רחותה) the time, from the conquest of Canaan until the apostasy of Eli, when the presence of God rested on Gerizim, and this they reckon as 260 years (cf. *Ma'lef*, Cod. Gaster 1169, fol. 88*a*). It has been suggested that this is simply a "reconstructed tradition," based on the duration of the Samaritan temple. If we deduct 260 years from the date of its destruction in 128 B.C., the edifice will thus have been founded in 388 B.C. An allusion to it is recognized by some scholars in Ps. 78:68-72.

3. Later times. The subsequent history of the Samaritans is related mainly by Josephus and by their own medieval chronicles, and the essential facts may be summarized briefly.

During the wars between the Ptolemies and the Seleucids, Samaria passed constantly from side to side: from Laomedon, governor of Syria, to Ptolemy Lagos in 320, then to Antigonus of Syria in 314, then back to Ptolemy in 311, then again to his enemy three years later. Once again it came under Ptolemy's sway by the terms of a treaty signed in 301, but three years later it was ravaged by Antigonus' son, Demetrius Poliorcetes.

Under the oppressive regime of Antiochus Epiphanes, the Samaritans appear to have quitted themselves with far less fortitude than the Jews, and it is perhaps for this reason also that they are characterized in Hellenistic Jewish literature as a foolish or churlish people.

Conquered by John Hyrcanus in 129/128 B.C., they were eventually liberated from the Jewish yoke by Pompey, while under Gabinius the territory was more adequately fortified. They lost some twelve thousand men in a revolt against Vespasian (Jos. War III.vii.32), while in the insurrection of Bar Cocheba they at first aided the Jews and then turned to the Roman side. For their assistance to his cause, Hadrian permitted them to rebuild their temple. After continuous oppression under the Christian emperors, they were finally suppressed by Justinian in 529.

In 636 they fell under Muslim rule, in 1099 under that of the Crusaders, and in 1244 (after the Battle of Gaza) again under the Muslims.

Medieval travelers report Samaritan communities in many places, even in Cairo, but these have long since disappeared. Only some two hundred souls remain, mainly at Nablus, under the shadow of Gerizim. In recent years, however, there has been a certain amount of migration to Jaffa and other Israeli cities.

Modern knowledge of the Samaritans dates only from the end of the sixteenth century, when Scaliger and other European scholars began a correspondence with them. Interest was fired especially when, in 1616, Pietro della Valle managed to procure from them a copy of the Samaritan Pentateuch and various other writings. In the late nineteenth century, Moses Gaster, A. E. Cowley, E. Kautzsch, M. Heidenheim, P. Kahle, and other European scholars spearheaded a revival of interest in the community, and MSS of their literature were acquired in increasing quantity. There are now extensive holdings in this field in the British Museum, the Bodleian, the Vatican, the Hebrew University, and the John Rylands libraries, as well as at the Hermitage in Leningrad. Scientific study of this material has been conducted especially by Cowley and Gaster, by Z. Ben Haim and S. Talmon in Jerusalem, and by the schools of P. Kahle and J. Bowman at Bonn and Leeds respectively. There is, however, a great deal of further work to be done before any adequate picture of the sect can be drawn; in the words of Chaucer, "God wot, there is a largë field to ear."

C. *THE SAMARITAN FAITH*. 1. Beliefs. The Samaritan faith is epitomized in five cardinal tenets: (*a*) belief in God; (*b*) acknowledgment of Moses as the supreme apostle of God and as a unique being; (*c*) acceptance of the Torah (Pentateuch) as the only authentic law of God; (*d*) recognition of Mount Gerizim as the chosen place of God, prescribed in scripture; (*e*) expectation of a final day of rewards and punishments.

a. God. God is unique and incorporeal, beyond time, space, and accident. He is without associate (שותף; Marqeh 183*a*); and, although he fills all things, he can be neither punctualized nor localized. He is beyond conception or description; but, as a poetic way of speaking, his glory (כבוד), power (חיל), and splendor (איקר) can be personified and hypostatized (e.g., Marqeh 15*a*). His essential being is epitomized in the words: "I AM WHO I AM" (אהיה אשר אהיה; Exod. 3:14), which are regarded as his most sacred designation. He is the creator and sustainer of all things, and is bound specifically to Israel by a covenant which has been affirmed on no fewer than ten occasions—viz., with Noah by the rainbow; with Abraham by circumcision; with Isaac and Jacob; with Moses by the sabbath; with the two tablets of the Ten Commandments; with the Passover; with the covenant of salt (Num. 18:19); and with the covenant of eternal priesthood made with Phinehas (Num. 25:12).

Like the Jews, the Samaritans refrain from pronouncing the Tetragrammaton, usually substituting the word *shēmâ*—i.e., "the Name." It has been stated that in some of their hymns they rhyme it with words ending in *-eh*, suggesting that they pronounced it "Yahweh." This, however, is doubtful.

b. Moses. Moses is not only the "exalted prophet" (הנבי הרם), the "seal [i.e., last, climax] of the prophets" (חותם הנביים), the "apostle" (שליח) par excellence, and the "choicest of creatures" (דמע הבוראים), but also an utterly unique being. He is a distillation (מפה) of the primordial light, itself none other than the holy light of God which illumines the saints. As such, he is the "light of the world," and all other lights derive from his. He therefore existed from the dawn of creation, and was only later incarnated as the offspring of Amram and Jochebed. The whole world was created for his sake (Marqeh 67*b*). He intercedes for the deserving and leads the prayers of the celestial congregation. He is the future prophet foretold in Deut. 18:18; for on any other interpretation, the promise contained in this verse would contradict the express words of Deut. 34:10—H 33:10 (as read in the Samar. text): "There shall not again arise [MT 'There has no more arisen'] in Israel a prophet like unto Moses"!

c. The Torah. The Torah was written by God in a MS (Arabic *madraja*) which was given to Moses on Sinai along with the two tablets (Arabic *ul-luāḥ*) of the Ten Commandments. It is permanent and immutable. The Samaritans often term it "the Verity" (קושטה), and they recognize no other part of the Bible.

d. Mount Gerizim. Mount Gerizim, not Zion, is the true chosen place of God prescribed in the Torah. According to the Samar. text, Deut. 12:5—H 12:4 declares that God "has chosen" it, not, as in the Jewish recension, that he "will choose" it. Moreover, after each version of the Ten Commandments (viz., after Exod. 20:17; Deut. 5:21), the Samaritans interpolate a paragraph (composed synthetically from Deut. 27:2-8; 11:30) ordering sacrifice on that mountain; and in Deut. 27:4 their text represents the curse as being pronounced on Ebal, and the blessing on Gerizim—rather than vice versa, as in the Jewish recension.

Gerizim existed before creation (Marqeh 68a; 71b). It alone escaped the Flood, and it alone will escape the destruction of all things on Doomsday. It is the center, or "navel" (טבור), of the earth, and Adam was fashioned out of its dust. It is the "choicest place in all the dry land" (רמע דיבשתה), and in the final age streams of living waters will issue from it. The ark of the covenant is hidden upon it (Marqeh 77b), but will be revealed in the last days.

In order to validate its claims, Samaritans identify Gerizim with several places mentioned in the Torah—viz., (a) the "ancient hill" (הר הקדם; RSV "hill country") of Gen. 10:30; (b) Bethel, the scene of Jacob's dream (Gen. 35:1); (c) the "house of divine beings" (i.e., angels; בית אלהים) and (d) the "gate of heaven" of Gen. 28:17; (e) Luz of Gen. 28:19—interpreted as Hebrew lô zeh (לו לה)—i.e., "to Him [i.e., God] it belongeth"; (f) the "sanctuary" (מקדש) of Exod. 15:17; (g) the "chosen place" of Deut. 12:11; (h) the "everlasting hills" (גבעת עולם) of Deut. 33:15; (i) "one of the mountains" and (j) YHWH-yir'eh, the scene of the intended sacrifice of Isaac, in Gen. 22 (Marqeh 71b-73a). It is said also to be the place where Abel built the first altar (cf. Gen. 4:4), where Noah sacrificed after the Flood (Gen. 8:20), and where the twelve stones were erected, in accordance with Deut. 27:4, after Israel had entered the Promised Land. In order further to authenticate their claims, the Samaritans read "Moreh" for "Moriah" in the story of the intended sacrifice of Isaac (Gen. 22:2), and identify it with a certain More, near Shechem. Similarly, they locate Abraham's encounter with Melchizedek king of Salem (Gen. 14:18), not at Jerusalem, but at Salim, also near Shechem.

e. The day of vengeance and reward. The day of vengeance and reward (יום נקם ושלם) derives its name from the Samar. text of Deut. 32:34-35 ("Is it not stored and sealed up in my treasuries, against the day of vengeance and reward?")—a reading supported by the LXX and by a fragment from Qumran. On that day God will inquire after the deeds of men. Scales will be set up, and angels will serve both as prosecutors and as defenders. God will cry out: "See now that it is I even I" (vs. 39 Samar.), and at that moment the earth will be split asunder, graves will open, and the dead will arise. Those that led worthy lives will be robed in clean garments and exude a fragrant aroma, whereas the wicked will be clad in tatters and emit a mephitic odor. After

judgment, the former will enter Eden, where Moses, Aaron, and the ancestral saints (זכאים) will greet them, whereas the wicked will be consigned to the devouring fire, and find themselves in the company of Cain, Lamech, Korah, Amalek, and other notorious sinners (Marqeh 189b-191a).

The day of doom is designated by a wide variety of names. Thus, in a single paragraph (190a), Marqeh the fourth-century theologian styles it: the day of resurrection (יום עמידותה); the day of reckoning (יום חושבנה); the day of judgment (יום דינה); the day of assembly (יום כנושה); the day of retribution (יום גזוו); the day of inquisition (יום שיאלה); the day when all feet shall quake (cf. Deut. 32:35); the day of the emergence from below the earth (יום המפוק מכתי ארעתה). In general, the description of it hews close to Deut. 32, and the latter is the ultimate (and oft-quoted) source of all doctrines concerning it.

f. The Taheb. Inextricably associated with the last day is the concept of the *Taheb* (תהב), or "Restorer," who is then to appear on earth to usher in the new dispensation. The *Taheb* is not a messiah in the Jewish sense of an anointed prince. Rather is he the prophet foretold in Deut. 18:18—the eschatological guide and monitor mentioned also in the Dead Sea Manual of Discipline (9.11), in the NT (Matt. 11:14; Mark 9:11 ff; Acts 7:37; etc.), and in the Pseudep. (Test. Levi 18), and identified by the Jews with Elijah (Men. 45a; B.M. 3a). Known also as the Star, in accordance with Num. 24:17 ("A star shall step forth out of Jacob"), the *Taheb* will restore the temple on Gerizim, reinstitute the sacrificial cult, and obtain the recognition of the heathen. He is destined to live 110 years. The date of his advent is disputed, but the Samaritans seem to have shared the Iranian and Jewish notion that the world will dissolve after six thousand years, and the *Taheb* is regarded as the herald of this event.

g. Ra'ūtah and Fanūtah. The Samaritans divide the history of their community into two major periods—viz., that of *Ra'ūtah* (רחותה), or "Favor," and that of *Fanūtah* (פנותה), when God turned away (פנה) from them. The former is said to have lasted for 299 years, of which 39 were passed in the wilderness, and the remainder when the temple stood on Gerizim unchallenged—i.e., before the apostasy of Eli.

The expression "era of favor" (קץ רצון) recurs in the Dead Sea Scrolls (1QH 15.15; fragment 9.8), as distinguished from the present "era of wickedness" (Zadokite Document 6.10, 14; 12.23; 14.19; 15.7, 10), and the penultimate "era of wrath" (Zadokite Document 1.5; 1QH 3.28; cf. B.B. 10a; Shab. 11a; cf. also Ecclus. 48:10).

h. The ancestral saints. No less important to the Samaritans than any of the foregoing is the concept of the ancestral saints (זכאים), who, in a successive chain (שלשלת), transmitted the divine "likeness" (צלם), first imparted to Adam (cf. Gen. 1:26-27). This likeness is interpreted metaphorically to mean something like prophetic inspiration or insight. It is identified with the "light of holiness" (אור הקודש)—i.e., the source of religious "illumination." Adam, it is said, passed it to Seth, Seth to Enosh, Enosh to Noah, and thence by successive stages it reached Abraham, Isaac and Jacob, Moses and Aaron, Eleazar and Phinehas, Joshua, Caleb, and the seventy elders, ceasing with the apostasy of Eli. The

Samaritans claim that, by virtue of it, the ancestral saints can intercede with God, and to this end pilgrimages are made to their reputed graves on Mount Gerizim.

2. Practices. The Samaritans are essentially a religious community, governed by a high priest.

The three seasonal festivals of Passover, Pentecost, and Booths are marked by pilgrimages to the summit of Gerizim, and on the eve of the first-named, the paschal lamb is slaughtered and consumed in accordance with biblical prescriptions. The name Passover (פסח), however, is reserved for this ceremony, the subsequent festival being known as that of Unleavened Bread (מצות). In agreement with the Sadducees and Karaites, the Samaritans observe Pentecost on the fiftieth day after the (first) sabbath in Passover-Maṣṣôth. It thus falls always on a Sunday, the word "sabbath" in the relevant law of Lev. 23:15 being taken literally, and not, as by the Jews, in the sense of "festival."

Sixty days before Passover and Booths occurs the so-called Day of Simmûth (צמות). The word means "conjunction," and originally bore an astronomical meaning. Today, however, it marks the dates of the semiannual payment of dues to the priests. Every Samaritan gives a half-shekel, and by way of receipt obtains a calendar for the ensuing six months, drawn up by the priests in accordance with the "correct computation" (חשבן קשטה) said to have been worked out by Phinehas from the meridian of Gerizim.

The Samaritans observe the sabbath rigidly; no one is permitted to stir from his house except to attend services at the *kinsha*, or synagogue. They allow no fire to burn on that day, interpreting the law of Exod. 16:23 to refer to the burning, rather than only to the igniting, of the flame. They also do not recognize the Jewish device of the ערוב, whereby the biblical law regarding the length of a sabbath-day's journey can be circumvented by the legal fiction of establishing an *ad hoc* residence on the perimeter of the city.

The holiest day of the year is the Day of Atonement, the fast of which is obligatory upon all. The high point of the service in the synagogue is the display of an ancient scroll of the Law, said to have been written by Abishaʿ, the grandson of Aaron. (Actually, it would appear to date from the twelfth century.)

Phylacteries are not worn by the Samaritans; the law of Deut. 6:8 is interpreted metaphorically. Similarly, prayer shawls are worn only by priests officiating at divine services, and this appears to be a modern innovation.

D. AFFINITIES WITH ISLAM. It is difficult to say how much of Samaritan belief, as recorded in the more recent sources, represents a genuine heritage from remote antiquity, and how much is simply borrowed from Islam. The parallels between technical expressions used by Samaritan writers and those found in the Quran and in such Muslim classics as the *Mishkāt al-Anwār* of al-Ghazzāli are indeed arresting, but the presumption of Samaritan priority is strengthened when we find them also in the works of the fourth-century Samaritan theologian Marqeh. It must not be overlooked, however, that the history of the text of Marqeh is as yet virtually unexplored,

and that most Samaritan writings show a constant process of adaptation and editorial manipulation. Hence we cannot be sure that Marqeh has not, in fact, been subjected to Islamizing redaction.

With this reservation, it is worth while to point out some of the more striking parallels.

a) Standard Samaritan epithets of God reproduce to a nicety some of those prominent in Muslim theology. Thus *Qaʾîm* (קעים), "the Permanent," corresponds exactly to Arabic *al-Baqī*, said by Abu Hurairah to have been one of the divine names revealed by Mohammed. *Hab-bôrē'* (הבורא), "the Creator," is the *al-Bāri'* of Quran 59.24. The statement that God has no *shāṭeph*, or "associate," accords with the common Muslim assertion that he has no *sharik*, of the same meaning.

b) The idea that Moses is a distillation of the primordial light finds its counterpart in Muslim notions associated with Mohammed, and the founder of Islam is likewise known as the "seal of the prophets." Moreover, the doctrine that the primordial light was transmitted through a chain of saints recurs in the writings of the Ikhwār al-Safā.

c) Several of Marqeh's designations of the day of judgment reappear verbatim in the Quran. Thus, the *yôm ḥušbanâ*, or "day of reckoning," is the *Yaumu 'l-ḥisāb* of Sura 40.28; the *yôm kinnûšâ*, or "day of assembly," is the *yaum 'l-jum'* of Sura 64.9, or the later *yaum 'l-ḥašr*. The *yôm 'amîdhûthâ*, or "day of resurrection" (also called explicitly *yôm giʾāmâ*) is the *yaumu 'l-giyāmah* of Sura 2.79; 83.5; and the *yôm dînâ*, or "day of judgment" (cf. Jewish *Yôm ha-Dîn*), is the *yaumu'd-dîn* of Sura 1.3; 83.17.

The scales (מוזן) of judgment are likewise mentioned in Sura 21.47 (*mizān*).

d) The notion that special waters flow from Gerizim is paralleled not only in Jewish ideas about Zion, but also in Muslim folklore concerning the holy rock at Mecca.

e) The use of the term בסר, "good news, gospel," in reference to the mission of Moses and the advent of the *Taheb* accords with the Arabic *bushrā* of the publication of Islam (e.g., *Mishkāt* XXIV, ch. 1); though the Christian εὐαγγέλιον is, of course, an equally striking analogue.

f) The statement of older writers that the Samaritans had no belief in angels is refuted by countless references to them from Marqeh onward, and a special group of four angels is said to have watched over Moses in the bulrushes. But the constant designation of the celestial powers as "the hidden ones" (כסיאתה) recalls at once the Islamic *al-ghaib* (or *al-ghiyāb*) in the same sense; while the מלאכי ערשו mentioned in a prayer and the נושאי ערשו of an unpublished Samaritan book of proverbs are surely the eight angelic *ḥamalatu 'l-ʿarš*, "throne-bearers," of the Quran (Sura 40.7; 69.17).

g) Lastly, the ancestral "saints" (זכאים), of varying number, bear a marked resemblance to the six ancient *'ūlū*, or "possessors of constancy"—viz., Adam, Noah, Abraham, Moses, Jesus, and Mohammed—of Sura 46.34.

E. KARAITE AFFINITIES. There are several curious affinities between the Samaritan exegesis of the Torah and that of the Karaites, the antirabbinical Jewish sect which rose to prominence in the eighth-ninth centuries of the Christian era. Thus, both interpret the law of levirate marriage (Deut. 25:5) to refer only to the betrothed but not to the fully espoused wife of a man's brother; both calculate Pentecost from the day after the (first) sabbath in Passover; both forbid the use of even the skin of carrion or of an animal not slain in accordance with Mosaic law; both insist that fires may not burn (let alone be kindled) on the sabbath. Both maintain, against the Jews, that by the law of Lev. 3:9 the fat tail of the sheep belongs to the priest alone; both render Exod. 20:26: "Thou shalt not go up towards mine altar in perfidy," rather than "by steps," taking the word במעלות as from מעל, "deal treacherously," rather than, as do the Jews, from עלה, "go up."

Now that it is becoming increasingly apparent, in the light of the Dead Sea Scrolls, that Karaite doctrines were to some extent a recrudescence of far earlier, nonnormative ideas, and did not always spring *ab ovo* in the eighth or ninth century, the possibility arises that the affinities between Samaritanism and Karaism may constitute links in the chain of an otherwise forgotten tradition—a view adumbrated by Geiger in the nineteenth century.

F. *LANGUAGE AND LITERATURE.* The traditional language of the Samaritans is a dialect of Western Aramaic (*see* ARAMAIC). It is written in the characters of the archaic Hebrew alphabet, resembling the script of the LACHISH ostraca and of Hasmonean coins (*see* MONEY). Since the Muslim conquest in 636, however, it has been replaced by Arabic, except for liturgical and learned purposes.

The earliest literature of the Samaritans has perished. It would appear that during the Hellenistic period they wrote, like the Jews, not only in their own tongue but also in Greek, for Eusebius and other writers preserve extracts from such compositions by the historiographers Artapanos and Eupolemos and from a metrical adaptation of Exodus by a certain Ezekiel. A Greek poem on Gerizim, obviously of Samaritan provenance, has also survived. In addition, there are sundry references to variant readings of the text of the Pentateuch contained in something styled τὸ Σαμάρειτικον. This is thought to have been a Greek rendering parallel to that of the LXX, or an adaptation of the latter to the Samar. Hebrew text. Others, however, believe that it is simply the Samar. Hebrew text itself.

Extant Samaritan literature falls into two major divisions: pre-Islamic, written in the native dialect; and post-Islamic, written (except for liturgical pieces) mainly in Arabic. The principal works of the former all date (approximately) from the fourth century and are: (*a*) a Targum, or translation, of the Pentateuch; (*b*) the treatises of the theologian Marqeh (i.e., Mark), known as the *Discourse of Marqeh* (מימר מרקה) or *The Book of Wonders* (ספר פליאתה); (*c*) the earliest portion of the Liturgy, called *Defter* (i.e., δίφθερα, "codex"), prominent elements of which are prayers by Marqeh himself and a series of hymns called the *Durrān*, or "String of Pearls," by one Amram Darah.

A striking feature of the Targum is its similarity to that of Onqelos (*see* TEXT, OT). This has been explained on the assumption that both ascend to a common oral version, variously "edited." An alternative view is, however, that the Samar. version was subsequently "corrected" from that of Onqelos.

Marqeh's disquisition is a prolonged (and tedious) homily on the career of Moses and on his final Song (Deut. 32). Not improbably, it was designed as a series of sermons.

Of the later works, written in Arabic, that which claims primary consideration is the book of Joshua, a version of the biblical text with midrashic (legendary) additions and interpolated hymns. The work is said to have been based in part on a Hebrew—i.e., Samaritan—original. A Hebrew version of this work was produced in the nineteenth century, and was claimed by Moses Gaster to be of remote antiquity. It is, however, quite demonstrably of far more recent origin, though the possibility must not be overlooked that the underlying scriptural text indeed reflects a pre-Masoretic recension. Moreover, the insertion of hymns attributed to Joshua now stands in a new light in view of the discovery of such apocryphal compositions, likewise attributed to him, among the Dead Sea Scrolls.

Noteworthy also is the so-called *Al-Asāṭir* [i.e., Stories] *of Moses*, probably of the twelfth or thirteenth century, written in Samaritan. The material contained in this work is often genuinely ancient, recurring in the Pseudep. of the OT and other early sources; and it is therefore a valuable repository of time-honored traditional lore. A distinction must be drawn, however, between the antiquity of the material and the date of the composition itself, and accordingly the claim of Moses Gaster that the latter is of the third century B.C. is untenable.

Of later works—many of them the product of a literary revival in the fourteenth century—mention may be made especially of a series of poems on the nativity and career of Moses, designed principally for recitation on the anniversary of his birth (*Mûlîd*) and on joyous occasions. The principal of these are by Ibrahim ibn Salamah, and Jacob the Rabban of Damascus; while the most elaborate and philosophical is the *Maulid an-Nashi'* ("Nativity of the Child"), composed in 1537 by Isma'il ar-Rumaihi.

An Arabic rendering of the Pentateuch, apparently drafted by a certain Abu-'l-Barakat in the twelfth century and later revised by Abu Sai'd, is also extant, and is remarkable for its similarity to the rendering of Saadya. Another, independent version is also known.

The principal expositions of Samaritan doctrine and practice are: the *Kafi* ("Compendium"), commenced by Joseph of 'Askar (a village near Shechem) in 1041, and the *Ṭabaḥ* ("Potpourri") by Abu-'l-Ḥasan of Tyre, written in the eleventh century. There are also numerous compositions on special portions of the Torah and a number of more extensive theological works. A good idea of these may be obtained from E. Robertson's detailed catalogue of the Crawford MSS in the John Rylands Library, at Manchester, England. It must be added, however, that the great bulk of Samaritan literature remains unpublished.

Concerning the Samar. Pentateuch, *see* TEXT, OT; VERSIONS, ANCIENT.

Bibliography. T. G. Juynboll, *Chronicon Samaritanum* (1848). J. Mills, *Three Months' Residence at Nablus* (1864). H. Heidenheim, *Bibliotheca Samaritana* (1884-85), includes large portions of Marqeh, though poorly edited. J. A. Montgomery, *The Samaritans* (1907). A. E. Cowley, ed., *The Samaritan Liturgy* (1909). M. Gaster, *Samaritan Eschatology* (1932). Y. Ben Zwi, *Sepher ha-Shômrōnîm* (1935; Hebrew). A. S. Halkin, "Samaritan Polemics Against the Jews," *Proceedings of the American Academy of Jewish Research*, 7 (1935-36), 13-59. Z. Ben Haim, "The Book of Asatir," *Tarbiz*, 14 (1943), 104-25; 174-90; 15 (1946), 71-87. S. Miller, ed., *The Samaritan Molad Môsheh* (1949), should be used with caution.   T. H. GASTER

SAMATUS. KJV form of SHEMAIAH 21.

SAMECH sä'měk [ס, *s* (*Sāmekh*)]. The fifteenth letter of the Hebrew ALPHABET as it is placed in the KJV at the head of the fifteenth section of the acrostic psalm, Ps. 119, where each verse of this section of the psalm begins with this letter.

SAMEIUS. KJV Apoc. form of SHEMAIAH 19.

SAMGAR-NEBO săm'gär nē'bō [סמגר-נבו] (Jer. 39:3). The name, or more probably the title, of a Neo-Babylonian prince who participated in the siege of Jerusalem in 588-586 B.C. The text probably mentions three, rather than four princes, the first of whom is "Nergal-sharezer the Samgar" and the second, "Nebo-sarsechim the Rabsaris." Both formations, then, represent Hebrew corruptions of Babylonian names, perhaps "Nergalsharusur the Sinmagir" and "Nebushazban the Rabsaris," respectively.   J. M. WARD

SAMI. KJV Apoc. form of SHOBAI.

SAMIS. KJV Apoc. form of SHIMEI 17.

SAMLAH săm'lə [שׂמלה] (Gen. 36:36-37; I Chr. 1:47-48). Fifth king in Edom "before any king reigned over the Israelites"; a native of Masrekah. Because of variant spellings in Hebrew and Greek, *cf.* SHALMAI.

SAMMUS. KJV Apoc. form of SHEMA 4.

SAMOS sā'mŏs [Σάμος, heights, lofty place (*according to* Strabo *Geography* VIII.3.19; X.2.17]. One of the Ionian islands, in the SE part of the Aegean Sea, only a mile from the promontory of TROGYLLIUM; it was SW of Ephesus and NW of Miletus. It measures *ca.* twenty-seven miles from E to W and *ca.* fifteen miles at its greatest width. Its chief city, also called Samos, was a free city in Paul's time. The

island was an important naval power in early times, especially in the sixth century B.C. under Polycrates. In 479 B.C. the Strait of Mycale, between Samos and Trogyllium, was the scene of the important defeat of the Persians by the Greeks. I Macc. 15:23 shows that Jews were settled there in the second century B.C. According to Acts 20:15, Paul's ship, on his final journey to Jerusalem, either "touched at" and anchored overnight at Samos (so RSV, though this is an unusual meaning for παρεβάλομεν) or "came near" to Samos and passed by it on the E or the W to anchor for the night at Trogyllium.

Bibliography. Strabo *Geography* XIV.1.12-18; V. Guerin, *Description de l'île de Patmos et de l'île de Samos* (1856); E. Kirsten and W. Kraiker, *Griechenlandkunde* (1955), pp. 333-51.   F. V. FILSON

SAMOTHRACE săm'ə thrās [Σαμοθρᾴκη, Thracian Samos(?)]. An island in the NE Aegean on the route of the apostle Paul's missionary travels.

1. Geography and history. The island, which lies off the coast of Thrace in the Grecian Archipelago, was probably settled by Samians in the eighth century B.C. They may have named it Thracian Samos (Homer *Iliad* XIII.12) because of a Thracian people they found there. Or it may have been settled by colonists from NW Anatolia or Lesbos. Lying on a sea lane which led from Greece to the Black Sea, it became a center of importance for travelers, colonists, and traders. Mount Phengari, the tallest of its four mountain summits, towers to a height of 5,250 feet, and served as a beacon for Aegean sailors. Poseidon was said to have watched the battle for Troy from its lofty peak.

Archaeological evidence indicates that the island was inhabited in the Neolithic Age. Greek colonists began to arrive *ca.* 700 B.C., gradually and peacefully assimilating a pre-Greek population of Thracian stock. Their town, which served as the center of the island city-state, developed into one of the major Greek cities, possessing lands on the Thracian coast opposite the island and thus controlling the sea lane between. The city was at its zenith of power in the sixth and fifth centuries B.C., declining somewhat thereafter with the loss of independence. Serving as a naval base in the Hellenistic period, it was known chiefly as the great religious center for N Greece. *See* § 2 *below.*

2. The Samothracian cult. The island held a special importance as an international religious center comparable to Olympia and Delphi as the home of a famous mystery cult which had secondary centers in many cities of Asia Minor and on the Boetian coast. Excavations, which began in the middle of the nineteenth century, following the discovery of the ship monument known as the Victory of Samothrace, commenced afresh after 1938 and unearthed the remains of the Sanctuary of the Great Gods, containing the ruins of twelve buildings from the time of Alexander and his successors. Renowned throughout the Greek world from the fifth century B.C. on, the cult of the Great Gods is referred to by Herodotus, Plato, and Aristophanes. To its public rites municipal ambassadors and pilgrims came from all over Greece and Asia Minor. Two of the pre-Greek divinities

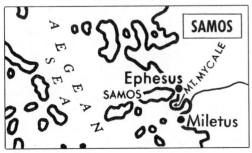

called *Cabiri* became identified by the Greeks with their twin-gods the Dioscuri, and were reverenced as the protectors and guides of sailors. The private mysteries of the Great Mother involved the familiar enactment of a ritual drama representing a sacred marriage; they were unique in their inclusive acceptance of all without restriction who desired initiation. Many prominent personages, including Philip of Macedon and Hadrian, were initiated into the Samothracian mysteries. With the banning of the cult in the fourth century A.D., the island declined in historical importance.

3. Paul's voyages. The ancient city located beside a small harbor on the N coast was visited by the apostle Paul on his way to Neapolis (Acts 16:11), and presumably on his return to Troas, as Acts 20:6 implies. An early Christian church, whose ruins were discovered in 1938 at the edge of the harbor, may commemorate the landing.

Bibliography. Pauly-Wissowa, *Real-Enzyklopädie,* 2nd Series, vol. I (1920), cols. 2223-26; K. Lehmann, *Samothrace, A Guide to the Excavations and the Museum* (1955), with an excellent bibliography.   E. W. SAUNDERS

SAMPSAMES sămp'sə mēz [Σαμψάμης, Σαμψάκης; Vulg. *Lampsacus*] (I Macc. 15:23). One of the places to which the Roman consul Lucius addressed a letter in order to further the interests of the Jews. It was perhaps a seaport on the Black Sea, the modern Samsun.   N. TURNER

SAMSON săm'sən [שִׁמְשׁוֹן, solar *or* sun's man; Ugar. *špšyn;* Σαμψών (Heb. 11:32)]. Hero or "judge" of the tribe of Dan, famous for his superhuman strength associated with his uncut hair as a Nazirite and for his exploits against the Philistines (Judg. 13–16).

1. Name
2. Narrative
3. Historical importance
4. The story as myth and folklore
5. Religious significance
Bibliography

1. Name. The Hebrew name Samson is clearly from the Hebrew root שֶׁמֶשׁ, "sun," but it is uncertain whether with the *-ōn* ending the word is to be understood as diminutive, hence "sun's child," or, more likely, simply as "solar," "sunny," or perhaps "sun's man." The ending *-ōn* may have originally been from the *-yanu* ending, frequent in Ugaritic personal names, and the form *shmshn* occurs as a Syrian place name. Josephus' derivation of the word as from שׁמֵן, "robust," and hence "strong," and its explana-

tion as from שָׁמַם, "be devastated," are probably attempts to avoid connecting the name with the sun.

Thus Samson seems clearly to have been a Canaanite personal name. Whether or not Samson is to be regarded as originally the hero of a sun myth (*see* § 4 *below*), the connection of his name with the sun is indubitable. His birthplace was across the Valley of Sorek (*see* SOREK, VALLEY OF) a short distance from the city Beth-shemesh, "house of the sun," the site of a shrine of the sun-god.

2. Narrative. The biblical account of Samson is a cycle of stories based on Hebrew folklore, doubtless told and retold orally for generations. While there are some inconsistencies in the narrative, the stories are probably all part of the earliest stratum in the book of Judges, perhaps an extension of the J document of the Hexateuch. There is here no so-called E material and remarkably little Deuteronomic or later editing (only 13:1; 15:20; 16:31*b;* and possibly 13:13*b*-14).

The present collection of Samson stories may have been included in the book of Judges in the following order: (*a*) the stories of his exploits in connection with or immediately following his intended marriage (chs. 14–15, ending with the brief editorial conclusion of 15:20); (*b*) another cycle of stories, also drawn from the earliest source, but perhaps deliberately omitted by the previous editor because based upon his nonmarital amours and culminating in his tragic death (ch. 16, with the editorial conclusion of 15:20 repeated in vs. 31*b*); (*c*) the story of the annunciation and birth of Samson, to account for his superhuman feats and his being worthy of inclusion among the "judges" (ch. 13).

The antiquity of these stories, in which is Hebrew storytelling at its best, is indicated not only by their character as true folklore, but also by their inclusion of bits of Hebrew poetry such as riddles and taunts (14:14, 18; 15:16; and probably 14:3, 16; 16:6, 15, 17, 23-24).

The successive events of the story are as follows:

a) Samson was born as the child of promise to a long-time barren woman who kept the vows of a Nazirite after an angel's appearance to her and her husband, MANOAH (ch. 13). The theme of the barren woman's at last giving birth to a promised son is common (cf. Sarah [Gen. 16:1; 18:1-15; 21:1-3]; Rebekah [Gen. 25:21-26]; Rachel [Gen. 30:1-2, 22-24]; Hannah [I Sam. 1]; Elizabeth [Luke 1:5-25, 57-80]). Unlike the similar appearance of Yahweh or his angel to Abraham (Gen. 18) or to Gideon (Judg. 6:11-24), it was not Manoah, but his wife, who played the chief human role in the event. The messenger spoke first to the woman, and it was by her logical reply that she calmed her husband's fears of death at having seen God. As the host, Manoah presented the sacrifice and asked about the divine name, but he received no answer (cf. Jacob [Gen. 32:29]). Yahweh, present in his angel in the miracle at the holy rock, disappeared in the ascending flame.

The whole experience was understood as promising divine power to the boy to be born. As he was to be a "Nazirite to God from birth," his mother was to prepare by carefully keeping the vows concerning food and drink: eat nothing unclean; have nothing to do with any product of the vine; drink no liquor

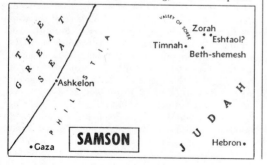

of any kind (cf. Amos 2:11-12). As for the son himself, from birth to death no razor dare touch his head (cf. the vow concerning Samuel [I Sam. 1:11], who is stated to be a Nazirite in a Dead Sea Scroll MS; for comparison of these lifelong vows, hair sacrifice, etc., in the later law, Num. 6, *see* NAZIRITE). In the subsequent story of Samson only the vow concerning uncut hair was observed, for wine flowed freely at the marriage feast, and the honey from the lion's carcass was hardly clean food, as the greatest source of uncleanness was any contact with a dead body. That, as expected, the son of promise had divine endowment was seen when, while he was yet at home, "the Spirit of the LORD began to stir him" (from פעם, "be or feel disturbed," especially by dreams; Judg. 13:25; cf. Gen. 41:8; Ps. 77:4—H 77:5; Dan. 2:1, 3). What this inner disturbance meant is told only in the subsequent episodes.

b) Samson's first adventures occurred in connection with his intended marriage with the Philistine woman at Timnah: after she had coaxed out of him the secret of his lion-and-honey riddle and he had paid his debt with the clothes of thirty Philistine victims, Samson discovered that she had been given to his best man and took prompt revenge by igniting Philistine crops with 150 live-fox-tail torches and by slaughtering many more Philistines (14:1–15:8).

Samson's would-be marriage was opposed by his parents as an undesirable union with "uncircumcised" pagans (cf. Esau [Gen. 26:34-35; 27:46]), but excused by the writer as Yahweh's scheme to discomfit the enemy (Judg. 14:3-4). It is obvious that, despite some confusion in the narrative, neither parent would have anything to do with the proposed marriage. Contrary to custom, then, Samson had to go after his own wife, procure Philistine instead of Israelite friends of the bridegroom (cf. Song of S. 3: 7), and hold the feast in the bride's, rather than the groom's, home. Some think he intended the unique type of marriage in which the husband occasionally visited the wife in her father's household (*sadiqâ;* cf. Gen. 2:24; *see* MARRIAGE § 1*f*), but more likely he planned to bring his bride home after the week's ceremonies were over. He had not intended to leave in a rage (Judg. 14:19).

The RIDDLE is an age-old form of mind-stretching and merrymaking suitable for the long hours of the festivities (cf. Ps. 19:1-4*a*—H 19:2-5*a*, based upon a riddle; 49:4—H 49:5; Prov. 1:6; Ezek. 17:2). Samson's riddle (Judg. 14:14) may have been an ancient one rephrased. If gastronomical, the expected answer: "Vomit," would have brought loud guffaws from the male drinking party. If astronomical, the answer: "The Lion sky constellation bringing the harvest," would have closely fitted the experience which had brought the riddle to Samson's mind. The reply given by the Philistines (vs. 18*a*) may have been another riddle whose answer only enraged Samson the more, for love, "sweeter than honey, stronger than a lion," had weakened him before his sweetheart's tears —and it was to bring his final destruction!

That the story tells of no reprisals against Samson for killing thirty men of Ashkelon in order to get the costly linen wrappers and the dress clothes to pay his wager may have been due to the distance of twenty-three miles. It is more likely typical of the

folklore nature of the tales. The hero, only temporarily outwitted, strode across the miles and single-handedly himself outwitted the enemy.

According to Canaanite law based upon earlier Sumerian and Babylonian legislation, the father had a right to give his daughter to someone else in order to save face when the bridegroom left the wedding festivities, but she should not have been given to the best man, for the latter's responsibility was to look after the groom's interests. Therefore, Samson's revenge was "blameless," with the law on his side, and the Philistines dealt with the bride and her father as with an adulterer (15:6*b*). Foxes with blazing torches attached to their tails were ceremonially hunted in the Roman circus centuries later, according to Ovid—a custom which had begun when grain-fields had been set afire by such a fox firebrand escaped from a farmer's boy. Samson's feat of catching three hundred such animals is another superhuman tale. This time Philistine anger forced him to find refuge in a cave.

c) Samson's next two exploits provide two etiological legends for place names: Ramath-lehi, the "Hill of the Jawbone," possibly originally so called because of its peculiar formation; and En-hakkore, the "Spring of Him Who Called," really "Partridge-Spring," named for a bird distinguished by its clear call-note (15:9-20).

Testimonial to fellow Judeans' fear both of Samson's mysterious power and of their Philistine overlords is the story that three thousand of them came and, humorously to Samson, bound him with new ropes to hand him over to the enemy. There is a bloody play on words in Samson's song of victory over his thousand Philistine victims—literally: "With the jawbone of a red ass I have reddened them bright red" (vs. 16). Afterward by a miracle God provided water for his thirsty hero (vss. 18-19; cf. Exod. 17:1-7).

d) The sheer strength of a superhuman giant is the point of the story of Samson's interrupting his night with a harlot at Gaza, the southernmost strong city of the Philistine pentapolis, pulling up the heavy city gates under the noses of sleeping guards, and striding off nearly forty miles to deposit them on a hilltop near Hebron (16:1-3).

e) The foolish weakness of the physical giant is the theme of the story of how, enslaved by passion in another illicit love, he toyed with his sacred vow and, sleeping on Delilah's lap, lost successively his hair, his power, his eyes, and his freedom (16:4-22). So valuable would Samson's capture be that the Philistine overlords offered Delilah a then enormous price, perhaps nearly four thousand dollars. Although she was deceived in turn by seven snapped bowstrings, broken new ropes, and an uprooted loom hanging to the seven locks of Samson's uncut hair, the woman readily recognized that her nagging had at last succeeded when he lay bare the essence of his being, "told her all his mind" (vss. 17-18). The Philistines inflicted customary revenge in gouging out his eyes (cf. the Ammonite threat [I Sam. 11:2] and Zedekiah's fate [II Kings 25:7]) and setting him to the hard labor of an ox or an ass, ironically for him, at previously gateless Gaza.

f) Samson's career ended in a final act of desperate heroism: his strength returning with his growing hair, brought into the temple of DAGON to provide amusement for the festival, uttering a prayer for vengeance for just one of his eyes, with a last surge of strength he pulled the supporting temple pillars and death down upon his head, but in this one deed accomplished more deliverance from the Philistines than in his whole life before (16:23-30). Thus he was rewarded with rest in the family tomb (vs. 31a).

3. Historical importance. The locale of the Samson stories was the border between the tribes of Dan and Judah, perhaps in the period after the migration of most of the Danites to their N home (Judg. 1:34; 18), only the remnants remaining in the S territory (see DAN). This was also the border between these Israelite tribes and the great Philistine plain to the SW. Samson's home at Zorah was some fourteen miles W of Jerusalem at the E end of the Valley of Sorek. The Philistine city of Timnah lay only four miles farther on. Probably because of their superior material civilization, including the use of iron, the Philistines in this border territory were increasing their control and expansion activities. But the conflicts with the Israelites in this period, perhaps the second half of the twelfth century, were only local disputes. As shown by the Samson stories, there were free communication and trade and even intermarriage between Israelites and Philistines.

Therefore, unlike Othniel or Gideon or Jephthah at the head of an Israelite army, Samson is never described as "deliverer" from the enemy. He was only to "begin to deliver Israel from the hand of the Philistines" (13:5) by feats of purely personal revenge. His anti-Philistine exploits strikingly resembled those of two other heroes with somewhat similar names, SHAMGAR (3:31) and SHAMMAH (II Sam. 23:11-12).

Thus the historical significance of the Samson stories lies not in his defeat of Philistines, for this became necessary only in the later era of Samuel and Saul (I Sam. 4-6; 13). It lies rather in its frank and colorful picture of life on the Philistine border in the period of the judges—wedding festivities and procedure and relationships with women, village heroism in feats of muscular strength and witty repartee, alternate free communication and sporadic clashes between Israelites and Philistines. Here is extraordinarily instructive sociological material, of more value to the historian, it has been suggested, than a list of conquered cities on such a significant monument as the Moabite Stone.

4. The story as myth and folklore. Samson's name, his home opposite the shrine to the sun-god at Beth-shemesh, and his adventures have given rise, beginning even with early Christian interpreters, to comparison with sun heroes of Greek, Phoenician, or Babylonian mythology—Hercules, Melkart, or Gilgamesh. His slaying of the lion, in method more marvelous than the similar deeds of David (I Sam. 17:34-36) or Benaiah (II Sam. 23:20), resembled that of such mythological persons. Striking parallels of features of Samson's career with the various roles of the sun have been enumerated: benevolently, his hair was the sun's rays giving daily agricultural life, but cut off by sleep-producing night (the name DELILAH, דלילה, may be a pun on Hebrew לילה, "night"); malevolently, the fox-tail firebrands were the sun-

withering blight on agricultural crops; Samson's solitary life, blinding, imprisonment, and hair regrowth were the sun's solo role in its annual waning and return in the season cycle, comparable to the death and resurrection of the god of vegetation (cf. the sun as bridegroom in Ps. 19:4b-6—H 19:5b-7). Some have interpreted Samson's adventures as numbering twelve, comparable to the twelve labors of mythical Hercules. Others have compared his career, from his slaying of the lion, his having seven locks of hair, and his fate at the hands of a woman, to that of Gilgamesh.

Such mythological parallels possibly indicate that certain of Samson's adventures originated from the heroes of mythology. His total career, however, is so earthy that he may better be interpreted as a folklore hero like a Paul Bunyan or a Peer Gynt. Samson is the rustic hero of frontier days. Although never described as a giant in stature, he was possessed of enormous muscular strength and given to selfish passion and feats of vengeance to restore injured honor. He was humorous trickster par excellence and conqueror of women, wild beasts, and warriors sent to capture him. The deeds of a historical Samson were probably enlarged to giant proportions by centuries of village storytelling.

5. Religious significance. Fortunately this primarily folklore hero was on the right side of the ethnological fence. Unlike Goliath, he was Israelite, not Philistine. His moral virtues and vices were those of the rough day in which he lived. But what gives the Samson cycle of stories religious significance is the fact that the story is tragedy. His selfish and uncontrolled passion, forgetful of sacred vows, brought him to disaster, even though in grim heroic climax. Thus he was a negative religious hero—an example of what God's charismatic individual should not be.

It is possible that in an earlier form of the story Samson's power lay only in the magic of seven unshorn locks of hair (cf. similarly Gilgamesh), and that the biblical account, by its addition of the Nazirite vow, partially transforms a folklore hero into a religious savior. In any case, the clear emphasis of the Samson stories as they stand is the working of Yahweh's spirit in his chosen hero, evident in his childhood (Judg. 13:24), exhibited in mighty feats of strength (14:6, 19; 15:14), withdrawn when in pursuit of his own passions he forgot his vow (16:20), but surging back again in response to prayer (16:28).

It was the interpretation of Samson's uniqueness in being devoted to God before birth and possessor of God's indwelling Spirit which inspired a gospel writer to write in language similar to that about Samson in the announcement of John the Baptist's birth (cf. Judg. 13:4-5 with Luke 1:15) and in the report of the growth of the child Jesus (cf. Judg. 13:24 with Luke 2:40). Thus Samson became one of the heroes of faith in the Letter to the Hebrews (11:32). His story has similarly inspired paintings by Rembrandt and Rubens, an oratorio by Handel, Saint-Saëns' opera Samson and Delilah, and Milton's Samson Agonistes.

Bibliography. G. F. Moore, *Judges*, ICC (1895), pp. 312-65. P. Carus, *The Story of Samson and Its Place in the Religious Development of Mankind* (1907). A. Smythe Palmer, *The Samson-Saga and Its Place in Comparative Religion* (1913).

P. Haupt, "Samson and the Ass's Jaw," *JBL*, XXXIII (1914), 296-98. M. Noth, *Die israelitischen Personnenamen* (1928), pp. 38, 223. C. F. Burney, *Judges* (1930), pp. 335-408. J. Pedersen, *Israel: Its Life and Culture*, I-II (1926), 72, 102, 222-24, 380-82; III-IV (1940), 35-37, 205-6, 264-65, 487-88, 493. A. Van Selms, "The Best Man and Bride—From Sumer to St. John," *JNES*, IX (1950), 65-75. W. F. Albright, *Archaeology and the Religion of Israel* (3rd ed., 1953), pp. 111-12; *From the Stone Age to Christianity* (2nd ed., 1957), pp. 283-84.   C. F. KRAFT

SAMUEL săm'yŏo əl [שמואל, name of God, *or* his name is God]. A prophet of the eleventh century B.C., who anointed first Saul and later David as king over Israel. The first book of Samuel in the OT canon reports his life and deeds.

A reconstruction of the historical data of the life of Samuel encounters great difficulties, for there are irreconcilable differences within the biblical tradition concerning Samuel. The sources of the books of Samuel (*see* SAMUEL, I-II, § C2) themselves introduce marked contrasts into the portrayal of Samuel. Therefore, a survey of the different biblical traditions is necessary prior to any attempt to discover the historical nucleus within the sources.

1. Biblical traditions
   a. E's portrait of Samuel
   b. J's portrait of Samuel
   c. L's contribution
   d. Other traditions concerning Samuel
2. Historical reconstruction
   a. Samuel's office
   b. Samuel's role in the establishment of the
      monarchy
Bibliography

1. Biblical traditions. Among the sources of the books of Samuel, the E source shows the greatest interest in Samuel; the J source is concerned with Saul rather than with Samuel; and the L source contributes only a shred of information to the enigma of Samuel.

a. E's portrait of Samuel. Elkanah, Samuel's father, was an Ephraimite from the town of Ramah in the territory of Zuph (I Sam. 1:1). At a family pilgrimage to the sanctuary of Shiloh, Hannah, Elkanah's wife, who was barren, besought the Lord in ardent prayer for a son, and she vowed to dedicate the child to the Lord if her petition were granted. When Samuel, this child of prayer, was born and weaned, Hannah entrusted him into the care of Eli, the priest of the sanctuary of Shiloh (1:19-28). Later, the Lord revealed to the boy Samuel the coming end of the house of Eli, and from that time Samuel was established as a prophet (3:3-21).

Samuel was the last "judge" of Israel, and he went out from his home town, Ramah, "on a circuit year by year to Bethel, Gilgal, and Mizpah; and he judged Israel in all these places" (7:16). Once, he called the people of Israel to Mizpah and bade them repent of their idolatry (7:3-6). There the Philistines attacked the unprepared gathering of the Israelites, but the entreaties of Samuel and the people's repentance moved the Lord to deliver Israel by a miracle (vss. 7-10). The Philistines were so completely defeated that they did not rise against Israel again in the days of Samuel (vss. 11-13).

As Samuel became old, he set his two sons in his stead as judges over Israel, but they turned out to be corrupt (8:1-3). Under these circumstances, the elders of Israel asked Samuel to appoint a king over the people. This request was an apostasy in the eyes of the Lord, but nevertheless he ordered Samuel to fulfil the wish of the people (ch. 8). Thus in a public festival at Mizpah, Samuel chose by lot the king over Israel, Saul (10:17-21*aba*). In a stern address Samuel warned King Saul and his people to remain faithful to the Lord (ch. 12).

In the next scene (ch. 15), the Lord, through his prophet Samuel, ordered Saul to engage in an expedition against the Amalekites and to consecrate for destruction all the captives and spoil. In spite of this divine command, after the successful campaign Saul spared the life of the king of the Amalekites. Also the best of the sheep and the oxen were spared from destruction by Saul's warriors for a sacrificial meal. When Samuel learned of the violation of the ancient custom, he himself slew the captive king and rejected Saul from kingship over Israel.

On a later date, Samuel secretly anointed David to be king of Israel (16:1-13). David, after his duel with Goliath, joined the royal court, but as his fame grew, he had to flee from the royal court because of Saul's jealousy and outbursts of rage. David escaped with the help of Samuel, who was the head of a prophetic guild (19:18-24).

Samuel's influence upon the life of Israel did not cease even with his death (25:1), for before the disastrous battle with the Philistines, Saul, beset by forebodings, consulted the ghost of Samuel with the help of a medium. The ghost conjured foretold the defeat of the Israelites and the deaths of Saul and his sons (28:3-19).

b. J's portrait of Samuel. The J source of the books of Samuel is interested in the life of Samuel insofar as it is involved with the career of Saul. Here Samuel is represented as a seer of Ramah to whom Saul turned for advice in his search for the lost asses of his father. Samuel invited Saul to participate as a guest of honor in a sacrificial meal (I Sam. 9). The next morning Samuel secretly anointed Saul to be king over Israel and sent him upon his way, with the admonition to wait at Gilgal seven days for the prophet's coming (10:1-16). After starting an uprising against the Philistines, Saul waited seven days for Samuel. But when Samuel did not arrive at the end of the appointed time and the people following Saul began to scatter, the king offered sacrifices in order to entreat the favor of the Lord before the impending combat with the Philistines. As soon as King Saul finished offering the sacrifice, Samuel arrived and, in the Lord's name, rejected Saul from kingship over Israel because of his disobedience (13:8-15*a*).

c. L's contribution. In the framework of this source Samuel makes his entry only within the short passage of I Sam. 10:21*b*β-27. It was Samuel's role to conduct the rites of the election of the king. He introduced Saul as the man who "was taller than any of the people from his shoulders upwards" and subsequently promulgated the laws of kingship and deposited them before the Lord.

d. Other traditions concerning Samuel. Samuel was remembered as a great intercessor, second only to

Moses (Jer. 15:1; cf. Ps. 99:6). The Chronicler's genealogical table lists Samuel as one of the "sons of Levi" (I Chr. 6:28). He and David are credited with the establishment of the office of gatekeepers who guarded the tent of meeting (9:22). The rabbinical tradition which ascribes the partial authorship of the books of Samuel to the prophet Samuel (B.B. 15*a*) also finds its roots in the Chronicles (I Chr. 29:29).

2. Historical reconstruction. Samuel's personality made a lasting impression upon his contemporaries. His office, his personality, and his role in the introduction of monarchy are shrouded by the presence of legendary elements and discrepancies within the tradition complexes. Therefore, any attempt at separating the historical data must consider the legendary character of the sources and will run the risk of rejecting historically sound data or admitting material of dubious historicity.

a. Samuel's office. Samuel belonged to a rich and important family of the town of Ramah, as the genealogy of his father, Elkanah, spanning over four generations, indicates (I Sam. 1:1). He was an Ephraimite, though the Chronicler lists him as one of the "sons of Levi" (I Chr. 6:28).

He was remembered as a "man of God," a "seer," a "prophet," and the last "judge" of Israel. He was, no doubt, more than a "seer" if the word "seer" meant a mere village clairvoyant who for a small fee gave information concerning the whereabouts of lost objects or animals (I Sam. 9:6-9). On the other hand, Samuel's office of "judge," conceived as an authority over the whole of Israel (8:4-5), must not be maintained either. Apparently he had authority in religious matters, as his connections with the cult, local and national, amply document. At the high place of Ramah, the people would not commence with the sacrificial meal before Samuel blessed it (9:13); he could invite guests, give orders, and determine the seating order of the worshipers at the sacrificial gathering (vss. 22-24). He had the oil for the anointment, or he could consecrate it so that it received some kind of potent sacramental character (10:1). He could also proclaim the consecration of spoils and captives for destruction (15:3) and deny the right of offering from the king (10:8; 13:13). All these cultic privileges and his role in the rites preparing the election of the king designate him as the leading religious personality of Israel in his own time.

Apparently Samuel had some connections with the prophetic guilds of Israel (10:5-6; 19:18-24). Whether or not he was a member or leader of the prophetic movement cannot be decided, but indubitably this man of God was one of the precursors of the great prophets of the eighth century B.C.

b. Samuel's role in the establishment of the monarchy. Samuel's role in the anointment of King Saul cannot be exactly defined, but it is exceedingly clear, in the light of the threefold witness of the sources (E: 10:17-21*aba*; J: 10:1-16; L: 10:21*bβ*-27), that his role was decisive in the introduction of monarchy into Israel.

A great difficulty arises from the fact that in the E source both the Lord and Samuel are opposed to earthly kingship, but in the J source their attitude is friendly. An attempt at historical reconstruction

might consider that Samuel could have opposed the introduction of kingship in the beginning. Later, however, under the influence of the growing menace of the Philistine power, he could have changed his position and taken an active part in the introduction of the monarchy. Samuel probably conceived kingship as an earthly vicegerency of the Lord's kingship over Israel (*see* THEOCRACY). Therefore, Samuel required from the king absolute obedience to the word of the Lord, as both rejection narratives reveal (I Sam. 13; 15). It is within the realm of probable historicity also that after he withdrew his support from Saul, Samuel searched for another theocratic vicegerent and found him in the person of the famed military leader David.

Bibliography. K. Budde, "Sauls Königswahl und Verwerfung," *ZAW*, VIII (1888), 223-48. E. König, *Der ältere Prophetismus bis auf die Heldengestalten von Elia und Elisa* (1905). S. R. Driver, *Notes on the Hebrew Text and the Topography of the Books of Samuel* (2nd rev. ed., 1913). H. Junker, *Prophet und Seher in Israel, eine Untersuchung über die ältesten Erscheinungen des israelitischen Prophetentums, insbesondere der Prophetenvereine* (1927). I. Hylander, *Der literarische Samuel-Saul-Komplex (I Sam. 1-15) traditionsgeschichtlich untersucht* (1932). R. Press, "Sauls Königswahl," *Theol. Blätter*, XII (1933), 243-48; "Der Prophet Samuel; Eine traditionsgeschichtliche Untersuchung," *ZAW*, LVI (1938), 177-225. W. A. Irwin, "Samuel and the Rise of the Monarchy," *AJSL*, LVIII (1941), 113-34. K. Möhlenbrink, "Sauls Ammoniterfeldzug und Samuels Beitrag zum Königtum des Saul," *ZAW*, LVIII (1940-41), 57-70. E. Robertson, "Samuel and Saul," *BJRL*, XXVIII (1944), 175-206. A. George, "Fautes contre Yahweh dans les livres de Samuel," *RB*, LIII (1946), 161-84. M. Buber, "Das Volksbegehren," *Lohmeyer-Gedenkschrift* (1951), pp. 53-66. G. von Rad, *Der heilige Krieg im alten Israel* (1952). M. Buber, "Die Erzählung von Sauls Königswahl," *Vetus Testamentum*, VI (1956), 113-73. M. Bič, "Saul sucht die Eselinnen," *Vetus Testamentum*, VII (1957), 92-97.

S. SZIKSZAI

***SAMUEL, I AND II.** The ninth and tenth books of the English Bible and the third and fourth books of the Former Prophets in the Hebrew Bible. They report the events of the period from the birth of Samuel, through the introduction of monarchy by Saul, and David's reign unto his old age.

A. Title
B. Contents
   1. Samuel (I Sam. 1-7)
   2. Samuel and Saul (I Sam. 8-15)
   3. Saul and David (I Sam. 16-II Sam. 1)
   4. David becomes king of Judah and Israel (II Sam. 2-8)
   5. The events of the Davidic court (II Sam. 9-20)
   6. Appendixes (II Sam. 21-24)
C. Composition
   1. Attempts to solve the problem
     a. Two-source theory
     b. Three-source theory
     c. Saga-cycle theory
   2. Demonstration of the three-source theory
   3. Source analysis of the books
   4. Evaluation of the sources
     a. Characteristics of the sources
     b. Dating of the sources
     c. Historicity of the sources

5. The history of composition
D. Text
Bibliography

A. TITLE. The names of the books in the Hebrew canon are I and II Samuel. These two books were originally one, and the LXX first introduced the division, naming them the books of the "kingdoms," βασιλειῶν α' and β'. The LXX has four books of "Kingdoms," the books of Samuel together with the

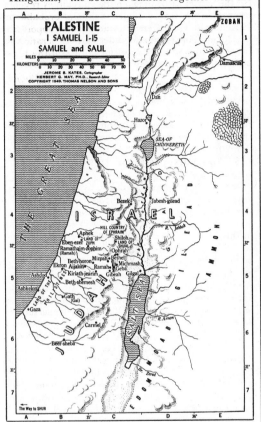

PALESTINE
I SAMUEL 1-15
SAMUEL and SAUL

MILES 0 10   20   30   40   50
KILOMETERS 0 10 20 30 40 50 60 70 80
JEROME S. KATES, Cartographer
HERBERT G. MAY, Ph.D. Research Editor
COPYRIGHT 1949, THOMAS NELSON AND SONS

two books of "Kings." Jerome preferred the designation *Regum* ("Kings"), in accord with the Hebrew מלכים, to *Regnorum* ("Kingdoms"), which name was customary then. The division into two books (in harmony with the LXX) appeared in the Hebrew Bible for the first time in a MS, A.D. 1448. The Bible of Felix Pratensis (1517-18) perpetuated this division in the printed editions.

The ascription of the books to Samuel as author is a Talmudic tradition (B.B. 14*b*), which also states that the events after the death of Samuel were related by the seer Gad and the prophet Nathan (B.B. 15*a*). This tradition is evidently based upon I Chr. 29:29.

B. CONTENTS. The two books can be divided into six parts:

1. Samuel (I Sam. 1-7). The birth of Samuel and his dedication to the service of the Lord at the ark sanctuary of Shiloh are the first events related (ch. 1). The child Samuel and an unknown man of God announced the downfall of the priestly family of Eli, the priest of Shiloh (chs. 2-3). The ark was captured by the Philistines in the battle at Aphek. Two sons

of Eli fell in this battle, and the news of the disaster killed Eli (ch. 4). But the captive ark brought calamity to the Philistines, who returned it to the land of Israel, where, at last, it found a home in Kiriath-jearim (chs. 5-6). In the seventh chapter Samuel, already the judge of Israel, called the people to a national repentance of sins. The Philistines' attack upon the people was deterred by a miraculous deliverance wrought by the Lord.

2. Samuel and Saul (I Sam. 8-15). The people of Israel desired to be like all the nations and have a king, in place of the judge Samuel. Though the Lord regarded the people's wish as an apostasy, he gave his consent to the designation of a king (ch. 8). Saul, a Benjaminite, in search of the lost asses of his father, came to Ramah, where Samuel secretly anointed him to be king over Israel, in accord with a divine command (chs. 9-10). In another scene Saul was publicly chosen to be king (10:17-27). In the next episode Saul, who did not seem to reign like a king, delivered Jabesh-gilead from the siege of the Ammonites. After this successful campaign, the army went to Gilgal to "renew the kingdom" (ch. 11). There, Samuel abdicated his office of judge and charged the people and King Saul to be faithful to the Lord (ch. 12).

Saul's military campaigns against the Philistines occupy chs. 13-14. In preparation for a battle, Saul offered a sacrifice. Because of this act, Samuel reprimanded Saul and rejected him from the kingship (ch. 13). Jonathan, Saul's son, prepared a great victory over the Philistines with a heroic feat, but unwittingly broke the fast which Saul had vowed for the army. Jonathan faced death for his breach of the vow, but the people ransomed his life (ch. 14). A summary account of Saul's military engagements and family closes this section. In a war against the Amalekites, Samuel had proclaimed a *ḥérem* or consecration for the destruction of all spoils and captives. Saul disobeyed the ban, and therefore Samuel again rejected him from the kingship (I Sam. 15).

3. Saul and David (I Sam. 16-II Sam. 1). Samuel had secretly anointed David to be the future king of Israel, and afterward David came to the court of Saul as a lyre player (ch. 16). David killed Goliath in a duel, whereupon the victorious youth was introduced anew to Saul (ch. 17). David won the friendship of Jonathan and the admiration of the people but awakened Saul's jealousy, and he attempted to kill David in a jealous rage. Later, Saul gave his younger daughter, Michal, to David in marriage (ch. 18). Jonathan succeeded in mollifying Saul's rage against David; in another scene Michal helped David escape from Saul. David found refuge within a prophetic group led by Samuel (ch. 19). Jonathan secretly met David and assured him of his unbroken friendship (ch. 20). Ahimelech, the priest of Nob, helped David in his flight, and for this reason Saul massacred the whole priestly colony of Nob. Abiathar, one of the priests of Nob, fled to David, who had, after a short stay with the Philistine Achish, gathered an army of freebooters and lodged with them in the mountains of Judah (chs. 21-22). Saul continued to pursue David in the wilderness of Ziph and Engedi. Once David spared the life of Saul, who had been in his power (chs. 23–24). David married Abigail, the widow of a rich Calebite (ch. 25), and he spared Saul's life again at Ziph (ch. 26). Later, he entered with his private army into the service of the Philistines, who entrusted to him the military outpost of Ziklag (ch. 27).

See map "Palestine: I Samuel 16–31, Saul and David," under SAUL.

The Philistine army encamped at Gilboa against the Israelites; Saul, in his despair, turned for advice to the ghost of Samuel, who foretold the defeat of the Israelites (ch. 28). David appeared at the Philistine mustering, but the distrust of his overlords, who sent him back to Ziklag, saved him from participation in the defeat of his own people (ch. 29). In the meantime, Ziklag was raided by the Amalekites. David found Ziklag burned and empty, but he pursued and overtook the Amalekites and rescued the captive women and children (ch. 30). In the Battle of Gilboa, the Philistines defeated Israel. Saul's three sons were slain, and Saul himself fell upon his sword (ch. 31). An Amalekite brought the news to David and reported that he had killed Saul on Mount Gilboa. David slew the Amalekite and sang a dirge over Saul and Jonathan (II Sam. 1).

4. David becomes king of Judah and Israel (II Sam. 2–8). After the death of Saul, the elders of Judah anointed David king in Hebron. In the N, Saul's son Ish-bosheth became king (ch. 2). Ish-bosheth's army commander promised to support David's claim for the suzerainty over the N, but Abner, the commander, was killed by Joab, the commander of David's army, in a private blood revenge (ch. 3). Soon Ish-bosheth was killed by two of his captains; the assassins expected reward from David but were executed by him (ch. 4). Being without a competitor, David also became the king of Israel. After the capture of the Jebusite city of Jerusalem, David established his own capital there (ch. 5). The ark was also brought to Jerusalem (ch. 6), but David's plan to build a temple for the ark was rejected by the Lord in the prophecy of Nathan, in which the Lord promised to establish the reign of the Davidic dynasty forever (ch. 7). In the eighth chapter a short summary of David's wars and a list of his chief officials are found.

See map "Palestine: II Samuel, The Kingdom of David," under DAVID.

5. The events of the Davidic court (II Sam. 9–20). David reinstated Mephibosheth, the son of Jonathan, into the estate of Saul and invited him into his court (ch. 9). The king of Ammon's humiliation of David's envoy led to repeated long wars with the Ammonites and their allies, the Syrians (ch. 10). During one of these wars David plotted the death of Uriah, one of his officers, with whose wife, Bathsheba, he had committed adultery. After her husband's death, Bathsheba became David's wife (ch. 11). When Nathan the prophet denounced David for the murder of Uriah, David repented, but the fruit of the illicit love died. Solomon was David and Bathsheba's second son (ch. 12). Amnon, the first-born son of David, raped his half sister, Tamar, whereupon her full brother, Absalom, killed Amnon in revenge. After this fratricide, Absalom fled to

Talmai, his maternal grandfather (ch. 13). As a result of Joab's reconciliating attempts between David and his son, after three years Absalom was allowed to return to Jerusalem, and after two more years David readmitted him to the court (ch. 14). Absalom successfully conspired against his father and finally started an open rebellion, which forced David and his army to flee from Jerusalem (ch. 15). The fleeing king kept his peace, even when he was humiliated by the curses of Shimei, a Benjaminite. Absalom listened to the wrong advice, deliberately given by Hushai, a friend of David, and delayed his attack on David. This tactical blunder enabled David and his army to retreat to Transjordan territory to rest and to rally new troops (chs. 16–17). In the ensuing battle the rebels were defeated, and Absalom was killed (ch. 18). The king mourned his son and pardoned Shimei, who prostrated himself before the victorious king (ch. 19). Later, Sheba, a Benjaminite, rallied the N tribes in a revolt against David, but the army of Joab successfully stifled this rebellion (ch. 20).

6. Appendixes (II Sam. 21–24). David, at one time during his reign, allowed seven of Saul's descendants to be put to death by the Gibeonites, who demanded their lives for obliteration of Saul's blood guilt. The seven Saulides were hanged. David, moved by the grief of Rizpah, who lost her two sons in this blood revenge, gathered the remains of the whole family of Saul and buried them in the tomb of Kish, Saul's father (ch. 21). Ch. 22 is a psalm attributed to David and identical with Ps. 18. Another poetical work, the "last words" of David, appears, together with a short summary of the feats of David's heroes, in ch. 23. The final chapter reports an episode from the life of David—that of the census of Israel. This census displeased the Lord, so that he sent pestilence upon the land. In order to avert the plague, David built an altar for the Lord on the threshing floor of Araunah as an expiation (ch. 24).

C. COMPOSITION. The books of Samuel are not the work of one writer, but they appear to be composed of different sources, as the parallel stories, incongruities, and discrepancies within the books indicate. Thus Saul is anointed to be king over Israel by Samuel secretly (I Sam. 10:1) and on two different occasions elevated to the same office in public ceremony (10:21; 11:15). Twice Samuel rejects Saul from kingship (13:14; 15:23). Twice David is introduced to Saul (16:21; 17:58). Twice David escapes from the court of Saul (19:12; 20:42); Saul knows of David's flight in the first case (19:17), yet he questions his absence from the court on a later date (20: 27). The slaying of Goliath is attributed both to David (I Sam. 17) and to one of his heroes, Elhanan of Bethlehem (II Sam. 21:19). These and many more similar instances establish beyond a doubt the composite character of the books.

Sharp differences can also be perceived in the religious outlook of several portions. Within I Sam. 7–12 there is an easily discernible shifting in the views concerning the evaluation of the institution of the monarchy. Kingship is alternately regarded as an institution favored by God, and condemned as an apostasy.

1. Attempts to solve the problem. The composite character of the books of Samuel presents a challenge to the scholarly world which advances three different theories in answer to the problem of the composition of the books of Samuel. All three theories recognize that the final composition of the books was the work of the Deuteronomic editors (*see* DEUTERONOMY), who, in order to document the Lord's reign and work in Israel's history, compiled and edited some extant literary material between 621 and 586 B.C. The difference between the three theories is in their separation and identification of the literary works utilized as sources by the Deuteronomic editors. Accordingly, one might distinguish between (*a*) the two-source theory, (*b*) the three-source theory, and (*c*) the saga-cycle theory.

a. Two-source theory. At the end of the nineteenth century some scholars suggested that two sources, J and E, were component parts of the books. Some of these scholars maintained that the J and E sources represent the actual continuation of the Pentateuchal sources marked with the same sigla. There were other scholars who accepted the two-source theory, but had some doubts concerning the connection of the sources of the books of Samuel with the sources of the Pentateuch. Others, in a mediating position, questioned the identity of these two sources and the Pentateuchal ones, but attributed the two sources to circles which stood near the Pentateuchal authors, J and E.

b. Three-source theory. A thoroughgoing analysis of the narratives of I Sam. 7–12, which report the institution of the monarchy, led several scholars to the recognition that, at least in the chapters in question, there are three easily separable sources. Two of these sources are favorably disposed toward the monarchy, and the third has a definitely antimonarchic attitude. These three sources are designated as "L," "J," and "E." Their identity with the Pentateuchal sources L, J, and E is not always asserted; however, the affinity with the sources of the Pentateuch is presupposed, as the use of the identical sigla indicates.

c. Saga-cycle theory. As a reaction to the sometimes exacting source-critical approach, several tradition-historical attempts were made to solve the problems of the books of Samuel. The tradition-historical school endeavors to trace individual traditions to their oral form and conception. The representatives of this school emphasize the decisive importance of narrative complexes centered around a single theme. They assume the independent existence of such saga cycles as the ark narratives (I Sam. 4–6; II Sam. 6) and the history of David's court (II Sam. 9–20; I Kings 1–2). The scholars belonging to this school of thought reject the separation of the book into sources. They explain the occasional doublets as the result of slow accumulation of MS variants, supplementations, and preservations of two different versions of the same oral tradition. Thus, the saga-cycle theory propounds that the books of Samuel were composed of narrative complexes, which were joined together, not by interweaving them along their full length, but by setting one after another and by connecting these parts loosely.

The apparent difficulty of the saga-cycle theory is in its lack of a sharp distinction between literary pieces and literary subjects. Apparently, the same literary piece might include several subjects—i.e., the shifting of interest from one topic to another does not necessarily mean a change of the narrator. The presence of a literary plan and the continuity of theological and historical views indicate that small, subject-centered literary units do belong in a larger whole, which deserves the name "source."

2. Demonstration of the three-source theory. The three-source theory seems to do the greatest justice to the books of Samuel because it offers the most probable explanation of some of the peculiarities of the books. This assertion can be supported by a validity of the three-source theory, which may be demonstrated within the narrative complex of Saul's elevation to kingship (I Sam. 7–12). This narrative complex can be unraveled into three separate threads.

One of these sources, designated with the sign "E" (7:2-17; 8; 10:17-21bα; 12), sharply condemns the institution of monarchy. The E source starts with the assumption that Israel did not need the military leadership of a king against the Philistines, for Samuel, the judge of Israel, had miraculously defeated the attacking troops of the Philistines (7:5-14). The defeat of the Philistine army was so complete that the Philistines did not again assault the nation of Israel within the lifetime of Samuel, and they restored all the former Israelite territories. Thus, in the opinion of the E writer, the introduction of kingship was not a national necessity arising from the pressure of the annihilating power of the Philistines, but a sheer apostasy of the obstinate people. For the Israelites rejected, with their demand for a king, not merely Samuel as the judge of Israel, but also the Lord's kingship over Israel (8:7). Samuel had warned the people of the despotic ways of the kings, but the people of Israel refused to listen. They stubbornly repeated their request to Samuel for a king, so that they might be like all the nations (8:10-19). Finally the Lord gave his consent to fulfil the foolish and rebellious desire of the people (8:19-22). Samuel called the people together at Mizpah for the selection of a king from the assembled tribes of Israel; there Samuel recounted the mighty saving acts of the Lord and contrasted them with the people's ungrateful desire for a king. The selection of the king was done by lot, and Saul became the king (10:17-21bα). The gathering at Mizpah was continued with Samuel's abdication of his office as judge and his farewell admonition to people and king. These farewell words (ch. 12) are also pervaded by the antimonarchic spirit, just as were the previously mentioned parts. The hero of the E source is apparently Samuel, beside whom King Saul is dwarfed.

The second strand of the narrative concerning the introduction of kingship in Israel is designated with the letter "J" (I Sam. 9; 10:1-16). In the J source Saul appears as a young man still living at his father's house and going on his father's errands. When Saul was sent in search of the lost asses of his father, he met Samuel, who anointed him to be king over Israel. In this source one does not hear the rebellious demand of the people for a king. Here, the introduction of the monarchy is not regarded as apostasy. On the contrary, it was the Lord himself who saw the affliction of his people under the Philistines and decided to deliver them by the hands of an anointed prince (9:16; 10:1 LXX). In this source Samuel does not have the same stature of national importance as in the E source but appears as a local seer, whose influence was most likely limited.

The third source, designated "L," appears in 10:21bβ–11:15. This source shows more sympathy toward kingship than does E. According to the account of the L source, the people did not desire a king so stubbornly as in E (ch. 8). The king apparently was appointed by the Lord, and the people's opinion concerning the necessity of the institution of the monarchy was mixed (10:26-27). The favorable attitude of the L source toward kingship is manifest in the fact that it calls those who voiced their derogatory opinion of Saul "worthless fellows" (10:27). That 10:21bβ-27 is not the direct conclusion of the E report in 10:17-21bα may be easily conceived. There is an abrupt change of the subject of action from Samuel (10:21a) to the people (10:22). The election to kingship by lot, as it is described in 10:20-21abα, presupposed the presence of Saul, but Saul was obviously not present (vs. 21bβ.) When the people inquired of the Lord, significantly they did not ask the question: "Did the man come hither?" (10:22 LXX), but, according to the MT: "Is there yet a man to come hither?" These facts and the emphasis on Saul's tallness (vss. 23-24) do not postulate the selection by lot, but rather the receiving of an oracle. This oracle would not have, necessarily, designated Saul to be king, but merely would have specified that the Lord's choice for kingship had to be one head taller than anyone else of the people. This presumed oracle would have been followed by a general mustering of the people, and when nobody had been found who could fulfil the requirements of the oracle (vs. 21bβ), the people would have had to inquire again (vs. 22) of the Lord. Obviously also, the divine answer: "Behold, he has hidden himself among the baggage" (vs. 22), could not have been obtained by the awkward oracle technique of the sacred lot, which was mentioned in the E account (vs. 21). The composition of the sources into one continuous narrative would have resulted in the present mutilated account. Also, in 10:25, the "law of the kingship" (MT; cf. RSV "rights and duties of the kingship") can hardly be identical with the "law of the king" (MT; cf. RSV "ways of the king") in 8:11. In L the law is divinely approved, and therefore it is laid before the Lord (10:25), but in E the "law of the king" is more or less the arbitrary way of the oriental despot (8:11-18). The dismissal of the people (10:25) prepared the scene for the deliverance of Jabesh-gilead (ch. 11). The continuity of the two episodes—i.e., Saul's election to kingship and the military deliverance of Jabesh-gilead within the L source—is established by the fact that, after the victory over the Ammonites, some of the warriors asked the death penalty for the "worthless fellows" (11:12) who, after Saul's elevation to kingship, doubted his ability to save Israel (10:27). But Saul showed clemency and declared that no man had to

be put to death on the day of deliverance of Israel (11:23).

Undeniably, the three-source theory can be best demonstrated within this complex, but the presence of the three sources can be traced throughout the books of Samuel.

3. Source analysis of the books. The separation of the three sources within the books of Samuel appears to be possible, and a short analysis will be presented.

I Sam. 1-6: Within chs. 1-3, two sources, J and E, might be separated, and some late additions and glosses (2:1-10, 27-36; 3:12-14) can be discovered. The J source (1:3b; 2:12-17, 22-25) does not mention the name of Samuel and speaks of Hophni and Phinehas, the sons of Eli, as the priests of Shiloh (1:3b). The E source, at the very start (1:1-3a, 4-28; 2:11, 18-21; 3:1, 2a, 3-11, 15-21), presents Samuel as the revered hero of the source, and his birth story and consecration (even as a child) to the service of the Lord in the sanctuary of Shiloh represent an appropriate prelude to the life of Samuel. The E source regards Eli as the only priest of Shiloh (2:20). The L source makes its first appearance in chs. 4-6. Its interest is focused upon the vicissitudes of the ark. The narrative is interwoven with the J source, which continues to follow the destiny of the sons of Eli in addition to its main interest in the fate of the ark.

For an analysis of I Sam. 7-12, *see* § C2 *above*.

I Sam. 13-15: Within these chapters, Saul's early wars and his rejection from the kingship are related. Apparently the E source could not have reported any of the Philistine wars, because E was convinced that after the victory at Mizpah the Philistines were subdued in Samuel's lifetime (7:13-14). Thus this story, which joins Saul's rejection from the kingship to a cultic offense during the punishing expedition against the Amalekites (ch. 15), must be E's version of Saul's rejection.

The rejection of Saul from kingship in ch. 13 (vss. 8-15a) originates from another source, J, which knows of Philistine wars even during Samuel's lifetime. To be sure, Saul's offense is cultic in its nature also, according to J. According to both E and J, King Saul had to bear a trial of faith, which he failed by sinning in the field of the cult. In ch. 14, L reports, significantly, a cultic offense of Jonathan, Saul's son, in connection with the Philistine wars; thus, this episode forms a partial parallel to the E (ch. 15) and J (13:8-15a) stories.

I Sam. 16-18: It is generally recognized that I Sam. 16:1-13, as the undisturbed continuation of Saul's rejection in ch. 15 (E), belongs to the E source. But also 16:14-23 belongs manifestly to E, as is shown by the organic connection between David's anointment and the coming of the Spirit of the Lord upon David on the one hand, and the Spirit's departure from Saul and his torment by an evil spirit on the other hand. Thus, David is brought, according to the E source, to Saul's court as a player of the lyre.

Some words, such as "a man of valor, a man of war" (16:18), and "he became his armor-bearer" (vs. 21), must be removed from the context, because they do not fit the E portrait of the youthful David. These words can be connected with 14:52: "When Saul saw any strong man, or any valiant man, he attached him to himself" (L). In this way, two accounts of David's coming to Saul's court can be established within ch. 16. But there is a third thread in ch. 17 (most clearly recognizable in 17:12-31, 55–18:4), according to which Saul did not know David before his duel with Goliath. This third thread is J, and it is conflated with the E source within ch. 17, so that sections could belong to both J and E. The E thread appears at its clearest in vss. 32-39. The musician David of the E source appears in 18:10-16 and the valiant warrior of L in 18:5-9, 20-29, while J is clearly seen in 18:17-19, which seems to allude to Saul's promise to give his daughter to the victor over Goliath (17:25).

I Sam. 19–30: Saul's jealousy of him forced David to flee from the presence of the king. He was helped in his escape by Michal, his wife, according to L (19:11-17). The same service was accorded to him in J's version (20:1*b*-42) by Jonathan. Finally, E reports that the escape of David was possible because of the help given by Samuel (19:18-24). The separation of the sources cannot be completed with precise finality in every case. Thus 21:1-9 might be L or J; the case is similar to 22:1-2, 6-23, but the Gath episode in which David feigns insanity before the Philistines (21:10-15) definitely points to E, for E does not recognize David's mercenary services to the Philistines. David's deliverance of Keilah from the hands of the Philistines in 23:1-13 is L; so are the Nabal and Abigail idyl in 25:2-44 and ch. 26, which reports David's sparing of Saul's life in the encampment at Ziph. The J source parallels L in 23:19-28; 24. In this account David spares the king's life in a cave at Engedi. E narrates about a secret covenant between David and Jonathan (23:14*b*-18) and thus supplies a doublet to J (20:41-42).

The next narrative complex is centered around David's association with the Philistines. The L source reports that David, after a short stay in Gath, received from Achish, king of Gath, the outpost of Ziklag (27:5-7). The J source, on the contrary, pictures David as staying in Gath with Achish and finally becoming Achish' bodyguard (27:8-12; 28: 1-2). Both the L and the J sources need 27:1-4 to introduce David's decision to become a mercenary of the Philistines. The events (at the mustering of the Philistine army at Aphek) which freed David from the danger of fighting his own people (ch. 29) were reported by both L and J, as traces of conflation show within the narrative. E (28:3-25) gives the memorable scene of Saul's consulting the ghost of Samuel with the aid of the medium of Endor. The L source, which is aware of David's manning of the fortress of Ziklag, relates the Amalekite raid on Ziklag and David's ensuing revenge and liberation of the captives (ch. 30).

I Sam. 31–II Sam. 6: The death of Saul and his sons on Mount Gilboa (ch. 31) is the L source, as the piety of the Jabeshites indicates (cf. ch. 11). The two sources L and J reappear in the composite II Sam. 1. Apparently the messenger who "escaped from the camp of Israel" (vs. 3) cannot be identical with the Amalekite who "by chance . . . happened to be on Mount Gilboa" (vs. 6). Also, the report of the young Amalekite (vss. 6-10) ought to be followed immediately by his questioning and execution (vss. 13-16). Instead, the continuity of this L narrative is interrupted by J's account of David's mourning (vss. 11-12). The dirge of David on Saul and Jonathan (vss. 17-27) belongs to J. Chs. 2–6 belong, in the main, to L, but there are small traces of foreign material present.

II Sam. 7-8: The seventh chapter starts with an oracle of Nathan (vss. 1-17), which prohibited David from building a temple for the Lord but promised establishment of the Davidic dynasty forever. This oracle is generally referred to as the dynastic oracle, which was repeatedly ascribed by biblical scholars to the Deuteronomic editor or was identified as a late midrash. However, if the central importance of the temple in late pre-exilic and postexilic periods is considered, it seems most unlikely that either the Deuteronomic editor or a late midrash would have expressed a prohibition in such terms, which not merely forbade David to erect a temple, but also discredited the necessity of building a temple (vss. 5-7). Because of the favorable attitude toward the institution of kingship, the dynastic oracle cannot belong to the E source, either (vss. 8-16). Thus the dynastic oracle might be assigned either to L or to J, or to an independent but ancient tradition, even though in a shorter form, for the whole seventh chapter is overladen with later additions. The eighth chapter has a definite similarity to I Sam. 14:47-51, for, as the latter summarizes the reign of Saul, so this chapter gives a short account of David's reign. Both sections are from the pen of L.

II Sam. 9-24: These chapters represent the so-called court narrative, which extends beyond the books of Samuel into the books of Kings (I Kings 1-2). This narrative of the Davidic court is the work of J. The chronological order might be restored by placing II Sam. 21:1-14—i.e., the vengeance of the Gibeonites on Saul's house—before ch. 9, where Jonathan's son, Mephibosheth, receives David's favor. Some scholars tried to discover traces of the E source within the court narrative, but the arguments enlisted do not bear out this contention. The occasional discrepancies (e.g., the conflicting reports on Absalom's offspring [cf. 14:27; 18:18]) must be explained by the presence of later accretions.

4. Evaluation of the sources. The use of the sigla of the Pentateuchal sources (L, J, E) for the sources of the books of Samuel does not necessarily imply their identity. Their use, however, expresses the conviction that the sources of the books of Samuel are related to the sources of the Pentateuch. The degree of relationship of these sources cannot be conclusively stated, and it will suffice to maintain that there are sufficient grounds in the similarities of style and outlook to assume that both the Pentateuchal sources and those of the books of Samuel originate from the same circle of authors.

a. Characteristics of the sources. Even a superficial comparison of the sources reveals that L (Lay source) is the least interested in theological thoughts, and that E approaches the events with a clearly definable "philosophy of history." Between the L and E sources, J has a middle place, its view on history being theocentric, though not always emphasized.

Also in the point of religious orientation, the sources differ markedly. An interest in the destiny of the holy ark is characteristic of L, which recognizes only the ephod and the oracle techniques (cf. I Sam. 23:6-13; 30:7-8) as God's means of communication with man. J also seems to take great interest in the fate of the ark but likewise in the destiny of the priesthood of Shiloh and Nob. J recognizes that, besides the oracle (II Sam. 21:1), men, too, are used by God to express, with unmistakable words, his will (I Sam. 9:1-10:16; 13:13-14). The rapture of the prophetic bands of I Sam. 10:10 does not arouse J's sympathy, but rather an indifferent attitude can be observed. E, however, seems sympathetic toward the same mass ecstasy (I Sam. 19:18-24), and is exceedingly interested in the person of Samuel, giving, in addition, his childhood idyl. E's religion, though it has cultic aspects, is not identical with cultic-ritual observance; obedience before the Lord is the decisive aspect of E's religion (I Sam. 15:22).

A difference between these sources can be clearly perceived in their individual concept of the "spirit of the Lord." For L, the spirit of the Lord meant an irresistible impulse for action and the communication of suprahuman power (I Sam. 11:6). J recognizes it as the force causing the mass ecstatic phenomenon (10:10). E, beyond the mass ecstatic aspect (I Sam. 19:18-24), also recognizes a constant leading and blessing spirit (16:13-14).

The most significant difference can be seen, as has been expounded already (*see* § C2 *above*), in the sources' views concerning the institution of kingship.

An investigation of the literary peculiarities of the sources reveals that the L source has an explicit preference for sagas presenting folk-tale motifs — e.g., Saul's hiding among the baggage (I Sam. 10:22) and his being called from behind the oxen (11:5). L enjoys reporting the bizarre marriage presents, when Saul asked for one hundred Philistine foreskins and David gave double the amount (I Sam. 18:25-27). David's flight, with the help of Michal, preserves a rough, peasant humor (19:11-17). L relates the Nabal episode with the sincere sympathy so characteristic of the folk tale toward the successful adventurer, and L even gives, with a rough sense of mockery, the name Nabal ("fool") to the extorted peasant (I Sam. 25:2-44). The stories which are not colorful enough for L's taste are given in short summaries (e.g., I Sam. 14:47-51; II Sam. 8). The circle from which the stories originate was close to the country folk. The place of origin is Judah, as is indicated by the unique traditions of L. These stories are: David's sojourning in Keilah (I Sam. 23:1-13), the Nabal episode in Maon (25:2-44), and David's presents given to the Judean elders from the Amalekite spoil (30:26).

The literary characteristics of J include a remarkably vivid, forceful style, elegance of expression, and a fondness for folk-tale or saga motifs. Folk-tale motifs appear in episodes such as that in which the young Saul starts out to look for the lost asses and finds a kingdom (I Sam. 9:1-10:16), and the fight of young David with Goliath (ch. 17). But the story of the ascendance of David and, especially, the court narrative assume the clarity of an eyewitness account. The apparent closeness to the court points to Jerusalem as the place of origin of the source.

It is characteristic of the E source that its literary material is mostly of the sacred, legendary nature. This source is not especially interested in the early kings, Saul and David. E's foremost hero is Samuel, the great intercessor, who, without battle, won a decisive victory over the Philistines (I Sam. 7). He was the judge of Israel, whom the people asked for a king (ch. 8); and after the rejection of Saul from kingship (ch. 15), he anointed David as the new king (ch. 16). Significantly enough, E alone includes Samuel's birth narrative (ch. 1), reports his childhood prophetic call (ch. 3), and relates that Samuel, even after his death, foretold Saul's defeat (ch. 28). The spirit of these legends has a degree of similarity with the medieval legends of the saints. The memories of the great man were probably preserved by the prophetic circles of the N empire, with which Samuel was associated, according to E (I Sam. 19:20). Therefore, the place of the origin of the E source was apparently the N, and there its native environment was located in the prophetic colleges.

b. Dating of the sources. In any attempt to find the date of the origin of any literary source, one encounters great difficulties. The dating of the sources of the books of Samuel can obviously not be divorced from the question of how far the sources extend beyond the conclusion of the court narrative of David (I Kings 1-2). Some scholars assume that the narrative extends to II Kings 17, relating the fall of Samaria. Accordingly, the earliest possible date of the writing of J would have been during the reign of Hezekiah (715-687 B.C.). Others think that J did not go beyond I Kings 12, which reports the separation of the two kingdoms. Consequently, the earliest date of J's writing would be after 922. E is traced by some scholars to II Kings 23 and is dated shortly after the Josianic reform (622). Others claim that E can be found throughout the books of Kings and find the date during the Exile, sometime after ·561. It appears, however, that there is little justification for tracing the sources of the books of Samuel beyond I Kings 1-2 — i.e., Solomon's ascension to the Davidic throne.

J, which extends to I Kings 1-2, seems to be closest to the happenings in the Davidic court; his account seems to be that of an eyewitness or, at least, based on an eyewitness' story. If this is true, J could be dated either during Solomon's reign or during Rehoboam's kingship — i.e., the late tenth century B.C. The L source's saga character must not be explained as being from a great remoteness from the events, but from L's connection to that cultural circle which is primarily responsible for the birth of sagas. The cultural environment of L is with the country folk, and there, among peasants and shepherds, the memories of events become sagas in a single generation. But L's closeness to the events of the Davidic reign can be assumed on the ground that David still did not become a stereotyped folk-tale figure, for his personality can be clearly observed. If all these factors are taken into account, the late tenth century B.C. seems to be the probable date for L.

The dating of E is dependent in large measure on its antimonarchic attitude. E's antimonarchic attitude is, in part, the authentic memory of the antimonarchic reaction at the time of the institution of kingship in Israel. This contemporary reaction was based upon this theological consideration: the Lord is the king of Israel; therefore the elevation of a human king is rebellious apostasy. This theocratic, antimonarchic view seems to be older than the monarchy itself (cf. Judg. 8:22-23; 9:7-15). But E's formulation of the "ways of the king" (I Sam. 8:11-18) points to some recent experience and concrete abuse of the royal power. The situation described in this "royal law" can hardly describe the reigns of Saul and David, for Solomon seems to be the first to have organized taxation (I Kings 4). The statement: "He will take the best of your fields and vineyards and olive orchards and give them to his servants" (I Sam. 8:14) could allude to the seizing of Naboth's vineyard (I Kings 21:1-16). If this is the case, the date of E would be after the reign of Ahab (869-850 B.C.), probably the end of the ninth or the beginning of the eighth century.

c. Historicity of the sources. The historical validity of these literary sources presents a very intricate problem. There are some scholars who, in a general, unqualified statement, endorse the historical reliability of the early source or sources but deprive the E source of historical validity. Against such generalizations, it must be maintained that, with the exception of the Davidic court narrative of J, all the sources are inclined to transcend the historical facts and prefer to convey the meaning of events in legends or sagas. On the other hand, the presence of an antimonarchic prophetic opposition in the time of the introduction of kingship is attested by the E source. Nevertheless, the fact that it is E's report will not detract from the historicity of the tradition. General statements on the historical reliability of any of the sources are unjustified, for a historical investigation must weigh, in each individual instance, the historicity of all the sources in question.

5. The history of composition. Any attempt to reconstruct the detailed history of the process of composition necessarily runs the risk of unwarranted speculation—at one or another point. However, it seems to be advisable to sketch, for the sake of clarity, a history of the composition. Approximately the following steps can be distinguished:

At first, some sagas were formed by utilizing folklore patterns and motifs; these sagas were transmitted in the channels of oral tradition. Such sagas were the origin of the kingdom (I Sam. 9:1–10:16), the wars of Saul (chs. 11–14), and the material concerning the ark (I Sam. 4–6; II Sam. 6). The dirges of David (II Sam. 1:17-27; 3:33-34) and the original pithy version of the dynastic oracle (II Sam. 7) belong to this period, and so do some original lists and annals such as those in II Sam. 8; 21; 23.

The second stage of the history of composition saw the emergence of the continuous historical works, L and J.

Later the E circle brought and joined together the original historical works of L and J and added to them its own prophetic point of view. This is especially clear in Samuel's birth and childhood narrative (I Sam. 1–3) and in the report on the rise of the monarchy (chs. 7–8; 12). E also contributed some independent tradition, such as the historically trustworthy episodes of the Amalekite war (I Sam. 15) and Saul's visit with the medium of Endor (I Sam. 28).

In the next stage, the Deuteronomic edition of the book took place. The Deuteronomist did not plow deeply into the already existent book, but added only some passages, such as I Sam. 2:27-36; 3:12-14; and some additions to the dynastic oracle (II Sam. 7).

The last step in the process of composition was the incorporation of such poetical material as I Sam. 2:1-10; II Sam. 22; 23:1-7 into the books of Samuel.

D. *TEXT.* The text of the books of Samuel is corrupt in many places, but occasionally a reconstruction of the text is possible by the utilization of the parallel accounts of the books of Chronicles and the ancient versions. Among the versions, the LXX is of foremost importance for the study of the text of Samuel. The LXX seems to point to a variant Hebrew text, nonextant at the present, which was unlike the MT. Some portions are missing from the LXX (e.g., I Sam. 17:12-31, 55-58; 18:1-5, 10-11, 17-19). The discoveries of MS fragments in the caves of Qumran also support the contention that the occasional divergence of the LXX text from the MT cannot be explained alone by the paraphrasing tendency of the LXX translators, or by their liberty with the text in general, but only by the former existence of non-Masoretic Hebrew texts. However, the Hebrew variants, revealing a higher degree of affinity with the LXX than with the MT, were apparently rejected and suppressed, probably during the second century A.D., as a result of Judaism's endeavor for a normative and authoritative text of the Scriptures.

Bibliography. Commentaries: A. R. S. Kennedy, ed., *New Century Bible* (n.d.); H. P. Smith, ICC (1899); O. Gressmann, *Schriften des AT* (2nd ed., 1921); G. B. Caird, *IB*, II (1953), 855-1176; H. W. Hertzberg, *Das AT Deutsch* (1956).

Special studies: This article follows, in its main lines, the analysis proposed by O. Eissfeldt, *Die Komposition der Samuelisbücher* (1931). The problems of composition are extensively discussed by R. H. Pfeiffer, *Introduction to the OT* (1941). See also: A. Lods, *Les sources des récits du premier livre de Samuel sur l'institution de la royauté israélite* (1901); L. Rost, "Die Überlieferung der Thronnachfolge Davids," *BWAT* (1926). The textual problems are discussed by J. Wellhausen, *Der Text der Bücher Samuelis untersucht* (1871); S. R. Driver, *Notes on the Hebrew Text and Topography of the Books of Samuel* (1913). For the Qumran texts, see: F. M. Cross, Jr., "A New Qumran Biblical Fragment Related to the Original Hebrew Underlying the LXX," *BASOR*, CXXXII (1953), 15-26.

S. SZIKSZAI

SANABASSAR, SANABASSARUS. KJV Apoc. forms of SHESHBAZZAR.

SANASIB. KJV form of ANASIB.

*SANBALLAT săn băl'ət [סנבלט; Akkad. *Sin-uballiṭ*, Sin (the moon deity) has given life]. The chief political opponent in Palestine of Nehemiah's efforts, as governor of Judah under the Persian Empire, to rebuild the walls of postexilic Jerusalem (*ca.* 445-437 B.C.; cf. Neh. 2:10, 19; 4:1, 7; 6:1-2, 5, 12, 14; *see* NEHEMIAH 3). Sanballat is referred to in a letter from Elephantine in Egypt (*see* ELEPHANTINE PAPYRI; *see also bibliography*) dated the seventeenth year of the Persian king Darius II (*ca.* 407 B.C.) as "Sanballat [סנאבלט] the governor [*peḥāh*] of Samaria," and as having two sons with the Hebrew names Delaiah and Shelemiah—suggesting that Sanballat observed Jewish faith and practice at least formally. *See* SAMARIA, TERRITORY OF.

While he does not call him "governor," Nehemiah also represents Sanballat as having substantial political power in the province of Samaria under Persian rule (e.g., Neh. 4:2). Nehemiah refers to him as "the Horonite," identifying him probably with Upper and Lower BETH-HORON, two towns in Ephraim overlooking the road from Jerusalem to Lydda and the Mediterranean coast—a position of considerable military strategic value which Sanballat must have controlled (cf. Josh. 10:10; I Macc. 3:16, 24; etc.). *See bibliography.*

The bitter opposition of Sanballat to Nehemiah's work was based presumably on the threat to the control of Judah enjoyed by Samaria to a greater or lesser degree ever since the fall of Jerusalem in 586 B.C. to Babylon. Nehemiah's uncompromising refusal to let his opponent's machinations deter him from his purpose to fortify Jerusalem (*see references above*) is the measure of Nehemiah's own political ability. The rivalry between the two leaders was primarily neither racial nor religious in nature, although such factors may have aggravated the mutual antagonism. As a matter of fact, Nehemiah's own account rather shows that Sanballat and his colleague Tobiah the Ammonite were on relatively good terms with influential segments of the Jewish community (cf. 6:10-14, 17-19), and the grandson of Eliashib, the Jewish high priest, took Sanballat's daughter in marriage during Nehemiah's absence from Jerusalem—for which, to be sure, Nehemiah on his return had him banished from the city (13:28). It is probable that the Jewish governor's adamant stand in this matter, as in others having to do with Sanballat, is responsible at this time in Jewish history for the very survival of the Jewish community itself.

The Jewish historian Josephus (*ca.* A.D. 100) implies that this last-mentioned affair—the expulsion of Sanballat's son-in-law from Jerusalem—brought about the Jewish-Samaritan schism (Antiq. XI.viii.2) and led to the building of the Samaritan temple on Mount Gerizim, but the biblical account gives no such indication. Moreover, Josephus places Sanballat himself, as well as these events connected with him, a century later than the time of Nehemiah, in the period of the change-over from Persian to Hellenistic rule over Palestine (333 B.C.; cf. Antiq. XI.vii.2; viii.2, 4). But Josephus' account at this point must be considered historically less trustworthy than that of Nehemiah. That there may have been two Sanballats has been suggested, and this is not impossible, but it is scarcely probable that their separate careers

should resemble each other in such detail as the accounts in Neh. 13:28 and Josephus do with regard to the marriage of Sanballat's daughter and the expulsion of his son-in-law from Jerusalem. The Josephus narrative is further suspect in this section for its being set in a context of much else that is historically questionable, if not plainly erroneous, in his narrative—e.g., the coming of Alexander to sacrifice in the Jerusalem temple and his being shown the book of Daniel, with its prophecies concerning him (Antiq. XI.viii.5).

See also GESHEM; TOBIAH 2.

Bibliography. A thorough review of the problem of Sanballat's role in Jewish history is given in H. H. Rowley, "Sanballat and the Samaritan Temple," *Bulletin of the John Rylands Library*, vol. 38, No. 1 (Sept., 1955), pp. 166-98. For text and translation of the Elephantine letter, with notes, see A. Cowley, *Aramaic Papyri of the Fifth Century B.C.* (1923), pp. 108-19; the translation alone is given also in J. B. Pritchard, *ANET* (2nd ed., 1955), p. 492. See also W. F. Albright, "The Date and Personality of the Chronicler," *JBL*, XL (1921), 111; *The Biblical Period* (1950), p. 52. See especially R. A. Bowman, Exegesis of Ezra-Nehemiah, *IB*, III (1954), 676, 817-18.   B. T. DAHLBERG

*SANCTIFICATION. The realization or progressive attainment of likeness to God or to God's intention for men. It may be regarded both as a status conferred by divine grace and as a goal to be aimed at. As a biblical doctrine it belongs more to the NT than to the OT, but it presupposes the fundamental OT conception of holiness.

1. OT background. Holiness in the OT, as in other sacred writings, relates to man's elemental reactions to that which is beyond his normal experience and control. It is to be classified as a category distinct from the intellectual and moral and aesthetic categories. But it must also be recognized that if this factor of human experience is not to be outgrown as man progresses from the primitive, it needs to be moralized and intellectualized. A main contribution of Hebrew religion was precisely this.

The basic sense of the Hebrew root קדש, *qadosh* (as of its Greek equivalent in the Bible, ἅγιος), seems to be "separateness"—i.e., from ordinary usage (*see* HOLINESS). In reference to God, the term "otherness" has been much used. What needs to be kept in mind, however, is not so much that God is essentially different from man as that he is God; the quality of the divine is positive. Modern thought, in contrast to biblical, is anthropocentric; and when we speak of God, we tend to describe him in negative, nonhuman terms. But the Bible retains the insight of primitive man, for whom the divine was not a hypothesis, but the primary reality, however indefinable. The word *qadosh* has this sense of reality in it; it is not a negative term. It is not taboo, the untouchable, but rather mana, superhuman potency; more correctly, it is both.

This is, of course, a primitive idea, and is applied to beings other than God, and to material things. Good examples of this sense in the OT are the narratives about the ark of the covenant in I Sam. 6:19-7:1; II Sam. 6:6-11 (cf. also Lev. 17-26; Ezek. 42:1-14; 44).

Real progress in religious thought arises when the

idea of holiness is lifted out of the impersonal. Two developments in particular are distinctive of the OT: (a) Holiness is conceived as referring pre-eminently to Yahweh (Job 6:10; Isa. 6:1-5; Hos. 11:9b), and all other persons and things are defined as holy only in connection with him, especially the priests and the temple (cf. Exod. 19:6; 29:42-44; Lev. 19:2; I Kings 9:3; Jer. 1:5). The books of Isaiah and Ezekiel are particularly significant here (cf. Isa. 5:16; 40:25, and the frequent reference to Yahweh as the "Holy One of Israel"). Ezekiel the priest-prophet thinks of God's action as specially motivated by concern for his holiness; and this finds expression in a curious use of the *niph'al* (passive) form of the verb *q-d-sh*, which the RSV renders "manifest" or "vindicate" (my) holiness (cf. Ezek. 20:41; 28:22, 25; 36:23; 38:16; 39:27). (b) The pre-exilic prophets moralized the notion of divine holiness—i.e., understood God's will as having moral implications. (This was somewhat obscured in the postexilic reorganization, but cf. Lev. 19:9-18.) Important chapters in this connection are Isa. 5; Jer. 5-7; Amos 4-5; Hos. 11; and even Ezekiel (cf. ch. 18).

2. **NT development.** *a. In the primitive church.* From Acts we learn that sanctification depends on reception of the Holy Spirit. This implies turning away from the world (Acts 2:40b), and presupposes forgiveness of sin (2:38; 26:18). More positively, reception of the Spirit confers power to perform miracles (2:43; 3:6; 4:12-16; etc.), moral power (4: 31-37), and generally the courage to witness to Christ (2:32-36; 4:31; 5:32).

Christians are called simply "saints," holy ones (ἅγιοι; 9:13, 32; 26:10). This is also regular Pauline usage (Rom. 1:7; 12:13; I Cor. 6:1; 16:1; etc.). Similarly, in Revelation the word is used fourteen times. For fuller emphasis, cf. I Cor. 7:34; Eph. 1:4; 5:27; Col. 3:12-17. Sometimes we have the present participle of the cognate verb in the same sense—e.g., I Cor. 1:2; Heb. 2:11; 10:14: "those who are being sanctified" (οἱ ἁγιαζόμενοι). The meaning in all these cases is not moral perfection, but consecration to Christ—i.e., a Christian appropriation of the original OT sense of separation. There is some overlapping of meaning with words implying cleanness or purification, whose basic notion is that of ritual purity, but which like sanctification easily pass over into a moral signification. See Acts 10:14-15, 28, which shows that Jews are no more "clean" than Gentiles, but all alike capable of being regarded by God as acceptable (cf. 10:34-35, 45; 11:17-18; 15:9; 28:28). For the collocation of purity and holiness, cf. Eph. 1:4; 5:26; Col. 1:22; I Thess. 4:7; II Tim. 2:21; Heb. 9:13-14. *See* SAINT.

This usage has two main implications: (a) it is the basis of the concept (more fully thought out in Paul) of the church as a holy society. This is a corporate ideal and needs to be kept in view if a too narrow and individualistic striving after sainthood is to be avoided. The original, semimagical concept of separateness is here fully personalized. Individual Christians enter the sphere of sanctification where with their fellow Christians they are united in worship of a Lord who is Head of the body and source of holiness and moral power. (b) The NT terminol-

ogy of sanctification implies that the church is a divinely controlled society. For the word "holy" (ἅγιος; קדש) is an attribute of God, and is applied in the NT to Christ also (Mark 1:24; John 6:69; Acts 3:14; 4:27; Rev. 3:7). See especially I Pet. 1:16; 2:9.

Church experience is described in Acts 20:32; 26:18 in terms of inheritance "among those who have been sanctified." The reference is not to the final inheritance of Christians, either here or in the similar passages Eph. 1:18; Col. 1:12. The perfect tense of the verb should be noted: the sanctification is already effected, even though not completed, when a man is gathered into the church; it is simultaneous with God's gift of forgiveness. This is clearest in Acts 26:18. Christians have entered upon an inheritance which may have appeared to many still future, beyond death. For the Christian who has begun to experience sanctification, the conventional distinction between here and hereafter, earth and heaven, becomes less absolute, and death itself loses significance.

b. In the Synoptic gospels. According to Mark, Jesus is God's Holy One (1:24), who drives out all that is unholy—e.g., the unclean spirits (1:23-26, 34, etc.). Even the holy temple has to be cleansed (Matt. 12:6; Mark 11:15-17; 14:58). He is not afraid of contamination by contact with uncleanness, for his holiness is positive and sovereign, not negative like that of the Pharisees (Mark 2:15-17; Luke 19: 5-10). He rejects their definition of what constitutes holiness and defilement, in order to diagnose the need of man more truly (Mark 7:1-23). Man's chief requisite is not warning against sinful actions so much as purification of heart where the overt sins are motivated (Matt. 5:21-32; 6:22-23; 7:17-18; 12: 34-35). Jesus understood his mission to be to cleanse men from that inward uncleanness which vitiates their life, issues in wrong deeds to their fellow men, and makes them unfit for fellowship with God. To this purpose he devoted his life, even to the ultimate sacrifice of death, believing that God would make this sacrifice potent for the emancipation and sanctification man needs (Matt. 26:28; Mark 10:45; 14:21-24).

c. In Hebrews. The main theme of the Letter to the Hebrews is the work of Christ as priest and sacrifice. It can be stated as the provision of "purification for sins" (1:3), implying the imagery of sacrifice, as in 2:17b; 5:1 and in the whole central argument of chs. 5-10. But the metaphor changes to that of sanctification when Christ is referred to as the sanctifier (2:11; 7:26-27; 13:12). These metaphors are used interchangeably, as we see from 9:11-14— a peak point in the argument—and 9:22-23. The point of contrast here between Christian and Jewish mediatory rites is that whereas the latter effected outward sanctification, Christ offers an inward one ("conscience"; vs. 14b) which fits men for God's service, or, more precisely, for the sharing of God's own holiness (ἁγιότης; 12:10), which is the greatest need of man. The vision of God is not possible for the unholy (12:14). "Sanctification" is a synonym for "perfection," a key word in this letter (2:10; 10:14; 11:39-12:2). This sanctification or perfection is due to Christ, who identified himself with man, made man fit for God's presence, and pioneered a way thither as "forerunner" (6:20; 10:19 ff; cf. 3:1*a*).

d. In John. The idea of sanctification does not occupy much space in the Johannine Gospel, but it can be related to the Johannine thought. Christ is the remover of the world's sin (John 1:29). Sin also is not much mentioned in this gospel (but cf. I John 1:7–2:2; 3:4-10). The narrative of the marriage at Cana seems to imply that Christ represents something more potent than Jewish "purification" (John 2:6); this, however, is described, not as purification (καθαρισμός) nor as sanctification (ἁγιασμός), but as a manifestation of glory (vs. 11). Almost in the same context Jesus protests against temple profanation, and exemplifies zeal for God's house (2:17). This means that in him is operating a power superior to the temple, and destined to replace it (cf. 4:20-26). The holiness of earthly temples such as those in Jerusalem and on Mount Gerizim—the best that men have developed in institutional religion—must give way when true spiritual worship is inaugurated.

Similarly, Jesus transcends the sacredness of the sabbath (5:9-18). In virtue of his contact with his Father, he can by-pass sabbath regulations in the performance of his divinely prescribed work. He does not cease work on the sabbath, but his work is part of God's (vss. 16-17; cf. 9:33). Nor can holy scripture be quoted to limit his freedom, for he is in communion with the Source of scripture, and his word is holier than the words of Moses (5:37-47). As Son of man, he is "from above"—i.e., from the source of holiness (3:12-13; 6:33-51; 8:23). He is God's "Holy One" (6:69).

Jesus' ministry is a continuation of God's own activity, and a revelation of God's glory; he represents God among men (13:31; 14:7-11). The terminology of sanctification is not used, but the essential thought can be expressed in it. Christ imparts holiness more effectively than all other media, personal or material. Those who believe in him are sanctified in the sense of being in communion with God himself (17:20-26; cf. "seeing" the Father in 14:9-10; 16:15, 25-28). They no longer simply exist; they live on a higher plane, eternally, not belonging any longer to the "world" of ordinary existence untouched by God's saving power. They possess the truth, and are sanctified by it (17:17); Christ's own sanctity is imparted to them (17:19). In the simpler thought of I John, they are children of God, and destined to be made like Christ; this very prospect is a means of purification (I John 3:3).

e. In I Peter. In I Pet. 1:2 sanctification is due to the Spirit, but is also connected with God's eternal purpose and the atonement effected by Christ (cf. 1:19; 3:18). It is a reproduction of the holiness of God himself (1:15-16), which distinguishes Christians from other men (2:9), and constitutes them a priesthood (2:5)—i.e., able to approach God and to facilitate the approach of others to him. The author comes near to defining this holiness as imitation of Christ. See 3:15*a*, where to "sanctify Christ as Lord in your hearts" must mean to acknowledge Christ's holiness (cf. Isa. 29:23; Matt. 6:9) and to appro-

priate it in the sense of letting it determine your own behavior (I Pet. 3:16, leading to vs. 18; cf. also 2:21 ff).

f. In Paul. In Christian experience sinful men are accepted by God. The limits imposed on human life by sin and death are broken. Sin is a powerful enemy but not sovereign, for God's grace is even more powerful (Rom. 5:20). This is the meaning of redemption and justification in Paul's writings. Is there need of sanctification as well? The Christian, freed from his past, walks in "newness of life" (Rom. 6:4). Negatively this involves avoiding former sinful behavior (Rom. 6:12-19). When Paul begins to speak of the positive implications of this, he uses the term "sanctification" (ἁγιασμός; Rom. 6:19, 22), which in this context means "righteousness," as contrasted with "sin," service of God rather than slavery to passion. In I Thess. 4:3, 7, it is contrasted with immorality and uncleanness. (The RSV alternates between "sanctification" and "holiness" in I Thess. 4:3, 4, 7, though the Greek ἁγιασμός is used in all three places, as also in I Tim. 2:15; Heb. 12:14. It would be preferable to translate "sanctification" in all these passages, and keep "holiness" as a rendering of the two cognate words which are more abstract—viz., ἁγιότης [II Cor. 1:12; Heb. 12:10] and ἁγιωσύνη [Rom. 1:4; II Cor. 7:1; I Thess. 3:13].)

The new moral emphasis is described in terms of the Spirit, which emphasizes its divinely given quality (Rom. 7:6*b;* 8:2-4, 11-13; Gal. 5:16-25; *see* HOLY SPIRIT). This Spirit terminology is, in fact, more frequent in Paul's references to the Christian development than the language of sanctification. For the two together, cf. I Cor. 3:16-17. Sometimes a reference to sanctification is conspicuously missing—e.g., Rom. 8:30 ("glorified" instead of "sanctified"); Gal. 3:26–4:7.

It is not sufficient, however, to take "sanctification" as a synonym for "moral growth," though this connotation is included. Sometimes "sanctification" refers to the original establishment of the believer in his new environment as a Christian who has broken from his sinful past—to his position at the start of the race, as it were, rather than to his progress as a runner in the race. Thus "sanctification" can be a synonym for "justification"—i.e., I Cor. 1:2: "sanctified in Christ Jesus, called to be saints"; 6:11; 7:14 (here note the original sense of holiness as separation from ordinary usage: the Christian, like the Jew, is a man apart; he belongs to Christ, and this determines all his conduct; cf. I Cor. 10:14-21; II Cor. 6:14–7:1; Eph. 1:4-5). The reference to Christ as our sanctification (I Cor. 1:30) is not to be taken exclusively in this sense, because a full exegesis would make Christ source of all the church's progressive attainment.

Against this reference of sanctification to the beginning of the Christian experience may be quoted passages which imply that sanctification is an aspect of the whole life of the Christian, or something the church contributes during the course of its service (cf. Rom. 12:1; 15:16*b;* II Cor. 7:1; Eph. 2:19-22). Even I Cor. 6:11 is in an ethical context. In I Thess. 3:13–4:7 "sanctification" means avoidance of gross sin, and in I Thess. 5:23-24 it is a process finally completed at the Parousia. Its connection with the

Spirit appears again in II Thess. 2:13-14, with the notion that it is part of God's original purpose for the church. The progressive moral and spiritual fitness of the church is due to Christ's cherishing rather than to her own self-culture (Eph. 5:25-30); but it is a gradual process not complete at the original calling of converts (cf. Eph. 4:12-13, 22–5:2; Phil. 1:9-11; 2:12-16).

In short, the experience Paul has in mind when he speaks of sanctification is too rich in significance to be confined to any single moment of the Christian career. If justification is taken to mean that act of God which starts a believer on his experience of salvation, sanctification has a much broader range. It is the process thereby inaugurated, presided over by the Spirit, and mounting up to a maturity definable in terms of Christ's own perfection (Eph. 4:16). Sanctification will be complete at the time of Christ's final intervention (I Thess. 5:23). See also JUSTIFICATION.

Bibliography. R. Otto, *The Idea of the Holy* (1923), pp. 1-11, 74-96; R. Asting, *Die Heiligkeit im Urchristentum* (1930); V. Taylor, *Forgiveness and Reconciliation* (1941), pp. 172-225; N. Snaith, *Distinctive Ideas of the OT* (1944), pp. 21-50; W. Eichrodt, *Theologie des alten Testaments* (4th ed., 1950), I, 131-38; E. Jacob, *Theology of the OT* (English trans., 1958), pp. 86-92.   E. C. BLACKMAN

*SANCTUARY [קֹדֶשׁ, sacredness, apartness, place apart; מִקְדָּשׁ, sacred place; ἱερόν; ναός; σκηνή]. Basically, a center of holiness. In the OT the word refers to heavenly or earthly sacred places, specifically the tabernacle, the temple, Jerusalem, Zion, etc. In the NT, ναός is used of the Jewish temple, the heavenly temple, and temples in general, including heathen sanctuaries. The word is also personalized for reference to the body of Jesus, to the spirit-filled life of the Christian, and for other applications. Ἱερόν is used of Artemis' temple and of the Jerusalem temple in whole or part.

See also TEMPLE, JERUSALEM; BAMAH; HIGH PLACE; TABERNACLE.   G. HENTON DAVIES

SAND LIZARD [חֹמֶט, *possibly* dark one; *cf.* Jewish Aram. חמם, to be dark; *cf.* Akkad. *hulmittu, species of lizard*]; KJV SNAIL. The ancient versions and the context in Lev. 11:30 favor some variety of LIZARD, but further identification is hazardous. Jewish Aramaic חוּמְטוֹן (*hûmṭôn;* "sandy soil") has been thought to place חֹמֶט (*hōmeṭ*) in the Skink family (Scincidae), whose haunts are sandy regions and who are often known as "sand lizards" (cf. Tristram, *NHB* 268-69).

See also FAUNA § C.   W. S. McCULLOUGH

SANDALS AND SHOES. Sandals apparently were worn in Palestine from the earliest times. The monuments of Syria and Mesopotamia depict numerous characters with footgear of various types, though ordinary persons are generally represented as barefoot.

1. Terms
2. Use
3. Types
4. Materials

5. Symbolic use
Bibliography

1. Terms. The general term for "sandal" or "shoe" in the OT is נַעַל, which occurs some twenty times. In Arabic it signifies that by which the foot is shielded, frequently the sole. In Hebrew it means footgear in a general sense and may be either "shoe" or "sandal," as distinguished from סְאוֹן, the Assyrian soldier's BOOT. The most common word in the NT is ὑπόδημα, a sole attached to the foot with straps (Matt. 3:11; 10:10; etc.). Σανδάλιον, specifically a protective sole bound to the foot, occurs only in Mark 6:9; Acts 12:8.

2. Use. Women's shoes appear to have been somewhat different from those worn by men. Shoes were designed for protection against cold and damp in winter and against the hot sand and sharp stones during the summer. They were especially useful for the shepherd, who had to be prepared to go through briers and over rough ground to care for the sheep. Foot protection was not required at home, and so shoes, being dirty, were removed upon entering the house (Luke 7:38, 44). Taking off one's shoes at the holy place was a mark of respect (Exod.3:5; Josh. 5:15; Acts 7:33) and is still practiced by Muslims when they enter their mosques. Footwear is not mentioned in connection with other priestly apparel, and the assumption is that the priests performed their ministrations barefoot. At other times they doubtless conformed to the general custom of wearing shoes. To go without shoes was a mark of poverty and destitution (Luke 15:22), or an outward sign of mourning (II Sam. 15:30; Isa. 20:2-4; Ezek. 24:17, 23). To put on one's sandals indicated readiness for a journey (Exod. 12:11; Acts 12:8) or for the discharge of a mission (Mark 6:9).

3. Types. As already noted, there is no way of distinguishing types of footwear from the biblical terminology. Our only sources are the monuments, descriptions in postbiblical literature, and present-day survivals. The earliest representation at Teleilat Ghassul (fourth millennium B.C.) is far from clear, and all that can be distinguished on a painted panel is some kind of low-cut boot. The Beni-hasan panel (early nineteenth century B.C.) depicts a group of Asiatics in Egypt (Fig. JOS 29). The men wear sandals composed of soles fastened by various methods—some with ankle and crisscrossed straps; others with, in addition to these straps, one running around the leg just above the ankle. The women have on a kind of low boot trimmed with a white band around the top which reaches above the ankle. The black obelisk of Shalmaneser III (854-824) depicts, on one of its panels, Jehu of Israel bearing tribute to the Assyrian king. The tribute bearers seem to be wearing shoes with upturned, pointed toes, though their height and method of fastening cannot be determined (Fig. INS 11). N Syrian monuments from Samal and Carchemish (ninth and eighth centuries) and a painting of Sargon II (721-705) show sandals with a high counter running from the arch on each side, held in place with a double strap over the arch and a single strap over the toes (Fig. SAR 27). But it must be remembered that these were probably not the shoes or sandals worn by ordinary

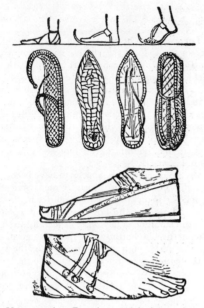

22. Upper: ancient Egyptian sandals; lower: Assyrian sandals

From Kurt Galling, *Biblisches Reallexikon* (Tübingen: J. C. B. Mohr)

23. Assyrian sandals fastened to the foot by means of thongs (latchets)

people. They probably had no more than a simple piece of leather or wood or fibrous material tied on with leather thongs (Gen. 14:23; Isa. 5:27 [שְׂרוֹךְ]; Mark 1:7; Luke 3:16; John 1:27 [ἱμάς; KJV "latchet"]) strung through ears or holes in the sides. Figs. SAN 22-23.

4. Materials. Leather was doubtless the regular material employed in the making of footwear. Shoemakers were probably included in the general class of leatherworkers. In later times wood was used, but leather bands or strings were generally supplied for them. Sometimes other material was used for such purposes (see S. Krauss, *Talmudische Archäologie*, I, 175-85). Worn shoes were mended with leather straps (Josh. 9:5, 13).

5. Symbolic use. Shoes were also of symbolic significance, as may be seen from the legal practice of presenting the shoe to confirm publicly the renunciation of levirate marriage rights or obligations (Deut. 25:9; Ruth 4:7-8). According to Amos 2:6;

8:6; the LXX of I Sam. 12:3; and some legal texts from Nuzi, shoes were obviously regarded as legal symbols—i.e., token payments necessary for strict legal transactions but often far from the spirit of the law (*see bibliography*). To be unsandaled was to be dispossessed (Deut. 25:10), and to cast one's sandals upon property signified possession (Pss. 60:8; 108:9).

Bibliography. E. A. Speiser, "Of Shoes and Shekels," *BASOR*, no. 77 (1940), pp. 15 ff, and references cited therein; R. de Vaux, *Les institutions de l'AT*, I (1958), 258-59.

J. M. MYERS

*SANHEDRIN săn hē′drən, săn′ə drĭn [סנהדרין, Heb.-Aram. *transliteration of* συνέδριον, *from* σύν, together, *plus* ἕδρα, seat; *the spelling* Sanhedrim *arose from a mistaken notion that the word derived from a* Heb. *masculine plural form*]. The supreme Jewish council of seventy-one members in Jerusalem during post-exilic times; or one of the lower tribunals of twenty-three members, of which Jerusalem had two, according to the Tosefta (Ḥag. 2.9; Sanh. 7.1; cf. M. Sanh. 1.6; 11.2). The supreme council had legislative and executive, as well as judiciary, functions, but the extent of its effective authority varied considerably under different political regimes.

Fig. ART 81.

A. Designations
   1. Greek
   2. Hebrew
B. History
   1. Origin and early history
   2. The Hasmonean regime
   3. The Roman period
     a. Early intervention
     b. Herodian rule
     c. Procuratorial government
     d. After A.D. 70
C. The Greek and the Hebrew sources
D. Competence
Bibliography

A. DESIGNATIONS. Both in the Greek and in the Hebrew sources various expressions are employed to designate the supreme council.

1. Greek. Five species of designation are to be distinguished under this head:

a) Συνέδριον occurs in the LXX version of the book of Proverbs in the sense of "deliberative assembly" (e.g., 15:17) and as an equivalent of "tribunal" or "court of justice" (e.g., 22:10). In point of historical reference, Josephus first uses the term in a passage concerning the Roman legate of Syria, Gabinius, who divided Palestine into five districts with a συνέδριον (Antiq. XIV.v.4) or σύνοδος (War I.viii.5) over each; but he first employs it to denote the supreme Jewish council in connection with certain Galilean activities of the youthful Herod (Antiq. XIV.ix.3-5). In the NT the term (especially in the plural) is sometimes used of any judicature (e.g., Matt. 5:22; Mark 13:9); but usually it refers to the supreme council before which Jesus, Peter, John, Stephen, and Paul had to appear (Matt. 26:59; Mark 14:55; 15:1; Luke 22:66; John 11:47; Acts 4:15; 5: 21; 6:12; 22:30; 24:20).

b) Γερουσία, "senate," is not infrequent in the

Apoc. (e.g., II Macc. 11:27). In the writings of Josephus the earliest historical appearance of the word to denote the supreme Jewish council is in Antiq. XII.iii.3, where Antiochus the Great (*ca.* 200 B.C.) uses it in this sense. In the NT the only occurrence of the term is in Acts 5:21, where we read "the sanhedrin [RSV 'council'] and all the senate [γερουσία] of Israel." This curious phrase may mean that the author of Acts had the erroneous notion that the sanhedrin was more comprehensive than the senate; alternatively perhaps the καί is explanatory, in which case the rendering should be "the sanhedrin, even the whole senate of Israel," the point being that the whole council, not merely the necessary quorum, was called together.

c) Βουλή is used fairly often by Josephus (especially in War; e.g., II.xvi.2) to designate the supreme council, but it is never so employed in the NT, although βουλευτής occurs in Mark 15:43 (where it means "councilor"); Luke 23:50 (where it definitely means "member of the high court," as the following verse shows). In Jos. War V.iv.2, βουλή apparently signifies the building in which the sanhedrin held its sessions.

d) Πρεσβυτέριον, "council of ELDERS," appears in Luke 22:66; Acts 22:5.

e) In his autobiography Josephus generally employs τὸ κοινὸν τῶν Ἱεροσολυμιτῶν or more briefly τὸ κοινόν to denote the supreme council (cf. Life 12; 38; 52; etc.).

2. Hebrew. Four types of designation are to be distinguished under this head.

a) סנהדרין is the usual word for the supreme council in talmudic literature; sometimes the ה is assimilated to the preceding נ, and sometimes the final ן is dropped; plural forms (feminine) are סנהדריות and סנהדראות. Such expressions as סנהדרין גדולה, "great sanhedrin," and סנהדרין של שבעים ואחד, "sanhedrin of seventy-one," serve to distinguish the high council from the lower assemblies of twenty-three members.

b) The expression בית דין גדול is also frequent (e.g., M. Sanh. 11.2); its meaning, "great house of justice," brings out the judicial function of the supreme council; the addition שבירושלים, "which is in Jerusalem," is not infrequently made.

c) The term חבר, "company" (*collegium*), is associated with the reigning high priest on certain Hasmonean coins, where it doubtless designates the supreme council; thus some of the coins minted in the reign of Alexander Janneus (103-76 B.C.) bear the legend: "Jehonathan the high priest and the senate [חבר] of the Jews."

d) כנישתא, "assembly," "meeting place," is used of the supreme council in the Megillath Ta'anith 10; cf. the employment of כנסת הגדולה, "the great synagogue," of the assembly under Ezra and Nehemiah (Neh. 8-10), which in the rabbinical tradition constitutes the connecting link between the last of the prophets and the first teachers of the law who are mentioned by name in the Greek period (cf. M. Ab. 1).

B. HISTORY. The sanhedrin remained basically an aristocratic body until the time of the great insurrection in A.D. 66-70, when, with the collapse of the Jewish state and the convocation of scholars at Jamnia, its whole character underwent a fundamental change. *See* ISRAEL, HISTORY OF.

1. Origin and early history. In rabbinical interpretation the sanhedrin had its origin in the council of seventy elders appointed to assist Moses in the business of government (M. Sanh. 1.6; cf. Num. 11: 10-24), and was reorganized by Ezra soon after the return from the Exile (cf. the Targ. to Song of S. 6:1). But the way in which the sanhedrin is thus connected with Moses and Ezra, and subsequently with the names of leading rabbis (cf. M. Ab. 1), betrays a concern to demonstrate that the council established at Jamnia had its roots deeply embedded in the soil of Israel's past. Actually, however, there is no trustworthy evidence for the early existence of the sanhedrin. The "elders" mentioned in such passages as I Kings 8:1; II Kings 23:1; Ezek. 14:1 scarcely constituted a regularly organized body; and the court of appeal presupposed in Deut. 17:8-13; 19:16-19, like the institution ascribed to Jehoshaphat in II Chr. 19:8, was merely a judiciary, not a legislative council largely responsible for the government of the country, as the sanhedrin evidently was in Greco-Roman times. Doubtless the returned exiles would require some form of political organization, and perhaps the "elders" of Ezra 5:5, etc., and the "nobles" and "officials" of Neh. 2:16, etc., represented the future sanhedrin in germ. In Greek sources the earliest mention of a Jewish γερουσία, "senate" (Jos. Antiq. XII.iii.3), has reference to the time of Antiochus the Great (223-187 B.C.). A Hellenistic γερουσία, however, was usually a democratic body, whereas the sanhedrin at Jerusalem was an aristocratic institution presided over by a hereditary high priest (*see* PRIESTS AND LEVITES), and this may indicate that the Jewish council goes back to the Persian period.

2. The Hasmonean regime. It would seem that this new dynasty had to enlist the support of experts in the interpretation of the law as well as that of certain influential priestly families, and that representatives of both sections were soon appointed to positions on the sanhedrin. This introduced an element of contrariety into government circles, and so the history of the sanhedrin during this period is largely bound up with the history of the conflicts between the SADDUCEES and the PHARISEES. According to Jos. Antiq. XIII.x.5-6, a Pharisee named Eleazar, having cast doubts on the legitimacy of the birth of John Hyrcanus I (135-104 B.C.), demanded that he should resign from the high priesthood and content himself with the civil leadership of the people, whereupon Hyrcanus joined himself to the Sadducees and declared the enactments of the Pharisees to be without validity—an action which must have entailed their expulsion from the sanhedrin (cf. the parallel in B. Ḳid. 66*a*). The conflict continued, and, according to Jos. Antiq. XIII.xv.5, Alexander Janneus (103-76) on his deathbed advised his wife Salome Alexandra to ally herself with the Pharisees. This she did (Simon ben Shetah, a leading Pharisee, was her brother), and during her reign (76-67) the Pharisees for the first time became the dominant party (Jos. War I.v.2).

3. The Roman period. The quarrel between Alexandra's sons, Hyrcanus and Aristobulus, led directly to the intervention of Rome in Jewish affairs of state.

a. Early intervention. Pompey in 63 B.C. abolished the monarchy and made Hyrcanus II high priest and ethnarch of the Jews (Jos. Antiq. XIV.iv.4; War I.vii.6). Gabinius, the proconsul of Syria (57-55), went further: he deprived Hyrcanus of civil power and degraded the sanhedrin of Jerusalem by dividing Jewish territory into five administrative districts with a council over each (Jos. Antiq. XIV.v.4; War I.viii. 5). A new order was introduced by Caesar in 47 B.C.: Hyrcanus again became high priest and ethnarch of the Jews, while Antipater was made governor of Judea (Jos. Antiq. XIV.viii.3; War I.x.3); and apparently the sanhedrin was restored to its former status as the supreme council over the whole extent of Jewish territory in Palestine, for Herod in his youth had to appear before it because he had trespassed on its authority by putting to death a rebel chief and many of his followers in Galilee (Jos. Antiq. XIV.ix.3-5).

b. Herodian rule. At the beginning of his reign Herod the Great (37-4 B.C.) sought to destroy the influence of the priestly aristocracy by taking bloody action against them (Jos. Antiq. XIV.ix.4; XV.i.2). Later he successfully prosecuted his capital charge against the aged Hyrcanus before the sanhedrin (Jos. Antiq. XV.vi.2). Not being qualified by his descent to assume the high priesthood himself, he reduced the importance of that office by making it no longer hereditary and tenable for life; no fewer than seven high priests were arbitrarily appointed and deposed during his reign (cf. Jos. Antiq. XV.iii.1, 3; ix.3; XVII.vi.4; etc.). The authority of the sanhedrin was curtailed, and Herod soon came to be hated as a cruel tyrant. After his death an embassy from Jerusalem went up to Rome and asked that Palestine be incorporated into the Roman province of Syria, contending that, with the greater autonomy this would bring, the Jews would quickly show that they were not really an unruly people (Jos. Antiq. XVII.xi.2). Despite this plea Augustus confirmed Herod's testament, save that Archelaus was appointed ethnarch until he proved himself worthy of the royal title. This he never did, and, after a delegation from Jerusalem and Samaria had complained of his misgovernment before Augustus, he was banished to Gaul (Jos. Antiq. XVII.xiii.2; War II.vii.3), and his ethnarchy (Judea, Samaria, and Idumea) was put under Roman procurators (A.D. 6).

c. Procuratorial government. With the introduction of the new system the territory over which Archelaus had ruled became an imperial province under a procurator of equestrian rank, and the taxes for which the sanhedrin was responsible (like the tolls collected by the *publicani*) would go directly into the *fiscus*, or imperial treasury. The Roman officials did not share the Herodian jealousy of the local aristocracy, representatives of which, together with leading scribes or learned lawyers, appear to have mainly made up the composition of the sanhedrin (cf., e.g., Mark 14:1, 53). The nobility being predominantly Sadducean and the lawyers predominantly Pharisaic, the sessions could be enlivened by stormy debates (cf. Acts 23:1-10). The internal government of the province seems to have been largely in the hands of the sanhedrin, and its authority in judicial matters finds recognition in many passages in the NT (cf. Matt. 5:22; Mark 14:55; John 11:47; Acts 4:15; 22:30; etc.). To what extent (if any) it had constitutional responsibility for the administration of justice in the tetrarchies of Antipas and Philip is disputed; but its religious authority would be recognized by Jewish communities even beyond the boundaries of Palestine (cf. Acts 9:2, etc.).

The high priest acted as president and convener of the sanhedrin (cf. Mark 14:53; Acts 24:1; Jos. Antiq. XX.ix.1; etc.), although, of course, it was in the power of the Roman authorities to proceed independently of the sanhedrin and to call the sanhedrin together to deal with any case they considered required their attention (cf. Acts 22:30; 23:26-30). The procurator (or the legate of Syria) exercised the right of appointing and deposing the high priest (cf., e.g., Jos. Antiq. XVIII.ii.2), but he would be careful to restrict his choice to members of the priestly oligarchy. Of the eighteen high priests who held office in A.D. 6-67, sixteen represented only five families, and those who belonged to such families played an important role in the public life of the time, though their effective power was curbed by the opposition of the Pharisees (Jos. Antiq. XVIII.i.4). Strictly there was only one high priest at a time, but the word "high priest" could be used in the plural (RSV "chief priests") in a general sense to denote the sacerdotal aristocracy (e.g., Luke 23:13; Jos. War VI.ii.2); and it is noteworthy that Josephus could complain that the Zealotic revolutionaries, by appointing Phanias to the high priesthood in 67, "had robbed of their dignity those families from which in their order the high priests had been selected" (War IV.iii.6).

A new regime was established by Claudius in 41, when Herod Agrippa I was made king of all the territory (save Iturea) which had been ruled over by his grandfather Herod the Great. After Agrippa's death in 44 the whole of his kingdom became an imperial province under a procurator of equestrian rank (as the Judean district had been previously). There were seven procurators before 41, and seven again after 44. In response to a Jewish petition Herod of Chalchis and, after his death in 49, Agrippa II were granted the authority to appoint high priests (Jos. Antiq. XX.i.1-3; viii.8; ix.7). There were seven high priests in 6-41, and eleven were appointed from 41 up to the time when the Zealots took charge of affairs during the great rebellion of 66-70.

d. After A.D. 70. Thanks to the insurrection, the large measure of autonomy which had hitherto been conceded to the Jewish people was taken away, and the sanhedrin as a political institution with authority other than purely religious ceased to exist. The sanhedrin founded at Jamnia (which after several migrations settled in Tiberias toward A.D. 200), though held in rabbinical literature to be a direct continuation of the old institution, established under Moses and reorganized by Ezra and the men of the Great Synagogue at Jerusalem (cf. M. R.H. 2.9; M. Ab. 1.1-2.8; etc.), was really an assembly of religious teachers, the effectiveness of whose pronouncements was limited by the willingness of Jewish communities to abide by their rulings. It was an ecclesiastical tribunal of an academic character and, despite the fact that it came to acquire much power and influence in Jewish circles (cf. Origen *Letter to Africanus* 14), talmudic literature still leaves traces of a deep-seated regret that the veritable sanhedrin was no more (e.g., M. Soṭ. 9.11).

C. *THE GREEK AND THE HEBREW SOURCES.* According to the Greek sources, the Apoc., the NT, and the writings of Josephus, the sanhedrin was basically composed of men drawn from the priestly nobility. On the other hand, according to talmudic literature, it was a court of experts in the interpretation of the law, the priestly element not appearing and the Sadducees scarcely taken into account save as exponents of unacceptable opinions; and pairs of famous rabbis, whose names can be given, filled the offices of president (נסיא) and vice-president (אב־בית־דין) from *ca.* 160 B.C. to the time of Hillel and Shammai (*ca.* 30 B.C.–A.D. 10). One possibility is that this difference in representation is to be accounted for by supposing that there were two sanhedrins in Jerusalem, one being a political, the other a religious, institution. It seems much more probable, however, that the rabbinical picture is due to a tendency to read the past in the light of the present, the sanhedrin as it existed prior to the great insurrection being thought of in terms of the court founded at Jamnia, the destruction of Jerusalem in 70 having eliminated the influence of the priestly aristocracy with its Sadducean traditions. Of course, this does not necessarily mean that talmudic literature preserves no trustworthy reminiscences concerning the sanhedrin of the period before 70; on many points of detail, indeed, it may well be reliable, but modes of representation having no corroboration in the Greek sources should always be treated with a certain reserve.

As regards the usual talmudic view that the sanhedrin was composed of seventy-one members (M. Sanh. 1.6; cf. Num. 11:16), it may be observed that Josephus appointed seventy elders when preparing for the rising in Galilee and that the Zealots established a tribunal of seventy members in Jerusalem during the great rebellion (Jos. War II.xx.5; IV.v.4). Among other points of interest we note that vacancies were filled by co-optation (M. Sanh. 4.4), and that membership was confined to Jews of pure Israelite descent (M. Sanh. 4.2). There were no sittings on sabbaths or on feast days (M. Yom. Tob. 5.2), and a capital case could not be tried on the eve of a sabbath or festival, as it was not legal to pass a sentence of death until the day following the trial; nor could a capital case be tried by night (M. Sanh. 4.1). The sanhedrin held its sessions in the "hall of hewn stone" (לשכת הגזית) on the S side of the great court of the temple (M. Mid. 5.4). On the other hand, we gather from Josephus that the council chamber was near the Xystos and outside the upper city (War V.iv.2; VI.vi.3), and this may be indicated by the rabbinical name (ξυστός = גזית); but some scholars conjecture that Josephus is referring to the locus of the later sittings, which, according to a tradition preserved in the Babylonian Talmud, was situated

outside the temple area (Sanh. 41*a;* 'A.Z. 8*b;* etc.). Also, according to the NT, the sanhedrin could hold its sessions in the residence of the high priest (Mark 14:53).

As to procedure, the members sat in a semicircle so that they could be seen by one another, and before them stood the two clerks who recorded the votes for and against acquittal (M. Sanh. 4.3). In capital cases certain special formalities had to be adhered to (M. Sanh. 4.1; 5.5). The sanhedrin does not seem to have been a court of appeal in the sense that a condemned person could appeal to it against the judgment of a lower court, but it could be requested to intervene whenever an inferior court was unable to agree as to the interpretation of the Mosaic law in any particular case (M. Sanh. 11.2; cf. Jos. Antiq. IV.viii.14).

D. *COMPETENCE.* There are several pieces of evidence which have to be considered in any discussion of the important question whether the sanhedrin during the procuratorial period was constitutionally competent to execute a capital sentence.

According to Mark's Gospel, which probably contains the passion narrative in its earliest extant form, Jesus was arrested at the order of the Jewish authorities, but executed at the order of Pilate; and this may be taken to imply that the sanhedrin was not authorized to inflict the death penalty without procuratorial consent. It is possible, however, that Jesus was handed over to Pilate on a political charge of sedition because he had not committed an obvious capital offense against the Mosaic law, and that Mark's account of the nocturnal trial (14:55-65) is anachronistic, a reflection of the fact that certain Christians had been condemned to death by the sanhedrin for committing blasphemy in identifying the crucified Jesus with the promised Messiah (cf. Deut. 21:23; Gal. 3:13; 5:11); Jesus had not yet been "accursed by God" on Calvary when he stood before his accusers.

In John 18:31 the Jews informed Pilate that it was not lawful for them to put any man to death. But is it likely that Jews would have reminded the procurator of the limitations of their legal authority, or that Pilate would have required any such reminder? The Fourth Evangelist here seems to have an apologetic aim in view—to show that a constitutional restriction was the only thing that prevented the Jews from putting Jesus to death; and vs. 32 suggests that a theological motive is also involved.

In J. Sanh. 1.1; 7.2 we read that the power to pass capital sentences was taken away from the Jews forty years before the destruction of the temple. But this may be an inference based (*a*) on a tradition that the sanhedrin ceased to hold its sessions in the temple forty years before its destruction, and (*b*) on a rule, which was apparently not laid down before *ca.* 150, that the sanhedrin could pass a capital sentence only when sitting in the temple chamber (cf. B. Sanh. 41*a;* B. 'A.Z. 8*b*).

In the *Pericope Adulterae* (John 7:53–8:11) the following dilemma may be intended: If Jesus pronounced against carrying out the requirements of the Mosaic law (Deut. 22:23-24), he would be discredited by the people; whereas if he counseled action contrary to the Roman imperial decrees (by pronouncing that the woman should be put to death), his enemies would secure material for a grave accusation against him. On the other hand, should a dilemma be involved, it could equally well be of the form: If Jesus declared that the prisoner should be released, he would be contravening the Mosaic law; whereas if he declared that the Mosaic ruling should be applied, he would stand condemned by his own ethical teaching concerning the necessity of love and forgiveness (cf. Luke 6:27-38).

In the Megillath Ta'anith 6 we read that five days after the withdrawal of the Roman troops in 66 the Jews were again able to put evildoers to death. But in the eyes of the Zealotic revolutionaries the greatest sin was committed by members of the chosen race who betrayed Israel by supporting the Roman government, and the passage may mean that soon after the removal of the occupation forces from Jerusalem, faithful Jews were free to deal with traitors and apostates after the manner required by divine justice.

From Jos. Antiq. XVIII.iv.1 we learn that Pharisaic pressure restrained the Sadducean magistrates who were wont to be harsh in their judgments; there is no suggestion in the passage that any restraint or restriction came from the side of the imperial authorities.

According to Jos. Antiq. XX.ix.1, James and certain other Christians were put to death at the order of the sanhedrin; and although objection was taken to the action, the critics do not contend that the sanhedrin was formally incompetent to inflict capital punishment. The objection may have come from certain Pharisees who disapproved of the arbitrary way in which Ananus, the Sadducean high priest, filled vacant seats on the sanhedrin, and who perhaps took the view that an identification of the crucified Jesus with the Messiah was not blasphemy in the strict sense of the law of Moses (cf. Gamaliel's warning in Acts 5:33-42).

According to Acts 6:8-8:1, Stephen was condemned by the sanhedrin and was duly stoned to death. The proceedings do not seem to have constituted a case of mob violence: thus the precept of Lev. 24:14 was observed, the prisoner being taken out of the town to be stoned (Acts 7:58); and the witnesses, who must cast the first stones (Deut. 17:7; cf. M. Sanh. 6.4), laid their clothes at the feet of a prominent member of the council (Acts 7:58).

In M. Sanh. 7.2 we read of a priest's daughter who was burned to death for committing adultery. On the basis of two other rabbinical passages (B. Yeb. 15*b*; T. Sanh. 9.11), however, it could be argued that this execution took place during the reign of Agrippa I (41-44), when the procuratorial system of government was temporarily suspended. On the other hand, these two passages do not exclude the possibility that the execution took place as late as 53.

In M. Sanh. 7.1 strangling is mentioned as one of the four authorized modes of capital punishment, although this punitive measure is nowhere referred to as a recognized Jewish practice either in the OT or in the Greek sources. It seems to have been introduced by the rabbis toward 100, perhaps in an effort

to avoid official detection of the fact that they continued in some degree to exercise judicial authority after 70, when the sanhedrin was deprived of all constitutional power.

According to Philo *Embassy to Gaius* 39, even the high priest was liable to the death penalty if he entered the holy of holies in the temple at Jerusalem at other than the prescribed times.

An inscription discovered in 1871 by Clermont-Ganneau definitely shows that the Jewish authorities were formally entitled by the imperial government to put any Gentile to death if he ventured to pass into the sanctuary beyond the second enclosure of the temple (cf. Jos. Antiq. XV.xi.5; War V.v.2; VI.ii.4; Philo *Embassy to Gaius* 31; Acts 21:29; Eph. 2:14). The ordinance doubtless implies that a special dispensation had been granted to the Jewish authorities. Generally the sanhedrin would be competent to deal only with religious offenses committed by Jews. The procurator would be ultimately responsible for the maintenance of public order, and he would be kept informed of the proceedings at Jewish courts. But it ought not to be inferred from the special character of the ordinance that the inscription has no bearing on the general question under consideration. For if in certain circumstances the Jewish authorities could have a Roman citizen put to death—a right not even enjoyed by the procurator himself—is it not likely that the sanhedrin would be empowered to execute any Jewish citizen accused and found guilty of a capital offense against the law of his religion?

Bibliography. E. Schürer, *A History of the Jewish People in the Time of Jesus Christ*, div. II, vol. I, 163-95 (or better, *Geschichte des jüdischen Volkes im Zeitalter Jesu Christi*, II [4th ed., 1907], 237-67).

For the view that there was a religious and a political sanhedrin, see: A. Büchler, *Das Synedrium in Jerusalem und das grosse Beth-din der Quaderkammer des jerusalemischen Tempels* (1902). J. Z. Lauterbach, "Sanhedrin," *Jewish Encyclopedia*, XI (1905), 41-44. S. B. Hoenig, *The Great Sanhedrin* (1953).

On the competence of the sanhedrin, see: J. Juster, *Les juifs dans l'empire romain*, II (1914), 127-62. F. Büchsel, "Die Blutgerichtsbarkeit des Synedrions," *ZNW*, XXX (1931), 202-10. H. Lietzmann, "Der Prozess Jesu," *SBA*, XIV (1931), 310-22. H. Lietzmann, "Bemerkungen zum Prozess Jesu," *ZNW*, XXXI (1932), 78-84. F. Büchsel, "Noch einmal: Zur Blutgerichtsbarkeit des Synedrions," *ZNW*, XXXIII (1934), 84-87. J. Jeremias, "Zur Geschichtlichkeit des Verhörs Jesu vor dem hohen Rat," *ZNW*, XLIII (1950-51), 145-50. T. A. Burkill, "The Competence of the Sanhedrin," *Vigiliae Christianae*, X (1956), 80-96; cf. XII (1958), 1-18. P. Winter, "Marginal Notes on the Trial of Jesus," *ZNW*, L (1959), 14-33, 221-51; *On the Trial of Jesus* (1960).

T. A. BURKILL

SANSANNAH săn săn'ə [סַנְסַנָּה]. A town in the S part of Judah in the neighborhood of Ziklag (Josh. 15:31). The parallel lists of the cities of Simeon give HAZAR-SUSAH; HAZAR-SUSIM; and are apparently the same as "Sansannah," a form which probably arose from a scribal error due to the preceding name, Madmannah.

S. COHEN

SAPH săf [סַף] (II Sam. 21:18). Alternately: SIPPAI sĭp'ī [סִפַּי] (I Chr. 20:4). One of the descendants of the giants. He was slain by a member of the

"Thirty," Sibbecai the Hushathite, in a Philistine encounter at Gob. Saph is included among the descendants of the giants who, probably as foreign mercenaries serving with the Philistines, took up their residence at Gath.   E. R. DALGLISH

SAPHAT. KJV Apoc. form of SHEPHATIAH 6.

SAPHATIAS. KJV Apoc. form of SHEPHATIAH 6.

SAPHETH. KJV Apoc. form of SHEPHATIAH 7.

SAPHIR. KJV form of SHAPHIR.

SAPPHIRA sə fī′rə [Σαπφείρη; Aram. שׁפּירא, beautiful; *related to* SHIPHRAH]. A member of the primitive Christian community in Jerusalem, wife of ANANIAS.

Acts 5:1-10 relates that Sapphira and her husband sold a piece of property and pretended to give the entire proceeds to the community while keeping part for themselves. When rebuked by Peter for this deceit, each in turn fell dead.   T. S. KEPLER

SAPPHIRE. A transparent rich-blue corundum. It is of the same chemical constituents as the ruby. There are also white, green, purple, and yellow sapphires. The word translates the following:

a) ספיר = σάπφειρος (RSV mg. "lapis lazuli," in accord with Theophrastus and Pliny). The biblical contexts suggest brilliance and preciousness, with no indication of color or hardness. God stands on a tile of sapphire (Exod. 24:10); his throne is sapphire (Ezek. 1:26; 10:1). It is one of the marvels derived from the earth (Job 28:6, 16). The New Jerusalem is laid in sapphire (Isa. 54:11). It is a stone in the breastpiece of judgment and the ephod (Exod. 28:18; 39:11), a stone in the covering of the king of Tyre (Ezek. 28:13). It is used of the girdle worn by the scribe (Ezek. 9:2 LXX). The beauty of the form of the princes of Jerusalem had been like sapphire (Lam. 4:7). The body of the lover is a column of ivory adorned with sapphires (Song of S. 5:14).

b) Σάπφειρος (RSV mg. "lapis lazuli"). It is the second jewel in the foundation of the walls of the New Jerusalem (Rev. 21:19).

c) Ὑακίνθινος (RSV mg. "hyacinth"; KJV "JACINTH"). Color of the breastplates of the riders in Rev. 9:17.

See also JEWELS § 2.   W. E. STAPLES

SARA. KJV Apoc. and NT form of SARAH.

SARABIAS. KJV Apoc. form of SHEREBIAH 2.

SARAH sâr′ə [שׂרה; Σάρρα, princess, mistress]; KJV alternately: SARAI sâr′ī [שׂרי; LXX Σάρα; Heb. 11:11; I Pet. 3:6; *see below*], SARA. **1.** The wife of ABRAHAM, and the mother of ISAAC.

The change from "Sarai" to "Sarah" at Gen. 17: 15, together with the change from "Abram" to "Abraham" at vs. 5, is a significant clue for literary criticism. This is apparently the work of a late writer, whether the author of Gen. 17 himself or a redactor, since all previous and subsequent occurrences of these names have been made to conform to this

change. It is noteworthy that Gen. 17:15 offers no etiological explanation of the meaning of "Sarai" and "Sarah." The former is probably the old Semitic feminine form, and "Sarah" was substituted for it as a later grammatical form. Both names evidently mean "princess" or "mistress" (cf. שׂר, "prince," from the root שׂרר, "to rule"), although there is a possibility that the root is שׂרה, "to strive" (as in "Israel"), with reference to Sarah's contentiousness toward Hagar. Once-popular identifications with Semitic goddesses have little value.

Sarai is first mentioned in Gen. 11:29-30, where it is stated that she was Abram's wife and that she was childless. According to 20:12, she was also Abram's half sister. She accompanied him to Haran (11:31) and subsequently to Canaan (12:5). Judging from 12:4; 17:17, Sarai was sixty-five years old at this time; but despite her age she had retained so remarkably a beauty that when Abram found it advisable to go to Egypt to escape famine in Canaan, he schemed with her to tell the half-truth that they were brother and sister, out of anxiety for his personal safety (12:10-13). As a result Pharaoh took her into his house, but plagues sent upon him caused him to understand that Sarai was really Abram's wife, and he expelled them together from his land (12: 14-13:1).

Gen. 16 recounts Sarai's strife with her maid HAGAR. Despairing of herself producing the heir which God had promised Abram, she gave Hagar to him with the hope that she might produce a child for them. However, Sarai could not suppress her resentment when Hagar conceived and became contemptuous toward her (vss. 1-5). In anger she had Hagar expelled from the camp, but after a vision of God in the desert her maid returned to bear ISHMAEL (vss. 6-15).

At the time that her name was changed to Sarah, God promised that she would have a great posterity through a son who would be born to her within a year (Gen. 17:15-21). This promise was repeated at the time of a subsequent visit to the patriarchal couple at Mamre by Yahweh and two angels in human form (18:1-10). Sarah overheard Yahweh speaking this; but because she was now ninety years old, she laughed in disbelief, and for this Yahweh reproved her (vss. 11-15).

At this point in the narrative a second account of Abraham and Sarah's dissembling about their relationship intrudes (ch. 20; cf. the parallel story involving Isaac and Rebekah in ch. 26). This incident took place in Gerar. Thinking them to be brother and sister, King Abimelech took Sarah into his house, but he was warned by God in a dream not to touch her (20:1-7); thereupon he reprimanded Abraham but gave Sarah a gift and sent them away with permission to live in his territory, and a curse of sterility which God had put upon his household and flocks was removed (vss. 8-18).

According to the divine promise, Sarah conceived in her old age and bore Isaac (21:1-3), whose name is explained from her joyous laughter at his birth (vss. 6-7). At Isaac's weaning feast, she jealously demanded the expulsion of Hagar and Ishmael, which this time was permanent (vss. 8-21). Sarah died at Kiriath-arba (Hebron) at the age of 127 (Gen. 23:1-

2) and was buried in a family cave at Mach-pelah purchased by Abraham from the Hittites (vss. 3-20; 25:10; 49:31). She is mentioned once more in the OT at Isa. 51:2, where she is recalled as an ancestress of the Hebrews.

The NT has several reminiscences of Sarah. In Rom. 4:19 her prolonged barrenness is cited as evidence of Abraham's faith. In 9:9 her conception of Isaac as the heir of promise in the place of Ishmael is mentioned as an instance of divine sovereignty in election. Her own faith is cited in Heb. 11:11, and her submissiveness to her husband is chosen in I Pet. 3:6 as an example of true godly adornment. Gal. 4:21-31 plainly refers to her in an allegorical contrast to the slave-girl Hagar, although it does not mention her name.

That postbiblical Judaism looked upon its first mother not only as an example of piety but also as a paragon of beauty may be observed in some of its legends and midrashes, but the most striking and detailed description of her charms has been discovered among the Dead Sea Scrolls. In a partially preserved Aramaic document dating from the first century A.D. an ancient scribe has pictured the retainers of Pharaoh praising Sarah to their lord, describing in detail her hair, her eyes, her mouth, and other parts of her body, and rising to a climax in the hyperbole: "Above all women is she lovely and higher is her beauty than them all."

Bibliography. The apocryphal material is published in N. Avigad and Y. Yadin, *A Genesis Apocryphon* (1956), col. xx:2-8. On etymology, see: T. Nöldeke, *ZDMG*, XLII (1888), 484; P. Jensen, *Die Keilinschriften und das Alte Testament* (3rd ed., 1902), pp. 364-65; E. Meyer, *Die Israeliten und ihre Nachbarstämme* (1906), pp. 269 ff; K. Tallqvist, *Assyrian Personal Names* (1914), p. 193. S. J. DE VRIES

2. The heroine of the book of Tobit; daughter of Raguel, and bride of Tobias after many tribulations (Tob. 3:7 and frequently throughout the book).
F. W. GINGRICH

SARAIAS. KJV Apoc. alternate form of SERAIAH 2.

SARAMEL. KJV form of ASARAMEL.

SARAPH sâr'ĭf [שׂרף, to burn] (I Chr. 4:22). A descendant of Judah. The note regarding his rulership in Moab and his return to Lehem adds little information, as Lehem is an unknown site. The text of the RSV is based upon the Vulg. The Hebrew is unintelligible. E. R. ACHTEMEIER

SARASADAI săr'ə săd'ī; KJV SALASADAI săl'—. Apoc. forms of ZURISHADDAI.

SARCHEDONUS sär'kə dō'nĭs. KJV translation of the Greek name of ESARHADDON, in one MS of Tob. 1:21 (ἐπὶ Σαρχεδόνος).

SARDEUS. KJV Apoc. form of Zerdaiah. *See* AZIZA.

SARDINE STONE. KJV translation of σάρδινος (following Vulg. *lapis sardinus;* RSV CARNELIAN). Theophrastus suggests the sardine stone is the male

of σάρδιον and is of a brownish color, while the transparent red variety is female and our carnelian.
W. E. STAPLES

SARDIS sär'dĭs [Σάρδεις]. A city in W Asia Minor; capital of ancient Lydia.

1. Location
2. Topography
   a. City and acropolis
   b. Temple of Artemis
   c. Churches
   d. Cemeteries
3. History
4. Excavations
Bibliography

1. Location. Sardis is located in the Hermus Valley (modern Gediz) on the banks of its S tribu-

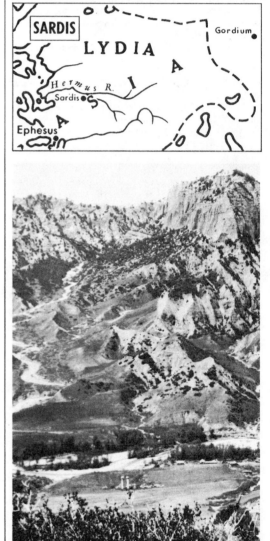

Courtesy of the Oriental Institute, the University of Chicago

24. General view of Sardis, showing the two high remaining pillars of the temple of Artemis

tary, the Pactolus (modern Sart Çay), N of the Tmolus Mountains (modern Bozdağ). The site is well known, as it contains a number of striking ancient landmarks: an acropolis formed by a craggy rock, actually a spur of the Tmolus, on the E side of the Pactolus; Roman and Byzantine ruins at the foot of the citadel; the temple of Artemis, and the cemetery of the "thousand hills" (Bin Tepe), across the Hermus. Fig. SAR 24.

2. Topography. *a. City and acropolis.* The acropolis is the most impressive feature in the present-day scenery.* Although heavily eroded, it still carries the ruins of fortification walls which are made of reused material of classical-to-Byzantine origin. The lower city was also fortified, but at present a poor Byzantine wall is the only known remnant of the lower circuit to the N of the citadel. Among the ruins of the city are a Roman theater and stadium, both constructed in concrete, and a large rectangular concrete building. Near the stadium there is a ruined

Courtesy of the Oriental Institute, the University of Chicago

25. A view of the citadel commanding Sardis

marble arch; to the W nearer the Pactolus a large building awaits further investigation. A Roman aqueduct can be traced leading from Mount Tmolus to the acropolis. Fig. SAR 25.

b. Temple of Artemis. The outstanding architectural relic is the temple of Artemis, to the W of the acropolis. Its original form is hardly known. The cult was dedicated to a local Asiatic goddess, identified with Artemis but sometimes referred to as Cybele. During Croesus' rule the temple must have been of Ionic appearance; but this archaic temple was destroyed in the Ionic revolt of 499 B.C. when the

Courtesy of Ahmet Dönmez

26. The temple of Artemis at Sardis

lower city of Sardis was burned (Herodotus V.102). The present building is a fourth-century reconstruction on the same monumental scale as the temple of Artemis at Ephesus, but it was never finished. Roman repairs were made to its E façade after an earthquake in A.D. 17 had brought a landslide from the acropolis down on the temple. Two columns of the ornate temple were still standing when the American excavations began in 1910, although the building had been in steady decay since the sixth century A.D. Fig. SAR 26.

c. Churches. A small brick church was built against the SE angle of the peristyle of the temple in the fourth century A.D. It is excavated and well preserved. There are some other ruins which may prove to be churches, although excavation would be needed to investigate whether any specific church can be identified and attributed to the period of Rev. 1:11. On the N side of the city eight large piers of white marble, sometimes attributed to a church, deserve examination.

d. Cemeteries. The cemeteries of ancient Sardis are twofold. Modest rock-cut tombs exist on the slopes of the hills across the Pactolus to the W and even on the E bank of this river. A characteristic element in the modern scenery of Sardis is the necropolis, which lies some seven miles to the NW of the ancient city across the Hermus River, S of the Lake of Gyges (modern Marmara göl). The modern name of the cemetery, Bin Tepe ("a thousand hills"), is a numerical exaggeration for the multiplicity of burial mounds visible on the horizon. There are *ca.* a hundred tumuli, round hills erected over chamber tombs. In general appearance Bin Tepe is related to the tumulus cemetery to the NE of the Phrygian city of Gordium, and to Etruscan cemeteries (cf. Caere). The largest tumulus is the "tomb of Alyattes," on the E side, some 150 feet high and surrounded by a stone retaining wall (Herodotus I.93). It covered a stone tomb chamber; but modern archaeological investigations of Bin Tepe have not yet been made, so that the whole complex is insufficiently known. It can be presumed to contain the royal and aristocratic burials of the Mermnad Dynasty.

3. History. The history of Sardis is closely tied up with that of LYDIA, whose capital it remained throughout the political vicissitudes of the region. There is some evidence for prehistoric habitation; but the leading position of the city must be a development of the Lydian period under the kings of the Mermnad Dynasty. Sardis appears in the royal inscriptions of the Persians as *Sparda* (Darius, Behistun § 6; Babylonian *Sa-par-du*), a name designating the Lydian land, as well as the city. Sardis became the most important Persian city in Asia Minor. It lay at the W end of the great royal road which went from Susa across the rivers and through Asia Minor. A branch road led from Sardis to Ephesus (Herodotus V.52-54). The wealth of the city of the Persian period can be gauged to some extent from the jewelry found in tombs of the Pactolus cemetery. Among the gold plaques, necklaces, pendants, bracelets, and seal stones there are excellent samples of Achaemenian artistry.

Sardis may appear in the OT in Obad. 20 as SEPHARAD (ספרד), as a place where exiles from

Jerusalem were living during the fifth century (?) B.C.

In 334 the city surrendered to Alexander, who left a garrison in the acropolis. Sardis remained the administrative center under the Seleucid Dynasty. In the struggle of the usurper Achaeus against Antiochus III the lower city was burned (216 B.C.). Sardis was yielded to the Romans in 189 and put under Pergamene rule until 133 (see LYDIA). Under the Romans, Sardis became the center of a *conventus iuridicus* which encompassed a large number of Lydian cities. It enjoyed great prosperity in the first three centuries A.D. Trade and industry flourished. After the earthquake of 17, Tiberius facilitated reconstruction by his munificence (Tac. Ann. II.47). Hadrian visited Sardis in 123.

From the first century on, Christianity gained in Sardis. Melito, bishop of Sardis in the time of Marcus Aurelius, wrote a large number of treatises, one of which, a sermon, has recently been recovered in the Chester Beatty Papyri. After the reorganization of Asia by Diocletian in 297, Sardis became the capital of the revived district of Lydia, seat of the governor and of the archbishop of Sardis, who was metropolitan.

Sardis was conquered by the Arabs in 716. It continued to be inhabited even after its destruction by Tamerlane in 1403. At present it is the site of a small village which still preserves the name of Sart.

4. Excavations. An expedition under Howard Crosby Butler worked at the site from 1910-14. A joint expedition of Harvard and Cornell universities in co-operation with the American Schools of Oriental Research started new excavations in 1958. The identification of the large Roman buildings will have to await the outcome of the architectural analysis now in progress.

Bibliography. Bürchner, "Sardes," *Realenzyklopädie der klassischen Altertumswissenschaft,* II, A (1920), 2475-78. *Sardis* (Publications of the American Society for the Excavation of Sardis; 1922—). F. G. Kenyon, *Chester Beatty Biblical Papyri,* vol. VIII (1941). K. Bittel, *Grundzüge der Vor- und Frühgeschichte Kleinasiens* (1945), pp. 78-82. A. Goetze, *Kleinasien* (Kulturgeschichte des alten Orients III.I; 1957), pp. 206-9. G. M. A. Hanfmann, "Excavations at Sardis, 1958," *BASOR,* 154 (April, 1959), 1-35.   M. J. MELLINK

SARDITES. KJV form of Seredites. *See* SERED.

SARDIUS sär'dĭ əs [םדא (CARNELIAN *in* Ezek. 28: 13; KJV *mg.* RUBY); KJV σάρδιον (Rev. 21:20); RSV CARNELIAN; KJV SARDINE STONE in Rev. 4:3)]. A deep orange-red variety of chalcedony, darker than carnelian. The root of םדא suggests "redness." It is a stone on the breastpiece of judgment and the ephod (Exod. 28:17; 39:10).

W. E. STAPLES

SARDONYX sär'də nĭks. KJV translation of σαρδόνυξ in Rev. 21:20 (RSV ONYX). A banded form of chalcedony. *See* JEWELS AND PRECIOUS STONES § 2.

SAREA sâr'ĭ ə (II Esd. 14:24). One of the five scribes who wrote rapidly for Ezra.   C. T. FRITSCH

SAREPTA. KJV form of ZAREPHATH.

SARGON sär'gŏn [ןוגרס; Akkad. *Šarru-kēn,* the king is legitimate]. **1.** Sargon of Akkad (Agade); *ca.* end of third millennium, king of Akkad.

With the exception of a few damaged lines on a stela found in Susa, all historical inscriptions referring to Sargon of Akkad are extant only on later copies made and found in Nippur. Besides this body of material we have a group of literary texts in Sumerian and, mostly, in Akkadian, containing legendary tales centering around Sargon, and also sections from late chronicles, as well as references to him in omens.

In his inscriptions Sargon claims to have extended his realm from the Upper to the Lower Sea (i.e., from the Persian Gulf to the Mediterranean Sea), specifically mentioning Elam (and Barahshum); Mari; and, farther to the W Tuttul, Jarmuti, Ibla, and the semimythical localities of the Cedar Forest and the Silver Mountain. From other sources, epigraphic and archaeological, we have evidence which places Sargon and his powerful grandson Naram-Sin as far abroad as Nineveh, Chagar-Bazar, and Tell Brak in Upper Mesopotamia, and Diarbekir on the upper Tigris. The legends, especially the historical epic, *šar tamḫari,* take him deep into Anatolia; and certain passages in the historical texts refer to peaceful commercial relations with the E regions, around the Persian Gulf, of Magan, Meluhha, and the island of Telmun. As to Babylonia proper, Sargon, a high court official of King Ur-Zababa of the N city of Kish, conquered first that city and defeated the powerful Lugalzagesi of Umma, who had succeeded, for the first time in Mesopotamian history, in reaching out beyond the conquests of neighboring city-states to extend his sway over the entire S part of the region. During the fifty-six years of ruling which the king list gives to Sargon, he built, in N Babylonia, a new capital, Agade, which so far has not yet been located, and succeeded, perhaps by means of a standing army and an effective bureaucracy, in organizing the core of his far-flung state and at least in policing the outlying territory. His success in this respect is borne out by the fact that his successors—i.e., his sons Rimush and Man-ishtisu, and the latter's son Naram-Sin—could hold on to their realms for nearly sixty years in spite of rebellions from within and the attack of external enemies.

The legends reflect the unique achievements of Sargon and elaborate on his far-reaching campaigns and marvelous prowess. They endow the story of his birth and rise to power with mythological trappings and attribute his success to the love of the goddess Ishtar.

Bibliography. T. Jacobsen, "Early Political Development in Mesopotamia," *ZA,* N.F. 18 (1957), pp. 91-140; W. Nagel, "Ein altassyrisches Königssiegel," *AFO,* 18 (1957), p. 100, note 15.

2. Sargon I (*ca.* 1850 B.C.), king of Assyria. Nothing is known of this king but the impression of his seal on Old Akkadian tablets from Cappadocia. He was the son of Ikūnum and the father of Puzur-Ashur, and the twenty-seventh king, according to the Assyrian king list, but only the fifth king of Assyria of whom we have any documentation.

3. Sargon II (722-705 B.C.), king of Assyria and Babylonia, son of Tiglath-pileser III, successor to his

Courtesy of the Oriental Institute, the University of Chicago

27. Restored painting showing Sargon II (722-705 B.C.) and attendant before a god Ashur, from Khorsabad

brother Shalmaneser V, and the father of Sennacherib. The circumstances of Sargon's accession to the throne remain obscure. When his brother Shalmaneser V was murdered during the siege of Samaria, certain events must have happened in Assyria which brought Sargon to the throne. The fact that Sargon refers to himself only once as the son of Tiglathpileser III and that there are some clearly derogatory remarks concerning Shalmaneser V in his inscriptions makes it clear that an internal conflict brought about the accession of Sargon. Fig. SAR 27.

Among his first acts was the granting of a new charter to the city of Assur and of important privileges to sanctuaries. In his first campaigns, fought to establish his dominion, he was defeated near Der by Merodach-baladan, then king of the small kingdom of Bit-Yakin, who had the assistance of the Elamite king Humbanigash I. Sargon then turned against Syria, where, since the death of his brother, Shalmaneser V, the Assyrian rule had collapsed at least as far N as Hamath. On the historic battlefields of Qarqar on the Orontes (where in 853 Shalmaneser III had fought a similar coalition) he met the kings of Hamath and Damascus and others whom the Egyptian general Sib'u had been able to muster. The defeat of the allies was complete, and Sargon pursued the Egyptian contingent as far as Raphia, from

where the general fled home after another defeat. Sargon did not cross the Egyptian border.

The next years were taken up by campaigns directed toward two main military objectives: first, the advance toward SE Asia Minor, the containment of Midas, king of the Muski, and whatever was necessary to secure Assyrian communications to that front; and second, the offensive against Urartu. In both endeavors Sargon was extremely successful. He reached Cilicia and the Mediterranean coast in 712, held Asia Minor as far as the Halys River, erected a stela on Cyprus (Kition near Larnaca) and conquered and destroyed Musasir, the capital of Urartu, in 714—an event of which we know more than we do of any other of Sargon's campaigns, because of a special report of it (found in Assur) in the form of a letter addressed to Ashur and the other gods of the capital and to its citizens.

The conquest or reconquest of Samaria spelled the end of the kingdom of Israel, whose inhabitants were deported, first to a region on the River Habur, and then still farther, into Media, where they disappeared. In their place were settled Arameans deported from just-conquered Hamath, later on Arabs were moved there, and eventually the defeated inhabitants of Cutha and Babylon.

Not until more than ten years after his accession to the throne did Sargon turn against Babylon, where Merodach-baladan's rule seems to have been beset by internal conflicts. Babylon was given up without a fight, but Merodach-baladan escaped into Elam. Sargon made himself king of Babylon in 709, fortified the frontiers toward Elam, and received tribute from Telmun, the principal island in the Persian Gulf. In 711 another insurrection, caused by the king of Ashdod, and, of course, supported by Egypt, was crushed (Isa. 20:1).

In the following years, campaigns were made mainly toward the W, and they led to the annexation of the region between the Euphrates and the Taurus (Commagene) and to the N of it. The menace of the Cimmerians appeared for the first time when they moved into Asia Minor after clashes with the kings of Urartu. On one of the rather minor campaigns against them, Sargon was killed; an eponym list reads laconically: "The king was killed, the encampment of the king of Assyria was [. . .]."

Courtesy of the Oriental Institute, the University of Chicago

28. Reconstructed drawing of the palace at Dur-Sharruken (Khorsabad), residence of Sargon II, surrounded by the Nabu temple and the official residences

Courtesy of the Oriental Institute, the University of Chicago

29. Gateway of two human-headed winged bulls at Sargon's palace in Khorsabad (722-705 B.C.)

With the exception of the customary rebuilding of the sanctuaries in Babylonia, Sargon's main interest was concentrated upon the building of his own city, called Dur-Sharruken (Khorsabad),* near Nineveh. It was begun in 713 and inaugurated in 707 but hardly ever really inhabited, and finally was abandoned at the king's death. It represents one of the most ambitious projects of any Assyrian king with regard to building a new city in which to reside in a new and splendid palace. Figs. SAR 28; JAC 3; SAR 29.

Bibliography. H. Tadmor, "The Campaigns of Sargon II of Assyria," *Journal of Cuneiform Studies,* 12 (1958), 22-40, 77-100.
A. L. OPPENHEIM

SARID sâr'ĭd [שָׂרִיד]. A border town in the territory of Zebulun (Josh. 19:10, 12). The LXX reading "Sedud" is more correct than the MT "Sarid." It is almost certainly to be identified with Tell Shadud, a small mound located on the N edge of the Valley of Jezreel, approximately six miles N-NE of Megiddo. Surface explorations have shown that the site was occupied in the Late Bronze, Iron I, Hellenistic-Roman, and early Islamic periods.

Bibliography. W. F. Albright, "Bronze Age Mounds of Northern Palestine and the Hauran," *BASOR,* 19 (1925), 9; F.-M. Abel, *Géographie de la Palestine,* II (1938), 449-50.
G. W. VAN BEEK

SARON. KJV NT form of SHARON.

SAROTHIE sə rō'thĭ [Σαρωθεί(B), Σαρωθιε(A)] (I Esd. 5:34). Head of a family of sons of Solomon's servants who returned with Zerubbabel. His name is omitted in the parallels Ezra 2:57; Neh. 7:59.
C. T. FRITSCH

SARSECHIM sär'sə kĭm [שַׂרְסְכִים] (Jer. 39:3). The name or title of one of the Babylonian princes participating in the capture of Jerusalem. If the word-division of the MT is incorrect, the name may be "Nebo-sar-sechim," a corruption of "Nebushazban" (vs. 13); or it may be a title, שַׂר־סֻכִּים (*sar sukkim*), "chief of the slaves"(?).
J. M. WARD

SARUCH. KJV NT form of SERUG.

SASH [קִשֻּׁר] (Isa. 3:20); KJV HEADBAND. Alternately: ATTIRE (Jer. 2:32). That which is bound on; a band around the waist. *See* DRESS AND ORNAMENTS § 6.

SATAN sā'tən [שָׂטָן]. The archfiend; chief of the devils; instigator of all evil; the rival of God; the Antichrist.

1. Meaning of the term
2. In the OT
3. In the Apoc. and the Pseudep.
   a. History of the concept
   b. Names of Satan
   c. Role of Satan
   d. Reinterpretation of OT legends
   e. Iranian influence
   f. Dissident views
4. In the NT
   a. Names of Satan
   b. Role of Satan
   c. Rabbinic parallels
   d. Satan in Revelation
   e. Folklore
Bibliography

1. Meaning of the term. The Hebrew root שָׂטָן (cf. Arabic *š-ṭ-n*), from which the name Satan derives, means primarily "obstruct, oppose." It is used in the OT of obstructing a man's path (Num. 22:22, 32), opposing in war (I Sam. 29:4), preferring charges in a court of law (Ps. 109:6), and playing the part of an adversary in general (Pss. 38:20—H 38:21; 109: 4, 20, 29). Cognate is the root שָׂטַם (Gen. 27:41; Job 16:9; Ps. 55:3—H 55:4; etc.), whence the noun מַשְׂטֵמָה, "hostility" or "hatred" (Hos. 9:7).

The LXX renders the term uniformly by διάβολος, except in I Kings 11:14, 23, 25 (and in Codex Alexandrinus at Job 2:3), where it is treated as a proper name. Aq., Symm., and Theod. follow suit, except in Zech. 3:1 (and in the first-named's rendering of Job 1:6), where the word is transliterated. The Vulg. usually has *diabolus;* but in the three passages (viz., I Chr. 21:1; Job 1-2; Zech. 3:1-3) where the term is applied to a superhuman being, it treats it as a proper name.

In the Apoc. the form σατανᾶς occurs only at Ecclus. 21:27, but the substitute διάβολος is found in Wisd. Sol. 2:24.

On the usage in the Pseudep. and the NT, *see* §§ 3*b,* 4*a, below.*

2. In the OT. Nowhere in the OT does Satan appear as a distinctive demonic figure, opposed to God and responsible for all evil. To be sure, the name is applied in three passages (all postexilic) to a superhuman being, but in each case it is simply an appellative, not a proper name—i.e., it merely defines the role which the being in question happens to play in a particular situation.

a) In the prose prologue to the book of Job (chs. 1-2), the member of the divine entourage who impugns the integrity of the pious man of Uz and receives permission from Yahweh to put it to the test is described as "the satan" (הַשָּׂטָן; LXX ὁ διάβολος; but Vulg. *Satan;* Syr. סטנא). Here the name means no more than "the one who acts as accuser, or prosecuting attorney, on a given occasion." It is not implied that this is his constant name or role, nor even that he is inherently evil. Moreover, far from being the antagonist of God and the chief of a rival dominion, he is his subordinate and can act only with his consent and in accordance with his orders.

b) In Zech. 3:1-2 (519 B.C.; cf. 1:7), the celestial being who challenges the fitness of Joshua (Jeshua) ben Jozadak to function as high priest at the time of the restoration from the Babylonian exile, is likewise styled "the satan" (LXX ὁ διάβολος). Here again, no more is implied than an *ad hoc* accuser; certainly not an inherently malevolent fiend or antagonist of God. The role of this satan (i.e., prosecutor) is, in fact, simply part of the prophet's vision of a divine tribunal.

c) In I Chr. 21:1, "Satan" (LXX ὁ διάβολος) is said to have incited David to the sin of taking a census. Although the term is here used without the definite article, it is nonetheless no proper name, but simply a common noun (i.e., "*a* satan"), denoting a spirit—in this case, virtually a personification of human frailty—who happened on that particular occasion to act with untoward effect. The book of Enoch speaks similarly (40:7) of "satans"—in the plural; and the word is likewise employed as a common noun in the Dead Sea Scrolls (1QH fragments 4.6; 45.3; Formulary of Blessings), in the Talmud (Ber. 60*b*; Shab. 39*b*), in early portions of the traditional Jewish prayerbook, and in later Mandean literature (e.g., Right Ginza 279.4: סמאנוא). Moreover, it is to be observed that in the earlier account of this incident, in II Sam. 24:1, it is Yahweh himself who is represented as having vengefully incited the king. Accordingly, the satan of the later version may well have been regarded as his instrument, rather than his rival.

3. In the Apoc. and the Pseudep. *a. History of the concept.* It is only in the Deutero-canonical scriptures that Satan begins to emerge as a distinctive personality. This development may be attributed to the special conditions that obtained during the Greco-Roman period, when the national fortunes of Israel were in eclipse.

The time-honored classic theory that disaster was a divine retribution for apostasy had become increasingly insupportable, both emotionally and intellectually. In the first place, it ran counter to the ineluctable fact of life that men who are visited with affliction will not readily reconcile themselves to the darkness unless confident of the dawn, nor be persuaded of God's justice unless convinced at the same time of his mercy (cf. Lam. 3:31-33). Secondly, unless there were some assurance that the misfortune was but temporary and that the promises of the covenant (cf. Deut. 30:3-5) would eventually be fulfilled, the Jews of that difficult time might just as well resign themselves to the fact that, its basic charter having thus been revoked, the *raison d'être* of Israel had come automatically to an end.

Judaism fought its way out of this dilemma by increasing recourse to the dualistic theory that the world was currently in the clutches of a demonic marplot who was responsible at once for the massive sinfulness that had occasioned God's displeasure and for the vicious malevolence of Israel's oppressors. On this theory, the current "dark night" was not so much an expression of God's irremediable vengeance as a temporary setback in his continuous battle against the Evil One—a battle which would assuredly issue in his eventual triumph, the reassertion of his obscured verities, the salvation of the faithful, and the redemption of the ancient pledge.

The concept of the demonic marplot was derived from two main sources. On the one hand, out of the individual casual devils ("satans") of popular belief there now emerged the figure of an archdevil, who was the ultimate cause of evil not only in the sense of misfortune but equally of sin and crime, and who was therefore the "onlie begetter" of the current afflictions. Just as demons in general came to be regarded in late Greco-Roman thought as "antigods" (ἀντίθεοι; cf. Heliodorus *Aethiopica* IV.7; Pseudo-Iamblichus *De mysteriis* III.31.15), so this archdemon was the direct antithesis of Yahweh. It must immediately be added, however, that just as the concept of a supreme deity may express itself in henotheism as well as in monotheism, so that of a supreme devil did not automatically eliminate the countless individual devils of popular lore, but merely reduced them, by what may be termed "henodaemonism," to the status of his agents and adjutants.

b. Names of Satan. The archfiend was not always called Satan (or "*the* Satan"; Greek ὁ διάβολος); indeed, in the Deutero-canonical scriptures this title is relatively rare. His more usual name was BELIAL—i.e., "the Worthless One"—a term expressive more of his pragmatic effect than of his disposition. (Exactly comparable is the Gaelic "the Worthless One" as a sobriquet of the Devil.) Alternatively, he was known as *Maśṭemah* (Jub. 10:8; 11:5, 11; 17:16; 49:2; Zadokite Document 4:13; 5:18; 8:2; 16:5)—a name related philologically to *śaṭan* and meaning "hostility." (This name, it may be added, reappears at a later date in the Ethiopic, Arabic, and Coptic versions of "The Prayer of the Virgin on Behalf of St. Matthias in the City of Bartos [i.e., among the Parthians]." Not impossibly, the feminine form *Maśṭemah* was chosen in preference to the masculine *Śaṭan* in direct imitation of the Iranian Druj, the spirit of deceit and unrighteousness, who was regarded as female; *see* § 3*e below*.) Furthermore, in special contexts the demonic marplot continued to be designated by the name of one or other angel considered in earlier folklore to be responsible for this or that particular form of misfortune. Thus, as the bringer of death he might be called Gadriel (Enoch 69:6)—a name best explained as a distortion of *Qaṭriel*, from the Aramaic *q-ṭ-r*, "intrigue"; or Sammael (e.g., Testament of Abraham 16)—i.e., "the angel of poison." It was said, in fact, that he had originally been an angel named Satanel, but that the divine element (*el*) had been cut from his name when he led a rebellion against God and was ousted from heaven (II Enoch 29:4).

c. Role of Satan. At the same time, whether or not he was actually called by that name, all the varying implications of the word שׂטן were indeed applied to him. He was the obstructor of men's happiness and prosperity in that he led them to discord and violence (Test. Gad 4:7; Test. Benj. 7:1), licentiousness (Test. Reuben 4:7; Test. Simeon 5:3), and duplicity (Test. Asher 3:2). It was he, e.g., who had emplanted corruption among the sons of Noah (Jub. 11:5; II Enoch 22:42; cf. Gen. 6:10-12), who had led Dan to conspire against the life of Joseph (Test. Dan 1:7; cf. Gen. 37:20) and Potiphar's wife to attempt to seduce him (Test. Joseph 7:4; cf. Gen. 39:7). It was he too that had prompted the initial sin of man and thereby brought death into the world (Wisd. Sol. 2: 24; II Enoch 11:74-80; 22:42). He was likewise the cause of sicknesses (Jub. 10:8); and, again, it was he that regularly sent ravens and other birds to peck the newly sown seed out of the earth (Jub. 11:11). Evil men were men who had fallen beneath his sway (Test. Asher 1:8; Test. Benj. 3:3, 8; 1QS 3.20-25). He was portrayed as flying through the air on his fell missions (Targ. Job 28:7), and all human tribulation was due to his malevolence (1QS 3.23).

Moreover, he was now represented as the obstructor (i.e., satan), not only of men, but also of God. He had been at work even before the creation of man (II Enoch 22:42), and he commanded his own rival hosts (Ascension of Isa. 2:9; Adam and Eve 16), though it was necessarily affirmed that he and they would eventually be worsted in a decisive combat (Enoch 67:6; 103:8; Test. Dan 5:10-11; Test. Judah 25:3; Sibylline Oracles 3:71 ff; 1QH 3.35; 6.29; 10.34-35; 1QM, *passim,* especially 1.10, 13-14; cf. also Mandean Ginza [trans. Lidzbarski; 1925], pp. 16, 23).

There was, however, a certain fluidity about the concept, for the Evil One sometimes retained his earlier character of a servant, rather than an opponent, of God, and divinely appointed dooms and trials were thought to be executed through him. It was he, e.g., that was said to have instigated Abraham to the proposed sacrifice of Isaac (Jub. 17:16-18:12), an act which the Bible (Gen. 22:1) represents as a test of faith imposed by God himself. It was likewise he that served as God's instrument in the slaying of the first-born of the Egyptians (Jub. 49:2) —a view which may well have been suggested in the first place by seeing in the Hebrew word למשחית, "to destroy you," in Exod. 12:13 an allusion to the term המשחית, "destructive angel," which was a common synonym or epithet of Satan at this period (cf. 1QH fragments 4.6; 45.3).

d. Reinterpretation of OT legends. As the figure of the Evil One developed, traditional legends were modified to accommodate him. Thus, as the ultimate source of death, he came necessarily to be identified with the serpent in the Garden of Eden (II Enoch 31:3; Adam and Eve 14-16; Sot. 9b; Sanh. 29a)— an identification which was probably influenced also by the common notion that serpents were demonic. Similarly, he was identified with the ringleader of the "sons of God" who had consorted with the daughters of men (Enoch 54:6; cf. Gen. 6:1-4), and with the angelic upstart who had been cast out of heaven (cf. Isa. 14:12-15). *See* Lucifer.

e. Iranian influence. The other source of the concept of the Evil One was that Iranian dualism by which the Jewish masses were increasingly influenced during the Greco-Roman period. Satan was, to a large extent, simply a Judaized version of the Avestan figures of Angra Mainyu (Ahriman), the inveterate foe of the supreme god Ahura-mazda (Ormazd); or of Druj, the spirit of deceit. Indeed, almost all the salient features of the Iranian myth were boldly transferred to him. Of Angra Mainyu it was likewise said that he had brought death into the world (Yasna 30.4), and that the devas, or evil spirits, were under his leadership (30.6). He too was represented as a father of lies (Yasht 31.3) and as the causer of bodily deformities and afflictions (cf. Vidēvdat 2.29, 37; 20.3; 22.2). Moreover, just as the Dead Sea Hymns assert repeatedly that Belial will eventually be worsted (e.g., 3.35; 6.29; 10.34-35) and God's truth (אמת) will emerge triumphant (e.g., 4.25), so the Avesta is insistent that Angra Mainyu and Druj will suffer a like discomfiture at the hands of Asha, the spirit of truth and normalcy (Yasht 19.96; Yasna 29.2; 30.8; 47.6). And just as the apocalyptic era of corruption is frequently described in the Deutero-canonical scriptures as the epoch of "wrath" (Ecclus. 48:10; Enoch 5:9; 69:18; 91:9; Testament of Abraham 19; cf. B.B. 10a; Shab. 11a; 'A.Z. 18b)—a term deftly referred to the wrath and indignation of God— so in the Avesta it is Aeshma, the spirit of wrath and fury, that is held to be responsible for the prevailing anarchy and chaos (Yasna 29.1).

f. Dissident views. There were, of course, dissident voices. In precisely the same way that the worship of angels was discountenanced by the rabbis and their very existence denied by the Sadducees (Acts 23:8) —evidently as an infringement upon the absolute sovereignty of God—so too was the tendency to resort to dualism as an escape from acknowledgment of God's chastisement. An echo of this protest may be heard in the declaration of Jesus ben Sirach (Ecclus. 21:27 [missing in the Hebrew text]) that "when an ungodly man curses Satan [τὸν Σατανᾶν], what he is really cursing is his own self." The passage is often rendered (as in the RSV):

> When an ungodly man curses his adversary,
>   he curses his own soul,

but it is difficult to see what this can mean; whereas in the alternative translation the sense is transparent: the writer is protesting against the view that men can attribute their misdeeds to an independent Evil One; that figure of popular fancy, he avers, is really but a personification of their own natures!

4. In the NT. a. Names of Satan. Satan (usually Grecized as Σατανᾶς) is mentioned by name thirty-three times in the NT, but he appears also (thirty-two times) in the translated form, ὁ διάβολος, "the Obstructor, Devil." He is likewise styled: "the tempter" (ὁ πειράζων; Matt. 4:3; I Thess. 3:5; cf. I Cor. 7:5), "the evil one" (ὁ πονηρός; Matt. 13:19; I John 5:18), "the accuser" (κατήγωρ; Rev. 12:10), "the enemy" (ἐχθρός; Matt. 13:39; Luke 10:19), "the Plaintiff" (ἀντίδικος; I Pet. 5:8; RSV "the devil"), "the prince of demons" (ἄρχων τῶν δαιμονίων; Matt. 9:34; 12:24; Mark 3:22; Luke 11:15), "the ruler of this world" (ὁ ἄρχων τοῦ κόσμου τούτου; John 12: 31; 16:11), and "the prince of the power of the air" (ἄρχων τῆς ἐξουσίας τοῦ ἀέρος; Eph. 2:2). In II Cor. 6:15 he bears the alternative proper name of Beliar (i.e., BELIAL), and on two occasions (Matt. 10:25; 12:24, 27; cf. Mark 3:22; Luke 11:15, 18-19) Jesus styles him BEELZEBUL, a quasi-mythological sobriquet which has thus far eluded satisfactory explanation.

b. Role of Satan. Satan appears invariably as a distinctive personality. He is represented as entering into men and as the responsible author (not merely the personification) of their evil deeds and passions. It is Satan that tempts Judas and Simon Peter (Luke 22:3, 31; John 13:27); that prompts Ananias to withhold his contribution (Acts 5:3); that incites incontinence (I Cor. 7:5); and that shuts men's hearts and ears to the message of God (Mark 4:15; cf. Rev. 2:9; 3:9). He maliciously obstructs Christian endeavor, preventing Paul from visiting the Thessalonians (I Thess. 2:18). Essentially a power of darkness, he is the inveterate enemy of the light and of God (Acts 26:18), though he sometimes cunningly disguises himself as an "angel of light" (II Cor. 11:14)—possibly, indeed, as *the* angel of lights mentioned in the Dead Sea Manual of Discipline (3.20). He is a father of lies, a murderer from the beginning (John 8:44), and it is he that brought death into the world (Heb. 2:14).

At the same time, Satan retains the more primitive character of a noxious demon who causes bodily pains and afflictions. A woman who has suffered such afflictions for twenty years is said to have been "bound" by Satan (Luke 13:16), and he is described expressly as "ruining" or "corrupting" human flesh (I Cor. 5:5); while the two blasphemers, Hymenaeus and Alexander, are consigned to him by way of punishment (I Tim. 1:20), where the implication probably is that they were visited with some form of bodily torment.

c. Rabbinic parallels. It cannot be said that the NT makes any appreciable advance in the concept of Satan upon the time-honored fancies of Jewish popular lore. Almost everything that is said about him can, in fact, be paralleled from Jewish sources. Thus, when he is described as wielding dominion over the air (Eph. 2:2), he is simply filling the standard role of Sammael, the angel of death, in rabbinic literature (cf. Targ. Job 28:7), and the air is probably conceived also as the region of darkness, in accordance with the tradition attested by Philo (*On the Creation of the World* 7). Again, when he is styled "the accuser, prosecutor" (κατήγωρ; Rev. 12:10), not only is this a literal translation of the Hebrew *śaṭan,* but the Greek word is itself employed in rabbinic sources as one of his standard epithets (e.g., M. Ab. 4.11; Targ. Exod. 32:19). So, too, when the wicked and recalcitrant are termed the "synagogue of Satan" (Rev. 3:9), the expression finds its exact counterpart in the "congregation of Belial" (עדת בליעל; cf. LXX συναγωγή=עֵדָה) in one of the Dead Sea Hymns (2. 22). Similarly, the reference to the "angels of Satan" in Matt. 25:41 is not without rabbinic parallels.

d. Satan in Revelation. Of especial interest is the role played by Satan in the apocalyptic visions of the book of Revelation. He is described as "the great dragon, the ancient serpent" (ὁ δράκων ὁ μέγας, ὁ ὄφις ὁ ἀρχαῖος), and is said to be vanquished by Michael (or by an "angel who comes down from heaven") and thrust into the bottomless pit, along with his confederates. At the end of a thousand years, however, he will break loose, but only to be defeated once again, this time forever (12:9; 20: 2-3, 10).

The epithet "the ancient serpent" recurs in rabbinic literature (נחש הקדמוני: Genesis Rabbah 22, 23c; הנחש הראשון: Deuteronomy Rabbah 5), but it is there applied to the serpent in Eden. Here, on the other hand, the term refers rather to the primordial Dragon (Leviathan, Rahab, Tannin), who was said in ancient Hebrew myth to have been subdued by Yahweh at the dawn of creation (*see* COSMOGONY). This myth, related only allusively in the OT (Job 7:12; 9:13; 26:12-13; Pss. 74:13-14; 89:9-10; Isa. 27: 1; 30:7; 51:9-10), is more clearly articulated in the Babylonian Epic of Creation, where the gods who rebelled against the sovereignty of Anu are indeed thrust by their conqueror, Marduk, into nether caverns (*ṭubqātê;* IV.113). These contumacious spirits were known in Mesopotamian folklore as the "bound gods" (*ilāni ṣabtûti,* or *kamûti*) and were sometimes identified as "devils" (*ašakkê*). Onto this ancient Semitic myth, however, has here been grafted the Iranian myth of Azhi Dahaka, the noxious serpent, defeated in primeval time by the hero Thraetaona and held captive in the bowels of the earth, only to break loose again after a prescribed period (variously defined) and then to be finally discomfited by Keresaspa (cf. Yasht 19.38-44). Moreover, Satan has here been identified with the rebel angel ("Lucifer") of Isa. 14:12-15—a tradition anticipated in the book of Enoch (54:5-6) and perpetuated in subsequent Christian literature (cf. especially, in English literature, the Anglo-Saxon poems *Genesis B* and *Christ and Satan; The Vision of Piers the Plowman,* book II, lines 105-11; and, of course, Milton's *Paradise Lost*).

e. Folklore. Lastly, two items of folklore relating to Satan may here fittingly claim our attention:

a) In Jude 9 reference is made to an altercation between Satan and the archangel Michael for the body of Moses. According to Origen (*De principiis* III.2), the story in question was related in the pseudepigraphic Assumption of Moses, but it is not to be found in the incomplete text of that work that has come down to us. There are, however, several later rabbinic legends (cf. *Midrash Peṭîrath Môšeh,* in A. Jellinek's *Bêth Ha-Midrash,* VI, 71-76) which tell how Sammael, the satanic angel of death, gaily embarked on the mission of calling forth the lawgiver's soul, after Michael and other angels had proved reluctant to do so. Moreover, it has long since been suggested that a somewhat similar incident in the Testament of Abraham (ch. 16) may well go back to a story originally related about the death of Moses.

b) In Barn. 4:9 Satan is described as "the Black One" (ὁ μέλας). In illustration of this epithet—which has since become commonplace—it may be observed that the concept of the devil as a swarthy "Ethiopian" recurs later in the apocryphal Acts both of Andrew (ch. 22) and of Thomas (55), as well as in the famous Paris Magical Papyrus (lines 1238-39: σαδανας εθηϊωθφ). So too, in the Gnostic *Pistis Sophia* (p. 367 of the Coptic text), the fiend who presides over one of the hells is called "the Ethiopian [i.e., sunburnt] Ariuth"; while in a Mandean magical incantation, demons in general are designated "black ones" (שחורין). In Jewish legend, the Devil is sometimes portrayed as clad in black silk, and a similar tradition obtains in French and German folklore. Furthermore, modern inhabitants of Mosul believe in a female demon called "the Black One" (Sôdâ), while in Gaelic folklore the Evil One is sometimes named "Black Donald."

Bibliography. P. Carus, *History of the Devil* (1900); A. Brock-Utne, "Der Feind: Die ATliche Satangestalt im Lichte der sozialen Verhältnisse des nahen Orients," *Klio*, XXVIII (1935), 219-27; R. Schärf, "Die Gestalt des Satans im AT," in C. G. Jung, *Symbolik des Geistes* (1948), pp. 153-319; K. L. Schmidt, "Luzifer als gefallene Engelsmacht," *Theologische Zeitung*, VII (1951), 261-79.   T. H. Gaster

SATHRABUZANES. Apoc. form of Shethar-bozenai.

SATIRE. *See* Irony and Satire.

SATRAP sā′trăp [אחשדרפנים, Aram. אֲחַשְׁדַּרְפְּנַיָּא, *a transcription of* Medic *khšatrapāvan;* Pers. *khšaçapāvan,* protector of the land]; KJV LIEUTENANT (Ezra; Esther); PRINCE (Daniel). A governor of a province in the Persian Empire.

The Greek and Latin versions vary in their translation of the word; the Vulg. has *satrapae* except in Esth. 8:9 (*principes*); 9:3 (*duces*). In Greek epigraphic and classical literature the Persian word is reproduced as ἐξατράπης, ἐξαιθραπεύων, ἐξσατραπεύων, and finally shortened to σατράπης. Herodotus, who has given us the standard list of the twenty Persian satrapies (III.89-94), uses therein the Persian word σατραπηία, but he usually used the Greek word ὕπαρχος and once νομοῦ ἄρχων (III.120), since νομός (III.90, etc.) is his usual term for "satrapy." Thucydides and Xenophon follow the terminology of Herodotus. Jerome in the Vulg. uses *satrapa* before the Persian period (Judg. 3:3; I Sam. 29:6; II Chr. 9:14). The word occurs in Latin literature as early as Terence (died 159 B.C.).

Bibliography. J. A. Montgomery, *The Book of Daniel,* ICC (1927), p. 199. O. Leuze, *Die Satrapieneinteilung in Syrien und im Zweistromlande von 520-320* (Schriften der Königsberger Gelehrten Gesellschaft, 11 Jahr, Heft 4; 1935). E. Meyer, *Geschichte des Altertums,* III (1901), 51-52; IV (4th ed., 1944), 45-50.   R. H. Pfeiffer

SATYR. *See* Demon.

SAUL sôl [שאול; Σαουλ; *see* Saul Son of Kish, § 1]. **1.** KJV form of Shaul 1.
2. The first king of Israel. *See* Saul Son of Kish.
3. *See* Paul.

SAUL SON OF KISH.
1. Name
2. Family
3. The times of Saul
4. Choice of Saul as king
5. Major campaigns of Saul
6. Saul and Samuel
7. Saul and David
8. An estimate of Saul and his kingdom
Bibliography

1. Name. The name of the first king of Israel appears nearly four hundred times in the OT and once in the NT (Acts 13:21). In the OT it is confined to the books of Samuel; I Chronicles; the titles of Pss. 18; 52; 54; 57; 59; and Isa. 10:29. The name (שאול, "asked, requested") is a hypocoristicon and is to be explained on the basis of הוא שאול ליהוה, "He is lent to the Lord" (I Sam. 1:28). It also occurs as a West Semitic name in Assyria (ša-u-li), at Palmyra in the third century A.D. (שאילא), and possibly on a seal of uncertain date. *See bibliography.*

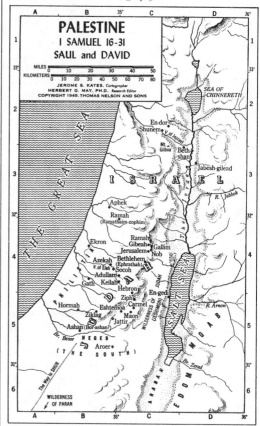

PALESTINE
I SAMUEL 16-31
SAUL and DAVID

MILES
0 10 20 30 40 50
KILOMETERS
0 10 20 30 40 50 60 70 80
JEROME S. KATES, *Cartographer*
HERBERT G. MAY, PH.D., *Research Editor*
COPYRIGHT 1949. THOMAS NELSON AND SONS

2. Family. Saul was a Benjaminite (I Sam. 9:1-2, 16, 21; 10:20-21). The family tree in Table 1 illustrates the family relationships of Israel's first king.

Table 1

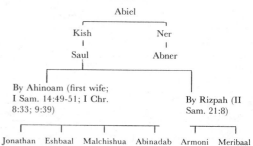

Abiel
Kish   Ner
Saul   Abner

By Ahinoam (first wife; I Sam. 14:49-51; I Chr. 8:33; 9:39)   By Rizpah (II Sam. 21:8)

Jonathan Eshbaal Malchishua Abinadab   Armoni Meribaal

The family home was at Gibeah in the tribal territory of Benjamin. The family was also somehow connected with Zela (II Sam. 21:14), for this was the

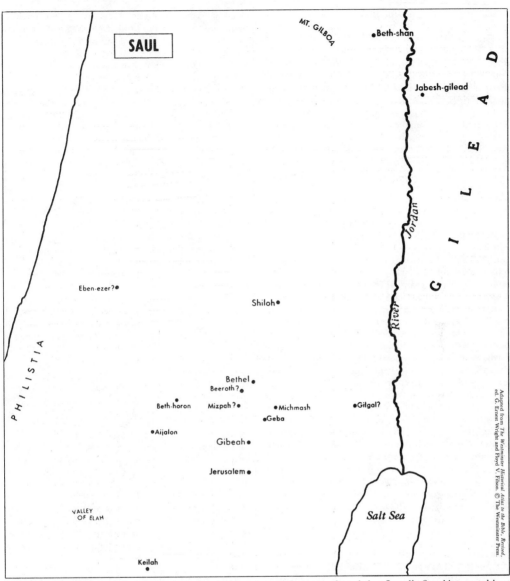

SAUL

MT. GILBOA

•Beth-shan

Jabesh-gilead
•

G I L E A D

Jordan River

Eben-ezer?•

Shiloh•

PHILISTIA

Bethel •
Beeroth?•
Beth-horon •   Mizpah?•   •Michmash
              •Geba
•Aijalon

•Gilgal?

Gibeah•

Jerusalem•

VALLEY
OF ELAH

Salt Sea

Keilah
•

Adapted from *The Westminster Historical Atlas to the Bible, Revised,*
ed. G. Ernest Wright and Floyd V. Filson. © The Westminster Press.

burial place of Kish and the place where the remains of Saul and Jonathan were interred. That the family was relatively well-to-do may be judged from the fact that it possessed asses, servants (I Sam. 9:3), fields, and oxen (11:5).

Gibeah of Saul, present Tell el-Ful ("hill of the beans"), is located *ca.* three miles N of Jerusalem and is a limestone mound of *ca.* two acres. The city in the time of Saul consisted of a village with a fortress of massive masonry, which may have been the castle of the king.* Excavations indicate that life was relatively simple, just what might be expected in the eleventh century B.C. At the time of Saul the Philistines maintained a garrison there with a governor or commander in charge (I Sam. 13:3). *See* GIBEAH 2. Fig. GIB 27.

See map "Palestine: I Samuel 1–15, Samuel and Saul," under SAMUEL, BOOKS OF.

3. The times of Saul. Saul was a creature of circumstances. He was the man of the hour. It must al-

ways be remembered that Israel's first king stood in a period of transition from a loosely organized group of tribes in the time of the judges to the larger and more effectively united confederation under David and Solomon. The times, therefore, played a most important role in the life and activity of the man concerning whom our sources do not speak too kindly.

From the religious point of view, the tribes had some measure of unity in Shiloh, as may be seen from the first chapters of I Samuel. Doubtless this fact made it easier for united political action later on. But in the wake of increasing Philistine pressure in the central highland, Shiloh had been laid in the dust, and the priestly leadership was apparently no longer adequate to meet the situation. Even the ancient symbol of the nation, the ark of the covenant, had virtually disappeared from the scene of action (I Sam. 6–7). Gilgal became the center of worship (10:8; 11: 14-15; 13:4, 8-15; 15:12, 21, 33).

On the political side, the Battle of Ebenezer ended tragically for Israel (I Sam. 4). The result was that all the central mountain territory, hitherto the center of Israelite cultic life, fell into the hands of the Philistines. The devastating blow struck at Shiloh was, of course, meant to wreck the rallying point of the tribes. A control center was set up by the enemy at Gibeah (10:5; 13:3) with a garrison and a governor. The heavy hand of Philistine hegemony is best illustrated by the monopoly on iron which they succeeded in imposing upon Israel (13:20-22). The Israelite farmers had to go to Philistine smiths for the making and sharpening of their plow points, colters, axes, and mattocks. No iron weapons were allowed, though Saul and Jonathan possessed them— how, we do not know. The success of the Philistines doubtless encouraged other enemies of Israel to take advantage of the situation to extend their holdings at the expense of Israel (ch. 11). Fortunately, the Philistines did not press their victory beyond the central highland, so that the Israelites were able to rally around the old shrine of Gilgal, where the kingdom of Saul was set up which marked the beginning of effective resistance against the Philistines.

4. Choice of Saul as king. There are at least two stories dealing with the choice of Saul as king. Both of them belong to the earlier source of SAMUEL. The first story centers in the episode of the lost asses of Kish, which Saul and a servant were sent to find. An exhaustive search in Benjamin and the surrounding area proved unfruitful. As a last resort they resolved to consult the seer in the town nearby. As they were about to enter the city, Samuel met them, though they did not recognize him. When they inquired after the whereabouts of the seer, Samuel informed them that he himself was the seer. He told them that the asses were found but pressed them to attend the sacrifice at the high place, where the best portion had been reserved for Saul. The next morning, in accordance with some cryptic intimations the day before (I Sam. 9:20, 22, 24), Samuel anointed Saul (10:1) and, with an extended discourse, sent him on his way. The sequel to the story of the lost asses and the private anointing of Saul belongs to the later source (10:17-25a); it relates the popular choice of Saul in a sacral meeting at Mizpah.

Apparently not all the people were convinced of the wisdom of the clamor of the majority (10:27; 11:12). Whether this opposition developed later or was present from the beginning is difficult to determine with certainty; doubtless there were misgivings on the part of the conservatives from the start.

The second story of Saul's rise to power is connected with the move of the Ammonites against Jabesh in Gilead (I Sam. 11). The people of Jabesh and the Benjaminites appear to have had a close affinity for each other after the episode detailed in Judg. 21, and because of what Saul did for them on this occasion they maintained this relationship (I Sam. 31:11-13; II Sam. 2:8 ff). In response to the threat of Nahash the Ammonite, an embassy was sent post haste to Gibeah to plead for help. The men of Gibeah could only lament the plight of their brethren. But "the spirit of God came mightily upon Saul when he heard these words, and his anger was greatly kindled" (I Sam. 11:6). He immediately sacrificed a "yoke of oxen" and sent the pieces to the people of the territory. This had the effect of binding them in a covenantal relationship and of pledging them to follow the inspired leader.

Here is a clear reflection of the charismatic principle operative in the time of the judges. This principle at work in the case of Saul is demonstrated elsewhere—e.g., in Saul's connection with the ecstatic prophets (ch. 10; 19:23-24). It is not difficult to understand how, after the incident at Jabesh, the events related in ch. 7 came to be associated with the selection of Saul as the chosen one of the Lord.

Immediately after Saul's return from the deliverance of the citizens of Jabesh, the people again raised their voices in behalf of making him king. Samuel yielded, and the ceremony of investiture was held at Gilgal in connection with a thanksgiving offering for victory over the Ammonites. These factors thus combined to put Saul in office: (*a*) the charismatic power which indicated the presence of the Lord, manifested in demonstration of skill and prowess, as shown by his defeat of the Ammonites; (*b*) the official act of anointing at Gilgal; (*c*) the popular demand and assent.

5. Major campaigns of Saul. The first act of Saul was the reduction of the Philistine outpost at Gibeah (I Sam. 13:1 ff), which he appropriated as his own seat of government and base of operations. The Gibeah exploit aroused the Philistines, who mustered their forces for war. Saul summoned his warriors to Gibeah, while the enemy encamped at Michmash, from which they raided Israel in several directions (vss. 17-18). Jonathan and his armor-bearer precipitated the battle by attacking the outpost of the Philistines (14:14 ff). The former's courageous exploit threw fear into the enemy camp and roused his fellows to action. The result was a telling local victory for the forces of Israel. But it did more than bring military success; it marked the beginning of Israel's earnest resistance against the foe. Those who for one reason or another had joined the Philistines (14:21) and those who hid out of fear joined hands with their brethren. There was a real revival of spirit in Israel that day, and the Philistines were driven out of the central highland as far as Aijalon (vs. 31).

To the early period of Saul's reign belongs also the raid on the Amalekites (ch. 15), the story of which comes from the later source. Like the Ammonites, the Amalekites, Israel's old enemy (Exod. 17:16), doubtless took advantage of the situation to expand its own territory at the expense of Israel. Saul, by his successful expedition against them, restored to Judah what they had taken.

The older source of Samuel says "there was hard fighting against the Philistines all the days of Saul" (I Sam. 14:52), which was probably all too true. Saul pressed his early local advantage and carried the war closer to their centers of population, and the next move we read about is that in the Valley of Elah,* some twenty miles to the SW of Gibeah. The Goliath episode is connected with this campaign (*see* § 7 *below*), which served to push the enemy still farther toward his own borders in the vicinity of Ekron and Gath (17:52). The effective operations of Saul appear to have cleared the Philistines pretty well from the extremities to which they had penetrated. The expansion of Saul's movements must have been keenly felt by the Philistines, especially as it developed toward the N. The threatened severance of their trade routes across the Plains of Esdraelon precipitated Saul's last battle with them at Gilboa.* This struggle, with its outcome, is described in I Sam. 29-31. The army of Saul suffered a severe defeat, and the enemy was victorious. The situation at Gilboa was similar to that which existed after the Battle of Ebenezer (ch. 4). However, Saul seems to have checked the immediate further advance of the Philistines, who never again penetrated the hill country beyond the W limits of Jerusalem, where they were dealt a powerful blow by David (II Sam. 5:17 ff). Thus, while they were not decisively beaten, they were definitely challenged and measurably weakened by Saul and his valiant followers. Figs. ELA 21; GIL 33.

6. Saul and Samuel. One of the most disconcerting episodes in the history of the early kingdom of Israel revolves around the increasingly strained relations between the "man of God" and the first king. Tradition has it that the popular clamor for a king arose because of the character and activity of Samuel's sons (I Sam. 8:2-3), which forced the old seer to yield; though, according to the much exaggerated Deuteronomic additions (10:18 ff; 12), which reflect later experiences, he had his misgivings about the whole affair. His first meeting with Saul occurred in connection with the lost asses of the latter's father (ch. 9). He is represented there as having reserved a special place of honor for Saul and then as having anointed him king in a private ceremony (ch. 10). Here there can be no doubt that Samuel was the responsible agent of Saul's inspiration, for "God gave him another heart" (10:9). At the time of public investiture Samuel again figured as the mouthpiece or representative of the Lord, though the ceremony was political in import (11:15). Moreover, he celebrated a great thank offering after the anointing. All this made a deep impression on the anointed king, who was utterly dependent upon Samuel. When Saul summoned the men of Israel to join him in delivering Jabesh from the Ammonites, he did it in his own name and in that of Samuel (11:7).

The first serious rupture between Samuel and Saul came just before the battle at Michmash (ch. 13). There was to be a sacrifice at Gilgal. Saul waited the number of days which had been agreed upon, but the Philistine pressure was mounting and the people became restless. When Samuel still delayed his coming, Saul took matters into his own hands and then overstepped his bounds. When the sacrifice was over, Samuel appeared and characteristically upbraided him for his rash act and informed him: "Now your kingdom shall not continue" (vs. 14). Saul was undoubtedly shaken by the prognostication, but, while Samuel left Gilgal apparently alone, "the rest of the people went up after Saul to meet the men of war" (13:15 Chicago Bible). The situation was thus not regarded yet as irreparable.

The final breach came after the Amalekite raid (ch. 15). At the instigation of Samuel, Saul undertook to liberate his brethren in Judah from the razzias of the Amalekites, who doubtless took advantage of the Israelite preoccupation with the in-

cursions of the Philistines. Saul was ordered to exterminate them ruthlessly, without mercy. The campaign proved quite successful, but Saul spared the king and the best of the sheep and cattle. Though Saul's explanation of his disobedience appears somewhat weak, the suggestion that he deviated a bit from the stern, conservative *ḥērem* of the old prophets may be correct. In any case, Samuel regarded this act of the king as rank insubordination to the will of the Lord and with his own hands slew Agag at Gilgal. Moreover, though Saul acknowledged his sin and begged forgiveness, Samuel refused to be appeased. He declared unconditionally that the Lord had rejected him in favor of "a neighbor of yours, who is better than you" (15:28). The best Saul could do was to persuade Samuel to remain for the sacrifice for the sake of appearance (vs. 30). The break was complete; "Samuel did not see Saul again until the day of his death" (vs. 35). Saul's last contact with Samuel came in the form of an uneasy conscience on the eve of his death in the Battle of Gilboa. A tired and beaten man, he sought out the witch of Endor in the last desperate hope for some word of encouragement from the spirit world from the man of God (28: 8-25). But to no avail, for the answer was the same as that given on previous occasions. The end had come; tomorrow he must die and Israel go down in defeat.

The attempt to combine the charismatic principle of leadership with a political kingdom thus ended in failure. The priesthood was probably kept on the side of Saul, since it was located at Nob, near Gibeah (I Sam. 21:1; 22:9, 11, 19), though he later alienated them (22:11 ff; 30:7-8). But Samuel could not be controlled. Obviously the lines between political and religious functions were not yet drawn and could not be at this stage. Conditions dictated that Saul carry out his responsibilities as king in accordance with demands. As later experiences testify, such a course did not always fit in with the principles and views of the prophets. Thus they were bound to clash sooner or later. Because Saul was a devoted person and deeply religious, the consequences of the breach with Samuel were demoralizing. Up to this point he had been fairly successful, but henceforth failure met him at every turn. "The Spirit of the LORD departed from Saul, and an evil spirit from the LORD tormented him" (16:14). In other words, the cessation of co-operation between him and the prophet was followed by a divided personality, which led to disaster for himself and the nation.

7. Saul and David. Two stories of David's coming to the attention of Saul are related in the sources of I Samuel. The first tells of the former's coming to the court as a skilled musician, sought out to calm the disturbed mind of the king after the rupture with Samuel (16:14-23). The other has David come to the notice of Saul in the Goliath episode (ch. 17), which is one of the most thrilling stories of the OT. But scholars generally regard the former story as the more authentic in detail of the two, mainly because in II Sam. 21:19 (cf. I Chr. 20:5) Goliath is said to have been slain by Elhanan. David certainly performed some heroic exploits—indeed, he may even have slain a giant too, but the account in part appears to have something of the character of sacred legend, the slaying of Goliath being a later attribution to DAVID.

Both narratives indicate the immediate rise to favor of the young Bethlehemite in the court of Saul. He became his personal attendant and armor-bearer (16:21). Not only so, but because he "was successful wherever Saul sent him" (18:5), he was soon made a lieutenant in the army, to the manifest satisfaction of all concerned. The rapid rise of David, together with the unstinted praise heaped upon him by the people, preyed on the already divided mind of the king. He was aroused to a jealousy which knew no bounds and which urged him to pursue the son of Jesse to the end of his life. It is not difficult to understand how Saul became a victim of desperation—in the wake of the withdrawal of prophetic support and the striking success of David, which could be due only, so Saul believed, to the transfer of the divine blessing from himself to David.

Chs. 18–24; 26–27 tell the story of the relentless efforts of Saul to do away with his young armor-bearer. First, in one of his melancholic fits he attempted to pin him to the wall with his spear (18:9-16). Then he exerted every effort to persuade him to marry his daughter, thinking perhaps to gain sympathy, on the one hand, or to spur David on in further exploits with the Philistines in the hope that he might be killed, on the other (18:17-18, 22-27). In each instance Saul's pains served only to thwart himself and enhance the prestige of David. The result was greater bitterness and hostility toward him (18:28-29). Next Saul tried to influence Jonathan and his servants to kill him (19:1); afterward Jonathan interceded with his father on behalf of his friend and secured a pledge from him that David should not be put to death (19:6). This pledge might have held had David not distinguished himself in further skirmishes with the Philistines. Again Saul attempted to thrust David through with his spear (19:9-10); failing this, he sent his police to David's quarters to take him while he slept (19:11-17), but Michal helped him escape. Another conference of David with Jonathan ended in a plan to discover once and for all whether it was safe for David to remain within reach of Saul (ch. 20). At the Feast of the New Moon, Saul flew into an uncontrollable rage when he discovered David's planned absence supposedly due to a visit with his family at Bethlehem, and Jonathan risked his own life in a futile endeavor to reason with him (20:23-33).

David's flight from the king and the latter's pursuit is one of the sorriest tales in the early history of the kingdom. Saul poisoned the minds of his bodyguard against David (22:7-8). Since the priests at Nob had unwittingly assisted David, he had them murdered in cold blood (22:11-20). With his army he prepared to follow David to Keilah (23:8), but when he discovered that David had fled, he gave up his plan. While David was in Horesh, informants brought word to Saul (23:19-23), who immediately went after him, only to find that he had escaped to the Desert of Maon (23:24 ff). He was compelled to give up the chase because of a Philistine raid (23:27-28). Thereafter Saul heard that David was at Engedi and set out to hunt him down there (ch. 24).* His life

was in David's hands there, but the latter demonstrated that Saul's fear of him was ill founded. Saul returned home once more after swearing an oath with David. Once more Saul pursued David, this last time in the Wilderness of Ziph (ch. 26), where the latter again could have put him out of the way. David and Abishai (26:7) stole into the camp by night and took the king's spear and jug of water as visible evidence of his exploit. Abishai wanted to thrust Saul through, but David would not be guilty of laying a hand on the Lord's anointed. When Saul was apprised of what had taken place, he acknowledged his error in attempting to kill David, especially in view of the fact that the latter had now twice spared his life. This was destined to be the last meeting between the two great rivals. "So David went his way, and Saul returned to his place" (26:25c). Fig. ENG 28.

8. An estimate of Saul and his kingdom. The Bible presents Saul as a rejected king because of his incomplete subservience to the prophetic commands. And certainly there was much to be desired in the way in which he carried out the commission laid upon him by Samuel and the times. But he was hardly to be blamed so severely as a cursory reading of the sources might indicate. He succeeded in checking the unhindered Philistine penetration of the central highlands of Israel. His expedition in Transjordan and his punitive raid on the Amalekites held the old enemies of his people in check and made his people relatively secure throughout his reign. He probably broke the monopoly on iron of the Philistines. He set the stage for his more sagacious successor, David, by developing a kind of separation of functions of church and state. To be sure, he was not very adroit in his relation with the religious authorities, but he broke the ice. The times demanded political leadership of a type that went beyond the old charismatic principle operative in the days of the judges. Saul took the step which marked the transition from judge to king, which was not fully realized until Solomon took over the kingdom.

As a person Saul was, first of all, a commanding figure. At times he could inspire his followers with unbounded zeal. He was also a man of conscience, or he never would have been so deeply troubled by prophetic opposition. This opposition was responsible for the indecision and fear so characteristic of him in later days. He admitted his guilt on numerous occasions but was met with stern refusal of mercy and forgiveness. This was enough to crush the stoutest personality. It interfered seriously with the progress of the kingdom. If Saul had had the sympathetic counsel of a Nathan, history might have presented an altogether different portrait of him.

The kingdom of Saul was only a loosely organized confederacy and of necessity so. It was modeled after the kingdoms of Israel's neighbors, Edom, Moab, and Ammon, rather than after those of the Canaanite city-states. Saul had the support of his own tribe—of Ephraim, Manasseh, and Judah, at least. He had a small standing army generaled by Abner, doubtless supported largely by gifts and booty. The capital, as shown by excavations, was not pretentious; it was just a fortress in the town and very modest indeed.

Bibliography. G. Beer, "Saul, David, Salomo," *Religions-geschichtliche Volksbücher,* II Reihe, Heft 7 (1906). W. F. Albright, "Excavations and Results at Tell el-Ful (Gibeah of Saul)," *AASOR,* vol. IV (1924). R. Kittel, *Geschichte des Volkes Israel* (6th and 7th eds., 1926), II, 78-102; *Great Men and Movements in Israel* (1929), ch. 5. A. Alt, *Die Staatenbildung der Israeliten in Palästina* (1930). A. T. Olmstead, *History of Palestine and Syria* (1931), ch. 20. F. James, *Personalities of the OT* (1939), ch. 6. W. F. Albright, *From the Stone Age to Christianity* (1940); *Archaeology and the Religion of Israel* (1942). M. Noth, *Geschichte Israels* (1950). A. C. Welch, *Kings and Prophets of Israel* (1952), ch. 2. E. Meyer, *Geschichte des Altertums* (3rd ed., 1955), vol. II, pt. II, pp. 239-48. J. Bright, *A History of Israel* (1959), pp. 163-74.

On occurrences of the name Saul, see: G. A. Cooke, *A Textbook of North-Semitic Inscriptions* (1903), p. 283. K. L. Tallquist, *Assyrian Personal Names* (1914). M. Noth, *Die israelitischen Personennamen im Rahmen der gemeinsemitischen Namengebung* (1928), p. 136. D. Diringer, *Le Iscrizioni Antico-Ebraiche Palestinesi* (1934), p. 247.   J. M. MYERS

SAVARAN. KJV form of AVARAN.

SAVIAS sə vī´əs [Σαουια (A)] (I Esd. 8:2 KJV). One of the ancestors of Ezra. The name is omitted by the RSV, which follows the LXX B at this point.
                                    C. T. FRITSCH

SAVIOR. *See* SALVATION; CHRIST.

SAVIOR, DIALOGUE OF THE. A Gnostic treatise in the form of a dialogue between Jesus and his disciples regarding cosmogony; one of the many Coptic documents discovered in 1946 at Chenoboskion in Upper Egypt. *See* APOCRYPHA, NT.
                                    M. S. ENSLIN

SAVOUR. *See* ODOR.

SAW [מְגֵרָה (*the second time in* I Chr. 20:3 *an error for* מַגְזֵרֹת, axes), *from* גרר, to drag(?); מָשׂוֹר; πρίζω]. In idea and primitive form, a knife with a notched blade, sometimes provided with a pistol-grip handle or an arched frame to enable the cutting edge to be applied more firmly. Early saws cut only on the push or the pull of the stroke, not on both. For cutting stone or other hard material, a copper blade provided with stone teeth was used, or powdered abrasive was run in under the cutting edge. The surgeon used the saw, especially for cutting bone.

The saw was a familiar implement of the Israelite woodcutter (Isa. 10:15), and stone-working with saws is referred to in the account of the building of Solomon's temple (I Kings 7:9). Heb. 11:37 alludes to the saw as an instrument for inflicting slow and painful death, and traditionally Isaiah's martyrdom was by this means. OT references to putting military prisoners "under saws" probably means only putting them to work (II Sam. 12:31).

Fig. CAR 13.   L. E. TOOMBS

SAYINGS OF JESUS, OXYRHYNCHUS. *See* OXYRHYNCHUS SAYINGS OF JESUS.

SCAB [יַלֶּפֶת; KJV גָּרָב (Deut. 28:27; RSV "scurvy"); מִסְפַּחַת (Lev. 13:6-8; RSV "eruption"); LXX λειχήν]. An itching DISEASE, perhaps *favus, tinea sycosis,* or *tinea tonsurans.*

SCABBARD (Jer. 47:6). An alternative form of SHEATH.

SCALES [פֶּלֶס] (Isa. 40:12). Alternately: BALANCE (Prov. 16:11); KJV WEIGHT. A plausible view holds this word, from the verb meaning "look at, examine," to be the indicator arm. *See* BALANCES; WEIGHTS AND MEASURES § 1.   O. R. SELLERS

SCALES (FISH). The translation of several Hebrew and Greek words in the Bible. *See also* BALANCE.

Only fish with both scales (קַשְׂקֶשֶׂת) and fins are permitted as food for the Israelite (Lev. 11:9-12; Deut. 14:9-10). The term is used figuratively in I Sam. 7:5 for scale armor (קַשְׂקַשִׂים), where the term otherwise would be דִבְקִים (II Kings 22:34; II Chr. 18:33; cf. θώραξ in Rev. 9:9).

מָגֵן, "shield," is used figuratively in Job 41:15—H 41:7 to mean the scales of Leviathan.

The LXX λεπίς, translated "scales" (of fish) in Lev. 11:9-12; Deut. 14:9-10, is used in metaphor to explain Paul's regaining his sight in Acts 9:18 (cf. Tob. 11:7-13).   J. A. SANDERS

SCALL, DRY. KJV translation of נֶתֶק (RSV ITCH).

SCAPEGOAT. *See* AZAZEL.

SCARAB. *See* SEALS AND SCARABS.

SCARECROW [תֹּמֶר, *properly* palm tree *or* pillar]. Probably a pillar, crudely shaped in human form and set up to frighten away birds or vandals, or possibly evil spirits. Jeremiah (10:5) compares pagan idols to "scarecrows in a cucumber field." Bar. (Letter of Jeremiah) 6:70—G 6:69 echoes Jeremiah's sentence (Greek προβασκάνιον). "Scarecrow" is the most apt translation; the KJV "upright as the palm tree" can hardly be correct in this context.
                                    L. E. TOOMBS

SCARF [רְעָלָה, veil] (Isa. 3:19); KJV MUFFLER. According to Arab tradition, a double veil, one part of which was placed around the head above the eyes and the other below the eyes, and the end of which was left hanging down over the chest.
                                    J. M. MYERS

SCARLET [שָׁנִי, תּוֹלַעַת, *or variant forms;* LXX *and* NT κόκκινος]. A highly prized brilliant red color obtained from the female bodies of certain insects and used for dyeing woven fabric, cloth, and leather. Coloring matter was extracted from the kermes (Sanskrit *krimja;* Ancient Persian *krmi;* Arabic *qirmiz*) insect, *Coccus ilicis,* which attached itself to the kermes oak, *Quercus coccifera,* a native of the Near East and the Mediterranean area. An insect similar to the true cochineal *Coccus cacti,* the source of a flourishing carmine dye industry later in the New World, was also found in the Ararat valleys and used for its coloring properties in antiquity. Shades of scarlet varied; results of dyeing were unpredictable. It is impossible to distinguish between the meaning of terms translated as "scarlet" or "crimson" in the Bible. Probably the more lasting hues were produced with the aid of a mordant such as alum.

In the OT תּוֹלַעַת is usually preceded or followed by שָׁנִי (*see* CRIMSON). The rendering of the latter word in Isa. 1:18 by φοινικοῦν in the LXX, and the identification of the kermes oak with Phoenicia by Theophrastus, the Greek botanist, suggest the likelihood that the Phoenicians developed the scarlet industry. Kermes was used not only for dyeing but also for medicinal purposes, and the Romans exacted it as tribute from conquered peoples. To the Hebrews scarlet was an important dye and color. Scarlet thread (Gen. 38:28, 30), cord (Josh. 2:18, 21), and cloth (Num. 4:8; II Sam. 1:24; Prov. 31:21; Nah. 2:3) are noted in the OT. Yarns dyed scarlet were used extensively alone and with linen and yarns of blue and purple for the tabernacle furnishings (Exod. 25:4; 26:1, 31, 36; etc.) and vestments of the priests (28:5-6, 8, etc.). According to the Dead Sea War Scroll (1QM 7.11), priests in time of battle were to wear girdles of linen, blue and purple and scarlet stuff, תּוֹלַעַת שָׁנִי (cf. Exod. 39:28-29). Scarlet clothing was associated with well-being (II Sam. 1:24; Prov. 31:21) and was also represented as the dress of the harlot Jerusalem (Jer. 4:30).

In the NT, "scarlet," as in the LXX, is a translation of κόκκινος. Reference is made to scarlet wool (Heb. 9:19), and the robe put on Jesus was scarlet (Matt. 27:28). The woman of Rev. 17:3-4 is dressed in purple and scarlet and is seated on a scarlet beast. Luxury is suggested by the allusion to Rome clothed in scarlet, purple, gold, and precious stones (Rev. 18: 16), and the economic import of the scarlet trade is implied in the statement that scarlet can no longer be bought from Rome because of her fall (vss. 11-12).

See also COLORS.

Bibliography. Pliny Nat. Hist. IX.140-41; XVI.12; XXI.45-46. Theophrastus *Inquiry into Plants* III.iv, xvi. A. Lucas, *Ancient Egyptian Materials and Industries* (2nd ed., 1934), pp. 36-39. J. R. Partington, *Origins and Developments of Applied Chemistry* (1935), pp. 522-23. H. Kurdian, "Kirmiz," *JAOS*, 61 (1941), 105-7. J. Laudermilk, "The Bug with the Crimson Past," *Natural History*, 58 (1949), 114-18. R. J. Forbes, *Studies in Ancient Technology*, IV (1956), 98-106.   C. L. WICKWIRE

SCENTED WOOD [θύων, *from* θύω, to offer burnt offerings]; KJV THYINE WOOD thī'ĭn. One of the imports prized by the apocalyptic "Babylon" and its peoples (Rev. 18:12). According to Pliny the Elder (*ca.* A.D. 23-79), who calls the tree "citrus" and says that it is known to the Greeks "by the name of *thyon* or sometimes *thya*," this fragrant wood, imported from Africa, was employed by the Romans in the manufacture of furniture, particularly tables. It took a high polish, and its grain ran in "waving lines" or "spirals like so many little whirlpools," which led to tables made of it being designated respectively as "tiger tables" and "panther tables." Because of its aromatic scent this wood was also used by the Greeks in connection with temple worship, whence the name θύων (see Homer *Odyssey* V.60). This large pinaceous tree (*Callitris quadrivalvis*) is called "sandarac" today (from σανδαράκη, realgar, orange pigment) from the resin (gum sandarac) furnished by the tree.

Bibliography. Pliny Nat. Hist. XIII.100; H. G. Liddell and R. Scott, *Greek-English Lexicon* (9th ed., 1940); L. H. Bailey, "Callitris," *New Encyclopedia of American Horticulture* (1947).
    J. W. BOWMAN

SCEPTER [מַחְקֵק (Num. 21:18; Pss. 60:7—H 60:9; 108:8—H 108:9; *cf.* KJV; RULER'S STAFF *in* Gen. 49:10); שֵׁבֶט, *and in* Esth. 4:11; 5:2; 8:4 *the expanded form* שַׁרְבִיט; ῥάβδος]; MIGHTY SCEPTER [מַטֵּה עֹז, rod of strength] (Ps. 110:2; Jer. 48:17; RULER'S SCEPTER in Ezek. 19:11). The official staff or baton of the king, emblematic of his authority

Courtesy of the Cairo Museum; photo courtesy of the Metropolitan Museum of Art

30. A guard with scepter in his left hand at the tomb of Tut-ankh-Amon (1361-1352 B.C.) at Thebes; in his right hand he holds a mace.

and, specifically, of his striking power; occasionally possessed also by a lesser dignitary (Num. 21:18). Figs. SCE 30; SEN 41.

A ceremonial staff—the stylized descendant of man's most ancient weapon, the club—is an almost invariable feature of Near Eastern royal portraits, and a similar object was undoubtedly part of the Israelite kings' royal regalia (Gen. 49:10; Pss. 45:6—H 45:7; 110:2; Ezek. 19:14). Scepters are mentioned in connection with the kings of Egypt, Moab, Damascus, and Ashkelon (Jer. 48:17; Amos 1:5, 8; Zech. 10:11).* The scepter of Yahweh, the supreme king, is the tribe of Judah, to which the Davidic monarch belonged (Pss. 60:7—H 60:9; 108:8—H 108:9); this is a metaphoric way of saying that the Davidic kingship is an extension of the divine au-

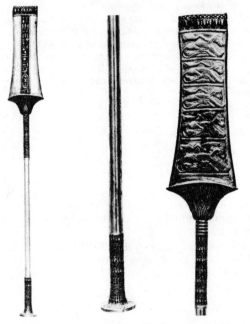

31. Three views of an Egyptian king's scepter, showing the elaborate use of gold, lapis lazuli, faïence, turquoise, and carnelian in inlays (Tut-ankh-Amon)

thority (*see* KING). The stafflike nature of the royal scepter is clear from the fact that the word translated "scepter" has a more general use for any kind of rod, as, e.g., the shepherd's club (Ps. 23:4) and the farmer's flail (Isa. 28:27), and is used in parallelism with the normal word for "staff" (מטה)—e.g., in Isa. 14:5. *See* ROD; CLUB. Fig. SCE 31.

Two main types of scepter are pictured in ancient art: a long, slender staff with an ornamented head; and a short-handled battle mace, with a pear-shaped stone head three or four inches long. The first is seen in a relief of the Persian king Darius, grasped in the right hand a little below the tip and with the butt resting on the floor between the king's feet, a position suggested by Gen. 49:10. The Persian royal scepter is mentioned in Esth. 4:11; 5:2; 8:4, where we are informed that it was made of gold and was extended by the king toward a suppliant who had won his favor. A scepter of this type is suggested by the metaphor in which the vine, Israel, grows tall and its strongest branch becomes a ruler's scepter (Ezek. 19:11). The mace type of scepter appears in a relief of Esarhaddon of Assyria; and, since this form of scepter is a stylized military weapon, it serves well to symbolize the king's striking power, as the scepter frequently does in the OT—e.g.:

> A scepter shall rise out of Israel;
> it shall crush the forehead of Moab
> (Num. 24:17; cf. Ps. 125:3;
> Isa. 14:5).

The only use of ῥάβδος in the NT is in Heb. 1:8, a quotation of Ps. 45:6—H 45:7.   L. E. TOOMBS

SCEVA sē'və [Σκευᾶς] (Acts 19:14). A Jewish high priest whose seven sons at Ephesus were exorcising evil spirits in the name of Jesus.

The story of Sceva and his seven sons ought to be understood in the larger context of Acts 19:11-20. Paul was just concluding two years of most successful missionary work at Ephesus when an outburst of remarkable healing miracles by his hands occurred. He was able to cure diseases and cast out demons at a distance by sending to the afflicted napkins and aprons which he had merely touched. Jewish exorcists there were so impressed that they undertook to cast out demons in the name of Jesus. The seven sons of Sceva attempted this. But the demon challenged their authority, and the possessed man leaped upon them and drove them away humiliated, naked, and wounded. People of Ephesus were so amazed that they began to revere the Lord Jesus, and many of the magicians abandoned their spells and destroyed their books of magic in a great bonfire.

The statement that Sceva was a high priest has caused difficulty. No record of the existence of a high priest by that name has been discovered. Codex Bezae reads "priest," but "high priest" is almost certainly the correct reading. Some have inferred Acts has reported an inaccurate popular tradition here; that these Jewish exorcists had falsely claimed to be sons of a high priest. But there is another reasonable possibility. Sceva was a name of Latin origin. It was common for a Jew to have both a Hebrew name and a Greek name. If we knew this man's Hebrew name, it might be possible to identify him.

Formerly a contradiction was felt between the statement in vs. 14 that there were seven sons and the report in vs. 16 that "both of them" (ἀμφοτέρων) were routed. But it has been learned from papyri and other sources that ἀμφοτέρων can mean "all," and so the RSV has translated it.

The reference to itinerant Jewish exorcists agrees with what we know otherwise of Jewish preoccupation with such matters. In Antiq. VII.ii.5, Josephus avers that King Solomon was a recognized authority on spells and incantations. Then he tells of one Eleazar who was famous for casting out demons. Jesus and his disciples, all of whom were Jews, were notable for their exorcisms. It is probable that this was one of the specialties of MAGI. We encounter SIMON MAGUS of Samaria in Acts 8:9-24; ELYMAS of Cyprus in 13:6-11; and Atomos, another magus of Cyprus, in Jos. Antiq. XX.vii.2.

That these Jews tried to cast out demons in the name of Jesus reminds us that the same thing occurred during the ministry of Jesus (Mark 9:38). The Paris Magical Papyrus 574, lines 3018 ff, gives a spell from the time of Hadrian or later, which begins: "I adjure you by Jesus, God of the Hebrews."

The healing power of faith has been known in many cultures. The temples of Aesculapius among the Greeks and Romans were hospitals. Testimonial inscriptions have been recovered from temple ruins in both Epidaurus and Rome. Christianity has shared this knowledge with other religions.

The narrative in Açts 19:11-20 may sound strange, perhaps incredible, to modern readers, because its ideas follow unfamiliar patterns. But in the real context of its time, there is not an item in the story which lacks authenticity.

Bibliography. K. Lake and H. C. Cadbury, *Beginnings of Christianity,* IV (1933), 239-42; S. V. McCasland, *By the*

Finger of God (1951); G. H. C. Macgregor, *IB*, IX (1954), 256-57. S. V. McCasland

SCHIN shĭn (Heb. shēn) [שׁ, *s̆*, *š* (*Śîn, Šîn*)]. The twenty-first letter of the Hebrew ALPHABET as placed in the KJV at the head of the twenty-first section of the acrostic psalm, Ps. 119, where each verse of this section of the psalm begins with this letter.

SCHOOL. *See* EDUCATION.

SCHOOLMASTER. *See* CUSTODIAN.

SCIENCE.

A. Egypt
   1. Mathematics
      a. Arithmetic and algebra
      b. Geometry
   2. Astronomy
      a. Calendar
      b. The "decans"
      c. Eclipse
      d. Astrology
      e. The "secret science of the pharaohs"
   3. Medicine
B. Mesopotamia
   1. Mathematics
      a. Arithmetic
      b. Algebra
      c. Geometry
   2. Astronomy
      a. The older period
      b. The Seleucid period
         i. The lunar calendar
         ii. The lunar ephemerides
         iii. Eclipses
         iv. Planets
         v. Astrology
   3. Medicine
C. Israel
   1. Mathematics
   2. Astronomy
      a. Sun and moon
      b. Eclipse
      c. Stars
      d. Constellations
      e. Astrology
   3. Calendar
   4. Medicine
Bibliography

A. *EGYPT.* **1. Mathematics.** In spite of the deep admiration expressed by Herodotus, Aristotle, and Democritus, the truth seems to be that Egyptian mathematics—and up to a certain extent the same is true for astronomy—has been a factor of only secondary importance in the civilization of Egypt. Its largely pragmatic and utilitarian character is the outcome of the general social and economic conditions of Egyptian society.

Among the sources are two fragmentary papyri from the Middle Empire (Papyrus Kahun and Berlin); two longer and slightly younger texts (Papyrus Rhind and Moscow), which seem to represent copies of older treatises; a leather document (British Museum leather roll); and two wooden tablets from Cairo.

a. Arithmetic and algebra. The Egyptian script possessed special signs for units, tens, hundreds, thousands, and millions. Addition and subtraction were made by the accurate counting of these signs. Multiplication and division were executed on the basis of the principle of duplication. The problem of multiplying 3 by 17 was realized as in Table 1:

Table 1

— 1	3
2	6
4	12
8	24
—16	48

               51 (sum total of 1 and 16, marked by — in the left-hand column, or 17 times 3, obtained by the addition of the corresponding numbers, 3 and 48, in the right-hand column).

In the case of division the inverse procedure is followed. If, e.g., 169 is to be divided by 8, the procedure in Table 2 is followed:

Table 2

— 1	8
2	16
— 4	32
8	64
—16	128

        21 (sum total of 1, 4, and 16, since the opposite numbers 8, 32, and 128 add up to 168).

In general, only fractions with the numerator 1 are used. Fractions such as (*a*) 2/5 are represented by $1/15+1/3$, or (*b*) 4/7 by $1/14+1/2$—general formula for (*a*) $2/n=1/3.1/n+5/3.1/n$; for (*b*) $4/n=1/2.1/n+7/2.1/n$. The Papyrus Rhind contains a table, from 2/5 to 2/101, for the reduction of a fraction of the type $2/n$ (*n* is an odd number) into two or more fractions with numerator 1.

The use of algebra of the empiric kind is shown by a problem like: "A number to which the fourth part of it is added becomes 15. Which is this number? [Answer] The number is 12, its fourth part is 3. Total 15. [Demonstration] Count with 4. Take one fourth, namely 1. Total 5. Count with 5 in order to find 15: —1   5

             —2   10
    result is 3.

                             Multiply 3 by

4:	1	3
	2	6
—4		12

    result is 12.

	1	12
1/4		3

         Total 15." (Papyrus Rhind, problem 26.)

Or: "How to divide 100 into two parts so that the square root of one part is ¾ of the other." This problem is solved by starting from the numbers 1 and ¾. These are squared (1, ½, and 1/16=1 9/16), and the square root is taken of the total (1¼). Then, the square root is taken of 100—namely, 10—which stands for 1¼ x 8. Finally, it is admitted that the original numbers (1 and ¾) have to be multiplied by 8 so as to become 8 and 6. It must be left to specialists to decide whether this solution is reached in a way similar to that used in modern algebra $(x^2 + y^2 = 100; y = \frac{3}{4} x; x^2 + 9/16\ x^2 = 100;$ etc.) or not.

b. Geometry. Besides being able to compute the areas of triangles, rectangles, and trapezoids, the Egyptians empirically found the relatively accurate value of 3.1605 for the number π. The problem runs as follows: "Method to compute a circular piece of land the diameter of which is 9 *khet*. What is its area of land? You should subtract its ninth (part) from 9. Rests 8. Then, you should multiply 8 eight times, which gives 64. See, its area is 6 *khâ* and 4 *setat*. Thus this is done:

1	9
1/9	1
Subtract from it, rests 8.	
1	8
2	16
4	32
—8	64

Its area in land is "6 *khâ* [written 60], 4 *setat*." (Papyrus Rhind, problem 50.) In more general terms, $A = (8/9\ d)^2$ if d is the diameter.

The same concise style appears in the computation of the volume of a truncated pyramid (with square base) with height h, a as the length of the lower and b as the length of the upper base. a is squared (a^2), a is multiplied by b (ab), and b is squared (b^2). All three are added $(a^2 + ab + b^2)$ and multiplied by ⅓ of h. The general formula ⅓h $(a^2 + ab + b^2)$ gives the correct volume of the truncated pyramid (Papyrus Moscow, no. 14).

"Problems concerning areas or volumes do not constitute an independent field of mathematical research but are only one of many applications of numerical methods to practical problems," O. Neugebauer has written.[1] The preceding examples will render evident the correctness of this characterization of Egyptian geometry.

2. Astronomy. The deficient nature of Egyptian arithmetic acted as a retarding force upon the development of astronomy. In another way, the scarcity and recent origin of the source materials are responsible for our imperfect knowledge of the achievements and the development of this branch of science.

a. Calendar. The Egyptian year consisted of 12 months of 30 days each; to the total of 360 days 5 *epagomenae* were added at the end of each year; the 12 months were divided into 3 seasons: inundation, winter, and summer. Its practical usefulness made it a model for Hellenistic astronomers, and it served as the basis for the lunar and planetary tables of Copernicus. Its origin, however, seems to have been rather of an agrarian practical—the more or less close coincidence of the annual rising of the water of the Nile with the heliacal rising of Sirius—than of an astronomical theoretical nature. Next to the civil calendar, lunar calendars for liturgical purposes were in use. A Demotic text of the Roman period (Papyrus Carlsberg no. 9) shows the way in which civil and lunar years were integrated. The procedure is

[1] *The Exact Sciences in Antiquity* (Providence, R. I.: Brown University Press).

based on the fact that 25 civil years are almost equal to 309 lunar months and contain 9,125 days, which are distributed over lunar months of 29 and 30 days. By means of this 25-year cycle it became possible to calculate the new and full moons without an error in excess of 2 days. The day was divided into 24 hours, 12 for the time of daylight and 12 for the time of night, originally of unequal length according to the change of the seasons, but later, in Hellenistic times, replaced by hours of equal length, each of which was divided into 60 minutes. Thus it was by a Hellenistic modification of an Egyptian practice combined with Babylonian numerical procedures that our present 24-hour day and 60-minute hour came into effect.

b. The "decans." Until the Hellenistic period there is no Egyptian evidence for the zodiac. By a special set of constellations, which first appear on coffin lids of the Middle Kingdom, the year is, however, divided into 36 "decans," each of which corresponds to ⅓ of the zodiacal signs and to 10 degrees of the ecliptic. The decans, of which only 2, Sirius and Orion, can be immediately identified and which in some cases represent groups of stars and in others a single star, rise in turn at a specific hour of the night during all the 36 periods of 10 days of the year. They are situated in a zone of the sky parallel to and S of the ecliptic. Every ten days a different star was chosen to mark the last hour of the night. The sequence of the decans is tabulated in "diagonal" fashion, which in the original documents runs from right to left. *See* Table 3.

Table 3

	Decades		Visibility
I	II	III	
		Star *A*	second to last hour
	Star *A*	Star *B*	next to last hour
Star *A*	Star *B*	Star *C*	last hour

c. Eclipse. In the existing documents only one doubtful reference to a partial solar eclipse of 610 B.C. has been discovered.

d. Astrology. It is only in the second century B.C. that texts of astrological content appear. It seems idle, therefore, to speculate on the astrological origin of Egyptian astronomy.

e. The "secret science of the Pharaohs." What has been called the "secret science of the Pharaohs," a general designation for the alleged astronomical and mathematical significance of the pyramids and of the pyramid of Cheops in particular, which supposedly included such knowledge as the exact value of π, the exact measure of the radius of the terrestrial globe and of the arc of the terrestrial meridian, is obviously not in accordance with the results of archaeological research.

The character and achievements of Egyptian astronomy are aptly summarized by Neugebauer (*The Exact Sciences in Antiquity* [1957], p. 91) as follows: "In summary, from the almost three millennia of Egyptian writing, the only texts which have come down to us and deal with a numerical prediction of astronomical phenomena belong to the Hellenistic and Roman period. None of the earlier astronomical documents contains mathematical elements; they are crude observational schemes, partly religious, partly practical in purpose. Ancient science was the product of a very few men; and these few happened not to be the Egyptians." [1]

3. Medicine. Until 1875 the achievements of Egyptian medicine were known only through the Greek writers such as Theophrastus, Dioscurides, and Galen. The discovery and subsequent publication of such documents as the Papyrus Ebers (a collection of medical prescriptions from the Eighteenth Dynasty), Kahun, Berlin (prescriptions from the Nineteenth Dynasty), and Smith (surgery from the Eighteenth Dynasty) thoroughly modified this situation.

The statement of Herodotus that "each physician treats one disease and not more . . . . Some are doctors of the eyes, others of the head, the abdominal region, and of diseases of uncertain localization" (II.84), seems to contradict the actual practice of general practitioners and specialists (oculists, dentists, surgeons) both.

Precise knowledge of the internal structure of the human body is lacking. Sicknesses of the respiratory system, larynx, bronchi, and pulmonary lobes are not kept apart but are classified after the common symptom of cough, for which a large number of remedies are given. Under sicknesses of the stomach are given gastric discomforts, dilatation, hemorrhage, and gastric fever, as well as cough, angina pectoris, and diabetes. In the same source, the Papyrus Ebers, afflictions of the intestinal system such as constipation and those caused by taenia and other parasites are mentioned, and the use of medicines (ricinus, honey, beer, poultice) is recommended; diarrhea and dysentery are, apparently, unknown. Both the Papyrus Ebers and the Papyrus Berlin deal with diseases of the urinary tract, among which is bilharziasis, the "hematuria of Egypt," and prescribe curative substances (beverages of different kinds, electuaries).

The knowledge of the exterior parts of the body, head and skull, and face (ears, mouth, eyes) is considerably more precise and advanced. Wounds of the skull and face (caused in battle), migraine ("pain in one side of the head"), alopecia, canities ("remedy to cause gray hair to disappear infallibly . . ."), head cold, fracture of the nose, inflammatory conditions of the ear, diseases of the teeth (filling of cavities, reinforcement of two teeth by means of a gold string, draining of an abscess through holes in the jawbone, treatment of the gums), conjunctivitis, trachoma, cataract, night blindness, are among the ills which can be determined with more or less certainty.

Considerable portions of the documents refer to matters which in modern terms would come under the heading of gynecology. For the determination of the sex of the unborn baby several methods were used. One of them, in the words of the Papyrus Berlin (no. 199), goes as follows: "(Put) barley and wheat (in two different sacks) to be aspersed by the woman with her urine, each day. . . . In case the barley germinates (first), it will be a boy; in case the wheat germinates (first), it will be a girl."

It is in surgery, the subject matter of the Papyrus Smith, that the achievements of the Egyptian physicians, obtained by a combination of common sense,

scientific method, and ingenuity, appear to be most advanced. Such devices as the use of some sort of adhesive tape, of stitches to close a wound, of splints, and of a tube to insert food into the mouth of a patient struck by tetanus, seem to be well attested. The following quotation from Papyrus Smith (no. 31) illustrates the process of examination, diagnosis, and prognosis practiced in the case of a dislocation of one of the cervical vertebrae: "[*Entitled*] Instructions concerning a dislocation of the neck. [*Examination*] If thou examinest a man having a dislocation in a vertebra of his neck, shouldst thou find him unconscious of his two arms (and) his two legs on account of it, while his phallus is erected on account of it, (and) urine drops from his member without his knowing it; his flesh has received wind [*abdominal tympany*]; his two eyes are blood-shot [*subconjunctival hemorrhage*]; it is a dislocation of a vertebra of his neck extending to his backbone which causes him to be unconscious of his two arms (and) his two legs. If, however, the middle vertebra of his neck is dislocated, it is an *emissio seminis* which befalls his phallus. [*Diagnosis* and *prognosis*] Thou shouldst say concerning him: 'One having a dislocation in a vertebra of his neck while he is unconscious of his two legs (and) his two arms, and his urine dribbles. An ailment not to be treated' " (J. H. Breasted, *The Edwin Smith Surgical Papyrus* [1930], pp. 324-25, 327, 452-53). [2]

B. MESOPOTAMIA. 1. Mathematics. The study of Mesopotamian mathematics is a recently developed branch of research. What is known of it is largely due to the pioneering efforts of O. Neugebauer and F. Thureau-Dangin (*see bibliography*). Generally speaking, the Mesopotamian mathematical documents fall into two groups, "table" texts and "problem" texts. They date from two periods, the "Old Babylonian" period, roughly contemporary with the Dynasty of Hammurabi (1800-1600 B.C.), and the "Seleucid" period (third, second, and first centuries B.C.). In the first, mathematics appears as a fully developed discipline. Though there is no evidence of earlier (Sumerian) stages, this naturally presupposes a period of undetermined length of development. The documents of the second period, posterior by over one thousand years, show little essential change (on the "zero" sign, *see below*) if compared with those of the first. The achievements of Mesopotamian mathematics are summarized by O. Neugebauer (*The Exact Sciences in Antiquity* [1957], p. 48): "We are dealing with a level of mathematical development which can in many aspects be compared with the mathematics, say, of the early Renaissance. Yet one must not overestimate these achievements. In spite of the numerical and algebraic skill and in spite of the abstract interest which is conspicuous in so many examples, the contents of Babylonian mathematics remained profoundly elementary." And again: "Babylonian mathematics never transgressed the threshold of prescientific thought." [1]

a. Arithmetic. The basic principle of Mesopotamian arithmetic is the consistent use, at least in mathematical and astronomical texts, of a positional sexagesimal system. In other words, a notation like 3, 4, 7, is equivalent to $(3. \ 60^2) + (4. \ 60) + 7$ or 11,047

---

[1] Used by permission of Brown University Press.

[2] Used by permission of the University of Chicago Press.

in the decimal notation. For a multiplication table for 10, as given in Neugebauer's transcription (*The Exact Sciences in Antiquity* [1957], p. 16), see Table 4.

Table 4[1]

1	10
2	20
3	30
4	40
5	50
6	1 (for 60)
7	1,10 (for 60+10=70)
8	1,20 (for 60+20=80)
9	1,30 (for 60+30=90)
10	1,40 (for 60+40=100)
11	1,50 (for 60+50=110)
12	2 (for 60+60=120)
13	2,10 (for 120+10=130)

A word of caution is, however, in place as to the exclusive use of the sexagesimal system, since clear evidence for other systems of notation has been found. The presence of special cuneiform signs for 1, 10, and 100 points toward the decimal system.

It is only in the Seleucid period that a special sign for "zero" is generally used. By this device, which in the older texts was already occasionally present in the form of an open space, the ambiguity of a notation 120 (as $1,20=60+20=80$ or $1,0,20=3,600 +0+20=3,620$) was avoided. The zero symbol is, however, never used at the end of a number. For this reason it would be wrong to accept the complete functional identity of the Mesopotamian and our zero.

"The advantages of the Babylonian place value system over the Egyptian additive computation [*see* § A1*a above*] with unit fractions are so obvious that the sexagesimal system was adopted for all astronomical computations not only by the Greek astronomers but also by their followers in India and by the Islamic and European astronomers. Nevertheless the sexagesimal notation is rarely applied with the strictness with which it appears in the cuneiform texts of the Seleucid period in Mesopotamia. Ptolemy, for example, uses the sexagesimal place value system exclusively for fractions but not for integers. . . . The same procedure was followed by the Islamic astronomers and it is the reason for our present astronomical custom to write integers decimally and then use sexagesimal minutes and seconds" (O. Neugebauer, *The Exact Sciences in Antiquity* [1957], p. 22).[1]

In order to divide a number a by a number b, the reciprocal of b $(1/b)$ as found in the tables of reciprocals which often accompanied the multiplication tables was multiplied by a. In the tables of reciprocals the numbers are arranged in such a way that the product of any number of the left-hand column and of the corresponding number in the right-hand column equals 1 (or any other power of 60): 2. $30/60= 1$; $3.20/60=1$, etc.), as in Table 5.

It is obvious that this procedure works only in case the number a contains the prime numbers 2, 3, and 5. For those numbers, absent from the table, which do not fulfil this condition, such as 7, 11, 13, 14, etc.,

[1] Used by permission of Brown University Press.

Table 5[1]

2	30	16	3,45	45	1,20
3	20	18	3,20	48	1,15
4	15	20	3	50	1,12
5	12	24	2,30	54	1,6,40
6	10	25	2,24·	1	1
8	7,30	27	2,13,20	1,4	56,15
9	6,40	30	2	1,12	50
10	6	32	1,52,30	1,15	48
12	5	36	1,40	1,20	45
15	4	40	1,30	1,21	44,26,40

(O. Neugebauer, *The Exact Sciences in Antiquity* [1957], p. 32; see also the same author's "Sexagesimalsystem und babylonische Bruchrechnung," *Quellen und Studien zur Geschichte der Mathematik*, Abteilung B, Band I-II [1930-32]).

sometimes the remark "7 does not divide," "11 does not divide," etc., is found. Other tables, however, give complete lists of reciprocals of both "regular" and "irregular" numbers (see A. Sachs, "Babylonian Mathematical Texts I," *Journal of Cuneiform Studies*, 1 [1947], 219-40).

Further proof of the skill of the Mesopotamian computers is found in the existence of tables of squares and square roots, of cubes and cube roots, etc. In most cases the roots are given for perfect squares and cubes only. As an approximation of $\sqrt{2}$, both 1.416 and the remarkably correct 1.414213 are given. The former is the same as found in the Indian *Śulvasūtras* (third or fourth century B.C.?). For lack of direct evidence, it is hard to say in which way these approximations were found. Similarly, it is hard to say whether the correct answer to the problem of computing the total sum (S) of the geometric series consisting of ten terms $(n=10)$ with first term (a) 1 and ratio (q) 2 was found by simple addition $(1+2+4+8+16+32+64+128+256+512=1023)$ or by the use of a formula similar to the modern formula

$$S = a\frac{q^n-1}{q-1},$$

since the Mesopotamian scribe prescribes only to take the last term (512) minus 1 and to add the last term to it $(511+512=1023)$.

An interest in number theory appears in the text known as Plimpton 322. Its numbers as arranged in the first three columns seem to have been obtained as a series of solutions of the Pythagorean equation $a^2=b^2+c^2$ (the first column list a^2/c^2; the second and third columns give the corresponding values of b and a). For a different interpretation, see E. M. Bruins, "On Plimpton 322. Pythagorean numbers in Babylonian mathematics," *Koninklijke Nederlandsche Akademie van Wetenschappen* (Amsterdam), *Proceedings*, vol. LII, no. 6 (1949), pp. 191-94; *Sumer*, 11 (1956), 117-21.

b. Algebra. Three preliminary remarks are in order. First, the use of the term "algebra" as applied to the contents of certain Mesopotamian mathematical texts seems to be justified by the fact that they contain problems resulting in equations of the first and second order, with one or more unknowns, which, but for the use of a symbolic notation, are solved by means of the systematic application of a developed combinatory procedure similar to that used in "modern" algebra. Furthermore, some of these texts seem to be the result of theoretical interest or to have, while repeating the original problem in a more complicated form, a didactic purpose, rather than to be the outcome of practical considerations. Finally, it should be kept in mind that the remarkable achievements of the Mesopotamian algebraists are to be taken as the result both of trial and error and of a rational theoretical effort.

Out of the numerous texts dealing with such problems as equations of the first, second, and, in special cases, of the third and fifth order, compound interest, consecutive powers of given numbers, and the determination of the exponents of given numbers, the following problem involving the solution of an equation of the second degree ($11x^2 + 7x = 6.25$ or, in the accepted form, $11x^2 + 7x - 6.25 = 0$) may serve as an example. For the sake of convenience the sexagesimal notation of the original text has been replaced by the decimal notation, and other slight changes have been made; the symbols a, b, and c have been used for 11, 7, and 6.25 respectively in order to show how the final formula

$$x = \frac{-b + \sqrt{b^2 + 4ac}}{2a}$$

was obtained:

"Multiply 11 [a] by 6.25 [c]: 68.75 [ac]. Take half of 7[b]: 3.50 $\left[\frac{b}{2}\right]$. Multiply 3.50 $\left[\frac{b}{2}\right]$ by itself: 12.25$\left[\frac{b^2}{4}\right]$. Add 12.25$\left[\frac{b^2}{4}\right]$ to 68.75 [ac]: 81 $\left[\frac{b^2 + 4ac}{4}\right]$ The square root of 81 is 9$\left[\frac{\sqrt{b^2 + 4ac}}{2}\right]$. Subtract 3.50 $\left[\frac{b}{2}\right]$ .... from 9 $\left[\frac{\sqrt{b^2 + 4ac}}{2}\right]$: 5.50 $\left[\frac{\sqrt{b^2 + 4ac}}{2} - \frac{b}{2}\right]$ or $\frac{-b + \sqrt{b^2 + 4ac}}{2}\right]$ ...." One final step, the division of the last formula by 11[a], is needed to obtain the correct answer: 0.50; the negative answer [−1.13636] is neglected.

c. Geometry. It would be somewhat wrong to consider geometry a special branch of Mesopotamian mathematics. Spatial relations were considered of importance only insofar as they led to algebraic equations. In other words, the "geometric" problems were of a primarily algebraic character.

Out of the large number of interesting problems only a few can be selected:

a) The rectangular triangle inscribed in a semicircle is understood in the following problem (*see* Fig. 1 *below*): "60 (is) the perimeter, 2 (the length of) the perpendicular (on the chord). Which is the length of the chord?" The solution says: "Square 2 [*a*]: 4. Subtract 4 from 20 [*d*, which, it should be noted, assumes a value 3 for π; *see below*]: 16. Square 20, the diameter [*d*]: 400. Square 16 [*d-2a*]: 256. Subtract 256 [(d-2a)²] from 400 [d²]: 144. The square root of 144 is 12. That is the length of the chord. Thus one should proceed." From Fig. 1 it will be seen without difficulty that the scribe follows the formula

$$l = \sqrt{d^2 - (d - 2a)^2}$$

in order to establish the length of the chord.

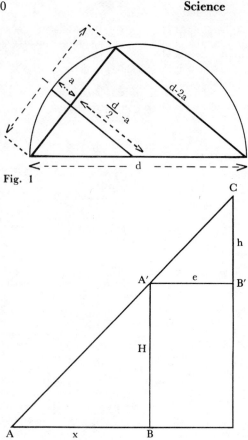

Fig. 1

Fig. 2

b) Knowledge of the Pythagorean theorem is also implied in the solution of a problem which involves the determination of the length (*L*), width (*l*), and diagonal (*d*) of a rectangle if $L + l + d = 40$ and $L.l = 120$. The correct answer ($L = 15$, $1 = 8$, $d = 17$), which is given without the intermediate steps, is based on the equation $d^2 = L^2 + l^2$.

c) That the concept of similarity of rectangular triangles was manipulated is apparent from the following problem (*see* Fig. 2 *above*). Height (*H*) and width (*e*) of a wall are given. A piece of wood (a tree?) sticks out above the wall at a height *h*. At what distance (*x*) does an observer have to be from the wall to see the top of the piece of wood? From the similarity of the triangles AA'B and A'CB' it results that

$$\frac{h}{e} = \frac{H}{x},$$

from which the formula

$$x = e - \frac{H}{h}$$

is derived by the scribe.

As to the circle, most documents give the crude value 3 to π. A better approximation of 3⅛, however, is given in a Susa text. (See E. M. Bruins, "Quelques textes mathématiques de la mission de

Suse," *Koninklijke Nederlandse Akademie van Weten- schappen* [Amsterdam], *Proceedings*, vol. LIII, no. 7 [1950], pp. 369-77.) As noted by Neugebauer, this approximation does not seem to be attested before Albrecht Dürer in 1525.

Among the other mathematical texts found at Susa in 1936 are tablets which give the computation of the radius r of a circle which circumscribes an isosceles triangle of sides 50, 50, and 60 ($r = 31.25$), the regular hexagon from which the approximation 1.75 for the square root of 3 can be deduced, a problem concerning the sides x and y of a rectangle with diagonal d with given values for xy and x^3d, which leads to a quadratic equation for x^4 ($x^8 + a^2x^4 = b^2$), etc.

The volume of cubes and parallelepipeds is correctly calculated (product of the base and the height). The volume of the truncated pyramid is calculated by the approximative formula: $V = \frac{1}{2}h\ (a^2 + b^2)$, a and b being the length of the lower and upper base and h the height. The volume of the cylinder is calculated with $\pi = 3$ (*see above*). No formula for the sphere has been found.

2. **Astronomy.** It is only since the careful investigations of such scholars as Epping, Kugler, Strassmaier, Schaumberger, Neugebauer, and others that a more precise view of Mesopotamian astronomy, free from misconceptions about the importance of magic, number mysticism, and astrology, has been reached. Chronologically the astronomical texts, the large majority of which originate from the archives in Uruk and Babylon and which were written by such professional scribes as Sudines, Naburianos, and Kidenas, as mentioned in the Greek and Latin sources, fall into several groups. As in the case of mathematics, evidence for the existence of a Sumerian astronomy is lacking.

a. The older period (1800-400 B.C.). The first texts based on observation, in this case of the planet Venus, date from the reign of Ammiṣaduqa (*ca.* 1650); they have proved to be of importance for the chronology of the period of Hammurabi. See Langdon, Fotheringham, and Schoch, *The Venus Tablets of Ammizaduga* (1928).

From a tablet from Nippur, written in the Cassite period but actually dating from an older period, it appears that the universe was conceived as consisting of eight concentric spheres with the moon in the center. (See O. Neugebauer, *Quellen und Studien zur Geschichte der Mathematik*, Abteilung B, Band 3 [1936], pp. 273 ff.)

In texts written *ca.* 700 B.C. though actually from an older age, the fixed stars, the planets, the moon, the seasons, etc., are mentioned. (See E. F. Weidner, "Ein babylonisches Kompendium der Himmelskunde," *AJSL*, 40 (1924), 186-208. B. L. van der Waerden, "Babylonian Astronomy II, The Thirty-six Stars," *JNES*, 8 (1949), 6-26; "Babylonian Astronomy III, The Earliest Astronomical Computations," *JNES*, 10 (1951), 20-34. From the same time date texts which deal with solar and lunar eclipses.

It seems safe to assume from these and other texts that by the end of the older period the Babylonian astronomers used "the zodiac of 12 times 30 degrees as reference system for solar and planetary motion," used "a fixed luni-solar calendar and probably some of the basic period relations for the moon and the

planets," and possessed "an empirical insight into the main sequences of planetary and lunar phenomena and the variation of the length of daylight and night." (O. Neugebauer, *The Exact Sciences in Antiquity* [1957], p. 103.)

b. The Seleucid period (third, second, and first centuries B.C.). The tablets of this period present the most mature achievements of Mesopotamian astronomical science.

i. **The lunar calendar.** It seems that from the beginning the Mesopotamian calendar has been lunar at all times. The beginning of the month was counted from the evening when the new moon could be seen again for the first time shortly after sunset. Apart from varying meteorological conditions during the observation of the horizon, a number of technical factors (the variable velocity of both the moon and the sun, the variation of the angles between the ecliptic and the horizon, the variation of the latitude of the moon) cause the length of the lunar months to be subject to variations. This length is actually comprised between 29 days plus 6 hours and 29 days plus 20 hours. A calendar of months of 29 and 30 days is only roughly in accord with the lunar cycle. Complete accordance would necessitate the addition of 1 day to 1 month of 29 days every 30 months. In addition to the variables mentioned above, the use of a calendar of this kind is accompanied by other inconveniences. There is, e.g., the fact that the lunar year of 12 average lunar months represents 354 days and is 11¼ days shorter than the solar year. After 3 such years the lunar year is over a month behind the solar (seasonal) year, and after 9 such years there will be a difference of a full season. A periodic adjustment becomes necessary in the form of the addition of a thirteenth month by royal decree. As Hammurabi puts it: "This year has a gap. The next month should be inscribed Elul II"; and, careful not to give the taxpayers an extra month, he adds that "the payment of taxes in Babylon will be terminated by the 25th of Elul II instead of by the 25th of Teshrît." Regularity in the intercalation of this thirteenth month is attested only from the fourth century B.C. onward; 7 intercalations are prescribed in 19 years, since 235 lunar months correspond exactly to 19 solar years or 19 lunar years plus 7 months.

ii. **The lunar ephemerides.** In order to cope with the difficulties connected with the variations of the length of the lunar month, a coherent system was developed by the Mesopotamian scribes predicting the effects of the above-mentioned variables on the visibility of the new crescent at the horizon. This theory lies at the basis of the composition of the so-called lunar ephemerides.

These documents, from Seleucid times, consist of columns of numbers and are of two types (I and II or A and B), of which, according to Kugler, the I or A type is more ancient and more primitive than the II or B type. Both types existed for unknown reasons simultaneously.

The main difference between the two types resides in the assumption, in the A-type texts, of a constant velocity of the sun, which runs contrary to actual observation but results in regular numerical progressions in the series of numbers on the tables. In the

B texts the numerical progressions show variations in accordance with the variability of the sun's velocity as confirmed by observation. Within the limits of this survey it is impossible to do justice to the contents of the ephemerides without assigning considerably more space than is available to technical discussion. Suffice it to say that the numerical data of these tablets refer to such topics as the year of the Seleucid era, the consecutive months, solar and lunar velocity, the length of daylight and night, the latitude of the moon, the evening of the first visibility of the new moon, the inclination between the ecliptic and the horizon, etc. (See further O. Neugebauer's chapter "Babylonian Astronomy," *The Exact Sciences in Antiquity* [1957], pp. 110-22.)

iii. Eclipses. With the data contained in the ephemerides it is possible to give an accurate computation of lunar eclipses. It seems likely that previously —as early, perhaps, as the time of Sargon I—lunar eclipses could be more or less precisely computed. A more refined method of computation became available only after the ephemerides were developed.

These same data, however, were insufficient for the computation of solar eclipses. The only question they are able to answer is whether a solar eclipse was excluded or possible.

iv. Planets. As in the case of the ephemerides, the planetary theory developed by the Mesopotamian scribes cannot be fully described within this framework. Several different systems were apparently in use simultaneously. They seem to have been modeled after the types A and B of the lunar ephemerides. In general it can be said that the procedure adopted in the planetary ephemerides is analytical. Each phenomenon regarding the planets was treated separately, just as if it concerned an independent body moving in the ecliptic. The planets of regular movement ("inner" planets), such as Venus, were studied without a division of the ecliptic; for others, like Mars ("outer" planets), a division of the ecliptic in six parts became necessary, and the movement of these planets within each of these six parts was considered as "regular."

The results of the Mesopotamian astronomers for the synodic revolutions of the planets are given in Table 6:

Table 6[1]

Planet	Number of revolutions	Years
Mercury	145	46
Venus	5	8
Mars	15	32
Jupiter	65	71
Saturn	57	59

(For detailed information see O. Neugebauer, *Astronomical Cuneiform Texts*, vol. II [1955].)

It should be stated that the conditions and the tools of observation (*alidade, gnomon, polos, clepsydra*) set limits to the precision of the celestial phenomena observed. It was their arithmetical skill and versatility which enabled the Mesopotamian astronomers to go beyond these limitations and to collect the precise numerical data contained in the ephemerides.

[1] O. Neugebauer, *Astronomical Cuneiform Texts* (London: Lund Humphries & Co. Ltd., 1955).

v. Astrology. From the older period (*see* § B2*a above*) date documents which deal with celestial omina which link important events in the life of the community (peace, prosperity; famine, epidemics, flood, war) and the king (universal dominion, victory; rebellion, usurpation) with certain celestial phenomena. The most important of these texts is known as *Enūma Anu Enlil,* "When Anu, Enlil . . ." (see E. F. Weidner, *Archiv für Orientforschung,* 14 [1942], 172-95, 308-18; 17 [1954], 71-89). This kind of omina texts may have served as the starting point for the horoscopic astrology of Hellenistic times.

In this connection and in connection with the wide spread of "Chaldean" astrology, it should be remembered that the rise of astrology in Mesopotamia and horoscopic astrology is rather recent. The earliest horoscope in Mesopotamia dates from 410 B.C., when Mesopotamia formed part of the Persian Empire; other cuneiform horoscopes belong to the Seleucid period; in Egypt the earliest horoscopes are from the reign of Augustus. Further, it should be kept in mind that the number of astrological texts, almost all of which belong to the Seleucid period, is very small if compared with the number of astronomical texts.

For detailed study of the older history of astrology and its subsequent popularity in Hellenistic and later times, see such works as F. Cumont, *L'Égypte des astrologues* (1937); A. Bouché-Leclerq, *L'astrologie grecque* (1899); A. Festugière, *La révélation d'Hermès Trismégiste,* vol. I; *L'astrologie et les sciences occultes* (2nd ed., 1950).

3. Medicine. The larger majority of medical texts comes from the royal library of Ashurbanipal (seventh century B.C.) and from temple archives. From the earliest times the art of medicine and the magical technique of the exorciser were well kept apart, and the former may be considered an objective science. A Sumerian text from *ca.* 2100 B.C. from Nippur contains a series of prescriptions without resorting to magical practices. In addition, this text gives the impression of being the result of long previous experience. In another, Assyrian text a repertory apparently composed by an individual physician is given which contains a list of plants with the corresponding disease and the proper method of preparation and application in three parallel columns.

To the Kassite period belongs a group of tablets which deal with diagnosis and prognosis. In them the practices of the magician and the physician appear together. *See* the work of R. Labat quoted in the *bibliography;* and for possible parallels between the Akkadian, Greek, and Indian procedure, see J. Filliozat, "Pronostics akkadiens, grecs et indiens," *JA* (1952).

In some texts a general classification after such symptoms as fever, skin disease, partial or general paralysis, troubles attributed to possession by a demon or witchcraft, is given. In other cases the Mesopotamian compilers introduced some kind of order among the medical documents by classifying them after the afflicted parts of the body. Thus, special collections of texts have been found which deal with diseases of the skull and face, the ears, the eyes, the respiratory organs, the liver (a particularly severe and often incurable kind of jaundice is called *aḫḫāzu* after the name of a demon), the genital organs, the urinary tract (a bronze tube was used for injections into the urethra), the intestines, the rectum, the lower extremities, etc.

Little direct information exists on surgery. In general it is clear from indirect evidence that serious and delicate operations (cataract[?], treatment of pleurisy by incision[?], trepanation[?]) were successfully executed. No document, however, describes the methods which were followed in such cases. The surgeon's art seems to have been handed down by direct oral instruction.

In spite of the fact that in many instances the documents deal side by side with magic and medicine, a distinct tendency to separate the two procedures and to adopt a more enlightened method of approach is apparent. Although the distinction between left (unfavorable) and right (favorable), all-important in divinatory practices, occurs also in medicine, it seems to have lost most of its force. Similarly, in the case of the symbolism of colors, so important in magic and divination, but explained in terms of their relation to certain facts confirmed by medical experience (red, inflammation; yellow, liver disease), a positivistic attitude of mind comes to the fore. The notion of the importance of the evolution of a disease, the recognition of the possibility of more than one diagnosis in the case of identical symptoms, the observation of a regular pattern in the condition of patients suffering from certain fevers, are so many indications of the same trend.

The products of Mesopotamian pharmaceutists and druggists enjoyed wide popularity in the Near East and were traded and used over an extensive area. The correct understanding of the plants and minerals used for them, their composition and formula, has been promoted by recent studies on chemistry, geology, and botany. (See R. C. Thompson, *A Dictionary of Assyrian Chemistry and Geology* [1936]; *A Dictionary of Assyrian Botany* [1949].)

C. ISRAEL. In our main source, the Bible, the data on ancient Hebrew science are incidental and very small in number. This is partly because of the character and purpose of the Bible. In addition, the political vicissitudes which accompanied the existence of Israel hardly ever permitted the creation of conditions favorable to scientific activity.

1. Mathematics. There is no evidence for anything even approaching an organized discipline of mathematics in the Bible. Scattered evidence for the use of both the decimal and the sexagesimal system can be found. The names of the numbers 30 to 90 are the plural forms of the numbers 3 to 9 (שלש=3, as against שלשים=30, etc.). Among the dry and liquid measures the proportion 1 to 10 occurs (Ezek. 45:11). Next to the sequence 1 talent=60 minas=3,600 shekels, based on the sexagesimal system, 1 talent is also equalled to 3,000 shekels (Exod. 38:25-26; cf. Ezek. 45:12). *See further* WEIGHTS AND MEASURES.

The extent of ancient Hebrew knowledge of (empirical) geometry can only be guessed from references to its use for surveying purposes which presuppose considerable practical skill.

2. Astronomy. The sum total of elementary observations of celestial phenomena found in the Bible can be summed up briefly.

a. **Sun and moon.** *See* SUN; MOON.

b. **Eclipse.** Eclipses of the moon may be alluded to in the expressions "to become dark, to be darkened," in Isa. 13:10 (חשך); Joel 2:10 (קדר); and "to turn into blood" in Joel 2:31. It should be noted that these same passages also mention the darkening of the sun. See also Matt. 24:29; Acts 2:20; Rev. 6:12.

c. **Stars.** "The stars" (כוכב; Ugaritic *kbkb;* Akkadian *kakkabu;* etc.) are created by God (Gen. 1:16); the "stars of heaven" are mentioned in Gen. 22:17 and elsewhere; the "shining stars" praise God (Ps. 148:3); the "stars of God" occur in Isa. 14:13; their multitude is mentioned in Gen. 15:5 and their height in Job 22:12.

Of individual stars, "Morning Star" or "DAY STAR" (הילל, *Hêlēl* [Isa. 14:12; KJV "Lucifer"]; *see* SHAHAR) and KAIWAN (i.e., Saturn; כיון [Amos 5:26]; Akkadian *kaiawānu; cf.* REPHAN [Acts 7:43]) deserve to be mentioned.

The star of Bethlehem (Matt. 2:2) was probably a comet or a meteor.

Worship of the stars and other celestial bodies was explicitly forbidden (Deut. 4:19; see also II Kings 17:16; Jer. 19:13; Ezek. 8:16).

d. **Constellations.** Among the constellations mentioned (Job 9:9; 38:31-32), only the identification of כסיל (Job 9:9; 38:31; Amos 5:8), "insolent, stupid, dull," with ORION (plural כסיליהם [Isa. 13:10; "their constellations"] may refer to Orion and its constellations), and of כימה (Job 9:9; 38:31; Amos 5:8), "heap, herd" (Arabic *kūmu*), with the PLEIADES seems to be reasonably certain. In the case of עיש (Job 9:9 [עש]; 38:32 [עיש על בניה]), "lion" (Arabic '*ayyūt*), there is doubt as to whether Arcturus (KJV), Ursa Major, the Pleiades(?), or Hyades(?) are meant (RSV "the Bear"). Even more uncertain are חדרי תימן (Job 9:9), the "chambers of the south" (i.e., the constellations of the S zodiac[?]); מזרות (Job 38:32), MAZZAROTH, a plural form, which has been taken as a reference to Venus as morning and evening star, the Hyades, or the S constellations of the zodiac; and מזרים (Job 37:9), *mᵉzārîm*, which is rather an expression for the cold N winds than a reference to the Hyades (RSV "whirlwind").

e. **Astrology.** "Astrology" as a designation for the art based on the assumption of an inescapable relationship between the celestial bodies and terrestrial happenings was obviously not officially at home in Israel. Isa. 47:13 exhorts Babylon to resort to astrologers, stargazers, and monthly prognosticators in a last effort to escape its doom (הברי שמים, lit., "dividers of the sky"; ἀστρόλογοι). In Dan. 1:20; 2:2 the translation "conjurer" (cf. RSV "ENCHANTER") for אשף (Akkadian *išippu*) is preferable to the KJV "astrologer." The same disregard for astrology appears from Jer. 10:2:

> [Be not] dismayed at the signs of the heavens
> because the nations are dismayed at them.

See also ASTROLOGER.

3. Calendar. *See* CALENDAR.

4. Medicine. *See* MEDICINE; DISEASES.

Bibliography. Only the bare essentials of a necessarily very extensive literature can be given. Such general works as A. Rey, *La science orientale avant les Grecs* (2nd ed., 1942); G. Sarton, *A History of Science,* vol. I (1952); B. L. van der

Waerden, *Science Awakening* (1954; English trans. by A. Dresden of the original version in Dutch under the title *Het ontwaken der wetenschap*); O. Neugebauer, *The Exact Sciences in Antiquity* (2nd ed., 1957); R. Taton, ed., *La science antique et médiévale* (1957), in *Histoire générale des sciences*, vol. I, may be supplemented by the following more specialized works.

For Egyptian mathematics texts, see: (*a*) Kahun: F. L. Griffith, *Hieratic Papyri from Kahun and Gurob* (1898). (*b*) Berlin: H. Schack-Schackenburg, *Zeitschrift für aegyptische Sprache*, 38 (1900), 135 ff; 40 (1902), 65 ff. (*c*) Rhind: A. B. Chace, H. P. Manning, R. C. Archibald, and L. S. Bull, *The Rhind Mathematical Papyrus* (2 vols.; 1927-29). (*d*) Moscow: V. V. Struve, *Quellen und Studien zur Geschichte der Mathematik*, Abteilung A, Band I (1930). (*e*) British Museum leather roll: S. R. K. Glanville, *JEA*, 13 (1927), 232 ff. *Catalogue générale . . . du Musée du Caire*, *Ostraca* (1901), pp. 95 f. (*f*) Cairo tablets, *Recueil de travaux relatifs à la philologie et à l'archéologie égyptiennes*, vol. 28 (1906).

For studies of Egyptian mathematics texts, see: O. Neugebauer, *Die Grundlagen der ägyptischen Bruchrechnung* (1926). T. E. Peet, *Mathematics in Ancient Egypt* (1931), *Bulletin of the John Rylands Library* 15, a concise and very good summary. B. L. van der Waerden, "Die Entstehungsgeschichte der ägyptischen Bruchrechnung," *Quellen und Studien zur Geschichte der Mathematik*, Abteilung B, Band 4 (1937), pp. 359-82: on fractions. On the 2/*n* table of the Papyrus Rhind, see also: E. M. Bruins, "Ancient Egyptian Arithmetic: 2/*N*," *Koninklijke Nederlandsche Akademie van Wetenschappen* (Amsterdam), *Proceedings*, Series A, vol. 55, no. 2, pp. 81-91. "Platon et la table égyptienne 2/*n*," *Janus*, XLVI (1957), 253-63.

On Egyptian calendars, see: O. Neugebauer and A. Volten, *Quellen und Studien zur Geschichte der Mathematik*, Abteilung B, Band 4 (1938): on the Papyrus Carlsberg No. 9. H. E. Winlock, "The Origin of the Ancient Egyptian Calendar," *Proceedings of the American Philosophical Society*, vol. 83 (1940). O. Neugebauer, "The Origin of the Egyptian Calendar," *JNES*, vol. I (1942). R. A. Parker, *The Calendars of Ancient Egypt* (1950): for the lunar calendars.

On the "decans," see: A. Beer, ed., *Vistas in Astronomy*, I (1945), 47-51 (article by O. Neugebauer).

On the eclipse, see: W. Erichsen, *Akademie der Wissenschaften und Literatur, Abhandlungen der Geistes- und Sozialwissenschaftlichen Klasse* (1956), no. 2.

On the "secret science of the pharaohs," see: L. Borchardt, *Gegen die Zahlenmystik an der grossen Pyramide bei Gise* (1922). N. F. Wheeler, "Pyramids and Their Purpose," *Antiquity*, 9 (1935), 5-21, 161-89, 292-304.

For Egyptian medical texts, see: (*a*) Ebers: W. Wreszinski, *Der Papyrus Ebers* (transliteration; 1913). B. Ebbell, *The Papyrus Ebers* (translation; 1937). (*b*) Kahun: F. L. Griffith, *Hieratic papyri from Kahun and Gurob* (1898). (*c*) Berlin: W. Wreszinski, *Der grosse medizinische Papyrus des Berliner Museums* (1909). (*d*) Smith: J. H. Breasted, *The Edwin Smith Surgical Papyrus* (1930).

For studies of Egyptian medical texts, see: H. Grapow, *Grundriss der Medizin der alten Ägypter*, vols. I (1954)-VII.1 (1961). G. Lefebvre, *Tableau des parties du corps humain mentionnées par les Égyptiens* (1952); *Essai sur la médecine égyptienne de la période pharaonique* (1956).

Most of the Mesopotamian mathematical texts are to be found in the following publications: O. Neugebauer, *Mathematische Keilschrifttexte* (3 vols.; 1935-37), in *Quellen und Studien zur Geschichte der Mathematik*, Abteilung A, Band 2. F. Thureau-Dangin, *Textes mathématiques babyloniens* (1938; *Ex Oriente Lux*, vol. 1). O. Neugebauer and A. Sachs, *Mathematical Cuneiform Texts* (1945; *American Oriental Series*, vol. 29). For further information, see the chapter "Babylonian Mathematics" in O. Neugebauer, *The Exact Sciences in Antiquity* (1957), pp. 29-48, with bibliography and notes. See also E. M. Bruins, "Areas in Babylonian Mathematics," *Janus*, XLVI (1957), 4-11.

For Mesopotamian astronomical texts see: O. Neugebauer, *Astronomical Cuneiform Texts* (3 vols.; 1955). T. G. Pinches, J. N. Strassmaier, and A. J. Sachs, *Late Babylonian astronomical and related texts* (1955). See further: F. X. Kugler, *Sternkunde*

und Sterndienst in Babel (2 vols.; 1907-10). E. Weidner, *Handbuch der babylonischen Astronomie* (1915). J. Schaumberger, *Sternkunde und Sterndienst* (1935). O. Neugebauer, "Babylonian Astronomy," *The Exact Sciences in Antiquity* (1957), pp. 97-138.

On Mesopotamian medicine, see: F. Kuchler, *Beiträge zur Kenntnis der assyrisch-babylonischen Medizin* (1904). H. Holma, *Die Namen der Körperteile im Assyrisch-Babylonischen* (1911). E. Ebeling, "Keilschrifttexte medizinischen Inhalts," *Archiv für die Geschichte der Medizin*, vol. XIII (1921); vol. XIV (1923). G. Contenau, *La médecine en Assyrie et en Babylonie* (1938). R. Labat, *Traité akkadien de diagnostics et' pronostics médicaux* (1951). H. E. Sigerist, *A History of Medicine*, I (1951), 377-497. S. N. Kramer, "The First Pharmacopoeia," *From the Tablets of Sumer* (1956), pp. 56-60.

On astronomy in Israel, see: G. V. Schiaparelli, *Astronomy in the OT* (1905).

See also the bibliographies under CALENDAR; MEDICINE; DISEASES.

                           M. J. DRESDEN

SCOFFER [לִיץ, *from* לִיץ, *originally* to be spokesman (KJV SCORNER)]; TAUNT [חרף, to be sharp, to say sharp things] (KJV REPROACH). One of several parallel expressions used, mostly in the book of Proverbs, to describe the man who rejects the path of WISDOM (*see also* PATH; WAY). In the OT the scoffer is numbered among the simpletons, the fools (Prov. 1:22), and the wicked (9:7), being the very opposite of the wise (13:1; 14:6; 15:12) and happy man (Ps. 1:1; *see* BLESSEDNESS). Although he is apparently often punished bodily (Prov. 19:25, 29; 21: 11; 22:10), this does not serve to improve him, since he will either abuse (9:7) or hate (vs. 8) his correctors, and will not listen in any case (13:1)! He scoffs at the way of wisdom and right, for the sake of scoffing (1:22), and is a source of strife, quarreling, and abuse (22:10).

His character is perhaps more acutely assessed in 21:24, where he is identified with the man of arrogant pride; this renders him incorrigible, and he seeks wisdom in vain (14:6; 15:12). He is an abomination to men because of his sinful folly (24:9), and thus incurs the dread "scoffing" of God (3:34). In Isa. 29:20 he shares the fate of the ruthless in the day when the meek and the poor are exulting in the Lord (cf. Prov. 3:34).

The word "taunt" describes the derisive mockery and scorn of an exultant enemy (cf. parallel words in Pss. 79:4; 89:51; 102:8). Thus, to be "made a taunt" implies utter defeat and oppression.

The psalmist describes his suffering in terms of the taunts of his enemies (Ps. 102:8) or of his friend (Ps. 55:12)! Nehemiah's enemies attempt a ruse to frighten him, thus putting him to scorn (Neh. 6:13). Pss. 44:13; 79:4 cry out that Israel has become the taunt of the neighboring people, while in Neh. 4:4; Ps. 79:12, Yahweh is bidden to turn their taunts upon their own heads; for Yahweh himself is the real object of this derision (Ps. 79:12; cf. 89:51). The scorn of the enemy against ruined Israel as well as Yahweh is expressed in the phrase: "Where is your God?" (Ps. 42:10). Zeph. 2:8 envisions retribution in the reversal of the "taunts of Moab" which have been heard by Yahweh. "Taunt" further appears in a series of synonyms for utter devastation by divine judgment in Jer. 24:9; 42:18; 44:8, 12; 49:13; Ezek. 5:15 (parallel to such words as "desolation," "reproach," "curse," "horror," BYWORD").

Bibliography. R. Pfeiffer, *Introduction to the OT* (1948), pp. 645-59; C. Fritsch, Introduction and Exegesis of Proverbs, *IB,* IV (1955), 767 ff.   J. A. WHARTON

SCORPION [עקרב; Arab. *'aqrab;* Assyrian *akrabu;* Ethio. *'aqrab;* σκορπίος]. An arachnid (not an insect), of which there are a dozen species in Palestine and ninety per cent of which are the yellow *Buthus quinquestriatus.* Scorpions are slow, nocturnal animals which prey upon insects and other arachnids, including other scorpions. Most species carry a poisonous sting at the end of the tail, which is fatal to their prey and extremely painful even to man.

According to Deut. 8:15, the wilderness abounded in both serpents and scorpions. The מעלה עקרבים, "Ascent of AKRABBIM," may have been so named because of an abundance of them.

Rehoboam threatens his people with a worse yoke than his father, Solomon, put upon them (I Kings 12:11, 14; II Chr. 10:11, 14). In fact, it will be as much worse as a scorpion is more dreaded than a whip.

Ezekiel is told not to fear his people even though their words and looks compare with briars, thorns, and scorpions (2:6).

Jesus, in giving the Seventy authority over serpents and scorpions, was referring to everything opposed to himself (Luke 10:19). He tells his disciples that earthly fathers know better than to give a child a stone, a serpent, or a scorpion when he asks for food (Luke 11:12). God, being wiser than men, knows even better how to answer requests addressed to him.

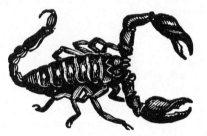

32. Scorpion

The first woe to strike those not sealed upon their foreheads is locusts, large as horses, equipped with stings like scorpions, which will torment them for five months (Rev. 9:3, 5, 10).

See also FAUNA § F3*a.*

Fig. SCO 32.

Bibliography. F. S. Bodenheimer, *Animal Life in Palestine* (1935); J. L. Cloudsley-Thompson, *Spiders, Scorpions, Centipedes, and Mites* (1958).   W. W. FRERICHS

SCOURGING. Beating with rod or staff (שבט, מטה) was a form of discipline and punishment dealt out to slaves, children, and—in the wisdom literature—to fools (Exod. 21:20; Prov. 13:24; 26:3; Isa. 9:4). More painful was the hide whip (שוט; I Kings 12:11, 14; properly for beasts [cf. Prov. 26:3; Nah. 3:2]), of which the עקרב, "scorpion"—so called because of its sting—was the cruelest type (II Kings 12:11, 14).

As a judicial penalty forty strokes are the maximum allowed by the law of Deut. 25:1-3, to prevent the undue humiliation of the culprit. The number varied in accord with the offense (vs. 2), but the laws fail to specify which crimes are punished by scourging (save, perhaps, for the case of defamation: ויסרו of Deut. 22:18 is understood by Jos. Antiq. IV.viii.23 and Sifre as "beat" [so RSV]). The offender was placed in a reclining position and beaten under the supervision of the judge.

Later Jewish law punished with scourging contraventions of biblical prohibitions not otherwise penalized (M. Mak. 3:1-9). The Mishna describes the procedure thus: After being examined to determine whether he could stand flogging, the culprit was bound by his hands to a pillar, and his back and chest were bared. The minister of the synagogue (חזן הכנסת; cf. Matt. 10:17) administered the flogging with a whip of calfskin, doubled twice and interlaced with two ass-hide straps (hence the verb μαστιγόω in Deut. 25:2-3 LXX; Matt. 10:17, from μάστιξ, by which the LXX renders שוט). One third of the strokes were laid upon the culprit's chest and two thirds on his back, to the total of thirty-nine (ארבעים חסר אחת=τεσσαράκοντα παρὰ μίαν, "forty less one"; II Cor. 11:24; cf. Jos. Antiq. IV.viii.21, 23)—one stroke fewer than allowed in Deuteronomy, to allow for error. If he befouled himself, the flogging was halted; if he died under the whip, there was no guilt for him (M. Mak. 3.10-14).

Roman practice in scourging varied with the status of the culprit. Freemen might be beaten with rods of elm or birch (*virga,* ῥάβδος; cf. I Cor. 4:21, whence ῥαβδίζω in Acts 16:22; II Cor. 11:25) by the lictors (ῥαβδοῦχος, "bearer of rods"; cf. Acts 16:35, 38). Slaves and non-Romans might be examined by scourging with a whip (μάστιξ in Acts 22:24, whence μαστίζω in vs. 25). The victim was stripped (16:22) and his hands tied to a post with thongs (22:25). Slaves, aliens, and criminals condemned to death might be beaten with a whip of knotted cord or leather straps, often weighted with pieces of metal or bone to aggravate the torture.* This worst form of scourging, known as *flagellum* (whence φραγέλλιον in

33. Roman scourges

John 2:15; φραγελλόω in Matt. 27:26; Mark 15:15], was administered upon the naked back, and was at times fatal. Fig. SCO 33.

Bibliography. "Stripes," *Jewish Encyclopedia,* XI (1905), 569-70; W. Smith, *et al.,* "Flagrum," *Dictionary of Greek and Roman Antiquities* (3rd ed., 1914). M. GREENBERG

SCREECH OWL. KJV translation of לילית (Isa. 34:14; RSV NIGHT HAG). *See* LILITH.

SCREEN [מסך, *from* סכך, to cover]; KJV HANGING. Alternately: COVERING. The priestly term for the three screens of the TABERNACLE furnishings.

It describes the screen separating the Holy of Holies from the rest of the TENT (e.g., Exod. 35:12 [LXX καταπέτασμα]; 40:21; etc.). For this screen the Hebrew also uses the word פרכת, "veil." The Greek does not distinguish consistently between the two Hebrew words. The Hebrew often uses both words of this screen. This screen was the richest material of all three, a colored linen with the same cherubic decorations on its inside as on the rest of the hangings of the Holy of Holies. It veiled the dwelling place of God, and on the Day of Atonement blood was sprinkled in front of the veil. *See* ATONEMENT, DAY OF.

The second screen was at the entrance of the tent itself (e.g., Exod. 26:36 [LXX ἐπίπαστρον], 37 [LXX καταπέτασμα]; etc.). This was the same linen material but without the cherubim and not of such excellent workmanship—i.e., of the embroiderer, not of the designer.

The third screen was at the gate of the court (Exod. 27:16 [LXX κάλυμμα]; 38:18 [LXX καταπέτασμα]; etc.). This was twenty cubits wide and was of the same material as the screen at the tent door.

No veil or screen is mentioned in Solomon's temple, but II Chr. 3:14 mentions the inmost veil (פרכת). If the P tabernacle imitates Solomon's temple, then the P veil and screen would confirm the Chronicles reference in part; otherwise the P veil and screens point to the second temple. For Herod's temple the evidence is not conclusive. Matt. 27:51 = Mark 15:38 = Luke 23:45 record the rending of the inmost veil when Jesus died. Heb. 6:19; 9:3 also refer to the veil of the Holy of Holies of the tabernacle. Heb. 10:20 uses the veil as a figure of the flesh of Jesus Christ, which is the only way believers enter into the presence of God. The NT Greek word for "veil" is καταπέτασμα. Since the law of the OT was canonical in NT times, Herod's temple certainly had the veils and Josephus' description of the two temple veils confirms this.

Bibliography. T. Zahn, "Der zerrissene Tempelvorhang," *NKZ,* XIII (1902), 729-56; H. Laible, "Der zerrissene Tempelvorhang und die eingestürzte Oberschwelle des Tempeleingangs vom Talmud bezeugt," *NKZ,* XXXV (1924), 287-314; H. L. Strack and P. Billerbeck, *Kommentar zum NT aus Talmud und Midrasch,* III (1926), 733-36.
G. HENTON DAVIES

SCRIBE [γραμματεύς]. A class of professional exponents and teachers of the law in postexilic Judaism.

1. Meaning of the term
2. Origins
3. Scribes and Pharisees
4. Scribes in the Sanhedrin
5. The scribes and Jesus
Bibliography

1. Meaning of the term. The original scribe, or *sôphēr,* was a person able to "cipher" (*sāphar*), and from this came the meaning of "secretary" or "scribe." At Jer. 36:26, the term is applied to an official who had charge of legal documents, such as deeds of purchase (cf. Jer. 32:12-15), and who had a special chamber in the royal palace (cf. II Kings 18:18; Jer. 36:12). At II Kings 22:3 ff, Shaphan the scribe appears to have been a kind of minister of finance, and, in the reign of Hezekiah, Shebna the scribe was secretary of state as well (Isa. 36:3; cf. 22:15).

Thus in pre-exilic times the term had no religious significance, but applied to a purely secular office.

There was another class, however, among whom the art of writing was cultivated, though the term *sophēr* never appears to have been applied to them before the Exile; this was the priestly caste, the first specialists in, and guardians of, the law. While the ancient class of professional scribes did no more than supply the name, the spiritual ancestors of the scribes of later Judaism were the pre-exilic priestly exponents of the law.

2. Origins. The scribes as a professional class of "doctors of the law" had their origins in the conditions of the Exile. It was then that the law became the center of all Jewish life and exiled Israelites occupied themselves in its study.

These early scribes cannot, however, have been simply jurists in the narrower sense (as they became in later times). They were also the wise men (*ḥakhāmîm*), the "men of understanding," the "just men," of Proverbs, Ecclesiasticus, and the book of Daniel (Dan. 11:33, 35; 12:3; cf. Ecclus. 38:24 ff; *see* § 3 *below*). It is also undoubtedly to this class of postexilic doctors of the law that we owe the selection and fixing of the canon of the OT. They were men of (sacred) letters, occupying themselves in gathering together Israel's sacred literature as well as interpreting it; in addition they were copyists, editors, and guardians of the textual purity of scripture.

It was at the time of the restoration under Ezra the scribe that the Sopherim emerged as a distinctive and influential professional class of teachers and interpreters of the law. Ezra is the type par excellence of these earliest postexilic doctors of the law (Ezra 7:6, 11-12; Neh. 8:1, 4, 9, 13; 12:26, 36). He is described as a "scribe skilled in the law of Moses" (Ezra 7:6), and as one who "had set his heart to study the law of the LORD, and to do it, and to teach his statutes and ordinances in Israel" (vs. 10). The twofold function of interpreter and teacher was characteristic of the profession. The (νομο)διδάσκαλοι, or "teachers (of the Law)," in the NT are identical with the νομικοί ("lawyers") or γραμματεῖς (Luke 5:17; cf. 2:46; 7:30).

3. Scribes and Pharisees. Like Ezra the priest-scribe (cf. Ezra 7:12), the scribes of the restoration were, according to our sources (Neh. 8:7; II Chr. 34:13), drawn from the families of the priests and Levites, forming themselves into guilds or clans (I

Chr. 2:55). The classic description occurs at Ecclus. 38:24–39:15.

> He will be filled with the spirit of understanding;
> he will pour forth words of wisdom
> and give thanks to the Lord in prayer.
> He will direct his counsel and knowledge aright,
> and meditate on his secrets.
> He will reveal instruction in his teaching,
> and will glory in the law of the Lord's covenant.
> Many will praise his understanding,
> and it will never be blotted out;
> his memory will not disappear,
> and his name will live through all generations.
> Nations will declare his wisdom,
> and the congregation will proclaim his praise;
> if he lives long, he will leave a name greater than
>   a thousand,
> and if he goes to rest, it is enough for him.
>   (Ecclus. 39:6b-11.)

According to rabbinic tradition, the period following the restoration was characterized by the rule of the Men of the Great Synagogue. The identity of these legendary figures cannot be certain, but it seems likely that they were scribes or leaders of the people drawn from the scribes. At the time of the Seleucid Hellenizing of Israel, it was a "synagogue of the scribes" (συναγωγὴ γραμματέων) which provided the religious backbone of the movement of popular resistance which culminated in the Maccabean Revolt (I Macc. 7:11-17). They belonged to the HASIDIM, "the pious," or "the loyalists" for the law; and they formed the spearhead of the Hasidean movement. (It is possible to interpret I Macc. 7:11 ff to mean that the "group of scribes" mentioned at vs. 12 as resisting Seleucid pressure represented at the time the entire movement or party of the Hasidim.)

It was sometime early in the Greek period that an influential group of lay scribes succeeded in forming a popular, democratic political party, consisting of themselves (at its head), with adherents and partisans from the people; they came to be known as the PHARISEES. The history of the scribes, or, at any rate, of the most influential section of them, the Pharisaic scribes, comes from now on to be the history of the Pharisaic party.

The important evidence for the position of the scribes in the time of Jesus comes from the gospels and Acts. The scribes (without further connection or qualification) are mentioned a number of times (e.g., Matt. 13:52; 9:3; Mark 9:11, 14). Individual scribes are featured in the gospel narrative at Mark 12:28 (cf. Matt. 8:19; Luke 10:25). The combination of σοφοί and γραμματεῖς at Matt. 23:34 (cf. I Cor. 1:20) reminds us of the connection between the *ḥakhamim* and the *sopherim. See § 2 above.*

These references to the scribes simply as such show clearly that they represented a distinctive class in the community. They practiced their legal profession throughout Palestine (and as certainly in the DISPERSION). Mark 7:1 refers to certain of the scribes from Jerusalem, and Matt. 7:29 to scribes of the masses outside Jerusalem; Luke 5:17 speaks of scribes drawn from every village in Galilee and Judea and from Jerusalem.

Most other references occur in combination with associated groups, in particular the "Pharisees and the scribes," or the "scribes and the Pharisees." The

evidence divides into two main categories: (a) that of Mark (and parallels) and Acts, and (b) that of Matthew and Luke.

Mark and Acts agree in making special mention of the "scribes of the Pharisees" (e.g., Mark 2:16 [cf. Luke 5:30]; Acts 23:9: lit., "some of the scribes belonging to the sect of the Pharisees"). Such passages are generally taken to imply that there were scribes with other sectarian affiliations, such as Sadducean scribes.

Mark agrees with Acts in the description of scribes in association with chief priests and elders (e.g., Mark 8:31; 10:33; 11:18, 27; 14:1; 15:31; cf. Matt. 2:4; 21:15; Luke 22:66; 23:10; Acts 4:5; 6:12). The usual order of the terms shows elders to have been the least important of the three groups; Schürer identified them with the lay members of the SANHEDRIN. For reasons not quite obvious (Matthew himself may have been a converted scribe), Matthew substitutes "elders of the people" for the Markan "scribes" at 26:3. The chief priests were the more important of the two remaining groups; they are not only almost invariably mentioned first, but the position of the scribes in relation to the "chief priests" is indicated at Mark 15:31: "the chief priests . . . with the scribes." The Lukan parallel uses ἄρχοντες ("rulers") for the entire group.

4. Scribes in the Sanhedrin. We evidently have to do with the composition of the Sanhedrin, the rulers of the people, consisting, in order of precedence, of chief priests, scribes, and elders. The chief priests were the heads of the priestly class, high priest, ex-high priests, and other leading members of the sacerdotal aristocracy (Acts 4:6: ὅσοι ἦσαν ἐκ γένους ἀρχιερατικοῦ). The scribes were obviously a special, high-ranking group in the Sanhedrin; they may have been identical with the scribes from Jerusalem mentioned at Mark 3:22; 7:1. Next to the high priest and his family, this group of Sanhedrin scribes represented the leading personages in the Jewish bureaucracy of the time.

The chief priests must have belonged, chiefly if not exclusively, to the party of the SADDUCEES. To which party did the Sanhedrin scribes belong? The accepted view is that they adhered strongly to the sect of the Pharisees, but also included Sadducean scribes. What is certain is that there were Pharisaic scribes in the Sanhedrin; Gamaliel (Acts 5:34 ff) was a Pharisee and a scribe. The only evidence we have for the existence of Sadducean scribes is the inference from the passages discussed above, referring to the "scribes of the Pharisees," together with one inconclusive reference in Josephus (War VI.v.3) to ἱερογραμματεῖς, where the context appears to favor "priestly scribes." But it is also possible to explain Josephus' term as a general description of Jewish scribes, intended for Greek readers, without any particular reference to priestly or Sadducean scribes. The Sanhedrin scribes may have been entirely Pharisees; they may have shared the rule of the people with the priestly aristocracy, mainly Sadducean, forming a Sadducean-Pharisaic coalition, extremely useful to Rome, with its policy of "divide and rule."

The next important evidence from the gospels is the combination of "Pharisees and scribes" found at

Mark 7:5 (=Matt. 15:1), and the much more frequent combination "scribes and Pharisees," never found in Mark but confined to Matthew, Luke, and to one occurrence in John (Matt. 5:20; 12:38; 23:2, 13-15, 23, 25, 27, 29; Luke 6:7; 11:53; John 8:3).

5. The scribes and Jesus. At Mark 7:5 the phrase "the Pharisees and the scribes" is not a stereotyped formula such as "scribes and Pharisees" has clearly become in Matthew. In the Markan passage it is a substitute for the earlier description "the Pharisees . . . , with some of the scribes, who had come from Jerusalem." This was a definite group of Pharisees with a certain number of Jerusalem scribes. It has all the appearance of having been an official deputation, and, since Jesus was being challenged on a point of law, his interrogators must have been the scribes from Jerusalem. It seems likely that the Pharisees belonged to a local group who had called in the scribes from the capital, possibly members of the Sanhedrin (or their deputies). The same kind of official visit is portrayed by Luke in his version of the healing of the paralytic (5:17 ff); Luke has also introduced his familiar motif of "representative universalism"—the Pharisees and "teachers of the law" (νομοδιδάσκαλοι) come from every village in Galilee and Judea and from Jerusalem (cf. also Luke 7:30 ff).

There is a quite different situation with the combination "scribes and Pharisees." At Luke 6:7; 11:53, the phrase may not yet have become a stereotyped one, but its use in Matthew (and at John 8:3) bears this character. It almost certainly represents a later historical perspective; the scribes are given precedence over the Pharisees, because, as professional lawyers, they were, in fact, much more important than the nonprofessional members of the party.

It might be objected that "scribes and Pharisees" occurs in the words of Jesus himself in the long denunciation of both at Matt. 23, and is therefore original. But in both the Markan and the Lukan parallels (Mark 12:38; Luke 20:45 ff; cf. 11:46) the denunciation is directed against the scribes alone; in Luke (11:39 ff) the Pharisees come in for a separate denouncing. This seems much more likely to reflect the historical situation.

The main business of the scribes was teaching and interpreting the law. This consisted mainly in the transmission of traditional legal judgments, known as HALACHAH, and distinguished from HAGGADAH, or edifying religious discourse. The scribes' real interest—and this applied especially to the Pharisaic scribes—was less in the plain meaning of the text than in the preservation of the legal system built upon it.

Their authority, but not their example, is recognized at Matt. 23:2-3. There are, however, also more spiritually minded scribes in the gospels (Matt. 8:19=Luke 9:57), and the gospel portrait of scribes, as well as Pharisees, requires to some extent to be corrected. It was to their faithful transmission of the religion of Israel in the Greek and Roman periods that we owe the preservation of our OT scriptures, together with the foundations in Judaism of the Christian religion.

Bibliography. E. Schürer, *History of the Jewish People in the Time of Jesus Christ* (1885), div. II, vol. I, pp. 306-51; W. R. Smith, *The OT in the Jewish Church* (1907), pp. 42-72; G. F. Moore, *Judaism in the First Centuries of the Christian Era* (1925-27); I. Elbogen, *Der jüdische Gottesdienst* (1931); C. Guignebert, *The Jewish World in the Time of Jesus* (1939), pp. 67-73; W. O. E. Oesterley, *The Jews and Judaism During the Greek Period* (1941), pp. 227-33; J. Lauterbach, *Rabbinical Essays* (1951), pp. 182 ff.   MATTHEW BLACK

SCRIP. A KJV archaism, referring to a wallet or a bag of a wayfarer; in I Sam. 17:40 a shepherd's bag (ילקוט; RSV "wallet") and in Mark 6:8; Luke 9:3; 10:4; 22:35-36, a traveler's bag (πήρα; RSV "bag").   J. M. MYERS

*SCRIPTURE, AUTHORITY OF. The Bible has been acknowledged as authoritative by Christians in every century, including the first. Even in apostolic days, when the NT was not yet written, the church had its Bible—namely, the scriptures of what we now call the OT. When in the course of time a NT had been added to the original Jewish Bible, the Christian Bible as a book of two testaments came to be accepted as authoritative in the same sense as the Jewish Bible had been authoritative both for Jews and for Christians in the apostolic age (*see* BIBLE; CANON OF THE NT). Thus, church and Bible are inseparable; there never was a time when the church existed without the Bible or when the church did not acknowledge the authority of the Bible. But though it is clear that the Bible is authoritative, it is not at all easy to define the nature of its authority. This question, to which little attention had been given up to the end of the eighteenth century, became one of the most urgent and difficult questions of theological discussion in the twentieth century. This was the direct result of the revolution in historical and literary scientific method which took place in the nineteenth century.

1. Authority of scripture in the apostolic church
2. From the apostolic age to the nineteenth century
3. Inadequate solutions of the problem of biblical authority
   a. The authority of plenary inspiration
   b. The authority of the church
   c. The authority of religious experience
   d. Rational and moral authority ("progressive revelation")
   e. The authority of poetic inspiration
4. Toward a more adequate view
   a. The authority of Christ
   b. The Scriptures as witness to Christ
5. The Word of God and the word of man
Bibliography

1. Authority of scripture in the apostolic church. The NT writers regard the scriptures of the OT as completely authoritative. They have unquestioningly taken over the view of rabbinic Judaism, that the Scriptures were given by God through his Spirit as the means by which the revelation originally imparted to the patriarchs and prophets of old might be communicated to the generations which came after them. The attitude of the whole apostolic church is epitomized in the words addressed by Paul (or his admirer) to Timothy: "From childhood you have been acquainted with the sacred writings which are able to instruct you for salvation through faith in

Christ Jesus. Every scripture inspired by God is also profitable for teaching, for reproof, for correction, and for training in righteousness, that the man of God may be complete, equipped for every good work" (II Tim. 3:15-17 RSV mg.). The ancient men of faith, to whom the original revelation had been given, had been moved by the Spirit to commit to writing the sacred truths which were to instruct the generations yet unborn (e.g., Acts 4:25). Thus, the words of scripture could be cited as the direct utterance of God (e.g., Heb. 5:5) or of the Holy Spirit (e.g., Heb. 3:7); sometimes a scriptural passage is quoted under the simple formula: "He says" (λέγει; e.g., Eph. 4:8; 5:14; RSV "It is said" is inaccurate). Moses and the prophets had spoken God's truth to every succeeding generation (Luke 16:29-31). The narrative of God's dealings with his people in past times was "written down for our instruction, upon whom the end of the ages has come" (I Cor. 10:11). Thus, the apostolic church believed that God had revealed his character and purpose to the patriarchs and prophets of Israel and that the Jewish scriptures were the written record of this revelation. But these scriptures could be understood only in the light of Christ's fulfilment of them (Luke 24:27, 44-45; John 5:39); the Jews themselves could not rightly comprehend them, because they did not possess the key to their mysteries—namely, Christ. Even the prophets themselves did not understand many of the things which they wrote, for such things could be apprehended only in the light of Christ's coming (I Pet. 1: 10-12). The Sacred Scriptures recorded the witness of the prophets to the Christ who was to come, while the preaching church bore its living testimony to the truth that Jesus of Nazareth was he.

Thus, the apostolic church, while it held no particular theory concerning the mode of the communication of the revelation recorded by the scriptural authors, believed that God had indeed spoken through the Scriptures. It worked out no theory of the "inspiration" of scripture; indeed, the word and the idea of inspiration are hardly biblical at all. (The word occurs only in the KJV of II Tim. 3:16, cited above from the RSV; the idea behind the phrase "every scripture inspired by God" is that God has breathed into the dry dust of the scriptural words the breath of life; cf. Gen. 2:7). In fact, the apostolic church did not believe in the "inspiration" of scripture in the sense in which later Christians, influenced by pagan ideas (cf. Vergil's Sibyl, *Aeneid* VI), came to believe in it. The veil which lies over the understanding at the reading of the Old Covenant is lifted only by Christ (II Cor. 3:14); the letter of scripture, even if engraved in stone, deadens, and the Spirit alone can breathe life into it. The Scriptures were not held to be authoritative on the ground that they were "inspired."

2. From the apostolic age to the nineteenth century. No official doctrine (dogma or church definition) of biblical authority was put forward during this whole period, because no heretic had arisen to dispute the authority of the Scriptures. Marcion (died *ca.* 160) questioned the authority of the OT, and the Alexandrians (Clement, Origen) during the next century found difficulties in its literal inter-

pretation, which they eased by their allegorical method (*see* ALLEGORY; CANON OF THE NT); but no major conflicts arose, and the authority of the Scriptures was accepted by all parties to the christological and other controversies of the ancient church. So matters continued through the Middle Ages and even through the Reformation period; Calvin would have agreed with Aquinas that theology was a matter of deducing and systematizing the truths which were contained in the inerrant words of scripture. It was the great revolution in historical method, which took place in the nineteenth century, that opened the question of biblical authority in its acute modern form. If, as a result of the application of scientific historical and literary methods (higher and lower criticism) to the books of the Bible, it was now no longer possible to believe in the literal inerrancy of scripture, in what sense could it still be believed that the Bible is authoritative? *See* BIBLICAL CRITICISM.

3. Inadequate solutions of the problem of biblical authority. *a. The authority of plenary inspiration.* An immediate consequence of the rise of the critical method was to provoke an extreme reaction in the form of theories of plenary inspiration. Frightened by the excesses of the Tübingen school of criticism and its successors, conservatives began to lay emphasis upon the literal inerrancy of the Bible, as inspired or even dictated by the Holy Spirit, in a manner that was novel in the history of Christian doctrine. Unbiblical notions of inspiration once more played a prominent part in the discussion, reviving the pagan conceptions of inspiration which had first entered Christian thought as a result of the Hellenization of the gospel in the second and third centuries A.D. The unbiblical word "inspiration" became the storm center of controversy, and the term "fundamentalism" has been widely applied to this type of view as a result of the appearance of a series of booklets on "the fundamentals" published in America from 1909 to 1915.

Nothing could better illustrate the devastating effects of this historical revolution upon traditional Christian belief than the triumphant recrudescence of fundamentalism, which has had a powerful appeal amid the very great religious confusion of the age, in the middle decades of the twentieth century. The widespread positivistic attitude of mind, which holds that scientific truth is the only kind of truth, is paradoxically the great strength of the fundamentalist position: since there is no other kind of truth than literal truth, either the stories of Gen. 1-3 are a literal, scientific account of creation, or they are false; there is no such thing as the truth of poetry for a generation brought up to believe that there is only one kind of truth. During the earlier years of the twentieth century, when biblical criticism seemed to be indissolubly bound up with liberal theology, the rejection of liberalism and belief in the biblical theology seemed to involve the repudiation of criticism altogether, but now it has been abundantly demonstrated that criticism and biblical theology are, in fact, not in opposition to each other, but belong together. *See also* INSPIRATION; REVELATION.

b. The authority of the church. Sometimes it is suggested that the Bible is authoritative because there stands behind it the authority of the church. The authority of scripture is therefore derivative from that of the church. It was the church (whether Jewish or Christian) which in the first place accepted the various books of scripture, while it rejected others, and thus the church is the supreme authority even over the Scriptures.

Now it is true that the relation of the church's authority to that of the Bible is a very complex and difficult problem; but this solution of it is altogether oversimplified and will not bear careful scrutiny. In the first place, it confuses authority with authorization; the church authorized the canon of the Bible, but it did not confer its authority upon it. In authorizing a canon of scripture, the church recognized an authority which it did not create. Secondly, having adopted a scriptural canon, the church must submit every question of faith and morals to the test of scripture and is no longer free to accept new doctrines which are not themselves demonstrable by scriptural warrant.

c. The authority of religious experience. In the earlier years of the twentieth century liberal theologians developed the view that the authority of scripture results from the fact that the Bible is the normative record of man's developing religious experience. The men of the Bible, especially the prophets, were religious geniuses, the fine flower of a people which enjoyed a national genius for religion, just as the Greeks had a genius for philosophy or the Romans for law.

This kind of theory, though still enjoying considerable popularity, is inadequate, primarily because it does not fit the biblical evidence itself: the Hebrew prophets do not fall easily into the class of "religious genius," and they would have been astonished to hear that their backsliding fellow countrymen had a genius for religion. Moreover, the theory does not account for the objectivity of scriptural authority: if we can say only that the Bible is authoritative because it is inspiring, what are we to say to those who declare that they are not inspired by it or about those parts of the Bible which we ourselves do not feel to be very inspiring?

d. Rational and moral authority ("progressive revelation"). Closely related to the foregoing theory and often compounded with it is the view that the progressive revelation of God's will and character, which the Bible enshrines, commends itself to the rational and moral consciousness of the human race and compels its assent ("We needs must love the highest when we see it"). God revealed himself as completely as the developing conscience of mankind was able to understand, and thus the Bible traces men's evolving ideas of God's character from primitive tribalistic notions to the ultimate conception of God as the Father of Jesus Christ. The Bible is thus the record of a progressive revelation which at each stage of human spiritual evolution is authoritative.

This theory is valuable insofar as it does away with the necessity of claiming that all parts of the record are equally "inspired," but it does not account for certain hard facts. Why, e.g., did the spiritual consciousness of mankind stop evolving about the end of the first century A.D.? Why may we not ex-

pect progressive revelation to continue, and why should we not look for new and greater Christs? And what are we to say to those good pagans, who are no less rational or moral than we, but who fail to be convinced by the biblical revelation?

e. The authority of poetic inspiration. Reaction from "liberal" views of this kind expressed itself in different ways, and toward the middle of the twentieth century a new conception of inspiration was put forward in certain quarters, notably by Austin Farrer (*see bibliography*). The inspired minds of the sacred writers perceived the truths of revelation and gave expression to them, not in literal prose (as fundamentalists insist), but in great prophetic images, which convey the biblical truth in much the same way as poetry, drama, or parable conveys truth in other fields. Those who (with Bultmann) would demythologize the gospel are as far as possible from the true scriptural method of imparting truth, for ultimate truth can be expressed only by means of the religious imagination, not by discursive reasoning. The NT writers themselves were aware of the nonliteral character of their imagery, and it is the modern demythologizers who have fallen into the error of literalism and have failed to understand the means by which religious truth can be expressed or communicated.

This theory has the great advantage of delivering us from literalism while yet at the same time it takes the biblical revelation very seriously; its danger is that it can easily fall over into an uninhibited proliferation of typological images and allegorical meanings, which recall the more luxuriant growths of Alexandrian speculation.

4. Toward a more adequate view. There is doubtless truth in each of the above kinds of view, but the defect of all of them is that they say little about God's action in history. A truer view would be one which starts from the fact that the history of Israel, culminating in Jesus Christ and his church, is a unique history with a significance paralleled by no other historical development.

a. The authority of Christ. The Scriptures (like the church) have no authority apart from Christ. They do not differ (as we now know) from other books because of the way in which they were written; they are amenable to the canons of literary and historical criticism just as other books are; they are not even distinctive on account of any ideas about God which they may contain—e.g., that he is love—for such ideas are found in other books which are not regarded as "scripture." The Bible must, then, derive its authority from the authority of Christ. If Christ is authoritative ("Lord"), then the Bible is authoritative; if Christ is just a man like other men, albeit a very good man, perhaps a religious genius, then the Bible is just a book like other books, doubtless a very good book and perhaps a work of religious genius. But if Christ is unique, then the Bible is unique. This is not because of the "ideas" which are found in the Bible, but because the Bible is a book of history.

b. The Scriptures as witness to Christ. The authority of scripture consists solely in the fact that the Bible is the authoritative historical witness to Christ. It is the testimony of those who actually saw and witnessed to the saving acts of God in history (Exod. 10:2; 12:26-27; 13:8,14-15; Deut. 4:34-35; 6:20-23; Judg. 6:13; Ps. 44:1; I John 1:1-3). This is the significance both of the OT and of the NT. Both testaments witness to Christ: the OT contains the testimony of the prophets to the Christ who should come; the NT contains the witness of the apostles to the fact that Jesus of Nazareth is he. Outside the Bible there is no historical testimony to Christ; everything that can be known about the Jesus of history is to be found in it. There is, of course, valuable testimony to Christ outside the Bible (e.g., in Augustine's *Confessions* or in Bunyan's *Pilgrim's Progress*), but it is not historical testimony, and therefore it is not "scripture."

This is why the canon of the NT closes about the end of the first century A.D.; there is no more historical witness to be had, for those who had been in touch with the original eyewitnesses were now almost all passed from the scene. It is not a question of the "progressive revelation" of ideas about God, but of the testimony of eyewitnesses to the unique and saving act of God in history, the Christ event, which is the theme of the Bible as a whole.

5. The Word of God and the word of man. The Bible is essentially a book of witness, and it is this in a twofold sense. On the one hand, it contains human witness to the events which the minds of the prophets and apostles, illuminated by God's Spirit, perceived to be the saving acts of God in Israel's history. On the other hand, it becomes the means through which the Holy Spirit bears his testimony in our hearts to the truth of God's salvation. The Bible is thus both the Word of God and the words of men, and each of these statements must be taken seriously. The Bible is the Word of God in that it contains God's saving Word to the world— namely, Christ—of whom it is the only authoritative historical record. In the strictest theological sense the "Word of God" is Christ, but in a derivative sense the Bible, qua witness to Christ, may be called the "Word of God." But its words are nonetheless human words—the poor, inadequate, stammering words of men who were subject to all the limitations of their historical situation, struggling to give expression to the truth which they had perceived.

Like all human words and sentences, the scriptural writings are historically conditioned and therefore fallible; yet they express the deepest truth about man and his relation to God that can be reached by finite and sinful beings. The testimony of the human writers becomes for us the means of our apprehension of God in Christ. In Luther's striking metaphor, the words of the Bible are the swaddling clothes in which the Christ is laid: "Poor and mean are the swaddling clothes but dear is the treasure which lies within." To deny the full humanity of the biblical words is error comparable to Apollinarianism in Christology; as in Christ God and man are joined in hypostatic unity, so in the Bible the testimony of the Holy Spirit is perfectly united with the human testimony of the prophetic and apostolic witnesses. Just as God could take a poor, uncouth slave tribe and make it the instrument of his saving purpose for the world, so he could take the fragmentary compositions of many writers and make of them one Book, through which the testimony of the Holy Spirit might bring conviction to the hearts of many.

In the last resort the authority of the Bible is apprehended by those to whom the Spirit of God has brought conviction through the words of its human writers; this double witness to Christ is the reality which gives to the Sacred Scriptures their sole and unique authority in the hearts and lives of all who confess that Jesus is Lord. To those who are not yet ready to acknowledge Jesus as Lord, the Bible may perhaps possess other kinds of authority— that of the insights of religious genius, that of compelling rational and moral conceptions of God's nature and purpose, or that of poetic imagination; but none of these admissions is equivalent to the authority acknowledged by the Christian believer who has found in the Scriptures God's authoritative, personal address to his own soul.

Bibliography. The literature on this subject is vast. Among modern books the following may be mentioned: G. E. Phillips, *The OT in the World Church* (1942). A. Richardson, *Preface to Bible Study* (1943). H. Cunliffe-Jones, *Authority of the Biblical Revelation* (1945). A. G. Hebert, *Authority of the OT* (1947). A. Richardson, *Christian Apologetics* (1947), ch. 9. A. Farrer, *Glass of Vision* (1948); *A Rebirth of Images* (1949). W. Vischer, *The Witness of the OT to Christ* (English trans., 1949), I, 7-34. J. Woods, *The OT in the Church* (1949). A. Richardson and W. Schweitzer, eds., *Biblical Authority for Today* (1951). H. W. Bartsch, ed., *Kerygma and Myth* (English trans., 1954). A. G. Hebert, *Fundamentalism and the Church of God* (1957). J. K. S. Reid, *The Authority of Scripture* (1957).

The following will also be found of great interest in the historical development of thought: W. Sanday, *Inspiration* (Bampton Lectures; 1893). J. E. Carpenter, *The Bible in the Nineteenth Century* (1903). C. Gore, *Doctrine of the Infallible Book* (1924). C. H. Dodd, *Authority of the Bible* (1928). E. Hoskyns and N. Davey, *The Riddle of the NT* (1931).

ALAN RICHARDSON

SCROLL [מגלה; ספר (Isa. 34:4), book; βιβλίον, βιβλαρίδιον]. A papyrus or leather book roll. *See* BOOK; ROLL; WRITING AND WRITING MATERIALS.

SCROLLS, DEAD SEA. *See* DEAD SEA SCROLLS.

SCULPTURE. *See* ART.

SCULPTURED STONES [פסילים] (Judg. 3:19, 26). The precise meaning of the Hebrew word translated thus is not evident. Elsewhere it refers to cultic representations of deities, which were prohibited by the First Commandment (*see* IDOL; IMAGE; GRAVEN IMAGE). It could refer simply to stone quarries which Ehud passed on the way to and from his fateful meeting with King Eglon. This seems unlikely, however, in view of frequent usage of the word with reference to idols (*see above*). More probably, the references in Judg. 3 are to hewn or dressed stones, or to sculptured stones (cf. פסל, "cut, hew"). These stones may have been set in a certain formation, as in the story about Joshua's taking stones from the Jordan (Josh. 4:20). They may have served as a boundary marker between Moab and the neighboring territory. If they were actually sculptured to a certain form or carved in relief, they probably had religious significance as well.

Boundary stones (Akkadian *kudurru*) bearing scenes in relief have been found in Mesopotamia dating from the seventeenth to the eighth century B.C. However, comparable remains have not been found in the Palestine area. Thus, no single interpretation of the Hebrew word translated "sculptured stones" in Judg. 3 can be regarded as securely established.

Bibliography. J. B. Pritchard, *ANEP* (1954), pp. 156, 176, 300-301, 310-11.

G. B. COOKE

SCURVY [גרב; LXX ψώρα ἀγρία; Vulg. *scabies*] (Deut. 28:27). Alternately: ITCHING DISEASE (Lev. 21:20). Not true scurvy, but a fungus disease such as *tinea* (ringworm). *See* ITCH.

SCYTHE [ἅρματα δρεπανηφόρα]. A curved blade attached to a war chariot. The military equipment marshaled by Antiochus V Eupator and Lysias against Judas at Beth-zur included three hundred chariots equipped with scythes, according to the account in II Macc. 13:2, although they are omitted in the list of I Macc. 6:30, which represents the total size of the army to be considerably smaller. The scythed chariot was a popular weapon among the Egyptians and the Persians, but it was not used by the Greeks and the Romans. It is known that the Seleucid kings used it at the Battle of Magnesia (190 B.C.), but Bevan (*see bibliography*) doubts that it was used after that (cf. Polybius V.53.10; Livy XXXVII.41); and it is unlikely that it would be used in a country like Judea.

Bibliography. E. Bevan, *The House of Seleucus*, II (1902), 290; F.-M. Abel, *Les Livres des Maccabées* (1949), p. 450.

E. W. SAUNDERS

*SCYTHIANS sĭth′ĭ ənz. A nomadic people speaking an Indo-Iranian dialect, originating in S Russia and moving through the Caucasus into the Near East. At the beginning of the eighth century B.C. the first waves of Eurasian nomads came on horseback into the Near East: first the Cimmerians (Akkadian *Gimirrai; see* GOMER), and then the Scythians (Akkadian *Ašguzai, Iškuzai*). Esarhaddon fought with the latter, naming Ishpaka as a king of the Scythians. While the Cimmerians, hard pressed by the Scythians as well as through Assyrian efforts, turned aside into Asia Minor, the sway of the Scythians extended farther to the E. The Scythians became the allies of Assyria—their king Bartatua requested a daughter of Esarhaddon in marriage—while the Medes sided with Babylonia. It remains uncertain as to whether the Scythians made any move to save their allies when Assyria was fighting her last battles. The Scythians seem to have gone, in a large-scale raid, along the Phoenician coast down to Egypt, where Pharaoh Psammetichus (663-609) turned them back by paying them off. They are supposed to have destroyed Ashkelon and Ashdod. Eventually the Medes turned against the Scythians and defeated and destroyed them, except for a remainder, which turned back toward the N.

The Scythians are referred to in the OT under the name ASHKENAZ (Gen. 10:3; I Chr. 1:6; Jer. 51: 27), and the threat of their raid through Palestine is often cited as the occasion for the book of ZEPHANIAH and some of the oracles in JEREMIAH (*see* § B1). The memory of their savagery persisted even to NT times, when Paul chose the name Scythian (Σκύθης) to represent the extreme of barbarism (Col. 3:11).

Bibliography. T. T. Rice, *The Scythians* (1957).

A. L. OPPENHEIM

SCYTHOPOLIS sĭth ŏp′ɔ lĭs [Σκυθῶν πόλις, city of Scythians]. Apoc. name of BETH-SHAN. *See also* DECAPOLIS.

SEA [ים; θάλασσα]. This term, with appropriate qualifying words, refers to a general gathering of water, specific bodies of water, and structures such as the bronze sea and the sea of glass.

According to the Priestly account of the Creation, God gathered together the waters apart from the dry land and called them "Seas" (ימים; Gen. 1:9-10). The sea is mentioned in the Bible as a body of water over which God's power extends (Job 26:12; Acts 14:15), where the fish dwell (Gen. 1:26, 28), where danger lurks (Jonah 1:4; Matt. 18:6), and from which great beasts of world power are pictured by the apocalyptic writers as coming (Dan. 7:3; Rev. 13:1). There is no evidence that the people of Palestine in biblical times sailed the Mediterranean Sea with fleets of ships, as did their neighbors the Phoenicians. *See* GREAT SEA.

Although the people of the Palestinian area were not primarily a seafaring people, they were acquainted with the most important seas of the region, and their history was often linked with them in some special way. The W border of the land was frequently designated as the Great Sea or the Western Sea; it was also mentioned simply as "the sea" (ים; θάλασσα; Josh. 16:8; I Kings 5:9; Acts 10:6; etc.). Among the other seas mentioned in the Bible are the RED SEA; the DEAD SEA; and the Sea of Galilee (*see* GALILEE, SEA OF). The Red Sea (ים סוף; "sea of reeds"; Exod. 10:19; 15:4; etc.) was the scene of the deliverance of the Hebrews in their flight from Egypt; the sea or a part of it is referred to in Isa. 11:15 as "the sea of Egypt" (ים מצרים). The Dead Sea is commonly referred to as the Salt Sea (ים המלח; Gen. 14:3; Num. 34:12; Deut. 3:17; Josh. 3:16; etc.). It was also described as the "sea of the Arabah" (ים הערבה; Deut. 3:17; 4:49; Josh. 3:16; KJV "sea of the plain"), and as the "eastern sea" (הים הקדמוני; Ezek. 47:18; Joel 2:20; Zech. 14:8). The Sea of Galilee (θάλασσα τῆς Γαλαίας), the largest fresh-water lake in Palestine, is frequently mentioned in connection with the ministry of Jesus (Matt. 4:18; 15:29; Mark 7:31; etc.). In the NT it is also called the Lake of Gennesaret (λίμνη Γεννησαρέτ; Luke 5:1) and the Sea of Tiberias (θάλασσα τῆς Τιβεριάδος; John 6:1; 21:1). In the OT it is designated as the Sea of Chinnereth (ים כנרת) in Num. 34:11; Josh. 13:27, and as the Sea of Chinneroth (ים כנרות) in Josh. 12:3.

The bronze sea (KJV "brazen sea") was a large basin made of bronze, located in front of the Jerusalem temple, and was, according to II Chr. 4:6, a storage place for water which the priests used in their ablutions. In addition to being called the "bronze sea" (ים הנחשת; II Kings 25:13; I Chr. 18:

8; Jer. 52:17), the vessel was also designated as the "molten sea" (ים מוצק; I Kings 7:23; II Chr. 4:2; *see* SEA, MOLTEN) and simply as "the sea" (הים; I Kings 7:24; II Kings 16:17; etc.).

The SEA OF GLASS (θάλασσα ὑαλίνη) is a term used in Rev. 4:6; 15:2 to refer to a kind of heavenly sea, like crystal, which was before the throne.

W. L. REED

*SEA, MOLTEN [ים מוצק-, cast, or poured, metal sea] (I Kings 7:24; II Chr. 4:2); BRONZE SEA [ים הנחשת] (II Kings 25:13; I Chr. 18:8; Jer. 52:17; KJV BRAZEN SEA); THE SEA [הים] (I Kings 7:24; II Kings 16:17). A large vessel made of cast bronze. It was cast by Hiram of Tyre, whom Solomon engaged for bronze work (I Kings 7:13-14); according to I Chr. 18:8, it was made from the bronze which David had taken as spoil (cf. II Sam. 8:8). If it stood in the place of the corresponding bronze LAVER of the tabernacle (Exod. 30:18), it may have been located at the entrance of the temple and before the altar.

The vessel was round, with a diameter of 10 cubits, its height was 5 cubits and its circumference 30 (LXX 33) cubits, and its volume was 2,000 baths (I Kings 7:23; in II Chr. 4:2 3,000). Its thickness was a handbreadth (3 inches), and its brim was turned outward, giving the appearance of a cup, "like the flower of a lily" (*see* LILY-WORK). Under the brim were two rows of ornamental gourds which were cast with the vessel. The basin rested upon twelve bronze oxen, facing at right angles in four directions. The oxen were probably only pediment figures, showing only their fore parts beneath the rim of the hemisphere.

Josephus assumed that the vessel was a hemisphere and its volume 3,000 baths. Others have taken the shape to be cylindrical and denied that from the given dimensions the volume of either 2,000 or 3,000 baths was possible, irrespective of whether its shape was hemispherical or cylindrical. C. C. Wylie suggests that the volume in I Kings was hemispherical and in II Chronicles cylindrical. Using the given dimensions in the respective formulas for volume of a hemisphere ($V = \frac{1}{3} Cr^2$), and of a cylinder ($V = \frac{1}{2} Crh$), and multiplying the result by 8 baths—a supposed rabbinical rule by which a cubic cubit equals 8 baths—he obtained the following results:

a) Volume = $\frac{1}{3} \times 30 \times 25 \times 8 = 2,000$ baths

b) Volume = $\frac{1}{2} \times 30 \times 5 \times 5 \times 8 = 3,000$ baths

The problem with this solution is the source of the supposed rabbinical rule which claims that a cubic cubit equals 8 baths. R. B. Y. Scott suggests that the capacities of the "sea" given in I Kings and II Chronicles were obtained by means of calculations rather than experimental measurements, and that the scribe who in I Kings calculated the capacity of the "sea" from its dimensions used in error the formula for the volume of a sphere instead of that of a hemisphere. On the basis of the estimate of a bath as 22 liters, and the value of the Hebrew cubit as 17.5 inches or 444.7 millimeters, Scott suggests that the volume of the sea in I Kings was actually 1,000 rather than 2,000 baths. This leaves unsolved the 3,000 baths in II Chronicles. The probable solution, if there is a solution at all, is that the volumes in both

Courtesy of E. G. Howland

34. The Molten Sea, a copper bowl 15 feet in diameter and 7½ feet in height; from model by E. G. Howland

I Kings and II Chronicles are later scribal additions.

The purpose for the molten sea is not given in the account of the Kings. II Chr. 4:6 states that it "was for the priests to wash in." However, the cosmic symbolism of the object has long been noted, and comparison has been made with the Babylonian *apsu,* a term used for the fresh-water "deep" from which all life and fertility were derived. Likewise the ornamental oxen (bulls?) on which the basin rested must have had originally some symbolic significance.

In the reign of King Ahaz, the sea was taken "from off the bronze oxen . . . , and put . . . upon a pediment of stone" (II Kings 16:17). When the Babylonians captured Jerusalem in 587 (586), the sea was broken up and its bronze pieces carried to Babylonia (25:13, 16).

Fig. SEA 34.

Bibliography. C. C. Wylie, *BA,* vol. XII (1949), no. 4, pp. 86-90; W. F. Albright, *Archaeology and the Religion of Israel* (3rd ed., 1953), pp. 148-50; R. B. Y. Scott, "The Hebrew Cubit," *JBL,* vol. LXXVII (1958). J. L. MIHELIC

SEA GULL [שחף; LXX λάρος, *a ravenous sea bird, perhaps* gull; Vulg. *larus (from* Gr.)] (Lev. 11:16; Deut. 14:15); KJV CUCKOO. Any of a family of web-footed sea birds (Laridae) of the subfamily Larinae, mostly of the genus Larus (of which there are *ca.* fifty species). These birds, which are gregarious and noisy, frequent sea-coasts and inland waters; their food is fish as well as various items picked up on shore such as worms, insects, bird eggs, young birds, refuse, etc.

The שחף is clearly a bird, and is unclean presumably because it eats live prey or carrion. The force of the argument that its place in the two bird lists (Lev. 11; Deut. 14) points to a land bird, and in particular to an owl (*see bibliography*), depends upon how confident we are that the lists have an intelligible arrangement which we can discover. That Driver finds eight owls in a list of twenty birds (or nineteen if we leave out the bat), raises some suspicion, in view of the variety of birds known in Palestine, that his method of identification is, in part, open to criticism.

The LXX's gull, in the light of Tristram's evidence for "many species of Sea-gull, common both on the coasts and on the Sea of Galilee" (*NHB* 211), is a reasonable surmise. Tristram mentions particularly the Common Gull (*Larus canus*), the Great Black-headed Gull (*Larus ichthyaëtus*), the Herring Gull (*Larus argentatus*), the Black-headed Gull (*Larus ridibundus*), and the Lesser Black-headed Gull (*Larus fuscus*). He also notes that petrels and shearwaters (of the family Procellariidae) abound in the E Mediterranean.

Bibliography. G. R. Driver, *PEQ* (April, 1955), pp. 13, 19.

W. S. McCULLOUGH

SEA MONSTER [תנין (Job 7:12). *See* DRAGON; LEVIATHAN; RAHAB.

SEA OF THE ARABAH ăr'ə bə [ים הערבה, sea of the desert, wilderness]. The lake equated in the OT with the Salt Sea (Deut. 3:17; Josh. 3:16; 12:3; see also Deut. 4:49; II Kings 14:25) and now generally called the DEAD SEA. This designation is derived from the situation of the sea in the deepest part of the Arabah depression.   W. H. MORTON

SEA OF CHINNERETH kĭn'ə rĕth. *See* GALILEE, SEA OF.

SEA OF GALILEE. *See* GALILEE, SEA OF.

SEA OF GLASS, GLASSY SEA [θάλασσα ὑαλίνη]. A vision of John the seer in Rev. 4:6; 15:2. In the vision of the heavenly throne room (4:6), this sea is described as "like crystal," an obvious borrowing from Ezekiel's characterization of the "firmament" appearing in his own throne vision (Ezek. 1:22); whereas in Rev. 15:2 the same glassy sea is "mingled with fire"—i.e., either reflecting the glow of the lightning playing about God's throne (4:5), or else (as is more probably meant) actually containing or even composed of the fire of judgment, through which all men must pass to attain the farther shore of salvation (cf. the "stream of fire" issuing before the throne of the "ancient of days" in Dan. 7:10).

The view is widely held that the prototype of John's glassy sea is to be sought in the Jewish teaching regarding an original creation pattern or cosmology (*einer alten Naturanschauung*) wherein it was said that there were "waters . . . above the firmament," and so in heaven, as well as below on earth (cf. Gen. 1:7; Ps. 148:4; I Enoch 3:3; Test. Levi 2:7; Jub. 2:4). But, while this further reference may lie in the background and furnish at this point the pattern for John's cosmological scheme, his more immediate thought centers in: (*a*) the furnishings of tabernacle and temple, where purification in the "laver" (Exod. 30:17 ff) or "molten sea" (I Kings 7:23 ff) was required of priests approaching the sanctuary to conduct the worship of Yahweh; and (*b*) the victory achieved at the crossing of the Red Sea, an event which for John symbolized man's passing through the eschatological fire of God's judgment, these two occurrences accordingly being fittingly signalized, respectively, by the "Song of Moses" and the "song of the Lamb" (Rev. 15:3 ff; cf. Exod. 15). It is likely, therefore, that we should see in this "sea of glass" the laver of cleansing—an integral part of the equipment of the heavenly tabernacle, and at the same time a representation or symbol at once of

God's wrathful judgment on man's sin and of that purifying process or "holiness without which no one will see the Lord" (Heb. 12:14; cf. Ps. 24:4; Matt. 5:8; I Cor. 10:1 ff; Rev. 22:3-4). This "sea of glass" is not to be confused with the "lake of fire" (Rev. 19:20), which symbolizes the "second death" (20:14).

Bibliography. Commentaries listed under REVELATION, BOOK OF. C. H. Kraeling, *John the Baptist* (1951), pp. 115 ff.

J. W. BOWMAN

SEA OF TIBERIAS tī bîr'ĭ əs. *See* GALILEE, SEA OF.

SEACOAST [חוף הים, *lit.* enclosure of the sea (Deut. 1:7; Ezek. 25:16; SEASHORE *in* Jer. 47:7; COAST OF THE SEA *in* Josh. 9:1); חבל הים, *lit.* territory of the sea (Zeph. 2:5-7); παράλιος (Luke 6:17)]. The fertile and populous E seaboard of the Mediterranean, inhabited in OT times by the Canaanites (Deut. 1:7) and later by the Philistines (Ezek. 25:16) and Phoenicians (Luke 6:17). *See* CANAAN; PHILISTINES; PHOENICIA.   L. E. TOOMBS

SEAH sē'ə. *See* WEIGHTS AND MEASURES § C4*f*.

SEALS AND SCARABS.

  A. Bible references
    1. Delegation of authority
    2. Assent to documents
    3. Sealing of masonry
    4. Metaphors
  B. Archaeology
    1. Iran and Mesopotamia
      a. Stamp seals
      b. Cylinder seals
    2. Egypt and the Aegean
      a. Cylinder seals
      b. Seal-amulets
      c. Scarabs
    3. Syro-Palestine
      a. Early clinder impressions
      b. "Hyksos" scarabs and cowroids
      c. Egyptian Empire scarabs and seals
      d. Hematite seals and bone scaraboids
      e. Gems and sealings
      f. Royal symbols and stamps
      g. "Rhodian" jar handles
  Bibliography

A. BIBLE REFERENCES. The first OT mention of a signet is preserved in the clan legend of Judah and Tamar (Gen. 38:18, 25). Two of the three pledges are relevant, Judah's SIGNET (חותם) and his CORD (פתיל; KJV wrongly "bracelet"). The association suggests that Judah may have owned a cylinder seal which he wore round his neck (*see* § B1*b below*), rather than a signet ring. However, the latter is clearly indicated when Pharaoh invested Joseph with royal power (Gen. 41:42), and the Hebrew word used is טבעת (cf. Egyptian *ḏbʿt*, current from at least Old Kingdom times). The same word is used for the various rings employed in the construction of the ark, its furniture, and Aaron's breastplate. It has therefore as wide a connotation as "ring" in English. The references in Genesis record events which traditionally took place within *ca.* a century of each other; the mention of Pharaoh's chariot shows that Joseph's appointment could not have preceded the Eighteenth Dynasty (ca. 1570 B.C.).

Passages referring to the Mosaic period which contain the word חותם, and in particular those which mention the engraving of onyx stones (Exod. 28:11, 21) and (vs. 36) of a gold FRONTLET (ציץ; KJV "plate") "like the engravings of a signet" (cf. Exod. 39:6, 14, 30), may be glosses of P documents in the Pentateuch. The ring (טבעת) is mentioned with other jewels among the free gifts offered for the tabernacle (Exod. 35:22; Num. 31:50). References to the act of sealing and to the use of seals and signets are discussed below.

1. Delegation of authority. As a conveyance of power, the use of a royal seal is attested from ca. 850 B.C., for Jezebel used Ahab's seal (חותם) to authenticate forged letters (I Kings 21:8). Postexilic sources referring to the period of the Exile give instances in which the king's ring (טבעת) was used (a) against the Jews (Esth. 3:10, 12) and (b) in their favor (Esth. 8:2, 8, 10). These sources may not be wholly historical, but the appointment of a regent for his son by King Antiochus IV Epiphanes, who was invested with the king's crown, his robe, and his signet, shows that the latter was one of the emblems of authority in the Seleucid Empire of the second century B.C. (I Macc. 6:15). Josephus refers to a similar investment in the first century A.D. (Antiq. XX.ii.2).

2. Assent to documents. The words of the prophet Jeremiah record the procedure for the legal purchase of land during the last days of the Judean monarchy, referring to a sealed deed of purchase and an open copy (Jer. 32:10-11, 14, 44). Cf. this account with the patriarch Abraham's purchase of the field at Hebron, when the payment of money before witnesses was sufficient (Gen. 23:2-20).

With the restoration of Jerusalem and its walls in the fifth century, the chief men of the city set their seal to a written covenant to keep its laws (Neh. 9: 38; 10:1).

3. Sealing of masonry. When Daniel was cast into the lions' den, the king sealed (Aramaic ḥᵃthām) it with his signet (Aramaic 'izqâ), and with the signets of his lords (Dan. 6:17—H 6:18). The only factual reference to sealing in the NT is contained in the account of the closure of the Holy Sepulchre (σφραγίζω, "to seal, impress"; Matt. 27:66).

4. Metaphors. The first reference to the subject in a figurative sense dates from the eighth century: "Bind up the testimony, seal the teaching" (Isa. 8: 16), referring, no doubt, to a scroll; cf. the passage from a postexilic pen: "like the words of a book that is sealed" (Isa. 29:11). The personal use of a signet, worn on the right hand (Jer. 22:24), and its choice (Hag. 2:23) are metaphors dating from the sixth century, while the simile "set me as a seal" (חותם) upon the heart and the arm occurs in a postexilic source (Song of S. 8:6). The same book (5:14) uses the word גלילים, geᵉlîlîm, from the Hebrew root gālāl, "to roll," apparently as a metaphor for the fingers of the hand, which may therefore be more correctly rendered "cylinders" than "rings" (KJV; in the RSV "גלילים of gold" is rendered "rounded gold"). The learned author of the book of Daniel also employs "seal" in a figurative sense (Dan. 9:24; 12:4, 9), while the editors of Job were definitely addicted to the use of this

metaphor (Job 9:7; 14:17; 33:16; 37:7; 38:14; 41:15).

References in the NT to a "seal," "impression," or "inscription" (σφραγίς) are general (Rom. 4:11; I Cor. 9:2; II Tim. 2:19; Rev. 5:1-2, 5, 9; 6:1, 3, 5, 7, 9, 12; 7:2; 8:1; 9:4), except for the description of the book with seven seals (Rev. 5). The verbs "to seal" or "to impress" are also used as metaphors (σφραγίζω; John 3:33; 6:27; Rom. 15:28; II Cor. 1:22; Eph. 1:13; 4:30; Rev. 7:3-8; 10:4; 20:3; 22:10).

B. ARCHAEOLOGY. Discoveries in Western Asia during the last hundred years provide more information than any other source about the use of seals in antiquity. Three main geographical divisions (§§ 1-3 below) correspond roughly to the spheres covered by those languages expressed in cuneiform writing, Egyptian and other hieroglyphic symbols, and Hebrew and Aramaic script; the development of seals and sealing will be followed in each area according to chronological order, as far as it can be established by comparative study. Fig. SEA 35.

1. Iran and Mesopotamia. The earliest attempts at the production of crude seals probably date from the fourth millennium.

a. Stamp seals. Stone "seal-pendants," which have been found in graves or in the debris of settlements, were either bored through the central axis or shaped and pierced like buttons, so that they could be strung on necklaces or cords; many impressions on clay of the designs engraved on the convex or flat surfaces of these seals have survived.

In ancient ELAM, now SW Iran, at the old capital of SUSA, stamp seals appear during an early phase of the city's growth contemporary with the introduction of metal. Both are found together on N Mesopotamian sites in the Tigris Valley (e.g., Arpachiyah, Gawra). The designs at Susa developed independently of the N, and show a preference for geometric stylization (Periods A-B=Early Uruk; see bibliography). So little is known of contemporary glyptic art in S Mesopotamia that it is not possible either to suggest the source or direction of cultural influence or to assess relative chronological priority.

The main event of the following phase was the invention of writing, represented at Susa (Period C=Late Uruk) by an apparently indigenous script, derived from pictographic symbols, while about the same time another pictographic script was employed in S Mesopotamia which was ultimately simplified into wedge-shaped strokes, now known as CUNEIFORM.

b. Cylinder seals. With the development of writing, seals in the form of a cylinder came into use. They were either provided with a loop at the narrow end, or were pierced longways for suspension; the outer face was engraved with patterns and signs in intaglio, worked in reverse; the design therefore read correctly when it was impressed on any flat or curved surface of moist clay, which was then sun-baked to preserve it. The seal could be worn on a necklace or wristlet of beads, or carried attached by a pin to some part of the owner's dress. See bibliography.

Fine seal-engraving was achieved by the Sumerians in the Proto-Literate (Jemdet Nasr) period, and was followed by increasing stylization in Early Dynastic times, the last phase of which is roughly equivalent to the date of the royal tombs at Ur (ca. twenty-fifth

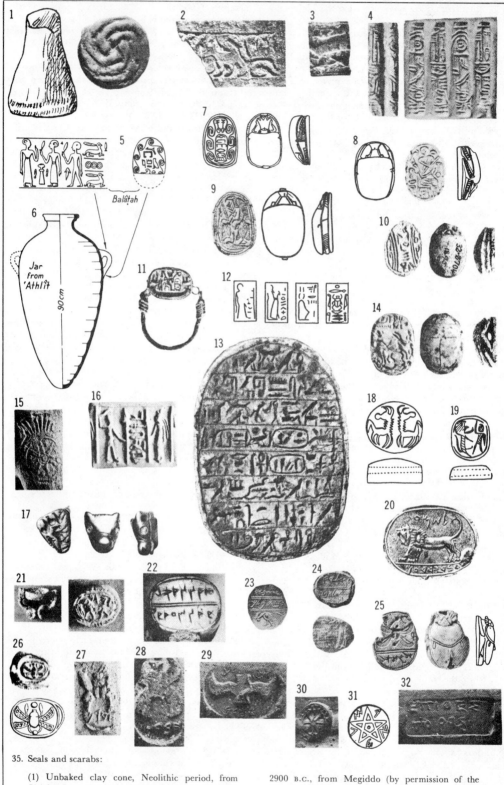

35. Seals and scarabs:

(1) Unbaked clay cone, Neolithic period, from Jericho (by permission of the Palestine Exploration Fund); (2) cylinder seal impression of pottery, ca. 2900 B.C., from Megiddo (by permission of the Oriental Institute, the University of Chicago); (3) ivory cylinder seal, ca. 2900 B.C., from Beisan (by

permission of the British School of Archaeology in Iraq); (4) steatite cylinder inscribed Ni-maat-Re (Amen-em-het III), *ca.* 1840-1790 B.C., from Tell el-'Ajjûl (by permission of the Palestine Archaeological Museum, Jerusalem, Jordan); (5) impressions on pottery handle of cylinder seal and scarab, from Balâṭah (by permission of the Palestine Archaeological Museum, Jerusalem, Jordan); (6) store jar to show approximate positions of sealings in no. 5, from 'Athlît (by permission of the Palestine Archaeological Museum, Jerusalem, Jordan); (7) steatite scarab, scroll pattern, *ca.* 1800 B.C., from Lachish (copyright: by permission of Oxford University Press); (8) steatite scarab, robed personage, *ca.* 1750-1650 B.C., from Lachish (copyright: by permission of Oxford University Press); (9) steatite scarab, hatched design, *ca.* 1750-1650 B.C., from Lachish (copyright: by permission of Oxford University Press); (10) steatite scarab, with name *Ỿqb(?)*, glyptic corruption of the correct *Ỿʿqb* (Hebrew Jacob), from Mirsim (by permission of the Palestine Archaeological Museum, Jerusalem, Jordan); (11) steatite scarab, set in bronze ring, inscribed Men-kheper-Re (Thut-mose III), *ca.* 1490-1436 B.C., from Tell el-'Ajjûl (by permission of the Palestine Archaeological Museum, Jerusalem, Jordan); (12) paste cuboid seal, inscribed Aa-khepru-Re (Amen-hotep II) with figures of three gods, their names written in characters allied to Early Canaanite script, *ca.* 1447-1421 B.C., from Lachish (copyright: by permission of Oxford University Press); (13) green glaze "lion hunt" scarab of Neb-maat-Re (Amen-hotep III), *ca.* 1413-1377 B.C., from Lachish (by permission of the Trustees of the late Sir Henry S. Wellcome); (14) steatite scarab, originally set in bronze ring, inscribed Usr-maat-Re, Setep-en-Re (Ramses II), *ca.* 1301-1234 B.C., from Tell el-Far'ah (by permission of the Palestine Archaeological Museum, Jerusalem, Jordan); (15) royal Hittite emblem impressed on jar handle, *ca.* 1400-1300 B.C., from Hazor (by permission of the Trustees of the British Museum); (16) impression of faïence cylinder seal, showing warrior-deity facing goddess, identified by her name inscribed in hieroglyphs, 'Astart (Astarte), *ca.* 1300 B.C., from Bethel (by permission of the American Schools of Oriental Research); (17) Haematite seal in shape of bull's head, obverse engraved with animals, *ca.* 1050-950 B.C., from Tell el-Far'ah (by permission of University College, Lon-

don, Department of Egyptology); (18) bone scaraboid, *ca.* 860-820 B.C., from Lachish (copyright: by permission of Oxford University Press); (19) bone scaraboid, *ca.* 810-710 B.C., from Lachish (copyright: by permission of Oxford University Press); (20) jasper scaraboid, inscribed *lšm 'bd yrb'm,* "(belonging) to Shema' the servant of Jeroboam [II?], king of Israel," *ca.* 786-746 B.C., from Megiddo (by permission of J. C. Hinrichs Verlag, Leipzig); (21) seal in copper mount, inscribed *lytm,* "(belonging) to Jôtham," (?) king of Judah, *ca.* 742-735 B.C., from Ezion-geber (by permission of the American Schools of Oriental Research); (22) carnelian(?) scaraboid in silver ring, inscribed *l'dnr 'bd 'mndb,* "(belonging) to 'Adoni-nur, the servant of 'Ammi-nadab" (by permission of the Palestine Exploration Fund); (23) onyx scaraboid, inscribed *ly'znyhw 'bd ḥmlk,* "(belonging) to Jaaza-niah, servant of the king," *ca.* 600 B.C., from Tell en-Nasbeh (by permission of the American Schools of Oriental Research); (24) clay sealing from document, marks of papyrus and thread on reverse, inscribed, upper register, *lgdlyhw;* lower register, (')*shr 'lhbyt,* "(belonging) to Gedaliah, he who is over the House," from Lachish (copyright: by permission of Oxford University Press); (25) steatite scarab: upper register, four-winged *scarabeus* with Hebrew letters *smk* above, and *ankh* sign between the wings; lower register, *l'ḥmlk,* "(belonging) to Semak Aḥimelek"; *ca.* 800 B.C., from Lachish (copyright: by permission of Oxford University Press); (26) clay sealing with impression of four-winged *scarabeus,* marks of papyrus document to which it was attached on back, *ca.* 850-700 B.C., from Samaria (by permission of the Palestine Exploration Fund); (27) royal jar stamp, class i, *ca.* 800-750 B.C., from Lachish (copyright: by permission of Oxford University Press); (28) royal jar stamp, class ii, *ca.* 750-700 B.C., from Lachish (copyright: by permission of Oxford University Press); (29) royal jar stamp, class iii, *ca.* 700-600 B.C., from Lachish (copyright: by permission of Oxford University Press); (30) jar handle with impressed rosette, *ca.* 600-500 B.C., from Lachish (copyright: by permission of Oxford University Press); (31) jar stamp, pentagram design, with Hebrew letters, *ca.* 600-500 B.C., from Ophel (by permission of Felice Le Monnier, Florence); (32) rectangular jar stamp, inscribed in Greek, from Lachish (copyright: by permission of Oxford University Press)

century). The cylindrical form remained typical of the seals classified, according to the main regional styles, as early Akkadian, Kassite, Assyrian, and late Babylonian (Herodotus I.195). The same shape enjoyed sporadic popularity whenever the influence of these powers extended to other lands of the E Mediterranean world (Fig. SEA 35, No. 3). The impression of a cylinder seal soon became, not merely a mark of ownership or security, but a form of legal assent to a written contract.

At the turn of the fourth-third millennium, Mesopotamian influence expanded in all directions; seals were carried by officials and merchants, and impressions from them found in many places are among the indications of far-reaching trade.

2. Egypt and the Aegean. Trade relations between Egypt and Crete in remote times seem to have existed, and a marked expansion of trade between the Nile Valley and the island is noticeable early in

the second millennium, when new influences were brought to bear on the intervening land routes through Asia.

a. Cylinder seals. However, the earliest seals to reach Egypt were cylinders based on Mesopotamian example, for the same distinctive symbols appear on both. But these Pre-Dynastic cylinders of black steatite were very lightly scratched, in comparison with Mesopotamian seals, and the most popular scene—a figure seated before a table of offerings—was entirely personal and religious in character (*see bibliography*). No impressions of this type of design have been found, and it is therefore concluded that these cylinders were traditional items which the deceased required to have with him in his tomb.

The situation had changed by the First Dynasty (*ca.* 2900 B.C.), when a pictograph of a cylinder seal was already established as an ideogram or determinative for words like "seal" and "treasurer" in hieroglyphic texts. During the first half of the third millennium cylinder seals were engraved with the names and titles of kings and officials, who used them in administrative business and sealed goods with them, which were intended for the royal tombs and pyramids. The collapse of the Old Kingdom was followed by a period of anarchy and a redistribution of wealth among the poorer classes, while the trade routes from the N were again open.

b. Seal-amulets. Stamp seals appear at this time, engraved with barbaric and geometric designs, which can be matched among the stamp seals of Syria and Crete. Described as "seal-amulets" to cover many varieties of form, including "button-shaped" seals, and the gradual emergence of scarab-shaped seals which ultimately replaced them, the majority were made of steatite, and the surface was sometimes covered with blue or green glaze, which occasionally filled the engraving, making it impossible to use them as seals. However, from the signs of wear and repair, it is considered almost certain that seal-amulets were not merely funerary, but were also worn as charms during life, chiefly by women and children. It is also clear from the continuity of design that the first scarabs were amulets in origin. *See bibliography.*

c. Scarabs. Various kinds of beetle were venerated in Egypt; among them the dung beetle (*Scarabaeus sacer*) became the emblem of resurrection and continual existence, because of its habit of carrying food in the droppings of animals, which it rolls into a ball. It has been known to lay eggs in the body of a dead companion, so that when the young emerged, the Egyptian saw life coming forth from death. In later times, he symbolized the scarab as the emblem of the Creator, *Kheper-Re*, rolling a ball—the sun—across the sky.

In the first centuries of the second millennium the emblem of a scarab was fashioned in stone to form the back of administrative seals. They were engraved on the flat surface with royal names and titles, or with those of government officials; a thin wire was passed through the length of the scarab, and was bound round the half-hoop of the ring, so that the flat surface of the stone swiveled in its setting when required for use as a seal (Fig. SEA 35, No. 11). However, the names of the earlier Middle Kingdom rulers also occur on cylindrical seals, though these soon became obsolete (No. 4). The revival of the upper classes under a vigorous Twelfth Dynasty (*ca.* 1900 B.C.) led to expansion toward the S, to periodic forays northward to Syria, and to reciprocal trade contacts with the Aegean (*see bibliography*). The resulting need of more officials holding authority under the king no doubt stimulated the production of scarabs, and many persons were styled "sealer" or "royal sealer," while among more unusual posts, one official was described as "guard of the 110 'Aamu" (*see* AMORITES). From the Twelfth or Thirteenth Dynasty onward, scarabs with designs and good-wish symbols became popular, and their history can be followed more closely in Palestine than in Egypt, where the majority were acquired by purchase toward the end of the nineteenth century, while in Palestine most of the scarabs now extant were found in excavations.

3. Syro-Palestine. Far removed in time from any other object which resembles a seal is an unbaked cone of clay with a swastika pattern on the base from Neolithic Jericho (Fig. SEA 35, No. 1). Apart from this isolated find, the E Mediterranean littoral added contributions of its own to cultural development, though it was inevitably influenced by the two great powers at opposing ends of the land bridge between Asia and Africa.

a. Early cylinder impressions. The habit of stamping jars and jar handles before kiln-firing is foreign to Mesopotamia, though the seals used were of cylindrical form (Fig. SEA 35, No. 2), and were probably carved from wood, though at least one ivory original is known (No. 3). They belong to Palestinian Early Bronze Age II (*ca.* 2900-2700), contemporary with the First–Third Dynasties in Egypt, and with Early Dynastic times in Mesopotamia. This valuable chronological link was broken in the troubled centuries which followed, and only an occasional seal-amulet (*see* § B2*b above*) has been discovered in Palestine.

The invention of a system of numerals and linear signs was not begun much before the last centuries of the Early Bronze Age in Palestine, but this significant development was followed, as it had been a thousand years before in Mesopotamia and Egypt, by the increased use of seals.

b. "Hyksos" scarabs and cowroids. Dating perhaps from *ca.* 1900 B.C., the impression of both a cylinder and a scarab seal and counterseal a jar handle (Fig. SEA 35, Nos. 5-6). The scroll border on the scarab is typical of contemporary Middle Kingdom date in Egypt, like the well-proportioned spirals of No. 7, though it is thought that Egyptian designers may have been stimulated by Cretan prototypes (*see bibliography*). More than one new cultural group penetrated into Palestine during the Middle Bronze Age, and each seems to have produced individual styles (contrast the back and sides of No. 7 with those of Nos. 8-10). The group which favored hatching in the design (as on No. 9) made only limited use of hieroglyphic signs, while there are indications (No. 10) that another group may have used them for the transcription of non-Egyptian names. These groups were known collectively to the Egyptians as HYKSOS, a term which is currently used for the period mid-eighteenth to mid-sixteenth centuries. During this phase some seals were made in which the back was shaped in imitation of a cowrie shell.

c. Egyptian Empire scarabs and seals. The military campaigns of Thut-mose III in the mid–fifteenth century established Egyptian rule over Palestine and part of Syria. Scarabs bearing his name are by far the most common (Fig. SEA 35, No. 11), and those of his immediate successors found in Palestinian tombs date them within a few decades, and confirm that some Egyptian control existed until the end of the Eighteenth or the beginning of the Nineteenth Dynasty (Nos. 12-14), though no doubt Hittite influence was stronger in the N (No. 15). Note in particular the names of Egyptian gods written in characters allied to Canaanite script (No. 12), and that of a Canaanite goddess transcribed in hieroglyphs (No. 16). The great age of scarabs in Egypt and Palestine ceased with the end of the Bronze Age, *ca.* 1200 B.C., but mass-produced reproductions became popular in the Mediterranean world in the centuries which followed.

d. Hematite seals and bone scaraboids. Because of unsettled conditions during the early decades of the Hebrew settlement, few cities recovered their former prosperity, and consequently few finds are datable to the first three centuries of the Iron Age. With the introduction of IRON, iron ore or hematite was used for making conoid seals, the bases of which were engraved with lifelike fauna. In this material a bull's head, pierced for suspension, is particularly fine (Fig. SEA 35, No. 17). Bone scaraboids with simple but lively designs of animals and men belonged to poorer individuals of the tenth-eighth centuries (Nos. 18-19).

e. Gems and sealings. Nearly two hundred gem seals carved in varieties of chalcedony have come to light in Israel and Judah, but none can be dated before the ninth century. Jezebel probably used a seal of this class when she forged letters in Ahab's name (I Kings 21:8), but the earliest gem now extant is that of Shema', who probably served Jeroboam II (Fig. SEA 35, No. 20). Among many beautiful seals, the following are of great historic interest: the seal of Jotham (No. 21); the name is not followed by a title or a patronymic, which suggests that it belonged to King Jotham of Judah [eighth century]); the seal of Adoni-nur (No. 22), "servant" of an Ammonite king, mentioned among his vassals by Ashurbanipal in Assyrian annals (mid-seventh century); and the seal of Jaazaniah (No. 23), possibly the individual mentioned in II Kings 25:22-23 who supported Gedaliah (No. 24) in his short governorship after the fall of the Judean monarchy early in the sixth century. Fig. GED 16.

f. Royal symbols and stamps. A four-winged scarabaeus engraved above an inscription reading *smk l'ḥmlk* (Fig. SEA 35, No. 25) on a scarab—the only one bearing characters in Early Hebrew script—is at least as early as the Shema' scaraboid on epigraphic grounds, while nine clay seals with a similar emblem (No. 26) found at Samaria, capital of Israel, may have come from correspondence sent from Judah. Jar handles stamped with a four- or two-winged symbol come exclusively from Judean sites and range between the eighth and sixth centuries. The Early Hebrew letters above the symbol read *lmlk*, "(belonging) to the king," while the name of one of four towns (Hebron, Socoh, Ziph, and Memshath) appears below (Nos. 27-29; *see* WEIGHTS AND MEASURES, § C4*e*). Over 550 of these stamps, supplemented by others found in 1956-57 at Gibeon, revive the E Mediterranean tradition of stamping jar handles (*see* § B3*a above*), which continued during the Exile (Nos. 30-31), and which finally became the hallmark of the wine exporters of the Hellenistic world (No. 32). *See bibliography.*

g. "Rhodian" jar handles. The largest class of these stamped handles comes from the island of Rhodes, which by virtue of its position as a key to the SE Aegean was able to export its inferior wine to Athens, Alexandria, Syria, and Palestine, also to places as far E as Susa and as far W as France and Spain; but other Greek islands, notably Chios and Thasos, shared in this trade, which flourished from the third to the second century B.C. Stamped from a die made of wood or clay, the inscription normally consists of two names, that of the "potter" or "manufacturer," followed by the name of an official, accompanied by

the word *epi*, "in the term of," which served to indicate a date. There can be little doubt that the Greek amphorae on which these stamps occur represent a late offshoot of an E Mediterranean trading system which originated in the fourth millennium B.C.

Bibliography. W. M. F. Petrie, *Scarabs and Cylinders* (1917): for early cylinders (§ B2*a above*), see pls. I-VI; *Buttons and Design Scarabs* (1925): see especially ch. 1. G. Brunton, *Qau and Badari*, vol. I (1927): see especially ch. XX, on seal-amulets. D. Diringer, *Le iscrizioni antico-ebraiche palestinesi* (1934): contains bibliography up to 1932, supplemented by S. Moscati, *L'epigrafia ebraica antica* (1950). A. Rowe, *Catalogue of Egyptian Scarabs* (1936). H. Frankfort, *Cylinder Seals* (1939): a survey of Mesopotamian and peripheral styles. O. Tufnell *et al., Lachish*, vol. II (1940): for "lion hunt" scarab (No. 13). H. Kantor, "The Aegean and the Orient in the Second Millennium B.C.," *AJA*, LI (1947), 1-32. O. Tufnell *et al., Lachish*, vol. III (1953): see ch. 10, pp. 340-48, for royal stamps; ch. 11, pp. 360-73, for scarabs and scaraboids. H. Goldman, Studies, *The Aegean and the Near East* (1956): for bibliography of early cylinder impressions (§ B3*a above*); see J. L. Benson on "Seal Impressions from Cyprus," p. 61; V. Grace on "The Canaanite Jar," pp. 80-109. L. le Breton, "The Early Period at Susa, Mesopotamian Relations," *Iraq*, vol. XIX, pt. 2 (1957), pp. 79-123: a useful illustrated summary. O. Tufnell *et al., Lachish*, vol. IV (1958): see ch. 7 and pls. 30-41.

O. TUFNELL

SEAMAN. *See* SHIPS AND SAILING.

SEASON. The translation of several words, all designating a period of time:

a) עֵת; καιρός. An annually recurring period distinguished by weather (חֹרֶף)—winter, late autumn cold (Prov. 20:4; Jer. 36:22), time of rain (Deut. 11: 14), of LATTER RAIN (Zech. 10:1), of dry summer heat (Ps. 32:4; Isa. 18:4); by behavior of animals and birds (Gen. 31:10; Isa. 18:6; Jer. 8:7); by features of the agricultural year—time of plowing (Exod. 34:21), of sowing (Lev. 26:5), of first leaves (Matt. 24:32), of barley harvest (Ruth 1:22), of wheat harvest (Gen. 30:14), of threshing (Job 5:26), of summer fruits (Gen. 8:22; Amos 8:1), of fig ripening (Mark 11:13), of grape harvest (Num. 13:26); by position of constellations (Job 38:32); by annual customs—pilgrimage (I Sam. 1:3; Luke 2:41), campaigning (II Sam. 11:1).

b) מוֹעֵד; καιρός; ἑορτή. A festival of the sacred lunar calendar (Gen. 1:14; Exod. 23:15; Ecclus. 47: 10; Gal. 4:10).

c) זְמָן (Hebrew and Aramaic); καιρός. A fixed, preordained time or period (Eccl. 3:1), especially in the phrase "times and seasons" (Dan. 2:21; Wisd. Sol. 8:8; Acts 1:7).

See also SUMMER AND WINTER; FEASTS; YEAR; CALENDAR. R. B. Y. SCOTT

SEAT [כִּסֵּא (*usually* THRONE; CHAIR *in* II Kings 4:10; KJV COVERING *in* Song of S. 3:10, STOOL *in* II Kings 4:10), *cf.* Akkad. *kussû*, seat, chair; מוֹשָׁב (SEATING, KJV SITTING, *in* I Kings 10:5), שֶׁבֶת (KJV DWELLING *in* Num. 21:15), *from* יָשַׁב, sit; מֶרְכָּב, *from* רָכַב, to ride; תְּכוּנָה, *from* כּוּן, be firm; καθέδρα, *from* κατά, down, *plus* ἕδρα, seat, chair; KJV *frequently for* θρόνος (RSV THRONE)]; BEST SEAT [πρωτοκαθεδρία, *from* πρῶτος, first, foremost, *plus* ἕδρα, seat, chair (KJV *variously* CHIEF, UP-

PERMOST, HIGHEST SEAT)]. The biblical data make it difficult to distinguish between "seat," "chair," and "stool," and in some instances the distinction between these terms and "throne" is not much clearer. כסא in most of its occurrences has reference to the royal or divine throne and is so translated.

Likewise we can say little about the materials and methods used in constructing this furniture. We know, mostly on the basis of Egyptian archaeology, that woodworking was a highly developed skill in the ancient Near East, but to what extent this was known in Palestine we can only surmise. It is instructive, however, that in Sennacherib's list of tribute received from Hezekiah of Judah *ca.* 701 B.C., both couches and chairs are mentioned (*ANET* 288).

The various uses of the word "seat" are:

a) Royal seats, court seats. These include the seat of Eglon, king of Moab (Judg. 3:20), dining couches at Saul's court (I Sam. 20:18, 25), a chair for Bathsheba beside Solomon's throne (I Kings 2:19*b*), the seat of Solomon's throne (I Kings 10:19*b*), the seating arrangement at court for Solomon's officials (I Kings 10:5), and Haman's seat at the Persian court (Esth. 3:1). *See* JUDGMENT SEAT. Figs. ART 70; DAR 4.

b) The seat of a palanquin (Song of S. 3:10).

c) Ordinary chairs or stools. These include Eli's at the door of the sanctuary at Shiloh (I Sam. 1:9) and by the roadside (4:13, 18), Elisha's in his roof chamber (II Kings 4:10), Job's in the town square (Job 29:7), and those of the pigeon sellers in the temple court (Matt. 21:12; Mark 11:15). Figs. BAN 19-20; COS 49.

d) Synagogue seats. No first-century synagogue has survived, but the synagogue at Capernaum, which has been excavated and is dated about the third century A.D., has two stone benches along each of two sides. People who could not be thus accommodated apparently stood or sat on the floor. The "best seats," of which the gospels speak (Matt. 23:6; Mark 12:39; Luke 11:43; 20:46), were the seats reserved for the elders who sat at the front with their backs to the ark and their faces to the congregation. "MOSES' SEAT" (Matt. 23:2) was a special chair (in some cases, at least, of stone) allotted to one of these elders who was presumably a scholar of distinction (*see* SYNAGOGUE). Fig. SEA 36.

e) Figurative. In Job 23:3 "seat" is used for God's dwelling place (cf. Isa. 18:4, where a cognate noun is translated "dwelling"), and in Ezek. 28:2 Tyre boasts that she sits in the "seat of the gods." In Prov. 9:14 folly, personified as a wanton woman, takes her seat in a public place. In Ps. 1:1 we have the "seat of scoffers," meaning the assembly of scoffers (in 107:32 the same word is translated "assembly"). In Amos 6:3 the "seat of violence" means the establishment of injustice in the land. In Ezek. 8:3 "seat" appears to be a base on which, or a niche in which, an image or some other idolatrous object rested. In Num. 21:15 the "seat of Ar," possibly so named because of a local seatlike land or rock formation, refers to some unidentified location in Moab.

f) The covering of the ark is called the MERCY SEAT.

Bibliography. For a discussion of woodworking in the time of Sennacherib, see C. Singer, E. J. Holmyard, and A. R. Hall, eds., *A History of Technology* (1954), I, 684-703.

W. S. MCCULLOUGH

SEAT, MOSES'. The scribes and Pharisees were said by Jesus to sit on Moses' seat (Matt. 23:2). The rabbis of a much later period had a transliterated word, קתדרא, to describe the seat which they declared had been made for Moses, like a scholar's seat in which one appeared to be standing while sitting. The SCRIBES were by long tradition the recognized exegetes of the LAW of Moses, and the seat meant by Jesus is the metaphorical *cathedra* of

From Sukenik, *Ancient Synagogues in Palestine and Greece* (The British Academy, Schweich Lectures, 1930); courtesy of the Hebrew University, Jerusalem, Israel

36. Seat of Moses, from the synagogue at Chorazin

the teacher. Only a few among the extensive body of holy people known as PHARISEES were actually scribes. But Matthew often classes them together as one unit for condemnation.

Fig. SEA 36.   N. TURNER

SEBA sē'bə [סבא]. Perhaps a Sabean colony in Africa. *See* SABEANS.

SEBAM. Alternate form of SIBMAH.

SEBAT. KJV form of SHEBAT. *See also* CALENDAR.

SECACAH sĭ kā'kə [סככה, thicket, cover]. A town of Judah in the "wilderness" district (Josh. 15:61), probably to be identified with modern Khirbet es-Samrah, *ca.* 3⅓ miles SW of Khirbet Qumran in the Buqe'ah (Valley of Achor). It is the largest of three fortresses in the Buqe'ah (*see also* MIDDIN; NIBSHAN). Typical Iron II remains (casemated walls, pottery, etc.) suggest that these cities may be among those fortified by Jehoshaphat (*ca.* 873-849; II Chr. 17:12). Some construction may date from Uzziah's reign (*ca.* 783-742; cf. II Chr. 26:10).

Bibliography. F. M. Cross, Jr., "A Footnote to Biblical History," *BA*, 19 (1956), 12-17; F. M. Cross, Jr., and J. T. Milik, "Explorations in the Judean Buqê'ah," *BASOR*, 142 (1956), 5-17.   V. R. GOLD

SECHENIAS. KJV Apoc. form of SHECANIAH 3.

SECHU. KJV form of SECU.

SECOND ADAM. A phrase used to describe the idea of Christ expressed in Rom. 5:14-19; I Cor. 15: 21-23, 45-50; and perhaps also Phil. 2:5-11. Christ, as the "second Adam" or the "second man from heaven," is a glorified, life-giving Spirit, in whom believers are made alive and glorified, in contrast to the first man Adam, who is of the earth, earthy, whose sin brought condemnation, and in whom all men die. *See* SON OF MAN § 3c. S. E. JOHNSON

SECOND COMING. A phrase used to refer to the future coming, or PAROUSIA, of Christ. Despite Heb. 9:28; II Pet. 1:16(?), the phrase does not occur in the NT, which omits "second"—e.g., Matt. 24:3; I Thess. 2:19; Jas. 5:7; II Pet. 3:4. Justin Martyr, *ca.* A.D. 150, supplies the first evidence for precisely this terminology (e.g., Dial. 14.8). H. K. MCARTHUR

SECOND QUARTER [משנה, second (district)]; KJV THE SECOND (Zeph. 1:10); THE COLLEGE (II Kings 22:14; II Chr. 34:22). A district of Jerusalem in which Huldah the prophetess dwelt, in the angle formed by the W wall of the temple and the first (oldest) N rampart of the city; subsequently included within the wall restored by Nehemiah (*see* OLD GATE). Fig. NEH 13.

G. A. BARROIS

***SECRET, MESSIANIC** mĕs'ĭ ăn'ĭk. The knowledge that Jesus was Messiah and Son of God, which according to several NT books was not disclosed until after the Resurrection except to a small group of disciples.

According to Mark, Jesus was not recognized as Messiah until Peter's confession at Caesarea Philippi (8:27-9:1), when Jesus also taught that he was the suffering Son of man. Even so, the disciples failed to grasp the import of this (cf. 8:31-32 with 9:30-32). The demons, however, being spiritual creatures, had earlier recognized him as Son of God; but he had bidden them be silent (1:24-25; 3:11-12). Even Jesus' parables were, according to Mark's theory, obscure until explained to the disciples (4:10-13, 33-34). The secret of his nature was made public only at the hearing before the high priest (14:62).

This theory explained to the evangelists the rejection of Jesus and the apparent obscurity of some of the teaching. Q likewise emphasizes his rejection and the messianic secret (Matt. 11:2-30=Luke 7:18-35; 10:12-15, 21-24). Paul believes that the secret had been withheld from both Gentiles and Jews (Rom. 11:25; I Cor. 1:18-24; 2:6-9), but for Christians it is a mystery no longer (II Cor. 3:12-18). According to Luke, the messianic prophecies of the OT are not understood until after the Resurrection (Luke 24:25-27, 44-48). In the Gospel of John, John the Baptist recognizes Jesus at once, and Jesus reveals himself to his disciples at the very first (1:29-51), but they are slow to realize the implications of his teaching, and chs. 13-17 portray him as explaining the mystery after Judas has left the Upper Room. *See* CHRIST § 5.

Bibliography. W. Wrede, *Das Messiasgeheimnis in den Evangelien* (1901). S. E. JOHNSON

SECRETARY. *See* SCRIBE.

SECU sē'kū [שכו, lookout point(?)] (I Sam. 19:22); KJV SECHU. A site on the route between Gibeah and Ramah where Saul, in pursuit of David, sought information relative to his whereabouts. Though the site has commonly been regarded as a village, there are indications that a place name is, perhaps, not to be preferred, for some Greek and Latin MSS—e.g., LXX B—read ἐν τῷξεφει, "on the bare hilltop," instead of the MT "Secu." The exact location is presently unknown, but a cistern on the ancient site apparently served as a well-known and much-frequented gathering place. W. H. MORTON

SECUNDUS sĭ kŏon'dəs [Σέκουνδος; Σεκοῦνδος; Lat. *Secundus,* second] (Acts 20:4). A Thessalonian, companion of Aristarchus. With others, they accompanied Paul from Greece (probably Corinth) on his final journey to Jerusalem, when he took his collection to be presented to the poor there. It is possible, but not probable, that Secundus went only as far as Troas. B. H. THROCKMORTON, JR.

SEDECIAS sĕd'ə sī'əs. ZEDEKIAH in Douay Version.

SEDUCTION. *See* CRIMES AND PUNISHMENTS § C3b.

SEED, SEEDTIME. Wheat, barley, and flax were planted between November and January; while chick-peas, cucumbers, lentils, melons, millet, and sesame were planted between January and March. *See* AGRICULTURE.

SEEING [ראה, חזה; ὁράω, βλέπω, θεάομαι, θεωρέω]. Some special biblical uses of this term are:

a) Experiencing (e.g., Pss. 16:10; 27:13; 34:8, 12 ["enjoy"]; 89:48; 90:15; John 8:51).

b) Seeing (one's desire) on an enemy (cf. Ps. 118: 7; found also on the MOABITE STONE).

c) Visionary seeing, foreseeing, etc. (cf. Num. 24: 4, 16; I Kings 22:19; Isa. 6:1; Ezek. 1:1; Zech. 1:8; Acts 9:10; 10:3, 11; 22:17-18; Rev. 1:12 ff). *See* PROPHET; VISION.

d) Recovering of sight by the blind, as a parable of spiritual enlightenment (Mark 8:18 ff; John 9) and a sign of the new age (Isa. 35:5a; Luke 4:18; 7:21-22). Living to see the dawn of the new age brings happiness (cf. Luke 2:26; 10:23-24) to those who respond. Those who "see and perceive" (cf. Mark 4: 12) will "see life" (John 3:36) or "see the kingdom of God" (Mark 9:1; John 3:3).

e) Seeing God. God is all-seeing but unseen—except to faith (Heb. 11:27). In earlier OT narratives seeing God is believed to be fatal, but there are exceptions (e.g., Exod. 24:10; the LXX spiritualizes: "They saw the place where the God of Israel stood"). Moses may see only God's back, since none can see his face and live (Exod. 33:20 ff). Cf. the NT affirmation: "No one has ever seen God"; but "the only Son . . . has made him known" (John 1:18), for he is the "image of the invisible God" (Col. 1:15). To see him and behold his glory (John 1:14) is to see the Father (John 14:9). "The pure in heart . . . shall see God" (Matt. 5:8); cf. Nathanael, whose introduction (John 1:47 ff) recalls an etymology of "Israel" as a "man who sees God" (איש ראה אל). Those who saw Jesus in resurrection (cf. Matt. 28:17; I Cor. 9:1; 15:5 ff;

etc.) had objectively real experiences, although others saw nothing (Acts 9:7; 10:41). To have seen the risen Christ was an indispensable qualification for apostleship (Acts 1:22). Cf. the emphasis on ocular testimony in John 3:11, 32; 8:38; 19:35; I John 1:1, 3 (*see* WITNESS). Yet a special beatitude is pronounced on "those who have not seen and yet believe" (John 20:29).   F. F. BRUCE

SEER. *See* PROPHET.

SEGUB sē'gŭb [שְׂגוּב, exalted]. **1.** The youngest son of Hiel, the man who rebuilt Jericho during Ahab's reign (I Kings 16:34). Segub and his eldest brother, Abiram, may have been offered as foundation sacrifices for the new city. Such practice occurred in the ancient world. This interpretation was first offered by the Targ. which remarked that Hiel had killed his sons. Many modern commentators dispute the theory, however, holding merely that the deaths in Hiel's family were popularly linked with his building project. In any case the editor of Kings considers their deaths the fulfilment of Joshua's curse against anyone who should rebuild Jericho (Josh. 6:26), and it was undoubtedly only because of that tradition that the historical detail of these deaths was remembered.

2. A great-grandson of the patriarch Judah (I Chr. 2:21-22).

Bibliography. J. A. Montgomery, *The Books of Kings,* ICC (1951), pp. 287-88.   J. M. WARD

SEINE [מִכְמֹרֶת; *cf.* Akkad. *kamaru,* net, snare] (Hab. 1:15-16); KJV DRAG. A large drawnet. *See* NET § 1*a.*

The context of Hab. 1:14-17 suggests that "hook," "net," and "seine" are used figuratively to designate the military power of Israel's enemies. The reference to worship in vs. 16 may be to some veneration accorded to weapons of war. The precise meaning of מִכְמֹרֶת is not clear.   W. S. McCULLOUGH

SEIR sē'ər [שֵׂעִיר, hairy, shaggy, covered with brush or forests]. **1.** The chief mountain range of Edom; modern Jebel esh-Shera'. It extends the entire length of the Edomite homeland from the Wadi el-Hismeh in the S to the Wadi el-Hesa in the N, though its elevation begins to decline N of esh-Shobek and then rises again, followed by another decline before reaching the Wadi el-Hesa. This N section is called Jebal (cf. Roman and Byzantine Gebalene, Gobolitis). Its extension to the SW to the Gulf of Aqabah is the Sha'fat Ibn Jad, and to the SE another lower range of hills overlooking the Hismeh Valley is the Ras en-Naqb. It reaches from the Arabah on the W to the desert on the E. Much of it is a high plateau (up to 5,600 feet above sea level) with rolling hills; the rest, especially as one approaches the edges, is very rough to nearly impassable. While heavily wooded at one time, the process of denudation was completed during World War I.

Seir became the home of Esau and his descendants, the Edomites (Gen. 32:3; 33:14, 16; 36:8; Josh. 24:4; Judg. 5:4; etc.), who displaced the Horites (Gen. 14:6; 36:20-21; Deut. 2:1-8, 12). "Seir" is also

used as an expression for the Edomite nation (e.g., Num. 24:18; Ezek. 35; cf. Ezek. 25:12-14).

See also EDOM; IDUMEA.

2. A mountain forming part of Judah's N border (Josh. 15:10; *see* JEARIM, MOUNT); usually identified with Saris near Kesla (Chesalon), *ca.* nine miles W of Jerusalem. It is probably the place of farthest penetration by the Israelites in their abortive effort to enter Canaan from the S (Deut. 1:44). They were chased back by the Canaanites and the Amalekites (Num. 14:45). Since Canaanites never lived in the region occupied by Edom and the combination of Canaanite (in the N) and Amalekite (farther S) fits the known situation W of the Jordan, it seems probable that "Seir" of Josh. 15:10 is meant in Deut. 1:44 as well. Furthermore, it is known that Israel attempted an invasion from the S of Palestine, but there is no implication of a campaign of occupation in the biblical narrative that would result in a flight from Seir (E of the Arabah) to Hormah (W of the Arabah).

It is also possible that it is this Mount Seir to which the Simeonites migrated in the late eighth century (I Chr. 4:42-43), though the Edomite Seir (*see* 1 *above*) is also possible.

Bibliography. F.-M. Abel, *Géographie de la Palestine,* I (1933), 390-91. A. Robert, "Idumée," *Dictionnaire de la Bible, Supplément,* vol. 4 (1949), cols. 195-99.   V. R. GOLD

SEIRAH sē'ə rə [שְׂעִירָה, wooded hills(?)] (Judg. 3:26); KJV SEIRATH. It is not clear from the context whether the word is the name of a city or a term applied to some topographical feature. Ehud, after assassinating Eglon king of Moab, "passed beyond the sculptured stones [הַפְּסִילִים; Amer. Trans. *Pesilim,* as though the name of a village] and escaped to Seirah." The association with the SCULPTURED STONES, possibly the weirdly shaped hills in the Ghor near the Jordan River, supports the interpretation of Seirah as a topographical feature in the same general area.

It has usually been assumed that Seirah is to be sought in the territory of Ephraim, but a location in the Jordan Valley or E of the Jordan River in Moabite territory is equally possible. If the tradition had intended to describe the route within Canaan of Ehud's return to Ephraim, it is probable that that reference would have been made to well-known places such as Jericho, Bethel, or Shiloh.   W. L. REED

*SELA sē'lə [סֶלַע, הַסֶּלַע, crag]; KJV *once* SELAH (II Kings 14:7). **1.** A fortress city of Edom, conquered by Amaziah of Judah and renamed by him Joktheel (II Kings 14:7). It is to be identified with Umm el-Bayyarah, the great acropolis which dominates the basin in which the Nabatean city of PETRA was built; this is proved by the quantities of sherds from the Early Iron I-II Age (1200-600 B.C.) which are found there. It is situated in the W boundary of Edom proper, *ca.* twenty miles from its S extremity, at the point where the road from Gaza climbs up the plateau from the Arabah, and was evidently intended to protect the S capital of Teman, located *ca.* three miles E. Figs. SEL 37-38; PET 41-42.

No details are given in the Bible as to the exact

From *Atlas of the Bible* (Thomas Nelson & Sons Limited)

37. Aerial view of Sela, Umm el-Bayyarah

Courtesy of the Palestine Archaeological Museum, Jerusalem, Jordan

38. Edomite mountain city of Sela, dominating the enclosure at Petra

course of Amaziah's campaign, but it is probable that, after defeating the Edomites in the Valley of Salt, he marched down the King's Highway as far as Teman, then turned westward and took the fortress in reverse. There is a possible reminiscence of this feat in passages that speak of Edom as living "in the clefts of the rock" (Jer. 49:16; Obad. 3), as the Hebrew word for "the rock" is the same as that translated "Sela."

Another Sela in Edom, marked by a village of the same name, is found a few miles W-NW of Buseireh (biblical Bozrah). This, however, was a Nabatean city and not the same as the Sela of the Bible.

2. A place on the border of the Amorites in the time of the judges (Judg. 1:36). It was apparently in Judah, but its site is unknown.

3. A place in Moab, mentioned rather obscurely in a prophecy of destruction (Isa. 16:1). Its site has not been identified.   S. COHEN

SELAH sē'lə. *See* MUSIC.

SELA-HAMMAHLEKOTH sē'lə hə mä'lə kŏth. KJV translation of סלע המחלקות (I Sam. 23:28; RSV ROCK OF ESCAPE). *See* ESCAPE, ROCK OF.

SELED sē'lĕd [סלד] (I Chr. 2:30). The first-born son of Nadab of Judah. He was childless—a terrible fate for a Hebrew, since immortality was known only in the perpetuation of one's name and honor through one's heirs.

SELEMIA sĭ lē'mĭ ə [Vulg. *Salemiam*] (II Esd. 14:24). One of five scribes Ezra was bidden to take with him, "because they are trained to write rapidly."

J. C. SWAIM

SELEMIAS sĕl'ə mī'əs. KJV Apoc. form of SHELEMIAH 6.

SELEUCIA sĭ lōō'shə [Σελευκία *or* Σελεύκεια, *according to MS preferred*]. The name of several cities, one of which (*see* SELEUCIA IN SYRIA) is mentioned in both the Apoc. and the NT; all situated in the Middle East and all founded during the Hellenistic period (*see* GREECE § 9) by Seleucus Nicator. In the Greek language "Seleucia" is the adjective formed from the noun "Seleucus," and so it means the "city belonging to Seleucus." *See* SELEUCUS 1.

There were nine ancient towns which bore this name, but only four of these are of great interest to the student of the Bible.

1. *See* SELEUCIA IN SYRIA.

2. Seleucia in Mesopotamia. This city was founded by Seleucus Nicator in 312 B.C. and was intended to be his capital in Mesopotamia, taking the place of Babylon as the center of the new Greek cultural interest in that part of the world. It was cosmopolitan, having a mixed population (*ca.* 600,000) of Macedonians, Greeks, Syrians, and Jews, in NT times. It was situated on the right bank of the River Tigris. When the city was destroyed (A.D. 164), there died with it all that was best of Hellenistic civilization in Mesopotamia.

3. Seleucia in Cilicia. This was an autonomous city, also owing its origin (300 B.C.) to Seleucus. It

Courtesy of the Department of Art and Archaeology, Princeton, University

39. The market gate at Seleucia

was situated on the River Calycadnus (now the Göksu) a few miles from its mouth, in the Roman province of Cilicia. It was anciently known as Seleucia Tracheotis or Trachea (the modern Icel, or perhaps Silifke). It was probably designed to protect Cilicia against attacks from the seaward side.

Fig. SEL 39.

4. Seleucia in Palestine. Josephus informs us that in the days of the ruthless and powerful Alexander Janneus (*see* HASMONEANS § 3*d*) a certain Seleucia was among the places which had previously belonged to the fast-disintegrating kingdom of Syria but were now in the hands of the Jews (Jos. Antiq. XIII.xv.4). This Seleucia was not the Syrian fortress (*see* SELEUCIA IN SYRIA), but was a city in Bashan, near GOLAN and Gamala, which too Alexander seized (Jos. War I.iv.8), and situated on the E side of Lake Merom in the extreme N of Palestine. Jewish occupation did little good to cities which had adopted Greek ways; much of the Greek culture was destroyed and nothing of comparable value substituted. When Pompey left the Middle East for home in 61 B.C., Seleucia once again enjoyed, in common with neighboring cities, virtually a complete freedom, in spite of the official subjection to a Roman governor; and the city magistrates were elected by the people on the Greek model and wielded wide powers of government in the city. Later on, Josephus fortified the place as a center of revolt against the Romans (Jos. War II.xx.6). The present site is unknown.

N. TURNER

SELEUCIA IN SYRIA. On or near the site of this Hellenistic city stands the modern Samandağ or Suediah, in Turkey, which is no longer a port, its importance as a trading center having been long ago usurped by the Turkish port of Iskenderun (or Alexandretta) much farther N. The constant depositing of silt, flowing down the river Orontes, has converted the ancient harbor into a level, marshy expanse. In the biblical period, from the third century B.C., Seleucia was a flourishing commercial city and frontier fortress on the seacoast of Syria and near Cilicia. It figured in the missionary journey of Barnabas and Saul. *See* PAUL § A2*d*.

1. Origin. There is no doubt that Seleucia and three other cities of N Syria, which together formed

a group known as the Seleucian Tetrapolis, were founded at the beginning of the third century B.C. by Seleucus Nicator, who was one of the generals of Alexander the Great and the first of the line of Seleucid rulers of Syria. It was five miles N of the mouth of the River Orontes, on which Antioch was situated. In the group were also Antioch, Apamea, and Laodicea. Antioch was built by Seleucus at the same time to form a new capital for his Syrian share of Alexander's empire, and the intention probably was that Seleucia should be an impregnable port serving the capital, from which ships might sail with passengers and merchandise along the coast as far as Egypt or westward to the island of Cyprus and Asia Minor. Seleucia, moreover, proved to be the fitting burial place of its founder, Seleucus.

The city is more strictly referred to as Seleucia Pieria in order to distinguish it from the many other Seleucias, especially the one in Mesopotamia and the one in Cilicia not far away. The name Pieria is mentioned by Strabo, the ancient Greek geographer of the first century B.C., who refers to a special kind of asphalt which was mined there. A monk named John Malalas, who was born in Antioch at the end of the fifth century A.D. and who spent most of his life there, has left in his *Chronicle* the interesting information that Seleucus Nicator had the desire to build many cities, and that he actually commenced with Seleucia, calling it after himself, and building it on the site of a previous trading center named Pieria. Malalas implies that Seleucia was older than Antioch, which was built next by Seleucus and called after his son Antiochus Soter. At all events, near the site of Seleucia today can be seen the ruins of the port of Al Mina, which traded with the cities of Greece until the time of Alexander the Great. Al Mina had been in very ancient times the capital of a small kingdom, Alalakh, which was destroyed *ca.* 1200 B.C. by invaders from the sea. It was probably with this old port as a nucleus that Seleucus founded the new Hellenistic port of Seleucia.

2. History. Early in its history Seleucia was lost by its Seleucid founders and went to Egypt, having been conquered by the Ptolemies. This was in the middle of the third century and was directly due to the conflict between the rival queens at the death of Antiochus II. At this point the new king of Egypt, Ptolemy III Euergetes, in order to take vengeance for the evil done by Laodice, wife and sister of Antiochus II, to his own sister Bernice, the second wife of Antiochus, came over from Egypt and eventually overran Syria, after he had first taken and entered in triumph the key fortress of Seleucia. The Egyptian force which achieved this, probably setting out from Cyprus, was designed to come to the aid of Bernice, who was already being supported by the city of Antioch. Seleucia surrendered willingly to Ptolemy, the garrison having declared in favor of Bernice, and the governor of Cyprus entered Seleucia with a squadron as he passed on his way to Antioch. Ptolemy came also, but too late to save his sister, who had been betrayed. The substance of Dan. 11:7-9 is to be interpreted in the light of these events; the "fortress" of vs. 7 is thought to be Seleucia, as being the fort of Antioch. The issue of this Third Syrian War was that Egypt retained Seleucia and all Phoenicia, although Laodice's son, Seleucus II Callinicus, had driven Egyptian forces from much of Syria. But it seems almost certain that this domination was short-lived in the case of Seleucia, because we find that in 229 Seleucus II is granting to the city its freedom. There must have been some form of counterattack and some attempt to regain Seleucia and other places, on the part of Seleucus, before he bowed to the inevitable and resolved on a ten-years' peace with Ptolemy. The words in Dan. 11:9 appear to hint at an unsuccessful counterattack of this kind at this point: "Then [the king of the north] shall come into the realm of the king of the south but shall return into his own land." It was not until the energetic campaigns of Antiochus III "the Great" that Seleucia was regained from Egypt by the Seleucids. By 219, Antiochus had decided it was time to regain the former Seleucid possessions; he attacked the strongly held Seleucia first of all, bribing some of the officers there, and speedily gaining control. On a later occasion in his reign, after great successes in the East in 205, he re-entered Seleucia in magnificent triumph as a second Alexander, bringing 150 elephants and enormous plunder. It was probably on this occasion, and actually in Seleucia, that he assumed the Achaemenid title of "great king," thus becoming known to the Greeks as Antiochus "the Great."

Seleucia increased in importance as a port and frontier fort until the Roman period. It was so well fortified, by nature as well as by man, that its advantages became obvious to potential foes of Syria. The fortress has therefore been well described as a kind of Ptolemaic Calais or a Syrian Gibraltar—a strong city which the Seleucid rulers valued highly in their constant struggles with the Ptolemies. This was particularly so when Ptolemy Philometor VI, ruler of Egypt in the mid–second century B.C., made an attempt to win Egypt's lost territories from Syria and, according to I Macc. 11:8, did succeed in 146 B.C. in capturing Seleucia and other coastal cities.

It was in Seleucia that the much-married and resourceful woman, Cleopatra Thea, was marooned during the subsequent period when Trypho was struggling to retain the throne of Syria. Cleopatra had first married Alexander Balas *ca.* 150 B.C.; but her father, Ptolemy Philometor, having decided to support Demetrius II, who was the rival of Balas and was trying to gain the throne of Syria, had proceeded to take her away from Balas and bestow her upon Demetrius. Her second husband was later captured by the Parthians, and it was while she was shut up in Seleucia (as Josephus states) that Cleopatra, living in dread lest the inhabitants should surrender to her husband's usurper, Trypho, sent a proposal of marriage to her husband's sixteen-year-old brother, Antiochus, along with the suggestion that he should usurp the kingdom himself, which he did in 138 B.C. (Jos. Antiq. XIII.vii.1). This seems to have been the end of Seleucia's domination by the Ptolemies forever; in 109 the Syrian ruler, Antiochus Grypus, again bestowed freedom upon the city—a privilege which apparently included the right to coin money.

Mithridates of Pontus and Tigranes of Armenia were at one in their suspicion of the encroaching power of Rome in the Middle East, and, before Pompey was entrusted in 66 B.C. with command of the Roman military maneuvers in the East, Armenian armies had invaded Syria and penetrated as far as Jerusalem. When Pompey arrived, he quickly drove the invading kings away and made himself master of everything in Asia W of the Euphrates. He granted to Seleucia, when it fell into his hands, the status of a free city (which privilege it had received on more than one occasion already) because of the stout resistance which it had shown against the invading Armenian king and his ally, the king of Pontus. On the collapse of the Syrian kingdom, the Romans improved it still more from a military point of view, increasing its already fine natural and artificial defenses.

At the time when Barnabas and Saul and John Mark, in A.D. 49, sailed away from here in a merchant vessel on the first Christian missionary voyage (Acts 13:4), and when, in the reign of Trajan at the end of the first century A.D., the holy martyr Ignatius, bishop of Antioch, passed through the port of Seleucia on his way to the wild beasts at Rome, Seleucia still enjoyed at the hands of the Romans the status of a free city. Although it is said that the missionaries returned to Antioch (Acts 14:26), with no mention of Seleucia, it is nevertheless beyond reasonable doubt that they landed at the port from which they had set out, rather than that they sailed up the River Orontes to Antioch itself. Beneath the sea, beyond the swampy ruins of Seleucia's port, two pieces of the old harbor which are, or were, locally known as Paul and Barnabas are reputed still to be visible, and in all probability these outer pillars of the harbor date at least from the apostle's period.

It is further most likely that it was from this same harbor of Seleucia that Paul set sail with Silas on his second missionary journey (Acts 15:40-41), and that Barnabas set sail from here with Mark on his second journey (vs. 39).

Its status as a free city was confirmed by the Romans in 70. It was the base of an imperial fleet, the *classis Syriaca,* early in the reign of Augustus and throughout the first century. Roman emperors attempted to improve the place as a port—never very successfully, for it was not really adapted geographically for the purpose. There is, however, one feat of Roman engineering which travelers may still see and wonder at. It is an enormous tunnel seven yards high, cut through the rocks at considerable depth for two hundred yards or so, apparently with the aim of deflecting the waters of a mountain stream—one of those "donkey-drowners" of which the ancient inhabitants complained—away from the harbor, to save the harbor district from floods and to form perhaps a reservoir of drinking water. At any rate, near the entrance the inscription "Divus Vespasianus et Divus Titus" has been discerned on a stone, and this suggests that the work had some connection with the visit of Titus to Palestine in order to quell the Jewish rising, or that at least it was contemporaneous with it (A.D. 66-70).

It is interesting to note that the harbor of Seleucia was the scene not only of memorable Christian journeys in the formative years of the new faith, but also of the journeys of one who must be regarded as a rival to the Christians, yet one who likewise set out to purify morals, to drive out demons, and to heal the sick wherever he went. The Greek author Philostratus tells us that Apollonius, the venerable sage of Tyana, and his fellow pagan evangelists, leaving Antioch, "went down to the sea of Seleucia, and finding a ship, they sailed to Cyprus" (*Life of Apollonius* III.lviii). Apollonius was a would-be reformer of paganism along Pythagorean lines. He was born at the beginning of the Christian era, and his journeys barefoot through the port of Syria must have coincided almost with those of Paul and Barnabas and Silas. Apollonius wrote letters, after the manner of the Christian apostle, and two of these were addressed to the councilors of Seleucia (almost certainly our Seleucia), who had asked him to visit them. From these letters we learn that the city was hospitable to man and devoted to the gods (*Epistles of Apollonius* XII; XIII).

3. Description. As is already clear, Seleucia Pieria was a valuable city-fortress in the N of Syria, high enough to make Cyprus visible on a clear day, situated in the bleakly mountainous frontier district between Cilicia and Syria. The city was established on a long, sloping S spur of Mount Pierius—or Mount Coryphaeus, as Polybius calls it—which broods over the Mediterranean, more than four thousand feet in height, just S of the Bay of Alexandretta, and now has the name of Jebel Mousa (or Mousa Dagh). It is the extreme S part of the long range known to the Romans as Mons Amanus.

Seleucia was surrounded by terraced cliffs on three sides and lay four or five miles N of the mouth of the River Orontes, sixteen miles W of Antioch. Its position reveals the astuteness of its founder, Seleucus, who appreciated the problems attendant on the constant heavy flow, down the river, of silt and sewage from Antioch which would quickly obstruct any harbor built at the river's mouth. Indeed, the silting has now finally completed its work, and the harbor, though five miles distant to the N of the mouth, lies at the present time beneath the swampy, malarial soil. It never ranked among the first-class ports of the world, but it was certainly the equal of Coptos, Myos Hormos, Aradus, and Berytus in the East.

From the sea the upper part of the city could be approached only by way of a steep and twisty stairway, still visible, cut in the rock (as Polybius tells us), but there was a lower part or suburbs, fortified strongly within the same walls, which was in reality the port and business quarter of the city. This lay on a table of level ground below the steep mountain on which the upper city and its acropolis stood.

The ancient city must have been a proud place, resplendent with many temples; and it had an amphitheater, partly cut out of the cliff, the ruins of which remain at the present time. The cities of the Syrian Tetrapolis, of which Seleucia was one, ever prided themselves during the Hellenistic period on their loyalty to Greek cultural ideals, and on coins dating from the middle of the second century B.C. there is stamped the high-sounding inscription ἀδελφοὶ δῆμοι ("brother townships"—a title with ancient Greek associations). Moreover, there is still to be seen the ruin of the ancient great road which connected Antioch with its port of Seleucia, running deeply through the rocks. There is also a lofty ruin of a great gate in the city wall, the market gate. In

addition, on the steep lower slopes of Mousa Dagh there is still visible a series of large caves, the ruins probably of ancient warehouses, and there are, moreover, desecrated tombs in the cliffs.

Extensive excavations have been carried out in modern times both in and around Antioch. These excavations, commenced in 1932 and interrupted by the outbreak of World War II, were conducted mainly under the auspices of Princeton University. Many of the remains of ancient Seleucia Pieria, which cover a very large area, began to be carefully unearthed and studied from July 17, 1937, and were excavated more extensively during the following spring and also in 1939. These included houses and the market gate, the large Doric temple in the upper city dating from the biblical period, and a memorial church, the Martyrion, in the lower city, dating from the fifth century A.D.

Bibliography. Polybius *Histories* 5.58.3–5.59.11. Strabo *Geography* 7.5.8. *Chronicle of John Malalas,* books VIII–XVIII. A. Holm, *The History of Greece* (English trans., 1894), vol. III, ch. 27; vol. IV, chs. 5, 13. V. Chapot, *Bulletin des Antiquaires de France, Mém.* (1906), pp. 149 ff. P. Jacquot, *Antioche* (1931), III, 479 ff. H. V. Morton, *In the Steps of St. Paul* (1936), pp. 98-101. R. Stillwell, ed., *Antioch-on-the-Orontes, Publications of the Committee for the Excavation of Antioch and Its Vicinity. III. The Excavations of 1937-1939* (1941). J. Finegan, *Light from the Ancient Past* (1946), pp. 257-59, 449. "Lands of the Bible Today" (National Geographic Society map; vol. CX [1956], no. 6). N. TURNER

SELEUCUS sĭ lōō′kəs [Σέλευκος]. The name of four kings of Syria belonging to the family known as Seleucidae. *See* ANTIOCHUS.

1. Seleucus I Nicator. One of Alexander the Great's generals, who after Alexander's death in 323 B.C. gradually made himself king of Syria, also ruling most of the Asiatic provinces which were once included in Alexander's empire. In 321 the satrapy of Babylonia was assigned to him; but in 316 Antigonus, ruler of Phrygia, drove him out. Seleucus placed himself under Ptolemy of Egypt (hence Dan. 11:5 calls him "one of his princes"), and assisted him in the defeat of Antigonus at the battle of Gaza in 312. After this, Seleucus regained his lost satrapy and established the Seleucid dynasty, which lasted

Courtesy of the American Numismatic Society

40. Coin of Seleucus I: obverse, head of Seleucus; reverse, Athena drawn in chariot by four elephants

until 65 B.C. After the Battle of Ipsus in 301 he received also Syria and much of Asia Minor. The Seleucid era, from which events are dated in I Maccabees and other histories, also began at this time. The founding of several great cities, including Antioch and Apamea, Laodicea, Edessa, Beroea, and Seleucia, centers of Greek culture, was his work. He was well disposed toward the Jews; indeed, he settled them in Antioch and several others of his cities, with rights of citizenship. He was assassinated in 282, while he was in the process of attempting to gain the whole of Alexander's empire.

Fig. SEL 40.

2. Seleucus II Callinicus (246-226 B.C.), son of Antiochus II of Syria. He is mentioned in Dan. 11: 6-9. He was engaged in a war, known as the Third Syrian War or Laodicean War, with Ptolemy Euergetes, who had invaded his dominions because his mother, the outrageous Laodice, had murdered the Egyptian princess Bernice. Ptolemy captured the city of Seleucia. When Seleucus tried to retaliate against Egypt, he was routed. It seems that Egypt captured Antioch and most of the Seleucid Empire. Seleucus entrusted much power to his younger brother Antiochus, who, however, proved to be treacherous until he was finally put down. Seleucus' reign ended in some uncertainty, and he died as the result of a fall from his horse.

3. Seleucus III Soter (or Ceraunus; 226-223 B.C.), son and heir of Seleucus II and brother of Antiochus III the Great. He did not wage war with Egypt, but his invasion of Asia Minor to put down Attalus—during which invasion he met his death—is thought to have been a prelude to future campaigns in Egypt on the part of his brother.

4. Seleucus IV Philopator (187-175 B.C.), nephew of Seleucus III and brother of Antiochus Epiphanes. He succeeded his father, Antiochus the Great. In II Macc. 3:7 he is mentioned in connection with an unsuccessful attempt to rob the temple at Jerusalem "for royal glory" (the reference is to him in Dan. 11: 20). Seleucus sent his chief minister, Heliodorus, to seize the funds which had been deposited in the temple. He was both avaricious and, at that time, in great need of funds. He had come to the throne in inglorious times, when his own country was weak and Rome was powerful in the East, and Seleucus owed much money to Rome in connection with a peace treaty made between them. Finally, his minister Heliodorus murdered him and attempted to seize the throne, but Seleucus was succeeded by his brother.

Bibliography. Jos. Antiq. XII.iii-iv. E. Bevan, *The House of Seleucus* (1900, 1901). G. A. Deissmann, *Bible Studies* (English trans., 1901), pp. 303-7. Histories of the Jews by Schürer and Juster. *Cambridge Ancient History*, vol. IX (1932). F.-M. Abel, *Les Livres des Maccabées* (1949). N. TURNER

SELF-CONTROL. The translation of several words in the Bible. The only occurrence of the word in the OT is as the translation of אֵין מַעְצָר לְרוּחוֹ in Prov. 25:28:

> A man without self-control
>   is like a city broken into and left without walls.

In some respects the KJV "he that hath no rule over his own spirit" is nearer the original. The picture is that of a city whose walls have been so nearly destroyed as to be without defense against an enemy; so is the man who has no restraint over his spirit, the "source of man's passionate energies" (*IB*, IV, 928). He has no defense against anger, lust, and the other unbridled emotions that destroy the personality. Prov. 16:32 gives the positive side:

> He who is slow to anger is better than the mighty,
>   and he who rules his spirit than he who takes a city,

although the same Hebrew word is not used. The virtue of self-control, a familiar one to Greek thought, is referred to in the OT only in the wisdom books.

In the NT "self-control" is used as a translation for words which come from two distinctly different Greek stems. In II Tim. 1:7 it translates σωφρονισμός, which occurs only once, and is used here as an equivalent of σωφροσύνη. Along with φρόνησις or σοφία ("good sense" or "wisdom"), ἀνδρεία ("courage"), and δικαιοσύνη ("justice"), σωφρονισμός was a virtue common to all Greek ethical thought since the days of Plato. It meant originally "soundness of mind as opposed to insanity," then "moderation," "good sense." The first meaning is found in Acts 26:25, and the second in I Tim. 2:9, 15. The cognate verb, σωφρονέω, appears in the first meaning in Mark 5:15; Luke 8:35; II Cor. 5:13; and in the second, "to exercise moderation," in Rom. 12:3; Tit. 2:6; I Pet. 4:7. Plato defines σωφροσύνη as "self-discipline in certain desires and pleasures"; and the corresponding adjective was often given the specific sense of "controlled in sexual desire," "chaste." Since in II Tim. 1:7 "self-control" is merely one of a list of three virtues, a "spirit of power and love and self-control," in contrast to a "spirit of timidity," it is somewhat difficult to determine the exact shade of meaning. Easton's translation, "sober wisdom," seems better than the RSV "self-control."

The other occurrences of "self-control" are translations of the noun ἐγκράτεια (Acts 24:25; Gal. 5:23; II Pet. 1:6) and the verb ἐγκρατεύομαι (I Cor. 7:9; 9:25), both meaning basically the control which one exercises over something or someone, including oneself. This last, ἐγκράτεια ἑαυτοῦ, played an important part from Plato on in the ethical systems of classical and Hellenistic teachers, who regarded it as one of the cardinal virtues. It represents the ideal of the free man's having power over his own desires and emotions, so that he does not become a slave to base pleasures (φαῦλαι ἡδοναί). Philo also uses it frequently, but he is influenced by his cosmological dualism, in which the material is to be avoided. Hence for him the goal of ἐγκράτεια is the avoidance of every physical act which is not absolutely essential to existence. In contrast ἐγκράτεια and ἐγκρατής appear very infrequently in the Greek Bible, and then only in the Apoc.

In the NT, Paul uses the verb in I Cor. 7:9 to mean the control of sexual desire, and in 9:25 of the athlete who exercises self-control over the bodily appetites as part of training for participation in the games. In Gal. 5:23 the noun is given in a list of virtues which are the "fruit of the Spirit"; and in much the same way it is found in II Pet. 1:6. In Acts 24:25 it, along with "justice" (δικαιοσύνη) and "future judgment," is the subject of Paul's discussion with Felix, but it is difficult to discover just what connotation the word has here. In I Cor. 7:5 "lack of self-control" is the translation for ἀκρασία, from the same root as ἐγκράτεια, and clearly means "incontinence."

Two things in particular may be said as one compares the idea of "self-control" in Greek literature and in the Bible. One is the fact of its rarity in the latter—a clear indication that it does not play an important part in the thinking of the biblical writers. The other is that, when it does occur, its meaning must be determined in the light of the whole biblical outlook. The Greek ideal looked toward a perfecting of the self into a harmonious whole—a man at peace with himself and with his environment, a work of which one might be justly proud and which justly claimed the respect of one's fellows. Hence ἐγκράτεια, "self-control," was the art of keeping all one's natural drives and instincts under one's command in order to produce a well-rounded personality. On the other hand, for the Christian, ἐγκράτεια is one of the "fruits of the Spirit," along with love, joy, peace, etc., whose essential meaning can be arrived at only in the light of the long history of the development of the idea that man can attain perfection only as he relies more and more upon God and not upon himself, and as he sees more and more clearly the meaning for himself of the work of Christ and of the Holy Spirit.

Bibliography. E. DeW. Burton, *Commentary on Galatians,* ICC (1920), p. 317. For a very good, although brief, treatment of the word, see F. D. Gealy, Exegesis of II Timothy, *IB,* XI (1955), 465. E. J. COOK

SELF-DENIAL. A concept which may be seen in both the OT and the NT. In general, self-denial is the rejection of self, the renunciation of one's personal desires or ambitions in favor of a higher goal. As the idea appears in the Bible, it is less prominent in the OT than in the NT, where it is portrayed as self-rejection in favor of personal loyalty to Christ (Matt. 16:24; Mark 8:34; Luke 9:23; *see below*).

1. Background in the OT
2. In early Christian piety
3. Radical self-denial in the NT
   a. In the teaching of Jesus
   b. In the thought of Paul
Bibliography

1. Background in the OT. In the OT there are forms of partial self-denial such as disciplinary restrictions and prohibitions for some individuals (*see* RECHABITE; NAZIRITE; ESSENES; FASTING; cf. also 1QS I.1-15, etc.).

Self-denial as such is not clearly expressed as a general principle in the main stream of OT thought. It is implied, however, to the extent that the vocation of Israel is understood in terms of subordinating national ambition to the purpose of God (*see* ELECTION; VOCATION; cf. Isa. 42:1-8; 52:13–53:12; etc.). Similarly, self-denial becomes the obligation of certain persons who must forego their own inclinations in favor of a special calling—e.g., Moses (Exod. 3:1-8), Jeremiah (Jer. 1:4-10; 15:15-18), and Amos (Amos 3:8).

2. In early Christian piety. One may describe as forms of partial self-denial certain acts of piety, fasting, charity, and self-restraint mentioned in the NT (Matt. 4:1-11; Luke 4:1-13; Acts 13:3; 14:23; I Cor. 7:5; 9:27; I Tim. 2:9; I Pet. 3:3-4; etc.; but cf. Mark 2:18-20). These practices, however, seem to be expressions of ordinary piety or SELF-CONTROL and do not receive a major emphasis in the NT.

In the Sermon on the Mount, an added dimension of self-denial is imparted to almsgiving and fasting when men are exhorted to carry out these duties in secrecy and without ostentation (Matt. 6:1-4, 16-18). Elsewhere in the NT, Christian life and piety are given a self-denying depth of meaning when the self-giving love of Christ is held up as the example (Matt. 20:25-28; Mark 10:42-45; Luke 22:25-27; John 13:12-17; II Cor. 8:9; Eph. 5:1-2; Phil. 2:5-11; I Pet. 2:21-23; etc.).

3. Radical self-denial in the NT. The strongest and clearest expression of self-denial in its radical and distinctive NT sense is found in the saying of Jesus: "If any man would come after me, let him deny himself [ἀπαρνησάσθω ἑαυτόν] and take up his cross and follow me" (Mark 8:34; cf. Matt. 16:24; Luke 9:23).

a. In the teaching of Jesus. The meaning of radical self-denial in the teaching of Jesus is clear: it is utter self-rejection in favor of following Christ. In Mark 8:34-35 (cf. Matt. 16:24-25; Luke 9:23-24; John 12:25-26), both the negative and the positive elements in the NT concept of self-denial appear. In its negative sense, self-denial is the rejection of one's own life, property, and welfare (Matt. 19:16-30; Mark 10:17-31; Luke 18:18-30; cf. Matt. 10:37-38; Luke 14:26-27). In its positive aspect, self-denial is but the first step in the total act of committing oneself to Christ. Thus, self-denial is not an end in itself; rather, it is the self-rejection which is incurred in the process of following Christ.

It is of significance that all three Synoptic gospels place the primary saying of Jesus about self-denial in the context of the first prediction of his own suffering and death. Seen in the light of this context, Christian self-denial is to be understood as participation in the cross of Christ (cf. Matt. 20:20-28; Mark 10:35-45).

b. In the thought of Paul. Even though self-denial as such is not mentioned in the writings of Paul, he nevertheless understands the Christian life in terms of sacrificial self-giving (Rom. 12:1). As far as Paul's personal life is concerned, the heart of his teaching is stated when he indicates his own desire to count all things as refuse for the sake of gaining Christ (Phil. 3:7-11). Even so, however, Paul does not think of the Christian life apart from the work of Christ himself. According to Paul, the Christian life has its focus and dynamic in the believer's dying and rising with Christ (Rom. 6). This spiritual-moral process of participating in the death and resurrection of Christ includes the renunciation of the old self in order that a new self might become a reality in and through Christ (Rom. 6:6-11; Gal. 2:20; cf. Eph. 4:20-24; Col. 3:5-11).

Bibliography. V. Taylor, *Jesus and His Sacrifice* (1937), pp. 268-73. R. Bultmann, *Theology of the NT* (trans. K. Grobel; 1951), I, 11-32, 239-46. See literature in W. F. Arndt and F. W. Gingrich, *A Greek English Lexicon of the NT* (1957), under "ἀπαρνέομαι," p. 80; "ἀρνέομαι," p. 107. R. L. SCHEEF, JR.

SEM. KJV NT form of SHEM.

SEMACHIAH sĕm'ə kī'ə [סמכיהו, Yahu has sustained] (I Chr. 26:7). One of the gatekeepers of the sanctuary.

Bibliography. M. Noth, *Die israelitischen Personennamen* (1928), pp. 70, 176.

SEMEI. KJV Apoc. form of SHIMEI 16.

SEMEIN sĕm'ĭ ən [Σεμεῖν=שָׁמְעִי (*e.g.,* Exod. 6:17)] (Luke 3:26); KJV SEMEI —ī. An ancestor of Jesus.

SEMELLIUS. KJV Apoc. form of SHIMSHAI.

SEMIS. KJV Apoc. form of SHIMEI 16.

SEMITE sĕm'īt. A person belonging to those peoples of mankind either having common descent from Shem the son of Noah (Gen. 5:32) or speaking one of the Semitic languages (*see* LANGUAGES OF THE ANCIENT NEAR EAST). This is a linguistic, and not a racial, classification.

The term was first used in 1781 by A. L. Schlözer to designate the descendants of Shem in the list of Gen. 10:21 ff. Geographically this list suggests that Shem's descendants spread from Lydia eastward through greater Syria, Assyria, to Persia. The N boundary was in Armenia; the S, on the Red Sea and the Persian Gulf. It is probable that EBER (Gen. 10:24) is to be related to those who spoke the HEBREW LANGUAGE. Curiously, the Canaanites and Abyssinians seem to be classified as sons of Ham (vss. 6-7), even though these languages are Semitic. This perhaps reflects the political situation in ancient Israel.

The original home of the Semites is difficult to assay. At the dawn of civilization traces of the Semitic languages are found all over the Fertile Crescent. They perhaps came originally from N Arabia but were already in the area of the Tigris and Euphrates before the great city-states were established. Waves of Semitic nomads (*see* NOMADISM) at various periods in prehistoric and historic times are thought by some to have successively engulfed the Fertile Crescent from the E deserts. It is impossible to prove this theory.

The Semitic family today includes most of the inhabitants of Syria, Iraq, Jordan, Israel, Arabia, and a high percentage of Turkey, Lebanon, and North Africa. Through the Jews they have influenced Europe and America, and through the Arabs they have penetrated deep into Africa.

The book of Genesis contains some suggestions of the pre-Mosaic Semitic religion. Even some of the practices of the patriarchs are not to be confused with orthodox Mosaic religion. There was belief in local deities (Gen. 16:13; 31:13; 35:7). Some of the names of the patriarchs and their relatives are not only place names but appear also as deities. The name El for "god" seems to have been widespread among the Semites and probably, as in Ugarit, indicates a great high god. The fertility cult was strong in pre-Israelite Canaan, and its survival during the monarchy caused the prophets from Elijah to Jeremiah much difficulty.

It is no longer necessary to argue the point that the Semites are not a race. It is a fallacy to apply eighteenth- and nineteenth-century linguistic studies to the field of anthropology. At best today they are a group of people speaking related languages. Already in the tenth century A.D. the language affinities of Hebrew and Arabic were recognized. In the sixteenth, Abyssinian (*see* ETHIOPIA) was added to this group. The OT has recorded the language of Canaan (Isa. 19:18), the Aramaic language (II Kings 18:26), that of Judah (II Kings 18:26, 28; Neh. 13: 24; Isa. 36:11; cf. "Jews" in Esth. 8:9), that of the Chaldeans (Dan. 1:4), and that of Ashdod (Neh. 13: 24). The NT speaks of Hebrew (Acts 21:40; 22:2; etc.). The eighth-century-B.C. siege of Jerusalem indicates that the ARAMAIC LANGUAGE was understood both by the inhabitants of the city and by the army of the enemy (II Kings 18:26-27). Aramaic may have been the language of diplomacy at the middle of the first millennium B.C.

Usually there are three divisions made in the list of Semitic languages: (*a*) Eastern: Akkadian (Babylonian and Assyrian); (*b*) Northwestern (sometimes subdivided): Aramaic, Syria, Samaritan, Palmyrene, Nabatean, Canaanite, Phoenician, Moabite, Hebrew (Amorite); (*c*) Southern: Arabic, Sabean, Minean, Ethiopic (Amharic).

There seems to be a basic common stock in vocabulary and a parallel structure to all the known Semitic languages, both ancient and modern. Yet the use of the definite article varies considerably. These languages popularly are considered to be consonantal, but internal vowel change is significant in all, and Akkadian and Ethiopic indicated vowels very early. Most of the languages added vowel signs late in their development. All the languages are written from right to left except Akkadian and Ethiopic. In all the languages the majority of the roots are triconsonantal, but a strong case has been made for biconsonantal roots. Parts of speech are formed by various affixes to these roots. The basic root form of the verb was the third person singular. The tense system is dissimilar to that in the Aryan languages. There is a multiplicity of verb forms, with Akkadian, Ethiopic, and Arabic having more than a dozen, and Hebrew and Aramaic having seven. The syntax is similar for all the languages. In Hebrew especially, subordination of clauses with conjunctions is rare. There is no neuter gender.

The influence of Semitic languages was spread by contact, invasion, and colonization into Egypt, Cappadocia, and Tunisia (Carthage), by early Christian missionaries to India, and by Islam throughout Africa and into Europe (Turkey, Spain).

From these Semitic-speaking peoples have come the three great modern, monotheistic faiths: Judaism, Christianity, and Islam. They seem to have been responsible for the invention of the ALPHABET sometime in the second millennium B.C. Situated astride the Fertile Crescent, for many years they were the middlemen of the world.

See also ASSYRIA AND BABYLONIA; CANAAN; EDOM; MOAB; PHOENICIA; SYRIA.

Bibliography. A. Scharff and A. Moortgat, *Ägypten und Vorderasien im Altertum* (1950); J. B. Pritchard, ed., *ANET* (2nd ed., 1955); S. Moscati, *Ancient Semitic Civilizations* (1957).
                                                      C. U. WOLF

SENAAH sĭ nā'ə [סְנָאָה; Apoc. Σαναάς]; KJV Apoc. ANNAAS ăn'ĭ əs. Alternately: HASSENAAH hăs'-ə nā'ə [הַסְּנָאָה] (Neh. 3:3). Head of a family or clan among the exiles returned from Babylon (Ezra 2:35; Neh. 7:38; I Esd. 5:23), and represented among those who aided Nehemiah with the repair of the Jerusalem wall (Neh. 3:3). Possibly the name is related to the "Tower of Sena'a" (Magdalsenna), which in ancient times controlled the road from the Jordan Valley to Baal-Hazor.

Bibliography. L. W. Batten, *Ezra and Nehemiah*, ICC (1913), p. 81; R. A. Bowman, Exegesis of Ezra, *IB*, III (1954), 582.

B. T. DAHLBERG

SENATE. In the Roman Empire, a hereditary legislative, administrative, and judiciary body made up of six hundred members of the aristocracy. Augustus set the property qualification for membership at a million sesterces. The group met twice a month in or near Rome to approve the emperor's report and to make decrees. By voting the deification or condemnation of dead emperors, and by choosing new ones, the Senate retained a kind of veto, but it gradually lost most of its powers. A few provinces away from the frontier remained under direct senatorial control, and certain religious and civil appointments were open only to Senators.

R. M. GRANT

SENATOR. According to II Macc. 6:1, Antiochus Epiphanes sent an "Athenian senator" (γέροντα Ἀθηναῖον; KJV "old man of Athens") to compel the Jews to apostatize and to rededicate their temple to Olympian Zeus. The Greek may also be translated "Geron the Athenian" (Geron was the name of several Athenians, see epigraphical evidence assembled by Wilhelm in *Anzeiger*, Akad. d. Wissensch. in Wien, Philos.-hist. Kl., 74 [1937], 20 ff). On the other hand, the context does not demand that γέρων be taken as a proper noun, and the parallel in I Macc. 1:41 refers merely to messengers sent by the king. The variant reading "a certain Antiochian senator" (Latin *senem quendam Antiochenum;* cf. RSV mg.), though superficially more appropriate, is not to be accepted against the combined testimony of all Greek MSS and all other ancient versions. Furthermore, since Antiochus built a magnificent temple to Olympian Zeus at Athens (Polybius XXVI.1, § 11), he may well have selected an Athenian to introduce the worship of the same deity at Jerusalem.

See also GERON.

B. M. METZGER

SENECA, EPISTLES OF PAUL AND. *See* PAUL AND SENECA, EPISTLES OF.

SENEH sē'nə [סֶנֶה]. A peak at the pass of MICHMASH, opposite another crag called BOZEZ. These crags are located *ca.* seven miles NE of Jerusalem along the Wadi es-Suweinit.

Seneh is mentioned only in an incidental way in the description of Jonathan's approach to the camp of the Philistines at Michmash (I Sam. 14:4). The following verse completes the description by locating one of the peaks "on the north in front of Michmash" and the other "on the south in front of Geba." If the order of these descriptions is the same as the order of the naming of the peaks, Seneh was on the S side of the pass. This would accord with the possible meaning of "Bozez" ("shining"), the peak on the N side, whose S slope would reflect the rays of the sun.

The etymology of "Seneh" is uncertain. One possibility is that it is from the root שֵׁן, "tooth," descriptive of the shape of the peak. Another possibility is that the word is from a root סְנֶה, "thorn," used because the area was noted for thorn bushes. Josephus' reference to the "Valley of Thorns, near a certain village called Gabaothsaul . . . from Jerusalem about thirty furlongs" (War V.ii.1), is often cited as having a possible reference to Seneh. The name of SENAAH (סְנָאָה), a city located in Judah and occupied by Jews returning from the Babylonian exile, may possibly be derived from the same root as Seneh (see Ezra 2:35; Neh. 7:38).

W. L. REED

SENIR sē'nər [שְׂנִיר]; KJV SHENIR shē'— in Deut. 3:9; Song of S. 4:8. According to Deut. 3:9, the Amorite name of Mount Hermon. In Song of S. 4:8 MT reads "Shenir," but some MSS have the reading "Senir" here also (so RSV; cf. I Chr. 5:23). According to this passage, Senir seems to have another designation than Hermon, since both names occur. Perhaps they refer to two different peaks (*see* HERMON, MOUNT). According to Ezek. 27:5, Senir was famous for its fir trees used for shipbuilding.

A. HALDAR

SENNACHERIB sə năk'ər ĭb [סַנְחֵרִיב; Akkad. *Sin-aḥḥē-rība*, Sin-Replace-the-(Lost)-Brothers!]. King of Assyria and Babylonia (705-681 B.C.); son of SARGON II, and father of ESARHADDON.

Sennacherib is one of those very few kings of the Neo-Assyrian Empire who came to the throne without any civil war or other complication. When his father died on the battlefield, the Empire was consolidated enough even to allow the new king some years of comparative peace. Although Sennacherib's policy toward Babylonia resulted in the destruction of that city, it should be stressed that he made every attempt to follow the example of his father by giving Babylon a special political status rather than incorporating it into the Empire. In general, Sennacherib adopted his father's policy of administrative integration of border states, though he was much more cautious in his military moves and resorted to warfare only when other means failed. It is somewhat puzzling that he mentions the name of his father only once in his numerous inscriptions.

The crucial event of Sennacherib's reign was certainly the destruction of Babylon and the years full of warfare, victories, and defeats which led up to it. All other campaigns of Sennacherib were, politically and militarily speaking, of minor importance, including the one against Hezekiah of Jerusalem, to which so much scholarly investigation has been dedicated.

In Babylon, two years after the accession of Sennacherib, a Babylonian, under the name of Marduk-zakirshumi II (703), ascended the throne, to which Sennacherib himself, as the son of Sargon II, had a definite claim. Merodach-baladan, the ruler of the powerful Chaldean tribe Bīt-Yakin, having returned from his exile in Elam, where he had been since his defeat by Sargon II, deposed the new king and took over Babylonia with Elamite military help. Merodach-baladan attempted to unite the warring Chaldean and Aramean tribal chieftains, and he seems also to have had as allies various Arab tribes and to have planned a diversionary maneuver by sending messages to the Assyrian vassals in the W to incite them to rebel. Sennacherib reacted with promptness and defeated the allied Elamites and Chaldeans near Kish, whereupon Babylonia surrendered. There he installed a native, Bel-ibni, as king (702-700). In the meantime the kings of Sidon and Tyre threw off the yoke of Assyria, rebelling thus openly for the first time, instead of paying tribute as had been their policy up to then. From farther S, where the proximity of Egypt apparently fostered the illusion of strength, we hear of offensive steps on the part of Hezekiah king of Judah, the most important prince of the region. He had received a letter from Merodach-baladan (II Kings 20:12-13) and had seized the pro-Assyrian ruler of Ekron. When Sennacherib appeared, all defiance collapsed quickly in Phoenicia, but the Assyrian army had to fight in the S (Ekron, Ashdod, Ashkelon), and it defeated with ease a sizable Egyptian army at Eltekiah. Camping most probably at Lachish,* Sennacherib summoned Hezekiah to pay tribute, which the latter seems to have done only after an Assyrian army started to lay siege to his city. Seen from the Assyrian military point of view, the purpose of the entire campaign, the third of Sennacherib, was to enforce the delivery of tribute and to make a show of military power toward Egypt, ruled at that time by the Pharaoh Shabaka. Even the action against Judah was only a typical punitive expedition and, as such, successfully handled in a minimum of time. Seen from the political point of view of the ruler of the small kingdom of Judah, who endeavored to maintain some independence by using Egypt's influence against that of more distant Assyria, it was a minor setback. In fact, the readiness of Sennacherib to take tribute instead of conquering the recalcitrant city actually saved it, in spite of the defeat of the Egyptian army and the foolish stubbornness of Hezekiah. This reluctance of Sennacherib cannot be explained; he may have had some respect for the tenacity of this people, in view of the long, drawn-out siege of Samaria; he may have realized that the rebellion in the W was but a diversionary move of Merodach-baladan; or he may have had other reasons to keep the campaign as short as possible. The OT report on these events is interwoven with a lively and anecdotal story centering around the prophet Isaiah, who is said to have kept Hezekiah from surrendering with the prophetic promise that the Lord would make Sennacherib return to his country because of some rumor. Then the text goes on to tell us that the "angel of the LORD" slew in one night 185,000 of Sennacherib's soldiers, thus forcing the king to return to Nineveh, where he was killed by his two sons. Obviously, two historical events have been telescoped in this report: the sudden departure of Sennacherib from Palestine and his death twenty years later. It has to be stressed that, however suddenly Sennacherib left for home, he cannot have suffered any patent losses through pestilence or the like, because the entire region would have rebelled immediately, and we know nothing about unrest in that part of the Assyrian Empire. The entire incident, and especially the story of the sudden death of the large Assyrian army, is, curiously

enough, reflected in Herodotus' report (II.141) on the conquest of Egypt by Ashurbanipal, whom the father of history insists upon calling Sannacharibos, when mice ate up the leather parts of the equipment of the Assyrian soldiers and thus compelled the invading army to retire. There are, of course, a number of difficulties in connection with Sennacherib's campaign in Palestine, such as the fact that the Bible mentions Tirhakah as pharaoh instead of his predecessor Shabaka, and the absence of any campaign reports of Sennacherib after the destruction of Babylon (689 B.C.). Still, from the extant cuneiform evidence, there was only one campaign of that king into Palestine. Figs. LAC 1-2.

Meanwhile, the Assyrian puppet Bel-ibni was no match for the wily Merodach-baladan, who set up a certain Shūzubu as king of Babylon and incited the inhabitants of that city, as well as the Aramaic tribes along the rivers, to rebellion. Again Sennacherib had to march as conqueror into Babylonia. He drove Shūzubu out of the capital but failed to capture Merodach-baladan, who fled again, with his family, by ship to Elam, leaving the Chaldeans to the mercy of Sennacherib, who deported a large number of them. Apparently with the intention of winning over Babylon by granting the city a special political position, Sennacherib made his own son Adadnadinshumi king of Babylon (700).

Six years later—rather peaceful years, with minor campaigns—Sennacherib realized the necessity of turning against Elam with drastic steps, caused most likely by the incessant attempts of the exiles in Elam to meddle in Babylonian affairs. Since Elam was always ready to support any insurrection in Babylonia with military forces and to offer asylum to defeated rebels, Sennacherib's intention was politically sound. In order to be able to attack the coastal cities on the Elamite side of the Persian Gulf, where most of the exiles lived, Sennacherib had sailors from Tyre, Sidon, and Cyprus build ships on the upper Euphrates, and on the Tigris near Nineveh. These were to float down the rivers, but those on the Tigris had to be transferred overland to the Arahtu Canal, obviously because the lower course of the Tigris was in enemy hands. Eventually these boats were to carry Sennacherib and his army across the gulf. In spite of a heavy storm, the coastal cities were attacked and taken, after heavy fighting. As we know only from the Babylonian Chronicle, the Elamite king, Hallushu, counterattacked swiftly, striking at Sennacherib's overextended supply lines. He took Sippar in the N and advanced downstream, took Sennacherib's son prisoner in Babylon, and made a certain Nergalushezib king of that city. Upon the Elamite's return, the new king was defeated by Sennacherib himself (693), who had turned back, conquered Uruk, and met the rebels near Nippur. Sennacherib, however, could not turn against Babylon, where Mushēzib-Marduk became king, but moved against Elam. Here, Hallushu's defeat had caused a rebellion; and the new king, Kudur-Nahhunde, avoided an engagement with the Assyrian army.

After having destroyed a number of smaller cities, Sennacherib was compelled by the bad weather of the advanced season to retreat (692). The new king of Babylon showed special skill in procuring Elamite military help—Sennacherib accused him of having handed over all the treasures of Esagila to buy this assistance—and a large army of Elamites, Babylonians, and their confederates from among the tribes of the mountains and the plains faced Sennacherib, when he returned to restore Assyrian prestige. The battle took place near Babylon at Hallule, and the Babylonian Chronicle calls it a defeat of Assyria—an impression which the excessively poetic and vague language used by Sennacherib in his description of the engagement underlines.

Although Sennacherib captured at Hallule the son of his old foe Merodach-baladan, the Babylonian king remained in power, and it took Sennacherib two years to prepare his revenge. Because of internal troubles in Elam, Babylon had to face the enraged Sennacherib alone, and he destroyed the city after a short siege on his eighth campaign (689). We know of this destruction only from the Bavian inscription of Sennacherib, in which as few as ten lines are devoted to this unparalleled act. The wording shows the still unabated angry mood of the king; he tells in the first person that he tore down the walls, the houses, palaces, temples, and temple towers of the city to their very foundations, including the earthen core of the towers; that he filled the Arahtu Canal with the rubble; and that he finally let the Euphrates flow over the city, so that no one should ever be able to discover its location. Only when Sennacherib reports that even the images of the gods were broken to pieces, does the style change from the first to the third person plural, and it is said that the soldiers committed this sacrilege.

For the eight remaining years of the king's reign we have no reports on warlike activities, except for a few lines on a broken alabaster slab which speak of a campaign against some Arab rulers. This reference does not entitle us to assume that Sennacherib went via Arabia to Lachish to receive tribute from Hezekiah.

On the fronts toward the N and the NW, Sennacherib's position was evidently consolidated, so that his reign represents a period of relative peace but for the Babylonian problem. His building activities were concentrated in the new capital of Nineveh, for which he erected an aqueduct unique of its kind and dimensions in the ancient Near East. His personal interest in technology is reflected in many of his inscriptions and shows also in his military planning.

His end is still shrouded in mystery. According to the Babylonian Chronicle, he was murdered in 681 by one of his sons. The Bible (II Kings 19:37) speaks of two sons, named Adrammelech and Sharezer, and localizes the crime in the "temple of Nisrokh." From Esarhaddon's inscription we learn that he was made crown prince over the opposition of the elder sons of Sennacherib, and from some indications in the inscriptions of Ashurbanipal (grandson of Sennacherib) it seems that Babylonians were implicated in the conspiracy. All this sheds suspicion on a number of people but is not definite enough simply to accuse Esarhaddon, who profited by the crime.

Figs. SEN 41; INS 12.

Bibliography. D. D. Luckenbill, *The Annals of Sennacherib* (1924): translation of the historical texts.

A. L. Oppenheim

SENTRY [בַּעַל פְּקִדֻת, lord of oversight]. A guard, usually armed, stationed at a specific point to oversee the passage of persons to and from that point. Irijah, son of Shelemiah, son of Hananiah, alone is called sentry in the Bible (Jer. 37:13-14). J. A. Sanders

SENUAH. KJV form of Hassenuah in Neh. 11:9.

SEORIM sē ôr′ĭm [שְׂעֹרִים] (I Chr. 24:8). A priest to whom the fourth lot fell, supposedly in David's organization of the temple. The lots separated the priesthood into twenty-four divisions, each serving in succession for a stated period. Actually the temple organization reflected is that in effect from the time of the Chronicler until A.D. 70. *See* Priests and Levites. E. R. Achtemeier

SEPHAR sĕ′fär [סְפָר]. A place mentioned as one of the limits of the settlements of the Joktanites, "from Mesha in the direction of Sephar to the hill country of the east" (Gen. 10:30). Since the former locality was in the N of Arabia (*see* Mesha 1), the latter must be sought somewhere to the S of the peninsula. Two cities, one in the interior of Yemen, the other on the coast of Mahra, have been identified with Sephar, but this equation is made difficult by the fact that both are written צפר. In postbiblical Hebrew, סְפָר means "border country," and it is possible that the phrase in Genesis does not mean a locality at all, but is to be rendered: "as far as the border country, that is, the hill country of the east." S. Cohen

*SEPHARAD sĕf′ə răd [סְפָרַד] (Obad. 20). Probably to be identified as Sardis, the capital of Lydia in Asia Minor. Obad. 20 refers to Jewish exiles in Sepharad. Linguistically the equation of סְפָרַד with Sardis is unobjectionable, since the Aramaic name of Sardis is spelled identically in a bilingual inscription found at Sardis itself. The name of Sardis contained a labial sound. It appears as *sparda* in Old Persian, *sapardu* in Babylonian.

The interpretation of Obad. 20 depends upon chronological problems. If the passage is of mid-fifth-century origin, it is an early indication of the presence of a Jewish colony at Sardis. The Aramaic

41. Sennacherib (705-681 B.C.) receives booty as he sits on his throne, at Lachish; from the Lachish Relief

text of the bilingual from Sardis may have been added to the Lydian version for the benefit of Jewish residents, but its date is disputed (455 or 394 or 349 B.C.), and Aramaic was current as the administrative language in W Asia Minor. Sardis as an oriental trade center, however, qualifies as a probable location for an early Jewish colony.

Bibliography. C. C. Torrey, "The Bilingual Inscription from Sardis," *AJSL,* 34 (1917-18), 185-98; P. Kahle and F. Sommer, "Die lydisch-aramäische Bilingue," *Kleinasiatische Forschungen* (1930), pp. 18-86; J. Friedrich, *Kleinasiatische Sprachdenkmäler* (1932), pp. 109-10.   M. J. MELLINK

*SEPHARVAIM sĕf'ər vā'əm [ספרוים]; SEPHAR-VITES sĕf'ər vīts [ספרוים]. A city of an unknown location, in Syria or Mesopotamia.

After the fall of the city of Samaria in 722 B.C., the Assyrian king Sargon II brought people from different places, including Sepharvaim, to the province (II Kings 17:24; 18:34; 19:13; Isa. 36:19; 37: 13). It is told that they used to burn their children in the fire to ADRAMMELECH and ANAMMELECH (II Kings 17:31). There may be a confusion with Sippar in Babylonia, but more probably it is here a distorted form of the Assyrian "Shabarain," the Hebrew equivalent of which is "Sibraim" (Ezek. 47:16). This town was situated between Hamath and Damascus, probably near Hums.

Bibliography. W. F. Albright, *Archaeology and the Religion of Israel* (1953), pp. 163, 220.   A. S. KAPELRUD

SEPHELA. KJV Apoc. form of SHEPHELAH.

*SEPTUAGINT sĕp'tōŏ ə jĭnt, —chŏŏ—. The name traditionally applied to the oldest Greek version of the OT. This name is apparently a shortened form of the title *Interpretatio secundum* (or *iuxta*) *septuaginta seniores.* The term *septuaginta,* or "seventy," is based on the ancient tradition (Exod. 24:1, 9) that seventy elders accompanied Moses up the Mount and saw the God of Israel, whereupon God gave the tables of the law to Moses. It was only fitting that seventy elders should in turn be responsible for translating the Torah into Greek. Aristeas increased the number to seventy-two in order to make six times twelve (tribes). The term "Septuagint," commonly abbreviated "LXX," should apply, strictly speaking, only to the Greek Pentateuch, but later the name served to embrace the whole OT. MSS commonly abbreviated the term οἱ ο'. Ancient Greek writers often refer to the LXX as ἡ κοινή (ἔκδοσις), or as ἡ ἐκκλησιαστικὴ ἔκδοσις.

1. Extent of the LXX. Besides a translation of the Hebrew OT canon, the LXX contained a number of other works. Though some variations do exist in the MSS, the following are usually found: I Esdras, Wisdom of Solomon, Wisdom of Jesus ben Sirach, Judith, Tobit, Baruch, the Letter of Jeremiah, and the four books of Maccabees. A number of cursives also include the Psalms of Solomon.

Certain canonical books also include a number of additions not found in the traditional Masoretic Text (MT). Some uncial MSS (A R T) as well as quite a few cursives append a number of canticles at the end of the Psalter. Greek Esther has also been considerably embellished; in fact, the Greek text is over twice as long as the MT. The book of Daniel (both LXX and Theod.) contains three extensive passages without MT counterpart. These are the story of Susanna, the story of Bel and the Dragon, and finally the Prayer of Azarias and the Song of the Three Children.

2. Date of translation. Just when the LXX was composed is not known, though it is probable that the Pentateuch was translated in Alexandria by the middle of the third century B.C.

a. The Aristeas romance. Traditionally the LXX was written during the reign of Ptolemy II Philadelphus (285-247 B.C.); this view is based on a work by a certain ARISTEAS written to a friend named Philocrates. The work, bearing the simple superscription Ἀριστέας Φιλοκράτει, is in the form of a narrative dealing with the "translation of the Law of the Jews" (Euseb. *Preparation for the Gospel* 9.38). It purports to give an eyewitness account written by a highly placed courtier in the court of Philadelphus of the translation of the Torah into Greek by seventy-two savants (six from each Hebrew tribe) sent by Eleazar the high priest at the request of the king.

The work tells of Demetrius of Phalerum, the royal librarian, reporting to the emperor that over 200,000 books had already been collected but that he was hoping to expand the collection to half a million volumes. Unfortunately, however, no translation of the Jewish Laws was contained in the library. Immediately the king addressed a letter to the high priest in Jerusalem (9-12). After a lengthy digression on the king's magnanimity in ordering the release of over 100,000 Jewish slaves in Egypt (13-28), the author continues with the text of a memo from Demetrius to the king setting forth the particulars which might be used for a letter to the high priest (29-32). The text of the actual letter follows (35-40), in which the king requests elders of blameless life, having experience in the law, and being able translators—six from each tribe—to be sent to his court in order to produce this work for his library. Aristeas and Andreas were sent by the king to deliver this letter, as well as numerous sacrifices and a hundred talents of silver. Eleazar the high priest responded courteously by a return letter (41-46), to which was appended a list of the names of the seventy-two elders (47-51). It might be noted that a few of the names are Hellenic (e.g., Theodosius *tris,* Theodotus, Dositheus), but the majority are typically Hebrew.

Detailed descriptions follow of the king's gifts to the temple, of the city, of parts of the temple and its service, of the citadel, of the city streets, and of general conditions of the country (52-120). The excellence of the elders selected by Eleazar is then set forth (121-27). After a lengthy statement by the high priest on the character of their religious beliefs and customs (128-71), it is related that Aristeas and Andreas returned to Alexandria along with the seventy-two elders, who were immediately received at court (contrary to royal custom), whereupon they showed the king the Hebrew parchments written with letters of gold. After seeing them the king bowed down seven times and assigned to them the finest of lodgings (172-81). Seven days of banqueting followed for the honored guests, in the course of which the king asked each of the seventy-two sages various ethical questions, the elders acquitting themselves in very fine fashion (182-300).

After a three-day interval Demetrius took the savants to the island of Pharos, where in a secluded but well-appointed house they set to work. The work of translation was finished in seventy-two days (301-8). Then Demetrius called the Jewish community together and had it read out to them; the LXX was received with a tremendous ovation, and copies were requested. Since it was so well and accurately done, no revision would ever be permitted, a curse being pronounced on anyone who would revise, add, or excise anything in the translation (309-11). Finally the king heard it read also, fittingly marveled at it, and urged that reverent care be exercised over the books and that the translators be dismissed with princely gifts (312-22).

b. Later embellishments. Later writers fit the story with certain miraculous elements. Philo, as well as later writers such as Pseudo-Justin, Irenaeus, and Clement of Alexandria, insist that the translators worked independently. When each had completed the entire translation the efforts of the several translators were compared and found to be completely identical. Even more fantastic is the story of Epiphanius (*On Weights and Measures*), in which the account has grown to include the entire OT and twenty-two books of the Apoc. In general it may be said, however, that all these accounts seem to go back to the Aristeas narrative, or at least to a closely related version of the same tale. This is particularly likely in view of the great popularity the Aristeas account had among Jews and Christians alike.

c. Critical evaluation. The Aristeas story is a historical romance written in the latter half of the second century B.C. or the first years of the first, by an unknown Jewish writer of Alexandria under the guise of a pagan member of Philadelphus' court. Ever since the conclusive statement of H. Hody in his *Contra historiam LXX interpretum Aristeae nomine inscriptam* (1705), it has been accepted that the author is not the person he presents himself as being. That he is a Jew is apparent from his devotion to Judaism,

his interest in Jerusalem's topography and in the temple and its rituals and furnishings, and his obvious subscription to Jewish religious customs and ethical outlook.

Furthermore, the narrative contains a number of inaccuracies impossible to an Alexandrian writer of Philadelphus' day. The most glaring error is the mention of Demetrius of Phalerum as chief librarian, which position he never occupied. Nor was he a member of Ptolemy II's court, since the latter, on his accession, banished Demetrius to exile— Demetrius was unfortunate enough to have supported the wrong son of Soter for the succession. Another lapse is the representation of Menedemus of Eretria as being present at the banquet though he had died *ca.* two years before the end of Ptolemy I Soter's reign. The work also contains a number of archaizing anachronisms. And the use of LXX phraseology throughout the description of the temple furnishings and ritual indicates that the LXX had been in use for a long time.

Finally, the whole tone of the work militates against its historicity. That the bibliophile king should have been interested in adding a translation of the Jewish law is not unlikely in itself, but that he should have elaborately honored the translators, engaged in theological speculations with them, and admitted the superiority of Jewish monotheism is most improbable. The actual origins of the LXX are rather to be seen in the linguistic needs of the Diaspora in Alexandria in the century following Alexander.

P. Kahle has suggested that Aristeas' work reflects Jewish propaganda for a recension of the LXX rather than for the original translation. He maintains that the *raison d'être* for the work was an official revision of the text carried out in the latter half of the second century. Propaganda is made only for something that is contemporary; thus the date of Aristeas would automatically give one the date of the LXX recension. Furthermore, Demetrius reports to the king (30) that the library does not contain a copy of the Jewish Laws. The reason for this is that they "are written in the Hebrew characters and language and ἀμελέστερον σεσήμανται κὰι οὐχ ὡς ὑπάρχει. ..." This obscure passage could be interpreted to presuppose the earlier existence of unsatisfactory translations, though it would be dangerous to press the point.

One objection to Kahle's reconstruction which apparently has never been raised is the unlikelihood of such a revision made *ca.* 130 B.C. being limited to the Pentateuch. Were Aristeas actually referring to an official or standard revision of the Greek text, it would almost certainly have contained the Prophets, as well as some of the Writings, at that late date. The canon for Alexandrian Jews in the latter half of the second century B.C. would hardly have been limited to the Torah.

Kahle's pupil A. Sperber has gone far beyond him in assessing differences between MSS obviously recensional or copyist in origin as evidence for different Greek translations or Targums. Kahle's thesis has found little acceptance among most contemporary LXX scholars, who are in the main continuing in the Lagarde tradition, for which see § 5 *below.*

3. Minor Greek versions. a. Aquila. By 132 B.C., when the grandson of Ben Sirach wrote the Prologue to the Ecclesiasticus, "the law and the prophets and the rest of the Bible" existed in Greek translation. The LXX soon became very popular among the Jews of the Diaspora for whom Greek was the familiar spoken language. When the Christian church began to spread beyond Jewish borders, it adopted the LXX as its Bible. By the end of the first Christian century the Jews were reacting against the use of the LXX, partly because it was not based on contemporary forms of rabbinic exegesis, and partly because of Christian apologetics against Judaism based on faulty LXX renderings. More and more the LXX became identified as the Bible of the Christians. To meet the growing need for a Jewish version, Aquila, a Jewish proselyte of Pontus and a relative of Hadrian, produced in A.D. 128 his version based on strict rabbinic laws of interpretation and slavishly literal to the Hebrew text. In fact, Aquila's text can be understood only by one who is familiar with the Hebrew. *See* AQUILA'S VERSION.

b. Theodotion. Possibly somewhat earlier (though this is by no means certain) was the LXX revision of THEODOTION. Nothing is certainly known of Theodotion except that he probably came from Ephesus. His revision is of great importance, since it was widely used and strongly influenced LXX MSS. In fact, in one case, the book of Daniel, Theod. became the official version. Theod., however, apparently revised a text somewhat different from the LXX; a pre-Theodotionic text existed already in NT times, since the writer of Revelation liberally quotes from Daniel according to Theod. rather than the LXX. This Theod. (or pre-Theod.) was a revision based on a consultation of the Hebrew.

c. Symmachus. A third Greek version was produced somewhat later than Aq. (toward the end of the second century) by the Ebionite SYMMACHUS. The work of Symmachus can easily be recognized by its elegant and bombastic style. Its periphrastic character renders it somewhat less useful than those of Aquila and Theodotion.

Other Greek versions are known to have existed, but of their origins nothing is known. Even Origen, who used three such others, simply called them *Quinta, Sexta,* and *Septima.* Only a few fragments of these are extant.

4. Recensions of the LXX. a. The work of Origen. Modern LXX criticism inevitably goes back to the prodigious work of Origen (d. 254), the father of LXX criticism. By the beginning of the third century the history of the Greek text was already complex. Origen accordingly determined to make a critical edition of the LXX. To this end he studied Hebrew already early in life. By 240 he had collected immense amounts of materials and began active work on his mammoth Hexapla, so named from the six columns of texts it contained. Column I contained the Hebrew text which served as the basis for his textual studies. The other columns contained the following texts: II—the Hebrew text in Greek transcription; III—Aq.; IV—Symm.; V—LXX; VI—Theod.

Of most interest is the fifth column. Origen realized that the LXX and the Hebrew frequently diverged. The LXX had numerous words, phrases, or even whole paragraphs with no counterpart in the Hebrew. On the other hand, the reverse was also often the case. In the former instance Origen marked the beginning of the intrusive text with an obelus and its end with a metobelus. For Hebrew materials not paralleled in the LXX, Origen inserted materials from the other columns, marking the beginning of the passage with an asterisk followed by an indication of the source (α'σ'θ' or οἱ γ'), and its end with a metobelus.

This huge work was completed in 245 at Caesarea. Its exact relation to the Tetrapla (the last four columns in an independent edition) is uncertain, though the latter was probably later. H. M. Orlinsky, on the other hand, maintains with some plausibility that Tetrapla was simply another name for the Hexapla, since the first two columns were of no use to monolingual Christians.

Obviously the work of Origen was too bulky to reproduce in its entirety, and so the fifth column alone was copied. In the course of time the Aristarchian signs (so called because they were used by Aristarchus in his great edition of Homer) used by Origen were no longer understood, and copyists either omitted some of them or put them into the wrong places. Origen could hardly have foreseen the textual chaos which has followed on his great work.

One of the best evidences for Origen's fifth column is the slavishly literal rendering of it into Syriac by Paul, bishop of Tella (618-19), known as the Syro-hexaplar, of which substantial portions are still extant. Pamphilus and Eusebius supplied Constantine with fifty copies of Origen's column for his use in the capital. This recension is usually called the Hexaplaric or Palestinian recension.

b. Hesychius. A second recension of the LXX was made *ca.* the end of the third century by the bishop Hesychius (died 311). Little is known about the Hesychian or Egyptian recension. The text can be identified in part from biblical quotations in the Egyptian fathers, especially those of Cyril of Alexandria (died 444). In the Prophets it appears that Codex Marchalianus (Q) is its chief textual representative. For large parts of the LXX this text group has not yet been identified.

c. Lucian. Better known is the Lucianic recension (also known as the Antiochian), which became the accepted text throughout Asia Minor. Lucian the Martyr (died 311) was reputed to have produced this text, but it is not at all clear what he did. Any revision done by Lucian was effected, not on the LXX in any pre-Hexaplaric sense, but on an Antiochian or pre-Lucianic text. It has long been recognized that the OL sub-version is a translation of a text very similar to that of Lucian with the hexaplaric plusses omitted. One therefore suspects that Lucian's work was mainly based on a comparison with Origen's Hexapla, which he is known to have used, and that his work was mainly additive. It is not at all certain that a recovery of Lucian would bring us nearer to the original LXX; the real question, which at the moment is wholly unsolved, is what was the relation of the pre-Lucianic Antiochian text to the pre-Hexaplaric text. If the former was a revision of the LXX, it is apparent that a fairly extensive revision of the LXX on the basis of a Hebrew text not always equal to the MT took place in or about Antioch at least 150-200 years before Lucian.

The Lucianic text can usually be identified from extensive biblical quotations found in Theodoret and Chrysostom. From these, in turn, certain MSS can be classified as Lucianic for certain books. E.g., it is clear that for the four books of the Kingdoms MSS *b* b' o r c₂ e₂ are clearly Lucianic, whereas MSS g i and H(olmes) P(arson) 246 have numerous Lucianic readings. Marginal Lucianic readings are to be found in the Syro-Hexaplar and in MSS M and j. It should be carefully noted, however, that this applies only to these books. For other LXX books the textual character is quite different.

5. Modern approach to LXX criticism. Modern LXX criticism may be said to have begun with Paul de Lagarde (died 1891). He maintained that the history of all extant LXX MSS is bound to these three recensions. From citations in the Fathers known to have used these recensions, these texts can be identified. Textual criticism therefore must begin by identifying and unscrambling these strata, before any further attempt at determining the actual text of the LXX can be made. Lagarde felt that textual labor should produce critical editions of these recensions on the basis of which the Ur-text, or LXX, might be established. He himself pioneered the plan by editing (somewhat prematurely, to be sure) a first volume (Genesis to Esther) of the Lucianic text. It should be added that sub-versions must be considered as MS evidence as well; e.g., for the books of Kings the Armenian text is good MS evidence for the Hexaplaric recension, whereas for Daniel the Bohairic (Coptic) is Hesychian. When Lagarde died, the work was taken up by his former pupil A. Rahlfs, who promoted and began the Göttingen LXX, on which *see* § *9a below.* Most later LXX scholars have followed the Lagardian principles, among the more notable of whom are Montgomery, Margolis, Kappler, Ziegler, Gehman, Orlinsky, and Katz; for bibliographies containing their works, *see bibliography* § *d.*

Since the early days of modern criticism a number of pre-Origenian LXX papyri have been found (such as Chester Beatty, Rylands, Scheide, and Murabba'at papyri), all of which demonstrate the complexities of the history of the text prior to Origen. The critic can evaluate these finds, however, only in the light of the later history of the text for which the Lagardian principles are sound. For the text, critical character, and value of these papyri, consult the bibliographies listed in *bibliography* § *d.*

6. Character of the LXX. The Greek OT as it exists today is a composite book, the work of various translators of varied ability who worked at different times. The whole OT was probably complete by the middle, certainly by the end, of the second century B.C. It is generally held that the provenance of all of them was Egypt, a likely though not fully certain presupposition. The Pentateuch was undoubtedly translated first, probably during the reign of Philadelphus, but not by a body of scholars who came to a common agreement for the entire Torah as Aristeas and later romancers maintain, but by separate translators.

In general it is a good translation, but each book has individual translation traits and must be individually studied.

The books of the Kingdoms reflect the work of five distinct translators, each with distinct characteristics. Their works comprise I Samuel; II Sam. 1:1–11:1; 11:2–I Kings 2:11; 2:12–21:43; 22:1–II Kings. That these represent distinctly different translations can easily be seen by comparing them. E.g., the Greek of II Kings is extremely literalistic, syntactically Semitic, and often gives evidence of a lack of understanding of the Hebrew *Vorlage*. The translator of I Kings 2:12–21:43, however, is much less slavish to the Hebrew, uses on the whole much better Greek, and often paraphrases the text by haggadic additions which obviously had no textual support. These additions are similar in character to the amplifications in the Hebrew texts of Samuel found in Qumran IV.

The LXX Psalter represents the Hebrew text more or less adequately. It was probably subject to numerous revisions in the course of its history because of its common liturgical use. On the other hand, Greek Proverbs and Job are inadequate to the MT, though their Greek is quite excellent; in fact, the suggestion that one translator was responsible for both translations has much to commend itself. In both cases the Hebrew *Vorlage* seems to have been considerably different from the MT. Greek Job is about one sixth shorter than the MT, the missing verses being supplied from Theod. in modern editions of the LXX. The Proverbs text has suffered considerable expansion through revisers who felt that the free translations were not sufficiently literal and therefore added doublet renderings which now stand side by side with the older stratum. The text of Ecclesiastes is extremely Hebraic in character and is a slavishly word-for-word rendering of the Hebrew. It is probably either the text of Aquila or very strongly influenced by his work. The reasons for the adoption of such a text (it must have been almost incomprehensible to a monolingual Greek reader) by the Christian church are not at all clear.

The later prophetical books are quite varied in character as well. The text of Ezekiel represents an attempt at a literal rendering of a Hebrew text at times apparently imperfectly understood and often corrupt. Greek Jeremiah is seemingly based on a Hebrew text recensionally at variance with the MT, since not only is the text markedly different but also the order of the materials varies considerably from that of the MT. The LXX of the book of Daniel is extant in only two MSS, an eleventh-century Chigi MS and in Chester Beatty 967/8, for which the only other text evidence to be found is in a Syriac MS housed in Milan (Codex Syr-hex. Ambrosianus C.313). The Christian church substituted an Ur-Theod. text of Daniel by the beginning of the second century, if not earlier. In fact, since the NT quotes mainly from Theodotion's Daniel, it has been suggested that two variant pre-Christian texts existed side by side, and that Theodotion simply adopted the one with little or no change in his revision.

Greek Isaiah has long been a favorite field of study for LXX scholars. The history of its text, partly because of its frequent use by NT writers and partly for reasons of early Christian and Jewish apologetics, is more complex than that of any other OT book. The translation is very free, at times almost wholly useless for MT text criticism. It remains valuable, however, as a source book for ancient Jewish exegesis. (On the Greek of the LXX, *see also* GREEK LANGUAGE § 4*a*).

7. Importance of the LXX. It is by now fully apparent that the LXX is more than simply a happy source for all kinds of proposed emendations of the MT. Its textual character constitutes a problem in itself. It is now assured that the LXX is of some use in restoring a Hebrew base (*Vorlage*) often at variance with the MT. The textual criticism of the MT will remain largely dependent on LXX studies.

But the LXX is of importance for its own sake as well. It is a translation document and as such is largely bound by its base, to be sure, but, especially in those books more freely rendered, it constitutes a valuable source for understanding the theological and ethical outlook of Alexandrian Jewry. Many of the attitudes betrayed by the writer of the Aristeas legend are clearly identical with those of some of the LXX translators, notably of Greek Isaiah.

Another point that needs continual stress is the importance of LXX research for NT studies. The LXX constitutes the bridge between the OT and the NT. It provides the thought world and vocabulary for the NT writers. Kittel's *TWNT* is an attempt to appreciate this intimate relation. NT Koine is not simply the everyday Greek of an Eastern people in the first Christian century; its religious vocabulary derives ultimately, not from the Greek world, but from the Hebrew world of the OT through the medium of LXX Greek.

8. Texts. For a discussion of the most important papyri finds since 1938, including Rylands 458, the Chester Beatty and John H. Scheide biblical papyri, and the Berlin fragments, cf. J. W. Wevers, "Septuaginta-Forschungen," in *Theol. Rundschau*, N.F. XXII (1954), 111-38. For earlier materials cf. F. G. Kenyon, *Our Bible and the Ancient Manuscripts* (4th ed., 1939), pp. 61-74.

LXX MSS are usually divided into uncials and cursives—the former, on vellum, using Greek capital letters throughout, whereas cursives are in minuscule script. Traditionally the former have, in view of their obvious costliness and importance in antiquity, been accorded a great deal of weight, whereas cursives are often by-passed. Actually the text of a cursive may be far more important than that of an uncial. For the books of Kings, e.g., the text of a_2 (Petrograd 62) is as important for establishing the earlier Egyptian text as Codex Vaticanus (B), whereas M (Codex Coislinianus) is a mixed text with a number of Lucianic readings on the margin. Obviously the cursive is here one of the most important MSS extant for establishing the text of Kings. In fact, the recovery of the Lucianic text of Kings can be made only by cursive texts (MSS b b o r c_2 e_2). The isolation of vellum or uncial texts for special consideration, though usually done, is in itself unwarranted.

For a description of all LXX MSS used by the Göttingen LXX Gesellschaft, one can consult A. Rahlfs, *Verzeichnis der griech. Handschriften des A. T. für das Septuaginta-Unternehmen aufgestellt* (*Göttingische gelehrte Anzeigen*. Phil.-Hist. Kl.; 1914). MSS not known to Rahlfs at the time of publication are listed and used in the various editions published by the Gesellschaft. *Cf.* § 9*b below.*

9. Printed editions. a. Early editions. The early history of complete LXX editions began with the Complutensian Polyglot, published in four (plus two NT) volumes (1514-21) under the auspices of Cardinal Ximenes. Its text was taken over by later Polyglots as well—viz., Antwerp (1569-72), Heidelberg (1586-1616), Hamburg (1596), and Paris (1645). Some of the MSS used for its preparation are now no longer extant, though a few have been identified (chiefly HP 68, 108, 248).

Contemporary with the Complutensian was the Aldine edition (Venice, 1518-19), edited by Andreas Asolanus and Aldus Manutius. Its text was apparently based on the MSS housed at St. Mark's in Venice, three of which (HP 29, 68 and 121) have been identified. It appears that HP 68 was a common textual source for the Complutensian and the Aldine edition.

By far the best-known edition was published at Rome in 1586 under orders of Pope Sixtus V, and accordingly known as the Sixtine text. Its great importance lay in the fact that it was based largely on Codex Vaticanus (or B—Vatican Greek codex no. 1209), its lacunae being filled in from other MSS. Almost all editions for the next three hundred years were based on the Sixtine text, including such important editions as that of the Walton or London Polyglot (1657), of Holmes and Parsons (the first major compilation of textual variants made), five volumes (1798-1827), and those of Tischendorf (1850, 1856, 1860, 1869).

A fourth edition was based on Codex Alexandrinus (known as A) and was produced by Grabe (1707-20). Grabe's edition is not a straightforward reproduction of A, but was intended as a critical edition. He adopted Origen's system for correcting a text by marking with an obelus all passages having no parallel in MT, and with an asterisk such passages as he considered to be Hexaplaric.

b. Modern editions. Modern scholarship has continued the work of producing editions along two distinctly different lines, each of which has certain advantages as well as defects. The British, or Cambridge, school began work on the production of the "Cambridge LXX" in 1883. The Cambridge school has continued, though on a much more modest scale, the Holmes Parsons tradition by reproducing as accurately as possible a text (in this case that of B), and carefully collating for a critical apparatus the texts of selected MSS, sub-versions, and patristic quotations. No attempt is made at assessing variants; the only evaluation that is made—and this is a responsible one—is in the selection of the materials to be collated. A manual edition of the text of B, along with the variants of a few of the more important uncial texts, was produced by H. B. Swete (*The OT in Greek*, 3 vols. Vol. I first appeared in 1887; subsequent revised editions in 1895, 1901, and 1909. Vol. II was published in 1891, later editions in 1896 and 1907. Vol. III went through four editions—1894, 1899, 1905, and 1912. The last editions have all been reprinted).

Another approach to the problem has been taken by the Göttingen school. The *Societas Litterarum Göttingen* has followed Lagarde's plan of producing critical editions. The printed text is the result of careful assessment of all available texts by the editor and purports to be the true LXX. MSS are classified according to recensional families. Many textual problems are by no means solved, and new papyri finds are showing the early history of the LXX text to be quite complex; the establishment of the LXX text appears far more difficult than it did to Lagarde. A manual edition was also produced by Rahlfs in 1935 shortly before his death (*Septuaginta; id est V.T. Graece iuxta LXX Interpretes*, II Tom.). This too is intended as a critical edition based mainly on Codices Vaticanus, Sinaiticus, and Alexandrinus with recensional variants from Lucian, Origen, and the later Catenae also cited in the apparatus.

Bibliography. (*a*) Texts of the Aristeas romance. These may be found in P. Wendlund, *Aristeae ad Philocratem Epistula* (1900); H. St. J. Thackeray, in H. B. Swete, *An Introduction to the OT in Greek* (2nd ed., rev. by R. R. Ottley, 1914), pp. 551-606; R. Tramontano, *La Lettera di Aristea a Filocrate* (1931); H. G. Meecham, *The Letter of Aristeas* (1935); M. Hadas, *Aristeas to Philocrates* (*Letter of Aristeas*) (1951). The editions of Meecham and Hadas reproduce the text of Thackeray. For a useful bibliography of Aristeas studies, cf. Hadas, *op. cit.*, pp. 84-90.

b) LXX texts. Only such texts as might be considered indispensable for LXX students are listed here. Others may be found in the bibliographies listed below. R. Holmes and J. Parsons, *V. T. Graecum cum Variis Lectionibus*, V Tomae (1798-1827). H. B. Swete, *The OT in Greek* (3 vols.; 1909, 1907, 1912). A. Brooke, N. McLean, and H. St. J. Thackeray, *The OT in Greek: Vol. I, The Octateuch* (in four parts); Vol. II, *The Later Historical Books* (in four parts); Vol. III, Pt. I, *Esther, Judith, Tobit* (1906-40). M. L. Margolis, *The Book of Joshua in Greek*, Pts. I-IV (1931-38). *Septuaginta V.T. Graecum Auctoritate Societas Litterarum Gottingensis editum:* Band I, *Genesis*, ed. A. Rahlfs (1926); IX, Pt. I, *Maccabaeorum liber I*, ed. W. Kappler (1936); X, *Psalmi cum Odis*, ed. A. Rahlfs (1931); XIII, *Duodecim Prophetae*, ed. J. Ziegler (1943). Ziegler also edited the following volumes: XIV, *Isaias* (1939); XVI, Pt. I, *Ezechiel* (1952); XVI, Pt. II, *Daniel, Susanna, Bel et Draco* (1954); and XV, *Jeremias, Baruch, Threni, Epistula Jeremiae* (1957). A. Rahlfs, *Septuaginta; id est V.T. Graece iuxta LXX Interpretes*, II Tom. (1935).

c) Indispensable tools for LXX research. For Hexaplaric materials, F. Field, *Origenis Hexaplorum quae supersunt; sive veterum interpretum Graecorum in totum V.T. Fragmenta*, II Tomae (1867-74).

For lexicon, I. F. Schleusner, *Novus Thesaurus philologico-criticus; sive Lexicon in LXX et reliquos Interpretes Graecos ac Scriptores apocryphos V.T.*, in five parts (1820-21), still an extremely useful, though antiquated, work. The best introduction to LXX studies is still H. B. Swete, *An Introduction to the OT in Greek* (2nd ed., rev. by R. R. Ottley, 1914).

For a concordance, E. Hatch and H. A. Redpath, *A Concordance to the LXX and the Other Greek Versions of the OT* (2 vols.; 1897), together with a supplementary volume in two fascicles (1900, 1906).

For grammars, H. St. J. Thackeray, *A Grammar of the OT in Greek According to the LXX*, I (1909), dealing with orthography and accidence. Attention should also be called to R. Helbing, *Grammatik der Septuaginta, Laut-und Wortlehre* (1907); see also his *Die Kasussyntax der Verba bei dem Septuaginta; ein Beitrag zur Hebraismenfrage und zur Syntax der* κοινή (1928). J. Psichari, *Essai sur le Grec de la Septante* (1908). F.-M. Abel, *Grammaire du Grec Biblique, suivie d'un choix de papyrus* (1927), also gives some useful information.

For papyri, E. Mayser's extensive *Grammatik der griech. Papyri aus der Ptolemäerzeit, mit Einschluss der gleichzeitigen*

Ostraca und der in Ägypten verfassten Inschriften, vol. I (1936); vol. II (3 pts.; 1926-34).

For LXX and NT vocabulary, Kittel, *TWNT*.

d) Bibliographies. For the extensive literature, see the bibliographies by E. Nestle at the end of the articles on "Bible Versions A. I" in *The New Schaff-Herzog Encyclopedia of Religious Knowledge*, II, 120-21; and on "Septuagint" in *HDB*, IV, 453-54. Also extensive bibliographies in H. B. Swete, *An Introduction to the OT in Greek* (*see* § 10*c above*); G. Bertram, "Zur Septuaginta-Forschung," *Theol. Rundschau*, N.F. III (1931), 283 ff; V (1933), 173 ff; X (1938), 133 ff. A complete bibliography of all the scholarly writings of M. L. Margolis was prepared by J. Reider in *Max Leopold Margolis Scholar and Teacher* (ed. R. Gordis; 1952), pp. 63-77. Extremely useful too are the references in H. M. Orlinsky, "On the Present State of Proto-LXX Studies," *JAOS*, LXI (1941), 81-91; H. R. Willoughby, ed., "Current Progress and Problems in LXX Research," in *The Study of the Bible Today and Tomorrow* (1947), pp. 144-61. A selected bibliography may be found in B. J. Roberts, *The OT Text and Versions; The Hebrew Text in Transmission and the History of the Ancient Versions* (1955), pp. 299-307. For an extensive bibliography of publications since 1938, see J. W. Wevers, "Septuaginta-Forschungen," *Theol. Rundschau*, N.F. XXII (1954), 85-138, 171-90.

J. W. WEVERS

SEPULCHRE. *See* TOMB.

*****SEPULCHRE, HOLY.** *See* HOLY SEPULCHRE.

SEPULCHRES OF DAVID, OF THE KINGS, ETC. *See* TOMBS OF THE KINGS.

SERABIT EL-KHADEM. *See* ALPHABET; INSCRIPTIONS.

SERAH sĭr'ə [שֶׂרַח; *cf.* S Arab. *shārih̬*, the one who explains, opens, extends]; KJV SARAH sâr'ə in Num. 26:46. A daughter (and probably a clan or family) of Asher; and a sister of Imnah, Ishvah, Ishvi, and Beriah, with whom she went into Egypt with Jacob (Gen. 46:17). According to Jewish tradition Serah was named with the sons of Asher because she was the head of a great family which was included among the recognized families of Asher. Her name occurs in connection with the census which Moses took in the wilderness (Num. 26:46). The prominence of Serah in the genealogical tables led the rabbis to infer that there was something extraordinary in her history; as a consequence she became the heroine of several legends.   H. F. BECK

SERAIAH sĭ rā'yə [שְׂרָיָה, שְׂרָיָהוּ, Y is prince; Apoc. Σαραιά, Σαρεά]; KJV Apoc. SARAIAS sə rā'yəs (I Esd. 5:5; 8:1; II Esd. 2:2); ZACHARIAS zăk'ə-rī'əs (I Esd. 5:8). **1.** The secretary to King David during the time when the Davidic kingdom was at its full height and power, and afterward (II Sam. 8:17). He is called Sheva in II Sam. 20:25, Shavsha in I Chr. 18:16, and Shisha in I Kings 4:3. Probably in all three of the latter passages the original Hebrew reading was שְׁוָא.

2. The chief priest who was serving in Jerusalem at the time when the city was captured and destroyed by King Nebuchadnezzar of Babylon in 587(6) B.C. (II Kings 25:18 = Jer. 52:24). According to the narrative, he was taken before Nebuchadnezzar at Riblah and there killed, in order to make Judah's subjection complete. He is mentioned in the list of the high priests, descendants of Levi and of Zadok, in I Chr. 6:14. There he is said to be the son of Azariah and the father of Jehozadak, who apparently escaped his father's fate at Riblah, but who nevertheless was taken into exile by Nebuchadnezzar. Ezra also claims descent from Seraiah in Ezra 7:1 (I Esd. 8:1), and thus it can be assumed that Ezra went into exile with his brother Jehozadak. However, Jehozadak was evidently Seraiah's first-born son.

3. One of the captains of Judean forces which still remained at large in the open country after the capture and destruction of Jerusalem in 587(6) B.C. (II Kings 25:23; Jer. 40:8). Upon hearing of Nebuchadnezzar's appointment of Gedaliah as governor of Judah in 586, Seraiah and his men, together with similar forces, submitted to Gedaliah at Mizpah in the assurance that Gedaliah would treat them in a wise and just manner. However, because of Ammonite intrigue, Gedaliah and his chief officials and guards were, after six months, assassinated by Ishmael of the royal Davidic house. Seraiah, the other captains, and their forces, fearful for their lives, fled to Egypt.

4. A quartermaster, the son of Neriah, who, according to the text, accompanied King Zedekiah on a journey to Babylon in 594 B.C., taking along an oracle of the prophet Jeremiah to be first read orally in Babylon and then sunk in the Euphrates (Jer. 51:59, 61). We have no certain knowledge that Zedekiah himself made this journey, but undoubtedly Seraiah was part of a caravan which made its way to Babylon to renew Zedekiah's pledge of loyalty to Nebuchadnezzar. According to Jer. 32:12, Seraiah was a brother of Jeremiah's secretary, Baruch. The oracle by the prophet which Seraiah carried with him had one purpose: to plant the Word of the Lord in Babylon, where, after many years of exile, it would take inevitable effect in the fall of Babylon. The sinking of the oracle in the Euphrates symbolized the fact that Babylon, like the written document, would never rise again.

5. The second son of Kenaz; the brother of Othniel; the father of Joab; and a member of the tribe of Judah (I Chr. 4:13-14).

6. A Simeonite; the father of Joshibiah; the son of Asiel; and the grandfather of Jehu (I Chr. 4:35). He was a prince in his tribe.

7. One of those who returned with Zerubbabel out of exile in Babylon to Judah (Ezra 2:2; I Esd. 5:8). He is called Azariah in Neh. 7:7.

8. One of those who set their seal to the covenant made between God and the people in the days of Nehemiah (Neh. 10:2).

9. One of the "chiefs of the priests" (Neh. 12:7) who returned with Zerubbabel out of exile in Babylon (11:11; 12:1, 12). Being a leader among the people, he was automatically granted residence in Jerusalem (11:1), while among the laity, lots were cast to determine who was to remain in Jerusalem and who was to dwell in the towns of the countryside. He is called Azariah in I Chr. 9:11.

10. An officer of King Jehoiakim of Judah in the days of the prophet Jeremiah (Jer. 36:26). In the winter of the year 604 B.C., he was commanded by the king to imprison Jeremiah and Baruch, after Jeremiah had caused to be read before the king a scroll bearing his prophecy of the judgment of Yahweh upon Judah. However, Jeremiah and Baruch escaped from their would-be captors.

E. R. ACHTEMEIER

SERAPHIM sĕr′ə fĭm [שרפים, *plural of* שרף, seraph]. Winged celestial beings, of uncertain identity; possibly, winged serpents. *See* ANGEL § A3.

SERED sĭr′ĕd [סרד] (Gen. 46:14; Num. 26:26—G 26:22); **SEREDITES** sĭr′ə dīts; KJV **SARDITES** sär′dīts. The oldest son of Zebulun; ancestral head of the "family of the Seredites."

SERGIUS PAULUS. *See* PAULUS, SERGIUS.

SERJEANT. KJV translation of ῥαβδοῦχος (RSV POLICE) in Acts 16:35, 38.

*SERMON ON THE MOUNT. A discourse of Jesus recorded by Matthew (chs. 5-7) as having been spoken to disciples and others in the hill country of Galilee in the early part of his ministry. It begins with a group of blessings (the Beatitudes), and then deals with social duties in a series of contrasts between the teaching of Jesus and the ancient legal traditions of the Jews. It next turns to the private religious duties of almsgiving, prayer, and fasting; and finally gives instruction about the inner quality of the religious life in a number of short parables, of which the last is the parable of the two houses. The Sermon is the first of five main discourses into which the bulk of the teaching of Jesus, as recorded by Matthew, has been collected. Each discourse ends with a formal phrase of the type: "When Jesus finished these sayings . . . ," and this provides the transition to the next incident or block of material.

In Luke there is a corresponding, but much shorter, discourse commonly called the Sermon on the Plain, from the statement in Luke 6:17 KJV that Jesus "stood in the plain." This also begins with beatitudes and ends with the parable of the two houses. Comparison of the two sermons suggests that they are elaborations of an earlier discourse contained in a source used by both evangelists. Study of the literary relations, and also of the form of the separate sayings, is a valuable preliminary to any discussion of the meaning of the Sermon on the Mount, which is generally held to have unique importance in disclosing the teaching of Jesus on matters of conduct and in presenting some of his most challenging demands.

1. Literary relations
   a. The written tradition
   b. The oral tradition
2. Form of the sayings
3. Interpretation
   a. The Beatitudes
   b. The sermon in Luke
   c. The sermon in Matthew
Bibliography

1. Literary relations. Matthew's account of the public ministry of Jesus begins after the death of John the Baptist. Jesus left the seclusion of Nazareth and began to announce in Capernaum the near approach of the kingdom of heaven. His first public act was the choice of four disciples; then he set out on a tour of Galilee, proclaiming the kingdom both by teaching and by healing various kinds of sufferers (Matt. 4:12-25). So far, Matthew follows the pattern laid down by Mark, though reserving Mark's examples of healing for later use; but now he expands the teaching theme and, between Mark 1:39 and 40, inserts the Sermon on the Mount. The discourse is absent from Mark, though there are parallels to six of the separate sayings in different Markan contexts. The effect of Matthew's procedure is to throw into great prominence the connection between the teaching of Jesus, the proclamation of the kingdom, and the gathering of disciples.

Luke's account of the public ministry begins in Nazareth itself with a synagogue sermon announcing the imminent fulfilment of promises made through Isaiah. The narrative shows how these promises were at once taken up in exorcisms and healings, and how Jesus' interpretation of them started a growing conflict between himself and the Jewish authorities (Luke 4:14-6:11). In all this Luke follows Mark quite closely, except that he has his own remarkable account of Peter's call; and at 6:12-16 Luke comes to Jesus' appointment of the Twelve after a night spent in prayer in the hills. Then the healing theme is again mentioned but not illustrated; it is now the turn of teaching in a short discourse (Luke 6:20-49), which was no doubt intended by the author to be closely related to the hostility which Jesus had encountered. Almost all the sayings in this discourse have parallels in the Sermon on the Mount, but in different order and sometimes differently phrased. Three verses have parallels elsewhere in Matthew; only four verses are quite without parallel. One brief saying has a Markan parallel.

a. The written tradition. The Sermon on the Mount is more than three times as long as the Lukan discourse. It has roughly twenty-eight verses with parallels in Luke 6, thirty-one verses with parallels elsewhere in Luke, and the remaining forty-seven verses are peculiar to Matthew. From this it follows that the two sermons cannot be independent. It is possible to hold the view that the Sermon on the Mount is the original form of a discourse which Luke shortened by dispersing some of the material throughout his gospel and omitting the rest; but it is not easy to give plausible reasons for this suggested procedure. It is more commonly held that both Matthew and Luke had access to a source which contained a teaching discourse, beginning with beatitudes and ending with the parable of the two houses. Each evangelist made his own modifications of the source. Most Protestant scholars use the symbol "Q" to designate the material common to Matthew and Luke but not found, with some exceptions, in Mark; and hold that the Q material, whether comprising one source or several, was used with Mark in the composition of the two gospels. Some Roman Catholic scholars take a not entirely dissimilar view, but regard the Q material as forming part of the Aramaic collection of sayings of the Lord made, according to the evidence of PAPIAS, by Matthew. *See* Q; SYNOPTIC PROBLEM; JESUS CHRIST § A.

An attempt to reconstruct the discourse as it stood in the source must begin with the verses common to both sermons as a nucleus, and then test the claims of the other material.

Among the materials peculiar to Luke the four woes (Luke 6:24-26) which correspond to the Lukan beatitudes are suited to the Semitic manner of speaking, but seem somewhat inappropriate when addressed to disciples, and necessitate a fresh start at Luke 6:27a. Hence they may have been introduced here from elsewhere or composed by Luke. The sayings of Luke 6:39-40 do not fit easily into their present context and are found separately elsewhere in Matthew. It is not easy to be certain about their proper position. The saying in Luke 6:45 is used elsewhere by Matthew in a rather forced manner; here it is not inappropriate to its context, though it makes a change of theme from actions in general to speech in particular. So it is possible that Luke slightly expanded the original discourse by a few sayings from elsewhere.

Other Lukan material in Matthew's sermon has parallels in Luke 9:51-18:14, Luke's great insertion in the Markan framework where he throws together a large number of sayings and incidents, often without any clear sequence. It is all the more notable when such a sequence does occur, as in the group of sayings on prayer in Luke 11:1-13. In Matthew, sayings from this group appear separated and in different contexts at Matt. 6:9-13; 7:7-11. Similarly, the sayings of Luke 11:33-35, joined by the catchword "lamp," appear separately at Matt. 5:15; 6:22-23. The Lukan context of these sayings seems more likely than the Matthean to represent the underlying source. The parable of the accuser (Matt. 5:25-26) seems to have been brought in from elsewhere to serve the purpose of moral instruction, whereas Luke 12:58-59 preserves its primitive eschatological meaning. Again, the saying on divorce (Matt. 5:32) is different from the other antithetical statements about the law. It does not indicate, as they do, a righteousness exceeding that of the scribes and Pharisees, but takes sides in a scribal debate (or, in the Lukan form, contradicts the law; *see* § 3c *below*). Further, the parallels to the sayings in Matt. 5:13; 6:19-21; 7:13-14, 22-23, are so different in wording that they seem to come from separate versions of the Q material, rather than from a common source. To these considerations must be added the fact that Luke is known (from his treatment of Mark) to handle his material in blocks, whereas Matthew often rearranges material and forms collections illustrating particular themes. Hence it is probable that the Q material with parallels in Luke 9:51-18:14 formed no part of the sermon as it stood in the source but was introduced by Matthew when he was compiling the Sermon on the Mount.

The material peculiar to Matthew comprises five beatitudes, a series of very distinctive verses relating the teaching of Jesus to the law (Matt. 5:17, 19-24, 27-28, 31, 33-39a, 41, 43; 6:1-8, 16-18), and a few other verses. It is not easy to be certain whether the sermon in the source contained this material or not. It may be held that the material was originally present and was omitted by Luke because its strongly Jewish interest would be uncongenial to Gentile readers. That Luke was prepared to make considerable omissions from his sources is known from his use of Mark. On the other hand, it may be suggested that the special Matthean material was absent from the Q discourse but came from another sermon-discourse which also, perhaps, began with beatitudes. In compiling the Sermon on the Mount, Matthew would have combined these two sources. In making a choice between these possibilities, the decision turns on the kind of issue presented by Matt. 5:38-48. This passage contains two examples of the formula: "You have heard that it was said . . . . But I say to you . . . ." The citations of the old law are Matthean only; but the corresponding commandments of Jesus have parallels, more or less close, in Luke. The correspondences are shown in Table 1.

Table 1

Matthew	Luke
5:38-39*a*	———
5:39*b*-40	6:29
5:41	———
5:42	6:30 with a possible reminiscence in 6:34
5:43	———
5:44	6:27-28
5:45	6:35 (in thought, not wording)
5:46-47	6:32-33 (in thought more than wording)
5:48	6:36 (with different key word)

In this passage it may indeed be that Luke performed a delicate surgery, excising some sayings, rearranging and rewriting the rest; but it seems a simpler and more understandable procedure if Matthew, in his familiar manner, was combining and reshaping material of two collections of sayings.

Thus it may probably, though not certainly, be held that Luke reproduced and slightly expanded a Q sermon whose extent is roughly indicated by the verses common to the Matthean and Lukan discourses. Matthew made a compilation from the Q sermon, other Q material, and an M discourse used only by himself. If this is so, it means that the original intention of the Q sermon should be more readily discernible in Luke than in Matthew. At least it cannot be assumed that Matthew's setting of the sayings provides the only or most important clue to their meaning. This does not imply, however, that the Matthean material and arrangement can be neglected; nor, when sayings differ considerably in wording, can it be taken for granted that the Lukan form is primary. Each saying must be judged on its own merits. There is little point in trying to decide between Matthew's "mountain" and Luke's "level place" as the scene of the discourse, since no doubt the evangelists indicated what seemed to them an appropriate location. Luke gave his sermon the character of a public manifesto (6:17; 7:1; and cf. the woes in 6:24-26), and Matthew was moved by the same impulse in his closing formula (7:28); but there are strong indications that the sermon in the source was addressed to disciples only (Matt. 5:1; Luke 6:20; and the wording of the Beatitudes, especially that on the persecuted; *see* § 3*a below*).

b. The oral tradition. It is open to question whether the sermon in Q represents a remembered discourse of Jesus or a collection of sayings preserved separately in the oral tradition from which all written sources arose. It is inherently probable that Jesus gave connected teaching; but all the Synoptic discourses are in part compilations. The Synoptic gospels are composed, largely though not entirely, of short units of teaching or narrative strung together by vague indications of time or place, by catchwords, or by common themes. The fact that some sayings in the Sermon on the Mount appear in totally different contexts in Luke shows that the evangelists lacked an authoritative tradition about their original contexts. Hence it is possible to examine the sayings in isolation, though their setting in the gospel narrative may be an important indication of their significance to the evangelist and the church tradition he reflects.

The relation of the sayings in the Sermon on the Mount to the church tradition may be studied by examining parallels in the letters.

It is clear from I Cor. 7:10-11 that a tradition of the teaching of Jesus was known to Paul, though he seldom quoted it directly. He could distinguish a commandment of the Lord (which here presupposes the form in Mark 10:11-12 rather than the variants in Matthew and Luke) from his own instructions, which were, in effect, a modification for the circumstances of Gentile life of Jesus' teaching on divorce. It may reasonably be supposed that sayings of Jesus were widely remembered throughout the early church, and were preserved (and sometimes adapted) to meet the needs of church life. They would have a semi-independent existence until written collections became authoritative.

Some sayings of Jesus were current in variant forms with identical meaning. Thus Matt. 7:16*b* has the same figure of trees and fruit as the differently worded Luke 6:44*b;* and there is a third form in Jas. 3:12, where it is used, without reference to Jesus, in a passage on control of the tongue. These are variations of a familiar proverb. Similarly, the differently worded but parallel sayings Matt. 5:48; Luke 6:36, as well as I Pet. 1:15 ("As he who called you is holy, be holy yourselves in all your conduct"), are adaptations of Lev. 11:45. Again, the thought of forbearance in judging in Matt. 7:1-2 is repeated with amplifications in Luke 6:37-38; and Paul appeals to it as a familiar principle in Rom. 2:1-3; 14:10. Hence it may be concluded that some of the sayings of Jesus existed alongside proverbial or traditional sayings and may have been influenced by them.

To some sayings, however, there are verbal parallels sufficiently close to suggest direct reminiscence. I Pet. 3:14: "Even if you do suffer for righteousness' sake, you will be blessed," echoes the distinctive words of Matt. 5:10. I Pet. 4:13-14: "Rejoice in so far as you share Christ's sufferings, that you may also rejoice and be glad when his glory is revealed. If you are reproached for the name of Christ, you are blessed," recalls the words of Matt. 5:11-12: "Blessed are you when men revile you . . . on my account. Rejoice and be glad, for your reward is great in heaven." ("Reproach" and "revile" represent the same Greek verb.) Further, I Pet. 2:12 seems to reproduce Matt. 5:16 in a form adapted to the

Gentile mission, and with a strong eschatological note, which may be original. In Rom. 12:14 the command: "Bless those who persecute you; bless and do not curse them," has words characteristic of both variant forms in Matt. 5:44; Luke 6:28. These similarities suggest that, at least in circumstances of hardship and persecution, the early Christians had for their encouragement a group of sayings of Jesus (in Greek) which could be woven into apostolic letters and recognized for what they were.

There are other possible parallels to sayings in the Sermon on the Mount which suggest greater freedom in adaptation. Thus Jas. 5:12 looks like a concise summary of Matt. 5:34-37, and may well preserve the saying: "Let your speech be, Yea, yea; Nay, nay" (ERV-ASV), in a more original form. The saying: "Repay no one evil for evil" (Rom. 12:17 and similarly I Pet. 3:9), may be said to convert Matt. 5:39; Luke 6:29 into a generalization. Possibly Phil. 4:6 generalizes the teaching against anxiety (Matt. 6:25-34; Luke 12:22-31); and it may be thought that the closing section of the sermon (Matt. 7:21-27) is summed up in: "Be doers of the word, and not hearers only" (Jas. 1:22 and similarly Rom. 2:13). The passage Jas. 5:1-3 has some verbal reminiscences of Matt. 6:19-20 and, indeed, of the Lukan woes. The setting is strongly eschatological and may be original; but it looks as if original sayings have here been, not abbreviated, but expanded. Similarly Jas. 1:5 could be an expansion of Matt. 7:7; Luke 11:9, with a more abstract version still in I John 5:14-15. The parenetical sections of the letters provide examples of an ethical tradition that could have developed by expansion or abbreviation of sayings of Jesus.

Consequently a study of the meaning of sayings in the Sermon on the Mount needs to take into account the intentions of the evangelists, the significance of the sayings in the sources, the modification of sayings in the course of their preservation by the primitive church, and the meaning of the sayings in their original setting in the ministry of Jesus.

2. Form of the sayings. The Sermon on the Mount contains sayings of various types. Some are simple commands such as: "If any one forces you to go one mile, go with him two miles" (Matt. 5:41). Force is given to such commands simply by the moral authority of the speaker. A special case of such authority is provided by the six antitheses—e.g., "You have heard that it was said to the men of old, 'You shall not kill; and whoever kills shall be liable to judgment.' But I say to you that every one who is angry with his brother shall be liable to judgment" (Matt. 5:21-22a). The formula is undoubtedly an adaptation of a common rabbinic device which contrasted what was "heard" in a particular passage of scripture (i.e., what might be understood in a narrowly literal sense) with broader interpretations that could be urged either from other passages of scripture or by logical demonstration. The Matthean formula lacks any such demonstration or scriptural argument, and the authoritative phrase: "I say to you," is more prophetic than rabbinic. Its setting is not so much exposition of the law as the utterance of a prophetic oracle, though the difference between the words of Jesus and the rabbinic formula must not be exaggerated.

To other commands a warning is added—e.g., "Make friends quickly with your accuser, while you are going with him to court, lest your accuser hand you over to the judge . . . , and you be put in prison; truly, I say to you, you will never get out till you have paid the last penny" (Matt. 5:25-26). The first part of the saying is no more than a piece of proverbial wisdom ("It is better to settle out of court if you can"); the second part, with its strongly prophetic tone, converts it into an eschatological warning. Promise and warning are found together in the wisdom saying in Matt. 6:19-21, the Lukan form of which (12:33-34) appears in an eschatological context. The sayings on almsgiving, prayer, and fasting (Matt. 6:1-4, 5-6, 16-18), with their deliberately formal and repetitive structure, also join warnings and promises in a manner recalling wisdom sayings. Closely related to the commandment with a promise is the commandment with a purpose—e.g., "Let your light so shine before men, that they may . . . give glory to your Father who is in heaven" (Matt. 5:16).

Other commandments are provided with various kinds of argument or demonstration. The passage Matt. 6:25-34 is a complex example, containing three types of justification for the general command: "Do not be anxious." There are pieces of proverbial wisdom: life is more than food or clothing; anxiety cannot add to your span of life; there is enough trouble today without worrying about tomorrow (vss. 25b, 27, 34). Then there is a simple argument by analogy from less to greater in familiar rabbinic style, which depends for its force on a vivid awareness of God: if God feeds the birds, he will certainly feed you whom he values much more (vss. 26, 28-30). Finally, there are prophetic sayings which criticize Gentile faithlessness and promise God's kingdom (vss. 32-33). Another example of the argument from less to greater appears in Matt. 7:9-11, which is both preceded and followed by prophetic imperatives. Somewhat more complex is the section Matt. 5:43-47; Luke 6:27-35. Matthew has a commandment with a purpose—to behave as God does—followed by the argument: If you love only those who love you, how are you better than tax collectors and Gentiles? Luke has a series of simple commands, followed by the Golden Rule (widely quoted in rabbinic and other writings), and then the direct commandment of love for enemies, with a promise of acting as God does. In both passages, the basic justification of the commands is given in prophetic disclosure of the nature of God (cf. Matt. 6:7-8).

Thus examination of the commands in the Sermon on the Mount discloses a dual kinship—with prophetic speech on the one hand and with wisdom sayings (proverbial or rabbinic) on the other. These two classes, broadly understood, account for the remaining material as well.

Among wisdom sayings may be included the sayings on serving two masters (Matt. 6:24), on trees and fruit (Matt. 7:16-20), two rabbinic-type rulings (Matt. 5:22b, 34b-36), the only liturgical instruction (Matt. 6:9-13), and a dark saying or riddle (Matt. 6:22-23). Here also belong the simple comparisons and parables—e.g., the speck and the log (Matt. 7:3-5), the salt and the lamp (Matt. 5:13, 15—used differently in Mark and Luke and so handed down without a standard application). The parable of the two houses (Matt. 7:24-27) doubtless conveys an eschatological warning, and therefore belongs to both wisdom and prophetic sayings.

So also do the BEATITUDES, a type of saying common in the Psalms (e.g., 40:4; 112:1-2). Here they are associated with future benefits (even the first) and so are akin to such oracles as Isa. 19:24-25; Dan. 12:12. Further prophetic-type sayings are found in Matt. 6:14-15; and possibly in 5:13a, 14a ("You are the salt of the earth; . . . the light of the world"), which have been compared to Isa. 61:6 but are not easy to place and are regarded by some scholars as compositions of the evangelist. The remaining prophetic sayings are dominated by the person of the speaker. They are Matt. 5:17, one of the notable "I have come" sayings which are scattered throughout the gospels, together with the appended sayings on eschatology and the law in 5:18-20; the closely allied sayings in 7:21-23, in which association with Jesus apart from performance of the known will of God is repudiated; and the closing parable, with the significance it attaches to the words of Jesus (cf. Isa. 8:16-18; Dan. 12:9-10).

Because the wisdom-type sayings can be paralleled from proverbial and rabbinic sources, it has been suggested that they may have been attributed to Jesus at an early stage in the tradition. The commandments also may have taken shape in the life of the primitive church. On this view the distinctive element in the teaching of Jesus was the prophetic utterance of immediately relevant warnings and promises, the eschatological announcement of the kingdom. Scholars who contest this view acknowledge the influence of the early Christian communities on the form of the sayings and would agree that some alien sayings have been attributed to Jesus; but they would question the exclusively eschatological emphasis. It may be forcibly argued that Jesus availed himself of familiar proverbial wisdom and simple rabbinic teaching devices in order to convey a primarily prophetic message. The wisdom sayings, as well as the commands uttered on his own prophetic authority, were drawn into the service of the proclamation of the kingdom. On either view, the speaker of the Sermon on the Mount is not so much lawgiver, teacher, or rabbi as prophet of the final will and action of God.

The Hebrew prophets frequently uttered their oracles in poetical form, with its characteristic and varied parallelism (*see* POETRY [HEBREW]). Examples are numerous in the sayings of Jesus. Matt. 7:7-11 is beautifully constructed in synonymous parallelism (in which one strophe balances and repeats another), together with a concluding saying in antithetical parallelism (in which one strophe is balanced by another in contrast):

> Ask, and it will be given you;
> seek, and you will find;
> knock, and it will be opened to you.
> For every one who asks receives,
> and he who seeks finds,
> and to him who knocks it will be opened.

> Or what man of you,
> if his son asks him for a loaf, will give him a stone?
> Or if he asks for a fish, will give him a serpent?

> If you then, who are evil,
> know how to give good gifts to your children,
> how much more will your Father who is in heaven
> give good things to those who ask him?

There are also examples of step parallelism, in which one strophe develops the thought of the preceding one (e.g., Matt. 5:17; 6:6). From these simple but flexible devices elaborate poetical units are built up, as may be seen in the varied correspondences of Matt. 6:25-30. It is of some importance to observe that the poetic form is not always exactly reproduced in the Matthean and Lukan versions of a saying. Thus Luke 12:24 runs:

> Consider the ravens:
> they neither sow nor reap,
> they have neither storehouse nor barn,
> and yet God feeds them.

Matt. 6:26 breaks the parallelism with: "They neither sow nor reap nor gather into barns." Again, the parallelism of Luke 12:28:

> which is alive in the field today
> and tomorrow is thrown into the oven,

is destroyed by a slight variation of the Greek in Matt. 6:30: "which today is alive and tomorrow is thrown into the oven." Thus the poetical structure of the sayings may be used with caution as one guide to their original form.

3. Interpretation. In both gospels (and in the source) the BEATITUDES have first place and provide the keynote. A comparative study of the two forms reveals the intentions of the evangelists and the original purport of the sayings. Then it becomes possible to examine the remainder of the two sermons and their various sections.

a. The Beatitudes. The four Lukan beatitudes are balanced by four woes, and differ somewhat from the corresponding Matthean sayings in wording. Luke uses the second person plural throughout, Matthew the third person for 5:3-10 and the second person for vss. 11-12. Opinion is divided on the original form. The Lukan beatitudes give a vivid impression of hearers' being directly addressed (reinforced by the repeated "now" in vs. 21); in Matthew they read like generalizations. But blessings in the OT are commonly expressed in the third person, and there is precedent for a change of person in the last blessing of a series. It is difficult to see why Matthew should have changed an original second person when the rest of his sermon preserves so forcibly the direct address. Woes, however, are often expressed in the second person, and it may be that Luke, in adding the woes, changed third to second person to secure uniformity. The decision is not of great importance, since both forms are in the prophetic manner. It is possible to translate: "How happy are they who . . . !" and: "Alas for you who . . . !" if it is understood that the blessings and woes are not simple comments of joy and grief but prophetic words intended to bring to pass the things about which they give promises or warnings. *See* BLESSINGS AND CURSINGS.

The beatitude on the poor (Luke 6:20b, 24; Matt. 5:3) reflects a strong characteristic of OT religion, in which God is the vindicator of the poor and needy (Ps. 107:39-43), and the king as God's agent has responsibility for the poor (Ps. 72:1-4). In biblical tradition the word "poor" even developed an almost technical meaning, deriving from the period of Seleucid rule, when it was poor men of firm and simple piety who maintained the faith against pagan enticements (cf. Ps. 86:1-2; Pss. Sol. 10:7). Matthew's phrase "the poor in spirit" is intended to make this fact clear. No doubt the Lukan beatitude has the same intention, though it is also closely related to Luke's familiar concern for the poor and reflects conditions in first-century Palestine, where a large class of destitute, unemployed, and landless peasants lived side by side with wealthy farmers, great landed proprietors, and rich bankers. *See* POOR; POVERTY.

There is no essential difference of meaning between "kingdom of God" and "kingdom of heaven," which reproduces more closely the first-century Jewish idiom. Both mean God in his sovereignty—i.e., God visibly exercising his sovereignty and the result of this exercise. The phrase "Theirs (yours) is the kingdom of heaven (God)" is of a type that implies possession of the kingdom and presupposes the double thought that God the king is actively at work and will shortly demonstrate his sovereignty with power; and that those who heed the promise and warning will share his sovereignty. *See* KINGDOM OF GOD.

The beatitude on the hungry (Luke 6:21a, 25a; Matt. 5:6) doubtless reflects the OT theme of God's readiness to relieve, not only physical, but also spiritual, hunger (Ps. 107:4-9; Isa. 55:1-2). In the gospels a dominant note is the importance of meals among the actions of Jesus (fellowship meals with his disciples, meals with sinners, the feeding of the multitude) and in his teaching ("A man once gave a great banquet . . ."; "Bring the fatted calf and kill it, and let us eat . . ."). It is notable that the spiritual and literal senses are held together, and neither is neglected for the other.

Matthew reads "hunger and thirst for righteousness." The word "righteousness" can mean right action on man's part, as it certainly does in Matt. 5:20; 6:1 (RSV "piety"). Some interpreters favor this meaning here and elsewhere in the sermon. By it the phrase would perhaps refer to an intense longing for an ideal of perfection surpassing the Jewish moral ideal and going beyond any conformity to rules of conduct. But "righteousness" can also mean right action on God's part, and in the later chapters of Isaiah often means the divine vindication and salvation. Such a meaning is appropriate in the present context: the phrase would refer to those who long intensely for the divine vindication. This interpretation would thus draw out the wider meaning of the Lukan phrase while maintaining its eschatological tone (cf. Matt. 6:33; and *see* RIGHTEOUSNESS IN THE NT).

The beatitude on the unhappy (Luke 6:21b, 25b; Matt. 5:4) may perhaps be illustrated in the OT poetry of the Exile and the return, where grief is turned into joy (e.g., Ps. 137 for the grief; Ps. 126 for the rejoicing). The Beatitudes as a whole are close to the promises of Isa. 61:1-2 (which Jesus expounded in the synagogue at Nazareth, according to Luke 4:16-21); and the Matthean beatitude, with similar meaning but different wording, reflects Isa. 61:2b. Its primary reference was wider than personal bereavement. This beatitude must be seen against the actual distress of an occupied country, and the devout Jewish expectation of the "consolation of Israel" (Luke 2:25) in the forthcoming mighty act of God. *See also* MOURNING.

The beatitude on the persecuted (Luke 6:22-23, 26; Matt. 5:10-12) predicts suffering for the disciples and draws an analogy with the fate of the prophets with whom they are compared. Since the mission charge in the Markan and Lukan traditions, though not in the Matthean (Mark 6:7-11; Luke 10:1-16; Matt. 10:5–11:1), lacks this note of suffering, it has been suggested that the beatitude belongs to a later stage in the ministry of Jesus when, according to Mark, the theme of suffering was uppermost in his mind. The argument is not decisive, since every version of the mission charge anticipates rejection of the messengers; though, indeed, the wording of the beatitude may have been influenced by later Christian experiences. Matthew's phrase "on my account" is perhaps a simplification (such as is found at Matt. 16:21 when compared with Mark 8:31; Luke 9:22) of Luke's "on account of the Son of man." This phrase brings to mind the eschatological figure in Dan. 7:13, who represents the saints of the Most High and receives a kingdom after experience of suffering (vss. 21-22, 25-27). Matt. 5:10 appears to be an alternative version of this beatitude, in which "for righteousness' sake" could mean either "for your loyalty to the law" (as of the Maccabean martyrs) or "for your reliance on God's vindication" (*see above*). The content of the blessing is a great reward in heaven (vs. 12), where "heaven" is a substitute for the divine name and not the future state of the righteous. It means that God will give a great reward to those who suffer, when his kingship is fully manifested; and thus is essentially the same as the promise of vs. 10 that they will share the kingdom of God. For the theme of reward, *see* §§ 3b-c *below*.

When these four beatitudes are regarded as a whole, it can be seen that they are addressed to people who are poor, hungry, and miserable and who expect to be harshly treated. To them is promised a share in the divine sovereignty, which will be their happiness and satisfaction. Both physical and spiritual senses must be included in these promises; and the whole forms a revolutionary messianic proclamation of the kind announced in Isa. 61:1-2 and in the Magnificat, Luke 1:50-53. The teaching thus introduced is not inaptly called an ethic of grace.

The remaining beatitudes in Matthew are spoken, not to people in certain situations such as poverty or persecution, but to people of certain character—i.e., who are humble, merciful, purehearted, and peacemaking. These are common themes in Jewish teaching. Matt. 5:5, a commendation of humility, is taken from Ps. 37:11. Matt. 5:7 could be a rephrasing of Prov. 19:17. The purity of heart required in Matt. 5:8 for seeing God (which, in Palestinian speech, is another way of saying "appearing before God") is required in Ps. 24:3-4 for appearing before God in the temple. Matt. 5:9 commends the peaceable character, as does Ps. 34:14, and says that God recognizes peacemakers as sharing his own character (being sons of God).

Only in the first of these beatitudes is there any

immediate suggestion of the reversal of situation characteristic of the Q beatitudes. It is true that the theme of inheriting (i.e., possessing) the land, which derives from the possession of Canaan, provided an eschatological image; and that the mercy, vision, and peace of God were regarded as complete only in the new age. But they were not confined to it; and the promises of these beatitudes cannot easily be pressed into the same mold as that of the prophetic beatitudes of Q. The M beatitudes are wisdom sayings which sum up a number of themes prominent in the teaching of Jesus. The Matthean beatitudes as a whole, with added sayings and changes of wording, lean somewhat heavily toward wisdom teaching and must be balanced by the eschatological proclamation in Luke; but neither can easily be discarded. One sort helps to interpret the other: both together make up the teaching of Jesus. The ethical instruction of Jesus cannot be divorced from his prophetic announcement of the kingdom of God, and his eschatological proclamation does not stand apart from his fargoing teaching on conduct.

b. The sermon in Luke. This passage may be analyzed as follows:

6:27-35, the radical demands of love

Vss. 36-45, consequences in word and deed

Vss. 46-49, the call to decision

The radical demands of love are stated with sharp clarity in vss. 27-28. These words, spoken first to peasants familiar with ill-treatment and robbery from soldiers and guerrilla bands, were easily adapted to Christian communities facing religious hostility. They are more than counsels of prudence for the weak before the strong. They require the positive action of love: praying for opponents and blessing them—i.e., counteracting the atmosphere of contempt, malice, bitterness, and hatred that marked relations in first-century Palestine. In vss. 29-30 there are illustrations of what could happen: a blow on the face and forcible theft of clothing and possessions. (The parallel verses in Matthew rephrase the illustrations so that they refer to court proceedings; *see* § *3c below*.) In these illustrations there is a touch of familiar proverbial exaggeration, in order to state with maximum emphasis the negative aspect of vss. 27-28—i.e., the principle of nonretaliation in injurious personal encounters. Then is stated the Golden Rule (vs. 31), not because it applies with any exactness to the preceding, but because anyone who acts accordingly must try to put himself in another person's place. It is, as it were, the minimum condition of a properly personal relationship; and it would appear that love demands a personal relationship even with a hostile opponent.

The argument in vss. 32-34 suggests that the original context of this group of sayings was in an exposition of the commandment: "Love your neighbor as yourself' (cf. Luke 10:25-37). If men do good only to their own circle of friends and lend only to those who can do them favors, they are no better than sinners ("Gentiles" is probably meant; cf. Matt. 5: 46-47) who act on the basis of mutual interest. Love for neighbor is to be so conceived that men do their acts of kindness without expecting any return. Their sufficient reward is that they are acting like God, who is kind to ungrateful and wicked men (cf. the

vivid illustration in Matt. 5:45). The concept of reward, as it is used here, does not imply receiving something, but becoming something—namely, sons of God, who share and reflect his character.

This extension of the meaning of "neighbor" also transforms the meaning of "love." In the teaching, and indeed the practice, of Jesus, love is not called forth by worth in the loved object, but is simply the overflowing of the divine nature which men are to share. Love of this kind is distinguishable from a love called forth by the inherent worth of the object, love which desires to possess and enjoy its object for its own self-satisfaction and fulfilment. Since God is absolutely sovereign, his love cannot proceed from self-interest, but is always outward-flowing in kindness and blessing to those who need it most. *See* LOVE IN THE NT.

Certain consequences in word and deed follow from the command to be merciful as God is merciful (vs. 36). They are illustrated in an assorted group of sayings which give the impression of having been collected with an eye on the inner life of the early Christian communities, but which may originally have been spoken to Pharisaic opponents. In vss. 37-38 four prohibitions (in the present tense) are matched by four passive verbs which, in the original Aramaic, would probably be understood as referring to God ("Judge not, and God will not judge you . . ."). The sayings are similar in meaning to Matt. 6:14-15 and were probably spoken in answer to Pharisaic criticisms of Jesus' association with and promises to sinners. The picture, typically Palestinian, of grain being measured out is an illustration of the overflowing mercy of God, which is neither arbitrary nor limited. The presupposition of these sayings, that men who have received God's mercy are bound to share and exercise it (cf. Matt. 18:23-35), made them readily adaptable for the Christian communities. They were probably understood as prohibiting censoriousness and encouraging generous forgiveness.

The proverbial parable in vs. 39 is used in Matt. 15:12-14 to characterize the Pharisees as "blind guides." Here it has the general meaning that men do not see the way sufficiently well to be able unerringly to condemn others. The saying of vs. 40 is used differently in Matt. 10:24-25, and the original meaning cannot be certainly decided. Its general sense is that men cannot expect to teach others to see further than they themselves see; and it may have had an application to teachers in the Christian communities. The parable of the speck and the log (vss. 41-42) betrays its polemical origin in the word "hypocrite," and means that men are not sufficiently free from prejudice and self-concern to correct others. The parable shows that a "hypocrite" is primarily, not someone who pretends to be godly, but someone sincere about his religion and blind to his faults. *See also* § *3c below*.

The parable of trees and fruit (vss. 43-44) appears at Matt. 7:15-20 as a test for false prophets (and looks like an adaptation to later church life), and at Matt. 12:33-35 as a test between Jesus and his opponents. Its more general meaning in the Lukan context is that as the fruit of a tree depends on the nature of the tree, so a man's actions depend on the "treasure of his heart"—i.e., the inner resources of his nature. As he is, so he speaks. A man's speech, harsh or charitable, demonstrates his own character (assuming some link in thought with vss. 37-39).

The question of vs. 46 introduces the call to decision. If men address Jesus respectfully as "Lord," they presumably assent to his teaching even though they do not put it into practice. They must therefore decide, under the pressure of a forthcoming crisis, whether they will allow his words to influence their inner life or not. The parable of the two houses dramatizes the decision and its consequences. Matthew's version is more rhythmical than the Lukan and corresponds well with the Palestinian scene. The point is that, in the Deluge, men who hear the words of Jesus and do them will be saved; those who hear and fail to perform will be lost. It is remarkable that this supreme position is given, not to scripture or scribal tradition, but to the words of Jesus.

The Sermon on the Plain begins and ends with the note of forthcoming crisis. The beatitudes and woes, with their reversal of fortune, are spoken in prophetic manner as words which go forth to effect what they promise. The concluding parable calls men to decide whether or not they will take their stand on the words of Jesus. This eschatological conception springs from the conviction that the kingdom of God is at hand, that the divine sovereignty is moving toward its full manifestation. Yet although this is the framework of the sermon, it is not its heart. The central teaching is a description of God's sovereignty as absolute love. In the conviction that the powers of the kingdom were already at work, Jesus bade men practice such love in the difficult relations of daily life. This central teaching confronts men with the kingdom of God as something to be shared and shown forth. In the sermon as a whole there is a duality which corresponds to the presentation of the kingdom elsewhere as "already here and still to be consummated." Even though the sermon is composite, with sayings taken from discussions about the law and controversy with the Pharisees adapted to Christian community use, there can be little doubt that it conveys the double emphasis of Jesus' teaching.

c. The sermon in Matthew. This may be analyzed as follows:

5:13-16, address to the new community
5:17-48, six antitheses on the fulfilment of the law
6:1-18, on almsgiving, prayer, and fasting
6:19-7:12, on possessions, anxiety and trust, behavior to neighbors
7:13-27, concluding challenge

The salt metaphor, handed down with different phrasings and applications (cf. Mark 9:50), was originally a warning to Israel (in Luke 14:25, 34-35, it is addressed to the multitude) and has been reapplied to the community of disciples. SALT was an essential constituent of Jewish meals and sacrificial offerings, and the parable means that Israel (or the new Israel) is essential to the world only so long as it performs its proper duty. The sense in which this is understood is given in 5:14-16. By mutual regard and practical kindness, the community is to demonstrate a quality of life which will prompt men to glorify God. (The perils inherent in such counsel are

in mind in 6:1-18.) The association of the light of the world and the hill city is perhaps explained by a similar combination in OT imagery of the community of the new age (e.g., Isa. 2:1-5; 60:1-3, 14, 19-20). The lamp parable has also been variously transmitted. The Matthean wording suggests the conversion of those within Judaism, the Lukan form (11:33) the conversion of the Gentiles. The odd wording in Mark 4:21 (lit., "Does a lamp come to be put . . . ?") suggests a reference to the Servant of God as light to the Gentiles (Isa. 42:6; 49:6). The original use of the parable by Jesus may therefore have been in answer to rebukes for making his message known indiscriminately.

This short complex of sayings from various contexts provides an introduction to the social duties of the new community.

There is clear evidence that Jesus disputed the oral tradition of the law, distinguished between one part of the written law and another, and uttered sayings that had the effect of undermining large sections of it (examples in Matt. 12:1-8; 19:3-9; 15:11-13; respectively). It is natural that some should have accused him of destroying the law, while others took advantage of its relaxation. Matt. 5:17-20, which introduces the antitheses, appears to rebuke those who thought that Jesus' chief intention was to relax the harshness of the law and modify the rigidity of the Pharisees. The passage is difficult to interpret, for it uncompromisingly asserts the validity of the law. Even minute details of the tradition are essential in this age, and entrance into the new age is by a loyalty to the law more intense than that of the Pharisees. One solution of this problem is to regard the passage, in whole or part, as a creation of the primitive Jewish Christian community either defending itself against Jewish criticism or, more probably, attacking teachers in the Hellenistic Christian communities. It is not easy, however, to suppose that Matthew was unaware of or indifferent to the contradiction between sayings of Jesus that rigidly maintain and that vigorously criticize the law. Also, even the Q tradition has sayings asserting the validity of the law. Matt. 5:18 appears more bluntly at Luke 16:17. And at Matt. 23:23; Luke 11:42, both the weightier matters of the law and the supererogatory practices of the Pharisees are commended. Hence it is permissible to look for an interpretation which will resolve the conflict (even though it cannot be confidently asserted that the sayings in their present form go back to Jesus).

Apart from vs. 17, the passage is dominated by eschatological language and seems to reflect a debate about the relation of the law to the age to come, which has also left traces at Matt. 11:12-15; Luke 16:16-17. The primary purpose of the (prophetic) coming of Jesus was to announce the nearness of the kingdom of God and so to confront men with God in his sovereignty. For the present age the law mirrors the holiness and sovereignty of God; the inauguration of the new age would mean that the grand design to which the law prophetically pointed (in ancient Hebrew tradition Moses was prophet, not scribe; Deut. 18:18) was brought to completion. The righteousness of the Pharisees set before men an elaborate and extensive but finite obligation; the proclamation of the kingdom set before them an infinite obligation. According to the outlook of Pharisaic righteousness it was possible, in principle, to satisfy God by keeping his law perfectly; according to the teaching of Jesus, God is not satisfied until men "enter the kingdom of heaven" and so share the divine sovereignty.

In the antitheses the teaching is given in a series of interpretations (not contradictions) of the law, though at each stage an attitude is indicated which cannot be prescribed by law at all. There is no reason to deny that Jesus taught in this manner, though the Matthean arrangement has been artificially elaborated. It is likely that an original nucleus contained simple antitheses to which illustrations and other relevant materials were later added.

The opening of the first antithesis (5:21-22a) can be understood in rabbinic manner to mean: "You have heard . . . 'You shall not kill,' and have understood that only he who kills is liable to judgment." When anger is classed with murder, not only the external act but also the springs of emotion are subjected to judgment. The meaning of vs. 22b is not certain. It is best understood as a scribal ruling with comment: the rule is that a man who insults his brother is liable to prosecution, but the truth is that he is in danger of destruction (*see* RACA; FOOL). Matt. 5:23-24 appropriately introduces the theme of reconciliation as a prerequisite for worship (cf. Matt. 6:14-15), and the same theme colors the interpretation of 5:25-26 as practical counsel for reconciliation within the community. In Luke 12:57-59 it is an eschatological parable.

The antithesis on adultery (5:27-28) asserts that the marriage bond is injured even by the thought of unchastity, so that MARRIAGE is judged by its inner quality as much as by its legal form. The sayings on renunciation (vss. 29-30) appear again at Matt. 18: 8-9, with more consistent eschatological language. Here the offending hand or eye refers to natural desires that become uncontrolled and destroy the "whole body"—i.e., ruin the whole personal life.

The antithesis on divorce in vss. 31-32 has parallels in Matt. 19:9; Mark 10:11; Luke 16:18, though the statements are not identical and present a delicate critical problem. Only in the Matthean versions is the excepting clause for unchastity present, and its effect is to rule that divorce is permissible for one cause. This is in harmony with the interpretation currently given by the school of Shammai and repudiated by the school of HILLEL. The Markan and Lukan forms of the saying do not recognize divorce for any cause, and must be original. The Matthean form is either an attempt to avert a direct conflict between the teaching of Jesus and the law, or the first stage in transforming an absolute statement about the divine intention of marriage into a rule of limited obligation.

The antithesis on oaths (5:33-34a) begins with the legal principle that a man who has taken an oath (i.e., called God as witness to the truth of his statement or promise) must not break his word. This opens up a wide area of debate (cf. Matt. 23:16-22), including the question whether all oaths—those made on the name of God and those in some other form—are equally binding. Jesus' ruling is that all equally involve God and his sovereignty; but his fundamental judgment is against taking oaths at all. He teaches men to be so aware of the presence of God that they are totally committed by "Yes" or "No." *See* OATH.

The antithesis on retaliation (5:38-39a) deals in fact with the law of compensation for injury. In the time of Jesus, and perhaps from early times, Exod. 21:24 was understood as allowing an injured man to claim damages. Jesus replaced this reasonable practice by the command: "Do not stand out for damages against the man who injures you" (to paraphrase vs. 39a; the KJV "resist not evil" is misleading). The principle is illustrated by four examples: the backhanded smack on the face (only Matthew has "the *right* cheek"), which the rabbis regarded as a very insulting assault punishable by a heavy fine; a lawsuit claiming clothing; compulsory service as baggage carrier for the army of occupation; and begging and borrowing. (All except the third have differently applied parallels in Luke.) Every injury or demand has its legal remedy or limitation. Jesus instructs men not to insist on their rights but to give more than is demanded of them.

The antithesis on love of neighbor (5:43-45) provides the climax and is elaborated, as the last member of a series, with a clause of purpose—namely, sharing God's nature in sonship. The Matthean section is similar to the Lukan version in purport (*see* § 3b above). The opening formula can be understood in rabbinic manner to mean: "You have heard . . . 'You shall love your neighbor,' and have concluded that you should hate your enemy." There is no explicit command in Jewish literature to hate enemies.

The final and summarizing sentence (vs. 48) means that men are to be all-inclusive in their love, as God is. The word translated "perfect" goes back to an Aramaic idea of wholeness or completion. *See* PERFECTION.

This section of the sermon has a number of absolute demands together with immediately practical applications, though sometimes stated in nonliteral and exaggerated forms. The author has used sayings and parables from various contexts, often eschatological, to serve this practical purpose. He portrays Jesus as consistently pressing behind the legal ruling to fundamental questions of personal relations raised by anger, contempt, infidelity, mistrust, revenge, and hatred. In all this there is nothing repugnant to rabbinic teaching at its best. The antitheses themselves are modified rabbinic formulas, and most of the sayings can be paralleled from rabbinic tradition which may reach back to the early first century. Jesus does not here contradict the law; nor does he make it more profound or more difficult. He is not fundamentally concerned with law at all, but with God's sovereign will, mediated directly by himself, and encountered in personal relations. The fundamental sanction is sharing the nature of God himself. This is the eschatological challenge, presented in the authoritative "I say to you" of Jesus.

The self-contained section 6:1-18 gives three examples of the general instruction (in agreement with the best rabbinic teaching) that religious duties are to be performed, not to impress people, but to please God. Jesus is not here criticizing contemporary teachers, but exposing the corruption of motives.

Religious duties, sincerely undertaken, can conceal an unacknowledged desire for human approval. This is the character of the hypocrite, the man who sincerely plays his part but is untouched in his real nature (*see* § 3*b above*). In the duties of almsgiving, prayer, and fasting, men must encounter the "Father who sees in secret"—i.e., who unerringly discerns the inner motive. Jesus employs the language of reward (*see* §§ 3*a-b above*), possibly in the sense that God will reward men at the judgment though his intention is far removed from an arbitrary future reward for piety. If the danger of religious duties conscientiously performed is the substitution of an abstraction for personal encounter, the reward promised by Jesus is the restoration of personal encounter with the Father. It is perhaps not accidental that in these verses God is frequently spoken of as "your (our) Father." *See* ALMS; FASTING; PRAYER.

The original simple scheme has been augmented by additional sayings on prayer. Matt. 6:7-8 warns, not against the repetition of familiar prayers (as the traditional "vain repetitions" might suggest; see the RSV translation), but against the Gentile custom of addressing many gods and using magical and meaningless formulas. (It can only be conjectured whether this saying originally took shape among the mixed population of Galilee or in the Gentile mission field.) A Christian, when he prays, relies on the sole sovereignty of God, who knows his need before he asks (cf. Matt. 6:32).

The LORD'S PRAYER, with an appended saying on forgiveness as a commentary on 6:12, is also an addition to the simple scheme. The prayer is found in a different context and with different wording at Luke 11:2-4. Yet it may be remarked how aptly the longer Matthean form suits the sermon as a whole. Every phrase of the prayer represents a theme of the discourse, and vs. 10:

> Thy kingdom come,
> *Thy will be done,*
>   *On earth as it is in heaven*

(the italicized words are in Matthew only), may be said to express the central motif of the sermon.

The section 6:19–7:12 consists largely of material found elsewhere in Luke, and lacks the clear arrangement of earlier sections, though some groupings can be discerned.

The sayings of 6:19-24 are loosely held together by the thought of possessions. A link with the preceding section is provided by vs. 21 ("What you value most determines your thinking"), and the same theme is carried on by the obscure saying in vss. 22-23, well translated in the RSV. By the unsound eye Matthew evidently meant greed or envy, though Luke's application is different. The choice between God and MAMMON in vs. 24 is followed by a section on ANXIETY and trust (vss. 25-34). It mixes earthy common sense with an insistence on God's providential care for ephemeral flowers and unclean birds (if Luke's word "ravens" is preferable to Matthew's "birds of the air"; cf. Ps. 147:9); but its distinctive note is a vivid awareness that the divine sovereignty and vindication are within the grasp of faithful men. (For an analysis of this section, *see* § 2 *above;* for "and his righteousness," in Matthew only, *see* § 3*a above*.)

The section 7:1-12 is an oddly assorted group of sayings of which vs. 6 is peculiar to Matthew; vss. 1-5, 12, appear in Luke's sermon; and vss. 7-11 elsewhere in Luke. It may tentatively be suggested that Matthew intended a balanced paragraph on the wrong and right attitudes toward one's neighbor. A censorious attitude is condemned, and illustrated by a parable, in vss. 1-5; while vs. 6, clearly a proverbial expression, may be an ironical comment on pious readiness to put others right though despising them. Some scholars regard this verse as a piece of apocalyptic Jewish exclusiveness adopted by extreme Jewish Christians and incorporated among the sayings of Jesus. The meaning of vss. 7-11, in their present setting, must be determined by the Golden Rule in vs. 12, which reads like a commentary on them. In Luke they illustrate the theme of diligent petition; but it is possible that they were originally directed against critics of Jesus who objected to his giving God's good things to unworthy people. His reply is that we should not attribute to God conduct that we should think monstrous in a father. Matthew uses this teaching about God to describe a right attitude toward one's neighbor.

The conclusion seems to have been carefully and deliberately arranged (mostly out of material from Luke 6; 13) to present a repeated call to decision. The theme of the two ways (7:13-14) is familiar in Greek and Jewish writing (e.g., Deut. 30:15-20; Jer. 21:8); and this saying may have grown out of Luke 13:23-24, which is an encouragement to enter the narrow door of the kingdom while it is open. The Matthean form, though it is despondent about men's response to the proclamation of the kingdom, may be understood as an invitation to "choose life," rather than an intimation that a few have life chosen for them. The trees-and-fruit parable assumes in Matthew the probably secondary form of a test of true and false prophets (*see* § 3*b above*), and is immediately followed by a qualification in vss. 21-23. The ability to prophesy and work miracles is no proof of genuine discipleship, but only a resolute determination to do the Father's will made known in the words of Jesus. The parable of the two houses (*see* § 3*b above*) presents the fundamental decision and leads neatly to the closing formula with its acknowledgment of the authority of Jesus.

This conclusion of the sermon—the call to decision and the portrayal of Jesus as prophet and teacher (rabbi)—is in accord with the adaptation of sayings to the needs of the early Christian communities. Yet it is not adequate to describe the sermon as the announcement of the new law, for by an interpretation of the law it overthrows a legalist attitude. It would be truer to say that the teaching of Jesus, just as much as his miracles and apocalyptic sayings, confronted men prophetically with the sovereignty of God. The sayings are signs of the kingdom. To discuss whether the sermon contains a practical rule of conduct or an ideal is beside the point; it brings men in decision before God and their neighbor, and so begins the process of setting them free to share God's sovereignty and do his will.

Bibliography. For commentaries see the bibliography under MATTHEW, GOSPEL OF; LUKE, GOSPEL OF. For the common critical view of the literary problem, see B. H. Streeter, *The*

Four Gospels (1924), pp. 249-54. For Roman Catholic views, see B. C. Butler, *The Originality of St. Matthew* (1951), ch. 3; J. Dupont, *Les Béatitudes* (1958), pt. 1, which is a rich critical and theological study. Different views on the forms of the sayings may be found in R. Bultmann, *Die Geschichte der synoptischen Tradition* (3rd ed., 1957-58); W. Manson, *Jesus the Messiah* (1943), especially ch. 5. Of value for exegesis are: H. Windisch, *Der Sinn der Bergpredigt* (1929; *The Meaning of the Sermon on the Mount*, English trans. S. M. Gilmour, 1951); M. Dibelius, *The Sermon on the Mount* (1940); T. W. Manson, *The Sayings of Jesus* (1949); A. N. Wilder, *Eschatology and Ethics in the Teaching of Jesus* (rev. ed., 1950). A good popular exposition is A. M. Hunter, *Design for Life* (1953). For rabbinic teaching, see B. H. Branscomb, *Jesus and the Law of Moses* (1935); D. Daube, *The NT and Rabbinic Judaism* (1956).

K. GRAYSTON

SERON sĭr'ŏn [Σήρων] (I Macc. 3:13, 23). Governor of Coele-Syria and general of the Syrian army. He boasted that he would make a name for himself in battle against Judas Maccabeus. He was defeated by Judas at the ascent of Beth-horon, *ca.* 12 miles NW of Jerusalem. With the defeat of Seron, Judas' military prowess was recognized as posing a serious threat to Syria.

S. B. HOENIG

*SERPENT. A scaly, limbless, elongate reptile of the genus Ophidia or Serpentes.

1. Names and identification
2. Literal usage
3. Figurative usage
4. Magical or supernatural occurrence
5. In mythology
6. Cultic significance
7. In eschatology
Bibliography

1. Names and identification. Serpents are mentioned often in the Bible, and a number of names are used for them. None of these names can be identified with precision from a zoological standpoint.

a) נחש (*nāḥāsh*) is the general word for all serpents, corresponding to ὄφις.

b) Two snakes of the Bible can only be regarded as legendary. These are the שרף (*śārāph*), the flying serpent of Num. 21:8; Deut. 8:15, which in the Sinai wilderness could have been identical with the אפעה noted below; and certainly שרף מעופף (*śārāph meʿophēph*), the fiery flying serpent of Isa. 14:29; 30:6 (*see* SARAPH; SERAPHIM). Either a legendary or an indeterminable snake is תנין (*tannîn*) of Exod. 7:9, in the incident where rods were transformed into snakes before Pharaoh; the same word is used to designate serpents in Deut. 32:33; Ps. 91:13, and the serpent DRAGON in Gen. 1:21; Ps. 74:13; 148:7; Isa. 27:1; 51: 9; Jer. 51:34; Ezek. 29:3; etc.

c) Various other words are synonymous with "serpent." On זחלי (Deut. 32:24), *see* CRAWLING THINGS. On ἑρπετόν (Jas. 3:7), *see* CREEPING THINGS.

"Viper" is used to render שפיפן (*shephîphôn;* Arabic *siff*, Akkadian *šippu;* Gen. 49:17; KJV "adder"), identified with Cerastes; and אפעה (*'eph'ê;* Arabic *'afʿā*) =ἔχιδνα, identified with *Echis carinatus* Schw., a viper living in sandy plains. Another word has been translated "viper" by error: עכשוב (*'akhshûbh;* Ps. 140:3—H 140:4; KJV "adder"), rendered in the quotation in Rom. 3:13 as ἀσπίς, "asp." According

to Tur-Sinai, עכשוב is an anagram (accidental transposition of consonants) from עכביש (*'akkābhîsh*), "spider," certainly also regarded as poisonous.

"Adder" is the translation of צפע (*sephaʿ;* Isa. 14: 29; KJV "cockatrice") and צפעני (*siphʿônî;* Prov. 23: 32; Isa. 11:8; 59:5; Jer. 8:17; KJV usually "cockatrice"). This name is applied today to the big viper, *Vipera palaestinae* Wern., which is the only poisonous snake in N and central Palestine, being less common in the hills.

"Asp" is the usual translation of פתן (*pethen*). This is the ἀσπίς of the NT (Rom. 3:13).

Thirty-six species of snakes are known in Palestine today, very few of which could have been assumed to have been known specifically to the ancient Hebrews. The common name *nāḥāsh* was probably applied to all snakes, but especially to the bigger species of Coluber, such as the common Syrian Black Snake (*Coluber jugularis* L.), the Diced Water Snake (*Natrix tesselatus* Laur.), the Montpelier Snake (*Malpolon monspessulanus* L.), or the Cat Snake (*Tarbophis fallax*). But there is no definite way to identify the poisonous species. Yet it is by no means sure that the present use is identical with the biblical usage, if in Bible times the species were separated at all. In Greek antiquity this was definitely not the case. The *shephîphôn*, if the interpretation is correct, would embrace the Cerastes vipers, *Cerastes cerastes* L., *Cerastes vipers* L., and *Pseudocerastes fieldi* Schm. Finally, there is the *pethen*, which is usually identified with the *Naja haje* L., the uraeus snake of ancient Egypt, the snake of the Egyptian snake charmers which inflates its neck when excited. This snake has not thus far been found in Palestine, but it could well be a memory from the early Egyptian associations of the Hebrews.

Serpents must have been held in abhorrence in general. Probably, as is often the case, all serpents were thought to be poisonous.

F. S. BODENHEIMER

2. Literal usage. Many of the serpent references call for no special comment: the bite of a serpent (Eccl. 10:8; Amos 5:19; fatal in M. Yeb. 16:6; Sanh. 1.4); the movement of a serpent over rocks (Prov. 30:19); the charming of serpents (Ps. 58:5—H 58:6; Eccl. 10:11; Jas. 3:7); the serpents sent by the Lord to afflict Israel in the wilderness (Num. 21:6-7; Deut. 32:24; Wisd. Sol. 16:5-14; I Cor. 10:9); etc. The "flying serpent" of Isa. 14:29; 30:6, if a real animal, is presumably a desert viper (*Echis carinata*), which popular imagination graced with the power of flight (cf. the "winged serpents" of Arabia mentioned by Herodotus II.75). The serpent in the sea, to which Amos 9:3 refers, is probably a large aquatic animal, perhaps credited with fabulous powers, though subject to Yahweh's will (cf. Ps. 139:9-10). The expectation that dust will be the serpent's food in the messianic age (Isa. 65:25; cf. Gen. 3:14), indicates that the serpent will have become innocuous and no longer a danger to man.

3. Figurative use. Although thirteen of the eighteen species of Palestinian snakes which Tristram mentions are in fact harmless, biblical writers usually treat the snake as dangerous and wicked (so also M. B.K. 1.4). Thus the serpent is used to represent evil men (Ps. 58:4), the Assyrians (Isa. 14:29), the Babylonians (Jer. 8:17), Israel's enemies (Deut. 32:

33), the effects of wine (Prov. 23:32), danger in general (Ps. 91:13), the scribes and Pharisees (Matt. 23: 33; *see* VIPER), etc. The reference to the nations' eating dust like a serpent (Mic. 7:17) points to their impending humiliation. A more favorable side of the serpent is its reputed shrewdness (cf. Gen. 3:1); hence the admonition to Jesus' disciples: "Be wise as serpents" (Matt. 10:16; cf. Midrash Rabba on Song of S. 2:14: "God saith of the Israelites: Towards me they are sincere as doves, but towards the Gentiles they are prudent as serpents"). The metaphor involving Dan in Gen. 49:17 is complimentary: Dan, though small and weak, can advance his cause by discreet, vigorous action (cf. Deut. 33:22; Judg. 18).

4. Magical or supernatural occurrence. The turning of a rod or staff temporarily into a serpent occurs only in connection with Israel's departure from Egypt (Moses in Exod. 4:3; 7:15; Aaron in 7:9-10; the Egyptian magicians in 7:12).

5. In mythology. The familiar mythology of the ancient Near East, with its primeval struggle between two opposing powers, has numerous echoes in the OT, where, of course, the contest is between Yahweh and his antagonist. One of the terms for the latter is the "fleeing serpent" (Job 26:13; cf. Pss. 74: 13-14; 89:9-10; etc.; Isa. 51:9); cf. the words of Mot in the Ugaritic text (I AB[i], lines 2-4):

> If thou smite Lotan, the serpent slant,
> Destroy the serpent tortuous,
> Shalyat (*šlyt*) of the seven heads
> (*ANET* 138).

See DRAGON; LEVIATHAN; RAHAB.

While the unique narrative of man's expulsion from Eden (Gen. 3) reflects Israel's basic theism, some of its details and undertones suggest connections with the mythology of Western Asia; the Sumerian tale of Enki and Ninhursag, the Adapa story, the Gilgamesh Epic, all offer at various points parallels to the biblical tradition. In the Gilgamesh Epic, e.g., in Tablet XI, Utnapishtim and his wife have the prospect of being like the gods (lines 193-96); there exists a life-giving plant (lines 266-70); a snake snatches this plant from Gilgamesh (lines 285-89).

In Gen. 3 the serpent is not only one of the Lord God's creatures, but it is also one of the craftiest (vs. 1) and best informed (vss. 4-5). For some unstated reason (a major theological problem is here evaded), the serpent opposes the Creator's purposes (cf. II Cor. 11:3), and the results (Gen. 3:14-19) are disastrous for all concerned, including the serpent. It is implied in vs. 14 that theretofore the serpent had not moved on its belly, though how it did get about is not indicated. In Enoch 69:6 (which R. H. Charles thinks is pre-Maccabean, but which C. C. Torrey places in the first century B.C.), an angel, Gadreel, is said to have led Eve astray; Wisd. Sol. 2:24 reads: "Through the devil's envy death entered the world," which some interpret as marking the identification of the serpent with the devil. Philo takes the serpent to be a symbol of passion and sensual pleasure (*Questions and Answers on Genesis* I.31). *See* EDEN, GARDEN OF; PARADISE.

6. Cultic significance. It is abundantly clear from a wide range of evidence that the snake was a symbol of deity and of fertility powers in the ancient Near East. In Egypt, where the veneration of serpents in one form or another was common (some serpents being good, and others harmful), the ancient serpent-goddess of Lower Egypt was the beneficent Buto or Wazit. In the form of a uraeus or cobra she became the symbol of royalty, and she was later attached to the royal crown as protectress of the king. On the other hand, the most important of all Egyptian demons (or evil gods) was Apophis, the supreme opponent of Re, and he also was represented by a serpent.

In Mesopotamia, too, the snake served as a religious symbol (for a group of such symbols, *see* bibliography). It was, e.g., associated with the god Ningizzida, a minor deity. *See* bibliography.

In late Canaanite and early Hebrew Palestine, evidence of the worship of a serpent-goddess has been uncovered at Beth-shan, Beth-shemesh, Gezer, Hazor, Shechem, and Tell Beit Mirsim. *See* bibliography.

In the account of Hezekiah's reforms in II Kings 18:4, we are told that "he broke in pieces the bronze serpent that Moses had made" (cf. Num. 21:8-9, where it is called a "fiery serpent"; John 3:14). Whatever the origin of this brazen object, in the eighth century it was looked upon by the prophetic party as idolatrous, and it was destroyed. That it should ever have been made by Moses is doubtful. It is more probable that this serpent was of Canaanite origin, representing a fertility deity recognized in Jerusalem long before David's time, and whose veneration continued under the Hebrew regime down to the reign of Hezekiah. *See* bibliography. *See also* NEHUSHTAN; SERPENT, BRONZE; SERPENT'S STONE.

7. In eschatology. As early as Isa. 27:1 a mythological motif is used for an eschatological purpose: in this passage "Leviathan the fleeing serpent" stands for the Lord's enemies, who "in that day" will be overthrown. It is not clear whether these enemies are terrestrial, celestial, or cosmic. *See* bibliography.

It remains for the Christian author of Revelation to identify "that ancient serpent" with the Devil or Satan (Rev. 12:9-15; 20:2). Thus the serpents of the primeval cosmic struggle, of the Garden of Eden, and of the ancient fertility cult are united with all that the Jewish SATAN had come to stand for, though this composite creature's ultimate end is to be cast forever into the lake of fire and brimstone (20:10; cf. Matt. 25:41).

Bibliography. For snakes as religious symbols, see: G. Contenau, *Everyday Life in Babylon and Assyria* (1954), plate XXIII. On the god Ningizzida in particular, see E. D. Van Buren, "The God Ningizzida," *Iraq*, I (1934), 89. In *Symbols of the Gods in Mesopotamian Art* (1945), p. 40, Van Buren says of the device of two serpents twisted together: "All the evidence tends to prove that the motive was a symbol, not of any particular divinity, but of the blessings of fertility ensured by the union of male and female."

On archaeological evidence of the worship of serpents, see: W. C. Graham and H. G. May, *Culture and Conscience* (1936), pp. 81-90. J. Finegan, *Light from the Ancient Past* (1946), pp. 139-46; Y. Yadin, "Further Light on Biblical Hazor," *BA*, XX (May, 1957), 43-44.

On the bronze serpent of II Kings 18:4, see: H. H. Rowley, "Zadok and Nehushtan," *JBL* (June, 1939), pp. 113-41.

For a possible astronomical meaning of Isa. 27:1, involving

the constellations Serpens, Draco, and Hydra, see: J. Skinner, *Isaiah I*, Cambridge Bible (1915), 212.

W. S. McCullough

SERPENT, BRONZE. The bronze figure of a snake made by Moses and erected by him in the wilderness (Num. 21:8-9). While in the wilderness on the way from Mount Hor, many of the wanderers were bitten by fiery serpents (vss. 4-7; *see* FIERY SERPENT). The ones who had been bitten were urged to look to the bronze serpent, that their wounds might be healed. A number of problems emerge from the story.

The KJV regularly speaks of brass, but brass is a carefully compounded alloy of copper and zinc, a combination not known to the ancients. The KJV is therefore incorrect in the use of the term "brass." Bronze is a common mixture of copper and tin, which are frequently found in proximity to each other.

The story comes from one of the early sources, probably E, in which the use of magic and magical cures are prominent, but the story is used by the later compiler to emphasize the importance of faith in God.

The snake was a well-known reptile of the wilderness, and was, in fact, worshiped by many of the neighbors of the Hebrews, and, indeed, later by at least one Christian sect, the Ophites (*see* NEHUSHTAN). The snake represented evil and destruction, but also healing and creativity. The symbol of the healing snake is still preserved in the physician's caduceus, which shows the snake entwined about the wand of Mercury.

The fact that the Hebrews continued to worship or venerate the symbol (see II Kings 18:4) indicates that the image had, or came to have, more than temporary healing properties. The biblical record is careful to emphasize that healing came from God, not from the bronze snake. The Fourth Gospel quotes Jesus as paralleling his own forthcoming experience with this incident in the wilderness (John 3:14). The Synoptics make no mention of this.

W. G. Williams

SERPENT'S STONE [אבן הזחלת, stone of the creeping one]; KJV STONE OF ZOHELETH zō'ə lĕth. A rock or stone near EN-ROGEL, by which Adonijah sacrificed victims in view of his clandestine coronation (I Kings 1:9). The name may either represent an indifferent toponym or suggest that the ground where the stone stood was consecrated to a divinity having the serpent as emblem. The figure of the serpent is found repeatedly on religious monuments or utensils in ancient Palestine (*see* SERPENT § 5). An alternate explanation of the name זחלת by means of a dialectal Arabic form *zaḥueileh*, "slippery scarp of rock," is most questionable.

Bibliography. G. A. Smith, *Jerusalem*, I (1907), 109-11; H. Vincent, *Jérusalem Antique* (1912), pp. 138-41; G. Dalman, *Jerusalem und sein Gelände* (1930), pp. 165-66; J. Simons, *Jerusalem in the OT* (1952), pp. 160-61.   G. A. Barrois

SERUG sĭr'ŭg [שרוג; LXX *and* NT Σερουχ; *for traditional etymologies, see* Jub. XI.1-2, 6]; KJV NT SARUCH sâr'ək. Son of Reu, of the line of Shem. Serug became father of Nahor at age thirty and then lived two hundred years longer and had other sons

and daughters (Gen. 11:20-23; I Chr. 1:26; Luke 3: 35). The name is identified with that of the Akkadian city and district Sarugi, situated W of Haran.

L. Hicks

SERVANT. A person of either sex who is in the service of a master. He is under obligation to obey, to work for the benefit of his master. He usually receives some protection in return. There are both voluntary and involuntary servants. There are native and foreign-born slaves, but the two are not to be equated with the previous grouping. The terminology of the Bible does not consistently distinguish "servant" from "slave" or "bondmaid." *See* SLAVERY.

The word נער refers to a boy and so an attendant (Num. 22:22). Joshua is Moses' helper (Exod. 33: 11). Elisha has an attendant who is probably a voluntary follower (II Kings 4:12). The term משרת is also used for both Joshua and the servant of Elisha. The נערים may be followers of a leader (Gen. 14: 24; I Sam. 25:5; II Kings 19:6; etc.). The feminine form of this word, "maiden," is also used (*see* MAID; Gen. 24:16; Ruth 2:5; Esth. 2:9; etc.).

The term משרת perhaps most closely approximates our concept of a free servant who ministers to another. The Levites are ministers of the Lord (Ezra 8:17; Isa. 61:6; Ezek. 44:11). So are the priests (Exod. 28:35; Joel 1:9; 2:17; cf. false priests in Ezek. 20:32). Officers are ministers of the king (I Chr. 27: 1; Prov. 29:2). Angels also minister before the Lord (Ps. 103:21; 104:4).

The שכיר is the hired servant, or HIRELING (Exod. 12:45; Job 7:1; Mal. 3:5; etc.). Unlike the slave, the hired servant could refuse to perform a task.

The Aramaic פלח in Ezra 7:24 is for the servant of God only, the priest who reveres God (Akkadian *palâḫu*, "revere").

In the KJV the most frequent use of "servant" is for עבד, but this is more properly "slave" (Gen. 9: 25; Exod. 21:2; Deut. 5:15; etc.). The sense is neither complete nor correct when the word is translated "servant." *See* SERVANT OF THE LORD.

The Greek word παῖς is primarily "child" and so related to the Hebrew נער. By extension and use in the LXX it has the meaning of "worshiper" and "slave" (Acts 4:27, 30). Thus in Matt. 8:6, 8-9, 13, this word is used interchangeably with δοῦλός. He is a king's attendant (Matt. 14:2) as well as a worshiper of God (Luke 1:54, 69).

Διάκονος is one who obeys and serves another. He is the king's servant or minister (Matt. 20:26; 22:13; 23:11; Mark 9:35; etc.). The magistrates and the teachers as well as all the followers of Christ are such ministers (Rom. 13:4; II Cor. 6:4; Col. 1:7; etc.). *See* DEACON.

In the LXX, θεράπων is used for the Hebrew עבד. Moses is such a servant of God (Exod. 14:31; Num. 12:7; cf. Heb. 3:5). The verb is frequently used of restoring someone to health (Matt. 12:10, etc.).

A domestic servant having a close relationship to the master's family is designated by the Greek word οἰκέτης. He probably lived with the family but need not be a slave, although this word also is used in the LXX for עבד. It is obvious that such a servant, who lives in, cannot have two masters (Luke 16:13; cf. I Pet. 2:18). Cornelius had such servants (Acts 10:7).

This servant is accountable only to his own master (Rom. 14:4).

The ὑπηρέτης is the "under rower," hence an attendant servant or minister. The word is used of magistrates, executioners, and officers of king and Sanhedrin. It is almost a synonym for "deacon."

The hired servant similar to שכיר is in Greek μίσθιος, μισθατός (Luke 10:7; LXX for שכיר). He worked for daily wages (Luke 15:17 ff). The sons of Zebedee had such servants in their fishing business (Mark 1:20). The parable of the wolf and the hireling has made this word a classic (John 10:12 ff).

In the LXX and the NT, δουλός is the direct equivalent of עבד. It really means "slave." He is completely in the service of another and has no freedom save to obey. It is unnecessary to indicate the frequency with which this concept is used in the Bible. The fellow slave or associate is rendered by the term σύνδουλος (Col. 1:7; Rev. 6:11; etc.).

In the OT covenant servants were to be protected (Lev. 25:42-55; Deut. 5:15; 15:15; etc.). There are no regulations about the hired servant in the Book of the Covenant (Exod. 21–23). The law tried to discourage voluntary servitude on the part of Hebrews. The distinction between the limited type of service and complete slavery is not clear, except that the duration of voluntary bondage is limited (Exod. 21:2; Lev. 25:39).

A servant could be trusted to seek out a wife for one's son (Gen. 24). Female servants or maids could become concubines and bear children for the master (ch. 16). They could also inherit property (15:2; cf. Nuzi). They could marry into the family (I Chr. 2:35). The hired servant was to be paid at the end of each day's work (Deut. 24:15; cf. Luke 15:17, 19).

The image of the servant of God as a worshiper (Lev. 25:55; Num. 12:7; Ps. 105:42; Jas. 1:1; etc.) is best understood in relation to עבד the "slave" of God; and to עבודה, "slavery," or "divine service." So also is the Suffering Servant of Isaiah. C. U. WOLF

SERVANT OF THE LORD, THE [עבד יהוה]. A title given to the figure whose call and mission, sufferings, death, and exaltation are depicted in Isa. 53 and related passages; sometimes called the "Suffering Servant." The expression "servant of Yahweh" is not actually used, but Yahweh calls him "my servant" (42:1; 49:3, 6; 52:13; 53:11), and he speaks of himself as "his [Yahweh's] servant" (49:5).

1. The title "servant(s) of Yahweh"
2. The Servant Songs
3. The problem
4. History of interpretation
5. Who was the Servant?
6. Religious significance of the Servant
Bibliography

1. The title "servant(s) of Yahweh." The word "servant" (עבד) properly means a slave (cf. NT Greek δουλος), but a slave need not have been contemptible to his master. We may compare the modern connotation of "knight," which in Old English denoted a menial (cf. German *Knecht*). Any servant of Yahweh was a privileged person. In general the word עבד expressed the relationship of the weaker to the stronger party in a covenant (ברית); the servant

was entitled to look to his lord for protection and—what is implied in the word חסד, the emotional bond which united the two parties to a covenant—"steadfast love" (e.g., Ps. 103:4; KJV usually "loving kindness" or "mercy").

The worshipers or devotees of any god were his "servants." (It is probable that the distinction between the 'ōbhᵉdhê, "worshipers of" Baal, and the 'abhdê, "servants of" Yahweh, in II Kings 10:23 is artificial and that the original was "servants of Baal"; so LXX and some Hebrew MSS.) In any case, individual Israelites were the "servants" and collective Israel the "servant" of Yahweh (Ps. 136:22; and note the association with "steadfast love").

Various classes of people, as well as individuals, are called "servant(s) of Yahweh." Prominent among the former are the prophets (II Kings 9:7; Ezra 9:11; Amos 3:7; seventeen times in all), and specifically Ahijah (I Kings 14:18), Elijah (II Kings 9:36), Jonah (II Kings 14:25), and Isaiah (Isa. 20:3). Others distinguished by the title are the patriarchs (Abraham [Gen. 26:24], Isaac [Gen. 24:14], Jacob [Ezek. 28:25]), Moses (Exod. 14:31; some thirty-six times), Joshua (Judg. 2:8), Caleb (Num. 14:24), Job (Job 1:8); and of kings, David (II Sam. 3:18; about thirty times), Hezekiah (II Chr. 32:16), and Zerubbabel (Hag. 2:23; cf. Zech. 3:8; 6:12, where the messianic צמח, or "Branch," refers to Zerubbabel). Even Nebuchadrezzar, king of Babylon, is called "my servant" in Jer. 25:9; 27:6; 43:10.

2. The Servant Songs. It is usual to denote certain passages in Deutero-Isaiah as the "Servant Songs." They are 42:1-4[9]; 49:1-6[13]; 50:4-9[11]; 52:13–53:12. (The figures in brackets indicate the extreme limits of the Songs; most scholars limit them to the unbracketed figures.) This is not to say that the Songs are from a different author: the majority opinion today is that they were composed by Deutero-Isaiah himself, though they may be later than the rest of his work. The first three are very similar in vocabulary to Deutero-Isaiah; the fourth is *sui generis* but more similar to Deutero-Isaiah's work than to that of any other writer. Isa. 42:5-9; 49:7-13; 50:10-11 may have been composed, or adapted, to relate the original Songs to their following contexts.

a) 42:1-4: Yahweh introduces his Servant as his chosen one, endowed with his spirit to bring forth "justice" (KJV "judgment") to the nations. (The Hebrew משפט appears here to mean something like "true religion.") He will work quietly and unobtrusively, and will not fail or be discouraged until he has established משפט in the earth.

b) 49:1-6: The Servant announces himself to the distant peoples as called by Yahweh from birth and kept in readiness for his mission. He is "Israel," in whom Yahweh will be glorified. So far he has labored in vain, but he is confident that his recompense is with his God. Now, he continues, Yahweh has assured him that it is not enough that he should be his servant to restore Israel; he is to be a light to the nations, that Yahweh's salvation may reach to the end of the earth.

c) 50:4-9: This passage does not contain the word "servant" (though cf. vs. 10), but it seems necessary to include it in the servant cycle as a middle term between the second song and the last. The speaker is the Servant. He describes how Yahweh wakens him morning by morning to hear as disciples hear. He has not turned back from his task, even though he has had to suffer violence and ignominy. But he is confident in the nearness of his divine vindicator; none shall be able to secure a verdict of guilty against him.

d) 52:13–53:12: This passage begins (52:13-15) and ends (53:11-12) with words of Yahweh. The "we" of 53:1-10 must be either Israelites or the Gentile nations, probably the latter. After Yahweh has announced the coming exaltation of his Servant, the "we" exclaim that the unbelievable has come to pass. The Servant had been disfigured and despised, and they supposed him stricken by God. They see now that it was for their sins, not his own, that the Servant died and was laid in a felon's grave. The resurrection of the Servant is more hinted at than described, but in the closing scene Yahweh recurs to the theme of the beginning: the "many" who were appalled at the Servant, the "many" whose sins he bore, will be apportioned to him as his "spoil." The meaning is in places obscure; this may be due in part to textual corruption.

3. The problem. It is not surprising (*see* § 1 *above*) that many answers to the question, Who was the Servant? have been proposed. The Servant could be Israel, or he could be an individual. If he is an individual, is he king or prophet? Again, if king or prophet, is he a historical individual, or someone still to come?

In the wider context, Israel is called "my servant" (41:8 ff), and in 49:3 the Servant is called "Israel." But since in the following context the Servant has a mission to Israel, he may be an individual or group in whom, so to speak, Israel is incorporated, as the king might be said to embody his people.

4. History of interpretation. The servant passages were understood by NT writers as prophesying Christ, and the general opinion is that Jesus regarded himself as their fulfilment. It is true that he nowhere quotes directly from the passages which modern scholars delimit as the Servant Songs, though he did say of Isa. 61:1-2*a*, which is so similar in spirit to the Songs that some scholars have included it in the song cycle: "Today this scripture has been fulfilled in your hearing" (Luke 4:21). It is clear that Jesus thought of his sufferings as having been "written of him" (Matt. 26:24, 54, 56; Mark 9:12; Luke 18:31; 24:25-27, 46), and it would be hypercritical not to include Isa. 53 and the related passages among "the scriptures" to which he referred. The "many" of Mark 10:45 is strongly reminiscent of the fourfold "many" in Isa. 52:14-15; 53:11-12. At the beginning of the Christian era there were also Jews who thought the Servant was the messiah, but since they found difficulty in conceiving of a suffering messiah, this interpretation was always qualified—e.g., in Targ. Isaiah the exaltation of the Servant is applied to the messiah, but his sufferings fall in part upon Israel, in part upon the Gentiles. Later, as Christians pressed the messianic interpretation, most Jews adopted the collective theory, that the Servant was Israel.

Few Christians dissented from the messianic interpretation until the end of the eighteenth century, when the Jewish view began to gain increasing currency. The full collective theory presents serious difficulties, since the character of the Servant in the Songs is different from that of Israel elsewhere in Deutero-Isaiah. Reaction from it began at the end of the nineteenth century; since then numerous "historical individual" theories have been put forward. Of kings, Hezekiah, Uzziah, Jehoiachin, Zerubbabel, and even Cyrus have been suggested; of prophets, Isaiah, Jeremiah, and even Deutero-Isaiah himself (the "autobiographical" theory). Moses was both ruler and prophet, but it is as the former that he has been named. Others have seen in the Servant an unknown contemporary of Deutero-Isaiah.

None of the historical individual theories has any wide following today. The Servant is not a direct portrait from life. The most attractive form of the collective theory is that associated with the concept of "corporate personality," according to which Israelite thought could pass easily from nation to individual and vice versa. "Israel" could have a mission to Israel, and the real mission of the Servant could even be concentrated in a single person, the prophet himself. One current form of the messianic interpretation is that which would see in the Servant the future messiah depicted in the role of the pre-exilic king, who, there is some reason to believe, annually "suffered" certain ritual penalties as the representative and embodiment of the people he ruled. In general, it may be said that the disjunctives collective *or* individual, prophet *or* king, are no longer so vigorously pressed as formerly. The Servant is too complex a figure to be fitted into any single category.

5. Who was the Servant? Assuming that the Songs are from Deutero-Isaiah, or, what is otherwise reasonably certain, from an intimate member of his circle; since, in Deutero-Isaiah, Israel is called Yahweh's servant, we must start from the equation the Servant = Israel. But since (except in 49:3-5, where "Israel" has a mission to Israel) the Servant of the Songs is anonymous, and since the anonymity of the Servant is accompanied by a progressively heightened individualization in the portrait of him, it is probable that the prophet looked for the coming of one who would more perfectly embody the ideal of what Yahweh's servant should be. (He is quite outspoken about the imperfections of Israel, and there is also every reason to believe that his expectations of Cyrus were only partially realized.) It is true that the Servant's sufferings are in the past (Isa. 53:1-10*a*), but the past is from the standpoint of speakers who are living in the future (52:13-15). This return to what is substantially the traditional Christian interpretation has met with increasing support in recent years. The Servant bears more the features of a prophet than those of a king, but much in the portrait could apply to both prophet and king, and he manifests exactly those qualities which accorded with messiahship as Jesus understood it. In this sense he is a messianic figure, although we should not attempt to apply every detail in the description of him.

6. Religious significance of the Servant. More important even than who the Servant was is the question, What was the Servant to do? Suffering is the great purifier, when it is accepted without bitterness. A prophet may encounter suffering in the course of his work; so Hosea and Jeremiah. The uniqueness of the Servant lies in this: he not only encountered and accepted suffering in the course of his work; in the final phase suffering became the means whereby he accomplished his work, and was effective in the salvation of others. He made himself an "offering for sin" (אשם; 53:10). This is vicarious suffering, but it is not crude substitution. What happens is that the "we" are moved to repentance, confession, and amendment: "Upon him was the chastisement that made us whole, and by means of his stripes there is healing for us" (53:5 orig. tr.). The Servant accomplishes this, not only for Israel, but also for "many nations," the Gentiles. There remained nothing more to be said about the vocation of suffering until Christ came and "served himself heir" to this, the sublimest utterance of prophecy. On all hands it is agreed that whoever was the original of the Servant, none except Christ was its fulfilment.

Bibliography. The literature on the subject is enormous. Of the Commentaries listed under ISAIAH, those by Duhm, Levy, Skinner, and Volz are important. Of articles and monographs the following are only a selection: S. R. Driver and A. Neubauer, *The Fifty-third Chapter of Isaiah According to the Jewish Interpreters,* vol. II (1877). K. Budde, "The So-called 'Ebed-Jahweh-Songs' and the Meaning of the Term 'Servant of Yahweh' in Isaiah Chaps. 40–55," *AJT* (1899), pp. 499-540. E. Sellin, *Serubbabel* (1898); *Der Knecht Gottes bei Deuterojesaja* (1901); *Mose und seine Bedeutung für die israelitisch-jüdische Religionsgeschichte* (1922). J. Fischer, *Isaias 40–55 und die Perikopen vom Gottesknecht* (1916). H. W. Robinson, *The Cross of the Servant* (1926). H. Gressmann, *Der Messias* (1929), pp. 287-339. A. S. Peake, *The Servant of Yahweh and Other Lectures* (1931). O. Eissfeldt, "The Ebed-Jahwe in Isaiah xl.-lv. in the Light of the Israelite Conceptions of the Community and the Individual, the Ideal and the Real," *ET,* XLIV (1932/33), 261-68. J. S. van der Ploeg, *Les chants du Serviteur de Jahvé dans la seconde partie du livre d'Isaïe* (1936). H. S. Nyberg, "Smärtornas man. En Studie till Jes. 52, 13-53, 12," *Svensk Exegetisk Årsbok,* VII (1942), 5-82. I. Engnell, "The 'Ebed Yahweh Songs and the Suffering Messiah in 'Deutero-Isaiah,'" *Bulletin of the John Rylands Library,* XXXI (1948), 3-42. H. W. Wolff, *Jesaja 53 im Urchristentum* (2nd ed., 1950). J. Lindblom, *The Servant Songs in Deutero-Isaiah* (1951). H. H. Rowley, *The Servant of the Lord and Other Essays on the OT* (1952). C. Lindhagen, "The Servant of the Lord," *ET,* LXVII (1955/56), 279-83, 300-302. V. de Leeuw, *De Ebed Jahweh-Profetieen* (1956), gives a summary in French. S. Mowinckel, *He That Cometh* (1956), pp. 187-257; C. R. North, *The Suffering Servant in Deutero-Isaiah* (2nd ed., 1956) contains a full bibliography. H. Ringgren, *The Messiah in the OT* (1956). W. Zimmerli and J. Jeremias, *The Servant of God* (1957).   C. R. NORTH

SESIS. KJV Apoc. form of SHASHAI.

SESTHEL sĕs'thĕl. In I Esd. 9:31 for BEZALEL 2.

SETH sĕth [שת, *see below;* Σηθ]; KJV SHETH shĕth in I Chr. 1:1. In the Yahwistic genealogy, the third son of Adam and Eve (Gen. 4:25). However, the Priestly genealogy, not mentioning Cain or Abel, allows the inference that Seth was Adam's first son (5: 3-8; supported by I Chr. 1:1; Ecclus. 49:16-17; Luke 3:38; *see* PENTATEUCH § A3, 5). The latter source furnishes the few statistics of Seth's life. Since both genealogies have Seth, Enosh, and Noah in common and exhibit other parallels, they may represent two versions of an earlier traditional list. But in the present

J narrative Seth appears as God's gracious gift to Eve as restitution for slain Abel.

Eve named him "Seth" (*shēth*), saying: "God has appointed [*shāth*] for me another child instead of Abel" (Gen. 4:25). Etymologically this explanation is inadequate, raising also grammatical questions, and may originally have rested merely on assonance (cf. 4:1*b*). The correct etymology is uncertain, though it may possibly be connected with the nomadic, Aramean *Suti.* But the theological importance for the Yahwist of the traditional etymology ensured its continuance.   L. HICKS

SETHUR sē'thər [סתור, concealed (by the deity)] (Num. 13:13). A member of the tribe of Asher sent to spy out the land of Canaan; son of Michael.

Bibliography. M. Noth, *Die israelitischen Personennamen* (1928), pp. 38, 158.

SEVEN, SEVENTH, SEVENTY. The number seven was sacred among the various Semitic peoples, as well as among many other peoples.

Among the Egyptians, seven gradually succeeded four as the favorite holy number. The deceased was met in the nether world by seven cows and one bull, and seven gods and seven serpents gave him audience. Isis was accompanied to the Delta by seven scorpions. The newborn's fate was told by seven Hathors. In magic and medicine seven was a potent number. Seven gods are invoked in incantation. Holy oils and ointments were seven. Seven was the correct dosage of pills, and seven stones were used in certain cures. Multiples of seven—fourteen, twenty-one, forty-two, seventy, seventy-seven—were also important.

In Mesopotamia seven was holy from earliest times, but the origin of its sacred character is problematic. It has been assumed generally that the observation of the moon's phases led to the hebdomadal division of the month. The lunar month, however, never has a whole number of days, so that the month and the seven-day week are actually incompatible systems of reckoning. The oldest reference to seven-day periods in cuneiform dates from the twenty-third century B.C. and has reference to seven-day religious festivals and observances and not to the division of the month. It appears that in Mesopotamia the seven-day week had its origin in the cult and was independent of the lunar month, which was the basis of time-reckoning in civil life. It has been suggested that the seven-day week had its beginning in the heptads of Sumero-Akkadian theology and cosmology. The seven planets were doubtless a factor in the sanctity of the number. The matter is too involved to be discussed here, and it must suffice simply to note the important role of seven in Mesopotamian religion.

Seven plays such an important role in the OT that only the chief features of its use can be noted here. Its symbolic use is so extensive that it is difficult to tell when it is intended merely as an ordinary specific number. As in Mesopotamia, seven days was the period for certain important festivals and cult procedures. Passover and Tabernacles are seven-day festivals. The New Year, the Day of Atonement, and Tabernacles all occur in the seventh month. The

Feast of Weeks (Deut. 16:9) and the Jubilee (Lev. 25:8-10) were based on the square of seven. Seven pervades every aspect of the cult. Seven days is the period for ordination of priests and consecration of altars (Exod. 29:35-37). The victims for sacrifice are often seven (Gen. 7:2; 8:20; 21:28-30; Num. 28:11; I Chr. 15:26; Job 42:8); the number of altars seven (Num. 23:1-2, 4, 14, 29; II Chr. 29:21). The sacrificial blood is sprinkled seven times (Lev. 4:6, 17; 14:7; 16:14; Num. 19:4), and so too the anointing oil (Lev. 8:11).

The furnishings and decorations of the temple were often in sevens (I Kings 7:17 [if the MT is retained]; Ezek. 40:22, 26; cf. Prov. 9:1). The seven-branched candlestick (Exod. 25:31-37; I Kings 7:49; Zech. 4:2, 11), except for the ark of the covenant, was the most sacred object in the temple. The OATH is connected with seven, and seven human victims atone for a broken covenant (II Sam. 21:6, 9). The seven locks of Samson's hair (Judg. 16:13, 19) were probably connected with the Nazirite vow. Seven was also a factor in vengeance and punishment (Gen. 4:24; Exod. 7:25; Lev. 26:18; Prov. 6:31; Dan. 4:16, 23, 25). Seven had special importance in connection with angels (Ezek. 9:2; Zech. 4:10b; Rev. 15:1, 6-8; see ANGEL). Evil spirits and infirmities also came in heptads (Luke 8:2; 11:26). Seven was effective in magic, as seen in Joshua's reduction of Jericho by means of a potent combination of sevens (Josh. 6:4, 8, 13) and Naaman's cure by seven baths in the Jordan (II Kings 5:10). Seven rawhide bowstrings, however, were not enough to hold Samson (Judg. 16: 7). The sneezes of the resuscitated child (II Kings 4: 35) were a good omen, whether the exact number seven was important or not. The ideal number of sons was apparently seven (Ruth 4:15; Job 1:2; II Macc. 7; Acts 19:14). Seven-day and seven-year periods are mentioned in numerous miscellaneous connections. Famine and plenty come in seven-year cycles (Gen. 41; II Kings 8:1). The common period for waiting is seven days (Gen. 7:3-4, 10; 8:10, 12; I Sam. 10:8; 11:3; Ezek. 3:16-17). Wedding festivals were celebrated for seven days (Judg. 14:12, 17; Tob. 11:19). Serious ritual defilements lasted seven days (Lev. 15:19, 28; Num. 19:11, 14, 16). In Deut. 7:1, seven is used as synonymous with "many," and in a number of cases it appears to be a round figure for a moderately large number (Gen. 31:23; Job 1:2; Ps. 12:6; Prov. 26:16, 25; Isa. 4:1; 11:15; 30:26; Jer. 15: 9; Matt. 12:45; Luke 11:26; Acts 20:6; 21:4; 28:14). Jacob's seven prostrations before Esau may not be intended as an exact figure (Gen. 33:3). In the Amarna Letters and in an Ugaritic letter suppliants speak of prostrating themselves seven times and seven times. The "seven ways" in which Israel's enemies will flee (Deut. 28:7, 25) perhaps harks back to the ancient Sumerian seven-direction system, which was superseded by the four-direction system.

Seven-year periods of tribulation are interrupted in the middle by divine intervention (Dan. 7:25; 9:27; 12:7; Luke 4:25; Jas. 5:17; Rev. 11:2). Multiples of seven are common. Seven is doubled for good measure (Gen. 46:22; Lev. 12:5; Num. 29:13; I Kings 8:65; Tob. 8:19). The neat division of time between Abraham and Christ into three periods of fourteen generations (Matt. 1:17) is clearly artificial. Seventy

is often an approximate figure (Gen. 46:27; Exod. 1: 5; 15:27; 24:1, 9; Num. 11:16, 24; II Sam. 24:15; II Kings 10:1; Ps. 90:10; Isa. 23:15; Jer. 25:11; 29:10; Ezek. 8:11; Dan. 9:2, 24; Zech. 1:12; 7:5; Luke 10:1). The Egyptians mourned Israel for seventy days (Gen. 50:3). The funerary offerings for Baal in Ugaritic myth were a series of seventy animals. The gods of Ugarit are collectively designated as the "seventy children of Asherah." The seventy-sevenfold vengeance of Lamech (Gen. 4:24) and the forgiveness seventy times seven which Jesus enjoined (Matt. 18: 22) are intended figuratively for a practically unlimited number. The seven thousand who never bowed knee to Baal (I Kings 19:18; Rom. 11:4) represent only a fraction of the number of apostates. In Rev. 11:13 the figure is explicitly designated as a tithe. In the Moabite Stone it comprises the total Israelite population of Nebo who were sacrificed to Mesha's god.

Besides the numerous explicit heptads in the OT and the NT, there also are many latent cases where one may count seven items—e.g., the seven characteristics of the Lord's spirit in man (Isa. 11:2); the seven petitions of Solomon's prayer (I Kings 8:29-53) and of the Lord's Prayer (Matt. 6:9-13); the seven parables of Matt. 13; the seven woes of Matt. 23; the seven utterances of Christ on the cross; a postresurrection appearance to seven disciples (John 21:2); seven afflictions (Rom. 8:35) and seven gifts (Rom. 12:6-8); seven qualities of heavenly wisdom (Jas. 3:17); seven virtues that supplement faith (II Pet. 1:5-8). The book of Revelation is especially rich both in explicit heptads (Rev. 1:4, 20; 3:1; 4:5; 5:1-6; 8:2; 10:3-4; 12:3; 13:1; 15:1; 17:7) and in latent ones (5:12; 6:15; 7:12; 19:18; 21:8).

It is hard to say what the numerous symbolic uses of seven in the Bible have in common. Perhaps the simplest and most comprehensive generalization that can be made is that seven denotes completeness, perfection, consummation.

Bibliography. P. Jensen, *Kosmologie der Babylonier* (1890); J. Hehn, *Siebenzahl und Sabbat bei den Babyloniern und im AT* (1907); J. Curtis, *A Dissertation upon Odd Numbers* (1909); H. and J. Lewy, "The Origin of the Week and the Oldest West Asiatic Calendar," *HUCA,* 17 (1943), 1-152.

M. H. POPE

SEVEN, THE. A name given in Acts 21:8 to the group ordained by the Twelve (see TWELVE, THE) to assist them in "serving tables" and distributing charitable offerings to the widows of the HELLENISTS (cf. 6:1-6). The narrative of their selection and ordination has commonly been taken, mistakenly perhaps, as the institution of the order of deacons. See DEACON.

The Seven all bore Greek names, and one of them was a proselyte from heathenism. It may be assumed that they were themselves Hellenists—i.e., Jews whose native tongue was Greek, and who tended to adapt themselves to Greek habits and ways of life. Their special appointment came about as a result of the difficulty of orthodox Jews, even though Christian believers, in sharing a common table with those of lax standards regarding the Jewish law. The charges of heterodoxy respecting the temple and the law, leveled against Stephen by Pharisaic rigorists, would seem to bear out this interpretation.

Acts tells us only about the activities of Stephen and Philip, whom it represents as preachers and evangelists (see EVANGELIST), rather than as agents of charity (cf. 21:8). Little more is known of these men. Philip and his daughters finally settled in Hierapolis in Asia Minor (Euseb. Hist. III.31.3-4; V.24.2). Clement of Alexandria (Misc. III.4.25-26) knew a story about the proselyte Nicolas and his jealousy over his beautiful wife; but Clement was kind enough to spare him the charge made by other church fathers of being the founder of the sect of Nicolaitans, first mentioned in Rev. 2:6, 15. Byzantine tradition made PROCHORUS the amanuensis of the Fourth Evangelist.

The number seven was probably symbolic, like the number twelve, and may have been associated in the mind of the Third Evangelist with his peculiar account of the sending forth of the Seventy (Luke 10: 1 ff), which is parallel to the sending forth of the Twelve (Luke 9:1 ff). As the latter represents the twelve tribes of Israel, so seventy may represent the Hebrew numbering of the nations of the earth (cf. Gen. 10:32). If this be the case, there is greater plausibility to the view of certain critics that the Hellenists were not Jews at all, but Gentiles (cf. the variant "Hellenists" for "Hellenes" in some MSS of ·Acts 11:20). M. H. SHEPHERD, JR.

SEVEN CHURCHES [αἱ ἑπτὰ ἐκκλησίαι]. "Seven churches" in cities of the Roman province of Asia are mentioned collectively in Rev. 1:4, 11, 20, and separately in chs. 2-3 as the recipients of the scroll of Revelation (cf. also 22:16). The theory is widely held that just these cities were selected for mention because they were the heads of postal and judicial districts; accordingly, they would be salient points of influence for the distribution of the book in the province. Another—and complementary—suggestion would be that the order of their mention in 1:11 is intended to suggest the lamps (λυχνίαι; cf. vs. 20) of the seven-branched LAMPSTAND (מנורה; LXX λυχνία) of the tabernacle (Exod. 25:31 ff).

Bibliography. In addition to the Commentaries listed in the bibliography under REVELATION, BOOK OF, see: W. Ramsay, *Letters to the Seven Churches* (1904), p. 191; J. W. Bowman, *The Drama of the Book of Revelation* (1955), p. 23.
J. W. BOWMAN

SEVEN WORDS FROM THE CROSS; SEVEN LAST WORDS. The sayings attributed to Jesus, by the canonical evangelists, during the hours of his CRUCIFIXION. The number seven is accidental, for only one of the sayings appears in as many as two gospels, and no gospel gives more than three. The traditional order, which depends on harmonizing at least three varying accounts (Matthew-Mark, Luke, John), is as follows:

a) "Father, forgive them; for they know not what they do" (Luke 23:34). This is absent from many of the best MSS. If authentic, it was apparently spoken early during the Crucifixion—perhaps, as often pictured, while Jesus was prone on the ground, his hands being nailed to the crosspiece. Cf. the words of Stephen (Acts 7:60).

b) "Truly, I say to you, today you will be with me in Paradise" (Luke 23:43). This was spoken to

that one of the two felons, crucified with him, who had said: "Remember me when you come in your kingly power." The other felon had joined in the derision of Jesus, and Matthew and Mark say that both had done so. Even in Luke, the thief's words may have been derisive, being transformed by Jesus' reply. The name Dismas, traditionally given the repentant criminal, has no sufficient historical warrant.

Some would punctuate: "I say to you today, you will be with me"—i.e., at some future time—on the ground that Jesus nowhere else taught the immortality of the soul apart from the body. The change, however, strains the Greek.

c) "Woman, behold your son! . . . Behold your mother!" (John 19:26-27). This was spoken to Jesus' mother and to the "disciple whom Jesus loved." Mary is never named in the Fourth Gospel. The identity of the Beloved Disciple is obscure (see JOHN, GOSPEL OF). Here, he takes Jesus' mother to his own home. Yet at Acts 1:14 she is apparently lodging with the whole group of Jesus' followers at Jerusalem.

d) "My God, my God, why hast thou forsaken me?" (Matt. 27:46; Mark 15:34), a quotation of Ps. 22:1. Several lines of this psalm recall the crucifixion story (see vss. 7-8, 15, 18), and the whole describes the agony of a man innocent of sin. It would naturally be in Jesus' mind as he was dying. This in no way lessens the desolation of his words.

e) "I thirst" (John 19:28). In response to the cry, a sponge full of vinegar was held to Jesus' mouth, and he apparently accepted it. This may conflict with Luke 22:18, where Jesus vows to drink nothing until the kingdom comes.

f) "It is finished" (John 19:30).

g) "Father, into thy hands I commit my spirit" (Luke 23:46). This prayer, based on Ps. 31:5, had long been used by Jews at evening. The whole of Ps. 31 expresses trust in God in the face of persecution and death. PIERSON PARKER

SEWING. Sewing of garments must have been practiced from MB, to judge from the needles and awls found in Palestinian sites. Words which refer to sewing are:

a) מפל (Job 14:17), "cover over" (KJV "sew up").

b) תפר (Gen. 3:7; Job 16:15; Eccl. 3:7; Ezek. 13: 18), "sew." In light of the LXX ῥάπτω (συρράπτω), "to stitch together," it probably means to sew together a rent or two pieces of cloth, rather than to sew on a patch.

c) Ἐπι(ρ)ράπτω (Mark 2:21), "sew on" (with ἐπί), used of sewing on a patch. J. M. MYERS

*SEX, SEXUAL BEHAVIOR.** Although there are many manifestations of sex in the Bible, there is no single word for it. Its importance is indicated, however, by the role it plays in the life of biblical people.

The centrality of religious faith in the Bible, as well as the prominence of sexuality in the pagan cults that competed with it, made inevitable the effort to work out a theology of sex. This theology has considerable biblical documentation. The long history covered by our sources provided for those inner and outer pressures upon biblical culture which resulted in certain changes in the patterns of sexual behavior that are noted in the Bible.

1. Place and role of sex in the Bible. While the Bible is not concerned with sex as such, allusions to it may be found on many pages. These allusions are expressed with considerable candor and freedom, although, paradoxically, circumlocutions are sometimes used in order to avoid a direct reference to a sexual act or organ (*see below*). The importance of reproduction, and therefore of sexual intercourse, constitutes one reason for the biblical emphasis. Sons are needed in order to preserve the father's name and personality. Thus sex relations are important to the entire family or clan group, even as the birth of a child is hailed by the entire community (Ruth 4:14, 17). One finds no condemnation of sex in the sources, for it is viewed as fundamentally good in serving an essential social purpose which is at the same time deeply personal (*see* MARRIAGE § 5). The function of sex in preserving and perpetuating the family name motivates a vigorous biblical rejection of its abuse and perversions. *See* BESTIALITY; SODOMITE; PROSTITUTION.

Sex on the animal level was recognized as the means of providing increase in flocks and herds (Gen. 30:35, 39), on which the population depended for clothing, shelter, food, and offerings to their God.

A third reason for the prominence of sex in the Bible is to be found in the threat to the integrity of Israel's life which the ancient Near Eastern cult of sex continuously posed. Some biblical writers were intensely conscious of this threat and sharply attacked the premises and practices which were seducing the men of Israel. The language of this attack therefore contains many specific references to the widespread sexuality which was popularly viewed as divine and as the source of man's salvation. *See* § 10 *below*.

2. Meaning of "male" and "female." The word "sex" refers primarily to the physical differences between male and female, to the character of being male or female. The word is therefore the symbol of a distinction which is universal.

a. Vocabulary. An ancient poetic oracle records the belief, which may have been widely held, that the words for "man" and "woman" in the Hebrew language are closely related—the second comes from the first:

> She shall be called Woman [אשה],
>   because she was taken out of Man [איש]
>   (Gen. 2:23).

Actually the words do not derive from the same root, although their origin is uncertain. The origin of איש, "man" or "male," can only be conjectured. One theory bases it upon the Assyrian root *isanu*, "strong," but this is improbable. Another, which is more generally accepted, bases this word on the root אנש (Assyrian *anašu*), "to be weak, sick"; or a root with the same spelling which means "to be inclined to, to be friendly, social" (Arabic *aniša*). A third root, the Arabic of which carries the meaning "soft, delicate," has the above Hebrew spelling. In favor of one of these possible roots is the plural form of איש, אנשים, "men," and the collective word for "man" or "mankind," אנוש.

While usually used to designate "man" in opposition to "woman," איש sometimes refers to the male of animals (Gen. 7:2). In its primary meaning its emphasis on the sexual distinction between man and woman can be seen in a number of passages (Gen. 19:8; 24:16; 38:25; Exod. 22:16; Lev. 15:16; 20:10-11; Num. 5:13-14; Deut. 22:22—H 22:15; etc.). Man is set over against women by the term איש also (Gen. 2:23-24; Lev. 20:27; Num. 5:6; Deut. 17:2-3; Josh. 6:21; 8:25; Jer. 40:7). Thus the word identifies a member of a class which is set over against another class on the basis of the possession of certain sexual characteristics and functions and which is distinguished as male or masculine.

Derived perhaps from אנש, with the root meaning of "soft, delicate," the word for "woman" is אשה. It may be translated "woman, female, wife." It too may designate female animals, as in Gen. 7:2-3. Elsewhere it appears to describe men who are feeble and timid (Jer. 50:37; 51:30). It particularly refers to woman in her sexual function of reproduction, as conceiving, bearing, and nursing children (Exod. 2:2; Lev. 12:2; Judg. 13:24; II Sam. 11:5; I Kings 3:18; Isa. 49:15; etc.). But the term may also indicate a harlot (Josh. 2:1; 6:22; Judg. 11:1; etc.; *see* PROSTITUTION) or a concubine (Judg. 19:1, 27), when the proper descriptive word is added to אשה. Woman's status as belonging to a man is likewise expressed by this word. A man takes a woman to wife (Gen. 12:19; 16:3; 20:12; Num. 36:3; etc.). *See* MARRIAGE.

Also used in juxtaposition to distinguish the two sexes are the words זכר, "male," and נקבה, "female." The origin of the first of these is obscure. The word is set over against אשה "woman," in the command against sodomy (Lev. 18:22; 20:13). It appears in contrast to נקבה several times (Gen. 6:19; 7:3, 9, 16; Lev. 3:1, 6; Deut. 4:16). Referring to animals, especially for sacrifice, it identifies the male of the species (Exod. 34:19; Lev. 1:3, 10; 4:23; 22:19; Mal. 1:14). The second word, נקבה, "female," is related to the root נקב, "pierce," in the judgment of many scholars, based possibly upon the nature of the act of copulation. Both women and female animals are designated by this term (Gen. 1:27; 5:2; Lev. 12:5, 7; 15:33; 27:4-5, 6-7; Num. 5:3; 31:15; cf. Gen. 6:19; 7:3, 9, 16; Lev. 3:1, 6; 4:28, 32; 5:6).

The words for "male" and "female" in the NT do not represent any departures from the meanings of terms found in the OT sources. The word ἀνήρ identifies the need of the male in causing pregnancy (Luke 1:34; cf. Matt. 14:21; 15:38). The word γυνή is commonly used for "woman," "wife," and "bride."

The meaning "wife" occurs most commonly (Matt. 5:28, 31-32; 14:3; 18:25; Luke 1:5, 13, 18, 24; I Cor. 7:2 ff; 9:5; Eph. 5:22-23; Col. 3:18-19). Where the distinction between the sexes follows the stereotype set by Gen. 1:27, the Greek makes use of θῆλυς, "female" or "woman" (Matt. 19:4; Mark 10:6; Rom. 1:26-27; Gal. 3:28).

b. Summary of meanings. The Bible contains terms which clearly distinguish the sexes from each other, on the human and also on the animal levels. While the origin of the terms used must be regarded as uncertain, the use to which they are put in the Bible reveals that they have distinctive meanings. They stress both the differentiation and the relation between the sexes which lie at the root of biblical society and which constitute its assurance of survival in history. This is true of the terms translated "man" and "woman," "male" and "female," "husband" and "wife."

3. The organs of sex. The literature of the Bible records a strange combination of frankness and reticence in its discussion of sex. This was due partly to powerful sex taboos (*see* § 4 *below*) and partly to the limitations of the Hebrew language and the peculiar nature of Hebrew psychology. Precise words for physical organs may be identified, but they carry a broader connotation than may be found in modern usage. The language is poetic and imaginative; the psychology is that of the whole man, who manifests his total self through each of his physical acts. Euphemisms are used to conceal in language what must not be exposed in fact—the male and female organs of sexual intercourse and reproduction. Exposure of these organs was held to be shameful.

a. Male organs of generation. The word בשׂר is a general term which sometimes simply indicates the male organ of generation. Literally it means "flesh," deriving perhaps from a root in Assyrian, *bišru*, "blood relation." It may be used of the bodies of animals (Gen. 41:2-19; Exod. 21:28; Num. 12:12; etc.) and of the bodies of human beings (Exod. 30:32; Lev. 6:10—H 6:3; 14:9; 15:13, 16; 16:4, 24, 26, 28; 17:16; Num. 19:7-8; Job 14:22; Isa. 10:18; etc.). It specifically refers to the male organ, however, in a number of instances (Gen. 17:11, 14, 23-25; Exod. 28:42; Lev. 15:2-18; Ezek. 16:26; 23:20; 44:7, 9). An example of the language of this euphemism is as follows: "You shall be circumcised in the flesh of your foreskins" (Gen. 17:11). Another passage whose meaning is equally clear reads: "You shall make for them linen breeches to cover their naked flesh; from the loins to the thighs they shall reach" (Exod. 28: 42). בשׂר is never used in connection with the female organs of reproduction.

In the NT the Greek term σάρξ may be translated "flesh." Thus it appears to be equivalent to בשׂר of the OT. It never, however, specifically singles out the male sex organ. As the term is used in Matt. 19: 5-6; Mark 10:8a-b; I Cor. 6:16; Eph. 5:31, it refers to the union of a man and a woman through the act of sex, whereby they become "one flesh." It is the source of the sexual urge, however, in one instance (John 1:13): "born, not of blood nor of the will of the flesh [σαρκός]." The word connotes the bearer of sinful feelings and desires and the means of sensual enjoyment, in various books of the NT and the Apoc.

(Rom. 8:3b; Gal. 5:16; Col. 2:18; II Pet. 2:18; I John 2:16; Ecclus. 23:17). Another word, σῶμα, means "body," viewed as the seat of the sexual function (Rom. 4:19; I Cor. 7:4a-b). As is evident from the references cited above, the Greek words for "flesh" and "body," while having a sexual significance at times, do not apply to the male sex only.

The term ירך has the meanings "thigh," "loin," "side," and is one of the general terms for the male organ of sex as well. It is so used in Gen. 24:2, 9 (some translate here "thigh"); 46:26; 47:29; Exod. 1: 5; Judg. 8:30. The Hebrew word denotes the seat of procreative power, so that we may translate the last-named reference "springing from his loins" for the RSV "his own offspring." The writer of the Letter to the Hebrews uses the Greek term ὀσφῦς when he names those who are descended from (the loins of) Abraham (Heb. 7:5). The LXX uses this Greek word also in translating the Hebrew ירך and related terms (Gen. 35:11). The meaning of "belly," "womb," or "body" is found in the Hebrew בטן in connection with men (Job 19:17; Ps. 132:11; Mic. 6:7). A related word is חלץ, which also means "loins" as the seat of virility (Gen. 35:11; I Kings 8:19; II Chr. 6:9).

Primarily associated with the male sex organs, another Hebrew root, meaning "feet," recurs in the OT. According to Exod. 4:25, Zipporah cut off her son's foreskin and touched Moses' genitals (RSV "feet") with it. Ruth uncovered the "feet" of her husband's kinsman Boaz and lay down (Ruth 3:7b), following the instructions of Naomi (vs. 4). Each of the seraphim in Isaiah's vision had six wings, with two of which he covered his "feet" (Isa. 6:2). The complete desolation of Judah by the Assyrian armies is compared to completely shaving the hair of a man's "feet"—pubic hair (7:20). Used of women, the word has a similar connotation (Deut. 28:57; Ezek. 16:25).

Other words occurring occasionally or only once include the term שפכה, from a root "to pour out," the male organ as a fluid duct (Deut. 23:1—H 23:2), and זרע, "seed" or "semen" (Lev. 22:4c [flow of semen]; Num. 5:28 [a woman made pregnant with semen; RSV "shall conceive children"]; Jer. 31:27 ["the seed of man and the seed of beast"]). The NT uses σπέρμα, which has the same meaning as the Hebrew word (John 7:42; Rom. 1:3, where the Greek reads "from the seed of David"; II Tim. 2:8; Heb. 11:11). Once in the statement of a law prohibiting the violent seizure by a woman of a man's sex organs (Deut. 25:11), they are referred to by a Hebrew expression meaning "that which excites shame," from the root מבושׁ.

b. Female sex organs. In addition to the euphemism "feet" to identify the female sex organs, a general term translated "nakedness" is also found. It is used in the context of shameful exposure, especially of woman's sex organs (Lev. 18:6-19; 20:17-21; I Sam. 20:30; Lam. 1:8; Ezek. 16:37; 23:10, 29). In Leviticus this word occurs in the phrase "uncover the nakedness of" and connotes sexual intercourse which is preceded by exposing the woman's sex organs (cf. Isa. 3:17). Used similarly only in Hosea is נבלות: "I will uncover her lewdness" (2:10—H 2:12). The LXX uses the term αἰδοῖον, "private parts," as a more precise translation of the Hebrew. The idea of disgraceful nakedness is indicated by the Greek γυμνότης (Rev. 3:18). Paul refers to the sex organs (both male and female) when he speaks of "our unpresentable parts," which are to be treated with greater modesty than is called for in connection with the more "presentable parts" (I Cor. 12:23-24).

A more specific word, רחם (perhaps from Assyrian *remu*, "be wide," or Arabic "be soft"), refers to the uterus or womb. With the meaning "go forth from the womb in birth," it appears in Num. 12:12; Job 38:8; Jer. 1:5; 20:18; while it is found in connection with opening the womb in order to give birth in Gen. 29:31; 30:22; Exod. 13:12; 34:19; Num. 18:15; Ezek. 20:26. The same root has likewise a figurative use, "compassion" or "to have compassion" (*see* § 9 *below*). As already noted, בטן sometimes means "womb" (Gen. 25:23-24; 38:27; Hos. 12:3).

The female breast is identified by שד occurring most often in the Song of Songs (1:13; 4:5; 7:4, 8-9; 8:8, 10). It appears with ינק, "to give suck" (Job 3: 12; Song of S. 8:1; Joel 2:16). With a sexual emphasis it is encountered in Hos. 2:2; and notably in Ezek. 16:7; 23:3, 21. Μαζός refers to a woman's breast (Test. Naph. 1:7), and to the breast of animals in I Clem. 20:10; but in Luke the word μαστός is used (11:27; 23:29), where it appears in relation to the breasts that give suck.

c. The sacredness of sex organs. The male sex organs were used in the making of an oath. Abraham commanded the oldest servant of his house to put his hand under his thigh and to swear by the Lord (Gen. 24:2-3, 9). When Jacob was about to die, he requested his son Joseph to put his hand under his thigh and to promise to deal truly with him (47:29). It is conceivable that the rite of CIRCUMCISION originally had a sexual significance. The rite performed upon Ishmael suggests a puberty rite preparatory to marriage. The fact that circumcision constituted a covenant bond between Yahweh and his people does not deprive it of this sexual significance. *See* § 10*c below*.

4. Sex taboos. Deeply entrenched attitudes toward forms of sexual behavior may take the form of taboos, whether crystallized into law or not. The exposure of one's private parts (nakedness) was one of these. It was shameful and abhorrent to the Hebrews to display the human sex organs except under rather strictly defined circumstances. A son of Noah violated this taboo when he beheld the nakedness of his drunken father (Gen. 9:21-23); David was denounced by his wife for exposing himself as he danced before the Lord (II Sam. 6:20); Hanun humiliated the servants of David by cutting off their garments at the hips, "in the middle" (II Sam. 10:4), with the result that the victims of this mistreatment "were greatly ashamed" (vs. 5). Nakedness was therefore a sign of humiliation and degradation. As such, war captives were compelled to submit to it (Isa. 20:2-4). A hated nation is taunted; she is thought of as a virgin whose nakedness will be displayed to all (47:3). One of the Dead Sea Scrolls refers to a fine that is levied for exposing one's nakedness (1QM VII.14).

Taboos against incestuous relations with women are formulated into law in the OT (*see* INCEST). They lie deeper than law, however. Intercourse with a woman in the kin group, with a woman in her menstrual period, with an animal (*see* BESTIALITY),

with a member of the same sex (*see* SODOMITE; HOMOSEXUALITY) is repugnant to the feelings of biblical man (Lev. 15:24; 18:23; 20:13; Deut. 27:20). There is horror at maimed or deformed sex organs (Lev. 21:20; Deut. 23:1). A woman must not wear male garments, nor must a man wear female garments (Deut. 22:5).

5. Regulation of sex behavior by law. The laws pertaining to sex are usually not concentrated in one portion of a biblical book. The various codes may repeat the same regulation (*see* LAW IN THE OT) on a number of subjects, including that of sex control.

Adulterous interest in another man's wife is prohibited (Exod. 20:14, 17; Lev. 18:20; 20:10; Deut. 22: 22-29). The codes note further the seduction of a virgin (Exod. 22:16); treatment of a female captive taken as war booty (Deut. 21:11-14); incest (Lev. 18:6-18; 20:11-12, 14, 20; Deut. 27:20, 22); causing one's daughter to become a harlot (Lev. 19:29); intercourse with a betrothed slave (19:20), with a menstruating woman (15:24; 18:19; 20:18); menstruation (15:19-24); a woman's abnormal hemorrhage (15:25-30); the discharge of semen (15:16; 22:4). Also included are laws against homosexuality (18: 22; 20:13); intercourse with a beast by members of either sex (18:23; 20:15-16); a woman's intervention in a quarrel between her husband and another man by seizing the latter's sex organ (Deut. 25:11); prohibition against the use of earnings from homosexual practices in the temple (23:18); laws in case of an amputated male sex organ (23:1), of crushed testicles (Lev. 21:20 [with respect to a priest]; Deut. 23:1); prohibition of cult PROSTITUTION among the sons and daughters of Israel (Deut. 23:17); and the treatment of a bastard (23:2). For laws pertaining to marriage, *see* MARRIAGE.

6. Sex segregation and discrimination. There is little direct evidence of the segregation of women in the biblical community. Susanna sought to bathe in privacy, when the elders tried to seduce her (Sus. 18-20). David's vantage point from his roof gave him the opportunity to observe what was doubtless intended to be a woman's private bath (II Sam. 11:2). Women seem to have had their own living quarters (see the expression "go in" to a woman's tent or apartment; Gen. 6:4; 16:2; 30:3; 38:8-9; 39:14; Deut. 22:13; Judg. 15:1; 16:1; II Sam. 12:24; 16:21; 20:3; Prov. 6:29; Ezek. 23:44). Noteworthy also is the clear indication in the book of Esther of the segregation of the women of the palace (1:9; 2:3, 9, 11, 14; etc.).

As to discrimination between the sexes in conduct covered by the law, there is more evidence for a definite conclusion. Because of her sexual function in a patriarchal society, a woman's violation of law and custom received harsher treatment than that of her male counterpart who might be involved in the same situation. Sexual infidelity was punished more severely (Deut. 22:13-21). The period of uncleanness after childbirth was seven days for a male child and two weeks for a female (Lev. 12:2-5). In making a special vow of persons to the Lord, there was a pronounced difference in the money value of a male and a female (Lev. 27:1-7). The differential narrows for the aged and the very young. Daughters did not automatically inherit from their father; they might do so only under special conditions (Num. 27:1-8; *see* INHERITANCE).

The force of a vow made by a woman depended upon the approval of her father or her husband; a man's vow must be kept regardless of the attitude of others (30:2-8). *See* WOMAN for other examples of her place in the community.

7. Sexual intercourse. Sexual intercourse took place principally for the procreation of children, but also for the sake of monetary gain (*see* PROSTITUTION § 2) and mutual pleasure. It had a further function in connection with the sanctuary of the fertility cult (*see* PROSTITUTION § 3). Sexual irregularities of the male were not condemned in themselves, provided ancient taboos and social customs were not violated.

The love of a man for a woman based on sexual attraction is indicated often by the root אהב in the OT. This "love" may relate to marriage or only to sexual intercourse (Gen. 24:67; 29:20, 30; Deut. 21: 15-16; Judg. 14:16; 16:15; I Sam. 1:5; 18:20; II Sam. 13:1, 4, 15; I Kings 11:1; II Chr. 11:21; Esth. 2:17; Eccl. 9:9; Song of S. 1:2, 4, 7; 3:1-4; Isa. 57:8; Jer. 2: 25; Ezek. 16:37; Hos. 3:1). Sexual passion may change to hate when resistance to the act of love is encountered (II Sam. 13:15). Sexual longing and love are capable of producing personal companionship which transcends its physical basis. The beloved is called a companion in the Song of Songs (1:9, 15; 2:2, 10, 13; 4:1, 7; 5:2; 6:4). The longing of a woman for a man (Gen. 3:16) is determined by God.

Sexual love in the NT is defined largely in the category of lust (Matt. 5:28; Rev. 14:8). Paul declares that the desires of the flesh must not be gratified (Rom. 13:14); it is well for a man not to touch a woman, but if he must, he should take a wife so as to avoid immorality (I Cor. 7:1-2). Thus strong passions will have a legitimate outlet. Self-control is best of all, for "the form of this world is passing away" (7:31). Younger men need this especially (Tit. 2:6). Husbands are to love their wives as they love their own bodies (Eph. 5:25, 28). This connotes the sexual union, which is described as becoming "one flesh" (Gen. 2:24; *see* LUST). The intimate relation that this union identifies is expressed by the word ידע with particular force, for the term means "to know" in a sexual and personal sense as used in this connection (Gen. 4:1, 17, 25; 24:16; 38:26; Judg. 19:25; I Sam. 1:19; I Kings 1:4; cf. Gen. 19:8; Num. 31:17; Judg. 11:39; 21:11). This meaning is emphasized in the account of the tree in the midst of the garden, the fruit of which would cause man to know good and evil. The Dead Sea Scrolls indicate that knowing good and evil signifies the entire range of sexual experience. *See bibliography.*

8. Sexual traits. Drawn from the experience of sex and of sex differences, descriptive terms of a general nature entered the biblical vocabulary. We may note "man's courage" as applied to the mother of the seven martyred sons (II Macc. 7:21). By far the most common term in biblical usage, which is drawn from the name for "womb" in Hebrew, is רחמים, "COMPASSION." While there is a question as to whether this comes from the idea of brotherly or of motherly feeling, the latter seems more likely. The word appears in relation to God (I Chr. 21:13; Neh. 9:19, 27, 31; Pss. 51:1—H 51:3; 77:9—H 77:10; 79: 8; 103:4; 119:77, 156; Isa. 63:7, 15; Jer. 16:5; 42:12;

Lam. 3:22). It is also used of man (Gen. 43:14, 30; I Kings 8:50; II Chr. 30:9; Neh. 1:11; Ps. 106:46; Prov. 12:10; Isa. 47:6; Dan. 1:9; Amos 1:11; Zech. 7:9). There is also a cognate verb, "to have compassion" (Deut. 13:17—H 13:18; Ps. 103:13; Isa. 9: 17—H 9:16; 49:15). Other words serving to characterize the apostate people addressed by the prophets in particular are taken from the sex vocabulary of the Bible. *See* MARRIAGE; PROSTITUTION; FAMILY; ADULTERY. *See also* such proper names as JERAHMEEL; JEROHAM; REHUM.

9. Theology of sex. The biblical interpretation of sex took the form of a reaction, not only to its abuse within the community, but also to its glorification in the culture that surrounded it. The reaction was presented in terms of biblical faith and the idealized pastoral life in which it was thought to have originated (Jer. 2:1). The principle of sex was embodied in the various fertility cults which confronted the people of the Bible. Sexual intercourse at the shrine was a part of the ritual related to the cycle of the seasons and the rebirth of vegetational and animal life (*see* PROSTITUTION § 3). This sensuality at the shrine was sternly condemned because of its threat to the ethical demands of Israel's faith (Amos 2:6-8). Yet its positive effect can also be seen in biblical theology: the God of Israel, not the gods and goddesses of the cult, is the source of fertility and fructification (Hos. 2:8). But God is Father and Creator without the aid of a female counterpart (Isa. 45:18; 63:16c). He is the source of sexuality and demands its use for the perpetuation of his people and the glory of his name. Maleness and femaleness reflect the image of God (Gen. 1:27). Man and woman become one flesh because of God's creative action (Gen. 2:21-24). When they use their sexuality apart from his relation to it, a curse falls upon them and upon their children (ch. 3). God creates and judges his people as Father (*see above*); he also loves them with the compassion symbolized by the womb of a mother. And man must turn to him with the personal, spiritual knowledge expressed in Hebrew by the word "to know," which is also used for sexual intercourse. See Isa. 11:2; Jer. 22:16; Hos. 4:1, 6, where there is a hint that the sexual "knowledge" of the Canaanite cult is undergoing a transformation under the influence of prophetic faith and teaching.

10. Changing patterns of thought and conduct. The developing biblical rejection of nature religions (fertility cults), as their threat to biblical faith became clear, involved also a development in the patterns of sexual control. Unlimited sex indulgence and pressures to restrict it, under the influence of both sociological and theological factors, created tensions that appear in the biblical records and in related writings. The powerful prophetic attack upon the abuse of sex has been noted; the demand for self-control in later writings can also be seen. To this end Gnostic asceticism is of no avail (Col. 2:23); only the life which is hidden with Christ can achieve this result. The control of sexual impulses through self-discipline is emphasized (Test. Naph. 8:8; I Cor. 7:9; Tit. 2:5-6). The entire book of IV Maccabees is devoted to a eulogy of the restraining power of reason over all of life; note especially how Joseph overcame sexual passion by reason (2:3). To look at a woman with lust in the heart may condemn a man to hell (Matt. 5:28-29). Yet the consummation of the meaning of sex in marriage provided an opportunity for Jesus to manifest his glory by his presence at a wedding feast (John 2:1-11).

Bibliography. Jos. Antiq. I.xii.2: evidence of circumcision among the Arabs at age thirteen; G. Aicher, "Mann und Weib, ein Fleisch," *BZ*, 5 (1907), 159-65; J. A. Montgomery, "Ascetic Strains in Early Judaism," *JBL*, 51 (1932), 183-213; W. A. Barton, *Archaeology and the Bible* (1941), pp. 365-66: "The Tale of the Two Brothers"; O. Piper, *The Christian Interpretation of Sex* (1941); L. M. Epstein, *Sex Laws and Customs in Judaism* (1948); P. Schempp, "L'homme et la femme d'après l'Ecriture Sainte," *Foi et Vie* (1948); P. Gordon, *Sex and Religion* (1949); O. A. Piper, *Die Geschlechter, Ihr Sinn und ihr Geheimnis in biblischer Sicht* (1954); R. Gordis, "The Knowledge of Good and Evil in the OT and the Qumran Scrolls," *JBL*, 76 (1957), 123-38; W. G. Cole, *Sex and Love in the Bible* (1959).

See also the bibliographies under MARRIAGE; WOMAN.

O. J. BAAB

SHAALBIM shā ăl'bĭm [שעלבים, place of foxes] (Judg. 1:35; I Kings 4:9). Alternately: SHAALAB-BIN shā'ə lăb'ən [שעלבין] (Josh. 19:42). An Amorite city which was assigned to Dan but which the Danites were unable to occupy. In time, however, the residents of Shaalbim became subject to forced labor for the house of Joseph. The city was finally occupied by Israelites and became a part of Solomon's second administrative district. Possibly SHAALBON and SHAALIM refer to the same place.

The Salaba in the territory of Samaria, mentioned by Josephus, may be identified with Khirbet Salhab at the head of the wadi of the same name, but not with Shaalbim. Jerome mentions a Selebi (Shaalbim?) along with Beth-shemesh and Aijalon. It is suggested that the name remains in modern Selbit, three miles NW of Aijalon and eight miles N of Beth-shemesh. Pottery picked up on the site indicates occupation during the period in question. For the present, most scholars identify Shaalbim with Selbit.

V. R. GOLD

SHAALBON shā ăl'bŏn (II Sam. 23:32; I Chr. 11:33); KJV SHAALBONITE —bə nīt [שעלבני]. The home of Eliahba, one of David's Mighty Men. Possibly it is to be identified with SHAALBIM.

V. R. GOLD

SHAALIM shā'ə lĭm [שעלים] (I Sam. 9:4); KJV SHALIM shā'lĭm. A region traversed by Saul in his search for the lost asses. Most scholars have sought its location in the territory of Benjamin. It has been conjectured that it may be an error for SHAALBIM or for SHUAL 2.

W. L. REED

SHAAPH shā'ăf [שעף]. The name of two descendants of Caleb, the brother of Jerahmeel:

1. The last-born son of Jahdai (I Chr. 2:47).

2. A son of Caleb and his concubine Maacah; the father of Madmannah (I Chr. 2:49).

E. R. ACHTEMEIER

SHAARAIM shā'ə rā'əm [שערים, double gate]; KJV SHARAIM shə rā'əm in Josh. 15:36. 1. A city of Judah in the Shephelah district of Azekah (Josh. 15:36). The pursuit of the Philistines after David's slaying of their hero, Goliath, reached from Shaaraim to Gath and Ekron (I Sam. 17:52 ff). Thus Shaaraim must be in or near the Wadi es-Sant (*see* ELAH, VALLEY OF), probably near Azekah. Eusebius mentions Σαραείν (Saraein) but gives no identification.

2. A city of Simeon (I Chr. 4:31) which appears as SHARUHEN in the parallel list (Josh. 19:6).

V. R. GOLD

SHAASHGAZ shā ăsh'găz [שעשגז] (Esth. 2:14). The eunuch in charge of King Ahasuerus' concubines.

Bibliography. On etymology, see L. B. Paton, *Esther*, ICC (1908), p. 69.

SHABBETHAI shăb'ə thī [שבתי, *possibly from* שבת, sabbath; Akkad. *šabbata'a;* Apoc. Σαββαταίος]; KJV Apoc. SABATEAS săb'ə tē'əs in I Esd. 9:48; SABBATHEUS —thē'əs in I Esd. 9:14. A Levite who assisted Ezra in the execution of the edict against having foreign wives (Ezra 10:15; I Esd. 9:14) and who was present at the reading of the law (Neh. 8:7; I Esd. 9:48). In Neh. 11:16 the same(?) man is called a "chief of the Levites."

J. M. WARD

SHACHIA. KJV form of SACHIA.

SHADDAI shăd'ī [שדי, the Mountain One]. *See* ALMIGHTY; GOD, NAMES OF, § C2a.

SHADE. *See* SHADOW.

SHADES. The belief that the shades of the dead were endowed with some vitality and that they possessed the power to inflict harm was widely held in the ancient Near East. Particularly feared were the shades of those who had been neglected by their kin or failed to receive the last rites of burial. Such shades could rise from the nether world to wreak vengeance upon the living, and great care had to be taken to nullify their malevolence.

The general term for "shades" in the OT is רפאים (to be distinguished from the other רפאים, which is an ethnic designation of the prehistoric inhabitants of Canaan; *see* REPHAIM). This word is used with the same connotation in Phoenician (*rp'm*) and in Ugaritic (*rp'um*). According to H. L. Ginsberg, the original meaning of the root *rp'* is "to mend, join," and hence the *rp'um* are a community of shades massed together in the nether world (cf. קהל רפאים, "the assembly of the shades," in Prov. 21:16; RSV "the assembly of the dead"). Rare terms for "shades" are אטים, אוב, רוח, and אלהים. The first of these is mentioned only once, in Isa. 19:3, and it is obviously the Akkadian *eṭimmu*, "the ghost of a dead person"; the word *'uṭm* is found also in Ugaritic and may be rendered "funeral meats." The term אוב, mentioned many times and usually translated "medium," has the meaning of "shades, ghost," in Isa. 29:4. The רוח in Eccl. 3:21 has the sense of "shades," and the אלהים seen by the witch of Endor (I Sam. 28:13) was clearly the apparition of the deceased Samuel. *See* FAMILIAR SPIRIT.

The aspect of fear of the "evil ghosts" (Akkadian

eṭimmu limnu), so prevalent in Babylonia, is not reported in the biblical literature. The shades are huddled together in שאול, "the nether world" (cf. Job 26:5-6; Prov. 9:18; Isa. 14:9; *see* SHEOL). They are called צהל רפאים, "the community of the shades" (Prov. 21:16; RSV "the assembly of the dead"); and the place is referred to as ארץ רפאים, "the land of the shades" (Isa. 26:19), or simply ארץ תחתיות, "the nether world" (Ezek. 26:20, etc.). Euphemistically שאול is called בור, "the Pit" (Isa. 14:15; Ezek. 32:23-31; etc.), or דומה (derived from דמם, "to be silent")—i.e., the abode of silence (Pss. 94:17; 115:17). It is a place of "darkness" (חשך), "forgetfulness" (נשיה), and "destruction" (אבדון; Job 26:6; Ps. 88:11-12—H 88:12-13).

In summary, the OT view is that the shades are lifeless, without any power to do good or evil.

See also IMMORTALITY. I. MENDELSOHN

SHADOW [צל (*alternately* SHADE); KJV טלל (RSV SHADE), צלל (RSV SHADE); ἀποσκίασμα, σκιά]. The shade of foliage (Jonah 4:6), clouds (Isa. 25:5), or a rock (Isa. 32:2) is welcome protection against the Near Eastern sun at midday, whose intensity was thought to be the work of demonic powers (cf. Pss. 91:6; 121:6). Consequently, צל may mean the shelter itself (Gen. 19:8), or, metaphorically, the protective power afforded by a man, a city, or a kingdom (under the metaphor of a tree: Song of S. 2:3; Ezek. 17:23; 31:6, 12, 17; cf. Isa. 30:2; of other foliage: Judg. 9:15; Ps. 80:8 ff; of a city: Jer. 48:45; of a rock: Isa. 32:2).

In other passages the shadow signifies transience and vanity (Job 8:9; 14:2; Pss. 102:11; 109:23; cf. I Chr. 29:15; Job 17:7; Eccl. 6:12; 8:13) or portends the coming night (Job 7:2; Jer. 6:4) or day (Song of S. 2:17; 4:6). For other, nonfigurative uses, cf. Judg. 9:36; II Kings 20:9-11; Isa. 38:8.

The CANOPY over Yahweh's GLORY will offer shade from the deadly rays of the sun (Isa. 4:6), and in his shadow the pious man is safe from mysterious, as well as familiar, threats (including the demon of noonday: Ps. 91:1, 6; cf. Ps. 121:5-6; Isa. 25:4-5). The shadow of Yahweh's hand (Isa. 49:2; cf. 51:16) and the shadow of his wings (Pss. 17:8; 36:7; 57:1; 63:7; cf. Ps. 91:1; Lam. 4:20; Hos. 14:7; *see* REFUGE; WINGS) are metaphors of his sovereign protection, the latter occasionally implying the temple at Jerusalem (cf. Ps. 63:7; *see* TEMPLE, JERUSALEM).

The familiar KJV phrase "shadow of death" is based upon a popular etymology of צלמות (צל, "shadow," plus מות, "death"), whereas the word is now seen as a form derived from צלם (unused in Hebrew; Akkadian *ṣalāmu*, "grow black") and should be translated with the RSV: "gloom," "deep darkness" (the RSV retains "shadow of death" in Ps. 23:4 for the sake of the traditional phrase, which is not seriously misleading in this verse; *see also* LIGHT). The error probably goes back to very ancient homiletical interpretation of the word, which is accepted by the Greek translations (σκιὰ θανάτου, "shadow of death") and appears in free adaptations of Isa. 9:2—H 9:1 in the NT (Matt. 4:16; Luke 1:79).

Except for Mark 4:32, which also recalls OT passages (cf. Ps. 104:12; Ezek. 17:23; 31:6; Dan. 4:11,

21), the NT usage reflects Greek, rather than Hebrew, thought. Col. 2:17; Heb. 8:5; 10:1 use the typically Hellenistic concept of a shadowy likeness which is the counterpart of true reality. The "shadow of turning" (Jas. 1:17 KJV; RSV "shadow due to change") refers somewhat obscurely to astronomical changes (perhaps eclipses or moon phases) by contrast to the constancy of God.

For "shades," *see* DEATH; IMMORTALITY.

Bibliography. M. Jastrow, *A Dictionary of the Targumim* (1950), II, 1285; W. Bauer, *Griechisch-Deutsches Wörterbuch* (1952), pp. 1374-75; L. Koehler and W. Baumgartner, *Lexicon in Veteris Testamenti Libros* (1953), pp. 803, 805; W. R. Taylor, Exegesis of Psalms, *IB,* IV (1955), 646-47.

J. A. WHARTON

SHADRACH, MESHACH, ABEDNEGO shăd'răk, mē'shăk, ə bĕd'nĭ gō [שדרך, מישך, (*in* Dan. 3:29 עבד נגוא), עבד נגו; *see below*]. The three companions of DANIEL. The names always occur together and in the same order (Dan. 1:7; 2:49; 3:12-30).

The youths were assigned these Babylonian names by Nebuchadnezzar's chief eunuch (Dan. 1:7), their Hebrew names being respectively Hananiah (חנניה, "Yahu has been gracious"), Mishael (מישאל, possibly "Who is what God is?"), and Azariah (עזריה, "Yahu has helped"). Cf. Dan. 1:6-7, 11, 19; 2:17; I Macc. 2:59; Song Thr. Ch. 1, 66; IV Macc. 16:3, 21; 18:12.

The etymology of the Babylonian names, as distinguished from the Hebrew, is obscure. The usual supposition is that the author of Daniel, or the tradition behind him, has with sardonic intent corrupted the forms of the names, each of which had originally contained the designation of a Babylonian deity as one of its constituent elements. "Shadrach" is conjecturally derived from the Akkadian *Shudur-Aku,* "Command of Aku [Sumerian moon god]," but it has also been read as a corruption of "MARDUK." "Meshach" has been dubiously explained as equivalent to the Akkadian *Mishaaku,* "Who is what Aku is?" (cf. "Mishael," *above*). "Abednego" is generally read with more assurance as a corruption of *Abed-nebo* = Akkadian *Abdi-nabu,* "Servant of Nabu [Babylonian god of wisdom]." But it is possible that the present form of the last of the names represents a merely philological dissimilation of consonants rather than intentional corruption for polemical purposes, which, if true, argues against the latter sort of motivation operating in the formation of the names Shadrach and Meshach as well. *See bibliography.*

The story of these companions of Daniel was eminently suited for inclusion in a work written to undergird the faith of beleaguered Palestinian Jews of 165 B.C. under the Seleucids (*see* DANIEL § 2; MACCABEES). The three men are presented as "youths without blemish, handsome and skilful in all wisdom, endowed with knowledge, understanding learning, and competent to serve in the king's palace" (Dan. 1:4). Consistent with the purpose of the writer of Daniel, the youths, with their more famous comrade, Daniel, demonstrate in their persons the superiority of traditional Jewish ways and convince their alien ruler of this by the excellence of their talents and by signs of divine favor toward them (1:19-20; 2:17, 47; 3:28-30). They are of stalwart faith and piety, withstanding all pressures to worship the pagan image set up by Nebuchadnezzar, even preferring the ordeal of the king's fiery furnace to apostasy (ch. 3). The apocryphal SONG OF THE THREE YOUNG MEN represents the heroes (vs. 1) as walking "in the midst of the flames, singing hymns to God and blessing the Lord," and engaging in prayer. The caliber of their faith is manifested with vigor and force, yet not without humility, in their classic reply to Nebuchadnezzar (in the canonical Daniel, 3:17-18): "If it be so, our God whom we serve is able to deliver us from the burning fiery furnace; and he will deliver us out of your hand, O king. But if not, be it known to you, O king, that we will not serve your gods or worship the golden image which you have set up."

The three friends' Hebrew names, as distinguished from their Babylonian names, occur separately in the OT elsewhere than in the passages cited above, but the persons who bear them cannot be identified with any of the three heroes in Daniel. The absence of genealogical data for the latter, beyond their association with the tribe of Judah (Dan. 1:6), points to the legendary framework in which the present tradition holds live. The renaming of the men (vs. 7) upon their entrance to a new position of status follows a pattern familiar from other personal histories in the Bible—the example of Joseph in the court of Pharaoh is directly analagous (Gen. 41:45; cf. also II Kings 23:34; 24:17). However, except for Dan. 1:7, the Hebrew names in the Daniel passages cited above are nowhere clearly associated with the Babylonian, and each self-contained narrative section uses one set of names to the exclusion of the other. It is possible, therefore, that in 1:7 the author explicitly identifies the one triad with the other in order to fuse two originally independent traditions, and this might be enough to account for the renaming of the young men.

Bibliography. J. A. Montgomery, *Daniel* (1927), pp. 119-25, 127-30, 193-219; R. H. Charles, *Commentary on Daniel* (1929), pp. 18-19; E. W. Heaton, *Daniel* (1956), pp. 116-21, 137-44; A. Jeffery, Exegesis of Daniel, *IB*, VI (1956), 367-68, 392-405. On the various etymologies, see, besides the foregoing: E. Schräder, *Cuneiform Inscriptions and the OT* (1888), II, 125-26 (German ed., pp. 429-30); E. König, *Hebräisches und Aramäisches Wörterbuch* (1910), p. 310; Gesenius-Bergstrasser, *Hebräische Grammatik* (29th ed., 1918), vol. I, section 20c; M. Noth, *Die israelitischen Personennamen* (1928), p. 249; A. Bentzen, *Daniel* (in German; 1952), p. 17.

B. T. DAHLBERG

SHAGEE shā'gĭ [שָׁגֵא] (I Chr. 11:34); KJV SHAGE. A Hararite; the father of Jonathan, one of the company of the Mighty Men of David known as the "Thirty." However, if in the parallel text (II Sam. 23:32b-33a) the word "son," which appears to have accidentally fallen out of the text after "Jonathan," is supplied in accordance with the Chronicler, the name of the father of Jonathan would be Shammah the Hararite (*see* SHAMMAH 3; cf. II Sam. 23:11), which appears preferable.

E. R. DALGLISH

SHAHAR shā'här. KJV translation of שחר in the title of Ps. 22 (RSV DAWN, as in several other occurrences of this word; alternately MORNING). Shahar is the Venus Star at dawn, in Canaanite mythology (*cf.* SHALEM [GOD], the Venus Star at close of day). The *locus classicus* for Shahar as a god is the Ras Shamra myth which describes the birth of Shahar and his twin Shalem to El, the senior god of the Canaanite pantheon.

The references to "eyelids of שחר" in Job 3:9; 41: 18 are probably not personifications of the dawn, but reflections of the Canaanite myth. The phrase "wings of שחר" in Ps. 139:9 is possibly a similar instance, though the reading שחר is less certain; the Syr. suggests that "as an eagle" (כנשר) should be read here.

Bibliography. C. H. Gordon, *Ugaritic Literature* (1949), pp. 60-62 (translation of Ras Shamra text); J. Gray, "The Desert God Attr in the Literature and Religion of Canaan," *JNES*, VIII (1949), 72-83; T. H. Gaster, *Thespis* (1950), pp. 249-54; G. R. Driver, *Canaanite Myths and Legends* (1956), pp. 22-23, 123.

J. GRAY

SHAHARAIM shā'ə rā'əm [שחרים] (I Chr. 8:8). A descendant of Benjamin. He had three wives, but banished two of them.

SHAHAZUMAH shā'ə zōo'mə [שחצומה] (Josh. 19:22); KJV SHAHAZIMAH —zī'mə. A border town in Issachar. No positive identification of the site of this town has been made. Tell el-Muqarqash, a mound situated on the promontory formed by the confluence of wadies Sirin and esh-Sherrar, approximately five miles E-SE of Mount Tabor, has been suggested. The site was occupied in the MB, LB, Iron I, and Byzantine periods, as shown by surface exploration. But others have tentatively proposed the identification of this mound with KISHION. It is possible that the Masoretic reading, "Shahazumah," is a conflation of two place names, Shahaz and Yammah.

Bibliography. W. F. Albright, "The Topography of the Tribe of Issachar," *ZAW*, 3 (1926), 232-33; A. Saarisalo, *The Boundary Between Issachar and Naphtali* (1927), pp. 68-69; A. Alt, "Die Reise," *PJ*, 24 (1928), 51.

G. W. VAN BEEK

SHALEM. KJV translation of שלם ("peace"), a word used only in Gen. 33:18. Commentators have taken it variously as the name of a city near Shechem (so KJV, after LXX; cf. versions), another name for Shechem, and a term describing Jacob's arrival at Shechem ("safely, in peace"; RSV "safely"). The context favors the RSV translation (cf. Gen. 28:21). It is not to be confused with SALEM (Gen. 14:18).

W. L. REED

*SHALEM (GOD) shā'ləm [שלם, he who brings to completion]. A deity now definitely known from the Ras Shamra Texts, especially that one describing the birth of Shalem and his twin, SHAHAR. The latter is the DAY STAR, and the pair are the Venus Star, which was regarded also by the Romans as a pair of twins. It has been suggested that Shalem signifies "the peace" of evening, but Shalem should be taken in its primary sense of "completion," signifying the star which completes the day, the Venus Star at evening, while Shahar is the Venus Star at DAWN.

In the OT, though Shalem is not recognized as a god, his name is compounded in the place name Jerusalem, which appears first in the Egyptian Execration Texts from Luxor (*ca.* 1850 B.C.) as *'urusha-limma* (suggested vocalization). This place name is abbreviated to Salem in Gen. 14:18 and in Ps. 76:2, where it is parallel to Zion. It seems likely that Shalem was the local god of pre-Israelite Jerusalem, and it may well be that the name Solomon was given to, or assumed by, the son of David (otherwise known as Jedidiah) out of respect to the local deity of Jerusalem. A dialectic variant of this name is Shalamanu, the name of a Moabite king mentioned by Tiglath-pileser III (743-726 B.C.). This suggests that Shalem, the evening manifestation of the Venus Star, was identical with Athtar, well known in Arabian mythology as the Venus Star. In the inscription of Mesha of Moab, Athtar is compounded with the national god CHEMOSH as Athtar-Chemosh. Further, in Judg. 11:24 the god of Ammon, Melech-ma ("the king"), distorted by Jewish scribes to "Milcom," is given as Chemosh. If these identifications are correct, the worship of MOLECH at Jerusalem was probably a relic of the pre-Israelite cult of the local god Shalem.

Bibliography. G. A. Cooke, *A Textbook of North Semitic Inscriptions* (1903), pp. 1-14 (Mesha Inscription); J. Gray, "The Desert God Attar in the Literature and Religion of Canaan," *JNES*, VIII (1949), 72-83; C. H. Gordon, *Ugaritic Literature* (1949), pp. 59-65 (translation of Ras Shamra text); G. R. Driver, *Canaanite Myths and Legends* (1956), pp. 22-23, 123 (translation of Ras Shamra text and introduction); J. Gray, *The Legacy of Canaan* (1957), pp. 136-37.   J. GRAY

SHALIM. KJV form of SHAALIM.

SHALISHAH shăl'ə shə [שלשה] (I Sam. 9:4); KJV SHALISHA. A region through which Saul passed in his search for the lost asses. Scholars have assumed that Saul was traveling N from Gibeah and that the listing of the land of Shalishah directly after the hill country of Ephraim indicates that Shalishah was either in or directly N of the territory of Ephraim. The reference to Benjamin at the end of the verse complicates ascertaining the direction of Saul's journey.

The city of BAAL-SHALISHAH (II Kings 4:42) may have been located in the land of Shalishah, which is perhaps to be sought in the vicinity of Kefr Thilth, SW of Shechem.   W. L. REED

SHALLECHETH, GATE OF shăl'ə kĕth [שער שלכת] (I Chr. 26:16). A gate in the W section of the temple enclosure in Jerusalem; a causeway led up to it from the city. This gate is tentatively identified with an ancient entrance twenty feet S of Bab el-Mutawada.   G. A. BARROIS

SHALLUM shăl'əm [שלם, שלום; Apoc. Σελλούμ, Σελλήμ, Σελώμ]; KJV SHALLUN —ən in Neh. 3:15; SALLUMUS săl'ə məs (I Esd. 9:25); SALOM sā'ləm (Bar. 1:7); SALUM (I Esd. 5:28). **1.** A son of Jabesh, apparently from Ibleam in the Plain of Esdraelon. He reigned as king over the N kingdom of Israel for one month in the year 747 B.C. (II Kings 15:10, 13-15).

He gained the throne by assassinating his predecessor, Zechariah, but was then in turn murdered by his successor, Menahem. Such royal murders were symptomatic of the deep decay which ate at the heart of the N kingdom from the time of Jeroboam II on, and which eventually led it to fall easy prey to the

Assyrian conqueror Sargon II in 721 B.C.—the date which marks the end of Israel. Both Amos and Hosea prophesied that the sins of Israel would result in such downfall; Hosea was actively engaged in preaching during Shallum's reign, or shortly thereafter.

2. Son of Tikvah (called Tokhath in II Chronicles), and husband of Huldah the prophetess (II Kings 22:14 = II Chr. 34:22).

3. The fourth son of King Josiah of Judah, and successor to his father in 608 B.C. (Jer. 22:11; I Chr. 3:15). He is usually called Jehoahaz.

4. An uncle of the prophet Jeremiah (Jer. 32:7). Shallum sent his son to the prophet, who was imprisoned in the king's court of the guard, in order to give Jeremiah the right to redeem a family field which had fallen to him at Anathoth. The prophet used the occasion to symbolize the fact that houses and fields and vineyards would in the future once again be bought in Judah, beleaguered though that country was by the Babylonians in the time of Jeremiah.

5. The father of Maaseiah, one of the keepers of the threshold of the temple in the time of the prophet Jeremiah (Jer. 35:4).

6. Son of Sismai; the father of Jekamiah; and a descendant of Jerahmeel of Judah (I Chr. 2:40-41).

7. A descendant of Simeon; son of Shaul; and the father of Mibsam (I Chr. 4:25).

8. The fourth-born son of Naphtali by his wife Bilhah (I Chr. 7:13).

9. A high priest; son of Zadok; and the father of Hilkiah (I Chr. 6:12-13; Ezra 7:2). Ezra claims to be descended from him. He is perhaps identical with Meshullam in I Chr. 9:11; Neh. 11:11; 12:13, although distinctions here are obscure.

10. A Levitic gatekeeper in the camp of the Levites, and one of the first to return to Judah from exile in Babylon (I Chr. 9:17). He is perhaps identical with Shallum the Korahite, son of Kore, mentioned in vss. 19, 31. According to Ezra 2:42 = Neh. 7:45, he was also the head of a family of gatekeepers in postexilic Judah. He is called Shelemiah in I Chr. 26:14, Meshullam in Neh. 12:25, and Meshelemiah in I Chr. 9:21. According to Ezra 10:24, he was also one of those who had married a foreign wife while in exile, but who, by the law of the new, postexilic community, was forced to put her away.

11. A member of the tribe of Ephraim, and the father of Jehizkiah (II Chr. 28:12).

12. An Israelite who had married a foreign wife while in exile (Ezra 10:42).

13. The son of Hallohesh, and one of those who helped to rebuild the wall of Jerusalem in the time of Nehemiah (Neh. 3:12). He had charge of half of one of the five governmental districts into which postexilic Judah was divided (the Jerusalem district formed the middle area). It can therefore be assumed that he belonged to a family which had remained in Judah after the downfall of the southern kingdom in 586 B.C.

14. Son of Colhozeh (Neh. 3:15). He repaired the Fountain Gate.   E. R. ACHTEMEIER

SHALMAI shăl'mī [שלמי, *perhaps hypocoristic for* (Yahu is) well-being] (Neh. 7:48). Alternately: SHAMLAI shăm'lī [שמלי (*Kethibh*), *probably an error for* שלמי (*Qere*); Apoc. Συβαΐ] (Ezra 2:46; I Esd. 5:

30); KJV Apoc. SUBAI sōō'bī. Eponym of a family of Nethinim, or temple servants, among the exiles returned from Babylon.

Bibliography. M. Noth, *Die israelitischen Personennamen* (1928), p. 165. B. T. DAHLBERG

*SHALMAN shăl'mən [שלמן] (Hos. 10:14). An unidentified foreign king; customarily considered an "abbreviation" of the name of an Assyrian king, SHALMANESER.

SHALMANESER shăl'mə nē'zər [שלמנאסר; Akkad. *Šulmānu-ašarid*, Šulmānu is leader]. **1.** Shalmaneser I (1274-1245 B.C.), son of Adad-nirari I. The first Assyrian king to leave detailed accounts of his campaigns, Shalmaneser I fought against the mountain people of the Zagros as far as Urartu, as well as against Shattuara of Hanigalbat and the Arameans along the Euphrates as far as Carchemish. His victories mark the return of Assyria to power after the Dark Age.

2. Shalmaneser II (1031-1020 B.C.). Nearly nothing is known of this king, who was one of the weak rulers who followed Tiglath-pileser I to the throne.

3. Shalmaneser III (858-824 B.C.), son of Ashurnasirpal II. Shalmaneser III represents one of those rulers who laid the foundations of the Neo-Assyrian Empire. He also was the first Assyrian king to come in contact with the kings of Israel. The three-front war which any Assyrian king of stature had to wage seems to have caused Shalmaneser III an immense amount of trouble. His wars against the kingdom of Urartu in the N were primarily defensive as to their goal, though necessarily offensive in manner. On the W front his motive was one of conquest. His stubborn push in that direction apparently took up most of his military effort, but failed to reach its ultimate objective, Damascus. For three years (858-856) Shalmaneser III struggled with the Aramean Ahuni to dislodge him from the left bank of the Euphrates and to establish Assyrian domination and administration again in the lands up to this river. The repercussions of these events made the rulers in Syria realize that only an alliance could muster enough military power to check the advance of the Assyrian army to the coast, and Irhuleni of Hamath and Adad-'idri of Damascus (called Ben-hadad in the OT) succeeded in forming such an alliance, a very rare feat in the history of that region. The kings of territories from Cilicia (Qu'e) to Ammon mustered an army of 63,000 men, not counting the pertinent chariotry and cavalry; and among these were 10,000 foot soldiers and 2,000 chariots sent by King Ahab of Israel. In spite of Shalmaneser III's claim of victory, he had to retreat (853) after having advanced as far as Qarqar, where the battle took place, though Aleppo had surrendered to him. In 848 the Syrian allies were again able to stand their ground against Shalmaneser III at Ashtamaku. In view of the danger implied in having to fight formidable adversaries in the N, as well as in the SW—adversaries that were bound to concert their efforts one day and to destroy Assyria— Shalmaneser III seems to have made extensive preparations up to 845 to assemble an immense army of

125,000 men. Even this effort did not suffice to crush the enemy. In addition to all these campaigns, Shalmaneser III and his officers were able to take Carchemish, thus bringing the Euphrates completely under Assyrian control, to be sufficiently active on the mountain front to keep Assyrian territory intact and protected, and furthermore to interfere in a fight for the Babylonian throne. There Shalmaneser III honored a treaty concluded with the Babylonian king, Nabuaplaiddin (885-852), by helping secure the throne for the son (Mardukzakirshumi) of the latter against the claim of a younger brother. In two small campaigns he defeated the pretender, pursuing him into the coastal regions of Chaldea. He entered Babylon as a welcome ally, participating in the rites of Marduk and Nabu. In the meantime, time and the ravages of continual warfare had changed the situation in Syria in Shalmaneser III's favor. The kings who had supported the alliance had died, and Hazael of Damascus had to face Shalmaneser III alone, at Mount Hermon, and was defeated. Although Jehu of Israel and the kings of Tyre and Sidon brought tribute to Shalmaneser III, he was still not able to conquer Damascus. In the remaining years of his reign, Shalmaneser III extended Assyrian domination deep into Cilicia and the regions to the N of it. A widespread rebellion in Assyria against his chosen heir, Shamshi-Adad V, marred the end of his reign. Fig. LEB 23.

4. Shalmaneser IV (782-772 B.C.), son of Adadnirari III. Throughout the duration of his reign, Shalmaneser IV had to fight a defensive war against the growing power of Urartu under its king, Argistis I. He was able to maintain only a foothold in that region, and he constantly had to yield territory to the enemy.

5. Shalmaneser V (727-722 B.C.), son of Tiglath-pileser III. His reign was short, and he left only one historical inscription. He ruled in Babylon under the name of Ululai and laid siege to Samaria when Hosea rebelled against Assyria upon the instigation of Egypt. We know of this event only from a mention in the Babylonian Chronicle. This siege may have lasted three years, if a quotation by Josephus of Menander of Tyre is to be believed, which speaks of a siege of Tyre lasting that long. At any rate, Shalmaneser V apparently died or was murdered during the siege, and the Assyrian army had to retreat quickly. Shalmaneser's brother, Sargon II, ascended the Assyrian throne. A. L. OPPENHEIM

SHAMA shā'mə [שמע] (I Chr. 11:44). One of the two sons of Hotham the Aroerite who were included among the members of the Mighty Men of David known as the "Thirty."

SHAMARIAH. KJV form of SHEMARIAH 2.

SHAME [*chiefly* בשת *and other derivatives of* בוש (be ashamed), חרפה (reproach, sexual shame), כלמה (humiliation), αἰσχύνη (shame), ἐπαισχύνομαι (be ashamed), *and* καταισχύνω (be disgraced); *also* חסד (derision), חפר (be abashed), ערוה (nakedness), קלון (disgrace), ἀτιμία (dishonor), ἐντροπή (misgiving), ὄνειδος *and* ὀνειδισμός (reproach), *and* παραδειγματίζω (hold up to public disgrace)]. The painful consciousness of guilt, unworthiness, or failure, and the ignominy often connected with it.

In the objective sense, shame is the disgrace which a sinner brings upon himself and those associated with him (Lev. 20:17; Prov. 14:34); or it may be the result of such natural calamities as barrenness (Gen. 30:23; Isa. 4:1; Luke 1:25) or widowhood (Isa. 54:4). Otherwise it is the opprobrium brought by one's enemies (Ps. 69:19—H 69:20; Mark 12:4), who often put outward marks of derision on their victims, either by exposure of their nakedness, which was a particularly painful form of disgrace for the Hebrews (cf. Isa. 3:17; 47:3; Ezek. 16:37), or by mutilation (Judg. 1:6-7; I Sam. 11:2; II Sam. 10:4-5; cf. also Jesus' abuse by his executioners). Shame comes as a divine judgment upon sinners (Ps. 44:9—H 44:10) and particularly upon Israel's foes (Isa. 7:20; Jer. 46: 24; 50:2; etc.). The devout soul prays for the shame of the wicked (Ps. 6:10—H 6:11; 31:17—H 31:18; 109:29). A frequent OT expression, adopted by NT usage, is "to be put to shame"—i.e., "disgraced, disappointed" (Ps. 35:26; Isa. 54:4; etc.; cf. Luke 13:17; II Cor. 7:14; Tit. 2:8). The cross on which Christ died was the symbol of his bitter shame (Heb. 6:6; 12:2).

Subjectively, shame is experienced as guilt for sin (Ezra 9:6; Prov. 6:33; Jer. 2:26; 31:19; Zech. 13:4), as a sense of defeat or failure (II Chr. 32:21; Jer. 9: 19—H 9:18; Mic. 3:7), as a violation of one's honor and modesty (II Sam. 10:5; 13:13; I Cor. 11:6 [contrast vs. 14]; 14:35), as embarrassment or exposure (Judg. 3:25; II Kings 2:17; Ezek. 36:30; Luke 14:9), or simply as the result of disappointment (Jer. 2:36; 14:3-4; 48:13; Hos. 10:6; and often). One may be ashamed of others, as some are of Christ (Mark 8: 38), but true believers are not ashamed of him and his gospel (Rom. 1:16; cf. Gal. 6:14), any more than he is of them (Heb. 2:11; cf. 11:16).

The experience of shame may be very painful (II Sam. 13:13; Ps. 69:20—H 69:21), and among the Hebrews it was manifested in face, bearing, and dress (II Sam. 13:19; 15:30; 19:5—H 19:6; Jer. 14: 3). Nonetheless it may lead to great good through repentance (I Cor. 4:14; 6:5; 15:34; II Thess. 3:14). There are always some, however, who are so depraved that they refuse to be ashamed (cf. Jer. 3:3; 6:15; Zeph. 3:5).

This word may also indicate the object of shame, thus nakedness and especially the pudenda (Gen. 9: 22-23; Rev. 3:18; 16:15); sin (Rom. 6:21; Eph. 5:12; Phil. 3:19; Jude 13); or idols and heathen gods, particularly Baal (Jer. 3:24; 11:13; Hos. 9:10). The scribes have substituted the word "shame" (*bosheth*) for "Baal" in the names Ishbosheth and Mephibosheth (cf. II Sam. 2:8; 4:4 with I Chr. 8:33-34).

S. J. DE VRIES

SHAMER. KJV alternate form of SHEMER 2-3.

SHAMGAR shăm′gär [שַׁמְגַּר; Hurrian *Shimig-ar(i)*, (the god) Shimike gave]. The "son of Anath," in whose days travel almost ceased in Israel because of the danger of marauding bands (Judg. 5:6), and who was said to have delivered Israel by killing six hundred Philistines with an oxgoad (3:31).

Although the non-Israelite name Shamgar has been explained variously as being originally Assyrian, Hittite, or Phoenician, it is most likely from the Hurrian equivalent mentioned above.

A certain Ben-Anath, "son of Anath," mentioned by Egyptian pharaoh Ramses II as a Syrian sea captain with whom he was allied, was at least a century too early to be Shamgar. "Son of Anath" probably refers, not to Shamgar's parentage, but to his community. He was "of Beth-anath," a Canaanite town in the Galilee area. The town itself bore the name of a Canaanite goddess ANATH.

The reference to Shamgar in the Song of Deborah should be of unique value because probably almost contemporary with the hero himself (Judg. 5:6). But unfortunately its only clear meaning is to date the dangerous public travel because of a menacing enemy as being in the pre-Deborah "days of Shamgar." Precisely opposite views as to Shamgar's role have therefore been understood of this passage.

One view is that Shamgar's anti-Philistine exploit was a campaign to clear the roads for resumption of travel. This interpretation is doubtful both because, although the Philistines had previously entered S Palestine, there was no Philistine menace in N Israel as early as 1125 B.C., and because the clear inference from the Song is that the time was one of continuous danger which was cleared up only by Deborah's action.

The other view is that Shamgar was therefore the cause of the serious travel conditions, being either a Canaanite chieftain or perhaps a Hurrian or Horite lord menacing the whole countryside. This is problematical because in the balance of the Song it is Sisera, not Shamgar, never again mentioned, who is the enemy, and the poetic parallel is with Jael, clearly pro-, not anti-, Israelite (unless the mention of Jael is a late metrical intrusion into the text).

The brief mention of Shamgar's deliverance of Israel by killing six hundred Philistines (Judg. 3:31) not only omits the customary statements about his judging and giving the land peace for so many years, but also it is apparently awkwardly inserted into the narrative at this point, for the beginning of the Deborah account (4:1) clearly implies that there was no deliverer between Ehud and Deborah. Some LXX MSS, however, omit the reference to Ehud in Judg. 4:1 and repeat this reference to Shamgar after the similar anti-Philistine exploits of Samson (i.e., after 16:31).

The instrument used by Shamgar was perhaps an eight-foot metal-tipped pole. His adventure is strikingly similar to the story of Samson and the ass's jawbone (Judg. 15:14-16), and his name as well to one of David's heroes, Shammah, also a slaughterer of Philistines (II Sam. 23:11-12).

On account of these similarities and the uncertainties concerning Shamgar, some scholars regard him as the invention of a later editor who substituted him for dishonorable Abimelech in order to complete the number of judges as twelve. Yet it is not unlikely that Shamgar was a local Galilean person of the middle twelfth century B.C. who was victorious, possibly not over Philistines, but more likely over some unknown foe. He may have been a tyrant plundering the caravans of prosperous foreign merchants and so regarded as a hero by the Israelites because he repulsed some of their enemies.

Bibliography. K. Tallqvist, *Assyrian Personal Names* (1914), p. 192; W. F. Albright, "Contributions to the Historical Geography of Palestine," *AASOR,* II (1921), 21-22; M. Noth, *Die israelitischen Personennamen* (1928), pp. 122-23; B. Maisler, "Shamgar ben 'Anat," *PEQ* (1934), pp. 192-94; R. M. Engberg, "Historical Analysis of Archaeological Evidence: Megiddo and the Song of Deborah," *BASOR,* LXXVIII (1940), 4-7; A. Alt, "Megiddo im Übergang vom kanaanäischen zum israelitischen Zeitalter," *ZAW,* N.F. XIX (1944), 67-85; W. F. Albright, "The Son of Tabeel (Isaiah 7:6)," *BASOR,* CXL (1955), 34-35; J. Bright, *A History of Israel* (1959), p. 157.   C. F. KRAFT

SHAMHUTH shăm'hŭth [שמהות]. An Izrahite or, preferably, a Zerahite (cf. I Chr. 2:6), who was the commander of a division of the Davidic militia for the fifth month (I Chr. 27:8). The name should, no doubt, be read as "Shammoth." *See* SHAMMAH 4.

SHAMIR shā'mər [שמיר, thorn]. 1. A Levite, son of Micah (I Chr. 24:24).
2. A village of Judah in the hill-country district of Debir (Josh. 15:48). Though Khirbet Somerah, *ca.* thirteen miles W-SW of Hebron, preserves the name, Shamir is probably el-Bireh, *ca.* a mile farther N.
3. A village in the hill country of Ephraim which became the home of the judge Tola, a man of Issachar (Judg. 10:1-2); possibly at or near the later site of Samaria.   V. R. GOLD

SHAMLAI. Alternate form of SHALMAI.

SHAMMA shăm'ə [שמא] (I Chr. 7:37). A member of the tribe of Asher, and the eighth son of Zophah.

SHAMMAH shăm'ə [שמה]. Alternately: SHIMEA shĭm'ĭ ə [שמעא] (I Chr. 2:13; 20:7); SHIMEAH [שמעה] (II Sam. 13:3, 32); SHIMEI shĭm'ĭ ī [שמעי] (*Kethibh*), שמעה (*Qere*)] (II Sam. 21:21). 1. An Edomite chief whose father, Reuel, was the son of Esau and Basemath daughter of Ishmael (Gen. 36:13, 17; I Chr. 1:37).
2. The third son of Jesse the Bethlehemite; the father of the wily Jonadab, the dubious friend of Ammon (II Sam. 13:3, 32), and of Jonathan the slayer of a Philistine giant (II Sam. 21:21; I Chr. 20: 7). Shammah was present at the sacrificial meal when Samuel was to anoint one of the sons of Jesse as king of Israel, but was not chosen by the prophet for the regal office (I Sam. 16:9). With his two elder brothers, Shammah was in the army of Saul during the Philistine campaign, and witnessed the defeat of the giant at the hands of his youngest brother (17:13 ff).
3. A Hararite, son of Agee, who achieved the unusual distinction of being the third in the high command of David, known as the "Three." An illustration of his heroism is preserved in the exploit when he defended singlehandedly a field of lentils from a foraging raid of the Philistines and egregiously defeated them (II Sam. 23:11-12; cf. I Chr. 11:12-14, where Shammah is omitted and where his feat is attributed in a garbled form to Eleazar the son of Dodo). His son Jonathan appears among the com-

pany of Davidic heroes known as the "Thirty" (II Sam. 23:32; I Chr. 11:34). *See bibliography.*

Bibliography. Cf. S. R. Driver, *Notes on the Hebrew Text of the Books of Samuel* (2nd ed., 1913), pp. 362 ff.
4. A Harodite who was a member of the Mighty Men of David known as the "Thirty" (II Sam. 23: 25). He was also commander of the 24,000 men of the Davidic militia, which served for the fifth month (I Chr. 27:8). His name is variously given as Shammoth of Harod (11:27) and Shamhuth, the Izrahite (27:8). "Shamhuth" appears to be a combination of the variants "Shammah" and "Shammoth," while "Izrahite" is read by Rudolph as "Zarhite."
E. R. DALGLISH

SHAMMAI shăm'ī [שמי]. 1. A descendant of Jerahmeel of Judah (I Chr. 2:28, 32); son of Onam; father of Nadab and Abishur; brother of Jada.
2. A descendant of Caleb of Judah (I Chr. 2:44-45); son of Rekem; father of Maon.
3. A descendant of Judah, and son of Mered by his Egyptian wife Bithiah (I Chr. 4:17).
E. R. ACHTEMEIER

SHAMMOTH shăm'ŏth [שמות] (I Chr. 11:27). A Harodite who was among the Mighty Men of David known as the "Thirty." In the parallel catalogue his name appears as "Shammah the Harodite" (II Sam. 23:25; *see* SHAMMAH 4), which may be presumed to be correct. The form "Harorite" (I Chr. 11:27) appears to be an error.

SHAMMUA shă mū'ə [שמוע]; KJV SHAMMUAH in II Sam. 5:14. 1. One of the sons of David who was born to him in Jerusalem by a concubine or wife. When David moved his capital to Jerusalem, he enlarged his harem from the residents of that city as a mark of his increased power and after the manner of oriental monarchs. Shammua here is identical with the Shimea mentioned in I Chr. 3:5.
2. A Reubenite; son of Zaccur (Num. 13:4). He was one of the twelve men sent out by Moses from the wilderness of Paran to spy out the land of Canaan before the conquest of that country by the Israelites.
3. A Levite; the father of Abda, and son of Galal (Neh. 11:17). He is called Shemaiah in I Chr. 9:16.
4. A priest; son of Bilgah; and the head of a priestly house (Neh. 12:18). There is some possibility that he is identical with 3 *above.*
E. R. ACHTEMEIER

SHAMSHERAI shăm'shə rī [שמשרי] (I Chr. 8:26). A Benjaminite; the first-born son of Jeroham.

SHAPHAM shā'fəm [שפם] (I Chr. 5:11-12). A Gadite dwelling in Bashan. He was second in authority in his tribe.

SHAPHAN shā'fən [שפן, rock badger, cony]. 1. The head of a family that figured prominently in the events of Josiah's reign and the last days of the Judean monarchy as well as the life of Jeremiah. He was secretary–financial officer to Josiah and was the bearer of the new-found "book of the law" from Hilkiah the priest to Josiah (II Kings 22:3-13; II

Chr. 34:8-20; *see* JOSIAH; DEUTERONOMY). He was also one of those sent by the king to consult Huldah the prophetess concerning the new book (II Kings 22:14). Shaphan and his sons seem to have been friends of the Josianic reform and were strong supporters of Jeremiah. Ahikam, one of the sons, who was also a court official and participant in the events surrounding the lawbook discovery (vss. 11, 14), saved Jeremiah from death at the hands of the mob during the critical days of King Jehoiakim (Jer. 26: 24). The prophet sent his famous letter to the exiles (ch. 29) via Elasah, another of Shaphan's sons (vs. 3). And it was from the house of yet another, Gemariah, that the scribe Baruch read Jeremiah's scroll to the people in Jehoiakim's reign (36:10-12). The family's sympathy with the prophet was further evidenced by the fact that Jeremiah was put under the guardianship of Shaphan's grandson, Ahikam's son Gedaliah, who was appointed governor of fallen Judah by the Neo-Babylonian captors of Jerusalem (39:14; 40:5). Some scholars question the identification of all these men as sons of the same Shaphan, but their contemporaneity and their common prominence in the life of the nation strongly imply that they belonged to the same family.

2. The father of the Jaazaniah whom one of Ezekiel's visions disclosed as an inciter of the people to idolatry (Ezek. 8:11). J. M. WARD

SHAPHAT shā'făt [שׁפט, judged]. **1.** A Simeonite; son of Hori (Num. 13:5). He was one of the twelve men sent out from the wilderness of Paran by Moses to spy out Canaan before the Israelite entrance into the land.

2. The father of the prophet Elisha. He is reported to have been from Abelmeholah, a town now thought to have been located on the E border of the territory of Manasseh, near the Jordan River. However, the site of the town is uncertain. Shaphat was living at the time Elisha was appointed the successor of Elijah (I Kings 19:16, 19; cf. vs. 20; II Kings 3:11; 6:31).

3. The last-born of the six sons of Shemaiah, and the grandson of Zerubbabel; a descendant of the royal line of David (I Chr. 3:22).

4. A Gadite chief who dwelt in the land of Bashan (I Chr. 5:12).

5. Son of Adlai. He was in charge of King David's herds in the valleys (I Chr. 27:29). E. R. ACHTEMEIER

SHAPHER. KJV form of SHEPHER.

SHAPHIR shā'fər [שׁפיר, beautiful] (Mic. 1:11); KJV SAPHIR sā'—. A place mentioned in the wordplay section of Micah's prophecy in alliteration with *shôfār*, "trumpet" (proposed textual restoration).

Eusebius mentions a Shafir between Eleutheropolis and Ashkelon, which has led many to suggest an identification with one of three neighboring villages called es-Suwafir *ca.* 6⅓ miles NE of Ashkelon, and 3½ miles SE of Ashdod. The identification with es-Suwafir would put Shaphir in Philistine territory, rather than Judean as the text seems to require. The LXX simply translates the word καλῶς, "beautiful."

A more likely tentative identification is a place W of Hebron, Khirbet el-Kom, on a hill *ca.* 3 miles E of Dawa'imeh, dominating the Wadi es-Saffar, which name would be an Arabic adaptation of Shaphir.

Bibliography. F.-M. Abel, *Géographie de la Palestine*, II (1938), 448; L. H. Grollenberg, ed., *Atlas of the Bible* (1957), p. 162. V. R. GOLD

SHARAI shâr'ī [שׁרי] (Ezra 10:40). One of the returned exiles, contemporaries of Ezra, who had married foreign wives. The name is absent from the parallel I Esd. 9:34.

SHARAIM. KJV form of SHAARAIM 1 in Josh. 15:36.

SHARAR shâr'är [שׁרר] (II Sam. 23:33). The father of Ahiam, who was one of the Mighty Men of David known as the "Thirty." In I Chr. 11:35 he is called Sachar. *See* SACHAR 1.

***SHAREZER** shə rē'zər [שׁראצר]. **1.** A god mentioned beside Regem-melech (Zech. 7:2).

2. A son of Sennacherib who, according to II Kings 19:37 (=Isa. 37:38; שׁראוצר in Isa. A 37:38), with Adrammelech murdered his father in the "temple of Nisroch"; probably abbreviated from Akkadian DN-*šar-uṣur*, "(name of a god) protect the king!" A. L. OPPENHEIM

SHARON shâr'ən [שׁרון, plain or level country(?); Σαρών, Σαρῶνα]; KJV NT SARON sâr'ən. The maritime plain extending approximately from Joppa to S of Mount Carmel.

1. Geographical features
2. In disputed passages
3. History
4. Figurative usage
Bibliography

1. Geographical features. The plain extends from a point near Joppa N to the Crocodile River (Nahr Zerqa), the S border of the Plain of Dor. It is *ca.* 50 miles long and varies from 8 to 12 miles in width. It is a well-watered region and is traversed by five streams, three of which—Nahr Zerqa, Nahr Iskanderuneh, and Nahr Mifjar—are perennial. The central part of the plain is characterized by an outcrop of Mousterian Red Sand, which rises to *ca.* 180 feet above the sea and causes the streams to flow to the N and to the S of it. The extensive sand dunes in the plain are a part of the Pleistocene hills which extend in places to the shore of the Mediterranean. The absence of any natural ports, and the presence of both marshes and sand dunes in the plain, made it a difficult area to colonize in OT times.

There were some small settlements in Sharon, such as that disclosed by the excavations N of Joppa at Tell Qasile, founded *ca.* 1200 B.C. However, the area was better known for its marshes and forests than for its cities during the early period of Israelite history. The reputation for fertility which the plain has enjoyed was doubtless the result of the presence of a forest of oak trees in the elevated areas, and of pastures and farming in the lower districts during years when the rainfall did not result in a seasonal flooding.

2. In disputed passages. There are three passages which have sometimes been interpreted as referring to a Sharon other than the maritime plain (Josh. 12: 18; I Chr. 5:16; Acts 9:35).

A city named Sharon is probably not meant by "LASHARON" in Josh. 12:18, where the reference is to the city of Aphek located in Sharon.

The "pasture lands of Sharon" in I Chr. 5:16 are mentioned in a context with Bashan and Gilead, E of the Jordan River. Since the Chronicler alone refers to a Sharon in this region, some scholars have questioned this reference to Sharon, which elsewhere in the same source (I Chr. 27:29; *see below*) designates the maritime plain. One interpretation emends שרון to שריון (with support from one LXX MS), "SIRION" (an alternate name of Mount Hermon, and so referring to the pasture lands of Mount Hermon; *see* HERMON, MOUNT). Another alternative is that שרון is a corruption of מישר, "tableland," as a designation of the S territory of the tribe of Gad between the River Arnon and Heshbon (cf. Josh. 13:9, 17, 21). In view of this uncertainty, and since no other source knows of a Sharon E of the Jordan, it is probable that the word was used exclusively to designate the maritime plain.

"Sharon" (Σαρῶνα) in the phrase "all the residents of Lydda and Sharon" (Acts 9:35) also refers to the coastal plain.

3. History. The armies of Thut-mose III probably skirted the plain at the E in order to avoid the difficult terrain near the shore (*see* EGYPT § 2*b*). There is no reference to an association with Sharon on the part of the Hebrews until the time of David; Shitrai the Sharonite was in charge of the herds that pastured in Sharon (I Chr. 27:29). This is perhaps based upon an old record which represented David as extending his influence over the Plain of Sharon. These pastures were most likely used only during dry seasons when pasture was scarce in the hills.

4. Figurative usage. Either the fertility or the somewhat forbidding nature of the plain may be implied in the figurative use of "Sharon" in the OT. The rose (a type of crocus which grows profusely in the area of Sharon) in Song of S. 2:1 may be interpreted in either way. The parallelism of vss. 1-2, especially the phrase "as a lily among brambles," may indicate that the author had in mind the image of a beautiful flower in the midst of a jungle. A similar interpretation may be placed upon the references in Isaiah, where the allusions may be to the forests rather than to the fertility of the plain. The phrases "Sharon is like a desert" (Isa. 33:9), "the majesty [הדר; cf. Lev. 23:40, where the word is used to refer to ornamental or goodly trees] of Carmel and Sharon" (Isa. 35:2), and "Sharon shall become a pasture for flocks" (Isa. 65:10) may be understood as having reference to the forests of the plain rather than to its fertility or productivity of crops. The use of ἐν τῷ δρυμῷ in the LXX to render השרון of Isa. 65:10, and possible references by Josephus to the wooded area of the plain (see "Drymus" in War I.xiii.2 and "Drymi" in Antiq. XIV.xiii.3) can be cited as further evidence that the ancients thought of Sharon as a forbidding forest rather than an attractive farming area.

Pls. XIV*a*; XVI*d*.

Bibliography. G. A. Smith, *The Historical Geography of the Holy Land* (1931), pp. 147-65; Y. Karmon, "Geographical Aspects in the History of the Coastal Plain of Israel," *IEJ,* 6 (1956), 33-50; D. Baly, *The Geography of the Bible* (1957), pp. 133-37. W. L. REED

SHARONITE shâr′ə nīt [שרוני] (I Chr. 27:29). A term applied to Shitrai, the person in charge of David's herds in the Plain of Sharon. *See* SHARON 3.
W. R. REED

SHARUHEN shə roo′ən [שרוחן] (Josh. 19:6). A city of Simeon located in the SW part of Judah. In the parallel lists of cities the name is given as Shilhim (Josh. 15:32) and Shaaraim (I Chr. 4:31).

Sharuhen is the same as the city of *Š*ʿ*raḥuna,* mentioned in Egyptian records as a town of the Hyksos, to which they retreated after the fall of their fortress at Avaris and their expulsion from Egypt. According to the memoirs of Ah-mose, the son of Ebana, inscribed in his tomb, this fortress was besieged for three years by Pharaoh Ah-mose I before being taken (*ca.* 1570 B.C.). *Ca.* ninety years later, when Thutmose III was invading Palestine to suppress a revolt, a civil war broke out in *Š*ʿ*raḥuna* between those who were favorable to the revolt and those who were loyal to the pharaoh; the latter won. The city was destroyed in the invasion of Shishak (*ca.* 925 B.C.) and does not seem to have been rebuilt.

Opinions have differed as to the location of Sharuhen. One of the most popular has placed it at Tell esh-Sheri′ah, *ca.* seventeen miles SE of Gaza. However, this identification is based on the similarity of the names, and Sheri′ah is an Arabic word that means "watercourse." In 1928 Flinders Petrie excavated Tell el-Far′ah, eighteen miles S of Gaza on the Wadi Ghazzeh, under the impression that this was the site of BETH-PELET. He found a fortress there protected by walls of rammed earth, a trench, and a counterscarp with a sloping glacis, typical of Hyksos defense works, as well as numerous articles characteristic of the people, including 114 scarabs, one of which bore the name of the Hyksos king Khian. Practically all the archaeologists have, therefore, identified Tell el-Far′ah with Sharuhen; and the government of Israel, in assigning names to localities in the country, changed the name of Tell el-Far′ah to Tell Sharuhen.

Bibliography. The Egyptian records are found in J. H. Breasted, *Ancient Records of Egypt,* II (1905), 13, 416. For the researches at Tell el-Far′ah, see *Beth-Pelet,* I (1930), and II (1932). S. COHEN

SHASHAI shā′shī [ששי; Apoc. Σεσίς] (Ezra 10:40; I Esd. 9:34); KJV Apoc. SESIS sē′sĭs. One of the returned exiles, contemporaries of Ezra, who had married foreign wives.

Bibliography. M. Noth, *Die israelitischen Personennamen* (1928), p. 41; R. A. Bowman, Exegesis of Ezra, *IB,* III (1954), 660-61. B. T. DAHLBERG

SHASHAK shā′shăk [ששק] (I Chr. 8:14, 25). A son of Elpaal of Benjamin. He had eleven sons.

SHAUL shôl [שאול, *traditionally* asked for, *but perhaps* dedicated (to God); *same as* SAUL; *cf.* שאל, שאלתיאל];

KJV SAUL sôl in Gen. 36:37-38; SHAULITES shôl'īts. **1.** The sixth king in Edom "before any king reigned over the Israelites" (Gen. 36:37-38; I Chr. 1:48-49). The identification of his territory is uncertain. Either "Rehoboth on the Euphrates" (RSV) or the less specific "Rehoboth by the river" (LXX and KJV) can be read. Mesopotamian *Raḥba;* the Palestinian REHOBOTH, *ca.* twenty miles SW of Beer-sheba; or probably an Edomite site now unknown may be indicated.

2. An Israelite; son of Simeon and a Canaanite woman (Gen. 46:10; Exod. 6:15; I Chr. 4:24); head of a clan of Shaulites (Num. 26:13).

3. A Levite, of the sons of Kohath (I Chr. 6:24—H 6:9; cf. Joel in vs. 36—H 21).

Bibliography. M. Noth, *Die israelitischen Personennamen* (1928), pp. 136, 216.   L. HICKS

SHAVEH, VALLEY OF shā'və [שוה עמק, *from* שוה, to be even] (Gen. 14:17). The valley in which Abraham, victorious over Chedorlaomer and his confederates, was met by the king of Sodom and by Melchizedek king of Salem, according to Gen. 14:17-18, where Shaveh is glossed as the "King's Valley" (KJV "King's Dale"). The mention of the "King's Valley" in II Sam. 18:18 points to a location in the immediate vicinity of Jerusalem, in relation to the royal estate known as the KING's GARDEN. Hence the Valley of Shaveh, or King's Valley, can be regarded as synonymous with the Kidron. *See* KIDRON, BROOK.

Bibliography. F.-M. Abel, *Géographie de la Palestine,* I (1933), 402-3. J. Simons, *Jerusalem in the OT* (1952), pp. 14-15, endeavors to locate the King's Valley N of the city.

       G. A. BARROIS

SHAVEH-KIRIATHAIM shā'və kĭr'ĭ ə thā'əm [שוה קריתים, the plain of Kiriathaim]. The location in Transjordan where CHEDOR-LAOMER subdued the EMIM (Gen. 14:5). Apparently it was the plain around KIRIATHAIM. Kiriathaim has frequently been identified with modern el-Qereiyat, 5½ miles W-NW of Dibon, but no remains have been found there from earlier than the first century B.C.

       E. D. GROHMAN

SHAVING. The custom of shaving the face and head was less common among the Hebrews than among the Egyptians and Romans (*see* BALDNESS; BEARD; HAIR; RAZOR). However, shaving was practiced by the Hebrews under certain circumstances. As a sign of mourning Job shaved his head (Job 1:20; the verb here is גז; it is used in Jer. 7:29; Mic. 1:16; in referring to the cutting of human hair and frequently in describing the "shearing" of sheep [Gen. 31:19; Deut. 15:19; etc.]). A more common term for shaving (lit., "to make bald") was גלח, rendered in the LXX as ξυράω (cf. Acts 21:24; I Cor. 11:5-6). Levites were instructed to "go with a razor over all their body" (Num. 8:7; KJV "shave all their flesh"). It was considered appropriate that Joseph should shave before appearing in the court of Pharaoh (Gen. 41:14). A person detected with leprosy of the head was instructed to shave, but avoiding the infected place (Lev. 13:33; 14:8-9). Priests were warned against shaving off the edges of their beards (Lev. 21:5). Nazirites (*see* NAZIRITE) were to let their hair

grow, but in case of defilement by contact with a dead body, and at the termination of the Nazirite vow, they shaved their heads (Num. 6:9, 18). Women taken captive in war, and before being married to an Israelite, were required to shave their heads, doubtless as a sign of mourning for their parents (Deut. 21:12-13). The shaving of Samson's head was a mark of his humiliation (Judg. 16:17, 19, 22), as was the case with the servants of David whose beards were shaved on one side by the Ammonites (II Sam. 10:4-5; I Chr. 19:4). The prophets saw the shaven head as a symbol of impending doom (Isa. 6:10; Jer. 41:5; 48:37); Levitical priests were forbidden both to shave their heads and to let their hair grow long (Ezek. 44:20).

Fig. RAZ 6.   W. L. REED

SHAVSHA shăv'shə [שושא] (I Chr. 18:16). Alternately: SERAIAH sĭ rā'yə [שריה] (II Sam. 8:17); SHEVA shē'və [שיא (*Kethibh*), שוא (*Qere*)] (II Sam. 20:25); SHISHA shī'shə [שישא] (I Kings 4:3). A high official who discharged the office of scribe (סופר; cf. Akkad. *sepēru*) in the royal court of David (II Sam. 8:17; 20:25; I Chr. 18:16). His sons ELIHOREPH and AHIJAH served in the same capacity during the reign of Solomon (I Kings 4:3).

Of the four variant forms of this name, the weight of the textual evidence inclines toward the assumption that Shavsha or Shisha is the original name. However, whether the name is of Babylonian origin (Shawshu = Shamshu, "sun") or is a hypocoristicon of an irrecoverable name is a presently unanswerable question. On the other hand, the secretariat of the united kingdom under David and Solomon assumed increasingly an international complexion.

       E. R. DALGLISH

SHEAL shē'əl [שאל, *possibly an error for* ישאל, May (God) grant! Apoc. Ἀσάηλος] (Ezra 10:29; I Esd. 9:30); KJV Apoc. JASAEL jā'sĭ əl. One of the returned exiles, contemporaries of Ezra, who had married foreign wives.

Bibliography. M. Noth, *Die israelitischen Personennamen* (1928), p. 257, no. 1295 (cf. p. 209); R. A. Bowman, Exegesis of Ezra, *IB,* III (1954), 659-60.   B. T. DAHLBERG

SHEALTIEL shē ăl'tĭ əl [שאלתיאל, שלתיאל (*probably the original form; see bibliography*), *perhaps* God is a shield, *or* God is victor; Σαλαθιήλ]; KJV SALATHIEL sə lā'thĭ əl in I Chr. 3:17; Matt. 1:12; Luke 3:27; Apoc. SALATHIEL (II Esd. 3:1). A son of King Jeconiah (Jehoiachin; cf. I Chr. 3:17; Matt. 1: 12), not of Neri (cf. Luke 3:27; *see bibliography*); the father of Zerubbabel the governor in postexilic Judah under the Persian king, Darius I according to all references (Ezra 3:2; Neh. 12:1; Hag. 1:1; etc.) except I Chr. 3:17-19, where he appears as his uncle. For various theories to account for the latter discrepancy, *see* ZERUBBABEL.

In II Esd. 3:1 he is identified with Ezra, but this is chronologically impossible (*see bibliography*) and is due probably to a redactor's gloss.

Bibliography. M. Noth, *Die israelitischen Personennamen* (1928), p. 63n. On the passage in II Esd. 3:1, see G. H. Box, "IV Esra," in R. H. Charles, *Apoc. and Pseudep. of the OT,*

II (1913), 549-50 (cf. p. 561n). On the ancestry of Shealtiel according to Luke 3:27, see J. Gabriel, *Zorobabel* (1927), pp. 37-38.   B. T. DAHLBERG

SHEARIAH shē'ə rī'ə [שְׁעַרְיָה] (I Chr. 8:38; 9:44). One of the six sons of Azel of Benjamin.

SHEARING-HOUSE. KJV translation of בֵּית עֵקֶד (RSV BETH-EKED) in II Kings 10:12, 14.

SHEAR-JASHUB shē'ər jā'shəb [שְׁאָר יָשׁוּב] (Isa. 7:3). The symbolic name of the first-born son of Isaiah (cf. Isa. 8:18). Its meaning could be either "(Only) a remnant will return (from exile)" or "A remnant will return (to God)" (cf. Jer. 3:7; Hos. 6:1). Contexts and the emphatic position of "remnant" indicate the former, though there are suggestions of both meanings: it will be a purified remnant that returns. Isaiah's doctrine of the remnant conveys both judgment and promise. It must have taken shape in his mind early in his ministry, since Shear-jashub was born by 737/736 B.C.

See also REMNANT; IMMANUEL § 1.

C. R. NORTH

SHEATH [תַּעַר, נָדָן (SCABBARD *in* Jer. 47:6; *cf.* Ugar. *t'rt*); θήκη]. The case or covering of a sword. The sheaths for the swords of David, Joab, and Peter (I Sam. 17:51; II Sam. 20:8; John 18:11) are mentioned; and figuratively, that for the sword of the threatening judgment of God (I Chr. 21:27; Jer. 47:6; Ezek. 21:3-5—H 21:8-10; cf. Ezek. 21:30—H 21:35). Stripping the bow naked in Hab. 3:9 (cf. KJV) is paraphrased as stripping it from its sheath in the RSV.   J. A. SANDERS

SHEBA shē'bə [שֶׁבַע]. **1.** The progenitor of a family in the tribe of Gad. He was descended from Abihail. According to the Chronicler the family was enrolled in the genealogical registry of the days of Jotham, king of Judah, and Jeroboam II, king of Israel (I Chr. 5:13).

2. A Benjaminite of the hill country of Ephraim; a member of the clan of the Bichrites (*see* BICHRI). He perished in an unsuccessful attempt to overthrow the throne of David (II Sam. 20:1-22).

In the troubled period that followed the suppression of the revolt of Absalom, when the ambiguous attitude of the king (II Sam. 19:1 ff), the jealousy between Judah and Israel (II Sam. 19:41-43), and the powerful faction that had anointed Absalom king (II Sam. 19:8, 10) provided the tinder for another political conflagration, Sheba became the spark for the new revolution against the house of David. As a Benjaminite he was, no doubt, able to secure the loyalties formerly attached to the house of Saul, and as an opponent of David he gave expression to the deep-seated hatred between the royal houses.

The utter seriousness of this extradynastic upheaval was immediately perceived by David, who ordered Amasa, the new commander of the army, to gather the Judean forces within three short days. When Amasa failed to appear on the third day, David commissioned Abishai to lead the royal guards in an attack upon Sheba. Joab, who appears to have been biding his time, accompanied his brother Abishai, but when an opportunity presented itself to liquidate his rival, he slew Amasa at Gibeon, where the latter had met up with his forces. Sheba had established himself in the meantime in Abel of Beth-maacah with a force of Bichrites. Joab, who now assumed command, besieged the city and spared it from destruction only because the inhabitants cast the head of Sheba over the wall.

E. R. DALGLISH

3. A town of Simeon in the S of Judah (Josh. 19: 2). In the passage in which the name occurs, the sum of the cities is mentioned as thirteen, but there are actually fourteen names. To account for this, some scholars have supposed that the words "and Sheba" are due to a scribal error from the preceding name, Beer-sheba. Others consider Sheba to be the same as Shema in the parallel passage in Josh. 15:26; the latter name could easily have arisen as a scribal error from Sheba. On this basis, it is plausible to suppose that Sheba and Beer-sheba (lit., "well of Sheba") were two parts of the same city, the former being the first settled and deriving its name from the seven (Hebrew *shebha'*) lambs with which Abraham made a covenant with Abimelech of Gerar (Gen. 21:28-29). Sheba would therefore be Tell es-Saba', where there are indications of settlement beginning with the Middle Bronze period (2100-1600 B.C.); it is located about two miles E of the modern Bir es-Saba'. *See also* SHIBAH.   S. COHEN

4. *See* SABEANS.

SHEBA, QUEEN OF shē'bə [שְׁבָא; Old S Arab. סבא] (I Kings 10:1-13). A queen who, having heard the fame of Solomon's wisdom, "came to test him with hard questions," and found that his wisdom and prosperity were such as to "surpass the report" which she had heard. She presented the king with gold, spices, and precious stones, received gifts in return, and "went back to her own land, with her servants." The exchange of goods mentioned in this account seems highly probable. The Assyrian Tiglath-pileser IV records tribute from an Arabian queen in his campaign of 732-731 B.C. and lists Sheba among the tribes of NW Arabia, while S Arabic inscriptions give evidence for Sabeans in S Arabia identical with those of the NW. The Sheba in the S was a center for overland trade, and the gifts described in Kings are ones which would come from the S. There is every indication that trading operations such as this were an important part of Solomon's economic wisdom (cf. I Kings 9:26-28; 10:11-12, 22-29). It is true that the recounting of riddles and stories was part of any cultured conversation among the Arabs, and that negotiation involved a great deal of such apparently unrelated conversation. The primary, although not necessarily so stated, objective of the meeting of Solomon and the Queen of Sheba was probably trade.

Josephus connects the Queen of Sheba with Ethiopia (Antiq. II.x.2; VIII.vi.5-6), and Arabic legends give considerable detail about the queen who married Solomon. It is true that the Sabeans founded colonies in Ethiopia. However, the tradition, apparently passed on from the Arabs to the Abyssinians, that the Abyssinian royal line has its direct descent from Solomon and the Queen of Sheba, is difficult to substantiate.   D. HARVEY

SHEBAH. KJV form of SHIBAH.

SHEBAM. KJV form of Sebam. *See* SIBMAH.

SHEBANIAH shĕb'ə nī'ə [שבניה, שבניהו]. **1.** One of the priests appointed to "blow the trumpets before the ark of God" as it was brought into Jerusalem during David's reign (I Chr. 15:24).

2. One of the Levites leading the worship at the public fast associated with Ezra's reading the Law (Neh. 9:4-5), and perhaps to be identified with one of the Levites of this name signatory to the covenant of Ezra (Neh. 10:10—H 10:11).

3. Another Levite signatory to the covenant of Ezra (Neh. 10:12). There is some MS evidence for reading "Shecaniah" (שכניה) either here or for 2 *above.*

4. A priestly house in the postexilic period (Neh. 12:14), a representative of which was among those signatory to the covenant of Ezra (Neh. 10:4—H 10:5). Numerous MSS, as well as the related list of Neh. 12:3, suggest the possibility that "Shebaniah" may in this case be a misreading for "Shecaniah" (שכניה).
                                    B. T. DAHLBERG

SHEBARIM shĕb'ə rĭm [השברים, quarries, *from* שבר, to break(?)]. A place between Ai and Jericho to which the men of Ai pursued the Israelites (Josh. 7:5). Alternately the word has been translated "the quarries" rather than as a proper name.

SHEBAT shē'băt [שבט; Apoc. Σαβάτ] (Zech. 1:7; I Macc. 16:14); KJV SEBAT sē'—; KJV Apoc. SABAT sā'—. The eleventh month in the Hebrew CALENDAR (January-February); the same as Akkadian *shabaṭu.*

SHEBER shē'bər [שבר, lion(?)] (I Chr. 2:48). Son of Caleb and his concubine Maacah, listed in the genealogy of the descendants of David.

Bibliography. M. Noth, *Die israelitischen Personennamen* (1928), p. 230.

SHEBNA shĕb'nə [שבנא, *abbreviation of* return now, O Yahweh!]. Alternately: SHEBNAH [שבנה]. State secretary in the court of King Hezekiah (II Kings 18:18 ff; Isa. 36:3 ff), and, if the man referred to in Isa. 22:15 ff is the same Shebna, at one time palace governor. The full form of the name was held by others in the OT—i.e., Shebaniah (שבניהו; Neh. 9:4, etc.). It was a common Palestinian name and occurs on seals from Lachish and elsewhere.

When Sennacherib of Assyria had captured most of the cities of rebellious Judah in 701 B.C. and, apparently unmoved by Hezekiah's tribute composed of the temple treasures, sought the capitulation of Jerusalem, Shebna was one of three emissaries sent by Hezekiah to negotiate with the Assyrians. Incensed by the Assyrian disdain for the power of Israel's God, these statesmen reported to Hezekiah (II Kings 18:37) and were then sent to the prophet Isaiah for the counsel of the Lord (19:1 ff). Isaiah prophesied severe chastisement for the city, as a consequence of its re-

fusal to heed the divine injunction against involvement in international power politics (Isa. 37:21-32; cf. ch. 7), but he also predicted the failure of the Assyrian siege (37:33 ff). There is an apparent condemnation of Shebna and the other officials in this oracle because of their counsel of an anti-Assyrian rebellion. It is possible that this attitude was one of the causes of Isaiah's earlier denunciation of Shebna (22:15-25).

According to some scholars, Jerusalem's immunity from Sargon's campaign of 711 B.C., when rebellious Ashdod was punished (Isa. 20:1), was due to the shift in Judean policy which accompanied the demotion of Shebna from palace governor to state secretary—i.e., the government returned to an attitude of submission. The oracle in Isa. 22:15 ff would then have been delivered prior to 711. But Shebna did not fall very far from his earlier post. The state secretary was second only to the "officer-over-the-year," according to the organization of Solomon's government (I Kings 4:2 ff), and, according to the account of the 701 episode, a ranking official in the later hierarchy as well. And further, Shebna's rebellious counsel was obviously still effective in 701 (Isa. 37:23 ff).

Some scholars have insisted that the Shebna of Isa. 22 and that of chs. 36–37 are different men. The stated cause of Isaiah's denunciation in the former passage is the official's preoccupation with the building of his own tomb, presumably to the neglect of his state duties.

Isa. 22:21-22 implies that the palace governor had broad powers over the nation at large (cf. Joseph's position in the Egyptian government in Gen. 45:8). He was apparently the king's chief lieutenant. The office referred to in Isa. 36–37 (II Kings 18–19) was also very important. The story shows that the state SCRIBE was one of the principal statesmen in Judah. He was not merely the "recorder," a title used in some English translations. Several commentators have preferred the translation "remembrancer" as an indication of the secretary's intimate role at the front of the king's retinue.

Bibliography. H. G. May, *AJSL*, 56 (1939), 147; J. A. Montgomery, *The Books of Kings*, ICC (1951), pp. 483-96.
                                    J. M. WARD

SHEBUEL shĭ bū'əl, shĕb'yōō əl [שבואל]. Alternately: SHUBAEL shōō'bĭ əl [שובאל]. **1.** Son of Gershom; a descendant of Moses; and a Levite in the temple. He assisted the priests in the temple service, the division of duties (I Chr. 26:26-32) reflecting the usage of the third century B.C. He also had charge of the temple treasuries (I Chr. 26:24). He is called Shubael in I Chr. 24:20.

2. A son of David's seer Heman (I Chr. 25:4). A Levite, he assisted with the temple music. He is called Shubael in vs. 20.   E. R. ACHTEMEIER

SHECANIAH shĕk'ə nī'ə [שכניה, שכניהו, Y has taken up his abode]; KJV SECHENIAS sĕk'ə nī'əs (I Esd. 8:29, 32), JECHONIAS jĕk'— (I Esd. 8:92). **1.** A descendant of David, of the exiled King Jehoiachin (Jeconiah), and of Zerubbabel (I Chr. 3:21-22); father of SHEMAIAH 10. *Cf.* 3 *below.*

2. A priest in the time of Hezekiah who assisted in distributing the temple offering among his fellow clergymen (II Chr. 31:15).

3. The father of HATTUSH 1, who returned to Judah with Ezra from the Exile (Ezra 8:3; I Esd. 8:29); probably to be identified with 1 *above. See* SHEMAIAH 10.

4. Son of Jahaziel, and one of those who returned to Judah with Ezra from the Exile (Ezra 8:5; I Esd. 8:32).

5. Son of Jehiel, and one of those who had married a foreign wife while in exile in Babylon (Ezra 10:2; I Esd. 8:92). It was he who suggested to Ezra that the returned exiles put away the foreign wives and children in the midst of the company of Israel, according to the commandments of the law.

6. The father of SHEMAIAH 22, one of those who helped to repair the wall of Jerusalem in the days of Nehemiah (Neh. 3:29).

7. The father-in-law of Tobiah the Ammonite (Neh. 6:18).

8. A priest who returned with Zerubbabel out of exile in Babylon (Neh. 12:3; I Chr. 24:11). He is probably identical with SHEBANIAH in Neh. 10:4; 12:14.   E. R. ACHTEMEIER

SHECHEM shĕk′əm [שֶׁכֶם]; **SHECHEMITES** —ə-mīts [שִׁכְמִי]. **1.** Son of Hamor the Hivite. His rape of Jacob's daughter DINAH was avenged by her brothers Simeon and Levi (Gen. 34; Josh. 24:32; Judg. 9:28). *See also* SHECHEM (CITY) §§ 1, 3.

2. One of the descendants of Joseph and of Manasseh, Joseph's first-born son (Num. 26:31; Josh. 17:2). The Shechemites derive their name from him as their progenitor.

3. The second-born son of Shemida of the tribe of Manasseh (I Chr. 7:19), perhaps identical with 2 *above.*   E. R. ACHTEMEIER

***SHECHEM (CITY)** shĕk′əm [שֶׁכֶם, shoulder *or* slope?; Συχεμ]; KJV alternately SICHEM sī′kəm (Gen. 12:6); SYCHEM (Acts 7:16). An ancient

SHECHEM

THE GREAT SEA

M A N A S S E H

●Thebez
●Samaria
Neapolis ●Tirzah?
MT. GERIZIM ● + MT. EBAL
Shechem●

Jordan

E P H R A I M
●Shiloh

Bethel
●●Ai

River

D A N

Jerusalem

J U D A H

●Hebron

Salt Sea

Adapted from *The Westminster Historical Atlas to the Bible, Revised,* ed. G. Ernest Wright and Floyd V. Filson. © The Westminster Press.

Canaanite city in the hill country of Ephraim (Josh. 20:7) near Mount Gerizim (Judg. 9:7); an important Israelite religious and political center.

1. The name. Since the time of Eusebius many have thought that the city received its name from Shechem son of Hamor (Gen. 33:18-19). It now seems more probable that the word meant "shoulder" or "slope" and that it derived from the geographical setting of the city, where the terrain can be thought of as the slope of Mount Gerizim* and Mount Ebal. (See Gen. 48:22, alluding to Shechem as one shoulder [שְׁכֶם אַחַד; RSV "one mountain slope"; KJV "one portion"].) Further evidence of an early Hebrew practice of designating a geographical feature near Shechem by means of anatomical terminology is the expression טַבּוּר הָאָרֶץ, "navel of the land" (Judg. 9: 37; RSV "center of the land"). The phrase refers either to one of the mountains overlooking Shechem —possibly Mount Gerizim—or to the plain W of the city. Fig. GER 24.

The appearance of the name in Egyptian texts which are usually dated in the nineteenth century B.C. makes it certain that the Hebrews acquired it from the Canaanites. The name designates the Canaanite city and its vicinity in two texts from the Twelfth Egyptian Dynasty and in one of the Amarna Letters, and is vocalized variously as Sakmemi, Sakmami, and Sekmem. Shechem is also mentioned on one of the early-eighth-century ostraca from Samaria in a context which suggests that the people of Shechem sent wine to the king of Samaria.

The Shechemites (הַשִּׁכְמִי; Num. 26:31) are said to be the family of SHECHEM (2), a descendant of Manasseh. The poetical form of Hos. 6:9 has made it difficult to translate the expression דֶּרֶךְ יְרַצְּחוּ שֶׁכְמָה (KJV "murder in the way by consent"; mg. "with one shoulder," or "to Shechem"), although most modern translations render it "murder on the way to Shechem." "SYCHAR" is thought by some scholars to be an error for "Shechem" (John 4:5); the Old Syriac gospels read "Shechem."

2. Location. Shechem is located *ca.* forty miles N of Jerusalem at the pass between Mount Gerizim and Mount Ebal where the main N-S and E-W highways converge. The many OT references to the city do not make it clear whether the city was located in the pass or near its E end. Following Josephus, who reports a visit by Vespasian to Shechem, which is also called Neapolis (War IV.viii.1), many geographers have placed the city in the pass where Nablus (modern form of "Neapolis") is located. However, as a result of a series of excavations at Tell Balatah, *ca.* 1½ miles E of Nablus, near the famous "Jacob's Well" at the E end of the pass, it is now certain that this mound is ancient Shechem. Fig. EBA 2.

The first excavations were conducted by German archaeologists who worked at various periods between 1913 and 1934. Beginning in 1956 with a preliminary re-examination of the site, the Drew-Mc-Cormick Expedition working in collaboration with the American School of Oriental Research, conducted a major campaign in 1957, and announced plans to continue the excavations. Significant discoveries have been made which supplement and clarify the biblical history of the city and leave no doubt that the great city walls, the temple (*see* SHECHEM, TOWER OF), and the houses were those of ancient Shechem. The excavations have demonstrated that the city reached its height during the Hyksos period, *ca.* the latter half of the seventeenth century B.C., in the patriarchal period. Although the chronology of Tell Balatah, especially during the Chalcolithic and Early Bronze periods (*ca.* 4000 to 2000 B.C.) and during the eighth to the fourth centuries B.C., is uncertain, archaeology has demonstrated the importance of the city, whose fortunes fluctuated with the political conditions operating in Canaan. It suffered a moderate decline at the time of the Hebrew conquest, a major destruction about the time of Abimelech (Judg. 9:45-46), and possibly a period of abandonment after the fall of the N kingdom, but was rebuilt in the Hellenistic period and occupied until *ca.* 100 B.C. *See* § 4 *below.*

A good water supply, a fertile plain directly E of the city, and control of the converging highways, especially the only E-W road through the mountains of N Canaan, combined to make Shechem a wealthy and powerful city. The fact that the city was not built on elevated terrain put it at a disadvantage from a military viewpoint, exposed as it was on the E and the W and overshadowed by Mount Ebal on the N. Large stone walls were constructed for the purpose of defending the city against attack. Their strength is attested by the fact that on one occasion the city was conquered by ambush (Judg. 9:35) rather than frontal attack, although the latter was possible with the use of siege methods.

3. History. Scholars do not agree on the dating of the OT sources which mention Shechem, but there is a trend toward the view that some must be dated as early as the ninth century B.C. and that they rest upon still earlier oral or written traditions. The city is referred to frequently in the patriarchal narratives. Abraham visited the place (מקום) of Shechem when the Canaanites were in the land (Gen. 12:6-7). The report of a theophany and the building of an altar, probably at the oak of MOREH nearby, suggest that the Shechem area, if not the city itself, was a religious center for Abraham.

Jacob, on his return from Paddan-aram, also visited Shechem and was kindly received by the inhabitants, who sold him land and permitted the building of an altar to honor his God, El-Elohe-Israel (Gen. 33:18-20). A part of the same tradition is the report of Jacob's return to the oak near Shechem, where he hid the foreign gods and earrings after a theophany at Bethel. An independent tradition in Gen. 34 reports the rape of Dinah by Shechem, the son of Hamor, followed, after a period of negotiation, by a surprise attack on the city by Jacob's sons, Simeon and Levi. The report of the killing of all the males and the plundering of the city has the appearance of a later embellishment, especially in view of Joseph's visit to Shechem, where his brothers were pasturing the flocks (Gen. 37:12-14). However, the peaceful intentions of Jacob and his desire to preserve amity with the Canaanites of the Shechem area are evident in all the narratives. Further indication of the importance of Shechem in the patriarchal period is the report that the bones of Joseph were buried there (Josh. 24:32; in the speech of Stephen there is an error in locating the burial place of all the patriarchs at Shechem rather than Hebron [Acts 7:16]).

Joshua is pictured as calling an assembly of the tribes at Shechem following the initial successes in the conquest of Canaan (Josh. 24:1). Because of the reports that assemblies were also held at SHILOH (18:1), there is some question of the relationship of the two cities. It has been argued that Shechem was a military-political center and Shiloh a religious center in the early period of tribal history. However, it is more probable that both cities served as headquarters and shrines for the tribes prior to the establishment of the capital at Jerusalem, although it is not possible to determine their relative importance. The covenant concluded by Joshua at Shechem, resulting in a twelve-tribe confederacy, rests on an authentic tradition and was an important factor in the survival of the tribes during the following centuries. Recollection of the religious significance of Shechem is preserved in the statement that after making the covenant there and recording the laws, Joshua placed a great stone under the oak "in the sanctuary of the LORD" (Josh. 24:26). The exact nature of the laws mentioned is uncertain, but it is thought that some of them, together with ancient Shechemite liturgies, have been preserved in Deut. 11:26-32; 27.

Aside from brief references to Shechem's place in the division of the land (Num. 26:31; Josh. 17:2, 7; 20:7) and its designation as one of the cities of refuge (Josh. 21:21; *see* CITY), it is not mentioned again until *ca.* 1100 B.C., the time of Abimelech. Although Shechem was his birthplace (Judg. 8:31) and the place where he was made king (9:6), he was not able to control the city. After ambushing its defenders he destroyed the city and sowed it with salt (9:45). It was to the men of Shechem that Jotham delivered his famous parable (9:7-20).

During the United Monarchy, Shechem is not mentioned, but it doubtless continued in a minor role. At the death of Solomon, Rehoboam went to Shechem to be crowned king (I Kings 12:1)—an indication of its political importance. After Rehoboam's failure to win support, Jeroboam "built Shechem" (vs. 25)—i.e., added to its buildings. However, he did not rule there long, doubtless because of difficulty in defending the city and a desire for a capital less accessible to Judean attack.

Other references to Shechem indicate only that the city continued to be occupied until the time of Jeremiah (Jer. 41:5); mention of it in alluding to the territory of Ephraim suggests that it had some importance both directly before and after the fall of the N kingdom (Pss. 60:6; 108:7; Hos. 6:9). The fate of Shechem during the Assyrian and Babylonian invasions is not described, and there is no mention in the OT of the city during the postexilic period. However, Josephus records that it was the home of the Samaritans (Antiq. XI.viii.6) and that it was destroyed by John Hyrcanus (Antiq. XIII.ix.1). The inhabitants of Shechem are called the "foolish people" (Ecclus. 50:26), and most scholars think that Bethulia in the book of Judith (4:6) is Shechem. A small community of Samaritans continue to dwell in the region; their synagogue is located on the S of Nablus *ca.* three miles from Shechem.

Bibliography. W. Harrelson, *The City of Shechem: Its History and Importance* (1953), Microcard Theological Series, no. 3, pp. 1-603. E. Nielsen, *Shechem, A Traditio-Historical Investiga-*

tion (1955), pp. 3-357. G. E. Wright, "The First Campaign at Tell Balatah (Shechem)," *BASOR*, no. 144 (1956), pp. 9-23; "The Archaeology of the City," *BA*, vol. XX, no. 1 (1957), pp. 19-32; "The Second Campaign at Tell Balatah (Shechem)," *BASOR*, no. 148 (1957), pp. 11-28. B. W. Anderson, "The Place of Shechem in the Bible," *BA*, vol. XX, no. 1 (1957), pp. 10-19. W. Harrelson, "Shechem in Extra-Biblical References," *BA*, vol. XX, no. 1 (1957), pp. 2-10. H. C. Kee and L. E. Toombs, "The Second Season of Excavation at Biblical Shechem," *BA*, vol. XX, no. 4 (1957), pp. 82-105.

W. L. REED

4. Addendum. In 1960 the third season of excavation (Fig. SHE 42) by the Drew-McCormick Expedition showed that the earliest occupation, immediately above bedrock, was a series of Chalcolithic

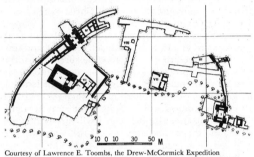

Courtesy of Lawrence E. Toombs, the Drew-McCormick Expedition

42. The excavations at Shechem after the 1960 season: I, the E gate; IV, the NE gate; V, the temple

camp sites (*ca.* 4000 B.C.), succeeded by a gap in occupation in the excavated areas until *ca.* 1800 B.C., although pottery of the intervening centuries was present. Soon after 1800 B.C. formidable defenses were erected and a palace, enclosed by a strong wall (formerly erroneously called the "temenos wall" on the assumption that it was primarily associated with the temple), dominated the city. The palace was rebuilt at least three times during the Hyksos period, and the street which skirted the temple inside the enclosure wall was rebuilt nine times. *Ca.* 1650 B.C. the palace area was filled over, the line of the city wall was moved to the N (the Cyclopean wall), and the great temple of Shechem was built over the buried palaces. Destroyed *ca.* 1550 B.C. during the Egyptian campaigns, the temple was rebuilt on a smaller scale and with a different orientation. This second and smaller temple, the existence of which was unrecognized before the 1960 excavations, was standing when the city passed peacefully into the hands of the invading Israelites and became the center of their tribal confederacy. Abimelek's destruction of the temple left the building a ruin and the site a place for storage pits until in the restoration of the city during the period of the monarchy a granary was built over the remains of the temple. The excavations have established a twelfth-century date for the period of the origin of the Abimelech story. There was no radical destruction of the city in the thirteenth century as was the case with Hazor and other N cities. Shechem enjoyed considerable prosperity in the ninth-eighth centuries, and the houses of the period were substantial structures. However, the Assyrian invasions of 724-721 B.C. totally destroyed the city, and left masses of fallen bricks and burned beams in all buildings excavated. Shechem reverted to the status of a village until the

Samaritan period, the houses of which showed that between *ca.* 325 and 100 B.C. Shechem was a prosperous city, probably rebuilt with the deliberate intent of making it a religious, if not political, rival of Jerusalem. The coin series found in the excavations ranges from the fourth century to *ca.* 110 B.C., and abruptly stops. This suggests the final destruction of Shechem may be attributed to John Hyrcanus, perhaps on the occasion of his destruction of Samaria in 107 B.C.

L. E. TOOMBS

SHECHEM, TOWER OF [מגדל שכם, *migdal sh⁺khem*, Migdal (Tower) of Shechem; *see* TOWER]. A place destroyed by Abimelech, whose attack resulted in the destruction of the stronghold of the house of El-berith and the death of *ca.* one thousand men and women who defended it (Judg. 9:46-47).

It was formerly thought that the Tower of Shechem was located some distance from Shechem, because of the statement that its people entered the stronghold only after hearing of the destruction of the city (vs. 46). It is more probable that the *Migdal* was on the acropolis in Shechem, where there was located the stronghold, or temple-fortress, of El (cf. 9:4, 6: "the house of Baal-berith" and "Beth-millo"). In the excavations at SHECHEM (Tell Balatah) a large building measuring *ca.* sixty-eight by eighty-four feet, with walls *ca.* seventeen feet thick, has been identified as the temple-fortress and the Tower.

W. L. REED

SHEDEUR shĕd'ĭ ər [שדיאור, Shaddai is light, *or* Shaddai is fire]. The father of Elizur, who was the leader of Reuben in the wilderness (Num. 1:5; 2:10; 7:30, 35; 10:18). The spelling of the name could suggest a derivation from either '*ôr*, "light," or '*ûr*, "fire." The former is the more probable in view of OT references to the light of the deity (e.g., Ps. 36:9—H 36:10; Isa. 2:5).

For the meaning of "Shaddai," *see* GOD, NAMES OF, § C2a.

Bibliography. M. Noth, *Die israelitischen Personennamen* (1928), pp. 130, 168-69.   R. F. JOHNSON

SHEEP [צון, small cattle; πρόβατον]; **SHEPHERD** [רעה; ποιμήν]. References to sheep in the Bible occur more than five hundred times, if one includes also allusions to LAMB and RAM. That the sheep was early domesticated in Palestine is suggested by the Cain-Abel story in Gen. 4. Sheep represented the chief wealth and the total livelihood of pastoral peoples, providing the peoples of the Bible with food to eat (e.g., I Sam. 14:32), milk to drink (e.g., Isa. 7: 21-22), wool for the weaving of cloth (e.g., Lev. 13: 47-48; Job 31:20; Ezek. 34:3), and even rough clothing (Heb. 11:37; cf. Zech. 13:4; Matt. 7:15) and covering for tents (Exod. 26:14). Inevitably also sheep served as a medium of exchange (see II Kings 3:4; Ezek. 27:18-19) and figured centrally in the sacrificial system (Exod. 20:24; Num. 22:40; John 2:14), being offered for a burnt offering (Lev. 1:10), a sin offering (4:32), a guilt offering (5:15), and a peace offering (22:21). Fig. SHE 43.

The chief Palestinian breed of sheep is today, and doubtless has been from the beginning, the so-called broad-tailed sheep (*Ovis laticaudata*). The tails, which commonly weigh ten pounds and even as

Courtesy of the Museum of the Ancient Orient, Istanbul

43. Lower register shows shepherds driving a sheep and
a goat; from Nippur

much as fifteen pounds, have always been regarded
as a delicacy, and, for their very choiceness, are
called for on occasion as a sacrifice (see, e.g., Exod.
29:22-25).

In view of the very nature of the sheep—affectionate (II Sam. 12:3), unaggressive (Isa. 53:7; Jer.
11:19; John 10:3-4), relatively defenseless (Mic. 5:8;
Matt. 10:16), and in constant need of care and supervision (Num. 27:17; Ezek. 34:5; Matt. 9:36; 26:31)—
and the corresponding relationship between the sheep
and the shepherd, it is not at all surprising that in
figurative-theological language the sheep and the
shepherd are repeatedly, and often movingly, employed. In the OT one thinks at once of such lines
as these: "The LORD is my shepherd, I shall not
want" (Ps. 23:1); or of Ezekiel (37:24 ff) looking forward to Israel's reconstitution: "They shall all have
one shepherd. . . . They shall dwell in the land where
your fathers dwelt . . . . I will make a covenant of
peace with them . . . ; and I will bless them"; or of
Jeremiah, earlier, looking in faith toward the same
event of Israel's re-creation: "I will gather the
remnant of my flock out of all the countries where
I have driven them, and I will bring them back to
their fold . . . . I will set shepherds over them who
will care for them, and they shall fear no more, nor
be dismayed, neither shall any be missing, says Yahweh" (23:3-4); or of the Second Isaiah, announcing
that very same redemptive event, and seeing Yahweh in the role of a shepherd:

> He will feed his flock like a shepherd,
>   he will gather the lambs in his arms,
> he will carry them in his bosom,
>   and gently lead those that are with young.

In the NT the figure of the shepherd and the sheep
finds in Christian faith its most profound application
in Christ as the good Shepherd of all sheep. This is
boldly articulated in the closing benediction of Hebrews in the simple phrase "our Lord Jesus, the
great shepherd of the sheep" (13:20). The shepherd/
sheep relationship between Christ and men is briefly
but powerfully expressed again in Mark 6:34, when
Jesus "saw a great throng, and he had compassion

on them, because they were like sheep without a
shepherd; and he began to teach them many things."

The two most extended biblical allegories of the
shepherd are in Ezek. 34; John 10. The OT passage
opens with the prophetic condemnation of the shepherds of Israel who have been feeding, not their
sheep, but only themselves, and moves on to the
declaration of Yahweh's own compassionate assumption of the role of shepherd over Israel: "I, I myself
will search for my sheep, and will seek them out. As
a shepherd seeks out his flock when some of his sheep
have been scattered abroad, so will I seek out my
sheep; and I will rescue them" (vss. 11-12). And
this, of course, recalls the more moving parable of
the ninety-nine sheep safely together and the one
sheep lost; and again the role of Christ as the Good
Shepherd (Matt. 18:10-14; Luke 15:3-6).

The allegory in Ezekiel continues: "I will feed
them on the mountains of Israel, by the fountains
. . . . I will feed them with good pasture . . . ; there
they shall lie down in good grazing land, and on fat
pasture they shall feed on the mountains of Israel. I
myself will be the shepherd of my sheep . . . . I will
seek the lost, and I will bring back the strayed, and I
will bind up the crippled, and I will strengthen the
weak, and the fat and the strong I will watch over; I
will feed them in justice" (Ezek. 34:13-16).

In the NT passage Christ is the shepherd, who
saves, sustains, and redeems the life of all who will
come into his fold. "I am the door of the sheep . . . .
If any one enters by me, he will be saved, and will
go in and out and find pasture." (John 10:7-9.)

But for what follows, the OT has no precedent.
Prophetic faith can conceive of Israel or the Servant
of Yahweh dying on behalf of the cause of the knowledge and reign of God in the world, but not God
himself, or the Son of God. Prophetic allegory never
sees the Shepherd dying for his sheep. The NT allegory of John 10 is unequivocal: "I am the good
shepherd. The good shepherd lays down his life for
the sheep. . . . So there shall be one flock, one shepherd" (vss. 11-18).   B. D. NAPIER

SHEEP GATE [שַׁעַר הַצֹּאן] (Neh. 3:1, 32; 12:39).
A city gate on the N side of Jerusalem, restored by
Nehemiah; implicitly referred to in John 5:2:
Ἔστιν . . . ἐπὶ τῇ προβατικῇ κολυμβήθρα, "There
is . . . by the sheep (gate) a pool." Fig. NEH 13.
See also JERUSALEM §§ 7b, 11.   G. A. BARROIS

SHEEPFOLD [גְּדֵרֹת, מִכְלָה; αὐλή]. An enclosure
for sheep against the night hazards of weather,
beasts, and robbers (e.g., Gen. 31:39; I Sam. 17:34);
sometimes jointly used by a number of shepherds for
a plurality of flocks and supervised by a single attendant through the night, each shepherd then calling forth again his own flock in the morning (John
10:1 ff). Such permanent enclosures are entered by
a gate (John 10:2) and may be an area enclosed by
stone walls, representing an effort comparable to
that of building a city (see Num. 32:16).
See also SHEEP.   B. D. NAPIER

SHEEPSKIN [תַּחַשׁ (Num. 4:25; KJV BADGERS'
SKINS), *see below;* μηλωτή (Heb. 11:37), *from* μῆλον,

sheep *or* goat]. The skin of a sheep, presumably tanned. As sheepskin must have been one of the commonest leathers of biblical Palestine, the paucity of references to it in the Bible is remarkable (cf. "tanned rams' skins" in Exod. 25:5; 26:14; 35:7, 23; 36:19; 39:34).

The RSV usually translates תחש as "GOATSKIN," and there is no reason for translating it differently in Num. 4:25.

In Heb. 11:37 being clothed "in skins of sheep and goats" is cited as illustrative of the destitution which the saints of the past had to endure.

W. S. McCULLOUGH

SHEERAH shē′ə rə [שארה, blood relationship, *or* a female relative] (I Chr. 7:24); KJV SHERAH shĭr′ə. Either the daughter of Ephraim and the sister of Beriah or the daughter of Beriah, the son of Ephraim. According to the MT, she or her descendants built Lower and Upper BETH-HORON and UZZEN-SHEERAH.

SHEHARIAH shē′ə rī′ə [שחריה] (I Chr. 8:26). A son of Jeroham of the tribe of Benjamin. He was a chief in his tribe, dwelling in Jerusalem.

SHEKEL shĕk′əl [שקל, *from root* to weigh]. A weight; later a coin. In early Babylonian times the shekel weight varied from 8.3 grams to 16.7 grams or *ca.* 0.3 ounce to 0.62 ounce. In Israelite times the shekel seems to have averaged *ca.* 11.424 grams or 0.403 ounce. At the time of the First Jewish Revolt (66-70) there was a silver shekel coin averaging *ca.* 14.27 grams, a little less than half an ounce.

See also MONEY, COINS; PIECE (OF MONEY) § 2; WEIGHTS AND MEASURES §§ B2-4*b*. O. R. SELLERS

SHEKINAH shə kī′nə [שכינה, that which dwells, *or* dwelling, *from* שכן, to dwell]. The word used in the Targums and rabbinic writings as a circumlocution to express the reverent nearness of God to his people. The word is not found in the Bible, but it is rooted in the OT, which frequently speaks of God's presence on earth, and is reflected in the NT, especially in the belief that God came to dwell in the flesh of Jesus Christ. The OT represents the presence of God in many ways, but the general idea is related to the teaching that Yahweh chooses to dwell with Israel by putting his "name" in a special place (Deut. 12:5, 11, 21). God, of course, also dwells in heaven and at times withdraws his presence.

The places chosen by Yahweh are also many, but a few are of special importance. In the time when Yahweh was described as a God of battle, the ark is represented as his place of abode (*see* ARK OF THE COVENANT). Num. 10:35-36 preserves this view in a vivid manner: "Whenever the ark set out, Moses said, 'Arise, O LORD, and let thy enemies be scattered; and let them that hate thee flee before thee.' And when it rested, he said, 'Return, O LORD, to the ten thousand thousands of Israel.'" Long before its removal to Jerusalem the ark was taken forth from Shiloh in the war against the Philistines. Yahweh's presence was so clearly associated with the ark that its capture was felt to be the departure of God (I

Sam. 4). One of the early narratives speaks of the ark guiding Israel through the wilderness (Num. 10: 33 E), but Yahweh comes down in a cloud to talk with Moses in the tent (Exod. 33:7-11 E). The earliest narrative tells how the cloud led Israel to Sinai (13: 21-22 J) and continued with the Israelites toward Canaan (33:1, 3). Both the ark and the cloud drop into the background as the place of Yahweh's presence after Israel is settled in the land and Jerusalem becomes the central sanctuary. In place of sanctuaries at Shechem (Gen. 12:6-7), Beer-sheba (21:33), Bethel (28:19), Peniel (32:30), and Shiloh, Jerusalem becomes the central sanctuary and the special abode of Yahweh.

The most frequent forms by which God makes his presence known are the ANGEL of the Lord, the face of God, and the glory of God. The relation between Yahweh and the angel of Yahweh is clearly indicated by the fact that Exod. 13:21 represents Yahweh as going before Israel, while 14:19 says it was the angel. Yahweh's name is in the angel (23:20-21). When Jacob saw the face of God, he met God himself (Gen. 32:30), and all who come to the sanctuary to worship seek the face of God (Ps. 24:6). Isa. 63:9 unites angel and face in the phrase "angel of his presence." However, the form that came to be most closely associated with the Shekinah was the glory of God. Ezekiel, who first introduced the term, saw the "appearance of the likeness of the glory of the LORD" (Ezek. 1:28), and in this form Yahweh moved from the temple to his people in Babylon (11:23). The priestly writers related this to the cloud.

The principal powers used to designate the presence of God are spirit, word, and wisdom. God takes his holy Spirit from those who are cast from his presence (Ps. 51:11), and it was by his holy Spirit that he dwelt with his people in the days of Moses (Isa. 63:10-11). God's word is at times the power by which God heals his people and delivers them from destruction (Ps. 107:20), but it is also personified as the strange power sent forth to accomplish Yahweh's purpose (Isa. 55:10-11). Prov. 8 presents wisdom both as the practical knowledge which guides men (vss. 5-11), governs society (vss. 12-16), and gives rewards (vss. 17-21), and as the personified power of God's creative activity (vss. 22-30).

The Targums first used "Shekinah," along with *yekara* ("glory") and *memra* ("word"), as a designation for God himself in his earthly dwelling. The Targ. of Onkelos, the Aramaic version of the Pentateuch arranged at Jabne *ca.* A.D. 100-130, replaces "name" in Deut. 12:5 with "Shekinah": "To the place which the Lord your God shall choose that his Shekinah may dwell there, unto the house of his Shekinah shall you seek." The Jerusalem Targ., a Palestinian version of the Pentateuch called Pseudo-Jonathan, relates "Shekinah," *yekara*, and *memra* to the "name" in Lev. 26:11. The Targ. of Onkelos identifies the Shekinah with the angel in the story of Hagar in Gen. 16:13 and with the face of Yahweh in Num. 6:25; Deut. 31:18. It is the Shekinah that passes before Moses in Exod. 34:6, and the Jerusalem Targ. speaks of the "glory of the Shekinah of Yahweh" in Lev. 9:6. In Num. 11 the Shekinah and the Spirit, though not identical, are closely associated.

The Aramaic for "tabernacle" is *mashkan,* formed from the same Hebrew verb (שׁכן) as that from which "Shekinah" comes, and George A. F. Knight links the idea of the "tabernacling presence" with that of the creative word or wisdom of God.

The TALMUD contains numerous references to the Shekinah, yet an interesting distribution is discovered. The Mishna, the oldest part of the Talmud compiled by Rabbi Judah the Patriarch (*ca.* A.D. 135-220), contains only two references to the Shekinah. The first says: "R. Meir said: When man is sore troubled, what says the Shekinah? My head is ill at ease, my arm is ill at ease" (Sanh. 6.5). Herbert Danby, before calling attention to the fact that the word "Shekinah" does not appear in some texts, remarks in a note that this is "an interpolated Haggadah." The second reference is: "If two sit together and words of the Law [are spoken] between them, the Shekinah rests between them" (Ab. 3.2). This raises the difficult question as to the relation between this statement and the statement of Jesus in Matt. 18:20 ("Where two or three are gathered in my name, there am I in the midst of them"), but it clearly has reference to God's presence.

Most of the references to the Shekinah are found in the HAGGADAH, the nonlegal portion of rabbinical literature, and it is here that a comprehensive expression of the immanence of the transcendent God is found. The presence of the idea in the popular literature of the Jewish people perhaps reflects the usage at the time of NT writings, especially when it is remembered that the Targums made appeal to the same type of people. God's nearness to man in a world of struggle and perplexities is stated both in a universal way and in particular ways. The universal presence of God is compared to light, a light that is said to be the food of angels (Num. Rabbah 21.16). The light is none other than God himself (15.5). In the same way that the sun in the sky illuminates the far corners of the earth, God, who dwells in the seventh heaven far above the limitations of the finite world, makes his presence known everywhere through the Shekinah (Sanh. 39a). If the earth shines with the glory of God, it is said to be the "face of the Shekinah" (ARN II), and the priestly benediction (Num. 6:25) is interpreted in a manner that identifies the face of the Lord with the "light of the Shekinah" (Num. Rabbah 11.5). When man is in trouble, there is heaviness in the head and arms of the Shekinah (Ḥag. 15b; cf. Sanh. 46a).

The particular presence of God is experienced most vividly in the sanctuary. God at first through the Shekinah spoke to Moses out of the burning bush (Exod. Rabbah 2.5), but he commanded Moses to make the tabernacle in which God could dwell (34.1). This special dwelling of God with his people was the supreme purpose for which the tabernacle was built (Num. Rabbah 13.6), and the candelabrum that burned "outside the veil" (Lev. 24:3) was a witness "that the Shekinah abides in the midst of Israel" (Shab. 22b). The statement that the day of the tabernacle's consecration was the first day of the Shekinah's existence in the universe (Shab. 85b) has reference to this special abiding of God, not to an idea that the Shekinah did not exist at all before that time.

The temple of Solomon also becomes a particular dwelling place for God. Even if God fills all space and the "heaven and the highest heaven" (I Kings 8:27) is unable to contain him, God can still descend and restrict his "Shekinah within a square cubit" (Exod. Rabbah 34.1). The windows of the temple were "narrow within but wide without" to let the light of the Shekinah illumine the world (Num. Rabbah 15.2). After the destruction of the temple the synagogue as a place of prayer and the study of the Torah is regarded as a special place for God to dwell. If ten assemble for prayer, or three sit to judge, or two sit, or even one sits, to study the Torah, "the Shekinah is in their midst" (Ber. 6a). Rabbi Simeon ben Jochai says: "Wherever the righteous go, the Shekinah goes with them" (Gen. Rabbah 86.6). And again: "Come and see how beloved are the Israelites before God, for whithersoever they journeyed in their captivity the Shekinah journeyed with them" (Bar. Meg. 29a). The Shekinah draws near to the righteous, but it departs from the sinful. At first the Shekinah dwelt in the lower regions, but between Adam and the time of Abraham it ascended, as sin increased, until it dwelt in the seventh heaven; however, because of the righteous, it descended to earth again between Abraham and Moses (Gen. Rabbah 19.7). Secret sins, pride, and pains caused to parents continue to drive the Shekinah away (Ḳid. 31a). Along with the concepts of *Ruach Hakodesh* ("Holy Spirit") and *Bath Kol* ("daughter of the voice"), the presence of God in the world and his nearness to his people was powerfully expressed by the idea of the Shekinah. It seems only a step from this belief that God could dwell in a particular place to the Christian belief that God dwelt in his fulness in Jesus Christ, but the employment of Greek terminology by the church fathers and the Jewish identification of Christians with the *Minim* (heresies) made it impossible for most Jews to take the step. The term *Minim* originally referred to the polytheism of Gnostic dualism, a heresy repeatedly condemned in early christological controversy.

The identification of CHRIST with the Shekinah is suggested in several places in the Pauline letters. In Colossians, God not only dwells in the fleshly body of Christ (1:19; 2:9), but the dwelling of Christ in the saints constitutes a spiritual body of Christ (1:18, 24; 2:19; 3:15). This dwelling of Christ in the saints described as the "riches of the glory" and as the "hope of glory" (1:27) may have reference to the Shekinah, although Lightfoot has suggested for the first phrase the "wealth of the glorious manifestation" (cf. Rom. 9:23; Eph. 1:18; 3:16). In Eph. 1:17 the "God of our Lord Jesus Christ" is parallel to the "Father of glory" to suggest "glory" as a title for Christ. Even if the genitive is here used adjectively to permit the translation "glorious Father," the term "Lord of glory," used nine times in Enoch, appears in I Cor. 2:8 as a title for Christ as the one in whom the wisdom of God is hidden. The Spirit, who makes known God's wisdom in the crucified Christ, brings freedom to those who turn to behold the "glory of the Lord" and are transformed "from one degree of glory to another" (II Cor. 3:18), and the rabbinical exegesis of Exod. 34:29-35 strongly suggests the Shekinah. Paul preached the "gospel of the glory of

Christ" (II Cor. 4:4), because God had made the light to shine out of the darkness "to give the light of the knowledge of the glory of God in the face of Christ" (vs. 6). In Romans the entrance of sin into the world causes man to "fall short of the glory of God" (3:23), but those who are justified by faith "rejoice in [the] hope of sharing the glory of God" (5:2). It was "by the glory of the Father" (6:4) that Jesus was raised from the dead, and those who live the spiritual life find the sufferings of the present unworthy to compare "with the glory that is to be revealed" (8:18). The glory which belonged to Israel (9:4) now belongs to all who are the children of Abraham by faith, because the Messiah has come and the glory of the Lord has already dawned (cf. II Macc. 2:8).

Some events in the Lukan writings are interpreted in language associated with the Shekinah. In the infancy narrative the angel Gabriel announced to Mary:

The Holy Spirit will come upon you,
and the power of the Most High will overshadow you
[ἐπισκιάσει] (Luke 1:35).

The LXX uses ἐπισιάξειν in Exod. 40:35 to describe the glory of the Lord in the tabernacle. The "glory of the Lord" shone round about the shepherds in the field when the angel appeared to them (Luke 2:9). At the Transfiguration "they saw his glory," Peter suggested that three tabernacles be built, and "a cloud came and overshadowed [ἐπισκίαξεν] them," before "they entered the cloud" and "a voice came out of the cloud" (Luke 9:32-35). The departure (ἔξοδος), about which Moses and Elijah spoke (vs. 31), was accomplished when Christ entered "into his glory" (24:26; cf. 9:26, 32) after his sufferings in Jerusalem. On the Damascus Road, Paul saw a "light from heaven, brighter than the sun," that blinded him with its radiance, and out of it a voice spoke (Acts 26:12-18; cf. 9:3-9; 22:6-11). It is not possible to demonstrate beyond doubt that the idea of the Shekinah colors the content of these narratives, but it is difficult to resist the conclusion that Hebraic roots are far deeper than the Hellenistic.

The Fourth Gospel has so many echoes of the Shekinah glory that it has been called the "Gospel of the glory." At first the theme of the tabernacling presence is prominent. Three terms found in the Targums appear in John 1:14: "The Word [memra] became flesh and dwelt [Shekinah] among us . . . ; we have beheld his glory [yekara]." The event of the Incarnation is nothing less than the glory of God pitching a tent (ἐσκήνωσεν) in human flesh. In the picture of Jesus as the dwelling place of the Spirit which descends and abides, the Ruach Hakodesh ("Holy Spirit") is associated with the tabernacle theme (John 1:33-34). The first of the seven signs (2:1-11; 4:46-54; 5:2-9; 6:4-13; 9:1-7; 11:1-14) in John's Gospel is an occasion for Jesus to manifest the glory that tabernacled in his flesh (2:11), and this is linked with the prediction of the destruction of the temple interpreted as the body of Jesus (2:21). Even if the temple of Jerusalem, long looked upon as a special dwelling for God, is destroyed, the true temple of God, the perfect presence of the Shekinah, is the body of Jesus. Later suggestions of the Shekinah

emphasize the idea of light. Num. Rabbah 15.5 bursts forth in praise of God with the words: "Thou art the light of the world." Jesus told his disciples: "I am the light of the world" (John 8:12). Readers familiar with the rabbinical ideas would not fail to make the connection. Direct evidence for a relation to the Targums is found in John 12:40-41. After the quotation of Isa. 6:10 the comment is made: "Isaiah said this because he saw his glory and spoke of him." The Targums on Isa. 6:1, 5, say: "I saw the yekara [glory] of the Lord resting on his throne—My eyes have seen the yekara [glory] of the Shekinah of the king of the ages." The very heart of the Fourth Gospel is the prayer of consecration in John 17, and there the glory of the Father in the Son comes to a climax with the petition that the disciples may behold the glory which the Father gave the Son before the foundation of the world (vs. 24). This gospel is seen in a new light when viewed against the Aramaic background.

The rest of the NT also reflects the idea of the Shekinah. Jas. 2:1 warns: "My brethren, show no partiality as you hold the faith of our Lord Jesus Christ, the Lord of glory." Christ is the Shekinah in the midst of the worshiping congregation, and his presence makes class distinctions absurd. Those who are reproached for the name of Christ are assured that the Spirit "of glory and of God" rests on them (I Pet. 4:14). On the Mount of Transfiguration, Jesus "received honor and glory from God the Father and the voice was borne to him by the Majestic Glory" (II Pet. 1:17). In the Old Covenant there was a "cherubim of glory overshadowing the mercy seat" (Heb. 9:5), but in the New Covenant the perfect revelation and the eternal purification for sin came through the Son of God who is the radiance of the glory of God (Heb. 1:3).

Bibliography. J. W. Ethridge, *The Targums of the Pentateuch* (2 vols.; 1862); R. T. Herford, *Christianity in Talmud and Midrash* (1903); H. L. Strack and P. Billerbeck, *Kommentar zum NT* (1922); G. F. Moore, *Judaism* (3 vols.; 1927); H. Danby, *The Mishnah* (1933); W. Eichrodt, *Theologie des Alten Testaments* (1933), vol. I; I. Epstein, ed., *The Babylonian Talmud* (34 vols.; 1948—); A. Cohen, *Everyman's Talmud* (1949); A. F. Knight, *From Moses to Paul* (1949); A. M. Ramsey, *The Glory of God and the Transfiguration of Christ* (1949); H. H. Freedman, *Mishnah Rabbah* (10 vols.; 1951).

D. MOODY

SHELAH shē′lə [שֵׁלָה (*in* 1 *below*), *apparently* javelin, LXX *and* NT Σαλα; שֵׁלָה (*in* 2 *below*), LXX Σηλωμ]; KJV OT SALAH sā′lə, NT SALA, in 1 below; **SHELANITES** shē′lə nīts. 1. A Shemite; father of Eber, and son of Arpachshad (Gen. 10:24; 11:12-15; I Chr. 1:18, 24); listed in Luke 3:35-36 as son of Cainan (Καιναμ; cf. LXX at OT passages; *see* KENAN).

2. The third son of Judah (Gen. 38:5, 11, 14, 26; 46:12; I Chr. 2:3); ancestor of the Shelanites (Num. 26:20; I Chr. 4:21).   L. HICKS

SHELAH, POOL OF [ברכת השלח, pool of the aqueduct]; KJV SILOAH sĭ lō′ə. A reservoir of the King's Garden in Jerusalem (Neh. 3:15), presumably the same as the King's Pool (2:14), in the lower tract of the Tyropoeon, toward the junction of this valley with the Kidron (*see* KIDRON, BROOK). It received the waters from Gihon (*see* GIHON, SPRING), by means of an aqueduct along the right bank of the Kidron. When the aqueduct was sealed off in view of the Assyrian threat, the pool was transformed so as to accommodate the water flowing from the tunnel of Hezekiah.

See also POOL; SHILOAH, WATERS OF; SILOAM; JERUSALEM § 7*b*. *See* map under SILOAM.

G. A. BARROIS

SHELEMIAH shĕl'ə mī'ə [שלמיהו, שלמיה, Y has recompensed, *or* Y has restored; Apoc. Σελεμίας]; KJV Apoc. SELEMIAS sĕl'ə mī'əs (I Esd. 9:34). Alternately: MESHELEMIAH mə— [משלמיהו].
1. A Korahite, of Levitical descent, chosen to be a gatekeeper of the sanctuary in I Chr. 23–26, which professes to give the arrangements made by David for temple officials (26:14). In 26:1 (cf. 9:21) he is called Meshelemiah.
2. Son of Cushi, and ancestor of Jehudi (Jer. 36: 14).
3. Son of Abdeel; one (LXX omits) of three men Jehoiakim sent to take Baruch and Jeremiah after the reading of the first scroll of Jeremiah's prophecies (Jer. 36:26).
4. The father of Jehucal (Jer. 37:3) or Jucal (38:1).
5. Son of Hananiah, and the father of Irijah (Jer. 37:13).
6. A son of Binnui in a list of those who put away foreign wives and their children, according to Ezra's reform (Ezra 10:39; cf. I Esd. 9:34).
7. Another son of Binnui in the list mentioned in 6 *above* (Ezra 10:41).
8. The father of Hananiah (Neh. 3:30).
9. A priest, one of three men appointed by Nehemiah to be in charge of the distribution among the Levites of tithes of produce brought to the temple (Neh. 13:13). These appointments were part of Nehemiah's action to restore cultic practice: the Levites thus were enabled to devote themselves again to the service of the temple.

Bibliography. M. Noth, *Die israelitischen Personennamen* (1928), p. 174; A. C. Welch, *The Work of the Chronicler* (1939), pp. 81-96. T. M. MAUCH

SHELEPH shē'lĭf [שלף]. A son of Joktan, and hence the name of an Arabian tribe (Gen. 10:26; I Chr. 1: 20). Since the name is mentioned just before Hazarmaweth (Hadramaut), it was evidently located in S Arabia. The word is the same as the Arabian Salaf or Salif, and occurs in Sabean inscriptions as the name of a Yemenite district. There is also a Sulaf, sixty miles N of Sanaa, the capital of Yemen. Thus, while it is impossible to fix the exact location of Sheleph, it is certain that the tribe lived somewhere in Yemen. S. COHEN

SHELESH shē'lĭsh [שלש, third(?), triplet(?); obedient *or* gentle, *according to* Arab. *salisun*(?)] (I Chr. 7:35). A head of a father's house in the tribe of Asher.

SHELOMI shĭ lō'mī [שלמי, peace(?)] (Num. 34:27). The father of the Asherite leader Ahihud, who was selected to help superintend the distribution of W

Jordanian Canaan among the tribes to occupy that territory.

Bibliography. M. Noth, *Die israelitischen Personennamen* (1928), p. 165. R. F. JOHNSON

SHELOMITH shĭ lō'mĭth [שלמית, *feminine of* שלמי, complete, *or* at peace]; KJV Apoc. ASSALIMOTH ə săl'ə mŏth. A name apparently sometimes confused with SHELOMOTH (שלמות), as illustrated in two instances: (*a*) the same man is called Shelomith in I Chr. 23:18 and Shelomoth in 24:22; (*b*) both names appear in reference to the same man in I Chr. 26:25-28. Noth suggests, with textual support in each case, that when the name refers to a man, Shelomoth is correct and Shelomith a textual error.
1. A Danite, daughter of Dibri, during the time of the wandering in the wilderness; the mother, by an Egyptian, of an unnamed man who as a sojourner went out among the Israelites and in a quarrel with an Israelite "blasphemed the Name, and cursed." He was stoned since repudiation of God whether by Israelite or by SOJOURNER was to be purged from the community (Lev. 24:11).
2. Daughter of Zerubbabel (I Chr. 3:19).
3. A Levite, the chief son of Izhar (I Chr. 23:18); called Shelomoth in I Chr. 24:22.
4. A son or daughter of Rehoboam, by his wife Maacah the daughter of Absalom (II Chr. 11:20).
5. Son of Josiphiah, head of a father's house that returned with Ezra from Babylon (Ezra 8:10, where the RSV reads, with the LXX and I Esd. 8:36, that he was of the family of Bani).

Bibliography. M. Noth, *Die israelitischen Personennamen* (1928), pp. 39, 165. T. M. MAUCH

SHELOMOTH shĭ lō'mŏth [שלמות, *see* SHELOMITH]; KJV SHELOMITH —mĭth except in I Chr. 24:22.
1. A Gershonite Levite, head of a father's house (I Chr. 23:9).
2. A Levite, son of Izhar (I Chr. 24:22). He is called Shelomith in I Chr. 23:18.
3. A descendant of Moses through Eliezer. In the account of David's arrangements for temple officials in I Chr. 23–26, Shelomoth and his brethren were in charge of all the dedicated treasures from the war spoil of Samuel, Saul, Abner, Joab, and David (26: 25-26, 28; the MT reads "Shelomith" in vs. 28).

Bibliography. A. C. Welch, *The Work of the Chronicler* (1939), pp. 81-96. T. M. MAUCH

SHELUMIEL shĭ loo'mĭ əl [שלמיאל; LXX Σαλαμιηλ, God is peace(?), *or* at peace with God(?), *or* my friend is God(?)]. Alternately: SALAMIEL sə lā'mĭ əl [Σαλαμιηλ, God is friendly(?)] (Jth. 8:1); KJV SAMAEL săm'ĭ əl. Leader of Simeon; son of Zurishaddai (Num. 1:6; 2:12; 7:36, 41; 10:19). He was one of twelve tribal leaders or deputies who assisted Moses in taking a census of Israel and in other tasks in the wilderness.

The ancestry of JUDITH is traced in Jth. 8:1 to this same person, whose name is given as Salamiel and whose father's name, as Sarasadai.

See also PRINCE.

Bibliography. M. Noth, *Die israelitischen Personennamen* (1928), p. 165. R. F. JOHNSON

SHEM shĕm [שֵׁם, *see* § 1 *below;* Σημ; Vulg. *Sem*]; KJV NT SEM sĕm. Eldest son of Noah (Gen. 5:32; I Chr. 1:4; Luke 3:36).

1. Etymology. The meaning of the name is uncertain. If originally Hebrew, it would seem to be the noun "name," "reputation," "fame." It might be a shortened form, lacking a verb or another noun as the second element (cf. personal names שְׁמִידָע, שְׁמוּאֵל, שְׁמִידָע). If originally Mesopotamian, it might be Babylonian *šumu*—"name," also used for "son."

The theory that Shem was a divine name or appellation is nowhere supported by the Genesis story.

2. In the J tradition. From the Yahwist (*see* PENTATEUCH § A) come an etiology of considerable antiquity and importance (Gen. 9:20-27) and a Shemite genealogy (10:21, 24-30).

When Noah became drunk and lay uncovered in his tent, "his youngest son" (Gen. 9:24) brought shame upon himself by seeing his father's nakedness. Shem and Japheth, by walking backward, covered their father without dishonoring themselves (vss. 20-23). When he awoke, Noah cursed Canaan—not HAM. Then he blessed "Yahweh, the God of Shem" (so MT, LXX, Targ., Pesh., Vulg., KJV), asked favor for JAPHETH (see §§ 1-2), and condemned Canaan to the menial service of the two brothers (vss. 24-27).

This etiological story indicates strongly that an earlier tradition knew Noah's three sons as Shem, Japheth, and Canaan, and that, to harmonize this version with the later tradition used by P, Ham was listed as the father of Canaan in vss. 18, 22. Further, the Shem of this story, rooted in Palestinian soil, seems quite different from the ancestor of the Mesopotamian families listed by P in 10:22.

9:25-27 is best viewed as an old ethnological piece used by J to explain why the Israelites (Shem) have to share the Promised Land (Canaan) with the Philistines (Japheth). Such was the divine will, as Noah had foreseen. The ancient ethnology thus received a valuable place in Israel's early history.

In the J genealogy Shem is the "father of all the children of Eber" (10:21; cf. vss. 25-30). He stands, therefore, as the eponymous ancestor of the Semites generally and the Hebrews specifically. *See* SEMITE; HEBREW.

3. In the P tradition. P's contribution consists primarily in linking Shem firmly to the Noah of the Flood, furnishing the statistics of his life, and expanding his narrow Palestinian locale into the arena of world history. Here Shem and his two younger brothers, Ham and Japheth, accompanied by their wives, join Noah in the ark (Gen. 5:32: 6:10; 7:13-15). After the Flood the sons share with their father in the divine covenant (9:1-17; *see* NOAH § 1). At the age of a hundred Shem begat Arpachshad, then lived five hundred years longer and had other children (11:10-11): Elam, Asshur, Lud, and Aram (10: 22; I Chr. 1:17 adds Uz, Hul, Gether, and Meshech; but cf. Gen. 10:23 and the LXX).

Bibliography. G. von Rad, *Das erste Buch Mose*, ATD, 2 (1949), 111-21.   L. HICKS

SHEMA shē′mə [שְׁמָע, he (God) has heard; Apoc. Σαμμούς]; KJV Apoc. SAMMUS săm′əs. **1.** Listed as part of the tribe of Judah in the genealogies of the Calebite-Jerahmeelite families: a son of Hebron and descendant of Caleb (I Chr. 2:43-44); possibly a geographical name: a town in the neighborhood of Hebron, perhaps the same as Eshtemoa (derived from the same stem).

2. A Reubenite, a son of Joel (I Chr. 5:8); possibly the same as Shimei or Shemaiah in vs. 4.

3. A Benjaminite, head of a father's house in Aijalon (I Chr. 8:13). In vs. 21 he is called Shimei.

4. One of the men, named without title or paternity, who stood with Ezra at the public reading of the law (Neh. 8:4; I Esd. 9:43).   T. M. MAUCH

5. A town in S Judah; probably the same as SHEBA.

SHEMA, THE shə mä′ [שְׁמַע, hear thou!]. The first word of Deut. 6:4: "Hear, O Israel . . . ," which became Judaism's confession of faith. The phrase, which probably originated during the time of Josiah (*ca.* 640-609), consists of six Hebrew words: שְׁמַע יִשְׂרָאֵל יְהוָה אֱלֹהֵינוּ יְהוָה אֶחָד. The dilemma of the translator is clear in the RSV, where four possibilities are suggested. Generally speaking, the alternative lies between an emphasis upon Yahweh's uniqueness and exclusiveness (cf. Deut. 4:39) and an emphasis upon Yahweh as an integral person, not divisible into a number of other gods or forces (cf. the Baal of Peor in Num. 25:2-3; the Baal of the covenant of Shechem in Judg. 8:33; 9:4; the Baal of Zebub, god of Ekron in II Kings 1:2-3 [NT βεελζεβούλ!]; the Baal of Tyre in I Kings 16:31-32). It is not impossible that both these distinctions are contained in the phrase. For a discussion of monotheism, *see* GOD, OT VIEW OF.

According to rabbinical tradition, the Shema originally contained only vs. 4, but was later expanded to include not only vss. 5-9 but also a second part (Deut. 11:13-21) and a third part (Num. 15:37-41). The first section includes the twofold injunction to love Yahweh utterly and to manifest this by perpetually calling to mind and inculcating his commandments. The addition of Deut. 11:13-21 serves to place this demand for obedience within the framework of blessing for its fulfilment and curse for its neglect. Num. 15:37-41 adds to the PHYLACTERIES of the first two sections the tassels (*see* TASSEL), which are also to aid in remembering the law, and concludes the whole with a statement derived from the introduction to the Decalogue (vs. 41; cf. Exod. 20:2; Deut. 5:6; *see* TEN COMMANDMENTS). Rabbinic law establishes the ancient ritual of reciting the Shema morning and evening (Deut. 6:7: ". . . when you lie down, and when you rise"), and Jewish literature contains a great deal of discussion about the forms of its use. As the classic statement of monotheism and the highest confession of Judaism, it has become a martyr's cry and an identifying mark of Jews through the centuries.

The dispute about which of the more than six hundred commandments of the Law was most important is characteristic of first-century rabbinical discussions. It was in this context that the delicate question about the "greatest commandment" was put to Jesus (Matt. 22:34-40; Mark 12:28-34). He answered with the unassailable Shema (the fuller form is in Mark 12:29-34), combining it with Lev. 19:18: "You shall love your neighbor as yourself," thus summarizing the "second table of the law"—i.e., the commandments of the Decalogue dealing with man's responsibility toward his fellows. For the complicated literary problem posed by Luke 10:27-28, see Commentaries.

Bibliography. *The Jewish Encyclopedia*, XI (1905), 266; W. Eichrodt, *Theologie des Alten Testaments*, I (1933), 85, 113; G. E. Wright, Exegesis of Deuteronomy, *IB*, II (1953), 372-75.   J. A. WHARTON

SHEMAAH shĭ mā'ə [שמעה] (I Chr. 12:3). The father of Ahiezer and Joash, who were among the disaffected Benjaminite warriors who joined the proscribed forces of David at Ziklag.

SHEMAIAH shĭ mā'yə [שמעיה, שמעיהו, Y has heard; Apoc. Σαμαίας, Σάματος, Σαμαίος]; KJV Apoc. MAMAIAS mə mā'yəs (I Esd. 8:44); SAMAIAS sə mā'yəs (I Esd. 8:39); SAMATUS —təs (I Esd. 9:34); SAMEIUS sə mē'yəs (I Esd. 9:21). Alternately: SABBAIAS să bā'yəs [Σαββαίας] (I Esd. 9:32); KJV SABBEUS să bē'əs. **1.** A chief of the tribe of Simeon (I Chr. 4:37).
2. Eponym of a Reubenite family (I Chr. 5:4).
3. Head of one of the fathers' houses of the Levites; chief of the sons of Elizaphan. In the account of the bringing of the ark from the house of Obed-edom to Zion in I Chr. 15:1-16:3, 43 (cf. II Sam. 6:12-19), he and two hundred of his brethren were among the Levites (*see* PRIESTS AND LEVITES) whom David charged with the transportation of the ark (I Chr. 15:8).
4. A Levite; son of Nethanel. He was the scribe who recorded the assignment by lot of twenty-four divisions of priests, in the account (I Chr. 23-26) of David's organization of the Levites according to their duties in the coming temple (24:6). *See* PRIESTS AND LEVITES.
5. A Levite; the eldest son of Obed-edom, and the father of valiant sons: a group of gatekeepers in David's temple arrangements (I Chr. 26:4, 6-7).
6. A prophet in the reign of Rehoboam who forbade the king to fight in order to suppress the revolt of the ten N tribes and reclaim them. The assembled warriors were to return to their homes, for Yahweh favored the revolt (I Kings 12:22; II Chr. 11:2). Since civil war continued throughout the reign of Rehoboam (I Kings 14:30), Shemaiah and his action probably are fictional. In a long insertion attached after I Kings 12:24, the LXX includes a brief version of the story of Ahijah the prophet and Jeroboam (cf. I Kings 11:29-39) and ascribes the prophetic activity to Shemaiah. The name occurs again in II Chr. 12:5, 7, in an elaboration (vss. 1, 2aβ, 3-8) inserted into the account in I Kings 14:25-28. In this elaboration the Deuteronomic interpretation of events, indicated in part by the juxtaposition of I Kings 14:22-24 and vss. 25-28, is stated explicitly in the words of the prophet Shemaiah: Judah sinned against Yahweh, so Yahweh permitted the invasion of Shishak; and when the king and princes repented, Yahweh exercised his grace by making the affliction lighter. The Chronicler concludes his account of Rehoboam by citing a history written by Shemaiah the prophet and Iddo the seer (II Chr. 12:15).

7. One of the nine Levites (cf. Deut. 6:6-9; *see also* the work of A. C. Welch in the *bibliography*) in a commission of sixteen men (of which only two were priests) sent by Jehoshaphat to teach the law in the towns of Judah (II Chr. 17:8). The story appears only in Chronicles.
8. A Levite of the family of Jeduthun; one of fourteen Levites who played a leading part in the cleansing of the temple during the reign of Hezekiah (II Chr. 29:14).
9. A member of a commission, composed of Levites and possibly priests, which distributed the first fruits, tithes, and offerings to the priests and Levites during Hezekiah's reign, according to the account in II Chr. 29-31.
10. One of the six sons of Shecaniah in a list of the descendants of David (I Chr. 3:21-22). Omit "and the sons of Shemaiah" (cf. Ezra 8:2-3), thus accounting for the number six at the end of vs. 22.
11. The father of Uriah the prophet (Jer. 26:20).
12. A leader in Babylonia; a Nehelamite; one of those among the exiles who proclaimed a speedy return from captivity. He wrote to the people in Jerusalem and to Zephaniah the priest, who was overseer of the temple, opposing Jeremiah for writing to the exiles as he had (see Jer. 29:4-7) and demanding that Jeremiah be imprisoned. Jeremiah denounced Shemaiah as a false prophet and foretold that neither he nor his descendants would live to see the Return (vss. 24, 31-32).
13. The father of Delaiah (Jer. 36:12).
14. A Levite, descendant of Merari, among those repopulating Jerusalem after the Exile (I Chr. 9:14; Neh. 11:15). According to Neh. 11:15-16, in Nehemiah's time he was one of the overseers of the noncultic affairs of the temple, such as maintenance. In the list in vss. 15-18, probably originally identical with I Chr. 9:14-16, he is called incorrectly a descendant of Bunni.
15. Another Levite who returned to Jerusalem after the Exile; a descendant of Jeduthun; the father of Obadiah (I Chr. 9:16). Perhaps he is identical with Shammua father of Abda in Neh. 11:17; the difference in names may be due to abbreviation, the longer forms having "iah" at the end: "Shammua" for "Shemaiah," and "Abda" for "Obadiah."
16. One of the chiefs of the Levites who liberally donated animals to the Levites for the celebration of the Passover held by Josiah (II Chr. 35:9).
17. A son of Adonikam; head of a father's house that returned with Ezra from the Exile (Ezra 8:13; I Esd. 8:39).
18. A leading man, one of a delegation sent by Ezra to Iddo at Casiphia to obtain Levites, when it was discovered en route that they were lacking in the group returning from Babylon (Ezra 8:16; I Esd. 8:44).
19. A priest, descended from Harim, in a list of those who put away foreign wives and their children according to Ezra's reform banning foreign marriage (Ezra 10:21; I Esd. 9:21).
20. A layman, descended from Harim, in the list mentioned in 19 *above* (Ezra 10:31; I Esd. 9:22).
21. One of the "sons of Ezora" listed among the laymen with foreign wives (I Esd. 9:34).
22. Keeper of the EAST GATE, and thus probably a Levite; son of Shecaniah. He repaired part of the

wall of Jerusalem in Nehemiah's time (Neh. 3:29).

23. Perhaps a prophet but probably a priest, since apparently he had access to the temple; son of Delaiah and descendant of Mehetabel. A prominent Jerusalemite, he was hired by Tobiah and Sanballat to fill Nehemiah with such fear of assassination that Nehemiah would go with him into the temple itself for refuge. The plot was intended to discredit Nehemiah as a coward and weaken him by the certain charge of sacrilege for intruding where only priests were allowed (Neh. 6:10).

24. The name of a priestly family occurring in three lists almost identical in outline and comparable in composition, citing: the priests who sealed the covenant in the days of Nehemiah (Neh. 10:8), the priests who returned with Zerubbabel (12:6), and the priests in the time of Joiakim (12:18).

25. A priest in the counterclockwise procession on the walls of Jerusalem during their dedication (Neh. 12:34).

26. Probably a Levite; a descendant of Asaph (Neh. 12:35).

27. A Levite musician in the counterclockwise procession on the walls of Jerusalem during their dedication (Neh. 12:36).

28. A Levite musician in the clockwise procession on the walls of Jerusalem during their dedication (Neh. 12:42).

Bibliography. A. C. Welch, *The Work of the Chronicler* (1939), pp. 55-77, 81-96, 110, 115-21, 129, 147; W. Rudolf, *Ezra und Nehemiah*, HAT (1949), p. 186; R. A. Bowman, Exegesis of Nehemiah, *IB*, III (1954), 719-21, 759, 784, 787, 794-99; W. Rudolf, *Chronikbücher*, HAT (1955), pp. 115-25, 172, 233-35, 251, 309.   T. M. MAUCH

SHEMARIAH shĕm'ə rī'ə [שמריה, שמריהו, Y has kept, preserved]; KJV SHAMARIAH shăm'— in II Chr. 11:19. **1.** One of the mighty Benjaminite warriors who joined David at Ziklag (I Chr. 12:5).

2. A son of Rehoboam (II Chr. 11:19).

3. A son of Harim in a list of those who put away foreign wives and their children according to Ezra's reform banning foreign marriage (Ezra 10:32).

4. A son of Binnui in the list mentioned in 3 *above* (Ezra 10:41).   T. M. MAUCH

SHEMEBER shĕm ē'bər [שמאבר, *in form resembles West Semitic names occurring in Hammurabi's time; cf. Su-mu-ebuḫ in Mari Texts* (ARM I, 24, 8); Samar. שמאבד; Dead Sea Genesis Apocryphon שמיאבד; Syr. שמאיר] (Gen. 14:2). King of Zeboiim; one of the five rebels defeated in the Valley of Siddim by a coalition of Eastern kings. *See* ABRAHAM.   L. HICKS

SHEMED shē'mĭd [שמד, destruction, *or* extermination; *many MSS read* שמר, Shemer] (I Chr. 8:12); KJV SHAMED shā'—. Head of a father's house of the tribe of Benjamin, descended from Shaharaim by Hushim. He built, or rather repopulated, the towns of Ono and Lod after the Exile.   T. M. MAUCH

SHEMER shē'mər [שמר, watch(?)]. Alternately: SHOMER shō'— (I Chr. 7:32); KJV SHAMER shā'— (I Chr. 6:46; 7:34). **1.** The original owner, or owners (i.e., the name may be that of a clan), of the hill upon which Omri built Samaria (I Kings 16:24).

The city was named after this clan (*shômerôn*, "belonging to Shemer").

2. An ancestor of a Levitical singer in the Jerusalem temple (I Chr. 6:46—H 6:31).

3. A remote descendant of Asher (I Chr. 7:32, 34).   J. M. WARD

SHEMIDA shĭ mī'də [שמידע, Eshmun (the Phoenician God) has known(?)]; SHEMIDAITES —dī-īts. Descendant of Manasseh, a Gileadite enumerated in the list of the second census taken by Moses in the wilderness (Num. 26:32; Josh. 17:2; I Chr. 7:19). The father of Ahian, Shechem, Likhi, and Aniam, he was the eponymous ancestor of the Shemidaites, one of the families of Manasseh to whom land was allotted by Joshua. The name has been found on eighth-century ostraca from Samaria.

Bibliography. M. Noth, *Die israelitischen Personennamen* (1928), pp. 123-24, 181; W. F. Albright, "The Site of Tirzah and the Topography of Western Manasseh," *JPOS*, XI (1931), 241-51.   R. F. JOHNSON

SHEMINITH shĕm'ə nĭth. *See* MUSIC § B1.

SHEMIRAMOTH shĭ mĭr'ə mŏth [שמירמות, name of heights *or* heavens(?); Akkad. *Sammurāmat*, goddess(?); *cf.* Σεμίραμις]. **1.** A Levite harpist among those whom David charged to provide music during the transportation of the ARK OF THE COVENANT from the house of OBED-EDOM to Zion (I Chr. 15:18, 20) and to maintain musical worship before the ark thereafter (16:5).

2. A Levite in a commission sent by JEHOSHAPHAT to teach the law in the towns of Judah (II Chr. 17:8).   T. M. MAUCH

SHEMUEL shĕm'yōō əl [שמואל, *same as* SAMUEL]. **1.** Son of Ammihud; the leader representing the tribe of Simeon in the commission appointed to divide the land of Canaan (Num. 34:20).

2. A son of Tola; head of a father's house in the tribe of Issachar (I Chr. 7:2).

3. KJV form of SAMUEL in I Chr. 6:33.   T. M. MAUCH

SHEN. KJV translation of השן (RSV JESHANAH).

SHENAZZAR shĭ năz'ər [שנאצר, *probably an error due to haplography for* שנאבאצר; Akkad. *Sin-ab-uṣur*, may Sin (moon deity) protect the father] (I Chr. 3:18). The fourth son of the exiled King Jehoiachin; probably to be identified with SHESHBAZZAR.

Bibliography. W. F. Albright, "The Date and Personality of the Chronicler," *JBL*, XL (1921), 108-10.   B. T. DAHLBERG

SHENIR. KJV alternate form of SENIR.

SHEOL shē'ōl. *See* DEAD, ABODE OF THE.

SHEPHAM shē'fəm [שפם] (Num. 34:10-11). A place not far from Riblah on the Upper Orontes, in the NE borderland of Canaan.

SHEPHATIAH shĕf'ə tī'ə [שפטיה, שפטיהו, Y has judged; Apoc. Σαφατία, Σαφαθι]; KJV Apoc. SA-

PHAT sā'făt (I Esd. 5:9); SAPHATIAS săf'ə tī'əs (I Esd. 8:34); SAPHETH sā'fĭth (I Esd. 5:33). **1.** One of the sons born to David at Hebron by one of his wives, Abital (II Sam. 3:4; I Chr. 3:3).

2. A Haruphite, one of the mighty Benjaminite warriors who joined David at Ziklag (I Chr. 12:5).

3. The leader of the tribe of Simeon during David's reign; son of Maacah (I Chr. 27:16).

4. A son of King Jehoshaphat (II Chr. 21:2).

5. A prince, son of Mattan. During the siege of Jerusalem by Nebuchadrezzar, he was one of four pro-Egyptian officials who charged Zedekiah to put Jeremiah to death because his prophecies were weakening the defenders of Jerusalem and his motives were traitorous. Unable to oppose them, Zedekiah handed Jeremiah over to them, and they tried to eliminate Jeremiah by leaving him to die in the bottom of a cistern (Jer. 38:1).

6. Founder of a family, of which 372 members returned from Babylonia with Zerubbabel (Ezra 2:4; Neh. 7:9), and 81 more with Ezra (Ezra 8:8). In I Esdras the respective numbers are 472 (5:9) and 71 (8:34).

7. Head of a family of SOLOMON'S SERVANTS which returned from Babylonia with Zerubbabel (Ezra 2:57; Neh. 7:59).

8. An ancestral eponym of the family of Meshullam, in a list of the Benjaminite families repopulating Jerusalem after the Exile (I Chr. 9:8).

9. An ancestral eponym of a Judahite family, descended from Perez, inhabiting Jerusalem in the time of Nehemiah (Neh. 11:4).   T. M. MAUCH

SHEPHELAH shǐ fē'lə [שׁפלה, lowland; Apoc. Σεφηλά]; KJV Apoc. SEPHELA sǐ—. Alternately: LOWLAND. A foothill region between the Philistine plain and the Judean highlands, severed from the latter by a series of longitudinal valleys.

The term designating this district appears twenty times in the Hebrew text of the OT. Ten times in the RSV it is transliterated "Shephelah"; in Joshua (eight times) and in Deut. 1:7; Judg. 1:9; Zech. 7:7 it is translated "lowland." The KJV translates it variously by "vale," "valley," "plain," "low plains," and "low country."

Despite this variety in translation, however, with the exception of Josh. 11:2, 16b (which seem to designate a similar "Israelite Shephelah" of low, rocky hills situated between the headlands of Carmel and the edge of the highlands of Samaria), all appearances of the term refer to the foothill district W of the Judean highlands. That a specific region is intended is indicated by the frequent OT reference to the Shephelah in company with the Negeb and the hill country, as one of the major geographical divisions of Judah (Deut. 1:7; Josh. 10:40; 12:8; 15:33; Judg. 1:9; Jer. 17:26; 32:44; 33:13). Further definiteness is given to this regional significance by references which distinguish between the Shephelah and the plain (II Chr. 26:10) or the seacoast (Deut. 1:7), or between the Shephelah and the coastal territory normally occupied by the Philistines (II Chr. 28:18; Obad. 19). This distinction is recognized in I Maccabees, which in one reference locates the town of Adida (see HADID) in the Shephelah (12:38) and in another describes it as "facing the plain" (13:13), and is also corroborated in the Mishna (Jerusalem

Sheb. IX.2), which locates LYDDA on the line of separation between the two sections.

The cities listed by the OT in the Shephelah (Josh. 15:33-42; II Chr. 28:18), insofar as they have been definitely located, are appropriately situated in this foothill district, with only Josh. 15:45-47 raising any question at this point. These latter verses refer exclusively to the Philistine coastland and have neither introduction nor summary characteristic of the regional listings which precede and follow them. This disruption of the general pattern of presentation, and their obvious and direct disagreement with the import of other passages, suggests that these verses either are out of place or imply an elasticity in regional definition which was not followed in other periods.

The extent of the Shephelah in the *Onomasticon* of Eusebius includes "all the low country about Eleutheropolis [Beit Jibrin] toward the north and west." The OT permits more definiteness and requires more inclusiveness. From the OT lists of cities ascribed to the region, its N and S limits are approximately defined by the Valley of Aijalon and the Wadi el Hesi, the latter leading past the great fortress of Eglon toward Debir in the hill country. However, for all practical purposes, Lachish on the Wadi Qubeiba became the chief fortress on the S frontier of the district. The northernmost Shephelah town cited is Adida (I Macc. 12:38), which served as a guardian of a N approach to the Valley of Aijalon.

A series of longitudinal valleys forming a "moat" of Senonian chalk severed the Shephelah's broad Eocene hills from the Cenomanian bulwark of the Judean mountains and made this a distinct district. Compared with the Judean highlands, which commonly range in height from two thousand to three thousand feet, this is a "lowland" region—its hills averaging from five hundred to eight hundred feet, but reaching a maximum of fifteen hundred feet in the S. The Shephelah, therefore, was not an integral part of the Judean highlands.

As a detached buffer zone between mountain ridge and coastal plain, it served as Judah's first line of defense against the Philistines and all who sought to attack the country from the W. Conquest of this region, however, was but a necessary preliminary to assault on the longitudinal moat and steep mountain scarp which served as the chief barrier to ascent into the hill country. This narrow zone of demarcation was Judah's true defense and, in keeping with its destiny, was dotted with a line of fortified towns.

A series of wide valleys cross the Shephelah horizontally and, as narrow defiles, ascend into the mountains beyond. These valleys form the natural routes by which access is gained into the Judean range. They were the avenues along which moved the tides of commerce and conquest, and near their termini were located some of the country's strongest fortresses; apart from them the history of Judah is not intelligible. From N to S they are Aijalon, Sorek, Elah, Zephathah (Zeita), and Qubeiba (Josh. 10:12; Judg. 16:4; I Sam. 17:2; II Chr. 14:10).

In addition to its strategic significance, the Shephelah was agriculturally important. The rich, red soil of its cross-valleys produced grain in abundance, and on its intervening slopes flourished olive and sycamore trees. So numerous were the latter that mere reference to their quantity served as a simile for a great plenty (I Kings 10:27; II Chr. 1:15; 9: 27; see also I Chr. 27:28). Grapes also flourished, and in some areas there was grass sufficient for grazing considerable herds (II Chr. 26:10). All in all, it was a very pleasant and temperate region, dotted with cities, and having neither the oppressive heat of the coastland in summer nor the penetrating chill of the highlands in winter.

Bibliography. G. A. Smith, *The Historical Geography of the Holy Land* (1931), pp. 197-240; F.-M. Abel, *Géographie de la Palestine*, I (1933), 416-18; G. E. Wright and F. V. Filson, *The Westminster Historical Atlas to the Bible* (1956), p. 19; D. Baly, *The Geography of the Bible* (1957), pp. 142-47.

                         W. H. MORTON

SHEPHER, MOUNT shē'fər [שפר הר] (Num. 33: 23-24); KJV SHAPHER shā'—. A stopping place of the Israelites in the wilderness. The location is unknown.

SHEPHERD. *See* SHEEP.

SHEPHERD OF HERMAS. *See* HERMAS, SHEPHERD OF.

SHEPHO shē'fō [שפו; LXX B Σωφ, LXX E Σωρ] (Gen. 36:23). Alternately: SHEPHI —fī [שפי; LXX A Σωφαρ, LXX B Σωβ] (I Chr. 1:40). Ancestor of a Horite subclan in Edom; fourth son of clan chief Shobal.

SHEPHUPHAM shĭ fū'fəm [שפופם, serpent(?)] (Num. 26:39); KJV SHUPHAM shoo'fäm. Alternately: SHEPHUPHAN shĭ fū'fən [שפופן] (I Chr. 8:5); SHUPPIM shŭp'ĭm [שפים, שפם] (I Chr. 7:12, 15); SHUPHAMITES shoo'fə mīts [שופמי] (Num. 26:39). A Benjaminite. The complicated and evidently disarranged Benjaminite genealogies in Gen. 46; Num. 26; I Chr. 7–8 present a varied pattern in respect to the name Shephupham. Although the name occurs in this form only in Num. 26:39, where it is the name of a son of Benjamin, the almost identical name Shephuphan appears in I Chr. 8:5, but here as a descendant, not a son, of Benjamin. In addition to this resemblance, the Benjaminite genealogies exhibit a striking pattern of "twin names" which incorporate some of the syllables of "Shephupham": Muppim, Huppim (Gen. 46:21); Shephupham, Hupham (Num. 26:39); Shuppim, Huppim (I Chr. 7:12); Shephuphan, Huram (I Chr. 8:5). These and other observations have led some scholars to conclude that the name Shupham (שופם) stood originally in the Benjaminite genealogies in Gen. 46; Num. 26; I Chr. 8, either as a son or as a grandson of Benjamin. The occurrence in I Chr. 7:12 is the result of alterations in what was once a Zebulunite list.

See also BECHER.

Bibliography. M. Noth, *Die israelitischen Personennamen* (1928), pp. 258-59.   R. F. JOHNSON

SHERAH. KJV form of SHEERAH.

SHERD. *See* POTSHERD; POTTERY.

SHEREBIAH shĕr'ə bī'ə [שרביה, Yahu has sent scorching heat(?); Akkad. *išribijama* (*a proper name*), *šarrabu* (*a demon*)]; KJV Apoc. ASEBEBIA ə sĕb'ə-bī'ə; ESEBRIAS ē'sə brī'əs; SARABIAS săr'ə bī'əs.

1. The "man of discretion," son of Mahli, who was provided for temple service during Ezra's encampment, and to whom the vessels of the sanctuary were entrusted (Ezra 8:18, 24; I Esd. 8:47, 54).

2. A Levite (according to I Esd. 9:48 and the Vulg.) who attended Ezra's public reading of the law (Neh. 8:7), shared in its exposition (9:4-5), and was a witness to the covenant renewal (10:12—H 10:13).

3. A Levite who accompanied Zerubbabel in the return from exile (Neh. 12:8) and became a chief of that rank (vs. 24). Some scholars believe that the name does not belong in this period but has been misplaced from Nehemiah's to Zerubbabel's time.

                         J. M. WARD

SHERESH shĭr'ĕsh [שרש, root(?); *cf.* Arab. *sarisun*, clever, *or* weak(?)] (I Chr. 7:16). A family of the tribe of Manasseh.

SHEREZER. KJV form of SHAREZER in Zech. 7:2.

SHESHACH shē'shăk. KJV translation of ששך, which is probably a cryptogram for BABYLON (so RSV; Jer. 25:26; 51:41). *See* ATHBASH.

SHESHAI shē'shī [ששי]. One of the three sons of Anak, or "giants," residing in Hebron when the Israelite spies reconnoitered the land (Num. 13:22; Josh. 15:14; Judg. 1:10). Named together with Ahiman and Talmai as a descendant of Anak, Sheshai was defeated in Hebron by the invading Israelites. The name Sheshai may be an abbreviated form of a once complete name, now reduced to a single reduplicated consonant.

Bibliography. M. Noth, *Die israelitischen Personennamen* (1928), p. 41.   R. F. JOHNSON

SHESHAN shē'shăn [ששן, *a short name formed by duplicating an abbreviation of a full name now unidentifiable; probably a name of endearment* (*cf.* bibliography)]. Head of a family in a genealogical list of the families descended from Jerahmeel, presented within a list of the descendants of Judah (I Chr. 2:31). According to subsequent verses, Sheshan had only daughters, one of whom he gave in marriage to his Egyptian slave Jarha (I Chr. 2:34-35). In vss. 34-41 the descent of Elishama (vs. 41) is being traced; his ancestor Sheshan is identified with Sheshan the Jerahmeelite, and this places Elishama in the line of Judah.

Bibliography. M. Noth, *Die israelitischen Personennamen* (1928), pp. 40-41.   T. M. MAUCH

SHESHBAZZAR shĕsh băz'ər [ששבצר, *apparently corrupted from* שנאבצר; Akkad. *Sin-ab-uṣur*, Sin (the moon deity) protect the father; Apoc. Σαναβάσ-σαρος]; KJV Apoc. SANABASSAR săn'ə băs'ər (I Esd. 2:12, 15); SANABASSARUS —ə rəs (I Esd. 6: 18, 20). A Babylonian Jew and "prince [*nāśî*] of Judah" (Ezra 1:8) with whom the first exiles returned to Jerusalem from Babylonia under the edict of Cyrus (538 B.C.; Ezra 1:11; *cf.* vss. 1-4). The "treasures of the house of the LORD" which had been carried off by Nebuchadnezzar (II Kings 24:13) were consigned to Sheshbazzar to be taken back with him to Jerusalem (Ezra 1:7-11). He was, moreover, the first "governor" (*peḥâ;* 5:14) of re-established Judah, now a province in the Persian Empire, and made an initial attempt—evidently abortive—at rebuilding the Jerusalem temple (vs. 16). If, as seems probable, he is to be identified with the "Shenazzar" of I Chr. 3: 18 (*see below and bibliography*)—a son of the exiled king of Judah, Jehoiachin—he was then a prince of the Davidic line and an uncle of Zerubbabel, who succeeded him as "governor" of Judah (cf. Ezra 5: 1-2; Hag. 1:1; the political denotation of the title *peḥâ* is somewhat ambiguous; *see* GOVERNOR). An inscription from the reign of Nebuchadnezzar refers to "the 5 sons of the king of Judah [Jehoiachin]," one of whom presumably would be *Sin-ab-uṣur* (Sheshbazzar), but unfortunately the sons are not mentioned there by name. *See bibliography.*

Beyond the foregoing account nothing else is presently known of Sheshbazzar. In the tradition his career has been overshadowed by that of his nephew and successor, ZERUBBABEL, who completed the rebuilding of the temple and became also the object of messianic expectations in Judah (Hag. 2:20-23; Zech. 4:6-10).

Zerubbabel's public career, which certainly began under Darius and not under the earlier Cyrus (Ezra 5:1-2; Hag. 1:1), is represented nevertheless by the self-contradictory and confusing narratives of the Chronicler in the book of Ezra as commencing under Cyrus (Ezra 3:1-4:4; cf. 2:2). Such confusion must represent the author's ignorance of the true chronology of Zerubbabel's work, or else his intentional disregard for it; or it suggests, even further, that he wrongly assumed Sheshbazzar and Zerubbabel to be the same person. In fact, many biblical interpreters down to the present time have argued that the two names belonged to one individual (*see bibliography*). The Jewish historian Josephus (*ca.* A.D. 100) scarcely relieves the confusion, associating the two names ambiguously in the same contexts but offering no indication of the relationship between them (Antiq. XI.i-iv).

Initially there seems to be reason for identifying Sheshbazzar with Zerubbabel. Both were called "governor" of Judah (Ezra 5:14; Hag. 1:1); both are identified with the return under Cyrus, if the account in Ezra is read uncritically (Ezra 1:11; 2:2; cf. 3:1-2); both are described as initiating the temple reconstruction (cf. Ezra 5:16 with 3:2, 8; 5:2; Hag. 1; Zech. 4: 9); and while I Esd. 6:18 relates that the temple vessels were consigned "to Zerubbabel and Sheshbazzar," thus clearly distinguishing between them, some MSS render this passage without an "and" between the names, supplying argument again for their identification. It has been supposed that Sheshbazzar was this individual's Babylonian name and Zerubbabel his Jewish name, after the analogy of Daniel and his three friends (Dan. 1:7).

A greater degree of probability attaches itself, however, to arguments for distinguishing between Sheshbazzar and Zerubbabel as two separate persons. Inscriptions from the neo-Babylonian period show that the relatively common name Zerubbabel is Baby-

lonian, while at the same time its syntactical form is not typical to Hebrew names generally. That the Jew Zerubbabel should have had two Babylonian names is therefore puzzling. Moreover, the books of Haggai and Zechariah are on critical grounds more trustworthy historically than the work of the Chronicler in Ezra-Nehemiah, and the former books clearly associate the public career of Zerubbabel with the reign of Darius, making no reference of any work of his earlier under Cyrus. Even the passages in Ezra 2:2; 4:1-4:4 do not explicitly place the beginning of Zerubbabel's work in the reign of Cyrus, while the material there seems clearly to describe events under Darius. More puzzling is it, if the two were really one, that no explicit identification of the two is made anywhere (unless I Esd. 6:18 be so emended; *see above*). There is, finally, the strong probability that the name Sheshbazzar is a corruption of "Shenazzar" due to a plausibly explained scribal error (*see bibliography*), which would identify Sheshbazzar as a son of the captive king, Jehoiachin (I Chr. 3:17-18), and therefore as an uncle of Zerubbabel, grandson of Jehoiachin. The LXX form, Σαναβάσσαρος (I Esd. 2:12, 15; 6:18, 20), reflects the original full Hebrew transliteration of the Akkadian (i.e., Babylonian, in this case) *Sin-ab-uṣur*, from which "Shenazzar" (שנאצר; I Chr. 3:18) is written defectively.

Accordingly, the major significance of Sheshbazzar lies in the fact that Cyrus the Persian ruler delegated authority again in Judah to a scion of the house of David, thus helping to prepare the way for hope in the restoration of the old kingdom, a hope which did indeed flourish in the days of Zerubbabel his successor.

Bibliography. On the identity of Sheshbazzar and the etymology of his name, see W. F. Albright, "Date and Personality of the Chronicler," *JBL,* XL (1921), 108-10; cf. also R. H. Charles, Introduction to I Esdras, *Apoc. and Pseudep. of the OT,* I (1913), 15-17. For a careful textual history of the name, see C. C. Torrey, *Ezra Studies* (1910), pp. 136-38. Detailed arguments in favor of the identification of Sheshbazzar with Zerubbabel are given in J. Gabriel, *Zorobabel* (1927; in German), pp. 48-79.

The inscription referring to Jehoiachin and his sons has been published by E. F. Weidner, "Jojachin, König von Juda," *Mélanges Syriens offerts à Monsieur René Dussaud,* II (1939), 925-26.

General: E. L. Curtis, *Chronicles,* ICC (1910), p. 101; L. W. Batten, *Ezra and Nehemiah,* ICC (1913), pp. 69-71; W. O. E. Oesterley and T. H. Robinson, *A History of Israel,* II (1932), 77-81, 89-90; W. F. Albright, *The Biblical Period* (1950), p. 49.

B. T. DAHLBERG

SHETH shĕth [שֵׁת, sons of tumult, *or* sons of pride (*reading* שְׁאֵת)]. **1.** The term "sons of Sheth" (Num. 24:17) is a descriptive term for Moabites. Their defeat at the hands of an expected Israelite ruler is foreseen in the oracle of Balaam (Num. 24:15-19).

2. KJV form of SETH in I Chr. 1:1.

SHETHAR shē'thär [שֵׁתָר] (Esth. 1:14). One of the seven princes of Persia under King Ahasuerus, and next to him in rank. The (Aramaic) Second Targum of Esther represents this individual as "from India." *See bibliography.*

Bibliography. On text, etymology, etc., see L. B. Paton, *Esther,* ICC (1908), pp. 68, 152-53.   B. T. DAHLBERG

SHETHAR-BOZENAI shē'thär bŏz'ə nī [שְׁתַר בּוֹזְנַי,
possibly delivering the kingdom (*see bibliography*)];
KJV SHETHAR-BOZNAI —bŏz'nī. Alternately:
Apoc. SATHRABUZANES săth'rə bū'zə nēz
[Σαθραβουζάνης] (I Esd. 6:3–7:1). An official, perhaps a royal scribe, in the Persian government for
the province "Beyond the River" (Trans-Euphratia),
which included Palestine. With Tattenai the governor, he wrote to the Persian king Darius inquiring
about the authority given to the Jews to rebuild the
temple at Jerusalem. The king's reply contained a
decree admonishing them to encourage and assist
this work (Ezra 5:3–6:13; cf. I Esd. 6:3–7:2).

Bibliography. On etymology, see R. A. Bowman, *Exegesis
of Ezra, IB,* III (1954), 608.   B. T. DAHLBERG

SHEVA shē'və [שְׁוָא, vanity(?)]; *or* like—*i.e.,* like the
father, *or* like the brother (*cf.* Arab. *sawā'un*)]. **1.** The
secretary in the list of David's administrative officials. He was in charge of the drafting and custody
of official documents and perhaps court records of
events (II Sam. 20:25). Each time this secretary appears, the name is different: Seraiah (II Sam. 8:17),
Shavsha (I Chr. 18:16), Shisha (I Kings 4:3). The
names in the LXX present another set of variations.
2. A man or family in the genealogy of Caleb;
founder of Machbenah and Gibea (I Chr. 2:49).

Bibliography. M. Noth, *Die israelitischen Personennamen*
(1928), p. 222; G. B. Caird, *Exegesis of II Samuel, IB,* II
(1953), 1091, 1154-55.   T. M. MAUCH

SHEWBREAD. *See* BREAD OF THE PRESENCE.

SHIBAH shī'bə [שִׁבְעָה, oath] (Gen. 26:33); KJV
SHEBAH shē'bə. A supposed name of a well dug
by Isaac; the source of the name Beer-sheba. This
tradition is in contrast to the account in Gen. 21:25-
31; in both cases a patriarch makes a covenant with
the king of Gerar, but in the case of Abraham the
name is derived from the seven lambs that were given
to seal the bargain, and in the latter from the oath
that Isaac and Abimelech took. Apparently there
were two cities which became one: SHEBA and BEER-
SHEBA; they are represented by the modern Tell es-
Saba' and Bir es-Saba', two miles apart. Since Beer-
sheba eventually became famous as the name of the
site, it was connected with both stories; but obviously it fits in better with the Isaac account.
                    S. COHEN

SHIBBOLETH shĭb'ə lĭth [שִׁבֹּלֶת, flowing stream,
or ear of grain; Ugar. *šblt;* Akkad. *šubultu, see below*]
(Judg. 12:6). The password whose mispronunciation
was used by the Gileadite sentries of Jephthah at
the fords of the Jordan to detect enemy Ephraimites.
This word or a cognate form is found in Ugaritic,
Phoenician, Judeo-Aramaic, and Syriac. Its meaning
was either "river" (Isa. 27:12; Ecclus. 4:26), "flood"
(Ps. 69:2, 15—H 69:3, 16), "ear of grain" (Job 24:
24; שִׁבֹּלִים in Gen. 41:5-7, 22-24, 26-27; Ruth 2:2;
Isa. 17:5), or "branches (or) bunch of twigs (of olive
trees)" (שִׁבֹּלִי in Zech. 4:12).

In the story the word could have been chosen for
either meaning. The meaning "flood" would have
been appropriate, although "ear of grain" as a
symbol of an agricultural goddess or a sign of the

zodiac could have been meant. Even so, it was the pronunciation which was most significant. In Gilead,
Jephthah's army had defeated the Ephraimites. Then
in order to prevent these one-time W Jordan soldiers
from escaping, every person was stopped as he attempted to cross the river and was asked by
a Gileadite sentry whether he was an Ephraimite.
Pretending to be a Gileadite or perhaps a Canaanite
—anything but what he was— each Ephraimite would
reply, "No." Then, required to say "Shibboleth"
(שִׁבֹּלֶת), if instead he said "Sibboleth" (סִבֹּלֶת) because
"he could not pronounce it right," he had betrayed
himself as an Ephraimite and was slain on the spot.

That difference in dialect is the basis of the story
is clear, but exactly what phonetics is involved may
still be an unsolved problem. On the face of it, the
distinction is simply between "sh" and "s." The
Ephraimites pronounced words beginning with "sh"
as though they began with "s," according to custom
common—e.g., in Arabic pronunciation of Hebrew
words (or cf. common Greek and English rendering of Hebrew names—e.g., שִׁמְשׁוֹן [shimshôn] becomes Σαμψών and "Samson"). In the Hebrew writing of the time this change could be expressed only
by writing the consonant *Sameq* (ס), "s," instead of
Shin (שׁ), "sh," for the system of pointing had not yet
been invented by which *Shin* (שׁ), "sh," may be written *Sin* (שׂ), "ś." While there is real phonetic distinction between these two unvoiced sibilants, the
palatal *Sin,* "ś," and the coronal-alveolar *Sameq,* "s,"
it would be much less distinguishable than that between either of these "s" sounds and "sh."

The point of the story may not be, however, that
the Ephraimites betrayed themselves by unwarily
saying "s" for "sh." Since both sounds were known
to all W Semites, under the circumstances the fugitives would have carefully imitated the sentry's word.
The point is that they could not pronounce it right.
Therefore, it is possible that whereas the Gileadites
in this case pronounced the "sh," unvoiced palato-
alveolar sibilant, as "th," unvoiced coronal-alveolar
spirant or fricative, the Ephraimites could not say
"th." Evidence from Phoenician, Aramaic, Old Akkadian, and elsewhere suggests both that these two
sounds were occasionally merged or alternatively
used and also that "th" was written as "sh." Thus
what is written as "sh" may have been pronounced
by the E Jordan peoples as "th," but, as the "th"
sound had been lost by the W Jordan peoples, they
could pronounce it only as "s," a phonetic difficulty
familiar today when Turks or Persians pronounce
Arabic *thalith* as *salis.*

This story constitutes evidence for early dialect
differences between E and W Jordan Israelites. Such
differences between N and S Palestinian Hebrew
dialects are known from comparison of the Samaritan
Pentateuch and Israelite ostraca with the primarily
Judean MT. The Danites recognized Micah's Levite
by his accent (Judg. 18:3; cf. Peter's Galilean accent in Matt. 26:73).

The use in wartime of speech peculiarities to detect fellow countrymen has been noted in Syrians'
replying "*Jemel*" instead of "*Gamel*," and their use
to discern enemies, in Frenchmen betraying themselves to Sicilians by pronouncing *ceci e ciceri* as *sesi
e siseri.*

This story is the origin of the word "shibboleth" as an English common noun meaning a criterion or test, as (a) a word or saying distinguishing adherents of a party or sect, or as (b) a sound in a given word which distinguishes persons of a particular nationality or district, or as (c) a peculiarity of speech distinguishing certain clans or groups.

Bibliography. R. Marcus, "The Hebrew Sibilant Sin and the Name Yisra'el," *JBL*, LX (1941), 141-50; E. A. Speiser, "The Shibboleth Incident (Judges 12:6)," *BASOR*, LXXXV (1942), 10-13; L. Koehler, *Lexicon in Veteris Testamenti Libros* (1953), p. 942.   C. F. KRAFT

SHIBMAH. KJV form of SIBMAH. ·

SHICRON. KJV form of SHIKKERON.

SHIELD. *See* WEAPONS AND IMPLEMENTS OF WAR § 4a.

SHIELD-BEARER [נשא הצנה] (I Sam. 17:7, 41). A warrior's attendant having the duty of carrying his master's shield. *See* ARMOR-BEARER.

SHIGGAION shĭ gā'yŏn, **SHIGIONOTH** shĭg'ĭ-ō'nŏth. *See* MUSIC § B1.

SHIHON. KJV form of SHION.

SHIHOR shī'hôr [שיחור, שחור, שחר]; KJV alternately SIHOR sī'—. A body of water in NE Egypt.

The term occurs four times in the MT as a geographical designation, intimately related to Egypt. A comparison of the LXX and the MT shows clearly that the name was not understood (if one accepts the MT as correct) by the translators of the LXX: (a) in Josh. 13:3 the LXX reads ἀοικήτου, "uninhabited"; (b) in I Chr. 13:5 the LXX has ὁρίων, "boundaries"; (c) in Isa. 23:3 comparison of the MT and the LXX requires special study; (d) in Jer. 2:18 the LXX has Γηων, which is known elsewhere (Gen. 2:12) as a transcription of Hebrew *Gîhôn*.

Shihor, which is localized in the passages cited above as being E of Egypt or belonging to Egypt, is thus generally identified with Egyptian *P³-š-Ḥr*, the Pool of Horus. The precise location of this Egyptian body of water is difficult, since it is closely connected to the problem of Per-Rameses (*see* ZOAN; PITHOM). Papyrus Anastasi III contains an encomium on this frequently mentioned residence of Ramses II in which *P³-š-Ḥr* is mentioned in parallelism with *P³-ṭwfy*, the Papyrus Marshes. Gardiner suggests that the latter name refers either to the swamps between Panamun (Diospolis Inferior, Tell el-Balamun) and the sea or to the neighborhood of Lake Menzaleh. If one accepts the identification of Per-Rameses with Tanis, or even the alternative site of Qantir *ca.* 12½ miles to the S, the approximate location of Shihor is secured. More specifically, Shihor (= *P³-š-Ḥr*) probably refers to the lower reaches of the Bubastite or Pelusiac Nile arm.

Bibliography. A. H. Gardiner, "The Delta Residence of the Ramessides," *JEA*, 5 (1918), 251-52; "The Geography of the Exodus," *JEA*, 10 (1924), 93.   T. O. LAMBDIN

SHIHOR-LIBNATH shī'hôr lĭb'năth [שיחור לבנת]. A place on the S boundary of Asher (Josh. 19:26).

It is sometimes identified with the Crocodile River, the Nahr ez-Zerqa, which flows into the Mediterranean six miles S of Dor. It is also possible that two sites, Shihor and Libnath, are intended, both of which remain unidentified.   G. W. VAN BEEK

SHIKKERON shĭk'ə rŏn [שכרון, drunkenness; *or possibly the plant,* Syr. שכרונא, henbane; σάκχαρον (*cf.* Jos. Antiq. III.vii.6; Vulg. *Sechrona*)]; KJV SHICRON shĭk'rŏn. A village on Judah's N border, rather near the Mediterranean Sea (Josh. 15:11). The site is probably Tell el-Ful, just N of the Valley of Sorek (*see* SOREK, VALLEY OF) and *ca.* three miles NW of Khirbet el-Muqanna (EKRON).

Bibliography. Y. Aharoni, "The Northern Boundary of Judah," *PEQ* (1958), pp. 27-31.   V. R. GOLD

SHILHI shĭl'hī [שלחי, javelin-thrower(?)] (I Kings 22:42; II Chr. 20:31). The maternal grandfather of King Jehoshaphat of Judah.

SHILHIM shĭl'hĭm [שלחים] (Josh. 15:32). A city in the S of Judah, not far from Ziklag. In the parallel passage in Josh. 19:6 it is called SHARUHEN and assigned to Simeon; in I Chr. 4:31 it is called Shaaraim. Since Egyptian texts invariably represent the Canaanite "l" by "r," it is possible that Shilhim is the Canaanite form of the name.   S. COHEN

SHILLEM shĭl'əm [שלם, requited, recompensed (*after the death of an older child?*); *see below*] (Gen. 46:24; Num. 26:49); **SHILLEMITES** —ə mīts (Num. 26:49). The fourth son of Naphtali; ancestral head of the Shillemites. The form of the name varies: Samar. שלום; LXX Συλλημ, Σελλημ, Σελλη; Syr. שלום, שלום (I Chr. 7:13; *see* SHALLUM).

Bibliography. M. Noth, *Die israelitischen Personennamen* (1928), p. 174.   L. HICKS

SHILOAH, WATERS OF shī lō'ə [מי השלח; LXX Σ(ε)ιλωάμ, Σιλωά] (Isa. 8:6). An aqueduct in Jerusalem. *See* SILOAM.

*****SHILOH** shī'lō. **1.** שלה, שלו, שילו. A city in Ephraim located N of Bethel and E of the main road from Shechem to Jerusalem (Judg. 21:19). It was an important Israelite center where the ark of the covenant and the tabernacle remained from the time of Joshua until the days of Samuel. A resident of Shiloh was a SHILONITE. A village N of Shiloh bore the name TAANATH-SHILOH.

Shiloh was identified with Khirbet Seilun,* *ca.* ten miles NE of Bethel, by E. Robinson, who visited the place in 1838; Eusebius, Jerome, and other early sources made the same identification. This identification, based upon surface exploration and the similarity of the ancient and modern names, was confirmed by the excavations of a Danish expedition at Seilun in 1926, 1929, and 1932. Although the excavations were never completed and much remains to be done, evidence of occupation by the Hebrews, during the periods when the OT refers to such occupation, was found. There were traces of occupation in the Middle Bronze period (*ca.* 2100-1600), but the archaeologists uncovered no evidence of a Canaanite city during the Late Bronze period (*ca.* 1600-1200).

The Israelites were the first to build extensively at this site, although a primitive Canaanite high place may have once existed there. The temple (I Sam. 1:9; 3:3) could not be located, but traces of a city wall and the remains of a synagogue and an early Christian church suggest that the traditions concerning Joshua, Eli, and Samuel at Shiloh were kept alive by pilgrimages to the city in later periods. Fig. SHI 44.

Shiloh was a suitable location for the Hebrews on their entrance into the land of Canaan, but less desirable in later periods when strategy required a control of the highways and more extensive farming areas. It is located on a low elevation overshadowed by hills on all sides except at the SW. Pastures and a water supply nearby were available, but the terrain prevented it from being easily defended against enemies.

The reasons for Joshua's choice of Shiloh as a headquarters following the residence at Gilgal are not clear (Josh. 14:6; 18:1); attempts to explain the move in terms of Jacob's remark in Gen. 49:10 are not convincing. Unlike Shechem and Bethel, which had figured in the traditions of the patriarchs, Shiloh appears to have had no significance prior to the Conquest. Its comparative remoteness and the absence of Canaanite occupation at the time may have recommended it as a political and religious center for the Israelite invaders.

In the time of Joshua, Shiloh was the scene of an assembly, and the tent of meeting was set up there (Josh. 18:1). From it representatives of the tribes set out to survey the land, and after they had returned to Shiloh with a written description of the region,

Courtesy of Harriet-Louise H. Patterson
44. Setting of Shiloh (modern Seilun)

Joshua cast lots to apportion the territory (Josh. 18:8-10; 19:51; for Shiloh as both a military and a religious center, see Josh. 22:9, 12, 29). Joshua's dates are uncertain, but there is archaeological evidence of the occupation of Shiloh as early as 1200 B.C. and continuing until *ca.* 1050 B.C., when the city was probably destroyed by the Philistines.

During the period of the judges, cities other than Shiloh began to assume importance, although the reference to the ark of the covenant as located at Bethel is either a late tradition or may indicate merely that the ark had been removed temporarily from Shiloh (Judg. 20:26-27). Judg. 18:31 implies that the temple remained at Shiloh for a long time. It was a shrine to which regular pilgrimages were made: "Behold, there is the yearly feast of the LORD at Shiloh" (Judg. 21:19). References to the dances of the daughters of Shiloh, and to the action of the Benjaminites who came from the vineyards nearby to seize them as wives, suggest the existence of some type of fertility cult at the city (vs. 21). The report of the bringing of four hundred young virgins to Shiloh following the defeat of Jabesh-gilead is also suggestive of such a cult, although the purpose of the narrative in both instances is to explain how the men of Benjamin were able to secure wives after their own had been killed in battle with other Israelites.

Further information about Shiloh can be gleaned from the traditions concerning the visit of Elkanah and Hannah to the city (I Sam. 1:1-2). It is not clear whether the man's custom of going to Shiloh "year by year" for the purpose of worship and to sacrifice implies an annual festival at Shiloh, or merely a pilgrimage that might occur at any time of the year. However, the references to Hannah's desire for a child (I Sam. 1:11), Eli's suspicion that she was drunk (vs. 13), her anxiety lest she be regarded as a base woman (בַּת־בְּלִיָּעַל; vs. 16), and the conduct of Eli's sons with the women who served at the shrine (2:22) suggest the presence of a Canaanite type of fertility cult at Shiloh.

The traditions concerning Eli's virtue, the Nazirite vow of Hannah (I Sam. 1:11), the theophany of Samuel (3:1-19), and the designation of Samuel as a prophet (נָבִיא; 3:20), at Shiloh make it seem probable that Shiloh was the scene of an early struggle on the part of the Israelites, who had an austere desert background, against the fertility cult of the Canaanites, which threatened to shape the Hebrew cult. With the loss of the ark of the covenant and defeat at the hands of the Philistines, Shiloh ceased to be an Israelite shrine, although a description of its destruction by the Philistines has not been preserved.

The priests of Shiloh settled in Nob (cf. I Sam. 14:3; 22:11). The report of the visit of Jeroboam's wife to the house of the prophet Ahijah at Shiloh (I Kings 14:2, 4) is evidence for the existence of a shrine there as late as 922 B.C., although the Danish excavations uncovered no extensive traces of occupation for this period. Shiloh never again regained its former importance. God had forsaken "his dwelling at Shiloh, the tent where he dwelt among men" (Ps. 78:60). The ruins at Shiloh were evidently well enough known to give meaning to Jeremiah's warning that the temple in Jerusalem would suffer a fate similar to that which befell the Lord's place in Shiloh (Jer. 7:12, 14). Although Jer. 26:6, 9, seems to imply that the city of Shiloh was a symbol of desolation, and itself in ruins, the reference may be merely to the ruins of the Shiloh temple. The city seems to have been occupied as late as the time of Gedaliah (41:5), although the report of eighty men coming from Shechem, Shiloh, and Samaria may refer merely to the region rather than to the city.

Bibliography. W. F. Albright, "The Danish Excavations at Seilun—A Correction," *PEQ,* 59 (1927), 157-58. A. T. Richardson, "The Site of Shiloh," *PEQ,* 59 (1927), 85-88. H. Kjaer, "The Danish Excavation of Shiloh. Preliminary Report," *PEQ,* 59 (1927), 202-13; "The Excavation of Shiloh 1929," *JPOS,* X (1930), 87-174; "Shiloh. A Summary Report of the Second Danish Expedition, 1929," *PEQ,* 63 (1931), 71-88.

W. L. REED

2. KJV translation of שׁילה, in the phrase "until Shiloh come," occurring in the Blessing of Jacob (Gen. 49:10) as a part of the oracle proclaiming the ascendancy of the tribe of Judah. The reference is probably to David, but it is hardly a proper name.

Shiloh is traditionally understood as a name of the MESSIAH, but the first evidence of such a title is late (Talmud Sanh. 98b), and the supposed derivation from *shālâ*, "to be at ease," makes doubtful sense. If the N city is intended (*see* SHILOH 1)—i.e., "until it [Judah or Judean rule] comes to Shiloh"—then the phrase might speak of the extension of Judean sovereignty over Israel, as actually occurred under David. Identification of the cryptic name as Shelah, third son of Judah (Gen. 38:5), is without basis.

The term is commonly read *shellô,* "to whom" or "that which is," a contraction of *'asher lô.* The RSV reads: "until he comes to whom it [the 'scepter' or 'ruler's staff'] belongs." Most of the versions read the word similarly, and the rendering is supported by Ezek. 21:27—H 21:32: "until he comes whose right it is." A major difficulty is syntactic, inasmuch as the phrase is left without a subject. The LXX seems to derive the meaning: "until the things reserved for him come."

There is no MS support for the emendation *mōshᵉlô,* "his ruler." The same sense may be derived, however, from Akkadian *shēlu* or *shîlu,* "prince, ruler." Repointed as *shayyālô,* "his ruler," it would admirably solve the semantic problem. Assyrian technical terms for civil and military office are found elsewhere in Hebrew (*see,* e.g., RAB-SHAKEH; TARTAN), although they occur in literature from the ninth century on—i.e., after Assyria came into direct contact with the Hebrews.

Most exegetes agree that a Judean leader is referred to in the verse; but whether he is a tribal head, a Davidic king, or a future messiah is problematic. The view that Gen. 49:10b is a later messianic gloss is presently less favored. The meaning of the Shiloh oracle must be sought, not only in the context of the Blessing of Jacob, but also in the light of the closely related Balaam oracles (Num. 22–24) and the Blessing of Moses (Deut. 33). All three reflect the political expansion of the United Monarchy. The person alluded to in Gen. 49:10 (cf. also the "star" and "scepter" of Num. 24:17-19) is David the conqueror. None of the ethico-religious aspects of the Davidic deliverer (e.g., Isa. 9:2-7; 11:1-9) is mentioned. Centuries later, when a messiah of Judean origin was expected, the passage was interpreted of the righteous offshoot of David (cf., e.g., Ezek. 21:27 and the "Messiah of Righteousness" in a Qumran commentary on Gen. 49:10). Although the NT ignores Gen. 49, Christian interpreters since the sixteenth century have frequently identified Shiloh with the Messiah.

Bibliography. A. Poznansky, *Schiloh: Ein Beitrag zur Geschichte der Messiaslehre* (1904); H. Gunkel, *Genesis* (4th ed., 1917), pp. 481-82; G. R. Driver, *JTS,* XXIII (1922), 70; F. Nötscher, *ZAW,* N.F. VI (1929), 323-24; J. Skinner, *Genesis,* ICC (2nd ed., 1930), pp. 518-24; E. Sellin, "Zu dem Judaspruch im Jakobsegen Gen. 49:9-12 und im Mosesegen Deut. 33:7," *ZAW,* LIX (1944), 57-64; J. Lindblom, "The Political Background of the Shiloh Oracle," *Supplements to Vetus Testamentum,* I (1953), 78-87; J. Allegro, *JBL,* LXXV (1956), 174-76; O. Eissfeldt, "Silo und Jerusalem," *Supplements to Vetus Testamentum,* IV (1957), 138-47.

N. K. GOTTWALD

SHILONITE shī'lə nīt [שׁילני, שׁילוני, שׁלוני]; KJV SHILONI shī lō'nī in Neh. 11:5. **1.** A designation of the prophet AHIJAH as a man from Shiloh (I Kings 11:29).

2. A designation of a member of one of the Judean families returning from exile (I Chr. 9:5; Neh. 11:5). There are numerous differences in the names of the families listed in I Chr. 9:5; Neh. 11:5. If "Shilonites" refers to persons from Shiloh, they traced their ancestry back to a place in the N kingdom. It is more probable that השׁילוני in both passages should be vocalized "Shelanite" to indicate a descendant of SHELAH (cf. Gen. 38:5; Num. 26:20).

W. L. REED

SHILSHAH shĭl'shə [שׁלשׁה, *see* SHELESH] (I Chr. 7:37). A division of the Zophah clan of the tribe of Asher.

SHIMEA shĭm'ĭ ə [שׁמעא, he (God) has heard] (I Chr. 2:13; 3:5; 6:30, 39; 20:7); KJV SHIMMA shĭm'ə in I Chr. 2:13. Alternately: SHAMMAH shăm'ə [שׁמה] (I Sam. 16:9; 17:13); SHAMMUA shă mū'ə [שׁמוע] (II Sam. 5:14; I Chr. 14:4); SHIMEAH shĭm'ĭ ə [שׁמעה] (II Sam. 13:3, 32), שׁמאה (I Chr. 8:32); שׁמעי (II Sam. 21:21 KJV; RSV SHIMEI)]; SHIMEAM —əm [שׁמאם, *from* שׁמע, to hear] (I Chr. 9:38). **1.** The third son of Jesse (I Sam. 16:9; 17:13); a brother of King David (I Chr. 2:13); and the father of Jonadab (II Sam. 13:3, 32) and Jonathan (II Sam. 21:21 KJV; I Chr. 20:7).

2. One of David's sons born in Jerusalem (II Sam. 5:14; I Chr. 3:5; 14:4).

3. A Levite of the family of Merari (I Chr. 6:30).

4. A Levite of the family of Gershom (I Chr. 6:39).

5. A Benjaminite, descendant of Jeiel (I Chr. 8:32; 9:38).

Bibliography. M. Noth, *Die israelitischen Personennamen* (1928), pp. 38, 184-85.   T. M. MAUCH

SHIMEATH shĭm'ĭ ăth [שִׁמְעָת] (II Kings 12:21; II Chr. 24:26). The mother (or father?) of one of the conspirators who murdered Joash king of Judah. The name of the murderer was Jozacar according to II Kings 12:21, Zabad or possibly Jehozabad according to II Chr. 24:26.

See also SHIMRITH.   D. HARVEY

SHIMEATHITES shĭm'ĭ ə thīts [שִׁמְעָתִים]. A subdivision of CALEBITES (I Chr. 2:55; see vss. 18-20, 50b-55), named in a list of three "families . . . of the scribes that dwelt at Jabez" (site unknown; perhaps somewhere in the center of Judah). The text is obscure and identification uncertain. The Vulg. reads *resonantes;* perhaps the name means "traditionists" (cf. שָׁמַע, "hear"). The name may be derived from an unknown person or place. According to vs. 55b the Shimeathites may have been one of the groups of KENITES who had participated in the northward movement to occupy S Palestine during the Conquest, or one of the groups of Kenites who were pushed northward by Edomite expansion during the Exile.

Bibliography. E. Curtis and A. Madsen, *Chronicles* ICC (1910), pp. 97-98; W. Rudolf, *Chronikbücher,* HAT (1955), pp. 22-23.   T. M. MAUCH

SHIMEI shĭm'ĭ ī [שִׁמְעִי, Y has heard (*a shortened form*); Apoc. Σομεείς, Σεμεί, Σεμείς]; SHIMEITES —īts (Num. 3:21; Zech. 12:13); KJV SHIMITES shĭm'īts in Num. 3:21. Alternately: SHEMA shē'mə [שֶׁמַע] (I Chr. 8:13). KJV alternately: SHIMEAH shĭm'ĭ ə (*Qere,* II Sam. 21:21); SHIMHI —hī (I Chr. 8:21); SHIMI shĭm'ĭ (Exod. 6:17); KJV Apoc. SAMIS sā'mĭs (I Esd. 9:34); SEMEI sĕm'ĭ ī (I Esd. 9:33); SEMIS sē'mĭs (I Esd. 9:23). **1.** A grandson of Levi; the second of two sons of Gershon. Thus he was the founder of a subdivision of the families of Levites descended from Gershon (Exod. 6:17; Num. 3:18; I Chr. 6:17; 23:7, 10). This subdivision of the tribe of Levi is read "the family of the Shimeites" in Num. 3:21; Zech. 12:13. In I Chr. 23:9 "Shimei" probably is a mistake for one of the sons in vs. 8. "Shimi" in Exod. 6:17 KJV must be an error.

2. A Benjaminite, descendant of Gera. He belonged to the family of the house of Saul, which had lost the kingship to David. When David was fleeing Jerusalem before the revolt of Absalom, at Bahurim on the way to the Jordan, Shimei cursed David and threw stones at him. Shimei voiced the protest latent in some Benjaminite quarters (see II Sam. 20:1) that David had supplanted the house of Saul, and he charged David with bloodguilt (cf. II Sam. 3:37; 4: 11; see 21:1-14; see also I Sam. 28-29). David prevented the killing of Shimei, taking the words of Shimei as sent by Yahweh and hoping that Yahweh would balance the curse with eventual blessing (II

Sam. 16:5-13). After the revolt of Absalom was overcome, Shimei with a thousand Benjaminites rushed to be among the first to meet David as he was about to recross the Jordan on his return to Jerusalem. He begged forgiveness, and David with an oath granted royal clemency on the occasion of Yahweh's grace reestablishing his reign (II Sam. 19:16-23). One of David's deathbed charges to Solomon was that he remove the curse of Shimei which still rested upon David's house and threatened the secure establishment of the dynasty. David's oath of clemency was not binding upon Solomon, and he was to watch for an opportunity to eradicate the curse by killing Shimei (I Kings 2:8-9). Solomon commanded Shimei to remain in Jerusalem, telling him that if he left Jerusalem on any pretext, it would mean his death, and Shimei agreed. Three years later Shimei violated his oath by going to Gath to bring back two runaway slaves. Thus freed from all taboos regarding Shimei, Solomon upon his return executed him (vss. 36-46).

3. A brother of King David (II Sam. 21:21).

4. One of those who did not support the usurpation attempted by Adonijah (I Kings 1:8). He probably was a man who had become prominent during David's reign. Possibly he is to be identified with the son of Ela who was one of Solomon's twelve administrative officers, in charge of the apportionment from the district of Benjamin (4:18).

5. A brother of Zerubbabel (I Chr. 3:19).

6. A family or clan of Simeon outstanding in its size (I Chr. 4:26-27).

7. Eponym of a family of Reuben (I Chr. 5:4).

8. A Levite of the family of Merari (I Chr. 6:29).

9. A Levite of the family of Gershom (I Chr. 6:42).

10. A Benjaminite, head of a father's house (I Chr. 8:13, 21). KJV "Shimhi" must be an error.

11. A postexilic family of Levitical singers of the Jeduthun group (I Chr. 25:3, 17); possibly of Davidic origin. *See* JEDUTHUN; MUSIC.

12. A Ramathite, one of David's officers over the king's possessions. He was in charge of the vineyards (I Chr. 27:27).

13. A Levite of the family of Heman. He took a leading part in the cleansing of the temple during the reign of Hezekiah (II Chr. 29:14).

14. A Levite, second official in charge of the overseers of the contributions, tithes, and dedicated things, securing their proper management for the support of the temple clergy. The account describes Hezekiah's reform but reflects postexilic times (II Chr. 31:12-13).

15. A Levite among those who put away foreign wives and their children according to Ezra's reform banning foreign marriage (Ezra 10:23; I Esd. 9:23).

16. A son of Hashum among those who put away foreign wives and their children according to Ezra's reform banning foreign marriage (Ezra 10:33; I Esd. 9:33).

17. A son of Binnui among those who put away foreign wives and their children according to Ezra's reform banning foreign marriage (Ezra 10:38; I Esd. 9:34).

18. A Benjaminite, a descendant of Kish and a remote ancestor of Mordecai (Esth. 2:5).

     T. M. MAUCH

SHIMEON shĭm'ĭ ən [שמעון, *perhaps diminutive for* (God) has heard (*same as* SIMEON)] (Ezra 10:31). Alternately: SIMON CHOSAMAEUS sī'mən kŏs'ə mē'əs Σίμον Χοσομαῖος (A), *see below*] (I Esd. 9:32); KJV SIMON CHOSAMEUS. One of the contemporaries of Ezra who are listed as having married foreign wives. CHOSAMAEUS, which appears as his second name in I Esdras, must not refer to this individual, but perhaps represents a corruption of one or more of the names of Ezra 10:32, omitted in I Esdras, or of Shemaiah (Ezra 10:31), or again of Hashum (vs. 33).

Bibliography. M. Noth, *Die israelitischen Personennamen* (1928), pp. 38, 60n, 185. B. T. DAHLBERG

SHIMHI. KJV form of SHIMEI 10.

SHIMI; SHIMITES. KJV forms of SHIMEI 1; SHIMEITES.

SHIMMA. KJV form of SHIMEA 1.

SHIMON shī'mən [שימון] (I Chr. 4:20). A family or clan of the tribe of Judah.

SHIMRATH shĭm'răth [שמרת, *from* שמר, watch over, preserve (*a shortened form*)] (I Chr. 8:21). A member of the tribe of Benjamin listed as one of the sons of Shimei.

Bibliography. M. Noth, *Die israelitischen Personennamen* (1928), pp. 38, 177.

SHIMRI shĭm'rī [שמרי, *from* שמר, watch over, preserve (*a shortened form*)]; KJV SIMRI sĭm'— in I Chr. 26:10. **1.** A Simeonite, an ancestor of Ziza (I Chr. 4:37).

2. The father of Jediael and probably Joha, two of David's Mighty Men (I Chr. 11:45).

3. The chief son of Hosah of the line of Merari, in a division of temple gatekeepers, in a postexilic alignment of Levites ascribed to David (I Chr. 26:10).

4. A Levite of the family of Elizaphan. He is ascribed a leading part in the cleansing of the temple during the reign of Hezekiah (II Chr. 29:13).
T. M. MAUCH

SHIMRITH shĭm'rĭth [שמרית, *probably* (God) has protected] (II Chr. 24:26). Alternately: SHOMER shō'mər [שמר, keeper, protector] (II Kings 12:21). The Moabite mother of Jehozabad, one of the conspirators who killed Joash, king of Judah.

See also SHIMEATH.

SHIMRON shĭm'rŏn [שמרון; *cf. place names* שמיר, שמרון, *and personal names* שמרי, שמרת, שמריה]; SHIMRONITES —rə nīts; KJV SHIMROM —rŏm in I Chr. 7:1. **1.** The fourth son of Issachar (Gen. 46:13; Num. 26:24; I Chr. 7:1); ancestral head of the Shimronites (Num. 26:24).

2. A Canaanite royal town (Josh. 11:1), later allotted to Zebulun (19:15). Its king joined Jabin's confederacy against Joshua and was defeated. Tell Semuniya, a site located approximately seven miles W of Nazareth, has been suggested as a possible identification. This is unlikely, since surface explorations have shown that the site was abandoned during

the period of the Israelite conquest and settlement.

Bibliography. W. F. Albright, "Bronze Age Mounds of Northern Palestine and the Hauran," *BASOR,* 19 (1925), 9-10; F.-M. Abel, *Géographie de la Palestine,* II (1938), 464.
G. W. VAN BEEK

SHIMRON-MERON —mĭr'ŏn [שמרון מראון]. A Canaanite royal town, whose king Joshua defeated (Josh. 12:20). It is probable that "Shimron" and "Meron" should be read separately, with the LXX.

SHIMSHAI shĭm'shī [שמשי, sun (-child); Apoc. Σαμέλλιος]; KJV Apoc. SEMELLIUS sĭ mĕl'ĭ əs. An official in the Persian government service for the province "Beyond the River" (Trans-Euphratia), which included Palestine. With his superior, Rehum, he cosponsored a letter to Artaxerxes opposing the rebuilding of postexilic Jerusalem by the Jews (Ezra 4:8-16; I Esd. 2:16-24). With a supporting reply from the royal court, they.with their associates forced this work to a halt (Ezra 4:17-24; I Esd. 2:25-30; *see bibliography*).

Bibliography. M. Noth, *Die israelitischen Personennamen* (1928), p. 223; R. A. Bowman, Exegesis of Ezra, *IB,* III (1954), 600. B. T. DAHLBERG

SHINAB shī'năb [שנאב; *cf.* Akkad. *Sin-a-bi,* (the god) Sin is my father (*Ur Excavation Texts,* V, 38, 3; 534, 3); *Adad-a-bi; Šamaš-a-bi;* LXX Σεννααρ] (Gen. 14:2). King of Admah; one of the five S Palestinian rulers who rebelled against Chedorlaomer, provoking his punitive campaign in which Tidal, Amraphel, and Arioch participated. L. HICKS

SHINAR shī'när [שנער]. A name for Babylonia. According to biblical tradition Nimrod ruled Babel, Erech, and Accad in the land of Shinar (Gen. 10: 10). These three cities can be identified: Erech as ancient Uruk, present-day Warka; Babel as Babylon; and Accad as the ancient Akkade, not yet located on the ground but to be sought for in the region between Babylon and Baghdad. The land of Shinar must accordingly have comprised the territories known anciently as Sumer and Akkad, later as Babylonia, and stretching from slightly N of modern Baghdad to slightly S of Nasiriyeh. Strangely enough, no indigenous term for these territories which could underlie the Hebrew term "Shinar" is known. Comparison with the term "Sumer" has been made, but the differences in form of the terms "Sumer" and "Shinar" have not been convincingly accounted for (*see* SUMER). Other geographical terms which have been adduced lack the proper geographical reference.

According to biblical tradition the tower of Babel was built in Shinar (Gen. 11:2). An as-yet-unidentified king of Shinar, Amraphel, is mentioned as an opponent of Abram in the problematical traditions of Gen. 14:1, 9. In Isa. 11:11 it is prophesied that the Lord will recover a remnant of his exiled people, in part from Shinar; and in Dan. 1:2 it is related that Nebuchadnezzar II of Babylon took temple treasures from the temple in Jerusalem to Shinar when he had captured the city. The "ephah" in Zechariah's vision was to be taken to the land of Shinar (Zech. 5:11). T. JACOBSEN

SHION shī'ən [שִׁיאֹן]; KJV SHIHON shī'hŏn. A border town in Issachar (Josh. 19:19). The exact location of the site is unknown. One suggested identification is 'Ayun esh-Sha'in, located *ca.* three miles E of Nazareth, but this is completely unsatisfactory. Another site, Sirin, located approximately fourteen miles SE of Mount Tabor, has also been proposed, because the writing of this name resembled that of Shion in one period. This identification is as yet archaeologically uncertain.

Bibliography. W. F. Albright, "The Topography of the Tribe of Issachar," *ZAW*, 3 (1926), 228-29; A. Saarisalo, *The Boundary Between Issachar and Naphtali* (1927), pp. 63-66; F.-M. Abel, *Géographie de la Palestine*, II (1938), 61, 464.

G. W. Van Beek

SHIPHI shī'fī [שִׁפְעִי, abundance, overflow] (I Chr. 4:37). A Simeonite descended from Shemaiah; the father of Ziza.

SHIPHMITE shǐf'mīt [הַשִּׁפְמִי] (I Chr. 27:27). A native of Shepham(?) or Siphmoth(?). *See* ZABDI 3.

SHIPHRAH shǐf'rə [שִׁפְרָה, *see below*] (Exod. 1:15). One of the two Hebrew midwives (*see also* PUAH) ordered by the king of Egypt to kill all male children (*see* MIDWIFE). The name appears as *Šp-ra* in a list of Egyptian slaves, and means "fair one." The Aramaic form is שִׁפּוּרָא, SAPPHIRA. Later Jewish legends identify Shiphrah with JOCHEBED.

Bibliography. L. Ginzberg, *Legends of the Jews*, II (1910), 251; W. F. Albright, "Northwest-Semitic Names in a List of Egyptian Slaves," *JAOS*, LXXIV (1954), 229.

J. F. Ross

SHIPHTAN shǐf'tăn [שִׁפְטָן, (the deity) has judged(?)] (Num. 34:24). The father of the Ephraimite leader Kemuel, who was selected to help superintend the distribution of W Jordanian Canaan among the tribes to occupy that territory.

Bibliography. M. Noth, *Die israelitischen Personennamen* (1928), pp. 38, 187. R. F. Johnson

SHIPMASTER [κυβερνήτης] (Rev. 18:17). The steersman or helmsman, the ship's pilot, who was sometimes also the owner of the ship.

In his vision of the mourning over the destruction of Rome, the author of Revelation records the cry which the shipmasters and other seafaring men uttered as they saw smoke rising from Rome while it was burning: "What city was like the great city?"

In Acts 27:11 the same Greek word was translated "CAPTAIN," signifying the one who was responsible for the navigation of the ship.

See also SHIPS AND SAILING.

B. H. Throckmorton, Jr.

***SHIPS AND SAILING IN THE OT** [*generally* אֳנִיָּה, ship; אֳנִי, fleet; סְפִינָה, ship (*only in* Jonah 1:5); צִי, ship (Num. 24:24; Isa. 33:21); כְּלִי גֹּמֶא, vessels of papyrus (Isa. 18:2)]. Because of the absence of good natural harbors on the Mediterranean S of the Carmel Range and also the domination of the coastal cities for a long period by the Philistines, the sea was a barrier and not a highway for Israel. Only during the period of Solomon did Israel engage in maritime enterprise, and then not from the Mediterranean but from the Gulf of Aqabah. However, throughout her history, Israel did know ships and sailing from contacts with the Phoenicians.

1. Biblical references to ships
2. Egyptian sources on Phoenician sailing
3. Assyrian ships and sailing
4. Pictures from Phoenicia and Palestine
Bibliography

1. Biblical references to ships. In the period of the judges the N tribes of Asher (Judg. 5:17) and Zebulun (Gen. 49:13; Judg. 5:18), as well as Dan on the Philistine coast (Judg. 5:17), appear to have sailed the Mediterranean. Solomon built a fleet of ships at EZION-GEBER at the head of the Gulf of Aqabah (I Kings 9:26-28; II Chr. 8:17-18), with the help of HIRAM, and engaged in trade with OPHIR. Sennacherib in an account of his sixth campaign (*LAR* II, 319) recounts a similar use of Phoenician builders and sailors: "Hittite [Syrian] people, plunder of my bow, I settled in Nineveh. Mighty ships (after) the workmanship of their land, they built dexterously. Tyrian, Sidonian and Cyprian sailors, captives of my hand, I ordered (to descend) the Tigris with them." Another reference in I Kings 10: 22 (cf. II Chr. 9:21) is to Solomon's "fleet of ships of TARSHISH at sea with the fleet of Hiram." Once again, in the time of Jehoshaphat, when Edom was weak, an attempt was made to revive the Ophir trade in "ships of Tarshish," but the ships were wrecked at Ezion-geber (I Kings 22:47-48; cf. II Chr. 20:35-37). In Ezek. 27, the lament over Tyre, there is a description of Phoenician ships with specific mention of nautical terms such as מָשׁוֹט (oar), חֶבֶל (pilot), מַלָּח (mariner), מִפְרָשׂ (sail), תֹּרֶן (mast), etc. Elsewhere in the OT there appear terms such as נֵס (sail; Isa. 33:23); חֹבֵל (mast[?]; Prov. 23:34).

2. Egyptian sources on Phoenician sailing. As early as the Old Kingdom of Egypt timber was shipped by sea from Phoenicia to Egypt. Annals of the reign of Snefru (*ca.* 2650) mention ships of over 170 feet in length and the bringing of forty ships filled with cedar logs to Egypt. A century later, at the time of Sahu-Re, there are pictured ships, one of which has a rudder of three oars and its mast lashed down, carrying Syrian captives (Fig. SHI 45). Pepi I took troops by sea and "made a landing at the rear of the heights of the mountain range on the north of the land of the Sand-Dwellers" (*ANET* 228), possibly the Carmel Range. Contacts between Egypt and Byblos in Phoenicia continued in the Middle Kingdom. An official of Thut-mose III of the New Kingdom tells of bringing timbers from Lebanon and of sailing on the Great Green Sea with a favorable breeze (*ANET* 243). From a little over a century before the time of Solomon comes the account of the Egyptian Wen-Amon's journey to Phoenicia to procure timber (*ANET* 25-28). In search of woodwork for the august bark of Amon-Re, he sailed from Tanis with a ship's captain and arrived at the harbor of Dor. From there he proceeded to Tyre and then to Byblos. The account speaks of twenty ships at Byblos and of fifty at Sidon.

Pictures of seagoing ships appear as early as the

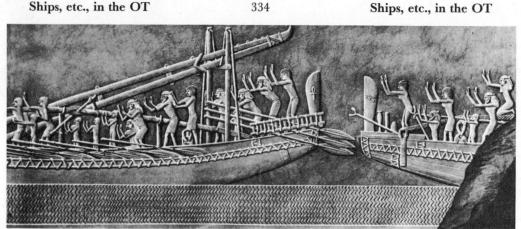

45. Cast of a relief showing ships carrying Syrian captives with hands raised to the Egyptian king Sahu-Re; Fifth Dynasty (*ca.* 2500-2350 B.C.)

Old Kingdom in Egyptian paintings and reliefs. In addition to the relief of ships with Syrian captives from the time of Sahu-Re, there is a tomb painting at Thebes, probably from the time of Amen-hotep III (1413-1377), showing two ships approaching an Egyptian port, where seven smaller, but similar, craft are already docked (*ANEP* 111). These sailing vessels have single masts with a crow's-nest at the top, and a large rectangular sail. High prows and sterns end in platforms. On the prow stands the pilot with a long sounding pole. The rudder consists of two oars, one on each side of the stern. A scene on the wall of the temple of Ramses III at Medinet Habu depicts the battle between the Egyptians and the Sea Peoples, the group to which the Philistines belonged. Both Egyptian and enemy craft are shown. The Egyptian ship consists of a crescent-shaped keel, a single mast topped by a crow's-nest, a yard arm with furled sail, a row of oars, and a paddle serving as a rudder. The boat's prow ends in a lioness' head. The ships of the Sea Peoples are similar except for the bird's head on both prow and stern (*ANEP* 341).

3. Assyrian ships and sailing. From the time of Tiglath-pileser I (1114-1076), who recorded a voyage off the coast of the Mediterranean at Arvad, Assyrian kings made expeditions westward to the sea (*ANET* 275). Shalmaneser III's (858-824) record of his conquest of Tyre on the bronze bands from Balawat shows booty being ferried from the island on which Tyre stood (Ezek. 27:4) to the mainland. The boats are small, guided by a helmsman with an oar at the stern, and propelled by an oarsman seated toward the bow (*ANEP* 356). The palace of Sargon II (721-705 B.C.) at Khorsabad had a relief depicting the transporting of logs by seagoing vessels (Fig. SHI 46). The ships have high, horse-headed prows and high sterns and are propelled by both oars and a sail which could be attached to a center mast crowned with a crow's-nest. Yet another type of seagoing vessel is pictured on a relief from Sennacherib's (704-681) time (Fig. SHI 47). A three-decked warship with sharply pointed prow is driven forward by oars arranged in two rows. Shields are hung around the upper deck, on which the armed warriors sit. Note the reference in

46. Six boats transporting logs in tow or aboard; from Khorsabad relief during reign of Sargon II (722-705 B.C.)

47. A three-decked Assyrian warship, from Quyunjiq

§ 1 to Sennacherib's account of making use of Phoenician builders and seamen in the construction and sailing of his warships. For a full description of the parts of Babylonian ships and a discussion of the terms used in the texts which describe them, *see* the work of A. Salonen listed in the *bibliography*.

4. Pictures from Phoenicia and Palestine. From Phoenicia itself representations of ships are few, and those which do exist come from later periods than those found in Assyria and Egypt. Coins of the fourth century found at Byblos show on the obverse a Phoenician war galley with a lion-headed prow (*ANEP* 225). Three soldiers sit on the deck. The ship is maneuvered by means of an oar which serves as a rudder. The most complete representation of a ship discovered in Phoenicia is found on a sarcophagus found at Sidon (Fig. SHI 48) and belonging to the first century A.D. It has a high, curved stern, to which is attached a flag. Unfurled on the mainmast is a large square sail, and on a foremast is a small square sail. In Palestine itself there has been found but one picture of a ship. This is crudely scratched on a stone found at Tell Sandahannah (Fig. SHI 49) and belongs, according to the excavator, to the period from 200 B.C. to A.D. 200. Like the Phoenician ships it carried a sail and was equipped with oars. The unique feature, however, is that it is anchored by two anchors at the stern (cf. Acts 27:29, where four anchors from the stern are mentioned).

Courtesy of the Librairie Orientaliste Paul Geuthner, Paris

48. Phoenician ship, from a sarcophagus of Sidon

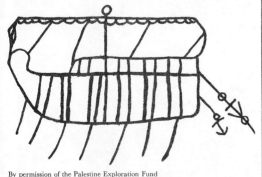

By permission of the Palestine Exploration Fund

49. Graffito of a ship, from Tell Sandahannah (Mareshah)

Bibliography. A. Köster, *Schiffahrt und Handelsverkehr des östlichen Mittelmeeres in 3. u. 2 Jahrtausend v. Chr* (1924). K. Galling, *Biblisches Reallexikon* (1934), cols. 453-56. A. Salonen, *Die Wasserfahrzeuge in Babylonien, Studia Orientalia*, vol. 8, pt. 4 (1939), contains a full bibliography. J. B. Pritchard, *ANEP* (1954), figs. 103-14; for literary references to Egyptian and Babylonian ships and shipping, *ANET* (2nd ed., 1955).
J. B. PRITCHARD

*SHIPS AND SAILING IN THE NT. This subject is an aspect of TRAVEL AND COMMUNICATION IN THE NT and has its setting in the larger Mediterranean world.

1. Vocabulary
2. Warships
3. Merchantmen
4. Ports
5. Sea lanes
6. Voyages
Bibliography

1. Vocabulary. The Greek ναῦς, which generally refers to large vessels, is used in Acts 27:41 of the merchant ship which is carrying Paul to Rome. It occurs nowhere else in the NT.

Πλοῖον is the common NT word for "ship." It means either a large ship or a small one. No fewer than thirteen times in Acts 27:6-44 it is applied to the same merchantman in which Paul is sailing. But the word is equally at home as a designation of fishing boats on the Sea of Galilee (cf. Matt. 14:22; Mark 1:19; Luke 5:2; John 6:19).

Πλοιάριον is a diminutive of πλοῖον and so should mean only "little boat," but it is also frequently used of Galilean fishing boats (Mark 3:9; Luke 5:2; John 6:22-24; 21:8). In the NT there is no longer a sharp distinction between ναῦς, πλοῖον, and πλοιάριον.

Σκάφη, "small boat or skiff," occurs only in Acts 27:16, 30, 32, where it refers to the ship's boat. When Josephus (War II.xxi.8) was defending Galilee, Tiberias revolted. Whereupon he brought it back into line by threatening an attack with 230 fishing boats which he had rounded up on the Sea of Galilee. He calls the boats σκάφη. Thus they could be called πλοῖον, πλοιάριον, or σκάφη. The words were popular synonyms. The episode from Josephus, as well as frequent references in the gospels, reveals a flourishing fishing industry on the Sea of Galilee. The boats were rowboats (Mark 6:48), but they probably used small sails also.

That the vocabulary of the NT agrees with Hellenistic usage in general is shown by Chariton's *Chaereas and Callirhoe* (ca. A.D. 150), where a small pirate vessel from Syracuse is called κέλης (I.vii.6; x.1; III.iii.13, 18; iv.8); κέλης μικρός (I.xi.2); πλοῖον (I.xiii.4; III.iv.6); ναῦς (I.xi.1; xiii.6; xiv.6). The great merchant ship Isis, described by Lucian (second century) in *Ship or Wishes*, is usually called ναῦς, but in the title and in 7, πλοῖον.

2. Warships. A relief found in Praeneste and now in the Vatican is thought to represent one of the ships used by Agrippa in the battle of Actium in 31 B.C.* Warships depended on oars rather than sails, for the sake of maneuverability. The most popular types at the time were biremes and triremes, although even quinqueremes and larger had been known. This one is a bireme. Only part of it is shown in the relief. It

50. Relief found at Praeneste, believed to be one of Agrippa's lighter ships at Actium; now in the Vatican

has been estimated that there were 18 oars on each side. With one man for each lower and two for each upper oar, there would be 108 rowers. The same estimate accounts for 25 mariners and 80 soldiers, thus a crew of 213. This particular ship has an outside gangway, main deck, and raised platforms, permitting three levels of fighting men. Those above could use arrows, darts, spears, etc. The length is estimated at 103 feet, the beam at 17; weight of cargo, *ca.* 61,770 pounds; and a displacement of 81 tons. Yet this is regarded as a warship of moderate size. Rams were standard equipment, as were grappling hooks to permit boarding and hand-to-hand fighting. Figs. SHI 50; OAR 1.

3. Merchantmen. Paul's famous trip to Rome (Acts 27) was made in three ships, at least two of which were grain ships operating between Alexandria and Rome. One of these was wrecked on Malta. Apparently there were no commercial passenger ships at the time. Passengers had to travel on freighters, whose main business was to carry grain and other cargo. There was a minimum of space left for passengers. Lucian (*Ship or Wishes* 5) mentions stern cabins (αἱ μετὰ τὴν πρύμναν οἰκήσεις) on the Isis. But it is not probable that any freighter had many cabins. These would be reserved for wealthy or official personnel. Travelers such as Paul and his companions would have to ride in steerage class. In fair weather they must have spent almost all their time on the main deck. It is difficult to see how they survived in storms. With hatches closed to protect cargo and prevent foundering, ventilation and living conditions in general below deck would have been exceedingly bad, even if passengers could get below. Acts 27:20 implies that the storm was accompanied by rain for many days. There were 276 persons aboard (27:37). Josephus (Life 3) tells of a wreck he experienced in the Sea of Adria with 600 aboard, 80 of whom were picked up, after a whole night of swimming, by a ship of Cyrene.

After seventy days of struggling with storms the Isis finally, far off course, put in at Piraeus, port of Athens. Lucian (*Ship or Wishes* 5) says that this ship was 180 feet long (εἴκοσι καὶ ἑκατὸν πήχεων) and over a fourth as wide, while its depth was 44 feet. It carried statues of Isis on each side of its prow. It had ornamental paintings, a scarlet topsail, and stern

cabins. The statement that it carried enough grain to feed Athens for a year might be hyperbole. Lucian mentions only the main deck and hold, saying nothing about decks in between, although it seems probable that there were such. He indicates (1) that the Isis was larger than most grain ships when he calls it a monster ship (ὑπερμεγέθη ναῦν καὶ πέρα τοῦ μέτρου).

The undersea photograph of a first-century B.C. wreck lying on the sea floor near the Phare du Titan off the French Riviera shows that the ship was carrying a great cargo of wine, oil, and other foods exported from South Italy to France. One sees an abundance of the jars (ἀμφορεῖς, πίθοι) in which such exports were packed. They were the casks, kegs, and barrels of that age. The hull of this ship—and of other wrecks like it—has disintegrated and disappeared. Only the picturesque containers lie there to indicate that the ships were over a hundred feet long. Grain was probably carried in bags. Rostovtzeff's *History of the Ancient World* (II, pl. lviv, 3) shows stevedores carrying grain up a gangplank in small bags and emptying them into a larger bag on deck.* The grain ships sailing from Italy, Greece, or any of the islands, such as Rhodes, would carry wine and similar items in the amphorae and *pithoi* standing in racks on all decks and in the hold. In Egypt this cargo was replaced by bags of grain for the return trip. Evidence of this commerce is provided by quantities of stamped wine-jar handles from Rhodes which have been found in such places as Asia Minor, North Africa, and Palestine. Fig. SHI 52.

Another good picture of a Roman grain ship is shown by Rostovtzeff (pl. lxiv, 1).* It has arrived in port with sails flying. The mainsail is ornamented with the traditional wolf and her young. Deck castles and many other features are visible. Pl. lxiv, 3, represents a steersman standing on the poop deck operating the rudder with a slender tiller. Rudders were

Alinari Photo
51. An Italian harbor

Alinari Photo
52. A small merchant ship

of the quarter type. Each ship had two. In the case of the Isis (*Ship or Wishes* 6) the rudders operated as a unit. Fig. SHI 51.

Each merchantman carried the statue of the deity from whom it got its name. The name of Paul's ship which was wrecked on Malta is not given, but that which carried him on to Puteoli in the spring was the Castor and Pollux. Lucian (9) relates that the Isis was saved from destruction on the Lycian coast by the intervention of the gods, who sent either Castor or Pollux as a bright star to appear at the masthead and guide the ship to the open sea. This reminds us of Paul's assurance in Acts 27:23-25 that God had sent an angel to inform him that there would be no loss of life of any of those sailing with him.

All the pictures of grain ships show a great square mainsail and a short, raked foremast with a small, square sail, which is the foresail (ἀρτέμων) mentioned in Acts 27:40. As all other tackling had been cast overboard, only this small sail could be hoisted to drive the ship on the beach.

Pliny (*Nat. Hist.* XIX) says that sails were usually made of linen, but apparently those of the Isis were of hides (*Ship or Wishes* 4). Roman grain ships generally carried a triangular topsail. Although something was known about tacking, it is evident that the type of sails used did not permit ships to make much headway in the face of a strong wind.

4. Ports. The only well-known port on the coast of Syria in antiquity was TYRE,* which for many centuries was the greatest center of shipping on the Mediterranean. Ezek. 27 gives a vivid description of this romantic city with its ships and commerce. Tyre continued to prosper and withstand all onslaughts until Alexander conquered it in 332 B.C. After that date it declined, as it was outstripped by Antioch, Ephesus, Corinth, Alexandria, and Rome, the centers of trade during the Hellenistic period. But that Tyre was still an active port in the first century A.D. is shown by the report in Acts 21:1-8 that when Paul was returning from his third missionary journey, he found a ship bound for Phoenicia at Patara on the S coast of Lycia, and sailed directly to Tyre, where passengers were disembarked for seven days, while the cargo was unloaded. Then they boarded ship again, heading S, and put in at Ptolemaïs for one day but the next day went on to Caesarea, the end of Paul's voyage. Fig. TYR 81.

Caesarea was the rival of Tyre at the time. Paul also landed there from his second missionary journey (Acts 18:22), and finally sailed from there to Rome (Acts 27:2). Caesarea had no natural harbor. Josephus (Antiq. XV.ix.6; War I.xxi.5-7) tells how Herod at great expense built this port on the old site of Strato's Tower as the show place of Judea. Josephus says Herod did this to protect ships bound for Phoenicia to Egypt from the stormy seas in this area. But Herod was, no doubt, also interested in strengthening his commerce in competition with Tyre, which was outside his kingdom. He constructed a breakwater two hundred feet wide of huge blocks of stone. The port became the seat of Roman administration of Judea (Acts 23:23-24; 25:1, 6).

5. Sea lanes. The best-known sea lanes of the time were those used by Rome to import grain from Egypt. Ships went directly to Alexandria. Its great light-

house was famous in the ancient world. Pliny (*Nat. Hist.* XIX.1) mentions a voyage from Messina to Alexandria in six days, another in seven, and one from Puteoli in nine. He also says the voyage from Gibraltar to Rome required seven days, from Hither Spain four, from Province Norbonne three, and from Africa two. But after reaching Alexandria, grain ships were compelled by unfavorable winds to return by the coasts of Syria and Asia Minor. Another famous sea lane was from Lake Maeotis above the Euxine to Alexandria. Diodorus of Sicily (III.34) says that with favorable winds ships reached Rhodes in ten days, then Alexandria in four, and from there up the Nile to Ethiopia in ten. The passage from Athens to Miletus was made in three days (Chariton *Chaereas and Callirhoe* I.xi.8). Paul sailed from Miletus to Rhodes in a day (Acts 21:1). Speed depended on wind and weather. Mediterranean winters were notoriously bad. Philo (*Embassy* 3, 29, 33) testifies to this. He remarks (*Embassy* 33) that warships are better suited to coastal voyages, while merchantmen prefer the open seas.

6. Voyages. Paul's journey to Rome (Acts 27:1–28:16) is the best-known voyage of antiquity, but the voyage of the Isis described by Lucian, as noted *above*, is worthy of comparison with it. Philo (*Embassy* 33) refers to a voyage of Petronius, a general from Caesarea, to Rome; he avoided Alexandria and followed the coast of Syria, spending each night ashore, as did Paul also (Acts 27:3). Because of inadequate lighthouses, ships avoided sailing at night when possible. Gregory Nazianzen (*Oration* XVIII.31) tells how he almost perished on a ship which dared in winter to go directly to Rhodes from Alexandria. Herod had a similar experience (Jos. Antiq. XIV. xiv.3). The Isis got into trouble by trying to sail W of Cyprus and was blown all the way back to Sidon. Then it almost came to grief following the coasts of Syria and Asia Minor. Chariton's romance (III.5.1) tells of a pirate ship which sailed from Syracuse to Miletus, but was caught in a winter storm off Crete and drifted helpless in the Sea of Adria until every member of the crew but one was dead. To encourage commercial shipping, Claudius offered substantial inducements to owners, including compensation for loss in storms (Suetonius *Claudius* XVIII).

Bibliography. C. Jacobitz, *Lucianus*, vol. III (1839). J. Smith, *The Voyage and Shipwreck of St. Paul* (1866). H. W. and F. G. Fowler, *The Works of Lucian*, vol. IV (1905). R. M. Blomfield, "Ships and Boats," *HDB*, ext. vol. (1909), pp. 359-68. M. Rostovtzeff, *A History of the Ancient World*, vol. II (1927), pls. lxiv, lxxiii. W. L. Rogers, *Greek and Roman Naval Warfare* (1937). W. E. Blake, *Charitonis Aphrodisiensis* (1938); English trans., (1939). L. Casson, "The Isis and Her Voyage," *Transcript*, American Philological Association, no. 81 (1950), pp. 43-56. E. G. Kraeling, *Bible Atlas* (1956). L. Casson, "More Deep-Sea Digging," *Archaeology*, vol. 10, no. 4 (1957), pp. 249-57; *The Ancient Mariners* (1959).   S. V. McCASLAND

SHISHA shī′shə. An alternate form of SHAVSHA.

SHISHAK shī′shăk [שׁישַׁק (*Qere*), שׁושַׁק (*Kethibh*); Akkad. *Susinḳu;* Egyp. *Šsnḳ;* LXX Σουσακ(ε)ίμ; *other Greek* Σεσώγχις, *etc.*]. An Egyptian pharaoh (*ca.* 940-915 B.C.), founder of the Twenty-second Dynasty, invader of Palestine, and plunderer of Jerusalem (I Kings 14:25-26).

When Solomon began to rule in Palestine, the central government in Egypt was weak. In the Faiyum there was a powerful family descended from Libyan chieftains. A prince of this family, Sheshonk, whom the Bible calls Shishak, became strong enough to be received on equal terms by a reigning pharaoh at Thebes. Soon Shishak claimed the rule of all Egypt, with his capital at Bubastis (PIBESETH) in the Delta. His rule was not easy, because the Delta contained many independent-minded Libyan chieftains, while Middle and Upper Egypt retained a tradition of separatism. However, he established his son as high priest of Amon at Thebes and succeeded in winning useful feudal recognition. Our chief Egyptian source of information on his Asiatic campaign comes from his building at the temple of Amon in Karnak late in his reign.

Solomon married the daughter of a pharaoh (I Kings 3:1), and this pharaoh later raided into Palestine, captured and burned the town of Gezer, and gave the city to his daughter, Solomon's wife (9:16). The pharaoh is unnamed and cannot be identified. He may have been one of the merchant-kings of the Twenty-first Dynasty residing at Tanis (Zoan) in the Delta. It would have been in character for them to secure good relations with the ambitious king at Jerusalem by such a marriage, and it may have been with such a Delta dynast that Solomon carried on his dealings in horses (I Kings 10:28-29). However, the sack of Gezer would be more like the Libyan war chieftain Shishak. Against the identification of Shishak as Solomon's father-in-law it may be argued that Jeroboam plotted against Solomon's life and then had to flee to Egypt, where Shishak gave him asylum (11:26, 40). Even though the institution of political asylum was safeguarded in the ancient Near East, the identity of Solomon's father-in-law must remain doubtful.

Ca. 920 B.C. or shortly thereafter, in the fifth year of Solomon's successor Rehoboam, Shishak made a gesture to restore some of Egypt's old glory. He led an army of Egyptians, Libyan scouts, and Libyan and Ethiopian mercenaries into Palestine for a wide-sweeping campaign. Among the cities which he captured was Jerusalem, where he looted the temple and the palace of the treasures upon which Solomon has laid out such great expenses. Some of Shishak's loot was later dedicated to the god Amon at Thebes.

Evidence for this Shishak raid into Palestine has

Courtesy of Gaddis Photo Stores, Luxor, Egypt

54. Inscription from a wall of the Amon temple at Karnak, listing the Palestine and Syrian towns taken by Shishak (Sheshonk I, in Egyptian; 940-915 B.C.)

been found at Megiddo in the fragment of a triumphal stela which he erected there.* On the walls of the temple of Karnak he listed the towns which he "captured." The list does not indicate that he went farther N than the foothills of Galilee. Thus the fragment of his seated statue found at Gebal in Phoenicia, if it was located there during his reign, must have been a gift from him to be dedicated to the local gods. The list of conquered towns runs to more than 150. *Ca.* two dozen identifications can be firmly made, most of them in the N kingdom. The section which apparently deals with localities in Judah is badly broken, but many of the towns seem to have been of minor importance. It is not known whether Jerusalem was listed in a section now broken. Figs. SHI 53, 54.

The relation between Shishak's raid and the split of the Hebrew kingdom into two realms is not clear. Rehoboam continued to sit upon the throne of Judah. Jeroboam, returned from exile, was on the throne of Israel. Biblical chronology places him there from Solomon's death, and not from the date of the Egyptian raid. Further, even though the city of Shechem has not been found in the list of conquered towns, Shishak specifically took cities in Israel, such as Megiddo. The evidence suggests that Shishak's purpose was not to support Jeroboam against Rehoboam, but to gain political and economic power.

The successors of Shishak did not have his energy or organizing ability. Two centuries were to pass before Egypt would again undertake major political and military activity in Palestine.

Bibliography. J. H. Breasted, *Ancient Records of Egypt,* vol. IV (1906), sections 709-22; H. R. Hall, in *Cambridge Ancient History,* III (1925), 257-61; A. T. Olmstead, *History of Palestine and Syria* (1931), pp. 354-56; P. G. Elgood, *The Later Dynasties of Egypt* (1951), pp. 36-45; W. F. Albright, *BASOR,* no. 153 (April, 1953), pp. 4-11. J. A. WILSON

SHITRAI shĭt′rī [שִׁטְרַי] (I Chr. 27:29). A Sharonite who was one of the royal stewards, in charge of David's herds that pastured in Sharon. The LXX B and Syr. (A) read the name as "Shirtai" (שִׁרְטַי).

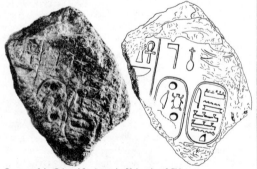

Courtesy of the Oriental Institute, the University of Chicago

53. Photo and drawing of fragment of Stele of Shishak, set up at Megiddo

SHITTAH TREE shĭt′ə [שׁטה]; **SHITTIM WOOD** shĭt′ĭm [שׁטּים]. KJV transliteration; now recognized as a kind of ACACIA tree or wood. *See* FLORA § A9*a*.

SHITTIM shĭt′ĭm [שׁטּים, acacia trees]. **1.** A place in the Plains of Moab (*see* MOAB 2), immediately NE of the Dead Sea, where the Israelites encamped before setting out to cross the Jordan. The camp was "by the Jordan from BETH-JESHIMOTH as far as Abel-shittim in the plains of Moab" (Num. 33:49). Abel-shittim seems to be the full name, while Shittim is the commonly used abbreviation.

Many important things happened while the Israelites encamped here. Balak of Moab tried to have Israel cursed by Balaam (Num. 22–24). The Israelites sinned with Moabite and Midianite women at Baal-peor and were punished (ch. 25). A census was taken (ch. 26). Joshua was publicly proclaimed as Moses' successor (27:12-23). Vengeance was taken on Midian (ch. 31). Reuben, Gad, and half-Manasseh settled E of the Jordan (32). Moses delivered his farewell address (*see* DEUTERONOMY), viewed the land from Mount Nebo, and died. Joshua sent two spies from Shittim to examine Jericho (Josh. 2). The people broke camp and moved from Shittim to the Jordan, preparing to cross over (3:1).

Mic. 6:5 speaks of "what happened from Shittim to Gilgal," probably referring to the Jordan crossing. In Hos. 5:2 the RSV emends an obscure passage to read: "They have made deep the pit of Shittim," perhaps remembering the episode of Baal-peor.

Abel-shittim has frequently been identified with Tell el-Kefrein, *ca.* seven miles E of the Jordan and *ca.* six miles N of the Dead Sea. Tell el-Kefrein is located on a completely isolated, cone-shaped hill, standing *ca.* 105 feet above the plain and commanding a splendid view of the Plains of Moab. It was occupied in OT times, since numerous Iron Age I-II (twelfth century through the beginning of the sixth century B.C.) potsherds were found. The site is small, the top of the hill measuring *ca.* 50 by 78 feet.

However, Nelson Glueck (*see bibliography*) argues convincingly that Tell el-Kefrein was only a small fortified police post and village on the way to the larger and stronger Abel-shittim, located at Tell el-Hammam, *ca.* 1½ miles E of Tell el-Kefrein. Tell el-Hammam stands on an imposing hill near the base of the hills rising to the Moabite Plateau. It commands the outlet of the Wadi el-Kefrein as it emerges from the hills, a very strategic position. On the flat top of the hill are remains of a large (*ca.* 460 by 80 feet), strongly fortified Iron Age I-II fortress. At each end was a massive tower. The fortification wall and other walls seem *ca.* 4 feet thick. There are traces of a strong glacis at one end, and it may encircle the outer wall. The entire top of the hill, inside the walled area, is covered with the foundation ruins of houses.

Bibliography. F.-M. Abel, *Géographie de la Palestine,* II (1938), 234. N. Glueck, "Some Ancient Towns in the Plains of Moab," *BASOR,* no. 91 (1943), pp. 13-18; *Explorations in Eastern Palestine,* IV, *AASOR,* XXV-XXVIII (1945-48), 221, 371-82.

2. A place name in Joel 3:18, which speaks of a fountain that will "water the valley of Shittim." If a particular valley is meant, it is probably the Wadi

en-Nar, the lower extension of the Kidron Valley. *See* KIDRON, BROOK.   E. D. GROHMAN

SHIZA shī′zə [שׁיזא] (I Chr. 11:42). The father of Adina, a Reubenite leader who was a member of the company of the Mighty Men of David known as the "Thirty."

SHOA shō′ə [שׁוע; LXX Σουε]. An unidentified people mentioned in Ezek. 23:23 after the Babylonians, the Chaldeans, and Pekod, as one of many who would rise against Judah.

SHOBAB shō′băb [שׁובב]. **1.** One of the sons of Caleb by his wife Azubah (I Chr. 2:18).

2. One of the four sons of David by Bathsheba who were born at Jerusalem (II Sam. 5:14; I Chr. 3:5; 14:4).

SHOBACH shō′băk [שׁובך] (II Sam. 10:16, 18). Alternately: **SHOPHACH** —făk [שׁופך] (I Chr. 19:16, 18). The commander of the Aramean forces marshaled by Hadadezer, king of Zobah, in his military campaign against David. After Israel's defeat of the Arameans in the first Syro-Ammonite war, Hadadezer augmented his allies with an additional complement of Aramean troops from beyond the Euphrates and placed Shobach in charge of the renewed military operations against Israel. In the ensuing battle at Helam in Transjordania, David inflicted such a crushing defeat upon the Aramean forces that the Syro-Ammonite axis was forever broken, the Aramean power was effectively curtailed, and the kingdoms lately tributary to Hadadezer became subject to David.   E. R. DALGLISH

SHOBAI shō′bī [שׁבי, *probably a shortened form, perhaps* one who leads captive; Apoc. Σαβεί]; KJV Apoc. SAMI sā′mī. One of the families of gate-keepers who returned from exile in Babylon (Ezra 2:42; Neh. 7:45; I Esd. 5:28).

SHOBAL shō′bəl [שׁובל, *perhaps nickname* basket; *cf.* Arab. *sābalun*]. **1.** The second son of Seir, and a clan chief (אלוף שׁובל, perhaps better "clan chief of Shobal") of the native Horite inhabitants of Edom (Gen. 36:20, 23, 29; I Chr. 1:38, 40).

2. Ancestor of a Calebite tribe settled in Kiriath-jearim (I Chr. 2:50, 52), apparently incorporated in Judah (I Chr. 4:1-2).   L. HICKS

SHOBEK shō′běk [שׁובק; *cf.* Arab. *sabiq,* victor] (Neh. 10:24—H 10:25). One of the chiefs of the people signatory to the covenant of Ezra.

Bibliography. M. Noth, *Die israelitischen Personennamen* (1928), p. 231.

SHOBI shō′bī [שׁבי] (II Sam. 17:27). An Ammonite prince, the son of King Nahash; with Machir the son of Ammiel from Lo-debar and Barzillai the Gileadite from Rogelim, he generously supplied David with food and equipment at Mahanaim during the rebellion of Absalom. Shobi was the brother of Hanun, the successor to his father's throne, whose scurrilous treatment of the good-will envoys of David precipitated the disastrous Ammonite wars and ultimately, with the fall of Rabbah, cost Hanun his throne. Shobi appears to have been, in his brother's stead, the Davidic nominee either as a tributary king or as a prefect (II Sam. 17:27-29; cf. II Sam. 10-12; I Chr. 19-20:3).   E. R. DALGLISH

SHOCHO, SHOCHOH, SHOCO. KJV forms of SOCO.

SHOE. *See* SANDALS AND SHOES.

SHOHAM shō'hăm [שהם, *a precious stone:* carnelian(?), beryl(?)] (I Chr. 24:27). A Levite, descendant of Merari; son of Jaaziah.

SHOMER shō'mər [שמר, keeper, watcher]. Alternately: SHEMER shē'— (I Chr. 7:34); SHIMRITH shĭm'rĭth [שלרית, *probably* (God) has protected] (II Chr. 24:26). **1.** The mother of Jehozabad, one of the servants who assassinated Joash (Jehoash) king of Judah (II Kings 12:21; II Chr. 24:26).
2. Eponym of a clan of the tribe of Asher (I Chr. 7:32, 34).   T. M. MAUCH

SHOPHACH. Alternate form of SHOBACH.

SHOPHAR shō'fär. *See* MUSICAL INSTRUMENTS § B2e.

SHOSHANNIM, SHOSHANNIM EDUTH shō-shăn'ĭm ē'dəth. *See* MUSIC § B1.

SHOULDER. Principally the translation of שכם and כתף, with nuances as in English—e.g., used in bearing burdens, supporting garments, thrusting; figuratively for the slope of a mountain jutting into the plain (cf. Shechem!), subjugation of peoples, etc.
The KJV "shoulder" of the sacrificial animal (Exod. 29; Lev. 7-10; Num. 6; 18) for שוק (with the LXX and the Vulg.) is better translated "thigh" (so RSV).   J. A. WHARTON

55. Incense shovel (Jewish?) from Palestine; Greco-Roman period

SHOVEL. 1. יעים (from יעה, "to collect"), one of the "utensils of the altar," mentioned in descriptions of the tabernacle (Exod. 27:3; 38:3; Num. 4:14) and of Solomon's temple (I Kings 7:40, 45 = II Chr. 4:11, 16). The shovels were made of bronze and were used for cleaning the altar and for removing the fat-soaked ashes and placing them into pots (Exod. 27: 3). They are listed among the booty carried off by the Chaldeans at the fall of Jerusalem in 586 B.C. (II Kings 25:14 = Jer. 52:18).
Fig. SHO 55.
2. רחת (Akkadian *rittu;* Ugaritic *rḥtm*), an implement mentioned with a FORK as used for WINNOWING (Isa. 30:34). It was a broad and shallow scoop with which threshed grain was caught up and thrown against the wind to remove the chaff.
Bibliography. G. E. Wright, *Biblical Archaeology* (1957), pp. 141-42.   J. L. MIHELIC

SHOWBREAD. *See* BREAD OF THE PRESENCE.

SHRINE. A consecrated structure housing the image of a deity or other cult object (ναός, as distinguished from the temple complex as a whole, ἱερόν).
The main room of the fosse temple at LACHISH contained an excellent example of a pre-Israelite shrine (LB II, the last phase of Canaanite culture, *ca.* 1400-1200 B.C.). It was a plastered recess in the temple wall with a wide platform to hold the cult objects. Immediately in front of the shrine was a stepped altar and a hearth. More elaborate temples, such as the later structures at Baalbek, devoted a separate building to the shrine, and placed the altars in an outer court. *See* TEMPLES.
"Shrine" appears in the RSV as an occasional translation for a number of Hebrew and Greek words or phrases. Micah's family shrine (בית אלהים; KJV lit., "house of gods"; Judg. 17:5) contained several images and was presided over by a priest. After the Assyrian conquest the semipagan population of Samaria erected shrines for their idols on the high places (בית במות; KJV lit., "houses of the high places"; II Kings 17:29, 32). These were demolished during Josiah's reform (23:19; *see* HIGH PLACE). Ezek. 16:16 refers to a shrine (במות; KJV lit., "high place") made of gaily colored cloth—probably a tent. Paul's proclamation that the true God does not live in man-made shrines (ναοί) brought him into conflict with the silversmith Demetrius, who made his living by selling models of the shrine of Artemis (Acts 17:24; 19:24).   L. E. TOOMBS

SHROUD. 1. A winding sheet for the dead. "Linen shroud" (KJV "linen cloth," "linen") is the translation of σινδών in Matt. 27:59; Mark 15:46; Luke 23:53. The word is used of a "linen cloth" used as a garment in Mark 14:51-52. *See* LINEN.
2. An archaism meaning "shelter, covert," used by the KJV to translate חרש in Ezek. 31:3 (RSV FOREST, with Akkadian and Arabic cognates).
                          H. G. MAY

SHUA shōō'ə [שוע, שועא, help; *cf.* אלישוע, אבישוע, מלכי־שוע, יהושוע; LXX Σαυα, Σωλα]; KJV SHUAH in Gen. 38:2, 12. **1.** A Canaanite, the father of Judah's wife (Gen. 38:2, 12; I Chr. 2:3 KJV). In I

Chr. 2:3 the daughter is referred to as בת־שׁוע הכנענית (KJV "the daughter of Shua the Canaanitess"), which the RSV treats as a proper name, BATH-SHUA.

2. Daughter of Heber, an Asherite (I Chr. 7:32).

Bibliography. M. Noth, *Die israelitischen Personennamen* (1928), p. 154.   L. HICKS

SHUAH shōō'ə [שׁוח; Assyrian *Šûḫu* (*an Aramean land on the Euphrates*); KJV שׁוחה (I Chr. 4:11; RSV SHUHAH), שׁוע (Gen. 38:2, 12; RSV SHUA)]; SHU-HITE —hīt. A son of Abraham by Keturah (Gen. 25:2; I Chr. 1:32). The name was probably connected with an Arab or Aramean tribe, that of the Shuhites, who later migrated near the land of Uz. Bildad the Shuhite (Job 2:11; 8:1; 18:1; 25:1; 42:9) was almost certainly a member of this tribe. The land of the Shuhites is sometimes identified with the Assyrian *Šûḫu* on the right bank of the Euphrates, S of Carchemish, between the mouths of the Balikh and Khabur rivers. An Edomitic location is also frequently suggested.

Bibliography. W. F. Albright, "The Name of Bildad the Shuhite," *AJSL,* XLIV (1927-28), 31-36.   H. F. BECK

SHUAL shōō'əl [שׁוּעָל, fox, *or* jackal(?)]. **1.** A region near OPHRAH (1), to which it is said that the first of three companies from the Philistine camp at MICH-MASH went (I Sam. 13:17). Since the second company went W toward Beth-horon, and the third went E toward the wilderness, it is probable that the first, in going "toward Ophrah, to the land of Shual," was moving in the region N of Michmash. Some have conjectured that it is the same as the "land of SHAALIM," where Saul sought the lost asses (9:4). Cf. the name of a town in S Judah, Hazar-shual, which has no apparent connection.

2. A division of the clan of Zophah of the tribe of Asher (I Chr. 7:36).   W. L. REED

SHUBAEL. Alternate form of SHEBUEL 1-2.

SHUHAH shōō'hə [שׁוחה, pit] (I Chr. 4:11); KJV SHUAH —ə. A brother of Chelub in fragmentary genealogical data concerning the tribe of Judah. Instead of "Chelub, the brother of Shuhah" (LXX BA), read: "Caleb the father of Ascha" (*see* ACHSAH).

SHUHAM shōō'hăm [שׁוחם] (Num. 26:42); SHU-HAMITES —ə mīts. Son of Dan, ancestor of the Shuhamites. Only a single Danite clan is named in the Danite genealogy here and in Gen. 46:23, where the name is give as Hushim.

SHUHITE. *See* SHUAH.

SHULAMMITE, THE shōō'lə mīt [השׁולמית] (Song of S. 6:13—H 7:1). The name or title of a maiden.

"Shulammite" is widely regarded as the equivalent of "Shunammite"—i.e., a woman from the town of SHUNEM. The interchangeability of liquids is a common linguistic phenomenon. This theory is still the most plausible. Sometimes the woman is identified with ABISHAG, the beautiful Shunammite brought to David in his old age (I Kings 1:1-4, 15; 2:17-22). If so, the usage is figurative of her legendary beauty.

The only other Shunammite specified in the OT is the wealthy woman visited by Elisha (II Kings 4:11, 25-26).

Many scholars conceive "Shulammite" to be the feminine form of "Solomon" or *sheˡlômô* (as "Judith" is feminine of "Judah"). Because of the definite article the term would likely be a title ("the Solomoness") rather than a proper name. It would designate the bride in her honorary role of "princess," companion to the bridegroom "king" (*see* SONG OF SONGS § 3*d*). In the context the Shulammite appears to dance, as the bride customarily did at the wedding ceremony.

Advocates of the cultic theory (*see* SONG OF SONGS § 3*b*) understand the Shulammite as consort of the Canaanite god of peace and well-being, Shalem, Shelem, or Shulman (*see* SOLOMON). She appears in nonbiblical sources as the goddess Shala or Shulmanitu, Ishtar of Uru-Silim-ma (Jerusalem?).

Since the *waw* is lacking in some Hebrew MSS, it is possible to read the original form as *sheˡlômîth*—i.e., the proper name SHELOMITH; or in Greek, SALOME.

Bibliography. C. Bruston, *La Sulamite* (1894); T. J. Meek, *AJSL,* XXXIX (1922), 5-7; H. H. Rowley, "The Meaning of 'The Shulammite,'" *AJSL,* LVI (1939), 84-91.   N. K. GOTTWALD

SHUMATHITE shōō'mə thīt [שׁמתי, *possibly a shortened form based upon* שׁמע, hear, *or* שׁמר, keep, watch over] (I Chr. 2:53). One of the Calebite families in Kiriath-jearim; descended from Shobal, a son of Hur.

SHUNEM shōō'nəm [שׁוּנם]; SHUNAMMITE shōō'nə mīt [שׁונמית, שׁונמית]. A border town in Issachar (Josh. 19:18), associated with the careers of Saul and Elisha. Shunem is identified with Solem, a village located *ca.* nine miles N of Jenin on the lower SW slope of Nebi Dahi, overlooking the Valley of Jezreel. Surface explorations have shown that the ancient site, which is beneath the modern village, was occupied from the Middle Bronze age through the Islamic period.

The town is first mentioned in the list of Syro-Palestinian towns conquered by Thut-mose III (1490-1435 B.C.), as Shunama. Early in the fourteenth century it was destroyed by Lab'aya, and it was rebuilt soon after by Biridiya, prince of Megiddo, according to the Amarna Letters. Thereafter, Shunem declined in importance, and it was one of the few towns in the plain captured by the Israelites (Josh. 19:18). In the late eleventh century the Philistines encamped at Shunem to do battle with Saul and the Israelites (I Sam. 28:4). It was raided by Shishak of Egypt *ca.* 918 B.C., according to the Karnak List, in which it is no. 15.

Abishag, the maiden who ministered to David in his old age (I Kings 1:3, 15) and whose hand in marriage was unsuccessfully sought by Adonijah (I Kings 2:17-22), was a Shunammite.

During the ninth century B.C., Elisha frequently stopped at Shunem, staying in the home of a good woman to whom he promised a male heir. It was here that he later revived her dead son (II Kings 4).

Bibliography. C. R. Conder and H. H. Kitchener, *SWP,* II (1882), 87; W. F. Albright, "The Topography of the Tribe of Issachar," *ŽAW*, 3 (1926), 226-34; F.-M. Abel, *Géographie de la Palestine*, II (1938), 470-71; J. B. Pritchard, ed., *ANET* (2nd ed., 1955), pp. 243, 485-86.   G. W. VAN BEEK

SHUNI shōō′nī [שׁוּנִי] (Gen. 46:16; Num. 26:15); SHUNITES —nīts. The third son of Gad; ancestral head of the "family of the Shunites."

SHUPHAM. KJV form of SHEPHUPHAM.

SHUPPIM shŭp′ĭm [שֻׁפִּים, שֻׁפָּם]. 1. A late, contracted form of SHEPHUPHAM.

2. A gatekeeper stationed on the W side of Jerusalem (I Chr. 26:16). The name appears here erroneously as a result of dittography from the last word of the preceding verse, as comparison with I Chr. 26:10 confirms.   R. F. JOHNSON

SHUR, WILDERNESS OF shōōr [מִדְבַּר שׁוּר, *see below*]. A place or a region on the NE border of Egypt, whither the Israelites went after they crossed the RED SEA (Exod. 15:22). The parallel account in Num. 33:8 has Etham instead of Shur.

Shur is also mentioned in several other passages. The angel of the Lord found Hagar "by a spring of water in the wilderness, the spring on the way to Shur" (Gen. 16:7). Abraham "dwelt between Kadesh and Shur" (20:1), the Ishmaelites "dwelt from Havilah to Shur, which is opposite Egypt in the direction of Assyria" (25:18). Saul "defeated the Amalekites, from Havilah as far as Shur, which is east of Egypt" (I Sam. 15:7), and "David and his men . . . made raids upon the Geshurites, the Girzites, and the Amalekites . . . , as far as Shur, to the land of Egypt" (27:8).

These references give us only the general direction—i.e., its location was somewhere in the proximate vicinity of Egypt and E of it. One can assume that it was a general designation for the Sinai wilderness E of Lake Timsah.

The "Way of Shur" (Gen. 16:7) is probably the ancient caravan route, called Darb el Shur, which went from Hebron by way of Beer-sheba, Khalasa, Ruheibeh, Bir Birein, Muweilleh, and on to the S into Egypt. Some believe that in biblical times "Shur" was a reference to a line of disconnected frontier fortresses which the Egyptians had erected to keep out the invaders from the E. Others claim that "Shur" denoted the long range of white cliffs, parallel to the coast, some twelve to fourteen miles E of the Gulf of Suez, and now called Jebel er-Rahah. These cliffs were given the name Shur ("Wall") because at a distance they have the appearance of a wall. It is claimed that the Arabs still call these cliffs Jebel es-Shur. The objection to this explanation is the fact that Shur means a "wall" only in Aramaic (Ezra 4: 12-13, 16). In biblical Hebrew it is used in this sense only in poetry (Gen. 49:22; Ps. 18:29 = II Sam. 22: 30). Moreover, as a proper noun, referring to topography and having appellative force, it lacks the definite article which is usual with such terms (cf. "the Jordan" [הַיַּרְדֵּן] in Josh. 3:1, 14; 4:1; and "the height" [הָרָמָה] in Josh. 18:25; Judg. 4:5; etc.).

Bibliography. C. L. Woolley and T. E. Lawrence, *The Wilderness of Zin* (new ed., 1936), pp. 57-62; E. G. Kraeling, *Bible Atlas* (1956), pp. 64, 69.   J. L. MIHELIC

SHUSHAN. KJV form of SUSA.

SHUSHAN EDUTH shōō′shăn ē′dŭth. *See* MUSIC § B1.

SHUTHELAH shōō′thə lə [שׁוּתֶלַח]; SHUTHELA-HITES —hīts; KJV SHUTHALHITES —thəl hīts. 1. The first son of Ephraim, and the father of Eran (Num. 26:35-36; I Chr. 7:20 [here, father of Bered]); ancestor of the "family of the Shuthelahites" (Num. 26:35).

2. A descendant of 1 *above* (I Chr. 7:21; LXX Σωθελε). However, the Ephraimite genealogy here is quite confused (perhaps containing three recensions of the earlier list in Num. 26:35-37), so that this Shuthelah may be only a repetition of 1 *above*.

Also, the LXX inserts Shuthelah (Σουταλααμ) and his son Edem into Gen. 46:20*b*.   L. HICKS

SHUTTLE [אֶרֶג] (Job 7:6; cf. Judg. 16:14). The tool used by a weaver to shoot the thread of the woof from one side to the other through the threads of the warp. In Judg. 16:14 (LOOM; KJV BEAM) the word might perhaps be read with different vowels, "weaver."   J. M. MYERS

SIA sī′ə [סִיעָא] (Neh. 7:47). Alternately: SIAHA sī′ə hə [סִיעֲהָא; Σουα] (Ezra 2:44; I Esd. 5:29); KJV Apoc. SUA sōō′ə. One of the temple servants, or NETHINIM, who returned from the Exile.

SIBBECAI sĭb′ə kī [סִבְּכַי]; KJV SIBBECHAI in II Sam. 21:18; I Chr. 20:4. A Zerahite of the town of Hushah who was included among the Mighty Men of David known as the "Thirty" (I Chr. 11:29; cf. II Sam. 23:27). Sibbecai is credited with the slaying of the Philistine giant Saph (II Sam. 21:18; Sippai in I Chr. 20:4) in a campaign against the Philistines at Gob (Gezer in Chronicles). He was the commander of the Davidic militia which served during the eighth month (I Chr. 27:11).

In II Sam. 23:27 his name is given as MEBUNNAI, but this appears to be an erroneous reading of the not-dissimilar word "Sibbecai."   E. R. DALGLISH

SIBBOLETH sĭb′ə lĭth [סִבֹּלֶת] (Judg. 12:6). Hebrew spelling of the Ephraimites' mispronunciation of the password SHIBBOLETH.

SIBMAH sĭb′mə [שִׂבְמָה]; KJV SHIBMAH shĭb′mə in Num. 32:38. Alternately: SEBAM sē′băm [שְׂבָם] (Num. 32:3); KJV SHEBAM shē′băm. A city of the pastoral tableland in Transjordan, given to the tribe of Reuben after the defeat of Sihon king of the Amorites (Num. 32:3, 38; Josh. 13:19). In the time of the oracles against Moab (Isa. 16:8-9; Jer. 48:32), it was in Moabite possession and was known for its vineyards, which were destroyed by the "lords of the nations." According to Jerome, it was located hardly five hundred paces from Heshbon. However, Sibmah was perhaps too important a place to be so near Heshbon, and some would identify it with Qurn el-Kibsh, between Heshbon and Nebo, overlooking the Wadi Salmah. This site is on a high, flat-topped hill, with an area of *ca.* 311 by 104 yards having been enclosed by a great wall.

Bibliography. N. Glueck, *Explorations in Eastern Palestine,* II, *AASOR,* XV (1934-35), 111: F.-M. Abel, *Géographie de la Palestine,* II (1938), 458.   E. D. GROHMAN

SIBRAIM sĭb rā'əm [סברים] (Ezek. 47:16). A place in the N borderland of Canaan, between Damascus and Hamath, probably in the neighborhood of Hums. It may be identical with SEPHARVAIM.

SIBYLLINE ORACLES sĭb'ə lēn. A collection of prophecies or wise sayings in Greek hexameter verse combining elements pagan, Jewish, and Christian. First mentioned by Heraclitus of Ephesus in 500 B.C., Sibyl (Σίβυλλα) was a prophetess of Cumae. Later, there came to be many "sibyls," and the term was sometimes employed to mean a diviner or seer in general. The collection of oracles attributed to Sibyl grew, under Jewish as well as Christian influences, from early times till the fourth century after Christ and eventually comprised fifteen books, most of which have been recovered. Hermas (*see* HERMAS, SHEPHERD OF) among Christian writers first mentions the Sibyl; but Justin, Theophilus of Antioch, Clement of Alexander, and other writers cite the oracles with respect.

Bibliography. J. Geffcken, ed., *Die Oracula Sibyllina* (1902); R. H. Charles, *The Apoc. and Pseudep. of the OT,* vol. II (1913). See also J. Moffatt, in *Dictionary of the Apostolic Church* (1915).   J. KNOX

SICHEM. KJV form of SHECHEM.

SICK, SICKNESS. *See* DISEASE.

SICKLE [מגל, חרמש; δρέπανον]. An implement for reaping standing grain. In the early periods it consisted of serrated flints inserted into a rounded

From Petrie, *Gerar;* by permission of the Department of Egyptology, University College London

56. Reconstructed arrangement of sickle flints, from Gerar; Eighteenth Dynasty

wooden frame; later it was made of metal with a wooden handle riveted on.

Fig. SIC 56.

SICYON sĭsh'ĭ ən [Σικυών, Συκυών, Σικιών, cucumber town]. A city of ancient Greece on the S shore of the Gulf of Corinth, eighteen miles NW of Corinth, and later a center of Roman power. In the Maccabean period it was granted the direction of the Isthmian games. The ancient city was on the shore, and on a terrace behind stood an acropolis. It was a busy place industrially and artistically, but it greatly declined during the first and second centuries A.D. According to I Macc. 15:23, Sicyon was one among many places to which the Roman consul Lucius wrote on behalf of the Senate, asking them not to fight against the Jews and to return all Jewish fugitives to Simon (139 B.C.). There must have been considerable Jewish populations in these places. Philo supports this latter supposition as far as Corinth is concerned (*Legation to Caius* 36).   N. TURNER

SIDDIM, VALLEY OF sĭd'ĭm [עמק השדים]; KJV VALE OF SIDDIM. A valley at the S end of the Dead Sea. It served as a battleground in the struggle of the five cities of the area (Sodom, Gomorrah, Admah, Zeboiim, and Zoar) to throw off the yoke of four Mesopotamian kings under the leadership of Chedorlaomer, king of Elam (Gen. 14:3, 8). This valley is specifically equated with the Salt Sea (vs. 3) —i.e., the DEAD SEA. The only suitable understanding of this equation interprets the valley in question to be covered by the shallow waters of the S embayment of the Dead Sea, S of the peninsula (el-Lisan) projecting from the Sea's E shore. Evidence from archaeology, topography, geology, hydrography, and classical tradition is in support of such a conclusion. The area is further described as containing numerous bitumen pits which served as death traps to some of the defeated and fleeing soldiers of Sodom and Gomorrah (Gen. 14:10). Chunks of bituminous material still, on occasion, rise to the surface of this S embayment.

Bibliography. J. P. Harland, "Sodom and Gomorrah: The Location of the Cities of the Plain," *BA,* V (1942), 17-32.   W. H. MORTON

SIDE sī'dĭ [Σίδη]. A port on a promontory on the coast of Pamphylia; a favorite haunt of Cilician pirates. The site now consists of extensive ruins at Eski Adalia. It had two harbors and was a useful refuge for those who wished to dispose of plunder. It was the scene of a sea battle between the Rhodians and Antiochus III the Great of Syria, wherein ships from Side and Aradus formed the left wing of the fleet of Antiochus. It was colonized originally by Cymeans and remained important as late as under the Roman emperors. This was one of the places to which the Roman consul Lucius is said to have written letters in 139 B.C. requesting kindly treatment for the Jews and the return of all fugitive Jews to Simon Maccabeus (I Macc. 15:23). Antiochus VII Sidetes was brought up here. Much coinage of Side is extant.

See also ANTIOCHUS 3, 7.   N. TURNER

SIDON sī'dən [צידון, צידן; Akkad. *and* Amarna *Ṣidun(n)u, Ṣa'idunu;* Phoen. צדן; Σιδών], SIDONIANS sī dō'nĭ ənz; KJV often ZIDON zī'—, ZIDONIANS. A Phoenician city between Tyre and Beirut.

1. Location. Sidon, now Saida, is situated on a small hill, projecting into the Mediterranean, *ca.* twenty-five miles N of Tyre. Behind the city is a fertile plain, which is now used for growing oranges and lemons. The city was protected on the side toward the land by a wall. There was a harbor on the N side, good and well protected, and another one on the S side. Some small islands help to keep heavy waves away. Like people in other Phoenician towns,

57. Air view of Sidon

the inhabitants of Sidon lived on agriculture, fishing, and trade, for which the city is well situated. The fishing fleet still uses the harbor, and a great shell mound by the city walls, consisting of millions of murex shells, tells about the important purple industry of ancient Sidon. *See* CANAANITES § 1; PURPLE. Fig. SID 57.

2. History. Like Tyre and Byblos, Sidon is a very old city. Little is known, however, about its most ancient times. The Amarna Letters (*see* TELL EL-AMARNA) from the thirteenth century B.C. reveal that while Tyre remained faithful to Egypt, King Zimreda of Sidon, in spite of his devoted letters to the Pharaoh, was an ally of King 'Aziru, the Amorite. Egypt at that time was losing its hold on Sidon, but it was still trading with it at the time of Wen-Amon (*ca.* 1100). Hittites and Hapiru, as well as the "Sea Peoples" from the N, tried to dominate Sidon in this time, but the city was able to keep a rather independent position.

The dominating position of Sidon is indicated also in the OT. In the genealogical lists in Gen. 10:15; I Chr. 1:13, Sidon is mentioned as the first-born of Canaan. In Gen. 10:15 it is implied that Sidon was at the N border of the territory of the Canaanites; so also Gen. 49:13 (cf. II Sam. 24:6). It is also called "Great Sidon" (Josh. 11:8; 19:28). It was never Israelite territory, but was close to the border of the tribe of Asher (Judg. 1:31). Sidon and Sidonians are often mentioned in a way which indicates that Phoenicia and the Phoenicians are meant (Deut. 3:9; Judg. 3:3; 10:6, 12; 18:7; I Kings 5:6; 11:1, 5, 33; 16:31; II Kings 23:13). This is especially clear in I Kings 16:31, where Ethba'al, the king of Tyre, is called "king of the Sidonians." The information here shows that at the time of Ahab (ninth century), Sidon was no longer the dominating Phoenician city; its hegemony had passed over to Tyre. But at this time the Assyrians pressed toward the W, and both Sidon and Tyre had to pay tribute again and again— to Ashurnasirpal II in 876; to Shalmaneser III (858-824); Tiglath-pileser III (744-727); and in 725 to Shalmaneser V (727-722), who invaded the Phoenician cities. The Assyrians were, however, interested in supporting Sidon against its rival, Tyre. In spite of this situation, Sidon and Tyre were considered as dangerous and arrogant by their neighbors. Especially the prophets of Israel saw them in this light and predicted their destruction (Isa. 23; Jer. 25:22; 27:3-6; 47:4; Ezek. 28:20-23; Joel 3:4). In the book of Ezekiel, however, the prophet seems to be aware that Tyre was dominating at this time and that the men of Sidon had to serve as rowers for the Tyrians (27:8).

The destruction of Sidon actually took place in 677. While Tyre had revolted several times against the Assyrians, it was first after the death of Sargon II in 705 that King Luli of Sidon, together with his allies, made an attempt to throw off the yoke. Sennacherib crushed the revolt in 701. Luli had to flee to Cyprus, and Sennacherib appointed Ethba'al as his successor, and inscribed his victory at the side of the inscription of Ramses II on the rock near the mouth of the River Nahr el-Kelb. But the son of Ethba'al, Abdimilkutte, also revolted, and this time the Assyrian king, Esarhaddon, preferred to destroy the city and kill its king.

Esarhaddon also tried to build a new city in the neighborhood, populated with deported people from around the Persian Gulf. But instead, Sidon grew up again. It was dominated by the Egyptians for a short time, 609-593, but was then conquered by King Nebuchadrezzar. The Babylonian sway did not last long, and under Persian domination Sidon regained some of its old importance and also a certain independence. It furnished ships for the navy of King Xerxes I and had them destroyed in the Battle of Salamis in 480. It may have been experiences like these which made the Sidonians revolt against Artaxerxes III Ochus in 351. They were encouraged by Egypt, but received no help when Artaxerxes advanced with a great army. King Tennes became

58. Sarcophagus of Eshmunazar, king of Sidon

frightened and fled, leaving the city to its fate. Its people burned all the ships in the harbor, so that nobody could flee. Then they went to their homes and stayed there when the city was burned. More than forty thousand are said to have lost their lives. It is no wonder, then, that Sidon surrendered to Alexander the Great without battle in 333.

The stone coffins of two of the succeeding Sidonian kings were dug out from the rock tombs near the city in the nineteenth century.* Tabnit and his son Eshmun'azar II reigned *ca.* 300 B.C. Tabnit called himself "priest of Astarte (Ashtart), king of the Sidonians," and Eshmun'azar II boasts that he and his family built temples for Astarte, Eshmun, and Baal. Fig. SID 58.

In the times of the Seleucids, Sidon again attained a rather independent position. There was a change in this after 64 B.C., when Pompey imposed Roman rule in Phoenicia, but Sidon still remained a prosperous and flourishing city for a long time. Its importance vanished slowly. The Phoenician monopoly in the purple industry was broken in Roman times, but the demand was still enormous for centuries. The cedar trees, which Sidon had used so freely in its trade (cf. I Chr. 22:4; Ezra 3:7), had also started decreasing.

In the NT, Sidon and the Sidonians are mentioned several times—e.g., Matt. 11:21, 22; Luke 4:26; 10: 13, 14; Acts 12:20. Jesus himself went to Sidon (Matt. 15:21; Mark 7:24, 31), and he preached to people from that city (Mark 3:8; Luke 6:17). Paul was there on his way to Rome (Acts 27:3).

Today Saida has *ca.* fifty thousand inhabitants. Its landmark is the big ruin of a Crusader castle.

Bibliography. G. A. Cooke, *A Text-Book of North Semitic Inscriptions* (1903), pp. 26-43; F. C. Eiselen, *Sidon: A Study in Oriental History* (1907); C. C. Torrey in *AASOR* (1919-20); G. Contenau, *La civilisation phénicienne* (1928); P. K. Hitti, *History of Syria* (1951); J. Huxley, *From an Antique Land* (1954), pp. 70-76.   A. S. KAPELRUD

SIDRACH sĭd'răk. Douay Version form of SHADRACH.

SIEGE. *See* WAR, METHODS OF, § 9.

SIEVE [כברה (Amos 9:9); נפה (Isa. 30:28)]. Isa. 30: 28 refers to a day of judgment when the Lord will sift the nations "with the sieve of destruction." In Amos 9:9 a similar sifting of the house of Israel is foreseen. *See* FAN; WINNOWING.

SIGNAL [מועד (KJV APPOINTED SIGN), משאת (KJV FLAME; SIGN OF FIRE), נס (KJV ENSIGN; BANNER; STANDARD), שרק (*verb;* KJV HISS)]. Clouds of smoke (Judg. 20:38), whistles (Isa. 5:26), cries and hand waving (13:2), trumpets (18:3), and flagstaffs (30:17) would seem to have been recognized signals in the OT. The terms "sign" and "signal" can be used interchangeably in rendering many of these Hebrew words. The signs of forthcoming events which were interpreted by priest and prophet were often intended as signals for concerted action. Such signs frequently conveyed some indication of the nature of the forthcoming event.

See also SIGNS AND WONDERS.   H. F. BECK

SIGNATURE [תוי] (Job 31:35); KJV DESIRE. This word is taken as the last letter of the Hebrew alphabet with the suffix of the first person singular: "my *tau*"—i.e., my "mark" or "sign." In biblical times the letter had the form of an "x" (cf. I Sam. 21:13; Ezek. 9:4). Job 31:35 then reflects a written legal process in which the defendant sets his signature upon a declaration of his innocence, and awaits the counter declaration of his accuser.

Bibliography. G. Hölscher, *Das Buch Hiob* (1952); L. Koehler and W. Baumgartner, *Lexicon in Veteris Testamenti Libros* (1953), p. 1020; S. Terrien, Exegesis of Job, *IB*, III (1954), 1124-25; G. W. Driver, *Semitic Writing* (1954), pp. 88-89 (but cf. p. 209, where he defends a different interpretation of Job 31:35).   J. A. WHARTON

SIGN IN THE OT [אות (*alternately* MARK; TESTIMONY; OMEN; GOOD OMEN; KJV TOKEN); את (Dan. 4:2-3—Aram. 3:32-33); ציון (Ezek. 39:15), *see* WAYMARK]; PORTENT [מופת; KJV *alternately* WONDER]; SIGNAL [משאת; KJV SIGN OF FIRE]; WARNING [נס]. A mark, symbol, or portent, serving to convey a particular idea or meaning. The various biblical words for "sign" usually take their meaning from their context, but in some cases their precise sense is uncertain. For "sign" as a miraculous act, *see* SIGNS AND WONDERS. *See also* SIGN IN THE NT.

1. A physical sign, something portentous
2. An identifying mark
3. A declaration
4. A warning
5. A proof of assurance
6. A reminder
7. A portent or object lesson
8. An omen
9. A witness or testimony

1. A physical sign, sometimes portentous. In Gen. 1:14 the heavenly bodies are to serve as signs— i.e., as directional, calendar, and weather indicators. In Jer. 10:2 the "signs of the heavens" suggest extraordinary celestial phenomena. In Ps. 65:8—H 65:9 "thy signs" seem to mean God's creative acts and his manifestations in nature. In Josh. 4:6; Ezek. 39:15 a sign is a cairn or a small heap of stones. In Ps. 74:4 military ensigns may be meant (cf. "signal," KJV "sign of fire," in Jer. 6:1). In Joel 2:30—H 3:3 "portents in the heavens and on the earth" mark the coming of the day of the Lord.

2. An identifying mark. The blood on the Hebrew houses is a sign to identify them (Exod. 12:13).

3. A declaration. The rainbow betokens God's covenant with Noah and all the earth (Gen. 9:12-13, 17); circumcision points to the covenant with Abram (Gen. 17:11).

4. A warning. The covering of the altar, made from the censers of Korah and his family, is to be a permanent warning to Israel (Num. 16:38), while the death of Korah and his company is to serve a similar purpose (Num. 26:10). Aaron's rod, kept before the ark, is to rebuke all potential troublemakers (Num. 17:10). In Ezek. 4:3 the sketch of the besieged city of Jerusalem on a brick is to warn Israel of what is soon to be a fact. The symbolic acts in Ezek. 12:1-16; 24:15-27 are signs in this sense.

5. A proof or assurance. In Josh. 2:12 Rahab asks for a "sure sign" that she and her family will be spared. A sign, meaning something which proves God's word or a prophet's to be true, is referred to in Exod. 3:12; I Sam. 10:7, 9; 14:10; I Kings 13:3, 5; II Kings 19:29 (cf. Isa. 37:30); 20:8-9 (cf. II Chr. 32:24, 31; Isa. 38:7); Isa. 7:11, 14; 38:22; Jer. 44:29. In Ps. 86:17 "sign" means a demonstration of God's favor.

6. A reminder. In Exod. 13:9 the Passover is to be like a sign on the hand: it will recall the deliverance from Egypt. Similarly in vs. 16 the sacrifice or redemption of the first-born in Israel has a commemorative purpose. In 31:17 sabbath-observance is to remind Israel of God's creative work and of the Creator's day of rest (cf. Ezek. 20:12, 20). In Deut. 6:8 God's words are to be bound as a sign upon the hand, so that they will never be forgotten. This passage and 11:18-20 were to serve as the scriptural basis for the later Jewish practice of wearing phylacteries.

7. A portent or object lesson. In Ps. 71:7 the psalmist claims to have been a portent to his contemporaries. Isaiah makes the same assertion about himself and his children (Isa. 8:18; cf. 20:3). The figure is used of an idolater in Ezek. 14:8.

8. An omen. The omens of soothsayers are mentioned in Isa. 44:25. Some take "signs" in Ps. 74:9 as a reference to priestly omens (others take as "ensigns," as in vs. 4). The phrase "men of sign" (Zech. 3:8) is thought to mean "men of good omen" (so RSV).

9. A witness or testimony. In Isa. 19:19 an altar in Egypt is to bear witness to the Lord in an alien land. The everlasting sign in Isa. 55:13 presumably means that the blessedness of the future will be a witness to the Lord's word and purpose (cf. 66:19). "Testimony" is used in this sense in Job 21:29.

W. S. McCullough

*SIGN IN THE NT [σημεῖον]. A word which occurs scores of times in the NT, and, as in the Bible generally, denotes an outward indication of an inner or hidden purpose, usually that of God himself. A sign is not necessarily supernatural in character, though frequently it is itself a prodigy (cf. the frequent combination σημεῖα καὶ τέρατα, "signs and wonders"), since in NT times it was considered reasonable to expect that God would authenticate any disclosure of his intention by means of supernatural occurrences.

1. The expectation of the signs of the Messiah
2. Jesus as himself the Sign
3. The miracles of Jesus as signs
4. The signs of the End
Bibliography

1. The expectation of the signs of the Messiah. In biblical times it would be a natural expectation that a true prophet should authenticate his message by showing signs; it was worthy of remark that John the Baptist had shown no sign (John 10:41). The Messiah, who was "the Prophet" par excellence (John 1:21; 6:14; cf. Deut. 18:15), would be expected to offer signs by which he might be recognized; but since there was considerable vagueness about the

Messiah's appearing, there would also inevitably be uncertainty about the signs he would show. It was wholly in keeping with the outlook of the age that the Pharisees should demand from Jesus a sign from heaven in order that he might authenticate himself, whether as prophet or as Messiah (Matt. 12:38; Mark 8:11; Luke 11:16; John 2:18). Thus, too, Paul speaks as if the Corinthians had every right to expect him to show the "signs of an apostle"—namely, σημεῖα καὶ τέρατα καὶ δυνάμεις (II Cor. 12:12). It was, in fact, regarded as axiomatic, at least until the nineteenth century, that a supernatural revelation should be attested by supernatural signs, although the sign itself need not be miraculous in character. The angel at the Nativity offered to the shepherds the σημεῖον of the babe in the manger (Luke 2:12), and Simeon spoke of the child Jesus as a "sign that is spoken against" (Luke 2:34). The manner of Jesus' birth is, for those who understand who he is, a sign of the divine initiative in our redemption, as also his resurrection from the dead is the sign of the divine authentication of his words and work (cf. Acts 2:22, 32-36). For the apostolic church the whole story of Jesus from his conception by the Holy Spirit to his ascension into heaven is a "sign" vouchsafed by God to those who will receive it; this attitude is especially characteristic of the Fourth Gospel. *See bibliography.*

2. Jesus as himself the Sign. Jesus condemned the attitude of those who demanded a sign in the heavens (Matt. 12:39; Mark 8:12; Luke 11:29; cf. Paul in I Cor. 1:22) and refused to give a sign. His point of view is that of the Bible generally. To demand a sign indicates lack of faith (John 20:24-30); thus the Israelites of old had tempted God in the wilderness by their demand for signs (Num. 11, etc.), and Paul reminds the Corinthians that the story of their fate was written for our admonition: "We must not put the Lord to the test, as some of them did and were destroyed by serpents" (I Cor. 10:9-11). It is highly significant that in the temptation story (Matt. 4:1-11; Luke 4:1-13) Jesus, the new Israel, refuses the suggestions of the devil and will not demand of God a sign; "You shall not tempt the Lord your God" (Matt. 4:7; Luke 4:12; quoted from Deut. 6:16). Forty years the old Israel had hardened its heart, as in the day of Massah (temptation) in the wilderness, and had tempted God (Ps. 95:8-10); but now the new Israel, Christ, being tempted to ask for a sign of God's favor, rejects the tempter in the wilderness during the forty days of testing. Thus, Jesus refused to ask for a sign and likewise to give a sign, since the demand for signs proceeds from unfaith. He would trust in God, and his followers must trust in him, apart entirely from supernatural signs.

Yet as God had given to the old Israel signs of his redemptive activity when he led his people forth from Egypt, across the Red Sea, and through the wilderness, so now God was giving signs that a mightier redemption was at hand. But they were signs of God's own choosing, not of man's. It seems clear that Jesus regarded John the Baptist as well as himself, his own preaching and healing works, as one of those "signs of the times" (Matt. 16:3) which the Pharisees ought to have understood. He himself performs prophetic signs, like those given by the prophets of old; such as, e.g., the great teaching sign of riding into Jerusalem upon an ass in fulfilment of Zech. 9:9 (Matt. 21:5). Even the pagan Ninevites had repented at the sign of Jonah's preaching, and the Queen of the South had recognized the sign of Solomon (Matt. 12:39-42; Luke 11:29-32); but the signs Jesus was showing, the signs of God's redemptive activity in this age (καιρός), were not the signs for which disobedient Israel was looking. Even heathen Tyre and Sidon would have understood and repented if they had seen the acts of power which had been done in Chorazin and Beth-saida (Matt. 11:20-24; Luke 10:13). But it was not so much his actions as his person which Jesus regarded as being primarily the sign of God's redemptive activity. The Son of man was himself the sign vouchsafed to that generation that the day of redemption was at hand; perhaps this was one of the reasons why Jesus adopted the title "Son of man" as his own personal self-designation. Ezekiel had, like other prophets (e.g., Isa. 8:18), regarded himself as a sign to his generation (Ezek. 12:6; 24:24), sent to speak God's word, whether they would hear or whether they would forbear (3:4, 11, etc.). So the Son of man, Jesus, is sent to proclaim God's word and to be a sign to a disobedient people; cf. Ezekiel's "He that will hear, let him hear" (3:27) with Jesus' "He who has ears to hear, let him hear" (Mark 4:9, etc.).

3. The miracles of Jesus as signs. Thus, Jesus refused to work prodigies (τέρατα) as signs in order to convince unbelievers, for he knew that such conviction was worthless (Matt. 4:5-7; Mark 15:32; Luke 16:27-31; John 6:26). Yet he regarded his miracles (δυνάμεις) as signs to those who already had the eyes of faith. His exorcisms were the sign that the kingdom of God was at hand and that Satan's kingdom was at an end (Mark 3:22-27); his preaching and his healing work were the fulfilment of the signs foretold by Isaiah concerning the days of the Messiah (Matt. 11:2-6; Luke 7:18-23; cf. Isa. 35:5-6, etc.). The significance of the miracles of Jesus as "signs" of the divine activity of redemption is understood only by those who believe in him; others are offended at him. "Blessed is he who takes no offense at me" (Luke 7:23). It is especially the Fourth Evangelist who develops the significance of the miracles of Jesus as signs (John 2:11, etc.); indeed, he never uses the word δύναμις but speaks many times of σημεῖα. *See also* MIRACLE.

4. The signs of the End. The person of the Son of man, as also his works (ἔργα), are in the view of the NT writers the signs of the end of the age, or of the dawning of the Day of the Lord. Nevertheless, Jesus had lived and died and risen again, and the Holy Spirit had been poured out in the latter days, but the world went on in very much the same way as before his birth. It was inevitable that there should be much discussion in the early church concerning the signs of the End, which in one sense had come already, but which in another sense was still to come. Tradition reported that Jesus himself had spoken of certain signs by which his followers might know when the End in this second sense was approaching (Mark 13:4-37). There would be wars, earthquakes, famines, and persecutions of the faithful, and with all these things there would be the sign of the preaching of the gospel to all nations, which would have to be

accomplished before the End could come (Matt. 24:14; Mark 13:10). The word of God must "smite the nations" before the End is consummated (Rev. 19:11-16). During the period before the End, the faithful must watch against temptations, closely connected, as we should expect, with false signs (Mark 13:6, 22; II Thess. 2:9; Rev. 13:13). Patient endurance is the quality required for such times; it is contrasted with the credulous looking for false signs by which even the elect may be deceived: "Watch and pray that you may not enter into temptation" (Mark 14:38).

Bibliography. A. Richardson, *Miracle Stories of the Gospels* (1941), ch. 3; C. H. Dodd, *Interpretation of the Fourth Gospel* (1953), pp. 297-389; E. J. Tinsley, "The Sign of the Son of Man," *Scottish Journal of Theology*, vol. 8, no. 3 (Sept., 1955); A. Richardson, *Introduction to the Theology of the NT* (1958), ch. 1.   ALAN RICHARDSON

SIGNET [חוֹתָם, חֹתֶם, חֹתֶמֶת (*alternately* SIGNET RING; SEAL); Aram. עִזְקָא (*only in* Dan. 6:17—H 6:18)]; **SIGNET RING** [טַבַּעַת (KJV RING)]. A ring used for impressing its owner's signature on the seals of documents and the like; often the mark of royalty or nobility. *See* KING.

An important person made his signature by pressing his ring into a plastic substance, such as wax, affixed to the document or other object being signed (Esth. 8:8; Dan. 6:17—H 6:18). Rings used for this purpose were normally made of gold and set with precious or semiprecious stones into which the name or personal insignia was cut by a skilled engraver, although ordinary stone or faïence scarabs set in gold or bronze might be used, and the signet could be carried on a cord around the neck instead of being set in a ring (*see* RING; SEALS AND SCARABS). The artistic ability of the signet maker set the standard for all delicate work with jewels, so that specific instructions are given that the inscriptions on the high priest's ephod, breastpiece, and crown should be engraved "as a jeweler engraves signets" (Exod. 28:11, 21, 36; 39:6, 14, 30). Since many influential citizens wore signets, they were common enough to be among the gifts of gold for the tabernacle (Exod. 35:22), and to be included in the booty of war (Num. 31:50), but they were rare and costly enough to be named by Isaiah among the signs of luxury and affectation in Israel (Isa. 3:21).

The signets of men of noble or princely rank, whose signatures carried authority, had a special importance (Gen. 38:18; Dan. 6:17); and the king's ring, with which he signed state documents, was particularly significant. The giving of this ring to a trusted counselor, as Pharaoh did to Joseph and the Persian king successively to Haman and Mordecai, was a mark of singular favor, since it conferred extraordinary powers upon the recipient (Gen. 41:42; Esth. 3:10; 8:2). The precious nature of the signet, together with the authority represented by the king's ring, gives rise to the striking metaphor by which a leader of Israel may be called the signet on Yahweh's hand (e.g., Zerubbabel in Hag. 2:23; and, ironically, Coniah in Jer. 22:24). A number of translations, including the RSV, read "signet" in Ezek. 28:12, where the Hebrew is obscure.

For archaeological examples of signet rings and

seals which were used as signets, *see* SEALS
AND SCARABS.   L. E. TOOMBS

SIGNS AND WONDERS. A word-combination
which appears many times in the Bible and may be
called a traditional formula. *See also* MIRACLE.

Of the approximately thirty-five occurrences of the
word "wonder" (מופת) in the OT, eighteen instances
are parallel to, and nine are practically synonymous
with, the' word "sign" (אות), for the meanings of the
words overlap (cf. Deut. 28:45-46; Ezek. 12:6, 11).
Israel's confession of faith, as expressed in the ancient cultic credo, included the affirmation that Yahweh brought his people out of Egypt "with signs and
wonders" (Deut. 6:20-24; 26:5-10; cf. Josh. 24:17).
This formula, which witnesses to Israel's faith in
Yahweh as the Lord of history (*see* GOD, OT VIEW
OF, § 1), is found again and again—e.g., in the
hortatory appeals of Deuteronomy (4:34; 7:19; 11:3;
29:3—H 29:2), in various summaries of *Heilsgeschichte*
(Neh. 9:10; Jer. 32:20-21; Acts 7:36), and in psalms
which recall Yahweh's marvelous dealings with his
people (Pss. 78:43; 105:27; 135:9).

In the NT the word "wonder" (τέρας) never
occurs by itself but always as a plural form in conjunction with "signs" (σημεῖα). Although the NT
word-combination σημεῖα καὶ τέρατα (Mark 13:22;
John 4:48; Acts 2:43; Rom. 15:19; etc.) has parallels in Greek literary tradition, the major point of
contact is with the LXX, where the expression occurs
frequently as a translation of אותות ומופתים.

1. The wonderful character of revelation. Theologically speaking, revelation and miracle are inseparably related. Whenever and wherever God reveals
himself in the world, the man of faith is conscious
of miracle. For REVELATION is not an event which
springs out of natural causes or explainable phenomena; God's holiness is otherworldly—i.e., beyond
anything known or conceivable in the ordinary world
'(*see* GOD, OT VIEW OF, § 4*a*). Thus the divine mystery is disclosed in happenings which evoke the response of awe, fear, and wonder (cf. Exod. 3:1-6).

The response to God's presence is indicated in the
vocabulary of miracles. God performs פלא, a wonder
or marvel which surpasses understanding (Exod.
15:11; Pss. 77:14—H 77:15; 78:12; 88:10, 12—H
88:11, 13; 89:5—H 89:6; Isa. 25:1); his acts of judgment and redemption are נפלאת, wonderful and extraordinary deeds (Exod. 3:20; 34:10; Josh. 3:5;
Judg. 6:13; Job 9:10; Pss. 78:4, 11, 32; 105:5; Jer.
21:2; etc.). Yahweh's marvels, insofar as they evoke
fear, may be described as נורא, a dreadful, awe-
inspiring thing (Exod. 34:10; II Sam. 7:23; cf. Ps. 66:
3, 5). Other terms for a miracle are "deed" or
"work" (עלילה, מעלל, מעשה; Deut. 3:24; Pss. 9:11—
H 9:12; 66:5; 77:12—H 77:13; 86:8; Isa. 12:4),
"great thing" (גדולה); II Sam. 7:23; II Kings 8:4; Job
9:10; Pss. 71:19; 136:4 ["great wonder"]), or "mighty
deed" (גבורה; Deut. 3:24 ["mighty act"]; Pss. 20:6—
H 20:7 ["mighty victory"]; 106:2 ["mighty doing"]);
the last term is comparable to the NT "mighty work"
(δύναμις; plural δυνάμεις; Mark 6:5; Luke 10:13;
Acts 2:22). The miracle may also be called a בריאה,
"creation" (Exod. 34:10; Num. 16:30; cf. Isa. 48:7;
Jer. 31:22). The deeds of Yahweh disclose the holi-

ness, greatness, and saving power of Israel's God,
according to Ps. 77:11-15—H 77:12-16, a passage
which employs several words for "miracle."

In the biblical sense, then, a miracle is an unusual,
marvelous event which testifies to God's active presence in the world. This does not mean, however, that
the miracle is a disruption of the natural order,
which, according to modern understanding, is governed by the law of cause and effect. To be sure, the
Bible bears witness to the regularity and depend-
ability of the natural order—"seedtime and harvest,
cold and heat, summer and winter, day and night"
(Gen. 8:22)—but this is the expression of God's covenant faithfulness and steadfastness (Ps. 148:6; Isa.
45:18; Jer. 5:24; 31:36). God is not outside and
bound by a system of law, but he is present any time
or anywhere (cf. Jer. 23:24) and is free to act as he
chooses, using the elements of the natural world to
accomplish his purpose. According to repeated statements in the Bible, "all things are possible with God"
(Gen. 18:14; I Sam. 14:6; Jer. 32:17; Mark 10:27),
although this is not construed to mean that he acts
in a capricious manner.

One of the basic tenets of biblical faith is the doctrine of providence, the conviction that the God who
is Creator and Lord shapes the events of history and
controls the powers of nature according to his sovereign purpose. Living within the sphere of God's action, the man of faith is alert for signs in the everyday world which indicate God's real presence in the
midst of his people. Indeed, the event which the
faithful Israelite or Christian may regard as wonderful may, from another point of view, seem quite
ordinary or may be regarded as an insignificant coincidence. Thus the miracle of the Red Sea may be
attributed to a strong wind which drove back the
shallow waters of the Sea of Reeds, the manna and
the quail were nothing more than phenomena familiar in the S wilderness of Palestine, or the crossing
of the Jordan was facilitated by seismic activity
which caused the waters to be dammed up temporarily. Similarly, some of Jesus' miracles—e.g., the
healing of the paralytic (Mark 2:1-12)—can be made
credible on the basis of modern psychological knowledge. Thus the element of wonder may be missed by
the observer, whether he belongs to the ancient time
or to the modern period. But within the biblical circle
of faith the question is not whether the miracle happened according to a particular description but
whether God was in the event, thus making it "wonderful." The conviction that God was wonderfully
present provided the motive for magnifying the event
further in the process of transmission; this is a phenomenon the biblical critic observes in the accretion
of the miracle tradition in the OT and the NT. It
must be admitted that other factors had a part too,
such as the literalistic misunderstanding of Joshua's
poetic command to the sun and the moon (Josh. 10:
12-13*a;* cf. vss. 13*b*-14), the attempt of Elisha's disciples to glorify their master with spectacular miracles, or the influence of Hellenistic wonder tales upon
the gospel tradition.

In a general sense, everything is miraculous to the
man of faith insofar as it is touched by the hand of
God. All of nature glorifies God, whose works are
wonderful (Job 38 ff; Ps. 139:14). But in certain

situations God's action coincides with a critical moment in the life of a person or a people, thus making it possible to speak of specific miracles.

In the OT the primary word for "wonder" is מופת, a word which, as already noted, has its counterpart in the NT τέρας. The word conveys the idea of something extraordinary or marvelous (Exod. 4:21; 7:9; 11:9-10; I Chr. 16:12; Ps. 105:5; Joel 2:30—H 3:3; cf. II Chr. 32:24), although the usage does not correspond to the idea of a miracle as a spectacular, abnormal event. Ezekiel's enactment of the fate of an exile was to be a מופת to the people, as was his tearless response to the death of his wife (Ezek. 12:6, 11; 24:24, 27). The term is close in meaning to אות (cf. NT σημεῖον; see below); hence it sometimes alternates with the latter (cf. II Kings 20:8; Isa. 38:7; with II Chr. 32:24), sometimes has an equivalent meaning (I Kings 13:3; Ps. 71:7; Zech. 3:8), and in the majority of cases is linked with אות (Exod. 7:3; Neh. 9:10; Pss. 78:43; 105:27; 135:9; Jer. 32:20-21; and nine times in Deuteronomy). It is noteworthy that Isaiah's act of going naked and barefoot during the siege of Ashdod (Isa. 20:2-4) is described as an אות ומופת, and that the prophet, together with his children, was לאתות ולמופתים in Israel (8:18). Ordinary and insignificant things may become extraordinary and "sign-ificant" if the light of divine revelation shines upon and transfigures them. God's presence may be detected in a casual remark, an untimely death, a turn of events, or the return of war-scarred land to normal (Gen. 24:10-21; I Sam. 2:27-36; 14:10; Isa. 37:30-32). The miraculous character of the event depends less upon its abnormal character than upon the time (kairos) of its occurrence—i.e., its happening at a particular juncture and with a particular meaning in the discerned plan of God. To the Egyptians, the crossing of the Red Sea was probably a freakish border incident; but to the Israelites, faced with a historical emergency and favored with a prophetic interpreter, the event disclosed the active presence of God. Similarly, the event of the Crucifixion and the Resurrection was a scandal to the Jew and foolishness to the Greek, while to the church it was the sign of God's wisdom and power (I Cor. 1:18-25).

In a broad sense, the history of God's action, as witnessed in the Bible, is miraculous from first to last. There were, however, decisive times in God's dealings with his people, and such times, according to the biblical tradition, were marked by an intensification of miracles, although due allowance must be made for the critical problems connected with individual miracle stories. Thus the time of Israel's early *Heilsgeschichte* (the Exodus, wandering in the wilderness, entrance into the Land of Promise) is portrayed as a time of many miracles. Similarly the rise of the prophets, by whom Yahweh spoke anew when Israel was engulfed in world politics, was marked by new miracles, according to the view of the prophetic schools (Elijah and Elisha narratives). And above all, the NT affirms that the inauguration of the New Age was accompanied by signs and wonders, which were performed, not only by Jesus himself (Acts 2:22), but also by his disciples and the church (John 14:12; Acts 4:16, 30; 5:12; 6:8; 14:3; I Cor. 12:10, 28; II Cor. 12:12; Gal. 3:5; Heb. 2:4).

2. Miracles as sign-events. The frequent association of biblical words for "wonder" with "signs" (אותות, σημεῖα) suggests another characteristic of biblical miracles. Not only do they witness to the wonderful character of God's actions, but they also have the effect of confirming the word of God, spoken in threat or promise, disfavor or favor. A sign stands in close, but subordinate, relation to the prophetic word, adding a kind of evidential support in experience. Thus men can not only hear God's word, but can also see it in action.

A sign makes an impact upon the senses, especially the sense of sight. In the OT the word אות is used with a variety of meanings, such as a marker, signal, token, ensign, omen, etc. (see SIGNS IN THE OT). A common denominator among all these meanings is that a sign is characterized by visibility or historical concreteness. When used in connection with "miracle," a sign is a visible indicator which points to the invisible power and activity of God in the world. Frequently signs are given in connection with a divine commission, as evidence of God's promise: "I will be with you." Thus, according to Exod. 3:12, Yahweh says to Moses: "This shall be the sign for you, that I have sent you: when you have brought forth the people out of Egypt, you shall serve God upon this mountain"—i.e., the very existence of Israel as a people, emancipated to serve Yahweh, will be historical confirmation of the commission. Quite apart from the question of the historicity of individual incidents, the intention of the other signs, whether given directly to Moses (Exod. 4:8-9, 17), or performed in the presence of the Israelites (4:28, 30) or the pharaoh (7:3; 8:23; 10:1-2), is to show that Yahweh's word is confirmed by visible signs which accredit Moses as his agent. (Note that in 4:21; 7:8-13 these אותות are called מופתים, showing that the two terms may alternate.) The same motif is present in the story of Gideon's commission at the time of Midianite oppression (Judg. 6:11-24). Gideon asks where are all the wonderful deeds (נפלאות) which have been recounted from the time of the Exodus. When Yahweh summons him to deliver Israel and promises: "I will be with you," Gideon asks for a sign which will show him that it is actually Yahweh who is speaking (vs. 17), and receives a sign in the form of the fire which consumes his offering. Similarly, in the early tradition of the origin of the monarchy (I Sam. 9-10), Samuel delivers to Saul the "word of God" (9:27)—namely, that Saul has been chosen to deliver Israel from its enemies—and promises that this word will be confirmed by signs (10:1-13). "When these signs meet you," says Samuel, "do whatever your hand finds to do, for God is with you" (10:7).

These passages not only show the close relation between word and sign but also suggest that a sign often has a predictive character. They point to what Yahweh is about to do in confirmation of his word of judgment or mercy spoken in the present. The prophets' primary function was to proclaim the "word of the Lord," which had the power to evoke repentance and faith; but they also pointed to signs, and even acted out signs, which demonstrated the effective power of the divine word in history. An important illustration is the Immanuel sign related in Isa. 7:10-16. Isaiah delivered to King Ahaz Yahweh's word that the Syro-Israelite alliance would not stand and that the attempt to put a puppet king on the throne of Judah would fail; and he further announced that Yahweh would confirm his word by any sign the king might choose, the assumption being that all things are possible with God. The sign which was predicted, despite the king's refusal to ask under the pretense of piety, is fraught with interpretive problems. Undoubtedly the sign was not associated with the manner of the child's conception, but rather with his imminent birth (probably in the royal line), his symbolic or significant name, and the meaning of the years of his childhood (*see* IMMANUEL). In any case, the wonder-child (cf. Isa. 9:2-7—H 9:1-6) would be concrete, visible evidence, to those who had eyes to see, that Yahweh was active in the historical situation to fulfil his purpose. Also, this demonstration may take the form of the prophet himself, who, together with his sign-children, withdraws into the prophetic community to wait for Yahweh in hope (Isa. 8:16-18), or the return of agricultural fertility (Isa. 37:30-32 = II Kings 19:29-31), or even "acted signs" (Isa. 20:3; Ezek. 4:1-3). Similarly, eschatological promises concerning the New Age are linked with predictions of signs which will take place (Isa. 45:1-8; 55:10-13) when the earth will be marvelously transformed (*see* CREATION § 3*b*). Indeed, the forecasting of wonderful portents in heaven and on earth was a prominent feature of apocalyptic (Dan. 4:2-3—A 3:32-33; 6:27—A 6:28; Joel 2:30—H 3:3). The NT, too, affirms that the end of the present age will be heralded by signs and wonders (Luke 21:11, 25; Rev. 12:1, 3; 15:1; cf. Acts 2:19).

The critical questions which arise out of specific miracle stories in the Synoptic gospels should not obscure the fact that, taken as a whole, they have their setting within the proclamation of the coming of the kingdom of God, the dawning of the messianic age. Jesus not only proclaimed the good news of the kingdom but also in his actions, especially his exorcisms, displayed the evidence that God's promises were being fulfilled. The gospel narrators regard his miracles as messianic acts, "mighty works" (δυνάμεις), which, viewed from the standpoint of faith, disclosed both God's action for man's salvation and the identity of Jesus as his appointed agent. Thus his preaching was accompanied by signs, enabling men not only to hear God's word but also to see its effectual power in the world (Matt. 11:4-5 = Luke 7:22; cf. Luke 10:23-24). His exorcisms were signs that the dominion of Satan was being broken and that God's kingdom was coming with power (Luke 11:20 = Matt. 12:28; Mark 3:22-30). His healings were signs of the immediacy of God's presence and power, manifest particularly in forgiveness (Mark 2:1-12). His nature miracles, such as the stilling of the storm at sea (Mark 4:35-41), portray the awe of those who sensed the majesty and power of divine sovereignty manifest in his words and works. In the Fourth Gospel, Jesus' miracles are essentially and exclusively signs —i.e., symbolic pictures which disclose, to those who see in faith, Jesus' δόξα and his identity as the Son of God (John 2:11; cf. 9:3; 11:4, 40). *See* SIGNS IN THE NT.

3. The ambiguity of signs and wonders. Implicit in the foregoing discussion is a further characteristic of biblical miracles—namely, their ambiguous character. While a sign is given to confirm the divine word, spoken in threat or promise, it does not in itself have the power to convince beyond a shadow of doubt. A sign supports or reassures faith, but not in such a manner as to take men out of the situation of faith—i.e., it does not provide the conclusive evidence which makes faith unnecessary. It would seem that various signs which Moses is reported to have performed in Egypt should have left no doubt in the mind of either the pharaoh or the Israelites, but tradition testifies that their evidential value was weakened by the ability of Egyptian magicians to perform similar feats, by the hardheartedness of the pharaoh, and by the Israelites' blind incapacity to see the proof of Yahweh's sovereignty in history. Despite all that had happened, the Israelites murmured: "Is Yahweh among us or not?" (Exod. 17:7). Similarly, in the NT, Jesus' signs and wonders did not lead irresistibly to faith (cf. John 12:37); rather, they too often merely aroused the curiosity of the crowds who flocked to him as they would to any wonder-worker. Even Jesus' enemies acknowledged that he performed miracles (Mark 3:22); and, according to the Fourth Gospel, his signs, being misunderstood, aroused the hostility which occasioned his death (John 11:47).

The ambiguous character of miracles is discussed in a Deuteronomic law (Deut. 13:1-5—H 13:2-6). It is said that if a prophet or dreamer gives a sign or wonder (אות או מופת), so that his words seduce Israel into the service of other gods, then he should not be heeded, even though the sign or wonder comes true, for in this way Yahweh tests the loyalty of his people. It is further stated that a sign must be congruous with the word of Yahweh as revealed historically in the event of the Exodus. Thus a sign is not in itself evidence of Yahweh's presence (for impostors or other "gods" may work miracles; cf. II Kings 3:27); it is significant only when seen in the context of Yahweh's saving history as interpreted by his prophets. Indeed, faith may discern visible signs of God's providence in history and nature, but fascination with prodigies does not lead to faith. In fact, the love of the miraculous may be a substitute for faith. In the late period of biblical Judaism, when prophecy was believed to have ceased (Ps. 74:9; I Macc. 4:46; 9:27; 14:41), there was a tendency to dwell upon spectacular wonders (II Chr. 20:20-30; 32:20-31; Bel 31-42; II Macc. 1:19-23; 3:22-40; 10:29-31; etc.).

The reluctance of the NT to stress the spectacular character of miracles is suggested, as noticed previously, by the fact that τέρατα is always combined with σημεῖα. Jesus himself constantly had to face the temptation of receiving the acclaim of a wonder-worker. The seeking after a "sign from heaven" could be a substitute for seeking God; hence he rebuked the skeptical Pharisees by saying: "No sign shall be given to this generation" (Mark 8:12; Matt. 12:39; Luke 11:29; cf. Matt. 16:1-4; John 4:48; 6:30). His mighty works, instead of evoking repentance and faith, met with hardness of heart; even pagan Tyre and Sidon, said Jesus, would have repented long ago had they witnessed such deeds (Matt. 11: 21 = Luke 10:13). Moreover, it is acknowledged in the NT that events which others regard as miraculous are not miraculous at all, for they do not disclose God's purpose but only deceive men. In the end time, according to the Little Apocalypse of Mark, "false Christs and false prophets will arise and show signs and wonders, to lead astray, if possible, the elect" (Mark 13:22; cf. II Thess. 2:9). It is said that even Satan and his helpers are able to work miracles (Rev. 13:13-14; 16:14; 19:20).

Nevertheless, although refusing to give his generation an unambiguous sign, Jesus' role involved the performance of the signs and wonders of the kingdom. To onlookers these acts were not different from the feats performed by any other wonder-worker; but to those who saw in faith, they were indications that the kingdom of God was coming. Above all, viewed from the church's standpoint of faith, Jesus himself was the sign of the kingdom. So Simeon declares (Luke 2:34) that the child Jesus is given "for a sign"; and the author of Matthew, relying on the LXX of Isa. 7:14, affirms that he fulfils the prophecy of the Immanuel sign (Matt. 1:22-23). In the faith of the church God's mightiest act, in the light of which all other signs and wonders of Jesus' career are understood, is the RESURRECTION, although the ambiguous character of this central sign is stressed especially by the Fourth Gospel (John 11:1-53; 20).

Bibliography. R. Bultmann, "Zur Frage des Wunders," *Glauben und Verstehen,* I (1933), 214-28; A. Guillaume, *Prophecy and Divination* (1938), Lecture 4, pp. 143-84; A. Richardson, *The Miracle-Stories of the Gospels* (1941); C. A. Keller, *Das Wort OTH als Offenbarungszeichen Gottes* (1946); P. Minear, *Eyes of Faith* (1946), pp. 143-45, 183-87; H. W. Robinson, *Inspiration and Revelation in the OT* (1946), pp. 34-48; W. Eichrodt, *Theologie des ATs,* II (1948), 83-87; H. Knight, "The OT Conception of Miracle," *Scottish Journal of Theology,* 5 (1952), 355-61; R. Bultmann, *NT Theology,* II (1955), 33-69; E. Jacob, *Theology of the OT* (1958), pp. 223-26.   B. W. ANDERSON

SIHON sī'hŏn [סיחן, סיחון]. Amorite king of Heshbon, a city E of the N end of the Dead Sea.

Num. 21:21-31 provides the primary information about Sihon king of the Amorites, and other OT references to him are principally dependent upon this source. However, Deut. 2:26, 30, preserves an apparently independent tradition which identifies Sihon simply as king of HESHBON. Deuteronomy also associates Sihon with Og king of Bashan, as the two Transjordanian kings whom Israel defeated in order to possess the entire region E of the Jordan (Deut. 1: 4; cf. Num. 21:33-35; Ps. 135:11).

Sihon is remembered by Israel because of his opposition to the passage of Israelite tribes, moving out of the wilderness toward Canaan, through his territory. Unlike Edom, which Israel by-passed when refused permission for transit (Num. 20:21), Sihon was attacked and defeated. The recollection of an Israelite victory in this area undoubtedly rests upon historical memory, as indicated by the brief poem embedded in the Sihon narrative (21:27-30). The poem implies the destruction of Heshbon, the city of Sihon and center of his power, and evidently summons victorious Israelites to its rebuilding:

> Come to Heshbon, let it be built,
> let the city of Sihon be established (21:27).

The extent of Sihon's power was certainly more circumscribed than Deuteronomy implies (Deut. 3:6-8), but the poem's allusion to Sihon's defeat of Moab need not be doubted, since the latter can well have consisted only of a small tribal coalition (Num. 21: 29; contrast vs. 26). Sihon is to be thought of, then, as controlling an area surrounding Heshbon, whose origins probably go back to the thirteenth century B.C. The more imposing title "king of the Amorites" would designate him only as one of the pre-Israelite inhabitants of Palestine.

OT references which imply a larger Sihonite domain, extending from the Jabbok to the Arnon but uncertainly bounded on the E (cf. Num. 21:24), most likely reflect the history of subsequent Israelite occupation of the region E of the Dead Sea. Both Reuben and Gad figure in this regional history (Josh. 13:8-28), with the role of Gad the more enduring as indicated by the use of its name for Solomon's administrative district in the area (I Kings 4:19 LXX; cf. II Sam. 24:5). Full occupation of the territory S of Heshbon and Medeba, to include Dibon and Aroer to the banks of the Arnon (Num. 21:30; Josh. 12:2), was hardly achieved before David's defeat of Moab (II Sam. 8:2) and, in turn, had been lost by the following century as indicated by the victory inscription of King Mesha of Moab.

The defeats of Sihon and Og persist, however, in the memory of Israel as monumental evidence of Yahweh's vindication of his people. As such they are recalled alongside the exodus from Egypt (Neh. 9:22; Pss. 135:11; 136:19-20).

Bibliography. M. Noth, "Num. 21 als Glied der 'Hexateuch'-Erzählung," *ZAW,* LVIII (1940-41), 161-89; "Israelitische Stämme zwischen Ammon und Moab," *ZAW,* LX (1944), 11-57.   R. F. JOHNSON

SIHOR. KJV alternate form of SHIHOR.

SILAS sī'ləs [Σιλᾶς]. Alternately: SILVANUS sĭl vā'nəs [Σιλουανός]. One of the leading men of the Jerusalem church; also called a prophet. He was associated with both Paul and Peter in apostolic missions.

1. The names
2. Journeys with Paul
3. Association with Peter
4. Character
5. Literary activity
Bibliography

1. The names. There seems little doubt that Silas and Silvanus are one and the same. The former appears in all the accounts of Acts and the latter in the letters. Luke retains the name which was known in the Jerusalem community, while Paul and Peter use the Latinized form as it appeared in Roman and Hellenistic circles. The Silvanus who was associated with Paul and Timothy (I Thess. 1:1) is certainly the same as Silas, the travel companion of Paul in Philippi (Acts 16:19 ff), whose imprisonment with Paul may be inferred from I Thess. 2:1-2.

2. Journeys with Paul. Silas first comes into notice in the Jerusalem church as companion of Judas Barsabbas (Acts 15:22 ff). He was chosen with Judas to bear the findings of the Jerusalem conference to Antioch. Paul and Barnabas were returning to Antioch, but it seemed fitting to send Judas and Silas as the special representatives of the church. After "exhorting" the church at Antioch, they returned to Jerusalem, although the Western Text adds: "But it seemed good to Silas to remain." However this may be, Silas was soon back in Antioch (vs. 40) and was chosen by Paul to accompany him on the mission to Asia and Macedonia in place of BARNABAS. Silas not only saw the S Galatian country on this journey, but quite likely the N Galatian as well, and from Troas set sail with Paul to the Macedonian country. He was in prison with Paul at Philippi and probably suffered as a Roman citizen the same as Paul (Acts 16:19 ff). He also went through the riots of Thessalonica and Beroea (17:1-15). But Silas did not seem to incur the same opposition as Paul, for he was left at Beroea while Paul departed to Athens. We next hear of Silas in Corinth, where he was reunited with Paul and Timothy. When Paul left Corinth after the Gallio incident, Silas remained, and this seems to have been the end of the relations between the two. Paul's mention of Silas in later writings only confirms the association in Corinth and throws no light on further relations.

3. Association with Peter. The First Letter of Peter mentions Silvanus in terms suggesting that he was an amanuensis of the apostle. It is conjectured that after he was replaced in Paul's company—Timothy, Aristarchus, and Tychicus being mentioned as Paul's helpers—he went to the areas of Pontus and Cappadocia, the N country with which I Peter is associated. His contact with this region on the way to Troas with Paul had given him the desire to do more work in it. In earlier days Silas and Peter had been apostles and prophets in the Jerusalem church, and this relationship was probably renewed and continued in the evangelization of the N country which was practically untouched by Paul.

4. Character. The Hellenistic character of Silas may be the reason for his selection as the successor of Barnabas, who had failed to measure up to Paul's expectations in that he had inclined to the Judaistic attitude toward Gentiles. But Silas was once paired with Judas Barsabbas, who was likely of the Judaistic party. The church at Jerusalem probably thought they would make a balanced team to make favorable contact between Jerusalem and Antioch. But if Silas was more liberal than Barnabas—enough so to replace him—his association with Peter presents another problem. It is evident that our knowledge of the temperament of these early personalities of the church is not complete. Silas was a minor character, it seems, whether associated with Paul or with Peter.

5. Literary activity. Paul's letters to the Thessalonians, written from Corinth, where Silas labored with him, contain salutations from "Paul, Silvanus, and Timothy." The use of "we" throughout the letters has been taken to mean that Silas and Timothy actually contributed to the writing. In the postscripts of both letters Paul uses the first person singular: "I adjure you," and "I, Paul, write." Possibly this indicates that Silvanus and Timothy were co-authors of the main sections of the letters. Those who object to Paul's apocalypticism in Thessalonians might want to assign the apocalyptic passages to Silas or

Timothy. The great literary activity of Silas which is usually pointed out is that of a scribe in the writing of the First Letter of Peter, based on the words: "By Silvanus, a faithful brother as I regard him, I have written briefly to you" (I Pet. 5:12). Silvanus was thus either a penman who merely took dictation, or a scribe who assumed much responsibility for the actual arrangement and content of the letter. The latter view is widely accepted by those who hold to Petrine authorship, but it must meet the objection that Peter was probably not capable of writing the kind of Greek found in the letter. It is altogether possible that Silas had the cultural qualifications to compose such a writing.

Bibliography. W. L. Knox, *St. Paul and the Church of Jerusalem* (1925), pp. 89 (note 3), 236 (note 42), 246 (note 5), 273 (note 13), 296 (note 30); E. G. Selwyn, *The First Epistle of Peter* (1947), pp. 9-17.   M. J. SHROYER

SILK [מֶשִׁי (Ezek. 16:10, 13); KJV שֵׁשׁ (Prov. 31:22), *properly* FINE LINEN; σηρικόν (Rev. 18:12)]. Silkworm culture originated in China, whence it spread through Korea to Japan. Sanskrit literature points to a silk industry in India in the first millennium B.C. A reference to it comes from Aristotle, who describes the silkworm with some detail (*History of Animals* 5.19). The juice of mulberries is referred to in I Macc. 6:34. In Ezekiel's oracle silk is the clothing of the maiden Jerusalem. Silk was a prized article of trade at Rome in the time of the author of Revelation.   J. M. MYERS

SILLA sĭl'ə [סִלָּא] (II Kings 12:20). Possibly a quarter or suburb of Jerusalem; mentioned in connection with the house of Millo (*see* MILLO 2), in which Joash king of Judah was murdered. The Hebrew text is uncertain.

SILO sī'lō. Douay Version form of SHILOH.

SILOAM sī lō'əm [Σιλωάμ]. A pool in Jerusalem, mentioned in connection with the healing by Jesus of a man born blind (John 9:7). The author of the Fourth Gospel interprets Siloam symbolically as "(the One who was) sent." The spellings Σ(ε)ιλωάμ, Σιλωά, are found in the LXX, the latter being a mere transcription of SHILOAH, which is the proper name of an aqueduct, meaning "the sender" of water (Isa. 8:6). It is rendered in the Latin versions by *Siloë* and in Arabic by *Selwan*, which is the name of the village opposite the SE hill of ancient Jerusalem. The complex relations between the aqueduct and the pool are considered here in their historical development and from the point of view of toponymy. For a detailed analysis of archaeological remains, *see* WATER WORKS. Fig. SIL 59.

1. Early aqueducts. Both the aqueduct and the pool belong to a system of canals and reservoirs in communication with the spring of GIHON, a system which was radically altered in the course of history. During the early phase of the monarchy, at the latest before the reign of Ahaz, the water was collected at the outlet of the spring in a reservoir originally dug out of the rock. This reservoir, scanty remains of which have been discovered beneath the modern steps leading to the spring, most likely represents

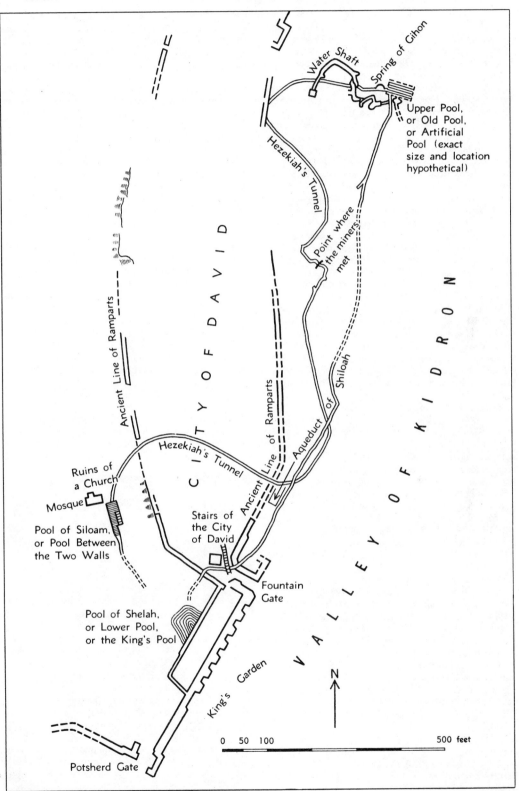

59. Water works of Jerusalem in the time of the Judean monarchy

the "Upper Pool" (II Kings 18:17; Isa. 7:3; 36:2), possibly also the "Old Pool" (Isa. 22:11), and the "artificial pool" (Neh. 3:16; KJV "pool that was made"). Some scholars, however, distinguish the Upper Pool from the Old Pool, and tentatively locate the latter, or both, in the Tyropoeon.

Two irrigation channels were fed from the reservoir by the spring. The older one has been followed on a short distance only. Several sections of a more recent aqueduct have been thoroughly explored. It followed the contours of the valley with a minimal slope, to make possible an extensive watering of terrace cultivations between the aqueduct and the bottom of the Kidron (see KIDRON, BROOK), which ran farther E and at a lower level than it does today. Some sections of the aqueduct were covered with slabs; some were underground on account of higher rock levels. The irrigation was effected by means of lateral openings in the E wall of the canal, which may be identified with the original Shiloah of the gently flowing waters (Isa. 8:6). It drained at first into a pool called the Pool of Shelah (see SHELAH, POOL OF), etymologically the Pool of the Aqueduct, in the lower tract of the Tyropoeon, toward the junction of this valley with the Kidron; the Pool of Shelah is presumably the same as the King's Pool (Neh. 2:14). Successive transformations of the lower Tyropoeon from Hezekiah to our day have made it impossible to ascertain the connecting link between the aqueduct and its ancient pool; the location of the latter corresponds roughly to that of the modern Birket el-Hamra.

2. Hezekiah's tunnel. When the armies of Sennacherib marched into Palestine, Hezekiah stopped all the springs (RSV), or fountains (KJV), outside the walls (II Chr. 32:4), by which are meant probably the openings of the Shiloah; there is ample archaeological evidence of a systematic obturation of the reservoir by the spring and of the aqueduct itself. The waters of Gihon were diverted by means of a tunnel to a point W of the City of David, well within the fortified perimeter of the capital (II Kings 20:20; II Chr. 32:30; Ecclus. 48:17). Hezekiah's tunnel is the S-shaped underground aqueduct cleared in 1910, and still in use.* Its measured length is 1,749 feet. The devious course of the tunnel has been variously explained, either because of the insufficient surveying methods of the tunnelers, or because of hard rock beds which made changes in orientation necessary, or because it was feared that the tunnelers might break through the tombs of the Davidic kings (see TOMBS OF THE KINGS). The tunneling was started from both ends by two teams of workers, as is evident from the examination of the tunnel itself and from a Hebrew inscription on the tunnel wall, which was removed in 1880 to the Imperial Museum at Istanbul, and is commonly known as the Inscription of Siloam. The translation by J. Simons (*Jerusalem in the OT*)[1] is:

"[This is](?) the boring through. This is the story of the boring through: whilst [the miners lifted] the pick each towards his fellow and whilst three cubits [yet remained] to be bored [through, there was hear]d the voice of a man calling his fellow, for there

[1] Used by permission of the publishers, E. J. Brill, Leiden, Netherlands.

was a split in the rock on the right hand and on [the left hand]. And on the day of the boring through the miners struck, each in the direction of his fellow, pick against pick. And the water started flowing from the source to the pool, twelve hundred cubits. A hundred cubits was the height of the rock above the head of the miners." Fig. HEZ 18.

3. The Pool of Siloam.* The Inscription of Siloam refers anonymously to the pool into which the tunnel drained. It is most likely identical with the "reservoir between the two walls" mentioned in connection with some work done to the Lower Pool (Isa. 22:9-11). The "two walls," however, are not identified with certainty as yet. They can scarcely be the parallel walls which once barred the Tyropoeon at its junction with the Kidron, as was assumed by some scholars; the interval between these structures was certainly never meant as a reservoir. All one dare say is that Isaiah's "two walls" were part of Hezekiah's program of fortification in a highly vulnerable part of the city. One may well assume that the name of the former aqueduct, the Shiloah, was transferred to Hezekiah's water system. There is, however, no early textual evidence for such a transfer. Josephus repeatedly refers to Siloam as a fountain, πηγή (War II.xvi.2; V.iv.1-2, 12), meaning, not the spring itself (Gihon), but the mouth of the tunnel. The first specific mention of the Pool of Siloam, ἡ κολυμβήθρα τοῦ Σιλωάμ, is in John 9:7. The construction of a church in the fifth century of the Christian era, to commemorate the miracle performed by Jesus, greatly altered the topography of the area adjacent to the exit of the tunnel. The pool was surrounded by porticoes and integrated in an architectural ensemble of which only scanty remains are visible today. Later on, a mosque was established over the ruins of the church, and a small minaret emerges

60. The Pool of Siloam

now above the portion of the pool which is still extant, and from which the women of neighboring houses draw their water. Fig. SIL 60.

As for the Lower Pool of Isa. 22:9, it is most certainly identical with the Pool of Shelah, at the outlet of the aqueduct put out of commission by Hezekiah, toward what is called today the Birket el-Hamra. It is not unlikely, although this cannot be proved conclusively on the basis of archaeological evidence, that it was remodeled to accommodate the surplus water discharged from the pool of Siloam. The Byzantine and medieval historical texts generally refer to this reservoir as distinct from the Pool of Siloam, and this duality may well go back to the reign of Hezekiah. *See* JERUSALEM § 5*b*.

Bibliography. G. A. Smith, *Jerusalem,* I (1907), 91-98; H. Vincent and F.-M. Abel, *Jérusalem Nouvelle,* IV (1926), 860-64; G. Dalman, *Jerusalem und sein Gelände* (1930), pp. 170-73; J. Simons, *Jerusalem in the OT* (1952), pp. 175-94; H. Vincent, *Jérusalem de l'Ancien Testament,* I (1954), 264-84, 289-97.   G. A. BARROIS

SILVANUS. *See* SILAS.

SILVANUS, TEACHINGS OF. A Gnostic apocryphon attributed to the companion of Peter and Paul; discovered in 1946 at Chenoboskion in Upper Egypt. *See* APOCRYPHA, NT.

SILVER [כֶּסֶף, pale, white; ἀργύριον, ἄργυρος, ἀργυροῦς].

1. In antiquity. Silver was known in the Near East as early as gold and copper. It normally surpassed in value all other metals until the Persian period (*ca.* 500 B.C.), when, with more abundant silver on the market, the silver-gold ratio was reversed. Silver was valued for jewelry, for charm AMULETS (e.g., "crescents"; Judg. 8:26), but mainly as a standard for business transactions; early appearances of the word in the Bible are with this meaning, as Gen. 23:15-16.

Egypt lacked native supplies of silver ore. In the period of her Asiatic conquests (1580-1350 B.C.), she obtained refined silver (cf. Joseph's cup in Gen. 44:2). The silver jewelry of the Egyptians (Exod. 11:2; 12:35) was their most expensive.

The Hittites and their successors in Asia Minor monopolized the world silver market from *ca.* the time of Abraham until *ca.* 1000 B.C. Mespotamian merchants engaged in silver and lead trading were established in Asia Minor *ca.* 2000, according to the Cappadocian Tablets.

In Palestine the small number of silver objects found in excavations suggests that from *ca.* 1400 B.C. silver was scarce except for Solomon's times, when it was "as common in Jerusalem as stone" (I Kings 10:27; II Chr. 9:27; Ecclus. 47:18). Silver is regularly given priority over gold in the OT; only in Chronicles and Daniel, as in the NT, is this order reversed. For silver in coins, *see* MONEY, COINS.

Phoenicia (II Chr. 9:21; Ezek. 27:12) and Arabia (II Sam. 8:10-12; II Chr. 9:14; cf. the N Arabian book of Job and its interest in silver mining) served as Israel's regional distributors for silver—e.g., TARSHISH (Jer. 10:9) and Tarshish ships (I Kings 10:22).

Courtesy of the Palestine Archaeological Museum, Jerusalem, Jordan

61. A silver bowl and a ladle in the form of a female figure, from Sharuhen (Tell el-Far'ah); Persian period

2. In the OT. The numerous OT references reveal the use of silver: (*a*) generally as a standard of wealth (Gen. 13:2; 24:35; Exod. 25:3; Num. 22:18; Deut. 7:25; Zeph. 1:18; Hag. 2:8; Zech. 6:11), as booty taken (Josh. 6:19; 7:21), as tribute paid (I Kings 15:19; cf. Song of S. 8:9), as payment of obligation in weight of metal—i.e., as money (Gen. 20:16; 23:15-16; 37:28; 45:22; Exod. 21:32; Lev. 27:16; Josh. 24:32; Judg. 17:10; II Sam. 24:24; Neh. 7:72; Job 28:15; Isa. 7:23; 46:6; Amos 2:6; 8:6); (*c*) as a noble's drinking cup (Gen. 44:2); (*d*) as a royal crown of gold and silver (Zech. 6:11); (*e*) as jewelry or personal ornament (Gen. 24:53; Exod. 3:22; 11:2; 12:35; Song of S. 1:11, where "ornaments of gold [are] studded with silver"); (*f*) in idol making (Exod. 20:23; Deut. 29:17; Judg. 17:4; Pss. 115:4; 135:15; Isa. 2:20; 30:22; 31:7; 40:19; Jer. 10:4; Dan. 2:32-33; 5:2-3; 11:8-9; Hos. 13:2); (*g*) in connection with the TABERNACLE, for trumpets (Num. 10:2), for bases (Exod. 26:19), for hooks and fillets and chapiters (Exod. 27:10, 17; 36:24, 26), for platters and bowls (Num. 7:13-14); (*h*) in connection with the Jerusalem TEMPLE (I Kings 7:51; I Chr. 28:15-16; II Chr. 2:7; Ezra 8:26, 28; Neh. 7:71); (*i*) as unmanufactured raw material (Exod. 31:4; 35:24, 32; I Kings 15:15). Fig. SIL 61.

The OT knows of mining for silver (Job 28:1), of the processes of refining (Zech. 13:9; Mal. 3:3; in Ezek. 22:20-22, the melting of scrap metals or jeweler's sweepings), and of multiple refinings in a crucible or fining pot (Prov. 17:3; 27:21) to produce "choice silver" (Prov. 10:20; cf. I Chr. 29:4; Ps. 12:6). Figuratively, refining silver is used for trying men's hearts (Ps. 66:10; Isa. 48:10), corrosion of silver for deterioration (Isa. 1:22; Jer. 6:30); while silver itself is used for bright color (Ps. 68:13), for the purity of God's word (Ps. 12:6), for great abundance (Job 3:15; 22:25; 27:16; Isa. 60:17; Zech. 9:3), and as of lower value than Wisdom (Job 28:15; Prov. 3:14; 8:19; 10:20; 16:16; 22:1; 25:11).

3. In the NT. In the NT silver is sometimes mentioned derisively (Matt. 10:9; Jas. 5:3; I Pet. 1:18), but also as wealth generally (Acts 20:33; I Cor. 3:12; Rev. 18:12) and as coins (Matt. 22:19; 26:15; 27:3-9; Luke 15:8-10), as required for tax payments (Matt. 17:24-27), and in connection with idol making (Acts 17:29; 19:24; Rev. 9:20). *See* ANTIOCH, CHALICE OF.

Bibliography. A. Lucas, *Ancient Egyptian Materials and Industries* (3rd rev. ed., 1948), pp. 278-83; C. Singer *et al.*, eds., *A

History of Technology I (1954), 582-88, and the Chronological Chart of Early Metallurgy, p. 575. P. L. GARBER

SILVERLING. KJV translation of כסף (RSV "SHEKEL of silver") in Isa. 7:23.

SILVERSMITH [צרף; ἀργυροκόπος] (Judg. 17:4; Acts 19:24); KJV FOUNDER in Judg. 17:4. One who works with silver, both refining the ore and casting or beating the finished product. There were smiths in Asia Minor early in the third millennium B.C. The smith was usually a "founder" who refined the ore and poured the metal into casts (Judg. 17:4). He also beat the silver (Jer. 10:9). The silversmith made musical instruments (Num. 10:2), trim and decorations (Exod. 26:19 ff), ware for the tabernacle and temple (Num. 7:13; II Sam. 8:11), and idols (Exod. 20:23; Acts 19:24). The lone NT passage involves the dispute of the guild of silversmiths with the iconoclastic threat in Paul's preaching. Demetrius was probably the master of the guild for that year.

See also METALLURGY; CRAFTS. C. U. WOLF

SIMALCUE. Alternate form of IMALKUE.

SIMEON sĭm'ĭ ən [שמעון] (the deity) has heard; *originally the name of a person; a short form with the diminutive ending -ôn;* Συμεων]. 1. The second son of Jacob by Leah (Gen. 29:33), and the *heros eponymos* of the tribe of Simeon. He is also always enumerated as the second in the lists of the descendants (Gen. 35:23; 46:10; Exod. 1:2; I Chr. 2:1). Joseph took him as a hostage (Gen. 42:24, 36; 43:23). In Gen. 48:5 he is an example of a full son. Gen. 34 makes it clear, above all, that the name Simeon refers to one of the twelve tribes.

Gen. 34:25, 30, changed from family history into tribal history, indicates that the tribe of Simeon, along with the tribe of Levi, which at that time was still secular, once settled in central Palestine but could not hold out against the superior strength of the Canaanites, especially those from Shechem. Gen. 34 provides an explanation for this fate, with which the Simeon-Levi passage in the Blessing of Jacob (49:5-7) agrees in its own way. Simeon belonged to that first wave of Israelites—namely, the Leah group —which had already occupied the entire Palestinian highland. In the S were Judah and, for a while, Reuben and Gad; in the N, Issachar, Zebulun, and Asher; and in the middle, Simeon and Levi. Obviously, many of the tribes were severely decimated in the course of the occupation (*Landnahme*) of the land. This is true, e.g., of the tribe of Reuben, which fell from its first-place position in the amphictyony and whose pitiful remnants finally came to rest E of the Jordan. The same thing is true of Simeon and Levi. Apparently they were not even without blame for the catastrophe which overtook them in central Palestine and caused Yahweh to "scatter them in Israel" (Gen. 49:7). They withdrew in the direction of the base in the S steppe from which they had started out. However, while Levi, in this fashion, got as far as Kadesh, where its last remnant finally met the Israelites, who were coming out of Egypt, and was gradually transformed into the priestly caste, the little band of Simeonites succeeded in establishing themselves on the most southerly border of the cultivated land. The city of Zephath, which they renamed Hormah (probably Tell es-Seba'), fell into their power (Judg. 1:17). The territory of an ancient Canaanite city-state was thus sufficient to receive their remnant. They were now a small group like the neighboring Kenites and Kenizzites and waited for the time when, with them, they would merge into Great Judah. From then on, their history is the history of Judah (Judg. 1:3). The Song of Deborah does not mention them, even as it does not mention Judah. In the Blessing of Moses (Deut. 33) a Simeon passage is missing, because the tribe had become too unimportant after the bloodletting and also because of the border situation, as in the case of Asher. What is enumerated in Josh. 19:1-8 as Simeon's property is an excerpt from the list of towns in the kingdom of Judah (cf. 15:26-32), dating from the time of Josiah, which the redactor took to be Simeonite but supplied with the significant postscript, 19:9. Simeon is missing completely from the system of boundary descriptions which originated in the period before the monarchy.

In the later literature Simeon appears almost exclusively in connection with statistics. In the P supplement to the Baal-peor tradition the evildoer who is caught in the act is a Simeonite. In the lists of the Priestly Code, Simeon's place is regularly after Reuben (Exod. 6:15; Num. 1:6, 22-23; 13:5; 26:12-14), even when both must give precedence to Judah (Num. 2:12; 7:36; 10:19). In Num. 34:20 the place immediately after Judah is geographically conditioned. In Deut. 27:12, Simeon leads the group of those who pronounce the blessing on Mount Gerizim. In the chapter on the Levite cities Simeon is associated with Judah (Josh. 21:4, 9; I Chr. 6:55, 65—H 6:40, 50, where in the former passage Judah and Simeon are replaced by "the land of Judah"). In Ezek. 48:24, Simeon is separated from Judah by Benjamin and receives only the second strip of land to the S of the sanctuary. In the list of gates, and as in vss. 24 ff along with Issachar and Zebulun, Simeon is put down still further (vs. 33). In the lists of Chronicles, Simeon always ranks second (I Chr. 12: 25; 27:16); likewise in the general structure (chs. 4–7). In the genealogy of Simeon (4:24 ff), which is expanded beyond the regular sources, the Chronicler is reworking an old account which indicates that conditions in Simeon were not settled for a long time still; as late as the time of Hezekiah one group wandered off into the region of Maon (vs. 41). Moreover, the fact that Simeon once occupied the same region in which Manasseh and Ephraim later settled is still echoed by the Chronicler in the strange phrase for N Israel, "Ephraim, Manasseh and Simeon" (II Chr. 15:9; and, similarly, with the addition "and as far as Naphtali" in 34:6). In the NT the tribe of Simeon appears in the seventh place on the list of the sealed (Rev. 7:7).

For the territory of Simeon, *see* TRIBES, TERRITORIES OF, § D1*b*. *See* the bibliography under ASHER.

K. ELLIGER

2. Grandfather of MATTATHIAS 1 (I Macc. 2:1).

3. A "righteous and devout" (δίκαιος καὶ εὐλαβὴς [cf. צדיק וחסיד]) man, living in Jerusalem at the time of the birth of Jesus (Luke 2:25-35). "Looking for

the consolation of Israel"—the fulfilment of Jewish messianic hopes which would bring salvation to Israel (cf. Isa. 40:1; 49:7-10; 51:3; 61:2; 66:13; also Mark 15:43; and *see* MESSIAH, JEWISH, § 4)—he had been promised that he should not die before he had seen "the Lord's Christ" (God's chosen and anointed One, the Messiah; cf. Luke 9:20). At the time of Jesus' presentation, which Luke apparently combines with the rite of purification after childbirth (*see* CLEAN AND UNCLEAN § 4), Simeon, inspired by the Holy Spirit, went into the temple (probably into the court of the women), took the child up in his arms, and blessed God, saying:

> Lord, now lettest thou thy servant depart in peace,
> according to thy word;
> for mine eyes have seen thy salvation
> which thou hast prepared in the presence of all peoples,
> a light for revelation to the Gentiles,
> and for glory to thy people Israel.

This blessing, called the NUNC DIMITTIS and used in the daily evening prayers of Western Christendom since the fourth century, expresses Simeon's gratitude for God's gift to him (vss. 29-30) as well as to Israel and all the world (vss. 31-32). The fulness of OT allusions in this brief canticle shows the central position which messianic expectations occupied in Simeon's faith (Isa. 40:3-5 and 52:10 [conflated in Luke 3:4*b*-6]; Isa. 42:6 and 49:6 [from the "Servant Songs"; *see* SERVANT OF THE LORD, THE, § 2]; Isa. 46:13; and for "revelation to" [ἀποκάλυψιν; Luke 2:32] meaning "unveiling of," Isa. 25:7; 60:2-3).

Then Simeon blessed the child's parents, saying also to Mary:

> Behold, this child is set for the fall and rising of many
> in Israel,
> and for a sign that is spoken against
> (and a sword will pierce through your own soul also),
> that thoughts out of many hearts may be revealed
> (Luke 2:33-35).

This saying introduces clearly the note of suffering which accompanies the appearance of the Messiah. His coming "for a sign" (σημεῖον; cf. Isa. 7:11, 14; Luke 11:30-32) will also bring judgment to "many hearts" (cf. Isa. 8:14-15; Matt. 21:42-43; John 9:39; 16:8-11; I Cor. 1:23; I Pet. 2:8) and even sorrow to his mother (Luke 2:35*a*).

4. An ancestor of Jesus, in the Lukan genealogy (Luke 3:30).

5. KJV form of SYMEON 1.

6. KJV form of SIMON in Acts 15:14 (RSV SYMEON 2). Peter's original Hebrew name is usually spelled Σίμων in the Greek NT, but here and in II Pet. 1:1 (MSS A and ‫א‬) it occurs as Συμεων. *See* PETER §§ 1, 7.   L. HICKS

SIMON sī′mən [‫שמעון‬, *a diminutive form of* ‫שמעאל‬, God has heard; Σίμων, snub-nosed(?)]. **1.** Simon II, high priest (died *ca.* 198 B.C.), son of Onias II and father of Onias III and Jason. His achievements are celebrated in Ecclus. 50:1-21.

2. The father of Judas Iscariot (John 6:71; 13:2, 26), who is called "Simon Iscariot" in the first and third of the Johannine passages cited. On the meaning of "Iscariot," *see* JUDAS (ISCARIOT).

3. Son of Jonah (Matt. 16:17) or John (John 1:42; 21:15-17), and brother of Andrew (John 1:40). Jesus

named him "Peter" (Πέτρος; Aramaic ‫כיפא‬, "rock"; Matt. 16:18; John 1:42). *See* PETER.

4. A brother of Jesus (Mark 6:3; Matt. 13:55), thought by some to be identical with the Simeon son of Clopas, mentioned by Hegesippus (Euseb. Hist. III.11, 32) as successor of James as head of the Jerusalem church.

5. Simon the Zealot (Ζηλωτής, "zealot, enthusiast"; Luke 6:15). Mark 3:18; Matt. 10:4 have "Cananaean" (Κανανᾶιος, not from "Cana" or "Canaanite" but from Aramaic ‫קנאנא‬, "zealot, enthusiast"). Luke has correctly translated the Aramaic word. Simon was probably thus designated because he formerly had identified himself with fanatical opponents of Roman rule in Palestine, called Zealots. He was selected by Jesus for apostleship. He is not mentioned again in the NT. Some early Christian writers identified him with Simeon son of Clopas, who was said by Hegesippus (Euseb. Hist. III.11, 32) to have become successor of James as head of the Jerusalem church.

6. The Pharisee in whose house Jesus was anointed by a sinful woman (Luke 7:36-50). The location of the house is not indicated, though it seems to have been in Galilee and possibly in Capernaum. Simon, thinking Jesus a prophet (vs. 39), invited him to dinner, apparently in order to converse at length with him. He was friendly to Jesus but somewhat casual, as is indicated by his failure to extend to Jesus courtesies customarily accorded guests (vss. 44-46). He was shocked at Jesus' sympathetic attitude toward and free relationships with sinners. Pharisaic tradition forbade contact with "unclean," law-neglecting people. Jesus rebuked Simon by means of a parable and commended the woman for her loving act.

7. A leper (the Aramaic word ‫גרבא‬ may mean "jar merchant"), at a dinner in whose home at Bethany Jesus was anointed by Mary (Mark 14:3-9; cf. John 12:1-8). It is possible that he was the husband of Martha or the father of Mary, Martha, and Lazarus. If he once was a leper, he obviously had been cured of his disease, possibly by Jesus. *See* MARTHA.

8. Simon of Cyrene, who was impressed into carrying Jesus' cross to the place of execution (Mark 15:21; Matt. 27:32; Luke 23:26). It is unlikely that he was a Negro. Many Jews lived in Cyrene, the capital city of the North African district of Cyrenaica. Simon was perhaps residing at this time in a country district of Palestine and was entering Jerusalem for the Passover. He is said in Mark (15:21) to be the father of Alexander and Rufus, persons obviously known to the readers of this gospel (cf. Rom. 16:13).

9. The tanner of Joppa in whose house by the seaside Peter stayed "for many days" (Acts 9:43; 10:6, 17, 32). He probably was a Christian. Tanning was odious to Jews because of the necessity of handling dead bodies (Lev. 11:39-40). Tanners, though avoided by the Pharisees, were accepted readily into the Christian fellowship.

10. *See* SIMON MAGUS.

Bibliography. "Σίμων" in Pauly-Wissowa, *Realenzyclopädie der klassischen Altertumswissenschaft*, Zweite Reihe, III (1929), 162-80; for Simon in Greek literature, M. Buchberger, ed., *Lexikon für Theologie und Kirche*, IX (1937), 570-73, and the literature therein cited; J. Blinzler, "Simon der Apostel, Simon der Herrenbruder, und Bischof Symeon von Jerusalem," *Festschrift Landersdorfer* (1953), pp. 25-55; O. Cullmann, *The State in the NT* (1956), pp. 8-23: on Simon the Zealot, and the Zealot movement in the time of Jesus.

E. P. BLAIR

SIMON MACCABEUS. A Hasmonean leader and high priest of Judea (lived *ca.* 200-136 B.C.). He was the second of Mattathias' five sons; he was nicknamed "Thassi(s)" (I Macc. 2:3), perhaps from תשיש, "weakling." Together with his father and two brothers, Judah and Jonathan, he was outstanding in the successful war of independence waged by Judea after 168 B.C. against Seleucid Syria under Antiochus IV Epiphanes. In his alleged testament to his sons (I Macc. 2:49 ff), Mattathias is said to have enjoined his sons (vs. 65): "Now behold, I know that Simeon your brother is wise in counsel; always listen to him; he shall be your father."

From the moment that Jonathan was chosen leader to succeed Judah, Simon became his closest associate and counselor in all political and military matters. Together they avenged the murder of their brother John; eluded the Syrian forces under General Bacchides; and, several years later, after defeating Bacchides' army, concluded a pact with him, to the consternation of the pro-Seleucid, Hellenized Jews in Judea (I Macc. 9).

In 147-146 B.C., during the Judean struggle against Demetrius II Nicator, Simon captured the fortified city of Beth-zur, and later took Joppa by surprise, thus acquiring a vital outlet to the Mediterranean Sea. Subsequently he built Adida (Hadid), NW of Jerusalem, and fortified it as a strategic defense for Jerusalem (I Macc. 12).

When Jonathan was taken captive by Trypho Diodotus, a notorious opportunist, Simon naturally assumed leadership of his faltering and frightened people. "By this speech of Simon's, the multitude was inspired with courage; and as they had before been dispirited through fear, they were now raised to good hopes of better things" (Jos. Antiq. XIII.vi.3-4). Simon rallied his forces and drove Trypho out of Judea; and while Trypho and Demetrius struggled for the throne of Syria, he built fortresses throughout the land.

Simon then proceeded to achieve a brilliant diplomatic victory. He sent a delegation to Demetrius and asked for relief of taxation. This was tantamount to asking for recognition of Judea as a sovereign state, and Demetrius knew it. But, being desperate for allies, Demetrius was forced to grant his request. Documents, coins, contracts, etc., now began with: "In the first year of Simon, the great High Priest and General and Ruler of the Jews." "Now the affection of the multitude toward Simon was so great that in their contracts one with another they wrote, 'in the first year of Simon, the benefactor and ethnarch of the Jews,'" is how Josephus put it (XIII.vi.7). Simon proceeded to capture Gazara, and he settled there. He took also the citadel of Jerusalem (Akra), purified and fortified the temple mount, and appointed his son John general of all his forces (I Macc. 13).

Simon's leadership brought Judea to such status

that both Sparta and Rome renewed their alliance of friendship with this little country. The Jews themselves then (141 B.C.) manifested their appreciation for Simon and their utter trust in him by taking a step unprecedented in their long history since becoming a sovereign people: "In the great assembly of the priests and the people and the rulers of the nation and the elders of the country, the following was proclaimed . . . . Simon should be their leader and high priest for ever, until a trustworthy prophet should arise" (I Macc. 14:27-48). This resolution they recorded on bronze tablets and put upon pillars on Mount Zion. Previously, the high priesthood had been hereditary, and it had been handed down in the family of Onias, which traced its lineage to Zadok, appointed by King Solomon for his temple. Simon was thus the first to be elected to this office.

Antiochus VII Sidetes renewed his predecessor's pact with Simon; he was at war with Trypho and needed allies. However, when he emerged victorious, Antiochus demanded from Simon the return of Joppa, Gazara, the citadel of Jerusalem, and some other places. Simon recognized these to be Judean by historical right, and rejected the claim. For the battle that ensued, Simon handed over leadership to his son John, who defeated Antiochus' forces. Simon himself came to an untimely end (136 B.C.) when he was assassinated by his treacherous son-in-law Ptolemy the son of Abubus, whom he had appointed general over the Plain of Jericho. Ptolemy aspired to succeed Simon, but John thwarted Ptolemy and himself succeeded Simon.

A good case has been made for identifying Simon the Just (M. Ab. 1) with Simon Maccabeus. *See* the work of S. Hoenig in the *bibliography*.

Bibliography. W. O. E. Oesterley, "The First Book of Maccabees," in R. H. Charles, *The Apoc. and Pseudep. of the OT*, I (1913), pp. 59-124; E. Schürer, *Geschichte des jüdischen Volkes*, vol. I (5th ed., 1920), pt. I, sec. 7; E. R. Bevan, "Syria and the Jews," ch. XVI in *Cambridge Ancient History*, VIII (1930), 495-533; F.-M. Abel, *Les Livres des Maccabées* (Études Bibliques; 1949), and see the Bibliographie, pp. LX-LXIV; S. Tedesche and S. Zeitlin, *The First Book of Maccabees* (Dropsie College Edition: *Jewish Apocryphal Literature*, 1950); S. Hoenig, *The Great Sanhedrin* (1953), pp. 31-35.

H. M. ORLINSKY

SIMON MAGUS sī'mən mā'gəs [Σίμων ὁ μάγος]. A Samaritan magician referred to in Acts and known in later legend.

1. The record of Acts 8:9-24
2. The Magus
3. The Christian
4. The heretic
5. The Antichrist
6. Interpretations
Bibliography

1. The record of Acts 8:9-24. Among the disciples driven out of Jerusalem by the persecution following the death of Stephen was Philip (not the apostle, but the deacon appointed in Acts 6:5), who went to a village of Samaria. This was probably the region of Samaria, not the capital Sebaste. One suggested site is Gitta, with which Justin (Apol. I.26, 56) associates Simon Magus. There Philip preached and made many converts. Among these was one Simon, a notable magician, who for some time had been amazing the Samaritans with his magic, saying that he was "somebody great," and his admirers proclaimed that he was the "power of God which is called GREAT." Simon was amazed by the miracles of healing which Philip performed.

When the church in Jerusalem heard about Philip's success, it sent down Peter and John to investigate. They laid their hands on the new converts and imparted to them the Holy Spirit, whom up to then they had not received. This apostolic ability to confer the Holy Spirit by laying on of hands so impressed the avaricious Simon that he offered to buy the power from Peter and John. But Peter bitterly denounced him, and Simon humbly repented.

This narrative has numerous obscurities. Just what had Simon been doing to amaze the Samaritans? What specific claims had he made for himself? What nature had his admirers ascribed to him? Was he an honest convert or a hypocritical deceiver motivated by avarice? What does the monopoly of the apostles on imparting the Holy Spirit by laying on of hands signify? Why is John a completely silent actor in the drama? These features indicate that the story is more complicated than it appears to be on the surface.

2. The Magus. While the word "magus" (ὁ μάγος) does not actually occur in the story, the participle μαγεύων ("practicing as a magus") and the noun ταῖς μαγίαις ("works of a magus") indicate clearly enough that Simon was a magus by profession. He ought to be compared with Elymas Bar-Jesus (Acts 13:6-12; *see* ELYMAS), called both a magus and a false prophet and associated with the Proconsul Sergius Paulus, who came into violent conflict with Paul at Paphos. Another magus of the island of Cyprus, whose name is Atomos and who is associated with Governor Felix, is mentioned by Josephus in Antiq. XX.vii.2. While MAGI are mentioned only three times in the NT, the word appears frequently in the Greek translations of the OT for such terms as "enchanter," "diviner," "necromancer."

Originally the Magi were a shaman caste of the Medes. Then they became Zoroastrian priests of Persia. But in the Mediterranean world the term had lost its national connotation and indicated a profession of persons engaged in astrology, necromancy, incantations, exorcism, etc. They were held in respect by such eminent men as Sergius Paulus and Felix; and even Philo in *Special Laws* III.101 speaks of a high type of magus with genuine appreciation, but of a lower kind as charlatans, mendicants, and parasites.

3. The Christian. That later generations of Christians regarded Simon Magus as an impostor who became a Christian only from base motives is obvious, but Acts states simply that Simon believed and was baptized and continued his association with Philip, deeply impressed by the signs which he did. His only mistake was that he thought he could buy ability to impart the Holy Spirit, on which the apostles held a monopoly. For this error Peter administered a merciless denunciation. Although Peter said: "You have neither part nor lot in this matter,

for your heart is not right before God," it appears that even Philip did not possess this power. One motif of the story seems to be that only the apostles could impart the Holy Spirit.

But Simon repented, so he was presumably still a Christian. A hundred years later, although Justin attacks the followers of Simon, Menander and Marcion, with all his power, he nevertheless admits in Apol. I.26.6 that their followers are called Christians. So we have to assume, not only that Simon became a Christian, but that he remained one.

4. The heretic. For *ca.* three centuries Simon Magus gripped the imagination of early Christians. They wove him into a romantic saga which expressed various Gnostic ideas. Eusebius (Hist. II.13. 1-8) was led to say that Simon was the author of all heresy. This view had its roots in Acts itself, as we have seen, but Justin (Apol. I.26) is the one who really got this speculation on its way. First he says that Simon carried about with him a woman named Helena, who had been a prostitute at Tyre; but that Simon, who was worshiped by nearly all Samaritans and some others as the first god, considered Helena his first idea, Ennoia, generated in his mind. Justin also says that the Romans worshiped Simon and had set up a statue to him on the island in the Tiber with the inscription *Simoni Deo Sancto*, a statement which is now thought to be an outright error. In 1574 a fragment of a statue was found on this island bearing the inscription *Semoni Sanco Deo Fidio*, etc., which had been erected to the Sabine divinity Semo Sancus.

As Justin appears to be the source from which most of his successors drew their information about Simon Magus, we need to be on guard as to the accuracy of anything they say. Eusebius, in the passage noted above, says Simon's followers worshiped him and Helena with pictures, images, idols, incense, sacrifices, and libations.

Irenaeus (Her. I.23.1-2) adds it was believed that Simon through Helena conceived in his mind the lower angels, archangels, and powers by whom the world was formed. Then Helena was held in captivity by these lower powers from jealousy, was abused, compelled to be reborn again and again as a female, until she became a professional prostitute. She was the lost sheep of the gospels, and Simon came down to redeem her. He had assumed the form of the lower powers in order to disguise himself. He appeared to be a man, while he was not. He was thought to suffer, but did not. This is a touch of Docetism. The OT scriptures were inspired by these low powers, which made the world. So both the world and the flesh, which they created, and the scriptures, which they inspired, are rejected by all who trust in Simon and Helena, who are saved by grace, free, and can do as they please. Hence the licentious practices to which Eusebius alludes. The Simonians, therefore, were like Marcion in rejecting the OT and considering the world evil. But whereas he emphasized celibacy, they turned to license. Irenaeus even ascribes a trinity to the Simonians: Simon appeared to the Jews as the Son; to the Samaritans as the Father; but to others as the Holy Spirit.

5. The Antichrist. In this strange creation of early Christian pseudepigraphy Simon acquires virtually all the features of the Antichrist. In imagination, at any rate, he is not only set up in a temple to be worshiped, but is also made the protagonist of evil. He is the "man of sin," the incarnation of Satan, who is determined to uproot the true faith. The gallant knight who defends the faith, on the other hand, is Simon Peter, who meets Simon Magus on every battlefield, according to the *Clementina*—first in Samaria, but then in Caesarea, Tyre, Tripolis, Laodicea, and Antioch, but not in Rome (a later addition). Justin said Simon went to Rome in the time of Claudius, but later legends put him there under Nero, and even bring in Paul along with Peter, as a kind of afterthought. But Peter always triumphs. Simon Magus is finally slain or is a suicide. One legend says he had himself buried with the promise of rising on the third day, which he could not do; another, that he tried to fly, and with the aid of demons was succeeding, when Peter's prayers forced the demons to let him fall and perish.

6. Interpretations. There is so much of symbol and allegory and Gnostic speculation in the Simonian legends that some have denied that Simon ever existed. F. C. Baur and his followers of the Tübingen School held that Simon and Helena were mythical; that they were based on the Phoenician sun cult; that Simon was Herakles or Baal, and Helena, the moon, as Selene, or Luna. In different legends she is called Ennoia, Sophia, Sapientia, etc. Baur even argued that Simon was Paul in disguise and that the story shows the struggle between Peter and Paul in the early church. George Salmon (*see bibliography*) recognized that Simon was historical, but held that he is not the same as Simon of Gitta, of whom Justin writes.

That there is a basis in the confusion of the stories for these different views cannot be denied. It is probable, however, that Simon Magus was an actual person. But even in the Acts there are incomprehensible features. No one knows beyond question what he means when he calls himself "Great," or what the people mean by the "power of God which is called Great." These very words, because of their mysterious character, were the fertile seed which germinated and developed into the luxuriant crop of legends of the later centuries. They tell more about the times when they were written than about Simon Magus himself. The *Clementina* and the apocryphal Acts were written for entertainment as well as instruction, and should be read in this light.

The mass of the Simon Magus literature was produced by an age which was interested primarily in signs, wonders, and miraculous displays as demonstrations of the truth of the Christian faith.

Bibliography. G. Salmon, "Simon Magus," *Dictionary of Christian Biography*, IV (1887), 681-88; J. H. Moulton, "Magi," in J. Hastings, ed., *Encyclopedia of Religion and Ethics*, VIII (1917), 241-44; R. P. Casey, "Simon Magus," *Beginnings of Christianity*, V (1933), 151-63; A. D. Nock, "Paul and the Magus," *Beginnings of Christianity*, V (1933), 164-88.

S. V. McCasland

SIMON PETER. *See* Peter.

SIMPLICITY [Lat. *simplicitas*]. A quality of being plain, uncompounded, and free from adornment or duplicity. In a moral sense, *simplicitas* is used in Latin literature to express such qualities as plainness, openness, directness, and naturalness. The most prominent motifs related to simplicity in the Bible are: (*a*) plain openness which is free from the complications of sophistication or duplicity; (*b*) moral uprightness and integrity of heart; (*c*) purity and loyalty in devotion to God, Christ, or one's fellow man; and (*d*) liberality which springs from simple goodness and willingness to give of the self without reservation.

1. In the OT. In the OT the dominant conceptions related to simplicity are innocence, integrity, uprightness, and simpleness. Several Hebrew terms are used to convey these ideas. The word םת is used to describe the simplicity (innocence) of the two hundred men who went with the rebellious Absalom to offer sacrifice at Hebron (II Sam. 15:11). Elsewhere, םת is employed to suggest such related ideas as integrity (Gen. 20:5; I Kings 9:4; Job 4:6; Ps. 7:8—H 7:9—G 7:9; Prov. 19:1), and uprightness of way or heart (Prov. 2:7; 10:9; cf. ישר, "uprightness," in Deut. 9:5; I Kings 9:4; Job 33:3). In the Psalms the word פתי, "simple," is used in a good sense to describe inexperienced or unsophisticated persons (Ps. 19:7—H 19:8—G 18:8). God preserves the simple (Ps. 116:6—G 114:6) and gives understanding to them (119:130—G 118:130). (With these expressions cf. the teaching of Jesus on childlike faith and trust in God [Matt. 19:13-14; Mark 10:13-16; Luke 18:15-17].) It should be noted, however, that the word פתי is sometimes used to suggest ignorance and folly (Prov. 1:22; 9:6; 14:15-18).

An instructive passage for the various shades of meaning related to the idea of simplicity is found in Test. Iss. 3:1-8. Here the description of a simple man is that of a responsible, frugal, pious, and generous person who walks in uprightness of heart and is never a busybody or malicious against his neighbor.

2. In the NT. In the NT the primary word for "simplicity" is ἁπλότης, which characteristically designates an undivided loyalty, purity in devotion as to Christ; but the term can also mean "wholeness of heart" in the sense of "generosity" or "liberality." Slaves are exhorted to be obedient to their earthly masters "in singleness of heart, as to Christ," and this exhortation is further explained as "doing the will of God from the heart," and "rendering service with a good will as to the Lord" (Eph. 6:5-8; cf. Col. 3:22). In II Cor. 11:3 simplicity is characterized as an attitude of Sincerity in devotion to Christ.

Perhaps ἁπλότης also suggests a quality of wholeheartedness, willingness to give of the self without reservation. Paul uses the term four times where the context demands the translation "generosity" or "liberality" (Rom. 12:8; II Cor. 8:2; 9:11, 13; cf. Jas. 1:5; Test. Iss. 3:8; Herm. Mand. 2:4).

In the metaphor about the eye in Matt. 6:22 (cf. Luke 11:34), the RSV translation for ἁπλοῦς "sound," is probably better than the KJV "single." The soundness of vision here probably symbolizes clarity and purity of moral perception which is free from duplicity, envy, and the like. The wholeness of vision in this passage is the opposite of an "evil eye" —i.e., inner perception beclouded and made unhealthy by envy, stinginess, or ulterior motives (cf. Ecclus. 14:9-10; Matt. 20:15).

Bibliography. W. Sanday and A. C. Headlam, *Romans,* ICC (1895), p. 357; C. Spicq, "La vertu de Simplicité dans l'A et le NT," *Revue des Sciences philosophiques et theologiques,* XXII (1933), 1-26; H. J. Cadbury, "The Single Eye," *HTR,* XLVII (1954), 69-74. See the several articles under the title "The Evil Eye," by C. R. Smith, C. J. Cadoux, and J. D. Percy, *ET,* LIII (1941-42), 181-82, 354-55; LIV (1942-43), 26-27.
                                                        R. L. SCHEEF, JR.

SIMRI. KJV form of SHIMRI 3.

SIN sĭn. KJV translation of סִין, the Hebrew name of PELUSIUM (so RSV).

SIN, SINNERS. The Bible takes sin in dead seriousness. Unlike many modern religionists, who seek to find excuses for sin and to explain away its seriousness, most of the writers of the Bible had a keen awareness of its heinousness, culpability, and tragedy. They looked upon it as no less than a condition of dreadful estrangement from God, the sole source of well-being. They knew that apart from God, man is a lost sinner, unable to save himself or find true happiness.

It is not difficult to find biblical passages referring to sin; as a matter of fact, there are few chapters which do not contain some reference to what sin is or does. It might even be said that in the Bible man has only two theological concerns involving himself: his sin and his salvation. Man finds himself in sin and suffers its painful effects; God graciously offers salvation from it. This is, in essence, what the whole Bible is about.

As might be expected, the biblical literature shows a marked development in its understanding of sin. As far back as the origin of man can be traced, he appears always to have been *homo religiosus,* and an unavoidable aspect of every religion has always been the realization of some kind of estrangement between man and the divine. Among primitive peoples this sin-consciousness and its remedy have been conceived dynamistically, and traces of dynamistic ideas remain as a primitive element in the OT notion of sin. There is reason, however, to believe that even in early times the Hebrews possessed at least the beginnings of a genuine awareness of the theological meaning of sin. As their understanding of Yahweh's being and personality developed, their recognition of the seriousness of sin increased. The prophets preached the tragic reality of the nation's sin, and the people learned it by experience, particularly in the events leading up to the Exile. The NT put sin in an even darker light as it simultaneously demonstrated God's amazing way of dealing with it in Christ.

1. In the OT
    a. Terminology
    b. Nature
    c. Origin, development, and extent
    d. Responsibility and personal awareness
    e. Penalty
    f. Remedy
2. In the Apoc. and the Pseudep.
    a. Nature and standard
    b. Origin, development, and extent
    c. Qumran dualism

3. In the NT
    a. Terminology
    b. Nature and standard
    c. Origin
    d. Extent and prevalence
    e. Remedy
Bibliography

1. In the OT. *a. Terminology.* It is no accident that the Bible, with its keen sense of moral and spiritual values, is particularly rich in the vocabulary of sin. This is especially true of the OT. Not being interested in offering a theoretical definition, the Hebrew writers only strove to reflect in their rich and vivid terminology the profundity and the widespread effects of sin as they experienced it. According to their basic orientation, the OT terms may be arranged as follows:

a) Formal words, indicating a deviation from what is good and right. The most common root is חטא, ("miss, fail, sin"; see its derivatives for "error, fault, sin," "sinful," "sinner"). It is the equivalent, even in etymology, of the NT word ἁμαρτάνω, ἁμαρτία. Unlike the English word "sin," it is one of the least theologically profound words for sin. The verb occurs in its concrete meaning of "miss" in Job 5:24: "You shall inspect your fold and miss nothing"; also in Judg. 20:16: "Every one could sling a stone at a hair, and not miss" (cf. also Prov. 8:36; 19:2). In the vast majority of passages, however, the verb indicates spiritual and moral failure, either toward one's fellow man (e.g., Gen. 20:9) or toward God (e.g., Lam. 5:7). It may also be extended to include the guilt and punishment accompanying sin (e.g., Gen. 43:9). In certain forms it also indicates the act of purifying from sin, particularly by means of prescribed offerings (e.g., Lev. 6:26—H 6:19). The noun חטאת is frequently used in cultic contexts as a technical designation for an offering for sin. *See* SACRIFICES AND OFFERINGS.

Formal and unexpressive is the verb עבר, when it means to overstep or transgress the word, command, law, or covenant of Yahweh (Num. 14:41, etc.).

Other formal roots are שגה and שגג (also שגגה, "sin of inadvertence"), which means to err through IGNORANCE. Similar in meaning is תעה, "wander" or "stray" (usually of physical straying, but of moral error in Ps. 58:3—H 58:4; Ezek. 44:10).

b) Theological terms, indicating sin as defiance against God. By far the most important is פשע ("to revolt, rebel, transgress"; with its cognate noun, "rebellion, transgression"). Although as compared with חטא this root occurs with relative infrequency, it is by all counts the OT's most profound word for "sin," indicating its theological meaning as "revolt against God." It cannot indicate a mere failure or mistake, like חטא, since it consists of wilful disobedience. Both the verb and the noun are used of revolt against nations or transgression against men (e.g., I Kings 12:19; Amos 1:3 ff), but generally they indicate transgression against God and defiance of his rule. They may also indicate the guilt accompanying such sin (e.g., Job 33:9). The active participle designates a rebel (equivalent to "sinner," "wicked") in several passages.

Revolt against God may likewise be expressed by the roots מרד and מרה with their respective nouns (cf. Ezek. 2:5-8). A weaker word is מאן, indicating refusal to obey Yahweh's commandments in such passages as Exod. 4:23.

Another strongly theological root is חנף ("be godless, profane"; with its derivatives for "profaneness, pollution"; "profane, godless"). It indicates ruthless violation of the holy. The verb means "to be impious or estranged from God," hence "polluted."

Still another root in this group is מעל ("act treacherously"; with its noun, "treachery"), indicating sacrilege toward and apostasy from God.

c) Terms describing a sinner's inner state. The root עוה ("be or act wrongly, pervertedly") expresses conscious and intentional badness. The verb occurs in a physical sense in Isa. 24:1: "He will twist its surface and scatter its inhabitants" (cf. Lam. 3:9). It may also refer to psychological dismay (Isa. 21:3). Otherwise it means "to act wrongly." The noun עון ("perversity, iniquity, guilt"), which occurs frequently, may indicate the iniquitous act, the guilt accompanying it, or its punishment. In many cases the three are indistinguishable (e.g., Gen. 4:13; 19:15).

The root רעע ("be bad"; with its cognates for "badness" and "bad") is generally used in a qualitative sense (see EVIL). An important meaning, however, is moral and spiritual badness, manifested in various forms of maliciousness and perversity. "Doers of evil" and "evil men" are expressive terms for sinners.

The precise opposite of צדק, "be righteous," is the root רשע ("be guilty, wicked"; with its cognates for "wicked and guilty act"; "guilty" or "wicked"). Despite its obvious juridical associations, it is not a merely legal word but indicates the corrupt inner nature of the guilty man. Ps. 1:4: "The wicked . . . are like chaff," and Isa. 57:20: "The wicked are like the tossing sea," provide vivid images of the looseness of character which the Hebrew mind associated with this word. The verb, usually in the causative, frequently means "to act guiltily" or "to condemn as guilty." The nouns and adjectives vacillate between the meanings of "guilt" and "wickedness," these being practically synonymous to the Hebrew mind. רשע is the most important OT (and Jewish) designation for "sinner."

A vivid term is בליעל, from which the proper name BELIAL has come. It indicates the worthlessness and unwholesomeness of a base and godless fellow (e.g., I Kings 21:10).

d) Terms in which the ethical aspect is prominent. Both רעע, "be bad," and רשע, "be wicked," have this meaning. Another word is חמס ("treat violently or wrongly"; with its cognate for "violent wrong"). Less descriptive and more juridical is עול ("do wrong, act perversely"; with its cognates for "injustice, wickedness"; "evildoer").

e) Terms indicating the baneful results of sin. עמל, "toil, trouble, mischief," is a late word similar in use to רעה, "evil." A parallel term is און, which often indicates the trouble and sorrow caused by wicked men (e.g., Job 4:8) and hence the whole disposition of sin leading to it (e.g., Isa. 1:13). Often, especially in the Psalms (e.g., 64:2—H 64:3), it is associated with deceit, lying, and malicious slander. It may be that the term bears reminiscences of the evil believed by superstitious minds to have been caused by magical spells (see MAGIC; SORCERY), but it is difficult to demonstrate that its employment in the OT refers to the active exercise of magical charms.

f) Terms for "guilt." Generally the Hebrews did not distinguish between the sin and its resultant guilt. Thus, as we have seen, all the leading words for "sin" also express "guilt." The OT has, however, a special word for "guilt," אשם ("be guilty, condemned"; with its cognates for "offense, guilt, guiltiness," and "guilty"). The primitive associations of this word are clearly apparent in I Sam. 6:3-4, 8, 17, where an אשם consists of the golden tumors and mice presented by the Philistines to ward off the baneful influences of the ark. There the word means "guilt offering," as it often does in the priestly legislation and in Ezek. 40 ff (see SACRIFICES AND OFFERINGS). Again, one word does service both for a spiritual condition and for the remedies employed to relieve it. In Lev. 4-5; Num. 5, where the verb refers to becoming guilty primarily in cultic transgression, the dynamistic associations are plainly present (cf. also I Chr. 21:3). As Israel's faith outgrew ideas of taboo, its concept of guilt became more ethical and spiritual. Thus in the majority of cases, particularly in late materials, this root conveys a personalized conception of culpability (cf. Gen. 26:10; II Chr. 24:18; Ezra 9:6; Prov. 30:10; Jer. 51:5; etc.).

This list does not at all exhaust the vocabulary of sin in the OT. Various other terms are employed to show that sin is obstinacy, PRIDE, BACKSLIDING, FOLLY, deceit, uncleanness (see CLEAN AND UNCLEAN), etc. In addition there is a name for every particular sin and crime. It is little wonder that various words for "sin" are often heaped together as synonyms (Exod. 34:7, 9; Lev. 16:16, 21; Ezra 9:6-9; Ps. 32:1 ff; 51:1 ff; Prov. 6:12-14; Isa. 1:4; Dan. 9:5; and elsewhere). When employed in poetic parallelism, the terms for "sin" often tend to lose the sharp edge of their distinctive meanings. In some cases, however, synonyms accentuate the peculiar qualities of one another (e.g., Job 34:36-37).

b. *Nature.* The predominant conception of the nature of sin in the Bible is that of personal alienation from God. Theologians have pointed out that all conceptions of sin appearing in human thought tend to reduce themselves to a basic three: the moralistic, in which sin is construed as deviation from an external norm; the monistic, in which sin is somehow equated with man's creatureliness or physical nature; and the personalistic, which is that of the Bible. To these might be added the dynamistic conception of primitive religions, in which sin is the transgression of a taboo or an offense against mysterious supernatural beings and forces; philosophically considered, this conception is basically a form of monism, as, e.g., an analysis of the dynamistic and Brahmanic elements in Hinduism will reveal.

There really can be no doubt that the intensely personalistic, or, better, theological conception of sin is the most characteristic view of the OT and the exclusive conception of the NT. This is, in fact, one of the most impressive triumphs of biblical religion, alongside the distinctive biblical awareness of the intensely personal character of God and of this God's intimately personal way of dealing with sin.

It is possible, however, to trace the influence of other modes of thought in the OT. These other conceptions rarely appear in pure form in the OT—or outside the Bible, for that matter. In the OT we often find dynamism developing into moralism or into a highly personal conception, or the personal conception degenerating into moralism. It is often very difficult to isolate each of these in a particular passage, yet it is possible to distinguish the basic orientation of these various conceptions and to show which represents the authentic idea of biblical thought.

The nature religions of the ancient Near East were essentially monistic in making man, the world, and the divine part of one identical process. For them the natural world was peopled with supernatural powers. Although sin was, to a degree, interpreted as a violation of the express will of the gods, it was often felt to be any impingement, known or unknown, upon the irrational prerogatives of the supernatural. This notion of sin has more of the quality of the violation of taboo than of the transgression of high moral and spiritual standards.

Survivals of taboo-consciousness are clearly present in certain early elements in the OT. Even though most of the old laws have undergone a Yahwistic reorientation, the taboo idea may still be traced in many passages (e.g., Lev. 19:9, 19). It is difficult to explain the prohibition against the eating of blood as arising from any other source (Lev. 17:3-4; cf. Gen. 9:4), and this is probably the basis also of the distinction between clean and unclean animals (Lev. 11; Deut. 14:3-21). It also lies behind the rules for ritual purification in Lev. 12–15 (see CLEAN AND UNCLEAN). Associated with this is the entire circle of dynamistic concepts which the early Hebrews received from their cultural heritage: the word, spirit, blessing, curse, oath, vow, etc., which were felt to have some kind of independent power; also the concept of immediate retribution (II Sam. 6:7), of communal guilt (Num. 16:32; Josh. 7:24), of culpability even for innocent transgressions of ritual (Lev. 4:3; 5:15), and of the need for the banishment or execution of notorious sinners (Gen. 4:13-14; Lev. 17:4; 20:3; 24:16; Num. 9:13; Deut. 17:7; etc.). Similar is the idea of the "devoted thing" (see DEVOTED), the spoils of a holy war which were claimed exclusively for Yahweh (Josh. 6:17-18, etc.).

It cannot be denied, however, that generally the OT conception of sin appears on a much higher moral and spiritual level. Apart from the cultic rituals, most of the laws contained in the Pentateuch and elsewhere evince a strong awareness of ethical right and wrong (see LAW IN THE OT). This awareness needs to be understood mainly in relation to the rising understanding of Yahweh's own supremely moral being. It was as he came to understand what was wrong in relation to the will of Yahweh that the Israelite understood what was wrong in relation to his neighbors. Sins of all kinds were rightly interpreted as, first of all, sins against God (Gen. 39:9; Ps. 51:4—H 51:6).

It was chiefly the great prophets who led Israel to see that sin is something intensely spiritual, and consequently deeply tragic. They proclaimed that sin in its awful reality involves, not the violation of a taboo or the transgression of an external ordinance, but that it touches upon a man's personal standing with God. "Woe is me!" cried Isaiah as he received his vision of

Yahweh high and lifted up, "for I am lost; for I am a man of unclean lips, and I dwell in the midst of a people of unclean lips" (6:5). Thus the sinner becomes particularly aware of his deep sinfulness in the awesome presence of the holy God (cf. I Kings 17:18; Ps. 51:4—H 51:6; Luke 5:8). Such sin *coram Deo* was rightly understood to be, in its deepest essence, estrangement or alienation from God resulting from man's distrust and disobedience. Sin is, above all, יֶשַׁע, "revolt," as the story of Adam's sin (Gen. 3) makes abundantly clear. This realization is often expressed by the prophets in words like these:

> Our transgressions are multiplied before thee,
>   and our sins testify against us;
> for our transgressions are with us,
>   and we know our iniquities:
> transgressing, and denying the LORD,
>   and turning away from following our God,
> speaking oppression and revolt,
>   conceiving and uttering from the heart
>   lying words (Isa. 59:12-13).

Thus the standard of moral good was Yahweh's revealed will, and sin against this was transgression against the covenant which he had made with his people (cf. especially Hosea for the development of this theme). This is the high theological conception of sin which dominates OT thought and is completely taken over by the NT.

It has been mentioned that there is a third basic conception of sin, the moralistic. Always the danger of descending into moralism was present with Israel. In the wisdom literature and especially in Proverbs a tendency toward an external, moralistic conception of sin appears, but this came to fullest development in later Jewish legalism, which identified every jot and tittle of the Torah, including the old taboos (although many now appeared in reinterpreted form), as the criteria of sin. The whole duty of man was circumscribed by the Torah, and accordingly the entire definition of sin. Thus almost as much as with the old dynamism, the legalist conceived of guilt as being incurred automatically and almost impersonally, but now through transgression of a written code (or, with the Pharisees, of its oral interpretation), with little consideration of the ethical and spiritual significance of the act involved. Of course, legalism could never be entirely divorced from the personalistic conception. The rationale of obeying the little-understood details of the Torah was the assurance that they authentically represented the divine will. To obey it was to obey God. Yet in adhering to the letter of the law Jewish legalism came to lose much of the true prophetic insight into the nature of sin as personal rebellion and estrangement from God.

c. Origin, development, and extent. The OT contains surprisingly little reflection on the origin of sin in the human race. It is true that the story of Adam's fall in Gen. 3 (see FALL) unmistakably intends to explain how sin began, even though the terminology of sin is lacking. It seems strange, however, that the rest of the OT shows such little acquaintance with this tradition; possible references to it appear only in two ambiguous passages: Job 31:33; Hos. 6:7 (Job 15:7-8; Ezek. 28:17 evidently presuppose a different fall tradition; Isa. 43:27 refers to Abraham or possibly Jacob). In Gen. 6:2, 4, an ancient myth of the sons of God corrupting the human race by marrying women is drawn into the Yahwistic account of the tragic deterioration of mankind after Adam's fall. Here it is not presented as an alternative explanation of the origin of sin, but as evidence for and impetus to the ongoing corruption of humanity resulting from the sin in the Garden. It inspired speculations in intertestamental Judaism, however, that these marriages were the origin of sin (*see below*).

Another explanation for the origin of sin was that of demonic influence. This explanation does not appear until late in the OT literature. With considerable justification, the SERPENT of Gen. 3 has been interpreted, both in Judaism and in Christianity, as representing demonic temptation, but there is no hint of this in the account itself. Demonology plays a very unimportant role in the OT. The "evil spirit from the LORD" which tormented Saul (I Sam. 16:14) is a remnant of dynamistic thought and does not represent a personal demon as conceived in later biblical thought. SATAN is mentioned, with the definite article and not as a proper name, but as a wicked supernatural adversary, in Job 1:6–2:7; Zech. 3:1-2. The only passage in which temptation to sin is ascribed to him is I Chr. 21:1, where he is said to have incited David to number Israel (cf. II Sam. 24:1).

The OT writers were more concerned to trace the source of sin "existentially" in human life than to indulge in historical and cosmological speculations. The notion that it arises either from creatureliness as such or from sexual generation does not appear in the OT. Such passages as Job 14:1; 15:14; Ps. 51:5—H 51:7 speak only of the fact that man is sinful from the time of conception and that frail "flesh" is prone to all the evils of life.

According to the Hebrew writers, and particularly Jeremiah, sin comes from the corrupt HEART of man. Here, at the center of his being, the sinner is at odds with his Creator. Yahweh says:

> This people draw near with their mouth
> and honor me with their lips,
> while their hearts are far from me
> (Isa. 29:13).

There is a depth of iniquity in the human heart:

> The heart is deceitful above all things,
> and desperately corrupt;
> who can understand it? (Jer. 17:9).

It is from this evil heart that all sin arises: "The LORD saw that . . . every imagination of the thoughts of his heart was only evil continually" (Gen. 6:5; cf. 8:21). There is therefore no hope of man's avoiding sin unless God gives him a new heart (Ezek. 11:19; 18:31; 36:26).

The heart is not so much the seat of the intellect as of the will, and it is man's will that has become corrupt and perverse. God showed man the way; he made a covenant with Israel; but man refuses to obey and continually rebels against God. It is thus basically his will that is at fault: "They say, '. . . We will follow our own plans, and will every one act according to the stubbornness of his evil heart'" (Jer. 18: 12). "They did not obey or incline their ear, but every one walked in the stubbornness of his evil heart" (Jer. 11:8; cf. 7:24; 11:9-10; 16:12; 23:17; Isa. 6:10; 63:10).

Thus sin's essence lies, not in isolated acts of transgression, but in the depth of man's being. As he fell into sin through an inordinate use of his will (Gen. 3), that same will, with its organ, the heart, has become so warped through estrangement from God that it henceforth gives rise to all sorts of evil. Thus sin becomes a fateful and tragic habitus leading at last to complete destruction. Sin begets greater sin; the sin of one individual involves everyone associated with him, through its evil influence; a sin of thought leads to transgressions in word and act. In short, the whole life, the whole being, of man has become sinful and corrupt. It has become his very nature to sin (Jer. 13:23).

Nowhere does the tragic course of sin appear more plainly than in the primeval history of Gen. 2–11. The main purpose of the Yahwistic writer particularly (the priestly interpolations have a less serious view of human sinfulness) is to indicate the spiritual degeneration of mankind resulting from the sin in the Garden. Not only are the immediate consequences of Eve and Adam's disobedience depicted, but the writer also shows how this led irresistibly to enmity and fratricide (4:3-8), then to mass murder and brutality, and to the invention of the instruments of civilization whereby evil could appear in greater refinement (vss. 17-26); further to the corruption of the race through marriage with supernatural beings (6:2, 4), until at last the wickedness of mankind became so great that it had to be destroyed with a flood (vss. 5 ff). This particular tradition does not claim that even Noah was sinless (he was preserved because he "found favor in the eyes of the LORD" [6:8; cf. vs. 9]), as appeared in his drunkenness after the flood had subsided (9:20-21). His descendants returned to the folly of the antediluvians, making use of the developing skills of civilization to erect a tower that was to be the symbol of their prideful defiance of God (11: 1 ff). *See* BABEL.

The pre-exilic history of Israel provided another vivid example of the tragic course of sin. As interpreted by the prophets, this sad history demonstrated that neither Yahweh's favor nor his chastisement could turn the people from their sins (Deut. 32:15; Jer. 11:9-10; Hos. 9:10; 11:2; 12:14; etc.). The people actually delighted in wickedness (Jer. 5:31). Thus Israel's perversity is depicted as brazen wantonness and shameless ingratitude (Ezek. 16; 20; 23; cf. Jer. 2–3; Hos. 1:1–2:13). The sinner spoils all good and sins against the grace of God. "God made man upright, but they have sought out many devices" (Eccl. 7:29). Sin is as a dreadful sickness, from which God alone can save (Pss. 6:2—H 6:3; 107:17-18; Hos. 5:13; 6:1; 7:1).

Two of the most notorious examples of hardened sinners were Pharaoh (Exod. 4:21; I Sam. 6:6) and Saul. Even though they temporarily showed outward signs of repentance (cf. I Sam. 15:24 ff), their hearts at last became completely hardened. There were many like them (e.g., Zedekiah [II Chr. 36:13]; cf. Isa. 63:17; Zech. 7:12). But all Israel needed constantly to be warned: "Harden not your hearts!" (Ps. 95:8).

Because sin is rooted in the heart, all of human life is liable to its taint. No area of activity is exempt from it. There are cultic sins; sins in social and political life; spiritual sins such as pride, hatred, and envy. Sin resides even in the intentions and desires (Exod. 20:17). There are sins of which no one else is aware (Pss. 19:12—H 19:13; 90:8) or of which the sinner himself is unconscious (Lev. 4:2 ff). Various lists of sins are to be found in the OT (Exod. 20:3-17; Deut. 5:7-21; 27:15-25; Job 31; Ps. 15; Prov. 6:16-19; Ezek. 18:5-8; etc.), but none of these exhausts the possibilities of evil.

Is there then no one who is not guilty of sin? Of "fools" and "evildoers," Ps. 14:1, 3 (=53:1, 3), says:

> There is none that does good.
>
> . . . .
>
> They have all gone astray, they are all alike corrupt;
> there is none that does good,
> no, not one.

Other passages extend this condemnation to all classes of men, even to the righteous: "Surely there is not a righteous man on earth who does good and never sins" (Eccl. 7:20);

> Who can say, "I have made my heart clean;
> I am pure from my sin"? (Prov. 20:9).

Other references to the universality of human sinfulness are in I Kings 8:46 ("There is no man who does not sin"); II Chr. 6:36; Ps. 143:2; Isa. 9:17; and also in Job 4:17-19; 14:4; 15:14, where it is closely allied with creatureliness but not identified with it. Since the Hebrew mind held to the solidarity of the human race (see MAN, NATURE OF), it should not be surprising that it included all of mankind under the condition of sinfulness.

As the Hebrew mind held to the solidarity of the race, it also believed in the essential unity of the life and being of the individual man. Therefore, as has been pointed out, a man's whole being and activity, beginning in his sinful heart and reaching out to all his thoughts, words, and deeds, are affected by sin. This also means that man is a sinner from his conception. It is said that

> The wicked go astray from the womb,
> they err from their birth, speaking lies
> (Ps. 58:3—H 58:4).

Another psalmist applies this to himself:

> Behold, I was brought forth in iniquity,
> and in sin did my mother conceive me
> (Ps. 51:5—H 51:7).

Thus the OT contains the elements of a doctrine of original sin. It does not theorize about the process by which humanity has become corrupt: all it knows —and it knows this for sure, through painful experience—is that all of mankind since Adam has been sinful, that the whole man is sinful, that man's entire life is sinful from its beginning.

d. Responsibility and personal awareness. Inasmuch as man cannot escape involvement in sin, it might seem logical to conclude that he ought not to be held responsible for it. Nothing, however, is further from OT thought. For one thing, since sin is rooted in the rebellious heart, the seat of the will, it is basically an act of perverted freedom, and hence man is always responsible for it, even though its effects overwhelm him and progressively enslave his will itself. For another thing, God offers grace as a remedy for sin

(*see below*) and urges the sinner to repent and forsake his evil ways. Among all the prophetic appeals for repentance, perhaps one that makes this clearer than any other is Ezek. 33:11: "As I live, says the Lord GOD, I have no pleasure in the death of the wicked, but that the wicked turn from his way and live; turn back, turn back from your evil ways; for why will you die, O house of Israel?" The fact that man is often warned against succumbing to sin (e.g., Gen. 4:6-7) and constantly urged to do the good (Deut. 30:11-20; Josh. 24:14; etc.) presupposes his entire responsibility.

God holds all men to account for their wrongdoing, even the Gentiles (Sodom [Gen. 19:13; Ezek. 16:49-50]; the Canaanites [Lev. 18:25]; Israel's neighbors [Amos 1:1–2:3; cf. Jonah, the oracles against the nations]). It stands to reason then that Israelites are answerable to him. Their sin is all the greater because they sin against his covenant and against better knowledge.

An important consideration is the distinction between corporate and individual responsibility for sin. In its early development Israel was very much influenced by a dynamistic concept of corporate guilt, as strikingly appears in the account of Achan's punishment (Josh. 7). Not only was the guilty man put to death, but all his goods, his flocks, and his family also perished with him (vs. 24). The family group was a much more significant entity than the individual person. When the head of such a group transgressed, he transmitted guilt to every member of it (cf. II Sam. 21:6; II Kings 9:8; etc.).

Even in official Yahwism this conception played an important role. In the great COVENANT formulations, however, its scope was somewhat restricted. Thus, according to the Decalogue (Exod. 20:5; Deut. 5:9; cf. Exod. 34:7; Num. 14:18), the iniquity of the fathers is to be visited upon the children, but only "to the third and fourth generation." Moreover, Deut. 24:16 provides a humanitarian rule against the blood purges which the Hebrews occasionally witnessed: "The fathers shall not be put to death for the children, nor shall the children be put to death for the fathers; every man shall be put to death for his own sin." This is a rule which King Amaziah of Judah is remembered as having honored (II Kings 14:6).

The corporate involvement of sin deeply impressed itself upon the people, however. The prophets proclaimed that it was not only a few wicked individuals, but the whole nation, that was laden with sin (Isa. 1:4). Generation after generation treasured up wrath. Thus it was easy for those who were finally forced to bear the painful consequences to protest that all the effects of corporate guilt were being visited upon them. The exiles lamented:

> Our fathers sinned, and are no more;
> and we bear their iniquities
> (Lam. 5:7).

They even had a proverb:

> The fathers have eaten sour grapes,
> and the children's teeth are set on edge.

Against this both Jeremiah and Ezekiel protested (Jer. 31:29-30; Ezek. 18; 33:10-20). No son was to be held accountable for his father's crimes. "The soul that sins shall die" (Ezek. 18:4). In saying this, they did not mean to deny corporate involvement in sin: this was beyond dispute. Their purpose was to accentuate individual responsibility, which was in danger of becoming submerged in a consciousness of overpowering national calamity. Even though the nation was now suffering a bitter corporate punishment, there was hope for the individual if he would repent.

It has been mentioned that guilt for sin came to be felt more personally as Israel's theological understanding of the real nature of sin developed. Wherever the concept of sin is associated with dynamistic thought and is conceived of, at least in part, as the transgression of an irrational taboo, its primary psychological effect is to produce, not a genuine sense of guilt, but an uncanny feeling of dread. The result is panic instead of godly sorrow. With masterful sureness, the writer of Gen. 4:13-14 depicts the blind terror of Cain, who cries in alarm at the mark of curse placed upon his forehead: "My punishment is greater than I can bear." Cain understood all too little the real seriousness of his sin. He was more afraid of its evil results for himself than sorrowful for the crime itself.

On the other hand, a true spiritual sense of guilt, which includes deep sorrow and shame, follows from the knowledge that sin is a personal affront against a holy and righteous God. Such guilt is felt as a heavy burden which oppresses the soul. It comes to vivid expression in such language as this:

> For my iniquities have gone over my head;
>   they weigh like a burden too heavy for me.
> . . . .
> I am utterly bowed down and prostrate;
>   all the day I go about mourning
>   (Ps. 38:4, 6—H 38:5, 7).

The sinner knows himself to be under the WRATH OF GOD (cf. Ps. 90:7-8). So long as he keeps his guilt to himself, there is no relief for his soul:

> When I declared not my sin, my body wasted away
>   through my groaning all day long.
> For day and night thy hand was heavy upon me;
>   my strength was dried up as by the heat of summer.
> I acknowledged my sin to thee,
>   and I did not hide my iniquity;
> I said, "I will confess my transgressions to the LORD";
>   then thou didst forgive the guilt of my sin
>   (Ps. 32:3-5).

It will be noted that this intense inward awareness of guilt is mainly expressed in texts dating from late periods of Israel's religious development, as in the Psalms cited above and in Ezra 9:6-15; Ps. 51; Isa. 59:9-15; 64:5-6; Jer. 14:7; Dan. 9:4-19. Many of these are prayers, in which the most saintly men of Israel—who know their sinfulness the most clearly because they live the most intimately with God—lay their sin before him whom it concerns the most and who has the only remedy for it.

This brings up the question of the sinfulness of those who are called perfect or righteous in the OT (see RIGHTEOUSNESS IN THE OT). It is significant that many of the most notable exemplars of piety are said explicitly to have committed sin: Noah (Gen. 9:21), Abraham (Gen. 12:11 ff), Moses (Num. 20:11-12),

David (II Sam. 11; 24), Elijah (I Kings 19:4), Isaiah (Isa. 6:5), Jeremiah (Jer. 15:19), and others. And yet it is said of Noah that he "was a righteous man, blameless in his generation" (Gen. 6:9; cf. 7:1); also that, like Enoch (5:24), he "walked with God" (6:9). The Prologue of the book of Job declares that its hero was "blameless and upright, one who feared God, and turned away from evil" (1:1; cf. vs. 8). In some of the Psalms (e.g., 18:20-24—H 18:21-25; 26; 41: 12) the writers claim complete purity and innocence. In the light of the universal sinfulness of humanity, which is the dominant teaching of the OT, how are such expressions to be understood?

It should be made clear that the terms involved in these claims of innocence are generally based on external standards of goodness. The leading words are: צדיק, "righteous"—i.e., not guilty of specific sins—a juridical term; ישר, "upright," as judged by external conduct; and תם, "perfect" as far as personal worth is concerned. (צדיק is the precise opposite of רשע, "guilty.") To be described as "righteous," one needs to conform, at least outwardly, to the commonly accepted standard of what is right. It is not so much a question of whether one ever commits sin as of one's basic walk of life and attitude toward the standard of right. In later Judaism this standard came to be, of course, the Torah.

On this basis all truly God-fearing men would qualify as righteous. As a matter of fact, an awareness of the antithesis between the righteous and the wicked in this sense plays a major role in many of the Psalms (e.g., Ps. 1) and in much of the wisdom literature. A wicked man is not just a sinner—i.e., one who from time to time falls into sin. He lives in sin; he adopts it as his way of life; his whole existence is under a dark cloud of guilt. On the other hand, a righteous man may occasionally fall into sins, but because his basic attitude is hatred toward sin, he is not charged as being "guilty" or "wicked."

This distinction probably accounts for such claims of innocence as are found in Ps. 18:20 ff. It is plain that these claims lack the deep inwardness of conscience which some of the other Psalms reveal (32; 38; 51; etc.). They ignore the more important question of whether one can really be right with God even though he may observe the outward norms of pious conduct. In spite of its naïve and artless Prologue, this is the real problem of the book of Job. His inquisitors accuse Job of all kinds of sin, while he stubbornly maintains his "righteousness" (27:6; cf. 11:4; 33:9; etc.), but the question which he himself knows he can never avoid is: "How can a man be just before God?" (9:2). Job abandons the norms of an easy moralism and reaches out into a dark unknown for that forensic righteousness which God imputes in spite of the sinner's personal guilt. Job was looking for a wonder which only the NT would make plain.

e. Penalty. Since Yahweh holds all men accountable to him for their sin, it is also he who brings their penalty upon them. As supreme Ruler over all the world, he announces the penalty of each nation's sin (cf. Amos 1:1–2:3). But his covenant people are not exempt from this judgment. Judah and Israel are also under indictment for their transgressions (Amos 2: 4 ff). The peculiar importance of Amos, the earliest of the writing prophets, is that he for the first time clearly announces Yahweh's judgment upon his own people:

> Behold, I am setting a plumb line
>   in the midst of my people Israel;
>   I will never again pass by them
> (7:8).

Again and again the prophets declare Yahweh's verdict (Isa. 2:10-21; 5:26-30; 7:17-25; 8:5-8; 10:33-34; Jer. 25:8-11; Ezek. 9; Hos. 13:16; Amos 3:10-11; 5: 27; 6:14; etc.; cf. Lev. 26:17, 25, 31-39; Deut. 28:25-68). In apocalyptic passages the imagery of Yahweh's judgment is set forth in lurid detail (Isa. 24:21-23; 63:1-6; 66:15-16; Joel 3:11 ff). Yahweh's purpose is to use Israel's enemies as the executors of his judgment (Isa. 10:5-11; Jer. 27:6 ff). But even these are subject to his condemnation (cf. Isa. 10:12-16).

Although forensic language is employed, it is plain that the penalty which results from transgressions has an internal connection with it. I.e., sin's penalty follows immediately and necessarily. For the Hebrew mind sin included, besides the act itself, the guilt attaching to it and its painful results, which might be called its judgment. Thus it is said that God judges a guilty man by bringing his conduct upon his own head (I Kings 8:32). Sin is never an isolated and easily forgotten act; it sets in motion a whole series of consequences; it begets more sin and more guilt and more pain, and then the whole series over again. This is the tragic course of sin which has been described above. Since this necessary involvement of act and consequence belongs to the essential nature of moral creation, it is indeed the judgment of God. Theologically speaking, since the sinner lives (at least to the extent that he sins) in estrangement from God, while God has created him to live in harmony with him and to enjoy all the consequent blessings of peace and well-being, it necessarily follows that his life apart from God will be filled with pain and misery.

He who digs a pit will fall into it,
  and a stone will come back upon him who starts it rolling.
A lying tongue hates its victims,
  and a flattering mouth works ruin (Prov. 26:27-28).

It is for this reason that the leading terms for "sin" in the OT include its penalty (see above). This is particularly true of חטא and עון. When Cain cries out: "My עון is greater than I can bear" (Gen. 4:13), it is the punishment of his crime that troubles him, not the evil deed in itself. The fire and brimstone which rains down upon Sodom is called the "עון of the city" (Gen. 19:15). Aaron protests to Moses: "Oh, my lord, lay not חטאת upon us [RSV 'do not punish us'] because we have done foolishly and have sinned [חטאנו]" (Num. 12:11).

Thus suffering comes to be interpreted as the penalty of sin, and great suffering as the penalty of great wickedness. The people see their land destroyed and go into captivity because of their sin (II Kings 17:6 ff). The First Psalm makes a sweeping generalization which ignores all conflicting experience: all that the godly man does shall prosper; the way of the wicked shall perish. Job's antagonists have made a rigid dogma of this. For them all suffering is the penalty of sin; hence it is indisputable that Job is guilty, however much he may protest his inno-

cence. Nowhere in the OT are the sorrows of the wicked, which are the penalties of sin, set out more luridly than in the speeches of Job's accusers (15:17-35; 18:5-21). They do not even imagine the possibility that Job's sufferings have been inflicted for some other purpose (1:6-12). Most Hebrew thinkers had sense enough not to make so exact an equation, however. They knew that the righteous did not always enjoy happiness, that the wicked did not always suffer (Job 21:17-26; Ps. 73; Jer. 12:1-4), that the intensity of suffering was not always in proportion to the sin (Hab. 1:13). Here was what was to become one of Israel's most agonizing problems. See SUFFERING AND EVIL.

The ultimate penalty for sin is death. This is given profound expression in the Eden prohibition: "In the day that you eat of it you shall die" (Gen. 2:17), and in the judgment imposed for transgressing this prohibition:

> You are dust,
>   and to dust you shall return (3:19).

Here human mortality is made into a punishment for sin. In the Pentateuchal laws the death sentence is required for the most flagrant sins (Exod. 21:15-17; Lev. 20:10-16; 24:10-17; Num. 15:30-31; Deut. 21: 18-21; 22:21-22; cf. Josh. 7:25). When the penalty of DEATH is declared upon the unrepentant wicked, this may be understood as a death which is spiritual as well as physical (Ps. 73:27; Ezek. 3:19).

f. Remedy. A discussion of sin, with all its woeful diagnosis, would not be complete without a consideration of the remedy that has been provided for it (see ATONEMENT; CONVERSION; CRIMES AND PUNISHMENTS; FORGIVENESS; REGENERATION; REPENTANCE; SANCTIFICATION). At any rate, the OT is not entirely clear about the ultimate cure of sin. For this it depends upon the fuller revelation of the NT. See § 3e below.

The Hebrew sinner sought relief in two separate directions. He sought atonement through the cultic rituals, and later, in Jewish legalism, in an attempt to keep the whole Torah and its interpretation. But men of deep spiritual perceptiveness could find no ultimate relief in these devices. They were led to cast themselves simply upon God's mercy in an act of confession and trust. Thus the highest insight of OT faith is that "deliverance belongs to the LORD" (Ps. 3:8—H 3:9).

> If thou, O LORD, shouldst mark iniquities,
>   Lord, who could stand?
> But there is forgiveness with thee,
>   That thou mayest be feared
> (Ps. 130:3-4).

2. In the Apoc. and the Pseudep. a. *Nature and standard.* Sin continued to be a burning problem in the intertestamental period. The literature of this period offers occasional examples of a sin-consciousness reminiscent of the prophets and of the great canonical Psalms. Both individual (Prayer Man. 9, 12) and national (Bar. 1:17-19; 2:12; 3:2, 7-8) guilt are confessed. There was a realization, especially in the early part of this period, that sin is, first of all, wilful defiance of and estrangement from God:

> The beginning of man's pride is to depart from the Lord;
>   his heart has forsaken his Maker.

For the beginning of pride is sin,
   and the man who clings to it pours out abominations
      (Ecclus. 10:12-13; cf. Wisd. Sol. 1:3).

However, the dominant conception of sin during this entire period was legalistic. The Torah, or Law, became the entire definition of the divine will and completely circumscribed sin. To sin was to break the law; to do righteousness was to keep it. Throughout the Apoc. and the Pseudep., from the earliest writings to the latest, as in all the rabbinical literature following, this was the practical standard of sin (cf. Tob. 3:4-5; 4:5; Wisd. Sol. 2:12; Ecclus. 10:19; 21:11; II Bar. 15:5; 19:3; Asmp. Moses 12:10-11; II Esd. 7: 72; 8:56; IV Macc. 5:17-21). The old idea that a person could sin in ignorance was retained (Test. Zeb. 1:4-5; cf. Slavonic Enoch 30:16; 31:7). The most heinous kind of transgression was, of course, that which was committed knowingly and deliberately against the law (II Bar. 15:6; II Esd. 9:36).

With increased sharpness the lines were drawn between the righteous, who were faithful to the law, and the wicked, who transgressed it. The latter were given the exclusive name "sinners." A work which strongly manifests the spirit of Pharisaism, the Psalms of Solomon, takes the view that a righteous man may sin, but this is through weakness and error, and not as the sin of the wicked, who transgresses wilfully and habitually:

The righteous stumbleth and holdeth the Lord righteous.
. . . .
  There lodgeth not in the house of the righteous sin upon sin.
The righteous continually searcheth his house,
  To remove utterly (all) iniquity (done) by him in error.
He maketh atonement for (sins of) ignorance by fasting and
    afflicting his soul,
  And the Lord counteth guiltless every pious man and his
    house.
The sinner stumbleth and curseth his life.
. . . .
He addeth sins to sins . . . .
  He falleth—verily grievous in his fall—and riseth no more.
The destruction of the sinner is for ever (3:5-13).[1]

Thus all of humanity is sharply divided into two classes (Ecclus. 33:12-15; Pss. Sol. 13:4; etc.). According to their attitude toward the law all men are judged and rewarded (Jth. 8:5-8; Ecclus. 40:8-11, 17; Asmp. Moses 12:10-11; Enoch 5:6-9; 22:9-13; 99–101; Pss. Sol. 9:15; 13:4-11; 14:2). The essence of piety is the doing of good works (II Esd. 8:36). This is the true wisdom and fear of God, which no ungodly man possesses (cf. Wisd. Sol. 1:4; Ecclus. 15:7).

b. Origin, development, and extent. The literature of the intertestamental period is rife with speculation concerning the origin of sin and evil. Since this was a time of recurring disillusionment and painful tension for Judaism, it is small wonder that many earnest souls were constantly seeking for answers to the urgent question of how this evil began, and at the same time were increasingly taking refuge in apocalyptic (see APOCALYPTICISM) as an ultimate solution for it.

Speculations concerning the origin of sin took their departure chiefly from the story of Adam's fall in Gen. 3, from the account of the marriage of the "sons

---

[1] R. H. Charles, ed., *The Apocrypha and Pseudepigrapha of the Old Testament* (Oxford: The Clarendon Press).

of God" with women in Gen. 6:2, 4; from the concept of an "inclination" or יצר that was "evil continually" according to Gen. 6:5; 8:21; and from various OT passages which speak of universal sinfulness and of the corruption of the heart.

Although II Esdras, a somewhat heterodox writing reflecting the anguish of Jewish piety in the years following the destruction of Jerusalem in A.D. 70, approaches very close to blaming God for sin (cf. 4:30), most of the literature of this period is very certain that it is not God (Wisd. Sol. 1:13-16; Ecclus. 15:11-13, 17, 20; cf. 31:13) but man (Enoch 98:4) who is responsible for causing it. In Hellenistic Alexandria the idea that the body is essentially evil apparently had some influence on Jewish thinking (Wisd. Sol. 9: 15; cf. 8:20); but generally the orthodox Hebrew view was maintained that man was created good and in God's image (Wisd. Sol. 2:23; 8:19-20; Test. Naph. 2:5; Slavonic Enoch 44:1; 65:2; II Esd. 3:4-6). Sin came into the human race when Eve was seduced by Satan and persuaded Adam to transgress with her (Enoch 32:6; 69:6; Jub. 3:15-35; Slavonic Enoch 31: 3-6; IV Macc. 18:8; cf. also the late Book of Adam and Eve and the Apocalypse of Moses). Although Eve was often given the primary blame for this, it came to be realized that Adam's sin was the more representative and destructive (cf. Ecclus. 25:24 with II Esd. 7:118).

In the early literature of the intertestamental period little consequence was drawn from Adam's sin, beyond that which Gen. 3–11 itself affirms (cf. Jub. 4:2-5). Wisd. Sol. 12:10 says only of the Canaanites that "their origin was evil and their wickedness inborn." In three apocalyptic writings of the first century A.D., however, the relation between Adam's sin and the sinfulness of all mankind is forcefully stated. These are the Slavonic Enoch, II Baruch, and II Esdras. The first of these posits a tragic connection without explaining its process: "I saw all forefathers from all time with Adam and Eva, and I sighed and broke into tears and said of the ruin of their dishonour: 'Woe is me for my infirmity and for that of my forefathers' " (41:1). According to the second, Adam plunged "many" into the darkness of sin (II Bar. 18: 2; 56:8-9), so that, even with the Law to illumine his descendants, they sinned and transgressed (19:3). Because of Adam's sin death came upon all mankind (23:4; 51:15; 54:15), together with all kinds of suffering and evil (56:6-7). All of mankind are going to destruction because of that first sin:

O Adam, what hast thou done to all those who are born from
  thee?
And what will be said to the first Eve who hearkened to the
  serpent?
For all this multitude are going to corruption,
Nor is there any numbering of those whom the fire devours
               (48:42-43).[1]

Yet individual men are responsible for their own transgression. Adam has somehow given them an evil propensity, but it is they who choose to do wrong:

For though Adam first sinned
And brought untimely death upon all,
Yet of those who were born from him
Each one of them has prepared for his own soul torment to
  come,

And again each one of them has chosen for himself glories to come (54:15; cf. 51:16).

Adam is therefore not the cause, save only of his own soul,
But each of us has been the Adam of his own soul (54:19).[1]

It is more universal death than universal sin that is attributed to Adam.

II Esdras likewise posits a close relation between Adam's transgression and the corruption of the human race (3:7-8; 7:11-12). This writer apparently believed that this exists as a hereditary connection between Adam's sin and the sin of mankind, similar to the growth of a grain of evil seed: "For a grain of evil seed was sown in Adam's heart from the beginning, and how much ungodliness it has produced until now, will produce until the time of threshing comes!" (4:30; cf. vss. 31-32). It is this that accounts for the death and universal suffering to which Adam's descendants are subject (3:7; 7:48, 120). In anguished tones similar to those of II Bar. 48:42-43 this writer cries out for the tragedy of Adam's fall: "O Adam, what have you done? For though it was you who sinned, the fall was not yours alone, but ours also who are your descendants. For what good is it to us, if an eternal age has been promised to us, but we have done deeds that bring death?" (II Esd. 7:118-119). All the pain and perplexity of a disenchanted Judaism are reflected in these lines. They were written, significantly, at the very period when the NT was coming into being.

From the tradition of the "sons of God" intermarrying with women and producing giants, intertestamental Judaism drew far-reaching speculations which were intimately connected with the developing angelology and demonology of the period (*see* ANGEL; DEMON). These speculations appear in various writings, but are most prominent in Enoch. The "sons of God" were identified with the fallen angels, or "Watchers," who were originally good (Jub. 4:15) but sinned (Test. Naph. 3:5; Slavonic Enoch 7:3; 29:4-5). It was they who entered into sexual relations with women and produced monsters, who corrupted the earth with their wickedness (Enoch 6:1-2; 7:1; 9:8-9; 10:11; 12:4; 15-16; 19:2; 69:4; 86; Jub. 5:1-4; Slavonic Enoch 18:3-5; II Bar. 56:12). Test. Reuben 5:3, 6, blames the women for seducing the Watchers, but in other passages it is the latter who are at fault. Associated with this tradition is the idea that sin continues to be the result of demonic temptation (Enoch 64:2; Jub. 7:27; 10:1; 11:4; 12:20; Test. Benj. 5:2).

Another tradition closely associated with the theory of demonic seduction was developed in the Testaments of the Twelve Patriarchs and apparently had important influence on the Qumran theology (*see* §2c *below*). This is the hypostatization of the "spirits of error," corresponding to the "spirits of truth," mentioned in Test. Reuben 2:2–3:8; Test. Simeon 6:6; Test. Judah 16; Test. Dan 5:5. These become practically equivalent to two opposing cosmic principles in Test. Judah 20:1.

Again a close connection can be drawn between the "spirit of deceit" and the "evil inclination" (יצר), particularly as these appear in the Testaments. The first mention of a controlling יצר occurs in Ecclus. 15:14, where it is not spoken of as necessarily being evil

(cf. 27:6). But in Ecclus. 37:3 its evil power is definitely emphasized:

> O evil imagination, why were you formed
> to cover the land with deceit?

This יצר must be controlled by keeping the law (21:11).

The Testaments develop the theory of the evil inclination as the source of sin (Test. Judah 18:3; Test. Joseph 2:6). But there is a good as well as an evil inclination in man (Test. Asher 1:3-9; 3:1-2). It is the duty of man to follow the good יצר (Test. Benj. 6:1) and to resist the evil. IV Maccabees, a late Alexandrian writing, reveals Greek influence in its claim that reason, aided by the law, can control the evil יצר (2:5-6, 21-23; cf. 7:16). The evil inclination is further mentioned in Jub. 7:24; Slavonic Enoch 53:3; II Esd. 7:92. Its further development in rabbinic Judaism, where it became very prominent, cannot be touched upon here, except to say that it was never construed as something radically and basically wrong at the core of man's being.

This last is forcefully expressed by II Esdras, which speaks of sin's arising from a "grain of evil seed" (4:30) or from the "evil heart" (3:20-22, 26; 4:4) within man: "For an evil heart has grown up in us, which has alienated us from God, and has brought us into corruption and the ways of death, and has shown us the paths of perdition and removed us far from life—and that not just a few of us but almost all who have been created!" (7:48). This reflects the teaching of the old prophets that man sins because his heart is corrupt at its very core. Various passages emphasize the depravity of fallen mankind (Enoch 16:3; Jub. 1:22; 10:8; II Bar. 56:10). Sin in the human heart is spoken of as a deadly poison (Test. Gad 6:3), producing all sorts of evil (Wisd. Sol. 4:12; Ecclus. 27:10). In a passage strikingly similar in expression to Rom. 1:18-32, which it may have influenced, the Wisdom of Solomon describes the blindness of idolatrous men and the spiritual corruption resulting from it (13:1-9; 14:22-31).

It necessarily follows from the hereditary transmission of sinfulness that all of humanity is corrupt, and this is a consequence drawn in a variety of intertestamental writings (Wisd. Sol. 13:1; Ecclus. 8:5; Enoch 84:4; Jub. 21:21; Test. Levi 2:3; II Esd. 7:46; 8:55-56). Again it is II Esdras that expresses this the most forcibly: "For all who have been born are involved in iniquities, and are full of sins and burdened with transgressions" (7:68). To some of the latter's most sweeping statements, however, it allows exceptions (3:36; 7:48, 140). Out of the corrupt mass of humanity there have been a few who have not sinned (Prayer Man. 8; Slavonic Enoch 41:2; II Bar. 9:1; 18:1; cf. Pss. Sol. 17:41).

Judaism never abandoned its belief in the freedom of the will, despite all this (cf. Ecclus. 15:15-17). Even as a sinner man is accountable for his actions (Wisd. Sol. 13:8-9; Enoch 98:4), which God will bring into judgment (Wisd. Sol. 4:20; Slavonic Enoch 65:4; II Esd. 3:34). The sinner's only recourse is to follow the prescribed ritual for atonement (Jub. 5:17-18; Pss. Sol. 3:9), and to cast himself upon God's mercy by repentance and confession (Wisd. Sol. 15:1-2; Ecclus. 5:4-8; 7:8; 17:25-27, 29; 21:1-2; Prayer Man. 13; Jub. 22:14; Pss. Sol. 9:11-15).

---

[1] R. H. Charles, ed., *The Apocrypha and Pseudepigrapha of the Old Testament* (Oxford: The Clarendon Press).

c. Qumran dualism. The discovery of the library of the ancient Qumran community (*see* DEAD SEA SCROLLS) has illuminated the concept of sin held by an important segment of Jewish society, and in doing this has indicated the probable origins of several distinctive aspects of NT hamartiology. The influence of this strain of Jewish thought has been almost entirely extinguished in rabbinical theology, but it now appears to have survived in the NT doctrine of opposing cosmic powers, as also in Paul's distinctive use of the term "flesh" as the virtual equivalent of "sin."

It is believed that some of the notions of the Qumran community were widely held during the time of Jesus and in the century preceding, but we now know them almost exclusively as they were built into a rigid system by the ascetic brotherhood living in isolation near the shore of the Dead Sea. This community shared much of the common stock of Jewish beliefs about sin. The law was also for them pre-eminent, and the practical criterion of sin. They spoke of the evil יצר (CDC II.16; 1QH VII.13, 16) and knew of the fall of the Watchers (CDC II.18). They too made a distinction between a deliberate sin and one of ignorance or inadvertence (1QS VIII.24). However, they took sin far more seriously than most of their contemporaries, as appears clearly in their Book of Hymns (*Hodayoth*, 1QH), and particularly in the very severe penalties which they inflicted on delinquent members (see the Manual of Discipline, 1QS). Believing that they were presently living under the "epoch of wickedness," they had separated themselves into a saintly brotherhood governed by rigid rules. They were seeking to overcome wickedness through strict observance of the law, through meditation upon the "secrets" of God, through ritual cleansings, and ultimately through an apocalyptic world-conflict.

To comprehend the entire rationale of this community, and especially its great preoccupation with sin, it is important to take note of the cosmic dualism which lay at the basis of its theology. We have seen that Judaism generally, already in parts of the OT, divided sharply between "the righteous" and "the wicked" as separate and antagonistic classes. The Qumran community made this antithesis absolute. In this they were almost certainly influenced by Iranian dualism, although they ultimately attributed both good and evil to God's creation. These were elemental world-forces under the control of divine determinism. The Qumran theology spoke of good and evil as opposing "spirits" (cf. Test. Judah 20:1): "God created man to rule the world, and appointed for him two spirits after whose direction he was to walk until the final Inquisition. They are the spirits of truth and of perversity. The origin of truth lies in the Fountain of Light, and that of perversity in the Wellspring of Darkness. All who practice righteousness are under the domination of the Prince of Lights, and walk in ways of light; whereas all who practice perversity are under the domination of the Angel of Darkness and walk in ways of darkness. . . . It is in these ways that men needs must walk . . . according as a man inherits something of each. . . . Between the two categories He has set an eternal enmity. . . . The spirits of truth and perversity have been struggling in

the heart of man" (1QS III.17-21; IV.15-17, 23).[1] Although it may be assumed, at least according to the more noble insights of the community, that some of the righteous are out in society, the ideal place for the "children of light" to oppose darkness is in the holy community. Here they are organized as an army against the hosts of evil. The initiate solemnly vows "to keep far from all evil and . . . to walk no more in the stubbornness of a guilty heart and of lustful eyes, doing all manner of evil; . . . to love all the children of light, . . . and to hate all the children of darkness" (1QS I.4, 6-7, 9-10).[1] Henceforth he spends his every moment in fighting wickedness. If he backslides, he is severely censured or even cast out of the community.

It is obvious that this artificial structure contained great dangers for hypocrisy and externalism; on the other hand, there is evidence that for many it promoted a deep spiritual sensitivity to the constant reality of sin. Despite the ideal of belonging entirely to the "spirit of truth," the covenanters experienced the cruel power of temptation. Their greatest dread was to fall into the power of the "Angel of Darkness," who is constantly bent on causing the sons of light to stumble (1QS III.21-24). A recurring theme in the Hymns, expressed in language reminiscent of some of the canonical Psalms, is the anguish of this bitter struggle.

The Qumran believer attributed his inability to fulfil the ideals of moral perfection, not only to temptation, but also to the weakness of his flesh. In his hymns he came to employ the Hebrew word for FLESH (בשר), which in the OT had been no more than a designation of creaturehood and mortality, as being also the occasion—though not necessarily the cause—of his transgression. Because his flesh is weak, the spirit of error often overwhelms him. Strong language is used:

> But I—I belong to wicked mankind,
> to the communion of sinful flesh.
>   My transgressions, my iniquities and sins,
> and the waywardness of my heart
> condemn me to communion with the worm
> and with all that walk in darkness
>   (1QS XI.9-10).[1]

The only hope is to cast oneself upon the mercy of God, who will grant forgiveness and provide his spirit (Spirit) to help. There can be little doubt that in this tradition, rather than in the theology of the rabbis, Paul's concept of an antagonism between flesh and Spirit originated (*see* § 3 *below*). Such an utterance as this would not have been (so far as it went) offensive to Paul:

> How can flesh have reason,
> or the earth-bound direct its steps,
> except that Thou hadst created spirit
> and ordained the working thereof?
>   (1QH XV.21-22).[1]

3. In the NT. The presence and the problem of sin are just as much a part of the NT as of the OT, and yet one who reads it is immediately struck by an astounding difference. All the old terms and concepts are here in the NT, but deepened and strangely

[1].From the book *The Dead Sea Scriptures* by T. H. Gaster; copyright © 1956 by Theodor H. Gaster, reprinted by permission of Doubleday & Company, Inc., and Martin Secker & Warburg Ltd., London.

transformed. The one factor which makes this great difference is the work of Jesus Christ. He provides something which the saints of the OT yearned for but could never find: real and certain victory over sin. The doctrine of sin in the NT is dominated by the assurance that Christ has come to conquer it. Thus, whatever is said to emphasize sin's deadliness and seriousness serves to magnify the greatness of the salvation from sin which Christ has obtained.

As we should expect, each of the NT writers has a characteristic way of speaking about sin. Paul is by all counts the most profound. But there is no essential disharmony amid the variety. Above all, they are all dominated by the assurance of Christ's effective answer to sin.

It needs to be emphasized while saying this that Hellenism has made little essential difference. Some have maintained that Paul, e.g., was much under the influence of Greek dualism in his association of sin with the body. We now see clearly, however, that the sources of his teaching are Hebraic, perhaps with traces of Iranian dualism by way of the latter's penetration into late Hebrew theology. Hellenism has, of course, contributed the heritage of its language as the vehicle of NT thought, but it is important to observe that the NT radically transforms the content of many of the Greek words for "sin" in keeping with its essentially different ideology.

a. Terminology. All the NT words for "sin" occur in classical Greek, but many of them were given new associations already in the LXX. They may be grouped as follows, according to their basic semantic orientation:

a) Formal terms, indicating "deviation from the good." By far the most prominent NT word for "sin," the equivalent of חטא in the OT, is ἁμαρτία, "sin, sinfulness" (also ἁμάρτημα, "sinful act"; ἁμαρτάνω, "miss the mark, sin"; ἁμαρτωλός, "sinner"). In classical usage this term indicated the missing of a target or road, hence also intellectual error and moral fault. In the NT it occasionally refers to wrong done to a fellow man, but generally it is used to express sin (with all its Hebraic connotation) against God. The NT seldom uses ἁμάρτημα, which is the most common in classical Greek, preferring ἁμαρτία, which in the Synoptics, Acts, Hebrews, the Pastoral and Catholic letters, and Revelation ordinarily indicates a sinful act (which points to the inward condition of sinfulness, however). Paul and John prefer to use the latter word to indicate the sinful quality of life and the state of alienation from God. In Rom. 5–7, ἁμαρτία is personified in poetic imagery to bring out its demonic power (cf. Gen. 4:7; Zech. 5:6-8; Ecclus. 27:10).

Ἁμαρτωλός (both as noun and as adjective) is frequently employed in the LXX as the translation of רשע, "guilty, wicked." In view of the sharp antithesis that Jewish theology had made between "the righteous" and "the wicked" as opposing classes, it is not surprising that the NT represents the Jews as applying the word ἁμαρτωλός, not to themselves, but to their enemies and to those who were not observing the law. The following meanings may be distinguished: (*a*) as a sociological-ethical term, it indicates a person of notoriously bad morals, such as a tax collector or harlot (Matt. 9:10-11; 11:19; Luke 7:37; 19:7; I Tim. 1:9; Jas. 4:8; 5:20); (*b*) in the mouths of the Pharisees it is a word of condemnation for any who do not follow their ritual (John 9:16 ff; cf. 7:49; Matt. 12:1 ff; 15:2; Luke 11:37-38); (*c*) as occasionally in the LXX, it designates the Gentiles (Matt. 26:45; Mark 14:41; Luke 6:32-34 [cf. Matt. 5:47]; Gal. 2:15); (*d*) in a more spiritual sense it applies to men outside of Christ under God's condemnation (Mark 8:38; Rom. 5:8; Gal. 2:17; Heb. 7:26; etc.), and is the self-designation of those who are under the conviction of guilt (Luke 5:8; 18:13; I Tim. 1:15).

Another formal word for "sin" is παράπτωμα, "trespass," indicating an individual lapse and not a condition of sinfulness (but cf. "dead through . . . "trespasses" [Eph. 2:1]). In Heb. 6:6 the verb παραπίπτειν means "to apostatize from God."

Similar is παράβασις, "transgression" (also παραβάτης, "transgressor"; παραβαίνω, "go beyond, transgress"). Occurring with the object stated or implied, it is a stronger term than παράπτωμα, indicating a deliberate breach of the law or morality.

Similar to the OT idea of שגגה are ἄγνοια and ἀγνόημα. *See* IGNORANCE.

b) Terms with theological orientation. Etymologically related to the above words is ἀνομία, "lawlessness" (also ἄνομος, "lawless"; ἀνόμως, "lawlessly"). It indicates an attitude or condition of contempt for and violation of law—i.e., "iniquity" or "wickedness" (ἄνομος may also indicate one who is ignorant of the law). A similar word is παρανομία, "wickedness" (also παρανομέω, "transgress the law").

Παρακοή, the regular term for "disobedience," is used occasionally in the NT (e.g., Rom. 5:19) to indicate disobedience toward God.

The most profoundly theological word for "sin" is ἀσέβεια, "ungodliness, impiety, sacrilege" (also ἀσεβέω, "act impiously"; ἀσεβής, "impious"). This is the word which the LXX often uses to translate פשע, and it indicates offense against God in distinction from ἀδικία (*see below*), which refers to wrongdoing against mankind. It occurs chiefly in Romans, the Pastoral letters, I and II Peter, and Jude.

c) Terms indicating spiritual badness. Κακία (also κακός, "bad") and πονηρία (also πονηρός, "bad") both indicate qualitative and moral evil. They translate the Hebrew רע, רעה, in the LXX, and in the NT they generally refer to moral and spiritual depravity. The neuter adjectives used substantively indicate moral evil. Ὁ πονηρός is pre-eminently the devil (Matt. 13:19, etc.). Κακία sometimes has the special meaning of "malice" or "evil disposition."

d) Ethical and juridical terms. A favorite word in classical usage for indicating wrongdoing toward mankind is ἀδικία, "injustice, unrighteousness." The NT employs it (also ἀδίκημα, "misdeed"; ἀδικέω, "do wrong or injustice"; ἄδικος, "unjust" or "sinful"; ἀδίκως, "unjustly") in the sense of crime toward a fellow man or, more theologically, of sin in general. I John equates ἀδικία and ἁμαρτία (3:4; 5:17).

Ἔνοχος, a forensic word meaning "guilty" or "liable" for a particular wrong, occurs a few times in the NT (e.g., Mark 3:29).

In Matt. 6:12 (cf. Luke 11:4) the term ὀφείλημα, "debt," indicates the burden of guilt which the sinner bears in the sight of God.

b. Nature and standard. In some of the NT writings (as Hebrews, James) the concept of morality and the definition of sin are still very similar to those of Judaism—i.e., sin is thought of in relation to the law. However, the NT in general strongly opposes the legalistic and impersonal conception. In the NT every vestige of the taboo concept is eliminated. Jesus refused to observe the scruples of the Pharisees concerning ritual cleanliness (Mark 7:2-5; cf. Matt. 15: 1 ff), making the pronouncement: "There is nothing outside a man which by going into him can defile him; but the things which come out of a man are what defile him" (Mark 7:15). This is probably also partially the intent of the story of Peter's vision of clean and unclean animals in Acts 10.

There were lively controversies in the early church over the keeping of the law (Acts 10–11; 15; Gal. 2; etc.), but the view eventually won out, chiefly through the work of Paul, that this was no longer the ultimate standard of morality (*see* LAW IN THE NT). Jesus kept the law (Matt. 5:17), but he made it clear that legalism, particularly as it was enforced by the Pharisees, had no place in his concept of righteousness. He refused to follow their tradition, condemning them in withering terms as hypocrites and blind leaders of the blind (Matt. 23:13-36). They had made the law an odious thing (vs. 4) and the occasion for all kinds of externalism and pretense. Jesus showed them that some parts of the law could be turned against other parts (Mark 10:2-12); he showed them that such ordinances as the keeping of the sabbath were intended for man's benefit and not as a burden (Matt. 12:1-14; cf. John 9:14, 16); he also reminded them that love was the real fulfilment of the law (Matt. 5:43-48; 22:36-40; cf. Rom. 13:9-10; Gal. 5:14; Jas. 2:8).

It is important to observe that Jesus did not count the righteousness obtained by keeping the law as worthless and meaningless; his claim, rather, was that this righteousness is not sufficient (Matt. 5:20), and, if substituted for true inward piety, becomes a horrible farce. Righteousness measured by such an externalistic standard leads to prideful boasting before God (Luke 18:11-12) while neglecting the duties which God really requires (Matt. 15:3-9; 21:30-31; 23:23-26). Thus the very righteousness of which the spiritual elite boasted was in Jesus' eyes the cause of their condemnation before God. Jesus looked for a consciousness of failure before the searching penetration of God's judgment, even when the law had been outwardly observed (Matt. 19:21). Even "the righteous" needed to understand that they were sinners in the sight of God (cf. Mark 2:17).

Jesus, according to the Synoptic writers, offered no statement on the nature of sin. He was not interested in sin in the abstract but rather in specific sins—or, more accurately, he was interested primarily in sinners. It may be assumed that his idea of the nature of sin was entirely Hebraic. This represented a return to the deep inward conceptions of parts of the OT. In repudiating a narrow legalism, Jesus showed that his understanding of the will of God was far wider, and of the darkness of sin far deeper, than the scribes and Pharisees imagined. In the Sermon on the Mount he showed that all the hidden attitudes and emotions are involved in sin, just as much

as the outward actions by which legalism judged a man (Matt. 5:21-48). It is what lies in the heart that counts the most in God's sight. It is sin in the depths of man's being that defiles him the most (Mark 7:21-23). On the other hand, the true quality of the outward life is determined by and is a manifestation of the spiritual attitude within, whether for good or for ill (Matt. 7:15-27; cf. Jas. 2:14 ff).

James shares the view that the law has to be taken more seriously (i.e., more inwardly) than in rabbinic Judaism (2:8, 10). The apostle Paul, however, goes completely beyond the law as a standard of sin and righteousness. Such a passage as Rom. 5:13: "Sin is not counted where there is no law," shows that he could not entirely escape his rabbinic habits of thinking, but for him the law led to condemnation rather than to self-righteousness. Having been a Pharisee himself, Paul knew by personal experience the hollowness of a righteousness measured by external standards. He had been "as to righteousness under the law blameless," even surpassing others in zeal (Phil. 3:6; cf. Gal. 1:14), but now he understood that this had been his very sin (I Cor. 15:9; Gal. 1:23; Phil. 3:7; I Tim. 1:15). As a converted man Paul could henceforth make no compromise with legalism (Gal. 2:11 ff; Col. 2:16), even though for the scruples of weaker brethren (I Cor. 8) and out of prudence and patriotism he was willing to fulfil the outward conventions of Jewish ritual (Acts 16:3; 21:20 ff). Paul knew that the law was impotent as a means of leading one to reconciliation with God (Rom. 8:3).

The Apostle does not deny that if a person could really keep the law perfectly, in spirit as well as in letter, he would be considered righteous in God's sight. The sad truth is that no one can keep it perfectly. Thus the law points out a man's failures. It shows the depth of his sinfulness. This function of the law is clearly expressed in Rom. 3:20; 5:20; 7:7-24; Gal. 3:19-24, and particularly in these words: "So the law is holy, and the commandment is holy and just and good. Did that which is good, then, bring death to me? By no means! It was sin, working death in me through what is good, in order that sin might be shown to be sin, and through the commandment might become sinful beyond measure" (Rom. 7:12-13).

It is thus in connection with the law that Paul's most characteristic understanding of sin appears. He often speaks of particular sins, but generally he speaks of sin as an evil power working against the law and against the influence of God's Spirit to drag a person into transgression. It is in this aspect that sin appears in the notable section Rom. 5:12–8:10, where it is personified as a cruel enemy of the soul, allied with the flesh (*see below*) and finding opportunity through the law to bring the soul into bondage and condemnation.

Thus the doctrine of two opposing cosmic principles, which has been observed in the Qumran theology (*see* §2c *above*), reappears in Paul. With Paul there is a constant struggle of sin versus Christ, of the flesh versus the Spirit, of darkness versus light. A person is in bondage to the one or to the other (Rom. 6:16). He is either a slave of sin or a slave of Christ, a child of light or a child of darkness (cf. Rom. 13:12; Eph. 5:8; I Thess. 5:4 ff). He does the work of his master, whichever this may be, and receives the appropriate recompense (Rom. 6:21-23). This whole world is presently in the hands of the powers of darkness, which Christ has come to destroy (Eph. 2:2; 3:10; 6:12; Col. 1:13; 2:15).

The Johannine literature manifests a similar indebtedness to the concept of hostile world-forces (I John 5:19). It speaks of a domain of sin, which is the realm of darkness (John 1:5; 3:19-21; I John 2:11). Those who oppose Christ are enslaved to this evil power (John 8:31-34; cf. Matt. 6:24).

The Jew looked upon Gentiles as slaves of darkness and evil. Paul agrees with this judgment; but in a notable passage (Rom. 1-3), where he explains how the Gentiles have perversely and rebelliously corrupted themselves in spite of the better knowledge that God had given them in his natural revelation, he includes the Jew under the same condemnation, because he sins against even greater light. Here the perversity of all kinds of sin is compellingly described. Although the Gentiles knew God, "they did not honor him as God or give thanks to him, but they became futile in their thinking and their senseless minds were darkened" (1:21). "For this reason God gave them up to dishonorable passions" (vs. 26). They have grown so wicked that they not only do evil things "but approve those who practice them" (vs. 32). Without mentioning him by name at first, Paul then addresses the Jew, who would instinctively resist being put in the same classification with the Gentiles: "Do you suppose, O man, that when you judge those who do such things and yet do them yourself, you will escape the judgment of God?" (2:3). "There will be tribulation and distress for every human being who does evil, the Jew first and also the Greek" (vss. 9). Paul shows that the sin of the Jew is even more heinous than that of the Gentiles, because while teaching others he does not teach himself (vss. 19-21), while preaching to others he forgets to follow his own admonition (vss. 21-22), while boasting in the law he dishonors God by breaking the law (vs. 23). This is the real essence of sin, both for the Gentile and for the Jew: to turn away from God's light in order to walk in the ways of evil.

Sin is therefore rooted in hatred toward God, as Paul (Rom. 8:7) and the Fourth Gospel (15:23-24) agree. The transfer of this hatred to Jesus is the Jews' greatest sin (cf. Matt. 21:33-39). The greatest sin of all is that of rejecting Jesus as the Son of God (John 15:22; cf. I John 2:22). The very serious sin of apostatizing from the gospel is prominently mentioned in the Letter to the Hebrews (2:3; 3:12; 6:4-6; 10:26; cf. I John 5:16). The unforgivable sin (Mark 3:28-30) is to oppose the work of the Holy Spirit with deliberate malice. Lists of various kinds of sins are to be found in Matt. 15:19; Mark 7:21-22; Luke 18:11; Rom. 1: 28-31; 13:13; I Cor. 5:9-11; 6:9-10; II Cor. 12:20; Gal. 5:19-21; Eph. 4:25-31; 5:3-5; Col. 3:5, 8; I Tim. 1:9-10; 6:4-5; II Tim. 3:2-4; Tit. 3:3; I Pet. 4:3; Rev. 9:21; 21:8; 22:15.

c. Origin. To a great extent, the NT gives the OT answer to the question of sin's origin. James approaches the Jewish doctrine of an evil inclination (יֵצֶר) in his explanation of the psychological process of sinning: "Each person is tempted when he is lured and enticed by his own desire. Then desire when it has conceived gives birth to sin; and sin when it is full-grown brings forth death" (1:14-15; cf. 4:1-2). Paul, however, while admitting that the "flesh" has passions and desires which entice to evil and hence must be resisted (Rom. 13:14; Gal. 5:16-21), makes the principle of sin which lies within the heart responsible for the unruliness of these desires. Indeed, so perverse is the heart of man that the very prohibitions of the law which are intended to keep the desires in check serve rather to arouse them (Rom. 7:7-8). As Jesus declared, sin lies deep in the corrupt heart of man (Mark 7:21-23). This is the OT view taken seriously once more (cf. Mark 7:6-7).

Very prominent in Paul's hamartiology is the concept of "the flesh," which is the ally and vehicle of sin. His employment of this term as a designation of the realm of evil in man, and as opposed to the realm of the Spirit, almost certainly has affinities with the ideology of the Qumran sect (*see* § *2c above*). In his list of the "fruits" of the flesh, Paul makes it plain that these are not merely sins of the body but of the mind as well (cf. Gal. 5:19-21). For a full discussion of the meaning of this term, *see* FLESH; BODY. Suffice it here to say that for Paul it evidently meant the realm of creaturely (and hence primarily. sensual) life, which, apart from the renewing and governing power of the divine Spirit, leads into all manner of sins.

In Rom. 7:5-8:13 the flesh is brought into close connection with the law and with sin. Here Paul is discussing the problem of how anything so good and holy as the law (7:12) can be the occasion for sin. As stated above, it is because of the sin lurking within, which is aroused by the knowledge of wrong provided by the law and works through the weakness of the flesh to the doing of evil: "For sin, finding opportunity in the commandment, deceived me and by it killed me" (7:11). The sinner rebels against the law because it is spiritual and he is fleshly (7:14), and these two are in deadly opposition to each other (8:7; cf. I Cor. 2:14). Even for a twice-born man like Paul, who had also received the Spirit, there is a constant struggle going on within (Rom. 7:15-24). In an autobiographical style reminiscent of some of the Psalms and of the Qumran Hymns—which is yet intended as typical of every man's experience—the apostle describes the agonies of this struggle. When he wants to do right, evil lies close at hand (vs. 21). His inmost self—changed in principle by the power of the Spirit —delights in God's law, but sin wages war with him and takes him captive (vss. 22-23). Because he is fleshly, he is weak. His will is unable to perform the good that his better nature chooses. "I can will what is right, but I cannot do it" (vs. 18). At last the apostle cries out in his anguish: "Wretched man that I am! Who will deliver me from this body of death?" (vs. 24). The answer is immediately given. It is the Lord Jesus Christ (vs. 25).

The NT inherits from intertestamental Judaism a belief in demonic temptation as a source of sin. This is closely associated with the notion of cosmic evil forces mentioned above. The devil is mentioned in John 8:44 as the originator of murder and deceit, and as the "father" of those who oppose the work of Christ (cf. I John 3:8). He is often mentioned (also as "the evil one," "the tempter," or "Satan") as the archopponent of God and the seducer of men. He appears as Jesus' tempter in Matt. 4:1-11; Mark 1:12-13; Luke 4:1-13. Christians are warned against him (I Pet. 5:8), are told to resist him (Jas. 4:7), and are admonished to watch and pray that they enter not into temptation, for "the spirit indeed is willing, but the flesh is weak" (Mark 14:38; cf. Matt. 6:13).

When the question of the ultimate origin of sin is raised, it is evident that the NT possesses a definite historical theory. No trace of the fall of the Watchers is to be found in the NT, except perhaps in II Pet. 2:4; Jude 6. It is rather to Adam's sin in Eden that mankind's depravity is traced. II Cor. 11:3; I Tim. 2:14 contain definite recollections of the serpent's seduction of Eve; the latter passage gives Eve, instead of Adam, the specific blame for the fall (cf. Ecclus. 25:24). But in Rom. 5:12-19, Paul blames Adam, setting forth a doctrine of racial involvement in sin similar to that found in Jewish apocalyptic writings of the first century A.D. (Slavonic Enoch 41:1; II Bar. 48:42-43; II Esd. 4:30; etc.). *See* § *2b above.*

Paul's teaching must, of course, be understood in the light of its context. In Rom. 5 he is writing about the representative work of Christ, of the fact that through his death sinners who believe on him are reconciled to God (vss. 6-11). Adam is brought in as a foil to Christ. He was the bringer of death, as Christ is the bringer of life: "If, because of one man's trespass, death reigned through that one man, much more will those who receive the abundance of grace and the free gift of righteousness reign in life through the one man Jesus Christ" (vs. 17). Paul really means to make a comparison here between Adam as the symbolic representative of all his sinful descendants and Christ as the representative of all who receive righteousness from him (vs. 14). In speaking of Adam, however, he cannot avoid making statements which strongly suggest that his first sin was the cause of all other sinning, and hence of death, which is the result of sin: "Sin came into the world through one man and death through sin, and so death spread to all men because all men sinned" (vs. 12). "As by one man's disobedience many were made sinners, so by one man's obedience many will be made righteous" (vs. 19). Whether this was through inheritance or through evil influence or through corporate guilt, Paul does not say, but that there is a necessary historical connection is unquestionably his meaning. There was something specifically ominous about Adam's transgression (vs. 14). The sins of his descendants were not like it, because it was the proto-sin which engulfed all the rest of mankind in death. Since Paul is more interested in making verbal parallels than in producing strict logic (cf. vs. 19), it is hardly fair to his intent to hold that vs. 18 indicates only the possibility of all men's being involved in Adam's sin, equivalent to the mere possibility of the salvation of all men in Christ. In I Cor. 15:45-47, where Adam and Christ are again contrasted, the important distinction is that between the natural and the spiritual life. *See* ADAM; FALL.

The primeval sin of unbelief and idolatry, which leads to all kinds of corruption and moral decay when God gives men up to the lusts of their hearts, spoken of in Rom. 1:18 ff (*see above*), does not necessarily refer to Adam's sin. This is not a historical ac-count but a description of the progress of depravity in humanity generally.

d. Extent and prevalence. Although Jesus made no sweeping statement of the universality of sin, it is apparent that he looked upon all men as sinful. It stood to reason, of course, that the Gentiles were sinful—Jesus would be the last one to argue against this fact. The significant thing is that he considered the most notable keepers of the law as sinful. He saw the sin deep in their hearts (John 2:25; cf. 8:7) and, like John the Baptist before him (Luke 3:7), denounced them as an evil and corrupt generation (Matt. 12:34-35; 16:4; 23:33; Mark 8:38; 9:19; Luke 9:41; cf. Acts 2:40). Even the ordinary people addressed by him in the Sermon on the Mount were described as being evil (Matt. 7:11; Luke 11:13). Jesus said that the victims of Pilate's brutality and the victims of the fallen Siloam tower were no more notorious sinners than the rest, but that all needed to repent lest they likewise perish (Luke 13:1-5). Several passages in the NT make it plain that the only exception to universal guilt is Christ himself (II Cor. 5:21; Heb. 4:15; 7:26; I Pet. 1:19; 2:22; I John 3:5).

We have observed that Paul includes all men, Jews as well as Gentiles, under the condemnation of sin (Rom. 1-3). He repeatedly asserts this in no uncertain terms: "I have already charged that all men, both Jews and Greeks, are under the power of sin" (Rom. 3:9). "No human being will be justified in his sight by works of the law" (vs. 20). "All have sinned and fall short of the glory of God" (vs. 23). "Now it is evident that no man is justified before God by the law" (Gal. 3:11). "But the scripture consigned all things to sin" (vs. 22; cf. also Rom. 5:12-19). So widespread, indeed, is the corruption of sin that even the natural creation is affected (Rom. 8:19-22).

As all men are sinners, according to Paul's doctrine, so also the whole being of man is infected with its poison. It is in all the organs and members of the body (Rom. 6:19; 7:23), in the intellect (Rom. 1:21; Eph. 4:17-18), and even in the will, since this is held captive by the desires of the flesh (Rom. 7:15-20). One of the results of sin is physical death (Rom. 5:12 ff; 6:23); but to "die in one's sins" (John 8:24) or to be "dead through trespasses and sins" (Eph. 2:1, 5) means something far more dreadful than this. It means to be dead to God, beyond hope of spiritual recovery apart from his grace. Paul understood that this was his natural condition when he learned the real intent of the law: "I was once alive apart from the law, but when the commandment came, sin revived and I died . . . . For sin, finding opportunity in the commandment, deceived me and by it killed me" (Rom. 7:9, 11).

Even though all this is true of the sinner, he is never excused of his responsibility, no more than he is considered beyond saving. Paul expressly combats moral determinism in Rom. 3:5-8. Ignorance is considered only a partial mitigation of responsibility (Luke 12:47), and it is excused only by divine grace (I Tim. 1:13-14). Sin is a debt that must be paid unless God mercifully forgives it (Matt. 6:12; cf. 18:27). The fact that the sinner is continually urged to repent is proof that he is responsible and that there is help for him if he sincerely seeks it.

The Hebraic notion that suffering is the result of

sin is put into Jesus' mouth in the Fourth Gospel (5:14); yet this same book combats an automatic connection between sin and suffering (9:3). The most characteristic NT view is that suffering is a means to spiritual improvement under God's fatherly hand (Heb. 12:10; cf. Rom. 5:3-5; 8:17-18).

One of the features of the last age, according to the Pastoral letters, II Peter, Jude, and Revelation, is that the corruption of mankind will increase enormously, until at last God intervenes with his judgment (cf. also Luke 17:26-30; 18:8).

e. Remedy. It appears that the NT takes at least as dark a view of sin's nature and effects as the OT does; indeed, it assumes all that the OT has said about sin, but makes it even more explicit and pointed. It is able to take sin as seriously as it does because it also knows the remedy for sin. The very purpose of its stern teaching is to convince men of their need for this remedy. God's effective answer to sin is Christ: "For God has done what the law, weakened by the flesh, could not do: sending his own Son in the likeness of sinful flesh and for sin, he condemned sin in the flesh, in order that the just requirement of the law might be fulfilled in us, who walk not according to the flesh but according to the Spirit" (Rom. 8:3-4). This is why Christ appeared: "He will save his people from their sins" (Matt. 1:21); he is "the Lamb of God, who takes away the sin of the world" (John 1:29); he "came not to call the righteous, but sinners" (Matt. 9:13); "the Son of man came to seek and to save the lost" (Luke 19:10).

This fully explains Jesus' attitude toward the notorious sinners in Jewish society, with whom he intimately conversed and even sat down at table (Matt. 9:10-11; 11:19; Luke 7:34; 15:1-2; 19:7). He really was a "friend of tax collectors and sinners." The proud and self-righteous Pharisees scorned him for this; it proved his own baseness in their eyes. But Jesus knew that the only way to help a needy sinner was to enter into close fellowship with him, confronting him with his own holy presence. This was not only psychologically sound but also theologically meaningful. It is in the presence of one who is holy, yet gracious, that a sinner will confess and abjure his sin (cf. Luke 5:8; 7:37 ff; 19:8).

Like John the Baptist (Matt. 3:2; Mark 1:4; Luke 3:3; cf. Luke 1:77), Jesus preached repentance and demonstrated God's forgiveness (Matt. 9:2; 18:3; etc.). Henceforth this was to be the urgent appeal of the church as it carried the gospel to many places (Luke 24:47; Acts 2:38; 5:31; 10:43). *See* REPENTANCE; FORGIVENESS.

In the letters Christ's work, and particularly the reconciliation which he obtained upon the cross, is set forth as the crowning victory over the power of sin (Rom. 3:25; 4:25; 5:21; 7:25; II Cor. 5:21; Gal. 1:4; Col. 1:14; Heb. 2:17; I Pet. 2:24; 3:18; I John 1:7; 2:2; 4:10; Rev. 1:5; etc.). As Paul makes so abundantly clear in Romans and Galatians, a sinner obtains JUSTIFICATION before God through faith in this Christ, apart from the works of the law.

This involves the REGENERATION and transformation of the sinner. The believing sinner is now a new man in Christ (Col. 3:10-11). He is nothing less than a new creature (II Cor. 5:17); it is no longer he who lives but Christ who lives in him (Gal. 2:20); because

of this the old, sinful nature is being put to death and a new, spiritual nature brought to life (Rom. 8:10; II Cor. 5:14-15; I Pet. 2:24; 3:18); it is his duty now to be completely transformed, rather than to continue in conformity to this natural world (Rom. 12:2). The believer has entered a new aeon: he has been transferred from the dominion of darkness into the kingdom of God's beloved Son (Col. 1:13).

All this puts the problem of sin into an entirely different light. The burning question is no longer how to obtain righteousness (this is God's free gift) or how to rid oneself of guilt (Christ has taken this upon himself), but how to live consistently in this new sphere of life. This is the problem of Christian SANCTIFICATION. It is absurd for a believer to go on in sin "that grace may abound" (Rom. 6:1). This grace comes only through being in Christ, and if one is in Christ, he has left the domain of sin and belongs entirely to Christ's domain (this is the theme of Rom. 6). The solemn word is addressed to him: "You are not your own; you were bought with a price. So glorify God in your body" (I Cor. 6:19-20).

But the purest saints are never entirely free from sin and from sins, as Paul himself experienced. I John puts this in its characteristic enigmatic way, stating that on the one hand a believer does not sin (3:6, 9; 5:18) and on the other hand he does sin (1:8, 10; 2:1; 5:16). The real difference lies in the principle of his life. A true Christian can never give himself over to sin; yet he will every day need to pray: "Forgive us our sins" (Luke 11:4). It is for this reason that he can never claim a righteousness obtained by his own efforts. His abiding consciousness is that of his debt to grace.

Bibliography. Of primary importance is the group of articles by G. Quell, G. Bertram, G. Stählin, and W. Grundmann on ἁμαρτάνω, etc., in G. Kittel, ed., *Theologisches Wörterbuch zum NT* (1933—); see English translation in J. R. Coates, ed., *Bible Key Words*, vol. III (1951), as also articles in this work on other words for "sin."

For both the OT and the NT a brief survey appears in M. Burrows, *An Outline of Biblical Theology* (1946), pp. 165-75 (sin in the OT). Important data appear in the Theologies of the OT by G. Oehler (1874), I, 229-45; A. B. Davidson (1904), pp. 203-35; O. Baab (1949), pp. 84-113; O. Procksch (1950), pp. 632-46; L. Köhler (English trans., 1953), pp. 166-81; W. Eichrodt (5th ed., 1957), I, 251-56; E. Jacob (English trans., 1958), pp. 281-97; G. von Rad (1958), I, 157-64, 262-67; T. C. Vriezen (1958), pp. 201-12; G. A. F. Knight, *A Christian Theology of the OT* (1959), pp. 124-27, 141-43. Also valuable are: J. Köberle, *Sünde und Gnade im religiösen Leben des Volkes Israel* (1905); W. Staerk, *Sünde und Gnade nach der Vorstellung des älteren Judentums* (1905); F. Bennewitz, *Die Sünde im alten Israel* (1907); J. Pedersen, *Israel*, I (1926), 411-37.

On sin in the Apoc. and the Pseudep., see: F. C. Porter, *The Yeçer Hara'* (1902); H. M. Hughes, *The Ethics of Jewish Apocryphal Literature* (1916), pp. 145-214; A. Büchler, *Studies in Sin and Atonement in the Rabbinic Literature of the First Century* (1928); G. F. Moore, *Judaism* (1932), I, 460-96; K. G. Kuhn, "New Light on Temptation, Sin, and Flesh in the NT," in K. Stendahl, ed., *The Scrolls and the NT* (1957), pp. 94-113.

For the NT, see the Theologies of B. Weiss (1882), I, 315-51; F. C. Grant (1950), pp. 170-82; R. Bultmann (English trans., 1951), I, 239-53; P. Feine (1953), pp. 188-200; E. Stauffer (1955); A. Richardson (1959). Also valuable are: R. C. Trench, *Synonyms of the NT* (1915), pp. 224-33; J. Freundorfer, *Erbsünde und Erbtod beim Apostel Paulus* (1927); W. D. Davies, *Paul and Rabbinic Judaism* (1948), pp. 17-35; W. D. Stacey, *The Pauline View of Man* (1956), pp. 154-73.

For a general discussion of sin, the following are useful: J. Müller, *The Christian Doctrine of Sin* (English trans., 1876); F. C. Tennant, *The Sources of the Doctrine of the Fall and Original Sin* (1903); N. P. Williams, *The Ideas of the Fall and of Original Sin* (1927); E. Hirsch, *Schöpfung und Sünde* (1931); R. Otto, *Sünde und Urschuld* (1932); S. Kierkegaard, *The Sickness Unto Death* (English trans., 1941); R. Niebuhr, *The Nature and Destiny of Man* (1943), I, 178-264; E. Brunner, *Man in Revolt* (English trans., 1947), pp. 114-211; C. R. Smith, *The Bible Doctrine of Sin* (1953); E. La B. Cherbonnier, *Hardness of Heart* (1955); F. Greeves, *The Meaning of Sin* (1956).

S. J. DE VRIES

SIN, WILDERNESS OF [מדבר סין]. A wilderness "between Elim and Sinai" (Exod. 16:1; 17:1; Num. 33:11-12). Exod. 17:1 locates Rephidim between the Wilderness of Sin and Sinai, while Num. 33:11-12 records two other stopping places between the Wilderness of Sin and Rephidim—namely, Dophkah and Alush.

The location of the Wilderness of Sin has not been established with certainty. It has been suggested that it may stand for the wilderness in the vicinity of Pelusium (which was called in Hebrew סין; Ezek. 30:15-16; LXX Σάιν). However, the statement in Exod. 16:1 that it is "between Elim and Sinai," and in Num. 33:11-12 that Rephidim is between the Wilderness of Sin and Sinai, demands that its location be sought in the proximity of Sinai, perhaps at Dophkah, which is probably connected with the ancient Egyptian mining region at Serabit el-Khadim. In this case the Wilderness of Sin would be located at Debbet er-Ramleh, on the W fringe of the Sinai Plateau.

There is a very close similarity between Sin and Sinai, and it is quite possible that the name Sinai (סיני) is derived from "Sin" (סין).

Because of the close similarity between the names Sin and Zin, these wildernesses are easily confused. The Wilderness of Zin is located S of Judah and NE of Sinai. The LXX and the Vulg. make no distinction in the names of the two wildernesses. Both of them spell "Zin" (צן) as "Sin" (סין).

J. L. MIHELIC

SIN OFFERING. *See* SACRIFICE AND OFFERINGS § A4*a*.

SINAI, MOUNT sī'nī, sī'nī ī [סיני, *sometimes with* הר, hill, mountain, *or* מדבר, wilderness; LXX Σ(ε)ινα]. The name of the sacred mountain in the Yahwist (J) and Priestly (P) strata of the Pentateuchal narrative, before which Israel encamped when God bound her to himself in COVENANT (Exod. 19-24). Moses as the mediator of the covenant went up into the mountain when he wished to speak with God (19:3, 10; 24:9), came down from it to communicate to the people what God had told him (19:14); and, after the rite which sealed the covenant was celebrated, ascended the mountain and remained there forty days and nights (24:18; cf. ch. 32). When Yahweh revealed his presence to the people from the mountain, he did so with "thunders and lightnings, and a thick cloud . . . , and a very loud trumpet blast. . . . And Mount Sinai was wrapped in smoke, because the LORD descended upon it in fire; and the smoke of it went up like the smoke of a kiln, and the whole mountain quaked greatly" (19:16, 18).

In the Elohist stratum and Deuteronomic literature another name for the sacred mountain appears: HOREB hôr'ĭb [חרב, "desolate region, desert, wilderness"; LXX Χωρηβ]. No geographical distinction between this term and "Sinai" is discoverable in the record, and the two must be reckoned as synonyms (cf. Exod. 3:1; 18:5; Deut. 1; 4:10; 5:2; etc.) A tradition in Deut. 1:2 states that it is "eleven days' journey from Horeb by the way of Mount Seir to Kadesh-barnea" (*see* SEIR; KADESH). Elijah, discouraged and fearful, made a pilgrimage to Horeb for enlightenment (I Kings 19:4-8), and it is not impossible that the detailed list of stations between the mountain and Kadesh in Num. 33:16-36 (P) was so carefully preserved because pilgrimages like that of Elijah were a frequent occurrence during the early days of the nation's history.

1. Traditional location. Since the fourth century A.D. the sacred mountain of the Exodus traditionally has been located in the high mountains at the apex of the Sinai Peninsula. The legend of Catherine of Alexandria affirms that after martyrdom her body was carried by angels to the top of the mountain that now bears her name (at the beginning of the fourth century). By the fourth century small communities of monks had retired to the region; and a certain Ammonius, a monk of Canopus in Egypt, after visiting the holy places of Palestine, made a pilgrimage to Mount Sinai *ca.* A.D. 373, reaching it eighteen days after leaving Jerusalem. While he was there, a massacre of the monks took place at the hand of the Saracens. Another monk, named Nilus, who lived at Sinai from *ca.* 390 on, recounts a second massacre by the same people. In 536 Theonas at the Council of Constantinople is listed as a presbyter and legate of the holy Mount Sinai, the desert Raithou (on the Red Sea coast) and the holy church at Pharan (modern Feiran by Jebel Serbal). The origin of the present Monastery of Saint Catherine on the NW slope of Jebel Musa is traced back to A.D. 527, when Emperor Justinian established it on the site where Helena, mother of Constantine the Great, had erected a small church two centuries earlier.

As one approaches the traditional Mount Sinai from the Egyptian mining center of Serabit el-Khadim to the N (DOPHKAH?), he enters a wide valley or

62. Jebel Musa (Mount Sinai?)

63. General view of Jebel Musa (Mount Sinai?)

small plain, called er-Raha, *ca.* two miles long and one third to two thirds of a mile wide. This would be the only natural place for the encampment of Israel before the sacred mount (Exod. 19:1-2; Num. 33:15). Before him rise the steep cliffs of Ras es-Safsaf, with a valley on each side. This is the NW summit of the range, of which Jebel Musa is the higher (*ca.* 7,500 feet) SE summit, while Jebel Katarin, SW of the latter, is higher still (*ca.* 8,500 feet). Between the latter mountains is the Monastery of Saint Catherine, from which it is a hard climb of over 1½ hours to the top of Jebel Musa. Whether Ras es-Safsaf or Jebel Musa is the sacred mount, or whether both are involved in the tradition, cannot now be decided, and is relatively unimportant. Christian tradition thinks of the former as Horeb and the latter as Sinai, though the latter is some three miles distant from the plain.

Figs. SIN 62-63.

2. Other theories. During the nineteenth century various attempts were made to locate Mount Sinai at Jebel Serbal, some distance to the W by the Wadi Feiran. Here was the early Christian center Pharan, and the seat of a bishopric. The *Peregrinatio Silviae*, edited from an imperfect MS in Rome in 1887, makes the presuppositions of this view impossible. Silvia's pilgrimage, which this work describes, is dated A.D. 385-88. In depicting the topographical details of Sinai, this pilgrim specifically says that the "mount of God" was thirty-five (Roman) miles from Pharan, the correct distance between the oasis in the Wadi Feiran and the traditional Sinai.

Other scholars during the nineteenth century and in the twentieth prefer to look for Mount Sinai in NW Arabia, near the biblical land of Midian. There are two reasons for this preference. One is the supposition that Exod. 19:16, 18, presupposes a volcanic disturbance, and the nearest likely volcanoes which in historical times have been active are in Arabia S of the Gulf of Aqabah. The other reason is that, after fleeing Egypt, Moses took up his abode with the Midianites and married into one of their families (Exod. 3:1; 18:1). The territory of MIDIAN is in NW Arabia. Against this view are these arguments: the family into which Moses married was a Midianite clan of wandering smiths, the KENITES

(Num. 10:29; Judg. 1:16; 4:11), a group whose presence near the Sinai mines would be scarcely surprising. As for the supposed volcanic features of Exod. 19:16, 18, it may be held that the language of theophany in the OT is so frequently drawn from weather phenomena, fire, and the shaking of the earth that it is difficult to historicize it in Exod. 19, so that one may conclude that a volcano is actually meant. J. Pedersen has aptly remarked: "A search might with equal justice be instituted for the mountains that melted like wax when Yahweh passed over the hills of the earth."

A third location for Mount Sinai, and one for which considerable support can be deduced, is with one of several mountains in the neighborhood of Kadesh-barnea (*see* KADESH). In two old poems (Deut. 33:2; Judg. 5:4-5), and again in Hab. 3:3, Sinai as the scene of God's revelation of himself and of his leadership in the wilderness is mentioned in association with SEIR, or Edom; PARAN; and even (Habakkuk) with TEMAN, a town in Edom. At the time of the Israelite wandering the term "Seir" was used in the biblical traditions for some part of the wilderness bordering Kadesh, and the king of Edom appears to have claimed territory on both sides of the Arabah (cf. Num. 20:16). To this evidence there may be added (*a*) the references to the three-day journey into the wilderness which Moses requests Pharaoh to permit Israel to make—a distance more in keeping with the area of Kadesh (though it is farther than three days' travel on foot) than with the traditional location (Exod. 3:18; 5:3; 8:27); and (*b*) the association of Rephidim with MERIBAH (Exod. 17:1-7), a site otherwise known to exist in the Kadesh area, where water from the rock is more easily obtained than at the traditional Sinai (cf. Num. 20:2-13). Against this view that Mount Sinai was in the Kadesh-Seir area, however, are the following observations: (*a*) The poetic allusions, above mentioned, to Yahweh's wondrous leading of Israel in the wilderness are more in the nature of summary statements than of precise geographical delineation, and one would hesitate to draw inferences from them as to the location of Sinai. (*b*) The Mosaic request for Israel to be permitted to go into the wilderness a three-day journey can actually be fitted into none of the proposed locations for Sinai. (*c*) There is, indeed, a discrepancy in the narrative as to the position of the water-from-the-rock tradition, since it is recounted twice (Exod. 17; Num. 20); in view of this fact it is doubtful whether too much reliance can be placed on the geographical implication of the location from Exod. 17, where the E story of the event appears to be coupled with Rephidim only by an introductory fragment of the itinerary being fitted into JE by the Priestly editor (vs. 1*a*). (*d*) None of the stations of the Israelite wandering in the wilderness can be meaningfully understood if their journey went directly either to Kadesh or to Midian. (*e*) A location of Sinai in either of the latter areas would leave the ancient tradition about Jebel Musa unexplained, for it appears at a time when holy places would be expected to be made easily accessible to pilgrims unless there were strong reasons to prevent this being done. (*f*) Finally, the tradition in Deut. 1:2 of an eleven-day journey from Kadesh to Horeb surely is best understood in relation to the S part of the Sinai Peninsula.

Bibliography. E. Robinson, *Biblical Researches in Palestine,* I (1841), 90-144; E. H. Palmer, *The Desert of the Exodus* (1871); A. Dillmann and V. Ryssel, *Exodus and Leviticus* (3rd ed., 1897; for a survey of rival views, see the discussion of Exod. 19:1-2); W. M. F. Petrie, *Researches in Sinai* (1906); H. Guthe, "Sinai," *The New Schaff-Herzog Encyclopedia of Religious Knowledge,* X (1911), 440-41; C. S. Jarvis, *Yesterday and To-day in Sinai* (1931); E. G. Kraeling, *Rand McNally Bible Atlas* (1946), pp. 107-13; M. Noth, *History of Israel* (trans. S. Godman; 1958), pp. 129 ff. G. E. WRIGHT

SINAITICUS sīn′ĭ ĭt′ə kəs. A fourth-century Greek codex MS of the Bible (symbol ℵ) discovered by Konstantin von Tischendorf in the Monastery of St. Catherine at the foot of Mount Sinai in 1859. It contains the entire NT—being the only early Greek MS so complete—but practically all the OT before Ezra 9:9, as well as certain later portions, has been lost. In addition it includes the Epistle of Barnabas and part of the Shepherd of Hermas. It is one of the primary witnesses to the text of both LXX and NT (*see* TEXT, NT; VERSIONS, ANCIENT).

The codex consists of 346½ sheets of high-quality vellum, probably made from antelope skins. Each page, 15 by 13½ inches, contains four columns with twelve to fourteen uncial letters to the line, except in the poetical books, which have two columns. Marks in the margins of the gospels showing divisions worked out by Eusebius (A.D. 260?-340?) set the earlier limit of its age. The script, by three hands of varying ability, was dated by Tischendorf about the middle of the fourth century; and comparison with other MSS of this period has confirmed his estimate. Many corrections were made soon after the writing, and a large additional number appear to come from the seventh century.

Tischendorf's story of the discovery of this codex has appealed to the general public and has often been retold to dramatize the need for revised versions. "In visiting the library of the monastery in the month of May, 1844," he relates, "I perceived in the middle of the great hall a large and wide basket full of old parchments; and the librarian, who was a man of information, told me that two heaps of paper like these, mouldered by time, had been already committed to the flames." Among the parchments Tischendorf recognized pages from an ancient Greek Bible. His enthusiasm betrayed to the monks their value; so he was allowed to take with him only forty-three sheets. These are now in the Court Library at Leipzig.

In 1853 Tischendorf was able to arrange a return visit, on which he hoped for at least permission to copy the remaining sheets. But the only trace of the codex he could find was a scrap, containing eleven lines of Genesis, which had been used for scratch paper many years before.

On a third visit in 1859, as he describes it, "after having devoted a few days in turning over the manuscripts of the convent, . . . I told my Bedouins, on the 4th of February, to hold themselves in readiness to set out with their dromedaries for Cairo on the 7th. . . . On the afternoon of this day, I was taking a walk with the steward of the convent in the neighborhood,

and as we returned towards sunset, he begged me to take some refreshment with him in his cell. Scarcely had he entered the room when, resuming our former subject of conversation, he said, 'And I too have read a Septuagint.' . . . So saying, he took down from the corner of the room a bulky kind of volume wrapped in red cloth, and laid it before me. I unrolled the cover, and discovered, to my great surprise, not only those very fragments which, fifteen years before, I had taken out of the basket, but also other parts. . . . Full of joy, which this time I had the self-command to conceal from the steward and the rest of the community, I asked, as if in a careless way, for permission to take the manuscript into my sleeping-chamber, to look over it more at leisure. There by myself I could give way to the transport of joy which I felt. I knew that I held in my hand the most precious Biblical treasure in existence."

After delays of several months Tischendorf was allowed to take the MS to Russia to have it copied,

64. Looking down on St. Catherine's Monastery from the NE, with Jebel Musa (Mount Sinai?) in the background

65. Codex Sinaiticus (fourth century A.D.)

and eventually it was presented to the czar. It remained in St. Petersburg (Leningrad) until 1933, when the British Museum purchased it from the Soviet government for £100,000.

Figs. SIN 64-65.

Bibliography. K. von Tischendorf, "The Discovery of the Sinaitic MS" in *When Were Our Gospels Written?* (1866). C. R. Gregory, *Canon and Text of the NT* (1907), pp. 329-40. F. Kenyon, *Our Bible and the Ancient MSS* (5th ed., 1958), pp. 66-67, 128-35. I. M. Price, *The Ancestry of Our English Bible* (3rd ed., 1956; rev. W. A. Irwin, A. Wikgren), pp. 60-63.
T. S. KEPLER

SINCERITY [תמים; εἰλικρίνεια; Vulg. *sinceritas* (Josh. 24:14; I Cor. 5:8; II Cor. 1:12; 2:17)]. A quality of personal character or action which is free from falsification, deceit, or wickedness, and is characterized by purity, genuineness, and the like. The various qualities associated with sincerity in the Bible are purity, genuineness, uprightness, truthfulness, and godliness. *See* SIMPLICITY.

The etymology of εἰλικρίνεια is uncertain. The idea behind the word, however, may have been that of being found true and pure when openly examined. This is expressed in Paul's claim for sincerity "in the sight of God" (II Cor. 2:17). The adjective εἰλικρινής, "sincere," is employed to express similar ideas in Wisd. Sol. 7:25; Phil. 1:10; II Pet. 3:1. Sincerity is also closely associated with the ideas expressed by γνήσιος, "genuine" (II Cor. 8:8); γνησίως, "genuinely" (Phil. 2:20); ἁγνῶς, "sincerely" (Phil. 1:17 [1:16 KJV]); and εὐθύτης, "straightness" (Josh. 24: 14 [תמים; cf. Judg. 9:16, 19, KJV]). Sincerity is associated with TRUTH in the sense of moral uprightness in I Cor. 5:8, where it is contrasted with wickedness. In Tob. 3:5 the Vulg. gives *sinceriter* for ἐν ἀληθείᾳ, "in truth" (BA), or ἀληθινῶς, "truly" (S).

A distinctive meaning imparted to the idea of sincerity in the Bible is that of godliness or holiness. In II Cor. 1:12 sincerity is mentioned in connection with holiness as being "godly sincerity." In this light, the "sincere mind" of II Pet. 3:1 may be understood in the sense of a devout and godly mind aroused to true piety. Such sincerity is especially important for those who preach the gospel (II Cor. 1:12; 2:17). By contrast, those who proclaim Christ with impure motives do not preach sincerely (οὐχ ἁγνῶς; Phil. 1:17 [1:16 KJV]).
R. L. SCHEEF, JR.

SINEW [גיד; Akkad. *gidu*]. In Job 10:11; Ezek. 37:6, 8, the reference is clearly to the tendons and other connective tissues forming (together with the bones) the framework which holds together the flesh with its covering of skin. Thus Gen. 32:32: "the sinew of the hip which is upon the hollow of the thigh" retains the anatomical vagueness of the text itself. The Talmudic identification of this "sinew" with the sciatic nerve rests upon ancient cultic practice, possibly influenced by the LXX translation νεῦρον (Vulg. *nervus*), which appears in the technical sense "nerve" (from "sinew," "cord," "fiber") after 300 B.C.

In Isa. 48:4 the neck as an "iron sinew" recalls the term "stiff-necked," figurative of obstinate self-will (e.g., Exod. 32:9). The "sinew of his thigh" (Job 40:17) seems to be a euphemism for the *membrum virile*.

Bibliography. The *Talmud* (Soncino ed., 1948): *Hullin* 89*b*, 90*b*, 100*b*; *Kiddushin* 25*a*. S. Terrien, Exegesis of Job, *IB*, III (1954), 1187.
J. A. WHARTON

SINGERS, SINGING, SONG. *See* MUSIC.

SINIM, LAND OF sī'nĭm. KJV translation of סינים (RSV SYENE).

*SINITES sĭn'īts [סיני]. A group mentioned as Canaanites in Gen. 10:17; I Chr. 1:15. Strabo knew a town called Sinna, on the slopes of Lebanon, and Hieronymus was of the opinion that the *civitas Sini* could be located in the foothills of Lebanon, possibly near Nahr el-'Arqa. Others have suggested the N Phoenician Sianu, mentioned in Assyrian inscriptions, but nothing can be said for certain.
A. S. KAPELRUD

SINNER. This word, usually a translation of חטא or ἁμαρτωλός, has four principal meanings in the Bible:

a) In the OT it usually means "godless one," or one who lives outside the law (Num. 16:38; Prov. 1: 10; and especially Pss. 1; 25–26; 51; 104). In the NT this is often expressed by "workers of iniquity" (ἀνομία)—i.e., workers of lawlessness. It includes harlots, murderers, and the like, but also tax collectors (*see* TAX COLLECTOR), who, because of their servitude to pagan rulers, placed themselves outside the law (Luke 7:37; Rom. 3:7).

b) A heathen or Gentile. This is a natural extension of the first meaning (Mark 14:41; Luke 6:32 ff; 24:7; Gal. 2:15).

c) One from the "people of the land," or 'AM HA'AREZ, who violated the traditions of the Pharisees or even, because of ignorance, provisions of the Mosaic code itself. Most of the common people were in this class. Jesus was particularly concerned for them, saying they were "like sheep without a shepherd" (Matt. 11:19; Mark 2:15 ff; 6:34; Luke 15).

d) One who is separated from God, whether aware of it or not. Paul, who seldom uses the word at all, gives it this meaning in a majority of cases (Rom. 5:8, 19; 7:13; Gal. 2:17).

See also LAW IN THE OT; LAW IN FIRST-CENTURY JUDAISM; LAW IN THE NT; SIN.
PIERSON PARKER

SION. KJV form of SIRION in Deut. 4:48; KJV form of ZION in Ps. 65:1 and the NT.

SIPHMOTH sĭf'mŏth [שפמות]. A village in S Judah to which David sent some of the booty taken from the Amalekites for kindnesses shown him and his men (I Sam. 30:28; cf. I Chr. 27:27). The site is unknown.

SIPPAI. Alternate form of SAPH.

SIR. The translation of אדני (*Adonai*) in Judg. 6:13 (usually translated "Lord"); and in the NT the occasional translation of κύριος (also usually translated "Lord"). In Acts 27:10, and in several other Acts passages in the KJV, the plural "Sirs" translates ἄνδρες, meaning simply "men."

The word κύριος was used to designate not only God (in the LXX and the NT) and Christ (in the

NT), but also a master (in contrast to a slave), or an owner (e.g., of a vineyard). It was also used as a term of polite address. In the gospels it is occasionally difficult to know whether the word means "Lord" or "Sir."

For the meaning of "Lord" as applied to God or as a title of Jesus, *see* GOD, OT VIEW OF; LORD (CHRIST). B. H. THROCKMORTON, JR.

SIRACH, SON OF sī'rək [υἱὸς Σειράχ *or* Σιράχ, *from* בן סירא]. Ben Sirach, the author of ECCLESIAS-TICUS, which is often called the Wisdom of Jesus the Son of Sirach, or simply Sirach. The final χ in Greek may be an attempt to represent a guttural sound in the pronunciation of א (cf. 'Ακελδαμάχ in Acts 1:19 for Aramaic חקל דמא), or it may be simply a sign that the word cannot be declined (cf. 'Ιωσήχ in Luke 3:26 for יוסי). T. A. BURKILL

SIRAH, CISTERN OF sī'rə [בור הסרה]; KJV SIRAH, WELL OF. A location from which Joab treacherously recalled Abner to murder him (II Sam. 3:26). Josephus (Antiq. VII.i.5) says that Besera (*Bôr-sīrāh*, "well of Sirah") was *ca.* 20 stades (2½ miles) from Hebron. The cistern of Sirah is probably to be identified with 'Ain Sarah, 1½ miles NW of Hebron. V. R. GOLD

SIRION sĭr'ĭ ən [שריון; Akkad. *perhaps Sirara*]; KJV SION sī'ən in Deut. 4:48; THE FIELD in Jer. 18:14. According to Deut. 3:9, the Sidonian name of Mount Hermon. In Ps. 29:6, Sirion is mentioned together with Lebanon:

> He makes Lebanon to skip like a calf,
> and Sirion like a young wild ox.

Since in this passage Sirion is mentioned together with Lebanon, the suggestion may not be implausible that Sirion is a designation of the Anti-lebanon Range (*pars peo toto?*).

See SISMAI. Cf. now also the Ras Shamra Texts. A. HALDAR

SISAMAI. KJV form of SISMAI.

SISERA sĭs'ə rə [סיסרא]. Leader of a confederation of Canaanite kings whose army was routed by the flooded River Kishon and the troops of Barak and Deborah, and who was himself slain in the tent of Jael (Judg. 4:1-22; 5:19-31).

The name Sisera is non-Semitic. Although formerly explained as Hittite, Assyrian, Egyptian, or N Arabian, it is now thought to have been Illyrian in origin, as closely related to Illyrian personal and place names with the element *ero*.

Sisera's city, Harosheth, is identified as Harosheth-ha-goiim, "Harosheth of the (foreign) nations" (Judg. 4:2, 13, 16), apparently to distinguish it from an Israelite community of the same name (cf. "Galilee of the nations" in Isa. 9:1—H 8:23). Its location, uncertain but possibly the site of the excavation at Tell 'Amr some twelve miles NW of Megiddo, was evidently at or near the NW end of the Plain of Esdraelon.

Both Sisera's name and his city seem to corroborate the suggestion that he was leader of W sea peoples, originally from Europe, like the Philistines but to be distinguished from them, who were penetrating eastward just N of the Carmel headland into the desirable plain at the same time that the Israelites were coming down from their mountain highlands to claim the same territory. This may then be the story of the crucial battle when invading sea peoples in league with native Canaanite defenders took their last stand against the Israelites and their God and were ingloriously defeated.

The tradition that Sisera was of foreign origin may lie behind the mention of the "sons of Sisera" in the postexilic list of temple slaves (Ezra 2:53; Neh. 7:55; I Esd. 5:32), for most of these "NETHINIM" were foreign captives of war.

The biblical story of Sisera appears in two forms: the poetic Song of Deborah, probably composed soon after the events described and therefore remarkably authentic (Judg. 5); and a late prose narrative (ch. 4) which seems to combine this account of Sisera with a different story of Jabin, who is given the unhistorical title of "king of Canaan." Therefore, in the latter, Sisera is relegated to the subordinate position of general in Jabin's army. These two men are similarly associated in the late source of Samuel, where their oppression is an example of God's judgment on Israel's apostasy (I Sam. 12:9), and in a psalmist's imprecatory prayer that God will do to his enemies as he did "to Sisera and Jabin at the river Kishon" (Ps. 83:9—H 83:10).

In the Song of Deborah, however, Jabin is not mentioned, while Sisera, evidently a powerful prince, is leader of a confederation of Canaanite kings, and his queen mother and her princesses expect rich booty as their accustomed spoils of war. Sisera's royal city, Harosheth, lay at a strategic spot in the conflict, whereas Jabin's center at Hazor was miles away NE of the scene of the struggle.

The circumstances of the battle are vividly set forth in both accounts. That the scene was "by the waters of Megiddo" (Judg. 5:19), and yet there is no evidence that this stronghold was involved, suggests the date of *ca.* 1125-1100 B.C., when the site of Megiddo had not yet been reoccupied after the city's destruction perhaps half a century before. According to the prose account, some ten thousand foot soldiers from Zebulun and from Barak's tribe of Naphtali were involved; but according to the more authentic Song, six tribes bordering on the plain put perhaps forty thousand men into the fray. It took a huge number of Israelites on foot to meet Sisera's 900 iron chariots (probably an exaggerated number, but to be compared with Egyptian pharaoh Thut-mose III's claim of capturing 924 chariots in his fifteenth-century-B.C. Megiddo battle).

The course of the battle is not clear, but its outcome is indisputable. Perhaps too great distance is involved for Barak's troops to have charged down from Mount Tabor to meet Sisera's chariots from Harosheth. Deborah's Song speaks only of Taanach, the waters of Megiddo, and the Kishon. There may be poetic license in the details—because of a sudden downpour in late winter the brook Kishon became a raging torrent drowning hundreds of charioteers seeking to squeeze through the narrow valley at the

W end of the plain—although experience in World War I showed that fifteen minutes' heavy rain on clay soil could convert charging cavalry into plunging horses' hoofs. In any case Sisera ran for his life.

Because of some differences between the poetic and the prose accounts of Sisera's fate, especially the manner of his death, some have suggested that the prose narrative confused the authentic Song portrayal, in which Jael struck down Sisera, with a story in which another heroic woman, known only as the "wife of Heber the Kenite," betrayed Jabin into the hands of Barak. In the prose narrative fleeing Sisera sought and received asylum at the tent of one whom he expected to be friendly, and so fell into exhausted sleep, but then was treacherously murdered and his corpse betrayed into the hands of the pursuing and coincidentally arriving Barak. On the other hand, as some interpret, in the Song fugitive Sisera paused at a tent only for the hospitality of a drink of water. Having brought him the typical bedouin drink of curdled sour milk, it was when he unguardedly buried his head in the large bowl that the woman, with skill mastered from driving tent pegs, struck the shattering blow with the mallet. Thus the brave woman, violating the law of hospitality—unless, as some would explain, Sisera had guiltily violated the women's quarters by entering—and not waiting for any soporific effect of the drink, showed her loyalty to Israel by striking her guest down. Then, straddled over him,

> she struck Sisera a blow,
> she crushed his head,
> she shattered and pierced his temple.

This gory picture is rivaled by the irony of the concluding scene, sometimes compared with Hector's mother in Homer's *Iliad*, in which Sisera's queen mother and her attendant princesses console themselves that the delay is only because their victorious men are gathering spoils, including a "wench [lit., 'womb'] or two" for each warrior.

Religiously, Sisera's defeat was the tale of holy war, in which Canaanite and foreign paganism were defeated, not simply by the human troops of Barak and Deborah, but by the judgment of the Lord, for "from their courses (the stars) fought against Sisera." Historically, Sisera's downfall, shortly after the days of Shamgar, was the end of the last full-scale native Canaanite uprising against the Israelites and their winning of the important Plain of Esdraelon.

Bibliography. E. Power, " 'He asked for water, milk she gave' (Judg. 5:25)," *Bibl.* (1928), p. 47; J. Garstang, *The Foundations of Bible History: Joshua, Judges* (1931), pp. 289-306; H. Bauer, "Die Gottheiten von Ras Schamra," *ZAW*, N.F. X (1933), 83-84; W. F. Albright, "The Song of Deborah in the Light of Archaeology," *BASOR*, LXII (1936), 26-31; A. Alt, "Megiddo im Übergang vom kanaanäischen zum israelitischen Zeitalter," *ZAW*, N.F. XIX (1944), 67-85; M. Noth, *History of Israel* (1958), pp. 36-38, 149-52, 162-63.
C. F. KRAFT

SISINNES sĭ sĭn′ĭz [Σισίννης]. Governor of Coele-Syria and Phoenicia. When returning exiles under Zerubbabel began to build the house of the Lord in Jerusalem, Sisinnes objected. Darius, quoting the decree of Cyrus, ordered Sisinnes to desist (I Esd. 6:

7 ff; 7:1; Jos. Antiq. XI.i.3; XI.iv.7). Cf. Tattenai (Ezra 5:3; 6:6).
J. C. SWAIM

SISMAI sĭs′mī [סמסם; *cf. name of a god* (ססם, *ssm*), *in* Phoen. עבדססם; Ugar. *'bd.-ssm;* Akkad. *Ša-aš-ma-a*] (I Chr. 2:40); KJV SISAMAI —ə mī. A postexilic name in a genealogy tracing the descent of Elishama. *See also* SHESHAN.

Bibliography. K. Tallqvist, *Assyrian Personal Names* (1914), p. 219; M. Noth, *Die israelitischen Personennamen* (1928), p. 252; W. Rudolf, *Chronikbücher*, HAT (1955), pp. 19-20.
T. M. MAUCH

SISTRUM. *See* MUSICAL INSTRUMENTS § B1c.

SITHRI sĭth′rī [סתרי, *perhaps* concealed (by the deity)] (Exod. 6:22); KJV ZITHRI zĭth′—. Son of Uzziel, and cousin of Moses, listed in the genealogy of Levi.

Bibliography. M. Noth, *Die israelitischen Personennamen* (1928), p. 158.

SITNAH sĭt′nə [שׂטנה, hostility]. A well dug by the servants of Isaac near Gerar (Gen. 26:21). It was given this name because the herdsmen of Abimelech, king of Gerar, disputed with them about it. It must have been in the vicinity of REHOBOTH, but the exact site is unknown.
S. COHEN

SIVAN sĭ′văn [סיון]. The third month of the Hebrew CALENDAR, Akkadian *simānu* (May-June).

SIX HUNDRED AND SIXTY-SIX [ἑξακόσιοι ἑξήκοντα ἕξ, *or* χξς′—*i.e.,* 666; *also* ἑξακόσιοι δέκα ἕξ, *or* χις′—*i.e.,* 616] (Rev. 13:18). The "number of the beast." The larger figure (666) is found in MSS א (feminine), A (masculine), P al (neuter), and as the number χξς′ in P⁴⁷ 046, 1 pm; the smaller figure (616) appears in MSS C and 11 (feminine), in authorities known to Irenaeus, and as the number χις′ in MS 5. (Unfortunately, the minuscule MSS 5 and 11 have been lost.)

The numerous attempts to solve the enigma presented by John's use of this number may be summarized as follows:

a) Theories assuming that the "number of the beast" represents a name to be discovered by the reader's ingenuity (cf. "let him who has understanding reckon" it; vs. 18). Since the day of Irenaeus students have employed the known numerical values of the letters of both Hebrew and Greek alphabets in the endeavor to discover a name whose total numerical value will equal the indicated sum. Such students assume that John has made use of the system known to the rabbis as *Gematria* (Hebrew for geometry), a system adopted by both Jews and Greeks when it appeared desirable that only the initiated should learn the name in question. Such attempts include the following proposals: (i) assuming "666" to be original, the "name" suggested is either "Latin" (λατεῖνος: λ = 30, α = 1, τ = 300, ε = 5, ι = 10, ν = 50, ο = 70, ς = 200), and so suggesting a reference to the Roman Empire and its emperor; or Neron Caesar (נרון קסר: נ = 50, ר = 200, ו = 6, ן = 50, ק = 100, ס = 60, ר = 200); and (ii) assuming the originality of "616," the "name" may be either "Caesar is God" (καῖσαρ θεός: κ = 20, α = 1, ι = 10, σ = 200, α = 1, ρ = 100, θ = 9, ε = 5, o = 70, ς = 200) or Gaius Caesar (γ = 3, α = 1, ι = 10, o = 70, ς = 200, κ = 20, α = 1, ι = 10, σ = 200, α = 1, ρ = 100). Those who employ the Hebrew characters as in Neron Caesar (above) suggest that "616" may be due to a scribe's dropping the final "n" in Neron, as in the Latin. (iii) Some have interpreted John's statement that "the number of the beast . . . is a human number" as a case of isopsephism (i.e., two words whose numerical values are the same, in this case that of a beast and that of a man).

b) Theories asserting the general or indeterminate nature of the number's symbolism; thus, (i) some conclude that "a human number" means one humanly intelligible; (ii) others suggest that "666," by the system known as triangulation (*Dreieckszahl*), equals the sum of all the numbers from 1 to 36, the latter figure in turn being the sum of all those from 1 to 8 (the number of the Antichrist; cf. 17:11); in consequence, both 8 and 666 represent anyone opposed to and less perfect than Jesus, whose name in Greek adds up to "888" (ι = 10, η = 8, σ = 200, o = 70, υ = 400, ς = 200).

Of these theories, that suggesting Neron Caesar as possessing the "number of the beast" and the one involving triangulation and the Antichrist appear to have most to commend them.

Cf. ATHBASH; REVELATION, BOOK OF.

Bibliography. See the Commentaries listed in the bibliography under REVELATION, BOOK OF; also Introductions, particularly that of T. Zahn (2nd English ed., 1917), III, 444 ff.

Special studies: A. Deissmann, *Licht vom Osten* (4th ed., 1923), pp. 276-78, especially p. 278[3]; A. Farrer, *A Rebirth of Images* (1949), pp. 257-60; N. W. Lund, *Studies in the Book of Revelation* (1955), pp. 151 ff.   J. W. BOWMAN

SKIFF [אניה in the phrase אניות אבה, skiffs (boats) of reed (KJV swift ships); cf. Akkad. *apu*] (Job 9:26); KJV SHIP. A kind of boat. Job likened the fleeting days of his life to swiftly passing skiffs of reed. See SHIPS AND SAILING.

SKIN [עוֹר; גלד (Job 16:15), cf. Arab. *jild*, skin; δέρμα (Heb. 11:37), δέρρις (Mark 1:6), *from* δέρω, skin, flay]. The outer covering of the body of a man or an animal.

1. Human. The skin, bones, sinews, and flesh make up the human body (Job 10:11; 19:20; Lam. 3:4; Ezek. 37:4-6), though skin sometimes designates the whole body (Exod. 22:27—H 22:26; cf. Job 19:26). The color of the Ethiopian's skin gives us Jeremiah's well-known question (Jer. 13:23). The variation in the hairiness of the skin is recognized in the story of Jacob and Esau (Gen. 27). Darkened, hardened, or feverish skin can be the result of hunger or disease (Job 7:5; 30:30; Lam. 4:8; 5:10). In Lev. 13:1-46 the treatment of certain abnormal skin conditions is indicated. In Mic. 3:2-3 the flaying of the skin of the people is a metaphor for their maltreatment by their rulers.

2. Animal. Apart from the allusion to Leviathan's skin in Job 41:7—H 40:31, all the biblical references to animal skin are to the hides of dead animals. As the principal domesticated animals of Palestine were

oxen, asses, sheep, and goats, it is probable that they furnished the hides in commonest use. There are allusions to the skins of kids (Gen. 27:16), of rams (Exod. 25:5), of goats (Exod. 25:5, but the meaning of תחשים is uncertain), and of sheep and goats (Heb. 11:37). The Mishna refers also to the skins of the pig, the camel, the gecko, the chameleon, the lizard, the land crocodile (Hullin 9.2). All such hides were doubtless tanned in some way before being used. *See* LEATHER; TANNING; GOATSKIN; WATERSKINS; WINE § 2c.

The hides of some sin offerings (those involving the priesthood or the whole community) had, like most of the carcass, to be destroyed (Exod. 29:14; Lev. 4:11, 21; 8:17; 9:11; 16:27; cf. Num. 19:5); the skin of other sin offerings, as well as that of all burnt offerings, became the property of the priests (Lev. 5:13; 7:8), and presumably had some economic value. The flaying of these animals is referred to in Lev. 1:6; II Chr. 29:34.

3. Proverbial expressions. *a. "Skin for skin!"* (*Job 2:4*). The original significance of this phrase is unknown. The context suggests that the meaning in Job is, "Skin on behalf of skin; an expendable asset will be surrendered for the sake of a less expendable one."

b. "By the skin of my teeth" (*Job 19:20*). Textual corruption has been suspected, and various emendations have been proposed, though none has gained general acceptance. If the text is sound, we may have a proverb, the meaning of which in Job would appear to be either "with the loss of almost everything" or "by the smallest possible margin."

W. S. MCCULLOUGH

SKIRT. 1. כנף ("wing"). The loose end, one of the four corners of a garment, usually the מעיל. The meaning is clear from I Sam. 15:27; 24:4-5—H 24:5-6, where David is said to have cut off the skirt of Saul's robe. Covering with the skirt of one's garment symbolized the right of marriage (Ruth 3:9). The term is also used symbolically of the corners or ends of the earth (Job 38:13).

2. שׁוּל. The part of a garment which hangs down loosely, perhaps the lowest part. In some passages it is apparently the loose outer garment of women, and it is used figuratively in connection with Jerusalem, whose skirts were lifted up in shame because of her illicit relationships (Jer. 13:22, 26; Lam. 1:9; Nah. 3:5). The term is also used to refer to the edge (KJV "hem") of the ephod, which was to be adorned with golden bells and pomegranates alternately (Exod. 28:33-34; 39:24-26), and to the "train" of the Lord in Isaiah's vision (6:1).

3. KJV translation of פה (lit., "mouth") in the expression "mouth [RSV 'collar'] of his robes" (Ps. 133:2). *See* COLLAR 1.   J. M. MYERS

SKULL, PLACE OF A. *See* GOLGOTHA; HOLY SEPULCHRE.

SKY. *See* HEAVEN.

SLANDER. In the OT several Hebrew words are used for evil talk intended to damage or destroy a neighbor (cf. II Sam. 16:1-4; 19:24-30; I Kings 21:

8-14 for classical examples, though the word itself does not appear). The close relationship of slander to the Ninth Commandment is seen in Lev. 19:16 (*see* TEN COMMANDMENTS). Such "character assassination" typically marks the man who has rejected God's law and stands under judgment (Pss. 50:20; 101:5; Jer. 6:28; 9:4; Ezek. 22:9). The tongue is regarded as an especially vicious instrument of evil (Ps. 57:4; Prov. 17:4-11 [cf. Jas. 3:1-12]; Jer. 9:8).

In the NT, καταλαλέω, "to speak evilly" of one's neighbor (I Pet. 2:1; καταλαλιά in II Cor. 12:20), includes not only untruthfulness, but perhaps primarily lovelessness. It is an identifying characteristic of the heathen world (cf. I Pet. 2:12; 3:16), intolerable within the household of faith (Jas. 4:11-12).

The RSV translates διάβολος (*see* SATAN) in its original meaning, "slanderer," in I Tim. 3:11; II Tim. 3:3; Tit. 2:3. Similarly, βλασφημία (*see* BLASPHEMY) is translated "slander" when verbal abuse of men is indicated (cf. the "catalogues of sin" in Matt. 15:19; Mark 7:21-22; Eph. 4:31; Col. 3:8-9; I Tim. 6:4-5).   J. A. WHARTON

*SLAVERY IN THE OT.** The ownership of man by man. OT Palestine, embracing a period of more than a thousand years, was economically, and to a large degree also socially, an integral part of the ancient Near Eastern world. Slavery was an economic institution, and in order to evaluate biblical slavery in its proper perspective, we must take into account the slave institutions as they existed in the other

Courtesy of the American Schools of Oriental Research

66. Earliest representation of war captives; drawing made from the impression of a cylinder seal found at Uruk in Babylonia, in the second half of the fourth millennium B.C.

parts of the Fertile Crescent. Frequent and extensive references to the slave systems of the neighboring peoples in a discussion of biblical slavery is also of paramount value for another reason, the availability of source material.

Fig. SLA 66.

1. Literary sources
2. Terminology
3. Sources of slavery
    a. Captives of war
    b. Foreign slaves
    c. Sale of minors
    d. Self-sale
    e. Insolvency
4. Legal status
    a. Branding
    b. The female slave
    c. Marriage between free and slave
    d. The house-born slave
    e. The fugitive slave
    f. Treatment
    g. Peculium
    h. Manumission
5. State slavery
6. Temple slavery
7. The economic role of slavery
Bibliography

1. Literary sources. The law codes and the vast number of private economic documents relating to slavery from Babylonia, Assyria, and Syria enrich and supplement the legal and extralegal information at our disposal in the OT. It is only by utilizing the inestimable treasures of the extrabiblical evidence that the similarities, as well as the differences, between the biblical attitude toward slavery and that of the neighboring peoples become apparent and meaningful. The most important sources for the study of slavery in the ancient Near East (excluding Pharaonic Egypt, where the available material is extremely scant) are: (*a*) the Ur-Namu Code (*ca.* 2050 B.C.), the Laws of Eshnunna (early twentieth century B.C.), the Lipit-Ishtar Law Code (middle of the nineteenth century B.C.), the Code of Hammurabi (*ca.* 1700 B.C.), and the Middle Assyrian Laws (fourteenth–twelfth centuries B.C.); (*b*) private and court documents from Babylonia and Assyria embracing the period from the end of the third millennium to the beginning of the Christian era; (*c*) the Hittite Laws (middle of the fifteenth century B.C.); and (*d*) the Akkadian documents from Alalakh and Ugarit (N Syria), dating from the eighteenth to the thirteenth century B.C. The biblical slave legislations are recorded in Exod. 21; Lev. 25; Deut. 15. In addition to these, there are references to slavery in many other books of the OT. The only extrabiblical data relating to Jewish slavery in the period under discussion are found in the Aramaic Papyri from the Jewish colony at Elephantine (Egypt), dated in the fifth century B.C.

2. Terminology. The earliest Sumerian terms for male and female slaves are the composite ideograms *nitá + kur* ("male of a foreign country") and *munus + kur* ("female of a foreign country"), indicating that the first human beings to be enslaved in ancient Babylonia were captives of war. In later Sumerian times the slave is referred to simply as *sag* ("head"), thus *sag nitá* ("male head") and *sag geme* ("female head"). In Akkadian the generic term for "slave," often preceded by the determinative *rēšu* ("head"), is *wardum* (feminine *amtum*). The alphabetic texts from Ugarit employ *'bd* for "male slave," and *amt* for "female slave." The OT terminology consists of three main terms: עבד for a male slave, אמה and שפחה for a female slave; infrequently, the descriptive designation מקנת כסף ("[persons] bought with money"), נער ("young man"), and נפש ("person") are also used to indicate slaves. (It should be pointed out that the Akkadian, Ugaritic, and Hebrew terms for "slave" are often employed to designate the inferior status of a freeborn person in relation to the king, or to a deity.) Unlike the Mesopotamian and Ugaritic usage of the term "slave" to denote any unfree person, whether native or foreign, the biblical legislations employ in some cases the adjective "Hebrew"—i.e., "a Hebrew slave" (עבד עברי), or "your brother, a Hebrew man or a Hebrew woman" (אחיך העברי או העבריה), and in other cases the unspecified terms "male slave" and "female slave." This distinction is interpreted in the Talmud to mean that in the former cases the laws apply to Hebrew slaves and in the latter cases to non-Hebrew slaves. This interpretation often leads to irreconcilable discrepancies, which will be pointed out in the discussion of the individual laws.

3. Sources of slavery. *a. Captives of war.* The Sumerian term for "slave" (*see* § 2 *above*) clearly indicates that the earliest source for slave supply was war. That captives of war, and in some cases also large segments of the defeated civil population, were reduced to slavery is amply attested in the war annals of the ancient Near East. The same method of enslaving war prisoners was used by the small city-states in Syria and Palestine during the middle of the second millennium B.C., and by the Israelites some centuries later (cf. Num. 31:7 ff; Deut. 20:10 ff; I Kings 20:39; II Chr. 28:8 ff; etc.). The Code of Hammurabi and biblical law take this universal practice of the enslavement of war captives for granted and seek to ameliorate the lot of some of those unfortunates and their immediate families. Paragraphs 32, 133-35, of the Code of Hammurabi decree: (*a*) that captive soldiers and state officials, who have no means of their own, shall be ransomed either by their city temple or by the state; and (*b*) that a woman whose husband has been taken prisoner may remarry in case she has no means to support herself and her children. Equally, the Middle Assyrian Laws (Tablet A, paragraph 45) provide that a wife of a captured soldier who cannot support herself shall become a ward of the palace. Deut. 21:10-14 prescribes that if a soldier sees among the captives a beautiful woman and takes her for a wife, she must be treated as a free person, and he cannot, after he no longer loves her, sell her as an ordinary prisoner of war.

b. Foreign slaves. Traffic in foreign slaves was an integral part of the merchant's activity in the ancient Near East. We have a large body of evidence concerning the import and export of slaves to and from various parts of Mesopotamia, but our information on this subject from biblical Palestine is exceedingly meager. Though foreign slaves, in small numbers, were undoubtedly imported into Palestine (cf. I Chr. 2:34-35), we have only two laws dealing indirectly with the export of Hebrew slaves abroad. Exod. 21:16; Deut. 24:7 prescribe the death penalty for the crime of kidnaping and selling of a freeborn person. The laws do not specifically state that the stolen person was sold into a foreign country, but we may assume that this was the case (cf. Gen. 37: 28). Also the Deuteronomic law (23:15-16—H23:16-17) prohibiting the extradition of fugitive slaves most probably has as its subject a Hebrew slave who has fled from a foreign country seeking asylum in his native land. We thus have some evidence for the import and export of slaves to and from Palestine in the biblical period.

c. Sale of minors. "Voluntary" sale of children by their parents, especially in times of economic stress and war, was not an uncommon practice in the ancient Near East (*see bibliography*). This may have happened, under similar circumstances, also in Israelite Palestine, but we have no proof of it. The law of Exod. 21:7-11 (which is not repeated in the later legislation of Deut. 15) and the cases reported in Neh. 5:1-5 represent no clear evidence of the outright sale of minors by their parents. Exod. 21:7-11 deals with the sale of a young girl by her father with the condition that the girl, after having reached puberty, be married off, either as a wife or as a concubine, to her master himself or to one of his sons. Similar conditional sales of young girls by their parents are known from the Hurrian colony at Nuzi. In some cases the sale contract provided that the girl was to be married off to a free person, and in others, to a slave. In the former situation it was not a sale into slavery, since the girl and her future children remained free; only in the latter case was it a sale into slavery. The law of Exodus clearly provides for the future marriage of the girl to her freeborn master or to one of his sons. It states explicitly that "the master shall have no right to sell her to a stranger" (RSV translates לעם נכרי lit. "to a foreign people"; Targum Onkelos renders it לגבר אחרן, "to another man"—i.e., to anyone outside the master's family); hence it was not a sale into slavery. That the law does not consider this transaction an outright sale (although it uses the terms מכר, "to sell," and אמה, "female slave") is evident from vs. 8, where it is clearly stated that if the master does not take her as his wife, he must let her be redeemed, and from vss. 9-11 that if he does not take her as his concubine or give her in marriage to one of his sons, "she shall go out for nothing, without payment of money"—i.e., the master forfeits the money which he had paid for the girl as a penalty for breach of contract (*see bibliography*). Neither can the reported cases in Neh. 5:1-5 be considered as "voluntary" sales of children by their parents. The economic depression at that time forced some farmers to hand over their land and their children as pledges for loans. When the debts were not paid, the creditors foreclosed the land and sold the pledged children—against the will of their parents.

d. Self-sale. Hunger or debt drove people to sell first their children and then themselves into slavery. Voluntary self-enslavement was a common phenomenon among strangers. This was particularly the case with the Habiru in Nuzi, who, being unable to secure employment, entered "of their own free will," singly or with their families, into the status of servitude (*see bibliography*). Of all the ancient law codes, the OT legislations alone mention the case of self-sale or voluntary slavery (Exod. 21:5-6; Lev. 25:39 ff; Deut. 15:16-17). Exod. 21:5-6 provides that if a Hebrew debtor-slave, to whom his master has given a wife, refuses to go out free after his six-year term of service has expired, he shall serve his master "for life," לעלם. The reasons for the action of the former slave are: (*a*) economic security ("I love my master"), and (*b*) the desire to remain united with his wife and the children she has borne him ("I love . . . my wife, and my children"). Deut. 15:16-17 (which is essentially a parallel to the earlier law of Exodus) does not mention the case of the master's having given his Hebrew debtor-slave a wife, and therefore bases his refusal to go out free on the economic reason only: "because he loves you and your household, since he fares well with you." While the subject of the laws of Exodus and Deuteronomy is the Hebrew debtor-slave, that of Lev. 25:39-55 is the Hebrew who because of poverty voluntarily enters into the status of slavery, either to a fellow Hebrew or to a resident alien: "If your brother becomes poor . . . and sells himself to you . . . [or] to the stranger or sojourner with you . . . ." Thus, all three slave legislations contain laws pertaining to self-enslavement of Hebrews, and we must assume, therefore, that such cases, in one form or another, were common in ancient Israel.

e. Insolvency. Although captives of war, foreign slaves, and children born of slave parentage made up a substantial part of the unfree population of the ancient Near East, the basic supply source for slaves was the freeborn native defaulting debtor. Mesopotamian law (cf. the Code of Hammurabi, paragraphs 114-19, and the Middle Assyrian Laws, Tablet A, paragraph 48) recognizes the right of the creditor to seize his defaulting debtor and force him to perform compulsory service.

Insolvency could be the result of many causes, but one of the chief factors was unquestionably the exorbitant interest rate charged on loans. In Babylonia, Assyria, and Syria, the average interest was 20-25 per cent on silver and 33⅓ per cent on grain. There is no information in the OT in regard to the interest rate charged on loans in Palestine. That interest was charged is evident, first, from the injunction, repeated in all three codes, against the taking of interest from a fellow Hebrew (Exod. 22:25—H 22:24; Lev. 25:35-37; Deut. 23:19-20—H 23:20-21), and secondly, from the references of the charging of interest in Ps. 15:5; Prov. 28:8; Ezek. 18:8-17; 22:12.

That the Palestinian creditor had the right to seize his defaulting debtor and reduce him to slavery is amply attested in the texts. Among those who joined David in the cave of Adullam were a number of defaulting debtors who had fled from their creditors (I Sam. 22:2). In II Kings 4:1 the creditor seized the children of his deceased debtor, and the widow appealed to the prophet Elisha for help: "The creditor has come to take my two children to be his slaves." Neh. 5:1-5 shows that pledged children were reduced to slavery if their parents failed to pay the debts. This practice is also reflected in the prophetic literature:

> Because they sell the righteous for silver,
> and the needy for a pair of shoes
> (Amos 2:6);

> Which of my creditors is it
> to whom I have sold you?
> (Isa. 50:1).

That the right of seizure of the defaulting debtor was recognized by the prevailing law is proved by Exod. 22:2. This law provides that the thief be sold into slavery, not as a punishment for stealing, but for his inability to compensate the owner for the loss of property. The subject of the laws of Exod. 21:2-4; Deut. 15:12 is the Hebrew defaulting debtor,

whom the laws are seeking to protect by limiting his term of forced labor to six years. *See* § 4h below.

4. Legal status. *a. Branding.* Legally the slave was a chattel. He was a commodity that could be sold, bought, leased, exchanged, or inherited. In sharp contrast to the free man, his father's name was never mentioned; he had no genealogy, being a man without a name. As a piece of property the slave was usually, although not universally, marked with a visible sign, just as an animal was by a tag or a brand. In ancient Egypt captives of war were branded and stamped with the name of the king, and privately owned slaves were marked by having their heads shaved, sometimes with a pigtail left (Bakir, *Slavery in Pharaonic Egypt,* pp. 31, 81, 110). In ancient Babylonia the slaves, particularly those who displayed a tendency to run away, were marked with an *abbuttum* (cf. B. Landsberger, *Materialien zum Sumerïschen Lexikon,* vol. I, Taf. 7, Kol. III, pp. 23-28; the Laws of Eshnunna, paragraphs 51-52; the Code of Hammurabi, paragraphs 146, 226-27). The precise character of the *abbuttum* is not clear. Some scholars maintain that it was a brand on the forehead; some interpret it to have been a special haircut; and still others consider the *abbuttum* to have been a small tablet of clay or metal suspended on a chain around the neck, wrist, or ankle of the slave. In the Neo-Babylonian period the prevailing custom was to tattoo the name of the owner on the wrist of the slave. This is described in slave-sale documents as: "A, whose left wrist is inscribed with the name of N," or "A, whose right wrist is inscribed with the name of N." Temple slaves were, as a rule, marked with the symbol of the god or goddess in whose temple they served.

The biblical law prescribes that he who, after his six-year term of service is over, voluntarily submits to perpetual slavery shall have his ear pierced with an awl (Exod. 21:6; Deut. 15:17). It is difficult to see what the purpose of this piercing was, since the hole was necessarily small and invisible. It may be suggested, therefore, that the hole was made in order to push through it a ring, or cord, on which was fastened a tag made of clay or metal. This does not exclude the possibility of the existence also of a tattoo mark. Cain's mark (Gen. 4:15), the writing of Yahweh's name on the hand (Isa. 44:5; 49:16), and the *tau* mark upon the forehead (Ezek. 9:4) clearly show that tattoo marks were used to signify possession. Privately owned slaves in the Jewish colony of Elephantine in the fifth century B.C. were marked on the wrist with the names of their owners (cf. A. E. Cowley, *Aramaic Papyri of the Fifth Century B.C.,* no. 28:4-6; E. G. Kraeling, *The Brooklyn Aramaic Papyri,* no. 5:3).

b. The female slave. The female slave, like the male slave, was treated as a commodity. She was leased for work, given as a pledge, or handed over as a part of a dowry. In addition to her routine duties as a maidservant, she was subject also to burdens peculiar to her sex. Ownership of a female slave meant, not only the right to employ her physical strength, but also, and in many cases primarily, the exploitation of her charms by the male members of her master's household, and the utilization of her body for the breeding of slave children. The highest position a female slave could achieve was to become a childbearing concubine to her master, and the lowest, to be used as a professional prostitute.

According to the Code of Hammurabi (paragraphs 146-47), a female slave who has borne children to her mistress' husband cannot be sold. Abraham and Sarah apparently acted in the case of Hagar in accordance with this ancient law. Hagar was the property of Sarah, and when, after she had given birth to Ishmael, she became "haughty," all her mistress could do was to embitter her life; she could not sell her (Gen. 16). We are not informed about the behavior of Zilpah and Bilhah, the female slaves of Leah and Rachel, after they had borne sons to Jacob, but we may assume that if they had acted the way Hagar did, the same law would have applied to them.

Female slaves were mated with male slaves for the purpose of giving birth to slave children. Exod. 21:4 provides: "If his master gives him [the slave] a wife and she bears him sons or daughters, the wife and her children shall be her master's and he shall go out alone." That the female slave was used promiscuously in her master's household may also be inferred from the statement in Job 31:10:

> Then let my wife grind for another [i.e., be reduced to slavery],
> and let others bow down upon her.

c. Marriage between free and slave. Marriages between freeborn women and slaves were common in ancient Babylonia. With the consent of his master, a slave could take a freeborn woman and conclude a legal marriage with her. According to the Code of Hammurabi (paragraph 175), the children born of such a union were free, and their father's master could not lay claim to their service. We have no information about such marriages in Israelite Palestine. The reference in Lev. 19:20 to a female slave שפחה, who is betrothed to another man, is not clear, since we do not know precisely the status of the female slave involved in the case, nor who the "other man" was. The case of Sheshan, who had no sons of his own and therefore married off one of his daughters to his slave Jarha (I Chr. 2:34-35), is no evidence for mixed marriages. In accordance with good Babylonian and Syrian usage, Jarha was most probably manumitted and adopted by Sheshan before the marriage was consummated, for otherwise Jarha would not have been listed in the genealogical record of Judah.

d. The house-born slave. Legally, the status of the house-born slave (יליד בית, "one born in the house," or בן בית, "a son of the house") differed in no way from that of the purchased slave (מקנת כסף); only socially was the position of the former better than that of the latter. The case of Eliezer, the trusted servant of Abraham, is a good illustration of the treatment accorded a house-born slave. The complaint of Abraham (Gen. 15:2-4) that Eliezer would be his heir, however, is no proof that house-born slaves inherited the property of their childless masters in Palestine (or anywhere else in the ancient Near East). What Abraham meant when he said:

"A slave born in my house will be my heir," was that if no son were born to him, he would have to adopt Eliezer and appoint him as his heir.

e. The fugitive slave. Harboring a fugitive slave was, like receiving and possessing stolen goods, punishable by law. The Laws of Eshnunna (paragraphs 12-13) impose a fine for harboring runaway slaves. The leniency of the early Babylonian legislation in this case stands in marked contrast to the harshness of the Code of Hammurabi. Harboring a fugitive slave is considered a capital offense: he who helps a slave escape from the city gate, or refuses to hand over a fugitive slave to the authorities, "shall be put to death" (paragraphs 15-16). A fugitive slave was as helpless as a stray animal, and anyone who seized him and delivered him to his master was entitled to a reward of two shekels of silver (paragraph 17). The custom of rewarding a person for apprehending a runaway slave was also known in Syria (D. J. Wiseman, *The Alalakh Tablets,* no. 3; see also the Hittite Code, paragraphs 22-23).

The OT slave legislations (Exod. 21; Lev. 25; Deut. 15) do not consider the case of the fugitive slave. This omission is rather remarkable, since the tendency of slaves to run away, for reasons of cruel treatment or a desire for freedom, was no less prevalent in Palestine than it was in the adjacent countries. Hagar ran away from her mistress, Sarah (Gen. 16). When David sent his young men to procure food from the farmer Nabal, the latter defiantly inquired: "Who is David? Who is the son of Jesse? There are many slaves nowadays who are breaking away from their masters" (I Sam. 25:10). Runaway slaves were handed over to their owners (cf. I Sam. 30:15), and fugitive slaves were extradited from foreign countries. When Shimei heard that his two slaves had run away to the Philistine city of Gath, he promptly went there and brought them back (I Kings 2:39-40). On the Deuteronomic ordinance prohibiting the extradition of fugitive slaves, *see* § 4h *below.*

f. Treatment. Although theoretically the slave was considered a mere chattel and classed with movable property, both law and society could not disregard the fact that he was human. We thus have the highly contradictory situation in which, on the one hand, the slave was recognized as possessing the qualities of a human being, while, on the other hand, he was considered as being void of these and was treated as a "thing." The slave's status as a chattel, deprived of any rights, is clearly emphasized in his relation to a third party. If he is maimed, killed, or, in the case of a slave girl, violated by a stranger, the master is compensated for his loss; the slave himself is never considered as an injured party (cf. the Laws of Eshnunna, paragraphs 23, 31, 55, 57; the Code of Hammurabi, paragraphs 116, 213-14, 219-20, 231, 252). Biblical legislation considers only two such cases, one in which a slave is killed by a goring ox and the other in which a stranger has carnal intercourse with a betrothed slave girl. In the first instance, the owner of the animal must compensate the slave's master by paying him thirty shekels of silver, the average price of an unfree person (Exod. 21:32). In the second instance, the offender escapes with the light penalty of bringing a "guilt offering," since "she [the slave girl] was not free" (Lev. 19:20). (For the meaning of נחרפת, "betrothed," cf. T.B. Kid., fol. 6a; B. Landsberger, *Archiv für Keilschriftforschung*, II [1925], 70).

Although both the Mesopotamian and the biblical laws treat the slave in his relation to a third party as a "thing," there is a fundamental difference in the attitude of these two legislations in regard to the status of the slave in relation to his own master. Mesopotamian law does not consider the latter aspect at all—the slave's fate is in fact, if perhaps not in theory, at the mercy of his owner. The biblical legislation, on the contrary, recognizes the humanity of the slave by restricting the master's power over him. A master may maltreat his slave, "for the slave is his money" (Exod. 21:20-21), but if, as a result of the beating, the slave is permanently maimed, freedom must be granted to him as a compensation for loss of limb (Exod. 21:26-27), and if the beating causes the immediate death of the slave, the master is liable to punishment (Exod. 21:20-21). (The MT reads: נקם ינקם, "It [the deed] shall surely be avenged"; the Samar. reads: מות יומת, "He [the master] shall surely be put to death.")

It should be stressed that slavery in biblical Palestine was of a domestic character. The slave worked shoulder to shoulder with his master in the field or at home, and hence he was treated as a member, albeit an inferior one, in the large household. The law requires that the non-Hebrew slave participate in the religious observances of his master, including that of the enjoyment of the sabbath rest (cf. Gen. 17:13, 27; Exod. 12:44; 20:10; 23:12; Lev. 22:11; Deut. 5:14; 12:12, 18; 16:11, 14). The prophetic literature, although recognizing the existence of economic servitude, insisted upon the humanity of the slave. Joel (2:29—H 3:2) proclaimed:

> Even upon the menservants and maidservants
>   in those days, I will pour out my spirit;

and Job (31:15) eloquently condemned the whole system of slavery by questioning its moral basis, for:

> Did not he who made me in the womb make him
>   [the slave]?
> And did not one fashion us in the womb?

g. **Peculium.** The privilege of accumulating a peculium was granted to the Babylonian, Assyrian, and Egyptian slave from early times. The Code of Hammurabi takes the existence of the peculium for granted and decrees the manner of its disposal at the death of the slave. According to paragraph 176, the property amassed by a slave jointly with his free-born wife is to be divided after his death in equal shares between the widow and the master. It is evident from this law that the master was the legal owner of the slave's property, and hence, if that property was the result of a joint effort of a free person and a slave, the master could claim his slave's share only. In late Assyria and in Neo-Babylonia slaves played an active part in the economic life of the two countries. Some of them were engaged as craftsmen, agents, and tenant farmers; they owned houses and land, and even possessed their own slaves. For this privilege to accumulate and enjoy property the slave paid a certain amount of his earnings to his master (called *mandattu*), but after the slave's death the master appropriated the peculium.

The same privilege of accumulating property was also granted to the Palestinian slave. Lev. 25:49 provides that if a Hebrew sold himself to a non-Hebrew, his kinsmen should redeem him, or: "If he grows rich he may redeem himself" (i.e., with his peculium). The slave of Kish (the term used is נער, "young man," which like the Akkadian *ṣuḫāru* often signifies a young servant or slave) had in his possession one fourth of a silver shekel (I Sam. 9:8); and Ziba, the slave of Saul, is reported to have had fifteen sons and twenty slaves (II Sam. 9:10). The legal owner of the slave's peculium was his master. This is clearly stated in vs. 12: "All who dwelt in Ziba's house became Mephibosheth's servants."

h. **Manumission.** The Code of Hammurabi recognizes four legal means by which a slave is entitled to his freedom: (*a*) a defaulting debtor and his family who have been sold or handed over to service are to be freed after three years of work in the house of their purchaser or obligee (paragraph 117); (*b*) a slave-concubine and her children are to be freed after the death of the master (paragraph 171); (*c*) children born of a legitimate marriage between a free woman and a slave are free (paragraph 175); and (*d*) a Babylonian slave bought by a merchant in a foreign country and brought back to his native land is to be unconditionally released (paragraph 280). The law set forth in paragraph 117 was promulgated by Hammurabi (we have no earlier parallels to this provision) in order to check the tendency of wholesale enslavement of defaulting debtors. Regardless of the amount of debt, three years of service in the house of the purchaser or creditor were deemed sufficient to work off any debt. Whether this law was ever enforced, however, is very doubtful. We have numerous documents from ancient Babylonia and Neo-Babylonia attesting to the selling or handing over of wives and children to creditors, but evidence of their release after a three-year term of service is conspicuous by its absence.

The most common methods of manumission in the ancient Near East (but not mentioned in the Code of Hammurabi) were release by adoption and by purchase. The Sumerian Lipit-Ishtar Law Code provides that if a slave has compensated his master, this slave shall be freed (paragraph 14). The purchase transaction could be carried out in two forms, by payment of the whole sum at once or by an obligation assumed by the slave to support his master for the duration of the latter's life. In the first case, the slave's release was effective immediately and made irrevocably; in the second case, the slave's freedom was conditioned upon the fulfilment of his promise. To make the release doubly safe, the manumitted slave was sometimes dedicated to a god—i.e., he was put under the protection of a deity against any future claim by the children of the manumitter.

According to biblical law there are five means by which a slave is entitled to his freedom. These are: (*a*) a Hebrew slave (עבד עברי) and his wife, or a Hebrew female slave (עבריה), are to be released after a six-year term of service (Exod. 21:2-4; Deut. 15: 12); (*b*) a Hebrew (the text has אחיך, "your brother") who has sold himself voluntarily into slavery, either to a fellow Hebrew or to a stranger, is to be freed in the year of the jubilee (Lev. 25:39-43, 47-55); (*c*) a Hebrew girl who had been sold by her father on the condition that she be married off to her master or to one of his sons, is to be freed if, after she has reached puberty, her master refuses to abide by the agreement (Exod. 21:7-11); (*d*) a "slave" (עֶבֶד) permanently maimed by his master is to be freed without compensation (Exod. 21:26-27); and (*e*) a fugitive "slave" (עֶבֶד) must not be delivered to his master; the right of asylum shall be granted him (Deut. 23:15-16—H 23:16-17).

The subject of the laws of Exod. 21:2-4; Deut. 15:12 is the Hebrew debtor-slave. Like the Code of Hammurabi (paragraph 117), the Hebrew lawgivers sought to check the ruthless power of the creditors by limiting the period of forced labor of the default-ing debtor to six years. (The Deuteronomic legislator, aware that in Babylonia the limit was three years, stressed the fact [15:18] that the Palestinian creditor was amply compensated, since "at half the cost of a hired servant he [the debtor-slave] has served you six years"). In essence the manumission laws of Ex-odus and Deuteronomy are alike (release after six years), but the latter introduces a new factor reflect-ing the changed economic conditions in the country: now women also are sold as debtor-slaves, and they are to be released in the same manner as the males. Whether the enforcement of the law of release of the debtor-slave was more successful in Palestine than its counterpart was in Babylonia is, in view of the lack of contemporary private documents and court records, hard to say. Jeremiah (34:8-16) ex-plicitly states that the Hebrew slaves in his time were not released in the seventh year. Nehemiah (5:5 ff) makes no direct reference to the laws of Exodus and Deuteronomy, but from the context of his hortatory speech it would appear that the law of manumission was not observed in his time either.

The subject of the Levitical law 25:39-43, 47-55, which decrees the manumission of the Hebrew slave in the year of the jubilee, is the poor Hebrew who has sold himself voluntarily into slavery. This law does not abrogate the earlier laws of the release of the debtor-slave in the seventh year. It is an exten-sion of, or addition to, those laws, applying to a case which had not been dealt with in the legislations of Exodus and Deuteronomy. Although literally the law of the jubilee applies only to cases of self-sale, it may be assumed from the concluding statement in vs. 42: "They [the Hebrews] are my servants, whom I brought forth out of the land of Egypt; they shall not be sold as slaves," that this law of release was meant to embrace all Hebrew slaves, regardless of the cause of their enslavement. If this interpretation is correct, it would include the debtor-slaves who chose to remain in perpetual slavery after the ter-mination of the six-year period. (Cf. Targum Jona-than, where the term לְעֹלָם, "for life," is interpreted to mean until the year of the jubilee; M. Kid. I.2: "He that has his ear bored through is acquired by the act of boring, and regains his freedom at the

year of the jubilee or at the death of his master"; see also Jos. Antiq. IV.viii.28.) Theoretically, the jubilee law, unparalleled in any other slave legislation of the ancient Near East and Greece (*see bibliography*), abolishes the institution of perpetual slavery for all members of the national community. It denies the right of any man to own a Hebrew forever: "For to me the people of Israel are servants, they are my servants whom I brought forth out of the land of Egypt: I am the LORD your God" (Lev. 25:55).

The law of Exod. 21:26-27 presents considerable difficulty of interpretation. The literal meaning of the law is, of course, quite clear. The loss of limb, caused by beatings administered by the master, is considered sufficient ground for the manumission of the slave. The ambiguity arises when we ask for the identity of the slave. Unlike the law of vss. 2-4 of the same chapter, which employs the adjective "He-brew" (עֶבֶד עִבְרִי, "a Hebrew slave"), vss. 26-27 use the general term "slave" (עֶבֶד), without specifying as to whether a non-Hebrew slave, a Hebrew slave, or both are meant. On the basis of the distinction in the text between "Hebrew slave" and "slave," Jewish tradition interprets the law of vss. 26-27 as applying to non-Hebrew slaves only. This view is hardly tenable. If this law is applicable to non-Hebrew slaves only, it would mean that when a master de-liberately maims his Hebrew slave, the deed goes unpunished, while when he maims a non-Hebrew, the latter is to be granted his freedom as a com-pensation for his loss of limb. Some scholars, on the other hand, try to overcome this inconsistency by assuming that vss. 26-27 are a continuation of vss. 2-6, and hence this law would apply to Hebrew slaves only (cf. J. Morgenstern, "The Book of the Covenant," *HUCA,* 7 [1930], 51 ff). However, taking into consideration (*a*) that the same general term "slave" is also used in vss. 20-21, where a severe penalty is prescribed for a master who killed his slave (which could not possibly be interpreted to mean a non-Hebrew slave only), and (*b*) the hu-manitarian spirit of biblical legislation, it would seem that the perplexing problem could be solved by as-suming that "slave" in vss. 20-21, 26-27, refers to any unfree person, Hebrew and non-Hebrew alike. Thus, the Book of the Covenant restricts the power of the master over his slave regardless of nationality and grants the slave legal protection in cases involv-ing loss of limb or death. (The Levitical pronounce-ment in 25:44-46 that, in contradistinction to the Hebrew slave, the non-Hebrew slave is to remain a "perpetual possession," merely indicates that the law of the jubilee does not apply to the latter; it does not imply that the Canaanite slave is to be regarded as a piece of property at the mercy of his Hebrew mas-ter. The Levitical attitude in regard to the foreign slave, therefore, does not contradict the laws of the Book of the Covenant.)

As already mentioned, the most common practice of release in the ancient Near East was manumission by purchase. The Mesopotamian codes, with the exception of the Lipit-Ishtar Law Code (paragraph 14), do not mention this practice, since release by purchase was a private matter between the master and his slave; if an owner was willing to let his slave go, the law did not interfere. That a Palestinian slave could buy his freedom if the master agreed to it is self-evident. Only in one case does the law explicitly demand of a master to let his slave be redeemed. Lev. 25:47-54 provides that if a Hebrew slave owned by a non-Hebrew has the means wherewith to buy his freedom, the master must grant his request; no such demand, however, is made of a Hebrew master (vss. 39-41), although he may have been morally obliged to comply.

The Deuteronomic provision 23:15-16—H 23:16-17, prohibiting the extradition of fugitive slaves, has been considered by some scholars as an unrealistic law reflecting the wishful thinking of reformers. This law (couched in the apodictic form in distinction to the casuistic formulation typical in civil legislation) reads: "You shall not give up to his master a slave who has escaped from his master to you. He shall dwell with you, in your midst, in the place which he shall choose within one of your towns, where it pleases him best; you shall not oppress him." If this law literally applied to any slave who had run away from his master, it certainly was unrealistic, for if put to practical use, it would have resulted in the immediate abolition of slavery. This, however, is not the case. Vs. 16 makes it quite clear that the law has in mind, not a local slave who escaped from one household and entered into another, but a fugitive slave from a foreign country seeking asylum in Palestine. If this is the intent of the law, the Code of Hammurabi and the Middle Assyrian Laws provide indirect precedents for the Deuteronomic provision. Paragraphs 280-81 of the Code of Hammurabi decree that if a merchant buys a Babylonian slave in a foreign country and brings him back to Babylonia (for sale) and his former owner recognizes him, then, if the slave is a native Babylonian, he must be freed without compensation, but if he is of foreign origin, his former master may recompense the merchant and take back his slave. The Middle Assyrian Laws (Tablet C, paragraph 3) prohibit the selling abroad of a pledged free man or woman. These two laws are limited to specific cases and, therefore, are not exactly parallel to the Deuteronomic provision, but they do demonstrate the general tendency of Semitic law to prohibit the sale of natives into a foreign country.

No Canaanite code of laws has as yet been recovered, and we do not know whether restrictions on the sale abroad of native-born people were imposed by local legislation. Among the tablets recently discovered at Alalakh are two treaties which were concluded between Syrian city-state kings. Both treaties contain extradition clauses according to which each party pledges to arrest in his country any fugitive slave from the other party's country and deliver him to his master (cf. D. J. Wiseman, *The Alalakh Tablets*, nos. 2-3). Assuming that these clauses represent the general practice in Syria in the middle of the second millennium B.C. and taking into consideration also the few incidents of extradition of foreign fugitive slaves recorded in the OT (*see* § 4e *above*), we may conclude that Canaanite law did not prohibit the sale abroad of native slaves; and if such slaves managed to return to their country of origin, they were

extradited. In contrast to this Canaanite practice, Deuteronomy demands that a fugitive slave from a foreign country who is a native of Palestine shall not be delivered to his master. The question now arises whether the unqualified term "slave" (עֶבֶד) in the text applies to any native slave or to Hebrews only. The aforementioned Babylonian and Assyrian laws applied to natives only—i.e., to former members of the respective national community. This is also implicit in the Deuteronomic law. 23:16 requires that the fugitive slave shall be accorded the protection of the community in which he chooses to live. This would suggest that the law has in mind a former member of the community—a debtor-slave or a minor who had been sold abroad—namely, a Hebrew. Thus Deuteronomy, for religious and national reasons, opposes the extradition of a Hebrew fugitive slave from a foreign country and demands that the right of asylum and freedom of movement be granted him. (Postbiblical law prohibited the sale of a Hebrew slave abroad, or to a stranger, for the same reason; cf. M. Git. IV.6: "If one sell his [Hebrew] slave to a non-Jew or to anyone outside the land [of Israel], he goes forth a freeman.")

5. State slavery. From time immemorial it was the fate of those who were spared on the battlefield to be reduced to slavery. War captives were the property of the victorious king—i.e., they became state slaves. It was these enslaved war captives who, with the assistance of *corvée* gangs recruited from the ranks of the native population, constructed roads, erected fortresses, built temples, tilled the crown lands, and worked in the royal factories connected with the palace. After the collapse of the Egyptian rule in Palestine and during the subsequent period of the "judges," there was no centralized power in the country, and as a result both the *corvée* and state slavery were nonexistent in Israel. With the emergence, however, of a new centralized power under David and Solomon, the institutions of *corvée* and state slavery were re-established. The main source whence the state slaves were recruited was again, as had been the case before, captives of war. Some of the captives were, in accordance with the usage of the time, presented to the temple as the victorious deity's share of the booty (cf. Num. 31:32-47; Josh. 9:23-27; Ezra 8:20; Ezek. 44:7-9); some were, again in conformity with the practice in the ancient Near East, distributed as gifts to military leaders and state officials in recognition of their services (cf. Deut. 20:10-14; 21:10; Judg. 5:30). The bulk of the captives, however, fell as share to the king—i.e., to the state.

Although the institution of state slavery was introduced after the initial military victories of David, it became an important economic factor only after the conquest of the Arabah. It is a well-established fact that slave labor (excepting household servants) is highly unprofitable unless employed on a large scale in nontechnical production. The natural field for the exploitation of unfree labor is, therefore, on large landed estates and in mining industries. The metallurgical industry in the Arabah presented such an ideal field (cf. N. Glueck, *BASOR,* 79 [1940], 4-5). David, Solomon, and the kings who ruled that region after them, put the state slaves to work in the mines and thus utilized them to considerable advantage.

That the institution of state slavery existed in Palestine from the days of David down to the period of Ezra and Nehemiah is attested by the two technical terms preserved in the OT designating this branch of slavery: the general term עֶבֶד מַס and the specific term עַבְדֵי שְׁלֹמֹה. The first, meaning "total slavery," is applied in I Kings 9:21 to the native Canaanites whom Solomon reduced to slavery, and since the new class of slaves was officially called into existence by Solomon, they were appropriately named "Solomon's slaves" (cf. I Kings 9:27; II Chr. 8:18; 9:10). Once established, this class of state slaves remained in existence, varying in number and economic importance, until the end of the Judean kingdom. Under the new ecclesiastical order created by Nehemiah and Ezra the בְּנֵי עַבְדֵי שְׁלֹמֹה, the "descendants of Solomon's slaves," were merged with the NETHINIM (נְתִינִים), the "temple slaves" (cf. Ezra 2:55-58; Neh. 7:57-60; 11:3). The end of independent statehood marked also the end of state slavery.

6. Temple slavery. Temple slaves were recruited in Mesopotamia from two sources: prisoners of war presented by the kings and dedications made by private individuals. Like the temples in the neighboring countries, the Palestinian sanctuaries also shared in the war booty (שָׁלָל), which included captives. After the successful campaign against the Midianites, Moses is reported to have presented a number of war captives as a gift to the temple (Num. 31:25-47). Joshua is said to have reduced the Gibeonites to "hewers of wood and drawers of water" in the sanctuary (Josh. 9:21-27). On the other hand, there is no evidence of the dedication of slaves to Palestinian sanctuaries by private individuals. The enumeration of monetary values as substitutes for persons or goods vowed to the temple in Lev. 27:2-9 does not mention slaves. The Palestinian temple slaves, the נְתִינִים, are first mentioned in the postexilic period, when they returned from Babylonia with Zerubbabel and Ezra (Ezra 2:43-54; Neh. 7:46-56). Their origin is traced back in Ezra 8:20 to the temple slaves whom "David and his officials had set apart to attend the Levites." (A class of temple servitors by the name of *ytnm* is mentioned in the Ugaritic texts; cf. C. H. Gordon, *Ugaritic Manual,* Text 301:1.) That the Nethinim, though probably not exclusively, were the descendants of war captives and hence non-Hebrews, is also attested by Ezekiel, who complained that uncircumcised foreigners served in the temple (44:7-9). The Nethinim, like the Neo-Babylonian temple slaves, the *širqu* (R. P. Dougherty, *The Shirkûtu of Babylonian Deities*), were housed in separate quarters and worked under the supervision of overseers (cf. Neh. 3:31; 11:21). They could marry outside their own class, but the children born of such marriages were claimed by the temple (cf. M. Kid. III.12).

7. The economic role of slavery. The evidence available to us from Babylonia, Assyria, Syria, and pre-Israelite Palestine (Tell el-Amarna period) indicates clearly that slave labor played a minor role in the fields of agriculture and industry. Unlike Egypt, where, theoretically, the land belonged to the crown, private ownership in land was the rule in the Semitic countries of the ancient Near East. With the

notable exception of the large holdings of the crown and the temples, the overwhelming part of the arable land was in the possession of small holders. These tilled their patches of ground with the assistance of their large families, and there was no pressing need for outside help, in the form of either hired laborers or slaves. Besides, slaves were expensive, and the average farmer could hardly afford to buy one. To be sure, there were large landowners who worked their estates with hired hands. This help, however, was primarily drawn from the ranks of the expropriated peasantry who remained on their ancestral land as dependent sharecroppers or tenants. Slave labor was not a decisive factor in the agricultural life of the ancient Near East, including Palestine.

The counterpart of the freeborn tenant farmer in agriculture was the freeborn artisan in industry. The evidence from Mesopotamia shows that very few slaves engaged in the skilled professions (cf. Mendelsohn, "Free Artisans and Slaves in Mesopotamia," *BASOR,* 89 [1943], 25-29). Palestinian industries (primarily weaving and dyeing, pottery making, and metallurgy) were located in places where the necessary raw material for the given industry was to be found in abundance. The skilled workers in these manufacturing plants were recruited from the free local population. Biblical data shows that some of those artisans even formed their own trade organizations. For details concerning participation of slaves in skilled work and in trade organizations, *see bibliography.*

To sum up: the economy of biblical Palestine (as well as that of ancient Mesopotamia) was based on free labor. The activities of the slave centered mostly in the household of the rich; he was, in the main, a domestic servant rather than an agricultural or industrial worker.

Bibliography. On the sale of children by their parents, cf. (for Babylonia): I. Mendelsohn, *Slavery in the Ancient Near East* (1949), pp. 5-10; A. L. Oppenheim, "Siege-Documents from Nippur," *Iraq,* 17 (1955), 69-89; and (for the Tell el-Amarna period in Syria): J. A. Knudtzon, *Die El-Amarna-Tafeln* (1915), no. 81.

On the Exodus law on the sale of a freeborn girl, see I. Mendelsohn, "The Conditional Sale into Slavery of Free-Born Daughters in Nuzi and the Law of Ex. 21:7-11," *JAOS,* 55 (1935), 190-95.

For cases of self-sale in ancient Egypt, see A. El-M. Bakir, *Slavery in Pharaonic Egypt,* Supplément aux Annales du Service des Antiquités de l'Égypte, no. 18 (1952), pp. 74-76, 81.

To compare the Levitical slave legislation with the slave legislation of other ancient civilizations, see W. L. Westermann, "Upon the Slave Systems of Greek and Roman Antiquity," *EOS Commentarii Societatis Philologae Polonorum,* 48 (1956), 20.

On the participation of slaves in skilled work, see I. Mendelsohn, "Free Artisans and Slaves in Mesopotamia," *BASOR,* 89 (1943), 25-29. On their formation of their own trade organizations, see I. Mendelsohn, "Guilds in Ancient Palestine," *BASOR,* 80 (1940), 17-21.

See further: B. J. Siegel, *Slavery During the Third Dynasty of Ur,* Memoir Series of the American Anthropological Association, no. 66 (1947); M. David, "The Manumission of Slaves Under Zedekiah," *Oudtestamentische Studiën,* 5 (1948), 63-79; I. Mendelsohn, *Slavery in the Ancient Near East* (1949); A. El-M. Bakir, *Slavery in Pharaonic Egypt,* Supplément aux Annales du Service des Antiquités de l'Égypte, no. 18 (1952); I. Mendelsohn, "On Slavery in Alalakh," *IEJ,* 5 (1955), 65-72;

E. Häusler, *Sklaven und Personen minderen Rechts im AT* (1956);
G. Kehnscherper, *Die Stellung der Bibel und der alten christlichen
Kirche zur Sklaverei* (1957).   I. MENDELSOHN

SLAVONIC ACTS OF PETER. *See* PETER,
SLAVONIC ACTS OF.

SLAVONIC VERSIONS slə vŏn′ĭk. One of the
earliest versions of the Bible, still in wide use tòday,
is the Slavonic translation made by the brothers
Cyril and Methodius, in the ninth century. *See*
VERSIONS, MEDIEVAL AND MODERN, § 9.

SLEDGE, THRESHING. An instrument made of
two planks, turned up slightly at the front, with
sharp stones set in holes in the bottom, weighted with

Courtesy of Herbert G. May

67. A Palestinian sledge

stones or the driver, and pulled by animals, to separate grain from straw. *See* THRESHING.

Figs. SLE 67; THR 60.

SLEEVES [פסים; LXX *and* Aq. ποικίλον, variegated
(Gen. 37:3, 23, 32), καρπωτός, reaching to the wrist
(II Sam. 13:18-19); Symm. χειριδωτός, sleeved];
KJV COLOURS. The distinctive feature of the robe
given to Joseph as a mark of his father's favoritism
(Gen. 37:3, etc.) and that worn by Tamar, the daughter of King David (II Sam. 13:18-19). The translation "with sleeves" is supported by the Greek
versions and by the consideration that a long garment with sleeves would indicate wealth and prestige
as over against the short sleeveless garment of the
ordinary person. On the other hand, the explanatory
gloss in the latter passage (vs. 18) may imply some
more unusual feature of dress during the early
monarchy which had become unfamiliar in the
glossator's day.   J. M. MYERS

SLIME [רור (Job 6:6), *cf.* Akkad. *lēru*, spittle; תמם
(Ps. 58:8—H 58:9), *from* מסס, to melt]. This word is
a simile for what is tasteless (Job 6:6), and it is used
to describe the trail left by a snail, in terms of the
snail's dissolving into slime. *See* BITUMEN; PITCH.

SLING [קלע; מרגמה; σφενδόνη]; SLINGSTONES
[אבני קלע, stones of a sling; אבן, stone]; SLINGERS
[קלעים]. The sling was carried by shepherds and warriors for hurling small stones or clay pebbles. It consisted of two narrow strips of leather or woven
textiles joined by a middle part (כף קלע, "hollow of
a sling"; I Sam. 25:29) which was flat and some-

what broader for holding the stone or pebble. One
end was tied to the hand or wrist and the other held
by the hand so that it could be released after being
swung.

The word מרגמה (Prov. 26:8) is a *hapax legomenon*
rendered in the LXX as σφενδόνη (probably correctly). The clause כצרור אבן במרגמה is rendered as
ὅς ἀποδεσμένει λίθον ἐν σφενδόνῃ (i.e., כצרור was
read as כצורר), "like one who binds the stone in the
sling." This was an act of folly, since the stone had
to be placed loosely in the sling to permit its release.

Pliny (Nat. Hist. VII.201 [57]) made the unlikely
suggestion that the sling was invented by the Syro-
phoenicians, whereas it was actually already used in
early times by foreign (Libyan?) soldiers according to
Egyptian reliefs; it was also well known to the Assyrians. The sling was a primitive weapon. At Tell
Hassuna (ca. 4500 B.C.) numerous baked clay pellets
were found which probably served as ammunition
for slings. Slingstones have been found at Tepe
Gawra (ca. 3500 B.C.) and at numerous other sites
in the Near East, as well as in Upper Paleolithic
sites in Europe. Round stone balls in great numbers,
usually identified as slingstones, are found in excavated sites in Palestine and are often two or three
inches in diameter. Figs. SLI 68-69.

Among the Hebrews the sling was used by shepherds (I Sam. 17:40) as well as by professional slingers in the Israelite and Judean armies (II Kings 3:25;
II Chr. 26:14). Smooth, rounded stones were used
as bullets (I Sam. 17:49), being carried in a bag
suspended from the shoulder, or as among the

Courtesy of the American Schools of Oriental Research

68. Above: a "smooth stone" (limestone) from the Valley
of Elah; below: a flint slingstone from the excavations at Tell Beit Mirsim

69. Flint slingstones from Lachish (*ca.* eighth century?)

Romans in the folds of the toga. Great accuracy could be achieved by slingers; in fact, the Benjaminites lefthanded "could sling a stone at a hair, and not miss" (Judg. 20:16; cf. I Chr. 12:2; and τοῖς ἀπὸ Συρίας σφενδονήταις of Jos. War III.vii.18). In describing the impervious Leviathan the poet declares that for him slingstones are turned to stubble (Job 41:28—H 41:20). If the RSV reconstruction of a corrupt passage is correct, Zech. 9:15 represents the Israelites overcoming their foes, devouring and treading down the slingers (perhaps reading בְּנֵי קֶלַע, "sons of a sling," for אַבְנֵי קֶלַע, "stones of a sling").

The Roman Army had slingers only in the *auxilia*, not in the legion itself.

Bibliography. H. Bonnet, *Die Waffen der Völker des alten Orients* (1926), pp. 114 ff. S. M. Cole, "Differentiation of Non-Metallic Tools," in C. Singer *et al., A History of Technology,* vol. I (1954), ch. 18; cf. also ch. 8: "Foraging, Hunting and Fishing." J. W. WEVERS

SLOTHFULNESS, SLUGGARD. The principal Hebrew root underlying these English words is עצל, "neglect," "be sluggish" (cf. Judg. 18:9, where the RSV is more accurate than the KJV), which in one of its forms is often translated "sluggard" in the RSV where the KJV has "slothful" (man; cf. Prov. 15:19; 19:24; 21:25; 22:13; 24:30-34; 26:13-15). The words "sloth," "slothful," "slothfulness," and "sluggard" are found only in the WISDOM literature of the OT and, with but one exception (Eccl. 10:18), in the book of Proverbs alone. "Slothfulness" describes the stupid indolence of the man who takes the course of idleness even when disaster threatens (cf. Prov. 24:30-34). In the thought of the wisdom movement, such a sluggard represents the opposite of the diligent man, who carefully plans his course according to the prudent wisdom of "enlightened self-interest." These opposites constitute one of the contrasting pairs which are used in the teaching of Proverbs to delineate the two ways of life open to every man: the way of wisdom and the way of folly. In Israel this teaching concerning the two paths (*see* PATH; WAY) is developed far more fully than in the corresponding wisdom movements of the ancient Near East— no doubt, under the influence of the Deuteronomic doctrine of retribution (*see* DEUTERONOMY), according to which obedience to divine law ensured prosperity and the good life, while disobedience entailed misfortune in every area of life. Thus in Israel the way of the sluggard and the fool is also the way of the unrighteous, while the way of the diligent and wise is also the way of the upright before God. From this standpoint there are serious theological implications in the sluggard's laziness, even when he is made the butt of raw humor. For this reason there is a somber note, something of the derision of God (cf. Ps. 2:4), in the caricatures of the sluggard: Prov. 10:26; 19:24 (cf. 26:15); 21:25; 22:13 (cf. 26:13); 26:14.

In the NT we find a clear echo of this concept in Matt. 25:26, where the "wicked and slothful servant" appears as the opposite of the ideal "good and faithful servant." In the entire chapter the "two paths" of the wisdom literature are placed in the framework of NT eschatology: the way of foolishness, sloth, and unrighteousness results at the latter day in the bitter laments of the "outer darkness" (vs. 30); while the way of wisdom, diligence, and righteousness results in the joyful participation in the eschatological feast (vs. 10), in the "joy of the master" (vss. 21, 23), and in the "kingdom prepared . . . from the foundation of the world" (vs. 34).

Bibliography. R. H. Pfeiffer, *Introduction to the OT* (1948), pp. 657-58. J. A. WHARTON

SMELL. *See* ODOR.

SMELT [צרף (Isa. 1:25), refine; צוק (Job 28:2), pour out]. The contexts clearly indicate the process of separating a metal from its ore by heat. *See* METALLURGY.

SMITH. *See* METALLURGY.

SMOKE [עשן, קיטור; καπνός]. As a phenomenon accompanying the appearance of God in acts of self-disclosure or in warlike anger, the word appears throughout the OT. The smoke ("like the smoke of a kiln") and FIRE that characterize the THEOPHANY on Mount Sinai, together with the quaking of the mountain, have caused exegetes to think of volcanic phenomena (Exod. 19:18; 20:18; cf. also Gen. 15:17 for an obscure but provocative parallel). In stylized form, the smoke and fire of Sinai becomes a stereotype of the presence of God in his GLORY (Isa. 4:5; 6:4; cf. Rev. 15:8).

In different contexts, smoke derives from the fire of God's anger, breaking forth in WRATH against his enemies (Deut. 29:20; Ps. 18:8; Isa. 30:27; cf. the smoke of cities and lands destroyed by God's judgment in Gen. 19:28; Isa. 34:10; Rev. 18:9, 18; 19:3).

The smoke of SACRIFICES AND OFFERINGS and of INCENSE is referred to in Ps. 66:15; Ezek. 8:11 (contrast Rev. 8:4). As a figure of that which is ephemeral, "smoke" appears in Ps. 37:20; 68:2; 102:3; Isa. 51:6; Hos. 13:3 (cf. other figurative uses in Ps. 119:83; Prov. 10:26; Song of S. 3:6; cf. apocalyptic imagery in Joel 2:30; Acts 2:19; Rev. 9:2-3, 17-18; 14:11). J. A. WHARTON

SMYRNA smûr′nə [Σμύρνα, Ζμύρνα]. A large and important city on the W coast of Asia Minor; the modern Izmir. It was in NT times, and has remained to this day, one of the largest and busiest commercial centers of the entire region of Asia Minor and the Aegean Sea. The city lay at the E end of a long, narrow gulf. The original city was a colony of Aeolian Greeks, but was soon taken over by Ionian Greeks and became part of the Ionian League. It lay two or three miles NE of the later site. King Alyattes

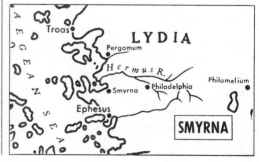

of Lydia destroyed the old city in the early sixth century B.C., and for several centuries there was only a group of villages at and near the site. At the end of the fourth and beginning of the third century B.C., Antigonus and Lysimachus refounded and fortified the city on its present site. It had a small landlocked harbor, as well as a spacious mooring area in the gulf. Its importance was due not only to its port facilities but also to the fact that the region around it was fertile and productive and that it was the terminal point of a key road that ran eastward up the Hermus Valley and through central Asia Minor. Its prosperity suffered at times, however, from earthquakes.

As early as 195 B.C., Smyrna put itself on the side of the Romans and built a temple for the cult of the city of Rome. Smyrna never wavered from her loyalty to Rome, and Rome protected and rewarded the city (except when one of Julius Caesar's murderers, Trebonius, took refuge there and Dolabella took the city and executed Trebonius). When the province of Asia, in 23 B.C., was given permission to build a temple to the Emperor Tiberius and eleven cities contended for the privilege, the Roman Senate decided in favor of Smyrna in view of its long loyalty and many services to Rome (Tac. Ann. IV.55-56). It vied with Ephesus and Pergamum for the title of first city of Asia. Strabo calls it the "most beautiful of all" the cities, and tells of its excellent city plan, its paved streets, and noteworthy public buildings, including the Homereium, for Smyrna was one of the cities which claimed to be the birthplace of Homer; however, Strabo notes the lack of proper drainage for the city's well-paved streets (*Geography* XIV.1.37).

The religious life of Smyrna included a variety of cults. The city took pride in the imperial cult. There was also the cult of the "mother of Sipylus," a form of Cybele-worship. Reverent honor was paid to Homer; this implied acceptance of the Homeric pantheon. The city was the home of a considerable number of Jews, who showed aggressive hostility toward the Christians.

How or when Christianity first came to Smyrna we cannot say. Our first information comes from the book of Revelation; Smyrna is one of the seven churches addressed (1:11; 2:8-11), and it and Philadelphia are the two churches which receive unqualified praise. The church at Smyrna was not outwardly wealthy; it was undergoing tribulation; a limited period of intense persecution (symbolized by "ten days") lay just ahead, and prison was to be the lot of some of the Christians; the slanders of the Jews, whose hostility to the church deprived them of all right to call themselves true Jews or their assemblies a true synagogue, seem to have been prominently involved in this satanic attack; but all Christians who proved faithful in this severe test would receive the "crown of life" and deliverance in the final judgment. Attempts have been made to connect phrases in this passage of Revelation with aspects of the life of Smyrna: Christ "the first" speaks to the church of the city which eagerly claimed to be "first of all"; Christ "who died and came to life" speaks to the city which was destroyed by Alyattes and refounded

under Antigonus and Lysimachus; the church in the city which had been steadfastly loyal to Rome is warned to "be faithful unto death," if need be, in its loyalty to Christ; the church in the city which was pulsing with life in its trade and civic activity is reminded that the "crown of life," true and eternal life, can come only from Him who died and is "alive for evermore" and has the "keys of Death and Hades" (1:18).

When Ignatius, bishop of Antioch in Syria, was being taken to Rome for martyrdom *ca.* the second decade of the second century A.D., he conferred with Christian leaders on his journey through Asia Minor, and later wrote letters to some of the churches there. Of the seven letters (including one to the church at Rome), four were written during Ignatius' stop at Smyrna; of the other three, written at Troas, two went to Smyrna, one to the whole congregation and one to the bishop Polycarp. They make clear the developed organization of the church at Smyrna; it had a bishop, a body of elders, and a body of deacons (Ign. Smyr. 12:2). They indicate, however, that a docetic tendency was strong in the Smyrnean church, and those of that docetic viewpoint rejected the leadership of the bishop, absented themselves from the Eucharist and common prayer, and were lacking in practical kindness to Christians in need.

Some forty years later, *ca.* A.D. 156, this same Polycarp, then at least eighty-six years old, was burned alive as the "twelfth martyr in Smyrna," after he had confessed being a Christian and refused the proconsul's appeal that he renounce his faith. The Jews again were prominent in the persecution, and although the day was a sabbath, they were active not only in the clamor for condemnation but

Courtesy of F. K. Doerner

70. View of Smyrna (modern Izmir) and the harbor

Courtesy of Ahmet Dönmez

71. Ancient Smyrna with aqueduct in the foreground and Mount Pagus in the distance

also in gathering wood for the fire. The Martyrdom of Polycarp, written soon after the event in the form of a letter from the church of Smyrna to the church of Philomelium, tells this story and is the first detailed account of a Christian martyrdom after that of Stephen (Acts 6:8-8:3).

Figs. SMY 70-71.

Bibliography. W. M. Ramsay, *The Letters to the Seven Churches of Asia* (no date), chs. 19-20; C. J. Cadoux, *Ancient Smyrna: A History of the City From the Earliest Times to 324 A.D.* (1938).

F. V. FILSON

SNAIL [שבלול, *possibly* moistener (*from* slimy trail); *cf.* Arab. *balla,* to moisten; KJV חמט (Lev. 11:30; RSV SAND LIZARD)]. Any of a group of mollusks of the family Helicidae, with and without external shells.

The meaning of שבלול (*shabbᵉlûl*) in Ps. 58:8—H 58:9 is obscure. The Jewish tradition has taken it to be "snail, slug" (which receives some support from the Arabic cited above); Jerome takes it as *vermis,* "worm," but the LXX, the Vulg., and the Peshitta interpret it as "wax." *See bibliography.*

See also FAUNA § G1.

Bibliography. On snails in Palestine, see Tristram, *NHB* (1867), pp. 295-97. On the meaning of שבלול, G. R. Driver, *JTS,* 34 (1933), 41-43, argues for an "efflux" (an early miscarriage); this is followed by Koehler, *Lexicon,* p. 942.

W. S. McCULLOUGH

SNAKE CHARMING. Serpents abound in Palestine, and the art of snake charming was known in the country (cf. Eccl. 10:11; Isa. 3:3; Ecclus. 12:13). The technical term employed for this activity was לחש, "to whisper, to charm." In two instances "snake charming" is used in biblical literature metaphorically: (*a*) to depict enemies, who are "serpents, and adders which cannot be charmed" (Jer. 8:17); and (*b*) to describe sinners, who are

like the deaf adder that stops its ear,
so that it does not hear the voice of charmers [מלחשים]
(Ps. 58:4-5—H 58:5-6).

I. MENDELSOHN

SNARE. *See* TRAPS AND SNARES; HUNTING.

SNOW [שלג; χιών]; FROST [קרח, *alternately* ICE; חנמל, *alternately* HAIL; כפור; קישור, HOARFROST]. Snow is relatively rare in Palestine, which is on the margin of the subtropical climatic zone. It falls in the hills on an average of three days annually, and sometimes there is a heavy fall (II Sam. 23:20; I Macc. 13:22). The snow cap on Mount Hermon (cf. Jer. 18:14), however, is visible from many parts of the land, and snow in the Bible is proverbial for its whiteness (Exod. 4:6; Num. 12:10; Ps. 51:7—H 51:9; Isa. 1:18; Rev. 1:14), for its cleanness (Job 9:30), for its beauty (Ecclus. 43:18), and, in the heat of harvest, for its refreshing coolness (with food or drink [?]; Prov. 25:13). Job speculates on the storehouses in the sky from which snow comes (Job 38:22; Ps. 147: 16). For its use in simile, see Prov. 25:13; etc.

The word קרח means either "frost, extreme cold" (Gen. 31:40; Jer. 36:30), or "ice" (Job 6:16; 37:10; 38:29; Ps. 147:17). In Job 37:10 water is said to harden like cast metal under the cold wind, which is God's breath (cf. Job 38:30; Ecclus. 43:20). The

"morsels" of ice in Ps. 147:17 would be hail. חנמל, "frost" (Ps. 78:47), more probably refers to severe hail or large hailstones (cf. Exod. 9:24-25). On the other hand, "frost" in Ps. 148:8 (קישור) resembles smoke and is associated with snow; it may mean "snow squall." "Hoarfrost" (כפור) is frozen dew (Exod. 16:14; Ps. 147:16; Ecclus. 43:19); and, like dew, it was believed to fall imperceptibly from the sky (Job 38:29).

See also PALESTINE, CLIMATE OF; SUMMER AND WINTER; HEAT AND COLD; HAIL; DEW.

Bibliography. D. Ashbel, *Introduction to Meteorology* (in Hebrew; 1940), pp. 246, 268; D. Baly, *The Geography of Palestine* (1957), pp. 50-52.

R. B. Y. SCOTT

SNUFFDISHES. KJV translation of מחתה (RSV "trays") in Exod. 25:38; 37:23; Num. 4:9. *See* SNUFFERS.

SNUFFERS [מזמרות, מלקחים]. Implements used in tending the lamps in the tabernacle and the temple. Though more often described as made of gold, they were more likely of bronze, as stated in II Kings 25:14=Jer. 52:18.

The use in I Kings 7:49-50=II Chr. 4:21-22 of both מזמרות ("snuffers") and מלקחים ("tongs") suggests that the words refer to two different instruments. The derivation of מזמרות from זמר, "to prune," points to some sort of scissors or similar cutting instrument, used for trimming the wicks of the lamps (II Kings 12:13; 25:14=Jer. 52:18). The derivation of מלקחים from לקח, "to take, grasp, seize," as well as the fact that its form is a dual, implying a thing consisting of two parts, indicates the meaning "tongs." This is borne out by the description in Isa. 6:6, where one of the seraphim uses "tongs" to take a burning coal from the altar. In Exod. 25:38; 37:23; Num. 4:9 "snuffers" (מלקחים; KJV "tongs" in Exod. 25:38; Num. 4:9) and "trays" (KJV "snuffdishes"; elsewhere "firepans" or "censers") are mentioned together as part of the equipment of the golden lampstand of the tabernacle. It may be inferred that they were used to remove and dispose of the burned portions of the wicks.

J. L. MIHELIC

SO sō [סוא; LXX Σηγωρ, Σωα, Σοβα] (II Kings 17:4). A "king of Egypt" *ca.* 725 B.C., who persuaded Hoshea of Israel to stop paying tribute to Shalmaneser of Assyria.

No known pharaoh of the time can be fitted to the name. However, the Assyrian annals about this time mention an Egyptian general in Asia by the name of Sib'e, and the Hebrew consonants could be differently pointed and read "Sive." If so, this Sive may have been commander for one of the many small dynasts in the Egyptian Delta, before that region was united by Ethiopian conquest a few years later.

Bibliography. J. B. Pritchard, ed., *ANET* (2nd ed., 1955), p. 285, with note 3. For the traditional view that this was the Ethiopian king Shabako, see M. F. L. Macadam, *The Temples of Kawa,* vol. I (1949), p. 124 (note 1), p. 132.

J. A. WILSON

SOAP [ברית; ברר, purify]; KJV SOPE. Cleansing substance obtained by decomposing oil, probably olive oil, with an alkali gotten by burning certain saliferous plants (e.g., *Salsala kali*). The two appearances of "soap" suggest that it was used for washing both the body (Jer. 2:22) and clothes (Mal. 3:2).

The infrequent use of terms which can confidently be translated as "soap" or a synonym reflects the fact that the ancients used other means of cleansing. The body was covered with oil and scraped or rubbed. Fabrics were cleaned either through the use of wood ashes or more often, as today in the Near East, by being pounded on stones while wet. Utensils were rubbed with LYE.   H. N. RICHARDSON

SOCKET [פֹת (KJV HINGE); KJV אֶדֶן (RSV BASE)]. Ancient doors and gates generally swung on pivots set in stone sockets, many of which have been

Courtesy of the Oriental Institute, the University of Chicago

72. An inscribed stone socket in which a door was pivoted, from Tell Asmar

found in excavations. Some sockets may have been of metal (I Kings 7:50; II Chr. 4:22).

See also ARCHITECTURE; DOOR; GATE.

Fig. SOC 72.   O. R. SELLERS

SOCO sō'kō [שׂוֹכוֹ, thorny place(?)] (I Chr. 4:18; II Chr. 11:7; 28:18); SOCOH [שׂוֹכֹה, שֹׂכֹה] (Josh. 15: 35, 48; I Sam. 17:1; I Kings 4:10); KJV SOCOH, SOCHO, SOCHOH sō'kō, SHOCHO, SHOCHOH, SHOCO shō'kō. **1.** A town in the SHEPHELAH between Adullam and Azekah (Josh. 15:35). When the Philistines, with Goliath, were preparing to attack, they took over Soco, and then encamped at Ephes-dammim, between Soco and Azekah (I Sam. 17:1). Rehoboam repossessed and fortified Soco (II Chr. 11:7). In the reign of Ahaz it was again taken over by the Philistines (II Chr. 28:18). The name was still known to Eusebius, Jerome, and the writers of the Talmud, and, in fact, has been preserved to modern times in Khirbet Shuweikeh, a site on the Wadi es-Sant (ancient Valley of ELAH). However, though Shuweikeh preserves the ancient name (in the diminutive form), the actual site is probably Khirbet 'Abbad, a short distance to the W, since pottery of biblical times has been found only at the latter site. One of the four royal potteries producing a standard-size jar (two baths) in the later Judean Monarchy was at Soco. *See* WEIGHTS AND MEASURES § C4e; POTTERY § 3.

2. A town in the S hill country of Judah, near Debir and Eshtemoh (Josh. 15:48). It is to be identi-

fied with another Khirbet Shuweikeh, some ten miles SW of Hebron, a little E of modern Dahariyeh.

3. A place in the third district of Solomon, under the administration of BEN-HESED (I Kings 4:10). This is probably the same as No. 67 in the great topographical list of Thut-mose III (*see* EGYPT) and No. 38 of SHISHAK. It has been identified with Tell er-Ras, near a third Shuweikeh, some ten miles NW of Samaria, just N of modern Tul-Karem.

4. Soco occurs in I Chr. 4:18 seemingly as a personal name, in a genealogy of the "sons of Judah." However, some of the names in the context are likewise place names in S Judah—e.g., Eshtemoh (Eshtemoa), Gedor, and Zanoah—found also in the context of Josh. 15:48. It is possible, therefore, that the origin of the name in I Chr. 4:18 is from the town in S Judah (*see* 2 above).   W. F. STINESPRING

SODERING. KJV form of SOLDERING.

SODI sō'dī [סוֹדִי, (one familiar with the) counsel of Y(?)] (Num. 13:10). The father of Gaddiel, who was sent from the tribe of Zebulun to spy out the land of Canaan.

Bibliography. M. Noth, *Die israelitischen Personennamen* (1928), p. 152.   R. F. JOHNSON

SODOM sŏd'əm [סְדֹם; Σόδομα]. One of the "cities of the valley." It is the most often mentioned of the five cities—thirty-six times in all, alone sixteen times. Sodom is the wicked city par excellence, and its destruction, along with that of GOMORRAH, is often held out as a warning of the punishment which the Lord will bring upon those who neglect or sin against God.

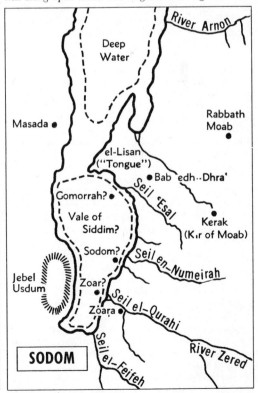

SODOM

The S boundary of the Canaanites ran from Gaza to Sodom, Gomorrah, Admah, and Zeboiim (Gen. 10:19), and this may indicate the topographical order of these cities from S to N. Lot, looking toward the Jordan–Dead Sea Valley, chose this region and moved his tent as far as Sodom (13:10-12).

CHEDORLAOMER, along with the three other eastern kings, made war on Bera king of Sodom and on the kings of the other four cities of the valley (Gen. 14: 2). Fourteen years later, the four eastern kings returned and put down the rebellion of the five cities and, after a raid to the S, returned and fought with the same five kings (vs. 8) in the Valley of SIDDIM. Those of the forces of Sodom and Gomorrah who did not fall into the pits of bitumen in this valley were driven into the mountains. It was on this occasion that Lot was captured, to be rescued subsequently by Abram (vss. 12-16).

So great was the sin of Sodom and Gomorrah that the Lord was determined to destroy them, especially after Abram could not find even ten righteous persons in Sodom (Gen. 18:20-33).

The two angels, who had gone from Abraham to Sodom, found Lot sitting in the gate of Sodom (Gen. 19:1). They revealed to him the Lord's intention to destroy the city. The next morning they induced Lot, his wife, and their two daughters to flee from Sodom to the hills. Lot begged that he be allowed to go to ZOAR and there be spared, and his plea was granted (vss. 12-23).

"Then the LORD rained on Sodom and Gomorrah brimstone and fire from the LORD out of heaven; and he overthrew those cities, and all the valley, and all the inhabitants of the cities, and what grew on the ground." (Gen. 19:24-25.) The next morning, from near Hebron, Abraham saw the smoke from the destroyed cities of the valley arising "like the smoke of a furnace" (vs. 28).

1. Location. No traces of the cities of the valley have been found, but the sites may with great probability be located in the area now submerged under the waters of the S part of the Dead Sea. Here, S of the peninsula el-Lisan ("the Tongue"), was doubtless the Valley of Siddim, which originally had been a fertile plain, well watered by the five streams, prolonged westward, which today flow from the E and the SE into this part of the Dead Sea.

It is implied in Gen. 14:3—"the Valley of Siddim (that is, the Salt Sea)"—that this valley came to be submerged under the surface of the Dead Sea. The parenthesis seems to have been added centuries later, after this part of the valley had become inundated.

Other evidence points to the location of Sodom and the other cities under what is now the S part of the Dead Sea. Jebel Usdum, a mountain *ca.* 5 miles long and over 700 feet high, largely a mass of crystalline salt, is situated along the S end of the W side of the Dead Sea. Its Arabic name, meaning "Mount of Sodom," may preserve the name of the ill-famed city, and this in turn may further suggest that Sodom lay near the S end of this valley.

The erosion of this salt mountain over the centuries has caused pinnacles to stand out, which ancient and modern writers have likened to Lot's wife. The myth of Lot's wife's being transformed into a "pillar of salt" (Gen. 19:26) may not only have arisen

Courtesy of the American Schools of Oriental Research

73. Pillar of salt on Jebel Usdum

to explain a natural formation resembling a human figure, but may indicate that Sodom was situated near this mountain of salt (Fig. SOD 73). Perhaps Sodom might be located on the (westward prolongation of the) stream, Seil en-Numeirah.

Further evidence of this location of the cities of the valley is provided by the site of Bab edh-Dhra', which apparently had been a pilgrimage place. It is situated *ca.* 5 miles from, and *ca.* 500 feet above, the shore of the Dead Sea, SE of el-Lisan. Since no traces of habitation have been found elsewhere in this region, we must conclude that the homes of these pilgrims who frequented Bab edh-Dhra' must have come from this area, once the Valley of Siddim. The fertile fields around the mouths of the streams which flow into this SE part of the Dead Sea suggest that the ancient Valley of Siddim had been even more fertile.

There are many reasons for believing that this submerged area had once been an inhabited plain. The maximal depth of the water in this S embayment is *ca.* 18 feet, whereas N of the peninsula of el-Lisan a depth of over 1,200 feet has been ascertained by soundings.

Sometime in our era some natural force, perhaps an earthquake, caused the water of the N part of the Dead Sea to flow over into the plain to the S, the Valley of Siddim. Then, too, evaporation has not kept pace with the inflow of the water of the Jordan. It is estimated that the rise of the water level of the Dead Sea amounts to *ca.* three inches annually.

2. Destruction. The manner of destruction of the cities of the valley is suggested by the accounts of ancient writers, and modern investigations furnish credence to their reports. That fire played a major part in the catastrophe is indicated by the biblical account (Gen. 19:24-28) and by the remarks of Strabo, Diodorus, Josephus, and Tacitus. Brimstone (sulphur) can hardly have played any appreciable part in this catastrophe. Rather, seepages of bitumen (or asphalt), petroleum, and the accompanying gases emanating therefrom may well have caused a great explosion and conflagration. The ancients were unacquainted with the properties of gases, but certainly the presence of gas must be indicated by the ancient writers in their mention of the soot which tarnishes, the deleterious atmosphere which withers plants, and the ill-smelling odors, all emanating from this Dead Sea region.

Investigations conducted by geologists for oil companies have revealed abundant traces of petroleum (as well as of gas and exudations of bitumen) in the area around Jebel Usdum.

Noteworthy is the statement in Gen. 19:28 that Abraham, looking from near Hebron toward Sodom and Gomorrah, saw that "the smoke of the land went up like the smoke of a furnace." For it to be seen from a distance, a heavy, black smoke seems indicated; and, with the ancient comments in mind, one may well associate the phenomenon with oil.

Thus it seems possible, even probable, that the destruction of Sodom and the other cities of the valley was brought about by a great conflagration caused by the ignition of petroleum seepages and accompanying gas. This may have been started by a stroke of lightning, which might be associated with the phrase "from the LORD out of heaven" (Gen. 19:24).

The approximate date of the catastrophe may be conjectured from the evidence afforded by the pottery found at Bab edh-Dhra'. This festival site seems to have been frequented from *ca.* 2300 to *ca.* 1900 B.C. The cessation of visits to this site may coincide with the destruction of Sodom and the other cities of the valley, whence came the "pilgrims" to this site. And the corollary would be that here also we would have evidence that Abraham was living *ca.* 1900 B.C., or *ca.* the end of the twentieth century B.C.

According to Stephanos of Byzantion (seventh century A.D.), among the bishops present at the Council of Nicaea in A.D. 325, there was a Severos, Bishop of Sodom. A strange title for a bishop! Could a Sodom have been rebuilt on the W shore of the Dead Sea? The same authority locates Engaddi (En-gedi) near "Sodom of Arabia." By A.D. 381, it is a Bishop of Zoar who appears to represent this region.

The modern state of Israel founded a town named Sodom just N of Jebel Usdum. Near here, in 1953, Israel's first oil well went into operation. So the association of Sodom with oil may be traced back over a period of four thousand years.

Bibliography. W. F. Albright, *BASOR,* 14 (1924), 5-7; *AASOR,* VI (1924-25), 58-62; M. G. Kyle, *Explorations in Sodom* (1928); F. G. Clapp, "The Site of Sodom and Gomorrah," *AJA* (1936), 323-44; "Geology and Bitumens of the Dead Sea Area," *Bulletin of the American Association of Petroleum Geologists* (1936), pp. 881-909; G. E. Wright, *The Pottery of Palestine* (1937), pp. 78 ff; "The Chronology of Palestine Pottery in Middle Bronze Age I," *BASOR,* 71 (1938), 27-34; F.-M. Abel, *Géographie de la Palestine,* II (1938), 467-68. N. Glueck, *AASOR,* XV (1934-35); XVIII-XIX (1937-39). J. P. Harland, "Sodom and Gomorrah: The Location and Destruction of the Cities of the Plain," *BA,* V (1942), 17-32; VI (1943), 41-54.   J. P. HARLAND

SODOM, SEA OF [*Mare Sodomiticum*]; KJV **SODOMITISH SEA** sŏd'ə mī'tĭsh. The name employed in II Esd. 5:7 for the lake called in the OT the Salt Sea and now commonly known as the DEAD SEA. The name "Sea of Sodom" is derived from the prominence of the metropolis of Sodom, which was situated near the lake's S shores.   W. H. MORTON

SODOM, VINE OF. *See* VINE OF SODOM.

SODOMITE sŏd'ə mīt. An English common noun, derived from the story of SODOM in Gen. 18-19, meaning a male person who engages in sexual relations with another male. The men of Sodom demanded that Lot surrender his two male guests (angels) to them for sexual purposes: "Bring them out to us, that we may know them" (Gen. 19:5; for the meaning of "know," *see* SEX). The wickedness of Sodom became proverbial (Isa. 3:9; Lam. 4:6; II Pet. 2:7-10; Jude 7). *See* HOMOSEXUALITY; PROSTITUTION § 3*b.*   O. J. BAAB

SOJOURNER [גֵּר, *see* GER; תּוֹשָׁב, from יָשַׁב, dwell; LXX πάροικος, *later* προσήλυτος]. A person living in mutually responsible association with a community, or in a place, not inherently his own.

The technical term in Hebrew is גֵּר, which is translated "sojourner" or "stranger" (Exod. 22:21; 23:9; Lev. 23:22), as in the case where the noun and a verbal form appear ("the stranger [גֵּר] who sojourns [הַגָּר] among you"; Exod. 12:49 P; cf. vs. 48; Lev. 19:33-34; etc.), or "alien" (Exod. 23:12; Deut. 1:16; 14:21; Jer. 22:3; Ezek. 47:21-23; etc.; *see* STRANGER; ALIEN). The term תּוֹשָׁב appears in H and P (I Chr. 29:15; Ps. 39:12), usually along with גֵּר (Lev. 25:47, etc.; Num. 35:15; I Chr. 29:15; Ps. 39:12). The LXX usually translates both גֵּר and תּוֹשָׁב by πάροικος, and in late texts frequently uses προσήλυτος. In the NT, παρῴκησεν is translated "he sojourned" (Heb. 11:9); πάροικον, "aliens" (Acts 7:6); ξένοι καὶ πάροικοι, "strangers and sojourners" (Eph. 2:19); παροίκους καὶ παρεπιδήμους, "aliens and exiles" (I Pet. 2:11).

In the basic meaning of the term, a sojourner is a person who occupies a position between that of the native-born and the foreigner. He has come among a people distinct from him and thus lacks the protection and benefits ordinarily provided by kin and birthplace. His status and privileges derive from the bond of hospitality, in which the guest is inviolable. The *ger* is everyone who comes traveling and, settling in a strange place for a shorter or longer period, has claims to protection and full sustenance (cf. Gen. 18: 1-8; 24; Judg. 19:16-21; Job 31:32). Placing himself under the protection of a particular clan or chieftain, or a person, the sojourner in turn assumes responsibilities. Abraham sojourned in Egypt (Gen. 12:10 J), and in Gerar in a relationship of loyalty to the chieftain Abimelech (20:1 E; 21:23 JE); as "a stranger and a sojourner" (גֵּר־וְתוֹשָׁב) among the Hittites he had no right to own land but asked for this right so that he might bury Sarah (23:4 P; cf. Heb. 11:9). Lot as a sojourner had no right to stand against the practices of the men of Sodom (Gen. 19:9 J). After going to Abimelech, Isaac became a sojourner there and Abimelech protected Isaac and his wife from maltreatment at the hands of the Philistines (26:1-11 J). Jacob was a sojourner with Laban (32:4 J) and claimed maltreatment (31:3-7 E). Esau and Jacob sojourned in the land of Canaan and so increased in property and flocks that Esau moved to Seir (36:6-8

P). The covenantal promise to Abraham (17:7-8 P), reiterated in Isaac's blessing upon Jacob (28:1-4 P) and in God's disclosure to Moses (Exod. 6:4 P), was that he would give to Abraham's descendants "the land of Canaan, the land in which they dwelt as sojourners" (cf. Ps. 105:6-15 = I Chr. 16:13-22). When the brothers of Joseph told Pharaoh that they had come to sojourn in Egypt, he granted their petition to dwell in the land of Goshen and asked them to supply him with overseers of his cattle (Gen. 47:1-6 J). Israel sojourned in Egypt (Isa. 52:4) and was oppressed (Gen. 15:13 J; Deut. 26:5-11; Ps. 105:23-25; Acts 7:6). According to popular etymology the name of Moses' son is interpreted as though it were Gersham—i.e., "sojourner there" (Exod. 2:22 J). A man from the hill country of Ephraim sojourned in Gibeah (Judg. 19:16). David as a sojourner made the interests of his Philistine patron Achish, king of Gath, his own (I Sam. 27:2-3, 12; 28:1 ff). The man who claimed he had dispatched Saul said: "I am the son of a sojourner, an Amalekite" (II Sam. 1:13). Elijah sojourned with a widow in Zarephath who acted for his welfare and he pleaded with God for hers (I Kings 17:20). The exiles in Babylon who had acquired wealth and position are referred to in Cyrus' decree as sojourners (Ezra 1:4). The worshiper in the temple is God's personal guest who receives divine protection and must do God's will (Ps. 15:1). Some of the reasons for a person's or group's becoming sojourners may be cited: to escape famine (Ruth 1:1; II Kings 8:1) or military attack (II Sam. 4:3); to find sanctuary after a land has been destroyed by conquest (Isa. 16:4); to be in Jerusalem for celebration of the Feast of Weeks (II Chr. 15:9); to maintain the nomadic ideal, the Rechabites dwelt as sojourners in Judah (Jer. 35:7); a Levite might settle down as a sojourner wherever he found a place or a person or group where he could perform his function (Judg. 17-18; 19:1; cf. Deut. 12:12; 16:11, 14; etc.). The basic meaning of גר, "sojourner," cited in the above passages, underlies Acts 7:6; Eph. 2:19; Heb. 11:9; I Pet. 2:11.

The above instances show that the root meaning of "sojourner" is especially evident in early texts, and that this basic meaning persists in the later stages of biblical history and literature. Two further connotations developed in the Covenant Code and D, and in the postexilic period.

In the Covenant Code (Exod. 20:22–23:33) and preceding decalogue (20:1-17) and D, *ger* ("sojourner," "stranger") designates, not the immigrant Hebrew, but the indigenous population of Palestine conquered by the Hebrews. The popular conception that close connection exists between a land and its tutelary deity, a connection which demands that whoever settles in a land must serve the national deity, had not been followed in the cosmopolitan syncretism prevailing in Israel before the Deuteronomic reformation (cf. I Kings 11:7-8; 16:31-33; 20:34). A check on syncretism, the Deuteronomic reformation renewed the popular conception just cited at the same time that it was primarily an attempt to make Israel's heritage with Yahweh the structure and content of life in Israel.

Three perspectives informed the laws concerning the sojourner: (*a*) Israel is to remember that once she was a sojourner in Egypt and that God saw her oppression, delivered her, and established her in a bounteous land (Exod. 22:21; Deut. 5:14-15; 10:17-22; 16:10-12; 23:7; 24:14-22; 26:5-11).

b) The God who saved Israel from bondage is the protector of the poor and weak and disinherited; the purpose of Israel's economy is to supply need, and special attention must be given to the welfare of those who need help. "You shall not oppress a stranger [*ger*]; you know the heart of a stranger, for you were strangers in the land of Egypt" (Exod. 23:9). "For the LORD your God . . . is not partial and takes no bribe. He executes justice for the fatherless and the widow, and loves the sojourner, giving him food and clothing. Love the sojourner therefore; for you were sojourners in the land of Egypt" (Deut. 10:17-19; cf. Exod. 22:21-24; Deut. 14:28-29; 24:14-22; see also Pss. 94:6; 146:9; Jer. 22:3; Zech. 7:10; Mal. 3:5).

c) The covenant between God and Israel depends upon the participation of all members of the community in its requirements and benefits; Israel is a holy people, the land is not to be defiled (Deut. 21:23), and the sojourner must conform as far as possible to the covenant regulations. "You shall rejoice in all the good which the LORD your God has given to you and to your house, you, and the Levite, and the stranger who is among you" (Deut. 26:11; cf. vss. 12-15; 29:10-13; Exod. 22:21-24). The sojourner is subordinate, dependent upon Israel's charity and forbearance; his position of inferiority is indicated: by the personal pronominal suffix "your" (of you) attached to גר (Exod. 20:10; Deut. 1:16; 5:14; 29:11), by the fact that he is classed with those occupying a position of dependence like the fatherless and the widow (24:17-22), he can eat the flesh of an animal that has died a natural death, forbidden to the Israelites (14:21), the *gerim* are called wood-gatherers and drawers of water for the Israelites (29:11). At the same time he is almost an Israelite (cf. 23:7-8); he participates in the assembly (29:10-13; Josh. 8:30-35); he is entitled to the benefit of the tithe (Deut. 14:28-29); he is to be judged the same way as an Israelite (1:16); he is entitled to equal justice (24:14); he is expected to keep the law and observe festivals along with the native Israelites, joining in the celebration of the sabbath, the festival of deliverance in the D decalogue (5:14-15), the Feast of Weeks (16:10-12), Tabernacles (16:13-14), the offering of first fruits (26:11).

In the postexilic period the trend in the D perspective (*c*) cited above is extended. Deutero-Isaiah takes up the promise to Abraham ("By you all the families of the earth will bless themselves"; Gen. 12:3*b* J) and sets forth the universal scope of Yahweh and Israel:

> This one will say, "I am the LORD's,"
> another will call himself by the name of Jacob,
> and another will write on his hand, "The LORD's,"
> and surname himself by the name of Israel
> (Isa. 44:5; cf. 42:1-4; 49:6; 55:4-5).

Also accentuating the D perspective (*c*) were the drastic reforms of Ezra and Nehemiah, which excluded from the community all who would not conform. In postexilic writings, *ger* ("sojourner," "stranger," "alien") designates a naturalized alien, a proselyte (in the Holiness Code and P, the LXX translates *ger* by προσήλυτος; cf. Aramaic גיור, "proselyte"; in the Mishna *ger* denotes one who has become incorporated into the covenant people by circumcision and adoption of Israel's laws, and the verb נתגיר means "to become a convert"). The PROSELYTE is as much a member of the community of Israel as the native-born. Again and again it is reiterated that there is one law for the native-born and the proselyte: "For the assembly [קהל], there shall be one statute for you and for the stranger [גר] who sojourns [הגר] with you, a perpetual statute throughout your generations; as you are, so shall the sojourner [גר] be before the LORD. One law and one ordinance shall be for you and for the stranger who sojourns with you" (Num. 15:15-16; cf. 9:14; Exod. 12:49; Lev. 17:15; 24:16, 22; etc.). For the proselyte equally as for the native-born, Israel was "his people" (Lev. 17:8-9). A sojourner is to show the same fidelity to Yahweh as an Israelite (Lev. 20:2; Ezek. 14:7). He has the same rights (Num. 35:15; Ezek. 47:21-23), and is bound by the same laws, whether civil (Lev. 24:13-22), moral and religious (18:26; 20:2; 24:16), or ceremonial (Exod. 12:19; Lev. 16:29; 17:8-15; 22:18; Num. 15:14, 26, 30; 19:10). Certain distinctions do persist: if he would keep the Passover, he must be circumcised (Exod. 12:48); a Hebrew sold into servitude to a *ger* may be released before the Jubilee year (Lev. 25:47-55); in certain passages where גר (19:10), תושב (22:10), גר and תושב (25:23, 35, 47; Num. 35:15) appear, the sojourner is in an inferior position.

The basic meaning of גר, "sojourner," is employed to express Israel's relation to God's favor. Israel lives by God's invitation, "Come and live over at my place," and by doing the will of the divine host: "The land shall not be sold in perpetuity, for the land is mine; for you are strangers [גרים] and sojourners [ותושבים] with me" (Lev. 25:23);

> Hear my prayer, O LORD,
>   and give ear to my cry;
>   hold not thy peace at my tears!
> For I am thy passing guest [גר],
>   a sojourner [תושב], like all my fathers
>   (Ps. 39:12);

> I am a sojourner [גר] on earth;
>   hide not thy commandments from me!
>   (119:19).

Bibliography. W. R. Smith, *Lectures on the Religion of the Semites* (1894), pp. 75-79. S. R. Driver, *Deuteronomy*, ICC (1895), pp. 126, 165. A. Bertholet, *Die Stellung der Israeliten und der Juden zu den Fremden* (1896). M. Guttmann, "The Term 'Foreigner' (נכרי) Historically Considered," *HUCA*, III (1926), 1-20. T. Meek, "The Translation of *Gêr* in the Hexateuch and Its Bearing on the Documentary Hypothesis," *JBL*, XLIX (1930), 172-80. E. W. Heaton, "Sojourners in Egypt," *ET*, LVIII (1946), 80-82. J. Pedersen, *Israel: Its Life and Culture*, I-II (1946), 40-42, 100, 356-57, 505; III-IV (1947), 92-93, 170, 522, 583-84, 603, 627-28. H. G. May, "Theological Universalism in the OT," *JBR*, XVI (1948), 100-107. G. E. Wright, Exegesis of Deuteronomy, IB, II (1953), 401, 476.   T. M. MAUCH

SOLDERING [דבק, to join, fasten, unite]. Soldering is mentioned in a context of idol making (Isa. 41:7). The broad meaning of the word includes "tacking," "riveting," "hammering," etc. (*see* ANVIL). Archaeology gives no evidence of soldering with alloys of lead, tin, etc., before Roman times. "Hard" solder (copper and zinc) was used in Egypt (2900-2750 B.C.), and soldering with pure silver was found in the tomb of Tut-ankh-Amon.

Bibliography. A. Lucas, *Ancient Egyptian Materials and Industries* (3rd rev. ed., 1948), p. 248; H. Maryon, "Fine Metal Work," in C. Singer *et al.*, eds., *A History of Technology*, I (1954), 649-54.   P. L. GARBER

SOLDIER. *See* ARMY; WAR, METHODS OF, §§ 4-7.

SOLEMN ASSEMBLY [עצרה, gathered assembly] (Lev. 23:36; Num. 29:35; Deut. 16:8; II Kings 10:20; II Chr. 7:9; Neh. 8:18; Isa. 1:13; Joel 1:14; 2:15; Amos 5:21). Alternately: COMPANY (Jer. 9:2—H 9:1). A term used mainly of the community of Israel gathered and separated for a solemn occasion, whether on a stated day of feasting or fasting, or for an extraordinary reason (cf. II Kings 10:20). Israel is always the "assembly of the LORD" (קהל; cf. Exod. 16:3; Lev. 4:13; Num. 20:4); but it is as a solemn assembly that it is in a state of ritual holiness and accomplishes its sacred functions. The term has virtually the same meaning as "holy convocation" (*see* CONVOCATION, HOLY) except that it stresses the fact of the assembly as such, while the latter emphasizes the summons to it. The term "solemn assembly" is used in a technical sense of the seventh day of the PASSOVER and of the eighth day of Booths (Lev. 23:36; Num. 29:35; Deut. 16:8; II Chr. 7:9; Neh. 8:18). In Isa. 1:13; Amos 5:21 the prophets use it to refer critically to the spirit in which similar stated observances were held. A solemn assembly can also be a special occasion at an extraordinary time, as a fast (Joel 1:14; 2:15); or, even as in Elijah's "assembly for Baal" (II Kings 10:20), a gathering summoned with malicious intent.

In Jer. 9:2—H 9:1 the term ("company") is used of Israel as gathered for purpose of rebellion against God and his prophet.   J. C. RYLAARSDAM

SOLOMON sŏl'ə mən [שלמה; LXX A *and* LXX B Σαλωμών; Luc. Σολομών, Σαλωμών; NT *and* Josephus Σολομών; Syr. *Sheleimun*; Arab. *Suleiman*]. The throne name of Israel's third king (962-922 B.C.). By revelation through Nathan he was given the name Jedidiah (II Sam. 12:25), "beloved of the Lord." According to the same passage, he was called Solomon by David. The name is probably a caritative from שלום (*shalom*), "peace" or "prosperity." The name of Solomon occurs nearly three hundred times in the OT and a dozen times in the NT.

Solomon was the second son of David and Bathsheba; their first son died soon after birth (II Sam. 12:18). Virtually nothing is known of Solomon's family. He was reputed to be a lover of women and the husband of many wives (I Kings 11:1; cf. Song of S. 6:8), particularly foreigners. His chief wife was apparently a daughter of the pharaoh (I Kings 3:1); for her he built a separate house (7:8*b*). One other wife is specifically mentioned—Naamah an Ammonitess (14:21, 31), who was the mother of Rehoboam, Solomon's successor. Two daughters are known—Taphath (4:11) and Basemath (4:15), both of them wives of Solomon's district supervisors.

1. Sources. The sources are limited to a few passing references in II Samuel, I Kings, and I and II Chronicles, all of the Kings materials being embedded in a Deuteronomic framework and those of Chronicles in priestly writings. The compiler drew on official sources for the most part, the "book of the

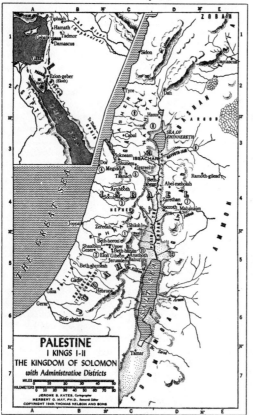

PALESTINE
I KINGS I–II
THE KINGDOM OF SOLOMON
with Administrative Districts
MILES
KILOMETERS
JEROME S. KATES, Cartographer
HERBERT G. MAY, PH.D., General Editor
COPYRIGHT 1949, THOMAS NELSON AND SONS

acts of Solomon" (I Kings 11:41), temple archives, and likely some prophetic reminiscences (II Chr. 9: 29). The first and second chapters of I Kings belong to the history of David.

There is no connected history of Solomon. There are only numerous individual stories and anecdotes, such as those of his securing of the kingdom for himself (I Kings 2:12-46), the organization of his kingdom (4:1-28), the plans for the temple and other building enterprises (chs. 5–8), the visit of the Queen of Sheba (10:1-13), the mercantile activities of Solomon (10:26-29), the prophecy of Ahijah of Shiloh in connection with the rebellion of Jeroboam (11:26-39), and some others often descriptive of the most intimate details of his rule. Perhaps some of the ex-

tended materials dealing with the temple are due to the special interests of the compiler, but this does not explain the broken character of the narratives concerned with other phases of his life and activity. These facts, however, do not mean that we do not have a great many priceless stories, detailed enough to give us an excellent picture of the period and the man.

2. Solomon's anointing. Normally Solomon would not have succeeded to the throne. The next in line after Absalom was Adonijah, who, however, acted prematurely in his bid to become king. He had provided himself with the proper accouterments for a crown prince (I Kings 1:5-6) and had won the support of two of the most powerful personalities in his father's kingdom—Joab, the commander of the army, and Abiathar, the priest who had been with the king since his outlaw days. Though Adonijah's attempt to gain the throne miscarried, it did bring the problem of succession to a head (vs. 11).

Thus, while the legitimate heir was in the act of having himself proclaimed king formally, another party was busy with other plans of its own. This party consisted of Zadok, Benaiah, Nathan and Shimei, and Rei (whose position is not given). Whether they had been inspired by Bathsheba or vice versa is not known, but in any case they now combined to put Solomon in the place of his father. There appear to be overtones of palace intrigue here, perhaps inspired by rivalry and suspicion between Abiathar and Zadok, Benaiah and Joab. Nathan the prophet was the prime schemer. He advised Bathsheba to approach the rapidly weakening king and remind him of the oath which he swore to her that Solomon should be king (I Kings 1:17) and to inform him of the movement of Adonijah, carefully pointing out the danger confronting her and her son should it succeed (vs. 21). She did as she had been instructed. When she withdrew from the presence of the king, Nathan, in accordance with a prearrangement, entered posthaste and confirmed her words. The dying king was too weak to resist such formidable pressure, had he even wished to do so. Bathsheba was summoned, and the oath with respect to her son's succession was confirmed. Then Zadok, Nathan, and Benaiah were instructed to carry out the order of the king (vss. 33-35). With as much pomp and ceremony as could be provided, the agents of David took Solomon to the spring of Gihon, where Zadok performed the official act of anointing him king (vs. 39). With them was the famous bodyguard of Cherethites and Pelethites (*see* DAVID), who held the real secret of power: Adonijah either had not taken them into his confidence or had failed to win them. In addition to the anointing, other symbols of royalty were present at the investiture of Solomon— riding on the king's mule and the sounding of the trumpet. As the popular response to their act proves (I Kings 1:40), Solomon's partisans were well organized.

Absent from Solomon's induction were the elders of Judah and Israel. The reason is not far to seek. This was a new way of kingmaking. There was no charismatic experience on the part of Solomon, no popular approval, and no demonstration of the ability of the anointed one. There was no specific divine act or precept, except possibly the oath sworn by David or the participation of the priest and prophet of God. It was only the word of David which brought the final solution to the problem of succession. Solomon owed his position to the fact that he was the son of the favorite wife of David, not to any marked gifts or military prowess. He was a victim of palace diplomacy and had not the slightest conception of the tremendous price paid by his father for the kingdoms over which he bore rule. Solomon was born with a silver spoon in his mouth, and this fact is apparent in almost every act recorded of his administration of the heritage of David. He had other qualities, however, which he doubtless developed in the atmosphere of his youth and which he would not have acquired had he not had the advantages of a favorite boy in the royal court.

3. Solomon takes over the kingdom. Solomon occupied the position of coregent with his father as long as the latter lived, though to all intents and purposes he was the real ruler; David was on his deathbed when Solomon was anointed. The first decision Solomon had to make as king concerned his brother Adonijah, whose movement to gain the throne collapsed as soon as the followers of Solomon shouted: "Long live King Solomon!" (I Kings 1:39). While Adonijah and his followers were celebrating what they thought was a triumph, they heard the acclaim of the crowd for Solomon (vss. 41-48) and were informed of the true state of affairs by Jonathan the son of Abiathar. The followers of Adonijah dispersed, and he himself laid hold of the horns of the altar, where he was given both assurance and warning by Solomon (vs. 52). He swore allegiance to the king and then was permitted to retire to his own house.

David is reputed to have given Solomon a charge, a kind of last will and testament (I Kings 2:1-9), in which he advised him to keep the commandments of the Lord, to avenge the deeds of Joab and Shimei, and to treat the sons of Barzillai the Gileadite with kindness because of the assistance their father had rendered to him during Absalom's rebellion. However that may be, Solomon was not long in dealing with his possible opponents. The result of Bathsheba's plea on behalf of Adonijah's request for Abishag (vss. 13-21) was a singular reversal for her, although she may have regarded the plea as harmless, since her son was well established in the popular mind as king. Abishag was not, in fact, one of David's concubines (I Kings 1:4), but the populace doubtless regarded her as a member of the harem. The harem was the sole possession of the king; it went with the kingdom. Solomon, recognizing at once that to accede to the request of Adonijah would undermine his own authority, had him executed by Benaiah (2:25). Abiathar, who was David's right-hand man so far as priestly matters were concerned, was unfrocked and banished to Anathoth (vss. 26-27)—the narrator generously regards this act as the fulfilment of the word of the Lord against the house of Eli (I Sam. 2:27-36). Next Solomon dealt with Joab, David's powerful commander of the army (I Kings 2:28-35). Finally, Shimei was kept under house restrictions. When he inadvertently went to Gath to bring back two of his slaves who had been apprehended there, he was called to account for violating the king's orders. The sentence, of course, was death.

Thus Solomon by virtually a single stroke had removed his opponents and rendered his position secure. It is interesting to observe that Benaiah, Joab's successor, was the chief executioner for the king. The ruthlessness and barbarity by which Solomon crushed the opposition are in marked contrast to the way in which his father handled his opponents. The method employed reflects the change both in the times and in the character of the man. As we shall see later, he made amends for his treatment of Abiathar by catering to the supporting elements of the priesthood. But such a course was not possible in the case of Joab, who was one of the most feared military leaders of his day. The news of Joab's death was in all probability the signal for the revolts of Hadad of Edom (I Kings 11:14-22) and Rezon of Zobah (vss. 23-25).

David's conquest of Edom had been quite thoroughgoing (II Sam. 8:13-14; I Chr. 18:12-13), but not to the extent that "every male in Edom" (I Kings 11:15) was slain, for some of the servants of the king of Edom had escaped to Egypt, taking along with them Hadad, an Edomite prince, who was but a child at the time. When news reached Hadad, now grown to manhood, that both David and Joab were dead (I Kings 11:21), he made preparations to return to his homeland. There is no reference to Solomon's resistance, and Hadad doubtless operated in the region most inaccessible to him. Hadad did not interfere, to our knowledge, with Solomon's vast industries and shipping interests at Ezion-geber, but that he did cut off a slice of the Edomite territory belonging to David's empire is beyond dispute.

Ominous stirrings also appeared at the extreme NE limits of the empire. Rezon, one of the chiefs of Hadadezer, whom David had subdued (II Sam. 10:15-19), broke away from Solomon and became the leader of a group of outlaws. Apparently he took Damascus (I Kings 11:23-25), where he and his men entrenched themselves. The narrator affirms that "he was an adversary of Israel all the days of Solomon, doing mischief as Hadad did" (vs. 25). This can mean only that he kept hammering away at the outlying districts of the Aramean states in the region of Damascus which Solomon could no longer control effectively. In any case Solomon was living on inherited prestige. He never conducted a serious military campaign, though he did a considerable amount of fortification (I Kings 9:15-19) along with his other building projects.

4. Organization and administration. The census of David and the recent uprisings demonstrated the need for some kind of effective organization of the empire. Probably there were other matters, such as preparation for building enterprises, administrative needs, and increasing popular dissatisfaction, which made some kind of closer control necessary. Tradition has it that the census came toward the very end of David's reign, when there was little or no time to carry out the fiscal and administrative policies growing out of the survey of his resources.

Consequently it fell to Solomon's lot to put into

Table 1			
Officials	*I Kings 4:2-6*	*II Sam. 8:16-18*	*II Sam. 20:23-25*
1. Commander	Benaiah	Joab	Joab
2. Chief of bodyguard	——	Benaiah	Benaiah
3. Recorder	Jehoshaphat	Jehoshaphat	Jehoshaphat
4. Scribe(s)	Elihoreph and Ahijah	Seraiah	Sheva
5. Tribute chief	Adoniram	——	Adoram
6. Chief of district governors	Azariah	——	——
7. Steward	Ahishar		
8. Priests	Zadok and Abiathar	Zadok and Ahimelech	Zadok and Abiathar
9. Personal priest	Zabud	Sons of David	Ira
10. Priest	Azariah	——	——

effect the program worked out by David's officials. The Chronicler (II Chr. 2:17-18) says Solomon took a census of the resident aliens in Israel, which may well be so. That Solomon's administrative policy was closely related to that of his father is shown by the fact that some of the officers of David were continued, together with all the offices; two more were added. Table 1 illustrates the situation.

The Solomonic list shows some expansion, as might be expected because of the extension of local controls and the growing requirements of the court for putting into effect its political and religious objectives. In constructing the table, the MT has been followed literally, though there are numerous variants in the Greek (for which see the Commentaries). There is some question also about items 1 and 2 of the first column. But the important fact is that we have two additional officials—i.e., the steward of the palace or royal chamberlain and the chief of the administrative district governors, a kind of governor-general or high commissioner. An interesting sidelight is the prominence of the Zadok and Nathan families, who were perhaps being rewarded for their earlier services to the king. Also to be noted is the merger of the royal bodyguard (Cherethites and Pelethites) with the army. The commander of David's bodyguard, who had taken over Joab's old position, had apparently made the bodyguard a part of the army, for it is not mentioned henceforth in the royal annals. The list clearly underlines the direction of the kingdom away from military operations and toward internal development.

For purposes of administration the nation was divided into twelve districts (I Kings 4:7-19). As it now stands, the list is incomplete, though originally it was not so. A prefect was placed in charge of each of the twelve districts. The list gives the names of the officers and the district for which each was responsible. The districts themselves cut across the old tribal boundaries deliberately, for one of the aims of the promoters of the scheme was to modify local loyalties and thus bind the nation more securely to the central government at Jerusalem. Because of the importance of this new arrangement, it may be well to outline the program presented in I Kings, as given

by W. F. Albright ("The Administrative Divisions of Israel and Judah," *JPOS,* V [1925], 17-54). *See* Table 2.

Table 2 [1]

1. ... son of Hur, in Mount Ephraim.
2. ... son of Deqer, in Maqats, and in Shaalbim and Beth-shemesh and Ayyalon (and) Beth-hanan.
3. ... son of Hesed, in Arubboth; he had Socoh and all the lands of Hepher.
4. ... son of Abinadab, all of Naphath-Dor (Taphath, daughter of Solomon, was his wife).
5. Baana, son of Ahilud, Taanach and Megiddo to beyond Joqneam, and all Beth-shean below Jezreel from Beth-shean to Abel-meholah contiguous to Zarethan.
6. ... son of Geber, in Ramoth-gilead; he had the tent villages of Jair (son of Manasseh which is in Gilead); he had the region of Argob which is in Bashan (sixty large cities with walls and bronze bars). Geber, son of Uri, in the land of Gilead (the land of Sihon king of the Amorites and Og king of Bashan).
7. Ahinadab, son of Iddo, (in) Mahanaim.
8. Ahimaats, in Naphtali [and Issachar?]; he also took Basemath, daughter of Solomon, as a wife.
9. Baana, son of Hushi, in Asher [and Zebulun].
10. Jehoshaphat, son of Paruh, Bealoth?
11. Shimei, son of Ela, in Benjamin.
12. One prefect was in the land of Judah.

The list in Table 2 reflects carefully planned divisions which were pretty largely retained subsequently and were of the utmost significance for the purpose for which they were instituted. The whole plan may have followed a general pattern of administration adopted by Egypt or similar methods employed in Mesopotamia. It is to be noted especially that two of the district administrators were directly connected with the royal family by marriage.

Over each district was placed a prefect whose duty was the handling of the business of the district as it concerned the central government at Jerusalem. His

[1] Used by permission of W. F. Albright.

chief responsibility was to see that the stipulated revenue which had to be paid in kind, not in money, was provided to meet the demands of the huge building undertakings of Solomon (*see below*). Each district had to supply one month's needs (I Kings 4:27), comprising rations for the king's tables, provender and grain for his horses, and manual labor for his local building projects. Besides these were the daily offerings, which required no small amount of revenue (II Chr. 8:12 ff).

The *corvée* also required careful organization; even then there were repercussions. As may be seen from Table 3, the numbers of forced laborers in the several accounts tally, though the numbers of officers over them do not. Only I Kings records a levy from Israel; the other forced laborers were aliens.

Table 3

	I Kings 5:13-18	II Chr. 2:17-18	II Chr. 2:2
Burden-bearers	70,000	70,000	70,000
Stonecutters	80,000	80,000	80,000
Levy from Israel	30,000		
Overseers	3,300	3,600	3,600
Total aliens in census		153,600	

According to I Kings 9:20-23; II Chr. 8:7-10, the levy was made from Amorites, Hittites, Perizzites, Hivites, and Jebusites. No Israelites were drafted for work. The Kings passage says Solomon appointed 550 overseers; the Chronicles passage says 250 were appointed.

As the passage from I Kings 9 indicates, Solomon continued the policy of David in converting captives from the surrounding areas into forced laborers. Forced labor, which was widespread in the ancient world, is illustrated by the practice of Mesha king of Moab (830 B.C.), who employed Israelite slaves to cut beans for Qarhoh. In the same manner, foreign groups within Israel were drawn into the *corvée* pool. For normal purposes these groups might have been adequate; but Solomon was not an ordinary king. He was not only extravagant in everything he undertook, but he had such a far-reaching program that normal methods and supplies soon ran out. Hence he was compelled to resort to an Israelite draft—the 30,000 noted in the preceding table (I Kings 5)—which must have been a severe strain on the economy of the country.

A very significant part of the administration of Solomon was the construction of a whole series of fortifications at strategic points in Israel and Judah (I Kings 9:15-19), as well as organization for trade and commerce (9:26-28; 10:22-29). These items will be discussed below and are mentioned here only because they reflect the careful and ambitious plans of the king, together with the enormous requirements of men and material with the consequent weakening of the economy of the empire.

Forced labor was one of the causes for the rebellion of the N tribes under Jeroboam, who was originally one of Solomon's officials (11:28). He is said to have been in charge of the Joseph levy and to have been an efficient servant. His position enabled him to observe the hardships of his people and per-

haps capitalize on them. That his flight had something to do with forced labor or heavy tribute is made evident by the complaints lodged with Rehoboam shortly after the death of Solomon and Jeroboam's return from exile (12:2-4). At any rate, Jeroboam fled to Egypt, where he remained as long as Solomon lived (11:27, 40).

5. Building enterprises. Organization, forced labor, and heavy taxation were demanded by Solomon's extensive building projects, which were so extravagant that they undermined the economic balance of the empire. Solomon inherited the Jerusalem built by David, which consisted of the citadel of Zion with a complex of buildings which surrounded it (II Sam. 5:9). The plans of David called for the building of the house of the Lord (II Sam. 7; hardly altogether midrashic), as hinted at in I Kings 5:3. Since David could not fulfil his desires in this respect, this was the first undertaking of Solomon, though some of the other building projects may have been carried on simultaneously.

Arrangements were made with Hiram of Tyre to supply the requisite lumber for the buildings (I Kings 5). The diplomatic agreements provided that the Tyrian king supply cedar and cypress wood from Lebanon. His men were to supervise the cutting and shipping of the lumber, the servants of Solomon to perform most if not all of the manual labor required (vs. 6). Shipping included transportation from the forests to the sea, the rafting of the logs, their floating to a port along the Mediterranean selected by Solomon, perhaps Joppa (II Chr. 2:16), where they were taken apart and dragged ashore. From thence they were in the hands of Solomon, whose men moved them to Jerusalem (I Kings 5:9). In exchange for services and materials, Solomon agreed to give Hiram "food for my household" (I Kings 5:9). As far as the records go, this agreement (vs. 12) is one of the only two formal treaties which the Israelites ever ratified with a foreign state; the other is the agreement between Asa and Ben-hadad (II Chr. 16:2 ff). After some years the amount of supplies which Solomon sent annually to Hiram, plus the requirements for his own needs, led to his bankruptcy; so that he was compelled to mortgage some of his cities in Galilee (I Kings 9:11). In addition to builders—i.e., the skilled mechanics of Hiram (5:18)—the architect or decorator was a Tyrian (7:13, 40, 45; cf. II Chr. 4:11, 16). There were also the men of Gebal (the Byblos of the Greeks), presumably contracted for on the same basis as the other skilled workmen.

The temple (*see* TEMPLE, JERUSALEM) was begun "in the four hundred and eightieth year after the people of Israel came out of the land of Egypt" (I Kings 6:1), which was also the fourth year of Solomon's reign (I Kings 6:1; II Chr. 3:2).

The temple was built on the old threshing floor of Araunah-Ornan (II Chr. 3:1), where David had erected an altar for sacrifice to the Lord for staying the plague (II Sam. 24:16-25; I Chr. 21:15-25). The location was somewhere in the present area of the Dome of the Rock. Its orientation was toward the E, with the rising sun visible between the pillars of Jachin and Boaz. Its prototype was the Syrian temple —e.g., at Ugarit, Qatna, Tainat, and Megiddo—with certain features such as the capitals and decorations explained on the basis of Egyptian and Assyrian contacts. This could be expected in view of the fact that Solomon employed a Phoenician architect to draw and execute the plans. Actually the temple was nothing more than a royal chapel, possibly patterned after Assyrian models. Along with the temple came a whole series of ritual innovations, which started the long process of institutionalism which the prophets so roundly condemned when it sublimated the stern religious ideals of the Mosaic cult. The temple and its cults thus were responsible to a large degree for the Canaanization of Israel's religion and for the drive toward a syncretism so apparent in later times when the line between cult symbol and the spiritual content of Yahwism became quite thin and in many instances seemed to vanish altogether.

The completion of the temple in the eleventh year of Solomon (I Kings 6:38) was the signal for a great celebration (ch. 8), greatly expanded by the editor. Solomon's dedication may well have been more elaborate than the ceremonial festivities surrounding the removal of the ark to Jerusalem (II Sam. 6:12-20). In any event, the ark was taken from the city of David and placed in the adytum, the most holy place in the temple (I Kings 8:6). Many sacrifices were offered, as when David brought the ark from the house of Obed-edom to the dwelling place he had made for it in his newly chosen capital. Solomon officiated as a priest both in blessing and in prayer. The poem of I Kings 8:12-13 (II Chr. 6:1-2), though not too clear as it stands, is very old and certainly reflects contemporary thought. Accordingly the temple was regarded as the dwelling place of the Lord, and when the ark, the symbol of his presence, was deposited therein, it signified that he had taken up his residence in the house which Solomon had built. And since the temple was part of the palace complex, the Lord now dwelt in the very house of the king.

The palace formed the second of Solomon's building operations (I Kings 7:1-8). The most celebrated portion of the palace complex was the House of the Forest of Lebanon (7:2-5), so called because of its cedar columns, beams, and paneling. Isa. 22:8 offers a hint as to the purpose of the structure—for the storage of weapons. The Arabic version adds here "a house for his weapons," probably on the basis of the Isaiah passage. The Hall of Pillars (7:6) was probably a portico before the House of the Forest of Lebanon. The Hall of the Throne or the Hall of Judgment (7:7) was completely paneled with cedar and was doubtless the audience room of the palace. The great ivory throne (I Kings 10:18-20) was located there. Solomon's house—i.e., his private residence (I Kings 7:8)—was part of another court, separated in some way from the public halls of the palace ("in the other court back of the hall"). Last of all was the house of Pharaoh's daughter (I Kings 7:8b), to which she was in due time ceremoniously escorted (I Kings 9:24) from David's city (I Kings 3:1; cf. II Chr. 8:11).

Other building operations at JERUSALEM were the Millo (I Kings 9:15, 24; 11:27b) and the "breach of the city of David" (11:27b), both mentioned in connection with the rebellion of Jeroboam. That Solomon constructed sanctuaries for his foreign wives is also a matter of record (I Kings 11:7-8). The narrator hints at the development of a kind of syncretism which is quite understandable in the light of other Solomonic tendencies. It may be that the shrines which he erected for some of his foreign brides were due to political expediency, though we cannot be certain of it.

Outside Jerusalem extensive projects were also carried out.* Solomon fortified a whole series of towns all around his land (I Kings 9:15, 17b-19; II Chr. 8:1-6). The list in I Kings follows geographical lines and indicates an excellent perception for the proper location of such fortifications. HAZOR (1) is in the extreme N, just S of Lake Huleh. MEGIDDO is located near the famous pass between the Carmel range and the highlands of Ephraim. Beth-horon the Lower was to the NW of Jerusalem. Baalath is unknown, but was probably somewhere in the S, possibly somewhere on the route to the Gulf of Aqabah. Tamar was just S of the Dead Sea. Gezer commanded the road between Jerusalem and the N Philistine country; but it is probably a mistake for Gerar, since it is said to have been a marriage dowry presented to Solomon by the pharaoh who had just taken it and since there is no sign of a destruction of Gezer by fire at this time. Fig. WAT 6.

The fortifications and the famous stables at Megiddo* may furnish the best example of the work of Solomon. The older portions of the gate of stratum IV are generally thought to belong to the Solomonic period. (*See*, however, MEGIDDO § 3d.) From the gate extends an excellent wall which encircled the whole city. There may even have been an outer wall as well. The main wall has been called a "remarkable piece of fortification, . . . an enduring tribute to the might of its constructor." At Megiddo there was also a well-constructed governor's residence. The stables, which are an example of the chariot cities referred to in I Kings 9:19; 10:26, were constructed in buildings stabling about 120 horses, each composed of five units containing twenty-four stalls. The floors were paved with stones. Each stall had its pillar properly holed for purposes of securing the horses, which also served as a support for the roof. Mangers were also provided for each stall. There appears to have been room for something like 300 horses. Similar installations were found at Tell el-Hesi, Gezer, Taanach, and possibly Hazor. In view of the archaeological materials, the numbers of Solomon's chariots and horsemen (I Kings 10:26) as 1,400 and 12,000 respectively, do not appear too extravagant. That he had horses and chariots at Jerusalem can hardly be doubted, but the stables of Solomon under the temple area shown to tourists were used for such purposes only in Crusader times and were certainly not from the Solomonic period. Figs. STA 78-80.

A type of fortification similar to that at Megiddo prevails at Hazor, Beth-shean, Gezer, Tell el-Hesi, Lachish, Ezion-geber, and other places, all of which tend to confirm the biblical tradition of Solomon's activity as a great builder, not only with respect to the palace-temple complex at Jerusalem but also in other centers of his empire. The same may be said with regard to the store-cities (I Kings 9:19).

Finally there is the great refinery at EZION-GEBER,

Solomon's seaport on the Gulf of Aqabah (I Kings 9:26; II Chr. 8:17), which was brought to light by Nelson Glueck in 1938-40. As noted above, the outer wall and gateway were the same type as those of Megiddo and Lachish. But the chief interest in the site is its industrial complex of huge copper and iron smelters where metal was extracted from ores for shipment to other centers of the empire and for export. Some of it was used also for the manufacture of metal articles of all kinds, also for export purposes. Only a king of Solomon's vision, organization, and wealth could develop such a project.

6. Solomon the diplomat and merchant. Such enormous building operations required both labor and materials of vast quantity. Stones for walls, paving, and pillars were abundant in the land. Cedar and cypress timbers were, of course, procured from the Lebanon Mountains under contract with Hiram of Tyre (I Kings 5:8), but as we learn from the elaborate decorations wrought out for his temple and palace, Solomon's predilection for luxury was not satisfied with plain buildings. All kinds of metals were required, some of which came from distant places, others from his own realm. Wide contacts are thus indicated on both the diplomatic and the trade levels.

It will be recalled that Solomon, early in his reign, entered into a marriage alliance with the pharaoh of Egypt in connection with which he received a city (I Kings 3:1; 9:16). Solomon continued the office of recorder (4:3), which had charge of foreign relations. There was the treaty with Hiram (5:1-12; 9:10-14) under which cedar and cypress were supplied for the various building projects of Solomon, for which the latter was compelled in the end to cede certain Galilean towns which proved very disappointing to the Tyrian king. Solomon also had a trade agreement with Hiram (9:26-28; 10:11-12) relative to his Red Sea fleet and possibly also to Mediterranean trade (II Chr. 9:21).

Political arrangements with foreign countries account for many, though not all, of Solomon's wives. His marriage relationships with Moab, Ammon, Edom, and others suggest some plan along the line of holding those states inherited from his father. Just how much is involved is not certain, but such practices were common. The mother of Rehoboam was an Ammonitess. The fact that Solomon built shrines for some of these wives is indicative of their importance for his relations with foreign countries. There are further hints of foreign alliances in I Kings 10:24-25; II Chr. 9:23-24 (though the reference in the latter passage may be tribute). Nevertheless, they do afford probably a true picture of his worldwide interests and alliances of one kind or another.

Solomon's diplomacy was directed primarily toward commercial ends. As observed above, this was the chief reason for his treaty with Hiram. More significant is the establishment of the great seaport on the Gulf of Aqabah, the home base for his fleet. Hiram and Solomon made a maritime agreement whereby a trade fleet was formed, probably manned by Phoenician sailors and financed by Israel. Once every three years (I Kings 10:22) the fleet made a round trip to Ophir, evidently on the E coast of Africa somewhere in Somaliland. From Ezion-geber they carried copper and iron and manufactured articles and in exchange brought back gold, silver, ivory, and two breeds of monkeys. In II Chr. 9:21, ships that "went to Tarshish" is generally regarded as an error for "Tarshish ships"—i.e., refinery ships which originally designated Mediterranean fleets, carrying metals from the mining and refinery centers of Sardinia, and possibly farther W, to E ports. It is possible, however, that Solomon had some arrangement with Hiram for mutual assistance by the sailors of their respective fleets on the Red Sea.

Solomon has been called a "copper king" because of his vast shipping and mining interests and his extensive needs for copper for temple utensils. Glueck's explorations in S Palestine have disclosed very extensive copper and iron mining and refining industry all through the great depression between the Dead Sea and the Gulf of Aqabah which is known as the Arabah. Glueck's investigations signally confirm the Deuteronomist's description of it as a "land whose stones are iron, and out of whose hills you can dig copper" (Deut. 8:9). The pottery evidence all points to the conclusion that virtually all the mines and smelters in the region were actively worked in the time of Solomon. David may already have exploited the mines of Edom (II Sam. 8:13-14; I Kings 11:15-16), and if he had done so, Solomon merely continued his father's plans and greatly expanded them. The ceramic remains prove that the operations were manned by Edomite slaves.

Solomon was not completely absorbed in mining, refining, and shipping by sea. According to I Kings 10:28-29, he was engaged in lucrative horse and chariot trade. Albright's translation of these verses makes the situation quite clear: "And Solomon's horses were exported from Cilicia; the merchants of the king procured them from Cilicia at the current price; and a chariot was exported from Egypt at the rate of six hundred shekels of silver and a horse from Cilicia at the rate of a hundred and fifty; and thus (at this rate) they delivered them by their agency to all the kings of the Hittites and the kings of Aram" (*Archaeology and the Religion of Israel*, p. 135). Thus Solomon was a great "horse trader," having actually a monopoly on the horse and chariot trade because he controlled the land trade routes between Syria and Egypt. Moreover, as the archaeological remains of his vast stable projects in many strategic locations in his empire show, he himself was vitally interested in horses and chariots. His military machine was completely modernized and mechanized by comparison with Saul's and David's. He adopted the horse and chariot as his chief weapons, being no longer content with his father's methods.

The visit of the Queen of Sheba (I Kings 10:1-13; II Chr. 9:1-12) was, in all probability, more of a trade mission than anything else, though, of course, diplomatic negotiations were involved. It has been suggested that Solomon's naval expansion stimulated S Arabian trade with the N, though it may actually have been a threat thereto. The queen's appearance at Solomon's court resulted in an exchange of goods from her country for goods which the king was able to provide and which she desired. Her quest of wisdom was also involved, but the main objective of her long journey was to observe for herself the wealth and power of the famous king who was competing for her trade, and to discover whether the rumors were true (I Kings 10:6). Solomon's commercial expansion was no idle threat; it was real, and he had the power and ingenuity to carry it through. The visit ended in a kind of treaty consummated by the exchange of goods. The sea trade initiated by Solomon vanished, and Jehoshaphat's attempt to revive it was abortive (22:47-48); nevertheless, the numerous references to Sheba indicate that some measure of trade continued over land (e.g., Job 6:19; Isa. 60:6; Ezek. 38:13).

Solomon was not only a trader in his own right, but he also regulated the trade of others by his control of the land routes. The domestication of the camel two centuries earlier made caravan trade much more practicable over long distances. In the N he ruled Zobah and probably, early in his reign, Damascus; in the S he had almost undisputed mastery in Edom, Moab, and Ammon. All trade caravans, therefore, had to cross his territory. He was thus in a position to collect toll and possibly also to determine the type of goods passing through his land. From such caravan traffic Solomon received a sizable amount of revenue (cf. I Kings 10:15), all of which helped to strengthen his economy and raise his prestige. His mercantile agents (vs. 28) too were present everywhere carrying out his trade policies to the same effect.

7. Dreams and visions. Solomon was a many-sided personality. There can be no question that on occasion he was deeply and genuinely religious. So much may be ascertained from his dreams and visions which are recorded in connection with certain specific religious acts or ceremonies, and their character is such that their authenticity cannot be disputed. That some phases have been magnified by the tradition goes without saying, but the absence of any hint of criticism against Solomon's dreams and visions such as Jeremiah (23:25 ff) and the Deuteronomist (13:1-5) leveled against the dreamers of their day is strong argument in favor of their authenticity.

The first dream of Solomon is recorded in I Kings 3:5-15 = II Chr. 1:7-13. It occurred in conjunction with a religious celebration at the old high place at Gibeon, present el-Jib, *ca.* five miles to the NW of Jerusalem. The Gibeon tradition is somewhat complicated by the older associations with the place itself. Gibeon was one of the cities of the Hivite tetrapolis (Josh. 9:17) respected even by David. The Chronicler places the tent of meeting there (II Chr. 1:3), as well as the brass altar of Bezalel (vs. 5). The ark was already in Jerusalem, but sacrifice there would hardly have been sufficient for Solomon's purpose at the time. The Jerusalem shrine at the threshing floor of Araunah was a local altar to which Israel had not yet become accustomed. Hence Solomon resorted to the sacred altar of burnt offering at Gibeon, outside Jerusalem, which had a much wider appeal and significance, for his sacrifice was for "all Israel."

Sometime during that sacrificial period the Lord appeared to Solomon in a dream with the offer to grant any request he made. The request of the king has become one of the celebrated passages of the Bible. Because he was young and inexperienced and had to take the place of his famous and respected father, he asked for an "understanding mind to govern thy people, that I may discern between good and evil; for who is able to govern this thy great people?" (I Kings 3:9). The Lord responded favorably to his prayer and promised not only wisdom for judgment (cf. the overtones of the Absalom rebellion [II Sam. 15:1-6]) but also riches and honor and long life if he was as obedient as David his father.

The conclusion of the story is confused; it has Solomon repairing to Jerusalem, where he also offers burnt offerings and peace offerings before the ark. This may, indeed, be a later observation, at least in part indicating the priority of Jerusalem. However, it may equally well be an authentic tradition pointing to the dual system of Jerusalem and Israel set up by David, requiring sacrifice for the city as was done for Israel at Gibeon.

The second vision occurs after the dedication of the temple (I Kings 9:1-9; II Chr. 7:11-22). Commentators are of the opinion that this is a Deuteronomic expansion of the dream described above. The theme, language, and spirit are comparable to Deuteronomy (e.g., cf. I Kings 9:8-9 with Deut. 29:25-26), and yet there is nothing inherently against the probability of a vision on such an auspicious occasion. In truth, it might be expected at a time when emotional currents were running so strongly and when the sense of achievement was so deeply felt.

Dreams and visions (*see* DREAM; VISION) played a significant role in ancient religion. And Solomon was a typical oriental ruler and thus might be expected to exhibit just such qualities as the Bible attributes to him. Since dreams (by incubation) were the normal method of revelation in his time, he understood and cherished their meaning.

8. Solomon's wisdom. The WISDOM of Solomon is celebrated in Bible and legend. The tradition is stated in I Kings 4:29-34—H 5:9-14. The story of Solomon's rule, after he had carried out his (or David's) plan of securing the kingdom, begins with his prayer for wisdom (I Kings 3:3-15; II Chr. 1:7-12), which was granted. Immediately after the theophany comes the passage dealing with the king's wisdom in handling the case of the harlots, as if in illustration of the wisdom conferred upon him by the Lord (I Kings 3:16-28). One of the reasons given for the visit of the Queen of Sheba (I Kings 10:1-13; II Chr. 9:1-12) was "to test him with hard questions" (I Kings 10:1*b*), which Solomon is reputed to have answered with distinction. His wisdom is said to have excelled rumor and her own expectations. The book of Proverbs begins with the following statement: "The proverbs of Solomon, son of David, king of Israel." A large section of the book is entitled: "These also are proverbs of Solomon which the men of Hezekiah king of Judah copied" (Prov. 25:1). The present introductory verse of Ecclesiastes is certainly meant to refer to Solomon. And, of course, he is credited with the Song of Solomon and the apocryphal book Wisdom of Solomon. The narrator of I Kings 4 says he was responsible for 3,000 proverbs and 1,005 songs—typically exaggerated, of course. Even the obituary of Solomon (I Kings 11: 41) refers to his wisdom as recorded in the Acts of Solomon, the official record in the royal archives.

To understand the meaning of the wisdom of Solomon, it is essential to investigate the terminology employed in the passages concerned and the general range of capabilities which the tradition assigns to him. In his prayer he asked for an "understanding mind to govern thy people, . . . to discern between good and evil" (I Kings 3:9). The Lord responded by giving him a "wise and discerning mind" (vs. 12). Here wisdom is applied to the judicial process whereby the king governed his people. It is illustrated by the court case which all Israel heard about. From that example all Israel heard about the "judgment which the king had rendered," and "that the wisdom of God was in him, to render justice" (I Kings 3: 28). The combination of the terms "to judge," "to discern between good and evil," "judgment," "the wisdom of God," all point to the king's ability to render judicial decision.

The famous (Matt. 12:42; Luke 11:31) Queen of Sheba came "to test him with riddles"; this points in another direction. Wisdom to solve riddles or outwit another person is quite different from that involved in court. It indicates skill along another line entirely. Recall the riddle of Samson (Judg. 14:12 ff), which was propounded by a man who had no judicial qualities at all so far as the records go. The חידה was an enigmatic saying or epigram (cf. Num. 12:8). Thus the Queen of Sheba came to try out Solomon's ability to answer witticisms, to match her wits against his. When she had concluded her series of tests, she not only affirmed the accuracy of the reports which had come to her "of your affairs and of your wisdom" (I Kings 10:6), but said: "Your wisdom and prosperity surpass the report which I heard" (vs. 7). She regarded as exceedingly fortunate those who "hear your wisdom" (vs. 8) and pronounced blessed the Lord who "made you king, that you may execute justice and righteousness" (vs. 9). Here we have a clear turn from riddles to the ability to govern judiciously.

The description of Solomon's wisdom in I Kings 4:29-34—H 5:9-14 is nothing more than a summary of the above-noted observations plus the addition of a few details. According to it, "God gave Solomon wisdom and understanding beyond measure" (4:29—H 5:9), which covers the judicial element. The statement that "Solomon's wisdom surpassed the wisdom of all the people of the east, and all the wisdom of Egypt" (4:30—H 5:10) relates to the realm of proverbs or wise sayings. The fact that "he was wiser than all other men, wiser than Ethan . . ." (4:31—H 5:11), is doubtless based on his supposed lyrical compositions. The "three thousand proverbs" (4: 32—H 5:12) connects him directly with the book of Proverbs. The phrase "the wisdom of Solomon, . . . his wisdom" (4:34—H 5:14), which all the peoples and kings of the earth who had heard about it came to witness, is a summary of a summary and includes all the elements noted thus far.

That there is Solomonic material in the collections of the book of PROVERBS can scarcely be doubted,

though there can at present be no certainty as to which one comes from the wise king. He is said to have surpassed in wisdom "all the people of the east, and all the wisdom of Egypt. For he was wiser than all other men, wiser than Ethan the Ezrahite, and Heman, Calcol, and Darda, the sons of Mahol" (I Kings 4:30b-31a—H 5:10-11). This description connects him at once with Mesopotamia, Egypt, and Canaan, whose wisdom must therefore have been known and recognized in Israel, and since in other areas there is definite knowledge of contacts with all these areas, one need not hesitate to believe that Solomon appropriated material in this category also. Tradition may magnify, but it does not originate. The commercial relationships of the period were conducive to all kinds of activities; and travel was extensive. To be sure, what we know of Solomon's administrative policies does not coincide with many of the moral proverbs of the Bible, but there are innumerable wise sayings which could easily have been current in his day.

It is rather significant that, according to the narrator, Solomon "spoke of trees, from the cedar that is in Lebanon to the hyssop that grows out of the wall; he spoke also of beasts, and of birds, and of reptiles, and of fish" (I Kings 4:33—H 5:13). Alt relates this verse to such passages as Job 38-41; Prov. 30:15, 18-20, 24-28, 29-31. Eissfeldt has already referred to some of the latter verses in connection with the statement of the narrator of I Kings just noted. From Egyptian and Mesopotamian sources we know that nature wisdom was as international in scope as the practical wisdom so frequently compared with the book of Proverbs. Since Solomon was concerned almost entirely with cultural interests there can be no doubt that he took great pains to imitate and amplify not only architectural interests but didactic interests as well. In view of the Egyptian and Babylonian-Assyrian lists or catalogues the numbers given in I Kings 4:32—H 5:12 no longer appear so utterly fantastic.

9. Summary. Solomon is said to have maintained his father's kingdom, which extended from the N and E limits of the Aramean state of Zobah to the border of Egypt (II Sam. 8:11-12=I Chr. 18:11-13; I Kings 4:20-25; II Chr. 9:26), though he did have some difficulties with Aramean guerrilla bands around Damascus and with Edomite rebel bands under Hadad (I Kings 11:14-25). How seriously they interfered with his administration is uncertain, but the progress of royal projects seems to indicate that they cannot have been too obstructive. A true assessment of the narrative in the light of archaeology and contemporary history proves that the historians of Israel cannot have exaggerated the splendor of his kingdom too greatly (I Kings 10:14-27; II Chr. 1:15; 9:13-27). His internal organization carried out the program of David, and he added thereto many features of his own design such as his fortifications, chariotry, and vast manufacturing enterprises.

The revolt of JEROBOAM (1) shows that these extensive interests were burdensome, but they had their constructive side. They provided far more security than the nation had known before or was to experience for many years. The nation's population grew;

new cities and towns sprang up everywhere. Religion was accorded a prominent place, though architectural and ritual innovations were not an unmixed blessing. The court records of David and the Gezer Calendar (*see* ALPHABET § A1*b;* CALENDAR § 3*b*), a schoolboy's exercise, demonstrate that cultural interests were advanced. Jesus was certainly right when he spoke of "Solomon in all his glory" (Matt. 6:29).

Bibliography. G. Beer, "Saul, David, Salomo," *Religionsgeschichtliche Volksbücher, 2 Reihe* (1906). W. F. Albright, "The Administrative Divisions of Israel and Judah," *JPOS,* V (1925), 17-54. R. Kittel, *Geschichte des Volkes Israel,* II (7th ed., 1925), 146-64. L. Rost, *Die Überlieferung von der Thronnachfolge Davids* (1926). P. L. O. Guy, *New Light from Armageddon* (Oriental Institute Communications, no. 9; 1931). A. T. Olmstead, *History of Palestine and Syria* (1931), ch. 22. C. Watzinger, *Denkmäler Palästinas* (1933, 1935). S. Yeivin, "Social, Religious and Cultural Trends in Jerusalem Under the Davidic Dynasty." *Vetus Testamentum,* III (1935), 149-66. F. James, *Personalities of the OT* (1939), ch. 8. R. S. Lamon and G. M. Shipton, *Megiddo I, Seasons of 1925-34. Strata I-V* (Oriental Institute Publications, XLII; 1939). N. Glueck, *The Other Side of the Jordan* (1940), chs. 3-4. W. F. Albright, *Archaeology and the Religion of Israel* (2nd ed., 1946). I. Mendelsohn, *Slavery in the Ancient Near East* (1949). J. A. Montgomery, *The Book of Kings,* ICC (1951). A. Alt, *Kleine Schriften zur Geschichte des Volkes Israel* (1953), II: "Die Staatenbildung der Israeliten in Palästina," 1-65; "Israel's Gaue unter Salomo," 76-89; "Die Weisheit Salomos," 90-99. E. Meyer, *Geschichte des Altertums,* vol. II, pt. 2 (1953), pp. 262-70. M. Avi-Yonah, *Sepher Yerushalayim* (the Book of Jerusalem), vol. I (1956; in Hebrew). G. E. Wright, *Biblical Archaeology* (1957), ch. 8. J. Bright, *A History of Israel* (1959), pp. 190-208. M. Noth, *The History of Israel* (1960).   J. M. MYERS

SOLOMON, PSALMS OF. *See* PSALMS OF SOLOMON.

SOLOMON, WISDOM OF. *See* WISDOM OF SOLOMON.

SOLOMON'S PORTICO (John 10:23; Acts 3:11; 5:12). A part of the outer court of Herod's temple. The KJV translates the word στοά as "porch" (not to be confused with the vestibule of Solomon's temple, also called a "porch" in I Kings 6:3 KJV). This portico was the E side of the colonnaded ambulatory that extended all the way around the outer court, as we learn from Josephus (Antiq. XX.ix.7). The colonnade on this side rested on a platform supported by a high retaining wall. According to Josephus, who reflects popular tradition, this device was first employed by Solomon (War V.v.1; Antiq. VIII.iii.9). The temple area of Zerubbabel may also have had a supporting wall and platform at this point, but it seems most likely that the portico and substructure of NT times were entirely the work of Herod's builders (War I.xxi.1).

See also TEMPLE, JERUSALEM.

W. F. STINESPRING

SOLOMON'S SERVANTS. All kings have servants. Who "Solomon's servants" were—his princes and officers—is shown by the lists in I Kings 4:1-19. Presumably "servants" in 3:15 means "ministers." In I Kings 5, Hiram and Solomon have servants (LXX usually δοῦλοι Σαλωμών); but it is clear from a comparison of vss. 6 and 13 that Solomon's servants and

laborers and, indeed, the *corvée* (מס; vss. 6, 13) reveal the presence of state slaves in Solomon's labor force. The purposes of the *corvée*—temple, palace, and fortifications in Jerusalem and other building elsewhere—are given in 9:15-19. To these must be added the industries of Ezion-geber, also manned by slaves. Vss. 20-22 point out that the *corvée* was raised, not from the Israelites, but from the pre-Israelite inhabitants of the land—Hittites, Perizzites, Hivites, and Jebusites (but cf. Deut. 7:1 for the usual seven). I Kings 9:22 appears to contradict 5:13, but "Israel" in 5:13 could include Israel and these other peoples. The phrase in 9:21: למס עבד (cf. Gen. 49:15; Josh. 16:10) appears to mean total enslavement. "Solomon's servants" (I Kings 9:27; II Chr. 8:18; 9:10) thus included state slaves. Perhaps Solomon even sold the people (freeborn Judeans or *corvée?*) to Egypt in exchange for horses (cf. Deut. 17:16).

For the "sons of Solomon's servants," *see* NETHINIM; SLAVERY.

Bibliography. I. Mendelsohn, "State Slavery in Ancient Palestine," *BASOR,* 85 (Feb., 1942), 14-17.

G. HENTON DAVIES

SOLOMON'S SONG. *See* SONG OF SONGS.

***SON OF GOD** [υἱὸς τοῦ θεοῦ, υἱὸς θεοῦ; Aram. בר אלהין]. A term used in the OT to denote a divine being, and in the NT to refer to Jesus.

1. OT usage
2. Apoc. and Pseudep. usage
3. Jesus as Son of God
   a. The Gospel of Mark
   b. Q
   c. Luke
   d. Matthew
   e. Jesus' use of the idea
   f. The Pauline letters
   g. Hebrews
   h. The Gospel of John
   i. The First Letter of John
   j. The Apostolic Fathers
Bibliography

1. OT usage. The only passage in the OT where this exact phrase is found is Dan. 3:25, where King Nebuchadnezzar sees in the furnace along with Shadrach, Meshach, and Abednego a fourth man whose appearance is that of a "son of the gods," or divine being. In this sense the phrase sometimes occurs in the plural. The SONS OF GOD, or godlike personages, see that the daughters of men are beautiful, and giants are born to their union with these mortal women (Gen. 6:2, 4). "Sons of God" appeared in the presence of the Lord at the time when Job was first put to the test (Job 1:6; 2:1), and at the Creation they all shouted for joy (Job 38:7; cf. Pss. 29:1; 89: 6; perhaps 82:1, 6). This usage reflects the older, polytheistic background.

In a different sense, Israel or Ephraim (i.e., the N kingdom) is called God's son or first-born son (e.g., Exod. 4:22-23; Deut. 1:31; 8:5; Ps. 80:16 MT; Jer. 3:19; 31:9, 20; Hos. 11:1; 13:13; Mal. 1:6). The term "son" is also used in reference to David (II Sam. 7:14) and the Davidic king (Ps. 89:26-27). The thought is that God has created and chosen the nation and its leader, who stand in a relation of filial dependence and obedience to God. In one of the psalms, God addresses his "anointed," a king not otherwise identified, with the words: "You are my son, today I have begotten you" (Ps. 2:7). The idea is also applied to faithful Hebrews in general (e.g., Deut. 14:1; Isa. 43:6; Hos. 1:10). God's loyal people therefore address God as their Father (Deut. 32:6; Isa. 63:16). It is difficult to say whether the words "today I have begotten you," when addressed to a king, originally bore any suggestion that the king so chosen received a nature and character different from that of other men. The only thought may be that at this time God has decided to be a Father to the king, and the king henceforth has the obligations of a son and some of his prerogatives. It cannot be denied, however, that in the later OT books the king has certain supernatural characteristics (*see* CHRIST § 1).

2. Apoc. and Pseudep. usage. The OT usages are characteristic of the intertestamental literature as well. Here Israel is God's Son (Ecclus. 36:12; Wisd. Sol. 18:13; Jub. 2:20; 19:29; II Esd. 6:58), God is Father (Ecclus. 23:1, 4; 51:10; Wisd. Sol. 2:16; III Macc. 5:7; Jub. 1:28), Jacob is his first-born son (Jub. 19:29), and Jacob's descendants are God's children (Jub. 1:24-25). The Israelites will be God's sons in the future age (e.g., Pss. Sol. 17:28-30); God, like a Father, punishes them for their sins (e.g., Wisd. Sol. 12:19-21); and occasionally the signally righteous are called "sons of God" (Ecclus. 4:10). "Son of God" is not a regular Jewish title for Messiah, although the messianic interpretation of Ps. 2:7, which was much used by Christians, might have suggested the designation of Messiah as Son of God. The occasional instances where the Messiah is addressed by God as "my son" (Enoch 105:2; II Esd. 7:28-29; 13:32, 37, 52; 14:9) may be due to Christian interpolation. There is an exceptional passage in Enoch 106:5 telling of the birth of Noah, who resembles the "sons of the God of heaven"—i.e., the angels. *See* CHRIST § 2.

3. Jesus as Son of God. Although occasionally the NT refers to Israel as God's Son (e.g., Matt. 2: 15, quoting Hos. 11:1), the "sons of God" in the plural are usually the followers of Jesus (but see Luke 20:36, where those who rise from the dead are sons of God). Jesus is the unique Son of God, and the most remarkable fact is that all the gospels, in contrast to Jewish literature, emphasize the point that the Messiah is also Son of God. The phrase, like most of Jesus' christological titles, takes on a number of associations. It is difficult to determine just what was in the minds of the earliest Christians when they used it. Did they think at all of the angels or divine beings of the OT? It can only be said that when the NT mentions the Son in connection with the angels, his superiority to them is generally emphasized (e.g., Heb. 1:4).

a. The Gospel of Mark. The oldest complete gospel preserved to us, that of Mark, uses "Son of God" as its favorite designation of Jesus. The first verse, which may be the gospel's original title, reads: "The beginning of the gospel of Jesus Christ, the Son of God." The phrase "the Son of God" is omitted by two important MSS, Sinaiticus (א) and Koridethi (Θ), by the church father Origen, and in part of the quotations in Irenaeus; but it is probably genuine, because it is in accordance with the evangelist's style. At the Cross the centurion who is probably a pagan, exclaims: "Truly this man was a son of God!" (Mark 15:39).

In Mark the phrase has several points of reference: (*a*) God proclaims Jesus as his Son. This occurs at the Baptism, where Jesus sees the heavens opened and the Spirit descending like a dove upon him, whereupon a voice comes from heaven: "Thou art my beloved Son; with thee I am well pleased" (1:11). "The Beloved" may be a designation of Messiah (cf. Eph. 1:6), or it may mean God's "only" or "unique" Son. The phrase translated: "With thee I am well pleased," might also be rendered: "I have decided on you"—i.e., chosen you. If the evangelist speculated about it at all, he may have thought that Jesus became Son of God at this moment. The first part of the voice from heaven seems to be a reminiscence of Ps. 2:7, and the "western" text of Luke— i.e., Codex Bezae (D) and the OL—in the parallel passage Luke 3:22 quotes the psalm directly: "To-day have I begotten thee." The second half of Mark's voice from heaven alludes to Isa. 42:1 and refers to the Servant whom God has chosen (*see* SERVANT OF THE LORD). The story of the Transfiguration is likewise climaxed by the words from heaven: "This is my beloved Son; listen to him" (9:7). Here the background is messianic and eschatological. Jesus is attended by Moses and Elijah, both of whom were regarded as forerunners of the Messiah and were sometimes believed to have ascended into heaven without experiencing death. For a moment the disciples are given a vision of the glory which Jesus will have in heaven and will bear with him when he returns. "Son of God" in these passages suggests not only Messiah but also the Lord of II Cor. 3:7–4:6, in whose face the glory of God shines out, not temporarily, as in the face of Moses, but permanently.

b) To be Son of God is also to be SON OF MAN. The Son of man comes in the glory of his Father with the holy angels (8:38). Indeed, the traits of the transfigured Christ are reminiscent of the glorified Son of man.

c) "Son of God" is used as a title of Messiah. At the hearing before the high priest, Jesus is asked: "Are you the Christ, the Son of the Blessed?" (14: 61)—"the Blessed" being used to avoid pronouncing the name of God. Jesus' answer is: "I am." One passage in Mark seems to reject the idea that the Messiah inherits his dignity as a descendant of David: "David himself calls him Lord; so how is he his Son?" (12:35-37).

d) "Son of God" is the title given Jesus by demons and pagans. Demons, presumably because they are spiritual beings, recognize the nature of Jesus before the disciples are able to do so (3:11; cf. 1:24: "the Holy One of God"). The insane man in the country of the Gergesenes or Gerasenes cries out: "What have you to do with me, Jesus, Son of the Most High God?" (5:7). "The Most High God" was a title which might refer to the God of Israel or, when used by pagans, to the highest god of their pantheon. Mark appears to have written his gospel primarily for former pagans, to whom the phrase "Son of God" would suggest a divine being like Asclepius—i.e., a divinized hero who healed men's diseases and was their savior. The term therefore suggests the whole miraculous side of Jesus' work, as in the story of the walking on the water, when Jesus says: "Take heart, it is I" (or "I am," ἐγώ εἰμι; 6:50; the phrase is used by God himself in Exod. 3:14-15).

e) "Son of God" suggests also the filial relationship of Jesus, who obeys God even to his death. In the parable of the wicked husbandmen (12:1-11) God finally sends his beloved Son, who is killed and cast out of the vineyard. In Gethsemane, Jesus prays: "Abba, Father, all things are possible to thee; remove this cup from me; yet not what I will, but what thou wilt" (14:36). There are some things that neither the angels nor the Son know, but only the Father (13:32). As Son of God in this sense, whoever does the will of God is Jesus' brother and sister and mother (3:35). God is the disciples' Father in heaven (11:25). *See* CHRIST § 5.

b. Q. In Q, the disciples are taught to love their enemies and thereby to become sons of their Father, who does the same. They must become "perfect" or "merciful" like their Father (Matt. 5:44-48=Luke 6:35-36). The prayer given them by Jesus begins with "Father" or "Our Father who art in heaven" (Matt. 6:9=Luke 11:2). If they, evil though they are, know how to give good gifts to their children, how much more will the heavenly Father give good things (or the Holy Spirit) to those who ask him (Matt. 7:11=Luke 11:13). *See* Q.

But while in Q those who depend on God and imitate his loving kindness are his sons, Jesus is uniquely the Son of God. The tempter so addresses him twice (Matt. 4:3, 6=Luke 4:3, 9). As Son of God he might have power to turn stones into bread and to cast himself down from the wing of the temple without hurt. These may be thought of as characteristics of the Messiah, who has miraculous powers, but the term "Messiah" is not used in Q, and the Christology of the Q tradition may center in an angelic Son of God. On the other hand, it is just possible that Mark's story of the Baptism was originally part of Q; or that at any rate the baptism and temptation stories are part of a single tradition in which Jesus is Son of God, chosen and beloved. It should be emphasized that in the temptation story Jesus, as God's true and obedient Son, will not violate his Father's teaching as found in holy scripture.

Q contains another highly significant passage, Matt. 11:25-30. Only part of this (vss. 25-27) is paralleled in Luke 10:21-22. Here Jesus addresses God as "Father, Lord of heaven and earth," and thanks him because the revelation has been hidden from the wise and understanding and revealed to babes. He then declares that all things have been delivered to him by his Father and that no one knows the Son but the Father, nor does anyone know the Father except the Son and anyone to whom the Son chooses to reveal the Father. This is more like the teaching of the Fourth Gospel than that of the Synoptics, for in Jesus' synoptic teaching it is gen-

erally presupposed that God the Father is known to all devout believers, whether they are disciples of Jesus or not. It has therefore been conjectured that the passage originally contained no reference to the hiddenness of the Father. The secret now being revealed would, on this theory, be the identity of the Son. The Messiah, according to Jewish teaching, could not be recognized until Elijah came to anoint him or until he was revealed in some other way (see, e.g., Just. Dial. 8.4). In the case of Jesus, the Son's identity was presumably first made known at the Baptism. Thereafter it is recognized by the "babes."

Matthew's passage concludes with an appeal to those who toil and are burdened to accept Jesus' yoke, which is easy, and to learn from him. The reference may be to the "yoke of the Torah" or the "yoke of the kingdom," phrases known in rabbinical literature. There is a further allusion to the great appeal made by wisdom in the conclusion to Ecclesiasticus (51:13-30). Sometimes, therefore, it is thought that in this passage Jesus embodies the heavenly wisdom of Prov. 8:22-31; Wisd. Sol. 7:22-8:1, through whom the worlds were created. The form of the passage also suggests that of certain divine self-revelations known in pagan literature. The wisdom ideas included here have parallels in the Pauline letters. In I Cor. 1:24, Christ is the power of God and the wisdom of God. This wisdom has been hidden from the rulers of the world (I Cor. 2:6-9) and is a stumbling block to the Jews and foolishness to the Greeks (I Cor. 1:23).

c. Luke. Luke clearly regards "Son of God" as a title of the Davidic Messiah. Gabriel, in his annunciation to Mary, says:

> He will be great, and will be called Son of the
>   Most High;
> and the Lord God will give to him the throne of his
>   father David,
> and he will reign over the house of Jacob for ever;
> and of his kingdom there will be no end
>
> (1:32-33).

This language is completely biblical and messianic and would seem to come from a very primitive Christian theology. In contrast to Mark and Q, which could be understood as teaching that Jesus became Son of God at his baptism, Luke appears to say that he is Son of God at least from his birth, even though his full investiture with messianic dignity may come later.

> The Holy Spirit will come upon you,
> and the power of the Most High will overshadow you;
> therefore the child to be born will be called holy,
> the Son of God (1:35).

This again is theologically undeveloped. Apart from Mary's question in 1:34: "How can this be, since I have no husband?" and the statement in 2:5 that Mary is still Joseph's betrothed, the story is very much like that of the birth of Samuel in I Sam. 1 (*see* VIRGIN BIRTH). The important point is that the birth of the Son of God is wondrous.

In other places Luke's editorial work shows that he identifies "Son of God" and "Messiah." The demons hail Jesus as Son of God, and he does not permit them to speak because they know that he is

Messiah (4:41). In the transfiguration story God addresses Jesus as his Son, his Chosen (ὁ ἐκλελεγμένος; 9:35), while in 23:35 the Messiah of God is called the Chosen (ὁ ἐκλεκτός). When, in 22:69-70, Jesus predicts that the Son of man will hereafter be seated at the right hand of God, his questioners say: "Are you the Son of God, then?" and he answers: "You say that I am."

The Son-of-God sayings in Luke, as in Mark and Q, sometimes strike the filial note. Mary reproaches the boy Jesus because she and his father (i.e., Joseph) have sought him sorrowing. Jesus answers: "Did you not know that I must be in my Father's house?" (2:49). Twice on the cross Jesus addresses God as Father (23:34, omitted by some MSS and versions; 23:46).

Luke also refers to Adam as son of God (3:38) and to God as the Father who will give the disciples the kingdom (12:32). In Luke's form of the controversy with the Sadducees, Jesus says that in the future age people will not marry or die, since they are equal to angels "and are sons of God, being sons of the resurrection" (20:35-36). This is very Semitic language, and the "sons of God" are practically identical with angels.

d. Matthew. An analysis of Matthew shows that he frequently adds to his sources, Mark and Q, the phrase "my Father" or "my Father who is in heaven" (e.g., 7:21; 10:32-33; 20:23; 26:29). Whereas Luke 12:8 reads: "Everyone who acknowledges me before men, the Son of man also will acknowledge before the angels of God," the parallel Matt. 10:32 is as follows: "Every one who acknowledges me before men, I also will acknowledge before my Father who is in heaven." Though both forms contain some Semitic traits, Luke's appears to be more primitive. Matthew has clearly replaced "Son of man" with the idea of Son of God. Matthew also adds "your Father who is in heaven" (18:14), but in one instance Mark (11:25) also has the phrase, and the later evangelist has simply taken it over in Matt. 6:14-15. "My Father" occurs frequently in places where Matthew may use a special source or oral tradition (e.g., 15:13; 16:17; 18:10, 19, 35; 25:34; 26:53), and "your Father" and related phrases in 5:16; 6:1, 4, 6, 18; 18:14; 23:9. It appears, therefore, that Matthew develops with equal emphasis the thoughts that God is Jesus' Father and that he is the Father of the disciples.

Into his sources at various points Matthew also inserts the phrase "Son of God." The demons address Jesus in this fashion (8:29; cf. Mark 1:24). Peter hails Jesus as "the Christ, the Son of the living God" (16:16; cf. Mark 8:29). The high priest adjures Jesus to say whether he is "the Christ, the Son of God" (26:63; cf. Mark 14:61), and twice while he is on the cross he is reproached for having said that he was the Son of God (27:40, 43; cf. Mark 15:29-32). Matthew's form of the Great Commission bids the disciples baptize into the name of the Father, the Son, and the Holy Spirit (28:19; see TRINITY).

Once in the special material it is implied that the disciples are sons of God (17:26). As sons of the King they are not required to pay the temple tax, but in order to avoid scandal, they should neverthe-less pay. This doctrine of Christian freedom is similar to that of Paul.

Matthew's story of the Annunciation and the Virgin Birth (1:18-25) curiously does not use the phrase "Son of God." But in the narrative of the flight into Egypt, Matt. 2:15 quotes Hos. 11:1: "Out of Egypt have I called my son," a passage that originally referred to Israel as God's son. It may be that the evangelist thought of Jesus as the true representative of Israel and his return to the homeland as typified by the Exodus. In any case, like Luke, he seems to have regarded Jesus as Son of God from the time of his birth or conception. The Synoptic gospels have no clear, explicit idea of Christ's pre-existence.

To both Matthew and Luke, then, the term "Son of God" is primarily one of Jesus' messianic titles, and it can be used almost interchangeably with "Messiah" and "Son of man." It calls attention, however, to his miraculous birth, to his filial relationship to God, and to his relationship to his disciples, who are also—in a true, though different, sense—sons of God.

e. Jesus' use of the idea. The foregoing provides the basis for consideration of Jesus' own possible use of the concept (see JESUS CHRIST). It is characteristic of the Synoptic gospels that they do not quote him as using the phrase "Son of God." The term is used by others, while he himself employs "Son of man." He is not often represented as speaking of "the Son" in an absolute sense, and scholars often question the genuineness of the passages where he is said to do so. Many of the references to God as "my Father" appear to have been introduced by Matthew. The theological tendency which produced the Gospel of John, with its numerous self-revelations, seems already to have been at work.

There is less reason to question the references to God as "your Father," though Matthew has increased the number of them, or the address "Father" or "Abba" in prayer. Jesus apparently had a strong sense of filial relation to God and emphasized God's fatherly relation to mankind (see, e.g., the Q passages Matt. 5:44-48; 6:9; 7:11 and parallels). This aspect of Jesus' teaching may be one of the principal factors which led to the development of Christology, and it probably explains why to the evangelists he is the unique Son of God.

f. The Pauline letters. Although Paul's letters are earlier in date than the Synoptic gospels, they usually represent a more advanced theology. This is true as regards Christology as in other respects. Paul uses the term "Son of God," often in connection with God's love and his adoption of believers as his sons, although he employs the titles "Christ," "Christ Jesus," "Jesus Christ," and "Lord" much more frequently.

In his earliest letter, I Thessalonians, Paul uses the term "his [i.e., God's] Son" in connection with the hope of Christ's return from heaven (1:10). This picture of the PAROUSIA is reminiscent of some of the Son-of-man passages in the Synoptics. A slightly later letter, I Corinthians, speaks of the Son as the Messiah. "When all things are subjected to him, then the Son himself will also be subjected to him who put all things under him, that God may be everything to every one" (I Cor. 15:28). Some church fathers omit the words "the Son," but the usual reading of the text may be genuine. The Son, according to this passage, will have a temporary messianic kingdom. See KINGDOM OF GOD; ESCHATOLOGY OF THE NT.

Another passage, Rom. 1:3-4, may be an example of Paul's missionary preaching. The apostle speaks of the good news of God "concerning his Son, who was descended from David according to the flesh and designated Son of God in power according to the Spirit of holiness by his resurrection from the dead, Jesus Christ our Lord." This is a careful statement. As compared with the speech attributed to Peter in Acts 2:36: "Let all the house of Israel therefore know assuredly that God has made him both Lord and Christ, this Jesus whom you crucified," the Pauline formula avoids the thought that Jesus became Son of God only after the Resurrection. He was marked out or declared as such by the Resurrection. A distinction is further made between what he was externally (κατὰ σάρκα) and what he was spiritually.

Paul probably believed that Christ, as Son of God, was pre-existent. When the full time had come, God sent out his Son, made from a woman, made under the law (Gal. 4:4; cf. Rom. 8:3). There is no suggestion here of the Virgin Birth; it is simply that when he sent his Son into the world, God made him subject to all human conditions, including membership in the Jewish community (cf. Phil. 2:5-11).

In other places Paul speaks of the Son in connection with his fundamental gospel. E.g., his call to be an apostle came when God decided to reveal his son in (or to) Paul (Gal. 1:15-16; cf. 1:1). Christ Jesus was proclaimed as Son of God to the Corinthians (II Cor. 1:19), and they were called into communion with God's Son (I Cor. 1:9).

Paul's principal contribution to the idea is in the working out of the relationship between Christ and other men as sons of God. God sent his Son under the conditions of human creatureliness to redeem those who were under the law and to make it possible for them to receive adoption. Because Christians are now sons, God has sent the Spirit into their hearts, crying: "Abba! Father!" (Gal. 4:4-6; cf. Rom. 8:14-16). Believers have been reconciled by the Son's death and will be saved by his life (Rom. 5:10). God sent his own Son in flesh like sinful flesh, and thus sin was condemned in the flesh (Rom. 8:3). Believers will therefore be freed from sin, and from its consequence, death, for adoption means the redemption of their bodies (Rom. 8:23). Indeed, it has been God's plan that they should be conformed to the image (εἰκών) of his Son, so that he should be the first-born among many brothers (Rom. 8:29). Through faith the believers are all sons of God in Christ Jesus (Gal. 3:26). All this was motivated by the love of God and Christ. God did not spare his own Son (Rom. 8:32); Paul says that the life he now lives he is able to live because of faith in the Son of God, who loved him and gave himself for him (Gal. 2:20).

"Son of God" in Paul therefore calls attention to the relation between God and Christ which existed even before Christ came into the world and which is manifested in Jesus' love and obedience. This and much more is summed up in Col. 1:12-20, where Paul develops his Christology most completely. Here he speaks of the Father, "who has qualified us to share in the inheritance of the saints in light. He has delivered us from the dominion of darkness and transferred us to the kingdom of his beloved Son, in whom we have redemption, the forgiveness of sins. He is the image [εἰκών] of the invisible God, the first-born of all creation; for in him all things were created. . . . He is before all things, and in him all things hold together. He is the head of the body, the church; he is the beginning, the first-born from the dead, that in everything he might be pre-eminent. For in him all the fulness of God was pleased to dwell, and through him to reconcile all things, whether on earth or in heaven, making peace by the blood of his cross." See INCARNATION, THE.

g. Hebrews. Toward the end of the first century, the Letter to the Hebrews develops further the idea of Paul that the world was created through the Son of God. The author's method is to start from the messianic texts, II Sam. 7:14; Ps. 2:7, and by making a christological use of numerous other OT passages, to establish his view of the person and work of Christ. In contrast to the former, partial revelation through the prophets, God has now spoken through his Son, who is heir of all things and through whom the aeons (ages or worlds) were made (Heb. 1:1-2). "He reflects the glory of God and bears the very stamp of his nature, upholding the universe by his word of power" (1:3), and is now enthroned at God's right hand, far above the angels (1:4). Here we find a doctrine similar to that of Philo's LOGOS and established by a method of scripture interpretation similar to that of Philo, the difference being that Christ is clearly a person distinct from God the Father. As Son, Christ is ruler over God's house, the Christian community (3:6); he is equated with the anointed king of Ps. 45 (Heb. 1:8-9); and as a great high priest who has passed into the heavens to offer a perfect sacrifice and intercede for his people (4:14), he is typified by Melchizedek (5:6; 7:3, 28). Despite his dignity as Son, or perhaps as a mark of his filial relationship, he learned obedience through suffering and was perfected (5:8-10). It is uncertain whether the author has in mind such parts of the gospel tradition as the Gethsemane story; at any rate, his doctrine of Jesus' sonship has two sides, and Christians are sons of God as in the gospels (2:10; 12:5-8).

h. The Gospel of John. "Son of God" is the title of Jesus most characteristic of the Gospel of John. It is coupled with the titles "king of Israel" (1:49), "Messiah" or "Christ" (11:27; 20:31), and "Son of man" (5:27-29), or rather these are parts of Jesus' divine sonship. Jesus is the unique Son of God and not of human origin (1:12-14, 18; 8:58; 13:1-3). As such he is unknown to the world until revealed (6:42; 8:19; 19:9). He has been sent to save the world, and one must believe in him to be saved (3:16, 18, 35-36). God has given all authority into his hands, so that he is equal with God (3:35-36;

5:18; 10:18, 30, 34-36; 16:32; 17:10; 20:28). Having been given this authority, as creator he bestows life and executes judgment (5:21-24). Another aspect of his sonship is his unfailing loyalty to the Father (2:16); in this world he imitates the Father by doing his work (5:17, 19-30). It is unnecessary for the Son to testify to himself (5:31-32), for the witnesses are John the Baptist, the work of Jesus, the Father, and the Scriptures (5:33, 36-37, 39); instead of seeking his own glory, he is glorified by God (8:50-54; 11:4; 12:27; 14:13, 28; 17:1). Those who believe in his name are given the authority to become children of God (1:12) or sons (8:35-36). They are thus branches of the true vine (15:5, 14-16). Their relation to Christ is analogous to the relation of Christ to the Father (10:14-15; 17:21; 20:17, 21). Thus the idea of the divine sonship is climaxed in the Fourth Gospel. This sonship is sometimes called "metaphysical," but since such categories of thought are foreign to the NT, it would be better to say that in John's mind the sonship of Christ is not moral or adoptive, but that Christ is fully the Son of God as human beings are children of their earthly parents. *See* CHRIST § 11.

i. The First Letter of John. The closely related First Letter adds very little to the doctrine. Its principal theme is its demand of full faith in Jesus as Son of God (I John 3:23; 4:14-15; 5:5, 20). This faith binds the church in union with the Father and the Son (4:14-15), and the church bears witness to it (1:1-3), as does the Father (5:9-12), while he who denies it is antichrist (2:22-24). As Son of God, Jesus destroys the works of the devil (3:8), cleanses his people with his blood (1:7), expiates their sins, and gives them life (4:9-10; 5:11-12).

j. The Apostolic Fathers. The somewhat confused Christology of the Shepherd of Hermas is based entirely on the idea of Christ as Son of God, the term "Christ" being used but once (Herm. Vis. II. 2.8) and the name Jesus not at all. The most difficult passage is the allegory of the slave in Herm. Sim. V.2-6, which tells how a certain man chose a slave and told him to fence his vineyard, promising him freedom as a reward. Since the slave weeded the vineyard and thus did more than he was commanded, the owner, after consulting his beloved Son, decided that the slave should be joint heir with the Son. In one passage (Herm. Sim. V.5.2) it is explained that the slave is the Son of God, and further that God made the Holy Spirit to dwell in the flesh of the slave, and since the flesh did not defile the Spirit, God chose this flesh as κοινωνόν, companion of or sharer in the Holy Spirit (Herm. Sim. V.6.5-6). This would seem to teach an adoptionist Christology and one which distinguishes between the eternal Son and the incarnate Son. On the other hand, the Shepherd tells Hermas that the Son of God is not given the appearance or guise of a slave but great power and lordship (Herm. Sim. V.6.1); a distinction is drawn between the Son and the slave in V.6.4, and in V.6.7 Hermas is taught that *all* flesh in which the Holy Spirit has dwelt, and which has been kept spotless, will receive a reward. Thus Hermas has probably confused the idea of the eternal Son of God with the adoption of Christians as sons of God.

In other passages the Son of God is identified with the law of God (Herm. Sim. VIII.3.2-3) and with the Holy Spirit, who speaks to Hermas in the form of the church (Herm. Sim. IX.1.1). The Son in one vision is identified with a rock which is very old, because he is older than all creation and counselor to the Father (Herm. Sim. IX.12.2; cf. IX.14.5, where it is said that the name of the Son of God is great and incomprehensible, and supports the whole world), and with a new gate because he was manifested in the last days of the consummation and one cannot enter into the kingdom of God or approach the Lord except through him (Herm. Sim. IX.12.3-6). Here there are apparent echoes of John 3:5; 14:6.

Other books of the Apostolic Fathers emphasize the idea of Jesus as Son of God but add no new teaching. In the letters of Ignatius, the Virgin Birth is taught (Ign. Eph. 18:2; 19:1; Smyrn. 1:1), as well as the Johannine idea of Christ's intimate union with the Father (Ign. Eph. 3:2; 5:1; Magn. 1:2; 7:1). The Epistle to Diognetus, in an eloquent passage reminiscent of Paul and John, speaks of God's sending Christ in gentleness and meekness and as a king might send his son (Diogn. 7:2-4).

Bibliography. E. Norden, *Agnostos Theos* (1913); E. D. Burton, *The Epistle to the Galatians* (1920), pp. 404-17; K. Lake and F. J. Foakes-Jackson, *The Beginnings of Christianity,* I (1920), 392-403; B. S. Easton, *The Gospel According to St. Luke* (1926), pp. 166-68; E. Huntress, " 'Son of God' in Jewish Writings Prior to the Christian Era," *JBL*, LIV (1935), 117-23; L. Bieler, *Theios Aner* (1935-36); T. Arvedson, *Das Mysterium Christi* (1937); W. L. Knox, *Some Hellenistic Elements in Primitive Christianity* (1944), pp. 6-7; C. H. Dodd, *The Interpretation of the Fourth Gospel* (1953), pp. 250-62; E. Stauffer, *NT Theology* (1955), pp. 108-11; F. C. Grant, Harper's Annotated Bible, No. 15 (1956), pp. 13-15, 20.   S. E. JOHNSON

*SON OF MAN [בֶּן־אָדָם, בֶּן אֱנוֹשׁ; υἱὸς ἀνθρώπου, ὁ υἱὸς τοῦ ἀνθρώπου; Aram. בַּר אֱנָשׁ]. A term for man; human being; an apocalyptic figure; in the NT, a title for Jesus.

1. In the OT
2. In Enoch
3. In early Christian literature
   a. The Synoptic gospels
   b. The Gospel of John
   c. The heavenly man of the Pauline letters
4. Origin and development of the idea
   a. Philo
   b. II Esdras
   c. Mandaean literature
   d. Manichean literature
   e. Early Gnosticism
   f. Relation to Judaism and Christianity
5. Jesus' use of the term
Bibliography

1. In the OT. The form is used frequently in Ezekiel as God's address to the prophet (e.g., Ezek. 2:1), and here it must mean "O man." Elsewhere in the OT it is in parallelism to אִישׁ, "man" (Num. 23:19; Job 35:8; Ps. 80:17; Jer. 49:18), or אֱנוֹשׁ, "man" (Job 25:6; Ps. 8:4; Isa. 51:12; 56:2); twice it is found alone (Ps. 146:3; Dan. 8:17, where it is addressed to the prophet). There is one occurrence of בֶּן אֱנוֹשׁ in parallelism to אָדָם, "man" (Ps. 144:3). The Aramaic בַּר אֱנָשׁ is found in Dan. 7:13, where one "like a son of man" is apparently contrasted with beasts which symbolize the monarchies of Babylonia, Media, Persia, and Greece (*see* ESCHATOLOGY OF THE OT). Rabbinical Aramaic uses the term בר נשא or בר נשא in the sense of "a certain man" to introduce an unnamed person at the beginning of a narrative (cf. ἄνθρωπός τις [Luke 15:11]). This is closely analogous to the usage in Daniel.

2. In Enoch. The Ethiopic version of Enoch, translated from a book written in Aramaic and Hebrew sometime in the first two centuries B.C., uses the phrase many times in that portion which is usually called the Similitudes of Enoch (chs. 37–71; *see* ENOCH, BOOK OF). Although parts of eight MSS of a form of Enoch have been found in the Qumran caves, these do not include the Similitudes. It is likely, nevertheless, that the Similitudes are pre-Christian and were written in Hebrew.

The Similitudes predict the coming of an Elect or Chosen One (*see* MESSIAH), in whose days righteousness shall prevail and in whose presence the righteous and elect will remain forever (Enoch 39:6*b*). This Elect One will sit on the throne of glory and "try the works" of the righteous (45:3). In him dwells the spirit of wisdom, understanding, and might (49:2-3). At the resurrection of the dead he chooses out the righteous and holy and sits on the throne of God (51:1-3; 61:8).

The Son of man appears in chs. 46–48; 62–71; and, while these chapters may represent a source separate from that in which the figure is called the Elect One, the final author of the Similitudes appears to regard the two as identical. Ch. 46 begins with the description of "one who had a head of days," as in Dan. 7:9, and also of one who had the appearance of a man, his face full of graciousness like one of the holy angels (46:1). The latter figure, the Son of man, is obviously a development of the one in Daniel. He "has righteousness," and he reveals treasure that is hidden, because the Lord of Spirits has chosen him (46:3). He will remove from their seats the kings and mighty who have persecuted God's congregations (46:4-8), and he will be a staff to the righteous and a light to the Gentiles (48:4). The mighty will suffer travail pangs "when they see that Son of man sitting on the throne of his glory" (62:2-5; a close parallel to Matt. 25:31). The Son of man was hidden from the beginning, and the Most High has preserved him and revealed him to the elect (62:7). All judgment is committed to the Son of man (69:27-29; cf. John 5:27). At the conclusion of the Similitudes, Enoch's "name" is raised, within his lifetime, to that of the Son of man, and in the present text of the book he seems actually to be identified with that figure (71:14-17). The book of Enoch appears to constitute the immediate background for some of the NT ideas of the Son of man (*see* ESCHATOLOGY OF THE NT).

3. In early Christian literature. The phrase occurs frequently in the gospels, always in sayings ascribed to Jesus or in indirect discourse reporting his words, and the evangelists always understand it as a self-designation of Jesus. Elsewhere in the NT it is found only in Acts 7:56, where the dying Stephen exclaims that he sees the heavens opened and the Son of man standing at the right hand of God, and

in Rev. 1:13; 14:14 (without the definite article), where the glorified Christ is portrayed as "like a son of man," there being a clear reminiscence of Dan. 7:13. The plural phrase "sons of men," meaning "human beings," and not referring to Jesus, is found in Mark 3:28; Eph. 3:5.

In the second century the apocalyptic force of the term "Son of man" appears generally to be lost. In Ignatius, Jesus is Son of man because he is of the family of David according to the flesh (Ign. Eph. 20.2), and in Barn. 12.10-11 Jesus' nature as Son of man is contrasted with his nature as Son of God. Hegesippus, quoted in Euseb. Hist. II.23.13, says that James the brother of the Lord, at the time of his martyrdom, cried out, "Why do you ask me about the Son of man, since he sits in heaven at the right hand of the mighty power, and shall come on the clouds of heaven?"

a. *The Synoptic gospels.* While the first three evangelists all identify Jesus with the Son of man, the associations of the phrase vary in the Synoptic tradition.

In the Gospel of Mark there are two passages where in the older tradition the phrase might possibly mean "a man"—2:10 (=Matt. 9:6=Luke 5:24): "that you may know that the Son of man has authority on earth to forgive sins"; and 2:28 (=Matt. 12:8=Luke 6:5): "The Son of man is lord even of the sabbath." At the same time, even when he writes the above passages, the evangelist himself must think of "Son of man" as referring to one who is more than human; he is the exalted Lord who will come in glory (*see* PAROUSIA). Such a figure is portrayed in three other passages. The first of these is 8:38 (=Matt. 16:27=Luke 9:26): "Whoever is ashamed of me and of my words in this adulterous and sinful generation, of him will the Son of man also be ashamed, when he comes in the glory of his Father with the holy angels." Here Jesus is practically identified with the Son of man, who is in turn SON OF GOD (cf. Mark 13:32). In 13:26 (=Matt. 24:30= Luke 21:27) the Son of man will be seen coming in the clouds with great power and glory. Finally, when the high priest at the trial asks Jesus whether he is Messiah, the Son of the Blessed (i.e., of God), the answer is given: "I am; and you will see the Son of man sitting at the right hand of Power [i.e., the power of God], and coming with the clouds of heaven" (14:62=Matt. 26:64=Luke 22:69).

The other instances of "Son of man" in Mark teach that the Son of man must suffer, be rejected, die, and rise again. All these sayings occur after Peter's confession at Caesarea Philippi, and they include the three "passion predictions" (8:31; 9:31; 10:33-34; and parallels); the striking saying that "the Son of man also came not to be served but to serve, and to give his life as a ransom for many" (10:45= Matt. 20:28; cf. Luke 22:27); the saying of 14:21 (=Matt. 26:24=Luke 22:22) that the Son of man goes (to his death) as it is written; and, finally, 14:41 (=Matt. 26:45), from the Gethsemane story: "The Son of man is betrayed into the hands of sinners."

Thus Mark's concept of "Son of man" is highly developed. It is Jesus' own designation for himself and denotes one who is a man but who will also come in angelic glory; who is also Messiah and Son of God; and who will suffer and give his life for others in accordance with scripture, and rise again. The suffering of the Son of man is apparently connected with the figure of the righteous servant of Yahweh in Isa. 52:13–53:12 (*see* SERVANT OF THE LORD). This idea that the Son of man suffers is apparently Mark's own contribution to the doctrine, for Matthew and Luke contain it only in passages which they derive from Mark (*see* CHRIST § 5).

The so-called Q passages in Matthew and Luke (*see* Q) are of two kinds: (*a*) In one group "Son of man" is a self-designation of Jesus ("I" or "I, a man"), with no clear implication that the Son of man will come in future glory. This, at least, is the case with Matt. 8:20 = Luke 9:58: "Foxes have holes, . . . but the Son of man has nowhere to lay his head"; and with Matt. 11:19 = Luke 7:34: "The Son of man came eating and drinking, and they say, 'Behold, a glutton and a drunkard, a friend of tax collectors and sinners!' " In their present setting in the gospels these, of course, have a certain pathos and irony—to the evangelists they mean that the heavenly Son of man is friendless and rejected—but the sayings themselves do not demand this. Matt. 12:32 = Luke 12:10 is of a slightly different character: "Whoever says a word against the Son of man will be forgiven; but whoever speaks against the Holy Spirit will not be forgiven." In its context the most natural reference is, "Whoever speaks a word against me," but if the saying is detached, it might conceivably refer to the angelic figure. Luke 11:30 preserves a more original form of a saying which in Matt. 12:40 has been edited to predict the death and burial of Jesus. Here the Son of man is a sign "to this generation" as Jonah was to the men of Nineveh. The "sign of Jonah" is evidently the preaching of repentance, which was more effective in Jonah's story than in the time of Jesus, though "something greater than Jonah is here." The total impression of these four passages is that Jesus, the Son of man, is a preacher and teacher with a decisive message, which is being rejected.

b) Other passages refer to the transcendent Son of man but do not definitely identify him with Jesus. In Matt. 24:27 = Luke 17:24, the Son of man (Matthew: "the coming [παρουσία] of the Son of man") will be like the lightning shining from one end of heaven to the other (*see* PAROUSIA). Luke 17:26 = Matt. 24:37 compares the days of the Son of man to the heedless days of Noah before the Flood. Matthew changes "days of the Son of man" to "coming of the Son of man." Luke 17:22 also speaks of the days of the Son of man and 17:30 of the "day when the Son of man is revealed." Though these verses do not appear in Matthew, they may be part of the Q discourse. The phrase "Son of man" apparently stood in this Q passage, therefore, but it may be a substitute for an earlier word, "Messiah," for "days of the Messiah" is a familiar expression in Jewish eschatology. Finally, in Matt. 24:44 (= Luke 12:40, omitted by one group of MSS) it is said that "the Son of man is coming at an hour you do not expect." These passages all teach that the appearance of the Son of man will be sudden and unexpected, and perhaps unmistakable.

There remain three Q passages in which only one of the evangelists uses the phrase "Son of man." Matt. 19:28 (cf. Luke 22:30) promises thrones for the Twelve when the Son of man sits on the throne of his glory. Since almost the identical phrase is found in Matt. 25:31, the mention of the Son of man is probably the editorial work of the evangelist. Luke 12:8 reads: "Everyone who acknowledges me before men, the Son of man also will acknowledge before the angels of God," while at this point Matt. 10:32 has: "Every one who acknowledges me before men, I also will acknowledge . . . ." In the Lukan saying, the Son of man is Jesus and also the eschatological figure; Luke may possibly have added "Son of man." A similar situation exists in Luke 6:22 (= Matt. 5: 11), except that "Son of man" here has no clear eschatological reference (*see* CHRIST § 6).

Matthew uses the phrase several times in sections of the gospel not paralleled by the other evangelists. The most striking occurrence is in 10:23: "You will not have gone through all the towns of Israel, before the Son of man comes." This probably refers to the heavenly judge, and so do 13:41; 24:30; 25:31; and perhaps 13:37. In all of these except possibly 25:31 the phrase is due to the evangelist's editorial work. Twice Matthew adds the words to Markan passages. "Son of man" is used in 26:2, where the reference is to Jesus' coming crucifixion. Matt. 16:28 (cf. Mark 9:1) predicts that some of the disciples will see the Son of man coming in his kingdom.

There remain several passages found only in Luke. In 18:8, at the conclusion of the parable of the unjust judge, the question is asked: "When the Son of man comes, will he find faith on earth?" This may come from the tradition, or be Luke's own comment. Luke 21:36, which is eschatological, appears to be an editorial passage. But in 22:48, Jesus says to Judas: "Judas, would you betray the Son of man with a kiss?" The story of Zacchaeus concludes with the words: "The Son of man came to seek and to save the lost" (19:10). Here it is a self-designation, as in the similar phrase added by some MSS to Luke 9:56; Matt. 18:11. Finally, there is a solitary instance in which the angel in the resurrection story refers to the prediction that the Son of man must die and rise again (Luke 24:7).

It appears, then, that the Q passages divide into two groups, those in which "Son of man" is the transcendent one, as in Enoch, and those in which it is Jesus' self-designation; and the situation is much the same in the special materials of Matthew and Luke, certain of which may, indeed, have come from Q.

b. The Gospel of John. In several ways the use of the term in the Fourth Gospel is like that in the other gospels. E.g., John emphasizes the point that he who is Messiah and Son of God is also Son of man; thus in John 1:51, after Nathanael has called Jesus rabbi, Son of God, and king of Israel, Jesus uses the designation "Son of man." Other instances are in 3:13-18; 5:25-27; 12:34. The phrase is used only by Jesus except in 12:34, where his questioners quote his words. Likewise John carries on and develops in his characteristic way Mark's teaching that the Son of man must suffer.

In saying that the Son of man will be glorified by his Passion (12:23; 13:31), the evangelist makes an apparent reference to the Servant (Isa. 49:3); so also with his exaltation or lifting up (12:32; cf. Isa. 52:13) and his gathering the scattered children of God (11: 52; cf. Isa. 49:5-6).

John, however, has independent knowledge of the Son-of-man tradition. More than the other evangelists he preserves the old idea of the Son of man as judge. As Son of God, Jesus calls the dead to rise because the Father has given him to have life within himself —i.e., the Son is, like the Father, a source of life; but as Son of man he is also given authority to execute judgment (5:25-27; cf. Enoch 69:27-29).

The most difficult problem in John's use of the term is raised by 1:51, where Jesus tells Nathanael that he will see the heavens opened and the angels of God ascending and descending upon the Son of man. Although the Fourth Gospel never explicitly mentions the baptism of Jesus, this looks like an allusion to that story. In 6:27 it is said that God the Father has set his seal upon the Son of man, and, of course, the verb σφραγίζω, "to seal," is used in the NT to refer to the gift of the Spirit (e.g., II Cor. 1: 22; Eph. 1:13; 4:30) and in later Christian literature in connection with Christian baptism. Finally, in 12:34 the phrase "Son of man" is used after a voice has come from heaven, as at the Baptism and the Transfiguration; and what this voice says can be described as a word of God setting his seal on Jesus. This suggests that John may know a story of the Baptism in which Jesus is called Son of man. Was Jesus "named in the presence of the Lord of spirits" as in Enoch 48:1-2?

There is some slight indication that for John the term "Son of man" carries also a reference to Jesus' humanity. The angels perhaps carry messages between God and the Son of man (1:51); thus the latter is thought of as a prophet. Jesus' believers must eat the *flesh* of the Son of man if they are to have life within them (6:53), and after the question as to the identity of the Son of man, Jesus answers: "The light is with you for a little longer" (12:35).

John's most distinctive contribution is the doctrine that the Son of man, who has come down from heaven, will ascend again. He was pre-existent in heaven (3:13), and he has come down from heaven and given life to the world, being the true bread and the food that endures to everlasting life (6:27, 32, 53). He is the only one who has ascended to heaven (3: 13); thus Enoch and others are left out of account. His Ascension occurs by his being lifted up (3:14). His disciples will see him ascend (6:62), and his lifting up will show them that he is Son of man (8:28) and will draw all men to him (12:32). The dramatic approach of the Greeks is the sign that the hour has come (12:23), and the withdrawal of Judas from the Last Supper—which ensures the Crucifixion—marks the glorification of the Son of man. Moses' lifting up of the bronze serpent Nehushtan (Num. 21:8-9) is used as the type of the Crucifixion (3:14). Seeing, for the Fourth Evangelist, is believing, and believing results in salvation. Thus John uses the metaphors of seeing and eating to express the relationship of the believer to the crucified and glorified Son of man. A Son-of-man tradition independent of the Synoptic gospels must underlie these Johannine passages, and the evangelist has synthesized this with his own

Christology, which is essentially the Son-of-God idea (see CHRIST § 11).

c. The heavenly man of the Pauline letters. Although Paul does not use the phrase "Son of man," his concept of Christ as the heavenly man may be related to it (see SECOND ADAM). The passages fall into two groups: (*a*) Adam and Christ are contrasted in Rom. 5:14-19; I Cor. 15:21-23, 45-50. Through Adam came condemnation and death, and in him all men die. He was made a "living soul" but had a natural body and was of the earth, earthy. In contrast, through Jesus came the free gift of grace which brought justification and resurrection. He is—at least in his future form as the Last Adam—not just a "living soul" but a "life-giving spirit"; he has a spiritual body and is the Lord from heaven. The contrast is between the beginning and the end, and between sin and grace. (*b*) In Phil. 2:5-11, there may be an implicit contrast to Adam, who had been made according to the εἰκών and ὁμοίωσις of God; who grasped at the fruit of the tree of life, and, being disobedient, was degraded and became a slave. Christ Jesus, however, who originally existed in the μορφή of God, did not grasp at equality with God. He took upon himself the μορφή of a slave and was made in the ὁμοίωμα of man. As he was obedient, even to death, God has exalted him and given him a name which is above every name. This is reminiscent of the naming of the Son of man in Enoch 48:1-2. Paul's speculation, however, appears to center in the biblical Adam rather than in the Son of man as known in Daniel and Enoch, although it may be influenced by the latter.

4. Origin and development of the idea. Several factors have led scholars to raise the question whether the Son-of-man idea can be explained solely from the OT and the Jewish tradition.

a. Philo. Enoch is not the only Jewish book that knows of a Son of man or a heavenly man. PHILO JUDEUS, the Alexandrian philosopher of the first century A.D., speaks of a heavenly man in his tractates *On the Account of the World's Creation* and *Allegorical Interpretation of Genesis.* He distinguishes between two men created at the beginning of the world —the heavenly man of Gen. 1:27, who is, so to speak, the pattern for all future humanity (*Creation* XXIII.69-71; XLVI.134); and the first earthly man, whose fashioning is related in Gen. 2:7 (XLVI.134 ff). In one passage (*On the Confusion of Tongues* 146) the Logos is called "beginning and name of God, and the man according to [God's] image, and he who sees, Israel." Thus the heavenly man or archetype of mankind is also the first-born Son of God and prototype of Israel.

b. II Esdras. IV Ezra, the II Esdras of the English Apoc., a Jewish apocalyptic work of the first century A.D. (see ESDRAS, BOOKS OF), to which Christian additions were made in later times, contains the figure of a man who rises from the sea and flies with the clouds of heaven (II Esd. 13:3). Enemies converge upon him from the four winds of heaven, but a flood of fire issues from his mouth and consumes them (13:5-11). This man had been kept hidden by God until the time for him to deliver the creation and to order those who are preserved after the great conflict (13: 26). The present text identifies him as God's Son

(13:32). This part of the apocalypse cannot have influenced the NT writings, nor can it have been influenced by them; it is an independent piece of Jewish speculation.

c. Mandaean literature. The ideal or heavenly man is also a feature of the Mandaean religion (*see* GNOSTICISM). The Mandaeans are a religious community located in two places, in lower Mesopotamia (Iraq) and in Iran. Their oldest literature dates from *ca.* the ninth century A.D. but contains ideas and traditions that are much older. Mandaeism is a non-Christian form of Gnosticism that contains Jewish, Christian, ancient Babylonian, and Parsi elements, the Parsi strand being the latest. The Mandaeans' knowledge of Christianity results from hostile contact, at a late date, with Orthodox or Nestorian Christianity. They regard Jesus as a false messiah, and his mother, Ruha d'Qudsha (Holy Spirit), as a demon; John the Baptist, however, is to them a true messiah. But most of the traditions of Jesus, and perhaps of John also, do not belong to the oldest strata of their writings. In the oldest portions the hero is a redeemer, Manda d'Hayye ("knowledge of life"). Through his voice and speech the first vines sprouted up. He created other human beings. He was the champion of light in its primordial conflict with darkness, and also the guardian of the soul in its descent and incorporation into humanity. He redeems man's soul—the divine element imprisoned in the body—and enables it to rise to the heavenly realm which is its true home. As a victorious figure he is probably modeled on the Babylonian god Marduk. The other Mandaean redeemer, Enosh-Uthra ("man-angel"), who figures prominently in the Right Ginza, the principal Mandaean book, duplicates most of these functions, but he is obviously also the Mandaeans' competitor with Jesus. It is said that he healed the blind, dumb, deaf, and lepers, put Jesus to flight, and returned to heaven. Obviously he is based partly on Marcionite ideas of Christ, and he is somehow related to Jewish ideas about Adam and his first descendants, including Enosh (Gen. 5:6).

d. Manichean literature. The Manichean religion, which is earlier than the Mandaean texts and may have influenced them, assigns a very important role to the Primal Man, produced from the Mother of Life, who in turn emanated from the king of the realm of light. This Primal Man is the champion of light against the powers of evil, who wound him and take part of his nature captive. It is from this captured divine element that the "archons," or commanders, of the evil power produce the created world, including humanity. Man, accordingly, is a twofold creature, fashioned partly in the image of the archons and partly in that of the power of light.

e. Early Gnosticism. Mani, the founder of Manicheism, lived in the third century A.D. In the second century, however, the figure of the Anthropos, or Man, is already an important feature of GNOSTICISM, both pagan and Christian. The *Poimandres,* the first tractate of the Hermetic Corpus, makes the Anthropos the offspring of Nous, or mind. Valentinus, the first great Christian Gnostic, places Anthropos and his consort Ecclesia ("Church") in the fourth position of the Ogdoad, or divine hierarchy, after the Ineffable, the Pater, and the Logos. The Gospel

of Mary, of the Barbelognostics, makes the First Man the fount of all existence.

f. Relation to Judaism and Christianity. All of the above suggests that speculations about the heavenly man arose independently of Judaism and Christianity. When the Anthropos first emerges as a mythological figure, he is a heavenly being who has some of the characteristics of humanity; he is the progenitor of the human race, and the champion of mankind in combat. He comes to be identified with the Messiah of Jewish expectation only in the book of Enoch and in the NT. The man of II Esdras has traits that are largely derived from the OT, but this does not altogether explain his mythological characteristics. The Son-of-man idea appears in Judaism at a time when Jewish thought is moving toward the strictest monotheism and angels and angelic figures are becoming, in rabbinic thought at least, more definitely subordinate to God. The Son of man is not characteristic of the rabbinic writings and has not been found mentioned in any of the Qumran literature hitherto published. Iranian religion, on the other hand, knows of a figure called Gayomart (*gayamaretan,* "mortal life"), who is very similar to the later Anthropos. Gayomart was the first human being to die. From his seed came the first man and woman. He is the first and foremost among the dead, and at the final resurrection his bones will be raised up first, then afterward those of other human beings. Certainly Iranian thought greatly influenced Jewish eschatology, even among the Pharisees and the Essenes, from 200 B.C. on, but to what extent it is difficult to say. *See* PERSIA, HISTORY AND RELIGION OF.

It is sometimes argued that Gayomart's trait of being champion of humanity was borrowed from the Babylonian god Marduk, and that this combined Anthropos idea furnished the inspiration for the Son of man of Daniel and Enoch. This could be true for Enoch, where the Son of man is pre-existent, concealed by God until the right time, and where it is said that he will reveal all hidden secrets and be the judge of mankind. But Daniel's Son of man does not have any of the characteristic Anthropos traits. He is not the judge; God himself is. He is only a symbol of the "saints of the Most High," the Jewish people, who in the future will have dominion. It seems better to suppose that Daniel's Son of man furnishes the author of Enoch with his basic picture, and that the book of Enoch then changes the Son of man from a symbol to an actual being who has the characteristics of the Primal Man.

The Gnostic tradition, which is a blend of Iranian, Egyptian, and Platonic elements, probably derives its Anthropos idea from Iranian sources. Philo and II Esdras receive it more indirectly, and in them it is synthesized with Jewish ideas about Adam. Jewish literature differs in its theological interpretation of Adam. In the Wisdom of Solomon, Jubilees, Enoch, Ecclesiasticus, and the Sibylline Oracles, Adam is idealized, and the tendency is to explain the origin of all evil as due to Cain, or to the angels or demons. II Esdras and the Apocalypse of Baruch are the only pseudepigraphic writings that ascribe to Adam the beginning of sin and evil.

Paul shows no clear sign of being influenced by the Anthropos speculation, except insofar as he may derive some ideas from Enoch. His comparison of Adam and Christ is independent even of Philo's tradition, for the heavenly man is not the first man but the coming Lord. To be sure, in Phil. 2:5-11 Christ is a pre-existent being, and in Col. 1:15-20 he is also the image of God, the first-born of all creation, through whom all things were created, the first-born from the dead, and the reconciler of all things. But, while some of this is parallel to ideas of the heavenly man, it may be because of his faith that Christ is the power of God and the wisdom of God (I Cor. 1:24); it is thus a wisdom type of Christology.

The Son-of-man idea in the Synoptic gospels seems to have no origin other than the book of Enoch and the familiar Semitic phrase that means "a man." Under the influence of Mark's thought it comes to be assimilated to the ideas of Messiah and the Servant of the Lord. The characteristic features of the Johannine doctrine can all be accounted for by the ideas of Enoch and the Synoptics and their development in the Christian tradition.

5. Jesus' use of the term. The double question, whether Jesus described himself as Son of man and what he meant by it, is of great importance. An answer, if it can be given, will help toward an understanding of his own view of his mission and person and also in reconstructing his teaching about the future (*see* JESUS CHRIST). The most powerful affirmative argument is that in the gospels the term is always found in words attributed to Jesus himself. One gains the impression that he used it without explanation and left it to his hearers to decide what meaning should be attached to it. It is a Semitic phrase that would be familiar to Jewish hearers, however ambiguous it was, but no Hellenistic Christian would be likely to insert it into the tradition.

On the other hand, it can be argued that the phrase is not found in all parts of Jesus' recorded teaching. It is conspicuously lacking in the parables, occurring only in the interpretation of the parable of the tares (Matt. 13:37, 41), at the beginning of the parable of the last judgment (Matt. 25:31), and at the conclusion of the interpretative sayings attached to the parable of the unjust judge (Luke 18:8). Interpretations attached to parables usually show marks of having arisen out of early Christian preaching; this is especially true of the explanation of the sower (Mark 4:14-20), and it probably explains the interpretation of the tares. The saying in Luke 18:8 may be genuine but a floating saying which did not originally belong with the parable. There are reasons for thinking that the great judge of Matt. 25:31-46 was not originally the Son of man but King Messiah. Thus "Son of man" is not integral to any of Jesus' parables, which are perhaps the most characteristic feature of his teaching.

Nor is the Son-of-man idea closely associated with Jesus' teaching about the KINGDOM OF GOD. The interpretation of the parable of the tares speaks of the Son of man's having a kingdom (Matt. 13:41), but the difficulty of this has just been mentioned. According to Matt. 16:28 the Son of man will be seen coming in his kingdom, but this is probably a result of Matthew's editorial work, since the parallel Mark 9:1 says only: "There are some standing here who will not taste death before they see the kingdom of God come with power." "Son of man" occurs in Luke 9:58, and in the immediate context the kingdom of God is mentioned (Luke 9:60, 62). The phrase "kingdom of God" does not, however, occur in Matt. 8:21-22, which parallels Luke 9:60.

It must, however, be granted that Jesus would not necessarily use the phrase "kingdom of God" every time he spoke about his mission. "Son of man" occurs in Matt. 12:32 in a context that has to do with Jesus' work of casting out demons; in the Lukan parallel (12:10) this is, however, not the case. The saying in Luke 11:30: "As Jonah became a sign to the men of Nineveh, so will the Son of man be to this generation," is part of a section in which Jesus defends his new mission. Preaching and casting out of demons were both signs of the advent of the kingdom of God.

The above evidence may mean that Jesus never used the phrase "Son of man," but that it was added to the tradition by Jewish Christians. But this is not the only possible interpretation. It is noteworthy that in the Gospel of Mark teaching about the kingdom of God is prominent in the story of the Galilean ministry, but the phrase does not appear in the words of Jesus recorded as spoken in Jerusalem. Paul, who has some knowledge of Jesus' life and teaching, not only does not use the phrase "Son of man" but speaks of the kingdom of God only occasionally. "Son of man" and "kingdom of God" might therefore belong to separate cycles of Christian tradition, both of them essentially genuine. Both phrases occur in Mark and Q, the two most important sources of the gospel tradition, and also in the special materials of Matthew and Luke (in Matthew, of course, in the form "kingdom of the heavens"). On this supposition, the two independent traditions at a very early date were brought together in the sources and yet not mingled until the later evangelists wrote their books.

The fact that in Q "Son of man" has two separate references is important in deciding whether Jesus used the phrase. Where it means "I myself" or "a man," its absence from the parables and the kingdom-of-God sayings creates little difficulty. If these were the only genuine Son-of-man sayings, then Jesus regarded himself as primarily the announcer—or even the bringer—of the kingdom. But if the apocalyptic Son-of-man passages are genuine, Jesus described his role in terms reminiscent of Enoch and made for himself the most exalted claim possible.

Two of the sayings where the phrase may mean "I" or "a man" are found in Mark. The first (2:10) occurs in the story of the healing of the paralytic: "That you may know that the Son of man has authority on earth to forgive sins," after which the narrative continues: "he said to the paralytic, 'I say to you, rise, take up your pallet and go home.' " The phrase could mean "man," for in the conclusion of his form of the story, Matthew says: "When the crowds saw it, they were afraid, and they glorified God, who had given such authority to men" (Matt. 9:8). Recent commentators object to this interpretation because the evangelist, with his doctrine of Son of man, would not have understood the saying thus, and because the idea of man's forgiving sins seems to introduce a modern theological note. On the other hand, if these are the words of Jesus, they could mean this: God has given man the authority to pronounce forgiveness of sins. Was not this part of Jesus' message? Was the prerogative of forgiveness reserved to him alone?

The situation is similar in the controversy over plucking grain on the sabbath. But here there are two sayings: "The sabbath was made for man, not man for the sabbath; so the Son of man is lord even of the sabbath" (Mark 2:27-28). Matthew and Luke omit the first of these verses but include the second. It has been suggested that Mark originally wrote only vs. 27, and that Matthew substituted the second saying for it; in this case the texts of Mark and Luke were later conformed to that of Matthew, for some MSS of Mark omit part or all of vs. 27. It still remains possible that vs. 28, in the sense of "man is master of the sabbath," is an explanation of vs. 27, but only if the verse belongs to an old tradition, since to the evangelists "Son of man" means the coming judge.

The "I" or "man" sayings in Q, and one in Luke's special material, seem less open to objection. Jesus, a man, unlike the animals, has nowhere to lay his head (Matt. 8:20=Luke 9:58). Because he is not an ascetic, he is stigmatized as an eater and drinker and a friend of the disreputable (Matt. 11:19=Luke 7:34). Words spoken against him can be forgiven (Matt. 12:32=Luke 12:10). He is a sign to this generation, but a greater sign than Jonah (Luke 11:30=Matt. 12:40). He has come to seek and save what was lost (Luke 19:10). To these we may add the beatitude in Luke 6:22 addressed to those who are hated and rejected for the sake of the Son of man.

This is a definite strand of tradition, consistent in itself and fitting in with parables and sayings that describe Jesus' mission, e.g.: (a) the three parables of Luke 15, the parable of the great supper (Matt. 22:1-10=Luke 14:16-21), and that of the laborers in the vineyard (Matt. 20:1-15), all of which are on the theme of forgiveness and acceptance; and (b) sayings and parables on the new age (Mark 2:18-22; Matt. 11:2-13=Luke 7:18-28; 16:16). The passages last named include the same theme as Matt.12:32—Jesus' willingness to bear adverse criticism.

The "Parousia" sayings fall into several groups:

The first group contains reminiscences of Dan. 7:13. The Son of man will be seen seated at the right hand of the power of God and coming with the clouds of heaven (Mark 13:26; 14:62). As in Enoch, Daniel's figure has ceased to be a symbol and is an actual being. These sayings are in a way parallel to the saying in Mark 8:31 about the future suffering of the Son of man, for both there and in 14:62 the Son-of-man statement comes after the suggestion that Jesus is, or claims to be, Messiah. Since it is Mark's basic theology that Jesus is Messiah only as Son of man, and since the tradition was fond of adding OT quotations and allusions, some doubt arises as to whether Jesus himself made the statement.

Closely related are the occurrences of Luke 17, which must be mainly from Q. Here it is said that days are coming when the disciples will desire to see one of the days of the Son of man but will not see it (vs. 22). They are not to go here and there where others say he may be found, for the Son of man will be like the lightning flashing under the sky (vss. 23-24)—sudden and unexpected, perhaps unmistak-

able (cf. vss. 26-30). Matt. 24:44 (=Luke 12:40, omitted by Codex 1 and its allies) also teaches that the Son of man comes at a moment when he is unexpected. Luke 18:8 also appears to belong to this group. Here Jesus does not identify himself with the coming one, and these sayings fit well with his general rejection of special signs (Luke 11:29-32; Mark 8:12; Luke 12:54-56; 16:27-31). There seems no adequate reason to doubt that this is his teaching.

Matt. 10:23: "You will not have gone through all the towns of Israel, before the Son of man comes," gives a definite prediction about the time of his coming, in contradiction to Luke 17:22, and must therefore be considered doubtful. Matt. 24:30 also speaks of a visible sign of the Son of man in heaven. This is a note added to his version of Mark's Little Apocalypse and may be a product of early Christian speculation.

In Matthew's special material, as in Mark 8:38, the Son of man is the Enochic judge, attended by angels and seated on his throne of glory (e.g., Matt. 13:41; 25:31). Matthew has added this touch to Matt. 19:28, while it does not appear in Luke 22:30. Luke also seems to picture the Son of man as judge in his editorial verse 21:28. Influence of Mark and—in Matthew's case—Enoch is sufficient to account for these instances.

Finally, there are the statements that in the future the Son of man will be ashamed of those who are ashamed of Jesus (Mark 8:38) and that he who acknowledges Jesus will be acknowledged by the Son of man (Luke 12:8). The beatitude on those who are hated and rejected for the sake of the Son of man (Luke 6:22) may be related to these, but it reverses the order of Mark; apparently it is the earthly Jesus who is Son of man. This group of sayings emphasizes the close bond between Jesus and his followers, and it is noteworthy that in the parable of the last judgment (Matt. 25:31-46) to do a human service to "one of the least of these my brethren" is to do it to the King or Son of man. One aspect of the concept of the Son of man in the gospels is his deep involvement in suffering or persecuted humanity, but this may be only because the personality of Jesus cannot be separated from the concept.

Although the gospel tradition has developed the Son-of-man concept, particularly by introducing the language of Daniel and Enoch, there can be little doubt that Jesus spoke of himself as the Son of man and also spoke of the future coming of the Son of man. Furthermore, as earthly Son of man, he was charged with a mission that brought new hope to the outcasts, represented the dawning of a new age, and was a sign to his own generation just as Jonah's message of repentance was a sign to Nineveh. Though we have only the evidence of Mark that he connected the humble, earthly Son of man with the one to come, none of his hearers could have failed to draw the conclusion. It is only Mark who states clearly that the Son of man must suffer, but there is good non-Markan evidence that Jesus considered himself rejected, and furthermore that he expected death (Luke 13:33: "It cannot be that a prophet should perish away from Jerusalem").

It has been objected that Jesus, being a Jewish prophet and a man of great humility, could not have ascribed to himself the glory of the heavenly Son of man. One answer must be that we cannot rule this out as psychologically improbable. If Enoch could be thought of as elevated to such a dignity; if Philo, being a Jew, could think of Moses as transformed into a new and almost divine being; and if it was not presumption—as it surely could not be—for a man to be a prophet or Messiah; then Jesus might have believed that his calling would lead to this heavenly office. His humility and reticence, however, seem to have kept him from making an open claim of this. His hearers evidently found his words enigmatic, and the gospel tradition has preserved the mystery in them (*see* JESUS CHRIST).

Bibliography. H. Lietzmann, *Der Menschensohn* (1896); K. Lake and F. J. Foakes-Jackson, *The Beginnings of Christianity,* I (1920), 368-84; B. W. Bacon, *The Story of Jesus* (1927), pp. 254-76; C. H. Kraeling, *Anthropos and Son of Man* (1927); J. Héring, *Le royaume de Dieu et sa venue* (1937); C. T. Craig, "The Problem of the Messiahship of Jesus," in E. P. Booth, ed., *NT Studies* (1942); R. Otto, *The Kingdom of God and the Son of Man* (1943); H. B. Sharman, *Son of Man and Kingdom of God* (1943); F. C. Grant, *The Earliest Gospel* (1943), pp. 63-69; G. S. Duncan, *Jesus, Son of Man* (1947); C. H. Dodd, *The Interpretation of the Fourth Gospel* (1953), pp. 241-49.

S. E. JOHNSON

SON OF PERDITION. *See* PERDITION; ANTICHRIST.

SONG OF DEGREES. *See* DEGREES, SONG OF.

***SONG OF SONGS** [שׁיר השׁירם]. The OT book normally appearing after Job in the Hebrew Bible and first among the Megilloth (*see* CANON OF THE OT), and after Ecclesiastes in the LXX. In Protestant and Roman Catholic Bibles it appears after Ecclesiastes. It is called SONG OF SOLOMON in the English versions from the KJV through the RSV, and CANTICLES in Roman Catholic versions (from *Canticum Canticorum,* Latin translation of Hebrew *shîr hashshîrîm*).

The Song of Songs is a collection of lyrics celebrating nuptial and prenuptial love. The tradition of Solomonic authorship does not stand scrutiny, for the work is an anthology of songs and song fragments. Although the book has been treated variously as an allegory of divine love, as a pagan liturgy in which the lover is the dying and rising god and the beloved the mourning goddess, and as a drama recounting the affairs of Solomon with a country maiden, it is best understood as a compilation of pastoral lyrics, some of which were intended for use in Hebrew weddings. In the Song the folk mind of Israel is expressed through simple delight in the beauties of nature and an ardent eroticism. The Song of Songs is not didactic. It does not teach promiscuity or monogamy. Its theological value is that it shows among the ancient Hebrews a fervent and candid pleasure in the psychophysical relations of man and woman.

1. Origin
   a. Authorship
   b. Locale
   c. Date
2. Canonical status
3. Interpretation
   a. Allegorical
   b. Cultic
   c. Dramatic
   d. Lyrical
4. Poetics
   a. Parallels
   b. Genre
   c. Imagery
5. Content
   a. Nature
   b. Courtship and marriage
Bibliography

1. Origin. As long as Solomon was considered the poet, the Song was treated as a unity dating from the tenth century B.C. The diverse geographical references to Jerusalem, Transjordan, and N Israel were all thought to cohere in the vast domain of the United Monarchy. But once Solomonic authorship is set aside, the provenance of the book is thrown into relative obscurity.

a. Authorship. The sole evidence for Solomonic authorship is found in the editorial introduction: "The Song of Songs, which pertains to Solomon" (the long form of the relative, *'asher,* betrays the notation as editorial, since throughout the poems the short form, *she,* is used without exception). The title was early interpreted to mean "The Song of Songs, *by* Solomon," but the Hebrew construction is ambiguous and may, quite apart from authorship, denote possession ("belonging to Solomon"), dedication ("in honor of Solomon"), style ("in the fashion of Solomon"), or subject matter ("concerning Solomon"). There is no way of knowing which interpretation the editor intended, and, even if we did know, his judgment could not be taken as infallible. Internal evidence must be examined.

Solomon's name appears six times in the text (1:5; 3:7, 9, 11; 8:11-12). The first and the last two occurrences are figurative allusions to the fabulous wealth of the king—i.e., the beloved describes herself as dark "like the curtains of Solomon," and the lover boasts that he would rather have his "vineyard" (his beloved) all to himself than divide with king and tenants the rich produce from Solomon's vineyard. In the third chapter, Solomon is mentioned three times as principal in a spectacular procession. Here it is possible that the historical Solomon is referred to (*see* § 1c *below*). Three references to "the king" (1:4, 12; 7:6) are generally associated with Solomon. But in none of these instances does Solomon speak. He can be made into the lover of the Song only on the assumption that the few offhand references to Solomon and the one poem in which he is prominent (3:6-11) are normative for a series of poems diverse in form and content. One may allow that in one or two of the poems Solomon is the chief figure, without assuming him to be the author. That no other name than Solomon's has been connected with the book is not surprising. The folk psychology of the Song is expressed in the anonymity of the speakers and the poets. The true hero and author is love.

b. Locale. The geographical setting for the Song is diverse. Northern locations are frequently named (Damascus, Tirzah, Sharon, Carmel, Lebanon, Amana, Senir, Hermon). Transjordan sites appear (Gilead, Heshbon, Mahanaim?). Judah is represented (Jerusalem, Engedi). Some of the allusions do not presuppose that the place names form the locale of the poem. They may be literary or idiomatic allusions. "I am a rose of Sharon" (2:1) indicates that the beloved is as unrivaled in her beauty as the exquisite flower from the Plain of Sharon. It does not necessarily mean that the poet is from that region or that the maiden's home was in Sharon. "Daughters of Jerusalem [or Zion]" (2:7; 3:5, 10-11; 5:8, 16) seems to be a stereotyped phrase for the female retinue (in a wedding party?) and does not afford prima-facie evidence of Jerusalemite setting.

The general atmosphere of the Song is such, however, as to support a N Israelite rural origin. Only the poem of 3:6-11, with its lavish *décor*, requires an urban setting, preferably Jerusalem. The others correspond to the agricultural life of the small towns and peasant holdings of the N. The preponderance of northern place names corroborates the mood and imagery of the poems. But there is nothing to preclude the presence of lyrics from the bucolic strata of society in Judah and Transjordan. It may be seriously doubted that the sophisticated Solomon would have composed songs so largely pastoral, and that his jaded and acquisitive tastes for women would have been content with the rather simple-minded sentiments of the majority of the lyrics. Although the Song uses lush imagery, the emotion behind it is naïvely intense, giving no hint of the satiety and power hunger of Solomon. There is nothing in the geographical setting, either in place names or in rural mood, that favors Solomon as poet or as subject (except 3:6-11), and there is much that contravenes the tradition. Those who insist on Solomonic authorship must assume that the king pursued his maiden into the N countryside.

c. Date. There are no historical allusions in the Song that conclusively date any part, but there are one or two clues.

Tirzah, capital of the N in the early ninth century, before Omri built Samaria, is mentioned in parallel with Jerusalem in 6:4. This reference might be dismissed as an attempt at verisimilitude, a deliberate archaizing, possibly to avoid naming the apostate Samaria (*see* SAMARITANS). Or it could have been employed simply because of the meaning of Tirzah, "charm, pleasure." The context, however, favors Tirzah as the capital of the N kingdom known to the poet, analogous to Jerusalem in the S.

The one poem in which Solomon is central (3:6-11) may be an epithalamium composed for one or more of his famous marriages. The possibility that Solomon is treated symbolically as the prototypical bridegroom and that the Song was composed for the marriage of commoners in later times (*see* § *3d below*) is not to be ruled out. The major objection is that the sumptuous appointments and attendants described seem ill suited to country weddings. The balance of evidence favors both the Solomon and Tirzah poems as tenth- and ninth-century compositions, even though the latter may have been later accommodated to general usage.

A considerable factor in dating the book is the peculiarity of its language. It possesses forty-nine terms peculiar to itself. Many words and stylistic

features are formed in accordance with Aramaic, the language that replaced Hebrew as the common tongue among the Jews sometime after the Exile. On account of the occurrence of foreign terms (Persian *pardēs*, "garden" [4:12—H 4:13]; Greek *'appiryôn*, "palanquin" [3:9]), many scholars date the Song in the Persian or the Greek period. But there are complicating caveats.

ARAMAIC as a language had a checkered history and was present in the ancient Near East from at least 1200 B.C. Aramaisms appear in several early OT compositions, and there is a growing feeling that Aramaic was a strong factor in N Israel (Jacob may have been an Aramean [*see* ARAMEANS], and the close contact between Israel and Syria encouraged linguistic interchange). In short, the Aramaic flavor of the Song may be more a matter of regional dialect than of date. But if the Song reflects genuine folk poetry which has not been translated, then it would have been written before Aramaic became the common language in late postexilic times.

The peculiar terms of the Song are often due to the novel subject matter. No other OT book is so replete with FLORA; FAUNA; PERFUME; and SPICES. The technical terms for many of these were of foreign vintage. The spice we know as cinnamon derives from the Far East and has simply been transliterated into other languages (κιννάμων; קִנָּמוֹן [4:14]). From the days of Solomon, Israel had trade contacts with India, and many of the luxuries in the Song have clear Sanskrit parallels—e.g., NARD (Sanskrit *naladu;* נֵרְדְּ [1:12; 4:13-14]) and purple dyed wool (Sanskrit *ragaman;* אַרְגָּמָן [3:10; 7:5 —H 7:6]). The supposed Grecism *'appiryôn* for "litter," PALANQUIN (3:9), may not have entered Israel in Hellenistic times but rather may have come direct from Sanskrit *paryanka*. Nevertheless, the technical terminology of the Song most often finds its parallels in literature regarded on other grounds as postexilic: the Priestly source; Prov. 1-9; Chronicles.

The outside chronological limits are the reign of Solomon (961-922 B.C.) and the period when Aramaic became the accepted peasant tongue in Palestine (450-300 B.C.?). At most, but one or two of the poems suit the time of Solomon. Several may have sprung from N Israel before 722. The extant form of the book, doubtless liberally supplied by compositions from intervening centuries, was edited in the fifth century. The argument that the fresh and sensuous spirit of the Song would be inconceivable in the prudish and rigid postexilic age is simply a reflection of the prevailing caricature of that era.

2. Canonical status. Dispute over the propriety of including the Song in the canon flared at Jamnia in A.D. 90, when Rabbi Akiba, in defense of the work, delivered his now famous dictum: "For all the world is not as worthy as the day on which the Song of Songs was given to Israel, for all the writings are holy, but the Song of Songs is the Holy of Holies" (M. Yadayim 3.5). Also well known is the rabbinic rebuke: "He who trills his voice in the chanting of the Song of Songs in the banquet-halls and treats it as a secular song, has no share in the world to come" (Tosef. Sanh. 12.10).

It is widely assumed that only the claim to Solomonic authorship and the allegorical interpretation of the Song rescued its canonicity. While there are hints of allegorical treatment in the latter half of the first Christian century (e.g., Josephus calls the work "hymns to God," and in IV [II] Esd. 5:24, 26; 7:26, "lily," "dove," and "bride" are used of Israel), it is not certain that Akiba interpreted the work symbolically. Objection to treating it "as a secular song" may have been aimed at the bawdy and vulgar renditions of those drinking copiously. It is probable that the allegorical interpretation followed canonicity, rather than preceded it. Once the Song was accepted as canonical, the rabbis would be tempted to look for esoteric religious meaning, especially if they had to counteract its frivolous employment. Their motivation was not to repress sex and the plain meaning of the Song, but to ensure a proper atmosphere for its contemplation. But allegory, once started, is hard to control.

Since the allegorical theory was in full sway by the time the Christian church made its canonical pronouncements, the Song was unquestioned. But as the clear meaning of the eroticism became apparent in modern times, there have been those militantly opposed to its inclusion in the canon—e.g., Sebastien Castellion (1544), W. Whiston (1723), J. G. Semler (1771), and Eduard Reuss (1879).

3. Interpretation. Roughly four schools of interpretation, with significant variations in each, have arisen to explain the moral and literary complexities of the Song: the allegorical, cultic, dramatic, and lyrical. While the allegorical and dramatic have sharply declined in popularity and the cultic and lyrical have waxed strong, all views are represented in contemporary scholarship.

a. Allegorical. This type of interpretation was predominant among Jews and Christians through seventeen centuries and is still favored by some Roman Catholic and orthodox Jewish interpreters. In the Jewish version the lover is Yahweh and the beloved is Israel. The details of their relationship are thought to set forth the history of God's people, generally from the Exodus to the coming of the Messiah. The fullest development is in the Targum, but variants may be found in the Midrash Rabbah to the Song of Songs, Saadia Gaon, Rashi, Ibn Ezra, and are followed by some modern Christian interpreters.

In Christian dress the terms of the allegory were shifted so that the bride was the church—a position easily adopted from key NT passages (John 3:29; Eph. 5:22-33; Rev. 18:23; 21:2, 9; 22:17). The earliest exposition was by Hippolytus of Rome, but it was Origen's twelve-volume commentary, probably his most immediately influential work, that displayed the fertile imagination of the adept allegorist. He was followed by Jerome, Athanasius, Augustine, Wesley, and innumerable others. In the main, Christian interpreters did not try to read into the allegory a connected history of the church, although Thomas Brightman followed the Jew Nicholas de Lyra in reading the Song as a historical allegory of Judaism and the church, while the antipapal Cocceius regarded it as a history of the church climaxed in the Reformation.

A common variation in the primary Christian alle-

gory was to see in the Song the relation of God and the individual soul. Origen had suggested this possibility, and it was adopted by Gregory of Nyssa and given its classic expression in the eighty-six sermons of Bernard of Clairvaux, in which he got barely beyond the second chapter! The high level of Bernard's mysticism was not maintained by all who followed him, for interpreters frequently fell into a morbidly pious eroticism. Another common form of Christian allegorizing (preferred by Ambrose, Cornelius a Lapide, and Richard of St. Victor) was to treat the bride as the Virgin Mary. Martin Luther held to the novel view that the bride was Solomon's kingdom personified and that the Song celebrated the loyalty of his subjects. Some have professed to see in the maiden of the Song a personification of wisdom (similar to Prov. 8).

It is typical of those defending the Song as allegory that they are able to see more than one level of meaning in the same symbols. The earlier allegorists, while conceding the presence of the literal, despised and discounted it (Origen: "The only sense of the Canticle intended by God is the spiritual or allegorical sense"). Modern allegorists are less averse to admitting the overt meaning of the text, although they stoutly insist that the Song's primary teaching is symbolic. Some interpreters recognize multiple identities in the bridal figure, she being by turns Israel, the church, the Virgin Mary, and the individual believer.

The objections to allegory center on the complete subjectivity of the method. Where the man-woman relation is used symbolically in the OT (Ezek. 16; 23; Hos. 1-3), the figure is unfailingly indicated, but there is no clue to allegory anywhere in the Song. Allegorists have been totally at variance in the meanings they have found. A few examples follow:

> My beloved is to me a bag of myrrh,
>> that lies between my breasts
>>> (1:13).

This phrase was understood by Rashi and Ibn Ezra as the tabernacling presence of God over the ark between the cherubim; by Cyril of Alexandria as Christ and the two Testaments; by Bernard as the crucifixion of Christ, which strengthens the believer in sorrow and in joy.

> Upon my bed by night
>> I sought him whom my soul loves;
> I sought him, but found him not
>>> (3:1).

Rashi applied this to the Israelites' wilderness wanderings; Cyril to the women who sought Christ on resurrection morning; and Joüon to the capture of the ark by the Philistines.

> Your navel is a rounded bowl
>> that never lacks mixed wine.
> Your belly is a heap of wheat,
>> encircled with lilies (7:2).

To Ibn Ezra the navel was the Great Sanhedrin and the mixed wine was the Law. Simon Patrick and the Westminster Assembly biblical annotators recognized the two Christian sacraments, the navel being the baptismal font and the belly the Lord's Supper!

The allegorical parallelisms adduced from Muslim Sufism and the Hindu cult of Krishna, the divine lover, are not true allegories, for, without exception, either the god is named or some clue is given to the mystical meaning. That the affinities of man and woman often serve to mirror the relation between man and God does not mean that every poet who touches the subject intends to use symbolism. The world's treasury of simple love poetry is a standing rebuke to the notion.

b. Cultic. A popular theory springing from the discovery of ancient Near Eastern cult liturgies is the assumption that the Song of Songs was a pagan ritual later secularized or perhaps accommodated to Yahwistic usage. The lover is the dying and rising god; the beloved is his sister or mother, who laments his passing and frantically searches for him. The Near Eastern mythical pairs known to Israel were the Canaanite BAAL (see BAAL [DEITY]) and ANATH and the Babylonian TAMMUZ and Ishtar (see ASSYRIA AND BABYLONIA). The pagan liturgy entered Israel in connection with the spring and fall festivals of agriculture (see PASSOVER; BOOTHS, FEAST OF)—i.e., as a part of the observance of the NEW YEAR.

External support for this interpretation is seen in the liturgical reading of the Song at Passover, practiced as early as the eighth Christian century, but lately omitted in public reading outside Eastern Europe. Also, a reference in the Mishnah to the daughters of Jerusalem dancing and singing in the vineyards at the Wood Festival (the Fifteenth of Ab) and after the Day of Atonement is said to attest the early entrance of pagan revelries into the harvest celebrations of Israel and thus to provide a milieu for the Song (M. Ta'an. 4.8). In fact, advocates of the cultic theory insist that the Song's acceptance into the canon was facilitated by its established liturgical use.

Internal evidence is cited in the titles of male and female (e.g., Solomon equated with the god Shelem and Dodh, "beloved" in the RSV, regarded as a form of Hadad [see HADAD 5] or Baal); the intense amours and erotic imagery; the vanishing lover and the searching beloved; the structureless conversations; the elaborate allusions to flora, fauna, spices, and perfumes; the woman dancing naked. All these are shown to be features of extant Tammuz liturgies.

But there are formidable problems. It is undemonstrated that the harvest festivals in Israel ever had dying and rising rituals connected with them. The Passover reading of the Song is paralleled in the reading of Ruth at Pentecost and Ecclesiastes at the Feast of Booths, and neither of these books has the slightest claim to origin in the cult. There are no unequivocally liturgical terms in the Song (e.g., zāmîr [2:12] has a clearly nonliturgical meaning in Tosef. Sanh. 12.10; see § 2 above). Exponents of the theory disagree as to whether the pagan ritual was revised for Yahwistic use. If it were, it is strange that the divine name is lacking. If not, the reader would expect more explicit reference to the dying and rising motif. The crowning objection is that, far from ensuring the book a place in the canon, its association with pagan religion would have barred it.

In effect, the cultic interpretation is a more sophisticated version of the allegorical approach, but it is no more successful in unlocking the book. On the other hand, it is possible that liturgical idioms from the northern fertility cult entered the common peasant speech and thus found their way into the Song. Yet the obverse is equally defensible: that the love language of the people found parallel expression in the Song and in the pagan liturgies.

c. Dramatic. When the allegorical view of the Song began to decline ca. 1800, the dramatic theory sprang up to fill the gap. After great favor in the nineteenth century, it has lost ground, and for good reasons.

The dramatic theory assumes that the Song involves plot and characterization, with Solomon and a rustic maiden, named in 6:13 as the SHULAMMITE, as principals. A three-character variation provided for a country lover, the shepherd, to whom the maiden remained faithful against all the king's blandishments. The practical effect of the third character is great, for it changes the whole tone and import of the Song. In its two-character form the book would extol the joys of conjugal love as exemplified in Solomon. In its three-character version it would celebrate premarital fidelity to true love, over against luxury and seduction. In one case Solomon is hero, and in the other, villain.

In accord with the dramatic instinct the conversations in the Song were divided among Solomon, the maiden, the shepherd and chorus (or choruses). It was often taken for granted that the maiden was ABISHAG the Shunammite of I Kings 1:1-4, 15; 2:17-22. The "daughters of Jerusalem" were identified as the Solomonic harem or a chorus of professional singers. Some "dramatic" interpreters do not think of the Song as staged but rather as a dramatic reading; this is an admission of the thinness of evidence for the theory.

The weaknesses in the dramatic theory are fatal. The analysis of the Song into acts or scenes, speeches and accompanying mimes, takes nearly as many turns as there are interpreters. The reconstructions are often ingenious and plausible, but the variant schemes cancel out one another as obvious figments of the imagination. There is no character development or psychological disclosure. Literary units are carved up to supply reasonably coherent repartee among the speakers. Stage directions are manufactured. Solomon is not a prominent figure in the book and the notion of the two-character theory, that he appears as the "shepherd" pursuing his beloved, is dubious. If the three-character hypothesis is thought preferable, then the resulting defamation of the king's character would hardly have been a theme to endear the work to later rabbis. Finally, none of the dramatic theories can trace a convincing development of plot. The lovers taste of full union, praise one another, recoil and are reunited again and again, without the slightest shred of story form. The dramatic theory is a vain attempt to salvage a moral point and structural coherence.

d. Lyrical. When the false leads are eliminated, the true interpretation is the simplest. It was doubtless the plain sense of the Song which the Jews before

Jamnia recognized but which the allegorical tide swamped (*see* § 2 *above*). The Song of Songs is a collection of love songs that do not have the least intent of symbolizing divine love, nor have they derived from pagan religious celebration. While loosely connected in tradition with Solomon (one of the poems appears to observe his wedding; *see* § 1c *above*), they are not the work of a single poet, much less a dramatist. The Song teaches no lesson and tells no story. It extols human love in courtship and marriage by letting the lovers speak for themselves.

Theodore of Mopsuestia, the literalist exegete of Antioch (360-429), was apparently the first to call the Song secular, and his view was declared heretical. A few Jewish medievalists, mostly anonymous, regarded it as a song written by Solomon for his favorite wife. Sebastien Castellion (1546) had to leave Geneva because, as Calvin said, "He considers that it [the Song] is a lascivious and obscene poem, in which Solomon has described his shameless love affairs." Luis de Leon (1567) fell into the hands of the Inquisition for similar effrontery. Grotius (1732) saw a mystical meaning but stressed the erotic sense. J. G. von Herder, with his fine sense of folk literature, gave a masterful exposition of the "secular" view.

A special form of the lyrical hypothesis was advanced by K. Budde (1893), who based his view on the work of J. G. Wetzstein, who in 1873 described the seven-day Syrian wedding festivals that he had witnessed. Budde saw the Song as a disordered cycle of songs for Jewish weddings in which the groom was "king" and the bride "maiden" for a week (not "queen"!), the girl danced for her lover on the eve of the wedding, and detailed erotic praises of the male and female bodies were offered (called *wasfs* in Arabic).

There are many attractive features to the wedding-song theory, but it cannot account for all the poems. It explains the allusions to the "king," but it hardly accounts for Solomon's centrality in 3:6-11. It provides the milieu for the rather unrestrained bodily descriptions, but the entire Song cannot be regarded as toasting marital love. In fact, Budde was forced to assume that the undoubted references to premarital love were sung at the wedding festivities by the young companions who intended to conjure and confirm the love that was only beginning to awaken, since courtship practice kept the bride and groom apart before the ceremony. But the Song gives the clear impression of the social mixing of the sexes.

Another difficulty with the wedding-cycle theory is that certain elements noted by Wetzstein are lacking in the Song—e.g., the war songs in which the groom's prowess is honored. At best, there is hardly enough material for seven days of celebration. It must not be forgotten also that the Syrians are a mixed people with no Jewish connections; like customs have not survived in Palestine. Nevertheless, the criticisms do not seem to invalidate the essence of the theory, but only its rigid application.

The lyrical theory, now widely held, is the only one that avoids the pitfalls of allegorical, cultic, and dramatic overschematizing. It recognizes an anthology of lyrics and lyric fragments, some for use at weddings, others singing the raptures of premarital love. The precise number of literary units assembled in the Song is much disputed. Those who have employed FORM CRITICISM have generally demarcated from twenty to forty poems.

Now that the allegorical interpretation is in decline among Roman Catholics and virtually extinct among Jews and Protestants, a number of interpreters have attempted a didactic redirection of the Song, emphasizing the purity and propriety of married love and the religious character of marriage (cf. Eph. 5:25-33). Since the Song is in the Christian canon, it is not amiss to see it in total context. But such reinterpretation sometimes rises from an uneasiness about the Song's frankness and is clouded by an overapologetic attitude. It is likely also to dismiss the ancient social setting of the Song in the desire for immediately applicable truth. The prude's discomfort and the censor's fear must not efface the simple delight of the Song in the sexuality of the race. "Love is strong as death" (8:6), and stronger than the reticence and embarrassment of interpreters.

4. Poetics. The Song of Songs shares with other biblical poetry the technical features of parallelism of members and mixed meters (*see* POETRY, HEBREW, §§ 3-4), as well as boldness of imagery. It is in subject matter that the Song diverges sharply from most extant pre-Christian Jewish literature.

a. Extrabiblical parallels. The most convincing parallels are from Egypt, where the lovers are called "my brother" and "my sister" and are compared with steeds and gazelles. There is the same delight in the beauties of nature and a reveling in the appeal of aromatic spices. Yet the bodily descriptions are lacking in Egypt, and traces of magic and polytheism appear. Modern Arabic poetry gives franker treatment to the body.

Since the Renaissance, comparisons with classical love poetry have been common. Sappho's marriage songs are too psychologically sophisticated to bear resemblance to the Hebrew work. The Idylls of Theocritus, especially the eighteenth and twenty-seventh (where Daphnis and Acrotime converse), are perhaps closest, but the self-consciousness of the lovers and the elegance of form produce a quite different effect. The erotic poets Meleager and Philodemus were still more ribald in their mood. It is interesting, however, that both men spent their youth in Transjordan in the first century B.C., thus affording evidence of a continuing Palestinian poetry of love.

b. Genre. Allegorists have seldom inquired about the genre, since in their view the Song's purport is on a plane entirely other than the literal. The dramatists see dramatic dialogue. The cult theorists locate the Song in a liturgical celebration of the death and rebirth of the god, later recast for Yahwism or else secularized.

Lyricists are inclined to see in the anthology epithalamiums (such as Ps. 45) or pure folk lyrics with no settled "situation in life." Much depends upon how seriously the wedding-cycle hypothesis is taken (*see* § 3d *above*). The only explicit epithalamium is 3:6-11, perhaps also 1:1-4. The praise of the bodies of the lovers may be understood also as wedding songs (*see* § 3d *above*), with an ultimately conjuring intent—i.e., to secure the fertility of the woman and the virility of the man. The female chorus and the addresses to the lovers may be the parts spoken by the young companions, who are given a prominent role in oriental weddings (*see* MARRIAGE). Some profess to see traces of an alluring call associated with the Bedouin custom of the bride's fleeing into the desert, pursued by the groom, who must win her through coaxing.

Many of the poems, however, must be forced if they are to fit into wedding recitation, and the parallels with modern Arabic practice should not be overdrawn (it should be noted that among the Arabs some of the *wasfs* are used in courtship). The situation for certain units seems less in community practice than in the excited psyche of the lover-poet. It does not take any elaborate theory to explain the upsurging emotion of love in the springtime. The dream sequences express poignantly the ambivalent experiences of erotic excitation and fear of separation, the latter hardly explicable as marital anxiety.

The love songs were reckoned as wisdom genre originally because the technical skill of the musician and singer was regarded as *ḥokmâ* (*see* WISDOM). The professional mourning women were called "wise women" (RSV "skilful women"; Jer. 9:17). With equal validity the hired wedding celebrants who rendered the Song could have been termed "the wise." Solomon was said to have displayed his wisdom in songs (I Kings 4:32), and the wise men Ethan and Heman (I Kings 4:31) were apparently identified as heads of guilds of temple singers (I Chr. 6:33, 44; 15:17, 19). Thus were wisdom and song connected. When the Song was attributed to Solomon, it was doubly confirmed as wisdom literature.

c. Imagery. The rich imagery springs mainly from the Song's constant interweaving of nature and love. The countryside, described in its own right, passes over into symbolic representation of love: the beloved is a spice-filled garden, a fruitful vineyard; the lover, a gazelle or an apple tree. The considerable imagery of perfumes and spices shows that the upper class set the mores of love. The more expensive spices and gums were named as erotic lures even in peasant singing. As water was at a premium in Palestine, ointments and oils were generally used for hygienic purposes. It is quite likely that for weddings even the poorer classes would manage to indulge in a few luxuries.

In estimating the aesthetic impact of the imagery, we should recall that standards of taste in women have changed so radically toward slimness that we easily forget the preference for plumpness in most cultures and eras, as a sign of ability to work and of sexual fecundity. Ungenteel imagery in the Song can often be accounted for by this ancient taste. Likewise, comparison of the beloved to such massive and solid things as towers, walls, and horses is regularly confined to some one feature—e.g., the tower's gracefulness, the wall's impregnability to frontal attack, or the horse's brightly ornamented head gear.

5. Content. *a. Nature.* The rapport and interaction between the external world and the psychic state of the lovers produces an almost un-Hebraic delight in nature for its own sake, or at least for

love's sake. Elsewhere in the OT, nature is mentioned incidentally as the vehicle or occasion for religious meaning, as when a prophet's call comes through an almond rod in bloom, or the objects of nature are called upon to join in praise of God, or the wonders of creation are cited to overawe a critic of the divine government (*see* WORLD, NATURE OF THE). But the projection of the love experience into nature and the reflection of nature's moods in the lovers is abundantly present in Near Eastern, classical, medieval, Renaissance, romantic, and modern poetry. It is a constituent element of human nature which did not perish among the Hebrews simply because their religion made no direct use of it.

The poems in which nature plays a prominent role are the summons to the beloved to come into the fields at springtime (2:8-17; 7:11-13). But the collection is permeated with direct and symbolic allusions to flowers (henna, wild rose, lily, fig and grape blossoms), trees (pine, cedar, apple, palm), agricultural produce (raisins, nuts, pomegranates, dates, figs, wheat, wine, honey), and animals (gazelle, stag, turtledove, sheep, horse).

b. Courtship and marriage. The Song supplies virtually no data on the mores or institutions of Hebrew marriage. Monogamy appears to be the ethos of the poems. Polygamy may even be rebuked by implication (6:9), but this does not make the book a social pamphlet.

The more subtle and ineffable attitudes of mind toward sex and marriage find forceful articulation. The poems deal with concrete cases, expressing the sensations and desires of lovers and their youthful friends. The Song ranges over the spectrum of coquetry and flirtation, lovesickness and fear of loss, sensuous longing and fulfilment. The candor about sexual desire and gratification is no proof of low standards of morality (*see* SEX AND SEXUAL BEHAVIOR). In fact, compared with the classical world, the Hebrews had a high level of sexual morality. The distinguishing feature of the corpus is the complete lack of self-consciousness about the man-woman relation, in sharp contrast to the Greek lyricists (*see* § 4*a above*). Although the work has not been censored, it is not lewd or crudely sensate. Man and woman are joined in a psychophysical unity which the poets neither hide nor exploit. Only one of the poems generalizes about its subject (8:6-7), declaring that love is mightier than death, natural catastrophe, or wealth.

Bibliography. History of interpretation: C. D. Ginsburg, *The Song of Songs* (1857). W. Rudolph, "Das Hohe Lied im Kanon," *ZAW*, XVIII N.F. (1942/43), 189-99. H. H. Rowley, "The Interpretation of the Song of Songs," *The Servant of the Lord and Other Essays* (1952), pp. 189-234.

Commentaries and special studies. (*a*) Allegorical: P. Joüon (1909). Bernard of Clairvaux, *On the Song of Songs* (1952).

b) Cultic: W. H. Schoff, ed., *The Song of Songs: A Symposium* (1924), discusses extrabiblical parallels. M. Haller, *HAT* (1940). H. Ringgren, "Hohes Lied und hieros gamos," *ZAW*, LXV (1953), 300-802. T. J. Meek, *IB*, V (1956), 91-148. H. Ringgren, *Das Hohe Lied* (1958).

c) Dramatic: H. Ewald (1826). F. Delitzsch (1877). S. R. Driver, Introduction (1913), pp. 436-53. W. Pouget and J. Guitton, *The Catholic Scripture Library* (1946). L. Waterman (1948).

d) Lyrical: J. G. Wetzstein (in the Appendix to Delitzsch's commentary, 1877). K. Budde, "The Song of Solomon," *The New World*, III (1893), 56-77; *KHC* (1898). P. Haupt (1907). M. Jastrow (1921). K. Budde, *Die Heilige Schrift des AT* (1923). W. Oesterley (1936). A. Feuillet, *Le Cantique des Cantiques* (1953). R. Gordis, *The Song of Songs* (1954). F. Landsberger, "Poetic Units Within the Song of Songs," *JBL*, LXXIII (1954), 203-16. H. Schmökel, *Heilige Hochzeit und Hohelied* (1955). V. Hamp, "Zur Textkritik am Hohen Liede," *BZ*, N.F. 1 (1957), 197 ff.   N. K. GOTTWALD

SONG OF THE THREE YOUNG MEN; KJV **SONG OF THE THREE HOLY CHILDREN.** The first of the apocryphal Additions to the book of Daniel, together with Susanna and Bel and the Dragon. This section, consisting of a hymn, is written between vss. 23 and 24 of the Hebrew text of the third chapter of Daniel. A prayer and confession of Azariah precedes the hymn. Here Azariah, one of the three men, prays for his people and seeks to probe into the sin which brought upon them the calamity of being thrown into the furnace. He seeks pardon and asks:

> Let all who do harm to thy servants be put to shame.
> . . . .
> Let them know that thou art the Lord, the only God
> (vss. 20, 22).

The Song, or Hymn, of the Three Young Men is very similar to Pss. 103; 148. It is the praise given by the three to the Almighty because they have been saved from the flames of the fiery furnace. In it there is an acknowledgment of his justice even when calamity is brought to the Jews, a prayer for deliverance because of his name's sake and because of his promise to the patriarchs that he would not destroy Israel follows. It includes also a prayer for the punishment of the enemies of Israel.

The fact that it is a prayer led many to believe that the original Addition was written in Hebrew, for this was the language of prayer.

The time and place of the writing of these Additions is not known. It is surmised that the story of saving from the fiery furnace was written, perhaps, in the time of Antiochus Epiphanes. The purpose of the author was to instill courage and to demonstrate that even as the fathers were saved, so would the present generations be saved.

The absurdity of idolatry is evident in the Song. Hence many have held that the original was not in Hebrew but in Greek, to emphasize the folly of pagan worship and to stress conversion.

Whether the entire story is historic or not is a debatable question.

Bibliography. R. H. Pfeiffer, *History of NT Times with Introduction to Apocrypha* (1949), pp. 444-48; B. M. Metzger, *An Introduction to the Apoc.* (1957), pp. 99-105.   S. B. HOENIG

SONS OF GOD [בני אלהים, בני אלין]. An ancient designation of heavenly beings, used vestigially in the OT in (*a*) a legend related in Gen. 6:1-4; (*b*) the prose prologue of the book of Job; and (*c*) three poetic passages (Job 38:7; Pss. 29:1; 89:7). In accordance with regular Hebrew usage, "sons of God" means simply "beings of the god-class"—i.e., members of the pantheon; and the expression actually occurs in this sense in the Ras Shamra Texts (e.g., 2.16, 23-34; 51.2-3; II AB, iii.15) and in a Canaanite magical in-

scription, of the eighth century B.C., from Arslan Tash (*cf. bibliography*). In their anxiety to avoid any suggestion of polytheism in Holy Writ, several ancient and modern translators have rendered the words as "sons of the mighty," "sons of potentates," and the like; but the discovery of the expression in the early extrabiblical texts has now put the true meaning beyond all doubt. In the OT, of course, it is simply a mythological relic, like Cupid or the Muses in English poetry.

In Job 38:7, "sons of God" stands parallel to "morning stars," and a similar parallelism occurs in a mythological text from Ras Shamra (IV AB, i.4-5: *b n i l=[p] ḥ r k k b m*). This suggests that the beings in question may sometimes have been regarded as astral or even identified with heavenly bodies.

According to the reading of the LXX, Symm., OL, and a fragment from Qumran (*cf. bibliography*) at Deut. 32:8, God (*'Elyôn*) originally apportioned territories on earth "according to the number of the sons of God [למספר בני אל]." This has been thought to foreshadow the later Jewish concept that every land and people is under the tutelage of a distinct patron angel (cf. Ecclus. 17:17). It has been suggested, however, that "sons of God" is there once more a mere paraphrase for "stars," and hence that the verse means simply that God made nations innumerable (*cf. bibliography*). The MT—perhaps in an attempt to palliate the seemingly pagan tone of the passage—reads incongruously: "according to the number of *the children of Israel* [למספר בני ישראל]."

See also ANGEL.

Bibliography. On the meaning of the phrase in Hebrew usage, see T. H. Gaster, *Orientalia*, XI (1942), 59. On the Qumran fragment of Deut. 32:8, see *Bibl.*, XXXVI (1955), 165. On the phrase as a paraphrase for "stars," see W. F. Albright, *From the Stone Age to Christianity* (2nd ed., 1957), pp. 295-96.   T. H. GASTER

SONS OF PROPHETS [בני הנביאים]. This phrase hardly denotes physical descent from a PROPHET, but rather members of a prophetic guild, or order, first appearing in the time of Saul and Samuel in the eleventh century B.C. and employing group ecstasy in the service of Yahweh. They are called a "band" of prophets (חבל הנבי) when first mentioned in I Sam. 10:5, and a "company" (read קהלת הנביאים) in 19: 20. The sons of the prophets appear again prominently in the ninth century B.C. in association with Elisha (II Kings 2:3; 3:11; 4:1, 38; 6:1-2). These guilds of professional prophets continue to appear variously indicated (I Kings 18:4, 19; 22:6; II Kings 23:2; Jer. 26:7-8, 11) until the fall of Jerusalem in the early sixth century B.C.

See also RECHABITE; NAZIRITE; SAUL; SAMUEL; ELISHA.

Bibliography. R. B. Y. Scott, *The Relevance of the Prophets* (1944), pp. 46-49; H. H. Rowley, *The Servant of the Lord* (1952), ch. 3.   B. D. NAPIER

SONS OF THUNDER. See BOANERGES.

SOOTHSAYER [עונן, מעונן]. A practitioner of divination, who foretells future events by means of omina derived from nature or artificially produced signs.

Acts 16:16-19 tells about a girl in Philippi who was possessed with a spirit of DIVINATION and practiced soothsaying (μαντεύομαι). Paul rebuked the spirit and drove it out of the girl.   I. MENDELSOHN

SOPATER sō′pə tər [Σώπατρος] (Acts 20:4). Son of Pyrrhus; a man from Beroea who, with others, accompanied Paul from Greece (probably Corinth) on his final trip to Jerusalem when he took his offering for the poor there.

See also SOSIPATER.   B. H. THROCKMORTON, JR.

SOPE. KJV form of SOAP.

SOPHAR sō′fər. Douay Version form of ZOPHAR.

SOPHERETH sŏf′ə rĕth [סופרת, scribe] (Neh. 7:57); **HASSOPHERETH** hă— [הספרת] (Ezra 2:55; I Esd. 5:33); KJV **AZAPHION** ə zā′fĭ ən [᾽Ασσαφιώθ] (I Esd. 5:33). Head of a family of the "sons of Solomon's servants" (*see* NETHINIM) who returned from the Exile with Zerubbabel.   G. HENTON DAVIES

SOPHONIAS. KJV Apoc. and Douay Version form of ZEPHANIAH.

SORCERY. *See* MAGIC.

SOREK, VALLEY OF sôr′ĕk [נחל שרק, a choice vine]. The valley in which Delilah, Samson's mistress, lived (Judg. 16:4). It is the modern Wadi es-Sarar, which begins *ca.* thirteen miles W-SW of Jerusalem and runs toward the Mediterranean in a northwesterly direction. Khirbet Suriq on the N side of the Wadi, to the N of Beit Jibrin and not far from Sar′ah (Zorah), preserves the ancient name and may be the site of ancient Sorek. Eusebius calls the place Capharsorech.

The valley itself is guarded by BETH-SHEMESH, a fortress city on the frontier between Israel and Philistia. Though it once belonged to the Danites (before the Philistine invasion) and was still occupied by Israelites, Beth-shemesh and the Valley of Sorek, or at least its W section, seem to have been under Philistine control during the period of the judges. Delilah's betrayal of Samson was tantamount to the surrender of the mountain fortress of Zorah to the Philistines. Later Zorah was incorporated into the kingdom of Judah and formed the N boundary for the Shephelah province of Azekah (see Josh. 15:33-36).

Bibliography. W. F. Albright, "The Fall Trip of the School in Jerusalem . . . ," *BASOR,* 17 (1925), 4-5.   V. R. GOLD

SORES [אבעבעת; LXX φλυκτίδες ἀναζέουσαι] (Exod. 9:9-10); KJV **BLAINS.** Cutaneous blisters or infections, mentioned only in connection with the sixth Egyptian plague. These vesicles were localized inflamed swellings, such as abscesses or boils. Perhaps the malignant pustule of cutaneous anthrax is meant, since the plague affected animals and men alike.   R. K. HARRISON

SORREL. *See* COLORS.

SORROW. There is no distinctive OT expression for "sorrow" (at least fifteen Hebrew root words are

translated "sorrow"), which suggests that it was never the object of reflective thought. Of greater concern are the events, often of theological significance, which occasion JOY or sorrow. The term itself is only one of a variety of expressions describing human suffering (*see* SUFFERING AND EVIL), for which a fairly comprehensive word is צר, צרה, "trouble." It is the opposite of שלום, "peace," meaning "wholeness," "harmony," "fulfilment of the goals of earthly existence." *See* PEACE IN THE OT.

Poignant descriptions of purely human sorrow occur in II Sam. 1:19 ff; 18. In early Israel one grieved, not so much over DEATH itself as over the untimely, violent death, or over death without the happy fulfilment of family relationships (cf. Gen. 42:38; 44:29 ff; 46:30). Israelite WISDOM knew that joy and sorrow are intertwined in human life (Prov. 4:13), sorrow often coming as the result of one's own folly (10:1) or that of another (23:29). The late pessimism of Job 7:1-10 (cf. Ps. 90:10); Eccl. 1:18; 7:3 is not characteristic of the OT as a whole, or of the wisdom movement (cf. Wisd. Sol. 20:21 ff; 38:18 ff).

Though trouble and sorrow are part of human existence, they do not belong to God's order, but are connected with human sinfulness (Gen. 3:16-17; Ps. 16:4), coming as the result of God's wrath (Ps. 88:7-9; Lam. 1:1-12; Ezek. 23:33-35), often for the purpose of chastisement (II Sam. 7:14; II Chr. 6:24-31; cf. Hos. 3:3-5; Amos 4:6-12; Heb. 12:3-11). Ultimately, they will also be removed by God (for the faithful: Pss. 13; 31; 107:39-43; in the new age: Isa. 51:11; cf. 25:8; Jer. 31:1-17; Rev. 21:4).

The cultic rites of repentance before Yahweh are patterned upon customs of MOURNING (Josh. 7:6; I Kings 21:27; Neh. 9:1), but such "official" sorrow for sins drew acid criticism from the prophets (Isa. 58:5; Hos. 5:15-6:4; Amos 4:6-12) who demanded genuine repentance (Joel 2:12-13) issuing in genuine obedience (Isa. 58:6-7; Hos. 6:6).

In the NT the characteristic word for sorrow is λύπη, which appears in the sense of general "pain" and "suffering" (Heb. 12:11; I Pet. 2:19), but more often of "inner anguish" (Luke 22:45; John 16: 6, 20; Rom. 9:2). As the "man of sorrows" (cf. Matt. 26:37; Mark 14:34; Luke 19:41; 22:44; John 11:35), Jesus recalls the SERVANT OF THE LORD of Isa. 52:13-53:12 (cf. Matt. 8:17; Luke 22:37; I Pet. 2:24-25).

The tension of the Christian community which is "in, but not of," the world (cf. John 15:19) is reflected in II Cor. 7:8-12 and, in a different way, in John 16:1-22. In the former passage, sorrow at the knowledge of one's own disobedience is called "godly grief" (ἡ κατὰ θεὸν λύπη), producing repentance, which leads to salvation; while "worldly grief (ἡ τοῦ κόσμου λύπη), apparently the anxiety and guilt of unfulfilled human ideals, leads to death. In John 16 the departure of Jesus will cause the "world" to rejoice because of its hatred of him (vs. 20; cf. 15:18), but for the disciples this means "sorrow," not only at his leaving (vs. 6), but also because the hatred and persecution of the world will come upon them as well (15:18-20). However, this "sorrow will turn into joy" (vs. 20) at their reunion with him (vs. 22; cf. Rev. 21:3-4).

Bibliography. J. Pedersen, *Israel* (1926), p. 332.

   J. A. WHARTON

SOSIPATER sō sĭp′ə tər [Σωσίπατρος, saving one's father] (Rom. 16:21). A Christian mentioned by Paul as sending greetings to the recipients of the Letter to the Romans. He is called a "kinsman" of Paul—i.e., a Jew. SOPATER is another form of the same name (Acts 20:4), and in all likelihood the two references are to the same man. F. W. GINGRICH

SOSTHENES sŏs′thĭ nēz [Σωσθένης]. **1.** The ruler of the SYNAGOGUE at Corinth (Acts 18:17); successor of Crispus, who had become a Christian (vs. 8). Sosthenes was the spokesman for the Jews in a legal action brought against Paul in the court of Gallio, proconsul of Achaia. When Gallio ruled that the matter was outside his jurisdiction, a crowd of on-lookers (probably Greeks; so KJV) proceeded to beat Sosthenes, and Gallio did not stop them.

2. Paul's Christian brother who was with him (in Ephesus) when he wrote I Corinthians; he is the only companion of Paul mentioned in I Cor. 1:1, though others are referred to in 16:17-19. He must have been known to the Corinthians, but need not have been one of them unless he was identical with 1 *above*.

The two men named Sosthenes have been considered the same by some scholars from Theodoret to modern times; but opinion is now sharply divided, and the evidence does not permit a definitive answer to the problem. If they are the same, Sosthenes must have undergone a dramatic conversion similar to that of Paul himself, turning from persecution of Christianity to missionary work in its behalf.

F. W. GINGRICH

SOSTRATUS sŏs′trə təs [Σώστρατος, Σόστρατος]. Governor of the citadel of Jerusalem in the time of Antiochus IV (II Macc. 4:28), who demanded from Menelaus the sums which the latter had promised to pay the king for his appointment to the priesthood. Antiochus finally called both Menelaus and Sostratus to account when the payments were not made.

S. B. HOENIG

SOTAI sō′tī [סֹטַי] (Ezra 2:55; Neh. 7:57). Head of a family of "sons of Solomon's servants" (*see* NETHINIM) which returned from the Exile with Zerubbabel.

SOUL. The translation of several words in the Bible. In the KJV of the OT (the clue is partly obliterated in modern translations) "soul" represents almost exclusively the Hebrew נֶפֶשׁ. The word "soul" in English, though it has to some extent naturalized the Hebrew idiom, frequently carries with it overtones, ultimately coming from philosophical Greek (Platonism) and from Orphism and Gnosticism, which are absent in נֶפֶשׁ. In the OT it never means the immortal soul, but is essentially the life principle, or the living being, or the self as the subject of appetite and emotion, occasionally of volition. Ψυχή in the NT corresponds to נֶפֶשׁ in the OT but is relatively infrequent. It continues the old Greek usage by which it means "life." Paul sometimes prefers σῶμα and πνεῦμα to express new psychological distinctions. Once or twice he depreciates ψυχή. A heightened meaning of the word appearing occasionally is to be noted (*see* § 3 *below*).

1. In the OT
   a. Etymology of נֶפֶשׁ
   b. Hebrew idea of "soul"
   c. *Locus classicus*
   d. Usage of נֶפֶשׁ
   e. Relation of נֶפֶשׁ to other terms
2. In the Apoc.
3. In the NT
Bibliography

1. In the OT. *a. Etymology of* נֶפֶשׁ. The Hebrew word is probably from Akkadian *napâšu*, "expand," giving *napištu*, "throat, neck," with a possible meaning "breath" (cf. Arabic) and then "breath-soul." The meaning "throat, neck," is suggested, not always convincingly, for sundry passages of the OT—e.g., Isa. 5:14; 29:8; Jonah 2:6; the clearest case is possibly Ps. 105:18. The meaning "breath" in the OT is doubtful.

b. Hebrew idea of "soul." Hebrew thought could distinguish soul from body as material basis of life, but there was no question of two separate, independent entities, except for a possible trace of the "Greek" idea in Job 4:19: "those who dwell in houses of clay, whose foundation is in the dust [is dust?]." The word נֶפֶשׁ designates the life principle, which always appears in some form or manifestation without which it would not exist. This is not contradicted by passages like Gen. 35:18; I Kings 17:21-22, which speak of the נֶפֶשׁ as departing or returning. The Hebrew could not conceive of a disembodied נֶפֶשׁ, though he could use נֶפֶשׁ with or without the adjective "dead," for "corpse" (e.g., Lev. 19:28; Num. 6:6).

c. Locus classicus. In Gen. 2:7 we read that "the LORD God formed man of dust from the ground, and breathed into his nostrils the breath of life [נִשְׁמַת חַיִּים]; and man became a living being [נֶפֶשׁ חַיָּה]." This latter expression is used collectively of the animals in Gen. 1. The qualification "living" in Gen. 2:7 emphasizes the contrast with the inert dust. The writer might have written רוּחַ instead of נְשָׁמָה for "breath" (see Gen. 7:15).

***d. Usage of* נֶפֶשׁ.** The Hebrew could speak of his flesh as we would say "body," but often he spoke of his נֶפֶשׁ—i.e., himself as a psychophysical organism. He did not *have* a body but *was* an animated body, a unit of life manifesting itself in a fleshly form. The life principle in man was sometimes linked with the blood (e.g., Gen. 9:4; Lev. 17:11, 14; Deut. 12:23). The word נֶפֶשׁ frequently means "life" (e.g., saving life [Josh. 2:13]; taking life [I Kings 19:4]; risking life [Judg. 5:18; II Sam. 23:17]; fear for life [Ezek. 32:10]). Life is always a totality, which may express itself in the body as a whole or concentrate itself in some part, member, or organ of the body (tongue, eye, ear, hand, heart, etc.), which by synecdoche can represent the whole in a certain aspect. To speak of a "diffused personality" is misleading. The use of the personal pronouns implies a sense of the unity of the self. The phrase acquires a profounder meaning in Isa. 53:12 (cf. vs. 11) in view of the value of what is surrendered (cf. II Sam. 23:13-17). The word נֶפֶשׁ often means "self," "person," and with pronominal suffixes can form an emotional substitute for the personal pronouns. It can express the reflexive idea and is used for "persons" in enumerations.

The soul, like the spirit, can increase or decrease in strength. When all the strength ebbs away, death intervenes. To pour out the soul is to stand forth as helpless (e.g., I Sam. 1:15; Ps. 42:5). A strong soul can surpass its apparent limits through persons and things connected with it. This has been called "extension of personality." With other selves it can form a psychic unity (e.g., Gen. 23:8; II Kings 9:15; Ps. 33:20).

e. Relation of שֶׁפֶּשׁ *to other terms.* שֶׁפֶּשׁ, as used of the human totality, was generally preferred when the self was thought of as having desire or appetite or emotional experiences (cf. English "soulful"). שֶׁפֶּשׁ can represent the totality of feeling (Exod. 23:9). The שֶׁפֶּשׁ hungers and thirsts; is greedy; is satisfied; feels joy, sorrow, love, hatred, hope, despair, etc. To express the energy or character of the self, the word SPIRIT could be used, unusual energy or insight or skill being attributed to the invasive spirit of God; while to express volition or the organization of the soul for action the word HEART was available, occasionally coupled with "soul." The three terms are frequently interchanged. God is to provide a new character and new energy (Ezek. 11:19; 18:31; 36:26). The heart also is the chief seat of the intelligence—thinking is practical rather than speculative, and thoughts readily pass into actions.

2. **In the Apoc.** The evidence yielded by the Apoc. is significant only in the case of the Wisdom of Solomon. In books like I–III Maccabees, Tobit, Judith, and in particular Ecclesiasticus the usage of ψυχή corresponds by and large to that of שֶׁפֶּשׁ. Occasionally in Ecclesiasticus ψυχή represents לֵב "heart." In the Wisdom of Solomon there are clear traces of Greek conceptions—e.g., reference to pre-existence of the soul (8:19), immortality of soul (3:1), soul as burdened by the body (9:15), ethical qualities attributed to the soul (1:4; 2:22; 7:27; 10:7; 17:1), the idea that soul goes to Hades (16:14). In II Esd. 7:102-15 there is evidence for belief in reservation of souls after death for judgment.

3. **In the NT.** The etymology of ψυχή is ψύχω, "to breathe." In the KJV it is translated sometimes by "soul," sometimes by "life."

As compared with שֶׁפֶּשׁ in the OT, ψυχή is relatively infrequent in the NT. This is partly due to the fact that so much of the OT is poetry, which encourages the use of synonyms and pathetic periphrases. Especially in Paul, who is introducing new psychological distinctions, the self-transcendent self can be expressed by σῶμα and the fact of consciousness by πνεῦμα. But ψυχή and πνεῦμα are sometimes synonymous.

Like שֶׁפֶּשׁ, we find ψυχή meaning "life," which can be cared for (Matt. 6:25), saved or lost (Mark 8:35), sought (Matt. 2:20), laid down (John 10:11), risked (Phil. 2:30), etc. שֶׁפֶּשׁ can be used reflexively (II Cor. 1:23; I Thess. 2:8) or as "persons" in enumerations (Acts 7:14) or as the subject of emotion (Mark 14:34; Luke 1:46; John 12:27). It can express unity when qualified with "one" (Acts 4:32; Phil. 1:27; cf. II Kings 9:15).

In general in the NT, ψυχή continues the old Greek usage (characteristic, e.g., of Homer) by which it means "vitality, life." When a contrast is intended, ψυχή is opposed to σῶμα and πνεῦμα to σάρξ. Heb.

4:12 probably does not imply a distinction between soul and spirit. In one place (I Cor. 2:14-15) there is more than a suggestion of depreciation of the ψυχή in Paul's use of ψυχικός to describe the "natural" (KJV) or "unspiritual" (RSV) man with no spiritual perception. The same attitude reappears in I Cor. 15:42-50. This is doubtless due to Paul's emphasis on the Spirit of God. He depreciates the living being of Gen. 2:7 (who on the OT view was God's vis-à-vis and therefore open to divine influence), because for him man is hopelessly in thrall to sin and needs Christ, the last Adam, to communicate to him the Spirit. The passage I Thess. 5:23 does not imply a trichotomy of spirit, soul, and body, but merely expresses the totality of the human personality as needing to be sanctified by God. Cf. Deut. 6:5.

In some passages of the NT, especially in Hebrews and the Pastoral letters, ψυχή seems to receive a heightened meaning (e.g., Heb. 6:19; 10:39; 13:17; Jas. 1:21; I Pet. 1:9, 22; 2:11, 25). This probably finds its explanation in certain passages in the gospels—e.g., Mark 8:35 (cf. Isa. 53:11-12); Luke 12:19-20, 22-23; 20:19—which turn the attention away from this world to life in the world to come.

Bibliography. C. A. Briggs, "The Use of שֶׁפֶּשׁ in the OT," *JBL*, vol. XVI (1897), pts. I-II, pp. 17-30. H. W. Robinson, *The Christian Doctrine of Man* (1911), pp. 1-150; *The Religious Ideas of the OT* (1913), pp. 79-83. E. de W. Burton, *Spirit, Soul, and Flesh* (1918), p. 214. L. Dürr, "Hebr. שֶׁפֶּשׁ=akk *napištu=Gurgel, Kehle,*" *ZAW*, Heft 3/4 (1925), pp. 262-69. H. W. Robinson, "Hebrew Psychology," *The People and the Book* (ed. A. S. Peake; 1925), pp. 353-82. J. Pedersen, *Israel I-II* (1926), p. 578. A. R. Johnson, *The Vitality of the Individual in the Thought of Ancient Israel* (1949), p. 107. C. R. Smith, *The Bible Doctrine of Man* (1951), p. 274. R. Bultmann, *Theology of the NT*, I (1952), 190-246.   N. W. PORTEOUS

SOUTH. *See* ORIENTATION.

SOUTH, THE. *See* NEGEB.

SOUTH RAMOTH. KJV form of Ramoth of the Negeb. *See* RAMAH 5.

SOW [ὗς; *cf.* Sanskrit *śūkara, sūkara,* wild boar, pig] (II Pet. 2:22). The mature female of the SWINE.

SOWER, SOWING. *See* AGRICULTURE.

SPAIN spān [ἡ Σπανία, *short form of* Ἱσπανία (I Macc. 8:3)]. A country in SW Europe which Paul hoped to visit (Rom. 15:24, 28).

The Spanish peninsula is bounded by the Pyrenees Mountains and the Bay of Biscay on the N, the Atlantic Ocean on the W and SW, and the Mediterranean Sea on the SE and E. The country is mountainous, with the main ranges running from E to W, and on the Mediterraean coast the land descends with relative abruptness toward the sea.

The first inhabitants of Spain lived in the Paleolithic period, and Cro-Magnon man is represented by the notable paintings in the famous cave of Altamira. Sometime within the succeeding Neolithic or Bronze ages a people known as the Iberians came in, probably from North Africa. From them the peninsula was anciently called Iberia (ἡ Ἰβηρία), a name attested as early as the sixth- or fifth-century his-

SPAIN

0 100 200 mi.

BAY OF BISCAY

ATLANTIC OCEAN

Altamira•

PYRENEES

Ebro

Numantia•

•Segovia

•Alcantara

Guadalquivir

•Seville

Cartagena

Cadiz•

MEDITERRANEAN SEA

Jack Finegan

torian Hecataeus (Arrian *Anabasis of Alexander* II. 16.5). Probably by the eleventh century B.C. the Phoenicians were establishing trading posts in Spain, of which the most important was Gadeis, or Gadira (Herodotus IV.8), on the site of present Cadiz (Velleius I.2). Within a few centuries the Greeks also were going to Spain. Herodotus tells of a Samian ship which was blown beyond the Pillars of Heracles to Tartessus, probably at the mouth of the Guadalquivir River (IV.152), and describes the Phocaeans as voyaging to Iberia and Tartessus in fifty-oared vessels (I.163). By the third century B.C. the Carthaginians had taken most of the peninsula and established their capital at Carthago Nova, now Cartagena (Polybius II.13). Here in 209 B.C. Scipio Africanus won an important victory over the forces of Hannibal (Polybius X.10), and within a few years the Carthaginians were driven out. Native forces long continued to fight against the Romans; but with the fall of the stronghold of Numantia to Scipio Aemilianus in 133 B.C., organized resistance finally ceased (Appian *Wars in Spain* 84-98).

By 197 B.C. two Roman provinces were established in Spain, each under a propraetor, one centering in the valley of the Ebro River, the other in that of the Baetis or Guadalquivir. The former, being nearer to Italy, was known as Hispania Citerior; the latter, Hispania Ulterior (Livy XXXII.28.11). Under Augustus, Spain was reorganized into three provinces (Pliny Nat. Hist. III-IV). Hispania Citerior retained its unity and was under a governor (*legatus Augusti pro praetore*). Hispania Ulterior gave way to two provinces. In the less urban W was the province of Lusitania under a governor. In the more thoroughly Romanized S was Baetica, a senatorial rather than an imperial province, under a proconsul. The ready reception of the imperial cult at this time shows the appreciation with which the administration of Augustus was regarded. The Romans also built an

excellent system of roads which encircled and crossed the peninsula, and their bridge at Alcantara and aqueduct at Segovia remain as well-known monuments. How thoroughly Roman Spain became is shown by the work of such persons as the writers Seneca, Martial, and Quintilian, and the emperors Trajan, Hadrian, and Theodosius I, all of whom were from Spain.

The chief evidence which suggests that Paul was able to fulfil his hope of visiting Spain is the statement of Clement, who, writing to the Corinthians (I.5) from Rome *ca.* A.D. 95, says that before his martyrdom Paul had "come to the extreme limit of the West [τὸ τέρμα τῆς δύσεως]." This phrase, which presumably could mean nothing less than Spain, correlates with the reference in the Muratorian Fragment a century later to the "departure of Paul from the city [of Rome] on his journey to Spain." The tradition, widely accepted in Spain, that the apostle James was the first to preach the gospel there, appears to be no earlier than a treatise called *De ortu et obitu patrum*, which is attributed to Isidore, bishop of Seville, 600-36. The first witnesses to the existence of Christianity in Spain are Irenaeus (*ca.* 180), who refers to the "churches . . . in Spain" (Iren. Her. I.10.2); Tertullian (*ca.* 200), who speaks of "all the limits of Spain" as "subjugated to Christ" (*An Answer to the Jews* 7); and Arnobius (*ca.* 306), who says that there were "innumerable Christians" in Spain (*Against the Heathen* I.16).

Bibliography. Schulten, "Hispania," *Pauly-Wissowa*, vol. VIII, pt. ii (1913), cols. 1965-2046; J. J. Van Nostrand, Jr., *The Reorganization of Spain by Augustus*, University of California Publications in History, IV, 2 (1916); C. H. Robinson, *The Conversion of Europe* (1917), pp. 268-83; J. J. Van Nostrand, "Roman Spain," in T. Frank, ed., *An Economic Survey of Ancient Rome*, III (1937), 119-224; R. Altamira, *A History of Spain from the Beginnings to the Present Day* (trans. Muna Lee; 1949); F. J. Wiseman, *Roman Spain* (1956).

J. FINEGAN

SPAN [זרת]. A measure based on the distance between ends of extended thumb and little finger; half a cubit, eight inches or a little more. In Lam. 2:20 the plural form טפחים is translated "a span long" in the KJV, taken to be related to טפח, HANDBREADTH (*see also* WEIGHTS AND MEASURES § D4c.). The RSV interprets "of their tender care" (lit., "of hands"[?]).

O. R. SELLERS

SPARROW [צפור (*alternately* BIRD), *see* BIRDS; στρουθίον, *diminutive of* στρουθός, sparrow]. Any bird of various genera of the finch family (*Fringillidae*).

Although צפור has a number of meanings in the OT, it appears to refer to one of the passerines in Pss. 84:3—H 84:4; 102:7—H 102:8; Prov. 26:2 (on the variety of the passerines in Palestine, see Tristram *NHB* 201-4). In these passages it is used along with "swallow," and it may indicate a type of sparrow. The altars mentioned in Ps. 84 mean, presumably, by metonymy, the various structures in the temple area which would be natural haunts for small birds. For efforts to discourage birds from perching on the sanctuary itself, see Jos. War V.vi.224; M. *Middoth* 4.6. In Ps. 102:7—H 102:8 the words "a lonely bird on the housetop" can hardly apply to any of the commoner sparrows. Tristram supposed that the bird intended was the blue thrush (*Petrocincla cyanea;* cf. G. R. Driver's "blue rockthrush").

Στρουθίον is used in Matt. 10:29; Luke 12:6 to point to an object of very little worth—viz., a sparrow sold as food in the market place. Jesus asserts that, as such an insignificant creature has its place in God's care and economy, so the disciples must not fear opposition, for "you are of more value than many sparrows" (Matt. 10:31; Luke 12:7).

See also FAUNA § B4.   W. S. McCULLOUGH

SPARTA spär'tə [Σπάρτη, *perhaps from* σπάρτος, Spanish broom, *or from* σπαρτή, sown *or* cultivated]; SPARTANS —tənz. The principal city in S Greece in ancient times, and capital of the region of Laconia; settled by a Dorian people also called LACEDAEMONIANS. After defeating Athens in the Peloponnesian War (431-401 B.C.), the city declined in population and influence until its independence was lost in 192 B.C., when it was compelled to join the Achaean League. Under Roman rule Sparta alone among the Greek cities was granted self-administration similar to the Maccabean state. The evidence of II Macc. 5:9 suggests that there was a colony of Jews there as early as the second century B.C.

Bibliography. R. Marcus, *Josephus,* Loeb Classical Library, vol. VII (1943), Appendix F, contains bibliography; S. Schüller, "Some Problems Connected With the Supposed Common Ancestry of Jews and Spartans," *Journal of Semitic Studies,* I (1956), 257-68.   E. W. SAUNDERS

SPEARS. *See* WEAPONS AND IMPLEMENTS OF WAR § 3*b.*

SPECK [κάρφος, *from* κάρφω, to shrivel, dry up] (Matt. 7:3-5; Luke 6:41-42); KJV MOTE. A minute piece of dried material from wood, straw, or wool, contrasted by Jesus with a log (δοκός; KJV "beam").

SPECKLED. *See* COLORS.

SPECKLED BIRD OF PREY; KJV SPECKLED BIRD. The translation of עיט צבוע (Jer. 12:9). For עיט, *see* BIRD OF PREY. צבוע means "dyed" (from צבע, "to dip, dye").

The text of Jer. 12:9*a* is admittedly difficult. The LXX ("hyena's cave") has led to two suggestions: Koehler (*see bibliography*) drops עיט and takes צבוע to be "hyena" (cf. Zeboim, "hyenas," in I Sam. 13:18); G. R. Driver (*see bibliography*) reads "hyena" and interprets עיט as "lair" (cf. Arabic *ghāṭa,* "to enter to hide oneself"; *ghaiṭ,* "garden, lowland").

Bibliography. E. Koehler, *Lexicon* (1953), p. 791; G. R. Driver, *PEQ* (May-Oct., 1955), pp. 140-41.
W. S. McCULLOUGH

SPELT [כסמת, *kussemeth;* כסמים, *kussᵉmîm;* Ugar. *ksmm*]. A kind of coarse, inferior WHEAT, *Triticum spelta* L. The Hebrew, however, may refer to *Triticum dicoccoides* (Koern.) Schulz (*see* FLORA § A1*b,* where it is called *Triticum dicoccum* Schrank), another similarly inferior wheat, called emmer (or amelcorn, a source of starch). Identification is uncertain, though emmer is present in the area today, while spelt is

not. That *kussemeth* was a kind of wheat seems likely from its use with WHEAT in the three biblical passages in which it is found. In a partially broken text in the Ugaritic Keret legend (Tablet 126:III:10), *ksmm* seems to be in poetic parallelism with "wheat." In Exod. 9:32 wheat and spelt (or emmer? KJV RIE) escaped the plague of hail in Egypt. Isa. 28:25 describes the work of the farmer who plants spelt (KJV "rie"; mg. "spelt") as a border around the more valuable wheat and barley. Spelt (KJV FITCHES; mg. "spelt") is included with an odd mixture of grains to make coarse bread in Ezek. 4:9.

More than a dozen species of wild and cultivated wheat are found in Palestine today. The presence of two Hebrew words for this staple GRAIN, therefore, may indicate quality more than species. Thus *kussemeth* may have referred merely to the inferior grades of wheat.   J. C. TREVER

SPICE [בשם, *bōśem;* סמים, *sammîm*(?); ἄρωμα]. Any of certain fragrant vegetable products highly prized in ancient times for cosmetics, sacred oil and incense, perfume, and burial preparations. The term seems not to be associated in the Bible with foods. Considerable difference exists between scholars about the meaning of *bōśem,* which is taken by some to be the generic term for "spice," while by others (*see* FLORA § A7*l*) it is considered to refer to the gum of the *Commiphora opobalsamum* (L.) Engl., an aromatic tree common to S Arabia. (*Ṣōrî* more likely refers to the gum of this tree; *see* BALM.) The majority of the occurrences of *bōśem* would tend to argue for a generic meaning. *Sammîm* is generally an adjective, "fragrant," but in Exod. 30:34 it is twice translated "sweet spices" (cf. II Chr. 2:4—H 2:3; 13:11, where the RSV is inconsistent). Even there, however, it could mean "fragrances" or "perfumes" (cf. Exod. 25:6; 30:7).

Spices formed an important part of the wealth of the ancient world. They were prominent among the gifts presented to Solomon (I Kings 10:25; II Chr. 9:24), and featured in the visit of the Queen of Sheba from S Arabia (I Kings 10:2, 10; II Chr. 9:1, 9). The land of Sheba gained great wealth from its control of the spice trade route across S Arabia. "There were no spices such as those which the queen of Sheba gave to King Solomon" (II Chr. 9:9). Tradition claimed that Solomon had spice gardens near Jericho (cf. Song of S. 4:14; Jos. Antiq. VIII.vi.6; War IV.viii.3), especially noted for their balsam trees (cf. Pliny Nat. Hist. XII.111). Several centuries later Hezekiah proudly showed his stores of spices to the envoys of Merodach-baladan of Babylon (II Kings 20:13=Isa. 39:2).

Spices were necessary for the temple cultus. Solomon is reported to have said to Hiram of Tyre that he would dedicate the temple to the Lord "for the burning of incense of sweet spices" (lit., "fragrant incense") before him (II Chr. 2:4—H 2:3). Certain Levites and sons of the priests were responsible for the spices and their proper mixing, after the return of the Jews from exile (I Chr. 9:29-30). The priestly writer gave lists of the spices used as the ingredients of the holy anointing oil (Exod. 30:23) and the fragrant incense (vs. 34), the spices being gathered from the people (35:8).

74. Ethiopian princess attended by bearers of spices, from an Eighteenth Dynasty (*ca.* 1570-1310 B.C.) wall painting of Thebes

The many references to spices in the Song of Solomon indicate specifically and figuratively the personal emphasis upon them. An orchard of fruit and spice trees does not do justice to the beauty of the bride (4:14-16), and the cheeks of the groom are like "beds of spices, yielding fragrance" (5:13; cf. 8:14). Beauty treatment with spices suggests their use in cosmetics (Esth. 2:12).

The use of spices in the preparation of a body for burial is mentioned in connection with the burial of Asa (II Chr. 16:14) and prophetically of Zedekiah (Jer. 34:5), but particularly of the burial of Jesus (Mark 16:1; Luke 23:56; 24:1; John 19:40).

For sources and description of specific spices, *see* ALOES; BALM; CALAMUS; CANE; CASSIA; CINNAMON; DILL; GALBANUM; GUM; HENNA; MYRRH; NARD; SAFFRON; STACTE; SWEET CANE; TRAGACANTH. *See also* COSMETICS; FRANKINCENSE; INCENSE; OINTMENT; PERFUME.

Fig. SPI 74.

Bibliography. I. Löw, *Die Flora der Juden*, vol. I, pt. 1 (1926), pp. 299-304; H. N. and A. L. Moldenke, *Plants of the Bible* (1952), Index; W. Phillips, *Qataban and Sheba* (1955), ch. 24.

J. C. TREVER

SPIDER [עכביש; Arab. *'ankabût, 'aknabût;* Yemen *ukkaš;* KJV שממית, *see below*]. An arachnid, not an insect, with hundreds of species in Palestine. However dissimilar in other respects, all are able to spin

From Bodenheimer, *Animals of the Bible* (Tel Aviv: Dvir Company Ltd.)

75. Poisonous spider (*Latrodectes tredecimguttatus*)

a kind of silk, from which many build webs. This web is the spider's sole claim to biblical importance (Job 8:14; Isa. 59:5). However, in each case, this web is an emblem of frailty and insecurity. The שממית (Prov. 30:28) is better translated "lizard" (so RSV). Job 27:18 has "spider's web" following the LXX and the Syr., but the MT and the KJV have "moth."

See also FAUNA § F3*b.*

See the bibliography under SCORPION.

Fig. SPI 75.   W. W. FRERICHS

SPIES [מרגלים, תרים; KJV אתרים, *see below; ἐγκάθετος, κατάσκοπος*]. Persons sent into hostile territory to gather information beneficial to the aggressors.

The usual Hebrew word for "spies" is מרגלים, a plural participle from רגל, "foot," hence "those who go about on foot (secretly)"; תרים (only Num. 14:6 in this sense; "those who had spied out") is a participle of תור, which originally probably meant "to turn, go about," hence "those who wander about, or spy out" (cf. Num. 14:6; in I Kings 10:15; II Chr. 9:14 "traders"; KJV "merchantmen"). The odd rendering of אתרים in Num. 21:1 as "spies" by the KJV may be due to confusion with תרים; it is probably simply a proper noun, Atharim (so RSV).

In ancient as in modern warfare, spies were often used to discover weaknesses in a country or town's defenses (Gen. 42:9, 12). Moses sent twelve spies into the Negeb and the hill country who reported on the fortifications as well as on the productivity of the land (Num. 13). In the Jericho campaign Joshua is reported to have sent two spies in advance (Josh. 2:1), though what they actually achieved is not clear from the narrative. Spies were used, however, not only to gain information, but also to spread rumors, as in the instance of Absalom's revolt (II Sam. 15:10).

There are only two NT allusions to spies—i.e., the spies sent by Jesus' enemies the scribes and chief priests (Luke 20:20), and a commendation of Rahab for welcoming the spies (Heb. 11:31; cf. Josh. 2:1-21).

J. W. WEVERS

SPIKENARD spīk'nərd, —närd. KJV translation of נרד, *nērd* (Song of S. 1:12; 4:13-14), and νάρδος πιστική (cf. Vulg. *spicatus,* "spikelike") in Mark 14:3; John 12:3 (RSV "pure nard"). *See* NARD; FLORA § A7*k.*

SPINDLE (פלך) (II Sam. 3:29; Prov. 31:19). *See* DISTAFF.

SPINNING. *See* CLOTH.

*SPIRIT [רוח; πνεῦμα; Lat. *spiritus*]. A term applied to God, gods, incorporeal beings generally, and to the divine element in human personality.

1. Terminology
2. God
3. Incorporeal beings
4. Manifestations of God
5. The divine element in man
6. Spirit versus flesh
7. Paul's triangle of personality
8. The spirit of man and the Spirit of God
Bibliography

1. Terminology. The root meaning of both רוח and πνεῦμα is "a movement of air," "breeze," or "wind," and so "breath." By extension it became the life principle. The original idea apparently survives in Gen. 1:2*b:* "The Spirit of God was moving over the face of the waters." "Spirit" here is רוּחַ (LXX πνεῦμα). The passage could be translated: "The wind of God was moving over the face of the waters." Indeed, in the Amer. Trans. T. J. Meek has rendered the passage: ". . . a tempestuous wind raging over the surface of the waters."

Something of the nature of wind survived in the concept of spirit as it was developed by biblical writers. Jesus says to Nicodemus in John 3:8: "The wind blows where it wills, and you hear the sound of it, but you do not know whence it comes or whither it goes; so it is with every one who is born of the Spirit." The saying involves a wordplay, for πνεῦμα means both "wind" and "spirit." If the passage were put into Hebrew, the word would be רוּחַ.

As the life principle, רוּחַ, πνεῦμα, "spirit," dwells in living, breathing beings, in the flesh of both men and animals. In this sense it is parallel to *nephesh* (נפשׁ) or *psyche* (ψυχή). In Job 27:3; Isa. 42:5; Zech. 12:1 it is said that God creates man's spirit, and in Job 10:12 that he preserves it. So the spirit belongs to God.

But ninety-four times in the OT רוּחַ occurs in the expression "the Spirit of God," where again the Greek translation is πνεῦμα. The Spirit of God is thought of as inspiring the prophets, especially the ecstatic type (Num. 11:17-29; I Sam. 10:6-10; 19:20-23). It inspires persons to deeds of frenzy and so at times is regarded as an evil spirit (I Sam. 16:15-16, 23; 18:10; 19:9; I Kings 22:21). It impels prophets to utter instruction or warning (Num. 24:2; II Sam. 23:2); or it imparts warlike energy and administrative power to the leaders of ancient Israel (Judg. 3: 10; 11:29; I Sam. 11:6; etc.). It rests especially on the messianic king (Isa. 11:2; 42:1). Ps. 139:7 indicates that רוּחַ and πνεῦμα finally came to mean the universal presence of God.

רוּחַ is apparently always used in an individualized sense, as was characteristic especially of early biblical thought, which is concrete rather than abstract. This statement applies almost equally well to πνεῦμα in the NT. But there one comes upon intimations of philosophical developments.

The study of "spirit" in the Bible must not be limited to consideration of particular words, such as those noted above. One needs to keep in mind the concepts of natural and supernatural, which were not characteristic of biblical thought, but are now essential to our thinking. "Spirit" is so intimately connected with the supernatural in our thought that we should look for expressions of this idea, as well as for words which are translated "spirit" in the English Bible.

2. God. When we say that GOD is spirit, a spirit, or spiritual, we usually mean, to say the least, that God has no physical body, that he is immaterial; and we say that he is pure spirit. In this sense, "spirit" indicates substance, the nature of God's being. But this is a philosophical type of thought which was unknown to early Hebrews. Some early biblical stories do not hesitate to attribute a physical body to God. In the creation story of Gen. 2:4–3:24 anthropomorphism is characteristic. According to Gen. 32: 24-30, Jacob wrestled with God in the form of a man, and saw him face to face. Exod. 33:11 states

that Moses saw God face to face; and vss. 12-23, that Moses was permitted to see God's back as he walked by.

But this idea that God has a corporeal body was left behind as the prophets acquired a belief that God is universal, eternal, and with no physical likeness whatever. This view is reflected in Isa. 40:18-26. Christianity inherited this prophetic conception, and in the NT it is assumed as a matter of course. True universality and immateriality are implicit in the words of Jesus in John 4:21, 24: "Neither on this mountain nor in Jerusalem will you worship the Father. . . . God is spirit, and those who worship him must worship in spirit and truth." It seems probable that "spirit" in this passage is intended to indicate "substance"—i.e., "immaterial being." The statement is as close as the Bible comes to working out a philosophical conception of God.

3. Incorporeal beings. Various types of these are mentioned in the Bible. Along with a fully developed monotheism, like fossils in rocks, embedded in early strata of the Bible are vestiges of older beliefs. Among these are dragons. There is a sea serpent named LEVIATHAN (Job 3:8; Ps. 74:13-14; Isa. 27:1); Rahab, a dragon which causes storms at sea (Job 9:13; 26:12; Ps. 89:10—H 89:11; Isa. 30:7; 5:19); a desert dragon BEHEMOTH (I Enoch 60:8; II Esd. 6: 49). Such Hebrew ideas should be compared with Vritra of the Indian Rig-Veda and Tiamat of Babylonian mythology. Lev. 16:26 ff refers to AZAZEL, a strange creature of the wilderness, to whom a goat was sacrificed on the Day of Atonement. This spirit appears to be similar to the satyrs of Greek mythology.

SATAN does not appear in the earlier part of the Bible. We encounter him first in I Chr. 21:1 ff; Job 1:6 ff; Zech. 3:1-2, all of which are fairly late. But he became firmly embedded in Hebrew faith and was inherited by Christianity. He appears under various names. In the DEAD SEA SCROLLS (CDC VI, VIII; 1QS I), as well as in II Cor. 6:15, he is called Beliel or Beliar. In Mark 3:22-27 the scribes call him Beelzebul. Matt. 4:1-11, which records the temptation of Jesus, refers to him as the devil. Satan's appearance on that occasion is not described, although supernatural power and knowledge are ascribed to him. But in Rev. 12:7; 20:2 he is called both a dragon and a serpent. Dragons are mentioned several times in Revelation, and there is the later story of Saint George and the Dragon, but eventually dragons were to disappear from Christian thought except insofar as they survive in the features of Satan, who is sometimes still portrayed with a barbed tail and a goatlike body.

Angels (*see* ANGEL) appear frequently in the OT, but they remain anonymous until Daniel (8:16; 10: 21; etc.) introduces Gabriel and Michael, who reappear in the NT (cf. Luke 1:19, 26; Jude 1:9; Rev. 12:7). Numerous other angel names are mentioned in such books as Enoch. While evil spirits or demons (*see* DEMON) are rare in the OT except in the forms of dragons, noted above (cf. I Sam. 16:14), they became prominent in the interbiblical period and are assumed in the NT, where they appear with great frequency.

Another category of spiritual beings is souls of the

dead. Dan. 3:86 LXX; Heb. 12:23 refers to souls of the redeemed as spirits. I Pet. 3:18-20 mentions a descent of Christ into Hades to preach to unregenerate spirits in prison, who had rejected Noah's call to repentance. *See also* SPIRITS, DISTINGUISHING.

4. Manifestations of God. Important special manifestations of God are the Spirit of the LORD; the Spirit of GOD; the Spirit of the Lord Jesus CHRIST; the HOLY SPIRIT; and the Spirit of TRUTH.

5. The divine element in man. The divine element in man is indicated first by the view that he is created in the image of God (Gen. 1:27), which means that man is by nature like God. This probably indicates that he has intelligence and free will and is a moral being. But the figure of an image is used in a Christian sense to indicate transformation of personality into the likeness of Christ (Rom. 8:29; I Cor. 15:49; II Cor. 3:18). Christ himself is also said to be the image of God (I Cor. 11:7; II Cor. 4:4; Col. 1:15; Heb. 1:3).

The Bible also indicates the spiritual nature of man by saying that he is a son of God. In Luke 3:38; Acts 17:28 this is taken in the ancient Stoic sense, and means that all men are by nature sons of God, a view which is essentially parallel to the idea that man is created in the image of God. But the Bible generally uses "image" rather than "son" to express the idea.

Gen. 6:2; Job 1:6 refer to angels as sons of God. This expresses their supernatural, immaterial nature. The Hebrew king (II Sam. 7:14) was regarded as God's son; this was a moral, covenant relationship, but it also involved the sacrament of anointing. Hos. 11:1 calls the nation Israel God's son. Yet the prophets commonly spoke of all Hebrews as God's sons (Isa. 43:6; Mal. 2:10). In the NT only believers are considered sons of God; Paul (Rom. 8:15, 23) speaks of them in terms of adoption, while John 3:7 speaks of a new birth.

6. Spirit versus flesh. In Pauline language there is a contrast between the Spirit of God and the spirit of the world (I Cor. 2:12; Eph. 2:2). Paul also likes to distinguish between the flesh and the Spirit (Rom. 8:4; Gal. 5:16-24), while in Rom. 8:10 the contrast is between spirit and body. John 6:63 is familiar with this distinction. In Rom. 2:29; 7:6; II Cor. 3:6, Paul distinguishes between the spirit and the letter; in I Cor. 2:5, between the Spirit and the wisdom of men.

7. Paul's triangle of personality. The spirit enters into Paul's triangle of personality, which is developed in Rom. 7:7-25; Gal. 5:16-24. In the former passage, especially in vs. 25, the three elements of personality turn out to be mind (νοῦς), flesh (σάρξ), and the conscious "I" (ἐγώ). The "I" must choose between the flesh and reason. But in Gal. 5:16 ff the mind (νοῦς) is replaced by spirit (πνεῦμα). We can harmonize the two passages by assuming that the πνεῦμα, or spirit, resides in the νοῦς, or intelligence.

8. The spirit of man and the Spirit of God. Paul's analysis of personality, one element of which is man's spirit, enables him to present his idea of the Christian's fellowship with Holy Spirit. According to Rom. 8:9-17, it is the spiritual nature with which God has endowed every man that makes it possible for the Spirit of God to dwell in man. It provides a

basis for the continuing conversation between man's spirit and the divine Spirit which comes to dwell within him.

Bibliography. F. Brown, S. R. Driver, and C. A. Briggs, *Hebrew and English Lexicon* (1907); E. D. Burton, *Commentary on Galatians* (1921), pp. 486-92; M. Burrows, *Outline of Biblical Theology* (1946), pp. 113-43; W. Bauer, *A Greek-English Lexicon of the NT* (ed. and trans. W. F. Arndt and F. W. Gingrich; 1957).   S. V. MCCASLAND

SPIRIT, HOLY. *See* HOLY SPIRIT.

SPIRITS, DISTINGUISHING. Paul places δια-κρίσεις πνευμάτων, "the ability to distinguish between spirits" (KJV "discerning of spirits"), among the SPIRITUAL GIFTS (I Cor. 12:10). Primitive Christian beliefs provide the background for this usage. There are two kinds of SPIRIT (§ 3), good and evil (I Cor. 12:3-11; II Thess. 2:11; Eph. 6:12). Inspired messages may come from either, genuineness being independent of externalities (I John 4:1). The spirits can be distinguished, and the validity of inspiration established (I Cor. 12:3; 14:32; I John 4:2-3; cf. I Cor. 2:12-15). Spiritual discrimination is essential to the maintenance of Christian truth (I Thess. 5:18-21), separating the "spirit of truth" from the "spirit of error" (I John 4:6). The tests are: (*a*) theological, affirming the lordship of Jesus and the apostolic witness (I Cor. 12:3; I John 1:1; 2:24; 4:2); and (*b*) moral and practical, the witness of the fruits (Matt. 7:15; Gal. 5:22-23), of the spirit of Christ (Rom. 8:9; I Cor. 13), and of usefulness to the church (I Cor. 14:14-26).   E. ANDREWS

SPIRITS IN PRISON [πνεύματα ἐν φυλακῇ] (I Pet. 3:19). A phrase which refers to Christ's DESCENT INTO HADES between the Crucifixion and the Resurrection. The spirits can be human beings—i.e., the souls of the departed who died before Christ—or angelic beings—i.e., the fallen angels of Gen. 6:1-7 (cf. I Enoch 15:8 ff; 54:5; Jub. 10). Even the thesis that our phrase embraces both human and angelic beings is not excluded. Behind the mythological setting is the idea that the event of Christ had a universal significance and that Christ as the Redeemer of all mankind opened the door of the prison of death. The myth is at home in ancient oriental and Greek texts and was applied to Jesus.

Bibliography. E. G. Selwyn, *The First Epistle of St. Peter* (1949), pp. 197 ff.   E. DINKLER

SPIRITUAL BODY [σῶμα πνευματικόν] (I Cor. 15:44-50). The resurrection body. In this life man's soul, the principle of his physical life, animates a body of flesh and blood. The Christian, who has entered upon the new life in Christ, indwelt by the HOLY SPIRIT, is more than "fleshly" or "soulish"; he is "spirit." "Spirit," when used of man, denotes man in his relation to God—i.e., as acted upon by the Holy Spirit. Insofar as the divine Spirit motivates him, he is "spiritual." As man now possesses a body corresponding to his "fleshly" or "soulish" condition, so in the resurrection he will possess a body corresponding to his condition of total redemption, a "spiritual body." This does not mean a body made of a "spirit substance," but a body wholly possessed by, and wholly an instrument of, the Holy Spirit, fully adapted to the resurrection life in Christ.

See also RESURRECTION.

Bibliography. H. A. A. Kennedy, *St. Paul's Conception of the Last Things* (1904); W. D. Davies, *St. Paul and Rabbinic Judaism* (1948); J. A. T. Robinson, *The Body* (1952); W. D. Stacey, *The Pauline View of Man* (1956).

G. W. H. LAMPE

*SPIRITUAL GIFTS. The term used in the NT to designate the special endowments of the members of the church for its service. (For the Greek terms so translated, *see below*.) The NT picture of the church from its earliest days is that of a community under the direction of the Spirit. Christians, being in the church, are "in the Spirit" and have tasted the "first fruits of the Spirit" (Rom. 8:9, 23). Extraordinary signs of the Spirit's presence and power are everywhere evident. The gospel of salvation first declared by Jesus, then proclaimed by those who had received it, has been confirmed by God himself "by signs and wonders and various miracles and by gifts of the Holy Spirit distributed according to his own will" (Heb. 2:4). Such phenomena are called "spiritual gifts." They vary in character from the strongly emotional outpourings of the ecstatic to the normal, everyday practice of God's will; from talents and activities contributing to worship to those equally necessary for meeting the general needs of the Christian community. All such powers and activities are given by God, and their worth is to be judged by the measure in which they promote the well-being of the church.

1. Nature and diversity
    a. General usage
    b. Particular usage
2. The eschatological setting
3. Evaluation and control
Bibliography

1. **Nature and diversity.** Though πνευματικά is sometimes used (I Cor. 12:1; 14:1) for "spiritual gifts," the distinctive and more frequently used term is χαρίσματα, plural of χάρισμα ("free gift"), a word very rare outside the NT. The term "spiritual" (πνευματικόν) is linked with it once only (Rom. 1:11). There are two usages: the general, of some favor (II Cor. 1:11) or capacity (I Cor. 7:7) or truth (Rom. 1:11) or endowment (I Cor. 1:7) shared by an individual through divine grace or providence; and the particular, of specific abilities used or responsibilities assumed for the well-being and growth of the fellowship (Rom. 12:3-8; I Cor. 12–14; Eph. 4:7-13; I Pet. 4:10-11; I Tim. 4:13), all of divine bestowing. NT writers, particularly Paul, hold a very democratic view of such gifts, believing that every Christian possesses some of them, with varying degrees of fulness (Rom. 12:6).

a. **General usage.** Spiritual gifts are "grace gifts." When man merited only condemnation and death, because of his sin, God by his free gift (χάρισμα) gave righteousness and life (Rom. 5:15-17). Death is sin's wages, but eternal life is the "free gift [χάρισμα] of God" (Rom. 6:23). Deliverance from peril is a gift (χάρισμα) calling for thanksgiving (II Cor. 1:11). The power to live a celibate life, thus giving all one's capacities and powers to one's vocation, is a gift (χάρισμα; I Cor. 7:7). One must not neglect the gift (χάρισμα), the talent, that is in him (I Tim. 4:13-14). He should, indeed, since human nature is capable of improvement, earnestly desire the "higher gifts" (I Cor. 12:31; cf. Matt. 25:14-30). Service to others must be in proportion to the gift (χάρισμα) that each has received (Rom. 12:6; I Pet. 4:10). The blessings and privileges and powers of the church are "spiritual gifts" (χαρίσματα), and are never repealed (Rom. 11:29; I Cor. 1:7). One may impart a gift (χάρισμα) to others, as the apostle wishes to impart the truth of the gospel (Rom. 1:11).

Such uses of the term "grace gift" indicate some favor given by God to the individual or to the church, with only secondary reference to the way in which individuals should exercise their gifts.

b. **Particular usage.** The focus of interest here is the church, the fellowship of those who are "in Christ Jesus," and the primary emphasis is upon its well-being and growth. The use of one's gifts must show no tinge of self-importance, but rather sincere humility as one renders service to the body of Christ, of which each is a member, and in which each is to fulfil his particular function (Rom. 12:3-5; I Cor. 12).

A list of "spiritual gifts" (χαρίσματα) follows this order: wisdom, knowledge, faith, healing, miracles, prophecy, discerning of spirits, tongues, and interpretation of tongues (I Cor. 12:8-10). Lists, though not identical (Rom. 12:6-8; I Cor. 12:28-30; Eph. 4:11), emphasize the same general categories, with some specific reference to the various ministries of the church. Attempts at classifying these gifts as natural or supernatural, miraculous or nonmiraculous, have not been too successful, because the NT draws no such distinction; it assigns all to the operation of the Spirit and co-ordinates the Spirit with the Father and with Christ (I Cor. 12:4-6; Eph. 4:4-6). Some would separate those most useful in worship (prophecy, teaching) from those more practical or ministering gifts (healing, administrations, service; I Pet. 4:10-11). All gifts—that moving to liberality (Rom. 12:8), as that issuing in tongues (I Cor. 14:13-19)—are related to the corporate body, the church, are diverse because its needs are so, and are assessed in the light of their contribution to that body's proper functioning (I Cor. 12:14-26).

The primary gift, source of all others, is the Spirit, whose genuineness is tested by the confession of Jesus as Lord (I Cor. 12:3). The exalted Lord, the Spirit, bestows gifts upon his church (II Cor. 3:17; Eph. 4:9-11; Phil. 2:9-11). He gives apostles, the Twelve and all who like them are sent to witness to the gospel and to lead the church at large (Rom. 16:7; I Cor. 9:5; II Cor. 8:23; Gal. 1:19).

He also gives prophets, men with the gift of utterance who speak the things they have "seen and heard" with boldness, freedom, and intelligibility, revealing insight (wisdom and knowledge) into the nature and practice of God's will (Acts 4:20, 31; I Cor. 1:5; 12:8; 14:29; II Cor. 8:7; Eph. 1:8-9, 17; Col. 1:9-10), as well as comforting, strengthening, and guiding the church in its work and worship (Acts 13:1-3; I Cor. 14:3).

He gives teachers, who instruct converts, and the church generally, in faith and practice, in gospel tradition, and in the Scriptures. They become increasingly important as discrimination between true and false teaching becomes essential. Bishops are expected to possess this gift to a superior degree (cf. Acts 20:28-31; Rom. 12:7; Col. 3:18-4:1; I Tim. 5: 17; Heb. 5:12; Jas. 3:1; I Pet. 2:18-3:7). With teaching, the service of pastoral care is sometimes linked (Eph. 4:11), suggesting perhaps the close relationship between them.

He gives evangelists, traveling missionaries, somewhat lower in standing than apostles and prophets, but noted for their special emphasis upon preaching the "good news" wherever opportunity offers (Acts 21:8; II Tim. 4:5). *See also* MINISTRY.

The gifts thus far defined are all related, though not exclusively, to the very fluid ministry of the early church, a ministry of varied functions inspired by the Spirit for the good of the corporate body. Functions, however, which gain place through effective and habitual exercise come to be recognized more formally (I Cor. 16:15; Eph. 4:7-16; I Thess. 5:12). From the first, the "laying on of hands" sets persons apart for particular work (Acts 6:6; 13:3), but later becomes a more official act, as in the Pastoral letters, where Timothy is given authority to do the work of an evangelist. The act does not bestow the gift (χάρισμα) but gives authority and confirmation to the zeal and capacity already evidenced by Timothy and which he is warned to rekindle (I Tim. 4:14; II Tim. 1:6).

There are also gifts which, though shared by the ministry, are not particularly of it. Faith is a gift (I Cor. 12:9; Phil. 1:29), and possibly prayer "in the Spirit," since the Spirit enables the believer to cry "Abba" (Rom. 8:16; I Cor. 14:14; Eph. 6:18-19). Christians believe that "the *dunamis* of God" (Mark 12:24) present in the Christ of the Gospels, and delegated to his apostles (Mark 6:7; Luke 9:1; 10:19), still operates in the church to impart the gifts of miracles and healings (Rom. 15:18; I Cor. 12:28; Gal. 3:5; Heb. 2:4; Jas. 5:13-16). Those performing works of charity or helping generally in the Christian community have the gift of service (I Cor. 12:28; cf. Rom. 12:8), while the leaders or overseers in church affairs, who may well be the forerunners of the later episcopal presbyters (Acts 14:23; 20:17), have the gift of administration. Since Christians are to distinguish truth from error in all things, especially in ecstatic utterances, to some is given the spirit of discernment (I Cor. 12:10; cf. I John 4:1). A gift greatly coveted, but placed by Paul last in value, as indeed in his list (I Cor. 12:28), is the glossolalia (unintelligible ecstatic speech), which, unless the gift of interpretation (some rational explanation) be applied to it, adds nothing, may even be detrimental, to the common good (14:18, 23).

Thus the NT confronts us with a Spirit-created, Spirit-endowed community, depending entirely upon the resources of God's grace in Christ. Quite probably at first, only the extraordinary gifts, glossolalia and kindred phenomena, were attributed to the Spirit. Soon it was believed that the Spirit is active in every aspect of the Christian movement. Believers have gifts to bring, e.g., to worship—"a hymn, a lesson, a revelation, a tongue, or an interpretation" (I Cor. 14:26)—while others exercise their gifts in the practical affairs of the church. As the Christian fellowship grew and understood more clearly its needs,

new capacities were found to meet them, clearly indicating the constant provision of the Spirit. Hence Paul speaks of "varieties of gifts," "varieties of service," "varieties of working," not so much distinguishing the gifts in kind as indicating how the rich and manifold operations of the Spirit find their expression in an equally rich and manifold diversity of effects (I Cor. 12:4-6), all stemming from the same Spirit, the same Lord, the same God, who is the source of "life in Christ Jesus" (I Cor. 1:30; cf. II Cor. 13:14).

2. The eschatological setting. Spiritual gifts in the NT presuppose the messianic community, the new Israel of God, furnished and sustained in every good and necessary function by the Spirit, inheriting the promises made to the old Israel concerning the Spirit's coming, and witnessing to their fulfilment (Acts 2:16-17; 3:25-26; Gal. 6:15-16; I Pet. 2:9-10). Marvelous signs demonstrate the Spirit's presence in power and that men are living "in the last days." The key, therefore, to an understanding of the Spirit's activity is eschatological. The Day of the Lord has dawned; the kingdom of God has come. The primitive kerygma is that through the ministry, death, and resurrection of Christ all that was anticipated in Israel's history is now being realized (Acts 2:17-21; 3:21, 24; 10:43; cf. Mark 1:14-15). As members of Christ's body, the church, Christians are constantly enriched with the blessings of the "new age" while they wait for the future consummation (I Cor. 1:7; 10:11; Heb. 6:5). They live in a fellowship created by the Spirit, filled with the Spirit, over which the Lord the Spirit reigns, and for which he bestows all the gifts and graces essential to its corporate life (Acts 2:33; Rom. 5; 8; I Cor. 1:9; II Cor. 3:17; Gal. 5:22-23). The Spirit is thus the "first fruits" (Rom. 8:23) or the "guarantee" (II Cor. 1:22; 5:5; Eph. 1:14) of the future inheritance which Christians already taste and share (Heb. 6:4; I Pet. 4:14). The reign of God, yet to be fulfilled, is now manifest in "righteousness and peace and joy in the Holy Spirit" (Rom. 14:17).

3. Evaluation and control. All spiritual gifts are valid, but not all are equally good. Their worth to the church determines their value. Paul, with the Corinthian church as background, where ecstatic powers, particularly "tongues," are given undue place and prominence, sees the necessity of guiding spiritual gifts into ethical and rational channels. He introduces the analogy of the body (I Cor. 12:12-26), with its organic unity, diversity of function, interdependence of members, to illustrate how the χαρίσματα are also diverse in function, interdependent, and designed to give unity, solidarity, and healthy growth to the Christian fellowship. All gifts, therefore, are to be subordinated to, and have value in proportion as they further, this purpose. The ministry is graciously given (Eph. 4:7-8) to bring the church "to mature manhood, to the measure of the stature of the fullness of Christ." Prophecy is given for "upbuilding and encouragement and consolation" (I Cor. 14:3). Every gift is justified in the measure that it contributes to the faith and knowledge, peace and order, of the church, and must be exercised with a deep sense of responsibility to God, who has called Christians to be "good stewards" of his "varied grace" (I Cor. 14: 33, 36; I Pet. 4:10-11).

Since all gifts are for the service of the church, how

can they be so used? Paul finds the answer in the "more excellent way" of love (ἀγάπη), the greatest of all "spiritual gifts" (Rom. 5:5; I Cor. 12:31–13:1), the undeserved grace bestowed on man that he might bestow it in complete self-giving upon his fellows. Since gifts fall into a scale of relative significance as the ends of love are promoted, this becomes both the criterion of value and the principle of control. By introducing this regulatory concept of love, his basic moral premise, Paul corrects the confusion and disorder of the Corinthian church and prepares the way for a more ethical apprehension of the Spirit's activity in those "fruits of the Spirit" which are the marks of Christian character (Gal. 5:22; cf. Eph. 5:9).

Bibliography. In addition to Commentaries on Romans and I Corinthians, see: H. B. Swete, *The Holy Spirit in the NT* (1910); C. A. A. Scott, *The Fellowship of the Spirit* (1921); E. F. Scott, *The Spirit in the NT* (1923); F. Büschel, *Der Geist Gottes im NT* (1926); R. B. Hoyle, *The Holy Spirit in St. Paul* (1927); F. J. Foakes-Jackson and K. Lake, *The Beginnings of Christianity*, vols. I, V (1933); J. Weiss, *The History of Primitive Christianity* (English trans.; 1937); C. K. Barrett, *The Holy Spirit and the Gospel Tradition* (1947); H. A. Guy, *NT Prophecy* (1947).   E. ANDREWS

SPIT. The act of spitting is uniformly a sign of the strongest rejection and contempt in the OT and the NT, apparently as part of quasi-legal formulas in Num. 12:14; Deut. 25:9.

None of the OT occurrences reflects directly the widespread superstition that human spittle contains the mysterious essence of the man himself and is therefore potentially usable in all kinds of magic and subject to strong taboo, with the possible exception of Lev. 15:8.

Jesus follows widespread Jewish practice in the use of spittle to heal in Mark 8:23; John 9:6 (*see* HEALING). Sabbath law is broken by Jesus in his mixing the clay in John 9:6, and this may constitute the main point of this action. In Mark 7:33 the act of spitting may entail the dispersal of demonic forces rather than an act of healing by means of the spittle. *See* DEMON; MIRACLE.

Bibliography. O. Weinreich, *Antike Heilungswunder* (1909), pp. 68, 97-98; H. Strack and P. Billerbeck, *Kommentar zum NT* (1924), II, 15-18; J. G. Frazer, *The Golden Bough* (1-vol. ed., 1930), pp. 13, 218, 233-37, 435-37, 568.   J. A. WHARTON

SPOIL [שָׁלָל; *see also below*]. Plunder taken as right of conquest.

The most common word, שָׁלָל, indicates goods, cattle, and captives subject to division among the victors (e.g., Gen. 49:27; Exod. 15:9), as distinguished from בַז and its later cognate בִזָּה, often translated "booty," which mean things taken by each warrior for himself (e.g., Num. 31:53; Jer. 15:13; Ezek. 25:7 [*Qere*]). Less common is מְשִׁסָּה (II Kings 21:14; Isa. 42:22; Jer. 30:16; also Isa. 42:24 *Qere* and KJV, where the *Kethibh* מְשׁוֹסֶה, parallel to בֹּזְזִים, "robbers," should rather be interpreted as a participle, "spoiler"). חֲלִיצָה refers to what is stripped from a slain warrior (Judg. 14:19; II Sam. 2:21). בֶּצַע (Judg. 5:19) means something obtained by violent means, often illegally, and elsewhere is usually translated "gain." גְּזֵלָה (Isa. 3:14) comes from a word with the root meaning "to rob"; and since the taking of spoil was considered to be a right of the victor, and hence

perfectly moral, the word might better be rendered "pillage." The KJV uses "spoil" for some occurrences of שֹׁד, "destruction," and טֶרֶף, "prey," and also in Isa. 25:11 for the *hapax legomenon* אָרְבוֹת, which comes from the root אָרַב, "to lie in ambush," and more probably means "artifice" or "trickery" (RSV "skill"). In the NT, σκῦλον (Luke 11:22) refers first of all to armor taken from a slain warrior, and by extension to any spoils taken by force; and ἀκροθίνιον (Heb. 7:4) means the best part, hence the "first fruits," or the choice portion of the plunder, which was given to the deity.

Warfare in the ancient Near East inevitably involved the rights of plunder. The victor automatically assumed his right to possess anything belonging to the vanquished enemy. This usually involved cattle (Deut. 2:35; 3:7; I Sam. 14:32; II Chr. 15:11; Jer. 49:32), clothing (Josh. 7:21; Judg. 5:30; II Chr. 20: 25; 28:15), precious metals (Josh. 7:21; Judg. 8:24-25)—in fact, anything that could be carried or driven away (II Chr. 20:25; cf. Gen. 14:11, 16), including women and children (Deut. 20:14), whereas the male populace was often exterminated (Num. 31:7, 17). The taking of spoil was a warrior's greatest pleasure (Ps. 119:162; Isa. 9:3—H 9:2).

The division of spoils followed certain general rules among the Hebrews. As among the later Arabs the leader probably received a special share, though he could also ask his warriors to give up some of theirs for a particular cultic purpose, as in the case of Gideon (Judg. 8:24-25). According to the Priestly account of Num. 31, Israel returned from their victory over the Midianites with "all the spoil and all the booty," and brought them to Moses and Eleazar into the camp for distribution. All male children were to be killed, and of women only virgins were to be kept alive. Thereupon the spoil was divided into two parts, one part to be equally distributed among the warriors and the other to the people at large. Furthermore, a levy for the deity was assessed. The warriors were to give up one person or beast out of every five hundred; the people, one out of every fifty. Beyond this, as a special offering each man brought "the LORD's offering"—namely "articles of gold, armlets and bracelets, signet rings, earrings, and beads." This was "booty" (בַז) taken by each warrior for himself, in distinction from "spoil" (שָׁלָל), which had to be divided. The actual division of the spoil was done by the chieftain, who was probably known as the אֲבִי עַד (Isa. 9:6—H 9:5, where "Everlasting Father" may rather mean "Father of spoils").

Choice plunder was often devoted to the deity; it then became part of the treasures of the sanctuary. Goliath's sword was housed at the sanctuary at Nob (I Sam. 21:9), whereas the armor of the defeated Saul was placed by the Philistines in their temple of Ashtaroth (31:9-10). In temple times parts of the spoil won in battle were dedicated "for the maintenance of the house of the LORD" (I Chr. 26:27), where special officers were charged with the care of all such gifts.

In special cases no spoil might be taken. Prior to an assault a city or tribe might be "devoted" to God. Such a vow meant that everything animate was to be destroyed, all precious metals and objects given to God, and the remainder, including the city with its dwellings and surrounding fields, burned or otherwise made useless. Jericho was placed under the BAN (i.e., devoted to destruction) at the time of the Conquest (Josh. 6:17-19).

See also BOOTY.

Bibliography. J. Pedersen, *Israel: Its Life and Culture,* vols. III-IV (1940), pp. 1-32; A. G. Barrois, *Manuel d'Archeologie Biblique,* vol. II (1953), ch. 16: "La Guerre."

J. W. WEVERS

SPONGE [σπόγγος]. The skeleton of a type of marine animal. The usefulness of the sponge is dependent upon its power to absorb liquids without losing its own toughness. The word is used in three NT passages (Matt. 27:48; Mark 15:36; John 19:29) in which Jesus is offered a sponge full of vinegar, or sour wine, to quench his thirst.   S. A. CARTLEDGE

SPOON. KJV translation of כַּף, more correctly rendered "dishes for incense" (so RSV). *See* INCENSE, DISHES FOR.

SPRING. The usual translation of עַיִן and מַעְיָן, but *see* FOUNTAIN.

SPRING RAIN [מַלְקוֹשׁ, benefiting לֶקֶשׁ, late-sown crops]; KJV and twice RSV LATTER RAIN. Showers of April and May which bring the rainy season to an end; linked with EARLY RAIN as a token of divine goodness. *See* PALESTINE, CLIMATE OF.

SQUAD [τετράδιον; Vulg. *quaternio*] (Acts 12:4); KJV QUATERNION kwə tûr'nĭ ən. A guard usually consisting of four soldiers, one for each of the night watches.

There is some evidence that even where the words *quaternio* or τετράδιον were not used, a guard was customarily made up of four soldiers: see Polybius VI.33, which indicates that when camp is pitched, the maniples "supply two guards [φυλακεῖα] for [the tribune] (a guard consists of four men) of which one [guard] is stationed in front of the tent and the other behind it next the horses." Cf. also Vegetius *De Re Militari* III.8; Philostratus *Vita Ap.* 7.31; Philo *Against Flaccus* 13; Gospel of Peter 9; John 19:23.

In Acts 12:1-11, Peter was guarded by four squads —i.e., by sixteen soldiers. Although vs. 4 suggests that Herod intended to keep Peter in prison for some time—until "after the Passover"—actually the four squads appear to be named with reference to the four watches of the night, a squad per watch. The narrative really has in mind only this one night. Peter was bound "with two chains"—i.e., to a guard on each side. The other two soldiers would be the "sentries before the door" of vs. 6 or the "first and the second guard" of vs. 10. Of course, Luke is not primarily concerned to show how many guards there were—when the angel "struck" Peter, there would be present only the four whose watch it was—nor to station them precisely in the prison, but to show that no matter how extravagantly Peter might be guarded, he could not be held.   F. D. GEALY

SQUARE [רְחוֹב]; KJV usually STREET; BROAD PLACE in Jer. 5:1. A word of uncertain meaning;

perhaps an open space where public gatherings could be held, inside the gate of a typical Israelite city, as found in the excavations (cf. II Chr. 32:6; Neh. 8:1, 3, 16; and perhaps Ezra 10:9; see also Deut. 13:16; Judg. 19:15; Esth. 4:6; 6:9, 11; Job 29:7).

See also CITY § B2*e*.   C. C. MCCOWN

STABLE. KJV translation of נָוֶה (RSV "pasture") in Ezek. 25:5. In modern (and probably in ancient) Palestine separate stables for domestic animals were practically unknown. At night they were sheltered in caves or in the house, rarely in a separate "basement." *See* STALL.

STACHYS stā'kĭs [Στάχυς, head of grain] (Rom. 16:9). A Christian man greeted by Paul and designated as "my beloved."   F. W. GINGRICH

STACTE stăk'tĭ [נָטָף, *nāṭāph, from root* to drip; στακτή]. One of the four aromatic ingredients of the holy INCENSE which was burned "before the testimony in the tent of meeting" (Exod. 30:34). The same list of ingredients is found in Ecclus. 24:15 (στακτή; KJV "storax") in a poem in praise of Wisdom. The LXX translates לֹט, *lōt,* in Gen. 37:25

76. Stacte

with σταχτή (*see* MYRRH). The Hebrew root meaning suggests the droplets of gum exuded from a number of shrubs and trees (cf. Job 36:27 for its association with water). The storax tree, *Styrax officinalis* L., and the opobalsamum (ASV mg. of Exod. 30:34), *Commiphora opobalsamum* L., are considered the most likely sources. Zohary (*see* FLORA § A9*p*) favors the *Styrax officinalis* L. also for לִבְנֶה, *libhnê* (*see* POPLAR), mentioned in Gen. 30:37; Hos. 4:13.

See also FLORA § A7*i*.

Fig. STA 76.

Bibliography. H. N. and A. L. Moldenke, *Plants of the Bible* (1952), pp. 224-25.   J. C. TREVER

STADIA stā'dĭ ə [στάδια]; KJV FURLONGS. *See* WEIGHTS AND MEASURES § D4*e*.

STAFF [מַטֶּה (*alternately* ROD; BRANCH; TRIBE); שֵׁבֶט, מִשְׁעֶנֶת, מַשְׁעֵנָה, מַקֵּל (*alternately* REED, SCEP-

TER, TRIBE; KJV ROD *in* Lev. 27:32, PEN *in* Judg. 5:14); KJV *occasionally* בד (RSV "pole"), חץ (RSV "shaft"), מוט (RSV "pole"), מוטה (RSV "pole"), עץ (RSV "shaft"), פלך (RSV "spindle"); ῥάβδος (KJV "rod" *in* Rev. 11:1); KJV ξύλον (RSV "club"]. In addition to many references to the literal use of a staff—by travelers, warriors, riders, shepherds, etc.—there are a number of figurative references to "staff." From the idea of a staff as support came the figurative use of "staff of bread" (Ezek. 4: 16; 5:16; 14:13; etc.). The staff, or ROD, of MOSES and that of AARON (Exod. 7:9 ff; Num. 17:5 ff), like those of the Egyptian magicians, were the instruments of miraculous powers (*see* MAGIC). The rod of Moses became his scepter in the desert, and in battle —especially when upraised—symbolized the presence of God among his people. Each of the tribes had a rod or staff (מטה) on which its name was written (Num. 17:2—H 17:17). According to II Kings 4:29, 31, the staff of ELISHA possessed healing power. Evidently the staff of the shepherd, on which he leaned, gave a sense of security to his flock (cf. Ps. 23:4). The Lord's staff is regarded often as a symbol of his presence and power (cf. II Sam. 22:19=Ps. 18:18—H 18:19; Isa. 3:1). Both rod and staff are instruments of divine judgment (Isa. 10:15; 30:32); and Assyria is like a staff in the Lord's hand against Israel (Isa. 10:15, 24; cf. Job 9:34; Ps. 2:9; Isa. 9:4; Ezek. 20:37). Old people who sit with staff in hand, unafraid and undisturbed, are a symbol of security (Zech. 8:4).

Jesus sent his disciples forth with the suggestion that they carry neither money nor extra clothes nor a staff (according to Matt. 10:10; Luke 9:3; but Mark 6:8 says he instructed them to take a staff). In Heb. 11:21 mention is made of the detail that Jacob had leaned on his staff while blessing the sons of Joseph (a reflection of the LXX rendering of Gen. 37:31, which translates "upon the head of his staff").

H. F. BECK

STAG. *See* HART.

STAIRS [מעלה, מדרגה, לולים; KJV מדרוה (Song of S. 2:14; RSV "cliff"); ἀναβαθμός]. Since the roof of a Palestinian house was the place for many family activities, stairs were a common feature. In the one-story house the stairs normally would be on the outside. They would be made of stone and without balustrade. In a two-story house, in addition to the stairs to the roof, there would be an inside flight to the second story. In city streets, as today, where there were steep hills, there would be stairs from one level to another (Neh. 3:15; 12:37). Stairs have been found leading down into deep wells or cisterns at Gezer, Megiddo, Beth-zur, Gibeon, and Qumran (Figs. STA 77; DEA 16). By NT times Greek and Roman theaters throughout the world had stairs. In I Kings 6:8 לולים, which occurs only here, is taken to mean "winding stairs." The other Hebrew and Greek words for "stairs" have the root meaning of "going up." There are stairs (RSV "steps") in Ezekiel's temple (Ezek. 40:6; 43:17). "Stairs of the Levites" are mentioned in Neh. 9:4. The "ladder" (סלם) in Jacob's dream may be a flight of stairs (Gen. 28:12).

See also ARCHITECTURE; HOUSE; LADDER.

Figs. PER 33; SAL 7; SAM 20. O. R. SELLERS

Courtesy of James B. Pritchard

77. Stairs descending to the pool at Gibeon

STAIRS OF THE CITY OF DAVID [מעלות עיר דויד] (Neh. 12:37). Alternately: STAIRS THAT GO DOWN FROM THE CITY OF DAVID [המעלות היורדות מעיר דויד] (Neh. 3:15). Stairs of rock mentioned in the records of the restoration of Jerusalem under Nehemiah, toward the S end of the City of David (*see* DAVID, CITY OF), in the vicinity of the TOMBS OF THE KINGS. Excavations have led to the discovery of such a flight of rock-cut steps on the hill wedged between the valleys of the Tyropoeon and the Kidron, and leading to a postern in the E fortifications of the city, possibly the FOUNTAIN GATE. Fig. NEH 13.

Bibliography. J. Simons, *Jerusalem in the OT* (1952), pp. 95-96, 449-50; H. Vincent, *Jérusalem de l'AT*, I (1954), 245, 251-52. G. A. BARROIS

STALL [רפתים, ארות, מרבק]. A place for tying and feeding cattle. In the average home animals were kept in the yard, or in the lower section of the house, or in a cave stable under the house or nearby. For further details, *see* MANGER.

In Amos 6:4; Mal. 4:2—H 3:20 the phrase "calves from the stall" (עגלי מרבק) means calves specially fattened with fodder in the stable, as contrasted with range animals. This is the meaning also of the ambiguous phrase "stalled ox" (שור אבום; RSV "fatted ox") of Prov. 15:17.

Both Hezekiah (II Chr. 32:28: "stalls for all kinds of cattle") and Solomon (I Kings 4:26—H 5:6: forty thousand horses; II Chr. 9:25: four thousand horses) had very extensive stalls or stables (ארות). Most scholars consider the forty thousand an exaggeration.

Courtesy of the Oriental Institute, the University of Chicago

78. Model of stables in the NE area at Megiddo (Stratum IVA)

Courtesy of Herbert G. May

79. Stalls with mangers, from Megiddo stables

Courtesy of the Oriental Institute, the University of Chicago

80. Stable at Megiddo in NE area of Stratum IVA, showing the arrangement of stalls

One Greek version (G^B) of I Kings 4:26 has four thousand. However, the very large extent of Solomon's stables has been strikingly substantiated by excavations at Megiddo and elsewhere. At MEGIDDO two separate groups of stable units have been excavated. Their plan was fairly uniform. On either side of passageways paved with hard lime were rows of stalls facing one another across the central aisles. The stalls were paved with cobblestones and rubble. At the head of the stalls, along the passageway, were pillars with mangers between. On the passageway side of the pillars, just above the tops of the mangers, were holes for the tie ropes of the horses. In all, there were about 450 stalls in the Megiddo stables (Figs. STA 78-80; MAN 8; MEG 33). Similar building arrangements have been found at Tell el-Hesi, Gezer, Taanach, and Hazor (though the most recent excavators do not interpret this last as a stable). Some of these may reflect Solomon's building activities. Hazor, Megiddo, and Gezer are mentioned in I Kings 9:15.

Bibliography. R. S. Lamon and G. M. Shipton, *Megiddo I, Seasons of 1925-34* (1939), pp. 32-44; J. A. Montgomery and H. S. Gehman, *Books of Kings*, ICC (1951), pp. 127-28.

S. V. FAWCETT

STANDARD [דגל, נס; KJV נום (Isa. 59:19; *cf.* RSV)]. A troop or tribal ensign used as a rallying signal. *See* BANNER.

STARS. *See* SCIENCE §§ A2, B2, C2.

STEADFASTNESS [ὑπομονή]. Alternately: ENDURANCE; PATIENCE; PATIENT ENDURANCE; PERSEVERANCE. A term which sometimes connotes reliability, constancy, fidelity, but which primarily means patient or steadfast endurance. In the Bible it is usually related explicitly to adverse circumstances, afflictions, persecutions, and even martyrdom. It has been well defined as denoting "an inward feeling, as well as outward conduct, but directed only against aggression." It connotes, not simply acceptance, or patience, but perseverance under trial. Often it is explicitly oriented to hope and describes a willingness to endure because of hope in what has been promised.

In Rom. 15:3-4 Paul, referring to Christ, quotes Ps. 69:9: "The reproaches of those who reproached thee fell on me," and then writes that this "was written for our instruction, that by steadfastness . . . we might have hope." Paul is telling the Romans that they must patiently endure reproaches as Christ endured them; and that if they do so, they may hope that the promises offered them in Christ will be fulfilled (cf. Rom. 5:3-4). The Christian endures (is steadfast) both because he hopes and in order that he may have hope.

In II Thess. 1:4 Paul writes: "We ourselves boast of you in the churches of God for your steadfastness and faith in all your persecutions and in the afflictions which you are enduring." The Thessalonians are "patiently enduring" (are steadfast in) persecutions and afflictions, and Paul boasts of this endurance (steadfastness) and faith.

Jas. 1:3-4 bids the brethren to rejoice when they meet trials, for the testing of faith "produces steadfastness." Trials are to be understood as testings, and testing leads to the ability to endure.

B. H. THROCKMORTON, JR.

STEALING. *See* CRIMES AND PUNISHMENTS § C7*b*.

STEED [אביר (Judg. 5:22; STALLION *in* Jer. 8:16; 47:3; 50:11), strong, powerful one; אמץ (Zech. 6:7; KJV BAY; *cf.* 6:3), strong one(?); קל (Isa. 30:16; KJV THE SWIFT), swift one; רכש (Mic. 1:13; KJV SWIFT BEAST; *in* I Kings 4:28—H 5:8, SWIFT STEED; KJV DROMEDARY)]. A HORSE which is especially strong, brave, swift, and of generally high mettle, suited particularly for battle.

J. A. SANDERS

STEEL. KJV translation of נחושה in II Sam. 22:35; Job 20:24; Ps. 18:34; Jer. 15:12 (RSV BRONZE).

STEER. A term used in the translation of פר, "young steer" (KJV "bullock"), in Isa. 34:7 (elsewhere "bull"; "calf").

STEPHANAS stĕf'ə nəs [Στεφανᾶς, crown, *either a shortened form of* Στεφανήφορος, crown-bearer, *or a development of* Στέφανος] (I Cor. 1:16; 16:15, 17). A man who, along with his household, is included among the very few individuals personally baptized by Paul. He and his household are described as the "first-fruits" of Paul's ministry in Achaia. They are here commended for their earnest and devoted service (διακονία) to the Christian community.

Paul urges the Corinthian Christians, in the light of their divisive tendencies (I Cor. 1:10-17), to follow the leadership of such men, and he rejoices in the pleasure of Stephanas' visit to him in Ephesus (16:17-18) along with Fortunatus and Achaicus. These latter two, since they are mentioned by name, were probably not members of Stephanas' household. Stephanas and his two companions seem to have constituted a delegation from the Corinthian church to consult with Paul. They probably brought the letter written to Paul by the Corinthian church (7:1) and took back with them to Corinth the document known as I Corinthians. It is not clear that Stephanas and his companions had any formal official churchly status, but their actions and the manner in which they are here mentioned represent a first step in the direction of a definite local ministry in the churches.

J. M. NORRIS

STEPHEN stē'vən [Στέφανος, crown, wreath] (Acts 6:5, 8-9; 7:1 [Codex Bezae], 59; 8:2; 11:19; 22:20). One of seven men "of good repute, full of the Spirit and of wisdom," who at the command of the Twelve were selected by the "body of the disciples" and set before the apostles, who prayed and laid their hands upon them, thereby appointing them to serve tables, or specifically to remedy the neglect of the widows of the HELLENISTS "in the daily distribution" (Acts 6:1-6). Stephen's name heads the list of the SEVEN; and he only is honored with a character qualification: "a man full of faith and of the Holy Spirit." Vs. 8 further describes him as being "full of grace and power" and as therefore doing "great wonders and signs among the people."

The only available information about Stephen is that which is found in Acts. "Crowned" with martyrdom and prominently displayed as the first Christian martyr, Stephen ("crown") is his appropriate name.

Acts gives us no biographical data about Stephen. Was he himself a Hellenist? If so, in what sense? Was he resident in Jerusalem? From whom did he receive his instruction in the faith? Luke does not call him a DEACON; yet, the question remains, does Luke intend here to set forth the origin of the diaconate? Or are the Seven elders, not deacons? *See* ELDER.

Did Stephen really "serve tables"—i.e., supervise the daily dole of the widows? Or, in spite of the fact that this problem was reputed to be the immediate cause of the setting apart (ordination?) of the Seven, was this charitable service only a minor part of their work, and had the Seven already distinguished themselves as preachers? It may also be asked, who had previously been responsible for managing the dole? And was the dole problem of such nature as to call for the selection and setting apart of seven men "full of the Spirit and of wisdom"? In the pre-Lukan form of the tradition, were the Seven "set apart" to be responsible for the dole only; and has Luke, in the light of the subsequent work of Stephen and Philip, and of his theory of the centralization of the control of the expansion of the church in all its activities in the apostles and the Jerusalem church, anachronistically made of the event a full ordination event?

Since Stephen and Philip (nothing is known about the other five named) are described as doing only the work of evangelists, we may suppose that Luke was concerned with the dole problem primarily because and to the extent that (*a*) it pointed to the existence within the church of a group moving away from the original Jewish Christian nucleus toward the inclusive church of the Greco-Roman world; (*b*) it was or was reputed to have been responsible for summoning Stephen to a position of official responsibility; (*c*) it provided an occasion for setting forth a new stage in the organization and expansion of the church (whether or not the Seven correspond to the Seventy of the gospel, or of Num. 11); and (*d*) it provided Luke an opportunity to set forth his theory of the primacy of the Twelve and of the church in Jerusalem relative to all subsequent church development, thus showing how the church was one, holy, catholic, and apostolic.

Stephen's disputants (vs. 9) are certainly intended to be Hellenists, meaning Diaspora (*see* DISPERSION) Jews representing the very areas in which the church was to win great victories—indeed, had already done so by Luke's time. Likewise the Hellenists of vs. 1 are most probably meant to be Greek-speaking, Greek-minded, Jewish Christians—not "Greeks," meaning "Gentiles." That Nicolaus is described as a proselyte (vs. 5) suggests that the events of 6:1-6 were intended to be viewed as a conflict, not between Gentile Christians and Jewish Christians, but between two diverging types of Jewish Christians, the one insisting on the necessity of keeping the whole law (is this why "Hebrews" is used?); the other facing toward the full Gentile Christian position, not yet having actualized it (therefore "Hellenists") but foreshadowing it, and so providing a proper introduction for Stephen. Further, the plan of Acts virtually requires that the "Hellenists" be, not "Greeks," but Jewish Christians with "Greek" upbringing.

Although it is probable enough that Luke regarded the conflict alluded to in Acts 6:1-6 as one between the two types of Jewish Christians described above, and that he thought of Stephen as a pro-Greek Jewish Christian, this, after all, is of minor concern in the total picture of Acts 6:1-8:3. For Stephen's real conflict is with the Jews, and, indeed, with Diaspora Jews, even in Jerusalem. Apart from any reasons of sheer historical fact—and Luke has carefully selected his facts—the first martyr's meeting death at the hands of Jews, even Diaspora Jews, is in accord with Luke's designs in Luke-Acts, both here and generally:

a) The resemblances between the accounts of the trial and death of Jesus in the Gospel and of Stephen in Acts are too great to be coincidental. Luke can scarcely have avoided assimilating them to each other, whichever may have been the model for the other. The Jews, he will say, are responsible for both deaths.

b) As described in Acts, Jewish hostility to the

expanding church, generally in the apostolic age and in all the extra-Palestinian centers of Paul's activity, and exclusively in Luke's own time after A.D. 70, was exerted by Diaspora Jews. Therefore, it is appropriate that such should be introduced into the story as early as ch. 6, and on so important an occasion as the death of the first martyr (vs. 9).

Apart from the details of the text, the speech of Stephen presents four problems: (a) How is it related to its literary context? (b) How are we to explain the fact that Stephen does not really speak to the charges brought against him? (c) What is its source? (d) What is its function, here and in Acts?

In Acts 6:1–8:3 there are certainly two, and most probably three, sources. Obviously, as noted above, 6:1-6 and 6:8 ff represent two different Stephen traditions, which are juxtaposed but unrelated, neither explaining or being explained by the other—in fact, each making a problem for the other. Vs. 7 functions as a bridge which both separates and joins them, but which is unrelated to the Stephen event.

Vs. 8 begins a new episode. It may well be that this tradition originally recounted only the trial and martyrdom (6:8-14/15; 7:55-60) but no speech. In this case 7:1-53 would be a third source, or, better, anti-Jewish polemic which Luke fashioned into a speech for his purposes in Acts.

If this is a correct analysis of the three sections of the narrative, then the fact that Stephen does not address himself to the charges preferred is to be explained by Luke's employing the occasion for another purpose. Luke's scheme in Acts appears to be this: first, the gospel is dramatically preached to the Jews (Acts 2: "Let all the house of Israel . . . know . . . . For the promise is to you . . ."; then, in ch. 3, the rejection takes place: "You denied the Holy and Righteous One, . . . and killed the Author of life"). Yet, the offer of repentance is again extended (3: 19 ff). But Jewish opposition continues (ch. 4; 5:17-32). And now Luke sees in the event of Stephen's martyrdom the proper occasion for giving the final *coup de grâce* to Jewish resistance in this his longest speech in Acts. He does this by setting forth the history of the people of Israel as a history of continual disobedience to God. First, they rejected Moses; they "refused to obey him" and "thrust him aside." Then they made their own gods. And finally they built a temple, although "the Most High does not dwell in houses made with hands." Then the speech turns from the third person to direct address, as Stephen draws the conclusion: "You stiff-necked people, . . . you always resist the Holy Spirit. As your fathers did, so do you." Luke understands the rejection to be a total one. The "people and the elders and scribes, . . . the council" (6:12), "brethren and fathers" (7:2), and the part of "the witnesses"—all indicate that to Luke the death of Stephen was not "mob" action; it was official. This gives point to Luke's insistence that the Israel that rejects radically is radically rejected. This prompts and justifies the final judgment.

Luke may or may not have composed the whole of the speech. His effective treatment of the material makes it impossible to determine in what form he may have found any of the traditions he used.

The function of the speech in Acts is sufficiently explained above. It may be further stated that by it Luke prepares the way for the ultimate abandonment of temple Judaism; and by hurling the charge of disobedience to the law back into the teeth of the Jews, he will win understanding for the Christian reinterpretation of the law, as being indeed God's law, but not as Jews read it.

Thus Stephen's speech does not account for his death; rather, his death provides Luke with an opportunity to show (a) that the church is a martyr church, (b) that the Christian is summoned to witness to his faith, even unto death, and (c) that the Israel which has rejected Christ has been rejected by God.

Stephen's death becomes an epiphany: "The heavens opened," revealing "the Son of man standing at the right hand of God" (7:56), ready either to receive or to show his approval of Stephen, or to come to establish his kingdom.

With unobtrusive skill and fine reticence Luke introduces into the scene a "young man named Saul," who also "was consenting to his death" (7:58; 8:1), and whose determination to "lay waste" the church only became intensified, until he too saw the heavens opened.

Since Luke was not concerned to enter into Stephen's historical situation in such a way as to make clear to us how Stephen was related to the evolving church in idea and practice, the historical value of the account remains in debate. For contemporary opinions, *see bibliography*.

Bibliography. W. Mundle, "Die Stephanusrede Apg. 7: eine Maertyrerapologie," *ZNW*, 20 (1921), 133-47; F. J. Foakes-Jackson, "Stephen's Speech in Acts," *JBL*, XLIX (1930), 283-86; H. J. Cadbury, "The Hellenists," in F. J. Foakes-Jackson and K. Lake, *Beginnings of Christianity*, V (1933), 59-74; E. C. Blackman, "The Hellenists of Acts vi.1," *ET*, 48 (1936-37), 524-25; J. Weiss, *The History of Primitive Christianity* (English trans., 1937), pp. 165-79; A. M. Farrar, "The Ministry in the NT," in K. E. Kirk, ed., *The Apostolic Ministry* (1946), pp. 113-82; B. S. Easton, "Deacon," *The Pastoral Epistles* (1947), pp. 181-85; W. Foerster, "Stephanus und die Urgemeinde," *Dienst unter dem Wort* (1953), pp. 9-30; M. Goguel, *The Birth of Christianity* (English trans., 1954), pp. 167-76; G. H. C. Macgregor, Exegesis of Acts, *IB*, IX (1954), 87-107; M. Dibelius, *Studies in the Acts of the Apostles* (English trans., 1956), pp. 167-70; E. Haenchen, *Die Apostelgeschichte* (1956), pp. 217-58; H. P. Owen, "Stephen's Vision in Acts vii:55-6," *NTS*, I (1956), 224-26; C. S. C. Williams, *The Acts of the Apostles* (1957), pp. 95-112; M. Simon, *St. Stephen and the Hellenists* (1958); J. Munck, *Paul and the Salvation of Mankind* (English trans., 1959), pp. 218-28.   F. D. GEALY

STEPHEN, REVELATION OF. An apocryphal apocalypse known to us by its condemnation, together with the Apocalypse of Paul and the Apocalypse of Thomas, in the so-called Gelasian Decree, and mentioned by Sixtus Senensis (A.D. 1593) in his *Bibliotheca Sancta:* "The Apocalypse of Stephen, the first martyr, who was one of the seven deacons of the apostles, was prized by the Manichaean heretics, as Serapion witnesses." It has been often surmised, but with little seeming justification, that the writing so referred to was in substance the tale told by Lucian (A.D. 415), a priest in Kaphargamala, a town near Jerusalem, of the discovery of the bodies of Stephen, Nicodemus, Gamaliel, and the latter's son Abibas, in consequence of a thrice-repeated vision to him of Gamaliel.

A romance, extant only in Slavonic and published by I. Franko in 1906 in *ZNTW*, provides a background for Lucian's narrative in the form of an elaborate and highly fanciful expansion and amplification of the story of Stephen in Acts, in which Saul plays a very prominent part as chief inquisitor. That this romance of uncertain date has a definite connection with Lucian's tale is certain—the detail of the several coffins is sufficient to prove this—but that it was prior to, and thus the real beginning of Lucian's narrative, as Franco argued, is far from sure. Thus the conclusion that any of this material was part of the apocryphon allegedly prized by the Manicheans would seem most hazardous.

See APOCRYHA, NT.

Bibliography. A résumé of the Slavonic romance is given by M. R. James, *The Apocryphal NT* (1924), pp. 564-68, while a convenient summary of Lucian's famous tale is to be found in the article "Stephen" in Smith and Cheetham, *A Dictionary of Christian Antiquities* (1880), II, 1929-33.   M. S. ENSLIN

STEPPE. A translation used twice for words more frequently translated "desert" or "wilderness" (מדבר in I Chr. 6:78—H 6:63; ערבה in Job 39:6; KJV "wilderness"; *see* DESERT). The references are to level, unforested land, receiving eight to sixteen inches of rain, and found in Palestine along the edge of the desert in S Judah and along the edge of the desert E of the Jordan. *See* PALESTINE, CLIMATE OF; PALESTINE, GEOGRAPHY OF.

L. E. TOOMBS

STEWARD, STEWARDSHIP. An official who controls the affairs of a large household, overseeing the service at the master's table, directing the household servants, and controlling the household expenses on behalf of the master. So Joseph's household affairs are in the care of a steward (Hebrew lit., "man over the house"; Gen. 43:19; 44:4; cf. I Kings 16:9). Eliezer, Abraham's steward, is also his heir (Gen. 15: 2). The kings of Israel had such officers over their households, perhaps "treasurer" or "prince" (I Kings 15:18; I Chr. 27:31; 28:1; Isa. 22:15). In Dan. 1:11, 16, the Hebrew מלצר is translated as a proper name in the KJV, but it seems to be properly "guardian" or "steward."

Bishops are stewards of the affairs of God. (Tit. 1: 7.) All Christians are to be stewards of God's mysteries (οἰκονόμος; I Cor. 4:1; Gal. 4:2; I Pet. 4: 10). The Christian concept of stewardship before God involves time, talents, possessions, and self (Luke 12: 42; Eph. 3:2). In the NT there are other stewards mentioned. They are not always slaves but may even be the treasurer of a city (Rom. 16:23). The parable of the unjust steward tells of their duties (Luke 16:1-8). Obviously a stewardship can be betrayed. The ruler at the wedding feast in Cana is a steward (John 2:8-9). The master of a vineyard is also a steward (ἐπίτροπος; Matt. 20:8; Luke 8:3).   C. U. WOLF

STIFF-NECKED. A metaphor for rebellion and unteachableness, taken from the use of domestic animals for various kinds of work (ערף, "neck," plus

קשה, "be hard" [in verb and noun forms]; σκληροτράχηλος). The ox "stiffens his neck" when he refuses direction, or "turns a stubborn shoulder" when offered the yoke (cf. Hos. 4:16; 10:11; Zech. 7:11-12; cf. Neh. 9:29).

The term typically describes Israel's rebelliousness against Yahweh during the wilderness wandering (Exod. 32:9; 33:3, 5; Deut. 9:13), which becomes a stereotype of apostasy (Jer. 7:26). Such rebellion consists in disobedience and idolatry (Exod. 32:9; Deut. 31:27), reversing the course of Yahweh's redemptive history (Neh. 9:16-17; Jer. 7:26). A chief characteristic of the "stiff-necked" is refusal to listen to the word of God delivered through the prophets (II Kings 17:13-14; II Chr. 36:12-13; Jer. 7:25-26; 19: 15; cf. Ezek. 3:7; Zech. 7:11-12), which in Acts 7: 51-53 is called "resist[ing] the Holy Spirit" (cf. Isa. 63:10). God's grace appears in sharp contrast to Israel's stubbornness in Exod. 34:9; Deut. 9:6; II Chr. 30:8; Neh. 9:16 ff. The opposite of this attitude is the transformation of the external forms of the covenant relationship (*see* CIRCUMCISION; COVENANT) into a profound inner motive of obedience (Deut. 10: 16), in willing submission to Yahweh's will (II Chr. 30:8).

Bibliography. R. Bowman, Exegesis of Nehemiah, *IB*, III (1954), 750, 754.   J. A. WHARTON

STOCKS [סד, מהפכת, בית המהפכת; ξύλον]. An instrument of punishment, in which the victim is confined to a given position by having his (hands and) feet locked in a wooden frame.

Of the several Hebrew words that have been rendered "stocks," סד of Job 13:27 (LXX κώλυμα, "impediment"); 33:11 (LXX ξύλον, "stocks") has the best claim to this rendering, on the basis of both context and cognates (see lexicons). מהפכת of Jer. 20:2-3; 29:26 (LXX καταρράκτης, "trap door"; the latter passage transposes the order of the Hebrew)—cf. בית המהפכת of II Chr. 16:10 (LXX φυλακή, "ward") —is rendered by the Targ. כיפתא, "vault," "prison." In view of the similarity of the roots (הפך; כפף; the meaning would appear to be "a cramped room") this rendering is attractive. צינק of Jer. 29:26 (LXX ἀπόκλεισμα, "guardhouse") has been variously rendered "stocks," "shackles," and "collar" (so RSV); cognates suggest some sort of fastening device (see the lexicons).

Roman incarceration was aggravated by chains and stocks (ξύλον; Acts 16:24). Roman stocks were wooden frames with several holes designed to force the legs apart. Eusebius speaks of the torture of imprisoned martyrs whose feet were stretched in stocks separated "to the fifth hole" (Hist. V.i.27).

M. GREENBERG

*****STOICS** stō'ĭks [στωικοί]. Adherents of a school of philosophy founded at Athens by Zeno, a Phoenician from Citium in Cyprus (*ca.* 332-262 B.C.). The school takes its name from the Painted Porch (ἡ ποικίλη στοά), an open colonnade in the Agora adorned with the frescoes of Polygnotus, in which Zeno began to teach in 302. From Athens, Stoicism spread through all the kingdoms of the Middle East, to become the dominant philosophy of the Hellenistic world and eventually, after its introduction to Rome in the second century B.C., of the whole Roman Empire. *See* GREEK RELIGION AND PHILOSOPHY § 8c.

When Zeno turned to philosophy, he became a follower of Crates, who was himself a disciple of Antisthenes, the first of the great Cynics; and from him he learned the Cynic spirit of inward freedom, austerity, and fearless devotion to duty in the scorn of consequences and of conventions. His wider interest in logic and in physical theory was fostered by a teacher of another school, the Megarian Stilpo. In its ethics, always the central interest of its masters, Stoicism was simply a broadened and humanized Cynicism; and Stoic and Cynic were alike in the burning missionary zeal to turn men's hearts to the pursuit of virtue. Zeno himself was the noblest example of his own teaching; the Athenian people honored him in life with the award of a golden crown and in death with a public funeral, a tomb in the Ceramicus, and an epitaph which lauded his fidelity to his own principles of virtue and temperance, and his good influence in leading the youth into the same way of life.

Stoicism had a succession of great teachers, extending over five hundred years from Zeno to the Emperor Marcus Aurelius Antoninus; and it was laid under contribution to a remarkable degree by Christian ethical theory, to some extent by Paul and much more extensively by some of the great Latin writers such as Ambrose of Milan (late fourth century). Zeno's immediate successor was Cleanthes (*ca.* 303-232 B.C.), author of a *Hymn to Zeus*, which gives expression to the profound religious sentiment that often marks this school. His contemporary Aratus published the philosophical poem *Phainomena*, which had an exceptionally wide circulation and is cited in the Areopagus sermon of Paul (Acts 17:28: "We are indeed his offspring"). Chrysippus of Soli, who succeeded Cleanthes, brought acute logical powers to the support of the system. In the second century the leadership of the school passed to Rhodes under Panaetius (185-109), who went to Rome in 144 B.C. and introduced Stoicism into the powerful aristocratic circle of Scipio Aemilianus. His disciple Posidonius of Apamea in Syria (135-51) succeeded him as head of the Rhodian school, where he was visited by Cicero in 78 B.C. He dominated the intellectual life of the first century, at Rome as well as in the Greek world. Under him, the severely rational Stoicism of Panaetius was popularized and degraded by the acceptance of star-worship and astrology and all forms of divination, and by a new tolerance of the ancient religion and its foulest myths —all the rubbish which Panaetius had sought to banish. At the same time, the interest in practical ethics was less pronounced in him than in any other Stoic teacher. His system was actually eclectic— owing as much to Plato as to Zeno and Chrysippus, and marked by a wide-ranging interest in the sciences which had hardly been equaled since Aristotle.

Unfortunately, all the works of the early Stoics have perished; they are known to us only in fragments, and from the accounts of later writers, such as Diogenes Laertius. For complete works of Stoic philosophers, we have to turn to the later exponents of the doctrine—chiefly Seneca, the tutor of Nero; the slave Epictetus, a younger contemporary of Paul; and the philosopher-emperor Marcus Aurelius. It is significant that Stoicism could be embraced with equal fervor by slave and emperor, by Phoenician, Syrian, Greek, and Roman; for it was from the beginning concerned with man as man, and with the cosmos as his only state.

The fundamental tenet of the Stoic philosophy is that virtue (ἀρέτη) is the only good, and vice the only evil. The wise man will be indifferent to pain and pleasure, to wealth and poverty, to success and misfortune; against all the vicissitudes of external circumstances he has fortified himself with the impenetrable armor of apathy (ἀπάθεια)—insensibility. Like the great apostle, he has learned, in whatever state he is, to be content (αὐτάρκης)—literally, self-sufficient, independent of everything that is not in his own power. He knows how to be abased and how to abound; in any and all circumstances he has learned the secret of facing plenty and hunger, abundance and want (Phil. 4:11-12).

Virtue consists in living conformably to nature (τὸ ὁμολογουμένως τῇ φύσει ζῆν), for virtue is the goal toward which nature leads us. "Wherefore the End is to live in keeping with Nature—that is to say, in accordance with our own nature and the nature of the universe [κατὰ τὴν τῶν ὅλων], doing nothing that is forbidden by the General Law [ὁ νόμος ὁ κοινός], which is the right Reason [ὁ ὀρθὸς λόγος] which pervades all things and is identical with Zeus, director of the government of the things that are. And this very thing is the virtue of the happy man and the smooth flow of life, when all activities promote the agreement of the spirit [δαίμων] in each individual with the will of the governor of the universe" (Diogenes Laertius *Lives of Eminent Philosophers* VII.88).

The course of the universe and of every individual life is determined by destiny (εἱμαρμένη), and man's whole freedom consists in accepting that which is ordained for him, in making his own will one with the will and purpose that governs the universe. But this destiny is no blind and cruel fate—it has decreed all things in wisdom and for the good of all; it is "good and acceptable and perfect" as the will of God (cf. Rom. 12:2). Yet this will and purpose in the universe is not personally conceived. Though the name of Zeus is retained and is often invoked in quasi-personal terms, it is in fact no more than a symbol for the power, itself material, which pervades the universe as ever-living fire, creative fire (πῦρ τεχνικόν), and germinative reason (λόγος σπερματικός), and is present in man as the soul. The essential nature of man is therefore one with the essential nature of the universe; and "to live in accordance with nature" can be interpreted to mean equally in accordance with one's own nature and in accordance with the nature of the universe. For man is related to the universe as microcosm to macrocosm, and the same fiery principle of life, law, and reason pervades both.

The creative fire or germinative reason which is the soul of the world and may be called Zeus and countless other names as well is also known as providence (Latin *providentia,* Greek πρόνοια), for it governs the world and all that is in the world by intelligence and wisdom. As evidence for this, the Stoics point to the order and regularity that reign in nature, especially in the movements of the heavenly bodies; to the adaptation of means to ends in the life of plants and animals; to the laws of cause and effect; and to the manifold beauty of the universe. It would be absurd to suppose that this mighty system, harmonious in all its parts, came into existence by chance or without conscious purpose. Above all, the high endowments of man show that it exists and is governed for his benefit. "The world itself was made for the sake of gods and men, and whatsoever is in it was prepared and contrived for the enjoyment of men. For the world is as it were a home common to gods and men, a city of which both are citizens; for they alone have the use of reason and live by justice and law" (Cicero *De Officiis* II.lxii).

Counting himself a member of such a commonwealth, a city of gods and men which embraces the whole world, the Stoic is no longer rooted in the life of a particular state or nation. His ideal republic is not, like that of a Plato or an Aristotle, conceived on the model of the Greek city-state, but is an empire of wisdom and justice embracing all mankind; and the wise man is a citizen of the cosmos (κοσμοπολίτης; the word is first used by the Cynic Diogenes). For the providence which governs all things is not concerned with man as Athenian or Spartan or Roman, as rich or poor, as slave or free, but with the entire human race and with every individual within it. Some sparks of the divine fire are in every human soul as germinative seeds of reason (σπερματικοὶ λόγοι), and therefore all alike are offspring of Zeus and brethren. Stoicism thus prepares the way for the magnificent structure of Roman law, to which the whole Western world is still indebted; and in a still more significant realm, it creates a climate of thought congenial to the individualism and universalism of Christianity, to its conception of brotherhood, and to its catholic church.

Bibliography. Primary sources: H. von Arnim, *Stoicorum Veterum Fragmenta* (3 vols.; 1903-5); Diogenes Laertius, *Lives of Eminent Philosophers,* bk. VII (text with trans. by R. D. Hicks; 1925). See also the philosophical writings of Cicero, especially *De Officiis, De Finibus, De Fato,* and *De Natura Deorum;* and the writings of Seneca, Epictetus, and Marcus Aurelius Antoninus.

Modern writers: E. Zeller, *The Stoics, Epicureans and Sceptics* (2nd ed. rev., 1880; trans. O. J. Reichel); E. V. Arnold, *Roman Stoicism* (1911); E. R. Bevan, *Stoics and Sceptics* (1913); G. Murray, *The Stoic Philosophy* (1915); P. Barth, *Die Stoa* (5th ed. rev. by P. Goedeckemeyer, 1941); M. Pohlenz, *Die Stoa* (2 vols.; 1948); E. Barker, *From Alexander to Constantine* (1956). F. W. BEARE

STOMACHER stŭm′ək ər. KJV translation of פְּתִיגִיל (RSV "rich robe") in Isa. 3:24. "Stomacher" was the name of a decorative covering worn in front of the upper portion of the body. *See* ROBE 5.

STONECUTTER [חֹצֵב אֶבֶן *or* חָרָשׁ (KJV HEWER OF STONE *in* II Kings 12:12; WORKER OF STONE *in* I Chr. 22:15), חֹצֵב (I Chr. 22:2; KJV MASON)]. One who quarries or cuts STONE for building, etc. Solomon had eighty thousand (eighty companies?) of such quarrymen in the hill country preparing stone for the temple (I Kings 5:15 ff). Styles of cutting, as well as masons' marks, are valuable clues to archaeological age. C. U. WOLF

STONES. Palestine is a stony country, and the bedrock is often not far beneath the surface of the ground or may be exposed on the hillsides (*see* PALESTINE, GEOLOGY OF). This very common feature of the terrain has had many and varied uses. The stones referred to in scripture are here classified according to the uses to which they were put.

Certain kinds of stones were general utility instruments.* Sharp stones were shaped into knives (Exod. 4:25; Josh. 5:2); some were used as flints to strike fire (II Macc. 10:3) or as weights for scales (Lev. 19:36; Deut. 25:13, 15; II Sam. 14:26; Prov. 11:1; 16:11; 20:10, 23; Mic. 6:11; Zech. 5:8).* Their weight (Prov. 27:3) made them convenient for use as plummets (Isa. 34:11; Amos 7:7-8). All these and millstones, whorls, rubbers and polishers, molds for casting, mortars and pestles,* loom weights, potter's wheels, etc.,* made of stone, can be illustrated in archaeological finds. Vessels for holding water were hewn from stone (Exod. 7:19; John 2:6). *See* KNIFE; FLINT; WEIGHTS AND MEASURES; VESSELS; MILL; PLUMBLINE. Figs. STO 81, 82; MOR 70; POT 61-62; VES 14.

Certain large stones served as landmarks, such as

81. Gray limestone razor handle with slit for a razor blade; from Tepe Gawra, "Uruk" period (end of fourth millennium)

82. Copy of one-mina weight of Nebuchadnezzar II (605-562 B.C.). The inscription says it is an exact copy which belonged to Marduk-shar-ilani.

the great stone in Gibeon (II Sam. 20:8), the stone of Bohan (Josh. 15:6; 18:17), the stone of Zoheleth (I Kings 1:9 KJV), and the stone Ezel (I Sam. 20:19 KJV). They also served as waymarks (Jer. 31:21) and to mark boundaries (Deut. 19:14). *See* BOHAN; ZOHELETH; EZEL; WAYMARK; LANDMARK. Fig. LAN 12.

The most important use of stone was for building. It was regarded as superior to brick (Isa. 9:10), which was substituted for it in Babylon (Gen. 11:3) and in areas of Palestine when stone was not readily available. Stone was among the materials collected by David (I Chr. 22:14-15; 29:2). The foundation of the temple consisted of great hewn stones (I Kings 5:17-18; 7:10), and the superstructure was also of stone (I Kings 6:18; 7:9, 11-12). The repairs made by Jehoash (II Kings 12:2) and by Josiah (II Kings 22:6; II Chr. 34:11) included hewn stones. They are also mentioned in connection with the materials used for the second temple (Ezra 5:8; 6:4; Hag. 2:15). The stones of Herod's temple are referred to in Matt. 24:1-2; Mark 13:1-2; Luke 21:5-6. Stones were used for city walls (Neh. 4:3), for dwellings (Lev. 14:45; Amos 5:11), for palaces (I Kings 7:1, 9), for fortresses, for a pavement (Exod. 24:10; John 19:13), and for columns (Esth. 1:6). They were used as dikes about vineyards (Prov. 24:30-31); also to close the mouths of wells and cisterns (Gen. 29:2-3, 8, 10), the mouths of caves (Josh. 10:18, 27), and the entrance of tombs (Matt. 27:60; John 11:38). In the Neolithic period massive stone slabs were used in the construction of burial chambers called DOLMENS. *See* ARCHITECTURE; HOUSE; CITY; TOMBS. Fig. DOL 35.

Stones had military uses. They were convenient missiles for the hand (Exod. 21:18; II Sam. 16:6, 13; Ecclus. 22:20; 27:25; II Macc. 1:16; 4:41; Mark 12:4) and for the sling (Judg. 20:16; I Sam. 17:40, 49-50; I Chr. 12:2; II Chr. 26:14; Prov. 26:8; Jth. 6:12; Ecclus. 47:4) or catapult (II Chr. 26:15; I Macc. 6:51). *See* INSTRUMENTS AND WEAPONS OF WAR.

Another use of stones was in the making of ornaments. The priests' breastplates were decorated with stones (Exod. 28:17, 21). Beads, a common article of adornment, were also made of many kinds of stones, such as onyx, quartz, agate, amethyst, opal, lapis lazuli, steatite, etc., illustrated from the excavations. *See* BEADS; JEWELS AND PRECIOUS STONES.

Stones were used to commemorate events (Josh. 7:26; 8:29; II Sam. 18:17). In some cases, a PILLAR served as a memorial (Josh. 24:26-27; I Sam. 7:12) or as a monument to the dead (II Kings 23:17; cf. Ezek. 39:15). Single stones were consecrated as memorials to God (Gen. 28:18-22; Isa. 19:19), and a religious name was given to the place (Gen. 35:7). The stones set up by Joshua at Gilgal (Josh. 4) were an example of a circle with memorial significance. A cairn, as well as a pillar, at Mizpah is mentioned in Gen. 31. *See* MEMORIAL.

Inscriptions might be placed on monumental stones (Deut. 27:4, 8), on altars (Josh. 8:32), or on stone tablets such as those on which the Law was written (Exod. 32:15-16, 19; 34:1, 4, 29), or engraved on cliffs, as by the Dog River, N of Beirut, where Ramses II carved the first of the many records

which make this a veritable outdoor museum. The rebellion of Mesha, king of Moab (II Kings 3:4), was recorded by the successful rebel on a memorial stone, and such inscribed steles are found throughout the Near East. Figs. MOA 66; STO 83. *See* INSCRIPTIONS.

The Israelites used unhewn stones for altars (Exod. 20:25; Deut. 27:5-6; Josh. 8:31). They might be natural rock (Judg. 6:20-21; 13:19; I Sam. 6:14; 14:33) or artificially built of stone. Elijah's altar on Mount Carmel (I Kings 18:31) was of this kind. Ezekiel's blueprint for the temple to come included hewn

Courtesy of the University Museum of the University of Pennsylvania

83. Black stone Sumerian tablet with pictographic signs; from the end of the fourth millennium

stone tables to be used for slaying the sacrifices (Ezek. 40:42). In Maccabean times, the stones of the altar were laid aside as defiled, and a new altar was built (I Macc. 4:46-47). Stones, both in their natural state and graven, served as idols (Lev. 26:1; Deut. 29:17; II Kings 19:18; Jer. 2:27; Hab. 2:19; cf. Isa. 57:6). It is quite possible that the Israelites shared the feeling common among other early Semites that stones, perhaps meteorites, partook of the nature of the divine. E.g., pre-Islamic Arabs engaged in the worship of stones; cf. the use of the Kaaba Stone in the corner of the Mosque at Mecca as an object of worship. Gilgal means "circle," and the stones set up by Joshua there (Josh. 4) may represent an early circle for stone-worshipers, recalling the megalithic remains at Stonehenge in England.

The hardness and strength of stones lent symbolic meaning to their use in metaphorical language (Exod. 15:5, 16; I Sam. 25:37; Neh. 9:11; Job 6:12; 38:30; 41:24; Ezek. 11:19; 36:26). The NT refers to them in object lessons as sterile (Matt. 3:9), dumb (Luke 19:40), or inedible (Matt. 4:3; 7:9). The good seed fell on "rocky ground" (Matt. 13:5, 20; Mark 4:16; Luke 8:4-8)—i.e., shallow soil with stone near the surface. Jeremiah buried stones in a dramatic action oracle (Jer. 43:9-10).

In Zech. 3:9 a stone with seven facets is set before Joshua, the high priest, and an inscription is placed upon it. This has been variously interpreted as meaning the foundation stone of the temple, the "top stone" of Zech. 4:7, a jewel in the high priest's breastplate or in Zerubbabel's crown, or the finished temple. A living stone is a stone that is sound, not broken. The Christians are so called in I Pet. 2:4-8 (cf. Eph. 2:20-22) because they are built into the spiritual temple of which Christ is the chief cornerstone. Jesus had thus applied the reference to the cornerstone in Ps. 118:22 to himself (Matt. 21:42;

Luke 20:17-18). Note also the figurative reference to cornerstone in Isa. 28:16.

In Rev. 2:17 a white stone is mentioned. This is an obscure symbol and has several possible interpretations. The thought intended here may be that of a charm or amulet bearing the victor's name as a secret writing. Only the bearer will know the name written thereon. It is white to symbolize the heavenly character of the victorious believer and marked with the name bestowed as a sure proof of his future triumph. The symbol is derived from familiar beliefs and practices concerning defense against evil and evil ones; through this the believers will have power against every enemy. D. M. C. ENGLERT

STONES, PRECIOUS. *See* JEWELS AND PRECIOUS STONES.

STONING [רגם סקל; λιθάζω, λιθοβολέω]. Biblical law punishes the following offenses with stoning: worship of other gods (Deut. 17:2-7), and incitement thereto (13:6-10—H 13:7-11); child-sacrifice to Molech (Lev. 20:2-5); prophesying in the name of another god (Deut. 13:1-5—H 13:2-6); spirit-divination (Lev. 20:27); blasphemy (Lev. 24:15-16); sabbath-breaking (Num. 15:32-36); homicide by an ox (Exod. 21:28-32); adultery (Deut. 22:22-23); filial insubordination (Deut. 21:18-21). According to Josh. 7:25, violation of the *ḥērem* was also punished with stoning. For the procedure in judicial stoning, *see* CRIMES AND PUNISHMENTS § D1.

As Palestine is a stony country, pelting with stones (sometimes leading to death) was a common expression of mob anger and hatred (I Sam. 30:6; I Kings 12:18). This appears several times in the NT (Matt. 21:35; 23:37; John 10:31; Acts 14:5). *See further* CRIMES AND PUNISHMENTS § E2*a*.

The procedure described by later Jewish law (M. Sanh. 6.1-4) is very deliberate, allowing for the last-minute appearance of new evidence in favor of the condemned, and for a confession before death. The culprit was stripped, and then knocked off a scaffold six cubits high by one witness to his crime. If he survived the fall, the other witness dropped a stone on his chest; if he still lived, all present stoned him. Since the stoning of Stephen (Acts 7:57-58) appears to have been more summary, the possibility that it was a lynching has to be considered. However, vs. 58, telling of the witnesses' disrobing before casting the first stone (a detail not mentioned in the Mishna) suggests something more deliberate than lynching. We have no knowledge of how early (if ever) the mode described in the Mishna was practiced.
M. GREENBERG

STOOL. KJV translation of כסא (RSV CHAIR) in II Kings 4:10 and of אבן (RSV BIRTHSTOOL) in Exod. 1:16. *See also* FOOTSTOOL (lit., "stool of the feet"). Fig. BAN 19.

STORAX stô'răks. KJV translation of στακτή in Ecclus. 24:15. A gumlike substance gathered from a tree. *See* STACTE; *see also* FLORA § A9*p*.

STORE-CITIES [ערי מסכנות]; STOREHOUSES [בית האוצר]. Sites on which were built warehouses

for the storage of government supplies of various kinds.

Egypt was well known for its store-cities, which have been excavated at Tell Retabah (Pithom) and Tanis (Raamses; Exod. 1:11). In Palestine, David had stores in various villages and cities (I Chr. 27:25). Solomon built storehouses in several areas of the country where the monthly supplies for the court were kept (I Kings 4:7-19; 9:19). Jehoshaphat built storehouses throughout Judah (II Chr. 17:12-13). Hezekiah likewise is well known for the storehouses and store-cities he built (32:27-29).

The storehouse was also a repository for the tithe (Mal. 3:10) and may have been at the temple presided over by Levites (I Chr. 9:26, 29). Large private storehouses also are not unknown.

See also TRADE AND COMMERCE.

H. N. RICHARDSON

STORK [חסידה, kindly, loyal one; LXX ἐρῳδιός, heron (Lev. 11:19; Ps. 104:17—G 103:17); πελεκάν, pelican (Deut. 14:18); ἀσίδα (*from* Heb.; Jer. 8:7); ἔποψ, hoopoe (Zech. 5:9); Vulg. *herodio* (Lev. 11:19; Ps. 104:17); *onocrotalus*, pelican (Deut. 14:18); *milvus*, bird of prey, kite (Jer. 8:7); *miluus* (*milvus;* Zech. 5:9); Targ. (Onq.) חוריתא, white one]. Any of a family (*Ciconiidae*) of large, long-legged wading birds of the genus Ciconia, related to the herons, whose food consists of fish (when available), as well as small mammals, birds, and reptiles. Their faithful tending of their young is proverbial, as is their habit of returning annually to the same nesting place. Tristram saw the white stork (*Ciconia alba*) as well as the black (*Ciconia nigra*) in nineteenth-century Palestine. While most of these birds were migrating northward to Europe, some remained at established nests in the Holy Land.

Although it cannot be conclusively established that חסידה (an unclean creature; Lev. 11:19; Deut. 14:18) is a stork, it is at least a reasonable supposition. This bird's practice of nesting in a treetop, when a suitable building is not at hand, may be referred to in Ps. 104:17; the allusion in Jer. 8:7 is apparently to its migratory habits. The somewhat similar appearance of the heron and the stork may have confused ancient observers, and it is possible, as G. R. Driver suggests (*see bibliography*), that sometimes חסידה was used for "heron."

Bibliography. G. R. Driver, *PEQ* (April, 1955), p. 17.
W. S. McCULLOUGH

STORM [זרם, storm of wind and rain (*see* RAIN); סופה, סער, windstorm, gale; שואה, devastating (storm); λαῖλαψ, windstorm, gale; σεισμός, disturbance, large waves]. *See* PALESTINE, CLIMATE OF; WHIRLWIND; THUNDER AND LIGHTNING.
R. B. Y. SCOTT

STOVE. *See* OVEN.

STRAIT OF JUDEA. KJV Apoc. form of RIDGE OF JUDEA.

STRANGER. A term which frequently appears in translations earlier than RSV for the technical term גר, for which the more adequate translation is

"SOJOURNER." In the RSV it is used in such phrases as "the stranger [גֵּר] who sojourns [הַגָּר] among you" (Exod. 12:49 P; cf. Lev. 19:33-34, etc.), and to translate the terms זוּר and ξένος where the basic meaning is "one who is strange, different, foreign."

T. M. MAUCH

STRANGLING. One of the four methods of capital punishment prescribed in rabbinic law. Unlike stoning, burning, and decapitation, this penalty is not mentioned in the OT. According to the Talmud, it is the most merciful form of execution and is therefore applicable to cases where biblical law does not specify some other method.

In Acts 15:20, James agrees that Gentile converts need not conform to the entire law, so long as they abstain from idolatry, fornication, and the eating of blood or of "what is strangled" (some MSS omit the last item). James here insists that Gentiles conform to the Jewish method of slaughtering, by cutting the throat of the animal and draining all the blood from the carcass. Philo (*On the Special Laws* IV.122) refers to the practice of killing animals by strangling or throttling them; but from other sources it appears that the term "strangling" was sometimes applied loosely to any form of slaughtering not approved by Jewish law. See M. Hullin 1.2.   B. J. BAMBERGER

STRAW [תֶּבֶן (KJV CHAFF *in* Jer. 23:28), מַתְבֵּן]. Wheat or barley stalks cut to 1½–2-inch lengths in the process of THRESHING.

Straw seems to have had several uses. Some passages (Gen. 24:25; Judg. 19:19; I Kings 4:28—H 5:8) mention straw along with provender or barley, suggesting its use for the bedding down of animals, but not necessarily for food. It thus served the purpose to which present-day hay is put, but whole stalks were not used in the ancient Near East. It was, however, also used for food (Isa. 11:7), either alone or mixed with grains. From both excavated remains and literary sources (Exod. 5:7-12) we learn that straw was used as a binder in brickmaking.

H. N. RICHARDSON

STREAM OF EGYPT. KJV Apoc. form of EGYPT, BROOK OF.

STREET. See CITY § B2*i; * BAZAAR; BROAD PLACE; SQUARE.

STRINGED INSTRUMENTS. See MUSICAL INSTRUMENTS § B6*a.*

STRIPES. See SCOURGING.

STRONG DRINK [שֵׁכָר; LXX *and* NT σίκερα]. A term with cognates in almost all the other Semitic languages. While it seems to have meant "barley beer" at one time, it later came to denote any intoxicating beverage prepared from either grain or fruit. As such it was forbidden to priests (Lev. 10:9) and Nazirites (Num. 6:3; cf. Judg. 13:4, 7, 14; Luke 1:15). It is mentioned only once (Num. 28:7) as a constituent of a DRINK OFFERING.

Strong drink often appears in parallel with wine

to refer to intoxicants in general. Thus Isaiah condemns those

> who rise early in the morning,
> that they may run after strong drink,
> who tarry late into the evening
> till wine inflames them!
>
> (Isa. 5:11).

Similarly Hannah protested to the priest at Shiloh that she had "drunk neither wine nor strong drink" (I Sam. 1:15). The sage warns: "Wine is a mocker, strong drink a brawler" (Prov. 20:1; cf. 31:4, 6).

See also DRUNKENNESS; WINE.

Bibliography. E. Busse, *Der Wein im Kult des ATs,* Freiburger Theologische Studien, 29 (1922), 12, 20; H. F. Lutz, *Viticulture and Brewing in the Ancient Orient* (1922), pp. 81-86.

J. F. ROSS

STRONGHOLD [מִבְצָר, מָעוֹז, מָצָד; ὀχύρωμα]. Alternately: FORTRESS. Like "fortress," "stronghold" is used figuratively to mean God as the refuge of the righteous (Ps. 9:9—H 9:10), a foreign country as a political ally (Ezek. 30:15), or even the temple as the symbol of a deceptive and false security (Ezek. 24:21-25; cf. Amos 6:8).

See also CITADEL; TOWER.   J. A. SANDERS

STUBBLE [קַשׁ]. Dry grain stalks considered as refuse or fuel. In Exod. 5:12 the word is distinguished from "STRAW" (תֶּבֶן), as requiring that the people be "scattered abroad through all the land of Egypt, to gather" it; and this has usually been taken to mean the stumps left in the field, whence the English translation "stubble." However, this meaning is not necessary here, and elsewhere the word seems to be synonymous with "straw" and "CHAFF" in indicating the refuse from THRESHING. All the other occurrences are in figures of speech. Such material is either quickly consumed by fire (Exod. 15:7; Isa. 5:24; 47:14; Joel 2:5; Obad. 18; Nah. 1:10; Mal. 4:1) or is blown away (Isa. 40:24; 41:2; cf. Job 13:25; Jer. 13:24; cf. Ps. 83:13, where קַשׁ is translated "chaff").

H. N. RICHARDSON

STUFF. The translation of several words in the OT:

a) An auxiliary used to designate "material" or "cloth" (perhaps "yarn") in passages mentioning blue, purple, or scarlet which was highly prized because of its color (the KJV does not insert the word "stuff" in these passages). Such material was contributed as offerings for the making of cult objects (Exod. 25:4; 35:6, 23, 25) such as curtains for the tabernacle (26:1; 36:8), the veil (26:31; 36:35), the screen (26:36; 27:16; 36:37; 38:18), the ephod (28:5-6; 39:1-3, 5), and decorations of the sacred vestments of the priests (28:33; 39:24, 29). Scarlet material (stuff) was one of the substances prescribed for use in the ritual for cleansing from disease (Lev. 14:4, 6, 49, 51-52; Num. 19:6).

b) גְּנָזֵי בְרֹמִים, carpets of multicolored material, a valuable article of trade (Ezek. 27:24).

c) כְּלִי, "vessel," "article." In Josh. 7:11 it refers to the articles or possessions of those who appropriated banned objects from Jericho.

d) מְלָאכָה, "work," "thing," "material"; used of offerings received for the sanctuary (Exod. 36:7).

e) צבע, "dyed stuff" (Judg. 5:30), colored material greatly prized.

f) בגד כלאים שעטנז, a garment of two kinds of material (Lev. 19:19); שעטנז, "mingled stuff" (Deut. 22: 11), refers to the law forbidding the wearing of a garment made of two kinds of material such as wool and linen.

See also SCARLET; DYEING; COLORS; VESSEL.

J. M. MYERS

STUMBLING BLOCK [מכשלה, מכשׁול; πρόσκομμα, σκάνδαλον]. That which causes one to stumble or fall; mentioned in both a literal (Lev. 19:14) and a figurative (Jer. 6:21) sense in the OT. A literary characteristic in Ezekiel describes the idols of silver and gold as the "stumbling block of their iniquity" (7:19; 14:3-4, 7; 44:12), yet God himself may be a stumbling block to his faithless people (Isa. 8:14). This last reference, which relates the meaning to a "trap" and a "snare," is of special importance, since in the NT it is applied twice to Christ (Rom. 9:32-33; I Pet. 2:8). The NT has only the metaphorical usage, but the most important Greek noun (σκάνδαλον) and verb (σκανδαλίζειν) have both a messianic and a moral application. Spiritual ruin may result from wrong relation either to Christ (noun: Matt. 16:23; Rom. 9:32-33; 11:9; I Cor. 1:23; Gal. 5:11; I Pet. 2:8; verb: Matt. 11:6=Luke 7:23; Matt. 13:21 =Mark 4:17; Matt. 13:57=Mark 6:3; Matt. 15:12; 17:27; 24:10; 26:31=Mark 14:27, 29; John 6:61; 16: 1) or to others (noun: Matt. 13:41; 18:7=Luke 17:1; Rom. 14:13; 16:17; I John 2:10; Rev. 2:14; verb: Matt. 5:29-30; 18:8-9=Mark 9:43, 45, 47; Matt. 18: 6=Mark 9:42=Luke 17:2; Rom. 14:21; I Cor. 8:13; II Cor. 11:29).   D. MOODY

SUA. KJV Apoc. form of Siaha. *See* SIA.

SUAH sōō'ə [סוּח] (I Chr. 7:36). A division of the clan of Zophah in the tribe of Asher.

SUBA. KJV form of SUBAS.

SUBAI. KJV Apoc. form of Shamlai. *See* SHALMAI.

SUBAS sōō'bəs [Σουβάς] (I Esd. 5:34); KJV SUBA —bə. Head of a family of sons of Solomon's servants who returned with Zerubbabel. His name is omitted in the parallels Ezra 2:57; Neh. 7:59.

C. T. FRITSCH

SUBURBS. *See* PASTURE LANDS.

SUCATHITES sōō'kə thīts [שוכתים]; KJV SUCHATHITES. One of three families of scribes who lived in Jabez of Judah. They traced their descent through Caleb and counted both the Kenites and the Rechabites in their ancestry (I Chr. 2:55).

W. H. MORTON

SUCCOTH sŭk'əth [סכות, booths]. **1.** A city of Gad, situated not far from the Jordan Valley, in E Palestine.

The name of the city is explained as being derived from the booths which Jacob made for his cattle on his way back from Paddan-aram (Gen. 33:17), but it is more probable that this is an old Canaanite place for the observance of the harvest festival which came to bear the same name. The city was a part of the kingdom of Sihon and was assigned to the Gadites (Josh. 13:27). When Gideon was pursuing the Midianites, he called upon the people of Succoth to supply food for his famishing army and was answered with derision; whereupon, on his victorious return, he caught a young man of the city, made him write down the names of the princes and elders of Succoth, and then inflicted a cruel punishment upon them (Judg. 8:5-9, 14-16). It was also near Succoth that the bronze vessels for the temple of Solomon were cast (I Kings 7:46; II Chr. 4:17). There are two references in Psalms to the Vale of Succoth as a desirable country for apportionment among the righteous (60:6; 108:7).

The site of Succoth has been identified as Tell Deir'alla, located *ca.* two miles N of the Jabbok (Nahr Zerqa) as it leaves the E hills and takes a winding way to join the Jordan. The tell completely dominates a very fertile region known as the Ghor Abu Obeideh, between the Wadi Rajeb and the Zerqa, which was evidently the Vale of Succoth mentioned in Psalms. There are evidences of settlement from at least Middle Bronze times, including the entire period of the Israelite settlement, and the site was apparently flourishing until the sixth century B.C. The identification is further confirmed by the Palestinian Talmud (Sheb. 9.2, 32*a*), which states that Succoth is the same as the contemporary Taralah. The nearby Tell el-Ekshas has been suggested because its name also means "booths"; but it is too far from the Jabbok, too small in size, and does not appear to have had the same length of settlement.

Bibliography. N. Glueck, *The River Jordan* (1946), pp. 110-11, 146-57; "Explorations in Eastern Palestine IV," *AASOR,* vols. XXV–XXVIII (1951), pt. I, pp. 308-10, 336-50.

S. COHEN

2. An Egyptian city mentioned in Exod. 12:37; 13:20; Num. 33:5-6 as a station on the route of the Exodus.

Succoth is mentioned as the first stop in the flight of the Israelites from Egypt. It has long been supposed that the Hebrew name is an adaptation of Egyptian *Tkw(t)*, the civil name of the capital of the eighth Lower Egyptian nome and generally identified with the modern site of Tell el-Maskhutah in the Wadi Tumeilat. This identification is both philologically and geographically acceptable, but it must be noted that the location is not absolutely certain. Tell el-Maskhutah was excavated in 1883 by Naville, who identified the site as biblical Pithom on the basis of favorable philological evidence and of certain architectural features, taken by him to be store chambers.

The identification of Succoth is intimately connected with that of Pithom and Rameses. For details and bibliography, *see* PITHOM.   T. O. LAMBDIN

*SUCCOTH-BENOTH sŭk'əth bē'nŏth [סכות בנות, *lit.* tabernacles, booths, of girls; *certainly a corruption*]. A deity or deities worshiped by colonists from Babylon settled in Samaria by the Assyrians after 722 B.C.

(II Kings 17:30). The association with Babylon has suggested that the deity was Ṣarpanitu, the consort of MARDUK, the city-god of Babylon. This goddess was popularly termed Zir-banitu ("seed-creating"). The first element of Succoth-Benoth suggests SAK-KUTH as in Amos 5:26, but this deity was Ninib, and the association with Babylon and Ṣarpanitu suggests that we might have expected Marduk here, and in fact Stade has suggested Marduk-Banit. It is possible that the whole phrase "Succoth-Benoth" is a corruption of "Ṣarpanitu." It is significant that the Greek versions, by their inclusion of a final vowel, support this view.

Bibliography. M. Jastrow, *The Religion of Babylonia and Assyria* (1898), pp. 121-23; J. A. Montgomery, *Commentary on Kings,* ICC (ed. H. S. Gehman; 1951), pp. 473-74.

J. GRAY

SUCHATHITES. KJV form of SUCATHITES.

SUD sŭd [Σούδ; Lat. *Sodi;* Syr. *Sur*]. A river, according to Bar. 1:4, which states that Baruch, after writing his book, read it to King Jeconiah and his sons, mighty men, elders, and people, while they were in exile "in Babylon by the river Sud." There is no other reference to a stream with this name. The Greek word translated "river" (ποταμός) may refer here to a river or to any other flowing stream. Sud probably is not an alternate name for the Euphrates. It may have been the name of a canal or branch channel of the Euphrates; in any case it was located in or near the city of Babylon.   F. V. FILSON

SUDIAS sōō'dĭ əs. In I Esd. 5:26 for HODAVIAH.

SUFFERING AND EVIL.

1. Evil
    a. Terminology
    b. Nature
    c. Origin
    d. Power
2. Suffering
    a. In the OT
    b. In the NT
Bibliography

1. Evil. *a. Terminology.* In the OT the two principal terms to express evil are רַע or רָעָה, on the one hand, and צַר and צָרָה, on the other. The former term is the opposite of טוֹב, which means "valuable" with reference to an end—thus either fit to promote an end, or a thing's being truly what it pretends to be. Accordingly, רַע designates a lack of fitness or usefulness for a goal, or indicates opposition to the goal of the object thereby characterized. The LXX renders it usually by κακός, or by πονηρός. While κακός emphasizes unfitness or worthlessness—i.e., devaluates an object in accordance with its own intrinsic standard or goal—πονηρός is "evil" in the sense of "dangerous," "perilous," or "harmful"—i.e., it characterizes an object with reference to the negative significance which it has for something or somebody else. In the Greek Bible, πονηρός designates the evils which created beings cause to one another, whereas κακός and κακία are especially used to designate the evils which God places upon man. The NT, how-

ever, shows a preference for πονηρός in the broad sense of רַע. The modern differentiation between natural and moral evils is alien to the Bible, the reason being that רַע measures both objects and persons with reference to God's ultimate purpose (cf. the phrase "He did what was evil in the sight of the LORD" [e.g., II Chr. 21:6; 22:4; 29:6]). The results of the divine curse (Gen. 3:14-19) are "natural" evils, but to the Hebrews they were evil primarily because their presence was an indication that man did not enjoy that unbroken fellowship with God for which he was destined.

צַר or צָרָה, another common term for evil in the OT, denotes, like its Greek equivalent, θλῖψις, something that hurts, limits, or oppresses people and makes them feel unhappy. It designates the evil condition in which men are, rather than the quality or action of beings. In Ps. 25:17-18—H 24:17-18, we find ἀνάγκη ("inescapable distress"), ταπείνωσις ("humiliation"), and κόπος ("toil") as synonyms. Another synonym is στενοχωρία ("hopeless situation"). Θλῖψις is one of the key words of Paul, who uses it twenty-four times out of forty-five in the NT.

b. Nature. The numerous references to evil found in both the OT and the NT indicate that the biblical writers were fully aware of its existence and took it seriously. The lengthy lists of evils (e.g., Ps. 25:17-18; Rom. 8:35; II Cor. 11:23-27; 12:10; Rev. 7:16-17) point to a literary or liturgical tradition. Evils that are particularly frequently mentioned are the inclemency of nature, diseases, want, distress, calamity, toil, hardship, hopeless situations, weakness, corruptibility, futility, insults, defamations, enmity, injustice, oppression, persecution, and sins, but also the state of mind created by these evils—e.g., hunger, thirst, sorrow, fear, anxiety, despair. Major calamities are often described by images of cosmic catastrophes, such as rushing water (e.g., Ps. 18:11, 15-16; Isa. 28:2; 43:2), the sea (e.g., Pss. 46:2; 89:9; Isa. 5:30; 43:16; Rev. 21:1), earthquakes (e.g., Isa. 29:6; Rev. 6:12; 16:18; cf. Pss. 46:2; 144:5; Isa. 34:3), tempest (e.g., Job 9:17; Ps. 55:8; Isa. 29:6; 54:11), fire (Isa. 5:24; 10:16; Jer. 4:4; I Cor. 3:13, 15; Jas. 5:3), darkness (e.g., Pss. 91:6; 97:2; Isa. 5:30; 9:2; Mic. 7:8; Rev. 16:10; *see* LIGHT), and the extinction of the stars (Ezek. 32:7; Dan. 8:10; Matt. 24:29; Rev. 6:13).

The evil character of the happenings and conditions is not seen, however, in their being obstacles to man's desire for happiness, but rather in their rendering faith difficult. When they occur, God hides his face from man (e.g., Pss. 22:24; 38:9; Isa. 54:8; Jer. 16:17)—i.e., makes it impossible for man to discern God's saving will. They also obscure the GLORY of God in this world (e.g., Pss. 25:3; 79:9; Isa. 42:8; cf. Pss. 6:5; 42:3; Isa. 35:2; 45:5); they create the impression that God is unable to overcome them. This is particularly the case with the evils with which God's chosen people are afflicted. Worse, however, than the evils which man suffers are those which he brings into being himself—e.g., his unrighteousness (*see* RIGHTEOUSNESS), lack of regard for his neighbor (*see* LOVE), and his unbelief (*see* FAITH) or worship of other gods (*see* IDOLATRY). To them the NT adds the stumbling block (σκάνδαλον)—i.e., actions through which the fellow man's faith is endangered (e.g., Matt. 16:23; 18:6; Rom. 14:13; I Cor. 8:9). These things the Lord hates (e.g., Isa. 1:14; 61: 8) and pours out his wrath (*see* WRATH OF GOD) upon those that do them (e.g., Gen. 6:7, 13; Pss. 21: 9-10; 60:1, 3; Isa. 5:25; Jer. 3:5; Matt. 3:7; Rom. 1:18). Consequently, biblical thought is not primarily preoccupied with escaping suffering or with seeking pleasure, but rather with shunning sin.

c. Origin. In spite of the fact that the Jewish rules governing the clean and the unclean had their historical roots in primitive taboos, the prophets had already interpreted them in a moral sense, and this view was re-emphasized by Jesus (e.g., Matt. 15:11-20; Mark 7:15-23; Luke 11:41). Nothing is evil in itself. The strong contrast between the world (*see* WORLD, NATURE OF THE) and the KINGDOM OF GOD, which characterizes particularly the Johannine literature but is present in the whole NT, cannot be interpreted in Manichean terms. The passage I John 5:19, which in the KJV reads: "The whole world lieth in wickedness," is in the RSV correctly rendered as: "The whole world is in the power of the evil one." Similarly, man cannot be considered as the cause of evil. While the depravity of man is already stated in the OT (e.g., Gen. 6:5, 12; 8:21; Pss. 38:3; 51:5), the fall of man (Gen. 3:1-7) presupposes the existence of evil, and the divine curse (Gen. 3:14-19), though increasing the evils in this life, does not bring them into being. Man has to bear the moral responsibility for his sinfulness and the reign of death over the whole race (Rom. 5:12-14; cf. 8:20-22), but the origin of these evils lies outside himself. Nevertheless, evil—i.e., the operation of factors by which the teleology and harmony of this world is disturbed—would never have changed from potentiality to actuality except for man's sin. Thus sin is considered in the Bible as the root of all evils.

Likewise, the biblical view differs from Iranian dualism. Belief in a personal devil (*see* SATAN) appears at a late stage in the OT, and while it became constitutive for the message of the NT, it did not impair the idea of God's exclusive work in creation. The devil has the power to bring forth evils in this world (e.g., I Pet. 5:8-9; I John 5:19; Rev. 2:9-10), and is their "father" as the "evil one" (e.g., Matt. 13:19, 38; Eph. 6:16; I John 2:13-14; 5:18-19). This view enhances the evilness of all evils, because it discovers behind them a malicious intention (e.g., John 8:44; I Pet. 5:8). But his power has been given to Satan by God, and thus it is not only limited but also lacks creativity (e.g., Matt. 12:26-28=Luke 11:18-20; John 12:31; Rev. 12:9; 20:1-3). Throughout the Bible, the view prevails that it is God the Creator who made the existence of evils possible in this world, and who not only allows them to develop (e.g., I Sam. 2:6-7), but also uses them to curb one another (e.g., Ps. 39:9-10). However, since the existence of evils is subservient to God's purpose, the biblical outlook maintains the basic difference between good and evil, though in a concrete case it may be difficult for the individual to tell what specific end certain evils serve (e.g., Job 42:2-3). Though it is by the will of the Creator that evils are found in this world, they do not originate, as is held in Stoicism,

out of a necessity inherent in nature. The differentiation of good and evil is therefore in the Bible not a merely subjective one, made with reference to man's desire for happiness, but rather has an objective reason.

d. Power. With God as Creator, evil remains constantly under divine control. In the OT this conviction expresses itself primarily in the many prayers in which God is requested to deliver the individual or his people from all kinds of evil. But only slowly does the idea dawn that God himself will eventually abolish all evils and that the believers shall live in a state of perfect harmony. The "eschatology of blessing" (*see* ESCHATOLOGY OF THE OT) anticipates originally a realm of peace and prosperity in which Israel is to live securely (so probably still in Isa. 11: 1-10; 25:8), rather than a universal period of bliss. Only in Daniel do we encounter the idea of a divine kingdom by which all injustice on earth will be destroyed and death will be overcome by resurrection; and only late in the intertestamental period, with the distinction between the present age and the age to come, could a hope for the complete annihilation of all the evils be entertained. In the NT, however, the view is commonly held that God himself will make an end to them (e.g., I Cor. 15:24-26; Rev. 7:17; 21:4), and that Satan will be chained and imprisoned (e.g., Rev. 20:2-3, 10). In its manifestations the power of evil is not free but must follow a divine program (e.g., II Thess. 2:3-11). Moreover, even at the present time, no evil, however mighty it may be, is powerful enough to prevent or thwart the execution of God's saving purpose (e.g., Matt. 11:25; John 5:44; 9:3; 11:4; Rom. 8:37-39; II Cor. 4:7-11; 12:9; Col. 2:15; I Pet. 3:22). Notwithstanding this hopeful outlook, however, the reality of evil is taken seriously. The Bible is pervaded by a sense of awe for the terribleness of the evils of this world, and particularly of sin, which is the root of all of them (*see* SIN, SINNERS). Evils are not interpreted, as in Neoplatonism, as mere lack of goodness, and they exist not "as rejected by God" merely, but rather as willed and sent by him to wherever sin is found. Nowhere does the Bible teach that good will always result from evil. It is in spite of evil that goodness asserts itself.

But evil is inferior in power to goodness, because it presupposes the existence of goodness. Unlike Zoroastrianism, which holds that evil exists of and by itself, the Bible teaches that evil comes into being only in opposition to the goodness of the Creation (Gen. 1:31). Hence, it cannot last forever, and individual evils go on only for "a little while" (e.g., Ps. 37:2; I Pet. 5:10; cf. II Cor. 4:17-18).

2. Suffering. a. In the OT. Evils cause suffering. The OT does not contrast physical and mental suffering, since man is seen in his totality. The same cause may underlie bodily pain and mental anguish. The biblical writers are not particularly interested in the origin of suffering either. Rather, as beings who believe in a final destination, they inquire into the reason and purpose of suffering. In the earliest stage of their faith, and in agreement with other Semitic religions, the Israelites interpreted suffering as a divine punishment for sin. They were firmly convinced that a moral order guided the destinies of man, and while the wicked might prosper for a long while (e.g., Job 21:28-33), they were sure that God's righteous judgment would eventually reach them (e.g., Pss. 7:15-16; 37:1-3; 52:1, 5; 73:12-20; 92:7). At times, however, they became impatient, when God's thunderbolts did not fall immediately upon the wicked one who prospered (e.g., Eccl. 7:16; Jer. 12:1-4; Hab. 1:2-4; Mal. 3:7-15). In turn, they took their own calamities as indications of God's wrath (e.g., Pss. 38:3; 42:5, 9). In agreement with their belief in collective life, the members of the nation might suffer for the wickedness of their king, or the descendants for the sins of their parents (e.g., I Sam. 22:18; I Kings 21:20, 22, 29; II Kings 21:10-11; cf. Exod. 20:5).

But if there were a moral order governing the universe, why did the righteous man suffer at all? (e.g., Job 3; 6–7; Pss. 22:1-18; 42:9). Various answers were given. Job, e.g., resigns himself to the wisdom of God, which is both undeniable and incomprehensible (Job 42:2-3). The author of Ps. 44 assails God violently for neglecting his people. Others found satisfaction in the idea that God would finally vindicate their cause (e.g., Pss. 22:19-20; 31: 9, 21; 34:6, 17, 19; 37:1-3; 43:1; 46:10; 50:15; 55:22; 77:2; Prov. 10:2-3) and mete out a terrible judgment upon the righteous man's adversaries or oppressors (e.g., Pss. 35:8-10; 37:1-2; 40:13-14; 58:6-7). As eschatological thinking began to prevail, however, they did not hope for immediate help, but looked forward to a more distant Day of Yahweh (see DAY OF THE LORD), when all human injustice would be straightened out (e.g., Isa. 3:14-15; Dan. 12:1; Amos 1–2; cf. Hab. 3:16). Intertestamental Judaism found consolation in the recompense of the righteous ones after death (e.g., Wisd. Sol. 3:1-5; 5:16-17).

Another answer to the problem of suffering consisted in accepting it as a divine education, by which people would be led away from their anthropocentric outlook back to God (Pss. 20:6; 39:7; 46:10-11; Isa. 49:26; Jer. 9:24), and from sinfulness, including unconscious sins, to obedience (e.g., II Chr. 20:9-10; Neh. 9:26-27; Job 5:17-18; 33:19-30; Isa. 1:5-9, 25; 26:16; 37:3; 63:9; 65:16; Jer. 6:27-30; 10:18; Hos. 5:15; Mal. 3:3). Yet the question remained, Why does the prophet, the messenger of God, also suffer, and even worse than other people? (e.g., Jer. 8:18-21; 15:15; cf. Ps. 44:23). This leads to a third interpretation of suffering—viz., that in solidarity with his people, the Servant of God has taken vicariously upon himself the punishment of his nation (Isa. 53: 2-12). Fourthly, we notice, parallel with this, in Deutero-Isaiah (40:2; 55:5) and II Maccabees (6:12-17) the idea of atoning suffering (see ATONEMENT). By accepting the Lord's punishment, one will be delivered of one's guilt (cf. Pss. Sol. 13:10; 18:4-6).

It is remarkable that, with all their experience of terrible suffering, the Israelites were never moved to take a pessimistic view of life. Since God is Lord, even Ecclesiastes, the gloomiest of the OT writers, counsels his readers to enjoy life (Eccl. 1:2-11; 9:7-10; 11:7-10).

b. In the NT. The primitive church adopted all the OT views of suffering, but modified them in the light of Jesus' passion and cross. Jesus himself had taught that his suffering was a divine necessity (δεῖ; e.g., Matt. 16:21 = Mark 8:31 = Luke 9:22; cf. Matt. 17:22-23 and parallels; Matt. 20:17-19 and parallels; Luke 17:25; 24:26; John 17:1), which had been laid upon the Son of man. This was a new and original idea. The atoning effect of his suffering (e.g., Rom. 3:25; Heb. 9:15; I John 2:2; 4:10; Rev. 5:6) rested upon his willingness as the sinless one to give his life for sinners (Rom. 5:6-8; I Pet. 2:24; 3:18; cf. Mark 10:45) in perfect obedience to God's judgment (Phil. 2:8; Heb. 5:8; cf. Heb. 2:18). This is the mystery of the Passion—that he, as Son of God, should take upon himself the burden of mankind. Thus, in accepting the necessity of his suffering, Jesus did not act under a compulsion placed upon him, but rather accepted it with the spontaneity of love. The judicial character of Christ's passion precludes the assumption that suffering is good or meaningful by itself.

From this interpretation of the passion of Christ, the primitive church approached its own suffering. The deepened understanding of the sinfulness of all men leads to the recognition that suffering is the rightful fate of all people in this evil age (Rom. 8:18; Gal. 1:4; cf. Eph. 5:16; 6:13). But, as Paul especially will point out, the believers who thus accept suffering not only serve Christ's cause (e.g., Phil. 1:29), but also, being united with the risen Lord, continue his suffering for mankind, because the church is his body (e.g., Rom. 8:31-39; 12:4-21; II Cor. 1:5; 4:10-11; Phil. 3:10; Col. 1:24; I Thess. 2:13-16; I Pet. 4: 12-13). In completing "what is lacking in Christ's afflictions" (Col. 1:24), the believers participate, though in an instrumental way only, in the atoning work of Christ. Thus suffering is the inescapable lot of the Christians (e.g., John 16:33; Acts 14:22; Rom. 8:17; I Cor. 12:26; Phil. 1:29-30; 3:10; I Thess. 2:14; 3:4; II Tim. 3:12; I Pet. 3:14; 4:13; 5:1), and particularly of the apostles (e.g., Acts 9:16; I Cor. 4:8-13; II Cor. 1:4-5; 4:8; 7:4-5; Phil. 3:10; Col. 1:24; I Thess. 3:7). The public confession (ὁμολογία) that Jesus is the Christ will result in tribulation and martyrdom (Mark 13:12-13 and parallels; Rev. 17:6; 20:4). The "great tribulation" (Dan. 12:1; Matt. 24: 21; Mark 13:19; Luke 21:23; Rev. 7:14) that is to come upon mankind has started with the passion of Christ and will continue until his PAROUSIA (e.g., Matt. 26:39; Mark 13 and parallels; II Thess. 1:5). By showing that suffering results, with equal necessity, from the sinfulness of mankind and from the missionary activity of God's people, the NT almost completely dismisses the question of the individual's fault for suffering (e.g., Luke 13:1-5; John 9:2-3; but see I Cor. 11:29-30).

In addition to its atoning function, the believers' suffering serves a twofold purpose. It brings into focus the suffering of the universe (e.g., Rom. 8:19-22), and it purges faith from the dross of self-love and love of the world (e.g., II Tim. 1:8, 12). By the way in which the believer accepts suffering, the transforming power of the gospel and the glory of Christ are brought to light (e.g., II Tim. 1:12; I Pet. 2:21-25). The suffering of the followers of Jesus is unavoidable, because the Savior's work runs counter to the aspirations of the world and its powers. Therefore, these powers hate his disciples even as they hated the master (e.g., John 15:18; I Cor. 2:8; cf. Matt. 5:10-12; I John 3:11-12).

Seeing suffering in the context of holy history, the NT is not, like Stoicism, interested primarily in man's ability to stand suffering physically and mentally, but rather in the spiritual aspects of suffering. Satan uses the suffering of our "flesh"—i.e., everything that ties us to this world (II Cor. 4:7, 10, 16-17; 7:5-6; Col. 1:24)—to tempt us—i.e., to destroy in us the desire for the new life in Christ (e.g., II Cor. 4:10-12; cf. Matt. 10:28; Rom. 8:36) and our faith (II Cor. 2:11; I Thess. 3:3; Rev. 2:10; cf. Mark 4:17 with Luke 8:13), either by making us shrink from the pain involved (e.g., Matt. 20:22=Mark 10:38; Rom. 8:18-24) or by persuading us to trust in our own superior strength and endurance (e.g., II Cor. 13:5-7; cf. Matt. 10:28). However, if the temptation has been overcome and the tribulation accepted as a divine education meant to reduce our trust in ourselves (e.g., Matt. 23:12; 26:33 = Mark 14:29; cf. Matt. 10:16; Luke 10:3; Rom. 8:17; Jas. 4:6; I Pet. 1:6-7; Rev. 3-9), it serves to strengthen our inner life (e.g., Rom. 6:4-8; II Cor. 4:17; 7:10; 12:7; Phil. 3:7-16; I Pet. 4:1; Jas. 1:2; Rev. 2:10; cf. Rom. 8:18-24; Heb. 12:11). Moreover, since the believers realize that their new life in the "flesh" is Christ's, no longer theirs (e.g., II Cor. 4:10-11; Gal. 2:20; Rev. 6:9-10), their suffering serves as evidence of Christ's triumph (Mark 13:9; I Cor. 1:26; II Cor. 4:16; 6:4; 12:9; I Thess. 3:3-4; II Thess. 1:5), as well as an unmasking of the wickedness of evil (Matt. 10:26 = Luke 12:2; Mark 4:22 = Luke 8:17; I Cor. 4:5; II Thess. 2:3). Suffering "for the name" is, therefore, a privilege (χάρις) and a sign of divine election (e.g., Matt. 5:12 = Luke 6:22-23; Acts 5:41; I Cor. 11:32; II Cor. 6:4-5; 11:23-29; Gal. 3:4; Col. 1:29; II Thess. 1:4-8; I Pet. 2:19-21; 4:12-16, 19), whereas self-inflicted suffering is worthless (Col. 2:23).

Christians, therefore, will endure suffering patiently instead of rebelling against the God who sent it (e.g., Rom. 5:3-4; I Thess. 3:3; I Pet. 2:21-23), and without fear or anxiety (e.g., Matt. 6:25-33; 10:26-31; Luke 12:4, 7, 32; I Cor. 7:29-32; Phil. 4:6; I Pet. 3:14; 5:7; Rev. 2:10; cf. Matt. 13:22). No matter how heavily he has to suffer, the believer can be sure of Christ's final triumph over all the powers of evil (e.g., Luke 11:22; John 16:33; I Cor. 15:27; Phil. 2:10-11; Rev. 5:5; 6:2; 17:14; 20:9, 14-15), because he experiences that victory in his own life (e.g., Rom. 8:37; I Cor. 15:57; I John 2:13-14; 4:4; 5:4-5; I Pet. 5:10; Rev. 2:7, 11, 13, 17, 26; 12:11; 21:7). Being sure that the evils of this world will never be able to crush him (e.g., II Cor. 6:9; II Thess. 3:3; II Tim. 4:18; cf. Matt. 6:13) and that the Tempter flees when firmly opposed (e.g., Jas. 4:7), the believer can look at all evils with equanimity and patience (e.g., Matt. 13:21=Mark 4:17; Rom. 5:3-4; 12:12; II Thess. 1:4; Rev. 1:9). In his sufferings he never ceases to entertain HOPE (Rom. 5:2, 4-5; 8:20; 12:12; I Thess. 1:3), not only because all evils are short-lived (I Pet. 1:6; cf. Rom. 8:18), but also because whatever he may lose in this life is like nothing in comparison with what he is to obtain with Christ (e.g., Matt. 16:26 and parallels; Matt. 19:29 and parallels; Rom. 8:17-18; II Cor. 4:17; Phil.

3:8; II Thess. 1:7; cf. Matt. 13:44-46). The follower of Jesus is capable of overcoming his anxious cares and his worries about the uncertainty of the future (e.g., Matt. 6:25-34; Jas. 4:13-15), because God provides whatever we really need (Matt. 6:32; Luke 12:30; II Cor. 7:6). Thus, notwithstanding the fact that evils and suffering are experienced with greater intensity under the New Covenant than under the Old, the faith of Christ attains to a level never reached in the OT—viz., joy over suffering (e.g., Matt. 5:12; John 14:28; 16:20, 22; Acts 13:52; Rom. 5:2; 12:12; Phil. 2:17; I Thess. 1:6; Jas. 1:2). Similarly, while in the OT the believer becomes so preoccupied with his own suffering that he seems to lose sight of the rest of the world, the follower of Christ feels as a result of his suffering a deep compassion for the suffering of others. Their calamity is a divine indication that we are to grow in helpful love (e.g., Luke 10:29-37; I Cor. 12:26; Gal. 6:2; I Pet. 4:1-4). Nor must the believer who has been harmed or wronged retaliate upon his adversary, because by so doing he would serve the ends of the devil, for it is Satan's device through evil to call forth new evils. Rather, a disciple of Jesus is to respond with love (e.g., Matt. 5:38-45; Luke 6:27-30; Rom. 12:14-20; cf. II Cor. 1:23), forgiveness, and reconciliation (e.g., Matt. 5:24; 18:21-22; Luke 17:3-4) to all acts of enmity, for he is called upon to imitate in a constructive manner the example of Christ (e.g., Matt. 20:22; I Cor. 4:16; 11:1; II Cor. 2:7; I Thess. 1:6). By such action the power of evil will definitely be broken in this world.

Bibliography. A. S. Peake, *The Problem of Suffering in the OT* (1904). H. Cremer, "πονηρός, πονηρία," *Biblisch-theologisches Wörterbuch* (10th ed., 1915), pp. 959-62. H. J. Wicks, *The Doctrine of God in the Jewish Apocryphal and Apocalyptic Literature* (1915). J. Y. Batley, *The Problem of Suffering in the OT* (1916). L. W. Batten, *Good and Evil: A Study in Biblical Theology* (1918). V. Ravi-Booth, *Why Do the Righteous Suffer?* (1920). J. Lindblom, *Skandalon: Eine lexikalisch-exegetische Untersuchung* (1921). R. Liechtenhan, "Die Überwindung des Leidens bei Paulus und in der zeitgeschichtlichen Stoa," *ZThK*, III (1922), 368-99. A. Juncker, *Jesus und das Leid* (1925). O. Schmitz, *Vom Wesen des Ärgernisses* (1925). H. Schmidt, *Gott und das Leid im AT* (1926). J. Schneider, *Die Passionsmystik des Paulus* (1929). W. Wichmann, *Die Leidenstheologie*, BWANT, IV (1930). A. P. Sheperd, *Sin, Suffering, and God* (1931). E. S. Jones, *Christ and Human Suffering* (1933). J. J. Stamm, *Das Leiden des Unschuldigen in Babylon und Israel* (1946). N. F. S. Ferré, *Evil and the Christian Faith* (1947). J. Coppens, *La Connaissance du Bien et Mal et le Péché du Paradis* (1948). A. D. Sertillanges, *Le Problem du Mal* (1948). C. R. Milley, "The Wrath of God," *ET*, LXVII (1951), 142-45. H. Rowley, *Submission in Suffering and Other Essays on Eastern Thought* (1951). M. Buber, *Images of Good and Evil* (1953). J. A. Sanders, *Suffering as Divine Discipline in the OT and Post-Biblical Judaism* (1955). E. F. Sutcliffe, *Providence and Suffering in the Old and New Testaments* (1955). C. R. North, *The Suffering Servant in Deutero-Isaiah* (2nd ed., 1956). H. W. Robinson, *The Cross in the OT* (1956). R. S. Siebeck, "Über den Schmerz," in *Antwort, Festschrift zum 70. Geburtstag von Karl Barth* (1956). O. A. PIPER

SUICIDE. The word "suicide" does not appear in the Bible, but there are several instances of the occurrence. In the OT there are the suicides of Saul and his armor-bearer (I Sam. 31:4-5), Ahithophel (II Sam. 17:23), and Zimri (I Kings 16:18). In the NT the single case is that of Judas (Matt. 27:5; *see* JUDAS 7).

There are no specific biblical prohibitions of suicide, nor is the act as such condemned. Nevertheless, its rarity reflects not only deterring sociological conditions but also an implicit attitude which can be inferred from religious tenets common to the OT and the NT. God is Creator and Sovereign of all creation who alone has authority to give and take away (Job 1:21). The Sixth Commandment and the regulations regarding shedding human blood (Gen. 9:5-6) undoubtedly influenced the attitude. Later rabbinic literature cites the latter passage in specifically prohibiting suicide (Gen. Rabbah 34.21*b*). Josephus expresses the Jewish attitude when he calls suicide an "impious act against God our Creator" (War III.viii. 5), though he tacitly approves the act of a large body of Jews who, surrounded by the Romans at Masada, took their own lives in patriotic and religious devotion (War V.II.viii.6-7).

While early Christians undoubtedly shared in the Jewish attitude, further theological implications may be inferred from such passages as Rom. 14:7-9; I Cor. 6:19; Eph. 5:29. In Acts 16:27-28 Paul prevents a suicide. However, the biblical attitude toward suicide can only be inferred.   F. W. YOUNG

SUKKIIM sŭk′ĭ ĭm [בים‎] (II Chr. 12:3); KJV SUKKIIMS —ĭmz. Part of the forces which Shishak brought up from Egypt in his attack against Jerusalem. They are probably to be identified with the *Ṯktn,* later *Ṯk,* known from Egyptian texts as a class of soldiers of Libyan origin.   T. O. LAMBDIN

SUKKOTH sŏok′ɔth [כות‎, booths]. *See* BOOTHS, FEAST OF.

SULPHUR. The translation of θεῖον (usually BRIMSTONE) in Rev. 9:17-18.

SUMER sŏo′mɔr [Sumer. *ki-engi(r);* Akkad. *šumerum*]; SUMERIANS sŏo mĭr′ĭ ɔnz. The land which came to be known in classical times as Babylonia (*see* ASSYRIA AND BABYLONIA), situated in the S half of modern Iraq in the alluvial valleys of the Tigris and Euphrates rivers, roughly between modern Baghdad and the Persian Gulf, an area of approximately eight thousand square miles. Its people, the Sumerians, developed what was probably the first high civilization in the history of man.

1. Prehistory
    a. The earliest inhabitants (*ca.* 4000-3300 B.C.)
    b. The coming of the Sumerians (*ca.* 3300-3000 B.C.)
2. History
    a. The early dynastic period (*ca.* 3000-2300 B.C.)
    b. The conquest by Akkadians and Guti (*ca.* 2300-2100 B.C.)
    c. The Sumerian revival (*ca.* 2100-1720 B.C.)
3. Social and economic institutions
    a. City-state and temple
    b. Government
    c. Economic life
    d. Law and justice

    e. Slavery
    f. Family life
    g. The physical appearance of Sumerian cities
4. Technological and scientific achievements
5. Religion
    a. Cosmology and theology
    b. The role of man
    c. Rituals and cult
6. Art
    a. Sculpture
    b. Cylinder seals
    c. Music
7. Invention and development of writing
8. Education
9. The Sumerian "national character"
Bibliography

1. Prehistory. The name Sumer is first found in a Sumerian inscription dating from *ca.* 2400 B.C., but there is no reason to doubt that it was current as far back as the beginning of the third millennium B.C., and perhaps even earlier.

a. ***The earliest inhabitants*** **(ca. 4000-3300 B.C.).** The Sumerians were not, however, the original inhabitants of Sumer. These were a people known archaeologically as "Ubaidians"—i.e., the people responsible for the cultural remains first unearthed at a tell, or mound, known as Tell al-Ubaid, and then in the very lowest levels of a number of other tells throughout ancient Sumer. They spoke a language now designated by some scholars as "Proto-Euphratean." It was this Ubaidian people which, as early as 4000 B.C. or thereabout, established the village settlements which gradually developed into Sumer's great urban centers: Eridu; UR; Larsa; Isin; Adab; Kullab; Lagash; NIPPUR; Kish. The Ubaidians were responsible for Sumer's earliest cultural advances: they were its first farmers, cattle raisers, fishermen, weavers, leatherworkers, carpenters, smiths, potters, and masons. They did not long remain the sole and dominant group in the land, however. For as the Ubaidian settlements thrived and prospered, Semitic nomads from the Syrian and Arabian desert lands to the W infiltrated them, both as peaceful immigrants and as warlike conquerors.

b. ***The coming of the Sumerians*** **(ca. 3300-3000 B.C.).** The Sumerians, on the other hand, probably did not arrive in Sumer until the very last quarter of the fourth millennium B.C. Anthropologically speaking, the Sumerians belong to the dolichocephalic Mediterranean race. They spoke a language which is agglutinative in character, but which seems to be unrelated to any other known language, living or dead. The location of their original home is quite uncertain, although the region of the Caucasus Mountains is a possibility. For, to judge from a cycle of Sumerian epic tales which has recently become available, some of the early Sumerian rulers seem to have had an unexpectedly close and intimate relationship with a city-state known as Aratta. Although this city-state was probably situated far to the NE of Sumer, to the E of the Armenian Mountains, and perhaps somewhere in the region W of the Caspian Sea, its rulers—at least, according to the Sumerian epic poets—had Sumerian names, and its people worshiped the Sumerian deities and spoke the Su-

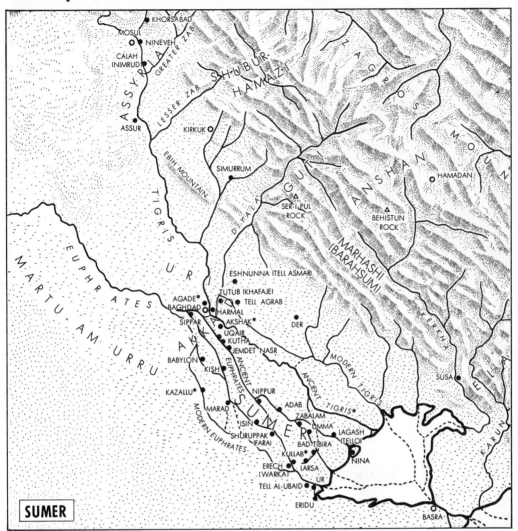

Courtesy of *Scientific American*

merian language. But wherever the Sumerians may have come from, and whatever type of culture they may have brought with them, this much is certain: their arrival led to an extraordinarily fruitful fusion —both racial and cultural—with the native population, and brought about a creative spirit fraught with no little significance for the history of civilization. In the course of the centuries that followed, Sumer reached new heights of political power and economic wealth, and witnessed some of its most significant achievements in the arts and crafts, in monumental architecture, in religious and ethical thought, and in oral myth, epic, and hymn. Above all, the Sumerians, whose language gradually became the prevailing speech of the land, devised a system of writing, developed it into an effective tool of communication, and took the first steps toward the introduction of formal education.

2. History. *a. The early dynastic period* (ca. 3000-2300 B.C.). The first ruler of Sumer whose deeds are recorded—if only in the briefest kind of statement —is a king of Kish by the name of Etana, who prob-

ably ruled at the very beginning of the third millennium B.C. In a document written centuries later, he is described as the "man who stabilized all the lands." It may thus be inferred that Etana of Kish held sway, not only over Sumer, but also over the lands surrounding it; in short, that he was the first known empire builder. Probably not very long after this, a king by the name of Meskiaggasher founded a dynasty at the city of ERECH and extended his rule from the Sea (possibly the Mediterranean) to the Zagros Mountains. Meskiaggasher's son, Enmerkar, conducted an expedition against the distant city-state of Aratta (*see § 1b above*), whose importance lay in its abundant resources of metals and stone. Fig. SUM 84.

One of Enmerkar's heroic heralds and companions-in-arms in the struggle against Aratta was a warrior by the name of Lugalbanda, who succeeded him on the throne of Erech. The victories and conquests of both Enmerkar and Lugalbanda sparked the imaginations of the Sumerian poets and minstrels to such an extent that a whole cycle of epic tales grew up

84. Tablet from Nippur with Sumerian epic poem, "Enmerkar and the Lord of Aratta"

about them. Four of these poems have been recovered and restored only quite recently, and at present they are our most important source of historical information about these early days.

By the end of Lugalbanda's reign, however, the power of the city of Erech was seriously threatened by its N neighbor, the city-state of Kish; for the last ruler but one of the "Etana dynasty," Enmebaraggesi by name, was not only a successful leader in war but was also the founder of Sumer's holiest shrine. On the military side, he was noted for his defeat of ELAM, the land directly to the E of Sumer. As a religious leader, he was the first to build a temple to the Sumerian air-god Enlil in the city of Nippur.* Since Enlil was the chief Sumerian god, the "father of all the gods," Nippur thereafter became Sumer's most important religious, spiritual, and cultural center. Figs. NIP 20-22.

Enmebaraggesi's son, Agga, tried to carry on in his father's footsteps, but by this time the city-state of Ur (the biblical Ur of the Chaldees) was ready to take over the rule of Sumer as a whole. Its first king was Mesannepadda, who is said to have ruled eighty years. Mesannepadda and the dynasty which he founded at Ur* were powerful rulers in firm control of important sources of raw materials located outside Sumer. The tombs of the royal cemetery at Ur,

85. Mosaic standard from Ur (*ca.* 2500 B.C.) showing celebration of a victory with music and feasting

which probably date approximately from this period, were filled with weapons, tools, vessels, and ornaments, fashioned of gold, silver, copper, and semiprecious stones. Fig. SUM 85.

Ur did not long remain the capital of Sumer. A short time after the death of Mesannepadda, the city-state of Erech once again came to the forefront as the leading city of Sumer, this time under the rule of the great Gilgamesh, whose deeds won him such wide renown that he became the supreme hero of Sumerian story and legend. Poems extolling Gilgamesh and his exploits were written and rewritten throughout the centuries, not only in Sumerian but in all the other more important languages of Western Asia. Gilgamesh became the hero par excellence of the entire ancient world: an adventurous, brave, but tragic figure symbolizing man's constant but hopeless drive for fame, glory, and immortality; so much so that Gilgamesh has sometimes been taken to have been a rather legendary figure who lived long before Mesannepadda of Ur. However, evidence has come to light proving beyond any reasonable doubt that Gilgamesh was, in fact, a younger contemporary of Mesannepadda!

The next great Sumerian ruler concerning whom we have any information is Lugalannemundu, a king of the city of Adab. He is reported to have ruled ninety years, and to have controlled an empire extending from the mountains of Iran to the Mediterranean Sea, and from the ranges of the Taurus to the Persian Gulf. Not long after him, a king of Kish by the name of Mesilim became the dominant figure in Sumer. According to his own surviving inscriptions, he built temples at both Adab and Lagash, far to the S of Kish. In fact, Mesilim, who probably lived sometime near the middle of the third millennium B.C., was responsible for the first case of political arbitration as yet known: a bitter border dispute between the two Sumerian city-states of Lagash and Umma was brought before him as the overlord of the

86. Eannatum leading his soldiers over bodies of the dead enemies (above); troops are led by Eannatum in his chariot (below); from Telloh, middle third millennium

entire land, and he proceeded to arbitrate the controversy by measuring off what seemed to him a just boundary line between the cities; he even had an inscribed stele erected to mark the spot in order to prevent future disputes.

But Sumer's political strength was waning; its cities were exhausting themselves by their incessant struggle for superiority and control, and a Semitic conqueror would soon appear on the scene. In Sumer's final spurt of power, it was the city of Lagash which played the predominant role. One of its rulers, Eannatum, actually succeeded in extending the sway of Lagash over Sumer as a whole, and even over several of the neighboring lands.* His success too proved to be ephemeral, and in a short while Lagash was reduced to its former boundaries. The Lagash dynasty is, in fact, memorable more for its literary achievements than for its military campaigns; for its archivists prepared commemorative inscriptions in a unique narrative style, marking them as man's earliest historians. Figs. SUM 86; NET 15.

The last ruler of this Lagash dynasty was a king by the name of Urukagina, noteworthy as man's first known social reformer. According to one of his inscriptions—one in which the word "freedom" appears for the first time in history—he set limits to the oppressive powers of a greedy bureaucracy; reduced taxes; put a stop to injustice and exploitation; and took special pains to help the poor, the widow, and the orphan. But after less than ten years of rule, Urukagina was overthrown by Lugalzaggesi, the ruler of the neighboring city-state of Umma, who put much of Lagash itself to the torch.

Lugalzaggesi in time became ruler of Erech, and he made such extensive conquests both to the E and to the W of Sumer that, as he claims in his records, fifty princes bowed to his authority.

b. The conquest by Akkadians and Guti (ca. 2300-2100 B.C.). But now the Semites from the W and the N of Sumer, under one of the more ambitious and capable of their leaders, found it possible to take over the rule of the country and establish a Semitic dynasty. Sargon, its founder, is usually referred to as Sargon the Great (*see also* SARGON 1) because of his extraordinary military and administrative achievements. In the course of his reign, which lasted more than half a century, he conquered almost all of Western Asia, and perhaps even parts of Ethiopia, Egypt, and Cyprus. Sargon also founded a new capital city by the name of Agade—whence the name Akkad for N Sumer, and Akkadians for its Semitic population—and made it, at least for a time, the richest and most powerful capital in the world. To Agade, according to the later Sumerian historiographers, came the nomadic Martu (*see* AMORITES) from the W, bringing choice oxen and sheep; to it came the people of Meluḫḫa, the "black land" (probably Ethiopia), with their exotic wares; to it came also the Elamites and Subarians from the E and the N, carrying loads "like load-carrying asses"; to Agade also came all the princes, chieftains, and sheiks of the plains, bringing monthly and yearly gifts.

Upon Sargon's death, two of his sons carried on in his footsteps, and tried, with some success, to hold on to their father's empire. But his grandson, Naram-Sin,* seems to have had his troubles in Sumer; in any

case, for some unknown reason, he destroyed Nippur, the holy city of Sumer, and desecrated and plundered Sumer's most sacred shrine, the "House of Enlil." Not long after this, Naram-Sin met a crushing defeat at the hands of the Guti, a semibarbaric people which inhabited the mountains of Iran. Sumer was overrun and laid waste, and all communications by land and sea were made impossible. Following the death of Naram-Sin's son, Agade itself was completely destroyed and never restored; according to Sumerian tradition, it became a city forever cursed. Thus, after less than a century, the mighty empire of Sumer, which had held such brilliant promise in the days of its Semitic ruler, Sargon, came to an abrupt and catastrophic end. Fig. ASS 96.

c. The Sumerian revival (ca. 2100-1720 B.C.). It took the Sumerians several generations to recover from the blow. Toward the end of the Guti terror, the city of Lagash once again came to the fore, particularly under the rule of an extraordinarily pious governor by the name of Gudea.* A score of the inscribed statues of this ruler—originally set up in the temples of Lagash, and unearthed by the French excavators—have made Gudea's the Sumerian face best known to the modern world. Moreover, the Gudea "cylinders," *ca.* twenty-four inches in height and covered from beginning to end with two of the longest Sumerian hymns as yet known, have provided a considerable insight into the range and scope

87. Statue of Gudea, king of Lagash, from Telloh

of Sumerian religious literature. The source and extent of Gudea's political power is as yet unknown, but his inscriptions indicate that he had, at the least, trade contacts in practically the entire world then known: he obtained gold from Anatolia and Egypt, silver from the Taurus, cedars from the Amanus, copper from the Zagros ranges, diorite from Ethiopia, and timber from Dilmun, which many scholars identify with the island of Bahrain, but which may actually turn out to be India. Fig. SUM 87.

88. Stele of Ur-Nammu, king of Ur (*ca.* 2060-1955 B.C.):
top register, the king stands before the deity
Ningal(?); the second register depicts two similar
scenes of the king making libation to a deity; on the
third register he is carrying a basket and building
tools; the fourth register shows a ladder. All scenes
here shown describe a king worshiping the gods at
Ur before building a ziggurat.

89. A stele of Ur-Nammu showing in the second register
a ritual sacrifice of a bull and a lamb; the fourth register depicts the musicians beating drums, perhaps
music accompanying the ritualistic sacrifice (twentieth century B.C.)

Not long after Gudea's rule over Lagash, the
Sumerians under the leadership of Utuhegal, king of
Erech, finally freed themselves altogether from the
Guti yoke. Soon afterward, there broke out a struggle
for power between the cities of Lagash and Ur for
the control of Sumer. Victory went to Ur-Nammu,*
the king of Ur, who founded a dynasty—the so-called
Third Dynasty of Ur—which ruled most of Mesopotamia for more than a century. Ur-Nammu was not
only a successful military man, but a social reformer
and lawgiver as well. Only recently part of a law
code compiled by his scribes has come to light. It tells
us that Ur-Nammu removed the "chiselers" and
grafters from the land, established and regulated
honest weights and measures, and saw to it "that the
orphan did not fall a prey to the wealthy, that the
widow did not fall a prey to the powerful, that the
man of one shekel [i.e., the poor] did not fall a prey
to the man of sixty shekels [i.e., the rich]." Three of
the laws found in the Code of Ur-Nammu are of
very special importance for the history of man's
ethical evolution; they lay down the rule that, in
cases where one man has done a bodily injury to another, the guilty party is simply to be punished by
the payment of a fine. Figs. LAW 16; SUM 88-89.

Ur-Nammu's son Shulgi was a skilful diplomat as
well as a successful soldier. Throughout his reign,

Sumer continued to prosper and to dominate at least
some of the lands around it. But time was running
out for the Sumerians. Hordes of Semitic nomads by
the name of Amurru (the biblical Amorites) kept
streaming in from the Arabian Desert to the W, and
in the course of time made themselves masters of
some of the more important cities, such as Isin,
Larsa, and BABYLON. Even in Ur itself, Semitic influence seems to have come into the ascendancy; for
at least two of Shulgi's three successors bore Semitic
Akkadian names, though they themselves were lineal
descendants of the Sumerian founder of the dynasty.
In any case, the Elamites to the E took advantage of
the growing Semitic strength, and of the political discord and confusion which presumably resulted from
it. They finally attacked and captured Ur itself and
carried off its last king, Ibbi-Sin, into captivity to
Elam.

During the 2½ centuries following the fall of Ur,
there was a bitter intercity struggle for dominance
and control over Sumer and Akkad, first between
the cities of Isin and Larsa, and later between Larsa
and Babylon. Finally, in the year 1720 B.C. or thereabout, HAMMURABI of Babylon defeated Rim-Sin,
the last king of Larsa, and emerged as the sole ruler of a
united Sumer and Akkad. This date may be said to
mark the end of ancient Sumer. By this time the
Sumerian people—i.e., the people which had spoken
the Sumerian language—were practically extinct, and
the Semites were in complete control. The kings were

all Semites, and the spoken language was the Semitic Akkadian. To be sure, the culture as a whole was still predominantly Sumerian in form and content. Not only that, but the schools and academies of Sumer and Akkad continued to utilize the Sumerian language and the Sumerian literature as the fundamental basis of their entire curriculum. So much so that the vast majority of the Sumerian literary works are known, not from originals going back to the date of their composition, but from copies prepared—presumably by Semites—during the first four centuries of the second millennium B.C.

3. Social and economic institutions. The Sumerian civilization was essentially urban in character, though it rested on an agricultural, rather than an industrial, base.

a. City-state and temple. Sumer, in the third millennium B.C., consisted of a dozen or so city-states, each comprising a large and usually walled city, surrounded by suburban villages and hamlets. The outstanding feature of each city was the main temple situated on a high terrace, which gradually developed into a massive stage-tower or *ziggurat,** Sumer's most characteristic contribution to religious architecture. The temple usually consisted of a rectangular central shrine, or "cella," surrounded on its long sides by a number of rooms for the use of the priests. In the cella there was a niche for the deity's statue, fronted by an offering table made of mud brick. The temple was constructed largely of mud bricks, and since these are unattractive in texture and color, the Sumerian architects beautified the walls by means of regularly spaced buttresses and recesses. They also introduced the mud-brick column and half-column, and covered these with colored patterns of zigzags, lozenges, and triangles, by inserting thousands of painted clay cones into the thick mud plaster. Sometimes the inner walls of the shrine were painted with frescoes of human and animal figures, as well as with a varied assortment of geometric motifs. The temple was the largest, tallest, and most important building in the city, in accordance with the theory current among the Sumerian religious leaders, that the entire city belonged to its main deity, to whom it had been assigned on the day that the world was created. In practice, however, the temple corporation owned only some of the land, which it rented out to sharecroppers; the remainder was the private property of the individual citizens. Fig. ASS 105.

b. Government. Political power lay originally in the hands of the free citizens and a city governor known as the *ensi,* who was no more than a peer among peers. In cases of decisions vital to the city as a whole, these free citizens met together in a bicameral assembly, consisting of an upper house of "elders" and a lower house of "men." As the struggles between the various Sumerian city-states grew more violent and bitter, and as the pressures from the barbaric peoples to the E and the W of Sumer increased, military leadership became a pressing need, and the "king"—or, as he is known in Sumerian, the *lugal* ("big man")—came to the fore. At first the king was probably selected and appointed by the assembly at critical moments for a specific military task. But gradually kingship, with all its privileges and prerogatives, became a hereditary institution; in time, it even came

to be considered the very hallmark of civilization. The kings established a regular army, with the chariot—the ancient "tank"—as the main offensive weapon, and a heavily armored infantry which attacked in phalanx formation. Sumer's victories and conquests were due largely to its superiority in military weapons, tactics, organization, and leadership. In the course of time, therefore, the palace began to rival the temple both in wealth and in influence.

c. Economic life. But priests, princes, and soldiers constituted, after all, only a small fraction of the cities' population. The great majority of the free citizens were farmers and cattle-breeders, boatmen and fishermen, merchants and scribes, doctors and architects, masons and carpenters, smiths, jewelers, and potters. There were, of course, a number of rich and powerful families who owned large estates; yet even the poor managed to own farms and gardens, houses and cattle, for in many respects the economy was free and uncontrolled. Riches and poverty, success and failure, were—at least to some extent—the results of private enterprise and individual drive. The more industrious of the artisans and craftsmen sold their handmade products in the free town market, receiving payment either in kind or in "money," which was normally a disk or ring of silver of a standard weight. Traveling merchants carried on a thriving trade from city to city, and with surrounding countries, both overland and by sea; and not a few of these merchants were probably private individuals rather than temple or palace representatives.

d. Law and justice. The economic life of Sumer was characterized by the key concepts of law and justice. Significant economic and legal reforms were already introduced by Urukagina (*see* § *2a above*) who lived at the end of the twenty-fourth century B.C., and law codes were compiled at least as early as the time of Ur-Nammu (*see* § *2c above*), who reigned in the middle of the twenty-first century B.C. Moreover, Sumerian legal documents have been excavated in considerable numbers: contracts, deeds, wills, promissory notes, receipts, and actual court decisions, some of which, at least, were actually studied as legal precedents. In theory, it was the king who was responsible for the administration of law and justice; in practice, it was the city governor or *ensi,* or rather his representative, the *mashkim,* who attended to the legal and administrative details. Court cases were usually heard by tribunals consisting of three or four judges. Suits could be brought either by private parties or by the government. Evidence was taken in the form of statements from witnesses and experts, or was obtained from written documents. Oath-taking played a considerable role in the court procedure, particularly the oath by the witnesses. The decisions of the judges were legally binding, unless new evidence came to light.

e. Slavery. While the vast majority of the inhabitants were free citizens, slavery was a recognized institution, and the temples, palaces, and rich estates owned slaves and exploited them for their own benefit. Many slaves were prisoners of war, and these were not necessarily foreigners, but might frequently be Sumerians from a neighboring city defeated in battle. Sumerian slaves were also recruited in other ways: freemen might be reduced to slavery as punishment for certain offenses; parents could sell their children as slaves in time of need; or a man might even turn over his entire family to creditors in payment of a debt, although for no longer than three years. The slave was the property of his master like any other chattel. He could be branded and flogged, and was severely punished if he attempted to escape. On the other hand, it was to his master's advantage that a slave stay strong and healthy, and slaves were therefore usually well treated. They even had certain legal rights: they could engage in business, borrow money, and buy their freedom. Furthermore, if a slave, male or female, married a free person, the children were free. The sale price of a slave varied with the market, as well as with the individual involved; the average price for a grown man was ten shekels, a sum which was at times less than the price of an ass.

f. Family life. The basic unit of Sumerian society was, as with us, the family, whose members were knit closely together by love, respect, and mutual obligations. Marriage was arranged by the parents, and the betrothal was legally recognized as soon as the groom presented a bridal gift to the bride's father; it was often consummated with a contract inscribed on a tablet. While marriage was thus reduced to a practical arrangement, there is some evidence to show that surreptitious premarital lovemaking was not altogether unknown. The woman in Sumer had certain important legal rights: she could hold property, could engage in business, and could qualify as a witness. But the husband could divorce her on relatively light grounds, or—if she had borne him no children—he could marry a second wife. Children were under the absolute authority of their parents, who could disinherit them or even sell them into slavery (*see above*). But, in the normal course of events, children were dearly loved and cherished, and, at the parents' death, inherited all their property. Adopted children were not uncommon, and these too were treated with the utmost care.

g. The physical appearance of Sumerian cities. There is no way of estimating, with any reasonable degree of exactness, the size of the population of Sumerian cities, since there was no official census; or at least no traces of any have as yet been found. Probably the number of people varied anywhere from ten to fifty thousand. The city streets were narrow, winding, and quite irregular, with high, blank house walls on either side. They were unpaved and undrained, and all traffic was either by foot or by donkey. The average Sumerian house was a small, one-story, mud-brick structure, consisting of several rooms grouped around an open court. The well-to-do Sumerian, on the other hand, probably lived in a two-story house of about a dozen rooms, built of brick and plastered and whitewashed both inside and out. The ground floor consisted of a reception room, kitchen, lavatory, servants' quarters, and sometimes even a private chapel. For furniture there were low tables, high-backed chairs, and beds with wooden frames. Household vessels were made of clay, stone, copper, and bronze; in addition, there were baskets and chests made of reed and wood. Floors and walls were adorned with reed mats, skin rugs, and woolen hangings.

Below the house there was often located the family mausoleum, where the family dead were buried. In early times, however, there were special cemeteries for the dead, located outside the cities. The Sumerians believed that the souls of the dead traveled to the nether world, and that life continued there more or less as on earth; they therefore buried with the dead their pots, tools, weapons, and jewels. In the case of kings, they sometimes even buried with them some of their courtiers, servants, and attendants, as well as their chariots and the animals which had pulled them. It is largely from the rich finds of tombs that the modern archaeologist has learned so much concerning the material culture of the ancient Sumerians.

4. Technological and scientific achievements. On the technological side, some of Sumer's most far-reaching achievements revolved about irrigation and agriculture. The construction of an intricate system of canals, dikes, weirs, and reservoirs demanded considerable engineering knowledge and skill. Surveys and plans were prepared, which involved the use of leveling instruments, measuring rods, drawing, and mapping. For mathematical and arithmetical purposes, a sexagesimal system of numbers was utilized, featuring a most useful device of "place-value" notation not unlike that of our own decimal system. Tables of square roots, of cube roots, and of exponential functions, as well as collections of algebraic problems involving the solution of complicated quadratic equations, were compiled for use in the Sumerian schools. Measures of length, area, capacity, and weight were effectively standardized. Farming, too, had become a complicated and methodical technique requiring foresight, diligence, and skill. A recently translated Sumerian essay—a veritable "farmer's almanac"—records a series of instructions and directions to be followed by the farmer from the first day to the last, from the watering of the fields to the winnowing of the harvested crops. Sumerian craftsmen were skilled in metallurgy; in the processes of fulling, bleaching, and dyeing; and in the preparation of paints, pigments, cosmetics, and perfumes. Pharmacology, too, had made no little progress; for, from a "prescriptions" tablet recently reinterpreted, we learn that the Sumerian physician made use of quite an assortment of botanical, zoological, and mineralogical "simples" for his materia medica, as well as of a number of elaborate chemical operations and procedures.

5. Religion. *a. Cosmology and theology.* On the intellectual and spiritual level, the Sumerian thinkers and sages evolved a cosmology and theology which became the basic creed and dogma of the entire Near East. They believed that sea and water surrounded the universe on all sides, and therefore concluded that a primeval sea had existed from the beginning of time and was a kind of "first cause" and "prime mover." In this primeval sea was engendered the universe, consisting of a vaulted heaven superimposed over a flat earth and united with it. In between, separating heaven from earth, was the moving and expanding atmosphere. Out of this atmosphere were fashioned the luminous bodies: the moon, the sun, the planets, and the stars. Following the separation of heaven and earth, and the creation of the light-giving astral bodies, animal and human life came into existence.

This universe, they believed, was under the charge of a pantheon, consisting of a group of living beings, manlike in form but superhuman and immortal, who —though invisible to mortal eyes—guide and control the cosmos in accordance with well-laid plans and duly prescribed laws. There were gods in charge of heaven, earth, air, and water; of the sun, the moon, and the various planets; of wind, storm, and tempest; of the rivers, the mountains, and the plains; of the cities and states, and of fields, farms, and irrigation ditches; of the pickax, the brick mold, and the plow. The leading deities of this pantheon were the four "creating gods" in control of the four major components of the cosmos: heaven, earth, air, and water; their Sumerian names were, respectively, An, Ki, Enlil, and Enki. Their creating technique consisted of the divine word: all the creating deity had to do was to lay his plans, utter the word, and pronounce the name. To keep the cosmic entities and cultural phenomena, once they were created, operating continuously and harmoniously without conflict and confusion, they devised the *me*, a set of universal and unchangeable rules and laws which were obeyed willy-nilly by everybody and everything.

b. The role of man. As for man, the Sumerian thinkers, in line with their world view, had no exaggerated confidence in him and his destiny. They were firmly convinced that mankind had been fashioned from clay and was created for one purpose only: to serve the gods by supplying them with food, drink, and shelter, so that they might have full leisure for their divine activities. Life, the Sumerians believed, is beset with uncertainty and haunted by insecurity, since a man does not know beforehand the destiny decreed for him by the unpredictable gods. When he dies, his emasculated spirit descends to the dark, dreary nether world, where life is but a dismal and wretched reflection of earthly life.

One fundamental moral problem—a favorite with Western philosophers—never troubled the Sumerian thinkers at all; namely, the delicate problem of free will. Convinced beyond all need for argument that man was created by the gods solely for their own benefit and pleasure, the thinkers accepted the divine decision that death is man's lot, and that only the gods are immortal. To the gods was attributed all credit for the high moral qualities and ethical virtues that the Sumerians had, no doubt, evolved gradually and painfully from their social and cultural experiences. It was the gods who planned; man only followed divine orders.

The Sumerians, according to their own records, cherished goodness and truth, law and order, justice and freedom, righteousness and straightforwardness, mercy and compassion. And they abhorred evil and falsehood, lawlessness and disorder, injustice and oppression, sinfulness and perversity, cruelty and pitilessness. The gods, too, preferred the ethical and moral to the unethical and immoral. Still, in their inscrutable way, they had created sin and evil, suffering and misfortune. The proper course for a Sumerian "Job" to pursue was not to argue and complain, but to plead and wail, to lament and confess his inevitable sins and failings. And since the great gods were far away in the distant sky, and might have had more important matters to attend to, the Sumerian thinkers evolved the notion that each individual had a special personal god—a "good angel," as it were—who would hear his prayer, and through whom he would find his salvation.

c. Rituals and cult. While private devotion and personal piety were important religious acts, it was the public rites and rituals which played the more prominent role in Sumerian religion. The center of the cult was, of course, the temple with its priests, priestesses, singers, musicians, eunuchs, and hierodules. Here sacrifices were offered daily, consisting of animal and vegetable fats, and libations of water, beer, and wine. In addition, there were the New Moon Feast and other monthly celebrations. Most important was the prolonged New Year celebration, culminating in the *hieros gamos* ceremony, when the reigning monarch married Inanna, the goddess of love and reproduction, and thus ensured fertility to the soil, and fecundity of the womb. This royal "holy marriage" ceremony was but one of a number of the more mystical Sumerian cult practices revolving about the notion of a "dying god" and his resurrection, which served to explain, at least to some extent, two theological inconsistencies which disturbed the rather tidy and methodical Sumerian mind. First was the bitter and incontrovertible fact that, in spite of the deity in charge, all vegetation died and all animal life languished during the hot, parched summer months. This led to the assumption that the god of vegetation had "died," or rather, that he had been carried off to the nether world, where he remained during those hot, lifeless months. He did not return to the earth until the autumnal equinox—the time of the New Year—when, as a result of his sexual reunion with his wife, fields and farms, plains and meadows, began to bloom and blossom again. The other difficulty concerned the death of the Sumerian king, who, in the course of time, began to be thought of as a deity, and therefore presumably immortal. This inconsistency was resolved, at least in part, by identifying the king with the vegetation-god, whose annual death, resurrection, and reunion with his wife were taken more or less for granted. Every New Year, therefore, the Sumerians celebrated with pomp and ceremony, with music and rejoicing, the union in marriage between the king (as the risen god) and the goddess who was the latter's wife. The origins and evolution of this remarkable fusion of myth and ritual, of cult and credo, are quite obscure. There were quite a number of "dying gods" in ancient Sumer, but the best known is Dumuzi, the biblical TAMMUZ, whom the women of Jerusalem were still mourning in the days of the prophet Ezekiel. Originally, the god Dumuzi was probably a mortal Sumerian ruler, whose life and death had, for some unknown reason, made a profound impression on the Sumerian thinkers and mythographers. His wife was Inanna, the ambitious goddess of love and war, who, according to the mythographers, was responsible for Dumuzi's forced sojourn in the nether world. In historical times, therefore, the *hieros gamos* at the New Year celebrated the marriage of the Sumerian king (as the god Dumuzi) to the latter's wife, the goddess Inanna.

6. Art. *a. Sculpture.* In the field of art, the Sumerians were particularly noted for their skill in sculpture. The earliest sculpture was abstract and impressionistic. The temple statues show great emotional and spiritual intensity, but indicate no marked skill in modeling. This came gradually, however, and the later sculptors were technically more superior, although their images lost in inspiration and vigor. The Sumerian sculptors manifested a considerable degree of skill in carving figures on stelae and

Courtesy of the Oriental Institute, the University of Chicago

90. Group of statues, from the Abu temple at Tell Asmar

plaques, and even on vases and bowls. It is from their sculpture that we learn a good deal abut the appearance of the Sumerians and their dress. The men were either clean-shaven, or they had long beards and long hair parted in the middle. The most common form of dress was a kind of flounced woolen skirt, over which long cloaks of felt were sometimes worn. Later, the "chiton," or long shirt, took the place of the flounced skirt; covering this shirt was a big, fringe-edged shawl, carried over the left shoulder and leaving the right arm free. Women, on the other hand, often wore dresses which looked like long, tufted shawls, covering them from head to foot, leaving only the right shoulder bare. Their hair was usually parted in the middle, and braided into a heavy "pigtail," which was then wound around the head; on important occasions, they wore elaborate headdresses consisting of hair ribbons, beads, and pendants.

Fig. SUM 90.

b. Cylinder seals. One of the most original art contributions of the Sumerians was the cylinder seal, a small cylinder of stone engraved with a design, which became clear and meaningful when rolled over a clay tablet, or over the clay sealing of a jar. The cylinder seal became a sort of Mesopotamian trademark, although its use penetrated Anatolia, Egypt, Cyprus, and Greece. The Sumerian artists were highly ingenious in devising suitable designs, especially when the seal was first invented. The earliest cylinder seals are carefully incised gems, depicting such scenes as the king on the battlefield; the shepherd defending his cattle from wild beasts; or rows of animals, or of fairy-tale creatures and monsters. Later the designs became more decorative and

formalized. Finally, one particular design became predominant, almost to the exclusion of all others: the "presentation scene," in which a worshiper is being presented to a god by his "good angel." *See* § 5*b above.*

c. Music. Both instrumental and vocal music played a great role in Sumerian life, and some of the musicians were important figures in temple and court. Beautifully constructed harps and lyres have been excavated in the royal tombs at Ur; and percussion instruments, such as the drum and tambourine, were also common, as were pipes of reed and metal. Poetry and song flourished in the Sumerian schools, but practically all the recovered works are hymns to gods and to kings, for use in the temples and palaces. Nevertheless, there is every reason to believe that music, song, and dance were a major source of entertainment in the home as well as in the market place.

7. Invention and development of writing. Probably the most important Sumerian contribution to civilization was the invention and development of the Cuneiform, or wedge-shaped, system of writing, which was borrowed, first by the Akkadians and afterward by many of the surrounding peoples, each of whom adapted it to their own language. Without it, the cultural progress of the entire ancient world would undoubtedly have been much slower than it was. The script began as a series of pictographic signs devised by temple administrators and priests for the purpose of keeping track of the temples' resources and activities. At first, therefore, it was used for the simplest administrative notations only. But in the course of the centuries, the Sumerian scribes and teachers so modified and molded the script that it lost its pictographic character, and became a purely phonetic system of writing, in which each sign stood for one or more syllables. Clay tablets, inscribed in cuneiform writing by means of a reed stylus, have been excavated by the tens of thousands in the ancient buried cities of Sumer, and are now found in museums the world over. More than ninety per cent of these tablets are economic, legal, and administrative documents not unlike the commercial and governmental records of our own day. But some five thousand tablets and fragments have been found inscribed with Sumerian literary works, consisting of myths and epic tales, hymns and lamentations, proverbs, fables, and essays. This is man's oldest collection of belles-lettres as yet known, antedating the Greek *Iliad* and *Odyssey* and the Hebrew Bible by close to a millennium. Moreover, there are quite a number of biblical motifs and ideas which have their prototypes and counterparts in the literature of Sumer. *See* Writing and Writing Materials § 1*a.* Fig. WRI 29.

8. Education. A direct outgrowth of the invention of the cuneiform system of writing (*see* § 7 *above*) was the introduction and development of the Sumerian system of education, a notable milestone in the history of man's intellectual advance. The main goal of the Sumerian school was "professional"; it aimed to train scribes, secretaries, and administrative personnel, much like our modern business schools. But in the course of its growth and development, and particularly as a result of its ever-widening curriculum, the Sumerian school came to be the center of culture and learning. Within its walls flourished the scholar, the "scientist," and the writer of poetry and prose. Its headmaster was known as the "school father"; his assistant was called the "big brother"; and the pupils were the "school sons." Other members of the faculty were designated the "man in charge of drawing," the "man in charge of Sumerian," and the "man in charge of the whip." Teachers' salaries were low; although the students all came from well-to-do families, the tuition fee was probably quite small. The curriculum, once the first steps in cuneiform writing had been passed, consisted of copying and memorizing "textbooks" containing long lists of words and phrases, including the names of trees, animals, birds, insects, countries, cities, villages, stones, and minerals. The Sumerian schoolmen also prepared a large and diverse assortment of mathematical tables and problems (*see also* § 4 *above*), as well as a variety of grammatical texts and Sumero-Akkadian dictionaries. On the literary side, the pupils studied, copied, and imitated the varied assortment of poetic narratives, hymns, proverbs, and essays, which for one reason or another had met with acceptance and approval throughout the land. School discipline was harsh and severe; there was no sparing of the rod. Most of the graduates probably became scribes in the employ of the palace, the temples, and the rich private estates. But there were also those who devoted their lives to teaching and learning, and can therefore be compared to our modern academicians.

9. The Sumerian "national character." To judge from several Sumerian essays recently pieced together, the educational system of Sumer—and, as a result, the Sumerian "national character"—was deeply colored by a psychological drive for superiority and pre-eminence, for prestige and renown. Indeed, the Sumerians, not unlike the Hebrews of a later day, considered themselves to be a "chosen people," a rather special and hallowed community in more intimate contact with the gods than the rest of mankind. They nevertheless had a high regard for humanity as a whole; so much so that the Sumerian word for "mankind"—like its English counterpart, "humanity"—came to mean "humaneness"—i.e., conduct worthy of a human being. The Sumerians even had a moving vision of all mankind living in peace and security, united by a universal faith, and perhaps even by a universal language. But, unlike the Hebrew prophets or the modern idealists, they never transformed this vision into a starry Utopia of the future; instead, they projected it back into the distant past, into man's long-gone Golden Age.

Bibliography. C. L. Woolley, *The Royal Cemetery, Ur Excavations*, vol. II, (1934); T. Jacobsen, *The Sumerian King List, Assyriological Studies*, vol. XI (1939); B. Landsberger, "Die Anfaenge der Zivilisation in Mesopotamien," *Ankara Üniversitesi Dil ve Tarih-Coğrafya Fakültesi Dergisi,* II (1944), 431-37; T. Jacobsen in H. Frankfort *et al., The Intellectual Adventure of Ancient Man* (1946), pp. 125-219; H. Frankfort, *The Birth of Civilization in the Near East* (1951); A. Falkenstein, "La cité-temple sumérienne," *Journal of World History,* I (1954), 784-814; H. Frankfort, *The Art and Architecture of the Ancient Orient* (1955), pp. 1-61, plates 1-69; R. J. Forbes, *Studies in Ancient Technology*, vols. I-IV (1955-56); S. N. Kramer, *From the Tablets of Sumer* (1956); A. Falkenstein, *Die neusumerischen*

Gerichtsurkunden, vols. I-III (1956-57); O. Neugebauer, *The Exact Sciences in Antiquity* (2nd ed., 1957).

For translations of Sumerian literary texts, see: A. Falkenstein in A. Falkenstein and W. von Soden, *Sumerische und Akkadische Hymnen und Gebete* (1953), pp. 1-231; S. N. Kramer in J. B. Pritchard, ed., *ANET* (2nd ed., 1955), pp. 37-57, 159-60, 382, 455-63, 496.

S. N. KRAMER

SUMMER AND WINTER [קַיִץ, heat, time of fruit, *also* summer fruit; חֹרֶף, harvest ending, time of cold and rain; θέρος, heat, time of fruit; παραχειμάζω, to winter, spend the winter (Acts 27:12; 28:11; I Cor. 16:16; Tit. 3:12); παραχειμασία, a wintering (Acts 27:12; for the purpose of wintering = to winter in); χειμών, winter, stormy weather]. The two principal SEASONS in Palestine. There is settled fine weather of the subtropical zone from about mid-May to mid-September, and a cool rainy season with intermittent fine periods beginning with the EARLY RAIN and ending with the latter rain (SPRING RAIN).

See also PALESTINE, CLIMATE OF; DROUGHT.

R. B. Y. SCOTT

SUN. References to the sun occur especially in passages dealing with the beginning or end of the world, but there are also divers allusions to the heathen worship of it and to popular lore associated with it. Occasionally, too, it is introduced as a symbol of permanence.

1. Terminology
2. In cosmogony and eschatology
3. Cult and worship of the sun
4. In biblical folklore
5. In idiomatic expressions
Bibliography

1. Terminology. The usual Hebrew term for "sun" is שֶׁמֶשׁ, a word common to all the Semitic languages but of uncertain etymology. It is most often treated as masculine, but sometimes (e.g., Exod. 22:3; Deut. 24:15; II Sam. 2:24; Ps. 104:22; Jonah 4:8; Mic. 3:6; Nah. 3:17) as feminine. This alternation of gender probably reflects variant traditions among the earlier and surrounding pagan Semites concerning the sex of the solar deity. Thus, while in the Mesopotamian pantheon Šamaš is always a god, the Ugaritic Š-p-š and the S Arabian S-m-s-m are goddesses, and in an Amarna letter from Ashkelon (232: 22, Kn.), the deity is likewise treated as female. Similarly, among the Hittites, there was both a male and a female solar deity.

Less common names of the sun are: (*a*) חֶרֶס (Job 9:7), of unknown etymology; and (*b*) חַמָּה, "hot one" (Song of S. 6:10; Isa. 24:23; 30:26). The former appears also in the toponyms, Heres (Judg. 8:13); הַר חֶרֶס, "mount of the sun" (Judg. 1:35); and, according to the Vulg., Targ., and Symm., עִיר חֶרֶס (MT הַתֶּרֶס; Judg. 19:18). On the other hand, the name "Timnath-heres" in Judg. 2:9 (MT and versions) is probably to be emended to "Timnath-serah." In Enoch 78:1, the names of the sun are given as Orjares and Tômas, which represent respectively אוֹר חֶרֶס and a corruption of חַמָּה.

2. In cosmogony and eschatology. The sun was fashioned and placed in the firmament on the fourth day of creation, to light the earth in daytime and to regulate the seasons (Gen. 1:14-19). At the end of the present era, when all things revert to primordial chaos, it will be darkened (Isa. 13:10; Ezek. 32:7; Joel 2:10; 2:31—H 3:4; 3:15—H 4:15; Zeph. 1:15; Matt. 24:29; Rev. 8:12), or reverse its course (Enoch 80:5). But at the final triumph of Yahweh, when a new order is brought to birth, it will shine sevenfold as bright as now (Isa. 30:26; Enoch 93:16; 1QH 7.24-25; T.B. Sanh. 91*b*).

A fanciful, astronomical description of the sun is given in Enoch 40:6-9; 72; 78.

3. Cult and worship of the sun. The sun (Shamash; Ugaritic Š-p-š) figures in all the Semitic pantheons. The popularity of the sun cult in early Palestine is attested by such place names as Beth-shemesh, "house of the sun" (Josh. 15:10; I Sam. 6:9; I Kings 4:9; etc.), and En-shemesh, "spring of the sun" (Josh. 15:7; 18:17). Sacrifices to the sun-goddess (Š-p-š) are prescribed in ritual tariffs from Ras Shamra–Ugarit (1.12; 3.47), and in one text from that site the worship of the sun on rooftops appears to be mentioned (3.50: *ṣ q r n b g g;* cf. Akkadian *ṣaqāru,* "be high"), comporting with the denunciation of this "heathen" practice in Jer. 19:13; Zeph. 1:15. The sun-god is associated with the "Lady of Byblos" in a letter from Tell el-Amarna (116:65, Kn.); and on inscriptions of the eighth century B.C. from Zenjirli, in N Syria, he is mentioned beside Hadad, El, Resheph, and a certain Rakkab-el (Hadad, 2; Pannamuwa, 22). Furthermore, a place named Šamaš-Edom occurs in the Syro-Palestinian list of Thut-mose III (no. 51) and in the Karnak stele of Amenophis III (*ARE* II, 783).

The worship of the sun, as of other heavenly bodies, was forbidden in the religion of Yahweh, as impugning the uniqueness of that deity (Deut. 4:19; 17:3). Nevertheless it was adopted officially by the apostatic king Manasseh of Judah (II Kings 21:3, 5) and was maintained by his immediate successors and by the populace in general (Jer. 8:2). Although formally proscribed in 621 B.C. as part of the religious reformation instituted by Josiah (II Kings 23:5), it seems still to have survived in popular practice in the days of Ezekiel (Ezek. 8:16).

A feature of this apostatic cult was the placing of

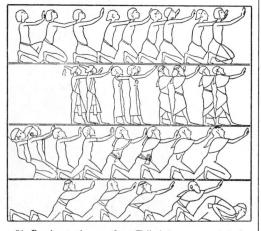

91. Praying to the sun; from Tell el-Amarna, period of Akh-en-Aton (*ca.* 1380-1362 B.C.)

model horses and of chariots (LXX a chariot) of the sun at the entrance to the sanctuary (II Kings 23:11). These doubtless represented the conveyance in which the solar deity was believed to traverse the heavens. In Akkadian hymns to Shamash, he is, indeed, described as "chariot-rider" (*rakib narkābti*), and it is probably to this that the divine name Rakkab-el on the inscriptions from Zenjirli really refers. Pottery models of horses and chariots have been found in pre-Israelitic levels at several Palestinian sites and have been interpreted as evidence of this custom. The underlying concept is paralleled, of course, both in ancient India (e.g., Rig Veda I, 115:3-4; VII, 60: 3; IX, 63:8) and in Greece (e.g., Homeric Hymns 2.63; 4.69; 28.44; 31.9; Hesiod, fragment 67 Rzach).

Fig. SUN 91.

4. In biblical folklore. Several items of popular lore relating to the sun are mentioned in the Bible:

a) In Josh. 10:12—a quotation from the lost Book of Jashar—the sun is said to have stood still, at the command of Joshua, until the Israelites had defeated their foes at Gibeon. This is a Hebrew version of a familiar *märchen* motif. In the *Iliad* (XVIII.239) Hera similarly advances the setting of the sun to confer an advantage upon the Greeks in battle; while stories of its miraculous retardation are to be found in Celtic mythology and among the New Zealanders and the Lilloeet Indians of British Columbia.

It has been suggested also that the well-known incident in the Rig Veda (I, 175:4; IV, 17:14; VI, 56:3) where Indra drags off a wheel of the sun's chariot in his fight against the devas, reflects an attempt to postpone sunset until victory has been won.

b) In II Kings 20:8-11; Isa. 38:7, the shadow of the sun is said to have receded ten degrees on a sundial as a sign that the ailing King Hezekiah would not die, as expected, but would live for a further fifteen years. This is a special application of the equally common motif that, at moments of crisis, the sun reverses its course.

c) In Mal. 4:2—H 3:20 it is said that on the Day of Judgment the "sun of righteousness shall rise, with healing in its wings." This picture is based on the widespread representation of the solar deity as a winged disk—a representation found throughout the ancient Near East (cf. *ANEP* 477, 486).

d) The midday sun was regarded as a DEMON (Ps. 91:6)—a belief which is virtually ubiquitous.

e) The gospels assert that the sun was darkened at the crucifixion of Jesus (Matt. 27:45-56; Mark 15:33; Luke 23:44-49; John 19:28-30). Here again we have a special application of a belief well attested in other cultures that the day is darkened at the death of an important personage or hero.

5. In idiomatic expressions. Like the moon, the sun was regarded as a symbol of permanence (Pss. 72:5; 89:37)—an idea well attested also in Akkadian literature.

The expression "under the sun" is used in Ecclesiastes (1:3, 9, 14; 2:11) to denote mundane existence. Considering the late date of the book (*see* ECCLESIASTES), it has been thought that this is an imitation of the Greek ὑφ' ἡλίῳ (e.g., *Iliad* IV.44; Euripides *Alcestis* 151, 394). But the expression occurs also in Phoenician inscriptions of the third century B.C.

(Sidon, Tabnith, 7-8; Eshmun'azar, 12) and has been recognized even in Elamitic (*na ḫ ḫ u n t e ir š a r ā r a*).

Bibliography. General: W. T. Olcott, *Sun-lore of All Ages* (1914). F. Boll, *Die Sonne im Glauben und in der Weltanschauung der alten Völker* (1922).

On the gender of the sun: J. Grimm, *Teutonic Mythology*, II (trans. F. Stallybrass; 1883), 703-4. K. Albrecht, *ZAW*, XV (1895), 313-25. H. Winckler, "Šams = Göttin," *ZDMG*, LIV (1900), 408-20.

On sun-worship at Jerusalem: F. J. Hollis, in S. H. Hooke, ed., *Myth and Ritual* (1933), pp. 89-110. W. C. Graham and H. G. May, *Culture and Conscience* (1936), p. 237-38. But see also: W. F. Albright, *JBL*, LIII (1934), 154-55. W. M. F. Petrie, "Supposed Sun-worship at Jerusalem," *Syro-Egypt*, III (1936), 11-13.

On chariots of the sun: G. A. Cooke, *A Text-Book of North Semitic Inscriptions* (1903), p. 165. For comparative material, see: K. Helm, *Altgermanische Religionsgeschichte*, I (1913), 178, 256. N. M. Penzer, *The Ocean of Story*, II (1923), 150-51 (Hindu). A. B. Cook, *Zeus*, I (1914), 205 ff; II (1925), 96, 552.

On the solar disk: S. A. Cook, *The Religion of Ancient Palestine in the Light of Archaeology* (1925), pp. 47-48. F. W. von Blissing, "Die älteste Darstellung der geflügelten Sonnenscheibe," *ZAS*, LXIV (1929), 112. B. Pering, "Die geflügelte Scheibe in Assyrien," *AFO*, VIII (1933), 281-96. O. Eissfeldt, "Die Flügelsonne als künstlerisches Motiv und als religiöses Symbol," *Forschungen und Fortschritte*, XVII (1942), 145-47.

T. H. GASTER

SUN, CITY OF THE [עִיר הַחֶרֶס or עִיר הֶחָרֶס, *see below*]; KJV **CITY OF DESTRUCTION**. Seemingly a city in Egypt, referred to in an oracle forecasting the expansion into Egypt of the worship of Yahweh (Isa. 19:18-22).

The difference between the KJV and the RSV reflects a variation in the textual tradition. About fifteen Hebrew MSS (as well as the Dead Sea Isaiah Scroll) and some versions, including the Vulg., read עִיר הַחֶרֶס. There is, however, considerable support for the reading הֶרֶס ("destruction," from הָרַס, "throw down"), and less support for חֶרֶס ("sun," as in Job 9:7, though the word is rare and its etymology uncertain). Oddly enough, the LXX reads "city of righteousness." The second reading, "city of the sun," makes good sense, for it can be taken as a reference to Heliopolis (cf. בֵּית שֶׁמֶשׁ, "house of the sun," in Jer. 43:13, which the RSV translates "Heliopolis"); this great center of Egyptian religion will become a city of Israel's God. Possibly this reading was the original text, and the replacement of חֶרֶס by הֶרֶס was due either to accident or to deliberate alteration. In the latter case some see an attempt by Palestinian orthodoxy to discredit the Jewish temple built by Onias in Egypt at Leontopolis (in the Heliopolis district) *ca.* 160 B.C. (Jos. Antiq. XIII.iii.1). *See* HELIOPOLIS.

W. S. McCULLOUGH

SUN, HORSES OF THE. *See* SUN § 3.

SUPERSCRIPTION ON THE CROSS. *See* INSCRIPTION ON THE CROSS.

SUPERSTITION [δεισιδαιμονία] (Acts 25:19); **SUPERSTITIOUS** [δεισιδαίμων] (Acts 17:22 KJV; RSV "religious"). An ambiguous word, which may be used (*a*) in a neutral sense; (*b*) in a

good sense to indicate proper respect, reverence, or fear of deity; and (*c*) in an unfavorable sense, indicating exaggerated or unfounded fear of the gods, or religious thought and practice judged to be crude and misinformed—i.e., superstitious. Such a word always has a relative meaning. A religious belief or practice toward which one man might be neutral, which another might approve, and another reject, might by all be called δεισιδαίμων. Since the word carries this variety of meaning, it has, strictly speaking, no English equivalent. Every English translation is an interpretation which presumes to know what the writer meant to say. Only if the context makes this clear is an adequate English translation possible.

Unfortunately, in the two instances in which the noun or its adjective occurs in the NT, the context is indecisive. E.g., in Acts 25:19, the RSV and the KJV prefer the unfavorable sense, "superstition," whereas many other translations use the word "religion," connoting one of the first two senses given above. The translation to be preferred depends less on the answer to the question, What would the pagan Festus say to the Jewish king Agrippa? than on the answer to the question, What does Luke intend that Festus shall say? Since it is Luke who is really speaking, we do not need to introduce into the argument the question whether or not Festus would be concerned to speak courteously of the Jewish religion before Agrippa. Here, Luke is speaking through Festus and past Agrippa to the reader. And since to Luke the Christian faith alone is the true religion, he can use δεισιδαιμονία of the Jewish faith, not in the neutral sense but only as, if not "superstition," then at least "scruples" (R. A. Knox). Thus Luke uses the word here to trivialize the Jewish complaint against Paul.

In Acts 17:22 the interpretation "superstition" appears to survive in translations only in the KJV ("too superstitious"), with its modification in the ERV-ASV ("somewhat superstitious"), and, among interpreters, in Zahn, who urges that Paul does not begin the speech with the usual oratorical flattery, but attacks the Athenians as polytheistic, demon-fearing idolaters. A rather subtle interpretation proposes that Paul chose the word as ambiguous and left it to the Athenians to decide whether it meant "religion" or "superstition." Another interpretation is that Paul suggests but will not express blame in choosing a word which points to a distinction between pagan and Christian piety. Most interpreters, however, whether regarding the speech as Pauline or as Lukan, accept the verse as a true *captatio benevolentiae*, and the words as meaning "religious" (favorable sense). R. A. Knox nicely interprets: "scrupulously religious." C. H. Rieu brings out the neutral sense: "very interested in religion."

If the speech was fashioned by Luke, "religious" is the preferable translation. If the words are Paul's words, the problem is more complicated.

Bibliography. See F. J. Foakes-Jackson and K. Lake, *Beginnings of Christianity*, IV (1933), 214-15, 311; and Commentaries on Acts.

F. D. GEALY

SUPH sōōf [סוּף, reeds, rushes]. One of the expressions describing the location of Moses' address to

Israel (Deut. 1:1). The place is "beyond the Jordan in the wilderness, in the Arabah over against Suph," but its precise location is unknown and is not clarified by the other places mentioned in Deut. 1:1. The KJV follows the LXX and the Vulg. and supplies ים, reading "the RED SEA," as ים סוף is regularly translated. Perhaps Suph, if it is a place name, is identical with SUPHAH.   E. D. GROHMAN

SUPHAH sōō'fə [סופה]. An area, apparently in Moab, probably near the Arnon (Num. 21:14), including the place WAHEB. In Num. 21:14 the RSV understands two proper names, "Waheb in Suphah," while the KJV translates: "What he did in the Red Sea," emending *sûphâ* to *yam sûph*, "RED SEA."   E. D. GROHMAN

SUPPER. *See* MEALS § 1*a*.

SUPPER, THE LORD'S. *See* LORD'S SUPPER.

SUR sōōr [Σουρ] (Jth. 2:28). A coastland city of Syria mentioned as sending envoys of peace to Holofernes. It has been identified with the port city of Dor near Carmel. Perhaps the name is a Greek transliteration of the Hebrew form of TYRE (צור), in which case it would represent an error by the translator or a later copyist, since Tyre has already been mentioned with Sidon in the same passage.

Bibliography. F. Stummer, *Geographie des Buches Judith* (1947), p. 28.   E. W. SAUNDERS

SUR, GATE [שער סור] (II Kings 11:6); KJV SUR, GATE OF. A gate in Jerusalem, possibly leading from the king's palace to the temple, mentioned in the narrative of the murder of Athaliah. The Hebrew text is probably corrupt. The parallel passage (II Chr. 23:5) reads: שער היסוד, "Gate of the Foundation." The identification of both structures is most probable.   G. A. BARROIS

SURETY [*in the translation of the verb* ערב, *to be* surety, *and of the derivate* ערבה, surety; ἔγγυος]. A person held as legally responsible for the debt, default, or failure of another, in contradistinction to a material or objective PLEDGE, which stands usually for חבל but also for ערבון (Gen. 38:17-18, 20), the latter being a derivative of ערב, "to be surety." The word "surety" is used technically in such texts of the OT as Gen. 43:9; 44:32, where Judah stands surety for his brother Joseph; and Prov. 6:1; 11:15; 17:18; 20:16; 22:26; 27:13. Failure to pay or to appear personally would have resulted in the surety's being compelled to assume the debt, or being deprived of his personal freedom and being reduced to the condition of a slave. Hence the Proverbs advise men against giving themselves a surety for others, especially for strangers, which indeed was most risky. The same legal term is used figuratively: God is said to be surety for the pious in the face of his oppressors (Ps. 119:122), and Jesus Christ shall be surety (ἔγγυος) for men in the New Covenant (Heb. 7:22).

For the legal aspects of the practice of holding a person, or of offering oneself as surety for others, *see* DEBT. *See also* SLAVERY.   G. A. BARROIS

SURGERY. *See* MEDICINE.

SURNAME [כנה; ἐπικαλέομαι, ἐπιτίθημι ὄνομα]. To add a name.

In Isa. 44:5 it is said that at the coming time of blessing some (Gentiles) will "surname" themselves Israel, as a sign of their oneness with the chosen people. In Isa. 45:4, God, speaking to Cyrus, says: "I surname you"—i.e., "I give you a title of honor."

In the NT four men are said to have been surnamed. Simon was surnamed by Jesus "Peter" (Mark 3:16)—i.e., Jesus "placed the name" upon him (cf. Matt. 16:18). To James and John, sons of Zebedee, Jesus gave the name of "Boanerges" (Mark 3:17). Mark interprets this surname to mean "sons of thunder," but this interpretation is not certain. The Hebrew for "sons" would be *bene*, but the Greek here is *boane*. Furthermore, we cannot be sure that the Greek *rges* equals the Hebrew *regesh* ("thunder"). It has been conjectured that the Greek transliterates the Hebrew *rgatz* ("wrath"), so that the word would mean "the hot-tempered"; and other conjectures have been made.

In Acts 1:23, Joseph called Barsabbas is surnamed "Justus." And in Acts 4:36 we are told that the apostles surnamed Joseph "Barnabas," by which surname alone he is called in the rest of Acts and in Paul's letters (cf. I Cor. 9:6; Gal. 2:1, 9, 13; Col. 4:10). Acts tells us that the name means "Son of encouragement," but this meaning is difficult to derive.

See also PETER; BOANERGES; BARNABAS.
     B. H. THROCKMORTON, JR.

SUSA sōō'sə [שושן; *cf.* Akkad. *šu-ša-an, šu-(ú)-ši;* Elam. *šu-šu-un;* Herodotus Σοῦσα, Aeschylus Σουσίς]; KJV SHUSHAN shōō'shăn. The ancient capital of ELAM, in SW Iran; the residence and court, "door," or "gate" (Esth. 2:19; cf. Xenophon *Anabasis* I.9.3: αἱ βασιλέως θύραι, "the king's door"; Old Pers. *duvarayāmaiy*, "at my door"), of the Achaemenian kings. Herodotus (V.49) mentions the presence of a royal treasury at Susa. Neh. 1:1; Esth. 1:2 speak of "Shushan the palace" (RSV "Susa the capital").

In a well-known inscription Darius the Great describes the building of his palace at Susa. Timber was brought from the Lebanon, from Gandhāra and Carmania; gold from Sardis and Bactria; lapis lazuli and carnelian from Sogdiana; turquoise from Chorasmia; silver and ebony from Egypt; ornamentation for the wall from Ionia; ivory from Ethiopia, Sind, and Arachosia; and stone columns from Elam. Among the craftsmen drafted into service were Ionian and Sardian stonecutters, Median and Egyptian goldsmiths, Sardian and Egyptian carpenters, Babylonian brickmakers, and Median and Egyptian wall-decorators. Fire wrought havoc to the royal buildings during the reign of Artaxerxes I (465-425); they were rebuilt under Artaxerxes II Mnemon (404-359). Its location made Susa a traffic center on the roads to Sardis, to Ecbatana through the Luristan Mountains, and to Persepolis.

Archaeological investigations conducted at Susa (modern Shūsh) since the middle of the nineteenth century (W. K. Loftus, M. Dieulafoy, J. de Morgan, R. de Mecquenem, R. Ghirshman) centered around four tells: (*a*) of the *apadāna,* or royal palace; (*b*) of the acropolis; (*c*) of the royal city; and (*d*) the "tell of the artisans." They have revealed the main features of Susa's history over a period of more than five thousand years, and show that the site was inhabited since the beginning of the fourth millennium (Susa I pottery). Comparison between the Susa pottery and ceramic ware from other sites in Mesopotamia and Iran permits the establishment of a fairly reliable chronology for the early periods. This and the discovery of Mesopotamian objects in Elam and of Elamite objects in Mesopotamia confirm the frequent political, military, commercial, and cultural relations between the two areas. Fig. PRE 67.

Susa's golden period was under Achaemenian rule. It was the scene of the mass marriages between some eighty of Alexander the Great's officers and ten thousand of his troops and Iranian girls in 324. Its importance declined under the Seleucids and the Parthians. The Sassanian king Shapur II (309-79) destroyed the city, allegedly because of a revolt of its large Christian population (Ghirshman), but it was rebuilt later under the name of Ērānshahr-Shāpūr. After it was captured by the Arab armies (ca. 638), a gradual decline set in. Today the site is not much more than a group of ruins.

In the village of Shūsh the alleged tomb of the prophet Daniel is the object of devout veneration on the part of the Shiite Muslims. References to Daniel's tomb as a site of pilgrimage are to be found in the Arabic authors from the ninth to the eighteenth centuries (Ṭabarī I.2566-67; Muqaddasī 407, 417; Ibn Ḥauqal [2] 255; Yāqūt V.172; Šūštarī 18). According to a story reported by Benjamin of Tudela, who traveled in Iran between 1164 and 1173, the Seljuq ruler Sanjar (1117-57) ordered Daniel's coffin encased in glass to be suspended from the center of the

Courtesy of the Oriental Institute, the University of Chicago

92. Air view of the mound of ancient Susa

bridge over the river in the middle of the city, in an effort to settle a dispute between the inhabitants of the two city halves.

Fig. SUS 92.

Bibliography. W. K. Loftus, *Travels and Researches in Chaldaea and Susiana; with an Account of Excavations at Warka, the "Erech" of Nimrod, and Shúsh, "Shushan the Palace" of Esther, in 1849-1852* (1857); M. Dieulafoy, *L'acropole de Suse* (4 vols.; 1890-92); J. de Morgan, *Mission scientifique en Perse* (1894-1904), vol. IV; V. Christian, "Susa," in *Pauly-Wissowa's Realenzyklopädie der klassischen Altertumswissenschaft,* Supplement Bd. VII (1940), pp. 1251-74; R. de Mecquenem, *Archéologie susienne* (1943), in *Mémoires de la Mission Archéologique en Iran,* vol. XXIX; R. Ghirshman, *Cinq campagnes de fouilles à Suse 1946-1951* (1952).

The building inscription is to be found in R. G. Kent, *Old Persian* (1950), pp. 142-44; Benjamin of Tudela's story in A. Asher, *The Itinerary of Rabbi Benjamin of Tudela* (1841), I.74, pp. 1 ff. M. J. Dresden

SUSANCHITES soo'sən kīts. KJV name for natives of Susa in Ezra 4:9.

SUSANNA soo zăn'ə [Σουσάννα]. An addition to the book of Daniel wherein the prophet displays his wisdom. The story is so well written, with so few characters and such impressive issues, that it is widely regarded as one of literature's great pieces, as the "first detective story."

Susanna was accused of adultery by two elders whose advances she had repulsed. She maintained her innocence, but when put to trial before the community on their testimony, she was about to be found guilty. Daniel shouted for true justice and was permitted to cross-examine the elders. He asked each elder separately under what tree the sin had been committed. The elders named different trees, thus contradicting each other. Susanna was then acquitted, and the elders were executed in accordance with the biblical law: "Then you shall do to him as he had meant to do to his brother" (Deut. 19:18-21).

It is believed that the story may have been written by a supporter of the Pharisees or particularly a follower of Simon Ben Shetah, who opposed the Sadducees. At the time the Sanhedrin flourished according to Pharisaic rule, and the book is believed to display a satire of the Sadducean practice. Yet, were this the case, the book would have been included in the canon.

The story of the trial indicates the value of cross-examination of witnesses. As narrated, the story is in direct contradiction to the Pharisaic practice and law that false witnesses can be put to death only on the basis of an alibi—i.e., other witnesses show that the first pair of witnesses were with them at the time of the committal of the crime; they were not at the scene of the crime and therefore have given false testimony. Thus the book of Susanna depicts only a contradiction of "witnesses in fact" and not in "matter of time." Because of this contradiction to Pharisaic, accepted law, the book was not included in the canon.

Because of the names of the trees and the play on words (paronomasia) many have thought that there was a Greek original of the book. Its general style, however, reveals that it was written first in Hebrew in Judea. Some scholars believe that it was written in Babylon, because that country is mentioned in the first six verses of the text. This is refuted by the fact that the name of the country Babylon is an addition found only in Theod. (second century), which is based on a later revision of the story.

Some believe that it was excluded from the canon because it reflected on the good name of the daughters of Israel and on the probity of the judges. Origen explains the exclusion of the book as a result of the few passages therein containing scandal. This is improbable, because even in the biblical books the ancient writers did not seek to hide scandal. It is felt that the work was penned by a pious Jew and its main motive was to teach that sinners and hypocrites are punished. One should prefer death to sin, but one will be rewarded if he maintains trust in God.

Among Jews in the Middle Ages the story may have been known vaguely. Nahmanides (Deut. 21: 14) mentions *Megillat Shoshan*. In Christian theology allegorical interpretations were given—Susanna prefigured the church. Origen maintained the historicity of the story, though Julius Africanus disagreed. Origen also believed that the names of the false elders were known; they conformed to the mention in Jer. 29:23.

Talmudically there is no basis for the story; it is only a moral fiction showing how a youngster refutes the falseness of elders. In this it is similar to the story in *A Thousand and One Nights* (Ali Chadsa).

The relationship of Daniel to the events in the story is most fitting, once one recalls that the name "El is my Judge" portrays Daniel.

Some scholars have seen in the story echoes of a myth, the virgin-swan or sun-goddess in her bath, or the story of the chaste wife. Another motif may have been that of the clever judge and his unique decision. Pfeiffer (*see bibliography*) believes that the story is pagan in origin, without any didactic purpose. Its religious teaching is like that of Tobit and Judith, illustrating God's vindication of the righteous and punishment of the wicked.

Bibliography. M. Gaster, *Chronicles of Jerahahmeel* (1899), pp. 1-9; L. Ginzberg, *Legends of the Jews*, I (1909), 426, 706; R. H. Charles, *The Apoc. and Pseudep. of the OT* (1913), I, 642; C. C. Torrey, *Apocryphal Literature* (1945); R. H. Pfeiffer, *History of NT Times* (1949), pp. 434-36, 448-54; S. Zeitlin, "Jewish Apocryphal Literature," *JQR,* vol. 40, no. 3 (1949-50), p. 236; B. M. Metzger, *Introduction to the Apoc.* (1957), pp. 107-13.   S. B. HOENIG

SUSI soō′sī [סוסי, horse] (Num. 13:11). The father of Gaddi, who was sent from the tribe of Manasseh to spy out the land of Canaan.

Bibliography. M. Noth, *Die israelitischen Personennamen* (1928), p. 230.

SWADDLE [חתל, to entwine, enwrap; σπαργανόω, to wrap up in swaddling cloths]. Primarily, to wrap a newborn infant in cloths. It is apparent that this custom was followed through the entire biblical period (*see* BIRTH). The Hebrew word refers to binding a broken arm with a bandage in Ezek. 30:21.

Bibliography. For comment on the Greek term, see E. J. Goodspeed, *Problems of NT Translation* (1945). Note also J. H. Moulton and G. Milligan, *The Vocabulary of the Greek NT Illustrated from the Papyri and Other Non-Literary Sources* (1914-30).   O. J. BAAB

SWALLOW [דרור (Ps. 84:3—H 84:4; Prov. 26:2), *cf.* Akkad. *durāru,* freedom, Arab. *darīr,* swift (horse); סוס, סיס (Isa. 38:14; Jer. 8:7; KJV CRANE), *see below;* KJV עגור (Isa. 38:14; Jer. 8:7; RSV CRANE)]. Any of a family (*Hirundinidae*) of small, long-winged passerine birds noted for their graceful flight.

We do not know what species of small bird דרור designated in OT times, but the allusions to its flying (Prov. 26:2) and to its nesting in the temple area (Ps. 84:3—H 84:4) make the identification with "swallow" not unreasonable. The LXX takes it to be a turtledove in Ps. 84:3 and sparrows in Prov. 26:2.

The meaning of סום, *sûs* (סים, *sîs*), is also uncertain; it may be onomatopoeic. The LXX takes it to be "swallow" (χελιδών). The references to its cry (Isa. 38:14) and to its migratory habits (Jer. 8:7) are frequently supposed to indicate some type of swift (of the family *Apodidae*), but in fact these data are inconclusive. *See bibliography.*

Bibliography. For Tristram's evidence about both swallows and swifts, see *NHB*, pp. 204-8. E. Koehler, *Lexicon* (1953), p. 656; G. R. Driver, *PEQ* (1955), p. 131, suggest the colloquial Arabic *sîs* to support the meaning "swift," but the relevance of such a colloquialism to ancient Hebrew is doubtful.   W. S. McCULLOUGH

SWAMP [בצה] (Isa. 35:7, *where the* MT *is corrupt;* Ezek. 47:11). Same as MARSH.

SWAN. KJV translation of תנשמת (Lev. 11:18; Deut. 14:16; RSV WATER HEN). There is no apparent reason for including such a bird as the swan (Genus Cygnus of the family Anatidae) among Israel's unclean birds. Moreover, while the swan was obtained by Tristram in Palestine, it was described by him as a rare bird. These and other considerations have led to the general abandonment of "swan" as a rendition of the obscure Hebrew word.   W. S. McCULLOUGH

SWARMING CREATURES [שרץ] (Gen. 7:21, etc.). *See* CREEPING THINGS.

SWARTHY [שחרחרת] (Song of S. 1:6); KJV BLACK. The sun-browned skin color of the peasant maiden, contrasted with the elaborately guarded complexions of the harem women.

SWEARING. *See* OATH.

SWEAT (NT) [ἱδρώς]. Luke 22:43-44 mentions the appearance of an angel to Jesus and that in his agony "his sweat became like great drops of blood," but this material is not found in other gospels. The absence of the passage from MSS Vaticanus, Alexandrinus, Freer, and others indicates that this is an apocryphal addition to Luke.

"Like great drops of blood" is ambiguous. It may mean either that the sweat formed in drops resembling large drops or clots (as Moffatt translates it) of blood, or that blood oozed through the skin to form bloody sweat. While some cases of this latter phenomenon are recorded, their authenticity has been strongly disputed. The Greek ὡσεί is often used to indicate simple comparison. The author probably meant to say only that the perspiration of Jesus formed in drops like blood. The breaking out of sweat on an individual under intense emotion is a familiar occurrence.

See also GETHSEMANE.

Bibliography. W. Bauer, θρόμβος, *Greek-English Lexicon to the NT* (1957), p. 364; A. Macalister, "Bloody Sweat," *HDB,* III (1900), 330, cites literature of alleged instances.   S. V. McCASLAND

SWEET CANE [קנה, *qānê*] (Isa. 43:24; Jer. 6:20). Alternately: AROMATIC CANE (Exod. 30:23; KJV CALAMUS); CALAMUS (Song of S. 4:14;

Ezek. 27:19). A species of REED (or grass) which yielded an aromatic oil used in holy oils and perfumes. The word literally means "reed," but in five OT references it is listed along with spices, implying an imported reed or product.

Sweet cane was used in the holy anointing oil (Exod. 30:23; *see* ANOINT) and in sacrificial offerings (Isa. 43:24; Jer. 6:20; *see* SACRIFICE AND OFFERINGS). It is included in a figure of a fragrant garden, to which the bride is likened (Song of S. 4:14). It was an important item of trade, along with CASSIA (Ezek. 27:19). Exod. 30:23 (cf. Jer. 6:20) informs us that it was "sweet-scented" (RSV "aromatic").

Identification with some of the aromatic reed grasses of India, as most botanists now agree (*see* FLORA § A7e), seems reasonable but is by no means certain. The context of Isa. 43:24 hardly justifies the identification with sugar cane, as some botanists suggest.

Bibliography. H. N. and A. L. Moldenke, *Plants of the Bible* (1952), pp. 39-41.   J. C. TREVER

SWINE [חֲזִיר, boar; LXX σῦς, boar; ὗς, boar, sow; NT χοῖρος, little pig; ὗς, sow]. The references to swine in the Bible show various applications:

a) Lev. 11:7; Deut. 14:8 forbid swine's flesh to Israelites. Both passages read: "The swine, because it parts the hoof . . . but does not chew the cud, is unclean to you," but Leviticus adds after "hoof": "and is cloven-footed" (the LXX and the Samar. of Deut. 14:8 is the same as the MT of Lev. 11:7). From the remains in the late Neolithic stratum at Gezer it would appear that the pre-Semitic inhabitants of Palestine killed and ate the pig freely. The pig was also the most sacrificed animal among the Greeks, and the popular agrarian rites of the swine-god Adonis must be recalled in this connection. By contrast, swine's meat is forbidden to many Semites. Among the Babylonians this meat was sacred to various gods and could be eaten at certain feasts, though it was prohibited at other times. Among the Syrians it was sacred to Tammuz. Among the Egyptians swine's meat was usually taboo, but could be eaten at certain times. Since the swine was thus generally prohibited, its occasional sacrifice must have signified the greatest holiness and potency. In turn, this probably explains such passages as Isa. 65:4; 66:3, 17, which show how apostate Jews indulged in heathen sacrificial rites presumably of great potency. It is, of course, possible that the OT prohibition of swine's flesh was originally a reversion from the known customs of certain of their predecessors in Canaan. Otherwise it is a custom which they share in common with other Semites, perhaps in revulsion from the habits of ancient Near Eastern men. The prophet condemns the eating of swine, dogs, and mice. The view that these animals were totems and originally associated with various Israelite and Jewish tribes or groups has not gained acceptance.

b) The remaining references in the OT show metaphorical usage. In Ps. 80, a community lament, an enemy who has ravaged Israel is likened to a wild boar out of the forest. It is a figure of destructiveness (vs. 13), and the identity of the ravisher is too vague to be significant. Wild boars are known for their capacity to destroy growing crops. In Prov. 11:22, a beautiful woman without discretion is likened to a golden ring in a swine's snout. II Macc. 6:18 shows how the Hellenizing party sought to compel Jews to eat swine's flesh (cf. I Macc. 1:47).

In the NT there is the same metaphorical usage. In Matt. 7:6, what is holy must not be given to the dogs, and pearls must not be thrown to swine. Religious truth must not be shared with certain kinds of men, heathen and irreligious. Similarly in the parable of the prodigal son, the younger son became a keeper of pigs, which expresses extreme degradation for a Jew, though it was by no means unknown for Jews to take such employment. That this son was compelled to consider eating swine's food is, of course, a figure of his poverty. Similarly in II Pet. 2:22 the inevitable dirtiness of the sow as an unclean animal is emphasized, as a figure of heresy. The association of dog and pig in some of these references accords with OT and certain classical authors.

The demons who as Legion possessed the Gadarene demoniac requested permission of Jesus that they might be transferred from the man to the large herd of swine feeding near at hand on the hillside. This was apparently done, for the swine were then set in motion and, rushing into the sea, were destroyed by drowning. The historical and moral difficulties are great, but the symbolism of the swine is clear. They are symbols of the unclean, whether of the Gadarene country itself and its inhabitants as non-Jewish or of the herdsmen who, if they were Jewish, were acting in unclean ways; or most probably the swine, as unclean, were regarded as fit bearers of the demons.

See also HOLINESS; CLEAN AND UNCLEAN.

Bibliography. W. R. Smith, *The Religion of the Semites* (3rd ed., 1927), pp. 290-91, 448-49, 475, 621; R. de Vaux, "Les sacrifices de porcs en Palestine et dans l'Ancien Orient," *Von Ugarit nach Qumran* (ed. J. Hempel; 1958), pp. 250-65.
                                        G. HENTON DAVIES

SWORD.
1. Terminology
2. Description
   a. Straight sword
   b. Sickle sword
3. Biblical usage
Bibliography

1. Terminology. The common Hebrew word for "sword" is חֶרֶב.

The word בָּרָק literally means "a flashing," hence "lightning." In Job 20:25 it is rendered by the KJV as "the glittering sword." Since vs. 24 refers to the bronze arrow striking one through, the RSV is probably right in understanding the word as referring to the "glittering point" of the arrow.

The word מְכֵרָה in Gen. 49:5 (KJV "habitation") is a *hapax legomenon* of unknown meaning.

The word רֶצַח in Ps. 42:10 is incorrectly rendered by the KJV as "sword"; the root means "to kill, murder," and it probably refers to a fatal disease or wound which, being inflicted by the enemy, is called "murder."

שֶׁלַח, translated "sword" in Job 33:18; 36:12, means "missile," "WEAPON" (cf. Joel 2:8).

פתחות (Ps. 55:21—H 55:22; also probable emendation in Mic. 5:6—H 5:5; KJV "the entrances thereof") is correctly rendered "drawn swords" (from the root פתח, "to open").

The NT uses two words for "sword": μάχαιρα and ρομφαία. The word ξίφος occurs only in the LXX. The exact difference between the two NT words is not clear, though originally ρομφαία was a large, broad-bladed sword especially used by the Thracians.

2. Description. Near Eastern swords were basically of two types: the straight, thrusting sword, and the bent (or sickle) sword.

a. Straight sword. Such swords have been found in Palestine from as early as the end of the Middle Bronze period at Tell el-'Ajjul. Archaeologists arbitrarily distinguish swords from daggers by length, forty centimeters being the point of division.

Straight swords had a triangular blade of bronze or iron, usually with a tang extending beyond the shoulder, which was inserted into a haft made of wood, bone, or ivory, or was riveted to it (Fig. WEA 11, c). The Egyptian sword was usually under a meter in length, pointed and double edged, and could be used for slashing or thrusting. The haft and blade were molded of one piece, and wood or ivory was inlaid in the haft. The Assyrians had both long and short swords, as the monuments attest.

b. Sickle sword. Sickle swords have been found as early as *ca.* 1800 B.C. in Palestine-Syria at Byblos, and, though not as common as the straight sword, became widely disseminated throughout the Near East, possibly through the Hyksos. They entered Egypt from Syria by the time of the Eighteenth Dynasty, and became the favorite weapon of the pharaoh. This was the *khopesh* sword (Egyptian *ḫ p š*, "foreleg"), so called because of its curved shape. (The Egyptians later also borrowed the Semitic name *ḥarb* for the straight sword; cf. Egyptian *ḫ r p*, as well as the Greek word ἅρπη). Its usual form consisted of a flat hilt with a rectangular recess for wood or ivory inlay, and a blade which began as a straight sword but eventuated in a sickle form. Fig. WEA 11.

3. Biblical usage. The straight-bladed sword is the only one recognized in the OT, unless the מכרה of Gen. 49:5 should mean "sickle sword." The sword could be used for slashing or cutting (I Sam. 17:51; cf. Ezek. 5:1), or for thrusting (I Sam. 31:4-5); hence one could "fall on the sword." It was double-edged (Judg. 3:16; Ps. 149:6) and consisted of a hilt (נצב; Judg. 3:22) and a blade (lit., "flame"; להב in Judg. 3:22; Nah. 3:3: RSV "flashing sword," KJV "bright sword," lit., "blade [flame] of a sword"; להט in Gen. 3:24: "flaming sword," lit., "blade [flame] of the sword"). It was worn in a leather sheath (תער in I Sam. 17:51; II Sam. 20:8; Jer. 47:6 ["scabbard"]; נדן in I Chr. 21:27), which was tied to the girdle (II Sam. 20:8), on the left side of the body (cf. Judg. 3:15-16, 21).

The חרב is commonly used in scripture as a symbol for violence and oppression.

Both μάχαιρα and ρομφαία are used literally as a weapon for warfare (Matt. 26:47, 55; Mark 14:43, 48; Luke 22:52; Rev. 6:4, 8; 13:10; 19:21). It was sheathed (Matt. 26:52; John 18:11), and could be "drawn out" (Matt. 26:51; Mark 14:47; Acts 16:27)

and used to strike (Luke 22:49) and kill (Acts 12:2; Heb. 11:37) or wound (Rev. 13:14). Reference to double-edged swords is also common (Heb. 4:12; Rev. 1:16; 2:12). "Sword" is also commonly used in a figurative sense. It is a symbol for war and dissension (Matt. 10:34), for divine judgment (Rev. 1:16; 19:15), for political authority (Rom. 13:4), or for a mother's anguish (Luke 2:35). In Eph. 6:17 part of the armor of God worn by the Christian is the "sword of the spirit"; this spiritual sword is further identified as being the Word of God (cf. Heb. 4:12; Rev. 1:16; 2:16; 19:15).

Bibliography. H. Bonnet, *Die Waffen der Völker des alten Orients* (1926), pp. 71 ff; W. Wolf, *Die Bewaffnung des altägyptischen Heeres* (1926), pp. 66 ff; P. Thomsen, "Schwert C," *RVG* (1927-28); A. G. Barrois, *Manuel d'Archéologie Biblique*, I (1939), 379 ff.   J. W. WEVERS

SYCAMINE [συκάμινος]. A tree referred to by Jesus in a statement concerning faith: "If you had faith as a grain of mustard seed, you could say to this sycamine tree, 'Be rooted up, and be planted in the sea,' and it would obey you" (Luke 17:6). The Greek word appears only here in the NT, but it is used to translate the Hebrew שקמה (*šiqmâ*), "SYCAMORE," regularly in the LXX. Luke uses συκομορέα, "sycamore," in 19:4, where it very probably refers to the sycamore-fig tree. Thus it is likely that "sycamine" was meant to refer to the MULBERRY TREE, to which the Greek word more often applied. In I Macc. 6:34, however, μόρον is used for "mulberry tree." In Greek συκῆ means "fig," and the FIG belongs to the mulberry family. The black mulberry (*Morus nigra* L.) is abundant in Palestine.

Since the context of Luke 17:6 gives no hint about the nature of the tree, it is possible that Luke did not intend to distinguish the trees of 17:6; 19:4. Thus the sycamore fig may have been meant in both passages.

See also FLORA § A2*e*.

Bibliography. I. Löw, *Die Flora der Juden*, I (1926), 266-74; H. N. and A. L. Moldenke, *Plants of the Bible* (1952), pp. 140-41.   J. C. TREVER

SYCAMORE [שקמה, *šiqmâ* (*always plural*); συκομορέα]; KJV SYCOMORE. A tree and its fruit associated particularly with the SHEPHELAH. The name in English was derived from the Greek σῦκον, "fig," plus μόρον, "mulberry," clearly indicating the *Ficus sycomorus* L., a type of fig tree with a leaf looking much like a mulberry leaf and belonging to the same family. The Greek, in turn, was derived from the Northwest Semitic name. The tree has no relation to the American sycamore, which is a plane tree, *Platanus occidentalis* L., or "buttonwood," *Platanus wrighti* (Arizona sycamore) or *Platanus racemosa* (California sycamore).

The LXX always translates the Hebrew with συκόμινος, which in the NT is thought to be the true MULBERRY, while συκομορέα in Luke 19:4 stands for the sycamore fig. The Arabs call this tree *ğimmeiz* today.

The importance of this tree in Bible times is indicated by David's appointment of an overseer for these trees in the Shephelah (I Chr. 27:28; Ps. 78: 47; cf. Isa. 9:10—H 9:9), while its abundance is sug-

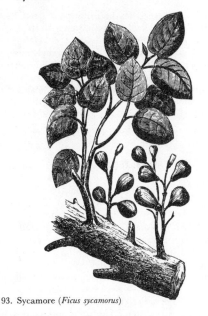

93. Sycamore (*Ficus sycamorus*)

gested in the phrase "plentiful as the sycamore of the Shephelah" (I Kings 10:27; cf. II Chr. 1:15; 9:27). Amos found employment as a "dresser of sycamore trees" (Amos 7:14), which involved puncturing the unripe fruit to make it more edible. The trees grow only in the lowlands and coastal plains, where they escape the frost (Ps. 78:47). Zacchaeus, short of stature, found a sycamore-fig tree in Jericho convenient for climbing to see Jesus (Luke 19:4). Even today this tree provides many a poor family with some food, for the tree bears fruit several times during the year, although it is inferior in quality to the common FIG.

See also FLORA § A2*j;* FRUIT.

Fig. SYC 93.

Bibliography. H. N. and A. L. Moldenke, *Plants of the Bible* (1952), pp. 106-8.   J. C. TREVER

SYCHAR sī′kär [Συχάρ] (John 4:5-6). A city of Samaria where JACOB'S WELL was located, probably the same as SHECHEM.

1. Biblical evidence. The gospel account locates Sychar "near the field that Jacob gave to his son Joseph" (John 4:5). Here "the field" must be a reference to Gen. 48:22, where Jacob gave Joseph "one mountain slope" (Hebrew *Shechem*). This appears to be the field at Shechem which Jacob purchased "from the sons of Hamor, Shechem's father" (Gen. 33:18-19; cf. Josh. 24:32). Thus Sychar must have been at or near both Shechem and Jacob's well. The chief problem concerning Sychar and its identification is whether or not Sychar and Shechem refer to the same place.

2. Sychar as 'Askar. Until recently most scholars regarded Sychar as a site distinct from Shechem and identified it with the village 'Askar. There is considerable evidence for this view. It is undeniable that the correct reading in John 4:5, as indicated by the best MSS, is "Sychar." The author of the gospel makes no mention of Shechem and would hardly confuse the two, for he had a good knowledge of the geography of Palestine. Jerome (*ca.* A.D. 400) quotes without any objection or comment the following statement from Eusebius (*ca.* 335): "Sychar is before [E of] Neapolis, near the piece of ground which Jacob gave to his son Joseph, where Christ, according to John, held discourse with the Samaritan woman by the fountain. It is shown to this day" (*De Situ et Nom. Hebr.* 279). The Bordeaux Pilgrim (*ca.* 333), like other travelers, describes Sychar as *ca.* a mile from Shechem. Epiphanius likewise distinguishes the two places (*Versio Antiqua* 253).

Those who distinguish Shechem and Sychar identify the latter with the Arab village of 'Askar, which is a half mile N of Jacob's well at the SE foot of Mount Ebal. A Samaritan chronicle of the fourteenth century or earlier speaks of a town called 'Ischar as near Shechem and the same as Sychar. It is said that the Samaritans pronounce it *'Askar*. The Talmud also mentions an En-Sikhar or Ein-Sokher, which must be the spring of 'Askar (J.T. Sheḳ. V.1 [48*d*]). So also the mosaic map of Madeba of the sixth century A.D. has at the site of 'Askar this note: "Sychar which is now Sychora."

3. Sychar as Shechem (Balatah). Although it is undeniable that Sychar appears in the best MSS, it is undoubtedly a textual error. The Sinaitic Syr. reads "Shechim" for "Sychar." The chief evidence for this textual error is the statement of Jerome that Sichem and Sichar are the same and that Συχάρ is a copyist's error for Συχέμ (*Quaest. in Gen.* 373). Since Jerome's time the reports of various travelers, beginning with Arculf (*ca.* 700), have asserted that the two words refer to the same place.

In much of the discussion about Sychar a basic error has been the common assumption that Shechem is to be identified with Neapolis (Nablus), but a careful reading of Eusebius and Jerome shows that they do not identify the two (*see above* and Jerome *De Situ et Nom. Hebr.* 266; *Epistle* CVIII [XXVII].13).

The question has been settled by excavations at Tell Balatah which have demonstrated that it is the Shechem of the OT and the city meant in the passage which has "Sychar" as a textual error. Tell Balatah is a mound 1½ miles SE of Nablus at the E edge of the pass between Mount Gerizim and Mount Ebal. At the SE edge of it is Jacob's well, which was at Sychar or Shechem (John 4:5).

Bibliography. G. A. Smith, *Historical Geography of the Holy Land* (1935), ch. xviii: "The Question of Sychar"; F.-M. Abel, *Géographie de la Palestine*, II (38), 458-60, 472-73; W. Harrelson, B. W. Anderson, and G. E. Wright, "Shechem, the Navel of the Land," *BA*, XX (1957), 2-32.   D. C. PELLETT

SYCHEM. KJV form of SHECHEM.

SYELUS. KJV Apoc. form of JEHIEL.

SYENE sī ē′nĭ [סונה; LXX Συήνη]. A village, now called Assuan, situated on the E bank of the Nile just N of the first cataract in Upper (Southern) Egypt. Its name, if we are to follow the generally accepted view, signifies "market" or "trading post," aptly reflecting the importance of this village and its neighbors as points of exchange in the commerce between inner Africa and Egypt proper. The Egyptian name *Swn* survives in modern Arabic as *'Aswān* or *'Aṣwān* through the intermediary of Coptic *Swan, Swēn*.

Located at the southernmost boundary of ancient Egypt, Syene is only naturally coupled with MIGDOL in the Delta to express the limits of Egypt in Ezekiel (29:10; 30:6): "from Migdol to Syene." The utter remoteness of Syene in terms of ancient geographical knowledge also accounts well for the use of the gentilic form in Isa. 49:12:

> Lo, these shall come from afar,
> and lo, these from the north and from the west,
> and these from the land of Syene.

The reading סונים is supported by the Dead Sea Isaiah Scroll and clarifies the hitherto enigmatic סינים, "Sinim," usually read here. Since the form is properly the plural of a gentilic adjective, it would be best translated "the people of Syene."

Mention of Syene is almost completely absent from Early Egyptian texts; and it is only after Elephantine, the true metropolis of the district, declined that Syene attained any great importance. Elephantine is a long, fertile island in the Nile at Syene and was for most of Egypt's long history the administrative and religious center of the first Upper Egyptian nome. The strategic location of the island, at a place in the Nile Valley where the arable land yields to the rugged cliffs of the river bank and the river itself to the S is hardly navigable, made Elephantine a natural frontier station against Nubia. As an island it afforded far better protection against the sudden attacks of the enemy than its sister settlement Syene on the shore; it is possible that the latter was at first only a supplementary site to the fortress on Elephantine.

Our most immediate early source of information concerning Syene and Elephantine is the corpus of Aramaic papyri originating in that district. These papyri (*see* ELEPHANTINE PAPYRI) date mainly from the fifth century B.C. and consist of business documents and letters of a Jewish colony established on Elephantine, the members of which manned a garrison in the military service of the Persians. Even in these documents, however, Syene does not seem to have the military importance of Elephantine, which is called יב (*Yēb*) after the Egyptian name of the island. Syene is usually mentioned merely as the residence of such and such a person; and although several individuals are known to have possessed houses both on Elephantine and in Syene, it is the former on which the main settlement of the colony was established and where the chief temples, of both the Egyptian god Khnum and the Jewish God Yahweh, were located.

In addition to the commercial and military significance of Syene and Elephantine, the proximity of extensive granite quarries used from the first dynasty onward and the continuous presence of the personnel necessary for working and hauling contributed much to the growing prosperity of the district. The stone quarried there, chiefly rose granite, bore the name Syenite; modern usage of this term is slightly at variance with the ancient.

Herodotus is the earliest classical writer to mention Syene, but only in an erroneous account concerning the sources of the NILE. That Syene, Ele-

phantine, and the neighboring island of Philae continued to be of strategic importance in the Greco-Roman period is confirmed by Strabo (17.1.53-54), who gives an account of the Ethiopic rebellion staged there in 25 B.C. and informs us that the Romans regularly maintained three cohorts at this place.

Syene (Assuan) today is famous as the site of the dam completed in 1902 for the control of the Nile for irrigation.

Bibliography. E. G. Kraeling, *The Brooklyn Museum Aramaic Papyri* (1953), pp. 21-26.   T. O. LAMBDIN

SYMBOL, SYMBOLISM. A representation, visual or conceptual, of that which is unseen and invisible. The religious symbol points beyond itself to reality, participates in its power, and makes intelligible its meaning. As such it goes beyond a sign or an image. The value of a symbol is its ability to elucidate; to compress into a simple, meaningful whole, readily grasped and retained; to provide a center for the shaping of conduct and belief.

Symbols are part of the language of faith, the means by which faith expresses itself when it interprets the holy, the eternal, the beyond; when it communicates the divine confrontation, claims, and demands. As such, symbolism is a part of biblical religion from its beginning.

Symbolism is the vehicle of revelation. Born in encounter, given during inspiration, symbols summarize and interpret the experience. They are created, are given, born, grow, and die amid changing circumstances. At times they appear as something new; at times they bring new significance to observances which have lost their meaning or which have been adapted from elsewhere. Taken from the realm of human experience, they relate man to that which is of ultimate concern.

1. In the OT
   a. Symbolic words
   b. Symbolic persons
   c. Symbolic objects
   d. Symbolic places
   e. Prophetic symbolism
   f. Cultic symbolism
2. In later Judaism
3. In the NT
   a. Symbolic titles
   b. Symbolism of Jesus
   c. Symbolism of salvation
   d. Symbolism of worship
   e. Symbolism of eschatology
Bibliography

1. In the OT. Among the Hebrews there was no clear-cut distinction between the sacred and the secular. The spiritual expressed itself in the physical. Thus nature and history became the spheres of revelation, and everything carried within itself the capacity for symbolic significance. Insofar as words, persons, events, or actions summed up the hopes and expectations, the meaning and significance, the past and future, of Israel's history and faith, they can be termed symbolic.

a. Symbolic words. Israel's religion was based on dialogue, a speaking-hearing relation. Her God was

(a) *"Absalom's Pillar"* in the Kidron Valley, opposite the S part of the temple's enclosure in Jerusalem. Some date it in the Maccabean period, as the burial place of Alexander Janneus; but more probably it was built in the Roman period, its architecture being Herodian. It is not, as some have suggested, a pillar erected by Absalom to immortalize himself (II Sam. 18:18).

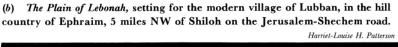

(b) *The Plain of Lebonah,* setting for the modern village of Lubban, in the hill country of Ephraim, 5 miles NW of Shiloh on the Jerusalem-Shechem road.

PLATE XXV

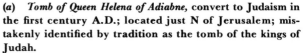

(a) *Tomb of Queen Helena of Adiabne,* convert to Judaism in the first century A.D.; located just N of Jerusalem; mistakenly identified by tradition as the tomb of the kings of Judah.

Herbert G. May

(b) *Acropolis,* or citadel of Athens, which included the Parthenon, Temple of the Wingless Victory, Erechtheum, and Propylaea.

Herbert G. May

Edward Capps, Jr.

(c) *The Great Pyramid of Gizeh,* built by Khufu in the Fourth Dynasty (*ca.* 2700 B.C.). It covers *ca.* 13 acres and is over 480 feet high, containing more than 6¼ million tons of stones.

PLATE XXVI

(a) *Temple of Bacchus,* erected at Baalbek in honor of the Roman god of the vine (Greek god Dionysus).

(b) *The Arch of Ecce Homo,* Triumphal Arch of Hadrian (A.D. 117-38), which tradition marks as the place where Pilate turned Jesus over to the Jews, saying, "Behold [here is] the man."

PLATE XXVII

(a) *Theater at Epidaurus,* considered the most beautiful in Greece with almost perfect acoustics; almost every seat in the theater remains in its original state.

(b) *Excavations at Pool of Bethesda,* where Jesus healed a man of 38 years; now identified in the Bezetha Quarter of Jerusalem, near the Tower of Antonia and the Sheep's Gate.

(c) *'Ain Feshkha,* a spring S of Khirbet Qumran, near which buildings used by the Qumran community have been excavated. The water of the spring served the community for agriculture and animal husbandry.

(d) *Bethany,* home of Mary, Martha, and Lazarus, *ca.* 1⅝ miles from Jerusalem, by the Mount of Olives; modern el-'Azariyeh.

PLATE XXVIII

Harriet-Louise H. Patterson

(a) *Jerusalem* from the Mount of Olives with the Dome of the Rock at the site of the temple, lower center of picture.

PLATE XXIX

(a)   *Temple of Apollo*, at Corinth.

(b)   *The Parthenon*, Temple of Athene on the Acropolis at Athens; built *ca.* 438 B.C. and considered the finest example of Doric architecture.

(c)   *Wadi Murabba'at* in the Wilderness of Judea, *ca.* 12 miles SW of Khirbet Qumran. From caves here have been recovered important MSS from the late first and early second centuries A.D., including a letter by Simon bar Cocheba.

PLATE XXX

(a) *Jacob's well,* scene of Jesus' conversation with a Samaritan woman, at the foot of Mount Gerizim.

Harriet-Louise H. Patterson

Joseph Saad

(b) *Cave XI,* one of the more recently discovered caves N of Khirbet Qumran, in which relatively intact MSS were discovered; looking from the inside of the cave toward the Dead Sea.

William L. Reed

(c) *Excavations* at Tell el-Far'ah (Tirzah).

PLATE XXXI

(a) *Temple of Apollo,* ruins of the most important temple erected to this god, at Delphi, Greece.

(b) *Excavations at Khirbet Qumran,* the "Dead Sea Scroll" sect community center. The round cistern (upper left of center) may go back to the time of the Judean kings, when the city was known as the "City of Salt."

(c) *Cave IV* in the vicinity of Khirbet Qumran; the largest depository of Dead Sea Scrolls.

PLATE XXXII

a speaking God. He addressed her with words. A word was more than a means of communication; it was a symbol—a dynamic, living reality—embodying the power, authority, and purpose of the speaker (Isa. 55:11; cf. Deut. 18:22; Jer. 28:9). A word was a thing, event, confrontation, claim, demand. It was this that made the work of prophet, priest, and lawgiver so significant. At climactic moments, Israel understood herself confronted by the divine word, a word promising grace and judgment, a word calling for a response—to hear and to obey. The words spoken were collected, preserved, studied, treasured; they became a lamp to the feet, a light to the path (Ps. 119:105). At the last God presented his ultimate word, the word made flesh, who fulfilled all previous words, and became the one, all-inclusive word of God to man.

The dynamic of a word is seen in BLESSINGS AND CURSINGS, which carry within them the ability to work good (Gen. 27:33-37; Num. 22:6; Ps. 129:8) or to work evil (Gen. 9:25; Num. 23:7-8; Isa. 24:6). Once the word has been spoken, the effect becomes assured.

Again, word symbolism is inherent in a NAME. A name is representative, an extension of the personality, carrying in it the soul, vitality, power, and authority of the person to whom it belongs (Exod. 3: 13-15; cf. Gen. 17:5; I Sam. 17:45). To speak in the divine name is to possess the divine Spirit (II Chr. 15:1; Isa. 61:1; Mic. 3:8), to speak with divine authority—"Thus says the Lord." To invoke the divine name is to call forth the divine power (I Kings 8:29, 33; 18:24; II Kings 5:11).

At times symbolic names were given to children, to indicate something had happened or was about to happen (cf. Shear-jashub, "a remnant shall return" [Isa. 7:3]; Immanuel, "God is with us" [Isa. 7:14]; Lo-Ammi, "not my people" [Hos. 1:9]).

Word symbolism further appears in the anthropo-, therio-, or sociomorphic manner of speaking of the deity. God could not be portrayed visually; hence he is described symbolically, so as to make comprehensible his nature and activity. He is represented with features of a man, a beast, of nature itself. His eye denotes his omniscience (Jer. 5:3; Amos 9:8) and favor (Deut. 11:12; Pss. 33:18; 34:15); his arm, his power (Exod. 15:16; Pss. Sol. 13:2); his right hand, victory, vindication (Exod. 15:6; Pss. 17: 7; 44:3). He comes in judgment like a roaring lion (Amos 3:8), an E wind (Jer. 18:17), a storm (Jer. 30:23). By all such descriptions God was made intelligible; his will and purposes made plain; and his activity, as a living force in the vicissitudes of life, made known.

b. Symbolic persons. From the beginning of Israel's history there were men who, as representatives of the tribe or nation, typified the hopes, strength, and characteristics of the group. Such were the patriarchs, as Abraham (Gen. 12:2-3; 17:4-8; Isa. 51:1-2; cf. Luke 3:8; Rom. 4:1-5, 9-12); the eponymous tribal ancestors, as Esau (Gen. 25:25; 27:39-40; Obad. 10; Mal. 1:2-5) and the sons of Jacob (Gen. 49; cf. Deut. 33); and in a minor way the charismatic leaders, as Barak, Gideon, Samuel, and Saul.

Again, the king, the anointed of the Lord, seated as regent on the divine throne (Pss. 2:6-7; 45:6), em-

bodied in himself the hopes of the nation, and was responsible for its destiny.

In a later age, despondent over her fate, bereft of faithful rulers, Israel idealized the great figures of her past and longed for their reappearance in an expected deliverer, the Messiah, who would restore her to favor with God, and to prominence among the nations. Such were Moses the lawgiver and prophet par excellence (Deut. 18:15; cf. Hos. 12:13; 1QS 9:11; John 1:21; 6:14; 7:40); Elijah the forerunner (Mal. 4:5—H 3:23; cf. Ecclus. 48:4-11; Matt. 16:14); David the king (Ezek. 34:23; 37:24; cf. Isa. 9:1-6; 11:1-5; Pss. Sol. 17:23-51); and Aaron (or Zadok) the priest (cf. Zech. 6:12-13; I Macc. 14:41; Zadokite Fragment 4:1; 1QS 9.11). The Prophet of the Exile saw the nation itself as emblematic of the coming deliverer (cf. Israel the Suffering Servant, in Isa. 49:1-6; 52:13–53:12; cf. Mark 10:45; Acts 8:32-35). All these individuals were related to Israel's destiny. Each, in his own way, represented God and man. Each was, in himself, a meeting place of the nation and God. Each carried within him all the tradition of the past, the experience of the present, and the hope of the future. And each pointed to that Coming One, who would embody all that for which they stood. The NT sees the culmination of these hopes fulfilled in Jesus. *See § 3b below.*

c. Symbolic objects. A certain symbolism, by way of association, or representation, was attached to numerous objects—objects of nature, as the pillar of witness, indicative of a covenant (Gen. 31:44-53; Josh. 24:26-27), the pillar of cloud, divine guidance (Exod. 13:21) and glory (Exod. 16:10), fire, the divine presence and glory (Exod. 3:2-6; 24:17; Lev. 16:2), guidance (Exod. 13:21), and wrath (Num. 11: 1; Deut. 4:24; cf. Heb. 12:29); cult objects, as the ark, symbolic of the covenant (Exod. 25:10-22) and the presence of God (Num. 3:31; I Sam. 4:3-8), the tables of testimony, the law (Exod. 25:16, 21; 31:18; 40:20), the altar of incense, prayer (Ps. 141:2), the altar of sacrifice, revelation (Gen. 12:7-8; 26:25; 35: 1; II Kings 16:15); personal objects, as phylacteries denoting service to God (Exod. 13:16; Deut. 6:8; 11:18), and fringes, the commandments (Num. 15: 37-41; Deut. 22:12).

Parts of the body also had certain spiritual significances. The intimate union of the spiritual and the physical in Hebrew psychology resulted in every physical organ having psychical and ethical attributes of its own: the eye, mental perception; the ear, obedience; the hand, strength; the nose, anger (cf. Exod. 15:8; II Sam. 22:9; Ps. 18:8); the heart, intellect (Prov. 14:33) and will (Prov. 16:9); the kidneys, emotions (Prov. 23:16); the bowels, love or sympathy (Song of S. 5:4); the liver, the center of life (Prov. 7:23; Lam. 2:11); blood, the principle of life (Lev. 17:11; Deut. 12:23).

d. Symbolic places. While such places as the Deep (Gen. 1:2; Prov. 8:28; Isa. 51:10; Amos 7:4), Sheol (Job 26:6; Pss. 16:10; 139:8; Amos 9:2), and the Pit (Pss. 30:3; 88:6; Isa. 14:15), as a remnant of mythology, had symbolical meaning, names of geographical sites at times became symbolic: e.g., Sodom, the seat of immorality and wickedness (Isa. 1:10; Ezek. 16: 46; Martyrdom of Isa. 3:10; cf. Rev. 11:8); Egypt, the place of bondage and evil (Hos. 11:5[?]; cf. Rev.

11:8); and Jerusalem, the holy city, God's dwelling place (Isa. 24:23; 62; Joel 2:32; Zech. 2:4, 12; 8:3; cf. Rev. 21:2, 10), also termed Zion (Isa. 2:3; 60:14; Jer. 31:6; 50:5; Joel 3:17; II Esd. 10:44). In NT times Babylon became symbolic for Rome, the seat of wickedness (cf. II Bar. 11:1; I Pet. 5:13; Rev. 17: 5; 18:10).

e. Prophetic symbolism. The prophets, more than anyone else, were responsible for the symbolism of the OT. The nature of the prophetic task and the prophetic experience, together with the intense and naïve realism of Semitic thought, made symbolism an essential element in the prophetic ministry. Visions, dreams, actions, as well as words, had an objectivity of their own enabling them to actualize the divine purpose and will. The visions of the prophets were the pledge of impending divine activity. An almond rod indicated the certainty of divine action (Jer. 1:11-12); a boiling pot, terror from the N (vss. 13-15); two baskets of figs, good and bad, the exiles and remnant in the land (ch. 24); a basket of summer fruit, the destruction of Israel (Amos 8:1-2); dry bones reclothed with flesh, Israel renewed by the Spirit of God (Ezek. 37:1-14).

Closely akin to vision are dreams which foretell the future (I Sam. 28:15; cf. Gen. 37:5-8; 40:7-13; 41:1-32; Dan. 4:13-27). Of religious significance is the dream of Nebuchadnezzar, in which a great image of gold, silver, bronze, iron, and clay is destroyed by a stone, leaving no trace, symbolizing the founding of the eternal kingdom (Dan. 2:31-45).

Of a similar nature were the prophetic actions which dramatized the divine message. We read of Samuel's tearing his mantle, a symbol that God had torn the kingdom from Saul (I Sam. 15:27-28); Ahijah's rending his garment into twelve pieces, the rending of Solomon's kingdom (I Kings 11:30-32); the striking of arrows by Joash at Elisha's command, Israel's victory over Syria (II Kings 13:15-19); Jeremiah's wearing of the yoke, Judah's bondage to Babylon (Jer. 27:2-7, 10-12); Isaiah's three-year walk in captive's garb, Egypt and Ethiopia's captivity by Assyria (Isa. 20:2); the inscribing of tribal names on wood by Ezekiel, the union of Judah and Israel (Ezek. 37:15-23). These mimetic actions indicated the future and effected its coming.

Again, the prophets made abundant use of symbolic imagery. Apart from numerous metaphors, there were figures which portrayed the meaning of Israel's existence. Such a figure was the VINE (and vineyard). The vine was an essential element in Israel's economy. It required constant care and pruning. It signified prosperity (I Kings 4:25; Mic. 4:4; Zech. 3:10) and fruitfulness (cf. Gen. 49:22; Ps. 128: 3). By means of the figure the prophets vivified the many facets of Israel's relation to God, his grace, and her apostasy. Israel was a choice vine brought out of Egypt (Ps. 80:8), the planting of the Lord (Jer. 2: 21), designed to bear fruit for God (Isa. 5:1-5). But Israel became degenerate and wild (Jer. 2:21), yielding wild grapes (Isa. 5:4, 7). Because of this she was destroyed by shepherds (Jer. 12:10) and becomes a desolation. This figure was adapted by Jesus to represent the relation between himself and his disciples. *See § 3b below.*

Another figure, as rich and versatile in depicting Israel's spiritual history, is that of a SHEEP. A sheep is dependent and helpless. It needs constant care, guidance, and protection. It is led by a voice. Without this it strays, becomes lost, a prey to the wild beasts. Israel is God's flock, the sheep of his pasture (Pss. 79:13; 100:3; Ezek. 34:6). God is their true shepherd (Ps. 23; Ezek. 34:12, 16). But he has entrusted them to the care of human shepherds (religious leaders) who have proved unfaithful and greedy (Ezek. 34: 1-10). As a consequence the sheep have gone astray, and have been scattered (Ps. 119:176; Isa. 53:6; Ezek. 23:1; Ezek. 34:5-6), doing what they desire (Ezek. 34:6), becoming lost (Jer. 50:6; Ezek. 34:11), counted for slaughter (Ps. 44:22). Finally, the Lord determines to search for them (Ezek. 34:11-16), and brings them back, carrying the lambs in his arms (Isa. 40:11).

A third figure, taken from everyday life, especially suited to convey religious truth is that of a WAY. A road, or path, indicates action (walking) and direction (conduct), and thus purpose (cf. Ps. 103:7; Isa. 26:8). The concern in life is to take the right road. For a way may lead to life (Prov. 6:23; 10:17; Jer. 21:8) or to death (Prov. 7:27; 14:12; Jer. 21:8). Israel's religious leaders were especially commissioned to point out the way she should go. Blessing was to be found in taking the right way (Ps. 1: 6; Prov. 12:28; Isa. 26:7), the way of holiness (Isa. 35:8) which leads to Zion, the way of the Lord. Israel's whole life was a walk—from Egypt to Canaan, from bondage to freedom, from death ·to life. When she lost her way, was taken captive, a way had to be prepared again (Isa. 40:3; Mal. 3:1) to enable her to come to the city of God (Isa. 35:8-9). This figure particularly emphasized that conduct had fateful implications for life. It found renewed emphasis among the Jewish sectarians (1QS 4.2; 8.13-14; 9.16-21) and the Christians. *See § 3b below.*

The lion, with its strength, its terrifying roar, its crouching and sudden leaping upon its prey, was used by the prophets to typify the divine wrath and judgment (Isa. 31:4; Hos. 5:14; 11:10). Yahweh roars from Zion (Jer. 25:30; cf. Joel 3:16[?]; Amos 1:2[?]; 3:8), striking terror in the heart of his enemies. Destruction will be sure and devastating. Only a few fragments will be left (Amos 3:12).

f. Cultic symbolism. The great cultic symbol, preempted from everyday life, was that of covenant. Covenant was the basic feature of life on all levels. Life consisted in the making of covenants. Israel's very existence was effected by a great covenant ceremony at Sinai. Here she heard the divine voice. Here she received the law. Here she knew herself to be the people of God, sworn to obedience, dedicated to service, subject to discipline, dependent on mercy. Her station in life depended on keeping covenant. Basic to her cultic and religious life, the bond of union, locus of loyalty, periodically renewed, broken, yet promised anew, the covenant became the vantage point from which the whole of Israel's history was viewed.

Cultic symbolism was often in the form of mimetic action, as the offering of first fruits, sanctifying the harvest (Exod. 23:16; 34:22; Deut. 26:1-11); the first-born, sanctifying the herds and flocks (Exod. 22:29-30; 34:19-20), bringing blessing and holiness (Deut. 15:19-23); the burnt offerings (Lev. 1:1-13) and sin offerings (4:6), renewing holiness; the Day of Atonement ceremonies (Lev. 16), bringing forgiveness.

At the great festivals, cult dramas were re-enacted which strengthened the foundation of national life. These FEASTS, of ancient agricultural origin, were adapted to Yahweh-worship and given historic and symbolic significance. Passover, thus, celebrated the exodus from Egypt and became prophetic of the new exodus and the dawn of the new day; the New Year Festival, the enthronement of God and the creation of the world, prophetic of the eschatological day of the Lord; the Feast of Weeks, the giving of the law; Tabernacles, life in the wilderness.

Closely related to ritual were the rite of CIRCUMCISION, a sign of the covenant and membership in the family of God; and the SABBATH, celebrating creation (Exod. 20:11), with its attendant rest (Deut. 5:15). Keeping sabbath later became one of the marks of true devotion to God. See WORSHIP IN THE OT.

2. In later Judaism. Postexilic and later Judaism, enhanced by allegorical exegesis, read much symbolic significance into the OT. Hidden truths were felt to lie behind the literal word (and grammar, at times) of scripture, which could be elicited only by the enlightened interpreter. The TEMPLE, its accessories, sacrifices, institutions, dietary laws, were all given symbolic import. A greater emphasis was placed on the meaning of numbers (e.g., three represents the holy, or divine; four, the earth; seven, heaven and earth, association with God; ten, completeness; see NUMBER). Figurative meaning was attributed to metals (e.g., gold, the glory of God; silver, moral innocence; brass, strength) and colors (blue, holiness; purple, royalty; white, purity; black, evil and disaster). The seven-branched candlestick was said to represent the soul; the ram's horn, the messianic; an ear of corn, the resurrection.

With the rise of apocalyptic, a weird and bizarre imagery was brought into being to describe past and future history. Historic kings and kingdoms were represented by weird beasts (Dan. 7:1-8) and horns of animals (7:24; cf. 8:8, 22). The horn of a he-goat signified Alexander the Great (8:5-8); a great ram's horn, Judas Maccabeus (Enoch 90:9); a lion's destruction of an eagle, the overthrow of Rome by the Davidic messiah (II Esd. 11). A further development was an extended angelology and demonology, and a developed eschatology with world holocaust, final judgment, and new world of bliss.

Among Jewish sects we have also a reinterpretation of certain prophetic books in line with the spiritual conditions of the day, symbolic significance being given to oracles to give them contemporary meaning (cf. the commentaries on Nahum, Habakkuk, and Micah of the Qumran sect).

3. In the NT. NT symbolism, for the most part, centers around the person of Jesus Christ, his identity, and the significance of his life and ministry. Much of the imagery has been borrowed from the OT and Jewish apocalyptic.

a. Symbolic titles. The one, all-inclusive symbol in the NT is Jesus Christ—the Anointed One, the Messiah—who sums up in himself the nation Israel, together with its expectations, the new covenant, and the new community. In him is fulfilled the function of king (Matt. 21:15; John 18:37), priest (Heb. 4:14-5:10), prophet (John 6:14; 7:40), cult (Heb. 9:1-10:25), and word (John 1:1; Heb. 1:1). By descriptive titles and figurative names, the apostles sought to convey the significance of Jesus to all classes of men, both Jew and Greek.

Most meaningful of these is perhaps that of Son (a term with Hebraic and Hellenistic affinities), by which the intimate relation of Jesus to God is typified. He is the one, unique Son, sent to gather the fruit of God's vineyard. He gives his life to redeem men and enable them to become sons of God. See SON OF GOD.

Another symbol which emphasizes Jesus' humility, and the sacrificial significance of his death, is that of the LAMB. He is the true paschal lamb (I Cor. 5:7), the "Lamb of God, who takes away the sin of the world" (John 1:29).

Closely connected with this figure is that of priest, the great contribution of the writer to the Hebrews. Christ is the one true high priest, who offers the one all-sufficient sacrifice providing permanent access to God. In him, thus, the whole of Israel's cultic religion finds its fulfilment.

Again, Jesus is termed the WORD (John 1:1), the agent of creation, revelation, and redemption. In him the power, promise, and claim of the divine word again find expression. He is the final word, to which men are challenged to respond.

Jesus is further termed Lord, a word with many religious and social affiliations. He is God in human form, Lord of the cult, the one true Master of men, claiming their allegiance, devotion, and service.

b. Symbolism of Jesus. That Jesus consistently used imagery and symbolism is the testimony of all the gospel writers. He used figures from the most common and elementary spheres of life to illustrate religious truth (see IMAGE). His primary symbol was that of the kingdom of God, the rule of God in men's hearts. This was the theme of his preaching (Matt. 4:17), the subject of his parables (ch. 13), the object of his concern. He was eager that men should see it, find the way to it, and enter it. This figure, recalling the covenant and theocracy, fulfilled in Jesus, who had come to gain a kingdom and turn it over to the Father, became the framework for viewing the whole of redemptive history, looking forward to the grand climax when Jesus shall be acclaimed "King of kings and Lord of lords."

Another symbol of Jesus is that of shepherd and sheep. To the meaning this figure had in the OT, Jesus added the significance of his mission, to give his life for those gone astray (John 10:11, 15). In distinction from the religious leaders, who were hirelings (vss. 12-13), and the false messiahs, who were thieves and robbers (vs. 8), he is the true shepherd. It is his voice they follow, he lays down his life for them, and he goes to gather other folds into the one flock of God (vs. 16).

Jesus emphasized the necessity of union with him under the symbol of the vine. His concern was for fruitful living. As branches receive life from the vine, so the disciple from Christ (John 15:4). The disciple's vitality depends on this relation; without Christ he can do nothing (vs. 5). Moreover, if there is no fruit, the branch is cut off and destroyed (vs. 6).

Again, he used the figure of the way (John 14:6). By this symbol Jesus indicated that he fulfilled the prophetic statements concerning the way (e.g., Isa. 35:8; 40:3; Mal. 3:1), provided the way of access to God, and manifested the type of conduct essential to fellowship with God (cf. Matt. 22:16). Thus Christianity became known as the Way (Acts 9:2; 19:9, 23; 22:4) and Christians, those of the Way.

c. Symbolism of salvation. The chief symbol of salvation is the Cross, in which much of the theology of the NT converges. The message of the Cross is the power of God (I Cor. 1:18), for the Cross is the way of salvation (Gal. 6:14; cf. Col. 2:14), the means of uniting the divided segments of humanity (Eph. 2: 16; cf. Col. 1:20), and the way of life for the Christian (cf. Matt. 10:38; 16:24; Mark 8:34; 10:39; Luke 9:23; 14:27). Since the NT era, the Cross has become the one universal symbol of salvation through Christ, emphasizing both his death for the sins of the world and the new life he gives to men.

When describing the reality of salvation, the NT writers use a variety of symbolic terms: "justification," a legal term for a sentence of acquittal (Rom. 4:25; 5:16, 18; cf. 3:24; 8:30; I Cor. 6:11); "adoption," a means of entering a family fellowship as a son (Rom. 8:15; Gal. 4:5); "ransom," manumission of a slave, or redemption of a prisoner (Matt. 20:28; Mark 10:45; cf. Eph. 1:7; Col. 1:14; I Tim. 2:6; Heb. 9:15); "expiation," restoration of fellowship, or removal of guilt, through sacrifice (Rom. 3:25; I Cor. 5:7).

The redeemed community is called the body of Christ, emphasizing: "Where Christ is, there is the church." By this figure is emphasized the church's corporate nature and servile function.

Again, the church is termed the bride of Christ, typifying its intimate union with Christ and its subservient status.

d. Symbolism of worship. The symbolism of worship comes to the fore in the sacraments. Each of the sacraments is a dramatic portrayal of the gospel, embodying mimetic overtones. In BAPTISM water signifies the triumph over the forces of evil (passing through the waters with its threat on life, reminiscent of crossing the Reed Sea; I Cor. 10:1-2; cf. Ps. 74:13; Isa. 51:9-10); the passing from death to life (cf. Rom. 6:4); the removal of defilement (as in the lustrations of the sectarians; cf. Acts 2:38; Tit. 3:5); and the giving of life (Rom. 6:4; Gal. 3:27; cf. John 3:5). Baptism takes the place of circumcision as the act of inauguration into the holy community (cf. I Cor. 12: 13). It is a participation in the death and resurrection of Jesus (Rom. 6:3-6; Col. 2:12). One is buried with Christ (Rom. 6:3), raised to newness of life (Rom. 6:4; Col. 2:12), and thus enters the body of Christ (I Cor. 12:13). It thus becomes an enactment of the drama of salvation.

In a similar manner the Eucharist (*see* LORD'S SUPPER) dramatizes the gospel. It is the mark of the new covenant (Matt. 26:26-29; Mark 14:22-25), recalls the fellowship meals of Jesus with his disciples (as in the love feast [Acts 2:42, 46]), proclaims the

Cross-Resurrection event (I Cor. 10:16-17; 11:23-30), and looks forward to the messianic banquet (cf. Luke 22:15-19; Did. 9-10). Here is dramatized the whole meaning of salvation, with an emphasis on the death of Christ and the new life of fellowship which follows from it.

e. Symbolism of eschatology. In the eschatology of the NT there is recourse again to apocalyptic, with its themes of heavenly worship, plagues, heavenly warfare, resurgence of evil and its destruction, resurrection, judgment scene, and restoration of bliss, under the figure of the New Jerusalem, together with weird animal symbolism and numerology. By this rewriting of history in cosmic terms, using symbolic imagery, the author sought to comfort and strengthen the church in the face of Roman persecution.

In subapostolic times one meets the symbol of a FISH (an acrostic on Ἰησοῦς Χριστός, Θεοῦ Ὑιός, Σωτήρ), representing Christ, baptism, the Resurrection, Eucharist, kingdom, and, perhaps, the power of the gospel (John 21:1-13); the SHIP, representing the church, in which the faithful are carried over the sea of life; and an elaboration of symbolic objects depicted in Christian art and architecture.

The word "symbol" has also been used to designate a summary statement of faith, as, e.g., the Roman Symbol, forerunner of the Apostles' Creed.

Bibliography. H. W. Robinson, "Hebrew Psychology," in A. S. Peake, ed., *The People and the Book* (1925), pp. 353-82; "Prophetic Symbolism," in T. H. Robinson, ed., *OT Essays* (1927), pp. 1-17. J. Pedersen, *Israel*, I-II (1926), 99-259; III-IV (1940), 112-17. A. Farrer, *A Rebirth of Images* (1949). J. Muilenburg, "The Ethics of the Prophet," in R. N. Anshen, ed., *Moral Principles of Action* (1952), pp. 527-42. A. N. Wilder, "Myth and Symbol in the NT," *Journal of Religious Thought*, vol. X, no. 2 (1953), pp. 105-23. F. E. Johnson, *Religious Symbolism* (1955)—a series of fourteen studies on symbolism by scholars in various fields. F. W. Dillistone, *Christianity and Symbolism* (1955). L. Koehler, *OT Theology* (1957), pp. 22-35, 119-26. P. Tillich, "The Word of God," in R. N. Anshen, ed., *Language, an Enquiry into Its Meaning and Function* (1957), pp. 122-33. V. H. KOOY

SYMEON sĭm'ĭ ən [Συμεών]; KJV SIMEON. **1.** With Barnabas and others, a Jewish Christian teacher and prophet in the church at Antioch, having the Gentile surname of NIGER (Acts 13:1). *See* MINISTRY; PROPHET IN THE NT.

2. The name of Simon Peter as used by James in Acts 15:14. N. TURNER

SYMMACHUS sĭm'ə kəs. A late-second-century Greek translator of the OT. According to Eusebius and Jerome, he was an Ebionite. His translation was used by Origen for the fourth column of his Hexapla.

Symmachus' translation (Symm.) shows acquaintance with and dependence on Aquila and Theodotion but constitutes a completely new, sometimes almost periphrastic, translation. Only fragments of Symm. are extant, though there are sufficient to give one an idea of his elegant, involved style.

See also SEPTUAGINT §§ 3c, 4a. J. W. WEVERS

*SYNAGOGUE [συναγωγή]. The place of assembly used by Jewish communities primarily for public worship and instruction, or the assembly itself. The Greek derivation of the term indicates simply a gathering, void of any religious connotation. With the exception of the much-debated מוֹעֲדֵי-אֵל (Ps. 74:8 Aq.), there is no mention of the synagogue edifice in the OT.

1. The name.
2. Origin
3. Expansion
   a. In Palestine
   b. In Babylonia
   c. Greco-Roman
   d. In Egypt
4. Location, orientation, architecture
5. Separation of sexes
6. Educational use
7. Furniture
8. Officers
   a. Archisynagogos
   b. Ḥazzan
   c. The "messenger"
   d. Herald of the Shema
9. Secular and semisecular use
Bibliography

1. The name. In the LXX, συναγωγή is used most frequently to render the Hebrew עֵדָה, "congregation"; occasionally it appears as the equivalent of קָהָל, "assembly." In the Hebrew ECCLESIASTICUS, עֵדָה does not always correspond to συναγωγή. Of its ten appearances, only five have συναγωγή in the Greek text. It should be noted, however, that the date of the Hebrew Ecclesiasticus is uncertain.

In the Aramaic versions of the Bible, עֵדָה is always rendered by כְּנִישְׁתָּא (Syr. כְּנִישְׁתָּא), which, like συναγωγή, means simply a gathering. The Aramaic and the Greek terms evince a close relationship of dependence; some scholars are inclined to consider the former as the model for the Greek translators.

Patterned after the Aramaic is the neo-Hebrew כְּנֶסֶת, which may mean simply a gathering. According to some writers, however, it acquired at a very early date the special meaning of an assemblage for worship and instruction, and this special sense might have been attached to the word when the gathering in Neh. 8-9 was later termed כְּנֶסֶת הַגְּדוֹלָה.

Of particular interest is the unusual form כְּנֵסִיָּה in Ab. 4.11. Some scholars see this form implied in the plural of כְּנֶסֶת, which sounds like כְּנֵסִיּוֹת; others consider the singular כְּנֵסִיָּה a later formation after the plural of כְּנֵסִיּוֹת. There is a consensus as to its meaning—namely, that it denotes association or society of any kind. However, the suggestion of Chajes that כְּנֵסִיָּה was patterned after the Greek (ek)klesia—nun and lamed being interchangeable—and has the same meaning as the Christian ekklesia, deserves consideration.

With the first century A.D. the term συναγωγή appears in Jewish sources (Philo, Josephus) and especially in the NT more and more in the sense of "place of assembly," "house of worship and instruction." About the same time the place for worship in Tannaitic literature is named בֵּית הַכְּנֶסֶת, "house of assembly." It is generally stated that in several instances the shorter form of כְּנֶסֶת alone is used; but in these places the word means the congregation, not the place of the assembly of the congregation.

It is different with the Aramaic equivalent of בֵּי כְּנִישְׁתָּא. Here, in the Palestinian sources the shorter form of כְּנִישְׁתָּא alone is predominant. The attempt to explain away the many instances in which כְּנִישְׁתָּא alone occurs is rather forced and hardly convincing. It seems that in Palestine, outside the school where בֵּית הַכְּנֶסֶת was used, the influence of the Greek term συναγωγή made itself felt and caused the people to drop the בֵּי in their own Aramaic tongue.

Another Greek name for the place of Jewish public worship is προσευχή, meaning "prayer." It is used metonymically in the sense of "house of prayer," corresponding to the Hebrew בֵּית תְּפִלָּה (Isa. 56:7). In synagogue inscriptions from Egypt (third to first century B.C.) προσευχή is the only name used. It predominates in the writings of Philo and Josephus and occurs also in the NT. The name was taken over by Latin writers of the first century A.D. under the form of proseucha (Juvenal Satires III.296).

Various scholarly attempts to construct a wall of separation between συναγωγή and προσευχή, so as to confine the latter to small chapels outside the city near the river and under open sky, fail to do justice to all the available data. Some sources seem to indicate that συναγωγή and προσευχή were used interchangeably, although this fact does not exclude the possibility that in certain sources προσευχή represents a special type of synagogue.

Probably the two terms originated in different cultural centers. Προσευχή seems to have been adopted by the Hellenistic Jews of Egypt and spread to Greece, Asia Minor, and Rome. Its use in Palestine, if any, must have been very limited. No parallel term in postbiblical Hebrew or Aramaic was coined. On the other hand, συναγωγή reflects the Palestinian scene, where we find a parallel neo-Hebrew as well as an Aramaic term adopted to designate the place of assembly for public worship.

While προσευχή is used in the third century B.C., the first mention of συναγωγή in the sense of "place of worship" is in the first century A.D. (Philo, NT). This can hardly suffice to determine the beginning of the use of the latter term.

Besides these two Greek names well known from literary and epigraphic sources, there are some names known almost exclusively from epigraphic material. They have Hebrew or Aramaic counterparts which are linked up with some biblical phrase traditionally associated with public worship. These are:

a) Τόπος, "place"; often ἅγιος τόπος, "holy place." Its Aramaic counterpart is אַתְרָא קַדִּישָׁא, found on inscriptions at ancient synagogues in Palestine. The name was suggested by certain impressive biblical scenes where מָקוֹם (Aramaic אֲתַר) appears almost as key word and is interpreted traditionally as referring to the "place of worship." The scenes are: the sacrifice of Isaac (Gen. 22:3-4, 9, 14); Jacob's dream (28:11, 16-17, 19); and the burning bush (Exod. 3:5). That these three scenes occupy a prominent place in the paintings of the Dura synagogue indicates that for Jews they were intimately associated with the synagogue.

b) Τὸ οἶκος, "the house." This term has been connected with the neo-Hebrew usage of הַבַּיִת for the temple of Jerusalem. The Aramaic counterpart is הָדֵין בֵּיתָא, which is found in two inscriptions of the Dura-Europos synagogue. The Aramaic byt' is retained in some of the Iranian inscriptions, which seems to indicate that *byt'* was a well-established technical term for "synagogue." The name might have been suggested by the scene of Solomon's prayer (I Kings 8:22 ff), where "this house" is repeatedly associated with "prayers and supplications." Also here "house" is alternated with "place," another name for "synagogue."

c) The name σαββατεῖον, mentioned in the edict of Emperor Augustus (Jos. Antiq. XVI.vi), is generally taken to mean "synagogue," and it is assumed that it owed its name to the fact that there were only sabbath services in connection with the reading of the Torah. At the beginning of the Christian era Valerius Maximus appears to have confused the Jews with the worshipers of the Phrygian deity Sabbazius. This confusion would be understandable if the Jewish place of worship in Rome had been known by the name of Sabbateion. No Hebrew or Aramaic counterpart of this name is known; only later Syriac has a corresponding name: בית שבתא (plural בית שבי).

Returning to συναγωγή and especially to its Hebrew counterpart, we note that כנסת ישראל is used to designate the whole body of Israel, the totality of the adherents of the Jewish faith. Similarly συναγωγή is used in the writings of the church fathers as meaning the totality of the Jewish world and forming an antithesis to the *ekklesia,* which was the whole body of the Christian world. The idiom כנסת ישראל, as well as its concept, is rare in the Tannaitic period but is a familiar feature in the post-Tannaitic haggadic and midrashic literature.

All available data point to the fact that συναγωγή obtained its final Jewish stamp during the rise of the Christian community, which assumed the name ἐκκλησία (*see* CHURCH, IDEA OF). By what means could these two neutral, seemingly synonymous, terms have become symbols of two opposite camps? This problem lies at the bottom of the best studies on the subject. Most scholars follow Vitringa's direction: they seek the solution by shifting our attention from the Greek terms to the corresponding Hebrew terms, עדה and קהל. With only slight variations in detail, they agree that the Christian choice of קהל (*ekklesia*) was due to its association with קהל יהוה ("the community summoned by Yahweh") and to the reminiscence of יום הקהל ("day of assembly"), the unique religious experience on Sinai. עדה–συναγωγή, they assert, was more fitting for a legalistic, semisecular Jewish community. But another and, in some ways, more plausible way of explaining the Christian choice, based on the Greek usage of the word, has been proposed by J. Y. Campbell (*see* bibliography under CHURCH, IDEA OF).

Jewish scholars endeavor to show that עדה and קהל, as well as their Greek counterparts, were used interchangeably and that the Christian choice of ἐκκλησία was due to the need of an external mark of distinction from the Jewish community. Attempts have been made to combine the two views as representing two stages in the development of the early Christian community in Palestine.

All these theories have this in common: they focus attention on the term ἐκκλησία adopted by the Christian community and take the use of συναγωγή for the Jewish community, or place of Jewish worship, as a

matter of course, which needs no further investigation. And yet if we bear in mind how little use Philo and Josephus made of συναγωγή, the later universal use of the term, especially in the relations between Christians and Jews, requires some explanation.

The following suggestion may be ventured: About the beginning of the first century A.D., the word συναγωγή came into disrepute and was used by Gentiles with an air of contempt, because it was considered as part of the Judeo-Greek lingo. One learns of the disrepute of the Greek language spoken by the Jews from the remarks of Cleomede (first century B.C.?) that Epicure's vulgar expressions derive in part from the very low Jewish jargon. Cultured Hellenistic Jews shunned the term, as did the Greek-speaking Christians; they preferred the more reputable synonym ἐκκλησία. But the Jews clung tenaciously to συναγωγή. Undoubtedly there were various emotional motives for this attachment, but one of them was probably the echo, the assonance of Sinai. One should bear in mind that assonance played an important role in the LXX. Through the association of συναγωγή with Sinai—the very symbol of the OT—the term lent itself perfectly as a shibboleth to distinguish the Jewish community and its place of worship from the new Christian community, which asserted that the Sinai covenant had been superseded by the new covenant. This surmise would explain satisfactorily the fact that, as reported by Epiphanius, the Ebionites, who were opposed to the rejection of the law or Sinai covenant, insisted on calling their congregations and places of worship "synagogues" and not "ekklesia." They wanted to proclaim their loyalty to Sinai thereby.

2. Origin. The beginnings of the synagogue cannot be certainly recovered; rabbinic sources offer no clue whatsoever. Various passages in the TARGUM, especially that of Pseudo-Jonathan, and in the MIDRASH imply the existence of the synagogue from the very inception of the Jewish people. The same idea is ascribed to the apostle James in Acts 15:21. Philo (*Life of Moses* III.17) and Josephus (Apion II.xvii.75) state clearly that the institution goes back to Moses.

None of these writers conceived the synagogue as a man-made institution, owing its existence to certain internal and external factors. It was in the sixteenth century that Carolus Sigonius, an expert in the field of political institutions of the Greeks and Romans, endeavored to treat the institutions of the "republic of the Hebrews" in the same perspective. His terse statement on the synagogue contains some of the salient points of the still dominant view: "The origin of the synagogue is by no means an old one. We find, indeed, no mention of it [in scripture] either in the history of the Judges or in the history of the Kings. If it is at all admissible to venture a conjecture in this kind of antiquity, I would surmise that synagogues were first erected in the Babylonian exile for the purpose that those who have been deprived of the TEMPLE of Jerusalem, where they used to pray and teach, would have a certain place similar to the temple, in which they could assemble and perform the same kind of service. The same, I think, did the other Jews in the DISPERSION, be it in Asia or in Egypt or in Europe. It was for this reason that the custom of synagogues was first established in the provinces where there was no temple. After the return from Babylon and the restoration of the temple of Jerusalem, the Jews still retained the well-established institution of the synagogue, namely so that while the residents of the city of Jerusalem attended the reading of the Law in the temple, all those coming to the city from the provinces attended the reading of the Law in their respective synagogues."

The Dutch scholar Hugo Grotius strenuously defended the traditional view of the Mosaic origin of the synagogue, and throughout the seventeenth century these two opposing views were kept in balance. Finally, through the work of Vitringa, the scales turned decidedly in favor of the school of Sigonius.

Though endorsing the main thesis of this school, Vitringa, and especially his followers in the nineteenth century, recognized that the Babylonian exile was not the proper place for the establishment of the synagogue as a universally accepted institution; more positive factors and more favorable circumstances were required. It was the Persian period, the period of the activities of Ezra and his successors, the scribes (*see* SCRIBE), which brought to fruition the work begun in the Babylonian exile. This theory is still the standard view among scholars. It should be noted that Krochmal, Zunz, and Graetz, on the one side, and Wellhausen and Schürer, on the other, have greatly contributed to this standardization. For one reason or another they all set the beginning of the synagogue in the Babylonian exile but its consolidation in Palestine as a result of Ezra's work.

What continued to baffle Vitringa and his followers was the fact that express mention of the synagogue could not be found in Hebrew literature before the last century of the second temple. This led some scholars to seek the origin of the synagogue in a much later period. According to them, the idea of regularly weekly assemblies was conceived first by the Jews living in the Hellenistic world, especially in Alexandria, where they came in touch with Greek religious associations (*thiasae*) and the collegia of the Romans, which held meetings every seventh day. The Jews organized sabbatical meetings in special assembly places after the pattern of the *thiasae*. This institution was transplanted first to Galilee, which had a considerable Hellenistic element, and finally, in the Maccabean period, to Jerusalem, where it underwent a profound transformation. This theory has been rejected generally, but it still deserves consideration.

Another discordant voice, this time in the opposite direction, was that of Leopold Löw. He challenged the very basis of the standard view—i.e., that from the beginning the synagogue was a place of worship, taking the place of the temple, the center of sacrificial worship. The origin, he said, is not to be sought in the sphere of religious ritual but in the secular realm of municipal life. Already in the pre-exilic period there was a special building in Jerusalem where public meetings of the city were held. There the prophets would deliver their orations, giving to the assembly a religious coloring. Gradually the meeting place was transformed into a synagogue. The name of the embryo synagogue was בֵּית עָם, "house of the people" (cf. Jer. 39:8).

Löw's suggestion was dismissed in passing by the representatives of the standard view. However, his main thesis of the secular origin of the synagogue has been revived and modified in certain scholarly circles in America.

The new trend in biblical studies toward a more conservative dating of portions of scripture could not fail to exercise an influence on the dating of the synagogue. Ps. 74:8 is almost the only constant in the flux of the arguments of the various theories. For nearly two centuries this psalm was assigned to the Maccabean period. Recently this date was challenged, and some scholars moved it to the fifth century B.C. Obviously, the date of the origin of the synagogue had to shift accordingly. Indeed, following a tip by Wellhausen that the synagogues represent a survival of the *bamoth* (local shrines), these scholars surmised that some of the *bamoth* never ceased to be places of worship but that soon after the reformation of 621 B.C. they underwent a transformation from sacrificial to synagogal worship. The synagogue is made a direct descendant of the reformation.

The tendency to deflate the importance of the Babylonian captivity for the history of Israel and to rehabilitate the people who remained in Palestine after the last deportation of 587 B.C. has affected our subject also. Aside from the extreme view, which would confine the whole Exile in the realm of fiction, there is the moderate school which, admitting that the deportation to Babylon was a substantial one and that the deported formed the backbone of the political and cultural life of the nation, nevertheless insists that Palestine remained the central scene of the history of Israel. There the Deuteronomistic work (*see* DEUTERONOMY) continued during the Exile, and its most impressive religious document was produced. In rehabilitating Palestine as the center of the Deuteronomistic activity, the representatives of this school of thought seek the origin of the synagogue here also. They aver that the well-marked features of the Deuteronomistic orations have all the appearances of institutional character and represent the prototype of synagogal worship.

In these several theories the temple of Jerusalem, with its sacrificial ritual, appears as a negative force which had to be curbed to make room for the synagogue. We may examine now an attempt to derive the synagogue from the ritual of the temple. According to this hypothesis, the synagogue owes its existence to the institution known by the name of *maamadoth*. It consisted in the division of the lay population into twenty-four groups (posts) whose task it was to send alternately every week representatives to the temple to be present at the daily sacrifices. Since they could not take an active part in the ritual, these lay representatives developed a parallel synagogal worship and gave rise to a synagogue within the precincts of the temple. Through the connection of these lay representatives with their constituents, the institution spread rapidly. The suggestion is hardly tenable, however, because the institution of the *maamadoth* is probably much later than the establishment of the synagogue.

The discoveries of the nineteenth century contributed little, if anything, to the formulation of the above theories. Noteworthy, therefore, is an effort to find a clue to the origin of the synagogue in the ELEPHANTINE PAPYRI,* discovered at the beginning of the twentieth century. These papyri brought to light two facts: (*a*) the existence of a Yahweh temple with sacrifices in Egypt during the fifth century B.C.; (*b*) strong, occasionally violent, opposition on the part of the local religious authorities to animal sacrifices. If one assumes that the Elephantine Yahweh temple was not an isolated relic of "old, popular religion," but rather the normal pattern of worship of the Jews in the Diaspora after the destruction of the first temple of Jerusalem, it seems logical to consider the synagogue as a transformed Yahweh temple. The process of transformation is explained as follows: The Yahweh temples in the Diaspora (*see* DISPERSION) did not pretend to be places of worship in their own right but merely representatives of the only rightful temple of Jerusalem. As such, the temples were supposed to be realistic copies of the temple with all its ritual. Only under the impact of external obstacles, as in Elephantine, and of internal development did the realism of the representation wane, to be replaced by one more spiritual and symbolical. Fig. ELE 25.

None of these theories tells the whole complex story of the origin of the synagogue, but each one throws some light on the subject and deserves consideration.

3. Expansion. Data concerning ancient synagogues are derived from the NT, Hellenistic writings (Philo and Josephus), earlier rabbinic writings, and archaeological and epigraphical material.

a. In Palestine. At the time of Jesus a synagogue within the precincts of the temple of Jerusalem, in the "hall of the hewn stones," is attested by Tannaitic texts (M. Yom. VII.1; Tosef. Suk. IV.5; P.T. Suk. 54*a*). It seems to have been primarily a place for the "reading of the Law" and adjoined a "house of study," where, it is surmised, Jesus was found "sitting among the teachers, listening to them and asking them questions" (Luke 2:46). The existence of several synagogues outside the temple is substantiated by Acts 6:9; 24:12; Tosef. Meg. III.6.

The Theodotus Inscription* found on the hill Ophel, SW of Jerusalem, points to a synagogue of a foreign group. It reads: "Theodotus, son of Vetenus, priest and archisynagogos, grandson of an archisynagogos, built the synagogue for the reading of the Law and for the teaching of the commandments and the guest house and the rooms and supplies of water as an inn for those who are in need when coming from

abroad, which synagogue his fathers and the elders and Simonides founded." The name Vetenus, as well as the special concern for those coming from abroad, gave rise to the much-debated hypothesis of the identification of the Ophel synagogue with that of the Libertini (or Freedmen). It would suggest also that the synagogue was built primarily for pilgrims coming from Rome. The titular head, Theodotus, might have been the recognized authority of the Jews of Rome and could well be identified with Theudas of Rome. Theudas, according to rabbinic sources, was not only the head of Roman Jewry, but he was also respected in Palestine for his generosity in supporting students and scholars there. Therefore, was the best-qualified patron of a synagogue with the explicit purpose of "reading the Law and teaching the commandments." Fig. SYN 94.

The later rabbinic tradition that at the time of the

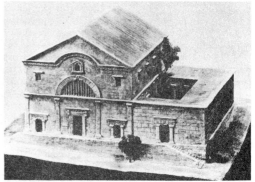

95. Model of an ancient synagogue at Capernaum, built in the third century A.D.

96. Interior of synagogue in Capernaum

94. Theodotus inscription, from a Jerusalem synagogue

97. Reconstruction showing the interior of the Capernaum synagogue

98. Wall benches in the Capernaum synagogue

destruction of the temple there were 480 synagogues in Jerusalem and that each of them had (probably in the sense of "consisted of") a house for reading the Law and a house of study of the Mishna echoes the formula of the Theodotus Inscription and probably refers mainly to synagogues of foreign groups.

In the first century A.D. most cities and bigger villages must have had some kind of synagogue (cf. Matt. 4:23; 9:35). Two of the Galilean synagogues are singled out: (a) The synagogue of Nazareth where Jesus went, "as his custom was, on the sabbath day. And he stood up to read" (Luke 4: 16); (b) The synagogue of Capernaum where "he was teaching them on the sabbath" (vs. 31). When ruins of the synagogue of Tell-Umm (Capernaum)* were discovered in the nineteenth century, few scholars

could resist the temptation of identifying the synagogue with that in which Jesus taught. Only a thorough examination revealed that the structure could not be dated earlier than the end of the second century. But it is possible, and even probable, that the earlier synagogue stood on the same site. Like the synagogues in Jerusalem, those outside appear in the NT mainly as places of "reading" and "teaching." Figs. SYN 95-98.

Two synagogues which played a part in the events of the last Jewish war against Rome are mentioned by Josephus: (a) The synagogue of Caesarea. Its desecration, perpetrated by the Greek population of the city, marked the beginning of the Jewish revolt in A.D. 66 (Jos. War II.xiv.4-5). (b) The great *proseuche* in Tiberias, a "huge building capable of accommodating a large crowd." Here the party hostile to Josephus held political assemblies disguised under the convocation of public fast ceremonies (Jos. Life LIV-LV). Tannaitic sources mention a synagogue in Tiberias as the subject of a heated halakic controversy (M. 'Er. X.10; P.T. Sheḳ. II.8). The number of synagogues in Tiberias increased in the third century, after it became the seat of Judah I, the Prince, and his academy. According to tradition, there were thirteen synagogues there in the fourth century (T.B. Ber. 8a). Some of these belonged to foreign groups.

The second major center in Galilee, Sepphoris, likewise the seat of Judah I for a certain period, presents a similar configuration of synagogues in the third century. There was a "great synagogue," which is mentioned in Tannaitic sources as having imitated

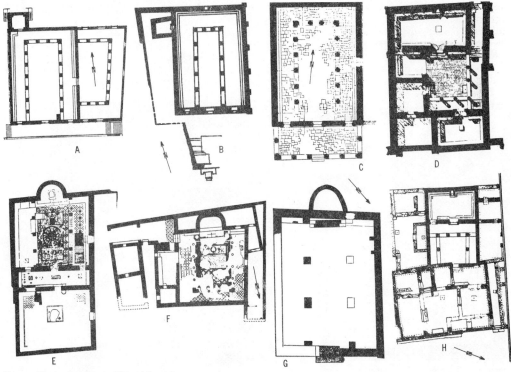

99. Plans of ancient synagogues: (A) Capernaum; (B) Chorazin; (C) Kefr Bir'im; (D) early synagogue at Dura-Europos; (E) Beth Alpha; (F) Hamath-by-Gadara; (G) near ancient Jericho; (H) later synagogue at Dura-Europos

Courtesy of the Magnes Press, the Hebrew University, Jerusalem, Israel

100. Mosaic in the synagogue at Beth Alpha, showing
the zodiac and seasons

From Sukenik, *Ancient Synagogues in Palestine and Greece* (The British Academy, Schweich Lectures, 1930); courtesy of the Hebrew University, Jerusalem, Israel

101. Reconstruction showing the interior of the Beth
Alpha synagogue, near Mount Gilead (sixth century A.D.)

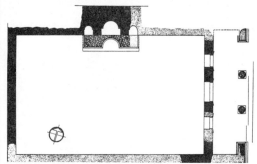

From Kohl and Watzinger, *Antike Synagogen in Galilaea* (Berlin: Der Deutschen Orient-Gesellschaft)

103. Floor plan of the Eshtemoa synagogue, Palestine

the temple worship on fast days (Tosef. Ta'an. I.10; Pesiḳ. dRK 136*b*). Sepphoris had synagogues of foreign groups also.

Archaeological excavations in Palestine have brought to light some odd remains of about fifty synagogues in smaller cities and villages.* Most of them are located in Galilee (Lower and Upper); a number are E of the Sea of Galilee in Transjordan. All indications are that they were erected after the bulk of the Jewish population moved to Galilee, with Tiberias as its center (end of the second century onward). Fig. SYN 99.

Of special interest are Capernaum and Chorazin, because, in addition to their role in the NT, they represent the earlier basilical type of synagogue without apse. On the other side, Beth-Alpha is the best-preserved representative of the later, Byzantine basilical type with apse.* Equally important is the synagogue in the S of Hebron, Eshtemoa,* because of

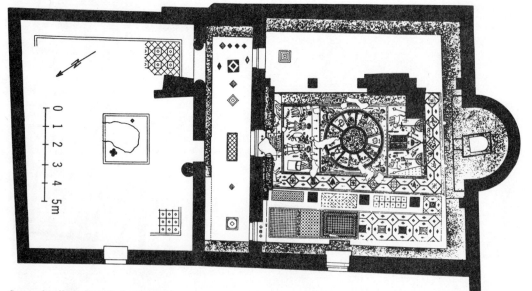

Courtesy of the Hebrew University, Jerusalem, Israel

102. Floor plan of the Beth Alpha synagogue

its deviations from the classical basilical type and its adoption of certain elements of the Babylonian non-basilical syhagogue. Figs. SYN 100-102, 103.

Data about these synagogues, including lists of them, can be found in works by S. Klein, J.-B. Frey, and E. Goodenough, listed in the *bibliography*.

b. In Babylonia. Very few literary records of ancient synagogues have come down to us from Babylonia. In the third century Nahardea, the Jerusalem of Babylonia, had, either in the city or nearby, a synagogue by the name of Shaf-Yetib (T.B. Meg. 29a). One tradition traces its origin to the exiled Judean king Jehoiachin, who allegedly built the synagogue with stones from the temple of Jerusalem. Some historians are inclined to believe that there is a historical kernel in this tradition. This synagogue

Courtesy of Yale University

106. Synagogue at Dura-Europos, showing the Torah shrine (*a*), elder's seat (*b*), and benches (*c*)

Courtesy of Yale University

104. Synagogue at Dura-Europos; the Torah shrine with the decorations of its façade

From *Syria*, III; by permission of the Librairie Orientaliste Paul Geuthner, Paris

105. Fresco from Dura-Europos synagogue

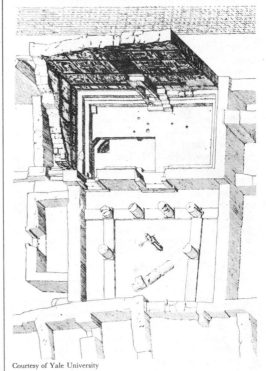

Courtesy of Yale University

107. Isometric drawing of the synagogue at Dura, by H. Pearson

had the reputation of the "presence of the Shekinah." Another synagogue with the same reputation was that of Hucal. Mention is made also of a Daniel synagogue where people used to come from distant places to attend sabbath services (T.B. 'Er. 21a). From the fourth and fifth centuries the following synagogues are mentioned: synagogue of Abi-Gubair ('Er. 61b); synagogue of the Jews of Rome in Mahuza (T.B. Meg. 26b); synagogue of Mata-Mehasya (T.B. Shab. 11a; Meg. 26a; B.B. 3b).

None of these was connected with teaching activity; almost always they appear as places for prayer. Only in Sura the "house of study" of Rab (first half of second century) seems to have been also the "synagogue of the school of Rab" (T.B. Meg. 29a). Rab transplanted many Palestinian customs to Sura.

Until recently no archaeological and epigraphical

material of any Babylonian synagogue was known. In 1934 excavations in Dura-Europos brought to light remains of a synagogue which are termed the "most revealing archaeological monument of the history of ancient synagogues." The preservation of the W orientation wall, with the *aedicula* (Torah receptacle) and the paintings, offers an insight into the making of the ancient synagogue in the East. Figs. SYN 104-107; ART 84.

c. Greco-Roman. The NT and abundant epigraphical material are the chief sources for the synagogues in the Greco-Roman world. The following synagogues are mentioned in Acts in connection with Paul's missionary activity: Damascus, Syria (9:2, 20); Salamis, Cyprus (13:5); Antioch of Pisidia (13:14); Iconium, Phrygia (14:1); Philippi, Macedonia (16:13); Thessalonica (17:1); Beroea (17:10-11); Athens (17:17); Corinth (18:4); Ephesus (18:19; 19:8). To these may be added Antioch, Syria. According to Josephus, the votive offerings carried off from the temple of Jerusalem by Antiochus Epiphanes were restored there by his successors and placed in the synagogue of Antioch (War VII.iii.3). The synagogue here took the place of the temple of Jerusalem.

d. In Egypt. Here the synagogue developed against the background of the Elephantine temple of Jao in the fifth century B.C. and the Onias temple in Leontopolis (165 B.C.–A.D. 73). Both left only slight marks on the synagogue.

Aside from the well-known "Great Basilica," of which a Tannaitic source of the second century (Tosef. Suk. IV.6) gives a vivid, though exaggerated, description and which was conceived as a counterpart of the Herodian temple, there were in the first century several other synagogues in the different quarters of the city of Alexandria (Philo *On the Special Laws* 20). They seem to have been dedicated to the ruling authorities.

Then there is epigraphical evidence of five synagogues in Lower Egypt and four in Middle Egypt. As far as we know, the earliest is the inscription from Schedia: "In honor of King Ptolemy and Queen Berenice . . . the Jews (dedicate) this *proseuche*." The consensus of scholars is that it refers to Ptolemy III (Euergetes I; 246-221 B.C.). Other dedicatory inscriptions of the same pattern are those of Xenephyris and of Nitri. All these commemorative inscriptions reflect clearly the sacral character of the *proseuche*-synagogue of Egypt.

There are a few examples from the Greco-Roman world outside Egypt. From Acmonia, Phrygia, comes this inscription: "This house, erected by Julia Severa, Gaios Tyrronios Klado, archisynagogos for life, and Lucius, son of Lucius, archisynagogos, and Popilios Rufus, archon, have restored, partly out of their own expenses, partly out of offerings [by others]. They repaired the walls and the roof; they consolidated the doors and refashioned the whole ornamentation. Wherefore the congregation [synagogue] honored them with a gilden shield because of their virtuous conduct and also because of their benevolence and zeal toward the congregation." The suggested date of this inscription is the first century. Another comes from Phokaia, Jonia, and is dated 60-80. In both of them the synagogue is called "the house" (τò οἶκος) and not *proseuche*. Two later inscriptions from Apa-

maia, Syria, and Sides, Pamphylia, show an interest in mosaic ornamentation.

No structural remains of any ancient synagogue have been discovered in Rome, but the rich epigraphical material from the catacombs yielded the names of thirteen synagogues in the first three centuries A.D. The four earliest are named after ruling persons: Augustus, Agrippa, Herod, and perhaps Voluminus, procurator of Syria and friend of Herod. These synagogues were probably built "in honor" of their patrons in the same way the earlier Egyptian synagogues were built "in honor" of the Ptolemies. A fifth synagogue of this kind, the "synagogue of Severus in Rome," where a special Torah scroll was preserved, is mentioned in rabbinic writings (Gen. Rabbati 45.8). It is assumed that it refers to Alexander Severus (222-35). The synagogue of the "people of Acra of Lebanon" has been also suggested to be identical with the "synagogue of Severus," since Acra was the birthplace of Alexander Severus. Three synagogues are named after various districts of Rome: Subura, Campi (Campo Marte), and Calcarenses. Then there are three of foreign groups: the Hebrews, the Tripolitanians, and the people from Acra of Lebanon, mentioned above. According to one scholar, the "synagogue of Elaia" found in the inscriptions refers to those coming from the province of Asia, also another synagogue of a foreign group. Much debated is the "synagogue of the *vernaculi*"; the same scholar claims that it was the synagogue of the natives of Rome, in contradistinction to the many synagogues of foreign origin.

In one respect these inscriptions reveal an affinity between Rome and Alexandria (or Egypt in general). In both places the synagogue in its earlier stage was built under the patronage of the ruling person. This bestowed upon the building a cultic character, a reflection of the temple of Jerusalem. On the other hand, there seems to be a difference between the synagogue in these two places: In Egypt the term *proseuche* is used exclusively, while in Rome the name *synagogue* seems to have been adopted. This latter term is always used, however, in the sense of "congregation" or "assembly" and not in the sense of "place of prayer." The building was called *proseuche* (Juvenal) among the native Jews, and *sinagoge* among the immigrants from Palestine, who belonged to the "synagogue of the Hebrews."

4. Location, orientation, architecture. Most of the controversies concerning these matters have to do with the interpretation of certain rabbinic rulings and their harmonization with archaeological finds.

The authoritative rabbinic canon, the Mishna, has no tractate dealing with the synagogue. Legislation regarding the synagogue is confined to a small fraction—the first three paragraphs—of the third chapter of Tractate Megillah, and here there is not a single regulation pertinent to position, orientation, and architecture. It seems to indicate that the central authorities in Palestine in the first century A.D., who laid the foundation of this code, did not consider these subjects a matter of their concern. The few earlier rabbinic rulings come from the Tosefta, a compilation which consists, in the main, of splinters of old, mostly rejected, rulings and customs, combined with later additions to the Mishna. Under no circumstances should these regulations be considered *eo ipso* authoritative.

One regulation fixes the "highest point of the city" as the site for the synagogue (Tosef. Meg. IV.23). Modern scholars consider it as the sanction of an ancient custom of selecting a place of worship on hills. It stems also from the endeavor to make the synagogue resemble the temple of Jerusalem, which stood upon the crest of a mountain. In accordance with this ruling, most of the ancient Galilean synagogues were built on high, commanding points. Yet the ruling did not find its way into the Mishna and is almost entirely ignored in Palestinian sources.

"Field synagogues," built on free places outside the city in the Amoraic period (third-fifth centuries), are asserted in some sources. Most modern scholars confine the custom to Babylonia and attribute its origin to the alleged destruction of the synagogues in the cities during the beginning of the Sassanian rule. But the existence of this custom is very doubtful; except for subtle Talmudic and midrashic "hints," there is no evidence to sustain it.

On more solid grounds rests the assertion that in the first century A.D. the custom spread of selecting the site of the synagogue in the proximity of water. The adduced rabbinic "hints" are vague and uncertain, but there are sufficient nonrabbinic sources attesting an ancient habit among Jews to recite prayers near rivers or the seashore (Acts 16:13; Philo *Flaccus* 14; Jos. Antiq. XIV.x.23). Since most of the evidence refers to communities in Egypt and Greece, scholars are inclined to confine the custom to Hellenistic Jewry. Generally it is traced back to the ancient belief of the presence of God in water; its attribution to the need of water for ablution is a later rationalization.

According to the general view, the orientation was determined from the very beginning by the principle of the orientation of the worshiper during prayer: "Those standing outside the land of Israel should turn their heart [='mind'; P.T. 'face'] towards the land of Israel; those in the land of Israel should turn their *heart* toward Jerusalem, etc. . . . As a result, those in the North [of Jerusalem] turn their face to the south; those in the south turn their face to the north; those in the east turn their face towards the west, those in the west, towards the east, so that all of Israel pray toward one and the same place" (Tosef. Ber. III.15-16). Thus it was thought that the wall opposite the entrance should face Jerusalem, in order that the worshiper, entering the synagogue, would face Jerusalem. This arrangement, which was dominant through the Middle Ages, still prevails.

Yet a different principle seems to be implied in this ruling: "The doorways of the synagogue should be made in the east side, in accordance with the entrance of the Tent of Meeting which was in the east" (Tosef. Meg. IV.22). Here the W seems to be set as the principle of orientation, irrespective of the position of the synagogue toward Jerusalem. Medieval Jewish authorities, as well as modern scholars, with the exception of Löw, could not conceive that there might have been a segment in the rabbinic world which would not recognize Jerusalem as the principle of orientation, and therefore they surmised that the ruling contemplates only Babylonian synagogues, E of Palestine. It seems more reasonable to admit that the ruling reflects the view of a certain group who considered the similarity of the synagogue with the sanctuary the overruling principle.

It should be noted that the ancient synagogues in Palestine were of two types: the earlier (second and third centuries) with orientation toward the entrance, marked by a monumental façade facing Jerusalem; the later type with orientation toward the side opposite the entrance, which was marked by a receptacle for the Torah shrine facing Jerusalem. The discovery of the synagogue in Dura-Europos showed that in the East orientation of the second type was well established already in the first half of the third century, at a time in which the earlier type of orientation was dominant in Palestine. The second type cannot be considered a "later" development of the first.

The search for a line of development of synagogal architecture which would enable us to assign to each of the discovered types its proper place and date is still at the stage of mere speculation.

It seems clear that any regulations which would promote specific synagogal architecture must have as point of reference the temple of Jerusalem or the Aaronic tabernacle. As long as the temple existed, Palestine had no need to endow its synagogues with features of the temple and to bestow upon them a sacral character. The synagogues were confined to "reading the Law and teaching the commandments." Hence, there is a lack of regulations concerning synagogal architecture in the Mishnaic code.

The Jews of the DISPERSION, deprived of direct contact with the temple, endeavored to establish contact through the synagogue by adopting certain stylistic features of the temple. Two areas came into consideration: the exterior—its architectural forms and ornamentation—and the interior with its sacred symbols.* In the Hellenistic world, especially in Alexandria, where the external splendor of the temple was highly appreciated and admired (ARISTEAS), the imitation of the architectural grandeur of the Herodian temple seemed to be the best link between temple and synagogue. This gave rise, probably at the beginning of the first century A.D., to the basilical style with its monumental façade, as we know it from the earlier Galilean synagogues. Indeed, in the rabbinic tradition the "basilica" of Alexandria, which was used also as a synagogue, appears in juxtaposition to the temple. At times this equation of temple and synagogue seems to have offered the Hellenized leaders an excuse to introduce animal and human figures in the ornamentation of the synagogue—a fact which could not fail to provoke the protest of the more conservative rabbinic teachers. An ultra-conservative circle in Palestine seems to have condemned not only the excesses of equation but also the very idea of similarity, which might cause the temple to be supplanted by the synagogue (cf. Josh. 22:7 ff). From this circle came the much-discussed halachah: "One shall not make a house after the pattern of the temple, nor a porch after the temple porch, nor a courtyard like that of the temple, nor a table like the temple table, nor a menorah like that of the temple" (T.B. Men. 28*b*). This halachah makes sense when directed against synagogues of the Gali-

From Kohl and Watzinger, *Antike Synagogen in Galilaea*
(Berlin: Der Deutschen Orient-Gesellschaft)

108. Stone from the synagogue at Eshtemoa, showing
seven-branched lampstand

From Sukenik, *Ancient Synagogues in Palestine and Greece* (The British Academy,
Schweich Lectures, 1930); courtesy of the Hebrew University, Jerusalem, Israel

109. Ark(?) on the frieze of the Capernaum synagogue

lean type, where the basilical "house" (οἶκος = "synagogue"), with its porch, courtyard, and Menorah,
was made after the pattern of the temple. This radical trend did not prevail, though it lingered on
to emerge again in the tenth century among the
Karaites. Figs. SYN 108-9; ART 82-83.

At the same time (*ca.* the first century A.D.)
another pattern of synagogue was taking shape in
Babylonia. Because of geographical, political, and
cultural circumstances, the external features of the
temple were not an effective medium of contact; so
the Babylonians turned to the interior and adopted
the holiest symbols, the ark and the Menorah, as the
most effective links between temple and synagogue.
Accordingly, the interior, where these symbols were
placed, became the focal point for the worshiper as
well as for the architect, whose artistic creativity concentrated on the aedicula, the repository of the holy
ARK OF THE COVENANT and the Menorah (*see* LAMP-
STAND). This type of synagogue was also opposed
strongly by the ultraconservatives (cf. the much debated saying of Rabbi Ishmaelben Eleazar in Shab.
32*a*).

The detached and at times hostile attitude of the
Palestinian authorities toward both types of synagogal structure underwent a basic change in the
middle of the second century, for after the suppression of the Bar Cocheba Uprising (135), Palestinian
Jewry also had to resign itself to organizing its reli-

gious life without temple. Thus the need was felt to
transform the simple "houses for reading the Law
and teaching the commandments" into "little sanctuaries." Of course, this called for a synagogal architecture similar to the temple, the "great" sanctuary,
and Palestine had two types from which to choose:
the monumental façade outside (Greco-Roman) and
the holy ark inside (Babylonian). As part of the
Greco-Roman world, Palestine adopted first, in the
main, that pattern. But there were also synagogues
of "Babylonians" in Palestine in the third century
which were probably built after the Babylonian pattern and could not fail to exercise considerable influence. Thus we find various tentative efforts to
combine the two basic elements, façade and ark (Eshtemoa, Nawa, Sheiq el-Abreik, etc.). Usually termed
"transitional forms," these specimens are, rather,
"hybrid" formations. With the decline of the Palestine center in the fourth and fifth centuries, the Babylonian influence gained the upper hand. As a result,
we have in the Byzantine period a complete fusion of
the two elements, façade and ark, in which the
former is subdued to the latter (Beth Alpha).

The two opposing and uncompromising views on
the synagogue found their clear expression in statements of the earlier Karaites. Anan, of the lineage of
the exilarchs, the highest dignitaries of Babylonian
Jewry, represents the genuine Babylonian attitude to
make the synagogue as similar to the temple as possible. The opposite view was represented by Daniel
Al-Kumisi, the champion of the Karaitic settlement
in Jerusalem.

5. Separation of sexes. Neither a ruling concerning, nor any clear allusion to, separation of sexes in
ancient synagogues in Palestine has yet been found in
earlier rabbinic sources. Among later authorities the
main basis for such a separation rests on the "great
enactment" (תיקון גדול) to erect a gallery in the
"women's hall" of the temple of Jerusalem, in order
to separate the women from the men during the celebrations of the "water-drawing" (P.T. Suk. V.1; 55*b*).
In Hellenistic centers of the first century separation
seems well attested by Philo. In the great basilica-
synagogue of Alexandria the women seem to have
been referred to as "those on the upper story,"
as against the men, designated as "those of the lower
level" (P.T. *ibid.*, according to Sukenik). A somewhat
similar picture is offered by the archaeological data.
The remains of the ancient basilical synagogues of
Galilee, with a distinctive Hellenistic stamp, show
unmistakable indications of the existence of galleries,
which probably were the place assigned women. But
no traces of a women's gallery have been found in
the well-preserved remains of the non-basilical, more
oriental synagogue of Dura-Europos. Scholars differ
in interpreting these facts. According to one school,
the silence of earlier rabbinic sources and the absence of a women's gallery in Dura reflect an earlier,
more liberal attitude toward women, allowing them
to sit in the main hall, though in a special part, together with the men. The other school suggests that
the silence of earlier rabbinic authorities implies that
in those circles no provisions were made at all for
women in the synagogue, because they were excluded
from active participation in public worship. For a
few special occasions, in which women might have

had access to the synagogue, a temporary, removable screen might have been sufficient.

Only the latter interpretation seems to fit the evidence that provisions for separation of sexes appear mainly in synagogues with a Hellenistic tinge. In the Hellenistic world women seem to have played an important role in the religious life of the Jews. Acts 16:12 ff is evidence that in Philippi women frequented the place of prayer during the sabbatical gatherings.

Another consideration should be borne in mind. It is probable that the basilical type of synagogue, which adopted architectural features of the temple, followed the example of the "woman's hall" in separating the sexes—i.e., by erecting galleries. The communities with a nonbasilical type of synagogue might have taken stricter measures of separation, confining the women to a separate, adjoining room, as seems to have been the case in the earlier building of the Dura-Europos synagogue.

6. Educational use. From the first, reading from the Scriptures and exposition of the Law constituted the focal point in the sabbatical gatherings, which gave the synagogue the character of an educational institution. This aspect is conspicuous in the Hellenistic world; to Philo and Josephus the synagogue is primarily a place of instruction, a "school of philosophy."

It is obvious, therefore, that educational institutions should have been closely connected with the synagogue. Reference has been made to the rabbinic tradition of the third century that there were 480 synagogues in Jerusalem, each of them housing a "house of the book" (בית הספר), for reading the Scriptures, and a "house of study" (בית המדרש), for study of the Mishna (P.T. Meg. III.1). The "house of study," generally conceived as the place of instruction for more advanced youth, is considered in the third century as a parallel institution to the synagogue rather than as a part of it. (Cf. the controversy about the rank relation of the two institutions in the Palestinian Talmud.) That this was the case in the first century A.D. is doubtful, however, since Jesus and Paul appear teaching in the synagogue, and no mention is made of the "house of study" in the NT. (The *schole Thyrannou* in Acts 19:9 can hardly be identified with a *Beth Hammidrash* at the side of the synagogue in Ephesus.)

Following certain rabbinic sources, most scholars agree that the synagogue was the place where children received their elementary instruction, perhaps in an adjoining room or in the courtyard. There is, however, some difference between the Palestinian tradition and the Babylonian. In the former the *Beth Ha-Sepher*, the alleged children's school, appears at the same level as the *Beth Hammidrash;* both are connected with the synagogue but locally separated. In the Babylonian tradition the alleged elementary school is often identified locally with the synagogue proper. The Palestinian tradition about "five hundred houses of teachers" in Bethar at the time of Bar Cocheba reads in the Babylonian version: "There were four hundred synagogues and in each of them there were four hundred teachers of children" (T.B. Giṭ. 58a). To understand the relation between school and synagogue in the first century A.D., we should take into consideration only the few earlier Pales-

tinian traditions. First, the term *Beth Sepher* must be clarified, for the usual rendering of "primary, elementary school," is somewhat misleading. The first education of children began, not with the reading of the Torah scroll, but with the reading from tablets, followed by rolls containing small portions from the Scriptures (Shema, etc.; cf. the Nash Papyrus). This instruction was probably imparted in the house of the teacher; children attending elementary schools are usually referred to as "sucklings of the house of their teachers." Only when the children reached the stage to be instructed in the reading of the sabbatical lessons were they introduced into the "house of the book." Unable to furnish the necessary scrolls, the teacher used the Torah scrolls of the synagogue. The children went to the room where these were kept, and there they prepared the sabbatical lessons under the supervision of the ḥazzan, the custodian of the scrolls (Shab. I.3). Thus the *Beth Sepher* seems not to have been a school in the strict sense of the word; nor was it confined to children. Rather, it was a place which afforded facilities for anyone eager to read the Scriptures. See EDUCATION, NT.

The term *Beth Hammidrash* should likewise be modified. It was hardly a "school of higher learning" but rather a place for anyone desiring to be an expert in the exposition of the Law. It might have housed various "secret rolls" of Midrashic or halakik nature and certain "Pesher" scrolls, accessible to a restricted circle.

These two kinds of facilities are probably referred to in Tannaitic literature (T.B. Ber. 4b). The only pertinent archaeological find, the Ophel Inscription, points in the same direction: The synagogue was to offer facilities "to read the Law and to teach the commandments." Whether these facilities were in the synagogue proper or in some adjoining buildings depended probably on the needs and the means of the various communities.

7. Furniture. The one indispensable piece of furniture in the ancient synagogue was the Torah shrine, in which one or more Torah scrolls and probably some prophetical rolls were kept to be used for the sabbatical and festival lessons.

The name of this repository underwent an interesting change ca. the second century A.D. תיבה, generally considered as an abbreviation of תיבהשל ספרים, "chest of books," is used almost exclusively in earlier rabbinic sources. The term is reminiscent of Gen. 6:14 (LXX κιβωτός); Exod. 2:3, and *passim* (LXX θίβιν). The second Greek rendering is obviously an adoption of the Hebrew term and may indicate that the Hellenistic Jews were familiar with the Hebrew תבה as repository for the law of Moses. This name would then be traced back at least to the second century B.C.

The synonymous ארון, "ark," associated with the "ark of the tent of meeting" (Exod. 25:10, and *passim;* LXX κιβωτός) appears rarely in rabbinic sources. A cryptical saying from the second century seems to imply that the name ארון הקדש ("the holy ark") was imposed by certain authorities but that it was rejected by the "people of the land" (Shab. 32a; cf. § 4 *above*). The inference that in the second century this name was a subject of controversy between various groups in Palestine suggests that it was an innovation introduced at that time. It is unlikely that the animosity of the opponents could have been provoked by the mere introduction of a new name; in all probability, an essential innovation in the role of the Torah shrine was associated with the new name.

Most scholars believe Talmudic sources make it clear that until the end of the fourth century the Torah shrine had no permanent place within the synagogue but that, as a simple portable chest, it was brought into the synagogue from an adjoining room, when required for public worship. Archaeological data seemed to confirm this at first. Later investigations, however, led experts to the reconstruction of a "small architecture," a shrinelike structure within some of the earlier synagogues (second century). This structure is considered as the "sanctuary" for the Torah shrine.

Attempts to adjust the archaeological data to alleged Talmudic tradition by asserting that the "small architecture" was a later addition or by challenging the existence of such an internal structure are not convincing. The discovery of the Dura-Europos synagogue has established definitely the existence of an aedicula for the Torah shrine in the third century (245), and it probably goes back to an earlier model. Scholars label it, as well as similar discoveries, as a transitional form, a fixed place in the synagogue to receive a portable Torah shrine during the reading of the lessons.

These efforts assume that the various forms represent various stages of the same type of synagogue. But it is equally possible that there were different types of synagogues side by side in the same period. There might have been a Hellenistic type beside a rabbinic type, or an exilic Babylonian type in juxtaposition to a Palestinian synagogue. There is no need to adjust the archaeological data to assumed rabbinic implications.

It seems reasonable to surmise that the name *tebah* was adequate for a Torah chest placed in some adjoining room. But when a "sanctuary" was erected to house the Torah shrine, the association with the ark of the tabernacle imposed itself and gave origin to the name. The name represented an innovation consisting in the building of a "sanctuary" for the Torah shrine and thus proclaiming the synagogue a substitute for the sanctuary of Jerusalem. Certain conservative circles in Palestine, who took offense at this claim, reacted strongly by labeling the *aron hakkodesh*, the "ark of holiness," as "coffin," which shares the name *aron* or *arona*. All through the second century, as long as the opposition was strong, the name was avoided in Palestine. When the permanent ark repository became dominant and the opposition lessened, *aron* or *arona* became the favorite name for the Torah shrine.

The assumption among scholars that the use of a portable תיבה is inconsistent with the existence of a permanent repository for the Torah shrine is far from obvious. There remains the possibility that at the side of the *aron* within the "sanctuary" the portable תיבה in the form of a Roman *capsa* existed for practical uses. Cf. P.T. Shek. II.18; VI.1; and parallels.

The fact that there is no reference to the Torah shrine in the NT might suggest that in the first century the shrine played no important role either in Palestinian Nazareth or in Hellenistic Antioch of Pisidia (cf. Luke 4:16-17; Acts 13:15-16). The earliest mention of the Torah shrine by the church fathers seems to be from the fourth century, where κιβωτός is used, probably in the sense of *aron*.

Like the ark of the tabernacle, the Torah shrine, especially the *aron* type, was covered and screened from the sight of the congregation. Rabbinic sources of the third century mention two kinds of screening: (a) *Paroket* or *parokta* (Aramaic), "veil" or "curtain" (P.T. Meg. IV.75b and parallels). It screened up the whole platform or aedicula where the ark was located, so that the ḥazzan was able to roll up the scroll behind the veil. This picture suggests a Babylonian type of synagogue; in fact, the alleged Palestinian source refers expressly to a "synagogue of the Babylonians." (b) *Killah*, a kind of baldachin spread over the ark, is mentioned in the Palestinian Talmud (Meg. III.73d; Shab. 17c). It probably reflects the way of screening the Torah shrine in the Palestinian type of synagogue. Whether the baldachin screen was also used in Babylonia under the name *pirsa* (Meg. 26b) is uncertain. Archaeological data have corroborated the existence of a *paroket* in Dura-Europos, but the attempt to find there traces of the baldachin on the top of the *paroket* is not convincing. The baldachin was spread over the ark proper and not in combination with the *paroket*.

Next to the Torah shrine and closely connected with it was the *bema*, an elevated podium used for the reading of the lessons and the recital of certain benedictions. Its name, as well as its use, is generally traced to the scene of Ezra's reading the Torah "on a wooden pulpit" (Neh. 8:4-5). The next mention appears in a Tannaitic tradition of the first century, where it is reported that a wooden *bema* was erected in the temple hall for Agrippa I to perform the prescribed reading of the Law by the king every seventh year at the Sukkoth Festival (Soṭ. VII.8). In the beginning of the third century we hear of a high *bema* in a synagogue in Simonia (Palestine) on the occasion of the installation of a famous preacher and teacher (P.T. Yeb. XII.13a; Gen. Rabbah 81.2). In all these cases the *bema* is improvised for a special occasion. As a permanent feature of the synagogue, it appears in a statement of Samuel (Babylonian teacher of the third century): "The *bema* and the boards—a kind of lectern—do not possess the sacredness of the ark (*aron*) but only that of the building." The need to rule upon its degree of sacredness would seem to indicate that the *bema* was newly introduced in Babylonia. The suggestion that it was near the *aron* is confirmed also by archaeological data.

There is no mention of the *bema* in the NT, although some scholars are inclined to consider the "Moses' SEAT" (Matt. 23:2) in the nature of a *bema*, serving the same purpose of an elevated chair for the reader.* In a larger sense this may be true; in a stricter sense, however, the *bema* is a raised place from which to speak in a public assembly and is thus an appropriate term for a pulpit from which the reading of the Torah takes place. On the other hand, *kathedra* points to a scholastic sphere, a raised chair for a prominent teacher. Fig. SEA 36.

Most of the excavated ancient synagogues were provided with one or two rows of stone benches running along two or three walls, exceptionally also along the entrance wall (Dura-Europos). No traces have been found of chairs in the center of the synagogue, though there are literary and archaeological indications that in the third century in Babylonia mats were spread out in the center for the people to sit upon. A Palestinian source (second century?) mentions wooden chairs, reclining chairs, and *kathedra* (P.T. Meg. 73*d;* Shab. 6*a*). Whether all these were honorary chairs for dignitaries and scribes in a prominent place (Matt. 23:6 and parallels), reminiscent of the seventy-one chairs for the members of the great council in the basilica of Alexandria, is uncertain. It might well be that in the Hellenistic synagogues the chairs (*subsellia*) took the place of the mats of Babylonia.

Rabbinic sources of the second and third centuries indicate that the Menorah was a favorite gift to be offered to the synagogue, even by non-Jews (Tosef. Meg. III.21; P.T. Meg. 74*a;* T.B. 'Arak. 6*b*). Earlier sources refer to lamps in the synagogue as practical objects. Later a. symbolic function is attached to them as reminiscent of the lights of the Menorah in the temple of Jerusalem. In the ornamentation of the earlier Palestinian synagogues the Menorah motif, though not entirely absent, remains inconspicuous. But in the Babylonian synagogue of Dura-Europos the Menorah, together with *aron*, is dominant, especially in the ornamentation of the aedicula. Later the Menorah became prominent in the ornamentation of the Palestinian synagogues, perhaps through the increase of Babylonian influence.

8. Officers. a. Archisynagogos. The highest officer is known as "head of the synagogue" (ראש הכנסת); the corresponding Greek title, "archisynagogos" (ἀρχισυνάγωγος), is used in the Greco-Roman dispersion, and rarely as "*archon* of the synagogue" (Luke 8:41) used. The Greek term was also used, though not so often, by non-Jewish religious associations. The NT, early Tannaitic tradition, and epigraphical material bear witness to the spread of this title all through the Greco-Roman world from the first century A.D. to the end of the fourth century.

Originally the archisynagogos was the presiding officer of the assemblies in the strict sense of the word, and probably the Hebrew name should also be rendered "head of the assembly." He was responsible for maintaining order during the meetings and removing disturbances (Luke 4:13); he was authorized to distribute honors, such as reading of the Torah, reading from the Prophets, and preaching (Acts 13: 15; M. Soṭ. VII.7-8). According to some scholars, in the first century the archisynagogos selected the prophetical reading on the sabbath and thus could fix the topic of the sermon. At one time he seems to have monopolized completely the honor of reading the Torah. Against such misuse of authority seems to have been directed the apocryphal halakah which forbids the archisynagogos to read the Torah unless he is asked by the assembly (Tosef. Meg. IV.21). The archisynagogos played an important role in mourning feasts—hence the custom, introduced in the second century A.D., of drinking at this occasion a cup to the health of the "head of the assembly" (P.T. Ber. 6*a*). Later the leadership of the archisynagogos extended beyond the limits of the meetings; he was probably the head of the synagogue building,

sharing its administration with the head of the council of the community, the γερουσιάρχης (cf. Ophel Inscription).

The office of the archisynagogos seems to have been at first elective for a limited time, probably one year. But the same person could be re-elected; sometimes he was elected "for life." Later we find in certain regions, especially Asia Minor, women and children called archisynagogos, an indication it had become a mere honorable and hereditary title.

Taking the term "head" literally, modern scholars are inclined to limit the office to one in each synagogue, and efforts are made to explain away the plural, *archisynagogoi*, in Acts 13:15. However, the inscription from Apamaea names expressly three *archisynagogoi*. Whether the number 3 is something more than accidental and whether the plurality of *archisynagogoi* in Apamaea is typical of Syria cannot be ascertained.

b. Ḥazzan. Like its corresponding Greek term ὑπηρέτης, "ḥazzan" has a variety of meanings in connection with the idea of service—hence the renderings "minister," "servant," "officer," etc. (Luke 1:2; Acts 13:5). There has been much discussion about the status of the ḥazzan of the synagogue in relation to the etymology of the term. The traditional derivation from חזה, "to see," misled some earlier scholars to elevate the ḥazzan to the rank of the Christian BISHOP, whose name likewise derives from a root meaning "to see" (ἐπίσκοπος). An examination of the rabbinic sources by Christian scholars of the seventeenth century resulted in downgrading the ḥazzan to the rank of the Christian DEACON. This equation is generally accepted, although some would assign to the ḥazzan only the rank of sexton. Also in the seventeenth century a new etymology was suggested—namely, the Arabic *khasin*, "storekeeper." A recent suggestion to trace the term to the Assyrian *hazanu*, "governor" or "overseer," may raise again the position of the ḥazzan.

In earlier rabbinic sources the ḥazzan appears at the most solemn religious ceremonies as an assistant to the archisynagogos. He takes the Torah and hands it over to the archisynagogos, who delivers the scroll to the captain of the high priest or to the king (Soṭ. VII.7-8). The ḥazzan performed most of the duties of the archisynagogos in the conduct of public worship. He assigned the functions during the worship, handed the Torah and the prophetic scroll to the reader (Luke 4:20; Sof. 14.3), and received them after the reading. At the proper moment he called upon the priests to pronounce the benediction (Sifre Num. 39). As assistant he accompanied the archisynagogos at funeral ceremonies and mourning feasts, probably reciting certain eulogies and benedictions; and also he had a cup drunk in his honor (P.T. Ber. 6*a*).

Some functions mentioned in the earlier sources seem to be of a different nature. The ḥazzan accompanied the members of the synagogue in their procession when they brought the firstlings to Jerusalem (Tosef. Bik. II.8). This duty is probably connected with the fact that at the Bikkurim ceremony the reading of Deut. 26:3 ff was essential. In the first century A.D. those who brought the firstlings were not supposed to read themselves (M. Bik. III.7). Thus, the ḥazzan went as reader. He appears also as officer of the law court, executing the sentence of scourging (M. Mak. III.12) and perhaps reading certain passages in Deut. 28:59 ff during the execution of the punishment. The advent of the sabbath and the festivals was announced by the ḥazzan from the roof of the synagogue by blowing the trumpet three times, the signal for the suspension of work (Tosef. Suk. IV.199; P.T. Shab. 16a).

While the early literary sources show the ḥazzan primarily as assistant to the archisynagogos in his role as head of the religious meetings, the scarce and late epigraphical material reveals him as assistant to the archisynagogos in his capacity as administrator (cf. inscriptions from the synagogues of Apamaea and of Umm el-Amed). There is no evidence that instruction of children was a duty inherent in the office of ḥazzan, though in small communities and under certain circumstances he did perform this function (P.T. Yeb. 13a).

c. *The "messenger."* Closely connected with the office of the ḥazzan was that of the "messenger of the congregation"—*sheliaḥ zibbur.* The name led older scholars to think of him in connection with the ἄγγελοι τῶν ἐκκλησίων in Rev. 1:20. His main assignment consisted in reciting the prayers aloud in order that the congregation could follow his lead. In earlier sources this messenger appears especially in connection with solemn occasions with a complicated order of prayers. From the beginning there seem to have been two opposing views about the role of the "messenger." The official one considered him as representative of the congregation, absolving its members from praying themselves. In offering prayers the messenger assumed the role of priest. The sages did not recognize this priestly role, however; they confined the messenger's task to leading the members of the congregation in prayer (M. R.H. IV.9; Tosef. IV.12). At first the function of reciting aloud the prayers was not assigned to any permanent officer but was performed voluntarily by any qualified member. As a rule, the person was called upon by the archisynagogos or by the ḥazzan. Since these two were in charge of the orderly conduct of public worship, the latter had to act as messenger of the congregation when no other qualified person could be found or when the person called upon declined. In the course of time the reciting of the prayers and the reading from the Scriptures became the main feature of the ḥazzan. The two terms, *ḥazzan* and *sheliaḥ zibbur,* became synonymous.

d. *Herald of the Shema.* The messenger who recited the prayer was preceded by one who recited the Shema with the blessings attached to it. In contradistinction to the private reading of the Shema, usually expressed by the verb *kara,* the recitation at public worship is represented by the verb *paras.* Most modern scholars agree to the Aramaic derivation of this term. They render the phrase *paras eth Shema,* somewhat literally, as the dividing of the verses of the Shema, to be recited antiphonally by the reader and congregation.

A more plausible explanation has been suggested. In connection with the idiom *paras diatagma,* which means to display an imperial edict for public promulgation, it is suggested that *paras* has become synonymous with "promulgate" and that *paras eth Shema* should be rendered "to promulgate the

Shema." One may go farther and suggest that, unlike the private reading of the Shema, which was usually recited by heart (M. Ta'an. 4.3), the recitation in the synagogue originally was made from a scroll. Probably this scroll contained not only the Shema proper but also the Decalogue (M. Tam. IV–V; Nash Papyrus). The reader of the Shema in the synagogue was called upon to unfold the scroll of the Shema and to promulgate the imperial edict, the Decalogue. He played the role of herald in the sense used in I Tim. 2:7; II Tim. 1:11. However, the promulgation of the Shema from a written scroll seems to have come into disuse, in Palestine at least, soon after the Decalogue had been eliminated from public worship.

Reading of scripture constitutes the principal part of public worship in the synagogue. This was especially true at the beginning of the Christian era, as witnessed by the NT, Philo, and Josephus. It is also indicated by the fact that in the Mishnaic code the rules concerning the synagogue are inserted in Tractate Megillah (III.1-3), which deals mainly with the reading from the Scriptures.

The sabbatical reading from the Pentateuch according to the triennial cycle seems to have been fixed in the first century B.C. The Pentateuch was divided into about 155 sections (Sedarim), one for each sabbath, so that the Torah was read through once in three years. At that time the reading from the Prophets (the Haftarah) shows no fixed scheme; yet it is unlikely that the lesson was left entirely to the free choice of the reader. Probably some control was exercised by the archisynagogos or by the ḥazzan. One of them would also call upon members of the congregation to read from the Scriptures.

In Palestine and Babylonia the reading was accompanied by an Aramaic translation (Targum) of the Hebrew text. Anyone who was capable, even a minor, was entitled to give the translation (Meg. IV.6). In certain important, learned centers there seems to have been a professional interpreter, called *Torgaman* or *Metorgaman.* As a rule, however, it was the schoolmaster, whose calling made him familiar with the translation of the Scriptures, who furnished orally the Aramaic interpretation.

When a competent person was present, the reading of the Scriptures was followed by an exposition of the lessons. To a certain extent this exposition was only an expansion of the Targ. In most cases it was based on the prophetical lesson (Luke 4:16 ff). It was customary to invite any stranger (teacher) who happened to attend the service to deliver this address (Acts 13:14). On synagogue worship, *see further* WORSHIP IN NT TIMES.

9. Secular and semisecular use of the synagogue. Modern historians tend to exaggerate the role of the synagogue as a communal center, the "house of the people"; but it has long been recognized that the synagogue was not confined to religious worship. It fulfilled some secular and semisecular functions. Already in the first century the synagogue seems to have been used as a law court where justice was administered. In the NT we find the synagogues in juxtaposition to the magistrates (Luke 12:11); rabbinic sources of the third century relate of Rabbi Yohanan and Rabbi Abahu that they have acted as judges and decided legal cases in the ancient synagogue of Caesarea (P.T. Ber. 6a and parallels; Sanh. I.18a). In particular, the carrying out of the sentence of scourging has been assigned to the ḥazzan of the synagogue (Matt. 10:17; 23:34; Mark 13:9; M. Mak. III.12). The reason for the choice of the synagogue might have been the fact that during the execution of this punishment certain passages from Deuteronomy were recited. The Torah scroll, of which the ḥazzan was custodian, was used also in civil processes such as oath-taking (Lev. Rabbah 6).

For a somewhat similar reason funeral services, especially the delivery of the eulogies, for deceased communal teachers were held in the synagogue (Tosef. Meg. III and parallels). The coffin (aron) of the teacher of the law was compared with the ark (aron) of the Law. Of course, as a rule the synagogue was also the largest building and could accommodate the crowd who would come to pay homage to the teacher.

The synagogue was used often for political gatherings because of its facilities. In the first century Josephus notes a political assembly in the great synagogue of Tiberias (Life LIV). In the third century rabbinic authorities permitted deliberations about public affairs in the synagogue on the sabbath (T.B. Keth. 5a).

As a meeting place, especially on sabbaths and festivals, the synagogue offered the opportunity to communal officers for various public announcements: lists of lost articles and similar communications (T.B. Yeb. 63b; B.M. 28b; Lev. Rabbah 6.2).

The use of the synagogue as an inn for itinerants is still a subject of discussion among scholars. There are various rabbinic utterances to the effect that travelers, especially teachers and students, were accommodated (P.T. Ber. 5d; Meg. III.74a; T.B. Pes. 101a). These seem to run against an explicit Tannaitic ruling which forbids eating, drinking, and sleeping in the synagogue (Tosef.; T.B. Meg. 28a-b). Most scholars take the term "synagogue" in this connection in its larger sense of comprising the precinct which contained a special guest room. Epigraphical and archaeological data seem to lend support to this view. The Theodotus Inscription speaks clearly of an inn for strangers beside the synagogue. Also remains of ancient synagogues (e.g., El-Hammeh and Dura-Europos) show a complex building with several adjoining rooms, one or two of which probably served as a guest house. Nevertheless, there seem to be some references which cannot be explained in this way; they indicate the use of the synagogue proper as a hospice. It seems plausible that the Tannaitic ruling mentioned above, like most of the earlier rulings about the synagogue based on the analogy with the sanctuary of Jerusalem, does not represent an official, binding rule but a kind of statute of a certain circle with Essene tendencies.

Between the two extremes, the one endowing the synagogue with all the attributes of the sanctuary of Jerusalem and the other denying the synagogue any claim to sacredness, there was in the first three centuries a great variety of attitudes and no definite official position.

Bibliography. C. Sigonius, De republica Hebraeorum libri VII (1583), pp. 63-65, 215-33, contains the earliest historical treatment of the synagogue. C. V. Vitringa, De synagoga vetere libri tres (1696). L. Herzfeld, Geschichte des Volkes Israel, III (1857), 129-37, 183-226. L. Zunz, Die gottesdienstlichen Vorträge der Juden (2nd ed., 1892). J. Wellhausen, Israelitische und jüdische Geschichte (1895). L. Löw, "Der synagogale Ritus," Gesammelte Schriften (1898), IV, 1-71; V, 21-33. W. Bacher, "Synagogue," HDB, IV (1905), 636-42. M. Rosemann, Der Ursprung der Synagoge (1907). M. Friedländer, Synagoge und Kirche in ihren Anfängen (1908). E. Schürer, Geschichte des jüdischen Volkes im Zeitalter Jesu Christi, II (4th ed., 1907), 497-544; III (1909), 1-96: still the most balanced exposition. I. Elbogen, Der jüdische Gottesdienst in seiner geschichtlichen Entwicklung (1913). J. Juster, Les Juifs dans l'empire Romain, vol. I (1914). H. Kohl and C. Watzinger, Antike Synagogen in Galilaea (1916), is fundamental for architecture and ornamentation. S. Krauss, Synagogale Altertümer (1922), is indispensable. W. O. E. Oesterley, The Jewish Background of the Christian Liturgy (1925). G. F. Moore, Judaism in the First Centuries of the Christian Era, vol. I (1927). H. Strack and P. Billerbeck, Kommentar zum NT nach Talmud und Midrash, vol. IV (1928). L. Finkelstein, "The Origin of the Synagogue," Proceedings of the American Academy for Jewish Research (1930), pp. 49-59. S. Zeitlin, "The Origin of the Synagogue," Proceedings of the American Academy for Jewish Research (1931), pp. 69-81. F. W. Foakes-Jackson and K. Lake, The Beginnings of Christianity, vol. I (1933). E. L. Sukenik, The Ancient Synagogue of Beth-Alpha (1932); Ancient Synagogues in Palestine and Greece (1934); The Ancient Synagogue of El-Hammeh (1935). L. Rost, Die Vorstufen von Kirche und Synagogue (1938). S. Klein, Jewish Settlements in Palestine (Hebrew Sepher Ha-Yishub), vol. I (1939), contains epigraphical and rabbinic data on ancient synagogues in Palestine. L. Ginzberg, A Commentary on the Palestinian Talmud (Hebrew), especially vol. III (1941). H. G. May, "Synagogues in Palestine," BA, VII (Feb., 1944). M. Noth, Geschichte Israels (1950). P. J.-B. Frey, Corpus inscriptionum Judaicarum, vol. I (1936); vol. II (1952). E. Goodenough, Jewish Symbols in the Greco-Roman Period, I (1953), 178-267. J. Morgenstern, "The Origin of the Synagogue," Studi orientalistici in onore di Giorgio della Vida, II (1955), 192 ff. C. H. Kraeling, The Excavations of Dura-Europos, Final Report VIII, Part I: The Synagogue (1956), discusses all aspects of the synagogue, with emphasis on architecture and ornamentation. S. W. Baron, A Social and Religious History of the Jews, vols. I-II (2nd ed., 1958).   I. SONNE

*SYNAGOGUE, THE GREAT. Traditionally, a council having Ezra as its founder and first president. It is not mentioned in the Bible (at I Macc. 14:28, μεγάλη συναγωγή means merely a large gathering).

According to legend, the Great Synagogue consisted of 120 (some say 85) men, who controlled Jewish affairs, particularly in the religious sphere, ca. 450-200 B.C. It is said to have played an important role in fixing the OT canon—an idea first suggested, it seems, in the sixteenth century. Some Talmudic writers add that it composed the books of Ezekiel, Daniel, Esther, and the minor prophets; and that it issued directions on how to read various portions of the OT. None of this is reflected in the OT or the Apoc. or by Philo or Josephus. The Talmudic writers knew little of their people's history after the Exile. The Great Synagogue appears to be wholly legendary, though perhaps based on stories, in Neh. 8–10, of a single great gathering.   PIERSON PARKER

*SYNOPTIC PROBLEM sĭ nŏp′tĭk [σύν-ὀπτικός, common view or viewed together]. The problem of accounting for the extensive and complex combination of similarities and differences in the first three gospels.

The first three gospels are designated as "synoptic" in order to indicate the common perspective in which they view the career and teaching of Jesus as distinguished from that of the Fourth Gospel (*see* JOHN, GOSPEL OF). There is overlapping between the first three and the fourth gospels, especially in the passion story, but only about nine per cent of the material in the Synoptics coincides with material in the Fourth. The coincidence of material as among the Synoptics is much higher. Approximately ninety-one per cent of Mark is paralleled in one of the other two gospels or in both. The same thing can be said of about fifty per cent of Matthew and about forty-one per cent of Luke. The distinction between the perspectives of the Synoptic gospels and the Fourth Gospel concerns, not only the amount of material involved, but also practically every other phase of their relationship: the order of events, style, the content and method of Jesus' teaching, and the theological outlook of the writers.

Despite the common characteristics of the first three gospels, which justify their being grouped as a unit over against the Fourth Gospel, their relationship each to the other creates a problem. When they are arranged in the parallel columns of a synopsis, there is revealed a curious and extremely complex combination of similarities and differences in their interrelationships which demands an explanation. They are very much alike at many points and yet very different at many other points, in both narrative and discourse material. And these characteristics appear consistently and all-pervasively, in the relationships of single sentences as well as of large blocks of material. Why is this so? How are these characteristics to be explained? This is the synoptic problem. A Greek synopsis of the first three gospels is required in order to observe the phenomena in their more minute ramifications, but an English translation will reveal the general nature of the problem.

A. *THE NATURE OF THE PROBLEM.* The combination of similarities and differences between the first three gospels may be observed both in their larger relationships and within single units.

1. Larger relationships. These have to do with three sets of data: material common to all three gospels; non-Markan parallels of Matthew and Luke; and material peculiar to each gospel.

a. Material common to all three gospels. A large body of material is common to all three gospels. It is similar in content and wording, and the units are arranged in approximately the same order. It contains some teachings of Jesus, but it is mainly narrative in nature.

With regard to the order of the units, one observes that it is Mark which appears to provide the framework. Matthew or Luke occasionally departs from this order, but they never agree against Mark in such a departure. If one of them differs from Mark, the other agrees with Mark (cf., e.g., Matt. 10:1-4 with Mark 3:13-19 and Luke 6:12-16; Luke 4:16-30 with Mark 6:1-6 and Matt. 13:53-58; Luke 13:18-19 with Mark 4:30-32 and Matt. 13:31-32; Luke 10:25-28 with Mark 12:28-34 and Matt. 22:34-40).

In regard to the contents of this material, the approximately ninety-one per cent of Mark which is paralleled in either Matthew or Luke or in both has the following relationships to the other gospels: about eleven twelfths of Mark parallels fifty-eight per cent of Matthew, and about one half of Mark parallels forty-one per cent of Luke.

This may be broken down still further. About sixty verses (nine per cent) of Mark are found only in this gospel. Twenty-one of these comprise peculiar Markan pericopes—mostly narrative (3:20-21; 7:2-4, 32-36; 8:22-26; 14:51-52), but with one teaching unit (4:26-29). The remaining thirty-nine verses consist of minor narrative touches (e.g., 1:1; 3:9; 11:11) and teachings (e.g., 2:27; 9:29; 10:24; 13:36-37) scattered throughout the gospel.

Of Markan material with an equivalent in either Matthew or Luke, it is the former which provides the greater number of parallels. Luke has only about 14 verses of Mark which are not in Matthew (Mark 1:23-28; 9:38-41; 12:41-44). On the other hand, Luke fails to parallel Mark at many points where Matthew does. There are in the neighborhood of 180 verses of Mark with parallels in Matthew but not in Luke. Seventy-four of these are in Mark 6:45–8:26, and 53 more are found in the passion story. Included in the total are some verses in which a somewhat different version of the Markan material appears in Luke (e.g., Luke 4:16-30). Also, there are some 36 Markan verses, both narrative and discourse, which in Matthew and Luke are expanded (e.g., parallels to Mark 1:7-8, 12-13; 3:28-29).

b. Non-Markan parallels of Matthew and Luke. Between 200-220 verses of Matthew and Luke parallel each other without corresponding parallelism in Mark. This material is mostly discourse, some very similar (117 verses) and some with greater divergencies (50-60 verses) in wording. About 55 verses contain narrative materials (e.g., Luke 7:1-10 = Matt. 8:5-10, 13). The best places to observe this material are in Matthew's Sermon on the Mount (Matt. 5–7 and parallels) and Luke's central section (Luke 9:51–18:14 and parallels).

c. Material peculiar to each gospel. The small percentage of material found only in Mark has already been noted. Matthew contains about 212 and Luke about 214 verses peculiar to each. The infancy stories of each gospel belong in this category; they overlap at few points. In addition, there are stories (17 in Matthew and 24 in Luke), parables (12 in Matthew and 19 in Luke) and teaching material scattered throughout each gospel (136 verses in Matthew and 85 in Luke). Examples of stories are those in Matt. 14:28-31; 27:3-10; 28:11-15; Luke 3:10-15; 4:28-30; 5:1-10; 7:11-17. Examples of parables are Matt. 13:45-46; 25:1-13, 31-46; Luke 10:25-37; 15:11-32; 16:19-31. The material peculiar to Matthew has a strong Judaistic flavor, that in Luke a more humanitarian and universalistic note.

2. Single units. The synoptic problem is more complex than is indicated by the foregoing data. Within each separate unit of the tradition recorded in more than one gospel there are similarities and differences which, generally speaking, correspond to the phenomena observed in the relationships of the larger blocks of material. These cannot be precisely observed in a comparison of English texts, but a few examples can indicate the characteristics which permeate the entire record.

a. Material common to the three gospels. The healing of a leper (Mark 1:40-45; Matt. 8:1-4; Luke 5:12-16) is related by Mark in 98 words, 38 of which are peculiar to him; by Matthew in 62 words, with 19 peculiar to him; and by Luke in 100 words, with 46 peculiar to him. Matthew and Luke have introductory sentences which differ from Mark and from each other. Matthew does not contain the closing verse of Mark (27 words); Luke has it, but only 6 of 27 words parallel Mark. The heart of the narrative (excepting Mark 1:43) finds Mark paralleled almost verbatim by either Matthew or Luke and often by both (cf. vss. 40*b*-44).

The healing of the palsied man (Mark 2:1-12; Matt. 9:1-8; Luke 5:17-26) illustrates a difference in introductory sentences but not in the conclusion of the incident, and a close similarity throughout despite some variations among the three. Vs. 10 of Mark (20 words) is paralleled in both Matthew and Luke practically verbatim (Luke has three grammatical variations).

In the story of the disciples' plucking corn on the sabbath (Mark 2:23-28; Matt. 12:1-8; Luke 6:1-5) Matthew and Luke both employ 92 words, against 100 in Mark, to relate the core of this incident in a manner very similar to Mark, and often with verbal equivalents. Two major differences exist, however: vs. 27 of Mark is not paralleled in either of the other gospels, and Matthew adds 44 words (vss. 5-7) which are peculiar to himself.

The story of Christ in Gethsemane (Mark 14:32-42; Matt. 26:36-46; Luke 22:40-46) is reported by Mark and Matthew with very close verbal similarity, but Luke's report is abbreviated and contains very few words employed by either of the others.

The sending out of the Twelve (Matt. 9:35–10:16) presents a very confusing combination of similarities and differences, not only in the relationship of the three gospels, but also with regard to materials paralleled only in Matthew and Luke or peculiar to Matthew (cf. parallels in Mark 3:13-19; 6:6-11, 34; Luke 6:13-16; 8:1; 9:1-5; 10:1-12).

b. Parallels of Matthew and Luke. Some of this material is almost verbally equivalent (e.g., Matt. 3:7-10 and Luke 3:7-9; Matt. 4:3-10 and Luke 4:3-10). The temptation of Jesus has as its core material in Matt. 4 and Luke 4 which is not in Mark at all, yet the beginning and the ending of the report have a relationship to Mark (cf. Mark 1:12-13; Matt. 4:1-2, 11; Luke 4:1-2, 13).

At other points there are interesting variations along with the similarities. The Beatitudes (Matt. 5:3-12; Luke 6:20-23) illustrate, not only a difference in the number reported by each evangelist (nine in Matthew and four in Luke), but also a difference in wording. Matthew's are in the third person, Luke's in the second person. As consistently elsewhere, Matthew has "the kingdom of Heaven"; Luke, "the kingdom of God." The last Beatitude carries the same thought in each gospel, but it is worded somewhat differently in each.

The Lord's Prayer (Matt. 6:9-13; Luke 11:2-4) is reported in Luke in a shorter form, with some differences in wording, at the same time that certain items are identically worded.

On practically every page of a synopsis this combination of similarities and differences, agreements and variations, is observed. The minute phenomena join with the larger blocks of material to confront the student with the synoptic problem.

B. *THE HISTORY OF THE STUDY OF THE PROBLEM.* Treatment of the issues on a scientific basis had to wait until the eighteenth century, and it has engaged the exhaustive attention of scholars ever since. Every conceivable combination of theories and guesses has been proposed, yet from the beginning there has been steady progress toward as much of a solution as the data will yield. Generally speaking, the line of progress moved from an oral hypothesis, along with hesitant feelers in the direction of written sources, to a full realization that the problem was a documentary one, the "two-document" hypothesis being the foundation upon which several "multiple-source" hypotheses were later developed.

1. Ancient solutions. The ancients contributed nothing substantial to the solution of the problem. On the assumption that the gospels were written by, or on the basis of material provided by, eyewitnesses, there was a tendency to produce an organization of parallel passages into harmonies such as Tatian's *Diatessaron* (170) and, much later, Osiander's *Harmonia Evangelica* (1537). The patristic tradition (see Augustine especially) considered Matthew to be the original gospel, Mark being a condensed version of it, and Luke being dependent upon both Mark and Matthew. This remained the orthodox position until 1863 and provided the foundation for the theory of the Tübingen scholars in the mid-nineteenth century and Zahn in 1897; it is still the official position of Roman Catholic scholars and is espoused by an occasional Protestant scholar (e.g., Jameson, in 1922).

2. The modern period to 1900. *a. The initial stage of the modern period (1750-1835).* The earliest attempts to deal scientifically with the synoptic problem produced three main hypotheses apart from the continuation of the patristic tradition. The first was the hypothesis of a primitive oral gospel formulated in Aramaic on the soil of Palestine by the apostles, or by one of them, which became stereotyped through constant repetition. According to this view, the differences among the three gospels were attributable to the variant forms under which the oral gospel reached the several evangelists, as well as to the various tendencies or interests of the early communities (cf. Herder, 1796-97; J. C. L. Giesler, 1818). Although this view persisted to a limited extent (cf. Westcott, D. Smith, A. Wright), scholars as a whole abandoned it in favor of the theory that between the oral stage and the finished gospels there was an intermediate stage in which most of the oral tradition was reduced to writing.

The second hypothesis was that of an original written gospel (*Protevangel*), in Aramaic or Hebrew, which was not identical with any known gospel and which each evangelist translated or from which he secured the material which he used (Eichhorn, 1804). This view collapsed of its own weight, after it was seen that successive recensions of the original were required to explain the differences among the gospels.

A third hypothesis was Schleiermacher's "fragment hypothesis" (1818), which explained the interrelationships of the gospels as due to the use by the evangelists of similar and dissimilar collections of material. This suggestion of Schleiermacher was destined to be more fully developed in the immediate future and also, much more extensively, by Schmidt, Bultmann, Dibelius, and other form critics after World War I.

b. The two-document hypothesis (1835-1900). The stage was now set for the development of the documentary hypothesis which was to crown the work of the nineteenth century, and which has remained the key to the basic literary relationships of the Synoptics. Swinging sharply away from patristic tradition, scholars concluded that Mark was the earliest gospel and that it had provided both the framework and the bulk of the narrative content of Matthew and Luke (cf. especially Lachmann, 1835; C. H. Weisse and C. G. Wilke, 1838; H. J. Holtzmann, 1863; and B. Weiss, 1886).

The other twin in the two-document hypothesis was concluded to be a collection of sayings of Jesus (LOGIA or Q), consisting of at least two hundred verses paralleled in Matthew and Luke, which each in his own way had combined with Mark, along with other fragmentary traditions, to produce the finished gospels (cf. especially Weisse, 1838; Weizsäcker, 1864; Hawkins and Wernle, 1899).

The two-document hypothesis may be diagramed as in fig. 1.

3. Since 1900. In certain quarters, notably in Germany, scholars turned away from an exclusive concern with literary problems to investigate the preliterary formation of the gospel tradition in conjunction with the theological import of the gospels (*see* FORM CRITICISM). The attention thus given to unraveling the immediate sources of Mark is alone

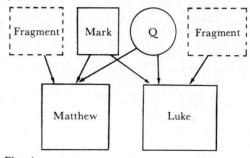

Fig. 1

relevant to this subject. At the same time lively discussion of the problems left unsolved by the two-document hypothesis continued in Europe and America. Largely in an effort to account for the materials peculiar to Matthew and Luke, there developed after World War I a trend in the direction of multiple-source hypotheses (cf. especially Streeter, Grant, Parker). In the several areas of discussion the main developments were as follows:

a. The Markan source. Because of the omission of Markan passages by one evangelist and not the other (Matthew 24-25 verses; Luke, 61 verses), especially Luke's omission of Mark 6:45-8:26, along with minor agreements against Mark, a theory of the use by Matthew and Luke of different editions or versions of Mark came into being early in the period (cf. Wendling, 1905; Bacon; Moffatt) and continued to have some appeal (cf. Goguel, Bussmann, Crum). The trend, however, was toward the view that Matthew and Luke had used Mark in substantially the form in which we now possess it (cf. Hawkins, Burkitt, Streeter, Turner, V. Taylor, Rawlinson, Cadbury, McNeile, Montefiore). This was based upon the uniformity of style in Mark, and the probability of accidental coincidence or the selective creativity of Matthew and Luke, as well as the probability of textual assimilation and emendation.

In the pursuit of the sources of Mark the tendency increased, while allowing Peter some influence upon the composition of the gospel (*see* PAPIAS), to emphasize the importance of other sources, either written or oral or both (cf. Goguel, T. Manson, Bussmann, Branscomb, Grant, Dodd, Guy). The use of Q by Mark was favored by some, but not by the majority.

There were also two-source theories (E. Meyer, Crum, Parker), a three-source theory (A. T. Cadoux), and multiple-source theories (W. L. Knox and V. Taylor). Roman Catholic scholars continued to assert the priority of Matthew (cf. Voste, Chapman, Vaganay, Levie).

See MARK, GOSPEL OF.

b. Q. The majority of scholars agreed that Q was primarily a discourse source, with little narrative and no passion story, its material being largely, if not exclusively, represented by the parallel materials of Matthew and Luke. A few considered it as a sort of Proto-Matthew (cf. Bacon, Kilpatrick, Parker). Most agreed that its original order was better preserved by Luke, but there was sharp disagreement as to whether Matthew or Luke better represented the original wording. To account for the differences in its use by Matthew and Luke, the theory of different recensions or parallel collections of sayings was favored by most over theories of oral tradition or different translations of an Aramaic document. A few proposed different sources of Q (cf. Burton, B. W. Robinson, Bussmann), while an occasional scholar renounced the theory of Q in favor of Luke's use of Matthew (cf. Enslin, Butler).

c. Other sources of Luke. The theory that Luke possessed a third cycle of tradition (*see* L), either written or oral, of a relatively homogeneous character and represented mainly by stories and parables, came to be generally accepted (cf. variant theories of Moffatt, Bussmann, Crum). The proposal by Streeter that Luke had combined Q and L into a Proto-Luke, prior to its conjunction with Mark, appealed to some scholars (cf. V. Taylor, W. Manson, Parker), but different explanations of the large amount of non-Markan material in Luke seemed to others more likely (cf. Perry, Grant, Cadbury, Hunkin, Montefiore, Goguel, Creed). Opposition was especially strong to the idea that Luke had substituted the framework of Proto-Luke for that of Mark. A still different source for the infancy narrative, either as a translated document or as the free composition of the evangelist, was generally taken for granted.

d. Other sources of Matthew. It was proposed that Matthew possessed a third homogeneous cycle of tradition comparable to Q and L, of a Judaistic cast, which he had conflated with Q (cf. Burton, Albertz, Bacon, Streeter, V. Taylor, McNeile, T. Manson, Kilpatrick, Parker, Vaganay), but there was great dispute over various aspects of this proposal. While the Judaistic atmosphere of the material peculiar to Matthew was generally recognized (Crum and Kilpatrick opposed), the literary homogeneity of the material was questioned (cf. Goguel, Scott, Grant, Parker), as was the theory that Matthew alone employed the method of conflating his sources (cf. Bacon, Easton, Kilpatrick). Some continued to think of this material as from Q (cf. Easton, Bacon, Scott) or due to different sources of Q (Bussmann).

Most scholars considered the infancy story to be from a different cycle of tradition than that of Luke, and probably the free composition of the evangelist. The use of a collection of messianic proof texts (*testimonia*), in written or oral form, was generally agreed upon.

e. Other theories. Theories of Aramaic originals persisted in the view that all the gospels were direct translations of Aramaic documents before A.D. 60 (Torrey) or in views which proposed the use by the evangelists of Aramaic sources (cf. McNeile, Vaganay). A general Aramaic background for the gospels was as much as most scholars believed the evidence warranted (cf. Black).

On the basis of the pronouncements of the Pontifical Biblical Commission (1911, 1912), supporting the patristic tradition, Roman Catholic scholars labored at the synoptic problem upon the premise that Matthew was the original gospel (cf. Voste, Chapman, Vaganay, Levie), at times making some concession to the theory of the priority of Mark.

f. Summary. There has emerged from all the laborious work devoted to the solution of the synoptic problem, as its most permanent result, the hypothesis of two major documents (Mark and Q) employed by Matthew and Luke in conjunction with bodies of tradition peculiar to each, a distinct third source for Luke (L) being the most definite of the latter. The continued disagreement over many details indicates that literary criticism has accomplished about as much as it can. The most promising aspect of criticism appears to be the effort to relate the cycles of tradition to distinct geographical localities and to conditions operative in the currents of life and thought of the primitive communities (cf. e.g., Streeter and Parker), and thus to the interests of form criticism and related disciplines designed to lay bare the secrets of the preliterary formation of the gospel tradition. *See also* MATTHEW, GOSPEL OF; MARK, GOSPEL OF; LUKE, GOSPEL OF.

Bibliography. Synopses: A. Huck and H. Lietzmann, *Synopsis of the First Three Gospels* (English trans. F. L. Cross; 9th ed., 1936). *Gospel Parallels, A Synopsis of the First Three Gospels* (1949), uses the RSV text, arranged on the model of the Huck-Lietzmann Greek synopsis.

General: J. Moffatt, *Introduction to the Literature of the NT* (1929)—valuable for the pre-1914 period. B. H. Streeter, *The Four Gospels* (4th ed., 1930)—one of the most influential multiple-source hypotheses. T. Manson, *The Teaching of Jesus* (2nd ed., 1935), pt. I. E. B. Redlich, *The Student's Introduction to the Synoptic Gospels* (1936). A. E. Barnett, *The NT: Its Making and Meaning* (1946), ch. 9—one of the best statements of the problem and of source theories in compact form. V. Taylor, *The Gospels* (6th ed., 1948). P. Parker, *The Gospel Before Mark* (1953)—a significant attempt to relate source study to currents of early church life. H. A. Guy, *A Critical Introduction to the Gospels* (1955). F. C. Grant, *The Gospels* (1957), represents a multiple-source theory and a good effort to relate gospel origins to early church life.

Historical surveys: M. Jones, *The NT in the Twentieth Century* (1914), pp. 189-226. C. J. Montefiore, *The Synoptic Gospels* (2nd ed., 1927), Introduction to vol. I. C. C. McCown, *The Search for the Real Jesus* (1940), ch. 10—the most up-to-date and inclusive survey of source study and much else involved in the quest of the historical Jesus.

On Mark's Gospel: B. W. Bacon, *The Gospel of Mark* (1925). A. T. Cadoux, *The Sources of the Second Gospel* (1936). A. E. J. Rawlinson, *Saint Mark*, WC (7th ed., 1949). V. Taylor, *The Gospel According to St. Mark* (1952). W. L. Knox, *Mark*, in H. Chadwick, ed., *The Sources of the Synoptic Gospels*, vol. I (1953).

On Matthew's Gospel: B. W. Bacon, *Studies in Matthew* (1930). G. D. Kilpatrick, *The Origins of the Gospel According to St. Matthew* (1946).

On Luke's Gospel: B. S. Easton, *Gospel According to Luke* (1926). V. Taylor, *Behind the Third Gospel* (1926). H. J. Cadbury, *The Making of Luke-Acts* (1927).

See also bibliography under the several gospels.

D. T. ROWLINGSON

SYNTYCHE sĭn'tĭ kĭ [Συντύχη, coincidence, success] (Phil. 4:2). A woman in the church at Philippi, advised by Paul to compose her differences with EUODIA.

F. W. GINGRICH

SYRACUSE sĭr'ə kŭs, —kŭz [αἱ Συράκουσαι] (Acts 28:12). A city on the E coast of the island of Sicily.

Thucydides (VI.2) and Diodorus of Sicily (V.6) state that the first inhabitants of Sicily were the Sicani (οἱ Σικανοί). Thucydides and Philistus (died *ca.* 365 B.C.), whom Diodorus cites, believed they came from Iberia; but Timaeus (died *ca.* 250 B.C.), whose opinion Diodorus prefers, thought they were indigenous. From them the island was called Sicania (ἡ Σικανία). After them came the Siceli (οἱ Σικελοί), who were said to have crossed over in a body from Italy, and from whom the island took the name of Sicily (ἡ Σικελία). Archaeologically and anthropologically the Sicani and Siceli seem to be branches of the same people, who probably came to the island from elsewhere at different times, and are represented by numerous finds of the Neolithic and Aëneolithic periods. Later, Phoenicians settled on Sicily, and then came Greek colonists (Thucydides VI.3-5).

The first Greek colony was Naxos; the second, established a year later, probably in 734 B.C., was Syracuse. Many ancient writers, including Clement of Alexandria (*Stromata* I.xxi.131, 8 [398]), name Archias of Corinth as the founder of Syracuse. The story is that he went to the oracle at Delphi and was asked whether he chose wealth or health; when he chose wealth, he was sent to found Syracuse, which became famously rich (Strabo VI.269; Συράκουσαι, in Stephen of Byzantium *De Urbibus*, ed. W. Xylander [1568], col. 267).

The new colony was planted on the island of Ortygia (Pausanias V.7.3), from which Archias expelled the Siceli there resident. Later this island was connected with the shore, and Syracuse included large tracts of mainland. Under the ruler Gelon the city won an important victory in battle with the Carthaginians, according to Herodotus (VII.166) on the very day the Greeks vanquished the Persians at Salamis (480 B.C.). When Syracuse attempted to dominate all Sicily, it was attacked by a large fleet from Athens, but again was victorious (413 B.C.) with the almost complete destruction of the attacking forces (Thucydides VI-VII; Diodorus XIII; Plutarch *Nicias*). With Dionysius the Elder, who obtained power in 405 B.C. (Diodorus XIII.109-14), a series of tyrants arose who ruled Syracuse with varying degrees of severity or mildness until the city was taken by the Romans in 212 B.C. (Livy XXV.23-31; Plutarch *Marcellus* 14-19).

Under the Romans, Syracuse became the residence of the governor of Sicily, and by Augustus in 21 B.C. the city was given the rank of a colony (Dio LIV.7.1). As described by Cicero (*Against Verres* II.4.117-19) in the first century B.C., Syracuse was the largest of the Greek cities and the loveliest of all cities. On the island were temples of Diana and Minerva, the palace of the governors, and the famous spring Arethusa. In the mainland quarter called Achradina were the forum, town hall, senate house, and temple of Olympian Jupiter. In Tycha were crowded habitations, and in Neapolis a great theater.* Long famed for fishing, shipbuilding (Athenaeus V.206-9), textiles, and bronze work (Cicero *Against Verres* II.4.58-60), Syracuse enjoyed great prosperity under the Roman Empire, and was allowed by Nero to conduct gladiatorial shows on a magnificent scale (Tac. Ann. XIII.49). The impressive ruins of ancient Syracuse include the temple of Athena, built probably by Gelon in the fifth century B.C. and transformed into

Courtesy of the Italian State Tourist Office
110. The theater at Syracuse

a Christian cathedral in the seventh century A.D.; the Greek theater, erected probably by Hieron I (478-467 B.C.) and enlarged by Hieron II two hundred years later; the large amphitheater, constructed in the time of Augustus; and the Christian catacombs of the third and fourth centuries. Fig. SYR 110.

Bibliography. Ziegler, "Σικελία," *Pauly-Wissowa*, Zweite Reihe, II, ii (1923), cols. 2461-2522. C. and I. Cafici, "Sikuler," *Reallexikon der Vorgeschichte*, XII (1928), 123-57. W. Hüttl, *Verfassungsgeschichte von Syrakus* (1929). G. Libertini, *Il Regio Museo Archeologico di Siracusa* (1929); excavation reports in *Notizie degli scavi di antichita* (Atti della Accademia Nazionale dei Lincei). D. Randall-MacIver, *Greek Cities in Italy and Sicily* (1931). K. Fabricius, *Das antike Syrakus*, Klio, Beiheft XXVIII, N.F. XV (1932). Wickert, "Syrakusai," *Pauly-Wissowa*, Zweite Reihe, IV, ii (1932), cols. 1478-1547. V. M. Scramuzza, "Roman Sicily," in T. Frank, ed., *An Economic Survey of Ancient Rome*, III (1937), 225-377. C. Anti, *Guida per il visitatore del teatro antico di Siracusa* (1948). H. Leclerq, "Syracuse," *Dictionnaire d'archéologie chrétienne et de liturgie*, XV, ii (1950), cols. 1840-55.   J. FINEGAN

SYRIA sĭr'ĭ ə; **SYRIANS** —ənz. Terms used in the LXX and in some English translations to render the names ARAM and ARAMEANS.

***SYRIAC VERSIONS** sĭr'ĭ ăk. The Syriac language, a member of the Semitic family of languages, became the vehicle of several important versions of the OT and the NT. *See* VERSIONS, ANCIENT, § 4.

SYROPHOENICIA sī'rō fĭ nĭsh'ə; **SYROPHOENICIAN** —ən [Συροφοίνισσα]. According to Mark 7:26, a Greek (or "pagan") woman of Syrophoenician origin heard of Jesus' mission in the boundaries of Tyre and Sidon. The parallel verse (Matt. 15:22) calls her a Canaanite (Χαναναία), which is the ancient name by which the Phoenicians called themselves. The name Syrophoenicia refers to the fact that in the time of Jesus, Phoenicia (including Tyre and Sidon) was included in the Roman province of Syria.   M. AVI-YONAH

SYRTIS sûr'təs [Σύρτις] (Acts 27:17); KJV **QUICKSANDS.** The Greek name of two shallow gulfs on the N coast of Africa. The larger, Syrtis Major, W of Cyrenaica, is now called the Gulf of Sidra; it is probably the Syrtis intended in this passage. The smaller, Syrtis Minor, is now called the Gulf of Gabes. Sailors feared these shallow waters, with their treacherous hidden rocks and sandbanks.   F. V. FILSON

*TAANACH tā'ɔ năk [תַּעֲנָךְ] (Josh. 12:21; 17:11; 21:25; Judg. 1:27; 5:19; I Kings 4:12; I Chr. 7:29); KJV once TANACH tā'năk (Josh. 21:25). A Canaanite and later Israelite Levitical town on the S edge of the Plain of Esdraelon.

Taanach is identified with Tell Ta'annak, a site located midway between Megiddo and Jenin overlooking the Plain of Esdraelon. In antiquity it commanded two trade routes, one connecting the hill country with the Plain of Acre, the other linking the Plain of Esdraelon with the Plain of Sharon across the Carmel Range.

Minor excavations at the site were made in 1901-4. The excavators neglected both stratigraphy and pottery chronology, with the result that only a sketch of the history of the site can be given.

The earliest occupation belongs to the end of EB II and the beginning of EB III (ca. twenty-sixth century B.C.). A noteworthy feature of this stratum is a tomb that resembles Egyptian tombs of the time of Djoser (Third Dynasty) in its style of masonry and techniques of construction; such similarity points to Egyptian influence in this period. The site was again occupied during MB IIC (late seventeenth and sixteenth centuries B.C.) and LB I (late sixteenth and early fifteenth centuries). In the latter period Taanach and the route linking it with the Plain of Sharon are mentioned in the account of Thutmose III's campaign against a coalition of Syro-Palestinian princes (ca. 1468).

The most important archaeological finds at the site, consisting of a dozen whole and fragmentary cuneiform tablets, belong to the occupation of the late fifteenth century B.C. These tablets—addressed to Rewashsha prince of Taanach and written by different persons, including Amanhatpa (Amenophis), the Egyptian governor of Gaza—contain a variety of requests and orders. During the Amarna Age (ca. fourteenth century B.C.) the site was inhabited, as shown by the appearance of Taanach (spelled Tah[nu-k]a) in one of the Amarna Letters. See TELL EL-AMARNA.

After the Israelite invasion of Palestine in the late thirteenth century B.C., Taanach was allotted to Manasseh (Josh. 17:11; I Chr. 7:29) and was assigned to the children of Kohath as a Levitical city (Josh. 21:25). Contrary to Josh. 12:21, which suggests that the Israelites captured Taanach, Judg. 1:27 makes it clear that Manasseh was unable to take full possession of the town, because of Canaanite strength. The site was probably occupied in the late twelfth century B.C., judging from the Song of Deborah (Judg. 5:19), which places the battle between Sisera and Barak "at Taanach, by the waters of Megiddo"; since this battle was fought nearer Megiddo, this description suggests that Taanach, not Megiddo, was the nearest inhabited town. Possibly to this occupation belongs a large clay incense altar found in the excavations, which is decorated on two sides with animals in relief stacked one above the other, some with human heads and some with animal heads modeled in the round (Fig. ART 66). Taanach prospered under David (ca. 1000-961) and Solomon (ca. 961-923), and during the latter's reign was governed by Baana, one of the twelve district officers over Israel (I Kings 4:12). This occupation was destroyed by Shishak of Egypt in the course of his Palestinian campaign (ca. 918), as shown by the appearance of Taanach (spelled t'nk in Egyptian) among other conquered towns in the Shishak list at Karnak.

Whether the site was inhabited during Iron II is uncertain; it was reoccupied during late classical times and again in the Arab period.

Bibliography. G. A. Smith, *The Historical Geography of the Holy Land* (1894), pp. 386-89. E. Sellin, "Tell Ta'annek," *Denkschriften der Kaiserlichen Akademie der Wissenschaften, Wien* 50:4 (1904); "Eine Nachlese auf den Tell Ta'annek in Palästina," *Denkschriften der Kaiserlichen Akademie der Wissenschaften, Wien* 52 (1906). J. A. Knudtzon, *Die El-Amarna Tafeln,* vol. I (1915), no. 248:14. J. Simon, *Handbook for the Study of Egyptian Topographical Lists Relating to Western Asia* (1937), Taanach no. 14, pp. 178-81. W. F. Albright, "A Prince of Taanach in the Fifteenth Century B.C.," *BASOR,* 94 (1944), 12-27. J. B. Pritchard, ed., *ANET* (2nd ed., 1955), pp. 235-36, 243, 490. G. W. VAN BEEK

TAANATH-SHILOH tā'ɔ năth shī'lō [תַּאֲנַת שִׁלֹה]. A village between Michmethath and Janoah on the NE boundary of Ephraim (Josh. 16:6). It is usually identified with the modern Khirbet Ta'nah el-Foqa, ca. seven miles SE of Shechem on a mountain where it may have served as a fortress in ancient times. Although uncertain, if Taanath is from אנה, "approach" (cf. Exod. 21:13), it might indicate the approach to Shiloh. W. L. REED

TABBAOTH tăb'ĭ ŏth [טַבָּעוֹת, *perhaps from* טַבַּעַת, signet, ring] (Ezra 2:43; Neh. 7:46; I Esd. 5:29); KJV Apoc. TABAOTH. Head of a family of temple servants, or NETHINIM, returned from the Exile.

TABBATH tăb'ɔth [טַבָּת]. A place E of the Jordan where Gideon ended his pursuit of the Midianites after routing them in the valley of Jezreel (Judg. 7:22). It must have been in the vicinity of KARKOR, where they rallied their forces (Judg. 8:10), and the ascent of Heres (see HERES, ASCENT OF), from which Gideon returned after defeating them for the second time (Judg. 8:13). Tabbath must therefore have been in the mountains of E Gilead, and would be a logical place for a defeated army to retire to in an attempt to recover. A probable identification of the site is Ras

Abu Tabat, on the slopes of the Jebel 'Ajlun, NW of Pakoris on the Wadi Kufrinjeh.   S. COHEN

TABEEL tăb'ĭ əl [טבאל, Aram. God is good; Apoc. Ταβέλλιος]; KJV TABEAL (no good) in Isa. 7:6; KJV Apoc. TABELLIUS tə běl'ĭ əs. **1.** Evidently an Aramean, the father of a man whom the allied kings Rezin of Damascus and Pekah of Israel intended to set up in Jerusalem as a puppet king in place of the Davidic king Ahaz (Isa. 7:6). Thus Judah was to be added to the anti-Assyrian alliance. Since the son of Tabeel probably was a Syrian, it may be that Judah was to be included in the domains of Damascus. The MT has vocalized the name "Tabeal," perhaps to express scorn.

2. An Aramean in Samaria who was a party to a letter to Artaxerxes I endeavoring to prevent Jewish reconstruction (Ezra 4:7; I Esd. 2:16).

T. M. MAUCH

TABER. KJV translation of תפף, meaning "to beat," as on a timbrel (תף), in Nah. 2:7—H 2:8 (RSV "beat"). The archaic English word "taber," or "tabor," means "to beat," as on a tabor, or little drum.

TABERAH tăb'ə rə [תבערה, burning] (Num. 11:3; Deut. 9:22). A stopping place of the Israelites in the wilderness. Here the people, complaining about their misfortune, provoked the Lord to anger. He sent his fire among them, destroying a part of the camp (Num. 11:1-2). The place received its name, Taberah, "because the fire of the LORD burned among them." In Deut. 9:22 it is mentioned with Massah and Kibroth-Hattaavah as the place where the Israelites "provoked the LORD to wrath." It is not listed in the itinerary of Num. 33. The location is unknown.   J. L. MIHELIC

TABERNACLE [משכן, dwelling, *from* שכן, to dwell]. A sacred tent, a portable sanctuary, said to have been erected by Moses. It was the place at which the God of Israel revealed himself to and dwelt among his people. It also housed the ark and accompanied Israel during the wilderness period. It is stated that it was located in several places in Canaan after Israel's settlement in that land and finally was replaced by Solomon's temple. It was thus Israel's portable sanctuary from Sinai to Solomon's temple.

1. Terminology
2. The tabernacle in P
   a. Materials and furniture
   b. The dwelling
   c. The furniture for the court
   d. Erection of the tabernacle and its consecration
3. The tabernacle in the early traditions
4. The problem of the tent and the tabernacle
5. Reassessment of P's account of the tabernacle
6. The tabernacle in the NT
Bibliography

1. Terminology. The tabernacle is known also by the two principal Hebrew words for "sanctuary"—i.e., מקדש (LXX ἁγίασμα; ἁγιαστήριον; ἡγιασμενον; τὰ ἅγια; Vulg. *sanctuarium*) and קדש—as well as by the following names:

a) "Tent of meeting" (אהל מועד), which occurs about 130 times in P and several times in E (Exod. 33:7; Num. 11:16; 12:4; Deut. 31:14). This is almost always rendered in the Greek by ἡ σκηνὴ τοῦ μαρτυρίου, "the tent of the testimony," and in the Vulg. by *tabernaculum testimonii* but in Numbers far more often by *tabernaculum foederis*. The Hebrew word for "meeting" means "to meet by appointment" —hence "tent of meeting"—i.e., where Yahweh meets with Moses and Israel (Exod. 29: 42-43; Num. 17:4). In Exod. 29:42; 33:11; Num. 7:89 the purpose of this meeting is further defined as communication, and so "tent of meeting" really means "tent of revelation," "tent of the oracle," "tent of the testimony" (*see below*). Similarly Westcott spoke of the three truths represented by the names of the tabernacle: God's presence; God's righteousness; and God's "conversableness."

b) "The tent" (19 times in P); "tent of Yahweh" (I Kings 2:28 ff); "house of the tent" (I Chr. 9:23); and "house of Yahweh" (Exod. 23:19); "tabernacle of the house of God" (I Chr. 6:48). The LXX employs for אהל ("tent") σκηνὴ (nearly 140 times) and σκήνωμα (44 times). The Vulg. uses *tabernaculum*, and less frequently *tentorium*. In Wisd. Sol. 9:8; Ecclus. 24:10 the name "sacred tent" (σκηνὴ ἅγια) appears.

c) "Tabernacle," "dwelling," "dwelling place," "habitation," "abode," "encampments." The Hebrew noun, משכן, is derived from the verb "to dwell." In Exod. 25:9 the word means the shrine as a whole, but in 26:1, etc., it means virtually the holy of holies. The LXX rendering is generally σκηνή (about 106 times), or σκήνωμα (17 times). The Vulg. uses *tabernaculum*.

d) The Priestly writer also uses the name משכן העדות, "tabernacle of the testimony" (Exod. 38:21, etc.), and more rarely אהל העדות, "tent of the testimony" (Num. 9:15, etc.), expressions paralleled by P's "ark of the testimony" (Exod. 25:22, etc.), and rendered in the LXX again by ἡ σκηνὴ τοῦ μαρτυρίου, where in all cases the reference is probably to the two tables of law. The Vulg. has *tabernaculum testimonii* except in Num. 10:11, where we read *tabernaculum foederis*.

2. The tabernacle in P. The biblical account of the tabernacle begins in the Priestly sources with Exod. 25–31, which contains (25:10–27:19) Yahweh's instructions to Moses in the form of a specification of sizes and materials, etc.; and continues with Exod. 35–40, largely a repetition in the past tense of Exod. 25–31, though the order of contents is different.

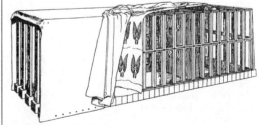

Reproduced from McNeile, *Book of Exodus*, by permission of the publishers, Methuen & Co. Ltd., London

1. The tabernacle, from the NE (A. H. McNeile, after A. R. S. Kennedy)

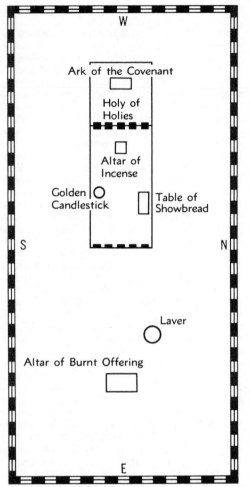

W

Ark of the Covenant

Holy of
Holies

Altar of
Incense

Golden
Candlestick

Table of
Showbread

S

N

Laver

Altar of Burnt Offering

E

Courtesy of the American Schools of Oriental Research

2. Plan of the tabernacle and its courts

There are also considerable differences as to order, extent, and translation in the LXX version of chs. 35–40. There are further references to the tabernacle and its furniture in Num. 3:25 ff; 4:4 ff; 7:1 ff. There are also striking parallels to the tabernacle in the account of Solomon's temple (I Kings 6 ff), and in the account of Ezekiel's proposed temple (Ezek. 40 ff). The Letter to the Hebrews offers the first Christian interpretation of the priestly tabernacle.

The writings of Josephus and Philo; the systematic Jewish account of Jewish views in the third century A.D., Baraitha; and the numerous and often conflicting views of Jewish and Christian commentators, reveal the difficulties of understanding the plan and specification of the structure, though fortunately main principles are clear. Figs. TAB 1-2.

a. Materials and furniture. God commands that the tabernacle is to be erected out of the voluntary gifts of the people. The materials are specified in Exod. 25:3 ff (cf. 35:4 ff): gold, silver, and bronze; blue and purple and scarlet stuff and fine twined linen; goats' hair, tanned rams' skins, goatskins, acacia wood, oil for the lamps (light), spices for the anointing oil and for the fragrant incense, onyx stones, and stones for set-

ting, for the ephod, and for the breastpiece. The three metals are used in descending value from the inmost sanctuary to the surrounding court. There was both ordinary and refined gold treated in various ways in special, hammered work for the cherubim and candlesticks, e.g. The bronze was an alloy of copper and probably tin. To the three colors (violet, purple, and scarlet) mentioned must be added, of course, the red of the rams' skins. There is no need to seek symbolical meaning in the colors. They simply represent what was available, though violet is prominent. Besides, the red of the goatskins finds a parallel in the pre-Islamic *qubbah*, which has been described as a small tent of red leather with a dome housing an idol which could be carried on a camel's back. Since black was the normal color for tents, the mention of red of the *qubbah* and the red of the goatskins shows that the tent of red leather is one of the oldest and most characteristic features of ancient Semitic religion. There was ordinary linen stuff, and the fine twined linen was a superior fabric from finer flax. Then tanned skins from rams and goats, and the durable wood of the acacia tree. The list of materials is followed by a definition of the purpose. The pattern is divinely revealed so that there can be made a dwelling place for the tabernacling presence of Yahweh (Exod. 25:8; 29:45; cf. Ezek. 37:27). It is this conception which dominates the Priestly account of the tabernacle and which is basic for the theology of the Jerusalem cultus.

The narrative proceeds in Exod. 25:10 with the construction of the ark, P's ark of the testimony, destined for the holy of holies. It had a more elaborate design than the ark of the other traditions, and was an oblong chest of acacia wood overlaid within and without with gold, approximately 3¾ by 2¼ by 2¼ feet, and it contained the testimony—possibly the Decalogue or possibly some other document of covenant requirements (cf., e.g., II Kings 11:12; Ps. 132:12). Before it were to be placed a pot of manna (Exod. 16:33 ff) and Aaron's rod that budded (Num. 17:10). Resting on the ark and on a gold molding around the rim of the ark, in the form of a solid slab of gold, was the mercy seat or propitiatory, כפרת. At each end of the golden slab and one piece with it were the little figures of refined gold known as the cherubim. With their faces toward the slab and their wings arching overhead, they surrounded the sacred center of the holy of holies. For between the cherubim and above the mercy seat was the dwelling of the God of Israel (Exod. 25:22; 30:6; Num. 7:89). This ark was carried by means of poles which were left permanently in four golden rings on the two short sides (corners) of the ark. This position ensured that Yahweh could always face the way the camp was going. The relation of P's ark to the ark of the earlier traditions will be considered below.

The sacred writer now turns to the furniture of the outer shrine, the holy place, the table of the shewbread (presence) and the lampstand. The table for the N side of the holy place was of acacia wood overlaid with fine gold, as high as the ark but not so wide or long, decorated with a gold molding. It had rings and poles for carrying, the rings being close to a frame or rail which connected the four legs. Accessories to the table were gold plates for carrying and holding the loaves of the presence, dishes or cups for the frankincense (Lev. 24:7), and large and small gold vessels for wine libations.

On the S side was to stand the seven-branched golden lampstand. The central stem stood on a tripod, and the stem extended to the first arm. The rest of the stem was the shaft, and from this six golden branches bent outward and upward. The almond was the model for the ornamentation, and there were two cups each on the base and the shaft, and three at intervals on each of the six arms, and a capital or knob—a rounded flower decoration—just below the place where each pair of branches joined the shaft. Each branch and the central shaft ended in a lamp, which either gave a perpetual light (Exod. 27:20; Lev. 24:2) or was lit at night only (I Sam. 3:3; cf. Lev. 24:3). The accessories, snuffers, snuff dishes, and oil vessels were also golden. A talent of gold (224.6 grams) was used to make the lampstand according to the divine pattern alluded to in Exod. 25:40.

According to Exod. 30:1-5 (=37:25-28), there was to be placed in front of the veil an altar of incense. There is, however, no mention of this in Exod. 25, where it should have occurred. There is, too, the persistent reference to the altar of burnt offering as "the altar" (100 times and more; e.g., Exod. 27:1); there is the reference in 30:10 to the Day of Atonement (Lev. 16), where no altar of incense is mentioned. There is also the probable absence of the incense altar from I Kings 7; Ezek. 41; and there are variants in the position and contents of Exod. 30:1-10 in the MT, Samar., and LXX versions. Probably, then, the section on the altar of incense is a later addition, for this incense altar is not mentioned in the LXX version of the recapitulation in Exod. 37. The altar was of acacia wood overlaid with pure gold, one cubit long and wide, and two cubits high. There were a golden molding, horns, rings, and poles. Perpetual incense was to be offered by the priests night and morning,* and annually atonement was to be made on its horns. Exod. 30:6 appears to suggest that the altar of incense was within the veil—i.e., in the holy of holies itself (cf. I Kings 6:22; Heb. 9:4). Fig. SHO 55.

b. The dwelling. The main narrative in Exod. 26 (=Exod. 36) turns to the tabernacle itself, and so to the curtains, for the tabernacle was a tent of ten curtains, each twenty-eight by four cubits. These ten curtains of violet, purple, and scarlet fabric with woven cherubim were to be joined in two sets of five, along each long side of which were to be sewed fifty loops of violet thread, and the two curtains were to be connected by fifty gold clasps, "that the tabernacle may be one whole" (26:6). Then over this there was to be a tent, a one-piece covering of goats' hair in turn made of five and six curtains coupled by hooks and clasps (bronze), of a total size of forty by thirty, so as to ensure that the tabernacle was completely covered. Again, the larger size meant that the goats'-hair covering overlapped the linen and allowed an extra fold in front (vs. 9). The two coverings could also be so arranged that the joins in each covering did not coincide. The tent was to have two coverings, one a covering of rams' skins dyed red, and the other a covering of skins of a dugong—unless one covering

of tanned rams' skins and goatskins is really intended (cf. 26:14; 40:19).

The curtains were supported by forty-eight acacia frames. For a long time it was thought that these frames were thick boards or beams, twenty on the N side, twenty on the S, and eight on the rear wall, each fifteen feet high, two feet three inches wide, and one foot six inches thick. These frames consisted of two long, light side arms, connected at top, middle, and foot by cross rungs, with two silver bases for each frame, each base having a mortise into which the extension of the side arms could fit. These silver bases were thus a continuous foundation around the dwelling. The frames were further held together by five bars, passing through golden rings and running along the three sides; the middle bar extending the whole length of the side, and the two members of the top pair and bottom pair alike running halfway along the side. The frames and the bars were plated with gold. The front, of course, had no frames, for it was simply enclosed by curtains. The interpretation of Exod. 26:22-25 is difficult, but the suggestion of a pair of frames fastened together at each corner of the W or rear end of the framework, and sloping upward and inward from their own bases to just under the top bar, is possible. These frames were thus projecting buttresses to strengthen the corners and to take the folds of the curtains. These four frames give the final total of forty-eight frames, and their eight bases, a total of a hundred bases. Fig. FRA 23.

Next came the veil, separating the holy of holies from the holy place, and the screen which served as the door of the holy place. The veil was of the best many-colored material, embroidered with cherubim, hanging from clasps and draped over four pillars of gold-plated acacia wood supported from four silver bases. Of the two parts thus separated by the veil, the outer was twice the size of the inner, just as Solomon's *hekal* was twice the size of the *Debir*—the oracle or inner part. Twenty cubits from the veil was the screen closing the dwelling on the E side. The screen was made of the same material as the screen at the entry of the court (27:16), was embroidered but not with cherubim, and hung from golden hooks on five gold-plated pillars of acacia wood supported by bronze bases, like the bronze bases of the court. The over-all structure of the tabernacle thus reveals three cubes, one for the most holy place, and the other two for the outer holy place. It has been much disputed whether these perfect cube measurements are internal or external measurements, for various indications support each point of view. Fig. TAB 1.

c. The furniture for the court. Having thus dealt with the furniture of the tabernacle and the tabernacle itself, the record now proceeds to the furniture of the court and the court itself. In each case the furniture is first treated as more important, for the dwelling and the court were but enclosures for the furniture. The first and most important item of the contents of the court was the altar (Exod. 27:1), the altar of burnt offering (30:28), the bronze altar (38:30). This altar was a hollow box of bronze-plated acacia wood, five cubits long and broad and three cubits high, with a horn projecting upward at each corner. Halfway down was a ledge (cf. Lev. 9:22), and below this a grating on all sides fitted with bronze rings and with bronze-plated poles whereby the altar was carried. The origin and purpose of the horns remain obscure, but they were used for asylum (I Kings 1:50-51, etc.), and they were also smeared with blood in the service of the consecration of the priests (Exod. 29:12); in connection with the sin offering (Lev. 4:18-34); and on the annual Day of Atonement (Lev. 16:18). The grating around the four sides of the foot of the altar allowed the sacrificial blood to be dashed against the base of the altar through the network. The altar was thus a hollow box with a thin sheaf of metal, and merely in this form, hardly suitable for the purposes of fire sacrifices and the like. It is probably a description based upon and an imitation of Solomon's massive bronze altar (II Chr. 4:1, but not in I Kings).

The altar was to stand at the center of the court—the court of the tabernacle, a rectangle on an E-W axis, 100 cubits (150 feet) long and 50 cubits wide, two squares of 50-cubit sides. In the western of these two squares was the tabernacle, and in the eastern the altar, the altar being in exactly the same position in its square as the ark was in the holy of holies in its square. The court itself was screened from the Israelite camp, which lay beyond, by five white curtains 5 cubits high but of varying lengths. The long curtains were on the N and S sides and were each 100 cubits long. The W curtain was 50 cubits long, and on the E side there were two curtains each 15 cubits wide, leaving an opening of 20 cubits which could be closed by an embroidered hanging. The six curtains hung from poles which rested on or in bronze bases, the bronze showing the grade of a third sanctity appropriate to the court. The poles were held in place by cords attached to bronze pegs on the ground, and according to Exod. 38:19 they had silver capitals with silver bands (fillets) at the base of the capitals. It was intended that there should be a pillar for every five cubits of hanging, but then this would not agree with the number of pillars which Exodus states as belonging to each side. No solution to preserve both the symmetry and the mathematics has been devised, whether the corner pillars be counted once or twice in the numeration.

In the record there now appears a paragraph dealing with the provision of the oil for the lampstand (Exod. 27:20-21), but it is a passage which presupposes both the erection of the tabernacle (40:1-17) and the consecration of Aaron and his sons (ch. 29). Ch. 28 deals with the garments of Aaron and his son, ch. 29 with their ordination, and in 29:43-46 there is a renewed summary of the purpose of the tabernacle and in vs. 45 of the real secret of Israel's religion in terms of the exodus from Egypt and of the tabernacling presence. The section on the altar of incense (30:1-10) is followed by the census of the people to determine the offerings for atonement and for the service of the sanctuary (vss. 11-16). The following section (vss. 17-21) describes the laver, a bronze bowl on a bronze base, to hold water for the ablutions of the priests during the ceremonial. The separation of the section on the laver from the other is often thought to raise difficulties. Presumably the choice was to put the laver with the altar of burnt offering, or to regard it as the furniture subordinate to the requirements of the priest. But the laver is

dealt with very briefly; it is not mentioned in the directions for the march (Num. 4), and it appears in what is probably a secondary tradition of P (cf. 30: 28; 31:9; etc.). There follow two sections concerned with the making and use of the priestly anointing oil (30:22-33) and of the incense (vss. 34-38). The remaining chapter of this first section deals with the appointment and investing of the foreman of the artisans, Bezalel, and his assistant Oholiab, and their able helpers, and with the law concerning sabbaths.

d. Erection of the tabernacle and its consecration. Like the pattern, place, and mode of erection, the time of erection of the dwelling is also revealed. The Lord instructs Moses to erect the tabernacle on the first day of the first month of the second year of the Exodus, nine months after the arrival at the sacred mountain (Exod. 19:1). Moses completes the erection, and then furnishes it with the various items in their appointed places. When all the work is finished, then the dwelling is ready for the divine Inhabitant, whose cloud now covers the tent of meeting and whose glory fills the dwelling. Henceforward Moses cannot enter, and the behavior of the cloud on or above the dwelling is the signal for Israel to advance or to remain encamped. When encamped, the tent of meeting is at the center of the camp with Levites on three sides, and with Moses, Aaron, and his sons on the fourth and E side. Then three tribes of Israel are on each side of the quadrilateral thus formed. One tribe in each of the four sides seems specially to be distinguished, and gives its name to that side of the camp. Judah occupies the center of the E side, the most sacred side. Ephraim is in the center on the W; Reuben in the S has the central position there. The number of Levites who served the tabernacle is no fewer than 8,580 (Num. 4:48).

These arrangements depict a diminishing of holiness from the center outward. At the center of the holy of holies is the mercy seat above the ark; then outside the veil is the less holy place; outside this again the court, then the dwellings of the priests, and then the main camp. In the same way there is a diminishing in the value of the metals used, fine gold at the very center, then ordinary gold, then silver, and lastly bronze. The best gold is used for the ark, for the mercy seat, for the plating of the table of the presence bread and its vessels; for the candlestick and its utensils; for the altar of incense, and for parts of the high priest's dress. Ordinary gold is used for the moldings and rings and staves of the ark, table, and incense altar, for the cherubim, for the hooks of the curtains, for the frames and bars, for the pillars of the veil and the screen, and for the other parts of the high priest's dress. Silver is used for the bases of the frames and of the pillars of the veil, for the hooks and moldings in the court. Bronze is used for the altar of burnt offering, for the bases of the court, and for the laver. The altar utensils, the firepans, the forks, the shovels, and the basins, are all likewise of bronze. The disposition of the altars shows the degrees of holiness and shows also the proper context of the various items. Just as the mercy seat is pure gold —for it is really the footstool of the presence—so the altar is of bronze, for it belongs to the court, to receive the offerings of the people. The same symbolic gradation is probably true of the dimensions and the figures employed. The chief numbers are 3 (divinity), 4 (humanity), 7 and 10 (completeness), and their fractions and multiples. The holy of holies, like the New Jerusalem, is a perfect cube matching the perfection of the presence. The holy place is two cubes; and various ratios, mainly 2 to 1, of the chief numbers are used—the court is 100 cubits by 50, etc. It is this graduated holiness and perfection which also explain why the people may come as far as the court, the priests alone may enter the holy place, and only the high priest the holy of holies but once a year. Worship for Israel is "to draw near," and the tabernacle's organization and specification are a commentary on this activity of drawing near.

A blast from the silver trumpets was the signal to strike camp (Num. 10:1 ff), whereupon the priests entered the tabernacle and, taking down the veil, wrapped it round the ark (4:5 ff), adding two further coverings. In the same way all the furniture of the sanctuary was to be wrapped (4:7-14), and then fully wrapped and protected; the carrying by means of the poles was entrusted to the first guild of the Levites, the sons of Kohath. Likewise the second guild, the Gershonites, transported the curtains of the tabernacle, the tent of meeting with coverings, the sheepskin covering, the screen, and the court hangings and screen and the altar and the equipment, in two covered wagons drawn by four oxen supplied by the heads of the tribes. The third guild, the sons of Merari, removed the frames, bars, pillars, and bases of the dwelling, and the pillars and bases of the court in four wagons drawn by eight oxen. Then on the march the Levites marched in the middle of the line, with six tribes in front and six behind (Num. 2:17; but 4:17 ff).

Such is P's account of the sacred dwelling of the wilderness period—it was the place of divine revelation; it was the one place for worship and sacrifice. This double character means that it was the focal point of P's view of the divine order of Israel's cult, for it was in the center of the camp and the people, as the temple is in Ezekiel. Hence its symbolism.

After Numbers there is very little to learn about P's dwelling. The ark is the leading feature in the passage of Jordan, but nothing is said of the tent of meeting. Then from Josh. 18:1; 19:51 we learn that the people of Israel set up the tent of meeting at Shiloh, where the arrangements for the division of the land were also made. Thereafter the ark is mentioned apart from the tent, though, of course, the tent may be assumed to be present (cf. I Sam. 2:22b, but this is not in the LXX). After the destruction of Shiloh, the ark eventually was deposited in the house of Abinadab at Kiriath-jearim, and this man consecrated one of his sons to tend it, presumably in the absence of the Levites, who alone were permitted to touch the ark. Following the destruction of Shiloh, the priests of Eli's house appear to have migrated to Nob. There emerges a priestly community of eighty-five persons, eventually slain by Doeg the Edomite as a punishment for their assistance to David (I Sam. 22:18-19). These priests had helped David by giving to him the bread of the presence and Goliath's sword, which was kept wrapped in a cloth behind the ephod. This story clearly implies a sanctuary. There is no reference to the tent, but it may be assumed (ch. 21).

3. The tabernacle in the early traditions. JE also speaks of the tent of meeting and of the tent in Exod. 33:7-11; Num. 11:16-17, 24, 26; 12:5, 10; Deut. 31: 14-15; but these passages reveal a different picture. In Exodus the tent of meeting is a simple tent pitched outside the camp (Exod. 33:7; Num. 11:26-27; etc.). Moses and other Israelites went out to this tent to seek their God, and it is clearly not Moses' tent but a divine tent different but parallel to P's tent. It had but one guardian, Joshua, an Ephraimite, whereas P's tent was tended by 8,580 Levites. The tent in E then was far simpler in every way than its counterpart in P. Further, it is claimed that the verbs in Exod. 33:7-11; Num. 10:17-21 are frequentative and describe what was customary. Further, if Exod. 33: 11 is literally meant, Moses was himself able to pitch the tent, whereas the elaborate, weighty, and fairly large tent of meeting in P must have required the combined efforts of many persons, though P claims in Exod. 40:16-34 that Moses erected the tent of meeting singlehandedly, which, in view of the size of the curtains alone, was a well-nigh impossible task. Substantially the same account of the tent appears in the stories of the seventy elders (Num. 11:16-17, 24-30), of Miriam's leprosy (ch. 12), and of Joshua's commission (Deut. 31:14-23).

It is reasonable to assume that the JE tent continued to shelter the ark at least until the days of Shiloh (cf. Ps. 78:60). The temple of Yahweh at Shiloh had a door and doorposts, and this suggests an edifice more like a temple than a mere tent, though Samuel's duties are reminiscent of those of Joshua (I Sam. 3:15). Thereafter the tent does not seem to have been mentioned with the ark, and it has been supposed that tent and ark had different locations and therefore different histories. But then David pitched a tent for the ark after he had brought the ark to Jerusalem. The narrative appears to imply that David's tent was not the tent of meeting, but a new tent which he had provided and pitched in readiness for the advent of the ark to his new capital (II Sam. 6:17; 7:2; I Chr. 16:1; 17:1). But testimony is not lacking to the presence of the tent continuously. From Egypt to David's day Yahweh had been moving about in a tent for his dwelling (II Sam. 7:6). The text should probably read: "from tent to tent and from tabernacle to tabernacle" (cf. I Chr. 17:5). Before David's tent stood the altar, with the customary right of asylum (I Kings 1:50), and within it there was at least the horn of oil (vs. 39). Following the erection of Solomon's temple, the tent of meeting and all its vessels accompanied the ark into the temple (8:4), though it has been usual to dismiss this verse as a gloss—a very arbitrary solution. It is possible that II Sam. 7:1-7 implies more than one tent and also correctly suggests that Yahweh was accustomed to dwell in a simple tent. It is therefore very likely that, after the settlement, the tabernacle was set up permanently at Shiloh as the amphictyonic shrine (Josh. 18:1; 19:51); and was later removed from there to Nob in the days of Saul. Then it was eventually removed to Jerusalem to be David's tent, unless that was a new construction, and thence into Solomon's temple.

4. The problem of the tent and the tabernacle. It would be natural and reasonable to infer or take for granted from the Pentateuch that the JE tent and the P tabernacle were really one and the same. But there are grave difficulties in the way of a simple identification. Thus, P's narrative of the structure and erection appears to be a very precise and matter-of-fact account, but a closer examination reveals that there are so many obscurities and omissions that it would not be possible on the basis of P's present instructions to erect such a structure as his tabernacle. No details are given for the making of the cherubim (shape); for the feet (or corners) of the ark and the table; for the thickness of the gold of the mercy seat, of the table, of the frames—and how the great weight of the overhanging curtains was borne without the whole structure falling inward. Then, too, nothing is known of the size of the two outer coverings of the tent, the material of the lamps on the lampstand, the various moldings, and the ledge around the bronze altar. Especially difficult is it to know how the hollow box sheathed in bronze serving as the altar could have withstood the heat necessary for the burning of animal sacrifices. Similarly the sons of Merari have but four wagons assigned to them for the transport of much bulky and heavy materials. There were, e.g., one hundred bases of solid silver which each weighed ninety-six pounds (Exod. 38:27)—a total of more than four tons—not to mention the hundreds of feet of curtain for the court and the three hundred bronze bases. If, therefore, the instructions to Moses are intended as a detailed specification, then the omissions, the obscurities, are a serious difficulty.

Also, the question arises whether the Israelites in the desert were in a position to erect such a sanctuary. There were gifted foremen who are mentioned by name, and with them a list of helpers. But even so, were all the skills of joinery, embroidery, casting, etc., present to the degree required for the erection of the tabernacle? Several centuries later, Solomon for his temple had to have recourse to Phoenician skilled labor for his metal work (I Kings 5:6; 7:13-14, 40, 45). Then, too, the amounts of the materials required are very considerable. Precious stones, linen, dyes, oil for the lamps, not to mention about 1¼ tons of gold, about 4 tons of silver, and about 3 tons of bronze. All this could have been readily forthcoming if the desert population of Israel had been upwards of two millions (Num. 1); but a smaller figure, and certainly at the very outside limit ten thousand people, is nearer the mark, and such a smaller group of people could not have possessed so much precious metal.

The third group of difficulties is seen in the many differences between the tent of E and the tabernacle of P already noted, and in the virtual silence of the traditions concerning the tabernacle from the settlement to Solomon's temple. It has been claimed that such references as occur are due to the Chronicles (I Chr. 16:39; 21:29), psalmists (Ps. 78:60, etc.), and editors of various glosses (e.g., I Kings 8:4).

It is such considerations as these that have led the critical movement to treat P's tabernacle as not historic and to find the explanation of the priestly portrait in ideal rather than in historical situations. As a corollary of the Graf-Wellhausen position and with the acceptance of P as a postexilic author devoted to priestly aims and ideals, P's tabernacle has been seen and explained as an ideal fiction based on Solomon's

temple. Wellhausen claimed that the tabernacle was a copy of Solomon's temple and not its prototype (cf. Wisd. Sol. 9:8). How else can one explain the giving of one direction about a simple earthen altar (Exod. 20:24-25), and then another and totally different instruction a few weeks later about a bronze altar (27: 1-8), without supposing that in fact a very long interval of time had passed, and Exodus' bronze altar was really not a sudden correction of text in ch. 24, but one much later and modeled on Solomon's bronze altar (II Chr. 4:1; cf. I Kings 8:22, 64; 9:25; II Kings 16:14-15)? The Graf-Wellhausen reconstruction has thus given a sequence in which E's tent is the shadowy original; then Solomon's temple, and then Ezekiel's ideal reconstruction, and lastly P's own tabernacle follow. After the end of Judah and the destruction of Solomon's temple, both Ezekiel in the Exile and P after it attempt the reconstruction of the relationship between Yahweh and Israel. Both see the problem as one of finding a worthy medium for the dwelling of Yahweh in the midst of his people—in short, the doctrine of the tabernacling presence. Accordingly, following on the extirpation of idolatry, Ezekiel sketches his ideal temple as the future location for the return and manifestation of the divine presence. His ideal is thus future, eschatological, and messianic. On the other hand, P describes his ideal in terms of the desert period of Israel, and his ideal is thus historical, classical, and Mosaic. But both representations are ideal transformations of Solomon's temple, P by diminution of dimension. The followers of the Graf-Wellhausen school then came to regard P's tabernacle as nonhistorical—largely an ideal fiction of the postexilic priestly writers.

It is, however, well known that the Graf-Wellhausen hypothesis is undergoing considerable modification. Its religious and evolutionary aspects are being rejected by an increasing number of scholars, and its literary aspects are being modified in a more conservative tendency. Its documents, J, E, D, and P, are no longer points on a date line, but represent streams of tradition, and in the flow of the stream is material both ancient and new. There is thus a new respect for the tradition of the P documents, as there is also a growing respect for some of the special standpoints of the Chronicler. It follows, therefore, that P's account of his tabernacle must be reassessed in the light of the new approach to and new understanding of Pentateuchal criticism. This may be achieved without abandoning the distinctive entities corresponding to the JE, D, H, P, symbols.

5. Reassessment of P's account of the tabernacle. This reassessment may perhaps be illustrated by the following examples. There is, e.g., the problem of access to the dwelling. As is well known, the priestly and Levitical system provides that the court may be visited by the people, the holy place by the priests, and the holy of holies by the high priest once a year. There is thus a threefold degree of access. This is reminiscent of the picture in the narrative portions of Exodus. The people at Sinai are gathered together near the altar at the foot of the mountain (Exod. 19:17; 20:21; 24:2-8). But Israelite representatives of the priesthood and seventy of the elders of Israel make a nearer approach. They go up to the Lord, they worship afar off, and they receive a vision of God (vss. 1-2, 9-11). But Moses goes farther—enters the cloud and goes on the mountain and is there for forty days and nights (vss. 12-18, etc.). People, priests and elders, and Moses represent degrees of access to God. It is clear that there is a rough parallel between the threefold narrative access of Exodus and the threefold Levitical access of P. It is accordingly claimed that the traditions of the exodus narrative reflect the stamp of postexilic Judaism, and in particular the degrees of access in the narrative reflect the Levitical degrees of access. But if this is so, how are we to explain the association of the elders with the priests in the second degree of access? We have to suppose that the priestly editors who prohibited the access of laymen to the holy place yet permitted the elders access to the mountain. But then why should they invent such a circumstance, which could constitute such a damaging precedent to their own rules? It is therefore much easier to suppose that, as elsewhere in judicial procedure, the elders were historically associated with the priests in this second degree of access at Sinai. It is easier to suppose that later Levitical degrees of access, which were stricter, were a development out of the exodus traditions of access, than to suppose that the priestly editors invented a picture of degrees of access at Sinai which contradicted their own privileges.

Again in regard to the tabernacle itself, there is the prior, simpler tradition of the tent of E. But it is almost universally supposed that P's tabernacle is based on Solomon's temple. But why should P project his ideal into the past behind Solomon's temple? In view of the fact that there was a tent in the tradition, it is equally feasible that P's tabernacle is an elaboration of E's tent, with, of course, much difference and even contradiction, which itself was the model from which Solomon in part drew the design for his own temple. No doubt, there was much cultic innovation in Solomon's temple and much Phoenician precedent, but there was probably much Israelite inheritance too. In fact, it seems possible to consider the tabernacle, not as a postexilic idealization of Solomon's temple, but as one of the missing links, even if in idealized form, between E's tent and Solomon's temple. To see the cherubim of Solomon's temple as taken from the cherubim of the tabernacle is to see the possibility of a new place and a new interpretation, not to say a new spirit, in the understanding of P's tabernacle. It is probable, therefore, that the hypothesis governing future study of the tabernacle will not be that it is the priestly idealization of an institution that preceded Solomon's temple. If credence can be given to the Chronicler's tradition that the tabernacle was in existence before Solomon's day and that it was in the great high place at Gibeon (I Chr. 16:39; 21:29; II Chr. 1:3; but cf. I Kings 3:4), then a new vantage point for the survey of the problem will have been gained.

This vantage point will have for its working hypothesis, not that E's tent and P's tabernacle are irreconcilable traditions, but that the two traditions are probably capable of closer integration, for if it is true that P's tabernacle ill suits the desert period, it is equally true that E's simple tent ill suits the conditions of the amphictyonic shrine which have been shown to be normative during the period of the judges. How far is it possible to progress in the reconciling of the divergent traditions? There are two extreme positions which probably cannot be sustained. The first is that P's tabernacle was a pious fiction projected by an exilic or postexilic writer into the Mosaic age. The second is that P's tabernacle was identical in every aspect with E's tent. Unlikely, too, is the view that E's tent was really Moses' tent, with which he made do until P's tabernacle was erected (cf. Exod. 33:7 LXX). E's tent was in existence after the tabernacle was erected. There is no suggestion that E's tent was temporary by intention. Further, Exod. 33:11 implies that Moses' own tent was in the camp.

Real substance remains in the difficulties which suggest desert Israel did not have the craftsmen, the materials, or the wealth to erect the tabernacle. There is not so much substance in the view that the instructions for erection are full of omissions, obscurities, and the like. These omissions may not be due to any ideal point of view, but may actually represent a summary statement of what was actually done, pointing to the fuller knowledge and actual skills which in part were not, and in part could not be, transferred to writing. This would be even more true if some of the written parts were contemporary with the structure itself. The argument that the tabernacle does not figure in Judges and in the early monarchy is at best an argument from silence, and there are pointers to the contrary. It is also probable that some of the arguments based upon the differences between E's tent and P's tabernacle have been overdrawn, particularly in relation to the supposed different location, one outside the camp, and the other central within the camp. It is claimed that Exod. 33:7-11 should be interpreted as Moses' normal practice. The verbs are taken as frequentative. It is also generally agreed that this passage presupposed an earlier passage in which the JE traditions spoke of the making of the tent. That missing passage might have the effect of showing that pitching the tent outside the camp was not Moses' habitual custom, but that it represented a temporary action. One scholar has shown the importance of understanding Exod. 33:7 in terms of the withdrawal of God's presence from Israel as a result of the golden-calf episode. Thus, in the context following Israel's wickedness at Sinai there is first the expulsion order (vs. 1); the denunciation of the people and denial of the "presence" (vs. 3); then the removal of the ornaments because of the bad tidings concerning Yahweh's denial of the presence (vss. 4-6); then presumably an instruction to erect a tent, which is to be a portable shrine and is to serve the people after they have left the mountain, as a substitute shrine for the mountain sanctuary. Then Moses pitched the tent outside the camp, thereby symbolically showing the denial of the presence to the camp. Even if the verbs are frequentative, and it was Moses' custom always to pitch the tent outside the camp, then it is clear that this was limited to his life in the desert. With the passing of the generation condemned to die in the desert and not to enter the land, the symbolism of the tent outside the camp was no longer necessary, and thereafter ark and tent resided and moved in the center of the camp. But it is probable that the pitching of the tent outside the camp was exceptional, for even this symbolism by inference shows that the proper place of the tent was in the camp. P, in carrying the central position back to the desert period, has simply extended to the desert what was actual after the settlement, because he has ignored the wickedness of Sinai and its consequences. Similarly the reference to the ark as setting out ahead of Israel in Num. 10:33 suggests that this only occurred when a camping ground had to be found. It even appears that in such movements the people were left behind, for it is an exceptional procedure, and, when accomplished, the ark, wrapped in the curtains of the tent, returned to the myriads of Israel. The normal procedure, then, on ordinary journeys, when ark (and tent) and people moved together, is described in Num. 10:17-21. These and other considerations suggest that the different locations of the tent in E and the tabernacle in P are more apparent than real, and that these differences are related to the theological ideas.

Of decisive importance too is the controlling doctrine of the tabernacling presence. Certainly this is central to the thought of Ezekiel and P, but it is also characteristic of Levitical theology at Jerusalem. It has also been shown that this doctrine is substantially older. It is related to ancient conceptions on Israel like the ark, the tent, and the experience of Moses and Israel (Exod. 17:7). If these traditions are reliable, then the tabernacling presence is probably best explained as Moses' greatest contribution to desert Israel's faith, and in that case P's traditions concerning the tabernacling presence are a later edition of an earlier and continuing fact. It is this doctrine of the presence which is the magnet that attracts P's tabernacle into the desert period. P's tabernacle is thus no pious fiction, but an ideal elaboration of an ancient doctrine and its accompanying institutions. After all, it is the Mosaic age which is the creative period of Israel's religious history, and it seems incredible that a doctrine like the tabernacling presence, which is characteristic of many periods and figures in many books in the OT, should not also be found in the desert period. It has been found possible to date early Israelite poetry to the thirteenth and twelfth centuries. Similarly, basic concepts of the prophets and Israelite apodictic laws probably belong to this desert period. Also, Israel's laws of sacrifice in Leviticus show affinity with common Semitic practice. It is not unreasonable to find the basic origin of the "presence" theology in the faith of Moses. Similarly again, efforts to trace a Proto-P show a new respect for the historical traditions of P, which are sometimes even more reliable than those of the older sources.

But when all is said and done, P's tabernacle, as now described in Exodus–Numbers, is hardly the desert structure with which Moses worked. But within P's account there are certain features which connect with the desert life. P's tabernacle is a tent, made of tent curtains: it has a covering of red leather which, like the acacia wood, is a product of the desert. On this basis one scholar has isolated all the typically desert characteristics of the tabernacle; and from these features considered to belong to the early source of P, he seeks to construct the actual Mosaic tabernacle.

In P's use of tabernacle terminology, such as the verbs "to tabernacle" and to "dwell," P's effort to find appropriate terminology for his doctrine of the presence may be detected. Wrestling as he was with the polarity of transcendence and immanence, P rescued and restored a desert vocabulary "genuinely archaic" to express this polarity. But the desert vocabulary itself points to a rudimentary apprehension of the doctrine. The desert nucleus of the tabernacle in P is now becoming apparent, and it centers in a doctrine and its terminology, and an institution of desert materials and construction which expressed this doctrine. One cannot even be certain that the cubelike dimension of the structure necessarily points to Solomon's temple as its original, for Moses and the Levites, as their names show, were assimilated in some degree to Egyptian culture. On the other hand, the frames of the tabernacle are reminiscent of the throne room of El at the source of the rivers, and it has been suggested that the occurrence of the same word in Ras Shamra suggests that El's room was something like a trellis pavilion.

Yet to say that there is a core of desert portrayal in P's tabernacle and that P's account must accordingly and in that sense be used to supplement E's picture of the tent, is not to claim that E's tent and P's tabernacle are identical. They were not and they never were. It has been suggested that the solution is to be found in II Sam. 7:6: "I have been moving about in a tent for my dwelling." The parallel in I Chr. 17:5: "I have gone from tent to tent and from dwelling to dwelling" (but not LXX), has been adopted as the correct text for II Sam. 7:6 also, and this would give a number of tents and dwellings. But though the text in I Chr. 17:5 is too uncertain for use, yet the idea of more than one historic tent may afford a solution.

There was, first, a tent erected by Moses which served as a portable shrine, normally housed at the center of the camp, but occasionally at least in the desert period pitched outside the camp to symbolize the withdrawal of Yahweh's presence. This tent, with its ark, at least, if no other pieces of furniture, was the dwelling of Yahweh and gave visible expression to the new doctrine and faith of Yahweh's tabernacling presence among his people.

There was next the sanctuary at Shiloh, which appears to have been a more permanent structure.* This suggests that the curtains and other fabric portions of Moses' tent had by this time decayed after the hard usage of the wilderness wanderings and the settlement in Canaan. But the ark remained and either old or new furniture, such as a lamp, a table of shewbread, and the like. The Shiloh sanctuary thus replaced the perishable parts of the old Mosaic tent in a shrine more suitable as an amphictyonic center for the Israel of that day. Fig. SHI 44.

The destruction of Shiloh was followed by the separate adventures of the ark: Philistia, Kiriath-jearim, Jerusalem; and of remnants of the tent and its furniture, such as the table of the shewbread, etc.

So far, then, there has been only one tent and its survival in remnants. The second tent is that of David. In bringing the ark to Jerusalem, David was reviving Mosaic tradition. But this ark was set "in its place, inside the tent which David had pitched for it"

(II Sam. 6:17). It is quite reasonable to see in this tent David's revival of the traditions of the tent. David's tent could hardly be Moses' tent after some centuries of use, so it was probably a new tent. If it was a new tent, then it is but a short and reasonable step to concur in the suggestion that P's tabernacle account reflects David's tent. It has been further suggested that "in its place" in II Sam. 6:17 suggests the royal tent had a holy of holies, דביר. Near to it must have been an altar of burnt offerings, where David, according to the same verse, offered burnt offerings and peace offerings before the Lord. From I Kings 1:50; 2:28-30 has been inferred at least an altar of burnt offering in the court, and possibly a second horned altar within the tent—i.e., either the altar of incense or else a table of presence bread. Perhaps II Sam. 7:18 implies the veil before the ark.

To associate P's tabernacle or something very like it with David's tent is part of an increasing tendency to date various documents and lists in the P document to premonarchic and early monarchy days. Thus the census lists of Num. 1; 26 and the lists of the cities of refuge and the Levitical cities (Josh. 21; I Chr. 6) almost certainly belong to the days of David, while the priestly list of stations of the Exodus (Num. 33:1-48) and the list of spies (13:4-16) also belong to the period of which they speak. In the same way then, and in view of the long history of transmission which Exod. 25–31 reveals, it is quite feasible that the tabernacle records of P could reflect the Davidic tent. Then, if this is true, P's tabernacle will not be an idealized copy of the temple of Solomon, but not less than one of its actual prototypes. On the older view the catastrophe of the Exile was seen to be an appropriate time for the flowering of the idealism of Ezekiel and P. The newer view, in suggesting the days of David, points to an actual revival of covenant theology in the Davidic kingship (II Sam. 7; Pss. 72; 89), and to the revival of Mosaic themes in ark and tabernacle and presence.

5. The tabernacle in the NT. The influence of the terminology is to be seen in such phrases as John 1:14: "The Word . . . dwelt [i.e., 'tabernacled'] among us," and the laver or "washing of regeneration" (Tit. 3:5). Then there are references to the tabernacle in Acts 7:44; Rev. 13:6; 15:5; 21:3. The Letter to the Hebrews sets forth the Christian interpretation of the Mosaic tabernacle. Its titles show the presence of God, his righteousness, and his "conversableness." The furniture of the court symbolizes man's approach to God, just as the furniture of the most holy place represents God's approach to man in holiness, grace, and sovereignty. According to Hebrews, the tabernacle is modeled on a heavenly pattern (8:5); it has its divine prototype (8:2, 5; 9:11), the "greater and more perfect tent"; it has a symbolic meaning for the writer's age (9:9), but the way into the sanctuary is not yet opened as long as the outer tent is still standing. But when Christ appeared, he entered once for all, not into the human sanctuary, but into heaven (9:24). Similarly in Rev. 21:3 the dwelling of God with men is identified with the Holy City, the New Jerusalem, coming down out of heaven, dwelling among men, and removing all tears, sorrow, pain, and death.

But even heaven and the New Jerusalem are not the real culmination of the tabernacle image. After all, the tabernacle and the New Jerusalem are only places. What is of chief significance is that the tabernacle is the place of the presence. The tabernacle thus properly belongs to the theology of the Incarnation. No doubt, the idea of the presence dwelling in a place had begun to give way even in the OT to the idea of the presence living in a person. But this personifying of the presence image of OT faith took place fully in the person of Jesus Christ, "for in him all the fulness of God was pleased to dwell" (Col. 1: 19; cf. 2:9). Thus in the NT the tabernacle finds a double fulfilment: as a place, in heaven and in the New Jerusalem; as a personified image, in the body of Jesus Christ (cf. Rom. 8:9; I John 3:2; Rev. 13:6). The tabernacle of the OT as the place of the presence is the principal bridgehead in the OT to the doctrine of the Incarnation.

See also ARK OF THE COVENANT; GLORY; PRESENCE OF GOD; TEMPLE, JERUSALEM.

Bibliography. A. H. McNeile, *The Book of Exodus* (1908), pp. lxxiii-xcii; S. R. Driver, *The Book of Exodus* (1911), pp. 257-62, 428-32; E. Sellin, "Das Zelt Jahwes," *BWAT*, 13 (1913), 168-92; R. Hartmann, "Zelt und Lade," *ZAW*, XXXVII (1917-18), 209-44; G. von Rad, "Zelt und Lade," *NKZ*, XLII (1931), 476-98; F. Bovet, "Sur le Tabernacle," *RHPR*, N.S. XXI (1933), 277-80; G. Beer, *Exodus* (1939), pp. 133-35; F. M. Cross, Jr., "The Tabernacle," *BA*, vol. X, no. 3 (Sept., 1947); M. Haran, "מהותו של אהל מועד (The Tent of Meeting)," *Tarbiz*, vol. XXV, no. 1 (Oct., 1955), pp. 11-20 (English summary on pp. iii-v); M. H. Segal, "למהותו של אהל מועד (On the Tent of Meeting)," *Tarbiz*, vol. XXV, no. 2 (Jan., 1956), pp. 231-33 (English summary on pp. viii-ix); G. von Rad, "Zelt, Lade und Herrlichkeit Gottes," *Theologie des ATs*, I (1957), 233-40; D. W. Gooding, *The Account of the Tabernacle* (1959); M. Noth, *Das zweite Buch Mose* (1959), pp. 171-74; M. Haran, "The Nature of the ''Ōhel Mô'ēdh'' in Pentateuchal Sources," *Journal of Semitic Studies*, V (1960), 50-65.

G. HENTON DAVIES

TABERNACLES, FEAST OF. See BOOTHS, FEAST OF.

TABITHA tăb'ĭ thə [Ταβιθά]. See DORCAS.

TABLE. The translation of many different words in the English Bible (*see* § 1 *below*). The word covers a variety of meanings. The tables mentioned in the Bible were used for eating, ritual, money-changing, and writing.

1. Terminology
2. Tables for eating
   a. Development
   b. Tables of kings
   c. Tables of commoners
   d. Manners
   e. NT tables
3. Tables for ritual
   a. The table of the bread of the Presence
   b. Other Hebrew sacrificial tables
   c. Idolatrous tables
   d. The table of the Lord
4. Tables of money-changers
5. Tables of the law
6. Figurative references
Bibliography

1. Terminology. The following words are translated "table":

Table   507   Table

a) שֻׁלְחָן, meaning: table for eating (Judg. 1:7 and often); table of the bread of the Presence (Exod. 25:23 and often); other temple tables (Ezek. 40:39-43); altar of burnt offerings (Mal. 1:7); heathen ritual table (Isa. 65:11).

b) לוּחַ, meaning: table of the law (Exod. 24:12 and often); TABLET (KJV "table" in Prov. 3:3; 7:3; Isa. 30:8; Jer. 17:1; Hab. 2:2).

c) מֵסַב, COUCH (KJV "table" in Song of S. 1:12).

d) Τράπεζα, meaning: table for eating (Matt. 15:27); communion table (I Cor. 10:21); pagan ritual feast (I Cor. 10:21); table of the bread of the Presence (Heb. 9:2); by metonymy, FEAST (KJV "table" in Rom. 11:9); table of money-changers (Matt. 21:12).

e) Πλάξ, meaning: TABLET of the law (KJV "table" in II Cor. 3:3; Heb. 9:4); writing "tablet" (KJV "table" in II Cor. 3:3).

f) Πινακίδιον, "tablet" (KJV "table" in Luke 1:63).

g) Some Greek MSS have κλινῶν (Mark 7:4; KJV "tables"; RSV mg. "beds" is better), not found in some of the best MSS (א B) and so omitted in the RSV text.

h) The RSV introduces the word "table" in translating: פָּנָיו (lit., "his face") in Gen. 43:34; II Kings 25:29; Jer. 52:33; יָשַׁב (lit., "he sat") in I Sam. 20:5; and various Greek words meaning "to recline or sit at table"; ἀνακλίνω (Matt. 8:11); ἀνάκειμαι (John 12:2; 13:28; in both verses the KJV also inserts "table"); κατάκειμαι (Mark 2:15); κατακλίνω (Luke 7:36); συνανάκειμαι (Luke 7:49); ἀναπίπτω (Luke 11:37).

2. Tables for eating. This is the most common meaning.

a. Development. The root meaning of שֻׁלְחָן, "skin, hide," indicates that it was originally a piece of leather like the *sufrah* which the Bedouin of today sometimes use as a table. Isa. 21:5 pictures the Medes and Elamites as using a leather or low table, for they sit on rugs. Significantly, tables are never mentioned in the patriarchal narratives. The earliest table for eating in the Bible is that of a Canaanite king at the time of the Israelite conquest (Judg. 1:7). In Egypt representations of tables for eating are rare before the New Kingdom. *See* the Tables on the Megiddo Ivory, *ca.* 1200 B.C., Fig. BAN 19.

b. Tables of kings. The table of Adoni-bezek (Judg. 1:7) was evidently large and elevated, for many of his conquered enemies ate scraps under it. King Saul's table was also large, for many of his court ate at it (I Sam. 20:29, 34). The Queen of Sheba was amazed at the food of Solomon's table (I Kings 10:5). Various people ate at the table of David (II Sam. 9:7), especially of Solomon (I Kings 2:7; 4:27—H 5:7), of Jezebel (I Kings 18:19), and of Nehemiah (Neh. 5:17). Sometimes this meant eating at the expense of the ruler, not literally at his table.

c. Tables of commoners. The prophet of Judah ate with the old prophet of Bethel at a table (I Kings 13:20). The family of Shunem provided a table among the furniture of Elisha's room (II Kings 4:10).

d. Manners. Jesus the son of Sirach condemns miserliness at table (Ecclus. 14:10), and he devotes a long section to table etiquette (31:12-32:13).

e. NT tables. The Greek words listed in § 1 *above* (under *h*), if taken with their root meaning, indicate

that reclining was the usual posture at table in NT times. Following the Greek example, at formal meals the table was U-shaped, to permit servants to enter with food. The guests reclined on couches around the outside of the table, so that the women mentioned in Luke 7:38 would have no difficulty in anointing the feet of the reclining Jesus and at the Last Supper John's head could naturally have been near Jesus' chest (John 13:23). The usual table was evidently quite high, for dogs could eat scraps underneath (Matt. 15:27).

3. Tables for ritual. *a. Table of the bread of the Presence.* The structure of this table in the tabernacle is described in Exod. 25:23-30; it was of acacia wood, 2 cubits long, 1 cubit wide, and 1½ cubits high, overlaid with gold, and provided with rings and poles for carrying. It was consecrated by the sacred anointing oil (30:27) and placed on the N side of the holy place, outside the veil of the holy of holies (26:35). On it every sabbath the priest placed the fresh BREAD OF THE PRESENCE (Lev. 24:5-7). The Kohathites were in charge of carrying this table (Num. 3:31), and its arrangement for transportation is described in Num. 4:7-8. Solomon made a new golden table for the bread of the Presence in the temple (I Kings 7:48). After Ahaz defiled the temple with idolatry, its furniture, including this table, was purified by Hezekiah (II Chr. 29:18). It was doubtless taken or burned by the Babylonians in the capture of Jerusalem. The table of the second temple was taken by Antiochus Epiphanes (I Macc. 1:23), and Judas Maccabeus made another one (I Macc. 4:47-51). The table was taken from Herod's temple by the Romans and was represented among the spoils on the Arch of Titus in Rome. The Mishna speaks of a complicated system of golden props and rods above the table to support and separate the loaves (Menahoth XI.6).

b. Other Hebrew sacrificial tables. According to I Chr. 28:16, David gave silver to Solomon to make tables for the temple, and II Chr. 4:8 says that Solomon made ten tables for the temple (which some think were for the bread of the Presence). Ezekiel lists twelve temple tables: eight for slaughtering the sacrifices (40:39-41) and four for the instruments of sacrifice and the pieces of flesh (vss. 42-43). Similarly the Mishna (Shek. VI.4) lists thirteen tables in the temple: eight of marble for rinsing the inward parts of the sacrifices, one of marble for parts of the offering, one of silver for the sacrificial instruments, one of marble on which the new bread of the Presence was laid, one of gold for the old bread, and the golden table of the bread of the Presence. It is uncertain what temple tables or altars are intended in Ezek. 41:22; 44:16.

c. Idolatrous tables. Isa. 65:11 condemns idolaters who "set a table" (perhaps a sacrificial feast) for Gad, the god of fortune. Bel 13—G 12 refers to a table on which food and drink were placed before the god Bel in Babylon. In I Cor. 10:21 the "table of demons" means a pagan sacrificial meal. E.g., Oxyrhyncus Papyrus 110 gives an invitation to supper "at the table of the Lord Serapis."

d. The table of the Lord. In Mal. 1:7, 12, this is the altar of burnt offering. In I Cor. 10:21 the phrase refers to the communion table.

4. Tables of money-changers. These were small trays on stands. Jesus overturned these tables in the temple in protest against cheating and commercialization (Matt. 21:12; Mark 11:15; John 2:15). *See* MONEY-CHANGERS.

5. Tables of the law. The two tables of the Ten Commandments are called "tables of stone" (Exod. 24:12), "tables of the testimony" (Exod. 31:18), and "tables of the covenant" (Deut. 9:9). God promised them to Moses (Exod. 24:12), wrote them with his own "finger" (Deut. 9:10), and gave them to Moses on Mount Sinai (Exod. 31:18). Because of the sins of the people, Moses broke these first tables (Exod. 32: 15-19; Deut. 9:9-17). Then Moses made new tables and went up the mountain; the Lord wrote on the new tables and gave them to Moses, who placed them in the ark (Exod. 34:1-4, 28-29; Deut. 10:1-5). The tables were still there in Solomon's day, according to II Chr. 5:10 (cf. Heb. 9:4). Perhaps these tables were like small Egyptian stone steles, which were often rounded at the top.

6. Figurative references. In Ezek. 39:20, God's table stands for the slain of Gog's army, who are eaten by birds and beasts. In Prov. 9:2, Wisdom's table symbolizes the benefits of godliness. The "tables" (KJV), or "tablets," of the heart in II Cor. 3:3 are a reference to the souls of the Corinthian Christians.

Bibliography. S. Krauss, *Talmüdische Archäologie,* I (1910), 58-60. A. Deissmann, *Licht vom Osten* (4th ed., 1923), p. 299, on the table of demons. A. Erman and H. Ranke, *Aegypten und aegyptisches Leben im Altertum* (1923), pp. 215, 219, 221. B. Meissner, *Babylonien und Assyrien,* I (1920), 248, 314, 406, 418; II (1925), 73, 87. G. Dalman, *Arbeit und Sitte,* VII (1942), 16, 127, 213-14, 218-24. J. A. THOMPSON

TABLELAND [המוישר, ארץ המוישר, the level place]; KJV PLAIN. The OT designation for that part of the fertile Transjordanian Plateau between the Arnon and Heshbon (Josh. 13:15-17; *see* PALESTINE, GEOGRAPHY OF). Although assigned to the tribe of Reuben (Deut. 4:43; Josh. 20:8), it was Moabite territory during the monarchy (Jer. 48:21-25). Among its famous cities (Josh. 13:15-21) Dibon and Medeba are well-known Moabite strongholds. *See* MOAB; PLAIN.
L. E. TOOMBS

TABLES OF DUTIES. *See* LISTS, ETHICAL.

TABLET. A translation of several words in the Bible:

a) לוח (Prov. 3:3; 7:3; Isa. 30:8; Jer. 17:1; Hab. 2:2) is usually translated "TABLE" (an archaism, meaning "tablet"). The word is also used to refer to wooden planks (Ezek. 27:5), metal plates (I Kings 7:36), and a writing surface of stone (Exod. 24:12; 31:18; etc.). The NT equivalent of לוח is πλάξ (I Cor. 3:3; KJV "table"; cf. Heb. 9:4).

b) The גליון (Isa. 8:1; KJV "roll") was probably a wooden tablet.

c) The πινακίδιον (Luke 1:63) was likely a wax writing tablet. *See* WRITING AND WRITING MATERIALS.

In the KJV "tablet" renders כומז in Exod. 35:22 (ARMLET); Num. 31:50 (BEADS), and בית נפש in Isa. 3:20 ("perfume boxes"; *see* PERFUME).
R. J. WILLIAMS

TABOR tā'bər [תבור]. A Levitical town in the territory of Zebulun (I Chr. 6:77—H 6:62). It does not appear in the parallel list in Josh. 21:34-35, which may indicate errors in one or both texts. If the Chronicles reading is correct and there was a town named Tabor, it must have been on or near the hill of the same name. *See* TABOR, MOUNT.
G. W. VAN BEEK

TABOR, MOUNT [הר תבור]. A hill in the Valley of Jezreel having important associations with the judges of Israel and with Christian tradition. Mount Tabor, known in Arabic as Jebel et-Tor, is an isolated hill situated in the NE corner of the Valley of Jezreel, approximately six miles E-SE of Nazareth and twelve miles W-SW of the S end of the Sea of Galilee. Its sides rise steeply from the Valley of Jezreel and curve gently in at the top to form a dome-shaped summit. The summit surface is roughly rectangular and measures slightly more than a half mile E-W and *ca.* one quarter mile N-S. Although Tabor reaches a maximum elevation of only 1,843 feet, its isolation and its steep sides combine to give it a majestic appearance which invites comparison with Mount Carmel and Mount Hermon (Ps. 89:12 —H 89:13; Jer. 46:18). Its summit commands a magnificent view of the entire valley, and it dominates two important routes: the E-W road connecting the Valley of Jezreel and the Sea of Galilee, and the N-S road between Beth-shan and Damascus.

It is possible that there was an early sanctuary on the summit of Mount Tabor, if Tabor is the mountain to which reference is made in Deut. 33:19. It is first mentioned by name, however, in connection with the division of the land among the tribes after the Conquest, as the meeting place of the territories of Issachar, Naphtali, and Zebulun (Josh. 19:12, 22, 34). It is not surprising, therefore, that Mount Tabor was selected by Barak as the base from which he and the men of Naphtali and Zebulun launched their successful attack against Sisera (Judg. 4:6-14). During the oppression by Midian, it was the place where the two Midianite kings, Zebah and Zalmunna, killed the brothers of Gideon (8:18). In the Hellenistic-Roman period, Antiochus III, the Great, is reported to have fortified Mount Tabor in 218 B.C., and Josephus claims to have erected a wall around its summit.

Mount Tabor's primary fame rests on its traditional identification as the Mount of Transfiguration. But whether it is the actual site of the Transfiguration cannot be determined with certainty, since the mountain is not named in the gospel narratives (Matt. 17: 1-8; Mark 9:2-8; Luke 9:28-36). On the strength of this identification, Helena the mother of Constantine built a church on Mount Tabor in A.D. 326, and by the seventh century A.D. there were three shrines on its summit, dedicated to Jesus, Moses, and Elijah. Other churches and monasteries were built during the next four centuries, and all these structures were destroyed in 1187 by Saladin, whose brother in turn erected a fortress on the hill in 1212. By the end of the thirteenth century, this structure had also been destroyed, and the summit was abandoned for six hundred years. In the late nineteenth century a

Courtesy of Herbert G. May

3. Mount Tabor rising above the Plain of Jezreel

church and a monastery were erected by the Greek Orthodox community; and a Latin basilica, designed in the old Syrian style, was built on the highest point of the summit by the Franciscans.

Fig. TAB 3.

Bibliography. C. R. Conder and H. H. Kitchener, *SWP,* I (1881), 367-68, 388-91.   G. W. VAN BEEK

TABOR, OAK OF [אלון תבור]; KJV TABOR, PLAIN OF. A place near Bethel. It was here that Saul was to meet three men going to the sanctuary at Bethel; this was Samuel's second sign confirming the mission of Saul (I Sam. 10:3). The exact location of this tree is unknown.   G. W. VAN BEEK

TABRET tăb'rĭt. *See* MUSICAL INSTRUMENTS § B3.

TABRIMMON tăb rĭm'ən [טברמן, (the god) Ram-mân (*cf.* II Kings 5:18) is good; LXX B ταβερέμα, LXX L ταβερεμμάν]. The father of Ben-hadad I, the king of Damascus whose own father was Ḥazyanu (biblical Hezion; cf. I Kings 15:18 and the Aramaic Melqart stele). The Rimmon of his name is the Ak-kadian god Rammân ("roarer"—i.e., "thunderer"), a manifestation of the god Hadad.

Tabrimmon was possibly the predecessor of Ben-hadad I as king of Damascus, but nothing more is known of him.

Bibliography. E. Kraeling, *Aram and Israel* (1918); W. F. Albright, "A Votive Stele Erected by Ben-Hadad I of Damascus to the god Melcarth," *BASOR,* 87 (1942), 23-29; A. Dupont-Sommer, *Les Araméens* (1949); M. F. Unger, *Israel and the Aramaeans of Damascus* (1957), pp. 57, 142.
                    R. A. BOWMAN

TACHE tăch. KJV translation of קרס (RSV "clasp"; "hook"). The word is a KJV archaism.

TACHMONITE. KJV form of TAHCHEMONITE.

TACKLE [חבל, cord (Isa. 33:23; KJV TACK-LINGS); σκευή (Acts 27:19; KJV TACKLING)]. The apparatus on a ship (ropes, pulleys, etc.) used in working the sails and handling cargo. In Isa. 33:23*a*, which is a nautical fragment entirely out of its context, the "tackle" (ropes) is said to hold the mast (such mast ropes are technically called "shrouds") and the sails. In Acts 27:19 σκευή presumably means all the ship's equipment (this would include the tackle) which could be dispensed with in an emer-gency. *See* SHIPS AND SAILING.   W. S. McCULLOUGH

TADMOR tăd'môr [תדמר, palm tree]. A city in the wilderness to the N of Palestine that was built by Solomon (II Chr. 8:4). In the parallel passage in I Kings 9:18, the Masoretic directions call for a read-ing "Tadmor," while the text itself has "Tamar" (RSV "Tamar . . . in the land of Judah," inserting "of Judah"). The distinction is not a real one, as both "Tadmor" and "Tamar" have the same meaning. If "Tadmor" is the correct reading in these passages, it is identical with the famous Arab city that was known as Palmyra by the Greeks, which was situ-ated in a fertile oasis in the Syrian desert, 120 miles NE of Damascus. The city is mentioned in Assyrian records beginning with Tiglath-pileser I (1115-1100 B.C.) as *Tadmar ša mât Amurri,* "Tadmor of the west-ern country" (*ANET* 275), and the site still bears the Arabic name Tudmur. The city reached the height of its power under Odenathus (A.D. 255-67) and his wife and successor, Zenobia, and was finally destroyed by the Roman emperor Aurelian in 273. The splendid old ruins from the period of its prosperity still attest to its former glory.

From *Atlas of the Bible* (Thomas Nelson & Sons Limited)

4. General view of Tadmor, called Palmyra by the Romans

Courtesy of the Arab Information Center, New York

5. Monumental arch and colonnade of the court of the temple of Baal at Tadmor

Biblical scholars are divided on the question of the identity of the Tamar or Tadmor mentioned in the Bible with the historical Palmyra. Some would identify the city of Solomon with a place of that name in the SE part of Judah (*see* TAMAR 5). On the other hand, it is notable that the building of the city is mentioned directly after the statement of Solomon's conquest of Hammath-zobah in Syria, and that the general direction of the cities in this section which Solomon is said to have built runs from N to S (II

Chr. 8:2-6). The prosperity which developed in Solomon's reign was primarily due to his control of the routes of trade between Egypt and Arabia on the one hand, and Asia Minor and Mesopotamia on the other. It would have been sound policy for him to establish such a station as Tadmor, which lay on the direct route from Zobah to Mesopotamia, and to place a garrison of soldiers there to ensure the safety of his caravans. After his death and the division of the kingdom, this outpost must have been abandoned to the Arameans.

Figs. TAD 4-5.

Bibliography. I. Starcky, *Palmyra* (1952).   S. COHEN

TAHAN tā′hăn [תחן]; **TAHANITES** —ə nīts. The third son of Ephraim; ancestor of the family of Tahanites (Num. 26:35). In the Ephraimite genealogy in I Chr. 7:20-29, which shows signs of disturbance, Tahath appears as the third son of Ephraim and Tahan as a descendant in a later generation (vs. 25).

             R. F. JOHNSON

TAHAPANES. KJV alternative form of TAHPANHES.

TAHASH tā′hăsh [תחש, porpoise] (Gen. 22:24); KJV **THAHASH** thā′—. The third son of Nahor and Reumah; identified with the place name Taḫši in the Tell el-Amarna Letters and in Thut-mose III's records; located N(?) of Damascus.

TAHATH tā′hăth [תחת, substitute, *or* compensation(?)]. **1.** A name in a genealogy of the family of Kohath, one of the three sons of Levi (I Chr. 6:24). The name occurs again in a subsequent list which traces both the Levitical descent of Heman and the Levitical line from Kohath (vs. 37).

2. Eponym of an Ephraimite family; son of Bered (I Chr. 7:20).

3. Eponym of another Ephraimite family; son of Eleadah (I Chr. 7:20).   T. M. MAUCH

4. A stopping place of the Israelites in the wilderness (Num. 33:26-27). The location is unknown.

TAHCHEMONITE tä kē′mə nīt [תחכמני] (II Sam. 23:8); KJV **TACHMONITE** tăk′mə nīt. A word identifying one of David's Mighty Men. The first consonant probably is an error; very likely a copyist mistook the Hebrew article ה ("the," in "the Hachmonite") for a ת. *See* HACHMONITE.   T. M. MAUCH

TAHPANHES tä′pə nēz [תחפנחס, *taḥpanḥēs; but in* Ezek. 30:18 *t^eḥaphn^eḥēs;* LXX Ταφνάς]. Alternately: TEHAPHNEHES tĭ hăf′ nə hēz (*t^eḥaphn^eḥēs;* Ezek. 30:18); KJV **TAHAPANES** tə hăp′ə nēz (Jer. 2:16); KJV **TAPHNEZ** tăf′nēz (Jth. 1:9). A city on the E frontier of N (Lower) Egypt.

Tahpanhes is almost universally identified with the classical site of Daphnai, modern Tell Defneh. The Hebrew consonantal spelling is an accurate transcription of the Egyptian name *T³-ḥ(t)-(n.t)-p³-nḥsy,* "the Fortress of Penhase." Penhase, which is also the origin of the biblical name Phinehas, means literally "the Nubian," but was the name of a powerful Theban general of the eleventh century B.C. whose success in suppressing rebellion in the Delta area resulted in the perpetuation of his fame in the names of several places. The LXX reading Ταφνάς is perfectly

correct, but through popular etymology the name was later altered by the Greeks to Δαφναι, the latter surviving in the modern Arabic name Tell Defneh.

The site known as Tell Defneh is an unimpressive mound in the desert bordering on Lake Menzaleh in N Egypt. According to the excavation reports of Flinders Petrie, who investigated the site in the latter part of the nineteenth century, there is little evidence of extensive occupation before the time of Psammetichus, founder of the Saïte Dynasty (*ca.* 663 B.C.). The importance of the city for some centuries after that time is clear, however, from its mention in the OT, as well as from the more specific information given by Herodotus (II.30), who names Daphnai, ELEPHANTINE, and Marea as the three important frontier stations during the reign of Psammetichus and during the Persian occupation.

From the biblical references we learn that Tahpanhes was a refuge city for the Jews who fled from Palestine before the successive Assyrian invasions. It was to Tahpanhes, e.g., that Johanan son of Kareah fled with the remnant of Judah, contrary to the oracle of the Lord as expressed by Jeremiah (42:19). The prophet followed them and delivered in that city a further promise of destruction for Egypt and the Jews who dwelt there.

Bibliography. W. M. F. Petrie, *Tanis II* (1888), pp. 47-96; W. F. Albright, "Baal-zephon," *Festschrift Alfred Bertholet* (1950), pp. 13-14.   T. O. LAMBDIN

TAHPENES tä′pə nēz [תחפנים; LXX Θεχεμείνα, Θεκεμείνα] (I Kings 11:19-20). An Egyptian ·queen of the time of David and Solomon.

In the time of David, young Hadad of Edom fled to Egypt. The reigning pharaoh received him cordially and wedded him to the sister of his queen, Tahpenes. After the death of David and Joab, Hadad returned to Edom and opposed Solomon. The unnamed pharaoh cannot be identified, but he was probably one of the Twenty-first Dynasty rulers at Tanis in the Delta. Although the name Tahpenes looks Egyptian, no such name has been found. Probably the LXX's use of -*m*- instead of -*p*- is correct. Then, as in the use of the title "pharaoh" as a proper name, we may have here the Egyptian title "the wife of the king" (pronounced something like *ta-him-nes*), treated as if a name. *See bibliography.*

Bibliography. The solution noted above seems to have been first offered by B. H. Stricker, *Acta Orientalia,* XV (1937), 11-12.   J. A. WILSON

TAHREA. Alternate form of TAREA.

TAHTIM-HODSHI tä′tĭm hŏd′shī [תחתים הדשי]. A place in the N, possibly between Gilead and Dan, visited by the census takers of David (II Sam. 24:6 KJV). The place is not mentioned elsewhere. Wellhausen suggested the reading החתים קדשה ("Hittites to Kadesh"), according to a Greek MS. This conjecture has been accepted in the RSV: "to Kadesh in the land of the Hittites." As the kingdom of David actually reached as far N as Kadesh, the conjecture is not unlikely.   A. S. KAPELRUD

TALENT [ככר; τάλαντον]. The standard large weight in Mesopotamia, Canaan, and Israel. It varied in weight, but may in biblical passages be considered as *ca.* seventy-five pounds. In NT times as money the talent was equal to six thousand drachmas. *See* WEIGHTS AND MEASURES §§ B2-3, 4*g, i.*   O. R. SELLERS

TALISMAN. An amulet or charm; an object having supposed magical power. *See* AMULETS.

TALITHA CUMI tăl′ə thə kū′mī [ταλιθά κοῦμι; Aram. טְלִיתָא קוּמִי]. The Aramaic words attributed to Jesus in the healing of Jairus' daughter and found only in Mark 5:41, where they are translated in expanded form as τὸ κοράσιον, σοὶ λέγω, ἔγειρε ("Little girl, I say to you, arise"). The Aramaic consists of the feminine of טַלְיָא (*talyâ*), meaning "lamb" or "youth," and the *piel* imperative feminine singular of קוּמִי (*qûmî*), "stand," "rise up." The latter may be a correction from the shorter, masculine form, קוּם (κοῦμ), which is read by the best Greek MSS and in some critical texts. The confusion is doubtless due to the fact that both forms were pronounced alike. The unusual reading of Codex Bezae (D) and the Washington Gospels (W), ραββι ταβιθα (D, θαβιθα), may be dialectical (for *râbithâ*, "maiden"), or a scribal corruption, involving assimilation to Acts 9:40. *Tabîthâ* is read by several Greek and by most OL MSS in Mark (cf. Luke 8:54).

The retention of the Aramaic in a healing story would enhance the miraculous aspect of the event for Gentile readers (*cf.* EPHPHATHA in Mark 7:34). The use of foreign words in such contexts was common in the magical papyri. It was thought that translation might impair their efficacy. In Mark, however, the characteristic preservation of Aramaic sayings in various contexts may also be attributed to an interest in retaining the actual words of Jesus.

Bibliography. G. Dalman, *Jesus-Jeshua* (1929), pp. 11-12, 203; K. Preisendanz, *Papyri Graecae Magicae* (2 vols.; 1928-31); L. J. McGinley, *Form-Criticism of the Synoptic Healing Narratives* (1944), contains a useful collection of parallels from rabbinic and Hellenistic sources; V. Taylor, *The Gospel According to St. Mark* (1952), pp. 296-97.   A. WIKGREN

TALMAI tăl′mī [תַּלְמַי]. **1.** One of the three sons of Anak, or "giants," residing in Hebron when the Israelite spies reconnoitered the land (Num. 13:22; Josh. 15:14; Judg. 1:10). Named together with Ahiman and Sheshai as a descendant of Anak, Talmai was defeated in Hebron by the invading Israelites.

2. King of Geshur; father of David's wife Maacah, who was the mother of Absalom (II Sam. 3:3; 13:37; I Chr. 3:2). When Absalom was forced to flee his father's court after the murder of Amnon, he took refuge with his grandfather in Geshur, a small Aramean kingdom NE of the Sea of Galilee.

There are close parallels to the name Talmai in Nabatean nomenclature.

Bibliography. L. Koehler and W. Baumgartner, *Lexicon in Veteris Testamenti Libros* (1953), p. 1030.   R. F. JOHNSON

TALMON tăl′mən [טַלְמוֹן, טַלְמֹן, *perhaps* brightness; *cf.* Arab. *zalmun;* Apoc. Τολμάν]. A Levite, and the eponym of a Levitical family of gatekeepers in the postexilic temple (I Chr. 9:17; cf. Neh. 11:19), listed among the returned exiles (Ezra 2:42; Neh. 7:45; 12: 25; I Esd. 5:28).

Bibliography. M. Noth, *Die israelitischen Personennamen* (1928), p. 223.   B. T. DAHLBERG

TALMUD tăl′mŭd [תַּלְמוּד, *from* לָמַד, *lāmādh,* to study, to learn]. The written story, in Hebrew and Aramaic dress, of biblical interpretation, of the making of bylaws, of the adding to the store of wise counsel, covering a period of almost one thousand years from the time of Ezra to the middle of the sixth century of the Christian era.

1. Repository of the oral law
2. Function and scope of the oral law
3. Talmudic antecedents: Midrash and Mishna
4. Division of Mishna and Talmud
5. Halachah and Haggadah
6. The two Talmudic versions
   a. Palestinian
   b. Babylonian
7. The influence of the Talmud
8. The burnings of the Talmud
9. Attacks on the Talmud in modern times
10. Editions
11. Commentaries
12. The Talmud in Jewish education
13. Significance of the Talmud in our times
Bibliography

1. Repository of the oral law. The Talmud, which was at first mainly oral, grew out of the conviction that besides the written Torah (Law)—the Bible—there had been from the first, from the divine communications to Moses at Sinai onward, an oral Torah, handed down from generation to generation, which lawgiver and prophets strove to engrave on the hearts of the people. As teacher succeeded teacher in synagogue and school, their teachings and often conflicting opinions, all based on the Bible, were treasured. Through long practice the power of memorizing had been greatly strengthened, but the accumulated mass of oral traditions and teachings became so unwieldy that the best memory could not be trusted. Then there came the necessity for a compilation which would summarize all that was most vital and essential in the teachings of preceding generations, and at the same time preserve for future generations the vast treasure house of thought and action, religious aspiration, and worldly wisdom, wherein they would find inspiration and guidance amid the persecutions and temptations they might have to encounter. Thus was the Talmud produced. As repository of the oral law it ranks, in Jewish eyes, second only to the Hebrew scriptures as a national-religious creation and possession, and throughout many generations has exercised an influence on the life of the Jewish people not inferior to that of the Bible itself.

2. Function and scope of the oral law. The oral law as embodied in the Talmud fulfils a twofold function. In the first place, it interprets the ordinances of the written law, explaining their contents and defining their scope. As such, the oral law forms an integral and indispensable part of the written law, for without the oral law it would be impossible to observe the written law. How, e.g., could the biblical sabbath law be observed if there were no oral law to define the term "work"? In the second place, the oral law adapts and modifies the ordinances of the written law to changes in conditions and circumstances—social, domestic, economic. As such the oral law serves to transform the Torah from a mere written document, liable to become obsolete, into a continuous revelation keeping pace with the ages. Included in the oral law, with all the authority it commends, are those numerous measures and enactments introduced by the recognized religious leaders either as a "fence around the law" (e.g., the prohibition of handling a working implement on the Day of Rest) or as an expression of religious devotion and loyalty (e.g., the kindling of lights on Hanukkah. *See* FEASTS AND FASTS).

3. Talmudic antecedents: Midrash and Mishna. The earliest method of teaching the oral law was by means of a running commentary, MIDRASH, on the biblical text. When the exposition yielded a legal teaching, the result was Midrash HALACHAH; if a nonlegal, ethical, or devotional teaching, it was Midrash Haggadah (הגדה, "narration"). The Midrash method was employed already by Ezra and his associates in the public reading of the Law which they held on that memorable convocation in the year 444 B.C., at which the Torah was enthroned supreme in the constitution of the new community in Judea. The Midrash method was followed by those generations of teachers who succeeded Ezra, the Soferim (סופרים, "bookmen," or "scribes"), whose activities came to a close *ca.* 270 B.C. After the Soferim came in succession the five "Pairs" (זוגות, *zûghôth*) of teachers, of whom the last and greatest were Shammai and Hillel (both at the end of the first century B.C.).

With the Zugoth a new method of teaching began to emerge as a rival to that of the Midrash—a method in which the oral law was taught without reference to the Holy Writ. This evidently represented a progressive method of teaching in that it enabled the teachers to put on the order of the day any such subjects as they desired, without being tied to the sequence of biblical texts. It would still have been possible, while retaining the Midrash form, to trace back every oral teaching to its respective biblical source. That this course was not resorted to, it may be assumed, was a result of the attitude of the SADDUCEES, who, by employing the very text of the written Torah to attack the validity of the oral law, weakened the biblical warrant claimed in support of oral traditions and teachings. On the other hand, deprived of the aid to memory which the Holy Writ could supply, the oral law could be imparted and retained chiefly by means of repetition. Hence the name Mishna (משנה, lit. "repetition") was given to the new method of teaching; and Tannaim (from Aramaic תנא, *t*ᵉ*nâ*, a variant of Hebrew שנה, *shānâ*, "to repeat," "to hand down orally") was the name by which Mishna teachers became known.

The adoption of the Mishna method did not, however, oust altogether the older Midrash form. Not only was it allowed to retain the Haggadic field almost to itself, but even in the realms of Halachah its sway, though disputed, did not entirely cease, with the result that Midrash and Mishna continued to exist side by side as media for teaching Halachah. Attempts at the compilation of Halachic teachings in Mishna form were made at an early stage of its development. There is strong proof of the existence of a codified body of Mishnaic lore as far back as the days of the schools of Shammai and Hillel (*ca.* 50), if not earlier. Foremost among the collections of the later period is that of Rabbi Akiba (died a martyr's death in 135 under the Hadrianic persecutions), which was subsequently developed by his disciple, Rabbi Meir (110?-75?). This later codification became the groundwork of the Mishna of Rabbi Judah the Prince (*ca.* 135-217), designated "rabbi par excellence," which presents a digest of the whole legal system governing Jewish life and action as taught and developed in the schools of Palestine throughout the period of Soferim, Zugoth, and Tannaim up to the beginning of the third century that followed the rise of Christianity. Rabbi Judah's Mishna soon gained wide recognition and became the authoritative canon of the oral law and the main basis of instruction and principal subject of study, investigation, and research for the schools, both in Palestine and in Babylon for several centuries. The Mishna of Rabbi Judah, however, contained only a minor fraction of the legal material current in the Palestine academies. There were many additional and rival collections that issued from contemporary authorities of Rabbi Judah, such as Bar Kappara, Rabbi Hiyya, and Rabbi Hoshaia, which preserved teachings which Rabbi Judah had for one reason or another thought fit to exclude and which often went counter to his teaching. These "external" or "additional" teachings, Baraitha (Aramaic ברייתא), or Tosefta (Aramaic תוספתא), could not, however, be ignored in the discussions of Rabbi Judah's Mishna; nor could the oral traditions and teachings transmitted in Midrash form. These discussions were carried on in the schools of Palestine and Babylon by scholars designated Amoraim (Aramaic אמוראים, "speakers"), whose activities stretched from the conclusion of the Mishna down to the end of the fifth century of the Christian era. Their endeavor was to interpret the Mishna, explain its obscurities, discuss its contents, trace back its teachings to the Bible, and harmonize contradictions in oral traditions as emanating from different authorities or schools. Theirs was also the task of making final decisions of Halachah as well as formulating new Halachoth (legal judgments) in answer to problems which arose out of changed conditions of life. This intellectual activity of centuries was crystallized in the Gemara (Aramaic גמרא, "completion"), which, together with the Mishna of Rabbi Judah, constitutes the Talmud.

4. Division of Mishna and Talmud. The Mishna and Talmud are divided into six Orders (סדרים, *S*ᵉ*dharîm*). Each Order is subdivided into tractates (מסכתות, *Massekhtôth;* singular *Massekhtâ*), of which there are sixty-three, and each tractate into chapters (פרקים, *P*ᵉ*raqîm*). The Orders are as follows:

a) Zeraim (זרעים, "seeds")—agricultural laws.

b) Moed (מועד, "appointed seasons")—laws concerning the sabbath, festivals, and fasts.

c) Nashim (נשים, "woman")—laws of marriage and divorce.

d) Nezikin (נזיקין, "damages")—civil and criminal laws.

e) Kodashim (קדשים, "consecrated things")—laws appertaining to the sanctuary and the sacrificial rites.

f) Tohoroth (טהרות, "cleanliness")—laws of levitical purity.

5. Halachah and Haggadah. Side by side with its legal material are the HALACHAH, the legal material of the Talmud, and the Haggadah, covering the whole field of ethics and religion. Moral reflections, homilies, apologues, maxims of worldly wisdom, metaphysical speculations, tales of Israel's past (both historical and legendary), visions of its future, and obiter dicta, often showing remarkable powers of observation on geometry, medicine, astronomy, physiology, botany, and other scientific subjects, are the constituents of the Haggadah. Its aim everywhere is to edify, inspire, elevate, and supply those finer qualities of heart and mind, moving man to that righteousness of action which the Halachah prescribes.

6. The two Talmudic versions. As a product of two distinct centers of learning, the Talmud appears in two versions: the Palestinian and the Babylonian, much dissimilar in subject matter, method, presentation, and language. The differences in the two versions extend to the very basic text common to both, the Mishna of the Rabbi Judah, readings in the one version often varying from those in the other. No satisfactory explanation has so far been found to account for these textual variants, but there is no doubt that in many cases they represent two recensions of the Mishna made by Rabbi Judah himself; the existence of these recensions is already indicated in the Babylonian Gemara.

a. Palestinian. The Palestinian Talmud is often referred to as the Yerushalmi (ירושלמי, "Jerusalemite"). The first designation is, however, the more accurate, as this Talmud is the product of the schools of Tiberias, Caesarea, and Sepphoris. It is also known as the "Talmud of the Children of the West."

The Palestinian Talmud was compiled hurriedly, because of the persecutions which the Jews in Palestine suffered throughout the third and fourth centuries at the hands of their Roman rulers. This fact may account for its incompleteness and its lack of unity, coherence, and profundity, as well as for the corrupt state of its text. The Palestinian Talmud has Gemara only for the first four Orders, and none for Kodashim and Tohoroth. The Palestinian Talmud on Kodashim, claimed to have been discovered by Solomon Friedländer and published by him in 1907-8, has been proved a forgery. In bulk the Palestinian Talmud is only about a third of its sister version, and its dialect is that of Western Aramaic. Tradition ascribes the redaction of this Talmud to Rabbi Johanan ben Nappaha (died 279). A disciple of Rabbi Judah the Prince, he excelled all his contemporaries by his great intellectual gifts and founded the Academy of Tiberias, which became the principal seat of learning in Palestine and the main "workshop" of the Palestinian Talmud. It is, however, a fact that the Palestinian Talmud contains material of considerable proportions of a much later date than Rabbi Johanan, and it is accordingly safe

to assume that, while Rabbi Johanan laid the foundation of the Palestinian Talmud, it took its present shape in all essentials sometime at the beginning of the fifth century, shortly before the closing of the Tiberias School and the extinction of the Patriarchate (425).

The Palestinian Talmud is generally regarded as subordinate to the Babylonian Talmud, on which all subsequent codifications of the law rest. The Palestinian Talmud is nevertheless indispensable for the study of the Halachah, as it represents the Halachah in its unbroken line of development in the home of the Mishna. It also derives additional importance from the Haggadic material it contains. Making up about one sixth of its total subject matter, the Haggadah of the Palestinian Talmud is a veritable mine of information on the internal and external relations of the Jews in Palestine; and, on account of its relative antiquity, this Haggadah is of great historical importance and value.

b. Babylonian. This version, written in Eastern Aramaic, records the discussions on Rabbi Judah's Mishna as carried on in the schools of Babylonia. Like its sister version, the Babylonian Talmud abounds in Haggadah, constituting about one third of its contents and mirroring the entire knowledge of the secular and religious rabbis of the time.

A constant intellectual intercourse and interflow of ideas, alike in the realms of Halachah and Haggadah, existed between Babylonia and Palestine, and statements of the Palestine Amoraim enjoy high authority and occupy an important place in Babylonian Gemara. The great teacher, who was responsible for the intellectual activity which gave birth to the Babylonian Talmud, was Abba Arika, "the Tall" (died 247), so called because of his high stature. He was of Babylonian origin but spent some years in Palestine, where he studied under Rabbi Judah. Returning to his homeland in the year 219, he founded the academy at Sura, on the Euphrates, where he taught his master's Mishna, which he had brought back with him. Thousands of disciples flocked to his lectures, and his reputation rose so high that he became known as Rab (Aramaic רב), "teacher par excellence." His famous contemporary and collaborator was Mer Samuel (died 254), who was likewise a disciple of Rabbi Judah and who on his return home to Babylon became the head of the academy at Nehardea. He was considered the leading authority in matters of civil law, in which his judgments were declared by later generations as binding, and he is the author of the well-known dictum: "The law of the land is law," which has proved of tremendous influence on the development of Jewish civil law.

The intensive activities of the Babylonian Amoraim reached their climax under Abbaye (280-338) and his colleague and Halachic opponent Raba (299-352), the respective heads of the academies of Pumbeditha and Mechuza. Both Abbaye and Raba were dialecticians of a high order, and their discussions in which they displayed much acumen occupy much space in the Babylonian Gemara. Layer upon layer of Halachic and Haggadic material continued to be added during the several generations that followed Abbaye and Raba, each generation interpreting, arguing, and debating the opinions and judgments of generations preceding. The mass of orally transmitted traditions and teachings accumulated through the centuries assumed such large proportions that the time came for a "redaction" involving the sifting, systematization, and orderly arrangement of the whole. This work of "redaction" was undertaken by Rab Ashi (died 427), who, elected at the early age of twenty-three as head of the Sura Academy, directed its affairs with singular brilliancy and success for fifty-two years. During all this time, he applied himself to the gigantic task of collecting, sifting, and arranging the vast store of Halachah and Haggadah that engaged the minds and hearts of the teachers and disciples in the Babylonian schools. The results of his enormous labors constitute the basic elements of the Babylonian Talmud. Rab Ashi's work of redaction was carried on by his successors, especially by Rabina bar Huna, known as Rabina II (flourished 488-99), who "redacted" the new material that had accumulated since Ashi's death. Rabina II is said to have been the last of the Amoraim to teach Torah on the basis of oral transmission, and with him the Talmud may be regarded as having come to a close. The finishing touches were supplied by the Saboraim (Aramaic סבוראי, from סבר, "reflect"), who flourished from the end of the fifth to the middle of the sixth century. They "reflected" upon the work of the Amoraim as crystallized in the Talmud, sifted it critically, and also made certain additions of an explanatory character.

7. The influence of the Talmud. The Talmud as a written book was closed just as the Dark Ages were beginning; but its greatest influence on the dispersed people of Israel merely began then. It contributed powerfully to the religious and national preservation of the Jew in that Judaism was able to adjust itself to every time and place, to every condition of society and stage of civilization. Furthermore, in times of stress and danger the Talmud offered the Jew a spiritual haven of tranquillity, a kind of "dreamland" into which he could always withdraw, oblivious of the outer world with its hate and its malice, its cruelties and its tortures. Poring over its pages, generations of Jews have found in the Talmud the satisfaction of their deepest religious yearnings, as well as an outlet for their highest intellectual aspirations. Thus did the Talmud accomplish, in the words of Felix Perles, "the historic miracle of injecting into Jewry, dispersed amidst a hostile world, again and again an indestructible vitality, and at the same time stamping it with that uniform character which it has preserved to this day despite all dissolving influences."

And not on Jews and Judaism alone did the Talmud exercise its beneficent influence. Through the intellectual and moral discipline it imparted, Talmudic thought helped to lead the thought of the Middle Ages into new channels and to prepare the way for what was of permanent value in the Renaissance, and through the Renaissance for influencing modern civilization.

8. The burnings of the Talmud. The "persecution" of the Talmud began before it was actually committed to writing. Hadrian (117-38), Antoninus Pius (138-61), and the Persian kings Yazdegerd II (438-57) and Peroz (459-84) forbade the study of the Law. During the Middle Ages, persecutions and burnings of the Talmud were of not uncommon occurrence. Very often these took place at the direct instigation of Jewish converts to Christianity, who made libelous statements about the Talmud. One of them was Nicholas Donin, a former Talmudist, who formulated charges against the Talmud in a document of thirty-five articles. As a result of his allegations, Pope Gregory II issued an order for the confiscation of the Talmud. Twenty-four cartloads of books were brought together and burned publicly in Paris in June, 1242. These persecutions and burnings of the Talmud continued throughout the following centuries up to the time of Reuchlin (1453-1522) and his fellow humanists, who fought against the destruction of "a book written by Christ's nearest relatives."

The Babylonian Talmud was also subjected, during the Middle Ages, to a censorship by the church, and passages regarded as objectionable to Christians were deleted. Later the Jews themselves, in order not to give offense to the church, exercised a censorship in MSS and in printed editions of the Talmud. These deletions have been preserved and published separately in a number of publications, the most noted of which is the one entitled *Sefer Chesronoth ha-shas* (The Book of the Lacunas of the Talmud).

9. Attacks on the Talmud in modern times. In modern times the Talmud in the hands of anti-Semites was turned into a weapon wherewith to attack the Jews and Judaism. In their endeavor to expose the Jews to obloquy and to provoke Gentile hostility against them, they claimed that the Talmud, which was the guide of Jewish life, condoned and sanctioned crimes of all sorts against non-Jews, such as theft, robbery, murder, and rape, and was to blame for the number of misdeeds of which the Jews were alleged to be guilty. Jewish and non-Jewish scholars have had no difficulty in showing that these attacks were based on falsification and perversion of texts, tendentious selections, and very often ignorance. The translations of the Talmud (*see bibliography*) have also contributed to dispel much of the mystery and absurd notions that seemed to surround it in the eyes of the non-Jewish world.

10. Editions. There is only one MS extant of the whole Babylonian Talmud—i.e., the Munich MS, written in the year 1343 and edited by Hermann L. Strack (1912). The first edition of the Palestinian Talmud, based mainly on a Leiden MS, was published in 1522-23, and that of the Babylonian Talmud in 1520-24, both in Venice by Daniel Bomberg, a non-Jew. Since then there have been numerous editions of both Talmuds. Most famous among these is the Vilna Romm edition of the Babylonian Talmud, first published in 1886 and since then reprinted several times with additional improvements; a new photostat edition of it has recently been produced in America.

11. Commentaries. The Talmud is by no means an easy work to study. Its peculiar style, pregnant in brevity and succinctness, as well as its method of presentation in which clauses, sentences, questions, and answers run into one another without any sign of demarcation, tends to make the Talmud almost a sealed book, difficult to understand without guide or commentary. The commentaries on the Talmud are legion. The oldest commentary, on practically the whole of the Talmud, is that of Hananel ben Hushiel (died 1050); only parts of it are extant. The most classical and universally adopted guide for Talmudic interpretation is that of Rabbi Solomon Yitschaki of Troyes, Rashi (1040-1105); this guide appears by the side of the Talmudic text in all printed editions.

To a different class of commentary belongs that of the French rabbis of the twelfth and thirteenth centuries, known as *Tosafoth* (Additions). The *Tosafoth*, which also appears by the side of the printed Talmudic text in the form of glosses, is distinguished for its detailed critical research, which has laid the Talmudic studies on a deeper and broader basis.

Nor is there a lack of supercommentaries. Of these may be mentioned the *Marshaa* (1612) by Samuel Edels, noted for its acute analytical method, and the *Maharam* (1619) by Meïr ben Gedaliah of Lublin, a commentary popular for its clarity.

The commentaries on the Jerusalem Talmud are the *Korban ha-Edah* (1743) by David Fränkel, and the *Pene Mosheh* (1750) by Moses Margolioth. Modern scholarship has also contributed richly to the elucidation of the Jerusalem Talmud, and outstanding in this connection is the *Commentary on the Palestinian Talmud* in three volumes (1941) by Louis Ginzberg, which has been hailed as a masterpiece of modern Halachic study.

12. The Talmud in Jewish education. The immense influence which the Talmud has exerted over the Jewish people is the result of an educational system in which the Talmud was made to occupy the most important place. With its redaction the Talmud became the principal subject of study in academy and school. Instruction in the Talmud was begun at an early age in the elementary schools, and continued in the *Yeshivah*, where the advanced student was introduced to the analytical method called "pilpul." The important place assigned to the Talmud in the curriculum of Jewish studies was the distinctive feature of Jewish education throughout the Middle Ages. The broadening of Jewish culture in consequence of the emancipation led to the gradual displacement of the Talmud by other subjects; yet the Talmud continued to play a major role in Jewish education. The mind of the child was fed by the stories of the Talmud, and its *Haggadah* instilled in him a high ethic and a loyalty to Jewish traditions and ideals. In our own days the trend is toward the revival of interest in the Talmud, even in quarters where hitherto it has been entirely neglected. More and more do Jewish schools include Talmud as a subject of instruction, and the number of adult groups meeting regularly for the study of the Talmud is steadily on the increase. Noteworthy in this connection is the *Daf Yomi* (Daily Folio), instituted in 1929 at the instance of Rabbi Meir Shapiro of Lublin, and adopted by a large number of orthodox Jews as their daily Talmudic lectionary. The causes for this revival are many and varied. Among them must be included the recognition of the Talmud as a unique preservative force of Judaism and of its importance as constituting the "humanities" of Hebraism which no Jew with a claim to Jewish culture dare ignore.

13. Significance of the Talmud in our times. Widely though the modern world is separated from the centuries that preceded it, the Talmud still remains, after the Bible, the most fruitful, spiritual, and moral force in Jewish life. Notwithstanding the changed conditions which make many of the laws inapplicable to our times, Jewish life even today is largely founded on Talmudic teachings and principles. The ritual, the liturgy, the festivals, the marriage laws, derive directly from the Talmud; even as it is the Talmud which inspires those virtues for which the Jew is conspicuous: his benevolence, compassion, strong affection for family ties, hatred of violence, and aversion to cruelty—even cruelty to animals.

The restoration of the Hebrew polity, after a submergence of two thousand years, is giving to the Talmud a new significance. Many of its laws rendered obsolete by reason of the fall of the Jewish state, particularly those referring to the *Jus* and to agriculture, are slowly coming once more into their own, and it is to the Talmud that the builders of the new social order in Israel are turning more and more for light and guidance in their manifold and stupendous tasks.

Bibliography. Translations of the Talmud: German: L. Goldschmidt, ed., the whole of the Babylonian Talmud (1897-1909). English: I. Epstein, ed., the whole of the Babylonian Talmud in English (36 vols.; 1935-48). French: M. Schwab, *Le Talmud de Jérusalem traduit pour la première fois* (11 vols.; 1878-90).

Special studies: G. F. Moore, *Judaism in the First Centuries of the Christian Era*, vol. I (1927). M. Waxman, *A History of Jewish Literature*, vol. I (1930). H. L. Strack, *Introduction to the Talmud and Midrash* (1931). J. Kaplan, *The Redaction of the Babylonian Talmud* (1933). I. Epstein, *Judaism* (1939). J. Z. Lauterbach, *Midrash and Mishnah in Rabbinic Essays* (1951). I. Epstein, "The Rabbinic Tradition," *The Jewish Heritage* (1955), pp. 51-69. I. EPSTEIN

TALSAS tăl'səs. KJV Apoc. form of ELASAH 2.

TAMAH. KJV alternate form of TEMAH.

TAMAR tā'mər [תָּמָר; Θαμάρ, date palm]. **1.** Daughter-in-law of Judah. The Canaanite wife of Judah's eldest son, Er, she remained a widow after Er's death, because the second son, Onan, refused to marry her and Judah withheld his third son, Shelah, beyond the promised time (Gen. 38:6-11, 14, 26). Out of impatience Tamar offered herself, disguised as a prostitute, to Judah (vss. 12-23), and bore his twins, Perez and Zerah (vss. 24-30). She is recalled as an ancestress of the tribe of Judah in Ruth 4:12; I Chr. 2:4; Matt. 1:3.

2. Daughter of David (II Sam. 13:1; I Chr. 3:9). Amnon, a half brother, was so infatuated with her beauty that he forcibly seduced her (II Sam. 13:2-14); afterward his lust turned to loathing as he drove her, shamed and weeping, from his house (vss. 15-19). Subsequently Absalom, her full brother, obtained revenge by having Amnon murdered (vss. 20-29).

3. Absalom's only daughter, renowned for her beauty (II Sam. 14:27). The LXX and the OL of this passage add that she became Rehoboam's wife and bore Abiathar. If this is correct, she is the MAACAH (10) of I Kings 15:2; II Chr. 11:20-22 (but cf. II Chr. 13:2). S. J. DE VRIES

4. A city built by Solomon, according to the actual text in I Kings 9:18. The parallel passage in II Chr. 8:4, as well as the Masoretic directions in Kings, reads TADMOR. Some scholars would identify this city built by Solomon with 5 *below* (so RSV, which reads "Tamar in the wilderness, in the land of Judah," presuming "of Judah" has dropped from the Hebrew text or interpreting "the land" as the land of Judah; cf. the KJV translation "Tadmor in the wilderness, in the land").

5. A city in the extreme SE part of Judah, near the S end of the Dead Sea. According to Ezek. 47:19; 48:28, it marked the E end of the S border of his ideal land of Israel, which is to run from there to the waters of Meribath-kadesh (*see* KADESH). The RSV also reads "Tamar" in Ezek. 47:18 instead of the Hebrew "and you shall measure" (תמדו). Tamar was evidently a well-known fortified town on the boundary between Israel and Edom. During the time of Solomon, since the Edomites were subdued, it may have been a supply depot for the mines in the Arabah region, which, like the mines of the Egyptians in the Sinai Peninsula, needed a steady supply of water and provisions in order to be worked regularly; later, after Edom recovered its independence, Tamar may have been a fortress protecting the border.

It may be the same as HAZAZON-TAMAR. According to Ptolemaeus, Tamar was fifty-five miles from Jerusalem; according to the Poitinger map, fifty-three. The site is uncertain; Qasr ej-Jeheiniyah, on the W side of the Arabah, and el-Qeriya, S of the Dead Sea, have been suggested. S. COHEN

TAMARISK tăm′ə rĭsk [אשׁל, *'ēšel;* Aram. אשׁלא, *'ešlâ;* Arab. *'athl*]. A distinctive tree or shrub with minute scalelike leaves pressed close to feathery branches. More than a dozen species are listed in Post's *Flora,* but there is some confusion among botanists concerning identifications and naming. The most common species is called *Tamarix pentandra* Pall. (also *Tamarix pallasii* Desv.). The *Tamarix mannifera* (Ehrenb.) Bunge, common to the Sinai Desert, exudes an edible resin which is considered one possible identification for the MANNA of the Exodus.

Abraham planted a tamarisk in Beer-sheba (Gen. 21:33; KJV "grove"). Saul sat under one in Gibeah (I Sam. 22:6), and his bones were buried beneath another one in Jabesh-gilead (I Sam. 31:13; KJV "tree"). The latter passage is repeated in I Chr. 10: 12, but אלה "OAK" (*see* TEREBINTH), is given as the tree. It is quite probable that a sacred tree or shrine is to be understood in each passage.

See also FLORA § A9*q;* ASHERAH.

Pl. XVI*b.*

Bibliography. I. Löw, *Die Flora der Juden,* III (1924), 398-404; G. E. Post, *Flora of Syria, Palestine and Sinai,* I (1932), 222-25; H. N. and A. L. Moldenke, *Plants of the Bible* (1952), pp. 227-28. J. C. TREVER

TAMBOURINE. *See* MUSICAL INSTRUMENTS § B3.

TAMMUZ tăm′ŭz, tä′mŏoz [תמוז; *with definite article,* התמוז (Ezek. 8:14)]. Alternately: THAMMUZ thăm′ŭz, thä′mŏoz. The Sumerian deity of spring vegetation; known from the Gilgamesh Epic as the lover of Ishtar, goddess of love, who had betrayed him. The anniversary of her betrayal was the occasion of an annual wailing for the god in the fourth month, which was named for him. Ezekiel attests a local variation of this rite practiced by the women of Jerusalem on the fifth day of the sixth month. The motif of a dying god is suggested by the annual wilting of vegetation in the Near East, and has sundry local variations—e.g., the cult of ADONIS in Syria, of Persephone and Dionysus in Greece, and of Osiris in Egypt.

Bibliography. S. A. Cook, *The Religion of Ancient Palestine in the Light of Archaeology* (1930), pp. 139-40; M. Witzel, *Tammuz-Liturgien und Werwandtes* (*Analecta Orientalia*), X (1935); A. Moortgat, *Tammuz* (1949); A. S. Kapelrud, *Baal in the Ras Shamra Texts* (1952), pp. 27-29; W. F. Albright, *Archaeology and the Religion of Israel* (1953), p. 167; E. O. James, *The Ancient Gods* (1960), pp. 78-80. J. GRAY

TANACH. KJV form of TAANACH in Josh. 21:25.

TANHUMETH tăn hū′mĭth [תנחמת, consolation] (II Kings 25:23; Jer. 40:8). The Netophathite (*see* NETOPHAH) whose son Seraiah was a captain who remained with Gedaliah after the Exile. A Lachish stamp contains this name.

TANIS tä′nĭs. A city in Egypt. *See* ZOAN.

TANNER, TANNING. The process of tanning, using lime, the juice of certain plants, or the bark or leaves of certain trees, has been known from ancient times.

In Exod. 25:5; 26:14; 35:7, 23; 36:19; 39:34 "tanned rams' skins" (KJV "rams' skins dyed red") are used as coverings for the tabernacle. The Hebrew word for "tanned" is מאדם, the *pual* participle of the regular word "to be red." The LXX has ἠρυθροδανωμένα, from the word "to dye red." The RSV translation "tanned" is due to the probability that the skins were reddened as a result of the tanning process employed.

In Acts 9:43; 10:6, 32, we have "Simon, a tanner" (βυρσεύς). Tanners were not held in good repute among the Jews, as we see often in the Talmud. It was customary for tanners to live outside the cities because of the nature of their work; Simon lived by the seaside. The fact that Peter was willing to stay with Simon was an indication of at least the beginning of a more liberal attitude on the part of Peter toward such ceremonial matters. The tanner's house was an excellent setting for the triple vision of a vessel filled with all kinds of animals.

S. A. CARTLEDGE

TAPESTRY. KJV translation of מרבדים (Prov. 7:16; 31:22; RSV COVERINGS).

TAPHATH tä′făth [טפת] (I Kings 4:11). A daughter of Solomon, and wife of Ben-abinadab, one of Solomon's officials in the district of Naphath-dor.

TAPHNES. KJV form of TAHPANHES in Jth. 1:9.

TAPHON. KJV form of TEPHON.

TAPPUAH tăp′yōō ə [תפח, apple(?)]. A Calebite family or person descended from Hebron (I Chr. 2: 43); possibly the name of a town in the vicinity of Hebron. *See* BETH-TAPPUAH.

TAPPUAH (PLACE) [תפוח, quince(?)]. **1.** A city in the Shephelah, one of the cities of the second district of Judah (Josh. 15:34). In the same list a BETH-TAPPUAH appears among the cities in the hill country of Judah (vs. 53). The exact location of the Shephelah Tappuah is unknown, although it has often been identified with Beit Nettif, *ca.* twelve miles W of Bethlehem.

2. A city on the N border of the territory of Ephraim (Josh. 16:8). Associated with EN-TAPPUAH and located on the (S) border of Manasseh, assigned to the Ephraimites; the region around it (the land of Tappuah) is assigned to Manasseh (17:7-8). Sheikh Abu Zarad, *ca.* eight miles S of Shechem, has been proposed as its location.

The king of Tappuah is mentioned among the Canaanite kings defeated by Joshua (Josh. 12:17). His city is perhaps to be identified with the Ephraimite Tappuah, since it is associated with Bethel, the land of Hepher, etc. A Canaanite king of Tappuah and the men of the city are mentioned in a late tradition about Judah (Test. Judah 3:2; 5:6), but without furnishing information concerning the location.

Tappuah may have been the scene of a ruthless attack by Menahem king of Israel (II Kings 15:16). The Hebrew text has תפסח (KJV TIPHSAH). The RSV reads "Tappuah" on the basis of the Greek (ταφωέ). Since Tirzah is mentioned in the same verse, probably the Ephraimite Tappuah is intended.

W. L. REED

TARAH. KJV form of TERAH.

TARALAH tär′ə lə [תראלה]. A town in the allotment to the tribe of Benjamin (Josh. 18:27). The identifiable sites in the list in which it appears suggest that it was in the hill country NW of Jerusalem (vss. 25-28). W. H. MORTON

TAREA tär′ĭ ə [תארע] (I Chr. 8:35). Alternately: TAHREA tär′— [תחרע] (I Chr. 9:41). A descendant of King Saul through Jonathan.

TARES. KJV NT translation of ζιζάνιον (RSV WEEDS).

TARGET. The translation of מטרה (KJV "mark") in Job 16:12 (elsewhere "mark"). The KJV incorrectly translates as "target" צנה in I Kings 10:16; II Chr. 9:15; 14:8 (*see* BUCKLER; SHIELD) and כידון in I Sam. 17:6 (*see* JAVELIN). W. S. McCULLOUGH

*****TARGUM** tär′gŭm [תרגום, translation; Aram. תרגום, תרגומא; *corresponding verb form in* Ezra 4:7]; plural TARGUMS or TARGUMIM —gŭmz, —gə mǐm. **1.** The Aramaic translation of scriptural books, especially the Pentateuch, as delivered orally in the synagogue during the period of the second temple and later, in accordance with a generally accepted, but by no means rigidly fixed, tradition of interpretation.

2. The written Targums now extant, which are for the most part editions of the old traditional rendering, made in Palestine and Babylonia at various times from the second Christian century and later. *See* VERSIONS, ANCIENT.

B. J. BAMBERGER

TARPELITES tär′pə līts. KJV translation of Aramaic טרפליא (LXX Ταρφαλ(λ)αῖοι; Vulg. *Terphalaei*) in Ezra 4:9 (RSV "officials"). The word is either a professional name (like Dinaites, judges) or an ethnic name (like Babylonians, Elamites). Besides the RSV and KJV translations, the following meanings have been suggested: *tabellarii*, "couriers" (improbable); "Tibarenes" (*Tubal*); "the men of the Tetrapolis" (Antioch, Seleucia, Apamea, and Laodicea; see Strabo XVI.749-50); Persian *tarapâra*, "beyond the river" (W of the Euphrates; i.e., Syrians).

R. H. PFEIFFER

TARSHISH tär′shĭsh [תרשיש, *perhaps* yellow jasper *or other gold-colored stone; in* Esth. 1:14 *perhaps for* Old Pers. *ṭrsus*, the greedy one]; KJV alternately THARSHISH thär′shĭsh (I Kings 10:22; 22:48; I Chr. 7: 10). **1.** A Benjaminite, son of Bilhan (I Chr. 7:10).

Bibliography. M. Noth, *Die israelitischen Personennamen* (1928), p. 223; F. S. Brown, S. R. Driver, and C. A. Briggs, eds., *Hebrew and English Lexicon* (1955), p. 1076.

2. One of the "seven princes of Persia and Media" next in rank to King Ahasuerus (Esth. 1:14). The (Aramaic) Second Targ. of Esther adds "from Egypt" after this name.

Bibliography. L. B. Paton, *Esther,* ICC (1908), pp. 68, 152-53. B. T. DAHLBERG

3. A far-off, and sometimes idealized, port that cannot be identified with any one location. The identification of the original Tarshish is unsettled, ranging from the Levantine ports (Tarsus is not out of the question) to Tartessus in Spain, which many authorities favor. Tarshish exported finely wrought silver, according to Jer. 10:9; and silver, iron, tin, and lead, according to Ezek. 27:12. When Jonah wishes to evade his mission to Nineveh in the E, he boards a ship at Joppa bound for Tarshish in the W (Jonah 1:3), evidently in the Mediterranean. "Ships of Tarshish" came to designate the larger seagoing vessels, regardless of their origin or ports of call. Yet it may be worth noting the places associated with the ships of Tarshish. Isa. 23:1 connects them with the lands of the KITTIM, pointing to Cyprus and the Aegean, and tying in with Gen. 10:4, where Tarshish is classified as Greek (cf. also Isa. 66:19). Yet I Kings 10:22 tells of Solomon's fleet of Tarshish that fetched gold, silver, ivory, monkeys, and peacocks, pointing to a route along the Red Sea and the Indian Ocean; II Chr. 9:21 has the same fleet going to Tarshish (tying in with Ps. 72:10) to bring back the same cargoes. I Kings 22:49 mentions Jehoshaphat's ships of Tarshish sailing for Ophir from Ezion-geber, which rules out any Mediterranean route; II Chr. 20:36 has the same ships made in Ezion-geber for sailing *to* Tarshish. It is important to note that Isa. 2:16 parallels Tarshish with "the pleasant place, desire" (RSV "beautiful craft"), suggesting that whatever the original identification of Tarshish may have been, in literature and popular imagination it became a distant paradise.

C. H. GORDON

TARSUS tär′səs [Ταρσός]. A city in the province of Cilicia on the SE coast of Asia Minor (Acts 9:11, 30; 11:25; 21:39; 22:3).

Tarsus is the historical capital of CILICIA and especially the chief city of the E fertile part of this country, Cilicia Pedias. The city is located on the right bank of the Tarsus River (ancient Cydnus) *ca.* ten miles from the present coast line. Its location has never changed, from its foundation in prehistoric times to the present day, and as a city with a continuous history of at least six millenniums it should have better claims than Damascus to being the "oldest city of the world."

1. Prehistory and early history
2. Iron Age, Assyrian, and Persian history
3. Hellenistic history
4. Roman history
5. Topography and archaeology
Bibliography

1. Prehistory and early history. The earliest settlement at Tarsus is contained in the prehistoric mound on the SW side of the city, called Gozlu Kule. The site was founded at least as early as Neolithic times, and was a fortified town in the third millennium B.C. It became an important center of coastal trade in the phase when Troy had its early *floruit, ca.* 2300 B.C. In the second millennium B.C., when Cilicia makes its appearance in Hittite records as the country of Kizzuwatna, Tarsus is one of its most important towns, under the name of Tarša. This name is therefore preclassical and probably as ancient as the site. A seal impression of one of the early kings of Kizzuwatna, Ishputahshu, was found at Tarsus. The presence of this and other early documents in hieroglyphic and cuneiform writing suggests that Tarsus may have been the capital of Kizzuwatna.

Excavations have produced evidence of architecture and objects of Hittite Empire type in Tarsus in the period 1400-1200 B.C. After the annexation of Kizzuwatna by the Hittites, the city was under firm control of central Anatolia.

2. Iron Age, Assyrian, and Persian history. Tarsus was overrun and destroyed by the Sea Peoples in their aggression of *ca.* 1200 B.C. The destruction is archaeologically attested, as is the arrival of Mycenean Greek refugees, who now settled in Cilicia. Greek legend confirms the diaspora of Mycenean Greeks after the Trojan War. Late legends refer to this first Greek colonization of Tarsus. It is not precisely remembered and is variously attributed to Perseus, Heracles, or Triptolemus and a group of Argives.

In Assyrian records Tarsus is first mentioned by Shalmaneser III (858-824), who captured the city in his twenty-sixth year (Black Obelisk 132 ff). The most specific Assyrian activity in Tarsus is reported for Sennacherib (704-681). During the Cilician campaign in 698 his army took Tarsus and carried off its spoil (*Annals* IV.66 ff). The same historical event is recorded in Greek sources, which preserve less accurate but interesting memories of the event. Sar-

danapallus (the mythical Assyrian royal name created by the Greeks) is said to have built Tarsus and Anchiale (to the W) in one day, Tarsus in the likeness of Babylon with the river flowing through the city. Whatever rebuilding took place under Assyrian auspices can only have continued the previous topography of Tarsus.

Sennacherib in his Cilician campaign also had to cope with Ionian attacks on the coast, as Greek historians report (Eusebius *Chronicle*). The archaeological evidence of Greek trade would confirm that renewed Greek colonization followed this endeavor, but no specific Greek contingent is attested to have settled in Tarsus in this period. Hellenization by contact and cultural influence increased from the seventh century on.

For the Persian period we lack detailed evidence. Tarsus was the capital of the kingdom of Cilicia and started issuing coins in the fifth century B.C. The city and the palace of King Syennesis are prominently mentioned in the account of the expedition of the younger Cyrus in 401 (Xenophon *Anabasis* I.2.23). The coinage after the defeat of Cyrus consists of Persian satrap issues until the conquest by Alexander. Baal Tars, the god of Tarsus, appears as a Zeus of Greco-Persian type on the obverse of fourth-century silver staters.

3. Hellenistic history. In 333 Alexander saved the city of Tarsus from being burned by the Persians. During his stay in Tarsus the king became severely ill from bathing in the chilly Cydnus River.

The fate of the town under the Seleucids is not known in detail. Its name was changed to "Antioch on the Cydnus" in the third century in honor of one of the early Seleucid kings. Its coins reappear under this name during the rule of Antiochus IV Epiphanes (175-163). A minor insurrection against this ruler, because Tarsus and Mallus were to be presented as a gift to the king's mistress in 171 B.C., is reported in II Macc. 4:30.

4. Roman history. The prominent status of Tarsus continued to be acknowledged in Roman times, when the city was made the capital of the province of Cilicia in 67 B.C. As the governor of Cilicia, Cicero stayed in the city in 50 and was admired for his liberal rule. After Pompey's death, and in order to settle matters in Cilicia, the representatives of the province met Caesar at Tarsus in 47. The city then assumed the title of Iuliopolis, in honor of Caesar. In the struggle after the murder of Caesar, Tarsus was involved in opposition against Cassius and was severely punished by him in 43, when a huge fine was imposed on the city and was ruthlessly collected. Tarsus was rewarded for its resistance to Cassius by Mark Antony in 41, and the city was exempted from taxes. The most spectacular and romantic event during Antony's visit was the arrival of Cleopatra, who sailed up the Cydnus River to Tarsus as a second Aphrodite in full regalia.

Under Augustus, Tarsus had its full rights restored as a free city. Boethus, one of Antony's appointees and a dishonest administrator, had been dismissed and exiled, thanks to the intervention of Athenodorus, a Stoic philosopher. This Athenodorus had been a teacher of Augustus. He was one among many outstanding philosophers to have come from Tarsus, which by this time had grown into a center of intellectual life. Strabo emphasizes the native interest in learning in Tarsus, where the schools were full of local students rather than strangers, such as was the case at Alexandria (XIV.673-74). Many of the Tarsian philosophers and philologists went to teach in Rome.

The general prosperity of Tarsus was based on the fertility of the Cilician plain. Special industries mentioned for the town are the weaving of linen and the making of tents. The raw materials were the flax of Cilicia and perhaps a goat's-hair fabric called *cilicium* for tents. Linen from Tarsus is often referred to, and the tentmaking industry acquired fame through Paul (Acts 18:3). Paul's pride in his birthplace as "no mean city" (21:39) is understandable on the basis of the political, economic, and intellectual prominence of Tarsus at this time.

How large a contingent of the citizens of Tarsus were Jewish in the days of Paul is unknown. The Greek names of the philosophers are not even a guarantee that their families were more than recently Hellenized. In general, the population must have continued as a mixed Anatolian substratum with Greek, Roman, and Jewish additions.

The later Roman history of Tarsus is peaceful in a general way. For a while the only troubles were local and connected with petty rivalries among the cities of Cilicia. Serious competition did not arise for the metropolis of Tarsus until the third century A.D., when Anazarbus became the counterpart of Tarsus in E Cilicia.

Tarsus was visited by several emperors and adopted a succession of honorary titles in the second and third centuries A.D. Hadrian was singled out for special honors, with the title of Hadriane for the city, the instituting of a festival Hadrianeia, and the erection of statues.

In the Parthian wars of Rome, Tarsus and Cilicia were again of strategic importance. The city was captured by Shapur after his victory over Valerian III in A.D. 260. In 363 the Emperor Julian the Apostate was buried in Tarsus after an unsuccessful campaign in Persia.

The later history of Tarsus is one of continued dispute between East and West. In the eighth century Harun er-Rashid refortified the city and left his mark on its architecture. After many vicissitudes it was incorporated in the Ottoman Empire by Beyazit I.

5. Topography and archaeology. The ancient appearance of Tarsus is hard to reconstruct, in view of the continuous habitation and remodeling. We know from Assyrian and Greek sources (Xenophon *Anabasis* I.2.23) that the Cydnus flowed through the city. It was navigable and connected Tarsus with its harbor, Rhegma, a coastal lagoon where the arsenals were located (Strabo XIV.672). The change in the course of the river was effected in the sixth century A.D. by the Emperor Justinian, who had the Cydnus led into a channel E of Tarsus, with various minor branches going through the city, as they do today.

The excavated part of Tarsus consists mainly of the preclassical levels on the mound called Gozlu Kule. This tell was a minor outpost of the Hellenistic and Roman city. It served conveniently for the build-

ing of a Roman theater on its N slope. The major civic buildings are buried under the modern town. We have references to agorai, stoai, avenues, bridges, baths, fountains, a gymnasium, a stadium, palestrae; but none of this former architectural glory has been located. The remnants of an aqueduct, baths, and a gateway are Byzantine and Arabic. The present level of habitation has risen far above the original one by filling in of the coastal plain and accumulation of habitation debris. When new construction is undertaken, excavation invariably produces Byzantine architectural remains. In the center of the modern town a large Roman building decorated with mosaics was found under the new courthouse in 1947.

The major remnant of Roman architecture is the colossal foundation of a pseudo-dipteral temple, the marble superstructure of which is entirely lost. Its concrete skeleton is often referred to as the "tomb of Sadanapallus" and is popularly called Donuk Tash (the "fallen stone").

Bibliography. W. M. Ramsay, *The Cities of St. Paul* (1908), pp. 85-244; D. Magie, *Roman Rule in Asia Minor* (1950), pp. 272, 1146-48; H. Goldman, *Excavations at Gözlü Kule, Tarsus,* vols. I-II (1950, 1956).   M. J. MELLINK

TARTAK tär'tăk [תרתק] (II Kings 17:31). A deity worshiped by the Avvites settled in Samaria after 722 B.C. No such deity is known, and the name is presumably a corruption of Atargatis (Hebrew עתרעתה or Aramaic עתרקתה), a goddess worshiped in Syria and by the Arameans in Mesopotamia. This deity is a composite figure—Athtar (*see* DAY STAR; SHAHAR; SHALEM; MOLECH), or his female counterpart Athtarat (*see* ASHTORETH), and Anath, the most active goddess in the Syrian fertility cult—in the Ras Shamra Texts.

Bibliography. J. Garstang, *The Syrian Goddess* (translation and commentary of Lucian, *De Dea Syria;* 1913); J. A. Montgomery, *Commentary on Kings,* ICC (ed. H. S. Gehman; 1951), pp. 474-75.   J. GRAY

TARTAN tär'tăn [תרתן, *from* Assyrian *turtānu, or tartanu*] (II Kings 18:17). Alternately: COMMANDER IN CHIEF (Isa. 20:1). The title of an Assyrian general in command of an army group.

The office is first attested under Adad-nirari II (911-891 B.C.) in historical texts. We know of such officials under Shalmaneser III, Tiglath-pileser III, Sargon II (Isa. 20:1), and Sennacherib (II Kings 18:17). There are tartan officials of the right and of the left wing, the Assyrian army being divided into two bodies called "right" and "left," and we also know of a "second *turtānu.*" The word, although late, seems to be of foreign origin and cannot be connected etymologically with *terdennu,* "second (in age or position)," in spite of the semantic and phonetic similarity.

Bibliography. E. F. Weidner, *Die Inschriften vom Tell Halaf* (1940), p. 12, note 44 (with previous literature).
     A. L. OPPENHEIM

TASKMASTER [נגשׂ]. One whose office it is to allot tasks and to enforce their performance by any means. He is the foreman or OVERSEER of labor gangs (Exod. 1:11). In Egyptian reliefs they are equipped with rods for discipline. Their cruelty is legendary (Exod. 3:7; 5:6-14; Job 3:18). In fact, the Hebrew root means "to oppress." The fact that David and Solomon had such superintendents over their enforced Israelite labor gangs was disruptive of the monarchy (II Sam. 20:24; *cf.* ADONIRAM [I Kings 4:6]; ADORAM [I Kings 12:18; II Chr. 10: 18]). Solomon used many such officers (I Kings 5: 16; *see* OFFICER) in the building of the temple. Any foreign ruler may be considered a taskmaster or oppressor by the prophets (Isa. 3:12; Zech. 10:4). The driver is a taskmaster for his beast (Job 39:7).

C. U. WOLF

TASSEL [ציצת (Num. 15:38-39; KJV FRINGE), *cf.* Akkad. *ṣiṣitu*, projection; גדל (Deut. 22:12; KJV FRINGE), Akkad. *gidlu*, plaited work (torque), bulb *or* string (of garlic)]. The Israelites were to make tassels or fringes on the four corners of their garments. *See* FRINGE; CLOTH. J. M. MYERS

TATIAN tā'shən. *See* VERSIONS, ANCIENT, § 4*a*.

TATTENAI tăt'ə nī [תתני] (Ezra 5:3, 6; 6:6, 13); KJV TATNI tăt'nī. The governor of the province "across the river" under Darius Hystaspes.

Bibliography. W. Eilers, *Iranische Beamtennamen in der keilschriftlichen Überlieferung* (1940), pp. 35 ff. For a possible rendering in cuneiform as "Tattanni," see A. T. Olmstead, "Tattenai, Governor of 'Across the river,' " *JNES*, 3 (1944), 46. A. L. OPPENHEIM

TATTOO [כתנת קעקע, *lit.* writing of incision, *in the phrase* make a writing of incision] (Lev. 19:28). A pattern made on the skin by making punctures and inserting pigments. Both the KJV ("print any marks") and the RSV ("tattoo any marks") paraphrase the literal Hebrew, in which the word "tattoo" appears as a noun. Tattooing is mentioned along with self-inflicted lacerations in the rites of mourning for the dead, probably because both practices were associated with the pagan cults. H. G. MAY

TAU tô (Heb. tou) [ת, *t* (*Tāw*)]. The twenty-second letter of the Hebrew ALPHABET as it is placed in the KJV at the head of the twenty-second section of the acrostic psalm, Ps. 119, where each verse of this section of the psalm begins with this letter.

TAUNT. *See* SCOFFER.

TAVERNER'S BIBLE tăv'ər nər. The first complete Bible printed in England (1539). The OT was that of the Matthew Bible; the NT was revised on the basis of the Greek text. The work was done by a layman, a lawyer and student of Greek, Richard Taverner.

See also VERSIONS OF THE BIBLE, ENGLISH, § 4*a*.

J. R. BRANTON

TAVERNS, THREE. *See* THREE TAVERNS.

TAWNY [צחרוח; *cf.* Sahara] (Judg. 5:10); KJV WHITE. The whitish-brown color of the she-ass.

TAX, TAXES. A compulsory contribution to the support of government, local or federal, civil or ecclesiastical. Terms which designate some form of

Courtesy of the Oriental Institute, the University of Chicago

6. Men flogged for nonpayment of taxes, as scribes record the details; from the tomb of Mereruka, Saqqarah; Sixth Dynasty (*ca.* 2350-2200 B.C.)

taxation are the following: ערך, "assessment" (II Kings 23:35); מס, "forced labor" (Deut. 20:11); מנדה, "tribute" (Ezra 4:13); בלו, "import duty" (Ezra 4:13); הלך, "toll" (Ezra 4:13); κῆνσος, "tax" (Matt. 22:17); φόρος, "tribute" (Luke 20:22); τέλος, "toll" (Matt. 17:25); δίδραχμον, "half-shekel tax" (Matt. 17:24); ἀπογραφή, "enrollment (for tax purposes)" (Luke 2:2; *see* CENSUS).

A heavy tax in kind was exacted of all Egypt during the seven years of plenty. Some twenty per cent of all the produce of the land during the prosperous years was kept aside and stored, particularly grain for making bread. Egypt was thus spared the worst consequences of her own years of leanness and became a source of supply for other countries during the famine (Gen. 41:25–42:5). While accruing to the benefit of all the people, such a tax was possible only in a country like Egypt, where the Pharaohs actually owned the state (Gen. 41:44). Fig. TAX 6.

During the period of the judges there was in Israel no army or royal court to support (I Sam. 8:10-18). David seems to have been able to maintain an army without taxing the people in money or in kind, having men of military age in divisions of 24,000 each ready for active service month by month (I Chr. 27:1). Eventually David's treasury grew to enormous proportions, principally because of booty of war and tribute exacted from those he subdued (II Sam. 8; I Chr. 27:25-31).

Forced labor was required by Israel of the various resident Canaanite peoples who were not driven out of the land (Josh. 16:10; 17:13; Judg. 1:28). Both David and Solomon pressed aliens into *corvée* labor (II Sam. 20:24) on the construction of the temple (I Chr. 22:2; II Chr. 2). On other projects, as well, Solomon forced "all the people who were left of the Amorites, the Hittites, the Perizzites, the Hivites, and the Jebusites" (I Kings 9:20; II Chr. 8:7) into slave labor.

Israelites themselves were compelled to do forced labor in building the temple (I Kings 5:13) under Solomon. In all probability it was Solomon who first introduced state taxes in Israel. During the period of Israel's aggrandizement David's court could live within whatever means the spoils of war and foreign tribute provided. During the subsequent period of stabilization Solomon's court depended partially on its own subjects for support, and Israel was taxed. "Solomon had twelve officers over all Israel, who provided food for the king and his household; each man had to make provisions for one month in the year" (I Kings 4:7). This was in addition to the tribute and gifts incoming from subject peoples and more or less dependent foreign governments, as well as tolls collected from caravans and traders (I Kings 10:14-29; II Chr. 9:13-28).

Recent archaeological discoveries, in particular the Samaria Ostraca dating from the early eighth century B.C., as well as the Lachish Ostraca from Tell ed-Duweir in S Palestine, dating from the early sixth century B.C., offer very scant though concrete data on taxes in kind paid to the Israelite kings. Jar handles from Gibeon and Lachish are stamped in Hebrew characters of the period, למלך, "to the king." These jars probably held a bath, *ca.* ten gallons, and may have been the type used by Solomon to levy payment for Hiram's servants (II Chr. 2:10). *See bibliography.*

The cause of the division of the kingdom is attributed by Jeroboam and his fellow Israelites to the oppressive taxation and *corvée* exacted by Solomon and attempted by Rehoboam (I Kings 12).

The Chronicler reports that Jehoshaphat was able to regain much the same prestige Solomon had enjoyed and received taxes from his own people (II Chr. 17:5) as well as tributes from foreign peoples (II Chr. 17:10 ff). Finally, however, it was Judah which paid tribute to the Assyrians (II Kings 18: 13-16), the Egyptians (II Kings 23:33), and the Babylonians (II Kings 24-25). In order for King Jehoiakim to pay the tribute exacted of him by Pharaoh Neco, landholders in Judah were taxed, each according to his assessment (II Kings 23:35). *See* TRIBUTE.

Under the Persians there was begun a system of taxation which reached into the purses of the common people. Differing from what is commonly understood as tribute to a foreign master, wherein indigenous princes were directly liable for regular payment (Esth. 10:1), this system was administered directly in each Persian province by a Persian satrap. By decree of Darius Hystaspis these satraps paid fixed sums into the royal treasury (Herodotus III.89). This royal revenue was exacted of the people in the form of "tribute, custom, or toll" (Ezra 4:13). Artaxerxes (II?) specifically, however, exempted all priests, Levites, singers, doorkeepers, and other temple servants from payment of the tax (Ezra 7:24). Besides the royal revenue there was as well a tax imposed on the people called "bread of the governor," which maintained the local governor's household. It consisted of food and wine taken from the people, besides forty shekels of silver daily (Neh. 5:14-15). Though Nehemiah in his governorship claims not to have exacted the "bread of the governor," the people were forced in hard times to mortgage their fields, vineyards, and houses to survive, as well as raise the money for the royal revenue (Neh. 5:3-4; 9:37). These burdens were in addition to those of supporting the sanctuary and rebuilding the walls of Jerusalem.

Later in Hellenistic times, under the yoke of the Ptolemies and the Seleucids the office of tax collecting was not assigned by the foreign king to his local representatives, as in Persian times, but rather was farmed out to the highest bidder, who had army help in collecting the taxes. Josephus' anecdote about Joseph the Tobiad is corroborated fully by external Egyptian sources insofar as the system of taxation is depicted (Jos. Antiq. XII.iv.1-5). Men of eminent rank from the various Ptolemaic provinces gathered in Alexandria to bid for the right to collect the taxes from their own people.

Though we know very little of the Seleucid system of taxation, it is likely that the same tax-farming practice persisted. From letters purportedly by the Seleucid kings Antiochus III (Jos. Antiq. XII.iii.3) and Demetrius (I Macc. 10:29-31; 11:34-35; 13: 37-39) we learn of a poll tax, salt tax, and crown tax. At times the Seleucids exacted as much as a third of all grain produced, half of the fruit grown, and a share of the tithes paid by Jews to support the temple.

When Pompey had captured Jerusalem in 63 B.C., a tax was imposed upon the Jews which soon amounted to more than 10,000 talents (Jos. Antiq. XIV.iv.5). Julius Caesar, however, reduced the amount of taxes in general and decreed that no tax should be farmed or levied in the sabbatical years, nor that more than a fourth of the produce of the year following (?) should be collected. He stipulated that tithes should be paid by the Jews to Hyrcanus as to their own rulers of times past. For the use of the port city of Joppa, Hyrcanus was liable to a tax of 20,675 *modii.* This amount was to be raised as a tax on the land, the harbor, and its exports, and paid to the Roman officials at Sidon annually, except in the sabbatical year (Jos. Antiq. XIV.x.5-6).

Herod the Great laid a tax on produce of the field (Jos. Antiq. XV.ix.1) and a sales tax on all items bought and sold (XVII.viii.4). Under the procurators the financial system of the Empire was introduced. As in Ptolemaic times, tax collecting was farmed out at auction to the highest bidder (*see* TAX COLLECTOR). There were four principal kinds of duties: a land tax payable in kind or in money, a poll tax and a tax on personal property (Matt. 22:17), export and import customs at seaports and city gates, and in Jerusalem a house tax (Jos. Antiq. XIX.vi.3).

Aside from the tribute and taxes due foreign powers, the Jewish people individually were subject to a half-shekel payment annually to the temple, in the NT called the DIDRACHMA (Matt. 17:24). The background of the temple tribute was undoubtedly the half-shekel atonement money required of all males twenty years and over (Exod. 30:11-16). In Nehemiah's time the Jews paid a third of a shekel to the temple (Neh. 10:32-33); this was later changed to a half shekel, collected annually of every Jew twenty years and over throughout the world (Jos. Antiq. XVIII.ix.1). After the fall of Jerusalem in A.D. 70 the Roman emperor Vespasian ordered all Jews, despite the destruction of the temple, to continue the tribute payable annually into the capital (Jos. War VII.vi.6).

In order to collect the half-shekel temple tax levied on all Jews twenty years of age and over (Matt. 17:24), tax collectors went from town to town annually to raise the money, and in the Diaspora tax houses were set up to receive the impost.

An enrollment for purposes of taxation was ordered by the Roman emperor Augustus. This decree brought Joseph and Mary to Bethlehem in Judea, where Jesus was born (Luke 2:1-7; *see* QUIRINIUS). Another enrollment recorded in the NT evoked protests from the Jews, and disturbances ensued (Acts 5:37).

Matthew was one of the customs officials (Matt. 9:9; cf. Mark 2:14). Jesus frequented their company despite the low regard in which they were held both by the populace and by the Pharisees (Matt. 9:10-13; Mark 2:15-17; Luke 5:29-32). During his ministry the Pharisees asked Jesus if it was lawful to pay taxes to Caesar. Jesus, recognizing that his interrogators were seeking some evidence of sedition against him whereby to cause him trouble with the Romans, answered that laws of state should be obeyed (Matt. 22:17-21; Mark 12:13-17; Luke 20:22-25). This logion is reflected in the advice issued by Paul, who insists that taxes and revenues be paid to the state without fail (Rom. 13:6-7).

Bibliography. On the ostraca see D. Diringer, in *PEQ* (1941), pp. 89-106; in O. Tufnell, *Lachish III—The Iron Age* (1953), pp. 331-39. J. B. Pritchard, ed., *ANET* (1955), pp. 321-22; *Hebrew Inscriptions and Stamps from Gibeon* (1959).

J. A. Sanders

TAX COLLECTOR [Τελώνης; Heb. מוכס; Aram. מוכסא]; KJV PUBLICAN. In NT times the Roman officialdom in Palestine had direct responsibility for collecting regular taxes, such as poll and land taxes. The collection of tolls from those transporting property (including slaves) by land or sea was still, however, farmed out to private contractors. The latter paid a stipulated sum in advance for the right to collect the tolls in a certain locality, and then tried to make a profit on the transaction. The Greek term τελώνης and the corresponding Latin *publicanus* apply in the first instance to such entrepreneurs. These "publicans" were sometimes, but not invariably, Romans. Apparently the Jew Zacchaeus (Luke 19:2-10, where he is called "chief tax collector") had amassed his wealth by farming the tolls in the region of Jericho. See Taxes.

Both the Roman officials and the tax farmers employed Jewish underlings to do the actual collecting. It is to such small fry that the term τελώνης is usually applied in the NT. The rendering "tax collector" in the RSV is therefore more exact than the "publican" used in the older versions.

Tax officers are never popular, even in free lands; but the Palestinian tax collectors were an especially degraded and despised lot. At the beginning of the Christian era, the Jews of Palestine were not reconciled to Roman domination, even though they recognized some of the benefits of the Roman system. They regarded themselves as an oppressed people under military occupation, and they looked forward to liberation in a not very distant future. The harshness of the procurators aggravated their resentment; messianic and revolutionary movements seethed under cover and at times boiled into the open. The extremists bluntly asserted that any act of submission to Caesar—such as paying a tax—was treason to God. The more responsible leaders did not go so far; yet they looked on the taxes and tolls as tribute exacted by a foreign conqueror, not as a legitimate requirement for the maintenance of social order. Besides, the sums wrung from them were often excessive, to fatten the purses of the Roman officers or swell the profits of the tax farmers.

The Jews who for pay participated in these operations were therefore regarded as doubly base and despicable. They had sold their services to the foreign oppressor as against their own people, and they were engaged in literal robbery. For they were helping their principals to mulct the public, and no doubt part of what they collected stuck to their own fingers.

The rabbinic sources repeatedly bracket tax collectors with robbers. They and their families are disqualified from holding communal office, and even from giving testimony in a Jewish court. Just as one may deceive a highwayman to avoid loss, so one may deceive a tax collector (M. Ned. 3.4). This decision, the details of which are discussed by authorities of the first Christian century, reflects the near-revolutionary mood of that time. Later scholars, who regarded the imperial taxes as morally and legally valid, drastically modified the older rule; the Babylonian Talmud, composed in a more settled society, permits evasion only if an unauthorized or arbitrary tax collector is himself flouting the established laws.

The Synoptic gospels (the only NT writings which mention the matter) hold the same opinion of tax collectors as the early rabbinic sources. As the latter name "robbers and tax collectors" together, the gospels speak repeatedly of "tax collectors and sinners" (Matt. 9:10-11; 11:19; Mark 2:15-16; Luke 5:30); tax collectors are classified with prostitutes (Matt. 21:31) as flagrant offenders against morality. A follower of the disciples who flouts the authority of the church is to be treated "as a Gentile and a tax collector" (Matt. 18:17)—i.e., he is to be completely ostracized.

The willingness of Jesus to eat in the company of tax collectors (see the passages cited above and Luke 19:11 ff) does not mean that he tolerated or condoned their activities. On the contrary, the extent of his compassion is displayed by his association with these depraved creatures, in the hope of winning them for a better life. Just as the prostitutes whom he befriended were expected to respond to his guidance and return to the way of decency, so the tax collectors were summoned to repent and reform. Matthew-Levi gave up his post as collector of tolls in order to become a disciple; the rich Zacchaeus undertook to restore fourfold whatever he had taken by fraud, and to donate half his capital to charity.

The rabbis also considered the possibility that tax collectors might turn over a new leaf; such repentance, they remarked, is difficult because the penitent cannot possibly make restitution to all those he may have mulcted (Talmud B.Ḳ. 94*a*). In later centuries, Jewish scholars drastically modified the requirement of monetary restitution in all cases of robbery, in order to encourage inner repentance.

Bibliography. E. Schürer, *A History of the Jewish People in the Time of Jesus Christ* (Eng. trans. 1897-98), div. I, pt. II, pp. 65-71; I. Abrahams, *Studies in Pharisaism and the Gospels, First Series* (1917), pp. 54-61.   B. J. Bamberger

TAX OFFICE [τελώνιον]. A place mentioned in Matt. 9:9; Mark 2:14; Luke 5:27, in connection with the call to Matthew-Levi. The tax office in question was probably a toll or customs booth, where duties were levied on merchandise in transit. See Tax Collector; Taxes.   B. J. Bamberger

TEACHER [διδάσκαλος, *from* διδάσκω, teach]; KJV usually MASTER. The term appears often in Greek literature. Frequently it is a title of respect, and is found coupled with κύριος, "lord," and βασιλεύς, "king."

In the NT the term is sometimes applied to non-Christian leaders such as John the Baptist (Luke 3: 12) or Jewish religious authorities (Luke 2:46; John 3:10). For teachers of the Mosaic law, however, the compound νομοδιδάσκαλος is often preferred, especially by Luke. See DOCTOR.

Of some sixty instances of διδάσκαλος in the NT, more than thirty are in reference to Jesus, mostly in direct address. Here it is the natural counterpart of DISCIPLE. John 1:38 equates the term with RABBI, and it is likely that διδάσκαλε usually represents "rabbi" in the underlying oral tradition. This implies no official position. Rather, it indicates Jesus' status as leader of a group; and also, perhaps, that the authoritativeness of his teaching was publicly recognized (cf. Matt. 7:29; Mark 1:22; Luke 4:32).

Elsewhere, the title "teacher" is given to leaders of the young church, nearly always with some hint of official position (Acts 13:1; Eph. 4:11; II Tim. 1:11; Jas. 3:1). Of those so designated just after the NT period, undoubtedly the most famous was Polycarp. In the Martyrdom of Polycarp he is called "the "teacher of Asia" (12:2), "apostolic and prophetic teacher" (16:2), "glorious teacher" (19:1). Paul ranks teachers next below apostles and prophets, and above miracle-workers, healers, administrators, and speakers with tongues. All these seem to have enjoyed church-wide recognition (Rom. 16:6-8; I Cor. 12:28-30), though, no doubt, several of the lesser functions could be embodied in one individual.

In the evolution of the church's threefold ministry, the exact place of the teacher is not clear (see CHURCH, LIFE AND ORGANIZATION OF; MINISTRY). The Didache clearly sets "prophets and teachers" off from "bishops and deacons" (Did. 15:1). Harnack supposed, from this, that the early church had two distinct series of orders: presbyter-bishops and deacons for local work, and apostles, prophets, and teachers for the work of the church universal. This, however, postulates a degree of systematization highly unlikely at so early a period. Far more probably, the situation in the first Christian decades was fluid, with "prophets and teachers" as recognized officials in some local areas but not in all. At Antioch, it seems, the earliest officers were called exclusively "prophets and teachers" (Acts 13:1 ff). Nearby churches may well have followed the same pattern, or at least have used the same terminology.

Unlike the Christian prophet (see PROPHET IN THE NT), the teacher had a contemporary model in the Jewish synagogue; and his office certainly inherited, from the synagogue, its position of high honor in the young church. The teacher was a herald of the gospel. His task was to address the church, and to engage in pedagogical instruction and, probably, rudimentary theological discussion. This work usually consumed all his time, so that the local congregation was held responsible for his livelihood.

PIERSON PARKER

TEACHING IN THE EARLY CHURCH. Instruction or exhortation on various aspects of Christian life and thought, addressed to men already won by the missionary preaching in order to strengthen them.

See also PREACHING; CHURCH, LIFE AND ORGANIZATION OF.

***TEACHING OF JESUS.** A body of teaching recorded almost exclusively in the four gospels. The rest of the NT seldom directly quotes sayings of Jesus (there is an example in I Cor. 11:24-25), and of these only one or two are unrecorded in the gospels (e.g., the saying mentioned in Acts 20:35). Sayings attributed to Jesus from other sources add little, even if agreement were possible about their genuineness, to the main outlines of his teaching (see AGRAPHA). The NT contains words attributed to the ascended Christ, communicated in prophetic manner to a Spirit-filled person (e.g., Rev. 1:10–3:22), and it is not impossible that the gospels include thoughts first recorded in the inspired gatherings of the early church, as well as the remembered words of Jesus before his death. The evangelists, or the traditions they drew on, were not dispassionate reporters of his sayings, but recorded his teaching, in part at least, to illustrate their own convictions about him and his message.

When the gospels are examined and compared by the methods of literary and historical criticism, certain themes appear which had central importance in the teaching of Jesus and gave coherence to his words and actions—e.g., the imminence of the kingdom of God, the offer of forgiveness to sinners, and the possibility of obedience to the point of suffering and death. Within the exposition of these themes must also be sought the teaching of Jesus about God and his will for us, as well as Jesus' own understanding of his person and work.

It has been the task of later generations to draw out the consequences of the teaching of Jesus, both the themes directly proclaimed by and the themes implicit in his sayings; and there is reason to suppose that the process had begun by the time the Synoptic gospels were being written. With the appearance of the Fourth Gospel the teaching of Jesus received its clearest and most coherent reformulation (or, as some would say, restatement) within the NT period. Whatever view is taken of the relation of the Johannine to the Synoptic record, most scholars would be unwilling to build up an account of the teaching of Jesus on a particular theme by bringing together sayings taken indiscriminately from Synoptic and Johannine sources, without at least first studying them in their separate settings.

1. Jesus as teacher
2. The forms of the teaching
3. Modifications in the tradition
4. Major themes
5. Developments
Bibliography

1. Jesus as teacher. Jesus was regarded as a teacher by his disciples, his opponents (e.g., Mark 12:14), and the people generally. All the evangelists except Luke preserve the Aramaic word RABBI or its variant "Rabboni." He taught publicly in the open air, in synagogues, and in the temple. Privately he taught his disciples (see DISCIPLE). Like contemporary Jewish teachers he gathered disciples, though, unlike them, he did not create a school of biblical interpretation but sent his disciples to share his own proclamation (Mark 6:7-13). As a recognized rabbi he was consulted on questions of conduct and doctrine. The gospels record that he was asked about the legality of divorce and gave distinctive teaching in reply (Mark 10:1-12), about a particular accusation of adultery (in the story which appears in many MSS at John 7:53–8:11), about a family quarrel (Luke 12:13-15), and about the legality of Jewish tribute to Caesar (Mark 12:13-17; see TRIBUTE). Among theological questions, he was asked to give his opinion about the most important commandment (Mark 12:28-34; cf. Luke 10:25-28; see LOVE [NT]), to answer a Sadducean objection to the doctrine of RESURRECTION (Mark 12:18-27), to lay down the conditions of possessing life in the coming age (Mark 10:17-22), to solve the disciples' perplexity about a man blind from birth (John 9:2-3), and to give some assurance about the number destined to be saved (Luke 13:23-24). Jesus himself is represented as initiating a debate on the Davidic origin of the Messiah (see MESSIAH [JEWISH]) by reference to a verse of Ps. 110 (Mark 12:35-37). In all these matters Jesus was moving entirely within the interests of contemporary teachers, and, on some points at least, his teaching was closely similar to theirs.

Jesus is also represented as giving teaching explanatory of his actions (e.g., in Mark 11:15-17), or in extended discourses such as the Sermon on the Mount and the apocalyptic address of Mark 13 (see APOCALYPTICISM). Study of the discourses suggests that they are, in part, compositions by the evangelists, and that the component sayings were probably uttered in response to questioning and criticism. Much the same is true of the collections of parables such as Mark 4:1-33, or the greatly extended group in Matt. 13. Jesus is represented as announcing the kingdom in parables, and the difficult sayings in Mark 4:10-12 draw a parallel between the task Jesus set himself and the dual responsibility of the prophet to utter public prophecy and to provide private instruction (cf. Isa. 6:9-10; 8:16). The pattern of "public retort and private explanation" is familiar from rabbinic Judaism (see bibliography), and examples have been found in the teaching of Jesus (e.g., Mark 7:1-23; 10:2-12); though many scholars regard its appearance in the Markan section on parables as an artificial device of the evangelist to account for the later obscurity of the parables (see PARABLE). However this may be, some parables were first spoken in reply to questions, and it is often possible to understand them more satisfactorily by detaching them from their present contexts and considering what questions they answer.

Despite the parallels between Jesus and the rabbis, the gospels preserve sayings severely critical of his contemporaries (e.g., the brief sayings of Mark 12:38-40, which are embedded in a long polemical discourse in Matt. 23:1-36). Their body of teaching is regarded as the "traditions of men" (Mark 7:7; RSV "precepts of men"). Further, Jesus' teaching provoked popular astonishment and sometimes disapproval (Mark 1:22, 27; 6:2; 11:18). In the synagogue at Capernaum, his words and exorcism caused the hearers to exclaim at this new teaching uttered with authority unlike that of the scribes (which probably

means that he taught like an ordained rabbi, with the privilege of introducing novel doctrines, and not like the ordinary elementary teachers; see bibliography). It is notable that his work as teacher was closely associated with healing (e.g., Luke 5:17; 6:6; 13:10-11), and that when requested to perform some act of power he was addressed simply as TEACHER (Mark 4:38; 5:35; 9:17, 38; 10:51; the point is made explicit in John 3:2). The title was thus wider than it is in modern usage; hence, no doubt, Luke's occasional substitution of MASTER. (The RSV sometimes translates "teacher" by "master" in Matthew and Mark.) The request of the sons of Zebedee for privileged places in the coming age (Mark 10:35-37) and Peter's bemused remark at the Transfiguration (Mark 9:5) also demonstrate a tendency in the primitive Christian tradition to press the title beyond its normal meaning, which becomes explicit in the Fourth Gospel, where not only is the "Rabbi" identified with Son of God and King of Israel (John 1:49), but also the content of Jesus' teaching is his self-disclosure (John 7:14-31; 8:12-30).

In all the gospels there is one further extension of the significance of this teaching activity. In popular estimation he was a prophet, a successor to John the Baptist or a reviver of the prophetic spirit of earlier times (e.g., Mark 6:15; 8:28). The proverbial saying that "a prophet is not without honor, except in his own country" (Mark 6:4), may imply that Jesus tacitly accepted this estimate; and the saying of Luke 13:33: "It cannot be that a prophet should perish away from Jerusalem," suggests that he identified himself with the prophets who suffered for the divine message. Much of his teaching had close kinship with that of the prophets in form, manner, and content (see SERMON ON THE MOUNT § 2). The initial summary of his message in Mark 1:15, by its choice of words, places Jesus at once in the prophetic tradition, as the herald of the fulfilment of prophecy. His undoubted sense of vocation cannot be adequately recognized by the title "teacher." Popular feeling came somewhat closer with "prophet"; he himself apparently chose SON OF MAN to indicate what he was doing.

2. The forms of the teaching. The forms of Jesus' teaching may be studied by the methods of FORM CRITICISM. There is a broad distinction between parables and sayings, though the two overlap. The sayings may be grouped according to their type (such as maxims, exhortations, and blessings), or according to the cultural milieu from which they came (such as the prophetic, apocalyptic, and wisdom traditions; see SERMON ON THE MOUNT § 2). Examination of the sayings in this manner gives some insight into the various categories of the recorded tradition of Jesus, and may permit a judgment about the originality of the sayings, and the influences at work upon them in the earliest period of transmission.

The sayings were originally spoken in Aramaic, and scholars have sought to show that there is clear evidence of Aramaic style, language, and idiom behind the Greek text of the gospels. Attention has been drawn to the frequent occurrence of the forms of Hebrew poetry (see POETRY [HEBREW]), with its characteristic and varied parallelism. Retranslation of the sayings into Palestinian Aramaic provides instances of deliberate wordplay, a common feature of Semitic poetry. It is said that in Aramaic the sayings give the impression of being carefully premeditated and studied deliverances, prophetic utterances of the style and grandeur of Isaiah. By this use of prophetic form and language, the teacher ensured that his words would not be forgotten.

Not all the teaching of Jesus is conveyed by parables, detached sayings, and discourses. A common unit in the Synoptic gospels is the "pronouncement story" or brief narrative (such as Mark 2:15-17), which sketches a situation in the barest outline, betrays no interest in the persons involved, but simply leads up to the pronouncement of Jesus in answer to a question or in response to an action. It is further to be noted that the teaching of Jesus was not confined to speech, but was partly declared by actions. When the Baptist sent messengers to inquire about the mission of Jesus, his reply pointed to his healing activity (Matt. 11:2-6; Luke 7:18-23). Thus it is relevant to take into account the "miracle stories" (*see* MIRACLE), which have a well-marked form in the Synoptic gospels; and also a number of "kyrios stories," which lack a common or well-marked form but all demonstrate Jesus as Lord. They include the calling of the disciples, the confession of Jesus as Messiah, the Transfiguration, the entry into Jerusalem, and the cleansing of the temple.

The Fourth Gospel lacks parables and has few aphorisms which, when they occur, are embodied in dramatic dialogues or long discourses. The dramatic dialogue (e.g., with Nicodemus in 3:1-15) appears to be a development of a less common Synoptic form. The long interwoven discourses are not closely allied to the loose Synoptic compositions and have their nearest, though not very close, parallels in the philosophical religious dialogues of the Hellenistic world. Although study of the Dead Sea Scrolls suggests that the "typically Greek" terminology of the Johannine discourses was more familiar in Palestine than has been supposed, yet forms in which the teaching of Jesus appears in the Fourth Gospel still look like a conscious modification or transformation of the simpler Synoptic forms.

3. Modifications in the tradition. Modifications may have taken place at a stage much earlier than the composition of the Fourth Gospel, though scholars are widely divergent in their judgments about the extent to which the sayings (and deeds) of Jesus have been reliably preserved. It is not easy to discover objective criteria by which the original can be separated from the secondary, without first assuming what needs to be proved. In setting out the teaching of Jesus it is necessary to remember that the customs and interests (not too narrowly understood) of the primitive Christian communities caused his words and actions to be remembered. From the beginning a process of selection must have taken place, and it is possible by comparing the written gospels to observe how sayings and themes were modified.

The influence of the changed circumstances of a later time may be detected in many of the parables (*see also* SERMON ON THE MOUNT, especially § 3). If, e.g., the parable of the marriage feast in Matt. 22:1-14 is compared with its equivalent parable of the great banquet in Luke 14:16-24, it at once appears that the kernel is a parable about a man who prepared a fine meal for invited guests and threw it open to all and sundry when the invited guests declined to come. The picture was immediately applicable to the Pharisaic opponents of Jesus, who refused to respond to him and criticized his offer of the gospel to sinners. The Lukan form has a repeated invitation to people outside the city (vss. 23-24), and this looks like an allegorical touch to represent the subsequent Gentile mission of the church. In Matt. 22:6-7 there is a more extensive allegorical development, which hints at the martyrdom of Christian missionaries and the destruction of Jerusalem, and so converts the parable into an outline of history from the prophets to the Last Judgment. The notoriously puzzling vss. 11-14 (absent from Luke) appear to have been originally a separate parable, possibly joined to the previous one in order to guard the primitive church against the admission of immoral and unrepentant pagans.

This example illustrates the tendency of the primitive church to use what was spoken to Jesus' contemporaries for their own concerns by adaptation, arrangement, and allegory. They transferred the eschatological challenge to the (near) future, made room for the Gentile mission of the church, and by means of a hortatory twist discovered rules for their own existence.

If now the individual strata of the Synoptic tradition are examined, it appears that certain traits predominate in each. Thus in the material peculiar to Matthew there is a notable concentration of teaching apparently directed to predicting the coming of the Son of man and much emphasis on the permanent importance of the Jewish law. The special Lukan material is particularly interested in the Christian mission to Gentiles and unfortunates. Similarly Mark and the sayings collection Q have their particular interests (*see* Q; MARK, GOSPEL OF; MATTHEW, GOSPEL OF; LUKE, GOSPEL OF). When, therefore, the sayings of Jesus are assessed, in order to form a picture of his teaching, it is necessary to give some weight to the stratum in which they are found and the influences that may have modified them.

4. Major themes. In the Synoptic gospels the teaching of Jesus is dominated by the kingdom of God. The fundamental content of this phrase is derived, by way of a rabbinic form of expression, from the OT (especially the Psalms and Deutero-Isaiah) where the dual conviction is maintained that God is already King and will finally reign in open triumph. This duality is present in those parables of Jesus which depend on the idea of growth. To the Hebrew mind the incomprehensible processes of nature (cf. Mark 4:27) were a sign of the mysterious sovereignty by which God maintained the daily life of his people. At the same time, the parabolic application of the metaphor indicates an effective working of this sovereignty in the course of history. Such a presentation seems almost a direct response to the eager expectation, in first-century Palestine, of an imminent victory of the divine sovereignty. It is noteworthy that both forms of this hope—i.e., pious quietism and revolutionary zealotism—were combined in the Qumran sectarian literature. Apocalyptic writings were widely popular and fostered such expectations (see APOCALYPTICISM). That Jesus was not insensitive to their appeal is shown by the influence on his teaching of Dan. 7, from which was probably derived the term SON OF MAN and possibly the necessity of suffering and the gathering of disciples to be the "saints of the Most High." On the other hand, Jesus by no means identified himself with apocalyptic sentiments. The distinctiveness of his teaching may be seen when it is recalled that the apocalyptic expectation of the historical kingdom of God required both the purification and the triumph of Israel, and also the conquest of an opposition. The opposition might be regarded as demonic forces or Gentile enemies, or the two together. Some Jews responded with denunciations of Gentile idolatry and morals, and launched a vigorous movement aimed at their conversion (cf. Matt. 23:15); others, less optimistic, believed that God had handed over the present age to the evil powers, so that nothing could be done until they received the signal for the coming age when God would intervene to make his triumph sure.

Jesus used these themes with a difference. In part he identified the opposition with demonic forces; for this, his exorcisms are clear evidence. He could use the kingdom metaphor of a rival kingdom of evil (Mark 3:24) in order to assert that it was fatally divided and coming to an end (cf. the vision of Satan's fall [Luke 10:18]). The narrative of the TEMPTATION OF JESUS preserves a tradition that he repudiated the doctrine of a present age handed over to the devil (Luke 4:5-8). Moreover, the healing activity of Jesus was wider than exorcism; he restored withered limbs and freed men from the indignity of unclean diseases. For Jesus the primary opposition to God's kingship was a distorted world, inhabited by distorted beings.

Toward Gentiles, especially those with whom Jews came into daily contact, Jesus counseled forbearance, forgiveness, and love (e.g., Luke 6:27-35; see SERMON ON THE MOUNT § 3b). He was notorious for his association with tax collectors and sinners (see SIN; the word "sinners" often means Gentiles, rather than Jews careless of the law). He neither despised Gentiles for their ignorance and wickedness nor approved their ways. (The best comment on the irony of Mark 7:27 is his repudiation of the separatist ritual food laws in Mark 7:15.) Except under pressure (e.g., Matt. 8:5-13), he confined his teaching to his own people and so instructed his disciples (Matt. 10:5-6); but at the same time he urged upon them a new response to Gentiles in their midst and warned them of the catastrophe that would result from a continued policy of hostility (so, in part, is to be explained the "apocalyptic" language of Mark 13).

In the teaching of Jesus it was not Gentiles who hindered the coming of the kingdom, but unrepentant Israelites. His primary announcement was that "the kingdom of God is at hand; repent, and believe in the gospel" (Mark 1:15). The demand for repentance was stock Jewish teaching, and had been already voiced by John the Baptist (cf. Matt. 3:2). With Jesus the distinctive and paradoxical feature was that he found the hard, unrepentant core, not among the "sinners," but among the "righteous" (cf. the irony of Mark 2:17). It was these who resented his offer of the gospel to sinners and heard his reply in such

parables as the prodigal son and the marriage feast (Luke 15:11-32; Matt. 22:1-10); who argued that the omens were wrong for a new divine act and heard themselves rebuked for inability to read the signs of the times (Luke 12:54-56). It was certainly Pharisees who regarded his healings on the sabbath as dishonorable to God, and so provoked the controversy about scribal rulings which produced Jesus' most vigorous rebukes (e.g., Matt. 23:1-36; Luke 11:37-52) for the way they had made the practice of the law external and destroyed its prophetic, personal challenge. See LAW (IN THE NT).

The yoke of Jesus, unlike the scribal yoke of the law, was easy (Matt. 11:29-30), because he did not make acceptance by God conditional on keeping the burdensome law; but, once accepted and made a disciple, it was necessary for one to become as a child (Mark 10:15), to cut off every wrong ambition (Mark 9:43-47), to renounce, if need be, personal possessions (Mark 10:17-27; see WEALTH) and even life itself (Mark 8:34-35; see SELF-DENIAL). No doubt these rigorous demands arose from the critical situation of Jesus' own ministry (cf. the instructions to disciples in Mark 6:7-11); but they had the effect of confronting men with no lesser standard than the holy God in his sovereignty. As the parables of the hidden treasure and the fine pearl show (Matt. 13:44-45), it was the intention of Jesus to bring men to the point of decision; and this, unlike the scribal tradition, was the common purpose of his ethical teaching (see SERMON ON THE MOUNT § 3). He held out to men the responsibility of "entering the kingdom of God," which means, in part, sharing God's sovereign attributes—as, e.g., the divine love and forgiveness (Matt. 18:23-35; for the equivalence of kingdom and life, see Mark 9:43-47; for kingdom and righteousness, Matt. 6:33). Renunciation is therefore not an arbitrary feature of Jesus' teaching; it is an inherent necessity if men are to receive and share the life of God.

The opportunity of decision is not indefinitely open. Jesus warned his contemporaries of the disastrous consequences of not responding to his appeal. The note of judgment was not only prominent in his teaching (often expressed by the metaphor of the reckoning [Matt. 25:14-30]), but also urgent. Israel was like a fruitless fig tree, in danger of being cut down (Luke 13:6-9); and in some sayings (such as Mark 9:1) Jesus appears to have looked for a rapid denouement that would both settle the fate of Israel and inaugurate the new age of the kingdom.

In all this teaching Jesus closely associated a body of disciples with himself. They were to learn his teaching and pass it on; they shared his work of proclamation, healing, and feeding. To receive or reject the disciples was to receive or reject Jesus himself (Matt. 10:40; Luke 10:16). This unity of master and disciples (which some scholars also detect in the corporate meaning of the title "Son of man," is the foundation, in the teaching of Jesus, of the church (see CHURCH, IDEA OF). They are the little flock which is to receive the kingdom (Luke 12:32), to share in the sovereignty and judgment (Luke 22:28-29), and, above all, to suffer with Jesus (Mark 8:34-35). At one point, at least, it seems that Jesus believed that some disciples would share the suffering of the Son of man (Mark 10:35-45), before which the kingdom would not come. (The connection of thought has been traced in Dan. 7; many scholars believe that Jesus was consciously taking the part of the Suffering Servant of Isa. 53, despite the scarcity of clear references to this passage in his teaching.) His words at the LAST SUPPER, when he gave bread and wine to his disciples, seem to mean that as a condition of sharing his life (his body) they must also share his sacrifice (his blood). In the end, he went to his death alone, convinced that it was God's will to bring about his sovereignty through total defeat, and persuaded that he died, not only for God, but also on behalf of "the many." *See* DEATH OF CHRIST.

There is little agreement among scholars about Jesus' expectation of what would happen after his death. By direct announcement, by parables, by actions (Luke 11:20), he had proclaimed the nearness of the kingdom, which would mean vindication for himself and his disciples and judgment for the unheeding. That he expected his death to be vindicated in resurrection (even though the disciples did not take his meaning) is firmly established in the tradition; what is not so clear is whether he expected the winding up of God's dealings with men to take place at once or after an interval of time, long or short.

For Jesus' teaching about God, which lies behind his preoccupation with the kingdom of God, *see* GOD (NT); for his teaching about his own person and work, *see* CHRIST; and the separate titles by which he was addressed, especially SON OF MAN. On Jesus' teaching generally, *see also* JESUS CHRIST.

5. **Developments.** Development of the teaching of Jesus takes place in the Fourth Gospel along three important lines. There is a revaluation of the Synoptic eschatology; "kingdom of God" is almost entirely replaced by "eternal life," and there is developed teaching about the Holy Spirit; there is explication of the Christology latent in the Synoptic records; and there is conscious reflection on the significance of the continuing community of disciples. For these themes, *see* JOHN, GOSPEL OF.

Bibliography. On Jesus as teacher: C. H. Dodd, "Jesus as Teacher and Prophet," in G. K. Bell and A. Deissmann, eds., *Mysterium Christi* (1930); D. Daube, *The NT and Rabbinic Judaism* (1956).

On the forms of Jesus' teaching and modifications in the tradition: C. F. Burney, *The Poetry of Our Lord* (1925); V. Taylor, *The Formation of the Gospel Tradition* (1935); M. Black, *An Aramaic Approach to the Gospels and Acts* (2nd ed., 1954); J. Jeremias, *The Parables of Jesus* (1954); R. Bultmann, *Die Geschichte der Synoptischen Tradition* (3rd ed., 1958).

On the major themes: A. Schweitzer, *The Quest of the Historical Jesus* (1910); R. Bultmann, *Jesus and the Word* (1935); T. W. Manson, *The Teaching of Jesus* (1935); C. J. Cadoux, *The Historic Mission of Jesus* (1941); W. Manson, *Jesus the Messiah* (1943); R. Bultmann, *Theology of the NT*, vol. I (1952), ch. 1; T. W. Manson, *The Servant-Messiah* (1953); H. E. W. Turner, *Jesus, Master and Lord* (1953).

On particular themes, see special bibliographies; see also the following: V. Taylor, *Jesus and His Sacrifice* (1937); R. N. Flew, *Jesus and His Church* (1938); C. K. Barrett, *The Holy Spirit and the Gospel Tradition* (1947); R. H. Fuller, *The Mission and Achievement of Jesus* (1954); J. Jeremias, *The Eucharistic Words of Jesus* (1955); W. G. Kümmel, *Promise and Fulfilment* (1957); J. A. T. Robinson, *Jesus and His Coming* (1957); W. Zimmerli and J. Jeremias, *The Servant of God* (1957); J. Knox, *The Death of Christ* (1959); M. D. Hooker, *Jesus and the Servant* (1959).   K. GRAYSTON

TEBAH tē'bə [טבח, *perhaps* born at the time (*or* place) of a slaughtering] (Gen. 22:24). The first-son of Nahor and Reumah; same as BETAH and TIBHATH; identified with the place name Tubiḫi of the Tell el-Amarna Letters, and probably with Dbḫ of Thut-mose III's Retenu list. It is located generally between Damascus and Kadesh.   L. HICKS

TEBALIAH tĕb'ə lī'ə [טבליהו, Y has dipped—*i.e.,* purified(?); *or* good belonging to Y(?)] (I Chr. 26:11). The third son of Hosah in the line of Merari; a temple gatekeeper in a postexilic alignment of Levites ascribed to David.

TEBETH tē'bĕth [טבת]. The tenth month in the Hebrew CALENDAR (Akkadian *ṭebītu;* December-January).

TEETH. *See* TOOTH.

TEHAPHNEHES. Alternate form of TAHPANHES.

TEHINNAH tĭ hīn'ə [תחנה, supplication] (I Chr. 4:12). A man or family of Judah, probably Calebite; founder of Irnahash.

TEIL TREE tēl. KJV translation of אלה (usually OAK) in Isa. 6:13. "Teil" is an obsolete name for the lime or linden tree, *Tilia europea. See* TEREBINTH.
    J. C. TREVER

TEKEL tē'kəl, tĕk'əl. *See* MENE, MENE, TEKEL, AND PARSIN.

TEKOA tĭ kō'ə [תקוע; Apoc. Θεκώε]; KJV alternately TEKOAH; KJV Apoc. THECOE thĭ kō'ē; TEKOITES —īts, OF TEKOA [תקועי, תקוע, *feminine* תקעית] (II Sam. 14:4, 9; 23:26; I Chr. 11:28; 27:9; Neh. 3:5, 27). A city in the highlands of Judah (cf. I Chr. 2:24; 4:5), identified with Khirbet Taqu'a, *ca.* six miles S of Bethlehem, ten miles S of Jerusalem. The ruins of the last occupation lie scattered on top of the hill which forms a small plateau of *ca.* four or five acres. Its height of *ca.* 2,800 feet is above that of Bethlehem and the Herodium to the N. It is surrounded by an area under cultivation; there are a couple of springs in the vicinity. Fig. TEK 7.

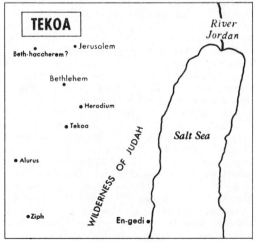

7. The Judean wilderness as viewed from Tekoa (modern Tequ'), with Herodium (Jebel Fureidis) circled

Eusebius says Thecua (Tekoa) was twelve (Roman) miles S of Aelia (Jerusalem), near a wilderness of the same name. Here a tomb of Amos the prophet was pointed out, a place of veneration also noted in Byzantine historiography. There was a church (a "Propheteum") of Saint Amos in Tekoa at which the monks of the New Laura worshiped and communed (*see below*). A remnant of this church may be the large baptismal font, three feet and nine inches deep and four feet in diameter at the top, cut out of a single limestone block. Jerome mentions that the people of Tekoa lived on a mountain twelve (Roman) miles from Jerusalem and that as he looked each day from Bethlehem, he could see the village of Tekoa. A medieval Jewish tradition pointed to one of the caves in the area as the grave of Amos.

In the royal administrative reorganization, Tekoa became a part of the highland district of Bethlehem (Josh. 15:59a LXX). One of David's Mighty Men, Ira son of Ikkesh, was a native of Tekoa (II Sam. 23:26). After Absalom's slaying of his half brother Amnon to avenge the latter's rape of Tamar, Absalom's sister, Absalom fled for safety to the home of his maternal grandfather, Talmai king of Geshur (cf. II Sam. 3:3). In order to effect an honorable *rapprochement* between David and Absalom, Joab sent for a woman from Tekoa to point out, through a ruse, the needlessness of carrying out the sentence of death which lay upon Absalom for the murder of Amnon. The stratagem succeeded, and Absalom was restored to favor—only to revolt against his father a short time later (II Sam. 13:37–14:24).

After the division of the monarchy, possibly soon after Shishak's invasion of *ca.* 918, Rehoboam (*ca.* 922-915) included Tekoa among the cities whose fortifications were to be strengthened (II Chr. 11:6). *Ca.* a half-century later, Jehoshaphat (*ca.* 873-849) met and defeated an army of Moabite, Ammonite, and Meunite invaders in the wilderness between Tekoa and En-gedi (II Chr. 20:20).

The prophet Amos, whose ministry included (roughly) the years 752-738, lived at Tekoa and was called from there to bring God's message to the N kingdom (Amos 1:1). In his oracle warning of the impending invasion from the N, Jeremiah calls for a trumpet blast from the walls of the fortress Tekoa and a fire signal from BETH-HACCHEREM. Though it may be but a play on words, it would appear that Tekoa was still an important post in the Judahite defense system on the edge of the wilderness which stretched eastward to the Dead Sea (Jer. 6:1).

People from Tekoa helped rebuild the walls of Jerusalem after the Exile, even though their leaders took little interest in the reconstruction program (Neh. 3:5, 27).

In 160 B.C., Jonathan and his brother Simon escaped from the Syrian general Bacchides by taking refuge in the wilderness of Tekoa, the name of a large section of the Judean wilderness. The white, hard limestone surface, with veins of flint in it, made it difficult to track anyone in this desolate region. Lookouts posted on the barren hilltops could easily spot any effort at a sneak attack or encirclement; the nature of the terrain itself made this sort of maneuver difficult. The communications with the S Judean rebels could be easily maintained. Thus the wilderness was a good place to go to gain time and reorganize one's forces, much as David did in the wilderness of Ziph and En-gedi at an earlier date. The pool of Asphar (Yellow Pool) was probably one of the reservoirs which Uzziah (*ca.* 783-742) had dug in the wilderness (II Chr. 26:10) to supplement the inadequate water supply. A little less than three miles S of Tekoa is Khirbet Bir ez-Za'faran (Saffron Well or Pool), perhaps suggesting the yellow color of the water, or that of some kind of flower which grew around the place in the spring). At Khirbet Bir ez-Za'faran, not far from Sheikh Ahmed Abu Safar, are remains of ancient wells near some cisterns dug into the rock. It may have been here that Jonathan and his troops pitched camp and from here made their raid against Madeba (I Macc. 9:32 ff; Jos. Antiq. XIII.i.2).

In A.D. 68 Simon, one of the Jewish revolutionaries, camped at Thecoue (Θεκούε, Tekoa) with his raiders. He sent a representative, Eleazar, to the Idumean garrison in the Herodium, *ca.* three miles to the NE, to demand the surrender of the garrison. The Idumeans killed Eleazar and then sent one James to ascertain Simon's strength. James, after visiting Simon in his camp, treacherously misrepresented the strength of Simon's army to the leaders of the Idumean army concentrated at Alurus (Halhul, four miles N of Hebron, seven miles SW of Tekoa) so greatly that when Simon approached with his forces, the Idumeans fled in panic (Jos. War IV.ix.5-6).

In 454-58 a Monophysite monk named Romanus established a convent near Tekoa, after being expelled from his home convent of Elpidius for his heterodoxy. *Ca.* thirty years later this community came to an end. In 508 some discontented monks from Mar Saba, a monastery E of Bethlehem, founded a New Laura (convent) in a wadi S of Tekoa, apparently near or in the ruins of the monastery of Romanus. The New Laura is remembered in history as a center of Origenism during the twenty years preceding the Fifth Ecumenical Council (Constantinople II, 553) after which those espousing Origenism were expelled and replaced by orthodox monks. The New Laura is perhaps to be identified with Qasr Umm Leimun, a ruin with a church built on a hill at the beginning of the Wadi el-Menka', from which position there is an excellent view of the watershed and the way to Tekoa, as the descriptions require. Nearby is the ruin of a smaller church called Qasr el-'Abd. The cells were not found, but they may have been less permanent structures and have disappeared.

During the Crusades (1132) Tekoa became a benefice of the Holy Sepulchre. In 1138 it was sacked by a band of Turks, but the populace found refuge in a large cave in the nearby Wadi Khareitun, which cuts through the hills to the Dead Sea. In the same year King Fulk gave the inhabitants the right to exploit the deposits of bitumen and salt from the Dead Sea.

The village plays no further role in the history of the region and is unoccupied today.

Bibliography. M. Marcoff and D. J. Chitty, "Notes on Monastic Research in the Judaean Wilderness, 1928-29," *PEQ* (1929), pp. 167-78, especially 171 ff. F.-M. Abel, *Géographie de la Palestine,* vol. II (1938); *Les Livres des Maccabées* (1949), pp. 166-67.   V. R. GOLD

TEL-ABIB tĕl'ə bĭb' [תל אביב; Akkad. *Til-abûbi,* mound of the flood]. A town in Babylonia, the home of Ezekiel and other exiles (Ezek. 3:15). It was near the canal CHEBAR, but its exact location cannot be determined. Some of the Jews who were exiled in 597 B.C. had made their home here, and the town took its name from the Akkadian name of the mound on which it was built, which was a designation of mounds containing buried cities believed to have existed before the Flood.   H. G. MAY

TELAH tē'lə [תלח, fracture(?)] (I Chr. 7:25). A family of the tribe of Ephraim, in a postexilic list tracing the descent of Joshua.

TELAIM tĭ lā'əm [הטלאם] (I Sam. 15:4). Alternately: **TELEM** tē'lĕm [טלם] (Josh. 15:24). A city of Judah, near Ziph and not far from the border of the Amalekites. It was here that Saul assembled his forces in his campaign against the city of the Amalekites who apparently were harassing the tribe of Judah, which had appealed for rescue, just as Jabesh-gilead had previously (I Sam. 15:4; cf. I Sam. 11:4-6). In I Sam. 27:8 it is better to read *miṭṭelem,* "from Telem" (cf. LXX), instead of the MT *mēʿôlām,* "from of old"; the passage would then indicate that the territory of the Amalekites extended from the vicinity of Telaim to the border of Egypt.

The site is uncertain; Abel suggests Khirbet Umm es-Salafeh, SW of Kurnub, and Press, Khirbet Abu Tulul, twelve miles SE of Beer-sheba.   S. COHEN

****TEL-ASSAR** tĕl ăs'ər [תלאשר]; KJV TELASSAR (Isa. 37:12); THELASAR thĭ lā'sər (II Kings 19:12). An Aramean site in N Mesopotamia, conquered by Sennacherib's predecessors on the throne of Assyria. II Kings 19:12 (=Isa. 37:12; תלשר) defines it as the abode of the people of Eden (*see* BETH-EDEN). "Tel" is the Semitic word for "mound," and its use shows that in OT times the site was ancient, with early strata already buried.   C. H. GORDON

TELEM tē'lĕm [טלם, brightness; *cf.* Arab. *ẓalmun;* Apoc. Τολβάνης]; KJV Apoc. TOLBANES tŏl'bə-nēz. 1. A Levite, and one of the contemporaries of Ezra listed as having married foreign wives (Ezra 10:24; cf. I Esd. 9:25).

Bibliography. M. Noth, *Die israelitischen Personennamen* (1928), p. 223.   B. T. DAHLBERG

2. Alternate form of TELAIM.

TEL-HARSHA tĕl här'shə [תל חרשא, the ruined city mound of the deaf-mute] (Ezra 2:59; Neh. 7:61); THELERSAS thĭ lûr'səs. A Babylonian place from which men unable to produce genealogies proving their Jewish lineage came to Jerusalem. The place, as yet unidentified, was apparently a Jewish settlement on the site of a ruined city.   R. A. BOWMAN

****TELL EL-AMARNA** tĕl ĕl ə mär'nə. The modern name of the site of Akhetaton, capital of Egypt during the reign of Amen-hotep IV (*ca.* 1375-1366).

  1. The site
    a. Location and name
    b. Historical context
    c. The Amarna Revolution
    d. Description of the site
  2. The Amarna Letters
    a. Discovery, disposition, and general content
    b. Historical significance
  Bibliography

1. The site. *a. Location and name.* Tell el-Amarna is the modern designation of the site in Egypt *ca.* two hundred miles S of Cairo on the E bank of the Nile, occupied in antiquity by the city called Akhetaton, capital and sacred precinct of Amen-hotep IV (Akh-en-Aton),* tenth ruler of the Eighteenth Dynasty. The modern name, originally the result of an error, is now sanctioned by common usage. Actually, el-Amarna is a roughly semicircular area bounded on its six-mile diameter by the Nile and on its periphery by an arc of high cliffs; it derives its name from the tribe of the Beni ʿAmran, who settled there in comparatively modern times. The villages found at present in the region are Hawata, el-Amarea, Hag Qandil, Esbi, and et-Till; it is from a chance combination of the name of the last-mentioned village with that of the area in general that the appellation Tell el-Amarna was formed by travelers who visited the site. For the meaning of the ancient name Akhetaton, *see* § *1b below.* Figs. AKH 8-9.

b. Historical context. Amen-hotep IV became pharaoh of Egypt *ca.* 1375 B.C. after a coregency of not more than twelve years with his father, Amen-hotep III, during whose reign Egypt had already begun to lose her hold on the large Asian and African empire conquered and controlled by his predecessors Thutmose III, Amen-hotep II, and Thut-mose IV. Recent study has cast considerable doubt on the period of coregency, which, if shortened or rejected completely, will force a change in the chronology; because a new chronology has not been worked out in detail, the commonly accepted datings are followed herein. The events of the new king's early years, so important for understanding his subsequent actions and policies, are difficult to reconstruct. The one fact which stands out clearly, however, is his indifference to the affairs of the Empire and his devotion to religious matters. He is depicted as physically malformed, ʻwith a thin, sensuous face; narrow, sloping shoulders; and un-

Courtesy of Foto Marburg

8. Painted limestone bust of Queen Nefert-iti, from Tell el-Amarna

usually large hips and abdomen. He married his sister Nefert-iti, who bore him six daughters. Figs. EYE 39; TEL 8.

In the sixth year of his reign, for reasons still only conjectured, he broke with the influential priesthood of Amon at Thebes, then the capital, and devoted himself exclusively to the worship of Aton, the sun-god, whose uniqueness and supremacy he proceeded to promulgate throughout Egypt. His disavowal of Amon in particular and of the other gods in general was violent and thorough. The name of Amon was excised from monuments in the entire land, and the king changed his name from Amen-hotep, "Amon is satisfied," to Akh-en-Aton, meaning either "the one who is beneficial to Aton" or "it goes well with Aton." The religious heresy and the political changes which accompanied it are often referred to as the Amarna Revolution.

Because Thebes was so intimately identified with Amon, Akh-en-Aton planned and built three cities, sacred precincts to his own unique deity, Aton, in the three principle regions of the Empire—i.e., in Nubia, in Egypt itself, and presumably in Syria. The Egyptian city, certainly the most remarkable of the three, was situated at el-Amarna and was named Akhetaton, meaning either "the horizon of Aton" or "place of the effective glory of Aton." When the palace and temples of the new city were completed, Akh-en-Aton moved there with his family and court; thus Akhetaton became the new capital of Egypt.

Few details of happenings in the rest of Egypt are available for the major portion of his reign, but in his twelfth year a genuine crisis seems to have been precipitated both by internal dissension created by the abrupt social, political, and religious reforms con-

nected with the revolution and by a growing concern over the rapid dissolution of the Empire which had been in progress during this time. Some attempt was made on the part of the Pharaoh to remedy this situation; his younger brother, Smenkhkere, whom he had married to Meritaton, his eldest daughter, and had made coregent with him, returned to Thebes in an effort to conciliate with the priesthood of Amon. This desperate reversion to the old order was not successful, and both Akh-en-Aton and his brother Smenkhkere disappeared from the historical scene. The kingship was assumed by the half brother of Queen Nefert-iti, Tutankhaton, who removed the capital to Thebes and submitted himself to the desires of the still powerful priesthood of Amon, even to the extent of altering his name to Tut-ankh-Amon. In spite of the extraordinarily lavish contents of this king's tomb and the material wealth such furnishings imply, his reign was not a successful one. After a short rule by Eye (Aya), another member of the Akhetaton court, the throne was turned over to the army general Hor-em-heb, and the records of the heretic kings from Amarna were erased from the Egyptian scene as violently and completely as had been those of Amon by the first of the aberrant line.

c. The Amarna Revolution. The central feature of the Amarna Revolution as brought about by Akh-en-Aton was, of course, its religious heresy, an essentially monotheistic cult devoted to the worship of Aton. The existence of Aton as the name of the sun disk in a physical sense is attested well before the Eighteenth Dynasty, but Aton as a god appears only shortly before the time of Akh-en-Aton himself. The evidence, however, is quite sufficient to show that the conception of the sun disk as a life-sustaining principle was not invented by the heretic king but was adopted by him from a previously existing tradition. It is reasonably conjectured that Atonism is an offspring of Heliopolitan theology and that its dominant position during the Amarna period represents a temporary victory of that venerable priesthood over the more recently established one of Amon at Thebes. It is reasonable too to suppose that Akh-en-Aton was reared under the influence of the Heliopolitan priests; otherwise his heresy is even more difficult to understand.

Because the evidence is so limited, some scholars feel that "monotheism" is not a satisfactory designation for the religion of Akh-en-Aton; they prefer "henotheism," suggesting that although other gods are not specifically mentioned in the Amarna texts, recognition of their existence, but on a lower level than that of Aton, may well have persisted. It is certainly true that most of Egypt, to judge from the monumental remains of prior and later dates, was ignorant of or indifferent toward the heresies of Akh-en-Aton and his family at Amarna. The sources and nature of this new religion have been a subject of great interest to OT scholars and to historians of religion in general, especially because of the often-cited relationship of Atonism to the religion of Moses. There is, however, no real evidence of direct transmission from the Egyptian to the Israelite, and even a cursory examination of the two will show that similarities between them are often superficial, tending to diminish as one probes deeper into the moral, legal, and philosophical aspects of each. The often-quoted parallels between Ps. 104 and the Aton Hymn of Akh-en-Aton provide a striking example of literary influence; but because the style and phraseology of the Aton Hymn survived Atonism itself, one may regard these literary resemblances as a result of adaptation on the part of early Hebrew poets of figures and types still current in Egypt at a much later date.

The Amarna period is equally remarkable for the changes which took place in art forms and in literary composition. The striking naturalism familiar from most of the Amarna portraiture, tending in some instances to caricature, represents a radical departure from the traditional forms of Egyptian art, although, depending on the status of the coregency mentioned above, it may have had some precursors in the reign of Amen-hotep III. Eccentricity of style is greater at the beginning of Akh-en-Aton's reign than toward the end, illustrating, perhaps, the setting in of reaction paralleling the religious reconciliations spoken of above. Realistic representation is coupled with an equally unusual choice of subject; for the first time in Egyptian history the mystery surrounding the pharaoh was abandoned, and we are confronted with innumerable scenes depicting the private life of the king and his family engaged in various civic and domestic activities at the palace and in the environs of Amarna. These representations show, in addition, a shift in emphasis from concentration on the eternal and the afterlife in the traditional art to an interest in the new for the living, current, and temporary. These changes are paralleled in the literature of the period; we find the colloquial speech invading and replacing the classical written form of the language, mainly a holdover from the late Middle Kingdom and widely separated at this time from the common speech of the people.

Closely associated with the new religion was an extraordinary emphasis on the concept of *maat*, "truth." Historians have often attributed to this concept the changes discussed in the preceding paragraph, but recent studies have shown rather conclusively that *maat* in the Amarna literature should be understood as a unifying force of rightness and order in all things and never as actuality or reality as comprehended by the senses. The *maat* of Akh-en-Aton is distinguished from that of previous times mainly in its intimate association with the pharaoh, to whom, according to the texts, it is sustenance, and in the lack of symbolism and personification of the concept in the Amarna milieu.

d. Description of the site. Extensive British and German excavations (*see bibliography*) during the second, third, and fourth decades of the twentieth century have made available much information concerning the plan of the city and its principal buildings, as well as a wealth of data bearing on the daily life and institutions of its inhabitants. The city extended over five miles from N to S but was hardly more than half a mile wide. This rather unusual shape was conditioned by the natural lay of the land: no part of the city could be inconveniently far from a source of water. On the basis of location or presumed purpose the excavators have given names to the separate quarters of the city; these include, from N to S, the following: (*a*) Customs House, (*b*) North City, (*c*)

North Palace, (*d*) North Suburb, (*e*) Central City, (*f*) Eastern Village, (*g*) River Temple, and (*h*) Maru-Aton, or the Precinct of the Southern Pool.

Although excavations have not been completed, it is apparent from what has been discovered that Akhetaton was a beautiful and impressive city. Most of its area, apart from that devoted to official buildings and temples, was occupied by estates, ranging from the sumptuous to the modest, of the nobles and middle-class residents of the city; all the houses show a striking uniformity of plan, with size the principal mark of the owner's importance. Though not haphazard, the city itself does not show careful planning beyond the main N-S streets.

The Central City consisted of the Great Temple and its dependencies, including the Hall of Foreign Tribute and several official residences, the Palace, and the Royal Residence. Associated with the latter were the usual storehouses, a small temple, and priests' quarters. The remainder of Central City consisted of administrative buildings, such as the Records Office, Military and Police Headquarters, and some private homes. Fig. TEL 9.

9. Model of a nobleman's house, Tell el-Amarna

The Precinct of the Southern Pool, which lies in the extreme S and includes a garden, a pool, a small temple, and several other buildings, appears to have been a resort area for the royal family. Eastern City, which is located in a central position back toward the arc of cliffs, was presumably the home of the tomb diggers and grave tenders for the royal city. This is indicated both by the nature of the finds there and by the proximity of the settlement to the famous rock tombs in the nearby cliffs. These tombs, with their rich wall paintings of buildings and activities in Akhetaton and their various inscriptions, have proved an invaluable aid for reconstructing the Amarna scene. The more modest tombs of the middle-class inhabitants were located on a hill slope just E of Eastern City; these are constructed mainly of mud brick, with some little limestone.

The life of this remarkable city, Akhetaton, was extremely short. With the exception of scattered Roman remains, there is no evidence either of prior or of subsequent occupation of the site, which appears to have been abandoned suddenly and completely at the fall of the Amarna court. In fact, the evidence indicates that skilled masons at the command of a later pharaoh carried out an orderly devastation of the city; this pharaoh was presumably Hor-em-heb, whose ascent to the throne marked the end of the Amarna line.

2. The Amarna Letters. *a. Discovery, disposition, and general description.* The Amarna Tablets consist almost entirely of diplomatic correspondence between the Egyptian courts of Amen-hotep III and Amen-hotep IV and the rulers of allied or vassal states in or bordering on the Asian section of the Empire. They were discovered by Egyptian peasants in 1887 in the ruins of el-Amarna near the above-mentioned village of et-Till. The tablets found at that time, together with a few which turned up later, are distributed at present among several European museums: the largest collection, of over two hundred, is in the Berlin Museum; over eighty are in the British Museum; and others are in Cairo and the Ashmolean Museum at Oxford.

Because the majority of the letters were sent to Egypt by princes and local rulers in Syria and Palestine and deal with various political, military, and economic problems, the Amarna Tablets* rank first among archaeological finds bearing on the topology and history of the biblical lands in the latter half of the second millennium B.C. Although written by officials whose native languages included a wide variety of Semitic and non-Semitic dialects, the tablets themselves are written mostly in cuneiform Babylonian, the diplomatic language of the entire Near East at this time. Frequent use of glosses, presumably to facilitate the understanding of difficult or ambiguous Babylonian words, as well as substratum influence of a more subtle nature, makes these texts an invaluable source for our knowledge of contemporary Canaanite. Fig. CLA 35.

The correspondents may be divided into three categories: (*a*) rulers of nations on a comparatively equal footing with Egypt; (*b*) vassal princes in Syria, Phoenicia, and Palestine directly under Egyptian control; and (*c*) various minor Egyptian administrative officials in the same areas. The first group includes (*a*) Kadashman-Enlil I and Burnaburiash II, kings of the Kassite Dynasty in Babylon; (*b*) Ashur-uballit I, king of Assyria; (*c*) Tusratta, king of Mitanni; (*d*) Suppiluliumas, king of the Hittites; and (*e*) an unnamed king of Alasya (Cyprus). *Ca.* forty letters may be assigned to this group with certainty. Most frequently heard from among the vassal princes are Akizzi of Qatna, Abdi-Ashirta of Amurru (land of the Amorites), Rib-Addi of Byblos, Ammunira of Beirut, Zimrida of Sidon, Abimilki of Tyre, Aziru of Amurru, and Abdi-Khepa of Jerusalem, with other letters from Hazor, Akko, Megiddo, Gezer, Ashkelon, and Lachish.

b. Historical significance. At the beginning of the fourteenth century B.C. five principal centers of power must be reckoned with in the Near East. In addition to Egypt itself, these include: (*a*) the Mitanni kingdom, a basically Hurrian population having a ruling class of Indo-Aryans, with its capital at Wassukkanni in the region of the Upper Khabur; (*b*) the Hittite kingdom, with its capital at Hattusa (modern Boğaz-köy) in Anatolia; (*c*) the Assyrian kingdom; and (*d*) the Kassite Dynasty in Babylon. A comparison of these dominant areas of control with the first group of correspondents cited above shows that each is represented to some extent in the Amarna correspondence, thus pointing out the extraordinary importance of these tables for reconstructing the historical scene.

Under the powerful leadership of Thut-mose III

(*ca.* 1482-1450) the borders of the Egyptian Empire had been extended northward to the Euphrates and southward to the Nubian city of Napata, above the Third Cataract of the Nile. During the rule of his successor, Amen-hotep II (*ca.* 1450-1425), Egypt was forced to withdraw from its northernmost Syrian provinces under the constantly expanding Mitanni kingdom. Toward the end of the reign of Amen-hotep III (*ca.* 1412-1375) Egypt's hold on its entire N empire had weakened; and the Amarna correspondence gives us a vivid, if not always too clear, account of the gradual loss of this vast area.

The most extensive correspondence from a single source is that of Rib-Addi,* prince of Byblos, from whom over fifty letters to the Egyptian court are extant—a singularly repetitious series of urgent requests for military aid, which, to judge from their number and common content, did not meet an enthusiastic response at Amarna. The main source of trouble was Abdi-Ashirta of Amurru, who, taking advantage of Egyptian weakness and nonsupport, was attempting to gain control over several adjacent principalities. Constant reference is made to the *Sa.Gaz* people, elsewhere mentioned as the Habiru (properly *'Apiru*), with whom Abdi-Ashirta was closely allied. The Habiru, who are generally associated, at least in respect to their name, with the Hebrews, first came to the attention of the scholarly world through the Amarna Letters; mention of them was subsequently discovered in texts as early as the twentieth century B.C., and they became a subject of intense investigation. Although many features of the Habiru problem remain obscure, it is clear from numerous references that they consisted mainly of unlanded vagrants who entered into a dependent status as agricultural laborers or soldiers in exchange for maintenance. The true urgency of Rib-Addi's requests is apparent from events mentioned in the texts themselves. In no. 74 he states that all his cities in the mountains and on

10. Tell el-Amarna tablet: a letter from Rib-Addi of Gebal to Amen-hotep III

the sea have fallen to the (*Sa.*)*Gaz* people, with the exception of Byblos and two others, and that even then Abdi-Ashirta was attempting to incite the other cities against Byblos. Later Byblos and only one other city remained his, and finally only Byblos. Eventually Rib-Addi was forced to flee to Beirut, whose prince, Ammunira, was related to him by marriage. Fig. TEL 10.

Mitanni control in the N was finally usurped by the Hittites under the command of Suppiluliumas, who *ca.* 1370 B.C. proceeded from his sacking of their capital, Wassukkanni, into Syria, where unexpected hostility from the king of Kadesh on the Orontes brought him directly into contact with the vassal states of the Egyptian Empire. Suppiluliumas completed his conquest of Syria in a second campaign *ca.* 1340 B.C., during which he subjected the powerful fortress of Carchemish.

Little is known of the extent to which Egyptian control survived in Palestine after the reign of Akhen-Aton. Certainly the civil strife indicated in the letters of Abdu-khepa of Jerusalem and of the other princes, if left unopposed, could have resulted only in a completely anarchic situation. It is not until the reigns of Seti I (1318-1299) and Ramses II (1299-1232) that Egypt once more became actively involved with her Asian empire.

Bibliography. W. M. F. Petrie, *Tell el Amarna* (1894). N. de G. Davies, *The Rock Tombs of El Amarna* (*Archaeological Survey of Egypt*) *I-VI* (1903-1908). H. Schafer, *Amarna in Religion und Kunst* (1931). T. E. Peet, C. L. Woolley, H. Frankfort, J. D. S. Pendlebury, *et al.*, *The City of Akhenaten I-III* (1923-51). R. Anthes, "Die Maat des Echnaton von Amarna," *JAOS*, Supplement no. 14 (1952). A. H. Gardiner, "The So-Called Tomb of Queen Tiye," *JEA*, 43 (1957), 11-25.

The standard edition of the Amarna Letters is that of J. A. Knudtzon and O. Weber, *Die El-Amarna-Tafeln* (1915), whose system of numbering the letters is universally followed. Several additional letters were published by F. Thureau-Dangin, "Nouvelles Lettres d'el-Amarna," *Revue d'Assyriologie*, 19 (1922), 91-108. For an English translation, see S. A. B. Mercer, *The Tell el-Amarna Tablets* (1939).

The following studies merit note: J. de Koning, *Studiën over de El-Amarnabrieven en het Oude-Testament inzonderheid uit historisch oog punt* (1940). W. F. Albright, "The Egyptian Correspondence of Abimilki, Prince of Tyre," *JEA*, 23 (1937), 190-203; "Cuneiform Material for Egyptian Prosopography, 1500-1200 B.C.," *JNES*, V (1946), 9-25. W. F. Albright and G. Mendenhall, "Akkadian Letters," in J. B. Pritchard, ed., *ANET* (2nd ed., 1955), pp. 482-90. M. Greenberg, *The Hab/piru* (1955).

T. O. LAMBDIN

TEL-MELAH tĕl mē'lə [מֶלַח תֵּל, the ruined city mound of the salt] (Ezra 2:59; Neh. 7:61); **THERMELETH** thûr mē'lĭth in I Esd. 5:36. A Babylonian place from which men unable to produce genealogies proving their Jewish lineage came to Jerusalem. The site, as yet unidentified, was probably a Jewish settlement on a ruined city which had been sown with salt (cf. Judg. 9:45). It has been suggested that it may have been the Thelma of Ptolemy (V.20), a place in the low salt tract near the Persian Gulf.

R. A. BOWMAN

TEMA tē'mə [תֵּימָא]. A son of Ishmael, and hence the name of an Arabian locality (Gen. 25:15; I Chr. 1:30). It is the same as the modern Teima, an oasis located *ca.* 250 miles SE of Aqaba, on the road to the head of the Persian Gulf, and *ca.* 200 miles N-

NE of Medina, on the road to Damascus. Lying as it does on the junction point of these two great highways, Tema was an important caravansary; the caravans of Tema, mentioned as traveling through long stretches of the desert (Job 6:19), are in reality the caravans that journeyed toward that city. The oracle in Isa. 21:14, which bids the inhabitants of Tema help their fugitive brethren with food and drink, probably refers to the campaign of Tiglath-pileser III of Assyria in 738 B.C.; part of N Arabia was conquered, and Tema escaped destruction by paying tribute. The dire predictions of Jeremiah against the inhabitants of Tema and nearby tribes (Jer. 25:23; cf. 49:28-33) may refer to the campaign of Nebuchadnezzar of Babylon against that region.

Nabonidus, the last king of Babylonia, seems to have set especial store upon Tema. In 552 B.C. he undertook an expedition against it, slaughtered all its inhabitants, and completely rebuilt and repopulated the city; he made it his residence for perhaps ten years, leaving his son Belshazzar as his deputy ruler in Babylon. The Teima Stele in the Louvre (sixth or fifth century B.C.), which deals with legal matters, is remarkable for the cosmopolitan nature of the names cited in its text. The exact reason for the long stay of Nabonidus in Tema is uncertain. His motive may have been a political one—to establish a point of contact with Egypt, Babylonia's sole remaining ally against the rising kingdom of Persia; or it may have been his desire to build up a great religious center in opposition to Babylon, with whose priesthood he was perpetually quarreling. In either case his attempt did not succeed, as *ca.* 540 Cyrus of Persia (according to Xenophon) conquered all that region of Arabia, and Babylon itself succumbed a year later.

See also TEMANITE 2.

Bibliography. R. P. Dougherty, "Nabonidus in Arabia," *JAOS* (1922), pp. 305-16; S. Smith, *Babylonian Historical Texts* (1924), pp. 98-123; J. A. Montgomery, *Arabia and the Bible* (1934), pp. 58-68.

S. COHEN

TEMAH tē'mə [תֶּמַח; Apoc. Θομοΐ]; KJV **TAMAH** tā'mə in Neh. 7:55; **THAMAH** thā'mə in Ezra 2:53; **THOMOI** thŏm'oi in I Esd. 5:32. Eponym of a family of Nethinim, or temple servants, among the exiles returned from Babylon (Ezra 2:53; Neh. 7:55; I Esd. 5:32).

TEMAN tē'mən [תֵּימָן, on the right side, southern]; **TEMANITES** —mə nīts; KJV **TEMANI** —nī in Gen. 36:34. A clan descended from Esau (Gen. 36:11, 15) and the place where it lived, identified with Tawilan, NE of Elji, on a shelf of land above Elji and below Jebel Heidan, which rises above it to the NE. Because only the outline of a circumvallation can be traced, the strength of the Edomite fortification cannot be determined, but the unusually large amount of Edomite Early Iron I-II (*ca.* 1200-600) pottery suggests a site of considerable importance, probably the largest and most important in the central Edomite area (cf. Jer. 49:7). It dominated the fertile, well-watered area, which was thickly settled in the Edomite period and the meeting place of important trade routes. One of the kings who reigned in Edom before there was a king over the Israelites was "Husham of the land of the Temanites" (Gen. 36:34; I Chr. 1:45).

Like "Bozrah," "Teman" is used as a parallel expression for the Edomite nation (Jer. 49:20; Ezek. 25:13; Amos 1:12).

Bibliography. N. Glueck, *Explorations in Eastern Palestine*, II, *AASOR*, 15 (1934-35), 82-83. V. R. Gold

TEMANITE tē′mə nīt [תימני, תמני, *gentilic of* Teman (תימן) *and* Tema (תימא)]. **1.** An inhabitant of the region occupied by the clan of Teman (Gen. 36:34; I Chr. 1:45).

2. The designation of Job's companion Eliphaz (Job 2:11; etc.). The term is usually understood as referring to Teman in Edom, but the context strongly suggests Tema in Arabia (cf. Job. 6:19). V. R. Gold

TEMENI tĕm′ə nī [תימני, on the right hand(?), southern(?)] (I Chr. 4:6). A man or family of Judah; son of Ashhur, a son of Caleb.

TEMPERANCE. *See* Self-control.

*TEMPLE, JERUSALEM.** There were in the biblical period three successive temples in Jerusalem on the same site: Solomon's, Zerubbabel's, and Herod's. The site is identifiable without question; it is that of the presently standing and justly famous Muslim shrine known as Qubbet es-Sakhra, the "Dome of the Rock" (sometimes incorrectly called the Mosque of Omar), completed in A.D. 691 (Figs. TEM 12-15). The religious importance of these temples is shown by their frequent mention in both the OT and the NT.

  A. The temple of Solomon
    1. Biblical data
      a. I Kings
      b. II Chronicles
      c. Ezekiel
      d. Other biblical data
    2. Archaeological data and special problems
      a. Ground plan
      b. The bronze pillars
      c. The bronze sea
      d. Miscellaneous items
      e. Building material
    3. Attempts at reconstruction
  B. The temple of Zerubbabel
    1. Biblical references
    2. References in the Apoc. and the Pseudep.
    3. Josephus references
    4. Rabbinic references
    5. Conclusion
  C. The temple of Herod
    1. NT references
    2. Josephus references
    3. Middoth references
    4. Archaeological data and modern study
    5. Attempts at reconstruction
    6. Summary and conclusion
  Bibliography

A. THE TEMPLE OF SOLOMON. This was the "first temple," according to Jewish nomenclature, and has naturally elicited the most interest and dis-

Trans World Airlines Photo

11. The wailing wall at Jerusalem, with typical Herodian masonry

cussion. Prior to its establishment as a symbol of the official state religion, there were smaller, local temples at various places (*see* Temples). Nevertheless, the recently nomadic Hebrews had had little architectural experience, and as we proceed to examine the biblical record, it is not surprising to learn that help was sought from the nearby Canaanites (Phoenicians; *see* Canaan; Phoenicia), who had a considerable tradition of material culture.

1. Biblical data. Although temple references are to be found in some twenty-three OT and eleven NT books, the chief sources of information about Solomon's structure are the descriptions in I Kings, mainly chs. 5-8, with parallels in II Chr. 2-7, and those in Ezek. 40-43, which are a dream of the future yet incorporate genuine reminiscences of the fallen first temple.

a. I Kings. The early tradition in II Sam. 24:16-25 relates that David purchased a threshing floor from Araunah the Jebusite upon which to build an altar. According to I Chr. 22:1; II Chr. 3:1 (where Araunah is called Ornan), this was the site of Solomon's temple. Some traditions (probably late) claim that David had hoped to build a temple (II Sam. 7:2; I Kings 5:3), even going so far as to collect a considerable amount of building material, artisans, and money for the project (I Chr. 22:2-16; *see* IB and other Commentaries). At any rate, Solomon took decisive action, calling upon Hiram (Huram, Ahiram) I, king of Tyre (*ca.* 968-935 B.C.; *see* Hiram 1), for workmen and materials. (The tradition that David early in his reign was helped by Hiram in building the royal palace [II Sam. 5:11] presents a chrono-

12. Aerial view of the temple area

13. The Dome of the Rock from the NW

logical difficulty; the reference is either to Abibaal, father of Hiram, or to events late in the reign of David; cf. I Kings 5:3.)

In addition to the skilled Phoenician workmen (called here SIDONIANS; I Kings 5:6), Solomon used thirty thousand forced laborers from his own country (vs. 13; vs. 15 appears to be a later exaggeration). A special contingent from Gebal (Byblos) is also mentioned (vs. 18). The work began, so it is said, 480 years after the Exodus (6:1). Unfortunately this item does not agree with information from elsewhere about the Exodus (see CHRONOLOGY OF THE OT); but fortunately, other data are added—namely, "in the fourth year of Solomon's reign . . . in the month of Ziv, which is the second month." Taking 961 as the accession date of Solomon, we have 957 as the date for the beginning of the temple. Josephus (Antiq. VIII.iii.1) puts the event in the eleventh year of Hiram; this agrees well with the biblical date. The month of Ziv (April-May; see CALENDAR), after the winter rains were over, was the proper time of year to begin.

In size the building was 60 cubits long, 20 cubits wide, and 30 cubits high (6:2). These are interior measurements. The cubit (see WEIGHTS AND MEASURES), a practical unit of measure taken from the human body (like the foot), is roughly the length of the forearm from the elbow to the finger tips. It is still much used in Bible lands. In ancient times there were three cubits, the ordinary of 17.6 inches, the royal of 20.9 inches, and a rarely used long cubit of 21.6 inches. It is now generally agreed that the royal cubit is the one intended in descriptions of the temple. Thus the rough equivalent of 1½ feet or ½ yard given in English is not quite sufficient. The metric equivalent of ½ meter is more nearly correct, though still a little short.

At the front of the temple was an 'Ûlām (or 'Êlām), variously translated "porch," "portico," "vestibule," or "entrance hall," 20 cubits wide, on the inside, corresponding to the inside width of the rest of the structure, and 10 cubits deep (6:3). There were windows, the number and size of which are not specified, but apparently belonging to the main part of the

Courtesy of Herbert G. May

14. The temple area with Jerusalem in the background, from the Mount of Olives

temple (vs. 4). Beyond the vestibule was the *Hêkhāl*, or main room (variously called "holy place," "temple proper," "main room," "nave," etc.), 40 cubits long (vss. 3, 17). Beyond the *Hêkhāl* was the *Debhîr*, the "holy of holies," "oracle," "shrine," "most holy place," "inner sanctuary," or "adytum." This room was an exact cube, 20 cubits in each dimension (vss. 5, 16, 19-20). Figs. TEM 16-18.

From Parrot, *Le Temple de Jérusalem* (Neuchâtel: Delachaux & Niestlé)

15. The temple area today from the SE

Around all of the outside of the building except the vestibule (vs. 5) there was a structure variously designated as a "side wing," "galleries," "side chambers," "side rooms," and the like. A few scholars regard this structure as a later addition, or even as a part only of the second temple, that of Zerubbabel (*see* § B *below*). Most, however, defend it as Solomonic. This side structure was arranged in three stories, the first 5 cubits broad, the second 6 cubits broad, the third 7 cubits broad, each story being 5 cubits high. Offsets in the main walls were made to accommodate these increasing widths of the stories, in order, so it was said, that supporting beams need not be inserted into the main walls. There is no reliable information as to how, or as to what extent, each story was divided into rooms (vss. 5-6, 10). Another uncertainty is as to how access to this side structure was gained. The entrance was on the "right shoulder" of the building, which could mean either the N or the S side, depending on where the observer was standing (but the S is more probable, since direction was usually indicated by facing E). Ascent was by *lûlîm*, translated "winding stairs" in the older versions, "trap-doors" in Moffatt, "a circular trap door" in the Amer. Trans., and simply "stairs" in the RSV (vs. 8). Reconstructions naturally

vary widely in this detail. Many assume two entrances, one on each side, variously located.

Another feature generally included in reconstructions of the ground plan of this temple is the pair of huge bronze pillars, mentioned in a description of the bronze objects in and around the building (7:13-22). The one on the right (or S?) was called Jachin, the other Boaz (*see* JACHIN AND BOAZ)*—the significance of these names being much debated (*see bibliography*). Their exact location is not given in the Hebrew of I Kings 7:15, but the Greek adds "for the porch of the temple" (so Amer. Trans.), and II Chr. 3:15 (cf. vs. 17) says they were "in front of the house." Thus they are usually placed just outside the entrance to the vestibule, in spite of the expression "in the vestibule" in I Kings 7:19 (which could be translated "at the vestibule," as in vs. 21). Their over-all height, including capitals of five cubits, was 23 cubits (nearly 40 feet), and their circumference is said to have been 12 cubits (*ca.* 20 feet), a large figure on which some doubt has been cast, but it is supported by Jer. 52:21. They were perhaps hollow, the metal being four fingers (*ca.* 3 inches) thick, or they may have had a wooden core. Fig. JAC 3.

On the basis of these data, plus Ezek. 41:5, giving the thickness of the temple walls proper as 6 cubits, and Ezek. 41:9, stating that the walls of the side chambers were 5 cubits thick, excellent reconstructions of the ground plan of Solomon's temple appeared a half-century ago (Fig. TEM 16). A recently

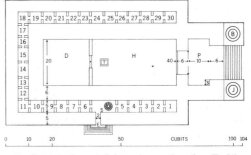

16. Ground plan of Solomon's temple, after T. W. Davies (1902), based on Stade (1887)

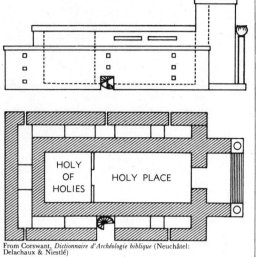

From Corswant, *Dictionnaire d'Archéologie biblique* (Neuchâtel:
Delachaux & Niestlé)

17. Ground plan and reconstruction of Solomon's temple,
after Corswant (1956)

published plan is very similar (Fig. TEM 17). From
Ezek. 41:8 it would appear that the building stood on
a platform 6 cubits high, with ten steps leading up
between the pillars to the entrance of the vestibule
(40:49). The steps were shown in the older plans
(*see* Fig. 4); a popular and widely copied plan adds
the platform, making the steps more logical (Fig. TEM
18). But this plan also extends the side structure to
each side of the vestibule and gives it an entrance on
each side, in contradiction to I Kings 6:5, 8. Recent
attempts at reconstruction reject these features (*see*
§ A3 *below*), probably rightly.

The interior walls were covered with cedar wainscoting; the floor was covered with boards of cypress.
Thus no stonework could be seen anywhere on the
inside of the building (6:14-18). According to the
English translations, much of this woodwork was
"overlaid'" with gold (vss. 19-22, 30): This seems
exaggerated, even in connection with wealthy Solomon; it has been suggested, with good reason, that
the proper word is "inlaid." It is unlikely that such
splendid woodwork would have been completely
covered, even with gold. Ivory INLAY is now well
known from Palestinian excavations at Samaria and
Megiddo; it is likely that gold was used in the same
way. Vss. 20, 22, mention an altar of cedar decorated
with gold (also 7:48; II Chr. 4:19). Perhaps it can

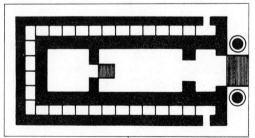

From C. Watzinger, *Denkmäler Palästinas* (Leipzig: J. C. Hinrichs Verlag, 1935),
vol. II

18. Floor plan of Solomon's temple, according to
Watzinger

be inferred from Exod. 40:26 (*see* TABERNACLE) that
this altar was placed in front of the entrance to the
holy of holies; this may be the altar mentioned in
Isa. 6:6.

The holy of holies contained two huge cherubim
(*see* CHERUB) of gold-trimmed olivewood, each 10
cubits high, with an equal wingspread. They faced
the front, so that a wing of each cherub touched the
wall, while the other two wings met in the center of
the room (6:23-28).* Beneath these wings was placed
the ARK OF THE COVENANT (8:6-7). The gold chains
of 6:21 are not in the LXX and are difficult
to visualize (*see* IB). Fig. ANG 26.

All the inside wainscoted walls were filled with
carved figures of gourds, cherubim, palm trees, and
open flowers (6:18, 29). Some have doubted the
authenticity of the report on this intricate art work;
but in general it is in agreement with the archaeological evidence. Fig. ANG 25.

Leading to the holy of holies there was a double
door of olivewood, decorated in the same way as the
walls, with lintel and doorposts in some sort of
pentagonal or fivefold arrangement, the nature of
which is not clear in the present, corrupt state of the
text (6:31-32). The nave or temple proper had much
larger double doors, each door divided into two folding leaves. These doors were also richly decorated
with carving and gold (vss. 33-35). There was no
door to the vestibule. In front of the building was
the "inner court," fenced about "with three courses
of hewn stone and one course of cedar beams" (6:36;
cf. 7:12), a type of construction found notably at
Megiddo.

Seven years were required to finish the temple
(6:38), but Solomon's building was not ended. He
continued for thirteen years more erecting a series
of palaces and other royal buildings adjoining the
temple, which thus became a part of the complex—
a royal chapel, as it is sometimes called (7:1-12).

In addition to the vast amount of stone- and woodwork already described, much artistry in bronze was
required. For the execution of this, Solomon hired
one Hiram of Tyre, bearing the same name as the
king, but also known as Huram-abi (7:13; II Chr.
2:13; 4:16). This man, represented as of great artistic
skill, was half Israelite, as his mother was from
Naphtali or Dan (I Kings 7:14; II Chr. 2:14). His
first task was to cast the great pillars Jachin and
Boaz, already mentioned above. The text emphasizes
the size of the columns, but even more the artistry of
the capitals, decorated with lily-work and hundreds
of pomegranates, though the details are confused (I
Kings 7:15-22). A number of modern artists have exercised their ingenuity trying to reconstruct them.
Since they seem to be represented as hollow bowls in
vss. 41-42, a few scholars have interpreted them as
cressets, great bowls filled with fire, giving off flames
by night and smoke by day. If this feature is correct,
it is strange that it is not mentioned somewhere in
the biblical accounts.

Another unusual, and even sensational, bronze
structure was the "molten sea," a huge tank or basin
10 cubits (*ca.* 17½ feet) in diameter and 5 cubits
deep. It is also said to have been 30 cubits in circumference, a rough estimate using 3.0 instead of the
more accurate 3.14159 as the ratio of circumference

to diameter; the more exact ratio would not have been known to the biblical writer. The bowl was decorated with two rows of gourds all the way around. It was a handbreadth thick, and had a cup-like brim resembling the flower of a lily. The capacity was two thousand baths (*see* WEIGHTS AND MEASURES), or *ca.* ten thousand gallons. This great basin rested upon twelve bronze bulls arranged in groups of three, each group facing a point of the compass; the whole structure was placed in the SE corner of the inner court before the temple (7:23-26, 39, 44). For problems of technique and interpretation, *see* SEA, MOLTEN. Fig. SEA 34.

Other bronze objects made by Hiram the artisan included ten ornate wagons (KJV "bases" and RSV "stands" are not good translations; Moffatt "trolleys" is better), carrying ten lavers (water basins; *see* LAVER), each having a capacity of forty baths, or *ca.* two hundred gallons (7:27-39). Again, questions of size and utility arise. It has been estimated that the "sea" would weigh nearly thirty tons, and one of the wagons with its basin of water *ca.* four tons. Granting that such large objects could have been made by Hiram and his men, how could they have been moved from their place of casting in the Jordan Valley (vss. 46-47), and how could they have been used? How could the "sea" have been filled, and how could the laver wagons have been moved about, weighing as much as a modern motor car, and certainly without ball bearings in the wheels? Five of them were placed on one side of the court and five on the other; perhaps they were seldom moved (vs. 39). Fig. LAV 15.

Smaller bronze objects, pots, shovels, and sprinkling bowls (RSV "basins"), are also mentioned (7:40, 45). A concluding statement, probably from a later editor, mentions certain inside furnishings, with heavy emphasis on the word "gold": the altar before the steps to the holy of holies (*see above*); the nearby table for the BREAD OF THE PRESENCE; ten lamp-stands, five on each side of the entrance to the holy of holies; artificial flowers, lamps, tongs, cups, snuffers, sprinkling bowls, incense dishes, firepans, all said to be of gold, some of pure gold; finally we are told that the very door sockets (some translate "hinges") were of gold (vss. 48-50). Door sockets in those days were normally of hard stone; a number of such sockets have been found in archaeological excavations. *See* HINGES; SOCKET. Fig. SOC 72.

b. II Chronicles. We learn here, and here only, that the temple mount was called Moriah (3:1).* But the chief "overlooked" item supplied by the Chronicler (*see* CHRONICLES, I AND II) is the large "bronze" altar, 20 cubits square and 10 cubits high, mentioned along with the two columns and the "sea" (4:1). The presence of an altar in the inner court is taken for granted in I Kings 8:22, 64; 9:25; II Kings 16:14-15. It probably was intended to supersede the altar built by David at this spot (II Sam. 24:25). The lack of any mention of its construction at the proper place in I Kings 7 (probably between vss. 22 and 23) has been the subject of fruitless speculation by various scholars. Fig. MOR 69.

Some of the Chronicler's contribution consists of exaggeration of the figures in I Kings. E.g., the height of the vestibule is said (II Chr. 3:4) to have

been 120 cubits (some 200 feet), an incredible figure that has caused certain credulous artists to draw the temple with a huge tower (or even two pylons) at the front. Actually, there is no reason to suppose that the front was higher than the rest of the building, which rose 30 cubits, inside measurement (I Kings 6:2).

Another exaggeration concerns the height of the pillars Jachin and Boaz.* According to Kings the columns were 18 cubits, the capitals 5 more, making a total of 23 cubits. The Chronicler (3:15) makes the total 35 plus 5 cubits, *ca.* 75 feet, a good match for the 200-foot tower! The circumference is not given, but this is already so great in Kings (12 cubits, *ca.* 20 feet) that some conservative scholars have suggested reducing it to 5, or even 2, cubits. Fig. JAC 3.

As to the "sea," the Hebrew says (II Chr. 4:3) its bowl was decorated with figures of bulls ("oxen") instead of gourds as in Kings, but the RSV changes the reading to "gourds" to conform to Kings. The capacity of the bowl is given as three thousand baths (fifteen thousand gallons) instead of two thousand (vs. 5). A note is added to the effect that the wagon-borne lavers were for washing the burnt offerings, while the "sea" was for the ablutions of the priests (vs. 6). This function of the "sea" has been doubted by many commentators, who prefer to see in this great tank what one has called a cosmic significance, a symbolizing not only of the cleansing power of water but also of the primeval ocean from which all life and fertility were thought to have been derived. This conception has parallels in Mesopotamian as well as in Canaanite culture. It would also explain the use of the name "sea." Certainly it is difficult to imagine the priests climbing to bathe in this tank, the rim of which probably stood some 15 feet above the pavement of the court.

The Chronicler is even more lavish with gold than is the author of Kings. The 120-foot vestibule was "overlaid [inlaid?] . . . on the inside with pure gold" (3:4). Everything was richly trimmed with gold, especially the holy of holies, wherein were used six hundred talents of fine gold, equivalent in value to *ca.* $20,000,000. Even the nails were of gold, some weighing as much as fifty shekels, perhaps equal in value to *ca.* $500 (vss. 8-9). For good measure, precious stones were plentifully sprinkled round about (vs. 6).

The veil mentioned in 3:14 was probably not a feature of Solomon's temple, but belonged to one of its successors (*see* §§ B-C *below*). The bronze platform of 6:13, upon which Solomon stood at the dedication of the temple, is also lacking in Kings. Its authenticity is uncertain, though there are archaeological parallels in which a king or votary stands upon a sort of box at a sacred ceremony.

c. Ezekiel. As noted above, the temple in the book of EZEKIEL is a vision of the future, projected by the prophet or by one of the editors of the book. Yet its basic plan seems to have been taken from the recently destroyed structure of Solomon, and some commentators have gone so far as to suppose that the author of the vision personally made measurements of the ruins of the old temple (cf. 40:4-41:15, in which the angelic guide does much measuring).

It is clear that Ezekiel's temple faced the E (8:16; 11:1; 43:1-4; 44:1-3), and there seems little reason to doubt that the Solomonic structure had a similar orientation, facing the sunrise. Solar elements in the religions round about caused many temples to be so oriented, and it has been plausibly claimed that such elements persisted in the religion of Israel, though they could be carried so far as to be productive of great evil (8:16-18). It should be borne in mind that Solomon's Phoenician architects would have followed current practices.

The altar in the inner court, "overlooked" in Kings but mentioned in II Chr. 4:1, is also mentioned here (Ezek. 40:47) and even described in some detail (43:13-17), though the material is not specified, and stone, not bronze, may be implied. There is no exact agreement with Chronicles as to over-all dimensions, and of course no certainty that a Solomonic altar is described. The size of the vestibule is 20 by 11 (Hebrew) or 20 by 12 (Greek) cubits, instead of 20 by 10, as in Kings. Steps leading to the vestibule are mentioned. The two pillars are just barely in evidence, but not by name (40:49).

The size of the nave agrees exactly with Kings, likewise the size of the adytum, though nothing is said about the height of either. The side chambers are more complicated, being divided into ninety rooms, thirty in each story; they also have two entrances instead of one; their manner of attachment to the walls of the temple is similar. The raised platform under the whole structure may be another "overlooked" Solomonic feature (*see above*). The outside length of the temple is given as 100 cubits, a round figure that would agree fairly well with an estimate based on the inside dimensions from Kings. An over-all roof is mentioned—an item lacking in Kings but surely to be taken for granted. It would have been flat, then as now (cf., e.g., Josh. 2:6; Judg. 16:27; II Sam. 11:2; *see* ARCHITECTURE). The inside arrangement, decoration, and furnishings are similar to those listed in Kings (Ezek. 41). The various courts and adjacent structures are different from those of Solomon (ch. 42). Conspicuous by its absence is the great "sea"; its place seems to be taken by the stream of living water flowing eastward from the threshold of the temple toward the Dead Sea, fructifying the barren land as it goes (47:1-12).

d. Other biblical data. The temple did not stand alone, but was part of a complex of royal buildings that took altogether twenty years to build (I Kings 7:1-12; 9:1, 10-11). For this reason some refer to the temple as a royal chapel. The king did have a private entrance from his palace, and especially in the early days of the monarchy he had sacerdotal functions; but the temple also had public and national significance, increasingly so as time went on.

According to I Kings 10:11-12 (=II Chr. 9:10-11) Solomon used rare "ALMUG wood" or "algum wood" (sandalwood?) brought by Hiram's fleet from the S to enhance further the richness of the temple. Treasure was kept in the temple, as we see from the account of Shishak's plundering (I Kings 14:25-26). There has been much discussion as to whether this treasure was kept in the main structure or in the side chambers. King Asa of Judah himself drew upon the temple treasury for a political purpose (I Kings 15:

15-19). The young King Joash was hidden somewhere in the temple during the usurpation of Athaliah, under the protection of the priest Jehoiada, who seems to have had control of the army (*see* JEHOIADA; PRIESTS AND LEVITES IN THE OT). When Joash was crowned, he stood by one of the pillars "according to the custom" in the presence of the people gathered in the inner court. Care was taken that Athaliah not be slain in the sacred precincts (cf. I Kings 2:28-33). The rival temple of Baal was destroyed (II Kings 11:1-20).

After the building had stood for a century, repairs were needed, and provision was made for this purpose by Joash. But Joash also was forced to draw on the temple treasury to pay an indemnity against invasion by Hazael, king of Syria (II Kings 12:4-18). Soon afterward Joash of Israel attacked Jerusalem and plundered the temple (14:11-14). King Jotham of Judah added an "upper gate," probably on the N side of the inner court (II Kings 15:35; cf. Jer. 20:2). Ahaz (*ca.* 735 B.C., some two centuries after the founding of the temple) took treasure from the sanctuary to pay Assyria for protection against Israel and Syria. He also had a new-style altar, which he saw in Damascus, copied for use in the temple court in Jerusalem; the original altar was pushed aside for minor uses. Finally, probably in order to eke out his tribute to Assyria, he broke up the bronze laver wagons and removed the bulls supporting the "sea," replacing them with a stone base or pedestal (not "pediment," as in the RSV!) and making certain other minor structural changes (II Kings 16:7-18). His son Hezekiah took further treasure from the temple and even stripped off gold trimmings to raise a sum to pay Sennacherib of Assyria as indemnity against attack (18:15-16).

The apostate King Manasseh installed various heathen altars, images, and utensils within the sacred precincts; Josiah in turn removed these and restored the proper worship of Yahweh, after repairing and refurbishing the misused structure (II Kings 21:3-7; 22:3-9; 23:1-4, 6-7, 11-12; note how the king stood by one of the pillars in the solemn act of rededication in 23:3; cf. 11:14). Nebuchadrezzar, following his first attack (598/597 B.C.), took vessels of gold and other treasure from the temple, but apparently did not damage the structure (II Kings 24:13; II Chr. 36:10). It was quite otherwise with the second attack. The temple was completely plundered and then burned, along with most of the rest of the city (587/586). Particular mention is made of the breaking up of the bronze pillars, of such of the laver wagons as were left (cf. II Kings 16:17), and of the "sea," and the transportation of the metal to Babylonia (II Kings 25:8-17; Jer. 52:12-23; an editor has added the bronze bulls in Jer. 52:20, overlooking II Kings 16:17; "three cubits" in II Kings 25:17 should, of course, be "five cubits"; cf. I Kings 7:16; Jer. 52: 22). Yet, in spite of the destruction, certain sacrifices continued to be offered (Jer. 41:5).

The description of the TABERNACLE in Exod. 25-31; 35-40 is to a certain extent based on reminiscences of Solomon's temple (e.g., the nave and the adytum are each exactly half the size of Solomon's, though there is no vestibule), but no additional information is afforded.

The description of Josephus (Antiq. VIII.ii-iv) may be included under biblical data, since he does not seem to have had additional sources. He inclines to exaggeration and was probably influenced by the Herodian temple, which he knew very well. *See* § C *below.*

2. Archaeological data and special problems. The older literature sought parallels and origins from Egypt and Mesopotamia. From these areas there were, no doubt, indirect influences. However, the biblical account makes it clear that Solomon's temple was built by Phoenician architects and artisans, with mainly unskilled help from Israel. Therefore, in the final analysis Phoenician (more properly Canaanite) and, in a larger sense, Syrian models must be sought (*see* CANAAN; PHOENICIA). It is at this point that recent archaeological research has made some further progress.

a. Ground plan. Essentially this plan consists of a vestibule, a main room, and an inner or back room arranged longitudinally. This simple and appealing arrangement, in which each unit becomes more esoteric as one penetrates the interior, has examples in sacred architecture all the way from ancient Egypt, through Greece and Rome, to modern churches of the very common basilica type, with, of course, many modifications and elaborations of detail. Since Egyptian antiquities have been known so long, it was not difficult for scholars of the later nineteenth century to argue for Egypt as the cultural source of Solomon's sanctuary, and to show good ground plans of, e.g., the temple of Amon-Re at Karnak, built by Ramses III, as proof, though the correspondence turns out to be inexact upon close examination.

With the rise of Assyriology, or, more properly, Anatolian and Mesopotamian studies, much effort was expended during the earlier part of the twentieth century in an attempt to show Mesopotamian or Anatolian parallels and prototypes with respect to the temple of Yahweh in Jerusalem. Two names of important parts of the building lend plausibility to this attempt: the word for "vestibule" in the Hebrew text, 'êlām or 'ûlām, seems to be borrowed from Akkadian *ellamu*, "front"; and *hêkhāl*, "main room," "nave," sometimes used for the whole structure, is clearly borrowed from Akkadian *êkallu*, "palace," which in turn is derived from Sumerian *e-gal*, "large house." The derivation of *debhîr*, "inner sanctum," "adytum," is not clear: it may be related to the common Hebrew verb *dābhar*, "to speak," and thus signify "oracle," "the place where God speaks"; or it may be connected with a Semitic root, found in Arabic, meaning "to be behind," thus signifying merely "rear room"; or it may be a loan word of unknown origin; even Coptic *tabir*, "interior," has been brought into the discussion.

Much of this research has to do with the "long room" or "long house," an oblong rectangle, originally open at one end (the *liwān* type), later with a door in one of the short sides. When such a structure was divided laterally into three parts with the largest part in the middle, a plan similar to that of Solomon's temple was achieved.

Other arrangements are the "broad room" or "broad house," with the entrance in the middle of a long side, and the "around-the-corner" type, with

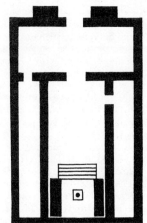

From K. Möhlenbrink, *Der Tempel Salomos* (Stuttgart: W. Kohlhammer Verlag)

19. Ground plan of Assyrian long room temple, after Andrae·

the entrance near one end of a long side—so called because the one entering must make a turn in order to get a full view of the room.

The long type was hardly known in Lower Mesopotamia, but it appears rather frequently in early Assyria and among the Hittites. Hence it is sometimes spoken of as being "northern" in origin (in reference to S Mesopotamia). Some have even suggested S Russia as the place of ultimate origin. Thus this "northern" long room would be the ancestor of the Greek megaron, as well as of similar types in Anatolia, Mesopotamia (especially Assyria), Syria, Palestine, and even Egypt. Fig. TEM 19.

A practical objection to all this is that simple types of construction like these might arise independently in different localities, though cultural connections and borrowings must not be ruled out altogether. Moreover, oft-mentioned Assyrian parallels, such as the temples of Anu-Adad and Nebo at Asshur, turn out to correspond rather inexactly with the Solomonic plan, as was the case with the Egyptian parallels mentioned above. Nevertheless, certain terms gained from this study are useful: the Solomonic temple as a whole is a "long house," the vestibule is a "broad room," the nave is a "long room," the adytum is the unusual "square room" type.

A "northern" origin may also be indicated by the wainscoting of wood. Neither Mesopotamia nor Egypt had sufficient wood for such lavish use, but this style is well attested for N Syria (Zenjirli), central Anatolia (Boghazköy), and W Anatolia (Troy). The Phoenicians could easily adopt this style because of their possession of the cedar wood of Lebanon.

Canaanite temples antedating the time of Solomon have been excavated in Palestine at Lachish, Bethshan, Megiddo, Shechem, and most recently at Hazor. They range in date from *ca.* 1500 to 1100 B.C. Only the one at Hazor, destroyed in the latter part of the thirteenth century, seems to resemble closely Solomon's structure in its ground plan, though it is only about half as large. What is needed is a Phoenician temple of the tenth century, but none has been found. We have instead, as our best parallel, almost a missing link, the small temple or chapel found in 1936 at Tell Tainat (or Tayinat),* ancient

Hattina, in N Syria between Aleppo and Antioch, dated in the ninth (or eighth) century, shortly after the time of Solomon. The size is about two thirds that of Solomon's temple, and the plan is remarkably similar, though with differences in detail: e.g., the columns are definitely within the portico, and the raised platform in the adytum does not extend over the whole area of the room (Fig. TEM 20). As with Solomon's temple, so was the Tainat chapel a part of a temple-palace complex. Fig. JAC 4.

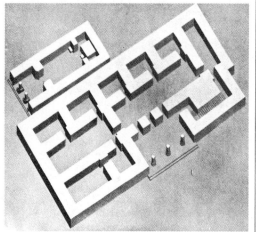

Courtesy of the Oriental Institute, the University of Chicago

20. Plan of the palace at Tell Tainat, with the small temple at the upper left

b. The bronze pillars. Some controversy exists as to whether these stood free, and hence were symbolical, or served functionally to support the roof or an architrave. It was pointed out above that I Kings 7: 19 may read "in the vestibule" and that the columns of the Tainat chapel are so placed. Nevertheless, an almost overwhelming body of opinion favors the free-standing hypothesis. Not only does the biblical text on the whole favor this, but the number of parallels is impressive, beginning with the New Kingdom in Egypt, where it was customary for the pharaohs on a festival anniversary to erect two obelisks as sun symbols before the temples of Amon-Re. The phenomenon is also attested for Assyria, Phoenicia, and Cyprus. The most striking extrabiblical literary parallel is that of Herodotus (II.44) in his description of his visit to the temple of Heracles in Tyre: "In it there were two pillars, one of refined gold, one of emerald, a great pillar that shone in the night-time." In each case such pillars would probably symbolize some divine or cosmic power relied upon to support the current dynasty or religious establishment (like the Assyrian holy tree or "tree of life"). One can also think of the cosmic significance traditionally attached to the so-called Pillars of Hercules.

The N Syrian *hilani* house, so often mentioned in discussions of the entrance to Solomon's temple, is not entirely relevant if Solomon's pillars were free-standing. The *hilani* pillars were functional, supporting a lintel.

c. The bronze sea. This, too, probably had symbolic significance with cosmic overtones. One thinks immediately of the "sacred lake" by Egyptian temples,

sometimes said to be designed merely for ablutions, sometimes said to be filled with *Nûn*, water from the subterranean Nile or ocean, with great cleansing and fructifying power. Also discussed in this connection is the Mesopotamian *apsû*, a word meaning both the subterranean ocean, the source of life and fertility, and the basin of holy water in a temple (*see* § A1*b above*). Another possibility is that the word *yam*, "sea," was applied by the Canaanite Phoenicians, to whom the Mediterranean was the chief source of livelihood. It must also be remembered that the great bowl was supported by bulls, the most popular animal representative of fertility in the ancient Near East, usually associated with the god Baal (or Hadad), by no means unknown to the Israelites. *See* Baal; Calf, Golden; Sea, Molten.

d. Miscellaneous items. The elaborate carving on the wood wainscoting, with figures of "cherubim, palm trees, and open flowers," finds its best counterpart in the richly carved ivories of pre-Solomonic and post-Solomonic dates discovered at such places as Nimrud, Khorsabad, Ras Shamra, Arslan-Tash, Samaria, and most recently Megiddo, all thought to reflect Phoenician or Syrian influence. Particularly striking are some of the cherubim from these collections. From the same cultural area come the pomegranates, gourds, netting, and lily-work of the pillars and the "sea"; likewise the "latticed windows" or "windows with recessed frames,"* though it must be recognized that the ultimate origin of the clerestory principle, still so important in modern churches, is to be sought in Egypt. Perhaps it can be said that the basic plan of the temple came from the far N, but that it took on Hittite, Assyrian, Syrian, Egyptian, and Phoenician elements as it traveled about in the movements and mixtures of peoples of the second millennium B.C. It would have been called "Tyrian" or "Sidonian" or "Canaanite" in its time, or, as we would say, "Phoenician"; but Phoenician culture at that time was a mixed culture, made up of the elements indicated above. Figs. TEM 21; WIN 22-23.

Many observers have been impressed with the great rock that is so prominently featured within the Dome of the Rock today, giving the structure its very

Courtesy of the Oriental Institute, the University of Chicago

21. Window with recessed frames, on ivory inlay from Khorsabad, showing Astarte at the window

name. Hence it has become the fashion to say that this was a "sacred rock" from time immemorial, even before Solomon, David, or Araunah, and that the rock was responsible for the choosing of this site for a sanctuary. But the biblical record says nothing about the rock; it may not have been regarded as important or significant; it may or may not have been a part of the threshing floor. Therefore, attempts by scholars to determine the relationship of Solomon's temple (or its successors) to the rock are beside the point. The two favorite hypotheses are that the rock lay under the holy of holies or under the great "overlooked" sacrificial altar in the forecourt. The rock is too large to have been restricted to these features. If it lay under the temple at all, and if we consider its size (58 by 44 feet) and its central location, the most plausible hypothesis would seem to be that it lay under the *hekhal,* or main room, or, we may as well say, under the temple as a whole.

e. Building material. While the wood for the temple had to be brought from the Lebanon, the bronze from Solomon's copper mines and smeltery in the ARABAH, the gold and ivory from far away in the S (I Kings 10:22; II Chr. 9:21), the basic building material, the stone, was immediately at hand, in the hills round about Jerusalem (I Kings 5:15), even in the city itself. The great stones were cut and finished in the quarries (I Kings 5:17; 6:7). The famous white limestone, called in Arabic *meleki,* the "royal" stone (or, according to some, *meleqeh,* the "smooth stone"), is familiar to every visitor to Jerusalem, and is still quarried from the great cavern under the Old City now known, perhaps with some justification, as Solomon's Quarries (called by Josephus the "Royal Caverns"). It has been reported that the beautiful white limestone facing on the Iraqi Parliament building was quarried near Hebron, S of Jerusalem, and transported to Baghdad along the desert road. This stone is reduced to lime in a hot fire; note the burning by the Chaldeans (II Kings 25:9).

3. Attempts at reconstruction. These attempts go back at least as far as that of Lamy (Paris, 1720) and Altschul (Amsterdam, 1724). During the nineteenth century a considerable number of major works bearing on Solomon's temple were published, along with numerous periodical articles; many of these works included sketches and plans, some of them fantastically imaginative. A notably accurate student of the subject was Bernhard Stade, whose *History of Israel,* containing a discussion of the temple, began to appear in 1881. Stade's plans and sketches have been copied more than any other in serious scholarly works, at least until very recently (*see bibliography*). On the other hand, the models and reconstructions of Conrad Schick (first published in 1896 after their author, a devout and distinguished architect, had lived in Jerusalem for fifty years) have had a great popular vogue, but are now known to be very inaccurate, especially in their portrayal of Solomon's temple. Indeed, Shick actually confused features of Solomon's temple with those of Herod's.* The famous works of Perrot and Chipiez (1887-89) were better based historically, yet they strike us today as more artistic than accurate. Fig. TEM 22.

As was pointed out above, the ground plan has occasioned little difficulty or difference of opinion,

22. Solomon's temple, front view, after Schick (1896)

and the older sketches, such as that of Stade (Fig. TEM 16), are as good as the most recent. The really serious problems arise when attempts are made to reconstruct the superstructure. As noted above in regard to the ground plan, Assyriological activity in the early part of the twentieth century brought an overemphasis on Assyrian parallels. This was the case with the nevertheless great contributions of Walter Andrae, beginning *ca.* 1908. Möhlenbrink (1932) and Galling (1928, 1931, 1937), two very important contributors, are still under this influence. Probably Carl Watzinger (1933, 1939) shows the best understanding of the need for fitting Solomon's temple into its immediate Phoenician and Syrian background, without neglecting the search for more remote origins, not so much in Assyria, but still farther N. His simple and convincing diagrams are now beginning to be highly praised and widely copied. However, as noted above, he seems to be wrong in bringing the side chambers all the way to the front of the building; nor is it likely that he can be right in assuming that the superstructure was made of mud brick, only the foundations and socles being of stone. His front towers, his stairways, and his side entrances can also be criticized without detracting from the solid value of his research and presentation.

In the American milieu, a new period of study on Solomon's temple began in 1941, when G. E. Wright reprinted a photograph of the Schick model as an example of inaccuracy, along with the diagrams of Watzinger,* as being approximately correct in "bare outline." The Tell Tainat chapel was offered as having the best parallel ground plan, while too much searching among the temples of Egypt and Assyria was declared unfruitful. A number of objects from Palestine, Phoenicia, and Syria were presented as being the kind of thing most likely to throw light on the decoration and equipment of Solomon's temple. In other words, the parallels should come from as

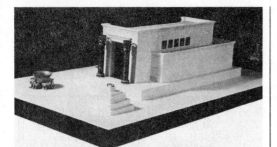

Courtesy of E. G. Howland

23. Howland-Garber model of Solomon's temple: a view from the right front

Courtesy of E. G. Howland

24. Carved wainscoting on the interior walls of the Holy Place, showing pilasters with palm trees flanked by cherubim; from model by E. G. Howland

close as possible in time and place; there has been too much ranging far afield. A year later W. F. Albright commended Wright, though he himself was willing to range farther abroad in attempting to explain the significance of such objects as the altar, the "sea," and the pillars. Both writers intimated that a new era for understanding the first temple had arrived. Fig. TEM 18.

Soon thereafter a college teacher, P. L. Garber, and a professional model maker, E. G. Howland, combined forces to meet the challenge suggested by the hopeful words of Albright and Wright. At considerable cost in time and money, these men produced the Howland-Garber model of Solomon's temple, first exhibited in 1950. This model, apart from the question of its accuracy, is something of a masterpiece,

Courtesy of E. G. Howland

25. Howland-Garber model of Solomon's temple: interior of the temple

the most serious effort of its kind since the days of Conrad Schick (another model was shown at the New York World's Fair in 1939, also one by Gottstein in the New York Jewish Museum in 1950, but published information about these is not readily available). Not only is published information on the Howland-Garber model available, but also filmstrips and photographs. It will probably become widely known, and its high cost will no doubt discourage rival efforts. Figs. TEM 23-26.

Certain features of this model may be pointed out to illustrate the problems of all makers of models and reconstructions. As was mentioned above, the construction of an altar of burnt offering in front of the temple is not mentioned in Kings, though its existence is taken for granted. The only descriptions are in II Chronicles and Ezekiel, and they are not in agreement. The Solomonic altar seems to have been made at least in part of bronze (I Kings 8:64; II Kings 16:14; II Chr. 4:1); there is no indication of its design. Ezek. 43:13-17 describes a three-stage structure, each stage smaller than the one below, like a Babylonian ziggurat or tower-temple; no material is specified, though one would naturally expect it to be stone. Howland and Garber have followed Ezekiel in rough outline in producing their controversial altar. Fig. TEM 27.

Courtesy of E. G. Howland

26. Howland-Garber model of Solomon's temple: front view of the temple, with "molten sea" at left, and altar of burnt offering at right

Courtesy of E. G. Howland

27. The altar of burnt offering (cf. Ezek. 43); from model by E. G. Howland

There is little controversy about the general design and size of the "sea"; hence most reconstructions are much the same. The problems are with respect to significance, use, and practicability.

The temple structure itself in this model stands upon a podium or platform 6 cubits high, necessitating a flight of ten steps to reach the vestibule. This feature is from Ezekiel (40:49; 41:8) and hence controversial; some would place the building flat on the court pavement, thus obviating the steps.

The pillars in this model are free-standing, according to a presently strong majority of opinion. The design of the capitals follows that of an incense burner from Megiddo as an aid to clarifying the rather puzzling description of I Kings 7, which has given rise to so many conflicting restorations on paper. But this procedure also to some extent involves acceptance of the debatable cresset theory mentioned above. Fig. TEM 28.

28. Detail of the pillars of capital of the Jachin and Boaz pillars of the Solomonic temple, by E. G. Howland

The side chambers stop short of the portico on each side, in accord with the biblical text, but contrary to Watzinger. There is no attempt to divide them into small rooms, as in Ezekiel, followed by many reconstructions on paper. They are not given windows, since none is mentioned in the biblical text except in connection with the main walls of the temple. The entrance to these side chambers (and there is only one in the biblical text, though many reconstructors have assumed two) is placed inside the temple, in the nave, on the theory that the side cham-

bers were for the storage of treasure, which could be more easily guarded if the front door of the temple were the only outside entrance. This seems to be the detail of the Howland-Garber model that has occasioned the most criticism.

On the question of a tower, or towers, or pylons above the portico, the solution is simple: no difference in height anywhere is mentioned in Kings; hence no tower or towers are to be assumed, in spite of the almost universal tendency of other reconstructors to add them, a tendency from which even Watzinger was not exempt.

With respect to the adytum, a perfect cube 20 cubits long in each direction on the inside, the chief problem is to explain the differences of 10 cubits in inside height between the adytum and the temple as a whole, which was 30 cubits high. One solution is to assume that the adytum was on the same level as the nave (nothing to the contrary appears in the biblical data), and then to make the roof or ceiling over the adytum 10 cubits lower than the roof over the rest of the temple. But the biblical text says nothing about a difference in height anywhere. Watzinger, following K. Galling, on the basis of archaeological analogies ranging all the way from early Assyrian sanctuaries to Roman temples in Syria, raises the floor of the adytum *ca.* 5 cubits and supplies the flight of steps for entrance thus made necessary. The remaining 5 cubits are incorporated in an unused space between the ceiling of the adytum and the temple roof (Fig. TEM 29). Garber and Howland have followed this well-documented suggestion.

At this point one thinks of the obscure and controversial verse, I Kings 6:31 (see RSV mg.). Something about the entrance to the holy of holies was "pentagonal" or "fivefold" (cf. "square" or "fourfold" in vs. 33). The most common explanation is that the door or at least its frame was gabled, thus producing five sides, in contrast to the square shape of the main door (vs. 33). Another suggestion is that the stairway was recessed, so that the top five steps were inside the back room, cutting into the raised floor, to give a better view of the interior of the adytum on occasion. A third suggestion is that the

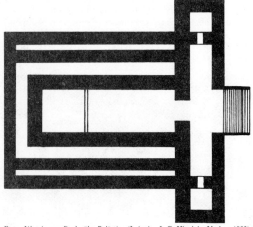

From Watzinger, *Denkmäler Palästina* (Leipzig: J. C. Hinrichs Verlag, 1935), vol. II

29. Floor plan of Herod's temple, according to Watzinger

doorposts themselves were pentagonal in cross-section, thus allowing the doors to swing open at a wider angle than ninety degrees, to allow a better view of the interior. The model follows the third of these hypotheses in this very uncertain matter.

The many intricate details of decorations and furnishings cannot be discussed here. One feature of the interior decoration of the model must be noticed, however. This is the use of the so-called proto-Ionic (or proto-Aeolic) volutes in the capitals of the wooden pilasters in the nave. This particular feature is, of course, not specified in the biblical text, but it represents the use of an authentic architectural theme of the time (as found, e.g., at Megiddo and Ramat Gan), which could hardly have been completely lacking in Solomon's very artistic structure. One should also notice the splendidly and authentically realistic cherubim in the adytum. *See* CHERUB.

Finally, a word must be said about the straight-edged cornice on the parapet. Every house was required to have a parapet, according to Deut. 22:8, and it is likely that this temple had one. But a parapet is not necessarily a battlement (though the KJV erroneously so translates in Deut. 22:8). Many of the older reconstructions, following Stade, supplied Solomon's parapet with "crow-step" crenelations. Watzinger would have none of these, and used simple, straight lines. Howland and Garber followed this idea; but, forced to be a little more specific because of the elaborateness of the model, they chose the "Egyptian streamlined cornice" as employed on the Karnak temple, but also attested in Palestine (Megiddo pottery shrines, of Solomonic date) and Phoenicia (Amrit). This item must be recalled in the following discussion.

Albright and Wright praised the Howland-Garber model but were not satisfied with some of its details, nor with the copyright restriction that forbade reproduction if any change were made, even the slightest. It was decided to "start afresh." An artist named Stevens was employed, who, after suitable briefing, produced a drawn reconstruction of Solomon's temple, plus a separate drawing of the altar of burnt offering according to the description in Ezek. 43:13-17. These were first published by Wright in 1955 (Figs. TEM 30; ALT 19). The drawing of the temple has already been copied in several books; it may be referred to as the Stevens-Wright reconstruction. Since it is an offshoot from, or reaction to, the Howland-Garber model, a few words of comparison and contrast must be undertaken.

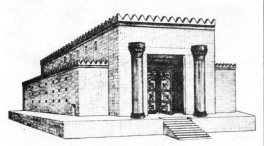

30. Stevens-Wright reconstruction of Solomon's temple (1955)

The Stevens-Wright altar follows Ezekiel as strictly as possible, showing three stages with a large platform at the top reached by a long, steep flight of steps. The Howland-Garber altar, following Ezekiel only impressionistically, tapers more steeply, with no steps but with a ramplike arrangement similar to that of some ziggurats. Both appear to be of stone, whereas the Solomonic altar was said to be bronze, in the biblical account (*see* § A1*b above*). Both altars have the usual horns (*see* ALTAR). The fact is that good information on this altar is lacking at the present time, so that neither of these attempts can lay strong claim to authenticity.

Stevens and Wright do not offer a "sea"; several other reconstructions of this object have proved satisfactory. Stevens and Wright show nothing of the interior arrangement, decorations, or furniture; they have only a front elevation of the altar and temple exterior drawn on paper. Their pillars are free-standing, the capitals being rendered impressionistically, whereas Howland and Garber used the Megiddo incense burner, an actual archaeological object, though perhaps not the capital of a column. Probably neither is very close to the original, and both accept the Robertson Smith–Albright cresset hypothesis.

The chief differences are in the side chambers and the parapet. Stevens and Wright reject the inside entrance to the side structure proposed by Waterman and adopted by Howland and Garber. They show an outside entrance near the front of the side structure on the right (S) side. There is no way of telling from the drawing whether there is proposed another, similar entrance on the other side, as Watzinger and others would have it; however, Stevens and Wright agree with Howland and Garber against Watzinger in stopping the side structures short of the vestibule or portico on both sides (I Kings 6:5). They also agree against Watzinger in having no towers at the front of the building. But Stevens and Wright put windows (many of them) into the side chambers, against Watzinger and Howland and Garber. None are mentioned in the biblical text.

The most striking disagreement to the eye is at the parapet. Here Watzinger and Howland and Garber have the straight-edge construction, while Stevens and Wright show a crow-step crenelated battlement very similar to that of Stade from 1881. A considerable controversy has arisen over this point. A battlement, by its very name and nature, belongs to a military fortification. The second temple was fortified in Hellenistic and Hasmonean times. Herod's temple was used as a fortress after Titus had taken the rest of the city. Does this prove anything with regard to Solomon's temple, designed by Phoenician architects? Some Assyrian temples had battlements, not surprisingly, as the Assyrians were such a warlike people. Does this prove anything with regard to Solomon's plan? No doubt, Phoenician architects knew about battlements; but did they put them on temples in general or on Solomon's temple in particular? Architects enjoy adding battlements to their reconstructions as a sort of eye-filling top dressing. On some expeditions this is routinely done, especially in those areas where very little is known about superstructures. But a good thing can be overdone.

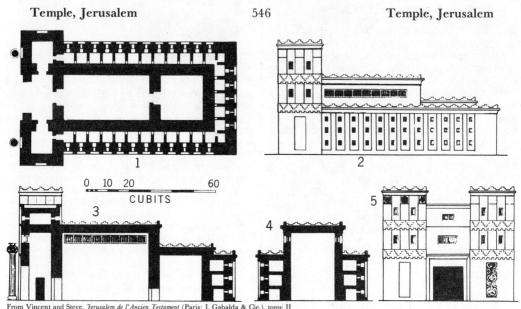

From Vincent and Steve, *Jerusalem de l'Ancien Testament* (Paris: J. Gabalda & Cie.), tome II

31. Vincent-Steve reconstructions of Solomon's temple (1956): (1) ground plan; (2) side view; (3) longitudinal cross-section; (4) breadth cross-section; (5) front view

Corswant's *Dictionnaire d'Archéologie Biblique* (1956) has a brief treatment of the temple of Solomon with a simple line drawing of the ground plan and a side elevation (S side; Fig. TEM 17). One notes the following features: there is a tower at the front; the pillars are free-standing; the cornice is straight-edged; the side structure does not come all the way to the front; it has only one entrance, on the S side, in the middle of the side, from which winding stairs go up; this side structure has windows, though not nearly so many as in the Stevens-Wright reconstruction; there are steps up to the vestibule, but none from the nave into the adytum.

In conclusion, there is the very serious work of Père L.-H. Vincent, who has devoted a lifetime to fruitful study of the archaeology of Palestine, and of Jerusalem in particular. He is not in what may be called the modern German tradition of Galling, Möhlenbrink, Watzinger, Albright, Wright, and Garber, but more in the French tradition of De Vogüé and Dieulafoy, adding mathematical calculations, particularly triangulation, to the biblical text and to archaeology as a means of determining some of the details of the building. The Egyptians are known to have used certain triangles (such as the "sacred" and the "Osirian"). Assuming that Solomon's (or rather Hiram's) architects used known principles of Egyptian mathematics, and given certain basic dimensions in the biblical account, unknown details can be calculated. Needless to say, there is in addition no lack in Vincent of attention to archaeology and the biblical text, the main resources of other scholars. But the results are somehow different and distinctive. The text is well supplemented with drawings by Père A.-M. Steve. Fig. TEM 31.

There is no reconstruction of the altar. The "sea" is about the same as the others except that the bowl seems larger, the bulls smaller, and they are lying down (couchant). The pillars are free-standing, but

are not cressets; their capitals are more bulbous, like some of the older restorations. There is no platform, nor are there any steps, either to the vestibule or to the adytum; everything is flat on the ground, so to speak. Behind the pillars are two towers, each 50 cubits high, arrived at by a process of triangulation aided by archaeological parallels, but not by the text of Kings. The roof is not in a straight line, but descends stepwise from the tower to the nave to the adytum to the rear part of the side structure, making four stages in all. Every stage is surmounted by battlements with crow-step crenelations, and the crow-step theme (curiously inverted) is used to decorate the front and sides of the towers. In addition to the clerestories, admitted by all, Vincent (or Steve) is more generous with small windows than Stevens and Wright. There is even a hint of the possibility of the use of glass. The three-story side structure is divided into thirty-odd rooms in each story (following Ezekiel, though not exactly), and each room has a window; there are also windows in the fronts and sides of the towers (*see plan*). The battlements suggest a fortification, but one wonders how a building with so many windows could be defended.

Finally, examination of Vincent's ground plan shows a different approach to the much-discussed problem of the entrance or entrances to the side structure, a medial position between the unprotected entrance or entrances on the outside found in most plans and the very much protected single entrance from the nave advocated by Waterman and adopted by Howland and Garber. Vincent (with his artist-collaborator, Steve) agrees with Waterman that the side structure housed treasures, and hence that the entrance or entrances should be protected. A side room is added to each end of the vestibule, and from each of these side rooms there is an entrance to the side structure (*see plan*). Most commentators would feel that there is little justification of this feature from the biblical text, and too much recourse to speculation on what might be logical, given a certain point of view. It might also be pointed out that such accommodation to the exigencies of the side structure is in sharp contrast to another extreme view, that of Möhlenbrink, who claims that the Solomonic building had no side structure at all, the side structure being a part of the second temple and its presence in the text of Kings being the work of an ill-informed late editor.

Perhaps it can be justly said in summary that it is fortunate that the only outstanding model of the twentieth century so far produced, which is likely to be viewed by large numbers of untrained persons seeking information, is that of Howland and Garber. This model, while inevitably manifesting certain questionable details, is a relatively sane and conservative product, resting solidly on the text of Kings, the only reliable literary source, while utilizing some of the less controversial finds of archaeology. An inexpert viewer is not likely to get a very wrong impression, such as that created by Schick's Solomonic model, so badly confused with the temple of Herod, to say nothing of its resemblance to a German castle.

On the other hand, there is every reason why scholars should continue to study the subject and produce books and relatively inexpensive plans drawn on paper, even if such books and plans sometimes espouse extremely debatable interpretations and reconstructions. Knowledge is often advanced by those who have the courage to be different.

B. THE TEMPLE OF ZERUBBABEL. In 539 B.C., Cyrus II, the Great, king of Persia (*see* CYRUS), captured Babylon, overthrowing the Chaldean or Neo-Babylonian Empire, and incorporating Mesopotamia, Syria, and Palestine into the new Persian Empire. Reversing the deportation policy of the preceding Assyrian and Chaldean empires, he issued his famous decree of amnesty, whereby the deported peoples were allowed to return to their own lands and to practice their own religious observances, so long as they did not engage in political rebellion against PERSIA. Judah seems to have been incorporated into the Persian province of Syria or Transeuphratia ("Beyond the River [Euphrates]"; Ezra 4:11-23), but with a considerable degree of local autonomy (6:6-8). As a result of these developments, a number of Jews returned to Judah and Jerusalem under SHESH-BAZZAR and ZERUBBABEL (some consider these two to be the same person). With the help of those who had never left, a temple was started on the old site, and finished probably *ca.* the year 516/15 B.C. This temple is often called after Zerubbabel, who seems to have been in charge of the Jewish community during most of the construction, but not at the end. Jewish writers call this the "second temple," and speak of the entire postexilic period, including the time of Herod and his new (third) temple, as the period of the second temple. Thus is shown how highly this temple was regarded. It is also well to remember that the second temple, in spite of paucity of information about it, stood for nearly five hundred years, more than a century longer than the life of Solomon's structure, and of course far longer than its magnificent successor built by Herod, which lasted less than one century.

1. Biblical references. Our earliest sources are Haggai (*ca.* 520 B.C.) and Zechariah (*ca.* 520-518), but they are very meager. The former complains that the people are now prosperous enough to live in paneled houses, but are procrastinating in building the "house of the LORD" (Hag. 1:1-4). He suggests that their economic difficulties, drought, inflation, and the like, are due to the ruined state of the temple (vss. 8-11). Within a month, this challenge stirs Zerubbabel, the governor, and Joshua (or JESHUA 5), the high priest, to lead the people in the work of construction (vss. 14-15*a*). Standing in the midst of the ruins and the confusion of reconstruction, the elderly prophet, who apparently had seen the former temple (2:3), encourages the builders and predicts a future for the new temple more splendid than the glory of its predecessor (vss. 4-9). Several months later the enthusiastic prophet predicts the greatest material and spiritual success for Judah under the leadership of Zerubbabel as an outgrowth of the refounding of the temple (vss. 15-23). Thus the temple plays its part in the earliest postexilic messianic prophecy.

Zechariah speaks of the temple very little. In 1:16 its rebuilding is predicted. The coming of the Lord to dwell in the midst of his people is mentioned in 2:10-11; this may refer to the temple. 6:11-14 is the enigmatic passage that prophesies of the coronation of Joshua, the high priest, his rebuilding of the temple, and his assumption of a messianic title and royal prerogatives. The person originally referred to would seem to have been Zerubbabel, whose name was removed after his political failure. 6:15 mentions the help of "those who are far off" in building the temple; this is a reference to the returned exiles or, very improbably, to Gentiles. 7:3 speaks of priests who belong to the "house of the LORD." 8:3 speaks of the sanctity of the temple mount, and 8:9-13 mentions the laying of the foundation of the temple and the blessings that soon will follow. 8:22 portrays Gentiles coming in the near future to seek the Lord in Jerusalem, presumably at the temple.

The Chronicler (*see* CHRONICLES, I AND II), writing perhaps two centuries later, though utilizing earlier sources, seems to be our next witness. I Chr. 23–26, setting forth the organization of the temple staff, the "courses" (KJV) or "divisions" (RSV) and duties of the Levites, the temple musicians, the gatekeepers, the treasurers, and the like—surely this passage reflects to some extent the temple organization of the author's own day, and it is plain that it was fairly elaborate. II Chr. 36:22-23 (end of the book) simply anticipates verbatim a few words at the beginning of the book of Ezra, which follows.

Ezra, usually regarded with Nehemiah as a continuation of the work of the Chronicler (*see* EZRA AND NEHEMIAH, BOOKS OF), yields valuable historical information, in spite of some chronological garbling. Ch. 1 tells of the decree of Cyrus as it related to the Jews and of the return of a small group under Sheshbazzar, with definite intent to rebuild the temple. They were even allowed to bring back the sacred vessels that remained (though one may doubt such figures as 5,400 [1:11; cf. II Kings 24:13; 25:15]). Ezra 2:68-70 speaks of freewill offerings by individual Jews to the temple fund, and of some of the officials who expected to serve in the sanctuary (cf.

vss. 36-54). Ch. 3 tells first of the restoration of the altar of burnt offering and resumption of its sacrifices, a few months after the first return. The leadership is already credited to Zerubbabel and Jeshua, and Shesh-bazzar seems to disappear (vss. 1-6). Next, the foundations of the temple are laid. Again leadership is credited to Zerubbabel and Jeshua (vs. 8), though another verse (5:16) makes it appear that Shesh-bazzar remained in charge at this early period (vss. 7-13).

4:1-5 tells of the offer of the Samaritans to join in the rebuilding of the temple, and its rejection by Zerubbabel and Jeshua, followed by continued attempts by the rejected neighbors to hinder the construction from the time of Cyrus to that of Darius. Ch. 5 brings us to the time of Haggai and Zechariah, who are mentioned by name as spurring Zerubbabel and Jeshua to the work of building (vss. 1-2). Tattenai, governor of Transpotamia (Syria), investigates sharply what is happening, but does not stop the construction. He is told by the Jews that they were given authority to build by Cyrus; he writes Darius to ascertain the correctness of this claim. In ch. 6 Darius replies that the claim is correct and that Tattenai is to appropriate royal funds from the taxes of his province for completion of the building and the maintenance of the sacrifices.

The project was completed in the month of Adar of the sixth year of Darius, presumably the first of that name, hence in the spring of 515 B.C. (6:15, a most valuable datum; a few have proposed Darius II, and hence a date *ca.* a century later). A dedicatory sacrifice followed, very modest in comparison with Solomon's (vs. 17; cf. I Kings 8:5; II Chr. 7:5). Doubtless the temple itself was also more modest, though 5:8; 6:4 speak of "huge stones" or "great stones" (but the translation has been challenged; cf. I Esd. 6:9, 25); and 3:7 claims that Phoenician help was enlisted, as in the days of Solomon. On the other hand, some of the old people who remembered the first temple were disappointed at the appearance of the new foundations (3:12-13; Hag. 2:3; though the latter verse may refer only to the ruined condition before rebuilding began). By and large, it is probable that recent writers have tended to overemphasize the inferiority of the second temple, especially if the reports of substantial financial aid by the Persian government (Ezra 1:4; 3:7; 6:4, 8-9) are correct.

Unfortunately, the only statement of dimensions of this temple given in a biblical passage, "height . . . sixty cubits . . . , breadth sixty cubits" (6:3), is both incomplete and unrealistic, so that nothing can be drawn from it except an impression of rather large size.

The book of Nehemiah mentions the temple only incidentally. 2:8 speaks of the "gates of the fortress of the temple," referring to nearby towers protecting the approach to the sacred precincts. 10:32-39 mentions the temple tax, first fruits, tithes, and other arrangements for financing the worship services. Chambers for the storage of contributions in kind are also mentioned here and in 12:44-47, along with treasurers and other members of the temple staff. In 12:40 the people stand at the "house of God" during the dedication of the new wall. 13:4-14, the story of the nepotism of Eliashib, mentions a "large chamber" in the "courts of the house of our God," formerly used for storage, in which Tobiah was living, and from which he was expelled.

Certain verses in Daniel (7:25; 8:11-13; 9:24-27; 12:11) contain veiled references to the desecration of the second temple and the stoppage of its services by Antiochus Epiphanes, *ca.* 168 B.C. For information in the Psalms on the history of the second temple, *see* PSALMS, BOOK OF.

2. References in the Apoc. and the Pseudep. I Esdras is essentially a parallel of the last two chapters of II Chronicles, the canonical book of Ezra, and Neh. 7:73–8:13*a*. It adds practically nothing to the canonical material except that the temple is finished on the twenty-third day of the month of Adar, in the sixth year of Darius, instead of the third day (7:5, probably the correct reading; cf. Ezra 6:15). In I Esd. 9:38, 41, Ezra reads before the people in the "open square before the east gate of the temple" instead of in the "square before the Water Gate" (Neh. 8:1, 3). These locations may or may not be the same; no further information is available, except that Josephus follows I Esdras.

Ben Sirach (*see* ECCLESIASTICUS), in his praise of famous men, mentions the work of Zerubbabel and Jeshua in building the temple (Ecclus. 49:11-12), very briefly. More extended is the description of the activities of Simon II or Simeon, son of Onias (Hebrew Yohanan), high priest near the beginning of the second century B.C. (50:1-21). Simon seems to have been in full charge of the city. He is credited first with repairing the temple, then fortifying it with great walls. Then he constructed a large reservoir and fortified the whole city. Vss. 5-21 contain a detailed and eloquent description of Simon's splendor in the performance of his duties; how richly dressed he was; how he came from behind the veil (vs. 5 RSV mg.) before the holy of holies (thus we know there was a veil); how he went up to the altar of burnt offering, receiving the portions of the animals from his assistant priests, and making the oblation before all the people assembled in the courtyard. Then he poured a libation at the foot of the altar; a fragrant odor arose; the priests shouted and blew trumpets; the people fell on their faces; the singers began a melodious song; the people remained in prayer. When the service was concluded, the high priest came down from the altar, lifted his hands, and pronounced a benediction upon the whole congregation, who bowed down a second time to receive the blessing. Lacking detailed information about the building itself, we are grateful for this description of one of its typical services.

I Maccabees (*see* MACCABEES, BOOKS OF) provides the most extensive apocryphal references because of its preoccupation with the attack of Antiochus. 1:20-24 gives a list of temple furnishings plundered by Antiochus; there is so much gold and silver that we are reminded of the days of Solomon (cf. vss. 21-23 with I Kings 7:48-50). The veil or curtain (probably lacking in Solomon's temple) is mentioned. Other verses in ch. 1 speak of the pollution of the sanctuary, and especially of the altar of burnt offering in the inner court (vss. 37, 39, 45, 54, 59; cf. 3:51). 4:36-59 tells the inspiring story of the purification and rededication of the temple, after the victories of Judas (*see* DEDICATION, FEAST OF). But the altar of burnt offering was so polluted by the heathen sacrifices that it had to be dismantled and a new one built in its place, of "unhewn stones," so it is said, "as the law [Exod. 20:25; Deut. 27:6] directs, . . . a new altar like the former one" (I Macc. 4:47). This is interesting, since neither Solomon's altar (I Kings 8:64; II Chr. 4:1) nor that of Ezekiel (43:13-17) seems to manifest regard for the Pentateuchal law. I Macc. 4: 51 mentions "curtains"; perhaps there were two, one before the nave, the other before the adytum. Vs. 57 speaks of the front of the temple being decorated with "golden crowns and small shields" (cf. 1:22), but this does not sound plausible. The same verse mentions the repair of the chambers of the priests, though without specifying whether these chambers were within the temple proper, within a side structure, or outside around the inner court. 6:7 mentions the restoration of high walls around the sanctuary, "as before"; these presumably had been first added by the high priest Simon II (Ecclus. 50:1-2; *see above*). Thus the temple became a stronghold in the battle against the foreign garrison in the nearby citadel (I Macc. 6:18, 26, 51-54, 62). After the death of Judas, the renegade high priest Alcimus attempted to dismantle the fortifications around the temple, but he died before the attempt could be completed (9:54-56). Jonathan repaired the damage, and he himself assumed the high priesthood *ca.* 153 B.C., in addition to his duties as military and political leader (10:17-21). Simon took over all these duties, strengthened further the fortifications of the temple, and refurbished the sanctuary and its equipment (13:8-9, 52; 14:15).

In spite of the obvious concern of the compiler of II Maccabees with the temple, and especially with its purification and rededication, his book yields very little further factual information about the structure itself, its history, or its services. Notable is the claim that the second temple is the most famous and the most sacred shrine in the whole world (cf. 2:19, 22; 3:12; 5:15-21; 14:31; 15:18; etc.).

The Letter of ARISTEAS contains a glowing description of the temple, presumably resulting from an official visit to the Holy City (vss. 84-104). There is also the story of the incredibly rich furnishings donated by Ptolemy Philadelphus to the high priest Eleazar for use in the sanctuary (vss. 51-82; note the emphasis on the table of the bread of the Presence). Unfortunately, the dating of this document is so debatable (ranging from 200 B.C. to A.D. 33) that it is uncertain whether the writer is describing the structure of Zerubbabel, that of Herod, or simply using his imagination, at least for the most part. Since some of the description surpasses in grandeur what we know even of Herod's magnificent structure, the third alternative would seem to be the safest. The great and beautiful curtain seems to be at the main entrance, not before the adytum (vs. 86); the costume of the high priest is rich beyond belief (vss. 96-98); the ritualistic skill of the assistant priests is uncanny, and they are seven hundred in number (vss. 92-95); but most remarkable of all is the inexhaustible water supply furnished by a copious natural spring within the temple area, supplemented by a vast system of connected reservoirs, so that the huge amounts of sacrificial blood could be washed away almost in-

stantly (vss. 89-91; cf. a similar tradition in Tac. Hist. V.12). The reservoirs or cisterns are credible enough; there are some under the area today; they have been explored archaeologically, and may date back to the time of Herod or before. But no spring, or trace of a spring, has ever been found in this area. We can only conclude that this spring is somewhat like the stream of fresh water flowing from the temple in the vision of Ezekiel (47:1), though Ezekiel's stream had a far grander purpose. On the other hand, we need not doubt that whatever temple Aristeas was describing stood on the highest point of the city, or nearly so (vs. 84), and was oriented toward the E (vs. 88).

3. Josephus references. Josephus (Apion I.xxii) quotes a description of Jerusalem from Hecateus of Abdera, a writer contemporary with Alexander the Great. Hecateus says that the temple enclosure was 5 *plethra* (*ca.* 500 feet) long and 100 cubits broad, was surrounded by a stone wall, and was entered by a double gate. The altar of burnt offering within this enclosure was constructed of unhewn stones (*see* § B2 *above* on I Macc. 4:47), 20 cubits on each side and 10 cubits high (same dimensions as the bronze altar in II Chr. 4:1). The temple itself is not described except as a "large building." Inside were an altar (of incense) and a lampstand, both of heavy gold (two talents!); and upon them was a light that was never extinguished. There is nothing unreasonable here except perhaps the amount of gold (which most ancient writers were prone to exaggerate).

Book XI of Josephus' *Antiquities* in general parallels the postexilic biblical material. In addition, we read of Alexander the Great's sanction of the building of the rival Samaritan temple on Mount Gerizim (Antiq. XI.viii.4), doubtless a historical fact; also the story of Alexander's reverent visit to the temple in Jerusalem and his sacrifice there (XI.viii.5), considered by most historians to be pure legend.

Book XII parallels the Letter of Aristeas and the books of Maccabees down to the death of Judas. According to XII.iii.3-4, Antiochus III, the Great (223-187 B.C.), was very friendly to the Jews and their temple. He subsidized the sacrifices, helped finance temple repairs and additional construction, including "porticoes," and reaffirmed the legal ban against the presence of foreigners and unclean animals within the sacred precincts.

Book XIII leads beyond the apocryphal material to that point where Josephus becomes almost our sole literary source. XIII.iii.1-3 tells of the building of the temple of Onias at Leontopolis in Egypt (*see* TEMPLES [THOSE BESIDES JERUSALEM]). It is said to have been similar to the one at Jerusalem, though smaller and less elegant. From this it would seem again that the second temple may have been underrated by some modern writers, as noted above. XIII.xiii.5 contains the well-known story of how Alexander Janneus was pelted by citrons by the people as he stood by the altar to offer sacrifice. After massacring six thousand of his subjects, the priest-king caused a wooden barrier to be erected about the altar in the court, so that the people no longer could come near at the time of sacrifice.

Book XIV begins with the civil war between ARISTOBULUS II and HYRCANUS II. The latter, at the instigation of Antipater, father of Herod the Great, enlisted the support of ARETAS, king of the NABATEANS. Aristobulus took refuge in the temple, which was besieged by Aretas during Passover (XIV.ii.1). The Roman general Scaurus favored Aristobulus, forcing Aretas to raise the siege (XIV.ii.3). Pompey reversed this policy, came in person, and captured Jerusalem *ca.* 63 B.C., restoring Hyrcanus to power. Pompey entered the temple—an act of impiety in the eyes of the Jews—but respected the sanctity of the place so much that he took no plunder (XIV.iii.1–iv.4; cf. War I.vii.6). Later, Crassus plundered the treasure left by Pompey, amounting to thousands of talents of gold, sent by Jews from all over the world (Antiq. XIV.vii.2; War I.viii.8). In the wars leading to the triumph of Herod, it was customary for the defenders of Jerusalem to barricade themselves in the temple as a last resort (Antiq. XIV.xiii.3-4; xvi.2). When Herod and his Roman supporters attacked the city in 37 B.C., some of the porticoes around the temple were burned (XIV.xvi.2); but Herod, after he controlled the city and with an eye to the future, held back all foreigners from entering, defiling, or plundering the sanctuary (XIV.xvi.3; War I.xviii.3).

In XV.xi.1 it is stated that the second temple was 60 cubits lower than that of Solomon. Such a statement is based on the legendary height of 120 cubits for Solomon's temple in II Chr. 3:4. We can only conclude that Josephus regarded the second temple as markedly inferior to the first.

From Jos. War I we learn that the fortress at the NW corner of the temple area, later called Antonia by Herod, was called Baris ("Tower") in Hasmonean times (I.iii.3; v.4). The brief reconciliation between Aristobulus II and Hyrcanus II took place in the temple (I.vi.1). The temple was so strongly fortified as to constitute a second line of defense (I.vii.1). A bridge connecting the temple with the city was cut for this reason by defending Jews during the attack by Pompey (I.vii.2). In the fifteenth year of his reign (*ca.* 20 B.C.), Herod began to dismantle the second temple in order to build a new and greater one (I.xxi.1).

4. Rabbinic references. In the Mishna, Yom. 5.2 tells of a stone remaining after the ark of the covenant disappeared in the destruction of the first temple. This stone was called *Shethiyah,* generally interpreted to mean "foundation stone," and projected a few inches above the floor or ground level. The stone in question may be the "sacred rock" (*see* § A2d *above*), in which case we have a tradition that at least a part of the rock lay under the adytum in all three temples. The "foundation stone" has also been interpreted as a movable stone brought in to replace the ark in Zerubbabel's temple. Later (or parallel) rabbinic references emphasize the importance of this stone and its position in the heart of the temple (of Herod), without yielding further information about its nature.

T.B. Yom. 21*b* has sometimes been interpreted as presenting a list of five things in Solomon's temple that were lacking in Zerubbabel's: the ark and its equipment, the sacred fire, the Shekinah, the Holy Spirit, and Urim and Thummim. Actually, the term "second temple" here refers to the Herodian sanctuary, as is usual in rabbinic literature. The whole point of the passage is the religious inferiority of Herod's temple, despite its physical grandeur, to that of Solomon.

5. Conclusion. Exact and reliable information about the details of Zerubbabel's temple are lacking. The probabilities are that it was similar in plan and size to Solomon's structure, since it was built on the same site and Phoenician workmanship was still the prevailing style. The new temple was somewhat less rich and costly than the old, though this difference has been exaggerated by some writers, both ancient and modern. Definitely lacking were the "sea" and wheeled lavers outside, the ark of the covenant and the cherubim within. Nothing is said of the pillars. The nave contained an altar of incense and a table for the bread of the Presence, but only one lampstand instead of the former ten. Use of curtains instead of doors may have been a new feature. The temple stood alone, not in a palace complex.

From time to time additions and changes were made. Notable was the fortifying of the temple by the high priest Simon II, continued by the Hasmoneans. The Letter of Aristeas (vs. 84) speaks of three encompassing walls, possibly fortifications, or perhaps only partitions separating the inner court from the outer court or courts (note the plural of this word in I Macc. 4:38, 48; cf. 9:54). In Hasmonean times a palace was built on the W hill overlooking the temple (Jos. Antiq. XX.viii.11). Perhaps at this time was constructed the bridge over the Tyropoeon Valley (*see* JERUSALEM), mentioned in connection with the attack by Pompey (Antiq. XIV.iv.2; War I.vii.2). But this Maccabean bridge is not to be connected with extant archaeological remains, such as Robinson's Arch or Wilson's Arch, as some have sought to do. Extant remains in the area belong to the Herodian, not the pre-Herodian period, as practically all archaeologists agree.

It will not be necessary to speak of reconstructions of Zerubbabel's temple; seldom are they attempted, because of scarcity of definite evidence. Most regrettable is the attempt of Möhlenbrink in the frontispiece of his useful monograph, reproduced by Vincent with a proper warning of its lack of value.

C. THE TEMPLE OF HEROD. As was pointed out above, this temple lasted a much shorter time than the other two. Begun *ca.* 20 B.C., the basic structure was completed in about a year and a half, but subsidiary construction was still in process a half-century later (John 2:20), and may not have been entirely finished when the destruction came in A.D. 70. Although on the same site as the two preceding temples, this one involved an almost complete rebuilding according to the new and then prevailing style of architecture, the Hellenistic-Roman, but with retention of the Solomonic arrangement of rooms within the sanctuary itself. It is logically absurd, therefore, to confuse Herod's and Zerubbabel's temples under the name of "second temple." Herod's was definitely the third temple, no matter what tradition may say.

Our chief literary sources are the NT, Josephus (principally Antiq. XV.xii; War V.v), and the Mishna tractate Middoth. The brief description in Philo *Special Laws* I.13 (*De Monarchia* II.2) is too vague and general to be of use. The descriptions of

Josephus and the Mishna are both in considerable detail, but unfortunately not in complete agreement with each other. Thus problems arise when reconstruction is attempted. Archaeology plays a valuable part in the extensive literature, since certain parts of the substructure of Herod's temple are still extant under the large area or court around the Dome of the Rock. This area, which to some degree corresponds to the area around Herod's temple, is now called el-Haram esh-Sharif, usually translated "the Noble Sanctuary," though "the glorious holy place" is perhaps a more exact rendering.

1. NT references. Although the NT contains more than a hundred references to Herod's temple, few of these are of such nature as to yield any detailed information about the dimensions or appearance of the structure itself. Most of these references have to do with attitudes on the part of the Jews or the early Christians toward the temple as an institution. A number of gospel passages portray Jesus as frequenting the temple, "teaching" or "walking" there; the same is true of the early Christians in the book of Acts. Clearly, Jesus and his immediate followers still considered the temple as the religious center of their communal life. Only later came the idea that the temple was unnecessary (Rev. 21:22).

Two words are used in the Greek: ναός, meaning the sacred building alone, and ἱερόν, the whole sacred area, including various auxiliary courts, side chambers, and porticoes. Both words are translated "temple," without distinction, but the reader needs to keep the difference in mind, especially since only priests could enter the ναός.

E.g., the expression "the pinnacle of the temple" (Matt. 4:5; Luke 4:9) refers, not to the top of the temple proper, but probably to the SE corner of the outer court, high above the Kidron Valley, very much as is the situation today. Likewise, such expressions as "the buildings of the temple" (Matt. 24:1), its "noble stones" (Luke 21:5; cf. Mark 13:1), "walking in the temple" (Mark 11:27), and "teaching" there (Luke 20:1) use the broader term, ἱερόν. Similarly, the money-changers were not within the building itself, but in one of the courts outside (Matt. 21: 12; Mark 11:15; Luke 19:45; John 2:14). By contrast, the curtain (the NT mentions only one, that before the adytum) was within the building (Matt. 27:51; Mark 15:38; Luke 23:45—using the word ναός), as was the altar of incense before which Zechariah (KJV Zacharias) was performing his sacerdotal duties, while the people remained outside (Luke 1: 8-11; cf. Rev. 11:1-2). In general, this distinction is clearly observed in the NT, likewise in Josephus, though there are certain borderline cases (since language is not an exact science like mathematics).

Only a few details are mentioned. There was a section of the temple precincts called SOLOMON'S PORTICO, where Jesus and the apostles walked (John 10:23; Acts 3:11; 5:12). The "Beautiful Gate" is twice mentioned (Acts 3:2, 10), but nothing is told of its location or design. An official of the temple called CAPTAIN appears several times (Luke 22:4, 52; Acts 4:1; 5:24, 26). Paul was accused of bringing Greeks into the "temple" (ἱερόν)—i.e., into a court forbidden to Gentiles (Acts 21:28; see § C2 below). We learn that in times of tumult the gates of the tem-

ple area (ἱερόν) could be quickly closed, but nothing is said about their number or location (vs. 30). Neither Jesus nor Paul, of course, ever entered the ναός or temple building proper (cf. 25:8; 26:21; the word in these verses is ἱερόν).

2. Josephus references. Antiq. XV.xi, written ca. A.D. 95, probably in Rome, will be considered first, since it gives a more generalized view.

The work of rebuilding was begun in the eighteenth year of Herod's reign (20/19 B.C.). Herod thought, according to Josephus, that Solomon's temple was 120 cubits high (cf. II Chr. 3:4); its successor was only half as high; Herod wished to redress the deficiency and restore the former glory (Antiq. XV.xi.1). Some feared that the old structure would be pulled down and not replaced, or that some profanation would occur. Herod reassured them by very careful preparations, such as providing a thousand wagons, hiring ten thousand workmen, and training a thousand priests to be superior masons and carpenters for work upon the most holy portions of the structure (XV.xi.2).

The old foundations were removed and new ones laid. The new building was 100 cubits long, and the same in height; a structural difficulty prevented attainment of the full height of 120 cubits. The middle of the structure was much higher than on each side. Huge white stones measuring 25 by 8 by 12 cubits were used. The double entrance doors were adorned with embroidered veils or curtains, above which the lintel was decorated with a golden vine bearing huge clusters of grapes. The entire temple was surrounded by a large paved court, which was bounded by extensive porticoes or colonnades, supported in part by great walls where the steepness of the hill made them necessary. The circumference of the area was 4 stadia (stades or furlongs in English), each side being one stadium (ca. 600 feet) long. (This does not agree with other data, representing the area to be larger; therefore some have assumed the 4 stadia to be a pre-Herodian dimension; see § C3 below.) On top of all was another wall inside the outer edge, which had on the E a double portico (stoa) of the same length as the wall. This portico faced the front gates of the temple proper (XV.xi.3). See SOLOMON'S PORTICO.

The fortress near the NW corner of the temple area, built or rebuilt in Hasmonean times (War I.iii.3; v.4) and called Baris ("Tower"), was strengthened by Herod and renamed Antonia, in honor of Antony (Antiq. XV.xi.4; cf. Neh. 2:8, possibly referring to the original structure at this location; Acts 21:34-40; 22:24; 23:10, where the "barracks" [KJV "castle"] probably is Antonia). The sacerdotal vestments were kept in this building.

The outer W side of the temple area had four gates. The first gate (probably in the center) led to the royal palace by a bridge over the Tyropoeon Valley. Two more (probably to the N) led to the suburbs; the last (most southerly) led into the city by a long flight of steps down into the valley and another long flight up again. The S side had gates (probably two), and a great portico, called the Royal Portico, with a triple ambulatory (walkway) as contrasted with a double ambulatory on the other sides (Fig. TEM 32). The valley below this portico was so deep that looking over into it caused giddiness (cf. the "pin-

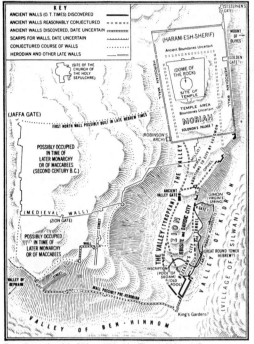

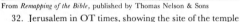

From *Remapping of the Bible*, published by Thomas Nelson & Sons

32. Jerusalem in OT times, showing the site of the temple

nacle" of Matt. 4:5; Luke 4:9). There were four rows of columns, the fourth being engaged with the S wall. Each column was 27 feet high and so thick that three men with outstretched arms were required to embrace it (an estimated 17 feet; cf. with Solomon's Jachin and Boaz). The total number of columns was 162, their capitals being of the Corinthian order. The two outer walkways were 30 feet wide, the middle one half again as wide; their length was a stade. The total height of the outside walkways was over 50 feet, but the height of the middle one was much greater, the roof being raised in the center (Antiq. XV.xi.5).

Inside this first enclosure, or outer court ("Court of the Gentiles"), was a smaller enclosure, to be reached by a few ascending steps. This inner enclosure was surrounded by a low stone wall (or balustrade) on which was an inscription (or inscriptions) warning foreigners to go no farther, on pain of death. The enclosure itself had three equidistant gates on the N side and three on the S. On the E there was one large gate where Jews might enter with their wives, since the area within this gate was the Women's Court. Beyond this was an area into which the women could not go ("Court of Israel"). Still closer to the temple proper, and immediately surrounding it, was the court which only the priests could enter ("Priests' Court"). Within all was the temple building itself, with an altar of burnt offering in front. These courts and enclosures required eight years to build (XV.xi.6).

The building itself was completed in a year and a half. As in the days of Solomon, a great dedicatory sacrifice was held. This dedication was held on the anniversary day of the king's inauguration, to make the occasion all the more notable (XV.xi.5).

The king had built for himself an underground passage from Antonia to the E gate of the inner enclosure. Over this gate was a tower. The tunnel was thought to be particularly useful in case there should be a rebellion (XV.xi.7).

In Antiq. XX.ix.7 we read that the construction of the temple precincts (ἱερόν) was "finished" during the time of Agrippa II, who, though not king of Judea, had charge of the temple. This was during the procuratorship of Albinus, ca. 63. The cessation of construction is said to have thrown eighteen thousand men out of work—an exaggeration, since the original project employed only ten thousand (*see above*). The king was urged to rebuild the E portico, which was reputed to have been constructed by Solomon (*see* SOLOMON'S PORTICO). This portico was 400 cubits long (or high), and because of the deep valley (Kidron) outside was supported by great walls built of huge white stones 20 cubits long and 6 cubits high. Although the temple treasury was well filled, Agrippa felt that this project was too vast to undertake and denied the petition, but allowed much paving to be done throughout the city. Later, Agrippa gathered material to increase the height of the sanctuary building by 20 cubits to bring it to the supposed Solomonic height, but the war intervened before this work could be begun (War V.i.5).

The *Jewish War* was written earlier than the *Antiquities;* in fact, it appeared shortly after the struggle was over (probably ca. 75). It affords us more details about the temple area, and especially about the sanctuary itself. War I.xxi.1 puts the beginning of construction in Herod's fifteenth year, as opposed to the eighteenth in Antiq. XV.xi.1. New foundations were laid, and the whole area was made double its former size. There were great colonnaded porticoes (stoas) around the whole, and a fortress called Antonia dominated the area on the N. This fortress was not attached directly to the temple area, but was separated by porticoes that could cut communication when destroyed (II.xv.6).

War V.v describes the sacred area just as it was before the attack of the Romans. Solomon had built a great foundation wall on the E side. Now, over a much greater area the top of the hill was leveled off, and foundation walls were built on the other three sides(?). There were upper courts surrounded by a lower enclosure; the foundations of the latter reached down in some places three hundred cubits or more (V.v.1).

Above the foundations and pavement rose all around the double porticoes supported by shining marble columns 25 cubits high. The porticoes were 30 cubits wide, and their total circumference, including the Tower of Antonia, was six stades (ca. 3,600 feet). The lower outer court was paved with varicolored stones. The inner area was surrounded by a stone fence or balustrade 3 cubits high, bearing at intervals inscriptions in Greek and Latin warning foreigners to proceed no farther (Fig. PAR 22). Beyond this, fourteen steps led up to the inner area, which was surrounded by a wall of its own 25 cubits high. A level terrace 10 cubits wide lay between the steps and the wall. From this, other flights of five steps led up to eight gates, four on the N and four on the S. The E part of this inner area was the Women's

Court. One gate on the N and one on the S led into this court. It also had a gate in front, on the E side, and another opposite, on the W, leading still closer to the sacred edifice; but the women could go no farther than their own court. The W wall of the inner area had no gate. Inside the wall of the inner area were storage chambers and single-columned porticoes, their columns being smaller but otherwise not inferior to those of the outer porticoes in the lower court (V.v.2).

Of the ten gates just mentioned, nine were overlaid with gold and silver, but the one on the E of the Women's Court, the E gate of the inner area (cf. II.xvii.3; VI.v.3), was of Corinthian bronze, far exceeding the others in value (probably the "Beautiful Gate" of Acts 3:2, 10). Each gate had two doors 30 by 15 cubits, except that the one leading into the sanctuary from the Women's Court was larger, having doors 40 cubits high, with more massive plates of gold and silver. Fifteen steps, shallower than at the other gates, led up to the more sacred area beyond the Women's Court (V.v.3).

The centrally located sanctuary building was reached by twelve steps. In front it was 100 cubits high and the same in width. Behind the vestibule it was 60 cubits wide, the two side wings of the vestibule being each 20 cubits wide. The entrance to the vestibule was 70 cubits high and 25 wide, had no doors, and was overlaid with much gold. The inside of the vestibule was 90 cubits high, 50 cubits in breadth, and 20 cubits deep. At the back of the vestibule was the main doorway of the temple. It had double doors, each 55 cubits high and 16 wide, overlaid with gold, as was the surrounding wall. Above it were golden vines, with clusters of grapes as tall as a man. Before it hung a full-length curtain of Babylonian tapestry, of various materials and colors, embroidered with a panorama of the heavens, typifying the universe. The building itself was in two stories (V.v.4).

The interior of the sacred building exclusive of the vestibule was 60 cubits high, 60 cubits long, and 20 cubits wide. The main room, corresponding to the Solomonic *Hekhal*, was 40 cubits long, and contained the seven-branched LAMPSTAND, the table for the BREAD OF THE PRESENCE, and the ALTAR of incense. The adytum, screened from the main room by a veil or curtain, was 20 cubits in depth (and the same in width). It was called "holy of holies" and contained no furniture whatever.

There were numerous side chambers in three stories around the lower part of the building, with entrances on either side of the main doorway. The upper 40 cubits of the building had no side chambers. Since the part surrounded by chambers was 60 cubits high, the total height of the central part of the building was 100 cubits (V.v.5).

The outside of the building was covered with so much gold that an onlooker could scarcely look directly at it in bright sunlight. All not overlaid with gold was of pure white stone like the snow on a mountaintop. Golden spikes prevented birds from defiling the roof. Some of the stones were 45 cubits long, 5 cubits high, and 8 broad.

The altar of burnt offering in front of the building was 15 cubits high, 50 cubits square. The top had horns at the corners, and was approached by a ramp on the S side. No iron was used in its construction. A stone barrier about a cubit high surrounded both building and altar to separate the laity outside from the priests inside (V.v.6).

No ritually unclean person was allowed near the sanctuary. Ordinary priests were clothed in fine linen; the high priest when ministering wore sumptuous vestments trimmed with gold and precious stones. He wore even more sumptuous garments on the Day of Atonement, the only day in the year when he, and he alone, entered the adytum (V.v.7).

The tower (or fortress) of Antonia, at the NW corner of the temple area, was built on a rock 50 cubits high covered with smooth stonework to make it more difficult to climb. Protected by a wall 3 cubits high, the tower itself was 40 cubits high. At each corner of the tower was a turret. Three of these were 50 cubits high, but the one on the SE corner was 70 cubits high, so as to command a view of the whole temple area. Stairways led up from the porticoes of the temple to the tower (cf. Acts 21:40). A Roman cohort was constantly quartered in the commodious interior of the fortress. The temple dominated the city; Antonia dominated the temple. N of Antonia was the hill Bezetha, cut off from the fortress by a deep fosse. This hill formed the only obstruction to the view of the temple from the N (V.v.8; cf. V.iv.2; Antiq. XVIII.iv.3).

3. Middoth references. The name of this tractate of the Mishna (*see* TALMUD) means "measurements"; the subject matter of the tractate is the details of the sanctuary itself rather than its environs. Since some dimensions and other details differ from those of Josephus, there is a considerable difference of opinion as to which source is the more reliable. The view assumed here is that JOSEPHUS is to be given the preference, since, as a citizen of Jerusalem and a priest while the temple was standing, he had firsthand knowledge. By contrast, the author of Middoth, writing *ca.* 150, was, with respect to Herod's temple, in a position similar to that of Ezekiel with respect to Solomon's structure: writing after the destruction of the sanctuary, he was inclined to idealize or even exaggerate with a view to possible future restoration. In this connection it is to be noted that Josephus, in spite of his well-known tendency to exaggerate, apparently gives a slightly smaller dimension for the entire sacred area than does Middoth.

The tractate opens with a statement of how the priests and Levites kept watch at various points around the holy place. The larger enclosed area is referred to as the Temple Mount; the smaller enclosure immediately surrounding the sacred building is called the Temple Court. The Temple Mount had five gates (Josephus implies seven or eight): the two Huldah gates on the S; the Kiponus gate on the W; the unused Tadi (or Todi or Tari) gate on the N; the Palace of Shushan (or Susa) gate on the E (cf. Neh. 1:1; Esth. 1:2, 5-9; Dan. 8:2). The Temple Court, or inner enclosure, had seven gates (Josephus nine)—three on the N, three on the S, and one on the E called the Nicanor gate (Midd. 1.1-4).

The Temple Mount was 500 cubits square (a circumference of *ca.* 3,400 feet; Josephus' larger figure is 6 stades, or *ca.* 3,600 feet, but he includes Antonia, and Middoth does not; hence Josephus has a smaller estimate than does Middoth). The largest open space was to the S, the next largest to the E; the N space was next in size, and the W space was the smallest. In other words, the temple was in the NW part of the area (Midd. 2.1).

As one approached the temple proper, there was a latticed partition (*Sŏregh*) 10 handbreadths high (the fence or balustrade according to Josephus was 3 cubits, or 18 handbreadths, high). Inside this was a rampart or terrace 10 cubits wide (Josephus agrees), reached by twelve steps (Josephus fourteen). All the inner entrances and gates were 20 cubits high and 10 cubits wide and had doors, except the entrance to the vestibule (Josephus 30 by 15 cubits). All the gates were overlaid with gold, except the Nicanor (E) gate, which had bronze (similar to Josephus). The E wall was lower than the others, so that the high priest at the proper time could look directly into the sanctuary from the Mount of Olives (Midd. 2.3-4).

The Women's Court was 135 cubits square (no dimensions in Josephus). Fifteen steps led up from this court to the Court of Israel, which was higher than the Women's Court (agrees with Josephus). The Court of Israel was 135 cubits long and 11 cubits wide. Next was the Court of Priests, of the same size as the Court of Israel. One tradition made the Priests' Court 2½ cubits higher than the Court of Israel. The whole of the Temple Court, exclusive of the Women's Court, was 187 cubits long and 35 cubits wide. Another tradition assigns thirteen gates to the Temple Court, in contrast to the seven of Midd. 1.4 (2.5-6).

In front of the building was the altar of burnt offering, 32 cubits square at its base (Josephus says 50 cubits square and 15 cubits high). It had a stepwise construction, the top level being 24 cubits square. There was a ramp on the S side (ditto Josephus), 32 cubits long and 16 wide. No iron was used in its construction (ditto Josephus). The place of slaughter ("shambles") was just N of the altar. The laver stood SW of the altar, between the ramp and the building (3.1-6).

It was 22 cubits from the altar to the vestibule. The latter was approached by twelve steps (ditto Josephus), arranged in groups with landings between. The entrance to the vestibule was 40 cubits high and 20 wide (Josephus 70 by 25). A golden vine hung over the main entrance of the sanctuary at the back of the vestibule (ditto Josephus). This entrance was 20 cubits high and 10 wide (Josephus 55 by 16). It had two sets of double doors opening inward, the wall being 6 cubits thick. The walls were covered with gold, but not the doors (Josephus says walls and doors were so covered). There were 38 side chambers or cells, arranged in three stories, with an entrance on the right of the main doorway, the left entrance being unused (Josephus mentions the three stories and says these chambers could be entered from either side). Each story was broader than the one below; there were offsets in the main building like those in Solomon's temple. Outside the cells was an ascending passageway around three sides of the building, by which the upper chamber over the main room and the holy of holies could be reached (3.6–4.5).

The greatest outside width, the greatest length, and the greatest height of the building were each 100 cubits (Josephus agrees). The upper chamber was 40 cubits high. On top was a parapet, surmounted by a scarecrow arrangement (Midd. 4.6; Josephus speaks of "sharp golden spikes").

The front wall of the vestibule was 5 cubits thick, the vestibule was 11 cubits deep, and the wall between the vestibule and the main room 6 cubits thick (Josephus has the vestibule 20 cubits, but says nothing about the thickness of the walls; Solomon's vestibule was only 10 cubits deep). The interior length of the main room was 40 cubits (Josephus agrees; Solomon's *Hekhal* had the same length). Between the main room and the holy of holies was a dividing space of one cubit. The holy of holies was 20 cubits square (ditto Josephus; Solomon's adytum was a cube of 20 cubits).

The outside width of the building behind the vestibule was 70 cubits (Josephus 60). The vestibule therefore had 15-cubit projections on each side (Josephus 20) to make up the 100-cubit width. Thus the building could be described as narrow behind and wide in front, "like a lion" (Midd. 4.7; contrast Solomon's plan, in which the front of the building was actually narrower than the rest).

4. Archaeological data and modern study. It has long been obvious that Josephus and Middoth cannot be made to agree. Neither presents an exact description in the modern sense of the word; both have value for achieving an approximate conception, though Middoth omits such characteristic features as the porticoes. For this reason, archaeological research has been helpful, especially since the Muslim structures now covering the enclosed site (the Haram esh-Sharif) retain some traces and features of the Herodian area, whereas it is hardly conceivable that any vestiges of the Solomonic or Zerubbabel buildings could have survived. This "Herodian thesis" has been widely held since the pioneer work of De Vogüé in 1864 (*see bibliography*). Even earlier, Edward Robinson (1838) had pointed out the now famous traces of "Robinson's Arch," still to be seen projecting from the W Haram wall, near the SW corner, and recognized as part of a Herodian structure (though of uncertain identification). Another American in 1851 pointed out the remains of an old gate ("Barclay's Gate") below the present Gate of the Moors, a short distance N of Robinson's Arch. Now walled up, this aperture probably marks the site of the most southerly of the four gates of Herodian times—the one mentioned above as opening to a long flight of stairs into the Tyropoeon Valley (Jos. Antiq. XV.xi.5).

Immediately to the N (*see plan*) is the Wailing Wall, or Western Wall, as it is called by the Jews. This stretch (*ca.* 50 yards) of the W wall of the Haram area was uncovered at some unknown time during the Turkish period, and has been viewed and commented upon by countless thousands of tourists, as well as by scientific observers (Fig. TEM 11). The lower courses are composed of large blocks of smooth-faced, marginally drafted limestone, usually *ca.* 15 feet long and 3-4 feet high, though one huge block is 16½ feet long. This type of stonework, found here and at other spots in Jerusalem and at Hebron, has become very well known under the name of "Herodian masonry," and the chronological implication is probably correct. At this spot there are smaller blocks of Roman masonry above the Herodian, and above the Roman rests Arabic and Turkish work. This pattern is more or less characteristic of the whole Haram enclosure, except on the N side, as will appear below. It must be borne in mind, however, that in many places the Herodian blocks are now below ground level, and hence cannot be seen without excavation.

A short distance N of the Wailing Wall is the principal modern entrance to the area, called in Arabic Bab es-Silsileh, or the Gate of the Chain. *Ca.* the middle of the nineteenth century, Titus Tobler had called attention to underground vaults in front of the Gate of the Chain. In 1865 Charles Wilson, working for the Palestine Exploration Fund, discovered, under the modern street and gate, an arch built against the Haram wall and linked up with the vaults. Further investigation was carried on by Charles Warren, but the name "Wilson's Arch" has persisted. The span of this arch is about the same as that of Robinson's, but Wilson's is practically intact. The arch is now several yards below the street level. Though showing evidence of rebuilding from time to time, this structure probably marks the site of Herod's route to the main entrance of the temple, which included a bridge at this point (Jos. Antiq. XV.xi.5; War II.xvi.3; VI.vi.2). Herod's bridge may have replaced a Maccabean bridge at the same location (Antiq. XIV.iv.2; War I.vii.2). *See* § B5 *above*.

Ca. 200 feet N of Wilson's Arch were found the remains of "Warren's Gate," just S of the modern gate called Bâb el-Mathara or Bab el-Mutawada. While the area has never been thoroughly studied, it appears likely that it contains traces of the more southerly of the two gates leading to the suburbs of the city (Antiq. XV.xi.5).

Turning to the E Haram wall, now constituting the SE part of the city wall, two features present themselves to the eye: the so-called Golden Gate, now walled up, a little N of center; and the great stones in the "Herodian masonry" at the SE angle (Fig. TEM 33). Although the gate in its present form is of Byzantine origin, it may be the successor of the Palace of Shushan gate of Middoth (Josephus does not mention an E gate). Later Christian traditions connected the Golden Gate with the Beautiful Gate of Acts 3:2 (probably incorrectly) and with Jesus' triumphal entry (more probable).

The great stones of the SE angle of the Haram wall constitute one of the readily accessible show places of Jerusalem, seen by every tourist and studied by every scholar. There are twenty-one courses of stone underground, discovered by excavation, and fourteen more above ground. The fifth row up of those above ground is the master course, with stones the largest and most impressive of all. There can be no doubt that we have here not only the SE corner of the modern city wall, but also the SE corner of the supporting structure of Herod's temple precincts.

In the S wall, the obvious noteworthy features are, from E to W, the great stones of the corner, just described in connection with the E wall, the small Single Gate, the Triple Gate, and the Double Gate. All these gates are now walled up. The Single Gate is of late date and has no relevance to our problem. The Triple Gate and the Double Gate (so named

From Simons, *Jerusalem in the Old Testament* (Leiden: E. J. Brill Ltd.)

33. The SE angle of the Haram Wall

from the number of arched entrances) probably mark the sites of the two Huldah gates mentioned in Middoth (and implied in Josephus). The Double Gate is now partially hidden by an unsightly structure built against the wall, but archaeological research has determined its main features.

If it is fairly clear that the E, S, and W sides of the present Haram largely coincide with the corresponding sides of Herod's temple area, the same is not true of the N side. Here there is no wall comparable to the others, nor is there any Herodian masonry. What remains of the rock upon which Antonia was built is now partly included in the sacred area, whereas formerly the rock and fortress were separate from the temple area, though connected by some sort of stairways (*see* § C2 *above*). The present circumference is *ca.* 5,000 feet, whereas the largest circumference given by Josephus is *ca.* 3,600 feet. These and other considerations make probable the suggestion first made by Conder, that the present circumference includes a post-Herodian N extension (probably made in the time of Justinian). Herod's N wall probably began a short distance N of the Golden Gate, where there is a slight jog or bend in the present wall, and continued W a short distance N of the present inner platform.

The quadrilateral Haram area is neither a true rectangle nor a parallelogram, and the same can probably be said of Herod's enclosure. Thus the archaeological investigation of the outside walls has been fruitful with regard to recovering the line of Herod's walls, and the traditional idea of the perfect square (as in Middoth) must be abandoned. But the inside of the sacred area is another matter. The cen-

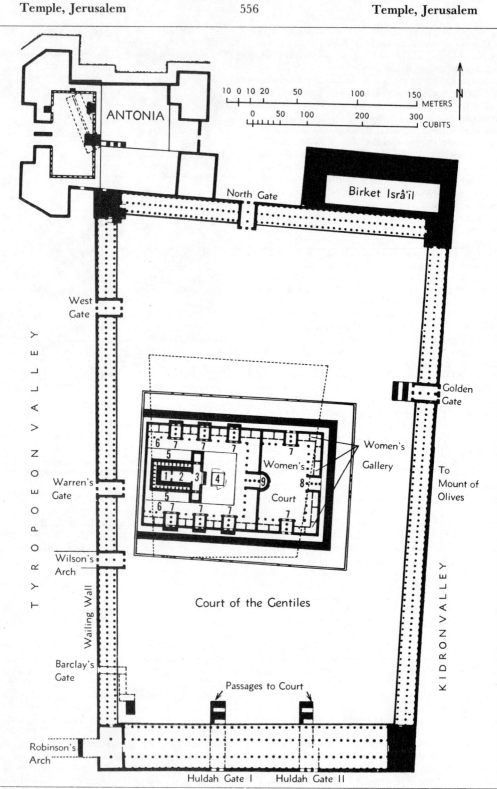

From Vincent and Steve, *Jerusalem de l'Ancien Testament* (Paris: J. Gabalda & Cie.)

34. Ground plan of Herod's temple and courts, based on Vincent-Steve: (1) holy of holies; (2) holy place; (3) porch; (4) altar of burnt offering; (5) court of priests; (6) court of Israel (men's court); (7) sanctuary gates; (8) Nicanor gate(?) or Gate Beautiful; (9) Nicanor gate

tral sanctuary has been completely changed, and what is there cannot be investigated very closely by scholars because of Muslim religious sensibilities. The Dome of the Rock bears no resemblance to Herod's temple. The only point in common is the sacred rock, which is now within the building, and may have been so in the buildings of Solomon, Zerubbabel, and Herod. The present raised platform around the inner sanctuary can only faintly suggest Herod's platform, which was different in size, shape, and orientation. Hence, for reconstruction of the sanctuary proper, recourse must be had to the literary sources and to comparative archaeology.

5. Attempts at reconstruction. Many have offered ground plans of the sacred enclosure; a few have attempted reconstruction of the building itself. Basic is the work of De Vogüé (1864), who presented both a ground plan of the area and a complete restoration of temple and environs in his magnificent folio publication. The restoration was deemed worthy of reproduction by Vincent and Steve in 1956. De Vogüé considered the Herodian area conterminous with the present Haram, Antonia being inserted into the NW corner. The plans of Vincent and Steve and the *Westminster Dictionary of the Bible* (1944) are similar, except that Antonia is outside the N wall, though contiguous to it. By contrast, *HDB* (1902), Hollis (1934), *Westminster Historical Atlas to the Bible* (rev. ed., 1956), *Harper's Bible Dictionary* (1952), and Simons (1952) suppose that Herod's N wall was S of the present N wall of the Haram, and thus that Antonia was some distance away, though connected by stairways; this is the view adopted here.

With regard to the placement of the sanctuary within the area there is a wide divergence of opinion. Here much depends on whether the sacred rock is supposed to have been under the adytum or the altar of sacrifice. One can only say with certainty that the building was near or over the rock, and that the entrance was toward the E.

The ground plan of the inner courts is controversial in details, though not in general conception. There was first the balustrade or fence, beyond which Gentiles could not go. Then a stairway on all sides except the W, then first on the E the large Women's Court, which all Jews could enter. Following that, at a slightly higher level, reached by a semicircular flight of steps, came the Court of Israel (i.e., Jewish men), perhaps surrounding the sanctuary on three sides. Finally, in front of and on both sides of the building was the Court of Priests. In the front part of this court were the altar in the center, the shambles on the right (N), and the laver on the left. Fig. TEM 34.

The ground plan of the sanctuary is little in question, since it was supposed to follow the traditional pattern set by Solomon, and apparently did so rather closely, except for the wider vestibule. There is little difference in reconstruction here all the way from De Vogüé to Watzinger and Vincent (Fig. TEM 29). Not so, however, is the situation with regard to the front face, or façade, of the building. The literary sources disagree as to size, and give no details of structure. De Vogüé shows a tetrastyle effect, with two pilasters at the sides of the entrance and two columns between, surmounted by a straight lintel or

From Parrot, *Le Temple de Jérusalem* (Neuchâtel: Delachaux & Niestlé)

35. A Bar Cocheba coin with a reproduction of the temple

architrave (without pediment) above. This conjecture is in the fashion of the fortress at 'Araq el-Emir (which also has "Herodian" masonry), and is somewhat similar to the much-discussed Bar Cocheba coin (Fig. TEM 35), which, however, may not represent the temple even schematically. Schick's offering (Figs. TEM 36-37) is quite incredible, being thoroughly un-Hellenistic and un-Roman. Watzinger's attempt (Fig. TEM 38), though based on excellent research, seems to go to the opposite extreme from that of Schick. The four columns, the great pediment, the smaller pediment over the door, the straight and simple lines—all are so reminiscent of the ordinary Greco-Roman temple that one wonders if perchance Herod did not take care to have something more distinctive, especially when the glowing quality of Josephus' description is considered. Incidentally, in support of a pedimented tetrastyle is the drawing on a fragment of glass from a Jewish catacomb of the third or fourth century A.D. (Fig. TEM 39). This drawing is usually cited in support of the free-standing feature of the pillars before Solomon's temple. The building represented is more likely that of Herod. Finally, attention may be called to the sketch of Vincent and Steve (Fig. TEM 40), also very simple in conception, but eliminating certain conventional Hellenistic-Roman features, such as pediment and tetrastyle. If Watzinger is too Hellenistic, perhaps Vincent and Steve are not quite enough so, but depend more on Anatolian and Mesopotamian analogies.

36. Herod's temple, front view, after Schick (1896)

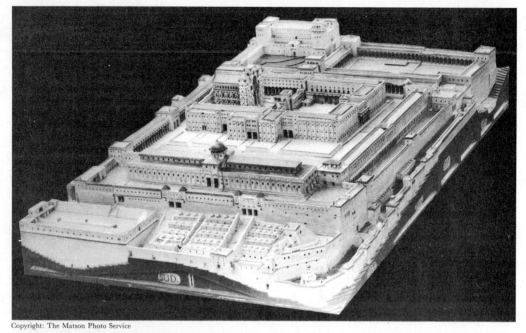

37. Reconstruction of Herodian temple area structures and arrangements, according to Schick

From Parrot, *Le Temple de Jérusalem* (Neuchâtel: Delachaux & Niestlé)

38. Reconstruction of the façade of Herod's temple, after Watzinger (1935)

Attention may be called to the golden eagle shown by both Watzinger and Vincent and Steve over the grand entrance to the vestibule. To Herod this was only a familiar feature of Hellenistic art, but to Jewish orthodoxy it was an outrage against the law, which prohibited images of any sort. Near the end of Herod's reign, when a report of his death had spread, a group of zealous students of the law, encouraged by two prominent teachers, invaded the temple area, had themselves lowered from the roof, and chopped down the offending image. The perpetrators and their teachers were executed, but the image was not restored, so far as we know (Jos. Antiq. XVII.vi.2-4; War I.xxxiii.2-4).

6. Summary and conclusion. By way of summary, it seems necessary only to point out again that Solomon and his architects determined the ground

plan of the sacred building itself from the prevailing temple styles of his day, and that this plan was maintained by Zerubbabel and Herod with little change. Herod greatly enlarged the temenos and surrounded it with the impressive system of porticoes or stoas in the Greek manner. Whether he also put a conventional Greek façade on the temple itself, or treated it more in the plain oriental manner, is still a problem for the reconstructionists, as noted above.

In connection with the destruction of the temple in A.D. 70, attention should be called to the Arch of

From Parrot, *Le Temple de Jérusalem* (Neuchâtel: Delachaux & Niestlé)

39. Glass fragment from Jewish catacomb showing the temple

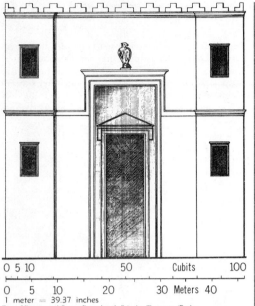

0 5 10   50   Cubits   100

0   5   10   20   30 Meters 40
1 meter = 39.37 inches
From Vincent and Steve, *Jerusalem de l'Ancien Testament* (Paris: J. Gabalda & Cie.), tome II

40. Front view of Herod's temple, after Vincent-Steve (1956)

Titus in Rome, upon which are sculptured some of the sacred objects taken from the temple (Fig. MUS 85): the golden lampstand, the golden table of the bread of the Presence with incense cups, two silver trumpets, and perhaps three tablets of the Law. These objects are depicted as being carried in the triumphal procession in honor of Titus (Jos. War VII.v.5). According to a later (and quite legendary) tradition, mentioned by Gibbon, and with which we may conclude, these objects (or at least the lampstand and the table) were deposited in the Temple of Peace. When Genseric sacked Rome in 455, he took the sacred objects to Carthage. In 533 Belisarius, the general of Justinian, took Carthage and transported the temple objects to Constantinople, where they were again displayed in a triumphal procession (in 534). Thence they were returned to a Christian church in Jerusalem, at or near the very spot from which they had been taken so long before. More realistic is the story that the objects fell or were thrown into the Tiber during the attack by Constantine in the year 312—and were never recovered.

Bibliography. Commentaries: ICC, *IB*, and HAT on relevant passages in I Kings, II Chronicles, and Ezekiel. M. Hadas, *Aristeas to Philocrates* (1951; Letter of Aristeas), pp. 13-15, 132-41.

The literature is vast. Among older works, see especially: M. De Vogüé, *Le Temple de Jérusalem* (1864): of small value for Solomon, basic for Herod. E. Robinson, *Biblical Researches in Palestine* (3rd ed., 1867), I, 238, 281-306; III, 163, 220-43: the permanent record of the famous visits of 1838 and 1852, including the discovery of "Robinson's Arch." C. W. Wilson and C. Warren, *The Recovery of Jerusalem* (1871): reports on the work of the Palestine Exploration Fund, "Wilson's Arch," etc. C. Warren, *Underground Jerusalem* (1876); shows some of the difficulties of early excavations undertaken by the Palestine Exploration Fund. C. Warren and C. R. Conder, *Jerusalem,* Survey of Western Palestine, vol. V (1884): a summary of the work of the Palestine Exploration Fund. B. Stade, "Der

Text des Berichtes über Salomos Bauten: 1 Kö. 5-7," *ZAW,* III (1883), 129-77; *Geschichte des Volkes Israel,* I (1887, in the series entitled *Allgemeine Geschichte,* ed. by W. Oncken), 311-43: the pioneer work on reconstruction of Solomon's building, with excellent plans, still useful. G. Perrot and C. Chipiez, *Histoire de l'Art dans l'Antiquité,* IV (1887), 159-338; remarkably artistic reconstructions, though somewhat confused historically. C. Schick, *Die Stiftshütte, der Tempel in Jerusalem und der Tempelplatz der Jetztzeit* (1896): based on assiduous and lifelong devotion to the subject, but historically confused, as noted above. I. Benzinger, *Hebräische Archäologie* (1st ed., 1894), pp. 239-49, 383-404: depends heavily on Stade; (3rd ed., 1927), pp. 211-19, 328-37: shows trend away from the use of Egyptian background. G. A. Smith, *Jerusalem,* II (1908), 48-82, 495-555: one of the best among the older popular works in English. C. R. Conder, *The City of Jerusalem* (1909): mostly concerned with history of the city, but the Frontispiece shows an oversimplified reconstruction of Herod's temple. M. Dieulafoy, "Le Rythme Modulaire du Temple de Salomon," in Académie des Inscriptions et Belles-Lettres, *Comptes Rendus* (1913), pp. 332-47: an important study of the use of triangulation in establishing the proportions of the temple. E. T. Richmond, *The Dome of the Rock* (1924), fig. 15: the best photograph of the sacred rock. G. B. Gray, *Sacrifice in the OT* (1925), pp. 133-47: supports the view that the adytum, not the altar, was over the sacred rock.

More recent literature: Among the work of L.-H. Vincent, see: *Underground Jerusalem* (1911); *Jérusalem Antique,* Recherches de Topographie, d'Archéologie et d'Histoire, vol. I (1912); "Jérusalem," in L. Pirot and A. Robert, *Dictionnaire de la Bible,* Supplément, IV (1949), 897-996; L.-H. Vincent and F.-M. Abel, *Jérusalem Nouvelle,* Recherches de Topographie, d'Archéologie et d'Histoire, vol. II (1914-26); L.-H. Vincent and A.-M. Steve, *Jérusalem de l'AT,* I (1954), 193-221, plates XIX, XLI, LIII; II-III (1956), 373-610, plates CI-CXLIX —particularly important. The articles of Vincent in *RB,* beginning *ca.* 1902 and continuing for more than half a century, should also be consulted to get the full force of this author's contribution. Among the works of K. Galling, whose total contribution to the modern understanding of the subject is great, see: "Tempel," *Religion in Geschichte und Gegenwart,* V (2nd ed., 1931), 1040-46; "Das Allerheiligste in Salomos Tempel," *JPOS,* XII (1932), 43-46; "Tempel in Palästina," *ZDPV,* LV (1932), 245-50; *Biblisches Reallexikon,* HAT, I (1937), 511-19; contribution to *Ezekiel,* HAT, vol. XIII (2nd ed., 1955). See also: W. Andrae, *Das Gotteshaus und die Urformen des Bauens im alten Orient* (1930), which served to turn attention from Egyptian to Mesopotamian backgrounds for the study of Solomon. A. Rowe and L.-H. Vincent, "New Light on the Evolution of Canaanite Temples," *PEQ* (1931), pp. 12-21. H. W. Hertzberg, "Der Heilige Fels und das AT," *JPOS,* XII (1932), 32-42. K. Möhlenbrink, *Der Tempel Salomos,* Beiträge zum Wissenschaft vom A und NT, Folge 4, Heft 7 (1932): a very useful work. H. Schmidt, *Der Heilige Fels in Jerusalem* (1933): Schmidt locates the rock under the adytum, in opposition to Hertzberg and others. F. J. Hollis, "The Sun-Cult and the Temple at Jerusalem," in S. H. Hooke, ed., *Myth and Ritual* (1933), pp. 87-110; *The Archaeology of Herod's Temple* (1934): an exhaustive study the value of which is much debated. G. Dalman, *Sacred Sites and Ways* (1935), pp. 285-308. C. Watzinger, *Denkmäler Palästinas,* I (1933), 88-95, Abb. 39; II (1935), 33-45, Abb. 25-28; *Handbuch der Archäologie,* I, in W. Otto, ed., Handbuch der Altertumswissenschaft, VI (1939), 805-15: Watzinger's ideas and reconstructions have been widely accepted. G. Loud, *Khorsabad,* I, Oriental Institute Publication XXXVIII (1936), especially fig. 98, for Assyrian parallels. C. W. McEwan, "The Syrian Expedition of the Oriental Institute of the University of Chicago," *AJA,* XLI (1937), 8-16: preliminary notice of the Tell Tainat (Tayinat) temple (see also *Oriental Institute Bulletin,* no. 1 [1937], p. 13). E. B. Smith, *Egyptian Architecture as Cultural Expression* (1938), pp. 147-85, for Egyptian parallels. R. B. Y. Scott, "The Pillars Jachin and Boaz," *JBL,* LVIII (1939), 143-49. V. Müller, "Types of Mesopotamian Houses," *JAOS,* LX

(1940), 151-80: an excellent summary of research from 1930 to 1940, with useful diagrams. W. Andrae, *Alte Feststrassen im Nahen Osten* (1941). H. G. May, "The Ark—A Miniature Temple," *AJSL*, LII (1936), 215-34; "The Two Pillars Before the Temple of Solomon," *BASOR*, 88 (1942), 19-27. W. F. Albright, "Two Cressets from Marisa and the Pillars of Jachin and Boaz," *BASOR*, 85 (1942), 18-27. G. E. Wright, "Solomon's Temple Resurrected," *BA*, IV (1941), 17-31; "The Temple of Solomon," *BA*, VII (1944), 73-77 (cf. 79-83). H. K. Eversull, *The Temples in Jerusalem* (1946): contains photographs of a number of plans and reconstructions. L. Waterman, "The Damaged 'Blueprints' of the Temple of Solomon," *JNES*, II (1943), 284-94; "The Treasuries of Solomon's Private Chapel," *JNES*, VI (1947), 161-63; further discussion with G. E. Wright, *JNES*, VII (1948), 53-55. J. L. Myers, "King Solomon's Temple and Other Buildings and Works of Art," *PEQ*, (1948), pp. 14-41. G. Contenau, *La Civilisation Phénicienne* (1949), pp. 140-52. C. C. Wylie, "On King Solomon's Molten Sea," *BA*, XII (1949), 86-90: discusses the cubit and the capacity of the "sea" (see further remarks in *JBL*, LXXVIII [1959], 75-77). C. G. Howie, "The East Gate of Ezekiel's Temple Enclosure and the Solomonic Gateway of Megiddo," *BASOR*, 117 (1950), 13-19. M. B. Rowton, "The Date of the Founding of Solomon's Temple," *BASOR*, 119 (1950), 20-22. J. Simons, *Jerusalem in the OT* (1952), pp. 1-59, 344-436: the most useful work in English, especially for Herod's temple, contrary to the title; excellent notes and bibliography. W. F. Albright, *Archaeology and the Religion of Israel* (1953), pp. 143-55. A.-G. Barrois, *Manuel d'Archéologie Biblique*, II (1953), 399-456. D. S. Robertson, *Handbook of Greek and Roman Architecture* (1954), pp. 70-105, for Greek parallels. R. Naumann, *Architektur Kleinasiens* (1955), pp. 338-432, for Anatolian and N Syrian parallels; good treatment of the Hilani house (reconstruction, p. 372). A. Parrot, *The Temple of Jerusalem*, Studies in Biblical Archaeology, no. 5 (1955): the best popular survey of all the Jerusalem temples. W. Corswant, *Dictionnaire d'Archéologie Biblique* (1956), pp. 289-95. Works by P. L. Garber, whose work is most helpful for an understanding of the Solomonic structure: "Reconstructing Solomon's Temple," *BA*, XIV (1951), 2-24; "A Reconstruction of Solomon's Temple," *Archaeology*, V (1952), 165-72; "Reconsidering the Reconstruction of Solomon's Temple," *JBL*, LXXVII (1958), 122-33, with comments by W. F. Albright and G. E. Wright; P. L. Garber and E. G. Howland, *Solomon's Temple: A Reconstruction* (1957). G. E. Wright, "The Stevens Reconstruction of the Solomonic Temple," *BA*, XVIII (1955), 41-44; *Biblical Archaeology* (1957), pp. 136-45. Y. Yadin, "The Third Season of Excavations at Hazor, 1957," *BA*, XXI (1958), 34-39; "The Fourth Season of Excavations at Hazor," *BA*, XXII (1959), 2-8: excavation of a temple similar in plan to that of Solomon. R. B. Y. Scott, "The Hebrew Cubit," *JBL*, LXXVII (1958), 205-14; "Weights and Measures of the Bible," *BA*, XXII (1959), 22-32.

Josephus: Editions of B. Niese and Loeb Classical Library; translations of Whiston, Bohn's Standard Library, and Loeb Classical Library.

Editions and translations of Middoth: *Mishnayoth*, standard editions, such as those of Wilna or Warsaw (1880 and later). O. Holtzmann, *Middot* (1913), in G. Beer and O. Holtzmann, eds., *Die Mischna*: text, German translation, and commentary. H. Danby, *The Mishnah* (1933), pp. 589-98: the standard English translation. I. Epstein, *The Babylonian Talmud, Seder Ḳodashim* (1948): another excellent translation. P. Blackman, *Mishnayoth*, V (1954), 503-33: text (not critical), English translation, and commentary.

References to the legend about the taking of the sacred objects of Herod's temple and their return to Constantinople and Jerusalem: E. Gibbon, *The Decline and Fall of the Roman Empire* (1st ed., 1776-81), chs. XXXVI, XLI. F. W. Far.ar, "Candlestick," in W. Smith, *Dictionary of the Bible*, I (American ed., 1880), 356. S. Reinach, *L'Arc de Titus et les Dépouilles du Temple de Jérusalem* (1890), pp. 22-26. T. Hodgkin,

"Vandals," *Encyclopaedia Britannica* (11th ed., 1911), XXVII, 884. H. Lamb, *Constantinople* (1957), pp. 130, 142.

W. F. STINESPRING

*TEMPLES. We are concerned here with those temples erected in Palestine, other than the Solomonic temple and the structures which were built in its place (*see* TEMPLE, JERUSALEM). Our chief sources of information are the Bible, which proceeds often by way of allusions, and the archaeological discoveries.

1. Definition and terminology
2. Canaanite and foreign temples
    a. Pre-Israelite
    b. After the Hebrew conquest
3. Hebrew sanctuaries and temples (those besides Jerusalem)
    a. The patriarchal era
    b. From the Hebrew conquest to the building of Solomon's temple
    c. From the building of Solomon's temple onward
Bibliography

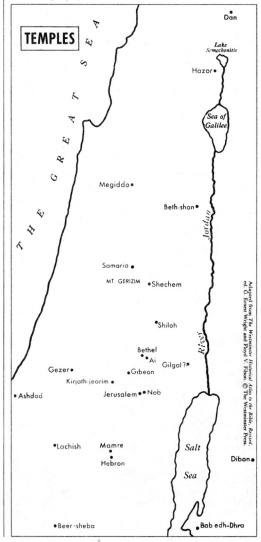

1. Definition and terminology. The word "temple," sporadically used in the English versions, specifically applies to man-made architectural structures built for the cult of God or the gods, as distinguished from the so-called high places, which normally do not consist of buildings of any sort except for an enclosure around the sacred territory (*see* BAMOTH; HIGH PLACE). This distinction, however, is somehow unessential. A temple may be erected in place of, or in connection with, or as a substitute for, an ancient high place. Meanwhile the basic concept remains the same—viz., that of a place where the god is believed to have manifested his presence and abiding virtue, and where men meet him in adoration and worship. Hence the Hebrews had no specific word for what we call "temple," but rather spoke of the "house" (בית, *bêth*) of such or such a deity. Solomon's temple is no exception. Its main hall is called in Hebrew היכל, *hêkāl,* a material transcription of the Sumerian *E-Gal,* which the Assyrians rendered by *bîtu rābu,* meaning "the Great House." The Hebrew expression בתי במות, *bātê bāmôth,* groups together the divine "houses" and the "bamoth" or "high places." The versions show a certain vagueness in their rendering; cf. the RSV "houses on high places" (I Kings 12:31), "houses of the high places" (I Kings 13:32), and "shrines of the high places" (II Kings 17:29, 32; 23:19).

2. Canaanite and foreign temples. We are especially concerned in this section with the temples and places of worship of the non-Hebrew population of Palestine, before and after the Conquest, excluding the sanctuaries related to the religion of Yahweh in its various forms. Most of the ancient temples of Canaan were connected with the religion of the Semites, although a few of them did belong to other cults. They are mentioned occasionally in the Bible, but never described in full; see, e.g., the references to the temple of El-berith in Shechem (Judg. 9:46), the temple or temples of Dagon in Ashdod and the Philistine districts (Judg. 16:23-30; I Sam. 5:2; I Chr. 10:10). In contrast with the scanty information from the texts, we are favored with an abundance of archaeological material. The identification of ruined buildings as temples, however, is always a delicate matter. It depends largely on considerations of plan and location, and still more on the examination of the objects found in the ruins. The structures

described in §§ 2*a-b below* may reasonably be regarded as temples and shrines. They are listed, as far as possible, in chronological order.

a. Pre-Israelite. The identification of a Chalcolithic structure from Megiddo (stratum XIX; *ca.* 3300-3000 B.C.) as a temple or shrine is possible, though by no means evident. It consists of a narrow hall with a row of stone bases along its longer axis, and a raised platform of adobe, which was subsequently remodeled. Fig. TEM 41.

The foundations of a small building discovered in the ruins of et-Tell, the biblical Ai, may be regarded with great probability as an ancient shrine or temple. It consisted of two rooms built against the inner facing of the city wall. Two steps gave admittance to a first room, rectangular in shape and measuring approximately twenty-five feet in width and eighteen feet in depth. A bench of masonry ran along two of its walls. Two earthenware stands, identifiable probably as incense burners, the ivory handle of a knife, jars and bowls of the Early Bronze Age, were found in this room; bones and ashes had been heaped in a corner. There is no evidence that a piece of charred wood lying in the middle of the room should be identified as part of an ASHERAH. It is just as probable that it was a post for supporting the roof. A narrow door opened into a second room of about the same size, but less regular in shape. In a corner of this room was a structure of masonry which has been described as an altar by archaeologists, although this is by no means certain. Fragments of Egyptian alabaster and stone vessels from the second or third

42. Shrine and altar at Ai (third millennium B.C.)

dynasty were found among remains of Early Bronze Age pottery. Miscellaneous refuse had been swept into three pits lined with stones. The building as a whole and its contents may be dated tentatively from the late phase of the Early Bronze Age (second half of the third millennium B.C.). Fig. TEM 42.

At Megiddo the remains of three temples were unearthed from stratum XV (Middle Bronze Age, *ca.* 1900 B.C.). Two of them stood side by side on the same alignment; the third was close to the first two, but at an angle. Each unit consists of a single room *ca.* forty to forty-five feet in width and twenty-seven to thirty feet in depth, with stone bases for the posts supporting the roof, and a raised rectangular platform against the back wall, where the image of the god presumably stood, and where offerings were

41. Shrine with large altar at Megiddo, Stratum XIX (*ca.* 3300-3000 B.C.)

placed before it. Four lateral steps led to the platform of the third unit. Each unit had a front portico of two columns. Close to the shrines and in obvious relation with them, a low enclosure surrounded a huge circular block of masonry, approximately thirty feet in diameter and more than six feet high, with a flight of steps leading to its top. A large amount of bones and ashes found in the enclosure offers good evidence that the structure thus described was an open-air altar for burnt offerings. Figs. ALT 20; MEG 27.

The ancient sanctuary of Gezer, often described as a "high place," consisted of an irregular row of eight rough pillars of stone unequal in size and in appearance, and ranging from approximately 5 to 10 feet in height. Their relation to the pavement of field stones which covered the area where they stood remains undefined. To the W of the row of pillars, but not toward its center, stood a large block of stone measuring about 6 by 5 feet and 2½ feet in height. The top of the block had been hollowed intentionally. This monument has been described often as an "altar," although it might have been equally well a pedestal for a statue or emblem, or a stand for placing offerings. Close to the pillars, in the layer of virgin soil above the rock and below the filling on which the pavement had been laid, the bodies of young children had been buried in earthenware jars. A natural cave in the rock E of the row of pillars contained another burial, while a circular pit nearby had been filled with miscellaneous potsherds, some

43. The alignment of standing stones of the "high place" at Gezer

of them dating from the Late Bronze Age (*ca.* 1500 B.C.), and a crude bronze figurine representing a serpent. The organic relationship of all these things to the row of pillars has not been conclusively established. It is about certain, however, that the pillars could not possibly have been meant as functional elements of an architectural structure, such as pillars to support the beams of a roof. They can be regarded most likely as good examples of the raised stones which we know from literary sources to have been characteristic elements of the early Semitic places of worship (*see* PILLAR). Unfortunately, defective tech-

niques used in the excavation of Gezer (in 1902) and the inadequacy of archaeological recordings leave us much in the dark as to the age and detailed interpretation of the so-called "high place." Dates ranging from the end of the Early Bronze Age to the Late Bronze Age have been advanced. (Fig. TEM 43.) A temple of Byblos on the Phoenician coast, dating from the Middle Bronze Age, with a row of raised stones in the rear of a two room shrine, constitutes thus far the closest analogy.

A shrine from the second half of the Middle Bronze Age (from 1800 B.C. onward) was discovered at Nahariya, five miles N of Acre. It consists of a long stone building at the E end of which was a small square room. The vestibule at the W entrance of the main hall seems to have been added at a later date. Several incense burners, miscellaneous pottery, a silver figurine representing a female deity, and clay figurines of doves, usually associated with the worship of Ishtar, were found in disorder among the ruins.

One of the buildings on the acropolis of Shechem has been recognized for a temple, with great probability. Its foundation rests on an artificial platform dating from the latter phase of the Middle Bronze Age (*ca.* 1800 B.C.). The building, which has unusually thick walls, is a rectangular hall of *ca.* thirty-three by forty feet divided into three aisles by columns, the stone bases of which were found in place. A little porch gave admittance to the hall. Great caution must be exercised in the evaluation of the detailed reports by the early explorers of Shechem. A re-examination of the ruins by G. E. Wright in 1956 would suggest a date possibly as low as the Late Bronze Age, and the possible identification of the shrine with the temple of El-berith or Baal-berith, referred to in Judg. 9:46.

A temple of Lachish, rebuilt several times, was discovered in a filled-in section of the ancient fosse which surrounded the ramparts of the city in the Middle Bronze Age. The original building had been in use from *ca.* 1475 to 1400 B.C. It consisted of a rectangular shrine, approximately fifteen feet in width and thirty feet in depth, with a square antechamber and a small room on one side. There was a long, narrow bench of adobe along the back wall of the sanctuary, with three small platforms which may have been used as altars or as the bases of stands for placing offerings. Two large jars were buried in the ground in front of the median "altar." The building, which shows no trace of violent destruction, was subsequently enlarged in such a way that the elaborate altarlike structures of shrines No. 2 and 3 were superposed over the bench of the early sanctuary. Shrine No. 2 was in use from *ca.* 1400 to 1325 B.C. In the main room, roughly square (slightly more than thirty feet in each dimension), were the stone foundations of the four pillars which had once supported the roof. A stone bench and a square altar with a hearth were built against the back wall, while long, narrow "tables" of adobe ran parallel to the three other walls. There were similar tables in an annex in the rear of the sanctuary. Numerous earthenware vessels had been buried—intentionally, so it seems—in the layer of earth between the floor of shrine No. 1 and the pavement of shrine No. 2.

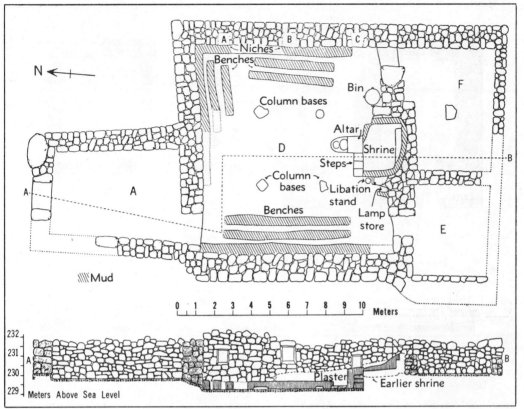

44. Plan for the temple at Lachish, Structure III (*ca.* 1350-1225 or 1200 B.C.).

Shrine No. 3 appears to be a mere remodeling of No. 2. An elaborate altar with three lateral steps stood on a broad adobe platform built against the back wall. There were two hearths in front of the altar, right and left of which respectively stood an earthenware stand and a large four-handled jar. Tables similar to those of shrine No. 2 ran in a double row along three sides of the room. Abundant pottery of the Late Bronze Age, jars, cups, bowls, and Cypriote water bottles, together with objects of ivory and of metal, were found in the sanctuary, its annexes, and the surrounding area. Some objects in this miscellany are of a specifically religious character—viz., a bronze figurine representing the Syrian god Reshef, gold leaves embossed with the figure of a female deity, and fragments from several earthenware stands usually found in the ruins of temples and places of worship. The sanctuary of Lachish was destroyed by fire toward the end of the Late Bronze Age, possibly when Merenptah raided Palestine in 1223 B.C. Fig. TEM 44.

A large building of Megiddo, identified as a temple, adds little to our information. Its thick walls, like those of a fortress, and its extremely simple plan —a single rectangular room, deeper than wide, with an entrance porch flanked by what seems to have been the foundations of two square towers—make it a striking replica of the temple of Shechem described above. The stratum in which it belongs dates from the fourteenth-thirteenth century B.C. Fig. TEM 45.

The excavation of Beth-shan has brought to light the remains of several temples built in succession like those of Lachish. The dates proposed at first, on the assumption of historical synchronisms deducted from Egyptian seals and scarabs discovered in the ruins, had to be lowered by a century or two, when a more accurate knowledge of the stratification of the site could be obtained. It is a fact, however, that Egyptian influences are most conspicuous in the architecture and the archaeological material of the temple, presumably on account of the intermittent occupation of the city by Egyptian armed forces from the Eighteenth to the Twentieth Dynasty. The architecture of the earliest temple, which would be more aptly described as a complex of open-air courtyards divided once by adobe walls, of which only the foundations and lower courses were left, shows little or no organic unity. The sanctuary was dedicated to Mekal, god of Beth-shan, as we learn from a stele of limestone where the god is represented with features borrowed from the iconography of Reshef, god of lightning, otherwise identified with the Egyptian god Seth (*see* ART § 2*b*). We have here an interesting instance of religious syncretism, when the Egyptian overlords vowed to the local deity as well as the indigenous population. Various structures and objects found in the sacred area were specifically related to religious worship—namely, a raised basalt stone on a platform of adobe, a stepped altar, and several trays or tables of basalt, together with miscellaneous

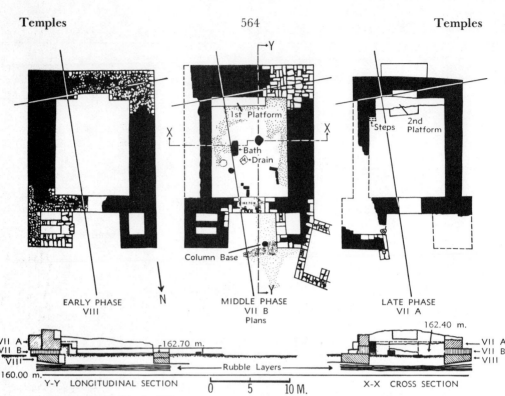

Courtesy of the Oriental Institute, the University of Chicago

45. **Phases of Late Bronze Age temple at Megiddo** (Strata VIII, VIIB, VIIA, fourteenth-thirteenth centuries B.C.; *ca.* 1400-1150)

vessels and figurines of a mythological character. A panel of basalt, representing the fight of a lion and a mastiff, was found nearby, but its relation to the sanctuary cannot be proved conclusively. *See* ART § 2*b*.

The stratum in which the buildings and objects just described were discovered dates from the fourteenth century B.C. In the course of the following century a small temple was built to replace the ancient sanctuary of Mekal. It consisted of a hall more wide than deep, with benches of adobe along the walls, and an altar. The stone bases of two columns for supporting the beams of the roof were found in their original position. Various objects found in the temple show that it was dedicated to Mekal and his consort.

Temple No. 3, dating from the twelfth century B.C., is very similar to the preceding temple, with, however, more regularity. Both structures show a striking analogy to the Egyptian shrines of the el-Amarna period. Fig. TEM 46.

Toward the eleventh century B.C., twin temples were built, differing from the earlier structures both by their orientation and by their plan.* Like the temples of Lachish, they were disposed in depth and divided by columns into three aisles, the central aisle being presumably higher than the others, for lighting purposes. In each temple, steps led from the central aisle to the altar platform. The N temple was dedicated to a female deity, presumably the Canaanite 'Anath, identified with her Egyptian counterpart, Antit, whose features are seen on a small stele discovered in the temple. The S temple continued to be the "house" of Mekal-Reshef. Earthenware offer-

ing stands and models of temples decorated with naked human figures, snakes, and birds, were found in the whole area. It is possible, and even probable,

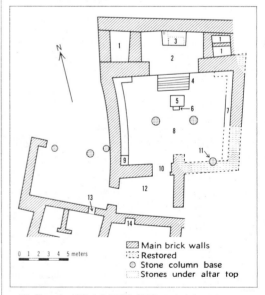

46. Temple of Seti I (1302-1290 B.C.): (*a*) store room; (*b*) altar room; (*c*) upper altar (brick); (*d*) steps leading to upper altar (brick); (*e*) lower altar (brick); (*f*) small stone; (*g*) mastaba (brick); (*h*) sanctuary; (*i*) high ledge; (*j*) entrance; (*k*) column base (doubtless from southern temple of Ramses X); (*l*) anteroom; (*m*) door; (*n*) niche

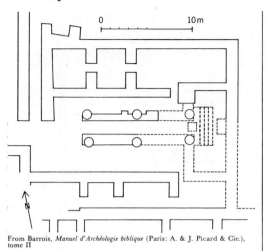

0   10m

From Barrois, *Manuel d'Archéologie biblique* (Paris: A. & J. Picard & Cie.), tome II

47. Beth-shan: plan of temple no. 5, the S temple (eleventh century B.C.)

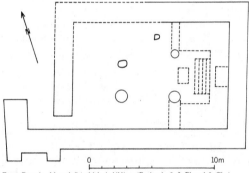

0   10m

From Barrois, *Manuel d'Archéologie biblique* (Paris: A. & J. Picard & Cie.), tome II

48. Beth-shan: plan of temple no. 4, the N temple (eleventh century B.C.)

that the twin temples of the eleventh century are those mentioned in the Bible as the temple of Ashtaroth (I Sam. 31:10) and the temple of Dagon (I Chr. 10:10), in reference to the exposition of the armor (or head) of Saul after he fell on Mount Gilboa. The substitution of Dagon for Mekal is probably due to the fact that Saul was defeated by the Philistines, and that the cult of Dagon, an old Canaanite deity, was popular in the Philistine districts. Figs. TEM 47-48.

The recent excavation of Hazor has led to the discovery of two Canaanite temples built in succession at the foot of the ancient earth wall of the city. It is best here to quote from the (provisional) report of Yigael Yadin, director of the Rothschild Expedition. The "Holy of Holies" contained "a basalt sculpture of a male (deity?), seated on a throne, holding a cup. A row of several stelae, with rounded tops, was placed just left of the sculpture.* All of these were devoid of reliefs, except for the central one which bears a very effective and simple design: two upstretched hands in prayer fashion, below the emblem of the deity—a crescent and a sun-disk within. The whole row was flanked by a basalt orthostat, bearing the head and forelegs of a lion on its narrow side, and a relief of a crouching lion—its tail coming up

from between its hind legs, on its wide side." On the basis of the many vessels found in place together with the sculptures and the clear stratification of the temple, Yadin predicates a date in the thirteenth century, or possibly the end of the fourteenth century B.C. Figs. TEM 49; ALT 21.

Courtesy of the American Schools of Oriental Research

49. Statue and stelae in the Late Bronze Canaanite temple at Hazor

b. After the Hebrew conquest. Canaanite cults continued normally in regions or single localities in which the Israelites were not able to establish themselves. The biblical records even suggest that many local shrines and high places remained open and retained a considerable popularity in districts completely subjugated, because of the complacency and at times the approval of the kings of Israel and Judah.

Several rooms on the acropolis of Megiddo (stratum V *a; ca.* 1000 B.C.) contained an unusual number of articles usually associated with Canaanite worship, such as small altars of limestone, offering stands, and incense burners. The religious destination of these rooms seems probable, but it is difficult to recognize in them a definite architectural formula. Two raised pillars of stone in a passage may have had a cultic significance, although they may have been mere supports for a lintel.

The texts give practically no information on the Canaanite and foreign temples of Palestine under the monarchy, and archaeological evidence is scarce. The Moabitic shrine at Dhībān (excavated in 1956) was found to be part of a palace-temple compound, and contained several utensils usually associated with Semitic religious worship.

Cults akin to the old Canaanite religion survived long in the cultures of neighboring countries, such as the districts of Transjordan controlled toward the beginning of the Christian era by the NABATEANS. The exploration of their places of worship proved most valuable for a better understanding of West Semitic cults and temples. It appears that open-air "high places" may have been used simultaneously with temple buildings. This is most probably the case at Petra. The high place on the summit of the Zibb 'Atuf is best preserved. It consists of a carefully leveled area accessible from the canyon of the Wadi Musa by means of stairs cut in the sandstone of the cliffs. A square block with free steps has been interpreted as an altar for burnt offerings. The victims were slain and prepared on a rocky platform left of the altar; the water necessary for the service was stored in vats dug out of the rock. Another open-air place of worship had a circular processional area around a rock presumably regarded as sacred. Pottery and coins make it clear that it was still in use in the first century of the Christian era. It is highly probable that the monuments known as el-Khazneh, in the upper canyon, and ed-Deir, at the head of a gully NW of the city, were temples, and not tombs, as it was believed. Their impressive façades had been carved out of the sandstone of the cliff. Unfortunately, they had been thoroughly emptied long before archaeologists discovered them, and the rare objects discovered in the vicinity did not add anything to our knowledge of these monuments.

The Nabatean site of the Djebel Ramm, NE of the Gulf of Aqaba, offers a good example of the duplication of a high place by a temple. The open-air sanctuary was located on a narrow cornice of rock at the foot of a high vertical cliff, and was approached from the valley floor by a steep footpath. The water of a spring was collected in a rock-cut basin, and votive inscriptions to Allat, a lunar deity, and Dusharra, a sun-god invoked here as "lord of the house," had been engraved in a long row along the cliff. The valley temple corresponding to the rock sanctuary was a square-shaped building adorned with columns. Inscriptions of a votive character in Nabatean cursive script had been written with a reed pen on the stuccoed and painted wall panels. The temple dates from the beginning of the second Christian century.

The duality of high place and temple is not equally apparent in the Nabatean sanctuary of Khirbet et-tannur, on the ridge of the Transjordanian plateau, S of the Wadi el-Hesa. The building was remodeled several times, the latest restoration dating from the end of the first century of our era.

It would be futile to venture an over-all theory on the functional difference between a high place and a temple on such insufficient premises. However, the exploration of the Nabatean places of worship makes it plain that the relationship between these two types of sanctuaries is not one of anteriority and posteriority, as if a regular temple would sooner or later supplant an ancient high place, the high place getting out of use as soon as the temple has been built.

In W Palestine, Herod and the tetrarchs built a series of shrines and temples in which the syncretistic tendencies of the art and religion of the Near East in Hellenistic and Roman times are clearly seen, such as the temple of Derketo, a female deity worshiped in Ashkelon, birthplace of Herod; the temple of Augustus on the hilltop of Samaria-Sebaste; and similar politico-religious foundations at Caesarea Philippi and Tiberias. These buildings are scarcely germane to a study of the development of Semitic sanctuaries in biblical Palestine.

3. Hebrew sanctuaries and temples (those besides Jerusalem). It must be kept in mind that a considerable interval of time elapsed between the first appearance of the Hebrew nomads, or semi-nomads, led by their patriarchs, the conquest of Palestine by Joshua, and the establishment of the monarchy. Thus the foundation of the temple of Jerusalem by Solomon is a relatively recent event in the whole history of the Hebrews, and it is almost inconceivable that their religious cult would not have materialized long before in places of worship and eventually in regional shrines or temples. Archaeological information concerning these is utterly lack-

ing, but biblical references make it possible to outline the history of the places of worship of the Hebrews in Palestine prior to the foundation of the Solomonic temple, as well as to follow some later developments of the Yahweh cult, which resulted in the establishment of sanctuaries adjudged heretical by the official body of priests attached to the temple of Jerusalem.

a. The patriarchal era. The book of Genesis lists the places where the patriarchs worshiped on the soil of Palestine. In each instance God is believed to have manifested himself to the founder or founders of the sanctuary, which consisted, as a rule, of an open-air area akin to the high places of the Canaanites, with the usual combination of sacred tree or trees, raised stones, and eventually an altar and a well or reserve of water. *See* HIGH PLACE; PILLAR.

The sancuary at SHECHEM (3), founded by the patriarchs by the oak of Moreh, had a stone altar (Gen. 12:6-7; 33:20). Jacob's well, mentioned in John 4:5-6, was in close relation to the place. The sanctuary of BETHEL, which is at the origin of the national shrine of the N kingdom, goes back to Abraham, who built there an altar (Gen. 12:8). It owes its very name ("house of El") to the stone pillar erected by Jacob as a mark of the divine presence which had revealed itself in this place (Gen. 28:18-22). The erection of such monuments is a distinctive feature of the narratives of the Jacob cycle. The manifestation of God to Abraham by the oaks of MAMRE resulted in the creation of a sanctuary which is not explicitly mentioned in the Bible, although its memory was kept alive in popular traditions to the days of Herod the Great, who built a monumental enclosure around what was believed to be the sacred area. The sanctuary by the wells of BEER-SHEBA marked the S limit of the territory where the patriarchs had dwelt. Abraham had planted there a tree (Gen. 21:33), and Isaac had built an altar (Gen. 26:25).

Although these sanctuaries of the patriarchs are not, strictly speaking, temples, in the sense of temple buildings, the narratives in which their foundations are recorded contain valuable information concerning the Hebrews' idea of the essential requirements for the foundation of a place of worship, from a theological point of view as well as with regard to the liturgical expression given to basic beliefs. Furthermore, some at least of these places of worship founded and visited by the patriarchs were to develop in later times into most popular shrines and sanctuaries.

b. From the Hebrew conquest to the building of Solomon's temple. The books of the Bible covering the history of the Israelites from the conquest of Palestine by Joshua to the establishment of the royal sanctuary in Jerusalem tend to project the state of affairs prevailing in the time of their composition back upon the period immediately following the Conquest, when the tribes settled on Canaanite soil and gradually adjusted themselves to the conditions of sedentary life. Now the exclusive monopoly of the temple of Jerusalem had become for the authors of the historical books a political as well as a religious dogma, which they traced back to the prophetic utterances of Moses. They were, of course, hard put to reconcile their views with historical reality, confronted as they were with the existence, not of one national place of worship prior to the reign of Solomon, but of several local sanctuaries. Figs. HIG 22-23.

The existence of these places of worship was duly acknowledged by the biblical authors, who were reticent on the tribal origins, or eventually on the Canaanite background, of provincial sanctuaries. The apparent conflict of the historical facts with the theory of the one sanctuary designated or to be designated by God was tentatively solved in three ways: (*a*) Such religious centers as Shechem and Gilgal (*see* GILGAL 1) were regarded chiefly as national memorials, respectively of Joshua's crossing of the Jordan (Josh. 4:19-24) and of the solemn liturgy of blessings and curses allegedly prescribed by Moses and conducted by Joshua (Deut. 27; Josh. 8:30-35), the latter occasion being considered as a particular event in the life of the people, and not as an institution to be repeated periodically, although various biblical references might support the second alternative, at least as a likely hypothesis. (*b*) The early centers of worship of the Israelites in Canaan were regarded as transitional between the period of the desert, when the tribes had the TABERNACLE of Moses at their national shrine, and the establishment of the royal sanctuary. (*c*) The same provincial sanctuaries were legitimized by the fact or the assumption that the ARK OF THE COVENANT had been housed in them at some time or other, or, if not the ark, at least some pieces from the furnishings of the tabernacle.

Our knowledge of these sanctuaries rests entirely on textual evidence from the Bible, short of archaeological confirmation. The first in date, according to the order of their appearance in the narratives of the books of Samuel, Kings, and Chronicles, is the sanctuary of SHILOH, in the territory of Ephraim. It consisted of a temple building, in which the ark had been placed, prior to its being carried away as war booty by the Philistines. Valuable details on the temple of Shiloh as a center of pilgrimage, on its ritual, and of its college of priests, officially a branch of the Levitic order, may be gathered from I Sam. 1; 3.

NOB (I Sam. 21:1-6), on the E slopes of the Mount of Olives, in the time when Jerusalem was still in the hands of the Jebusites, had also a small temple served by Levitic priests. The text makes reference to a table for bread offerings, believed to be the very table of the showbread of the tabernacle. *See* BREAD OF THE PRESENCE.

KIRIATH-JEARIM, one of the four cities of the Gibeonites which formed an enclave in Israelite territory (Josh. 9:17), had been an indigenous—i.e., Canaanite—place of worship, as may be inferred from its aliases: Baalah, Baale-Judah, Kiriath-Baal. It housed the ark of the covenant after it was recovered from the Philistines, and turned into a Yahwistic holy place, for some twenty years; the mention of Eleazar's being consecrated to have charge of the ark is probably aimed at removing the objectionability of the place, in the eyes of priests (I Sam. 7:1-2).

GIBEON itself, an ancient Canaanite high place, is mentioned in relation with Solomon's offering of sacrifices prior to the building of the temple (I Kings 3:4-5), and is credited with the custody of the tabernacle and its bronze altar (I Chr. 21:29; II Chr. 1:3, 5).

The historical books of the Bible assume, of course, that the official cult ceased in these various sanctuaries as soon as the temple of Jerusalem was open for worship.

c. From the building of Solomon's temple onward. It may be surmised from incidental passages of the Bible, chiefly from the prophetical books, that at least some of the provincial sanctuaries of the Israelites continued in competition with the temple, just as Canaanite and foreign cults and places of worship had defied every effort of the Jerusalem priestly circles to uproot them. It is also most likely that the distinction between the surviving centers of worship of the Israelites and the local shrines of the Canaanites became less and less perceptible.

The Bible gives some incomplete, yet valuable, information on two Hebrew sanctuaries regarded as heretical in the religious circles of Jerusalem. The first one is the sanctuary of Laish-Dan, by the spring of the Jordan at Tell el-Qadi. The story of the foundation of the sanctuary (Judg. 18) makes it plain that the cult rendered there was that of an adulterated form of Yahwism, as divine images were being used. Its personnel claimed Levitic origins. The choice of the place, however, suggests an undefined relation to local cults—namely, that of the Baal of Mount Hermon, and of the anonymous deity worshiped in the grotto of Baniyās (Caesarea Philippi), and subsequently identified with the Greek god Pan.

The other dissident sanctuary is that of BETHEL. While its first origin can be traced back to the time of the patriarchs (*see* § 3*a above*), it is represented as a recent foundation of Jeroboam (I Kings 12:28-33), and it became in fact the national shrine of the kingdom of Israel, rival of the temple of Jerusalem. The anniversary of its foundation was celebrated on the full moon of the eighth month of the year, to offset the popularity of the Feast of Tabernacles, observed in Jerusalem on the fifteenth of the seventh month. The Levitic origin of the Bethel priesthood is categorically denied by I Kings 12:31. Most objectionable to the Jerusalem priestly circles was the erection in the temple of Bethel of a golden calf (*see* CALF, GOLDEN). It does not seem, however, that the "golden calves" were really idols, but rather parts of the pedestal or throne of the deity, as is suggested by the religious iconography of West Asia during the first millennium B.C., which shows the gods standing on some animal figures. The "calf" of Bethel was involved in the same reprobation as Aaron's golden calf (Exod. 32:4), in the eyes of the Jerusalem priesthood as well as of the prophets, and became the symbol of heresy. Reference is made to a similar figure set by Jeroboam in the temple of Dan (I Kings 12:29-30), although the cult at Dan is reported to have ceased at the time when Shiloh was ruined in the days of Samuel (Judg. 18:31). The cliché "from Dan to Beer-sheba," meaning all of Palestine from N to S, may be accountable for the tradition of another "calf" being worshiped at Beer-sheba. Amos mentions the cult at Beer-sheba with reprobation (Amos 5:5; 8:14).

Later sanctuaries had some indirect connections with the religion of Yahweh. Such is the temple of the SAMARITANS, on Mount Gerizim. It was turned by Antiochus Epiphanes into a temple of Ζεύς Ξένιος (167 B.C.), while the temple of Jerusalem was dedicated to Ζεύς 'Ολύμπιος, possibly at the request of strong local parties desirous to Hellenize every institution, including religion (II Macc. 6:1-2; Jos. Antiq. XIII.v.5). The Samaritan temple was destroyed by Hyrcanus in 108 B.C. (Jos. Antiq. XIII.x.2-3; War I.vii.7), and rebuilt, possibly under Hadrian, in honor of Ζεύς "Υψιστος.

Outside Palestine, a Judeo-Aramaic colony which had left the mother country toward the seventh century B.C. had founded a temple at Elephantine in Upper Egypt, where they worshiped Yahweh jointly with other gods. *See* ELEPHANTINE PAPYRI.

According to Josephus (Antiq. XIII.iii.1-2; x.4; xiii.1-2; XIV.viii.1; War I.ix.4; VII.x.3), a party of Jewish refugees in Egypt was granted by Ptolemy VI Philometor (181-145 B.C.) the use of an ancient temple in Leontopolis in the Delta, where they instituted an unofficial Yahweh cult.

See WORSHIP IN THE OT.

Bibliography. General: K. Galling, *Biblisches Reallexikon* (1937), cols. 511-16. G. A. Barrois, *Manuel d'Archéologie Biblique*, II (1953), 342-75.

Detailed information on ancient temples discovered in W Palestine can be gathered from the following, arranged in the order in which they are discussed herein: G. Loud, *Megiddo II: Seasons 1935-1939* (1948; quoted repeatedly; see Index at the end of the volume of text). J. Marquet-Krause, "La deuxième campagne de fouilles à Ay," *Syria*, XVI (1935), 330-33. R. A. S. Macalister, *The Excavation of Gezer II* (1912), pp. 381-406. I. Ben-Dor, "A Middle Bronze Age Temple at Nahariya," *QDAP*, 14 (1950), 1-41. O. Tufnell, C. I. Inge, and L. Harding, *Lachish II: The Fosse Temple* (1940). A. Rowe, *Beth Shan Topography and History* (1930); *The Four Canaanite Temples of Beth Shan I* (1940). Y. Yadin, "Excavations at Hazor," *BA*, XIX (1956), 2-12. G. Dalman, *Petra und seine Felsheiligtumer* (1908).

Concerning the places of worship of the Hebrews in the patriarchal age, see E. Dhorme, *La Religion des Hébreux Nomades* (1937).

On the dedication of the Jerusalem and Gerizim to Jupiter, see E. Bikermann, *Der Gott der Makkabäer* (1937), pp. 92-94.

On the cult and temple of Elephantine, see A. Vincent, *La religion des Judéo-Araméens d'Eléphantine* (1937).

G. A. BARROIS

TEMPT [πειράζω, ἐκπειράζω; נסה]; TEMPTATION [πειρασμός; מסה]. To test, try, put to the proof. "Tempt" and "temptation" are used in the Bible characteristically of the testing of man or of God.

In the OT, a wide variety of things can be tested: a sword (I Sam. 17:39), a reputation (I Kings 10:1; II Chr. 9:1, for wisdom), or convictions (Dan. 1:12, 14). But the most characteristic use is of God's testing man, or man's testing God. God tests individuals (Abraham [Gen. 22:1]; Hezekiah [II Chr. 32:31]) and nations (Israel [Exod. 15:25; Deut. 33:8]). God's purpose in this is clearly stated in Deut. 8:2: "You shall remember all the way which the LORD your God has led you . . . , testing you to know what was in your heart, whether you would keep his commandments, or not." God's testing is always for the good end of exposing loyalty and disloyalty, faith and unbelief, for what they are; it is never an enticement to evil. God's testing could include exposing false prophets for the liars they were (I Kings 22:21-23),

or permitting Satan to afflict Job (Job 1:6-22; 2:1-7). Later writers of sacred history were careful to revise their story to make it clear that Satan, and not God, entices men to evil (cf. I Chr. 21:1 with II Sam. 24:1).

In the NT, God still tests men's faith and understanding (cf. Jesus' testing Philip [John 6:6]). He still permits human (Matt. 16:1; etc.) and superhuman (I Thess. 3:5) agents to test men.

Perhaps the typical "temptation," the inner core of all forms of testing, is the enticement to apostasy found in persecution (I Pet. 4:12). This understanding of temptation underlies the petition in the Lord's Prayer: "Lead us not into temptation" (Matt. 6:13). But, like the OT saint, the Christian knows that it is not God who entices him to evil, but his own desires that produce sin (Jas. 1:12-15); he also knows that God will not let him be tempted beyond his strength (I Cor. 10:13).

Jesus has "in every respect . . . been tempted as we are" (Heb. 4:15), and this enables him to help us in our temptations (2:18). Even when we fall, he acts as our High Priest, and we receive forgiveness in him (Col. 1:12-13; Heb. 4:14-16). His victory over the powers of evil is final and representative (Col. 2:13-15); though "the whole world is in the power of the evil one" (I John 5:19), Christ shares his victory with his people, who have been "delivered . . . from the dominion of darkness and transferred . . . to the kingdom of [God's] beloved Son" (Col. 1:13).

In both OT and NT, men put God to the test—i.e., seek to discover whether his purposes are good and merciful. But while God has cause to test the faith and loyalty of fickle men, man has no ground whatever to test God, whose purposes are ineluctably gracious and loving. Testing God is thus tantamount to an assertion of unbelief, and it is always condemned, both in the OT (cf. Ps. 95, etc.) and in the NT (Ananias and Sapphira [Acts 5:9]; Peter's plea for the Gentiles [Acts 15:10; I Cor. 10:9]). It was the core of the temptation which Jesus resisted in the wilderness (Matt. 4:7).   J. MARSH

TEMPTATION OF JESUS. The forty-day period of testing in the wilderness where Jesus, led by the Spirit, was tempted by the devil (Mark 1:12-13; Matt. 4:1-11; Luke 4:1-13; Heb. 2:18; 4:15; *see* JESUS CHRIST). The Greek verb πειράζω, "tempt," means "to try" or "to test." This testing may have a good intent, to prove the true nature of a person; or an evil intent, to incite a person to sin.

Jesus, as SON OF GOD and Messiah, was both tried and tempted. According to Jewish thought, a man of God could prove his faith through trials. Empowered by the Spirit, which came upon him at baptism, Jesus faced and defeated his adversary. The writer of the Letter to the Hebrews declares that Jesus is able to help and sympathize with others because he was tempted in every respect but without sin (4:15).

The Gospel of John omits the Temptation, but the other gospels agree on five points: (*a*) that Jesus faced temptation (*b*) in the wilderness (*c*) for forty days; (*d*) that he was directed by the Spirit and (*e*) enticed by Satan. Mark's brief and starkly pictorial story alone mentions wild beasts and omits the fasting of Jesus. Matthew and Luke present a dramatic dialogue between Jesus and the devil (*see* SATAN), in which three plausible proposals by the devil are decisively rejected by Jesus with quotations from Deuteronomy (6:13, 16; 8:3). As Son of God, he refused to use his powers to foster living by bread alone, to test God by a specious miraculous leap, or to surrender his complete loyalty to God.

The narratives of the Temptation are variously understood:

a) The accounts are said to be autobiographical. Only Jesus could have told his experiences to his disciples to illustrate his messianic mission. This is possible, though Jesus seldom is autobiographical in his teaching. Moreover, the literary forms of these stories indicate reflective thought about Jesus rather than reports of Jesus.

Courtesy of Denis Baly

50. Monastery of the Temptation, showing the cultivation in the Jordan Valley below with the wilderness in the background

b) The narratives are said to be devout imaginative illustrations intended to show that the Son of God faced decisions about his use of supernatural power before he began his public ministry; that he found in the Scriptures an arsenal and aid; that he rejected a faith founded on sensational appeals to God; that he endured a testing season of solitude and fasting; and that he was victor over the deceptive assaults of Satan.

c) A third theory is that the events, in which Jesus shows victory over the devil and his demonic powers, act as a prologue for Jesus' public ministry.

Fig. TEM 50.

Bibliography. W. J. Foxell, *The Temptation of Jesus* (1920); J. Vogels, "Die Versuchungen Jesu," *BZ* (1926), pp. 238-55; E. Fascher, *Jesus und der Satan* (1949); F. C. Grant, *Introduction to NT Thought* (1950), pp. 207-11; W. F. Arndt and F. W. Gingrich, *A Greek-English Lexicon of the NT* (1957), p. 646.   D. M. BECK

***TEN COMMANDMENTS.** The summary statement of the covenant requirements between Yahweh and Israel, consisting primarily of prohibitions. The term is derived from Exod. 34:28 (see also Deut. 4:13; 10:4), where Moses is commanded to write the Ten Commandments (lit., "ten words") on two tables of stone. The Ten Commandments, or the Decalogue, have been of inestimable significance for the history and development of contemporary religious and cultural existence. They have been called the Magna Charta of the social order.

1. Outline of contents
   a. Historical-theological prologue, Exod. 20:1-2
   b. Man's relation to God, Exod. 20:3-12
   c. Man's relation to his neighbor, Exod. 20:13-17
2. Literary examination
   a. Various versions of the Ten Commandments
   b. Literary analysis of Exod. 20:1-17
   c. Relation to the major traditions of the Pentateuch
3. The contents of the Ten Commandments
4. Date and authorship
5. Later history and significance
Bibliography

1. Outline of contents. *a. Historical-theological prologue, Exod. 20:1-2.* The Ten Commandments are presented in the form of a direct address of God to his people. Moses is not the intermediary (Exod. 20:19-20; but contrast Exod. 34:28). The prologue is an essential part of the commandments. Yahweh identifies himself and states the premise on the basis of which he addresses his people and calls them to obedience to his law: "I am Yahweh your God, who brought you out of the land of Egypt, out of the house of bondage." The saving action of Yahweh is the prior reality; grace is prior to law.

b. Man's relation to God, Exod. 20:3-12. Many attempts have been made to divide the contents of the Commandments into two types of law, suitable for division between the two stone tablets. The Roman Catholic and Lutheran, the Reformed, and the Jewish communities differ in their division of the commandments. While the question of their division is not of basic significance, it is defensible to distinguish between those commandments more directly concerned with man's relation to God and those concerned with relations between man and his neighbor.

The first five commandments (according to the Reformed tradition) may be described in short form as follows: (*a*) against polytheism; (*b*) against idolatry; (*c*) against dishonoring of God's name; (*d*) on sabbath observance; and (*e*) on honoring of parents. The last of these, on honoring of parents, belongs, strictly speaking, to the following commandments dealing with relations between men. Yet it is clear that the relation between a man and his parents in the OT is particularly close. The obligations of son to parents is a deeply religious one and comes to be used to describe the relation between Israel and her God (Jer. 31:20; Hos. 11:1). This commandment thus provides a good "bridge" between the two parts of the Ten Commandments.

c. Man's relation to his neighbor, Exod. 20:13-17. These commandments sum up, in negative but inclusive fashion, the basic social and moral requirements for the Israelite community.

2. Literary examination. Literary analysis of the Ten Commandments has not led to any scholarly consensus. Opinions are divided as to whether or not one ancient form of the Ten Commandments underlies the various versions. Opinions also differ as to the number of such versions. Nor has any consensus been reached concerning the relation of these laws to the major sources or traditions of the Pentateuch.

a. Various versions of the Ten Commandments. The Ten Commandments appear, with variations, in two places within the Pentateuch: Exod. 20:1-17; Deut. 5:6-21. The major variations occur in the sabbath command and in that against covetousness. (An explanation of the variations is suggested in § 4 *below.*) Exod. 34:11-26 is set forth as though it were intended to comprise the contents of the previous Ten Commandments given to Moses on the mountain, after he had broken the first tablets. Yet this collection can be divided into a set of ten commandments only with difficulty; furthermore, its contents differ basically from the contents of Exod. 20:1-17. This collection is more closely related to the Covenant Code (*see* LAW IN THE OT) than to the Ten Commandments. It is better understood as a festival calendar than as a variant form of the Ten Commandments.

The catalogue of curses pronounced by the Levites at the tribal gathering between Ebal and Gerizim (Deut. 27:15-26) contains twelve curses, not ten. It also differs widely in content from the Ten Commandments. It may be concluded, then, that only two listings of the Ten Commandments have been preserved in the OT. It is a separable question, however, how the various law collections are to be related to the Ten Commandments, and whether or not different decalogues existed in early Israel, arising out of different religious and historical contexts, and designed to serve varying purposes. Such questions are dealt with briefly in § 4 *below. See also* LAW IN THE OT.

b. Literary analysis of Exod. 20:1-17. The Ten Commandments in Exod. 20:1-17 are only loosely related to their literary context. Exod. 19:25 depicts Moses as having returned to the people at the foot of the holy mountain, once again to warn them against drawing too near to the revelatory scene about to be enacted. Further, as indicated above, Moses plays no direct role in the giving of the law as here described. Aaron, who was to have accompanied Moses to the mountain (Exod. 19:24), is not mentioned. The verses following the end of the Ten Commandments indicate that God has not yet given the law at all. In short, the Ten Commandments could be removed from their present literary context without damage to the literary connection between Exod. 19:25; 20:18; indeed, the connection between

these verses would be improved by the removal of the Ten Commandments.

The literary form of the Ten Commandments is of considerable importance for their understanding. There is general agreement that the early form of the Ten Commandments is best preserved in the first, sixth, seventh, eighth, and ninth commandments. These commandments are in the form of a strong negative particle, לֹא, followed by an active verb in the indicative, plus occasionally an object or an explanatory phrase. The explanations, justifications, and promises connected with the second, fourth, and fifth commandments and the itemization in the tenth commandment of persons or objects which are not to be coveted are considered to be later additions. It is precisely in respect to these additions that the differences between the two forms of the Ten Commandments are found.

It is not certain, however, whether the original form of the commandments was that of single verbs preceded by the negative particle—thus constituting a Decalogue of precisely ten words (Exod. 34:28)—or whether the original form consisted of short, categorical statements of varying length. The latter is the more probable. *See* LAW IN THE OT.

The early form of the Ten Commandments thus may be presumed to have consisted of short, categorical statements, primarily or perhaps exclusively in negative form, outlining the kinds of action disallowed within the Israelite community.

c. Relation to the major traditions of the Pentateuch. Literary-historical analysis of the Pentateuch during the nineteenth and early twentieth centuries led to the conclusion that the Ten Commandments arose under the influence of the great eighth-century prophets and were most closely related to the N Israelite document designated by the symbol "E" (*see* PENTATEUCH). More probably, however, the Ten Commandments have no direct literary connection with any one of the major Pentateuchal sources or traditions. *See* § 4 *below.*

3. The contents of the Ten Commandments. The first commandment states the unconditional and exclusive claim of Yahweh upon his COVENANT people. The existence of other gods is not called into question, but they are to count for nothing with the people of Yahweh. The expression translated "before me," or "besides me," might better be rendered "in opposition to me." Yahweh will tolerate no rivals to his authority. Implicit in this commandment is the Israelite understanding of the unity of God (Deut. 6:4).

The second commandment prohibits all forms of IDOLATRY. No image of the deity is to be made. The commandment is not merely directed against the religious practices associated with temple worship in Canaan or elsewhere. More fundamental is the conviction on the part of the Israelite community that Yahweh cannot be controlled by man. The making of images is designed to express more than an act of worship and devotion; it arises out of the desire to ensure the blessing and protection of the deity who is represented in the form of wood or clay or stone. Although ancient man no doubt was able to distinguish between the deity and his representation, such a distinction would be difficult to maintain in practice. The prohibitions against idolatry here and throughout the OT have been of inestimable significance in the preservation of the religious understandings of the Israelite community. Yahweh is not to be coerced into blessing his people or destroying their enemies. He remains free and sovereign even over the forms through which his people seek to worship him.

The third commandment extends the argument expressed in the second. Just as idolatry leads to the notion that the power of the deity can be controlled and put in man's service, so also does the use of the divine NAME. The ancient Near Eastern peoples considered the names of persons and things to be expressive of their nature or character (Gen. 2:19; 32:27-29; etc.). Once one knew the name of a person or thing, one had entered into relationship with and had a certain control over this person or object. In the case of Yahweh, however, this was not true. The name of Israel's God, Yahweh, is nowhere fully explained in the OT (Exod. 3:14 is best considered as the denial of an etymological explanation). Yahweh discloses his nature in his historical deeds.

The commandment is, accordingly, a prohibition of the use of the divine name to invoke curses or blessings or to reinforce one's own false oaths by the invoking of the divine name. God's name is not to be placed, by man, into man's service and control.

The fourth commandment authorizes one day in seven as a day of rest. The background of the Israelite SABBATH is probably to be found in the ancient oriental notion of days of ill omen, days on which it was considered dangerous to undertake important ventures. The Israelite sabbath, however, is a day of reflection and rejoicing, on which man and beast are to gain refreshment from the week's labors (Exod. 34:21; Deut. 5:12-15). In particular it is a day for holy remembrance, for reflection on Yahweh's deliverance of Israel from Egypt (Deut. 5:15). The basis for sabbath observance is more strictly religious in Exod. 20:11 and more socially oriented in Deut. 5:14-15. The two motivations are not, however, sharply distinguished in the OT.

It should be noted that this commandment authorizes both labor and rest from labor. No other commandment in the OT, apart from the first, has had as significant an effect upon the development of contemporary social life and thought. Slave as well as master, animal as well as man, is to be given due time for rest from toil. God himself rested on the seventh day, upon the completion of the works of creation (Gen. 2:2-3; Exod. 20:11). In the Bible the sabbath is never surrounded by strict rules for its proper observance. The fundamental commandment is quite simply that one day in seven is to be a day of holy rest.

The fifth commandment provides for the maintenance of the most fundamental unit of society, the FAMILY. The OT is quite explicit in describing what it means to honor (כבד) parents: they are not to be struck (Exod. 21:15); they are not to be cursed (Exod. 21:17; Lev. 20:9); they are not to be dishonored or despised, but are to be submitted to and obeyed (Deut. 21:18-21; 27:16). Such a commandment aims at the maintenance of family life in general; it is not merely intended as a commandment

for young children. The admonitions to parents to deal properly with their children are proper implications from this commandment (Eph. 6:4; Col. 3:21). The promise contained in the commandment indicates that the maintenance of the family is understood to relate to the promise of God: Israel is to be a holy people, faithful to the covenant, through whom God's purpose for mankind is to find fulfilment. Dishonoring of parents thus implies contempt for God's people and for his purpose through this people.

The remaining five commandments also aim at the preservation of the holy community. The commandment against taking human life is not to be limited to wilful homicide or murder; the Hebrew word (רצח) means either to kill or to murder, without distinction. The fundamental assertion is that life belongs to God; if human life is taken, it is to be taken in full awareness of this fact (Gen. 9:5-6). The commandment may have specifically in view the prohibition of the individual exercise of blood revenge: only the community may take the life of one of its members, under the divine sanctions provided. Such a specific interpretation, however, does not exhaust the meaning of the prohibition. The one who kills is acting as if he were God; all life is God's creation.

ADULTERY is categorically prohibited, since it also represents an act in defiance of God. God made mankind male and female; in marriage the two become one (Gen. 1:27; 2:18, 21-24; I Cor. 6:15-17). The act of adultery constitutes a denial of the unity of the relationship between man and woman, a unity affirmed by Yahweh and not understood to be compromised by occasional polygamous marriages. In the original setting of the commandment the emphasis probably lay upon the necessity to protect the objective character of the marriage relationship.

The commandment against theft rests on no biblical understanding that the right to private ownership of property is inviolable. Rather, the OT conceives of property as a kind of extension of the "self" of its owner (Josh. 7:24). Thus acts of theft are violations of the person. It may be that the commandment has in view the theft of a man (Exod. 21: 16—H 21:17) as a slave, rather than theft of property. In any case, the short, categorical prohibition draws the line between person and person, family and family, and forbids any trespass of these bounds.

False witness also destroys the wholeness of the covenant community. The neighbor (רע) is anyone with whom one has dealings and relationships, of either a more permanent or a more casual sort. Later distinctions between the brother and the stranger do not obtain in this commandment. Falsehood before the judges not only damages the person against whom the evidence is given; it is falsehood before Yahweh, the ultimate lawgiver and judge in the OT.

The commandment against covetousness involves more than a lustful or avaricious desire for the person or the property of someone. The Hebrew verb חמד means to desire to take pleasure in someone or something; it also means to set about to secure these for oneself (Exod. 34:24). In this commandment, therefore, both an inward desire for persons and things not one's own and the objective actions planned or taken to secure them are condemned. The maintenance of the wholeness of the covenant community is once again the object in view.

It should be noted that these commandments, although formulated primarily as prohibitions, carry direct implications for positive action. Furthermore, by their largely negative cast they provide the largest possible area of freedom for the community to give implementation to them in their common life and under changing circumstances. The Ten Commandments give no warrant whatever for a legalistic religious orientation.

4. Date and authorship. As indicated above, the Ten Commandments are only loosely connected with the narrative and legal context in which they are found. It has often been contended that the lofty moral and spiritual teaching contained in them must be a product of a much later time, under the influence of the great prophets of the eighth century B.C. The present form of the Ten Commandments may safely be assigned to the exilic period (587-530 B.C.) or to the century following. No sound reason exists, however, for dating the commandments in their presumed shorter form to such a late period. The prophet Hosea appears to have quoted the beginning of the Ten Commandments (12:9; 13:4). The same prophet summarizes the sins of Israel in terms highly reminiscent of the prohibitions of the second part of the Ten Commandments (4:2). No sound arguments have been offered which support the conclusion that any one of the commandments must be later than the age of Moses.

Positive evidence confirming a date in the period before the conquest of Canaan is, however, not at hand and is not to be anticipated. The most important information concerning date and authorship is provided by studies of early Israelite history and religion which indicate the connection between law of the type found in the Ten Commandments and covenants or treaties in the ancient Near East. The formal characteristics of certain Hittite suzerainty treaties are in a number of respects strikingly similar to those of the covenant ceremonies of the OT. In the Hittite treaties the major elements of comparison with OT covenant forms are: the preamble (containing the name, titles, and attributes of the king), the historical prologue (sketching previous relations between the two parties), the stipulations of the treaty (detailed lists of the requirements of the vassal to the king), and the curses-and-blessings formula. Such points of comparison are the more striking when the ceremony at the ancient city of Shechem is examined in their light (Josh. 24). Here appear preamble (vs. 2*a*), historical prologue (vss. 2*b*-13), and covenant stipulations (vss. 14-25). The curse formula, closely related to Josh. 24 and enacted in the region of Shechem, appears in Deut. 27. Further details of comparison between the Hittite treaties and the Israelite covenants are also found in Josh. 24.

Considerable evidence exists to support the conclusion that the covenant between Israel and Yahweh was regularly renewed (perhaps annually; perhaps once every seven years; see Deut. 31:10). The Ten Commandments would have provided an exceptionally fine summary of the covenant stipulations

suitable for these ceremonies of covenant renewal. Other legal materials would also have been useful in this connection; it need not, therefore, be concluded that the Ten Commandments alone were employed to define the covenant requirements. Once the connection between covenant and law has been seen, there appears to be no reason to assign the Ten Commandments to a date later than the early tribal confederacy under Joshua (and perhaps already under Moses).

The Ten Commandments were useful, however, in other connections. They may appear separately in Deuteronomy because of their employment in the "catechetical" instruction of priests and Levites in the Israelite towns and villages throughout the centuries (*see* DEUTERONOMY; PRIESTS AND LEVITES). The Exodus version of the commandments would then have its present location as a result of its connection with the Sinai covenant and with the regular ceremony of covenant renewal, while the Deuteronomy version would have found its present place because of its use in the teaching of religious leaders in town, village, and rural areas.

As to authorship, nothing positive can be said. No argument against Mosaic authorship is decisive, but none supporting Mosaic authorship can be taken to be more than a plausible possibility. The OT documents in many ways the critical importance of MOSES for Israelite faith and history. No more appropriate author can be suggested. This, however, does not constitute proof that the Ten Commandments came from his hand. If Moses was not their author, he was the one who provided the understanding of the relation between Yahweh and Israel which was to issue in this incomparable compendium of a people's responsibility to its sovereign God.

5. Later history and significance. As Israelite legal materials grew and developed, the Ten Commandments continued to have a decisive place. In a hymn associated with the later ceremony of covenant renewal (Ps. 81) the Ten Commandments are reflected, both as demand and as promise to this later generation. In the NT, the Ten Commandments are referred to by Jesus as simply "the commandments" (Mark 10:19 and parallels). They are and remain the fundamental policy statement in light of which the community of Israel and the Christian church discern their religious obligations. Furthermore, the Ten Commandments are from first to last theocentrically oriented. They give no basis whatever for a religious understanding of law which relates obedience to the divine command to divine favor and blessing. Such categorical, unconditional specifications of the divine will cannot easily be transformed into an instrument used to coerce or compel God's blessing. The Ten Commandments are rooted in the covenant relationship. This relationship is understood to have been initiated by a saving God who has demonstrated his graciousness and his authority in the deliverance of his people from Egyptian slavery. Obedience to this fundamental covenant law is thus an obedience born of gratitude and praise, not servile submission to an arbitrary or capricious deity. Despite the dangers inherent in any legal specifications of religious duties, the Ten Commandments give less warrant to legalism than any other collection of laws in the OT. It is a free, sovereign, gracious God who addresses his covenant people, defining the character of his relation to them, and of theirs to him, and calling for free and grateful obedience.

Bibliography. S. Mowinckel, *Le Décalogue* (1927). L. Köhler, "Der Dekalog," *Theol. Rundschau,* I (1929), 169-84. A. Alt, *Die Ursprünge des israelitischen Rechts* (1934). S. Mowinckel, "Zur Geschichte des Dekalogs," *ZAW,* 55 (1937), 218-34. J. Begrich, "Berit, ein Beitrag zur Erfassung einer alttestamentlichen Denkform," *ZAW,* 60 (1944), 1-11. H. H. Rowley, *Moses and the Decalogue,* Bulletin of the John Rylands Library, 34 (1951), 81-118, contains full bibliography. K. H. Barnhardt, *Gott und Bild, ein Beitrag zur Begründung und Deutung des Bilderverbotes im AT* (1952). G. E. Mendenhall, *Law and Covenant in Israel and the Ancient Near East* (1955). E. Jenni, *Die theologische Begründung des Sabbatgebotes im AT* (1956). W. Keszler, "Die literarische, historische und theologische Problematik des Dekalogs," *VT,* VII (1957), 1-16.

W. J. HARRELSON

TENANT. *See* FARMER.

TENON [ידות, *feminine plural of* hand]. A projection on the end of a piece of wood or other material, intended to fit into a hole or socket in another piece, to form a joint. The wooden frames of the TABERNACLE were held in place by two tenons on each frame (mortised into silver sockets? Exod. 26:17, 19; 36:22, 24).

L. E. TOOMBS

TENT [אהל; σκηνή, οἶκος, *see* TABERNACLE]. A movable habitation used by nomads, shepherds, and soldiers (Gen. 4:20; 25:27; Judg. 8:11 KJV), but distinct from hut or BOOTH.

Originally animal skins, the coarse cloth of present-day Bedouin tents, probably similar to those of the early biblical patriarchs, is hand-woven black goat's hair (Song of S. 1:5). Allowance was made for shrinkage after rain, rendering the cloth taut as it was stretched over the tent poles (Exod. 27:10). Addition of fresh material, which became discolored in the heat of the sun as the tent was being made, probably accounts for the striped appearance of the cloth. Stone spinning whorls and loom weights of clay and stone dating from *ca.* 3000-2000 B.C. have been recovered through archaeology. New tents added to the enclosure of clan encampments after weddings gave rise to the "bridal canopy" (חפה; Ps. 19:5—H 19:6; Joel 2:16), a continuing feature of the Jewish wedding ceremony.

The center pole was often higher than those at the sides of the tent; this afforded the simile of the heavens' being like a tent spread out (Isa. 40:22). Cords, used to hold the covering in place (Exod. 35:18; Job 4:21; Isa. 54:2; Jer. 10:20), were fastened to wooden pegs in the ground (Judg. 4:21). A curtain hanging from the center poles divided the larger tents into two rooms, with the back portion reserved for women (Judg. 15:1; cf. Gen. 43:30). Abraham's tent at Mamre would have had such an arrangement, whereby Sarah was able to overhear the conversation with the three visitors (Gen. 18:10). At other times it would appear that the patriarchs were wealthy enough to afford separate tents for their wives (Gen. 24:67; 31:33). Such wealth in patriarchal times was in dire contrast to the poverty of the exodus and wilderness period, when tents were very few.

The furnishings of such nomadic tents were, and are, very meager. The stove or oven consisted of a few stones placed at the tent entrance, or simply a hole in the ground. Coarse straw mats served as beds, which could be rolled up during the day, and even as chairs. A piece of leather spread on the floor was the table (Ps. 23:5; Isa. 21:5). Bags of goatskins, earthen pots, bowls and water jars, a stone grain mill, simple lamps, and other crude instruments completed the chattels of the ancient tent dweller.

The best single picture of tent life in the Bible is offered in Gen. 18. Camp sites such as that at Mamre were choice indeed where trees offered shade and a water supply was nearby (cf. Isa. 13:20).

After settlement in Canaan the Israelites would return at harvest time to their tents, encamping near the crops. This ancient custom in Israel became associated with the annual celebration of the Exodus and became known as the festival par excellence (החג; *see* BOOTHS, FEAST OF). The Rechabites, however, continued for religious reasons to live in tents the year round (Jer. 35).

Long after the Israelites became a settled people living in more permanent kinds of dwellings, the word "tent" was still used in the common language to mean "home" (I Kings 8:66; 12:16; Isa. 38:12; Jer. 4:20), "household" or "people" (Zech. 12:7; Mal. 2:12), or even "sanctuary" (Ezra 9:8).

Paul, originally from Tarsus of Cilicia, known for its *cilicium,* or goat's-hair cloth, was a tentmaker. While in Corinth, Paul stayed in the home of Aquila and Priscilla, who plied the same trade (Acts 18:1-3).

J. A. SANDERS

TENT OF MEETING [אהל מועד]. A designation of the TABERNACLE from the E and P strata of the Pentateuch.

TENTMAKER [σκηνοποιός]. Paul's trade, according to Acts 18:3. We are told that Paul and Aquila, and probably also Priscilla, Aquila's wife, worked together at this trade in Corinth.

There is a question, however, as to whether "tentmaker" is the best translation of the Greek term. The etymological meaning of the word is, to be sure, "tentmaker"; and if this is the meaning of the word in Acts, then the reference is to tents made out of the felted cloth of goat's hair, still used by the Bedouins for tents. This cloth was a product primarily of Cilicia, and so was called *cilicium* in Latin. Paul, of course, came from Cilicia.

But there is evidence for believing that the term meant "leatherworker." The earliest Latin translation we have bears *lectarius,* which means one who makes beds or bedsteads, and probably also leather cushions. The Peshitta used a word which transliterated the Latin *lorarius,* meaning "harness worker." Chrysostom, Theodoret, and probably Origen called Paul a "leatherworker." So that it is quite possible, and many would say probable, that to the readers of Acts in the early church the word meant "leatherworker."

B. H. THROCKMORTON, JR.

TEPHON tē'fŏn [Τεφών] (I Macc. 9:50); KJV TAPHON tā'—. A Judean city fortified by Bacchides. It may perhaps be TEKOA, because Josephus names it Tochoa (Antiq. XIII.i.3); but it was more probably TAPPUAH (Josh. 17:7) or perhaps NETOPHAH. N. TURNER

TERAH tĭr′ə [תרח = Akkad. *turaḫu*, ibex; LXX Θαρα (*in 1 below*), Τάρα (*in 2 below*); NT Θαρα]; KJV TARAH târ′ə in 2 below; KJV NT THARA thâr′ə. **1.** A descendant of Shem; the father of Abram (Abraham), Nahor, and Haran. Terah died at 205 (Gen. 11:24-32; I Chr. 1:26; Luke 3:34).

This OT personal name cannot be separated from Akkadian *Til ša turaḫi* ("the mound of Terah"), a city located on the Baliḫ River in Upper Mesopotamia (*see* ARAMEANS). Quite probably Terah either took his name from, or gave it to, that region.

According to P, Terah's home was Ur, in S Babylonia. Taking Abram, Lot, and Sarai, Terah left Ur for Canaan; but when he reached Haran, he settled there and died (Gen. 11:31-32). However, the earlier J source points strongly to Aram-naharaim as the original home of the patriarchs (Gen. 24; 27:43; 28:10; 29:1-14; 31:46-49, 51-53a; Deut. 26:5a). *See* UR; HARAN 4; ABRAHAM § C1.

Josh. 24:2 speaks of Terah as worshiping pagan deities. Since both Ur and Haran were flourishing centers of the moon-god Sin, Terah has often been associated with this particular cult. But this should be viewed in the light of the implications of the Abrahamic tradition. *See* PATRIARCHS § 4; NAHOR 2.
L. HICKS

2. A stopping place of the Israelites in the wilderness (Num. 33:27-28). The location is unknown.

TERAPHIM tĕr′ə fĭm [תרפים]. Though plural in form, this word may designate either one or more idols. In Gen. 31:19, 34-35, the teraphim are small and portable, and easily stolen and concealed. They are the household gods of Laban (31:30). The Nuzi Tablets (*see* NUZI) make it clear that not Jacob, but only Laban's sons were entitled to inherit Laban's teraphim, thus elucidating Rachel's impulse to steal them. The paternal household gods were eagerly sought after by the heirs for reasons that were basically religious but may have had ramifications of power and property rights as well.

The teraphim in I Sam. 19:13, 16, is an idol of the size, and in the shape, of a man. It was in the house of David and Michal.

Teraphim were used by Israelites cultically in the period of the judges (Judg. 17:5; 18:14, 17, 20). Along with other elements inherited from the pre-Israelite past, the teraphim came to be condemned in the biblical writings (I Sam. 15:23; II Kings 23:24). Hosea (3:4-5) predicts a period when teraphim (along with other cultic trappings) will cease—thus indicating the use of teraphim in the Israel of his time. Ezekiel (21:21) lists teraphim among the Babylonian media of divination. Zechariah (10:2) includes teraphim among the sources of false predictions.

Bibliography. C. H. Gordon, "Biblical Customs and the Nuzu Tablets," *BA*, III (1940), 1-11; *Introduction to OT Times* (1953), pp. 116-17; A. E. Draffkorn, "ILANI/ELOHIM," *JBL*, LXXVI (1957), 216-24. C. H. GORDON

TEREBINTH tĕr′ə bĭnth [אלה, *'ēlâ* (*alternately* OAK); τερέβινθος]. A large, common tree, probably

Courtesy of Denis Baly

51. A terebinth, probably here a sacred tree, growing in the ruins of a Roman temple, at Yajuz in Gilead

Pistacia terebinthus L. or *Pistacia palaestina* Boiss., or perhaps some other species (*cf.* NUTS; MASTIC). Isaiah said Judah's destruction would be like the burned stump of "a terebinth [KJV TEIL] or an oak ['*allôn*]" (Isa. 6:13). Hosea condemns the high-place worship "under oak ['*allôn*], poplar, and terebinth" (Hos. 4:13; KJV ELM). The occurrence of *'allôn* and *'ēlâ* together in these passages makes clear the original distinction of meaning. Ben Sirach gives a fitting description of the terebinth in his poem in praise of Wisdom:

> Like a terebinth I spread out my branches,
> and my branches are glorious and graceful

(Ecclus. 24:16; KJV "turpentine"; Syr. "oleander").

The RSV mg. gives "terebinth" (KJV "plain of") for *'ēlôn* in Gen. 12:6; and for *'ēlōnîm* in Gen. 13:18; 14:13; 18:1; Deut. 11:30. Not only do these passages very probably refer to the terebinth, but also the following references in which "oak" is used: *'ēlâ* in Gen. 35:4; Judg. 6:11, 19; I Kings 13:14; I Chr. 10:12; Isa. 1:30; Ezek. 6:13; *'allâ* in Josh. 24:26; *'ēlôn* in Judg. 4:11 (KJV "plain"); and *'ēlîm* in Isa. 1:29; 57:5 (KJV "idols"). *'Ēlâ* in II Sam. 18:9-10, 14 (the account of Absalom's death), probably refers to some deciduous OAK, common to Gilead, which was mistaken for the terebinth. The Valley of Elah (I Sam. 17:2, 19; 21:9; *see* ELAH, VALLEY OF) probably refers to a valley noted for its terebinths, though there are none there today.

Fig. TER 51; Pl. XIa.

See also FLORA § A9r; MAMRE; OPHRAH; ZAANANNIM.

Bibliography. I. Löw, *Die Flora der Juden*, vol. I, pt. 1 (1926), pp. 191-95; G. E. Post, *Flora of Syria, Palestine and Sinai*, I (1932), 285-86; H. N. and A. L. Moldenke, *Plants of the Bible* (1952), pp. 178-79. J. C. TREVER

TERESH tĭr′ĕsh [תרש, *perhaps from* Pers. *tarsha*, desire; *see bibliography*]. One of King Ahasuerus' two royal eunuchs, guards at his private chambers, who plotted his assassination. The matter was discovered by Mordecai, who informed Queen Esther and thereby saved the king's life; the two guards were hanged (Esth. 2:21-23). The event was later recalled to Mordecai's advantage with regard to the royal favor (6:2).

Bibliography. L. B. Paton, *Esther*, ICC (1908), pp. 69, 189-90.
B. T. DAHLBERG

TERRESTRIAL BODIES [σώματα ἐπίγεια]. In I Cor. 15:40 Paul contrasts "terrestrial" or "earthly" bodies with "celestial" or "heavenly" bodies. Terrestrial bodies are bodies which exist here on earth, while celestial bodies exist in heaven and are of a different substance. Paul is making the point that there are different kinds of bodies, and that the resurrection body has its own unique character. *See* CELESTIAL BODIES; RESURRECTION IN THE NT.

B. H. THROCKMORTON, JR.

TERTIUS tûr'shĭ əs [Τέρτιος; Lat. *Tertius,* third] (Rom. 16:22). The person to whom Paul dictated the Letter to the Romans. It is abundantly clear that Paul often, if not always, dictated his letters to a secretary. This is to be inferred from his statements that he wrote a small part of certain letters with his own hand (I Cor. 16:21; Gal. 6:11; Col. 4:18; II Thess. 3:17). No doubt, many of Paul's friends in various places wrote to his dictation in order to save him time and trouble. The only one whose name we know is Tertius, who interposes a greeting of his own in Rom. 16:22 between the apostle's salutations. It seems unlikely that the style or thought of Paul was significantly altered by those who wrote for him.

F. W. GINGRICH

TERTULLUS tər tŭl'əs [Τέρτυλλος, *diminutive from* Lat. *Tertius*]. The prosecutor of Paul before the Roman governor of Judea. He began his accusation (Acts 24:2-8) by flattering the governor, Felix. His charge against Paul was that he had been found to be a public nuisance, a disturber of the peace, and a leader of the sect of the Nazarenes. In the eyes of a provincial governor, this was a serious charge.

It is not clear whether Tertullus was a Roman, a Greek, or a Jew. As the authenticity of Acts 24:6*b*-8*a* is doubtful (the RSV prints this in the mg.), the major argument for his being a Jew (his reference to "our law" and to Lysias' coming and taking him "out of our hands") loses most, if not all, of its weight. No other words in his brief accusation require us to assume he was a Jew.

He might have been a professional Roman advocate who offered his services at the tribunals of provincial magistrates where the forms of Roman laws, of which non-Romans would know little, were followed.
B. H. THROCKMORTON, JR.

TEST. *See* TEMPTATION.

TESTAMENT [διαθήκη]. Properly, a written instrument by which a person disposes of his estate, to take effect after his death.

The Hebrew language seems to have no word for "testament," though the law of inheritance seems to have been the subject of customary legal procedures in OT times. The blessing of Isaac (Gen. 27), the request of Elisha for a "double portion" of Elijah's spirit (II Kings 2:9), and the case of Zelophehad's daughters (Num. 36) are all connected with disposal of estates, but give little information. Israelite legal custom may have dictated concerning disposal of an estate, and even the rabbinic writings took over the word דייתיקי as a term for "testament," in which a testator disposes of his property after death. The same word was used to designate the spiritual legacy of a wise man or philosopher, and the custom of leaving such a document was followed by eminent scholars as late as the Middle Ages in Islam.

The Greek διαθήκη was thus essentially an arrangement, a dispensation in normal colloquial usage of NT times, but one passage in Aristophanes shows that it could have the meaning "covenant," an agreement between two parties in which at least one is bound by oath (*see* COVENANT). The LXX translated ברית with the word διαθήκη. Consequently this is the normal word for "covenant" in the NT, translated into Latin subsequently as *testamentum*.

The NT follows the OT (LXX) meaning for διαθήκη throughout, as a "covenant," except in Heb. 9, where the usual colloquial Greek meaning "will" is used to support the argument for the abrogation of the OT. As a will becomes effective only at the death of the testator, so the death of Christ established the new covenant, put it into effect, just as the death of sacrificial animals in the OT established the old covenant. In Gal. 3:15-18, Paul makes use of the same analogy. The covenant with Abraham was an arrangement which was binding; subsequent generations could not change it. Therefore the Christ, heir of the testament, receives the promise ("In thee shall all the nations be blessed"), regardless of the subsequent addition of the law.

These two meanings from διαθήκη—the normal Greek usage "testament," and the OT-LXX meaning "covenant," derived from ברית—thus both appear in the NT; but there can be no doubt that the fundamental meaning of "covenant" in the NT is derived from, and is a highly creative reinterpretation of, the OT ברית, a two-party arrangement in which one is bound by oath. The two uses are similar only in that both represent an arrangement binding upon the recipient which he cannot change.

G. E. MENDENHALL

*TESTAMENTS OF THE TWELVE PATRIARCHS, THE [Διαθῆκαι τῶν Πατριαρχῶν]. A pseudepigraphic work which probably reached its present form in the second or third century A.D., though it includes material which seems to have been put into writing as early as the beginning of the second century B.C. The present form consists of twelve sections, each entitled a "testament," purporting to record the deathbed speeches of the twelve sons of Jacob. These sections are all of (roughly) the same structure: The patriarch calls together his sons; tells them of his life; warns them against some particular vice or recommends some particular virtue; prophesies their future sins, punishments, and ultimate salvation; and finally dies and is buried by them in Hebron. The individual speeches develop the biblical form found in Josh. 23-24; I Kings 2; the collection of them is inspired by Gen. 49 (cf. Deut. 33), and is the chief preserved example of a large Judeo-Christian literature of "testaments," attributed usually to OT worthies but also to Orpheus and to Jesus Christ. (These generally differ from the NT by using the word "testament" [διαθήκη] in the sense of "last words," rather than of "covenant" [*see* TESTAMENT].)

In the Testaments of the Twelve Patriarchs, the individual sections are composed of (a) narrative material closely related to JUBILEES and the rabbinic midrashim (see MIDRASH); (b) eschatological and demonological material related to the Enoch tradition (see ENOCH, BOOK OF) and to the Qumran literature (see DEAD SEA SCROLLS); and (c) homiletic material related to that of the WISDOM literature, the Qumran literature, rabbinic literature, the NT (see SERMON ON THE MOUNT; JAMES, LETTER OF), and a group of early Christian works: the DIDACHE; the Epistle of Barnabas (see BARNABAS, EPISTLE OF); and the Shepherd of Hermas (see HERMAS, SHEPHERD OF). At the same time, many of the sections are examples of the confession of sins, which had come to play a large part in Judaism and is represented by a long series of works (Ezra 9; Neh. 9; Bar. 1–3; Prayer of Manasseh; etc.; see CONFESSION). These various elements enabled the work to appeal to many different groups, and it evidently enjoyed considerable circulation. Though no list of canonical books (see CANON OF THE OT) includes it, several take the trouble to state explicitly that it is not canonical. Nevertheless, especially in the Armenian church, it was often included in MSS of the OT and was certainly read in church services during the Middle Ages. For its further history, see § 1 below.

1. History of the text. Much of the material in the present work was originally written in Hebrew or Aramaic, as shown by many evident Semitisms in style and content, and some probable mistranslations. What form this material first had is uncertain. The Qumran sect (see ESSENES) possessed a work so closely related to the preserved Testament of Levi that it must have been either the source or a variant form of the preserved testament. Of this work we have sixty minute fragments of one MS from Qumran Cave 1, and slightly larger fragments of three MSS from Qumran Cave 4, one of them in a hand which allegedly dates from the late second or early first century B.C. Further, we have two fragments— one extending to eight columns—of an eleventh-century Cairo Genizah MS which was probably copied from one found near Qumran. This (proto?) Testament of Levi had been translated into Greek— two extensive fragments of it are interpolated into a tenth-century Greek MS of the preserved Testament of Levi—and probably into Syriac; a fragment of it is found in a ninth-century Syriac miscellany in the British Museum. The Qumran sect also possessed a work closely related to the Testament of Naphtali. Of this a few small fragments have been found in the caves. From later medieval Hebrew midrashic material we have further evidence of the existence of extremely variant forms of the preserved text, or independent developments of its sources: a late Hebrew Testament of Naphtali, which differs widely from that in the Testaments of the Twelve Patriarchs, and several amplified versions of the stories of the wars of the sons of Jacob, which are now found in the Testament of Judah, but evidently circulated independently, as well.

So long as no fragments of any testament save that of Levi had been found in the Qumran material, this fact was taken as evidence that the Qumran sect did not possess the other testaments. Since the Testament of Naphtali, as noted, certainly circulated apart from the others during the Middle Ages, it is still possible that the sect possessed only the Testament of Levi and the Testament of Naphtali. But this notion is made unlikely by the frequent occurrence in the other testaments of terms and concepts characteristic of the literature of the Qumran sect. These, however, may have come from a source common to it and to the Testaments. Apart from such literary parallelism (and from the Qumran-sect material) the first evidence for the preserved work's existence is generally thought to be a reference by Origen in his fifteenth homily on Joshua (section 6) to a "certain book which is called 'The Testament [sic] of the Twelve Patriarchs,' although it is not accepted in the canon." But the teaching which he attributes to this book— that a different demon acts in each different sinner —is not clearly stated in the preserved text. (The passage usually cited, Test. Reuben 2–3, lists fifteen or sixteen spirits, meaning psychological powers, which supposedly act in all men.) Jerome (*Tractatus sive Homiliae in Psalmos XIV*) refers to the "book of Patriarchs, although it is reckoned among the apocryphal [books]," as containing material now found in Test. Naph. 2:8. There is every probability that the preserved text had by this time reached substantially its present form, since within about a century of Jerome's lifetime it was translated into Armenian from a MS which lacked, at most, only a few of the latest Christian interpolations. However, the fact that variant forms of the work and independent fragments of cognate material were also in circulation, makes it unsafe to take references to such material in patristic authors, Byzantine historians, and rabbinic literature, as proofs of a knowledge of the Greek text we have.

This text was apparently popular in the tenth century, from which come the three earliest preserved Greek MSS of it. These represent two textual families, separated by considerable differences; therefore, it seems likely that the text had been copied often in the interval which separated them from their common original. No doubt, many copies were even less faithful than these. A later Venetian MS, transcribed by James, shows the text reduced to a series of excerpts. Similarly, a translation into Slavonic (of uncertain, but medieval, date) is also represented by two families of MSS, one of which shows large Christian interpolations. Reported translations into Georgian and Serbian have not yet been investigated. The Latin translation—by exception, faithful—was made in the thirteenth century by Grosseteste, bishop of Lincoln, with the assistance of a Greek cleric. It has been retranslated since the Renaissance into many modern European languages. For the scholarly editions of the earlier texts, see bibliography.

2. History of the criticism. The tenth-century interest in the text may have been connected with the Byzantine renaissance (cf. Photius' interest in early works and apocryphal traditions). Further, the Middle Ages and the Renaissance generally had a weakness for secret books, apocalyptic prophecies, special revelations, and the like. In these periods, therefore, the Latin version enjoyed great popularity both in England and on the Continent, as the many MSS and translations of it show. With the rise of rationalism this popularity waned. The scholarship of the seventeenth century—primarily concerned with authorities for dogmatic controversy and institutional practice—barely produced an edition of the Greek text (by Grabe, in his *Spicilegium SS. Patrum*, 1698), and the eighteenth century paid this text almost no attention.

With the increasing study of church history in Germany during the early nineteenth century came a series of attempts to treat the book as a product of one or another party of the early church. The discussion thus aroused led to a realization that the text contained apparently contradictory elements, notably about the Gentiles—some passages were extremely hostile to them; others predicted their salvation and praised Paul—and about the Messiah—some passages described him as a man filled with the Spirit, others as God in human form. Hence came various makeshift theories of interpolation and eventually a study of the whole text's integrity: F. Schnapp, *Die Testamente der Zwölf Patriarchen untersucht* (1884). Schnapp concluded that the work had originally been a collection of purely moral disquisitions—a dramatization of material from the wisdom literature (like AHIKAR). Later students were to explain it as a collection of synagogue homilies. All the eschatological material, and much of the haggadic (*see* HAGGADAH), was explained as interpolated.

Schnapp's conclusions were generally accepted—though with reservations—on the Continent (Schürer, Baljon, de Faye), but were sharply criticized in England, where the Colenso controversy had left an absurd hostility to theories of interpolation. Deane, e.g., refused to see the obvious incoherences and contradictions in the work, and laid great emphasis on the claim that the MSS then known showed no considerable textual divergences. This emphasis shaped the history of the criticism by giving undue importance of Conybeare's discovery, at the turn of the century, that one version of the Armenian text was considerably shorter than the Greek and in particular lacked a number of the passages or words which had been generally recognized as Christian interpolations. This discovery was taken as confirming the theory of interpolation. On the other hand, as remarked above, even the shorter version of the Armenian text agreed with the Greek in almost all major elements, and in particular contained most of the apocalyptic material which Schnapp had eliminated. When Schnapp, translating the text for Kautzsch's *Apokryphen und Pseudepigraphen des AT* (1900), continued to follow his former theory, he was taken to task by Bousset for neglecting the evidence of the Armenian. Hence came a reconsideration of the problem and, in 1908, Charles's edition of the Greek text.

Charles's work is largely explicable as a vector of two forces: On the one hand, his own examination had convinced him that the Testaments were basically Hebrew in language and Jewish in composition; therefore, whatever elements seemed undoubtedly Christian had to be supposed interpolations. On the other hand, the record of English criticism and the influence of Bousset made him anxious to find MS evidence for the interpolations he had to suppose. Therefore, he usually preferred the shorter texts of both the Greek and the Armenian versions. Thus he

got rid, by textual criticism, of as much apparently Christian material as possible. The rest had to be dealt with by higher criticism. Part of it he interpreted as expression of Jewish messianic hopes, part as expression of Jewish piety. (To account for the similarities of the Testaments to the gospels, he had recourse to a special, Galilean, pietistic, universalistic Judaism, otherwise unknown and not very likely in Galilee on the eve of the Maccabean conquest—which was where he dated the Testaments.) Finally, what he thought the irreducible remainder, he bracketed. Having thus secured a Jewish text, he found that it still contained contradictions. Notably, some passages expected a messiah from Levi; others from Judah; others, apparently, from both Levi and Judah. Also, many passages glorified the descendants of Levi, but others denounced them as destined to lead Israel to sin and ruin. Therefore, Charles concluded that the basic text was a pro-Hasmonean work of the latter years of John Hyrcanus, which had been interpolated, after the fall of the Hasmoneans, by writers opposed to them and concerned to revive the earlier hope for a messiah from Judah. These conclusions were accepted—with some reservations—by Schürer, and have since been generally repeated, with only minor modifications, by the writers of "standard works."

Almost all subsequent study of the Testaments has been based on Charles's collection of material, especially on his account of the MSS. This has never(?) been checked, and we can only hope that his accuracy was better than his judgment, for his "explanations" of readings, by supposed MS corruptions in the Armenian and the Hebrew, are often fantastic. His apparatus (if correct) is invaluable and (whether correct or not) has made all students of the subject his debtors, but his conjectures must be viewed with suspicion. Since the appearance of his work, the major developments of the study have been two:

a) Charles's preference for the shorter versions of the Greek and Armenian texts has been successfully attacked. It has been shown that the longer versions of both texts are superior (Burkitt, Hunkin, De Jonge). Further, it has been shown that neither text of the Armenian version is a reliable guide for the elimination of most of the Christian interpolations (Messel, De Jonge). However, there remain some instances when the longer versions do contain interpolations which the shorter lack. Hunkin, who did the essential work here, contented himself with proving that the longer texts were good copies, the shorter ones slovenly abbreviations; he did not give enough attention to the possibility that the good copies might be good copies of texts in which the process of interpolation had been carried further than it had in the texts from which the slovenly abbreviations were made.

b) Serious attempts have been made to redate some of the material. Parts, at least, of the haggadah have been shown to come from the first quarter of the second century B.C. (Bickerman; cf. E. Meyer). The Qumran documents have provided important parallels to the moral, demonological, and messianic passages, and in particular have made it probable that the juxtaposition of Levi and Judah in messianic passages represents, not interpolation, but an original expectation of two messiahs (Kuhn, anticipated by Beasley-Murray; cf. Dupont-Sommer and Otzen). At the same time Leivestad has revived Schnapp's theory of interpolation in its most drastic form, and the same theory has been turned inside out by De Jonge, who maintains that our present work was compiled by a second- or third-century Christian from earlier materials, thus making the early passages, as it were, interpolations in a Christian framework.

3. Upshot of the criticism. These attempts at redating testify to what was remarked in § 1 *above,* the extreme fluidity of the literary forms which have embodied this tradition. These texts have evidently been excerpted, abbreviated, expanded, interpolated, and, at least in places, practically rewritten. Further, it is quite probable that, whenever they were originally composed, the author(s) worked into them elements from other written sources or relatively fixed oral traditions, and that these elements continued to circulate apart from the Testaments, both independently and in other works, from which they had been taken or into which they had likewise been inserted. Given such a history of the text, it is apparently hopeless to try to unscramble the present omelet. On the other hand, along with this fluidity of literary forms has gone a surprising fixity in the preservation of details: the figures reported apropos of the purchase of Joseph still reflect the units of Seleucid currency; many terms and concepts are exactly paralleled in the Manual of Discipline; the Hebrew Testament of Naphtali, which shows a thorough medieval reworking of one of the original testaments, has yet, in certain places, preserved the wording of the original so faithfully that misreadings and mistranslations in the Greek can be corrected from its text. Because of this fixity it is sometimes possible to date particular elements in the present text, or, at least, to associate them with particular literary traditions. However, we know too little of ancient Judaism and of ancient Christianity to be quite sure about the possible limits of the variations of either religion. Therefore, identification of particular passages as "Jewish" or "Christian" is necessarily somewhat hazardous.

Because of this uncertainty it is tempting to say of the Testaments, as one might say of certain midrashim, that they were never written; they grew. But this would not be correct. The Testaments have an external, narrative, consistent, literary frame, which is almost certainly the work of one editor (or author, or compiler—it is difficult to choose between such terms for such a work) and the result of a single literary operation which, at least theoretically, might be dated. But this frame is so nondescript that it is extremely difficult to date, especially when there is no assurance as to what elements may have been worked into it from older material, or added to it, by glossation, later on. (It is significant that De Jonge has devoted the least of his attention to the dating of the frame, though this would have been most important for his theory.) And even if one could date the frame, any one of the pieces framed might be several centuries older or younger than the framework.

Therefore, the Testaments' historical value is that, not of a landmark, but of a stream bed. They show us the confluence and direction of certain elements in the religion of Palestine during the two centuries before and the two centuries after the Christian era. It is a remarkable conjunction: Hellenistic culture (Braun has shown that the story of Joseph owes much to the Hellenistic romances); biblical learning; pride in the tradition of Israel and an exclusive attitude toward the Gentiles; faith in the future of Israel and in the ultimate salvation of the Gentiles; concepts of the messiah as both priest and king; conflicting attitudes toward the Maccabees, seen now as the instruments of God's salvation, again as corrupters of the nation, who led it to its ruin; intense awareness of the influence on man of spiritual or psychological forces outside his personality; resolute adherence to the belief in human freedom and moral responsibility; a (bucolic?) idealization of rural simplicity and a wisdom tradition promising to make its students citizens of the world; a morality of asceticism, self-sacrifice, and brotherly love; and the expectation of a kingdom very much of this world, where even God will come down to dwell among men. This list is not intended to be exhaustive and certainly is far from being so; it is merely a sampling of the variety.

Besides distinguishing these elements, we can trace the stream in which they sooner or later converged. It rose in the pre-Maccabean period, from the pious study of the OT and the haggadic development of bare OT narratives into stories filled with Hellenistic detail. In the early Maccabean times it received a great afflux of national feeling, reshaping its folk tales to reflect the achievements of the Maccabean wars and the hopes of final national salvation which those wars both expressed and encouraged. For a brief period this tradition of the pious came very near to the tradition of the people. But when the Maccabean regime led to the inevitable disillusionments of human politics, the original current and direction of the stream of pious tradition reasserted itself; the primitive piety cut for itself ever deeper, but narrower, channels, became more and more the tradition of special groups—Essenes, Pharisees, Christians—and split into various branches, each of which was augmented and diversified by the special interests of the group through which it flowed. In the Testaments of the Twelve Patriarchs we have the Christian branch of the stream, as it was eventually frozen when Christianity lost touch with the haggadic tradition from which it had emerged, and substituted a literature of relatively fixed, written works, for an oral tradition incidentally expressed in written forms. In spite of many parallels of terminology which this Christian material shows to that of the Dead Sea finds, it is by no means certain that the Dead Sea sect either shaped the elements of the book we now have or contributed largely to them. For the present book shows no trace of the communal organization and compulsory discipline characteristic of the Dead Sea sect. Instead, it speaks of personal piety and self-discipline. This difference may be explained by difference of interest and/or editorial elimination of earlier traits, but not until several scholars have reworked the material independently and in detail will it be possible to say with any confidence whether or not such explanations are adequate.

Bibliography. Texts: R. Sinker, *Testamenta XII Patriarcharum* (1869), is a careful transcript of the best MS of the long text. R. H. Charles, *The Greek Versions of the Testaments of the Twelve Patriarchs* (1908), includes, besides the readings of nine Greek MSS, the Genizah fragments, the Hebrew Testament of Naphtali, some of the midrashic parallels, and the variant readings of the Armenian and Slavic versions. The Qumran fragments published to date are in D. Barthélemy and J. Milik, *Discoveries in the Judean Desert* (1955), I, 87 ff; J. Milik, "Le Testament de Lévi en Araméen," *RB*, LXII (1955), 398 ff.

Translation and commentary: R. H. Charles, *The Testaments of the Twelve Patriarchs Translated from the Editor's Greek Text* (1908), with a fuller commentary than that in his *Apoc. and Pseudep. of the OT* (1913), II, 282 ff. Retroversion into Hebrew, with commentary, by I. Ostersetzer, in A. Kahana, *Hassepharim Hahiṣonim* (2nd ed., 1957), I, 142 ff.

Bibliographies are to be found in R. H. Charles, *The Testaments of the Twelve Patriarchs . . .* (1908), pp. xl-xli; M. de Jonge, *The Testaments of the Twelve Patriarchs* (1953), pp. 170-71; O. Eissfeldt, *Einleitung in das AT* (2nd ed., 1956), pp. 780-81. None of these is exhaustive, even for the periods professedly covered. They do, however, contain references to the critical works referred to in the above text, except: E. Meyer, *Ursprung und Anfänge des Christentums* (1925), II, 12, 44, 167-68, etc.; A. Dupont-Sommer, *Nouveaux aperçus sur les MSS de la Mer Morte* (1953), pp. 63 ff; K. Kuhn, "Die beiden Messias Aarons und Israels," *NTS*, I (1954-55), 168 ff. Discussions of Kuhn's article have usually paid some attention to the Testaments. E. Ehrlich, "Ein Beitrag zur Messiaslehre der Qumransekte," *ZNW*, LXVIII (1956), 234 ff, contains a brief bibliography. Of the works which have appeared since this article went to press, see especially M. Philonenko, *Les interpolations chrétiennes des Testaments des douze Patriarches et les Manuscrits de Qumran* (1960).

For rabbinic parallels to the Testaments, see especially L. Ginzberg, *The Legends of the Jews* (1909-46), vols. II, V.
                                                    M. SMITH

TESTIMONY. Evidence given by a witness or witnesses, orally or in written form, primarily to the action and requirements of God.

In the OT, two Hebrew nouns are generally translated by the term "testimony." The more common is עֵדוּת, derived from the verb עוּד, "to repeat," "to affirm," "to reprove or admonish," and always used in reference to the testimony of God. Its most frequent occurrences are in connection with the ARK or the TABERNACLE. Less frequent is the term עֵדָה, probably derived from the above verb, also in reference to the testimony (testimonies) of God. This word also refers to the law in general; it appears several times (Deut. 4:45; 6:17; etc.) in connection with other terms for the law of God: "statutes" (מִשְׁפָּטִים) and "judgments" (חֻקִּים). The verb עָנָה, "to answer," may also designate the testimony of Yahweh against sinners (II Sam. 1:16; Isa. 59:12; etc.; see also the verb עוּד). In Isa. 8:16, 20 (see also Ruth 4:7), the noun תְּעוּדָה designates, not the Torah, but the particular prophetic testimony of Yahweh given through Isaiah to Judah during the early years of the ministry of Isaiah.

In the NT, the verb μαρτύρειν in its various nominal and verbal forms provides the terms for "testimony" and "WITNESS." The nouns μαρτυρία and μαρτύριον refer to the testimony of eyewitnesses to the revelation of God in Jesus Christ in both word (II Tim. 1:8) and deed—particularly in suffering (Matt. 10:18; Luke 21:13). Christ himself bears testimony to God's work, but his testimony is rejected (John 3:11, 32-33).

In the OT, the term refers particularly to the written words of the law, while in the NT the testimony to God's action is provided in the proclamation of the gospel in word, deed, and suffering. The contrast must not be drawn too sharply, however; in the OT, the testimony to God's action calls for decision and action on the part of his people (see Josh. 24:15, 22: "You are witnesses" [עֵדִים]).

See also WITNESS; MARTYR.   W. J. HARRELSON

TETA. KJV Apoc. form of HATITA.

TETH tĕth (Heb. tāth) [ט, *ṭ* (*Ṭêth*)]. The ninth letter of the Hebrew ALPHABET as it is placed in the KJV at the head of the ninth section of the acrostic psalm, Ps. 119, where each verse of this section of the psalm begins with this letter.

TETRARCH tĕt'rärk, tē'trärk [τετράρχης, τετραάρχης, *from* τετράς, four, *plus* ἀρχή, rule]. Originally, the ruler of a fourth part of an area; losing its original sense, the word came to mean a "petty ruler." As a title it is lower than "king," and implies limitations and dependency. Thus, e.g., when Herod the Great died in 4 B.C., his domains, entrusted to him by the Romans, were divided among three of his sons. Of these, Archelaus received the title ETHNARCH, while Herod Antipas and Philip each became a tetrarch. The term is found frequently in the NT and in Josephus, as well as in pagan sources and inscriptions.

Precisely what the privileges and limitations of the tetrarch were is difficult to say; it was a title lower than the infrequent "ethnarch," which in turn was lower than the frequent "king." Herod the Great was first named a tetrarch by Mark Antony (Antiq. XIV. xiii.1; War I.xii.5), but was later named king. In general, the size of the domain and the amount of independence granted and tolerated by the Romans dictated which title was to be bestowed. Of such bestowed titles, ethnarch was presumably the lowest royal one.

Mark 6:14, 26, speak of Antipas as king rather than as tetrarch. Matt. 2:22 speaks of Archelaus as king rather than as ethnarch (so, too, Jos. Antiq. XVIII.iv.3). While some commentators believe that those instances are errors, it is likely, rather, that the titles of tetrarch, ethnarch, and king were somewhat fluid, and not strictly fixed.

The puzzle as to why Luke 3:1 singles out Lysanias of Abilene for mention is frequently accounted for by supposing that since Luke used the title τετράρχης he needed to specify four territories.

Bibliography. E. Schürer, *A History of the Jewish People in the Time of Jesus Christ*, div. 2, vol. II (1891), pp. 7-8, footnote 12 cites examples of the use of the term, as in Euripides and Demosthenes, and others. J. M. Creed, *The Gospel According to St. Luke* (1930), p. 49.   S. SANDMEL

TETTER [בֹּהַק; LXX ἀλφός] (Lev. 13:39); KJV FRECKLED SPOT. An obsolete term which originally indicated the presence of unspecified dermatological conditions of obscure etiology. It evidently describes acquired leucoderma (vitiligo), a cutaneous condition marked by the rise of depigmented patches without other trophic changes. The skin assumes a piebald appearance, as opposed to the whiteness of albinism (congenital leucodermia).

See also LEPROSY.

R. K. HARRISON

*TEXT, OT. Traditionally, the textual study of the Hebrew OT has been twofold: the history of the transmission of the text and a classification of scribal errors with their emendation; but, although basically the same division still obtains, recent developments have seen a far greater emphasis on the former and a corresponding tendency to regard textual corruption as incidental to, and even conditioned by, the history of the transmission itself. To some degree this change of emphasis is reflected in standard editions of the MT, particularly in Kittel's *Biblia Hebraica* (third edition, 1937, and subsequently).

Likewise, in the study of the versions (*see* VERSIONS, ANCIENT) we find strong contemporary indications of a change of general standpoint as a result of a more adequate application of historical criticism than was formerly practiced. There is a persistent stress on the individuality of each version, especially as an interpretation of the parent text, and the versions are no longer thought of simply as a storehouse of possible "readings," to be used for retranslation into an "original" or at least pre-Masoretic Hebrew text. Consequently, the application of the versions is rendered more complicated than it was in the past, and everywhere—from the direction of the MT and of the versions—caution is called for. Nevertheless, the Dead Sea Scrolls imply that in some cases the LXX followed a different, pre-Masoretic Hebrew text. Used judiciously, the versions can be of greater importance than ever before.

A. The Hebrew text
  1. The Dead Sea Scrolls
    a. Qumran
    b. Murabba'at and others
  2. The question of an early standard Hebrew text
    a. Evidence against
    b. Evidence for
  3. The scribes
    a. Scribal activity
    b. Rabbi Akiba
  4. The Masoretes
    a. The Masoroth
    b. Vocalization
  5. The Cairo Genizah
  6. The ben Asher and ben Naphtali texts
  7. Post–ben Asher texts
    a. MSS
    b. Printed editions
    c. Biblia Hebraica
B. The Samaritan recension
C. The evidence of the versions
  1. LXX
    a. The question of proto-LXX
    b. The character of the LXX
    c. Hermeneutics in the LXX
  2. Non-LXX Greek Bibles
  3. The Targums
  4. LXX-daughter translations
D. The classification of scribal errors and their emendation
  1. The MT as a recension

  2. Accidental errors
  3. The restoration of the text
    a. The MT
    b. The hypothetical "original Hebrew"
Bibliography

A. *THE HEBREW TEXT.* 1. The Dead Sea Scrolls. Superlatives have become common in evaluating the Scrolls, both as the earliest extant source material for the text of the OT and as the literature of the sect of the Scrolls, and it is well nigh impossible to exaggerate their value.

Our interest, obviously, lies in the former aspect, and in this matter it appears necessary to mention two simple facts which are frequently forgotten. The first is that the scrolls from Qumran are essentially different from those of Murabba'at and other sources; the second is that the biblical scrolls from Qumran themselves are not homogeneous, but contain texts whose divergences are both numerous and very important.

a. Qumran. Pride of place goes to the Qumran (Essene?) Scrolls, but their significance will be modified as the number of texts increases, and as the close scrutiny and comparison of each text-form produces a better assessment of individual scrolls and fragments. Not all biblical fragments are as yet available for study, and it must be emphasized that whereas reports and conclusions offered by the scholars who have been able to study the documents are largely drawn upon here, they may well have to be modified when other scholars have been able to examine the actual documents or facsimiles of them.

In general, two introductory observations may be made: (*a*) There is in all the Qumran Scrolls, biblical and others, a marked absence of any sign of rigid transmission of a uniform or standardized text. It has often been remarked that the text of most, if not all, the larger Qumran biblical MSS suffers from scribal corruption, and this in itself suggests that the scribes and the sect of the Scrolls were not by tradition scrupulous in the transmission of the text. The same conclusion is indicated by the fact that numerous divergent text forms of the same book were transmitted by the same sect. (*b*) The Qumran Scrolls obviously all belong to one sect, and the possibility of sectarian and deliberate intrusion of textual changes must be borne in mind when we deal with the biblical MSS. Consequently, it might well be wrong, and it is certainly illogical, to conclude that the evidence supplied by Qumran documents is immediately and generally applicable to the whole history of the Hebrew text in pre-Christian times. Nevertheless, the Qumran biblical MSS are about a thousand years earlier than the previously oldest extant Hebrew Bibles, and as such they are actual copies of texts which were current in the period before Christ, and before the period when rabbinic teaching claims the Hebrew text was standardized.

It is impossible in the present context to indicate the significance of each text of the Qumran Scrolls, and premature to indicate any definitive conclusion about the whole collection. Nevertheless, some tentative conclusions should be available for the general reader, and a selection of the more interesting documents is outlined here from this standpoint.

a) 1QIs[a]. The text of this scroll is published in

facsimile, *The Dead Sea Scrolls of St. Mark's Monastery*, vol. I: *The Isaiah MS and the Habakkuk Commentary* (edited by Millar Burrows; published by the American Schools of Oriental Research; 1950 and subsequently), and the original scroll is now in the Hebrew University at Jerusalem, Israel. It contains the whole text of Isaiah and is in a well-written script, which does not, however, belie the large number of textual corruptions contained in it. There are fifty-four columns, with an average of thirty lines per column; and the text is divided into paragraphs of two kinds, open and closed. The principle of paragraph division is also found in Masoretic transmission, but it is significant that the general pattern of paragraph division in 1QIs^a does not coincide with that of the MT.

An interesting feature is the orthography of the text; compared with the MT, it is particularly abundant in *scriptio plena*, in the full form of the second and third person masculine plural suffixes and second masculine singular suffixes, and in some verbal forms. To what extent these orthographic variations can be useful for the reconstruction of the history of Hebrew grammar still remains debatable. On the one hand, they are not unparalleled in other possible sources of comparison, especially the Samar. Pentateuch. On the other hand, the grammatical forms of other scrolls do not all show the divergences, and it is natural to assume that 1QIs^a, together with a few other fragments, belongs to a variant transmission of the text. A comparison of the orthography with that of the Greek transcription of the MT in col. 2 of Origen's Hexapla (as found, particularly, in col. 1 of thirty-five palimpsest sheets of Psalms in Origen's Hexapla discovered in 1894 by Mercati in the Ambrosiana in Milan) will immediately show how marked is the divergence between the Origenic and the sectarian traditions, despite occasional similarities. Likewise, sporadic similarities with later Masoretic vocalizations—e.g., some of the pointing attached to Cairo Genizah MSS with Palestinian vowel marks (*see* § A4*b below*), lose in significance when it is remembered that the Masoretic vocalization itself lacks uniformity.

A remarkable feature of 1QIs^a is that it reveals, albeit in a uniform script and probably copied by the same scribe, two quite distinct scribal traditions in the two halves of the scroll—indeed, the division occurs halfway through the scroll (cols. 1-27: Isa. 1-33; and cols. 28-54; Isa. 34-66). The text in the first half is much more nearly free from corruption, and the characteristic orthography mentioned above is more commonly and more consistently found in the second half.

Another important feature is that the scroll shows signs of having been corrected, sometimes by a later scribe, and additions, ranging from single consonants to lengthy passages, have been inserted in the space between lines and even running into the margins. The most important additions are in Plate XVI, line 14 (Isa. 21:1), line 32 (21:15); Plate XVII, line 2 (21:17); Plate XXII, line 20 (28:16, where the divine name *Adonay* is added to the Tetragrammaton); Plate XXIV, line 25 (30:15, an addition to the divine name); Plate XXVIII, lines 18-20 (34:17–35:2), line 26 (35:8); Plate XXIX, line 16 (36:15); Plate XXX,

lines 11-12 and marginal overflow (37:6-8), line 21 (37:14); Plate XXXI, line 10 (37:31); Plate XXXII, line 14 and margin (38:21-22); Plate XXXIII, line 7 and margin (40:7-8), line 13 (40:13), lines 15-16 (40:15-16), line 19 (40:20); Plate XXXIV, line 14 (41:11), line 25 (41:20); Plate XXXVI, line 12 (43:3); Plate XXXVII, line 9 (44:3), line 15 (44:9), line 22 (44:16), line 2 (44:25), line 3 (44:25), line 17 (45:11, addition to the divine name); Plate XL, line 29 (49:2); Plate XLI, line 14 (49:14, variant to the divine name); Plate XLIII, line 15 (52:1); Plate XLVI, line 26 (56:12); Plate LII, line 17 (65:12), line 18 (65:13, addition to the divine name); Plate LIV, line 10 (66:20). In most of these passages the corrections bring the text, though not the orthography, into agreement with the MT, but significant exceptions are in 43:3; 44:3, the latter indicating a departure from the MT. In 44:9 the scroll is emended to include a word which in the MT is marked as doubtful (*puncta extraordinaria; see* CORRECTIONS OF THE SCRIBES). Special interest attaches to the insertions which deal with the divine name. They are sufficiently numerous to attract attention, and in four out of the five cases the text is expanded. But the whole problem of the divine name in Hebrew MSS needs separate treatment, for a study of Genizah fragments and even of the textual variants in the later MSS and Hebrew printed Bibles will show that here, above all other places, there does not seem to have been a rigid adherence to a traditional form.

An enigma in 1QIs^a is the presence in the margins of a number of signs and crosses.

Scholars have been interested in the character of the textual divergences which occur in this scroll. There are numerous readings which vary from the MT (in the seventh edition of Isaiah in *Biblia Hebraica* they are printed in a third section of the critical apparatus), and it is claimed that in some instances they confirm conjectural emendations, in others they offer improvements on the Textus Receptus, while in yet others they are obviously the result of textual error and corruption. It is interesting to note that the RSV has included as many as thirteen changes mainly based on the readings of this scroll, and five of them without any support from ancient versions. They are: 3:24; 14:4, 30; 15:9; 21:8; 23:2; 33:8; 45:2, 8; 49:24; 51:19; 56:12; 60:19.

b) 1QIs^b. The second scroll of Isaiah—so-called simply because 1QIs^a was the first to be unrolled and published—is in many respects a more interesting scroll than its sister, and the whole study of the biblical scrolls would be in better perspective had it been given the same intensive study. It was one of the more difficult scrolls to unroll, but it has now appeared in *Ozar ha-Megilloth ha-Genuzoth*, the Scrolls in the Hebrew University (published by Sukenik and produced by the Bialik Foundation and the Hebrew University, 1954) with fifteen plates of facsimile. This material is augmented by a plate of seven fragments, presumably from the same scroll, published in *Discoveries in the Judaean Desert*, vol. I: *Qumrân Cave I*, by Barthélemy and Milik (pp. 66-68, Plate xii), with facsimiles and full annotation. Taking both sources together, there are available for study some twenty-two fragments from Isa. 1–30; the main bulk of the material, however, is from chs. 38–66, with gaps where the leather of the scroll, especially at the bottom of the columns, has rotted.

There are a few readings in the scroll which disagree with the MT; and a scrutiny of them will serve to underline what is probably one important feature of this scroll. In 53:11 the scroll, as does 1QIs[a], supports the reading preserved in the LXX and advocated by many modern scholars (although others disagree), and the phrase should be translated: "After the travail of his soul he shall see light." Again, in the next verse, 53:12, the scroll has, again with 1QIs[a] and the LXX, "their transgressions" instead of the MT "the transgressors."

There are nine other textual divergences, but without giving the detailed reasoning in each case, it may be noted here that they are all capable of explanation on other grounds than as variant readings. It is also to be noted that of two lists of variants which have hitherto been published, Sukenik mentions some seven dozen, and S. Loewinger (see bibliography) in a most thorough collation—which, however, errs on the side of exaggeration—lists about three hundred. But the very great majority are concerned with waw and yodh, especially waw. Nor is this a matter of a divergent orthography as in 1QIs[a], for it is seldom indeed that the insertion of the consonant waw does not coincide with a vowel of the o class in the printed MT. The same phenomenon occurs in some Cairo Genizah MSS, and an examination of MSS and editions such as is given in the collations of Kennicott, De Rossi, and C. D. Ginsburg will show precisely the same kind of deviation and in roughly equally abundant proportions.

The only hypothesis which has been based on the textual witness of the two Isaiah scrolls is the one put forward by Kahle, and this, backed by the immense learning and prestige of the author, has been accepted and elaborated by other writers. Kahle argues that the presence of variants in both texts, supported by the pre-Masoretic date of the scrolls, confirms the view that he has always expounded— namely, that in pre-Masoretic times the Hebrew text was transmitted only in popular, unauthorized forms, which he calls *vulgärtexte*, and that there was no standardized text (indeed, such a detailed, definitive text cannot be visualized until the Middle Ages).

Obviously the hypothesis is a plausible one, but a possible modification may be mentioned here— namely, that since 1QIs[b] is so essentially similar to Masoretic texts in the Cairo Genizah fragments and to later Masoretic MSS, it may be claimed that in the MS we find a text form which points to the existence of a pre-Masoretic "Masoretic" text. It must not be thought that 1QIs[b] was an authoritative text among the sectarians; it is unlikely, in view of the multiplicity of text forms among the scrolls, that they had any fixed standardized text. But it is very significant that among the Qumran texts one has turned out to be as similar as is humanly possible to what later became the rabbinic standard, orthodox text. As has been noted, the only notable textual variants between the MT and 1QIs[b] are in Isa. 53:12-13, and they have also the support of the LXX, and consequently point to a possible error in the MT transmission itself. The near-identity of orthography, too,

points to a close affinity with the MT. If, then, such a text can be shown to have existed in pre-Masoretic times and in non-Masoretic circles, is it likely that rabbis at a later date chose this particular text to be adopted as their own, or that in the MT they aimed at producing a text similar to it? 1QIs[b] suggests that the textual tradition which led to the MT was in existence in orthodox Judaism before the time of the Masoretes, and that the Masoretes perpetuated, rather than created, a standard text form in the days after the fall of Jerusalem in A.D. 70.

c) 4QSam[a] and [b]. The present assessment of these scrolls is wholly dependent on information supplied by F. M. Cross in various articles (see bibliography). According to his statement there were in Cave IV some MSS of Samuel, in addition to fragments of the historical books Joshua–Kings, which stand in close relationship with one another and which belong to a text form which is reflected by the LXX rather than the MT. One of these MSS, 4QSam[b], Cross estimates to be the most archaic of the Qumran scrolls, going back to *ca.* the end of the third century B.C., and is an earlier exemplar of the textual type discovered in 4QSam[a]. The MS 4QSam[a] is well preserved and contains a substantial amount of text.

If Cross is correct, the significance of the Samuel texts appears to be twofold: (*a*) The affinities between 4QSam[a] and [b] point, even more clearly than the Isaiah texts, to the existence of "types" of text among the Qumran biblical scrolls. There were minor deviations among scrolls of the same "type," as witness the Samuel scrolls themselves, and, again, 1QIs[a] and [b]; but it is now possible to speak in terms of recensions, with affinities with one out of a number of quite different text forms. (*b*) The second feature is one that is also underlined by Cross himself. It is that the question of the Hebrew parent text of the LXX is still unsettled, and that although recent trends to explain textual divergences on the ground of "inner-Greek" tendencies is legitimate, the fact remains that by means of judicious retranslation the LXX can sometimes suggest a Hebrew text which might be at least a form of the pre-Masoretic text, and in a recension which diverges considerably from the present MT.

d) 4QEx[a]. Yet another scroll which relates to previously known text forms is this Exodus Scroll, which has affinities with the SAMARITAN PENTATEUCH and the LXX. The preliminary account by Patrick Skehan (see bibliography) states that the extant text in the scroll ranges from Exod. 6:25 to 37:15, and the material and columnar order of 6:25–18:21 and 28:39–32:30, twenty-four columns in all, can be reconstructed in considerable detail. I.e., the amount of text is sufficient to indicate definite conclusions. The script is Paleo-Hebrew, the orthography varies from both the Samar. Pentateuch and the MT, but has affinities with 1QIs[a]. The important feature, however, is the degree of textual agreement with the non-Masoretic Pentateuch, including such characteristics as the intrusion in Exod. 32:10 of a part of Deut. 9:20. (There is a lacuna in the facsimile, and only part of the quotation has survived, but it is sufficient to warrant the conclusion.)

e) 1QLev. These fragments of Lev. 19–23 in Paleo-Hebrew script have paleographic interest as well as textual. It was originally thought that the script indicated an association with the Samar. Pentateuch, but the nature of the text pointed away from it, and the text was regarded as akin to the Masoretic. Thus, in script, both 4QExᵃ and the Leviticus fragments are Paleo-Hebrew and not Samar. But it still remains impossible to give a positive answer to the question of the date of this "ancient" hand. Many prominent scholars are convinced that the script is genuine pre-Aramaic, and consequently the age of the fragments is older than any other MSS in the whole collection—even as old as the fourth or third century B.C. The other answer is based on the possibility that the script is archaized. It is well known that the Mishnah (Yadaim 4.5) and Talmud (T.B. Zeb. 62a; Shab. 115b) proscribe the use of Paleo-Hebrew script for Holy Writ, and it is tacitly implied that such a practice was current. There is thus ample evidence, which might well be still further supported by these fragments, for the view that among the Jews the two alphabets existed side by side for centuries, even into the Christian era, though they did not enjoy equal prestige.

The general picture that emerges from the Qumran biblical scrolls is that the sectarians, obviously intent on transcribing biblical texts, had no fixed text form, nor did they regard divergent forms in any sense as disturbing. The only possible exception is that corrections in 1QIsᵃ seem to postulate as archetype a text form similar to the MT. An examination of the MSS shows, however, that near-prototypes of the LXX, on the one hand, and the Samar. Pentateuch, on the other, were known and transmitted by them, and it would appear pedantic to deny the existence also of an equally near-prototype of the MT, as witness 1QIsᵇ, and the numerous fragments of the Pentateuch which also diverge from the MT but very rarely. It is a remarkable coincidence that the accidental discovery of divergent text forms in Qumran should agree to a marked extent with recensions previously so well known as the LXX and the Samar. Pentateuch. But it still remains pertinent to ask whether a similar multiplicity of recensional text forms had been transmitted within Judaism itself. It is one thing to think of an element of freedom (i.e., *vulgärtexte*) within a given text form, be it Masoretic, proto-LXX, proto-Samar.; what the scrolls have produced goes beyond this, by demonstrating the existence of distinct recensional text forms.

b. Murabba'at and others. When we turn to the Wadi Murabba'at biblical scrolls, the textual setting is very different. From a couple of letters found in caves in the region and from coins we see that the MSS in general belong to the period of the Bar Cocheba Revolt in A.D. 132-35.

The biblical Hebrew texts consist of fragments of the Pentateuch and of Isaiah, and scholars are united in stressing the uniformity with the MT that characterizes them. Rabbi Akiba's close relations with the revolt are well known, also the part he played in the fixing of the Textus Receptus of the Hebrew Bible. But the fact that these texts were current in Akiba's time points to their existence well before the second century A.D., and serves to underline the suggestion already made that Akiba's text form was not created by him or his successors, but merely more

carefully transmitted, and stripped of traces of the earlier *vulgärtexte*. In any case, it is noteworthy that the Murabba'at Hebrew texts, which belonged to orthodox Judaism, are those which correspond most closely to the MT of all the Dead Sea biblical MSS.

Greater interest attaches to a leather scroll in Greek from a cave in the same area. It contains fragments of the minor prophets, with the books of Jonah, Micah, Nahum, Habakkuk, Zephaniah and Zechariah represented. The best-preserved column, Hab. 1–2, is given in facsimile, with a discussion by Barthélemy, in *RB*, Lx (1953), 18-29; and this article has been further discussed by Kahle, in *TLZ*, no. 2 (1954), cols. 81-94. Barthélemy finds that the MS, from the late first century A.D., consists of a revision of the old LXX, from the pre-Christian era, similar to the basis of the renderings by Aq., Symm., and Theod. in the second century A.D., and is also the text used by Justin Martyr, in the same century, in his Dialogue with Trypho, in which he refutes Christian interference with the LXX. I.e., the Murabba'at Greek text shows that there was in currency, among Jews and Christians in the second century A.D., a common text form, accepted by both parties, which was itself a revision of the earlier LXX.

Kahle, however, insists on a different significance for the text of this scroll. Firstly—and this is important for his argument—he accepts the independent evidence of the paleographer C. H. Roberts, that the scroll belongs to a period between 50 B.C. and A.D. 50—i.e., up to a century earlier than Barthélemy's date. In quality, the text agrees with Aq., Symm., and Theod. only sporadically, and also shows divergences from the MT. It is yet another *Vulgärtext*, which, Kahle insists, were abundant in Judaism before the texts of both Hebrew and Greek Bibles were fixed. Similarity with the text of Justin Martyr, which Kahle allows, indicates, however, that Justin's quotations from the minor prophets belong to the Lucianic recension, a text form which is also represented in the Rylands Papyrus 458 from the second century B.C. I.e., there is here still further evidence, even in the fathers, that a variety of text forms of the Greek Bible were current among Jews in the pre-Christian era. Thus, in Kahle's view, the Murabba'at Greek minor prophets belongs to the type of texts which shows an attempt to establish alignment between the Greek and Hebrew Bibles.

2. The question of an early standard Hebrew text. Thus the fundamental problem which is posed anew by the Qumran scrolls is whether or not a standardized text existed among Jewish orthodoxy in pre-Christian times. Alternatively, is it likely that from among a chaos of divergent popular texts current at that time, a text form emerged which in due course became the standard and authoritative text? In the absence of direct evidence, all we can do is to state the arguments for each alternative.

a. Evidence against. There are three witnesses:

a) The witness of the LXX is clear that its parent text frequently diverged from the classical text. From time to time scholars protest vigorously that too much is made of apparent differences, that more notice should be taken of the interpretive element in the version, which, of course, minimizes the extent of textual divergence between the two. Again, the history of LXX transmission is itself complex, and apparent divergences may be explained on the ground of inner-Greek corruption. But despite all these caveats, it is quite obvious that for many books there are readings which postulate a different *Vorlage,* and in some cases, such as Samuel, Jeremiah, and Job, the divergences are substantial.

b) The witness of the SAMARITAN PENTATEUCH.

c) The witness of the Hebrew text itself. There are a number of duplicated passages which show minor textual variation: II Sam. 22 = Ps. 18; II Kings 18: 13–20:19 = Isa. 36–39; II Kings 24:18–25:30 = Jer. 52; Isa. 2:2-4 = Mic. 4:1-3; Ps. 14 = Ps. 53; Ps. 40:13-17 = Ps. 70; Ps. 57:7-11 + 60:6-12 = Ps. 108.

b. *Evidence for.* (*a*) It appears implicit in such passages as Deut. 17:18-19; Josh. 1:8, that at least the Torah was sacrosanct and inviolable in text form even before the close of the OT.

b) Rabbinic reference in Midrash Rabbah (Num. 11:3) to payment from temple funds for those "who checked the Law Scroll in the Temple court"; i.e., there was an authorized Scroll of the Law which was accepted as archetype for other scrolls. So also T.B. Keth. 106*a*. T.B. Soṭ. 20*a* reports that Rabbi Ishmael (first century A.D.) said to a scribe: "My son, be careful, because thy work is the work of Heaven: if thou omittest a single letter or addest a single letter, thou dost as a consequence destroy the whole world." J. Ta'an. 4.2 says that three scrolls of the Torah were kept in the temple after the return from exile, and in case of divergence the correct reading was that which was given in two of them. Other slightly divergent references to the same principle occur in the Talmudic tractate Sopherim (eighth century) and Siphre (Midrash to Numbers and Deuteronomy) whose authorities go back as far as any rabbinic writing.

c) References outside rabbinic writings which, however, support the theory of a fixed text for the Pentateuch alone (cf. Aristeas 176-79), and the general impression left by the writings of Philo and Josephus.

d) The probable textual implications of the Qumran and Murabba'at MSS, as already indicated.

The whole problem would be simpler if the evidence of the history of the canon were more direct (*see* CANON OF THE OT). The commonly accepted view has been that though the Torah was fixed, there were still minor controversies among the rabbis about the Prophets (e.g., Ezekiel) and the Writings (e.g., Song of Songs) until well into the Christian era. It follows that the transmission of the text would indicate similar conditions. The evidence points to the likelihood that there was a fixed, standard text for the Torah in pre-Christian times, though it is obvious from the divergences in all extra-Masoretic material, the LXX, Samar., Targums, DSS, that there existed also other text forms. But it is likely that the other portions of the OT, the Prophets and Writings, not only had minor divergent forms, but diverged considerably. The Isaiah scrolls from Qumran are sufficiently near the MT to point to a "Masoretic recension" in contrast to other recensions in the pre-Christian period. But it is natural to assume that canonicity involves at least a degree of standard-

ization of the text, and the rabbinic debates in the Mishnah, as well as other references in Josephus and Philo, do presuppose a tripartite division of the OT by the end of the first century B.C.

3. The scribes. From the earliest times, the transmitting of scripture was the work of SCRIBES—*Sopherim;* in the NT, γραμματεύς ("learned in holy scriptures"). They were professionals, and the title is current from the time of Jeremiah (8:8), where the scribe is assumed to be learned in the law and capable of proclaiming its precepts. The office is associated in a technical way with Ezra and with Simeon the Just (Simon the High Priest; *ca.* 300 B.C.), but whether this means more than a unique rabbinic office associated with the "Great Synagogue" (*see* SYNAGOGUE, THE GREAT), is questionable. It is certainly true that the office of scribe, in the sense necessary for our reconstruction, must include a great number of people in each generation and cover a long period, coming down well into the Christian era.

a. Scribal activity. In another respect rabbinic information is important. It derives the Hebrew word *sopher* from סָפַר, "to count," and indeed the scribes did count: they counted the number of letters in the Torah, the number of words, the number of passages, and the number of times certain words or forms of words occurred. This may reflect the inordinate feeling of adoration of the "word" which characterizes much of rabbinic thought and teaching, but it also has a rational justification, for it became a safe means of checking MSS and ensuring a standard transmission. T.B. Kid. 30*a* states that the "early scholars were called *sopherim* because they used to count all the letters of the Torah. Thus, they said, the ו in גחון (Lev. 11:42) marks half the letters of the Torah; דרוש דרש (Lev. 10:16) half the words; והתגלח (Lev. 13:33) half the verses. The ע of מיער (Ps. 80: 14) marks half of the Psalms, and Ps. 78:38 marks half the verses in the book." Though Talmudic references generally belong to a later period, the antiquity of this passage justifies its inclusion here in support of the view that the scribal activity was always concerned with the need for a correct transmission. Gradually the technical efficiency of the scribe's art separated him from the scholar, although some theological significance always attached to the office.

Another feature of scribal activity which presumably goes back to an early period is the division of the text into pericopes. A section, *pisqa,* was marked with a letter פ (פתוחה, "open") or ס (סתומה, "closed") according to whether the next paragraph was begun with a new, indented line, or on the same line after a space, or with a new line without indent where the paragraph ends near a full line. It might appear that this work should be placed in the Talmudic period, but the presence of paragraph division—without the letters—in the Qumran biblical MSS and in early MSS of the LXX draws attention to its probable existence in rabbinic texts at an equally early date. There is considerable divergence between the paragraph division in the scrolls and the MT, and it is likely that it represents sectarian diversity rather than, as was thought at one time, diversity of date.

The scribes, however, did more than simply transcribe texts: by means of various marks and signs they indicated passages in the text concerning which there was traditional doubt. Midrash Rabbah to Num. 3:13 says that in certain words dots are entered over or under consonants which are not to be read, or conversely, over or under consonants which are to be read and the other consonants ignored; and the custom is attributed to the time of Ezra. Other scribal marks, which are to be found even in many printed editions of the MT, include the following:

a) *Puncta extraordinaria* (*see* CORRECTIONS OF THE SCRIBES), found in ten passages in the Pentateuch (Gen. 16:5; 18:9; 19:33; 33:4; 37:12; Num. 3:39; 9: 10; 21:30; 29:15; Deut. 29:28), and five other places (II Sam. 19:20; Ps. 27:13; Isa. 44:9; Ezek. 41:20; 46:22); they are obviously old, and are referred to in Siphre, a rabbinic commentary on Num. 3:39 from the early third century A.D., and in M. Pes. 9.2.

b) *Paseq*, "divider"—a perpendicular stroke between two words. It occurs in about 480 places in the OT, but its antiquity has been doubted, and its function seems to be associated with accentuation.

c) The inverted *Nun*, found nine times (Num. 10: 35-36; Pss. 107:21, 26, 40). Its function was argued among the rabbis: Simon ben Gamaliel in the second century A.D. said it signified textual dislocation, but his son, Judah ha-Nasi', would not admit there was dislocation in the sacred text.

d) Scribal emendations, *Tiqqune Soph*ᵉ*rim* (*see* EMENDATIONS OF THE SCRIBES). These are not indicated by a sign but are listed in Masoretic records, which trace them back to Ezra. The number also varies, but it is usually given as eighteen. They are mostly attempts to avoid anthropomorphisms, and, as a rule, consist of a change of suffix to avoid direct reference to God.

e) Omissions of the scribes, '*Itture Soph*ᵉ*rim*. A list is given in T.B. Ned. 37*b*, and consists of five instances where a word not written is to be read, five instances where a word written is not to be read. The lists of *Tiqqunim* and '*Itturim* are far from complete, and there is still doubt about their real significance.

f) *Sebirin*, "unexpected forms." These, too, are given only in Masoretic lists—they may also be found in the marginal Masora of *Biblia Hebraica* (e.g., Gen. 49:3). The readings are not actually corrected, but simply marked as "unexpected."

g) *K*ᵉ*thîbh* (*see* KETHIBH), and *Q*ᵉ*rê* (*see* QERE). A word in the text in MSS and printed texts is very frequently marked and annotated in the margin with a reference to *Q*ᵉ*rê*. I.e., what is written in the text (*K*ᵉ*thîbh*) should be enunciated differently. Instances of this are innumerable, and range over the whole period of scribal and Masoretic activity.

b. Rabbi Akiba. The one person who stands out in this period of scribal activity is Rabbi Akiba, born *ca.* A.D. 50, martyred *ca.* A.D. 132. In many respects he was responsible for the rehabilitation of the whole religious life of Judaism after the crisis between the collapse of the state of Judea (A.D. 70) and the time of the Bar Cocheba Revolt (132-35). True, there had long been an indirect and unconscious preparation within Pharisaism for the survival of Yahwism independently of worship at the Jerusalem shrine; indeed, such a survival was inherent in the Pharisaic

attitude toward scripture. Consequently, after the collapse of the temple shrine the Bible took over the authority of the shrine, and its prestige increased even beyond that of the Maccabean period, which produced the Pharisaic movement itself. The letter of the Scriptures, particularly of the Torah, was of consequence even in its *yodh* and tittle, its particles and vocalic consonants. Small wonder, then, that rabbinic teaching, and subsequent Christian interpretation, worked out a theory that in Akiba's time, and under his influence, a standard archetype and authoritative text-form of the Hebrew Bible was created, and that this archetype was carefully and scrupulously transmitted by all scribes, because no other text would be tolerated. Furthermore, it is a development that can be seen as part of a yet greater movement during the emergence of Judaism from the greatest crisis in its whole history. It is natural to think of the final fixing of the canon and the codification of the Mishna as part of the program—and it is not less natural to think of the final fixing of the text in the same way.

4. The Masoretes. a. The Masoroth. To Rabbi Akiba the Mishna attributes one of the key words of the whole story of the Masoretic activity. "The tradition is a fence around the Torah" (Pir. Ab. 3.14), and the Hebrew word for tradition is MASORA. From the way it is used, the word was well known by the time of Akiba, and a tradition in the Jerusalem Talmud (Meg. 4.1) associates with it the interpretation of Torah to which Neh. 8:8 refers.

The use of the term "fence" in connection with formal study of the Torah is instructive: it implies that the Masora had a restrictive, as well as an interpretive, application. But in its later, and more common, usage, Masora refers to the massive compilations assembled by rabbinic copyists and text editors, who were called בעלי המסורת, those who controlled and transmitted the Masora, the tradition of the text.

Before we can correctly reconstruct its nature, one other important piece of the history of Judaism must be stressed—namely, Akiba's death and the collapse of the Bar Cocheba Revolt, and the consequent scattering of the Jewish community. Its spread was in two main directions: E and W, Babylonian and Palestinian, technically known as Madinchae and Ma'arabe. There had probably been a die-hard core of Judaism in Babylon since the Exile, and it is a historical possibility, though not well authenticated, that the Jews there had maintained a strict, exclusive type of Judaism of which, in their time, Nehemiah and Ezra had been worthy representatives. From the pre-Christian period we have the divergent interpretations associated with the schools of HILLEL and SHAMMAI, who were representative of the Babylonian and Palestinian traditions respectively. From a later period we have considerably divergent traditions and interpretations incorporated in the Babylonian and Palestinian Talmud and Targums, again reflecting the different schools. It is quite in keeping with this —indeed, it is necessary—that we find also Babylonian and Palestinian Masoroth.

This distinction—whose establishment was one of the main and early discoveries of Paul Kahle—provides a simple and adequate explanation for a confusing feature in the study of the Masora since the Middle Ages. It was assumed that since Akiba had, apparently, established an authoritative text form, a Masora—i.e., a corpus of traditions relative to its transmission—would have accompanied it. But since the extant copies of Masoroth produced at a later period are known to have shown divergence among themselves and also with the MT itself, it was assumed that the uniform Masora had become corrupted in the course of time. What Kahle has shown is that the disagreements reflect earlier divergent traditions, traceable to different Masoroth—namely, those in Babylon and those in Palestine. The reconstruction is rendered still more plausible by reference to two especially important centers of transmission in Babylon, the one at Nehardea and later at Pumbedita, and the other at Sura. Nehardea, which both rabbinic writings and Josephus describe as a strong center of Judaism in Hellenistic and early Christian times, became a prominent academy in the second and third centuries, and is claimed as the place from which emerged an ancient tradition relating to the number of verses in the Bible, which is, as we have seen, one of the main features of scribal activity. Sura's importance came later and was more concerned with Talmudic study than the actual transmission of the Bible, if, indeed, the two should be separated. The Palestinian center was, of course, at Yabneh (Jamnia), whither Judaism moved its seat of learning after the fall of Jerusalem in A.D. 70. After Bar Cocheba's Revolt, the center there died down, and rabbinic pursuits were taken up at Usha in Galilee, where Rabbi Akiba had lived; but by the late third century Tiberias had gained eminence, and though other centers were prominent from time to time, Tiberias succeeded in retaining its place as successor to the Great Sanhedrin, and it was from there that the Palestinian version of the Talmud was issued.

Various collections of Masoroth are in existence; some recent editions are invalidated by the fact that their composition is artificial and based on the wrong conception of an originally uniform corpus, which the authors have attempted to reconstruct by an artificial eclecticism. Of genuine collections the most important is *Ochlah we Ochlah* (*see bibliography*). As a result of Kahle's insistence on separating E and W transmissions, however, interest has turned more on the Hebrew MSS themselves, and the Masoretic notes incorporated in their margins.

The annotation is divided into two classes: *Masora magna*, written on the upper and lower margins of a sheet, and *Masora parva*, on the side margins and between the columns. At the end of each book in the printed rabbinic Bibles other notes are collected and arranged lexically. They are known as *Masora finalis*.

The Masora *magna* and *parva* contain much the same kind of information—e.g., they state the number of times a certain form or a certain word is used, and draw attention to abnormal forms of script, *scriptio plena* and *defectiva*. More significant are the annotations concerning scribal interference with the text. Some of them have already been mentioned, but a further classification belongs to this later period of Masoretic activity.

Among the *literae majusculae, minusculae, suspensae,* the following illustrate the kind of use to which the Masoretic notes were put: Gen. 1:1 begins with an enlarged ב as the initial consonant of the Torah, and other enlarged initial consonants are found in I Chr. 1:1; Prov. 1:1; Eccl. 1:1; Song of S. 1:1; an interesting one, though it is not consistently found, is in Isa. 40:1. The final consonants of Gen. 50:26, and of the Pentateuch (Deut. 34:12), are enlarged. An interesting case is the enlargement of consonants of the Shema (Deut. 6:4), for they are not the first and last letters of the whole formula, which would attract attention to a form שׁד—being the Hebrew word for "demon"—but the letters עד (ע being the last letter of the first word), which, says the Masoretic note, "calls God to 'witness' that the formula is duly recited." Enlarged letters in the middle of words generally have an enumerative significance: thus, the middle consonant of the Torah, the middle consonant of the middle verse. Not all MSS have these special forms, and it will be noticed that they are frequently omitted from the text of *Biblia Hebraica*. *Literae minusculae*, rarer than *majusculae*, sometimes suggest variant readings, or, as in Gen. 23:2; 27:46, the insertion of a letter. *Literae suspensae* include נ in Judg. 18:30, where it is virtually a futile scribal attempt to change the name of Moses into Manasseh to avoid an unfavorable reference to the former.

Thus the interest of the Masoretes seems to have centered on peculiar and irregular forms, for the guidance of the professional scribe. For our purposes, however, they can have but little significance, and even for the most orthodox of Jewish biblicists, they can be of no great value except antiquarian. Indeed, this was the case long before the stabilization and mass production of the text by means of the printing press; even comparatively early MSS from the period following the final appearance of vocalized texts show a tendency to disregard the Masoretic notes of the margins and ends of the column. Or rather, the notes were used by the scribe to give expression to his artistic talent and were transformed by him into ornamental figures, with weird and sometimes beautiful designs, particularly when geometrical patterns were used.

b. Vocalization. But we must go back some centuries in the history of the MT in order to see another, and more important, side to their work—namely, the vocalization of the text. The consonantal text had been supplied with *matres lectionis,* as the vowel-bearing consonants א, ה, ו, and י are called, throughout the centuries of its transmission, and, apparently, the later the text form, the more abundant the *matres lectionis.* In the course of time, and largely under the influence of outside stimuli, the rabbis invented a scheme whereby a detailed and authoritative system of vocalization and accentuation was attached to the text. This could not have taken place until early in the Middle Ages, for neither Talmud seems to know of any system of vocalization. T.B. B.B. 21*b* tells of a debate about the correct pronunciation, and consequently the meaning, of זכר in Deut. 25:19, which can be *zékher* ("remembrance") or *zākhār* ("male"). Tractate Sopherim, attributed to the eighth century A.D., and mainly devoted to scribal activity, seems to mention everything except a scheme of vocalization. Even after vocalization had been generally adopted, there are indications that there was strong opposition to it even as late as the twelfth century, for in *Maḥzor Vitry,* a prayer book from that period, Rabbi Simha, head of the academy at Sura, said that the Pentateuch should not be supplied with vowel points because they were "not derived from Sinai," but a contrary assertion was also expressed, for another rabbi, of the eleventh century, said that the marks of vocalization were "revelation, given to Moses on Sinai; God had not created the Torah lacking in anything."

The first indications of vowel marks are in Masoretic notes and refer to dots or strokes attached to the conjunction and to inseparable prepositions. They are called Mil'el and Milra', according to whether the consonants were to be vocalized with a full vowel (later a *páthaḥ*) or a weak vowel (*sheʷâ*) respectively. This custom of attaching vowel signs—נִקּוּד, "pointing"—was basic to the whole scheme of vocalization. The subsequent story of pointing texts emerges clearly for the first time as a result of the discovery and elucidation in the nineteenth century of Cairo Genizah fragments. The above-mentioned *Maḥzor Vitry* says that three systems of vocalization had been in use at various times for the Hebrew text: the Tiberian, Babylonian, and that of the "land of Israel." It is now apparent that behind this statement lies the complicated story of rival formations and developments in the Babylonian and Palestinian academies, and the final supremacy of the latter, though not before considerable modification had taken place within it. The Babylonian method consisted of inserting above the text the consonants א (=ā), ע (=a), י (=i), ו (=o), but in the course of time they were written small and horizontally, so that they look like a newly devised convention. It came to be known as supralineal pointing, and is still used in some editions of Targum, and in Yemenite texts. More important, however, is the way the Babylonian scheme was modified during the few centuries it flourished. At first, probably in the sixth century A.D., the vowel marks were sporadically attached to consonants to indicate the type of vowel sound preserved in the traditional pronunciation. But in the latter part of the eighth century, a Jewish sect appeared (or made a reappearance, for there are some who claim that their history goes back into the pre-Christian period and is connected with the Qumran sect), called Qaraites, who laid great emphasis on the transmission and recitation of the text. Under their influence, despite their anti-rabbinic and anti-Talmudic teaching in matters of doctrine, a scheme of pointing was invented which was more refined and more scrupulously arranged; and in due course it replaced the earlier scheme. The two types of Babylonian pointing are indicated in Kahle's textual notes in *Biblia Hebraica* as *Einfach* (*E*), "simple," and *Komplizierte* (*K*), "complex," for there are extant MSS among the Genizah fragments which belong to each type; and in the Prolegomena, a list is given of over twenty MSS of Babylonian provenance, with variants cited in the critical apparatus of the text as $V(ar)^{ka}$. In the list a small "a" indicates the Pentateuch, "b" the Prophets, "c" the Writings.

The development of W vocalization can likewise be traced through two different stages. The earlier, known as the Palestinian, has been recovered from a few biblical fragments, again from the Cairo Genizah, and, to a greater extent, from liturgical texts from the same source. When they were first discovered, in 1894, they were tentatively identified as specimens of primitive Palestinian pointing; Kahle, indeed, was able to subdivide the specimens into three groups which he called P1, P2, and P3. This system, moreover, has basic affinities with that preserved in the Samar. Pentateuch and is discussed by him in *Masoreten des Westens,* vol. II (1930), and is referred to in *Biblia Hebraica* under the siglum Var^{Pal}.

Like the Babylonian, the Palestinian vocalization is supralineal, and has eight vocalic signs, though two of them appear to be alternatives. *Dāghēsh* and *Rāphē'* are used sporadically, and, again as in the Babylonian vocalization, they were limited to cases where the text was ambiguous. Dots were placed over different parts of words to indicate disjunctive and conjunctive accents.

The influence of the Qaraite movement caught up with the Palestinian vocalization, as it did with the Babylonian, and forced the Masoretes to produce a more complicated and refined form of pointing. But in one important respect the result was more far-reaching, at least in appearance, than happened in the Babylonian academies. A completely new scheme was invented, consisting of marks which had nothing to do with the Hebrew alphabet, but was composed of dots and dashes. It is the system with which every student becomes familiar as soon as he has learned the Hebrew alphabet. Because its development was in the control of Masoretic families in Tiberias, it has always been known as the Tiberian pointing, and the main period of its activity was between *ca.* 780 and 930, the period during which six generations of a family of Masoretes, ben Asher, flourished. Some members of the family are especially renowned, particularly the last, Aaron ben Moshe ben Asher, who produced an edition of the Masoretic text, fully marked with vowels and accents, and, of course, supplied with its appropriate Masora. In addition, he collected a Masoretic grammar, and published the rules under the title דקדוקי־ הטעמים, "grammatical rules of the accents." It is claimed that a copy of Aaron's Bible was kept in the Sephardic Synagogue at Aleppo, but during the fighting in Syria in 1949-50 the synagogue and its MS treasures were destroyed. The scroll, however, had always been carefully guarded, and only very rarely was even a Jewish scholar allowed to consult it, and that only visually, for a few minutes at a time. Consequently, any real use was denied it, and a collation of it with other texts was virtually impossible.

There was a contemporary Masoretic family of considerable renown in Tiberias, that of ben Naphtali, but its tradition and teaching are not nearly so well known. What is known is that the vocalization transmitted by them varied in details from that of ben Asher: there is a tradition that there are 875 such divergences. More significant is the fact that ben Asher and ben Naphtali variations postulate two distinct traditions of text transmission. The former became the classical and standard form, at least in name. The latter has been preserved in statements and in tabulations handed down in Masoretic collections and references. The most recent is that by C. D. Ginsburg, published in his great work, *The Masorah* vol. I, pp. 571-78 (ח; paragraphs 589-98), and discussed in his *Introduction*, pt. II, ch. X, pp. 241-86. The basis for Ginsburg's list is a British Museum MS, Or 2482-4, "The Mukaddimât or introductions (in Arabic and Hebrew) to the weekly Parashiyyoth of the Pentateuch," by Samuel ha-Rofe al Maghribi, written *ca*. 1380, with a number of other MSS.

Kahle, however (*Masoreten des Westens*, II, 50 ff), discusses the matter further, and demonstrates the importance of getting nearer the time of ben Naphtali himself, as was done by Derenbourg, "Manuel du Lecteur" (*JA*, Series VI, vol. 16 [1870], pp. 309-550), and in a later work by L. Lipschütz, *Ben Ascher—Ben Naftali. Der Bibeltext der tiberinischen Masoreten* (1937). Both these works deal with the list given by a Masorete, Mishael ben Uzziel, who lived in the tenth or eleventh century.

Traditionally, it has always been maintained that the ben Asher–ben Naphtali divergences deal with minutiae, such as the vocalization of יששכר and of the verb אכל when preceded by a preposition; the quiescing of י with an inseparable preposition; the use of *daghesh lene* after ויהי; and one or two points of accentuation. But on the basis of a Cairo Genizah fragment at Hebrew Union College, Cincinnati, S. H. Blank (*see bibliography*) has argued for the existence of a complete recension of the text, which should be attributed to ben Naphtali. The case may be regarded as proved, inasmuch as the details of vocalization seem to have been consistently worked out, but its significance is that it shows that the whole level of the transmission had now reached such a height of refinement that not only the text, but also its pointing, was being finally established among the Masoretes.

5. The Cairo Genizah. Until early in the twentieth century the reconstruction of the history and transmission of the MT was almost wholly dependent on rabbinic statements and traditions, helped by what could be implied from comments by occasional Christian teachers such as Jerome. MSS were limited to late and, as it now appears, confused products of the late Middle Ages; transmitted by scribes who were themselves often ignorant of what had happened to the text before it came to their hands. It was the Cairo Genizah fragments, and their elucidation largely at the hands of Paul Kahle, which first enabled the traditional story to be modified and, obviously, corrected. Kahle's account *The Cairo Geniza* (Schweich Lectures, 1941; published 1947) is the best available treatment in any language of this fascinating and fundamentally important collection of Hebrew MSS.

The synagogue in which the fragments were discovered belongs to A.D. 882, and was rebuilt in 1890, when its MSS first became available in considerable number. Later they were acquired by major libraries throughout the world, but the vast majority are in Britain, in the University of Cambridge, the British Museum, the Bodleian in Oxford, and the John Rylands Library in Manchester—probably in this order. The last-mentioned has about 11,000 fragments, and it is estimated that there are in all well over 200,000 texts; they relate to all aspects of synagogue life and worship (*see* GENIZAH); some date from the eighth century, though others belong to an earlier period and still others are later. There is one MS of the fourth or fifth century which is a palimpsest, and contains as nether script a portion of Aq.'s Greek translation (*see* AQUILA'S VERSION), but this MS is not really relevant to the question of dating the Genizah fragments, as its main use was in the ninth or tenth century for Yannai's Piyuttim. Indeed, J. L. Teicher has argued strongly (*see bibliography*) against dating any Genizah fragments earlier than about the first half of the ninth century.

For the present purpose, it is the biblical fragments that are important. They are mainly from codices; this fact immediately means that they were not official scrolls to be used in synagogue worship but were for the instruction of cantors, worshipers, and probably children. There are some MSS which contain occasional, yet significant, textual variations from the MT: divergences in the form of the divine name—Yahweh, Adonay, Elohim—are fairly common. Again, many MSS are pointed, and it is mainly by means of the various types of pointing that Kahle has reconstructed the history of vocalization outlined above. Targumic renderings accompany the text in many cases, and these again have been of great importance for the history of Aramaic translations (*see* TARGUM). Finally, the importance of marginal Masoretic notes, which sometimes accompany the text, has already been shown. Without the Genizah fragments it would have been well nigh impossible to prove the local character of the E and W transmissions, and this may be regarded as one of the main results of the Genizah fragments.

6. The ben Asher and ben Naphtali texts. The supremacy of the ben Asher edition of the text over that of ben Naphtali was acclaimed by Maimonides (died *ca*. 1204), and from that time on, it has enjoyed the prestige of textus receptus—at least in theory. It is generally assumed that four extant MSS can claim to be ben Asher texts, and they also are the oldest extant MSS of the MT of any considerable length. They are the Cairo Codex of the Prophets, Former and Latter (A.D. 895); the Aleppo Codex (first half of tenth century), partly damaged by fire in 1949; the Leningrad Codex, B 19a (completed 1008), now used as the text for Kittel's *Biblia Hebraica*. Another MS, British Museum, Or 4445, which contains Gen. 39:20–Deut. 1:33, has the name ben Asher entered on its margins, and consequently is traditionally associated with him. Kahle attributes this MS to the period when ben Asher was alive and when his text "was a great authority for the copyist." On the other hand, the text of Or 4445 does not correspond exactly with the final text form of ben Asher. In a critical analysis of Kahle's assessment by Teicher (*see bibliography*), however, points of detail are raised which suggest that the authenticity of all the supposed ben Asher MSS is not yet completely established.

Nevertheless, the general adoption in 1937 of the Leningrad Codex B19a as the basic text form for a critical edition of the Masoretic Bible marks an important step forward in the story of Hebrew textual study, for the history of the text from the eleventh century onward clearly shows that no attempt was made to maintain the textual integrity of the ben Asher text and punctuation.

7. Post-ben Asher texts. *a. MSS.* There is no paucity of MSS from the eleventh century and later. C. D. Ginsburg (*Introduction,* pp. 469-778) has given a detailed description of sixty important MSS, but the fullest lists come from the eighteenth-century collations of Kennicott (*Vetus Testamentum Hebraicum cum variis lectionibus;* 2 vols.; 1776, 1780), and De Rossi (*Variae lectiones Veteris Testamenti . . . ;* 4 vols.; 1784-88, with a supplement, 1798).

It is possible to show that the text form transmitted in these MSS contains, not only a departure from the ben Asher text, but even a tendency to include hybrid readings and, particularly, traces of the transmission of ben Naphtali. Thus, in the collection of MSS known as Erfurt 1, 2, 3, from the eleventh-fourteenth centuries, the tradition is that of ben Naphtali, or at least it is closely associated with him; similarly, the Reuchlin Codex of the Prophets (A.D. 1105), now at Karlsruhe. When Ginsburg was engaged in editing his list of ben Naphtali divergences, he employed, in addition to the Mukaddimat, the following Hebrew MSS, among others: B. Mus. Add 21161, CDG 28 (mid–twelfth century); Add 15250, CDG 21 (thirteenth century); a Toledo MS, Or 2201 (dated A.D. 1246); B. Mus. Or 2348, CDG 40; and Or 4227, CDG 50; where not only are the usual list of variants included, but also additional details about their occurrence.

b. Printed editions. The position was in no way improved when printed Hebrew Bibles began to appear. The Psalms were printed in 1477, the Pentateuch in 1482. Ginsburg (pp. 779-976) has described twenty-two of the most important early editions, and special significance attaches to the following: (*a*) the second rabbinic Bible of Jacob ben Chayim (1524/5), which has largely been used since that time as the text for printed editions, but which was based, as ben Chayim himself declares, on late and unsatisfactory MSS; (*b*) the Complutensian Polyglot (1514-17; published 1520), whose text was merged with that of ben Chayim in the subsequent Polyglots of Antwerp (1569-72), Paris (1629-45), and London (1657-69); (*c*) Kennicott (1776-80) and de Rossi (1784-88), whose importance, as has been noted, is the collation of MSS and printed editions; (*d*) Baer and Delitzsch (1869-92), which was criticized by Ginsburg and by Kahle because of unscientific treatment of the Masora; (*e*) Ginsburg (1894, 1908, 1926), which Kahle has again criticized as showing faulty assessment of unevenly assembled material; (*f*) Kittel, *Biblia Hebraica* (editions 1 and 2; 1906, 1912), whose main drawback, according to present standards, is that the basic text is that of ben Chayim, and the emendations included in the footnotes are too frequently conjectural and lack textual support from the versions.

c. Biblia Hebraica. The principle of editing the text was radically changed for the third edition of *Biblia Hebraica* (1937 —). The text is based on the ben Asher text of Leningrad, B 19a. Its dual critical apparatus has the MSS and versional variants separated from textual emendations, and, for the separate edition of Isaiah, the variants from 1QIs^a are entered in a third section. Furthermore, the *Masorah parva* of the Codex has been entered alongside the margins of the text, and although it does not seem to be widely understood by students, it is certainly of some value in that readers of the text are at least introduced to one of the major features of Masoretic activity.

B. *THE SAMARITAN RECENSION.* The Samar. Pentateuch, at least in theory, goes back to the time of the Samaritan schism. *See* § A1*b; see also* SAMARITAN PENTATEUCH.

C. *THE EVIDENCE OF THE VERSIONS.* Despite the full treatment of the ancient VERSIONS, an assessment of their witness to, and bearing on, the history of the OT text is in order here.

1. LXX. In actual importance, pride of place belongs to the LXX (*see* VERSIONS, ANCIENT, § 2*a*). There are numerous points in the consideration of the LXX which have a direct bearing on the Hebrew text. First, there is the question of whether it is even correct to talk of an "original" LXX text for the OT in the pre-Christian period.

a. The question of proto-LXX. The Letter of Aristeas (*see* ARISTEAS) describes what has traditionally been understood as the origin of the versions, but recently the view has been put forward that Aristeas actually refers to a revision of already existing renderings in order to produce a standard Greek Bible for the use of Jews in the Hellenistic Diaspora. Thus Kahle refers in *The Cairo Genizah* and elsewhere to a "Greek Targum" in the sense of a number of renderings in Greek, which were by no means uniform following. In this view he has had a considerable following.

It can further be shown that alongside, and possibly preceding, the Greek translation there was a transliteration, traces of which are still to be found in proper names and in individual words and phrases. In 1937, F. X. Wutz (*see bibliography*) developed a thesis that the present LXX postulates such a transliteration, and H. M. Orlinsky (*see bibliography*) has shown that transliterations of the Prophets and some of the Writings, as well, were used for lectionary purposes in the synagogues by Hellenistic Jews who were unable to read Hebrew. Despite the failure of Wutz's theory in detail, the basic assumption to the thesis remains true, for it not only explains the forms of proper names, but also provides the best, if not the only, reason for some of the textual variations between the MT and the LXX. On the other hand, there is in the LXX evidence that it was translated directly from the Hebrew. This is seen in innumerable examples of confusion of Hebrew letters, whose Greek equivalents have no resemblance (e.g., אדם and ארם, Edom and Aram), and it can also be shown that at the time the Pentateuch LXX was produced, the writing was in the process of transition from Paleo-Hebrew to the Aramaic square script, and for the later books it can be shown that the script was Aramaic.

The problem, however, is wider than one of transliteration and relationship between alphabets. The NT, quite obviously, still retains many divergent readings which testify to the existence of a variety of Greek translations or of Hebrew text types in the first century A.D. E.g., the text behind Acts 7 and sometimes behind the Letter to the Hebrews has affinities, not with the LXX or the MT, but with the Samar. Pentateuch. Again, there are similar indications within the LXX transmission itself—e.g., in two almost contemporary codices, Alexandrinus and Vaticanus, divergent readings in the book of Judges are almost strong and numerous enough to postulate two different recensions, and one of the natural explanations for such variation is that the two codices preserve two forms of an OT Greek Targum.

What Kahle has demonstrated is the possibility of applying to the LXX his general theory of the history of textual transmission. There is, according to his view, an emergence of the Masoretic standard Hebrew text from the numerous pre-Masoretic variant forms; again, there is in the Aramaic Targums (see TARGUM) an emergence of the standard texts of Onkelos and Jonathan from earlier paraphrases. Likewise, he maintains, the Christian LXX emerged as a standard text out of a number of free and paraphrastic renderings from an earlier period. The Jews, after the fall of Jerusalem, refused to accept the Christian Greek Bible, and produced Aq.'s translation, and the development of the LXX then became an essentially Christian affair. The logical conclusion of Kahle's view—and he has insisted on it—is that any attempt to reconstruct an "original," pre-Christian LXX is futile, because, at least for the books outside the Torah, it is impossible to show that any such text ever existed.

To some degree Kahle's thesis must be accepted, for it cannot be assumed that the LXX was an authoritative text so far as the NT is concerned. In its quotations from the OT, although the LXX predominates, there was freedom to quote from other renderings, and some of these can be identified (e.g., pre-Theod. in the book of Revelation). Yet Kahle has not been convincing in the whole of his reconstruction, and the most cogent counterargument is the appearance of modern critical editions of the LXX, particularly the Göttingen LXX. It is, admittedly, a critical and eclectic text, and scholars often challenge the judgments on which a particular reading is based, but in principle and in its critical apparatus, a method is followed which shows how, behind the largely identifiable recensions of Origen, Hesychius, and Lucian, and the more amorphous Catena group, there is a text which forms the LXX version. The Chester Beatty and Scheide papyri support this contention for the pre-Origen period. Furthermore, in the NT usage the LXX is predominant over all other Greek versions, and obviously proves the existence of such a version. It appears to be overstating the case to argue that the existence of other Greek versions disproves the existence of the LXX for the time immediately prior to the NT.

b. The character of the LXX. The comparison of the LXX text with the present MT raises yet another problem of basic importance. It is demonstrable that in the Pentateuch, though minor variations are legion and despite displacements in Exod. 30 ff and Numbers, the parent text of the LXX basically coincides with the present Hebrew. But for the historical books Joshua–Kings, the Qumran Samuel MSS show that the LXX reflects a parent text which diverges so much that the existence of a different Hebrew recension must be assumed. The conclusion was offered as far back as the late nineteenth century, that, compared with the LXX, the book of Joshua in the MT had been expanded in certain sections, and the additional readings were later incorporated in some LXX recensions—e.g., the Lucianic. The view that textual additions in the LXX are to be attributed to inner-Greek tendencies must consequently be modified. There are further complications. The problem of the basic Hebrew text of Chronicles, Ezra-Nehemiah, involves not only the rendering of those books in the LXX but also their relationship to the apocryphal I and II Esdras. The Greek text of Esther again appears in two forms in the Greek Bible, the ordinary LXX and the Lucianic, and both forms have additions which bear no relationship to the Hebrew text. Incidentally, it is significant that whereas in the Greek Bible the additions are interspersed among the chapters of what correspond to the Hebrew Esther, in the Vulg. they are placed at the close of the book. Again, the Greek text of Job is interesting. As they stand, the LXX and the MT are more or less in agreement, but this is because of Origen, who took over about a sixth part of the whole Greek version from the version of Theod. The question, then, is whether it is even approximately correct to use both Greek renderings indiscriminately for the textual reconstruction of the Hebrew Job on the basis of the LXX. Some aspects of the problem have been discussed by D. H. Gard, other aspects by Gerleman; and a general review by Wevers (see bibliography) emphasizes that the problem is still an open one. The great difficulty with the Psalter is to establish the LXX text itself, for as the hymnbook of the Hellenistic Diaspora and of the Christian church, the text was inevitably subjected to innumerable changes. In LXX Proverbs there are grounds for thinking that, when compared with the order in the MT, the various collections of Proverbs incorporated in the book had at one time an independent existence. In the book of Ecclesiastes it appears that the version of Aq. had ousted the original LXX at an early period.

For the Prophets the text of Jeremiah stands out as the most difficult to outline. The text of the LXX is shorter than the MT by about an eighth, and it can be shown that the Greek version not only is homogeneous, but also provides a metrical regularity which is lacking in the MT. Textual transpositions, too, reflect a diversity of tradition, and we are left with the obvious conclusion that there were originally two independent Hebrew recensions, the one reflected in the present LXX and the other retained in the MT. For Isaiah, the latest examination of the text, by Seeligmann (see bibliography), shows that the version is far from being an adequate translation, and that its author had not intended it to be a literal rendering. Consequently, it has but little to contribute to the textual treatment of the MT. For the remainder of the Prophets, the LXX has comparatively little to offer apart from individual passages. The book of Daniel, of course, constitutes a different problem, for the LXX has traditionally transmitted the text of Theod., and the genuine LXX was unknown, apart from the eleventh-century Chigi MS, until the discovery in 1930 of the Chester Beatty Papyrus 967 from the third century A.D. *See* VERSIONS, ANCIENT.

c. Hermeneutics in the LXX. Another, probably more profitable, aspect of the study of the LXX text in relation to the Hebrew deals with the presence in the version of hermeneutic principles. Interpretations and elaborations of the text show far-reaching inner-Greek influence. Study of this feature is well organized and can be conveniently observed when applied to the main sections, the Pentateuch, the historical books, Isaiah, the wisdom literature. An important fact which is emerging is that conclusions relating to one section do not necessarily apply to the others. Thus, it is misleading to speak of anti-anthropomorphisms in the LXX generally, because, even within one section, the Pentateuch, it becomes clear by analysis that this trait is strongly represented in Exodus, whereas it is practically nonexistent in Leviticus. By the same token, it is wrong to generalize about the nature and provenance of any particular hermeneutic scheme, and to insist that it is everywhere either Jewish-rabbinic or Hellenistic. It can be either. E.g., Gerleman has shown that in the LXX of Proverbs the translation reflects considerable familiarity with Greek tradition and style, even in matters of meter and assonance, on the one hand, and Stoic philosophy, on the other. In a critical survey, however, Wevers says that most of the instances quoted by Gerleman are capable of easier and more natural explanation as Jewish interpretation. Obviously there is considerable disagreement among scholars on the general approach to the subject. The first to emphasize its importance was Fränkel, but its main growth has taken place more recently, with H. S. Gehman and his school, including Wevers as a prominent member, in the U.S.A., and Georg Bertram, followed to some extent by Gerleman, in Europe; it may also be mentioned that C. H. Dodd in Great Britain gave some interesting pointers in the same direction.

2. Non-LXX Greek Bibles. The non-LXX Greek renderings of the first two centuries, Aq., Symm., and Theod., have a direct bearing on the history of the MT. The first, of course, reflects the standardized Masoretic text and the determination of Judaism to reject all nonconformist texts, especially the LXX. The basic affinity between Aq. and the Targum of Onkelos is significant, just as is the similarity in the two names. The exact place and function of Theod. is not clear, nor the extent of its similarity with Targum Jonathan. The likelihood that the Symm. translation is a Christian (Ebionite) product tends to place it outside the present survey. But the whole question arises afresh because of the discovery of the MS containing sections of the minor prophets in Greek in the Wadi Murabba'at caves (*see* § A1*b*). Mention must also be made of the Aq. fragments in the Cairo Genizah palimpsests from the fifth-sixth centuries A.D. which contain passages of I-II Kings and Ps. 22.

3. The Targums. Next to the Greek Bible and possibly contemporary and parallel to it are the Aramaic Targums (*see* TARGUM; VERSIONS, ANCIENT), and once again, from the standpoint of their relevance to the Hebrew text, an important problem is whether or not Kahle is right in his hypothesis that a number of free paraphrastic Aramaic renderings emerged in a standardized and authoritative text form. The material at our disposal consists of two fairly well-defined groups: (*a*) the literal official translation of the Pentateuch in Targum Onkelos and of the Prophets in Targum Jonathan; and (*b*) free interpretations, with sometimes lengthy interpolations of a Midrashic character, with a didactic purpose, which are available for Pentateuch, Prophets, and Hagiographa. They consist of Targums for the Pentateuch, Jerusalem I (Pseudo-Jonathan) and II, as well as the other sections of the OT. How far back they go is not known, but there is evidence of their existence in pre-Christian times. An Aramaic Targum of Job was found at Qumran (Cave XI) in 1956. The synagogue officials opposed the use of any Targum in written form; but M. Meg. 4.4 states that the oral translation follows the reading of the Torah verse by verse and the reading of the Prophets after every three verses. From numerous fragments from the Cairo Genizah which contain text and Targum, it would appear that at a later time not only were written Targums permitted in the synagogue, but also Prophets and Writings were rendered verse by verse.

It is assumed that the free paraphrastic Targums are older than the literal renderings; and consequently, of the two types of Targum for the Pentateuch, the former are the more valuable for the treatment of the text and the linguistic study of Aramaic. Particular intrinsic interest attaches to the Targum known as Jerusalem Targum II, or the Fragment Targum published by Ginsburger in 1899 (*Das Fragmententhargum, Targum Yerushalmi zum Pentateuch*), and this has been enhanced by an announcement which not only proclaims the discovery of a complete new MS (*Neofiti* 1) of this Targum in the Vatican Library, thus rendering the name Fragment Targum obsolete, but also states that despite its late date—fifteenth century A.D.—it will provide important evidence for the degree of "infiltration" of the Onkelos text into the text of the freer Targums. This feature was already known from the way the text of Onkelos replaced the quotations from the Torah in Targum Jonathan, which explains why this Targum too might be regarded as an official text.

In their present form Onkelos and Jonathan presuppose a long period of revision, and in spite of the names having been identified with Aq. and Theod. and consequently their date pushed back to the second century A.D., it can be shown that the final revision took place in Babylon in the fifth or sixth century. I.e., their emergence as revised, standardized text form is explained as the end of a long process. It is Kahle's hypothesis. What is still a problem, however, is that if Kahle is right, how were the unofficial Targums of Jerusalem I and II and others allowed to survive, indeed to flourish, if the purpose of the official Targums was to replace the free paraphrases? It seems reasonable to assume that both types of Targum, free and official, were current long before that time, and that the final revision of the latter does not preclude their existence at least as far back as the second century A.D. There is more justification for the production of Aramaic translations at that time than in the sixth century, by which time Judaism was everywhere familiar with the Hebrew of the Mishna and Talmud. Furthermore, the analogy of the Greek Bible is relevant. The post-70 Judaistic enthusiasm produced Aq.'s translation, which was totally independent of the LXX and other Greek versions; likewise Onkelos was independent of Jerusalem I and II and others. But the new translations did not necessarily abolish the already existing renderings, and the paraphrastic Targums were transmitted alongside the other.

It remains likely, however, that it is the paraphrastic Targums which retain pre-Masoretic material, and the new complementary material provided by *Neofiti* 1 is extremely welcome.

4. LXX-daughter translations. Other translations, the Peshitta, the daughter translations of the LXX, Old Latin and Vulg. Arabic, have various incidental contributions to make to the textual study of the MT, but they do not substantially affect the general story of the Hebrew textual transmission.

D. *THE CLASSIFICATION OF SCRIBAL ERRORS AND THEIR EMENDATION.* 1. The MT as a recension. The story of the Masoretic transmission of the text makes it clear that there are sporadic traces of scribal interference with the text, which are in accordance with preconceived theological standpoints or, more important, with liturgical needs. Indeed, the invention of both the Babylonian and the Tiberian vocalizations and accents is part of the Masoretic recensional activity. They form part of the legitimate development of the text and should not be subject to critical treatment solely as instances of scribal errors; their parallel would be the rabbinic and prerabbinic glosses and interpolations within the text itself.

2. Accidental errors. The scribes, however, were aware of accidental textual corruption, particularly where at the end of a line part of a word was written, to be repeated at the beginning of the following line. In order to avoid the inevitable dittography, any vacant space at the end of the line was filled with an elongated form of one or other of the five *literae dilatabiles,* א, ה, ל, ת, ם; and Genizah fragments and later MSS and printed editions show how widespread the custom had become. Sometimes other consonants were also used for this purpose.

Nevertheless, scribal errors do occur within the Masoretic tradition, and lists of types of error and instances are available in a number of books (*see bibliography*). In a recent treatment, *The Text of the OT* (1952; English translation 1957), E. Wurthwein has obtained excellent instances of the various classes of errors in the Isaiah scroll 1QIsᵃ, a text which is admittedly one of the most notorious examples of careless scribal work. The only caveat which might be entered against the use of this scroll is that it is not representative of the Masoretic scribal activity, and an examination of the Genizah fragments will show that the incidence of scribal errors is far less common. The main sources of error include the following:

a) Confusion of similar consonants. It should be noted that as a result of the Qumran Scrolls discovery, the question of Hebrew writing and paleography has been opened wider than ever before. Until 1947 the Aramaic script as used for the Hebrew Bible in the pre-Christian era was unknown. The Nash Papyrus was generally regarded, until 1937, as representing the script of the late first or early second century A.D.—i.e., a period well after the Aramaic script had become finally established. Albright's discussion of the papyrus in 1937 (*see bibliography*) caused a change in the attitude of most scholars, and a date early in the first century B.C. is now generally accepted. The Qumran Scrolls obviously contribute immensely to our knowledge of Aramaic paleography, and it is an added advantage that the script in the scrolls—in contrast to the text —is careful, highly developed, and apparently professional. But the result of the paleographical studies is to underline the dangers of relying solely on script to claim confusion between similar consonants in the MT. At best this should be used only as secondary support when there are other grounds for assuming scribal error.

There are instances of confusion which are well established. ב and ד in Gen. 9:7; ב and ר in I Kings 22:32; כ and מ in II Kings 22:4; מ and שׁ in Num. 24:19; א and ד in II Chr. 22:10; ה and שׁ in Num. 26:38-39; ד and ר frequently, and can be presupposed for both Paleo-Hebrew and Aramaic square scripts.

b) Corruption due to confusion in word-division. An instance of two words rendered as one occurs in Ps. 45:3; three words as two in Hos. 7:4; three words as one in Ps. 90:11; two words as one in Isa. 2:20 (which is supported by 1QIsᵃ, with an interesting change of plural ending); two words as three in Jer. 23:33.

c) *Matres lectionis.* The history of the textual transmission, especially since the Qumran discovery, shows that the use of vowel letters varied considerably and was a fruitful source of scribal error, as can be seen in the very frequent divergence between *Qere* and *Kethibh* readings (see F. M. Cross, Jr., and D. N. Freedman, *Early Hebrew Orthography* [1952]).

d) Dittography and haplography. Leaving aside the possibility that a case of dittography is responsible for a grammatical howler in II Kings 15:16, it is clear from MS evidence in II Kings 18:17 that the repetition of the word "Jerusalem" has caused a dittograph of two complete words; in II Kings 11:17 we have a possible dittograph of four words; II Kings 7:13 has, again demonstrated by MSS, a dittography covering a full clause of seven words. Such instances as I Kings 7:42; Isa. 17:12-13 should be regarded as variant marginal readings which have infiltrated into the text, rather than as mere dittographs. An interesting case of haplography causing confusion between two words may be found in Ps. 17:10 (cf. footnote in *Biblia Hebraica*). The omissions of sections of text, such as those in Gen. 4:8; I Kings 10:15 (cf. II Chr. 9:14); Josh. 21:36-37, are surprising because the sense is disturbed. In I Sam. 13:1, however, the omission of the number may be deliberate. In some places—e.g., Judg. 20:13; Ruth 3:5—the vocalization of omitted words has been regularly entered in the text by scribes and printers.

e) Homoeoteleuton. Whereas in the preceding

group dittographs and haplographs occur frequently with identical words or parts of words, this next class is much wider, because all that is involved is an ocular slip between two words whose endings are similar. Acknowledged instances occur in Gen. 1:9; I Sam. 14:41.

f) Errors due to dictation. It was commonly assumed that scribes wrote out their MSS by dictation, which would, consequently, have been a fruitful source of error, especially by confusion between both the gutturals and the sibilants. But there is no rabbinic reference to any custom of dictation, and it seems wise not to include this class of possible *lapsus,* especially since the existence of visual errors is so incompatible with it.

3. The restoration of the text. a. The MT. Regarded as a whole, the discipline textual criticism of the Hebrew OT has in principle two quite different purposes, which reflect the objective of the critic, and in this respect the critical apparatus of *Biblia Hebraica* may be regarded as roughly indicative of the method of their implementation. On the one hand the critic may be involved in no more than the establishment of the MT, and producing a list of possible variants. For this purpose extant MSS in the Masoretic tradition should be brought into considerable use; and Ginsburg, Kennicott, and De Rossi resume their legitimate function. In addition, the biblical MSS from the Cairo Genizah should be collated, and due attention paid to quotations in rabbinic sources, Talmudic, Midrash, Mishna— they all have their special contributions. From the DSS, the MSS from Murabba'at belong to the same tradition and should also be collated.

b. The hypothetical "original Hebrew." The problem becomes complicated when the other scrolls, the extremely important Qumran documents, are considered. If we are to be guided by other textual criticisms—e.g., the NT and LXX—great care should be taken to keep apart all textual evidence of divergent recensions. If Kahle is right, even the MT itself is hybrid, and was never ideally free of mixed readings or vocalizations except possibly in the strictly ben Asher MSS. But if, for convenience, it is allowed that the Masoretes did transmit a standard text from the time of Akiba, it should follow that all text forms for the pre-Masoretic period are non-Masoretic, and do not provide material for this particular section of the textualist's work.

Nevertheless, the need for the textualist to deal with the hypothetical pre-Masoretic text is manifest. It is he alone who is capable of assessing the text forms supplied by Qumran on the one hand, and the ancient versions on the other. His starting point is in the MT, together with the variants in the above-mentioned first critical apparatus. He proceeds with the greatest caution, and deals with the text piece-meal. Before venturing on emendation, the textualist observes that latterly, great progress has been made in the study of Hebrew lexicography, both in relation to cognate languages and its own semantics, and new meanings have been established for words which in the past were confusing. Even readings well established as accidental textual errors have from time to time been justified, and the production of at least two major Hebrew dictionaries during

the past few years proves that all was not well with the lexicography of the past.

Emendation, however, is still necessary, and the Hebraist draws on the resources of the versions specialist. Here again—indeed, above all other places— he realizes how gingerly he must proceed. It is utterly naïve and anachronistic simply to take a LXX reading, even from Swete or Rahlfs, turn it into Hebrew, and claim that it represents the text of the Hebrew in its pre-Masoretic "original" form. The second critical apparatus of *Biblia Hebraica* has frequently been criticized on this score, and it must be admitted that it does fail to reflect very much of the highly specialized work that has been devoted especially to the LXX.

As a result of all the safeguards to the text and versions, conjectural emendation must needs play a far less prominent role in textual criticism, and it is admittedly at best subjective. But it is still legitimate. The textual critic is an interpreter of the text, and aims to produce a rendering that makes the message of the Scriptures intelligible. If he finds that despite the sources available to him, the passage with which he deals still defies explanation, he must resort to manipulation, and emend according to his understanding. But he does not present his emendation as an authoritative reading, and for this reason he knows that in any printed edition of the MT conjectural emendation cannot be placed anywhere other than in a secondary section of the critical apparatus.

Bibliography. General: OT Introductions by R. H. Pfeiffer (2nd ed., 1948); A. Bentzen (2nd ed., 1952); O. Eissfeldt (2nd ed., 1956). Introduction to the RSV (1952). P. Kahle, *The Cairo Geniza* (1947). D. W. Thomas, "The Textual Criticism of the OT," in H. H. Rowley, ed., *OT and Modern Studies* (1951), pp. 238-63. B. J. Roberts, *The OT Text and Versions* (1951). H. W. Robinson, ed., *The Bible in Its Ancient and English Versions* (2nd ed., 1954). P. Kahle, *Opera Minora* (1956). I. M. Price, *The Ancestry of Our English Bible* (3rd ed., by W. A. Irwin and A. P. Wikgren; 1956). E. Würthwein, *The Text of the OT* (English trans. P. R. Ackroyd; 1957). F. G. Kenyon, *Our Bible and the Ancient MSS* (1958).

On the Dead Sea Scrolls: O. Eissfeldt, *Variae Lectiones . . . ad Jes 1–66 et Hab 1–2* (1951). P. Kahle, *Die hebräischen Handschriften aus der Höhle* (1951). C. Kuhl, "Schreibereigentümlichkeiten. Bemerkungen Zur DSIa," *VT,* II (1952), 307-33. D. Barthélemy, "Redécouverte d'un chainon manquant de l'histoire de la LXX," *RB,* LX (1953), 18-29. F. M. Cross, "A New Qumran Biblical Fragment Related to the Original Hebrew Underlying the LXX," *BASOR,* 132 (1953), 15-27. R. de Vaux, "Quelques textes hébreux de Murabba'at," *RB,* LX (1953), 268-75. P. Kahle, "Die im August 1952 entdeckte Lederrolle mit dem griechischen Text der Kleinen Propheten und das Problem der LXX," *TLZ,* 79 (1954), 82-94. S. Loewinger, "Variants of DSIii," *VT,* IV (1954), 155-63. M. Burrows, *The Dead Sea Scrolls* (1955). F. M. Cross, "The Oldest MSS from Qumran," *JBL,* LXXIV (1955), 147-72. P. Skehan, "Exodus in the Samaritan Recension from Qumran," *JBL,* LXXIV (1955), 182-87. P. Benoit, "Le travail d'édition des fragments MSS de Qumran," *RB,* LXIII (1956), 49-67 (English trans., *BA,* XIX [1956], 75-96). P. Skehan, "The Qumran Manuscripts and Textual Criticism," *Vetus Testamentum,* Supplement IV (1957), pp. 182-87. M. Burrows, *More Light on the Dead Sea Scrolls* (1958). F. M. Cross, *The Ancient Library of Qumran* (1958). M. Martin, *The Scribal Character of the Dead Sea Scrolls* (2 vols.; 1958). J. T. Milik, *Ten Years of Discovery in the Wilderness of Judaea* (1959). B. J. Roberts, "The Second Isaiah Scrolls from Qumran (1QIs^b)," *Bulletin of the John Rylands Library,* 42 (1959), 132-44.

On the MT: S. Frensdorff, *Ochlah we Ochlah* (1864). C. D.

Ginsburg, *Introduction to the Masoretico-Critical Edition of the Hebrew Bible* (1897). C. Levias, "Masorah," *JE,* VIII (1904), 365-71. P. Kahle, *Masoreten des Ostens* (1913); "Die masoretische Uberlieferung des hebräischen Bibeltextes," in H. Bauer and P. Leander, *Historische Grammatik der hebräischen Sprache* (1922), pp. 71-162; *Masoreten des Westens,* I (1927); II (1930); "Der AT Bibeltext," *Theol. Rundschau,* V (1933), 227-38. S. H. Blank, "A Hebrew Bible MS in the Hebrew Union College Library," *HUCA,* VIII–IX (1931-32), 229-55. W. F. Albright, "A Biblical Fragment from the Maccabean Age: The Nash Papyrus," *JBL,* LVI (1937), 145-76. R. Gordis, *The Biblical Text in the Making: A Study of the Kethib-Qere* (1937). P. Kahle, *Prolegomena to Kittel's Biblia Hebraica*[3] (1937). A. Sperber, "Problems of the Masora," *HUCA,* XVII (1942-43), 293-394. E. Brønno, *Studien über hebräische Morphologie und Vokalismus auf Grundlage der mercatischen Fragmente der 2 Kol. der Hexapla des Origenes* (1943). J. L. Teicher, "The Oldest Dated Document in the Genizah," *Journal of Jewish Studies,* I (1949), 156-58; "The ben Asher Bible MSS," *Journal of Jewish Studies,* II (1950), 17-25. C. Brockelmann, "Das Hebräische," *Semitistik,* vol. III (1953), pp. 59-69. M. H. Segal, "The Promulgation of the Authoritative Text of the Hebrew Bible," *JBL,* LXXII (1953), 35-47. W. F. Albright, "New Light on Early Recensions of the Hebrew Bible," *BASOR,* 140 (Dec., 1955), 27-33. M. Greenberg, "The Stabilization of the Text of the Hebrew Bible . . . ," *JAOS,* 76 (1956), 157-67. F. M. Cross, Jr., "The Dead Sea Scrolls," *IB,* XII (1957), 645-67, especially "The Early History of the [OT] Text," pp. 655-57.

On ancient versions: H. A. Redpath, "A contribution towards settling the dates of the translation of the various books of the LXX," *JTS,* VII (1906), 606-15. H. B. Swete, *Introduction to the OT Greek* (rev. R. R. Ottley; 1914). J. Fischer, *Zur LXX Vorlage im Pentateuch* (1926). C. H. Dodd, *The Bible and the Greeks* (1934). G. Bertram, "Zur LXX-Forschung," *Theol. Rundschau,* III (1931), 283-96; V (1933), 173-86. H. M. Orlinsky, "The Columnar Order of the Hexapla," *JQR,* XXVII, NS (1936-37), 137-49. F. X. Wutz, *Systematische Wege von der LXX zum hebräischen Urtext* (1937). G. Bertram, "Zur LXX-Forschung," *Theol. Rundschau,* X (1938), 69-81, 133-67. V. Hamp, *Der Begriff "Wort" in den aramäischen Bibelübersetzungen* (1938). C. T. Fritsch, *The Anti-Anthropomorphisms of the Greek Pentateuch* (1943). J. Ziegler, *Studien zur Verwertung der LXX im Zwölfprophetenbuch, ZAW,* XIX (1944), 107-33. G. Gerleman, *Studies in LXX: Job* (1946); *Chronicles* (1946). H. M. Orlinsky, "Current Progress in Problems in LXX," in H. R. Willoughby, ed., *The Study of the Bible Today and Tomorrow* (1947), pp. 144-61. G. Gerleman, *Synoptic Studies in the OT,* Lunds Universitets Årsskrift 44 (1948). I. L. Seeligmann, *The LXX Version of Isaiah* (1948). F. Stummer, "Zur Stilgeschichte der alten Bibelübersetzungen," *ZAW,* 20 (1945-48), 195-231. P. Katz, "Das Problem des Urtextes der LXX," *Theologische Zeitschrift,* V (1949), 1-24. H. M. Orlinsky, *The LXX, The Oldest Translation of the Bible* (1949). D. H. Gard, *The Exegetical Method of the Greek Translator of the Book of Job, JBL* Monograph no. 8 (1952). H. S. Gehman, "Hebraisms in the Old Greek Version of Genesis," *VT,* III (1953), 141-48; "Ἅγιος in the LXX and Its Relation to the Hebrew Original," *VT,* IV (1954), 337-48. J. W. Wevers, "LXX Forschungen," *Theol. Rundschau,* 22 (1954), 85-138, 171-90. D. W. Gooding, *Recensions of the LXX Pentateuch* (1955). G. Gerleman, *Studies in LXX: Proverbs* (1956). D. Macho, "Una copia completa del Targum palestinense al Pentateuco en la Biblioteca Vaticana," *Sefarad,* XVII (1957), 119-21. M. Black, "The Recovery of the Language of Jesus," *NTS,* III (1957), 305-13.

On restoration of the text: F. Delitzsch, *Die Lese-und Schreibfehler im AT* (1920). F. Perles, *Analekten zur Textkritik des AT* (1895; new ed., 1922). A. Geiger, *Urschrift und Übersetzungen der Bibel* (1857; new ed., 1928). J. Kennedy in N. Levison, ed., *An Aid to the Textual Amendment of the OT* (1928). J. Reider, "The Present State of Textual Criticism of the OT," *HUCA,* VII (1930), 285-315. H. S. Nyberg, "Das textkritische Problem des AT am Hoseabuch demonstriert," *ZAW,* XI (1934), 241-54. P. Ruben, "A Proposed New Method of Textual Criticism in the OT," *AJSL,* LI (1934-35), 30-45, 177-88; LII (1935-36), 34-42. P. Volz, "Ein Arbeitsplan für die Textkritik des AT," *ZAW,* XIII (1936), 100-113. E. Robertson, *The Text of the OT and the Methods of Textual Criticism* (1939). R. Marcus, "On the Textual Criticism of the Hebrew Bible," *JBL,* LXVIII (1949), 29-34. J. Morgenstern, "The Loss of Words at the Ends of Lines in MSS of Biblical Poetry," *HUCA,* XXV (1954), 41-83. J. Weingreen, "Rabbinic Type Glosses in the OT," *Journal of Semitic Studies,* II (1957), 149-62.   B. J. ROBERTS

*TEXT, NT. No other writing which has come to us from the ancient world has had so great an influence upon Western life and culture as has the NT. And yet, the text of no other body of ancient literature exists in so many different forms. This variety is, in the main, the result of the almost embarrassing number of copies of the NT that have been preserved from ancient times and from the Middle Ages. The ultimate task of textual criticism is to recover, with as much precision and assurance as possible, the original text.

A. The problem
B. Sources
  1. Ostraca and talismans
  2. Papyri
  3. Uncials
  4. Minuscules
  5. Lectionaries
  6. Versions
  7. Quotations of the Church Fathers
C. Written text of the NT
D. Printed text of the NT
  1. The Complutensian Polyglot
  2. Erasmus
  3. Other early editions
  4. Modern critical editions
E. Theory and method
  1. From Origen to Bentley
  2. The work of Richard Bentley
  3. Bengel and Wettstein
  4. Beginnings of modern criticism
  5. Westcott and Hort
    a. Internal evidence of readings
    b. Internal evidence of documents
    c. Genealogical evidence
    d. Internal evidence of groups
  6. Von Soden and later developments
F. Conclusion
Bibliography

A. **THE PROBLEM.** The NT is now known, in whole or in part, in nearly five thousand Greek MSS alone. Every one of these handwritten copies differs from every other one. In addition to these Greek MSS, the NT has been preserved in more than ten thousand MSS of the early versions (*see* VERSIONS, ANCIENT) and in thousands of quotations of the Church Fathers. These MSS of the versions and quotations of the Church Fathers differ from one another just as widely as do the Greek MSS. Only a fraction of this great mass of material has been fully collated and carefully studied. Until this task is completed, the uncertainty regarding the text of the NT will remain.

It has been estimated that these MSS and quotations differ among themselves between 150,000 and 250,000 times. The actual figure is, perhaps, much higher. A study of 150 Greek MSS of the Gospel of Luke has revealed more than 30,000 different readings. It is true, of course, that the addition of the readings from another 150 MSS of Luke would not add another 30,000 readings to the list. But each MS studied does add substantially to the list of variants. It is safe to say that there is not one sentence in the NT in which the MS tradition is wholly uniform.

Many thousands of these different readings are variants in orthography or grammar or style and have no effect upon the meaning of the text. But there are many thousands which have a definite effect upon the meaning of the text. It is true that not one of these variant readings affects the substance of Christian dogma. It is equally true that many of them do have theological significance and were introduced into the text intentionally. It may not, e.g., affect the substance of Christian dogma to accept the reading "Jacob the father of Joseph, and Joseph (to whom the virgin Mary was betrothed) the father of Jesus who is called 'Christ' " (Matt. 1:16), as does the Sinaitic Syriac (see VERSIONS, ANCIENT); but it gives rise to a theological problem.

It has been said that the great majority of the variant readings in the text of the NT arose before the books of the NT were canonized and that after those books were canonized, they were very carefully copied because they were scripture. This, however, is far from being the case.

It is true, of course, that many variants arose in the very earliest period. There is no reason to suppose, e.g., that the first person who ever made a copy of the autograph of the Gospel of Luke did not change his copy to conform to the particular tradition with which he was familiar. But he was under no compulsion to do so. Once the Gospel of Luke had become scripture, however, the picture was changed completely. Then the copyist was under compulsion to change his copy, to correct it. Because it was scripture, it had to be right.

Many thousands of the variants which are found in the MSS of the NT were put there deliberately. They are not merely the result of error or of careless handling of the text. Many were created for theological or dogmatic reasons (even though they may not affect the substance of Christian dogma). It is because the books of the NT are religious books, sacred books, canonical books, that they were changed to conform to what the copyist believed to be the true reading. His interest was not in the "original reading" but in the "true reading." This is precisely the attitude toward the NT which prevailed from the earliest times to the Renaissance, the Reformation, and the invention of printing. The thousands of Greek MSS, MSS of the versions, and quotations of the Church Fathers provide the source for our knowledge of the earliest or original text of the NT and of the history of the transmission of that text before the invention of printing.

B. *SOURCES*. It does not lie within the scope of this article to discuss in detail all the sources for the study of the text of the NT. Actually, no complete catalogue of the thousands of MSS of the versions has ever been published, nor, indeed, has one ever been compiled. For information on the Church Fathers, many excellent patrologies and special studies are available.

The official list of Greek NT MSS which is now accepted by all scholars was drawn up by C. R. Gregory and has been kept up to date by Ernst von Dobschütz, Walter Eltester, and Kurt Aland. This official list divides the MSS into six quite arbitrary and sometimes quite meaningless classifications according to the material upon which they are written, the kind of writing used, and the use for which they were intended. These classifications are: ostraca; talismans; papyri; uncials; minuscules; and lectionaries. To these Greek MSS as thus classified must be added the evidence of the versions and of quotations from the fathers.

1. Ostraca and talismans. Twenty-five OSTRACA and nine talismans (*see* AMULETS) containing small portions of NT text are now known. They are of no importance for the recovery of the original text or for the history of the transmission of the text. It will, therefore, suffice here to note that the ostraca are designated by the letter "O" and an index figure (e.g., O^1, O^2) and that the talismans are designated by the letter "T" and an index figure (e.g., T^1, T^2).

2. Papyri. Less than a century ago, not one fragment of PAPYRUS was known which contained any NT text. Today, sixty-four papyrus NT MSS (all fragmentary) have been catalogued, and several others, which have not yet been given official listing, are known. These papyrus fragments are designated by the letter "P" with an index figure (e.g., P^1, P^2). Portions of twenty books, just over forty per cent of the entire NT, are now known on papyrus. The papyri date from the second to the eighth centuries, with more than half of them dating from the third and fourth centuries.

Among the most interesting and the most important of the papyrus NT MSS are:

a) P^{52} (Manchester, John Ryland's Library, P. Ryl. Gk. 457). This small fragment is the oldest known extant MS of any part of the NT and dates from *ca.* A.D. 140. It measures *ca.* 3½ by 2½ inches and contains parts of John 18:31-33, 37-38. Because of its very fragmentary nature, it is of no great value in establishing the second-century text of the Fourth Gospel. The MS was published by C. H. Roberts in 1935.

b) P^{46} (Dublin, private library of Chester Beatty, Beatty Biblical Pap. II; and Ann Arbor, University of Michigan, Pap. 222). Forty-six leaves of this MS are in the private library of Chester Beatty in Dublin, and thirty leaves are in the library of the University of Michigan. (Some other fragments are known to be in private hands.) All the leaves are somewhat mutilated, but they originally measured *ca.* 11 by 6½ inches and contained 25-32 lines of writing per page. The MS was a single quire codex of *ca.* 104 leaves. It dates from very early in the third century, probably from *ca.* 200. It contains the Pauline letters (in whole or in part) in a very unusual order: Romans, Hebrews, I and II Corinthians, Ephesians, Galatians, Philippians, Colossians, and I Thessalonians. Originally, it may have contained II Thessalonians and Philemon. Most certainly it never contained the Pastoral letters. It was published by F. G. Kenyon (1934-37).

c) P⁶⁶ (Cologny, Switzerland, private library of M. Martin Bodmer, Pap. Bodmer II). This MS contains chs. 1-14 of the Gospel of John, with but few lacunae, and fragments of chs. 15-21. It dates from very early in the third century, probably from *ca.* 200. The MS is made up of several quires containing varying numbers of leaves. It measures *ca.* 6½ by 5½ inches and originally contained 146 leaves. The script is in a good literary hand, although it contains many errors, which are apparently due to carelessness. In most cases these errors have been corrected by the original scribe. The MS was published by V. Martin (1956-58).

d) P⁴⁵ (Dublin, private library of Chester Beatty, Chester Beatty Biblical Papyri I; and Vienna, Austria, Österreichische Nationalbibliothek, Pap. Graec. Vindob. 31974). Portions of 30 leaves of this MS are preserved in Chester Beatty's private collection in Dublin, and a fragment containing Matt. 25:41-26:39 is preserved in the National Library in Vienna. The Dublin leaves contain parts of Matthew, Mark, Luke, John, and Acts, all very much mutilated. Originally the MS contained *ca.* 110 leaves measuring *ca.* 10 by 8 inches and containing *ca.* 39 lines of writing on each page. It is written in a small, even hand and dates from just after the middle of the third century. The MS was published by F. G. Kenyon (1933-34) and by Hans Gerstinger (1933).

e) P⁴⁷ (Dublin, private library of Chester Beatty, Chester Beatty Biblical Papyri III). It contains portions of Rev. 9:10-17:2 on 10 leaves. Originally the MS was a single quire codex of 32 leaves measuring *ca.* 9½ by 5½ inches and containing 25-30 lines of writing on each page. It is written in a rough hand and probably dates from the last third of the third century. It was published by F. G. Kenyon (1934-36).

Without exception, the papyrus NT MSS which are extant today were found in Egypt and undoubtedly were written there. Many of them are too small to be of much value textually. Their cumulative evidence, however, is of value. They prove conclusively that in Egypt, particularly in the second, third, and fourth centuries, no one type of NT text was dominant. In those early centuries many types of text flourished side by side.

3. Uncials. The MSS that are referred to as UNCIAL are written on parchment in a style that ultimately descended from the capital letters used in Greek inscriptions—large, rounded Greek and Latin characters. The style owes its immediate origin, however, to the hand that was used in the literary papyri. This style of writing was used exclusively in the NT MSS until the ninth century, and it persisted until considerably later in the lectionaries. The official list of MSS now contains 241 uncials. Each is designated by an Arabic numeral preceded by a zero (e.g., 01, 02). It is customary, however, to designate several of these uncial MSS by the Hebrew, Latin, or Greek letters, by which they were earlier, and are still more familiarly, known.

Among the more important uncial MSS are the following:

a) 01 (ℵ; London, British Museum, Add. MS 43725), known as SINAITICUS. This is a fourth-century vellum MS of the Bible. The OT contains 199 leaves, and the NT contains 147½ leaves. An additional 43 leaves of the OT from this MS (known as Codex Friderico-Augustanus) are now in the University Library, Leipzig, and there is a small fragment in the Library of the Society of Ancient Literature, Leningrad. This MS contains the Epistle of Barnabas and the Shepherd of Hermas in addition to the canonical NT books. Each page of the MS measures *ca.* 15 by 13½ inches and, with the exception of those containing the poetical books, has four columns of writing, each containing forty-eight lines. The pages containing the poetical books (Psalms, Proverbs, Ecclesiastes, Song of Songs, Wisdom of Solomon, Ecclesiasticus, and Job) each have two columns of writing. The MS was written by three different scribes; nine correctors made corrections in it between the fourth and the twelfth centuries.

This MS is one of the most important witnesses to the text of the NT. Tischendorf relied heavily upon it for his eighth edition. Mark ends at 16:8; the *pericope de adultera* (John 7:52–8:11) is omitted; the doxology of Romans appears after 16:23.

The dramatic story of Tischendorf's discovery of this MS and of its eventual purchase by the British nation and government has often been told. *See* SINAITICUS.

b) 02 (A; London, British Museum, Royal MS I D V-VIII), known as ALEXANDRINUS.* Originally this early-fifth-century codex contained the whole Greek Bible and, in addition, I and II Clement and the Psalms of Solomon. Fig. ALE 15.

The OT has suffered some mutilation, and the NT now lacks Matt. 1:1–25:6; John 6:50–8:52; I Cor. 4:13–12:6. The Psalms of Solomon also have been lost from the MS. The codex contains 773 vellum leaves (630 in the OT, perhaps written by two scribes; 143 in the NT, perhaps written by three scribes), each measuring 12¾ by 10¼ inches. The text is written in two columns to the page with 46-52 lines per column.

c) 03 (B; Vatican City, Biblioteca Vaticana, Cod. Vat. Gr. 1209), known as VATICANUS. This early-fourth-century Greek uncial codex originally contained the whole Greek Bible with the exception of the Prayer of Manasses and the books of Maccabees.

The codex has suffered considerable mutilation. It now lacks Gen. 1:1–46:28; II Sam. 2:5-7, 10-13; Pss. 106:27–138:6; Heb. 9:14–13:25; the Pastoral letters; and Revelation. It contains 759 leaves (617 in the OT, 142 in the NT) of very fine vellum out of an original total of *ca.* 820. Each leaf measures 10½ by 10 inches. Each page of the poetical books of the OT contains two columns of text with 40-44 lines to the column. The rest of the codex contains three columns of text to the page with 40-44 lines to the column.

d) 04 (C; Paris, Bibliothèque Nationale, Cod. Gr. 9), known as EPHRAEMI-SYRI.* This early-fifth-century palimpsest originally contained the entire Bible. Only parts of Job, Proverbs, Ecclesiastes, Wisdom of

Solomon, Ecclesiasticus, and Song of Songs are now extant from the OT. Portions of every NT book except II Thessalonians and II John are extant. It contains 209 leaves (64 in the OT, 145 in the NT) measuring 12¼ by 9½ inches. There is one column of writing containing 40-46 lines per page. The upper writing contains a twelfth-century Greek translation of some writings of Ephraem Syrus. Fig. EPH 34.

e) 05 (D; Cambridge, University Library, Nn. 2.41), known as BEZAE.* In this fifth- or sixth-century uncial codex MS of the gospels and Acts in Greek and Latin, the gospels are arranged in the Western order: Matthew, John, Luke, Mark. The codex apparently originally also contained the Catholic letters, as the end of III John is preserved before the beginning of Acts. Fig. BEZ 41.

The codex contains 406 vellum leaves (plus 9 leaves that have been added by later hands) measuring 10 by 8 inches. Originally it probably contained 510 leaves or more. The Greek and Latin texts face each other on opposite pages—the Greek text on the left and the Latin text on the right. Each page contains one column of text with 33 lines of varying length (sense lines) per column.

f) 06 (D^p; Paris, Bibliothèque Nationale, Cod. Gr. 107), known as CLAROMONTANUS. This is a sixth-century uncial codex MS of the Pauline letters in Greek and Latin, containing 533 vellum leaves measuring 9⅝ by 7⅝ inches. Leaves 162 and 163 are palimpsest. Their under writing contains fragments of the *Phaethon* of Euripides. The Greek and Latin texts face each other on opposite pages—the Greek text on the left and the Latin text on the right. Each page contains one column of text with 21 lines of varying length (sense lines) per column. The MS contains all the letters traditionally assigned to Paul (Hebrews follows Philemon). It has suffered some slight mutilation.

g) 07 (E; Basel, University Library, Cod. A.N. III.12), known as Codex Basiliensis. This is an eighth-century MS of the gospels containing 318 leaves measuring *ca.* 9 by 6¼ inches. The text is written in a single column containing 23-25 lines of writing on each page. The MS allegedly was taken to Basel in 1431 and presented to the Dominican convent by John of Ragusa. It became a part of the University Library in 1559.

h) 08 (E^a; Oxford, Bodleian Library, MS Laud. Gr. 35), known as Codex Laudianus. This is a sixth- or seventh-century bilingual MS of Acts containing 227 leaves measuring *ca.* 10½ by 8⅝ inches. The text is written in two columns (the lefthand column is Latin, and the righthand column is Greek) containing 22-26 lines of writing in each column. The MS is known to have been in Sardinia sometime after the destruction of the Vandal kingdom in Africa by Belisarius. Early in the eighth century it was at Jarrow (England), where it probably had been taken by Ceolfrid, Abbot of Wearmouth and Jarrow. It was used by Bede when he wrote his commentary on Acts. Later the MS was taken, probably by the great missionary Boniface, to Germany, where it remained for several centuries. When the monastery at Würzburg was sacked by the Swedes in 1631, the MS was taken as part of the booty of war. Eventually it fell into the hands of Archbishop Laud, who presented it to the Bodleian Library in 1636.

i) 015 (H^p), known as Codex Coislinianus. This is a sixth-century MS of the Pauline letters containing 43 leaves. The codex has been mutilated, and the 43 extant leaves are divided among several libraries as follows: Paris, Bibliothèque Nationale, Cod. Gr. 202 Coislin, Suppl. Gr. 1074, Suppl. Gr. 1155. III, 24 leaves; Athos, Laura, no library number, 8 leaves; Kiev, Archaeological Museum, 154, 3 leaves; Leningrad, State Public Library, 14, 3 leaves; Moscow, Lenin State Library, 526.1 and Holy Synod Library, 563, 3 leaves; and Turin, National Library B.I.5, 2 leaves. Each leaf measures *ca.* 10¾ by 7⅝ inches. The text is written in a single column with 16 lines of writing on each page. The lines are short sense lines in accordance with the edition which was prepared by Euthalius in the fourth century. A subscription in the MS states that it was compared with a copy which was written by Pamphilus and preserved in his library at Caesarea.

j) 017 (K; Paris, Bibliothèque Nationale, Cod. Gr. 63), known as Codex Cyprius. A ninth- or tenth-century MS of the gospels containing 267 leaves measuring *ca.* 10 by 7⅜ inches. The text is written in a single column containing 16-31 lines of writing on each page. The MS was taken from Cyprus to Paris in 1673 and was placed in Colbert's library.

k) 019 (L; Paris, Bibliothèque Nationale, Cod. Gr. 62), known as Codex Regius. This is an eighth-century MS of the gospels containing 257 leaves measuring *ca.* 8⅝ by 6½ inches. The text is written in two columns with 25 lines of writing on each page. The most notable features of this MS are that it contains both the longer and the shorter endings of Mark and that it does not contain the *pericope de adultera* (John 7:53–8:11), although a space large enough to contain it is left blank.

l) 027 (R; London, British Museum, Add. MS. 17211), known as Codex Nitriensis. This is a sixth-century palimpsest MS of the gospels. It now contains only 53 leaves, on which is preserved a portion of the Gospel of Luke. The upper writing is part of a treatise of Severus of Antioch against John the Grammarian, written in Syriac in the early ninth century. The leaves measure *ca.* 11⅝ by 8⅞ inches. The under writing (i.e., the NT text) is written in two columns with 25 lines of writing to the page. The MS once belonged to the Convent of St. Mary Deipara in Nitria, but it was taken to the British Museum *ca.* 1847.

m) 032 (W; Washington, Freer Gallery of Art, 06.274), known as Codex Washingtonianus. This is a fifth-century MS of the gospels containing 187 leaves measuring *ca.* 8⅛ by 5⅝ inches. The gospels are arranged in the Western order: Matthew, John, Luke and Mark. The text is written in a single column with 30 lines of writing to the page. The MS was purchased by Charles L. Freer in Egypt in 1906. Without doubt, this is the most important MS of the NT, with the exception of the University of Michigan leaves of P^{46}, that is to be found in any American collection.

n) 037 (Δ; St. Gall, Stiftsbibliothek, Cod. 48), known as Codex Sangallensis. This is a ninth- or tenth-century MS of the gospels containing 195 leaves measuring *ca.* 8⅞ by 7¼ inches. The text is written in a single column with 17-29 lines of writing to the page. A Latin translation is written between the lines of Greek text. It was written by an Irish scribe in the monastery of St. Gall.

o) 038 (Θ; Tiflis, Georgian Museum, Cod. Gr. 993), known as Codex Koridethianus. This is an eighth- or ninth-century MS of the gospels containing 249 leaves measuring *ca.* 11 by 9 inches. The text is written in two columns with 19-32 lines of writing to the page. It was evidently written by a scribe who knew very little Greek. The MS once belonged to a monastery at Koridethi near the E end of the Black Sea. It was first discovered in 1853 and was taken to St. Petersburg, only to be returned to the Caucasus *ca.* 1870. The location of the MS was unknown for over thirty years. In 1901, it was rediscovered by Bishop Kirion, who took it to Tiflis.

p) 044 (Ψ; Athos, Laura, Cod. 172 [B′. 52]), known as Codex Laurensis. This is an eighth- or ninth-century MS of the NT (without Revelation) containing 261 leaves measuring *ca.* 8¼ by 6 inches. It is defective from Matt. 1:1 to Mark 9:5. The text is written in a single column with 30-31 lines of writing to the page. It contains both the shorter and the longer endings of Mark. The *pericope de adultera* (John 7:53–8:11) is omitted. The doxology of Romans comes after 14:23.

The uncial MSS date from the fourth to the tenth or eleventh centuries. Many of them are fragmentary. Because of the antiquity of many of them they were once looked upon as being the most important sources for the study of the text of the NT. Textual scholars today, however, are more prudent, and they do not hesitate to decide against an uncial reading if other evidence so warrants.

4. Minuscules. The minuscule MSS are those written in a cursive or running hand. They date from the ninth to the seventeenth or eighteenth centuries. A total of 2,533 minuscules have thus far been catalogued. They are designated simply by Arabic numbers (e.g., 1, 2). No attempt can be made here to describe in any detail even the most important of these hundreds of MSS. Only a few of the best known of the minuscules can be mentioned in the following list:

1. Basel, University Library, A.N. IV.2. A group of closely related MSS, including this one, is called "Family 1."

2. Basel, University Library, A.N. IV.1. This MS was Erasmus' chief source for his gospel text.

13. Paris, Bibliothèque Nationale, Gr. 50. A group of related MSS, including this one, is often called "Family 13" or the "Ferrar group."

28. Paris, Bibliothèque Nationale, Gr. 379, a member of the so-called Caesarean family.

33. Paris, Bibliothèque Nationale, Gr. 14, which contains the so-called Neutral or Alexandrian type of text. This is often called the "Queen of the cursives."

69. Leicester, Municipal Museum, a member of Family 13 (the Ferrar group).

81. London, British Museum, Add. MS. 20003, considered the best minuscule witness to the Acts.

118. Oxford, Bodleian, Misc. Gr. 13, a member of Family 1.

124. Vienna, Österreichischen National-bibliothek, Gr. 188, a member of Family 13 (the Ferrar group).

209. Venice, St. Mark, 10, a member of Family 1.

346. Milan, Ambrosiana, S. 23 supra, a member of Family 13 (the Ferrar group).

543. Ann Arbor, University of Michigan, 15, a member of Family 13 (the Ferrar group).

565. Leningrad, State Public Library, Gr. 53, a member of the so-called Caesarean family.

579. Paris, Bibliothèque Nationale, Gr. 97, a witness to the so-called Neutral or Alexandrian type of text.

700. London, British Museum, Egerton 2610, a member of the so-called Caesarean family.

826. Grottaferrata, A.a.3, a member of Family 13 (the Ferrar group).

828. Grottaferrata, A.a.5, a member of Family 13 (the Ferrar group).

892. London, British Museum, Add. MS. 33277, a witness to the so-called Neutral or Alexandrian type.

1071. Athos, Laura, A. 104, an important witness to von Soden's I° text.

1241. Sinai, 260, a witness to the so-called Neutral or Alexandrian type of text.

1582. Athos, Vatopedi, 747, a member of Family 1.

5. Lectionaries. The lectionaries are the service books that contain lessons to be read on every day of the calendar year and of the church year. Lessons are read from the Gospel (Matthew, Mark, Luke, and John) and from the Apostle (the rest of the NT outside the gospels, with the exception of Revelation). The official catalogue of MSS now contains 1,838 lectionaries. Many of them are uncials, although the majority of them are minuscules. They are designated by an italicized, lower-case "l" followed by an Arabic number (e.g., *l* 1, *l* 2). They date from the third or fourth century to the seventeenth century.

The lectionaries have long been considered of no value for the study of the text of the NT, and, for this reason, they never have been adequately represented in any critical apparatus. Recent textual research, however, has shown that the lectionaries are of great value for the study of the history of the transmission of the text of the NT. Unfortunately this research work is only in its initial stages, and not enough is yet known to justify any definite conclusions as to the part the lectionaries have played in the development of the NT text. All that can now be said is that in the future the lectionaries will play an ever-increasing role in the study of the text.

6. Versions. The most significant versions for the study of the NT text are those which were made before the year 1000 and which are direct translations from the Greek. The most important of these are: (*a*) Latin (OL and Vulg.); (*b*) Syriac (Old Syriac, Peshitta, Philoxenian, and/or Harclean and Palestinian); (*c*) Coptic (Sahidic, several Middle Egyptian versions, and Bohairic); (*d*) Armenian; (*e*) Old Georgian; (*f*) Old Slavic; (*g*) Gothic. Of less importance are: (*a*) Arabic (those translations made directly from the Greek); (*b*) Ethiopic; (*c*) Nubian; (*d*) Sogdian; (*e*) Frankish; (*f*) Anglo-Saxon; (*g*) Persian.

It is often affirmed that the versions are of great importance for the recovery of the original text of the NT because they often represent translations that were made in very early times. It must be remembered, however, that there are no extant MSS of the versions that date earlier than the fourth century. The MSS of the versions were subject to the same changes as they were copied and recopied as were the Greek MSS. A sixth-century Latin MS, e.g., is no better witness to an early-third-century text than is a sixth-century Greek MS. Both have been changed in the process of transmission.

For a complete discussion of the versions, *see* VERSIONS, ANCIENT.

7. Quotations of the Church Fathers. The NT quotations of the Church Fathers are of importance for the study of the NT text primarily because they can be definitely located as to time and place. It is of particular importance for the study of the transmission of the text to know, e.g., that a certain reading was known and used by Origen in Egypt in the first half of the third century. By this means, it has been possible to determine that the text of Family 1 (MSS 1 and 1582), at least in Matthew, was current at that early date.

The quotations of the Church Fathers should be taken only from critical texts of the Fathers. Unfortunately, too few such texts are available. In the absence of critical texts, it must be kept in mind that the Fathers did not always quote accurately. They harmonized their texts, and they misquoted just as often as does the modern writer. They made allusions and references to the NT text, and they often paraphrased.

There is no one source to which the student of the text of the NT can go for the quotations of the Church Fathers. Even the sixteen handwritten volumes of the *Index Patristicus,* compiled by J. W. Burgon and now housed in the British Museum, is incomplete, though it contains 86,489 quotations.

C. *WRITTEN TEXT OF THE NT.* The original copies of the NT books have, of course, long since disappeared. This fact should not cause surprise. In the first place, they were written on papyrus, a very fragile and perishable material. In the second place, and probably of even more importance, the original copies of the NT books were not looked upon as scripture by those of the early Christian communities. To the early Christians, the books that are now the NT books were only a few among many pieces of occasional writing. A letter of Paul, e.g., would at first have been valued, perhaps only because it came from the founder of some local church. Only after that letter had been read and reread, only after it had been copied and recopied, only after it had proved its worth, would it have been looked upon as scripture. Were it possible to recover or to reconstruct the original texts of the NT books, the resulting texts would be texts that never were looked upon as scripture.

Whenever any document is copied by hand, the copy differs from the exemplar. Many of the changes are accidental. Such changes are usually easy to detect and do not cause the textual student a great deal of trouble. They can be identified as various types of errors of the eye or ear. But many of the changes are intentional. It has been pointed out above that even after the NT books were canonized, they were often changed intentionally as they were copied. During the MS period, the interest of the copyist was in the "true reading" and not in the "original reading."

As far as is known, during the MS period no rigid control ever was exercised over the copying of MSS, nor was an official revision ever made in any great ecclesiastical center. Perhaps no more can be said about the MS period than that the great mass of evidence that comes from the Greek MSS, the MSS of the versions, and the quotations of the Church Fathers represents the various interpretations, the various doctrines and dogmas, the various theological interests, and the various worship habits of many different Christians in many different times and places. Before the Renaissance and the Reformation and the invention of printing, the NT was a living body of literature which was constantly being enriched as it was interpreted and reinterpreted by each succeeding generation.

D. *PRINTED TEXT OF THE NT.* The first portions of the Greek NT to be printed were the Magnificat (Luke 1:42-56) and the Benedictus (vss. 68-80). These passages were attached to a Greek Psalter which first appeared in Milan in 1481. The same passages were printed a second time in 1486 in Venice. They appeared again in Venice in 1496 or 1497 in a volume that came from the famous Aldine press. In 1504 the Aldine press printed the first six chapters of the Gospel of John. Sometime later, in 1514, John 6:1-4 appeared in print in Tübingen. Since these beginnings, literally hundreds of editions of the Greek NT have been printed. Only those which have been of major significance for the history of the printed text will be discussed here.

1. The Complutensian Polyglot. The first printed edition of the complete Greek NT contained the Greek and the Latin Vulg. texts arranged in parallel columns. It was vol. 5 of the edition of the Bible that is known as the Complutensian Polyglot, which received its name from Complutum, the Latin designation for Alcala in Spain, where it was printed. The NT volume was completed on January 10, 1514. The entire edition was completed on July 10, 1517. Permission for its publication, however, was not given by Pope Leo X until March 22, 1520, and it was not put into circulation until 1522.

The editors of this edition did not indicate which MSS they used in its production. In their preface, however, they said: "Ordinary copies were not the archetypes for this impression, but very ancient and correct ones; and of such antiquity, that it would be utterly wrong not to own their authority; which the Supreme Pontiff Leo X, our most Holy Father in Christ and lord, desiring to favor this undertaking sent from the apostolical library to the most reverend lord the Cardinal of Spain [i.e., Francis Cardinal Ximines], by whose authority and commandment we have had this work printed." Cardinal Ximines himself, in his dedication of the edition to Leo X, said: "For Greek copies indeed we are indebted to your Holiness, who sent us most kindly from the apostolic library very ancient codices, both of the Old and the

New Testament; which have aided us very much in this undertaking."

Although it cannot now be determined which MSS were used by the editors of the Complutensian Polyglot, it is evident that they used their MSS well. They did, however, "correct" their Greek text to the Latin Vulg. in a few places. E.g., they included I John 5:7-8 in their Greek text. This passage is unknown in any Greek MS with the exception of Codex Montfortianus (Greg. 61; Dublin, Trinity College, A. 4. 21), which was written early in the sixteenth century, after work on the Complutensian Polyglot had been completed.

The text of the NT in the Complutensian Polyglot is a better text than those of Erasmus, Stephanus, and the Elzevirs (see §§ D2-3 below). Had the Complutensian Polyglot been the first Greek NT published as well as printed, it might well have become the *textus receptus* upon which the KJV was based. Had that been the case, the entire history of the English NT after 1611 would have been vastly different.

2. Erasmus. The first complete Greek NT to be published, although it was the second one to be printed, was that of Erasmus. It contained the Greek text and a revised Latin Vulg. text in parallel columns. This edition was published by Joannes Froben, a German-born printer of Basel, who was evidently a very enterprising businessman. He heard of the work that was being done on the Complutensian Polyglot under the direction of Cardinal Ximines at Alcala and conceived the idea of getting an edition of the NT on the market before the Spanish edition could be published. Accordingly, on April 17, 1515, Froben sent a message to Erasmus, who was then in England, asking him to come to Basel for the purpose of editing the Greek NT. Erasmus arrived in Basel sometime during the summer of 1515. But as late as September 11, it was still being debated as to whether the Latin texts should be published in parallel columns to the Greek or in a separate volume. In less than six months, however, in March, 1516, the entire NT had been printed, and it was released immediately for publication. The volume was dedicated to Pope Leo X, and a copy was sent to him. All the evidence points to the fact that the enterprising Froben was given exclusive rights to publish the NT for a period of four years. (This fits well with the fact that Leo X did not give permission for the Complutensian Polyglot to be published until March 22, 1520.)

As we have seen, Erasmus' NT was prepared in great haste. Erasmus himself said later that it was "precipitated rather than edited." He depended largely upon late Greek MSS which he found in the University Library. In fact, a twelfth-century MS of the gospels (Greg. 2; Basel, University Library, A.N. IV.1) was sent to Froben to be used as printer's copy. The MS of Revelation which he used was mutilated at the end, and Erasmus translated the last six verses from Latin into Greek for his edition. In many places where it was not necessary, he "corrected" the Greek text to conform to the Latin (e.g., Acts 8:37; 9:5-6). He did not, however, include I John 5:7-8 in his Greek text. In answer to those who criticized him for this "omission," Erasmus said if he were ever shown one Greek MS that contained those verses, he would include them in his text. Later, he was shown Codex Montfortianus, which evidently had been written for the purpose, and he included I John 5:7-8 in his third edition (1522). Thus, those verses came, through the Greek texts of Stephanus and the Elzevirs, into the KJV, and there they remained for three centuries. The haste with which Erasmus' NT was prepared was reflected in its printing as well as in its use of MSS. It contained hundreds of typographical errors. Scrivener once said: "In that respect it is the most faulty book I know."

The second edition of Erasmus' NT appeared in March, 1519. The first two editions sold more than 3,300 copies. Other editions appeared in 1522, 1527, and 1535. The third and fourth editions contained the Greek text, the Latin Vulg. text, and Erasmus' own edition of the Latin text in parallel columns. These various editions contained only slight changes from the first, with the exception of the correction of typographical errors.

Erasmus' work met with some criticism, but not on the basis of what he had done to the Greek text. He was criticized for having dared to change the Latin text. In spite of this criticism, Erasmus' NT was immediately accepted. Thus, a text of the Greek NT which had been "edited" on the basis of late MS evidence and which too often had been "corrected" to the Latin text became stereotyped in man's mind. It was assumed for over three centuries to possess some prescriptive right, just as if "an apostle had been the compositor."

3. Other early editions. In 1546 and 1549, Robert Stephanus, a scholar-printer of Paris, published two editions of the NT. They contained a Greek text that was blended from those of the Complutensian Polyglot and Erasmus. In 1550 he published a folio edition (his third edition) which followed the text of Erasmus' fifth edition almost without variation. This edition contained marginal readings that were taken from some fifteen MSS, mostly from the Royal Library in Paris, and from the Complutensian Polyglot. The MSS (which include Greg. 05[D], 019[L], 4, 5, 6, 7, 8, 9, 38, and 120) were collated for him by his son Henry. Often the marginal readings were supported by all the MSS, but the text itself was not changed. Nearly six hundred readings from the Complutensian Polyglot were included in these marginal variants, but often they were cited incorrectly. More than seven hundred other readings in which Stephanus' text differed from the Complutensian Polyglot were not noted. This 1550 edition became the *textus receptus* for Great Britain.

Robert Stephanus left Paris late in the year 1550 and went to Geneva, where the next year (1551) he published his fourth edition of the NT. The text of this edition was exactly the same as that of his third edition. It contained the Greek text, the Latin Vulg. text, and Erasmus' Latin text in parallel columns. In this edition, however, for the first time our modern verse divisions appeared.

The French theologian Theodore Beza edited an

edition of the Latin NT (1556) and ten editions of the Greek NT (1565 [2], 1567, 1580, 1582, 1588, 1591, 1598, 1604, and 1611). All these Greek editions contained the Greek text, the Latin Vulg. text, and Beza's own Latin text arranged in parallel columns. For his Greek text, Beza relied upon the 1550 edition of Stephanus. Upon occasion, he mentioned variant readings in the margin, but only rarely did he ever introduce them into his text. Two ancient MSS, Codex Bezae and Codex Claromontanus, were at that time in Beza's possession; but he evidently made little, if any, use of them. Beza's editions of the NT are of no great value for the history of the printed text, but they are of interest because of the influence they exerted on two English translations, the Geneva Version (1557 and 1560) and the KJV (1611).

The Elzevirs were a famous Dutch family of scholar-printers. Of all the family, the Leyden Elzevirs are probably the best known. In 1624 they published their first edition of the Greek NT. Their basic text was that of Stephanus' third edition. They introduced into the text an occasional reading which they found in one of Beza's editions and which they took to be corrections of Stephanus. In some places, however, their text differs from both Stephanus and Bezae.

In 1633 the Elzevirs published the second edition of their Greek NT. It is in the introduction to this edition that was printed the statement: "You have the text, now received by all: in which we give nothing altered or corrupted." It was this statement which gave rise to the phrase *textus receptus*. The Elzevir text became the *textus receptus* for the Continent, just as the Stephanus text did for Britain. These two editions differ from one another in only 287 places.

In 1657, Brian Walton, later bishop of Chester, published his famous Polyglot. It was an edition of the entire Bible in six volumes. Vol. 5 contained the NT. The Greek text that Walton used was the text of the 1550 Stephanus edition. Beneath the Greek text were given the readings of Alexandrinus, which was designated by the siglum A. This marked the first time that a capital letter had been used to designate an uncial MS. In addition to the Greek text and the Latin Vulg., Walton also printed the Peshitta, the Ethiopic, the Arabic, the Persian (of the gospels), and the later Syr. of the NT books that are not to be found in the Peshitta (II Peter, II and III John, Jude, and Revelation), each accompanied by a Latin translation. In vol. 6, in an appendix, there appeared the collations of sixteen MSS that had been prepared under the direction of Archbishop Usher, the collations that had been collected by Stephanus and several other collations that had been prepared at Walton's request.

John Fell, bishop of Oxford, in 1675 published an edition of the NT which contained the 1550 text of Stephanus and some variant readings from MSS at the bottom of the page. But the importance of Fell's edition lies in the fact that he also published some evidence from the Coptic and the Gothic versions in his notes.

One of the most important of the earlier editions of the NT appeared in 1707. It was that of John Mill, who had spent more than thirty years in its preparation. The text that Mill used was that of the Stephanus (1550) edition. The notes and appendices contained the variant readings that had appeared in earlier editions, the readings that Mill had collected by collating such MSS as were available to him, readings that were taken from collations that were made for him by his friends, and many readings from the ancient versions and the Church Fathers. Altogether, Mill was able to cite *ca*. thirty thousand variant readings. He was the first to see the real value and the importance of the ancient versions and the Church Fathers for the study of the text of the NT.

Not only did Mill cite more variant readings than had ever been cited before, but he also dared to express his own opinion of the value of many of these variants. His mature judgment on the value of certain readings is to be found in his *Prolegomena*, written after the entire work was completed. Here he often reversed an earlier opinion on the value of the variants which he had collected.

In 1734, at Tübingen, John Albrecht Bengel published his edition of the NT. His text did not precisely follow the *textus receptus;* but, except in Revelation, he did not include a single reading that had not appeared in some earlier printed edition. He did, however, include, at the end of his volume, a critical apparatus in which he listed the MS evidence for his text as well as the evidence for variant readings. In addition to the apparatus at the end of the volume, he placed selected variant readings in the margins and indicated his opinion of them by means of Greek letters: α indicated readings decidedly better than in his text; β indicated readings somewhat more likely than those in his text; γ indicated readings equal to those in his text; δ indicated readings slightly inferior to those in his text; and ε indicated readings considerably inferior to those in his text.

John James Wettstein's great two-volume edition of the NT was published in Amsterdam in 1751-52. The text which Wettstein printed was, with very few exceptions, the text of the Elzevir edition of 1624. The value of the edition was in the great mass of new material it made available. On the upper part of the page stood the text itself. Below the text were printed those MS variants of which the editor approved. Next came other variant readings, with the MSS which contained them. Because Wettstein had examined so many MSS, this part of the evidence often filled most of the page. On the lower part of the page was printed a mass of quotations from Greek and Latin classical authors, Talmudic and Rabbinic writings, etc., which in Wettstein's opinion illustrated some passage, elucidated the use of some word, or presented an instance of a similar grammatical construction. Wettstein, for the first time, used capital letters as sigla for the uncial MSS (with the exception of Walton's use of "A" as a symbol for Alexandrinus) and Arabic numerals as sigla for the minuscule MSS.

Johann Jakob Griesbach published a three-volume edition of the NT in 1775-77. He printed the Elzevir text of 1624 with a few changes. Most of his critical materials were drawn from Wettstein, although he added some evidence from his own collations. Griesbach's second edition was published in 1796-1806.

Christian Frederick Matthaei published a twelve-volume edition of the NT at Riga in 1782-88. Because of his lack of knowledge of the principles of textual criticism, his text, which was "molded on his own views," was of little value. Matthaei's NT was of importance, however, because of the many MSS which it accurately cited. Bishop Middleton once characterized Matthaei as the "most accurate scholar who ever edited the NT." Many of the MSS he cited are known even today only through his publication.

John Martin Augustine Scholz published his two-volume edition of the NT in 1830-36. His text was a critical text—i.e., it was based upon his own critical principles, although it did not depart radically from the *textus receptus*. Scholz's chief claim to fame lay in the fact that he cited more than six hundred MSS—many times more than ever had been cited before. Only twelve of them, however, were cited with anything that approached completeness. In contrast to Matthaei, Scholz was perhaps the most inaccurate scholar who ever edited the NT.

4. Modern critical editions. Charles Lachmann was the first to publish an edition of the NT that ignored completely the *textus receptus*. His aim was to publish the text of the NT as it was known in the fourth century. He relied entirely upon ancient witnesses. His first edition was published in 1831; and his second edition, in two volumes, was published in 1842 and 1850. Lachmann's work stands as a landmark in the history of the printed text of the NT.

The critical text of the NT of Samuel Prideaux Tregelles was published between 1857 and 1872. In the construction of his text, Tregelles relied upon "ancient authorities" alone and refused to allow either the *textus receptus* or the great mass of late MSS to have any voice in determining the true reading. All his ancient Greek MS authorities were uncials, with the exception of the minuscules 1, 33, and 69 of the gospels and 81 of the Acts. Tregelles' critical apparatus, which gives the evidence for his text and for variants from his text, is a model of accuracy.

Lobegott Friedrich Konstantine von Tischendorf published no fewer than twenty-four editions of the Greek NT, if the reissues of his stereotyped *Editio Academica* (1855) are included. For our purposes, however, only his last and greatest edition need be considered. It was his eighth major edition (*Editio Octava Critica Major*), published in eleven parts between 1864 and 1872. Tischendorf's death prevented him from preparing the Prolegomena to his eighth edition. This task was undertaken by C. R. Gregory and Ezra Abbot. After Abbot's death, Gregory completed the Prolegomena volume, and it was published in 1894. Tischendorf's aim was to recover the best text of the NT, even though this might not necessarily be the oldest text. The text of his eighth edition was based upon ancient evidence, especially of the Greek MSS, but without neglecting the evidence of the versions and the Fathers. His text showed signs that he was greatly influenced by the evidence of Codex Sinaiticus, which was his greatest MS dis-covery. Even yet, Tischendorf's critical apparatus to his eighth edition is without parallel, and it is indispensable to the textual student.

After more than thirty years of labor, in 1881, Brooke Foss Westcott and Fenton John Anthony Hort published their critical text of the NT, *The NT in the Original Greek*. Unfortunately they published no MS evidence except that for a few readings which is to be found in their "Introduction and Appendix," which appeared in 1882. They relied heavily for their text upon Codex Vaticanus. The Westcott and Hort text has become, in effect, a new *textus receptus;* its hold upon textual scholars today is just as strong as was the hold of the Stephanus and Elzevir texts upon textual scholars between 1550 and 1831.

The most recent major edition of the text of the NT was that published by Hermann von Soden between 1902 and 1913. Von Soden adopted a new system of MS notation; he developed a new theory of the history of the text; and, of course, he constructed a new critical text. He has been often criticized for the incompleteness and the inaccuracy of his MS citation. In all fairness, it should be said that in this he was no worse, nor was he any better, than most other editors of the NT. He cites a great amount of minuscule MS evidence that is not available anywhere else. James Moffatt's English translation of the NT was based upon von Soden's text.

Under the auspices of a committee of British scholars, S. C. E. Legg published the Gospel of Mark in 1935 and the Gospel of Matthew in 1940. He used the text of Westcott and Hort and provided it with a critical apparatus. This edition was often referred to as the "new Tischendorf." Legg resigned from the editorship of this new edition in 1948. At that time his committee invited a committee of American scholars to join with them in completing the edition. The American-British undertaking is known as the International Greek NT Project. The "Project" will publish the *textus receptus* (Oxford, 1873) and provide it with a critical apparatus that is based upon new collations of all available MSS and upon new studies of the versions, the lectionaries, and the quotations of the Church Fathers. The two volumes that were published by Legg will be revised on the basis of the *textus receptus*. The new edition is designed as a tool to be used in future critical studies of the NT text.

In addition to the major editions of the Greek NT which have been listed above, many minor editions have been published. Among the more important of these are: J. M. Bover, Greco-Latin (1st ed., 1943); A. Merk, Greco-Latin (1st ed., 1933); E. Nestle (1st ed., 1898); A. Souter (1st ed., 1910); and H. J. Vogels, Greco-Latin (1st ed., 1920). By far the most popular of these minor editions is that of Nestle. It has been published in many editions since 1898. The text of the first two editions was based on the majority reading of Westcott and Hort, Tischendorf, and Weymouth. Beginning with the third edition (1903), Weiss was substituted for Weymouth. The apparatus in the Nestle NT has been revised in each succeeding edition. In 1904 the British and Foreign Bible Society published the Nestle third edition as its first edition. In 1958 the second British and Foreign Bible Society edition was published with a revised apparatus, although its text was still essentially the Nestle text.

E. *THEORY AND METHOD.* 1. From Origen to Bentley. Any study of the text of the NT, apart from the preliminary study of MSS, paleography, grammar, etc., should properly begin with Origen, the first great textual critic of the church.

Frank Pack (*see bibliography*) has shown that Origen's textual work should be conceived as a part of his larger conception of scripture. The same thing could be said of any textual critic, ancient or modern. There is no question but that the work of Tregelles, Tischendorf, von Soden, Legg, the Lakes, and others would be better understood if more were known regarding their larger conception of scripture.

Pack showed in his study that Origen's conception of scripture was based upon three major beliefs: (*a*) the tradition of the church is the framework within which all teaching, belief, and activity must be done; (*b*) scripture is a unity with light given from God equally in the OT and in the NT; (*c*) all scripture is inspired, so that whether every part of it looks important to the reader or not, it is important, and is to be interpreted in such a way that God is not dishonored.

Origen attributed the great variety of readings which he found in his MSS of the NT to four causes: (*a*) carelessness in scribal transmission; (*b*) conscious alteration made in a rash and daring manner (these are the more serious dogmatic corrections); (*c*) addition and subtraction made in an "arbitrary" way (these are the more simple, detailed corrections which are made in the interest of clarification of meaning or harmonization of accounts); (*d*) the corrupting influence of the heretics.

In those places where he called attention to the existence of more than one reading and indicated his preference for one or the other, Origen seems to have based his choice upon (*a*) dogmatics; (*b*) geography; (*c*) harmonization; (*d*) etymology; (*e*) the majority of MSS known to him.

Origen's main controls in the handling of variants in the text, then, may be summed up as: (*a*) contextual meaning and internal probability; (*b*) harmonization; (*c*) the tradition of the church. As Pack puts it, Origen's methodology was a process of: (*a*) correction; (*b*) the knowledge, use, and conflating of different textual traditions; (*c*) the handling of the text with the interests of teaching and preaching in mind. Even in those cases where he judged that the text had been corrupted by the heretics, Origen sought, because of his great respect for tradition, to avoid the task of having to change the copies of the NT in actual use.

By and large, this seems to have been the method used in handling the text of the NT until after the Reformation and the printing of the Greek NT. Chrysostom, in his homilies, was no mere follower of a traditional text, but a writer who consciously altered the text in an attempt to make more lucid certain passages of scripture. Bishop Theophylact of Bulgaria, who wrote in the eleventh century, treated his NT text in precisely the same way.

As we have seen, those who edited and published the early editions of the Greek NT (i.e., Cardinal Ximines, Erasmus, Stephanus, the Elzevirs, Beza, etc.) depended in the main upon late Greek MSS, which they used uncritically. Most of them did, to be sure, as, e.g., Stephanus, print variant readings. But as someone has said, these marginal notes seem to be more ornamental than anything else. Those readings which were debated were usually those in which the late Greek text differed from the late Latin Vulg. text which was in common use. Not always, but too often, the Greek text suffered by being "corrected" to the Latin.

In spite of the fact that materials were not used critically, however, an accumulation of variant readings was built up by those early editors. They collated MSS and recorded their readings. Usually such variant readings were relegated to prolegomena or appendices, as was the case in the editions of Walton, Fell, Mill, and others. It was, of course, easier to print the text "received by all" and to record variant readings in prolegomena or appendices. At least by using this method the editor did not leave himself open to all manner of charges of heresy. As it was, most of these early editors were subject to vicious attack. If Erasmus, e.g., had been content to publish the Greek text, or if he had printed beside his Greek text only the Latin Vulg., as was then in common use, all might have been well. But his own revised Latin version was regarded as such an innovation that every variant from the text in common use was regarded as presumption or even as heresy.

Stephanus was condemned by the theological faculty at the Sorbonne for publishing an amended Latin text several years before his first Greek text appeared. No wonder, then, that he did not try to publish an amended Greek text. His critics could make nothing of what they found in the margins of his 1550 edition, but they prohibited it because of its "annotations." When Stephanus told them that there were no annotations in the margin, but only variant readings, they demanded to see the MS from which the variants were taken. They were told that there was not one MS but several MSS and that they had been returned to the Royal Library. So severe did the criticism of Stephanus become that he fled to Geneva—some say that flight was necessary for him to escape death at the stake.

The early editors and printers of the Greek NT were motivated by the new interest in humanistic studies and by a desire to set the Greek text over against the Latin text in common use. Perhaps this latter motivation was tied up with the whole complex of the Reformation, the new Protestant movement, the break with Rome, etc. Without doubt, however, in some cases financial motivation entered in as well.

Gradually, as men saw not only that the Greek text of the late MSS differed from the Latin text in common use, but that it differed from the early Greek MSS and from the text of the ancient versions (other than Latin) and from the quotations of the early Church Fathers as well, they began an attempt to make a better Greek text. But still, they hardly dared to publish an amended text. As has been shown, their variant readings were relegated to marginal notes, prolegomena, and appendices. The text they printed was the text "commonly received by all." In no other way could they escape the censure of their fellow churchmen.

Even the great Mill, who had published practically unchanged the Stephanus text of 1550, was severely criticized. His crime was not that he had changed the text of the NT, but that he had made this text precarious. Not only the clergy, but university professors in England and Germany as well, declared that because he had found thirty thousand variant readings in the NT, his work was a work of evil tendency and inimical to the Christian religion. Fortunately for his peace of mind, Mill did not live to hear these attacks. He died only two weeks after his NT was published.

In the early part of his work Mill placed great value on the number of MSS supporting a reading, but later he became more aware of the value of the testimony of authorities of different kinds.

The principal attack upon Mill was made by Whitby in 1710. He charged Mill with making the text of the NT uncertain and insisted that in every case the text of Stephanus could be defended. Whitby seems to have thought that the evidence of numbers of MSS should outweigh all other considerations except when those numbers of MSS read against the *textus receptus*.

In 1713, Anthony Collins in his "Discourse of Free Thinking" used Whitby's attack on Mill as an argument for rejection of the authority of scripture.

2. The work of Richard Bentley. In answer to Collins' book, Richard Bentley published under the name of Phileleutherus Lipsiensis his "Remarks upon a Late Discourse of Free Thinking." In section 32, part 1, of his "Remarks," Bentley took up the subject of the various readings of the Greek NT. In this section he made some observations that were made a part of the later method of textual study. He said: " 'Tis a good Providence and a great Blessing, That so many Manuscripts of the New Testament are still amongst us; some procur'd from *Egypt*, others from *Asia*, others found in the *Western* Churches. For the very Distances of Places, as well as Numbers of the Books, demonstrates that there could be no Collusion, no altering nor interpolating One Copy by another, nor All by one of them." Further, "the lesser matters of Diction, and among several synonymous Expressions the Very Words of the Writers, must be found out by the same Industry and Sagacity that is used in other Books; must not be risk'd upon the credit of any particular MS or Edition, but be sought, acknowledg'd, and challeng'd, where-ever they are met with."

In 1713, Francis Hare, writing under the name of Philo-Criticus, published a pamphlet entitled "The Clergyman's Thanks to Phileleutherus for His Remarks on the Late Discourse of Free-Thinking." In this pamphlet he urged Bentley to edit an edition of the NT. He said, in part: "The *present* Text is not the Text as left us by the Apostles in their *Autographum*, but as it was settled about two hundred years ago by Robert Stephens, that learned Printer; whence it follows that if the Text should be revis'd now by an *abler* Hand, and by the help of *more and better Manuscripts,* such an Edition of it ought to be prefer'd; but such undoubtedly would that be which

you could give, would you, upon the Materials your Friend *Dr. Mill* has with so much Labour brought together, exercise the Critik, you, and you alone are Master of."

On April 16, 1716, Bentley wrote to Archbishop Wake and unfolded his plan for a new edition of the NT. In this letter he gave an account of some of his studies, and said that he had found a close agreement between the oldest Latin and Greek MSS. By means of this agreement he believed that he would be able to restore the text of the NT to what it had been at the time of the Council of Nicaea. He then spoke of the formation of the common text of the Greek NT.

"After the Complutenses and Erasmus," Bentley said, "who had but very ordinary MSS, it became the property of booksellers. Robert Stephen's edition, set out and regulated by himself alone, is now become the standard. The text stands, as if an apostle was his compositor.

"Pope's Sixtus and Clement, at a vast expense, had an assembly of learned divines to recense and adjust the Latin Vulgate, and then enacted their new edition authentic: but I find, though I have not discovered anything done *dolo malo,* they were quite unequal to the affair. They were mere *theologi,* had no experience in MSS, nor made use of good Greek copies, and followed books of 500 years before those of double age. Nay, I believe, they took these new ones for the older of the two; for it is not everybody knows the age of a manuscript.

"To conclude: in a word, I find that by taking 2000 errors out of the Pope's Vulgate, and as many out of the Protestant Pope Stephen's, I can set out an edition of each in columns, without using any book under 900 years old, that shall so exactly agree word for word, and, what at first amazed me, order for order, that no two tallies, nor two indentures, can agree better."

In 1720, Bentley issued his *Proposals for Printing.* These proposals were accompanied by the last chapter of Revelation as a specimen. They are contained in eight paragraphs as follows:

"(*a*) The author of this edition, observing that the printed copies of the New Testament, both of the original Greek and ancient vulgar Latin, were taken from manuscripts of no great antiquity, such as the first editors could then procure; and that now by God's providence there are MSS in Europe (accessible, though with great charge) above a thousand years old in both languages; believes he may do good service to common Christianity if he publishes a new edition of the Greek and Latin, not according to the recent and interpolated copies, but as represented in the most ancient and venerable MSS in Greek and Roman capital letters.

"(*b*) The author, revolving in his mind some passages of St. Jerome; where he declares, that (without making a new version) he adjusted and reformed the whole *Latin Vulgate to the best Greek exemplars,* that is, to those of the famous Origen; and another passage, where he says, that a verbal or literal interpretation out of Greek into Latin is not necessary, *except in the Holy Scripture, ubi ipse verborum ordo mysterium est,* where the very order of the words is mystery; took thence the hint, that if the oldest copies of the original Greek and Jerome's Latin were examined and compared together, perhaps they would be still found to agree both in words and order of words. And upon making the essay, he has succeeded in his conjecture beyond his expectation or even his hopes.

"(c) The author believes that he has retrieved (except in very few places) the true exemplar of Origen, which was the standard of the most learned of the Fathers, at the time of the Council of Nicaea and two centuries after. And he is sure that the Greek and Latin MSS, by their mutual assistance, do so settle the original text to the smallest nicety, as cannot be performed now in any *classic* author whatever: and that out of a labyrinth of thirty thousand various readings, that crowd the pages of our present best editions, all put upon equal credit, to the offense of many good persons, this clue so leads and extricates us, that there will scarce be two hundred out of so many thousands that can deserve the least consideration.

"(d) To confirm the lections which the author places in the text, he makes use of the old versions, Syriac, Coptic, Gothic, and Aethiopic, and of all the Fathers, Greeks and Latins, within the first five centuries; and he gives in his notes the various readings (now known) within the said five centuries. So that the reader has under one view what the first ages of the church knew of the text; and what has crept into any copies since is of no value or authority.

"(e) The author is very sensible, that in the sacred writings there's no place for conjecture or emendations. Diligence and fidelity, with some judgment and experience, are the characters here requisite. He declares, therefore, that he does not alter one letter in the text without the authorities subjoined in the notes. And to leave the free choice to every reader, he places under each column the smallest variations of this edition, either in words or order, from the received Greek of Stephens, and the Latin of the two popes Sixtus V and Clement VIII. So that this edition exhibits both itself and the common ones.

"(f) If the author has anything to suggest towards a change of the text, not supported by any copies now extant, he will offer it separate in his *Prolegomena;* in which will be a large account of the several MSS here used, and of the other matters which contribute to make this edition useful. In this work he is of no sect or party; his design is to serve the whole Christian name. He draws no consequences in his notes; makes no oblique glances upon any disputed points, old or new. He consecrates this work, as a κειμήλιον, a κτῆμα ἐσαἐι, a *charter,* a *magna charta,* to the whole Christian Church; to last when all the ancient MSS here quoted may be lost and extinguished.

"(g) To publish this work, according to its use and importance, a great expense is requisite: it's designed to be printed, not on the paper or with the letter of this *Specimen,* but with the best letter, paper, and ink that Europe affords. It must therefore be done by subscription or contribution. As it will make two tomes in folio, the lowest subscription for smaller paper must be three guineas, one advanced in present; and for the great paper five guineas, two advanced.

"(h) The work will be put to the press as soon as money is contributed to support the charge of the impression; and no more copies will be printed than are subscribed for. The overseer and corrector of the press will be the learned Mr. John Walker, of Trinity College in Cambridge; who, with great accurateness, has collated many MSS at Paris for the present edition. And the issue of it, whether gain or loss, is equally to fall on him and the author."

Although Bentley's proposed edition was never published, it is important for the study of the history of the NT text. He saw that it was necessary to use some discrimination in the choice of Greek MSS and that the ancient MSS are the witnesses to the ancient text. It must be kept in mind that a late MS may also be a witness to an ancient text; but, generally speaking, the older the MS, the older the text to which it witnesses. After the ancient text had been established through the general agreement of the ancient MSS with the ancient versions and the quotations of the Church Fathers, Bentley was ready to discard from consideration the whole mass of late witnesses. In this, of course, he was wrong. The late witnesses are of value for the history of the transmission of the NT text, and they may preserve an ancient reading that has been lost in the earlier MSS.

Bentley formed two other conclusions, in which he was wrong: (a) that Jerome used the Greek MSS of Origen in making his revision—the Vulg.; (b) that there had been *one* known and received Latin version, which was altered and revised to produce the confusion that Jerome found.

Had Bentley's edition been published, it would have shaken the foundations of the *textus receptus.* It was long before scholars again adopted the principle of selecting from among the mass of available materials.

3. Bengel and Wettstein. With the work of John Albrecht Bengel, there was a revival of interest in the study of the text of the NT on the Continent. Bengel was born in Würtenberg in 1687. During his student days at Tübingen (1703-7) he became interested in the variant readings in the text of the Greek NT. He had learned to value the NT as the declaration of God's revealed will, and he was anxious to know the precise form in which it had been given.

Bengel's difficulty in regard to the text of the NT was caused by the fact that before Mill's edition there were only partial collations of the variant readings which raised doubt in his mind. After much study, he came to the conclusion that the variant readings were less numerous than might have been expected and that they did not shake any article of evangelic doctrine. He also came to the conclusion that a Greek text was needed which was based upon sound principles of criticism applied to accurate and complete collations.

At first Bengel gathered materials for his own use, but he was encouraged by his friends to complete his work for publication. The collations which were made by Bengel and for him, unfortunately, do not meet the requirements of modern research.

Bengel's chief importance lies in the critical principles which he evolved. The great principle he fol-

lowed was: "The more difficult reading is to be preferred." This is an idea which is to be found in some
places in Mill's *Prolegomena*. Bengel attached high
value to the Latin versions as witnesses to the original text. Here, too, he followed Mill, as well as
Bentley.

Most important of all, it was Bengel who first advanced the theory of textual families or recensions.
He hoped to reduce all extant witnesses (Greek MSS,
versions, and quotations of the Church Fathers) into
"companies, families, tribes, and nations." He tried
to divide all extant Greek MSS into two families:
(*a*) the Asiatic, chiefly written in Constantinople and
its vicinity; (*b*) the African, comprising a few MSS
of the better type.

The next important step in the study of the text of
the NT was taken by John James Wettstein (not
Wetstein; *see bibliography*). Wettstein was born in
Basel in 1693. By the age of twenty, when he was
ordained a pastor, he was interested in biblical
studies. At that time he delivered a disputation on
the various readings of the NT. His love for this subject became a passion, the "master-passion which
consoled and dignified a roving, troubled, un-
prosperous life."

In 1714, Wettstein's search for MSS of the NT
led him to Paris; in 1715 and again in 1720, it led
him to England. On his second visit to England, he
was employed by Bentley to collate MSS, but he
seems to have learned but little from the great British
scholar.

Wettstein lived at a time when the textual critic
was suspect. Anyone who suggested changes in the
textus receptus was accused of tampering with the pure
Word of God. In spite of the fact that he was subjected to persecution, Wettstein fought constantly
for honest and free criticism. It should be noted, however, that Wettstein was constantly being accused of
holding unorthodox beliefs and that he was always
protesting his orthodoxy. Such constant protestations
of orthodoxy are usually open to some suspicion. In
insisting upon the fact that textual study should be
made free from theological bias and yet in insisting
upon his own orthodoxy, Wettstein was, in effect,
taking a theological position.

In 1730, while Wettstein in Basel was waging his
"fight for freedom," he published anonymously at
Amsterdam his famous *Prolegomena*—a quarto volume
of 201 pages. Even though it was published anonymously, no one who read it could doubt that it was
his.

The first five chapters of the *Prolegomena* dealt with
MSS and their authority. The codices which Wettstein had examined personally were marked with a
star; the MSS which had been examined and reported to him by his friends were marked with a
cross; the others had no mark. He discussed MSS in
general, the material on which they were written,
the method of writing, the form of the letters, accents, breathings, abbreviations, orthography, and
corrections. "The Apostles," he said, "were not literary purists. They spoke and wrote according to the
manner of the common people." Wettstein divided
the materials for the formation of the text of the NT
into four classes: (*a*) eight MSS written in the oldest

lettering; (*b*) twelve MSS of a later uncial type; (*c*)
MSS written by Latin copyists, accompanied by a
Latin version; (*d*) 152 minuscule MSS. He passed
judgment on many MSS. The place of honor he gave
to Alexandrinus, even though he confessed that it had
many faults introduced by copyists. He suspected
that it was the work of a female scribe. In spite of its
faults, Wettstein intended to use it as the base for
the text of his proposed edition of the NT.

Chs. 6-7 of the *Prolegomena* dealt with the Church
Fathers who have quoted the NT from the earliest
times to the invention of printing. He implied that no
edition of any Father which had not been edited
critically was of value for the textual criticism of the
NT.

Ch. 8 dealt with the Latin versions.

In ch. 9, Wettstein expressed his belief that the
Bohairic and Syriac versions were of great value.
The Syriac was of especial value, he thought, even
more trustworthy than the Greek text, as it represented the language in common use in apostolic
times.

The next five chapters (10-14) dealt with various
editions of the NT.

Ch. 15 pointed out that the Protestant commentators recognized and dealt with the various readings
to be found in the text of the NT.

In the last chapter of his *Prolegomena,* Wettstein
set down nineteen rules which he proposed to follow
in his own edition of the NT: (*a*) every effort should
be made to edit the NT as correctly as possible; (*b*)
all critical aids should be employed for the elucidation of the text; (*c*) the prescription of the *textus receptus* should have no authority; (*d*) editors must form
their own judgment as to accents, breathings, punctu-
ations, and orthography; (*e*) conjectural emendations
are never to be hastily admitted or rejected; (*f*) the
distinction of readings into those more or less weighty
is useless—i.e., all varieties of readings must be im-
partially considered by the critic; (*g*) between two
readings, the one which is better sounding, or more
clear, or better Greek, is not to be at once chosen but
more often the contrary; (*h*) a reading which exhibits
an unusual expression, but which is in other respects
suitable to the matter in hand, is preferable to another which, though equally suitable, has expressions
such as are not peculiar; (*i*) of two readings, the
fuller and more ample is not at once to be accepted,
but rather the contrary; (*j*) if of two readings one is
found in the same words elsewhere and the other is
not, the former is by no means to be preferred to the
latter; (*k*) a reading altogether conformable to the
style of each writer, other things being equal, is to be
preferred; (*l*) of two various readings, that which
seems the more orthodox is not to be forthwith preferred; (*m*) of two various readings in Greek copies,
that which accords with the ancient versions is not
easily to be considered the worse; (*n*) the witness of
the ancient Church Fathers has great weight in proving the true reading of the NT; (*o*) the silence of the
Fathers as to readings of importance in the controversies of their own times makes such readings
suspect; (*p*) great care should be taken not to adopt
as true readings the errata of collectors of readings
or of printers; (*q*) the reading which is proved to be

the more ancient, other things being equal, must be preferred; (r) the readings of the majority of MSS, other things being equal, must be preferred; (s) there is no reason why a reading should not be received into the text, not only if it is suitably attested, but even when it is doubtful which reading is preferable.

The *Prolegomena* formed a landmark in the history of textual criticism. It is to be regretted that Wettstein did not proceed immediately to the editing of the NT along the lines which he laid down. Unfortunately, however, as has been indicated, his NT did not appear until 1751 and 1752.

During the twenty-one years that elapsed between the publication of his *Prolegomena* and the publication of the first volume of his NT, Wettstein became obsessed by his theory of the Latinization of the early Greek MSS. It had long been recognized that the Greek text in the bilingual Greek-Latin MSS showed a remarkable resemblance to the Latin text. The suspicion arose that in such cases the Greek text had been "corrected" to the Latin text. Erasmus had suggested that at the Council of Florence, in 1439, it had been agreed that the Greeks who then united with the Roman church should alter their MSS to make them conform to the Latin Vulg. If any Greek MSS resembled the Latin in their readings, it was thought that this agreement might explain them. Erasmus had, of course, applied this principle to the late MSS. Wettstein, however, applied it to all the early codices and thus vitiated all the earlier principles he had laid down. He lamented the fact that all the most ancient MSS had been interpolated from the Latin and that it should be necessary to descend several centuries from the date of the oldest copies before any could be found which could be used for establishing a pure text.

4. Beginnings of modern criticism. It was with Johann Jakob Griesbach (born 1745) that real critical texts of the NT began. He recognized the value of the ancient MSS and approved, in principle, Bengel's theory of a twofold division of the Greek MSS into families: one African, and one Byzantine. Griesbach, however, divided the African family into two parts so as in fact to maintain that there are three classes of text—two ancient, and one more recent. The names assigned by him to these three classes of MSS were: (a) Western; (b) Alexandrian; (c) Constantinopolitan. The Western class contained the text which had been in circulation in the early periods and which because of the errors of copyists required much correction. The Alexandrian was an attempt to revise the old corrupt text. The Constantinopolitan flowed from the other two. Griesbach believed that the Western and Alexandrian recensions, as he called them, existed as distinct recensions in the latter part of the second century.

In deciding upon the value of a reading, Griesbach relied chiefly upon the evidence furnished by agreement of families. Agreement between the Western and Alexandrian he considered to be of great importance. It should be emphasized that he placed importance on the evidence of families and not upon the evidence of individual authorities, however important.

Griesbach laid down five canons of criticism: (a) no reading must be considered preferable unless it has the support of at least some ancient witness; (b) all criticism of the text turns on the study of recensions or classes of documents; not single documents but recensions are to be counted in determining readings; (c) the shorter reading is to be preferred to the longer; (d) the more difficult reading is to be preferred to the easier; (e) the reading which at first sight appears to convey a false sense is to be preferred to other readings.

Griesbach has never received the credit due him for his contributions to the study of the NT text. In many ways, he laid the foundations for the work of later scholars. The work of Westcott and Hort and of von Soden, e.g., was based upon precisely the principles which he laid down.

To Charles Lachmann, a classical philologist, must go the credit of being the first editor of the NT to break the sway of the *textus receptus*. His edition of 1831 was the first Greek NT after the invention of printing to be edited wholly on the evidence of ancient authorities, irrespective of later traditions.

Lachmann set out to edit the Greek NT as if the *textus receptus* had never existed. His object was to give the text of the Greek NT in that form in which the most ancient documents are known. His aim was purely historical; it was to recover, not the original text, but the text of the fourth century. He professed implicitly to follow ancient copies so far as then-existing collations made this possible. The oldest Greek MSS, compared with the citations of Origen, were the basis of his text. The readings of the OL, as found in unrevised MSS, and the citations of the Latin Fathers were his secondary sources.

Where the principal authorities agreed in an error (i.e., in a certain unquestionable error) Lachmann included this error in his text. He regarded such errors to have been a part of the textual tradition of the fourth century.

Lachmann recognized only two types of text: oriental and occidental. His witnesses for the gospels were 02 (A), 03 (B), 04 (C), 024 (P), 026 (Q), 029 (T), 035 (Z), and sometimes 05 (D). For Acts, they were 05 (D) and 08 (E^a). For Paul, they were 06 (D^P), 012 (G^P) and 015 (H^P). These witnesses were supplemented with the Greek remains of Irenaeus, the OL MSS *a, b, c*, the citations of Cyprian, Hilary of Poitiers, Lucifer of Cagliari, and Primasius.

Lachmann developed six canons of criticism for determining the readings of his text: (a) nothing is better attested than that in which all authorities agree; (b) the agreement has less weight if part of the authorities are silent or in any way defective; (c) the evidence for a reading, when it is that of witnesses of different regions, is greater than that of the witnesses of some particular place, differing either from negligence or from set purpose; (d) the testimonies are to be regarded as doubtfully balanced when witnesses from widely separated regions stand opposed to others equally wide apart; (e) readings are uncertain which occur habitually in different forms in different regions; (f) readings are of weak authority which are not uniformly attested in the same region.

After Lachmann, the next great opponent of the *textus receptus* was the British scholar Samuel Prideaux Tregelles. He was born into a Quaker family in 1813. At an early age he became a member of the Plymouth Brethren. The last years of his life were spent as a lay member of the Church of England. He at one time assured the bishop of Marlborough that he had become a member of the Church of England as a result of his study of the Greek NT. The only formal education that Tregelles ever had was received at the Falmouth Classical School. In spite of his lack of formal education, at the age of twenty-five he was deeply interested in the critical study of the Greek NT. This interest became the main occupation of his life.

Tregelles traveled extensively on the Continent and examined and collated many MSS of the NT. He developed a method for textual study which he called "comparative criticism." He defined this method by saying: "As a preliminary definition of terms, I state that by *'Comparative Criticism'* I mean such an investigation as shows what the character of a document is,—not simply from its age, whether known or supposed,—but from its actual readings being shown to be in accordance or not with certain other documents. By an estimate of Mss. through the application of comparative criticism, is intended merely such an arrangement as may enable it to be said, that certain Mss. do, as a demonstrated fact, present features of classification as agreeing or not agreeing in text with ancient authorities with which they are compared" (*An Account of the Printed Text of the Greek New Testament*, 1854).

In the same book he set forth and explained in detail his canons of criticism. They may be summarized as follows: (*a*) readings whose antiquity is proved apart from MSS are found in repeated instances in a few of the extant copies; (*b*) as certain MSS are found, by a process of inductive proof, to contain an ancient text, their character as witnesses must be considered to be so established that, in other places, their testimony deserves peculiar weight; (*c*) the concurrence of two versions in a definite reading excludes the supposition that the reading is merely an accident of transcription or translation; and that the accordance with them of certain MSS is likewise the result of fortuitous circumstances or of arbitrary alteration; (*d*) although patristic quotations are often modernized to suit the Greek text to which the copyist was accustomed, yet when the reading is such that it could not be altered without changing the whole texture of their remarks, or when they are so express in their testimony that such a reading is that found in such a place, we need not doubt that it was so in their copies; and so, too, if we find that the reading of early Fathers agrees with other early testimonies in opposition to those which are later; (*e*) the antiquity of documents is to be preferred to their number as a basis of testimony.

The greatest of the Continental students of the text of the NT was the "fabulous Tischendorf," a contemporary of Tregelles. Tischendorf was born in Saxony in 1815. His greatest contributions to the study of the text of the NT were made as a collector and publisher of MSS and as an editor of the NT.

He discovered and published more Greek uncial MSS than did any other man. His greatest discovery was, of course, Codex Sinaiticus. It has been noted above that he edited no fewer than twenty-four editions of the NT.

Tischendorf made but few, if any, improvements in the methods of textual criticism. He drew up six canons of criticism, but they contained no new suggestions for determining the oldest or the best readings. His canons were: (*a*) the text is only to be sought from ancient evidence, and especially from Greek MSS, but without neglecting the testimonies of versions and Fathers; (*b*) a reading altogether peculiar to one or another ancient document is suspect, as also is any, even if supported by a class of documents which seems to show that it has originated in the revision of a learned man; (*c*) readings, however well supported by evidence, are to be rejected when it appears that they have proceeded from errors of copyists; (*d*) in parallel passages, whether of the NT or the OT, especially in the Synoptic gospels, those testimonies are to be preferred in which there is no precise accordance of such parallel passages, unless there are important reasons to the contrary; (*e*) in discrepant readings, that reading should be preferred which may have given occasion to the rest, or which appears to comprise the elements of the others; (*f*) those readings must be maintained which accord with NT Greek, or with the peculiar style of each individual writer.

5. Westcott and Hort. B. F. Westcott and F. J. A. Hort finally dealt the death blow to the *textus receptus*, but in doing so they set up what has come to be a new *textus receptus* and "canonized" a new method for textual studies, the genealogical method.

B. F. Westcott (1825-1901) was one of the most amazing men of the nineteenth century. He was an educator, a churchman, a humanitarian, and a scholar. In 1870 he was elected Regius Professor of Divinity at Cambridge, and in 1883 he became a professorial fellow at King's College. He was appointed by the crown to a canonry at Westminster, and in 1890 he became bishop of Durham. He took a practical interest in the affairs of the British coal miners and of the employees of the shipping and artisan industries. He was a stanch supporter of the British co-operative movement. He was one of the main founders of the Christian Social Union. Among his scholarly publications were *History of the NT Canon*, *Characteristics of the Gospel Miracles*, *Introduction to the Study of the Gospels*, *The Bible in the Church*, *The Gospel of the Resurrection*, *History of the English Bible*, and *The Gospel of Life*. He also published commentaries on the Fourth Gospel, on Hebrews, and on the Johannine letters. He served as a member of the committee that was engaged in the revision of the NT (the Revised Version). During all this time, he and Hort were at work on their edition of the Greek NT.

In his *Bible in the Church* (1864), Westcott made two statements that reveal more about his interest in the text of the NT than any other words that ever came from his pen. In the Preface to that book, he said: "A corrupted Bible is a sign of a corrupted Church, a Bible mutilated or imperfect, a sign of a

Church not yet raised to the complete perception of Truth. It is possible that we might have wished . . . this otherwise: we might have thought that a Bible of which every part should bear a visible and unquestioned authentication of its divine origin, separated by a solemn act from the first from the sum and fate of all other literature, would have best answered our conceptions of what the written records of revelation should be. But it is not thus that God works among us. In the Church and in the Bible alike, He works through men. As we follow the progress of their formation, each step seems to be truly human; and when we contemplate the whole, we joyfully recognize that every part is also divine." In the final paragraph of this same book, he said: "The Bible, no less than the Church, is Holy, Catholic, and Apostolic: Holy, for they who wrote it were moved by the Holy Spirit: Catholic, for it embraces in essence every type of Christian truth which has gained entrance among men: Apostolic, for its limits are not extended beyond that first generation to which was committed the charge of preaching the Gospel in the fulness of its original power."

F. J. A. Hort (1828-92) was a fellow and lecturer in Emmanuel College and, later, Lady Margaret reader in divinity. He, like Westcott, was a member of the committee for the revision of the NT.

In Part II of their *NT in the Original Greek: Introduction and Appendix*, Westcott and Hort pointed out that "every method of textual criticism corresponds to some one class of textual facts," that "the best criticism is that which takes account of every class of textual facts and assigns to each method its proper use and rank," and that "the leading principles of textual criticism are identical for all writings whatever." They then set forth the methods of textual criticism in their "natural order" so that what they considered to be the higher methods came last into view. The following paragraphs represent a condensation, as far as possible in their own words, of Westcott and Hort's longer discussion:

a. Internal evidence of readings. This is the most rudimentary form of criticism. It consists in dealing with each variation independently and adopting at once in each case, out of two or more variants, that which looks most probable. It takes no account of any relative antecedent credibility of the actual witness. Internal evidence of readings is of two kinds, having reference respectively to the author and to copyists:

a) Intrinsic probability. The first impulse in dealing with a variation is usually to lean on intrinsic probability—i.e., to consider which of two readings makes the best sense, and to decide between them accordingly. The decision may be made either by an immediate and, as it were, intuitive judgment, or by weighing cautiously various elements which go to make up what is called sense, such as conformity to grammar and congruity to the purport of the sentence and of the larger context; to which may be rightly added congruity to the usual style of the author and to his matter in other passages. These considerations afford reasonable presumptions, presumptions which in some cases may attain such force on the negative side as to demand the rejection or qualify the acceptance of readings most highly commended by other kinds of evidence.

The assumptions involved in intrinsic probability are not to be implicitly trusted. There is much literature, ancient no less than modern, in which it is needful to remember that authors are not always grammatical, or clear, or consistent, or felicitous; so that not seldom an ordinary reader finds it easy to replace a feeble or half-appropriate word or phrase by an effective substitute; and thus the best words to express an author's meaning need not in all cases be those which he actually employed. It should be noted, however, that in the highest literature, and notably in the Bible, all readers are peculiarly liable to the fallacy of supposing that they understand the author's meaning and purpose because they understand some part or some aspect of it, which they take for the whole; and hence, in judging variations of text, they are led unawares to disparage any word or phrase which owes its selection by the author to those elements of the thought present to his mind which they have failed to perceive or to feel.

b) Transcriptional probability. The next step in criticism is the discovery of transcriptional probability, and is suggested on the reflection that what attracts us is not on the average unlikely to have attracted transcribers. If one variant reading appears to us to give much better sense or in some other way to excel another, the same apparent superiority may have led to the introduction of the reading in the first instance. Mere blunders apart, no motive can be thought of which could lead a scribe to introduce consciously a worse reading in place of a better. This does not mean that intrinsic inferiority is evidence of originality.

Transcriptional probability is not directly or properly concerned with the relative excellence of rival readings, but merely with the relative fitness of each for explaining the existence of the others. Every rival reading contributes an element to the problem which has to be solved; for every rival reading is a fact which has to be accounted for, and no acceptance of any one reading as original can be satisfactory which leaves any other variant incapable of being traced to some known cause or causes of variation. If variants are binary, ternary, or more complex, each in its turn must be assumed as a hypothetical original, and an endeavor made to deduce from it all the others, either independently or consecutively; after which the relative facilities of the several experimental deductions must be compared. Hence, the basis on which transcriptional probability rests consists of generalizations as to the causes of corruption incident to the process of transcription. Even at its best, this class of internal evidence, like the other, carries us but a little way toward the recovery of an ancient text, when it is employed alone. The number of variations in which it can be trusted to supply by itself a direct and immediate decision is relatively very small, when unquestionable blunders—i.e., clerical errors—have been set aside.

Readings which are certified by the coincidence of both intrinsic and transcriptional probability are of the utmost value in the application of other methods of criticism.

b. Internal evidence of documents. It is precarious to attempt to judge which of two or more readings is most likely to be right, without considering which of the attesting documents or combinations of documents are the most likely to convey an unadulterated transcript of the original text. In other words, it is precarious, in dealing with matter purely traditional, to ignore the relative antecedent credibility of witnesses, and trust exclusively to one's own inward power of singling out the true readings from among their counterfeits. The comparative trustworthiness of documentary authorities constitutes a fresh class of pertinent facts. The first step toward obtaining a sure foundation is a consistent application of the principle that knowledge of documents should precede final judgment upon readings.

The most prominent fact known about a MS is its date. Relative date affords a valuable presumption as to relative freedom from corruption, when appealed to on a large scale. But the occasional preservation of comparatively ancient texts in comparatively modern MSS forbids confident reliance on priority of date unsustained by other marks of excellence.

The first effectual security against the uncertainties of internal evidence of readings is found in what may be termed internal evidence of documents—i.e., the general characteristics of the texts contained in them as learned directly from them by continuous study of the whole or of considerable parts. This and this alone supplies entirely trustworthy knowledge as to the relative value of different documents. If the readings of two documents in all their variations are compared successively, ample materials for ascertaining the leading merits and defects of each are obtained.

Readings authenticated by the coincidence of strong intrinsic and strong transcriptional probability, or it may be by one alone of these probabilities in exceptional strength and clearness and uncontradicted by the other, are almost always to be found sufficiently numerous to supply a solid basis for inference.

Where one document is found habitually to contain morally certain or at least strongly preferred readings, and another habitually to contain their rejected rivals, there can be no doubt that the text of the first has been transmitted in comparative purity, and that the text of the second has suffered comparatively large corruption; and that the superiority of the first must be as great in the variations in which internal evidence of readings has furnished no decisive criterion as in those which made it possible to form a comparative appreciation of the two texts.

By this cautious advance from the known to the unknown it is possible to deal confidently with a great mass of those remaining variations—open variations, so to speak—the confidence being materially increased when, as usually happens, the document thus found to have the better text is also the older.

The use of internal evidence of documents is really a threefold process: (a) on the basis of internal evidence of readings, material is tentatively gathered. The results are not final, as they would be if internal evidence of readings alone were used. On some variations, at this stage, an ultimate conclusion can be predicted; on many more, only various degrees of probability can be estimated; on many more, any decision must be withheld. (b) Documents are investigated on the basis of what has been learned from the investigation of readings. In this step, it is determined which documents contain the best readings. (c) The readings are again investigated, but this time a tentative choice of readings is made simply in accordance with documentary evidence. Where the results coincide with those obtained at the first stage, a very high degree of probability is reached, resting on the coincidence of two and often three independent kinds of evidence. Where they differ at first sight, a fresh study of the whole evidence affecting the variation in question is secured.

c. Genealogical evidence. The first great step in rising above the uncertainties of internal evidence of readings was taken by ceasing to treat readings independently of one another, and examining them connectedly in series, each series being furnished by one of the several documents in which they were found. The second great step consists in ceasing to treat documents independently of one another, and examining them connectedly as parts of a single whole in virtue of their historical relationships.

Documents are not so many independent and rival texts of greater or less purity. By the nature of the case they are not independent; they are all fragments, usually casual and scattered fragments, of a genealogical tree of transmission, sometimes of vast extent and intricacy. All trustworthy restoration of corrupted texts is founded on the study of their history—i.e., of the relations of descent or affinity which connect the several documents.

Knowledge of the genealogy of MSS is chiefly gained by study of their texts in comparison with one another. The process depends on the principle that identity of reading implies identity of origin. Mixture, of course, confuses the picture. One source of knowledge concerning mixture is conflate readings.

d. Internal evidence of groups. In one sense, this is an intermediate step between the internal evidence of documents and genealogical evidence, but in order of discovery it naturally comes last.

When the internal evidence of documents was investigated, only single documents were considered; but the method is equally applicable to groups of documents. Just as the characteristics of any given MS can be noted by observing successively what readings it supports and rejects (each reading having previously been the subject of the tentative estimate of internal evidence of readings, intrinsic and transcriptional), and by classifying the results, so can the characteristics of any given group of documents be noted by similar observations on the readings it supports and rejects, giving special attention to those readings in which it stands absolutely or virtually alone.

As a result of their investigations, Westcott and Hort found many passages in the NT in which there are three forms of the text. Two of these forms were short, and the third was long, a combination of the two shorter forms. These longer readings (conflate readings) must be late, they argued, particularly since they are found only in the Church Fathers who wrote after the fourth century. The MSS which contained these conflate readings were grouped together under the name Syrian and were presumed to represent the recension of the NT which is attributed to Lucian of Antioch at the end of the third or the beginning of the fourth century. This Syrian text is characterized by stylistic changes, conflate readings, the tendency to make obscure words and phrases more lucid and the harmonizing of parallel passages. This type of text Westcott and Hort considered to be the least valuable of all. They then identified three pre-Syrian types of text: (*a*) the Neutral text, which is the primitive text that has been preserved in relative purity, if not in its original form; (*b*) the Western text, which was made in the second century by scribes who made interpolations, harmonized parallel passages, and suppressed certain details; and (*c*) the Alexandrian text, which was the work of "purists" trying to mold the NT text to classical standards.

Westcott and Hort never applied the genealogical method to the MSS of the NT. They used only the idea of applying the method to the NT MSS, and even then it was only a secondary element in their procedure. They actually applied the genealogical method only to individual passages and to individual variants. The genealogical method itself fails the NT textual student on two important counts: (*a*) it cannot adequately account for mixture which is so prevalent in the NT; and (*b*) it cannot get beyond a two-branched family tree. For an ultimate decision on the originality of any given reading, the student must rely upon what Westcott and Hort called the internal evidence of readings.

In spite of the fact that Westcott and Hort did not apply the genealogical method to the MSS of the NT, and in spite of the method's shortcomings, it has been the "canonical" method for studying the NT text since their time. Many scholars have made use of the method, and, almost without exception, they have come to a clearer understanding of its limitations and failures. As long ago as 1904, Kirsopp Lake called the method "a failure, though a splendid one."

6. Von Soden and later developments. Perhaps the most outstanding work since Westcott and Hort that has made use of the genealogical method is that of Hermann Von Soden (1852-1914). In Von Soden's opinion, all existing Greek MSS belong to one of the three great recensions which he designated as I, H, and K. The text of each of these recensions, he believed, can be reconstructed with tolerable, though not complete, certainty. He classified the MSS into groups according to: (*a*) their text; (*b*) their form of the text of the *pericope de adultera;* (*c*) their chapter divisions; and (*d*) their lectionary apparatus. Naturally, the text was the most important, and Von Soden was principally guided by it. The other points, however, were of value to him in distinguishing among groups of MSS which textually are almost identical.

Von Soden held that the I (Jerusalem) recension was made by Origen in the third century and was later published by Eusebius and Pamphilus of Caesarea. The H (Hesychian) recension was made in Egypt by Hesychius in the third century. The K (Koine) recension was made by Lucian of Antioch at the end of the third or the beginning of the fourth century.

The I recension corresponds roughly to Westcott and Hort's Western text. According to von Soden, it represents a recension of the Greek text which was made at a time posterior to the Latin and Syr. versions. These versions, therefore, represent a type of text that is earlier than and different from the I recension. Von Soden found the I recension nowhere in a pure form. He divided his I witnesses for the gospels into the following subgroups: I^a, I^η, I^ι, I^ϕ, I^β, I^o, I^π, I^σ, I^k, and I^r. He also found many MSS which preserved I readings but which would not fit into any of his subgroups. These MSS he called I^z.

I^a is the best representative of the I recension. All its MSS have suffered some corruption from K^1 but independently of one another. Codex Bezae, the oldest I^a witness, besides being corrupted by K^1, was influenced by parallelization, by omission due to paleographical causes, and by the African Latin and the Old Syr. versions.

I^η is essentially Family 1. It is a relatively pure form of the I recension that has been corrupted but very little by K. Originally, it had a critical note attached to the end of Mark. The *pericope de adultera,* with a critical note attached, originally appeared at the end of the Gospel of John. Since Von Soden's time, it has been demonstrated that this was the type of Matthean text used by Origen in his commentary on Matthew.

I^ι is essentially the Ferrar group or Family 13 and is a very valuable witness to the I recension. It has been corrupted by K (but probably not by K^x) and by the harmonization of parallel passages. It had the *pericope de adultera* after Luke 21:38.

I^ϕ has been greatly corrupted by K, but it still preserves the original readings of the I recension in many places where they have disappeared from I^η and I^ι. It is, therefore, an important I witness. In its original form, it did not contain the *pericope de adultera.*

I^β is a less important subtype, and it contributes nothing to the knowledge of the I recension that is not known from other sources. It has been greatly contaminated by K^1.

I^o is a mixture of K^1 and I. It contains some interesting readings but is of no great importance as a witness to the I recension.

I^π is a mixture of I with K^1 and K^x. It is found in the Purple Codices: 022 (N), 023 (O), 042 (Σ), 043 (Φ), and 080. The Cappadocian Fathers probably used this type of text.

I^σ is a mixture of I and K. It is of no particular value as a witness to the I recension.

I^k (or K^a) represents a form of the I recension that has been made to conform almost entirely to the K recension. It does, however, preserve enough I readings to show its original form. It is an I text that has been corrected to K^1 on the principle that the text should be followed which showed the greatest number of harmonizations of parallel passages.

I^r is another mixture of K^1 and I. According to Von Soden, it consists of nine parts K^1 and one part I. It probably, however, contains some K^x readings. There is a close agreement between the I^r MSS and the MSS of the A^a type of the Antiochene commentary text. (The Antiochene commentary is the

widely found commentary on the gospels of which
the basis in Matthew and John is Chrysostom; in
Mark, Victor of Antioch; and in Luke, Titus of
Bostra.) Typical MSS of both groups contain a note
to the effect that they have been compared with Jerusalem codices.

Von Soden reconstructed the original I recension
by comparing all these groups and subgroups. He
concluded that it was the type of text that was used
by Cyril of Jerusalem and by Eusebius of Caesarea.
All these subgroups of the I recension he regarded
as a compromise between Constantinople and
Antioch.

Von Soden's H recension corresponds to Westcott and Hort's Neutral and Alexandrian texts. It is
found in eleven MSS in varying degrees of purity.
The most important extant witnesses to this recension
are Sinaiticus and Vaticanus. The most important
witness, however, is ℵ-B, the archetype of those two
MSS. But even this archetype has been contaminated
by the Egyptian versions, by Origen, and by the K
and I recensions. Vaticanus more often represents the
archetype than does Sinaiticus.

The K recension of Von Soden approximates the
Syrian text of Westcott and Hort. In the gospels, Von
Soden divided his K witnesses into six subgroups:
K¹, Kᵃ, Kˣ, Kʳ, Kⁱ, and Kⁱᵏ.

K¹ is the oldest and the most important witness to
the K recension. Originally it either omitted the
pericope de adultera altogether or had it marked with
an asterisk to indicate its doubtful origin. K¹ seems
to have been the base text used by the Aᵃ MSS of
the Antiochene commentary on Matthew, Luke, and
John. On the basis of MS evidence, the existence of
K¹ cannot be demonstrated before the eighth century.

The remaining K witnesses are of much less importance than is K¹. Kᵃ was discussed above under
Iᵏ. Kˣ is an intermediate type of text lying between
K¹ and Kʳ. Its critical value is but slightly greater
than is that of Kʳ. Kʳ is a late type of text which
probably came into existence in the twelfth century.
It probably was made in Constantinople for ecclesiastical use. It is valueless insofar as the reconstruction of an early text is concerned. Both Kⁱ and
Kⁱᵏ are a mixture of K¹ and Kˣ with other recensions. Kⁱ is either K¹ influenced by Iⁱ or, more probably, Iⁱ corrected to a K¹ standard. Kⁱᵏ is a mixture
of Kˣ and Iᵏ. It is fairly common, but it is valueless
for critical purposes.

Although Von Soden was not able to produce any
direct evidence that the K recension was in existence
before the eighth century, he believed that he could
find traces of it in 02 (A), 04 (C), the Peshitta, the
Gothic, and, as has been pointed out above, in the
archetype of Sinaiticus and Vaticanus. If this were
true, it would place the K recension at least as early
as the fourth century.

After he reconstructed the texts of the three great
recensions, I, H, and K, Von Soden proceeded to reconstruct their archetype, which he called I-H-K.
This archetype is purely hypothetical; there is no objective proof that it ever existed, as it is not identical
with the text of any known MS, version, or quotation of a Church Father. In order to reconstruct I-H-
K, Von Soden followed a series of rules which he had

set up: (*a*) those readings are rejected which are explicable as due to harmonization; (*b*) if there are two
readings, both explicable as due to harmonization,
the one with Matthew and the other with another
gospel, the non-Matthean reading is to be preferred
on the ground that Matthew was the "norm gospel"
in early times; and (*c*) when there is no question of
harmonization, that reading is to be preferred which
is found in two out of three recensions, unless there
is some reason against it, as there often is when the
smaller linguistic points are in question. The result of
this process was to show that of the three recensions,
K is the least true and I is the most true to I-H-K.
But H is not far behind I in value as a witness to
I-H-K.

The reconstruction of I-H-K took Von Soden back
only to the end of the third century. He then had
to take into account the evidence of the Latin and
Syr. versions. He recognized two OL versions, the
African and the Italian. Originally they were two
separate versions. The African Latin represents I-
H-K with some corruption from Tatian; the Italian
Latin represents I-H-K with a much greater amount
of Tatianic corruption. The Old Syr. versions represent I-H-K with some corruption from Tatian and
some Origenian readings.

Von Soden concluded that the differences between
I-H-K and Tatian were not due to the text which
Tatian had before him but to his method of handling
that text. In the end, I-H-K proved to be the very
text to which Tatian himself bears witness.

Since the days of Von Soden, many significant
works on the text of the NT have appeared (for the
more important ones, *see bibliography*). But none of
them has contributed materially to the theory and
method of textual criticism. It is now generally agreed
that the genealogical method does not meet the needs
of the student of the text of the NT.

Among the textual scholars of today, the tendency
is to follow an "eclectic" method in order to reconstruct the earliest possible text of the NT. This
method can perhaps best be summarized by listing
the canons of criticism which are most commonly
used: (*a*) the shorter reading is to be preferred; (*b*)
the more difficult reading is to be preferred; (*c*) the
reading which best suits the author's characteristic
tendencies is to be preferred; and (*d*) the reading
which best explains the origin of all other variants in
a given passage is to be preferred. In other words,
the emphasis today is upon the internal evidence of
readings.

F. *CONCLUSION.* At the beginning of this article,
it was pointed out that the text of the NT contains
more variants than that of any other body of ancient
literature. It is generally considered that the task of
deciding among these variants is the task of the
textual critic. His task, it is usually said, is to choose
that reading which, among all those to be found in
the various sources, is most likely to be the original
or most primitive form. To be a textual critic in this
limited sense, however, is not enough for a NT
scholar. If he were working on the text of a Greek
or Latin classic, or, indeed, if he were working on
the text of a document from any other body of sacred
literature, he could function as a technician and

nothing more. The NT textual scholar who is working from within the Christian tradition must be more than a textual critic in the narrow sense of the word. He must be, in a certain sense, not only a textual critic but a church historian, a historian of Christian thought, and a theologian as well. The textual critic who works from within the Christian tradition works, not with documents which are like all other ancient documents, but with documents which are for him scripture, and his attitude toward that scripture is determined by the time and place and religious community from which he comes.

If the textual critic happens to be a Protestant, his task is complicated by the fact that he has to work with MS materials which were produced by those whose attitude toward scripture was vastly different from his own. He may be fully cognizant of the fact that the writers of the NT books were proclaiming the faith of the church as it was their faith; that they were concerned with the present, their present; that they selected from the already growing tradition of the church, both oral and written, those items in that tradition which would enable them to "bear witness to the revelation of God"; that they did not tell us all that had happened, nor did they tell us all that the church had thought and said; or, as someone has said, that "they did not scrape the bottom of the barrel." He may also be fully aware of the process by which the NT books were finally accorded canonical status. But what the Protestant text historian, with his post-Reformation attitude toward scripture, may not be aware of, or at least what he may not give due consideration to, is the fact that tradition and scripture, after the autographs were written and after they were accorded canonical status, continued to stand side by side, each supplementing the other, and each influencing the development of the other.

The task of the textual critic is at least a fourfold one:

a) The textual critic must fully collate, carefully study, and classify all the thousands of Greek MSS, MSS of the versions, and quotations of the Church Fathers. The completion of this task will, of course, require the combined labors of several generations of scholars. The only consolation is that if this work is done accurately and well, it will not have to be done again.

b) The textual critic must reconstruct the text of the NT autographs. If this proves to be impossible, he must strive constantly to approximate the autographs as closely as possible. But to do this, he must develop a new theory and a new method to supplant the largely discredited genealogical method of the past. The autographs must be recovered because the NT books are the documents which bring us closest to the historical events which are the great doctrines of the Christian faith. These historical events—the Incarnation, the Crucifixion, and the Resurrection—may all be subsumed under one, the "Christ event," which is the source and the norm of the life of the church. We are put in direct touch with the primitive church's experience of that event through the documents—the books of the NT—which she produced.

c) The text historian must reconstruct not only the text of the autographs, but many other texts as well.

The type of text represented by Codex Bezae was scripture for some Christians at some time, as was the type of text represented by Sinaiticus and Vaticanus. Even the late medieval MS that was used by Erasmus as printer's copy was scripture for some. As complicated as is the history, e.g., of the so-called Neutral text, the textual critic's task would be a fairly simple one if he had but to recover such easily distinguishable texts as those that are known as Neutral, Western, Caesarean, and Koine. But, to complicate his task, he finds that he has to recover many texts of but portions of his documents. In other words, his documents have been altered piecemeal. One MS, e.g., may show the result of intentional alteration in one pericope under the influence of some particular time and place, and in another pericope under the influence of some entirely different time and place.

d) The textual critic must place some evaluation upon the readings which he finds in his documents. He might well venture to say that a certain reading can be accepted, not as an original reading, but, nevertheless, as a part of the NT, because it comes to him in the stream of tradition. The textual critic is better equipped to pass such value judgments on texts or readings than is anyone else. Supposedly he knows the Greek MSS, the versional MSS, and the quotations of the Church Fathers. Supposedly he is at home in church history, the history of Christian thought and theology. Why then should he not be urged to do more than work on the assumption that the oldest NT is necessarily the best NT? The textual critic should take it upon himself to give to his contemporaries not only an original text but also many readings which have been examined and criticized in the light of the tradition of the church and of the underlying themes of the Bible. These readings and these texts need not be only the oldest possible texts and readings. If they proclaim the faith of the church, they are scripture.

Bibliography. For the published text of P[52], see: C. H. Roberts, *An Unpublished Fragment of the Fourth Gospel in the John Ryland's Library* (1935). For the published text of P[66], see: V. Martin, *Papyrus Bodmer II* (1956); *Papyrus Bodmer II, Supplement* (1958). On Chester Beatty Papyri (P[45], P[46], P[47]), see: F. G. Kenyon, *The Chester Beatty Biblical Papyri* (1933-37). H. Gerstinger, "Ein Fragment des Chester Beatty-Evangelienkodex in der Papyrussammlung der Nationalbibliothek in Wien," *Aegyptus* (1933), pp. 67-72.

On the history of the text, see: S. P. Tregelles, *An Account of the Printed Text of the Greek NT* (1854); *The Greek Testament Edited from Ancient Authorities* (1857-72). C. Tischendorf, *Novum Testamentum Graece . . . Editio octava critica maior* (2 vols.; 1869-72). F. H. A. Scrivener, *A Plain Introduction to the Criticism of the NT* (4th ed., rev. E. Miller; 1894). J. W. Burgon, *The Causes of the Corruption of the Traditional Text of the Holy Gospels* (ed. E. Miller; 1896); *The Traditional Text of the Holy Gospels* (ed. E. Miller; 1896). E. Miller, ed., *The Oxford Debate on the Textual Criticism of the NT held at New College on May 6, 1897* (1897). M. R. Vincent, *A History of the Textual Criticism of the NT* (1899). K. Lake, *Codex 1 of the Gospels and Its Allies. Texts and Studies*, vol. VII (1902). C. R. Gregory, *Canon and Text of the NT* (1907), pp. 297-598. H. von Soden, *Die Schriften des Neuen Testaments in ihrer ältesten erreichbaren Textgestalt* (2 vols.; 1902-13). H. J. Hoskier, *An Indictment of the Codex B and Its Allies* (1914). J. R. Harris, *On the Origin of the Ferrar Group* (1925). B. H. Streeter, *The Four Gospels* (1925). J. H. Ropes, "The Text of Acts," in F. J. Foakes-Jackson and K. Lake, eds., *The Beginnings of Chris-

tianity, pt. I: *The Acts of the Apostles*, vol. III (1926). K. Lake and S. New, "The Caesarean Text of the Gospel of Mark," *HTR*, vol. XXI (1928), no. 4. H. J. Hoskier, *Concerning the Text of the Apocalypse* (2 vols.; 1929). P. Collomp, *La Critique des textes* (1931). C. E. Legg, *Novum Testamentum Graece, Secundum Textum Westcotto-Hortianum, Evangelium Secundum Marcum* (1935). S. Lake, *Family II and the Codex Alexandrinus: Studies and Documents V* (1937). L. Vaganay, *An Introduction to the Textual Criticism of the NT* (trans. B. V. Miller; 1937). W. H. P. Hatch, *Principal Uncial MSS of the NT* (1939). C. E. Legg, *Evangelium Secundum Mattheum* (1940). K. Lake and S. Lake, *Family 13 (The Ferrar Group): The Text According to Mark, Studies and Documents XI* (1941). B. M. Metzger, "The Caesarean Text of the Gospels," *JBL*, LIV (1945), 457-89. E. C. Colwell, "Genealogical Method: Its Achievements and Limitations," *JBL*, LXVI (1947), 109-33. A. F. J. Klijn, *A Survey of the Researches into the Western Text of the Gospels and Acts* (1949). M. M. Parvis and A. P. Wikgren, eds., *NT MS Studies* (1950). M. M. Parvis, "The Nature and Tasks of NT Textual Criticism: An Appraisal," *JR*, XXXII (1952), 165-74. G. Zuntz, *The Text of the Epistles . . . Corpus Paulinum* (1953). A. Souter, *The Text and Canon of the NT* (2nd ed., rev. C. S. C. Williams; 1954), pp. 3-133. I. M. Price, *The Ancestry of Our English Bible* (3rd ed., rev. W. A. Irwin and A. P. Wikgren; 1956), pp. 153-224. F. G. Kenyon, *Our Bible and the Ancient MSS* (5th ed., rev. A. W. Adams; 1958).

On Origen as a textual critic, see F. Pack, *The Methodology of Origen as a Textual Critic in Arriving at the Text of the NT* (unpublished Ph.D. dissertation, University of Southern California Graduate School of Religion; 1948).

On Wettstein, see C. L. Hulbert-Powell, *John James Wettstein* (ca. 1937), p. 1, note 2.

For a thorough criticism of Westcott and Hort, see E. C. Colwell, "Genealogical Method: Its Achievements and Its Limitations," *JBL*, LXVI (1947), 109-33. M. M. PARVIS

*TEXTUS RECEPTUS tĕks'təs rĭ sĕp'təs. Latin for "received [or accepted] text," used especially of the 1550 edition of the Greek NT published by Stephanus, which came to be known as the "received text" in Britain, and of the 1633 edition of the Elzivir Greek NT, which was accepted on the Continent.

See also TEXT, NT, § D3. J. KNOX

THADDAEUS thă dē'əs, thăd'ĭ əs [Θαδδαῖος] (Matt. 10:3; Mark 3:18). *See* JUDAS 8.

THADDAEUS, ACTS OF [Θαδδαῖος]. A fifth-century version or parallel of the Syriac *Doctrina Addaei*, containing the local Edessene legends about Thaddeus and the correspondence between Abgarus and Jesus. *See* ABGARUS, EPISTLES OF CHRIST AND. M. S. ENSLIN

THAHASH. KJV form of TAHASH.

THAMAH. KJV alternate form of TEMAH.

THAMAR thā'mər. KJV NT form of TAMAR 1.

THAMMUZ. Alternate form of TAMMUZ.

THAMNATHA. KJV Apoc. form of TIMNAH.

THANK OFFERING. *See* SACRIFICE AND OFFER-INGS § A1d.

THANKSGIVING. An expression of thanks to God, which, with prayers on behalf of persons ad-dressed in letters, forms a regular part of Greek epistolary style, exemplified in the Egyptian papyri as well as in the NT. Among Paul's letters, Galatians is exceptional in the omission of such an opening (but see Gal. 1:3-5). *See* LETTER.

See also GRATITUDE.

Bibliography. P. Schubert, *The Form and Function of the Pauline Thanksgivings* (1935). O. J. F. SEITZ

THARA. KJV NT form of TERAH.

THARSHISH. KJV form of TARSHISH.

THASSI thăs'ī [Θασσί, zealous; Vulg. *Thasi*] (I Macc. 2:3). Surname of Simon, one of the five sons of Mattathias (cf. Jos. Antiq. XIII.i.2). Following Jonathan's defeat at Ptolemaïs and his ultimate death, Simon, the last survivor of the "glorious brothers," negotiated a treaty for Judean independence and became the founder of the Hasmonean Dynasty.

J. C. SWAIM

THEATER [θέατρον]. Structures taking advantage of natural land formations were designed as early as the fifth century B.C. in Greece for the presentation of dramatic performances which issued from the religious songs and dances in honor of Dionysus. The municipal theater also served as a center for the assembly of citizens (Acts 19:29-41). In its metaphorical use the Greek noun and corresponding verb for "theater," denoting the play itself, are found both in the NT (I Cor. 4:9; Heb. 10:33) and in Stoic teaching (Epictetus *Discourses* II.19, 25; III.22, 59).

1. History. Rival dramatic contests, held annually at the chief festival of the god Dionysus in Athens during the time of Peisistratus, involved choric readings and a spoken dialogue between the chorus leader and a person called the ὑποκριτής, or "answerer" (*see* HYPOCRISY). Dramatic action, made possible by the addition of several answerers and the introduction of themes drawn from national history or folklore, flowered into drama or τραγῳδία (lit., "goat song"). Comedy, which had its origins in odes called κωμῳδίαι sung to Dionysus at vintage time, often caricatured political events and personages of the day. In the Hellenistic age both tragedies and comedies were produced in quantity and presented before large audiences; there arose the so-called New Comedy, which did not use the chorus, and which took the form of a comedy of manners. Menander (died 292 B.C.), the best-known comic dramatist of the time, gave bawdy descriptions of private life, which have influenced drama up to the present time. The apostle Paul quotes from Menander's comedy *Thais* in I Cor. 15:33.

2. Buildings. Hellenistic theaters were built on natural ground slopes, with tiers of seats cut from rock, stone, wood, or marble slabs, arranged in ascending concentric crescents and separated into two or more sections by gangways. Unlike the amphitheaters, which were enclosed about an elliptical center or arena, the theater auditorium (*cavea*) was semicircular in form, with a circular orchestra or chorus space in the center and a raised wooden stage for the actors. The best-preserved theater of this type

Courtesy of the Arab Information Center, New York

52. Outer structure of the ancient Roman theater at Sabratha, Libya, *ca.* forty miles from Tripoli, built to hold five thousand people; erected not later than A.D. 180

Courtesy of the Arab Information Center, New York

53. Ancient Roman theater at Leptis Magna, *ca.* eighty miles from Tripoli, with its semicircular colonnade around the top

is that at Epidaurus in the Peloponnesus, dating from the fourth century B.C., which may have accommodated up to fourteen thousand spectators.* Roman theaters were often complete buildings; often the larger theaters had partly roofed auditoriums and semicircular orchestras with roofed stages.* The ruins of three great theaters at Rome date from the first century B.C. The amphitheater as the scene of spectacular professional combats finds first mention *ca.* 30 B.C. Pl. XXVIII*a;* Figs. THE 52-53; NAB 5.

3. The NT period. Herod the Great, loyal patron of the imperial cultural program, built theaters in Caesarea (recently discovered by Israeli archaeologists), Damascus, Gadara, Kanatha, Scythopolis, and Philadelphia,* where impressive ruins survive. According to Josephus (Antiq. XV.viii.1), Herod built a theater and an amphitheater in Jerusalem. A theater S of this city was discovered by C. Schick in 1887, but it is not certain that it is Herodian. Quinquennial and quadrennial games in the emperor's honor were celebrated in chief Palestinian towns throughout the Roman period, especially in the third and fourth centuries A.D. Remains of Greek and Roman theaters survive today in the Pauline cities of Philippi,* Athens, Corinth, Miletus,* and Ephesus* (cf. Acts 19:19, 31); the latter is said to have accommodated 24,500 persons. Figs. RAB 2; PHI 47; MIL 47; EPH 31.

Bibliography. For an interesting inscription of A.D. 103-4 found in the theater at Ephesus, see A. Deissmann, *Light from the Ancient East* (1927), pp. 112-13. M. Bieber, *The History of the Greek and Roman Theater* (1939). S. E. Johnson, "Laodicea and Its Neighbors," *BA,* XIII (1950), 1-18. E. Frézouls, "Les théâtres romains de la Syrie," *Ann. Arch. de Syrie,* II (1952), 46-100.   E. W. SAUNDERS

THEBES thēbz [נא; LXX Διὸς πόλις, *see below*]; KJV NO nō. The chief city of Upper (S) Egypt and capital of Egypt during most of that nation's periods of political unity from the Middle Kingdom (*ca.* 2000 B.C.) to the Assyrians' invasion under Ashurbanipal (*ca.* 661 B.C.).

In Egyptian texts Thebes is commonly referred to simply as *niwt,* "the City," but also, more explicitly, as *niwt rsyt,* "the Southern City," and *niwt 'Imn,* "the City of Amon." The simple designation *niwt* is reflected in the Hebrew transcription נא, while *niwt 'Imn,* referring to the fact that Thebes was the cult center for the worship of Amon, is echoed by Nah. 3:8: *Nō' 'Āmôn.* Extrabiblical attestations of the word *niwt,* both as the name of Thebes and otherwise, include (*a*) *Ni-i'* in the Late Assyrian annals; (*b*) Old Coptic *Ne;* (*c*) and less specific forms such as -*nē,* -*nā,* and *nau-,* elicited from the compound names *Panās, Psousennēs,* and the hieroglyphic spelling of *Naukratis.* These various forms have led scholars to believe that the Hebrew vocalization of *Nō'* is incorrect, but recent investigations in Egypto-Coptic phonology indicate that the Hebrew spelling may well be correct and may reflect an earlier Egyptian pronunciation of *Nu'wa(t)* or similarly. The problem is further complicated by uncertainty on the part of Egyptologists re-

Trans World Airlines Photo

54. Avenue of the sphinxes, temple of Karnak

Trans World Airlines Photo

55. The temple of Luxor, at Thebes

Trans World Airlines Photo
56. Massive columns in the temple of Karnak at Thebes

garding the precise consonantal reading of the Egyptian word itself.

The LXX renderings of this place name are not consistent. Twice (Ezek. 30:14, 16) *Nō'* is translated by Διὸς πόλις, "the City of Zeus," the name applied to Thebes by the Greeks after the identification of Zeus with Amon. The three other occurrences of *Nō'* in the MT are not so translated by the LXX: (*a*) Ezek. 30:15 LXX, Μέμφις implies נף, not נא, in the Hebrew *Vorlage;* (*b*) in Jer. 46:25—G 26:25, τὸν Ἀμμὼν τὸν υἱὸν αὐτῆς suggests that instead of אמון מנא, "Amon from Thebes," there stood in the text אמון בנא, "Amon in [or from] Thebes," and that this was misconstrued as אמון בנה, "Amon her son"; (*c*) in Nah. 3:8 LXX, μερίδα results apparently from a confusion between מנא, from Thebes, and the word מנת, "part, portion."

During the Eleventh Dynasty, Thebes, termed the world's first great monumental city, rose from relative obscurity to become the capital of Egypt. The city lost this prominent position with the coming of the HYKSOS at the close of the Middle Kingdom but regained its supremacy at the beginning of the New Kingdom. In both these instances Egypt was reunited from the S following a period of local rule and political confusion. A third but less impressive resurgence took place under the Ethiopian rulers of the Twenty-fifth Dynasty (715-663 B.C.), but the short-

57. The temple of Deir el-Bahri, at Thebes

lived success of these kings before the onslaught of the Assyrian invasion of Ashurbanipal was crowned

with the sack of Thebes by the Assyrian ruler *ca.*
661 B.C. The prophet Nahum is certainly speaking
with reference to this most thorough destruction of
Thebes when he announces the coming destruction
of Nineveh with the words:

> Are you better than Thebes
> that sat by the Nile . . . ?
> (Nah. 3:8).

Thebes is surrounded by an unrivaled aggregate of
sacred precincts and temples, attesting the religious
importance of the city. Among the more impressive
of these monuments are (*a*) at Karnak, the temples
of Monthu, Khons, Amon, and Mut; (*b*) at Luxor,
the temple of Amon-Min, chiefly the work of
Amenophis III and Ramses II; (*c*) across the Nile
(on the W bank), the magnificent Deir el-Bahri temple of Queen Hatshepsut, the Qurneh Temple of
Seti I, and the Ramesseum of Ramses II.
Figs. THE 54-57.

Bibliography. For an extensive bibliography of the archi-
tectural and epigraphical finds, consult B. Porter and R. Moss,
Topographical Bibliography of Ancient Egyptian Hieroglyphic
Texts, Reliefs, and Paintings, I: *Theban Necropolis* (1927); II:
Theban Temples (1929). For a survey of Thebes in Egyptian
history see H. E. Winlock, *The Rise and Fall of the Middle
Kingdom in Thebes* (1947); A. Scharff and A. Moortgat,
Ägypten und Vorderasien im Altertum (1950), *passim*, where
further bibliographies may be found.   T. O. LAMBDIN

THEBEZ thē′bĭz [תבץ]. A town which was attacked
by Abimelech and where he was fatally wounded by
a woman who threw an upper millstone on his head
(Judg. 9:50; II Sam. 11:21). Because the attack upon
Thebez is described in connection with Abimelech's
attack upon the Tower of Shechem, it is probable
that Thebez had previously been under his jurisdiction and had joined in the revolt against him instigated by the men of Shechem.

Thebez is usually identified with Tubas, *ca.* thirteen miles NE of Shechem. Important roads from
Shechem and Dothan converge at this point on the
way to the Jordan Valley; and Abimelech, in addition to seeking revenge on the people of Thebez, was
perhaps also interested in controlling a place of strategic military and commercial value.   W. L. REED

THECLA, ACTS OF PAUL AND thĕk′lȧ [Θέκλα].
A part of the apocryphal Acts of Paul, long circulated as an independent treatise. *See* PAUL, ACTS OF.

THECOE. KJV Apoc. form of TEKOA.

THEFT. *See* CRIMES AND PUNISHMENTS § C7*b*.

THELASAR. KJV form of TEL-ASSAR.

THELERSAS. KJV Apoc. form of TEL-HARSHA.

THEMAN thē′mȧn. KJV Apoc. form of TEMAN.

THEOCANUS. KJV Apoc. form of TIKVAH 2.

THEOCRACY thē ŏk′rȧ sĭ. The government of a
state by God; also, a state so governed. The word is
not biblical in its origin, but the idea was one of the

main tenets of the Hebrew people during their historical existence. The word "theocracy" occurs for
the first time in Josephus (Apion II.xvi), who contrasted it with other forms of government such as
oligarchy, monarchy, and republic. The concept of
theocracy involved the thought of God as the lawgiver, judge, and ruler of Israel and, in a wider sense
of the word, of the world. God's reign in human history does not appear as unmediated theocracy. But
biblical hope envisions God's government of his people also at the consummation of history (*see* ESCHA-
TOLOGY OF THE OT). These eschatological expectations follow two patterns. In the first pattern the
eschatological theocracy appears as a direct, unmediated reign of the Lord (cf. Isa. 2:2-4; 24:23; Zeph.
2:8-13; *see* KINGDOM OF GOD). In the other pattern
the eschatological monarchy is conceived to be under
the theocratic vicegerency of the Messiah (*see* MES-
SIAH [JEWISH]; cf. Isa. 9:2-7—H 9:1-6; 11:1-9; Amos
9:11). Here only the theocracy within history is
considered.

Within Israel's history, three different kinds of
theocracy can be distinguished: (*a*) the charismatic,
(*b*) the monarchic, and (*c*) the priestly theocracies.
These roughly correspond to the three main periods
of Israel's history, the premonarchic, the monarchic,
and the postexilic. There are some scholars who
identify theocracy with the priestly rule and thus
recognize its existence only in the postexilic period.
Others think that a theocratic outlook presupposes
the rule of an earthly monarch, from whence the idea
of divine rule could be derived, and they date the
origin of the concept of theocracy as coincident with
the rise of the Israelite monarchy. Yet it seems that
the recognition of the Lord's reign over his people
is premonarchic in its origin, for in a kingless society the Lord could easily be conceived as the single
ruler of Israel.

1. Charismatic theocracy. God was the ruler and
the king of Israel from the moment when, in the
covenant of Sinai, the people became a "kingdom of
priests" and a "holy nation" of the Lord (Exod.
19:6), and promised allegiance to the Lord (vs. 8).
At Sinai, Israel entered into the covenant which
transformed them into the covenantal people. The
people became an amphictyony, a religious confederation united in reverence of and service to Yahweh. The system of the twelve tribes of Israel can
be meaningfully interpreted only as a premonarchic
amphictyony (cf. Gen. 29:31–30:24; 49:2-27; Num.
26:5-51; Deut. 33:2-29). This religious league was
the only organization, as far as is known, transcending the tribal limitations of the premonarchic Israelites. The king of this politically unorganized
amphictyony was the Lord (Judg. 8:23; I Sam. 8:7).
Accordingly, the central sanctuary of the Israelite
amphictyony was nothing other than the ark, which
was recognized to be the empty throne of the Lord
(Num. 10:35-36; Jer. 3:16-17). The amphictyony
did not have a political or military organization controlled by some central, earthly organ of the ruling
Lord. Only occasionally, in time of national disaster,
did the Spirit of the Lord come upon some elected
hero who, through the divine gift of grace (charisma),
was able to perform the act of military deliverance
(e.g., Judg. 3:10; 6:34). These heroes, generally

called "judges," were charismatic leaders who, under the influence of the Spirit of the Lord, served as his representatives, and, in forming the nation's history, they brought the Lord's theocratic reign to fulfilment. They were the organs of Yahweh's reign, fought his wars (cf. Judg. 4–5), and appeared as deliverers of his chosen people (Judg. 6:14; 8:22). These men, under the influence of the Spirit of the Lord, had an almost prophetic certainty concerning the will of the Lord, as can clearly be perceived by their rallying proclamation: "Follow after me; for the LORD has given your enemies . . . into your hand" (Judg. 3:28; 7:7, 9, 15; 8:7).

Apparently there were, occasionally, amphictyonic wars, during which the whole tribal federation was called upon and acted as one (Judg. 4–5). The Lord and Israel were inseparably connected. The ancient "Song of Deborah" (Judg. 5) witnesses to this prevalent theocratic conviction of the age. Yahweh was not merely the God of Israel, but his triumphs were identical with the triumphs of Israel (Judg. 5:11). The marching army was the people of Yahweh (vs. 13); they marched down for him against the mighty (vs. 13); Meroz was cursed because its inhabitants did not come "to the help of the LORD" (vs. 23).

Besides the "judges," the prophets and the priests who proclaimed the divine will might be regarded as organs of the premonarchic theocracy. In the war against Sisera, the prophetess Deborah appeared beside Barak the judge. She called Barak to be the organ acting for God's deliverance (Judg. 4:4-7). The priests, as proclaimers of the Lord's will, were consulted (Judg. 20:28; I Sam. 14:41). Characteristic of this period is the fact that there was no institutionalized representative of the theocracy.

2. Monarchic theocracy. At the time of the introduction of kingship into Israel, there was opposition to the introduction of the monarchy. The introduction of the earthly kingship appeared to some as an apostasy which attempted to dethrone the Lord and to replace his freedom to elect instruments for his theocratic service with a dynastic sequence of kings (I Sam 8:7; 10:27). This antimonarchic, protheocratic attitude remained vocal enough to be echoed by the eighth-century prophet Hosea (Hos. 9:9). The apostasy of the people in making kings was emphatically denounced by this prophet (Hos. 8:4; 13:10-11). A slightly different protheocratic outlook can be discerned in the antimonarchic source of the books of Samuel. The opposition to the earthly kingship is prevalent, but there is also the conviction that the king was chosen by the Lord (I Sam. 12:12-15). To be sure, it was against the Lord's will, but he had consented, even if with resignation (I Sam. 8:9). Samuel the prophet claimed the right and had the power to reject Saul from being the king in the name of God (I Sam. 13:14; 15:23). The prophetic appointment of the king was recognized in the Northern Kingdom even centuries later, as Jehu's anointment proves (II Kings 9:1-13).

The king was the representative of Yahweh's theocratic rule; therefore he was not called "king" in religious context. His titles were "the LORD's anointed" (Pss. 2:2; 20:6—H 20:7; etc.) and the "prince" (נָגִיד) of the Lord (I Sam. 10:1; II Sam. 5:

2). The king ruled over the Lord's heritage (I Sam. 10:1); the people of Israel were not the king's but Yahweh's people (I Sam. 13:14; II Kings 9:6); the king is Yahweh's shepherd (II Sam. 5:2). Even the royal throne itself was considered the throne of the Lord (I Chr. 29:23). The kingship of the king is derived from the Lord's adoption of the king as his son (II Sam. 7:14; Ps. 2:7). In the case of Judah, the Lord pledged his blessing (in the so-called dynastic oracle) to the house of David (II Sam. 7). Thus, a new concept, the dynastic charisma, appeared beside the divine appointment of a single person for kingship. However, the Lord remained the king who sat high and lifted up (Isa. 6:1); his kingship was accepted as a tenet of faith (Isa. 43:15; 44: 6; Zeph. 3:15). In Ezekiel's plans for the restoration of the nation, the king is repeatedly called "prince" (נָשִׂיא; Ezek. 34:24; 46:12). The Deuteronomic legislation defines the king's duty as that of a pious student of the commandments of the Lord (Deut. 17:14-20).

3. Priestly theocracy. In the early postexilic period, Zechariah had envisioned equal roles for the king and the priest as the Lord's theocratic representatives (Zech. 4:14; 6:12-13), but the evidently deliberate exchange of the name of Zerubbabel prince for Joshua the high priest in 6:11 mirrors the history of the subsequent years. The restoration of the religious community in Judah, authorized by Cyrus' decree (Ezra 6:3-5), had enhanced the importance of the priest. The absence of a Jewish monarch during the Persian occupation contributed to the increasing of the priest's authority. The title "high priest" appears for the first time in reference to the postexilic Joshua (Hag. 2:2; Zech. 3:1). During the Persian, Hellenistic, and Roman periods, the Jewish hierocracy maintained its role as arbiter of, and mediator in, spiritual and religious affairs. The theocratic views of the NT community were predominantly eschatological. *See* KINGDOM OF GOD.

Bibliography. C. Eissfeldt, "Jahwe als König," *ZAW,* XLVI (1928), 81-105. M. Noth, *Das System der zwölf Stämme Israels* (1930). C. R. North, "The OT Estimate of the Monarchy," *AJSL,* XLVIII (1931), 1-19; "The Religious Aspects of Hebrew Kingship," *ZAW,* L, N.F. IX (1932), 8-38. M. Buber, *Das Kommende, Untersuchungen zur Entstehungsgeschichte des messianischen Glaubens,* I: *Königtum Gottes* (1932). A. Alt, "Gedanken über das Königtum Jahwes," *Kleine Schriften zur Geschichte des Völkes Israel,* I (1953), 345-57. J. Bright, *The Kingdom of God, The Biblical Concept and Its Meaning for the Church* (1953). J. Gray, "The Hebrew Conception of the Kingship of God: Its Origin and Development," *VT,* VI (1956), 268-85. A. A. Koolhaas, *Theocratie en monarchie in Israël: Eenige opmerkingen over de verhouding van de theocratie en het israëlitische koningschap in het OT* (1957).   S. SZIKSZAI

THEODOTION thē′ə dō′shən. According to ecclesiastical tradition, a second-century translator of the OT into Greek. Nothing certain is known of him. Irenaeus identifies him as a proselyte from Ephesus; Epiphanius, as a native of Pontus, who after following Marcion for a period of time became a Jewish proselyte. Jerome (probably through confusion with Symmachus) calls him an Ebionite.

His version (or revision) became exceedingly popular and was used most heavily by Origen for filling in LXX lacunae in his Hexapla. In fact, the text of

Theodotion (Theod.) actually supplanted that of the LXX in the case of Daniel, and large lacunae in other parts of the LXX are filled in with Theod. in the MSS (e.g., that of Job).

The origins of the version are, however, completely obscure. NT writers quoting the Greek OT often quote Theod. rather than LXX (cf. the numerous quotations from Daniel in Revelation). Thus there was obviously a Theodotionic text before the second century. Possibly there existed by NT times two Greek versions of the OT, to one of which the name of a second-century Theodotion later became attached. Another possibility is the suggestion that this pre-Theodotion may have been an oral Targ. which existed for correcting LXX and for filling in lacunae. This would then later have been put into writing by Theodotion.

See also SEPTUAGINT §§ 3*b*, 4*a*.   J. W. WEVERS

THEODOTUS thē ŏd′ə təs [Θεόδοτος] (II Macc. 14:19). One of the ambassadors (the others being Posidonius and Mattathias) sent by Nicanor to Judas Maccabeus for the purpose of establishing peace. The Greek phrase (δοῦναι καὶ λαβεῖν δεξιάς), meaning literally "to give and receive right hands," is translated in the KJV as "to make peace," in the RSV as "to give and receive pledges of friendship" (cf. Gal. 2:9).   J. C. SWAIM

*THEOPHANY [Θεοφάνεια, *from* Θεός, God, *and* φαίνειν, to make shine, to show; Lat. *theophania*]. An appearance or transient manifestation, unsought, of a divine being or of God to man. The interpretation of the biblical material in the light of such a definition suggests that this material may be graded as follows. There is (*a*) the theophanic material of the temporary manifestation; then (*b*) the material relating to the so-called "tabernacling presence" through the "name" and "glory" conceptions. This material is not strictly theophanic material, for it suggests a more permanent form of manifestation—almost a dwelling of God among men. There is (*c*) the most advanced material, which is concerned with the Incarnation, the manifestation of God in an entire human life. This article is concerned only with the first kind of material. For the second kind, *see* PRESENCE.

Transient appearances are recorded almost without detail in Gen. 3:8, where the voice of Yahweh walks in the garden and asks questions and pronounces judgments; in the Hagar stories at 16:7-14; 21:17, though the voice from heaven in the latter passage and again in 22:11, 15, hardly amounts to theophanies; and in the Balaam story in Num. 22:21-35, where the angel of the Lord is an obstructing presence. Similarly P uses the characteristic word "appear" without further detail (cf. Gen. 17:1; 35:9; Exod. 6:3). The attacks on Jacob (Gen. 32:22-32) and on Moses (Exod. 4:24-26; cf. Gen. 38:7) are really examples of skeuomorphy, whereby, as in the first of these passages, an old story of a defeated demon has been transferred to Yahweh, and whereby as in the latter two passages, illness and death have been interpreted as acts of Yahweh. Likewise dreams (Gen. 20:3; 28:10-17) do not properly rank as

theophany, but it is not always possible to distinguish between vision and theophany.

Thus the theophany in Gen. 15 is described as a vision. There is the characteristic formula: "Fear not," to introduce Yahweh's words. Abraham, deeply asleep after dark, sees a smoking fire pot and a flaming torch pass between the halves of the slain covenant animals. The deep sleep of vs. 12 is often a supernatural sleep (cf. e.g., Gen. 2:21; Job 4:13 = 33:15), and smoke and FIRE (Gen. 15:17) are characteristic of theophany. Yet the vision of the word of the Lord (15:1), the deep sleep (vs. 12), and the pot and torch symbolism (vs. 17) remove the story from the category of theophany. Similarly Gen. 18 is a story that belongs rather to the class of divine metamorphoses. The polytheistic background of the tradition is clear. Three men appear to Abraham, and the Lord appears to him and speaks. Either a Yahweh-appearing and -speaking story has been superimposed upon a polytheistic story of three gods' appearing as men, or else Yahweh is disguised in one of these three men.

1. Theophanies in nonhuman form
2. Theophanies in human form
3. Literary theophanies
4. Theophanies in the NT
Bibliography

1. Theophanies in nonhuman form. Exod. 3 describes how Yahweh's angel appeared to Moses in a flame of fire in a bush. The theophany thus includes a vision of the god and an account of his words (audition). No doubt, in many of these angel-of-the-Lord stories, the angel is a later interpretation and the story was first told of Yahweh himself. Characteristic in this passage is the flame of fire (cf., e.g., Exod. 13:21; 19:18; 24:17; Lev. 10:1-3; Num. 11:1-3; 16:35). The appearance of fire is characteristic of the Elijah stories (I Kings 18-19; II Kings 1; 2:11) and in the "literary" theophanies and in the NT (*see* §§ 3-4 *below*). Most of the references to the GLORY of God are not truly theophanic, but the sudden punishing eruptions of the glory (Num. 14:10; 16:19; 20:6) are parallel to the sudden fire noted above. Thus the fire, like the glory, is stationary in the sanctuary, but suddenly erupts to execute Yahweh's anger.

"The cloud" (Exod. 24:15-18; 40:34-38; Num. 9:15-23; etc.), with the article, describes the tabernacling presence rather than the theophanic manifestation (*see* PILLAR OF CLOUD AND FIRE). Similarly the "name" material is more characteristic of the tabernacling presence, because the "name" dwells rather than appears. Yet in Isa. 30:27-28 Yahweh's name comes from the E, burning and in smoke, to judge.

In the majestic theophany of Exod. 19 Yahweh comes personally to Israel disguised in the cloudiest(?) part of the cloud (vs. 9). To a people ritually prepared (vss. 14-15), at the appointed time (vs. 16), to the accompaniment of thunders, lightnings, thick cloud (no article), and a continuing trumpet, Yahweh came down in fire upon the mountain to speak. The people are not allowed to go up, lest they gaze, but Moses goes up. Natural elements, cultic features, and mythological language combine to set forth the supreme theophany of the OT. From this and other theophanic passages the following characteristic features emerge: the divine initiative; various revelatory formulas; the encounter and the relationship between God and the human party; the account of the purpose of the theophany and the reverential awe of the human party.

2. Theophanies in human form. The Sinai theophanies are the real theophanies of the OT. Exod. 24:9-11 records how Moses, Aaron, Nadab, Abihu, and seventy Israelite nobles saw the God of Israel. The implication is that they saw a form, and the reference to feet suggests a human form. The story is noteworthy in that they beheld God and were quite unharmed. This is contrary to the view that to see God or even hear his voice (Deut. 4:33; 5:24) was dangerous, if not fatal (e.g., Exod. 33:20; Judg. 13: 22; etc.); though, of course, as these passages also show, men often saw and heard God and lived (Exod. 3:6; 19:21; Num. 12:6-8; Judg. 6:22-23; Isa. 6:5). The story is unique in that it is the only theophany in the OT which is silent—no words of Yahweh are recorded. It is a theophany and not an audition. Perhaps the story is simply intended to set side by side important physical and spiritual activities.

In Exod. 33:17-23 Moses is promised a sight of God's back, but not his face (his glory?); but 33:11, like Gen. 32:30; Num. 12:6-8; Job 4:12-16, tells a different story. In Num. 24:4; Isa. 6; Ezek. 1; Dan. 7, the human form of God is seen in a vision or dream—i.e., only partially theophanic material. There are, besides, many stories which speak of Yahweh's appearing with human attributes as the "angel of Yahweh" or "of God." These are really stories about Yahweh, as the narratives often indicate (cf. Gen. 16:13; Exod. 3:2, 5-7; etc.).

3. Literary theophanies. Judg. 5:4 (cf. Ps. 114:5-8) speaks of the earthquake and the thunderstorms. Natural features are also seen in Pss. 18:7-15; 29; 68: 7-9; 77:16; 97:4-6; 144:5. It is difficult to see how these can be explained by cultic practices only. For eschatological theophanies see, e.g., Isa. 30:27; 63:1-6; Zeph. 1:14. See also Deut. 33:2; Hab. 3.

4. Theophanies in the NT. The NT refers in such passages as Acts 7:30; Heb. 12:18, 29, to OT passages. There are also the accompaniments of theophany, as in (*a*) the fire (Acts 2:3; I Cor. 3:13; II Thess. 1:7); (*b*) angels (II Thess. 1:7). There are, of course, a number of angelophanies in Acts (5:19; 8: 26; 10:3; 12:7; 27:23; cf. Matt. 4:11=Mark 1:13; Luke 22:43); (*c*) cherubim of glory (Heb. 9:5); (*d*) glory (Luke 2:9; I Cor. 15:40; II Cor. 3:7). In reality there are no true theophanies in the NT, for their place is taken by the manifestation of God in Christ (John 1:14; Col. 1:15; Heb. 1:1-3). The second advent of Jesus Christ is virtually an impending theophany, and is described in the terminology of theophany (Matt. 16:27; 24:30; 26:64; Mark 8:38; 13:26; Luke 9:26). The resurrection appearances and the Transfiguration are not properly theophanies.

See also ANGEL; CLOUD; FACE; FIRE; VISION.

Bibliography. A. Lods, "L'ange de Yahweh et l'âme extérieure," *Studien zur semitischen Philologie* (1914), pp. 263-78. J. Morgenstern, "Biblical Theophanies," *ZA*, XXV (1911), 139-93; XXVIII (1914), 15-60. W. W. von Baudissin, " 'Gott schauen' in der alttestamentlichen Religion," *Archiv für Religionswissenschaft*, XVIII (1915), 173-239. L. Dürr, *Ezechiels Vision von der Erscheinung Gottes* (1917). E. G. Gulin, "Das Antlitz Jahwes im AT," *Annales Academiae Scientiarum Fennicae*, Series B, vol. XVII, no. 3 (1923). F. Nötscher, "*Das Angesicht Gottes schauen*" *nach biblischer und babylonischer Auffassung* (1924). F. Stier, *Gott und sein Engel im AT* (1934). W. Baumgartner, "Zum Problem des Jahwe-Engels," *Schweizerische theologische Umschau,* XIV (1944), 97 ff. A. Weiser, "Die Darstellung der Theophanie in den Psalmen und im Festkult," *Festschrift A. Bertholet* (1950), pp. 513-31. W. Zimmerli, "Ich bin Jahwe," *Geschichte und AT* (1953), pp. 179-209. K. Elliger, "Ich bin der Herr, euer Gott," *Festschrift für K. Heim* (1954), pp. 9 ff. E. Jacob, "Manifestations of God," *Theology of the OT* (1958), pp. 73-85. T. C. Vriezen, *An Outline of OT Theology* (1958), pp. 233-49.

G. HENTON DAVIES

THEOPHILUS thē ŏf'ə ləs [Θεόφιλος, friend of God]. The person to whom Luke (1:3) and Acts (1:1) are addressed. These books are introduced by primary and secondary prefaces such as are characteristic of extended and well-written Hellenistic writings. Theophilus has the honor of being the only person mentioned in the NT to whom writings have been dedicated.

Who was Theophilus? No answer is available except on the basis of conjecture from the literary conventions of the time and the purposes for which Luke-Acts may be supposed to have been written.

It has been supposed, on the one hand, that Theophilus was not an individual person, but any "friend of God." In this case, Luke-Acts would be written for all devout Christians who were eager for more detailed and accurate information concerning the origin, history, and meaning of their faith. In support of this supposition it may be argued that Luke certainly expected the generality of Christians to be his chief readers, and that, so far as we know, at this time Christians wrote only for Christians.

On the other hand, and more probably, Theophilus is taken to be a real person. The name was a common one used by both Greeks and Jews. Writings were commonly dedicated to real persons, not fictitious or symbolic ones, even though the contents of the book may have been no particular concern of theirs, and the reading of it was certainly not intended to be limited to them. Also, if Theophilus was not a real person, he would hardly have been addressed as "most excellent" or "noble."

But if a real person, who was Theophilus? Sometimes the two possibilities have been combined in the view that, although Theophilus pointed to a real person, it was not his real name. In this case it may be thought of as a cover-up name, a prudential pseudonym intended to conceal the real identity of the individual in order to protect him from the persecution which might readily fall on any pagan or Christian official of high standing who would allow his name to be used in connection with a movement regarded as offensive if not subversive. It has been argued that the person meant was a Roman official such as a governor or procurator (for Luke's use of "most excellent," see Acts 23:26; 24:2; 26:25); or some person (perhaps several) of standing in Rome whose influence was sought for Paul's trial; or even the magistrate who was due to hear Paul's case when it came up for final adjudication. An ingenious proposal, which is usually mentioned but rejected as running too far beyond the evidence, is that Theophilus was the secret name by which the Roman church knew the cousin of the Emperor Domitian, T. Flavius Clemens, whose wife Domitilla was an adherent if not a baptized member of the church, and who himself may have had some instruction in, or been attracted to, the Christian faith.

If any of these four theories is accepted as true, Theophilus can hardly have been a Christian. Nevertheless, this point remains in dispute, and there are those who speak of him as a "Christian of prominence." The validity of this description depends on Luke's understanding of the words "most excellent" (κράτιστος; Luke 1:3) and "you have been informed" (κατηχήθης; vs. 4), and also on one's judgment as to why Luke invokes Theophilus. On the one hand, it is urged that a Christian would not have addressed a brother Christian by so honorific a title as "your excellency"—whence a surmise that Theophilus was baptized between Luke's Gospel and Acts. On the other hand, it is urged that κράτιστος is not always used in an official sense; it need not refer to equestrian rank; it occurs in conventionally formal, friendly, or flattering speech; and therefore Christians could have so addressed one another.

Likewise the significance of κατηχεῖν, "to instruct," is disputed. Does it mean that Theophilus had been under instruction as a catechumen and was on the way to being, or was now, a Christian? Or is the word much less technically used? Some think this word precludes Theophilus' being a pagan, yet so much weight can hardly be put on it. On the other hand, it has been proposed that here it may well not mean Christian instruction at all but on the contrary imply that Theophilus had received hostile reports of Christianity, which Luke writes to correct.

Finally, it is proposed that the fact that Luke's literary preface could have had slight meaning for the Christian communities of *ca.* A.D. 90 shows that Luke wrote for two markets: for the Christian community, and for the private reading of people of literary education. Theophilus represents this cultured class. He may or may not have been a Christian. In any case, as a person of high importance, whether of rank or not, he would be obligated to aid in the distribution of the work dedicated to him.

The chief importance of the variety of points of view presented in the above debates over Theophilus lies in the reflections on the early church which they stimulate. Who Theophilus was remains obscure.

Bibliography. H. J. Cadbury, *The Making of Luke-Acts* (1927), pp. 201-5; A. H. McNeile, *An Introduction to the Study of the NT* (2nd ed., 1953), pp. 94-95; M. Dibelius, *Studies in the Acts of the Apostles* (1956), pp. 88, 124, 146-47.

On the identity of Theophilus, see: D. Plooij, *Exp.*, vol. VII, no. 8 (1914); J. Weiss, *Die Schriften des Neuen Testaments* (3rd ed., 1917), 395; J. I. Still, *St. Paul on Trial* (1924); B. H. Streeter, *The Four Gospels* (1924), pp. 534-39; K. H. Rengstorf, *Das Evangelium nach Lukas* (1937), p. 11; E. Haenchen, *Die Apostelgeschichte* (1956), p. 106.

On the meaning of κατηχεῖν, see: E. Meyer, *Ursprung und Anfänge des Christentums*, I (1921), 5-11; F. J. Foakes-Jackson and K. Lake, *Beginnings of Christianity*, II (1922), 178-79, 508-10; F. H. Colson, "Notes on St. Luke's Preface," *JTS*, XXIV (1923), 300; J. M. Creed, *The Gospel According to St. Luke* (1930).   F. D. GEALY

THERAS thĭr'əs. Apoc. alternate name of AHAVA.

THERMELETH. KJV Apoc. form of TEL-MELAH.

*THESSALONIANS, FIRST LETTER TO THE thĕs'ə lō'nĭ ənz [Θεσσαλονίκεις]. A letter written by the apostle Paul and his associates Silvanus and Timothy to the church which they had recently founded at Thessalonica; now placed as the thirteenth book of the NT canon. It is generally regarded as the earliest Pauline letter extant.

The theological content is relatively slight, but it is plain that a rich complex of doctrine lies beneath the surface, assumed to be the common basis of belief. The most striking feature is the dominance of the expectation of the return of the Lord Jesus in heavenly glory, toward which all the thought is oriented. Apart from and also through the medium of the teaching and exhortation, the letter is of exceptional human interest for the attractive light which it throws upon the character and personality of the great apostle and for the singularly vivid picture it gives of the joy, confidence, mutual love, and assured hope of future blessedness which mark the life of the nascent church. The very absence of controversy enables the positive aspects of the new faith to shine forth all the more clearly.

1. Authorship
2. Destination: Thessalonica and its church
3. Occasion and character of the writing
4. Outline of contents
5. Doctrine
   a. Elements of the common faith
   b. Eschatology: The Parousia of the Lord Jesus
6. Text
Bibliography

1. Authorship. The authenticity of this letter is no longer seriously challenged and scarcely requires to be discussed. It is, in fact, quite impossible to account for it as a pseudonymous work of a later period. The very slightness of the theological exposition, once advanced as ground for denying that Paul could be the author, is, on the contrary, a powerful argument against pseudonymity—surely the composer of a pseudepigraph would have something weightier than this to attribute to the great apostle. There is no sign here of a theological ax to grind! The spontaneous and open warmth of the personal greetings and references is sufficient of itself to convince us that we are reading a genuine letter, not an artificial literary construction. The vividness of the eschatological expectation, undimmed by any trace of disappointment over the delay of the Parousia, speaks unmistakably for a date in the first generation of the Christian mission; and it is inconceivable, above all, that a later writer, composing in Paul's name after his death, should represent him as including himself among those "who are alive, who are left until the coming of the Lord" (4:15). No grounds of objection to the Pauline authorship can be laid in peculiarities of vocabulary or style, and the lack of doctrinal exposition is a problem only if we make the mistake of regarding Paul's letters as theological treatises. External evidence is less abundant than in the case of the major letters, but wholly supports the case for acceptance. First Thessalonians is found (in fragmentary form) in the earliest MS of the letters which we possess, the Chester Beatty Codex of *ca.* A.D. 200; and it is included in every canonical list that has come down to us, and in the oldest versions; it is cited by name in Irenaeus (*ca.* 180), and by countless writers after him.

A question of minor importance is the part that may be assigned to Silvanus and Timothy as co-authors. The first person plural is used throughout the letter, except for a few passages where the writer slips into the singular (2:18; 3:5; 5:27); in the first of these, he identifies himself as Paul ("We wanted to come to you—I, Paul, again and again—but Satan hindered us"). It is not to be taken for granted that Paul mentions Silvanus and Timothy merely out of courtesy. Both of them were men of weight. Timothy was, indeed, a very young man—years later Paul reminds the Philippians "how as a son with a father he has served with me in the gospel" (Phil. 2:22; cf. Acts 16:1-3); but he was already capable of being entrusted with a delicate and dangerous commission (I Thess. 3:1-6), and Paul does not hesitate to call him "God's fellow-worker in the gospel of Christ" (3:2 [D, and others]; *see* § 6 *below; see also* TIMOTHY, TIMOTHEUS). Silvanus, who is almost certainly to be identified with the Silas of Acts (15:22-18:5), had been a tried and trusted leader of the mother church in Jerusalem and was Paul's partner, rather than his assistant, in the conduct of the mission. (*See* SILAS, SILVANUS.) The use of the plural, then, is to be taken seriously as reflecting Paul's sense that all the responsibilities of the mission and of the teaching that still requires to be given are shared with his colleagues, junior and senior; he writes as a member of a group that is engaged in a common task and works in a true partnership. At the same time, the letter is substantially the work of Paul, and it is his accents that sound through its words. The writing is too spontaneous and spirited to allow us to suppose that its phrases were hammered out in a committee of three.

2. Destination: Thessalonica and its church. The church of the Thessalonians, to which the letter is addressed, had been founded by Paul and his colleagues only a few months, perhaps only a few weeks, earlier. They had come to Thessalonica from Philippi, the scene of their first mission in Macedonia, where they had established a loyal community of believers before being forced to leave the city by the governing authorities. They had been brutally treated at Philippi—assaulted by the crowd in the streets, beaten with rods at the command of the magistrates, and thrown into prison (Acts 16:22-24; cf. I Thess. 2:2). For all that, they were not discouraged from continuing work in Macedonia. Once released from prison, their only thought was to penetrate more deeply into the province, and they made straight for its capital city, Thessalonica.

The city of THESSALONICA had great strategic importance, which it has retained to our own day; known now as Saloniki, it was a base and supply port for the Allies in the First World War, and again, briefly, in the Second. With a good natural harbor on the Thermaic Gulf, it carried the trade of the valley of the Strymon and of three lesser rivers which flow into the same gulf nearby; and it lay on the Via Egnatia, the great Roman highway which was the principal artery of communication between Rome and her E provinces. Here the proconsul, the Roman governor of Macedonia, had his headquarters. Its fidelity to the cause of Octavius and Antony in the conflict which followed the assassination of Julius Caesar earned for it the privileges of a free city; it was governed by its own magistrates, known as "politarchs" (Acts 17:6, 8), with its council and popular assembly. Mingled with the old Macedonian population were considerable numbers of Greeks and Romans and many of other nationalities, including a substantial body of Jews.

It was the Jewish community, with its synagogue, which provided the apostles with their initial avenue of approach to the people of Thessalonica. For in the synagogue they encountered not only the Jews of the city, but a certain number of Gentiles—"devout Greeks," as they are termed in the book of Acts—who had been attracted in some measure to Judaism and had some knowledge of the Scriptures. It was chiefly among these Gentile adherents that the gospel message awakened the response of faith. Jewish converts were few, and the very success of the appeal to the Gentiles aroused jealousy among the Jewish community as a whole and caused it to harden in an ever fiercer opposition to the mission. This hostility at last found expression in violence. The vivid narrative of Acts pictures the rabble of the market place rioting under Jewish incitement, attacking the house in which the apostles were living, and when they could not find them, hustling their host and his friends before the politarchs and accusing them of subversive activities. "These men who have turned the world upside down have come here also, and Jason has received them; and they are all acting against the decrees of Caesar, saying that there is another king, Jesus" (Acts 17:6-7). The upshot was that Jason and his friends were obliged to give security against any further disturbance of the peace; and it was necessary for Paul and Silas and Timothy to escape from the city by night.

The story of Acts leaves us with the impression that the apostles were able to remain in Thessalonica for only three weeks, which were devoted chiefly to work in the synagogue and resulted in the conversion of some few Jews, together with "a great many of the devout Greeks and not a few of the leading women" (Acts 17:4). But Paul's own references to the Thessalonian church seem to indicate a mission that lasted for a considerable time and issued in a church composed in the main of converts from outright paganism. The "devout Greeks" of Acts hardly correspond to Paul's description of his converts as people who "turned to God from idols, to serve a living and true God" (I Thess. 1:9). These words point rather to a mission that has gone out from the synagogue into the streets and lanes of the city and has brought in men and women who had never come under the influence of Judaism. Moreover, the pastoral care with which the apostles had followed up their evangelism (see especially 2:9-12) and the strength of the affection which they had developed toward their converts (2:8; 3:6-10) would suggest, if not absolutely require, a period of months rather than weeks. Again, in its references to the persecutions which have come upon the Christians of Thessalonica, the letter gives no indication that these were instigated by the Jews. The Thessalonians have suffered at the hands of their own countrymen; it is in Judea, not in Macedonia, that the churches of God have been persecuted by the Jews (2:14). In fact, one would never learn from reading the letter that there was a Jewish community in Thessalonica at all, much less that it had been the center of the mission and had provided the apostles with the nucleus of the church.

It seems probable, therefore, that Acts gives us only half the story. That the mission began in the synagogue and that its first converts were drawn mainly from Gentiles attached to the synagogue—this we need not doubt. But following this initial success, there will have been a much longer period of missionary activity in the city streets, making its approach directly to the pagan population and gradually building up a Christian body in which the initial group of converts from the synagogue became an indistinguishable minority: the church would now consist in the main of people who had "turned to God from idols." It was the lot of such people to suffer persecution at the hands of their unbelieving neighbors (cf. 3:3-4); no Jewish prompting was needed. It may even be suspected that the author of Acts has exaggerated the part played by Jewish hostility in the expulsion of the apostles from the city; there may be an apologetic impulse at work here, seeking to take advantage of anti-Semitic feeling by suggesting that opposition to the church arose only as a result of Jewish misrepresentations of the gospel and its preachers. At all events, there is nothing in the letter itself to suggest that the life of the church in Thessalonica is affected in any degree by the continuing enmity of the synagogue.

3. Occasion and character of the writing. The apostles had left Thessalonica against their will, forced to escape by night in order to avoid further mob violence and danger to their friends. They could not fail to be anxious about the welfare of the fledgling church, exposed to the continuing attacks of hostile neighbors and deprived of strong and experienced leadership. They had made every endeavor to return—Paul affirms that he himself had wanted to come back, to see them face to face, again and again; but hindrances which he could only ascribe to Satan had made this impossible (2:17-18). They had indeed been hard pressed. At Berea, where they first attempted to renew their missionary activity, they had great initial success; but soon the instigators of the rioting at Thessalonica came to renew their incitements of the street crowds in the neighboring town also, and Paul was again forced to flee. For a time, he was separated from his two companions, leaving them in Beroea while he was escorted by sea to Athens (Acts 17:10-15). At length, they came together in Athens, but their concern over the situation in Thessalonica had now become so intense that they made the bold decision to send Timothy back to visit the city in person, to exhort and strengthen the church (I Thess. 3:1-5).

The letter was written immediately upon his return, and is primarily a fervent expression of the relief and joy which possessed the apostles on hearing from him that the church of Thessalonica was standing firm in the face of all it had to endure from pagan hostility. They thank God for the "work of faith and labor of love and steadfastness of hope in our Lord Jesus Christ" which the converts have so conspicuously maintained (1:2-3). They take pleasure in recalling and dwelling upon the memory of their own sustained and devoted efforts to teach the ways of Christ and to exhort and encourage their followers "to lead a life worthy of God, who calls you into his own kingdom and glory" (2:12); the word of God has worked effectually among them, as is shown by the very persecutions which they have endured. They speak of the depth of their affection and of their concern for the Thessalonian believers and of the great joy that has come to them through Timothy's good report. "Now that Timothy has come to us from you, and has brought us the good news of your faith and love . . . , we have been comforted about you through your faith; for now we live, if you stand fast in the Lord" (3:6-8). And they pray that God the Father and Christ the Lord may direct their way again to Thessalonica; and that the Lord may bring to fuller development the love and holiness of heart which will make the readers ready for his Parousia (vss. 11-13).

These personal recollections and assurances make up the greater part of the letter, occupying the whole of the first three chapters. The remainder is given to moral instruction along lines that Timothy's visit had shown to be particularly needed, together with a brief paragraph of an apocalyptic character (4:13-18), designed to remove the fear that believers who had passed away in the interval would fail to have part in the joys and glories of the coming Parousia. This second part of the letter (chs. 4–5) follows up the mission of Timothy. It has been suggested by some scholars that it may have been called forth, at least in part, by a letter brought back by Timothy from the leaders of the Thessalonian church, perhaps seeking guidance more authoritative than could be given by the youthful Timothy. There is, however, no hint of such correspondence in the letter itself, and there is really nothing in its words which could not equally well have been called forth by Timothy's report on the conditions in the church.

The date of the letter can be determined only in relation to the dating of Paul's first mission in Corinth; for if Timothy was sent to Thessalonica from Athens (I Thess. 3:1), he must have rejoined Paul and Silvanus either in Athens or, more probably, at the beginning of their mission in Corinth (Acts 18:5). During this mission, Paul was haled before GALLIO, the proconsul of Achaia (Acts 18:12-17), who held office in 51-52; on the basis of the statements of Acts, then, our letter will have been written in 50 or 51. *See* CHRONOLOGY OF THE NT.

4. Outline of contents. The letter falls into two main divisions, with the salutation at the beginning and a benediction at the close.

I. The Salutation, 1:1
II. Personal, chs. 1–3
   A. Thanksgiving, 1:2-10
   B. Retrospect on the mission, 2:1-16
     1. Pastoral labors of the apostles, 2:1-12
     2. Response of the believers, 2:13-16
   C. The mission of Timothy, 2:17–3:10

5. Doctrine. The letter is not in any sense a theological treatise, and it is only incidentally that reference is made to any of the doctrines of the Christian faith. Yet even these incidental references are sufficient to give some indication of the wealth of the apostolic teaching, and of the substance of the instruction given to these early converts.

a. Elements of the common faith. In their conversion, the Thessalonians have "turned to God from idols, to serve a living and true God" (1:9). He is known to them as "the Father" (1:1, 3; 2:11). It is he who has chosen them (1:4); called them into his own kingdom and glory (2:12); destined them, not for wrath, but to obtain salvation through the Lord Jesus Christ (5:9). Now his will is to govern all their life; their aim must be "to lead a life worthy of God" (2:12), just as it is the ambition of the apostles themselves "not to please men, but to please God, who tests our hearts" (2:4). The message which they preach has been entrusted to them by God (2:4); it is the "gospel of God" (2:2) or the "word of God," which works effectively in those who believe (2:13). The believers are "brethren beloved by God" (1:4), and it is God who teaches them to love one another (4:9) and gives them his Holy Spirit (4:8).

The thought of the apostle is clearly theocentric, but it will quickly appear that it is at the same time Christocentric, for the name of Christ is constantly linked with the name of God. The church is "in God the Father and the Lord Jesus Christ" (1:1); if the apostolic message can be called the "gospel of God" and the "word of God," it can likewise be called the "word of the Lord" or the "gospel of Christ" (1:8; 3:2); the men who "have been approved by God to be entrusted with the gospel" are at the same time "apostles of Christ" (2:4, 6); "our God and Father himself and our Lord Jesus" are invoked together in prayer (3:11); the salvation for which God has destined us is to be obtained "through our Lord Jesus Christ" (5:9); it is "in Christ" and "through Jesus" that Christians die and are assured of rising from the dead, that they may always be with their Lord (4:14, 16-18); it is "in Christ" that God makes known his will (5:18); and he is "our Lord Jesus Christ, who died for us so that . . . we might live with him" (5:9-10). Paul speaks of him under many names and titles—"the (our) Lord Jesus Christ," or "Christ Jesus," or "the (our) Lord Jesus"; sometimes as "Christ" or as "Jesus"; most frequently he calls him simply "the Lord" (Kyrios). He is the Son of God whom he raised from the dead, "Jesus who delivers us from the wrath to come" (1:10); and Christians await his coming from heaven. He commands the absolute allegiance of Christian believers, the commands and instructions of the apostles are given "in the Lord Jesus" (4:1 ff), and he punishes the wrongdoer (4:6). The faith, the hope, and the love of believers are directed toward him in the sight of God (1:3), and the supreme assurance and aspiration is that we should live together with him, that we should be always with the Lord (5:10; 4:17). There is nothing here that resembles a formal christological statement, yet we have unquestionably the reflection of a highly developed and many-sided doctrine of the person and work of Christ. It should be remarked that there is no indication that we have here a peculiarly "Pauline" theology; Paul is not engaging in a work of theological construction, but making use of the common elements of the early Christian teaching.

Further indications of a rich doctrinal content in the teaching which the Thessalonians have received also lie behind the references to the Holy Spirit and to the church (or churches), but these are not sufficient in themselves to give more than a hint of the range of conceptions involved.

b. Eschatology: The Parousia of the Lord Jesus. The most striking feature of the letter is the dominance of eschatological motifs, which certainly reflects the emphasis of the early preaching. The familiar OT theme of the "day of the Lord" is basic, first of all in the menacing sense given to it by Amos (Amos 5:18-20) and developed in all its somberness by later prophets (cf. Zeph. 1:14-15). It is the day of the Last Judgment, of the "wrath to come" (I Thess. 1:10); it comes "like a thief in the night" (5:2; cf. Matt. 24:43-44; Paul is here echoing words of Jesus), and brings "sudden destruction" to those who are assuring themselves of "peace and security" (5:3). Against this background of menace, Jesus is proclaimed as the one hope of deliverance—for it is "Jesus who delivers us from the wrath to come" (1:10). For those who are Christ's, the "day of wrath" is transformed into the day of light and of salvation. "You are all sons of light and sons of the day" (5:5), and "God has not destined us for wrath, but to obtain salvation through our Lord Jesus Christ" (5:9). It is the day of the "coming of our Lord Jesus Christ with all his saints" (3:13).

The primary sense of "parousia" is simply "presence" (παρουσία; cf. πάρειμι, "I am present"); but it is already found in authors of the classical period with the meaning "arrival," especially the arrival of a god or of a king. In Hellenistic times, it has acquired a technical sense in connection with the state visit of a king or emperor, sometimes of a general or of a high official. The parousia of such a dignitary involved much advance preparation, and often a good deal of expense, to provide the paraphernalia of a worthy welcome to the great man and a fitting expression of the people's loyalty. At the actual time of his coming, it was usual for the inhabitants to go out to meet him along the highway, to greet his appearance with shouts of acclamation, and to join his cortège for its entrance into the city, where he would distribute rewards and honors to the deserving citizens. The whole atmosphere of such an occasion was one of splendor and joy. These are the terms in which Paul thinks of the coming of Jesus. Since he has ascended into heaven, his coming must of necessity be conceived as a descent from heaven; and if his faithful subjects are to go out to meet him on the way, they must of necessity "meet the Lord in the air" (4:16-17). The cry of command, the call of the archangel, and the sound of the trumpet of God seem also to belong to the same Hellenistic ceremonial, suggesting the approach of the heavenly hosts which attend the descending King; the imagery of Hebrew apocalyptic is combined in a most unusual way with imagery drawn from a quite different tradition. It is not possible for us to define too precisely the relation of the various symbols to the reality of the future hope; but there is no mistaking the notes of triumph and joy, and the significance of the supreme assurance: "So we shall always be with the Lord" (vs. 17). See also PAROUSIA.

6. Text. The Greek text of the letter is exceptionally well attested, like that of all the Pauline writings. Papyrus evidence is scanty, being limited to three fragments of codices, containing, in all, parts of eighteen verses. It is found in part or in whole in twenty-two uncial MSS and about six hundred cursives, ranging in date from the fourth to the fifteenth centuries; and is represented in all the ancient versions. Citations are found in a good number of the early fathers, though they are naturally less abundant than those from the major letters. With all this wealth of evidence, there are only thirty instances in which the major modern editions (from Tischendorf's eighth edition to the twenty-second of Nestle and the commentary of Rigaux) give the slightest difference of text. Of these, only three are of more than technical interest:

a) In 2:7, Westcott and Hort read νήπιοι, "infants," and are followed by many other editors and commentators; this reading must be regarded as having much the weightier attestation, and can be rejected only on the ground that Paul never speaks of himself as an "infant." The reading ἤπιοι, "gentle," has reasonably strong support in the MSS and versions, is read by Nestle and most other modern editors of the text, and is favored, not without hesitation, by most recent editors; the word occurs in only one other passage of the NT (II Tim. 2:24), but is not uncommon in Greek literature.

b) In 3:2, Timothy is described as "our brother and God's fellow worker" (συνεργὸν τοῦ θεοῦ). This reading, adopted by Nestle and by Rigaux, rests upon quite limited evidence (D* 33 d e, and a very few patristic citations); B has συνεργόν alone; some good witnesses (א A P, the Latin Vulg. and the Harkleian Syr.) read διάκονον τοῦ θεοῦ, and this is the reading adopted by nearly all other editors and commentators; the Byzantine text conflates the two —διάκονον τοῦ θεοῦ καὶ συνεργὸν ἡμῶν, "minister of God and our fellow labourer" (KJV).

c) In 5:4, instead of ὡς κλέπτης, "as a thief," B and A read ὡς κλέπτας, "as thieves." Westcott and Hort, alone among editors, adopt this reading, swayed by their predilection for B.

Bibliography. G. Milligan (1908), notable for illustrations of usage drawn from Greek papyri; E. von Dobschütz in Meyer, *Kritisch-exegetischer Kommentar über das NT* (7th ed., 1909); J. E. Frame, ICC (1912); M. Dibelius, in Lietzmann, *Handbuch zum NT* (3rd ed., 1937); W. Neil, in the Moffatt NT Commentary (1950); surpassing all these, B. Rigaux in *EB* (1956), with exhaustive bibliography.   F. W. BEARE

*THESSALONIANS, SECOND LETTER TO THE. A letter written by, or in the name of, Paul and his associates Silvanus and Timothy to the church of the Thessalonians; now placed as the fourteenth book of the NT canon. Its authenticity is often called in question, but is defended by virtually all recent commentators.

It lacks the warmth of affection and the triumphant assurance of the first letter, tending rather to a certain somberness and formalism. The eschatological outlook is again paramount, but stress is laid more on the menacing judgments that await the ungodly than on the joys and glories which the day of the Lord will bring to the faithful—a complete reversal of the emphasis in the first letter. It is now taught that the parousia of the Lord Jesus, the vivid expectation of which pervades I Thessalonians, will not take place until the powers of evil in the world have come to a head in the parousia of an antichrist equipped with satanic powers of miracle and deceit. This is the theme which gives the letter its main interest and saddles the interpreter with his most difficult problems.

1. Authenticity
2. Destination
3. Occasion and purpose
4. Outline of contents
5. Main theme: The mystery of lawlessness
6. Text
Bibliography

1. Authenticity. The authenticity of the letter is in dispute, though it has been defended by all recent commentators. There is no weakness in the external attestation, which is, if anything, better than that of I Thessalonians. It appears to have been laid under contribution in Ephesians and in I Peter; its language is distinctly echoed in Polycarp and somewhat less certainly in Ignatius; it was included in Marcion's collection of the Pauline letters (before the middle of the second century) and is found in all subsequent canonical lists. The difficulties of attributing it to Paul arise chiefly from the comparison with I Thessalonians, both in the similarities and in the differences; indeed, if the first letter were not in existence, it is unlikely that the authenticity of the second would be questioned. The main difficulty is to see how the same writer could dispatch the two letters to the same congregation within the space of a few weeks, which is all the time that can be allowed to have elapsed between the two. Certain earlier lines of objection have been abandoned—as, e.g., the theory of F. H. Kern that the antichrist passage of ch. 2 is an adaptation of the Nero-redivivus myth, and therefore could not be earlier than 68-70. Kern found many followers among scholars of the nineteenth century, but his theory was demolished in the last decade of the century by the studies of apocalyptic literature made by Gunkel, Bousset, and Charles.

The main objections which may still be raised to the authenticity of the letter are the following:

a) It is surprising, if not altogether inconceivable, that at this early date Paul should have to warn his readers against allowing themselves to be led astray by letters circulated in his name without his authority (2:2), and should be obliged to devise means to guarantee the authenticity of his own letters (3:17). In the latter passage, the words "the mark in every letter" are puzzling. How many letters had Paul written at this time? From this period, only the two Thessalonian letters have come down to us; but the phrase "every letter" and the very need to provide signs of authenticity imply an extensive correspondence. Is it possible that Paul was already known as a letter writer in 50 or 51, and that an agitator could hope to win credit for his message by embodying it in a letter put out under the name of the apostle? This is a startling thought; but on the other hand, it must be admitted that it is at least equally hard to imagine a forger's seeking to authenticate his forgery by adding so bold a piece of deception as this.

b) The second objection to be raised is the inconsistency between the eschatological outlook of I Thessalonians, with its stress on the imminence of the Parousia, and the explicit teaching of II Thessalonians that the Parousia will not take place until after "the rebellion," and the revealing of the "man of lawlessness, the son of perdition," after some restraining force or person has been taken away. To this it is replied that such apparent discrepancies are a common feature of apocalyptic writing; premonitory signs of the end are not regarded as incompatible with its sudden and unexpected coming "like a thief in the night." In the gospels themselves, a succession of signs of the coming of the Lord and of the end of the age (Matt. 24 and parallels) are accompanied by warnings to be constantly ready and watchful, "for you do not know on what day your Lord is coming" (vs. 42). Accordingly, no great weight can be attached to this objection.

c) It is the problem of the literary relationships between the two letters that is now put forward as the chief stumbling block. The similarities of language and of general structure are so great as to suggest literary dependence of some kind; and it is more natural to think of another writer's copying Paul than of Paul's copying himself. The relationship is so close that it has even been suggested that Paul kept a copy of the first letter and read it over before writing the second, and drew freely upon its phrases. It is generally admitted that we have here a literary problem of unusual difficulty, which may even be regarded as "insoluble" without more knowledge of the circumstances than we now possess. It may at least be said that Paul does not elsewhere repeat himself and copy the structure of a previous letter in any comparable way. Let us remark that the argument could be turned in reverse; if we were to start by admitting the authenticity of II Thessalonians, we could allege the similarities as evidence casting doubt upon the Pauline authorship of I Thessalonians.

We are left with a measure of uncertainty, but it cannot be claimed that the case for rejection is strong enough to justify us in denying the traditional attribution of the letter to Paul, especially as no plausible occasion for its publication has yet been indicated. If the letter is pseudonymous, it is an outright forgery, intended to represent Paul as teaching an apocalyptic doctrine which is not his, but the product of the forger's imagination. Where are we to look for the circles, presumably late in the first century, which had become unduly excited over a report or a prophetic utterance to the effect that the day of the Lord had already come? Why would such a letter be addressed to the Thessalonians? And how would it gain acceptance as Paul's? On the whole, the difficulties in the way of accepting the letter are less serious than those which are raised by the attempt to account for it as pseudonymous writing of a later period.

2. Destination. For a discussion of the "church of the Thessalonians," *see* THESSALONIANS, FIRST LETTER TO THE, § 2. In the attempt to overcome some of the difficulties raised by the literary relationships between the two letters to the Thessalonians, a number of scholars have resorted to the hypothesis that they were written at approximately the same time, but to different groups or to different churches. Harnack proposed to treat the first letter as written to the Gentiles, the second as written to the Jewish Christians of the city. Apart from the impossibility of imagining a Pauline church split on lines of racial origin, it is not easy to see why the apostle should write so much less warmly to the Jewish section than to the Gentile group. Goguel suggested the possibility that II Thessalonians might have been addressed to Beroea, where there was a strong and well-disposed Jewish group, eagerly interested in the prophetic scriptures (Acts 17:10-11). Starting from Polycarp's passing reference to "letters" written by Paul to the Philippians, Schweizer offered the conjecture that II Thessalonians was actually written to the Philippian church. All these conjectures are indications of the straits to which excellent scholars feel themselves reduced by the difficulties of the literary problem. In themselves, they are far from convincing. It is best to accept all the difficulties, and to make the attempt to reconstruct the circumstances in which Paul may have sent such a letter to Thessalonica.

3. Occasion and purpose. A great part of our difficulty in dealing with this letter is due to our ignorance of the conditions of communication between Paul and his churches. It is clear that Paul has received further reports on the state of the Thessalonian church, but we have no knowledge of the means by which they were brought to him. We know that I Thessalonians depends upon a report brought by Timothy after a personal visit (I Thess. 3:1-8); but we know nothing of how the letter was transmitted, or by what messenger. It is not to be taken for granted that it had been received in Thessalonica by the time that II Thessalonians came to be written. All that we know is that some brief time after Timothy's visit, word came to Paul by some unknown channel from the Thessalonian church, and it is in response to this second report that he writes his second letter. He hears again of the persecutions which his converts are undergoing; and it may be that they are described in such harrowing terms as to account for the general somberness of the letter and for its emphasis on the dreadful punishments which will be meted out to the persecutors by the just judgment of God at the Parousia of the Lord. He is told that some have been persuaded that the day of the Lord has come already, and have been "shaken in mind" and unduly "excited" about it (2:1-2); and he seeks to remove this understanding by reminding them of his own previous teaching about the chain of events which are to precede and accompany the Parousia (2:3-12). And the later report leads him to view more seriously the tendency of some to live lazy and disorderly lives, imposing upon the charity of their hard-working brethren while they blissfully await the dawning of the glorious day (3:6-15).

The letter, accordingly, is written in response to a second report on the state of the Thessalonian church, and it has a threefold purpose: (*a*) to encourage and strengthen the readers to stand steadfast in the faith, unmoved by persecution; (*b*) to correct the erroneous notion that the day of the Lord has come, by showing that the events which must precede its coming have not yet been accomplished; and (*c*) to advise the church on the severe yet affectionate discipline that should be used in the case of lazy and disorderly members.

The date of the letter cannot be exactly determined, but it was probably written at no long interval after I Thessalonians—i.e., in 50-51. The general circumstances of the Thessalonian church have not greatly changed; the similarities of language in the two letters, if both are authentic, forbid us to think of them as separated by any long period of time; and the fact that Paul and Silvanus and Timothy are still together points to the early months of the mission in Corinth. After that, Silvanus (Silas) disappears from the narrative of Acts, and he is never again mentioned in the Pauline correspondence.

4. Outline of contents. The letter falls into three main divisions, in keeping with its threefold purpose, with the opening salutation and the closing benedictions and greetings, as follows:

I. The Salutation, 1:1-2
II. Thanksgiving, and affirmation of the righteous judgment of God, 1:3-12
   A. Thanksgiving for the growth of the readers in faith and love, and for their steadfast patience under persecution, vss. 3-4
   B. The righteous judgment of God (at the Parousia of the Lord Jesus, his afflicted followers will be granted rest, while the persecutors will pay the penalty of eternal destruction, vss. 5-10
   C. Prayer for the readers, that God may make them worthy of his call, 1:11-12
III. The parousia of antichrist and his overthrow, 2:1-3:5
   A. Plea against being excited by pretended revelations that the day of the Lord has come, 2:1-2
   B. Events that must precede the coming of the day, 2:3-5
   C. The restraining power, 2:6-7
   D. The parousia of the antichrist (the "lawless one"); his destruction by the Lord "by the manifestation of his Parousia";

his powers of deception, and the certain condemnation of those whom he deceives, 2:8-12
   E. Assurance and encouragement for the readers, 2:13-3:5
IV. Discipline, 3:6-15
   A. Warning against tolerating idleness, vs. 6
   B. Example of the apostles, vss. 7-9
   C. "No work, no food," vs. 10
   D. Appeal to the idlers themselves, vss. 11-13
   E. Idlers must be treated sternly, yet not as enemies but as brothers, vss. 14-15
V. Conclusion: Benedictions and greetings, vss. 16-18
   It may be remarked that the paragraph 3:1-5 has all the marks of a conclusion to the letter, and that the section on the discipline of the idlers is added almost as a postscript.

5. Main theme: The mystery of lawlessness. The chief interest of the letter lies in the central apocalyptic passage (2:1-12), where Paul gives us some indications, not always entirely clear to us, of the program of events which are to usher in the end of history, according to his prophetic vision. The theme is introduced, as so often happens in his letters, in relation to a practical problem which has arisen in the church to which he is writing, and his treatment presupposes a measure of previous instruction in the matter, as he expressly tells us (vs. 5). For this reason, he feels no compulsion to give a complete account of his apocalyptic doctrine, but only to stress again the aspects of it which his readers seem to have forgotten. The teaching here given is therefore fragmentary, and for us who lack the previous instruction given by him at Thessalonica, it presents some uncertainties of interpretation.

He is here dealing with a strange misunderstanding which has arisen in the Thessalonian church. Some of its members have been led to believe, on the strength of what they take to be a revelation— embodied, it may be, in a letter purporting to be from the apostles—that the day of the Lord has come (ἐνέστηκεν, "is present"). How they could entertain such a notion we cannot tell, but its effect has been to shake them out of their senses and leave them in a state of alarm and excitement (vss. 1-2). Perhaps they fear that they have been passed by, deprived of their part in the glory and joy of the day, and left to bear the fearful judgments that are to come upon the earth. Paul warns them against falling into any such error, bidding them remember what he has already taught them—that before that day comes, there must be a great rebellion against God led by a figure of towering arrogance, the "man of lawlessness, the son of perdition," who is the enemy of all religion and "takes his seat in the temple of God, proclaiming himself to be God" (vss. 3-4). This will be the final and total manifestation of the principle of evil which is already at work in hidden ways, the "mystery of lawlessness" (vs. 7). It is as yet held in restraint; Paul speaks in curiously cryptic terms of "that which restrains," as of some power known to the readers; and in the next verse, of "he who restrains," as of a person (vss. 6-7). By this power or person, the forces of evil are kept under until the time appointed for the revelation of the "lawless one" (vs. 8). Only then will the Lord come, and will "slay him with the breath of his mouth and destroy him by his appearing and his coming" (vs. 8).

The appearance of this master of evil is also called a "parousia," as it were a satanic caricature of the parousia of the Lord; given supernatural powers by Satan, he will work all manner of lying miracles, by which he will deceive those who are perishing "because they refused to love the truth and so be saved" (vss. 9-10). But this is not the state of the Thessalonians: "God chose you from the beginning to be saved, through sanctification by the Spirit and belief in the truth . . . , so that you may obtain the glory of our Lord Jesus Christ" (vss. 13-14). Thus Paul seeks to calm their excited minds with words of assurance.

At least three phrases in this passage are susceptible of more than one interpretation: (a) "the rebellion"; (b) "the man of lawlessness"; and (c) "what [or 'he who'] now restrains" (τὸ κατέχον, ὁ κατέχων). The first two can be set in the light of the standard patterns of Jewish apocalyptic; the third has no parallel to help us; in no case can the meaning be determined with certainty. Paul uses language which his readers will understand without difficulty, because they have received previous instruction from him (vs. 5); we are left uncertain of his meaning, because we have no means of recovering the substance of that previous teaching. "The rebellion" probably takes up the thought of a mustering of the nations against God, based upon such passages as Ps. 2; Ezek. 38-39; but it is not impossible that Paul should be thinking of a vast and violent uprising against the authority of Rome. Ancient interpreters nearly all take him to mean, however, a general defection from faith among the people of God. Jewish apocalyptic writings include widespread apostasy among the signs of the end; and it is remarkable that in the Dead Sea Scrolls the theme of treason to the covenant is linked with the "man of the lie." Many of the early fathers interpret the word to mean a general apostasy of Christians, which they tend to link with the heretical movements of their own time. Against such interpretations, it may be pointed out that Paul does not regard the hardening of Israel as an apostasy—he will "bear them witness that they have a zeal for God, but it is not enlightened" (Rom. 10:2); and it is quite impossible that as early as 50-51 he should have taught that a general apostasy of Christians from the gospel would be a sign of the end.

The "man of lawlessness," or the "lawless one," is depicted in terms which are drawn from Jewish apocalyptic, primarily from the description of Antiochus Epiphanes in Dan. 11:36-37. Though the term "antichrist" is not used (it occurs first in Christian literature in the Johannine letters), it conveys the essential notion of the figure here presented. Here again we encounter a variety of interpretations. Some take it in a collective sense, allowing the interpretation to be determined by the Johannine teaching (especially I John 2:18); "antichrist" or the "man of lawlessness" is not a particular individual but a principle of error or of evil which appears in many embodiments. In the later Middle Ages (Wycliffe) and the Reformation, the term is often

applied to the papacy as an institution, and to individual popes. It is clear, however, that Paul is thinking in terms of an individual who is to appear at the very end of the age; like the Lord, he is to have his own "parousia"—like a king making a splendid entry into his realm. Some interpreters have held that he is conceived by Paul as a supernatural being; but it seems evident that Paul presents him as a human being possessed of supernatural powers "by the activity of Satan." Attempts have been made to identify virtually all conspicuous enemies of the church and the gospel with antichrist, and such identifications continue to this day. See also ANTICHRIST; PAROUSIA.

The restraining power has generally been taken to mean the Roman Empire as "that which restrains," and the Roman emperor as "he who restrains"; this interpretation is found as early as Tertullian (ca. 200) and is still prevalent. Despite its long acceptance, this is nothing more than a conjecture, and one that will not stand up under scrutiny. If Paul entertained any idea that the coming of the Lord would take place while he himself was still alive, he cannot have held that the power of Rome must first crumble to clear the way for the revelation of antichrist.

A different line of interpretation, going back to the Antiochian theologians of the fourth century, has been revived: that which restrains is the divine decree that the gospel must "be preached throughout the whole world, as a testimony to all nations; and then the end will come" (Matt. 24:14); "he who restrains," in this view, is Paul himself, the apostle to the Gentiles. This hazardous conjecture would also seem to make shipwreck on the observation that if Paul is to be removed from the scene (vs. 7) before antichrist is revealed, then he cannot also include himself among those "who are alive, who are left unto the coming of the Lord." And surely it would be sheer affectation for him to speak of himself in such cryptic terms.

Others have imagined the restraining influence to be some angelic being—Michael and the armies of heaven; or the angel of the bottomless pit (Rev. 20:1-4); or even the Holy Spirit. It should be recognized that the apostle does not provide us with any key for solving his cryptic phrases; and it may be that he is simply saying that something or someone is delaying the final outburst of evil until the time that God has appointed, that the lawless one "may be revealed in his time" (ἐν τῷ ἑαυτοῦ καιρῷ; vs. 6).

6. Text. The Greek text offers no major problems, and there are only three readings of more than technical interest which call for consideration.

a) In 2:3, the witnesses are fairly evenly divided between ἀνομίας, "lawlessness" (RSV), and ἁμαρτίας, "sin" (KJV). Most editors favor the former reading, and suspect that ἁμαρτίας has been introduced as an explanation of ἀνομίας. On the other hand, it is possible that ἀνομίας has replaced an original ἁμαρτίας, to make an assimilation to the ἄνομος of vs. 8.

b) In 2:13, for ἀπ' ἀρχῆς, "from the beginning," many excellent witnesses read ἀπαρχήν, "as firstfruits" (Vulg. primitias). Modern editors are about evenly divided in their choice.

c) In 3:6, for παρελάβετε, "you received," the Byzantine text reads παρέλαβον, a typical stylistic correction of παρελάβοσαν, "they received," which is found in ℵ, A, D (—παρ), 33. Most of the patristic evidence supports the Byzantine reading, and thus, indirectly, the παρελάβοσαν from which it derives. Accordingly, παρελάβοσαν is to be preferred.

Bibliography. Monographs: W. Bousset, *The Antichrist Legend* (trans. A. H. Keane; 1896); "Antichrist," in *Encyclopaedia Biblica* (1899-1903); B. Rigaux, *L'Antéchrist et l'opposition au royaume messianique dans l'Ancien et le NT* (1932).

Articles: W. Wrede, "Die Echtheit des zweiten Thessalonicherbriefs," *Texte und Untersuchungen*, N.S. IX.2 (1903): the weightiest statement of the case against. A. von Harnack, "Das Problem des zweiten Thessalonicherbriefs," *Sitzungsberichte der Königlichen Preussischen Akademie der Wissenschaften, Phil.-hist. Klasse* (1919). M. Goguel, "L'énigme de la seconde épître auz Thessaloniciens," *RHR*, LXXI (1915). E. Schweizer, "Der zweite Thessalonicherbrief ein Philipperbrief?" *Theologische Zeitschrift*, vol. I (1945). (The preceding three articles propose a different destination for II Thessalonians.) On the theory of F. H. Kern that the antichrist passage represents an adaptation of the Nero-redivivus myth, see *Tübingen Zeitschrift für Theologie*, II (1839), 145-214. On reversing the order of I and II Thessalonians, see T. W. Manson, "St. Paul in Greece: the Letters to the Thessalonians," *Bulletin of the John Rylands Library*, vol. XXXV (1952-53). On the restraining agency, see O. Cullmann, "Le caractère eschatologique du devoir missionnaire et de la conscience apostolique de saint Paul. Étude sur le κατέχον (-ων) de II Thess. 2:6-7," *RHPR*, vol. XVI (1936), with a shorter statement in "Eschatology and Missions in the NT," in W. D. Davies and D. Daube, eds., *The Background of the NT and Its Eschatology* (1956).

F. W. BEARE

*THESSALONICA thĕs'ə lə nī'kə [ἡ Θεσσαλονίκη] (Acts 17:1, 11, 13; 27:2; Phil. 4:16; II Tim. 4:10). An important city of Macedonia, known today as Salonika.

The city was located on the Thermaic Gulf, now the Gulf of Salonika, at the W side of the peninsula of Chalcidice, and from the beginning has been the chief seaport of MACEDONIA. According to Strabo (VII.330, fragments 21, 24) this metropolis owed its foundation to Cassander, who named it after his wife, Thessalonica, daughter of Philip and sister of Alexander the Great. This was probably in 316 or 315 B.C. The settlers of the new city were the former inhabitants of some twenty-six villages in the region which Cassander destroyed. Among these towns was Therma, some seven miles to the SE; this doubtless accounts for the loose statement of Strabo that Thessalonica was formerly called Therma.

When Macedonia was divided into four districts in 167 B.C., Thessalonica was made the capital of the second district, that which extended from the River Strymon to the River Axius (Livy XLV.29-30). In 148 B.C., Macedonia was made a Roman province, and Thessalonica became the chief city of the province and the seat of Roman administration. Under the Romans it was declared a free city (Pliny Nat. Hist. IV.36), and in the time of Strabo (VII.323) it was the most populous of all the Macedonian towns. Later under the Emperor Gordian III (A.D. 238-44) Thessalonica was given the title Neokoros which indicated its oversight of a temple of the imperial cult, and under Decius ca. 250 it was made a colony.

Thessalonica was surrounded by a city wall, of which N and E stretches still stand. The extant portions are of Byzantine date, but rest at least in part upon more ancient foundations. The Via Egnatia ran through the city from SE to NW. This way was later called Vardar Street, from the River Vardar (Axius), but now again has its ancient name. Two Roman arches spanned the Via Egnatia, one at the W entrance to the city, known until its demolition in 1876 as the Vardar Gate, and the other near the E wall, the Arch of Galerius, built to celebrate the triumph of that emperor over the Persians in A.D. 297. A round Roman building N of the latter arch, and probably contemporary with it, was later transformed into the Church of St. George. The agora probably lay in the middle of the city, N of the Via Egnatia; the place of the hippodrome was near the SE wall.

An inscription from the Vardar Gate, now in the British Museum, and several other inscriptions found at Thessalonica, mention officials called politarchs. The Vardar Gate inscription probably dates between 30 B.C. and A.D. 143; one of the other inscriptions belongs to the reign of Augustus; and yet another, which was brought to Thessalonica from an outlying village, is dated under Claudius. This is significant because in Acts 17:6 the title "politarch" (ὁ πολιτάρχης) is applied to the city authorities of Thessalonica, and the word was otherwise previously unknown. *See bibliography.*

Bibliography. On "politarch," see E. D. Burton, "The Politarchs," *AJT*, II (1898), 598-632. See also C. Diehl, M. Le Tourneau, and H. Saladin, *Les Monuments chrétiens de Salonique, Monuments de l'art Byzantin* IV (2 vols.; 1918); O. Tafrali, *Thessalonique des origines au XIVᵉ siècle* (1919); E. Oberhummer, "Thessalonike," *Pauly-Wissowa*, Zweite Reihe, VI, i (1936), cols. 143-63.

J. FINEGAN

THEUDAS thōō'dəs [Θευδᾶς]. **1.** Theudas I, a pseudo messiah during the consulate of Cuspius Fadius (*ca.* A.D. 44). He promised to lead followers across the Jordan by dividing its waters by mere words, and thus to prove his divine powers. Cuspius apprehended him and decapitated him; he sent his head to Jerusalem as a sign of victory (Jos. Antiq. XX.v.1).

An allusion to Theudas is found in Acts 5:36, where Gamaliel makes reference to Theudas long before his appearance. This is, however, explained as referring to an event of A.D. 6 and to another rebel by the name of Theudas.

2. Theudas II, a Roman rabbi who lived *ca.* 133. He arranged that monies previously given to the temple be used for schools (Yer. Moed Katan 81*a*). He also introduced the practice of eating roast lamb in remembrance of the paschal feast. This was in opposition to the Palestinian rabbis, who declared: "Were you not Theudas, we would excommunicate you" (Pes. 53*a*). Theudas preached as *archisynagoge* (ruler of the synagogue) that a Jew should be a martyr rather than abandon his faith (Pes. 53*b*). The Talmud associates Theudas with Simon ben Shetah, who lived *ca.* 80, but this association is an anachronism.

Bibliography. E. Schürer, *History of the Jewish People in the Time of Jesus Christ* (1891), div. 1, vol. II, p. 168; R. H. Pfeiffer, *History of NT Times* (1949), p. 38. S. B. HOENIG

THIEF. See CRIMES AND PUNISHMENTS § C7*b*.

THIGH [ירך, μηρός]. The flank of the lower part of the trunk of the human body; the upper part of the leg.

The term is used frequently simply for this physical component of man; it is a part of the beautiful body of the maiden (Song of S. 7:1—H 7:2); it is that place where the sword is worn (Judg. 3:16; Ps. 45:3 —H 45:4; Song of S. 3:8; cf. Exod. 32:27 ["side"]). Used in this physical sense, the word was transferred by the priestly writers from the human body to physical objects, particularly those of cultic use—e.g., the "side" of the altar (II Kings 16:14) and the "base" of the golden lampstand (Exod. 25:31).

The more characteristically biblical usage is that which views the thigh as a dynamic part of the living organism, man. As such, it is not merely a physical element, but is important to the vitality of man. It is regarded as the seat of procreative powers. Sons are regarded as "offspring of the thigh" (יצאי ירכו; Gen. 46:26; Exod. 1:5: the sons of Jacob; Judg. 8:30: the seventy sons of Gideon). The use of this expression is derived from an unreflective notion that the reproductive organs are by proximity related to the thigh: because this is clearly the place where life originates, this part of the body was important as the seat and source of life. In Num. 5:16-21, the thigh is related to the birth, being involved in the question of illicit sexual intercourse. The implication of the phrase "your thigh fall away" is obscure. The word is to be understood in terms of its parallel, "belly" (בטן)— i.e., the punishment is related to the birth or loss of the child. The Mishna comments on this that the sin began with the thigh, therefore the thigh must be punished—an allusion to the thigh as related to sexual organs and therefore the seat of life.

This dynamic view of the thigh as the locus of life power is related to other practices in Israel's life. The slapping of the thigh was understood as an expression of shame, sorrow, and remorse (Jer. 31:19; Ezek. 21:12—H 21:17). The fact that it is the thigh which is employed may give expression to the notion that the most profound sorrow and remorse are bound up with life itself. In Gen. 32:25-32—H 32:26-33 there is mentioned a dietary practice which is here given its etiological explanation. This is the only mention of the practice in the OT, and is the basis for subsequent Jewish discussion. The reference may be more than etiological: the injury of the thigh may refer to the damaging of the vitality of Jacob, signifying some degree of mastery, even though "he did not prevail."

A more important usage is the role of the thigh in the swearing of an oath. The sealing and assuring fidelity to an oath were consummated by putting the hand under the thigh (Gen. 24:2; 47:29). Clearly this is an act relating the oath taker to the seat of life in the other party. Likely this was contact with the genital organs. Two interpretations of the act are plausible. On the one hand, there is recognition of the power and presence of the life-giving deity. God is then invoked as the guarantor of fidelity by the oath taker. On the other hand, this may be a pledge relating to the descendants of the man whose thigh is involved. The seed of the man is to enforce loyalty and to act as avenger if the oath is broken. By the time the narratives were recorded, the original meanings of the act may have been forgotten. But the practice nonetheless served to emphasize the life-and-death importance of the oath.

Related to "thigh" is a less important term, מתנים (see LOINS). This part of the body is also the place where man's vitality is most keenly felt, as the locus of strength (Prov. 31:17), and the place where anguish and pain are most sharply felt (Isa. 21:3; Nah. 2:10—H 2:11).

Thus the thigh is a physical part of the body of man which, in terms of dynamic and vitality, is regarded as the seat of life for the whole personality and the source of life for those it produces. As such, the scope of concern involved is that of the whole life of the organism.

Bibliography. P. Dhorme, "L'emploi métaphorique des noms de parties du corps en Hébreu et en Accadien," *RB,* 32 (1923), 202-3. W. BRUEGGEMANN

THIMNATHAH. KJV form of TIMNAH in Josh. 19:43.

THIRD DAY. Jesus' resurrection "on the third day" was an element in the earliest apostolic faith. There are two postresurrection references to Jesus' resurrection "on the third day"—in a speech by Peter (Acts 10:40) and in Paul's account of the kerygma he had received (I Cor. 15:3-4).

The gospels record Jesus' prediction of his resurrection on the third day (Matt. 16:21; 17:23; 20:19; Luke 9:22; 18:33; cf. Luke 13:32; 24:7). Scholars are divided as to whether these words were spoken in their present form by the historical Jesus, or were later made to conform to the experience of the church.

Mark's expression is always "after three days" (8: 31; 9:31; 10:34; with which cf. Matt. 27:63-64). It may be that originally "after three days" and "on the third day" meant the same thing; but the former is surely less precise, and the latter expression displaced it.

John does not use either phrase in connection with the Resurrection; but note John 2:1, 11: "On the third day . . . Jesus . . . manifested his glory." *See* RESURRECTION IN THE NT.

B. H. THROCKMORTON, JR.

THISBE thĭz'bĭ [Θίσβης] (Tob. 1:2). A place in N Galilee referred to as that from which Tobit was taken captive by the Assyrians (cf. II Kings 15:29; 17:6). The site is unidentified, but it is described in Tobit as lying S of Kedesh Naphtali (probably KEDESH) and above Asher (i.e., HAZOR). The Sinaiticus text adds that it is N of Phogor (unidentified). It is not named in the Hebrew and Aramaic texts. The Vulg. mentions Sephet (cf. medieval Safed?) as in the vicinity (cf. Josh. 19:37-39; 20:7; I Macc. 11:63; Jos. War II.xviii.1; Antiq. V.i.10; XIII.v.6; etc.).

Bibliography. J. Simons, *The Geographical and Topographical Texts of the OT* (1959), pp. 502-4. A. WIKGREN

THISTLE, THORN. Types of wild flora characterized by·sharp projections on stems, branches, or leaves. Seventeen different Hebrew words have been translated "thistle" or "thorn," "bramble," "brier," or "nettle," with little consistency in any of the ancient or modern versions (*cf.* FLORA § A12). Confu-

Courtesy of Winifred Walker

58. Thistle (*Silybum marianum, Centaurea calcitrapa*)

Courtesy of Winifred Walker

59. Thorn (*Zizyphus spina-christi*)

sion concerning the meaning of the Hebrew words apparently began very early. Arabic usage offers only a little help. The RSV follows the KJV with very few changes. The most common terms meaning

"thistle" are דרדר (*dardār*), חוח (*ḥôaḥ*), and τρίβολος; for "thorn," קוץ (*qôṣ*) and ἄκανθα are the most common.

Dardār appears to be the generic word for "thistle," and *qôṣ* for "thorn" (Gen. 3:18; Hos. 10:8; but cf. Isa. 34:13). Attempts to identify species only lead to confusion. It is doubtful that there was any attempt in Bible times to designate the many kinds of weeds and thorny flora with any degree of consistency.

Biblical references to thistles and thorns are mostly found in metaphors describing punishment for sin (Gen. 3:18; Josh. 23:13; Job 31:40; Isa. 5:6; 32:13; 34:13; Hos. 9:6; 10:8; Mic. 7:4) and those emphasizing anything that is generally worthless (II Sam. 23:6; II Kings 14:9; II Chr. 25:18; Prov. 15:19; Isa. 7:23-25; 55:13; Heb. 6:8; Letter of Jeremiah 6:71 [ῥάμνος]). As a symbol of evil they appear in the familiar saying: "Are grapes gathered from thorns, or figs from thistles?" (Matt. 7:16; cf. Prov. 22:5; Jer. 4:3; 12:13; Ezek. 2:6). Common experience made the thorn a symbol of pain (Prov. 26:9; Ezek. 28:24). Paul's reference to some chronic physical ailment as a "thorn in the flesh" (II Cor. 12:7; σκόλοψ) has defied attempts to define it. Gideon punished the men of Succoth with "thorns of the wilderness" (Judg. 8:7, 16). In the familiar parable of the sower, the seed which fell among thorns was choked out by thorns, which symbolize the preoccupation of man with the "cares of the world and the delight in riches" which "choke the word" (Matt. 13:7, 22; Mark 4:7, 18; Luke 8:7, 14).

It is a common sight in Arab lands to see a donkey piled so high with dried thorn bushes that the animal is barely visible as he trudges the dusty road to the Bedouin encampment. One will see the piles of thorns and briers beside black goat's-hair tents, ready for use as fuel for cooking (Ps. 58:9—H 58:10; Eccl. 7:6; cf. Ps. 118:12; Isa. 27:4). It is easy thus to imagine how the sight of fire rapidly consuming the thorns became a metaphor for wickedness and its destruction (Isa. 9:18; 10:17; 33:12; Nah. 1:10).

Thistles (particularly the *Centaurea* L. and the *Silybum* Adans.) seem to grow everywhere in the Holy Land, but they are particularly profuse in the plains areas. Close study of the dominant pink-lavender flower heads reveals intricate beauty; but where crops are essential, thistles are a troublesome nuisance and a symbol of neglect (cf. Prov. 24:31).

In ancient times various thorny bushes were used as hedges between plots of ground, but today the golden yellow-flowered *Acacia farnesiana* L., introduced from America (and other species from Australia), has become the common HEDGE. It, too, however, is thorny (cf. Isa. 5:5; Hos. 2:6; Mic. 7:4; Mark 12:1).

See also BRAMBLE; BRIER; NETTLE.

Figs. THI 58-59; Pl. XIV.

Bibliography. H. N. and A. L. Moldenke, *Plants of the Bible* (1952), pp. 70-72, 153, 165-66, 202-3, 206-7, 245, 248-49.

J. C. TREVER

THOMAS tŏm'əs [Θωμᾶς; Aram. תאומא, twin]. One of the twelve apostles, mentioned about midway in the four NT lists (Matt. 10:2-4; Mark 3:16-19; Luke 6:14-16; Acts 1:13).

His position in the lists may indicate that he was

regarded in the early church as neither the most nor the least important of the Twelve.

In the Fourth Gospel the name Thomas is three times (11:16; 20:24; 21:2) followed by the Greek name DIDYMUS, obviously the name by which he was known by Greek-speaking Christians.

"Thomas" in Aramaic (תאומא) and Hebrew (תאם) seems to be an epithet meaning simply "twin," not a personal name. Some Syriac Christians knew him as Judas—Judas Thomas (Judas the twin)—as is clear from the apocryphal Acts of Thomas and the appearance of "Thomas" and "Judas Thomas" for "Judas (not Iscariot)" in John 14:22 in Syr. MSS (sy[s] and sy[c]). These variants in John 14:22 may suggest that Thomas was early identified with the "Judas of James," of the lists of Luke 6; Acts 1.

It is startling to find that in the Acts of Thomas, Judas Thomas is regarded as the twin of our Lord himself, a suggestion which has been taken seriously by some modern scholars, and held as fact by the Mesopotamian church. If "Thomas" means simply "twin" and the suggestion of the Acts of Thomas is rejected, as it seems it must be, we are quite at a loss to know whose twin the man designated by "Thomas" was, or even his actual name.

This apostle's character is quite clearly delineated in the Fourth Gospel. When Jesus resolves to run the danger of returning to Judea from beyond the Jordan, Thomas' comment reveals both a pessimistic outlook and a spirit of intense loyalty and bravery (11:16). When Jesus assumes that the disciples know the way to the Father's house to which he is going soon, Thomas is humble and candid enough to confess openly his ignorance of Jesus' meaning (14:5). He can be convinced of the reality of the Resurrection only by incontrovertible evidence (20:24-28). When such evidence is produced, he is represented as capable of lofty expressions of faith (vs. 28). His incredulous attitude has won for him the characterization "doubting Thomas." Altogether it may be said that he is portrayed as a deeply devoted, but somewhat dull, disciple whose lack of understanding provides Jesus an opportunity to disclose the truth more fully; but when he understands, he responds with stubborn loyalty.

Traditions concerning Thomas' postresurrection missionary activities are of questionable value. One reported by Eusebius (Hist. III.1) has him working in Parthia. The third- or fourth-century Acts of Thomas claims that he worked and suffered martyrdom in India and that his body was carried to Mesopotamia. The present-day Christians of St. Thomas of India base their claim to descent from this apostle largely on this book or on documents derived from it.

It is inherently likely that Christianity was carried to India by the third century A.D., but how it got there is quite unknown. Contemporary scholars can neither prove nor disprove the claim that Thomas evangelized there.

Bibliography. F. C. Burkitt, "The Original Language of the Acts of Judas Thomas," *JTS*, I (1900), 280-90; T. K. Cheyne and J. S. Black, eds., *Encyclopedia Biblica*, IV (1903), 5057-59; J. R. Harris, *The Twelve Apostles* (1927), pp. 23-28 and *passim;* C. K. Barrett, *The Gospel According to St. John* (1955), pp. 327, 382, 475-77; L. W. Brown, *The Indian Christians of St. Thomas* (1956).   E. P. BLAIR

THOMAS, ACTS OF. One of a long series of early romances, styled apocryphal Acts (*see* ACTS, APOCRYPHAL), and among the latest of the five principal works of this sort, containing a very lengthy account of the travels, exploits, and miracles of Thomas in India.

The writing is the only one of its sort to have come down in essentially complete form. Its present length is nearly double the 1,600 lines ascribed to it in the Stichometry of Nicephorus. Since it consists of a long series of incidents, for the most part but loosely braided together, it is entirely conceivable that in the early years it circulated in a shorter form, together with the Martyrdom, which, as is true of all these writings, undoubtedly circulated separately.

In addition to versions in Armenian, Ethiopic, and Latin—all of which are palpably secondary—it is extant in both Syriac and Greek. Which of the two latter is to be regarded as the original is disputed. The commonly accepted view that it was composed in Syriac, very possibly in Edessa in the third century, by disciples of Bardesanes (Bardaisan), is in no small part due to the statement by Ephrem Syrus in his commentary on the apocryphal III Corinthians (*see* CORINTHIANS, THIRD EPISTLE TO) that this sect in its apocryphal Acts had turned the apostles of the Lord into preachers of their own impious views. Some of the mystic hymns in this apocryphon, notably the one styled the "Hymn of the Spirit," which are present only in the Syriac version, have actually been ascribed to Bardesanes himself. Occasional voices, notably of Max Bonnet and M. R. James, have been raised in favor of a Greek original, now for the most part lost, early translated into Syriac and subsequently from Syriac back into Greek. The eleventh-century Greek MS V (Vallicelian) is certainly a direct translation from the Syriac and contains—alone among Greek MSS—the Hymn to the Soul. In addition, several Greek MSS show such marked differences in the form of the concluding Martyrdom and the location of Thomas' lengthy prayer as to suggest the possibility that here we have vestiges of the original text. Other scholars, notably Harnack and Goodspeed, have suggested the possibility that the writing was issued in both languages. Occasional attempts, notably by Gutschmidt, to view the book as an early Christian adaptation of a series of Buddhist tales have been made, but have seemed to most investigators quite unsupported by the evidence.

To what extent the common reference to this apocryphon as Gnostic is justified is far from certain. That it is distinctly ascetic is obvious. The description of Thomas' mode of life in an early chapter (20): "He fasteth continually and prayeth, and eateth bread only, with salt, and his drink is water, and he weareth but one garment alike in fair weather and in winter, and receiveth nought of any man, and that he hath he giveth unto others," is reflected throughout the book, but would scarcely have seemed to orthodox Christians of the third century as indications of heresy. Thomas' chief object in his missionary adventures is severely restricted to the highly successful attempt to alienate wives from husbands, sweethearts from lovers. The only husband a Christian woman may have is Christ, the heavenly bridegroom. This theme, common in all these apocryphal

Acts, may well have led such groups as those easily dubbed Gnostics, Encratites, Apostolics, and Priscillians, as well as Manicheans, to approve the writing. The writing manifests little interest in doctrine.

Thomas is several times styled (in the Greek but not in the Syriac) the "twin brother of Christ." Christ appears in various forms—once in the likeness of his "twin brother." But this is probably not to be understood as a sign of Docetism. Actually it may be nothing more than the result of toying with Thomas' nickname, "the twin," together with the tradition that Jesus too had been a carpenter. The brief description of the ministry of Jesus, ending with the Lord's Prayer in its severely (unemended) Matthean form (chs. 143–44), shows no departure from the most orthodox appraisal. Unless our extant versions have been very drastically and successfully edited to rid the earlier writing of emphases which orthodoxy regarded as perverse, it is hard to avoid the feeling that the common term "Gnostic" for this compilation is actually unwarranted. Like many of the later Acts, there is far less interest in proclaiming doctrine, orthodox or otherwise, than in braiding together a long string of wonder tales about the ancient hero. Sexual intercourse and covetousness are, as already indicated, always to be combatted. They, not unorthodox doctrines, are the constant concern of the author. It may even be wondered if these themes, so common in pagan romances of the period, were not unnaturally shoved to the fore in stories intended as Christian substitutes for the popular literature. In none of the apocryphal writings is dependence upon the canonical writings more marked. Many of these fantastic tales, with their talking animals (asses and serpents), exorcisms, cures by relics of the long-dead Thomas, are little more than the reworking of familiar biblical stories.

A brief summary of the several episodes of the book may suggest in part the reason it proved so popular to many early readers and continued to be copied, although not infrequently officially condemned. The scene opens in Jerusalem with the apostles assembled to apportion the sections of the world in which each is to labor. India falls to the lot of Thomas. He refuses, but is forced by none other than Christ himself to go, for the latter sells him to a merchant who chances to be in Jerusalem in search of a carpenter to work for his king, Gundaphorus. Forthwith they depart (somewhat surprisingly) by ship (!) for India. En route they stop at Andrapolis, where a wedding is under way. At the feast, to which all must go, Thomas abstains, in a manner not unreminiscent of Daniel, from all the dainties; when approached by a Hebrew flute girl, he averts his eyes and sings a mystic bridal hymn, reminiscent of the Song of Songs, and apparently intended to suggest that the only proper marriage for a Christian is of the soul to Christ. After Thomas has departed from the bridal pair, the wedding is subsequently broken off by Christ, who appears in the form of "his twin brother Thomas."

Having arrived at the court of Gundaphorus, Thomas is directed to build for the king a palace. Instead, he spends the lavish funds on the poor and tells the angered king that a palace has been built

and awaits him in heaven. The king's brother, Gad, enraged at Thomas' effrontery, dies that night, sees the palace in heaven, is so enamored of it that he contrives to be restored to life, and returns to tell his brother. Then follows the episode of the serpent who has slain, out of jealousy, a woman's lover. The serpent is forced to confess this and his other, earlier evil deeds (from the days of Adam and Eve on) and dies. Later Thomas meets the colt of a she ass who, able to talk, identifies herself as of direct descent from Balaam's ass. At her bidding Thomas mounts her and rides to the city gate. As he humbly dismounts, to enter the city on foot, the ass drops dead. A lustful demon, who has long tormented a woman, is exorcised and departs in a cloud of fire and smoke. A young man, impressed by Thomas' preaching, murders his mistress because she will not agree to live in perfect continence. Later, as he eats the Eucharist, his hands wither. Thomas heals him and restores to life the murdered woman. After recounting her experiences while dead—she had been taken on a tour of hell, which she describes in great detail in words drawn from the Apocalypse of Peter—she, with many others, is converted and baptized.

Next a pious captain asks Thomas' help in curing his wife and daughter, long possessed by devils. Thomas sets out with the captain. Their horses fail. Four wild asses are summoned to draw the chariot in their stead. One of them, upon arrival at the captain's house, is endowed with speech and summons the devils, who are speedily banished and flee. Then the scene changes to another part of India, where the final event, replete with many details and ending with Thomas' martyrdom, takes place. It is in essence the same story, so common in all these apocryphal Acts. Mygdonia, the wife of a wealthy courtier, is converted to celibacy, despite the pathetic and moving pleas and finally the threats of her husband, who at last enlists the aid of the king, Misdaeus. But all, of course, to no avail. Not only is Mygdonia obdurate, but others, including the king's wife and son, are similarly converted. Finally, after Thomas has been several times warned and imprisoned, only to leave the prison whenever he desires through self-opening doors (all highly reminiscent of stories in the canonical Acts), the king attempts to torture him with plates of red-hot metal placed at his feet, only to find a flood rising from the plates, a flood which, had it not been for Thomas' gracious intervention, would actually have drowned him.

Finally Thomas is taken onto a mountain, is pierced by four spears, dies, and is nobly buried by his converts. Eventually the king too is converted, after his demon-ridden son has been cured by dust from Thomas' grave.

While extended sermons and other exhortations seem definitely subordinated to the somewhat light, flimsy, and at times clogged and slow-moving story, there are many mystic hymns and prayers replete with honorific titles. The most famous of these is the so-called Hymn of the Soul (chs. 108–13), which has received high praise by many critics through the years, even being styled the "most beautiful piece of literature produced by the early church." Nor is this any new discovery. Nicetas of Thessalonica in the eleventh century wrote an extended and enthusiastic paraphrase and commentary on it. The precise meaning of the poem is far from clear. The usual interpretation of it is that it is an allegory of the soul, which, of heavenly origin, is sent to earth to secure the pearl of price. Forgetful of its origin and mission, it is finally awakened by a revelation from on high, secures the pearl, and returns to heaven to don its former glorious heavenly robe, which—being his own strange counterpart—has wondrously grown with the growth of his own stature.

Not infrequently attempts have been made to interpret the hymn as a mystic portrayal of the Incarnation. Some have seen it as derived from the story of Joseph in Egypt and his coat of many colors. Whatever its precise purpose, it is manifestly not the composition of the author of the romance and is actually quite irrelevant in its context. Quite regardless of one's verdict regarding the book as a whole, all agree that the hymn was composed in Syriac and is older than its context. There seems little reason to question that it was inserted by the original author of the Acts, not later by an interpolator, into its present position—not that it was particularly apt, for it is not, but simply as a pretty decoration which had caught his fancy.

The writing, while devoid of historical value for the reconstruction of the life of Thomas, is not without value in its side lights on early Christian practices, especially in its detailed and vivid accounts of the way in which the Christian sacraments were at the time practiced: the anointing with oil before baptism, the subsequent immersion of the candidate, who had stripped naked save for a girdle; the immediately following Eucharist, with its elements, wine mixed with water, and bread signed with the cross. It also exhibits, as already remarked, a very wide, if superficial, knowledge of the content and phraseology of the canonical Testaments, both Old and New, but never suggests that they were employed or even possessed by the zealous missionaries, to say nothing of being used in services of worship.

For further details, including the large critical literature, see APOCRYPHA, NT.

Bibliography. A convenient English translation of the Greek text prepared by Bonnet, with constant attention to the variants in the Syriac version, is to be found in M. R. James, *The Apocryphal NT* (1924), pp. 364-439.   M. S. ENSLIN

THOMAS, APOCALYPSE OF.

One of the comparatively few apocalypses attributed to persons prominent in the NT. While condemned, along with the Apocalypse of Paul and the Apocalypse of Stephen, in the sixth century in the so-called Gelasian Decree, it remained but a name until the discovery in the early years of the twentieth century of what appears to have been its text, or portions of it, in two MSS—one of the eighth century, the other of the eleventh or twelfth—and a leaf of a fifth-century Vienna palimpsest.

Unlike the apocalypses of Peter and Paul, which are visions of the next world, this apocalypse is a prophecy of the end of this one, as revealed to Thomas by the Lord, who identifies himself as the "Son of God the Father . . . and the father of all spirits." In addition to a description of what actually appear to be contemporary events (in the guise of

prophecy in a style reminiscent of Daniel) is a series of the seven signs which will precede the ending of this world.

The writing was known in England in the ninth century and was apparently the source of the widely circulated "Fifteen Signs of the Last Days," commonly attributed to Jerome. From a clear reference to the deaths of Arcadius and Honorius, who died in A.D. 408 and 423 respectively, the apocalypse is commonly dated in the early fifth century. It was apparently written in Latin, although the possibility exists that a shorter version of it, as represented by the text of the later (eleventh-twelfth century) MS, may have been originally composed in Greek.

Bibliography. A translation of the portions of the text now available is given in M. R. James, *The Apocryphal NT* (1924), pp. 555-62. See also M. R. James, "Revelatio Thomae," *JTS,* 11 (1910), 228 ff; P. Bihlmeyer, "Un texte non interpolé de l'Apocalypse de Thomas," *Revue Bénédictine,* 28 (1911), 27-82.
    M. S. ENSLIN

*THOMAS, GOSPEL OF.

An early apocryphal, probably Gnostic, gospel, frequently referred to adversely by early Christian writers. The well-known infancy gospel of the same name may well be a drastically expurgated recension of this work.

The first to mention this gospel by name is Hippolytus (*Heresies* V.2), who says it was in use among the Naasenes, who found support in it for their view of the "nature of the inward man." He quotes from it: "He who seeks me will find me in children from seven years old; for there will I, who am hidden in the fourteenth aeon, be found." Origen (*Homily on Luke* 1) mentions without comment a gospel by this name as current. Eusebius (Hist. III.25.6) names it, along with the Gospel of Peter, as spurious. Cyril of Jerusalem (*Catechetical Instructions* V.36) ascribes it to the Manicheans, saying it was written "by one of those wicked disciples of Mani" and of a nature to corrupt the souls of the simple. According to the Stichometry of Nicephorus it contained 1,300 lines.

Irenaeus (Her. I.20.1), in his account of the Marcossians, states that they supported their doctrine by an unspeakably vast number of apocryphal writings, and refers to the story of the Lord, when a child, confounding his teacher by his esoteric knowledge of the nature of the letters of the alphabet. Since the story is found in our copies of the Gospel of Thomas, the apparent source of all subsequent infancy gospels, it has been often assumed that Irenaeus thus bears indirect testimony to its antiquity. All these references may well be to the same work, originally a Gnostic production and subsequently revised by the Manicheans. In what must be assumed to be its original form it has not come down to us. Among the MSS found in 1945 at Chenoboskion (see APOCRYPHA, NT) is one containing, along with other material, three writings: the Gospel According to Thomas, the Gospel According to Philip, and the Book of Thomas. It has been provisionally conjectured that this material may be a copy of the hitherto lost gospel, or at least may eventually throw light on the nature of this Gnostic gospel and on its relation to the collection of legendary stories of the infancy of Jesus long known to us under the same title.

This latter, the infancy gospel, is extant in two

Greek versions, a Latin version and a much-abbreviated Syriac revision from Greek, which carries with it the ascription to Thomas, described as "the Israelite, the philosopher," "the holy apostle," or simply "the Israelite" (variously "Ismaelite"). The Greek MSS are late, as are also the rather more abundant Latin. A Syriac MS is perhaps to be dated in the sixth century. In addition there is a Latin palimpsest, never published or even fully deciphered, of approximately the same age.

While the forms of the two Greek versions and the one Latin version exhibit many variations—one form of the Greek is much shorter than the other; the Latin has prefixed a short account of the flight to Egypt and a few of the miracles wrought there by the wonder child—they are plainly modifications of the same book: a compilation of stories of the superhuman power and wisdom of Jesus as an infant and small boy. Based upon nothing but unbridled imagination, they represent an early attempt to fill in the hidden years, which from the very beginning piqued the curiosity of readers of the canonical gospels, and to extend back into his infancy the superhuman powers which the more restrained canonical gospels ascribe to him as a man.

Jesus molds twelve little mud sparrows on the sabbath day, after gathering together into pools the water of a brook, and by clapping his hands causes them to fly away, to the amazement of Joseph and of a Jew who has chided him for profaning the sabbath. He withers the son of Annas the scribe, who has dispersed the water which Jesus had collected; causes a child who runs against him to drop dead; leaps down from the roof of a house and restores to life another child who has fallen off and whom Jesus has been accused of pushing; heals a workman's foot, cut by an ax; gathers water for Mary into his cloak (upon breaking the water jar); reaps a hundred measures of wheat from one kernel which he has sown; stretches out to the proper length a bed which Joseph has clumsily made too short; confounds his teacher, Zacchaeus, when the latter seeks to teach him the letters of the (Greek!) alphabet from Alpha to Omega (apparently the story to which Irenaeus referred). In the story of the twelve-year-old Jesus in the temple (which the longer Greek version repeats and which subsequent infancy gospels, notably the ARABIC GOSPEL OF THE INFANCY, greatly expand) the original nature of that tale—told with such restraint in Luke 2:41-51—is evident—namely, of the superhuman knowledge of the young child, who "put to silence the elders and teachers of the people." One and all, the stories depict an arrogant little wonder-worker, destitute of all save a high opinion of himself, the miraculous power to wreak vengeance on all who oppose him, and the ability to escape the consequences of his deeds.

This gospel, together with the Protevangelium of James (see JAMES, PROTEVANGELIUM OF), was used again and again by subsequent writers, and the contents of these two basic infancy gospels appear in even more garish form in such writings as the Gospel of Pseudo-Matthew, the Gospel of the Birth of Mary, the History of Joseph the Carpenter (see PSEUDO-MATTHEW, GOSPEL OF; MARY, GOSPEL OF THE BIRTH OF; JOSEPH THE CARPENTER, HISTORY

OF), and many others, both medieval and modern. To what extent this present mélange of wonder tales was a part of the earlier Gnostic Gospel of Thomas, to what extent interpolations and additions have crept in, is impossible to say. Save in the story of Jesus' esoteric knowledge of the nature of the letters, it is manifestly free from distinctive Gnostic speculation, while the longest of our recensions is less than half the length ascribed to its namesake in the traditional stichometry.

Attempts have been made to explain these stories as deliberately produced by orthodox Christians in opposition to the Gnostic heresy that it was not until baptism that the supernatural Christ descended upon Jesus and equipped him with miraculous power. It is not to be denied that these stories would provide a ready answer to such claims. Nevertheless, at our present stage of knowledge such speculation is at best uncertain, and it would seem possible to explain them more naturally as the forthright attempt to make explicit what seemed to be implied by the intriguing word of Luke: "The child grew and became strong, filled with wisdom; and the favor of God was upon him" (2:40; cf. vs. 52).

Bibliography. Texts of the apocryphon are available in C. Tischendorf, *Evangelia apocrypha* (2nd ed., 1876); P. Peeters, *Évangiles apocryphes* (1914), vol. II. An English translation is provided by M. R. James, *The Apocryphal NT* (1924), pp. 49-70. For further bibliography, *see* APOCRYPHA, NT.

M. S. ENSLIN

THOMOI. KJV Apoc. form of TEMAH.

THONG [אגדה, *in the phrase* אגדות מוטה, the thongs of the yoke (Isa. 58:6; KJV the heavy burdens); מוסר (KJV BOND); ἱμάς (KJV LATCHET *except in* Acts 22:25)]. A narrow strip of leather used as a cord or band for lashing a yoke (Isa. 58:6; Jer. 27:2); for tying prisoners (e.g., Paul in Acts 22:25); and, in early use, especially as the latchet or lace of a shoe (Mark 1:7 = Luke 3:16; John 1:27). Such strips were also used as instruments of flagellation. *See* WHIP.

H. F. BECK

THORN. See BRAMBLE; BRIER; FLORA § A12; THISTLE, THORN.

THORNS, CROWN OF. *See* CROWN OF THORNS.

THRACE thrās [Θρᾴκη]. In its early, definite meaning, Thrace was the area S of the River Danube; W of the Black Sea and Bosporus; N of the Propontis, Hellespont, Aegean Sea, and E Macedonia; and E of the River Strymon or, later, the Nestus. The Romans divided this region into two parts; that N of the Haemus Mountains was called Moesia, and the S area was called Thrace. After Roman control over Thrace had been growing for over two centuries, Claudius made it a province *ca.* A.D. 46. The Thracians, a fierce and warlike people, served many foreign rulers as mercenary soldiers. II Macc. 12:35 reports that a Thracian horseman helped Gorgias escape danger in a battle with Judas Maccabeus *ca.* 163 B.C.

Bibliography. Cambridge Ancient History, 10 (1934), 678-82; 11 (1936), 570-75. A. H. M. Jones, *The Cities of the Eastern Roman Provinces* (1937), ch. 1. F. V. FILSON

THRASEAS thrā sē'əs. KJV translation of Θρασαῖος, as the name of the father of Apollonius, in II Macc. 3:5. The RSV translates as a place name, TARSUS.

J. C. SWAIM

THREAD. See CLOTH.

THREE CHILDREN, SONG OF THE. See SONG OF THE THREE YOUNG MEN.

THREE DAYS. See THIRD DAY.

THREE TAVERNS [αἱ Τρεῖς Ταβέρναι]. A halting place on the road to Rome, through which Paul passed (Acts 28:15).

Three Taverns was thirty-three miles from Rome (*Corpus Inscriptionum Latinarum*, X.685), ten miles nearer the city than the Forum of Appius. Cicero mentions Three Taverns several times (*To Atticus* I.13; II.10, 13) and indicates (*To Atticus* II.12) that this was the place where the road to Antium intersected the Appian Way.

Bibliography. Philipp, "Tres Tabernae," *Pauly-Wissowa*, Zweite Reihe, IV, ii (1932), col. 1875.   J. FINEGAN

THRESHING. The separating of the kernels of grain from the straw. The stalks were laid out on a threshing floor, a flat surface of rock or pounded earth located in an open place exposed to the wind. The floor was usually at the edge or gate (I Kings 22:10) of the village or town and was owned either communally or privately (II Sam. 24:16 ff).

Several different methods of threshing were used. When there was a small quantity, the stalks were beaten with a stick or flail (Judg. 6:11). At other times animals were driven around over the grain, trampling it with their feet (Deut. 25:4).

More commonly, however, some kind of machine was used. One of these (עֲגָלָה, "cart") was a frame with rollers into which were fastened sharp stones or pieces of metal (Isa. 28:27-28). Another machine (מוֹרַג, "threshing sledge")* was made of planks turned up a little at the front with sharp stones or pieces of metal fixed into holes bored in the bottom (II Sam.

Courtesy of Herbert G. May

60. Palestinian threshing scene

24:22; I Chr. 21:23; Isa. 41:15). These machines were pulled by animals around and around over the grain. The vehicles might be weighted with stones or by the driver to make them more effective. Today in Palestine it is a common sight to see two or three children sitting on a sledge, enjoying the ride. The stalks are constantly turned over and the process goes on for several hours, depending on the amount to be threshed, until all the kernels can be seen to be separated from the stalks. Figs. SLE 67; THR 60.

The term חָרוּץ (Job 41:30; Isa. 28:27) also refers to some kind of threshing instrument made with iron (Amos 1:3) and perhaps a sledge in type.

Bibliography. K. Galling, *Biblisches Reallexikon* (1937), pp. 137-39; G. E. Wright, *Biblical Archaeology* (1957), p. 182.

H. N. RICHARDSON

***THRESHOLD** [סַף (KJV *alternately* DOOR, GATE); מִפְתָּן]. A word used for several kinds of entrances; usually a sacred place.

There is no doubt that in I Kings 14:17 סַף means the door of Jeroboam's house or the entrance to the women's quarters, and in Esth. 2:21; 6:2 it is also used of the royal palace. Similarly in Ezek. 43:8 "their threshold" is mentioned along with "my threshold."

In Judg. 19:27 the threshold of a house is meant (but the slain woman's hands were on the threshold; this was probably an accidental position).

Other references are to the temple. Certain priests were keepers of the threshold (II Kings 12:9; Ps. 84: 10 — H 84:11), and sometimes three are specially mentioned (II Kings 25:18=Jer. 52:24). Presumably the three principal entrances to the temple are intended. In II Chr. 34:9 these priests are named Levites. The word is found in the plural in a number of passages relating to the temple (I Chr. 9:19, 22: keepers of thresholds; II Chr. 3:7; Isa. 6:4; Amos 9: 1: Bethel [?]). It is not always clear whether the thresholds of the gates to the temple court or whether the temple thresholds are intended.

מִפְתָּן is used of Dagon's temple at Ashdod (I Sam. 5:4-5); of one of the resting places of Yahweh's glory (Ezek. 9:3; 10:4); of the place where Ezekiel's prince is to render him worship (46:2), and of the temple threshold from which the life-giving waters are to flow to fertilize the Arabah.

Leaping over the threshold is condemned in Zeph. 1:9 as an idolatrous custom, and this same custom is said to have arisen among the Philistines at Ashdod. Dagon's members rested on the threshold, so thereafter his worshipers leapt over the threshold. Cf. "pass over the door" in Exod. 12:23, and the bearing of this on the meaning of the Passover.

"Threshold" in the OT thus most often designates a sacred place, and sacrifices at foundations and doors confirm this.

See also DOOR; FOUNDATION; PASSOVER; TEMPLE, JERUSALEM.

Bibliography. H. C. Trumbull, *The Blood Covenant* (1887); *The Threshold Covenant* (1896).   G. HENTON DAVIES

THRONE [כִּסֵּא, כִּסֶּה; Aram. כָּרְסֵא; βῆμα, *properly* judgment seat; θρόνος]. The ceremonial chair of a king, so closely connected with the royal office that it becomes symbolic of kingship in all its aspects; associated also with God as supreme king and with the Messiah as his vice-regent. See KING.

Fundamentally כִּסֵּא is a seat of honor for any distinguished person: a governor (Neh. 3:7; lit., "to the seat of the governor," interpreted "under the jurisdiction of the governor"), a priest (I Sam. 4:13, 18, KJV; RSV "seat"), or a favored guest (II Kings 4:

10; "chair"; KJV "stool"). English translations normally do not use the word "throne" in these instances, but reserve it for the ceremonial chair of a king from which, equipped with the other symbols of his office, he discharges his duties. Fig. SEN 41.

The thrones of many foreign kings are mentioned in the OT (e.g., Exod. 11:5; Jer. 43:10; Jonah 3:6), but attention naturally centers on the Hebrew throne, and particularly on the throne of David, which was established by divine covenant. The description of Solomon's throne in I Kings 10:18-20, combined with representations of thrones found on ancient monuments, gives us an idea of the physical appearance of the Hebrew throne. Like Darius' throne, pictured on a relief from Persepolis,* Solomon's throne is a high-backed chair; but, unlike the Persian model, it has wide arm rests, exactly as shown on the sarcophagus of Ahiram, king of Byblos in Phoenicia (*ca.* 1000 B.C.), and on an ivory from Megiddo (Figs. GEB 15; ART 70). In both cases the lions have wings extended backward in the attitude of flight, and are, therefore, cherubim of a well-known type (*see* CHERUB). The lions on the Israelite throne were probably of the same kind. On the back of the throne was a carved bull's head, the ancient symbol of strength. Four such heads adorn the corners of a backless throne on a stele from Samal (Zinjirli). Although not mentioned in the description in I Kings, a FOOTSTOOL was an indispensable part of the throne (Isa. 66:1). Ivory inlay carved in animal or human shapes or in intricate geometric designs, and gold leaf into which similar designs were hammered (*repoussé*), increased the splendor of the throne, which was set on a dais reached by a flight of six steps, each with two standing lion figures, resembling the avenues of sphinxes common in ancient art. Fig. DAR 4.

God's throne was early represented by the ARK OF THE COVENANT. The divine throne could be seen in prophetic or apocalyptic visions (Isa. 6:1-3; Ezek. 1:4-28; Dan. 7:9-10; Rev. 4). Ezekiel describes it as made of lapis lazuli and set on a hemisphere of transparent crystal (Ezek. 1:26). The cherubim associated with the royal throne appear around Yahweh's throne as well, either supporting it (Ezek. 1:22) or flying around it (Isa. 6:2). In Daniel's vision (7:9) the divine throne is composed of flames, while in Revelation it stands in heaven, flanked by the twenty-four thrones of the elders, with an emerald rainbow around it, seven torches and a crystal sea in front, and four living creatures on each side. God's throne is spiritualized in a variety of ways in the Bible. Usually it is heaven, or *is* heaven (Ps. 11:4; Isa. 66:1; Matt. 5:34), but occasionally Jerusalem (Jer. 3:17), the temple (Ezek. 43:7), or the nation (Jer. 14:21) may be called the throne of God.

By metonymy "throne" represents royalty in all its aspects, and often specifies the king's function as judge (Ps. 122:5). Both Yahweh's throne and David's are seats of judgment (Ps. 9:4—H 9:5; Isa. 16:5), and the usage is continued in the NT, where the apostles and the Messiah will sit on thrones to judge the world (Matt. 25:31; Luke 22:30). The everlasting and divine throne of David (II Sam. 7:16; Ps. 45:6—H 45:7) gives rise to the concept of the Messiah's throne, rare in the OT (Isa. 9:7—H 9:6; Jer. 17:25) but frequent in the NT, where Christ is represented

as heir of the line of David (Luke 1:32; Acts 2:30).

Bibliography. K. Galling, *Biblisches Reallexikon* (1937), p. 520. *See also* the bibliography under KING.   L. E. TOOMBS

THUMMIM. *See* URIM AND THUMMIM.

THUNDER, SONS OF. *See* BOANERGES.

THUNDER AND LIGHTNING [רעם (Job 26:14; Ps. 77:18—H 77:19; Isa. 29:6; etc.), βροντή (Mark 3:17; John 12:29; etc.), thunder; קול, noise of thunder (Ps. 104:7), voice (Deut. 4:12); φωνή (Rev. 14:2), sound; ברק (Exod. 19:16; Jer. 10:13; etc.), ἀστραπή (Matt. 24:27; 28:3; etc.), lightning; אור (Job 36:32; 37:3, 11, 15), φῶς (Acts 9:3), light; אש, fire (Exod. 9:23), fire of Yahweh (I Kings 18:38); לפדים, *lit.,* torches (Exod. 20:18), lightnings; להבות אש (Ps. 29:7), flames of fire]. A familiar but awe-inspiring and sometimes dangerous natural phenomenon, often interpreted in the Bible as a visible manifestation of divine power. Electrical storms occur in Palestine and the adjacent deserts, especially in the spring and autumn months, when moist air from the sea is heated and forces its way rapidly upward into the cold upper air.

A cumulo-nimbus or thundercloud is, in effect, an atmospheric explosion in slow motion. Strong electrical charges are built up by friction of raindrops and ice particles, carried by the violent updrafts of warm air and downdrafts of cold air within the cloud. Two thirds of the ensuing discharges of lightning take place within the cloud itself or between clouds. The flashing discharges between the cloud and the ground release tremendous energy. Objects which are struck are shattered or set on fire, unless they are good conductors of electricity. Thunder is the noise of air exploding in the intense heat of the lightning's path.

The glitter and flash of the lightning (Ps. 144:6; Ezek. 21:10—H 21:15), its sudden illumination of the earth (Matt. 24:27), its darting movement (Nah. 2:4 —H 2:5), its spectacular fall to earth (Luke 10:18), its striking a target (Job 36:32), and the crash (Ps. 29:8) and reverberation (Isa. 6:4[?]; 29:6) of the thunder—all these are among the vivid impressions of the biblical writers. The lightning is the sword (Deut. 32:41), the spear and the arrows (Hab. 3:11), of Yahweh. Thunder is his voice, both figuratively and literally (Deut. 5:22; Ps. 29:3-9; Ecclus. 45:5; John 12:28-29). The awful majesty and power of the thunderstorm suggest a theophany (Exod. 19:16-20; Ps. 18:7-15—H 18:8-16; Hab. 3:4-15). Hence thunder and lightning become part of the imagery in descriptions of the heavenly throne (Ezek. 1:4-28; Enoch 14:8-22; Rev. 4:5). The storm displays Yahweh's control of natural forces (Job 28:26; Jer. 10: 13). It is the instrument of his power (Ps. 104:4), especially in the chastisement of his enemies (Deut. 32:41; Rev. 16:18). In Judg. 5:4-5; Hab. 3:3 it is perhaps not accidental that the thunderstorm comes from the direction of Edom, since such storms do come to Palestine from a southerly direction when low pressure is centered over Abyssinia.

R. B. Y. SCOTT

THUT-MOSE thŭt′mōs [Egyp. *dḥwty-ms,* (the moon-god) Thoth is born]. A name borne by four pharaohs of the Eighteenth Dynasty, including Thutmose III, founder of Egypt's Asiatic empire. *See* EGYPT § 2.

THYATIRA thī′ə tī′rə [Θυάτειρα]. A city in W Asia Minor. It was near the S bank of the Lycus River, and on the road between Pergamum on the NW and Sardis on the S-SE. It lay in the N part of ancient Lydia; at times, however, it was considered to be in the southernmost part of Mysia.

Little is known of the early history of Thyatira. The city grew in importance when, at the beginning of the third century B.C., Seleucus Nicator refounded it and, as it appears, settled a group of Macedonian soldiers there. It was never a great city, but it was the chief city of the Lycus Valley and developed profitable industries and trade. Inscriptions show that there were at Thyatira numerous trade guilds, including coppersmiths, tanners, leatherworkers, dyers, woolworkers, and linenworkers. Such guilds must have played a prominent part in the political, economic, social, and religious life of the city.

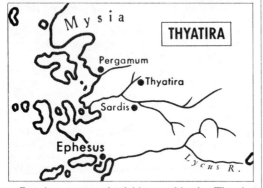

Prominent among the deities worshiped at Thyatira were Tyrimnos, who became identified with Apollo the sun-god, and Boreitene, a goddess identified with Artemis. It is possible that the references to the Son of God with "eyes like a flame of fire" and feet "like burnished bronze" are a conscious reference to the claims of the sun-god at Thyatira (Rev. 2:18). Under the Roman Empire the worship of Apollo Tyrimnaios was joined with the emperor-worship cult. Another religious cult at Thyatira was that of the Sibyl Sambathe or Sambethe, whose shrine was situated "before" rather than in the city. The theory that the woman called Jezebel in Rev. 2:20 was a priestess at this shrine can hardly be true, since Jezebel was evidently tolerated by the church at Thyatira as a member and was accepted by a minority of these Christians as a prophetess.

It is highly probable that there was a Jewish settlement at Thyatira. Acts 16:14 supports this conclusion. When at Philippi, Paul, Silas, and Timothy, seeking on the sabbath the Jewish place of prayer, came "to the riverside" "outside the gate," they found a group of "women who had come together," and among them was "Lydia, from the city of Thyatira." She was there as a "seller of purple goods" made in Thyatira, and she was a "worshiper of God," a Gentile who had been drawn to Judaism, probably through contact with Jews at Thyatira, but

who had not become a proselyte. The "purple" of the cloth or garments she was selling was probably the color known as "Turkey red," made with madder root for use by the guild of dyers at Thyatira.

It is not clear when or by whom the Christian gospel was first preached in that city. One possibility, suggested by Acts 19:10, is that during Paul's ministry at Ephesus one or more of his helpers or converts went to Thyatira and founded the church there; this hypothesis is far from certain. What is clear is that when the book of Revelation was written, *ca.* A.D. 95, there was a rather strong church in Thyatira (Rev. 2:18-29), with a commendable record of "love and faith and service and patient endurance," and with a history of growth in which the church's "latter works exceed the first." At the time of this report, however, the church was seriously threatened. A part of the church, apparently a minority, were following a woman symbolically described (with a reminder of I Kings 16:31 ff) as Jezebel. She was a member of the church and claimed to be a prophetess, and some of the Christians accepted her claim. She taught and led them "to practice immorality and to eat food sacrificed to idols." Though given time to "repent of her immorality," she had refused to do so, and she continued to lead others to "commit adultery with her." The rest of the church was tolerating her activities.

Three interpretations may be given to these scathing words:

a) The writer may be denouncing a teaching that physical indulgence has no effect on Christian faith (cf. Acts 15:29). On this false view, sexual libertinism and eating food offered to idols do not affect the Christian's faith or standing with God.

b) Since in the OT idolatry and worship of other gods is described as "fornication," and since wild feasting and sexual orgies were part of some pagan cults, the writer may be denouncing a laxity in which physical indulgence occurs during active participation in such pagan religions.

c) The "Jezebel" at Thyatira may have been promoting a sophisticated tolerance toward the many guilds of the city. Every such guild had its patron god, its feasts, its social occasions which could at times become immoral revels. "Jezebel" may have argued that these patron deities need not be taken seriously and these revels need not be condemned, since every workman, to make a living, had to join a guild, and he could take its religious rites lightly

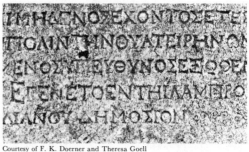

Courtesy of F. K. Doerner and Theresa Goell

61. A Greek inscription on a sarcophagus on the acropolis containing the name "Thyatira"

and would learn to know the realities of life if he shared in the revels and so by actual experience learned the "deep things of Satan."

The problem was not confined to Thyatira. It was found at Ephesus and Pergamum (Rev. 2:6, 14-15). So it cannot be explained simply by the presence in Thyatira of numerous guilds. Libertinism was a threat to Christian faith encountered by Paul and continually in later decades. The pagan world usually lacked a clear sense of monotheism and of the indissoluble tie between faith and moral living. At times it defended itself by a dualism which excused all physical indulgence as unrelated to spiritual life. It was hard for a small minority movement such as the Thyatira church to be cut off from the friendships and social life that assumed the legitimacy of polytheism and undisciplined physical indulgence. But the Christian faith was at stake in this decision, and the writer of Revelation pointed to the necessity of breaking with polytheistic and immoral practices. Fig. THY 61.

Bibliography. W. M. Ramsay, *The Letters to the Seven Churches of Asia* (no date), chs. 23-24; A. H. M. Jones, *Cities of the Eastern Roman Provinces* (1937), pp. 44-45, 54-55, 83-85.

F. V. FILSON

THYINE WOOD thī'ĭn. KJV translation of ξύλον θύϊνον (RSV SCENTED WOOD).

TIAMAT tĭ ä'mät [Akkad. *ti'amtu, Ti-'amat; tamtu, tamdu,* sea, ocean]. The goddess of the DEEP; consort of Apsu; mother of the gods of the Babylonian pantheon (Enuma Eliš, Tablet I:4 *passim*). A. Heidel (*see bibliography*) claims that Ti-'amat and תהום go back to a common Semitic form. She was a female dragon (*ANEP* 523, 670, 691; *see bibliography*) or a woman (*see bibliography*). Mummu (Tablet I:4) is an epithet (parallel to Mother Hubur, I:132?) of Ti-'amat (*ANET* 61), or a separate deity, the first-born son of Ti-'amat and Apsu. *See bibliography.*

Bibliography. On Tiamat as a female dragon, see A. Jeremias, *The OT in the Light of the Ancient East* (1911), vol. I, figs. 53-57. A. Heidel, *The Babylonian Genesis* (1942), pp. 98-101 (on Tiamat as a woman, see pp. 83-88); "The Meaning of 'Mummu' in Accadian Literature," *JNES,* VII (1948), 98-105.

J. J. JACKSON

TIBERIAS tī bĭr'ĭ əs [Τιβεριάς]. A leading city on the W coast of the Sea of Galilee. The name is still preserved for the modern town on this site, Tabariyeh. Figs. TIB 62; GAL 4.

Courtesy of the Israel Office of Information, New York

62. Sea of Galilee with town of Tiberias in the background

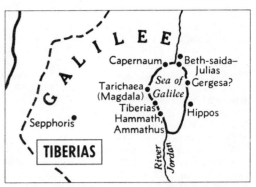

1. The site. This city was built by the tetrarch Herod Antipas *ca.* A.D. 25 to serve as the capital of his tetrarchy of Galilee and Perea, succeeding Sepphoris, which he also had built for a capital in 4 B.C. Tiberias was more conveniently located for reaching both districts of his rule. It was also at a focal point in the system of roads, both locally and internationally. It was named to honor Tiberius Caesar (A.D. 14-37), and its importance soon extended the name also to the lake (John 6:1; 21:1).

As the site of his city, Antipas chose a natural acropolis overlooking the activity around the Sea of Galilee (*see* GALILEE, SEA OF). This was on the W coast, S of centrally located Magdala (el-Mejdel), where the coastline curves inward, *ca.* five miles N of the outlet. It had a magnificent panorama. Magdala-Tarichaea was easily observed two miles N, and Capernaum lay less than five miles N across the arc of the lake. Somewhat farther and at different points of the compass a direct line of five or six miles across the lake would reach Bethsaida, Gergesa, and Hippos. The city itself included the palace on the acropolis, the castle at the N, and a narrow, rectangular town between rock and lake. Although open to the sea, on the land side it was walled round.

When the city was under construction, the workmen came upon a necropolis, which had the result of banning all Jews for fear of contamination by a corpse. Josephus relates that the population was heterogeneous, composed of both foreigners and Galileans, high and low, the poor and the newly freed, many of them settled here by force or under the inducement of a house and land (Jos. Antiq. XVIII.ii.3).

It must be remembered that the site is almost seven hundred feet below sea level, and lies inside a great bowl of mountains. Consequently, its climate is semitropical, humid and oppressive. Tiberias especially is blocked off from the W breeze, and affected also by the steaming sulphurous springs about it. These warm baths were really in a suburb to the S, called Ammathus (θερμά) by Josephus (War IV.i.3) and identified with the old fortified city of Hammath in Josh. 19:35. It was this ancient town whose cemetery was disturbed.

2. History. Tiberias was governed by a Council of six hundred with an Archon and a "Committee of Ten" (Jos. War II.xxi.3-9). Its population was Gentile, which may be the chief reason Jesus never visited this new city. There is only one reference to the city of Tiberias in the NT, where it is reported that following the episode of feeding a multitude somewhere on the E coast (the disciples and Jesus having already departed) some small Tiberian boats appeared at this isolated beach, in which the people embarked to follow on to Capernaum (John 6:23). Many of the Gentile residents held Jewish sympathies when revolt broke out here against the Romans in A.D. 65. Josephus destroyed the palace on the acropolis and proceeded to strengthen the defenses of the city. Unfortunately, Tiberias became involved in the feud between John of Gischala and Josephus; and when Vespasian laid siege to the towns of Tarichaea and Tiberias in 67, the latter opened its gates and capitulated. Tiberias had remained under the rule of Antipas and Agrippa I until 44, when the Romans set a procurator over Galilee. But in 59 Nero was disposed to present Agrippa II, now puppet king E of the Jordan, with the Galilean towns of Tiberias and Tarichaea as well as Bethsaida-Julias with fourteen villages. Thus Tiberias remained under Jewish rule until 100, though no longer a capital.

After the fall of Jerusalem in 135, Tiberias became a strong Jewish center and was recognized as one of four sacred cities in Palestine. The Sanhedrin was moved from Sepphoris to Tiberias in *ca.* 150, and schools of rabbinic study were established. When the Talmud (Ber. 8*a*, 30*b*) reports thirteen synagogues in Tiberias, this can apply only to this later flourishing of a Jewish metropolis. The Palestinian Talmud and the Tiberian vowel-pointing were here developed, and it is noteworthy that later Maimonides was entombed here. Once again in the twelfth century Tiberias was involved in the conflict between Saladin and the Crusaders. A few miles to the W, S of the Horns of Hattin, Saladin won his historic victory in 1187. The city and the larger area about it have suffered repeated earthquakes—e.g., in 1759 and 1837. After the First World War, British troops took Tiberias in October, 1918. When the British mandate ended in 1948, modern Tabariyeh was allotted by the United Nations to the new state of Israel.

Bibliography. E. Robinson, *Biblical Researches in Palestine* (1867), II, 368-87; E. Schürer, *History of the Jewish People in the Time of Jesus Christ* (1901), div. 2, vol. I, pp. 143-47; G. A. Smith, *Historical Geography of the Holy Land* (1931), pp. 448-51.

K. W. CLARK

TIBERIAS, SEA OF. *See* GALILEE, SEA OF.

TIBERIUS tī bîr′ĭ əs. Tiberius Claudius Caesar Augustus, the successor of AUGUSTUS as Roman emperor. He was born in 42 B.C. to noble parents, who were soon afterward divorced so that his mother, Livia, could marry Octavian (Augustus). From his twenty-third to his fifty-fourth year Tiberius was occupied with military affairs along the E and N frontiers of the Empire, except for an eight-year interval (6 B.C.–A.D. 2) when, out of favor with Augustus, he lived in Rhodes. In 12, Augustus had forced him to divorce his wife and marry the emperor's daughter Julia, in order to produce an heir to the throne. Julia's scandalous behavior led Augustus to banish her, in 2 B.C., and the subsequent deaths of two of her sons by a previous marriage meant that Tiberius had to be adopted by the emperor as his heir (A.D. 4); the Senate gave him

tribunician power and proconsular authority. When Augustus died, the Senate decided to name Tiberius emperor (September 17, A.D. 14). The Gospel of Luke dates the beginning of Jesus' ministry in the fifteenth year of Tiberius' reign (Luke 3:1).

His reign was conservative rather than innovating; he intended to preserve what Augustus had left, rather than to increase it. By severely limiting expenses he was able to leave an estate of two billion sesterces. Because of his advanced age there was almost constant intrigue concerning the succession; a leading part was played by the praetorian prefect Sejanus, who in 27 persuaded the emperor to live in seclusion on Capri. Sejanus, according to Philo a militant anti-Semite, was presumably responsible for the appointment of Pontius Pilate as procurator of Judea. When he became consul in 31, he apparently planned to have Tiberius deposed, but from Capri the emperor informed the Senate of the conspiracy, and Sejanus was executed.

Throughout Tiberius' reign there were trials for sedition and treason; some cases were genuine, while others seem to have been trumped up. Tiberius refused to accept divine honors in Italy, though even at Rome sacrifices were offered to his Genius, and in the E provinces worship was given him. On the other hand, he encouraged the worship of Augustus as a focal point of loyalty to the state. Like Augustus, he was unenthusiastic about foreign cults. Probably at the beginning of his reign, he forbade the practice of Druidism throughout the Empire. After a scandal at the temple of Isis in 19, involving Romans of high rank, the temple was destroyed, and the priests were crucified. About the same time, after a few Jews had defrauded a Roman matron, Tiberius forbade the observance of the Jewish law in Italy, and many Jews were deported.

Tiberius died, almost insane, on Capri on March 16, 37. His successor, Augustus' great-grandson, was hailed by the people with relief. The question of deifying Tiberius was raised by Caligula, but the Senate withheld approval (*see* EMPEROR-WORSHIP). Contemporary historians (Velleius Paterculus, Valerius Maximus) are quite favorable toward the emperor, perhaps out of necessity; later senatorial historians (Tacitus, Suetonius, Dio Cassius) are extremely hostile. To paint his character either white or black does injustice to the sources; and it must be remembered that Tacitus is a master of subtle vilification.

In the gospels he is named once (Luke 3:1), and the references to "Caesar" in the gospels allude to him (Matt. 22:17-21; Mark 12:14-17; Luke 20:22-25, 23:2; John 19:12-15). The denarius, or "tribute penny," to which the Synoptic gospels refer probably bore his portrait and the inscription TI.CAESAR. DIVI.AUG.F.AUGUSTUS ("Tiberius Caesar, son of the divine Augustus, Augustus").

Bibliography. F. B. Marsh, *The Reign of Tiberius* (1931). R. S. Rogers, *Criminal Trials and Criminal Legislation under Tiberius* (1935); *Studies in the Reign of Tiberius* (1943).

R. M. GRANT

TIBHATH tĭb′hăth [תבחת]. A town mentioned in I Chr. 18:8. In II Sam. 8:8 we find the reading בטח, which should probably be read טבח. *See* BETHER.

TIBNI tĭb′nī [תבני, *probably originally* Tabni] (I Kings 16:21-22). One of the three ninth-century commanders who fought for the throne of the kingdom of Israel after the fall of Baasha's short-lived dynasty. A three-year civil war with Omri, following Omri's defeat of Zimri, ended with Tibni's death and Omri's ascent of the throne.   J. M. WARD

TIDAL tī′dəl [תדעל; LXX θαργαλ; Genesis Apocryphon תרעל; Jubilees Têrgâl; Syr. תרעיל; Vulg. *Thadal*] (Gen. 14:1, 9). An ally of Chedorlaomer. Neither his name nor his country has been identified with certainty (for the latter, *see* GOIIM). In respect to form, "Tidal" is usually compared with "Tud'alia" (or "Tudḫalias"), a name borne by several Hittite kings. In respect to date, Tudḫalias I (*ca.* 1700-1650 B.C.?) best fits other historical allusions in Gen. 14: 1-12 (*see* ABRAHAM). Nevertheless, the identification remains uncertain.

Bibliography. R. de Vaux, "Les patriarches hébreux et les découvertes modernes, I," *RB*, LV (1948), 331-34; F. M. T. Böhl, "King Hammurabi of Babylon," *Opera Minora* (1953), pp. 352-53.   L. HICKS

TIGLATH-PILESER (III) tĭg′lăth pĭ lē′zər, —pī— [תגלת פלסר; Akkad. *Tukulti-apil-Ešarra*, my trust is (in) the son of (the temple) Ešarra] (II Kings 16:7). Alternately: TILGATH-PILNESER tĭl′găth pĭl nē′zər [תלגת פלנאסר] (I Chr. 5:6; II Chr. 28:20). King of Assyria and, under the name Pul, king of Babylonia (745-727 B.C.); son of Adad-nirari III; father of Shalmaneser V.

Tiglath-pileser III's accession to the throne of Assyria, either as a descendant of a collateral royal line or as a usurper, ended a period of political and military weakness in Assyrian history which had begun with Adad-nirari III (810-782). By means of systematic large-scale transplantations of subjected peoples and by a change from the policy of keeping up independent tribute-paying rulers at the frontiers of the Empire to one of complete annexation under the rule of an Assyrian official, he succeeded in creating the basis for the Assyrian Empire as it was maintained, defended, and extended by the kings of his family, the so-called Sargonides.

The containment of the kingdom of Urartu, which not only threatened Assyrian domination in the mountain regions but also extended its political influence into Upper Syria by supporting the ever-rebellious kings there, was the main goal of Tiglath-pileser III's military policy. His signal successes against Syria, highlighted by the fall of Damascus (732), were possible only after a series of campaigns (744, against Sarduris; 739, 736, siege of Turushpa) had forced the rulers of Urartu to relinquish their political aspirations beyond the borders of their country. Against Babylonia—i.e., against the unruly large tribes of the Arameans and Chaldeans—Tiglath-pileser was able to secure for himself the allegiance of the great cities. After the death of King Nabu-nasir of Babylon (734), he had to interfere and eventually to resort to the expedient of making himself king of that city. This he did under the rare Assyrian name of Pūlu (729-728).

Tiglath-pileser's first campaign was into the region to the E of the Tigris, where he built a fortress; then he turned N against Urartu and dispatched a general to penetrate even farther N, deep into the region of the Medes. The next year he won a battle in Commagene against an alliance of Urarteans under Sarduris and various rulers of Upper Syria. This victory brought Urartean influence in that region to an end, and Tiglath-pileser could use the next years (742-740) to lay siege to and eventually conquer Arpad, in N Syria. The effect of this victory was far-reaching (cf. II Kings 19:13 = Isa. 37:13); and tribute came in from Tyre, Damascus, Cilicia, Carchemish, etc. After having thus demonstrated the military power of Assyria, Tiglath-pileser turned toward the N but was again compelled to move against Syria, fighting and defeating an alliance of its kings. The threat posed against Damascus and Israel was considered rather serious there (I Kings 15:19), and the Assyrian inscriptions mention the tribute of Menahem of Samaria and Rezon of Damascus in a long list of such items, which even includes that of Zabibi queen of the Arabs. The region of Hamath was definitely pacified by the deportation of more than thirty thousand inhabitants to the mountains of Nairi. After a series of attacks against Urartu, which restrained the enemy but failed to achieve any signal victory, Tiglath-pileser had to turn his attention once more toward Syria, where Damascus was becoming increasingly powerful, mainly as a rallying point of all the anti-Assyrian forces of the Levant. Tiglath-pileser acted in his characteristic indirect way; instead of attacking Damascus, he advanced along the coast, accepting the submission of the Phoenician towns; but he had to conquer Gaza, whose king fled to Egypt. Ahaz of Judah turned to Tiglath-pileser for help against Pekah of Israel and his ally Rezon of Damascus. Pekah surrendered quickly, thus saving Samaria from destruction (II Kings 15:29). Consequently Rezon had to meet Tiglath-pileser without an ally. The fall of Damascus in 732 turned the entire region to Tiglath-pileser. When Pekah was murdered, the new king of Israel, Hoshea, paid tribute, and so did the kings of Ashkalon, Tyre, etc.

63. Tiglath-pileser III, from Nimrud

From *Atlas of the Bible* (Thomas Nelson & Sons Limited)

64. Inhabitants of a conquered city being deported; from a bas relief from the palace of Tiglath-pileser at Calah

From *Atlas of the Bible* (Thomas Nelson & Sons Limited)

65. The Tigris River emerging from the mountains near Ibn 'Omar

Damascus ceased to be a political power, after having withstood Assyria ever since the time of Shalmaneser III.

The death of the king of Babylon, Nabunasir, in 734, caused civil war to break out in Babylonia; and Tiglath-pileser had to fight, without much success (731), with the large Chaldean tribe Bit-Amukkani; while other tribal kings, among them Merodach-baladan, paid homage to the Assyrian king. In 729, Tiglath-pileser made himself king of Babylon and remained so until his death, in spite of an insurrection in that region. In Calah, Tiglath-pileser built himself a palace, the first to be constructed in a new style introduced from Syria. Historically most important was his extension of Assyrian administration into Syria and Palestine, which was bound to cause deep concern to Egypt once that country was able to afford a more aggressive foreign policy. Thus the conflict with Egypt began to shape up as a potential danger, and Esarhaddon and Ashurbanipal had to accept the military consequences and to attack Egypt. In Babylonia, Tiglath-pileser inaugurated the policy of siding with the cities against the unruly tribal kinglets, adhering thus in principle to the attitudes of Shalmaneser III and Adad-nirari III.

Figs. TIG 63-64.   A. L. Oppenheim

TIGRIS tī'grĭs [Τίγρις, *from* Old Pers. *Tigra*, *from* Assyrian-Babylonian *Idiglat*/*Idignat*, *also the source of* חדקל, HIDDEKEL hĭd'ə kĕl; *earliest form* Sumer. *Idigna*]. A major river in Western Asia. According to biblical tradition the Tigris was one of the branches into which the river issuing from the Garden of Eden divided: "Hiddekel, which flows east of Assyria" (Gen. 2:14). According to the book of Daniel, that prophet had his major vision on the bank of the Tigris (Dan. 10:4).

The Tigris originates in Armenia in the region NW of Diyarbekir and flows in a southeasterly direction, passing in its course Mosul, Tekrit, Samarra, Baghdad, Kur-el-Amara, and Amara, until, N of Basra, it joins with the Euphrates to form the Shatt-el-Arab, which empties into the Persian Gulf. Major tributaries are the Upper and Lower Zab, the Adheim, and the Diyala, which all join the Tigris from the E at points on the stretch from Mosul to Baghdad. S of Amara it receives the Kerkhah. The Tigris

is navigable up to Mosul, and a considerable body of river traffic moved on it in antiquity. Many important ancient cities were situated on the Tigris. On the E bank opposite Mosul are the ruins of ancient Nineveh, capital of Assyria during the time of the Assyrian Empire. Farther S, on the W bank, lies Qal'at Shergat, site of ancient Asshur, the original capital of Assyria and center of the cult of the national god Asshur. Still farther S, in the region of Baghdad, lay Opis, which became an important commercial center in Neo-Babylonian and later periods. At Sulman Pak on the E bank stood Ctesiphon, capital of the Parthians and Sassanians; and across the river from it, at Tel Umar, are the ruins of Seleucia, capital of the Seleucid rulers of Mesopotamia.

Fig. TIG 65.   T. Jacobsen

TIKVAH tĭk'və [תקוה, hope; Apoc. Θεκουέ]; KJV Apoc. THEOCANUS thē ŏk'ə nəs. Alternately: TOKHATH tŏk'hăth [תוקהת] (II Chr. 34:22). **1.** The father-in-law of Huldah the prophetess under King Josiah (II Kings 22:14; II Chr. 34:22).

2. The father of the Jahzeiah who opposed the plan for dealing with those with foreign wives (Ezra 10:15; I Esd. 9:14).   J. M. Ward

TILE [לבנה; κέραμος]. KJV form of BRICK in Ezek. 4:1. Also, Luke 5:19 refers to tiles on a ROOF, through which the palsied man was let down. This is the only reference to a tiled roof in the Bible. In the parallel account in Mark 2:4 the roof was broken up.   O. R. Sellers

TILGATH-PILNESER. Alternate form of TIGLATH-PILESER.

TILON tī'lən [תילון] (I Chr. 4:20). A family or clan of the tribe of Judah.

TIMAEUS tĭ mē'əs [Τιμαῖος] (Mark 10:46). The father of blind BARTIMAEUS the beggar.

TIMBER. *See* WOOD.

TIMBREL. *See* MUSICAL INSTRUMENTS.

TIME. The biblical conceptions of time and their terminology can be adequately understood only if one takes care not to assume unconsciously our modern Western scientific or philosophical interpretation of time in the Bible or to carry it over into the Bible. This will be made clear at the beginning by two examples:

a) We usually conceive of time as an abstract dimension, as a frame within which events take place. In this we were influenced, in the last analysis, by Greek thought. The OT, and also the NT, does not know this abstract phenomenon "time" as an idea of general validity. "Time" is understood there essentially from the point of view of time content, not as a dimension in itself, which is filled with all kinds of content. Let I Chr. 29:30: "the times [הָעִתִּים] that went over him" (KJV), serve as a graphic example. The text becomes more intelligible if one substitutes for "time" the content of the time, which is included with it in the Hebrew word: "the circumstances that came upon him" (RSV).

b) We like to consider time in contrast to eternity. In this usage the term "eternity" is usually understood, not only quantitatively as endless time, but also qualitatively as timelessness. The OT and the NT are not acquainted with this conception of eternity as timelessness. God, according to Rev. 1:4, is the one "who is and who was and who is to come"; and if in Rom. 16:26 (the only time in the NT) he is called the "eternal [αἰώνιος] God," this does not mean that as a timeless God he would have nothing to do with time, but rather that he is also Lord of the greatest spans of time, which he uses in his revelation (vs. 25).

As these examples show, it is necessary to clarify carefully the linguistic usage of the OT and the NT with regard to time, eternity, and related concepts. On the basis of this investigation it will then, perhaps, be possible to make some statements as to the biblical conception of time as compared with ours and that of the old oriental cultures or Hellenism.

1. Terminology
   a. In biblical Hebrew
   b. In LXX Greek
   c. In NT Greek
2. In the OT
   a. Concept of time in the OT
   b. Time and revelation
   c. God and time (eternity)
   d. Man and time
3. In the Apoc. and the Pseudep.
4. In the NT
Bibliography

1. Terminology. Only the more important and more general concepts of time are to be discussed here, not the times of the day and the seasons of the year, the division of time, the adverbs of time, etc. (for these, see HOUR; DAY; NIGHT; WEEK; YEAR; CALENDAR). The passages cited present, in most cases, only selected examples, without claim to completeness.

a. In biblical Hebrew. The Hebrew OT has no general word for "time," and likewise no special term for the categories of time—past, present, future. The Aramaic עִדָּן (Dan. 2:8-9, 21; 3:5, 15; 7:12) still comes closest to our general expression "time."

The most widely used word we can translate with "time" is עֵת (about 290 times). It means, not time in its duration—as a dimension—but rather the moment or point of time at which something happens (Exod. 9:18: "Tomorrow about this time I will cause very heavy hail to fall"; II Chr. 25:27). Moreover, whether the event which characterizes this point of time is of longer or of shorter duration remains irrelevant. Thus the point of time can change over into a longer period of time (I Kings 11:4: "when Solomon was old"—lit., "at the time of Solomon's growing old"; Jer. 50:16: "time of harvest"). Our differentiation between point of time and period of time already presupposes, however, time as a measuring tape which can be applied to events. This idea is not yet contained in the Hebrew word; time and time content still remain side by side without logical distinction (Esth. 4:14; Jer. 49:8). In many cases עֵת with qualitative coloring designates the right time for something, the suitable, favorable time (II Sam. 11:1: "In the spring of the year, the time when kings go forth to battle"; I Chr. 12:32: "men who had understanding of the times, to know what Israel ought to do"; Ps. 119:126; Eccl. 3:1-8; Hag. 1:2, 4—here עֵת approaches the Greek καιρός idea). On the basis of this linguistic usage passages like Ps. 104:27 become intelligible:

These all look to thee,
   to give them their food at its time [RSV "in due season"].

In an eschatological context עֵת may designate the coming hour of judgment (Isa. 13:22; Jer. 27:7; Ezek. 7:7, 12; 30:3; see DAY OF THE LORD). In the later language the plural seems sometimes to add up the single points of time to make periods of time, without, however, renouncing the basic meaning of the singular (Ezek. 12:27; Dan. 11:14). Here, too, the time content sometimes, outweighs the purely temporal meaning; it is better to translate it then with "fate" or "fortunes" (I Chr. 29:30; Ps. 31:15—H 31:16: "My times are in thy hand").

The word מוֹעֵד, derived from the verb יָעַד, "appoint (a time, a place)," means "place of meeting," "meeting," and, used with reference to time, "appointed time," "fixed term" (Exod. 9:5; II Sam. 20:4). In contradistinction to עֵת, "point of time," מוֹעֵד emphasizes more strongly conscious designation and arrangement; however, the two expressions can sometimes also be used as parallel synonyms in poetic language (Jer. 8:7; Hos. 2:9—H 2:11; cf. Dan. 8:19 with 8:17). The plural frequently means specifically the time of feasts (Gen. 1:14; Lev. 23:2, 4, 37, 44; Ezek. 46:9, 11). The use of the word in Dan. 12:7 is peculiar: "a time, two times, and half a time."

The word זְמָן occurs only three times, in the latest period of biblical Hebrew (Neh. 2:6; Esth. 9:27, 31). It is a loan word from the Aramaic and, like מוֹעֵד, means "the appointed time," "the fixed day."

Frequently the indication of the point of time of an event is by יוֹם, "day" (see DAY). In the process the original meaning of "day" (in contrast to "night" or a twenty-four-hour day) loses much color (Gen. 39:11; Jer. 36:2). "On the day when" is often synonymous with simple "when" (Lev. 14:57; Ps. 102:2—H 102:3). The use of יוֹם as an indication of a point of time forms the basis for the custom of designating decisive events as "the day of" (Isa. 9:4—H 9:3 [day of Midian]; Ezek. 34:12; Hos. 1:11—H 2:2 [day of Jezreel]; Obad. 12 ff). The decisive eschatological intervention of Yahweh is the "day of Yahweh," "that day" (*see* DAY OF THE LORD). Without more precise designation, "his day" in Job 3:1 KJV means "the day of his birth"; otherwise, however, "the day intended for someone," the day of death or of judgment (I Sam. 26:10; Job 18:20; Ps. 37:13; Ezek. 21:25—H 21:30). Instead of "day" we would probably use "hour" in similar contexts. The Hebrew of the Bible has no word at all for "hour."

In the cases in which we use "time" to mean a more or less exactly limited space of time, biblical Hebrew usually speaks of ימים, "days" (Gen. 26:1: "in the days of Abraham"; I Sam. 2:31: "the days are coming, when"). This usage is so familiar to us that in the translation of the OT we often prefer the phrase "in the days of" as the more solemn and venerable over our commonplace, everyday "at the time of." ימים, after an indication of time such as month or year, puts emphasis on the expiration of the full time in question (Gen. 29:14; 41:1: "after two whole years"). "All the days" is a common expression for "always," "forever" (Deut. 4:40; I Sam. 2:35).

The smallest possible space of time in contrast to a longer duration is designated in Hebrew by רגע, "moment" (Exod. 33:5; Ps. 73:19; Lam. 4:6), which is apt to be used hyperbolically (Job 20:5; Ps. 30:5—H 30:6; Isa. 54:7-8), once even with the quantitative adjective קטן, "brief" (Isa. 54:7).

A few other words which do not fundamentally designate specific spaces of time, but which can under certain conditions be so used, are still to be discussed:

קץ means, first of all, the "end," derived from the root קצץ, "to cut off." In its eschatological meaning (since Amos 8:1-2; then again especially Ezek. 7:2-3, 6) the word is the key word for the extreme (final) judgment. In Dan. 8–12 in the combination עת קץ (8:17; 11:35, 40; 12:4, 9), קץ הימין (8:19), מועד קץ (12:13), or alone (8:19; 11:27; 12:6, 13), it has become the term for the point of time at the end, the final time (*see* ESCHATOLOGY OF THE OT). Furthermore, קץ in the language of the Dea Sea MSS now also becomes the general and not necessarily eschatological designation for "time," "point of time," and "period of time" (cf. קץ, "to cut off"). The word can be put into the plural (1QS I.14, etc.); the "final time" then is called קץ אחרון, "the last time" (1 QS IV.16; 1QpHab VII.7, etc.).

Another word for "end," "close," is אחרית, "that which comes afterward." In certain cases one must actually translate it by "future" (Prov. 23:18; 24:14; Jer. 29:11: "to give you a future and a hope"). But here, too, a pure concept of time is not developed. The significance of the phrase באחרית הימים, "in days to come," "in the latter days," is disputed. The context usually shows whether this phrase is to be translated simply in analogy to the Akkadian expression *ina aḫrāt ūmē* by "in the future," henceforth "in the time to come" (thus probably in Gen. 49:1; Num. 24:14; Deut. 4:30; 31:29) or whether it is a prophetic-eschatological term "in the latter days" (Isa. 2:2; Ezek. 38:16; Dan. 10:14; Hos. 3:5; Mic. 4:1).

קדם constitutes an opposite to אחרית, and is likewise used with reference to both time and space: "at

the beginning," "the East," and "earlier," "of old," "primitive times," "olden times" (Deut. 33:27: "God from of old"="the eternal God"; Isa. 19:11: "ancient kings"). For our concept "the past," the Hebrew otherwise uses הימים הראשנים, "the days that are past" (Deut. 4:32), or similar turns of expression.

For the period of a GENERATION the Hebrew language uses the word דור. This also is not a pure concept of time, since the thought is primarily of the human beings who live in the period of time. With the double expression דור ודור, "generation after generation"; מדור לדור, "from generation to generation"; etc., we approach the expression for unlimited, infinite time.

The OT has not developed a special term for "eternity" which one could contrast with "temporality." However, it does, to be sure, have several possibilities for expressing the unending, incalculable, unchangeable duration of something, from the most distant past as well as until the most distant future, or also in both directions. Reference has already been made to כל הימים, "all the days," above. Most frequently עולם is used for this (440 times; in addition, the Aramaic עלם 19 times); the etymology of this word has not yet been explained. The basic meaning is probably "most distant time." This explains the fact that עולם (except in Eccl. 1:10; 3:11; *see below*) is never used as an independent substantive, but always in combination with the prepositions מן, "from"; עד and ל, "until"; or in substitution for these prepositional constructions as an adverbial accusative or as the second element of a made-compound. The meaning of past time (Gen. 6:4; Isa. 51:9) is less frequent in the OT, as compared with its use for the incalculable future (Gen. 9:16; I Kings 2:33) and for the total duration of time (Isa. 40:28; Jer. 31:3). As an expression of an extreme limit, עולם can, according to the "horizon" of the speaker with regard to time, refer to a variety of remote times (Deut. 15:17: "your bondman for ever"=lifelong; Isa. 63:16: "our Redeemer from of old"; Amos 9:11: "as in the days of old"=as at the time of David). Only in the connection "from עולם and until in עולם" (Ps. 90:2), as well as in the genitive compound, when according to the context both future and past are included, does the meaning "eternity" equal total duration of time. In addition to the temporal meaning, it often also contains a qualitative overtone in the sense of permanence or finality (II Sam. 23:5; Ps. 78:69). The special quality, however, is attached to the object, and is not implied in עולם of itself. The plural עולמים does not designate (except in Eccl. 1:10; *see below*) a plural of "aeons." It is, as an intensifying plural, quite similar to the singular in meaning (I Kings 8:13; Isa. 26:4). The late liturgical language, especially, shows the tendency toward intensification, doubling and piling up of the expressions with עולם (Pss. 106:48; 136; Isa. 45:17; Dan. 7:18). The conception of "eternity" is not changed by this. Probably under the influence of the Greek αἰών, new meanings for עולם come in in the latest biblical Hebrew and in Middle Hebrew—namely, "space of time," "age," "time" (Eccl. 1:10 and perhaps 3:11), "aeon," and "world" (*see* § 1c below). Only here can עולם appear as an independent substantive and as the subject.

In addition to עולם, both עד and נצח occur in

similar use and meaning, but more rarely. עַד is used with prepositions (Job 20:4 of the past; Isa. 26:4 of the future) or as a prepositional genitive (Hab. 3:6 of the past; Isa. 47:7 of the future); cf. also אֲבִי־עַד, "Everlasting Father" (Isa. 9:6—H 9:5). The situation is similar in the case of the least frequent נֶצַח (Ps. 74:3 of the past, otherwise of the future or the total duration of time; intensified in Isa. 34:10).

b. In LXX Greek. Greek has a general word for "space of time," "time": χρόνος. The word is clearly used for time as a measurable quantity, as is shown, indeed, by the quantitative adjectives such as πολύς, "much," or μικρός, "small," which often accompany it. In the LXX this word is used relatively seldom, usually as a translation of יוֹם/יָמִים, "day(s)." The Hebrew of the Bible has, to be sure, as we have seen, no corresponding word for "time" and says simply "day(s)." In most cases, however, in general designations of time in the LXX (likewise in our translations!) the Greek word for "day," ἡμέρα, has been used for יוֹם/יָמִים "day(s)," although this usage is rather unusual in nonbiblical Greek. The influence of the Hebrew original is clear here.

For the translation of עֵת, "point of time," καιρός serves in by far the most cases; less often, ὥρα, "hour," or ἡμέρα, "day." Καιρός is originally "the decisive thing," "the essential point." The word can be interpreted with reference to place, to an object, or to time. In the LXX the temporal meaning prevails almost completely; it is the established, correct, or decisive "point of time." The word serves also for the translation of מוֹעֵד זְמָן and עִדָּן. In some cases, but especially in the plural, καιρός or καιροί also is used a little less precisely for an interval of time, so that one can add in the genitive how long this interval of time is (a year's time, etc.) The noun αἰών or the adjective αἰώνιος, which belongs to it, almost always occurs in the LXX for עוֹלָם and עַד. The word αἰών originally means "vital force," "life," then "age," "lifetime." It is, however, also used generally of a (limited or unlimited) "long space of time." In many cases it should then be translated by "eternity." To be sure, naturally, one cannot assume a philosophical concept of eternity here either. The LXX goes even beyond the foundation laid by the Hebrew OT in doubling and plural formation.

c. In NT Greek. In the NT, too, χρόνος is comparatively rare. It represents the basically Greek conception of time as measurable duration. Characteristically the word is most frequently used by the proselyte Luke. The singular means "space of time," "period of time," and is very often accompanied by quantitative adjectives (Matt. 25:19: "a long time"; Rev. 20:3: "a little while"). The plural, likewise, designates a (usually longer) space of time (Luke 23:8; II Tim. 1:9). Both singular and plural may be more specifically defined as to content (Acts 17:30: "times of ignorance"; I Pet. 1:17: "time of your exile"). Nowhere is time interpreted abstractly as temporality, not even in Rev. 10:6, where the statement "that there should be time no longer" (KJV) is not announcing a future suspension of time. The word χρόνος means "delay" here, as in Rev. 2:21. Accordingly, the RSV translates: "that there should be no more delay."

In using ἡμέρα, "day," for "point of time" (Matt.

26:29; Col. 1:6, 9) and the plural ἡμέραι, "days," for "space of time" (Matt. 2:1; 9:15; II Tim. 3:1; Heb. 12:10) the NT also follows Hebrew-Aramaic usage. Of special importance are the passages in which ἡμέρα (in various combinations, and sometimes also absolute) is used for the eschatological time of judgment and time of salvation (Luke 17:24; Phil. 1:6, 10; I Thess. 5:2, 5; Rev. 6:17). *See* DAY OF THE LORD; ESCHATOLOGY OF THE NT.

Among the time concepts of the NT the word καιρός is particularly important. In Heb. 11:15 ("they would have had opportunity to return") it means the God-given possibility; otherwise the temporal conception is present everywhere. As in the LXX, καιρός specifies the established, favorable, or decisive point of time: it can, however, also be used to express a shorter (I Cor. 7:5) or a longer (Acts 17:26) length of time, a regular fixed time (Luke 12:42) or a general statement of time (Matt. 11:25: "at that time"). In the specific meaning of the word (favorable, decisive point of time) one can distinguish a secular from a Christian usage, according to whether the choice of the point in times lies within the discretion of men or whether the *kairos* is determined by God. An example of the secular use is the promise of the governor Felix to Paul: "Go away for the present; when I have an opportunity I will summon you" (Acts 24:25). The Christian significance is found in connection with what happens with reference to Christ (Matt. 8:29; 26:18; I Tim. 6:15; I Pet. 1:11). But men also have times of decision fixed by God (Luke 19:44; Rom. 13:11; Col. 4:5). Finally, καιρός also becomes an eschatological *terminus technicus* (Luke 21:8; Rev. 1:3; 22:10).

The use of the word αἰών in the NT is determined very much by the OT and the LXX. Αἰών means "long, distant, uninterrupted time," in the past (Luke 1:70) as well as in the future (John 4:14). The adjective αἰώνιος, "eternal," especially, serves for the actual statements of eternity (II Cor. 4:18; Heb. 9:12, 15), but nowhere is a clear distinction made between limited and unlimited duration of time. The idea of duration of time is fundamentally inherent in αἰών, as it is not in עוֹלָם, "most distant time." The intensifying plural occurs frequently in the NT, especially in the doxologies (Rom. 1:25; 9:5; Heb. 13:8), but it adds no new meaning. Here, as also in the doubling (Heb. 1:8 in the singular; Rom. 16:27; Eph. 3:21; Phil. 4:20 in the plural), the pattern of the LXX is likewise evident, only that the tendency toward more complicated forms is still more marked. New, as compared with the עוֹלָם of biblical Hebrew (except for Eccl. 1:10), is αἰών in the meaning, which can easily be explained from the basic meaning, "world epoch": συντέλεια τοῦ αἰῶνος, "close of the age" (Matt. 13:39-40, 49), having the same meaning in the plural (I Cor. 10:11; Heb. 9:26). Beyond that, in the Judaism of NT times the new meaning "world" develops, by means of which αἰών approaches the idea of κόσμος (Mark 4:19; I Cor. 2:6). This development parallels the appearance, which is to be observed since the first century B.C., of the meaning "world" for עוֹלָם in Hebrew and Aramaic, where, up until then, the missing idea "world" had been periphrased with the expressions "heaven and earth" or "the universe." Temporal and spatial meanings cross over into one another in the Jewish apocalyptic doctrine of the two aeons; the existence of this doctrine has been attested ever since the first century B.C. (*see* ESCHATOLOGY OF THE APOCRYPHA AND PSEUDEPIGRAPHA). In addition to II Esdras and the rabbinical literature (עוֹלָם הַזֶּה, "this aeon"; עוֹלָם הַבָּא, "the coming aeon"), the NT also uses these concepts (Matt. 12:32; Eph. 1:21: "not only in this age but also in that which is to come"). *See* ESCHATOLOGY OF THE NT.

2. In the OT. Of special interest, in addition to the secular understanding of time in the OT, is the relationship between time and revelation, which one can investigate further theologically in relation to God and his people or men. *See also* ESCHATOLOGY OF THE OT.

a. Concept of time in the OT. The OT is not alone in antiquity in its lack of a general concept for the dimension of time. The Egyptians and the Babylonians also know only expressions for the right, established point of time or for the long, unlimited duration, and use the word "day(s)" for the most varied designations of time. The abstraction "time" belongs among the accomplishments of Greek culture. If, however, time (as a dimension) is not abstracted from the abundance of individual events, then, naturally the events and their time constitute, to a large extent, a unit in OT thinking. It has been observed again and again how closely the Hebrew conception of time is bound up with its content, or even identified with it (Gen. 1:5: "God called the light Day, and the darkness he called Night"; Lam. 5:21: "Renew our days as of old"). Hence the frequency with which יוֹם, "day," and עֵת, "point of time," are combined with genitives which indicate the content of the time; hence also the importance which is given to the "right point of time" in OT statements of time generally. In order to underline the precedence of the time content as opposed to the chronological statement of time, it has often been pointed out that the Hebrew verb does not have any real tenses. Actions are determined primarily by the content-aspect of being completed or not being completed, not by the time categories past, present, and future (*see* HEBREW LANGUAGE). However, one must not draw too sweeping conclusions from this fact. Hebrew also has secondary possibilities for expressing the three degrees of time, as, conversely, Greek and our modern languages can also very well take into consideration the manner of action. It is questionable, generally, whether, when we have confirmed the lack of an abstract—let us say an "Aristotelian"—concept of time and the shaping of many OT statements of time from the point of view of content, we should go still further with the assertion that the OT possesses a conception of time which is entirely unlike ours and therefore a completely different understanding of reality. Such attempts (e.g., Pedersen, Marsh, Boman; *see bibliography*) make chronological order very much a matter of relativity in its significance for the consciousness of the men of the OT. Individual events, it is said, are arranged and differentiated in the OT, not according to their position in chronological sequence, but according to the nature of their content, fixed by God or psychologically perceived.

Matters which are widely separated with reference to time can, if their content coincides, be identified and regarded as simultaneous. The linear scale of time is replaced by the rhythm of time with the incessant return of the same time content. In worship the pious man experiences past acts of salvation as contemporary. A prophet like Amos assumes the synchronism of his hearers with the events of Exodus (Amos 2:9-11). One speaks of "contraction of time" and "fulness of time."

However, in relation to such attempts, it should be observed that the OT in many passages discloses quite ingenuously a naïve conception of chronological time, also in the realm of religion and in prophetic proclamation. In the presentation of the commandments and of the exodus events celebrated in worship the succession of the generations plays an important role (Deut. 6:7; 11:2-7, 18-21). The OT attaches great importance to genealogies and chronologies, although the people of God are frequently, throughout all the ages, interpreted as a "corporate personality" (*see* GENEALOGY). Then, too, the writing of history as highly developed as that of the OT is scarcely imaginable with an absolutely nonchronological feeling for time (*see* HISTORY). The prophets not only count on the coming again of the old times of salvation, but also on new, greater deeds of God (Isa. 43:18-19). On the whole, then, one must probably assume that the OT had an unconsidered chronological, linear conception of time.

b. Time and revelation. The OT attests God's action of revelation in history and thus in time (*see* REVELATION; HISTORY). In carrying out his plan by actions of judgment or salvation (Isa. 14:24-27; 46: 9 ff) God picks out certain points of time and gives them special significance for salvation. God is not by nature bound up with his people from the very beginning. The selection of Israel for the salvation of mankind (*see* ELECTION) has its beginning with the patriarchs and in the events of Exodus. The people have to adapt themselves to this; at the same time, however, new acts of God are promised, fulfilled, and promised again (Gen. 12:1-3; 13:14-17; 17:6-8; Josh. 21:43-45; Judg. 4:6-7, 14; 13:5; I Sam. 9:16; II Sam. 7; I Kings 14:6 ff; 15:29; Isa. 11:1 ff; 45:18-25; Jer. 23:1-8; Amos 9:11-12). Thus there comes into existence a history of salvation with a beginning and a goal, always through the free appointment of God and, therefore, not to be confused with a legality which might be calculated by men or with a development in the history of religion which leads higher and higher. Nevertheless, the individual acts of God do have a connection with earlier ones and drive the whole work of God closer to the final goal.

This OT interpretation of history as the history of salvation of necessity had an influence on the understanding of time. On the one hand, special emphasis falls on the *kairos*, the "today," on which the decision in favor of obedience is demanded (Deut. 11:2, 26, 32; Ps. 95:7). On the other hand, the course of time acquires its unified alignment toward a *telos* (goal) set by God. This becomes clear in a comparison of the OT understanding of time with that of the old oriental surrounding world. The Egyptian is conscious of the continuity of time, which presents itself in an unending repetition of the same thing. The course of the world does not lead to a goal or an end; periods of time repeat and renew themselves again and again. The situation is similar in the case of the Babylonians; their sense of time is marked by the constant rhythm or cycle of nature. It is cyclical and advances in speculation, at the most, to a theory of periods, not to one of a world history which is aimed at a goal and is irretrievable, in which each point of time has its unique significance.

This linear, goal-directed line of time is not quite so clear in all portions of the OT. In ECCLESIASTES historical revelation withdraws considerably before the emphasis on the omnipotence and the inscrutability of the Creator. Correspondingly the understanding of time is oriented in nature and therefore cyclical and static (Eccl. 1:2-11; 3:1-15). The eternal cycle gives rise to weary resignation:

> What has been is what will be,
> and what has been done is what will be done;
> and there is nothing new under the sun
> (1:9).

Elsewhere in the OT, on the other hand, motifs of the cyclical concept of time were taken over, but stripped of their original meaning and fitted into the view of the time of salvation. Thus, e.g., the motif of the return of a primitive paradise was taken over by the prophets in their eschatological proclamation (Isa. 11:6-8; Hos. 2:18—H 2:20). The latter days, however, are not regarded as the beginning of a new age, but as having a final character. The Priestly document divides history into four periods, beginning with the Creation, covenants with Noah, with Abraham, and at Sinai. Presumably there is a connection with an ancient oriental theory of four world periods of a world year, but the concept of time as a cycle and the cosmological speculation have been done away with. The same is true of the visions in Dan. 2; 7. The nonbiblical theory of world epochs or world dominions (cf. Hesiod *Erga* 106 ff), which was probably basic for the historical view of the apocalyptic writers, has been turned around in such a way here that the course of the world periods does not conclude in a new cycle, but in the kingdom of God of the latter days.

c. God and time (eternity). Just as the OT has no abstract term for "time," so also it has no theological dogmas on time and its relation to God. Nevertheless, certain theological principles can be deduced from OT texts. God reveals himself now and then *in* time as the sole Lord and thereby also as Lord *over* time. Only by thinking of the essence of God as the sole Lord (also over time), not on the basis of any kind of philosophical concept of time and eternity, can one understand the OT statements on time and God. God's dominion over time is most clearly revealed by the fact that he created time along with the universe as its creature form of existence (*see* CREATION). Time has its beginning, from which point the days can be numbered (Gen. 1). Time is something positive, not something which came into the world only with the fall of man. Temporality, the breaking up of time into past, present, and future, distinguishes the creature from his Creator, who is not bound by the limits of time (Ps. 90:4), who gives time and takes it again. Together with the created world, earthly time, determined by the stars (Gen. 1:14),

will also end or be absorbed in God's eternity (Isa. 60:19-20). Passages such as Isa. 65:20 ff; 66:23, which assume a continuation of time, merely point out the difficulty of imagining God's eternity; in any case, it is not the same as timelessness.

The transcendence of God over all time was probably first fully recognized and expressed by Deutero-Isaiah. To be sure, even in Gen. 21:33 the name of God, אל עולם, "the Everlasting God," appears at the sanctuary at Beer-sheba. The designation, which is surely pre-Israelitic, was transferred to Yahweh by the immigrants. Parallels to it are found in certain Phoenician inscriptions (Karatepe, Arslan-Tash, recently Ugarit) where "eternity" (in the sense of the unchangeable power, of the unbroken continuity of effectiveness) is ascribed, above all, to the sun. In the last analysis, then, the expression stems from the Canaanites' nature religion, with its cyclical idea of time, and has nothing to do with Deutero-Isaiah's thought on eternity, which is marked by faith in revelation and creation. Circumlocutions such as "I am the first and I am the last" (Isa. 44:6) are much more characteristic for this (41:4; 43:10-13; 48:12). For the despondent, disheartened exiles, who no longer consider a new intervention in history by Yahweh for their deliverance possible (40:27), the prophet points out the unique greatness of his Lord (vs. 28):

> The LORD is the everlasting God [אלהי עולם],
> the Creator of the ends of the earth.
> He does not faint or grow weary.

As Yahweh, the Creator, is Lord over the ends of the earth—how much more, therefore, also over the regions in which scattered Israel lives—just so he, as the eternal God, is also Lord over the history of all peoples—how much more so, therefore, also over the fate of Israel. Untiringly he will remain true to his redemptive purpose. A metaphysical timelessness, like that of the Platonic ideas, cannot be found here. Precisely as Lord over time, God injects his promise (40:8), his salvation (45:17), redemption, and righteousness (51:6, 8), his goodness (54:8), and his covenant (55:3) into the transitory creation as eternal values. In the postexilic period, since God's uniqueness was established, "eternity" became more and more a synonym for "godliness," soon a somewhat worn symbol for God's world and his activity (Ps. 90:2; 102:12-13, 25 ff; Isa. 35:10; 60:15, 19 ff; 61:7-8). With the increasing development of eschatological concepts in apocalyptic writings, עולם becomes the permanent attribute of the life to come (Dan. 12: 2: "everlasting life," "everlasting contempt").

d. Man and time. Temporality is the God-given form of existence for the creature world (Job 1:21; Ps. 90:3-12; Isa. 40:6-8). Man is not immortal (Gen. 3:22; 6:3), even though a long life is considered ideal (I Kings 3:11-14); and the decline of the span of life in primitive history (Gen. 5; 11:10 ff) expresses the separation of mankind from God, the source of life (Ps. 36:9—H 36:10; *see* AGE, OLD). Formal phrases such as: "May my lord King David live for ever!" (I Kings 1:31; cf. Neh. 2:3; Pss. 21:4—H 21:5; 61:7; 72:5; Dan. 2:4; 3:9; 5:10; 6:7, 22), stemming from oriental court style, have long since been separated from their source, the old oriental royal ideology, and are now merely to be considered as hyperbolic expressions (*see* KING). In the Royal Psalms, partly under the influence of the prophecy of Nathan (II Sam. 7) and the conception of an eternal covenant with David (II Sam. 23:5), they have been associated with the king's name, his throne, or his dynasty (Pss. 18:50—H 18:51; 45:2, 6, 17—H 45:3, 7, 18; 72:17; 89:4, 36-37—H 89:5, 37-38; 110:4; 132:12), and were later given an eschatological-messianic meaning. To be sure, OT man is keenly aware of the transitory nature of human life (especially after the breakdown of the old collective bonds), which he can interpret as the consequence of sin and God's wrath (Gen. 3:19; Ps. 90:7 ff). However, he does not seek refuge in a wishful dream of an endless life, but accepts time from the hands of Yahweh and subjects himself completely to him (Pss. 31:15—H 31:16; 73: 23, 26; 139:16; Eccl. 3:2, 14). *See* LIFE; DEATH.

Into this temporality of man, intended by divine creation and marked by sin, there now comes at certain points of time chosen by God in free sovereignty (I Sam. 3:1; Amos 8:11-12) revelation as an offer of GRACE, to which man must respond with FAITH. Thus God takes seriously the creature with his temporality, in that he himself permits his revelation to enter into time. Time and history are, therefore, in the OT not a matter of indifference, but are of decisive importance, because they must afford the means of salvation. Only in this way does time become meaningful and lose its oppressive enigmatic quality. It is given to man so that he can seize the opportunity and not pass up salvation (Deut. 27:9 ff; Ps. 95:7-9). Because time is not reversible, man cannot have divine revelation at his free disposal; he is constantly called upon to be vigilant and keep himself ready for God's call. Yet he is not handed over to the arbitrary action and caprice of God. The continuous sequence of God's acts, in which God's faithfulness and purposive will with regard to the accomplishment of salvation are recognizable, guides man educationally to an understanding of the coming periods of decision and the coming salvation. The peculiar realization of the exodus events in later generations (Deut. 29:14-15; Josh. 24:17) and the certainty of the prophets who see what is to come as already present, is determined by the conviction that God's salvation is the same wherever he grants communion with himself through his Word and his Spirit. It does not become thereby a timeless, mystic salvation, release from time, but is supratemporal (without the limits of the not-yet and the no-longer), as is God himself.

3. In the Apoc. and the Pseudep. Much of what was said about the conception of time in the OT is likewise true of the late Jewish Apoc. and the Pseudep., although a Hellenistic way of thinking also appears now to some extent. Time and time content can be kept apart, as in II Esd. 13:58. One moves in the categories past, present, and future (II Esd. 5:43). Measuring and comparing periods of time plays a greater role (Ethiopian Enoch 72-82). More than any others, the apocalyptic writings provide material on the concept of time (*see* APOCALYPTICISM). For their manifold content, especially the idea of the two aeons (II Esd. 7:50) with the whole apocalyptic reckoning of time (II Esd. 14:10-12; II Bar. 20:1; 85:10), *see*

ESCHATOLOGY OF THE APOCRYPHA AND THE PSEUDEPIGRAPHA.

Let us examine just a few conceptions of time which lead beyond the limits of the OT. God's dominion over time is expressed in new forms (II Esd. 4:36-37; *see* PREDESTINATION). The idea of preexistence is developed (Ecclus. 1:4; II Esd. 8:52; *see* PRE-EXISTENCE OF SOULS). Expressions for "eternity" are manifold (Bar. 3:10, 14, 20 ff; "the Everlasting" =God). One struggles with the difficulties of imagining eternity. Enoch 10:10 naïvely visualizes an eternal life with a life span of five hundred years. Ecclus. 18: 9-10 compares human life with eternity conceived as endless time. It is not quite clear whether time will still play a role in the new aeon (II Bar. 44:11-12), or whether it will be timeless (Slavonic Enoch 65).

4. In the NT. The NT builds on the OT understanding of time, which is linear and bears the stamp of the story of salvation, and develops it further consistently. All expressions of faith, in particular, have a temporal character, which would have been impossible in Hellenism, with its mythical-cyclical or philosophical-timeless thinking. There one does not expect deliverance through God's action within time, but one strives for release from the cycle of time in a timeless world beyond. Hence in Gnosticism, where the Christian faith appears decidedly Hellenized, decisive presuppositions of NT theology are abandoned: the OT view of history as determined by God's creative action; the redemptive significance of the unique dying of Christ, who was incarnated and thus entered into time (*see* INCARNATION); and the expectation of the PAROUSIA (*see also* DAY OF CHRIST) in the future. *See* GNOSTICISM.

The salvation-historical view is not marked by the same emphasis in all parts of the NT, but it is basic everywhere. The pronouncement of Jesus: "The time is fulfilled, and the kingdom of God is at hand; repent, and believe in the gospel" (Mark 1:15), is naturally more keenly interested in the present, decisive *kairos* than the reflections of Paul on the history of salvation in Rom. 9–11, e.g., or Luke's historic narrative in Acts. It would be a mistake, however, to play the one against the other. Just as one may not lose himself in apocalyptic calculations on the course of the history of salvation and thereby evade decision for the present (Luke 17:20-21; Acts 1:7), so it would be unbiblical to reinterpret the expectation of the kingdom of God which is to come in the sense of a "constantly pending decision" without expectation of a future realization.

It is not necessary here to go into the content-aspect of the story of salvation, with its center in the death and resurrection of Jesus Christ (*see* JESUS CHRIST; CHRIST), nor into the question of the connection between the OT and the NT and the problems of NT eschatology (*see* ESCHATOLOGY OF THE NT). On the other hand, a few more formal time categories which play a role in the NT story of salvation and in early Christian faith should still be mentioned. The realization of the story of salvation is bound up with καιροί (I Tim. 6:15; Tit. 1:3; I Pet. 1: 11), which God has established in his full authority (Acts 1:7) and suddenly causes to set in (I Thess. 5: 1-2). Because of this the νῦν, "now" (Col. 1:26), and the σήμερον, "today" (Heb. 3:7, 13, 15), take on tremendous importance for the community; it is a matter of making the most of one's time (Eph. 5:16; Col. 4: 5). God alone has command over the καιροί (Mark 13:32-33; Acts 1:7), but to those who believe in Christ he gives insight into the continuity of the divine plan of salvation: "to make all men see what is the plan [οἰκονομία] of the mystery hidden for ages in God who created all things" (Eph. 3:9). In doing so the mission of Christ in the fulness of time (πλήρωμα τῶν καιρῶν [Eph. 1:10]; πλήρωμα τοῦ χρόνου [Gal. 4:4]) is the center which is decisive for all times (*see* FULNESS OF TIME; PLEROMA). Christ's work is unique and occurs once for all (ἅπαξ, ἐφάπαξ; Rom. 6:10; Heb. 7:27; 9:12, 28; I Pet. 3:18). The time between Easter and the Parousia acquires its singular suspense between οὐκέτι, "no longer" (Gal. 3:25; Eph. 2:19), and οὔπω, "not yet" (Phil. 3:13; I John 3:2), from this. On the one hand, II Cor. 5:17 applies: "Therefore, if any one is in Christ, he is a new creation; the old has passed away, behold, the new has come," but, on the other hand, also Phil. 3: 12: "Not that I have already obtained this or am already perfect; but I press on to make it my own, because Christ Jesus has made me his own."

Bibliography. On terminology, see: C. von Orelli, *Die hebräischen Synonyma der Zeit und Ewigkeit genetisch und sprachvergleichend dargestellt* (1871). E. Jenni, "Das Wort ʿōlām im AT," *ZAW,* 64 (1952), 197-248; 65 (1953), 1-35.

On time in the OT, see: J. Pedersen, *Israel, Its Life and Culture,* I-II (1926), 487-91. J. Schmidt, *Der Ewigkeitsbegriff im AT* (1940). W. Eichrodt, "Offenbarung und Geschichte im AT," *Theologische Zeitschrift,* 4 (1948), 321-31. S. G. F. Brandon, *Time and Mankind* (1951). W. Vollborn, *Studien zum Zeitverständnis des AT* (Mikrokopie; 1951). J. Marsh, *The Fulness of Time* (1952). M. Noth, "Die Vergegenwärtigung des AT in der Verkündigung," *Evangelische Theologie,* 12 (1952), 6-17. G. Pidoux, "A propos de la notion biblique du temps," *RTP,* vol. III, no. 2 (1952), pp. 120-25. T. Boman, *Das hebräische Denken im Vergleich mit dem Griechischen* (2nd ed., 1954). E. Otto, "Altägyptische Zeitvorstellungen und Zeitbegriffe," *Die Welt als Geschichte,* 14 (1954), 135-48. C. H. Ratschow, "Anmerkungen zur theologischen Auffassung des Zeitproblems." *ZThK,* 51 (1954), 360-87. G. E. Wright, *God Who Acts* (2nd ed., 1954). M. Burrows, "Ancient Israel," in R. C. Dentan, ed., *The Idea of History in the Ancient Near East* (1955), pp. 99-131. W. Eichrodt, "Heilserfahrung und Zeitverständnis im AT," *Theologische Zeitschrift,* 12 (1956), 103-25. M. Noth, "Das Geschichtsverständnis der atl. Apokalyptik," *Gesammelte Studien zum AT* (1957), pp. 248-73.

On time in the NT, see: H.-D. Wendland, *Geschichtsanschauung und Geschichtsbewusstsein im NT* (1938). G. Delling, *Das Zeitverständnis im NT* (1940). O. Cullmann, *Christ and Time* (1950). E. Brunner, "Das christliche Verständnis der Zeit und der Ewigkeit," *Das Ewige als Zukunft und Gegenwart* (1953), 46-62. E. Dinkler, "Earliest Christianity," in R. C. Dentan, ed., *The Idea of History in the Ancient Near East* (1955), pp. 169-214.   E. JENNI

TIMNA tĭm′nə [תמנע, *perhaps originally Tamna'*; LXX Θαμνά (Ναμνά in I Chr. 1:39)]; KJV TIMNAH in Gen. 36:40; I Chr. 1:51. Two persons. Cf. the Qatabanian capital Timna', which existed in S Arabia from *ca.* the ninth to the first century B.C.

1. Sister of the clan chief (of) Lotan (אלוף לוטן), one of the native Horite inhabitants of Edom (Gen. 36:22; I Chr. 1:39). She is given as the concubine of Eliphaz son of Esau, and the mother of Amalek, in Gen. 36:12, to indicate a close relationship between Edomites and Horites.

2. A clan chief of Edom (אלוף תמנע; Gen. 36:40; I Chr. 1:51); given in I Chr. 1:36 as a son of Eliphaz (for Korah, cf. Gen. 36:16). This Timna may be either the name of the ancestor of the Edomite clan or the geographical designation of the territorial subdivision occupied by the clan (note "according to . . . their dwelling places" in Gen. 36:40; and cf. Israel's conquest of Edom in II Sam. 8:14).

Bibliography. W. F. Albright, "The Chronology of Ancient S Arabia in the Light of the First Campaign of Excavation in Qataban," *BASOR,* CXIX (1950), 8-10.   L. HICKS

TIMNAH tĭm′nə [תמנה, allotted portion] (KJV alternately TIMNATH tĭm′năth, THIMNATHAH thĭm′nə thə); TIMNATH [Θαμνάθα] (I Macc. 9:50; KJV THAMNATHA thăm′nə thə); TIMNITE tĭm′nīt [תמני] (Judg. 15:6). **1.** A town on the N border of Judah, near Beth-shemesh (Josh. 15:10). It was assigned to the territory of Dan (19:43). It is identified with Tell el-Batashi, in the Wadi es-Sarar, *ca.* four miles NW of Beth-shemesh.

During Samson's career Timnah was occupied by the Philistines. Samson married one of the women of Timnah but later lost her to his best man when he left her in a rage after she had betrayed the secret of his riddle (Judg. 14:1 ff).

Uzziah (*ca.* 783-742) apparently recaptured Timnah from the Philistines (cf. II Chr. 28:17). In 701 it was captured by Sennacherib (*ca.* 705-681), along with Eltekeh, Ekron, and other cities.

2. A village of Judah in the highland province of Maon (Josh. 15:57). This Timnah is probably the place referred to in the events described in Gen. 38: 12-14. It is probably to be identified with Tibnah, which lies on a slope below el-Khader, *ca.* four miles E of Beit Nettif and just NW of Jeba', which may correspond to the Gibeah mentioned as the neighboring town (Josh. 15:57).

3. A town, Θαμνάθα (KJV Thamnatha), fortified in 160 B.C. by the Seleucid general Bacchides, along with other cities including Emmaus and Bethel (I Macc. 9:50). In 43 B.C. the town Thamna (Θαμνα) became tributary to Cassius, one of the conspirators in the assassination of Julius Caesar (Jos. Antiq. XIV.xi.2). At the outbreak of the First Revolt, John the Essene was assigned as commanding officer of the province of Thamna (which included Emmaus; cf. I Macc. 9:50; Jos. War II.xx.4; III.iii.5). In the spring of A.D. 68, Vespasian captured the province (Jos. War IV.viii.1).

Eusebius says that Thamna was a large city in the territory of Diospolis between the latter and Aelia (Jerusalem). The present location is Khirbet Tibneh, a strategically located site in the rugged hill country of Ephraim, N of Mount Ga'ash, on the road from Lydda and Antipatris to Jerusalem. It is *ca.* 9 miles NW of Bethel and 7½ miles W-NW of Jufna (Gophna, chief city of a neighboring toparchy).

Bibliography. F.-M. Abel, *Géographie de la Palestine,* II (1938), 483; *Les Livres des Maccabées* (1949), p. 172. Y. Aharoni, "The Northern Boundary of Judah," *PEQ* (1958), pp. 27-31.
                                           V. R. GOLD

TIMNATH-HERES, TIMNATH-SERAH tĭm′năth hĭr′ĭz, —sĭr′ə [תמנת חרס, תמנת סרח]. The place of Joshua's inheritance and burial.

1. **Name.** According to Judg. 2:9, Joshua was buried "within the bounds of his inheritance in Timnath-heres, in the hill country of Ephraim, north of the mountain of Gaash" (*see* GAASH). In Josh. 19:50; 24:30 the place of Joshua's inheritance and burial is Timnath-serah. It is probable that Timnath-heres is the older form of the name, on the supposition that its meaning is "portion of the sun" (חרם), and that as such it was a place of sun-worship. Rabbinic tradition connects the origin of the name with Joshua's act of causing the sun to stand still (Josh. 10:13, where שמש is read; see Judg. 14:18; Job 9:7 for חרם), and claims that Joshua's tomb had a symbol of the sun on it. It has been suggested that the spelling of the name in Josh. 19:50; 24:30 (תמנת סרח) was a scribal error for תמנת חרם. The alternative is that an intentional change was made to remove the stigma of sun-worship which the older name would connote; Timnath-serah would not be inappropriate, since it might refer to the "portion remaining" to Joshua after the division of the land (Josh. 19:49).

2. **Location.** The Samaritan tradition which locates the tomb of Joshua at Kefr Haris, *ca.* nine miles SW of Shechem, is considered a late tradition and without archaeological substantiation. Most commentators locate the site at Khirbet Tibneh, *ca.* seventeen miles SW of Shechem. The modern name preserves the first part of the ancient name. Late Bronze Age and Early Iron Age potsherds from the surface of an impressive tell located there indicate a period of occupation at the time of Joshua. Eusebius and Jerome name the place Thamna, stating that the tomb of Joshua existed there in their day. It is probable that Timnath (Θαμναθα) in I Macc. 9:50 is to be identified with Timnath-heres; it was fortified with other Palestinian villages by Bacchides for the purpose of defense against the forces of Jonathan.

W. L. REED

TIMNITE. *See* TIMNAH.

TIMON tī′mən [Τίμων] (Acts 6:5). One of the seven men chosen by the HELLENISTS to look after the Hellenistic widows and also, probably, to engage in missionary work. His name is Greek, and he may have grown up in the Greek diaspora.

B. H. THROCKMORTON, JR.

TIMOTHY tĭm′ə thĭ [Τιμόθεος, one who honors God]; KJV **TIMOTHEUS** tĭ mō′thĭ əs. 1. A leader of the Ammonite forces who opposed Judas Maccabeus and his followers *ca.* 164 B.C. He was defeated by Judas in several encounters (I Macc. 5:6 ff; II Macc. 8:30 ff; 9:3 ff; 10:24 ff; 12:2 ff).

B. M. METZGER

2. A trusted and faithful associate of Paul, with whom he is linked in the address of several of Paul's letters, and who was the purported recipient of two of the NT letters: I and II Timothy.

Among Paul's letters, Timothy first appears as a youthful associate of Paul and Silvanus (*see* SILAS) at Corinth. All three are linked in the address of the First Letter to the Thessalonians (1:1), and the "we" phrases continue throughout the letter. Not long after they had left Thessalonica and had reached Athens, Paul's concern for the Thessalonian Christians be-

came so great that he sent Timothy back to them, so that he might confirm them in the faith. Paul knew that they had been undergoing a time of persecution, and he was eager to have them encouraged in their period of difficulty. And above all, Paul was anxious to have a direct report about the spiritual welfare of the young converts who made up the church at Thessalonica. Timothy had been sent (3:1-5), and had returned with the good news of their steadfastness in the faith, and of their continued affection for Paul (vss. 6-9).

In writing to the Thessalonians, Paul describes Timothy as a brother (I Thess. 3:2), as God's servant in the gospel of Christ, and by implication even ranks him among the apostles (2:6). II Thessalonians adds nothing to our knowledge of Timothy or of Paul's estimate of him, since in it Timothy is simply linked again with Paul and Silvanus in the address. Timothy's association with Paul at Corinth is probably confirmed by his being mentioned in the series of greetings that Paul wrote from the church at Corinth to the church at Rome in Rom. 16 (vs. 21). Even if one were to assume that Rom. 16 is a fragment from a letter written to Ephesus, the reference there to Timothy serves to underscore his close association with Paul in his missionary work.

The portrait of Timothy, as not only an associate of Paul but also his emissary, finds support in other letters of Paul. In the Corinthian letters we have another record of Timothy's assignment to be Paul's representative, but in this instance there is a suggestion of doubts Paul may have had about Timothy's effectiveness in a leadership capacity. As soon as Paul mentions that Timothy has been sent to the Corinthian church—apparently as the bearer of this letter (cf. I Cor. 16:10)—he hastens to comment on the arrogance of the Corinthian Christians who will complain because Paul himself has not come to them. The inference is that Paul had sent the young and inexperienced Timothy in his place. The apostle tries to offset the lack of confidence in Timothy by referring to him as "my beloved and faithful child in the Lord" (4:17). Timothy was commissioned to remind them of Paul's ways.

But the concluding mention of Timothy betrays that Paul had misgivings about his young colleague (I Cor. 16:10-11). The Corinthians are urged to put him at ease—as though he were bashful, or at least lacking in self-confidence. They are exhorted not to despise him—as though he had met with such a response on previous occasions. They are to send him back in peace—as though he had been involved in conflict in other situations. Paul must underline the fact that Timothy was doing the Lord's work just as much as he (Paul) was.

In the opening address of II Corinthians (1:1), Timothy is once again associated with Paul, presumably back in Ephesus. (Even if II Corinthians be regarded as a composite of several letters of Paul to the Corinthians, one would assume that all were written from Ephesus during Paul's protracted stay there.) Now, however, it is not Timothy who is to be Paul's messenger to the church at Corinth, but TITUS. The inference is clear: Timothy had been at Corinth, had preached there the same message that

Paul and Silvanus had proclaimed (1:19), but the inner difficulties of the church remained unresolved. It is Titus who figures prominently in the correspondence with the church at Corinth from this point on. Specifically, there are more references to Titus in II Corinthians than there are to him in all the rest of the NT. The implication is that Timothy could no longer serve as Paul's deputy in Corinth.

In spite of what appears to be a failure on the part of Timothy, the later letters of Paul continue to picture him as a close associate of Paul, and as one who was sent by Paul to strengthen the Gentile churches. The addresses of Phil. 1; Col. 1; Philem. 1 all link the names of Paul and Timothy. In Phil. 2:19, Timothy is about to be sent to Philippi to bring back to Paul an eyewitness report of the state of the church there. In spite of any ineffectiveness as a leader that we may infer from I and II Corinthians, Timothy remained to the end a faithful companion of Paul and one who was able to enter fully into an understanding of the people who made up the various Gentile churches. Paul describes him as "genuinely anxious for your welfare" (Phil. 2:20), and commends him for his faithful service, which can only be compared to that of a son serving with a father (vs. 22).

Although Paul's letters are the primary source for our knowledge of Timothy, Acts provides interesting detail, which will be credited in direct proportion to one's estimate of the historical reliability of Acts. According to Acts 16:1 ff, Timothy first appeared as a disciple at Lystra. Whether he had been converted by Paul, or was already a believer when Paul arrived, is not clear, although the references in the NT to Timothy as Paul's child in the Lord would suggest the former alternative (I Cor. 4:17; I Tim. 1:2). Timothy's father was a Gentile, and presumably a pagan. His mother was a Jewish Christian, although surprisingly her name is given in II Tim. 1:5 as Eunice, the daughter of a Christian lady named Lois. While it is conceivable that these women were Jewish in spite of their Gentile names, it seems likely that Acts and the Pastorals represent two divergent traditions about Timothy's family. The fact that Timothy had not been circumcised (Acts 16:3) indicates that his mother did not take seriously her religious responsibilities as a Jew; as a matter of fact, if she had, she would not have married a Gentile.

Acts reports that Timothy was circumcised by Paul in order to silence Jewish opposition; and together with Silas, they journeyed westward toward the Aegean Coast of Asia Minor (Acts 16:3). Nothing more is recorded in Acts of Timothy until the evangelists reached Beroea (17:14), when it was agreed that Paul would go on to Athens, leaving Silas and Timothy behind. Paul went to Athens and then on to Corinth, where Silas and Timothy joined him (18:5). The next we hear of Timothy, he was in Ephesus with Paul, and was sent from there to Macedonia, along with Erastus (19:22). The last report of him in Acts is in 20:4, where he appears in a large company of the brethren who were accompanying Paul through Macedonia and down the Ionian coast on the way to Jerusalem.

Even if one were to assume the authenticity of the PASTORAL LETTERS, they provide little in the way of specific information about Timothy, except that they purport to give the names of his mother and grandmother (II Tim. 1:5). The writer refers to "Timothy's" having been set aside by prophetic utterance for the work to which he was called. He is given instructions about the requirements for bishops, deacons, elders. He is warned against false teachers. But most of the letter consists only of general exhortations to endure suffering, seek righteousness, shun controversies, fulfil his ministry. The words spoken about Timothy in Paul's genuine letters are echoed in phrases that speak of him as "my true child in the faith" (I Tim. 1:2) and tell him not to be discouraged by his youthfulness (4:12). Timothy emerges as a much more real person in the indirect references to him in II Corinthians than he does in this letter which purports to have been addressed to him. Almost certainly the letters to Timothy are pseudonymous writings from the third generation of the church's life (II Tim. 1:5), a period in which the earlier spiritual enthusiasm had waned, and in which there was urgent need for regulation of doctrinal and ecclesiastical authority. The Pastorals are of no help, therefore, in reconstructing the portrait of Paul's youthful associate, Timothy. *See* PASTORAL LETTERS.

H. C. KEE

TIMOTHY, FIRST AND SECOND LETTERS TO.

Two letters found as the fifteenth and sixteenth books in the NT canon, purporting to have been written by the apostle Paul to his associate in work, Timothy.

Both letters are closely related in style, purpose, and content to the Letter to Titus. Together the three letters are called the PASTORAL LETTERS, the name indicating the ecclesiastical purpose of the correspondence: a chief pastor giving advice to pastors of the church. The letters are primarily concerned with church order, and are probably directed to churches in Asia Minor in the beginning of the second century. I and II Timothy give practical advice to a church which is consolidating its position in the world. Two emphases stand out: (*a*) The clergy must be selected carefully, its authority recognized, and its guidance in forms of worship followed (I Tim. 2-3; 4:12-6:2; II Tim. 1:6-2:13). (*b*) Heretics must be shunned or excommunicated (I Tim. 1:3-20; 4:1-11; 6:20-21; II Tim. 2:14-4:8).

II Timothy resembles the genuine Pauline letters more closely than does I Timothy or Titus. On this basis many scholars have concluded that the author has incorporated in his letter Pauline fragments.

J. C. BEKER

TIN [בְּדִיל, *from* Sanskrit *pātîra*]. As distinguished from other metals, tin appears in late OT passages (Ezek. 22:18, 20; 27:12; but cf. Num. 31:22). It was imported to the Near East by the Phoenicians (Ezek. 27:12) in TARSHISH ships from places not now certainly identifiable—the Balkans, Spain, and Cornwall have been suggested. That tin, probably in ore form, was employed in early BRONZE making has been established. Caucasia is considered as the earliest source of tin ore (cassiterite; SnO_2); the Midianite caravan merchants (Num. 31:22) were middlemen. בְּדִיל apparently could be applied to tin ore as to refined tin, and was sometimes confused with lead (cf. Zech. 4:10, where "plummet" is literally "the stone the tin"). *See also* PLUMBLINE.

Bibliography. R. J. Forbes, *Metallurgy in Antiquity* (1950), pp. 231-54; C. Singer *et al.,* eds., *A History of Technology,* I (1954), 563-92. P. L. GARBER

TINDALE'S VERSION. *See* TYNDALE'S VERSION.

TIPHSAH tĭf'sə [תִּפְסַח]. A place mentioned twice in the OT; probably two different places. **1.** A city in the NE corner of the border of Solomon's kingdom (I Kings 4:24 — H 5:4). It was an important city, situated on the W border of the Euphrates, where the river turns its southward course to an eastward course, about seventy-five miles S of Carchemish. It is most probably identical with Thapsacus, a trade center which is mentioned by Xenophon (I.4.11). In Seleucid times it was called Amphipolis, now Dibseh. **2.** Tiphsah is mentioned in II Kings 15:16 (so Hebrew text; see KJV-RSV mg.) as a place near Tirzah in Samaria. In a Greek MS the place is called Ταφωε, and תִּפְסַח here is therefore usually supposed to be a miswriting of תַּפּוּחַ, "Tappuah," a place about thirty miles N of Jerusalem, not so far from Tirzah. The RSV has preferred this conjecture and translates as "Tappuah." A. S. KAPELRUD

TIRAS tī'rəs [תִּירָס]. A subdivision of the Japhethites (Gen. 10:2; I Chr. 1:5), which has been compared to the τυρσηνοί and the Egyptian *Turusha* of Ramses III's records. The *Turusha* "from the sea" in the records of Ramses III are the same as the τυρσηνοί of Greek saga, where they appear as sea raiders in the Aegean.

Bibliography. Cf. especially the Homeric Hymn to Dionysos in E. Meyer, *Geschichte des Altertums* (2nd ed., 1928), vol. II, pt. 1, pp. 555-65, 578-79, 588. C. H. GORDON

TIRATHITES tī'rə thīts [תִּרְעָתִים]. A family of scribes of the Kenite tribe, dwelling at Jabez (I Chr. 2:55).

TIRE. KJV obsolete term meaning "headdress," used to translate פְּאֵר in Ezek. 24:17, 23 (RSV "turban"), and שַׂהֲרֹנִים in Isa. 3:18 (RSV "crescents").

TIRHAKAH tûr hā'kə [תִּרְהָקָה; LXX Θαρά, Θαρακά; *elsewhere* Ταρακὸς, *etc.;* Assyrian *Tarḳū;* Egyp. *Thrḳ*] (II Kings 19:8-9; Isa. 37:9). A king (689-664 B.C.) of Ethiopia and Egypt in the Twenty-fifth Dynasty; opponent to the Assyrian kings for the domination of Palestine.

Ca. 720 B.C., Egypt was broken up into many small principalities. Then an Ethiopian king, Piankhi, came N from his capital near the Fourth Cataract, and conquered and unified Egypt. His third successor in the rule of Egypt was his son Tirhakah (or Taharka). According to the biblical account, Tirhakah supported Hezekiah of Judah in revolt against Sennacherib of Assyria, which was another example of the futility of local reliance upon Egypt against Assyria or Babylonia.

Recent excavations in the Sudan have increased our knowledge of the reign of Tirhakah. As a pro-

vincial admirer of Egyptian culture, he was scrupulous in maintaining old rituals and repairing old temples. He was born *ca.* 709 B.C., and at the age of twenty became coregent with his brother Shabataka. At the same time he made his first visit to Egypt from Ethiopia. This means that when, in 700 B.C., Sennacherib defeated the Egyptians and Ethiopians at Eltekeh and then shut up Hezekiah in Jerusalem "like a bird in a cage," Tirhakah could not have been active in the campaign.

Possibly the biblical text has inadvertently substituted the name of Tirhakah for a previous Ethiopian pharaoh. The sudden destruction of the Assyrian army before Pelusium will also have preceded the reign of Tirhakah (II Kings 19:35; Herodotus II.141). However, the biblical account may be correct if Sennacherib undertook two campaigns against the West. In 700 he defeated Egypt and Ethiopia at Eltekeh, and perhaps in 688 moved against Tirhakah and the rebellious Hezekiah, at which time the Assyrian army was smitten with plague before Pelusium. In that event, the solution would be that the Deuteronomic compiler of the account simply telescoped two campaigns into one.

Tirhakah's later career is better known. He attempted to defend Egypt against the Assyrian kings Esarhaddon and Ashurbanipal, but was defeated in the Delta and driven S into Upper Egypt, where he maintained a rule of some dignity at Thebes.

Bibliography. *Cambridge Ancient History,* III (1925), 70-75, 84-86, 277-84; M. F. L. Macadam, *The Temples of Kawa,* I (1949), xii, 17-19; W. F. Albright, *BASOR,* 130 (1953), 4-11. J. A. WILSON

TIRHANAH tûr hā'nə [תִּרְחֲנָה] (I Chr. 2:48). A son of Caleb by Maacah his concubine; apparently part of a subordinate branch of Calebite families.

TIRIA tŭr'ĭ ə [תִּירְיָא] (I Chr. 4:16). A family or clan of the tribe of Judah.

TIRSHATHA tûr shā'thə. KJV translation of תִּרְשָׁתָא (RSV GOVERNOR) in Ezra 2:63; Neh. 7:65, 70; 8:9; 10:1. This title is the equivalent of פֶּחָה (from the Akkadian *piḫatu,* "governor"; cf. Neh. 12:26), and is generally derived from the Persian passive participle of the verb *tarš* ("to fear"), Avestan *taršta* ("the revered"), less probably from Old Persian *antare-kšathra* ("royal representative"). R. H. PFEIFFER

TIRZAH tûr'zə [תִּרְצָה]. One of the five daughters of Zelophehad who asked for and received an inheritance, although their father was dead and they had no brothers (Num. 26:33; 27:1-11; 36:10-12; Josh. 17:3-6).

TIRZAH (PLACE). A Canaanite city whose king was defeated by Joshua (Josh. 12:24); and later, the capital of the N kingdom from the time of JEROBOAM I until OMRI moved the seat of government to SAMARIA (I Kings 16:23-24). **1. Location.** The precise location of Tirzah cannot be determined from the biblical evidence. On the reasonable supposition that the capital would not be moved any great distance, a location in the general vicinity of Samaria has been sought. Early explorers of this region, aware that the city must have rivaled Samaria and Shechem in importance, searched for a large tell whose modern name would resemble the ancient name. Tulluza, a modern town on a hill N of Mount Ebal, and Teyasir, a fortress still farther N, have been identified as Tirzah.

Archaeological evidence, however, resulting from surface exploration of the region and from a series of excavations under the auspices of the Dominican École Biblique in Jerusalem since 1946 at Tell el-Far'ah, tends to support the identification of this site with Tirzah. No inscriptions have been found at Tell el-Far'ah, identifying the city, but the geographic location, *ca.* seven miles NE of Nablus, its strategic position on the road from Shechem to Beth-shan, and its size, *ca.* 1,968 feet by 984 feet, making it larger than Megiddo and almost twice the size of OT Jericho, make plausible the identification of this site with Tirzah. The chronology of Tell el-Far'ah, as determined by the excavators on the basis of stratification of architectural remains, and a study of the pottery, corresponds exactly with the chronology of Tirzah. Evidence of destruction at Tell el-Far'ah, and a later, incomplete construction of palace and fortifications, is in remarkable agreement with the record of Omri's reign at Tirzah (I Kings 16:17, 23). A comparison of the levels of occupation at Tell el-Far'ah and Samaria tends to suggest that the two sites complement each other in a way which is in accord with the biblical evidence relating to the chronology of Tirzah.

Several scholars have proposed that modern Jemma'in, *ca.* seven miles S of Shechem, is Tirzah. Such an identification rests in part on an interpretation of II Kings 15:16, which reports Menahem's attack on Samaria and TAPPUAH, a city usually located S of Shechem. However, it is probable that the reference to Tirzah in this case is merely a way of indicating the general region under attack by Menahem, which could have included territory both to the N and to the S of Samaria.

2. History. After the conquest of the Canaanite city, there is no mention of Tirzah until the time of Jeroboam (*ca.* 920 B.C.), although it is probable that the Israelites occupied the place during the intervening years as their power extended over the territory of Manasseh. The statement that Jeroboam's wife came to Tirzah and his son died there is an indication that the capital was moved, early in the reign, from Shechem to Tirzah (I Kings 14:17). Such a change may have been dictated by political and military factors which operated in Israel's relationships with Syria.

For a period of *ca.* forty years Tirzah was the capital of the N kingdom, serving as the residence of Baasha (I Kings 15:21, 33), who was buried there (16:6); Elah (vss. 8-9), who was slain in the city while in a drunken stupor; and Zimri, whose reign of seven days came to an end when Tirzah was besieged by Omri, and Zimri died by burning the palace over himself (vss. 17-18). After reigning in Tirzah for six years, Omri moved the capital to Samaria (vss. 23-24), as political and military orientation toward Phoenicia became desirable.

Tirzah then disappears from Israelite history, except for a reference to it in the time of Menahem (*see above*), and a simile which mentions the beauty of Tirzah, as "comely as Jerusalem" (Song of S. 6:4) —probably a saying originating at a time when both cities were capitals (i.e., before 880 B.C.), although preserved in a much later source. Tirzah, if it is Tell el-Far'ah, was occupied by Israelites until the fall of Samaria at the hands of the Assyrians, and later until *ca.* 600 B.C., when the Babylonians conquered the land.

Pl. XXXI*c*.

Bibliography. W. F. Albright, "The Site of Tirzah and the Topography of Western Manasseh," *JPOS,* XI (1930), 241-51; G. E. Wright, "The Excavation at Tell el-Far'ah," *BA,* XII (1949), 66-68. See also articles in *RB* by R. de Vaux and A. M. Steve, beginning with vol. LIV (1947), especially "Les Fouilles de Tell el-Far'ah, près Naplouse," LXII (1955), 587-89.   W. L. REED

TISHBE tĭsh'bĭ [תשבי]; **TISHBITE** —bīt. The supposed name of the native city of Elijah and the descriptive adjective presumably derived from it. The name of Elijah's father and tribe are never given, but he is six times described as *hattishbî* (I Kings 17:1; 21:17, 28; II Kings 1:3, 8; 9:36); in the first of these references the explanation is added that he was מתשבי גלעד, *mittōshābhê ghil'ādh,* "of the sojourners of Gilead." The LXX translators took the term "Tishbite" to be an adjective descriptive of locality, and so accordingly vocalized the consonants as *mittishbê ghil'ādh,* "of Tishbe in Gilead," and the RSV has followed them in its version (KJV "of the inhabitants of Gilead" is entirely wrong). This "Tishbe" has been identified with Listib, situated near the Wadi el-Masquf, one of the branches of the Wadi el-Yabis, far E in the mountains of N Gilead. However, this identification cannot be traced back further than Byzantine times and is based on a mere similarity of names and the nearby Mar Ilyas; it is entirely confuted by the fact that there is no evidence whatsoever of a settlement at Listib during the Israelite period. N. Glueck, therefore, is of the opinion that there was an early corruption of both names, and proposes to read instead in I Kings 17:1: "Elijah the Jabeshite [ובשי] of Jabesh-gilead [מיבש גלעד]." This would be entirely plausible, as much of Elijah's activity took place in the region of the Wadi el-Yabis.

Another possible explanation is to suppose that *hattishbî* is to be vocalized as *hattôshᵉbhî,* "one of the *tôshāb* class." This type of descriptive adjective is found in an old Mishna (Kid. 4.1) which enumerates ten classes into which the Jews who returned from the Babylonian Exile were divided—e.g., *kôhᵃnî,* "priestly class," and *nᵉthînî,* "temple-slave class." The word *tôshāb* has a specific meaning in biblical texts; it refers to one who was originally not a native, but who has been granted permanent right of settlement, in contrast to the *gêr,* who is a temporary guest. The most important *tôshāb* group in the time of the judges and the kings was that of the Kenites, a nomadic tribe which served as smiths, cattle dealers, and musicians (cf. the descendants of Cain in Gen. 4:20-22). When Solomon engaged in the importation of horses and chariots (I Kings 10:26-29), these Kenites, with their experience with animals and in smithcraft, would naturally be foremost in this service; they would give themselves the new name of Rechabites, meaning those who had to do with chariots and with the horses that drew them. This presumes that the term "Son of Rechab" in II Kings 10:15-17 means "the Rechabite" and that Jonadab's title of "father" in Jer. 35:6-10 means that he was the regenerator and reformer of the Rechabite group. Other Kenites, who may have followed some such occupation as that of scribe (cf. I Chr. 2:55), could have been known as *toshabim*. We know of the Rechabites that they lived in tents like the Kenites (cf. Gen. 4:20; Judg. 5:24), and that they refrained from agriculture and the drinking of wine (Jer. 35); they also aided Elisha, the disciple of Elijah, in his struggle against the Baal-worship that accompanied the Israelites' settling down to agriculture (cf. II Kings 10:15). ELIJAH, the outstanding opponent of the Baal-worship introduced by Ahab, could well have been acting in the tradition of these naturalized nomads, and therefore the passage in I Kings 17:1 can mean as much as "Elijah the Kenite, of the Kenites of Gilead."

Bibliography. N. Glueck, "Explorations in Eastern Palestine IV," *AASOR,* XXV–XXVIII (1951), pt. I, 218, 225-27; J. D. Michaelis, *Eibel fuer die Ungelehrten,* to I Kings 17:1.

S. COHEN

TISHRI tĭsh'rĭ [תשרי]. The seventh month of the Hebrew CALENDAR; formerly ETHANIM.

TITHE [עשׂר, to give *or* take the tenth of; מעשׂר, tenth part; δεκατόω, ἀποδεκατόω, to give or take the tenth of; δεκάτη, tenth part]. To give a tenth of property or produce for the support of a priesthood or other religious institution or purpose; also, the tenth given for such a purpose. Tithing was an ancient and widespread practice; reference to it is found in other religions and cultures than those of Israel or the Semitic peoples alone. The references to tithing in the OT apparently reflect differing customs in differing times and places, and make it impossible to reconstruct any clear-cut picture of the practice or history of tithing in Israel.

1. Earlier references to tithing in the OT
2. Tithing in Deuteronomy
    a. Deuteronomic provisions for tithing
    b. The relation of the tithe to the offering of first fruits
3. Tithing in the Priestly Code
4. Tithing in later Judaism
Bibliography

1. Earlier references to tithing in the OT. When the various parts of the OT are arranged in their most probable chronological order, the earlier references to tithing are casual ones which seem to connect it, for the most part, with N sanctuaries. The E narrative of Jacob's vision of the heavenly ladder, as well as the prophet Amos, mentions tithes in connection with the sanctuary at Bethel (Gen. 28:22; Amos 4:4). Furthermore, the late source of I Samuel, probably northern in origin, mentions tithes as one of the abuses Israel is to suffer under a king (I Sam. 8:15, 17). Whether or not the latter reference reflects any actual practice is open to question. It has been conjectured that the tithe was originally paid to the

king for the support of the royal sanctuaries, and came later to be paid directly to the officials at the sanctuaries. The strange source, peculiar to Gen. 14, which recounts the payment of tithes to Melchizedek by Abraham does connect tithing with Jerusalem (vs. 20). It is, however, difficult to date this source. Moreover, the tithe here is connected with booty gained in war rather than with the produce of the land as elsewhere (cf. Heb. 7:2, 4). Neither the account in Gen. 28 nor the one in Gen. 14 can be taken necessarily to reflect the practice of the age in which the patriarchal legends are set.

Tithes are not mentioned at all in the Book of the Covenant (*see* COVENANT, BOOK OF), the earliest written collection of laws preserved in the OT; Deuteronomy is the earliest code which provides for them. The most probable explanation of this is that tithes and the offering of the FIRST FRUITS, which is mentioned in the Book of the Covenant, are ultimately of common origin. If this is true, it may be that the need for a stricter definition of what was to be offered caused the appropriation of the tithe, an offering which had originated in N sanctuaries.

2. Tithing in Deuteronomy. Provisions for the offering of the tithe are first found in DEUTERONOMY; and, in the light of more recent views of the origin of this book, this fact would serve as further evidence for a N origin of the tithe.

a. Deuteronomic provisions for tithing. The tithe is mentioned in two ways in Deuteronomy. On the one hand, the tithe, the tenth of the yield of agricultural products, is to be used, year by year, in an offering culminating in a sacrificial meal in which the household of the farmer is to share (Deut. 14:22-27; cf. 12:6-19). Although the meal is a household affair, it is to be held at the sanctuary, and to it the Levite (*see* PRIESTS AND LEVITES) is to be invited. The offering and the meal are, however, a household affair, and their primary purpose is not the support of the Levite. It has been conjectured that this provision was a reform which was the result of such abuses as those condemned by the prophet Amos (Amos 4:4; cf. 5:11). Whether or not this is so is impossible to say on the basis of the evidence and in view of the uncertainty of the date of origin of the regulations in Deuteronomy.

On the other hand, Deuteronomy speaks of a tithe to be offered for charitable purposes every third year (14:28-29; 26:12-15). This tithe is to be distributed to the Levite, the SOJOURNER, the fatherless, and the widow—those without land to produce crops for themselves. The question of whether or not Deuteronomy is thus contemplating two separate tithes naturally arises, and the answer to the question is probably a negative one. The use of the tithe merely differed in the third year. The confusion that results from a comparison of the passages in Deuteronomy in which the tithe is mentioned is due to the fact that liturgical usage is a constantly developing thing, producing confusion in any code or manual in which it is reduced to written provisions. The tithe in Deuteronomy is, thus, something which may have different purposes. It is an offering which acknowledges God's ownership of the soil and its fruits, a means of support for the Levite, and an offering for the sake of charity.

b. The relation of the tithe to the offering of first fruits. The question of whether or not the tithe and the FIRST FRUITS are the same thing in Deuteronomy is one to which it is not possible to give an entirely satisfactory answer. The fact that Deut. 26:1-15 mentions the two quite closely together can be cited in support of an affirmative answer. The basket of first fruits could be taken to be a symbolic portion of the tithe (vss. 1-4), and the command to "rejoice in all the good which the LORD your God has given to you" could be taken to require a meal such as the one connected with the offering of the tithe elsewhere in Deuteronomy (vs. 11; cf. 14:22-27). Further support for the position that the tithe and the first fruits are the same thing could be found in the fact that a double tribute would not be expected. The term "tithe" could have been introduced at some point to define first fruits more precisely.

The difficulty with the equation of the two lies in the provision of Deuteronomy that the first fruits shall be given to the priests (18:4)—a provision nowhere made in connection with the tithe. The problem is one which cannot logically be solved. Here, as in the case of the question of whether or not Deuteronomy contemplates two tithes (*see* § *2a above*), the confusion is due to the fact that a code such as that of Deuteronomy preserves cultic customs from different ages and places and that actual usage was a living, developing thing. Undoubtedly the origin of both tithe and first fruits was the urge to express the conviction that all man's possessions belonged, ultimately, to God. Such expression used various forms.

3. Tithing in the Priestly Code. Between Deuteronomy and the PRIESTLY CODE no regulations with regard to tithing are found. The word used for "tithe" does occur twice in the legislative section of the book of Ezekiel, but here it is used simply. in the nontechnical sense of "a tenth" (Ezek. 45:11, 14). The provisions for tithing in the Priestly Code represent a development that had taken place since Deuteronomy. The later code stipulates that the tithe is to go exclusively to the Levites, who, in turn, are to give a tenth of what they receive to the priests (Num. 18:20-32). In the Priestly Code the tithe is associated with the heave offering (*see* SACRIFICES).

The Priestly Code, like Deuteronomy, usually considers the tithe as an offering of agricultural produce, not of cattle (Lev. 27:30-31), and that this was the practice is corroborated in references to the tithe in the book of Nehemiah (Neh. 10:37-38; 12:44; 13:5, 12). One passage, however, includes cattle in the tithe (Lev. 27:32-33), and this passage is corroborated in II Chr. 31:5-12. The discrepancy here is due, again, to development in cultic practice, which continued even in postexilic times. How the tithe was taken for granted in later times is illustrated by late, prophetic reference to it (Mal. 3:8, 10).

4. Tithing in later Judaism. In line with the tendency to regard the entire law as binding, two tithes were required in later times. In accord with the Priestly Code, the tithe for the Levites was collected, and was the chief source of their income. The Mishna (*see* TALMUD) stipulated that everything used for food, that was cultivated and grew from the earth, was subject to the tithe (Ma'as. I.1). How strictly this could be observed is seen in Jesus' condemnation

of the Pharisees for their lack of a sense of proportion with regard to what was important in religious observance (Matt. 23:23; Luke 11:42). In addition to the tithe for the Levites, a second tithe, which was consumed by the offerer in accord with the provisions of Deuteronomy, was required. The cattle tithe was reckoned in this second tithe. The charity tithe, in effect a third tithe, was also levied annually for the relief of the poor.

Bibliography. O. Eissfeldt, *Erstlinge und Zehnten im AT* (1917); A. Wendel, *Das Opfer in der altisraelitischen Religion* (1927), pp. 99, 174 ff.   H. H. GUTHRIE, JR.

TITIUS JUSTUS tĭsh'ĭ əs jŭs'təs. *See* JUSTUS 2.

TITLE. KJV translation of צִיּוּן (RSV MONUMENT) in II Kings 23:17.

TITLE ON THE CROSS. *See* INSCRIPTION ON THE CROSS.

TITTLE. *See* DOT.

TITUS tī'təs [Τίτος]. **1.** Titus MANIUS.

2. A co-worker of Paul. *See* TITUS COMPANION OF PAUL.

3. Titus Flavius Vespasianus, son, namesake, and successor of the Emperor VESPASIAN. He was born in A.D. 39, and after military service in Germany and Britain he went with his father to participate in suppressing the Jewish revolt in 66. After his father left to become emperor at Rome, Titus brought the war to a successful conclusion in 70. Thereafter he joined Vespasian as his coadjutor, and in 79 he came to the throne. His brief reign was remembered, especially in contrast to the succeeding reign of his brother

Courtesy of the American Numismatic Society
66. Coin of Emperor Titus

DOMITIAN, as a time of tranquillity and rather expensive public works. On his death in 81, he was deified by the Senate, with which he had been on the best of terms.

Figs. ROM 18; TIT 66.

4. A name given in some apocryphal works to the penitent thief of Luke 23:39-43. *See* DYSMAS.

R. M. GRANT

TITUS, EPISTLE OF. A Latin apocryphon purporting to be a letter of Titus, but in reality a dull declamation about virginity and a denouncement of "spiritual marriages," in which men and women (*virgines subintroductae;* συνείσακτοι) lived together but without sexual contacts. In addition it contains fragments from the apocryphal Acts of Andrew, of Peter, and of John. Probably written in Greek, it is extant in one eighth-century Latin MS. It is probably a production by Priscillianists, perhaps in Spain. *See* APOCRYPHA, NT.

Bibliography. D. de Bruyne, "Epistula Titi, discipuli Pauli, de dispositione sanctimonii," *Revue Bénédictine*, 37 (1925), 47-72; A. von Harnack, *Sitzungsberichte* of the Berlin Academy (1925), pp. 180-212.   M. S. ENSLIN

TITUS, LETTER TO. A letter found as the seventeenth book in the NT canon, purporting to have been written by the apostle Paul to his associate in work, Titus.

It is closely related in style, purpose, and content to the First Letter to Timothy, less so to the Second Letter to Timothy. Together the three letters are called the PASTORAL LETTERS, a name indicating the ecclesiastical purpose of the correspondence: a chief pastor giving advice to pastors of the church.

The relative priority of the letters is difficult to determine. Titus is probably the first, since it is difficult to imagine that this letter could have been written after I Timothy which treats the same topics more extensively.

Titus is primarily concerned with church order. Paul addresses Titus, whom he has left in Crete to organize missionary districts into churches. He advises that the clergy must be selected carefully, its authority acknowledged, and its guidance in matters of worship followed (1:5-9; 2:1–3:8). This task is especially urgent in the face of the heretics who threaten to destroy the church and its confession (1:10-16; 3:8-11).   J. C. BEKER

TITUS COMPANION OF PAUL. A Gentile protégé and aide of Paul; the purported recipient of one of the NT letters, which bears his name. Most of our information about Titus comes from two of the letters of Paul, Galatians and II Corinthians. Beyond this, there is brief mention of him in II Timothy and in the Letter to Titus, both of which almost certainly come from later than the time of Paul. Attempts to identify Titus with Titius Justus (Acts 18:7) have proved to be quite inconclusive.

1. In Galatians. On the occasion of Paul's second visit to Jerusalem after his conversion, he was accompanied by his co-worker Barnabas, and by a Gentile Christian named Titus (Gal. 2:1-10). The Jewish Christians of Jerusalem insisted that Titus should be circumcised, but Paul chose to make a test case of Titus, and refused to submit to their urging. Although the MS evidence is divided at this point—some of the MSS and some of the church fathers record that Paul *did* yield on this issue momentarily —the text usually translated is most probably correct, and Titus was accepted as a member of the Christian community without having been circumcised. That this incident established a precedent is evident from the fact that Paul appeals to it as the chief ground for his refutation of those who are insisting that the Galatian Christians must be circumcised.

2. In II Corinthians. Word had come to Paul that the Corinthian Christians had defied his instructions, and were in a hostile mood toward him and his apostolic leadership. He sent his associate Titus ahead of

him to see if the reports were true. The arrangement was that Paul would move slowly westward toward Corinth along a prearranged route, and Titus, returning eastward from Corinth, would meet Paul. Paul was at first disappointed that Titus had not arrived at Troas when Paul himself reached that city (II Cor. 2:13), but he was overjoyed to meet him in Macedonia (7:6), especially since Titus brought the news that the reports from Corinth were not true, or rather that they were no longer true. The Corinthian church was once again reconciled to Paul and willing to acknowledge his apostolic authority (7:9). Titus reported that the Corinthian Christians were as noble and as obedient as Paul had said they were (vss. 13-14).

On the strength of this report, Paul sent Titus back to Corinth to continue the work that he had so effectively begun there (8:6). Paul reminded the Corinthians that Titus had a deep concern for them, and urged them to complete the project of making a contribution to the church at Jerusalem. The way in which they responded to Titus' leadership in supervising the collection would give proof of their love for the saints and of the grounds for Paul's confidence in them, about which he had boasted to Titus (8:23). Titus was accompanied on his journey to Corinth by an unnamed brother who was "famous . . . for his preaching of the gospel" (8:18), together with some brethren from the other churches to assist in the collection. Later in the letter (12:17-18), Paul reminds the Corinthians that Titus has given no evidence of wanting to take advantage of them, just as Paul himself has had only their best interests at heart.

3. In the Pastorals. The impression that we gain of Titus in the letter that purports to have been written to him by Paul is that of a rather different person, who needs to be reminded to exercise his authority in ecclesiastical, doctrinal, and moral matters. The fact that this portrait of Titus varies so markedly from the vigorous, resourceful, strong right arm whom Paul pictures in Galatians and II Corinthians is one of the reasons most scholars now view this and the other Pastorals as pseudonymous. From this standpoint the challenge to "Titus" is recognized as simply a literary device by which to underscore the need of the churches to submit to ecclesiastical authority. *See* PASTORAL LETTERS.

Titus is addressed as "my true child in a common faith" (Tit. 1:4), which is intended to mean that he was converted to the faith by Paul himself. The word translated "true" often carries the meaning of "legitimate." The implication of this phrase that there was a close, filial relationship between Titus and Paul is borne out by the references to Titus in Galatians and II Corinthians. According to 1:5, Paul had sent Titus to Crete, to supervise the work of the churches there in Paul's name. Paul instructs Titus to meet him at NICOPOLIS, probably the Nicopolis located NW of the mouth of the Gulf of Corinth, where Paul expects to spend the winter. Such a journey does not fit well with what we know of Paul's travels, either from our primary source, Paul's letters, or from Acts, unless we suppose that Paul went N to Nicopolis after the brief visit to Corinth mentioned in II Cor. 2:1.

In the personal notes at the end of II Timothy, Titus is reported to have gone to still another field:

DALMATIA, in what is now Yugoslavia. Even those scholars who deny the authenticity of the Pastorals as a whole, acknowledge that the personal remarks at the end of II Timothy and Titus may well include fragments of otherwise unknown correspondence from Paul. One plausible conjecture is that these notes come from the time of his imprisonment in Caesarea, although they may also come from either Rome or Ephesus.

4. In Acts. The attempt has been made to identify Titus of Paul's genuine letters with Titius JUSTUS of Acts 18:7, since Codex Sinaiticus and other important ancient authorities have "Titius" in place of "Titus." But even if the text were certain—which it is not, since some MSS (e.g., A D) omit the first name entirely—there would be no warrant for associating an unknown man of Corinth, bearing a common name like Titus, with Paul's companion of the same name. In fact, it is not at all likely that Paul would have sent a native of Corinth back to the city to report to him on the troubled state of the church there.   H. C. KEE

TIZITE tī′zīt [תיצי] (I Chr. 11:45). A designation of Joha, one of David's Mighty Men; probably derived from a place, now unknown.

TOAH tō′ə [תוח] (I Chr. 6:34). A name in a list which traces both the Levitical descent of Heman and the Levitical line from Kohath. In a preceding list (vs. 26) this name is Nahath.

TOB tŏb [טוב, Apoc. Τουβίον]; KJV TOBIE tō′bĭ. Apoc. TOUBIANI tōō′bĭ ā′nĭ [Τουβιανοί, men of Tob]; KJV TUBIENI —ē′nĭ (II Macc. 12:17). KJV once ISHTOB ĭsh′tŏb (II Sam. 10:6-8; a mistaken rendering for "men of Tob"). A city in S Hauran; also the district surrounding it. It is mentioned in Egyptian sources as *tu-by* (no. 22 in the list of Thut-mose II), and as *Dubu* in the Amarna Letters. Jephthah fled to Tob when he was driven away by his half brothers, and it was from this country that he was recalled to lead the E tribes against the Ammonites (Judg. 11:3-5). The country was regarded as Aramean; and when Hanun, king of Ammon, sought allies in his war against David, Tob sent twelve thousand warriors, who were defeated with the other Arameans by the prowess of Joab (II Sam. 10:6-13).

Another name for Tob seems to have been TABEEL, one of the princes of which was chosen by Rezin of Damascus and Pekah of Israel to replace Ahaz on the throne of Judah (Isa. 7:6). In the postexilic period a number of Jews settled in Tob and had to be rescued by Judas Maccabeus when they were attacked by their Greek neighbors (I Macc. 5:13; II Macc. 12:17).

The name and site of the city of Tob are probably preserved in the village of et-Taiyibeh between Bozrah and Edrei, near the sources of the River Yarmuk.   S. COHEN

TOBADONIJAH tŏb′ăd ə nī′jə [טוב אדוניה] (II Chr. 17:8); KJV TOB-ADONIJAH. According to the MT, one of the Levites sent by Jehoshaphat to teach among the people of Judah. But the name is probably to be deleted as an error due to dittography and homoeoteleuton following the two preceding names in the list, Adonijah and Tobijah.

B. T. DAHLBERG

TOBIAH tō bī′ə [טוביה, Yahu is good; *same as* טוביהו, Tobijah; Apoc. Βάν (*emended by* RSV)]; KJV Apoc. BAN băn. **1.** Head of a family or clan of returned exiles that was unable to prove its Israelitish descent (Ezra 2:60; Neh. 7:62; I Esd. 5:37). The family may be related to the Tobiads described below, but clear evidence for such a relationship is presently lacking.

2. One of the chief opponents (along with SANBALLAT) of the successful efforts of Nehemiah the Jewish governor to rebuild the walls of postexilic Jerusalem (*ca.* 445-437 B.C.; Neh. 2:10, 19; 4:3, 7; 6:1, 12, 19; etc.). That he was called "the Ammonite" indicates his connection with the territory of Ammon across the Jordan River from Palestine, N of the Dead Sea. Extrabiblical records attest to the prominence of a family of this name in Ammon in the Persian period (*see bibliography*). The reference to him as "the servant" probably signifies his official title in the provincial government under Persian rule; perhaps he was "governor" of Ammon, as Sanballat was of Samaria and Nehemiah of Judah (cf. Neh. 2:10, 19).

Whether or not Tobiah was of Israelitish descent has not been established, but he could be a descendant of those Jews who fled to Ammon after the fall of Jerusalem in 586 B.C., who are mentioned in Jer. 41:15. The name Tobiah itself suggests at least a formal attachment of his parents to the Jewish cultus, and he himself appears to have observed Jewish faith and practice to some degree, for he was admitted to residence in a chamber of the Jerusalem temple during Nehemiah's absence from Jerusalem (Neh. 13:4-9). Whatever this episode involved—he was ejected by Nehemiah on the latter's return—it attests to the friendly relations existing between Tobiah and an influential portion of the Jewish nobility, to whom he was related also by marriage, and by whom he was well spoken of (6:17-19). Again, whether or not he was of mixed blood, scholars believe him to have been an ancestor of the house of Tobiah (Tobias) which in the third century B.C. became a rival of the house of Onias for the Jewish high priesthood in Palestine (cf. II Macc. 3:11; Jos. Antiq. XII.iv).

Nehemiah's unswerving opposition to Tobiah and Sanballat—and theirs to him—appears to have rested on neither religious nor personal grounds primarily, although these factors doubtlessly aggravated the antagonism between them. But it appears to have been based on Nehemiah's appreciation of what we should only expect to be true in the nature of the case, that Tobiah and Sanballat could be expected to subvert by every practical means available the restoration of Jerusalem to a position of strength that would curtail the influence and authority heretofore enjoyed by them in a relatively unorganized territory.

See also NEHEMIAH; GESHEM; SAMARITANS.

Bibliography. M. Noth, *Die israelitischen Personennamen* (1928), pp. 18n, 19n, 110n, 153; W. O. E. Oesterley and T. H. Robinson, *A History of Israel,* II (1932), 123-24, 154-

55, 200, 210-11; W. F. Albright, *Archaeology and the Religion of Israel* (1942), p. 222. For further historical data and a useful list of primary and secondary sources, see R. A. Bowman, *IB*, III (1954), 676-77, 804-8.   B. T. DAHLBERG

TOBIAS tō bī'əs [Τωβίας, God's goodness, *or* my good is Yahweh]. **1.** A "man of very prominent position," father of Hyrcanus (II Macc. 3:11).

2. Son of Tobit, and one of the principal characters in the book of Tobit. *See* TOBIT, BOOK OF.

      J. C. SWAIM

TOBIE. KJV form of TOB.

TOBIJAH tō bī'jə [תוביהו, Yahu is (my) good; *see also* TOBIAH]. **1.** One of King Jehoshaphat's Levites who traveled through the cities of Judah teaching the law of God (II Chr. 17:8).

2. One of the four men, returned from Babylon, whose contributions were to be used to make the crown for the high priest Joshua, according to a vision of the prophet Zechariah (Zech. 6:10, 14). The LXX takes the name as an appellative, "the useful men."   J. M. WARD

TOBIT, BOOK OF tō'bĭt [Τωβίτ, *see* § 1 *below*]. A didactic romance concerning a devout Jew of the Dispersion, Tobit, whose faithfulness and good deeds result in a supernatural deliverance from affliction for himself, his son Tobias, and Tobias' wife, Sarah. The book reflects a genuine Jewish piety mixed with elements of folklore from various sources, which the author has effectively woven into an artistic work of high quality and wide appeal. It was an invariable part of the APOCRYPHA, both as contained in the LXX and as adopted and circulated by the early Christians, and it was among the "deuterocanonical" books recognized officially as canonical by the Council of Trent in 1546.

The exact circumstances of the origin of the writing are in doubt, but there is general agreement on a date of *ca.* 200-170 B.C., and the weight of scholarly opinion probably inclines to composition in Aramaic or Hebrew in Syria or Mesopotamia. The chief alternative view preferred a Greek, Alexandrian original; and while there was much to be said for this, it has been rendered less likely by the discovery of Hebrew and Aramaic fragments of the book among the Qumran scrolls.

The Greek is a simple and fairly idiomatic, colloquial type, but it abounds in Semiticisms, whether these be translation phenomena or the reflection of the author's native idiom. The form of the text itself also presents a problem, for it exists in two chief and often quite different recensions (*see* § 2*b below*). While scholars have been rather evenly divided regarding which of these is prior, opinion now tends to favor the longer Sinaiticus text, supported also by the OL and the Qumran fragments, as the more primitive. The other text, however, read by codices Vaticanus (B) and Alexandrinus (A) generally has been made the basis of published editions and of translations of the Apoc. into English and other modern languages.

      1. Title and contents
      2. Text
         a. Extant texts
         b. The Greek recensions
         c. Original language
      3. Place and date
      4. Sources and unity
      5. Purpose
      6. History and influence
      Bibliography

1. Title and contents. The composition describes itself as the "book of the acts [lit., 'words'] of Tobit." The Hebrew version calls it the "book of Tobi," and the Aramaic the "history [act] of Tobiyah." The name Tobit (Τωβίτ; Τωβ(ε)ίθ) is a Greek form for Hebrew *Tôbî* ("my goodness"), itself doubtless an abbreviation of *Tôbîyâh* ("the goodness of Yahweh") as read in the Aramaic. Cf. Zech. 6:10 (Tobijah). The Latin Vulg. used "Tobias" (a Grecized form of Tobiyah) for both father and son, and thus popularized this usage, although it is somewhat confusing.

The story concerns Tobit, a devout and loyal Jew of THISBE and the tribe of NAPHTALI, who with his wife, HANNAH, and their son Tobias had been taken captive to Nineveh in the reign of Shalmaneser (*see* SHALMANESER 4) in the eighth century B.C. In Nineveh he continued his good deeds, especially in almsgiving and in giving decent burial to those of his own race who were slain by King Sennacherib (*see* SENNACHERIB). When the king learned of this practice, Tobit had to flee Nineveh; but after ESARHADDON succeeded to the throne, he was enabled to return, through the aid of Ahikar, his nephew and the chief minister to the new king. Tobit continued his burial of the dead, and one night, after such an act had made him "unclean," he slept in the courtyard. As he slept, the droppings of sparrows fell into his eyes and blinded him. In this situation, after being blind for four years, he in despair prayed fervently for divine help. *See* ANAEL; DEBORAH 3.

At this very time, in ECBATANA, Sarah (*see* SARAH 2), daughter of RAGUEL and EDNA, also uttered a prayer for deliverance from an unhappy plight in which her seven husbands had been successively slain in the bridal chamber by the evil and jealous demon ASMODAEUS. The prayers of Tobit and Sarah were heard by God, who dispatched the angel RAPHAEL to aid them. *See* ANGEL; DEMON.

Tobit, believing that his time of death was near, planned to send Tobias to RAGES to recover from a kinsman, GABAEL, a sum of money (about $20,000) which had been deposited with him years before. Raphael, posing as a dependable kinsman who knew the way, was employed to guide Tobias on the journey. In bidding them farewell, Tobit unwittingly prayed that God's angel might attend them. The travelers set out, accompanied by Tobias' dog (S text), and camped at the Tigris River, where a large fish leaped from the water as if to eat Tobias (or bite his foot). At Raphael's suggestion he caught the fish and saved the heart, liver, and gall for later use. The rest of the fish they ate. *See* GABRIAS; JATHAN; SHEMAIAH 17.

Before they arrived at Ecbatana, Raphael told Tobias about the attractive daughter of Raguel, Sarah, and indicated that by reason of kinship Tobias was now the only eligible husband left for her. He also induced him to enter into the marriage, instructing him to exorcize the demon by burning the heart and liver of the fish on the incense fire in the bridal chamber. After the arrival, exchange of greetings, and consummation of the marriage, Tobias carried out the instructions of the angel, and the smoke from the fire drove Asmodaeus away into Upper Egypt, where Raphael quickly followed and bound him. Meanwhile, Raguel, fearing the worst and unaware of these happenings, had had a grave dug during the night. But the next morning he was elated to find the young man alive, and at his insistence the wedding celebration was carried on for fourteen days. During this time Raphael went on alone and obtained the money from Gabael, and Tobias grew anxious to return home.

Back in Nineveh, Tobit and Hannah were in despair at Tobias' long absence; but at last he returned with his wife and Raphael, and they were overjoyed. Then Tobias, as Raphael had instructed him, placed the gall of the fish upon his father's eyes, and his sight was immediately restored. In gratitude for everything, they offered Raphael half the money; but at this point the angel made his true identity known, bade them thank God for his mercies, and disappeared. Tobit then uttered a long prayer of praise and rejoicing. The book closes with instructions from Tobit to Tobias and his predictions of the future, and with indications that both lived to a good old age and were buried with honor after enjoying many blessings, including, in the case of Tobias, the news of the destruction of Nineveh.

2. Text. *a. Extant texts.* The oldest complete text of the book is found in Greek. Of this there are two chief recensions, and a third which is derived from them and is definable in roughly chs. 6–13. Of the first two, the one (Rs) is represented mainly in Codex Sinaiticus, the other (Rv) in codices Vaticanus, Alexandrinus (A), one other uncial MS (V or Venetus), and several minuscule MSS. The third (Rc), a mediating type based mainly on Rs, is found in three minuscules and, for ch. 2, in Papyrus Oxyrrhyncus 1076. Important supplementary evidence comes from the ancient versions. The Old Latin (OL) is found in four MSS (α β γ δ in Charles, *Apoc. and Pseudep. of the OT*), and strongly supports the Rs text except that δ is Rc in part. The Vulg. is also basically of this type, although it is possible that a Semitic text was known to Jerome. He tells the story of receiving assistance from someone who was translating an Aramaic text into Hebrew. An Aramaic version of unknown origin exists which supports the Rs text. It was published in 1878 by A. Neubauer from a fifteenth-century Bodleian MS, but appears linguistically to reflect the period A.D. 300-700. Whether this depends upon an earlier Aramaic has been debatable; but the existence of such a version is attested by the Qumran fragments, three in Aramaic and one in Hebrew. These are probably from the first or second century B.C. and are all Rs in character. A free Hebrew version (HM) from the edition by Münster in 1542 appears also to depend upon an older Aramaic form of Rs type. Three other late Hebrew texts exist. That of Fagius (HF), from his edition of 1542, is apparently a free twelfth-century translation from Rv. But the "London" Hebrew (HL), edited by Moses Gaster from a late British

Museum MS in 1896-97, is close to the Vulg.; and the "Gaster" Hebrew (HG), copied by Gaster from a midrash on the Pentateuch, has affinities with Neubauer's Aramaic and the Vulg. Other versions are of less significance. Two fragmentary Syr. MSS of the seventh century A.D. support respectively the Rv to 7:11 and the Rc from there on. Related to Rv are a fragmentary Sahidic version, an abbreviated and faulty Ethiopic, and translations into Armenian and Arabic. *See also bibliography.*

b. The Greek recensions. The question of the relationship between the two principal Greek recensions constitutes a very difficult problem. Extensive identity in vocabulary and word order seems to point to dependence of the one upon the other, but the quantity and quality of disagreement are such as to suggest a common Greek exemplar instead. Even this may involve, in the opinion of some, divergent influences from Semitic documentary sources. Rs is much longer than Rv, *ca.* 1,700 more words in its total of *ca.* 7,200. While Rs has been alleged to be a deliberate expansion of Rv which adds nothing of significance to the narrative, Rv on the other hand gives evidence of being a reduction of the longer text (e.g., in 1:7-10; 2:10; 3:10; 5:3; etc.) which makes various improvements (1:4; 3:11; 12:5; 14:3; etc.) but at the same time results in a loss of vivid and appropriate detail and in certain questionable alterations or even violations of the real sense (e.g., in 1:4; 2:12; 3:10; 9:6; 12:6; etc.). The Rv text may be described as more stable than Rs and as showing less fluctuation among the versions which are related to it. However, a simpler and more direct relationship among the witnesses would suffice to explain this. It is true that Rv, in spite of its shorter character, fills in two major gaps in the Rs text (4:7b-18; 13:8-11a) and several minor ones. But these may be explicable as accidental omissions in S or its exemplar. The OL, which is related to Rs, fills in both the longer lacunae, and the Qumran Aramaic fragments attest one of them. Rs appears to reflect an earlier historical, political, and religious situation than Rv. This involves such things as geographical details, Jewish customs, and a more accurate list of Assyrian kings. Rv exhibits a later standpoint in theology and in such religious customs as tithing and fasting. Traces of liturgical and devotional use of the book also appear, including a tendency to assimilate the text to the OT (e.g., 2:6; 13:2). While Rv may show better transmission of some Hebrew names, Rs is in general closer to Hebrew or Aramaic in style, and one may argue with more cogency that it rests upon a Semitic original.

c. Original language. The question of priority of texts involves the problem of the original language of Tobit. This too has been much debated, with past opinion rather evenly divided between Greek and a Semitic form. While there has been a tendency toward favoring a Semitic original as time went on, among those who supported the Greek were such older scholars as Fritsche, Nöldeke, Schürer, Zöckler, and André. The external evidence for this view is scanty and inconclusive. Origen says that he did not know of a Semitic text and that the Jews did not have one among their apocryphal writings (*Epistle to Africanus* XIII). But Jerome in his prefatory remarks to Tobit in the Vulg. implies that he knew and used a "Chaldee" (i.e., Aramaic) text. This aspect of the problem is at least partly settled by the Qumran fragments. With respect to internal evidence, it has been argued that much of the book's phraseology is purely Greek idiom with no necessary relationship to a Semitic document (e.g., in 1:6 ff; 3:8; 4:6; 7:7; 12:7; etc.), and that the style is not typically that of translation Greek, lacking certain common expressions found in such compositions. The forms of proper names in the first part of the book are the usual Greek equivalents of the Hebrew. Such Semitic expressions as are reflected in the Greek may be explained from the author's native idiom. If the book was composed in Alexandria or some other Diaspora situation, it would probably be in Greek.

Scholars favoring a Semitic original contend that the style and phraseology of the book, especially in the Rs form, have a definitely un-Greek and Semitic character; certain constructions seem to demand an author who not only thought but also wrote in a Semitic language. Various alleged mistranslations are explained on this basis. Parallels in source materials are best so explained. The names of the characters and other particulars of the story fit better into a Semitic context. Those who favor an Aramaic original as against Hebrew—where opinion again has been sharply divided—indicate that this would explain a variability in word order, the absence of certain common Hebraisms (e.g., the καὶ ἐγένετο construction), and the presence of "mistranslations" explicable only from Aramaic. The form of Greek names in 14:4, 15, suggests Aramaic. It is further contended that Tobit's use of Ahikar as a source (see § 4 below) reflects the latter's primitive Aramaic form. From his first examinations of the Qumran fragments, Milik concluded that they suggested Aramaic as the original language. In the period of the book's probable composition (i.e., ca. 200 B.C.) Aramaic was a lingua franca which would naturally be used by a Jewish writer in Mesopotamia or even in Egypt.

Some of the arguments on all sides are subjective in character; but there seems to be a definite disposition to favor Aramaic. While a number of scholars were content to support a Semitic original as against Greek, certain investigators may be mentioned who specified either Hebrew or Aramaic. The former was favored by Bickell, Graetz, Levi, Heller, Joüon, and Müller; the latter by Fuller, Harris, Marshall, Torrey, Pfeiffer, and Zimmerman. Simpson left the matter an open question, and Zimmerman preferred to posit a Hebrew form of text mediating between the Aramaic and Greek.

3. Place and date. The circumstances of the composition of Tobit merit further consideration in view both of the bearing of this matter upon this question of language and of the unsolved problems that here exist. With the exception of a very few scholars, who regarded Palestine as a likely place of origin, there has been general agreement that a Diaspora situation is reflected in the book. Earlier critics, probably influenced mainly by the general contents and the supposition of a Semitic original, looked to Mesopotamia or the East as the place of origin. The demonology and magic, among other things, suggested a "liberal," extra-Palestinian milieu. But opinion

tended more and more to favor an Egyptian provenance as explaining various features of the contents, the sources used (see § 4 below), the earliest extant version—i.e., the Greek text—and the author's ignorance of Eastern history and geography. The existence of Aramaic and Hebrew texts in Palestine in the first or second century B.C. will have some influence on the linguistic argument as it affects place and date. The question of a date in the Persian period has again been raised, but comes up against the matters of internal evidence (see below; see also bibliography).

Bearing on the place and date of the book is the question of its "historicity." Luther was apparently the first to challenge the book as history; and it is clear from the errors to which we have alluded that it could not have come as we have it from the period of the events depicted. Some Roman Catholic scholars have tried to defend a date in the seventh century B.C. and to explain certain of the errors through highly questionable linguistic manipulations. But the author was simply not interested in the accuracy of the "history" which served as a framework for his story. It was Tiglath-pileser III (II Kings 15:29) who took Naphtali and Zebulun in 734 B.C., and not Shalmaneser; Sennacherib was not Shalmaneser's son, but Sargon's; Cyaxares and NABOPOLASSAR, rather than Assueres and Nebuchadnezzar, were responsible for the capture of Nineveh; the Tigris is not between Nineveh and Ecbatana (unless a tributary is in mind), and Rages is not a "two-days" journey from Ecbatana. The last statement (only in Rs) has often been regarded as an interpolation. See AHASUERUS.

There are, of course, other factors which make a later dating necessary, and which make possible a fairly definite indication of the time of composition. The knowledge of events of subsequent centuries (14: 4-5, 15), the references to Rages, to tithing (1:7 in Rs), the use of the Greek drachma (5:14—G 5:15) and of a Greek name (Dystros) for a month (2:12 in Rs), and the use of the OT, especially the quotation of the prophetic books, are some of the other evidences of a later date and probably one not earlier than ca. 200 B.C. The book, however, does not seem to reflect the situation of crisis which developed under Antiochus Epiphanes (see ANTIOCHUS 4), and it is therefore generally dated before this time—i.e., between 200 and 170 B.C. A later date also seems to be questionable, in view of the absence of certain developments in religious doctrines, such as apocalypticism, with its descriptions of the messianic age and beliefs in resurrection and immortality, or such as are reflected in the later rise of Pharasaic and Sadducaic parties. External evidence, specifically the Qumran documents, would give a terminus ad quem of whatever date is determined for the fragments. This has ranged from the sixth century B.C. down to the absolute limit of the period just before A.D. 70, but a date in the second or first century B.C. seems most likely, and nothing here precludes the dating of the book suggested above.

4. Sources and unity. The use of various earlier sources also throws light upon the problems of origin, as has been briefly intimated, and is of interest in connection with the composition of the work and its thought. The OT is, of course, an unmistakable ingredient; the book contains reflections of biblical ideas and events, biblical phraseology, frequent allusions to specific passages, and a few quotations or near quotations. Examples of the last category may be seen in 1:21 (II Kings 19:37); 2:6 (Amos 8:10); 4:14 (Lev. 19:13); 8:6 (Gen. 2:18); 13:2 (I Sam. 2:6; cf. Wisd. Sol. 16:13). Rather definite allusions occur in 1:4 (Wisd. Sol. 9:8); 1:5 (I Kings 12:28-30); 1:6 (Deut. 12:6; 16:16); 1:7 (Deut. 14:25-26); 1:8 (Deut. 14:28-29; 26); 1:10-13 (Dan. 1:8-9); 1:16-17 (Isa. 58:7; Ezek. 18:5-9); 1:17; 4:17 (I Kings 13:28-29; II Esd. 2:23; Ecclus. 7:33; 30:18; 38:16 ff); 1:18 (Isa. 37:36-37; Ecclus. 48:18, 21; I Macc. 7:41; II Macc. 8:19); 3:10; 6:15 (Gen. 42:38; 44:29, 31); 3:11 (Dan. 6:10); 3:17; 6:11; 7:13 (Num. 27:8; 36:6-9); 4:3; 10: 12 (Exod. 20:12; Prov. 23:22; Ecclus. 7:27-28); 4:10 (Prov. 10:2; 11:14); 4:7, 16 (Ecclus. 14:8-9); 4:7 ff; 12:8-9; 14:11 (Deut. 15:7-11; Ecclus. 17:22; 29:11-13; 35:2); 7:3-5 (Gen. 29:4-6); 7:11 (Gen. 24:33); 8:6 (Gen. 2:7, 18, 22); 11:15 (Deut. 32:39); 12:10 (Wisd. Sol. 1:12); 13:5 (Deut. 30:3; Jer. 29:14; etc.); 13:11 (Dan. 4:37); 13:12 (Gen. 27:29; Num. 24:9); 13:16-17 (Isa. 54:11-12); 14:4, 8 (Jonah 3:4); 14:4-5 (Ezra 1:1; Jer. 25:11-13; 29:10, 14; Dan. 9:2). But in some of these, as well as in other passages, common tradition rather than literary dependence may suffice to explain the parallelism. The quantity and nature of the data are nonetheless indicative of a date such as is generally proposed for the book. In particular a number of correspondences with ECCLESIASTICUS point to a similar period of origin for these two books.

Among the extrabiblical sources the popular Wisdom of Ahikar (*see* AHIKAR) is evidently used. Our author apparently knew the story in written form and assumed that his readers were acquainted with it. Direct borrowing may be posited in 1:21-22; 2:10; 11:18; 14:10, 15. Its most primitive form was Aramaic, an indication to some, again, of Aramaic as the original language of Tobit; but this earliest attestation is Egyptian (Elephantine Papyri of sixth-fifth centuries B.C.). In the story Ahikar was a prominent official under Sennacherib, king of Assyria. He adopted his nephew, Nadan (cf. Tob. 11:18), and arranged for the young man to succeed him upon his retirement. The nephew, however, lived riotously and plotted his uncle's overthrow by forging a charge of treason against him. Ahikar was condemned to be executed, but the executioner was his friend and kept him safely hidden. When trouble with the king of Egypt later called for wisdom such as only Ahikar had, Sennacherib repented of his act. The executioner then produced Ahikar alive, to the king's great joy. After he had outwitted the Egyptian king, Ahikar returned home in honor, while Nadan was reviled and imprisoned and eventually swelled up, burst open, and died. Ahikar, as Tobit, was vindicated because of his righteousness. In the Tobit story Ahikar is presented as a prominent official and a nephew and benefactor of Tobit. *See* HAMAN; NADAB 5; NASBAS; MANASSES.

Tobit also reflects the knowledge and use of the so-called Fable of the Grateful Dead. This is really a cycle of well-known stories, many variants of which have been collected. In the usual form the corpse of a debtor is rescued and buried, at great personal risk, by a traveling merchant. A mysterious stranger comes to his aid, who turns out to be the dead man's spirit returned in human form. He delivers the merchant from mortal danger and arranges a bride for him. Another variant makes the bride a princess whose bridegrooms successively have been slain by a dragon or monster, which the hero is empowered to kill. He is sometimes assisted by a dog. The common dragon-slayer theme also becomes involved in these forms. A similar type of story probably known to Tobit, especially if the latter's provenance is Egyptian, is the Tractate of Khôns, attested as early as 500 B.C. This recounts that at "Bchtn" (cf. Ecbatana?) in Egypt there was a princess possessed by a demon and that Khôns, agent of the god of Thebes, was sent to expel the demon and heal the maiden. It has, in fact, been suggested that Tobit was written to counteract this fable. The parallels in these various tales are obvious. Other minor sources of similar kind have been identified with some plausibility; and among these will be found such items as the fish, the magical properties of gall, etc. The name of the demon in Tobit, Asmodaeus, is Persian in origin, the suffix representing the Iranian *daeva* or *daiva* (Old Persian), usually meaning "demon," occasionally "god" (cf. Θεός). The meaning of the prefix has been much debated, but has (questionably) been referred either to Persian *Aesma* ("anger," "fury") or to the Hebrew root *shāmad* ("destroy"; cf. Aramaic *sh^emad*, "apostatize").

The various sources have been so skilfully woven into the story that most scholars regard the book as a unity. A very small minority would see in it a long process of elaboration and accretion. It is true that this element of possible elaboration and interpolation explains certain features, especially in the versions, and that the textual situation leaves the exact form of the original uncertain. But aside from the possible addition, or expansion, of the material in chs. 13–14, there is no conclusive evidence against the general integrity of the composition.

5. Purpose. The author's purpose has been characterized in both general and particular terms. But while his work may be designed specifically to emphasize the obligation of burial of the dead, or almsgiving, or fidelity to the Mosaic code in some particular situation, the contents may indicate the more comprehensive purpose of inculcation of general piety, or of showing the faithfulness of God to those who are faithful to him. Aside from certain extraneous elements noted above, the book reflects the conventional theological doctrines of Judaism. An incipient apocalypticism is present in ch. 13. Honesty, justice, sobriety, purity, and faithfulness to the law are stressed. In the practical sphere emphasis is given to almsgiving and charitable deeds, tithing, fasting, filial and marriage obligations, marriage to kin, observance of the feasts, and conduct toward the dead. The generous spirit of the book is illustrated in its citation of the "golden rule" in negative form in 4:15: "What you hate, do not do to any one." *See* ETHICS IN NONCANONICAL JEWISH WRITINGS; FEASTS AND FASTS; ALMS.

6. History and influence. The character of the book, together with its interesting story, ensured its preservation and use; and it became, as we have seen, a firm and undisputed part of the Apoc. in the LXX version. This fact doubtless militated against its use in orthodox Jewish circles; but there is evidence that it was highly regarded in both early and late Judaism. It was apparently used by the author of JUBILEES; traces of it are found in other Jewish writings and in the midrashim; and the Qumran fragments attest its use in Palestine at least among the sectaries of this community. It is not quoted in Josephus, Philo, or the NT; but there are possible reminiscences in the last, and among Christians it is commonly known and used as part of the LXX. It is alluded to or quoted in the DIDACHE, POLYCARP, II Clement, Clement of Alexandria (who cites 4:16 as "scripture"), Origen, Hippolytus, Cyprian, Athanasius, Ambrose, Jerome, and others. The Vulg. indicates that "the church reads it, but does not receive it among her canonical scriptures" (doubtless reflecting Jerome's attitude toward the Apoc.); but this opinion was modified by the Council of Trent in the decision favorable to certain of the apocryphal books already noted. It holds a similar position in the Eastern Orthodox and the Anglican communions; the latter continues to read lessons from it in the lectionary. As part of the LXX and the Vulg. it appears in biblical studies, and its influence may also be seen in the liturgy, in the arts, and in literary allusion. Raphael, Rembrandt, Titian, Botticelli, and other masters painted scenes from it. It was part of the early vernacular Bibles, including the English down to the early printing of the KJV. Beginning in 1629, the Apoc. were more and more frequently omitted from printings of the KJV, and the influence of the book of Tobit diminished correspondingly in Protestantism. *See also* APOCRYPHA.

Bibliography. Text and commentary: A. E. Brooke, N. McLean, and H. St. J. Thackeray, *The OT in Greek,* vol. III, pt. I (1940), gives the Rv text with fullest critical apparatus and prints separately the Rs text and the OL of Sabatier (1751) with critical apparatus. A. Neubauer, *The Book of Tobit, A Chaldee Text . . .* (1878), also gives the rabbinical texts and the OL. J. M. Fuller, in H. Wace, ed., *The Holy Bible with an Explanation and Critical Commentary. Apoc.,* vol. I (1888). D. C. Simpson, in R. H. Charles, ed., *Apoc. and Pseudep. of the OT,* vol. I (1913), is a thorough study of all aspects of the subject, with an annotated English translation of the Rs text. A. Rahlfs, ed., *Septuaginta,* vol. I (3rd ed., 1949), gives both Greek texts with variant readings of the uncial MSS and chief versions. *Biblia Sacra . . . , Libri Ezrae, Tobiae, Iudith* (1950), is an edition of the Vulg. with a full critical apparatus. F. Zimmermann, "The Book of Tobit," in S. Zeitlin *et al.,* eds., *Jewish Apocryphal Literature* (1958), is an excellent treatment, which gives the Rs text with an annotated English translation, and the Rv text in an Appendix. For other English translation of Tobit, see APOCRYPHA.

Special studies: J. R. Harris, "The Double Text of Tobit," *AJT,* III (1899), 541-54. G. H. Gerould, *The Grateful Dead* (1907). E. Schürer, *Geschichte des jüdischen Volkes,* III (3rd ed., 1909), 237-58. F. C. Conybeare, J. R. Harris, and A. S. Lewis, *The Story of Ahikar* (2nd ed., 1913). M. Schumpp, in A. Schulz, ed., *EH,* vol. XI (1933). R. H. Pfeiffer, *History of NT Times with an Introduction to the Apoc.* (1949). J. T. Milik, "Cave 4 of Qumran (4Q)," *BA,* XIX (1956), 88.

A. WIKGREN

TOCHEN tō'kən [תכן]. A village of Simeon in the S of Judah (I Chr. 4:32). The parallel list in Josh. 19:7 has in its place the village of ETHER, and the list of cities in Josh. 15 omits both names. The site of Tochen is unknown.

S. COHEN

TOGARMAH tō gär'mə [תגרמה]. Alternately: BETH-TOGARMAH bĕth'—. A region in Asia Minor associated with such known ethnic groups as Gomer (Cimmerians) and Ashkenaz (Scythians; Gen. 10:3; I Chr. 1:6; Ezek. 38:6) and referred to as supplying horses, horsemen, and mules (Ezek. 27:14). The context fits a city in Asia Minor which the Assyrians call Til-Garimmu, a name derived from Hittite Tegarama and carried into classical times as Gauraena (modern Gürün), some seventy miles W of Malatya. The best-known phase in the history of the city is the late eighth century B.C., when it was involved in Assyrian military campaigns. The Assyrians destroyed the city in 695 B.C.

Bibliography. E. Forrer, *Die Provinzeinteilung des assyrischen Reiches* (1921), pp. 74-75, 85; P. Naster, *L'Asie Mineure et l'Assyrie aux VIIIᵉ et VIIᵉ siècles avant Jésus-Christ* (1938), pp. 48, 74-75.

M. J. MELLINK

TOHU tō'hū [תהו]. One of the ancestors of the prophet Samuel (I Sam. 1:1). In the Levitical genealogies he appears as a Kohathite under the name of Nahath (*see* NAHATH 2; I Chr. 6:26—H 6:11) and Toah (I Chr. 6:34—H 6:19). Tohu, or possibly Toah, appears to be the original name.

E. R. DALGLISH

TOI toi, tō'ī [תעי] (II Sam. 8:9-10). Alternately: TOU tōō, tō'ū [תעו] (I Chr. 18:9-10). King of Hamath on the Orontes. The defeat of Hadadezer of Zobah by David removed from Toi the threat which the Aramean king had posed to his territory. For this reason he sent David gifts by his son Hadoram. Perhaps the embassy was also a token of the submission of his kingdom to Israel, since the gifts which he had sent are listed among the spoil of the nations which David subdued (II Sam. 8:11).

R. W. CORNEY

TOKHATH. Alternate form of TIKVAH.

TOLA tō'lə [תולע, crimson worm; Akkad. *tultu, see below*]; **TOLAITES** —īts. Two individuals or clans of the tribe of Issachar.

The Hebrew word is used in Isa. 1:18 ("crimson"); Lam. 4:5 ("purple"; KJV "scarlet") to refer to the crimson-colored cloth made by the use of a dye from a cochineal. The same or a cognate word is found in Judeo-Aramaic, Christian Palestinian, Mandaic, Syriac, and Ethiopian. Two derivative words (תולעה, תולעת) are used to mean either "worm" (Exod. 16:20; Deut. 28:39; Isa. 14:11; 41:14; 66:24; Jonah 4:7) or "scarlet (stuff)" (lit., "worm of scarlet"), mentioned frequently in the tabernacle furnishings (Exod. 25:4; 26:1, 31, 36; etc.). As a proper name the word may be a complimentary personification or may represent a totem animal (or plant in the case of Puvah; *see* 1 *below*).

1. According to the Priestly genealogies (Gen. 46:13; Num. 26:23) and the Chronicler's copy (I Chr. 7:1-2; so also in Jub. 44:16), the first of the four sons of Issachar. The others were Puvah, Jashub (Iob in Gen. 46:13), and Shimron. Tola was thus the chief of four clans, as in the census in Numbers (26:23-25), where the sons are designated as fathers respectively of the Tolaites, Punites, Jashubites, and Shimronites, making a total number of 64,300. It is doubtless not coincidental that Tola's brother was named Puvah, "madder" (technically *Rubia tinctorum,* a plant from which red dye was made). Nothing is known of the six sons of Tola listed by the Chronicler (I Chr. 7:2) in what may be an amplification of David's census (II Sam. 24) as mighty warriors, heads of subclans numbering 22,600.

The striking similarity between the names of Issachar's four sons—Tola, Puvah, Jashub, and Shimron—and the essential facts given concerning the judge Tola—viz., that he was "Tola the son of Puah, . . . [living, *yôshēbh*] at Shamir" (Judg. 10:1)—suggests that possibly these names were a late tradition derived from the statements concerning the judge.

2. A judge, identified as the son rather than the brother of Puah, and the grandson of DODO. "Puah" (פואה; Judg. 10:1; I Chr. 7:1) is an alternative spelling of "Puvah" (פוה; Gen. 46:13; Num. 26:23). While the versions render "Dodo" as "his uncle," the word seems clearly to be a proper name, judging by the same or similar words in the Moabite Stone, the Tell el-Amarna Tablets, and elsewhere, and in the Hebrew names David and Jedidiah.

The site of Shamir, scene of Tola's twenty-three-year career as judge and presumably the location of his tomb, is unknown. It may have been Samaria, but as seat of the chief clan of Issachar it was more likely located in the hill country of Ephraim not far S of the Plain of Jezreel.

As no details of the career of this judge are given except his genealogy, location, and length of service, some commentators consider Tola to be an unhistorical invention of a late editor to fill in the chronological space between Abimelech and Jephthah (so also, before Jephthah, Jair; and Ibzan, Elon, and Abdon, between Jephthah and Samson). Others consider that what is given on these minor judges is exact and authentic chronological information, probably based on official records, as to those who occupied the central office in Israelite society before the rise of the monarchy.

See also JUDGE; JUDGES, BOOK OF, § E1.

Bibliography. G. F. Moore, *Judges,* ICC (1895), pp. 270-73; M. Noth, *Die israelitischen Personennamen* (1928), pp. 7, 225, 230; C. F. Burney, *Judges* (1930), pp. 289-92; M. Noth, *History of Israel* (1958), pp. 99-102.   C. F. KRAFT

TOLAD. Alternate form of ELTOLAD.

TOLBANES. KJV Apoc. form of TELEM.

TOLL, PLACE OF. *See* TAX OFFICE.

*TOMB. A natural or artificial cave shaped as a burial place for the deceased. Burial places for the dead are mentioned frequently in biblical and contemporary extrabiblical literature. Thousands of tombs of various types have been excavated in the regions both E and W of the Jordan River, often several hundred at a single site like Jericho (Tell es-Sultan) or Gezer. The study of them is important, not only for what they suggest concerning belief in a future life, but also for what their contents reveal about cultural levels of ancient peoples, since objects

of daily use were customarily interred with the deceased. For further discussion of places of burial, *see* BURIAL; DOLMENS; MONUMENT; OSSUARIES; PIT; TOMBS OF THE KINGS. For rituals and significance, *see* BIER; EMBALMING; IMMORTALITY; MOURNING; RESURRECTION; SHEOL. For important tomb groups, *see* BETH-SHAN; BETH-SHEMESH; DIBON; GEBAL (CITY); GEZER; JERICHO; JERUSALEM; LACHISH; MACH-PELAH; MARESHAH (CITY); MEDEBA; MEGIDDO; MIZPAH; UGARIT; SELA.

1. Terminology
   a. In Hebrew
   b. In Greek
2. Location
3. Types
4. Contents
5. Significance
Bibliography

1. Terminology. *a. In Hebrew.* The two most common Hebrew words for "tomb" are קבר and קבורה, from קבר, "to bury." Because the use of English terms for burial places has not been standardized, both words are rendered by various English words. E.g., the KJV translates קבר as "grave" (Gen. 50:5; Num. 19:16; II Sam. 3:32; etc.) and "sepulchre" (Gen. 23:6; I Kings 13:22; Isa. 22:16; etc.); the RSV renders it as "grave" (I Kings 13:30; II Kings 13:21; Jer. 20:17; Ezek. 32:23; etc.), "tomb" (Judg. 8:32; II Sam. 17:23; Isa. 22:16; etc.), and "sepulchre" (Gen. 23:6; Ps. 5:9; Isa. 14:19; etc.). The same terms are used to translate קבורה (Gen. 35:20; I Sam. 10:2; II Kings 9:28; 23:30; Ezek. 32:24; etc.); it is also rendered as "burial" and "burial place" (Deut. 34:6; II Chr. 26:23; Eccl. 6:3; Isa. 14:20; Jer. 22:19; etc.). The KJV regularly renders שאול as "grave" (Gen. 37:35; I Sam. 2:6; Job 7:9; etc.) where the RSV transliterates as SHEOL (cf. I Kings 2:9, where the RSV translates "grave"). Other Hebrew words which doubtless referred to graves or tombs are: עי (Job 30:24; "heap of ruins"; KJV "grave"); שחת (Job 33:22; "Pit"; KJV "grave"); בור (Isa. 38:18, "pit"); בית (Isa. 14:18; "tomb"; KJV "house"; cf. Job 30:23 ["house appointed for all living"]; Eccl. 12:5 ["eternal home"], where there may be allusions to tombs).

Mishnaic Hebrew employs the same terms and also the word כוך (plural כוכים; B.B. VI.8; Oh. XVII.2); it has been adopted by archaeologists in the plural form, *kôkhîm,* as a technical term to designate Jewish and Christian tombs which contain loculi or niches opening from a central chamber, each large enough to hold a single body.

b. In Greek. The Greek words for "tomb" or "sepulchre" are μνῆμα (Luke 23:53; Acts 2:29; Rev. 11:9), μνημεῖον (Matt. 23:29; Mark 15:46; John 11:17; etc.), and τάφος (Matt. 23:27; 28:1). Like the Hebrew terms, these are translated variously as "grave," "tomb," "sepulchre," "burial place," and "monument." Contexts of the biblical references in which the various terms appear do not make clear whether the tomb involved was a natural cave, an excavated underground chamber, a trench-type grave, or a tower-type structure. It is probable that they might refer to any of these or to others which have been excavated in Palestine in great numbers.

2. **Location.** In biblical, as in modern, times in Palestine, cemeteries were usually located near cities and villages, often in a type of terrain, such as the rocky slopes of valleys, that was not suitable for agriculture, but where natural or artificial caves were available for tombs. Hebrew law did not prescribe the precise location of tombs, but on account of the belief in the defiling effect of contact with the dead (Lev. 21:1; Num. 6:6; 19:13; etc.), one may conclude that cemeteries were usually situated beyond the borders of a city or village. This practice has been illustrated by the discoveries of the excavators at such places as Jerusalem, Gezer, Jericho (Tell es-Sultan), Lachish, Megiddo, and other cities where the tombs were found to be located outside the city walls, at distances varying from city to city but sometimes, as at Jericho, in areas extending from one hundred yards to a half mile or more W and N of the walled city.

However, the discovery of human skeletons and skulls carefully buried beneath the floors of houses and in adjacent courtyards in Neolithic and Chalcolithic levels at such places as Wadi el-Mugharah,* Teleilat el-Ghassul, and Jericho suggests the practice of providing a place for the dead within the community. The cave of MACH-PELAH was the tomb of the PATRIARCHS (Gen. 23:9 ff; 25:9; 49:30; 50:13), but the traditions about it do not report its exact location with reference to ancient Hebron. Because it has not been possible to excavate beneath the floor of the great Hebron mosque where it is now thought to be located, archaeologists have not been able to determine whether its situation was originally within or outside the settled community. It seems probable that in ancient times, as in Palestine today, burials of important people were permitted within the cities, and the tombs became popular shrines. In death, as in life, provision was made for continued association with the family or clan. Jacob's prayer was characteristic: "I am to be gathered to my people; bury me with my fathers in the cave that is in the field of Ephron the Hittite, in the cave that is in the field at Mach-pelah" (Gen. 49:29-30). Figs. MUG 75-76.

After the Hebrews settled in Canaan, they followed the Canaanite practice of using natural or artificial caves, located near cities, for tombs. Gideon was buried in the tomb of his father, Joash, at Ophrah (Judg. 8:32); Samson was buried by his family in the tomb of his father, Manoah, "between Zorah and Eshtaol" (Judg. 16:31); and Asahel was buried in the tomb of his father at Bethlehem (II Sam. 2:32). The report that the Hebrews in the time of Saul concealed themselves from the Philistines by hiding in tombs, as well as in caves, holes, and cisterns, suggests that the tombs were in rural regions and that some of them were doubtless merely open caves (I Sam. 13:6). David was buried "in the city of David" (I Kings 2:10), Ahaziah is said to have been buried "in his tomb with his fathers in the city of David" (II Kings 9:28), and other kings are said to have been buried at Jerusalem (see TOMBS OF THE KINGS). Such tombs were located, as is still the practice, in uninhabited terrain adjacent to the cities.

Tombs were located in gardens (II Kings 21:18, 26; John 19:41), on elevated places (II Kings 23:16; Isa. 22:16), on the slopes of hills (II Chr. 32:33), and

beneath the ground (II Kings 13:21; II Chr. 34:4). Individual graves in cemeteries with family plots, as today in the Kidron Valley E of Jerusalem, were probably not common in biblical times, although such a cemetery has been found at Qumran* (see DEAD SEA SCROLLS) containing more than one thousand graves. A prerequisite for a tomb area was a type of rock formation suitable for caves or carved chambers. E.g., the tombs at Jericho were cut into the soft stone beneath the surface; they were approached by shafts which opened into caverns of various shapes and sizes. At Lachish (Tell ed-Duweir) burial caves, tombs, and single graves were located on the slopes and valleys of the city at the N, W, and S. At Tell en-Nasbeh some Early Bronze tombs were found on the mound, but others from the same period, and many from the Iron Age and later, were located in cemeteries N, NE, and W of the city. At Megiddo a necropolis containing tombs extending in date from the Chalcolithic through the Roman period was excavated on the E slope of the mound. Doubtless in most cases the presence of natural caves suitable for burials was a factor in determining the original location of a necropolis; these were reused and new chambers were hewn in the rock of the same region by succeeding generations. Fig. BUR 57.

3. **Types.** Although modern terminology employed to describe various types of tombs has not been standardized, it is often possible to recognize and classify burial places by the form of their entrances and chambers, as well as by their decoration, and the date of the objects, especially the pottery, that were interred with the dead. In many cases classification by form is impossible because some tombs were reused over many centuries, and others were damaged as a result of earthquake, later building, and the natural disintegration of the rock. However, the main features of tomb construction and the general development of types from simple pits of the Chalcolithic period to the elaborate subterranean chambers containing scores of kôkhîm that were characteristic of the Hellenistic, Roman, and Byzantine periods can be traced.

The earliest tombs in Palestine were simply holes into which the bodies were carefully placed, often in a flexed position but sometimes on their backs in an extended position. Examples may be cited from the caves at Wadi el-Mugharah, where such burials were found both within the caverns and beneath the debris, and outside near the entrances. They dated from the Paleolithic and Mesolithic periods, and are paralleled by those at similar cave settlements in Galilee, NW of Jerusalem, and E of Bethlehem.

As early as the Neolithic period, tombs were fashioned by lining and covering a pit with stones in such a way as to form a cist (from Latin, meaning "box") type of structure. Specimens have been found at Teleilat el-Ghassul that are dated in the Chalcolithic period. Similar in formation, but much larger in size, are the DOLMENS* which are scattered through Palestine; a large field of them is at el-'Adeimeh, E of the Jordan River, opposite Jericho. Although there has been some uncertainty as to their date, they are now generally considered to be Neolithic. A dolmen was constructed probably in imitation of a primitive house, by placing large stone slabs on end to form the sides, and a large stone on the top as a roof. Some of the structures have one side pierced by a rectangular opening large enough to have served as an entrance; there is no way of determining whether these were cut when the tomb was originally constructed or at a later date. The absence of pottery in the tumuli and the presence of flints characteristic of the Neolithic period suggest that they were the tombs of a nomadic people who expended considerable effort in preparing burial places for their dead. The practice of constructing tombs in imitation of houses is paralleled in the Chalcolithic period by the pottery house-urn chests found in a cave burial at Khudheirah. *See* OSSUARIES. Figs. DOL 35; OSS 13-15.

Beginning in the late Neolithic and Chalcolithic periods and continuing in succeeding periods through the Iron Age at Gezer, Megiddo, and Jericho, subterranean hewn chambers were often approached by a shaft-type entrance.* A typical tomb at Jericho consisted of a vertical shaft in the soft stone, at the bottom of which there was an opening into a cavelike structure. The shafts varied in diameter from three to ten feet; in depth, from three to

fifteen feet. The chambers also varied considerably in height and diameter; a typical one was *ca.* fifteen feet across and *ca.* four feet high. The earliest shafts were round in shape, usually containing at the bottom a large stone which sealed the entrance to the tomb. Rectangular shafts have also been found at Jericho, Tell el-'Ajjul, and other cities where Early and Middle Bronze Age tombs have been found. Some of the tombs contained a single burial, others as many as forty or fifty. In some cases there were openings from one chamber leading into two or more similar caverns in a kind of family vault. Figs. TOM 67-68.

At Byblos (ancient Gebal) pottery-storage jars, large enough to contain the flexed body of an adult, were used as tombs or coffins. Smaller jars containing the skeletons of infants and small children have been found at several biblical cities. A more common practice was to place the deceased in the tomb without enclosing it in any kind of box. At the end of the Late Bronze and beginning of the Early Bronze period, *ca.* 1200 B.C., some Canaanites adopted the practice of burying their dead in anthropoid clay coffins on the tops of which were molded in relief human features such as the face and hands. Excellent specimens found at Beth-shean are now in the Palestine Archaeological Museum in Jerusalem. Dating *ca.* three centuries later, and from Dibon, onetime capital of Moab, comes a terra-cotta coffin having on the lid a similar type of representation of the human features.

In this connection mention should be made of the stone sarcophagi,* like that of King Ahiram of Byblos.* Dated by some scholars as early as the thirteenth century B.C., they were carved from natural rock, sculptured on the sides and ends with scenes depicting the deceased ruler and his attendants, and inscribed on the edge of the massive lids with a Phoenician inscription. In the Hellenistic and Roman periods, similar stone sarcophagi of marble were beautifully carved on the outside surfaces with representations of human figures and symbols of the deities. Figs. SID 58; GEB 15.

There appears to have been a degeneration in the

Courtesy of the Oriental Institute, the University of Chicago

67. Middle and Late Bronze Age furnishings in shaft tomb at Megiddo

Courtesy of the Oriental Institute, the University of Chicago

68. Interior of Middle Bronze I shaft tomb at Megiddo, which shows the large size of certain tombs

Trans World Airlines Photo

69. Tomb of Tut-ankh-Amon (1352-1344 B.C.) at Thebes

construction of tombs about the beginning of the
Early Iron Age, coinciding with the period of Israelite settlement in Canaan. Caves continued to be used
as tombs, and even where there is evidence of some
attempt to shape the cave, the result was a plain
cavern without decoration or individual loculi. However, before the end of the Early Iron period, *ca.* 900
B.C., tombs were carefully hewn, usually in rock formation near the surface of sloping hills. Examples
excavated at Megiddo, Lachish, Tell en-Nasbeh, and
elsewhere follow a pattern of a small courtyard outside a shaped entrance which led down several steps
into a rectangular or oval chamber on the sides and
ends of which were shelves or ledges cut from the
native rock. The preparation of such a tomb would
have required considerable time and labor; this suggests that Hebrew leaders, like the Egyptian Pharaohs,* who could afford the cost, arranged for the
construction of their tombs during their lifetime. See,
e.g., the report of Asa's burial: "They buried him in
the tomb which he had hewn out for himself in the
city of David" (II Chr. 16:14). Fig. TOM 69.

Beginning in the Hellenistic period and continuing
through the Roman period, tombs became larger and
more elaborate in their construction. Of course, for
burial of the poor of the land in every generation,
pits, caves, and cisterns continued in use; see, e.g.,
a reference to the "graves of the common people"
(II Kings 23:6) in the Kidron Valley E of Jerusalem
in the time of Josiah. Just as the style of construction
of Jewish houses and public buildings (I Macc. 1:14;
II Macc. 4:9-15) was influenced by Hellenistic architecture and art, the building of tombs was similarly
affected. Before the destruction of the second temple,
several tomb complexes were carved in the rock formations N and E of Jerusalem. Among them were
the mausoleum of Queen Helena of Adiabene* (Jos.
War V.iv.2), the tombs of James and Zacharias in
the Kidron Valley near the "Tomb of Absalom,"* and
the so-called "Tombs of the Judges."* The front of
the latter included an inscribed architrave, porch,
and doorways, all carved from the native rock into
which were cut six chambers on two levels containing ledges and *kôkhîm* to accommodate seventy bodies
at one time. Some smaller tombs of the period, and
also in Byzantine times, were carved with rectangular
entrances into which a stone could be set, or with
grooves in front where a rolling stone could be placed*

Courtesy of Herbert G. May

  70. Hellenistic and Roman period tombs in the Kidron
     Valley: (*a*) "Tomb of Absalom"; (*b*) "Tomb of
     James"; (*c*) "Tomb of Zacharias." *B* and *c* belong to
     the tomb of the Hezir family, identified by an
     Aramaic inscription.

From *Atlas of the Bible* (Thomas Nelson & Sons Limited)

  71. Tomb cut in the rock, in Palestine

(Matt. 27:60; Mark 15:46; Luke 24:2; John 20:1). At
the time of new burials, such entrances were opened,
the bones from previous burials were placed in stone
boxes (*see* OSSUARIES)* for which small niches were
often carved in the walls, and the body was placed
on a ledge, or in a *kôkh* that projected into a wall
and could be sealed on the end from the main chamber by a stone slab. Pl. XXVIa; Figs. TOM 70;
ART 81; TOM 71; OSS 13-15.

Among the most elaborate tombs excavated thus
far in Palestine, Syria, and Jordan are those at
Marissa, Palmyra, and Petra. The famous painted
tombs of Marissa, dating from the Ptolemaic period
and showing Egyptian and Phoenician influence,
were of the *kôkhîm* type. The walls were richly decorated with brightly colored paints, which have faded
considerably since the discovery of the tombs *ca.*
1902. The paintings include representations of various types of animals, objects such as vases, and
musical instruments carried by human figures. Greek
inscriptions and graffiti, as well as an Aramaic inscription, offer some information about the owners
of the tombs, including the name of one Apol-
lophanes, head of a Sidonian colony at Marissa. The
necropolis included at least four tomb complexes.
The largest was approached through a court and
door over which there was a Greek inscription. From
the antechamber there radiated three large chambers
like the arms of a cross. In the walls of these rooms
were cut *kôkhîm* for forty-one burials and three other
recesses for large sarcophagi.

Tombs at Palmyra, some of which date during the
second and third centuries A.D., varied considerably
in style; the two chief types were the great subterranean "houses of eternity" and the equally impressive tomb towers. Both were located W of the city.
The former were often beautifully painted and contained skilfully carved statues and reliefs representing the members of the family buried in the tombs—
Aramaic inscriptions often mention their names. The
towers, some of which were four stories high, built
of carefully hewn stone blocks, were richly decorated
with colors and contained sculptures of the deceased.

Tombs at Petra varied considerably in size and
shape; most of them date from the late first century
B.C. and the first two centuries A.D. Pylon (tower)
tombs were carved from the native sandstone and
were usually surrounded by simple shaft graves;
sometimes graves of a later period were sunk into the

Courtesy of the Oriental Institute, the University of Chicago

72. Royal tombs, carved out of the rock, of Darius I,
Artaxerxes I, and Darius II; at Naqsh-i-Rustam in
Iran

roofs of the pylons. Even more impressive were the
great rock-hewn mausoleums, like el-Khazneh, the
Corinthian tomb, and the Tomb of the Urn, whose
architectural façades, containing doors, columns,
niches, and sculptures, were all cut from the colorful
sandstone. Constructed by the Nabateans, whose control of caravan traffic through the region resulted in
the wealth of which the tombs are a lasting memorial, the architecture shows Roman influence; one of
the tombs was that of a Roman soldier. Some of the
buildings, one of which was used in later times as a
Christian chapel, contained large chambers extending more than forty feet into the mountains from
which they were cut. Doubtless the large chambers
were used as mortuary chapels. In their walls were
cut niches for sarcophagi, and in the stone floors
were carved loculi for individual graves. A large
columbarium was carved in the face of one of the
mountains (el Habis); its numerous niches once contained small burial urns; traces of ashes testify to the
local practice of cremating the dead. A similar columbarium at 'Araq el-Emir (W of Amman) may be
seen near the rock-cut chamber tombs, one of which
has the name "Tobiah" inscribed on the outside
surface near the large doorway. *Cf.* Fig. TOM 72.

Trans World Airlines Photo

73. The so-called "Garden Tomb" at Jerusalem

The type of tomb used as the burial place for the
body of Jesus cannot be identified with certainty.
Tradition dating back to the early fourth century
A.D. has located the tomb in the edicule beneath the
dome of the Church of the Holy Sepulchre (*see* SEP-
ULCHRE, CHURCH OF THE HOLY).* Excavations in
Jerusalem have demonstrated that the city walls in
the Herodian period were situated so that the tomb
was outside the city; this discovery enhances the traditional location, although positive proof of the
identification is lacking. The Garden Tomb,* located
outside the present N wall of Jerusalem near "Gordon's Calvary," is a rival site. This tomb—a rock-
hewn chamber, the door of which was originally
sealed with a large rolling stone—has been identified
by archaeologists, since its discovery in modern times,
as a Jewish tomb of the Roman period; there is no
literary or archaeological evidence to identify it as
the burial place of Jesus. The gospels record the information that the tomb was a new one located in a
garden (John 19:41); it was the property of Joseph
of ARIMATHEA (Luke 23:50); it was sealed by a rolling stone, and the chamber was large enough for
Jesus' followers to enter (Luke 24:2-3). Figs. HOL
29-30; TOM 73.

Certain features of tomb construction are mentioned in the Mishna. Exact dimensions in terms of
cubits are specified for the size of the vault or chamber, the niches (*kôkhîm*), and the courtyard, although
Rabbi Simeon ben Gamaliel held that "all depends
on the nature of the rock" (B.B. VI.8). A tomb might
be sealed with either a wooden beam or a stone (Oh.
XV.8). It was a custom to mark the graves in order
to give warning of uncleanness by pouring over them
whiting mixed with water (Ma'as Sh. V.1; Sheḳ. I.1;
M.Ḳ. I.2; cf. Matt. 23:27).

Finally, mention may be made of the catacombs,*
the most famous of which are in the vicinity of Rome
and include both Jewish and Christian burials.
Among the catacombs there is considerable variety
of form, depending on the nature of the rock formation and the number of burials. However, the basic
pattern was that of a large, subterranean network of
corridors and chambers carved with burial niches
large enough to contain a single body. The corridors,
usually *ca.* three feet in width and in some cases
forty or fifty feet high, are lined with several tiers of
loculi, each a square-cornered, horizontal recess,
which could be sealed with bricks or a marble slab.
Interspersed among the labyrinthine corridors were
chambers to which Christians fled in time of persecution and where worship was conducted. The walls
were often decorated with paintings representing
Christian and Jewish symbols, as well as scenes from
the Bible. With the catacombs at Rome may be compared those found in Palestine at Sheikh Abreiq
(identified as Beth-shearim, a city mentioned often
in the Talmud). The entrances, corridors, and chambers were carved in imitation of Roman buildings;
the walls were inscribed with many Jewish symbols,
including several varieties of the *menorah* (*see* LAMP-
STAND). Greek, Latin, and Aramaic inscriptions identify by name some of the persons buried in the
catacombs. Fig. DES 27.

4. **Contents.** In addition to the objects mentioned
in the preceding sections, many others are often

found in excavated tombs. The number and type vary greatly, according to the degree of wealth and the cultural backgrounds of the persons who were buried in the tombs. In general, they may be classified as objects of personal adornment, military equipment, household use, and AMULETS of various kinds. Of course, tombs of the poor were devoid of valuables, or contained a few simple pieces of pottery beside the body; the tombs of the wealthy were often robbed of their treasures by later peoples.

Among the objects of personal adornment may be mentioned necklaces, bracelets, anklets, finger rings, earrings, pendants, and headdresses. Bone, bronze, iron, silver, gold, and semiprecious stones were used in the making of such objects. Great numbers of scarabs are often found in Palestinian tombs that were used during periods of Egyptian influence. The presence of mirrors, combs, and cosmetic palettes indicates further·an interest in personal appearance.

Military equipment of the "dagger type" in the Jericho tombs usually included a single copper dagger in a grave. Others at Jericho and elsewhere contained bronze daggers as well as javelin heads, flint arrowheads, and stone blades.

Even more numerous are the objects of household use. These include pottery lamps, jars, bowls, pitchers, cups, and other vessels which were used in the homes of the deceased. Small juglets contained oil or perfume; they were doubtless fashioned in imitation of the pottery jugs used for storage purposes in the home. Some Jericho tombs of the Middle Bronze Age, of which scores were excavated beginning in 1952, were found to contain materials that are, under ordinary circumstances, perishable. These included pomegranates and raisins or grapes, bones of sheep, and fragments of flesh; with such food were also found wooden stools, boxes, a bed, a table, and woven mats and baskets. Fig. ARC 43.

Miniature figurines of bone or clay in the shape of animals, birds, and human figures attest the custom of burying amulets of various kinds with the dead.

5. Significance. It is certain that ancient peoples did not all attach the same significance to the practice of burying their dead in tombs. Although the difference between the tombs of the poor and the rich in ancient Palestine can often be determined, there is uncertainty regarding the motivation and the ceremonies relating to burial practices. Scholars do not agree concerning the religious views evidenced by the custom of building tombs in the shape of houses and of depositing food and other objects in them. It is possible that the worship of the dead was involved, that the dead were feared and needed to be placated so as not to harm the living, or that a belief in physical resurrection led to an effort on the part of the living to make provision for the comfort and happiness of the dead in a future life.

Finally, attention may be called to several biblical references which shed some light on the significance of Palestinian tombs and graves. The burial of Deborah, Rebekah's nurse, under an oak tree may reflect a belief in sacred trees and the custom of locating graves near them (Gen. 35:8). In exceptional cases it was thought that the sin of a man might prevent him from having a burial in the tombs of his fathers (I Kings 13:22). It was considered a suitable

reward for a righteous ruler to "lie in glory, each in his own tomb," but to be removed from a sepulchre was a sign of great evil (Isa. 14:18-19). To be deprived of burial was considered a great calamity (II Kings 9:36-37; cf. Ezek. 32:27, which may imply that a punishment was involved when a warrior was buried without his weapons). It was an act of piety to protect the bodies of slain warriors until they could be buried (II Sam. 21:1-14), and to bury those who were killed during times of persecution (Tob. 1:18-19; 2:8-9). It is reported about Jason, who slaughtered many of his fellow countrymen and left them unburied, that he "had no one to mourn for him; he had no funeral of any sort and no place in the tomb of his fathers" (II Macc. 5:10). It was a mark of honor to have a watch kept over one's tomb (Job 21:32), but the practice of sitting in the tombs was condemned (Isa. 65:4; the reason for such a custom is not specified, although the context suggests a pagan practice). Persons thought to be possessed by demons lived in or among the tombs (Matt. 8:28; Mark 5:1-5; Luke 8:27). Well-known tombs such as those of Rachel* (I Sam.10:2) and David (Acts 2:29) were important landmarks. Jesus' rebuke of the scribes and Pharisees as hypocrites for building the tombs of the prophets and adorning the monuments of the righteous was doubtless not directed against these practices as such, but against those who ignored the living prophets while honoring the dead. Fig. RAC 3.

Bibliography. G. A. Barton, *Archaeology and the Bible* (1933), pp. 228-33; K. Galling, *Biblisches Reallexikon* (1937), cols. 237-52, 445-51; M. S. and J. L. Miller, *Encyclopedia of Bible Life* (1944), pp. 396-403; J. Finegan, *Light from the Ancient Past* (1946), pp. 353-98; A. G. Barrois, *Manuel d'archéologie biblique*, II (1953), 274-323; K. Kenyon, *Digging Up Jericho* (1957), pp. 6-65, 95-102, 194-209, 233-55. For detailed descriptions of tombs excavated at well-known biblical cities, see the official reports such as: J. H. Peters and H. Thiersch, *Painted Tombs in the Necropolis of Marissa* (1905), pp. 1-101, pls. I-XXI; P. L. O. Guy, *Megiddo Tombs* (1938), pp. 1-224, pls. 1-176; C. C. McCown, *Tell-en-Naṣbeh* (1947), pp. 67-128; O. Tufnell, *Lachish III, The Iron Age* (1953), pp. 169-254.

W. L. REED

TOMBS OF THE KINGS [קברות המלכים] (II Chr. 21:20; 24:25). Alternately: TOMBS OF THE KINGS OF ISRAEL [קברי מלכי ישראל] (II Chr. 28: 27); SEPULCHRES OF DAVID [קברי דויד] (Neh. 3:16); TOMBS OF THE SONS OF DAVID [קברי בני דויד] (II Chr. 32:33); KJV always SEPULCHRES. The tombs of the Judean kings of Davidic descent.

1. Biblical data. The necrological formulas with which the authors of Kings and Chronicles conclude their notices on the kings of Judah refer to burial grounds in the City of David (*see* DAVID, CITY OF), where the rulers of the Davidic dynasty were interred, apparently each one in his own tomb, as may be inferred from II Chr. 16:14; II Kings 9:28. References to the tombs of the sons of David (II Chr. 32:33), or to the sepulchres of David (Neh. 3:16), taken collectively, do not imply that there was a family vault in which the bodies were laid to rest, but rather a reserved area within the walls of the city, in which individual graves were provided.

The notices in Kings are stereotyped. Those in

Chronicles are generally freer, and record with greater detail the circumstances of the royal interments, especially when, by way of exception for such reasons as violent death, leprosy, or notorious impiety of the deceased, the interment did not take place in the royal necropolis. Here is the list of these exceptions: Jehoram was buried "in the city of David, but not in the tombs of the Kings" (II Chr. 21:20)— i.e., within the precincts of the city, although not in the royal enclosure; for Joash (II Chr. 24:25), we find the same formula; Uzziah was interred "in the burial field which belonged to the kings, for they said, 'He is a leper' " (II Chr. 26:23), a formula which has been diversely interpreted, but which suggests a contrast with the usual mode or place of royal interments; Josephus states that Uzziah "was buried alone in his gardens" (Antiq. IX.227), perhaps the gardens surrounding the house in which he was confined (II Chr. 26:21); Ahaz was buried in the city, but not in the "tombs of the kings of Israel" (II Chr. 28:27), where "Israel" is obviously a scribal error; Manasseh was interred "in the garden of his house, in the garden of Uzza" (II Kings 21:18), "in his house" (II Chr. 33:20); Amon, "in the garden of Uzza" (II Kings 21:26); in the last two instances, it is questionable whether the garden of Uzza ought to be identified with the burial place of Uzziah. The place of interment of the last four Davidic kings is not mentioned in the Hebrew text and its derivatives. Exceptionally Jehoiada, who had exercised the regency of the kingdom during the minority of Joash, was buried "in the city of David among the kings" (II Chr. 24:16).

2. Localization. The notice relative to Hezekiah in II Chr. 32:33 states that his tomb was "in the ascent" (מעלה) of the burial ground of the kings. This piece of information ought to be pieced together with the topographical data of Neh. 3:15-16, where the sepulchres of David are mentioned in geographical sequence after the "stairs [מעלות] that go down from the City of David." These texts point to the hill wedged between the valleys of the Tyropoeon and the Kidron, where excavations have led to the discovery of a flight of stone degrees leading to a postern of the E fortifications, possibly the FOUNTAIN GATE, and of much-dilapidated rock-cut tombs, the original disposition of which was diagnosed with some difficulty. It seems that individual burial chambers, in the shape of barrel vaults, were accessible from the surface through sunken rectangular shafts similar to those of the dynastic tombs of early Phoenician rulers. These chambers were distributed along a strip of ground, some 350 feet in length from N to S. Their identification as the tombs of the kings, even though not certain, is at least probable.

There are no positive clues to the localization of the garden of Uzza, nor of the private burial ground of Uzziah. One would incline to seek the latter out of town. An Aramaic inscription on a stone tablet refers to a possible transfer of Uzziah's remains at a later date. It reads as follows (translation by E. L. Sukenik): "The bones of Uzziah, King of Judah, were brought hither; not to be opened." The script is very similar to that used on ossuaries immediately before or around the beginning of the Christian era. Unfortunately the tablet was not found in its origi-

nal location, but among curios collected by an archimandrite of the Russian monastery on the Mount of Olives. The authenticity of the inscription, although not generally contested, has not been established beyond doubt. *See* INSCRIPTIONS. Fig. UZZ 19.

3. Late traditions. Miscellaneous traditions have diversely located the tomb of David in Bethlehem, in the domain of Gethsemane, or on the SW hill of Jerusalem, the Christian ZION. The latter tradition is based on an abusive exegesis of Acts 2:29, following which David's tomb was shown to pilgrims in the medieval chapel of the Upper Room, which has now become a mosque.

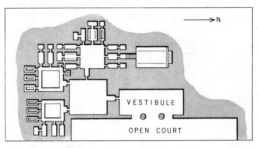

74. Plan of tomb of Helene of Adiabene, the so-called Tombs of the Kings

The so-called Tomb of the Kings of Judah, in the N suburb of Jerusalem, E of Nablus Road and close to the Anglican cathedral of Saint George, is in reality the hypogeum of Helen, queen of Adiabene, a district in Upper Mesopotamia. This monument antedates the ruin of Jerusalem in A.D. 70 by one or two decades. It is mentioned by Josephus (War V.147), in relation to the N wall of Jerusalem or wall of Agrippa.

Figs. NEH 13; TOM 74; Pl. XXVI*a*.

Bibliography. R. Weill, *La Cité de David* (1920), pp. 103-4, 157-83, 190-92; S. Krauss, "The Sepulchres of the Davidic Dynasty," *PEQ* (1947), pp. 102-11; S. Yeivin, "The Sepulchres of the Kings of the House of David," *JNES*, VII (1948), 30:45; J. Simons, *Jerusalem in the OT* (1952), pp. 194-225; H. Vincent, *Jérusalem de l'Ancien Testament*, I (1954), pp. 313-23. See also E. L. Sukenik, "Funerary Table of Uzziah King of Judah," *PEQ* (1931), pp. 217-21; (1932), pp. 106-7. On the late Christian and Muslim traditions concerning the tomb of David, see H. Vincent and F.-M. Abel, *Jérusalem Nouvelle*, III (1922), 457-58. On the monument of Helen (so-called Tombs of the Kings of Judah), see H. Vincent, *Jérusalem de l'AT*, I (1954), 346-62.   G. A. BARROIS

TONGS [מלקחים]. Gold tongs (or SNUFFERS) were among the articles of temple equipment (I Kings 7: 49; II Chr. 4:21). Seraphim used tongs to take a

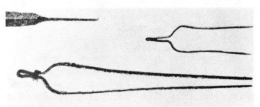

Courtesy of the Oriental Institute, the University of Chicago

75. Tongs from Megiddo tombs, Middle Bronze II or Late Bronze II (*ca.* seventeenth century or thirteenth century B.C.)

burning coal from the altar (Isa. 6:6). Bronze and iron tongs of tweezer or forceps type are known archaeologically (Fig. TON 75). *See also* SNUFFERS.

P. L. GARBER

TONGUE [לָשׁוֹן, γλῶσσα]. The biblical understanding of "tongue" includes: (*a*) its function as a part of the physical make-up of man whereby he eats and drinks (Judg. 7:5; Isa. 41:17); (*b*) its employment as a term for "language" and therefore "nation" (*see* TONGUES, CONFUSION OF); (*c*) a mode of the working of the Spirit (*see* TONGUES, GIFT OF); (*d*) its usage for the action and dynamic of the whole life of man; and (*e*) its use as a figure for that which has extension in a material sense.

Because it is the agent of speech, the tongue represents the various languages and dialects which men used. Men were recognized as being different in an essential matter when they spoke another language. Indeed, not only different; this difference is a part of a vague threat (Jer. 5:15). It is a synonym for "people" and "nation" (Isa. 66:18).

The more general and characteristic meaning of "tongue" begins with the recognition that the primary function of the tongue is to speak. While this in the most fundamental way is a function parallel to eating, the activity of speaking assumes a much greater significance. Speaking is not a mere verbal activity; it is an expression of the totality of man, his purposes and values. The tongue is the agent through which what is in man is effectively released into the world (Ps. 39:3—H 39:4). It is the agent to make manifest man's inward character. Thus "tongue" and "bitter words" stand in close relation to "secret plots of the wicked" and "scheming of evildoers" (Ps. 64:2-3—H 64:3-4). Frequently the tongue is an agent closely related to the HEART (לֵב) of man (Ps. 45:1—H 45:2; Prov. 10:20; 17:20). The tongue, as other members of the body, is a way of acting for the whole man. In the speaking of the tongue, all the powers of intellect and will are given expression.

The wisdom literature regards this from a utilitarian point of view. Man's speaking may bring upon him either good or ill: "Death and life are in the power of the tongue" (Prov. 18:21). A tongue which speaks words of kindness and courtesy may enhance the well-being of the speaker (12:18). In a negative way, the same possibility is stated:

> He who keeps his mouth and his tongue
> keeps himself out of trouble (21:23).

On the other hand, he who speaks carelessly or irresponsibly is sure to bring trouble upon himself (21:6; 26:28; 28:23).

So also, as a possible means to good or bad, in Ecclesiasticus: "A man's tongue is his downfall" (5:13). But the tongue need not lead to ruin:

> A pleasant voice multiplies friends,
> and a gracious tongue multiplies courtesies
> (6:5).

This same awareness of the great potentialities of the tongue is clear in James. The tongue, as the rudder of a ship, or the bit in the mouth of a horse (Jas. 3:3-8), is able to determine the whole course of one's life.

The thought of James, however, is not based simply on utilitarian motives. The ethical context in which James writes gives expression to a deeper dimension, which permeates the biblical understanding. Because the tongue reveals what is in the heart, there are moral implications to the speaking of the tongue. It is related to the doing of good (Ps. 34:13—H 34:14), not for the sake of personal benefit, but because the ethical life is man's way of seeking God. The tongue is the way man "speaks justice" (37:30). Much more often it is the instrument of acting wrongly in human relations. By the tongue, man boasts as he ought not (12:4); he slanders (Prov. 25:23); he speaks deceitfully (Pss. 109:2; 120:2). This is not simply speaking maliciously. The tongue is also the agent of cunning and scheming, which is more than outward action; it is setting one's heart, one's very life, against another to his damage (Ps. 140:2-3—H 140:3-4; Isa. 59:3). The tongue has related to it all the potentialities for the right or wrong ordering of life. It is an effective tool in the role of creating or destroying community. *See* WORD.

This suggests the profound implications involved in the biblical concept, which never separates ethical behavior from religious life. Indeed, "he who mocks the poor insults his Maker" (Prov. 17:5). The use of one's tongue in "speaking justice" or practicing deceit and slander have to do with the religious potentialities of the tongue. It, as all of human life, can be an instrument in expressing praise to God (Pss. 35:28; 51:14—H 51:16; 71:24; Rom. 14:11; Phil. 2:11). What proceeds from the tongue can cause alienation from God—i.e., SIN (Job 15:4-5; Pss. 39:1—H 39:2; 78:35-37). The tongue possesses all the potentialities for goodness and all the possibilities for badness which belong to man's createdness. "With it we bless the Lord and Father, and with it we curse men, who are made in the likeness of God. From the same mouth come blessing and cursing." (Jas. 3:9-10.)

The tongue, which is alive to all the possibilities of life, reveals the essential unity of man's life. Man's self-interest, his relation in the community of men, his relation with his God, all prosper or suffer as he affirms or denies the order of life which his Sovereign has willed. The tongue is an instrument man has been given (Isa. 50:4), that he might give expression to his affirmations and denials of the God of Israel as the Lord of all life.

The tongue is the means of expressing the total character of the person. God also is a conscious, willing personality, who by his tongue is able to release his power and purpose into life (Isa. 30:27). As the Bible understands man as being equipped to act freely and effectively, so much more God, who has given tongues to men.

Aside from this personal dynamic usage, "tongue" is also employed in a figurative sense as a projection, or extension, of that which in the material world is elongated. Examples of this are to be found in Josh. 7:21-24, which speaks of a "tongue" ("bar"; KJV "wedge") of gold; and Isa. 11:15, which refers to the "tongue of the sea." Clearly these usages disregarded the dynamic character of the term in its personal nuances, using it rather in a physical sense.

Bibliography. P. Dhorme, "L'emploi métaphorique des noms de parties du corps en hébreu et en accadien," *RB*, 30 (1921), 536-37; A. R. Johnson, *The Vitality of the Individual in the Thought of Ancient Israel* (1949).   W. BRUEGGEMANN

TONGUES, CONFUSION OF. *See* BABEL.

*****TONGUES, GIFT OF** [γλῶσσα, tongue; λαλεῖν, to speak]. Speaking in tongues, also called "glossalalia," glŏs'ə lā'lĭ ə, a striking phenomenon of primitive Christianity. It consisted in articulate, unintelligible speech issuing from Christians who, in a state of ecstasy, believed themselves to be possessed by the Spirit. It was prevalent in the Pauline churches, particularly at Corinth (I Cor. 12–14), but appeared earlier when the church was constituted in history and began its expansion into Judea and Samaria (Acts 2:1-42; 10:44-48; 11:15-17; 19:2-7).

This phenomenon was not limited to Christianity but was found in many of the religions of the ancient world. Wherever it appeared, the common element was the belief that the spirit of the god worshiped took possession of the devotee, spoke through him, and often produced bodily movements of abnormal character. During such ecstatic states the vocal organs were affected, the tongue moved as if by the operation of a power beyond the mental control of the subject, and utterances poured forth which, to the observer, were as impressive as they were incoherent.

    1. The tongues at Pentecost
    2. The Lukan account
    3. The glossolalia in Pauline churches
    4. Parallel phenomena
    Bibliography

1. The tongues at Pentecost. The glossolalia first appeared in the Christian church at Pentecost, when the apostles, and those associated with them, became convinced, after much rethinking and prayer (Acts 1:24), that the risen Jesus was God's Anointed (Acts 2:36), that the messianic age had begun (Acts 2:29-33), that they were the people of the New Covenant inheriting all the promises made to the people of the Old (Acts 2:16-17; 3:25). They were so overwhelmed by the force of these convictions that, with all their inhibitions released, resources of spiritual power became available to them, creating new levels of spiritual experience which found abnormal channels of expression. Luke, describing this momentous event, says: "They were all filled with the Holy Spirit and began to speak in other tongues, as the Spirit gave them utterance" (Acts 2:4). Similar manifestations continued, for the converts at Caesarea and Ephesus also "spoke in tongues" when they received the Spirit (Acts 10:46; 19:6), and Peter declared that the experience was similar to that at Pentecost (Acts 10:47). Glossolalia seems to have been the sure, to many perhaps the surest, evidence of the Spirit's indwelling. Note also that in some texts of the late addition to Mark at 16:17 there is reference to speaking "in new tongues."

A number of explanations, or rationalizations, of the "tongues" at Pentecost have been offered:

a) For the purpose of evangelization a miracle of language is said to have taken place, whereby the audience heard what was said in a number of foreign languages. Many of the early church fathers held this view.

b) The multitude, all of whom spoke either Greek or Aramaic, and many of them both, would understand, particularly those who knew the various dialects, what Peter and the others were saying.

c) It has been suggested that the speech of the apostles was filled with foreign phrases and idioms, heard over the years, which, under the intense emotion and excitement, began to pour forth automatically from the subconscious. Precedents are cited to illustrate this.

d) Another view is that because of the close spiritual rapport, the thoughts and feelings of the speakers were transferred to the hearers, and there was general understanding of what was said.

All attempts at rationalization are conjectural and are dubious especially when viewed in the light of what is said about glossolalia elsewhere in the NT.

2. The Lukan account. The story in Acts is clear. The "tongues" spoken on the day of Pentecost are foreign languages, understood by a bewildered and astonished crowd. But when "tongues" were spoken at Caesarea and Ephesus (Acts 10:46; 19:6), Peter equated the experience with his own, without any reference to a linguistic miracle. There is no evidence later that the apostles enjoyed the benefit of such a miracle, nor was there need of it, since Greek and Aramaic were sufficient to meet the needs of the church. Moreover, long before Luke completed Acts, the phenomenon of tongues was common in Pauline churches, but was certainly not thought of as the ability to speak foreign languages. Paul, indeed, declared that the glossolalia was not intelligible speech, would not be understood, and might even be construed as insanity (I Cor. 14:9, 23). Plainly an irreconcilable difference exists between the Lukan account in Acts 2:4 and Pauline accounts. The widely accepted view is that both writers were dealing with the same ecstatic phenomena.

What then has Luke done? Certain suggestions have been made. According to one view, Luke has taken the older and more reliable tradition concerning glossolalia, in which emphasis was mainly on the ecstasy of the disciples—as witness the reference to drunkenness (Acts 2:13)—and on the revival of the prophetic spirit (Acts 2:15; 3:24-25), and transformed it, shaping and dramatizing the event according to the rabbinic tradition of the giving of the law in every language, and in the interests of Luke's own emphasis on the universal appeal of Christianity.

Another suggestion is that, under Pauline influence, Luke sought to reinterpret the original speaking in tongues with a view to reducing the prestige of the current glossolalia, which had become damaging to the church.

Again, it is said that Luke has literalized the glossolalia, or perhaps has taken the view that, though unintelligible, it was nevertheless a form of language which, under the right conditions and by the proper people, could be understood.

3. The glossolalia in Pauline churches. Speaking in tongues was so well known at Corinth and elsewhere that Paul did not explain or describe it but simply stressed its unintelligible ecstatic character. There were "various kinds of tongues" because of differences of native language or diversity of spiritual mood (I Cor. 12:10, 28). Some Christians did not possess the gift (I Cor. 12:30), and others, wishing to safeguard the purpose of worship, sought to curb it

(I Cor. 14:39; Col. 3:16; I Thess. 5:19-20; cf. Eph. 5:18-20). Many believers (possibly members of the Cephas party [I Cor. 1:12]), tremendously impressed with it as convincing evidence of Spirit-possession, gave it primary value and eagerly desired it.

This Pauline glossolalia has been described as angelic speech (I Cor. 13:1), a heavenly language beyond human eloquence in which God is praised by the heavenly hosts; or again as antiquated or unusual speech, unintelligible because archaic, known only to someone with expert philological knowledge. This is meaningless speculation. Quite possibly, among the ecstatic outpourings, sounds which resembled syllables and words from current tongues gave the impression of a real language. This could hardly have been otherwise, and proves little.

Because of the exaggerated emphasis upon glossolalia at Corinth, Paul was compelled to deal with it. He does so by recognizing it as: (a) a genuine gift of the Spirit, not to be forbidden, and acknowledges that he shares the gift himself (I Cor. 14:5, 18, 39); (b) an aid to private devotion, a means of personal communion with God, an opportunity to express thoughts and feelings which could find no outlet through ordinary channels (I Cor. 14:4; cf. Rom. 8:26-27); (c) a sign to unbelievers (I Cor. 14:22), an evidence of divine power which, like the "sign of Jonah" (Matt. 12:39), though genuine enough, was yet unrecognized by the hardhearted and unbelieving scoffers and critics.

Paul saw the dangers in the practice even more clearly than its values. He gave it no precedence or encouragement in public worship (I Cor. 14:19, 28). It is last in his list and in point of value (I Cor. 12:10, 30; 14:19). He indicates methods of control:

a) By applying regulatory principle. The use of spiritual gifts must be determined by their worth in building up the church "in love" (I Cor. 13; 14:4-5, 17-19; Col. 3:14; cf. Eph. 4:16). Tongues are too individualistic, encourage self-centeredness and self-importance, and are detrimental to the solidarity of the Christian fellowship (Rom. 12:3; I Cor. 13:5; Phil. 2:3-4).

b) By maintaining orderly worship. The edification of the church is primary. The glossolalist must restrain himself and keep silent unless interpreted (I Cor. 14:27-28). When worship is not understood, or repels seekers after truth, it fails. Order and decency are of first importance (I Cor. 14:13-19, 23-33, 40).

c) By exercising the gift of interpretation. The capacity to interpret tongues was the special gift of some (I Cor. 12:10, 30; 14:28)—the ability to convey a supposedly rational account of what was said, possibly by thought-transference effective through spiritual rapport. The ecstatic lacking this gift should pray for it, since he has a responsibility both to himself and to the church (I Cor. 14:13-14).

4. Parallel phenomena. Such ecstatic speech as described above prevailed among the earliest Hebrew prophets, the professionalized nᵉbi'im (בני הנביאים), who, as Yahweh enthusiasts, wandered about the country in bands, working themselves into religious frenzy by means of music and dancing (I Sam. 10:5-13; 19:18-24; II Sam. 6:13-17; I Kings 20:35-37). The word nabi (נביא), by which they were called,

was probably suggested by their ecstatic babblings, and their hith-nabbe (התנבא), "prophesying," may well have corresponded to the glossolalia, though scholars are not agreed upon this. In Hellenistic circles also, followers of the Dionysian cult, or of some mystery religion, under powerful emotional pressures of ceremonial rites, often slipped into ecstatic states bordering on frenzy, and expressed themselves in forms intelligible only to the initiated. Through the centuries glossolalia has frequently reappeared among Christian groups, the Montanists, the Camisards, the Irvingites, and many modern sects given to emotional extremes. The psychological aspects are patent.

Bibliography. In addition to commentaries on Acts and I Corinthians, see: P. Volz, Der Geist Gottes (1910); K. Lake, The Earlier Epistles of St. Paul (1911); S. Angus, The Mystery-Religions and Christianity (1925); G. B. Cutten, Speaking with Tongues (1927); P. G. S. Hopwood, The Religious Experience of the Primitive Church (1936); A. L. Drummond, Edward Irving and His Circle (1937); A. Guillaume, Prophecy and Divination (1938); E. T. Clark, The Small Sects in America (1949); M. Barnett, The Living Flame (1953). E. ANDREWS

TONSURE. See BALDNESS.

TOOTH [שׁן; ὀδούς]. Biblical references to tooth and teeth are many and varied. Under OT law the loss of a tooth was considered equally as grave a matter as the loss of an eye (Exod. 21:24, 27; Lev. 24:20; Deut. 19:21; Matt. 5:38; on the lex talionis, see also LAW IN THE OT), and perfect teeth are a mark of special beauty in Song of S. 4:2; 6:6 (cf. Gen. 49:12).

The teeth of voracious animals, both real (Deut. 32:24; Job 41:14) and visionary (Dan. 7:5 ff; Rev. 9:8), signify predatory power (Job 29:17; Ps. 124:6; Dan. 7:5; Zech. 9:7). Thus the "enemy" or the "wicked man" may be characterized as a gnashing beast (typically the lion; Pss. 35:16-17; 57:4; 58:6; cf. also Ps. 37:12; Prov. 30:14; Lam. 2:16; Joel 1:6; Acts 7:54).

In Job 29:17 the righteous man breaks the "fangs" (lit., "jawbone") of the unrighteous, releasing the defenseless from his "teeth." Similarly, Yahweh is called upon by the psalmist to break the teeth of the wicked (Pss. 3:7; 58:6); but in his wrath he himself may be likened to a ravening beast (Job 16:9; Lam. 3:10-11; cf. also Lam. 3:16).

In other figures, the teeth may represent pain (Prov. 25:19) or distaste (10:26). The proverb in Jer. 31:29; Ezek. 18:2 ("set on edge"; lit., "become dull, insensitive") refers to the doctrine of corporate guilt and retribution (cf. Lam. 5:7), which was being strongly challenged in the seventh and sixth centuries (cf. Deut. 24:16; Ezek. 14:13-20).

The "gnashing of teeth" in Matt. 8:12; 13:42; 13; 24:51; 25:30; Luke 13:28 (cf. Ps. 112:10) has no close parallel in other literature, but clearly describes the despairing rage and remorse of those excluded from the kingdom.

Bibliography. On the obscure idioms in Job 13:14; 19:20, see S. Terrien, Exegesis of Job, IB, III (1954), 1003-4, 1047-48. J. A. WHARTON

TOPARCHY tŏp'är kĭ [τοπαρχία]. A small district administered by a toparch. In the time of Josephus and Pliny, Judea was divided into ten or eleven top-archies. The word (translated "district"; KJV "government") is used in I Macc. 10:30, 38; 11:28 to denote three provinces, in 11:34 called APHAIREMA; LYDDA; and RATHAMIN, which were added to Judea from Samaria by Jonathan. *See also* PROVINCE.

N. TURNER

TOPAZ [פִּטְדָה, *cf.* Sanskrit *pita,* yellow; τοπάζιον; Vulg. *topazius*]. An orthorhombic mineral, frequently occurring in transparent prismatic crystals. It is characteristically yellow to orange in color. The topaz is a stone in the breastpiece of judgment (Exod. 28:17; 39:10), a stone on the covering of the king of Tyre (Ezek. 28:13), and the ninth jewel in the foundation of the wall of the New Jerusalem (Rev. 21:20). Job 28:19 declares that the topaz of Ethiopia is of less value than wisdom. *See also* JEWELS AND PRECIOUS STONES § 2.

W. E. STAPLES

TOPHEL tō'fəl [תֹּפֶל] (Deut. 1:1). One of the limits of the general locality where Moses addressed the Israelites "beyond the Jordan in the wilderness, in the Arabah over against Suph, between Paran and Tophel, Laban, Hazeroth, and Dizahab." Tophel has been usually identified with modern eṭ-Ṭafileh, a village located in a fertile valley on the road from Kerak to Petra, *ca.* fifteen miles SE of the Dead Sea. However, this identification has been questioned on phonetic grounds; the Arabic "ṭ" does not correspond with the Hebrew "t." Although not mentioned elsewhere, Tophel may have been one of the stopping places of the Israelites in the wilderness.

Bibliography. N. Glueck, "Explorations in Eastern Palestine," *AASOR,* XVIII-XIX (1939), 42-43.

J. L. MIHELIC

TOPHETH tō'fith [תֹּפֶת]; KJV TOPHET —fit in Isa. 30:33; Jer. 7:31-32; 19:6. A place in the Valley of Hinnom (*see* HINNOM, VALLEY OF THE SON OF), close to the POTSHERD GATE, and in the vicinity of the Potter's Field (Jer. 19; *see* AKELDAMA). There is a general agreement as to its location in the lower tract of the Wadi er-Rababi, toward its junction with the Kidron (*see* KIDRON, BROOK). The name To-pheth is derived from the Aramaic תְּפָא and meant originally a hearth or a fireplace, previous to being used as a toponym. The Masoretes gave it the vowels of *bōsheth,* "shameful thing," on account of the shocking associations of the place. Topheth is described as an illicit open-air sanctuary or HIGH PLACE in the Valley of Hinnom, which became involved in the same reprobation (Jer. 7:31). Children were sacrificed as burnt offerings in honor of Baal, who is mentioned in parallelism with MOLECH (Jer. 32:35). It is not altogether clear whether these practices were those of a foreign cult, or of a corrupted form of Yahwism. They were popular under the reigns of Ahaz and Manasseh, who are recorded as having offered of their own children (II Chr. 28:3; 33:6). The high place of Topheth was desecrated by Josiah, in execution of his program of religious reformation (II Kings 23:10). Jeremiah, denouncing the past sins of the nation, cursed Topheth and the Valley of Hinnom, which he foretold would be called appropriately "valley of Slaughter," because of the number of men

and women slain in the day when God would exercise his vengeance on Judah and Jerusalem, and when the corpses should be interred in Topheth, for lack of vacant burying grounds. This, according to Semitic ideas, would be the ultimate profanation of the high place (Jer. 7:32; 19:6-7, 11). An oracle of Isa. 30:33 contains an uncertain reference to Topheth either as a toponym (KJV "Tophet"), or as a common name (RSV "a burning place"); the Hebrew has here תָּפְתֶּה.

See Map I under JERUSALEM.

Bibliography. H. Vincent, *Jérusalem Antique* (1912), pp. 127-30; W. R. Smith, *Religion of the Semites* (3rd ed., 1927), p. 377; G. Dalman, *Jerusalem und sein Gelände* (1930), pp. 206-7; J. Simons, *Jerusalem in the OT* (1952), p. 12.

G. A. BARROIS

*TORAH tôr'ə [תּוֹרָה, *presumably from* ירה, to direct, point the way; Apoc. νόμος]. General OT term for divine instruction and guidance, particularly through the law (*see* LAW IN THE OT); translated "law." The promulgation of Torah is particularly associated with the tribe of Levi and appears in an early text in connection with the oracular use of Urim and Thummim, the sacred lots (Deut. 33:8-11). Torah, while not the exclusive concern of the priests, is their particular responsibility (Jer. 2:8; 18:18; Hos. 4:6).

The term appears to have developed in meaning in the following way: (*a*) In early passages, priestly instruction is provided on the basis of oracles and traditional understandings of the requirements of Yahweh; (*b*) by the time of the later monarchy, "Torah" refers to the basic instruction and direction provided to Israel by Yahweh, particularly in the legal materials; (*c*) in the postexilic period (certainly by the time of Ezra, last half of the fifth century B.C.), "Torah" means the substance of the Pentateuch (Neh. 8:8), the book of Moses (Ezra 3:2; 7:6; Neh. 8:1; etc.); (*d*) finally, "Torah" becomes the standard term for the Pentateuch in its entirety, as distinguished from the Prophets and the other books (Prologue to Ecclesiasticus).

Bibliography. G. Östborn, *Tōrā in the OT* (1945), contains a full bibliography.

W. J. HARRELSON

TORCH [לַפִּיד; λαμπάς]. A brilliantly burning flame produced primitively by a highly combustible stick of wood or by an absorbent combustible material tied on the end of a rod or stick and dipped into oil and ignited. Yahweh signifies his commitment to the covenant with Abraham, he seals the covenant, by passing between the severed halves of animals in the form of a torch (Gen. 15:17; cf. for the significance of the account, Jer. 34:18). By the strategic use of torches, Gideon wins his incredible victory (Judg. 7:16 ff). In the poem on Leviathan, in Job 41, the remarkable description includes the lines:

> Out of his mouth go flaming torches;
> sparks of fire leap forth (vs. 19).

Zion's redemption is assured by the prophet in Isa. 62:1 in these terms:

> Her vindication goes forth as brightness,
> and her salvation as a burning torch.

The Greek term is ambiguous, sometimes (as in

the story of the virgins in Matt. 25) denoting the more sophisticated oil lamp and wick; but it is clearly the dramatic torch in John 18:3.

See also LAMP IN THE NT; LANTERN.

B. D. NAPIER

TORTOISE. KJV translation of צב (Lev. 11:29; RSV GREAT LIZARD).

TORTURE. The translation of two Greek words in the Bible. In Heb. 11:35 the word translated "tortured" (ἐτυμπανίσθησαν) refers to a method of torture or execution by some instrument (τύμπανον) now unknown. In Rev. 9:5 the word translated "torture" is βασανισμός, which has both a verb and a noun form. It is rendered differently elsewhere (usually "torment"). *See* CRIMES AND PUNISHMENTS.

B. H. THROCKMORTON, JR.

*****TOTEMISM.** A primitive social system based on belief in kinship with animals or plants. Members of the totem clan ascribe their origin to an animal or plant and regard themselves as related by mystical descent from it. The clan bears the name of the totem animal or plant, which is also its ethnic emblem, painted or tattooed on the bodies of the individuals and engraved on the clan shield. The sacred character of the totem excludes the species from use as common food, but the totem animal is the victim in the ritual meal of the clan. Kinship is reckoned through the mother, and marriage is exogamous—i.e., one belongs to his mother's totem and may not marry a member of his own totem.

The view that totemism was the original religion of the Semites and persisted among the early Hebrews was developed chiefly by W. R. Smith. The arguments can be noted only briefly here.

1. Animal and plant names
2. The worship of animals
3. Exogamy and kinship through the mother
4. Food taboos
5. Clan markings and standards
Bibliography

1. Animal and plant names. These are common in the OT, but constitute less than one per cent of the total personal names. Moreover, animal names are everywhere common—they were frequent even among the early Christians. Greater weight is to be given to animal names of clans. In the genealogies of the Edomites (Gen. 36), more than a third of the clans have animal names. The Edomites, according to tradition, were hunters, and totemism in full force has been found only among hunters. Some of the Israelite clans also had animal and plant names, the Arodites (ass clan; Num. 26:17), the Tolaites (worm clan; Num. 26:23), the Elonites (oak clan; Num. 26:26), the Becherites (camel clan; Num. 26:35), the Shuphamites (viper[?] clan; Num. 26:39), and the Calebites (dog clan; I Sam. 25:3). Such names may be survivals of totem-clan systems, but hardly more than that. *See* AROD; TOLA 1; ELON 1; BECHER 1; SHEPHUPHIM; CALEB.

2. The worship of animals. Persistently practiced despite the Second Commandment, animal-worship has been connected with totemism. The worship of powerful or mysterious animals, such as the bull or the serpent, is intelligible without resort to totemism, but the worship of a great variety of creatures may best be explained by totemism. The numerous theriomorphic gods of Egypt are strong evidence that the Egyptians passed through a true totemic stage, but among the Semites the evidence is meager. Perhaps the most striking example that can be adduced from the OT is Ezekiel's vision (8:7-11) of abominations committed in the temple, of "all kinds of creeping things, and loathsome beasts, and all the idols of the house of Israel" portrayed on the temple walls, with Jaazaniah the son of Shaphan (rock badger) leading the worship. This has been seen as a reversion to totemism in a time of stress. For J. Jacob's arguments against this view, however, *see bibliography.*

3. Exogamy and kinship through the mother. There are in the OT many instances of marriage outside the clan or nation, but Hebrew marriage was generally endogamous. In Judg. 12:9 there is explicit reference to exogamy. Traces of kinship reckoned through the mother may be seen in Gen. 22:22; Judg. 8:19; Ruth 1:8; II Sam. 17:25; Song of S. 1:6. In such a system, half brothers and sisters have no relation and may marry, as in the case of Abraham and Sarah (Gen. 20:12), or Amnon and Tamar (II Sam. 13:13). In the genealogies of temple servants in Ezra 2:43-60; Neh. 7:46-59, most of the ancestors have names with the Hebrew or Aramaic feminine ending. It has been suggested that these ancestors with ostensibly feminine names were temple prostitutes whose offspring became temple servants. The paternity of such offspring would naturally be indeterminate, and the reckoning of descent through the mother would have no connection with totemism.

4. Food taboos. These are an integral part of totemism, and it has been supposed that the OT dietary laws have this origin. There are apparent references to eucharistic eating of unclean animals, swine and mice, in Isa. 65:4; 66:17. Lists of forbidden foods such as those of Lev. 11; Deut. 15 may in part derive from totemism. The evidence, however, is equivocal, since of the animals that occur as personal or clan names in the OT, the proportion of clean and unclean is about equal.

5. Clan markings and standards. Incising or tattooing the body is forbidden in Lev. 19:28, but there are allusions to such practices in Gen. 4:15; Isa. 44:5; Ezek. 9:4; Zech. 13:6. There is no evidence that the marks in question were connected with totemism. In Ezek. 9:4 the purpose of the mark is to identify and protect those who shun animal worship. However, it may be that the animal-worshipers also had their own distinctive markings. In Revelation the different markings—the name of the Lamb and the Father (Rev. 14:1; 22:4) and the name or the number of the beast (Rev. 13:16-17; 17:5)—served to distinguish the worshipers of God and his Christ (Rev. 7:3; 9:4; 14:1; 22:4) and the worshipers of the beast (Rev. 14:9, 11; 16:2; 19:20). The symbolism, however, is explicitly connected with the marking of slaves (Rev. 7:3).

The Israelites had tribal standards (Num. 1:52; 2:2). According to tradition (Midrash Rabbah Numbers), some of these flags had animal representations. The symbolism is derived from the blessings of Jacob (Gen. 49) and Moses (Deut. 33), where several of the tribes are equated with animals. The symbolism, however, is not entirely consistent in the two poems. In Gen. 49:17 Dan is a serpent, while in Deut. 33:22 he is a lion's whelp. The symbolism seems to be mere poetic metaphor rather than vestigial totemism. The evidences for totemism among the Israelites seem to be mere vestiges of the prehistoric past.

See also CLEAN AND UNCLEAN; FAUNA; MAN AND SOCIETY; MARRIAGE.

Bibliography. W. R. Smith, "Animal Worship and Animal Tribes Among the Ancient Arabs and in the OT," *Journal of Philology*, 9 (1880), 75-100; J. Jacobs, *Studies in Biblical Archeology* (1894), pp. 64-103; V. Zapletal, *Der Totemismus und die Religion Israels* (1901); W. R. Smith, *Kinship and Marriage in Early Arabia* (1907); J. G. Frazer, *Totemism and Exogamy* (1910); S. Freud, *Totem and Taboo* (1918); W. R. Smith, *The Religion of the Semites* (1927); H. Findeisen, "Das Tier als Gott, Dämon und Ahne. Eine Untersuchung über das Erleben des Tieres in der Altmenschheit," *Kosmos-Bändchen* (1956); J. Henninger, "Le problème du totémisme chez les Sémites," *Sacra Pagina*, I (1959), 253-58.   M. H. POPE

TOU. Alternate form of TOI.

TOUBIANI. *See* TOB.

TOUCH [ἅπτεσθαι]. The verb which is always used of Jesus' "touching" or being "touched." It implies a touch which tends to hold and even sometimes to cling.

This is not the same as handling or feeling (as if in search of something), as when Jesus invited the Eleven to "handle" (ψηλαφᾶν) him after the Resurrection (Luke 24:39). Much less is it the more casual brush of contact. We may therefore suppose that Jesus really held the leper and was not quick to withdraw from contact with him (Matt. 8:3; Mark 1:41; Luke 5:13), and that he gripped the fevered hand of Peter's mother-in-law (Matt. 8:15). There was nothing remote, therefore, in his handling of the infants (Mark 10:13; Luke 18:15) or the bier (Luke 7:14), or the injured ear of the high priest's slave (Luke 22:51), the mute's tongue (Mark 7:33), or the eyes of the blind men (Matt. 9:29; 20:34); and probably, therefore, he did more than merely prod the disciples out of their fear at the Transfiguration (Matt. 17:7). Moreover, the woman with a flow of blood and other diseased folk took a good grip on his garment (Mark 5:27, etc.) and probably upon his person (Mark 3:10; Luke 6:19), a grip as real and restraining as that of the woman who anointed his feet (Luke 7:39).   N. TURNER

TOWEL [λέντιον, *borrowed from* Lat. *linteum*] (John 13:4-5). A linen cloth. Jesus' washing his disciples' feet and drying them with a towel was an act, not of degradation, but of humility.

TOWER. The translation of several words in the Bible. Towers were a common feature of the biblical landscape, and were located in cities, pastures, vineyards, and farm lands. Built of brick or stone, towers varied greatly in size; they served chiefly for refuge or defense against military attack. *See also* CITY;

FORTIFICATION; WAR, METHODS OF; WATCH TOWER.

The usual word translated "tower" is מִגְדָּל, *migdāl* (Gen. 11:4; II Kings 9:17; Isa. 2:15; etc.). Translators render the same word, where the context requires it, as the name of a city, MIGDOL (Ezek. 29:10; 30:6; KJV "from the tower"; RSV "from Migdol"; the latter is preferable and is a reference to an Egyptian city). מִגְדִּיל, *Qere* מִגְדּוֹל, in II Sam. 22:51 is used figuratively of God as a tower of salvation (so KJV; the RSV, with Kethibh, versions, and Ps. 18:50—H 18:51, renders the word as a verb).

Other words for "tower" are: בָּחוּן (Jer. 6:27; KJV "tower"; RSV "assayer"); בָּחִין (Isa. 23:13; KJV "tower"; RSV "siege tower"); בַּחַן (Isa. 32:14; KJV "tower"; RSV "watchtower"); מָצוֹר (Hab. 2:1); עֹפֶל (II Kings 5:24; KJV "tower," KJV mg. "secret place"; RSV "hill"); פִּנָּה (Zeph. 1:16 [KJV "tower"; RSV "battlement"]; 3:6 [KJV "tower," KJV mg. "corner"; RSV "battlement"]); מִשְׂגָּב (II Sam. 22:3; Ps. 18:2—H 18:3; 144:2; KJV "tower"; RSV "stronghold"); πύργος (Matt. 21:33; Mark 12:1; Luke 13:4). עֵץ מִגְדָּל (Neh. 8:4; KJV "pulpit of wood," "margin," "tower of wood"; RSV "wooden PULPIT") is a wooden platform which could be ascended by stairs (Neh. 9:4).

Towers mentioned by name include the following: tower of David (Song of S. 4:4); tower of EDER (Gen. 35:21; "tower of the flock" in Mic. 4:8); Tower of the Ovens (Neh. 3:11; 12:38 [KJV "Furnaces"]); Tower of Hananel; tower of Lebanon; Tower of the Hundred (KJV "Meah"); tower of PENUEL (1); Tower of Shechem. Towers in Jezreel, Tyre, and Siloam and others in Jerusalem are mentioned. Gen. 11:4 has usually been interpreted as indicating Hebrew knowledge of the Babylonian temple towers, the *ziqqurat* (*see* BABEL). Uzziah built towers, not only in Jerusalem (II Chr. 26:9), but also in the wilderness (II Chr. 26:10). Jotham built them on wooded hills (II Chr. 27:4), and Hezekiah constructed towers in Jerusalem (II Chr. 32:5). *See* SHECHEM, TOWER OF; OVENS, TOWER OF; HANANEL, TOWER OF; HUNDRED, TOWER OF THE.

Some towers were large enough to serve as citadels or fortresses into which the population of a village could retreat at a time of danger (Judg. 9:51). Others were doubtless nothing more than small stone rooms which served as watch towers in vineyards (Mark 12:1); such towers can still be seen in Palestine. *See* WATCH TOWER.

Towers are mentioned figuratively in references to God's protective power (Ps. 61:3—H 61:4), and as a symbol of human strength (Song of S. 4:4) and feminine beauty (Song of S. 7:4: "Your neck is like an ivory tower"; 8:10).

Archaeologists have excavated many city towers from as early as the Neolithic period; *see* JERICHO; BETH-SHAN; MEGIDDO; LACHISH; MIZPAH; SAMARIA; SHECHEM; etc. Explorations have disclosed the towered fortresses and fortress towers which guarded the E frontiers of Edom, Moab, and Ammon.

     W. L. REED

TOWER OF BABEL. *See* BABEL.

TOWER OF SHECHEM. *See* SHECHEM, TOWER OF.

TOWN CLERK. The term used to translate γραμματεύς in Acts 19:35. This is the one appearance in the Bible of this word in a non-Jewish context. The Greek term, appearing constantly in the gospels, elsewhere designates the Jewish SCRIBE.

1. The problem of translation. Because of the shifting patterns in civic administration and the concomitant fact that names of offices are frequently retained although function and status may greatly vary, the translation of γραμματεύς in Acts 19:35 is very difficult. Since Ephesus was a "free city," by the same token it was a city-state. Therefore, either city or state terminology could be appropriate. And since γραμματεύς roots in the meaning "scribe," "secretary" (English "clerk"), the translation "town clerk" is possible on the one hand, as is that of Moffatt, "secretary of state," on the other. Yet neither of these terms is very satisfactory: American cities have no official designated as "town clerk." Towns do have secretaries, keepers of records, but their functions are hardly those of the "town clerk" in Acts 19. And if the functions of the officer in Acts 19 are more than those of a town secretary as we know him, they are less than those of our "secretary of state." Nor does Goodspeed's choice, "recorder," help. *The Twentieth Century NT* (1900), and more recently C. H. Rieu (1957), translate "mayor." French and German translators more commonly prefer "chancellor" (*chancelier, Kanzler*). The difficulty here is that the word "chancellor," like γραμματεύς, has an extended history of meanings. Both words began humbly and increased in function and prestige. The office of chancellor arose from the Roman *cancellarius*, originally an usher or doorkeeper stationed at the lattice bar or chancel of a basilica or other law court; then, in the Eastern Empire he became a notary or secretary with judicial powers; finally, in the kingdoms of the Western Empire, he became an officer of increasingly important functions. Hence the title was used of the chief minister of state in Austria-Hungary (where it survived from the Holy Roman Empire) and in the German and Austrian republics of recent times. The objection to "chancellor" would be the same as that to "secretary of state."

Nevertheless, even if both these translations are overtranslations, they have the merit of suggesting that the γραμματεύς was the chief executive officer of the city (-state), the most important Ephesian official. Zahn urges that "Luther's *Kanzler* is still the best translation for it at least permits one to think of a high civil official—which can hardly be said of the *scriba* of the Latins, the city-*secretary* of Bengel and Weizsaecker, . . . or the *town clerk* of KJV."

2. Status and functions. It is clear from Acts 19 that the γραμματεύς was the principal municipal officer of Ephesus, the executive officer under whose immediate responsibility such situations as the riot over Paul would fall. His high status in the community is confirmed by coins and inscriptions from Ephesus, and by the fact that generally in Asia Minor his administration dated the year. Also, on occasion he might be an ASIARCH.

His functions in general would fall under three heads:

a) He would be responsible for keeping the records of the city, for taking the minutes of the council, or senate, and the assembly; he would file copies of decrees, of treaties, of edicts of emperors and governors—indeed, of the mass of miscellaneous documents which are involved in city and state administration.

b) He might be called upon to draw up the official decrees as approved by the senate and present them to the assembly, sometimes being himself the chairman, directing the debates. He might have charge of the endowment for doles to be given the citizenry, or distribute the annual money gifts from the public treasury on Antoninus' birthday, or direct the erection of statues decreed by senate and people in honor of emperors or other notables. The clerk was in a position to know much about affairs of state. Hence he became a more and more dominant figure in these affairs; and in the Roman period he, either alone or with the support of the leading magistrates, often moved decrees and took the lead in council and assembly.

c) As executive officer he would be the liaison officer between the civil administration and the Roman provincial administration, the headquarters of which were also in Ephesus. Since he would be held responsible for any riot, he naturally took hold of the situation quickly and quieted the mob by calling to their attention that "the courts are open, and there are proconsuls." Thus for Luke's purposes in Acts it is very important that the chief executive of Ephesus should declare himself for Paul and against Demetrius the silversmith, whose opposition to Paul was on economic grounds, and against the partisans of Artemis, whose opposition was on religious grounds. If, on the one hand, Luke describes the Ephesian incident in such a way as to show that Christianity is the end of paganism (vss. 26-27), on the other hand the town clerk will assure the Ephesians that their own special deity, Artemis, is really in no danger (vss. 35-37)! It is no less a person than the γραμματεύς who exonerates Paul from the charges of economic and religious subversion.

Bibliography. A. H. M. Jones, *The Greek City* (1940), pp. 238-39; D. Magie, *Roman Rule in Asia Minor* (1950), pp. 60, 645, 848-49, 1510-11. F. D. GEALY

TRACHONITIS trăk'ə nī'tĭs [Τραχωνῖτις, rough, stony district] (Luke 3:1). A district in N Transjordan, mentioned in the Bible only in connection with the dating of John in the reign of Herod Antipas "and his brother Philip tetrarch of the region of Ituraea and Trachonitis."

1. Location
2. Description
3. History
4. Economy
Bibliography

1. Location. Ancient Trachonitis can be defined only in the general terms given by Josephus. It lay *ca.* twenty-five miles S of Damascus and the River Pharpar. To the W the boundary was Gaulanitis, and to the NW Ulatha and Paneas at the foot of Mount Hermon (Jos. Antiq. XV.x.3).* On the SW the border was along Batanaea and Auranitis (Jos. Antiq. XVII.ii.1; War I.xx.4). To the E there was an indefinite border along the mountainous area now called Jebel Druze. Fig. HER 15.

2. Description. The area is a portion of the N Transjordan plateau which was known as BASHAN in the OT, in modern times called the Hauran. The most distinctive feature of Trachonitis, which gave it its name, is a large pear-shaped mass of black basalt covering *ca.* 350 square miles. This congealed flood of volcanic lava rises to a more or less uniform height of twenty to forty feet above the plateau. In the course of cooling, deep fissures and holes appeared in the lava. This formed the heart of Trachonitis, although portions of the surrounding plain were also included in the district. The Greek word for Trachonitis is properly an adjective, though the name of the district is at times given as a noun, the Trachon (ὁ Τράχων; e.g., Jos. Antiq. XV.x.1, 3; Strabo XVI. ii.16, 20).

This portion of the Hauran, so wild and rugged that it is difficult to enter, has always been an excellent refuge for robbers and rebels; hence the Arabic name, *el Leja,* "the Refuge." The first mention of Trachonitis seems to be in Strabo. He writes of "the two Trachones," referring to both Trachonitis and a similar but uninhabited area farther E, known today as *es-Safa.* He mentions the wildness of the terrain and its inhabitants (XVI.ii.20). Josephus speaks of it as habitually inhabited by robbers: "The inhabitants of those places lived in a mad way and pillaged the country of the Damascenes. . . . It was not an easy thing to restrain them since this way of robbery had been their usual practice, and they had no other way to get their living" (Antiq. XV.x.1; cf. XVII.ii.1-2).

3. History. This area, like the mountains of Jebel Druze to the E, has always been difficult to rule. The first mention of the ruler of Trachonitis comes from *ca.* 25 B.C., when it was ruled by Zenodorus with the tacit consent of Rome (Strabo XVI.ii.20; Jos. Antiq. XV.x.1-2). Later it was given by Augustus to Herod the Great, who was forced *ca.* 9 B.C. to assert his authority with troops to suppress a revolt (Jos. Antiq. XV.x.1; XVI.iv.6; ix.1). At the death of Herod in 4 B.C., and in accordance with his will, Trachonitis was given to his son Philip to form part of his tetrarchy, as is indicated in Luke 3:1 (Jos. Antiq. XVII.viii.1; xi.4; War II.vi.3). Philip seems to have been a strong ruler and able to maintain the peace for nearly forty years. Philo wrongly uses the name Trachonitis for the whole territory of Philip (*Legation to Caius* 41). After Philip's death in A.D. 34 it was included in the Roman province of Syria (Jos. Antiq. XVIII.iv.6). In 37 it was given by the Emperor Caligula to Herod Agrippa I, who ruled it until 44 (Jos. Antiq. XVIII.vi.10). Following Agrippa's rule it was governed by Roman officials until it was ruled by Herod Agrippa II (53-100). It was then placed under the direct rule of Roman officials as part of the province of Syria or Arabia, the latter becoming a Roman province in 106. The peak of prosperity for Trachonitis seems to have begun with the reign of Trajan (98-117).

4. Economy. In spite of the rugged terrain, some agriculture has always been possible in Trachonitis. There are springs and sufficient rainfall for the meager crops grown in the small patches of soil strewn with rocks. Although better suited to vineyards than to grain, the land is best suited to raising sheep and goats. The surprising number and size of the ruins of ancient cities indicate that it supported a much larger population then than now, especially in the early Christian centuries. These are the famous "black cities" of the *Arabian Nights.* Because of the almost complete absence of wood suitable for building, these ancient cities were built entirely of stone. Even the roofs, stairs, windows, and doors were made of the gloomy black basalt. Some of the doors are still in place and in working condition.

Bibliography. F.-M. Abel, *Géographie de la Palestine* (1938), I, 47; II, 156. D. Baly, *The Geography of the Bible* (1957), pp. 222-23. D. C. PELLETT

TRADE AND COMMERCE. Our sources of information concerning the development of trade and commerce in biblical antiquity are references from the Bible; parallels from the literature of neighboring countries; specific documents such as contracts, archives, etc.; and archaeological evidence with regard to imports, exports, and trade routes.

1. Real-estate transactions
2. Local trade
3. Import-export in Canaanite and Israelite Palestine
    a. Wares of importation and exportation
    b. Trade routes
    c. Royal enterprises
    d. Means of transaction
4. Import-export in Hellenistic and Roman Palestine
    a. Wares of importation and exportation
    b. Trading centers and trade routes
    c. Money and banking
Bibliography

1. Real-estate transactions. The Law and the Prophets are not favorable to unlimited freedom of transaction in matters of real estate. There is a strong feeling in Yahwistic circles that earth belongs to God, and that men are only his tenants. On the other hand, the strong organization of the family as a social unit tended to prevent the alienation of family property, or at least to keep real-estate transactions within narrow limits. To achieve this, the Law contained provisions for the privilege of the next of kin to redeem the land of an impoverished relative compelled to sell out (Lev. 25:25-34; *see* REDEEM). Such a privilege amounted in certain circumstances to a moral obligation. The institution of the Jubilee (*see* JUBILEE, YEAR OF) also tended toward the stabilizing of family ownership, although its modes of execution remain obscure to us (Lev. 25:10, 13-16). In spite of their late formulation, the laws on real-estate deals originated in ancient customs, as may be inferred from such texts as Ruth 4:3-4; Jer. 32:7-8, and from parallel documents found in the archives of NUZI (fifteenth century B.C.).

The transformation of social and economic conditions under the monarchy resulted in many transgressions of the old customs, and in a general neglect or outright contempt of the contemporary legislation. Kings were among the worst offenders, either when they usurped by violence the family estate of their subjects (I Kings 21:1-16), or when they acquired lands through forced purchases to grant them to members of the royal household, state officials, or tenants of fiefs, just as the rulers of the Canaanite city-states had done before them (I Sam. 8:14). The prophets condemned the greed of rich owners who seized the heavily mortgaged land holdings of poorer neighbors (Isa. 5:8). The rise of sects like that of the Rechabites toward the middle of the ninth century B.C. must be interpreted in part as a protest against the unethical business practices of the ruling class (Jer. 35:1-11). *See* RECHAB.

Biblical references to the legal instruments of transmission of real estate are scarce and much involved. The discussion between Abraham and Ephron the Hittite for the purchase of the cave of Mach-pelah, and the record of the business as it was understood by the author of Genesis, suggest that the legal acquisition of what was to become the burial ground of the patriarchs constituted a symbolic title to the occupation of the soil of Canaan by the Israelites (Gen. 23:3-18). Hence Abraham's insistence that all forms be observed. The entire episode, however, ought to be reconsidered in the light of Hittite laws, according to which the act of securing a full title to land property bound the purchaser to various feudal obligations. If these legal clauses really apply to the case, one might be led to reconstruct the narrative as if Abraham, who was understandably anxious to avoid any kind of servitude, and only interested in the acquisition of a burial plot, finally had to submit to the formal procedure.

A passage of Jeremiah describes in detail the writing of a real-estate contract (Jer. 32:9-14). Unfortunately, the text is corrupt, and the prophet was less interested in the accurate description of the procedure than in its symbolical application. We may gather, however, that, in usual practice, the contract would have been written in duplicate, the original sealed and kept in an earthenware vessel as a document of archive, while the purchaser retained the copy at hand.

A contract of sale of land, written in Babylonian cuneiform script and dating apparently from the fourteenth century B.C., was found at Shechem. A similar document from Gezer, written in Assyrian, dates from the seventh century B.C.

The gesture of the purchaser's setting his foot on the land marked the act of taking possession. There are indirect references to this usage in Pss. 60:8; 108:9. This symbolic gesture may be at the origin of the ritual of taking off one's shoe, by which a man would signify the transmission of his right (or obligation) to his kinsman in procedures of redemption or of levirate (Ruth 4:7-8; *see* MARRIAGE § 1*g*). The ritual, however, was interpreted desultorily in later times (Deut. 25:9-10).

2. Local trade. The predominantly rural economy of Palestine in antiquity gave the local trade its distinctive character. The bulk of the wares brought to market consisted of agricultural produce not actually consumed by the peasants, who traded it on regional markets for a few indispensable artifacts manufactured by town craftsmen, insofar as these artifacts could not possibly be homemade.

There was a steady trade in barley and wheat, olives and olive oil, grapes and wine, as well as in lentils, dried peas, raisins, dried figs and dates, almonds and other nuts. The demand for fresh vegetables and fruit varied according to local conditions, since all towns and villages were not equally endowed in gardens and orchards, because of unequal water supply.

Livestock was offered principally by nomads and seminomads, and by those peasants who owned extensive pastures or pasture lands—e.g., in the villages located on or by the N-S crest of the Palestinian highlands, with the wastelands sloping down toward the Valley of the Jordan, the Dead Sea, and the Negeb, as their grazing grounds. The trade in saddle or pack animals was naturally limited, while the sale of oxen, sheep, and goats, went on extensively, with a seasonal peak in the late spring, when lambs and kids were brought to market. Dairy products, such as milk (sweet and sour), cheese, butter fat, were sold to city people the year around.

Wild game and the catch of fishermen were not an important item on the food market in Canaanite and Israelite Palestine. Fishing and the preparation of salted fish, however, took a considerable extension in Hellenistic and Roman times, as one may gather from miscellaneous references in the NT, especially in the gospels, and from the Aramaic and Greek surnames of the little town of Magdala on the W shore of the Lake of Tiberias: respectively Migdal Nunayâ, "Migdal of the fish," and Ταριχεῖαι, "the salting houses."

The sale of agricultural products from the royal domains influenced the conditions of the market. Already Canaanite rulers had traded extensively in grain and olive oil, stored in the cellars of their palaces or in special warehouses. Similar activities on the part of the Hebrew kings must have created a very serious competition to private business. The promotion of agriculture and animal husbandry by Uzziah king of Judah was not altogether disinterested (II Chr. 26:10), and the kings of Israel had a quasi monopoly on oil and wine, as may be inferred from the extensive storehouses of the palaces at Samaria, in which they stocked the produce of the crown lands and the taxes of private landowners, which were levied in kind.

The market place was usually located at the gate of the city, where peasants from nearby villages or farms brought their produce (II Kings 7:1), and where foreign merchants offered their wares (Neh. 13:16). Quite often, the market of one particular gate was reserved for one or several categories of wares, while livestock was sold at another gate.

Craftsmen established in the towns supplied the local trade with pottery and textiles, chiefly wool and woolens. Much of the textile, however, was homespun, at least in Canaanite and early Israelite times. At a more advanced stage of the monarchy, some cities specialized in the weaving and dyeing industries, as archaeological discoveries at Tell ed-Duweir (Lachish) and Tell Beit-Mirsim (Kiriath-sepher) abundantly show. This, of course, made it necessary that the goods be offered to the buyers by the intermediary of merchants. Utensils of metal, such as kettles, tools, and weapons, as well as silver and gold ornaments, were sold by itinerant distributors or were manufactured locally.

Each branch of these trades or industries was usually carried in a specialized quarter of the town. In Jerusalem, potters had their workshops in the S suburbs, as one may infer from such toponyms as the Potter's Field (*see* AKELDAMA), the Gate of Potsherds (*see* POTSHERD GATE). Bakers had their street (Jer. 37:21), presumably in the vicinity of the Tower of the Ovens (*see* OVENS, TOWER OF THE). Josephus mentions also the wool market and the quarter of the smithies (War V.viii.1).

Barter was the primitive means of transaction on the city market or in the shops. A head of cattle constituted the basic standard of value, as one may infer from the Hebrew word קשׂיטה for a monetary unit referred to in RSV as "piece of money," while the Greek and Latin versions have ἀμνόν, *ovis*, according to etymology (Gen. 33:19; Josh. 24:32; Job 42:11). Objects of metal, and bars or rings or ingots of gold and silver in the case of important deals, soon replaced cumbersome bartering methods. It must be kept in mind, however, that money as we understand it did not appear in Palestine prior to the Persian and Hellenistic periods, and that, consequently, earlier texts mentioning a number of silver shekels—e.g., Gen. 23:16; 37:28; Judg. 16:5; etc.— refer in reality to corresponding amounts of silver counted on the basis of the shekel as unit of weight, and not of coinage. *See* MONEY.

3. Import-export in Canaanite and Israelite Palestine. Any level of industrial development, howsoever mediocre, and the unavoidable specialization of certain crafts which attends growing standards of living, make it necessary, as a rule, to import both raw materials and wares not readily found on the local market. These importations suppose, in return, balancing exports. This elementary principle of economics can be verified in Canaanite, as well as in Israelite, Palestine. Furthermore, it was natural that Palestine, by reason of its geographical location at the crossroads of trade routes between Mesopotamia, Syria, Asia Minor, the Mediterranean isles and lands, Egypt, and the countries beyond the Red Sea and the Persian Gulf, would have become involved in international commercial transit.

A good index of the participation of Syro-Palestine in international trade is the very fact of the technical and artistic syncretism characteristic of the industrial products of these countries during the Middle and the Late Bronze Age, which implies manifold exchanges, generally on the increase, between the various regions of the Near and Middle East. In particular, the composite style of the ivories of Megiddo and of Samaria, as well as of miscellaneous artifacts, shows a standardization of artistic methods and patterns which is obviously the result of intensified trade relations. *See* ART §§ 2*c*, 3*b*.

a. Wares of importation and exportation. The raw materials or produce and wares imported in, or exported from, Canaanite and Israelite Palestine are known to us through biblical references and archaeological discoveries. The principal exports from Palestine proper and the Transjordanian and Negeb districts were agricultural products, such as olive oil and cereals (I Kings 5:11; Ezek. 27:17). Some spe-

cialties of Palestine seem to have been much in demand on foreign markets: costly balm, odoriferous resins, gum, myrrh, and also honey, dried nuts, pistachios, and almonds, such as Jacob sent to Joseph as a present (Gen. 43:11; Ezek. 27:17). One may surmise that wine, pressed figs, raisins, and dates were also shipped abroad. Industrial exports were raw wool, woolen cloth, and embroidered or woven garments of many colors. Exporters from the region of Damascus, with their overseas expeditions of dried fruits, wine from Helbon, and fine woolens (Ezek. 27:18), must have been serious competitors to Palestinian traders.

The main articles of importation are industrial raw materials: tin, lead, and silver from Khurasan (?), Italy, Spain, Brittany, and Great Britain; copper from Asia Minor and Cyprus; iron from Asia Minor, inasmuch as the demand for copper and iron ores may have exceeded the production of the mining centers of the Arabah, which at any rate were not exploited intensively prior to the reign of Solomon (Ezek. 27:13); gold from S Arabia (Gen. 2:11; I Kings 9:28; 10:10-11, 14-15; II Chr. 8:18; 9:9); timber from Lebanon (I Kings 5:6, 8-9).

A certain amount of white linen was probably imported at all times from Egypt and from Syria (Exod. 9:31; Ezek. 27:7, 16), to supplement the limited supply of flax fiber which was harvested in Palestine and which was of inferior quality. Palestinian flax is mentioned in the so-called Calendar of Gezer (*see* AGRICULTURE; INSCRIPTIONS) and in Josh. 2:6; Hos. 2:5, 9. Purple-dyed wool and cloth came from Phoenicia, which had always had the *de facto* monopoly of this industry. The mantle from Shinar which Achan appropriated to himself after the conquest of Jericho (Josh. 7:21) may have been an isolated piece of curiosity, and there is as yet no evidence of a regular importation of textiles from this country, which is to be identified with Lower Mesopotamia.

Pottery from Cyprus, the Aegean isles, and continental Greece had been much in demand in Palestine during the latter part of the Late Bronze Age. The little port of Tell Abu Hawam, near Haifa, specialized in this importation. Under Solomon, and intermittently under his successors, shipments of precious woods, gems, ivory, spices, drugs, and exotic curiosities were brought from S Arabia, Ethiopia, and India by land caravans and by sea (I Kings 10:2, 10-11, 22; II Chr. 9:9-10, 21).

b. Trade routes. Prior to the advent of Hellenism, tribesmen from the Syro-Arabian desert had monopolized the organization of land caravans for the transportation of foreign goods. They are referred to in the Bible as Ishmaelites—a most general term, which may have included as well the early guilds of traders from Midian (Gen. 37:25-28), unless Ishmaelites and Midianites competed in long-distance convoys. At a lower level, local peddlers in Israelite Palestine were nicknamed Canaanites (Prov. 31:24; RSV "merchants").

Caravans from Asia Minor, once they had crossed the Taurus Mountains, followed the W border of the Syrian Desert and supplied the markets of Aleppo, Hama (Hamath), and Damascus, before they reached Palestine. Convoys from central and S Mesopotamia also had to take the devious road detouring to the N of the Syrian Desert, through Harran and Aleppo, since a direct crossing was, if not impossible, at any rate hazardous. It is possible, however, that direct connections were achieved, at least for some time, under the reign of Solomon, if there is any historical truth in the report that he fortified TADMOR (Palmyre) in the desert, according to II Chr. 8:4, and to a variant of the Hebrew of I Kings 9:18, usually read "Tamar" and translated accordingly in the versions.

The importance of the trade routes to and from the S of the Arabian Peninsula, and eventually Ethiopia and India, is well illustrated by the semi-legendary account of the visit of the Queen of Sheba to Solomon (I Kings 10:1-10; II Chr. 9:1-9). The route of gold and spices ran parallel to the Red Sea shore. From Aqabah, the caravans either continued N to Damascus via Moab and the tableland of Gilead, or NW to Jerusalem through the Negeb.

Transports by sea had always been in the hands of the Phoenicians, who succeeded in maintaining their monopoly on the traffic of tin ore, indispensable for bronze industry, even in the face of Aegean and, later, Greek competition. Phoenician sailors had been instrumental in making possible the lively exchange of ideas, arts, and crafts, which took place between the Asian mainland, Cyprus, the Aegean isles, and Greece during the latter half of the second millennium. Their so-called "ships of Tarshish" (*see* TARSHISH 3) continued to ploy the Mediterranean and East Atlantic sea lanes as late as Roman times. Their coastal vessels carried timber from Lebanon to Palestinian and Egyptian seaports, as may be gathered from such documents as the Egyptian tale of Wen-Amon, which dates from the Ramesside period, and from the biblical accounts of rafts of cedar and cypress wood shipped from Tyre for the construction of Solomon's temple.

The list of the ports of call of the Phoenician mariners along the Palestinian coast line can be drawn from ancient geographical documents, Greek authors, and archaeological information. From N to S, these ports and landings were: Minet el-Baida (the port of Ugarit), Byblos, Beirut, Sidon, Tyre, Acco, Tell Abu Hawam near Haifa, 'Atlit, Dor (which is mentioned in the texts of el-Amarna, and may have been controlled by Solomon; see I Kings 4:11), Caesarea, Jaffa, and the ports serving the inland towns of Ashdod, Ashkelon, Gaza, Raphia, and el-'Arish at the Egyptian border. Under the Hebrews all the coast line S to Jaffa was under the domination of the Philistines, with whom the Phoenicians had presumably a treaty of commerce. The same ports continued to be prosperous in Hellenistic and Roman times, and in many instances the shore accommodations, wharves, warehouses, etc., were substantially improved. Phoenician merchantmen may have sailed on the Red Sea and the Indian Ocean perhaps as early as the second millennium, as some texts of Ugarit would suggest; yet no sites of the Bronze Age have been discovered thus far on the shores of the Gulf of Aqabah. At any rate, there is ample evidence, textual and archaeological, of a brisk commercial traffic on the Red Sea during the first millennium B.C., at least intermittently. The

fluctuations of the maritime trade in these parts were due to the insecurity of the land link between the landings of the Gulf of Aqabah and the commercial cities of Palestine and Syria. See SHIPS AND SAILING (OT).

c. Royal enterprises. Rulers and kings have always played an important part in the foreign trade. The documents of TELL EL-AMARNA show them in active communication with one another concerning the delivery of raw materials and industrial metals or artifacts. The tale of Wen-Amon pictures the king of Gebal (Byblos) refusing to deliver price timber from his mountains to an Egyptian envoy who had had the misfortune of being robbed by pirates, and had become unable to pay cash. On the contrary, the king of Tyre agreed to sell cedar wood for the construction of the temple of Solomon against payments in kind, consisting in territory and foodstuffs (I Kings 5:11; 9:11). Solomon is reported to have engaged in the importation of horses and chariots (I Kings 10: 28-29). The MT is certainly corrupt, and its rendering in the RSV "from Egypt and Kue" ought probably to be emended and read "from MUSRI and KUE" (or Qoa, cuneiform *Qu'e*), which are two well-known districts of Cilicia, from which the Hittites and the Syrians also purchased horses and war chariots. Such importations, however, were not of an outright commercial character, as the text seems to suggest, but rather were means of securing suitable teams for the chariot forces of the king.

It may be inferred from a reference to store cities in the kingdom of Hamath (II Chr. 8:4), that Solomon also took part in strictly commercial activities. This became standard practice for the kings of Israel, who obtained from the Syrian kings a franchise for the establishment of commercial quarters (חוצות, bazaars) in Damascus, similar to the concessions which Syrian traders had in Samaria (I Kings 20:34). A valid analogy in modern times is that of the concession by the Ottoman government of bazaars to European traders in the ports and commercial centers of the Levant. The Bible refers to the commercial agents of the king as the סחרי המלך ("traders"), who were carrying on his business in foreign lands (I Kings 10:29).

Solomon and the kings of Judah became the principal partners of the Phoenicians in the commercial enterprises of the Red Sea and the countries beyond. These, indeed, were possible only if the wastelands between the Gulf of Aqabah and the S of Judah, as well as the routes of Edom, were adequately policed, so as to guarantee the safety of the caravans to and from the base of ELATH. Elath is identified with Tell el-Kheleifeh on the NW shore of the Gulf of Aqabah. The exploration of this site shows that it was occupied first during the Early Iron Age; Aramaic ostraca found in the ruins range from the sixth to the fourth century B.C. The toponym EZION-GEBER may well be an alias of Elath, although certain texts seem to refer to two different places. The creation of the base and the details of the joint enterprise of Hiram and Solomon are recorded in I Kings 9:26-28; 10:11-12, 22; II Chr. 8:17-18; 9:10-11, 21. Later, Jehoshaphat declined, at least for a time, the participation of Ahaziah of Israel in the Red Sea expeditions to Ophir; some of his own ships were wrecked at

Ezion-geber (I Kings 22:48-49; II Chr. 20:36-37). Uzziah restored Elath, which seems to have been abandoned in the meantime (II Kings 14:22; II Chr. 26:2). It finally fell into the hands of the Edomites during the reign of Ahaz (II Kings 16:6).

d. Means of transaction. The development of international trade in Canaanite and Israelite Palestine implies a considerable traffic of gold and silver, as is also evidenced by the repeated references to the abundance of precious metal under the reign of Solomon. The handling of gold and silver as the regular means of exchange was in the hands of a fast developing class of merchants and professional changers who weighed the ingots and tested their purity. Some system of banking and of credit may have been devised by the king's commercial agents before the Exile, in order to avoid the risky transfer of large amounts of metal; however, documentary evidence to this point is still lacking or inconclusive. Elaborate banking methods, letters of credit, and the like were in regular use in Mesopotamia. Many of the Jewish exiles took to these methods and turned in increasing numbers to the commercial professions and to international trade for their living, as one may infer from the names found in the documents of large commercial firms of Nippur and Babylon. It seems, however, that commerce and international trade in postexilic Palestine were still largely in the hands of foreigners—Phoenicians, Arabs, and Idumeans—as if the successful Jewish businessmen had voluntarily remained abroad.

Regular money appeared in Palestine under the Persian domination. Gold darics (אדרכנים) are mentioned by anachronism in I Chr. 29:7, while Ezra 2:69; Neh. 7:70-72 seem to have confused the Persian darics with Greek drachmas (דרכמונים), which do not fit in the historical context. The silver shekels and minas mentioned in these passages and in Neh. 5:15; 10:32 may be Persian silver coined in connection with the gold daric. The Persian province of Judea had even received and exercised the privilege of having its own silver coinage. Money, however, was still something of a rarity in Palestine, and it became abundant only under the Hellenistic rulers. *See* Money.

4. Import-export in Hellenistic and Roman Palestine. The conquest of Western Asia by Alexander and the subsequent Hellenization of Syria and Palestine brought about important demographic and economic changes. To be sure, the regional production, based as it was on agriculture, and thus depending on geographical and climatic conditions, remained more or less what it had always been, with perhaps three exceptions: an intensified cultivation of flax in the Valley of the Jordan and the region around Beth-shan, a notable increase in the production of chickens and eggs, and the essentially local development of fisheries on the Lake of Tiberias. These changes did not alter much the character of the regional market, and it is in the participation of Palestine in international trade—viz., export, import, and transit—that modifications are most significant.

a. Wares of importation and exportation. The exportation of Palestinian olive oil must have been affected, to a degree which cannot be evaluated easily, by the institution of a state monopoly in Ptolemaic Egypt. The oil shipped from Palestine was stored in the government warehouses of Pelusium in the Delta.

For the first time in its commercial history, Palestine began to export high-grade linen, as a result of the increased and improved production of flax fiber, so that linen from Beth-shan–Scythopolis was at a premium on the international market.

Meanwhile, new textiles were imported in increasing quantity. Cotton (כרפס), imported from India, was considered a luxury article (Esth. 1:6); rabbinical texts call it "shrubbery wool." Silk was brought from China in increasing quantities, and was not produced in Palestine until after the Arabic conquest, when mulberry trees were planted to provide food for the silkworms.

New fashions in the feeding habits of the population were the cause of a massive importation of Greek wines, which were shipped in large earthenware containers manufactured by Rhodian potters, whose marks were stamped on the handles or shoulder of the containers (Fig. POT 63, no. 8*d*). Salted fish from the Mediterranean, as well as sharp condiments and spices imported from Greece, were particularly appreciated by winebibbers. The Hellenized Sidonians established at Marissa in Idumea were among the traders specializing in this type of imports. They seem also to have dealt, at least occasionally, in exotic curiosities from Arabia, as may be inferred from the papyri of Gerza. Some of these are lists of animals, wild and domestic, shipped to Egypt for the stables of the Ptolemaic kings, and for the menageries which they maintained in the gardens of their palaces: Arabian horses, white camels, greyhounds, panthers, onagers, and hybrids of onagers and asses.

The trade of slaves, male and female, became a significant feature of Palestine economy in the Hellenistic and Roman periods. The principal factor which contributed to this development was the substitution of a pagan, secularized culture, for the civilization of the Canaanites and of the Hebrews, in which slaves, who for the major part were refugees and members of the community fallen into despondency, did not constitute really a caste. In the culture of Greece and Rome, however, slavery was a firmly established institution, and accordingly slaves were marketed, sometimes in the most literal sense, like merchandise or livestock.

Ptolemaic papyri contain much concrete evidence with regard to shipments of slaves, particularly young boys, from the Transjordanian districts to Egypt, via Idumea, where the Sidonians of Marissa took an active part in this kind of commerce. Among the women that were sold as slaves, some seem to have specialized in entertainment, not unlike the Japanese geishas. A tomb in the Hellenistic necropolis of Marissa had been reserved for such persons, whose names suggest that a strong proportion of them were of foreign origin, the Semitic names being in a minority.

Palestinian slave trade was particularly active under the Seleucid domination. Dealers followed advancing armies and bought at low price war prisoners, as well as the women and children whom soldiers captured as booty (I Macc. 3:41). According to II Macc. 8:10-11, Nicanor, the commander of the expeditionary corps of Antiochus IV Epiphanes in Palestine, advertised a huge sale of Jewish prisoners, to be held in the thoroughly Hellenized cities of the Mediterranean seaboard, at the rate of ninety "bodies" (σώματα) for one talent. *See* SLAVERY.

b. *Trading centers and trade routes.* Archaeology and historical research have made available some concrete information on the material equipment of trading centers and the organization of commercial routes during the Hellenistic and Roman periods.

The excavation of Tell Sandahannah, the acropolis of Marissa in Idumea, has brought to light the foundations of large buildings most similar in plan to modern khans or caravansaries, consisting of storerooms distributed along the four sides of a square courtyard, the gate of which could be closed at night. The pack animals were herded into the courtyard and unloaded, the goods stored in the cubicles of the ground floor, whereas the personnel took their quarters in the rooms on the second-floor gallery.

The network of overland trade routes passed under the control, amounting to a monopoly, of the NABATEANS and of the Palmyrenians, originally guilds of caravan leaders established along the borders of the Syro-Arabian Desert, who organized themselves as autonomous states, distinct from the nomadic tribes of the Arabian Peninsula. They had their own idioms, derived from Aramaic, and their government and religion. From the second century B.C. to the beginning of the second century of the Christian era, the Nabateans controlled the N-S trunk road from Hamath and Damascus to the SW corner of Arabia. Petra, conquered over the Edomites, was their capital and main center, from which the merchandise brought from Arabia, or from India and Ethiopia, was directed northward toward Damascus through the Hellenized district of the Decapolis, or westward to Palestine and Egypt. The Nabateans competed fiercely and successfully with the maritime routes developed by the Ptolemies, by pillaging vessels forced by the weather to the Arabian coast, and controlling the port of Leukè Komè, from which their privateers set out to intercept the merchantmen sailing on the Red Sea. The establishment of a system of customs by the Emperor Trajan broke the monopoly of the Nabateans and freed the sea lanes again.

In the N part of the Syrian Desert, the oasis of TADMOR became the capital of the Palmyrenian state, which flourished during the second and third centuries of the Christian era, at first under the protectorate, and later under the direct rule, of the Romans. Palmyre controlled the N Syrian traffic and the caravans to and from Central Asia. It became the chief emporium for Chinese silk. Palmyrenian caravan leaders cut straight across the wilderness, instead of detouring to the N by the antique road of the patriarchs, via Harran and Aleppo.

Sea transports continued in the Mediterranean in the hands of the Phoenicians and of the Greeks, whatever were the vicissitudes of their political allegiance. The harbor facilities of such cities as Tyre, 'Atlit, Dor, Caesarea, and Ashkelon were

greatly increased, as evidenced by historical accounts or archaeological exploration. In Egypt, the Ptolemies and their successors strove to develop relations by sea with the countries bordering the Red Sea and the Indian Ocean, but were hampered for a long time by the fierce opposition of the Nabateans (*see above*). The decline of the latter by reason of economic and political measures taken by Trajan resulted in an unprecedented activity in the maritime traffic, the cargoes being unloaded at the Egyptian ports of the Red Sea, and at the renovated base of Aila, formerly Elath, on the N shore of the Gulf of Aqabah.

c. *Money and banking.* The intensification of international trade relations during the Greco-Roman period was accompanied by the appearance of local currencies throughout the Mediterranean world and the Near and Middle East, and the generalization of banking procedures.

In addition to the Persian money which was still found on the market, Macedonian, Ptolemaic, Seleucid, and Roman coins were legal tender, as well as the bronze coins issued by the Maccabean and Herodian princes, the money of the franchised towns of the coast, and the coinage of the Jews during the first and second insurrections. The fact that the relative value of these various currencies was subject to continuous fluctuations according to denominations, the varying proportion of precious metal in the alloy, and the actual credit value on the market, made the profession of MONEY-CHANGER all-important. The gospels make a special reference to the changers established in the courtyards of the temple of Jerusalem, whose office it was to exchange the foreign coins of the pilgrims against the half shekels of the head tax, weighed according to the "shekel of the sanctuary" (Matt. 21:12; Mark 11:15; John 2:14; cf. Exod. 30:13). The money-changer was called in Greek κολλυβιστής, from κόλλυβος, which was the name of a small coin changers used to charge as their fee for the exchange of a given sum of money. Another term for "money-changer" was κερματιστής, from κέρμα, "small change." The Greek term for "banker" was τραπεζείτης, from τράπεζα, "table, counter," and, by extension, the banking house itself (Matt. 25:27; Luke 19:23). *See* MONEY.

The expatriation of Palestinian Jews by reason of deportations or of political and religious persecutions had as its consequence the fact that the exiles, unable as they were to continue in the rural occupations which had been their fathers' on the soil of Canaan, increasingly turned to international commerce and banking. This movement, which had begun in the time of the Babylonian exile, became generalized and gave the Jewish colonies of the Diaspora, in Egypt, Asia Minor, Greece, and Italy, the character which they retained for centuries. This factor was influential in the development of the Christian church, inasmuch as some of its earliest congregations outside Palestine grew out of Jewish communities.

Bibliography. Generalities in G. A. Barrois, *Manuel d'Archéologie Biblique*, II (1953), 207-73.

On real-estate transactions and the organization of commerce in Palestine and Western Asia prior to Hellenism, see: D. Cross, *Movable Property in the Nuzi Documents* (1937). I. Mendelsohn, "Guilds in Ancient Palestine," *BASOR*, no.

80 (1940), pp. 17-21. M. R. Lehmann, "Abraham's Purchase of Machpelah and Hittite Law," *BASOR*, no. 129 (1953), pp. 15-18.

The shore establishments of the Hebrew kingdoms in the vicinity of Aqabah are described and identified in N. Glueck, "The First Campaign at Tell el-Kheleifeh (Ezion geber)," *BASOR*, no. 71 (1938), pp. 3-18; "The Topography and History of Ezion geber and Elath," *BASOR*, no. 72 (1938), pp. 2-13; *Explorations in Eastern Palestine*, III (1939), 3-7; "The Second Campaign at Tell el-Kheleifeh," *BASOR*, no. 75 (1939), pp. 8-22; *The Other Side of the Jordan* (1940), pp. 89-113; "The Third Season of Excavations at Tell el-Kheleifeh," *BASOR*, no. 79 (1940), pp. 2-18; "Ostraca from Elath," *BASOR*, no. 80 (1940), pp. 3-10; no. 82 (1941), pp. 3-16; cf. *BASOR*, no. 84 (1941), pp. 4-5; no. 85 (1942), pp. 8-9.

On the maritime enterprises of the Phoenicians and the Greeks in the Mediterranean and the Red Sea: G. Contenau, *La Civilisation Phénicienne* (1928), pp. 287-308. A. Kammerer, *La Mer Rouge, l'Abyssinie et l'Arabie depuis l'Antiquité* (1929-35). F.-M. Abel, "L'Ile de Jotabé," *RB*, XLVII (1938), 510-38. A. Poidebard, *Un Grand Port Disparu, Tyr* (1939).

On commerce and slave trade in Idumea under the Ptolemies, see the sections relative to Marissa (Tell Sanda-hannah), in F. J. Bliss, *Excavations in Palestine* (1902). J. P. Peters and H. Thiersch, *Painted Tombs in the Necropolis of Marissa* (1905). L. H. Vincent, "La Palestine dans les Papyrus Ptolémaïques de Gerza," *RB*, XXIX (1920), 161-202. F.-M. Abel, "Marisa dans le Papyrus 76 de Zénon et la traite des esclaves en Idumée," *RB*, XXXIII (1924), 566-74; "Tombeaux récemment découverts à Marissa," *RB*, XXXIV (1925), 267-75. C. Edgar, *Zenon Papyri* (1925-1931).

On the overland trade by caravans, see: A. Kammerer, *Petra et la Nabatène* (1929). M. I. Rostovtzeff, *Caravan Cities* (1932). N. Glueck, "Nabataean Syria," *BASOR*, no. 85 (1942), pp. 3-8. J. Starcky, "The Nabataeans: A Historical Sketch," *BA*, XVIII (1955), 84-106. G. A. BARROIS

TRADER [*chiefly* סחר, *active participle of* סחר, go around travel]; KJV MERCHANT. One whose business is TRADE AND COMMERCE; in the OT, usually a traveling MERCHANT or peddler. He might travel far (Gen. 37:28), overseas (Isa. 23:2), form partnerships (Job 41:6), or even work in the temple (Zech. 14:21). Canaanites were the ancient traders and gave their name to the occupation (*see* CANAAN § 1). Rich and important traders were known (Isa. 47:15; Ezek. 17:4). Although not all were honest (Hos. 12:7), their extinction would be a time of catastrophe (Zeph. 1:11). C. U. WOLF

TRADES. *See* OCCUPATIONS.

***TRADITION, ORAL.** Tradition is the foundation of culture, a spiritual bond between the present and the past, between the individual and the greater fellowship in space and time, of which he is an integrated member. What man knows, his experiences and insights, what he has felt and thought and expressed in words, has, as far as it has been deemed important for the life and welfare of the community, been handed down by the tradition of mouth and example. This means also in rather fixed forms, but nevertheless always gradually and unconsciously adapted to the changing circumstances and interests of the changing ages. Man's memory of the past and his religious ideas and usages make no exception.

1. OT tradition
2. Local origin
3. Fixity and development
4. Genuine and secondary tradition
5. Tradition and texts
6. The transition from tradition to script
7. Traditio-historical and literary criticism
Bibliography

1. OT tradition. The OT includes many "memories" older than script, and many stories stamped by the storytellers' oral style. In fact, behind every type of LITERATURE represented there, lies a longer or shorter time of oral tradition. This is (since Gunkel) one certain result of the use of FORM CRITICISM and its methods: the definite type (*Gattung*) has sprung from a definite need in a definite "situation in life" (*Sitz im Leben*), and its forms have been created out of this necessity.

Many of the characteristics of the style forms point clearly back to the oral origin of the species. Both the priestly "decision" and the prophetic "oracle" are a "word" (דבר); the artistic mastership of the old tales of Genesis, Judges, Samuel, is just due to the fact that they were given their form by the storytellers, not by the rhetoric "literates" of that time, the scribes.

This applies to MYTH; LEGEND; historical narratives; and all sorts of popular stories; to customs, morals, and law; to geographical and cosmological knowledge; to individual and tribal GENEALOGY; to popular and sacral POETRY; and to cultic rituals and prayers and PSALMS.

The bearers of the tradition were those persons or circles who were especially concerned with the area of life and interests in question—the elders of the clan, or tribe, or city (*see* ELDER); the JUDGE of the tribal amphictyony; the priests with their "instructions," ordeals, and oracles, their rituals and cultic words (*see* PRIESTS AND LEVITES); the prophets (*see* PROPHET); the wise scribes of court and temple (*see* SCRIBE); and last but not least, the professional "storytellers," known in the Orient unto this day, and the "bards" or "rhapsodes" (מושלים).

Accordingly the "places in life" were the many different occasions where people met—the cultic feasts, where the legends about the foundation of the sanctuary and the traditions from the foundation of the people (Exodus, covenant, etc.) were retold; "in the gates," where judicial affairs were settled according to old custom and law, and where stories from old times, the deeds of the tribal heroes, were told in the council (סוד) of the community. But also there were private feasts such as nuptials, and vintage, and sheep-shearing, where love songs and other songs were sung, riddles put forth, etc.

2. Local origin. Every tradition that has come to us has passed through Jerusalemite mouths and pens; very much of it is, however, older than the Davidic "Great Israel." As "Israel" before that time was the N Israelite ten-tribe amphictyony, it makes no wonder that practically all pre-Davidic historical and quasi-historical tradition is of N Israelite origin. (This fact, thus, does not prove a N Israelite origin of the supposed book "E"—if it ever existed.) In the Davidic kingdom some Judean traditions, such as in Gen. 38; Judg. 1:9-17; and the interesting Hebron tradition in Num. 13:22*b*, were included. The Saul tradition and the Saul-David tradition lived at the courts of Saul and David respectively. The patriarch tales (*see* PATRIARCHS) lived partly in the N, partly in the S, among the pre-Israelite, originally Mesopotamian, Hebrew tribes, with which the Israelites fused. This does not preclude that the connection of Abraham or Jacob with this or that famous cult place may have taken place in Israelite times. Myths and legends about the primeval times, Creation, the Sea Monster, the Flood, etc., may partly have come in with the patriarchal tribes, and may partly have been taken over from the Canaanites, in both cases often with Mesopotamia-Babylonia as the ultimate source. The oldest law traditions probably were collected at the central sanctuary of the tribal amphictyony Shiloh or Shechem; in the later evolution Jerusalem no doubt played the greatest role. The same is certainly the case with the "wisdom" tradition (*see* LITERATURE § 2), and with most of the sacral poetry, while the priestly rituals and "rights" represent a fusion of old Israelite and pre-Davidic Jerusalemite tradition and later development. Jerusalem is also the place where the prophetic tradition and sayings, even from the N, were transmitted and collected, and got their present shape. Even the love poetry in the SONG OF SOLOMON, which is at least partly of Israelite origin, got its last "redaction" in Jerusalem.

3. Fixity and development. There are areas, such as cultic rituals and words, the wording of a traditional "law," etc., where conscious stress is laid upon accuracy, both of content and of form; the tradition must consciously be learned by heart. Within a definite circle and milieu the fairy tales, e.g., keep their relatively fixed form for centuries. But the same story often exists in many rather different variants in the different regions and circles. Fixity is often the last stage of a development.

First there is the selection. A tradition lives as long as any practical, sociological, or ideological interest is connected with it; without this interest it will die. A narrative must also appeal to the fancy and the emotions of the audience; it must have a thrill. Thus the immanent poetic and aesthetic forces, the "epic rules" of the human mind, always are at work, even in the mouth of the first narrator. The heroes and the events told become points of crystallization for all sorts of current anecdotes and motifs and interesting stories. In addition there is the unconscious modernization according to the changes of the material culture and of the religious and moral ideas.

Already in the oral stage the collecting of the originally separate and independent stories, law paragraphs, etc., begins. This also means that, to some degree, they must be adapted to one another, the variants must be combined, connecting links must be inserted, etc. Local "schools" of storytellers and "traditionists" thus may have created different forms of composition as well—a fact with which we have to reckon when we are dealing with the different forms represented by the MT and the LXX in Jeremiah and Proverbs.

Investigations of old Norwegian family traditions from isolated districts, the legendary content of which could be controlled by official documents, long forgotten by the "traditionists," have shown that after *ca*. three hundred years, tradition still could tell the historian something about the "what" of the events,

but very little or nothing about their "how" and "why."

Tradition thus is not only the process of transmission, but also that of development and creation as well. Before using a tradition as a historical source, one must discuss the literary type (*Gattung; see* LEGEND; LITERATURE) to which it belongs. The question to put to the Ai history (Josh. 8) is not: What is its historical content? but: To which literary type does it belong? With the correct answer: An etiological *sagn* (*see* LEGEND § 2*d*), the answer to the other question is given: The factual "kernel" is the Tell! This is the answer that has been corroborated by archaeology.

4. Genuine and secondary tradition. A genuine tradition has its point of departure in something "real"—an event, a locality, a sociological and political relation, etc. Through a traditio-historical investigation and literary documentation it can with greater or lesser certainty or probability be traced back to its origin. But a tradition can also have its origin in some "learned" theory or combination or speculation of later times, and "tradition says" may often not mean more than that. Every visitor to Palestine knows from the stories of the guides this sort of tradition.

5. Tradition and texts. Even long after the more occasional use of script (*see* LITERATURE § 1) the oral transmission of "spiritual" knowledge was considered normal. In the East learning by heart is unto this day the normal way of transmitting even the longest written texts, as the Koran and its commentaries. With the Jews both Mishna and TALMUD were orally transmitted for centuries; in the synagogue it was long forbidden to say the Torah from a written scroll; also the Aramaic and Greek translations (*see* TARGUM) were originally given orally, but in a traditional fixed form.

The whole "authorship" of ISAIAH was restricted to some six words (8:1-2; 30:7); the transmission of his sayings he, as he metaphorically says, "bound together and sealed in my disciples"—i.e., committed to their memory. The prophets' use of the script was only occasional, for special reasons and circumstances, as the letter of JEREMIAH to the exiles (ch. 29) and the writing down of his oracles (ch. 36). The "writing" in Hab. 2:2 refers only to the oracle in vss. 4-5. The common memory of the circle and the "chain of traditionists" were for long considered to be securer than the script. (It must be remembered that here we have to do with generations whose memory was not spoiled by magazines and dictionaries.)

The first writings thus do not put an end to the development of the tradition. After Baruch had written and rewritten the book of Jeremiah's *ipsissima verba* in their original poetic and metrical form, the same sayings continued to live in oral form, and under the influence of Deuteronomistic theology and phraseology they were reshaped as longer Deuteronomized "sermons," which now are found side by side with the original short sayings. Also the words of other prophets continued to live as spiritual forces in the Isaian circles, sometimes being adapted to new circumstances, inspiring additional and new prophecies. In this way the Judean additions to the collections of AMOS and HOSEA, the "anti-Assyrian" oracles in Isaiah, or the transformation of the "Woe" against ARIEL 1 (Isa. 29:1 ff) into an oracle of salvation may be explained.

The many variants now included in the saga of J that have given rise to the hypothesis about a contingent parallel "source" E are better explained as the result of the development of the existing oral tradition beside the written J. The selection of the matter and the pragmatism of J "made school"; the still orally transmitted material, however, continued its life and underwent the inevitable development, being adapted to the religious ideas and spiritual interests of later times. Of this younger form parts were incorporated in the J—perhaps partly already during the oral transmission of the "genuine" line. There can scarcely be any doubt that, e.g., the Sinai story (Exod. 19–24; 32–34) or the Balaam story (Num. 22–24) is braided together of two variants respectively, which already had acquired their fixed form, which the "redactor" wanted to respect as far as possible.

In the same way the separate material in CHRONICLES must be explained. Traditions which the Chronicler's main written source, Samuel-Kings, had not taken up, continued their oral life and more and more developed into legends. These, however, in many cases may include a historical kernel, and in some cases have certainly preserved definite historical knowledge—e.g., the tunnel of Hezekiah, or the captivity of Manasseh. Written pre-exilic records, older than Samuel-Kings, scarcely existed any more at the time of Chronicles.

We are thus confronted with an interaction of oral and written transmission.

6. The transition from tradition to script. The fundamental, conscious transition from oral transmission to script is done when critical outer and/or inner circumstances threaten to break off the living tradition. This happened with Israel at the fall of state, city, and temple and the deportation of the leading classes in 587 B.C. Both archaeology (Ingolt) and modern experiences from the deportations during the two world wars show that at such a catastrophe it is practically impossible for the exiles to save such luxuries as books, let alone tables; what existed of such things in the archives of Jerusalem was destroyed, and many of the bearers of tradition killed. The remnant of Israel was obliged to have the old sacral tradition written down in order to keep the connection with its spiritual foundations.

But even learning by heart continued to be the normal form of transmission, and the development of tradition could still take place (see § 5 above).

The idea of the primacy of the written text and of its unchangeability is the result of canonization. See CANON OF THE OT; TEXT, OT.

7. Traditio-historical and literary criticism. The interaction between oral tradition and written texts (see § 5 above) demonstrates that both traditio-historical and literary methods are necessary in OT science, and they must be in constant interaction. Clear instances are the Sinai story, the Saul-Samuel complex, and the flood story.

See FORM CRITICISM.

Bibliography. A. Olrik, "Epische Gesetze der Volksdichtung," *Zeitschrift für deutsches Altertum,* 51 (1909), 1 ff; *Nogle grundsaetninger for sagnforskning* (ed. H. Ellekilde; 1921).

K. Liestøl, *Norske aettesogor* (1922). H. Krohn, *Die folkloristische Arbeitsmethode* (1926). K. Liestøl, *The Origin of the Icelandic Family Sagas* (1930). H. S. Nyberg, *Studien zum Hoseabuche* (1935). H. Birkeland, *Zum hebräischen Traditionswesen* (1938). S. Mowinckel, "Oppkomsten av profetlitteraturen," *Norsk Teologisk Tidsskrift,* 43 (1942), 65 ff. I. Engnell, *Gamla testamentet,* vol. I (1945). S. Mowinckel, *Prophecy and Tradition* (1946). G. Widengren, *Literary and Psychological Aspects of Hebrew Prophets* (1948). J. Laessö, "Literary and Oral Tradition in Ancient Mesopotamia," *Studia Orientalia Joanni Pedersen . . . Dicata* (1953), pp. 205 ff. E. Nielsen, *Oral Tradition* (1954).

S. MOWINCKEL

TRADITION OF THE ELDERS [παράδοσις τῶν πρεσβυτέρων]. Jewish oral law intended to expound the written law by applying it to new circumstances or finding in it support for long-accepted custom (*see* HALACHAH; LAW IN FIRST CENTURY JUDAISM; TRADITION, ORAL). Developed by an elaborate commentary on OT texts (*see* MIDRASH), either legal or homiletical (*see* HAGGADAH, NT), it was also arranged topically, somewhat apart from its scriptural base, for teaching and discussion (*see especially* MISHNA; *also* GEMARA; TALMUD).

"Tradition of the elders" occurs only in Matt. 15:2; Mark 7:3, 5 (cf. Acts 6:14; Gal. 1:14). The rejection of unwritten tradition by Jesus here recorded is not fully supported elsewhere. He often ignored (Mark 2:13-17) rabbinic custom (*see* TAX COLLECTOR; SINNER), and so freely interpreted the written law that he often transgressed rabbinic principles (*see* SABBATH; DIVORCE; CLEAN AND UNCLEAN). But he also respected Jewish tradition (Mark 1:44), and his teaching (*see* SERMON ON THE MOUNT) was certainly influenced by it (Mark 12:28-34). Scholars are divided on the question of Jesus' treatment of the "tradition of the elders." Rabbinic tradition was in flux (*see* CORBAN), Jesus' attitude was complex, and the evangelists' later reporting of both was often unduly biased (Mark 7:3, 19*b*).

Bibliography. H. L. Strack and P. Billerbeck, *Kommentar zum NT aus Talmud und Midrasch,* I (1922), 691-720; G. F. Moore, *Judaism,* vol. I (1927); B. H. Branscomb, *Jesus and the Law of Moses* (1930); H. Danby, trans., *The Mishnah* (1933); W. G. Kümmel, "Jesus und der jüdische Traditionsgedanke," *ZNW,* 33 (1934), 105-30; D. Daube, *The NT and Rabbinic Judaism* (1956), pp. 55-300; M. Smith, "The Jewish Elements in the Gospels," *JBR,* XXIV (1956), 90-96.

I. W. BATDORF

TRADITIONS OF MATTHIAS. *See* MATTHIAS, TRADITIONS OF.

TRAIN. The translation of שׁוּל, meaning a trailing extension of a robe or skirt, in Isa. 6:1 (elsewhere "skirt"; KJV alternately "hem"). In Isaiah's vision the train of the enthroned Lord filled the temple.

TRANCE [ἔκστασις] (Acts 10:10; 11:5; 22:17). Alternately: AMAZEMENT (Mark 5:42; Luke 5:26; Acts 3:10); ASTONISHMENT (Mark 16:8). The state of mind of one who is receiving revelation.

The Greek term was used with a variety of meanings—e.g., literally, a change of place, or to put or be put outside; then, to mean the state in which one is "beside oneself," to indicate an intense but temporary emotional reaction to the presence of anxiety, terror, or the uncanny, the numinous; or, if the state was permanent, to signify insanity. In a more mystical sense, the term could stand for a prophetic rapture or trance, in which the body and its functions become quiescent and the soul withdraws or is released from the bonds which fetter it to earth and is ushered into the direct presence of the divine and made to hear the "words of God," and see the "vision of the Almighty" (Num. 24:4, 16).

In his use of ἔκστασις in Acts, both with Peter (10:10; 11:5) and with Paul (22:17), Luke is concerned with the trance only as a state which was commonly recognized as being a vehicle of revelation. By the form and sobriety of his language, he makes it clear that the trances into which Peter and Paul "fell" *happened* to them; they were not induced by orgiastic frenzy. Both Peter and Paul are described as at prayer, Peter on the housetop, alone, and Paul in the temple—i.e., they were in readiness for revelation.

In summary, Luke employs the trance pattern to show (*a*) that the free admission of the Gentiles to the Christian fellowship was an act of God, not of man: as a revelation event, it was commanded; and (*b*) that neither Peter nor Paul could have arrived at the decision to bring about such a radical shift in his own behavior or have dared to proclaim it in the church on the basis of his own experience or will. The Gentile mission is thus declared to be the work of God.

Bibliography. M. Joseph, *Universal Jewish Encyclopedia*, III (1941), 623. F. D. GEALY

TRANSCENDENCE. *See* GOD, OT VIEW OF.

TRANSFIGURATION. The transforming event in the life of Jesus, when his appearance became glorious in the presence of three disciples on a mountaintop (Matt. 17:1-9; Mark 9:2-10; Luke 9:28-36; II Pet. 1:16-21).

1. The event
2. The time
3. The place
4. The significance
Bibliography

1. The event. Three wonders occurred in this mysterious event: (*a*) Jesus was transfigured or changed by an unusual radiance or GLORY of face and garments; (*b*) Elijah and Moses, long dead, appeared; (*c*) a divine voice spoke from a cloud.

The gospels agree that Jesus took Peter, James, and John to a mountain; that Peter said it was good to be there and that they should make three booths (KJV "tabernacles") for Jesus, Moses, and Elijah; that the disciples were beset by fear; that the voice from the overshadowing cloud assured them about Jesus: "This is my (beloved) Son," and that they should hear him; that they were to say nothing of what they had seen until the resurrection of the Son of man (Matthew and Mark); and that they told no man about their experience (Luke).

Matthew omits Mark's statements about the fuller and about Peter's ignorance, but he adds details: Jesus' face "shone like the sun"; the "bright" cloud; the words "with whom I am well pleased"; the disciples fell on their knees; Jesus touched them and bade them rise with no fear. Luke also amplifies

Mark: Jesus was praying, and his countenance was altered; the conversation of Moses and Elijah with Jesus concerned his coming death in Jerusalem; "my Chosen"; glory attended both Jesus and these men; the disciples were heavy with sleep but awoke fully and witnessed the radiance.

2. The time. The Transfiguration shortly (six days, Matthew and Mark; eight, Luke) follows the famous declaration of Peter that Jesus was the Christ, after which Jesus first forecast his sufferings, death and resurrection, the necessity of a cross for his disciples, and the coming of the kingdom (Mark and Luke) or of the Son of man (Matthew). This is the decisive period during a northward trip in Jesus' ministry immediately before he began his final journey to Jerusalem. On the minor point as to whether the Transfiguration took place during day or night, Luke infers it was night (9:32).

3. The place. The mountain is not named. Matthew and Mark state that it was "high"; II Pet. 1:18 says that it was "holy." The events preceding the Transfiguration took place near CAESAREA PHILIPPI. Following the Transfiguration, Jesus and his disciples passed through Galilee (Mark 9:30). If the mountain is to be named, it is probably one of the S foothills of lofty Mount Hermon,* which rises N of Caesarea Philippi. This location is usually accepted, though Mount Tabor (*see* TABOR, MOUNT)* has its advocates. Cyril of Jerusalem and Jerome (fourth century) claimed Tabor for the Transfiguration. Since the sixth century, churches have been erected at intervals and pilgrimages made to commemorate the event. This identification with Tabor is improbable, because the Synoptic setting for the story is near Hermon (*see* HERMON, MOUNT), because Tabor is not high, because the Gospel of Hebrews (second century) and other writings were understood to refer to Tabor as the scene of the Temptation, and because the entire top of Tabor was walled (Jos. War II.xx.6; IV.i.8). Figs. HER 15; TAB 3.

4. The significance. "The Transfiguration is the paradise and the despair of commentators." (*a*) The Fourth Gospel omits the Transfiguration because the glory of God in Jesus is not centered in one event but is manifested throughout his life, death, and resurrection (1:14; 2:11; 5:44; 7:18, 39; 11:4, 40; 12:16, 23, 28, 41; 13:31; 17:1, 4-5, 10, 22, 24; 21:19).

b) II Peter contains the earliest reference, after the Synoptics, to the Transfiguration. The writer, using the name and the authority of Peter, cites the incident as an eyewitness of Christ's majesty to prove that Christians do not believe in myths; that they believe in God's gift of honor and glory to his beloved Son, and that this made more sure the prophetic words about Christ's coming. This interpretation of the story verifies the second coming (*see* PAROUSIA) of Christ.

c) The second-century Apocalypse of Peter rehearses the transfiguration story and interprets it as descriptive of paradise and of the Second Coming.

d) The church fathers frequently allegorized the Transfiguration. In the Eastern church the story became a mystical symbol of the transformation of this world and of the world to come. The celebration of the day (August 6), by the eighth century, equalled any other holy day except Easter. In the Western church the day was not ordered for general observance until the fifteenth century.

e) Faced with the complexities of the narratives, modern commentators vary widely in their interpretations. Orthodox defenders accept the account as historical and credible. Oppositely stand those who rationally reject any objective aspects of the story and prefer a symbolical treatment which illustrates theological motifs of the early church. Others view it as a postresurrection story of an appearance of Jesus to Peter, which has been misplaced in the gospel records. But the present position of the story in the gospel narratives is preferable, because it may represent a real and decisive experience of Jesus and his disciples. Matthew's report that Jesus called the experience a "vision" (17:9) is best accepted, although the term has many meanings. The actual historical circumstances can probably never be recovered or explained for entire satisfaction. The gospel narratives, laden with later meanings, unite facts and symbols. We may, however, distinguish some probable significance for the disciples and for Jesus: It was a visionary moment that revealed to his disciples Jesus' true nature (symbolized by the light) and his future glorious state after death. Their vision of Moses and Elijah, most notable in law and prophecy in Israel, signifies that law and prophecy support Jesus and his mission. The cloud and the voice are well-known symbols which localize the presence of God, who repeats Jesus' baptismal blessing so that the disciples may hear him. Only after the coming death and resurrection could they explain what their vision meant. Luke places more emphasis on Jesus, who, facing death, found in prayer the support, "with him," of great spiritual leaders and especially of God, who chose him for the way of suffering, death, and resurrection. A divine glory illumines these transforming moments and confirms Jesus for the hard days ahead. *See* JESUS CHRIST.

Bibliography. A. S. Martin, "Transfiguration," *HDCG* (1908), II, 742-46; E. Lohmeyer, *Das Evangelium des Markus* (1922), pp. 173-81; G. B. Bernardin, "The Transfiguration," *JBL*, 52 (1933), 181-89; J. Blinzler, *Die neutestamentlichen Berichte über die Verklärung Jesu* (1937); R. Höller, *Die Verklärung Jesu* (1937); G. H. Boobyer, *St. Mark and the Transfiguration Story* (1942); H. Risenfeld, *Jésus transfiguré* (1947); A. M. Ramsey, *The Glory of God and the Transfiguration of Christ* (1949); W. E. and M. B. Rollins, *Jesus and His Ministry* (1954), pp. 184-203; G. B. Caird, "The Transfiguration," *ET*, LXVII (1956), 291-94.   D. M. BECK

TRANSGRESSION. *See* SIN.

TRANSJORDAN trănz jôr′dən. The general term for the area that lies immediately E of the Jordan Valley, the Dead Sea, and the Arabah, roughly equivalent to the kingdom of Transjordan as constituted in 1923. It comprises the biblical areas of BASHAN; GILEAD; AMMON; MOAB; EDOM; as well as the desert regions to the E. The term is not used in the RSV-KJV, but the general area is often designated "beyond the Jordan" (עֵבֶר הַיַּרְדֵּן), which may also refer to the land W of the Jordan (nine times).

1. **Description.** The Transjordan is an elevated plateau, rising in height from N to S. Bashan is a level plain, with mountains to the E; Gilead, Ammon, and Moab contain hills that rise to three thousand to four thousand feet, intersected by valleys; Edom is a tableland that is for the most part five thousand feet or more above sea level. The region is intersected by numerous rivers and wadis that run across it in the general direction of E to W: the Yarmuk, Arab, Jurm, Jabis, Rajib, Jabbok (Zerqa), Nimrim, Zerqa Ma'in, Arnon (Mojib), and Zered (el-Ḥesa), as well as numerous smaller streams. The entire region is generally well watered, especially toward the N; Bashan was famous for its wheat, oaks, and cattle, Gilead for its grapes, olives, and balm, and Moab for its sheep. The King's Highway, starting at Damascus, ran the entire length of the area N to S.

2. **History.** There were well-developed settlements in Transjordan at least as far back as the Early Bronze period, in the third millenium B.C. In that part of the region which was below the Jabbok, however, there was a period of depopulation which lasted from the twentieth to the thirteenth century, possibly because of the destructive raid of Chedorlaomer (Gen. 14). After that the lower portions were settled by the Moabites and Edomites and the N parts were in the hands of the Amorite kings Sihon and Og, who were in turn dispossessed by the Israelites (Num. 21). The Ammonites began moving in from the desert not long after the Israelite conquest, probably in the twelfth century.

During the next four centuries the possession of the parts of the Transjordan area was fiercely contested by the various nations that lived there. Under David and Solomon the entire Transjordan was under Israelite rule, but after the division of the kingdom (*ca.* 935 B.C.) the struggle began anew and was complicated in the ninth century by the invasion of the Syrians of the kingdom of Damascus. The wars continued with varying results until 732, when the entire region was either annexed or made tributary to the Assyrian Empire. When the latter fell, it was succeeded by Babylonian (604-536) and Persian (536-332) rule.

The conquest of Persia by Alexander the Great brought a new element into the population of Transjordan, for numerous Greek colonists settled in the cities of the DECAPOLIS. About the same time the NABATEANS had extended their rule into Edom and were pushing northward into Moab. During the period of the Maccabean rulers (165-37 B.C.) the N portions of the region were resettled by Jews and became part of the kingdom of Herod. In NT times this part of Transjordan, known as PEREA, was ruled by the latter's son Herod Antipas, and was part of the kingdom of Herod Agrippa I and II until the end of the Jewish state in A.D. 73.   S. COHEN

TRANSLATIONS. *See* VERSIONS, ANCIENT; VERSIONS, MEDIEVAL AND MODERN; VERSIONS, ENGLISH.

TRAPS AND SNARES [פַּח, *properly* a bird trap, πάγις; מוֹקֵשׁ, *properly* the bait for a trap, *hence* trap; מְצוֹדָה ,מָצוֹד ,יָקוּשׁ ,חֶבֶל, שְׂבָכָה (*in this sense only in* Job 18:8); θήρα; βρόχος (snare *in* I Cor. 7:35 KJV; RSV "restraint"); קוּשׁ ,נָקַשׁ ,יָקַשׁ, *verbs for* setting traps]. Contrivances for catching birds or animals; frequently used metaphorically to describe sudden and unexpected death or disaster. *See also* HUNTING.

The numerous, but scattered, biblical references to traps, most of them poetic or metaphorical, give no precise picture of the instruments used in trapping, but three types of trap may be distinguished:

a) The most common is the automatic bird trap (פח), the familiar "snare of the fowler" (Pss. 91:3; 124:7). It is used by present-day Arabs and called *faḥḥ*. An Egyptian device, which corresponds closely to the biblical data, consisted of a roughly circular wooden base on which two nets were mounted.

76. Ramses II (1290-1224 B.C.) snaring birds with the gods Horus and Khnum, from Karnak

When the trap was set, the nets were drawn down to one side and held in place by a trigger, which, when released, allowed the nets to spring up and envelop the victim. The trigger could be released by hand, or sprung when the victim touched the bait attached to it. One scholar sees in this the original distinction between מוקש and פח, although in common OT usage the two are virtual synonyms. The מוקש was the manned, and the פח the self-springing, trap. The netlike nature of these traps (Job 18:8) and the suddenness with which they spring up (Amos 3:5) are repeatedly referred to in the OT. Fig. TRA 76.

b) Some traps for animals were nets (Ps. 141:9; Ezek. 12:13) or nooses of rope (Job 18:10) concealed in the bushes or along the paths which the animals frequented (Prov. 22:5; Hos. 9:8). They either fell upon the animal from above or trapped it by the feet (Job 18:9; Ezek. 17:20; I Cor. 7:35). Presumably the net or noose might sometimes be thrown by hand like a fish net or a lasso.

c) A third type of trap was the pit, covered with a camouflaged net which gave way when the victim walked upon it (Isa. 42:22; Jer. 18:22; 48:43-44).

Metaphorically "snare" is used of peril or death which strikes suddenly from hiding (Job 22:10; Ps. 18:5—H 18:6; Luke 21:34). There are overtones of maliciousness when the trap is set by an enemy (I Sam. 28:9; Ps. 140:5—H 140:6). Because of its association with the bait of the trap, מוקש has the distinctive connotation of that which first attracts and then destroys (e.g., false gods [Exod. 23:33], or the friendship of a hothead [Prov. 22:25]).

Bibliography. G. Gerleman, *Contributions to the OT Terminology of the Chase* (1946).   L. E. TOOMBS

TRAVEL AND COMMUNICATION IN THE OT.

From early times the inhabitants of Palestine were road-conscious. The country—whether organized in small city-states as in the Tell el-Amarna pe-

riod, or in a united state as under the Hebrew monarchy—was geographically a bridge between the great empires of the Nile Valley and the fertile plains of Mesopotamia. Its position astride the vital international roads linking Africa with Asia made the country into what was aptly called an "apple of discord" among the nations. Egyptian, Assyrian, and Babylonian armies bringing death and destruction in their wake, as well as caravans carrying goods from many parts of the then-known world, traversed its borders on routes along the Mediterranean Sea coast, on paths through mountain ranges, and on highways and byways.

Although most of the caravans crossed the country in transit to distant destinations, Palestinian merchants, either on their own account or as agents of the king, engaged actively in the export of agricultural goods and in the import of raw material and luxury articles. All these activities, military and commercial, presuppose not only the existence of roads in the middle of the second millennium but also a conscious effort to maintain them in serviceable order (cf. Tell el-Amarna Letter 199:10-13, in which an unnamed local prince writes to the pharaoh that he "made ready all the ways of the king, the lord, as far as Busruna"; see also the Moabite Stone Inscription, line 26, where Mesha king of Moab says: "I built Aroer, and I made the highway in the Arnon [Valley]").

1. Roads. The disruption of roads, or the inability to use them, was a portent of great misfortune. The Song of Deborah characterizes the chaotic situation in the country in the complaint that "caravans ceased and travelers kept to the byways" (Judg. 5:6); as did Isaiah (33:8) later when he exclaimed:

> The highways lie waste,
>   the wayfaring man ceases.

Conversely, felicitous times are distinguished by well-constructed roads. Isaiah (40:3-4) expressed this fact eloquently when he proclaimed:

> A voice cries:
> "In the wilderness prepare the way of the LORD,
>   make straight in the desert a highway for our God.
> Every valley shall be lifted up,
>   and every mountain and hill be made low;
> the uneven ground shall become level,
>   and the rough places a plain."

The term "way" is often used figuratively in the Bible in the sense of "justice," "righteousness," and the "good life" (cf. Prov. 2:13; 15:19; Isa. 26:7), and Jesus referred to himself in the words: "I am the way, and the truth, and the life" (John 14:6).

The OT employs the following terms for "road":

a) דרך, "way, road, route," is the most common word, and it is used in such expressions as דרך הים, "the way of the sea" (Isa. 9:1—H 8:23); דרך המלך, "the king's highway" (Num. 20:17); אם הדרך, "crossroads" (Ezek. 21:21 KJV—H 21:26; RSV "the parting of the way").

b) מסלה, "highway" (and once מסלול, in Isa. 35:8; cf. Akkadian *sullū* and *muslalu*, "main road").

c) ארח, "path, way."

d) נתיב and נתיבה, "path" (cf. Ugaritic *ntb*), used in such expressions as נתיבות עולם, "ancient paths" (Jer. 6:16), and בית נתיבות, "crossroads" (Prov. 8:2 KJV; RSV "in the paths").

e) שְׁבִיל, "path, road" (cf. שְׁבִילֵי עוֹלָם, "ancient roads" [Jer. 18:15]).

f) מִשְׁעוֹל, "narrow path" (Num. 22:24), and מַעְגָּלָה מַעְגָּל, "track [of wagon], course" (Ps. 104:5; Prov. 2:15 [RSV "path, wayside"]; Isa. 26:7).

Road building in the classical sense began with the appearance on the scene of the Romans. The ancient routes linking one community with another, or connecting one country with another, were originally trodden paths made by the feet of men and animals. The common Hebrew word for "road" is derived from the root דָּרַךְ, "to tread." The Egyptian author of the famous Satirical Letter (*ANET* 478a) describes the roads in Palestine as being filled with boulders and pebbles and overgrown with reeds, which made the passage of chariots extremely hazardous. In the course of time some roads, particularly those forming part of the international highways, were improved by government efforts in order to facilitate traffic and the movements of troops. The necessity for road construction may have arisen with the building of the cities for chariots and horsemen by Solomon (I Kings 9:19).

The texts refer to the following methods of improving the "ancient paths": (*a*) פָּנָה, "to prepare" (Isa. 40:3; 57:14; 62:10; Mal. 3:1; lit., "to make clear, clear the ground" of obstacles); (*b*) יָשַׁר, "to make straight, smooth" (Prov. 3:6; Isa. 40:3); (*c*) סָקַל, "to remove stones" (Isa. 62:10); (*d*) פָּלַס, "to level" (Ps. 78:50; Isa. 26:7); and (*e*) סָלַל, "to build up" (Isa. 57:14; 62:10). The latter term indicates that road construction—i.e., the artificial "casting up" of a trodden path for the traffic of passengers and vehicles—was practiced in biblical times. (Cf. the expressions אֹרַח יְשָׁרִים סְלֻלָה, "The path of the upright is paved" [Prov. 15:19; RSV "is a level highway"], and דֶּרֶךְ לֹא סְלוּלָה, "an unpaved road" [Jer. 18:15; RSV "not the highway"]).

The reference in Deut. 19:3 to the preparation of roads to the cities of refuge so that a person who killed without intent might find his way to one of them, and Jeremiah's advice to the exiles (31:21) to set up waymarks and to make guideposts on the road in the desert, show familiarity with road signs in the period of the monarchy.

2. International routes. The international highways of the ancient Near East linked together the great powers of Egypt, Assyria, and Babylonia, and the important cities of Syria and Asia Minor. One main route led from the Persian Gulf N to the cities of Ur, Babylon, and Ashur; then, turning W, to Harran; and from there SW to Carchemish, Halab, and to Ugarit on the Mediterranean coast opposite Cyprus. From Carchemish a route led NW to Kanish in the Hittite country. A parallel road led from Babylon along the Euphrates River to Mari, from there to Tadmor "in the wilderness" (built by Solomon, according to II Chr. 8:4), and thence turning SW to Damascus. From Damascus two great roads branched out to the S. One ran through the territory E of the Jordan to Elath on the Gulf of Aqabah and thence to Arabia; and the other ran through the territory W of the Jordan to Megiddo, Gaza, and from there to Egypt. With the domestication of the camel (sometime during the eleventh century), a road led from Tema (a rich oasis in the heart of the Arabian Desert) to Dumah in the Syrian Desert; from there it branched off into two sections, one leading E to Babylon and the other W to Damascus.

During the period of the monarchy the kings took advantage of the country's geographical position as a link joining Babylonia and Syria with Egypt and Arabia by levying a toll on goods in transit, and also by taking an active part in international commerce. David's conquests of the lands lying to the N and the S gave him mastery of the most vital arteries of commerce. Solomon's control of Ammon, Moab, and Edom in the S, and of the territories northward to Damascus, actually meant that he monopolized the entire caravan route between Arabia and the N. From Arabia routes of commerce led northward to Damascus, westward to Gaza and Egypt, and eastward via Dumah and Tema to the Euphrates and the Persian Gulf. Hence the strengthening by Solomon of the defenses of Hazor, Megiddo, Gezer, Beth-horon, Baalath, and Tamar (I Kings 9:15, 17-18), cities lying along a route leading from Edom to Damascus, undoubtedly had, besides strategic, also commercial purposes. The commendation of Balaam (Num. 23:9) that the Hebrews were a "people dwelling alone, and not reckoning itself among the nations," giving the impression that Israel was cut off from all contact with the surrounding world, does not reflect the situation of the monarchic period.

The two central international highways which passed through Palestine were the "King's Highway" (Num. 20:17) and the "way of the sea" (Isa. 9:1—H 8:23). The King's Highway,* a N-S route, starting at the great communication center of Damascus, led to Ashtaroth in Bashan and from there, through the territories E of the Jordan, to Ramoth-gilead, Rabbath Ammon, Heshbon, Rabbath Moab, Kir-Hareseth, and then along the way of the Desert of Edom, to Elath. Many of the cities mentioned in Num. 21:21-35 which the Israelites conquered on their way from Egypt (such as Edrei, Jazer, Heshbon, Medeba, and Dibon) were situated along this road. The way of the sea, a road trodden by Egyptian, Assyrian, and Babylonian armies, led from Damascus SW to Hazor, and from there, running along W of the Sea of Galilee, turned to Mount Tabor and thence to Megiddo in the Plain of Jezreel. From Megiddo a side road led N to Mount Carmel and Acco, where it joined the road along the Phoenician coast to Tyre and Sidon. The main highway continued from Megiddo along the Plain of Sharon to Japho and thence by the "way of the land of the Philistines" (Exod. 13:17) to Ashdod, Gaza, and Raphia to Egypt. S of the Sea of Galilee a branch of the Damascus highway proceeded W of the Jordan to Beth-shean, Jericho and from there to Jerusalem; another branch, starting at Beth-shean, ran to Shechem, Bethel, Gibeah, Jerusalem, and thence along W of the Dead Sea to En-gedi and Tamar. From Jerusalem two side roads branched off, one leading N to Japho and the other S to Gaza. From Bethlehem a road led to Beer-sheba, where it joined the road of Shur (Gen. 16:7) to Egypt. The country, particularly the N part, was crisscrossed with numerous ways and by ways connecting the major cities of the land. Fig. KIN 7.

It should be noted that the great international highways passed through Israel, while Judah was removed from the main stream of communication. The relative position of the two kingdoms to the great highways may have been one of the reasons why Judah was able to maintain its independence *ca.* 120 years after the fall of Israel. *See also* ROAD; SHIPS AND SAILING.

Bibliography. G. Dalman, "Palästina als Heerstrasse im Altertum und in der Gegenwart," *PJ*, 12 (1916), 15-36; N. Glueck, *The Other Side of the Jordan* (1940), especially pp. 15-16, 84, 145; M. Avi-Yonah, *A Geographical and Historical Atlas of Israel* (Hebrew; 1956); L. H. Grollenberg, *Atlas of the Bible* (1956); E. G. Kraeling, *Rand McNally Bible Atlas* (1956); G. E. Wright and F. V. Filson, *The Westminster Historical Atlas to the Bible* (rev. ed., 1956).   I. MENDELSOHN

TRAVEL AND COMMUNICATION IN THE NT.

This article emphasizes travel in Palestine and of early Christians generally; but it also deals with the importance of travel and communication in the Roman world as a whole. For a fuller account of travel by sea, *see* SHIPS AND SAILING.

1. NT journeys
2. Occasions of travel
3. Means of travel
4. Highways
5. Other means of communication
Bibliography

1. NT journeys. The journeys that first come to our attention in the NT are those which involve the child Jesus and his parents. Luke 1:39-56 records that shortly after his mother, Mary (*see* MARY MOTHER OF JESUS), had conceived the child at NAZARETH of GALILEE, she went to Judah to visit ELIZABETH and spent three months with her. According to 2:1-7, Jesus was born in BETHLEHEM because Joseph had taken his wife, Mary, with him to register in compliance with a decree of AUGUSTUS. Vss. 22-39 relate that the parents took Jesus to Jerusalem to comply with the Jewish law of purification (*see* CLEAN AND UNCLEAN), which occurred, according to Lev. 12:2-5, when the child was forty days old. Thus between the time of the conception and the purification Mary made no fewer than three trips to Jerusalem. As the distance from Nazareth to Jerusalem is *ca.* seventy-five miles, the journey on foot each way must have required five days; this indicates something of the importance of these journeys, and the difficulty with which they were executed. According to Luke 2:41, the parents of Jesus went to Jerusalem every year for the PASSOVER. Vss. 42-51 tell of a trip they made when Jesus was twelve. It is evident that Joseph and Mary were zealous in keeping the law, especially in attending the festivals. As there were several festivals each year, we may assume that during his youth Jesus went to Jerusalem many times. We might infer also that this pattern of travel was characteristic of every devout family of Palestine, and beyond also, insofar as they were able to go up to the Holy City.

John 2:13 mentions a trip of Jesus from Galilee to Jerusalem for a Passover; 5:1 tells of his going up to another feast; 7:1-14 says that Jesus and his brothers went up to Jerusalem for the Feast of Tabernacles; 10:22, that Jesus was at the Feast of Dedication; 12:1, that he was back at Passover again

(which is mentioned also in Matt. 26:17; Mark 14: 12; Luke 22:7). Matt. 28:16-20 relates that after the Crucifixion the eleven disciples returned to Galilee, and that Jesus himself went there and appeared to them after his resurrection. But Acts 1:12 ff indicates that the disciples shortly thereafter had reassembled in Jerusalem. The trip from Galilee to Jerusalem was one of the most frequent journeys of early Christians.

The journey of the MAGI (Matt. 2:1-12) is only alluded to, with no indication of the land from which they came. No details are recorded concerning the flight into Egypt (vss. 13-23), but the casual way in which it is introduced shows that such a journey would not have been considered unusual. The distance was two hundred miles or more each way.

We do not know the exact location on the Jordan where John was baptizing (Mark 1:1-11) when Jesus made the journey there; but if it was near JERICHO, it was *ca.* seventy miles from Nazareth. The excursion which Jesus made into the region of TYRE and SIDON (7:24-30), which is *ca.* thirty miles from Galilee, as well as the similar retreat to CAESAREA PHILIPPI (8:27-30), shows freedom and ease of travel in these areas. Jesus was almost constantly on the move from one village to another. Once or twice he was in SAMARIA (Luke 17:11; John 4:4). Several times he crossed the SEA OF GALILEE in fishing boats (Mark 4:35-41; 5:1-20; *see* FISHER). His last journey to Jerusalem was down the Jordan Valley (*see* JORDAN), by Jericho, and up through the hills to the Holy City (Mark 10:1, 46; 11:1). Once or twice he visited LAZARUS and his sisters, MARTHA and MARY 2, in BETHANY, just over the crest of the Mount of Olives from Jerusalem (Matt. 21:17; 26:6; John 11:1; 12:1).

The location of Emmaus, where the walk of two disciples with the risen Christ culminated (Luke 24: 13-35), is uncertain. But JOSEPHUS (War VII.vi.6) speaks of an Emmaus sixty furlongs from Jerusalem where Titus established a colony of eight hundred soldiers after the Jewish war, which may have been on the site of the modern village of Kolonieh in a valley *ca.* four miles W of Jerusalem.

We note in Acts 8:5 that Philip went down to Samaria, that he was joined there by Peter and John (vs. 14), and that he went next toward Gaza (vs. 26). Peter then went to LYDDA (9:35), JOPPA (vs. 39), and from there to CAESAREA (10:1). Gal. 2:11 informs us that Peter was at ANTIOCH of Syria, *ca.* 350 miles N of Jerusalem; and from I Cor. 1:12 we learn that he got as far away as Corinth, some eight hundred miles from Jerusalem across the Mediterranean. There is a tradition that Peter went as far W as ROME, but of this we are not certain.

The best-known Christian traveler of the period was Paul. Although born at Tarsus of Cilicia, on the S coast of Asia Minor, as a young man he went to Jerusalem as a student (Acts 22:3). As a persecutor he visited DAMASCUS (9:2). After returning to Jerusalem, he was sent back to TARSUS (vs. 30). Later he was brought to Antioch of Syria to assist the church (11:25-27). With this church as a base, he then became the greatest missionary.

On the first of Paul's missionary tours (Acts 13-14), accompanied all the way by Barnabas and part of the way by Mark, he sailed to CYPRUS; and from there to ATTALIA on the coast of PAMPHYLIA. Then he went *ca.* a hundred miles N through rugged hills to Antioch of PISIDIA, SE some seventy miles to ICO-NIUM, *ca.* twenty miles SW to LYSTRA, and some thirty miles SE to DERBE. Retracing his course to Attalia, he sailed back to Antioch. Acts 15:1-35 reports a journey of Paul and Barnabas to Jerusalem.

Paul's second missionary journey is recorded in Acts 15:41–18:22. The first part of this journey was overland from Antioch of Syria to TROAS on the Aegean. It is a difficult route of more than 600 miles. His way probably led to Tarsus, up through the Cilician Gates (*see* CILICIA) of the Taurus Mountains; by his Galatian churches at Derbe, Lystra, Iconium, and Antioch; turning at Tralla; through Philadelphia, Sardis, Pergamum, Adramyttium; and on to Troas. He went by ship to Neapolis; overland to Philippi, Thessalonica, and Beroea; by ship from there down to Athens; and by land to CORINTH. On his return he sailed to EPHESUS, *ca.* 250 miles, and then continued to Jerusalem, a voyage of some 600 miles.

The third missionary journey is reported in Acts 18:23–21:17, the first part of which was through Asia Minor to Ephesus, *ca.* five hundred miles. Then by land and sea he visited all his churches on the Aegean until he got to Corinth. After a time he retraced this course, bidding farewell to the churches, and sailed from Miletus to Jerusalem.

Then followed the trip to ROME of Acts 27:1–28:16, which was by sea, with the exception of the short distance from Puteoli to Rome. In this voyage he was shipwrecked on Malta.

Even this list does not exhaust Paul's travels. Acts does not give us a complete record. In II Cor. 11:25, Paul himself refers to three shipwrecks, all of which had occurred before the one which took place on his final voyage to Rome. Only the latter is mentioned in Acts. Gal. 1:17 notes a trip into Arabia about which Acts is silent. Further travels of Paul are indicated in the Pastoral letters, which may or may not be Pauline. I Tim. 1:3 speaks of a trip from Ephesus into Macedonia. II Tim. 4:13 knows of a sojourn in Troas; and vs. 20 of a visit at Miletus. Tit. 1:5 shows knowledge of a trip to Crete, while 3:12 seems to indicate that he visited Nicopolis and wintered there.

There were interesting travels also by less-known early Christians. Acts 18:24 tells of Apollos, an Alexandrian (*see* ALEXANDRIA), who preached in Ephesus even before Paul did. Acts 20:4 lists seven men from churches of Macedonia, Asia, and Galatia, who accompanied Paul on his last swing around the Aegean. Rom. 16:1-25 appears to be a letter of introduction, written by Paul, for Phoebe of CENCHREAE, as she was leaving on a visit to Asia. I Cor. 1:11 suggests that I Corinthians was occasioned by news Paul had received from persons of the household of Chloe of Corinth, who visited him in Ephesus. Phil. 2:25-29; 4:18 indicate that Philippians was written in response to a visit of Epaphroditus, who went from Philippi to Rome to see Paul in prison and care for his needs. Col. 1:2; 4:12 show that Epaphras had gone from Colosse in ASIA·to visit Paul. Eph. 6:21 probably

indicates that Tychicus had come from Ephesus for the same purpose. The Letter to Philemon seems to mean that the slave Onesimus had deserted his master, Philemon, at Colossae in Asia, and succeeded in getting to Rome, where he became stranded, and then attached himself to Paul, whom he may have known first in Asia. One of the most fascinating journeys is that of Tychicus as he returned from Paul to Asia, apparently carrying in his brief case letters from Paul to Ephesus (Eph. 6:21), Colossae (Col. 4:7), Laodicea (Col. 4:16), and Philemon, and probably with the slave Onesimus in his care. But on these matters *see* the articles on the various letters.

2. Occasions of travel. Then as now there were many reasons for travel. Various enterprises of religion were among the most important. This is further illustrated by Acts 2:5-13, where it is said that devout Jews from every nation under heaven were in Jerusalem at Pentecost. While this statement is hyperbolical, it is nevertheless essentially true. No fewer than sixteen areas are mentioned as places from which these pilgrims had come. They extend from ROME to ELAM and MEDIA, and from PONTUS to ARABIA. Yet this is only a selection of places where Jews lived at the time; such important centers as SYRIA, CYPRUS, and GREECE are not included.

At any time of the year, but especially during festivals, Jerusalem had a cosmopolitan character. One of the chief industries of the city must have been the entertainment of pilgrims. This was true to some extent of all the cities through which these pilgrims passed year by year. Inns and hostels were largely dependent on pilgrims. So also were Palestinian agriculture, which provided food, and shepherds and cattlemen, who afforded animals for sacrifices. Jerusalem was a center, not only of religion, but also of economic life and travel.

But similar situations prevailed in other nations of the time. Religion was as essential in them as it was in Palestine. Whether in Egypt, Italy, Greece, or Asia Minor, e.g., the construction, operation, and use of temples not only inspired and sustained the religious life of the people, but also provided for expression of their artistic talent and were a basis for important trades and industries. Vivid pictures of contemporary life and institutions of Greece and adjacent lands are given by Strabo's *Geography* and the *Description of Greece* by Pausanias. As Greek religion was a polytheism, it had many temples. Some of them, such as the Parthenon at Athens, were of exceptional beauty. The Eleusinian mysteries of S Attica drew initiates and pilgrims from all over that world. The cult of Dionysus inspired the Greek theater, which migrated far beyond Greece. Two of these were built at Gerasa (modern Jerash), and one at Philadelphia (modern Amman), whose remains stand to this day.

The Greeks also had religious festivals. The Panathenea were celebrated annually at Athens in honor of Athena, and all the people of Attica joined as pilgrims. But popular festivals also brought together people from all Greek states. The Olympian games occurred every four years in Elis, and the Nemean in Argolis every two years, in honor of Zeus; the Isthmian, every other spring at Corinth for

Poseidon; and the Pythian, every fourth year at Delphi for Apollo. All of them attracted visitors and pilgrims.

Greek religion was famous for its interest in healing, which was usually associated with temples of Asclepius. Pausanias (I.21.7) mentions temples of Asclepius at Athens, Cenchreae, Epidaurus, Smyrna, Pergamum, and in such remote places as North Africa and Crete. As they were the hospitals of that world, such temples attracted numerous pilgrims.

Wars continued to be important reasons for travel. The Hellenistic period was ushered in by the conquests of Alexander the Great. After first overrunning Greece, his armies marched through Asia Minor, Syria, and Palestine to Egypt, and back through Mesopotamia and Persia all the way to India. Then followed the less co-ordinated campaigns of his successors, until Rome emerged as the world power, absorbing all lands bordering the Mediterranean and extending from Spain and Britain to Mesopotamia, and from Cappadocia to Ethiopia. Palestine was taken over in 63 B.C.

The organization and government of this empire was possible only because of efficient means of travel and communication. Transportation of food, raw materials, and manufactured goods by both land and sea was indispensable. Travel by students to university centers, such as Athens and Tarsus, and to Jewish teachers at Jerusalem, as in the case of Paul (Acts 22:3), was common. Pliny's *Natural History* is evidence of travel for scientific reasons. That there was travel also just to see the world is indicated by such men as Strabo, Pausanias, and Diodorus of Sicily, whose works are little more than guidebooks.

3. Means of travel. The most common means of travel on land was to walk. This was the usual way in which Jesus traveled about during his ministry. The disciples often walked on longer journeys. It is related in Acts 8:26-31 that Philip encountered an Ethiopian on the way to Gaza who invited him to get into the chariot and ride with him, which Philip did. Saul of Tarsus went on foot even to Damascus, as indicated in Acts 9:8, where it is said that after he was blinded by a vision, his companions led him by the hand. It is probable that Paul went by foot on many strenuous journeys during his career. But this is the method of travel to which common people were accustomed.

Animals were also used for transportation. The most common animal was the donkey (Ass). It was used not only to carry baggage and other heavy burdens, as modern persons use pick-up trucks, but also to ride upon. The entry of Jesus into Jerusalem on a donkey (Mark 11:1-11) was unusual only in the sense that the action had a ceremonial meaning. It was based on the Hebrew custom of causing the crown prince to ride on the king's mule (I Kings 1: 32). While πῶλον, used in Mark 11:2, is ambiguous, and might mean "young horse," the author of Matt. 21:2 has rendered it ὄνον, "ass"; and in John 12:14 it is ὀνάριον, "young ass" or "little donkey." These writers were familiar with customs of the time. In Luke 10:34, where the Samaritan places the wounded man on his own κτῆνος, the animal is probably a donkey. Common use of donkeys is indicated by the ease with which they enter into the conversation of Jesus (13:15; 14:5). In such journeys as that of Mary to Bethlehem just before Jesus was born (2:5) and the earlier visit with Elizabeth (1:39), presumably donkeys were used. The Near Eastern donkey is strong, sure-footed, good-natured, and inexpensive, and he travels at a comfortable gait.

That camels* were widely used for transportation is also to be presumed. References to them are frequent in the OT (cf. Gen. 24:10; I Kings 10:2; *see* CAMEL). They were especially useful for caravans which carried heavy loads through regions where food and water were scarce. They are still used extensively in the Near East. Yet there are only incidental references to them in the NT. Mark 1:6 states that John wore a camel's-hair garment, a prophetic garb apparently reflected in II Kings 1:8; Zech. 13:4. This indicates that camels were to be found in the area. The picturesque sayings of Jesus in Matt. 19:24; 23:24 are likewise evidence that the camel was well known at the time. Otherwise Jesus could not have used them in this familiar way. In any case, camels were not so widely used as donkeys. They were more expensive, less docile, and altogether less reliable for general use. Fig. CAM 6.

The HORSE was well known among Hebrews at least from the time of Solomon (I Kings 4:26). But because of cost their use was limited mainly to persons of wealth, government officials, and military personnel. In the days of Judas Maccabeus the Syrians sent to invade Judah an army which contained a contingent of 7,000 horsemen (I Macc. 3: 39). When Theudas, who claimed to be a prophet, gathered a disturbing band of fanatical followers, Cuspius Fadus, the procurator, sent a troop of horsemen who cut off the prophet's head and dispersed those who had been excited by him (Jos. Antiq. XX.v.1). In organizing the defense of Galilee against the Romans in A.D. 66, Josephus was able to muster only 350 horsemen (War II.xx.8). His description of the Roman forces (War.III.iv.1) mentions three different units of 1,000 horsemen each, not including mules and other beasts of burden (War III.v.4). Moreover, 120 horsemen appear to have been attached to each legion (War III.vi.3). Josephus indicates a similar extensive use of horses in Adiabene and Parthia (Antiq. XX.iii.2; iv.2). The poetic language of the Revelation of John reflects the elaborate use of horses in military communications and operations (6:1-8; 9:16; 14:20).

Acts 23:23-32 states that after Paul's arrest in Jerusalem, he was sent to Caesarea with an escort of two hundred soldiers, two hundred spearmen, and seventy horsemen, with a mount for himself. They left Jerusalem at 9 P.M. and arrived at Antipatris forty miles away by dawn; the horsemen continued on to Caesarea the next day. As a forty-mile journey is too great for foot soldiers in one night, the text must be confused. It probably means that they turned back when it was certain that the horsemen could safely go the rest of the way alone. Acts 8:26-39, which tells of the Ethiopian pilgrim returning along the road to Gaza, shows that there was a chariot road from Jerusalem via Gaza and Egypt to

Ethiopia. The chariot was, no doubt, drawn by horses.

Elephants* were too ponderous for much practical use in travel, but they found a place in military campaigns (see ELEPHANT). Antiochus of Syria invaded Egypt with a force of chariots, cavalry, elephants, and a fleet (I Macc. 1:17). Syrians appeared in Judah at one time with an army which had thirty-two elephants (I Macc. 6:30-35). Mounted on each elephant was a tower carrying four soldiers and the Indian driver. The formation assigned to each elephant a thousand armored footmen and five hundred horsemen. Fig. SEL 40.

4. Highways. Highways of the NT period traversed both land and sea. SHIPS AND SAILING were fundamental in the life of the NT world. Romans considered the Mediterranean their sea, and it was a life line of the Empire. Roman food ships followed all sea lanes from Italy to ports of the Mediterranean, Aegean, Euxine, Adriatic, and even into the Atlantic along Africa and toward Britain. Ships also provided the most convenient means of transportation for individuals from E Mediterranean ports to Rome, and between the various cities on the shores of adjacent seas. Claudius offered commercial ship operators substantial inducements and subsidy against losses (Suetonius *Claudius* 18).

But Romans were also good road builders. They realized the strategic importance of land highways for military, commercial, and other purposes. Their policy was to build and maintain good roads into every new area as the Empire expanded. Unification of the various lands under Roman rule eliminated most border difficulties, and their police power maintained peace. Travel by land in the Empire was generally safe. Inns for travelers were frequent, but not always good. Christians usually depended on hospitality of their own brethren for entertainment (Acts 16:5; 17:7; 21:16; 28:7, 14; Heb. 13:2).

A traveler by land from Rome to Syria and Egypt set out on the Appian Way. He went via Capua and Tarentum to Brundisium, 360 miles; by ship across the Adriatic to Dyrrachium or Aulona, two days; by the Egnatian Way across Macedonia to Neapolis, port of Philippi, 381 miles; by ship usually to Troas, three days; to Antioch of Syria by Philadelphia and Julia, 880 miles; or to Antioch of Syria by Laodicea, 930 miles; to Caesarea, 365 miles; and to Alexandria, 435 miles—total, five days by sea and 2,420 miles by land, or, if by Laodicea, five days by sea and 2,470 miles by land. As travel on foot averaged *ca.* 16 miles per day, such a journey from Rome to Alexandria would have required *ca.* five months. By horse or carriage, time would have been cut at least in half. For roads and sea routes of the Roman period, *see* Map XXI, Vol. I. Figs. SHI 50-51.

5. Other means of communication. As travel was slow, difficult, and expensive, other means of communication were essential. One of the most popular was letter writing. Readers of the NT learn this first from the letters of Paul. But according to Acts 15:23-29, the first Christian letter was written by the apostles and elders at Jerusalem to the churches of Asia Minor. This was delivered by Paul and Barnabas as couriers—a method which Paul himself later employed. Such persons as Timothy (I Thess. 3:2), Tychicus (Col. 4:7), and Epaphroditus (Phil. 2:25; 4:18) served as messengers for Paul. This same custom was followed by Ignatius bishop of Antioch of Syria, on his journey as a prisoner through Asia Minor to Rome, where he became a martyr in 108. From Smyrna he wrote letters to Ephesus, Magnesia, Tralles, and Rome. Then from Troas he wrote to Philadelphia and Smyrna, and to Polycarp, bishop of Smyrna. Usually he mentions his messenger in the letter. As time is short, he asks Polycarp himself to write to churches ahead of him, requesting that they send him either messengers or letters by Polycarp's messengers.

The Roman government had its own official postal service, whose messengers went by both land and sea, depending on the season of the year and the destination. But there was no government post for private persons. If they wrote letters, they had to find their own ways of sending them.

Bibliography. W. M. Ramsey, "Roads and Travel (NT)," *HDB*, Extra Volume (1904), 375-402; G. E. Wright and F. V. Filson, *Westminster Historical Atlas of the Bible* (1945); S. V. McCasland, "The Greco-Roman World," *IB*, VII (1951), 75-99; E. G. Kraeling, *Bible Atlas* (1956).

S. V. McCASLAND

TRAVELERS, VALLEY OF THE [גי העברים] (Ezek. 39:11); KJV VALLEY OF THE PASSENGERS. A valley E of the Dead Sea—therefore outside the Holy Land proper (Ezek. 47:18)—to which the slain forces of Gog, with whom Israel will be at war in the latter days, are to be brought for burial by their Israelite vanquishers (Ezek. 38-39). Thereafter the place is to be known as the Valley of Hamon-gog (39:11-15). H. F. BECK

TRAY [מחתה, *lit.*, a thing for snatching up (live coals)] (Exod. 25:38; 37:23; Num. 4:9). Alternately: FIRE PAN (Exod. 27:3); CENSER (Lev. 10:1). A word representing a group of utensils used for handling fire or live coals. The translation "tray" refers specifically to the golden bowl on which the implements used for adjusting the wicks of the lamps in the tabernacle were placed.

See also CENSER; SNUFFERS. L. E. TOOMBS

TREASURE, TREASURER, TREASURY. Wealth in general, the sacred vessels and objects of the temple, the possessions of a king or of an individual. Wherever these are kept, there is a treasury; the OFFICER in charge is the treasurer.

1. Treasure
   a. General definitions
   b. Symbolic treasures
   c. Treasure during war and defeat
   d. Protecting treasure
2. Treasury
   a. General definitions
   b. Temple treasury
   c. Royal treasury
3. Treasurer
   a. In the OT
   b. In the NT

1. Treasure. *a. General definitions.* All wealth, regardless of the owner, is a treasure. Any valuable gift, silver or gold as well as any possession, may be called a "treasure" (מַטְמֹן [Gen. 43:23]; אוֹצָר [Isa. 30:6; Nah. 2:9]). In WISDOM literature it was axiomatic that the righteous would gain much treasure and be prosperous, while the wicked would suffer poverty (Ps. 17:14; Prov. 8:21; 15:6 [אוֹצָר]; 21:20; cf. Luke 16:25). Those who gain through unrighteous means shall lose their treasure (Prov. 10:2; 21:6). Yet Jesus sees such earthly treasures (θησαυρός) as transitory and vain (Matt. 6:19 ff; Luke 12:33 ff; cf. Prov. 27:24 [חֹסֶן]; Jer. 48:7; 49:4). In fact, such seeking after earthly treasures may lead to idolatry (Matt. 6:21; Luke 12:20-21). So Jesus urges they be given up in order to have wealth in heaven (Matt. 19:21; Mark 10:21; Luke 18:22). Job in his affliction seeks death like a treasure (Job 3:21).

Temple treasures are listed in Ezra 1:9-11 (cf. Ezra 2:69-70; Neh. 7:70 ff) and include basins of silver and of gold, bowls of silver and gold, miscellaneous vessels, priestly garments, money. The decoration and trim, the candlesticks, altars, etc., were also considered treasures by plunderers.

The royal treasures are listed in II Chr. 32:27-29 (cf. II Kings 20:13 ff; Eccl. 2:8), including silver, gold, precious stones, spices, shields, costly vessels, and probably grain, wine, oil, cattle, and sheep. Solomon's wealth is described in I Kings 10:10-25. The Wise Men presented royal treasures to the child Jesus (Matt. 2:11). The disaster impending upon Judah would involve the loss of all treasures to Babylon (II Chr. 36:18; Jer. 20:5; 50:37).

Gifts presented to the temple were considered treasures (Neh. 10:39). Joshua dedicated the booty from Jericho to the Lord (Josh. 6:19 ff). Such gifts, as well as the tithes and taxes, could be used for many purposes, including the cost of repairs (II Kings 12:9-16).

b. Symbolic treasures. Figuratively the forces of nature are treasures (Job 38:22; Ps. 135:7; Isa. 45:3; Jer. 10:13; etc.). So wisdom is a hidden treasure (Prov. 2:4; cf. Isa. 33:6). Israel is the treasured possession of God (Exod. 19:5; Ps. 135:4). Man should store up in heaven good treasures of salvation by faith and loyalty (Matt. 6:20-21). The gospel of salvation is a treasure for Paul (II Cor. 4:7; cf. Matt. 13:44, 52). Ultimately all treasuries and wisdom belong to and are found in Christ (Col. 2:3). To possess these eternal treasures is greater joy than having even a royal treasure (Heb. 11:26). Out of the good treasure ("treasury"? θησαυρός) of their hearts good men bring forth more good (Matt. 12:35; Luke 6:45).

c. Treasure during war and defeat. In warfare all treasure of whatever kind was fair game for the conqueror (Isa. 39:6 ff). So SHISHAK took away the temple treasures, the royal treasures, everything (I Kings 14:26). Plunder was a normal method for the international exchange of wealth (I Kings 15:18; II Kings 14:14; 24:11-13; Isa. 10:13; 23:18; etc.). TRIBUTE was a partial transfer of such wealth to the more powerful ruler (II Kings 12:18; 16:8; 18:13 ff; etc.). The fall of Jerusalem meant that all temple treasures, royal treasures, and private wealth went to Babylon (Jer. 15:13; 17:3; 51:13; Ezek. 22:25; Dan. 1:2; cf. II Chr. 36:18). In the last times plunder will be frequent (Dan. 11:43; cf. Hos. 13:15).

d. Protecting treasure. The possession of wealth caused care and trouble (Prov. 15:16). Guards, sentinels, treasurers (*see below*), and strong treasure houses (*see below*) were needed. Wealth was defended by one's life. Personal treasure was usually carried on the person for safekeeping (Luke 10:30 ff; cf. Matt. 6:19) or buried in the ground (Matt. 13:44; cf. Job 3:21; Jer. 41:8). Archaeologists frequently find hoards or caches of coins hidden beneath floors.

2. Treasury. *a. General definitions.* In the plural of the KJV "treasuries" may mean wealth or treasures of various kinds (*see above*) or the places for storing such treasures. A CHEST may be used for storing personal possessions (Ezek. 27:24). The casket of the wise men could be a treasury (θησαυρός; Matt. 2:11). God's grace and providence exercised through nature reveals the treasury of his blessings (Deut. 28:12; 33:19; cf. Isa. 45:3).

b. Temple treasury. The earliest temples of Sumer were rich and had treasuries. Some consider them to be the first capitalistic institutions. Tyre is said to have a city treasury (Ezek. 28:4), but this may mean the general personal wealth of the merchant city. The TABERNACLE seems to have had a treasury (Josh. 6:19). The TEMPLE in Jerusalem had rooms for various kinds of treasure (I Kings 7:51; I Chr. 28:11 ff). Solomon stored treasure in the temple treasuries (I Kings 7:51; II Chr. 5:1). Excavation of Canaanite temples reveals grain pits and other places that could be treasuries.

In Herod's temple tithes and taxes were paid at the treasury. Josephus (War V.v.2) mentions thirteen boxes for the receipt of the temple tax. The Mishna describes the treasure chests as trumpet-shaped receptacles in the Court of the Women. Judas returned the pieces of silver, but the priests would not put it into the treasury (Matt. 27:6; κορβανᾶς). Jesus often seated himself in the vicinity so he could watch the contributions to the treasury (γαζοφυλακεῖον; Mark 12:41 ff; Luke 21:1 ff; John 8:20).

c. Royal treasury. The temple treasury and the royal treasury in Solomon's day may have been identical. But Hezekiah had treasuries and storehouses for his wealth (II Chr. 32:27-28; Isa. 39:2). Records and tax receipts have come from the palace in SAMARIA. Documents and decrees may have been kept in the royal treasury (Ezra 5:17 [גִּנְזַיָּא; LXX γάζα; "royal archives"; *see* ARCHIVES, HOUSE OF THE]). In Persia bribes went to the royal treasury (Esth. 3:9; 4:7; *see* GENIZAH). Nehemiah followed the Persian customs concerning public treasures (Neh. 10:37; 13:7; LXX γαζοφυλακεῖον). Public records were kept there in Maccabean times (I Macc. 14:49). "Treasury" may at times not refer specifically to a place but to the accumulated assets of the king, wherever they may be (Ezra 7:20). The granary and the treasure or store-cities were also royal treasuries (Neh. 13:12; cf. Gen. 41:48 ff; Exod. 1:11 [מִסְכְּנוֹת]; I Kings 9:19; II Chr. 8:4-6; etc.). *See* STORE-CITIES.

3. Treasurer. *a. In the OT.* The treasurer is the officer in charge of royal or sacred treasures composed of goods, documents, money, and jewels. He is STEWARD of the possessions of the king and OVERSEER of the treasury (*see* § 2 *above*).

AZMAVETH was treasurer for David (I Chr. 27:25). He was in charge of the royal treasury. Probably ranking below him was Jonathan son of Uzziah (*see* JONATHAN 7), who was over treasuries throughout the kingdom. He was probably watchdog and overseer for royal tax collections, and supervisor of royal lands. Both are called stewards as well (I Chr. 27:31). AHIJAH is listed as treasurer over the treasury of the house of the Lord under David (I Chr. 26:20). Jehiel was over the same treasury in Solomon's day (I Chr. 29:7-8; *see* JEHIEL 2). Isaiah speaks of SHEBNA as "steward" (Isa. 22:15; KJV "treasurer") in the time of Hezekiah.

Nebuchadnezzar also had treasurers among his officers (Dan. 3:2). MITHREDATH was treasurer for Cyrus and was in charge of the booty captured and then returned to the original peoples (Ezra 1:8). Artaxerxes commanded all his financial representatives beyond the river to help Ezra with material aid in re-establishing the devastated land (Ezra 7:21-22). Nehemiah appointed several treasurers to care for the contributions (Neh. 13:13; I Chr. 9:26; cf. Neh. 12:44).

b. In the NT. The Ethiopian EUNUCH was in charge of the treasury of Candace the queen (Acts 8:27). The CHAMBERLAIN of Corinth in charge of that city's finances was Erastus (Rom. 16:23; *see* ERASTUS 1). C. U. WOLF

TREASURE CITIES. *See* STORE CITIES.

TREE OF KNOWLEDGE, TREE OF LIFE. Two miraculous trees which stood in the garden of Eden. The relationship between the two is difficult to determine because of conflicting sources used in Gen. 2–3. The significance of the expression "the tree of the knowledge of good and evil" is also much debated. The tree was the means to a knowledge which was, by right, a divine prerogative. The disobedient eating resulted in man's shame and guilt and his expulsion from the garden. The tree of life plays a significant role only after the Fall. Man is driven from the garden to prevent his attempting to gain immortality through the false means of this magical tree.

1. Terminology and usage
2. Parallels in comparative religion
3. Literary analysis
4. The tree of knowledge
   a. Moral judgment
   b. Secular knowledge
   c. Sexual knowledge
   d. Universal knowledge
   e. Summary
5. The tree of life
6. The theological significance
Bibliography

1. Terminology and usage. The expression "the tree of the knowledge of good and evil" (עֵץ הַדַּעַת טוֹב וָרָע) appears only twice in the OT (Gen. 2:9, 17). The same tree is presupposed, however, in Gen. 3:1-21 and is designated merely as "the tree which is in the midst of the garden" (vs. 3). One's eating from it brings the knowledge of good and evil (vss. 5, 22). A more exact translation of the expression is "the tree of the knowledge good and evil." According to Hebrew grammar, the noun is not in the construct state

followed by a genitive. Rather, it is an infinitive construct preceded by an article and followed by two accusatives. The syntax is important in indicating that the study of this difficult expression must be concerned with the entire phrase and not merely with "good and evil."

"The tree of life" (עֵץ הַחַיִּים) appears in Gen. 2:9; 3:22, 24; Prov. 3:18; 11:30; 13:12; 15:4; and four times in the NT (τὸ ξύλον τῆς ζωῆς; Rev. 2:7; 22:2, 14, 19). It occurs occasionally in the Jewish noncanonical books (I Enoch 24:4 ff; II Enoch 8:3 ff; II Esd. 8:52). Ezekiel possibly alludes to the tree of life without naming it (31:3-9; 47:12).

2. Parallels in comparative religion. The description of the trees in Eden stems from traditions which are not indigenous to Israel. The material belongs to that part of Israel's inheritance of Near Eastern mythology which either was transmitted directly from N Mesopotamia by the Hebrew ancestors during the Middle Bronze Age or was mediated through Canaanite culture. The parallels in comparative religion are significant in showing the peculiar form into which Israel reworked these ancient mythical motifs. *See* MYTH.

The tree of life belongs to that category of objects which have the power of bestowing eternal life, such as life-giving plants, water, and fruits. The mythical idea conceives of life in terms of a material substance which can be possessed through eating. This belief is manifest everywhere in the history of religion. In Egypt the tree of life is pictured as a tall sycamore upon which the gods sit and obtain immortality from eating. The mythology of India describes a tree in heaven from which Yama and the other gods partake of the life-giving drink, "soma." "Ambrosia," the sacred food of the Greek gods, also belongs to this class.

In Sumerian mythology the evidence is too scanty for certainty; however, the *gishkin* tree in the temple at Eridu may well represent a mythical tree of life. Its appearance is like a shining stone with roots reaching to the subterranean ocean. The presence of a life-giving plant is more certain. In the Babylonian-Assyrian literature there are no direct parallels to the tree of life; however, reference to magical plants which bestow immortality are frequent. Utnapishtim promises eternal life to Gilgamesh from a magical plant growing in the sea. In the Adapa myth it is magical bread and water which bestow the gift of immortality. These myths offer etiologies to explain why man has failed to attain immortality. They are an early witness to man's concern with the problem of life and death.

Ancient Near Eastern literature offers no parallels to the tree of knowledge. The earlier attempt to find a reference to a "tree of truth" in the Sumerian name *gishzida* must be abandoned as a mistranslation. It is highly significant that the biblical writer has refashioned his material in such a way as to shift the emphasis away from the Near Eastern concern with life and death to the question of man's obedience, which is without ethnic parallels.

3. Literary analysis. OT scholarship has long recognized the difficulty of understanding the role of the two trees in Gen. 2–3. According to 2:9*b* the tree of life stood in the midst of the garden along with the tree of knowledge. Gen. 3:1-21, however, speaks of only one tree in the midst of the garden, which is the tree of knowledge. The sudden introduction of the tree of life into the story (3:22-24) only increases the difficulty. If this tree was also forbidden, why was the writer silent about it? If it was not forbidden, how is one to understand man's free access to it?

The older literary criticism tried to solve this problem by unraveling two accounts within Gen. 2-3, J[1] and J[2]. Each source was assigned one tree. This solution seemed to have much in its favor, since there are abundant signs pointing to a composite source: (a) the double name, Yahweh Elohim, is peculiar to these chapters; (b) the tree of knowledge in 2:9b is tacked on the verse in a manner which is syntactically clumsy; (c) 3:22, 24, offer a doublet to 3:23. Many literary critics felt that the tree of life was secondary and should be eliminated entirely from the story.

More recent scholarship also has recognized the composite nature of the biblical account. Instead of attempting a mechanical division, it has traced the internal friction in the story back to its stage of oral tradition. The gradual process of assimilating older material did not succeed in eliminating all the discrepancies. In the opinion of most modern scholars a division of the story into two independent sources has not commended itself. The elimination of one of the trees has also not been successful.

4. The tree of knowledge. The tree of KNOWLEDGE presents such great problems in understanding that no generally acceptable solution can be offered. The following are the chief theories which have arisen in the history of interpretation:

a. Moral judgment. The tree of knowledge is the means to moral judgment, by which man distinguishes right from wrong. This traditional interpretation rests upon the frequent OT usage of the terms "good and evil" in an ethical sense (Isa. 5:20; Amos 5:14; Mic. 3:2). However, it raises the problem of whether there could have been real disobedience without a prior sense of right and wrong. It is difficult to reconcile the fact that God sought to prevent man from acquiring a sense of moral judgment with the Hebrew concept of the Deity.

b. Secular knowledge. The tree of knowledge is the means to secular knowledge, culture, and reason. This view recognizes that good and evil in the OT frequently have a far broader meaning than the merely ethical. Good and evil can mean salutary and harmful (II Sam. 13:22). Gen. 2-3 is interpreted as the first step toward wider knowledge, which means a retreat from the fear of God. In this view Gen. 3:24 reflects the familiar Promethean theme.

Several objections have been raised to this interpretation: There is no indication that Adam's sin caused an increase in worldly knowledge. The change is rather in terms of a sense of shame and guilt. Again, the discovery of the arts and crafts is not attributed in the OT to Adam, but to his descendants (Gen. 4:20 ff).

c. Sexual knowledge. The tree of knowledge is the means to sexual knowledge. The advocates of this interpretation have pointed out that the verb יָדַע, "know," occurs frequently as a euphemism for sexual

relations (Gen. 4:1; 19:5). When Adam and Eve acquired the knowledge of good and evil, they recognized their nakedness and experienced feelings of shame. Finally, several parallel passages containing the phrase "knowing good and evil" can be reasonably interpreted as referring to sexual knowledge (Deut. 1:39; II Sam. 19:35; 1QSa I.9-11).

The chief objections leveled against this interpretation are as follows: Gen. 2:23-24 already includes the idea of sexual knowledge and presents the etiology of the sexual relationship. Nowhere does the writer equate insensitivity to nakedness with lack of sexual knowledge. Nakedness is not merely shame before the other sex, but the exposure of oneself. Also the word טוֹב, "good," appears very infrequently with an exclusively sexual connotation. Finally, in Gen. 3:22, Yahweh affirms that man has become as "one of us" through this knowledge. This can hardly be reconciled with a similarity in sexual knowledge. Nor can this difficulty be avoided by understanding human procreation as a counterpart of divine creation.

d. Universal knowledge. The tree of knowledge is the means to universal or divine knowledge. The defenders of this interpretation point out that it is idiomatic in Hebrew to express a totality by using two extremes, "downsitting and uprising" (Ps. 139:2 KJV), "neither good nor bad" (Gen. 31:24). Furthermore, the totality of knowledge appears in II Sam. 14:17, 20, which is a close parallel. David is described as being "like the angel of God to discern good and evil." The commentary in vs. 20 adds that the angel of God knows "all things that are on the earth."

The following argument has been raised in objection to this interpretation: Unless the element of discernment is allowed within the idea of totality, the interpretation of 3:22 becomes extremely artificial. Man did not achieve omniscience from the tree. This difficulty cannot be evaded by understanding vs. 22 as an ironical statement.

e. Summary. The question can be seriously raised as to whether the uncertainty of the interpretation of the tree of knowledge does not stem ultimately from the fact that the author does not say precisely what he means anywhere. The error comes about when commentators attempt to solidify a concept which was originally fluid. Perhaps one should be satisfied with drawing a few broad lines: (a) Knowing good and evil is, in some sense, to be like God (Gen. 3:5, 22); (b) the knowledge brought a new relationship between God and man (3:8 ff); (c) the effect of the knowledge was not beneficial, as man had expected, but resulted in shame and guilt (3:7 ff).

5. The tree of life. What is the role of the tree of LIFE in the story? Gen. 3:22 clearly depicts the tree as being a means to immortality. Yet, if man had had access to it, why had he not already obtained eternal life? Some have tried to solve this dilemma by claiming that immortality was possible only in the continual eating the fruit. When man was driven out of the garden and cut off from the source of the fruit, immortality was forfeited. This interpretation cites as support the many parallels from comparative religion where immortality rests on continual nourishment. Further proof is offered by translating גם in 3:22 as "again" instead of "also." This theory has not met with general acceptance among scholars. It neglects to take into account the urgency of man's expulsion from the garden, which rested on the real possibility of his obtaining immortality through a single eating.

In attempting to understand the role of the tree of life in the story, it is important to find the point of view of the biblical writer. Many of the logical questions of the modern reader are simply not answered by the saga. Nor can the several discrepancies be completely resolved. What is significant is that the biblical writer presents the tree of life as an important factor only after man's disobedience.

Gen. 2, in spite of its naïve language, is a highly theological description of the Hebrew's understanding of the ideal life. The life intended for man by God is depicted as a quality of harmonious existence. Man became a "living creature" (נפש חיה) when first infused with the breath of God. He has life in obedient dependency upon God (2:7), within a human group (2:18 ff), performing an assigned task (2:15, 19-20).

Through disobedience man lost this kind of life. God said: "In the day that you eat of it you shall die" (2:17). Death is characterized as shame, guilt, and expulsion. God then feared lest man seek to substitute immortality through the tree of life for the loss of genuine life. This mythical idea is rejected as a false substitute. True life is not gained through a magical tree, but only through the proper relationship to God. It is because he has lost this relationship that man is expelled from paradise. The Genesis writer has skilfully employed this older mythical motif to symbolize a false solution to man's ultimate problem of life and death.

The tree of life reoccurs in the NT in the book of Revelation. Using the language of apocalypticism, the writer pictures man's restoration to fellowship with God in terms of the return of the blessings of Eden. The NT emphasis no longer rests on the magical qualities of the tree, but focuses on its purposes as a means to the healing of the nations (Rev. 22:2).

6. The theological significance. To tell his story, the biblical writer of Gen. 2-3 used ancient mythical motifs, one of which is the magical tree of paradise. Although the foreign material contained ideas generally strange to the OT, the writer has skilfully reworked this material to give a genuine Hebrew witness.

The story of Gen. 2-3 is a theological etiology explaining man's separation from God and the loss of the full life. The writer has broken the typical Near Eastern pattern by shifting the focus away from the loss of the mythical tree of life as the reason for death. Instead, he has placed the full emphasis on man's disobedience as the cause of his plight. He has created a vehicle for this theological message in the tree of knowledge. In the final analysis, the tree has become merely a stage setting for the real action between God and man.

Bibliography. A complete bibliography up to 1937 is given by T. C. Vriezen, *Onderzoek naar de Paradijsvoorstelling bij de oude semietische Volken* (1937), pp. 137 ff.

For the material of comparative religion, see: U. Holmberg,

Der Baum des Lebens (1922); A. Brock-Utne, *Der Gottesgarten* (1936); A. Bergema, *De Boom des Levens in Schrift en Historie* (1938); G. Widengren, *The King and the Tree of Life in Ancient Near Eastern Religion* (1951).

The following important exegetical studies: P. Humbert, *Études sur le récit du paradis et de la chute dans la Genèse* (1940); J. Coppens, *La connaissance du bien et du mal et le péché du paradis* (1948); H. J. Stoebe, "Gut und Böse in der jahwistischen Quelle des Pentateuch," *ZAW*, 65 (1953), 188 ff; B. Reiche, "The Knowledge Hidden in the Tree of Paradise," *Journal of Semitic Studies,* I (1956), 193 ff, with a bibliography from 1935-56; R. Gordis, "The Knowledge of Good and Evil in the OT and the Qumran Scrolls," *JBL*, 76 (1957), 123 ff.   B. S. Childs

TREES. *See* Flora.

TRELLIS [סבך עץ, *lit.*, interweaving of wood] (Ps. 74:5). Although Ps. 74:5 is corrupt, the words translated "trellis" most probably refer to the elaborately carved woodwork on and around the main entrance to the sanctuary in the temple. This trellis was hacked down by invaders for its gold overlay. *See* Temple (Jerusalem).   L. E. Toombs

TRESPASS OFFERING. *See* Sacrifices and Offerings § A4*b*.

TRESSES. The translation of a difficult word, רהט (KJV GALLERIES), in Song of S. 7:5.

*****TRIAL OF JESUS. 1. Before the Sanhedrin.** It is often asserted that the Sanhedrin trial, as depicted in the gospels, was illegal. Then, since the Jews were meticulous about judicial process, the NT accounts must be erroneous. Two answers may be made: (*a*) The destruction of Jerusalem, in A.D. 70, erased records for the very period in which we are interested. If NT records do not accord with earlier or later practices, this may prove little regarding Jesus' own time. (*b*) The gospels all make this a preliminary hearing, for binding Jesus over to Pilate. In that case, and considering the intense anger the Jewish hierarchy felt toward Jesus, full judicial procedure would probably have been thought unnecessary.

Their real complaint against him cannot have been his claim to messiahship. This was no crime in Jewish eyes. Nor, apparently, had he personally violated the Mosaic law, though he had proposed other than Pharisaic interpretations of it, and had befriended law-violaters. He was regarded, however, as a sorcerer (Matt. 10:25; Mark 3:22 ff; cf. Mark 6:14); this charge reappears in the Talmud (Sanh. 43*a; 107b*). He had defied the priests by cleansing the temple (Mark 11:15-19), refusing to account to them for his actions (Mark 11:27-33), and, perhaps, making them appear ridiculous by his answer on the resurrection (Mark 12:18-27). According to John 11:47 ff, the Sanhedrin also feared that Jesus might cause a popular uprising, and bring retaliation from Rome. Finally, they found him guilty of blasphemy. In Matthew and Mark this is fused with the question of his messiahship (Matt. 26:63-64; Mark 14:61-62), but in Luke, which is certainly more accurate here, the two are kept separate (Luke 22:67-69). By Jewish custom one tore one's garments on hearing blasphemy. The high priest did so now. This, and not the messianic claim, was the crime deserving of death under Mosaic law (Lev. 24:16; John 19:7).

Most of this would be meaningless to Pilate, however, and the Sanhedrin apparently lacked authority to sentence to death (cf. John 18:31; the killing of Stephen [Acts 7:54 ff] was in the nature of a lynching). So, according to Matthew and Mark, the council sought vainly for testimony regarding acts that Pilate might deem criminal. The gospels do not agree as to whether Jesus spoke during most of this. Finally, adjured in a manner that no Jew could refuse to answer (Matt. 26:63), he declared his own claim. This claim, which was not the ground on which the council itself condemned him, could nevertheless be laid before Pilate.

2. Before Pilate. The NT gospels, and particularly Luke, are kinder to the Roman authorities than they may have deserved. Doubtless this was to shield the feelings of Gentiles whom NT writers wished to convert. Certainly PILATE was not more lenient toward Jesus than he is here pictured. A harsh man, he had more than once so flouted Jewish sensibilities that bloodshed had ensued. During the Passover, Jewish patriotism was at fever pitch, and the governor would be especially on the alert to suppress any sign of rebellion.

Of the "many things" of which Jesus was accused before Pilate (Mark 15:3), only three are named, all at Luke 23:2:

a) Perverting the nation. This vague expression could mean any of the offenses listed in § 1 *above*, but more likely means that Jesus had excited the crowds. Cf. Luke 23:4.

b) Forbidding the giving of tribute to Caesar. In the light of Luke 20:25, this reads like false witness. However, Jesus' words on the earlier occasion are somewhat ambiguous, and might have been understood to mean, "Give Caesar not one whit more than his bare due."

Had the foregoing charges been true, they would make Jesus a sympathizer with the revolutionary Zealots. See ZEALOT.

c) Claiming to be a king—the only accusation that appears in all four gospels. Each repeats the word at least four times (John twelve times) in recounting Jesus' trial and crucifixion. In pressing this charge, the Fourth Gospel says, the accusers avowed their own exclusive loyalty to Caesar (John 19:12, 15).

All the gospels depict Pilate as perplexed, uncertain, and anxious to shift the decision to others. He sends Jesus to Herod Antipas (Luke 23:6-13), who is visiting Jerusalem, but who has no jurisdiction here. He seeks to release Jesus instead of BARABBAS, but is overruled by the clamor of the accusers and of the mob that, gathering meanwhile, has been stirred up by the priests. So he washes his hands, as a public disclaimer of responsibility for his own decision (Matt. 27:24).

In the Synoptics, Jesus is silent during most of this trial. Confronted with the direct question, however: "Are you the King of the Jews?" he replies: "You are saying [it]" [σὺ λέγεις]. Whether these words are a refusal to answer, or an acknowledgment, in any case he is delivered to execution. The INSCRIPTION ON THE CROSS shows him guilty of insurrection against Rome, in his claiming to be king.

Bibliography. T. Innes, *The Trial of Jesus Christ* (1899); M. Brodrick, *The Trial and Crucifixion of Jesus* (1908); J. Stalker, *The Trial and Death of Jesus Christ* (1909); B. S. Easton, "The Trial of Jesus," *AJT*, XIX (1915), 430-52, and attendant references; R. W. Husband, *The Prosecution of Jesus* (1916), probably the most widely used study in English; G. A. Barton, "On the Trial of Jesus Before the Sanhedrin," *JBL*, XLI (1922), 205-11; G. W. Thompson, *The Trial of Jesus* (1927); M. Radin, *The Trial of Jesus of Nazareth* (1931); A. Zeitlin, *Who Crucified Jesus?* (1942); G. D. Kilpatrick, *The Trial of Jesus* (1953).

Virtually all lives of Jesus deal with the trial. The following will be particularly useful: J. Mackinnon, *The Historic Jesus* (1931), pp. 238-75; M. Goguel, *The Life of Jesus* (1932), pp. 498-530; V. Taylor, "The Life and Ministry of Jesus," *IB*, VII (1951), 140-42.   PIERSON PARKER

*TRIBE. The normal social unit among Semitic nomads and seminomads, especially Israel before the conquest of Canaan. The basic unit was the family or household. It was a corporate personality consisting of clans and families held together by kinship. The belief in kinship by blood, marriage, adoption, or covenant is essential to the life of the tribe. Interest in genealogy is common to all tribal societies.

1. Tribes in the ancient Near East
2. Tribes in the Bible
   a. Terminology
   b. Origin, division, and growth
   c. Associations of clans
   d. Number of tribes
   e. Government of tribes
   f. Tribal boundaries
3. History or myth: individuals and tribes
Bibliography

1. Tribes in the ancient Near East. The earliest records of Semitic nomads (*see* SEMITES; NOMADISM) show that the tribal structure is common to all. The Amorites and Arameans set a pattern early in history. Edom (Gen. 36:15 ff), Midian (Num. 25:15), Ishmaelites (Gen. 25:16), and Arabians (Gen. 25:1; Isa. 13:20) have a tribal organization similar to that of Israel. In the OT ancestors are given for most of these tribal kingdoms, as well as for Ammonites and Moabites (Gen. 19:37-38). They were ruled by a PRINCE or chief, seldom a king. With settlement and the pursuit of agriculture, the tribal organization tended to fall apart. This is true of Amorites in Mari as well as Israel in Canaan. Perhaps only pasturage remained tribal after the establishment of the monarchy. David and Solomon, like the monarchs in other countries, deliberately undercut the tribal loyalties in order to develop nationalism. When they are first met, the Canaanites do not seem to have a tribal organization but are more in a city-state and monarchic pattern.

2. Tribes in the Bible. *a. Terminology.* The fullest description of Israel's early tribal organization is in Josh. 7:16-18, where four subdivisions are incidentally listed as follows: (*a*) nation (בני ישראל; οἱ υἱοὶ Ἰσραήλ); (*b*) tribe (שבט and מטה; φυλή); (*c*) clan (משפחה; δῆμος); (*d*) household or family (בית־אב; οἶκος; I Sam. 9:21; 10:20 ff). Thus Achan is reached, "son of Carmi." Although this schematization is clear and logical, the use of the terms is not fully consistent in the OT.

The "children of Israel" constitute a people or nation (עם). The term occurs in the Code of Hammurabi and in Aramaic; it is a cognate to Arabic 'amm(un), "community," and the Akkadian ummanu, "troops" and "people." The root originally meant "to join." The Greek in the LXX is usually λαός. The foreign nations are usually גוי (LXX ἔθνος). The term "people" is not limited to a nation, but could be the population of an area. Even ants are a people (Prov. 30:25-26), as is true of locusts (Joel 2:2).

The Greek word φυλή is commonly used to translate the Hebrew words for "tribe" and "clan." Obviously this is too broad to be of value. The שבט was the over-all social group. It considered itself to be one family or unit (Jer. 33:24; Amos 3:2). In the late writings—e.g., Chronicles—מטה appears. Both these Hebrew words have the meaning "staff." The concept of "tribe" is thus apparently derived from the ruler's or commander's staff, a symbol of authority and order. Occasionally these words are used for the subdivision of the tribe—namely, a clan (Num. 4:18; Judg. 20:12; I Sam. 9:21).

A "clan" (משפחה) was a group of households or an expanded family (Exod. 6:14; Num. 3:24). Usually they claimed a common ancestry (Gen. 24:27; 29:15; I Sam. 20:29). Usually the father lived on in the clan (Josh. 7:18; Judg. 9:1). The clan was the link between the family and the larger unit, the tribe (Num. 2:34). In the Priestly Code this Hebrew word is regularly and consistently used for a subdivision of the tribe. A stranger could be adopted into the clan. At one time Dan and Judah are called "clan" (Judg. 17:7; 18:1, 11; etc.). The אלוף was probably the same as a clan (Judg. 6:15; I Sam. 10:19; Mic. 5:2). Perhaps these could be considered clans before federation into a tribal unit had taken place. The LXX translates משפחה at least thirty-seven times with φυλή and more than two hundred times with δῆμος, "district" or "people."

In the strict language of the Chronicler the clan was subdivided into the "father's house" (בת-אב). This is almost a compound noun and occurs in the plural in many passages in Numbers. The father's house, or family, was usually larger than a modern Western European family because of polygamy, concubinage, and possession of servants and slaves. A family could therefore include what we might call several families living as one household (Num. 3:24; 34:14). They might include persons who were not kin by blood, such as the association of the Rechabites (Jer. 35:18). Strictly speaking, the father's house was the group centering around the father or grandfather and could be further subdivided into the individual families. In Josh. 7:18, Achan belonged to the household of Zabdi (his grandfather), but he was the son of Carmi. It is difficult except in such passages to distinguish the father's house from the individual family (Gen. 24:38-41; Deut. 29:18; I Sam. 9:21). A man took his own household with him wherever he went (Gen. 12:1; I Sam. 27:3). It is probable that the term מולדת in the Hebrew Bible has a nontechnical sense with reference to the nearest blood relation or kinfolk. It is literally the "breeding group" (Gen. 12:1; 31:3; 32:9; etc.).

b. Origin, division, and growth. Tribes, clans, and families normally developed from an original breeding group or family unit. A prominent man, perhaps the patriarch himself, gathered his own close kindred around himself. Here was almost an absolute blood unit. Only a few slaves and daughters-in-law were not blood kindred. As the group grew in wealth, size, and power through birth and conquest, smaller and weaker family groups of similar origin were attracted to or subjugated by the more prominent and more powerful group, and the family extended beyond pure blood kinship, eventually including a strong territorial tie as well. It is probable these alliances were within a similar language group. Tribes might also arise from common occupation and from contiguity. Thus the Arab group, the herders' Anazeh, were not necessarily from a common ancestor. There may be traces of such an associational origin reflected in the names Rachel and Leah. The tribes of Caleb may have been ass nomads with both common life and common ancestors. It is dangerous to oversimplify tribal origins.

In the early wanderings of the Israelites, old tribes seemed to disappear and new ones arise. In the first stages of the Conquest each may have lived relatively isolated from the other among the hills of Canaan. The tribes changed in importance and relative strength. Reuben, once first, was replaced by Judah. Benjamin is significant because of the role of Saul, and because of David's capital on the edge of their territory. Some, like Simeon and Levi, became territorially insignificant. Others, like Dan, might change territory. A clan might grow into a tribe. It might become so large that it divided, as did Joseph. Tribes could originate out of other tribes as the earlier ones increased in size and perhaps became too unwieldy for the political organization. Such was the origin of Ephraim and Manasseh, originally clans or even families of Joseph. These groups became tribes which were independent and controlled a large territory. Ultimately the territorial tie became as strong as the original blood kinship. There are those who believe that all three of these tribes were originally independent and that they coalesced through an alliance. The origin of Benjamin may be similarly a breaking off of one portion, the right hand or S portion of Joseph, after the entry into the Promised Land.

c. Associations of clans. Mutual affinity, common ancestry, a common enemy, as well as a religious covenant, may bring tribes together. The attachment of the family of Lot to Abraham may be an example of a coalition on a family basis. Abraham allied with similar tribes to fight a common enemy in Gen. 14. It is quite possible that some non-Israelitic groups made coalitions with Israel as the Conquest became more complete. The basic coalition within Israel was that based on the amphictyonic covenant at Shechem (Josh. 24:1 ff; cf. II Chr. 10), and Shiloh (Josh. 18:1 ff; 21:2; I Sam. 1-4). Similar amphictyonies have been noted in the first millennium B.C.

d. Number of tribes. The lists of the tribes in the OT vary in number (Num. 1; 26; etc.). There are ten in Deut. 33:6 ff; II Sam. 19:43; eleven in I Kings 11:31; but thirteen in Gen. 46:8 ff; 48:5 ff. There are more than twenty variant lists in the OT. Certain of these lists are geographical (Num. 2–3; 34:14; Deut. 27:12; I Kings 4:7; I Chr. 6:54; Ezek. 48:1 ff; etc.). Some are genealogical (Gen. 35:23; I Chr. 2–3; etc.). The tradition of the twelve is maintained in most of the lists (Gen. 35:22-26; Deut. 27:12-13; I Chr. 2:1-2; Ezek. 48:1 ff). This seems to be an artificial arrangement established after the tradition had arisen or after the twelve tribes had suffered a varied career. Thus we have twelve divisions in Gen. 29–30 only by including Dinah in place of the missing Benjamin. Likewise in I Chr. 2–3; 6:54-80, the twelve is maintained only by doubling or by counting both halves of Manasseh. In Deborah's Song, however, there are only ten tribes, who rallied to help her against the enemy (Judg. 5:14 ff). Warriors came from only some of the tribes. This may be because the S tribes were too far away from the battle scene or were not yet involved in Israel's federation. Simeon is omitted in two lists (Deut. 33:6 ff; Judg. 5:14 ff). There are no lists in II Kings, Ezra, or Nehemiah.

This artificial schematization is maintained in almost all the lists from the book of Numbers. There is artificiality in finding twelve clans for Levi and Judah. There are also twelve tribes of Nahor (Gen. 22:20), of Ishmael (Gen. 17:20; 25:13-16), of Esau (36:9-14; cf. vss. 40-43). Solomon had twelve administrative districts (I Kings 4:7-19). Some believe he used twelve to complete the tribal tradition. Others feel it is the twelve districts that are projected back into the other lists that caused the confusion in number. If Solomon's plan for redistribution was successful, the absence of lists in II Kings is a historical result. Nevertheless, the ideal of twelve remains (Ezek. 48). In the NT many people are still concerned with their tribal connection: Anna out of Asher (Luke 2:36), Barnabas out of Levi (Acts 4:36), Paul out of Benjamin (Rom. 11:1), and Jesus out of Judah (Heb. 7:14). Jesus promised his apostles that they would judge the twelve tribes, probably meaning all Israelites (Matt. 19:28). James writes to the twelve tribes in the Diaspora (Jas. 1:1). Paul likewise uses the term to mean all Israel (Acts 26:7). John in his vision has the list of twelve tribes, but Dan is missing (Rev. 7:1 ff).

The frequent use of the number twelve throughout the Bible and the Near East is perhaps based on the signs of the zodiac.

e. Government of tribes. The prince, elder, patriarch, or sheik was the tribal ruler. In his own clan or family he had almost absolute rule. The council of elders, consisting of the heads of all households, directed the affairs of the larger tribe (Gen. 36:15; Exod. 34:31; Num. 1:16). See ELDER.

Tribal customs readily became fixed, and government by customary law was simple. In the desert there was a deep-seated loyalty to the tribe, and a sense of brotherhood was firm. Solidarity and vengeance went hand in hand. Tribal government usually enforced a strict moralism, the nomadic ideal See NOMADISM.

f. Tribal boundaries. Some of the names reflect location, such as Benjamin. Some of the tribes, as

noted in § 2b *above,* moved. Many of the tribes continued only as territorial designations long after the tribal organization had disappeared. The allotment of tribal territory is given in several lists (Josh. 13–19). Other geographical lists have been noted above. It is obvious that some of the tribes were given a specific territory to have and to hold. Certain tribal names occur again and again for a territory or district and not for the tribe or individual—e.g., Ephraim and Gilead. In Judg. 6:35, Manasseh and Asher are treated as place names. In Manasseh we have a good evidence of personal names used for place names recurring in the Samaritan ostracon. Some place names occur in the genealogies under more than one tribal name, so that they may have belonged to more than one tribe or territory at various times.

3. History or myth: individuals and tribes. Israel traces its tribal unity to a common ancestor through the genealogy of Jacob and his sons. Some stories can hardly be interpreted mythologically or allegorically—e.g., Joseph's robe (Gen. 37:3) and Potiphar's wife (Gen. 39:7). Yet Gen. 49 is clearly tribal in character. Marriages among the individuals may be symbolic of other covenant relationships. We cannot say positively that the marriages in the early patriarchal stories and in the early chapters of Chronicles were not marriages of persons at all but solely alliances and coalitions of tribes. Judah married Canaanite wives (Gen. 38:1). Undoubtedly this caused Judah's family or tribe to increase and even to envelop some Canaanite enclaves, but to say that this represents the fusion of Judah with a specific Canaanite tribe is more than the record allows. The handmaid tribes—i.e., those tribes whose namesakes were the children of Bilhah and Zilpah—are sometimes considered as originally non-Israelite and late additions to the confederation. The record is clear that Asher, Naphtali, Dan, and Gad were weaker, less significant tribes, but this does not mean that they became handmaid tribes because of their weakness.

The relationship of tribes through their reputed mothers is not at all clear. Reuben and Zebulun are of a common mother, but they give evidence of no geographical, historical, or religious affinities beyond that of any random pair of the sons of Jacob. Benjamin is the only one of the sons of Jacob born in Palestine (Gen. 35:16-18). This may mean that Benjamin was the youngest and weakest of the tribes. All the tribes after the coalition and federation considered themselves as brothers (Exod. 2:11; Lev. 10:6; II Sam. 19:9; etc.). The significance of the first-born has been noted above. Yet there is no extra-biblical evidence that Reuben was ever the most powerful of the tribes. Judah was the first-born in prominence and power, at least in the days of the kingdom (I Chr. 2:3–9:1, etc.).

The death of an individual was sometimes explained as the disappearance of a tribe or clan. The deaths of Er and Onan are reported in Gen. 38:7-10. The fact that other names in the genealogy of I Chr. 2–3 also appear as clans does not prove that Er and Onan once existed as clans and were lost. The others may have originated out of the families or individuals surviving these two.

Corporate personality affords an explanation of this enigma. The one is the many and the many are the one. The tribe, the father, the chief, and the eponymous ancestor were all the same. When the father of a tribe died, he still lived on in the experience of his tribe. To distinguish a tribe from the individual is not within the provenance of the OT. The OT does not acknowledge such sharp classifications. The patriarch is neither an individual nor the personification of the tribe. He is the father who forever participates in the ongoing life and destiny of the tribe. Gen. 48 reflects what we would consider both traditions. In Gen. 48:21 Israel speaks as a person concerning his death, but in vs. 22 he speaks of his tribal accomplishments. Whether these are accomplished in person or not is irrelevant.

Bibliography. B. Luther, "Die israelitischen Stämme," *ZAW* (1901), pp. 37 ff. G. B. Gray, "Lists of Twelve Tribes," *Exp.* (March, 1902), pp. 225 ff. E. Meyer, *Die Israeliten und ihre Nachbarstämme* (1906). W. F. Albright, "The Administrative Divisions of Israel and Judah," *JPOS*, vol. V (1925). A. Alt, *Die Landnahme der Israeliten in Palästina* (1925); "Die Gaue Judas unter Josia," *PJ* (1925), pp. 100 ff; "Das System der Stammesgrenzen im Buch Josua," *Sellin Fest* (1927); *Der Gott der Väter* (1929); *Die Staatenbildung der Israeliten in Palästina* (1930). M. Noth, *Das System der Zwölf Stämme Israels* (1930). A. R. Johnson, *The One and the Many* (1942). T. Jacobsen, "Primitive Democracy in Ancient Mesopotamia," *JNES*, vol. II (1943). C. U. Wolf, "Terminology of Israel's Tribal Organization," *JBL* (1946), pp. 45 ff; "Some Remarks on the Tribes and Clans of Israel," *JQR* (1946), pp. 287 ff.

C. U. Wolf

*TRIBES, TERRITORIES OF. The territories of the tribes do not represent areas which can be defined once and for all; on the contrary, they have been subject to historical change, particularly during the beginnings of the history of Israel. In the course of time, the tribe of Judah incorporated the groups of Caleb, Cain, Kenaz, and Jerahmeel, as well as the remnants of the tribe of Simeon; in this way its territory grew even after the time of the occupation of the land proper; and one must distinguish between Judah in the narrower and Judah in the broader sense. The tribe of Dan gave up the territory NW of Judah to which it had initially aspired, and finally established itself in the extreme N of Palestine. Together with Levi, the tribe of Simeon was driven out of its original domain in central Palestine; and even though it was not forced to forgo the possession of land entirely, like the tribe of Levi, which was entirely obliterated, it could, with its remnant, just barely gain a foothold at the S border of Palestine. Similarly, after failures in the W, the stunted tribe of Reuben finally found refuge beyond the Jordan in the territory of Gad, where its own settlements, interspersed among those of Gad, can be regarded as tribal territory only in a modified sense. For these and similar separate fates of the tribes, information is provided in the respective articles on the individual tribes.

The question of the extent of the tribal territories is vexed by still another difficulty; this lies embedded in the nature of the sources. Fortunately, we possess among the pertinent materials one presentation which attempts to picture the state of affairs when the situation had been somewhat solidified. This con-

sists of a system of a series of fixed boundary points which outline fairly precisely the territories of the tribes still existing at that time. It is very probable that this system dates back to the time before the monarchy, although not (as later tradition believes) to the generation following directly after Moses. Nevertheless, the figure of Joshua, who also took an active part as a mediator of territorial claims in Josh. 17:14 ff, is probably not associated with it merely by accident and may not be too far removed in point of time. If, therefore, there is no objection to the usefulness of this source from the historical point of view, there is all the more, from a literary point of view. That is to say, it has not been preserved in its original state but has been revised repeatedly in later times. First of all, the mere lists of names were changed into an actual description of the boundaries by means of a connective text, which takes account of the direction in which the boundary runs, its situation in the terrain, and the like. As an example we may take the following, in which the old fixed boundary points are italicized: "The boundary on the north side runs from the bay of the sea at the *mouth of the Jordan*; and the boundary goes up to *Beth-hoglah*, and passes along north of *Beth-arabah* . . ." (Josh. 15:5 ff). Unfortunately, the transformation of the text did not take place regularly; and since, apparently simultaneously, regular lists of town names were worked in in order to fill out the framework with content as much as possible, it is not always easy to distinguish the original text of the fixed boundary points from the original text of the lists of town names. At this point, particularly, the differences of opinion among the scholars appears.

The difficulty is still further increased by the fact that this combined text, in the process of being worked into the Deuteronomic historical work, has undergone transpositions, abbreviations, additions, and other retouchings. On the other hand, precise isolation of the old boundary-description text is necessary, because the lists of place names (town lists) are in part considerably more recent in date. So, e.g., the Judean list of place names (Josh. 15:21 ff), parts of which are also in the description of Benjamin (18: 21 ff) and constitute the whole of the present description of the territory of Simeon (19:1-9) and Dan (vss. 40-48), dates from the time of Josiah, as Alt has plausibly demonstrated. Alt's line of argument has not been invalidated by the recently expressed doubts of Cross and Wright, or of Kallai and Aharoni, who suggest a dating in the ninth century.

Another difficulty is inherent in even the older system of boundary points insofar as it notes not only the actual property of the tribes but, in addition, certain territorial claims, without indicating the transition from reality to theory. Here, to be sure, a second early document is of assistance, one whose origins go back to the period before the monarchy and is based upon the same conviction that Yahweh had promised the land of Canaan to his people without any reserve. This "negative inventory of possessions," as Alt called it (Judg. 1:27 ff; also vss. 18-21), lists those territories, particularly in the great plains, which single tribes could not wrest from the Canaanites. It corrects, therefore, those overextended

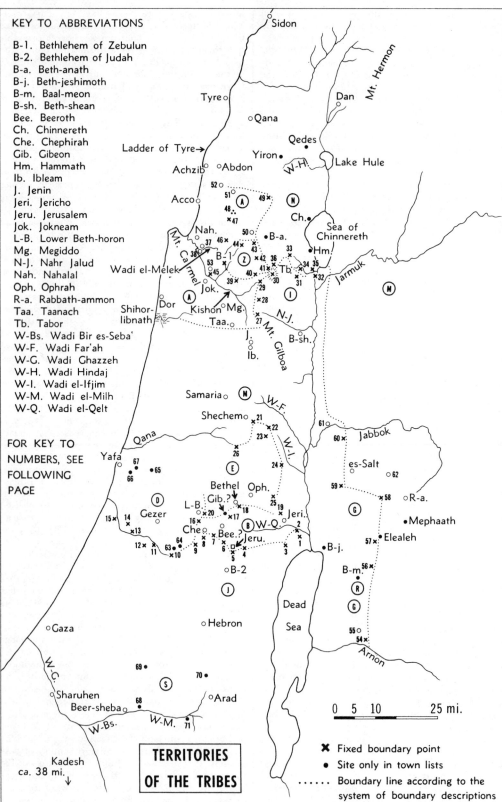

KEY TO ABBREVIATIONS

B-1. Bethlehem of Zebulun
B-2. Bethlehem of Judah
B-a. Beth-anath
B-j. Beth-jeshimoth
B-m. Baal-meon
B-sh. Beth-shean
Bee. Beeroth
Ch. Chinnereth
Che. Chephirah
Gib. Gibeon
Hm. Hammath
Ib. Ibleam
J. Jenin
Jeri. Jericho
Jeru. Jerusalem
Jok. Jokneam
L-B. Lower Beth-horon
Mg. Megiddo
N-J. Nahr Jalud
Nah. Nahalal
Oph. Ophrah
R-a. Rabbath-ammon
Taa. Taanach
Tb. Tabor
W-Bs. Wadi Bir es-Seba'
W-F. Wadi Far'ah
W-G. Wadi Ghazzeh
W-H. Wadi Hindaj
W-I. Wadi el-Ifjim
W-M. Wadi el-Milh
W-Q. Wadi el-Qelt

FOR KEY TO
NUMBERS, SEE
FOLLOWING
PAGE

TERRITORIES
OF THE TRIBES

✗ Fixed boundary point
• Site only in town lists
..... Boundary line according to the
      system of boundary descriptions

0 5 10   25 mi.

KEY TO NUMBERS FOR MAP ON PRECEDING PAGE

1. Beth-hoglah	25. Khirbet el-'Oja el-Foqa	49. Ramah
2. Beth-arabah	26. Tappuah	50. Khirbet Qana
3. Stone of Bohan	27. Jezreel	51. Yerka
4. En-shemesh	28. Shunem	52. 'Amqa
5. En-rogel	29. Hapharaim	53. Sheikh Abreik
6. Waters of Nephtoah	30. Tabor	54. Aroer
7. Mount Ephron	31. Shahazumah	55. Dibon
8. Kiriath-jearim	32. Beth-shemesh	56. Medeba
9. Chesalon	33. Adami-nekeb	57. Heshbon
10. Beth-shemesh	34. Jabneel	58. Ramath-mizpeh
11. Timnah	35. Lakkum	59. Betonim
12. Ekron	36. Aznoth-tabor	60. Mahanaim
13. Shikkeron	37. Tell el-Far	61. Sukkoth
14. Mount Baalah	38. Tell Harbaj	62. Jogbehah
15. Jabneel	39. Shadud	63. Zorah
16. Ras en-Nadir	40. Chisloth-tabor	64. Eshtaol
17. Ataroth-addar	41. Daberath	65. Jehud
18. Burj Beitin	42. Gath-hepher	66. Azor
19. 'Ain ed-Duq, Naarah	43. Rimmon	67. Bene-berak
20. Upper Beth-horon	44. Hannathon	68. Zephath-Hormah
21. Michmethah	45. Helkath	69. Ziklag
22. Taanath-shiloh	46. Beth-emek	70. Bethul
23. Janoah	47. Cabul	71. Moladah
24. Tell Sheikh edh-Dhiab	48. Khirbet Yanin	

TERRITORIES OF THE TRIBES

A — Asher	E — Ephraim	J — Judah	R — Reuben
B — Benjamin	G — Gad	M — Manasseh	S — Simeon
D — Dan	I — Issachar	N — Naphtali	Z — Zebulun

boundary demarcations; but since that is accomplished in bold outlines and in part deviating from the system of fixed boundary points, all kinds of questions remain as to details.

In spite of intensive work in the field, in which, since the twenties, the American and the German School of Archaeology in Jerusalem under Albright and Alt have especially taken part, the purely topographical questions which arise from location of biblical sites and boundary lines in the present-day topography are by no means all solved. Especially for Galilee, the earliest redactor of the source material was obviously not very well oriented. For this reason there is many a factor of uncertainty when an attempt is made in what follows to assign the territories of the Israelite tribes to the modern map. The basis is the system of tribal boundaries in the book of Joshua, which reproduces, in general, the situation shortly before the beginning of the period of the kings. We shall proceed in geographical sequence from the S to the N and consider first of all the land on the W side of the Jordan and then that to the E. *See* map "Territories of the Tribes." (Numerical superscriptions in this article refer to points on this map.)

1. Judah
2. Benjamin
3. Joseph
   a. Ephraim
   b. Manasseh
4. Issachar
5. Naphtali
6. Zebulun
7. Asher
8. The Transjordan tribal territories
   a. Gad
   b. Reuben
   c. The half-tribe of Manasseh
9. The remaining W Jordanian tribes
   a. Dan
   b. Simeon
Bibliography

1. Judah. There can be no doubt that what is described in Josh. 15:1-12 as the territory of Judah is the territory of Great Judah; for it already includes in its N-S dimension the settlements of the Calebites, the Kenites, the Kenizzites, the Jerahmeelites, and the Simeonites, from Hebron to Beer-sheba. The settlement area proper of the Judeans extends only approximately from the Siret el-Bella', the highest point of the principal watershed N of Hebron, to the height of Mar Elias between Jerusalem and Bethlehem. In vss. 2-4 even the wilderness (steppe), controlled by Judah and its friends, is included if the S boundary runs from the S tip of the Dead Sea past the Ascent of Akrabbim (Naqb es-Safa), thus roughly along the Wadi Fiqra, toward Kadesh-barnea to the oasis area of 'Ain Qedeis, 'Ain el-Qudeirat, and 'Ain el-Qeseimeh, and then bends around to reach the sea with the Brook of Egypt (Wadi el-'Arish). In the E the Dead Sea forms the undisputed natural boundary (vs. 5*a*). This boundary runs alongside the E slope of the mountains, the "wilderness of Judah," useful, in general, only as pasture land. But if it goes as far N as the mouth of the Jordan, it includes also a tip of the Jordan Valley. The course of the N boundary fully confirms the latter fact (vss. 5*b*-11). It begins in the vicinity of the mouth of the Jordan (hardly just at the southernmost point) and, passing by Beth-hoglah[1] ('Ain Hajlah), protrudes even up to the Wadi Qelt at Beth-arabah[2] ('Ain el-Gharabeh), but then swings back, apparently, to the general line of the Wadi Mukelik. At the point where this valley emerges from the mountains, "the stone of Bohan[3] the son of Reuben" should most likely be sought. The hinterland (דביר, "Debir," is a descriptive name) of the Achor Valley (el-Buqei'ah) and the region (read הגמימות, "Gilgal"; see Josh. 18:17) across from the Ascent of Adummim (Tal'at ed-Damm) likewise point to the mountain ranges along the Wadi Mukelik and its most northerly upper course, the Wadi es-Sidr. At En-shemesh[4] ('Ain el-Hod) the boundary reaches the last rise before Jerusalem, but then bends S around the city to En-rogel[5] (Bir 'Ayyub) and along the S slope of the Valley of Hinnom to the elevation at 3,212 feet between the railroad station and the Convent of the Cross. From there it extends N-NW to the spring of the Waters of Nephtoah[6] ('Ain Lifta), to again turn back—with a bulge at Mount Ephron[7], S of Bet Suriq, and near Kiriath-jearim[8] (Tell el-Azhar)—in a westerly direction and to arrive along Mount Seir on the N side of the "Forest Range" (Mount Jearim; still extant today in splendid remnants, between the Wadi el-Ghurab—or its many-named upper course stretching up to Kiriath-jearim—and the railroad valley) past Chesalon[9] (Kesla), at the descent to the so-called 'Artuf fault line. In the hill country the boundary goes through Beth-shemesh[10] (Tell er-Rumeileh) and Timnah[11] (Tell el-Batashi) to the "shoulder of Ekron"—i.e., in all probability to the hills NE of Khirbet el-Muqannah (=Ekron[12]), around which the Wadi es-Surar bends from the NW in a westerly direction—and arrives by way of Shikkeron[13] (Tell el-Ful) and Mount Baalah[14]—i.e., the hills by el-Mughar(?)—at Jabneel[15] (Yebna) and at the Mediterranean Sea. It is surprising that this description of the N boundary—apart from meticulously bypassing the territory of the city of Jerusalem—can present a relatively large number of points in the mountains, but then contents itself with a few main points along the not very much shorter way through the hill country and the coastal plain. The contrast is even greater if Ekron is identical with 'Aqir and if we agree that Shikkeron and Mount Baalah in Josh. 15:11 are secondary. Obviously only the stretch in the mountains represents the historical boundary of the tribal territory of Judah at the end of the period before the monarchy, while the rest exists as a boundary in idea only. Actually, even Beth-shemesh (HAR-HERES), according to Judg. 1:35, belonged to the cities which were not conquered. Furthermore, Kiriath-jearim may probably have defended itself for a relatively long time against the loss of its autonomy (Josh. 9), as it is unlikely that the Jebusites were quick to permit to be disputed their rights to the possession of the Plain of Rephaim, im-

mediately to the S of their city. In fact, the forward movement of the Judean settlement to the NW probably belongs to the movements of the tribe when it had already gained strength. From the foregoing it is automatically apparent that the "Great Sea" (Josh. 15:12) is once more merely the theoretical W boundary. The true boundary was formed for a long time by the wooded mountain slope along the 'Artuf fault line. Only gradually did the Judeans succeed in pushing their settlements forward to the edge of the hill country so that these areas then belonged to the permanent holdings of the state of Judah in the period of the kings. Cf., in addition, the location of Rehoboam's fortresses (II Chr. 11:6-10) and, finally, Josiah's division of the country into districts (especially Josh. 15:33-44).

2. Benjamin. Benjamin adjoins Judah on the NE. As a consequence its S boundary (Josh. 18:15-19) is identical with Judah's N boundary, but essentially only with its E tract; for Benjamin's settlement extended barely across the main watershed toward the W. As the W boundary, to be sure, a line is given (vs. 14) which runs from the "mountain [Ras en-Nadir[16]] that lies to the south, opposite Beth-horon" (i.e., Lower Beth-horon), almost due S to the mounds of the Judean city Kiriath-jearim[8] (Tell el-Azhar). In that way, however, the territories of Canaanite cities like Chephirah (Khirbet Kefireh, close to this border), Gibeon (el-Bireh? ej-Jib?), and Beeroth (ej-Jib? el-Bireh?), which were able to preserve in part their autonomy (Josh. 9) even until Saul's time, are, in the beginning, only ideally ascribed to Benjamin. That the same is true for Jerusalem is expressly confirmed by Judg. 1:21. In fact, the names of the Benjaminite list of towns in Josh. 18:21 ff, which originally constituted a portion of the list of districts in the kingdom of Judah at the time of Josiah, generally lead close to the main watershed or on across it toward the E. The N boundary (vss. 12-13) goes from the above-mentioned border mountain in the NW corner toward Ataroth-addar[17] (Khirbet 'Attarah; perhaps more to the W), consequently, up to the Wadi Selman rather directly toward the E. On the ridge of the mountains it swings toward the N, but leaves out the city of Bethel, earlier called Luz (cf. Josh. 16:2), and includes only the sanctuary (Burj Beitin[18]) which lies one kilometer to the SE on a knoll. From there it runs in a southeasterly direction through the "Wilderness," unfavorable to any settlement, down to the "shoulder of Jericho," whereby the last steep slope of the mountains is probably meant, and N past Jericho to the Jordan. Also in the Jordan Valley the Benjaminite settlement was probably rather feeble in the early period (cf. 6:26). The editor, who added the list of places in 18:21 ff, can, at a later period, name only Keziz, in addition to Jericho, and, according to its place in the list Keziz is more likely to have belonged to the tribe of Judah. Besides, the editor overextends the territory of Benjamin in the S by taking in Jerusalem, and, likewise in the N, by including Bethel (Beitin) and even Ophra (et-Taiyibeh), perhaps also Chephar-ammoni, if this name has been preserved in bowdlerized form in that of the present-day village of Rammun.

3. Joseph. The oldest form of the series of fixed boundary points appears to have treated Ephraim and Manasseh as a unit. The special development of Ephraim resulted in a special description of its boundaries—the heading now in Josh. 16:9*a*.

a. Ephraim. Ephraim's S boundary appears twice in Josh. 16: in vss. 1-3, as Joseph's boundary; in vss. 5-6*a*, as Ephraim's boundary. Its E portion (vs. 2) coincides naturally with the N boundary of neighboring Benjamin and lays claim expressly for Ephraim only to the "waters of Jericho," the oasis area of the 'Ain ed-Duq[19] and the 'Ain en-Nu'eimeh at the foot of the N "shoulder of Jericho." On the mountain ridge the city of Bethel (Beitin) across from the border sanctuary (el-Burj) falls to the Ephraimite side. The W part of the S boundary, then, runs N from Ataroth-addar[17] (Khirbet 'Attarah) across the Arkite territory along the transverse ridge later used by the most northerly Roman road from Jerusalem to Lydda, on which both Beth-horons lie, and presses forward to the sea by the way of Gezer (Tell Jezer). Again it follows from Judg. 1:29 (=Josh. 16:10) that the boundary, even in the hill country, is only theoretical; for this reason, as in the case of Judah, additional points to fix the boundary are lacking here. Otherwise, it is significant that this boundary does not coincide with that of the S neighbor, Judah. It is clear that the later redactor has saved the space here, which in his opinion belonged to the tribe of Dan and for which his sources provided no boundary description (*see* § *9a below*). From Judg. 1:35 one can conclude that this territory, too, was theoretically ascribed to "Joseph" when the series of fixed boundary points came into existence and that in no case did Benjamin's strip reach to the sea, but only in theory. In the severely abbreviated special description of Ephraim, Upper Beth-horon[20] (Beit 'Ur el-Foqa) occurs as an addition, while the detailed description of the complete Josephite S boundary names Lower Beth-horon (Beit 'Ur et-Tahta) at this point. Obviously the old series of fixed boundary points outlined only the area of the actual settlement of Ephraim, which, as was the case with Judah, found its limit first of all at the step downward from the hill country to the Shephelah. The actual W boundary ran along this rim, which with its forests constituted a good natural boundary, northward to the River Kanah. In just the same way the E boundary specified for Ephraim (Josh. 16:6-7) obviously follows the actual edge of the settlement when it runs from the most northerly point, Michmethah[21] (Khirbet Juleijil across from Shechem) SE to the landmark of the Taraniq (elevation *ca.* 3,400 feet) in the immediate vicinity of which both Taanath-shiloh[22] (for the early period probably Khirbet Ta'nah et-Tahta rather than Khirbet Ta'na el-Foqa) and Janoah[23] (Khirbet Yanun) lie. The boundary then is not drawn generously to the Jordan but goes down the Wadi el-Ifjim to Tell Sheikh edh-Dhiab[24] (Ataroth?), if not still farther along the edge of the mountains toward the S, not coming down into the Jordan Valley until the Khirbet el-'Oja el-Foqa.[25] Even then the boundary is not the Jordan, but Naarah[19] (Tell ej-Jisr at the "waters of Jericho") where it runs into the Plain of Jericho, which was first resettled under Ahab, from Ephraimite Bethel (I Kings 16:34). Ephraim's N boundary (Josh. 16:8; 17:7) turns S from Michmethah first and does not

turn off toward the W until near Tappuah[26] (Tell Sheikh Abu Zarad near Jasuf) to reach, with a great sweep back to the N, the Brook Kanah (Wadi Qanah)—and along this deep-cut valley, the edge of the plain (and across it, the sea). On the Brook Kanah the new 1:100,000 map records in grid 159-174 a Khirbet Qanah, *ca.* two miles SW of Jinn Safut. At what point the actual W boundary met this N boundary cannot be said. The mention of the sea in Josh. 16:8 is to be credited to the redaction, as also that in vs. 6 and the mention of the Jordan River in vs. 7.

b. Manasseh. The territory of the tribe of Manasseh is more difficult to ascertain. The S boundary (Josh. 17:7-10*a*) naturally corresponds to Ephraim's N boundary. Ephraim's E boundary must also be considered Manasseh's S boundary; here on the far side of the main watershed a broad wedge of Manassite territory pushed forward toward the S, at least as far as the latitude of Qarn Sartabeh, thus including the mouth of the Wadi Far'ah, and possibly even that of the Wadi el-Ifjim, in addition. That the Jordan constitutes the E boundary is obvious; but the question is, How far N? The description of this boundary was a victim of redaction and is replaced by the note that "on the east Issachar" is reached by Manasseh (vs. 10*b*). The additional note of the redactor in vs. 11 states that Manasseh still had towns in Issachar (and Asher), evidently Beth-shean (Tell el-Husn) and Ibleam (Khirbet Bel'ameh); with Dor (et-Tanturah) the list of places in Asher begins (Endor is secondary; cf. LXX). From this it may be concluded that the old description of the boundaries theoretically ascribed these unconquered Canaanite towns, or more precisely only Beth-shean (not Ibleam, which only the redactor took to be Issacharite because he confused the En-gannim mentioned in Josh. 19:21 with Jenin) to Issachar. The "negative inventory of possessions" (Judg. 1:27) awarded them to Manasseh—probably at the time of the temporary decline of Issachar, as Issachar is not mentioned at all in Judg. 1 and its Beth-shemesh is included in Naphtali. The redactor resolved the contradiction after the manner of Solomon. Most probably, however, the actual E boundary of Manasseh ended already at the S end of the Plain of Beisan. The description of the N boundary again is replaced by the note that "on the north Asher is reached" by Manasseh (Josh. 17:10*b*). Once more the comment following (vs. 11) permits the conclusion that along with Dor, and also with Taanach (Tell Ta'annak) and Megiddo (Tell el-Mutesellim), unconquered Canaanite towns, were theoretically included in Asher in the original boundary description. The later redactor took care of the matter in the same manner as in the case of Issachar. While the possession of the Plain of Jezreel continues to be largely theory in any case for the period before the monarchy, the boundary description of Asher (*see* § 7 *below*) seems to show that Manasseh's settlement actually did not include the Carmel area (for the more exact course of the N boundary, *see also* §§ 4, 7, *below*). That the sea constitutes the W boundary only in theory and that Manasseh's settlement scarcely advanced into the coastal plain, although the crossings are easier everywhere here, requires no discussion.

4. Issachar. Here the problem becomes urgent as to how much of Josh. 19:17-23 is boundary description or the text of a town list (*see above*). It is certain that the available series of boundary points has been supplemented by other place names; it is not so certain that the names there only concern the Levite towns in Josh. 21:28-29. Some possibilities of the identificaton of sites lying to the side of the presumed boundary lines are very tempting (Hapharaim = et-Taiyibeh; Beeroth = el-Bireh; Anaharath = en-Na'urah; En-hadda = Kerm el-Hadetheh); they are by no means conclusive. A boundary line appears clearly in the W (Josh. 19:18-19); from Jezreel[27] (Zer'in), which evidently is the corner point (this makes either the equation of En-gannim [vs. 21] with Jenin or the inclusion of En-gannim in the boundary fixed points series impossible) by way of Chesulloth, which is not identical with Chisloth-Tabor[40] (et-Tireh) near Iksal, toward Shunem[28] (Solem) and northward on toward Hapharaim[29] (cf. Bir el-Hufeijir) up to Tabor[30], which the system of boundary descriptions ascribes to Issachar. Also the N boundary (Josh. 19:22) is recognizable to some extent. It runs from Tabor eastward by way of Shahazumah[31] (probably Kerm el-Hadethe, rather than Tell Mekarkash, if not still farther N; *see § 5 below*) and thus to the Jordan immediately to the S of the Sea of Chinnereth. The Jordan naturally formed the E boundary, at Beth-shemesh[32] only in theory, since the town could not be captured (Judg. 1:33). The question is only how far the E boundary extended to the S before it joined Manasseh. However, if Issachar could still be considered Manasseh's E neighbor (Josh. 17:10; *see § 3b above*), the whole Plain of Beisan up to the Wadi el-Malih must be included in its territory, at least theoretically, but the "slave at forced labor" (Gen. 49:15) already had more substantial relations with the Canaanites of the plains. Whether Issachar also possessed land on the top of the mountains bordering the plain on the W is open to question. In any case, the equation Rabbith = Rabe at Ras Ibziq is no proof, since הרבית is merely an error in writing הדברת, "Daberath," and thus represents the Zebulunite town (Josh. 19:12) which, deviating from the old series of fixed boundary points, is added to Issachar in the list of the Levite towns (ch. 21), just as En-gannim (if this is Jenin) probably is. The actual settlement territory of Issachar is the fertile basalt plateau to the N of the Nahr Jalud up to the Tabor line.

5. Naphtali. Naphtali is Issachar's N neighbor, although, strange to say, Josh. 19:34 names Zebulun specifically as Naphtali's S neighbor. Did the redactor merely forget to mention Issachar, or does Josh. 19:33 contain the rest of the S-boundary fixed points, which then in vs. 22 were given only insofar as the places are Issacharite? There are, indeed, remarkably few points on the long stretch in vs. 22! In the second case, if one accepts the generally well-founded identification suggestions of Saarisalo, one gets a line which runs from the Tabor district first of all toward the NE to Khirbet Damiyeh (= Adaminekeb[33], surely not Adamah of vs. 36, which is to be found N of Chinnereth = Tell el-'Oreimeh), then along the SW edge of the Sahl el-Ahmah back toward Yemma, in the vicinity of which (Tell

en-Na'am? Khirbet Shemsin?), Jabneel[34] is probably to be sought, and by way of Khirbet el-Mansurah (= Lakkum[35]) across from el-'Abeidiyeh (= Beth-shemesh[32]) along the N side of the Wadi Fejjas out to the Jordan. Against this solution speaks the fact that the second point named in 19:33, Elon-be-Zaanannim (RSV "the oak in Zaanannim"), lies near Kedesh according to Judg. 4:11. If that is not an incorrect gloss or does not imply a Kedesh other than the one to be identified with Qedes near Lake Hule, one would have to regard Josh. 19:33 as, not the S, but rather the N, boundary, and, of course, to assume a mistake on the part of the redactor when he thinks of the series as running toward the E instead of toward the W, since it would be impossible to find room for three additional villages between an Elon near Tell Qades and the Jordan. The W boundary of Naphtali (vs. 34) must coincide with a part of the way with the boundary of Zebulun, which is directed from Tabor toward the NW. This is revealed in the summarized statement of the redactor that Naphtali borders on Zebulun in the S. But beforehand he mentions by name two points, of which at least the first is probably, although not necessarily (cf. I Sam. 10:3), to be sought in the vicinity of Tabor, while the second might lie on the common boundary with Asher, for which, otherwise, the corresponding summarizing formulation must again suffice. For the first, Aznoth-tabor[36], Alt suggested Khirbet Umm Jebeil, which might be considered for Heleph (Josh. 19:33), if Saarisalo's suggestion of Khirbet 'Arbathah is not adequate. Perhaps, however, Aznoth-tabor lies still farther to the W or even the NW. The other, Hukok, is hardly the well-known Jaquq, but presumably at the angle in the curve of the W boundary, where it turned away from the part common to it and Zebulun directly toward the N as the part common to it and Asher. Thus Hukok should probably be sought on the Sahl el-Battof. The point corresponds farther N to Ramah (er-Rameh), allotted by the redactor to Asher, whereby the Wadi Sellameh appears as a border valley. In the forests of the interior of Galilee the boundary was probably to a large extent a theoretical matter, as a continuation of the fixed-boundary-point series in Upper Galilee appears to be lacking altogether. Naphtali pushed its settlements out mainly from the Valley of the Jordan, which is given as the E boundary (Josh. 19:34; ביהודה is a corruption of בירדן; cf. LXX), up into the Galilean highland and in the old period scarcely advanced far beyond the edge, as the town list appended in vss. 35b-38 shows. The towns enumerated here from Hammath (Hammam Tabariyeh) in the S to Kedesh in the N hardly lead out of the Jordan Valley. Qedes lies *ca.* 3.1 miles to the W of the edge of the valley. If Yiron should actually be identified with Jarun, that shows a route up the Wadi Hindaj, rich in water, and along which the name Merj el-Hadireh could reflect En-hazor, which in the list precedes Yiron! Besides, the last two names on the list are taken over secondarily from the "negative inventory of possessions" (Judg. 1:33), where Beth-shemesh is included with Naphtali, in contradiction to the boundary description of Issachar (Josh. 19:22). Issachar's claims were evidently divided among his two neighbors during a period of temporary weakness (cf. Judg. 1:27, where Beth-shean is Manassite). Beth-anath could be el-Eb'eineh on the E part of the S edge of the Sahl el-Battof and thus the Canaanite counterpart of the Naphtalite Hukok, as Beth-shemesh is to Naphtalite Lakkum at the outlet of the Wadi Fejjas.

6. Zebulun. Among the Galilean tribes Zebulun is the only one whose territory is provided with a relatively complete boundary description (Josh. 19: 10-14). In this instance the redactor of the old fixed-boundary-point series, as in the case of Ephraim, found no theoretical overextension of the boundaries. That Zebulun did, nevertheless, at one time lay claim to the S Plain of Acco is shown by the other old document (Judg. 1:30) which is brought in at the beginning of the town list in Josh. 19:15 as a supplement. Nahalal is Tell en-Nahl and Kattath or Kitron probably Tell el-Far[37] or Tell Harbaj[38]. The system of boundary descriptions leaves the whole Plain of Acco and the Carmel area, in addition, to Asher, and it confines Zebulun within easily recognizable boundaries which amount to only its actual settlement area. Accordingly, the S boundary (Josh. 19:10-12) runs at an obtuse angle from the vertex Shadud[39] (Tell Shadud) westward to the "brook which is east of [lit., 'opposite'] Jokneam"—i.e., the brook which to the NE across from the Tell Qeimun, comes down from the region between Bethlehem and Umm el-'Ammad, and eastward by way of Chisloth-Tabor[40] (et-Tireh N of Iksal) toward Daberath[41] (Khirbet Dabureh). It keeps strictly to the N mountain rim of the Plain of Jezreel between Bethlehem in the W and Tabor in the E. Bethlehem (Beit-lahm) is first brought up, strange to say, in the town list in vs. 15, perhaps because it belongs with the unconquered Canaanite cities. From the foot of Tabor the E boundary (Josh. 19:13) turns inward into the hilly country by way of Japhia (which has nothing to do with Yafa SW of Nazareth) toward Gath-hepher[42] (Khirbet ez-Zerra' near el-Meshed) and Eth-kazin (Kefr Kenna or already at the Sahl Tur'an) and on farther, always north-northwestward, toward Rimmon[43] (Rummaneh) at the S edge of the Sahl el-Battof. Beyond this plain Zebulun's settlement did not extend to the N at the time of the old boundary description. The N boundary (vs. 14) is fixed by Hannathon[44] (in all probability Tell el-Bedewiyeh) at the W end of the plain and, in addition, by the "Valley of Iphtahel," the upper course of the Wadi el-Melek, which drains the Sahl el-Battof toward the SW and, with a bend to the W, N past Bethlehem on to the coastal plain. A W boundary is not explicitly named; it resulted of its own accord from the two "brook" valleys complementing each other by following the same direction, behind which a protective forest belt spread out to the coastal plain. Thus Zebulun's territory is a model of settlement by an Israelite tribe which worked its way into the hill country away from the great plains ruled by the Canaanites.

7. Asher. Asher's territory is the most difficult to reconstruct, because in Josh. 19:25-30 the fusion of the boundary description text with extraneous material is simply indissoluble, and, in addition, the topography at this very spot is still in a sad state. It is clear that the boundaries, as in the case of Judah

and Joseph, are again theoretically extended through to the sea. And indeed, as the SW point, Shihor-libnath is specified (vs. 26)—i.e., the swamp which fills the narrow strip of coastal plain S of Dor, shortly before the mountains recede from the sea. The NW point cannot be determined with the same certainty, since Hosah (vs. 29), mentioned before the end of the boundary at the sea, is not known. Tyre, which is named before Hosah, and which is itself already situated on the coast, and likewise Sidon in vs. 28 have come in secondarily. Asher's dreams hardly went farther N past Ras en-Naqura. The E boundary (Josh. 19:27-29) is also clear to some extent. It touches the territory of Zebulun—i.e., the SW corner —in all probability from the same point of departure as the boundary described in vss. 26-27, thus from Helkath[45] (perhaps Tell Harbaj[38] in the SE corner of the Plain of Acco, but more likely at the opposite end of the Kishon Gorge and closer to Jokneam), perhaps Tell el-Qassis and the Valley of Iphtahel (i.e., that part of the Wadi el-Melek which runs E-W, since a section which runs N-S cannot "touch" [reach] a line leading "northward" [vs. 27a]), and goes on beyond the valley "toward the north," through Beth-emek and Neiel, to come out first at Cabul (Kabul), "to the north" of the town (vs. 27b). Beth-emek[46] is thus not to be sought on the Sahl el-Battof but possibly on the Sahl et-Taiyibeh, ca. 3.1 miles farther W, and Neiel is S of Cabul[47], so that Khirbet Yanin[48] is eliminated. Since the list of names which follows in vs. 28 seems to be secondary and can be interpreted in connection with the extension of the Asherite territory northward to Tyre and Sidon, Ramah (er-Rameh below the Jebel Heidar) might well be the next point in the original description of the E boundary. The change in direction would be expressed appropriately in "turns" (vs. 29). But it is strange that the border contact with Naphtali, which is to be expected from Josh. 19:34, is not mentioned; presumably the mention of Ramah sufficed for this. Or is one, after all, to regard the Kanah mentioned in vs. 28, not as the Qana in the vicinity of Tyre, but rather as Khirbet Qana[50] on the N edge of the Sahl el-Battof? The boundary with Naphtali in the early period is to a large extent theoretical, but nevertheless an advance by Asher into the interior of the land along the great rise or fault from Lower to Upper Galilee is quite conceivable, and would then lead to that definition of claims over against Naphtali. From Ramah the boundary leads back toward Hosah and comes to an end at the sea. One does not have the impression from vs. 29b that it makes a special bend near Hosah, and can conclude from this that it actually represents already the N boundary of Asher. Thus a location for Hosah on the edge of the mountains may be considered perhaps in the vicinity of Yerka[51]-'Amqa[52]. The old system of boundary descriptions does not seem to have gone so far N with the N boundary as the somewhat later list of the unconquered cities which is worked into Josh. 19:29 (at the end), 30, from Judg. 1:31, and which claims for Asher N of Acco in addition: Achzib (ez-Zib), Mahalab (Mahalib between Tyre and the Nahr el-Qasimiyeh), and even Sidon; nor so far as the other secondary series (Josh.

19:28), which keeps then to the same latitude with Abdon (Khirbet 'Abdeh) but goes beyond the Ladder of Tyre with Hammon (on the Wadi Hamul?) and Kanah (Qana, *ca.* 7 miles SE of Tyre). The older boundary system did not need to go so far to the N because it could already satisfy Asher's claims in the S. The shifting of Asher's claims to the N is evidently only compensation for the fact that Asher had to relinquish to Manasseh (Judg. 1:27) the strip from Dor to the peak of Carmel, and to Zebulun (vs. 30) the southernmost part of the Plain of Acco.

The S boundary of Asher presents problems in other respects. It is described in Josh. 19:25-26 in such a way, unfortunately, that the redactor gives the series of fixed points with the exception of the end without connecting text and thus leaves the reader without indication as to the position of the places with regard to one another. The reason for this procedure is probably the fact that he had to reconcile sources which differed among themselves. It is clear that if the boundary "touches [lit., 'reaches'] Carmel on the west," it must come from the E. It is also clear that whether one puts Helkath to the N or to the S of the Kishon ravine, there is no room for the series of six towns between it and Carmel in a straight line. If one considers further that, according to Josh. 7:10, Manasseh borders on Asher in the N, but not on Zebulun, and that in the list of Thut-mose III the towns of Achshaph, Mishal, and perhaps Allammelech, which also figure in Josh. 19:25-26, stand in close proximity to Taanach and Ibleam, then one cannot avoid the conclusion that the series in vss. 25-26*a* is to be sought on the Plain of Jezreel and therefore belongs naturally to those places which Manasseh claimed afterward (Judg. 1:27) and which the redactor likewise conceded to it in Josh. 17:11 with the conciliatory formula "in Asher." Perhaps a series of villages is meant, running diagonally across the SE tip, which reached the W mountains somewhere near Taanach, thus allocating the large portion of the plain, including Taanach and Megiddo, to Asher. The fact that the redactor has ignored the border contact with Zebulun and Issachar on the N and E edges of the plain is not stranger than the same situation with Naphtali on the N part of Asher's E boundary. Thus Asher becomes Manasseh's N neighbor (Josh. 17:10) already at the SE tip of the Plain of Jezreel. Asher finally becomes Manasseh's neighbor—and here the boundary is no longer theoretical—in the section of the boundary which leads diagonally through the mountains to Shihor-libnath and includes Dor, on the coastal plain, and, in the mountains, even the so-called Bilad er-Ruha, S of the present Jebel Karmel. It is in this area that Asher's origins seem to have lain, which provided the tribe at first with claim upon the Plain of Jezreel, until it pushed its settlement across the bridge of woods N of Sheikh Abreik[53] westward past Zebulun farther N and could lay claim to the Plain of Acco as compensation when the stronger Joseph group contested its claim to the Plain of Jezreel.

8. The Transjordan tribal territories. The land E of the Jordan, like the territory of Joseph, is treated as a uniform territory in the old system of the series of fixed boundary points. But, while the description of Joseph was supplemented already in the older period by an appropriate special description of Ephraim, the division of the land E of the Jordan among Reuben, Gad, and the half-tribe of Manasseh is the work of later redaction and just as unreliable historically as carving out the so-called tribal territories of Simeon and Dan in the land W of the Jordan.

a. Gad. Originally Gad may have given its name to this whole area. The list of places in Num. 32:34-38, far from being systematized and therefore not suspect, shows Gadites in the S as well as in the N and the Reubenites, who had apparently immigrated later, only in the middle in mingled settlement with the Gadites. According to the text of the boundary description, the S boundary (Josh. 13:16) is evidently formed by the Arnon, on the N side of which lies Aroer[54] (Khirbet 'Ara'ir) and in whose broad ravine, though probably downstream, the "city that is in the middle of the valley" is probably to be sought. The E boundary (Josh. 13:16, at the end [read עַד], 26-27*aδ, b*) leads from Aroer straight N at first (rather along the present-day pilgrimage road) by way of Medeba[56] (Madeba) and Heshbon[57] (Hesban) toward Ramath-mizpeh[58] (Khirbet es-Sar). The list of places in Num. 32 mentions Dibon[55] (Dhiban) here as Gadite. Then the boundary turns westward toward Betonim[59] (Khirbet el-Batneh, S-SW of es-Salt) and from there runs N again toward the Jabbok, where, on the S side, Mahanaim[60] (Tell Hejjaj) is situated and, on the N side, Lo-debar may be sought. Then the boundary shifts a bit to the W and proceeds along the Jordan Valley close to the edge of the mountains, to reach the S end of the Sea of Chinnereth, including the plain to the E of the Jordan outlet from the sea. The narrow strip in the Jordan Valley opposite the Canaanite cities of Beth-shean and Beth-shemesh, which were still independent when the old boundary system originated, was Gadite only in theory; it is not by chance that town names are missing here. Even the more recent list of towns which has been worked into the description of the boundaries (Josh. 13:17-20, 25, 27*a*; cf. Num. 32:3, 34-38) mentions N of Sukkoth[61] (Tell Deir 'Alla), in addition, at most, Zaphon. It was the "half-tribe of Manasseh" that crossed the Jordan here and pressed ahead into the mountains (for this, *see § 8c below*). Gad's settlement territory was limited to the lower Jordan Valley and to the S part of the mountain ascent up to the line designated above. The lists of places, which do not coincide completely with the E boundary, show that Gad, too, went beyond this line in the course of time—e.g., up to Jogbehah[62] (Khirbet Jebeihah). That Gad also included primarily the mountains of Gilead (in the narrower sense, the forest district to the N and NE of es-Salt up to the Jabbok) in its expansion, is attested by the not-infrequent equation of the names Gad and Gilead.

b. Reuben. The position of Reuben's territory is fixed only by the town list. There is better or worse recollection according to whether one must date the list early or late. In any case, the redactor of Josh. 13 apportions the places differently from Num. 32:

34-38, which probably belongs to one of the older Pentateuchal sources. If one relies on the latter, the Reubenite settlements lie between the latitude of Elealeh (Khirbet el-'Ale, two miles N-NE of Heshbon-Hesban) and that of Baal-meon (Ma'in), and extend westward from the *ca.*-eleven-mile-long route between these two places, not as far W as that distance: Kirjathaim, according to Euseb. Onom. 112.16-17, was only ten Roman miles westward from Medeba. The list in Josh. 13 (aside from the insertion of the Levite cities [vs. 18=Josh. 21:36-37], which assumes an extension of Reuben in the E to Mephaath [Khirbet Nefa'a, S of 'Amman] as in the S to the Arnon) holds to the same general latitude, so far as the additional towns can be located, and adds Beth-jeshimoth (Tell el-'Azeimeh near Khirbet Suweimeh) in the Jordan Valley. Even thus there was scarcely a compact Reubenite area of settlement between a N and a S portion of Gadite property, a fact which follows from the uncertainty of the apportionment. But the later references may be correct in indicating that in the designated area the majority of the stunted tribe of Reuben could finally settle down among the Gadites.

c. The half-tribe of Manasseh. The wooded mountain country between the Jabbok and the Jarmuk, the so-called 'Ajlun, is designated in the later literature as the territory of the "half-tribe of Manasseh" (also in Josh. 13:29-31). In the system of the series of fixed boundary points the corresponding description is lacking; it is not to be expected, in view of the route of the Gadite boundary in the Jordan Valley (*see* § 8*a* above). The area became colonial land in the strict sense. The settlement, which certainly began even before the period of the kings (*see* MANASSEH), probably did not take place from the first by the same tribe. Even more in the period of the kings, all the N Israelite tribes certainly had a part in opening up the territory until it embraced "from Mahanaim, through all BASHAN," or "half GILEAD."

9. The remaining W Jordanian tribes. There are also no boundary descriptions in existence which make it possible to discern the actual extent of the territory of these tribes in the premonarchical period. What the place lists in Josh. 19 present is the artificial concept of a much later time.

a. Dan. It has been established above that the S boundary of Joseph does not coincide with the N boundary of Judah in the hill country and that the redaction artificially created a space for Dan here, although there was no corresponding boundary description at its disposal. Evidently when the system of the boundaries was set up, the little tribe had already migrated to the N or was on the way there, where, on the other side of the closed Israelite settlement territory (Kedesh in Naphtali appears to be the most northerly point, which at that time had perhaps not yet even been reached), it established itself in a city-state at the foot of Mount Hermon (Josh. 19:47). Boundaries could not be determined there. As a substitute the later redactor felt he should describe the territory of Dan, known from the traditions of Judg. 13-18, and for this purpose used a portion of the district list of Josiah in which the new acquisitions of the king in this area were already specified (Josh. 19: 41-46). At the beginning he placed the two towns

Zorah[63] (Sar'ah) and Eshtaol[64] (Eshwa'), which were well known from the Danite story of Samson (Judg. 13:2, 25) and were named in the second district in Josiah's list (Josh. 15:33), and he attached to them the whole series of the fifth district, after he had filled in the gap, which arose in Josh. 15:45, by taking in the entire land of the Philistines with the use of the catchword "Ekron." In so doing it did not matter in the least to him that places which were claimed for Judah in the boundary description in vss. 10 ff suddenly become Danite (Beth-shemesh[10], Timnah[11], Ekron[12]), nor did it matter that the northward curve of this incomplete tube-shaped district toward Jehud[65] (el-Jehudiyeh) or Azor[66] (LXX Jazur) and Beneberak[67] (Ibn Ibraq) transgressed the old boundary of Joseph or Ephraim, which runs from Beth-horon to the sea by way of Gezer. There is no need for further proof that this reconstruction of the tribal area of Dan can make no claim to historical probability.

b. Simeon. The case of Simeon is like that of Dan. Here, too, later redaction first created out of Joseph's list of districts a substitute for the missing old boundary description. Only this time the redactor did not simply make use of a whole district, but, instead, made an extract of the district in question (cf. Josh. 19:2-7 with 15:26-32) and reused it as the territory of Simeon, with the express statement that this was a portion of Judah's territory (19:9). For this, too, there is a historical fact to start with, insofar as the remnant of Simeon, after the catastrophe at Shechem, was actually able to gain a foothold once more in the extreme S, in the territory of the town of Zephath-hormah (Judg. 1:17). Hormah[68] is probably Tell es-Seba', three miles E of the sanctuary of Beer-sheba (Bir es-Seba'), which likewise grew into a town in the period of the kings, and because of its religious importance was moved up by the redactor to first place in the Simeon list. The territory stipulated by the list appears not to go beyond the Wadi es-Seba' or el-Milh in the S, and the ridge of Khashm el-Buteiyir running northward from Beer-sheba and its continuation to Ziklag[69] (Tell el-Khuweilfeh) in the W, and to keep to the edge of the mountains of Judah in the N; while in the E the ridge extending from Darejat to the SW and perhaps the Wadi el-Qarjetein, which accompanies it on the E side, could be considered the border (Moladah[71] = Tell el-Milh? Bethul[70] = Khirbet el-Qarjetein?). Sharuhen (Tell el-Far'ah) is an outpost and definitely not an old Simeonite possession. In other respects, too, doubts arise as to the historical knowledge of the redactor, for his Simeon list probably does not represent an "extract" which has been carefully considered in its details: the three names of Josh. 15:27 are omitted in 19:2, probably only because they have the same beginning (וחצר), and likewise Iim (עיים) of Josh. 15:29 in 19:3 (וע), while מרכבות (ביתה) and (חצר) סוסה in 19:5 are attempts to correct מדמנה and סנסנה, but only made changes for the worse. If this is so, then the redactor has given as Simeonite the second part of the list of the southernmost district of Josiah just as it was. He was approximately correct in so doing. To be sure, a place like Hazar-gaddah, "above the Dead Sea" according to Euseb. Onom. 68.17 ff—in fact, everything beyond Arad

(Tell 'Arad) to the E—was Kenite and thus belonged to larger Judah (Great Judah) but not to Simeon. But the tract of Beer-sheba certainly identifies Simeon's old territory in a way which is essentially and historically correct.

Bibliography. General: There are many papers and notes in the periodicals of the Palestine societies and schools, especially *AASOR, BASOR, IEJ, PEQ, PJB, RB, ZDPV.* See also commentaries on the book of Joshua and general works on biblical geography. See specifically: A. Alt, "Das System der Stammesgrenzen im Buch Josua," *Sellin-Festschrift* (1927), pp. 13-24 = *Kleine Schriften,* I (1953), 193 ff. M. Noth, "Studien zu den historisch-geographischen Dokumenten des Josuabuches," *ZDPV,* 58 (1935), 185-255. J. Simons, *The Geographical and Topographical Texts of the OT* (1959).

On the S tribes: W. F. Albright, "Egypt and the Early History of the Negeb: The Topography of Simeon," *JPOS,* 4 (1924), 149-61. A. Alt, "Judas Gaue unter Josia," *PJB,* 21 (1925), 100-16 = *Kleine Schriften,* II (1953), 276 ff. M. Noth, "Die Ansiedlung des Stammes Juda auf dem Boden Palästinas," *PJB,* 30 (1934), 31-47; "Zur historischen Geographie Südjudäas," *JPOS,* 15 (1935), 35-50. A. Alt, "Bemerkungen zu einigen judäischen Ortslisten des Alten Testaments," *BBLAK = ZDPV,* vol. 68, no. 3 (1951), pp. 193-210 = *Kleine Schriften,* II (1953), 289 ff. F. M. Cross and G. E. Wright, "The Boundary and Province Lists of the Kingdom of Juda," *JBL,* 75 (1956), 202-26. Z. Kallai-Kleinmann, "Notes on the Topography of Benjamin," *IEJ,* 6 (1956), 180-87; "The Town List of Judah, Simeon, Benjamin and Dan," *VT,* 8 (1958), 134-60. Y. Aharoni, "The Northern Boundary of Judah," *PEQ,* 90 (1958), 27-31. Z. Kallai, *The Northern Boundaries of Judah* (1960).

On the central tribes: W. J. Phythian-Adams, "The Boundary of Ephraim and Manasseh," *PEQ,* 61 (1929), 228-41. K. Elliger, "Die Grenze zwischen Ephraim und Manasse," *ZDPV,* 53 (1930), 265-309. W. F. Albright, "The Site of Tirzah and the Topography of Western Manasse," *JPOS,* 11 (1931), 241-51. A. Fernandez, "Los limites de Efráin y Manasés," *Bibl.,* 14 (1933), 22-40. K. Elliger, "Neues über die Grenze zwischen Ephraim und Manasse," *JPOS,* 18 (1938), 7-16. J. Simons, "The Structure and Interpretation of Josh. XVI-XVII," *Orientalia Neerlandica* (1948), pp. 190-215. E. Danelius, "The Boundary of Ephraim and Manasseh in the Western Plain," *PEQ,* 89 (1957), 55-67; 90 (1958), 32-43. E. Jenni, "Historisch-topographische Untersuchungen zur Grenze zwischen Ephraim und Manasse," *ZDPV,* 74 (1958), 35-40. P. N. Simotas, *E perigraphe ton synoron Ephraim kai Manasse* (1959).

On the N tribes: W. F. Albright, "The Topography of the Tribe of Issachar," *ZAW,* 44 (1926), 225-36. A. Saarisalo, *The Boundary Between Issachar and Naphthali* (1927). A. Alt, "Eine galiläische Ortsliste in Jos. 19," *ZAW,* 45 (1927), 59-81. Y. Aharoni, *The Settlement of the Israelite Tribes in Upper Galilee* (1957; in Hebrew).

On the E tribes: A. Bergmann, "The Israelite Tribe of Half-Manasseh," *JPOS,* 16 (1936), 224-54. M. Noth, Beiträge zur Geschichte des Ostjordanlandes, I: "Das Land Gilead als Siedlungsgebiet israelitischer Sippen," *PJB,* 37 (1941), 50-101; II: "Israelitische Stämme zwischen Ammon und Moab," *ZAW,* 60 (1944), 11-57; III: "Die Nachbarn der israelitischen Stämme im Ostjordanlande," *BBLAK = ZDPV,* vol. 68, no. 1 (1949), pp. 1-50. J. Simons, "Two Connected Problems Relating to the Israelite Settlement in Transjordan," *PEQ,* 79 (1947), 27-39. M. Noth, "Gilead und Gad," *ZDPV,* 75 (1959), 14-73.   K. Elliger

TRIBULATION [צרה, תלאה; θλῖψις, pressing, squeezing]. A term denoting affliction of various kinds. The Greek word is used especially to refer to the "great tribulation" of the end time, from which the elect will be rescued, as foretold in Dan. 12:1, where the LXX and Theod. render צרה by θλῖψις

(cf. Mark 13:19 and parallels; Rev. 7:14). The sufferings of Christians in apostolic times signified that the "great tribulation" was approaching. *See also* Suffering and Evil.   F. F. Bruce

TRIBUNAL [βῆμα]. An alternate form of Judgment Seat.

TRIBUNE trĭb'ūn [χιλίαρχος, commander of a thousand]; KJV CHIEF CAPTAIN. A Roman military officer in charge of a Cohort, such as that in Jerusalem at the time of Paul's visit (Acts 21-25). The Captain who seized and bound Jesus (John 18:12) was likewise a tribune.   N. Turner

TRIBUTE [מכס (Num. 31:28); מנחה (Judg. 3:15); ענש (II Kings 23:33); משא (II Chr. 17:11); מדה (Ezra 6:8)]. A compulsory contribution exacted by one prince or state of another, or by a superior power of an inferior, as in a suzerainty treaty.

Samuel clearly warned Israel what it would mean in terms of taxation and oppression if they set up a king to rule over them (I Sam. 8:10-18). One does not present himself empty-handed before his own king or other rulers (I Sam. 10:27). To submit to a king's rule is to recognize his sovereignty or to enter into a suzerainty covenant; to do so is to accept the obligation of rendering tribute. Such giving of gifts, we know from the tablets from Tell el-Amarna,* was mutual to overlord as well as vassal. When Hezekiah king of Judah was ill, his superior, Merodach-baladan prince of Babylon, sent gifts to him (II Kings 20:12; Isa. 39:1). Figs. CLA 35; TEL 10.

Usually, however, the tribute was paid by the inferior power in the treaty or covenant to the superior. Insofar as Israel's Covenant was of the suzerainty type, her sacrifices and offerings to Yahweh are to be viewed in this light. *See* Sacrifice and Offerings.

Aside from what the kings of Israel and Judah exacted of their own people for support of the royal court (*see* Tax), these Israelite rulers not infrequently received tribute from foreign princes and peoples. It is specifically said that the Syrians brought tribute to David (II Sam. 8:6) and that "all the kingdoms from the Euphrates to the land of the Philistines and to the border of Egypt" brought tribute to Solomon (I Kings 4:21—H 5:1).

In N Israel the house of Omri, especially Ahab, received tribute from Israel's weaker neighbors. On Ahab's death Mesha king of Moab ceased to pay tribute and rebelled against Israel (II Kings 3:4-5; *see* Moabite Stone). When Judah was defeated by Jehoash of Israel, the latter exacted gold and silver from temple and palace in Jerusalem (II Kings 14:14). Jehoshaphat as well received tribute from the Philistines and Arabs (II Chr..17:11), and Uzziah accepted tribute from the Ammonites (II Chr. 26:8). Among the royal psalms is a prayer for the prosperity of the king to whom all nations should render tribute (Ps. 72:10).

Tribute is to be distinguished from the booty which the conqueror forcefully takes in war. However, from the spoils of war a certain amount may be levied as tribute to God (Num. 31).

Apart from certain periods of national aggrandizement Israel was accustomed in her turn to give tribute to foreign powers. Israel was more often in the position of vassal than of overlord. The sons of Jacob, when they went to Egypt to seek relief because of famine, took with them tribute gifts (Gen. 43:11-12). Ehud, one of the judges in Israel's early history, carried tribute on a visit to Eglon king of Moab (Judg. 3:15-18).

Soon after the N kingdom, Israel, broke away in independence of the Davidic monarchy in Judah, Shishak king of Egypt invaded the S kingdom and took away both temple and palace treasures, as well as the shields of gold Solomon had made. Archaeological evidence from Megiddo in Palestine and Byblos in Phoenicia attest to Shishak's prestige and the tributes paid him. *See bibliography*.

When the house of Omri in N Israel waned in power, it was Syria which was in a position to command tribute (II Kings 12:18).

When the new Assyrian Empire asserted itself in the ninth and eighth centuries, Israel frequently felt the burden of its expansion in the form of tributes paid, to Adad-nirari III, to Tiglath-pileser III, to Shalmaneser V (II Kings 17:3; cf. Hos. 10:6), to Sargon II, and to their successors until Babylonia arose to weaken Assyria's hold, when tribute was exacted either by Egypt (II Kings 23:33) or by the Neo-Babylonian Empire (II Kings 16–25). For extrabiblical sources on Assyrian and Babylonian dominance, *see bibliography*.

Judah was normally obligated to Egypt for its military security (II Kings 18:21) but at times was forced, as was Ahaz, to appeal to Assyria for help. Tribute was the price for the help Tiglath-pileser afforded (II Kings 16:5-9). After the defeat of Samaria by Shalmaneser V and Sargon II, Judah was subject to Assyria's ambitions and was forced to withstand siege by the Assyrian forces under Sennacherib. Whatever was the cause of the failure of the siege (II Kings 19:7, 35-36), Hezekiah was forced to pay heavy tribute to Sennacherib, who states in what is now called the Sennacherib Prism (*see bibliography*) that he exacted a second tribute in addition to the former mentioned in the book of Kings (II Kings 18:13-16; cf. Isa. 36–39).

Though Hezekiah opened his storehouses as a gesture of submission to Merodach-baladan of Babylonia (II Kings 20:12-15), it was still Assyria which held the dominant position in the seventh century until near the close of the century, when Judah's allegiance was constantly torn between the new Babylonian power and her old friend Egypt. In all these positions Judah was the debtor, and tribute was the price of military and political stability. Pharaoh Neco laid a tribute on Jehoiakim, to be paid in silver and gold (II Kings 23:33-35). When Nebuchadnezzar defeated Judah in 597 B.C., it was Babylonia which reaped Judah's substance. However, as is now known, Egypt was by no means a weak power, and both Jehoiakim (II Kings 24:1) and Zedekiah (24:20) turned toward Egypt for help (Ezek. 17). However, Babylonia finally dominated the picture and absorbed as tribute the last of Judah's wealth (II Kings 25).

For the subsequent history of the tribute obligations of the Jewish people and the half-shekel temple tax, *see* TAX.

Bibliography. J. B. Pritchard, *ANET* (1955), pp. 263-64, 281-301, 307-11, contains Egyptian, Babylonian, and Assyrian historical texts where exaction of tribute is a recurring boast of the conqueror.   J. A. SANDERS

TRIGON trī'gŏn. *See* MUSICAL INSTRUMENTS § B4*b*.

TRINITY [Lat. *trinitas, coined by* Tertullian; *cf.* τριάς, *first used in this sense by* Theophilus of Antioch]. The coexistence of Father, Son, and Holy Spirit in the unity of the Godhead. While not a biblical term, "trinity" represents the crystallization of NT teaching. Thus, in I Cor. 12:4-6, Paul correlates "Spirit," "Lord," and "God" (cf. Eph. 4:4-6); a similar correlation appears in the benediction of II Cor. 13:14. Cf. the trinitarian baptismal formula of Matt. 28:19 (echoed in Did. 7:1), which may have replaced the earlier formula "into the name of the Lord Jesus" for purposes of the Gentile mission. See also Acts 2: 33; I Pet. 1:2; Rev. 1:4-5*a*. The text about the three heavenly witnesses (I John 5:7 KJV) is not an authentic part of the NT. A further adumbration is provided by the logion concerning the Father and the Son in Matt. 11:27 = Luke 10:22, alongside the parallelism of the "Son of man" and the "Holy Spirit" in Matt. 12:32 = Luke 12:10. The OT concepts of the Wisdom and Spirit of God (cf. especially Prov. 8:22 ff) have influenced many NT passages used as foundations for the later formulation of trinitarian doctrine (e.g., John 1:1 ff; Col. 1:15 ff; Heb. 1:2-3).

Bibliography. J. R. Harris, *The Origin of the Doctrine of the Trinity* (1919).   F. F. BRUCE

TRIPOLIS trĭp'ə lĭs [Τρίπολις, three cities]. The Greek name of a Phoenician seaport N of Byblos, representing a league of three cities dating from the fourth century B.C.; the modern Tarabulus.

Neither the founding nor the original name of the city is known. Older views related its origins to the decline of BYBLOS; others, which connect it with the colonization of Aradus in the eighth century B.C., are no longer considered tenable. The Canaanite name אתר has been found on a coin dated 189-188 B.C., but the interpretation is highly uncertain. Probably during the late Persian period the city became a center of conclaves for Phoenician cities in this region, the name signifying that it was a joint colony founded by peoples from the three cities of Sidon, Tyre, and Aradus. Strabo (Geography XVI.2.15) and Pliny (Nat. Hist. V.78) describe the three walled sections as separated a stadium's distance from one another. After the Battle of Issus more than four thousand Greek mercenaries in the Persian army fled to Cyprus and Egypt in boats seized in the harbor at Tripolis. In 162 B.C., Demetrius I came to Tripolis, and after killing Antiochus V and Lysias regained his father's kingdom (II Macc. 14:1-2; cf. I Macc. 7:1-4; Jos. Antiq. XII.x.1). The city gained its freedom from Seleucid control in 111 B.C.; under Pompey's reorganization it became a city-state. According to Josephus (War I.xxi.11), Herod built a gymnasium at Tripolis. Christianity is said to have been established here by the apostle Peter (Clementine *Homilies*

From *Atlas of the Bible* (Thomas Nelson & Sons Limited)

77. Tripolis, with snow-covered Lebanon Mountains in the background

11:36; *Recognitions* 6:15), and the list of bishops in the Christian community is known from A.D. 325 on.

Fig. TRI 77.

Bibliography. A. H. M. Jones, *The Cities of the Eastern Roman Provinces* (1937), pp. 231, 251; Pauly-Wissowa, *Real-Enzyklopädie*, Zweite Reihe, vol. VII A1 (1939), cols. 203-7.

E. W. SAUNDERS

TRIREME trī'rēm [τριήρης]. A galley with three men on each bench, each rowing one oar. The three oars passed together through the oar box. *See* SHIPS AND SAILING.

Jason sent sacred ambassadors to the games at Tyre, with three hundred silver drachmas, for the sacrifice to Hercules; but those who took the money used it instead to outfit triremes (II Macc. 4:18-20).

B. H. THROCKMORTON, JR.

TRIUMPH. The translation of a number of different words and expressions (nouns and verbs). It is difficult to isolate "triumph" from such other words as "victory" and "overcome."

In the OT "triumph" is usually God's triumph on behalf of Israel, over her enemies (cf. Exod. 15:1, 21 [גאה]; Deut. 33:29 [גאוה]; I Kings 22:12, 15 [צלח]; Pss. 18:50 [ישע]; 60:8=108:9 [רוע]; Isa. 45:25 [צדק]; Zech. 9:9 [צדיק]). The word also appears, especially in the Psalms, to describe known or hoped-for personal triumphs over enemies (Pss. 41:11 [רוע]; 54:7; 118:7 [ראה]; cf. Job 17:4 [רום]; Prov. 28:12 [עלץ]).

The most important passages in the NT are Col. 2:15, where God triumphs (in the Cross, or in Christ) over hostile supernatural powers; and II Cor. 2:14, which may be translated as in the RSV or as follows: "causes us to triumph," or "leads us in public procession." The Greek verb in both passages is θριαμβεύω.   B. H. THROCKMORTON, JR.

TRIUMPHAL ENTRY. The approach and entrance of Jesus, riding on a colt, into Jerusalem at the beginning of his last days; signifying an aspect of his messianic mission (Matt. 21:1-11; Mark 11:1-11; Luke 19:28-44; John 12:12-19). Mark indicates little messianic triumph in this event, but Matthew shows the city stirred at the coming of the "Son of David." In Luke the disciples hailed Jesus as "King," a title which John emphasizes, though the disciples did not at first understand "these things." John alone reports palm branches (12:13), from which the later term "Palm Sunday" originated. The

entry has been variously interpreted: (*a*) that Jesus, knowing messianic prophecy, fulfilled it in symbolic actions as he presented himself to Jerusalem; (*b*) that the event was originally an enthusiastic greeting of disciples, rejoicing over their leader coming to the Holy City, and was later filled with messianic meanings.   D. M. BECK

TROAS trō'ăs [Τρωάς, 'Αλεξάνδρεια ἡ Τρωάς]. A city located in Mysia in NW Asia Minor, on the shore of the Aegean Sea. It was opposite the island Tenedos and lay *ca.* ten miles S of ancient Troy (Ilium).

The ancient name of the site was Sigia (Strabo *Geography* XIII.1.47). The city was founded by Antigonus, one of the successors of Alexander the Great, and named Antigonia Troas. Later, *ca.* 300 B.C., Lysimachus king of Thrace added improvements and renamed it Alexandria Troas (Troas was originally the name of the region around ancient Troy). It was for a time the residence of Seleucid kings, and then for a time a free city. In 133 B.C. it came under Roman control, and was a large and important city.

Julius Caesar, according to Suetonius (*Julius Caesar* 79), thought of moving his capital to "Alexandria or Ilium," and similar hints are given of Augustus and Constantine. These stories at least show the prominence of Troas in Roman times. Under Augustus, Troas received a Roman colony, and Strabo called it "one of the renowned cities" of his time (*Geography* XIII.1.26). In the early second century an aqueduct was built to bring water into the city from Mount Ida. Its ruins and the ruins of baths, theater, etc., can still be seen. The city walls can be traced; they are *ca.* six miles in length.

Paul visited Troas at least three times, but never stayed long. After being turned away from Bithynia as a possible field of work, he passed through MYSIA and came to Troas, still uncertain where to go. A vision at night gave him a call to Macedonia, and he and his helpers promptly sailed from Troas to Neapolis, stopping overnight at the island of

Samothrace (Acts 16:7-11; here in vs. 10 begins the first of the "we passages" of Acts).

When Paul left Ephesus on his so-called third missionary journey, he went northward and "came to Troas to preach the gospel of Christ," and found "a door was opened for me in the Lord"; but because of uncertainty about the rebellious church at Corinth his "mind could not rest," and he "went on to Macedonia" to meet Titus and learn how things were at Corinth (II Cor. 2:12-13).

After his visit to Macedonia and Greece, Paul returned through Macedonia and crossed to Troas to meet a party of his friends who had assembled there and were waiting for him. This time Paul stayed seven days, and "on the first day of the week, when we were gathered together to break bread, Paul talked with" his companions and the church people of Troas (Acts 20:1-12). A second "we passage" (*see* ACTS OF THE APOSTLES) begins at Philippi and includes the report of the stay at Troas; Luke was familiar with Troas, though it is odd that he does not say whether Paul made any converts there on his first stop, just as Paul says nothing of converts in II Cor. 2:12-13. The existence of a church there, however, is clear in Acts 20:11-12. If II Tim. 4:13 is part of a letter Paul wrote during the period covered by Acts, he must have left his cloak and books with Carpus at Troas on this third visit. But if Paul was released from imprisonment at Rome and traveled again in Asia Minor, this verse will indicate that he again visited Troas.

In later times Troas became the seat of a bishopric.

Bibliography. D. Magie, *Roman Rule in Asia Minor* (1950), Index under "Alexandria Troas."   F. V. FILSON

TROGYLLIUM trō jĭl'ĭ əm [Τρωγύλλιον, Τρωγύλιον, Τρωγυλία, *etc.*]. A promontory formed by the W part of Mount Mycale on the W shore of Asia Minor. Near it on the W was the island of SAMOS, whose E end lay just N of the end of the promontory; a strait less than a mile wide separated island from mainland.

According to the Western and Syrian texts of the "we narrative" in Acts 20:15 (DHLP, etc.; cf. RSV mg.), "we crossed over to Samos, and having tarried (overnight) at Trogyllium we came on the next day to Miletus." The usually superior early MSS (א ABC, etc.) omit the reference to anchoring at Trogyllium; they indicate that Paul's ship anchored overnight at Samos and the next day reached Miletus (so RSV). If the reference to Trogyllium is original, the ship could have reached it from "opposite Chios" by sailing either along the W and S sides of Samos or through the strait on its E side.

An anchorage just E of the W tip of Trogyllium is today called "St. Paul's Bay."

Bibliography. Strabo *Geography* XIV.1.12-13; W. M. Ramsay, *St. Paul the Traveler and the Roman Citizen* (1896), pp. 292-94; J. H. Ropes, *Beginnings of Christianity*, III (1926), 194-95.   F. V. FILSON

TROPHIMUS trŏf'ə məs [Τρόφιμος, nutritious]. An Ephesian (Acts 21:29) who, with Tychicus, met Paul at Troas on his final visit to Jerusalem (20:4-5) and accompanied him to Jerusalem, where he represented

the Asian churches in the presentation of the collection for the church there.

Jews from the province of Asia saw Paul and Trophimus together in Jerusalem and supposed that Paul had taken him into the temple—i.e., within the barriers which separated the Court of the Gentiles from the Court of Israel (Acts 21:29). As Trophimus was apparently an uncircumcised Gentile convert to Christianity, Paul was accused by these Jews of defiling the temple (Gentiles were absolutely forbidden to enter the Court of Israel). This was the occasion of Paul's arrest.

II Tim. 4:20 says: "Trophimus I left ill at Miletus." If this is the same Trophimus, the statement is not reconcilable with Acts, according to which Trophimus was not left behind in Miletus on the trip to Jerusalem, but was seen there with Paul (Acts 21:29); and according to which Paul did not pass through Miletus on the trip from Jerusalem to Rome (cf. 27:7-8) and so could not have "left" Trophimus there.

         B. H. THROCKMORTON, JR.

TROUGH [רהט]; **WATERING TROUGH** [שׁקת]. A watering receptacle for animals. *See* RUNNEL.

TRUMPET. *See* MUSICAL INSTRUMENTS.

TRUSTEE [οἰκονόμος] (Gal. 4:2); KJV GOVERNOR. An administrator or manager. In both the KJV and the RSV the word is usually translated STEWARD.

TRUTH.
1. Terminology
2. In the OT
3. In the NT
   a. General
   b. John
   c. Paul
Bibliography

1. Terminology. The understanding of the biblical view of truth encounters special difficulties on account of the long and intricate history of the terminology. To most modern people, truth is the agreement between the intended subject matter of a word or a sentence, on the one hand, and the nature of the fact to which the word or sentence refers, on the other. But such a definition fails to do justice to what is designated as truth in the Bible. The English word "truth" is the common rendering of ἀλήθεια in the NT and the LXX. However, in both of them the term corresponds frequently to the Hebrew אמת, a noun derived from the verb אמן, which means "to sustain, to support." The basic meaning of the root is most clearly seen in the adjectival *Niph'al* participle נאמן, which is rendered "firm, solid, reliable" (Gen. 42:16), "faithful, tested" (Deut. 7:9; Isa. 1:21), "perceptible" (especially painfully so; Deut. 28:59), "true" (Ps. 19:9), and "lasting" (Ps. 89:29). The multiplicity of the renditions is an indication of the complexity of the fact to which they refer. Accordingly, אמת designates a reality, which is firm and unchanging. But these are not abstract properties. As synonyms indicate, the noun implies the ability to keep unchanged and whole and to be firm on account of an intrinsic energy. Consequently it is capable of imparting itself to other entities. Thus in legal language, אמת designates the factual action or an ascertained condition (e.g., Deut. 13:14), as contrasted with unfounded statements, and as modifier of other nouns it characterizes them as "right, correct, genuine, moving toward their intrinsic goal."

Thus, according to context, אמת should be translated "steadiness," "unchangeableness," "stability," "soundness," "faithfulness," "constancy," "truth," "loyalty," or "justice." The LXX has therefore considerably narrowed down the meaning of the word by rendering it in four fifths of all passages by ἀλήθεια and congeners, and twelve times by δικαιοσύνη ("righteousness"). The revised versions have frequently replaced the "truth" of the KJV by "faithfulness" (e.g., Gen. 24:27; 32:10; Exod. 34:6; Deut. 32:4; Josh. 24:14; I Sam. 12:24; II Sam. 2:6; 15:20). Similarly in Exod. 18:21, the "men of truth" of the KJV has given room to "men who are trustworthy" in the RSV; in Isa. 39:8 the text refers to "peace and security" rather than "peace and truth"; Isa. 42:3 says that God will "faithfully bring forth justice" (RSV) or probably "a justice the results of which cannot be broken." Josh. 2:12 does not speak of a "true token" (KJV) but rather of a "sure sign" (RSV), which is not misleading, or perhaps a "reliable sign," in which one can trust on account of the circumstances in which it has been given. On account of the complex meaning of the root אמן, the noun אמונה is rendered in the LXX both πίστις ("trust, trustworthiness, faith") and ἀλήθεια, and thus its meaning often merges with that of אמת.

2. In the OT. Though the noun originally designates a property of things, it is found in the OT applied to God as well as to human beings. God is a God of truth (Deut. 32:4; II Chr. 15:3), not "the true God" as contrasted with false ones, but rather one upon whom his people can rely. He "keepeth truth [RSV 'faith'] for ever" (Ps. 146:6 KJV). In Ps. 85:11 the rendering "Truth [RSV 'faithfulness'] will spring up from the ground" is in either case inadequate. The passage states that God's will shall be manifested everywhere without meeting opposition, just as a plant grows up naturally. The fact that in not a few passages God's אמת is coupled with his חסד ("steadfast love") indicates that his "truth" is not so much contrasted with falsehood as with fickleness (cf. Gen. 32:10; Pss. 25:10; 26:3; 40:11).

With reference to God, "truth" designates a quality of his nature or will—viz., constancy and unchangeableness. His actions give full and adequate expression to his nature, and this is to be so permanently, because he does not want it to be otherwise. Thus he can rightly be called a fortress, a refuge, or a rock, and his "truth" is the reason why people can trust in him. In a universe which is constantly in flux and change (it "floats upon the waters"), he proves to be the only unchanging reality. Thus, while in the Greek view of truth the cognitive element predominates, it is the ontological one in the OT. The fact, nevertheless, that אמת was rendered in the LXX by ἀλήθεια is best explained by the tendency inherent in God's אמת to manifest itself or rather to manifest himself as a person who is known by the way he acts (Exod. 3:14: "I AM WHO I AM"). Since this "truth"

of God is not an incidental property, but rather the very nature of God's will, which cannot be altered by changing circumstances, it follows that God's commandments are not arbitrary demands, but rather have "truth" in them (Neh. 9:13; Hos. 4:1). Such usage implies that the OT standard of justice is not found in an abstract sociological or ethical principle but in God's way of dealing with this world. Hence, belief in whatever is contrary to God's truth —e.g., false gods, false prophets, false doctrine—is not to be considered as regrettable ignorance but rather as something which ought not to be and therefore is to be stamped out.

Since according to the OT everything in this world is created by God and has its destination through the divine purpose, for which it has been brought into being, God's "truth" is to reflect itself in man's life. Thus the king, e.g., who is God's representative as ruler, must show אמת (e.g., Ps. 45:4), not "truth" (RSV) but rather unwavering adherence to the standards of the law (cf. Prov. 29:14). Likewise, the covenant demands of the Israelites to serve God in constancy, not to fall away (I Sam. 12:24, where the KJV has "in truth," the RSV, more appropriately, renders "faithfully"; cf. I Kings 2:4; II Kings 20:3; II Chr. 32:1). In Hos. 4:1 ("There is no truth [RSV 'faithfulness'] . . . in the land"), the RSV is probably correct in rendering "faithfulness." The prophet seems to allude to Israel's marital relationship with God.

As the manifestation of God's will, אמת is therefore synonymous with his commandment (e.g., Ps. 43:3), and thus in turn with man's appropriate response to it—e.g., "Thou desirest truth in the inward being" (Ps. 51:6), or "Truth has fallen in the public squares" (Isa. 59:14; cf. vs. 15: "Truth is lacking"). Thus while "truth" implies veracity, truthfulness, it is not confined to it, but rather designates the whole field of religious and moral life, as it agrees with God's will. This usage has become dominant in rabbinical Judaism. The man "who speaks truth from [or in] his heart" (Ps. 15:2) is a person whose thoughts and aspirations, which according to the OT originate in the heart, are directed toward God's אמת. Similarly the "men of truth" (Exod. 18:21 KJV; RSV "men who are trustworthy") are, as the context shows, people who in their judgments are eager to bring the facts to light. Calling upon the Lord "in truth" (Ps. 145:18) is not contrasted with hypocrisy, but rather, as the parallels in Josh. 24:14; Isa. 10:21 show, refers to a devotion in which the God of the covenant is worshiped—i.e., which is in accordance with what God has done for his people.

In addition to this specifically religious usage of אמת, the term is also found in the OT in a general sense. Thus the "right seed" (Jer. 2:21 KJV; RSV "pure seed") is one that will not deteriorate but will reproduce a plant having the same qualities as that from which it was taken; and Joseph wants to find out whether in his brothers there is "truth"—i.e., truthfulness (Gen. 42:16). In other instances, "truth" designates the actual fact over against mere contentions, particularly in a trial (e.g., Deut. 13:14; Zech. 8:16). "True" judgment (e.g., Zech. 7:9) is therefore one which is based upon established facts and cannot be disputed. In other instances, "truth" is contrasted with appearance or pretense (e.g., Judg. 9:15: "if in truth [RSV 'in good faith'] you anointed me." The "true" laws of God (Neh. 9:13) are laws which suit the actual conditions (cf. Pss. 19:10; 119:160).

3. In the NT. *a. In General.* In the NT, usage of ἀλήθεια and congeners goes back to the OT. However, under the influence of the LXX, and probably also the Hellenistic environment in which the Jews had lived for more than three hundred years, when the NT was written, the cognitive element is predominant in the Christian writings. However, particularly in references to God, not only do OT phrases recur, but also in the newly coined ones the ontological element is an essential ingredient. Failure to notice this fact has here, as in the case of "knowledge," led to seriously wrong interpretations.

The ontological aspect of truth is emphasized in phrases such as: "You . . . are established in the truth that you have" (II Pet. 1:12), which does not refer to doctrines but rather to saving facts, though known ones. In Hebrews, I and II Peter, and James (e.g., 1:18; 3:14; 5:19-20) this connotation is particularly outspoken. "Truth" is the true and eternal reality. Similarly truth is reality as contrasted with imagination and mere appearance —e.g., in Acts 12: 9, where the KJV rendering: "[Peter] wist not that it was true," has been correctly altered by the RSV into: "He did not know that [it] . . . was real" (cf. I John 2:27). The RSV has improved the rendering of John 7:26, by altering the KJV rendition: "Do the rulers know indeed that this is the very Christ?" into: "Can it be that the authorities really know that this is the Christ?" In I Pet. 5:12 the "true grace" does not designate a grace that is in accordance with a true proposition, nor is it contrasted with hypothetical "false" graces, but rather Peter points out that despite the oppression and persecution which the readers experience, God's grace is the real and solid foundation of their faith. In other passages the true is the genuine over against the conventional or the pretended—e.g., in Luke 16:11, where the "unrighteous mammon" is confronted with the "true riches," or, more exactly, the "true good" (e.g., Weymouth). Often truth is contrasted with error, falsehood, or lies (e.g., Mark 5:33; John 4:18; 10:41; Rom. 9; II Cor. 6:8; 7:14; 12:6; Phil. 1:18; I Tim. 2:7; I John 2:27; cf. Matt. 22:16; Mark 12:14).

A true Hebraism in the NT is the frequent use of *amen* or its Greek equivalent, ἀληθῶς, particularly as introducing words of Jesus, and commonly rendered "truly" or "verily" (e.g., Matt. 14:33; 26:73; John 4:42; 17:8). It characterizes a statement as being beyond doubt and irrefutable. Another Hebraism is probably the characterization of the Christian witness as true (e.g., John 5:31-32; 8:13-14; 21:24; Tit. 1:13; III John 12; *see* TESTIMONY; WITNESS). The phrase describes the testimony, not only as being in agreement with the facts, but also as based upon facts that are reliable, so that others can use it as the foundation of their life. In John 7:18 the rendition of the RSV obscures the Hebraic background by reading: "He who seeks the glory of him who sent him is true, and in him there is no falsehood." The KJV translates the last word correctly as "unrighteousness." But "true" also follows OT usage. It does not mean "truthful" but rather, as evidenced by its opposite,

"complying with the will of God." In a few instances "truth" denotes "veracity" (e.g., Mark 12:14; I Cor. 5:8), but more sparingly than the older exegetes assumed. Greek influence is also noticeable in Rom. 1:25, where Paul charges the pagans that "they exchanged the truth about God for a lie." The truth here designates that which lies hidden behind the appearances yet can be apprehended by the mind (vs. 20). But here, too, the modern translation detracts from the Hebraic background of the phrase by reading "truth about God," where the KJV has correctly "truth of God." The RSV thinks of a propositional truth which, however, could not be contrasted with the "lie" which consists in "worshiping and serving the creature rather than the Creator." The "truth of God" is the true nature of God, which all men apprehend intuitively, but which idolaters adulterate by wrongly interpreting it.

Particularly controversial in recent exegesis are those passages in which the "way of truth" or "the truth" in an absolute sense is referred to. The prevailing tendency was to understand these expressions as referring to a set of propositions, or to the supreme idea of truth in a Platonic sense. There can be no doubt but that both in the OT and in the NT truth is expressed in verbal statements, and that none of the NT writers refers to a truth or knowledge that is purely mental and without, or above, words. This fact implies, especially in the NT, the intrinsic consistency of the statements expressing the truth, and the absence of contradiction. However, whereas in Greek philosophy and science a true statement is one whose subject is a general concept, the truth of which the NT speaks describes a particular fact. In Heb. 10:26, e.g., acting contrary to the "knowledge of the truth" is explained as "spurn[ing] the Son of God and profan[ing] the blood of the Covenant" (vs. 29). Furthermore, this truth is characterized as a "present" one, or probably one that has come to the believers (II Pet. 1:12). This is not a Greek mode of expression, as little as the phrase "being established in the truth." A Greek philosopher would speak of a truth which had been established by means of demonstration, and of a thinker who establishes himself by means of right thinking. The phrase in II Peter points rather to an intrinsic dynamic of the truth, as in the OT. The "way of truth" (II Pet. 2:2) is obviously a reminiscence of Ps. 119:30 and designates primarily the conduct that is in keeping with the divine אמת. It is identical with the "way of God" (Matt. 22:16; Mark 12:14; Luke 20:21) which, according to the Pharisaic interlocutors, Jesus was "teaching in truth"—i.e., in accordance with God's אמת. But when it is said in II Pet. 2:2 that on account of the licentiousness of some members of the congregation the way of truth will be reviled, the author can hardly think of a doctrinal system. The term "way of truth" is obviously here a self-designation of the church, reminiscent of the simple "Way" found in Acts 9:2; 19:9, 23; 24:14 (cf. 16:17; 18:25-26). The addition of "truth" intimates its self-realization in the life of the church.

b. John. More frequently than all the other NT writers together, John and Paul use ἀλήθεια and its congeners—an indication of the importance they assigned to this concept. Both are also aware of the fact that they are moving in a world in which truth is conceived of in terms of philosophy, mythology, or mystagogics. Thus as they present their views, they are engaged in polemics against those approaches to the truth. It is obvious that to John ἀλήθεια is the OT אמת. He adds two new features to it, however—viz., the identification of Christ with the truth, and the description of the appropriation of the truth. That the problem of truth occupies the central place in John's Gospel is indicated by the fact that the judge Pilate, who represents the powers of this world, asks the question: "What is truth?" (John 18:38). Jesus reiterates constantly that God is "true" (John 3:33; 7:28; 8:26; 17:3; I John 5:20; cf. Rev. 6:10). Hereby he does not want to say that God is sincere, nor that he is the true God, but rather that he acts in accordance with the relation which prevails between the Creator and a sinful world. God never loses sight of the goal which he had "from the beginning"; this is evidenced by his sending the Son. Accordingly his ways (Rev. 15:3), his judgments (Rev. 16:7), and his words (John 17:17; cf. Rev. 19: 2; 21:5; 22:6) are true—i.e., in accordance with his plan. Thus, as the one who determines himself and is not deflected from his course by the things of the world, he is the only one that may be called God.

Whereas the OT places the emphasis upon God's being unchangeable and unchanging and thus the determining center of the universe, John lays stress upon the intrinsic energy of the divine truth, which comes to men and wants to be known (e.g., I John 5:20; cf. John 5:33; 18:37). While John shares with certain tendencies in Hellenism the conviction that God's truth is in opposition to a world which is under the Devil (John 12:31; I John 5:19) and thus lacks truth (John 8:44), he differs from Hellenism in describing God as one who saves this world and makes this fact universally known. There is no Gnosticism in John. It is against this background that Jesus calls himself the Truth (John 14:6; cf. 16:13), not for what he is, but for what he does—viz., as one "who has told you the truth which I heard from God" (John 8:40; cf. 5:33; 8:13-14). All that he does originates in the divine truth and makes the latter real in this world. The intimations of God's saving plan, which were given in the history of Israel, have now become actuality in Jesus. Thus he is the "true light" (John 1:9); the "true vine" (John 15:1, referring to Jer. 2:21), which bears fruit; and the "true bread from heaven" (John 6:32), which, unlike the manna in the wilderness (Exod. 16), will never perish, but rather sustain life everlasting in all who eat of it (John 6:55). All the "I am" predications of John's Gospel proclaim the same truth. Unlike the beings of this world, which come into existence and pass away again, Jesus, like the Yahweh of Exod. 3:14, has being in himself. He IS.

This is not Platonism, with its contradistinction between the idea and its imitation in concrete reality, but rather the contrast between the provisional and the final. Thus Christ is not the "essence of all truths," because he is not a truth that is distilled from the things of this world, but rather his ministry indicates the goal for which this world is destined. Truth has therefore an eschatological character in John, though the evangelist places more emphasis

upon the contrast between announcement and fulfilment than on that between past and future. As the truth Jesus is not simply disclosing what is in God; he is the manifest saving presence of God in this world. As a result, all that Jesus does and offers is true (e.g., John 7:18; 8:16)—i.e., in accordance with his nature and with God's plan. But this is not "realized eschatology." As the operation of God's presence in this world, the Truth is engaged in a battle against all falsehood (e.g., John 8:40, 44). Furthermore, far from being a static "principle" of truth, Jesus as the Word that was in the beginning (John 1:1) communicates himself to other people by consecrating them (John 17:17) and making the truth known to them (John 1:17). In accordance with his function of communication, Jesus can therefore promise that his work will be continued by the "Spirit of truth" (John 14:17; cf. 15:26; 16:31; I John 4:6; 5:7). Through him people will not only be familiarized with the truth, as in Greek mystagogics, but also be transformed according to their divine destination—i.e., to become like Christ (e.g., I John 3:1-2).

In order to reach this goal, people must accept or receive Christ (John 1:11-12), so that the truth is "in us" (I John 1:8; cf. III John 4) as the "true imperative" (I John 2:8; RSV "commandment") which determines our self. In this way we are "of the truth" (e.g., John 18:37; cf. I John 3:12)—i.e., the truth becomes our very nature, we are "true worshipers" (John 4:23), whom this indwelling truth (John 14:17) has delivered from the slavery of sin (John 8:34) and the Devil (John 8:44). These effects presuppose a knowledge of God and of Christ (e.g., I John 2:22-23; cf. John 8:19) and thus of the Bible (e.g., John 5:39), but it is the truth, or the unction of the Holy Spirit (I John 2:20, 27), which by its intrinsic energy (III John 8) leads man from confused knowledge to insight (e.g., John 8:32; III John 12) and from sin to love (e.g., I John 1:8; II John 1-3) and sanctity (John 17:17). Thus we "walk in the truth" (II John 4 KJV; III John 3-4 KJV) or "in the light" (I John 1:7), and worship "in spirit and truth" (John 4:23-24)—namely, in Him, who is the Truth (*see* LIGHT).

Most characteristic of John's view of truth is the phrase "to do the truth" (John 3:21; I John 1:6). It indicates that the truth is not a proven proposition, in consequence of which one does certain things, but rather a divine impulse, which the believer actualizes (cf. Rev. 22:7). Accordingly all progress in the apprehension of truth depends on one's willingness to accept the indwelling truth as the regulatory principle of both knowledge and actions.

c. Paul. Like John, Paul adopts the OT view of truth. This is particularly obvious when he speaks of God. In the argument of Rom. 3:1-7, the apostle has the אמת of God in mind, when he uses πίστις ("faithfulness"; vs. 3) and ἀλήθεια ("truthfulness"; vs. 7) as synonyms, and characterizes God as being "true" (vs. 4)—i.e., as keeping his covenant. In I Thess. 1:9 the "true" (ἀληθινός) God is the "real" God, as contrasted with idols. Similarly, in the contrast between iniquity and truth (RSV "right") in I Cor. 13:6, the latter term is used as indicating God's demanding will (cf. Rom. 2:8, 20; Eph. 5:9; 6:14; Phil. 4:8). Christ, who as a servant of the circumcised "shows God's truthfulness" (Rom. 15:8), manifests not so much God's truthfulness (RSV) as his faithfulness. But Paul comes closer to Greek mentality, when, e.g., in Rom. 1:18 he speaks of suppressing the truth of God by means of iniquity. Yet even here the emphasis falls not so much upon the conceptual content as upon the will to manifest itself implied in truth (cf. Rom. 1:25 and the "wicked deception" [II Thess. 2:10]).

An original feature in Paul is his view of the truth as a historical process, which reaches its climax in Christ and the church. In Christ the hidden or veiled aspects of God's reign of mankind come to light (e.g., Rom. 1:1-6; 16:25-26; II Cor. 4:6). When Paul says that the "truth is in Jesus" (Eph. 4:21), he thinks in the first place of the realization of God's redemptive work in Christ. Hence "truth" does not so much designate the demanding will of God, but rather the gospel (e.g., Gal. 2:5, 14; Eph. 1:13; 4:20; Col. 1:5). Like the former, it has an intrinsic energy which is divine (Rom. 1:16; II Cor. 6:7), thus overcoming the resistance of sin (II Cor. 13:8) and moving people to propagate Christ's cause (II Cor. 11:10). The truth of the gospel, according to Paul, is therefore not simply the message about Christ or salvation, but rather the process in which Christ and the church are jointly engaged in bringing salvation to mankind. The truth is God's saving work made manifest (II Cor. 4:2); in it one believes (II Thess. 2:12-13) and one loves it (vs. 10). For in hearing the "word of truth" one is in Christ (Eph. 1:13; cf. II Cor. 11:10: "The truth of Christ is in me"). Thus one can "obey the truth" (Gal. 5:7) without falling into the works of the law. In turn, a false gospel is one which cannot save, because Christ is not in it (Gal. 2:5; cf. 1:6-7). The same usage is found in the Pastorals (e.g., I Tim. 3:15; 6:5; II Tim. 2:15, 18; 3:8; 4:4; Tit. 1:14).

Bibliography. F. J. A. Hort, *The Way, the Truth, and the Life* (Hulsean Lectures, 1871; 1908); F. Büchsel, *Der Begriff der Wahrheit in dem Evangelium und den Briefen des Johannes,* Beiträge zur Förderung Christlicher Theologie, vol. XIV, no. 6 (1911); C. A. Scott, "Eph. IV, 21. As the Truth Is in Jesus," *Exp.,* vol. XIII, no. 3 (1912), pp. 178-85; G. Storz, *Gebrauch und Bedeutungsentwicklung von* ἀλήθεια *und begriffsverwandten Wörtern* (1922); A. Schlatter, *Der Glaube im NT* (4th ed., 1927), pp. 551-61; F. J. Briggs, "Eph. IV, 20, 21," *ET,* 39 (1928), 526; R. Bultmann, "Untersuchungen zur johanneischen 'Αλήθεια," *ZNW,* 27 (1928), 113-63; C. H. Dodd, *The Bible and the Greeks* (1935), pp. 42-75; W. Luther, *Wahrheit und Lüge im ältesten Griechentum* (1935); J. Pedersen, *Israel, Its Life and Culture* (1946), I, 339-48; C. K. Barrett, "The Holy Spirit in the Fourth Gospel," *JTS,* N.S. I (1950), p. 8; D. J. Theron, "Paul's Concept of ἀλήθεια"—a comparative study with special reference to the LXX, Philo, the Hermetic literature, and Pistis Sophia (Th. D. dissertation at Princeton Theological Seminary; 1950).　　O. A. PIPER

TRYPHAENA AND TRYPHOSA trī fē′nə, trī fō′ sə [Τρύφαινα, dainty; Τρυφῶσα, delicate]. Christian women, recipients of a greeting in Rom. 16:12, where Paul also calls them "workers in the Lord"; the word indicates that they were "toilers." Because their names come from the same Greek root (meaning "to live luxuriously"), it has been inferred that they were sisters, or even twin sisters.

Both names are found in Greek and Latin sources; Tryphaena is used of Jewish women in the papyri. Tryphaena is also the name of a queen who be-

friended the heroine Thecla in the Acts of Paul and Thecla 27 ff.　　F. W. GINGRICH

TRYPHO trī′fō [Τρύφων]; KJV **TRYPHON** —fŏn. A murderous upstart who usurped the throne of Syria for three years (142-138 B.C.). As Diodotus, he had been a general of ALEXANDER BALAS, and after the latter's overthrow he took advantage of unrest among the soldiers of the next king, Demetrius II Nicator, to strengthen his own position, and in the S he also gained the support of Jonathan and the Maccabean party (I Macc. 11:57 ff).

Trypho had already brought from Arabia the young son of Balas, in pretense of placing him on the throne instead of the now defeated Demetrius II, but in reality Trypho was after the throne for himself. He felt that Jonathan and the Maccabees might be a hindrance rather than a help to him, and he marched with an army toward Jerusalem. Jonathan met him at BETH-SHAN in 143 B.C., but he was induced by promises and flattery to go to Ptolemaïs and was there imprisoned (I Macc. 12:39-53). Simon, who succeeded Jonathan, in Jerusalem, tried to effect his brother's release by sending hostage money, but Trypho did not keep his word. Instead, he invaded Judea, and had Jonathan put to death at Bascama after he had twice tried to reach Jerusalem.

78. Trypho

According to 13:31, which there is some reason to distrust on this point, Trypho then murdered the young king whom he had brought from Arabia, Antiochus VI, and took the throne. He did not keep it long, for he now found Simon and Demetrius united against him.

It was Demetrius' younger brother, Antiochus VII Sidetes, who finally forced Trypho to flee to ORTHOSIA (I Macc. 15:10-37). Trypho committed suicide (Strabo XIV.5.2).

Fig. TRY 78.

See also ANTIOCHUS 6-7; HASMONEANS.

N. TURNER

TRYPHOSA. *See* TRYPHAENA AND TRYPHOSA.

TUBAL tōō′bəl [תֻּבַל, תֻּבַל]. Son of Japheth (Gen. 10:2; I Chr. 1:5); hence a country in Asia Minor. The name is usually referred to in conjunction with MESHECH 1 (Ezek. 27:13; 32:26; 38:2-3; 39:1) or other nations of Asia Minor (Isa. 66:19). The equation with Tabal of the Assyrian sources is as evident as the correctness of the association with Meshech-Mushki (Μόσχοι). Herodotus still lists the Tabaleans (Τιβαρηνοί) with the Μόσχοι (III.94; VII.78). Tubal and Meshech traded in bronze (copper) vessels

(Ezek. 27:13). Archaeology has confirmed that metallurgy was one of the outstanding industries of these two countries, and Assyrian texts refer to precious metal vessels of Tabal (Sargon, eighth campaign; 358, 361).

Although the exact location of Tabal is disputed, it is clearly a region in the Cappadocian part of Asia Minor, which played an important political role in the ninth and eighth centuries B.C. Under Shalmaneser III (859-824) twenty-four kings of Tabal sent presents to Assyria. In the eighth century the country was united under one king, Uassurme, whom the Assyrians dethroned in 732 B.C. A later king, Ambaris, conspired unsuccessfully against Sargon with Mushki (Meshech) and Urartu (Ararat).

Bibliography. P. Naster, *L'Asie Mineure et l'Assyrie aux VIIIᵉ et VIIᵉ siècles avant Jésus-Christ* (1938), pp. 24, 67, 83-89; B. Landsberger, *Sam'al* (1948), pp. 17, 19-20.

M. J. MELLINK

TUBAL-CAIN tōō'bəl kān' [תובל-קין, *see below;* θοβελ καὶ ἦν (*for* καιν?)] (Gen. 4:22). Son of Lamech and Zillah; brother of Naamah.

The name is often identified with Akkadian *Tabal* (*see* TUBAL), but this is uncertain here. Mowinckel interprets *tûbhal* as "one who brings forth, produces, property," from יבל, thus meaning the same as its second element, קין, "smith" (perhaps a gloss). The name Tubal-cain is intentionally similar in form, as possibly in meaning, to the names of the half brothers, Jabal and Jubal (vss. 20-21).

In its immediate context Gen. 4:22 serves to include smithery in the arts and crafts associated with early man. That "Tubal the smith" is the eponymous ancestor of ancient metalworkers is clearly the intent of the sentence, despite textual difficulties. In its wider context this sentence serves the Yahwist's general theme in Gen. 1-11 by showing that as mankind developed in civilization, he progressed also in sin. For Tubal-cain looks both backward to Cain's homicide (4:1-17) and forward to Lamech's unsavory boast (vss. 23-24).

Bibliography. S. Mowinckel, *The Two Sources of the Predeuteronomic Primeval History (JE) in Gen. 1-11* (1937), pp. 81-82; W. F. Albright, *JBL,* LVIII (1939), 95-96.

L. HICKS

TUBIENI. KJV form of TOUBIANI. *See* TOB.

TUMORS [מחרים, עפלים] (I Sam. 5:6, 9, 12; 6:4-5, 11, 17); KJV EMERODS ĕm'ə rŏds (archaic form of "hemorrhoids"). A dreaded infection of high mortality, transmitted by rodents. The chief symptom was an inflamed enlargement of the inguinal glands (buboes). The narrative indicates an epidemic more characteristic of bubonic plague than hemorrhoids (cf. KJV). *See* PLAGUE. R. K. HARRISON

TUNIC [כתנת (Job 30:18), *see* COAT 1; Aram. פטיש (Dan. 3:21; KJV HOSEN); χιτών]. An undergarment. *See* DRESS AND ORNAMENTS § A2.

TURBAN. The translation of several words:

a) פאר (from Egyptian *pjr;* alternately "headdress"), an ornamental head-covering, made of linen or fine linen, for men. It was removed at periods of mourning (Ezek. 24:17, 23; KJV "tire"). In Ezek. 44:18 (KJV "bonnet") this is the turban of the priest, and in Isa. 3:20 ("headdress"; KJV "bonnet") the finery of women (cf. Exod. 39:28). The Hebrew word is used figuratively in Isa. 61:3, 10 (*see* GARLAND 2; cf. Pss. Sol. 2:22).

b) צניף (alternately "crown"; "diadem"), something wrapped around the head. This was the turban of priest and king. In Zech. 3:5 (KJV "mitre") it refers to the clean headgear for Joshua the high priest. It is a special mark of royalty in Ecclus. 11:5; 40:4 ("crown"); 47:6 ("diadem"; KJV "crown"). In Job 29:14 it is a metaphor for "justice." In Isa. 62:3 (Qere) it appears to refer to a figure for the redeemed group in relation to other peoples. In general, this term appears to be parallel to 1 *above,* though it may refer to a headcloth more frequently wrapped around the head. Fig. AKH 10.

c) מצנפת (KJV "diadem"; "mitre"), a term related to *b above,* but confined to the headdress of the high priest (Exod. 28:4, 37, 39; 29:6; 39:28, 31; Lev. 8:9; 16:4) with the exception of Ezek. 21:26—H 21:31, where it is used in parallel with עטרה, the crown of the prince of Israel. It was made of fine linen (Exod. 28:39; 39:28) and was an article of priestly attire for the Day of Atonement (Lev. 16:4). Josephus (Antiq. III.vii.3, 6) says that the headgear of the priests was seamed at the folds and so became a cap.

d) סרוחי טבולים (Ezek. 23:15; "flowing turbans"; KJV "dyed attire"), the long, flowing hoods of the Chaldeans.

e) Κίδαρις (Jth. 4:15; Ecclus. 45:12; KJV "mitre"), the priestly turban; the reward for the winner of a contest, who would sit next to the king (I Esd. 3:6; KJV "headtire").

See also CAP. J. M. MYERS

TURPENTINE TREE. A KJV form of TEREBINTH.

TURQUOISE. A blue, bluish-green, or greenish-gray hydrous basic aluminum phosphate containing a little copper. The most famous mines are in Persia. It was used in Egypt from early Neolithic times, and came from Wadi Maghara and Serabit el Khadim in Sinai. The gem must have been favorably known in Palestine, yet no English version has noted it. Egyptian *mfkʒt* may have become נפך, *nōphekh,* CARBUNCLE. The Arabic version renders שפיר (Isa. 54:11, etc.; usually "SAPPHIRE") "turquoise," also אחלמה (Exod. 28:19; AMETHYST).

See also JEWELS AND PRECIOUS STONES § 2.

Bibliography. A. Lucas, *Ancient Egyptian Materials and Industries* (1948). W. E. STAPLES

TURTLEDOVE [תור, תר (KJV TURTLE *in* Song of S. 2:12; Jer. 8:7), *probably onomatopoeic,* cf. Akkad. *turtu,* Lat. *turtur;* τρυγών, *from* τρύζω, to make a low murmuring sound]. Alternately: DOVE (Ps. 74:19). Any of the smaller varieties of PIGEON. Tristram noted three species of turtledove in Palestine (probably *Streptopelia turtur turtur, Streptopelia decaocto decaocto,* and *Streptopelia senegalensis aequatorialis*). The seasonal appearance of some turtledoves seems to be referred to in Song of S. 2:12; Jer. 8:7.

In the OT the turtledove is, for the most part, grouped with the pigeon in a cultic or sacrificial role. This is reflected in Luke 2:24 when Mary, observing the requirements of Lev. 12, made the usual bird offerings after the birth of Jesus.

The use of the word as a metaphor for Israel appears only in Ps. 74:19.   W. S. McCullough

TUTOR. KJV translation of ἐπίτροπος (RSV GUARDIAN) in Gal. 4:2.

TWELVE. The special significance of this number may have derived from several factors: the divisions of the lunar year, the signs of the Zodiac (cf. II Kings 23:5; Job 38:32), or the fact that it is the sum of five and seven and the product of three times four. The practical advantage of the number, its maximum divisibility, as well as its importance in the Sumerian duodecimal or sexagesimal numerical system, must have contributed to its development of symbolic significance.

The fact that the tribes of Israel were twelve (Gen. 35:22; 42:13, 32; 49:28; Num. 1:44) was enough to give the number religious significance for the Israelites. The tribes of Ishmael were also twelve (Gen. 17:20). There is something important about the number itself, as indicated by the effort to retain it in spite of losses or gains in the actual number of the tribes. When the tribe of Levi disappeared, the Joseph tribes Ephraim and Manasseh were counted separately to preserve the sacred number, and so also in the NT it was necessary to find a replacement for Judas Iscariot in order to keep the proper number of disciples. Often representative persons and things in the OT are explicitly chosen in accord with the number of the tribes (Exod. 24:4; 28:21; Num. 7:3; 17:2, 6; Josh. 4; I Kings 18:31; Ezra 6:17; 8:35; Ezek. 48:31); and so too in the NT the disciples are related to the tribes of Israel (Matt. 19:28). The twenty-four classes of priests and Levites (I Chr. 24:4; 25:31), the twenty-four elders round the heavenly throne (Rev. 4:4; 5:8; 11:16; 19:4), and the forty-eight Levitical cities (Num. 35:7) are implicitly correlated with the twelve tribes. The seventy-two elders, counting Eldad and Medad (Num. 11:24-26), presumably were chosen equally from each of the tribes. The number of the young men who fought and died at the Pool of Gibeon, twelve each from Israel and Judah, may have symbolized the issue at stake, which was the unity of the original twelve tribes (II Sam. 2:12-17). The twelve gates of heaven (cf. Ethiopian Enoch 34:2; 35:1; 36:1), the celestial Jerusalem (Rev. 21:12-14), are inscribed with the names of the tribes of Israel, and the twelve foundations of the city wall with the names of the twelve apostles. The twelve kinds of fruit of the tree of life, however, are related to the months of the year (Rev. 22:2). Solomon's twelve officers who supplied food for the royal household, each for one month of the year, were only partially assigned according to the tribes (I Kings 4:7-19). The Chronicler attributes to David also a monthly system of royal service, each division consisting of 24,000 men (I Chr. 27:1-15). Of the 144,000 servants of God (Rev. 7:4), 12,000 are taken from each of the tribes. Twelve occurs in many other relations, ritual and otherwise, without explicit or implicit connection with the tribal system (Exod. 15:27; Lev. 24:5; I Kings 10:20; Jer. 52:20; Ezek. 43:16; Matt. 14:20; Rev. 12:1).

The "more than twelve legions of angels" (Matt. 26:53) suggests that the number may sometimes be merely an inexact round figure, as is probably the case with the twelve baskets of scraps picked up after the feeding of the five thousand (Matt. 14:20).
                                                    M. H. POPE

TWELVE, THE. A group of disciples especially selected and instructed by Jesus to assist him in his earthly mission (Matt. 10:1-4; Mark 3:13-19; Luke 6:12-16; cf. John 6:70), and at the coming judgment (Matt. 19:28; Luke 22:30). The number was symbolic of the twelve tribes of Israel (cf. Rev. 21:12-14). After the Resurrection, the vacancy left by the defection of Judas was made up by the choice and inclusion of Matthias (Acts 1:15-26). The number of the group was thereby closed, and no further additions to it were ever made. According to Paul, the Twelve (minus Judas) were among the first recipients of the appearances of the risen Lord (I Cor. 15:5; cf. Mark 16:7); and this tradition is confirmed by the resurrection narratives of Matthew, less precisely by Luke and John. In Acts 1-6, the Twelve are portrayed as the initial leaders of the church; but they were soon merged into a larger company of apostles. *See* APOSTLE; MINISTRY.

The lists of names of the Twelve in the Synoptic gospels do not exactly correspond. The Fourth Gospel introduces the name of Nathanael; and other variants in the names occur in uncanonical sources. All attempts to harmonize the lists are speculative. The NT tradition that Simon Peter was the first to be chosen by Jesus, as he was the first to see the risen Lord, is indisputable; but the nature of Peter's pre-eminence in the group, other than that of a ready spokesman for his colleagues, has been a constant subject of controversy among biblical critics and theologians (cf. Matt. 16:18; Luke 22:32; Acts 1:15; 2:14; 5:3; Gal. 2:8; *see* PETER).

Almost nothing of a trustworthy nature is known about the lives and labors of the Twelve, other than what is told in the NT—e.g., the martyrdom of James son of Zebedee in Acts 12:2. (*See* APOCRYPHA, NT.) The tradition of Peter's martyrdom and burial in Rome is doubtless authentic (cf. I Clem. 5.4; Dionysius of Corinth and Gaius in Euseb. Hist. II.25. 7-8). But much obscurity surrounds the tradition concerning the residence and death of John in Ephesus (*see* JOHN THE APOSTLE).

Bibliography. E. J. Goodspeed, *The Twelve* (1957).
                                              M. H. SHEPHERD, JR.

TWIN BROTHERS [διόσκουροι; Lat. *dioskuri*, sons of Zeus] (Acts 28:11). Castor and Polydeuces (Latin *Pollux*), who have an ancient and widespread history in classical mythology. Their mother was Leda, wife of Tyndareos, king of Sparta in legendary times. Hence they are sometimes called Tyndaridae. More often and after Homer's time they are called "Sons of Zeus." In the traditions they are one or both his sons, and one, both, or neither immortal.

As tutelary deities they served a variety of functions. Castor the horse-tamer became the god of horsemen (in iconography the two gods are commonly accompanied by their horses); Polydeuces, the master of the art of boxing, became the god of wrestlers. However, their chief function came to be as saviors (θεοὶ σωτῆρες) of mariners. Poseidon had rewarded their brotherly love by giving them power over wind and waves. Having attained a blessed immortality, they were identified with the constellation Gemini (the Twins, the third sign in the Zodiac), the two brightest stars of which are known as Castor and Pollux. They are therefore in a position to look down upon and save those in peril on the sea. Indeed, they might show themselves in the form of "St. Elmo's fire," the glow accompanying the brushlike discharges of atmospheric electricity appearing as a tip of light on the ends of pointed objects such as masts of ships, during storms.

Since Castor and Pollux were the tutelary deities of the navigators, many a ship would bear their insignia. This might mean that symbols or images of the Twins would be affixed as figureheads to the prow, perhaps with the name or names carried beneath.

Courtesy of the Italian State Tourist Office, New York

79. Holy precinct of the temple of Castor and Pollux at Agrigento, Sicily

The translation "with the Twin Brothers as figurehead" doubtless gives the sense of Acts 28:11, although the language of the text presents some difficulty. *See bibliography.*

Castor and Pollux were adequately honored in Rome. Their worship was early introduced following their assistance to the Romans at the Battle of Regillus, *ca.* 496 B.C. Temples were subsequently built in the Forum, the Circus Maximus, and the Circus Flaminius. A ship plying between Alexandria and Rome and bearing their insignia might well expect to be favored with a prosperous voyage. But Luke knows who the true Savior of mariners is.

Fig. TWI 79.

Bibliography. W. Smith, *Dictionary of Greek and Roman Biography and Mythology,* I (1859), 1052-54. J. R. Harris, *The Dioscuri in the Christian Legends* (1903); *The Cult of the Heavenly Twins* (1906). L. R. Farnell, *Greek Hero Cults and Ideas of Immortality* (1921), pp. 175-228. Dölger, "Dioskuroi, Das Reiseschiff des Apostel Paulus und seine Schutzgötter," *Antike und Christentum,* VI (1950), 276-85. W. Krauss, "Dioskuren," *Reallexikon für Antike und Christentum,* III (1957), 1122-38, contains an important recent bibliography of German and French items.

For a discussion of the problem of Acts 28:11, see: F. W. Blass and A. Debrunner, *Grammatik* (1913), section 198.7. H. H. Wendt, *Die Apostelgeschichte* (9th ed., 1913), p. 362. F. W. Foakes-Jackson and K. Lake, *The Beginnings of Christianity,* IV (1933), 343-44. E. Haenchen, *Die Apostelgeschichte* (1956), p. 650. Παράσημος, in W. F. Arndt and F. W. Gingrich, *Greek-English Lexicon* (1957).

F. D. GEALY

TWINED LINEN [שֵׁשׁ מָשְׁזָר]. A superior quality of LINEN made from yarn whose threads were composed of numerous fine strands. The curtains of the tabernacle (Exod. 26:1; 36:8), the veil (26:31; 36:35), the hangings for the door of the tent (26:36) and of the tabernacle (36:37), the hangings for the court of the tabernacle (27:9; 38:9, 16), the hangings for the gate of the court (27:16, 18; 38:18), the ephod (28:6; 39:2, 24), the girdle of the ephod (28:8; 39:5, 29), and the breastplate (28:15; 39:8) were made of this exquisite linen material. *See also* CLOTH.

J. M. MYERS

TYCHICUS tĭk'ə kəs [Τύχικος] (Acts 20:4; Eph. 6: 21; Col. 4:7; II Tim. 4:12; Tit. 3:12). A man described as a beloved brother and fellow slave of Paul's and as a faithful minister of the Lord, and who—together with Onesimus—is the bearer of the Colossian letter. Tychicus and Onesimus are to make known all matters concerning Paul, who is imprisoned, probably in Rome.

Eph. 6:21-22, with one slight omission and one slight addition, is a letter-for-letter copying of the Colossians passage. The setting in Colossians is natural, but that in Ephesians is quite artificial—constituting a part of its Pauline pseudepigraphical presentation.

In Acts 20:4, Tychicus, along with Trophimus, is designated a native of the province of Asia, who was with Paul in Greece and accompanied him overland to Troas at the end of the third missionary journey. Though not mentioned again in Acts, he was probably one of the "we" who traveled subsequently with Paul. II Tim. 4:12 tells only that Paul had sent Tychicus to Ephesus—probably an authentic Pauline word, but there are no means for determining when or from where Tychicus was sent. Tit. 3:12, probably a genuine Pauline word, indicates only that Tychicus was a possible replacement for Titus in the work in Crete, but there is nothing to indicate when and from where Titus was written.

Some suggest that Tychicus was the unnamed "brother" in II Cor. 8:22, and tradition says that Tychicus was later a bishop of Colophon and a martyr, but this is based on conjecture.

J. M. NORRIS

TYNDALE'S VERSION tĭn'dəl. William Tyndale published his translation of the NT in 1525, an octavo edition without notes and a quarto edition with marginal notes. In 1530 he published his translation of the Pentateuch with marginal notes of a highly controversial nature, and in 1535 his revised NT with a brief introduction to each book (except Acts and Revelation) and with softened marginal notes. Tyndale's Version provides the basic text of

80. From Tyndale's NT (A.D. 1525), beginning of the
Sermon on the Mount (Matt. 5)

the KJV and is the most important of the early versions.

Fig. TYN 80.

See also VERSIONS, ENGLISH, § 3.   J. R. BRANTON

TYRANNUS, HALL OF tī răn′əs [Τύραννος] (Acts 19:9). The place at Ephesus where Paul preached daily for two years. When Paul first reached Ephesus for a settled period of preaching, he worked in the synagogue for three months. At the end of that time the opposition to him had grown so strong that he withdrew, taking with him the disciples he had won during the three-month period. He continued his preaching in the hall of Tyrannus.

The Greek word for "hall" is σχολή. It means "leisure" or "rest"; then the activity for which leisure from work is used, such as discussion, debate, or lecture; or the group to which lectures are given ("school"); or the place where such a school meets.

This last meaning appears in Acts 19:9. The place could hardly have been a public building provided for the use of lecturers; since it is connected with an individual, Tyrannus, and since Paul was not disturbed in his daily preaching for two years, it is quite unlikely that the meeting place was a public forum or building. The fact that "all the residents of Asia heard the word of the Lord" suggests that the place was not a private residence but a well-situated hall which could house a well-attended preaching service.

Nothing definite is known about this Tyrannus. The name, as ancient inscriptions show, was common. If the place where Paul preached was a public building, Tyrannus was most likely the donor. If it was a private residence, Tyrannus was, no doubt, the owner. If, as is probable, it was a privately owned hall for lectures, he could have been the owner, or the lecturer whose name had become attached to the hall, or both. Unless he had become a Christian— and there is no evidence that he had—he must have rented the hall to Paul. That he did so shows at least a tolerance of Paul's preaching.

In the usually superior MSS (אAB), Acts 19:9 ends with the words "in the hall of Tyrannus." The "Western" type of evidence offers two additions. One addition is τινός after Τυράννου, "a *certain* Tyrannus," making clear that an individual is meant and per-

haps implying that he was not a prominent public figure. The other addition, made by some "Western" authorities, is ἀπὸ ὥρας πέμπτης ἕως δεκάτης, "from the fifth to the tenth hour"—i.e., from *ca.* 11 A.M. to 4 P.M. This was the period of the midday rest, and since we have evidence that school began in the early morning and that school and business broke off *ca.* 11 A.M. (Juvenal VII.222 ff; Martial IX.68; XII.57), this addition in Acts would mean that Paul could rent the hall, probably for a modest cost, at the hours when the usual lecturer, whether Tyrannus or some other, no longer wished to use it. While this time of day would conflict with the normal schedule of lunch and rest, it had two advantages for Paul: he could work to support himself in the early morning (cf. Acts 18:3), and he could reach many workers in trades and business during the time they were free to hear him. Whatever the disadvantages of the hour, Paul's strategy, if the "Western" reading is accepted, was eminently successful in reaching great numbers and winning many to faith in Christ. It is not at all certain that this "Western" reading is original in Acts, but it accords with the ancient living schedule and explains easily how Paul could get a hall for so long at a cost he could afford. It may well be a part of the original text of Acts, though it is hard to see why it was omitted in so many good ancient MSS and versions.

Bibliography. F. J. Foakes-Jackson and K. Lake, *The Beginnings of Christianity,* IV (1933), 239.   F. V. FILSON

TYRE tīr [צר, צור; Phoen. צר; Ugar. *Ṣr-m;* Amarna *and* Akkad. *ṣurru;* Τύρος]; **TYRIANS** tīr′ĭ ənz. An important Phoenician city in the southernmost part of the country, famous for its navigators and traders.

1. Location. Tyre was situated on a small island which was originally unconnected with the mainland. The rocky isle is *ca.* twenty-five miles S of Sidon, close to the borderland of the Israelite tribe of Asher (Josh. 19:29). Excavations indicate that the main harbor was probably on the S side of the island. It was protected by a breakwater, traces of which can now be found fifty feet below the surface. It was built in the tenth century B.C. by King Hiram, who was a contemporary of King Solomon. The breakwater was 820 yards long and *ca.* 9 yards thick. Behind it was one of the best harbors in Phoenicia. The mainland settlement of Tyre was called Ushu

From *Atlas of the Bible* (Thomas Nelson & Sons Limited)

81. Aerial view of Tyre

in cuneiform records. King Sennacherib (704-681) and King Ashurbanipal (668-633) both boast that they captured Ushu, which at least Ashurbanipal treated hard, but they were not able to get over to Tyre.

Tyre is now connected with the mainland. The first connection was made by Alexander, who built a mole, *ca.* half a mile long, when he besieged the city in 333 B.C. Tyre's location on a rocky isle gave it a strong position in cases of siege, and it was very hard to conquer in the time before Alexander.

Fig. TYR 81.

2. History. It is supposed that Tyre is an old city, but very little is known about its foundation. The Greek historian Herodotus has suggested that Tyre was founded in the twenty-eighth century. More reliable information is found in the Tell el-Amarna Letters, from the fourteenth century. At a time when several Phoenician princes allied themselves with the Amorites, the king of Tyre, Abimilki (Abimelek), remained faithful to the former lord of the country, the Egyptian Pharaoh. From this time also comes the Ugaritic Keret epic (*see* UGARIT), which mentions the "shrine of Asherah of Tyre," an indication that the Asherah temple of Tyre was already famous then.

Phoenicia had been firmly connected with Egypt since the sixteenth century, when Pharaoh Ah-mose drove the Hyksos out of Egypt and conquered the countries along the Mediterranean coast. Thut-mose I and III in the sixteenth and fifteenth centuries made several campaigns in Syria. Egypt's hold loosened in the Amarna period under Amen-hotep IV (1370-1353), but then Ramses II (1290-1224) marched as far as Beirut. However, *ca.* 1100 Wen-Amon, who also visited Tyre, is a witness to how far Egypt had lost the respect of the Phoenician governors. Tyre was on its way to attaining an independent position and the leadership among the Phoenician cities. It played a great role in trade and shipping, and its navigators and craftsmen were known to be excellent.

Also, Israel used craftsmen from Tyre in the time of David and Solomon. The border of the Israelite kingdom extended to Tyre (II Sam. 24:7). King Hiram of Tyre (981-947) sent messengers to David, along with cedar trees, and carpenters and masons who helped to build his palace (II Sam. 5:11; I Chr. 14:1). Hiram, who was considered a friend of David, was also in contact with his successor, King Solomon, whom he also supplied with timber of cedar and cypress (I Kings 5; I Chr. 22:4; II Chr. 2:3-18). Solomon paid with wheat and oil. Another Hiram from Tyre, a skilled bronze worker, made most of the molten objects in the new temple (I Kings 7:13-45). Solomon also gave King Hiram twenty cities in Galilee, but they did not please him (I Kings 9:11-14). Hiram sent able seamen to the new fleet which Solomon built at Ezion-geber to sail in the Red Sea and to Ophir (I Kings 9:26-28).

It was Hiram who built the big breakwater in Tyre, which made the harbor one of the best in the E Mediterranean. He developed the trade with Cyprus and Spain. His successor reigned only for a short time; then there was a revolution. Later the dynasty was restored.

In the time of Ahab of Israel (875-852) Ethbaal was king of Tyre and priest of Ashtart. He married his daughter Jezebel to Ahab (I Kings 16:31). She and her daughter, Athaliah, who was married to King Joram of Judah, tried to introduce Phoenician religion in Israel and Judah. It was, however, not because of these attempts that the prophets prophesied the imminent destruction of Tyre by Nebuchadrezzar (Jer. 27:3-6). The wealth and the pride of Tyre made it a dangerous opponent, and therefore Tyre would surely be doomed (Isa. 23:1-17; Jer. 25:22; 27:3; 47:4; Ezek. 26:2–29:18; Joel 3:4-8; Amos 1:9-10; Zech. 9:2-4). The psalmists saw Tyre in the same way (Pss. 45:13; 83:7—H 83:8; 87:4). Characteristic are the words of Ezek. 26:17:

> O city renowned,
> that was mighty on the sea,
> you and your inhabitants,
> who imposed your terror
> on all the mainland!

So are also the words of Zech. 9:3:

> Tyre has built herself a rampart,
> and heaped up silver like dust,
> and gold like the dirt of the streets.

Tyre played an important role in purple production, and its purple was the most famous and precious of the dyes of ancient times. Tyrian ships sailed to Egypt, Cyprus, Rhodes, Sicily, and the colonies in North Africa and Spain. In addition to dyed cloths they delivered timber, wheat, oil, and wine. Also, metal, slaves, and horses were sent to Egypt. Carthage, the most famous of the colonies which Tyre founded, dates from *ca.* 850. The gold mines of Thrace, N of Greece, were first worked by men from Tyre, according to Strabo.

The main deity in Tyre in this period was Melqart, actually an aspect of Baal, whose cult was taken over also in Carthage. It was probably the same god whom Jezebel wanted to introduce in Israel and against whom Elijah was fighting (I Kings 18).

The Assyrian king Tiglath-pileser I raided Syria in 1094, but first King Ashurnasirpal in 876 was able to have tribute from Tyre and other Phoenician cities. In 853 King Shalmaneser III (at Qarqar) defeated the army of the allied states and cities, of which Tyre was one. Tyre had to pay tribute, but retained so much of its independence that Tiglath-pileser III and Shalmaneser V had to try to break it again. Tyre was besieged for five years but was able to endure and to press through a treaty in 722. The defense was planned and led by King Elu-eli, whose aspirations did not stop with Tyre. He dominated most of Phoenicia, and also tried to extend his authority to Cyprus. He got there at last, after having been driven out of Phoenicia by King Sennacherib of Assyria (705-681), who replaced him with the king of Sidon, Ethba'al. However, when Sennacherib's son Esarhaddon destroyed Sidon in 677, King Baal of Tyre made a treaty with him and paid tribute.

The Neo-Babylonian Empire also tried to extend its domination to the coast of Phoenicia. Tyre was still hard to subdue. King Nebuchadrezzar besieged it for thirteen years before it yielded to the conqueror. The long struggle had exhausted its power, and the defeat of Tyre in 572 meant the end of Phoenician national life. When Cyrus of Persia conquered Babylon in 539, Phoenicia also came under his sway. Tyre lost its dominating position on the coast to Sidon, and Carthage detached itself politically from Tyre in 520. But Tyre was still active in trade and shipping, in spite of the loss of the colonies. Cedar trees and other products were exported (cf. Ezra 3:7; Neh. 13:16).

When Sidon revolted against Artaxerxes III Ochus (358-338), it was supported by Tyre and other Phoenician cities. The terrible destruction of Sidon in 351, however, was a warning to the other cities, which did not hesitate to capitulate. The whole situation was soon changed when Alexander arrived in Asia, swept through Asia Minor, and defeated the Persians at Issus in 333. Sidon, which had been crushed by Artaxerxes, surrendered at once, and so did also the other Phoenician cities, with the exception of Tyre, which again relied on its favorable position on an island and chose to resist the conqueror. Tyre received no help from the other Phoenician cities; on the contrary, their ships were used against it. Alexander did not want to besiege Tyre for years, so he conceived a device which made him able to attack the city without a long wait. He had a mole built from the mainland to Tyre, *ca.* half a mile long and two hundred feet wide. He pressed against Tyre for seven months, and then the city was no longer able to resist this persistent opponent. Its fate was hard. *Ca.* thirty thousand of the inhabitants were sold as slaves, and two thousand of the leaders were hanged. Victory celebrations took place in the Melqart temple, with sacrifices, rites, and processions. The mole which Alexander built, partly from houses and monuments torn down on the mainland, remained and connected Tyre with the coast for all the future.

Under the Seleucid kings who followed after Alexander, Tyre rose again slowly, though it never attained its former power and glory. Hellenistic culture was gradually adopted. Trade and industry were again developed. Pottery and glassware were produced. The glass from Sidon and Tyre was excellent and had a high reputation in all countries of the Western world. The production of dyes and of wine continued. Tyre was relatively undisturbed by the later Seleucid rulers, and in 126 B.C. it acquired a status of independence. It was able to retain this status when Pompey conquered the country in 64 B.C., but it was constantly under some kind of control by the Roman legate in Syria.

Tyre is mentioned in I Macc. 11:59; II Macc. 4:18. Also in the NT we hear about it several times (Matt. 11:21-22; Luke 10:13-14; Acts 12:20). Jesus withdrew to the district of Tyre (Matt. 15:21; Mark 7:24, 31), and he preached to people from that city (Mark 3:8; Luke 6:17). In the time of Paul, Christians were living there, and he visited them and stayed with them seven days while the ship with which he sailed unloaded its cargo (Acts 21:3-7).

Tyre remained a center of trade and industry in Roman times. Philosophy and poetry also had a home there. Eastern and Western influences met, and in the fourth century A.D. it glided definitely into the Byzantine sphere. In A.D. 636, Tyre was conquered by the Arabs. Today Tyre is only a minor town, called Ṣur, with *ca.* six thousand inhabitants.

Bibliography. E. Renan, *Mission de Phénicie* (1864); W. B. Fleming, *The History of Tyre* (1915); D. le Lasseur in *Syria,* III (1922), 1-26, 116-33; G. Contenau, *La civilisation phénicienne* (1928); A. Poidebard, *Un grand port disparu: Tyr* (1939); P. K. Hitti, *History of Syria* (1951).

          A. S. KAPELRUD

TYRE, LADDER OF. *See* LADDER OF TYRE.

TYROPOEON VALLEY tī rō′pĭ ən [φάραγξ τῶν τυροποιῶν, valley of the cheesemakers]. The Greek name of the small N-S valley in JERUSALEM dividing the Hill of Ophel, site of the City of David, from the Western Hill or Upper City. Known today as el-Wad, it is only a shallow depression from the debris dumped into it for centuries. In Herod's day two bridges probably spanned the valley connecting the W hill to the temple platform.

Bibliography. G. E. Wright, *Biblical Archaeology* (1957), pp. 126-27.   E. W. SAUNDERS

TZADDI tsä′dĭ, zä′— (Heb. tsä′thĕ) [צ, ṣ]. The eighteenth letter of the Hebrew ALPHABET as it is placed in the KJV at the head of the eighteenth section of the acrostic psalm, Ps. 119, where each verse of this section of the psalm begins with this letter.

UCAL ū′kəl [אֻכָל] (Prov. 30:1). A name in the title of a collection of proverbs: one of two pupils or contemporaries to whom Agur addressed his reflections. The address "Surely you know!" (vs. 4) confirms the reading of names in this difficult Hebrew verse. The LXX finds no proper names in the verse and translates here according to the verb כלה ("and I cease"). The Hebrew consonants can be retained and still provide variant reading by altered punctuation (ASV mg. "and am consumed").   T. M. MAUCH

UEL ū′əl [אוּאֵל, *see below;* LXX A Οὐήλ] (Ezra 10:34). Alternately: JOEL jō′əl ['Ιουνήλ (L)] (I Esd. 9:34); KJV JUEL jōō′—. One of the contemporaries of Ezra who are listed as having taken foreign wives. The name as given in the MT is unusual and may possibly be corrupted or contracted from אֲבִיאֵל, "God is father"; cf. the analogous "Iezer" (אִיעֶזֶר; Num. 26:30) for "Abiezer" (אֲבִיעֶזֶר; Josh. 17:2). For other conjectures, *see bibliography.*

    Bibliography. M. Noth, *Die israelitischen Personennamen* (1928), p. 235; R. A. Bowman, Exegesis of Ezra, *IB,* III (1954), 660; F. S. Brown, S. R. Driver, and C. A. Briggs, eds., *Hebrew-English Lexicon* (rev. ed., 1955), p. 15.
                               B. T. DAHLBERG

*UGARIT ōō′gə rĭt [Amarna *Ugarit*]. A city-state near the Mediterranean coast in N Syria.

1. Location
2. Excavations
3. History
4. Texts
Bibliography

1. Location. Ancient Ugarit was located *ca.* half a mile from the coast of the Mediterranean, in a valley through which the little river Nahr el-Fidd flows. It was situated *ca.* seven miles N of Laodicea ad Mare on the Syrian coast, straight E of the easternmost point of Cyprus. In the bay where Nahr el-Fidd runs into the sea, Ugarit had a port which could be used by seagoing tradeships. There was a harbor town here which was of considerable dimensions in the best time of Ugarit. In Greek times it was known as Leukos Limen, the White Harbor. It is now called Minet el-Beida and is used only by small fishing boats. Ugarit itself had a favorable position between the low hills. It is now a tell, lying between the two arms of the Nahr el-Fidd. It is called Ras Shamra, "Hill of Fennel," because fennel is growing there. The tell which comprises the ruins of the ancient city has the form of a trapezium, where the longest side is *ca.* 670 yards (N-S) and the longer diagonal *ca.* 1,100 yards. The hill is *ca.* 22 yards high. Fig. UGA 1.

Located close to the coast, Ugarit was an important center of trade. The road along the coast, from Egypt to Asia Minor, went through Ugarit. Another trade way went from Ugarit to Aleppo, Mari on the Euphrates, and Babylon. Export articles from the Eastern countries came this way. From Ugarit the sea route over to Alashiya (Cyprus) was a short one, and Ugarit very early traded with the Aegean islands. It became an important transit harbor. One of the main export articles was copper, which was used for the production of bronze. It was imported from Asia Minor and from Cyprus, and bronze was produced in Ugarit. Like other Phoenician cities, Ugarit delivered timber to Egypt; not only cedars, but also other kinds of wood. There were factories of

From Schaeffer, *The Cuneiform Texts of Ras Shamra–Ugarit* (The British Academy, Schweich Lectures, 1937)

  1. Air view of Ras Shamra (Ugarit), with the mound outlined in black and showing excavated areas on the mound

purple dye, as great heaps of murex shells indicate. These shells are found in abundance in the E Mediterranean.

2. Excavations. The exact location of Ugarit was unknown till 1928. In the early spring of that year a Syrian peasant was plowing his field a little N of Minet el-Beida. Suddenly his simple plow struck a stone, which no doubt looked like a tombstone. As was his duty, he notified the French *Service des Antiquités en Syrie et au Liban* in Beirut, at that time in charge of such matters. The tomb was of a Mycenean character,* as was found out by L. Albanèse, whom the director, Charles Virolleaud, sent to Minet el-Beida to investigate the place. It was also likely that here was an ancient cemetery, which might be worth digging up. But farther to the E was the tell, Ras Shamra. If there was a cemetery here, it was probable that there had once also been a city, and that city could only be hidden in the tell. The *Académie des Inscriptions et Belles-Lettres de Paris* decided to start diggings here, and on April 2, 1929, work began at Minet el-Beida, under the direction of Claude F. A. Schaeffer. After a month's work he changed over to Ras Shamra. Only a few days' work was sufficient to show how important the new site was. On May 20 they found the first tablets, twenty of them,

From Schaeffer, *Ugaritica*, III; courtesy of the Librairie Orientaliste Paul Geuthner, Paris

2. Late-Mycenean-period tomb at Ugarit (fourteenth-thirteenth centuries B.C.)

From Schaeffer, *The Cuneiform Texts of Ras Shamra–Ugarit* (The British Academy, Schweich Lectures, 1937)

3. Clay cuneiform tablets as originally found at Ugarit

written in a hitherto unknown cuneiform writing.* They were dug out from the corner of a room which had been burned black by a devastating fire. That was the beginning of a series of important finds which have yielded texts of enormous value for the study of Phoenician and Canaanite religion. The tell of Ras Shamra contained the ruins of a city which had been destroyed and rebuilt several times. The deepest layer, next to virgin soil, goes back before the Copper Age. Figs. UGA 2, 3, 4.

The cuneiform writing and the language of the tablets were not known. The tablets were made of clay and were technically produced in the same way as the Akkadian tablets. The signs were not Akkadian, and there were only about thirty of them— a fact which revealed that this was an alphabetical writing. The words were separated by a vertical stroke, which was of great help for the decipherment. The length and type of the words indicated that the language was Semitic. These facts were the starting point for the scholars who tried to decipher the writing on the tablets.

The first texts were published in the French archaeological journal *Syria* in 1930. The first scholar to publish an attempt at a solution was the German Hans Bauer, on June 4, 1930, in a German newspaper. He was followed immediately by two French scholars, Edouard Dhorme and Charles Virolleaud. Their solutions were not quite identical, but they worked their systems together and attained a solution which has since undergone only minor alterations.

In one of the texts which were found in the beginning of the campaign, there was a colophon which attested that the copy was made in the reign of Niqmad king of Ugarit (Gordon 62.56). Also other indications make it completely sure that the ancient city hidden in the mound of Ras Shamra is Ugarit, a city which was already known from the TELL EL-AMARNA Letters.

Schaeffer and his archaeologists had struck a complete library, with hundreds of tablets. Some of them had been used for teaching and practice, and there was sufficient reason to assume that there had been a scribes' school in the house where they found the library. The house was a great building, with many rooms. It was an official building, where also the chief priest (*rb khn*) had lived. Under the stone floor in one of the rooms a whole collection of tools and weapons was found. The collection had probably been given to the chief priest as a kind of offering or simply as a gift. It was made of bronze, and some of the weapons had dedications showing that they were gifts to the chief priest.

The building which housed the library, the scribes' school, and the chief priest was situated between two other great buildings which were soon excavated. They were well built and had a dominating position on the top of the hill. They had the same size and ground plan. Dedications show that one of them was a temple built for Baal, the other one for Dagon. They had a great inner room, the "holy of holiest," where the images of the gods were placed. Before it was another room, an anteroom for the inner room. Outside this was a forecourt with the remains of an

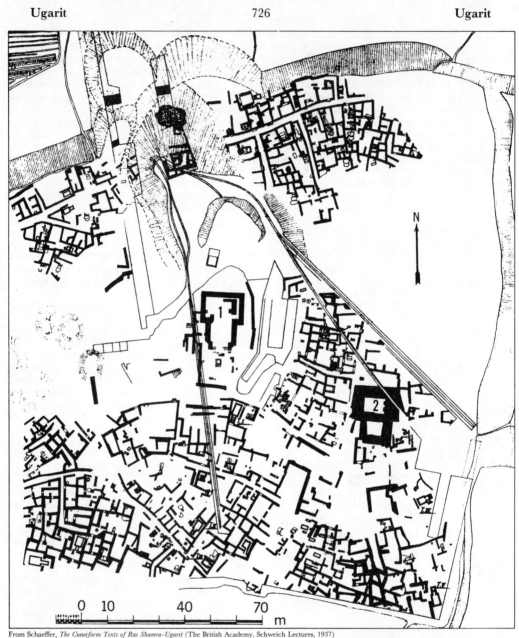

From Schaeffer, *The Cuneiform Texts of Ras Shamra–Ugarit* (The British Academy, Schweich Lectures, 1937)

4. Plan of the excavations of the NE section of Ugarit: (1) temple of Baal; (2) temple of Dagon

altar. Here the people are supposed to have gathered. The construction of the Baal temple is much the same as that of King Solomon's TEMPLE in Jerusalem. A staircase led up to the tower, where offerings were brought on the open terrace.

The texts give indications about the cult. So do also several objects which have been found in Ras Shamra and Minet el-Beida. Small golden amulets, in the shape of a naked woman, reveal that the fertility cult was popular and widespread. In a tomb there was found an ivory box, on whose lid the picture of a goddess was carved.* She wears a skirt in Cretan-Mycenean style. In her hands she holds ears of corn, and two goats, standing on their hind legs,

attempt to reach them. Also a little statue of a sitting fertility goddess was found, probably showing Anath, the consort of Baal. The goddess was wearing a stylized sheaf of corn on her head. So were also two other statuettes of bronze, representing the weather and fertility god Baal. One of them has horns on the helmet. On a great stone stele Baal is shown with ox horns on his helmet and brandishing a club in his right hand.* In his left hand he holds a stylized thunderbolt ending in a spearhead. Like some of the statuettes, the figure on the stele has a certain Egyptian character. Some features, such as the sword and the helmet, are not Egyptian but are clearly Asiatic. This is characteristic, not only for the composite

From *Syria*, X; courtesy of the Librairie Orientaliste Paul Geuthner, Paris

5. The goddess, "queen of the wild beasts," an ivory from Tomb III at Minet el-Beida (fourteenth century B.C.; excavator)

Courtesy of the Librairie Orientaliste Paul Geuthner, Paris

6. Baal with mace and spear; from Ras Shamra

where the deceased members of the family were buried. The tombs were built in Cretan style. Stairways of stone led down to the vault, where the corpses were placed, wrapped in reed mats, with tools, weapons, ornaments, and pottery around. Much had been stolen or broken when Ugarit was destroyed, but much of the pottery and some other objects were left. The pottery is of late Mycenean type and had probably been imported from Cyprus or Rhodes. It is not only these objects which indicate that the people of Ugarit took good care of their dead. In many tombs there are arrangements with a pit, or close to the grave there was a gutter which could lead the water down to the pit and had its opening level with the ground. Here water could be poured down as libations for the deceased. There are so many of these and similar arrangements in Ugarit that it is obvious that this funerary rite must have been widely observed. It is well known also from Mycenean tombs in Greece and Crete. Some other jars which have been found point in the direction of fertility cult; they are big jars which have had their bottoms knocked out and which have been placed over libation channels.

During war times there were no excavations at Ras Shamra, but they were resumed in 1948 and have been going on regularly since. Work has been concentrated on uncovering the great palace,* under the direction of C. F. A. Schaeffer. The palace is *ca.* 130 yards long, in the N-S direction, and *ca.* 90 yards E-W. It thus covered a large area. The most important discoveries in the palace were the royal archives. The so-called central archive, the S archive, and the E and W archives were found here, and were named after the part of the building in which

Courtesy of the Librairie Orientaliste Paul Geuthner, Paris

7. Two views of a statue of Baal, found at Ugarit in a tomb

character of Ugaritic art, but for Ugaritic culture on the whole. Figs. UGA 5, 6 (*cf.* UGA 7).

The houses which were found in the first layer were built in the fifteenth and fourteenth centuries. Many of them were spacious and well built, around an open court and with a flight of stairs leading up to the first floor. They had many rooms, even bathrooms and sanitary arrangements. Waste water could be led away into cesspits. Under many of the houses or under the courtyards were found funeral vaults, they were found. While nearly all texts found in the library in the first years of excavation were of a mythological-ritual kind, the archives in the palace yielded the historical material which had been lacking till then. The archive in the W wing contained largely administrative documents relating to the royal estates, that in the E wing had documents relating to the capital city, while those in the central archive were mainly legal documents. In addition there were letters in the archives. Almost all documents were written in the international language of these centuries, Akkadian, and only a few in Hurrian and Ugaritic. The script is Middle-Babylonian, with a few peculiarities. Twelve names of Ugaritic kings are found in the documents, which date from the eighteenth to the thirteenth century. The seals on the royal acts are remarkable, as they all bear the same design at the top, without regard to the identity of the reigning king. The motif is well known from Babylonian glyptic art; it is that of homage to a deified king. The seal was so well known in Ugarit that some rascals tried to forge it. One of the letters of the collection tells about this episode. Fig. UGA 8.

By permission of Prof. C. F. A. Schaeffer, Director of the Ras Shamra Expedition, Professor au College de France

9. The royal couple, on an ivory plaque, from the palace

Another remarkable piece, found in the season of 1952-53, is the ancient Ugaritic alphabet, with thirty letters, written probably in the fourteenth century and thus the oldest known ALPHABET in the world. Like the previous piece, it is now found in the National Museum of Damascus.

3. History. Civilization on the E shore of the Mediterranean goes very far back in time. N of Ugarit traces of Early Paleolithic civilization have been found. Nothing as old has been dug out in Ras Shamra. Excavation down to the bottom rock has taken the excavators down to the earliest level (V) where no pottery was found, only flint and bone tools. These tools indicate that stratum V belongs to Neolithic times. They were found twenty yards down from the surface of the tell. On the same level, but a little higher up, sherds of simple pottery were found. They have some linear decorations and seem to be of a type analogous with pottery found in N and E Syria, and also in Jericho. The level above this (IV) can be dated *ca.* 4000-3500. It shows a finely developed civilization from the Chalcolithic or Copper Age, with beautifully painted pottery, of a type well known from other sites in Syria and Palestine. It is often connected with the name of Tell Halaf.

In the next level (III), *ca.* 3500-2100, the pottery has again changed character. This was the period of the Early Bronze Age, from which historical docu-

From *Syria*, XXXI; courtesy of the Librairie Orientaliste Paul Geuthner, Paris

8. Plan of the palace at Ugarit, showing location of the royal archives

Many fine objects have been recovered from the palace. The ivory pieces from the king's bedroom are among them.* The foot panel of the bedstead of the king is supposed to be the largest single piece of ivory carving hitherto unearthed in the Near East. It is more than a yard wide and *ca.* twenty inches high. It is divided into sixteen panels, beautifully carved with pictures from the king's private and official life. Figs. UGA 9; ART 67.

ments are existing. Here is pottery of types connected with al-Ubaid and Jamdet Nasr. Influence from Mesopotamia can be seen clearly in this period. This is no wonder, as there was direct contact. King Sargon I of Agade and his successor Naram-Sin marched with their armies toward the W and reached the coast of the Mediterranean in the twenty-fourth century. Trade contacts had been established before this time, and they were developed further after the conquest of Sargon. Pottery, poorer in quality than previously, shows that a cultural downfall followed the fall of the Dynasty of Agade. This was the time of the ethnic movements in many parts of the Near East. The Amorites were streaming northward and established themselves in Syria and N Mesopotamia. They also reached Ugarit, probably coming along the coast.

Level II in Ras Shamra comprises the centuries 2100-1500, the Middle Bronze Age, one of the most turbulent periods in the history of the Near East. The excavations show that Ugarit already at this time had grown to a city of importance. The temples which have been unearthed seem to go back to this period, and there is no doubt that it was a city with a lively commerce. The royal seal, used by the Ugaritic kings, seems to be from this time. Several stylistic features point to the nineteenth or eighteenth century. The inscription "Yaqarum, Son of Niqmad, King of Ugarit" may indicate that this king and his father had been brought into their dominating position by the Amorite migration wave, which flowed into N Mesopotamia and Syria in the beginning of the second millennium B.C. It was in this time that the Hittites were building up their state too, and Hurrians (Horites) and Mitannians caused disturbances. Indo-European tribes came plundering along the coast of the Mediterranean. Also the Egyptians were active, and there are proofs that they played a role in Ugarit. Pharaoh Sen-Usert I (*ca.* 1971-1928) sent presents with his ambassadors, and a statuette of Princess Khnumit, who later married Sen-Usert II (nineteenth century). It is not unlikely that the princess was of Syrian origin. From about the same time is the stele of Sen-Usert-Ankh, an Egyptian representative at the court of the king of Ugarit. But this situation did not last long. The Hyksos overran Egypt, and also Ugarit was shaken, probably by Hurrites, but it soon recovered. Its ancient relations with Crete were developed. Trade was increased, new cultural influences absorbed, and Ugarit prospered. New houses were built, often in Cretan style, and a new rampart and wall were erected. After the fall of the Hyksos, Thut-mose I and III tried to re-establish Egyptian domination over Syria. Archaeologically this has left its traces in Ugaritic level I (*ca.* 1500-1100), Late Bronze Age and Iron I. Thut-mose III (1490-1435) stationed an Egyptian garrison in Ugarit in order to keep the area under control. The Egyptians first had trouble with the Mitannians, but from the time of Thut-mose IV there came a change in this. From 1440 to 1380 an Egyptian-Mitannian alliance existed. After that time the Hittites soon took the place of the Mitannians. King Suppiluliumas (1375-1335) conquered Mitannians and dominated N Syria. King Niqmad II of Ugarit, whose city-state had risen to great wealth at this time, could only nominally accept the rule of Pharaoh Amen-hotep IV; actually he sided with the Hittites. So did also his successors, Niqmepa and Ammistamru II. Letters written to the Pharaoh, found in TELL EL-AMARNA, witness to this double-dealing.

In the fourteenth century Ugarit was shocked by a catastrophe, an earthquake, which devastated the city and the port. They were rebuilt, but never attained their former splendor. The Egyptians tried to resume their domination, especially after the battle at Kadesh, where Pharaoh Ramses II (1290-1224) fought against the Hittites. In 1276 the two combatants made a treaty, and the relatively peaceful conditions which followed gave Ugarit a new opportunity to develop its trade. The Mycenean influence was great in this time, so extensive that Ugarit tended in the direction of becoming a Mycenean colony. But in the twelfth century Ugarit came to its end. Along the coast from the N came new invaders, the so-called Sea People. On their way toward the S they burned and destroyed Ugarit, which was never rebuilt. The harbor was used by Greek sailors in the sixth century B.C.; they called it Leukos Limen.

4. Texts. Already in the first season the excavators of Ras Shamra happened to strike the library in the house of the chief priest. Most of the texts were of a mythological character, and they have yielded a wealth of new information on the religion of Syria and CANAAN in the first half of the second millennium. The historical texts which were found later in the royal palace have been mentioned above. The tablets containing the mythological texts can be arranged in groups according to their contents. In the case of the long Baal-Anath text there is some discussion among scholars about the arrangement of the tablets. An additional difficulty is also that different scholars use variant designations of the tablets.

The liveliest picture of the Ugaritic gods and their life is given in the Baal-Anath text cycle. Here we meet El (or Il),* the leading god of the Ugaritic pantheon. He is represented as king of the gods. He is old and wise, the "Father of Years" (though *ab.šnm* may as well mean "Father of Shunem"). Several times in the texts he is characterized as *tr*, "Bull," a well-known symbol of masculine fertility. His procreative power was indicated also in the title *ab*, "Father." He was considered to be the father of the other gods, with the exception of Baal, who was called Dagon's son. El was the leader of the assembly of the gods, and the other gods needed his permission to start new enterprises. To him came Prince Sea, who asked permission to build a palace. Prince Sea also asked another favor in the assembly of the gods—namely, that Baal, Dagon's son, should be delivered into his hands. In this case we meet another side of El. He had grown old and anxious and was on the verge of yielding, together with the other gods, who were no better. This made Baal furious. Baal was the real hero of this cycle, the active, fighting god. One large temple in Ugarit was dedicated to him, another one to his father, Dagon. Baal was a rain, storm, and fertility god, "Lord of the Plowed Furrows." He was also seen as a bull, living in the good and beautiful fields, where he met the goddess

Anath, in the figure of a cow. Baal was identified with Hadad, the W Semitic storm and rain god. The designation Hadad is used of him several times in the text. Fig. UGA 10.

Baal was a hard fighter. Therefore he wanted to meet Prince Sea in an open fight. He got two magic clubs from the craftsman-god Kothar-wa-Khasis, and with the help of these he destroyed Prince Sea. This victory was claimed also by the goddess Anath, as is the case also with Baal's victory over Lotan, the

From Schaeffer, *The Cuneiform Texts of Ras Shamra–Ugarit* (The British Academy, Schweich Lectures, 1937)

10. El seated on a throne accepting an offering from the King of Ugarit; from Ras Shamra (fourteenth century B.C.)

"crooked serpent" (cf. Ps. 74:12-14). Baal and Anath may have been regarded as a unit in their capacity as fighters. We can see this also in the standing struggle with Mot, the god of the dry half of the year.

Prince Sea, who was defeated, did not get his palace built. Instead, Baal let Kothar-wa-Khasis build a palace for him on the mountain of the gods, Sapan, the "Mountain in the North." Through the help of the goddesses Anath and Asherah he was able to obtain the permission of El, and the palace (and temple) was erected. Then it was solemnly dedicated through a great banquet for the gods, with great sacrifices. The rites indicated in the text point in the direction of a New Year festival, of which Baal was considered founder.

But Baal was not always victorious, in spite of his fighting capacity. In a certain period he was unable to fight Mot, his ancient opponent. He sent his messengers to Mot and claimed the domination, but his time was up and he was no longer able to act. Mot knew that his time had come, that victory would be his without battle. Baal had to go into the earth, taking with him the clouds, the wind, the rains. A dry

period was coming over the earth while Baal was away. As soon as El and Anath heard of the disappearance of Baal, they mourned and sacrificed. Their mourning is described in a way which makes the text look like a ritual manual.

The throne of Baal was taken in possession by one of Asherah's sons, Athtar, who acted as a substitute king. But Anath, Baal's consort and cofighter, did not give in. She attacked Mot: "She seizes the god-son Mot, with a sword she splits him, in a sieve she scatters him, with millstones she grinds him, so that the birds may eat his remains." Mot is here treated like grain, and this fact may give a clue to the understanding of the character of this god. He may have represented the dry season with its drought but also with its ripening fruits and grain. Likewise, Baal may have represented the rainy season. In any case, after a while he returned to the earth with his rain and fertility. He drove away the substitute king, Athtar, and fought a terrible fight with Mot, whose turn it was now to go into the earth. Baal resumed his kingship and entered his throne in the palace on Mount Sapan. He was saluted with the cult cry: "Our king is Aliyan Baal, our judge, and none is above him!" The term "Aliyan" was used to denote Baal as the strong one, the one who prevailed. The cult cry clearly pointed out Baal as the dominating god; the words are without any reservations. This raises the question of his relationship to El. To this question different answers have been given. Some scholars see in the cult cry only an exalted expression of the power and the glory of the victorious young god, without any relation to the position of the leading god, El. Others hold that Baal challenged El and wanted to take over his position. They find analogies to this situation in other religions—e.g., Hurrian and ancient Greek. Every god had his worshipers, and changes in historical or ethnic circumstances may have changed the accent on the importance of the different gods. The texts indicate that while Baal was a young and active god who was popular in the Ugaritic cult, El was a more remote and shadowy figure. The Baal-Anath cycle has given much new information on the character of El and Baal, and also about Anath and Asherah.

The Legend of Aqhat,* Danel's son (previously called the Legend of Danel), is tolerably well preserved. After prayers to El and Baal, King Danel was blessed with a son, Aqhat. On a visit by Kothar-wa-Khasis, Aqhat was bestowed with a bow of unusual quality. The warlike and impetuous goddess Anath coveted this bow, but Aqhat was not willing to sell it, in spite of the offer of Anath to make him immortal. She had Yatpan transformed into an eagle, and he killed Aqhat. Aqhat's connection with fertility can be seen from the fact that "Baal failed for seven years," "without dew, without showers." Even the bow was lost at his death. Danel, the father of Aqhat, let Baal bring down the eagles and opened them, in order to find the remains of his son. He found them, buried them, punished the town where the murder had taken place, and had professional mourners to bewail the death of Aqhat for seven years. Pigat, Aqhat's sister, painted her face and went out with sword and dagger to avenge her brother. She met

From Virolleaud, *La Légende Phénicienne de Danel;*
courtesy of the Librairie Orientaliste Paul Geuthner, Paris

11. The legend of Aqhat

Yatpan, who betrayed himself under the influence of wine. But here the text breaks off. It seems to be a myth which tells about the death and resurrection of Aqhat, but nothing more definitely can be said. Fig. UGA 11.

The Legend of King Keret is harder to interpret, and several attempts have been made. In the first interpretations a series of biblical names was found in this text, but they mainly rested on a number of mistranslations which have now been abandoned. The hero of the story is King Keret of Hubur, who moans over the loss of his palace, his wife, and his children. El, the supreme god, comes to his help and shows him what to do. Keret invades the country of Udum and marries Huriya, the daughter of the king there. Baal urges El to bless Keret, and the king gets new sons and daughters. After a time Keret falls seriously ill, and his son Elhu wonders how he could really be a son of El, as the king was supposed to be. The king's illness influences the fertility of the field, and Elhu makes an offering to Baal. El finds it necessary to act, and with the help of Sha'taqat he restores Keret to his health. King Keret's son Yassib, who covets the throne of his father, is too late with his demands and is cursed by his father.

Some scholars think there is a nucleus of historical facts in the Keret story; others consider it a pure cultic myth. Most usually it is seen as a mythic hero legend, but it has also been characterized as some kind of social myth.

Some of the minor texts are of great interest, but very often hard to interpret. In the myth of the Rephaim, El summons the "Shades" (Rephaim) to a sacrificial feast, and on this occasion he announces that the victorious Baal is to be anointed with oil and become king and occupy his throne. The role of the Rephaim is not clear, but there are parallels with the Rephaim of the OT. The tablet which tells about Hadad-Baal has also new features about the "Bull Baal," "Dagon's son." Baal fights against devouring beasts, but is caught in a swamp. For seven years he is kept there while "the watercourses are parched dry," until his friends find him and help him out.

Two other texts worth mentioning are Shahar and Shalim, and Nikkal and Kathirat. The first one opens with a solemn declaration that glory shall be given to the gracious gods. A hymn shall be recited to the lute, in praise of the milk flowing from the breasts of the goddesses Athirat and Rahmay, who are in search of divine children to suckle. Seven times the sacrificers cook a kid in milk over the fire. Then it is told how the supreme god El comes to the shore of the great sea. Two women also arrive, and it is stated that "the organ of El grows long as the sea." Words are exchanged between El and the women. Then he kisses and embraces them. They bear two children— Shahar, "Dawn," and Shalim, "Dusk." The two sons are born in one day and suck the breasts of the goddesses. The words of the two women seem to indicate that they tease the aging god with his growing impotence, and the text will show how El is rejuvenated. It is a text connected with a feast with a sacred marriage and certain sacrifices, possibly of first fruits in early summer.

Nikkal and Kathirat is a song of Nikkal-and-Eb, the moon goddess and goddess of fruit, daughter of Hirhibi, king of summer, and of her marriage with Yarih, the West Semitic moon-god. The Kathirat, "shining daughters of the crescent moon," are asked to give their support when a son is going to be born. Yarih asks Hirhibi to give him his daughter Nikkal, pieces of silver, ten thousand pieces of gold, brilliant stones of sapphire, vineyards and orchards. Hirhibi wants to give him Pidriya, the daughter of Baal, but Yarih wants Nikkal. "Thereupon Yarih brings the betrothal gift for Nikkal; her sire sets the standard of the scales, her mother the tray(s) of the scales, her brethren arrange the plummets(?), her sisters (attend) to the weights of the scales" (Driver's translation; *see* Weights and Measures § A). So Nikkal-and-Eb became "the light of Yarih." The poem ends in an appeal to "let her dowry and her wedding gifts be weighed out unto her with shouts of applause." In some way the poem reflects ancient marriage customs as they were in use in the Middle East (*see* Marriage § 2c). It may possibly have been used at weddings, ensuring fertility for the bride and the bridegroom through the story of the divine marriage.

On the whole, the minor texts present additional features of the picture of the Ugaritic pantheon painted in the long texts. Through all these texts new light has been thrown on gods mentioned in the OT, such as El (*see* God, OT); Baal (4); Anath; and Asherah.

The historical texts found in the royal palace have been mentioned above. They consist of juridical and economical documents and a large collection of letters which give valuable information about the last centuries of Ugarit's history. They have yielded exact dates and details about ancient Ugarit and have confirmed the dating previously given to the mythical and cultic texts.

Bibliography. A bibliography of the enormous literature in the Ugaritic field can only be selective and will even then have to leave out works well worth reading. Nearly all the mythological texts were originally published by C. Virolleaud in the French journal *Syria* from 1929 on.

Decipherment: H. Bauer, *Entzifferung der Keilschrifttafeln von Ras Schamra* (1930).

Translations: C. H. Gordon, *Ugaritic Literature* (1949). T. H. Gaster, *Thespis* (1950). H. L. Ginsberg in J. B. Pritchard, ed., *ANET* (2nd ed., 1955), pp. 129-55.

Texts: C. H. Gordon, *Ugaritic Handbook* (1947); *Ugaritic Manual* (1955). J. Gray, *The KRT Text in the Literature of Ras Shamra* (1955). G. R. Driver, *Canaanite Myths and Legends* (1956).

Monographs: C. F. A. Schaeffer, *The Cuneiform Texts of Ras Shamra-Ugarit* (1939). R. Dussaud, *Les découvertes de Ras Shamra (Ugarit) et l'AT* (1941). R. de Langhe, *Les textes de Ras Shamra-Ugarit I-II* (1945). J. Obermann, *Ugaritic Mythology* (1948). O. Eissfeldt, *El im ugaritischen Pantheon* (1951). A. S. Kapelrud, *Baal in the Ras Shamra Texts* (1952). M. H. Pope, *El in the Ugaritic Texts* (1955). J. Gray, *The Legacy of Canaan. The Ras Shamra Texts and Their Relevance to the OT* (1957).

A. S. KAPELRUD

UKNAZ ŭk′năz [וּקְנַז]. KJV marginal note at I Chr. 4:15. The LXX and the Vulg. omit the וּ. Read with the KJV text "even KENAZ," though possibly a preceding name has dropped.

ULAI ū′lī [אוּלַי] (Dan. 8:2, 16). An artificial canal near SUSA, where Daniel received the vision of the ram and the he-goat. It is the Akkadian *U-la-a,* whose waters Ashurbanipal claims to have reddened with the blood of his enemies on his invasion of Elam. By the classical writers it was known as the Eulaeus. Near ancient Susa were three rivers—to the SW the Kerkha (ancient Choaspes), to the E the Abdizful (ancient Coprates), which flowed into the Karun (ancient Pasitigris). The Ulai was a wide artificial canal which connected the Kerkha and the Abdizful, and passed close by Susa on the N or the NE.

The word translated "river" in Dan. 8:2-3, 6 (אוּבָל in vs. 2, but אֻבָל and with the definite article in vss. 3, 6), is variously interpreted by scholars. Some derive it from a Semitic root "to bring, carry," yielding a noun "conduit" or "artificial canal." Others read the word as אֲבוּל (Aramaic אֲבוּלָא; cf. Akkadian *abullu*), "gate," and this reading is supported by LXX. In the latter case the reference in Daniel would be to the Ulai gate, probably so named because it faced the Ulai canal.

Bibliography. L. Waterman, "A Note on Daniel 8:2," *JBL,* LXVI (1947), 319-20; H. L. Ginsberg, *Studies in Daniel* (1948), pp. 57, 84.

R. F. SCHNELL

ULAM ū′lăm [אוּלָם, first, leader]. **1.** Eponym of a clan or family of Manasseh (I Chr. 7:16-17).

2. The first son of Eshek; head of a Benjaminite family famous as archers (I Chr. 8:39-40). Benjaminite archers are mentioned in II Chr. 14:8.

Bibliography. M. Noth, *Die israelitischen Personennamen* (1928), p. 231.

T. M. MAUCH

ULCER [עֹפֶל] (Deut. 28:27; I Sam. 5:6-12; 6:4-5); KJV EMEROD. A lesion of the skin or mucous membranes. עֹפֶל was generally used to describe inguinal buboes or "plague boils," rather than staphylococcal swellings or hemorrhoids.

R. K. HARRISON

ULLA ŭl′ə [עֻלָּא] (I Chr. 7:39). A family of the tribe of Asher. Various scholars suggest the name be read "Shua" (שׁוּעָא; cf. vs. 32), "Shual" (שׁוּעָל; cf. vs. 36), "Amal" (עָמָל; cf. vs. 35), or "Ara" (אֲרָא; cf. vs. 38).

Bibliography. W. Rudolf, *Chronikbücher,* HAT (1955), p. 74.

T. M. MAUCH

UMMAH ŭm′ə [עֻמָּה] (Josh. 19:30). A town in the territory allotted to the tribe of Asher. Ummah is generally regarded as an error for ACCO, which is conspicuously absent from the list (cf. Judg. 1:31). This reading is supported by several Greek MSS.

G. W. VAN BEEK

UMPIRE [מוֹכִיחַ, *Hiph'il participle from* יכח, *commonly Hiph'il,* to decide, adjudge] (Job 9:33); KJV DAYSMAN. A mediator suggested for resolving the conflicts of God and man.

Bibliography. S. Terrien, Exegesis of Job, *IB,* III (1954), 985.

B. D. NAPIER

UNCIAL ŭn′shəl. The form of letters—large and rounded—characteristic of most Greek and Latin MSS of the Bible between the fourth and ninth centuries, after which the MINUSCULE style became more common. Both terms are therefore applied to MSS written in the respective styles. The use of the word "uncial" has been traced to Jerome, who speaks disapprovingly of many books in his day as written in *"uncialibus . . . litteris."* His meaning has been much disputed; but since the Latin word *uncia* means a "twelfth part," and therefore an inch or an ounce, it seems likely that he is saying derisively that books were being written with letters an inch wide.

For descriptions of the great uncial MSS, *see* TEXT, NT, § B3.

J. KNOX

UNCIRCUMCISED, UNCIRCUMCISION. See CIRCUMCISION.

UNCLEAN, UNCLEANNESS. *See* CLEAN AND UNCLEAN.

UNDERSETTERS [כָּתֵף]. KJV obsolete term (I Kings 7:30, 34; RSV SUPPORTS) for the supports at the four corners of the bronze stands in the temple. *See* LAVER.

UNDERSTAND, UNDERSTANDING. Words which belong to the distinctive vocabulary of the wisdom literature (although they also appear occasionally in the Prophets), and which translate a number of Hebrew and Greek words that mean, in varying degrees, either "to grasp the full meaning of something said or done" or—in the context of action—"to have the knowledge and skill requisite for accomplishing a desired end." In the latter sense "understanding" is pre-eminently characteristic of the activity of God (Job 26:12; Prov. 3:19), and all understanding ultimately has its source in him (Prov. 2:6; II Tim. 2:7).

For "understanding" in its simplest and most superficial sense, that of being able to comprehend words spoken in a foreign language, the Hebrew word in the OT is always שׁמע (lit., "to hear"; Gen. 11:7; Ezek. 3:6; cf. the use of ἀκούω in I Cor. 14:2). Since the dividing line between KNOWLEDGE and "understanding" is a fairly fluid one, the English versions must sometimes translate "understand," where the Hebrew is content to say merely "know" (ידע; II Sam. 3:37). In the great majority of passages in the English OT, however, the words "understand" and "understanding" translate the various stems and cognates of the Hebrew roots בין and שׂכל. The root בין means primarily "to discern with the senses," "to perceive distinctions," then "to give close attention to," and finally—particularly in the derived stems—"to gain comprehension" or "give" it to others. The root שׂכל seems likewise originally to have expressed the idea of "paying close attention to," although in OT usage it has come to mean specifically "to have insight" or "to be prudent"; consequently it and its derivatives are often translated by some form of the word "wise" or "WISDOM" (Ps. 2:10; Prov. 23:9), as well as by "understand" and "understanding" (Ps. 111:10; Isa. 41:20). Both these basic words imply an active and habitual effort at comprehension rather than a mere passive state of possessing knowledge, and so they have connotations which are important for the moral as well as the intellective life.

It is significant for OT anthropology that the noun "understanding," besides being used to translate several words that have a specific connection with man's intellectual life, must also be used in some instances in the wisdom literature to translate the Hebrew word for "heart" (לב or לבב), which is often used in a figurative sense to denote the deepest recesses of the human personality where man's being centers and where the issues of his life are determined. (It is therefore sometimes translated in the English versions by "mind"; see HEART; MIND.) Typical passages where the sense of "understanding" seems the most appropriate are Job 34:10; Prov. 6:32 KJV; 9:16 KJV, in all of which the translators of the LXX also render the Hebrew word "heart" by a Greek word denoting "understanding" or the absence of it. This use, rather than indicating that the heart was regarded as the special "seat" of the intelligence, is perhaps best understood in the light of such English idiomatic expressions as "a deep person," "a shallow person," "a person lacking in depth," which are closely parallel in meaning to the Hebrew phrases "a man of heart" (Job 34:10) or "(a man) deficient in heart" (Prov. 6:32).

In the NT, the English verb "understand" is used to translate a large variety of words with varying shades of meaning: συνίημι, meaning specifically "to understand" (Matt. 16:12); νοέω, "to think or consider" and so "to arrive at understanding" (Matt. 15:17 KJV); γινώσκω, properly "to know, to be cognizant of" (John 8:27); ἐπιγινώσκω, "to recognize" (I Cor. 13:12; RSV-KJV "know"); εἶδον, "to see or perceive" (i.e., with the mind; I Cor. 13:2). The following verbs are also each translated at least once in the English NT by "understand": ἀκούω, "to hear" (I Cor. 14:2); γνωρίζω, "(to make) to know" (I Cor. 12:3); ἐπίσταμαι, "to know, or know about" (Mark 14:68); and φρονέω (I Cor. 13:11 KJV; the RSV more accurately translates "to think"). The noun "understanding" in the NT translates either σύνεσις, a Greek word of precisely equivalent meaning (Col. 2:2); διάνοια, "thought," "thinking" (I John 5:20); καρδία ("heart"; Eph. 4:18); or νοῦς, literally "MIND" (Phil. 4:7).   R. C. DENTAN

UNFORGIVABLE SIN.

A concept resting, first of all, on Jesus' words in Mark 3:29-30: " 'Whoever blasphemes against the Holy Spirit never has forgiveness, but is guilty of an eternal sin'—for they had said, 'He has an unclean spirit.' " This passage which refers to the scribes is commonly connected with Paul's word in II Thess. 1:8-9 about those who do not obey the gospel and who will suffer the punishment of eternal destruction. The writer of the Letter to the Hebrews declares that the apostate ones who crucify the Son of God and hold him up to contempt cannot be restored (6:4-6); he also says that deliberate sin after baptism cannot be forgiven and that rejection of the Son and the blood of the covenant and the Spirit of grace can merit only fiery judgment (10:26-31). The author of I John encourages prayer for a sinning brother, but he hesitates to encourage prayer for a brother whose sin is mortal (5:14-17).

Thus the unforgivable sin is not an "erratic boulder" appearing in a single passage of the Bible. In general, it fits into the threat of stern judgment, which is a persistent feature of the biblical background (Num. 15:30-31; Matt. 11:21-24; Mark 14:21; Luke 10:13-15; Rev. 14:9-11).

On the other hand, no emphasis on the unforgivable sin should be allowed to obscure or limit God's purpose to forgive, which is a constant note in the gospel message. In the Lord's Prayer, Christians are to pray for forgiveness. Jesus asked for forgiveness even for those who crucified him. Peter was restored after his threefold denial.

Negatively, the unforgivable sin does not describe a single act that merits eternal judgment. Certainly it does not refer to an inadvertent word or deed which might be the result of thoughtlessness. And it does not concern the unevangelized heathen who have never heard the Word.

The unforgivable sin applies to those who, after knowledge, deliberately and persistently reject Christ and refuse to recognize his work as the work of God. In its extreme and radical character the term points up the life-and-death claims of Jesus in his words and work as a Revealer of God. To reject him after knowledge is to shut oneself from the gospel truth and to condemn oneself to utter loss. As such, these harsh prophecies serve as warnings to men not to reject so great a salvation. Loss and destruction are the only alternative to the grace of God in Christ.

For men to deny what the Spirit attests is to make God a liar (I John 5:10). It is to pervert the whole spiritual order and to disqualify oneself from the kingdom of righteousness. In this perversion men lose the capacity to accept God's free offer of grace.

Bibliography. J. Müller, *The Christian Doctrine of Sin,* II (1883), 475-83; A. E. Brooke, *The Johannine Epistles* (1912); J. E. Thomas, *The Problem of Sin in the NT* (1927); E. B. Redlich, *The Forgiveness of Sin* (1937); C. H. Dodd, *The Johannine Epistles* (1946); C. R. Smith, *The Bible Doctrine of Sin* (1953), pp. 176-83.   P. E. DAVIES

UNGODLY. *See* GODLY.

UNICORN. KJV translation of רְאֵם, רֵים, and רְמִים (RSV WILD OX). The unicorn, a fabulous beast, was said to have a single horn on its forehead. The KJV derived "unicorn" from the LXX μονόκερως, "single-horned" (ἁδροί, "strong ones," in Isa. 34:7), and the Vulg. *unicornis* and *rhinoceros*. The LXX translation may have been based on accounts traceable to remarks by Ctesias (fourth century B.C.) on the Indian rhinoceros, a beast which Ctesias had never seen. The legend of the unicorn grew to vast proportions in the Middle Ages.

Bibliography. W. Ley, *The Lungfish, the Dodo, and the Unicorn* (1948), pp. 19-34, gives a sprightly history of the unicorn legend. See also: E. Schrader, *Keilinschriften und der AT* (2nd ed., 1883), p. 256; O. Shepard, *The Lore of the Unicorn* (1930).   E. M. GOOD

UNIVERSE. The translation of κόσμος (elsewhere WORLD) in Gal. 4:3; Col. 2:8, 20; and of τὰ πάντα (lit., "all things") in Heb. 1:3.

UNKNOWN GOD, ALTAR TO AN. Paul's sermon on the Areopagus (Acts 17:22-31) takes for its text an altar inscription "To an unknown god" ('Αγνώστῳ Θεῷ). No other evidence for the existence of such an inscription has ever been found, and most classical scholars hold that the use of this exact wording on a Greek altar is inconceivable. In the late fourth century Jerome had already affirmed that it actually ran: "To gods of Asia and Europe and Africa, gods unknown and alien." Accordingly, most modern commentators, whether they regard the speech itself as Pauline or not, follow E. Norden in holding that the dedication was in the plural: "To unknown gods"; and that it has been transposed into the singular to make it conform to the monotheistic doctrine of the author. For inscriptions worded in this way there is plenty of evidence; according to Pausanias (second century A.D.), there were "altars of unknown gods and of heroes" along the way from the harbor of Phalerum to Athens, and one such inscription has actually been found. There are also references in literature to sacrifices made to "a nameless god," and "to the appropriate god."

In all these instances, the significance seems to be the same: men are honoring a god whose name is unknown to them, for benefits received at his hands. The phrase cannot be taken as reflecting the notion of a god unknowable. Of course, the maker of the sermon was not concerned to expound the original intent of the inscription, but only to adapt the words to his own exposition of the revelation of God in Christ.

Bibliography. E. Norden, *Agnostos Theos* (1913); T. Birt, "'Αγνώστοι Θεοί und die Areopagrede des Apostels Paulus," *Rheinisches Museum*, 69 (1914), 349-92; K. Lake, "Note XIX. The Unknown God," in F. J. Foakes-Jackson and K. Lake, eds., *The Beginnings of Christianity*, pt. 1, vol. V (1933), pp. 240-46; B. Gärtner, *The Areopagus Speech and Natural Revelation* (trans. C. H. King; 1955), ch. 9: "The altar inscription."   F. W. BEARE

UNLEAVENED BREAD [מַצּוֹת, *from* מַצָּה, drained out, unfermented; LXX ἄζυμα]. Bread or cakes baked without yeast; mandatory for certain cultic occasions and uses but also utilized as ordinary food (Gen. 19:3; Judg. 6:19; I Sam. 28:24).

Unleavened bread is most intimately associated with the Feast of Unleavened Bread (*see* PASSOVER AND FEAST OF UNLEAVENED BREAD), for the duration of which only unleavened bread was permitted. It was eaten with bitter herbs (Exod. 12:8; Num. 9:11) and commemorated the haste in which Israel left Egypt. All the *matsôth* prepared for this feast were to be consumed within the seven-day period; the Samaritan Passover specified a quota for each of the seven days.

All baked cereal offerings brought to the altar were also always unleavened bread (Lev. 2:5 ff, etc.), and what remained of these offerings was to be eaten by the priests (Lev. 10:12).

Beginning with the offering of the sheaf at the beginning of the harvest (Lev. 23:11; Deut. 16:9), it was permissible to bake unleavened bread from the grain of the new crop (cf. Josh. 5:11); but until the Feast of Weeks (*see* WEEKS, FEAST OF), fifty days later, concluding the harvest, the use of the new crop for leavened baking was prohibited. This prohibition came to an end with the special cereal offering of two leavened loaves of bread at Weeks, consumed by the priests (Lev. 23:17).

The absence of leaven was a mark of separateness or holiness; leaven was kept from the holiness of God's altar, and, in times of states of special sanctity, from his people also. Just as the blood is drained (Lev. 1:15; נמצה) from the sacrificial animal, so the life or power of leaven is kept separate from the bread offered to God.   J. C. RYLAARSDAM

UNNI ŭn'ī [עֻנִּי, *probably hypocoristic for* (Yahu) has answered; *cf.* עֲנָיָה, ANAIAH] (I Chr. 15:18, 20). Alternately: UNNO —ō [עֻנּוֹ (*Kethibh*), עֻנִּי (*Qere*)] (Neh. 12:9); KJV UNNI. 1. A Levite; one of the musicians who accompanied the ark of the covenant when David had it brought up to Jerusalem (I Chr. 15:18-20).

2. A Levite of the postexilic period, contemporary of the high priest Jeshua (Neh. 12:9, where read "Unni" with the KJV).

Bibliography. M. Noth, *Die israelitischen Personennamen* (1928), pp. 39, 185. On text and etymology in Neh. 12:9, see R. A. Bowman, Exegesis of Nehemiah, *IB*, III (1954), 786.   B. T. DAHLBERG

UNPARDONABLE SIN. *See* UNFORGIVABLE SIN.

UNTIMELY BIRTH [נֵפֶל; LXX ἔκτρωμα] (Job 3:16; Ps. 58:8; Eccl. 6:3; I Cor. 15:8). In antiquity a birth which occurred before the full gestation period of approximately forty weeks had been completed was regarded as "fallen" or "miscarried," regardless of whether the fetus was nonviable or capable of independent existence. Modern medicine has made a distinction between abortion, in which the uterus is evacuated prior to the fourth month of pregnancy; miscarriage, where the uterus discharges the fetus during the fourth, fifth, or sixth month of gestation; and premature delivery, in which a fetus capable of independent life is born after the beginning of the seventh month but prior to full term. Since the OT untimely births "never see the light," it can be assumed that the references are to abortion or miscarriage. Num. 12:12 may indicate a missed abortion, in which a dead embryo is retained for a prolonged period in the uterus before being expelled. The rendering in Isa. 14:19 is an attempt to clarify a textual obscurity, the Hebrew being "a loathed branch."

Paul's use of ἔκτρωμα (I Cor. 15:8) suggests the unusual nature of his entrance into Christianity. He was a miscarriage of Judaism, precipitated suddenly from an alien, moribund mother and transformed from persecutor into apostle. The other apostles experienced a normal spiritual birth at a time when Paul could not be called an apostle any more than a miscarriage or an abortion could be regarded as a living child. Paul was keenly sensitive to the errors of earlier days, and consequently was overwhelmed by his dramatic conversion through divine grace.

R. K. HARRISON

UNWRITTEN SAYINGS. *See* AGRAPHA.

UPHARSIN ū fär′sĭn. *See* MENE, MENE, TEKEL, AND PARSIN.

UPHAZ ū′făz [אוּפָז]. A place mentioned as a source of gold (Jer. 10:9; Dan. 10:5). Its location is unknown. The suggestion has been advanced that "Uphaz" is an error for "OPHIR," which is also noted for its gold, and this suggestion is supported by the Targ. and the Syr. Hexapla, which read "Ophir" in Jer. 10:9.

G. W. VAN BEEK

UPPER BETH-HORON. *See* BETH-HORON.

UPPER CHAMBER. *See* CHAMBER.

UPPER GATE [שַׁעַר בֵּית יהוה הָעֶלְיוֹן, the upper gate of the house of Yahweh] (II Kings 15:35); KJV HIGHER GATE. A gate built by Uzziah for the temple of Jerusalem. The exact location is unknown. *See* TEMPLE (JERUSALEM).

G. A. BARROIS

UPPER ROOM [ἀνάγαιον, ὑπερῷον]. The place chosen by Jesus for his last meal with his disciples (Mark 14:14-15; Luke 22:11-12). Here it is called ἀνάγαιον. This commonly is taken to be the same room, ὑπερῷον, in which the disciples gathered after the Ascension (Acts 1:13) and which now they were using as a common living room. This would be a room in the upper story of a large house or a room on the roof, as the room which the wealthy woman made for Elisha (II Kings 4:10), probably like the upper chamber (עֲלִיָּה) of the widow's house where Elijah lodged (I Kings 17:19). In the home of the mukhtar or the principal house in an Arab village today there is likely to be an upper room, *medhafeh,* for the entertainment of guests.

According to Epiphanius, Hadrian found the building of which the Upper Room was a part still standing when he visited Jerusalem in A.D. 135. The building was identified by Cyril of Jerusalem, the Bordeaux Pilgrim, Sylvia, and others. The room,

called the Cenacle, is now on the first floor of the mosque En Neby Daud, remodeled from a fourteenth century church, S of the modern Zion gate. A Christian church adjoining the Cenacle existed as early as the fourth century.

Eglon was sitting in a roof chamber when he was slain by Ehud (Judg. 3:20). Josiah in his reform pulled down the altars on the roof of the upper chamber of Ahaz (II Kings 23:12). Daniel prayed in his upper chamber with his window open toward Jerusalem (Dan. 6:10). *See* ARCHITECTURE; CHAMBER; HOUSE; ROOF.

O. R. SELLERS

UPRIGHT. *See* RIGHTEOUSNESS.

UR ûr [אוּר, flame *or* light]. The father of Eliphal, one of the company of the Mighty Men of David known as the "Thirty" (I Chr. 11:35). However, there are indications that the name has suffered corruption, since in the parallel catalogue the father of Eliphelet (=Eliphal) is AHASBAI (II Sam. 23:34).

E. R. DALGLISH

UR (CITY) [אוּר; Assyrian-Babylonian *Uri,* from Sumer. *Urim*]. An ancient city on the Euphrates in Lower Mesopotamia (present-day Iraq), mentioned in the Bible as Ur of the Chaldees, home of Abraham.

The ruins of Ur, known as al-Muqayyer, were first investigated by the English archaeologists Loftus and Taylor in 1854; later explorations were made by Campbell Thompson in 1918 and Hall in 1918-19. Systematic excavations on the site were undertaken in 1922 by a joint expedition of the British Museum and the University of Pennsylvania, University Museum, under the direction of Leonard Woolley. The expedition, after completing twelve highly successful campaigns, ended its work on the site in 1934.

The site of Ur is roughly oval in shape, with the long axis of the oval pointing N-S. At the N end of the oval and at the middle of its W side are the remains of harbors for the river traffic, called by the excavators the North Harbor and the West Harbor respectively. An imaginary line drawn NW-SE through the mound would soon reach and pass along the main axis of the rectangular walled sacred area of the city, which occupies the middle third of the N half of the site. This area was very fully explored by the expedition. Continuing beyond the sacred area, the line drawn would pass in front of a large excavated area of private dwellings of the Isin-Larsa Period (twentieth-nineteenth centuries). A similar area of private houses was excavated between the S corner of the sacred area and the West Harbor. Immediately to the S of the North Harbor a large Neo-Babylonian palace was excavated. S of this palace a Neo-Babylonian temple, the Harbor Temple, was cleared. Two smaller temples on the E and SE edges of the site were likewise cleared.

The sacred area of Ur is, as mentioned, roughly rectangular. It contains in its NW part the main temple of the city, E-temen-ni-guru, dedicated to the moon-god Nanna (Akkadian Sin). Entrance to the temple was through a great towered gate in the NE side which led into a large rectangular forecourt surrounded by rooms of various kinds. In the NW corner of this court the excavators found a group of

From *Atlas of the Bible* (Thomas Nelson & Sons Limited)

12. Ziggurat at Ur. Notice its size in comparison with the person at its foot.

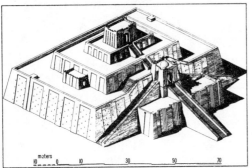

Courtesy of the University Museum of the University of Pennsylvania

13. Isometric projection of the ziggurat of Ur-Nammu restored

throne daises, presumably for the use of various gods when they met in assembly with Nanna. Across the court from the entrance, stairs led up to a larger rectangular inner court on a higher level. This court was also surrounded by rooms serving ritual and practical purposes such as temple kitchen, etc. In the middle of this court stood the temple tower, or ziggurat (Figs. UR 12-13).* It was at the time of Ur III (*ca.* twenty-second and twenty-first centuries) a stepped pyramid with three massive steps. The core was constructed of mud bricks, but the outer surfaces were encased in a skin of burned bricks. A long, monumental free staircase led up to the first stage at the middle of its E façade, while two flanking staircases led up along the façade from the right and left corners to join the middle stairway in a gate room at the top. Further, smaller stairs led from here up to the second and on to the third stage, on top of which stood the temple of the moon-god itself. From the court in which stood the ziggurat a gate and stairway at the SE corner led down to a lower terrace. This gate, venerated as the place where the god rendered judgment, was in the Ur III period closed and converted to serve as a separate temple, the E-dublal-mah. To the left of this converted gate, in the corner between the smaller forecourt and the wall of the ziggurat terrace, the excavators found the main storehouse of the temple, known as the Ga-nun-mah. It consisted of huge, narrow, rectangular storerooms for wool, cloth, and other goods, and had in its center

a double cella, possibly for Nanna and his consort Ningal, possibly for deities of the storehouse. To the right of the Dublal-mah, adjoining the SE side of the ziggurat terrace, lay another, different structure, the Giparku. This large complex housed in its SE part a temple for Ningal, the divine consort of Nanna. Behind this, in the SW corner of the building, was an elaborate temple kitchen with fireplaces, work tables, well, etc.; and in the NW part of the complex were located the quarters of the *entu*-priestess, a girl of royal descent chosen as the human bride of the moon-god and officiating at the yearly ritual of the sacred marriage. To the SE of the Dublal-mah the excavators came upon the scant remains of the royal palace of Shulgi of the Third Dynasty of Ur, and SE of this the magnificent mausoleum of the kings of the Third Dynasty of Ur. The mausoleum was solidly built of baked bricks laid in bitumen. Its plan was that of a private house, but the recessed outer wall and rebated doorways, characteristic of temples, made it a suitable resting place for deified rulers. Below the floors of the rooms in the back of the building two brick stairs led down to corbeled underground tomb chambers. The doors of these chambers had been bricked up and the stair well filled in after the burial ceremony. The central and earliest part of the mausoleum was built with bricks of King Shulgi. On the SE and NW smaller, similar buildings, built with bricks of Amarsin, had been added; they had much the same plan as the central unit and likewise contained subterranean tomb chambers. The buildings and tombs had all been thoroughly plundered in antiquity. Fig. ASS 105.

The mausoleum of the kings of the Third Dynasty of Ur was the last tomb in a royal cemetery located in this area and dating back to the middle of Early Dynastic times (*ca.* 2600 B.C.). This cemetery, carefully and skilfully explored by the excavators, yielded a wealth of treasures and threw new and unexpected light on ancient Sumerian burial customs and beliefs. Most striking were the royal tombs of Early Dynastic III date.* The findings left little doubt that the kings and queens of Ur were followed in death by their courtiers and personal attendants, who, dressed in their best, the soldiers with their spears, the musicians with costly harps, the grooms leading the royal ox cart, entered the grave chamber or the sloping ramp that led into the burial pit in order to follow their master into the world beyond. The peaceful sleeping positions of their bodies when found suggest that they had voluntarily let themselves be killed, possibly by drinking poison or by taking a strong sleeping draught before the burial pit was filled in over them. This custom—that the retinue of a ruler followed him in death—is now attested also in literary texts. The story of the death of Gilgamesh and his burial, told by an ancient Sumerian poet, relates that Gilgamesh' closest servants entered the grave with him. A variant interpretation of the findings at Ur, much in vogue in the years just after the discovery, assumed that the chief occupants of the royal graves were not actually kings and queens of Ur, but rather participants in a fertility rite who had to be killed after completion of the rite. This interpretation accords less well with the data, especially after further finds have shown that several of the occupants of the tombs were directly designated as "king" and "queen" on seals found in the cemetery, and since the literary evidence mentioned above has shown that the findings accord with Sumerian custom. Figs. UR 14-18; GAM 6; WEA 9.

At the site of the royal cemetery and at other points of the mound deep soundings were made to

Courtesy of the University Museum of the University of Pennsylvania

16. Head model of Queen Shubad of Ur, showing elaborate headdress and jewelry, from the royal tombs at Ur; Early Dynastic III period

Courtesy of the University Museum of the University of Pennsylvania

14. Statuette of a he-goat standing by a tree; made of gold, silver, lapis lazuli, and white shell on a wooden core; from Ur, Early Dynastic period

Courtesy of the University Museum of the University of Pennsylvania

17. The gold lyre from the great death pit at Ur, Early Dynastic period

clarify the stratigraphy of the site. It was found that occupation at Ur went back beyond the Early Dynastic Period to the Proto-literate Period, the Warka Period, and the Al-Ubaid Period (see SUMER). The last-mentioned period is the one in which S Mesopotamia generally seems to have been first settled. In two of these soundings the excavator found, separating the early and later layers of the Ubaid Period, a heavy deposit of silt laid down by water. Since the Euphrates in antiquity flowed close by the site, such a layer can fairly easily be accounted for by changes in the course of the stream bed or local inundations. Similar layers datable to various archaeological periods have been found in other ancient settlements in Mesopotamia. In the case of the silt layer at Ur, however, the excavator saw it as evidence, not of a change in the river bed or a local inundation, but of a catastrophic flood covering all of S Mesopotamia in Ubaid times. He further assumed that memories of this event were handed down to take the form which we have in the Sumerian and Assyro-Babylonian flood stories, stories

Courtesy of the University Museum of the University of Pennsylvania

15. Gold helmet from the tomb of Mes-kalam-dug; found at Ur, Early Dynastic period

Courtesy of the University Museum of the University of Pennsylvania

18. Gold cup and lamp, from Ur royal tombs, Early Dynastic period

which would have spread by oral tradition to underlie the biblical story of Noah and the Flood. Few Mesopotamian archaeologists have accepted this interpretation.

In an area SW of the sacred area and in an area between it and the West Harbor sections of private houses of the Isin-Larsa (twentieth-nineteenth centuries) and Old-Babylonian periods (nineteenth-sixteenth centuries) were excavated. In the preliminary reports these were named private houses of Ur in the times of Abraham, a designation which begs the question whether Abraham and the biblical tradition about him may be considered historical and, if so, which date may be assumed for his *floruit*. The houses were generally two stories high. A central court surrounded by rooms, a staircase in the corner leading up to an upper story with rooms opening upon a balcony around the court supported on wooden pillars, were the basic features. The roofs seem to have been flat. The plan is remarkably similar to that of older Iraqi houses of today. The streets along which the houses lay were narrow, winding lanes opening now and again on irregularly shaped open spaces. Here and there among the houses small public shrines dedicated to minor deities were found. Fig. SUM 85.

Bibliography. C. J. Gadd, *The History and Monuments of Ur* (1929). L. Woolley, *Ur of the Chaldees* (1929); *Excavations at Ur* (1954). For further details see Woolley's preliminary reports published regularly in *The Antiquaries Journal* during the years the expedition was in the field.　　　T. JACOBSEN

URBANUS ûr bā'nəs [Οὐρβανός; Lat. *Urbanus*, refined, elegant] (Rom. 16:9); KJV URBANE ûr'bān. A Christian man greeted by Paul. He is referred to as a "fellow worker" (συνεργός) of Paul, together with Prisca and Aquila in vs. 3 and Timothy in vs. 21 of the same chapter; this puts him in exceptional company.　　　F. W. GINGRICH

URI yōōr'ī [אוּרִי, fiery; *perhaps a contraction of* אוּרִיָּה, URIAH]. 1. A Judahite; the father of Bezalel, one of the builders of the tabernacle (Exod. 31:2; 35:30; etc.).

2. A gatekeeper in the restored temple (Ezra 10:24).

3. The father of Geber, the district officer in Gilead under Solomon (I Kings 4:19).　　J. M. WARD

URIAH yōō rī'ə [אוּרִיָּה, אוּרִיָּהוּ, Y is a light; *cf.* Hurrian *Ariya*, Akkad. *U-ri-ia-a*; Οὐρίου]; KJV alter-

nately URIJAH —jə; KJV NT URIAS —əs. 1. A Hittite; one of the Mighty Men in David's select order of the "Thirty," many of whom were foreigners (II Sam. 23:39; I Chr. 11:41). It is possible that his name originally was Ariya, which popular etymology transformed into Uriah. It is more probable either that he received the name Uriah from a sojourning father, or that he himself took the name Uriah, already current in Israel, when he became a SO-JOURNER in Israel and joined in the worship of Yahweh. His wife was Bathsheba, perhaps a daughter of that Eliam who like Uriah was a member of the Thirty (II Sam. 23:34), in which case she was a granddaughter of Ahithophel. King David summoned Uriah from the battlefield at the siege of Rabbah, the Ammonite capital, in order to make it appear that Uriah was the father of the child that would be born to Bathsheba. However, Uriah conducted himself according to the campaigning army's discipline for psychic integrity and strength in combat. He observed the taboo which forbade sexual intercourse to warriors consecrated for battle (cf. I Sam. 21:4; *see* BAN). His words express loyalty to the ark, to his commander Joab, and to David. Even when David made him drunk, he maintained his identity with the army in the field, sleeping with the royal guard. Uriah carried to Joab the letter in which David told Joab to place Uriah in the front of a sortie, and then to retreat from him so that he would be slain. When Bathsheba heard that he was dead, she lamented for her husband; afterward David took Uriah's wife to be his wife (II Sam. 11). Nathan declared to David that his action was a sin against Yahweh, and David agreed with the prophetic evaluation (II Sam. 12:1-15; cf. the comment of a scribe in I Kings 15:5*b*β). In a genealogy of Jesus Christ, "David was the father of Solomon by the wife of Uriah" (Matt. 1:6).

2. A priest; one of two reliable men, evidently prominent and trusted citizens, whom Isaiah got as witnesses to a prophetic oracle written on a tablet (Isa. 8:2). Either their action added to the oracle the weight of legal formality; or, especially when it was fulfilled, they could support the evidence showing that Isaiah had indeed delivered a sign from God (cf. Deut. 18:22).

3. Chief priest in the reign of Ahaz; almost certainly the same as 2 *above*. While meeting Tiglath-pileser king of Assyria at Damascus, Ahaz sent him detailed instructions to build a new altar for the temple exactly like the altar he saw at Damascus. It was ready when Ahaz returned, and the king gave the high priest directions for its use (II Kings 16:10-16). Perhaps Uriah subjected himself to the king's command when he should have protested (which might account for the omission of his name in I Chr. 6:4-15). Isaiah's evident estimation of the integrity of this priest (*see* 2 *above*) suggests the possibility that the motive behind the addition of this altar to the temple was not wholly wrong: the reason may have been, not political (if it was an Assyrian altar), but aesthetic enrichment of the ritual.

4. A prophet, son of Shemaiah of Kiriath-jearim. His story is told in an appendix added to show the grave danger facing Jeremiah after his temple

sermon (Jer. 26:20-23). Uriah was remembered as having been killed for declaring a message similar to Jeremiah's temple sermon. When King Jehoiakim sought to kill him, he fled in fear to Egypt. Elnathan the son of Achbor (cf. 36:12, 25) headed a mission that brought him back, and Jehoiakim slew him and cast him into the common graveyard. The only other OT record of an execution of a prophet is II Chr. 24:20-22.

5. The father of Meremoth; a descendant of Hakkoz (Ezra 8:33; Neh. 3:4, 21).

6. One of the men, named without title or paternity and thus probably laymen, who stood with Ezra at the public reading of the law (Neh. 8:4).

Bibliography. K. Tallqvist, *Assyrian Personal Names* (1914), p. 243; M. Noth, *Die israelitischen Personennamen* (1928), pp. 18, 168.   T. M. MAUCH

URIEL yŏŏr′ĭ əl [אוריאל, El is light]. **1.** The chief of the sons of Kohath in the time of David. He assisted in the bringing up of the ark of the covenant from the house of Obed-edom to Jerusalem (I Chr. 6:24—H 6:9; 15:5, 11).

2. A resident of Gibeah whose daughter Maacah was the mother of Abijah, king of Judah, according to II Chr. 13:2. In this verse the MT represents the name of the daughter of Uriel as Micaiah (so RSV), but this is certainly erroneous, since Maacah appears in the LXX and Syr. as well as in the seven other instances in the MT where she is mentioned. However, Maacah is represented to be the daughter of Absalom (II Chr. 11:20-21; Abishalom in I Kings 15:2, 10). The explanation most generally given to account for this difficulty proposes that Maacah was the granddaughter of Absalom and had for her parents Uriel and Tamar, daughter of Absalom (II Sam. 14:27 LXX; Jos. Antiq. VII.viii.5; VII.x.3; VIII.x.1). Maacah appears to have maintained her position in the Judean court as queen mother (גבירה) until she was deposed by her (grand)son Asa (I Kings 15:10, 13; II Chr. 15:16).   E. R. DALGLISH

URIEL (ANGEL) [Οὐριήλ = אוריאל, flame of God]. One of the four chief angels (the others being MICHAEL; GABRIEL; and RAPHAEL) mentioned in Enoch 9:1 (but cf. 40:9, where Uriel is replaced by Phanuel). Uriel figures prominently in various parts of the book of Enoch, serving as God's messenger to Noah, the "watcher" over "the world and Tartarus," and the principal guide of Enoch in his visions (10:1; 19:1; 20:2; 21:5 ff; 27:2; 33:4; 72:1; 74:2; 75:3-4; 78:10; 79:6; 80:1). He also appears in II Esdras, as sent to enlighten Ezra in his perplexity about the problem of evil and the ways of God (II Esd. 4:1; 5:20; 10:28). In midrashic literature Uriel is associated with light and is called the "one who brings light to Israel" (Num. Rabbah II.10).

S. B. HOENIG

URIJAH. KJV alternate form of URIAH.

URIM AND THUMMIM yŏŏr′ĭm, thŭm′ĭm [אורים; תמים]. Oracular media by which the will of God in relation to particular problems was ascertained. The initiator in this process of communication was man— he laid before God a question couched in precise words and expected an answer, or decision, in like manner, usually in the form of "yes" or "no" (in some of the Babylonian omen literature the supplicant's prayer is answered by the deity either with *anna*, "yes," or *ulla*, "no"; cf. *bibliography*).

Clear examples of the direct question-and-answer type of procedure are I Sam. 23:9-12; 30:7-8. In the first instance David asked the priest Abiathar to bring the ephod (in these two cases the term "ephod" is substituted for the "Urim and Thummim"; *see below*). After the ephod was brought, David addressed two direct questions to God: "Will Saul come down, as thy servant has heard?" and "Will the men of Keilah surrender me and my men into the hand of Saul?" Both inquiries were answered by the Lord in the affirmative: "He will come down"; and "They will surrender you." In the second instance the ephod was brought again, and David inquired: "Shall I pursue after this band? Shall I overtake them?" The answer was: "Pursue; for you shall surely overtake and shall surely rescue."

There are no explicit examples of a negative answer to an inquiry, but in two cases the refusal of God to respond was tantamount to a "no." In I Sam. 14:36-37 we are told that "Saul inquired of God, 'Shall I go down after the Philistines? Wilt thou give them into the hand of Israel?' But he did not answer him that day." The other case is recorded in 28:6. The large army of the Philistines encamped at Shunem frightened Saul, and he tremblingly inquired of the Lord in the hope of receiving some sign of encouragement. However, "the LORD did not answer him, either by dreams, or by Urim, or by prophets." (For a similar case where a refusal to answer was understood to be a negative response, cf. the incident reported about Ah-Mose I [*ANET* 448b]. The pharaoh, acting in the role of a deity, was asked for a decision, but he remained silent; when asked a second question, "the god nodded very much"—i.e., the answer was a "yes.") According to Num. 27:21, Joshua was commanded to direct his questions to the priest Eleazar, who in turn "shall inquire for him by the judgment of the Urim before the LORD; at his word they shall go out, and at his word they shall come in, both he and all the people of Israel with him, the whole congregation." It seems plausible to assume that in matters of military strategy some answers must have been in the negative.

Other instances of the use of oracular media are mentioned in I Sam. 14:18, 41. The first is an inquiry about a missing person, and the other is concerned with the detection of guilt. When Saul was informed that Jonathan was missing from the camp, he said to the priest Ahijah: "Bring hither the ark of God," in order to inquire about the whereabouts of his son. (The term "ark of God," or "ark of the covenant of God" [Judg. 20:27], is another name for the ephod or Urim and Thummim. This is evident from I Kings 2:26, where it is said of Abiathar that he "bore the ark . . . before David"; the ark could not possibly have been "borne" by a priest.) In the second case, Saul wanted to find the guilty person who had broken his oath forbidding the people to partake of food until evening. He said: "O LORD God of Israel, give *thāmîm* [so vocalized instead of the usual *thum-*

mîm] and Jonathan and Saul were taken, but the people escaped." The RSV, following the LXX, reads I Sam. 14:41: " 'O LORD God of Israel, why hast thou not answered thy servant this day? If this guilt is in me or in Jonathan my son, O LORD, God of Israel, give Urim; but if this guilt is in the people of Israel, give Thummim.' And Jonathan and Saul were taken, but the people escaped." *See bibliography*.

There are a number of cases where the question laid before God is introduced by the technical term שאל ביהוה, "to inquire of the LORD." Although no mention is made in these references to the ephod, the ark, or the Urim and Thummim, they may be considered in the category of oracular inquiries (e.g., Judg. 1:1-2; 20:23; I Sam. 10:22-23; 23:2-3; II Sam. 2:1; 5:19, 23-24).

The functionary in charge of the divinatory implements was a priest, and inquiries could be directed to any place where one carrying an ephod was present. According to Exod. 28:30; Lev. 8:8, the chief priest carried the Urim and Thummim on his body; Deut. 33:8 implies that the whole tribe of Levi—i.e., all members of the priestly class—had access to the Urim and Thummim (see also Ezra 2:63 = Neh. 7: 65). It was to the chief priest that the leaders of the people and the kings turned when a decision of national importance was to be made. This was done by Joshua (Num. 27:21), by Saul, and by David. Whether the Urim and Thummim were made use of in behalf of private individuals is not known. David consulted them when he was a leader of a small band (I Sam. 23:10-13). The five representatives of the tribe of Dan asked the Levite in the employment of Micah (who had an ephod): "Inquire of God . . . that we may know whether the journey on which we are setting out will succeed"; and the priest said: "Go in peace. The journey on which you go is under the eye of the LORD" (Judg. 18:5-6).

The Urim and Thummim are not mentioned after the period of David (the reference in I Kings 2:26 to Abiathar, who "bore the ark"—i.e., the ephod—relates to the reign of David). The passage in Ezra 2: 63 = Neh. 7:65 is ambiguous. It is doubtful whether Ezra meant to emphasize the need for the Urim and Thummim under the new dispensation, or whether he had in mind to introduce them anew after a lapse of *ca*. five centuries. Josephus' statement (Antiq. III.viii.9) that the "oracle" had been silent for two hundred years before his time, is not supported by the facts. It is the opinion of some scholars that the rise of prophecy, the new medium through which the word of God was communicated to the people and the kings, made the use of the Urim and Thummim unnecessary, and hence they are not mentioned in the texts since the time of Solomon. However, the protest of Hos. 4:12 that "my people inquire of a thing of wood, and their staff declares unto them" (the RSV renders לו יגיד "gives them oracles"), Ezekiel's remark (21:21—H 21:26) that the king of Babylon consulted the teraphim, and Zechariah's statement (10:2) that the teraphim "utter nonsense," would seem to point to the continuous use of the oracular media throughout the pre-exilic period.

The exact meaning of the words "Urim" and "Thummim" is not known. They are mentioned as a hendiadys five times (Exod. 28:30; Lev. 8:8; Ezra

2:63; Neh. 7:65; and in reverse order "Thummim and Urim," in Deut. 33:8), twice only "Urim" is given (Num. 27:21; I Sam. 28:6), and once *thâmîm* (I Sam. 14:41). The etymologies that have been suggested are unsatisfactory, nor are the interpretations of the LXX and the Vulg. of any help. The same uncertainty exists concerning the material the Urim and Thummim were made of, their shape, and the signs or symbols impressed on them. According to the texts the Urim and Thummim were deposited in the "breastpiece" (חשן), a small, square pocket made of multicolored stuff and twined linen, which the chief priest carried on his "heart" above the ephod (Exod. 28:16, 29-30; 29:5; Lev. 8:8). The "breastpiece" was attached to the ephod, and hence the latter term was in some cases used as a synonym for the Urim and Thummim. This information would suggest that the Urim and Thummim were small objects, perhaps in the shape of dice, made of metal or precious stones and having some symbols impressed on them (somewhat similar to the two onyx stones set on the shoulder pieces of the ephod, on which were engraved the names of the twelve tribes as described in Exod. 28:9-10). The symbols were necessarily reduced to a single letter or sign on each object—e.g., "a" representing an affirmative response and "b" a negative one—and accordingly interpreted by the priest in charge.

In complicated issues the divinatory media were used several times in order to decide the case in the most precise manner. In the Saul-Jonathan case they were used twice: first, to decide whether the guilt was with the people or with Saul and Jonathan; and the second time, to determine which of the latter two was the offender (cf. the case of Achan in Josh. 7:16-18, where the lot was cast four times until the guilty person was apprehended).

The technique employed by the priest in handling the Urim and Thummim is not stated. Since they were kept in a pocket, the priest either shook them in the receptacle and then pulled one out or used the same method as in the case of the "lots"—namely, he "cast" both of them on the ground or on any other surface.

Bibliography. G. Klaiber, *Das priesterliche Orakel der Israeliten* (1865); A. Jeremias, "Urim und Tummim," *H. V. Hilprecht Anniversary Volume* (1909), pp. 223-42; H. G. May, "Ephod and Ariel," *AJSL*, 56 (1939), 44-69.

On the deity's answer in Babylonian omen literature, see F. Nötscher, "Die Omen-Serie šumma âlu ina mêlê šakin," *Orientalia*, nos. 51-54 (1930), Tafel 95*a*, pp. 218 ff.

On Saul's use of Urim and Thummim, see S. R. Driver, *Notes on the Hebrew Text and Topography of the Books of Samuel* (2nd ed., 1913), p. 117.   I. MENDELSOHN

UR-MARKUS ŏŏr mär′kəs. A primitive form of the Gospel of Mark affirmed in some theories of the origin of the gospels. *See* MARK, GOSPEL OF, § 6; SYNOPTIC PROBLEM.

URN [στάμνος]; KJV POT. The term used in Heb. 9:4 in reference to the golden jar which held the manna. There is no archaeological clue to the form of the original OT vessel referred to, but it was probably a modified Egyptian pattern of the period of Ramses II, the time of the Exodus.   J. L. KELSO

USURY. KJV translation of נֶשֶׁךְ and τόκος (RSV INTEREST; *see also* DEBT).

UTENSILS [כֵּלִים]. A general word for implements, vessels, weapons, instruments, etc.; translated "utensils" with particular reference to the gold and bronze instruments of the tabernacle service: the snuffers, trays, shovels, pots, basins, forks, firepans, hooks, etc., particularly the instruments of the table, the lampstand, the altar of burnt offering, the altar of incense (Exod. 25:39; 27:3, 19; 30:27-28; 31:8-9; etc.). The word is also used of the utensils of the temple (I Chr. 9:28-29; II Chr. 24:14-19; "vessels" in I Kings 10:21; II Chr. 9:20; Jer. 27:18-21).   H. G. MAY

UTHAI ū'thī [עוּתַי, *perhaps hypocoristic for* (Yahu) has shown himself supreme; *cf.* Arab. *'atā;* Apoc. Οὐτά (I Esd. 5:30); Οὐθι (I Esd. 8:40)]; KJV Apoc. UTA ū'tə; UTHI. 1. A descendant of Judah resident in postexilic Jerusalem (I Chr. 9:4; cf. Neh. 11:4, where Athaiah [עֲתָיָה] apparently stands for this name).
2. Son or descendant (*see* ZACCUR 5) of Bigvai; listed as having returned from Babylon with Ezra (Ezra 8:14; I Esd. 8:40).
3. According to the RSV, the head of a family of temple servants who returned with Zerubbabel (I Esd. 5:30; but read correctly "Uta" with the KJV, omitted in the parallels Ezra 2:46; Neh. 7:48; cf. Οὐτά in LXX Neh. 7:48 Codices A א). *See* NETHINIM.

Bibliography. M. Noth, *Die israelitischen Personennamen* (1928), pp. 40, 191. On 3 *above*, see W. Rudolph, *Esra und Nehemia* (1949), p. 12.   B. T. DAHLBERG

UZ ŭz [עוּץ]; KJV HUZ hŭz in Gen. 22:21. An undefined territory in the Syrian Desert E of Palestine between, roughly, the latitudes of Damascus and Edom. Lam. 4:21 speaks of the daughter of Edom as living in Uz. Job is, according to the Prologue (1:1), native to the "land of Uz," quite possibly a purposely vague designation of the scene of the drama, which is elsewhere indicated as lying to the E of Palestine (vs. 3), as essentially a part of the desert (vs. 19; see also vss. 15, 17) yet comprising farming areas (vs. 14) as well as towns of considerable size (29:7).

Other OT references tend to confirm this general location. In Gen. 10:23, Uz is an Aramean tribe, counting, according to 22:21, their descent from Nahor, and, in 36:28, in some way related to the HORITES.   B. D. NAPIER

UZAI ū'zī [אוּזַי, *perhaps hypocoristic for* (Yahu) has heard; *cf.* אֲזַנְיָה (AZANIAH)] (Neh. 3:25). The father of a certain Palal, one of those helping Nehemiah with the repair of the Jerusalem wall.

Bibliography. M. Noth, *Die israelitischen Personennamen* (1928), pp. 40, 185.   B. T. DAHLBERG

UZAL ū'zəl [אוּזָל]. A son of Joktan and hence the name of an Arabian locality (Gen. 10:27; I Chr. 1: 21). According to Arabic tradition, Uzal, or more properly Auzal, was the original name of Sanaa, the capital of Yemen in both Himyarite and modern times; the present name means "beautiful" in Ethiopic and was given to the city by its Abyssinian conquerors. Glaser, however, found inscriptions that indicate that the original name of Sanaa was Tafidh

and holds that the name Auzal was not applied to the city until as late as the third century A.D. and then under the influence of the Arabian Jews, who made the identification from the Bible. He suggests for Uzal a town in the neighborhood of Medina, named Azalla, and mentioned as having been reached by Ashurbanipal of Assyria in his campaign in Arabia. Furthermore, that king mentions two nearby towns, Yarki and Hurarina, which recall the two sons of Joktan who are mentioned just before Uzal: Jerah and Hadoram, the latter possibly having been an original "Haroram," which was changed to its present form because of a confusion of ד and ר.

Ezek. 27:19, which occurs in the midst of a passage describing trading relations between Tyre and a number of other nations, has an especial bearing on the identification of Uzal. The opening words of this verse in the present MT are: "And Dan and Yavan going to and fro gave (products) for your wares" (וְדָן וְיָוָן מְאוּזָּל בְּעִזְבוֹנַיִךְ נָתָנּוּ). This, however, is surprisingly different from the rest of the passage (vss. 12-23), in which no verse begins with a conjunction, but always with the name of a country. A widely accepted emendation (RSV), following the LXX, is: "And wine from Uzal they exchanged for your wares" (וְיַיִן מֵאוּזָל בְּעִזְבוֹנַיִךְ נָתָנּוּ). This also contradicts the strict form of the passage, in which no verse begins with a product. It seems better, therefore, to regard the first three words of the verse as names: Waddan, Javan, and Uzal. Waddan is known as a station on one of the pilgrim roads between Medina and Mecca. On another pilgrim road between these two cities is a place called Yayn, somewhat to the SW of Waddan. "Yayn" could easily have arisen as a corruption of "Javan" (Hebrew *yāwān*), which would then be a designation for a Greek colony from Asia Minor, of which there were several in Arabia in ancient times. Since the Azalla of Ashurbanipal is located in the same region, it is probable that this is the best identification for the biblical Uzal.

Bibliography. E. Glaser, *Skizze der Geschichte und Geographie Arabiens*, II (1890), 309-12, 427-33.   S. COHEN

UZZAH ŭz'ə [עֻזָּא, עֻזָּה]. Alternately: UZZA. KJV Apoc. AZIAS ə zī'əs. 1. A Levite of the family of Merari. His father was Shimei, and his son was Shimea (I Chr. 6:29-30—H 6:14-15).
2. An obscure Benjaminite (I Chr. 8:7).
3. A son of Abinadab. He was fatally smitten while he was driving the oxcart which conveyed the ark of the covenant in its journey toward Jerusalem (II Sam. 6:1-7; I Chr. 13:1-10).

When David arranged to transport the ark to Jerusalem from the house of Abinadab, where it had remained for two decades after the disaster at Beth-shemesh (I Sam. 6:19–7:2), Uzzah drove the oxcart bearing the ark amid the accompanying festal procession. When they arrived at the threshing floor of Nacon (II Sam. 6:6; Chidon in I Chr. 13:9), the oxen stumbled. Uzzah put out his hand to secure the ark and suddenly died. In the popular mind his death was attributed to his violation of the sacrosanct character of the ark (II Sam. 6:7; I Chr. 13:10; 15:13). Greatly displeased at this incident, the king immediately canceled the journey, depositing the ark nearby, in the house of Obed-edom, and called the name of the place Perez-uzzah—"the breaking forth upon Uzzah."

4. The owner of the garden where kings Manasseh and Amon of Judah were buried (II Kings 21:18, 26).

5. Ancestor of temple servants who returned from exile with Zerubbabel (Ezra 2:49; Neh. 7:51; I Esd. 5:31).   E. R. DALGLISH AND J. M. WARD

UZZEN-SHEERAH ŭz'ən shē'ə rə [אֻזֶּן שֶׁאֱרָה, ear of Sheerah(?)]; KJV UZZEN SHERAH shǐr'ə. A village built by Sheerah, daughter of Ephraim (or Beriah), along with Upper Beth-horon and Lower Beth-horon (I Chr. 7:24). Though Beit Sira, three miles SW of Lower Beth-horon, has been proposed for Uzzen-sheerah, most scholars feel the site has yet to be identified.   V. R. GOLD

UZZI ŭz'ī [עֻזִּי, (Y is) strength; *a shortened form*]; KJV Apoc. EZIAS ĭ zī'əs; OZIAS ō—. **1.** A priest in lists of the Aaronite line descended from Eleazar (I Chr. 6:5-6, 51); an ancestor of Ezra (Ezra 7:4; I Esd. 8:2; II Esd. 1:2).

2. A descendant of Tola; eponym of a clan of the tribe of Issachar (I Chr. 7:2-3).

3. A name in what may be a tripartite grouping of postexilic Benjaminite families, or a list of families of Zebulun otherwise lacking in the lists of the tribes in Chronicles (I Chr. 7:7).

4. A postexilic Benjaminite family name (I Chr. 9:8), a datum which perhaps supports the first identification suggested in 3 *above*.

5. A Levite, descendant of Asaph (Neh. 11:22). He was overseer of the Levites in Jerusalem during a time considerably later than the return from exile, since he was a great-grandson of Mattaniah the son of Mica (vs. 17).

6. A priest, head of the priestly family of Jedaiah during the time of the postexilic high priest Joiakim (Neh. 12:19).

7. A Levite individual or division, in a group probably of musicians, in the clockwise procession on the walls of Jerusalem during their dedication (Neh. 12:42).

Bibliography. M. Noth, *Die israelitischen Personennamen* (1928), pp. 18, 38, 160.   T. M. MAUCH

UZZIA ə zī'ə [עֻזִּיָּא] (I Chr. 11:44). An Ashterathite whose name is among the sixteen additional ones the Chronicler adds to the lists of the Mighty Men of David known as the "Thirty."

UZZIAH ə zī'ə [עֻזִּיָּה(וּ), Yahu is (my) might; 'Οζίας]; KJV Apoc. and NT OZIAS ō zī'əs. Alternately: AZARIAH ăz'ə rī'ə [עֲזַרְיָה(וּ)]. **1.** A Kohathite of the tribe of Levi (I Chr. 6:24). Cf. AZARIAH 10.

2. The father of Jonathan, who was one of the twelve stewards of King David's property. Jonathan's task was the oversight of the king's treasuries in the country, in the cities, in the villages, and in the towns (I Chr. 27:25).

3. King of Judah *ca.* 783-742 B.C.; son and successor of Amaziah.

It is to be noted that in the two names of this king,

עֻזִּיָּה(וּ) and עֲזַרְיָה(וּ), there is a difference of only a single consonant. The meaning is practically the same in both cases—"Yahu is (my) might," and "Yahu is (my) strength." To explain the two names, however, as due to textual corruption is inadequate. They may be accounted for by the suggestion that one is a throne name, the other a personal name. In view of the fact that the prophetic references (Isa. 1:1; 6:1; 7:1; Hos. 1:1; Amos 1:1; Zech. 14:5) all use the name Uzziah, one might assume that this was the throne name and Azariah the personal name. But both names were used—Azariah in II Kings 15:1, 6-8, 17, 23, 27; Uzziah in 15:13, 30, 32, 34. The explanation is probably to be found in the king's leprosy. In the circumstances he was no longer able to perform his royal duties and so became a private citizen again, while his son Jotham acted as regent in his stead. The textual evidence seems to indicate that an attempt was made to substitute the throne name for the personal name. In the Peshitta the name Uzziah is used throughout.

Uzziah was sixteen years old when he came to the throne, and he is said to have reigned for fifty-two years. His mother was Jecoliah of Jerusalem (II Kings 15:2; II Chr. 26:3). It is noteworthy that he became king by action of "all the people of Judah" (II Kings 14:21; II Chr. 26:1; cf. II Kings 11:17 ff.). The figure of fifty-two years for his reign cannot be correct. The evidence of the Annals of Tiglath-pileser III of Assyria indicates that Uzziah disappeared from the scene *ca.* 742. Thus he seems to have reigned *ca.* forty-two years.

The Assyrian Annals mention a contemporary figure, Azriau from Ia-ú-da-a-a, in telling of events connected with the year 743. The identification with Azariah (Uzziah) of Judah gives a different picture both of the power and of the position of Judah from that which could be gathered from the biblical record, but it may very well be true. With the death of Jeroboam II of Israel, *ca.* 746, Azariah was probably the outstanding leader in the West. He was a leper and so was prevented from exercising kingly functions; but he still seems to have been the power behind the throne, and he became the center of opposition to Assyria during the period 743-742. Presumably he died soon afterward, as no further mention of his name occurs in the Assyrian records.

As in the case of Jeroboam II of Israel, the writer of Kings records but little of the long and prosperous reign of Uzziah. Fortunately, the Chronicler has preserved a long list of his achievements. These indicate the power and wealth of Judah during his reign. They are generally accepted as reliable history, although set in the familiar theological framework of the writer. This is clearly seen in the Chronicler's arrangement. Like his grandfather Joash (II Chr. 24:2), Uzziah had a tutor whose name was Zechariah (26:5), and he became strong; but with strength came pride, and the king proved false to Yahweh. The result was that he was stricken with leprosy.

The Chronicler reports a successful campaign against the Philistines in the West (II Chr. 26:6). The walls of Gath, Jabneh, and Ashdod were demolished. The following words: "and he built cities in the territory of Ashdod and elsewhere among the

Philistines," are difficult. The most likely explanation is that Uzziah subdued the N and E parts of Philistia. In this territory he established fortified posts which enabled him to maintain control over the caravan routes which passed through the Philistine Plain. The MT of II Chr. 26:7-8a is again difficult. "Gurbaal" is unknown; the LXX reads here "Petra." For "Ammonites" the LXX reads "Meunites," perhaps in both cases correctly. The general emphasis of the Chronicler here seems to be on military campaigns in Arabia—against the Arabs who dwelt in Petra, and the Edomite Meunites, who paid tribute to Judah. Uzziah's purpose in these campaigns would again appear to have been control of the trade routes from Arabia. This seems to be borne out by the datum that "he [presumably Uzziah] built Elath and restored it to Judah, after the king slept with his fathers" (II Kings 14:22; II Chr. 26:2). The wording of this verse, however, is obscure, with its strange chronological reference. It seems to be out of place in its present context. That Judah controlled Elath at this time has been verified by archaeological investigation which brought to light a seal bearing the inscription: "Belonging to Jotham" (Uzziah's son), in the excavations at Ezion-geber–Elath. Uzziah was so successful in all the military activities which he undertook that his reputation extended as far as the borders of Egypt (II Chr. 26:8). It is interesting to note that no interference or activity is recorded on the part of the powerful N kingdom. Fortress towers were built in Jerusalem (vs. 9) and also "in the wilderness" (vs. 10)—i.e., the Negeb. The term may possibly also include the Moabite Plain. It is probable that these latter were established to control the trade routes from Arabia. At the same time they served as a means of defense for flocks and herds. Under Uzziah agriculture prospered and livestock increased. For the latter the king had great water cisterns hewed out. He seems to have had a personal interest in farming. The general picture is one of prosperity throughout the country. Archaeology furnishes an interesting confirmation of the situation, for it indicates that the eighth century B.C. was the period of greatest building activity in the Negeb.

The king also built up his army and supplied the troops with weapons and equipment (vss. 11-14). As usual, the numbers given cannot be regarded as historical. Special attention is drawn to a new type of weapon, which has usually been understood as a kind of catapult mounted on a tower, capable of shooting arrows and great stones (vs. 15) against an attacking enemy. Such a weapon is known also from Egyptian and Assyrian inscriptions of this period. It has been plausibly argued, however, that the new weapon was not a catapult at all, but a shield for protecting slingers and bowmen. *See* WEAPONS AND IMPLEMENTS OF WAR.

Ca. 750, Uzziah was stricken with leprosy (cf. for the date I Chr. 5:17, where Jotham, Uzziah's son, and Jeroboam II of Israel are mentioned as contemporaries). Jotham, therefore, must have been acting as regent before the death of Jeroboam, which occurred *ca.* 746. From the Chronicler's point of view Uzziah must have been guilty of some serious crime to have become the victim of this disease. This crime

the Chronicler found in an invasion of the temple by the king "to burn incense on the altar of incense" (II Chr. 26:16b-20). The story is told in very dramatic fashion. The writer of Kings makes no mention of this incident, but it seems clear that the Chronicler found it in his source and used it because it suited his purpose. Its historicity, however, is questionable. That it was a popular tradition which lent itself to later embellishments can be seen in the additions in Josephus (Antiq. IX.x.4). At the same time, a historical reminiscence may lie behind it of a break between the king and the priesthood. The latter challenged the king's right to burn incense, claiming that this was the prerogative of the priests, the sons of Aaron, alone. However this may be, Uzziah contracted leprosy. This prevented him from carrying out his royal duties. In the circumstances he "dwelt in a separate house" (II Kings 15:5; II Chr. 26:21). The literal meaning of the MT is "a house of freedom." This is usually understood in the sense that he was isolated because of his disease and through fear of contagion. But a better suggestion seems to be that it means rather that he was relieved of his official duties because of his affliction. That this is so is indicated by II Kings 15:5b: "Jotham the king's son was over the household, governing the people of the land"—i.e., Jotham was appointed as regent for his father. He continued to act as regent until the latter's death *ca.* 742, but the reputation which Uzziah had won was remembered, and his influence was still felt in state affairs.

The Chronicler adds, probably with more exactness than II Kings 15:7, that on Uzziah's death "they buried him with his fathers in the burial field which belonged to the kings, for they said, 'He is a leper' " (II Chr. 26:23). Archaeology has provided a remarkable confirmation of this. In 1931 a carved stone tablet was found on the Mount of Olives, which dated from post-Maccabean times. It bore this inscription in Aramaic: "Hither were brought the

Courtesy of the American Schools of Oriental Research

19. First-century-A.D. stone tablet marking the burial place of the bones of King Uzziah

bones of Uzziah, king of Judah—do not open!" Fig. UZZ 19.

In the memory of later generations Uzziah's reign was exceeded in glory only by Solomon's. This period marked the zenith of Judah's power.

Bibliography. M. Noth, *Die israelitischen Personennamen* (1928), pp. 109 ff. W. F. Albright, "The Discovery of an Aramaic Inscription Relating to King Uzziah," *BASOR*, 44 (1931), 8-10. J. Morgenstern, "The Sin of Uzziah," *HUCA*, XII-XIII (1938), 1 ff. N. Glueck, "The Topography and History of Ezion-geber and Elath," *BASOR*, 72 (1938), 7 ff; "The Third Season of Excavation at Tell el-Kheleifeh," *BASOR*, 79 (1940), 13 ff. M. Noth, *Überlieferungsgeschichtliche Studien* (1943), pp. 182-84. W. F. Albright, "The Chronology of the Divided Monarchy of Israel," *BASOR*, no. 100 (1945), p. 18, note 8; *From the Stone Age to Christianity* (2nd ed., 1946), p. 217. Y. Sukenik, *Bulletin of the Jewish Palestine Exploration Society*, XIII (1947), 19-24. A. M. Honeyman, "The Evidence for Regnal Names Among the Hebrews," *JBL*, LXVII (1948), 13-25. E. R. Thiele, *The Mysterious Numbers of the Hebrew Kings* (1951), pp. 78-98. J. B. Pritchard, ed., *ANET* (2nd ed., 1955), pp. 282-83. W. Rudolph, *Chronikbücher* (1955), pp. 283-87. G. E. Wright, *Biblical Archaeology* (1957), pp. 156-60.

4. A priest who had married a non-Israelite wife in the time of Ezra (Ezra 10:21). Cf. AZARIAH 19.

5. A Judahite; father of Athaiah, who lived in Jerusalem at the time of Nehemiah (Neh. 11:4).

6. Chief elder of Bethulia (Jth. 6:15, etc.).

H. B. MacLean

UZZIEL ŭz'ĭ əl [עֻזִּיאֵל, El (God) is strength]; UZZIELITES —ə līts. Alternately: AZAREL ăz'ə rĕl [עֻזְרִאֵל] (5 *below*); KJV AZAREEL —rĕl. **1.** A grandson of Levi; one of the four sons of Kohath. As a son of Kohath he was a brother of Amram the ancestor of Aaron and Moses, and a brother of Izhar the ancestor of Korah (Exod. 6:18; Num. 3:19; I Chr. 6:2, 18; 23:12). He was the father of Mishael, Elzaphan, and Sithri (Exod. 6:22), and the founder of a subdivision of the families of Levites (*see* PRIESTS AND LEVITES), descended from Kohath (Exod. 6:22; Lev. 10:4; Num. 3:19, 30; I Chr. 6:18; 15:10; 23:20; 24:24). This subdivision of the families of Levites is called Uzzielites in two places: Num. 3:27, where "the families of the sons of Kohath were to encamp on the south side of the tabernacle" (vs. 29) and their role in the service of the ark and tabernacle is described (vs. 31); and I Chr. 26:23, where citation of their activity, probably concerning temple treasuries, has been lost. Members of this subdivision were among the Levites who transported the ark when David brought it to Zion (I Chr. 15:10), and they were among the Levites whose functions in the cult were ascribed to David's preparatory arrangements for the temple (23:12, 20; 24:24).

2. One of the captains of a successful expedition of Simeonites against the Amalekites at Mount Seir, expanding their territory, possibly during the reign of Hezekiah (I Chr. 4:42).

3. A Levite of the family of Jeduthun, in a list of Levites with which the Chronicler sets forth the cleansing of the temple by Hezekiah (II Chr. 29:14).

4. A name in what may be a tripartite grouping of postexilic Benjaminite families, or a list of families of Zebulun otherwise lacking in the lists of the tribes in Chronicles (I Chr. 7:7).

5. A postexilic family of singers of the Heman group (I Chr. 25:4). In vs. 18 he is called Azarel (cf. Uzziah and Azariah as names for the same king). *See* HEMAN; MUSIC.

6. A member of the guild of goldsmiths. He helped to rebuild the wall of Jerusalem (Neh. 3:8).

Bibliography. M. Noth, *Die israelitischen Personennamen* (1928), pp. 18, 160.   T. M. MAUCH

VAIL. KJV alternate form of VEIL.

VAIN [הֶבֶל, רִיק, תֹּהוּ, שָׁוְא; κενός, μάταιος, εἰκῆ, δωρεάν, *etc.*]. The commonest modern sense of "vain"—"conceited," "given to empty personal pride"—is expressed in the NT by· κενόδοξος, "self-conceit" (Gal. 5:26; KJV "desirous of vainglory"); cf. κενοδοξία, "conceit" (Phil. 2:3; KJV "vainglory"). Otherwise the term renders a variety of Hebrew and Greek words expressing something ineffective, unreliable, insubstantial, transient, like vapor. Paul's statement (Rom. 8:20) that the creation was subjected to "futility" (KJV "vanity") may echo Eccl. 1:2, etc., where "vanity" is הֶבֶל ("vapor"; *see* VANITY). In general, all resources or enterprises from which God is excluded are vain (Ps. 127:1). To resist God or attempt to frustrate his purpose is a particularly vain thing (Ps. 2:1, quoted in Acts 4:25). God's own work is never vain, nor is he sought in vain (Isa. 45:18-19).

In Acts 14:15 pagan gods or their cults are called "vain things" (μάταια), by contrast with a "living God"; the same implication of idolatry may be present in the "futile· ways" (KJV "vain conversation") of I Pet. 1:18, addressed to converts from paganism. This use of μάταιος appears in the LXX in I Kings (III Kingdoms) 16:2 (חַטָּאת), 13, 26; II Kings (IV Kingdoms) 17:15; Jer. 2:5; 8:19 (הֶבֶל); Add. Esth. 14:10 (LXX, expansion of Esth. 4:17); III Macc. 6:11.

To take Yahweh's name "in vain" (Exod. 20:7; Deut. 5:11) is to invoke it lightly or to no purpose, especially in blasphemy (cf. Lev. 24:10 ff) or perjury (Ps. 24:4).

The "empty phrases" (Matt. 6:7; KJV "vain repetitions") which Gentiles use in prayer (βατταλογέω, "heap up empty phrases") are meaningless babblings, sounds without sense. To approach God with lip service only, neglecting true heart obedience, is to worship him "in vain" (Mark 7:7, quoting Isa. 29:13 LXX). To turn away from Christianity is to "receive the grace of God in vain" (II Cor. 6:1; cf. I Cor. 15:2; Gal. 3:4); to have evangelized such people is to have run or labored in vain (Phil. 2:16; cf. I Cor. 15:10; Gal. 2:2).   F. F. BRUCE

VAIZATHA vī'zə thə [וַיְזָתָא] (Esth. 9:9); KJV VAJEZATHA və jěz'ə thə. One of the ten sons of Heman slain by the Jews in the general reprisal that followed Haman's frustrated attempt to destroy all Jews in the Persian Empire.

Bibliography. On text and etymology, see L. B. Paton, *Esther*, ICC (1908), pp. 71, 284.   B. T. DAHLBERG

VALIANT MAN. *See* MIGHTY MEN.

VALLEY. The translation of several words in the Bible, referring to depressions between mountains, broad plains or plateaus, narrow ravines, and low terrain. (*See also* PLAIN; SHEPHELAH.) The RSV uses "vale" twice (Pss. 60:6; 108:7) where the KJV has "valley"; "vale" is used frequently in the KJV (Gen. 14:3; 37:14; Deut. 1:7; I Kings 10:27; Jer. 33:13), where the RSV translates variously as "valley," "lowland," and "Shephelah."

The following words are usually translated "valley":

a) עֵמֶק (Num. 14:25; Josh. 8:13; I Sam. 6:13; etc.). The same word is mentioned in designating the level areas or valleys adjacent to the following places: ACHOR; AIJALON; BACA; BERACAH; ELAH; GIBEON; HEBRON (1); JEZREEL (1); KEZIZ (*see* EMEK-KEZIZ); REPHAIM; SHAVEH; SIDDIM; SUCCOTH (1). It designates also the valley of DECISION; the King's Valley (*see* SHAVEH), and the valley of JEHOSHAPHAT (Gen. 14:17; II Sam. 18:18; Joel 3:2, 12, 14).

b) בִּקְעָה (Deut. 8:7; Isa. 41:18; Ezek. 37:1; etc.). The same word is employed to designate the level areas or valleys in the vicinity of JERICHO; LEBANON; MEGIDDO. Cf. the Valley of Mizpeh (*see* MIZPAH 2).

c) גַּיְא (Num. 21:20; Deut. 34:6; II Kings 2:16; Ps. 23:4; etc.). The same word occurs in expressions referring to the valleys of the CRAFTSMEN; HINNOM; IPHTAH-EL; Mountains; SALT; Slaughter; TRAVELERS; Vision; ZEBOIM (2); ZEPHATHAH.

d) נַחַל (Gen. 26:19; Num. 24:6; Deut. 21:4; I Sam. 15:5). It also is used with the following place names: ESHCOL; GERAR; SHITTIM; SOREK; ZERED. Although it usually refers to a level area such as a valley, it may also designate the water flowing in the valley (*see* BROOK; RIVER).

e) שְׁפֵלָה (Josh. 9:1; 10:40; Judg. 1:9; etc., where the KJV has "valley" and "vale"; the RSV, "lowland" and "Shephelah"). The reference is to the foothills between the central highlands and the Philistine coastal plain.

f) φάραγξ (Isa. 40:4 LXX; Luke 3:5; Jth. 2:8; 7:4; etc.).

The contours of Canaan are such that valleys are located in every part of the land and vary considerably in shape and size. Ones like those running between Bethlehem and the Dead Sea are precipitous canyons or narrow gorges. Others, like those in the vicinity of Jezreel, are broad plains noted for their fertility.

Valleys are mentioned in designating geographical boundaries (Deut. 3:16); as well-watered regions (Gen. 13:10); and as the location of cities (Gen. 19:29) and springs (I Kings 18:5). They were also scenes of military combat (Gen. 14:8); the location of vineyards and orchards (Num. 13:23); the traditional home of the Canaanites (Num. 14:25) and their deity (I Kings 20:28). Valleys were grazing areas for herds (I Chr. 27:29); sites for the growing of grain (Ps. 65:13 — H 65:14) and the harvest of wheat (I Sam. 6:13); the habitat of ravens (Prov. 30:17) and doves (Ezek. 7:16). The destruction or filling of the valleys is used in figures of speech referring to God's judgment upon an unfaithful people (Mic. 1:6; Zech. 14:5). The "valley of deep darkness" ("shadow of death") symbolized the dangers of life (Ps. 23:4), and the "valley of the son of Hinnom" became a designation of the place of eternal punishment (see GEHENNA).　　　　　　　　W. L. REED

VALLEY GATE [שער הגיא]; KJV GATE OF THE VALLEY in Neh. 2:13. A gate of Jerusalem, leading W or SW into the Valley of Hinnom (see HINNOM, VALLEY OF), a thousand cubits from the DUNG GATE, and in the vicinity of the JACKAL'S WELL; restored by Nehemiah (Neh. 2:13, 15; 3:13). Its towers had been built by Uzziah (II Chr. 26:9). Fig. NEH 13. See also JERUSALEM §§ 6*b*, 7*b*.

　　　　　　　　　　　　　　　G. A. BARROIS

VALLEY OF DECISION. See DECISION, VALLEY OF.

VALOR, MAN OF. See MIGHTY MEN.

VANIAH və nī'ə [וניה, *possibly* Pers. *Vānyah*, worthy of love; *see bibliography*; Apoc. ῏Aνως]; KJV Apoc. ANOS ā'nŏs. One of the Jews, contemporaries of Ezra, who are listed as having married foreign wives (Ezra 10:36; I Esd. 9:34).

　　Bibliography. R. A. Bowman, Exegesis of Ezra, *IB*, III (1954), 660.　　　　　　　B. T. DAHLBERG

VANITY. A word used to translate several biblical terms. It has a variety of meanings, ultimately deriving from physical concepts of insubstantiality, inanity, nothingness, or chaos, but never connoting the subjective attitude of false pride as in modern English. "Vanity" often connotes "idolatry" or "idols."

The most common word translated "vanity" in the OT is הבל, meaning primarily, as the Arabic cognate suggests, "vapor, breath" (e.g., Prov. 21:6, comparing wealth accumulated through lies to a "fleeting vapor"; Isa. 57:13, where הבל is parallel with רוח, "wind"). In Eccl. 1:14; 2:11, 17; 4:16; 6:9, הבל stands in apposition to the phrase "striving after wind" and preserves a nuance of its primary meaning (cf. Ps. 144:4, comparing man to הבל and צל, "shadow"). Breath suggests evanescence, and in Ps. 39:11 man is הבל, and his comeliness passes away as a moth. The word expresses that which is light and insubstantial, which will always be outweighed (e.g., Ps. 62:9). In Ps. 39:5 הבל stands virtually parallel to אין, "nothingness." Ps. 62:9 describes men of low degree as הבל and men of high degree as כזב, "lie, delusion." In Prov. 13:11 הבל as a means of acquiring wealth is contrasted with solid work, and refers to appearance or pretension apart from substance.

The notion of delusion or unreality underlies the use of הבל to describe the life of the Gentiles (II Kings 17:15) or of the man who is indifferent to divine law (Ps. 94:11) or has deliberately rejected it (Ps. 78:33). This way of life, unregulated by divine discipline, is haphazard and futile, the prey of chance rather than governed and stabilized by the moral law; and the state in which there is no discrimination between righteous and wicked, wise and foolish, is described as הבל (Eccl. 2:17; 8:14).

Specifically הבל refers to idolatry (Jer. 16:19) or to idols or pagan gods (Deut. 32:21; I Kings 16:13, 26; Ps. 31:6; Isa. 57:13; Jer. 2:5; 8:19; 10:8; 14:22; 51:18; Jonah 2:8). In Jer. 51:18 there is a wordplay—the graven images are said to be without רוח (primarily "wind," secondarily "spirit") and to be הבל (lit., "vapor"). "Vanities" in Acts 14:15 (μάταια; RSV "vain things") similarly refers to pagan deities, for whom the people of Lystra mistook Paul and Barnabas.

"Vanity" may also be expressed by ריק (lit., "emptiness"). This may mean "annihilation" (e.g., Hab. 2:13) but generally, as הבל, expresses the futility of life apart from the guidance of God (e.g., Pss. 2:1; 4:2, where it is in parallelism with כזב, "delusion").

The word שוא, used apparently in its primary sense of "nothingness" in Job 15:31, may mean the frustration of a futile life (e.g., Job 7:3, where it is parallel to עמל, "trouble") but generally means "unreality" which a man creates for himself by dissembling (לב ולב; e.g., Pss. 12:2; 41:6), by deceit (מרמה; e.g., Job 31:5; Ps. 24:4), or by lying (שקר; e.g., Ps. 144:8). It may mean simply "lie, delusion" (Prov. 30:8; Ezek. 13:6, 8-9, 23; 21:29; 22:28). As הבל, it denotes that life outside the positive purpose of divine providence, to which the Gentiles were condemned (Isa. 30:28; possibly Hos. 12:11), and, like הבל, it may denote "idols" (Jer. 18:15).

"Vanity" is expressed also by תוהו, "chaos," found in parallelism with אין, "nothing," in Isa. 40:17, 23, and in Isa. 40:17 with אפס, referring to idols and their makers. It is found in parallelism with "lying" in Isa. 59:4.

As the Arabic cognate suggests, און should probably be translated "trouble" or "mischief" rather than "vanity"; its parallels in Job 15:35; Ps. 10:7; Prov. 22:8 also suggest this. In Isa. 41:29, where און, like הבל, שוא, and תוהו, denotes "idols," it is parallel to אפס, "nothing," which suggests that it may be a corruption of אין.

In the NT "vanity" (ματαιότης) has a similar range of meaning, from "nothingness" (II Pet. 2:18) to "chaos" (Rom. 8:20), and the futile life without the law of God (Eph. 4:17). The neuter plural of the adjective μάταια in Acts 14:15 refers to idols.

　　Bibliography. E. Podechard, *L'Ecclésiaste* (1912), pp. 171-73, 232-33.　　　　　　　J. GRAY

VASHNI văsh'nī [ושני] (I Chr. 6:28 — H 6:13). See JOEL 5.

VASHTI văsh'tī [ושתי, *possibly* Pers. *vašti*, one who is desired].

The wife of Ahasuerus (Xerxes I), according to the book of ESTHER (1:9-22). King Ahasuerus, on the seventh day of a banquet, sent for Queen Vashti to show off her beauty to the guests. When Vashti refused to come, the king banished her and proclaimed the edict throughout his empire "that every man be lord in his own house" (vs. 22). It was this deposal of Vashti which led to the search for other beautiful maidens, and eventually to the choice of Esther as the new queen.

The historicity of this account is questionable. Xerxes' queen was Amestris and not Vashti (Herodotus VII.61; IX.108-12). The attempt to identify Vashti with Stateira, the wife of Artaxerxes II, does not seem wholly successful. If the origin of Purim is found in Babylonian mythology, it is possible that Vashti represents an Elamite goddess allied with Haman and Zeresh against the Babylonian Marduk and Ishtar (*cf. bibliography*). On the other hand, the role of Vashti in the book of Esther may be simply a fictional device for introducing Esther.

Bibliography. L. B. Paton, *Esther*, ICC (1908), pp. 88-89.
D. HARVEY

VASSAL. A subject or subordinate ruling under another. Frequently the vassal was the defeated king appointed to rule in a subservient position over his own people or territory as a GOVERNOR. The Hebrew words for PRINCE and SERVANT are used for such vassals. This fall from rank and power is described in Lam. 1:1, although some scholars would emend the text and translate "labor gang" or "slave" instead of vassal. Vassals usually had some dignity and wealth left to them in spite of TRIBUTE required by the conqueror.
C. U. WOLF

VAT, WINE VAT. A square or circular cavity cut into the rock, in which grapes and olives were pressed into wine and oil. *See* OIL § 1; WINE §§ 2, 5.

VATICANUS văt′ĭ kăn′əs, —kā′nəs. An early-fourth-century Greek uncial codex MS of the Bible (symbol "B"). Originally it contained the whole Greek Bible, with the exception of the Prayer of Manasses and the books of Maccabees. It is one of the most important witnesses to the text of both the LXX and the NT. *See* VERSIONS, ANCIENT; TEXT, NT.

The codex has suffered considerable mutilation. It now lacks Gen. 1:1–46:28; II Sam. 2:5-7, 10-13; Pss. 106:27–138:6; Heb. 9:14–13:25; the Pastoral

letters; Revelation. It contains 759 leaves (617 in the OT, 142 in the NT) of very fine vellum out of an original total of *ca.* 820. Each leaf measures 10½ by 10 inches. Each page of the poetical books of the OT contains two columns of text, with 40-44 lines to the column. The rest of the codex contains three columns of text to the page, with 40-44 lines to the column. The MS was written by two scribes.

The codex has been in the Vatican Library since before the publication of the earliest catalogue of that library in 1475. When or how it came to the Vatican is unknown.

Fig. VAT 1.

Bibliography. A photographic reproduction of the MS was published by the authorities of the Vatican Library, *Bibliorum SS. Graecorum Codex Vaticanus 1209* (1904-7). See also: F. H. A. Scrivener, *Plain Introduction to the Criticism of the NT* (4th ed., rev. E. Miller; 1894), I, 105-21; C. R. Gregory, *Canon and Text of the NT* (1907), pp. 343-48; W. H. P. Hatch, *Principal Uncial MSS of the NT* (1939), plate XIV; I. M. Price, *Ancestry of Our English Bible* (3rd ed., rev. W. A. Irwin and A. P. Wikgren; 1956), pp. 56-58; F. G. Kenyon, *Our Bible and the Ancient MSS* (5th ed., rev. A. W. Adams; 1958), pp. 121, 202-6.
M. M. PARVIS

VAU vô (Heb. wou) [ו, *w* (*Wāw*)]. The sixth letter of the Hebrew ALPHABET as it is placed in the KJV at the head of the sixth section of the acrostic psalm, Ps. 119, where each verse of this section of the psalm begins with this letter.

VAULTED CHAMBER; KJV EMINENT PLACE. The translation of גב (lit., "something convex," "back") in Ezek. 16:24, 31, 39.

VEGETABLES [זרע[נ]ים (Dan. 1:12, 16; KJV PULSE; ירק (KJV HERBS); λάχανα (KJV HERBS)]. The vegetables most commonly cultivated in Palestine were LENTILS; CUCUMBERS; ONIONS; LEEKS; and BEANS. But Palestine was inferior to Egypt as a vegetable land; in Egypt one merely sowed the seed and watered it, and a vegetable garden appeared (Deut. 11:10). Vegetables were generally planted in gardens; Ahab demands Naboth's vineyard for such a purpose (I Kings 21:2). Of course, vegetables alone provided an insufficient diet; Paul can compare the man who eats only vegetables to the man who is weak in faith (Rom. 14:2). For the vegetables eaten by Daniel and his friends, *see* PULSE.
J. F. ROSS

VEIL; KJV alternately VAIL. There is relatively little material on veils worn by women in the OT. The Talmud has no designation for "veil." The veiled ladies in the present-day Muslim communities would have been out of place, for the most part, in OT times. It follows that several of the terms rendered "veil" in the Bible do not really refer to veils but to ornamental coverings of one kind or another, and their specific meanings are far from clear. Terms translated "veil" are:

a) צעיף, the veil or shawl mentioned in connection with Rebekah, who put it on when she approached Isaac before her marriage (Gen. 24:65). Here the veil appears to have been the mark of the marriageable maiden, and was removed in connection with the marriage ceremony (cf. Akkadian *kallatum kutumtum*, "veiled bride"). Such a veil was used by

1. Codex Vaticanus (fourth century A.D.)

Tamar to trick Judah (Gen. 38:14, 19); here it was a device to conceal her face.

b) רדיד, the veil-like garment worn by the women of Jerusalem (Isa. 3:23) and the maiden in Song of S. 5:7 ("mantle"). The LXX understood it as being a thin summer garment (θέριστρον), probably something like the stoles worn by women today.

c) צמה (KJV "locks"), a face veil, probably of ornamental character (Song of S. 4:1, 3; 6:7; Isa. 47:2).

d) מסוה, the mask wherewith Moses covered his face so that the Israelites were able to abide in his presence after he returned from the mount of God (Exod. 34:33-35). In the NT, Paul, referring to this incident, uses the word κάλυμμα, "hood" or "veil" (II Cor. 3:13-16), as a metaphor for that which conceals a thing from being understood.

e) מסכה (Isa. 25:7), probably some sort of cover, as indicated by its parallelism with "covering." In Isa. 28:20, where the word refers to a bedcover, it is translated "covering."

f) מספחות (KJV "kerchief"), a covering for the head. In connection with the activities of sorceresses (prophetesses), Ezekiel describes the making of these veils for the heads of persons of every stature (Ezek. 13:18).

g) KJV translation of מטפחת (RSV CLOAK) in Ruth 3:15.

On רעלה (Isa. 3:19), which is literally "veil," *see* SCARF.   J. M. MYERS

VEIL OF THE TEMPLE [פרכת, *perhaps from* Akkad. *paraku*, bar, *or parakku*, shrine; KJV κατα-πέτασμα (LXX *for* פרכת; Matt. 27:51; Heb. 6:19; RSV "curtain")]. The veil which hung at the entrance to the Most Holy Place in the temple (II Chr. 3:14) and before the inner room containing the ark and the mercy seat in the tabernacle (Exod. 26:33; 35:12; 39:34; Lev. 24:3). It was figured with cherubim on blue, purple, and scarlet material and fine twined linen (Exod. 26:31; 36:35; II Chr. 3:14) and was hung by clasps from four pillars of acacia wood (Exod. 26:32). In early days no one could enter through the veil except Levitical priests (Num. 18:7), in later times no one but the high priest on the Day of Atonement (Lev. 16:2). The veil was said to be taken down when the tabernacle was to be moved, and used to cover the ark (Num. 4:5).

At Jesus' death (Matt. 27:51; Mark 15:38) or during the Crucifixion (Luke 23:45), the veil of the temple was rent from top to bottom, thus exposing the Most Holy Place to view. The meeting place of God with man (Exod. 30:6) was now open to all. The veil is used in Hebrews as a symbol of the flesh of Christ (10:20), by which believers enter into the inner shrine of faith (6:19; 9:3).

See also TEMPLE, JERUSALEM; TABERNACLE; MOST HOLY PLACE.   E. M. GOOD

*VENGEANCE. The restoration of wholeness, integrity, to the community, by God or man. The various terms translated "vengeance" are a part of the legal terminology of the Bible.

The chief OT terms for "vengeance" are the nouns נקם (Judg. 16:28) and נקמה (Jer. 50:15). The verb from which they are derived is נקם, generally trans-

lated "avenge" (Num. 31:2). The AVENGER OF BLOOD (גאל הדם) is the next of kin of a slain man who is required by law to requite the life of his kinsman (Num. 35:9-34). Other terms for "vengeance" include ישע (lit., "to assist, save"; I Sam. 25:31), ריב, הריב ("to plead the case of someone"; vs. 39), השיב (lit., "to cause punishment to return"; II Sam. 16:8), and שפט ("to judge," "to vindicate"; Ps. 26:1).

The LXX shows considerable variety in the rendering of these Hebrew terms into Greek, but the most common translation is given by the verb ἐκδικέω and its derivatives. The same verb and its derivatives, ἐκδίκησις and ἔκδικος, lie behind the translations "to vindicate" (Luke 18:3, 5), "to avenge" (Rom. 12:19), "vengeance" (Heb. 10:30), and "avenger" (I Thess. 4:6).

Seldom does "vengeance" in the Bible carry the connotation of "vindictiveness" or "revenge." Only twice does the noun "revenge" occur (Prov. 6:34; Jer. 20:10), and only two occurrences of the adverb "revengefully" are found (Ezek. 25:12, 15), both in reference to the actions of Israel's enemies. Vengeance was understood to be a necessary means for the healing of the breach made in the solidarity of the family or the community as a result of manslaughter. The avenger of blood was considered to be acting, not only in behalf of family or community, but in God's stead (Gen. 9:5-6). Yet in times of despair, God the vindicator could be counted on as the avenger. When Second Isaiah refers over and over again to Yahweh as Israel's REDEEMER (גאל), he has in view Yahweh's coming restoration of his people to their land and the fulfilment of the promise to their forefathers. I.e., Yahweh is Israel's vindicator and avenger (Isa. 41:14; 43:1, 14; 44:6; etc.). The cries to Yahweh for vengeance, therefore, are cries for redemption, restoration, health, and healing, even though such redemption and healing may involve Yahweh's retributive justice (Jer. 15:15; 20:12).

In the NT, however, vengeance is reserved to God alone for its execution: "Vengeance is mine, I will repay, says the Lord" (Rom. 12:19; cf. Deut. 32:35; Heb. 10:30). God will vindicate his elect who cry to him day and night (Luke 18:7-8; cf. Rev. 6:10). At the last day, he will execute vengeance upon all who stand in opposition to his purpose (Luke 21:22; II Thess. 1:8), thus publicly displaying that redemption, that vindication, which has already been provided in Jesus Christ.

Bibliography. E. Merz, *Die Blutrache bei den Israeliten,* BWAT, vol. XX (1916), is the most complete and pertinent study. E. N. Haddād, "Blood Revenge Among the Arabs," *JPOS,* I (1920), 103-12. J. Pedersen, *Israel,* I-II (1926), 378-410. S. Nyström, *Beduinentum und Jahwismus* (1946), pp. 31-40. R. H. Swartzback, "A Biblical Study of the Word, 'Vengeance,' " *Interpretation,* VI (1952), 451-57. K. Koch, "Gibt es ein Vergeltungsdogma im AT?" *ZThK,* 52 (1955), 1-42. F. Horst, "Recht und Religion in Bereich des ATs" *Evangelische Theologie,* 16 (1956), 49-75. J. Scharbert, *Solidarität in Segen und Fluch im AT und in seiner Umwelt* (1958), pp. 90-100, 119-24.   W. J. HARRELSON

VENISON. KJV translation of ציד, צידה, in Gen. 25:28; 27:3, 5, 7, 19, 25, 31, 33 (RSV GAME).

VERMILION [ששר; *cf.* Akkad. *šaršarru, šaršeru;* LXX μίλτος]. A mineral product obtained from the widely used red (hematite) ocher; an ideal pigment for painting or "illumination." For the interior of rooms a renewable coat of pigment was spread over plaster. For exterior surfaces and more permanent requirements, ocher combined with clay was fired to produce a solid enamel. Probably a foreign import, it was highly resented by the prophets. Jehoiakim was condemned for neglecting justice while painting the palace with vermilion (Jer. 22:14). Jerusalem, pictured as the prostitute Oholibah, whose lovers were the Egyptians and Babylonians, "saw men portrayed upon the wall, the images of the Chaldeans portrayed in vermilion" (Ezek. 23:14; LXX ἐν γραφίδι).

Wooden idols were painted with vermilion (Wisd. Sol. 13:14; "red paint"). The Greeks employed it for the making of pottery (Pliny Nat. Hist. XXXV.152), and the Athenians attempted to monopolize its production (*Inscriptiones Graecae* II.1.546). The earths *sinopis* and *rubrica* used for pigment by the Romans (Pliny Nat. Hist. XXXV.13-15) were doubtless red ocher.

Bibliography. G. Perrot and C. Chipiez, *A History of Art in Chaldaea and Assyria* (1884), I, 286-87; G. M. A. Richter, *The Craft of Athenian Pottery* (1923), pp. 53-59, 96-97; A. Lucas, *Ancient Egyptian Materials and Industries* (2nd ed., 1934), pp. 282-92, 326-32; R. J. Forbes, "Chemical, Culinary and Cosmetic Arts," in C. Singer *et al.*, eds., *A History of Technology*, I (1954), 238-43.   C. L. WICKWIRE

VERSIONS, ANCIENT. Translations of the Scriptures or of some part of them, produced in ancient times for those who found it difficult or impossible to read the original language or languages. During the last centuries B.C., when certain congregations of Aramaic-speaking Jews became less and less familiar with the classical Hebrew of the OT, paraphrases in Aramaic, called Targums, were produced. About the same time other groups of Jews rendered the OT into Greek, both for themselves and for Gentile readers, who, of course, knew no Hebrew or Aramaic. Subsequent versions into other languages were made, either from the original Hebrew or from the Old Greek translations.

In the early Christian church, a similar need arose for rendering the NT from the original Greek into various other languages. In order to assist in the missionary work of the early evangelists, and to provide converts with the Scriptures in their mother tongue, versions of the NT were made into the languages of the major ethnic groups of the Near East and Southern Europe. In some of these cases the OT had already been available; in other cases the NT was followed by a translation of part or all of the OT.

1. Aramaic Targums of the OT. After the Exile the practice arose among Palestinian Jews of accompanying the public reading of the Hebrew scriptures in the synagogue with an oral paraphrase in the Aramaic vernacular for the benefit of a growing number of Jews who were more familiar with Aramaic than with Hebrew. The beginnings of this custom may be reflected in Neh. 8:8, which refers to the explaining of obscure words and phrases in the Hebrew of the Pentateuch. At first this oral interpretation was a simple paraphrase, but later it became more elaborate, and the various explanations tended to become fixed and traditional. Still later these Aramaic Targums (or Targumim)* were reduced to writing. Subsequently, however, by a strange irony of fate, the fact that they were now in a relatively fixed written form operated to abolish their use in the synagogue. As it had been ignorance of Hebrew which had called the Targums into existence, so Aramaic, in the course of time, shared the same fate as Hebrew and was as little understood. Even where Aramaic continued to be the spoken language, it altered its character, so that the dialect of the

From Tisserant, *Specimina codicum orientalium* (Berlin: A. Marcus and E. Weber, 1914); by permission of Alfred Töpelmann, Berlin

2. Scroll of Hebrew text with Aramaic Targ. in alternate verses, written *ca.* the eleventh century A.D. (Vatican Hebrew MS 448 [Kennicott 283]), showing Targ. of Exod. 40:9 ff

Targums became archaic and difficult to understand. Fig. VER 2.

Today Targums exist for the Pentateuch, the prophetical books, and most of the Hagiographa. Characteristics common to all these paraphrases include the following: (*a*) a tendency to avoid direct reference to the ineffable name of God, frequently by the use of the word *Mēmrā* ("the Word"); (*b*) in passages referring to God, anthropomorphisms and anthropopathisms are usually avoided and the narrative is recast; (*c*) some of the Targums include longer or shorter stories (similar to the Midrashim) that serve to illustrate the scripture text.

a. The Pentateuch. There are three Targums for the Pentateuch. The oldest appears to be the so-called Palestinian Pentateuch Targ., which until recently was known only through fragments but now is available in its entirety through the Codex Neofiti I of the Vatican. It preserves the idiomatic Aramaic used in Palestine perhaps as early as the first centuries of the Christian era. Secondly, the Jerusalem Targums of the Pentateuch (I and II), also called the Pseudo-Jonathan Targums, exhibit many of the linguistic and theological characteristics of the Palestinian Pentateuch Targ., but surpass it in the elaboration of angelology and demonology. Thirdly, the Targ. of Onkelos, which became the official Targ. of the synagogue, dates from perhaps the second or third century A.D. Though originally based on Palestinian traditions, in its present form it discloses many marks of Babylonian re-editing. It is quite literal, and of all the Targums is the most restrained in the introduction of extraneous matter. The Hebrew text from which it was made was in all essentials the MT. Gen. 49:10; Num. 24:17 are interpreted messianically.

Reference may be made here to the Samaritan Targ.* Early in the Christian era the Samaritan Pentateuch (i.e., Hebrew written in Samaritan characters) was translated into the Aramaic dialect used by the Samaritans. This version differs from the Jewish Targums in being considerably less literal than they. Fig. SAM 21.

b. The Prophets. The official Targ. on the Prophets is known as Targ. Jonathan bar-Uzziel. Like Targ. Onkelos, this one also had its origin in Palestine but was given final form in Babylonia. On the whole, it is not so literal as Onkelos, adhering more closely to the text of the Former Prophets (i.e., Joshua, Judges, I and II Samuel, I and II Kings) than to the text of the Latter Prophets (i.e., Isaiah, Jeremiah, Ezekiel, and the twelve minor prophets). A messianic interpretation is given to numerous passages, including Isa. 53.

c. The Hagiographa. One or more Targums exist for all books of the Hagiographa except for Ezra, Nehemiah, and Daniel. In general, these Targums differ widely among themselves as to dialectal peculiarities, as well as the degree of freedom of paraphrase (some are not translations but commentaries). None of the extant Targums on the Hagiographa is older than *ca.* the fifth century, and most of them are much later. It is likely, therefore, that they were never meant for public use in the synagogue or school, having been composed after the need of Aramaic translations had ceased.

2. Greek versions of the OT. *a. The LXX.* The word SEPTUAGINT (LXX) means "seventy" and refers to the legend that seventy (or seventy-two) Jewish scholars prepared a Greek translation of the Hebrew OT at Pharos in the harbor of Alexandria in Egypt. The story is first told in the so-called "Letter of Aristeas"; ARISTEAS pretends to be a contemporary of the translators during the reign of King Ptolemy Philadelphus (285-246 B.C.). Amid many unhistorical details in this story, the nucleus of fact appears to be that the Pentateuch was translated into Greek in Egypt sometime during the first half of the third century B.C. During the following two centuries the rest of the OT was translated, as well as certain noncanonical books (Sirach, Tobit, etc.). To all these, along with still other apocryphal books composed in Greek, the name LXX came to be given. When the NT authors quote from the OT, most of them quote it, not from the original Hebrew, but from the LXX or other Greek versions. In the early church, Gentile converts (who, of course, were ignorant of Hebrew) made use of the OT exclusively in its Greek form. As a result of the widespread use of the LXX by Christians, the Jews repudiated this version, and other Greek translations were prepared for their use. Notable among these were the renderings made by Aquila, Theodotion, and Symmachus. *See § 2b below.* Fig. VER 3.

In the course of the transmission of MS copies of the LXX, its text underwent several major changes

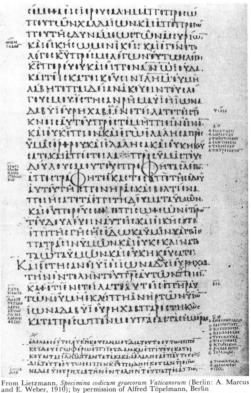

From Lietzmann, *Specimina codicum graecorum Vaticanorum* (Berlin: A. Marcus and E. Weber, 1910); by permission of Alfred Töpelmann, Berlin

3. Codex Marchalianus of the LXX, written not later than the sixth century A.D. (Vatican Greek MS 2125), showing Jer. 42:11 ff

beyond the usual amount of alteration inevitable in copying by hand. The first of these modifications was occasioned by the production at the beginning of the third century of Origen's famous Hexapla. This monumental work, the product of twenty years of stupendous energy on the part of the greatest Christian scholar of his time, was a sixfold version of the OT. In parallel columns, at each opening of his book, stood the following different texts: (a) the Hebrew text, written with only one or two words per line; (b) a transliteration of the Hebrew into Greek letters; (c) Aquila's Greek version; (d) Symmachus' Greek version; (e) the LXX; (f) Theodotion's Greek version.

The text of the LXX which Origen provided was a revised text. He marked with an obelus (— or ÷) Greek words which were not in his Hebrew text. Words occurring in the Hebrew but not in the LXX were inserted in the latter from Theodotion's Greek version, such insertions being marked by an asterisk (*). A metobelus (: or ⸓ or ⸔) marked the conclusion of the passage to which the asterisk or obelus referred.

So enormous was the Hexapla (containing, as it did, the OT copied out six times, involving perhaps seven thousand pages), that it probably was never recopied as a whole. Fragments of his magnum opus, however, are preserved in quotations made by various church fathers, and several editions of the fifth column, containing the LXX, were subsequently made. In recopying this column, however, it was inevitable that scribes would misunderstand the several critical symbols which Origen had used, and, as the LXX was now separate from the Hebrew column, would misplace them or, more often, omit them entirely. Thus the additions from Theodotion's version were confused with the LXX text, and Origen's painstaking labors unwittingly worked to introduce chaos into the text of the original LXX.

During the century following Origen's researches, three editions or recensions of his LXX text were published: (a) Eusebius of Caesarea, with the assistance of his friend Pamphilus, supplied Constantine the Great with fifty copies of the Greek Bible, containing in the OT Origen's fifth column, with alternative readings from the other versions in the margins.

b) Lucian of Samosata, a presbyter of Antioch who died a martyr's death at Nicomedia in A.D. 311 or 312, issued a revised text of the LXX, of which the most distinctive characteristic was his habit, when he found different words or phrases in different copies, of combining them into a conflate reading, and so of preserving both.

c) A third edition of the LXX was prepared by a certain Hesychius, who, so it is thought, was the martyr-bishop in Egypt mentioned by Eusebius (Hist. VIII.13).

Thus it came about that, at about the same time (ca. 300), three forms of the LXX were circulated in different regions: the edition of Eusebius and Pamphilus was generally used in Palestine; that of Lucian was accepted, not only at the place of its origin in Antioch, but in Constantinople and Asia Minor as well; while the Hesychian recension was disseminated in Egypt.

Even from this abbreviated account of the history of the transmission of the LXX, it will be readily perceived that many problems confront the scholar who seeks to recover the earliest Greek translation (or translations) of the OT. There is much mixture in extant MSS of the several earlier editions of the LXX, and only by patient comparison of readings in the MSS with the quotations of the Greek OT which church fathers made in Palestine, Constantinople and Asia Minor, and Egypt can one ascertain the recension to which each MS belongs. Furthermore, it is only by comparing the evidence of early versions made from these forms of the LXX, or made from the pre-Origenian form of the LXX, that progress can be made in charting the history of its transmission. At each stage of its transmission, the possibility of fresh corrections made from a Hebrew text that may have differed from the MT must be taken into account. Finally, the investigation becomes still more complicated if it be true, as some present-day scholars urge, that in various localities Greek-speaking Jews were accustomed to make renderings of the OT, after the manner of a Greek Targ., for the use of the local congregations. Thus, the MSS of the so-called LXX would not go back ultimately to one archetype made in Egypt, but to a multiplicity of renderings made at various localities. To the extent that this may be the situation, the task confronting the modern scholar in seeking to chart the vicissitudes of the transmission of the Greek OT, and to ascertain its earliest form, becomes one of bewildering proportions.

Fig. VER 4.

b. Other Greek versions. When the Christian church began to make large use of the LXX, par-

From E. von Dubschütz, Eberhard Nestle's Einführung in das Griechische Neue Testament (4. Auflage; Göttingen: Vandenhoeck & Ruprecht)

4. Greek Gospels MS with an OL interlinear, written during the ninth century A.D. (Codex Sangallensis, Greg. Δ), showing Luke 2:51 ff

ticularly in polemics against the Jews, the latter repudiated it as an inaccurate version of the Scriptures. Of several rival renderings of the OT that were produced, three are known today by the name of their translators, and three others must be referred to anonymously. Unfortunately all these are preserved only in relatively small fragments and in a limited number of patristic citations.

Ca. A.D. 130, Aquila, a native of Pontus and a proselyte to Judaism, completed an extremely literal rendering of the OT (*see* AQUILA'S VERSION). It was evidently his aim to find a Greek equivalent for every word in the original and to translate the derivatives of a Hebrew root by derivatives from the corresponding Greek root. As a result, his work was so slavishly literal as often to be unintelligible to readers who did not already know Hebrew as well as Greek. Aquila expressed his opposition to the Christians by rendering some of the messianic passages differently from the translation given by the LXX and upheld by the church.

Sometime during the second century A.D., THEODOTION, a Jewish proselyte of Ephesus (so Irenaeus; but Jerome says he was an Ebionite Christian), produced what seems to be a free revision of the LXX on the basis of the Hebrew. In Job it follows the MT much more closely than does the LXX, which is about one sixth shorter than the Hebrew text. In Daniel, Theodotion's Version lacks certain midrashic expressions which are present in the LXX, and, probably for this reason, his rendering became the accepted text used by the church. A characteristic of this version is the frequency with which Hebrew words have been transliterated and not translated.

One of the problems relating to Theodotion's Version arises from the circumstance that several quotations of the OT occur in the NT in a form differing from the LXX and agreeing with his rendering. The usual explanation is that Theodotion made use of some earlier version, perhaps a Greek Targ., oral or written, current in Ephesus during the first Christian century.

Toward the end of the second Christian century an Ebionite named SYMMACHUS produced a Greek translation of the OT quite different from Aquila's literalistic rendering. It is, in fact, distinguished by the purity of its Greek and the absence of Hebraisms. At the same time the freedom of his rendering sometimes lapses into paraphrase marked by anti-anthropomorphic renderings under the influence of the later Jewish tendencies.

The researches of Origen brought to light three anonymous Greek versions of portions of the OT. These are generally called, from their position relative to the four Greek versions in his great Hexapla, the Quinta, the Sexta, and the Septima versions. According to Eusebius, Origen found Quinta at Nicopolis, near Actium, and one of the other two near Jericho buried in a clay wine jar, partly sunk in the ground. To judge by the fragmentary quotations which survive, Quinta was written in very elegant Greek, comparable to the best Greek authors of the period. Sexta also shows some command of Greek and is marked by occasional tendencies to paraphrase.

Several Greek patristic writers of the fourth and fifth centuries quote non-Septuagintal renderings of the OT from a translator who is called "the Hebrew." "The Syrian" is also cited, who sometimes is said to agree with "the Hebrew." Nothing definite is known of these.

3. Latin versions. *a. Old Latin versions*. The name "Old Latin" is used here to denote the Latin translations of the Bible which existed prior to, or independent of, the great revision made by Jerome at the close of the fourth century. It appears that the Scriptures were translated into Latin first in North Africa sometime during the last quarter of the second century A.D. The OT was not translated from the Hebrew, but was based on the Old Greek text; it therefore is of importance in determining the pre-Origenian form of the LXX. In the third century A.D. several Old Latin versions circulated in Europe, including versions current in Italy, in Gaul, and in Spain. Divergent renderings of the same verse (at least eight variant renderings exist at Deut. 31:17, and at Luke 24:4-5 there are at least twenty-seven variant readings) bear out Jerome's complaint that there were almost as many readings as copies of the Old Latin. Undoubtedly what Augustine called the "infinite variety of Latin translations" (*On Christian Doctrine* II.11) arose from the circumstance that "in the early days of the faith, every man who happened to gain possession of a Greek MS and who imagined that he had any facility in both languages (however slight that may be) dared to make a translation" (II.13). The language of the Old Latin fragments corroborates this information as to their origin; instead of being the polished, literary language of that time, it is the vernacular and sometimes uncouth dialect of the common people.

To what family or text type do the Old Latin versions belong? It is easier to answer this for the NT than for the OT. In the NT the Old Latin witnesses support the so-called "Western" text, which is reflected in the bilingual MS Codex Bezae (*see* TEXT, NT). In the OT, where the textual families of LXX MSS have not been as fully worked out, it appears that in the historical and prophetic books the Old Latin not infrequently supports the Lucianic recension of the LXX.

b. The Latin Vulg. The Latin Vulg. Bible, prepared by Jerome at the end of the fourth century, has exerted a pervasive and profound influence throughout Western Europe. Not only did it become the authoritative text of the Roman church, influencing ecclesiastical terminology, but even in the secular world its Latinity left its mark as Latin developed into the Romance languages.

By the close of the fourth century the limitations and imperfections of the Old Latin versions had become evident to the leaders of the Roman church. In the OT the renderings rested on the Greek of the LXX instead of the original Hebrew, and in both testaments scribal corruptions had disfigured still further what had never been scholarly translations. It is not surprising, therefore, that *ca.* 382 Pope Damasus requested the most capable biblical scholar then living, Eusebius Hieronymus, known today as Jerome, to undertake a revision of the Latin Bible. Jerome accepted the task, and in 383 he sent

Damasus the first installment of his work, the four gospels. In his prefatory letter Jerome explains that he made a careful comparison of the ancient Greek MSS and altered the current Old Latin only when it seemed absolutely necessary, retaining in all other cases what had become familiar Latin phraseology. This procedure probably accounts for the presence of quite diverse renderings of identical expressions in Greek (thus, "high priest" is translated in Matthew by *princeps sacerdotum,* in Mark by *summus sacerdos,* in John by *pontifex*). When and how thoroughly he revised the rest of the NT has been debated by scholars. The commonly accepted opinion is that he performed his work in a much more cursory manner. Several scholars, however, have argued that Jerome had nothing to do with the making of the Vulg. text of the rest of the NT, but that, by a curious twist of literary history, the work of some other translator came to be circulated as Jerome's Vulg. text.

Jerome's first work on the OT was a revision of the Psalter on the basis of the LXX, undertaken soon after he had finished the gospels. Known as the Roman Psalter, it was introduced immediately into the liturgy (it is still used at St. Peter's in Rome and in Milan). A few years later in Palestine, Jerome revised the Psalter a second time. Dissatisfied with the Greek text he had used previously, for this revision Jerome obtained from the library at Caesarea a copy of the Psalms in the fifth column of Origen's Hexapla (*see* § 2*a above*). Known as the Gallican Psalter, because it was first used chiefly in Gaul, this version came to be incorporated in the traditional Vulg. Bible, and thus was the basis of Coverdale's English translation, which, through the "Great Bible" of 1539, passed into the Psalter of the Book of Common Prayer. Sometime later, as it seems, Jerome made a third translation of the Psalms, this time from the original Hebrew. In spite of its superior accuracy, this version never circulated widely and is found today in only a limited number of MSS. The text of the Gallican Psalter differs from the Hebrew at many places, perhaps the most noteworthy being the addition of three verses (from Rom. 3:13 ff) after Ps. 14:3, an interpolation which is still reproduced in the Prayer Book.

After revising other OT books from the LXX, Jerome came to realize that the only satisfactory procedure was to translate the *Hebraica veritas.* In his labors Jerome frequently consulted Jewish rabbis, whose influence is to be seen in occasional coincidences between the Vulg. and the Targums.

Outside the circle of Jerome's friends and admirers his revision was greeted with suspicion and even hostility. The sweeping nature of some of the changes that he introduced, as well as the marked difference of the text which he translated, alienated those who loved the older Latin renderings and could not understand the critical reasons for the alterations. Even Augustine was troubled that, by choosing the Hebrew OT as the basis instead of the LXX, Jerome seemed to cast doubts upon the divine inspiration of the latter! Jerome's naturally irascible temper showed little patience with his critics; in a letter to one of his friends he describes them as "two-legged asses." During subsequent centuries, however, the intrinsic

worth of Jerome's version came to be more widely appreciated, and eventually it was accepted throughout Western Christendom, thus earning for itself the name Vulg. (*vulgata* [*versio*], "the common version").

It was perhaps inevitable that, in the course of its transmission, scribes would corrupt Jerome's original work, sometimes by carelessness in transcription, sometimes by deliberate conflation with copies of the Old Latin versions. In order to purify Jerome's text a number of medieval recensions or editions were produced. Notable among these were the editorial work of Alcuin, Theodulf, Lanfranc, and Stephen Harding. In the thirteenth century numerous "Correctoria" of the Latin Bible were collected by scholars at the University of Paris and elsewhere. Unfortunately, however, each of these several attempts at purifying current copies of Jerome's versions resulted eventually in still further textual corruption. As a result, the more than eight thousand MSS of the Vulg. known today exhibit the greatest degree of bewildering cross-contamination of textual type.

The decision at the Council of Trent (1546) to prepare an authentic edition of the Scriptures in Latin was finally taken in hand by Pope Sixtus V, who issued an edition in 1590. After his death, in 1592 Pope Clement VIII called in all copies he could find and issued another authentic edition—differing from the former in some three thousand variants. This latter edition has remained the official text of the Roman church until today. Since 1907 work has been going forward among Benedictine scholars on a revised edition of the Latin Vulg.; most of the

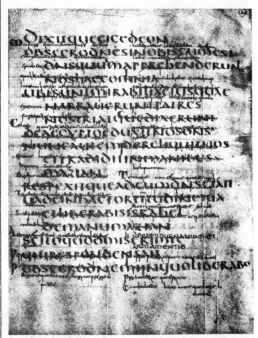

From Dold, *Zwei Bobblenser Palimpseste mit frühestem Vulgatatext* (Texte und Arbeiten I: Beuroner Kunstverlag Gmbh), pl. 1

5. Palimpsest Latin MS of Jerome's Vulg., written in the fifth century A.D., erased and reused in the eighth century for the writings of Isidor of Seville (the underwriting has been restored by ultraviolet photography), showing Judg. 6:13 ff

volumes of the OT have now been finished. A critical edition of the NT has been published at Oxford by several Anglican scholars. Begun by John Wordsworth and H. J. White, the first fascicle (Matthew) appeared in 1889; the last fascicle (Revelation), the work of H. F. D. Sparks, was issued in 1954.

Fig. VER 5.

4. Syriac versions. Syriac, a Semitic language, was the Aramaic dialect used at Edessa and in W Mesopotamia. It was similar to, but not identical with, the Aramaic dialect used in Palestine during the time of Jesus and his apostles.

a. The Old Syriac (and Tatian's Diatessaron). The oldest translation of part of the NT into Syriac was made sometime during the second century. Except for quotations by Syriac patristic writers, this version has been preserved in only two MSS; they are fragmentary copies of the four gospels, usually designated the Sinaitic Syriac MS (dating from *ca.* the fourth century) and the Curetonian Syriac MS (*ca.* the fifth century). The form of text in these MSS belongs in general to the "Western" family (*see* TEXT, NT), and is characterized by many striking omissions. Fig. VER 6.

6. MS of the Old Syriac Gospels written during the early part of the fifth century A.D. (Curetonian MS; Brit. Mus. Add. 14451), showing John 6:30 ff

Related to the Old Syriac version (but whether antecedent or subsequent is debated) is Tatian's famous Diatessaron, or Harmony of the Gospels. Drawn up *ca.* A.D. 170, it circulated widely in the Near East until zealous Syrian ecclesiastics sought out and destroyed copies after Tatian had been adjudged heretical. Unfortunately no MSS of the complete Diatessaron are known to exist today; except

for a tiny Greek fragment dating from *ca.* 220, our knowledge of Tatian's work rests only on secondary sources (e.g., quotations preserved in Ephraem's Syriac Commentary on the Diatessaron, and an Arabic translation of a form of the Diatessaron, the text of which had been partially conformed to the Peshitta Syriac Version).

b. The Peshitta. The word "Peshitta" means literally "the simple [version]," in contradistinction to more elaborate forms of Syriac text, such as the Hexaplaric Version of the OT and the Harclean Version of the NT, both of which had marginal variants and other critical apparatus. The origin of the Peshitta Version is obscure, both as to date and as to identity of the translators. The OT Peshitta was the work of many hands. Perhaps the Pentateuch was translated first, sometime in the second or third century A.D. Since its text follows closely the Masoretic Hebrew and resembles the Targ. Onkelos, many scholars have surmised that it was produced by Jews or by Jewish Christians. Subsequently the other books of the OT were added, some rendered freely after the manner of Targumic paraphrases. Later some of the biblical books were sporadically revised to conform to the LXX. The oldest extant MS of the Peshitta has the distinction of being the oldest copy of the Bible in any language of which the exact date is known; it is a MS of the Pentateuch dating from A.D. 442.

The Peshitta Version of the NT appears to date from the latter part of the fourth century. By this time the Old Syriac, like the Old Latin, had come to exist in a variety of forms. A uniform Syriac version was desirable, and as Jerome made a Vulg. text for the Latin church, so someone produced a common text for the Syrian churches. It was not a new translation, but a revision of the Old Syriac on the basis of the Greek text. The version was adopted by both Jacobite and Nestorian branches of the Syrian church, and has been transmitted very faithfully with a minimum number of scribal variants in the MSS.

Since the Syrian church did not accept as canonical the four minor Catholic letters (II Peter, II and III John, Jude) and the book of Revelation, the Peshitta did not include these five books.

c. The Philoxenian and/or Harclean. Among the Jacobites (a Monophysite branch of the Syrian church) several attempts were made to displace the popularity of the Peshitta Version. At the beginning of the sixth century Philoxenus, bishop of Mabbug, commissioned his coadjutor Polycarp to prepare a translation of the Greek Bible (LXX and entire NT). Very little of this version, which was finished in 508, has survived. To judge by extant fragments of Isaiah, a Lucianic text was used as the basis of revision of the OT. For the first time the minor Catholic letters and Revelation were included in a Syriac Bible. Printed editions of the Peshitta NT frequently contain these five books in the Philoxenian Version. No other part of the NT in this version appears to have survived.

Ca. a century after Philoxenus, the work of revision was resumed. Thomas of Heraclea (Ḥarkel of Mesopotamia) published a version equipped with marginal notes of variant readings found in several Greek MSS. Scholars are not agreed as to whether

Thomas' work involved a complete revision of the Philoxenian Version, or whether he merely reissued the earlier version with the marginal additions. It is, especially for Acts, one of the most important witnesses to the "Western" form of text.

d. The Palestinian Syriac. Toward the close of the fourth century the Melchite Christians of Palestine appear to have reduced to writing the version which heretofore had been provided orally when the Greek scriptures were read in church services (Aetheria [Silvia] *Peregrinatio* XLVII.3). The dialect, which differs slightly from Syriac, should more properly be called Palestinian Aramaic; its chief resemblance to Syriac is the form of script in which it is written. Of the OT only fragments remain of several books; of these the Psalter is best represented with forty-two psalms complete and stray verses of others. The general view is that the OT version was made from the

7. Palestinian Syriac lectionary of the Gospels, written A.D. 1104 (MS B; Monastery of St. Catherine on Mount Sinai), showing John 12:24 ff

LXX, though a few scholars have thought that in the Pentateuch it rests upon a Jewish Palestinian Targ. Of the NT the most extensive remains are in the form of gospel lectionaries. Here the text, while not free from the influence of the Peshitta, reflects a form of Greek text current in Palestine during the fourth and fifth centuries.

Fig. VER 7.

e. Paul of Tella's Syro-Hexaplar. Corresponding to the Harclean revision of the NT was the version of the OT known as the Syro-Hexaplar. This was made by Paul, bishop of Tella de-Mauzeleth near Alexandria, who undertook the work at the request of Patriarch Athanasius I. Finished in 616/617, it is a translation of the LXX text in the fifth column of

Origen's Hexapla with the asterisks and obeli preserved (*see* § 2a *above*), together with many marginal renderings from other Greek translators, such as Aquila, Symmachus, and Theodotion. Happily the version is extant for most of the books of the OT. The oldest Syro-Hexaplar MS (now in the Ambrosian library at Milan) is only a century younger than the original translation. It contains the poetical and prophetical books and has been published in a photolithographic edition. The importance of this version is very great, for it is an early and extensive witness to the Hexaplaric text of the LXX along with the Hexaplaric signs. It also witnesses to the original LXX text of the book of Daniel, a text which was almost totally supplanted in the church by Theodotion's version.

5. Coptic versions. Coptic is the latest form of the ancient Egyptian language, which until Christian times was written in hieroglyphs and their two derivatives, hieratic and demotic. During the early Christian era the language came to be written in the Greek alphabet, with the addition of seven characters taken from demotic. During the course of the centuries several dialects of Coptic developed at settlements along the Nile River. Today portions of the Bible are extant in six dialects: (*a*) Sahidic, formerly called Thebaic, used in Upper (i.e., S) Egypt; (*b*) Bohairic, formerly called Memphitic, used in Lower (i.e., N) Egypt, including Alexandria; (*c*) Achmimic, used in Upper Egypt around Achmim, the ancient Panopolis; (*d*) sub-Achmimic, used S of Asyut; (*e*) Middle Egyptian; and (*f*) Fayyumic, formerly known as Bashmuric, used W of the Nile and S of the Delta.

Of these dialects the first two are the most important for the study of the early versions of the

8. Coptic papyrus codex of John, written in the sub-Achmimic dialect *ca.* the third quarter of the fourth century A.D. (now in the Library of the British and Foreign Bible Society), showing John 6:14 ff

Bible. Portions of the NT were first rendered into Sahidic by *ca.* the beginning of the third century. By perhaps a century later, most of the books of the Bible were translated. Indeed, if one may judge on the basis of the existence of widely divergent Sahidic texts, some books were translated several times by independent translators.

The Bohairic Version, which appears to be one of the latest of the Coptic versions, came in the course of the centuries to supersede the use of the other versions. More MSS in this dialect have been preserved than in any other, but almost all of them are relatively late in date (twelfth to fourteenth centuries).

For the OT the Coptic translators utilized the LXX. In the Sahidic Version of Job, it appears that the translator used a pre-Hexaplar copy of the Greek, for it lacks about 375 lines (i.e., half-verses) which Origen inserted into the LXX text from Theod. The Sahidic Version of Daniel, on the other hand, was made from Theodotion's text. The Bohairic version of the Prophets discloses textual affinities with the Hesychian recension of the LXX.

In the NT both the Sahidic and the Bohairic versions agree often with the Alexandrian type of text. Except for an important MS of the Gospel of John in sub-Achmimic,* dating from the fourth century, only relatively small fragments have been preserved in the other dialects. Much study remains to be done on questions of date, mutual relationships, and textual type of the Coptic versions. Fig. VER 8.

6. The Gothic Version. The Gothic Version is noteworthy in several respects: it is the earliest one of which we have information regarding the identity of its translator; it is one of a few versions for which an alphabet is said to have been invented by the translator; it is the oldest surviving literature in any Teutonic language; and it is the only version of any considerable extent of which all the known MS evidence has been utilized. Produced by the learned Bishop Ulfilas, the apostle of the Goths of the Danubian provinces during the mid–fourth century, this version survives today in only six MSS, all of them fragmentary. The most complete is a deluxe copy dating from the fifth or sixth century and containing portions of all four gospels, which stand in the so-called "Western" order (Matthew, John, Luke, and Mark). It is written on purple vellum in large letters of silver ink, whence the name that is commonly given to this MS: Codex Argenteus (i.e., the Silver Codex).

Of the OT very few fragments survive (namely, Gen. 5:3-32; Ps. 52:2-3; and portions of Nehemiah). The translation is based on Lucian's recension of the LXX (*see* § 2a above). Of the NT more or less extensive remains are extant for all the books except the Acts, the Catholic letters, and Revelation. The character of the text appears to be similar in certain respects to the form of the Old Latin that circulated in Italy.

Fig. VER 9.

7. The Armenian Version. In the early years of the fifth century of the Christian era, Mesrop, the inventor of the Armenian alphabet, and Sahak the Patriarch began a translation of the Bible and of the liturgy into the national language as a reaction

Courtesy of the Universitetsbiblioteket Uppsala

9. Deluxe Gothic MS of the Gospels, written in the fifth or sixth century A.D. (Codex Argenteus of Uppsala), showing Mark 5:18 ff

against the prevailing use of Syriac in the worship.

Tradition is divided as to the textual basis of the rendering of the OT. Moses of Chorene (said to have been a nephew of Mesrop) states that the work was made, at least at the beginning, from the Syriac Version, because the Persian king Meroujah had burned, thirty years before, all the Greek books of the Armenians. Other early Armenian historians, however, declare that the rendering was made at the outset from Greek copies which had been secured at Constantinople and Alexandria. In any case, an examination of surviving Armenian MSS indicates that the OT rests upon the Hexaplaric recension of the OT. On the other hand, certain passages (notably in Jeremiah) disclose evidence of a (later?) revision from the Syriac.

Whether the NT was translated from the original Greek or from an intermediate Syriac version has been debated by scholars. The inclusion of the apocryphal Third Letter of Paul to the Corinthians in the early canon of both the Syrian and Armenian churches, and the presence of traces of Syriac orthography of proper names and Semitic syntax in the older Armenian patristic quotations of the NT, suggest a strong influence from Syria. On the other hand, most extant MSS embody a more Hellenized form of text. Probably, therefore, the original Armenian Version underwent a subsequent revision sometime between the fifth and eighth centuries. There is also a certain amount of evidence that the earliest form in which the gospels circulated in Armenian was that of a harmony, modeled upon Tatian's Diatessaron. *See* § 4 *above*. Fig. VER 10.

The book of Revelation underwent a remarkable series of revisions, of which Conybeare thought he could distinguish at least five. First rendered into Armenian in the fifth century (perhaps from an Old Latin original; so Conybeare), the most thorough-going revision was made during the twelfth century by Nerses of Lambron, bishop of Tarsus.

On the whole, the Armenian Version is unsurpassed for beauty of diction and accuracy of rendering. Called the "queen of the versions" (La Croze), it deserves far more attention than scholars have been accustomed to devote to its study.

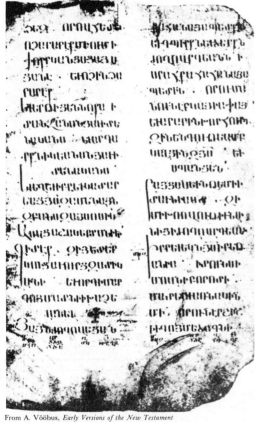

From A. Vööbus, *Early Versions of the New Testament*

10. Armenian MS of the Gospels, written A.D. 887 (Codex Lazareff), showing Matt. 25:45 ff

8. The Georgian Version. The Georgian language, used by a strong and vigorous people living in the Caucasus between the Black Sea and the Caspian, appears to be unrelated to any other known tongue. After Christianity had been introduced among the Georgians in the fourth century, Mesrop, according to Armenian traditions, invented and introduced an alphabet in Georgia. Who it was that made the earliest translation of the Scriptures into Georgian, what portions were first to be rendered, and what the textual basis was (Greek, Syriac, or Armenian), are questions more easily asked than answered. Probably the gospels and the Psalter were translated during the first part of the fifth century;

the book of Revelation, on the other hand, was not rendered until the end of the tenth or beginning of the eleventh century.

As regards the Georgian OT, the evidence of the MSS indicates that different parts were translated at different times and from different archetypes. One version of the Octateuch was made from the LXX. Another version, in the Prophets at least, was made from the Armenian. The NT, on the other hand, despite an ecclesiastical tradition which asserts that it was made directly from the Greek, is believed by those who have studied the version to rest either upon a Syriac or (more probably) an Armenian basis. Scholars have distinguished five versions or recensions of the Old Georgian gospels prior to a thoroughgoing revision made by Euthymius at the close of the tenth century. During the following century George the Hagiorite completed on Mount Athos a revised version of the Georgian NT which, in substance, has remained the basis of various printed editions.

Fig. VER 11.

9. The Ethiopic Version. The origins of Christianity in Ethiopia are hidden in the mists of history. How far the Ethiopian eunuch whom Philip baptized (Acts 8:26-39) may have spread the faith in his own country, we have no knowledge. The first definite historical figure in the Christianization of that land is Frumentius, whom Athanasius, patriarch of Alexandria, consecrated bishop of Aksum sometime *ca.* the middle of the fourth century. Presumably at or soon after this date a need was felt for translating por-

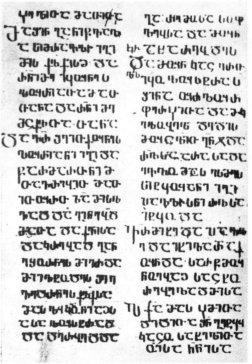

From A. Vööbus, *Early Versions of the New Testament*

11. Georgian MS of the Acts and the Catholic letters, written A.D. 974 (Monastery of St. Catherine on Mount Sinai), showing Acts 14:4 ff

tions of the Scriptures into the native tongue. It is not known whether Frumentius began the work of translation or whether (in accord with Abyssinian traditions) this was done by a group of nine Syrian monks who as Monophysites fled after the Council of Chalcedon in 451 from Syria to Egypt, whence they made their way to Ethiopia.

Wide textual differences exist among the extant Ethiopic MSS, none of which is known to antedate the thirteenth century. Most MSS after the fourteenth century preserve a text which has been extensively revised on the basis of the medieval Arabic text current at Alexandria. In the OT it appears that the original Ethiopic Version was made in the main from the LXX (though some scholars have thought they could discern influence from the Hebrew). In I Kings the type of text resembles the Greek of Codex Vaticanus, with strong Lucianic influence. The Ethiopic text of the NT is quite variegated: at times the translators followed the Greek text slavishly, even as regards the order of words, but at other times, perhaps where the Greek proved to be too difficult for them, they paraphrased wildly. The earlier type of text is predominantly Antiochian, but with occasional agreements with certain early Greek MSS (P[46] and B) against all other witnesses. Fig. VER 12.

10. Arabic versions. Opinion differs as to when the first Arabic translation of the Scriptures was made. Most scholars believe that not until after the death of Mohammed (A.D. 632), when the success of the Koran had made Arabic into a literary language, was the need for an Arabic version of the Bible really felt. (Prior to this time, it appears, Syriac was the ecclesiastical language among Christians in Arabia.) Other scholars, however, maintain that it is improbable that missionaries, who had introduced Christianity into Arabia long before this date, would have neglected to provide their converts with sacred literature in the vernacular. However this may be, the earliest extant biblical references are in quotations made by ninth-century writers.

13. Arabic MS of the book of Job, written in the first half of the ninth century A.D. (British Museum add. 26116), showing Job 22:12 ff

The Arabic MSS of the Bible preserve a multiplicity of versions, made from Hebrew, Greek, Samaritan, Syriac (several forms), Coptic (several dialects), and Latin. Some of the more interesting are the following:

The first and most important rendering from Hebrew was made by Sa'adya the Ga'ôn, a learned Jew who was head of the rabbinic school at Sura in Babylon (died 942). The translation discloses traces of Talmudic exegesis (such as the removal of anthropomorphisms) and of Sa'adya's own philosophy.

In 946 Isaak the son of Velásquez, a Spanish Christian of Córdoba, made a translation of the gospels on the basis of a Latin MS that contained Old Latin and Diatessaric readings.

12. Ethiopic MS of Job and Daniel, written during the fourteenth century A.D. (Paris, Bibl. nat., Eth. 11), showing text of Sus. 1 ff

In Alexandria during the thirteenth century two Arabic recensions of the gospels were produced. *Ca.* 1250 a Christian named Hibat Allâh ibn al-'Assâl revised an Arabic text translated from Coptic, using other Arabic translations made from Greek and Syriac, also furnishing his revision with a complicated critical apparatus. This proved to be too cumbersome for popular use, and was superseded at the close of the century by what has come to be termed the modern "Alexandrian Vulg." While depending chiefly upon the Coptic, it takes into account texts translated from Greek and Syriac. The unknown translator combined general fidelity to the original with a certain smoothness of style.

Fig. VER 13.

11. The Old Church Slavonic Version. *See* VERSIONS, MEDIEVAL AND MODERN, § 9a.

12. Other ancient versions. The Anglo-Saxon Version can be treated best as the historical antecedent to the English versions.

The Sogdian Version and the Nubian Version were made sometime during the sixth or seventh centuries, the former for Christians of Central Asia, the latter for the flourishing church of Nubia, between Egypt and Ethiopia. All that survives today of each version is a fragmentary lectionary MS.

Bibliography. General: E. Nestle *et al., Urtext und Übersetzungen der Bibel* (1897). F. C. Burkitt, "Text and Versions," *Encyclopaedia Biblica,* IV (1903), 4977-5031. F. F. Bruce, *The Books and the Parchments* (1950). B. M. Metzger, "The Evidence of the Versions for the Text of the NT," in M. M. Parvis and A. P. Wikgren, eds., *NT MS Studies* (1950), pp. 25-68, 177-208. B. J. Roberts, *The OT Text and Versions* (1951). I. M. Price, *The Ancestry of Our English Bible* (corrected ed. by W. A. Irwin and A. P. Wikgren, 1951). H. W. Robinson, *The Bible in Its Ancient and English Versions* (2nd ed., 1954). A. Vööbus, *Early Versions of the NT, MS Studies* (1954). B. M. Metzger, *Annotated Bibliography of the Textual Criticism of the NT* (1955), pp. 27-65; "A Survey of Recent Research on the Ancient Versions of the NT," *NTS,* II (1955), 1-16. E. Würthwein, *The Text of the OT* (1957). F. G. Kenyon, *Our Bible and the Ancient MSS* (5th ed., 1958).

Aramaic Targums: A. Berliner, *Targ. Onkelos* (2 vols.; 1884). M. Ginsburger, *Pseudo-Jonathan* (1903). A. Levy, *Das Targ. zu Koheleth nach südarabischen Handschriften* (1905). E. Brederek, *Konkordanz zum Targ. Onkelos* (1906). P. Churgin, *Targ. Jonathan to the Prophets* (1927). P. E. Kahle, *Die Masoreten des Westens,* vol. I (1927); vol. II (1930). E. Silverstone, *Aquila and Onkelos* (1931). P. Churgin, "The Targ. and the LXX," *AJSL,* L (1933), 41-65. A. Sperber, "The Targ. Onkelos and Its Relation to the Hebrew MT," *Proceedings of the American Academy for Jewish Research,* VI (1934-35), 309-51; "Peschitta und Onkelos," *Jewish Studies in Memory of G. A. Kohut* (1935), pp. 554-64. S. Wohl, *Das Palästinische Pentateuch-Targ.* (1935). V. Hamp, *Der Begriff "Wort" in den aramäischen Bibelübersetzungen* (1938). A. Wikgren, "The Targums and the NT," *JR,* XXIV (1944), 89-95. J. F. Stenning, *The Targ. of Isaiah* (1949), Alejandro Díez Macho of Barcelona is preparing an edition of Codex Neofiti I; see *Estudios bíblicos,* XV (1956), 446-47.

The Greek versions: *See* the bibliography under SEPTUAGINT.

The Old Latin versions: P. Sabatier, *Bibliorum Sacrorum Latinae versiones antiquae* (Rheims, 1739-43; Paris, 1751). A. M. Ceriani, *Critici Biblici. Le recensioni dei LXX a la versione latina detta Itala* (1886); F. C. Burkitt, *The Old Latin and the Itala* (1896). H. von Soden, *Das lateinische Neue Testament in Afrika zur Zeit Cyprianus* (1909). A. Jülicher, *Itala, das Neue Testament in altlateinischer Überlieferung nach den Handschriften* (1938—). B. Fischer, *Vetus Latina. Die Reste der altlateinischen Bibel*

(1949—). T. Ayuso Marazuela, *La Vetus Latina Hispana:* I, *Prolegómenos* (1953).

The Latin Vulg.: S. Berger, *Histoire de la Vulg. pendant des premiers siècles du moyen âge* (1895). P. Corssen, *Bericht über die lateinischen Bibelübersetzungen* (1899). J. Chapman, *Notes on the Early History of the Vulg. Gospels* (1908). P. Capelle, *Le Texte du Psautier latine en Afrique* (1913). H. Quentin, *Mémoire sur l'établissement du texte de la Vulg.* (1922). A. Allgeier, *Die altlateinischen Psalterien. Prolegomena zu einer Textgeschichte der hieronymianischen Psalmenübersetzung* (1928). H. J. Vogels, *Vulgatastudien. Die Evangelien der Vulgata untersucht auf ihre lateinische und griechische Vorlage* (1928). H. H. Glunz, *History of the Vulg. in England from Alcuin to Roger Bacon* (1933). P. Salmon, *La Revision de la Vulg., état des travaux difficultés et résultats* (1937). J. O. Smit, *De Vulgaat* (1948). J. H. Marks, *Der textkritische Wert des Psalterium Hieronymi juxta Hebraeos* (1956).

The Old Syriac: F. C. Burkitt, *Evangelion da-Mepharreshe* (2 vols.; 1904). A. S. Lewis, *The Old Syriac Gospels* (1910). C. H. Kraeling, *A Greek Fragment of Tatian's Diatessaron from Dura* (1935). A.-S. Marmardji, *Diatessaron de Tatien* (1936). C. Peters, *Das Diatessaron Tatians; seine Überlieferung und sein Nachwirken im Morgen- und Abendland, sowie der heutige Stand seiner Erforschung* (1939). B. M. Metzger, "Tatian's Diatessaron and a Persian Harmony of the Gospels," *JBL,* LXIX (1950), 261-80. A. Vööbus, *Studies in the History of the Gospel Text in Syriac* (1951); *Neue Materialen zur Geschichte der Vetus Syra in den Evangelienhandschriften* (1953).

The Peshitta: A. Rahlfs, "Beiträge zur Textkritik der Peschitta," *ZAW,* IX (1889), 161-211. G. H. Gwilliam, "The Place of the Peshitta Version in the Apparatus Criticus of the Greek NT," *Studia Biblica et Ecclesiastica,* V (1903), 187-237. A. Mingana, "Syriac Versions of the OT," *JQR,* N. S. VI (1915/16), 385-98. G. H. Gwilliam, ed., *The NT in Syriac* (1905-20). L. Haefeli, *Die Peschitta des Alten Testaments mit Rücksicht auf ihre textkritische Bearbeitung und Herausgabe* (1927). J. van der Ploeg, "Recente Pešitta-Studies (sinds 1927)," *Jaarbericht van het Vooraziatisch-Egyptisch Gezelschap, Ex Oriente Lux,* X (1948), 392-99. A. Vööbus, *Studies in the History of the Gospel Text in Syriac* (1951).

The Philoxenian and/or Harclean: J. White, . . . *Versio Syriaca Philoxeniana* . . . (2 vols.; 1778-1803). J. Gwynn, *The Apocalypse of St. John, in a Syriac Version Hitherto Unknown* (1897); *Remnants of the Later Syriac Versions* (1909). S. New, "The Harclean Version of the Gospels," *HTR,* XXI (1928), 376-95. W. H. P. Hatch, "The Subscription in the Chester Beatty MS of the Harclean Gospels," *HTR,* XXX (1937), 141-55. G. Zuntz, *The Ancestry of the Harklean NT* (1945); "Die Subscriptionen der Syra Harclensis," *Zeitschrift der deutschen morgenländischen Gesellschaft,* CI (1951), 174-96. A. Vööbus, "New Data for the Solution of the Problem Concerning the Philoxenian Version," *Spiritus et Veritas* (K. Kundzinš' Festschrift; ed. Auseklis; 1953), pp. 169-86.

The Palestinian Syriac: A. S. Lewis, ed., *A Palestinian Syriac Lectionary, Containing Lessons from the Pentateuch, Job, Proverbs, Acts, and Epistles* (1897). A. S. Lewis and M. D. Gibson, eds., *The Palestinian Syriac Lectionary of the Gospels* (1899). M. J. Lagrange, "L'origine de la version syropalestinienne des évangiles," *RB,* XXXIV (1925), 481-504. H. Duensing, "Zwei christlich-palästinisch-aramäische Fragmente an der Apostelgeschichte," *ZNW,* XXXVII (1938), 42-46. M. Black, *A Christian Palestinian Syriac Horologion* (1954).

Paul of Tella's Syro-Hexaplar: A. M. Ceriani, *Monumenta sacra et profana,* vols. I, II, V, VII (1861-74). P. de Lagarde, *Bibliothecae Syriacae* (1892). J. Gwynn, *Remnants of the Later Syriac Versions of the Bible* (1909), pt. II.

Coptic versions: H. Thompson, *The Coptic (Sahidic) Version of Certain Books of the OT from a Papyrus in the British Museum* (1908). G. Horner, *The Coptic Version of the NT in the Northern Dialect* (4 vols.; 1898-1905); *The Coptic Version of the NT in the Southern Dialect* (7 vols.; 1911-24). H. Thompson, *The Gospel of St. John According to the Earliest Coptic MS* (1924).

W. Till, *Die achmîmische Version der Zwölf Kleinen Propheten* (1927). F. H. Hallock, "The Coptic OT," *AJSL*, XLIX (1933), 325-35. A. Boehlig, *Untersuchungen über die koptischen Proverbientexte* (1936). W. Grossow, *The Coptic Version of the Minor Prophets* (1938). W. Kammerer, *Coptic Bibliography* (1950). P. E. Kahle, *Bala'izah* (2 vols.; 1954), especially pp. 10-14, 193-290.

The Gothic Version: J. Mühlau, *Zur Frage nach der gotischen Psalmenübersetzung* (1904). H. Lietzmann, "Die Vorlage der gotischen Bibel," *Zeitschrift für deutsches Altertum*, LVI (1919), 249-78. G. W. S. Friedrichsen, *The Gothic Version of the Gospels, a Study of Its Style and Textual History* (1926). *Codex argenteus Upsaliensis, jussu senatus universitatis phototypice editus* (1927). G. W. S. Friedrichsen, *The Gothic Version of the Epistles, a Study of Its Style and Textual History* (1939). W. Streitberg, *Die gotische Bibel* (3rd ed., 1950). F. Mossé, "Bibliographia Gotica, a Bibliography of Writings on the Gothic Language," *Mediaeval Studies*, XII (1950), 237-324.

The Armenian Version: A. Abeghian, *Vorfragen zur Entstehungsgeschichte der altarmenischen Bibelübersetzungen* (1906). F. C. Conybeare, *The Armenian Version of Revelation* (1907). F. Macler, *Le texte arménien de l'évangile d'après Matthieu et Marc* (1919). H. S. Gehman, "The Armenian Version of Daniel and Its Affinities," *ZAW*, N. F. VII (1930), 82-99. S. Lyonnet, *Les origines de la version arménienne et le Diatessaron* (1950).

The Georgian Version: A. Palmieri, "Le Versione Georgiane della Bibbia," *Bessarione*, Second Series, V (1903), 259-68, 322-27; VI (1904), 72-77, 189-94. F. Zorell, "Ursprung und Eigenart der georgischen Bibelübersetzung," *Handes Amsorya*, XLI (1927), 669-80. R. P. Blake, "Ancient Georgian Versions of the OT," *HTR*, XXII (1929), 33-56. G. Garitte, *L'ancienne version géorgienne des Actes des Apôtres* (1955). D. M. Lang, "Recent Work on the Georgian NT," *Bulletin of the School of Oriental and African Studies*, XIX (1957), 82-93.

The Ethiopic Version: H. S. Gehman, "The Old Ethiopic Version of I Kings and Its Affinities," *JBL*, L (1931), 81-114. S. A. B. Mercer, *The Ethiopic Text of the Book of Ecclesiastes* (1931). J. A. Montgomery, "The Ethiopic Text of Acts of the Apostles," *HTR*, XXVII (1934), 169-205. A. Vööbus, *Die Spuren eines älteren äthiopischen Evangelientextes im Lichte der literarischen Monumente* (1951).

The Arabic Version: P. Kahle, *Die arabischen Bibelübersetzungen* (1904). J. F. Rhode, *The Arabic Versions of the Pentateuch in the Church of Egypt* (1921). H. S. Gehman, "The 'Polyglot' Arabic Text of Daniel and Its Affinities," *JBL*, XLIV (1925), 327-52. B. Levin, *Die griechisch-arabische Evangelienübersetzung* (1938). G. Graf, *Geschichte der christlichen arabischen Literatur*, I (1944), 85-195. A. S. Atiya, *The Arabic MSS of Mount Sinai* (1955). J. A. Thompson, "The Major Arabic Bibles," *The Bible Translator*, VI (1955), 1-12, 51-55, 98-106, 146-50 (also published separately).

Other ancient versions: B. M. Metzger in M. M. Parvis and A. P. Wikgren, eds., *NT MS Studies* (1950), pp. 49 ff; and in *Twentieth Century Encyclopedia of Religious Knowledge*, I (1955), 142-43.   B. M. METZGER

*VERSIONS, ENGLISH.

The first English version of the complete Bible appeared in 1382, although Christianity had entered Britain more than a thousand years earlier. This early date for the beginnings of the church there rests on a statement of Tertullian (*Against the Jews* 7) that the gospel had progressed in Britain beyond the limits of Roman arms. Origen also (before A.D. 230) makes references in his homilies that support this early date. In 314 three bishops of Britain attended the Council of Arles. But while we can speak with assurance of the Christian movement in Britain probably earlier than the third century of the Christian era, there is no evidence of translation of the Bible. We may assume that the work of the missionaries was carried on by means of a running oral paraphrase of the biblical text. No written version was required at first. Moreover, the mingling and commingling of languages on the Isles of Britain placed a barrier to earlier translations of the Bible.

1. Anglo-Saxon beginnings
2. Wyclif's Version
3. Tyndale's translation and early related versions (1525-35)
   a. The Coverdale Version
   b. The Thomas Matthew Bible
4. The period of the Great Bible (1539-68)
   a. The Taverner Bible
   b. The Geneva Bible
5. The Bishops' Bible (1568)
6. The Douay (Douai) Version (1609-10)
7. The KJV (1611)
8. Other translations
9. The ERV (1881-85) and the ASV (1901)
10. Modern-speech translations
11. The RSV (1946, 1952)
Bibliography

1. Anglo-Saxon beginnings. There was no translation of the Bible into Anglo-Saxon, but there were poetic versions of biblical stories, such as those ascribed by Bede to Caedmon, who died in 680. Caedmon listened to biblical stories and set them forth in poetic paraphrase, sung to the accompaniment of the harp. Aldhelm Abbot of Malmesbury was also cleverly doing the same kind of thing. But there was no idea of translation of the Bible in its entirety; indeed, there were not many who could have read it. Not long afterward certain favorite sections began to be translated for the use and edification of the priest and for use in preaching. In the eighth century a number of translations of the Psalms appeared, and other small sections like the Decalogue and the Lord's Prayer. Bede is credited with a translation of the Gospel of John, completed at the very moment of his death. It may be assumed that by the time of the death of Bede in 735 the four gospels were in Anglo-Saxon. We know that Aldhelm, then bishop of Sherborne (died 709), translated the Psalms into Anglo-Saxon English, and that at his request Egbert, bishop of Holy Island, translated the gospels. In the next century King Alfred (848-901) took an active interest in the Bible and its translation, causing a translation of the Psalms to be made, and using the Ten Commandments and other sections of the Pentateuch in his code of laws.

Several MSS of the Psalter in the vernacular are extant, but they probably stem from the next two or three centuries. Ca. 950, the priest Aldred wrote a paraphrase of the gospels between the lines of a Latin text. It was during this century that translations of the gospels appeared without the Latin text, the earliest coming at *ca.* 1000 through the work of the Abbot Alfric of Bath. The translation of the Psalms into English by William de Shoreham of Kent in 1325 ought to be mentioned, as well as that of Richard Rolle of Hampole in 1330.

Yet all these translations, important as they are from a historical point of view, are relatively unrelated to the great stream of English translations, which began in a serious way with the work of William Tyndale but which had definitely been set under way by John Wyclif. Before Wyclif the sporadic and piecemeal efforts at translation were not designed primarily for the use of the average man, nor produced in quantities that would touch him. They were not complete Bibles but small sections. They were designed for few readers, principally among the clergy. Moreover, they did not create the ecclesiastical problems later translations often produced, probably because of the very nature of the sections translated and because the laity had so little access to them in any case.

2. Wyclif's Version. The first complete Bible in English appeared in 1382. The work of John Wyclif is different from any translations before him. He planned and executed the translation of the entire Bible with the average man in mind and for the specific purpose of placing the Bible in the hands of laymen. His work of translation was a part of a more comprehensive effort to reform the church which caused him to be called the "morning star of the Reformation." He was assisted by Nicholas of Hereford, who is credited with having translated the OT before he was excommunicated. Wyclif carried the task forward, and the finished NT appeared in 1380 and the complete Bible in 1382. John Purvey may have assisted in this work also. At any rate, he is credited with the revision of the entire work, which appeared in 1388. In line with his pastoral purpose of putting the Bible into the hands of laymen, Wyclif organized the "Poor Priests" or Lollards, who went forth teaching the Bible and delivering it to lay people. It was joyfully received.

Wyclif died in 1384, but his body was exhumed and burned in 1428, just as in 1415 his Bible had been condemned and consigned to the flames. His work, however, stands as a beacon, and greatly influenced later translations. In spite of the fact that reproductions of this translation were terribly expensive, since they were hand written, and in spite of the opposition of the church and state authorities, who ruled that anyone who read the Scriptures in the mother tongue "should forfeit land, catel, life, and goods from their heyres for ever," at least 170 MS copies of this first English Bible have survived; and several have been traced to the royal family and other prominent persons. Other, less pretentious MSS, written in small hand and crowding the page, were obviously the property of individuals of the common people.

For 150 years this Bible enjoyed a wide usage and was the only complete English Bible in use. Yet it had its weaknesses. For one thing it was based on the Latin Vulg. and made no use of older texts. Again, it was already archaic in language, using the earliest style of the language, which was rapidly changing as it blossomed into a literary vehicle. The OT translation especially was stiffly literal. John Purvey, who calls himself "this simple creature," attempted to revise the OT to harmonize with Wyclif's better version in the NT. Nevertheless, when printing was discovered, no one thought of publishing the translation of Wyclif. It had served its purpose magnificently, but the times demanded a better version of the Scriptures. Fig. WYC 43.

3. Tyndale's translation and early related versions (1525-35). Exactly a hundred years after the death of Wyclif in 1384, William Tyndale was born. During this century between Wyclif and Tyndale the printing press had appeared. The Turks had driven the Christian Greek and Hebrew scholars of Constantinople into Western Europe. Greek and Hebrew then began to be taught in the universities of Europe. It was inevitable that these events, along with the electrifying atmosphere of the sixteenth century with all its intellectually stimulating factors, should greatly affect the study of the Bible. Tyndale was reared in the midst of these exciting events. He studied at Oxford under the classical scholars Grocyn, Latimer, Linacre, and at Cambridge came under the influence of Erasmus, the great NT Greek scholar, who in 1516 was to publish the NT in Greek (*see* TEXT, NT). As a matter of fact, it was at Cambridge between 1511 and 1514 that Erasmus prepared his epoch-making edition for publication.

Having been ordained, Tyndale became chaplain and tutor in the family of Sir John Walsh. It was in his pastoral work that he said he "perceaved by experyence how that it was impossible to stablysh the laye people in any truth excepte the scripture were playnly layde before their eyes in their mother tonge" and added "which thynge onlye moved me to translate the NT." He began to discuss his project with clerical acquaintances and met with serious opposition. He was a man of inflammable spirit, as the notes in the margins of his translation of the NT were later to reveal, and he replied to one of his opponents, called a "learned man": "If God spare my lyfe, ere many yeares I wyl cause a boye that dryveth the plough shall know more of the scripture than thou doest."

The bishop of London, Cuthbert Tunstall, had the reputation of being a friend of learning, but when Tyndale asked for his approval and support, the bishop affirmed that his house was full and that "he had more than he could well finde." The bishop may have been afraid of the ecclesiastical attitudes of Tyndale rather than of translation itself. At any rate, no help came from Tunstall. Nevertheless, an alderman of London, Humphrey Monmouth, took Tyndale into his home and agreed to pay him a stipend of ten pounds. Tyndale remained under his roof for a year and worked diligently at his task, and at the same time met merchants from the Continent who brought him information which would be of value to his later work. At the end of one year he said: "In London I abode almoste an yere . . . and understode at the laste not only that there was no rowme in my lorde of londons palace to translate the new testament, but also that there was no place to do it in all englonde." Therefore he left England and went to the free city of Hamburg in 1524. He soon went to Wittenberg and was in close fellowship with Luther. He returned to Hamburg in the spring of 1525, where he received funds from his London patron, Monmouth. He hurried to Cologne in 1525 and began the printing of his finished NT translation in a quarto edition. Cochlaeus, an enemy of Luther, in a clever move discovered Tyndale's project and reported it to the authorities. Tyndale fled with some printed sheets to Worms. Here an octavo edition without notes was completed, and the quarto edition, which had been started in Cologne, was also completed with marginal notes. These editions were shipped into England hidden away in cases of merchandise. Three thousand copies of the octavo edition were shipped to England.

The Tyndale Version was eagerly purchased by the people to be read—and by Archbishop Warham to be burned. Funds were raised to be used in buying copies for the archbishop's fire; speeches were made against it. Bishop Tunstall said he had found two thousand errors in it—referring, no doubt, to the many changes made by Tyndale on the basis of the Greek text as over against the Vulg. The speech of Cochlaeus against it is a classic and shows the spirit of the opposition to any translation. "The NT translated into the vulgar tongue," said Cochlaeus, "is in truth the food of death, the fuel of sin, the veil of malice, the pretext of false liberty, the protection of disobedience, the corruption of discipline, the depravity of morals, the termination of Concord, the death of honesty, the well-spring of vices, the disease of virtues, the instigation of rebellion, the milk of pride, the nourishment of contempt, the death of peace, the destruction of charity, the enemy of unity, the murderer of truth."

The opposition was so strong that only a fragment of the quarto edition survived, now in the British Museum; and of the three thousand copies of the octavo edition only two are extant, one in the Baptist College in Bristol, England, and another in the library of St. Paul's, London. These few fragments are all that remain of the eighteen thousand copies printed 1525-28.

As soon as Tyndale had finished translating the NT, he began at once to translate the OT from Hebrew. In 1530 he published the Pentateuch with marginal notes of a highly controversial nature. He also translated Jonah. But he interrupted his work to revise the NT translation, probably to answer some of his critics and to forestall his erstwhile colleague George Joye from issuing an unauthorized edition in which he planned to present Tyndale's Version without notes, restoring the much-loved ecclesiastical terms, more in harmony with the Vulg., and more in line with his own theological ideas. Joye did indeed publish his version and did translate the OT from Psalms through Lamentations from the Hebrew, and Isaiah from the Latin. But Tyndale's revision also appeared in 1535 with brief introductions to each NT book except Acts and Revelation. He softened his marginal notes and added "extracts" (lections) for certain days of the church year—these were a sort of church service book. (See pp. 247-48 in the work of I. M. Price in the bibliography.)

It was soon after this that Tyndale, living at the English House, an English merchant's club at Antwerp, was betrayed by a supposed friend; and on October 6, 1536, he was strangled and burned. As he died, his last words were: "Lord, open the King of England's eyes."

The Tyndale translation is significant far beyond the fact of its being the first in a line of translations. It was the work of a man who was capable of handling seven languages with ease, whose knowledge of Greek especially is unquestioned, and whose style was so impressive that eighty per cent of the KJV is Tyndale. He knew how to consult freely Luther's translation, the Vulg., and the Latin translation of Erasmus, and yet remain gloriously creative. He was forced to do his work under most adverse circumstances and in the midst of the most serious threats of his life. But he persisted and accomplished the great purpose of his life, to give the Bible in the vernacular to the layman. And he also did more: he created such a desire and demand for the Bible that church and state at the very time of his death were moving toward the admission that there was need for a legal translation. So indeed the Lord opened the eyes of the King of England, and Tyndale's life ambition was fulfilled and his dying prayer was answered. Moreover, his translation remained the model, as to both style and content, so that all the translations from his day to the advent of modern-language translations are, in fact, revisions of his work. Also, his translation played a vital part in making the English language an able literary vehicle. Such is the importance of the Tyndale English Bible.

Fig. TYN 80.

a. *The Coverdale Version (1535).* Miles Coverdale (born 1488), who is said to have become acquainted with Tyndale in Hamburg, was himself busy with the production of a translation of the Bible. He stood in favor with King Henry VIII, and was also aided by Thomas Cromwell in gaining approval for his projected English Bible. It was published on the Continent, probably at Zurich in 1535, and was dedicated to Henry VIII. There is no word about a license by the King, but the 1537 edition distinctly says: "set foorth with the Kynges moost gracious license." In his 1535 dedication to the King, Coverdale identifies his sources: "Douche and Latyn." He mentions "fyue sundry interpreters" in this same document. These have been identified as the Swiss German Bible of Zwingli and Leo Juda, Luther's Bible, the Vulg., the Latin version of Pagninus, and Tyndale's NT and Pentateuch. Since he did not know Hebrew, he obviously was leaning on the Latin translations for his OT text where he did not have Tyndale's translation of the Hebrew. He was greatly influenced by the German translations, of which he was very fond. He was more of an editor and compiler than a translator, yet his text contains many phrasings of surpassing beauty, especially in the Psalms. His effort was very successful, perhaps because he was conciliatory in spirit, and because he was ready to make concessions in the interest of his primary goal: the complete Bible in English, with governmental license. He restored many of the ecclesiastical terms which had been rejected by Tyndale as incorrect translations of the Greek text. He omitted the caustic, controversial elements in the marginal notes and introductions. His character shines through these elements of his work as that of a gentle, sympathetic, and agreeable person. He shows great modesty and insists that he had "nether wrested nor altered so moch as one worde for the mayntenaunce of any maner of secte, but have with a cleare conscience purely and faythfully translated this out of five interpreters, havyng onely the many-fest trueth of the scripture before myne eyes." This he said in his Preface to the King, and in his Address to the Reader he considered "how excellent knowledge and lernynge an interpreter of scripture oughte to have in the tongues and ponderyng also myne owne insufficiency therein and how weake I am to performe the office of translatoure, I was the more lothe to medle with this worke." These quotations describe the attitude and spirit which aptly fitted Coverdale to fulfil the task needed in his day. So within the year of Tyndale's arrest his work appeared with strong support. Leaning on Tyndale's scholarly work and supplementing it, where it had not been finished, by his own translation from German and Latin, he presented to England her first complete English Bible in print.

b. The Thomas Matthew Bible (1537). The next version to appear was more of a revision of Tyndale than a new translation. It was printed on the Continent, perhaps at Antwerp, in the year 1537. It came out under the name of Thomas Matthew, though it has long been ascribed to John Rogers, chaplain of the English House in Antwerp and a close friend of William Tyndale. When Tyndale was arrested in 1535, he turned over to Rogers his work, including the translations of books of the OT. During his imprisonment he did further work, and this too was placed in Rogers' hands. Rogers was an able man for this task of editing and completing Tyndale's work. He was an Oxford graduate of 1525 and had served in the English House, where he had met and come to sympathize with Tyndale and his views; but it was also true that he stood in the midst of the crosscurrents of thought on the Continent, where Luther and other Reformers were working. He adopted Reformation views, and eventually under Bloody Mary became a martyr, being burned at the stake on February 4, 1555.

Rogers does not seem to have been a creative scholar, but he was a faithful editor and a courageous Christian, devoting his life to the propagation of the English Bible. He used Tyndale's translation wherever it was available. In other areas he used Coverdale's Version. His astute editing may be seen in the Psalms, where various readings are introduced in the margin and technical expressions carefully explained. He made use of extensive notes. His outlook is boldly Protestant, but he does not seem to have suffered for this at first, nor did his translation fail to gain a wide reading. His Dedication may have helped: "Dedicated to the moost noble and gracyous prynce Kyng Henry the Eyght and Queen Jane." Also, Cranmer and Cromwell gave his work their unreserved support. Cranmer wrote to Cromwell: "You shall receyve by the bringer herof a Bible in Englishe, both of a new translacion and of a new prynte, dedicated unto the Kinges majestie . . . and as for the translacion, so farre as I have redde therof, I like it better than any other translacion heretofore made. . . . I pray you, my Lorde, that you woll exhibit the boke unto the Kinges highnes, and to obteign of His Grace, if you can, a license that the same may be sold and redde of every person, withoute danger of any acte, proclamacion, or ordinance heretofore graunted to the contrary, astill such tyme that we, the Bishops shall set forth a better trans-

lacion, which I think will not be till a day after domesday." This request was made on August 4, 1537, and on August 13, 1537, Cranmer wrote a note of appreciation to Cromwell that he had "not only exhibited the Bible I sent unto you to the Kinge's Majestie, but [had] also obteigned of his grace that the same shal be alowed by his auctoritie to be bowght and redde within this realm." So less than a year after the martyrdom of Tyndale, his translation was authorized by the king at the request of Cranmer, the archbishop of Canterbury.

From Cranmer's note it is evident that the bishops had projected a Bible, but that Cranmer felt deep pessimism about the success of the project. He may not have recognized the true nature of the Matthew edition when he gave it the status of a new translation and a "new prynte." Or he may have been motivated by the desire to secure royal support for a Bible for the period before the appearance of the Bishops' Bible. He obviously feared a long delay—"not till a day after domesday." Thus we may feel that Cranmer was seeking to meet a need as soon as possible. The Matthew Bible was a better version than Coverdale's, and so the best available to Cranmer. But Cromwell knew of the danger that the dependence of Matthew's Bible on the Tyndale Version might well become an issue. The notes, too, could cause some trouble because of their controversial nature.

4. The period of the Great Bible (1539-68). With this danger in mind, Cromwell urged Coverdale to prepare a new Bible. It may be that churchmen were not too well pleased with the Matthew Bible, either because they saw Tyndale's hand in it or because of its caustic marginalia. At any rate, Coverdale was assigned the task of producing a new revision. John Rogers' edition of Tyndale was, without doubt, the work back of this Great Bible, so called because of its size. Other helps were Münster's Latin OT, a translation from the Hebrew in 1534-35; the Vulg.; and Erasmus' Latin NT. But the Matthew Bible was the basic text, and the other resources were used as supplementary factors. It is then a revision of Tyndale. Coverdale mentioned the work of "diverse and learned men." This might refer to earlier translators or to employment of scholars proficient in Hebrew, Greek, and Latin to help him with the preparation of the text, as some think. Foxe, in *Acts and Monuments (see bibliography)*, gives a real understanding of the legal hurdles and ecclesiastical problems encountered in this venture. It was carried out by Coverdale successfully. After the text had been prepared, he was forced to take the project to Paris printers, since no press in England could handle such a large page.

The work was begun with the license of the French king, Francis I, at the request of Henry VIII, and the printer Regnault began his work in 1538 on massive pages 15 by 9 inches with the text 13 by 8½ inches. But the work had hardly begun when the officers of the Inquisition stopped the printing and attempted to seize the pages which had been completed. But most of the printed materials had been shipped to England, and of the pages seized, "four great dryfattes full" were sold to a haberdasher "to lap in caps." These were afterward recovered and transported to England. When the trouble began, Coverdale and his colleague Grafton fled back to England. Shortly the large press in Paris was itself removed to London, where the printing was resumed. And so the large Bible was completed in the spring of 1539 and presented to the clergy with an order from Cromwell that it be "set up in summe convenient place within the church that ye may have care of, whereat your parishioners may most commodiously resort to the same and rede it."

It was largely Tyndale's Version with the marginal notes removed. Coverdale objected to the removal of some of them, but they were never included. The chapter summaries of the Matthew Bible were retained with slight changes. The work was enthusiastically received by the people, and the Bible passed through seven printings within three years. The second edition appeared with a long introductory Preface by Archbishop Cranmer, and has often been called the Cranmer Bible. Even Bishop Tunstall, the man who opposed Tyndale so fiercely, spoke in its favor. The popularity of this Bible among the lay people caused the clergy trouble, for while the clergy were still the official and most able interpreters of the intent of scripture, the readers would crowd around the Bible and noisily discuss it among themselves and also in their own houses. The clergy became so aggravated that Henry VIII had a warning issued against such debates and enjoined the people to seek the aid of "learned" men wherever the text was not clear. When the Roman Catholic reaction began, Coverdale fled to the Continent, while Cromwell and the Archbishop were both executed. Fig. GRE 39.

a. The Taverner Bible (1539). At the very time that the Great Bible was being completed, another revision of Tyndale was ready for the press. This was the work of a layman, Richard Taverner, a graduate of Oxford, a good student of Greek, and a man with a gift for writing. While the OT follows the text of the Matthew Bible, with only slight changes due to a comparison with the Vulg., the NT shows clearly the editorial hand of one who knew the Greek text. This work in the NT exerted an influence upon later translations. It contained no notes of a controversial nature. It has the distinction of being the first complete Bible printed in England, since it appeared before the Great Bible. Because this work appeared alongside the official publication of the Great Bible, it did not make the impression which otherwise it might have made. There were two editions of the whole Bible, a folio and a quarto, and the NT was published separately in two editions, a quarto and an octavo.

b. The Geneva Bible (1560). 1525-39 was a period of translation and revision, with a growing spirit of toleration on the part of the king. However, a strong Roman Catholic reaction brought the downfall and execution of Cromwell in 1540. Henry VIII was forced to reverse his more tolerant policies, and in 1543 "all translations of the Bible bearing the name of Tyndale" were proscribed. All notes were expunged from other versions. No laboring man or woman was allowed to read the Bible, under pain of imprisonment. Finally all Bibles were proscribed except the Great Bible, and it was available only to the upper classes.

The death of Henry in 1547 was followed by the reign of Edward VI (1547-53), who was a Protestant, and who sought to restore the Bible to the people. Archbishop Cranmer was active in this program. Reformers who had fled began to return, but Edward's reign was short, and he was succeeded in 1553 by Mary Tudor. She was fiercely Roman Catholic, and three hundred Reformers and Bible students were martyred, among them Cranmer and John Rogers. Coverdale managed to escape and wandered across the Continent, finally stopping in Geneva, a free and liberal city where many British scholars had congregated.

This was the home of the NT scholar Theodore Beza and of John Calvin the theologian. The brother-in-law of Calvin, William Whittingham, who was John Knox's successor at the English church in Geneva, was most responsible for the preparation and publication of the Geneva NT in 1557. The complete Bible appeared in 1560, sometimes called the "Breeches Bible" because of the translation of Gen. 3:7: "They sewed fig leaves together and made themselves breeches." Coverdale assisted with this translation; but Whittingham in his Preface says that a group of scholars worked on it night and day for two and a half years. This version used for the first time in English the verse divisions of Robert Estienne, originally employed in his Greek NT in 1551.

The Geneva Bible was a revision of the Great Bible. Tyndale's contribution was basic, but the OT was thoroughly revised on the basis of the Hebrew text with appeal to the Latin text of Münster, Leo Juda, and Pagninus. The OT work, headed by Anthony Gilby and Thomas Sampson, was ably done. The NT was largely a revision of Tyndale, but had a new set of marginal notes, Protestant in emphasis, but generally not as polemical as Tyndale—though one does recall that in Rev. 9:11 the pope is identified as the "angel of the bottomless pit," the "anti-Christ, King of hypocrites, and Satan's ambassador." The Bible was issued in a smaller, less expensive form than earlier English Bibles. It was printed in the Roman type as in our day, instead of the old block letter, the so-called Old English type.

It was simply dedicated to Queen Elizabeth, who came to the throne in 1558 with strong Protestant sympathies. She neither licensed nor condemned the Bible, but it enjoyed a wide popularity. The printing cost was assumed by the congregation in Geneva.

While this version did not displace the Great Bible in the churches, nevertheless it was extensively used by the people, so that the two Bibles stood side by side until the Bishops' Bible made its appearance. As a matter of fact, it passed through about 140 editions before it was eclipsed by the KJV. It was the Bible of Oliver Cromwell and of his army, of the Pilgrim fathers and the Mayflower Compact, of John Bunyan, of Shakespeare, and even of King James himself. This is by far the best edition which had been produced and amply justified the claims made for it in the Preface: "It was diligently revised by the moste approved Greke examples, and conference of translations in other tonges as the learned may easely judge, both by the faithful rendering of the sentence, and also by the proprietie of the wordes, and perspicuitie of the phrase." But it was designed that "both the learned and the others might be holpen." The Preface emphasizes the intention of the editors that the Bible must be in the hands of the people, accurately and clearly translated, with difficult passages clarified by means of notes.

The Geneva NT was revised in 1576 by Laurence Tomson with a commentary accompanied by the claim "that there is not one hard sentence, nor dark speech, nor doubtful word, but is so opened and hath such light given to it that children may go through with it, and the simplest that are, may walk without guide, without wandering and going astray." It claims to be a translation of Theodore Beza's Greek. But it seems to lean most heavily on Beza's Latin translation. In later printings of the Geneva Bible this revision is sometimes substituted for Whittingham's of 1560.

5. The Bishops' Bible (1568). The Geneva continued to be the Bible of the people, while the Great Bible was the pulpit Bible for the churches. The superiority of the Geneva Bible was evident, and because of this, Archbishop Parker took steps to revise the Great Bible, with the hope that it would take the place of both the Great Bible and the Geneva Bible. This was, in fact, the project which several years before had been in the mind of Cranmer, but which had come to nought, even as he had feared. The hope of Parker was that this new version would be so good that it would unite the churches and the people with one official, universally used Bible. Many of the scholars who participated in this project were bishops, and hence the name "Bishops' Bible."

Parker began his work by organizing the committee in 1564. His method was to parcel out to a large number of individuals portions of the Bible for revision, and to himself he assigned the position of general editor and director of publication. He asked that each man sign his initials at the end of his work, which he says, "I thought a polecie to show them, to make them more diligent as answerable for their doinges." They were directed to follow the text of the Great Bible except where "it varieth manifestly" from the Greek or Hebrew, or as he says to the Queen, "where the text was by sum negligence mutilated from the originall." They were to make use of the Latin texts of Pagninus and Münster "and generally others learned in the tonges." They were to make "no bitter notis upon any text, or yet to set downe any determinacion in places of controversie." Matters of genealogies and "other such places not edefieng" were to be indicated so that the reader may "eschue them in his publike readinge." Language that "gave any offence of lightnes or obsenitie [should] be expressed with more convenient termes and phrases." "Ink-horn terms" were to be avoided in favor of "usual English words." These directions clearly indicate the policy of Parker. The various books were parceled out and the work began. The fault in Parker's method was that it allowed men to work in isolation, so that the resultant text ran the risk of being uneven. This is precisely what resulted.

In the OT the text is that of the Great Bible, with slight changes, and the Apoc. is also almost identical with it. In the NT, where Parker himself did a large share of the work, there is evidence of real scholarship. A large share of the marginal notes was taken from the Geneva Bible in the NT, as much as two thirds. Yet even in this area the Bishops' Bible did not measure up to the Geneva Version. It resorted to an older version of the Lord's Prayer, chose "charity" in I Cor. 13, and in general used less accurate language than some earlier translations. The verse division of the Geneva Bible was followed.

Parker appealed to Queen Elizabeth for authorization of the text, and for some reason this was never given; yet because of the sanction of the bishops, this became the second authorized version. It was endorsed by the Convocation of 1571, and its possession and use by bishops and archbishops was ordered. In time it displaced the Great Bible as that version "appoynted to be read in the churches," and from 1577 it was "set forth by authoritie." However, it was never able to displace the Psalter of the Great Bible, which had now been in use for about thirty years. Archbishop Parker in the 1572 edition published in parallel columns the Psalter of the Great Bible and that of the Bishops' Bible, with a strong appeal: "Now let the gentle reader have this Christian consyderation within himselfe that though he findeth the Psalmes of this later translation folowing, not so to sounde agreeable to his eares in his wanted woordes and phrases, as he is accustomed with: yet let him not be to much offended with the worke, which was wrought for his owne commoditie and comfort. And if he be learned, let him correct the woorde or sentence (which may dislike him) with the better, and whether his note ryseth either of good wyll and charitie, either of envie and contention not purely, yet his reprehension, if it may turne to the finding out of the truth, shall not be repelled with griefe, but applauded to in gladnesse." But this appeal did not increase the popularity of the Bishops' Psalter. Perhaps the reason was largely that the Prayer Book had used the Psalter of the Great Bible, and people had become familiar with it through long usage and were unwilling to change. Moreover, this version did not displace the Geneva Bible in popular usage. It did, however, continue for forty years as the authorized version and pass through twenty editions before 1606, and was actually the basis of the KJV, which did win its place with the people. But the Bishops' Bible was never satisfactory to many scholars.

6. The Douay (Douai) Version (1609-10). While these versions were pouring forth from the presses, Protestants were extensively using the text in preaching and debate, while the Roman church simply fretted and exerted every effort to stop the work. At the time of the Diet of Worms in 1540, Surius said: "The heretics want the Bible to be the authority, but only on condition that it shall be for them to interpret it. We have no controversy with the heretics about the Bible, but about the meaning of the Bible. They want to unearth its meaning by aid of their own none too erudite brains; we say that that meaning is to be discovered in the perpetual agreement of the Catholic Church. They continue to spread the Bible abroad among the illiterate." Cardinal William

Allen wrote to the professor of canon law at Douay in 1578: "Catholics educated in the academies and schools have hardly any knowledge of the scriptures except in Latin. When they are preaching to the unlearned and are obliged on the spur of the moment to translate some passage into the vernacular, they often do it inaccurately and with unpleasant hesitation because either there is no English version of the words or it does not then and there occur to them. Our adversaries on the other hand have at their fingers' ends from some heretical version all those passages of scripture which seem to make for them, and by a certain deceptive adaptation and alteration of the sacred words produce the effect of appearing to say nothing but what comes from the Bible. This evil might be remedied if we too had some catholic version of the Bible, for all the English versions are most corrupt. . . . If his Holiness will permit (we) will endeavor to have the Bible faithfully, purely and genuinely translated according to the edition approved by the Church—perhaps indeed it would have been more desirable that the scriptures had never been translated into barbarous tongues; nevertheless at the present day, when either from heresy or other causes, the curiosity of man, even of those who are not bad, is so great, and there is often such need of reading the scriptures in order to confute our opponents, it is better that there should be a faithful and catholic translation than that men should use a corrupt version to their peril or destruction; the more so since the dangers which arise from reading certain more difficult passages may be alleviated by suitable notes."

Further light is shed upon the Roman position in the Preface to the Rheims NT: "Which translation we do not for all that publish upon erroneous opinion of necessitie that the holy scriptures should alwaies be in our mother tonge, or that they ought or were ordained by God to be read indifferently of all, or could be easily vnderstood of every one that readeth or heareth them in a knowen language; or that they were not often through man's malice or infirmitie, pernicious and much hurtful to many; or that we generally and absolutely deemed it more convenient in itself and more agreable to God's word and honour or edification of the faithful to have them turned into vulgar tonges, than to be kept and studied only in the Ecclesiastical learned languages: not for these nor any such like causes doe we translate this sacred booke, but vpon special consideration of the present time, state, and condition of our countrie, vnto which, divers thinges are either necessarie or profitable and medicinable now, that otherwise in the peace of the church were neither much requisite nor perchance wholy tolerable."

The Roman church then submitted to this work of translation as a tolerated necessity. The version would be based on the official Latin of the church, the Vulg., which was itself a translation. The work was projected by Allen, an Oxford scholar and a canon under Queen Mary and later a cardinal; however, Gregory Martin carried the translation to its completion. The work was started at the English College, Douay, France, but political upheavals caused it to move to Rheims, where the NT was completed. In 1593 the college returned to Douay,

where the OT was completed, but publication was delayed because of a lack of funds till 1609-10. Thus we see why the NT is known as the Rheims NT, and the whole Bible as the Douay Version. It was a translation of the Vulg.—or, as it says, "of the authenticall Latin"—and, while no reference is made to the Geneva Bible, there is unmistakable evidence of its influence. Hebrew and Greek originals are mentioned, but the use of these does not seem to be extensive. The translation is woodenly literal in numerous places, and often obscure in meaning. The Psalter is especially defective. It made extensive use of Latin words which had become the ecclesiastical terms of the Roman church. It used peculiar transliteration of feasts, money, etc., without an effort at translation. It used technical terms of Catholic doctrine where the meaning was not clear (e.g., "supersubstantial" bread, "exinanited himself," "do penance," "for which hostes God is promerited"). So on the basis of the Vulg. text this translation abounds in terms from the Latin language. These were influential in the writing of the KJV.

7. The KJV (1611). The long reign of Queen Elizabeth came to an end in 1603. During her reign the Catholic-Protestant struggle was largely settled. The propriety of Bible translation was accepted, and even the Roman Catholics had published a NT in English. Education had advanced, and England had produced men of letters whose names are among the greatest in English literature. In 1604 James VI of Scotland came to the throne as James I of England. He was a religious man, and was also interested in Bible translation, having himself attempted to translate some psalms and to write a paraphrase of the book of Revelation.

In the year of his accession he summoned a conference of high and low churchmen to meet at Hampton Court to consider complaints of the Puritans regarding matters alleged to be amiss in the church. Four Puritans were summoned before nine bishops, seven deans and archdeacons, five ecclesiastical lawyers, and the king himself. The complaints presented did not make much impression on the group; but James is reported to have spoken for five hours on the corruptions in the church. One bishop (Andrewes) said: "On that day his majesty did wonderfully play the puritan." But he ended his speech by attacking powerfully the Puritans, so that the bishops were highly pleased, at length, with his peroration. While the necessity for Bible revision was not on the list of Puritan complaints, Dr. Reynolds, the Puritan president of Corpus Christi College, Oxford, proposed that the English Bible be revised. There does not seem to have been great enthusiasm for this proposal in the conference, if we may judge from the tone of the Preface to the KJV. However, the idea appealed to the king, as the Preface says: "And although this [the motion to revise the English Bible] was judged to be but a very poor and empty shift, yet even hereupon did his majesty begin to bethink himself of the good that might ensue by a new translation, and presently after gave order for this translation."

On February 10, 1604, the king ordered "that a translation be made of the whole Bible, as consonant as can be to the original Hebrew and Greek, and this to be set out and printed without any marginal notes and only to be used in all churches of England in time of divine service." By July, 1604, King James says that he had "appointed certain learned men to the number of four and fifty for the translating of the Bible." These men were to be the "best learned" in Westminster and in "both the Universities" and their work was to be "reviewed by the bishops and the chief learned of the church," and "to be ratified by Privy Council and by royal authority." The men appointed were to be able, efficient biblical scholars and were chosen from among Anglican churchmen, Puritans, and laymen. Only forty-seven names have been included on the list of those who actually worked on the edition. Those men divided into six groups, four working on the OT and two on the NT.

In the OT the Westminster group worked through the Pentateuch to I Chronicles; one Cambridge group took II Chronicles through Ecclesiastes, the other Cambridge group to the Prayer of Manasseh and the rest of the Apoc. One Oxford group took all the Prophets; the other Oxford group took the four gospels, Acts, and Revelation; and the other Westminster group took the NT letters. The rules by which these were to proceed were as follows:

a) "The Bishops' Bible [is] to be followed, and as little altered as the truth of the original will permit."

b) Proper names were "to be retained as nigh as may be as they were vulgarly used."

c) "The old ecclesiastical words [are] to be kept, viz. the word *church* not to be translated *congregation,* etc."

d) When a word had "divers significations, that [is] to be kept which hath been most commonly used by the most ancient fathers, being agreeable to the propriety of the place and the analogy of the faith."

e) No change was to be made in chapter divisions "unless necessity so require."

f) "No marginal notes at all [are] to be affixed, but only for the explanation of the Hebrew or Greek which cannot without some circumlocution, so briefly and fitly be express'd in the text."

g) Cross references were to be inserted.

h) "Every particular man of each company [is] to take the same chapter or chapters, and having translated or amended them severally by himself, where he thinketh good, all to meet together, confer what they have done, and agree for their parts what shall stand."

i) "As any one company hath dispatched any one book in this manner they shall send it to the rest to be considered of seriously and judiceously, for His Majesty is very careful in this point."

j) "If any company upon the review of the book so sent, doubt or differ upon any place to send them word thereof; note the place, and withal send the reasons, to which if they consent not, the difference [is] to be compounded at the general meeting, which is to be of the chief person of each company, at the end of the work."

k) "When any place of special obscurity is doubted of, letters [are] to be directed, by authority, to any learned man in the land for his judgment of such a place."

l) Bishops were to send letters to their clergy requesting the assistance of men "skilful in the tongues," and to report to Westminster, Oxford, or Cambridge.

m) "Directors in each company [are] to be the Deans of Westminster and Chester for that place; and the regius [King's] professors in Hebrew or Greek in either University."

n) "These translations [are] to be used when they agree better with the text than the Bishops' Bible: Tindoll's, Matthew's, Coverdale's, Whitechurch's [the Great Bible was called Whitechurch's because Whitechurch was the publisher of the fifth edition] and the Geneva."

o) "Besides the said Directors before mentioned, three or four of the most ancient grave divines in either of the universities not employed in translating [are] to be assigned by the Vice Chancellar upon conference with the rest of the heads to be overseers of the translations as well Hebrew as Greek, for the better observation of the 4th rule above specified."

So the work went forward, and when it was finished, two members of each of the three centers were a committee of six to pass upon the final revision before it went to press. We have no reliable information about how carefully the fifteen rules were applied nor how completely the committee of six edited the work. But the version itself is a testimony to what was accomplished.

Internal evidence shows that the Tyndale-Coverdale versions are predominantly the source, but great use was made of Latin versions of Pagninus, Münster, Tremellius, Junius, and Beza, and of the Greek and Hebrew texts, which were available only in limited numbers and quality. The Rheims NT was certainly consulted on several occasions, and Luther's German version exerted some influence. The revisers made their own particular contribution in their critical linguistic work and in maintaining and heightening literary polish, especially in vocabulary, majestic quality, clear sparkling English style, and force of utterance.

This version met with opposition, as the editors expected when they said in the Preface: "Many men's mouths have bene open a good while (and yet are not stopped) with speeches about the translation so long in hand or rather perusals of translations made before and ask what may be the reason, what the necessitie of the employment." As soon as the version appeared, it was sharply criticized, and for forty years had to fight for its position. The Long Parliament in 1653 passed a bill for its revision and even had a committee formed, but the dissolution of the Parliament ended the action. But the King James was winning the day. The conciliatory attitude expressed in the Preface may have been of great help. It says: "We never thought from the beginning that we should neede to make a new translation, nor yet to make of a bad one a good one—but to make a good one better, or out of many good ones, one principall good one, not justly to be excepted against; that hath bene our indeavour that our worke." Ten pages earlier in the Preface they frankly state the relationship between earlier translators and themselves: "We are so farre off from condemning any of their labours that traveiled before us in this kinde—that we acknowledge them to have beene raised up of God for the building and furnishing of his church and that they deserve to be had of us and posteritie in everlasting remembrance . . . so if we building upon their foundation that went before us, and being holpen by their labours, doe endevour to make that better which they left so good; no man, we are sure hath cause to mislike us; they, we perswade ourselves, if they were alive, would thank us." So the excellent attitude of those who prepared this version, coupled with its own excellence, made for the victory which was to make this version the Bible of the English-speaking world for more than 250 years and makes it still perhaps the best loved and the most widely used. It belongs among the great treasures of English prose.

The KJV used the chapter divisions of Stephen Langton, archbishop of Canterbury in the thirteenth century, and the verse divisions of Robert Estienne of 1551. As was first done in the Geneva Bible, each verse was printed as a paragraph. This led to fragmentation of the original documents, and to the interpretation of verses out of context. On the other hand, the verse divisions as separate paragraphs had the advantage of "giving light" to the page. The version was first printed as a folio Bible, larger even than the Great Bible, the pages measuring 16 by 10½ inches. It was regarded as the authorized version, but though it was promoted by King James and executed by leading churchmen, there is no evidence of any official decree regarding it. It included about seventeen thousand cross references and footnotes.

There were weaknesses in the version from the beginning. The second rule was not carefully followed, so that the OT spelling of names does not agree with those in the NT. "Isaiah" is the spelling in the OT, "Esaias" in the NT; "Jeremiah" in the OT and "Jeremias" in the NT; "Hosea" in the OT and "Osee" in the NT; "Jonah" in the OT and "Jonas" in the NT. Again, the same Greek or Hebrew word was often unnecessarily translated by a variety of English words. Identical passages in the Synoptic gospels were often translated differently, thus distorting literary relationships. Often one English word was used to translate two entirely different Greek words in a short passage, and so real meaning was obscured. There were awkward passages: "I am verily a man which am a Jew." "Whom do men say that I am?" There were misprints, the most famous of which was corrected early. At Ruth 3:15, "he" was printed for "she" in the final clause. On this basis copies of the earliest printings are distinguished as "He" and "She" Bibles. Another glaring misprint, which was never corrected, is in Matt. 23:24: "straining at a gnat" (which the Douay Version also reads, when the reading should be "straining out a gnat"). There were other obscurities and mistranslations. The text of the Hebrew and Greek versions which were reverently mentioned as the "originalls" were not the relatively good texts we know today. Nothing better than the texts of Erasmus and Beza was available (*see* TEXT, NT; TEXT, OT). There is too much use of terms of Latin derivation which fail to translate the original Hebrew and Greek accurately. These and other weaknesses of the version could be emphasized. Some of them could not have been avoided—as, e.g., those due to faulty Hebrew and

Greek texts. Some were due to slips in editorial work —e.g., the variety of spellings and the misprints. Some must be attributed to a failure to distinguish between the true meaning of the original biblical terms and ecclesiastical usage—e.g., the use of "justification," "propitiation." Some were the result of failure to come to a clear understanding of the text, as in the case of Job 31:35.

Yet in spite of these faults, so clear after 350 years of study, the KJV came in one generation to stand as the greatest Bible of its day, rapidly displacing the Bishops' Bible as the pulpit Bible, and capturing first place in popular usage over the long-established favorite, the Geneva. It was revised several times, first in 1615, when a small edition containing hundreds of changes, mostly in spelling, was issued. Again in a new edition in 1629 the Apoc. were omitted, and in 1638 another revision appeared. The attempted sweeping revision of 1654 failed. The famous chronology of Archbishop Ussher (died 1656) —which dates the Creation in 4004 B.C.—was used in 1701 in Lloyd's edition. In 1762 the KJV was issued by Dr. Paris as the Cambridge Bible, with 383 marginal notes and other changes. In 1769 the Oxford Bible, issued by Dr. Blayney, appeared with 76 changes and corrections dealing with weight, measurements, and money. This edition remained as the standard version. Down through the years changes were made, generally of an explanatory character, or in the form of attempts to modernize spelling, and to provide marginal notes, but the essential text of the KJV remained unchanged.

8. Other translations. While the KJV reigned supreme between 1611 and 1881, when the ERV of the NT appeared, this does not mean that there were no efforts at translation during this long stretch of time. As a matter of historical fact, a rather large number of translations were published. In the seventeenth century there were publications of the Bible in paraphrase like those of Henry Hammond in 1653; of Woodhead, Allestry, and Walker in 1675; and of Richard Baxter in 1685. In the eighteenth century More's translation of the NT in 1729 was noteworthy, as were Wheaton's in 1745 and John Wesley's in 1755. There were others of considerable value, such as Purver's in 1764, Harwood's "Liberal translation" of the NT in 1768, Worsley's in 1770, Wakefield's in 1791, Newcome's in 1796, Scarlett's in 1798. The nineteenth century saw many more, among which were Charles Thomson's entire Bible from Greek and Hebrew texts (1808), Alexander's complete Bible (1822), Noah Webster's entire Bible (1833), Penn's NT (1836-37), Kenrick's NT (1842), Brenton's OT (1844), Norton's four gospels (1855), Conant's NT and parts of the OT (1857-61), Bromfeld's gospels (1863), Anderson's NT (1865), Bower's NT (1870), Alford's NT (1870), Rotherham's NT (1872), Julia Smith's Bible (1876). There were many more translations from the pens of Protestants, and several independent Roman Catholic translations, including Nary's NT of 1719, which had church approval, and two which were not sanctioned by the ecclesiastical authorities, Gedde's whole Bible in 1802 and Lengard's four gospels in 1836.

Important in stimulating this ever-growing stream

of translation was the discovery and publication of MSS of the Bible, especially of the NT. On the basis of these discoveries better reconstructions of the Hebrew and Greek texts of the Bible were published. The availability of such ancient MSS as Vaticanus and Alexandrinus made textual study and revision a necessity. Lachmann, on the basis of the wide variation between MS evidence and the "received" text, totally disregarded the "received" text in 1831. The discovery and publication of Sinaiticus by Konstantin von Tischendorf in 1859 caused renewed emphasis to be placed on textual study. Tischendorf edited a text, and so did Tregelles. Dean Alford in England did extensive work in Greek. Westcott and Hort spent about thirty years studying the Greek text of the NT before they finally published their important text in 1881. By the end of the nineteenth century the text which lies at the basis of the KJV was widely discredited. During this same period progress was being made on the text of the OT also. The essentially noncritical text of the Hebrew OT was being corrected by translations in the Latin, Greek, Syriac, Armenian, and other versions. The tenth-century MT of Ben Asher, which is a copy "of the men of Tiberias" of the eighth century, was accepted as basic. Work on the nature of Hebrew poetry, and archaeology and the study of comparative religion of the surrounding civilizations, threw light upon the OT. New translations were clearly demanded.

9. The ERV (1881-85) and the ASV (1901). For years there had been talk of a revision of the Authorized Version, but always strong opposition defeated any serious consideration of such an undertaking. However, the mounting evidence of need for such a revision reached such proportions that action could no longer be delayed. On February 10, 1870, a move was made in the upper house of the Convocation of Canterbury. Bishop Wilberforce presented a resolution that a committee of both houses be appointed to report on the desirability of a revision of the Authorized Version of the NT. An amendment to include the OT in the proposed action was adopted. The committee was appointed and unanimously recommended that the revision be attempted. The work was begun almost immediately by this committee, and others of capable scholarship were invited to participate regardless of nationality or religious affiliation. Consequently, with the Anglicans leading, Baptists, Congregationalists, Methodists, Presbyterians, and Unitarians participated in the work. Roman Catholics were invited, but none accepted. Fifty-four scholars were asked to form two divisions of twenty-seven members each for the work on the two testaments. By June of 1870 the two companies had begun their work.

Eight principles were drawn up for the work: (a) to introduce as few alterations as possible into the text of the Authorized Version consistently with faithfulness; (b) to limit, as far as possible, the expression of such alterations to the language of the authorized and earlier English versions; (c) each company to go twice over the portion to be revised, once provisionally, the second time finally; (d) that the text to be adopted be that for which the evidence is decidedly preponderating; and that when the text

so adopted differs from that from which the Authorized Version was made, the alteration be indicated in the margin; (e) to make or retain no change in the text on the second final revision by each company, except by two thirds of those present approving of the same, but on the first revision to decide by simple majorities; (f) in every case of proposed alteration that may have given rise to discussion, to defer the voting thereupon till the next meeting, whensoever the same shall be required by one third of those present at the meeting, such intended vote to be announced in the notice of the next meeting; (h) to revise the headings of chapters, pages, paragraphs, italics, and punctuation; (i) to refer on the part of each company, when considered desirable, to divines, scholars, and literary men, whether at home or abroad, for their opinions.

The OT company began with the Pentateuch and the NT company with the Synoptic gospels. Each company was urged to confer with the other as sections of work were completed, so as to guarantee uniformity in language and style. In August, 1870, American biblical scholars were invited to participate in the project with the eight principles of the British committee governing their work also. The British committee promised to send confidentially their revision at its various stages to the American committee, who would in turn send their criticisms and suggestions to the British companies before the second revision. The final revision was to be submitted to the American committee before publication, and the latter were to be allowed to publish in an appendix those readings of theirs which the British committee should decline to adopt. The American committee agreed not to publish a revision of their own for fourteen years.

The work of the NT was completed first and was published in England on May 17 and in America on May 20, 1881. It was enthusiastically received. One million copies were ordered in advance from the Oxford University Press and almost as many from that of Cambridge. Three million copies were sold in Britain and the United States in the first year. Chicago newspapers published the entire text for their readers on May 22, 1881. Such a reception was without precedent. The OT was completed four years later and was published in 1885 without so much excitement.

The ASV was published in 1901 incorporating many of the readings listed in the Appendix of the ERV. A large number of antiquated words were replaced, and an even larger number of purely British words were replaced by more American English words. Other changes took the form of the removal of archaisms and old expressions. The revision was widely acclaimed in America, and often described as the "most perfect English Bible in existence."

The Revised Version of the NT made about 30,000 alterations in the Authorized text, about 4½ per verse. Verse paragraphs were abandoned for sense paragraphs, with verse numbers in the margin. Cross references were not used. Italics were systematized and reduced in number. Poetry was more clearly indicated. The Greek text upon which it was based was much better than that used by the KJV.

Greek grammars and syntax were taken into consideration. The version omitted the liturgical conclusion of the Lord's Prayer, and deleted the additions of Erasmus to I John and Revelation. Many archaisms, obscurities, and inconsistencies were removed from the text. There is no doubt that this was a decided improvement over the older versions. It was immediately adopted for use in schools and churches and displaced the KJV in Canterbury and Westminster.

The initial popularity of the version soon began to wane. Criticisms mounted, and opposition to any revision of the Authorized Version, which had existed before the publication itself as a general prejudice, now became a specific attack upon this version. This antagonism was so pronounced that Gladstone spoke against its authorization. Canterbury, which had sponsored it, coolly accepted it. Charges were made that it had departed unnecessarily from the KJV in phraseology and had created an awkward literalism devoid of beauty, and that in this revision there was actually an impoverishment of the English language. Serious objections were raised against changes in the text, especially the changes in the Lord's Prayer and in some of the nativity passages, and to the version's way of handling the conclusion of Mark, the woman taken in adultery in John 7:53–8:11, etc. Many of these criticisms are now thoroughly discredited.

10. Modern-speech translations. The increasing number of NT Greek MSS had been an important factor in the background of the Revised Version. New study of Greek grammar had also played a part. But now something happened which would make sweeping changes in the understanding of the Bible in general and of the NT in particular. This was the discovery and study of ancient Greek papyri. Adolf Deissmann and others saw at once that the language of the papyri was exactly that of the NT (*see* GREEK LANGUAGE). It became clear that the language of the NT was not a sort of "holy dialect" or "Holy Ghost Greek," but the language of ordinary people. Since the NT was obviously written in popular nonliterary Greek, it seemed to many that it ought to be translated into nonliterary and modern English.

The recognition of this fact gave rise to a veritable flood of modern-speech translations of the NT; and similar attempts were made to translate the OT into modern speech. Mrs. Helen Spurrell of London in 1885 published a translation of the OT. Ferrar Fenton published his translation of the NT in 1895 and his OT in 1905 in the style of modern English in Great Britain. While these two translations are Protestant, it is worth while to note that the Catholic scholar Father F. A. Spencer published a modern-speech translation of the four gospels in 1901 and completed the translation of the entire NT in 1912, just before his death; but this was not published till 1937. During the first half of the twentieth century numerous translations were made, among the most important of which are: *The Twentieth Century NT* of 1899-1901, anonymously published; *The NT, A New Translation,* by James Moffatt in 1913, and the complete Bible in 1924-26; *The NT in Modern Speech* in 1903 by Richard Francis Weymouth, a layman of Mill Hill School, England; *The NT, an American Translation,* in 1923 by Edgar J. Goodspeed, and *The OT, an American Translation,* by J. M. P. Smith, A. R. Gordon, T. J. Meek, and LeRoy Waterman in 1927; the Centenary translation of the NT in 1924 by Helen Barrett Montgomery; *The Riverside NT* in 1923 by W. G. Ballantine; and more recently the NT translations of J. B. Phillips, beginning with *Letters to Young Churches* in 1947. Roman Catholic scholars began producing *The Westminster Version of the Sacred Scriptures* in 1913. A small edition of this, with 479 pages, was published in 1948. Monsignor Ronald Knox in 1944 published a modern-speech translation of the NT and in 1947 of the Psalms. There are many other Roman Catholic translations available.

11. The RSV (1946, 1952). Within ten years after the ASV was published, there was serious talk of a revision. The papyri discoveries, the great popularity and obvious value of some of the modern-speech translations, new MS finds, and developments in the textual criticism of the Bible, not to speak of the faults in the ERV and ASV, helped create the demand for a new version, so that when the International Council of Religious Education in 1929 secured the copyright covering the ASV of the Bible, it took steps to produce a revision. The American Standard Bible Committee was formed to consider the advisability of revision, and if it were advisable, to propose what principles should govern such a project. Thirteen leading biblical scholars constituted the committee and after two years of discussion and debate reached an almost unanimous conclusion favoring revision. It was prescribed that "the revision should embody the best results of modern scholarship as to the meaning of the scripture," and that it should be "designed for use in public and private worship," and that it should be "in the direction of the simple classic English style of the KJV." It was planned that from three to five members of the revision committee should be selected for their competence in English literature, in the conduct of public worship, or in religious education. All other members were to be chosen for their competence as biblical scholars.

After delays caused by the financial depression and by the death of some members of the original committee and the retirement of others, the committee, revitalized by new appointments, met in 1937 for serious work of revision. By agreement the task was outlined as revision of the ASV in the light of the KJV, and not a new translation, but as Dean Weigle of Yale, the chairman of the committee, said: "It was in effect a new translation, and for three reasons. The first is that no adequate revision can be made except upon the basis of a thorough study of the Greek text, and as careful procedure in putting its meaning into English, as would be required in the case of a new translation. The second is that the committee has used the new evidence concerning the Greek text and the new resources for understanding the vocabulary and grammar of the Greek NT which have been afforded by the remarkable discoveries of the past sixty years since the revisions of 1881 and 1901 were made. The third is that the present committee was not obliged, as the former committees were, to maintain the peculiar forms of Elizabethan English in which the KJV is cast." So in many areas the revision was a new translation.

The consonantal Hebrew text of the OT and the Westcott and Hort's Greek text of the NT were the authoritative original texts employed. Textual emendation on the basis of ancient versions was admissible, but conjectural emendation must be rarely and cautiously practiced. The use of "Jehovah" was to be rejected, and "Lord" was accepted. Archaic forms were discarded, including the archaic forms of the pronouns. Quotation marks and sense paragraphs were adopted as a policy. The translation of any given word was not necessarily limited to one word but was to be determined by usage in its context. Changes from the ASV were to be made only for good reason. A majority vote determined the change, but in the final action a two-thirds vote was required.

The OT section began at once with Genesis and the NT section with the Gospel of Matthew. These sections were subdivided into three pairs of two each. These pairs of scholars were supposed to prepare their revisions of assigned portions of scripture and to submit them to other members in previously arranged order of rotation, and these were to return their criticisms and comments to the revisers. This plan failed to work; so the individual member mimeographed his results and forwarded these to other members, who in turn mailed their criticism back to the reviser, so that at the meetings discussions in detail could at once take place. Each member took fifteen chapters as an assignment. The individual revisions were well prepared, but wide differences of opinion required lengthy meetings before agreement could be reached. It was obvious that the task, conducted in this fashion, would require far more time than could be given to it. So geographically sectional meetings were arranged for revision of assigned bodies of text to be submitted to the general meetings. This procedure proved effective, and in this manner the work proceeded.

The NT was completed in August, 1943, and was published on February 11, 1946. It was splendidly printed. On each page the name of the book and chapter appeared at the outside top margin. Chapter numbers were indented, and verse numbers in small figures were used in the text. Footnotes of two types were used, first, to cite variant readings, meanings, or other explanations, and second, to list parallel passages. This RSV was joyfully received and enjoyed great popularity. The OT was published September 30, 1952, and was equally well received. Though the task of the committee of revisers was completed, the group was maintained as a committee to receive suggestions and ideas for reconsideration.

Bibliography. J. Foxe, *Acts and Monuments* (ed. H. Seymour; 1855); A. W. Pollard, *Records of the English Bible* (1911), in which may be found many of the sources quoted herein; E. J. Goodspeed, *The Making of the English NT* (1925); M. M. Commack, *John Wyclif and the English Bible* (1938); L. A. Weigle, *The English NT from Tyndale to the RSV* (1949); H. Pope, *English Versions of the Bible* (rev. S. Bullock; 1952)— a Roman Catholic presentation; I. M. Price, *The Ancestry of Our English Bible* (3rd rev. ed. by A. Wikgren and A. W. Irwin; 1956).   J. R. Branton

*VERSIONS, MEDIEVAL AND MODERN (NON-ENGLISH).** By the middle of the twentieth century the Bible, or a significant portion of it, had been translated into more than one thousand different languages and dialects. Less than a score of these translations were made prior to the year 1000; all the others fall into the period to be comprehended herein. Furthermore, within some of the languages (e.g., French and German) the different renderings are numbered by the hundreds. Several of the more significant versions in certain representative European languages will be described. The languages (or groups of languages) are arranged alphabetically; the versions within each language are dealt with chronologically.

1. Dutch (and Flemish) versions
2. French versions
3. German versions
4. Greek (modern) versions
5. Hungarian versions
6. Italian versions
7. Portuguese versions
8. Scandinavian versions
   a. Danish (and Norwegian)
   b. Icelandic
   c. Swedish
9. Slavic (Slavonic) versions
   a. Old Church Slavonic
   b. Bohemian (Czech)
   c. Bulgarian
   d. Polish
   e. Russian
   f. Serbo-Croatian
   g. Slovak
   h. Slovenian
10. Spanish versions
Bibliography

1. Dutch (and Flemish) versions. From a philological point of view, the term "Dutch" includes both Dutch proper—i.e., the N Dutch of Holland— and Flemish, the S Dutch of Belgium.

The earliest rendering which is still extant of the Scriptures into a Dutch dialect appears to be a paraphrase of the Psalms dating from *ca.* the beginning of the tenth century. The translator is unknown, but, to judge from the dialect, he seems to have lived in Limburg. The precursors of versions properly so called are the *Bibles historiales* (*see § 2 below*). The most ancient of these, the metrical or Rijmbijbel of Jacob von Maerlant, dates from 1271. This is a rather free paraphrase in verse imitating Peter Comestor's *Historia scholastica* (a digest of parts of Bible history, with many legends and a good deal of secular history). Of literal translations of the whole or of parts of the Bible, the oldest, dating from the fourteenth century, is the work of an unknown translator; certain lexicographical features suggest an origin in Holland. From about the same century there originated several harmonies of the gospels in a dialect that is associated with Alost in Flanders. Some of these harmonies preserve Tatianic readings mediated through the Old Latin versions.

Ca. 1300 a translation was made from the Latin Vulg. by a Fleming, perhaps a layman, for the benefit of those unlearned in Latin. Some parts, which the unnamed translator was unwilling to popularize (as Deut. 22:13-21), are passed over with merely a reference to the Latin text. Difficult passages have explanations drawn mostly from Comestor's *Historia scholastica;* these are distinguished from the text by being written in a different character. After circulating in MS for several generations, this translation was made the basis of the first printed scriptures in Dutch; this was an edition of the OT (lacking the Psalms) which appeared at Delft in 1477. The comments of Comestor are omitted. The Psalms were issued in 1480.

The first NT printed in Dutch was published at Antwerp in 1522. This was translated from the Latin Vulg., but with reference to the Greek. Luther's German version of the NT (1522) was soon rendered into the Dutch language by various unknown translators, who published their work at Antwerp and at Amsterdam in 1523, as well as at several other places during the immediately succeeding years. Other versions were made from Erasmus' Greek text and Latin version, and were published at Delft in 1524 and at Antwerp in 1525 and 1526.

The earliest complete Bible in Dutch was prepared by a group of scholars whose names have escaped record. The section from Genesis to the Song of Solomon and the whole of the NT are based on Luther's German version; the other books appear to follow the Low German Bible published at Cologne *ca.* 1480. The honor of printing this first Dutch Bible (1526) goes to J. van Liesvelt, who, it should be mentioned, subsequently printed half a dozen other editions of the Bible. The publication of his edition of 1542 cost him his life.

Among Roman Catholic translations, mention should be made of renderings of the NT which appeared in 1527, 1530, and 1533, and in Dutch and Latin in 1539. The complete Roman Catholic Bible in Dutch did not appear until 1548, when a revision of the early version from the Vulg., first issued in 1477, was prepared by Alexander Blankaert, a Carmelite monk, and others, and was published at Cologne under the supervision of the authorities of the university at that place. In the same year another revision of the same early version was published at Louvain. It was prepared by Claes (Nicholas) van Winghe, one of the canons regular of Louvain, and contained a vigorous Preface in which Protestant Bibles were condemned. This version passed through many revisions, and for several centuries remained the standard Bible for Dutch Roman Catholics.

After Dutch Protestantism divided into various groups (Lutheran, Mennonite, Reformed, and Remonstrant), each group wished to have its own version; as a result, many translations of the Scriptures competed for supremacy. Among these was the so-called States-General Bible. It was proposed first in 1594, the rules for translators were discussed at the Synod of Dort in 1618-19, and the work was finally published at Leyden in 1637. This version became the standard Bible for the Dutch Reformed Church, corresponding to Luther's Version in Germany and the KJV in England.

The most important versions of the nineteenth and early twentieth centuries include the translation prepared by members of the theological faculty at Leyden. The NT was published in 1866; after several interruptions the OT was finished in 1901. In 1928 an interdenominational committee, which had been at work since 1911, was formally commissioned by the Netherlands Bible Society to produce a version in accord with modern Dutch idiom and based upon the oldest attainable text. The NT was published at Amsterdam in 1939, the Bible in 1951.

Among renderings by Roman Catholics is the translation by R. Jansen, B. Alfrink, J. Cook, and others. It was published in five volumes in honor of the Jesuit Peter Canisius (Amsterdam, 1936-39). Another version, *De katholieke Bijbel,* somewhat less satisfactory than the "Canisius" edition, is the work of the two Franciscans, Laetus Himmelreich and Crispinus Smits, who translated the OT and the NT respectively (Brugge, 1938).

2. French versions. The extant MSS of the earliest translations of parts of the Bible into French dialects date from the twelfth century. These include the Psalter (in two forms, each with the Latin and French text interlinear), the books of Kings, Revelation, and five chapters of John's Gospel. Toward 1170 Peter Waldo and several of his followers produced vernacular translations of the gospels, Paul, and other portions of the Bible. Despite the efforts of Pope Innocent III to suppress these Waldensian MSS, several escaped the vigilance of the Inquisitors at Metz and Liége.

Sometime between 1226 and 1250 the first complete French Bible was made by a corps of translators working at the University of Paris and using several Latin MSS. The style and accuracy of the translation vary widely in different parts of the Bible. Another version was begun between 1291 and 1295 by Guyard (Guiars) des Moulins of Aire, in the NE of France. Taking Peter Comestor's *Historia scholastica,* he made a free translation of it, adding or substituting other résumés of other parts of Bible history. Subsequent editions were made more and more complete and received the title *Bible historiale.* In *ca.* 1487 what is generally regarded as the first complete Bible was printed at Paris by the order of Charles VIII. This was called *La Grande Bible;* twelve editions appeared between 1487 and 1545.

At the beginning of the sixteenth century the distinguished Renaissance humanist Jacques Lefèvre d'Étaples (Faber Stapulensis) produced a literalistic revision of the *Bible historiale.* His translation of the NT was published anonymously at Paris in 1523. Because the marginal notes were thought to be biased toward Protestantism, the French clergy attempted to suppress the book, and Lefèvre's version of the complete Bible had to be issued at Antwerp (1530).

The first French Protestant version was the work of Pierre Robert Olivétan, a cousin of John Calvin's. Published in 1535 at Serrières near Neuchâtel in Switzerland, at the expense of the Waldensians, this translation, judged by the standards of the time, represents an "erudition really prodigious" (Reuss). Calvin himself wrote for it the Latin Preface and an Introduction to the NT, and introduced several emendations into the revision issued in 1545. Another revision of Olivétan's work, brought out by the Protestant printer Robert Stephanus (Estienne) at

Geneva in 1553, is said to be the earliest entire Bible, in any language, to contain Stephanus' division of the text into chapters and verses familiar to us. The first definitive revision of Olivétan's translation, undertaken by a group of pastors at Geneva, appeared in an edition, published in 1588, which was very frequently reprinted during the next two centuries. In this edition the divine name Yahweh was translated by *l'Éternel*, a rendering which has been retained in the Protestant Bible of France, and which was also adopted by James Moffatt in English.

Among half a dozen other revisions of Olivétan's version made by various scholars, the careful work of J. F. Osterwald, a pastor at Neuchâtel, is the most important. Publishing the version at Amsterdam in 1724, Osterwald continued to labor at the task of revision, and issued a much more thorough revision in 1744, embodying the results of the exegetical science of the time. Toward the latter part of the nineteenth century Louis Segond, a professor at the University of Geneva, published a translation of the OT (Geneva, 1874) and the NT (1879).

During the twentieth century the "Synodal Version," a revision of the Osterwald text, was sponsored by the Synod of the Reformed Churches of France and published by the Bible Society of France (Paris, 1910). This has been revised several times. A modern, vernacular version of the NT, prepared by several prominent scholars (including Maurice Goguel and Henri Monnier), was published in 1929. In 1947, the Protestant Bible Society of Paris issued the Bible du Centenaire de la Jeunesse, which embodies the latest results of scholarly investigation.

Of the many French versions made by Roman Catholics, the most important include Richard Simon's rendering of the NT, published anonymously at Trévoux in 1702, and a series of versions which proceeded from Port Royal and the Jansenist school. Perhaps the most idiomatic of the latter is that associated with Louis Isaac le Maistre, better known as De Sacy. The NT, based chiefly on the Greek, appeared at Mons in 1667; the OT, translated from the Latin Vulg., was finally authorized in 1695. This version was republished many times, even by Protestant Bible societies. Among twentieth-century Roman Catholic versions, mention must be made of Abbé Crampton's *La sainte Bible*, revised by the Jesuit fathers with collaboration of the professors of St. Sulpice (Paris, 1907); the version of the Latin Vulg. issued by the Pieuse Société Saint Paul (1932); a modern vernacular rendering by the Belgian Benedictine, Paul George Passelecq (Brussels, 1950); a revision of Crampton's OT, made by J. Bonsirven, with a new rendering of the NT by A. Tricot (Paris, 1952); and the translation, with excellent textual and exegetical notes, prepared by the professors at École Biblique in Jerusalem (Paris, 1949-54).

3. German versions. After the Gothic version of Ulfilas (*see* VERSIONS, ANCIENT, § 6), the oldest fragments of the Bible in a Germanic language are probably the Frankish version of Matthew made at the Bavarian monastery at Monsee in the year 738. The MS is bilingual, with Latin on the left-hand page and Frankish on the right. The unknown translator strove after an idiomatic, rather than a literalistic, rendering.

What has been called the "German Tatian" is a bilingual MS of the ninth century, originating at Fulda and now at St. Gall. This is a translation of Tatian's harmony of the gospels (*see* VERSIONS, ANCIENT, § 4a) in two columns per page, left in Latin, right in German. The Latin version rests on that of the Fulda codex of the sixth century, and the German rendering is in an East Frankish dialect, being clear and smooth but not so vigorous as that of the Monsee fragments.

Passing over many other Germanic versions made by known and unknown translators during the following centuries, preserved today in more than two hundred MSS (most of them from the fifteenth century), we turn to printed editions of the German Bible. It is not generally realized that eighteen editions of the complete German Bible (fourteen in High German and four in Low German) were published prior to Luther's translation. The first, which was also the first Bible printed in a modern European language, appeared in 1466 at Strassburg from the printing press of Johann Mentel. All fourteen editions in High German give, in the main, one and the same version, and all contain the apocryphal Epistle of Paul to the Laodiceans. Who made the version originally is not known, but it was already more than a century old when first printed; to judge on the basis of linguistic considerations, it probably originated near Prague. Perhaps interest in vernacular Bibles was stimulated by the Hussite movement.

The translation by Martin Luther marks an epoch in the history, not only of the German Bible, but of the German language as well. Based upon the court tongue of electoral Saxony, Luther's rendering was enriched from a number of other German dialects. He completed the first draft of his translation of the NT (from Erasmus' Greek Testament, second edition) in three months; it was published September 21, 1522. The entire Bible was finally translated and published by Hans Lufft of Wittenberg in 1534. Luther's rendering, noted for its majesty of diction and sweep of vocabulary, exerted a profound influence upon the rise of modern German literature. Never satisfied with having achieved the most felicitous translation, to the day of his death Luther continued to polish and revise his work. Though portions of the Bible had been previously translated from the Hebrew and the Greek, this was the first complete Bible translated from the original languages into a modern European vernacular. It became popular immediately; eleven editions were published during Luther's lifetime, besides numerous reprints. It formed the basis of several other versions, including the first translation of the Bible into Swedish (1541), Danish (1550), Icelandic (1584), and Slovenian (1584).

So influential was Luther's rendering that for almost a century other attempts at translation were few. The next complete Bible appeared at Herborn in 1602, being the work of the theologian Johannes Piscator (Fischer). Unlike Luther's rendering, this was scholastic in tone and abounded in Latinisms. In the following century Johann H. Haug, who introduced into Germany the mysticism of the Philadelphian sect (founded by Jane Lead of England), prepared a version on the basis of Luther's in comparison with the Zurich Bible and several English and French versions. It was published at Berleburg in eight folio volumes (1726-42), the last of which was devoted to the Apoc., Pseudep., and postapostolic books. It was partly from this edition (which contained the "missing" section in II Esd. 7) that Christoph Saur of Germantown, Pennsylvania, printed the first Bible in a European language to be published in America (1743).

During the centuries various attempts were made to revise Luther's translation, ridding it of obsolete words and expressions. By the middle of the nineteenth century six or seven recensions of his version were in circulation in Protestant Germany, but none of them had found widespread acceptance. In 1863 a committee, representative of different theological views, was appointed in order to undertake a revision involving only the very minimum of necessary changes. The NT appeared in 1867, and the complete Bible in 1883. This was issued as a *Probe-Bibel* ("Test Bible"), and additional comment and criticism were solicited from the church at large. Finally, after reviewing all proposals, a definite revision was issued by the Canstein Bible Press at Halle in 1892.

Among modern vernacular versions, special mention must be made of the "Menge Bible." Generally recognized to be one of the best of contemporary German versions, this was published by Hermann Menge at Stuttgart in 1926 after twenty years of unremitting labor. Like Luther, Menge continued to improve his work, and, a few months before his death in 1939, in his ninety-seventh year, he gave to the printer his final revision, which was incorporated into the eleventh edition and represents the "textus receptus" of the Menge Bible.

In 1931, on the four hundredth anniversary of the death of Zwingli, a committee which had been appointed by the Synod of Churches of the Canton of Zurich published a revision of the old Zwingli Version. Particularly in the OT, this version is generally regarded as one of the most satisfactory of modern German versions.

Another revision of Luther's Version was undertaken by the Evangelical Church of Germany in conjunction with the Union of German Bible Societies. In 1938 a "test edition" of the NT was issued, and in 1951 a "test edition" of the OT. After prolonged discussion and diverse criticism, a definitive revision of the NT was published in 1956.

Among Roman Catholic versions of the Bible, in German, of which there have been many, reference should be made to the following: In 1527 Hieronymus Emser, secretary to Duke George of Saxony, published a translation of the NT which was merely a slight revision of Luther's NT (1522), made to conform here and there to the Latin Vulg. In 1534 a Dominican, Johann Dietenberger, issued a revision of Emser, following Luther in the OT and the Zurich Bible in the Apoc. This version, revised in 1630 by Caspar Ulenberg and in 1662 by the clergy of Mainz, came to be called the "Catholic" Bible. The version made by Johann Eck, Luther's famous antagonist, was in the NT based closely on Emser and in the OT followed the pre-Lutheran rendering from the Vulg. His idiom, in the Bavarian dialect,

was so awkward and difficult to understand that his own biographer, Wiedemann, calls it the "worst of all Bible translations in the German language." First issued in 1537, it was not very successful and saw only two editions and seven printings, the last being in 1555.

H. Braun's work, which appeared in thirteen volumes from 1788 to 1805, was revised by J. F. Allioli and published in six volumes (1830-32). This translation, as well as that of J. H. Kistemaker (1825), achieved an even wider circulation by being issued by the British and Foreign Bible Society.

During the twentieth century Fritz Tillmann translated Vogels' edition of the Greek NT (Munich, 1927), and in 1937 Peter Ketter revised his earlier translation (Stuttgart, 1915) on the basis of Merk's edition of the Greek Testament.

Two members of the Order of Capuchian Monks, Konstantin Rösch and Eugen Henne, prepared a translation of the Bible, the former being responsible for the NT (Paderborn, 1932), and the latter for the OT (1936). Two other Roman Catholic scholars, P. Riessler and R. Storr, translated respectively the Old and New Testaments (Mainz, 1949). One of the most successful of modern Roman Catholics to put inexpensive copies of the Scriptures into the hands of the laity was Pius Parsch, a monk at Klosterneuberg, Austria. His translation of the Bible, from the original languages, was finished in 1952.

German translations of the OT by Jewish scholars have been made from time to time. Mention may be made of those prepared under the direction of L. Zunz (Berlin, 1837), S. Bernfeld (Berlin, 1902), N. H. Tur-Sinai—i.e., Harry Torczyner (four volumes; Frankfurt am Main, 1935-37; revised edition, Jerusalem, 1955—). Publication of the paraphrastic rendering by Martin Buber and Franz Rosenzweig was begun in Berlin in 1926 (new edition, Cologne, 1954—).

4. Greek (modern) versions. Modern colloquial Greek, which began to appear as early as the eleventh century, is the natural development of the Koine Greek of the Hellenistic age. Syntax underwent noticeable simplification; many new words were borrowed from Turkish, Slavic, and other languages; and the inflectional endings were greatly modified or eliminated altogether.

The first printing of a modern Greek version of any portion of the Scriptures was in a polyglot issued by the E. B. G. Soncino Press at Constantinople in 1547. This contained the Pentateuch and was prepared for the use of Jews who had been driven out of Spain. The Hebrew text is flanked by a Spanish translation in the right-hand column and by a modern Greek version in the left-hand column. The Targ. of Onkelos is above and the commentary of Rashi below. All these versions and texts are printed in Hebrew characters.

The first publication of a modern Greek version printed in Greek characters was issued in 1638. It is the NT in modern Greek and was prepared by Maximus, a Greek monk of Kallipolis (i.e., Gallipoli). The illustrious Cyril Lukar, patriarch of Constantinople, contributed a Preface to the volume. It was printed at Geneva by Pierre Aubert, and Lukar himself revised the proof after the death of the translator.

A revision of Maximus' rendering, based on orthographic and lexical corrections made by Anastasius Michael, was edited by the German theologian August H. Franke. It was published at Halle in 1710, largely at the expense of Sophia Louisa, queen of Prussia.

Another translation was made by Hilarion, head of the monastery of Mount Sinai at Constantinople. The NT was published by the British and Foreign Bible Society in 1828. As regards the OT, certain difficulties arose regarding the Bible Society's decision not to circulate the books of the Apoc. Hilarion was basing his translation on the LXX, which contains the Apoc.; the Bible Society decided that the version should be made from the basis of the Hebrew. Another committee was formed, composed of two English scholars, with a knowledge of Hebrew, and several learned Greeks, notably N. Bambas. Their version of the OT was published in 1840, of the NT in 1844. The Greek church, however, would not circulate the version lacking the Apoc. Hilarion's version of the NT was also revised by Bambas (1848), but this also, because of certain political reasons, found only limited approval, even though both ancient and modern Greek texts were printed in parallel columns.

A similar fate befell the modern Greek version of the gospels which was published at Athens in 1900, under the auspices of Olga, queen of the Hellenes. In the following year Professor Alexander Pallis published a frankly vernacular version of Matthew's Gospel in *The Acropolis,* an Athenian newspaper. What was considered to be undue license in his version aroused bitter hostility, which extended to Queen Olga's version also. The populace connected the latter book with a supposed Panslavist conspiracy, and riots broke out in the streets of Athens. This agitation led the government to issue a decree prohibiting the use of any modern Greek version of the Scriptures. (The prohibition was repealed in 1924.) Pallis published his completed version of the gospels (based on the Vatican Codex, B) at Liverpool in 1902.

In 1927 the Psalms in modern Greek were published at Athens by K. Kalinicos. Twenty years later two other renderings of the Psalter were issued at Athens, one by K. Phrilingos, and the other, which is designated a poetical metaphrase, by T. B. Konstantinos. Still other renderings of the Psalms appeared in 1950 (by T. Gritsopoulos) and in 1953 (by A. Kalamboussis).

In his commentary on the minor prophets (Athens, 1947), B. Vellas of the University of Athens included a new rendering of the Hebrew text into modern Greek. In 1954-55 Athanasios Chastoupsis and Nikolaos Louvaris published at Athens the complete Bible in Greek, the NT of which is a paraphrase rather than a strict translation. Similarly the versatile and energetic P. N. Trembelas issued the textus receptus of the Greek NT with a modern Greek paraphrase in parallel columns (two volumes; second edition, 1955). In 1955 Trembelas also published the LXX text of the Psalms (including the 151st Psalm) with a modern Greek paraphrase. A paraphrase of the Gospel of Luke and of the Acts was prepared by Bishop Athenagoras of Elaias and published in

Greek under the title *A History of Jesus Christ and of the Apostles* (Brookline, 1957).

5. Hungarian versions. The earliest Hungarian version of which any fragments survive dates from the beginning of the fifteenth century, and is the work of two Franciscan monks, Thomas and Valentine, who found asylum in Moldavia from Hungary, where they had been persecuted for Hussite doctrines. The translation, which is based on the Latin Vulg., is described as terse and exact. Also to the first half of the fifteenth century belongs the translation of Ladislas Batori, who, though from the family of princes of Transylvania, became a hermit in the Order of St. Paul. The first book printed in Hungarian was an edition of Paul's letters, translated from the Vulg. by Benedek Komjáthy. It appeared at Cracow in 1533. A translation of the gospels, prepared by G. Pesti, was published at Vienna in 1536. This is said to be a more free and independent rendering than that of Komjáthy. The first complete NT in Hungarian was the work of János Erdösi (Silvester), who had been a pupil of Melanchthon at Wittenberg. Translated from the Greek, it was printed on the first Hungarian Protestant printing press and published at Uj Sziget in 1541. The sixteenth century was marked by great literary activity in Hungary, and several other translations of the NT and of most of the OT appeared from various presses.

The first complete Bible in Hungarian was the work of Gáspár Károli, a pupil of Melanchthon and Reformed pastor of the little town of Göncz in Upper Hungary. It was rendered from the original languages, with reference to the Latin Vulg. and other versions. Since it was first printed at Visoly near Göncz in 1590, it is frequently known as the Visoly Bible. The appearance of this version exerted a notable influence, not merely on the spiritual life of the Magyar people, but on their national life and literature as well. More than one hundred editions of Károli's translation, often in revised forms, had appeared before the tercentenary of its publication was celebrated at Göncz in 1890.

During the Counter Reformation in Hungary, the printing of the Bible in the vernacular was prohibited, and consequently Hungarian Bibles had to be printed in other countries. One of these, a version prepared by a Reformed pastor of Debreczen, György Csipkés, who had studied Hebrew under J. Leusden at Utrecht, was completed in 1675, but arrangements for it to be printed could not be consummated until 1719. When the edition was crossing the Hungarian frontier, most of the copies were seized by the intervention of the Jesuits and were eventually burned.

At the beginning of the seventeenth century, in order to counteract the influence of Károli's Bible, the Roman Catholic archbishop of Esztergom (Gran), Péter Pásmány, had the Bible translated by a Jesuit scholar named György Káldi, who produced a vigorous and faithful rendering of the Vulg. This appeared at Vienna in 1626. It was revised several times, notably by the learned Béla József Tárkányi, who brought the version into conformity with the modern form of Hungarian speech. This version was published in 1865 at Eger (Erlau) with a Preface by Béla Bartakovics, archbishop of Eger.

In 1886, at the initiative of Theodore Duka, Hungarian patriot and scholar, a revision of Károli's Bible was undertaken. The OT, which was published at Budapest in 1898, aroused so much adverse criticism that another revision committee was appointed to bring the work into general accord with the ERV. The work of this committee, published in 1908, was no more successful than that of its predecessors. Several other attempts were made to produce a version that would be satisfactory to all Hungarian Protestants. The most recent of these is the work of a Joint Bible Commission composed of representative Reformed and Lutheran scholars, seven for the OT and seven for the NT. Taking as a textual basis the latest editions of Kittel's Hebrew Bible and of Nestle's Greek Testament, the Commission declared its aim to render as faithfully as possible the original languages into a modern Hungarian language which incorporates all that is best and still alive in the idiom of the old translation. The NT was completed in 1952, and several books of the OT have been published.

6. Italian versions. The earliest surviving portions of scripture in Italian are in the form of harmonies of the gospels. One such harmony, in the Tuscan dialect, is preserved in twenty-four MSS dating from the thirteenth and fourteenth centuries; another harmony, in the Venetian dialect, is extant in a MS dating from the fourteenth century. The first printed Bible in Italian appeared at Venice in 1471; it was the work of a Benedictine monk named Nicolo di Malherbi (Malermi). A champion of Florentine liberty, Antonio Brucioli, who was accused of Protestant leanings, published the NT at Venice in 1530, and two years later the complete Bible appeared. Though on his title page Brucioli claims that his version was made from the original languages, his knowledge of Hebrew was not great, and he probably relied upon Paginus' Latin version of the OT and that of Erasmus for the NT.

A new translation of the NT was made from the Greek by M. Teofilo, and printed at Lyons in 1551. The Preface is from the Preface by Calvin in Olivétan's French Bible. A revision of Brucioli's Version, prepared for the Protestant refugees in Geneva, was printed by F. Durone at Geneva in 1562.

The first Protestant translation of the Bible into Italian was prepared by Giovanni Diodati, whose family was compelled by religious persecution to flee from Italy. He was a very able scholar and when only twenty-one was appointed by Beza to teach Hebrew in the Academy of Geneva. His translation of the Bible from the original languages, rendered into pure Tuscan, the standard of Italian style, was published at Geneva in 1607. Despite the prohibition of Pope Pius IV, in 1564, of the reading of the Bible in the vernacular, Diodati's version met with a success comparable with that of Luther's German version.

In 1757 Pope Benedict XIV gave a qualified permission for the laity to read the Scriptures, and in 1776 Antonio Martini, who later became archbishop of Florence, published a translation of the Latin Vulg. in elegant Italian.

During the nineteenth century portions of the Bible, in the majority of cases a gospel, were translated into more than a dozen Italian dialects. Most of them were prepared at the instance of Prince Louis Lucien Bonaparte. During the twentieth century a number of fresh translations, many in inexpensive form, have been issued by Roman Catholic scholars. Most of them are based on the Latin Vulg., and all of them have, of course, notes and comments. Martini's Version, revised and corrected, was published at Turin in 1920. In 1929 the Cardinal Ferrari Society issued at Florence a version of the Bible prepared by Giuseppi Ricciotti and a group of other scholars. Although based on the Vulg., variations from the Hebrew and Greek are noted in the margin. An excellent translation in modern, dignified, and simple Italian, prepared under the care of the Pontifical Biblical Institute, and directed by Alberto Vaccari, began to appear in separate volumes in 1922. Another version, prepared by a Dominican scholar, Marco Sales, was published at Turin in 1931.

Among Protestant efforts, that of Giovanni Luzzi of the Waldensian theological faculty, Rome, has been most prominent. He served as the head of a committee which revised the old Diodati Version; this was published by the British and Foreign Bible Society in 1925. In 1930 he published at Rome his own translation of the Bible.

7. Portuguese versions. The earliest printed scripture in Portuguese is a harmony of the gospels, prepared by order of Leonora, wife of King John II of Portugal, and published at Lisbon in 1495. It was based on the popular Latin *Vita Christi* by Ludolphus of Saxony. Incredible though it may seem, the complete Bible has been available in Portuguese for only *ca.* two hundred years. This was the translation made by a Roman Catholic priest, João Ferreira d'Almeida, who, upon going as a missionary to the East Indies, became a Protestant. His rendering of the NT was published at Amsterdam in 1681, and the entire Bible, completed by other missionaries, was published at Batavia in 1753.

The first translation of the Bible in the vernacular to be printed in Portugal itself (where, despite several centuries of a flourishing literary productivity, the Scriptures remained unavailable in the language of the people) appeared in 1783-90. It was the work of a Roman Catholic priest named Anton Pereira de Figueiredo, and was published, with copious annotations, at Lisbon in twenty-three volumes. Obviously a Bible in such an expensive format remained inaccessible to all except the wealthy. Both these versions have been revised several times, and both (Pereira's minus the notes) have been printed by the British and Foreign Bible Society.

During the nineteenth and twentieth centuries several Portuguese versions of the NT were published in Brazil. A revision of the d'Almeida Version of the entire Bible was undertaken by an interdenominational committee, which patterned its work upon the American Standard Version of 1901. The NT of this revision (called the Versão Brasileira) was published at Rio de Janeiro in 1910, the entire Bible in 1914 (corrected edition, 1926). In 1951 the Bible Society of Brazil issued an "authorized revision" of the d'Almeida NT, which seeks to preserve in modern orthography much of the familiar and beloved phraseology of the older rendering. The revision of the OT appeared in 1958.

8. Scandinavian versions. *a. Danish (and Norwegian).* Prior to the Reformation portions of the Scriptures in Danish were to be found chiefly in parish churches and in the monasteries. The first complete translation of the NT was prepared under the auspices of the Danish king Christian II, who, a friend of the Reformation, had to leave his country as a refugee (1523). His secretary, Hans Mikkelsen, a former mayor of the Swedish city of Malmö, and Kristian Winther prepared the translation from the Latin Vulg. and Luther's German translation. It was published at Leipzig in 1524. The language of the version was a mixture of Danish and Swedish, and for this reason, as well as the fact that in the Preface King Christian II was defended and his enemies attacked, the version was not well received in Denmark. The first idiomatic Danish version of the NT was the work of Christen Pedersen (1480-1554), who may be said to be the father of Danish literature. His translation was published at Antwerp in 1529 and again in 1531. In the latter year he also issued a metrical version of the Psalms.

These and several other translations of parts of the Scriptures were preliminary to the appearance of the complete Bible in Danish. The Lutheran Church in Denmark, established in 1537, received a translation of the whole Bible in 1550. The work of preparing the version was entrusted by the Danish king Christian III to the bishop in Copenhagen, two professors at the university, and two ministers. These five, who made use of a draft of the entire Bible prepared by Pedersen, finished their work in 1548. In accordance with the command of Christian III, Luther's German translation was to be followed as closely as the Danish would allow. The German printer Ludvig Dietz was secured to print the edition, and in eighteen months after he had come to Copenhagen three thousand folio copies were ready for the binder. When it was published in 1550, the edition was distributed to the parish churches in both Denmark and Norway, the price being the cost of a good steer. In 1589 a second revised edition, the so-called Frederick II Bible, was issued, in which many of the archaisms of the first edition were removed.

All these translations were made from Latin and/or German versions; the first Danish Bible to be translated from the original languages was completed in 1607 by Hans Paulsen Resen, bishop of Zealand. Resen's translation, however, erred on the side of literalism and was lacking in respect of Danish idiom. It was subsequently revised by Bishop Hans Svane (Swaning) in 1647, and remained in wide use up to the middle of the nineteenth century.

In 1814 Norway was separated politically from Denmark, and certain creative forces in language and literature began to assert themselves. The rise of a composite of various rural dialects, called Landsmaal or New Norwegian, developed side by side with the official Norwegian language (Riksmaal). During subsequent generations significant changes in both forms of language, as well as the awakening of new spiritual life in both Denmark and Norway, called forth several new translations of the Bible. In Denmark, Jacob Christian Lindberg, a disciple of the prominent bishop, poet, and hymn writer, Grundtvig, published a translation of the OT in 1837-53 and of the NT in 1856. Among noteworthy versions of the NT that of Axel Sorensen, who prepared the first translation or paraphrase into the modern spoken vernacular (1881), and that of Bishop T. Skat Rördam, who used a better Greek text established by modern critical scholarship (1886), deserve special mention. The first translation of the entire NT into Landsmaal appeared in 1889, the work of several scholars (Belsheim, Skard, and Blix); the OT was finished in 1921. During the twentieth century a Royal Commission, consisting of prominent Danish scholars, issued in 1931 a new and excellent rendering of the OT which was authorized to be read in churches. In 1942 a "test revision" of the NT was circulated, looking forward to eventual authorization. Several Norwegian translations of parts of the Bible also appeared, including work by Buhl, Mowinckel, and Schjott. In 1938 the Norwegian Bible Society published a revised version of the Bible in "New Norwegian," prepared by Pastor R. Indrebö.

b. Icelandic. The earliest rendition of portions of the Scriptures into Icelandic exists in a work entitled *Stiorn* (or *Stjórn,* "Dispensation" [of God]) and dates from the thirteenth century. Attributed to Brandr Jónsson, who became bishop of Hólar in Iceland (1263), this version is in part translation and in part paraphrase of a portion of the OT (from Genesis to II Kings) and is based on the Latin Vulg., with explanatory remarks drawn from various authors.

The first printed portion of the Bible to appear in Icelandic was published at Roskilde, Denmark, in 1540; this was a translation of the NT made by Oddur Gottskálksson from the Vulg. and with reference to Luther's German version.

The *editio princeps* of the Bible in Icelandic was due to Gudbrandur Thorláksson, bishop of Hólar. After sending a man to Copenhagen to learn the art of printing, and another to Hamburg to learn bookbinding, he finally published the Bible at Hólar in 1584. The cost of printing was mainly defrayed by the financial assistance of King Frederick II of Denmark, who ordered that every church in Iceland should have a copy. In the opinion of many, this version is marked by a singular beauty of language and faithful simplicity of style, worthy to stand beside the work of Ulfilas, Luther, and Tyndale. This version has been revised many times, the most recent being in 1908. This revision was the result of a resolution of the Icelandic Bible Society, at Reykjavík in 1897, to sponsor the preparation of a translation based upon the original languages. The OT is the work chiefly of Haraldur Nielsson; the books of the NT were assigned to several translators connected with the theological seminary at Reykjavík.

c. Swedish. The first printed translation of the NT in Swedish was issued at Stockholm in 1526. At the request of King Gustavus Vasa, the version was prepared by Olaus Petri, who had attended Luther's lectures at Wittenberg, and by others who assisted in establishing the Reformation in Sweden. It was based on Luther's German translation of 1522, with reference to the Latin Vulg., and compared throughout with Erasmus' Greek text of 1522.

The complete Bible in Swedish was published in 1541; it was prepared by Laurentius Petri, archbishop of Uppsala, in collaboration with his brother Olaus Petri, assisted by other colleagues. The translation of the OT was based on Luther's Version, with reference to the Latin Vulg. The NT is a thorough revision of the text previously published in 1526. By royal decree a copy was provided for every church throughout the country. In the next century several attempts were instigated to revise the Gustavus Vasa Bible, but these came to no fruition. It was finally resolved to reprint the text of the 1541 Bible with corrections in orthography and the introduction of verse numbers, chapter headings, marginal subject headings, and other aids for readers. This edition, called the Gustavus Adolphus Bible, was published at Stockholm in 1618. In 1703 a revised edition appeared under the supervision of Eric Benzelius, archbishop of Uppsala. Very few changes were made in the text, but the chapter headings, notes, marginal matter, etc., were more extensively revised. It is known as Charles XII's Bible.

A new version of the Bible, based on the original texts and Luther's German version, was prepared by H. M. Melin, professor of theology at Lund. It was published at Lund in six parts between 1858 and 1865.

Several translations of the NT, prepared by individual scholars, both Protestant and Roman Catholic, appeared during the late nineteenth and twentieth centuries. The most recent revision of the text of the complete Bible, approved by the Church Diet of the Lutheran Church, was published in 1917. This final approval was given after several Bible commissions had been laboring for 140 years and had submitted many specimens of their work to the members of the Church Diet, which had rejected some and authorized others.

9. Slavic (Slavonic) versions. a. Old Church Slavonic. Slavonic, the ancient form of Slavic speech still used ecclesiastically in Russia and other Slavic countries, was one of the earliest languages in Europe to possess a Bible. In the second half of the ninth century Cyril (Constantine the philosopher, an erudite polyglot, formerly professor at the University of Constantinople) and his brother Methodius went as missionaries from Macedonia (Salonika) to Great Moravia. Here they organized a national church with services in Slavic. For this purpose they translated portions of the Scriptures, writing it in an alphabet which Cyril created for the purpose. Since at this time there was very little dialectic differentiation of the primitive Slavic languages throughout Central Europe, there were no linguistic obstacles to the spread of the literary language (which is called today Old Church Slavonic) among the great majority of the Slavs. Though the Moravian mission was forcibly terminated by the Roman clergy of S Germany in 885, after some two decades of work enough impetus had been given to continue the circulation of the Scriptures in Slavonic. During the next few centuries the original version underwent certain modifications reflecting the development of local Slavic dialects. Thus, Old Church Slavonic MSS of the gospels, the Psalter, and other portions of the Bible, are extant in several distinct recensions, including the Bohemian, Bulgarian, Croatian, Macedonian, Russian, and Slovenian. During subsequent centuries the several Slavic languages developed to such an extent that the Old Church Slavonic Version, used in the church liturgy, came to be less and less understood by the common people in the various Slavic countries.

The first printed edition of the complete Bible in Slavonic was prepared under the auspices of Konstantin, prince of Ostrog, in Volhynia, Russia. This edition was published at Ostrog in 1581 on the basis of a Slavonic MS dated 1499 and named after Gennadius, archbishop of Novgorod. For the OT it follows the text of the Greek LXX. A revision of the Ostrog Bible, prepared by Arsenios, a Greek, and by several others, was published at Moscow in 1633. This, in turn, was revised during the following century at the behest of the emperor, Peter the Great, in 1712. After many vicissitudes, and upon the issuance of a ukase by the Empress Elizabeth, the work was finally completed and issued at St. Petersburg in 1751. This edition, known as the "Bible of Elizabeth," takes into account the Hebrew text of the OT. Reprinted many times, it has remained the standard edition of the Slavonic Bible.

b. Bohemian (Czech). During the fourteenth century several unknown translators rendered the Psalter and other parts of the Bible from the Vulg. into Bohemian. The Reformer Ján Hus (1369-1415) made use of these versions in his revision of the Old Church Slavonic text. Later this version was revised by several of Hus's followers. The NT in this revision was issued in 1475, being the first printed scripture in the language, and the complete Bible, the fifth Bible printed in a modern European language, appeared at Prague in 1488. During the sixteenth century, when about three fourths of the country was Protestant, this Bible was revised and reprinted many times in various cities. Toward the end of the century a new rendering was prepared by members of the United Brethren from the Hebrew and Greek originals by a committee of eight distinguished scholars under the chairmanship of Bishop Blahoslav, and was issued in six volumes as fast as completed from 1579 to 1593. The translation came to be called the Kralitz Bible, from the Moravian castle where it was printed at the expense of Baron von Zerotin, and has remained the standard version for Protestants.

After the year 1620 the publication of non-Catholic Bibles in Bohemia and Moravia was prohibited, and efforts were made to prepare a translation from the Latin Vulg. for Roman Catholics. After some fruitless beginnings the work was entrusted to several Jesuits. The NT appeared in 1677, the complete Bible in 1715. It was called the Wenceslaus Bible because it was published at the expense of the society founded to honor Wenceslaus. This was subsequently revised on the basis of the text of the Kralitz Bible; several other Roman Catholic versions likewise made large use of the Protestant rendering.

During the twentieth century F. Zilka, a pastor of the Evangelical Church of the Czech Brethren and professor at the Hus Theological Faculty, Prague, published a translation of the NT (1933).

c. Bulgarian. "Old Bulgarian" is a designation sometimes given to Old Church Slavonic, and translations into this language are mentioned above (*see* § 9*a*). The first printed version of the NT in modern Bulgarian was published at Smyrna in 1840. It was translated from the ancient Slavonic Bible by a schoolmaster of Gabrova named Neophytus Papa Petros (or Neophyte Rilski). The first translation of the NT to be made from the original Greek was published at Bucharest in 1859, and the first translation of the OT from the Hebrew appeared in three parts between 1862 and 1864. In 1891 the Synod of the Bulgarian Orthodox Church appointed a committee, headed by Metropolitan Boris, exarch of Bulgaria, to prepare a revision. After five committees had worked successively on the project, the translation was published at Sofia in 1925. Another Bulgarian version was made by a committee under the leadership of Robert Thomson; the NT was issued at Sofia in 1921 and the Bible in 1923.

d. Polish. The earliest translation of any part of the Bible into Polish was the Psalter. Several MSS of this version survive, the oldest dating from the second half of the fourteenth century. The first printed NT was issued in two volumes in 1553; it was translated from the Greek by a Lutheran pastor at Königsberg, Jan Sieklucki (generally called Seklucyan), a friend of Luther.

Early Polish Bibles are associated with the names of the towns where they were published. The first edition of the entire Bible is known as the Cracow Bible (1561). Its origin is very obscure. It purports to be a rendering from the Latin Vulg. made by an anonymous translator, revised and prepared for the press by Jan Lwowczyk (i.e., John of Lemberg), a Roman Catholic theologian. Remarks in the Preface regarding persecution and intrigue have led some to suggest that the translation was really of Protestant origin, foisted upon Roman Catholics by the printer's trick of having the MS revised by Lwowczyk, whose orthodoxy was above suspicion. It has been observed that the translation does not adhere closely to the Latin, and that its idiom and orthography bear clear traces of influence from the Bohemian Bible of 1557. Other theories of the origin of the Cracow Bible have also been advanced. Curiously enough, the wood cuts in Revelation are borrowed from Luther's German Bible; in two of the cuts representing the dragon, the triple crown of the Papacy placed on his head has obviously been altered to a double crown, while in the cut representing Babylon, the triple crown has been altered to a single crown.

The second edition of the Bible in Polish, this one made from the original languages, was prepared by a group of eighteen or more scholars, gathered for this purpose by an eminent Polish prince, Nicolas Radziwiłł. Finished after six years of work, it was published in 1563 at Brest, Lithuania. Unfortunately this translation was not generally welcomed: adherents of the Lutheran and Reformed confessions suspected it of Socinian influence, and the Socinians complained that it was not accurate enough. After the prince's death (1565), a Roman Catholic member of his own family sought out and burned all copies he could locate. Subsequently a Socinian pastor at Łosk, Simon Budny, prepared a revision of the Brest Bible; this was published at Nesvizh in 1572.

What became the standard Roman Catholic version of the Bible in Polish was translated from the Latin Vulg., with reference to the original texts, by a Jesuit, Jakub Wujek. It was published at Cracow in 1599 with an Introduction by Stanisław Karnkowski, archbishop of Gnesen and primate of Poland. In 1935 a revised edition was published.

The Brest Bible was superseded by the so-called Danzig Bible, which finally became the edition used by all Evangelical Poles. It was prepared by ministers of the Reformed, Lutheran, and Moravian churches, and was published at Danzig in 1632. The archbishop of Gnesen, having discovered a trifling error (*do* for *od*) in Matt. 4:1, used this as a pretext for suppressing the edition, and all the copies of this Bible which could be seized were burned. The version was reprinted many times both in and outside Poland.

In 1928 the Mariavite archbishop O. J. M. Michal Kowalski published his translation of the NT at Płock.

e. Russian. Since Church Slavonic is not intelligible to the Russian people, the Ostrog Bible of 1581, as well as its revisions in 1633 and 1751, was not satisfactory for the laity. An effort was made to produce a version in the White (or Polish) Russian dialect by Franciscus Skorina, a native of Polotsk in White Russia. He translated from the Latin Vulg., but used also the Slavonic Version and the Bohemian Bible of 1506. Probably his intention was to translate the whole Bible, and he may have succeeded in doing so, but only portions of his version are extant today. These are twenty-two books of the OT and the Acts and letters of the NT. Most of these books were printed in Prague in 1517-19; two parts were printed at Vilna a few years later.

No other editions in the vernacular appeared until the nineteenth century, when they were published in connection with the founding of the St. Petersburg Bible Society in 1813. In 1821 the NT in Slavonic and in Great Russian was issued, translated by a committee appointed by the Holy Synod at the request of Czar Alexander I. The work had been undertaken by a group of professors at the theological academy at St. Petersburg, under the direction of the eminent churchman and scholar Vasily M. D. Philaret, afterward metropolitan of Moscow. In 1820 the translation of the OT from the Hebrew was begun, and the portion from Genesis to Ruth was finished. In 1825 this was printed by the Bible Society at St. Petersburg, apparently just before it was compelled to cease operations, in accord with a ban by Czar Nicholas I upon all private associations, even when nonpolitical. All copies of the Scriptures in stock were ordered burned. It may be mentioned here that during the short period of its existence, the Russian Bible Society had opened 290 depots in different parts of the Empire, portions of the Bible were translated and edited in fourteen new languages, and more than 876,000 copies of the Bible, or of some part of it, were printed in 26 different languages and dialects.

The accession of Czar Alexander II in 1856 made it possible for the Holy Synod, under the leadership of Philaret, to resume the work of translating the Scriptures. Under the general editorship of E. I.

Loviagin, professor of Greek in the theological academy at St. Petersburg, a group of scholars from this and three other theological academies (at Moscow, Kiev, and Kazan) began a fresh translation of the gospels, which appeared in 1860. The Synod also appointed a committee (including Loviagin and D. A. Chwolson, professor of Hebrew) to prepare a version of the OT. This appeared in installments in a church magazine and later was printed in one volume (St. Petersburg, 1875). As in the case of the Slavonic Bible, the apocryphal books form part of the Russian Bible. This has been reprinted at various times, the most recent edition being published at Moscow in 1956 with the authority of Alexei, the patriarch of Moscow and All Russia.

The Little Russian, or Ruthenian, dialect, which is used by people in the Ukraine, Galicia, and Bukovina, was employed as a vehicle for the Scriptures first in 1869. In that year P. A. Kulisch, a Ruthenian litterateur, published at Lemberg his translation of the Pentateuch. Continuing his work, with the assistance of D. I. Puluj, Kulisch prepared a translation of the entire Bible, conforming it to the ERV. After his death his MS was supplemented by I. C. Levitsky and edited for printing by Alexander Sluszarczyk. It was printed (in Russian characters) at Vienna in 1903. In 1921 another version of the NT in Ruthenian was published at Ždłgief (near Lemberg). This was made by Yaroslav Levitsky, and revised by a committee of professors and officials of the Greek Orthodox Church.

f. Serbo-Croatian.

f. Serbo-Croatian. Today Serbo-Croatian is the standard language of most of the inhabitants of Yugoslavia. The Serbs belong almost entirely to the Greek Orthodox Church and use the Cyrillic characters in writing; the Croats belong to the Roman Catholic Church and use the Roman characters in writing.

The first publication of portions of the Bible was an edition of the liturgical letters and gospels, translated by a Franciscan, Bernardinus Spalatensis, and published in 1495 at Venice. The first entire NT was translated from Erasmus' Latin version and Luther's German version by Antonius Dalmata and Stephanus Consul Istrianus. This was issued from the press of Baron Jan Ungnad, at Urach, near Tübingen, in 1563. One edition was printed in Glagolitic and one in Cyrillic characters. Though the Prophets were issued in Roman characters the following year (the identity of the translator is doubtful), the entire Bible in Serbo-Croatian was not published until the beginning of the nineteenth century. The Bible in Cyrillic characters was published at Budapest in 1804; the name of the translator is unknown. *Ca.* a quarter of a century later the Bible in Roman characters, translated from the Vulg. by Matia Petar Katančić, a Franciscan, was issued at Budapest in 1831.

The purest tradition of the Serbo-Croatian language was preserved orally during the centuries in folk stories and ballads. Until the nineteenth century, however, the literary language was not modeled on this tradition, but rested upon a Serbianized form of Church Slavonic. Through the efforts of the linguistic and literary reformer, Vuk Stefanović Karadžić (1787-1864), though without academic training himself, the language of the common people came to be regarded as a suitable vehicle for polite literature. In the interests of literary reform, Vuk issued his translation of the NT at Vienna in 1847.

Other translations and several revisions of Vuk's rendering have been published. The most important of these is the Bakotić Bible, prepared by Dr. Lujo Bakotić, a minister of high cabinet rank; it was published in Roman characters at Belgrade in 1933. His translation is said to be "inescapably lucid." A translation of the original languages into Croatian was undertaken by Ivan E. Šarić, archbishop of Sarajevo. The first fascicles of the OT appeared in 1941; a second edition of the NT was published in 1953.

g. Slovak.

g. Slovak. The Slovak language, which is the predominant native language of Slovakia (an autonomous part of Czechoslovakia), though existing for hundreds of years, first became stabilized and a vehicle of literary composition in the late eighteenth century. At the beginning of the nineteenth century the Bible was translated from the Latin Vulg. by Jiři Palkovič, a Roman Catholic canon of Gran. It was published in Gothic character in two volumes at Gran in 1829 and 1832. This version was replaced in 1926 by a translation made by Ján Donoval and a group of Roman Catholic scholars, revised by Richard Osvald. It was published by the Vojtech Union in Trnava in 1928.

A Protestant translation appeared in the work of Josef Rohaček, a Lutheran pastor, whose NT was published in Budapest in 1913, and whose complete Bible was issued at Prague in 1936.

The most recent version of the NT is that prepared by Stefan Žlatoš and Anton Jan Surjanský; it was published at Trnava in 1946.

h. Slovenian.

h. Slovenian. Slovenian is used in the Slovenian People's Republic (an autonomous unit within Yugoslavia) and in small adjacent areas of Austria and Italy. For centuries the Slovenes have enjoyed the reputation of being a hard-working, intelligent, and reliable people. The first publication of any part of the Bible in Slovenian was the Gospel According to Matthew, translated in 1555 by Primož Truber, a Reformed minister in Carniola in S Austria. His translation of the entire NT was completed in 1577. The OT was translated by a Lutheran pastor, Jurij Dalmatin, whose work was reviewed by a commission of Lutheran Church authorities of Carniola, Styria, and Carinthia. This first Slovenian Bible was printed at Wittenberg in 1584 under the patronage of the elector of Saxony. In the Preface it is stated that the version was made from the original languages and other versions (meaning particularly Luther's Bible, which it follows closely, even as regards the prefaces to the books of the Apoc.).

As in other countries, the Reformation in Slovenia was followed by a vigorous Roman Catholic counter-reformation in which Protestant clergy were persecuted and their Bibles burned. Toward the end of the eighteenth century several Roman Catholic ecclesiastics prepared the first version of the Bible for Slovenian Catholics. From 1784 to 1802 the parts of this translation, which was made from the Vulg., were issued at Laibach by Jurij Japelj, Blaž Kumerdey, and five others. At the middle of the nineteenth century another Roman Catholic version appeared at Laibach; this was translated from Allioli's German Bible by a group of priests (1856-59).

During the first part of the twentieth century, under pressure for Yugoslav political unity there was some agitation to drop the Slovenian language in favor of Serbo-Croatian. The tide of popular opinion among Slovenes rallied strongly in favor of retaining their own Slavic dialect, now somewhat modified through the centuries. Two revisions of the Scriptures were carried out. The British and Foreign Bible Society published Anton Chraska's version of the NT at Laibach in 1908, and of the Bible in 1914. The bishop of Ljubljana (Laibach), Antona Bonaventura Jeglíča, issued a translation of the NT in 1929.

10. Spanish versions. The earliest allusion to the existence of a Spanish version is the decree of John I, king of Aragon, issued in 1233 at Tarragona, that no one, clergy or laity, was to keep in his house any translation of the OT in the vernacular tongue. This implies the existence of such a translation. Later in the thirteenth century King Alphonse X not only relaxed this prohibition but ordered, it is said, that a translation be made of Jerome's Latin Vulg.

An unusual feature in the history of the Spanish version of the Bible, as compared with those made in other countries, is the large proportion of early translations made by Jewish rabbis from the Hebrew text. Some of these were made in the Castilian dialect and others in Judeo-Spanish, or Ladino, a dialect used by Jewish exiles from Spain, who settled in Turkey, Italy, and the Netherlands in the latter part of the fifteenth century. The first printed edition of the OT in Spanish appeared in 1553 and is a revision of an old Jewish version, made from the Hebrew and existing previously in MS form. Since the edition was produced under the protection of the Duke of Ferrara, it is generally called the Ferrara Bible.

The first printed NT in Spanish was translated from the Greek by Francisco de Enzinas, a young Spanish student at Wittenberg, in the house of his tutor and friend, Melanchthon. A few weeks after it came from the press in 1543, and before many copies had been circulated, Enzinas was arrested and the printed copies suppressed because of alleged heretical leanings. After a year's imprisonment Enzinas managed to escape; thereafter he lived in exile until his death at the age of thirty-two. Only a few copies of his translation have survived.

The second edition of the NT in Spanish was translated from the Greek by Juan Perez de Pineda. It was published in 1556 at Geneva, where Perez had fled to escape the Inquisition. Copies of this edition, which is regarded as a model of Castilian style, were smuggled into Spain by Julian Hernandez, who later was apprehended by the authorities and executed.

The first complete Spanish Bible was the work of Cassiodoro de Reina, one of the Spanish Reformers who had escaped from Spain *ca.* the year 1557. Soon afterward he began his translation, which was based on the original languages, with comparison made of other versions. It appeared at Basel in 1569. This version was later revised by another refugee from Spain, Cipriano Valera, who had been a monk but had come under the influence of the Reforma-

tion. The NT was published at London in 1596, and the complete Bible at Amsterdam in 1602. In this edition the books of the Apoc. are placed between the OT and the NT and are prefaced by a discussion of their authority. Many editions of this and other Spanish versions were published at various places outside Spain.

It was not before 1793 that the complete Bible in Spanish was printed on Spanish soil. This was the work of Felipe Scio de San Miguel, who later became bishop of Segovia. It was translated from the Latin Vulg. and was printed at Valencia in ten volumes. A second and revised edition appeared at Madrid, 1794-97, in nineteen volumes. Naturally few individuals could afford to buy such expensive editions, which contain many annotations. During the years a need was felt for a rendering that would take some account of the original languages. This was produced in 1825 by Felix Torres Amat, afterward bishop of Astorga, who made a fresh translation of the Vulg., with comparison of the Hebrew and Greek. Though often reprinted, it did not supplant Scio's rendering.

Since the Spanish used in Latin America differs not a little from that of the Iberian Peninsula, almost insuperable difficulties stand in the way of producing a version satisfactory to the whole Spanish-speaking world. An attempt to achieve this goal was made by a joint committee of Spanish and South American translators meeting in Spain, who prepared a rendering of the Nestle text of the Greek NT. It is called the Hispano-Americano NT and was published at Madrid in 1916.

The first complete translation of the Scriptures into Spanish made directly from the original languages by Roman Catholic scholars was published at Madrid in 1944. It was prepared by Canon Eloíno Nácar Fuster and Alberto Colunga under the auspices and direction of the Pontifical University of Salamanca. In 1947 another version from the original languages was published at Madrid, translated by Francisco Cantera and José Maria Bover. During the twentieth century several Roman Catholic renderings into modern, vernacular Spanish have appeared in South America.

Bibliography. General: [E. Nestle *et al.*], *Urtext und Übersetzungen der Bibel* (1897). T. H. Darlow and H. F. Moule, *Historical Catalogue of the Printed Editions of Holy Scripture in the Library of the British and Foreign Bible Society* (2 vols. in 4 pts.; 1903-8). R. Kilgour, *The Gospel in Many Years* (1929). O. M. Norlie, *The Translated Bible, 1534-1934* (1934); *The Bible in a Thousand Tongues* (1935). British Museum, *General Catalogue of Printed Books*, vols. XVI-XVIII (1936-37). E. M. North, *The Book of a Thousand Tongues* (1938). R. Kilgour, *The Bible Throughout the World* (1939). E. E. Flack, B. M. Metzger, *et al.*, *The Text, Canon, and Principal Versions of the Bible* (articles reprinted from *Twentieth Century Encyclopedia of Religious Knowledge;* 1956).

Dutch (and Flemish) versions: I. Le Long, *Boek-zaal der Nederduytsche Bybels* (1732; 2nd ed., 1764). H. van Druten, *Geschiedenis der Nederlandsche Bijbelvertaling* (2 vols.; 1895-1905). C. C. De Bruin, *De Statenbijbel en zijn voorgangers* (1937).

French versions: E. Reuss, "Fragments littéraires et critiques relatifs à l'histoire de la Bible française," *RTP*, vols. II, IV-VI, XIV; N. S., III-V (1851-67). G. Strümpell, *Die ersten Bibelübersetzungen der Franzosen, 1100-1300* (1872). S. Berger, *La Bible française au moyen âge* (1884); and several important articles in *Romania*, vol. XIII (1889). D. Lortsch, *Histoire de la Bible en France* (1910). A. Malo, "Traduction catholique de la Bible au Canada," *Culture*, XII (1952), 231-40. E. P. Arbez, "French Language Translations," *Catholic Biblical Quarterly*, XVII (1955), 76-87.

German versions: J. J. Mezger, *Geschichte der Bibelübersetzungen in der schweizerischen reformierten Kirche* (1876). W. Walther, *Die deutsche Bibelübersetzung des Mittelalters* (3 vols.; 1889-91). W. Kurrelmeyer, *Die erste deutsche Bibel* ("Bibliothek des litterarischen Vereins in Stuttgart"; 10 vols.; 1904-15). J. M. Reu, *Luther's German Bible* (1934). M. Buber and F. Rosenzweig, *Die Schrift und ihre Verdeutschung* (1936). H. Rost, *Die Bibel im Mittelalter* (1939). J. C. Gasser, *Die Neue Züricher Bibelübersetzung: Ein historischer Rückblick* (1945). W. Michaelis, *Übersetzungen, Konkordanzen und konkordante Übersetzung des Neuen Testaments* (1947). G. Eis, *Frühneuhochdeutsche Bibelübersetzungen: Texte von 1400-1600* (1949).

Greek (modern) versions: E. Legrand, *Bibliographie hellénique, ou description raisonnée des ouvrages publiés en grec par des Grecs* (1885-1903).

Hungarian versions: F. Verseghi, *Dissertatio de versione Hungarica scripturae sacrae* (1882). B. Vasady, ed., *Károlyi Emlékkönyv: A vizsolyi biblia megjelenésének háromszázötvenedik évfordulójára* (1940). K. Karner, "Die Bemühungen um einen zeitgemässen ungarischen Bibeltext," *ZST*, XVIII (1941), 28-32. L. M. Pákozdy, "The New Revision of the Hungarian Bible," *Bulletin of the United Bible Societies*, No. 6 (1951), pp. 11-15.

Italian versions: S. Berger, "La Bible Italienne au moyen âge," *Romania*, XXIII (1894), 358 ff. J. Carini, *Le Versione della Biblia in volgari italiano* (1894). E. P. Arbez, "Modern Translations of the OT," *Catholic Biblical Quarterly*, XVI (1954), 455-57.

Portuguese versions: C. Michaëlis de Vasconcellos and S. Berger, in *Romania*, XXVIII (1899), 543-67. G. L. Santos, *A Biblia em Portugal* (1906).

Danish (and Norwegian) versions: C. Molbech, *Bidrag til en historie af de Danske Bibeloversaettelser* (1840). C. W. Bruun, *Biblioteca Danica* (1872). P. Otzen, *Hvorledes danskerne fik deres Bibler* (1949). B. Molde, ed., *Bidrag till den Danske Bibels Historie: Festskrift in Anledning af den Danske Bibels 400 Aars Jubilaeum* (1950); *Källorna till Christian III:s bibel 1550: Textfilologiska studier i reformationstidens danska bibelöversättningar* (1950). E. Mollard, *Norske og danske Bibeloversettelser brukt i Norge* (1951). P. H. Vogel, "Dänische und norwegische Bibelübersetzungen seit der Reformation," *Internationale kirchliche Zeitschrift*, XLIV (1954), 235-40.

Icelandic versions: J. Belsheim, *Af Bibelen i Norge og paa Island i Middelalderen* (1884).

Swedish versions: E. Eidem, *Vår svenska Bibel* (1923). R. Gyllenberg, *Våra fädars bibel 1541-1941: Minneskrift utgiven av teologiska fakulteten vid Åbo akademi* (1941); *Festskrift utgiven av teologiska fakulteten i Uppsala 1941 till 400-årsminnet av bibelns utgivande paa svenska* (1941). J. Lindblom, *Psaltaren 1560 (Studier till 1541 års bibel;* 1943). G. Sjögren, *Om språket i de svenska bibelöversättningarna 1526-1541* (1949). Å. V. Ström, "Ett nyfunnet provtryck till Gustav Adolfsbibeln: Tillika ett moment i en apokryf bibelboks historia," *Kyrkohistorisk Årsskrift*, LIII (1953), 134-47.

Slavic (Slavonic) versions: J. Bonfante and B. M. Metzger, "The Old Slavic Version of the Gospel According to Luke," *JBL*, LXXIII (1954), 217-36 (with a survey of previous literature).

Polish versions: S. Zwolski, *De Bibliis polonicis quae usque ad initium saeculi XVII in lucem edita sunt* (1904). S. Kol, *Szymon Budny* (1956). P. Nober, "Elenchus biblicus polonus, 1940-1956," *Salmanticensis*, IV (1957), 667-95. L. Stephaniak, "Die polnischen Bibelübersetzungen," *NTS*, V (1959), 328-33.

Russian versions: E. Henderson, *Biblical Researches and Travel in Russia* (1826), pp. 69-136. L. J. M. Bebb, "The Russian Bible," *Church Quarterly Review*, XLI (1895), 203-25. I. A. Tchistovitch, *The History of the Translation of the Bible in the Russian Language* (in Russian; 1899). I. E. Evseev, *The Centenary of the Russian Translation of the Bible* (in Russian;

1916). Bp. Cassian, "The Revision of the Russian Translation of the NT," *Bible Translator*, V (1954), 27-35. A. Osipoff, "Publication of the Russian Bible," *Bible Translator*, VII (1956), 56-65, 98-101. J. F. Clark, "The Russian Bible Society and the Bulgarians," *Harvard Slavic Studies*, III (1957), 67-103.

Spanish versions: G. Borrow, *The Bible in Spain* (1842). J. E. B. Mayor, *Spain, Portugal, and the Bible* (1895). B. F. Stockwell, *Prefacios a las biblias castellanas del siglo XVI* (1939). J. Llamas, *Biblia medieval romanceada Judía-Cristiana; Versión del Antiguo Testamento en el siglo XIV, sobre los textos hebreos y latinos* (2 vols.; 1950, 1955).   B. M. METZGER

VESPASIAN vĕs pā′zhĭ ən, —zhən. Titus Flavius Vespasianus, Roman emperor (A.D. 69-79), founder of the Flavian Dynasty. He was born into a prosperous but undistinguished Italian moneylending family on November 17, A.D. 9. Passing through the normal equestrian offices, he became praetor in the reign of Caligula, commanded a legion under Claudius, and became *consul suffectus* in 51. *Ca.* a dozen years later he was proconsul of Africa, and in 66 accompanied Nero to Greece.

Vespasian was given command of three legions in order to suppress the Jewish Revolt, and he set about his task slowly and systematically. After Nero's murder, while Otho and Vitellius were contending for power, Vespasian came to believe that he himself should become emperor. The Jewish historian Josephus had already predicted this event (War III.viii.9); and on July 1, 69, the ex-Jew Tiberius Julius Alexander, nephew of Philo and prefect of Egypt, had his legions swear allegiance to Vespasian. The emperor-designate left the Jewish war to his son Titus and proceeded in leisurely fashion to Rome, winning popular support along the way and arriving in September, 70. Meanwhile Titus had taken Jerusalem, and in the early summer of 71 he joined his father at Rome, where they celebrated a joint triumph. Vespasian made Titus his partner in the imperial government, denying his other son, Domitian, any real power.

An excellent administrator, he recognized Rome's need for financial stability and therefore increased taxes—a small price to pay for order after anarchy. His way of life was simple and he treated the notion of deification with ridicule; when his last illness began, he said, "Unfortunately I suppose I am becoming a god." He died on June 24, 79, and was succeeded by Titus. The Senate consecrated him without hesitation.

In his reign, as far as we know, there were no persecutions of either Jews or Christians, though he expelled Cynic and Stoic philosophers from Rome because of their seditious statements. Josephus' devotion to him doubtless improved the position of Jews in the Empire, and Jewish Christians had been fortunate to leave Jerusalem on the outbreak of the revolt. It is only in Christian legend that we hear of Vespasian's seeking to have all the members of the family of David killed (Euseb. Hist. III.10.12).

On the other hand, he retained Palestine as part of the imperial estate, and the head tax of two drachmas, previously paid to the temple by adult male Jews, was transferred to the temple of Jupiter Capitolinus.

Since he became emperor as a result of crisis and civil war, he tried to provide a new solution for the problem of the succession, but it lasted only a genera-tion because of Domitian's despotism. Vespasian's real contribution was conservative: he saved the Empire at a time when it seemed to be perishing.

Bibliography. Josephus *Jewish War;* M. P. Charlesworth, *Cambridge Ancient History,* vol. XI (1936); R. L. James, *Oxford Classical Dictionary* (1949).   R. M. GRANT

VESSELS. Hollow utensils used for holding any sub-stance, dry or liquid. In Bible times pottery was the most common material so used, followed in turn by baskets, metalware, leather material, cloth bags, and wooden containers. The archaeologist seldom finds anything but pottery. The tombs around Jericho have furnished the best finds in basketry, leather, cloth, and wood. Metal would have lived through, but it was one of the first objects plundered in war, and tomb robbers soon removed metalware from the graves. The Hebrew term for vessels of all kinds is כְּלִי; the NT does not have a similar broad term.

1. Leather, cloth, wood, basketry. Vessels made of these materials were necessities for nomadic peo-ples, for pottery was too fragile and metal wares were too expensive. Only a small percentage of Bible people were nomads. For a sedentary people, as most of the Israelites were, leather's chief uses as a vessel were: (*a*) the leather bucket with which water was drawn from the well, (*b*) the waterskin in which it was carried, (*c*) the wineskin, and (*d*) the butter churn. The main use of cloth was the bag, which served primarily in transportation rather than storage. Cloth was not only expensive, but also easily subject to accident. The modern reader of the Bible seldom realizes how expensive cloth was in those days. Grain would be transported in sacks but not stored in them. Wood was used far less often than now, because of the expense of working it. The basket was a good, cheap container for many mate-rials and could be used both for transportation and for storage.

2. Ceramic and metal wares. Pottery* was in most cases the best container. (For a detailed description of pottery vessels, *see* POTTERY.) It is much harder to identify metal vessels with accuracy than it is to identify ceramicware. The largest metal bowl used in sacrifice was the אַגָּן, "basin" (Exod. 24:6; KJV "bason"). A related bowl was the מִזְרָק, also "basin." It came in copper (Exod. 27:3; KJV "bason"), silver (Num. 7:13; KJV "bowl"), and gold (II Chr. 4:8; KJV "bason"). אַגַרְטָל (Ezra 1:9; RSV "basin"; KJV "charger") is a postexilic synonym for מִזְרָק. The כְּפוֹר, which came in silver and gold (I Chr. 28:17; Ezra 1:10; 8:27; RSV "bowl"; KJV "bason"), seems to have been a smaller bowl in temple usage. This category included the rarest of all metal vessels men-tioned in the Bible—namely, those made of brass (Ezra 8:27; RSV "bronze"; KJV "copper"). This passage is one of the earliest references to this copper-zinc alloy that we have anywhere in litera-ture. יָע (SHOVEL; Exod. 38:3 ff; I Kings 7:40, 45, etc.) seems also to have been a member of the bowl family, but it cannot be definitely placed. In general, metal cooking pots and metal cups bear much the same names as their ceramic counterparts (*see* POTTERY). A number of metal vessels were used only in the sacrificial system (*see* SACRIFICES AND OFFER-

Courtesy of the Palestine Archaeological Museum, Jerusalem, Jordan

14. A basalt tripod for grinding cereals, from Palestine

Courtesy of the University Museum of the University of Pennsylvania

15. A variety of stone vessels, from the Pre-dynastic period and the Old Kingdom (before 2280 B.C.)

INGS). For a detailed vocabulary of metalware, see *BASOR* Supplementary Studies, nos. 5-6. Fig. POT 63.

3. Stoneware. Before metals came into common use for household dishes, some of the most expensive ones were made of stone.* The Egyptians were the best craftsmen in this field.* As soon as metal became cheap, however, it replaced stone in most instances. Alabaster, nevertheless, was so beautiful a stone that it continued to be the container of the finest-grade perfumes (Matt. 26:7). Glass was only coming into use by NT times. Large stone vats were used in the dyeing industry in OT times. John 2:6 speaks of large stone jars for purification purposes. For various kinds of vessels, *see* BASIN; BOWL; CALDRON; CRUSE; FLAGON; FLASK; GOBLET; POTTERY; etc. Figs. VES 14-15.   J. L. KELSO

VESTIBULE [אוּלָם, אֻלָם, אֵילָם, that which is in front, *see* 1 *below;* מִסְדְּרוֹן, *perhaps* pillared hall, balustrade, *see* 2 *below*]. **1.** A room at one end of a structure, serving as an entry room. The term is used once (I Kings 7:6; "porch") of such a room in Solomon's Hall of Pillars (*see* HALL). Elsewhere it is always as-sociated with the TEMPLE in Jerusalem. It is used of the first room in the main building of the temple of Solomon (I Kings 6:3; 7:12, 19, 21; I Chr. 28:11; II Chr. 3:4; 8:12; 15:8; 29:7, 17), Ezekiel (Ezek. 40:48-49; 41:15, 25-26), and Zerubbabel (Joel 2:17). The dimensions of the vestibule of Solomon's temple are given as 20 by 10 cubits (*ca.* 30 by 15 feet), with the height presumably 30 cubits (*ca.* 45 feet), as already stated of the temple as a whole (I Kings 6:2-3). How-ever, II Chr. 3:4 MT gives the height as 120 cubits (*ca.* 180 feet), for which the LXX and the Syr. have 20 cubits. Ezekiel's measurements, which are said to be in "long cubits, each being a cubit and a handbreadth in length" (Ezek. 40:5), are 20 by 12 (vs. 49 LXX; MT has 11). Each of the gates to the outer court of Ezekiel's temple is also described as having a vestibule at its inner end measuring 20 by 8 cubits (vss. 7-26), while each of the gates to the inner court had a vestibule at its outer end measuring 25 by 5 cubits (vss. 29-37). One of these contained four tables where the animals for the offerings were to be slaughtered, as well as the door to a room where the offerings were to be washed (vss. 38-39); and additional tables were outside the vestibule of the N gate (vs. 40). The prince was to enter for sacrifice by way of the vestibule of the E gate (44:3; 46:2, 8).

2. An antechamber(?) outside the roof chamber of the palace of Eglon king of Moab (Judg. 3:23).

E. M. GOOD

VESTMENTS. Translation of three related Hebrew words, derived from לבש, "to put on": לבוש and מלבוש (II Kings 10:22) referring to special dress of devotees of Baal; מלבשים (lit. "attired"; Ezra 3:10) to the clothing of priests. *See also* DRESS AND ORNAMENTS.

J. M. MYERS

VIAL. 1. The container (פך) from which Samuel anointed Saul (I Sam. 10:11). The same word is translated "flask" (KJV "box") in the account of the anointing of Jehu (II Kings 9:1, 3). It denotes the small Hebrew perfume juglet. *See* POTTERY § 3*b*.

2. KJV translation of φιάλη (Rev. 5:8; 15:7; 16:1-3, 17; 17:1; 21:9). The Greek word means a broad shallow cup or "bowl" (RSV). *See* POTTERY § 3*a*.

J. L. KELSO

VICES. *See* LISTS, ETHICAL.

VILLAGE. A collection of dwelling places and other assorted buildings having a simpler organization and administration than a CITY. In the OT the distinction between city and village is generally maintained (Lev. 25:29, 31; Deut. 3:5; I Sam. 6:18; I Chr. 27:25). The city was larger and walled. The village was unwalled, and in it the simple one-room house prevailed. Mud huts are still common in villages of the Near East, and grass huts are found in the Arabian Peninsula. The village did not have moats, ramparts, or a strong defense (Ezek. 38:11). It was an open town (Esth. 9:19). It probably had a guest house, but no temple. In Talmudic times a village was defined as a place without a synagogue. The NT did not keep this religious differentiation (Mark 1:38-39), but the OT duality persists in the Synoptics (Matt. 9:35; 10:11; Mark 6:56; Luke 8:1; 13:22).

In biblical times, especially in the OT, even the city was small. Megiddo and Jericho covered *ca.* twelve to thirteen acres, Lachish fifteen, and Debir less than eight. Jerusalem was a walled city, yet "bound firmly together" (Ps. 122:3). Perhaps it could be said that Israel inherited or captured its cities, but established its own villages in the hill country during the Conquest.

A village could grow over the years. Thus a village might be fortified (I Sam. 23:7). The size varied perhaps with the general security of the times. In years of peace, the people did not hesitate to live outside the fortified city walls. The growth of a village into a city is perhaps reflected in the proper names CAPERNAUM ("village of Nahum") and HAZAR-ADDAR ("village of Addar"). BETHLEHEM is called both a city (πόλις; Luke 2:4) and a village (κώμη; John 7:42). A destroyed city could become a village (Zech. 2:4). Many of the villages in Galilee in NT times were walled.

Often the village was dependent upon the city for protection and certain economic and political matters. This is perhaps indicated by the word בת, "daughter." In such instances jurisdiction of the village was controlled by the city-state; however, the council of elders was the local court and board. This dependency is evident in the distribution of the land under Joshua; 114 cities are listed as all allotted to Judah "with their villages" (Josh. 15:32-62; cf. 18:24, 28; I Chr. 6:54 ff; etc.).

Villages were close to the city wall (perhaps even built against the wall, as in medieval times in Europe). They can be likened to modern city suburbs (note, however, the KJV use of "suburb" for "open field" or PASTURE; e.g., Lev. 25:34). Often city dwellers would go out into villages for recreation and rest (Song of S. 7:11). It is possible that the village outside the wall may be later have been walled in, as some double-walled towns suggest. A group of villages may indicate a district or region —e.g., Amorite villages (Num. 21:32), those of Caesarea Philippi (Mark 8:27), and those of the Samaritans (Acts 8:25). Many cities are spoken of as having such villages: Beth-shean (Josh. 17:11; Judg. 1:27), Shechem (I Chr. 7:28), Gezer (7:28), Gath (18:1), Dor (7:29), Taanach (7:29), Megiddo (7:29), Rabbah (Jer. 49:2), Heshbon (Num. 21:25; Judg. 11:26), etc. Beth-saida, Bethany, Emmaus, are villages in the NT.

The villages were mainly involved in AGRICULTURE. The surrounding lands were variously shared by the inhabitants of the village. It was thus a farming center and a gathering place for shepherds in the winter. One or more threshing floors were the common property of the village. The farmers and shepherds were often away from the village in the spring and summer. The Near East still knows this seasonal alternation. The pasture land is specifically noted as belonging to the village in I Chr. 6:54 ff.

Nomadic enclosures or encampments are called villages. So the circle of tents of the Ishmaelites (Gen. 25:16; cf. Kedar in Isa. 42:11) make up a village. Such an encampment is clearly intended by the poetic parallelism in Ps. 69:25. The proper name HAVVOTH-JAIR suggests a similar collection of tents in a temporary camp (Num. 32:41).

Out of the villages came many great men in Israel. Saul and David were both villagers. The peasant was not the least in Israel (Judg. 5:11).

C. U. WOLF

VINDICATE. The translation of several Hebrew and Greek words used when the text emphasizes the successful establishment of a man's cause as just. The KJV uses "judge," "justify." *See* REDEEM; JUDGMENT; JUSTIFICATION.

VINE, VINEYARD. Along with the olive and fig trees, the grapevine is one of the most characteristic plants of Palestine. The three are mentioned together in Jotham's fable (Judg. 9:8-13), and elsewhere they symbolize the fruit of the land (cf. Josh. 24:13; I Sam. 8:14; II Kings 5:26; Jer. 5:17; 40:10; Hos. 2:12—H 2:14). In biblical times many individuals had no other financial resources than their vineyards; this in part accounts for Naboth's refusal to sell his vineyard to Ahab (I Kings 21:1-4).

1. Terminology of viticulture. The usual Hebrew word for "vine" is גפן, and the standard Greek term is ἄμπελος. Although these usually denote the grapevine, other vines were also known. Melons and cucumbers are mentioned in Num. 11:5, and gourds are specifically associated with vines in II Kings 4:39. Similarly, although כרם usually means "vineyard" (ἀμπελών), it may also refer to a garden in general; Ahab wanted Naboth's vineyard so that he could plant a vegetable garden (I Kings 21:2). Other terms used are: (*a*) שריג, "tendril," from the root שרג, "to interweave"; (*b*) שורק or שרקה, "choice vine," a superior vine producing grapes with a rich, dark hue; and (*c*) בצר, "to gather grapes." For the terms used for grapes, *see* § 3*e below.*

2. Antiquity of viticulture. The J source presents Noah as the father of viticulture (Gen. 9:20), and thus preserves the tradition that the growing of grapevines reaches back to the origins of civilization.

Courtesy of the Cairo Museum; photo courtesy of the Metropolitan Museum of Art

16. Gathering of grapes from an arbor, treading of grapes, and storing of wine in jars; from an Egyptian wall painting in tomb of Nakht at Thebes (fifteenth century B.C.)

Indeed, there are references to viticulture from the reign of Gudea, and the vine was cultivated in predynastic Egypt. Egyptian military inscriptions from the Old Empire refer to the vine in Palestine, and Sinuhe tells of the grapes of Syria-Palestine. Although the above-mentioned story of Noah implies that the vine was imported to Palestine from Armenia, it is probable that it had a spontaneous origin in many regions. However this may be, it is certain that viticulture is one of the oldest forms of AGRICULTURE. Fig. VIN 16.

3. Planting of vineyards. Isaiah provides us with a detailed description of the planting of a vineyard (Isa. 5:1-6), and much of the following material is derived from this account.

a. Location. The climate of Palestine is particularly well suited for the growing of vines. There is enough heat, but not too much; the rainfall, although scanty in certain areas, is generally sufficient. Ordinarily vineyards were planted on hills, since this land was less used for cereal crops (cf. Ps. 80:10—H 80:11; Isa. 5:1: "on a very fertile hill"; Jer. 31:5; Amos 9:13). But occasionally flat land was used, particularly the Philistine plain. Although vineyards were usually to be found in the open country, they were sometimes attached to houses; Naboth's vineyard was beside Ahab's palace (I Kings 21:1).

b. Preparation of ground. Before the vines themselves could be planted, a careful preparation of the plot was necessary. The larger stones were cleared away, and the first plowing was done. Furthermore, every vineyard was provided with a stone wall or HEDGE, to protect the vines from foxes (Song of S. 2:15), boars (Ps. 80:13—H 80:14), and thieves (Jer. 49:9). Finally, each vineyard had a stone watchtower (Isa. 5:2; *see* TOWER). During the vintage season the vinedressers and the guardians of the fruit lived in these towers; sometimes the ground floor was used for a wine press or a stable.

c. Planting of vines. The usual method of planting vines was to place them in rows from eight to ten feet apart. The stems were allowed to trail on the ground, but the clusters of grapes were propped up with forked sticks. Occasionally, however, the vine was allowed to climb a nearby tree; Ezekiel refers to a vine which

> towered aloft
>   among the thick boughs;
> it was seen in its height
>   with the mass of its branches
>   (Ezek. 19:11).

It was therefore possible for a man to sit under his vine (I Kings 4:25—H 5:5). Artificial trellises were not used until Roman times.

d. Pruning. After the vine had budded and the blossoms had become ripening grapes, the vinedresser cut off the nonbearing branches (Isa. 18:5; cf. John 15:2). The result was that the remaining branches were stronger and thus produced more fruit.

e. Harvesting of grapes. Although the grapes began to ripen toward the end of July, the actual harvest did not take place until August or September. The early grapes (בסר) were, of course, quite sour and set the teeth on edge (Jer. 31:29-30; Ezek. 18:2). The fully ripe grapes (ענבים) were either: (*a*) eaten in their natural state, (*b*) dried and made into RAISINS, (*c*) boiled down into a thick grape syrup (*see* HONEY), or (*d*) made into WINE. There is no evidence for the normal yield of a vineyard; we are merely told that as a result of Yahweh's anger "ten acres of vineyard shall yield but one bath [of wine]" (Isa. 5:10). A bath was approximately six gallons. According to Isaiah, each vine was worth a shekel.

4. Use of vineyards. Most vineyards were cultivated either by the owners themselves or by hired laborers (Matt. 20:1-16). But it was also a common practice for a large landowner to rent out his vineyards to a tenant (Song of S. 8:11; Matt. 21:33-43 and parallels). The owner would, of course, receive a share of the harvest (Matt. 21:34). Furthermore, in OT times various laws governed the use of vineyards. The owner was not allowed to reap a vineyard twice; rather, the gleanings were to be left for resident aliens, widows, and orphans (Lev. 19:10; Deut. 24:21). Vineyards were to lie fallow in the sabbath year (Exod. 23:10-11; Lev. 25:3-5), and were not to be sown with other seeds (Deut. 22:9); the latter rule was apparently not enforced in NT times, however, since we read of a man who had a fig tree planted in his vineyard (Luke 13:6). The importance of a vineyard is seen in the law that he who has planted one is exempt from military service (Deut. 20:6).

5. "Vine" and "vineyard" in biblical imagery. Viticulture has provided an abundant store of images in both the OT and the NT.

a. In the OT. "Vine" and "vineyard" are often used as symbols of Israel. She was brought out of Egypt and planted by Yahweh (Ps. 80:8-13—H 80:9-14); although she was a "choice vine" (*see* § 1 *above*), she became a "wild vine" (Jer. 2:21; cf. Isa. 5:1-7; Hos. 10:1). Just as the "wood of the vine" is useful only as fuel, so the inhabitants of Jerusalem will be destroyed (Ezek. 15; cf. 19:10-14). Similarly an individual can be referred to as a vine. Ezekiel (17:1-8) propounds an allegory in which the "seed of the land" (Zedekiah) is planted by a "great eagle" (Nebuchadrezzar) and grows up to be a "spreading vine." However, it is transplanted by another eagle (Hophra). Again, the wife of one who fears Yahweh will be like a fruitful vine (Ps. 128:3).

Naturally an abundance of vines and vineyards is an expression of Yahweh's favor. Forgiven Israel will be given vineyards (Hos. 2:15—H 2:17), and in the days to come "the treader of grapes [shall overtake] him who sows the seed" (Amos 9:13). Of course, the vineyards will yield miraculous fruit in the eschatological age; according to the Apocalypse of Baruch, each vine will have 1,000 branches, each branch will produce 1,000 clusters, each cluster will contain 1,000 grapes, and each grape will give 120 gallons of wine (29:5). Similarly grapes are used in metaphorical expressions. Yahweh found Israel "like grapes in the wilderness" (Hos. 9:10), and the remnant is compared to a cluster of grapes (Isa. 65:8).

b. In the NT. Jesus often mentions vineyards in his parables. He compares the kingdom to a vineyard for which its owner hired laborers; some worked all day, and some only a short time, but all received the same pay (Matt. 20:1-16). Those who will enter the kingdom are also compared to the son who first refused to work in his father's vineyard but then repented and went (Matt. 21:28-32). And the Jews are symbolized by wicked tenants of a vineyard who beat those sent by the owner (God) to collect some of the fruit; finally they killed even the owner's son (Christ) in order to gain control of the vineyard. Naturally the tenants were put to death and the vineyard was rented to others (the Christians; Matt. 21:33-43; Mark 12:1-11; Luke 20:9-17).

Of even greater significance, however, is Jesus' description of himself as the "true vine" and his Father as the vinedresser (John 15:1-11). Jesus is probably comparing himself to the vine of the Jews, which has become degenerate (*see* § 5a *above*). The main point, however, is that the Christian must "abide in [Christ]" if he is to bear the fruit of faith; otherwise he will be cast aside. Furthermore, the intimate bond between Christ and the church is strongly emphasized: "I am the vine, you are the branches."

Bibliography. L. Anderlind, "Die Rebe in Syrien, insbesondere Palästina," *ZDPV,* XI (1888), 160-77; V. Zapletal, *Der Wein in der Bibel,* Bibl. Stud., XX.1 (1920), pp. 103-6. E. Busse, *Der Wein im Kult des ATs,* Freiburger Theologische Studien 29 (1922); H. F. Lutz, *Viticulture and Brewing in the Ancient Orient* (1922); J. Döller, "Der Wein in Bibel und Talmud,"·*Bibl.,* IV (1923), 143-67, 267-99; A. C. Bouquet, *Everyday Life in NT Times* (1954), p. 78; R. J. Forbes, *Studies in Ancient Technology,* III (1955), 70-78; E. W. Heaton, *Everyday Life in OT Times* (1956). See also the commentaries on John 15.

J. F. Ross

VINE OF SODOM [סדם גפן; ἄμπελος Σοδόμων]. A vine with bitter clusters of poisonous grapes, to which Moses compares Israel (Deut. 32:32). Ancient and modern writers describe an orange-colored fruit which, because of its black, powdery interior, was taken as indicative of the destruction of the "cities of the Valley." *See* APPLE.

Bibliography. J. P. Harland, "Sodom and Gomorrah," *BA,* V (1943), 49-52.   J. P. HARLAND

VINEDRESSER. *See* FARMER.

VINEGAR [חמץ, *from the root* to be sour; ὄξος, *related to the adjective* ὀξύς, sharp (of taste)]. In biblical times vinegar was most commonly procured from grape WINE which had gone sour or had been overfermented (Num. 6:3; KJV "vinegar of wine"; however, this passage may also refer to "vinegar of STRONG DRINK"). It was also prepared by pouring water over the skins and stalks of grapes left over after the juice was pressed out (*see* WINE § 2) and allowing the whole to ferment.

When diluted, vinegar was regarded as a refreshing drink. It provoked thirst, however; the psalmist complains that his enemies gave him "poison for food, and . . . vinegar to drink" (Ps. 69:21—H 69:22). More commonly it was used as a condiment, particularly as a seasoning. Thus Boaz invites Ruth to "dip [her] morsel [of bread] in the vinegar" (Ruth 2:14 KJV; RSV "wine"; חמץ). Vinegar was, of course, forbidden to the Nazirites because of its association with wine and strong drink. *See* NAZIRITE.

The acrid qualities of vinegar are mentioned in Proverbs. It stings when poured on a wound (25:20, following the LXX; KJV "upon nitre"), and its effect upon the teeth is like that of smoke upon the eyes (10:26).

In the NT vinegar is mentioned only in connection with the CRUCIFIXION. In all four gospels (Matt. 27:48; Mark 15:36; Luke 23:36; John 19:29-30) we read that Jesus was offered vinegar shortly before his death. The evangelists do not cite the OT in this connection, but the event was probably interpreted as a fulfilment of Ps. 69:21—H 69:22 (*see above*). Possibly, however, the drink was the Roman *posca,* made of vinegar, water, and egg, a customary drink of soldiers and slaves; Luke specifically mentions "soldiers." In this case the act would be one of mercy.

According to Matt. 27:34 KJV, Jesus was offered "vinegar . . . mingled with GALL" just before the Crucifixion. This was intended as a drug. The RSV, however, follows the earlier MSS and reads "wine" instead of "vinegar." *See* DRINK.

Bibliography. V. Zapletal, *Der Wein in der Bibel,* Bibl. Stud., XX.1 (1920), p. 37; R. P. Forbes, *Studies in Ancient Technology,* III (1955), 78.   J. F. Ross

VINEYARDS, PLAIN OF THE. KJV translation of אבל כרמים (RSV ABEL-KERAMIN).

VIOL vī'əl. *See* MUSICAL INSTRUMENTS §§ B4*c*, B5*b*.

VIOLET [תכלת; LXX ὑάκινθον] (Jer. 10:9); KJV BLUE. A purple-blue color obtained from a Mediterranean mussel. Elsewhere in the OT the translation of תכלת (nearly fifty references) is "blue." The exact shade is uncertain. *See* BLUE; COLORS.

C. L. WICKWIRE

VIPER [אפעה (Job 20:16; Isa. 30:6; 59:5), *cf.* Arab. *'af'ay,* viper, LXX (*three different words*) snake; עכשוב (Ps. 140:3—H 140:4; KJV ADDER), *in Jewish tradition* spider (*cf.* עכביש, spider), *followed by Bodenheimer* (*see* FAUNA § C), LXX ASP (*so also Paul in* Rom. 3:13); שפיפן (Gen. 49:17; KJV ADDER), *cf.* Akkad. *šeppu,* snake, viper, Arab. *shipp* (Lane 1368), snake, LXX LYING (*verb*); ἔχιδνα (Matt. 3:7, etc.), *cf.* ἔχις, viper]. Any of a family of poisonous snakes (*Viperidae*), of which the Old World vipers (*Viperinae*) are the most representative.

The meanings of the three Hebrew words cited above are not certain. That עכשוב and שפיפן are used in parallel constructions with נחש, "serpent," appears to indicate that both point to some variety of snake, but more particular identification is hazardous. The desert saw viper (*Echis colorata*) and the common Palestine viper (*Vipera palaestinae*) are found in the biblical lands, as is the horned viper (*Cerastes cerastes cornutus*), the latter being known to attack even horses (*cf.* Gen. 49:17; Tristram, *Natural History of the Bible,* pp. 273-74). The viper of Acts 28:3 was probably the *Vipera aspis* of the Mediterranean region. For "viper" as a term of reproach (Matt. 3:7, etc.), *cf.* Aeschylus *Choëphoroe* 994; Euripides *Ion* 1262; Sophocles *Antigone* 531. For Rabbi Eliezer's favorable comparison of the Jewish sages with jackals, scorpions, and serpents, see M. Ab. 2.10.

W. S. McCULLOUGH

*VIRGIN [בתולה; παρθένος]. One who has had no sexual intercourse. The word usually refers to a woman.

1. Terminology
2. The identification of a virgin
3. The value of a virgin
4. The protection of virgins
5. A unique term for "virgin"
6. "Virgin" applied to communities
Bibliography

1. Terminology. The word בתולה, translated "virgin," may derive from a Semitic root בתל, which

in Arabic means "sever," "separate." These words signify that an individual has arrived at the age when he or she is capable of sex relations but has not yet had this experience. The Greek equivalent for this Hebrew word is παρθένος, also translated "virgin." Its use in the NT supports the meaning indicated by the Hebrew term. E.g., before Joseph and Mary "came together she was found to be with child"; being a virgin (Matt. 1:18), she had had no intercourse with a man (vss. 18-25). The Greek word is translated "unmarried" in I Cor. 7:25 (cf. vss. 28, 34). Again, applied to men, it describes those who are chaste because they "have not defiled themselves with women"—i.e., have not had intercourse with them (Rev. 14:4*a*).

Derived from the Semitic root עלם, perhaps meaning "be mature sexually," the word עלמה appears several times in the OT. In most instances it is used of young women who are ready for sexual relations and for reproduction, although it does not reveal whether or not they are virgins. In one case, however, the translation "virgin" appears in the LXX (Isa. 7:14). In the masculine gender, the word עלם usually means "youth" and fails to reveal whether there has been previous sexual experience (I Sam. 20:22; cf. 17:42).

2. The identification of a virgin. Proof of virginity may be demanded before the consummation of a MARRIAGE. If the bridegroom becomes suspicious, he may require her parents to exhibit suitable evidence that the bride is in fact a virgin (Deut. 22:13-21). A root which signifies both "pierce" and "profane" in the Hebrew is used (Lev. 19:29; 21:7, 14) in such a way as to suggest that the "piercing" is the result of sexual intercourse with a virgin. If she is unpierced, then she is obviously still a virgin. There was public evidence of virginity. Her garb probably showed that she had such a status. Tamar, raped by her brother Amnon (II Sam. 13:2-19), was a virgin (vs. 2*b*). The writer of the story adds that "she was wearing a long robe with sleeves; for thus were the virgin daughters of the king clad of old" (vs. 18*a*). Josephus says of this story that virgins in ancient times wore loose coats tied at the hands and reaching down to the ankles, so that their long, tight-fitting inner garment might not be seen (Antiq. VII. viii; *see* DRESS AND ORNAMENTS § B2). It may be that the veil was another means of identifying a virgin. When Rebekah the virgin (Gen. 24:16) saw Isaac, she took a veil and covered herself (vs. 65). This act may have simply been one of conformity to the custom which forbade a woman to show her face to a stranger, however.

3. The value of a virgin. In justifying his righteousness on the basis of the ideals by which he has lived, Job declares that he has avoided looking "upon a virgin" (31:1). A virgin was also a likely candidate for royal honors, as seen in the story of Esther. A virgin's greatest value, however, was her usefulness as a producer of children, especially sons who could carry on their father's name and give him a continued existence. For this purpose the full use of a woman's unimpaired sexuality was imperative. To carry on the line of Abraham, the story of Isaac's marriage stresses the fact that Rebekah was a virgin

(Gen. 24:16). His daughter's virginity was important to the father, and if it was lost, the offender must pay him the marriage price and make her his wife (Exod. 22:16). If a man falsely swore that his bride was not a virgin, he must pay the father one hundred shekels of silver and marry the woman, "because he has brought an evil name upon a virgin of Israel" (Deut. 22:19). The importance of virgins to the life of the community is underscored when destruction overtakes a population in a time of disaster. Virgins, together with young men, were to be destroyed by the wrath of God (Deut. 32:25). On the other hand, because of their value, conquerors did not kill virgins, although the other women were destroyed (Num. 31:17-18).

4. The protection of virgins. It was the duty of the family, especially the parents, to protect the virginity of their daughter. Legislation showing this may be noted: The father is to be compensated when a charge of unchastity against a daughter is not sustained; but, if it is sustained, the daughter shall be stoned to death at the door of her father's house (Deut. 22:19-21). If a man seizes and lies with an unbetrothed virgin and they are caught, the man must pay the father fifty shekels of silver (vss. 28-29). If a man seduces an unbetrothed virgin, he must pay the bride price to the father and marry her. If her father does not consent to this marriage, the guilty party must nonetheless pay the marriage present (Exod. 22:16-17).

While protected because of their value to their families and to society, virgins in biblical times were given considerable freedom. A parable about a marriage feast includes several allusions to virgins who prepare to meet the bridegroom (Matt. 25:1, 7, 11). In the day of restoration "the maidens [virgins] [shall] rejoice in the dance" (Jer. 31:13).

5. A unique term for "virgin." Isa. 7:14 reads in part: "Behold, a young woman [עלמה] shall conceive and bear a son, and shall call his name Immanuel" (for the root of this Hebrew term, see § 1 *above*). The LXX reads "virgin" (παρθένος), as does also the quotation of this passage in Matt. 1:23. An examination of the occurrences of עלמה in the OT does not remove the possibility of the meaning "virgin." E.g., Abraham's servant speaks of the "young woman" who comes out to draw water as the one appointed to be the bride of his master's son (Gen. 24:43-44). From the context, it is certain that this עלמה is a virgin. To be a bride of Abraham's son would be inconceivable had she not been a virgin. Again, in the story of the infant Moses placed in a basket in the river, we read that "the girl" (Moses' sister) went to call his mother (Exod. 2:8). The sister is called עלמה. While there is no indication that she was not a virgin, the text does not directly affirm that she was.

"The way of a man with a maiden [עלמה]" is strange and wonderful (Prov. 30:18-19). In contrast to her, the writer names the way of an adulteress, who, of course, was not a virgin. In the Song of Songs "maidens," the ecstatic lover declares, love her beloved; and rightly so, she adds (1:3-4). The "darling of her mother," the writer of these love poems asserts, is observed and praised by maidens [עלמות], and by the queens and concubines also.

Finally, at Ugarit, the word *ĝlmt* is placed in parallelism with the word *btlt*, "virgin," precisely in a story of annunciation.

In none of these references is the meaning "virgin" precluded, although in none is it specifically affirmed. One authority connotes the meaning of "virgin" when he identifies the young woman in Isa. 7:14 as a supernatural woman, the birth of whose son would be an omen of a wonderful transformation (*see bibliography*). He adds that this meaning was sensed by the translators of the LXX when they used the Greek word for "virgin," παρθένος.

6. "Virgin" applied to communities. By far the most frequent use of the word "virgin" is in the Bible's figurative description of cities, nations, and communities. The usage "virgin daughter" occurs often. This phrase describes Jerusalem/Zion (II Kings 19:21; Isa. 37:22; Lam. 2:13); "my people" (Jer. 14:17); Judah (Lam. 1:15); Egypt (Jer. 46:11); Sidon (Isa. 23:12); and Babylon (Isa. 47:1). Without the word for "daughter," biblical writers speak of "the virgin Israel" (Jer. 18:13; 31:4*b*, 21; Amos 5:2). The word "virgin" is applied by Ignatius in his Letter to the Smyrnaeans to those women who are admitted to the church office of "widows," an office which is described in the NT as available to women sixty years of age or older and who have been married only once (I Tim. 5:9). The later order or community of virgins which appeared in the church may rest upon the practice disclosed in Acts 21:9, where we read that Philip the evangelist had four unmarried (virginal) daughters who prophesied. The Christian church is figuratively addressed by Paul as one who is betrothed to Christ "as a pure bride" (παρθένος ἁγνή; lit., "an undefiled virgin"; II Cor. 11:2).

See also VIRGIN BIRTH.

Bibliography. J. L. Burckhardt, *Notes on the Bedouins* (1830); E. J. Dingwall, *The Girdle of Chastity* (1931); S. Mowinckel, *He That Cometh* (1956), pp. 110 ff, 184-85: interpretation of Isa. 7:14.

See also bibliographies under MARRIAGE; SEX; WOMAN.

                         O. J. BAAB

VIRGIN, APOCALYPSES OF THE ə pŏk′ə lĭps ĭz. Two unrelated apocalypses, the one extant in Greek, the other in Ethiopic, in which the Virgin is shown the torments of the damned. Both writings are late and of but antiquarian interest.

In the Greek apocalypse the Virgin, in answer to her query as to the torments of hell, is conducted by Michael to see the torments of the wicked—a strange medley of unbelievers: those who did not worship the Trinity, wicked priests, nuns who did not arise at the entrance of the priest, Jews who crucified Jesus, those who denied baptism, sorcerers, and murderers. The Virgin is pained at the sight, entreats the saint to aid her in intercession, and is finally met by the Son, who appoints all subsequent days of Pentecost to be times of rest for the tormented.

The other apocalypse, now extant only in Ethiopic but not improbably composed in Greek and subsequently translated into Arabic and from Arabic to Ethiopic, is scarcely more than a plagiarized transcript of the central section (chs. 13–44) of the Apocalypse of Paul (*see* PAUL, APOCALYPSE OF). There are some alterations and several additions, especially having to do with the torments of nuns guilty of abortion and infanticide. The setting for this tasteless plagiarism is John's account of the story the Virgin had told him of what had recently happened to her as she had been praying at Golgotha. The Son had appeared and had promised to show her a great mystery. After the tour the Virgin asks: "Wilt thou not forgive them?" and receives the answer: "Yes, if they repent from their heart. But as for their pastors, who did not admonish them, their part shall be with Eli and Fola. Eli did not reprove his sons; Fola sold his daughters for an ox."

See also APOCRYPHA, NT.

Bibliography. A brief but more than adequate summary of these two tasteless writings is provided by M. R. James, *The Apocryphal NT* (1924), pp. 563-64. For the Greek text, see M. R. James, *Apoc. Anecdota* (1893), vol. I; for the Coptic, M. Chaine, *Corpus scriptorum christianorum orientalium* (1909), Series I, vol. I.

For special study: M. A. A. Jugie, "La mort et l'assomption de la Sainte Vierge," *Studi e Testi* (1944), p. 114.

M. S. ENSLIN

VIRGIN, ASSUMPTION OF THE. *See* ASSUMPTION OF THE VIRGIN.

*VIRGIN BIRTH.** The doctrine, based on the narratives in Matt. 1:18-25; Luke 1-2 and related passages in the Scriptures, that Jesus was miraculously conceived by the Holy Spirit and born of a virgin mother. Problems both literary and theological have been debated in early and modern controversy over this critical point.

The literary questions, rooted in the quotation of the annunciation formula of Isa. 7:14 in Matt. 1:23, are complicated by the parallels in the Ugaritic literature, as well as in the OT. Since the excavation of the Nikkal poem at Ras Shamra (UGARIT) in 1933, the following lines have produced a small literature: (a) 77:5: "a virgin [*bethulah*] will give birth"; (b) 77:7: "Lo, a young woman ['*almah*] bears a son."

Similar wonder births are found in Gen. 16:11 (Ishmael); 17:19 (Isaac); Exod. 2:2 (Moses); Judg. 13:3, 5, 7 (Samson); I Sam. 1:20 (Samuel); Isa. 8:3, 18 (Maher-shalal-hash-baz); but Isa. 7:14 has received most attention because of its messianic associations. One interpretation, calling attention to the promise of immediate fulfilment in Isa. 7:14-24, has denied any messianic reference altogether. Another view appeals to certain words in the formula to defend an exclusive reference to the Messiah. Delitzsch says *hinneh* ("behold") "is always used by Isaiah to introduce a future occurrence," but this is difficult to maintain in the light of 5:7; 8:18; 12:2; 20:6; 21:9; 37:36; 40:9-10; 47:14; 48:10; 51:22; 59:9; 62:11; 65: 6. Machen, insisting on the miraculous meaning of '*oth* ("sign"), has followed early Christian apologists (Justin, Irenaeus, Origen) by failing to note the usage in the immediate context (8:18) and other OT passages. The most vigorous discussion has been centered around the meaning of '*almah,* which means a "marriageable girl, young woman (until the birth of her first child)" (Koehler and Baumgartner, *Lexicon,* p. 709). Those who hold that it always carries the connotation of an untouched virgin have great difficulty with Gen. 24:43; Exod. 2:8; Ps. 68:25; Prov. 30:19; Song of S. 1:3; 6:8, as well as with the usage

of the Greek word παρθένος in the LXX (cf. Gen. 34:3). The case is even more difficult when the adjective *harah* ("conceive") is examined (cf. Gen. 38: 24; II Sam. 11:5). Since the time of Jerome a number of Christians, recognizing fully the immediate reference to a fulfilment in the time of Ahaz, have found it tenable to defend both the messianic reference of Isa. 7:14 and the virgin birth of Jesus, by noting the use of typological interpretation in the Gospel of Matthew (e.g., 2:6, 15, 18, 23).

There is no decisive evidence that the narrative in Matthew based the virgin birth on Isa. 7:14. The quotation of the promise in Matt. 1:23 is only one of a number of OT proof texts in this gospel, and the teaching about the miraculous conception does not require the verse. Two facts establish the miracle: (*a*) after the betrothal and (*b*) before they came together, Mary was found to be with child "of the Holy Spirit" (1:18, 20). Strack and Billerbeck have pointed out that this idea of the life-giving and creative power of the Holy Spirit is absolutely new and has no parallels in Jewish thought.

The Eshnunna Law Code (3800 B.C.) required "bride money" of the prospective groom and provided for a refund with twenty per cent interest if the betrothed virgin died before the consummation of marriage. In early OT times betrothal was effected by payment of *moher* (fifty shekels) to the bride's father as a compensation for loss (Gen. 34:12; I Sam. 18:25) and presentation of gifts to the prospective bride (Exod. 22:16-17; 34:12; Ruth 4:5, 10). The bride used the time of betrothal to collect her trousseau and property, and the groom was exempt from military service for the year (Deut. 20:7). The marriage was complete after a marriage feast of joyous celebration (Matt. 25:1-13; John 2:1-11). Only after this ceremony could they live together as husband and wife (Matt. 1:18, 25), although they were considered husband and wife from the time of betrothal (Matt. 1:19-20), and the woman was considered a widow if her husband died.

It is the statement that Jesus was conceived (Matt. 1:18) and born (Matt. 1:25) to Mary "before" she and Joseph had sexual contact that constitutes the second evidence for belief in the virgin birth. Even if Joseph knew he was not responsible for the conception, there was the law that demanded death by stoning for both man and woman in cases of seduction (Deut. 22:23-24) and death for the man in cases of rape (Deut. 22:25-27). Joseph was not only "unwilling to put her to shame" (Matt. 1:19), but he also feared for his life. The strong verb in the phrase "as he considered this" (ἐνθυμηθέντος), in Matt. 1: 20, suggests this and explains why Joseph wanted to divorce her quietly (Matt. 1:19). This was difficult to do quietly, since an engagement could be terminated after betrothal only by divorce and the payment of the dowry. The narrative teaches clearly that the Holy Spirit, not Joseph, was the agency of the conception.

In the nativity narrative in Luke 1-2, in which Mary is the central figure, a more complete presentation of the miraculous conception is found. Here again questions both linguistic and literary emerge. Some scholars view Luke 1:34-35 as an interpolation into the Lukan text, an attempt to strengthen the idea of the virgin birth. The linguistic study is in favor of the virgin birth, but this is not so strong as the literary factors. The word παρθένος ("virgin"; Luke 1:27) appears a second time in the Lukan writings in reference to Philip's "four unmarried daughters, who prophesied" (Acts 21:9). The "bridesmaids" of Matt. 25:1, 7, 11, who were also unmarried, are called παρθένοι. In the writings of Paul παρθένος not only has the connotation of the unmarried status, but also the associated idea of purity is present. In I Cor. 7:25, 34, 36-38, the word is used six times. Here the translation of the RSV rightly recalls the marriage customs discussed as the background of Matt. 1:18-25, with the additional factor of "spiritual marriage." It seems that ἄγαμος ("unmarried") and παρθένος are used as synonyms in vs. 34. At least the parallels of vss. 32-33, where the contrast is between the unmarried and the married man, would suggest a parallel contrast in vss. 34-35 between the unmarried and the married woman. Furthermore, the singular verb (μεριμνᾷ) is most natural with the singular subject (ἡ γυνὴ ἡ ἄγαμος καὶ ἡ παρθένος). In II Cor. 11:2, Paul is jealous for the church of Corinth, which he has betrothed to Christ in order to present her "as a pure bride [*parthenon hagnen*] to her one husband." Paul fears "that as the serpent deceived Eve by his cunning," false teachers (vss. 13-15) would lead the church "astray from a sincere and pure devotion to Christ." This emphasis on purity develops into an ascetic meaning in Rev. 14:4, where chaste men who had not been defiled with women are also called παρθένοι. This emphasis of the NT on the unmarried status which develops into ascetic purity is certainly in favor of the spotless virginity of Mary, but classical and Koine Greek at times have only the idea of the unmarried status. An example from the papyri says: "I have charged you more than once, 'take away your virgin-born [παρθένεια] children.'"

The literary factors in favor of the virgin birth in the Lukan narrative may be most forcefully seen by comparing the annunciation to Zechariah (Luke 1:5-7, 11-20) with the annunciation to Mary (vss. 26-38):

a) Vss. 5-7: "In the days of Herod, king of Judea, there was a priest named Zechariah, of the division of Abijah; and he had a wife of the daughters of Aaron, and her name was Elizabeth. And they were both righteous before God, walking in all the commandments and ordinances of the Lord blameless. But they had no child, because Elizabeth was barren, and both were advanced in years."

Cf. vss. 26-27: "In the sixth month the angel Gabriel was sent from God to a city of Galilee named Nazareth, to a virgin betrothed to a man whose name was Joseph, of the house of David; and the virgin's name was Mary."

b) Vs. 11: "And there appeared to him an angel of the Lord standing on the right side of the altar of incense."

Cf. vs. 28: "And he came to her and said, 'Hail O favored one, the Lord is with you!'"

c) Vs. 12: "And Zechariah was troubled when he saw him, and fear fell upon him."

Cf. vs. 29: "But she was greatly troubled at the saying, and considered in her mind what sort of greeting this might be."

d) Vss. 13-17: "But the angel said to him, 'Do not be afraid, Zechariah, for your prayer is heard, and your wife Elizabeth will bear you a son, and you shall call his name John.

> And you will have joy and gladness,
> and many will rejoice at his birth;
> for he will be great before the Lord,
> and he shall drink no wine nor strong drink,
> and he will be filled with the Holy Spirit,
> even from his mother's womb.
> And he will turn many of the sons of Israel
>   to the Lord their God,
> and he will go before him in the spirit and power
>   of Elijah,
> to turn the hearts of the fathers to the children,
> and the disobedient to the wisdom of the just,
> to make ready for the Lord a people prepared.'"

Cf. vss. 30:33: "And the angel said to her, 'Do not be afraid, Mary, for you have found favor with God. And behold, you will conceive in your womb and bear a son, and you shall call his name Jesus.

> He will be great, and will be called the Son of
>   the Most High;
> and the Lord God will give to him the throne of
>   his father David,
> and he will reign over the house of Jacob for ever;
> and of his kingdom there will be no end.'"

e) Vs. 18*a*: "And Zechariah said to the angel, 'How shall I know this?'"

Cf. vs. 34*a*: "And Mary said to the angel, 'How can this be . . . ?'"

f) Vs. 18*b*: "For I am an old man, and my wife is advanced in years."

Cf. vs. 34*b* KJV: "seeing I know not a man" (RSV "since I have no husband").

g) Vss. 19-20: "And the angel answered him, 'I am Gabriel, who stand in the presence of God; and I was sent to speak to you, and to bring you this good news. And behold, you will be silent and unable to speak until the day that these things come to pass, because you did not believe my words, which will be fulfilled in their time.'"

Cf. vss. 35-38: "And the angel said to her,

> The Holy Spirit will come upon you,
> and the power of the Most High will overshadow you;
> therefore the child to be born will be called holy,
> the Son of God.

And behold, your kinswoman Elizabeth in her old age has also conceived a son; and this is the sixth month with her who was called barren. For with God nothing will be impossible.' And Mary said, 'Behold I am the handmaid of the Lord; let it be to me according to your word.' And the angel departed from her."

Special attention should be given to three units of contrast. The first is the contrast between Luke 1:5-7 and Luke 1:26-27. Elizabeth was an old woman, but Mary was a παρθένος. The second contrast is between vss. 18*b* and 34*b*. The great age of Zechariah and Elizabeth raised Zechariah's question: "How shall I know this?" Mary's question was raised by the fact that she had never had sexual relations with any man (Luke 1:34*b*). Mary's question cannot be avoided: "How can this be?" Here the manner of the miraculous conception is attributed to the

Holy Spirit, in contrast to the conception of John through the agency of an aged man. A third contrast is between vss. 15 and 35. John the Baptist was filled with the Holy Spirit even while he was in his mother's womb (vs. 15), and this apparently took place when "the babe leaped in her womb; and Elizabeth was filled with the Holy Spirit" (vs. 41) three months before John the Baptist was born. The greatest of the prophets was *filled* with the Holy Spirit six months after he was conceived by natural generation, but the Son of God was *conceived* by the Holy Spirit by supernatural generation. Therefore, by the miraculous work of the Holy Spirit, Mary became the tabernacle of the SHEKINAH glory of God as the "power of the Most High" overshadowed her (vs. 35). The word ἐπισκιάσει ("will overshadow") has these associations.

The problem of the virgin birth has brought forth claims of parallels in literature outside the Scriptures. Philo Judeus (*On the Cherubim* 40-52) uses the ideas, but he is speaking of the begetting of the soul or the virtues of the soul. Plutarch (*Numa* 4.4) suggests that a woman can be approached by a divine *pneuma* (spirit) and made pregnant, as he tells the legend of Numa, who, after the death of his wife, withdrew into solitude to have intercourse with the divine being Egeria; but he is speaking of real sexual intercourse, and the *pneuma* he mentions is none other than the Egyptian designation for Zeus (Amon; cf. *Isis and Osiris* 36). This and other stories about how Zeus begat such persons as Hercules, Perseus, and Alexander constitute nothing more than mythological fornication. The same sordid state is found in the stories about Apollo's begetting Ion, Asclepius, Pythagoras, Plato, and Augustus. The yawning chasm between these pagan myths of polytheistic promiscuity and the lofty monotheism of the virgin birth of Jesus is too wide for careful research to cross.

Bibliography. More detailed discussions and bibliography may be found in articles by D. Moody in *Review and Expositor,* 50 (1953), 61-68, 453-62; 51 (1953), 495-507; 52 (1953), 44-54, 310-24. See also: W. G. Machen, *The Virgin Birth of Christ* (1932); D. Edwards, *The Virgin Birth in History and Faith* (1943).　　　　　　　D. MOODY

VIRTUES. See LISTS, ETHICAL.

VISION. In general, the communication of that which is not otherwise accessible, divinely imparted to the man of God, most often the prophet. In Hebrew the terms employed are immediately related to the two OT designations of "seer" (*see* PROPHET). The most common words for "vision" are חָזוֹן (cf. חֹזֶה, "seer") and slightly variant forms; but מַרְאָה (cf. רֹאֶה, also "seer") appears not uncommonly in Ezekiel and Daniel and in Gen. 46:2; Num. 12:6; I Sam. 3:15. In the NT, "vision" is ὅραμα in Matt. 17:9 and in Luke-Acts; uncommonly ὀπτασία (Luke 1:22; 24:23; Acts 26:19; II Cor. 12:1) and ὅρασις (Acts 2:17; Rev. 9:17).

In Daniel the term is employed in varying forms some thirty times and denotes the marvelous disclosure of that which purports to be knowledge of the future. In Ezekiel, where, after Daniel, the terms for "vision" are most frequently used, the content of

vision ranges from the "appearance of the likeness of the glory of Yahweh" (1:28) to the disclosure of the nature and meaning of present Israel and her times (e.g., ch. 8) and on to the idealized organization of the redeemed Israel in the future (chs. 40-48). It may be that the vision in Ezekiel is an accompaniment or product of the abnormal psychical experience (certainly so, from the point of view of our psychological norms, which, however, are hardly those of the ancient East); but it is hazardous to attempt firm validation or invalidation of Ezekiel's visions in psychological terms.

Among the earlier classical prophets, the vision is a conventional (in prophetism's understanding) means of Yahweh's communication to the prophet of the meaning of immediate events in Israel's immediate history. The vision is at one with the disclosure of the Word of Yahweh. So we understand Amos 1:1: "The words of Amos, . . . which he saw concerning Israel in the days of Uzziah king of Judah and in the days of Jeroboam . . . king of Israel." So, too, we understand Isa. 1:1: "The vision [חָזוֹן] of Isaiah . . . , which he saw [חָזָה] concerning Judah and Jerusalem in the days of Uzziah, Jotham, Ahaz, and Hezekiah, kings of Judah." Even more pointedly equating vision and Word is the opening of Obadiah: "The vision of Obadiah. Thus says Yahweh . . . ."

In prophetism (in both OT and NT) the mystery of the vision is the mystery of the Word—the mystery of God's disclosure of himself and of the meaning of history in the light of his effective impingement upon it, his reign over it, and of his purpose ultimately to redeem all history.　　B. D. NAPIER

VOCATION [Lat. *vocatio*]. The biblical doctrine of God's call to his people to become instruments of his purpose at work in history and to be the recipients of his grace and salvation. In the OT, vocation is the calling of Israel to be the people of God; and in the NT, the doctrine refers to the calling of men to follow Christ, to become incorporated in the fellowship of the church, and to share in the Christian hope. Strictly speaking, these biblical ideas are quite different from the modern understanding of vocation as a job, position, or profession. *See bibliography.*

1. In the OT. The primary word used to express vocation in the OT is the Hebrew verb קָרָא, "to call" (LXX καλέω). The term is frequently used in an ordinary sense meaning "to call," or "to cry out" (Judg. 9:7; Isa. 6:4); but it may also mean "to invite" (I Sam. 16:3), "to summon" (II Sam. 1:15), or "to name" (Gen. 11:9). The word is used in a "vocational" sense when God as the subject invites, summons, or names his people and thus claims them for his service (Isa. 43:1; 49:1; Hos. 11:1-2; etc.).

In the thought of Second Isaiah, the vocation of Israel is understood in terms of a God who enters into a personal relationship with the people of Israel, names the nation as "his son," and claims Israel as his own (Isa. 43:1-7; 48:12; 49:1-4; 51:2; 54:6-8; *see* ELECTION; SELF-DENIAL § 1). Within the context of this national vocation, God calls certain individuals for a particular task, such as in the case of Moses (Exod. 3) and the prophets (Isa. 6; Jer. 1:4-10; Amos 7:14-15; etc.).

2. In the NT. The NT word corresponding to קָרָא in the OT is the verb καλέω, "to call," "to invite," "to summon," or "to name" (cf. προσκαλέω, "to summon" or "to call to oneself"; Matt. 10:1; Mark 3:13; Acts 2:39). While καλέω is used throughout the NT in a technical sense (except in the Johannine literature), referring to an action of God or Christ in calling men, the term is thus employed most frequently and with special emphasis by Paul and in the literature which bears his influence. The adjective κλητός, "called," and the noun κλῆσις, "calling," are used to designate some aspect of vocation almost exclusively in the literature written and influenced by Paul. Thus, the doctrine of vocation as it appears in the NT finds its most articulate expression in Pauline theology.

a. In the gospels and Acts. Insofar as the idea of vocation appears in the gospels and Acts, it is portrayed as the call, invitation, or summons of God or Christ to men (Acts 2:39). The call of Jesus is given to sinners rather than to the righteous (Matt. 9:13; Mark 2:17). Outside the parallel passage in Luke 5:32 (and some MSS of Matt. 9:13; Mark 2:17), where the words "to repentance" are added, the specific nature of this calling is not defined. A similar general calling or invitation of God is portrayed in the parable of the banquet (Matt. 22:1-14; cf. Luke 14:16-24 [these passages may have been preserved in the gospel tradition in order to explain how and why God's call to Israel was rejected by the Jews and then was extended to others; cf. Rom. 9-11]).

More specifically, Jesus called his disciples (*see* DISCIPLE) to follow him (Matt. 4:21-22; Mark 1:19-20; cf. Luke 5:1-11), and he sent them out to preach and cast out demons (Matt. 10:1-4; Mark 3:13-19; 6:7-13; Luke 6:12-16; cf. Acts 13:2; 16:10; *see* SELF-DENIAL § 3a). In the Fourth Gospel, the call of Jesus to the disciples is described with the verb ἐκλέγομαι, "to choose" (cf. John 6:70; 13:18; 15:16, 19); but the meaning of the relation between Jesus and the disciples is very similar to that in the Synoptic gospels.

These scattered references in the gospels and Acts seem to be based upon a general understanding of vocation as the call, invitation, or summons given by God, Christ, or the Holy Spirit to men to participate in some way in the work of God, to become followers of Christ, or to benefit from the promise of divine blessing.

b. In Pauline literature. In the Pauline literature (including those documents influenced by Paul), vocation is the calling of God to men which has its origin in the divine purpose of election; it is a call to participate in the Christian fellowship, and it includes an invitation to share in the Christian hope. The grand sweep of God's purpose and action is set forth in Rom. 8:28-30, where Paul's description moves from predestination, through calling (vocation), to final glorification. The movement of God's purpose in history as related to Israel and the Gentiles is then elaborated upon in Rom. 9-11. To participate in this glorious design for the salvation of men, God has called both Jews and Gentiles (Rom. 9:24).

Since Christian vocation, according to Paul, has its origin in God himself, it is appropriately described as a "holy calling" (II Tim. 1:9). Because it is a vocation which looks forward in hope (Eph. 4:4), it may also be designated as a "heavenly call" (Heb. 3:1). While the vocation of Christians is thus rooted in the divine purpose and looks forward in hope, it has at least these implications for the present life of those who are called: (*a*) The assumed context of Christian vocation for this present life is the church (I Cor. 1:9, 26; Eph. 4:1-7; I Pet. 2:9-10). In this fellowship, church members are called to be saints (Rom. 1:7; I Cor. 1:2; cf. the various functions of Christian members in the body of Christ [I Cor. 12:28-30; Eph. 4:11]). Similarly, Paul himself was called to be an apostle (Rom. 1:1; I Cor. 1:1). (*b*) Those who are called must live morally upright and responsible lives (Eph. 4:1; I Thess. 4:7; II Thess. 1:11). (*c*) Christians will ordinarily remain in the status in which they were called (I Cor. 7:17-24). They will pursue their normal occupations, remembering that their principal duty in every situation of life is to regard themselves as servants of the Christ who called them (I Cor. 7:22-23). (*d*) Those who are called according to the divine purpose know that "in everything God works for good with those who love him" (Rom. 8:28).

Bibliography. K. Holl, "Die Geschichte des Worts Beruf," *Gesammelte Aufsätze zur Kirchengeschichte,* III (1928), 189-219. E. Brunner, *The Divine Imperative* (trans. O. Wyon; 1937), pp. 198-207. K. Barth, "Der Beruf," *Die Lehre von der Schöpfung* (*Die Kirchliche Dogmatik,* III/4; 1951), pp. 683-743. A. Richardson, *The Biblical Doctrine of Work* (1952). J. O. Nelson, ed., *Work and Vocation* (1954); see especially the Bibliography, pp. 213-24.   R. L. SCHEEF, JR.

VOPHSI vŏf'sī [וּפְסִי; LXX Ιαβει] (Num. 13:14). The father of Nahbi, who was sent from the tribe of Naphtali to spy out the land of Canaan. The LXX reading suggests that the text containing this obscure name is uncertain.

Bibliography. M. Noth, *Die israelitischen Personennamen* (1928), p. 241.   R. F. JOHNSON

VOTIVE OFFERING. *See* Vows.

VOWS [אֵסָר, pledge; נֶדֶר; εὐχή]. The terms employed suggest the spoken word, the promise, or the "outgoing from the mouth" (cf. Num. 30:13). *See also* OATH; CORBAN; NAZIRITE.

1. Kinds of vows
   a. Bargains
   b. Unselfish devotion
   c. Abstinence
2. Laws concerning vows
3. Vows in the Psalms
   Bibliography

1. Kinds of vows. *a. Bargains.* In return for God's presence, protection, provision, etc., Jacob at Bethel promised worship, shrine, and tithe (Gen. 28:20-22[E]). Jephthah promised a living sacrifice for military victory and fulfilled his vow though it meant the sacrifice of his daughter (Judg. 11:30-31). Hannah prayed for a son, promising him to the temple at Shiloh (I Sam. 1:11). Absalom vowed sacrificial worship on condition of his return to his father's favor (II Sam. 15:7-12). Jonah's shipmates made vows in the hope of safety (Jonah 1:16). The vows of the four men in Acts 21:23 were probably of this kind.

b. Unselfish devotion. David sought to further his plan of establishing the ark at his new capital, Jerusalem, and so identifying divine and human rule, by undertaking not to go home, or go to bed, or sleep, until the ark was housed in Jerusalem (Ps. 132:2-5; cf. the vow of Paul in Acts 18:18).

c. Abstinence. Israel undertook to put the people and cities of Arad to the ban—i.e., to "devote them," to gain no advantage of spoil or renown from the battle—provided that Arad was delivered into their hands (Num. 21:1-3). Similar vows, oaths, of abstinence are recorded of Saul and his people (I Sam. 14:24) and of the forty Jews who compassed the death of Paul (Acts 23:21). In all three classes it is clear that a vow accompanies or is intended to strengthen prayer. It is possible that "his vow" in I Sam. 1:21 and "my vows" in Prov. 7:14 do not mean particular vows, but are general terms descriptive of the duties of worship in general (cf. Prov. 31:2; Nah. 1:15). When the Egyptian people will worship the Lord, they will, like Israel, offer sacrifices and will make vows and perform them (Isa. 19:21). Similarly, apostate Israelites will sacrifice and perform their vows to the queen of heaven (Jer. 44:25). In Mark 6:23 "he vowed" simply means "he promised faithfully."

For votive offerings or gifts promised to God, *see* SACRIFICES AND OFFERINGS.

2. Laws concerning vows. The laws of the OT and of Mishna tractate Nedarim—vows—also illustrate how constant a feature the vow is of Israel's life. The main sources are:

a) Lev. 7:16-17, which ordains that a vowed peace offering must be eaten within two days or what is left burned on the third (cf. Prov. 7:14, where this has been carried out).

b) Lev. 22:17-25, which prescribes that all sacrifices in fulfilment of vows must be without blemish (cf. Mal. 1:14).

c) Lev. 27, which is an appendix of laws relating to vows and tithes with instructions how these may be commuted or redeemed. Money values to rank as a fixed rate of exchange for vows are placed on men and women of different ages and wealth, on animals, on a man's house, and on his inherited land in relation to the year of Jubilee. But things or people devoted—i.e., put to the ban—cannot be redeemed. But neither firstlings of animals (Lev. 27:26), which already belong to the Lord (but contrast Hannah), nor the hire of sacred prostitutes, female or male (Deut. 23:18), may extinguish a vow.

d) Num. 6, laws regarding Nazirite vows.

e) Num. 15:1-10 (cf. 29:39), which lays down what must be sacrificed for, among other things, fulfilling a vow.

f) Num. 30, which requires that vows must be fulfilled, though the vows of an unmarried woman still at home, or of a married woman in her husband's house, depend upon the will of her father or husband respectively. A widow or divorced woman can make a binding vow. Like Num. 30:3; Deut. 23:21-23 de-

mands the fulfilment of vows, though in the latter passage not to vow is no sin (cf. Prov. 20:25; Eccl. 5:4-6).

g) Deut. 12, which holds that vows are also controlled by the law of the central sanctuary.

3. Vows in the Psalms. Gunkel has re-emphasized the place of the vow in those psalms known as laments of the community, and of the individual. Such laments frequently use the vow as an expression of hope of and thanksgiving for deliverance. Thus in 56:12-13 the worshiper says:

> My vows to thee I must perform, O God;
> I will render thank offerings to thee.
> For thou hast delivered my soul from death.

Even clearer are these verses from an individual thanksgiving (66:13-15):

> I will come into thy house with burnt offerings;
> I will pay thee my vows,
> that which my lips uttered
> and my mouth promised when I was in trouble.
> I will offer to thee burnt offerings of fatlings.

This passage shows the vow at its inception—something promised in trouble—and then later in its fulfilment, when it is not merely the fulfilment of a promise but is also the expression of thanksgiving to God, and is, in fact, accompanied by the appropriate sacrifices. Other passages are 22:25; 50:14; 61:5, 8; 65:1; 116:14, 18. But, of course, the making and fulfilling of vows does not necessarily require the use of the word "vow." "Heart's desire" in 20:4 could mean a royal vow, and in the community lament the vow appears thus:

> Then we thy people, the flock of thy pasture,
> will give thanks to thee for ever;
> from generation to generation we will recount thy praise
> (79:13),

where the first word "then," as in 80:18, makes the transition to the vow (cf. 20:6; 21:13—H 21:14; 54:6; 89:1-2; 144:9; etc.). Similarly, Ps. 101 could be considered as a statement of the king's duties in the form of a vow. Correspondingly, divine promises, oaths, and covenants to individuals and to Israel could be described as God's vows (cf. Gen. 12:2-3, 7; 15:5-6; II Sam. 7; and parallels in the Psalter—e.g., 89:3-4).

See also WORSHIP; CULTUS; TEMPLE, JERUSALEM.

Bibliography. J. Pedersen, *Der Eid bei den Semiten* (1914), pp. 119-27; A. Wendel, *Das israelitisch-jüdische Gelübde* (1931); H. Gunkel and J. Begrich, *Einleitung in die Psalmen* (1933), pp. 247-50.   G. HENTON DAVIES

*VULGATE vŭl'gāt [Lat. *vulgata (versio)*]. The term which, during the Middle Ages, came to be applied

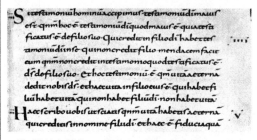

17. Alcuin's Vulg., a ninth-century-A.D. version

to Jerome's Latin translation of the Bible when its circulation had become so widespread as to be recognized as the "common" version. *See* VERSIONS, ANCIENT, § 3. Fig. VUL 17. B. M. METZGER

VULTURE [נשר (Prov. 30:17; Lam. 4:19; Hos. 8:1), *see* EAGLE; פרס (Deut. 14:12), *see* OSSIFRAGE; קאת (Ps. 102:6—H 102:7; Zeph. 2:14), *see* PELICAN; רחם (Lev. 11:18; KJV GIER EAGLE) *and* רחמה (Deut. 14:17; CARRION VULTURE; KJV GIER EAGLE), *cf.* רחם *Pi'el*, to have compassion; Arab. *rakham, rakhama,* vulture; LXX κύκνος, swan (Lev. 11:18), ίέραξ, hawk, falcon (Deut. 14:17); Vulg. *porphyrio,* water hen; Targ. (Onq.) ירקרקא, *possibly* gier eagle; KJV איה (Job 28:7; RSV FALCON); דיה, דאה (RSV KITE)]. Any of several large diurnal carrion-eating birds of prey of the family Accipitridae of the subfamily Aegypiinae, of the genera Gyps, Gypaëtus, etc.

Vultures quite surely existed in Palestine in the biblical period, but it is impossible from the biblical data to offer more than a tentative identification of those which were known. The word נשר may have designated vultures as well as eagles (*see* EAGLE); Tristram, Bodenheimer, and G. R. Driver propose that in some cases this word refers to the Griffon Vulture (*Gyps fulvus fulvus*), which in Tristram's time was the commonest of all the large birds of prey in the Holy Land (cf. Prov. 30:17; Lam. 4:19; Hos. 8:1). A larger vulture, but less frequently found in Palestine, is the Lammergeier (*Gypaëtus barbatus aureus*), known for its partiality for marrow bones and tortoises; this may be the unclean bird designated פרס (Lev. 11:13; Deut. 14:12). Another vulture seen by Tristram (but not in the rainy season) is the Egyptian Vulture (*Neophron percnopterus*), a true scavenger. Possibly רחם (Lev. 11:18) and רחמה (Deut. 14:17) refer to this bird, though G. R. Driver favors identifying these words with the osprey. *See bibliography.*

Bibliography. G. R. Driver, *PEQ* (1955), pp. 16-17.

W. S. MCCULLOUGH

WAFERS [רְקִיקִים, *from the root* רקק, to be thin; צַפִּיחִת (Exod. 16:31), *cf.* Arab. *root* make broad]. With one exception (*see below*), wafers are always mentioned in connection with offerings: (*a*) those made on the occasion of the consecration of priests (Exod. 29:2, 23; Lev. 8:26), (*b*) cereal offerings in general (Lev. 2:4; *see* CEREAL OFFERING), (*c*) thank offerings (Lev. 7:12; *see* THANK OFFERING), (*d*) NAZIRITE offerings (Num. 6:15, 19), and (*e*) Levitical offerings as a whole (I Chr. 23:29; KJV "cakes"). *See* SACRIFICES AND OFFERINGS.

Wafers were also eaten as a part of the everyday diet, however, as may be seen from the comparison of the taste of MANNA with that of "wafers made with honey" (Exod. 16:31). *See also* BREAD § 1*d*.

J. F. ROSS

WAGES [שָׂכָר (*śākār, śeker*), מַשְׂכֹּרֶת, *from* שׂכר, to hire; פֹּעַל, פְּעֻלָּה, (compensation for) a piece of work; μισθός; *rarely* ὀψώνια (*always plural*)]. Alternately: HIRE; RECOMPENSE; REWARD. The compensation given to a person hired for performing some work or service. In a primitive economy, like that of the nomadic Hebrews of the patriarchal era, or among the Israelite peasants, wage earners did not form a distinct social class. They worked for their maintenance, to which some wages paid in kind would be added (Gen. 29:15; 30:32-33; 31:7, 41). The complexity of urban civilization and the development of specialized crafts and trades, however, tended to increase the number of salaried auxiliaries, who received at least part of their wages, or even the entire amount, in weighed bronze or silver, during most of the period covered by the historical books of the OT. It should be remembered that coined money as we know it did not appear in the lands of the Bible before the Persian period, and that not before Hellenism did it become the normal means of payment.

The Bible mentions or implies the paying of wages to hired shepherds (Gen. 29:15; 30:32-33; John 10: 12), laborers and farm hands (Matt. 20:1-16; Luke 10:7; 15:17; John 4:36; Jas. 5:4), crewmen on fishing boats (Mark 1:20), mercenary soldiers (Luke 3:14), nurses (Exod. 2:9). The hire of a harlot is mentioned in Deut. 23:18; Isa. 23:17; Ezek. 16:31; Hos. 9:1;

Mic. 1:7; etc., and the prophet Micah speaks of the (illegal) hire of priests (Mic. 3:11). The above list of occupations for which wage earners were engaged is far from complete. Industrial and commercial concerns certainly employed a large number of wage earners, but the Bible has few direct references to the guilds of workers, and the references found in the Prophets, as well as in the NT, are mostly borrowed from agriculture and husbandry.

Wage earners as a class intermediary between the landowners and slave labor were known in Assyria as the *ḫupšû*, a term corresponding to the Hebrew חָפְשִׁי (*hophshî*). The latter applies to an emancipated slave who earns his living by hiring his services to an employer, without reference to any specific type of work (Exod. 21:2, 26-27; Deut. 15:12).

The determination of wages was debated informally between the master and the person whom he wished to engage. The story of Jacob offers a good example of the type of bargaining and of the many ways in which both parties tried to get the best of each other by cheating or deceit (Gen. 30:31-43; 31: 6-7). In the parable of the laborers in the vineyard (Matt. 20:1-16) the master shows an unusual liberality; the reference to the men standing idle in the market place would find an apt illustration in pre-Fascist Rome, when unemployed workers used to gather near the Ponte Fabricio in the hope of getting hired.

The law had some provisions to prevent or restrain the exploitation of wage earners by greedy masters. The wages of the hireling, whether he were an Israelite or a foreigner, must be paid daily before sunset (Lev. 19:13; Deut. 24:14-15). But the law was often ignored or flouted, and the prophets repeatedly condemned the foul practices of the employers (Jer. 22:13; Mal. 3:5). As a whole, the condition of a wage earner was not considered a happy one, while he was in continual anxiety concerning his meager retribution, and had to live from hand to mouth (Job 7:1-2; 14:6).

In figurative usage, the Hebrew or Greek terms rendered in English by "wages" and also by "recompense" and "reward" apply to the favors God grants to men (Isa. 23:18; 40:10; 62:11), and to the retributions of divine justice (Ps. 109:20; Rom. 6:23; II Pet. 2:15).

See also SLAVERY; TRADE AND COMMERCE.

Bibliography. For generalities, see G. A. Barrois, *Manuel d'Archéologie Biblique*, II (1953), 214-15. Information on some classes of wage earners in the ancient Near and Middle East may be gathered from the following articles: I. Mendelsohn, "Guilds in Ancient Palestine," *BASOR,* 80 (1940), 17-21; "The Canaanite Term for Free Proletarian," *BASOR,* 83 (1941), 36-39. E. R. Lacheman, "Note on the Word Ḫupšu at Nuzi," *BASOR,* 86 (1942), 36-37. I. Mendelsohn, "New Light on the Ḫupšu," *BASOR,* 139 (1955), 9-11.

G. A. BARROIS

WAGON. *See* CART.

WAHEB wā′hĕb [וָהֵב; Ζωοβ] (Num. 21:14). A place, apparently in Moab, probably near the Arnon. The RSV understands two proper names: "Waheb in SUPHAH," while the KJV translates: "What he did in the Red sea." The Hebrew (אֶת וָהֵב) shows that Waheb is the object of a verb, but this bit from the Book of the Wars of the Lord does not include the verb in question. E. D. GROHMAN

WAILING. *See* MOURNING.

WAISTCLOTH [אֵזוֹר] (Job 12:18; Isa. 5:27; Jer. 13:1-2, 4, 6-7, 10-11). Alternately: GIRDLE; KJV always GIRDLE. The innermost garment, worn around the loins and ordinarily never removed. It was made of leather (II Kings 1:8) or linen (Jer. 13: 1). Workmen removed their outer garments and wore only the waistcloth when on the jobs. *See* DRESS AND ORNAMENTS § A2. J. M. MYERS

WAIT. Both the Hebrew and the Greek language have a number of words which often or on occasion mean "wait," sometimes in the passive sense of "remain" or "defer" and sometimes with the active meaning of "expect" or "look for."

In the OT there are many references to "waiting" in the sense of "remaining" (cf. Judg. 3:25 [חוּל]; Ruth 1:13 [שׂבר]; I Sam. 14:9 [דָּמַם]; etc.); or of "lying in wait" (cf. Num. 35:20 [צְדִיָּה]; Judg. 16:2; I Sam. 15:5; Ps. 59:3 [אָרַב]). But it is pre-eminently for God that the Jew of the OT waits. The word often used of "waiting for God," קוה, has an active meaning. Its root connotes "tension" and "endurance." In waiting for God the Hebrew was in tense anticipation, full of hope, and willing to endure till God should come (cf. Pss. 25:3, 5, 21; 27:14; 39:7; Isa. 26: 8; 33:2; 49:23; 51:5; 60:9). To wait for God is to set one's hope on him (cf. Jer. 14:22, where the Hebrew verb for "wait for" is translated "set hope on"; and see the relation of "waiting" to "hoping" in Pss. 39:7; 130:5; Isa. 8:17). But to wait or expect is not enough: one who waits (קוה) must "keep to his [God's] way" (Ps. 37:34), must "hold fast to love and justice" (Hos. 12:6). And this one "shall not be put to shame" (Isa. 49:23); God will renew his strength (Isa. 40:31), and will help him (Prov. 20:22). God will incline to one who waits and will hear his cry (Ps. 40:1); and "those who wait for the LORD shall possess the land" (Ps. 37:9); they shall rejoice in God's salvation (Isa. 25: 9; cf. Gen. 49:18). Finally, God himself waits for ("looks for"; קוה) Israel to bear fruit (Isa. 5:2, 7).

In the NT the root of the most frequently used words for "wait" (ἐκδέχομαι, ἀποδέχομαι, and προσδέχομαι) has the active connotation of "take" or "receive." The same word means either "wait" (cf. Mark 15:43) or "receive" (Rom. 16:2). One who waits is expecting to receive; and in the NT waiting usually is related to salvation. There are exceptions to this (cf. Acts 17:16; I Cor. 11:33; Jas. 5:7); but Christians wait for "adoption as sons" (Rom. 8:23) or for a Savior from heaven, the Lord Jesus Christ (Phil. 3:20; see also Mark 15:43 = Luke 23:51; Acts 1:4 [περιμένω]; Rom. 8:19, 25; I Cor. 1:7; Gal. 5:5; I Thess. 1:10 [ἀναμένω]; Tit. 2:13; Heb. 9:28; 10:13; 11:10; Jude 21). And God's patience is said to have "waited in the days of Noah" (I Pet. 3:20).

See also HOPE. B. H. THROCKMORTON, JR.

WALLET [יַלְקוּט] (I Sam. 17:40); KJV SCRIP. A receptacle used as a shepherd's bag. David put the pebbles for his sling "in his shepherd's bag or wallet."

WALLS. Walls are mentioned often in the OT. Vineyards and fields have walls (גָּדֵר [Isa. 5:5]; שׁוּר [II Sam. 22:30]), made of unhewn stones set in mud or mortar. House walls* were of unhewn stones, mud, or brick. City walls,* normally of rough-hewn stones with upper courses of brick, were often of great height and breadth. The walls of houses and cities are generally designated by the Hebrew words חוֹמָה and קִיר, without sharp distinction in usage or meaning (Josh. 2:15; 6:5). Figs. JER 12; WAL 1, 2.

Courtesy of James B. Pritchard
1. Foundation walls of building at NT Jericho, Herodian period

Courtesy of the Oriental Institute, the University of Chicago
2. An Early Bronze Age city wall at Megiddo (*ca.* 3000-2500 B.C.)

References to walls in the NT are few (see Acts 9:25; II Cor. 11:33; Heb. 11:30; Rev. 21:12; etc.; τεῖχος). The term τοῖχος always has a pejorative sense in the NT (Acts 25:3; Eph. 2:14; μεσότοιχον).

Bibliography. J. B. Pritchard, *ANEP* (1954), pp. 224-36; G. E. Wright, *Biblical Archaeology* (1957), pp. 184-87 and *passim.* W. J. HARRELSON

*WAR, IDEAS OF. The concept of the holy war, declared, led, and won by Yahweh himself, governs

OT military thinking. Originating in Israel and reaching its greatest influence during the period of the judges, the concept was overshadowed in the monarchy by considerations of political expediency. The prophets, while supporting the holy-war ideology, thought of war primarily as the judgment of God against rebellious Israel or against the haughty Gentile nations. The apocalyptists saw in war a testing of faith and a sign of the end of the age. They held also that the final era of peace would be preceded by a massive holy war. Jesus taught little directly concerning war, but directed his mission toward creating the conditions of peace. The early church spiritualized the holy war and saw in it a struggle against sin, Satan, and the demonic forces of the cosmos, the decisive battle of which had been won in the death and resurrection of Jesus Christ.

1. The holy war
   a. Preparation
   b. Personnel
   c. Conduct
   d. Outcome
2. Historical sketch
   a. During the monarchy
   b. After the Exile
3. Prophetic ideas
4. Apocalyptic ideas
5. The teaching of Jesus
6. War and the NT church
Bibliography

1. The holy war. The concept of a holy war demands the presupposition stated in Exod. 15:3: "Yahweh is a man of war [אִישׁ מִלְחָמָה]." When the conviction that Yahweh is a warrior is joined to the confidence that he has the power to win victories (I Sam. 17:47), a holy-war ideology is not only possible but inevitable. I Sam. 17:47 declares precisely this faith: "The battle [הַמִּלְחָמָה] is Yahweh's." The separate elements in the Israelite practice of the holy war have been isolated and studied by Gerhard von Rad (*see bibliography*), and the treatment given here is based on his work.

a. Preparation. By its nature the holy war must have the sanction and active participation of the national god. He declares the war (Exod. 17:16; Num. 31:3). Consultation of the deity by one of the numerous methods available was, therefore, a necessary prelude to battle. Dreams, Urim, the ephod, or the word of the prophet was employed for this purpose (Judg. 7:9-14; I Sam. 28:6; 30:7; II Sam. 5:19, 23; I Kings 22:5, 7-8). Since no step could properly be taken without divine approval, "inquiring of the LORD" was an important means of determining strategy while the war was in progress (II Sam. 5:19-23; *see* WAR, METHODS OF). In general, any defense of Israelite territory against foreign invasion was *ipso facto* a holy war. The enemy, thrusting itself into the sacred land given to Israel in her covenant with Yahweh, would perforce bring the wrath of Israel's God against the invader. This breaks down only when the invader has been called in by Yahweh himself in order to punish his people. Both aspects of war are repeatedly illustrated in the book of JUDGES.

b. Personnel. The military commander did not lead in his own name or by his own genius. He was prepared for his office by a special gift of the Spirit of God, and by virtue of this gift he held his command (Judg. 6:34; 11:29; etc.). If for any reason the Spirit was withdrawn from him, his authority to lead went with it (Judg. 16:20; I Sam. 16:14). *See* SPIRIT.

The men who served under the charismatic leader were required to show complete single-mindedness in the service of Yahweh. The fearful, the newly married, and those entangled in financial or domestic worries were invited by the commanding officers to go home (Deut. 20:5-9). Their presence in the army would break the unity of those who "offered themselves willingly" (Judg. 5:2). The holy war was conducted with the full support of the priests and the cultus (Deut. 20:2; I Sam. 10:1), and the soldier, since he was offering service to Yahweh, took on a priestly quality, becoming for the duration of the war a holy person (I Sam. 21:14; Isa. 13:3). The military camps were places where Yahweh himself "walked" (Deut. 23:14), and, like any shrine, had to be kept ritually clean. Excrement was buried outside the camp area (Deut. 23:12-13), and any soldier who contaminated himself with a bodily discharge underwent a one-day purification ritual outside the camp (vss. 10-11). For a man to have intercourse with a woman would disqualify him from entering the encampment (I Sam. 21:4; II Sam. 11:11). Theologically the holy war appears as a responsibility of the Israelite under the COVENANT, and cultically as a sacrificial act, initiated by the will of Yahweh, and carried out by people devoted to his service and ceremonially pure.

c. Conduct. For the conduct of a holy war the number of soldiers in the army is of little importance (Judg. 7; I Sam. 14:6). The soldiers do not fight alone, for "Yahweh your God is he that goes with you, to fight for you against your enemies, to give you the victory" (Deut. 20:4; cf. Exod. 14:14; Deut. 9:3; Judg. 4:14). The holy war was called "Yahweh's war" (I Sam. 18:17; 25:28), and its battle cry was one of the numerous variants of the expression: "Yahweh has delivered them into our hand" (cf. Judg. 3:28; 7:15; I Sam. 7:8). The ram's-horn trumpet (*see* MUSICAL INSTRUMENTS), symbolic of the voice of Yahweh, sounded the assembly and the attack (Num. 10:9; 31:6; Judg. 3:27; I Sam. 13:3). The familiar divine name, Yahweh of hosts, has overtones of the holy war (*see* LORD OF HOSTS). In the Song of Deborah the Lord comes into battle from his mountain home and marshals the natural and cosmic powers against Sisera (Judg. 5:4, 20-21). Elisha sees the heavenly army of Yahweh drawn up on the hills around besieged Samaria (II Kings 6:15-19). At a crucial point in the battle the "terror of Yahweh" falls upon the enemy, throws them into confusion, and leaves them an easy prey to the numerically inferior Israelites, whose main function is "mopping up" after the victory, which is won by Yahweh alone (Josh. 10:10; Judg. 4:15; II Sam. 5:24; 7:10). The forty years of wilderness wanderings were a punishment for the people's lack of trust in Yahweh's ability to win the victory in spite of the physical size and military equipment of the Canaanite cities (Num. 14:1-12). David's willingness to go against Goliath (I Sam. 17:41-47) and Jonathan's singlehanded attack on the Philistines (I Sam. 14) are equally evidence of complete confidence in this premise.

Since the holy-war ideology was not confined to Israel, but was shared by her neighbors, it is not surprising that warfare often resolved itself into a power struggle between the gods of the warring nations, the victory going to the nation with the most powerful god (I Kings 20:28; II Kings 18:28-35). When the hard-pressed Israelites brought the ark of the covenant into battle, the Philistines exclaimed: "The gods have come into the camp. . . . Woe to us! For nothing like this has happened before" (I Sam. 4:7). The Philistines naturally accepted the defeat of the Israelites and the capture of the ark as evidence that Dagon was stronger than Yahweh. Accordingly they presented the ark as a gift to Dagon in his temple. The reader is made aware that the victory of the Philistines is not genuine evidence of the weakness of Yahweh. Dagon fell on his face before the ark (I Sam. 5:1-5). At a later date Mesha, king of Moab, attributed his defeat to the weakness of his god, Chemosh, and sacrificed his son on the city wall in an effort to revitalize the deity. When the Israelites were defeated, he ascribed the victory to the power of Chemosh (II Kings 3:21-27). *See* MOABITE STONE.

d. Outcome. Deuteronomy envisages three possible results of a holy war (20:10-20). A city brought under attack is to be offered terms of peace. If these are accepted, the citizens are enslaved but not killed. If the terms are rejected, the males are put to the sword, but the other occupants and the property of the city become booty for the victors. Exception is made of enemy cities within the boundaries of the Holy Land, which are to be utterly destroyed. This practice, known as "the ban" (חרם; *see* DEVOTED), in either the partial or the complete form is a common feature of OT narratives (Josh. 6:17; I Sam. 15:3), and serves to emphasize the sacrificial character of the holy war, which makes a whole city a sacrifice to Yahweh.

It should be emphasized that the holy war, although an important part of Hebrew theology, is never represented as an end in itself. The war looks beyond the day of battle to the time of peace which the victorious conclusion of hostilities will bring. The war itself is an instrument of the delivering God of the covenant by which he brings his people into that condition of well-being and prosperity which in the OT is called "Peace" (שלום; *see* PEACE, OT; REST). The holy-war ideology is, therefore, an integral part of OT covenant theology, emphasizing the sovereignty of God, his initiative, his concern for his people, and his activity as deliverer and preserver.

2. Historical sketch. The holy-war concept was developed and reached its greatest influence during the period of the judges. In that age the tribes were held together in a loose confederacy for the common worship of Yahweh and for common military action. The semi-independent tribal leaders could not be brought into united action unless they were assured that Yahweh was himself their leader. The cultic aspects of the holy war were reinforced by the fact that the rallying point of the tribes was at such a religious center as SHECHEM or SHILOH.

a. During the monarchy. With the coming of centralized administration under the monarchy the holy war lost much of its vital power as a living concept, although as an idea or ideal it exercised a profound influence throughout biblical times. During the reign of Saul, who was a rural monarch and desirous of preserving the traditional ways of his people, the holy war remained as active a concept as in the days of the judges, but with the rule of David the tribal organization of Israel was broken down, and Solomon's policies dealt a final blow to tribal society (*see* DAVID; SOLOMON). Warfare was transformed into an instrument of national policy, declared at the wish of the king to serve his purposes. Lip service might be paid to the older traditions, the king "inquiring of the LORD" before going into battle, or offering a prayer for victory (I Kings 8:44-45; 22:5); but the prophets who gave the divine verdict were creatures of the court (I Kings 18:19; 22:5-6), and only an occasional devoted man like Micaiah ben Imlah dared to stand out against them (I Kings 22:16-23). The king's mandate to control warfare was undergirded by a court theology which saw the monarch as the appointee of Yahweh, and his earthly representative; indeed, his son (II Sam. 7:14-17; Pss. 2; 72; *see* KING). Symptomatic of the changed outlook is the increasing importance attached to international treaties as a means of guaranteeing security (I Kings 15:18-19; 16:31; II Kings 15:19; 16:5-9; 17:4). The power of Yahweh needed to be bolstered by the might of one of the great powers.

Nevertheless, throughout the monarchy the ancient tradition of the holy war survived. The ordinary citizen and the common soldier were apparently more loyal to its principles than the court officials and generals. Uriah the Hittite, e.g., was faithful to his status as a consecrated warrior when he refused to go down to his house while on leave from the army. By contrast, David was willing to sacrifice this principle for his own convenience (II Sam. 11:6-13).

Holy-war thinking figures prominently in the book of DEUTERONOMY, where in five passages rules of warfare are given in a form which breathes the spirit of the holy war (20; 21:10-14; 23:10-14; 24:5; 25:17-19). The priestly historians in NUMBERS and JOSHUA are controlled by the same tradition. They regard the exodus from Egypt as the holy war par excellence. They report the events of the conquest and settlement of Palestine as the irresistible, triumphant march of the armies of Yahweh (Num. 21:21-35; 31:1-12; Josh. 6:1-21; 8:1-29; 10; etc.), checked only when the nation temporarily lost its faith in the complete sufficiency of Yahweh (Num. 14:39-45; Josh. 23:9-13). The holy-war tradition was thus preserved in that part of the Israelite cultus least dominated by the royal court. It may, like Deuteronomy, have belonged to the specific teaching of the country Levites (*see* the works of G. von Rad in the *bibliography*), as well as to that of the prophetic schools.

b. After the Exile. With the fall of the Israelite kingdoms another radical change in the idea of war took place. The nation ceased to exist as a political entity, and, therefore, lost its capacity to wage war either as an instrument of policy or as a response to the call of Yahweh. The only conceivable form of holy war in the postexilic period was revolt against the ruling power of the day.

To a remarkable degree the Maccabean revolt against Seleucid rule (*see* MACCABEES) reflects the ideology of the holy war. Its initiator and first leader, Mattathias of Modin, is described in terms reminiscent of the inspired military commanders of the period of the judges, although in the case of Mattathias the Spirit is not specifically mentioned as the inspiring agent (I Macc. 2:24-26). Judas' exhortation to his troops expresses the leading principles of sacral warfare. "It is easy for many to be hemmed in by few, for in the sight of Heaven there is no difference between saving by many or by few. It is not on the size of the army that victory in battle depends, but strength comes from Heaven" (I Macc. 3:18*b*-19). "He himself will crush them before us; as for you, do not be afraid of them" (vs. 22). The prayers offered before battle are part and parcel of the same conceptual framework (I Macc. 4:30-32 [note the appeal to the "terror of the Lord" in vs. 32]; 7:41-42). Characteristics of holy-war thought can be detected in accounts of the first and second Jewish revolts against Rome (A.D. 66-73 and 132-35 respectively; Jos. War IV; Dio Cassius LXIX). The fact that none of these revolts was wholly successful prevents them from being presented as thoroughgoing representatives of the holy war.

The foregoing historical sketch omits the important contribution made to the OT view of war by the prophetic and apocalyptic movements. This must now be considered.

3. Prophetic ideas. While the prophets regarded universal peace as a goal to be realized in the "latter days" (Isa. 11:6-9; Jer. 32:36-41; Ezek. 39:25-29; Mic. 4:3-4), they were not opponents of war as such. The earlier prophets were more than once engaged in stirring up internal strife (I Kings 1:11-14; 11:29-39; 16:1-4; 18:17; II Kings 9), or in supporting the king in his military ventures (I Kings 20:22-25, 26-28; 22:13; II Kings 3:13-20; 6:11-12). Elisha was such an active participant in the planning of strategy that King Joash called him "the chariots of Israel and its horsemen" (II Kings 13:14), and he died condemning the king for not wishing to strike down the Syrians more than three times (II Kings 13:14-19). As men of Yahweh these prophets were stanch adherents to the holy war, and if from time to time they did raise their voices against the king's military plans, it was because they felt that the conditions necessary for a holy war were not being met (I Kings 22).

The so-called writing prophets sometimes supported the king in war (Isa. 37:5), but they were far more often opponents than advocates of war. This does not mean that they transcended the traditions of the holy war, but rather that they felt it to be the only type of war in which Israel could validly engage. Since in their analysis of the situation the grounds for such a war were entirely lacking, they were compelled to speak against the participa-

tion of Israel in the power struggles among the great empires of the day.

The necessary prerequisite of holy war is uncompromising trust in the power of Yahweh to give victory. Precisely this quality was missing in Israel. The people trusted in wealth, in the strength of the army, in such alliances as they were able to conclude with foreign powers, and in the apparatus of diplomacy and compromise (Isa. 30:1-5; Jer. 9:23; Amos 2:13-16). Jeremiah declares:

> Cursed is the man who trusts in man
> and makes flesh his arm (17:5),

and Isaiah's oracle shows the impossibility of a holy war in Israel:

> Woe to those who go down to Egypt for help
> and rely on horses,
> who trust in chariots because they are many
> and in horsemen because they are very strong,
> but do not look to the Holy One of Israel
> or consult the LORD! (31:1).

> The Egyptians are men, and not God;
> and their horses are flesh, and not spirit
> (vs. 3).

Hosea speaks with the same accent:

> Ephraim is like a dove,
> silly and without sense,
> calling to Egypt, going to Assyria
> (7:11).

By taking up the religious practices of the nations around her, importing their gods, and abandoning or corrupting the worship of Yahweh, Israel has lost the true source of her strength, the presence of Yahweh with her armies is unthinkable, and the theological basis of the holy war is absent from her life and thought.

In allowing herself to come into this position Israel has denied her covenant vocation—viz., to be a nation marked off from other peoples by her devoted service to Yahweh. She has chosen to "mingle with the nations" (cf. Hos. 7:8), and has taken on their coloration and characteristics. Thus, the people of God stand under judgment, and, in typical biblical fashion, the punishment fits the crime. Yahweh permits them to be a nation like the nations of the earth, and, caught between the great world powers, their tiny army is helpless, and they become a spoil of war. In this way war takes on a new meaning for the prophets. It becomes the judgment of Yahweh on the apostasy and lack of trust of the nation. Striking illustrations of this prophetic reinterpretation of the theological significance of war may be found in Isa. 5:26-30; 10:5-11; Jer. 5:29-31; 6:1-5; Ezek. 5; Hos. 10:7-10; Amos 3:12; Mic. 1:10-16; Hab. 1:5-17. To give an exhaustive list of passages would be virtually to reproduce the prophetic books. The prophetic view of war as divine judgment is a leading idea in the Deuteronomic history work from Judges to the end of Kings, where national disaster and disobedience to Yahweh always go hand in hand.

The OT prophets applied their belief in war as Yahweh's instrument of judgment to other nations as well as Israel. God's control is sovereign over all human history, and he punishes evil where it appears beyond the bounds of Israel (Amos 1–2:3). Usually the destructive judgment of war is visited upon the foreigner because of his oppression of Israel (Jer. 46:10; Obad. 10-14; Nah. 1:2-3); but often the foreigner is condemned for his overweening pride and his confidence in his own power (Isa. 16:5-7; 19:11-15; Jer. 49:16), or for his brutality and lack of humanity (Jer. 51:25-26; Amos 1:13-14; Nah. 3:5-13). There is a reverse side to the coin. As Yahweh may use war to punish his own people, and to work out his vengeance against the foreigner, so he may use a warrior-king for the deliverance of his own people. Isaiah of Babylon saw in Cyrus of Persia the anointed servant of the Lord whose military campaigns would clear the way for Israel's return from exile (Isa. 45). When we enter this circle of thought, prophecy is passing over into apocalyptic.

4. Apocalyptic ideas. Three elements may be distinguished in apocalyptic ideas of war: it is evidence of the control of demonic powers over the present world order; it is a sign of the impending end of that order; and in the form of a final great holy war it will precede the era of peace and of the rule of God.

The apocalyptists considered the present world order to be under the control of demonic powers, who, using the godless rulers of world empires as their instruments, were leading it toward destruction. The wars engaged in by such rulers are, thus, demonic things, spawned by supernatural powers and carried out by their human servants, or originating in an insensate lust for power on the part of the human ruler himself. The pseudepigraphic book of Enoch traces the origin of war to one of the fallen angels, Gadreel, who "showed the children of men all the blows of death" (Enoch 69:6-7), and Jubilees traces it to the rebellious sons of Noah, who "began to war on each other" and "to teach their sons war" (15:2). Since the course of history is a record of increasing degeneration and decadence (Dan. 2:31-45), wars will increase in intensity, brutality, and destructiveness, and an uncontrolled outburst of warfare is a sign of the imminent end of the age (Dan. 8:23-26; IV Esd. 9:1-3; Mark 13:7-8). The demonic powers, whether human or divine, take special delight in directing their attacks against the people of God (Dan. 7:24-25; 8:23; Enoch 91:5-19). Thus war and persecution test the faith and endurance of the covenant community.

The most characteristic apocalyptic teaching about war is, however, a direct derivative from the ancient Israelite conception of the holy war. When God acts to assert his final control over the cosmos, the people of God will march under the messiah of the line of David against the forces of the pagan world and their demonic masters (II Esd. 12:31-39; 13:5-50; Syr. Apocal. Bar. 72; Pss. Sol. 17:23-24; Test. Levi 18:11-12; Test. Dan 5:10-12; Test. Reuben 6:12; Zadokite Document 9:10-20). This idea begins to appear in postexilic prophecy, where it is a working out of the prophetic view that war may be a judgment on the Gentile nations as well as Israel (Isa. 63:1-6; Joel 3:9-21; Hab. 3). Ezekiel's prophecy of the destruction of Gog is the most complete presentation of the theme in the OT (chs. 38–39). After the

cleansing of Israel and her reconstitution as a united nation under one king, Gog and his hosts invade the land, and Yahweh's wrath flames out against them (38:14-23). The divine call to war (vss. 19-23), the victory won by Yahweh's power alone (39:1-6), and the sacrificial nature of the war (vss. 17-20) are all present in Ezekiel's account, but the whole is highlighted by apocalyptic imagery, and the human forces play no more than a passive role.

The idea of the holy war at the end of the days became a common feature of apocalyptic thought, and continues to the present day in the doctrines of apocalyptically minded groups. The War of the Sons of Light and the Sons of Darkness provides a detailed description of such a war, conducted under messianic leadership, with an army composed of men and angels, engaged in a sacrificial battle against human enemies and their demonic allies (*see* DEAD SEA SCROLLS). OT quotations and allusions in this document show that it is self-consciously in the tradition of the holy war.

NT apocalyptic passages follow the typical apocalyptic views of war. War is seen as an evidence of demonic forces in action, and as a portent of the end of the age (Matt. 24:6-8; Mark 13:7-8; Luke 21:9-11). It provides the setting in which faith is put to the supreme test (Matt. 24:9-28; cf. Mark 13:9-13; Luke 21:12-24). While the Markan apocalypse is about a final holy war, Revelation alludes to it as the victory of the Lamb over the ten kings allied to the beast (Rev. 16:14-16), and locates the final battle at ARMAGEDDON. The same book contains a reference to the struggle against Gog and Magog in which the ideology of the holy war is strongly in evidence (20:7-9).

5. The teaching of Jesus. War is, rather unexpectedly, not a central concern in the ministry of Jesus. Insofar as he made messianic claims for himself, Jesus would be compelled to consider the traditional function of the messiah as leader of the final war. There is NT evidence that the disciples tried to cast their Master in this role (Matt. 20:20-27; Mark 10:35-45; Acts 1:6), and some scholars have attempted to show that Jesus accepted it, at least for a time. The weight of evidence indicates that as early in his career as the temptations Jesus rejected war as a means of carrying out his work (Matt. 4:8-10; Luke 4:5-8; *see* TEMPTATION OF JESUS), and defined his office in terms of the Suffering Servant of Deutero-Isaiah. His rebuke of Peter's use of the sword at the arrest (Matt. 26:51-54; Mark 14:47-48; John 18:10-11) is consonant with this view. Although not considering the figure of the warrior-messiah as applying to himself, Jesus indicates that he could have been such a messiah had he wished to do so (Matt. 26:53).

Jesus never spoke directly against war as an instrument of national policy. In his day war was the business of the Roman Empire and was conducted mainly on the frontiers, so that it could not have been immediately relevant to a Palestinian Jew living in a peaceful province of that empire. Jesus spoke as freely with soldiers as with others. He sometimes illustrated his teaching with an example drawn from war (Luke 14:31). He once called on his disciples to produce swords (Luke 22:36), and declared that he had "not come to bring peace, but a sword" (Matt. 10: 34). In the light of his total message this element seems little more than an honest recognition of the divisive nature of his teaching (Matt. 10:34-39).

The teaching of Jesus is strongly directed toward peace and peacemaking. The kingdom of God needs no force to establish or maintain it. The peacemaker is blessed (Matt. 5:9), and the enemy is to be met with love and good deeds instead of hate and violence (Matt. 5:43-44; Luke 6:27, 35). The ethic of Jesus is the antithesis of the warlike mood, and, if universally accepted, would create an ethos in which war was impossible.

6. War and the NT church. The church, the community of the new Israel, was basically different from OT Israel. The latter was a national structure, a political organism, and was, therefore, by its nature thrust into war. The church was an international and interracial body, and was by this fact delivered from engagement in warfare as a church. Individual Christians might serve in national armies, but a Christian armed force or a Christian military campaign was an impossibility. A doctrine of war like that found in the OT was not a pressing necessity for the NT church.

Consequently the NT writers reinterpret the holy war in a spiritual way (I Cor. 14:8; II Cor. 10:3; I Tim. 1:18-19). The church's struggle is not against human beings but against the demonic powers ruling a disordered cosmos (Eph. 6:10-12; *see* DEMON), and its weapons are entirely of the spiritual kind, to be used against the powers of evil, not against human enemies (II Cor. 10:4; Eph. 6:13-17). The basic Christian warfare is against sin in any of its manifestations.

Physical warfare belongs to the province of the state, not of the church. It originates in greed and lust for power and is one of the implements by which the demonic powers bring sin and death upon the present world order (Jas. 4:1-2). The Christian's struggle with his appropriate spiritual weapons is, therefore, against the very powers which bring war into existence; and when this struggle is consummated, war will be at an end.

Victory in Christian spiritual warfare, as in the OT holy war, is given by God, not achieved by men. But unlike the Jewish apocalyptists, the Christians did not have to wait until the end of the age for an intervention of God in history. (In the crucifixion and resurrection of Jesus Christ, God had won the decisive battle against the demonic, war-making powers, had broken their control over mankind, and guaranteed their ultimate overthrow.) While the doctrine of the second coming of Christ (*see* PAROUSIA) made it possible for the NT church to retain the idea of a holy war in the end of the days (*see* § 4 *above*), the vital theological importance of such a war was not felt by the Christian, and it became a minor motif in NT thought.

In the period of waiting between the act of God in Christ and the final total victory the Christian's duty was not military action, but endurance and witness to the gospel. In calling men to reconciliation with God in Christ the Christian was calling them to reconciliation with one another, and hence making peace (Rom. 5:1-5; II Cor. 5:16-21; Eph. 2:11-22; etc.). *See* ATONEMENT; RECONCILIATION; PEACE IN THE OT.

Bibliography. G. von Rad, *Der Heilige Krieg* (1951); W. Bienert, *Krieg, Kriegsdienst, und Kriegsdienstverweigerung nach der Botschaft des NT* (1952); G. H. C. Macgregor, *The NT Basis of Pacifism* (1953); G. von Rad, "Deuteronomy and the Holy War," *Studies in Deuteronomy* (1953), ch. 4; J. Lasserre, *Der Krieg und das Evangelium* (1956); S. Mowinckel, "The National Messiah," *He That Cometh* (1956); ch. 9; K. M. T. Atkinson, "The Historical Setting of the 'War of the Sons of Light and the Sons of Darkness,'" *Bulletin of the John Rylands Library*, 40 (1958), 272-98.   L. E. TOOMBS

WAR, IMPLEMENTS OF. *See* WEAPONS AND IMPLEMENTS OF WAR.

WAR, METHODS OF.

1. Terminology
2. Geographical conditions of Palestine
3. Military routes
4. Fortresses
5. Razzias
6. Ruses
7. Preparation for war
8. Open warfare
9. Siege warfare
10. Consequences of war
11. Wars of liberation
Bibliography

1. Terminology. The regular words for "war" in the Bible are מלחמה and πόλεμος, along with their corresponding verbs נלחם and πολεμέω. The word חיל is incorrectly rendered "war" by the KJV at Deut. 3:18 (RSV "[men of] valor"); II Chr. 33:14 (RSV "army"). Literally it means "strength"; by extension it also means "wealth," either economic or military, therefore "army" (cf. the English word "force"). The word לחם occurs only in Judg. 5:8 in an unintelligible phrase. The root צבא, "to wage war," is most commonly found in its substantival form, צבא ("host of warriors," "war service"). The word קרב derives from קרב, "to come near, approach"; it thus means "an approach with hostile intent"—i.e., "war."

In the NT the following words are used: ἀντιστρατεύομαι, "to war against" (Rom. 7:23; cf RSV "at war with"); πόλεμος, "war" (Matt. 24:6; Mark 13:7; I Cor. 14:8 ["battle"]; Heb. 11:34; Jas. 4:1, etc.); πολεμέω, "to war, battle, wage war" (Jas. 4:2; Rev. 2:16; 12:7, etc.); στράτευμα, "army, troops, soldiers" (Matt. 22:7, etc.; Luke 23:11; Acts 23:10, 27); στρατεύομαι, "to serve as soldier, wage war" (Luke 3:14; I Cor. 9:7, participle "soldier"; II Tim. 2:4; Jas. 4:1, participle "soldier in service"; II Tim. 2:4; I Pet. 2:11, etc.).

2. Geographical conditions of Palestine. To understand Hebrew battle tactics, it is necessary to examine briefly the terrain of Palestine (*see* Map I). Palestine is divided into four extremes: the coastal plains, the central ridge (the S extension of the Lebanon range), the Jordan Valley, and the Transjordanian Plateau (an extension of the Antilebanons).

The coastal plain, the most fertile and arable part of Palestine, was never completely occupied by the Hebrews—the Canaanites and Phoenicians held the N, the Philistines the S, part. The center of Hebrew culture lay in the central ridge, an almost unbroken range of hill country extending southward to the Negeb. This ridge is broken between the hills of Galilee and of Samaria by the large Plain of Esdraelon, a fertile plain of great strategic importance since the armies of antiquity (Egyptian and Assyrian, e.g.) most naturally traversed this plain. Megiddo (and Taanach to the S) was located at the juncture of this plain and the Plain of Sharon on the coast, thus constituting from earliest historical times a place of outstanding strategic importance from a military point of view. Westward the plain issues in the Jordan Valley through passes above and below the Hill of Moreh.

The Samaritan hills extend from Mount Gilboa overlooking the Plain of Esdraelon southward, with Mount Ebal and Mount Gerizim overlooking the Plain of Shechem. Passes from this plain run in all directions, giving to the plain and the city of Samaria, built by Omri, military significance. The S hill country was Judah, with the bleak Wilderness of Judah toward the E and the Shephelah to the SW. In the Shephelah fortress cities were built by the Israelites to protect their frontier against the Philistines, as well as the marauding tribes of the desert.

The Jordan Rift continues the depression of Coele-Syria southward to its lowest point at the Dead Sea (1,290 feet below sea level), through the Arabah until it issues in the Gulf of Aqabah. E of the Jordan is plateau land dissected by large E-W rifts: the Yarmuk, which flows into the Jordan just below its rise at the Sea of Galilee; and the Jabbok, which rises near Amman and divides ancient Gilead. The Arnon runs through an impressive gorge on the N border of ancient Moab into the Dead Sea. The S border of Moab was probably Wadi el-Hesa (the River Zered?), flowing into the Dead Sea just above its S tip.

3. Military routes. Palestine constituted the land bridge between the valleys of the Nile and the Tigris-Euphrates. The favorite route lay along the coastal trade route, as the inscriptions on the left bank of the Nahr el-Kelb show. Another route branched off at Megiddo through the Esdraelon Plain to the Jordan and from there northeastward to Damascus. Of some importance for later times was the Transjordan trade route from Damascus to Petra to the head of the Gulf of Aqabah.

For the invading nomads from the desert (Midianites, Ammonites, Moabites, Israelites) these great routes were of no importance. Once the Jordan was crossed, the Jericho Plain gave access to Palestine westward over the central ridge by way of Bethel to Lower and Upper Beth-horon to the coastal regions. Access to the central regions around Shechem was most easily gained from the Jordan Valley through the broad Wadi Far'ah.

4. Fortresses. Prior to the monarchy the Israelites had no walled cities for defense; and as a result, when raiding bands invaded the country, they had to hide in mountain caves (Judg. 6:2) and in holes, rocks, tombs, and cisterns (I Sam. 13:6). Saul forti-

fied his rude capital at Gibeah (Tell el-Ful), but defensive fortifications had their actual beginnings under David with the capture of Jerusalem. Eventually such defense posts as Libnah, Lachish, Gezer, and Beth-horon (especially Upper Beth-horon) constituted a series of fortified cities along the SW border. Omri built and fortified Samaria as the strong capital of the N kingdom. On opposite ends of the Plain of Esdraelon lay the fortresses of Megiddo and Jezreel, both admirably suited for defense. After the division of the monarchy, lines of defense were built on the borders. Baasha attempted to build Ramah as a frontier post, but Asa of Judah, with the bought help of the Arameans, was able to destroy Ramah and build Geba and Mizpah as Benjaminite border fortresses (I Kings 15:16-22).

5. Razzias. The razzia or raid has been from time immemorial the military form of the nomad and seminomad. The Ayyam el-'Arab in the Jahiliyah period find their modern counterparts in clan raids among the tribes of the Arabian Peninsula. Settled states found the sudden raids of such tribes highly disconcerting. Witness the complaint in the Instruction for King Meri-ka-re (twenty-second century B.C.) in Egypt: "Lo, the wretched Asiatic—it goes ill with the place where he is, afflicted with water, difficult from many trees, the ways thereof painful because of the mountains. He does not dwell in a single place, (but) his legs *are made to go astray*. He has been fighting (ever) since the time of Horus, (but) he does not conquer, nor yet can he be conquered. He does not announce a day in fighting, like a thief who . . ." (*ANET* 416). The ill-starred expedition of Aelius Gallus in 24 B.C. against the Bedouins was obviously not the first to suffer because of the mobility of the desert nomads.

Palestine in the pre-monarchical period was perennially subjected to tribal razzias; in fact, the tribe of Gad itself was a גדוד, a "raiding troop" (Gen. 49:19 RSV mg.). Thus the Israelites suffered from inroads by the Moabites, Amalekites, and Ammonites (Judg. 3:13), the Midianites (6:1-5), the Ammonites (10:9; cf. vs. 12), the Moabites (II Kings 13:20), the Amalekites (I Sam. 30:1-2), and the Philistines (Judg. 15:9; I Sam. 13:17-18). David also made intermittent raids on tribes in the desert S of the Negeb (I Sam. 27:8, 11).

Such raids, aside from the desire for plunder (שלל [II Sam. 3:22]), were often occasioned by disputes about wells (Gen. 26:17-22), or about rights of pasturage (Gen. 13:5-7). Raids naturally involved plunder and captives, and it would be the business of the raided village to attempt to recapture what had been lost. Such a raid undoubtedly lies behind the puzzling account in Gen. 14 in which a coalition of E kings are represented as raiding the Cities of the Plain. Abraham with a raiding party of 318 men gave chase and, by dividing his forces in a night attack, repossessed the stolen goods and liberated the captives. Such raiding bands were inevitably small, thereby allowing greater mobility as well as the element of surprise; cf. the story of Gideon and his 300 men who overcame the Midianites and their allies (Judg. 7-8) or the 600 men of Dan who captured Laish (Judg. 18:11-29).

6. Ruses. The success of an attack could often be ensured by the element of surprise. In the account of the capture of Ai (Josh. 8), Joshua lured the inhabitants out of the city by a pretended retreat while a large AMBUSH, hidden near the city, captured the defenseless city and sacked it. Shechem was similarly taken by Abimelech (Judg. 9:34-45), as was Gibeah of Benjamin by the Israelites (Judg. 20:29 ff).

The most favorable time of attack was either during the latter half of the night or immediately before dawn. The invading tribes are described as marching all night to surprise a strong Amorite coalition attacking Gibeon at dawn (Josh. 10:9). Saul surprised the Ammonites by a split-troop predawn attack (I Sam. 11:11), and Gideon fell on the Midianites just after midnight (Judg. 7:19) also in a split (three-group) attack. King Mesha of Moab captured Nebo from Israel by a night attack which began at the break of dawn (cf. Moabite Stone, line 15, *ANET* 320).

7. Preparation for war. The spring of the year was the "time when kings go forth to battle" (II Sam. 11:1). Once enemy territory was invaded, the army would live off the land; but in the case of defensive warfare, before the establishment of the Davidic dynasty, troop provisions were the responsibility of the soldiers' families (I Sam. 17:17-18), or of clans (I Sam. 25:18; II Sam. 17:27-29). Under Solomon, levies were made to provide food for the "king and his household" (I Kings 4:7, 27-28).

War was seldom declared, since this would eliminate the element of surprise. The declaration of war by Amaziah of Judah against Jehoahaz of Israel (II Kings 14:8) was unusual, and had disastrous consequences for Judah (cf. vss. 12-14). Negotiations were sometimes attempted in order to avoid actual conflict (Judg. 11:12 ff), but the demands made were often so preposterous that acquiescence was impossible (I Sam. 11:1 ff; I Kings 20:2 ff).

Troops were mustered in various ways: (*a*) by blowing the שׁופָר (a curved war horn; Judg. 3:27; 6:34); (*b*) by visible signals set on a hill (*see* BANNER); (*c*) by sending messengers throughout the land (Judg. 7:24), often with some symbol of a bizarre imprecatory rite appealing to the people's emotions, such as pieces of dismembered oxen (I Sam. 11:7) or the body of the ravished concubine cut into pieces (Judg. 19:29 ff).

Before engaging in war, Israel, like other nations, consulted their God to determine whether the times were favorable for the project. Yahweh was אלהי צבאות ("god of hosts"), which in early days certainly meant "God of the hosts of Israel." Yahweh is called a "man of war" in Exod. 15:3; he trains hands for war, even fingers for battle (Ps. 144:1). War might be undertaken only by divine sanction (Num. 14:40 ff); Yahweh gave heavenly help in times of battle (Josh. 10:11; Judg. 5:20). A favorable oracle might be sought from prophets (I Kings 22:5 ff; II Kings 3:11 ff). Joash, on Elisha's orders, resorts to arrow divination (II Kings 13:15 ff), and Saul illegally consults familiar spirits through necromancy (I Sam. 28:6 ff), more orthodox means (dreams, Urim, or prophets) having failed. Priestly oracles were probably the most commonly sought. Inquiry

was made before the ark (Judg. 20:27), or the ephod (I Sam. 30:7-8; *see* EPHOD 1), or the URIM AND THUMMIM (I Sam. 28:6; cf. 14:41). Priests would accompany the army into battle, as did the ark (I Sam. 4:4; 30:7; cf. Num. 31:6; II Sam. 11:11). The Philistines brought their idols along into the field (II Sam. 5:21). Jewish soldiers were known to carry charms to ensure their safety during the Maccabean Wars, according to II Macc. 12:40.

Before battle, sacrifices had to be made to gain God's favor (Judg. 6:20, 26; 20:26). This was "consecrating war," קדש מלחמה—i.e., translating the war and its instruments out of a profane into a sacred state (Jer. 6:4; Joel 3[4]:9; Mic. 3:5; cf. Josh. 3:5; Isa. 13:3). Such sacrifices were usually holocausts (*see* BURNT OFFERING; I Sam. 7:9). In particularly grave crises a human sacrifice was considered very potent (II Kings 3:27).

8. Open warfare. The battle array (מערכה) was of the simplest kind. A solid line of shield-bearing spearmen held the first line of defense, with the archers in the rear. Once battle was engaged, the whole mass of troops joined in hand-to-hand combat. The sounding of the trumpet gave the signal for attack (II Chr. 13:12; I Macc. 16:8) as well as for retreat (II Sam. 2:28; 18:16; 20:22). The army would often be divided for split attack (Gen. 14:15), usually into three parts (Judg. 7:16; I Sam. 11:11; II Sam. 18:2; I Macc. 5:33). Attack was often accompanied with a prearranged war cry, as: "A sword for Yahweh and for Gideon!" (Judg. 7:20; cf. I Sam. 17:52; Isa. 42:13; Amos. 1:14).

Bedouin battles, as in the War of the Basūs or the day of Dahis during the Ayyam el-'Arab, were often settled by the single combat of opposing champions. In similar fashion David killed the Philistine giant Goliath in such an encounter (I Sam. 17:48-51), whereupon the Philistines fled. In a later encounter between the forces of Ish-bosheth and David such a contest was arranged between twelve champions for each side (II Sam. 2:12 ff; cf. HELKATH-HAZZURIM).

The Israelites did not master the art of open warfare before the time of David. Saul was outmaneuvered by the Philistines in his last encounter with them when he allowed his army to be lured into open warfare at the base of Mount Gilboa on the Esdraelon Plain (I Sam. 28:4). The Israelites were more at home guarding Benjaminite, Judean, or Ephraimite passes; in fact, such passes as the one at Michmash could be held by very few men (I Sam. 14). Even as late as the ninth century the Syrians thought of Yahweh as a god of the hills (I Kings 20:23).

It was the Philistine crisis which brought about a unification of the tribes and a reorganization of military affairs. The charismatic chieftains (*see* JUDGE) of the premonarchical age were men of the moment, indulging in guerrilla tactics when the need arose. David himself was well versed in these tactics, but after his coronation he appointed as commander in chief of his forces Joab, a man of outstanding military genius. Through a stratagem Joab captured Jerusalem, the Jebusite stronghold, which David thereupon made his capital city. Joab was a master at siegework (II Sam. 11:1; 20:15), and it is doubtful whether this art was well known to the Israelites before this time.

Furthermore, David created an empire by incessant warfare with the Philistines, Moabites, Syrians, Edomites, and Ammonites (cf. especially II Sam. 8); in the course of this warfare horses and chariots were captured, and the methods of both open and siege warfare were developed. Under Solomon, cities to house these accouterments of battle were built (*see* CHARIOT), and a standing ARMY of mercenary troops became the accepted practice.

9. Siege warfare (מצור, "siege"; צור, "besiege"). Though siege warfare was already known to the Egyptians of the Middle Kingdom, it was actually the Assyrians who became masters of this type of warfare. It was, however, known throughout the Near East. To avoid a long siege, spies might be sent in advance to discover a city's weaknesses (Judg. 1:22 ff; *see* SPY).

An effective siege cut off all communications of a city without outside help and occupied all the water supplies in the neighborhood. When Joab had once taken the "city of waters" (cf. Polybius 5.71) at Rabbah of the Ammonites, he could send David word that the army was ready for the assault (II Sam. 12:27). Actually the siege of Rabbah is the first recorded siege of the Israelites; prior to this, direct assault was the usual means the Israelites employed in capturing a city. Once a place was invested, a fortress could communicate with other places of defense only by such means as flares, as is known from the fourth Lachish Letter (lines 10-13).

When the Israelites besieged a walled city, they built a siege wall (סללה; cf. דיק, which occurs as a synonym. The difference between the two words is not known. The latter word occurs only with reference to the investiture of Jerusalem by Nebuchadrezzar [II Kings 25:1; Jer. 52:4; Ezek. 4:2; 17:17; 21:22—H 21:27; 26:8; translated "siege walls" and "siegeworks" in the RSV], whereas סללה is used also of the Israelite siege; cf. II Sam. 20:15; the word occurs also in II Kings 19:32; Isa. 37:33; Jer. 6:6; 32:24; 33:4; Ezek. 4:2; 17:17; 21:22—H 21:27; 26:8; Dan. 11:15; translated "mound," "siege mound," "siege wall," "siegeworks" [Dan. 11:15], in the RSV). Such an earthen mound served as a protection particularly for the archers.

The Assyrian siege methods are well known from both cuneiform sources and the bas-reliefs. War machines were usually constructed of materials on hand for which trees in the vicinity would be hewn down (cf. Jer. 6:6). Then causeways would be built

3. City attacked with battering ram, from Nimrud

so that the siege machines, mounted on four or six wooden wheels, could be rolled up to the immediate area of the wall. Such machines were of two kinds: the movable siege platform from which one could shoot directly at the defenders on the walls, and the BATTERING RAM, operated by hand and so constructed as to give room for a body of archers on its tower (Fig. WAR 3). The defenders would try to neutralize the battering ram by chains and grapnels.

Meanwhile, the walls would be further weakened by the digging of a tunnel. Such a long trench approach was found in the Hyksos embankment at Tell ed-Duweir. Once the besiegers felt that the defense was sufficiently weakened to permit a concerted attack, the general assault was made. The first to advance were the heavy armed infantry, equipped with shields and spears. It was they who were to mount the tall scaling ladders. Meanwhile, crouched behind mantelets were the archers, who kept up a heavy barrage of arrows to protect the invading forces. The besieged, defending with the energy of despair, hurled boiling oil and shot burning arrows at the invaders.

The methods of siege warfare so well understood by the Assyrians and the later Babylonians were also adopted by the Seleucids of the second century B.C. in their siege of Jerusalem (I Macc. 6:48 ff). Specialized machines for hurling fire (πυροβόλα) and stones (λιθοβόλα) were used by the besiegers, as well as slings and σκορπίδια εἰς τὸ βάλλεσθαι βέλη σφενδόνας (some type of shooting device for hurling arrows). The catapult may have been known to the Assyrians (if the interpretation of *nimgalli*—lit., "large flies"—as a catapult in Sennacherib's Annals is correct; cf. Luckenbill, vol. II, p. 62, col. IV, 79). Just what σκορπίδια were is not known, though it has plausibly been suggested that they were small crossbows. According to Josephus, slingers were used for investiture by the Romans as well (War I.vii.3).

10. Consequences of war. Once a city was taken, the defenders were put to the sword. The narratives of the Conquest (Josh. 5–12) show complete ruthlessness on the part of the conquerors. Since war was believed to be a sacred duty, divine favor might be assured by declaring the *ḥērem* (חרם), a pact with the deity by which everything animate was devoted for destruction (cf. Josh. 6:17-21; I Sam. 15:3). Breaking such a promise was a major sacrilege and might involve defeat, as in the story of Achan (Josh. 7). Captured kings and leaders were usually slain. The male populace was often completely exterminated (I Kings 11:15), or mutilated (Judg. 1:6), or taken as slaves (Deut. 20:11). Women and children were the spoils of war, though pregnant women were often disemboweled (II Kings 8:12; 15:16; Amos 1:13).

The cruelty of the Assyrian conquerors was proverbial. Large numbers were impaled or decapitated, the dissevered heads being thrown together in large heaps. Principals were often drawn and quartered. Shalmanezer III boasted of having burned boys and girls alive in the city of Aridi (Monolith Inscription, line 17). Captives were mutilated by cutting off hands, feet, nose, ears, or tongue. Infants were dashed to pieces (Ps. 137:9; Nah. 3:10), and the able-bodied were taken into slavery. Native peoples in the West were deported to the East and replaced with loyal subjects (II Kings 17:6, 24; cf. 24:14; 25:11).

In the event of a successful siege the walls were broken down (II Kings 25:10), and the city and especially its temples were burned with fire (cf. vs. 9). Anything of value became BOOTY for the pillaging soldiers. Should a city submit voluntarily, however, a heavy tribute (II Kings 18:14-16) was imposed, and hostages might also be taken to ensure submission.

11. Wars of liberation. The revolt of the Maccabees originally had the character of partisan warfare. With the exception of a few sieges (such as the Jerusalem Akra and Beth-zur) the rebels engaged in guerrilla warfare, suddenly appearing seemingly out of nowhere, attacking, and then withdrawing, as suddenly as they had appeared, into the hills. These enervating tactics forced the Syrians to come to Palestine with huge forces including infantry, cavalry, and a scythe-chariot corps (*see* CHARIOT), as well as an ELEPHANT corps (II Macc. 13:2). In hilly Palestine such an unwieldy group, accompanied as it was with a large train, lacked maneuverability, and small guerrilla bands were able to make raids on it almost at will.

Bibliography. Josephus *Wars of the Jews.* B. Meissner, *Babylonien und Assyrien* I (1920), ch. 4. F.-M. Abel, "Topographie des Compagnes Machabéennes," *RB*, 32 (1923), 495 ff; 33 (1924), 201 ff, 371 ff; 34 (1925), 194 ff; 35 (1926), 206 ff, 510 ff. J. Kromayer and G. Veith, *Heerwesen und Kriegführung der Griechen und Römer* (*HAW* IV, 3.2 [1928]). A. Götze, *Kleinasien* (*HAW* III, 1.3, pt. 3, 1 [1933]), pp. 114 ff. A. G. Barrois, *Manuel d'Archéologie Biblique,* II (1953), 87 ff.

J. W. WEVERS

WAR CLUB. *See* CLUB.

WARDROBE, KEEPER OF THE [שֹׁמֵר הַבְּגָדִים]. A servant in the royal household who had charge of the robes of the king. In the time of Josiah's reform (II Kings 22:14) one is mentioned named Harhas (Hasrah in II Chr. 34:22). In II Kings 10:22 the robes for royal worship were in his care. Perhaps there was a special room in the palace for storing the royal robes.

C. U. WOLF

WARE (MERCHANDISE). *See* TRADE AND COMMERCE.

WARS OF THE LORD, BOOK OF THE. A document mentioned in Num. 21:14 (*see* NUMBERS, BOOK OF) as the source of the poetic quotation which immediately follows (vss. 14-15). It is possible that the two other poems quoted in this chapter (vss. 17-18, 27-30), or at least the first of them, are to be attributed to the same source; although this is by no means certain, since they are quite different in character.

The fragment which is explicitly assigned to the book gives no clue as to the book's nature or contents, being merely a geographical note from which even the main verb has disappeared. From the title, however, it may be safely presumed that the book was a collection of ancient folk poetry relating certainly to the wars of the conquest in the time of Joshua and perhaps also to those of Saul and David, which led to the establishment of the kingdom and

the empire. The mention of this book is important as confirming the view that the traditions embodied in the present biblical documents are derived in part from older written sources as well as from oral tradition. There is mention elsewhere (Josh. 10:13; II Sam. 1:18) of what is presumably another document of this kind, the "Book of Jashar" (*see* JASHAR, BOOK OF), which obviously cannot be older than the time of David and may therefore give a hint as to the date of the Book of the Wars of Yahweh.

The "wars of Yahweh" are the wars which were fought on his behalf and in which he personally took part; the interests of the god among ancient peoples were identical with the interests of the nation. For the early Hebrews war was a sacred activity ("to prepare war" is literally, in Hebrew, "to consecrate war" [Jer. 6:4]), and Yahweh himself was the God "of ṣᵉbhā'ôth"—i.e., "of armies" (Ps. 24:10; cf. vs. 8).

R. C. DENTAN

WASH, WASHINGS [כבס, *lit.* to trample, *usually of garments;* רחץ, bathe, *usually of persons*]. *See* BATHING.

WASHBASIN [סור רחץ]; KJV WASHPOT. The use of this word in Pss. 60:8; 108:9 is most interesting. The Hebrew term used here normally refers to a wide-mouth cooking pot. In these passages the cooking pot, which must be kept ceremonially clean, has degenerated into a washbasin. In these identical passages Moab is described as God's washbasin, perhaps because of its proximity to the Dead Sea.

J. L. KELSO

WASP [σφηξ] (Wisd. Sol. 12:8; cf. LXX at Exod. 23:28; Deut. 7:20; Josh. 24:12). Any of numerous species of insects of the order Hymenoptera, divided into two groups, the Diploptera (or *Vespoidea*) and the Sphecoidea (or *Fossores*). Most of the wasps are solitary in their habits (e.g., the *Eumenidae*, the mudwasps), but others are social (e.g., the Vespidae), and among the latter is the common hornet (Vespa crabro).

See also BEE; HORNET.

Bibliography. For Aristotle's discussion of wasps, see *Hist. Anim.* 554 *b* (V.23); 627 *b*–628 *b* (IX.41); cf. Tristram, *NHB,* pp. 321-22.

W. S. MCCULLOUGH

WATCH, WATCHES. *See* NIGHT.

WATCHER. The conventional rendering (following Aq., Symm., ἐγρήγορος; Vulg. *vigil*) of the Aramaic term עִיר, used in Dan. 4:13, 17, 23, to designate a certain type of celestial being. The rendering is based on derivation of the word from the root עוּר, "be awake."

The beings in question are more fully described in the pseudepigraphic book of Enoch (second century B.C.), where they are identified (21:10) specifically with the angels, and again (1:5; 10:9, 15; 12: 2, 4; 13:10; 14:1, 3) more generally with those denizens of heaven that were expelled for their waywardness and rebellion (cf. Gen. 6:1-8). The latter identification occurs also in the book of Jubilees (4: 15, 22; 7:21; 8:3), in the Testaments of the Twelve Patriarchs (Test. Reuben 5:6; Test. Naph. 3:5), in the so-called Zadokite Document (A ii, 17-19), and in the Genesis Apocryphon discovered among the Dead Sea Scrolls (II.1).

The exact meaning of the term עיר is uncertain. The LXX renders loosely "angel," and Theod. is content with mere transliteration (ειρ). As early as the second century B.C., however, it was already understood in the sense of "wakeful," for it is often paraphrased in Enoch by the expression "those that sleep not" (e.g., 39:12-13; 40:2; 71:7). If this view be correct, the name would reflect a common ancient belief that celestial beings are sleepless; this is said, e.g., of the Vedic Adityas (Rig Veda II, 27:9), of the Iranian Mithra (Yasht 10.7) and Ahura-mazda (Videvdat 19.20), of the Greek Zeus (Sophocles *Oedipus at Colonus* 702), and—in the OT itself—of Yahweh (Ps. 121:4). Considering the lateness of its appearance in Hebrew and Aramaic, and the acknowledged indebtedness of Jewish angelology to Iranian sources (*see* ANGEL), it is not improbable that the term reproduces a yet unidentified Iranian expression (e.g., *axvafnō*, "sleepless one") for some such mythological being as a fravashi. T. H. GASTER

WATCHMAN. One who keeps vigil, who guards a person or property, usually at night; hence, a sentry or keeper of the gate. In the NT the guard or sentries posted around prisons were acting as watchmen, although not designated as such (Acts 5:23; 12:6, 19).

Watchmen over fields and vineyards were posted usually only during the time of harvesting. They erected booths to serve as shelter from the heat and built watchtowers to facilitate observation (נצר; II Kings 17:9; II Chr. 20:24; Job 27:18; etc.).

The watchman (שמר, צפה) of the city kept the walls safe from the enemy at night and called out the safety of the city like a sentry (I Sam. 14:16; II Sam. 18:24; II Kings 9:17; Song of S. 3:3; 5:7; etc.). He was especially valuable in time of siege (Jer. 51: 12). Yet the biblical belief in providence was such that no watchman could protect the city unless God kept it (Ps. 127:1). Figuratively the pious are watchmen who await the Lord's blessings (Ps. 130:6).

The prophets as watchmen of God observed the impending doom on the nation as well and announced it to the sleeping, indifferent people (Hos. 9:8). The commission of a prophet was to be a watchman over God's people (Isa. 21:6; Jer. 6:17; Ezek. 3:17). Preachers and prophets do not always bring bad news to the people (Isa. 52:8; 62:6). The oracle concerning Dumah has become a familiar Advent or Epiphany pericope (Isa. 21:11-12). So the prophet is concerned to bring the people back to God (Jer. 31:6). This burden of responsibility is heavy on God's watchmen (Ezek. 33:2, 6). False prophets or the prophets of false gods are blind watchmen (Isa. 56:10).

An agent of God from heaven is called a "watcher" (עיר; LXX ἐγρήγορος) in Dan. 4:13 ff. Probably this agent is considered an angel. God is also a watcher over men (Job 7:20). In the apocryphal books the term "watchman" is used to designate fallen angels (ἐγρήγορος; Enoch 1:5; 10:9) and archangels (Enoch 20:1; 39:12).

See also OVERSEER; OFFICER; GUARD.

C. U. WOLF

WATCHTOWER [מגדל (II Kings 18:8; Isa. 5:2); מצפה (II Chr. 20:24; Isa. 21:8); בחן (Isa. 32:14)]. A structure from which a certain area of land could be guarded.

Towers were built in the fields from which the owner of the land or his workmen could watch the crops as they ripened and thus keep them from being stolen. The towers were generally constructed of stone and usually provided temporary living quarters, since the fields would have to be watched night and day for a period of time.

From *Atlas of the Bible* (Thomas Nelson & Sons Limited)
4. Watchtower in a Palestinian field

In present-day Palestine watchtowers are usually round and may be as high as ten feet. Often they consist of two levels—a ground level, where there will be living quarters, and the top level, surrounded by a low wall, from which there is a good view of the entire field.

Fig. WAT 4. H. N. RICHARDSON

WATER [מים; ὕδωρ]. In many instances, of course, this word is used in the ordinary sense, thus referring to springs, lakes, seas, rain, etc. In other cases the characteristics of water provide the basis for metaphor—e.g., "Unstable as water, you shall not have pre-eminence" (Gen. 49:4); "We are like water spilt on the ground, which cannot be gathered up again" (II Sam. 14:14);

> As in water face answers face,
> so the mind of man reflects the man
> (Prov. 27:19);

or "He who doubts is like a wave of the sea that is driven and tossed by the wind" (Jas. 1:6). Moreover, because of its cleansing power, water figured prominently in ritual usage and symbolism, as indicated by the references to "living" (i.e., fresh, running) water in the priestly literature (Lev. 14:5-6, 50-52; 15:13), WATER FOR IMPURITY (Num. 19:13, 20-21), holy water (Num. 5:17), and, in a special sense, the water of bitterness that brings the curse (Num. 5:18, 23-24). The prophets, critical of the efficacy of external rites, insisted that an inner cleansing was necessary (Isa. 1:16; cf. Ps. 51:7—H 51:9); and the priestly prophet, Ezekiel, proclaimed that this cleansing would take place in the new age, according to Yahweh's promise: "I will sprinkle clean water upon you, and you shall be clean from all your uncleannesses" (Ezek. 36:25). The cultic significance of water is further expounded in the NT, where the people of God are said to be cleansed "by the washing of water with the word" (Eph. 5:26; cf. Tit. 3:5), and individual baptism by water is the sign of baptism by the Spirit (John 3; cf. Heb. 10:22). In I Pet. 3:18-22 it is held that baptism is typologically foreshadowed in the story of the Flood, when "eight persons were saved through water"; and in I Cor. 10:1-5 the crossing of the Red Sea is taken to mean that the Israelites "were baptized into Moses in the cloud and in the sea," even as their thirst was quenched from Christ, the "supernatural Rock which followed them" (cf. Exod. 17:6; Num. 20:11). *See* BAPTISM.

The symbolism of water, however, is by no means exhausted by these cultic meanings. In a land where existence was often precarious, men knew in an elemental sense their dependence upon "bread and water" (I Kings 13:18; Isa. 3:1) as the basic necessities of life (the value of water is exquisitely portrayed in the Davidic episode, II Sam. 23:13-17), and in such a situation were prompted to confess their utter dependence upon God, who supplies man's daily needs (*see* BREAD). The theological meaning of the image of water comes to expression in Israel's ancient traditions concerning the sojourn in the wilderness. The lack of water invariably was the occasion for murmuring and doubt; and in these times of trial, according to tradition, faith was given the assurance of Yahweh's presence, for, in a miraculous manner (*see* SIGNS AND WONDERS), he provided his people with water (see the food-and-water traditions in Exod. 15:22-17:7; Num. 20-21; cf. I Kings 19:6; Neh. 9:15, 20; Pss. 78:15-16, 20; 105:41). According to Deuteronomic interpretation, the people were providentially led through these trying experiences in order that they might come to know that man lives only by the word of God (Deut. 8; note vss. 15-16). From the same viewpoint, the entrance into the Land of Promise would be attended by signs of Yahweh's goodness, "for Yahweh your God is bringing you into a good land, a land of brooks of water, of fountains and springs, flowing forth in valleys and hills" (vs. 7).

In contrast to the alluvial plains of Mesopotamia and Egypt, Palestine is by and large a hilly, rocky country whose fertility is dependent upon annual rainfall. It is, as Deuteronomy states, a "land . . . which drinks water by the rain from heaven" (11:11). Water, therefore, is an element friendly to man, rather than an enemy as in the extraneous flood tradition (*see below*). Thus the major contrast is between the desert and the fertile ground, as can be seen from the Yahwist's story of the Creation (Gen. 2). There it is said that, before Yahweh caused rain to fall, the earth used to be watered by a "mist" or "flood" (אד) which gushed up from the subterranean fresh-water stream (vs. 6), and Paradise is conceived as an oasis from which issued a river to irrigate the surrounding desert. Since Palestine itself is a kind of oasis on the fringe of the Arabian Desert, Israel was tempted to believe, on coming out of the wilderness, that rainfall and fertility were dependent upon the nature gods (*see* BAAL; RAIN). Elijah threw down the challenge to the Baal by announcing a famine in the name of Yahweh (I Kings 17:1), and the contest on Mount Carmel is best understood as a demonstra-

tion of Yahweh's power to bring rain (I Kings 18:20 ff; see especially vss. 41-46). Hosea declared that Israel had to learn her dependence upon Yahweh, who provides the gifts of fertility (Hos. 2:1-23—H 2:3-25), and criticized a superficial repentance, expressed in the confident testimony that Yahweh

> will come to us as the showers,
> as the spring rains that water the earth
> (6:3).

It is the God of Israel who blesses his people

> with blessings of heaven above,
> blessings of the deep that couches beneath
> (Gen. 49:25)—

i.e., he controls the heavenly and subterranean waters. Thus it came to be a cardinal tenet of Israel's faith that Yahweh waters the earth by sending rain and causing springs to gush forth in the valleys (Pss. 65:9-10—H 65:10-11; 104:10-13; 147:18; Amos 5:7-8; 9:6; cf. Job 5:10; 12:15; 26:8; 28:25-26; 36:27-28).

The significance of water in the Palestinian locale often provided the metaphors of religious language. Amos insisted that justice should "roll down like waters" and righteousness "like an ever-flowing stream" (5:24), rather than like the wadis that dry up quickly when the rainy season is over. Using the same figure, Jeremiah queried whether Yahweh would be to him "like a deceitful brook, like waters that fail" (Jer. 15:18). The gentle waters of Shiloah —an aqueduct which carried water from a spring to a pool inside the Jerusalem walls—were to Isaiah a symbol of quiet and confident faith in Yahweh, the spurning of whom would result in an overflowing flood from the Euphrates (Isa. 8:5-8). Water, therefore, could be a symbol of Yahweh's salvation, as in the summons to "draw water from the wells of salvation" (Isa. 12:3) or to "come to the waters" (55:1), even as the absence of Yahweh's word could be regarded as thirst and famine (Amos 8:11). Jeremiah rebuked the people for relying on water stored up in leaky cisterns and for rejecting Yahweh, the "fountain of living waters" (Jer. 2:13; 17:13; cf. Ps. 36:8-9—H 36:9-10). This theme finds new expression in the story of Jesus, who, at Jacob's Well, promised to provide "living water," in the drinking of which man would never thirst, for it would become in him a "spring of water welling up to eternal life" (John 4:10-15; cf. 6:35; 7:37-38). The book of Revelation affirms that Christ dispenses "water without price from the fountain of the water of life" (Rev. 21:6; 22:17; cf. Isa. 55:1).

Moreover, the contrast between the fertile ground and the wilderness often provides the imagery for expressing the blessing and salvation which God bestows upon his people. In the oracles of Balaam it is said that Israel is

> like valleys that stretch afar,
> like gardens beside a river,

for "his seed shall be in many waters" (Num. 24:6-7; cf. Gen. 49:22-26; Ps. 107:33-38; Ezek. 19:10-14). The divine Shepherd leads his flock "beside still waters" (Ps. 23:2), and the wise man, who meditates upon the law, is likened to a "tree planted by streams of water," fruitful in its season and evergreen even in the summer heat (Ps. 1:3; cf. Jer. 17:7-8). In eschatological literature, especially in the prophecy of Second Isaiah, the dawn of the new age is portrayed in terms of the fertility of an oasis. Not only will Israel be

> like a watered garden,
> like a spring of water,
> whose waters fail not
> (Isa. 58:11; cf. 27:2-3;
> Jer. 31:10-14);

but the whole arena of nature, affected by Yahweh's redemptive work in history, will be so transformed that springs will gush forth in the desert and the wilderness will blossom like the rose (Isa. 41:17-20; 43:19-21; 44:3-4; 48:21; 49:10; cf. 35:5-7). In the book of Ezekiel this eschatological motif finds expression in the vision of a river of life, issuing from below the threshold of the temple and having its source doubtless in the subterranean Deep; as the river flows down into the Arabah, it brings forth life on every hand, and even the stagnant waters of the Dead Sea are made fresh (Ezek. 47:1-12; cf. Ps. 46:4—H 46:5; Joel 3:18—H 4:18; Zech. 14:8). Also the image of the "river of the water of life" reappears in a NT vision of the end time (Rev. 22:1-2).

In these instances, water is a friendly element which symbolizes divine blessing and redemption, and this is true even when the source of the water is the primeval Deep (as in Gen. 2:6; 49:25; Deut. 33:13; Ezek. 47:1). But in another tradition, derived ultimately from the mythological views of Egypt, Mesopotamia, and Canaan, water is regarded as a foe which God overcomes.* The ancient *Weltbild,* which is taken for granted throughout the Bible, portrayed the universe as a three-storied structure: heaven, earth, and underworld. According to ancient mythology, this structure arose as a result of a primordial battle between gods who emerged from uncreated chaos. Victorious in the struggle, the hero-god split the body of the dragon of chaos (Tiamat in the Babylonian myth) and separated the two halves by a firmament. Thus the waters of chaos were not destroyed but pushed back, with the result that man's world was situated between the "waters above" (the heavenly ocean) and the "waters below" (the Deep; cf. Exod. 20:4; Deut. 4:18; 5:8; Pss. 104:3; 136:6; 148:4). The mythological ideas associated with this world view were undoubtedly mediated to the Israelites through the Canaanites. Ugaritic (Ras Shamra) mythology, which represents variations on themes familiar in ancient Egypt and Mesopotamia, relates that the storm-god Baal entered into conflict with the formidable water dragon known as Prince Sea and Judge River and that he was victorious in the struggle, thereby taking his "eternal kingdom" (*see* BAAL). This "twisting serpent" (cf. Isa. 27:1), known as Leviathan among the Canaanites, is portrayed on a cylinder seal which depicts two deities in the act of vanquishing a seven-headed monster. Concrete evidence of the influence of mythological thinking upon Israel is found in the fact that Solomon installed in the Jerusalem temple a bronze sea, which represented the subterranean fresh-water stream from which all life and fertility were derived (II Kings 25:13, 16; *see* SEA, MOLTEN).* Moreover, in the OT there are specific references to this dragon under the names Leviathan or Rahab (Job 3:8; 9:13; 26:12;

41:1—H 40:25; Pss. 74:14; 89:10—H 89:11; 104:26; Isa. 27:1; 51:9). Figs. LEV 27; SEA 34.

Faint echoes of this mythology are found in the priestly creation story (Gen. 1:1–2:4*a*), which begins with a portrayal of uncreated watery chaos (the Hebrew word for "Deep," תהום, is cognate with Babylonian Tiamat) and speaks of the interposition of a firmament to separate "the waters from the waters" (*see* CREATION §§ 1*a*, 3*a*). Furthermore, the priestly version of the Flood portrays the near return of the earth to pre-creation chaos as a result of the waters which poured down through the windows of the firmament and gushed up from the fountains of the Great Deep (תהום רבה; Gen. 7:11; cf. Isa. 54:9). Against this background of thought we may understand some of Israel's language of praise. Yahweh is king over the whole creation, for he has founded the earth upon the seas, and established it upon the rivers (Ps. 24:1); "the sea is his, for he made it," and "in his hand are the depths of the earth" (95:4-5); he has laid the beams of the heavenly chambers on the waters (104:3) and spread out the earth upon the waters (136:6); he has put the deeps in storehouses (33:7) and has commanded the waters above the heavens to praise him (148:4). Those who go down to the sea in ships may see the "deeds of Yahweh, his wondrous works in the deep," how he makes the waves to mount up to the heavens and to plunge to the depths (107:23-32). Indeed, the sea is full of God's creatures, even Leviathan which he formed (104:24-26). Let the sea roar, then, and let the floods clap their hands, for Yahweh comes to rule the earth (Ps. 98:7-9; cf. 96:11; Isa. 42:10; *see* ABYSS).

This language not only reflects the ancient *Weltbild,* but it also implies, and often articulates, a dramatic conflict between Yahweh and the waters of chaos. This is frequently the case with the expression "many waters" (מים רבים). In the psalm found in Hab. 3, it is said of Yahweh:

> Thou didst trample the sea with thy horses,
> the surging of mighty waters (vs. 15).

In the same poem Yahweh's anger was against the rivers (נהרים) and the sea (ים; Ugaritic *ymn*) when he rode forth on his chariots of victory (vs. 8) and that "Deep" (תהום) cried out in panic (vs. 10). The restless, rebellious character of the waters is portrayed in other poetic or liturgical contexts (e.g., Ps. 77:16-20—H 77:17-21), where "waters" is used in parallelism with "deep" and "sea"; 93:3-4, where "many waters" is parallel to "floods" (נהרות) and "sea"; 104:6-7; cf. 46:2-3—H 46:3-4; 114:3-5), and in some instances the waters are explicitly identified with the dragon of the Deep, called Leviathan or Rahab (Job 26:10-13; Pss. 74:12-14; 89:9-10—H 89: 10-11). It is said that at the time of the Creation, Yahweh set a bound which the waters should not pass (Ps. 104:5-9), that he shut the sea with doors so that its proud waves might be restrained (Job 38:8-11), and that he drew a circle on the face of the Deep so that the waters might not transgress his command (Prov. 8:22-31; see also Ps. 65:5-8—H 65: 6-9; Isa. 50:2-3; Jer. 5:22; 31:35).

In the religions of the Fertile Crescent the theme of the dramatic conflict with the waters was part of a pattern of myth and ritual which was re-enacted each year in connection with the seasonal cycle of fertility and summer barrenness, of death and resurrection. When Israel appropriated the theme, however, it was torn out of the cyclical pattern of polytheistic nature religion and was radically reinterpreted within the context of exclusive faith in Yahweh, the Lord of history. It may be, as some scholars hold, that Israel held a New Year's Festival (*see* New Year) at which time Yahweh's kingship was celebrated by rehearsing his victory over the waters of chaos. Some psalms may come out of such a cultic situation—e.g., Ps. 93, which affirms that Yahweh is enthroned in majesty above the thunder of "many waters" and the restless waves of the sea (cf. also Ps. 29, which may be as old as the tenth century in view of affinities with Canaanite literature; note especially vss. 3-4, 10-11). In any case, the mythological language was historicized. Yahweh's victory "in the beginning" was the evidence of his lordship over history, the assurance of his historical sovereignty in the present, and the prototype of his victory in the end, when all powers opposing his kingship would be vanquished.

The tendency to historicize mythological motifs is evident in the association of the chaotic waters with the Red Sea. Yahweh's victory at the Red Sea was a primary element of Israel's kerygma (Josh. 24:6-7; Neh. 9:11; Pss. 78:13; 106:7-12; etc.). In the Song of the Sea (Exod. 15), a poem which in its original form may date back to the premonarchic period in view of its consonance with early Hebrew and Canaanite poetic style, Yahweh is praised thus:

> At the blast of thy nostrils the waters piled up,
> the floods stood up in a heap;
> the deeps congealed in the heart of the sea
>   (vs. 8).

Here Yahweh's enemies are not the rebellious waters, but the hosts of the pharaoh. The sea is merely the passive instrument by which Yahweh wins his victory on behalf of Israel. But in other poems, of a later origin, the waters of the Red Sea are none other than the waters of chaos. Yahweh's battle was not fought in the timeless realm of mythology, but in the arena of history—namely, at the beginning, when Israel was created to be his people. Thus Ps. 77, recalling Yahweh's mighty deeds of old when he redeemed his people, says that

> When the waters saw thee, O God,
> when the waters saw thee, they were afraid,
> yea, the deep trembled (vs. 16—H vs. 17);

and, as the conclusion of the psalm indicates, the victory at the Red Sea is clearly in the poet's mind when he says:

> Thy way was through the sea,
> thy path through the great waters
>   (vs. 19—H vs. 20).

The identification is also clear in the message of Second Isaiah, who appeals to Yahweh to arouse himself "as in days of old" when the sea dragon Rahab was slain and a path was cut through the Great Deep (i.e., the Red Sea) in order that the redeemed could pass over (Isa. 51:9-10; cf. 43:16-17; 63:11-14). And what Yahweh did in the past he is about to do again. The God who commanded the Deep, "Be dry," is on the verge of inaugurating a new creation and establishing his kingly rule over Israel and all peoples (Isa. 44:24-28). In other passages we read that Yahweh rebuked the Red Sea and led his people through the Deep, that he divided the Sea and thereby performed an awe-inspiring deed, and that the Sea looked and fled (Pss. 66:5-7; 89:9-10—H 89:10-11, where Rahab is mentioned; 106:8-12; 136:13-15; cf. 114:3-5).

To Israel, the raging, unruly waters symbolized the powers which are opposed to God's sovereignty and therefore threatened to destroy the meaningfulness of history, as though the world ever had the possibility of returning to pre-creation chaos (cf. Jer. 4:23-26). These demonic powers could manifest themselves in Israel's historical enemies. Thus the "many waters" are sometimes equivalent to the "many peoples" or the foes who threaten Israel's existence (Ps. 144:5-8; Isa. 17:12-14; Jer. 6:23; Hab. 3:12-15). However, Israel could go through the "deep waters" (Pss. 69:1-2, 14-15—H 69:2-3, 15-16; 124:1-5; Isa. 43:2) in the confidence that Yahweh is Lord over the Deep. For he could bring the Deep over proud Tyre (Ezek. 26:19-21; cf. 27:26) or destroy the Egyptian pharaoh,

> the great dragon that lies
> in the midst of his streams
>   (Ezek. 29:3-5; 31-32).

Moreover, the nearness of death—the eschatological event which threatens to separate man from God—is sometimes described as a descent into the waters of the Deep. This is the case in the psalm inserted into the book of Jonah and occasioned by his sojourn in the belly of a fish (Jonah 2:2-9). Another psalmist tells how, when the snares of death confronted him, Yahweh came to the rescue in an earth-shaking storm. At his rebuke the channels of the sea were laid bare, and, reaching from on high, "he drew me out of many waters" (Ps. 18:7-19—H 18:8-20 =II Sam. 22:8-20; cf. Job 26:5; Pss. 42:7—H 42:8; 71:19*b*-21; 88:6-7—H 88:7-8). Thus "at a time of distress, in the rush of great waters" (Ps. 32:6), man could turn to God, confident of his saving power.

Since the Sea symbolizes chaotic, demonic powers that are subdued but not finally vanquished, apocalyptic writers looked to the future when the history-long conflict would be brought to an end. In the end time Yahweh with his victorious sword "will punish Leviathan the fleeing serpent, Leviathan the twisting serpent, and he will slay the dragon that is in the sea" (Isa. 27:1; cf. Ps. 74:12-17). According to Dan. 7, the seer beheld the four winds of heaven stirring up the "great sea" (cf. the wind that moved upon the waters of chaos in Gen. 1:2), and from this tempestuous deep came four beasts (or kingdoms), each of whom was judged by the Lord of history. The Testament of Levi associates the coming Day of Judgment with the breaking of the rocks, the extinguishing of the sun, and the drying of the waters (4:1). Similarly in the Assumption of Moses it is said that

> the sea shall retire into the abyss,
> and the fountains of waters shall fail,
> and the rivers shall dry up (10:6).[1]

[1] R. H. Charles, ed., *The Apocrypha and Pseudepigrapha of the Old Testament* (Oxford: The Clarendon Press).

According to the Sibylline Oracles: "In the last time the sea shall be dry" (V.447), and "the deep sea and Babylon itself" will be burned up (V.159). In an eschatological passage in the Gospel of Luke it is said that upon the earth there will be "distress of nations in perplexity at the roaring of the sea and the waves, men fainting with fear and with foreboding of what is coming on the world" (Luke 21:25-26). The book of Revelation draws freely upon this mythopoeic imagery. Satan is identified with the "great dragon, . . . that ancient serpent" (Rev. 12:9); a new version of the beasts rising out of the sea is presented (ch. 13); and the apocalypse reaches its climax in the vision of the new heaven and the new earth, wherein there will be no more sea (Rev. 21:1). Thus history is viewed as a dramatic conflict between the divine and demonic, creation and chaos, God and Satan; and, in the Christian faith, God's victory in Christ is both a foretaste and promise of the everlasting reign of the Lord God omnipotent.

Bibliography. H. Gunkel, *Schöpfung und Chaos in Urzeit und Endzeit* (1895); H. Frankfurt *et al., The Intellectual Adventure of Ancient Man* (1946), chs. 1-2, 5; H. Galling, "Die Chaosschilderung in Genesis 1," *ZThK* (1950), pp. 145 ff; H. G. May, "Some Cosmic Connotations of *Mayim Rabbim,* 'Many Waters,'" *JBL,* LXXIV (1955), 9-21; P. Reymond, *L'eau, sa vie, et sa signification dans l'AT,* Supplement to *Vetus Testamentum,* vol. VI (1958); G. A. F. Knight, *A Christian Theology of the OT* (1959), pp. 107-18. B. W. ANDERSON

WATER FOR IMPURITY [מי נדה, *lit.,* waters of impurity, *properly* waters for removing impurity]; KJV WATERS OF SEPARATION. A cleansing agent, described in Num. 19 in two slightly divergent accounts (vss. 1-13, 14-22) and used to purify those unclean by contact with the dead (*see* CLEAN AND UNCLEAN; cf. "water of expiation" [Num. 8:7], "water of bitterness" [5:18]). Elsewhere in the OT where uncleanness associated with death is described (Lev. 5:2; 11:8, 24-28; 21:1-4, 10-11; Num. 5:2; 9:6-7, 10-11; 31:19-24), the "water for impurity" is not mentioned, and the Nazirites had a special ritual which did not include its use (Num. 6:6-12).

An unblemished red cow, which had never been yoked, was presented to Yahweh, and then burned outside the camp together with cedar wood, hyssop, and scarlet thread (Num. 19:1-6; for the use of the last three ingredients in cleansing lepers, see Lev. 14:1-9). The composite ash, mixed with stream water, constituted the "water for impurity" (Num. 19:17), and was sprinkled from a bunch of hyssop on a dwelling in which death had occurred and on a person who had been in contact with a human corpse, a human bone, or a grave (vs. 18). Failure to undergo the sprinkling on the third and seventh days of the week-long period of impurity meant expulsion from Israel (vss. 11, 13, 20). All who took part in the ceremony incurred uncleanness "until evening" (vss. 7-8, 10, 21).

Although no exact parallel to the "water for impurity" is known (for approximate parallels, see RED HEIFER), the ritual use of magical ingredients mixed with water is widely attested in nonbiblical sources and argues an ancient, non-Hebrew origin for the ritual (*see* WATER OF BITTERNESS; and cf. Exod. 32: 20; Lev. 14:49-52; Num. 5:16-18). The choice of the

components of the "water for impurity" was apparently governed by the principle of opposites. The cow, an ancient fertility symbol; the red color of the thread and the animal, suggesting blood; the wood of the long-lived cedar; and the "living water" (מים חיים) provide a powerful combination of symbols of life to counteract the uncleanness caused by DEATH.

Bibliography. G. B. Gray, *Numbers,* ICC (1903), pp. 241-56. L. E. TOOMBS

WATER GATE [שער המים]. A gate on the E side of Jerusalem, restored by Nehemiah (Neh. 3:26; 12:37). Presumably located in the rampart above the spring of GIHON. Ezra read the Law to the people gathered at the entrance of the gate, where also booths were erected for the Feast of Tabernacles (Neh. 8:1, 3, 16). Some scholars identify the Water Gate with one of the S gates of the temple area. Fig. NEH 13. *See also* JERUSALEM § 7*b.*

G. A. BARROIS

WATER HEN [תנשמת (Lev. 11:18; Deut. 14:16), *perhaps* the heavy-breather; *cf.* נשם, to breathe, pant; LXX πορφυρίων, water hen; Vulg. *cygnus,* swan (Lev. 11:18); LXX-Vulg. ibis in Deut. 14:16; Targ. (Onq.) בותא, night bird, owl]; KJV SWAN. A member of the Rail tribe of birds (*Rallidae*), which frequent ponds, rivers, and marshes; the order includes rails, water hens, gallinules, and coots, and totals *ca.* two hundred species. Tristram says nothing about water hens in Palestine, but he does refer to the Purple Gallinule (*Porphyrio porphyrio*) as being common in the marshes of that country, and he suggests that, as it is omnivorous in its eating habits, it "might reasonably find a place in the catalogue of unclean birds" (*NHB* 249-51). It is purely conjectural that תנשמת designates one of the Rail birds. Koehler, Bodenheimer (*see* FAUNA § B2), and G. R. Driver (*see bibliography*) take it to be an owl.

Bibliography. G. R. Driver, *PEQ* (April, 1955), p. 15.
W. S. McCULLOUGH

WATER OF BITTERNESS [מי המרים המאררים, water that causes pain (bearing a curse; Num. 5:18-19, 24); מי המרים (vs. 23); המים המאררים, curse-bearing water (vss. 22, 24)]. A quasi-magical drink, consisting of dust from the sanctuary floor, ink from a parchment on which a curse had been written, and holy water, employed in the "ordeal of jealousy" to test a suspected adulteress (*see* JEALOUSY). Num. 5: 11-31, where the ordeal is described, has extensive glosses which make it appear that the potion was administered twice.

A husband who suspected his wife of infidelity, but had no legal proof, could bring her to the sanctuary, where, under conditions calculated to terrify the guilty, her innocence was tested. She was seated before the sanctuary facing the altar (in later times at the E gate of the temple; M. Soṭ. 1.5), where she would be exposed directly to Yahweh's power of blessing and cursing (*see* BLESSINGS AND CURSINGS). Her hair was unbound as a sign of her shame, and, according to the Mishna, she was clothed in black and had her bosom bare (Soṭ. 1.5-6). The priest placed in her hands her husband's cereal offering, called an "offering of remembrance" (*see* SACRIFICES

AND OFFERINGS); took dust from the floor of the sanctuary to enhance the sacredness of the potion (*see* HOLINESS); placed it in "holy water" (LXX "living"—i.e., running—water); and, standing before the woman, pronounced a terrible curse, with which she irrevocably identified herself by a double "Amen." The words of a written copy of the curse were washed into the water, the cereal offering made, and the woman compelled to drink. If she was guilty, the lower part of her body became distorted; if innocent, she was unharmed and received the blessing of bearing children. Ordeals by water, fire, battle, oath, etc., are pre-Hebraic and possibly older than belief in personal deities. Oaths of purgation taken before Yahweh (Exod. 22:9-11—H 22:8-10; I Kings 8:31; *see* OATH; WORD), the cultic use of semi-magical liquids (Lev. 14:49-52; Num. 19:17-19, *see* WATER FOR IMPURITY), and testing by sacred dust mixed with water (Exod. 32:19-20) are found in the OT, but genuine ordeals are rare (see Num. 16). For the Israelite the decision in all such tests rested with Yahweh, but the ritual of the "water of bitterness" shows clear traces of the more primitive conception that the water itself was able to destroy a perjured adulteress (vss. 22, 24, 27, and cf. vs. 21). *Protoevangelium* 16 describes how the test was applied to the mother of Jesus, and M. Soṭ. 9.9 indicates that it went out of use in the first century A.D.

Bibliography. Jos. Antiq. III.xi.6; G. B. Gray, *Numbers*, ICC (1903), pp. 43-56; R. Press, "Das Ordal im alten Israel," *ZAW*, 10 (1933), 121-40.   L. E. TOOMBS

WATER SHAFT. A system providing access for water from a spring into a city. Underground shafts or tunnels have been found at a number of excavated sites, such as GEZER; GIBEON; JERUSALEM; MEGIDDO. The word צנור in II Sam. 5:8, a difficult passage, is usually rendered "water shaft," although some scholars have understood this term as referring to the persons of the Jebusites. *See* WATER WORKS § 5; WELLS.   W. L. REED

WATER WORKS. Man needs water, whether to quench his own thirst and that of his beasts, to grow edible plants, to supply industries, or to scour the dust from himself and his possessions, at the surface of the ground. When nature, as in biblical lands, has confined to relatively few points the places where water is so found, man may either restrict his habitation to those places or use intelligence and skill to bring water from its natural sources to where he can best use it.

In the earliest times, before the arts of building and metallurgy were developed, while the digging of cisterns or the construction of wells and channels was too laborious a task to be undertaken, or even thought of, we find the settlements of men grouped in the neighborhood of springs and lakes or on the banks of perennial streams; or we may picture groups of nomads moving from one source of surface water to another. But as man learned to master new materials and fashion better tools, his command of nature's riches increased; and among these, in Southwest Asia, water was the most vital.

We are concerned, then, with the means by which man in ancient Palestine contrived to conduct the water provided by nature—underground, in springs and streams, or as rain—to receptacles of his own choice and construction on the surface of the land.

1. Earliest irrigation works
2. Assyrian irrigation projects
3. Springs and wells in Palestine
   a. Natural springs
   b. Built wells
4. Water storage
   a. Cisterns
   b. Pools
   c. Aqueducts
5. Water shafts
   a. In Jerusalem
   b. In Megiddo
   c. In Gezer, Ibleam, Gibeon
Bibliography

1. Earliest irrigation works. There can hardly have been a time when man had not noticed that water flows downhill, and can be held up or diverted by any solid obstacle in its path. These obvious facts will have suggested to the most primitive of Stone Age men the simple ideas of digging runnels, scooping out basins, or piling up barriers to guide, check, or store the rain or spring water that flowed by their early encampments. We cannot expect to find or recognize the traces of these earliest experiments. But we can be sure that they were made; and it is safe to infer that the rough stone terrace walls and unrevetted ditches and channels, which are still today a feature of the fertile lands wherever they rise above the alluvial plains, have been developed from simple irrigation works as old as agriculture itself.

It is not, however, these humble peasant structures, too common to be mentioned by early writers, which need concern us now. We read in biblical literature of springs and wells, but little or nothing of irrigation. For then as now, in all but the great river valleys, cultivators were content to raise such seasonal crops as would germinate in the winter and spring rains, and rarely attempted to extend by irrigation the range or seasons of cultivation. It was not agriculture, in fact, but town life that evoked from early man his most strenuous efforts to conserve and control his never-too-abundant supplies of water.

2. Assyrian irrigation projects. There are two important exceptions to this generalization. In the alluvial plains of Mesopotamia and Egypt, where powerful states ruled over large populations, things could be different. The cuneiform texts of Mari, touching affairs in the Euphrates Valley during the eighteenth century B.C., reveal the existence of an extensive system of irrigation canals maintained by the administrative energy of a dynasty of Amorite rulers, and by the labor of many subject villages and tribes. In later Assyrian times Sennacherib (705-681) created a gigantic system of weirs and canals, and a monumental bridge built of masonry, to irrigate with the waters of several rivers wide tracts of land containing fields, orchards, and a game park, round his capital at Nineveh; and in this enterprise he followed and surpassed the example of a ninth-century predecessor, Ashurnasirpal II (883-857), who had tunneled the rocky bank of the Upper Zab River, and dug a canal, to bring water to the fields of Calah.

3. Springs and wells in Palestine. Such spectacular agricultural projects were possible in the great river valleys, where water abounded, and powerful rulers commanding unlimited man power could harvest the fruits of their enterprise from vast tracts of irrigable land. But for Israel and Judah, and for their Canaanite predecessors, inhabiting a geographically and politically fragmented region, devoid alike of great rivers and of wide tracts of alluvial land, no such ambitious projects were feasible. For the society depicted in the OT, part urban, part agricultural, and part seminomadic, the best that could be done was to maintain or increase the yield of natural springs and wells, and protect them from hostile interference; to catch and store for domestic or communal use the periodic rainfall; and, lastly, to reduce the human labor involved in bringing the water from these sources to the homes of the people.

The task that confronts us, then, is to see what can be learned from the literary and archaeological record of the ancient use of springs and wells; of storage in pools and cisterns; and of the methods devised for improving for friends, and denying to foes, the access to those water supplies on which life and prosperity in Bible lands precariously depended.

a. Natural springs. We can be sure that the presence of natural springs was by far the most potent single factor determining the location of the earliest settlements. Certainly the oldest of those which have been archaeologically investigated, Jericho, owed its existence, in early Neolithic times, to the powerful spring, now 'Ain es-Sultan, which the folklore of a later age coupled with the miraculous career of Elisha (II Kings 2:19-22); and there are few perennial springs in biblical lands beside which there cannot be seen a "tell," or city mound, concealing the ruins of innumerable successive habitations.

Such springs are likely to generate a rich folklore; and the tale of Elisha at Jericho is a good example. But whether because the townspeople of Israel and Judah as a whole lost interest in such tales, or for some other reason, the fact is that in the Hebrew writings the scanty folklore of springs turns almost exclusively on the personalities of Israel's early tribal history. Thus in Exod. 17:6; Num. 20:11, the divine revelation through Moses' rod of the springs of Massah and Meribah concerns the anxieties of a nomadic nation seeking water in the desert; and in Josh. 15:19, the simple secular tale of Caleb adding two springs to his daughter's dowry recalls the allocation of lands in the earliest days of tribal settlement. But of the springs at which, day by day for centuries, the women of Israelite towns and villages drew water, no stories but that of Elisha have been preserved.

b. Built wells. The built wells feature, on the whole, more prominently; but of these too it may be said that the stories about them relate to tribal and pastoral society more than to city and village life. It is not known when man first discovered that reserves of water lay hidden beneath the earth and could be reached by his digging deep enough. The discovery is not likely to have been made very early; and the Bible tradition which attributes the oldest

Courtesy of Herbert G. May

5. Well at Beer-sheba, showing modern use of ancient water wheel

wells to the patriarchs, living in the second millennium B.C., may well be correct. The tales told of the famous wells round Beer-sheba* and Gerar (Gen. 21:30; 26:18; etc.), of the disputes that arose when they were first dug, and of the courtesies by which these were settled, seem all to be drawn from life; and if their association with Abraham and Isaac was indeed based on tribal memory, an origin about the middle of the second millennium may be inferred. It would be impossible, unfortunately, to recognize in the present wells at Beer-sheba or elsewhere the actual handiwork of the patriarchs; for none has been closely enough examined, and all have undergone many repairs since they were built. Fig. WAT 5.

Of the ancient town wells that have been examined, the most spectacular is the well of Lachish (Tell ed-Duweir); but others have been found at Beth-shemesh, Beth-shean, and Tell el-'Ajjul. The well at Lachish was sited high up the slope of the mound on which the city stood, close beside the wall. It was carried down to the immense depth of 144 feet beneath a circular wellhead in the stone revetment of the mound; and of that depth the first 25 feet, above bedrock, were lined with heavy stone blocks. All that can be said of the date of the well is that it was dug before the wall was built, and that was in the second phase of the Iron Age (*ca.* 900-600). The well of Haran, as we read in Gen. 29:2, was closed with a stone that could be rolled aside. It was outside the city, and the flocks gathered to it to be watered, probably from stone troughs (Exod. 2:16). So it was, too, at the city of Nahor in the same Mesopotamian region (Gen. 24:11), and so also at Bethlehem in Judah (II Sam. 23:15). Water was drawn from these wells by hand in pitchers or skins (Gen. 24:14-20); there is no evidence for the use of pulleys or any other mechanical device.

The finding of water where there were no springs was neither an easy nor a commonplace achievement; and there was a note of triumph in the servants' message to Isaac at Beer-sheba (Gen. 26:32): "We have found water." The actual digging, too, with the bronze tools available, was no light matter; and one may doubt that the patriarchs, half-nomads as they were, and unaided by professional masons, would have attempted anything so ambitious as the well of Lachish. The successful sinking of a well was therefore a feat worthy to be ascribed to the national heroes of the past.

> Spring up, O well!—Sing to it!—
> the well which the princes dug,
> which the nobles of the people delved,
> with the scepter and with their staves.
> (Num. 21:17-18.)

4. Water storage. The long summer of Palestine, where from May to October no rain falls, makes the climate seem dry. But in fact, from November to April the average rainfall in the hill country, from Judea in the S to Galilee in the N, is *ca.* twenty-five inches, or the same as in the center of England, commonly thought a wet country. Efficient storage of rain water can therefore do much to overcome the habitual summer drought; and for the common man the possession of a cistern may make all the difference between peace of mind and the direst hardship. Thus in 701 B.C. the Assyrian spokesman at Jerusalem thought to win over the common people by promising to each man his own vine and fig tree and his own cistern (II Kings 18:31); and similarly, *ca.* 830 B.C., King Mesha of Moab proclaimed on the monument which he set up in Dibon: "In the town of Qarhoh there was no cistern; so I said to all the people, let each of you make a cistern in his house for himself." (*See* MOABITE STONE.) So it has been ever since: until the introduction in modern times of piped municipal supplies, all but the poorest houses, in the towns and villages of Palestine not favored by springs, have possessed cisterns, where rain falling on roofs and courtyards in the winter is stored for use in the summer. Larger cisterns, too, have habitually been built beneath the courts of public and religious buildings. Thus in Jerusalem, beneath the temple area and the Church of the Holy Sepulchre, vast subterranean reservoirs—some vaulted in masonry, some hewn entirely in the rock; some medieval or Christian in origin, some much older—hold a perpetual supply of many millions of gallons.

a. Cisterns. It is not easy to say when the first cisterns were made, for the simplest of them have changed little in form since the earliest times. They are roughly bell-shaped chambers, hewn deep in the rock, with a narrow vertical shaft at the top for letting down pitchers. If the rock lies far below the soil, the shaft from the surface is lined with masonry of rough-hewn stones, to which successive generations add a few courses as the surface of the ground rises. At the top there may be a heavy ring stone, grooved by many ropes. In the floor, beneath the shaft, there will be a sump for removing the last drops of water at the periodical cleaning or replastering of the cistern. In Hellenistic or Roman times there was introduced a type of open storage tank, rectangular, and reached by broad or narrow flights of steps, the latter descending to the bottom along one side, the former stretching across the full width of one end. These tanks varied greatly in size; they would be filled by means of conduits brought from far or near, according to circumstances, and fitted with settling tanks near the inlet to retard silting. Since the limestone rock on which most Palestinian towns were built is more or less porous, a cistern to hold water through the summer must be plastered;

and it has been suggested that the great multiplication of domestic cisterns that archaeologists have observed during the Iron Age (from 1200 B.C.), and indeed the spread of population at that period into hilly regions remote from springs, was made possible by the discovery that a waterproof plaster could be made from burnt and slaked lime. This must have greatly increased the efficiency of existing cisterns and encouraged the construction of new ones. It is thought to have happened about the end of the Late Bronze Age, perhaps a little before 1200 B.C.

In the Canaanite town of Gezer, in the Shephelah of Palestine, excavation revealed the rock to be honeycombed with cisterns, one for each group of houses. The walls were covered by a cement of coarse plaster, but of a composition not recorded. Beth-shemesh, likewise, was described by its excavator as a "city of cisterns." This was in the Late Bronze Age (1600-1200 B.C.), and the cisterns are described as lime plastered. But in the earlier periods of the city there were none, and the inhabitants must have relied entirely on the yield of the neighboring spring. So it was until even later at the more remote and isolated town of Debir, in S Judah, where many lime-plastered domestic cisterns constructed after *ca.* 1000 B.C. were found, but none at all of earlier date.

Some Iron Age towns were almost or entirely devoid of spring water, like Samaria, first settled in the ninth century, or the Judean fortress of Mizpah. Such places, uninhabited or nearly so until Israel settled them, must from the first have relied on the efficient and adequate storage of rain water; and the development of the mortar which made this possible must be counted among the notable achievements of the Early Iron Age.

The building of cisterns was a mark of progressive government, benefiting not only the towns but also the countryside. Thus we are told that the active Jewish king Uzziah (*ca.* 783-742 B.C.) "built towers in the wilderness, and hewed out many cisterns, for he had large herds, both in the Shephelah and in the plain, and he had farmers and vinedressers in the hills and in the fertile lands" (II Chr. 26:10). Many such rural cisterns, of great capacity but easily filled in a normal year, may still be found in use by cultivators and shepherds; and many others are now derelict. Of these by far the most impressive that may be explored today are found among a group of monumental chambers, with spiral staircases and connecting galleries, that have been hewn to a great depth at various times, for varying purposes including water storage, in the soft limestone slopes and valleys round the Judean city of Mareshah.

b. Pools. King Mesha bade the men of Qarhoh be self-dependent and dig their own cisterns; but he himself built two pools within that city, together with its gates and towers; and another at Baal-meon. Several famous biblical cities had their pools: Hebron (II Sam. 4:12); Gibeon (II Sam. 2:13; perhaps also Jer. 41:12); Samaria (I Kings 22:38); and Jerusalem (II Kings 20:20). Many of these still exist, but not all can be recognized, as they have many times been repaired or replastered, and the rough masonry or lime plaster with which this was done has not much varied from age to age.

At Gibeon (el-Jib)* there may be seen today, in a valley near the ancient site, a rectangular pool lined with masonry and coated with mortar. Excavation has shown this to be probably of Roman origin; and the same is perhaps true of a similar impressive pool at Hebron, also constructed in a valley and lined with masonry. The ancient pool of Hebron cannot now be identified; but it seems likely that the "pool of Gibeon" (II Sam 2:13) was revealed in a sensational discovery made by excavation at el-Jib in 1956. This took the form of a vast circular pit, thirty-eight feet in diameter and of unknown depth, hewn in the rock close within the city wall; it was served by a spiral staircase, also rock-hewn, which descended, apparently, to the bottom. It was a riddle how the pool was filled, for there were no signs of any inlet. Yet marks of water on the wall, and wear

Courtesy of Herbert G. May

6. Solomon's pool, S of Bethlehem

and tear of the steps, proved that the pit was indeed a pool and kept well supplied with water. The sides were not plastered, but the rock is hard and, if not fissured, would have retained water. Pottery in the rubbish suggested that the pool had fallen into disuse by the sixth century B.C. See GIBEON § 3b. Fig. GIB 29.

At Gezer a similar great rock-cut pool, oblong with rounded corners, and furnished with steps along the side, existed within the wall. There the soft rock was rendered with lime cement. Its capacity has been reckoned at about 600,000 gallons; but again there is mystery how it was filled. See GEZER 2.

For Hezekiah's pool at Jerusalem, see below and also SILOAM § 3.

c. Aqueducts. The pool of Samaria has not been found. Waterless by nature, the city in Israelite times depended on rain caught in cisterns; for it was isolated by low ground from the nearest springs. It was only under the Roman Empire, after the city had been refounded under a new name by Herod the Great, and much rebuilt ca. A.D. 200, that the engineers of the day brought spring water to Sebaste by a masonry and rock-cut conduit partly hewn as a tunnel through the mountain, partly carried across the valley by a bridge. Only the foundations of the bridge remain; but it can be reckoned to have stood more than 160 feet high.

In the Roman and Hellenistic provinces aqueducts were not uncommon; they were open plastered channels following the contours or crossing low ground on walls or bridges. In Palestine another foundation of Herod's, Caesarea, was supplied by such an aqueduct from springs at the foot of the Carmel Range. It was built of concrete faced with masonry, and it

still bridges the dunes and marshes that surround the site of the ancient city. Where the ground level falls, the open channel is carried on arches.

At all flourishing periods from the Hellenistic to the present age, builders and cultivators in the lands of Jericho have made use of the powerful springs which rise in the Wadi Qelt; and water still rushes down rock-cut, or rubble-built and plastered, channels whose history, through many changes, may be traced perhaps to Herod the Great, the builder of a residence (now Tell Abu el-'Alayiq) overlooking the Jericho Plain. At about the same period similar aqueducts brought spring or flood waters to storage cisterns at the waterless castles of Alexandrium (Qarn Sartabeh) and Masada, and to the desert retreat of the Jewish sect of Qumran. See MASADA; DEAD SEA SCROLLS.

At Jerusalem for many generations the Jebusite inhabitants and the early Israelites could subsist on the yield of the spring Gihon,* which rose in the Kidron Valley at the E foot of the city mound. But as the population grew under the Jewish kings, and the temple became the scene of crowded festivals, a time came when it was determined to supplement the local supply with water brought fresh from springs in the higher hill country some fifteen miles to the S. It is still a moot point when this was first done. There exist today in a valley about halfway between the city and Hebron, three great reservoirs enclosed by three masonry barriers, which are popularly called King Solomon's Pools.* They are linked by a system of contour aqueducts, on the one hand with two groups of springs that feed them, on the other with subterranean reservoirs beneath the temple area. From the same valley a separate and lower aqueduct can be traced to the desert castle of Herod the Great (30-4 B.C.; see HERODION). The Jerusalem aqueducts, built at different levels, are two in number: rock-hewn conduits made up, where they cross hollows, in rubble concrete, or, at one point, siphoned in a pipe of rebated stone drums set in a concrete wall. One conduit has more recently been replaced by a line of earthenware pipes laid in its old channel. Figs. GIH 32; ETA 6; WAT 6.

Many hands have contributed through the ages to these aqueducts: Herod the Great, Pontius Pilate (Jos. Antiq. XVIII.iii.2), the Roman legion at Aelia Capitolina (inscriptions of Leg. X Fretensis), and the Saracenic sultans. These builders are known from written texts. We have no record of earlier builders; but the rough workmanship and archaic-looking tooling visible on some rock-hewn sections of the lower aqueduct have suggested that it may have been the work of one or another of the kings of Judah, designed to give its own supply of running water to the temple of Jerusalem. Of this there can be no certainty on present evidence, and the Bible does not state that Solomon or any of his successors brought water to the temple.

The conduit of King Hezekiah (ca. 715-687 B.C.), to which there is reference in II Kings 20:20, and which was rediscovered in 1838, was no less ambitious a project. The purpose of this was to supply, not the temple, but the city, with a safe reserve of water run by gravity from the Gihon spring to a new pool conveniently formed behind a barrage built across the central valley of Jerusalem. To achieve this, it was necessary to tunnel through the mountain spur on which the ancient city lay. The task was made difficult by strata of hard limestone, and the tunnel consequently traced a wavering S-curve, nearly doubling its length to something over 560 yards. An inscription describing the achievement was engraved on the rocky wall of the tunnel near its outlet. This was rediscovered in 1880 and is now to be seen in a museum in Constantinople (*see* SILOAM). The author of II Chr. 32:30 writes: "Hezekiah closed the upper outlet of the waters of Gihon and directed them down to the west side of the city of David"; and in poetical language Ecclesiasticus says:

> Hezekiah fortified his city,
> and brought water into the midst of it;
> he tunneled the sheer rock with iron
> and built pools for water (48:17).

Closing the "upper outlet" presumably meant that Hezekiah blocked the natural flow of the waters into the Kidron Valley, where from earlier times, perhaps from the reign of Solomon until his own day, two open-air channels, the one built, the other rock-hewn, had carried the "softly flowing" waters of Gihon, the "brook that flowed through the land" (II Chr. 32:4), to irrigate, through spaced apertures, the terraced gardens of Siloam. Of these the higher channel, after passing through a rock-cut tunnel beneath the S end of the city of David, helped to fill an older pool than Hezekiah's, which before his time had existed embanked behind a thick barrage near the issue of the central valley (cf. the "old pool" of Isa. 22:11).

These early aqueducts, like Hezekiah's tunneled conduit, both started from an enlargement and deepening of the cavern in which the Gihon rises; and this is the probable meaning of the "upper pool" of Isa. 7:3, with its conduit in the Fuller's Field. Fig. SIL 59.

5. Water shafts. *a. In Jerusalem.* Hezekiah's conduit was hewn at a time of danger to ensure the people of Jerusalem the use of their sping and to deny it to an enemy. The project was helped by the existence of some much earlier workings dug by the old Jebusite inhabitants of the city, centuries before, to bring the waters of Gihon toward the foot of a vertical shaft sunk to water level from above. Through this shaft citizens could draw water without leaving the shelter of the walls. The rock was excessively hard, but the Jebusites had succeeded, after some abortive attempts, in driving a flight of steps and a sloping passage to the head of a vertical chimney, which they bored down through the rock to reach an artificial extension of the cavern in which the spring rose. It was the workings at water level that Hezekiah was able to use for the start of his conduit. But his aim was not merely to bring water within the city, but to store it there in quantity, and to stop the flow outside. *See* JERUSALEM § 6c. Fig. HEZ 18.

b. In Megiddo. Other Bronze Age cities that were founded close to springs had made similar tunnels designed to make their water accessible with safety at all times. Some of these have been explored. One of the most instructive was found at Megiddo.* The

spring there rose in a small cave at the foot of the hill on which the city stood; and this had been deepened and extended from time to time as the water table fell. To draw from this spring, the women would leave the city, walk down the hill carrying their water jars, and reach the water by a flight of steps. At some time during the Bronze Age a covered way lined with masonry was excavated in the side of the hill to give them shelter as they went. This was no protection in time of war; and *ca.* the twelfth century a more efficient and much more ambitious project was undertaken. The plan, as at Jerusalem, was to tunnel inward from the spring, and downward from a point inside the city. The vertical part of the workings began as a great square well with a flight of rock-cut steps descending round its four sides. The well started at least twenty-four feet across, but the stairs caused it to contract so rapidly that there were still thirty feet or more to go to water level when it had grown too narrow to continue. Undeterred, the masons continued with a stepped sloping passage, which duly met a tunnel driven horizontally inward from the spring.* At this stage the staircase and tunnel served simply as a safe approach to the original springhead; but this could still be attained from the outside, and was vulnerable. Consequently it was soon decided to close the exit and prolong the horizontal tunnel inward, by hewing away the sloping passage. At the same time the tunnel was deepened so that the water could flow right in beneath the vertical shaft and be drawn up direct in buckets without the labor of climbing down the stairs. Figs. MEG 30; WAT 7.

For a time this system worked; but it probably failed in dry weather, because water then ceased to reach the bottom of the shaft. So it became necessary in early Israelite times to re-establish internal access to the spring by building up a new staircase where the old sloping tunnel had been cut down.

c. In Gezer, Ibleam, Gibeon. Similar but less ambitious water systems existed at Gezer and Ibleam

7. A tunnel of the Megiddo water system

Courtesy of James B. Pritchard

8. Tunnel of the water system at Gibeon

(Tell el-Bal'ameh); and the men of Judah made another at Gibeon (el-Jib).* In each case the aim was simple: to enlarge and deepen the actual springhead, and make it accessible underground from within the city. No attempt was made at these sites to bring and store the water, as Hezekiah was later to do at Jerusalem, within the walls of the city itself. Fig. WAT 8.

At Gezer the tunnel consisted of a short flight of steps leading down 20 feet to a landing, from which a much longer flight at right angles descended a further 75 feet on a straight run of 112 feet. There it entered a long cave containing the waters of the spring. Today there is no visible exit; but one must assume that in ancient times the spring came to the surface, and that the people of Gezer knew, before starting their gigantic task of tunneling, that they would strike water.

At Gibeon the system was identical in character. The outer approach to the spring was a deep cave artificially prolonged as a tunnel, which followed the water some forty feet into the hillside. During the Bronze Age, as far as we know, and in the early Israelite period, no special trouble was taken either to protect the spring or to save the women the trouble of carrying their pots down to it; only *ca.* the ninth century or later, when the city was fortified by a wall, was a special postern gate built above the spring to shorten the journey. The tunnel was a later defensive measure undertaken some time after the wall had been built. First, the opening of the cave was fitted with grooves so that it could be barred on the outside or built up; then a steep, dog-

legged staircase of ninety-three rock-cut steps, with a total length of more than fifty-five yards, was tunneled upward to emerge, after two turns, in an open space within the town walls. Two sections of this tunnel, instead of being bored through the rock, were excavated from above and roofed over with slabs.

It is a strange fact that these impressive water shafts, which played a vital part in the daily life of Canaanite and Israelitish cities, have passed almost unnoticed by ancient writers. Besides the Chronicler's laconic references to Hezekiah's great conduit, and the poet's brief commendation in Ecclesiasticus, there is only one allusion, enigmatic though dramatic, to the old Jebusite shaft. In II Sam. 5:8, David before Jerusalem says to his men: "Whoever would smite the Jebusites, let him get up the *ṣinnôr*." The discovery of the shaft leading from Gihon up into the Jebusite citadel gives support to the interpretation of this rare word as "water tunnel," or something of the sort; and the passage is an intriguing hint that the very strength of the Jebusite position proved, by the irony of fate, to be the Achilles' heel of their stronghold. That is all the historians tell us; but the wording of Ps. 42:7—H 42:8, where the same *ṣinnôr* recurs, is significantly reminiscent of the cavernous rumblings heard, as Jerome tells us in the fourth century, when the waters of Siloam periodically gushed forth into the pool where the blind man was healed (John 9:7).

Bibliography. Beth-shemesh: E. Grant and G. E. Wright, *'Ain Shems Excavations,* V (1939), 41-43.

Debir: W. F. Albright, *The Excavations of Tell Beit Mirsim,* III (*AASOR,* XXI; 1943), 63.

Gezer: R. A. S. Macalister, *The Excavation of Gezer,* I (1912), 256-64, 268.

Gibeon: J. B. Pritchard, *BA,* XIX (1956).

Jerusalem: L. H. Vincent, *Jérusalem de l'AT,* vol. I (1954), ch. 11.

Lachish: O. Tufnell, *Lachish,* III (1953), 92.

Megiddo: R. S. Lamon, *The Megiddo Water System* (1935).

Nineveh: T. Jacobsen and S. Lloyd, *Sennacherib's aqueduct at Jerwan* (1935).

Samaria: J. W. Crowfoot, K. M. Kenyon, and E. L. Sukenik, *Samaria-Sebaste,* I: *The Buildings at Samaria* (1942), 74-81.   R. W. HAMILTON

WATERCOURSE. The translation of אָפִיק (alternately "channel") in Ps. 126:4 (KJV "stream"); Ezek. 31:12 (KJV "river"); 32:6 (KJV "river"), where a dry stream bed (wadi) is indicated.

WATERPOT(S). *See* POTTERY; VESSELS.

WATERS, MANY [מים רבים]. An OT expression which often designates the waters of chaos, upon which, according to the ancient world view, the earth is founded. *See* CREATION §§ 1*a,* 3*a;* WATER.

WATERS OF MEROM. *See* MEROM, WATERS OF.

WATERSKIN [נבל, wineskin, waterskin, storage jar] (Job 38:37); KJV BOTTLE. A poetic designation of rain clouds in the phrase "waterskins of the heavens" (cf. Job 26:8). For animal skins as containers for liquid, *see* WINESKIN.

WATERSPOUT. KJV translation of צנור (RSV "cataract") in Ps. 42:7—H 42:8. *See* CATARACT.

*WAVE OFFERING [תנופה, *from* נוף, to wave to and fro; *cf*. Isa. 13:2 *for another use of the verb*]. A cultic act of offering agricultural produce before the altar by the Israelite worshiper.

This rite formed a small part of the complex system of sacrifice which developed in the late period of Israel's canonical history (*see* SACRIFICES AND OFFERINGS). The term gives no information about the motivation or meaning of the practice, but points to "the waving" before the altar of that which is being offered "before Yahweh." It has been suggested that the action was a waving toward the altar to signify the offering to Yahweh, then waving away from the altar. Perhaps the offering was returned to the worshiper. This, however, is an unproved conjecture. What might be offered was not uniformly regulated. A variety of items could be included: i.e., various parts of a ram, together with various kinds of "breads" (Exod. 29:22-24); the sheaf of the first fruits (Lev. 23:9-10; *see* FIRST FRUITS). The earliest practice was probably symbolic and later became an actual presenting of the real things which were being offered for the priests. At various occasions, both animal and grain offerings were offered in this way. Special emphasis was laid upon the breast of the ram as an important element (Exod. 29:26; Lev. 7:30; 10:14).

The wave offering is closely related to the other more prominent sacrifices of the cult; from the sparse evidence, it appears that the offerings "waved" were parts of the more important sacrifices. The priest was to wave before the altar in connection with (*a*) the sheaf of the cereal offering; (*b*) loaves of bread of the first-fruits offering; (*c*) seven lambs, one young bull, and two rams, which are a burnt offering; (*d*) the drink offering; (*e*) one male goat for a sin offering; and (*f*) two male lambs as a peace offering (Lev. 23: 15-20). It is not clear whether all these were directly a part of the wave offering, but they were closely related to it.

As a part of the intricate priestly system of sacrifice, this offering was to be done by the priests, as indicated by the phrase "Aaron and his sons" (Exod. 29:24), though Moses also made such an offering (Lev. 8:29). The reference of Lev. 7:28-34 is less explicit on this point. However, since the priest officiated in the peace offering, it is rightly inferred that the priest also acted in this instance. The wave offering was brought by the worshiper, but was offered only in co-operation with the priest, who must participate (Exod. 29:24-25). It has been proposed that the priest placed his hands upon those of the worshipers who held the offering and caused the waving movement (cf. Num. 6:19-20).

This offering was before the altar—i.e., "before Yahweh." As such, it was holy and could no longer be used for any "unclean purpose" (*see* CLEAN AND UNCLEAN). Among the "clean" usages, indeed, the primary usage of the offering was the support of priests and their families. The rite is among those in the media of alimentation (*see* SACRIFICES AND OFFERINGS). According to another form of the rite, the offering was taken from the priests after they had finished the waving, and was burned on the altar with the burnt offering (Exod. 29:25; Lev. 8:28).

W. BRUEGGEMANN

WAX [דונג, *probably* beeswax; κηρός (Jth. 16:15)]. The ordinary uses of wax—e.g., in sealing documents—are not mentioned in the Bible. Wax appears only in poetry, where its property of melting when exposed to heat provides a metaphor for wasting away and destruction. The heart of the persecuted man (Ps. 22:14—H 22:15), the wicked before God's judgment (68:2—H 68:3), and the mountains in the presence of the Lord (Ps. 97:5; Mic. 1:4; Jth. 16:15) "melt like wax."

L. E. TOOMBS

WAY [ארח, דרך; ὁδός]. A common biblical metaphor for courses of nature, modes of human and divine conduct, attitude, habit, custom, undertaking, plan, purpose, fate, and the like.

The flight of the eagle, the locomotion of the serpent, the navigation of a ship, the sex urge, are each a "way" (Prov. 30:19). Menstruation is the "way of women" (Gen. 18:11; 31:35). Two universals, procreation and death, are called alike the "way of all the earth" (Gen. 19:31; Josh. 23:14; I Kings 2:2). Human conduct is a way (I Kings 2:4; 8:25; II Chr. 6:16; Ps. 119:1, 9; Jas. 5:20) or ways (Job 4:6; 13:15; 22:3; Pss. 39:1; 119:5, 26; Ezek. 16:47; Acts 14:16; I Cor. 4:17; Jas. 1:8). There are for men two ways: (*a*) the good and the right way (I Sam. 12:23), or the way(s) of the Lord (Gen. 18:19; Pss. 18:21; 25:9), and (*b*) the way of evil (Prov. 2:12; 8:13; Jer. 18:11; Ezek. 3:18; Jonah 3:8, 10; Zech. 1:4), the way of sinners and the wicked (Ps. 1:1, 6). The Lord's way(s) and man's are radically different (Isa. 55:8-9). The Lord's ways are perfect (Deut. 32:4; II Sam. 22: 31; Ps. 18:30), right (Hos. 14:9), just (Dan. 4:37), and true (Rev. 15:3). Man's way may be either good (I Kings 8:36; II Chr. 6:27; Ps. 101:2, 6; Prov. 2:20; 29:27; Isa. 26:7; Matt. 21:32; Rom. 3:17; I Cor. 12: 31; II Pet. 2:15, 21) or evil (Gen. 6:12; Num. 22:32; Judg. 2:19; I Kings 13:33; Job 22:15; Ps. 36:4; Prov. 4:14, 19).

Man has freedom of the will (Ps. 119:59; Prov. 7:25; 21:29; 23:19) to avoid the evil way (Ps. 119: 101, 104, 128), or to follow it (Isa. 53:6; 57:17; 59:8; 65:2; 66:3; Jer. 3:21). Men or nations may change their ways for good or ill (Jer. 18; Ezek. 18). Discipline is effective (Prov. 22:6). Good example may be followed (I Kings 22:43; II Kings 22:2; II Chr. 11:17; 17:3), or evil (I Kings 15:26, 34; 22:52; II Kings 8:18, 27; 16:3; II Chr. 22:3; Prov. 16:29; Jer. 10:2; Ezek. 23:13, 31; II Pet. 2:15; Jude 11), or may not (I Sam. 8:3, 5; II Chr. 21:12). One can be misled (Isa. 3:12).

God observes and knows all man's ways (Job 24: 23; 31:4; 34:21; Pss. 119:168; 139:3; Prov. 5:21; Jer. 16:17) and requites each man according to his way(s) (I Kings 8:32, 39; II Chr. 6:23; Job 34:11; Ps. 146:9; Prov. 14:14; Jer. 4:18; 17:10; 32:10; Ezek. 7:3, 27; 11:21; 16:43; 18:30; 22:31; 24:14; 33:20; 36:19; Hos. 4:9; Zech. 1:6; 3:7), in spite of appearances to the contrary (Ps. 37:7-8). Yet the Lord will deal with Israel, when she shows remorse, not according to her evil ways, but for his name's sake and the covenant's (Ezek. 16:61; 20:43; 36:31-32). The Lord desires men to amend their ways and turn from evil and live (II Kings 17:13; II Chr. 7:14; Isa. 55:7; Jer. 7:3, 5; 18:11; 25:5; 26:3, 13; 35:15; Ezek. 18:23;

33:8, 11; Jonah 3:8, 10; Zech. 1:4). The Lord is ever ready to teach man and lead him in His way(s) (Pss. 16:11; 23:3; 25:8-9, 12; 27:11; 32:8; 86:11; 119: 27, 29, 33, 35, 37; 143:8; Isa. 30:21; Jer. 32:39; 42:3; Mic. 4:2). To follow the way of the Lord is to observe the Mosaic law (Exod. 18:20; 32:8; Deut. 5:33; 8:6; 9:12; 10:12; 11:22; 19:9; 26:17; 28:9; 30:16; Josh. 22:5; Pss. 18:21; 25:4; 51:13; 81:13; 95:10; 103: 7; 119:1, 3; Isa. 2:3; 42:24; 58:2; Jer. 7:23; Mark 12:14; Luke 20:21). Of the two ways open to man, one leads to life and peace (Ps. 16:11; Prov. 3:17; 4:18; 6:23; 8:32; 10:17, 29; 11:5; 12:28; 13:6; 15:24; 16:7, 17; Jer. 21:8; Matt. 7:13-14; Acts 2:28; Rom. 3:17) and the other to death and misery (Prov. 7:27; 13:15; 14:12; 16:25; 21:16; 22:5, 25; Isa. 59:7). Man may be under the illusion that he controls his own destiny and may do as he pleases (Prov. 12:15, 26; 16:9; 21:2; Jer. 10:23), but it is the Lord who guides and guards man's way (Pss. 37:23; 91:11; Prov. 2:8; 16:9; Jer. 10:23; Dan. 5:23) and to whom man should commit his way (Ps. 37:5; Prov. 3:6). Nevertheless, man's final way is a way of no return (Job 16:22). The "way of the LORD," God's purpose, which the prophets proclaimed (Isa. 40:3; Mal. 3:1), is fulfilled in Christ (Matt. 3:3; Mark 1:2-3; Luke 3:4; 7:27; John 1:23; Acts 18:25-26). It is the way of peace (Luke 1:79), of truth (II Pet. 2:2), of salvation (Acts 16:17). Christ has opened the "new and living way" to God (Heb. 10:20). He *is* the way (John 14: 4-6). Thus Christianity came to be designated as "the Way" (Acts 9:2; 19:9, 23; 22:4; 24:14, 22).

Bibliography. B. Couroyer, "Le chemin de vie en Egypte et en Israël," *RB*, 56 (1949), 412-32; A. Kuschke, "Die Menschenwege und der Weg Gottes im AT," *Studia Theologica*, 5 (1951), 106-18.   M. H. POPE

WAYFARER. A traveler by road, especially one who journeys on foot. These travelers could be merchants, smiths, musicians, returnees from the Exile, sojourners, or beggars. In times of war it was often unsafe to be a wayfarer (Judg. 5:6; 19:17 ff; Isa. 33:8). He often, however, received good Semitic hospitality (II Sam. 12:4; Job 31:32; Jer. 14:8). One of the families returning from the Exile are children of ARAH, "wayfarer" (Ezra 2:5; Neh. 6:18; 7:10). Jer. 9:2 refers to desert-caravan people as wayfarers.

See also SOJOURNER; TRAVEL AND COMMUNICATION; TRADER.   C. U. WOLF

WAYMARK [ציון, *ṣî-yûn; cf.* Arab. *ṣuwwah*, stone heap, *and* Jewish Aram. *ṣayyēn,* put up a pile]. Alternately: MONUMENT (II Kings 23:17; KJV TITLE); SIGN (Ezek. 39:15). A sign set up along a path or road.

In Jer. 31:21 "waymarks," probably small heaps of stones (the handiest objects), are to be used to mark the route of exile so that Israel can return by the same road. In Ezek. 39:15 the term designates a few stones to mark the location of an unburied human bone. In II Kings 23:17 "MONUMENT" is misleading; this grave would likely be marked only by a pile of stones.   W. S. McCULLOUGH

WAYSIDE [דרך, road, way, *from* דרך, tread, march; מעגל (Ps. 140:5—H 140:6), track, *from* עגל, roll; יד, hand, side]. The side of a road or path.

We find the following expressions: "by the wayside" in Gen. 38:21 and "by the way" in I Sam. 24: 3—H 24:4 (על הדרך); "at the road side" (KJV "by the way") in Gen. 38:16 (אל הדרך); "by the road" (KJV "by the wayside") in I Sam. 4:13 (יד דרך, "side of road," for יד דרך); "by the wayside" in Ps. 140:5 —H 140:6 (ליד מעגל, "at the side of a track").

           W. S. McCULLOUGH

***WEALTH.**

1. In the OT. In the OT wealth must be considered in relation to the synonymous term "riches." Both designate abundance of property (land, buildings, agricultural commodities, livestock, slaves), the basic economic commodity in an agricultural economy such as prevailed in Palestine (for another type of wealth, *see* MONEY).

"Wealth" is used to translate two Hebrew words, הון and חיל, both meaning "faculty," "ability," or "power," which come to have the metaphorical meaning "wealth"—the observable and tangible evidence of the ability to acquire and the power it gives over others. The term "riches" is regularly used to translate the Hebrew root עשר. Originally this root probably meant "abound," but in OT usage the abundance so consistently signifies riches that metaphorical meaning has been lost to literal meaning.

The distinctive OT attitude toward wealth is largely determined by religious understanding. Since Yahweh is Creator and Sovereign over all creation, all things belong to him. "The earth is the LORD's and the fulness thereof" (Ps. 24:1). Such an affirmation is understood by Israel through her particular historical and religious experience. It was Yahweh who had given his people the land of Palestine after the exodus from Egypt (Num. 34–36; Josh. 13–19). As Yahweh graciously gave Israel her inheritance in the Promised Land, so also he blesses individuals with wealth, foremost examples being Abraham (Gen. 13:2; 14:23) and Solomon (I Kings 3:13). Yahweh has given the wealth of the earth to his people for their enjoyment. They, in turn, must not forget or say: "My power and the might of my hand have gotten me this wealth" (Deut. 8:17). Israel's overlooking her resources as the sign of her dependence on God is inextricably related to her breaking the covenant and going after other gods. When Israel did forget and break the covenant, then her land and wealth were taken from her and she was sent into exile. Throughout Israel's history stern warnings are directed against those who strive for wealth through greed, trickery, and treachery, and against the pride and glory in it (II Sam. 12; Isa. 10:3; Jer. 5:27; 15: 13; 17:3; Ezek. 7:11; 28; Hos. 12:8; Mic. 6:12). Their end was destruction. And yet, to a faithful Israel, Yahweh promises that even the wealth of the nations will be brought to Zion (Isa. 45:14; 60:5, 11; Mic. 4:13). Wealth and riches may be a sign of God's blessing or the cause of God's wrath. Israel's faithfulness or unfaithfulness is central in the determination of which it shall be.

The book of Job strongly protests against the view that goodness brings wealth and wickedness brings poverty (*see* JOB, BOOK OF). And in a number of psalms (10; 12; 14; 37; 40; 41; 52; 70; 72; 74) "rich" is synonymous with "wicked" and "poor" with "righteous and godly" (*see* POOR). While the term "poor" is to be understood as a religious term, it undoubtedly reflects an economic situation in postexilic Judaism in which there was a growing concentration of wealth among those who were increasingly secularized (or Hellenized), especially the priestly aristocracy. Even so, there is the hope that God will vindicate himself and the righteous poor by a complete reversal of the situation. A more prudential, less theological attitude toward wealth is found in Proverbs. Riches are the reward of man's diligence (10:2, 27), a source of security (10:5; 18:11), protect a man's life (13:8), win friends (19:4). And yet, "a good name is to be chosen rather than great riches" (22:1). The desire for wealth may make men greedy (28:22), overconfident (28:11), arrogant (18:23), and eventually lead to loss of wealth (13:11; 22:16). For the explanation of this atypical attitude, *see* PROVERBS, BOOK OF.

2. In Jesus' teaching. The NT term for "wealth" or "riches" is usually ὁ (τὸ)πλοῦτος; occasionally τὰ χρήματα. Its attitude toward wealth, while consistent with that of the OT, lays added emphasis on its dangers. This emphasis derives from Jesus' own teaching. The saying: "How hard it will be for those who have riches to enter the kingdom of God!" (Mark 10:23) clearly illustrates his point of view. It is in relation to his proclamation of the kingdom that Jesus' words on riches must be understood. Jesus is frankly pessimistic about the ability of men who possess wealth to escape being beholden to it. The rich fool is a fool because the security and meaning of his life are rooted in his riches (Luke 12:16 ff). The rich young man finds his zeal for "eternal life" quenched when he is told to give away his possessions and follow Jesus (Mark 10:17 ff). Jesus believed that possessions invariably lay a man in bondage. In his saying: "You cannot serve God and mammon" (Matt. 6:24), Jesus draws a sharp line between service to God and service to mammon. He actually personifies riches (*see* MAMMON), probably to heighten his emphasis on the demonic power which mammon exercises over man. In view of such language it is questionable to speak glibly of riches as a "neutral" quantity in Jesus' view. The facts betray the probability that the person with possessions will fail to commit himself in thought and action to the truth that "a man's life does not consist in the abundance of his possessions" (Luke 12:15). And so Jesus positively taught his disciples: "Provide yourselves with purses that do not grow old, with a treasure in the heavens that does not fail . . . . For where your treasure is, there will your heart be also" (Luke 12:33-34). This was not economic reform in any technical sense. Jesus was combatting the insidious power of possessions to enslave men and destroy their ultimate trust in God and his kingdom. He did not condemn possessions as such. There is no reason to believe he expected the publicans he befriended to quit their remunerative occupation, nor did he expect all who heard him to give up working. The special demands on his close disciples were necessitated by the nature of a particular task. Neither did he commend poverty as such. The poor widow who gave the penny was not praised for her poverty but for the freedom with which she could give all she had in devotion to God (Mark 12:41-44). It was this freedom to sit lightly to one's possessions in wholehearted service to God that was the heart of the matter. Historically speaking, it was the poor of the land who responded to Jesus. When he said: "Blessed are you poor" (Luke 6:20), the word "poor" (*see* POOR) undoubtedly reflects the religious meaning of the Psalms: Blessed are you who in your destitution humbly await God's gracious action. But more than Jesus' words, his life itself carried his message. For he was a living renunciation of all that might stand between himself and complete trust, devotion, and service to God.

3. In the early church. The early church's attitude consistently reflects Jesus' teaching. This is vividly illustrated in the account of the sharing of possessions in Acts (4:32-35). This communal sharing was not communistic in any modern sense, but shows the early Christians' desire to express their love for one another and their self-abandonment in service to God while they hopefully awaited Christ's imminent return. The apostle Paul urged Christians to work, not only to provide for their own needs (I Thess. 4:11; II Thess. 3:12), but primarily in order that those who had more might help those who had less (II Cor. 8:13-15). Even so, the process of acquiring possessions was to be carried on as if they were not acquiring possessions (I Cor. 7:30-31). I.e., they were to avoid enslavement to either the process or the possessions, both of which were passing away. The Letter of James deplores obsequious praise and deference for the rich—which inevitably breaks the bond of fellowship of the church (2:1-7). The same letter sternly warns the rich who have gained their wealth through questionable means and who live in luxury and pleasure. A day of reckoning is coming (5:1-6). And so the words: "Come now, you rich, weep and howl." In I Timothy, Christians are admonished to be content with the necessities of food, clothing, and shelter. Those who desire to be rich fall into temptations and snares that plunge men into ruin (I Tim. 6:8-9). The rich are warned against pride and "setting their hopes on uncertain riches" rather than on "God who richly furnishes us with everything to enjoy" (6:17). "They are to do good, to be rich in good deeds, liberal and generous, thus laying up for themselves a good foundation for the future, so that they may take hold of the life which is life indeed" (vs. 18). The book of Revelation strongly denounces the church at Laodicea for its lukewarmness. "For you say, I am rich, I have prospered, and I need nothing; not knowing that you are wretched, pitiable, poor, blind, and naked" (Rev. 3:17). The same author paints a vivid, prophetic picture of the collapse of the whole economy of the Roman world, built, as he believed, on the false grounds of "impure passion," "wantonness," "self-glory," and "deception" (ch. 18). "In one hour all this wealth has been laid waste" (vs. 17). It is a sharp warning against the inevitable idolatry of riches which accompanies denial of God as the supreme source of and answer to man's deepest needs.

In the NT, then, while wealth is not condemned as such, there is a strong pessimism over the possibility of its being a blessing rather than a demonic snare to man. Unfortunately, later efforts to accommodate and rationalize its rigor drastically obscure the stark NT attitude.   F. W. YOUNG

WEAPONS AND IMPLEMENTS OF WAR.
Weapons among the Hebrews can best be discussed
in the light of what is known of weapons in the Near
East in general.

1. Development of weapons in the Near East.
a. Stone Age weapons. Weapons in some form or
other are as old as man himself. Early man may
simply have heaved unfashioned rock as an offensive
weapon, but as far as is known, man has always
used weapons of some sort, both in search of food
and against inimical forces.

Exactly at what time prehistoric man began
fashioning tools and weapons is not known. In fact,
it is often very difficult to determine whether a stone
used as tool or weapon found in the earliest sites
was fashioned or natural. .

Up to the latter part of the fifth millennium B.C.
all tools and weapons were made of stone, hence the
use of the terms Paleolithic, Mesolithic, and Neolithic (Old, Middle, and New Stone Age) to designate the periods of man's development up to the
introduction of metal. These divisions are merely for
the sake of convenience, and what is intended by
them will become clear below.

Stone Age man made tools and weapons of various
kinds of stones: of flint, obsidian, coarse granite, and
quartzite, though flint was on the whole most popular for finer work. These were fashioned by varied
techniques of chipping and flaking, and in later
developments of these techniques involved a fairly
extensive knowledge, not only of the properties of
the kind of stone to be worked, but also of the physical laws of angles and pressures involved in the
process of shaping a stone instrument into its
desired form.

It ought also to be stated emphatically that a carefully drawn distinction between tool and weapon is
quite impossible to delineate for the prehistoric Near
East. An axe, e.g., though normally used for felling
trees and shaping wood, could also be used for
hunting in hand-to-hand combat with some animal,
as well as for warfare. Even in the metal ages a
clear-cut distinction is not always possible. The bow
and arrow was certainly an implement of warfare,
but it was used for hunting food as well.

What man's first fashioned weapon may have
been cannot be known. Certainly the spear (wooden)
is an old weapon. From a clear-cut hole in a thigh
bone extending into the pelvis in a Neanderthal
skeleton at Mount Carmel, it has been suggested that
wooden spears were known to Neanderthal man.
He also appears to have used hafted narrowed flint
points as detachable spearheads. The simple club
must range as one of man's earliest tools as well.
The mace, a stone bound with thongs in tomahawk
style to a wooden handle, must have been in use
from time immemorial. In the nature of the case it
is impossible for prehistoric archaeologists or anthro-
pologists to answer this question. In the main, only
stone objects have remained intact as silent witness
to the use they may have had. Wood and leather,
both certainly used, have disintegrated throughout
the succeeding millenniums, and only shrewd reconstruction can approximate the use to which certain
stone objects found in Paleolithic levels may have
been put. In any event, the oldest occupied caves in
Palestine show evidence of a fairly extensive flint
industry. Hand axes which may be even earlier than
the cave deposits have also been found. During the
Middle Paleolithic period flake tools appear to
replace in part the hand axes of the Lower period.
This is the age of the Neanderthal skulls found at
Mount Carmel.

Exactly when the Paleolithic Age ended and the
Mesolithic began, or more particularly what the
chronological dimensions of the Mesolithic Age were
—i.e., the beginnings of agriculture—is becoming
increasingly difficult to determine, since the pre-
pottery Neolithic Age is being pushed back in time
with each successive expedition to the early Neolithic
site at Jericho. It now appears that Mesolithic cultures were practically contemporaneous to the early
Neolithic Age at Jericho. The most characteristic
Mesolithic culture thus far found in Palestine was
the Natufian (*ca.* 8000-6000 B.C.), in which grain
cultivation was well known, though the Natufians
were still mainly food-gatherers. The Natufians as
well as the Helwanians (near Cairo in Egypt) were
a microlithic culture. These microliths were of varied
types, including lunate, triangular, and trapeziform
shapes. Arrowheads particularly of the last-named
type were mounted on shafts of wood or bone for use
as arrows. Agricultural implements of various kinds
(sickles, pestles, and mortars) were also found in
abundance, indicating their essential Mesolithic
character. Incidentally, the oldest known fishhooks
come from the later Natufian period.

The beginnings of the Neolithic Age in Palestine
cannot as yet be determined chronologically. The
Neolithic Age has usually been thought of as the
beginnings of village life, usually about some shrine.
It was the age of the domestication of cattle
(although the dog apparently had already been
domesticated by the Natufians), of the invention of
pottery, and of the manufacture of ground and
polished stone celts. Actually pottery was not invented until late in the Neolithic period, so that
archaeologists usually divide it into pre-pottery and
pottery Neolithic.

The stone implements of this period are much
better than those of the Mesolithic. This marked
improvement was due to a major discovery. It was
found that grinding the edge of a stone celt and then
polishing it created a much finer edge than that of

a merely flaked tool. This meant that felling trees and shaping wood and bone became much simpler and more accurate. The process of grinding also meant that holes could be bored in stone during this period; this was particularly advantageous for shafting handles for axes—shafting being much superior to hafting with thongs for certain implements. In a sense, ground celts, found throughout Neolithic Egypt and the Near East as early as 5000 B.C., go hand in hand with agricultural pursuits. (Mixed farming seems to have started in Egypt by *ca.* 5000 B.C.) After all, a hoe culture depends in large part on ground celts. On the other hand, polished stone celts were abandoned in Egypt already in predynastic times, since the increasing aridity of the climate created a greater scarcity of trees for cutting. In dynastic times almost all wood had to be imported, mainly from Syria.

In contrast to the axe, which was either hafted into the end of a wood or bone handle or shafted (as was the mace), the adz was usually thonged. The adz differs from the axe in that the blade runs at ninety degrees to the handle. Since its blade was usually much narrower, the perforation of the adz seriously weakened the stone, thereby making shafting impractical.

Stone arrowheads are ancient, but the tanged variety was probably invented in Late Paleolithic times by the Aterians in North Africa, from which it quickly spread. The tanged arrowhead was particularly well adapted to the use of reed shafts. By the advent of the metal age a large variety of arrowhead types is attested. Already mentioned are the triangular (probably the most popular of all) and the lunate, both known from the Natufians. The transverse or chisel-end type is attested from Uruk times in the Mesopotamian Valley in the E, and in Egypt in the W. Similarly widespread is the leaf-shaped type found as far E as Susa, and as far W as Badari in Egypt. The tanged and the hollow-based varieties were both found in Egypt, particularly in the Fayyum.

Other stone weapons from the Neolithic (as well as the Chalcolithic) period are daggers, slingstones, maceheads, and battle-axes. At Tell el Hassuna (fifth millennium) baked clay pellets, probably for sling ammunition, were found in quantity. Many slingstones have also been found throughout Phoenicia and at Tepe-Gawra (*ca.* 3500 B.C.). Hassuna also produced a number of points of imported obsidian, possibly for ammunition for reed darts. Early daggers of flint with hollow-based hilts were used in predynastic Egypt and are of exceptionally fine workmanship. Maceheads of various types were common in Western Asia and in Egypt, as were battle-axes. The latter weapon is a celt of which the butt end is elongated and carefully shaped. Stone battle-axes are known, but it is uncertain whether they are copies of earlier metal weapons or simply a development of early antler axes. The earliest specimens of battle-axes known are clay models from the Ubaid period (*ca.* 3500 B.C.).

b. The Chalcolithic period. The latter part of the fifth millennium is usually known to archaeologists as the period in which copper tools and weapons began to replace stone, although the latter remained

in common use as late as the Iron Age. Metallurgy was widely practiced in the Near East from *ca.* 4000 B.C. onward, but metal replaced stone slowly. Even in Assyria polished stone celts were not largely replaced by metal (bronze) ones until a millennium later, whereas in Egypt this did not occur until *ca.* 2000 B.C., and in the Aegean, *ca.* 1500 B.C. Thus it is convenient to refer in general terms to a Chalcolithic Age, when metallic and nonmetallic tools and weapons occur side by side. In the Third Dynasty in Egypt soldiers were often equipped with metal weapons, whereas laborers still used stone tools. In fact, it was really for battle that the advantages of metal weapons became fully apparent. Such early metal weapons were at first copied from stone, but gradually the greater flexibility of metal allowed for the evolution of new forms as well. The advantages of metal weapons were quickly seen. Not only is a variety of new forms now possible, but they are much more durable. Stone edges if broken were useless; even if the stone were of some use, a tedious process of reflaking, grinding, and polishing was necessary before the instrument could again be used. On the other hand, a metal-edged instrument seldom broke, and the dulled edge could be quickly resharpened by hammering.

The earliest metal tools were made of native copper; this was before smelting was understood. Ancient native copper was of very high purity and as a result extremely soft. It could, however, be hardened by cold-working, especially by hammering. The earliest copper tools were the flat celts (axes and adzes). Metal celts with shaft holes were much superior to the old hafted stone implements; examples of the oldest found appear in the Sumerian hatchets and the adzes at Susa.

Daggers also constitute one of the earliest metal weapons. These were usually flat and triangular, the latter being necessary to provide lateral strength. Already before the Third Dynasty, Egyptian daggers were provided with a midrib both for giving firmness and allowing for a finer blade.

Metal was, of course, exceedingly precious, and hurling weapons would only be provided with metal tips. Whether spearheads evolved simply from the idea of a dagger mounted on a long shaft, as some have suggested, is not known, but already in early dynastic times in Egypt copper-tanged spearheads were fairly numerous, whereas copper arrowheads are very rare, probably because metal was too expensive simply to be thrown away and not recovered. For the evolution of the battle-ax the use of metal was all-important. It commonly consisted of a rounded body with a splayed blade and a cylindrical butt behind the shaft hole. Such a weapon was almost impossible to make from stone.

c. The Bronze Age. The most important discovery for the evolution of metal tools prior to the use of iron was the discovery of hardening copper by the addition of tin alloy to the copper, usually about five to fifteen per cent, thereby creating bronze. A greater amount of tin made the metal harder but also more brittle; a proper balance between flexibility and hardness had to be found (*ca.* ten per cent being the best amount). Furthermore, bronze can also be work-hardened, whereupon it yields about twice the tensile strength of copper. Pure copper is also almost impossible to cast except for flat celts, whereas bronze is easily adaptable to casting.

Bronze was particularly useful for the longer piercing weapons. The dagger with or without tang now became common in Western Asia. By casting the dagger with a hilt, the blade could also be kept slender throughout. The SWORD is simply the evolution of the dagger at the beginning of the Bronze

Courtesy of the Oriental Institute, the University of Chicago

9. Bronze weapons (*ca.* fifteenth-fourteenth century B.C.): (1, 4) spearheads; (2-3) dagger pommels; (5-7) dagger blades; (8) dagger

Courtesy of the Palestine Archaeological Museum, Jerusalem, Jordan

10. Weapons found in Palestine: (*a*) Hittite axe head; (*b*) sickle sword; (*c-d*) daggers (or swords); (*e-f*) spearheads; (*g-j*) arrowheads; (*k*) blunted arrowhead; (*l*) piece of armor

Age. The earliest common form was triangular with a riveted hilt. With the development of the midrib the dagger/sword gradually became longer and more slender. The casting of a bronze sword called forth all the skill of the ancient workman. The sword necessarily had to be made of good metal, and any nonmetallic materials or flaws had to be avoided. The proper balance between hardness and flexibility had to be found. Then after casting, the cutting edge had to be carefully work-hardened.

As stated above, copper spearheads were normally tanged. With the advent of bronze and the consequent possibility of casting metal in more complex molds, socketed spearheads made their first appearance. As in the Copper Age, metal arrowheads were still rather rare, still normally being made of flint or bone.

Figs. WEA 9-10.

d. The Iron Age. The earliest iron implements were made of meteoritic rock, as is apparent from their high nickel content. At first such implements, because of the rarity of the metal, were used only for ornamental or magical purposes.

Ancient smelting techniques would only produce wrought iron, which was not hard enough for swords or ancient cutting implements. To overcome this difficulty, the implement was first shaped and then carburized or case-hardened. This technique consisted of heating the object in contact with carbon, thereby in effect transforming the surface into steel.

The chief advantage of iron over bronze lay in its great hardness and strength. The sword in particular benefited from the use of iron, since the blade could be made almost unbreakable. Short swords or daggers also became common with the advent of the Iron Age, as may be seen from the excellent dagger found in the tomb of Tut-ankh-Amon.

2. Classification of weapons. Implements of warfare may be divided according to the use for which they are intended—i.e., as either offensive or defensive weapons. Many offensive weapons are naturally also used for defense. Defensive weapons consisted mainly of shields (of various forms) and protective armor. Defense in warfare consisted rather in strategic location of cities, walled defenses (such as already attested by 6000 B.C. at Jericho), moats, and the like. *See* WAR, METHODS OF.

Generally speaking, offensive weapons can be classified into three types: (*a*) The basic and undoubtedly the earliest type are the various hand-wielded weapons. These in turn are used in different ways. Some weapons are used for crushing the skull. Included in this category are clubs, battle-axes, and maces. Other weapons such as the ordinary ax (primarily used domestically) are intended for cleaving. Closely related to this is the cutting weapon exemplified by knives and edged swords. Still another type is the thrusting weapon, by which the wielder attempts to pierce or stab his opponents. This includes the dagger, lance, and pointed sword. In all these the weapons remains in the possession of the wielder.

b) A second type is the missile weapon. These are not retained in the hand, but the entire weapon is discharged by hand or arm action. It was suggested above that when man first emerged, an unfashioned stone probably constituted such a missile weapon. Included here are darts, spears, and javelins, all of which are attested from Paleolithic times.

c) Probably later in the evolution of weapons is the third type, in which the weapon discharges the missile. Here the discharging weapon is retained but the ammunition is propelled. As this type becomes more effective, the distance between the enemies becomes greater, until in modern times battle lines may be at quite some distance from each other. Examples of this type are slings (cf. Judg. 20:16), bows (and arrows), and catapults.

3. Offensive weapons. *a. Dagger* (חרב). This is a short sword used for stabbing. The word occurs only in the KJV of the Ehud story in Judg. 3 (vss. 16, 21-22) as a rendering of חרב, more commonly

Courtesy of the University Museum of the University of Pennsylvania

11. Gold dagger, from Ur, early Dynastic period

rendered "sword" in English versions. In form it is a sword, but shorter, probably of the dirk type.* Weapons under *ca.* 16 inches in length are usually called "daggers" by archaeologists, though, as far as is known, the Hebrews made no such distinction. Since the weapon which Ehud made for himself in order to assassinate Eglon was a cubit in length (*ca.* 17½ inches), it is properly rendered "sword" (RSV). Fig. HUN 36.

On the other hand, the Hebrews undoubtedly knew the shorter, stabbing sword as well, and it is quite possible that the original writers may often have intended "dagger" by the word חרב. Innumerable daggers have been found on Bronze and Iron Age sites throughout Egypt, Palestine, and Mesopotamia.* The dagger worn in a small scabbard is today a favorite weapon of the Bedouins in Transjordan. Fig. WEA 11.

b. Spear (חנית, כידון, צלצל, קין, רמח; λόγχη; cf. δεξιολάβος ["spearman"; Acts 23:23]). This is an offensive weapon consisting of a long wooden shaft (עץ) on which was mounted a (spear) head of stone or metal (להבת [I Sam. 17:7] or להב [Job 39:23]).

The חנית is the spear proper, whereas the כידון, also a hurling instrument, is translated "javelin" in the RSV (except in Jer. 6:23; 50:42). The רמח is a longer weapon and was used for thrusting; this might better be rendered by the word "lance." Both the words חנית and רמח were borrowed from Canaanite into Egyptian as *ḥnyt* and *mrḥ*. The word צלצל is a *hapax legomenon* in Job 41:7—H 40:31, where it occurs in the phrase צלצל דגים, probably a technical word for "fish spear" or "harpoon." Another *hapax legomenon* is the word קין at II Sam. 21:16. Ishbibenob, a Philistine champion, had a קין weighing three hundred bronze shekels. The word literally means "a forging," and the LXX interpreted it as δόρατος, "spear," a tradition perpetuated to the present day. The tradition is almost certainly wrong, however, since only the spearhead would have been made of bronze.

The spear is a very ancient weapon, probably as early as the Middle Paleolithic Age. The stone spear-

heads were normally tanged, and the wooden shaft would be split or bored to take the tang. The advent of the metal age made the spear more popular, since it permitted a socketed spearhead which could be riveted to the shaft. Most bronze (and iron) spearheads are of this latter type. Bronze heads are usually longer and narrower than the stone ones, which in the Syrian type were often triangular in shape. The tip was often equipped with two sharp hooks or barbs which rendered the extraction of the spear from a wound dangerous. The opposite end of the shaft was sometimes equipped with a socketed shoe used for setting the spear in the ground (cf. I Sam. 26:7).

Such spears were often carried by royalty, military leaders, or champions (I Sam. 17:45; 19:9; 20:33; II Sam. 2:23), as well as being equipment of the guard (II Kings 11:10). In fact, together with the shield (צנה), the spear constituted the tribal weapon of the Naphtalites. Mention is made of giants carrying extra heavy spears (I Sam. 17:7; II Sam. 21:16). It has been conjectured that the spear of Goliath was equipped with a thong (μεσάκυλον) at the middle of the shaft. The shaft of his spear is said to be like a מנור ארגים, "weaver's heddle rod" (not "beam"), so called from its shape rather than its size. If this is correct, the Philistine's hurling spear was of the *amentum* or ἀγκύλη type, which when released would revolve, thus giving a greater force for throwing.

The λόγχη which pierced Jesus' side (Matt. 27:49 RSV mg.; John 19:34) was undoubtedly the Roman *pilum*, a javelin consisting of a long, thin iron shaft about three feet long, inserted at one end in a wooden shaft of the same length. All legionnaires in imperial times were equipped with such *pila*.

The word δεξιολάβος in Acts 23:23 is a *hapax legomenon* of uncertain meaning. The rendering "spearmen" in the KJV and the RSV is simply based on the Vulg. interpretation of this word (*stipatores*). According to Theoph. Simocatta (*Hist.* 4.i), a seventh-century writer, it meant a light-armed soldier. A scholion from Matthaei refers to such as παραφύλακες ("bodyguard"). An earlier textual variant reads δεξιοβόλους, from which it has been inferred that they were javelin-throwers. Two hundred δεξι and two hundred soldiers and seventy horsemen were ordered by a tribune to guard Paul and bring him to Felix in Caesarea. Fig. ELA 23.

c. Javelin (חנית [KJV]; כידון [RSV]; סגר [Ps. 35:3 RSV]; רמח [Num. 25:7 KJV]). The RSV translates כידון "javelin" except in Jer. 6:23; 50:42, where it has "spear." In all places where the KJV has "javelin" (חנית or רמח), the RSV has "spear." In Ps. 35:3 the word סגר occurs in the difficult line והרק חנית וסגר לקראת רדפי ("And draw forth the spear and סגר to meet my pursuers"). Many scholars have thought of the word σάγαρις, a Scythian and Persian weapon—a rather unlikely suggestion in view of the vocalization. It is not at all certain that a weapon is intended; since the root סגר means "to shut, close up," it might simply be a pregnant construction for "closing up ranks."

The כידון was certainly a different weapon from the חנית, but what the exact difference was is unknown. All that can be definitely known from the biblical evidence is that it was stretched out in the hand (Josh. 8:18-19, 26), carried by a rider (Job 39:23), and quivered (רעשׁ; Job 41:29—H 41:21). It was carried along with the bow (Jer. 6:23; 50:42). It has been suggested that it was a light form of the חנית carried by riders and commonly used on the chase. This could, however, not apply in the case of Joshua against Ai.

d. Lance (כידון [Jer. 50:42 KJV]; רמח [I Kings 18:28 RSV]). For כידון, *cf.* § *3c above.* The רמח was a spear with a longer shaft and used for thrusting rather than for hurling (Num. 25:7-8). It was a weapon also in use by Egyptians (Jer. 46:4), as well as being the favorite offensive weapon of the Gadites (I Chr. 12:8) and the Judeans (vs. 24; II Chr. 14:8). It is often referred to together with the "shield," since the lance was used in battle array. The front line would be drawn up closely shield to shield with lances protruding, a formation well known from Assyrian monumental reliefs. The Arabs still use the *rumḥ* today, though they commonly use it in charging from the saddle.

e. Lancet (רמח [I Kings 18:28 KJV; RSV "lances"]). The word "lancet" is a textual error in modern editions of the KJV for the original "lancers," an Old English word adapted by the KJV translators from the Bishops' Bible's reading "launsers," meaning "lances." The change to "lancet" did not occur before the latter half of the eighteenth century.

f. Maul (מפיץ [Prov. 25:18 KJV; RSV "war club"]). The word מפיץ literally means "shatterer, disperser," as in Nah. 2:1. The rendering "maul," or "war club" as in the RSV, in the Proverbs passage is apparently based on understanding מפיץ as מפץ (*mappēṣ*). *See* CLUB § 2.

4. Defensive weapons. *a. Shield* (*buckler, target*) (כידון [KJV]; מגן, צנה, סחרה, רמח, שׁלט; θυρεός). The word כידון is incorrectly interpreted by the KJV as "shield" in I Sam. 17:45; Job 39:23, and as "target" in I Sam. 17:6. The RSV renders it correctly as "javelin" (*see* § *3c above*). The KJV renders רמה wrongly as "buckler" in I Chr. 12:8 (RSV "spear"). The two common words for "shield" and "buckler" are מגן and צנה (*see below*). Since two different types of shields are obviously intended by these words, one might expect the rendering "buckler" to be retained for צנה, and "shield" for מגן, but the English versions are quite inconsistent. (*See* BUCKLER.) The word סחרה occurs only in Ps. 91:4 in the statement describing God's faithfulness: צנה וסחרה אמתו. Both the KJV and the RSV render the word "buckler." The root סחר means "to go around"; hence a סחרה must be a protection which surrounds. In view of the Akkadian *seḥertu*, "enclosure," it has been suggested that the words mean either "armor" or "wall of defense." The word שׁלט occurs seven times in the OT. It may simply be a synonym for מגן, but this is uncertain; others suggest that the word means "armor" or "armaments." Fig. HUN 36.

Unfortunately, ancient Near Eastern shields were usually made of perishable materials, and thus no shield has as yet been found in Palestine. Both Egyptian and Assyrian reliefs give us numerous illustrations, however, of the various forms employed.* In Egypt a wooden shield covered with skin seems to

have been the only defensive weapon in the oldest period. The Egyptian shield was rounded at the top and square at the bottom. The Assyrians had many different types of shields. Common was the large rectangular shield (but rounded at the top like a Gothic arch).* These were made of wickerwork and leather. For siege warfare they used massive shields of this type to serve as protection for the bowmen. Figs. LAC 1; ASS 99, 102.

Syrian shields are attested in the tribute lists of Thut-mose III's thirteenth campaign ("bronze spears, shields, bows—all weapons of war"—*ARE* II, 509). Such Syrian shields were probably of the same type as the Egyptian, as may be seen from the representations of the Syrian god Resheph on Egyptian reliefs. The Amarna Letters mention no Syrian shields, though Tushratta of Mitanni does refer to leather shields decorated with silver or bronze as being included among gifts sent to Amen-hotep III. The Hittites also had simple rectangular shields curving inward. The Mitannians also used the smaller round shield. It has been suggested that this type of shield was due to Indo-Aryan influence, since the Philistine shields were also apparently round.

Among the Hebrews both types of shields were known. The smaller and more common round type was the מגן, known from the Lachish relief and frequently mentioned in the OT. This shield was used by the light-armed infantry and by chieftains. The large rectangular shield was the צנה, used to erect a solid-front battle line behind the protruding lances (רמחים). Goliath is said to have had an attendant for carrying his shield.

Shields were made of leather stretched over a wooden frame (like the well-known Roman *scutum*), or of wickerwork. The surface, being made of leather, had to be oiled regularly to guard against cracking (II Sam. 1:21; Isa. 21:5). On the march the shield was covered (Isa. 22:6), and in peacetime hung in arsenals (Song of S. 4:4; Ezek. 27:10). Metal shields were rare and probably used only for ceremonial purposes. Such were undoubtedly the gold-plated shields and bucklers which Solomon had made (I Kings 10:16-17), later carried off by the invading Shishak and replaced by bronze substitutes by Rehoboam (14:26-27). Ordinary soldiers, however, had the simpler and more practical leather shields, often bedecked with a heavy boss at the center to give added protection (Job 15:26), and equipped with a handle on the inside. That shields were usually nonmetallic is apparent from the fact that they were combustible (Ezek. 39:9).

The shield is often used figuratively to denote God's relation to his people. He is a shield about his servants (Gen. 15:1; Ps. 3:3; cf. Pss. 18:2, 30; 33:20; etc.). It is the symbol for divine deliverance (Ps. 18:35) as well as of God's anointed (84:9). In the NT the word θυρεός occurs but once (Eph. 6:16), as a symbol for the faith as being the vital defense for the Christian.

b. Armor (זנות [KJV]; חגורה [II Kings 3:21]; חליצה [II Sam. 2:21 KJV]; נשׁק, מד, כלי; ὅπλα, πανοπλία). According to I Kings 22:38, after Ahab's body was brought back to Samaria, his chariot was washed out and the dogs lapped his blood, והזגות רחצו ("and the harlots washed themselves [in it]").

Early Jewish (and Christian) interpreters found this repugnant and avoided it by finding an Aramaic root זין, "armor"; hence Targ. מני זינא; Peshitta *zayneh*, "his armor"; and Vulg. *habenas*, "thongs, reins" (the LXX, however, correctly reads αἱ πόρναι). The KJV perpetuated this wrong tradition by its "and they washed his armour."

The most common word for "armor" is כלי, a general word for "article," "vessel"; thus by extension it is used of the range of equipment carried by a warrior. (For נשק, *see* COAT OF MAIL.) The word הגורה properly means "girdle belt," an important part of a soldier's defensive armor, and in II Kings 3:21 is probably used by metonymy for the entire equipment. The KJV incorrectly renders חליצה by "armour" in II Sam. 2:21, whereas the RSV rightly uses "spoil." The word refers to that which is stripped off a slain warrior for plunder. The only word in Hebrew which is actually known to designate military dress is מד, literally meaning "measure" and by extension "garment." This usage is apparent from I Sam. 17:38-39, where Saul clothed David in his מד, which included a bronze helmet and a coat of mail. The same usage appears in 18:4, where, however, the KJV renders by "garments." The NT seldom refers to "armor" (Luke 11:22; Rom. 13:12; Eph. 6:11, 13); two words occur: ὅπλα, which like כלי is a general word for "weapons," and πανοπλία. The latter word refers to the "whole armor" of the Roman soldier, and is used by Paul as a figure for the defensive armor of the Christian in the world (Eph. 6).

Little is known of Hebrew armor. Saul and Jonathan both had armor, which must at least have consisted of a HELMET; a breastplate or coat of mail; GREAVES; and a shield. Probably a girdle belt (הגורה) was used for tying down the breastplate.

A puzzling bit of information occurs in I Kings 22:34; II Chr. 18:33. Ahab was struck by an arrow בין הדבקים ובין השריון ("between . . . and the breastplate"). The word דבק etymologically means "a thing joined"—hence, an appendage. It thus probably refers to the scale armor covering the abdomen, which was joined to the coat of mail or breastplate. It thus appears that Hebrew armor consisted of two parts: the שריון, "breastplate," and the דבקים, "lower scale armor," the whole cuirass also being known as שריון.

Roman armor in NT times consisted of helmet, cuirass, and greaves. Greaves were usually made of bronze and molded to fit the leg, with a cloth, felt, leather, or sponge lining to prevent chafing. Greaves (*ocreae*) consisted of two parts and covered the forepart of the leg only (in distinction from the Greek type, which encircled the leg) from knee to ankle. According to Arrian, the Roman warrior wore only one πρὸ τῆς κνήμης τῆς ἐν ταῖς μάχαις προβαλλομενῆς.

The earliest Roman helmet was a leather cap (*galea*), whereas later the metal helmet (*cassis*) became more prominent (though in later Roman times the two terms were no longer clearly distinguished). It consisted of various parts: the protective cap itself, a highly decorative and elaborate crest, two cheek pieces (*bucculae*), and a hinged visor. For comfort the helmet was normally lined with felt or sponge.

The cuirass or body armor (*lorica*) was of various kinds, but the simplest and most common consisted of a leather corselet made of strips of leather faced with metal and wrapped around the torso. These strips were then wired together to form a flexible and protective corset. Two shoulder pieces (*humeralia*), possibly of the same material, were hung over the shoulder and wired to the corset itself. This made a kind of sleeveless coat which after being donned would be laced at the back like a corset. Underneath the *humeralia* a plate of bronze was worn "a square span in size" and called a "heart guard" (Polybius 6.23).

Other types of armor made of metal were also known, though they were not so common as the simple *lorica*, probably because of their cost. Such were chain-mail armor (*lorica hamata*), already known to the Greeks in early times but likely oriental in origin. Another type was made of scale armor (*lorica squamata*), made of scales of bronze or iron and tied together with wire. Metal armor was worn by the praetorian guard in imperial times.

Bibliography. W. M. F. Petrie, *Tools and Weapons* (1917); B. Meissner, "Das Heer und das Kriegswesen," *Babylonia und Assyria,* vol. I (1920), ch. 4; H. Bonnet, *Die Waffen der Völker des alten Orients* (1926); W. Wolf, *Die Bewaffnung des altägyptischen Heeres* (1926); D. A. E. Garrod and D. M. A. Bate, *The Stone Age of Mount Carmel* (*Excavations at the Wady el-Mughara*), vol. I, pt. 1 (1937); A. G. Barrois, "L'Outillage et la Metallurgie," *Manuel d'Archéologie Biblique,* vol. I (1939), ch. 9; A. L. Oppenheim, *JCS,* IV (1950), 191-95; E. A. Speiser, *JAOS,* LXX (1950), 47-49; C. J. Singer *et al., A History of Technology,* vol. I: *From Early Times to the Fall of Ancient Empires* (1954), chs. 1, 3, 6, 8, 12, 18, 22; Y. Yadin, *PEQ,* LXXXVI (1955), 58-69.   J. W. WEVERS

WEASEL [חלד (Lev. 11:29); *cf.* Syr. *ḥlad,* to crawl, creep, burrow; Arab. *khuld,* mole, field rat; LXX, Vulg., Targ., Peshitta, *support* weasel]. A small carnivorous mammal, of the genus *Mustela,* which includes the martens and polecats (some use the genus *Putorius* for the smaller members of this group).

While the precise identity of חלד cannot be established, the ancient versions point to the weasel family. Koehler favors "mole-rat" (probably *Spalax typhlus*). *See* MOLE.

See also FAUNA § B2g.

Bibliography. On weasels and polecats in Palestine, see H. B. Tristram, *NHB* (1898), p. 151.   W. S. McCULLOUGH

WEATHER. The Bible has no word for "weather" but many references to weather phenomena. These may be classified as (*a*) incidental references in narrative (e.g., I Kings 18:45); (*b*) similes (e.g., Prov. 16:15); (*c*) figurative language in poetry and prophecy (e.g., Ezek. 1:4); (*d*) popular weather lore (e.g., Prov. 25:23); (*e*) meteorological speculations (e.g., Job 38:22). *See* PALESTINE, CLIMATE OF.   R. B. Y. SCOTT

WEAVING. *See* CLOTH.

WEDDING. *See* MARRIAGE.

WEEDS. The translation of several words in the Bible:

a) באשה (Job 31:40), "foul weeds" (KJV "cockle"). Since the word is derived from a root meaning "to stink," it may refer (so RSV) to foul weeds in general. Others have suggested a useless grass having the appearance of barley. A third possibility is the corn cockle (*Agrostemma githago* L.), a common grainfield pest in Palestine.

b) סוּף (Jonah 2:5—H 2:6). Elsewhere in the OT the word is translated "reed"; here it seems to mean some kind of seaweed. The Targ. and Aq. read "sea of reeds" or "Red Sea"; the LXX repoints *sûph* as *sôph* ("end," "period") and treats the word as a verse-divider.

c) רֹאשׁ (Hos. 10:4), "poisonous weeds" (KJV "hemlock"). *See* GALL.

d) Ζιζάνιον (Matt. 13:25-27, 29-30, 36, 38, 40; KJV "tares"). These weeds, probably darnel (*Lolium tremulentum*), grow in grainfields and resemble wheat. Because they cannot be distinguished easily from wheat, they are sometimes left to grow until the harvest approaches, when women and children weed them out by hand.

In the so-called parable of the tares, found in Matt. 13:24 ff, Jesus teaches his disciples to be patient until the final judgment. Premature separation of the wheat from the weeds is rejected (cf. I Cor. 4:5), and patience until the harvest is urged. Jesus offers two reasons for this: (*a*) men root up the wheat along with the weeds (Matt. 13:29) because they cannot know the hearts of others; and (*b*) God has determined the time of separation, which is not to be foreshortened (cf. 13:48*a*). The parable of the seine net (Matt. 13:47-48) teaches the same thing. These two parables are an example of Jesus' use of a double parable to emphasize an idea.

The interpretation of the parable of the tares in Matt. 13:36-43 is late and was probably composed by Matthew himself. It allegorizes the parable and interprets it as concerned primarily with the Last Judgment.

Bibliography. H. N. Moldenke, *Plants of the Bible* (1952), pp. 29-30.

R. W. CORNEY AND B. H. THROCKMORTON, JR.

*WEEK. A period of seven days, a basic unit of time reckoning current in various calendric systems, both ancient and of the present day. An institution of early Semitic origin, its use was mediated to the modern world by the Bible and by Jewish and Christian religious practice.

The customary term in biblical Hebrew for "week," שָׁבוּעַ (Gen. 29:27-28; Lev. 12:5; Dan. 9:24-27; 10:2-3), characterized it as "a seven" (שֶׁבַע)—i.e., a time unit of seven days. The days of the week were designated in biblical usage by number, "first day," "second day," etc. However, the final day of the week, originally referred to as "seventh day" (Exod. 20:10; 23:12; 31:15; 34:21), came eventually to be known as the SABBATH. Accordingly in late biblical writings the term שׁבת has occasionally the connotation "week" (Lev. 23:15; Isa. 66:23), and correspondingly also in Aramaic, rabbinic Hebrew, and NT Greek (τὸ σάββατον; Mark 16:9; Luke 18:12).

The week, just as the sabbath, had its origin in the ancient Semitic pentecontad calendar. Of this calendar the week was, in a very positive sense, the primary unit of time reckoning. Actually, under the conditions that produced this calendar, the week was originally an institution of primitive Semitic agricultural civilization, a time unit consisting of six days of field labor plus a seventh and culminating day of complete desistance therefrom. Furthermore, in this calendar seven weeks plus one additional day, a day of festal character, constituted a pentecontad, a second and larger time unit, one of fifty days. And, in turn, seven pentecontads plus two festival periods, each of exactly one week's duration, plus one further festal day—that of the NEW YEAR—365 days in all, constituted the year. From all this it is clear that in this pentecontad calendar the week, despite its basic role, did not run consecutively through the year, but was interrupted in its course by the seven one-day festivals, one at the conclusion of each pentecontad, and also by the New Year's Day, all of which, designated each by its particular name, stood outside, and so were not reckoned as integral with, the week.

Inasmuch as the Babylonians of the third millennium B.C. employed this pentecontad calendar, it is a reasonable inference that they were acquainted with the week as a time unit. This inference finds a measure of support in the ancient Babylonian custom, well attested for this relatively early period, of observing various religious festivals each for a period of seven days, and by the additional fact that in the later Babylonian luni-solar calendar the seventh, fourteenth, twenty-first, and twenty-eighth days of certain months, and also the nineteenth day of those same months—i.e., the forty-ninth, the seven-times-seventh, day from the commencement of the preceding month, and, not at all improbably, even though not yet attested in Babylonian literature, likewise the corresponding days of all months—were regarded as taboo days, upon which, much as on the biblical sabbath, certain specific forms of labor were interdicted. Certainly a seven-day week seems to have been basic here. But beyond this little is known of the role which the week may have played in Babylonian time reckoning and religious practice.

With the erection and dedication by Solomon of the first TEMPLE in Jerusalem in the second quarter of the tenth century B.C., and in response to changing political organization, increasing international contacts, and expanding commercial activities on the part of the Israelite nation, the solar calendar supplanted the pentecontad calendar as the official system of time reckoning for Israel. In this calendar the seven-day week had no logical and essential place as a unit of time reckoning. Instead, this solar calendar reckoned time, quite naturally, in terms of days, months, solar seasons, and solar years. But between the day and the month the seven-day week was a convenient, and even a more or less needed, unit of time reckoning. Moreover, so firmly rooted were the ancient sabbath and, as a corollary thereof, the week, in the tradition and practice of the Israelite people at large, and especially of that major section thereof whose primary occupation continued to be tilling the soil, that the sabbath lived on as a fundamental institution in the religious observance of Israel, and with it the seven-day week persisted as a convenient instrument of time reckoning, especially for fixing the incidence of the two annual seven-day agricultural festivals, ULEAVENED BREAD and Ingathering (*see* BOOTHS, FEAST OF), and also that of the one-day Feast of Weeks (*see* WEEKS, FEAST OF).

Eventually—though just how early, and whether under the influence of this solar calendar or of that of the luni-solar calendar (*see* CALENDAR), officially adopted by the Jewish religious community at some time during the final quarter of the fifth century B.C., we do not know—the seven-day week, with its culmination upon its final day, the sabbath, came, in Jewish usage, to run uninterruptedly through the year and the years, with complete disregard of the incidence of festal days, even those of the ancient, pentecontad calendar which had originally stood outside the week; these days were now largely discarded or radically changed in character and manner of observance. And so the week has continued to function, not only in Jewish, Christian, and Muslim religious practice, but also in general and conventional time reckoning.

Bibliography. See bibliography under SABBATH.

J. MORGENSTERN

WEEKS, FEAST OF [חג שבעות (Exod. 34:22; Num. 28:26; Deut. 16:10; II Chr. 8:13); *cf.* LXX ἑορτή ἑβδομάδων]. The second of the three great festivals in Israel, often treated as the conclusion of the cycle that began at Passover; celebrated after the fall of the temple to commemorate the giving of the law.

Other names by which this festival is known are: "Feast of Harvest" (חג הקציר, "feast of reaping/binding"; Exod. 23:16 [cf. LXX ἑορτή Θερισμοῦ]; ἡ πεντη-κοστή [ἡμέρα]); "Pentecost" (חמשים יום, "fifty days"; Tob. 2:1; II Macc. 12:32; Jos. Antiq. III.x.6; XIII. viii.4; XIV.xiii.4; XVII.x.2; Jos. War II.iii.1; VI.v.3; Philo *De Septen.* 21; Acts 2:1; 20:16; I Cor. 16:8; cf. Lev. 23:16); "Assembly" (עצרה, Aramaic אתא, "restraint" [?]; especially in Targ., Mishna, and Talmud; cf. Jos. Antiq. III.x.6: ἀσαρθά); "Day of First Fruits" (יום הבכורים; Num. 28:26; cf. LXX τῇ ἡμέρᾳ τῶν νεῶν).

Weeks was basically a harvest festival, and throughout its biblical history it maintained its original character in this respect. Exod. 23:16 designates it as the "feast of harvest," and this is probably its oldest title. The term "Weeks," while used as a title for the special festival day on which the first fruits of the wheat harvest were presented to the Lord, actually has reference to the entire period of the grain harvest, beginning with the first cuttings of barley and ending with the completion of the wheat harvest, about seven weeks in all. This entire period was one of special sanctity in which Israel was called to recognize God as the source of rain and agricultural fertility (Jer. 5:24). The feast is also known as the Day of First Fruits (Num. 28:26; cf. Exod. 23:16; 34: 22; Lev. 23:17), and it really marked the beginning of the season in which it was appropriate to bring the voluntary offerings of first fruits, a season which ended with the Feast of Booths (*see* BOOTHS, FEAST OF). Among Greek-speaking Jews the feast was known as the (Day of) Pentecost (lit., "the fiftieth [day]" and having reference to the seven-week period of harvest). It is an interesting fact that in secular Greek usage the adjective πεντηκοστή was a technical

tax term, deriving originally from a two–per-cent cargo tax in the harbor of Piraeus. There is, however, apparently no evidence that the term was selected as a title for the Jewish feast to suggest the "tax" of the first fruits as well as the duration of the cereal harvest, of which it marked the conclusion. Jub. 6:21 says: "This feast is twofold and of a double nature," and it explains this with reference to the weeks and the first fruits. The term עצרת, "assembly," focuses on the ceremonial of the feast day as such, thus comparing it to special days in the feasts of Passover and Booths (cf. Lev. 23:36; Deut. 16:8; *see also* CONVOCATION, HOLY). However, the Talmud, in which this occurrence is common, occasionally interprets this as the Assembly which closes the Passover cycle, thus also relating it to the harvest season. The feast, therefore, both by virtue of its relation to Passover and the entire harvest period, and as the season of the offering of first fruits, is agricultural in character. Neither the OT nor Josephus and Philo hint that it memorialized events in Israel's history. The book of Jubilees also treats the feast as a harvest observance (22:1) but makes it a covenant-renewal ceremony for the covenant of Noah founded on its day (6:1-21). It is possible that connection with the covenant of Noah facilitated its association later with the revelation of the law on Sinai. What is apparently the oldest reference to this is a saying in the Talmud (Pes. 68*b*) attributed to Rabbi El'azar ben Pedath (*ca.* A.D. 270): "Pentecost is the day on which Torah is given."

In Palestine, Weeks proper lasted only one day. In the Diaspora, to avoid not celebrating on the correct day, the duration was extended to two days. The date was set as the fiftieth day "from the morrow after the sabbath, from the day that you brought the sheaf of the wave offering" (Lev. 23:15). I.e., the ceremony of the sheaf fell on a day immediately after a sabbath; counting this day as the first, we find that Weeks fell on the fiftieth day. But there is a historic disagreement about what the term "sabbath" implies: does it refer to a weekly sabbath? or to some other day of rest? The phrase "after the seventh sabbath" (Lev. 23:16) speaks strongly for the former alternative. On this basis Weeks would always occur on the same day of the week, Sunday. This computation was adhered to by the Sadducees and the literalistic Karaites. It also has a parallel in the Christian day of Pentecost, though the "morrow after the sabbath" with which the count for it began was the "first day of the week" (Mark 16:2)—Easter Day, rather than the Day of the Sheaf. But according to the rabbis this "sabbath" was not a weekly day of rest, specifically that one which fell in the week of the Feast of Unleavened Bread; it was the first day of this feast, the fifteenth day of the month of Nisan, which is described as a day of "holy convocation" and of the cessation of work (Lev. 23:7). The Day of the Sheaf, accordingly, fell on the following day, the sixteenth of Nisan. Moreover, the Jews actually celebrated Weeks on the basis of this computation. This is still true, except that the Falashas place it fifty days after the seventh day of Unleavened Bread (vs. 8).

The sheaf presented as a wave offering (Lev. 23:

11) was the fistful of stalks produced when, in ceremonial fashion, the sickle was first put "to the standing grain" (Deut. 16:9). It was brought to the altar as the ἀπαρχή of both the country and all mankind (Philo *De Septen.* 2.20; cf. I Cor. 15:20, 23). It paid tribute to God as the owner of the land and the source of its products; and until its offering it was unlawful either to begin reaping or to use the new harvest as food (Lev. 23:14; M. Men. 10.6-7). Its offering by the priest was a communal rite in behalf of all the people, which opened the harvest season. Part of it was put on the altar; and the priest consumed the remainder. A male lamb was offered as a burnt offering (Lev. 23:12). The ceremony of the sheaf was integrally a part of the Feast of Unleavened Bread. *See* Passover and Feast of Unleavened Bread.

The day of the feast was one of solemn joy and thanksgiving that God's protection had watched over and brought to successful completion the activities of the cereal harvest season begun seven weeks before. It was a day of "holy convocation" (Lev. 23:21). Work was to cease; through its male representatives, and, especially in later periods, through the temple priesthood, the whole community of Israel presented itself before the Lord. As at the other great feasts, in addition to the daily burnt offering, offered at sunrise, there were other festal offerings (Num. 28:26 ff). But central to the significance of the day was the special cereal offering, consisting of "two loaves of bread" (Lev. 23:17). These loaves, from flour milled from the new wheat crop, and baked with leaven, were presented by the priest as a wave offering in behalf of all the people. Since the bread was baked with leaven, none of it was put on the altar; it was consumed by the priests. Along with the two loaves two lambs were presented, also as a wave offering. The presentation of the sheaf, seven weeks earlier, was the mark permitting the use of the new grain as food; beginning with this sacrifice, it was permissible to use it also for liturgical purposes. All males attending the ceremonies assisted by dancing an "altar dance," during which they sang the Hallel (Pss. 113-18). The feast was brought to a conclusion by the eating of communal meals to which the poor, the stranger, and the Levite were invited. Thus a basically agricultural rite honored the God of Israel and also recognized the fraternal bond of responsibility uniting the community bound by his covenant.

Weeks was also the Feast of First Fruits (Num. 28:26). After the sacrificial presentation of the loaves it was possible for individual worshipers to make offerings of the new grain crop as personal sacrifices of first fruits. The season for this apparently came to a close at the Feast of Booths (*see* Booths, Feast of). It seems that the private offerings could be made at any time during the season now begun, not only at the high feasts. These offerings were ceremonially presented by the worshiper to the priest, accompanied by the moving confessional recital of thanksgiving which recalled the great acts of God in Israel's deliverance from slavery and its inheritance of Canaan as the Land of Promise (Deut. 26:1-11). Weeks, therefore, not only celebrated God as the giver of grain but also, in the ceremony for the offering of first fruits, interpreted the meaning of harvests in the light of Israel's sacred history.

Following the destruction of the temple, Weeks continued to be observed by its gradual transformation into a feast commemorating the gift of the law. The joy of the feast was for the sake of the law. A compendium of Torah readings arose, to be read in preparation for the eve of the feast. The Zohar reinterprets the fifty days of the harvest season as the "courting days of the bridegroom Israel with the bride Torah" and makes the further statement that "in the third month (Siwan) the table of the Law was given to the third people" (Yitro 78*b*).

But, as already noted, the association of the revelation of the law with Weeks is a later development. The custom of the reading of Exod. 19 on this day seems to have begun *ca.* A.D. 200. Long before this it was customary to read the book of Ruth, with its characteristic harvest setting; and this custom has been maintained, despite the reorientation of the observance of a feast of the law. It is historically incorrect to describe Weeks as a "feast of revelation" at the time of Jesus, as has sometimes been done (cf. the work of I. Elbogen in the *bibliography*); and it is consequently misleading to attempt an interpretation of Acts 2 and of the meaning of Pentecost in the Christian church on the assumption that it constitutes a literal displacement of, or substitution for, a feast of the law. And, indeed, there is no evidence for this in the NT. Its allusions to Weeks are in terms of the symbolic meaning of the sacrificial loaves as first fruits (Rom. 8:23; 11:16; I Cor. 15:20, 23).

Bibliography. J. D. Eisenstein and J. L. Magnus, "Pentecost," *Jewish Encyclopedia*, IX (1905), 592 ff; G. B. Gray, *Sacrifice in the OT* (1925), pp. 323 ff; G. Dalman, *Arbeit und Sitte in Palästina* (1928), pp. 455-68; I. Elbogen, *Die Feier der drei Wallfahrtsfeste im zweiten Tempel* (1929); H. Schauss, *The Jewish Festivals* (1938), pp. 86 ff; M. Lohse, "πεντηκοστή," *Wörterbuch zum Neuen Testament*, VI, 44-53; E. Auerbach, "Die Feste im alten Israel," *Vetus Testamentum*, VIII, 1 ff.

J. C. Rylaarsdam

WEEPING. *See* Mourning.

WEIGHTS AND MEASURES. In early days of human communication standards of metrology by which weights, capacities, and distances could be understood became necessary. Long before any part of the Bible was written, man had learned to count and to exchange commodities. When trade advanced beyond the stage of simple barter, there developed means to determine the amount of goods involved beyond merely considering items that met the eye. At first measurements were probably made by reference to well-known physical phenomena. Weight was determined in terms of such objects as grains of a standard cereal or eggs of a common fowl, capacities by such estimates as the handful, distances by such expressions as "day's journey," "flight of an arrow," and lengths by references to parts of the body— finger, palm, span, or space between elbow and finger tip.

For weighing there were necessarily balances, and in prehistoric times stones came to be used as standards, instead of the less durable grains and eggs. Undoubtedly from the first attempts at measurement there was great variety in the objects used for weighing and measuring. Ur-Nammu, founder of the Third Dynasty of Ur, *ca.* 2050 B.C., in the earliest law code known up to 1960, established official weights and measures to curb dishonest merchants. And in an old Sumerian hymn to the goddess Nanshe, who was concerned with justice, there is a passage denouncing evildoers, among whom are those "who substituted a small weight for a large weight, who substituted a small measure for a large measure." So there was a long ancestry before the "two kinds of weights, a large and a small," and the "two kinds of measures, a large and a small," which are forbidden in Deut. 25:13-14.

There had been weights and measures in the civilizations around the E end of the Mediterranean in the two millenniums before the appearance of the Israelites, and their systems affected the Hebrew and Jewish standards as did the Persian, Greek, and Roman in later times.

A. BALANCES. For the use of weights, balances (מאזנים; Ugaritic *mznm*) were necessary. In Bible times and previously the balance consisted of a beam either suspended on a cord held in the hand* or mounted on an upright support. Both hand balances and standing balances are mentioned in Egyptian literature. A pan was suspended by cords from each end of the beam.* In Egypt some pictures show the cords passing into a tubular beam.* A fixed descend-arm at right angles to the beam indicated when the pans were at equal height; the standard weight and the object to be weighed would be equal. In Egyptian judgment scenes the heart of the deceased is pictured being weighed in the balance against the feather denoting truth or a full figure of the deity Ma'at.* The graduated scale using the principle of leverage apparently did not appear before the fourth century B.C. References to just balances in the literature of the ancient Near East show that dishonest manipulation of balances was not uncommon. Just balances are prescribed in Lev. 19:36; Job 31:6; Prov. 16:11; Ezek. 45:10. False or deceitful balances are denounced in Prov. 11:1; 20:23 ("scales"); Hos. 12:7; Amos 8:5; Mic. 6:11 ("scales"). Ezekiel was ordered to divide his hair into equal parts by the use of a balance (Ezek. 5:1). Balances are mentioned figuratively in Job 6:2; Ps. 62:9; Dan. 5:27. In Isa. 40:12 *peles* (פלס), like *mōz^enayim* (מאזנים), is an instru-

Courtesy of the Oriental Institute, the University of Chicago

12. Egyptian relief from the temple of Hatshepsut (1486-1469 B.C.), showing scale with bull weights against metal rings

13. Egyptian papyrus of the "Book of the Dead," showing the weighing of the heart of the deceased; from Milbank papyrus, second-first century B.C.

ment for weighing. The two are translated "scales" and "balances." The *peles* may be the indicator arm. *See* BALANCES. Figs. GOL 34; BAL 13; WEI 12-13; BAL 14.

B. WEIGHTS. What we know of weights in the ancient Near East comes from literary references and objects of stone, metal, or glass which evidently were used in balances. Most of these weights are uninscribed and have been the source of many conjectures and arguments. The few that are inscribed give us information, but even this is not definitive; for there is considerable variety in some weights with the same inscription.

1. Egyptian. Much that has been written about Egyptian weights is conjecture. Sir Flinders Petrie collected and classified more than 5,400 weights from Egypt and Palestine and assigned to them names taken from Egyptian, Hebrew, Greek, or Persian weights. While his work is important in showing the widespread use of weights, it does not prove that the Egyptians had an elaborate system. Egyptian numbering was in the decimal system, with hieroglyphs for the powers of ten up to a million. There were also hieroglyphs for the fractions from half to sixty-fourth. Earliest Egyptian weights from prehistoric times were of various stones, generally in blocks. Later they appear as cubes, spheres, cones, cylinders, domes, animals (bulls, cows, ibexes, hippopotamuses, ducks), or parts of animals.* Many reliefs show the weighing of metal rings in a balance against the animal-form weights.* Three weights are mentioned in Egyptian texts—the *dbn* (generally called "deben"), the *ḳdt* (referred to as "qedet" or "kitĕ"), and the *š·ty* (seal). From known examples the *dbn* weight in the form of cows is found to be *ca.* 91 grams, approximately 3.2 ounces avoirdupois or 3 ounces troy. One weight in the Metropolitan Museum, New York, inscribed "Sesostris, given life eternally, 70 gold *dbn*,"

14. Bronze weights inlaid in gold with the figure of a beetle, found at Nimrud, but probably of Egyptian origin; smaller weight is 5 oz., 296 gr.; larger weight is 8 oz., 263 gr.

weighs 945 grams, which indicates a Middle Kingdom weight of only 13.43 grams or 0.474 ounces avoirdupois for the *dbn*. Apparently the *dbn* varied greatly during Egyptian history. The *ḳdt* was a tenth of a *dbn*, *ca.* 9.1 grams. A *š·ty* was a twelfth of a *dbn*. Smaller measures were indicated by fractions. While there was considerable commerce between West Asia and Egypt and accountants of one country may have known something of the system of another country, the Egyptians kept their records in *dbn*. In the Bible there is no reference to the Egyptian weights. Figs. WEI 14, 12.

2. Mesopotamian. The weights of Babylon and Assyria conformed to no general standard through the ages. Changes in government brought about changes in standards. The Semitic verb meaning "weigh" is *šql*, and from this we get the noun "shekel," which from early days was a standard of weight and at the development of coinage came to designate the basic piece of silver money. In Akkadian this was *šiqlu*, in Hebrew שקל. There were two other common weights: the mina (Akkadian *manû*, Hebrew מנה) and the talent (*biltu*). "Talent" is from the Greek τάλαντον, once meaning "balance" and then applied to a weight. Apparently this measure is meant by the *gaggaru* in the Amarna Letters; the Hebrew word is ככר.

These weights varied greatly. The Babylonian-Assyrian method of counting was sexagesimal, with the number sixty used in computation instead of ten as in our system and that of ancient Egypt. Our division of the hour into sixty minutes of sixty seconds each comes from ancient Babylon. This standard has the advantage of easy division by three or four.

Ordinarily the talent consisted of sixty minas and the mina of sixty shekels; but there were also minas of fifty shekels. Moreover, there were "heavy" and "light" standards, with the heavy weighing twice as much as the light. And each of these seems to have varied as much as has the ton or the pound in England and America. There has been diversity of opinion among scholars as to what was the most generally accepted standard for these weights. Now it is evident that the ancient systems were loose and that the best we can do is to accept the evidence of inscribed weights and the testimony of later Greek writers.

An early Babylonian oval stone is inscribed "one half mina true weight." Its weight is 244.8 grams. This would make the mina 489.6 grams, approximately 1.08 pounds avoirdupois. Another, slightly damaged, cone-shaped stone, inscribed "one mina true weight . . . ," weighs 978.3 grams and is presumed to have weighed, undamaged, 979.5 grams, approximately 2.16 pounds avoirdupois. Clearly the first represents the light mina and the second the heavy mina. Some lion-shaped weights bear, in addition to the mina designation, the phrase "of the king." They represent both light and heavy standard, but they were some five per cent heavier than the ordinary weights. So it has been supposed that the "royal standard" indicated that payments to the royal treasury were slightly larger than the same sums used in ordinary transactions.

Since it is impossible, from the literature and the

artifacts now available, to give a definitive calculation of the Babylonian and Assyrian weights, and it is certain that these weights varied, only a rough estimate of them may be presented. *See* Table 1.

Table 1

COMMON WEIGHT

	Light	
Talent	30 kilograms	66 pounds
Mina	500 grams	1.1 pounds
Shekel	8.33 grams	0.295 ounce
	Heavy	
Talent	60 kilograms	132 pounds
Mina	1 kilogram	2.2 pounds
Shekel	16.67 grams	0.6 ounce

ROYAL WEIGHT

	Light	
Talent	30.6 kilograms	69.6 pounds
Mina	525 grams	1.16 pounds
Shekel	8.37 grams	0.31 ounce
	Heavy	
Talent	61.2 kilograms	138 pounds
Mina	1.05 kilograms	2.32 pounds
Shekel	16.74 grams	0.62 ounce

Figs. WEI 15-17.

3. Canaanite. The term "Canaanite" here is understood as applying to the ancient inhabitants of the land at the E end of the Mediterranean other than the Israelites. Thus it includes the Ugaritic and the Phoenician. It has long been known that the weights in this territory were in general the same as those of Mesopotamia, except that the mina in many instances consisted of fifty rather than sixty shekels (cf. Ezek. 45:12). In Ugaritic texts discovered at RAS SHAMRA there are references to the *kkr* Hebrew כבר, "talent") and the *ṯkl* (Hebrew שקל, "shekel"). There

15. Duck weights from Ishchali, Iraq

16. A weight of thirty minas, carved from black basalt in the shape of a duck; from the palace of Eriba-Marduk II(?; 688-680 B.C.)

17. Bronze lion-weights of two-thirds mina, from palace of Shalmaneser, king of Ashur

is an occurrence of -*mn*, which possibly means "mina"; but this is uncertain. It is doubtful that the mina was in common use, for large weights are given in such expressions as "eight talents, one thousand heavy shekels, two hundred shekels." The count of so many shekels, instead of twenty or twenty-five minas, would show that talents were reckoned directly in shekels (cf. Exod. 38:24: "twenty-nine talents and seven hundred and thirty shekels"). The talent probably was 3,000 rather than 3,600 shekels. Specification of heavy shekels shows that, as in Babylonia and later in Israel, there were two standards of weight, and it was important in transactions to specify the standard to be used. As in Babylonia, there was variety in the weight of the shekel, which we may roughly estimate as 8 or 10 grams for the light and twice that for the heavy.

Ras Shamra has produced weights of *ca.* 470 grams, one of which in the form of a lying ox has the hieroglyphic notation for "twenty," indicating a unit of 23.5 grams, which would approximate the heavy shekel of Palestine (*see below* § 2*d, i*). From the same location also are many uninscribed weights of 44 or 45 grams, indicating the same unit.

4. Israelite. In Israel computation was in the decimal rather than the sexagesimal system; but the weights were reckoned in the Babylonian and Canaanite units, and there is indication that in some instances, at least, the weights were identical. E.g., in II Kings 18:14 we read: "The king of Assyria required of Hezekiah . . . three hundred talents of silver and thirty talents of gold." In Sennacherib's prisms recording the same incident the amount of gold is the same thirty talents, though he claims eight hundred talents of silver. The discrepancy may be due to the Assyrian habit of boastful exaggeration, but the similarity of the two accounts is noteworthy.

a. Shekel. In the West Asian systems the shekel was the basic weight; but besides the differences represented by light and heavy, common and royal, there are marked variations shown in objective evidence from weights which have been found. No two inscribed weights with the identical notation measure exactly the same. The Hebrew shekel has been computed by various authorities as slightly over 11 (11.3-11.47) grams. At Tell Beit Mirsim (*see* KIRIATH-SEPHER) from an Iron II stratum there was found an uninscribed spherical weight of polished limestone weighing 4,565 grams. It is proposed that this is eight minas, and on the basis of fifty shekels to the mina (in the Ugaritic and Israelite systems) therefore four hundred shekels. According to this the shekel was 11.41 grams.

b. Inscribed weights. Objective evidence comes from inscribed weights found in excavations at Lachish, Zahariyeh, Samaria, Tell en-Nasbeh (Mizpah?), Beth-zur, Gezer, Silwan, and Salah, and acquired in Anathoth and Jerusalem. These are marked in old Hebrew characters and provisionally are dated seventh-sixth century B.C. There are three groups of these weights, nearly all of dome-shaped stone, marked נצף (*netseph*), פים (*pîm*, or according to some *payem*), and בקע (*beqa'*, "beka"; KJV "bekah").

c. Netseph. The netseph is not mentioned in the Bible. From its similarity to the Arabic *nusf*, "half,"

Courtesy of the Oxford University Press

18. Inscribed weights from Lachish: (*a*) "netseph"; (*b*) "pim"; (*c*) "beka"; (*d*) "8 shekels"; (*e*) two parallel hooks, meaning uncertain

it has been thought by some that the netseph was half of something. A shuttle-shaped weight purchased in Nablus in 1890 was marked רבע נצף (one fourth of a netseph) and רבע של (one fourth of a shekel, surmising that של was an abbreviation of שקל). According to such interpretation "netseph" and "shekel" were synonyms, with the netseph as the common shekel, but this is doubtful, and the meaning of "netseph" may be called uncertain. *See* § B4*f below.* Fig. WEI 18*a*.

d. Pim. Discovery of the pim cleared the meaning of a hitherto obscure passage in I Sam. 13:19-21, where there is recorded the trouble of the Hebrews because "there was no smith to be found throughout all the land of Israel" and it was necessary to go to the Philistines for the sharpening of implements. In the KJV the word was translated "file," and in some margins there was the notation "a file with mouths," based on the supposition that *pîm* was the plural of Hebrew *pê*, "mouth." Samuel Raffaeli surmised that the pim was the amount of weight (paid in silver) used in the transaction. This conjecture was confirmed when a pim weight was found. So the RSV has: "The charge was a pim for the plowshares and for the mattocks." The pim may be two thirds of a shekel. Fig. WEI 18*b*.

e. Beka. The בקע in Gen. 24:22 is translated "half shekel" on the basis of Exod. 38:26, where it is defined as "half a shekel, by the shekel of the sanctuary." The noun is related to the Hebrew verb *bāqā'*, which means "split." The bekas found so far are slightly heavier than half the shekel as estimated

above, but not enough to invalidate the calculation. Fig. WEI 18*c*.

f. Variations. In grams the netsephs found weigh 10.515, 19.210, 10.160 (on the basis of a fourth of a netseph at Samaria weighing 2.540), 10.105 (estimated from the Anathoth specimen weighing 8.680, but with a hole bored to make it a bead), 10.04, 9.998, 9.946, 9.935, 9.8, 9.76, 9.54, 9.447, 8.324, 9.28—average, 9.84.

The pims weigh 8.591, 8.13, 7.805, 7.75, 7.61, 7.27, 7.18—average, 7.762.

The bekas weigh 6.65, 6.15, 6.11, 6.095, 5.87, 5.8, 5.66 (possibly not a beka)—average, 6.11 or 6.05.

These weights, about only a few of which there can be any question, demonstrate the inexactness of the Israelite weight system. It would be gratuitous to say that the average represents the standard; doubtless the average will be changed as more inscribed weights are found. The difference between the heaviest netseph and the lightest is greater than the difference between the lightest netseph and the heaviest pim, and the difference between the heaviest pim and the lightest is greater than the difference between the lightest pim and the heaviest beka.

There are also inscribed weights with what appears to be the sign for shekel followed by the sign for a numeral—2, 4, 8,* or 16. From Lachish come weights marked by two parallel strokes with a hook on the end of each. Figs. WEI 18*d-e*.

g. Weights in the OT. Weights mentioned in the OT are the gerah, which is a twentieth of a shekel (Exod. 30:13; Lev. 27:25; Num. 3:47; 18:16; Ezek. 45:12); a third of a shekel (I Sam. 13:21); the beka or half shekel (Gen. 24:22; Exod. 30:13, 15; 38:26); the shekel (*passim*); the mina (I Kings 10:17; Neh. 7:71; Ezek. 45:12; "pounds" in I Kings and Nehemiah and "maneh" in Ezekiel); the talent (*passim*); and the kesitah, translated "piece of money" (Gen. 33:19; Josh. 24:32; Job 42:11).

The qesitah (קשיטה) is an enigma. The LXX translates by ἀμνός ("male lamb") in Gen. 33:19 and by ἀμνάς ("female lamb") in Josh. 24:32; Job 42:11. The weight may have been in metal in the form of a lamb. Another suggestion is that ἀμνάς is an expanded form of μνᾶ ("mina"). Jacob paid Hamor of Shechem a hundred qesitahs for a parcel of land. In Job's final state all his relatives and friends came to him, each bringing a qesitah and a gold earring. The Arabic *qesita* has been estimated at 1,429 grams or 3.15 pounds. Still another suggestion is that it was a quantity of silver equal to the price of a lamb.

Taking the shekel as 11.424 grams, the OT weights may be estimated as in Table 2.

Table 2

Gerah, 1/20 shekel	0.571 gram	8.71 grains
⅓ shekel	3.808 grams	0.134 ounce
Beka, ½ shekel	5.712 grams	0.201 ounce
Pim, ⅔ shekel(?)	7.616 grams	0.268 ounce
Shekel	11.424 grams	0.403 ounce
Mina, 50 shekels	571.2 grams	1.26 pounds
Talent, 3,000 shekels	34.272 kilograms	75.6 pounds

The Hebrew of Ezek. 45:12, followed by the KJV, calls for a mina (KJV "maneh") of "twenty shekels, five and twenty shekels, fifteen shekels," which would indicate that Ezekiel was following the Babylonian sixty-shekel system rather than the common or Phoenician system of fifty shekels to the mina. Following the LXX, the RSV has "fifty shekels." If the Hebrew of Ezekiel is correct, his mina would be *ca.* 685.44 grams or 1.536 pounds, and his talent 41.126 kilograms or 90.7 pounds.

According to Maimonides, the early Hebrew shekel weighed 320 grains of barley. If these grains are equivalent to troy grains, the shekel was *ca.* 0.292 ounce avoirdupois or 6.57 grams, considerably lighter than the shekel as computed above. Maimonides says that in the second temple this was supplanted by the *sela‘* (סלע), the equivalent of the heavy Phoenician shekel.

In II Sam. 14:26 the yield of the annual cutting of Absalom's hair is stated as two hundred shekels "by the king's weight." This, by various estimates, would be from 3½ to 4 pounds. Some commentators assume that twenty shekels was meant. One LXX MS has "one hundred."

Goliath's coat of mail (I Sam. 17:5), weighing five thousand shekels of bronze, has been variously estimated from 90 to 220 pounds; according to the table given above, it would be *ca.* 126 pounds. His spearhead (vs. 7) was "six hundred shekels of iron." Estimates of this have varied from 11 to 27 pounds. According to the table above, it would be *ca.* 17.12 pounds.

The "shekel of the sanctuary" (Exod. 30:13, 24; 38:24-26; Lev. 5:15; 27:3, 25; Num. 3:47, 50; 7:13-86; 18:16) is an expression peculiar to P. Repeatedly it is said to be equal to twenty gerahs. Some authorities translate "sacred shekel" and presume that it was different from the ordinary shekel. On occasion transactions with the priest involved adding a fifth to the normal value (Lev. 27:13, 15). On the other hand, it may refer to a standard weight which was kept in the sanctuary. The LXX has "sacred didrachma" (τὸ δίδραχμον τὸ ἅγιον) and takes the gerah to be an obolus. A didrachma is *ca.* 8.72 grams, lighter than the ordinary shekel. And the Attic obolus is a sixth of a drachma, so that the didrachma would contain twelve oboli. It appears, then, that the Greek translators were dealing in approximations, as were the English translators who reckoned the mina as a pound.

For convenience we may think of the Israelite shekel as weighing *ca.* as much as an American half dollar, the mina as *ca.* 1¼ pounds, and the talent as *ca.* 75 pounds.

In Dan. 5:25 the words "Mene, mene, tekel, and parsin" are sometimes interpreted as a play on the words "mina, mina, shekel, and a half [shekel]," with references to the Babylonian rulers Nabopolassar, Nebuchadnezzar, Nabonidus, and Belshazzar, indicating that the first two were great, the third much smaller, and the fourth still smaller. For other explanations, *see* MENE, MENE, TEKEL, AND PARSIN.

h. Weights in the Apoc. The Apoc. mentions shekels (I Macc. 10:40) and minas (I Esd. 5:45; KJV "pounds"). Bel 27 in the LXX, which the RSV follows, has "thirty minas of pitch." The "thirty minas" is not in Theod., which the KJV follows. Talents

are mentioned in I Esd. 1:36; 4:51-52; 8:56; Tob. 1:14; II Macc. 3:11; 4:8; 5:21; 8:10-11.

i. Weights in the NT. The talent in the NT parables was used to represent a large sum of money (Matt. 18:24; 25:15-28) or an indeterminate large weight (Rev. 16:21), as the heavenly hailstone weighed a talent (the RSV "hundredweight" gives the idea but certainly is not to be taken as the exact equivalent). The mina (μνᾶ), translated "pound," in Luke 19:13-25, like the talent in Matthew, doubtless represents a sum of money. "Pound" (λίτρα, Latin *libra*) as weight or possibly as a measure of capacity appears in John 12:3; 19:39, to indicate an amount of precious ointment. This was doubtless the Roman pound of twelve ounces.

C. MEASURES OF CAPACITY. 1. Egyptian. The standard measure of capacity in ancient Egypt was the *ḥḳt*, which has been estimated as 5.03 liters, amounting to slightly more than the English gallon or 1¼ American gallons. This measure was used for grain or metal. It was divided into fractions of one half, one fourth, one eighth, one sixteenth, and one sixty-fourth. In one *ḥḳt* there were 320 "ro" (*r*) measures. Occasionally there is mention of a third and a tenth of a *ḥḳt*. There were also the double *ḥḳt* and the quadruple *ḥḳt* and the "sack," *ẖ'r*, which amounted to four quadruple or sixteen single *ḥḳt*. In the Rhind Mathematical Papyrus the "sack" was five quadruple or twenty single *ḥḳt*. For liquids such as beer, milk, and honey there was the "hin" jar, *hnw*, which from inscribed examples is shown to be *ca.* 0.503 liter, or a little more than a pint. It was used also for a dry measure and was considered one tenth of a *ḥḳt*. Other vessels named in inscriptions are the *ds* jar, specially for beer, the *hbnt* jar for wine or incense, the *st'* jar for a small amount of beer, and the *mny* for incense. Their capacities are undetermined.

2. Mesopotamian. Names of measures for capacity abound in the Sumerian, Assyrian, Neo-Babylonian, and Nuzian texts. From the references it is evident that there was considerable variation in standards, which changed from country to country and from time to time. The evidence is highly complicated, and widely differing inferences have been drawn by scholars. Some of them have changed their opinions as new evidence has appeared or as they have examined the old.

Among the ancient Mesopotamians the basic measure of capacity seems to have been the Semitic *qa*, the equivalent of the Sumerian *sila*. The next higher unit was the *sutu*, which in the Old Babylonian period contained ten *qas*. (Later there are references to *sutus* of six, eight, and twelve *qas*.) Many of the calculations of the capacity of the *qa* are based on a ritual text which refers to the "*sutu* of ten minas." Since the mina was a weight, the cubic capacity of a *sutu* would depend on the material used in the calculation. First calculations were on the supposition that the material was water, which was used in the establishment of the metric system; but later calculations have been on the basis of barley, since this was the most commonly cultivated grain and the substance most frequently designated in connection with measures. Two most recent evaluations of the *qa* are

1.004 liters and 1.34 liters, roughly 1 or 1.33 dry quarts.

In the Middle Assyrian and Nuzian texts there is a third unit, *imeru*, which means "ass" and is represented in the cuneiform ideogram derived from the picture of an ass. Presumably it was the normal load an ass was expected to carry. This has been reckoned as *ca.* ninety kilograms, which would be about 138 liters of barley, roughly a hundred *qas*. Thus for Middle Assyrian and Nuzian times we may provisionally consider the standard measures of capacity: the *qa* (*ca.* 1.34 liters or 1.22 dry quarts), the *sutu* of ten qas (*ca.* 13.4 liters or 1½ pecks), and the *imeru* (134 liters or 3.8 bushels).

3. Canaanite. In the Ugaritic literature there are occurrences of a few units of measure. The *ḥmr* (homer) means "ass" and, like the Akkadian *imeru*, is used as a unit of dry measure. The *ltḥ*, corresponding to the Hebrew lethech (לתך), also is a unit of dry measure. The *lg,* corresponding to the Hebrew log (לג), may be a liquid measure. It is probable that the Canaanites had measures essentially like those in Mesopotamia; but there is not enough evidence to hazard any calculations about them.

4. Israelite. Undoubtedly the Hebrew measures of capacity never were finally fixed. They were related mostly to the Assyro-Babylonian system rather than the Egyptian. In several instances two names were used for the same unit.

a. Homer. The homer (חמר; Akkad. *imeru;* Ugar. *ḥmr*) was a standard dry measure (Ezek. 45:11), the normal load of an ass, and, on the basis of the reckoning given above, would be *ca.* 134 liters or 3.8 bushels. Other calculations make this measure considerably more than this amount—229.9 liters or 6.524 bushels, and in some of the older commentaries 11 bushels. References in the OT indicate that it was a fairly large measure. A homer of barley was worth fifty shekels of silver (Lev. 27:16). Divine punishment would reduce the yield of a homer of seed to an ephah (Isa. 5:10). The homer was equal to the cor and contained ten baths or ephahs (Ezek. 45:11-14). In the story of the miraculous provision of quails in the desert (Num. 11:32), when the people gathered the birds all day, all night, and the next day, "he who gathered least gathered ten homers." Even conservatively this would be 38 bushels.

b. Cor. Equal to the homer was the cor (כר; Sumerian GUR; Akkadian *kurru;* KJV usually "measures"). It was used both for dry measure (I Kings 4:22; 5:11—H 5:2, 25; II Chr. 2:10—H 2:9; 27:5) and for oil (Ezek. 45:14, where it is said like the homer to contain ten baths). Only in Ezek. 45:14 does the KJV use "cor." The cor may have contained 3.8-6.524 bushels or 35.4-60.738 gallons.

c. Lethech. The lethech (לתך; Ugaritic *ltḥ*) was a dry measure, mentioned only in Hos. 3:2, where Hosea is told to buy the woman for fifteen shekels of silver and a homer and a lethech of barley. The LXX omits the word, and the Vulg. has *dimidio coro.* The Mishna also evaluates the lethech as half a cor, and accordingly the KJV translates "a half homer." If this is correct, the lethech was 1.9-3.26 bushels.

d. Ephah. The ephah (איפה, אפה; Egyptian *'pt;* Coptic *uoipa;* LXX οἰφί) was a dry measure equal

to a tenth of a homer (Ezek. 45:11). It would then be 1.52-2.42 pecks, roughly three eighths to two thirds of a bushel. Evidently the ephah was in common use, as it is frequently mentioned in the OT (Exod. 16:36; Lev. 5:11; 6:20; 14:10, 21; 19:36; 23:13; Num. 5:15; 28:5; Judg. 6:19; Ruth 2:17; I Sam. 1:24; 17:17; Isa. 5:10; Ezek. 45:10-11, 13, 24; 46:5, 7, 11, 14; Amos 8:5; Zech. 5:6-10). The term is used to indicate the amount of cereal such as flour, barley, parched grain, wheat; or the container in which the cereal was measured, as in the prophetic demand for a just ephah. In Zech. 5:5-11 there is described an ephah with a lead weight on the mouth and the woman "Wickedness" inside. If this woman is considered life-sized, Zechariah's ephah would have to be considerably larger than the ephah estimated above. There are passages where the RSV inserts the word "ephah" to give the full meaning, as in Lev. 24:5: "Two tenths of an ephah shall be in each cake." The Hebrew has merely: "Two tenths will be the one cake." Other passages where the word "ephah" is inserted in the RSV are Lev. 23:17; Num. 15:4, 6, 9; 28:9, 12, 20, 28; 29:3, 14. In such passages the KJV inserts "deal," an indefinite amount.

e. Bath. Throwing some light on the ephah is the bath (בת), a liquid measure said to be equal to the ephah (Ezek. 45:11, 14). At Tell Beit Mirsim there was found a fragment of an amphora with the inscription "bath" (בת) and at Lachish the neck of a jar marked "royal bath" (בת למלך).* On epigraphic evidence these jars have been dated in the eighth century B.C. By extrapolation from the fragments it is estimated that each of these jars contained 21-23 liters, *ca.* 5½ gallons, corresponding roughly to the ephah of three eighths to two thirds of a bushel. The bath was used to indicate both small and large quantities (from one to thirty thousand) of liquids (I Kings 7:26, 38; II Chr. 2:10; 4:5; Isa. 5:10), and a just bath, like the just ephah, was prescribed (Ezek. 45:10). Fig. WEI 19.

19. Fragmentary jar from Lachish, bearing the inscription "royal bath" (lit., "bath to the king"; eighth century B.C.)

f. Seah. The seah (סאה; Akkadian *še'u;* Greek σάτον[?]) was a dry measure, about the size of which there are divergent opinions. In the KJV-RSV (Gen. 18:6; I Kings 18:32; II Kings 7:1, 16, 18; Isa. 27:8), after the LXX μέτρον, the word is translated by the noncommittal "measure." If the Greek is an exact equivalent, its capacity would be 1½ modii or 0.367 bushel or 1.452 pecks. By some it is proposed that the seah is the equivalent of the *šālîš* of Isa. 40:12, which means "a third," is translated "measure" in the KJV-RSV, and is supposed to be a thirtieth of a cor or a third of an ephah. According to the reckoning above, this would be 0.127–0.217 bushel.

g. Hin. The hin (הין; Egyptian *hn, hyn, hnw,* represented by a jar and by actual examples shown to be *ca.* 0.46 liter) was a liquid measure, according to Josephus (Antiq. III.viii.3), containing two Athenian choas, which equalled twelve sextarii. The bath (Jos. Antiq. VIII.ii.9) was seventy-two sextarii, so that the hin was a sixth of a bath. Accordingly the hin should be 3.5–3.9 liters, 3.68–4.22 quarts, or *ca.* a gallon. Besides the whole hin (Exod. 30:24; Ezek. 45:24; 46:5, 7, 11) there were fractions of the hin, one half (Num. 28:14), one third (Num. 28:14; Ezek. 46:14), one fourth (Exod. 29:40; Lev. 23:13; Num. 15:4; 28:5, 7, 14), and one sixth—the daily ration of water, *ca.* two thirds of a quart (Ezek. 4:11). There was prescribed a just hin (Lev. 19:36).

h. Omer. In the story of the gathering of manna (Exod. 16:13-36) the measure used was the omer (עמר; LXX γομορ), not to be confused with the homer. One omer was the daily ration (vss. 16, 18), with two omers to be gathered for the sixth day and the sabbath (vs. 22). One omer was to be kept as a memorial (vss. 32-34). The omer was a tenth of an ephah (vs. 36). Hence it would be *ca.* 2.3 liters, a little more than two dry quarts.

i. Issaron. Probably another name for the omer was the issaron (עשׂרון), which means a tenth, evidently of an ephah. Like the omer, it was a dry measure. In Exod. 29:40 the RSV has merely "tenth measure." In other passages (Lev. 14:10; 23:13, 17; Num. 15:4) the RSV adds "of an ephah," while the KJV uses the indeterminate word "deal."

j. Kab. A measure mentioned only once in the Bible (II Kings 6:25) is the kab (קב, KJV cab, possibly Egyp. *ḳb*). During the Syrian siege of Samaria an ass's head brought eighty (shekels?) of silver, and the fourth part of a kab of what seems to have been dove's dung brought five (shekels?). The Hebrew of this verse is corrupt, and there is no conclusive evidence as to what a kab was. Josephus (Antiq. IX.iv. 1) takes the fourth of a kab as a sextarius (ξέστης). According to rabbinical sources it was an eighteenth of an ephah, or about 1.16 dry quarts.

k. Log. The smallest biblical measure of capacity was the log (לג; Ugaritic *lg;* Coptic *lok*). It is named only in Lev. 14:10, 12, 15, 21, 24, and only as a measure of oil. The LXX translates κοτύλη, *ca.* half a pint. The Vulg. translates *sextarius.* It appears, then, that the log was equal to a fourth of a kab, or 0.67 pint.

l. Table of OT measures of capacity. Obviously measures of the Bible varied, as today the English gallon is different from the American gallon and the Connecticut bushel of 2,748 cubic inches is different from the Colorado bushel of 2,500 cubic inches. There was no absolute standard of measurement until the introduction of the metric system. So, with only a provisional attempt at approximate evaluation, we can give a table with the supposition that

sometime somewhere some of these estimates would be good. (*See* Table 3.

Table 3

Dry Measures

kab	1.16 quarts
omer, issaron, 1/10 ephah	2.09 quarts
seah, ⅓ ephah	⅔ peck
ephah	½ bushel
lethech, ½ homer	2.58 bushels
homer, cor	5.16 bushels

Liquid Measures

log	0.67 pint
hin	1 gallon
bath	5½ gallons
cor, homer	55 gallons

It is possible that all these measures, like our liter, were used for both dry and liquid substances.

m. Handful. The handful gives a general impression of quantity, though it could hardly be called an exact measure. We have it in such expressions as "handfuls of barley" (Ezek. 13:19), "handfuls of ashes" (Exod. 9:8), "handful of quietness" (Eccl. 4: 6), "handful of meal" (I Kings 17:12), "handful of the fine flour and oil" (Lev. 2:2), "handful of it" (Lev. 5:12), and "handful of the cereal offering" (Num. 5:26).

n. Later Jewish measures of capacity. In Bel 3 it is told that the Babylonians offered daily to their idol Bel twelve ἀρτάβαι of fine flour and six μετρήται of olive oil (KJV-RSV "wine," following Theod.). The artabe was a Persian measure estimated as 1 4/5 bushels. The metretes, which means "measurer," was an Attic vessel containing eight to ten gallons. The KJV translates "great measures" and "vessels" respectively; the RSV performs a calculation and arrives at "bushels" and "fifty gallons."

Postbiblical Jewish literature contains considerable discussion of measures of capacity using material objects, such as grains (of barley) and eggs, to determine amounts. The Talmud mentions the "desert measure," the "Jerusalem measure," and the "Sepphoris measure."

o. NT measures of capacity. Measures of capacity listed in the NT are Greek or Roman. The ξέστης (Mark 7:4, and some MSS of vs. 8) is the sextarius of *ca.* a pint, but here it is probably a general term for a small vessel, and the translation "pot" is justified. The μετρητής (John 2:6) is definitely a measure, as described above. It is translated "firkin" in the KJV. In the RSV the two or three metretai are "twenty or thirty gallons."

The bushel of Matt. 5:15; Mark 4:21; Luke 11:33 is the Greek μόδιος, a measure of 0.245 American bushel, meaning here a vessel which could cover a light.

The amount of ointment Mary used to anoint the feet of Jesus (John 12:3) was a λίτρα, the Roman pound of twelve ounces, used as a measure of both capacity and weight (cf. our two-ounce bottle). The mixture of myrrh and aloes which Nicodemus brought for the dressing of Jesus' body weighed *ca.* a hundred of these pounds. See § B4*i* above. The χοῖνιξ (Rev. 6:6; "quart"; KJV "measure") was *ca.* a quart.

D. *MEASURES OF LENGTH*. 1. Egyptian. In ancient Egypt small objects were measured by dimensions of the lower arm. The cubit, *mḥ*, length from the elbow to the tip of the middle finger, was represented by the hieroglyph showing the horizontal forearm with the palm down. It was *ca.* 52.3 centimeters or 20.6 inches. The Egyptian cubit, however, was variable.* Graduated scales found by archaeologists show a "strong" cubit of 52.5 centimeters divided into seven palms or twenty-eight fingers and a "weak" cubit of 45 centimeters equal to six palms or twenty-four fingers. The palm, *šsp*, width of the hand not including the thumb, pictured as an arc, was a seventh of a cubit, *ca.* 7.47 centimeters or 2.67 inches. The finger, *db'*, pictured by an upright finger, was a twenty-eighth of a cubit or a fourth of a palm, *ca.* 1.82 centimeters or 0.67 inch. Fig. WEI 20.

For longer measures there was the rod, *ḥt*, represented by the hieroglyph of the branch of a tree. It was a hundred cubits, *ca.* 52.3 meters or 57.2 yards. It was called also "rod of cord," *ḥt n nwḥ*. There was a much larger measure called the "river," *ytrw*, the hieroglyph of which contains the picture of a channel filled with water. Its length is uncertain, but it is presumed to be at least two kilometers.

2. Mesopotamian. Like the Egyptian, the Sumerian and Akkadian small measures for length were based on parts of the forearm with the cubit (Sumerian *kus;* Akkadian *ammatu*) as a standard. It is thought that the Mesopotamian cubit was a bit shorter than the Egyptian, *ca.* 50.1 centimeters or 19.7 inches. Also, the Mesopotamian cubit varied. Graduated rules on statues of Gudea show that one cubit of Lagash was 49.584 centimeters and another 49.574 centimeters. While the difference is not large,

it shows that the standard was not absolute. The Sumerian ideogram *ŠU BAD* represents the open hand or span from the tip of the thumb to the tip of the little finger. It is a half of a cubit, *ca.* 25 centimeters or 8.8 inches. The finger (Sumerian *šusi;* Akkadian *ubânu*) was a thirtieth of a cubit, 1.67 centimeters or 0.66 inch. In Neo-Babylonian times the finger was a twenty-eighth of a cubit.

For larger measures there was the rod (Sumerian *gi;* Akkadian *qanû*) containing 6 cubits and equal to *ca.* 3 meters or 3.27 yards. A Sumerian measure *ninda* was 12 cubits, *ca.* 6 meters. The rope (Sumerian *zer;* Akkadian *ašlu*) was 120 cubits, *ca.* 60 meters, corresponding possibly to the Egyptian "rod of cord." The double stadion (Sumer. *giš*) was 720 cubits, *ca.* 360.7 meters. The walk of a Babylonian hour, equal to two hours of our time (Sumerian *danna;* Akkadian *bêru*), was 1,800 *NINDA*, equal to 21,600 cubits, *ca.* 11.82 kilometers or 7.35 miles.

3. Canaanite. Evidence of Canaanite measures of length are scarce, but in all probability they corresponded to the measurements of ancient Mesopotamia and later Israel. Ugaritic *'mt* is like Akkadian *ammatu;* but where it occurs, it means "elbow," as do the Akkadian and Hebrew words for "cubit."

4. Israelite. Like the Egyptians, the Sumerians, and the Assyro-Babylonians, the Israelites used the cubit as a standard.

a. Cubit. Undoubtedly the cubit (אמה; Akkadian *ammatu;* Ugaritic *'mt*) was the length of the forearm to the tip of the middle finger; but, as human arms are of different lengths, the Israelite cubit was not absolute. There are more than a hundred occurrences of the word for "cubit," including the dual אמתים and the plural אמות, and four occurrences of the Aramaic plural אמין in Ezra 6:3; Dan. 3:1. Also there are instances where the word "cubit," like "shekel,"

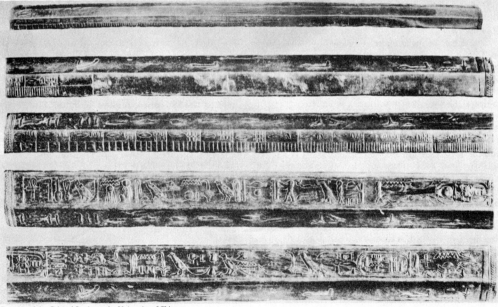

20. Cubit measuring stick covered with gold overlay and containing the name of Amen-hotep II; New Kingdom, Eighteenth Dynasty (*ca.* 1570-1310 B.C.)

is implied and is inserted in the RSV and italicized in the KJV. E.g., in Ezek. 43:16-17a the Hebrew has: "The altar hearth shall be square, twelve long by twelve broad. The ledge also shall be square, fourteen long by fourteen broad." Since the word "cubit" is used in vss. 15, 17b, it is evident that the dimensions are in cubits. And in Ezek. 46:22 the Hebrew has: "In the four corners of the court were small courts, forty long and forty broad." In both instances the LXX adds the word "cubits."

Ehud's sword (Judg. 3:16) was a gōmed (גמד) in length. This is the only occurrence of the word in the OT. It is translated "cubit" in the KJV-RSV, but the LXX has σπιθαμῆς ("span") and the Vulg. palmae manus ("palm of a hand"). A weapon of a cubit or a span in length would be lethal; but, in view of Eglon's corpulence, one of only a palm in length might not have reached a vital spot.

In Palestine as yet there have been found no cubit measures. One bit of objective evidence is in the SILOAM INSCRIPTION, giving the length of Hezekiah's tunnel as 1,200 cubits. The survey of this aqueduct has put its axial length as 533.1 meters. According to this calculation the cubit was 17.49 inches. It is evident, however, that 1,200 is a round number, and the points considered as the starting of the digging at the ends of the tunnel are not certain. Other calculations have placed the Siloam cubit at 17.58 inches. The inscription's 100 cubits from the tunnel to the surface is clearly a round number.

Jehoash king of Israel, after capturing Amaziah king of Judah, broke down the wall of Jerusalem for four hundred cubits, from the Ephraim Gate to the Corner Gate (II Kings 14:13; II Chr. 25:23). Hanum and the inhabitants of Zanoah repaired the Valley Gate and repaired a thousand cubits of the wall as far as the Dung Gate (Neh. 3:13). If archaeologists ever locate these gates, there will be more evidence on the length of the cubit, though four hundred and a thousand seem to be round numbers.

The cubit is used extensively in giving dimensions of Noah's ark (Gen. 6:15-16); of the ark of the covenant and other paraphernalia of the tabernacle as ordered by the Lord through Moses (Exod. 25:10-27:19; 30:1-5) and executed by Bezalel and Oholiab (Exod. 36:1-39:30); of Solomon's temple and its paraphernalia (I Kings 6:2-7:38); of the city, the temple, and the land in Ezekiel's visions (Ezek. 40:5-43:17; 45:1-5); and of the second temple (Ezra 6:3).

That there were different cubits in Israel is clear. The bed of Og king of Bashan (Deut. 3:11) is said to have been nine cubits long and four cubits broad "according to the common cubit" (KJV lit., "after the cubit of a man"). This suggests that there was another cubit. If one of the Egyptian cubits is meant, the bed was from thirteen to sixteen feet long and from six to seven feet wide. The measuring reed of Ezekiel's escort in his visions extended in length "six long cubits, each being a cubit and a handbreadth in length" (Ezek. 40:5). The word "long" (RSV) is not in the Hebrew, but clearly the text implies that there was a short cubit, the more common one, and that Ezekiel's cubit was this short one plus a handbreadth. The length of this cubit again is specified in Ezek. 43:13. If we take the common cubit, like

the short Egyptian cubit, to consist of six palms, Ezekiel's cubit would be, like the long Egyptian cubit, seven palms, so that the six-cubit measuring reed would be seven ordinary cubits long. This would be, according to the foregoing calculation, 51.829 centimeters or 20.405 inches.

In many cases cubits are named in round numbers. The waters of the Flood covered the mountains fifteen cubits (Gen. 7:20). Quails on the ground were two cubits deep (Num. 11:31). The people were to follow the ark at a distance of ca. two thousand cubits (Josh. 3:4). When his guide led Ezekiel E of the temple, it was by four stages of a thousand cubits each (Ezek. 47:3-5). Benaiah slew an Egyptian five cubits tall (I Chr. 11:23). Zechariah's flying scroll had a length of twenty cubits and a breadth of ten cubits (Zech. 5:2). The gallows that Haman erected was fifty cubits high (Esth. 5:14; 7:9). The image that Nebuchadnezzar built was sixty cubits high and six cubits broad (Dan. 3:1). With more of an attempt at exactness, Goliath's height is given as six cubits and a span, which would be ca. 9½ feet.

The two bronze pillars, Jachin and Boaz, were eighteen cubits high (I Kings 7:15; II Kings 25:17; Jer. 52:21). The capitals upon them were five cubits high according to I Kings 7:16; Jer. 52:22, but only three cubits high according to the account in II Kings 25:17.

The NT word for "cubit," like that of the LXX, is πῆχυς. In Matt. 6:27 (=Luke 12:25) the RSV has: "Which of you by being anxious can add one cubit to his span of life?" The KJV translates: ". . . unto his stature?" In both versions "cubit" is incongruous. It is not a measure of time, and a smaller measure would make better sense as an addition to the human stature. The Greek ἡλικίαν can signify either stature or a time of life.

When the disciples started to bring in the boat after their large catch (John 21:8), they were not far from land, but "as it were two hundred cubits" (KJV) or "about a hundred yards off" (RSV). The RSV interpretation illustrates the popular conception of the cubit. Most people are content to think of it as 1½ feet, which is about right, though probably a little less than the actual cubit when in biblical times it was used for accurate measure. It is easy to think of Solomon's temple, sixty cubits long, twenty cubits wide, and thirty cubits high (I Kings 6:2), as ninety feet long, thirty feet wide, and forty-five feet high.

b. Span. The distance between the extended thumb and the little finger was the span (זרת), the next inferior measure. While the LXX translates correctly σπιθαμῆς, the Vulg. mistakenly translates palmus, which belongs to the next lower category. Both the ephod (Exod. 28:16) and the breastpiece (Exod. 39:9) were a span square. Goliath's height exceeded six cubits by a span (I Sam. 17:4). In the poetic verse Isa. 40:12 there is asked who has marked off the heavens with a span. That the span was half a cubit is shown by Ezek. 43:13, where the border of the altar is given as a span, and in vs. 17, where it is given as half a cubit. According to Ezekiel's scale it would measure 25.914 centimeters or 10.202 inches. On the common scale it would be ca. 22.212 centimeters or 8.745 inches.

c. Handbreadth. The handbreadth or palm (מפח, vocalized *ṭephach* or *ṭōphach*), breadth of the hand at the base of the fingers, generally is considered a sixth of a cubit, which would be 7.404 centimeters or 2.915 inches. With the vocalization *ṭōphach*, the measure is given as the thickness of Solomon's molten sea (I Kings 7:26; II Chr. 4:5) and is used figuratively in "made my days a few handbreadths" (Ps. 39:5). With the vocalization *ṭephach*, it is used to define Ezekiel's cubit (Ezek. 40:5; 43:13), and it is given as the length of some pieces of equipment (RSV "hooks") in Ezekiel's temple (Ezek. 40:43). It was the width of the frame around the acacia table made by Bezalel (Exod. 25:25; 37:12). The LXX word is παλαστῆς. The Vulg. translates by *palmus* except in Exod. 25:25 (*quatuor digitis*); 37:12 (*quatuor digitarum*); I Kings 7:26 (*trium unciarum*, "three inches"); Ps. 39:5 (*mensurabiles*, "small measures").

d. Finger. The smallest Israelite linear measure was the finger (אצבע; Egyptian *db'*), a fourth of a handbreadth. As a measure the finger in the MT occurs only in Jer. 52:21, where the thickness of the two hollow pillars is given as four fingers. In the LXX of I Kings 7:15—G 7:3, followed by the RSV, the four-finger thickness of these pillars is mentioned; but the clause is not in the Hebrew or the KJV. The finger would be 1.85 centimeters or 0.728 inch.

With the understanding that there was variation, the small units of linear measure are listed in Table 4.

Table 4
Linear Measures

Common Measures

Finger	0.728 inch
Handbreadth, 4 fingers	2.915 inches
Span, 2 handbreadths	8.745 inches
Cubit, 6 handbreadths	17.49 inches

Ezekiel's Measures

Span, 3½ handbreadths	10.202 inches
Cubit, 7 handbreadths	20.405 inches

e. Uncertain measures. For distances there are several words for which no exact value is certain. There is the "pace" (צעד), so translated in II Sam. 6:13 but elsewhere translated "step."

The fathom (ὀργυιά), a measure for depth of water (Acts 27:28), is considered to be four cubits or six feet.

The stadion (στάδιον; II Macc. 12:9-10; Luke 24:13; John 6:19; 11:18; Rev. 14:20; 21:16) contained four hundred cubits, which would be 215.5 yards in our estimate of the Israelite measure. According to the Greek standard it was 200 yards, according to the Roman 206.3 yards. In Rev. 14:20; 21:16 the RSV has "stadia." In other occurrences it converts loosely into miles; e.g., sixty stadia (Luke 24:13) are "about seven miles." This would be according to the Roman unit. The KJV regularly uses "furlong."

The mile (μίλιον) in Matt. 5:41 probably was the Roman mile of 1,000 double paces, 5,000 Roman feet, or 1,618 yards.

A day's journey (דרך יום, מהלך יום, ἡμέρας ὁδός) was a general term (Gen. 30:36; 31:23; Exod. 3:18;

5:3; 8:27; Num. 10:33; 11:31; 33:8; I Kings 19:4; II Kings 3:9; Jonah 3:3-4; Luke 2:44). Its length would depend on the method of transportation and the kind of terrain covered. A fair estimate is that under ordinary conditions it would be *ca.* twenty to twenty-five miles. A day's journey, three days' journey, and seven days' journey are mentioned.

A sabbath day's journey (σαββάτου ὁδός) is given as the distance between Olivet and Jerusalem (Acts 1:12). According to Josephus this was six stadia, which would be 1,237.8 yards. Another explanation is based on Exod. 16:29, which forbids a man's leaving his "place" on the sabbath, and Josh. 3:4, where the distance between the people and the ark is given as *ca.* two thousand cubits. Presumably some could go to the ark to worship on the sabbath. So the sabbath day's journey would be *ca.* two thousand cubits.

E. MEASURES OF AREA. 1. Egyptian. In Egypt the cubit (*mḥ*) was used in computing areas. A strip of land one cubit wide and a hundred cubits long was reckoned as a cubit in area. A hundred cubits—i.e., an area a hundred cubits square—was a *st't*, like the Greek aroura. This is estimated as *ca.* 2,735 square meters or approximately two thirds of an acre. A half *st't* was a *rmn*, a quarter a *ḥsb*, and an eighth a *s'*. Ten *st't* were a *ḫ'*, which means a thousand—i.e., a thousand cubits, as above.

2. Mesopotamian. In Babylonia and Assyria it was customary to measure land by units of capacity; an area was measured by the quantity of seed (presumably barley) necessary to sow it properly. Thus we have such expressions as an *imeru* of land. There would be variations depending on the rate at which the seed was distributed and the distance between furrows. On occasion areas are described by linear measures. Thus a piece of land could be described as a *NINDA* square. The relative literature is complicated, as the measures varied in different times and places.

3. Israelite. There is no special terminology for measures of area in the OT. The word צמד, *ṣemedh* (Ugaritic *ṣmd*), means "stick" or "yoke," by metonymy a pair of oxen. The *ṣemedh* is presumed to be what a yoke of oxen could work in a day. In I Sam. 14:14, Jonathan and his armor-bearer are said to have killed *ca.* twenty men within *ca.* half a furrow's length (KJV half an acre) in a *ṣemedh* of land. The Hebrew of the clause is not clear; the LXX indicates a different text; the Vulg. translates צמד by *jugerum* (etymologically related to *jugis*, "yoke," which means a measure of land containing 28,000 square feet, approximately five eighths of an acre). In the KJV the word מענה, *ma'anâ*, is translated "acre," and *ṣemedh* regularly "a yoke." In Isa. 5:10 the word צמד is interpreted "acre" in the KJV-RSV, *jugerum* in the Vulg., and "yoke of oxen" in the LXX. Clearly it indicates a measure of land.

Elijah's trench about his altar on Mount Carmel was as great as would contain two seahs (KJV-RSV "measures") of seed (I Kings 18:32). *See* § C4*f above.*

From Talmudic sources it is evident that the Israelites and Jews, like the Babylonians and Assyrians, estimated acres by processes of seeding.

F. CONCLUSION. No weight or measure in biblical times was sufficiently fixed to enable us to give its exact metric equivalent; but there were ideals for just balances, just weights, and just measures. There were different standards in the various countries of the Near East; and frequently two standards, such as short and long, light and heavy, common and royal, were used simultaneously in the same country. Generally the evidence is clear enough to give us approximate values for the metrological terms.

Bibliography. A. R. S. Kennedy, "Weights and Measures," *HDB*, IV (1902), 901-13: a comprehensive article containing the pertinent information at the time of its publication. D. D. Luckenbill, *The Annals of Sennacherib* (1924), p. 34. W. F. Albright, *The Excavation of Tell Beit Mirsim*, AASOR, XII (1932), 77; XXI-XXII (1943), 58-59. H. Lewy, "Assyro-Babylonian and Israelite Measures of Capacity and Rates of Seeding," *JAOS*, 64 (1944), 65-73: a thorough study based on literature and experiment. A. Segrè, "Babylonian, Assyrian, and Persian Measures," *JAOS*, 64 (1944), 73-81; "A Documentary Analysis of Ancient Palestinian Units of Measure," *JBL*, LXIV (1945), 357-75. C. H. Gordon, *Ugaritic Handbook* (1947); *Ugaritic Literature* (1949). A. Gardiner, *Egyptian Grammar* (2nd ed., 1950), pp. 197-200. A. G. Barrois, Chronology, Metrology, Etc.," *IB*, I (1952), 153-57, with most of the relevant data in the book and article; *Manuel d'archéologie biblique*, II (1953), pp. 348-58, pls. 49, 51. S. N. Kramer, *From the Tablets of Sumer* (1956), pp. 50, 100, 223. R. B. Y. Scott, "Weights and Measures of the Bible," *BA*, XXII, 2 (May, 1959), 22-39. O. R. SELLERS

WELLS. Because of the scarcity of rainfall, wells have always been important in Bible lands, and they are mentioned frequently in the Bible. Their depth and shape often vary in accordance with the type of soil and the water level, some being shallow pits and others great shafts many feet deep. This variety makes it difficult to choose the most descriptive English word for translation. *See* CISTERN; FOUNTAIN; PIT; RESERVOIR; WATER; WATER WORKS.

The most common word for "well" is באר (Gen. 21:30; Num. 21:18; etc.; but see Gen. 14:10; Pss. 55:23—H 55:24; 69:15—H 69:16, where the meaning is "pit"). The root באר occurs in several place names such as BEER (Num. 21:16); BEER-ELIM (Isa. 15:8); BEER-LAHAI-ROI (Gen. 16:14); BEEROTH (Deut. 10:6); and BEER-SHEBA (Gen. 21:14), where famous wells were located.

Other words for "well" are: בר, בור (I Sam. 19:22; II Sam. 23:15; the RSV often uses "cistern" where the KJV has "well"—e.g., Deut. 6:11; II Chr. 26:10; Neh. 9:25), מעין (Isa. 12:3; the RSV often uses "spring" where the KJV has "well"—e.g., Josh. 18: 15; II Kings 3:19); מקור (Prov. 10:11 KJV [RSV "fountain"]); עין (Neh. 2:13, with RSV "Jackal's Well"; the RSV usually uses "spring" where the KJV has "well"—e.g., Gen. 24:13; Exod. 15:27). Greek words are πηγή (John 4:6) and φρέαρ (John 4:11).

Biblical wells were located in the wilderness (Gen. 16:14), in valleys (Gen. 26:17), near cities (Gen. 24: 11), in fields (Gen. 29:2), and in courtyards (II Sam. 17:18). They were especially important in a nomadic society (Gen. 26:18), supplying water for both families and flocks (Gen. 29:2). The water supply of villages and cities from cisterns and springs was often supplemented from wells (I Sam. 19:22; II Sam. 23: 15; John 4:6). Because of their importance the possession of wells was frequently a cause of strife (Gen.

26:20-21), one which has continued among the Bedouins.

Some wells were large enough for men to enter as places of concealment (II Sam. 17:18-19). The mouths of the wells were covered, doubtless to keep the water clean and to prevent persons or animals from falling in (Gen. 29:3; Exod. 21:33, where "pit" refers to a type of well). Water was carried from the wells in jars (Gen. 24:16) and doubtless was removed from the deeper wells by means of jars or waterskins attached to ropes (John 4:11).

In a primitive society wells, like springs and streams, were thought to be places inhabited by spirits (Gen. 16:14); the Song of the Well (Num. 21: 17) is an early Hebrew folk song which suggests the Lord's power over the well. According to Gen. 26: 20-22, wells were named (*see* ESEK; SITNAH; REHOBOTH 2) to commemorate events in tribal history. Among the figurative uses of "well" may be cited the comparison of a harlot or adventuress to a narrow well (Prov. 23:27), and that of a wicked city which keeps fresh her wickedness as a well keeps its water cool or fresh (Jer. 6:7). W. L. REED

WEN. KJV translation of יבלת (RSV DISCHARGE; *see also* PLAGUE) in Lev. 22:22. The reference is to a cattle disease marked by suppurating sores, perhaps symptomatic anthrax or malignant anthrax. R. K. HARRISON

WEST. *See* ORIENTATION.

WESTERN SEA [הים האחרון, *lit.*, the sea behind]. The designation of the Mediterranean in Deut. 11:24 (KJV "uttermost sea"); 34:2 (KJV "utmost sea"); Joel 2:20 (KJV "utmost sea"); Zech. 14:8 (KJV "hinder sea"). *See* GREAT SEA. W. L. REED

WHALE [κῆτος (Matt. 12:40); KJV תנין *in* Job 7:12 (RSV SEA MONSTER); Ezek. 32:2 (*erroneously* תנים; RSV DRAGON)]. Any of several species of large warm-blooded, air-breathing sea mammals of the order Cetacea.

Quite apart from any belief they entertained about mythical monsters in the seas, the biblical Hebrews may have known or heard about various large marine animals, any one of which could be referred to as a "great fish" (Jonah 1:17) or as a "sea monster" or "whale" (Gen. 1:21). These terms might refer to a true fish such as the shark, some species of which attain lengths of over thirty feet. They might also designate the whales and dolphins. The whales most likely to be encountered in the Mediterranean, Arabian, and Red seas would be the humpback whale (*Megaptera böops*) and the fin whale (*Balaenoptera*); the dolphins (*Delphinidae*) might be Risso's dolphin (*Grampus griseus*), the common dolphin (*Delphinus delphis*), and the bottle-nosed dolphin (*Tursiops tursio*). W. S. McCULLOUGH

WHEAT [חמה, *ḥiṭṭâ* (*cf.* Aram. חנטין, *ḥinṭîn*; Ugar. *ḥṭṭ*; Arab. *ḥinṭa*); בר, *bar* (*alternately* GRAIN; KJV *alternately* CORN); KJV דגן, *dāghān* (RSV GRAIN); KJV ריפות, *rîphôth* (Prov. 27:22; RSV CRUSHED GRAIN; *in* II Sam. 17:19, RSV GRAIN; KJV GROUND CORN); σῖτος]. An annual grass, *Triticum aestivum* L. or *Triticum durum* Desf., which produced one of the most important grains for food in ancient biblical times. It has been cultivated for food in the area at least since Neolithic times.

The KJV translates *bar* with "wheat" in Jer. 23: 28; Joel 2:24; Amos 5:11; 8:5-6 (the RSV retains "wheat" in Jer. 23:28 and the passages in Amos, while elsewhere the word is given its more general meaning, "corn" (i.e., "grain"; so RSV). "Wheat" is also found in the KJV for *dāghān* in Num. 18:12; Jer. 31:12, where "grain" (so RSV) is expected. *Rîphôth,* which probably meant "crushed grain," is translated "wheat" in Prov. 27:22 KJV (cf. II Sam. 17:19, where the KJV has "ground corn" for the same word). For related words, *see* BREAD; FLOUR; GRAIN; SHIBBOLETH.

Botanists have disagreed concerning the identification of the many species and subspecies of wheat, but recent studies have classified them according to chromosome count—i.e., I Einkorn, 14; II Emmer, 28; and III Spelt, 42. Zohary (*see* FLORA §§ 1*a-b*) claims that the biblical wheats were from the emmer class, *Triticum dicoccoides* (Koern) A. Schulz and *Triticum durum* Desf.; but other botanists identify them with the spelt class, *Triticum spelta* L. and *Triticum aestivum* L. (common bread wheat). The former is common to Egypt and southerly areas, while the latter is common to Asia Minor and more northerly areas. The absence of wild specimens of the spelt group in Palestine today (they are common to N Syria) argues in favor of Zohary's position (cf. references to wheat in Egypt: Exod. 9:32, etc.). Gen. 41:5-7 clearly refers to *Triticum compositum* L. (spelt group), club wheat, in Egypt.

The presence of both *ksmm* (Hebrew *kussemeth*) and *ḥṭṭ* in Ugaritic texts from N Syria, where the spelt group is common, implies that there the words referred to that group of wheats. Thus it seems probable that *ḥiṭṭâ* was used for both kinds of wheat, and *kussemeth* for inferior varieties of them. *See* SPELT.

The harvest of wheat was an ancient time reference (Gen. 30:14; Exod. 34:22; Judg. 15:1; *cf.* GEZER CALENDAR), the Feast of Weeks (i.e., of the wheat harvest; *see* WEEKS, FEAST OF) being one of the three principal ancient yearly festivals (Exod. 34: 22; Num. 28:26-31). There are frequent references to the processing of wheat: harvesting (Ruth 2:23; I Sam. 6:13), threshing (Judg. 6:11; I Chr. 21:20), cleaning (II Sam. 4:6), and winnowing (Matt. 3:12). Wheat was an important item of trade with Tyre (I Kings 5:11—H 5:25; II Chr. 2:10, 15—H 2:9, 14; Ezek. 27:17 [cf. Acts 12:20; Rev. 18:13]). Poetically, wheat appears as a symbol of God's care (Ps. 81: 16—H 81:17; 147:14) or of a curse (Job 31:40; Jer. 12:13), and of the beauty of the bride (Song of S. 7:2—H 7:3). In the NT wheat is mentioned in allegory (Matt. 3:12; Luke 3:17) and parable (Matt. 13:25-30; Luke 16:7). Paul (I Cor. 15:37) and John's Gospel (12:24) use the sowing of the wheat kernel to illustrate the transformed spiritual life.

Grains of wheat, mostly carbonized, have been discovered in several excavations in the Holy Land (frequently in the tombs of ancient Egypt). About a bushel of what was probably wheat has come from Dhiban (ancient Dibon, capital of Moab), illustrating the importance of Transjordan as a grain-producing country (Gen. 30:14; II Chr. 27:5).

See also BREAD; FLOUR; GRAIN; MILLSTONE; SACRIFICES AND OFFERINGS; SHIBBOLETH.

Bibliography. Pliny Nat. Hist. XVIII.63-70 (xii), 81-93 (xix-xxi); G. E. Post, *Flora of Syria, Palestine and Sinai,* II (1933), 781-83; I. Löw, *Die Flora der Juden,* I:2 (1928), 779-98; H. N. and A. L. Moldenke, *Plants of the Bible* (1952), pp. 228-33; W. L. Reed, "A Recent Analysis of Grain from Ancient Dibon in Moab," *BASOR,* 146 (April, 1957), 6-10.

J. C. TREVER

WHEEL [אוֹפָן, *'ôphan;* Heb. *and* Aram. גַּלְגַּל (*usually* galgal; cf. gilgal in Isa. 28:28), *from* גָּלַל, roll; τροχός (Jas. 3:6), *from* τρέχω, run]. A disk or circular object capable of turning on a central axis. The OT writers took the wheel for granted and were probably unaware that it had been invented in Mesopotamia before 3000 B.C.

1. Structure
2. Vehicles
3. Temple stands
4. Yahweh's throne
5. Figurative use

1. Structure. Early wheels were of solid wood, and were often in three parts, plus rim, perhaps because of the scarcity of wide planks (Fig. WHE 21; *cf.* CHA 23). Doubtless this type of wheel survived into the biblical period. But the spoked wheel, which was developed *ca.* 2000 B.C., is well known in the

Courtesy of the University Museum of the University of Pennsylvania

21. A plaque found at Ur, showing a war chariot with wooden wheels

OT, and in I Kings 7:33 certain wheels (*see* § 3 *below*) are reported to have had axles, rims, spokes, and hubs, in this instance of cast bronze. Figs. CAR 15; CHA 24.

2. Vehicles. The wheel was used on wagons or carts (Isa. 28:27-28) and also on chariots (Exod. 14: 25; Isa. 5:28; Jer. 47:3). "Wheel" by metonymy may designate any of these vehicles (Ezek. 23:24; 26:10; Nah. 3:2).

3. Temple stands. In the account of Solomon's temple, ten "stands" are described, each with four wheels (1½ cubits in diameter), and upon these stands were placed the ten lavers of the temple court (I Kings 7:30-33). *See* TEMPLE, JERUSALEM, § A1*a*.

4. Yahweh's throne. In Ezekiel's visions of the Divine Presence (1:4-28; 10) there appear the four cherubim who support Yahweh's throne, beside each of whom is a gleaming wheel (possibly a double wheel) equipped with eyes. The significance of these wheels can only be surmised: perhaps we have an echo of the chariot of the sun-god (*cf.* II Kings 23: 11). In Dan. 7:9 these wheels have become the wheels of God's throne, as they are in Enoch 14:18. Later, however, in Enoch (61:10; 71:7), the wheels of Ezekiel (*'ôphannîm*) have been transformed into the angels Ophannin, who like the Seraphim and Cherubim guard the divine throne.

5. Figurative use. A broken wheel at a cistern or well, making it impossible to draw up the life-giving water, supplies a metaphor for death in Eccl. 12:6.

In Ps. 77:18—H 77:19 "wheel" (*galgal*) appears to mean "whirlwind." In Ps. 83:13—H 83:14; Isa. 17:13, the same word (RSV "whirling dust") may refer to the "wheel-shaped dried calix of the thistle *Gundelia Tournefortii*."

Driving a wheel (of a royal chariot) over the wicked (Prov. 20:26) is presumably a figure for their punishment.

Ben Sirach alludes to the heart of a fool as a "cart wheel" (Ecclus. 33:5).

The meaning of the phrase "wheel of origin (or creation)" in Jas. 3:6 is uncertain. Moffatt renders it the "round circle of existence," the RSV the "cycle of nature," and Arndt and Gingrich "course of life."

W. S. McCULLOUGH

WHEEL, POTTER'S. *See* POTTER'S WHEEL.

WHELP [גוּר (CUB *in* Nah. 2:11—H 2:12; young (*of jackal*) *in* Lam. 4:3); בֵּן, *lit.* son (*of a lioness*) *in* Job 4:11)]. One of the young of a lion.

In Jacob's blessing (Gen. 49:9) Judah is praised as a lion's whelp, presumably because of his strength and alacrity in leadership (cf. Deut. 33:2, a reference to Dan). When judgment befalls Babylon, her residents

> shall roar together like lions,
> they shall growl like lions' whelps
> (Jer. 51:38).

Judah is personified as a mother lioness, Jehoahaz and Jehoiachin as her whelps (Ezek. 19). Nineveh is compared to a lions' den in which whelps were raised (Nah. 2:11-13—H 2:12-14). Eliphaz uses figures of the lion and the lioness and her whelps for the wicked and violent (Job 4:10-11).

See also LION; DEN OF LIONS.   H. F. BECK

WHET [לטשׁ, *also* hammer, strike, tap, sharpen (Ps. 7:12—H 7:13); שׁנן (Deut. 32:41; Ps. 64:3); קלקל (Eccl. 10:10)]. "Whet" is used in allusive and figurative phrases—e.g., to whet the tongue or the sword —expressing incitement and preparation for attack or other action. In Deut. 32:41; Ps. 7:12 it indicates the Lord's preparation for judgment.   H. F. BECK

WHIP [שׁוֹט (I Kings 12:11, 14; II Chr. 10:11, 14; Prov. 26:3; Nah. 3:2; *alternately* SCOURGE; DISASTER); φραγέλλιον (John 2:15; KJV SCOURGE)]. An instrument of punishment or of coercion, both of men and of animals. According to John 2:15, Jesus used a whip to drive the sellers, the money-changers, and the sheep and oxen from the temple. *See* SCOURGE.   H. F. BECK

WHIRLWIND [סַעַר, סְעָרָה, high wind, windstorm; סוּפָה, destructive wind; גַּלְגַּל, whirling wind (Ps. 77: 18—H 77:19; Isa. 17:3)]. The designation of several types of winds. סַעַר and סְעָרָה are roughly synonymous and designate a violent wind or windstorm, but not specifically a whirlwind or tornado, unless the context demands it. Even Jer. 23:19 (סַעַר מִתְחוֹלֵל, "whirling tempest"; KJV "grievous whirlwind") may mean no more than the swirling eddies which mark the approach of a stormwind; cf. Isa. 17:13: "whirling dust [גַּלְגַּל] before the storm [סוּפָה]."

Stormwinds are not unusual in the rainy season, but true whirlwinds or tornadoes are rare and occur chiefly near the coast in early winter when the air is unstable. Such whirlwinds as have been recorded are destructive along a narrow path, and it may be that the סְעָרָה which swept up Elijah (II Kings 2:11) was thought of as sucking him up in the funnel-shaped vortex. The chariot and horses of fire, in II Kings 2:12; Hab. 3:8, are a figure for thunder and lightning, expected to accompany a tornado.

Whirlwinds of a lesser sort are the "dust devils" or whirling columns of dust which sometimes are drawn up from a hot, dry surface in unstable air; these are probably meant by the "palm-columns [תִּימָרוֹת; RSV "column"; KJV "pillars"] of smoke" in Song of S. 3:6. *See* PALESTINE, CLIMATE OF.

Bibliography. D. Baly, *The Geography of the Bible* (1957), pp. 65-66; D. Nir, "Whirlwinds in Israel in the Winters 1954-55 and 1955-56," *IEJ*, VII (1957), 109-17.

R. B. Y. SCOTT

WHITE. The translation of a number of biblical words, chiefly לבן and λευκός. In the OT "white" generally describes the natural color of an object— animals (Zech. 1:8), the results of leprosy (Lev. 13), stripped branches (Joel 1:7), milk (Gen. 49:12), snow (Isa. 1:18). White garments are also mentioned (Eccl. 9:8); the cloth would be washed with a detergent, bleached in sulphur fumes, and left to dry in the sun. This process is used as an analogy for the purification of the sinful man (Ps. 51:7—H 51:9; Isa. 1:18; Dan. 11:35; 12:10). In the NT white garments indicate the glory of their wearer: the transfigured and risen Lord (Matt. 17:2; 28:3), angels (John 20: 12; Acts 1:10), and the various inhabitants of heaven in Revelation are so attired.

The NT also speaks of "whitewashed" (κονιάω) objects in much the same way we use the word today; on the outside everything looks fine, but within there is uncleanness and corruption (Matt. 23:27; Acts 23:3).

See also FULLER; TEXTILES; COLORS.

Bibliography. R. J. Forbes, *Studies in Ancient Technology*, IV (1956), 83.   R. W. CORNEY

WHORE. *See* PROSTITUTION.

WICK [פשתה (FLAX *in* Exod. 9:31; KJV FLAX; TOW); λίνον (KJV FLAX)]. *See* FLAX; LINEN.

WIDOW [אלמנה; χήρα]. Many references to the widow indicate that hers was an unfortunate state and that she was frequently subjected to harsh treatment. As an object of public concern she is often linked with the orphan or fatherless. When judgment and destruction threaten or are imagined as having come, she is included among its victims. A special class of widows is found in the early Christian community. Cities may be symbolically designated as widows.

1. Laws concerning widows
2. Harsh treatment of widows
3. The widow as an object of compassion
4. Special class of widows in the Christian community
5. Symbolical use of the term
Bibliography

1. Laws concerning widows. "In every code except the Hebrew, the widow has rights of inheritance but in Hebrew law she is completely ignored" (*see* the work of T. J. Meek in the *bibliography*). One reason for this strange neglect may be the Hebrew belief that death before old age was a calamity, a judgment for sin which was extended to the wife that was left. It was therefore a disgrace to be a widow (Ruth 1:20-21; Isa. 54:4: "the reproach of your widowhood"). On the other hand, several laws do consider her plight or recognize her existence. The law of levirate marriage, whatever its primary purpose, gives her considerable security (*see* MARRIAGE § 1g; INHERITANCE). A childless widow could return to her father's house, at least if she was the daughter of a priest (Lev. 22:13; cf. Ruth 1:8), where she might wait for a levirate marriage, even with a late husband's brother who was too young for marriage or not yet born (Gen. 38:11; Ruth 1:11). But if there were no brothers or if they were too poor to support the widow, she was without other recourse. The law gave her some recognition, nonetheless. If she took an oath, it stood, since she had no husband who might revoke it (Num. 30:9). The widow could remarry (Lev. 21:14; Ruth 1:9, 13; I Sam. 25; Ezek. 44:22).

2. Harsh treatment of widows. The stern condemnations voiced by the prophets and other writers against injustice include attacks upon the mistreatment of widows (Isa. 1:23c; 10:2; cf. Job 22:9; 24:3; 31:16; Ps. 94:6). In the day of judgment God will take swift action against those who oppress hired laborers and the widow and the orphan (Mal. 3:5). The prominence of these strong words of denunciation abundantly testifies to the prevalence of oppressive treatment of the widow in biblical society. "Widow" in Hebrew resembles the word meaning "be mute," אלם, suggesting the muteness induced by disgraceful widowhood. Her plight may have been aggravated by the possibility that she wore identifying garments (Gen. 38:14, 19).

3. The widow as an object of compassion. The biblical concern for the widow is evidence that she needed it because of her inferior position in the com-

munity. She evidently had only the protection which public compassion afforded her by acts of charity and justice. The Law and the Prophets, as well as some of the Writings of the OT, contain evidence of this situation. It appears also in NT writings. As a member of the covenant community the widow must receive the same merciful treatment as that which is given to the sojourner and the fatherless (Deut. 14:29); her garment must not be taken in pledge (24:17; cf. Amos 2:8), because she may own only one, in all likelihood. The process of gathering grain and grapes should take into account the hunger of the widow and leave some of the harvest for gleaning purposes (Deut. 24:19-21). The Levite, the sojourner, the fatherless, and the widow are to be given the tithe of the produce in the third year (26:12; cf. 27:19).

The widow is under the special care of God, who provides her with food and clothing (Deut. 10:18). So gracious will be the kindness of God that he will sustain the fatherless children and preserve the widows if they put their trust in him (Jer. 49:11). God is declared to be the "father of the fatherless and protector of widows" (Ps. 68:5). He watches over the forlorn and needy, the fatherless and those without husbands (146:9). Jesus reaffirmed the biblical view of God's concern for the widow by speaking with anger of those who devour widow's houses and then make long prayers (Luke 20:47). This biblical emphasis is interestingly paralleled by a passage in the so-called "Legend of King Keret" (*see bibliography*): "Thou [the king] didst use to judge the cause of the widow . . . to drive out them that prey upon the poor" (Krt. C:45). God's compassion for the widow must be reflected in the concern of the faithful for her welfare (Jas. 1:27).

4. Special class of widows in the Christian community. Judging from the language of I Tim. 5:3, 9, there appeared in the early church a group of women called "real widows" (cf. Acts 6:1; 9:39). This was a group to which not all women who were widows could belong. The passage cited states that the "real widow" is to be honored. She must learn her religious duties as these relate to life in her own family, and help her parents. She sets her hope on God and engages in prayer day and night. She must be at least sixty years of age and married only once. Her duties include rearing of children, showing hospitality, "washing the feet of the saints," and helping the needy. Younger widows should not be enrolled as "real widows," for they will desire to marry again (I Tim. 5:11). The existence of this order of widows is attested by early church leaders, such as Ignatius (Smyr. 13:1) and Polycarp (Phil. 4:3).

5. Symbolical use of the term. The term for "widow" is applied to the city of Babylon. To her will come both widowhood and loss of children (Isa. 47:9)—loss, i.e., of her population. Desolated Israel is to be of good cheer and to forget the "reproach of [her] widowhood" (54:4d). Sad at heart, one poet says that Jerusalem sits lonely; she has become like a widow (Lam. 1:1). Another cries out: "Our mothers are like widows," and then mentions poverty and servitude as proof of this (5:3-4). A Christian seer hears an angel cry out that Babylon is fallen and another voice exclaim that she is complacent, confidently declaring: "I am no widow, mourning I shall never see" (Rev. 18:7*d*).

See also MARRIAGE; FAMILY; WOMAN; INHERITANCE.

Bibliography. L. Zscharnack, *Der Dienst der Frau* (1902), pp. 100 ff. A. Kalsbach, *Die altkirchliche Einrichtung der Diakonissen* (1926). H. L. Ginsberg, "The Legend of King Keret, A Canaanite Epic of the Bronze Age," *BASOR,* Supplementary Studies, nos. 2-3 (1946), p. 32. For the status of the widow in nonbiblical codes, see T. J. Meek, *Hebrew Origins* (2nd ed., 1950), p. 77.

See also the bibliographies under MARRIAGE; FAMILY; WOMAN; INHERITANCE.   O. J. BAAB

WIFE. *See* MARRIAGE.

WILD ASS [עָרוֹד (Job 39:5; *also* SWIFT ASS), Aram. עֲרָד (Dan. 5:21), *cf.* Arab. *'arida,* flee; *'ard,* ass; פָּרֶא in Jer. 2:24; KJV WILD MAN *in* Gen. 16:12), *cf.* Arab. *fara'a,* wild ass; Akkad. *parū,* mule]. A wild quadruped, *equus hemionus hemihippus,* of the horse family, known also as the onager. For the domesticated animal, *see* Ass.

In the biblical period and for centuries later, wild asses roamed the less settled parts of Western Asia. Xenophon (end of the fifth century B.C.) refers to these animals in the Mesopotamian region (*Anabasis* I.5), as does A. H. Layard in the nineteenth century (*Nineveh and Its Remains* [1849], I, 324-25). For H. B. Tristram's account of wild asses in the deserts of North Africa, see *NHB* 41-43.

Wild asses, swift and untamable, are usually referred to in the OT either to reinforce a point that is being made, or in a figure of speech. In Gen. 16:12 the intractable Ishmael is described as, literally, the "wild ass of mankind." In Isa. 32:14 the presence of wild asses in what was formerly a human habitation suggests the complete absence of men, and in Jer. 14:6 the threatened drought will be so complete that even the wild asses will suffer. Hosea compares Israel to a solitary wild ass wandering off to Assyria (Hos. 8:9), and Jeremiah takes up this figure to assert that the people's devotion to the baals is like the lust of a wild ass in heat (Jer. 2:24). The reference to wild asses in Dan. 5:21 emphasizes the extent of the change in Nebuchadnezzar's fortunes. In Ps. 104:11 wild asses share with other animals in the waters provided by the Lord. It is in Job that we find more allusions to the wild ass than in any other OT book: to its braying (6:5), its colt (11:12), and the Lord's giving it freedom to roam the steppe (39:5-8); this wilderness, however, is the proper habitat of wild asses and the like, and poverty-stricken men who go there do so only in desperation (24:5).

Fig. ASS 94.   W. S. McCULLOUGH

WILD GOAT [אָקוֹ, *possibly* suckling; *cf.* יָנַק, to suck; Akkad. *unîqu,* kid; יָעֵל; *cf.* Ugar. *y'l,* wild goat; Arab. *wa'l,* wild goat, *from wa'ala,* to ascend, climb]. An untamed horned ruminant mammal of the genus Capra, with backward-curving horns. It is believed that the wild goat of biblical Palestine was the Nubian ibex (*capra ibex nubiana; see* FAUNA § A2*fiii*). The allusions in the OT indicate that these animals were known to the Hebrews as living in rocky re-

gions (I Sam. 24:2—H 24:3; Job 39:1; Ps. 104:18). The feminine word, יַעֲלָה ("doe"; KJV "roe"), is used in a complimentary sense of one's wife in Prov. 5:19.

Bibliography. Rock drawings from Petra and vicinity (probably pre-Islamic but later than A.D. 100) point to the ibex as a common game animal hunted with the dog and the bow. See *BASOR,* no. 142 (April, 1956), p. 30; *BA,* vol. XIX, no. 2 (May, 1956), p. 33. Somewhat similar drawings in the Negeb are described by E. Anati as pictures of antelopes in *Archaeology,* VIII (1955), 31-42. For wild goats in Palestine in the nineteenth century, see Tristram, *NHB* (1867, pp. 95-97.

W. S. McCULLOUGH

WILD GOATS' ROCKS [צוּרֵי הַיְּעֵלִים] (I Sam. 24:2—H 24:3); KJV ROCKS OF THE WILD GOATS. The location of a cave where David showed magnanimity to Saul. Although the site is not precisely known, it was in the limestone wilderness near En-gedi, *ca.* halfway up the W shore of the Dead Sea, where ibexes are still plentiful.

L. E. TOOMBS

WILD GOURDS [פַּקֻּעֹת, bursters]. A plant with trailing, vinelike shoots, usually identified as the colocynth. It produces a fruit resembling an orange in color and shape and could easily be mistaken, as by the prophets associated with Elisha (II Kings 4:39), for an edible melon. A powerful purgative, it could be poisonous and fatal if eaten in quantity.

See also FLORA § A14*d*.

Bibliography. J. P. Harland, "Sodom and Gomorrah," *BA,* VI (1943), 49-52.   R. F. SCHNELL

WILD GRAPES [בְּאֻשִׁים, stinking or worthless things] (Isa. 5:2, 4). An expression used in Isaiah's imagery of the vineyard: in response to God's kindness and mercy, Israel has brought forth wild grapes —i.e., she has repaid him with ingratitude and rebellion.

See also VINE.   H. F. BECK

WILD OLIVE [עֵץ שֶׁמֶן; ἀγριέλαιος]. *See* OIL TREE; CYPRESS; FLORA § A9*m*.

WILD OX [רְאֵם (רֵים *in* Job 39:9; *plural* רְמִים *in* Ps. 22:21—H 22:22; KJV UNICORN), *cf.* Akkad. *rēmu,* wild bull; KJV תְּאוֹ (Deut. 14:5; RSV ANTELOPE)]. A wild two-horned quadruped, *bos primigenius,* called in Europe the aurochs, thought to be the stock from which the domesticated ox was derived.

The nine references in the OT to wild oxen would appear to indicate that the biblical Hebrews had some knowledge of these beasts. Not only are their horns alluded to, but their great strength is recognized (cf. Job 39:9-12). Thus the psalmist praises the Lord for having exalted his horn "like that of the wild ox" (Ps. 92:10—H 92:11; cf. Num. 23:22; 24:8; Deut. 33:17). Contrariwise, when in Isa. 34:7 it is prophesied that even the wild oxen of Edom will fall, the terrible thoroughness of the Lord's judgment on this nation is emphasized.

Wild oxen were known in ancient Mesopotamia and are mentioned in the Assyrian records (*see* bibliography). For allusions to such oxen in classical literature, see Herodotus VII.126 (in Macedonia);

Aristotle *History of Animals* 488*a*, 499*a;* Pliny Nat. Hist. VIII.30 (in Ethiopia).

Bibliography. A. T. Olmstead, *History of Assyria* (1923), pp. 64, 78, 92, 95, 240. For an illustration of the hunting of these animals, see Figure 49 opposite p. 92.

W. S. McCullough

*WILDERNESS. The translation of several different words (מדבר, ישימון, ערבה, ἐρημία, etc.); often used interchangeably with "DESERT." An accurate translation is difficult, because the so-called wilderness regions included arid and semiarid territory as well as sandy desert, rocky plateaus, pasture lands, and desolate mountain terrain. Such regions existed in Canaan (*see* PALESTINE, GEOGRAPHY OF) and beyond its E and S borders (*see* ARABIA; SIN, WILDERNESS OF). "Wilderness" is mentioned also in connection with the following: BEER-SHEBA; BETH-AVEN; DAMASCUS; EDOM; ENGEDI; ETHAM; GIBEON; JERUEL; JUDAH, HILL COUNTRY OF; KADESH; KEDEMOTH; MAON; MOAB; PARAN; SHUR; SINAI; TEKOA; ZIN; ZIPH 2.

W. L. REED

WILL. The translation of διαθήκη in the NT. The word does not occur in the OT, but a common Hebrew term, ברית, meaning "covenant, agreement, alliance," is translated by διαθήκη in the LXX. This Greek word had the meaning of "will" exclusively in Hellenistic times. When it is used for ברית, the sense of "will" is lost, although one aspect is retained—namely, the idea that the διαθήκη is the declaration of the will of one person and not the result of an agreement between two parties; God alone determines the conditions of the covenant.

In the NT a man's "will," in the human context, may not be annulled once it has been ratified (Gal. 3:15; RSV mg. "covenant"). This reference deals primarily with the appointment of an heir. Irrevocability was a characteristic of such a will in Greek communities, while in Roman practice a will could be revoked by the testator at any time before his death. In another passage, "where a will is involved, the death of the one who made it must be established" (Heb. 9:16) before the promised inheritance can become effective (vs. 17). Apart from these passages, διαθήκη regularly expresses the idea of COVENANT (Luke 1:72; Acts 3:25; Rom. 11:27).

O. J. BAAB

WILL OF GOD. "Will" as applied to God must be understood in terms of its meaning with reference to man. It is an act or process of volition; something wished by a person, especially one with power or authority; strong purpose, intention, or determination; power of self-direction, or self-control; conscious and deliberate action or choice; disposition or attitude toward others.

The intention herein is to note how this concept is applied to God by biblical writers, and to observe also how they relate it to the will of man, to phenomena of the natural world, and to the course of history, as well as to discuss the views of science and philosophy concerning the issues raised.

1. Terminology
2. The Creator
   a. The natural world

   b. The creation of man
   c. The kingdom of God
   d. Satan overcome
3. The humanity of God
4. Will of God and will of man
5. Will of God and moral law
6. Is anthropomorphism true?
Bibliography

1. **Terminology.** Biblical Hebrew contains a variety of verbs carrying such meanings as "to determine," "to desire," "to take pleasure in," "to favor," "to love," "to choose," "to please," "to covet"; and nouns for "favor," "grace," "purpose," "delight," "pleasure," and "will." These words are applied to God as well as to man, carrying the implication of full personality. But there is no word in biblical Hebrew for "will" in the technical psychological sense in which it is used in scientific studies of personality.

E.g., the noun חפץ is used with reference to God in Isa. 44:28; 46:10; 48:14. In each case it is translated in the RSV as "purpose," and in the Vulg. as *voluntas*. In 44:28; 48:14 the LXX uses θέλημα, but in 46:10, βουλή. "Will" is used here in the objective sense of "purpose," or "commandments which one can keep."

Another Hebrew word for "will" is רצון, which occurs in Ezra 10:11; Pss. 40:9; 103:21; 143:10. In every case it is rendered as "will" by the RSV. In Ezra 10:11 the LXX uses ἀρεστόν, and the Vulg. has *placitum*. For all the passages from Psalms the LXX gives θέλημα; the Vulg., *voluntas*. Here also the reference is to the objective will of God, which a person can keep, not to will as a subjective psychological process. There is no indication of an effort to distinguish between will, feeling, and intellect. There is no speculation about the psychological constitution and nature of human personality.

Biblical language with reference to man is functional and practical. Without being critically concerned about it, ancient Hebrews tended to treat personality as an unanalyzed unity, with no interest along philosophical lines. Their language contains no words for abstractions. They were familiar with will as desire and as an act of desire, but not with will as a faculty of the mind as contrasted with intellect, feeling, or emotion. Our study of the will of God, so far as Hebrew is concerned, therefore, is not based on Hebrew words, but on actions ascribed to God, and various roles attributed to him by Hebrew writers in the course of the development of their culture. and religion.

Almost the same situation is found in the Greek of the NT. The will of God is usually expressed by θέλημα, and in most cases it means God's objective will, which one can keep. In Matt. 7:21, Jesus speaks of ὁ ποιῶν τὸ θέλημα τοῦ πατρός μου, "he who does the will of my father." In John 4:34 he says: ποιήσω τὸ θέλημα τοῦ πέμψαντός με, "[I] do the will of him who sent me." These passages use "will" with the meaning which we have noted in the LXX.

However, there is evidence of the beginning of a use of θέλημα in the psychological sense. E.g., I Pet. 3:17 says: εἰ θέλοι τὸ θέλημα τοῦ θεοῦ (lit., "if the will of God should desire it"). Even more to the point is II Pet. 1:21: οὐ γὰρ θελήματι ἀνθρώπου ἠνέχθη προφητεία ποτέ, "No prophecy ever originated by the will of man." In these words from the latest document of our NT, we probably have the closest approach to the true psychological concept of will which occurs in biblical literature. It is, of course, a reference to the will of man, but it would imply by contrast the will of God. It shows that by the middle of the second century Christian thought was beginning to adapt itself to the abstract pattern of psychology. But generally speaking, θέλημα and related nouns and verbs are used in the NT with essentially the same meanings which they have in the LXX, and in their Hebrew prototypes. Although there are minor exceptions, on the whole, NT thought remains prephilosophical.

2. The Creator. There are at least four distinct strands in biblical thought which present God as Creator. Each of these in its own unique way reveals a conception of the will of God. The idea is derived from attitudes and actions attributed to God in the different phases of creation. The role which God takes in each case is like that of a man, and his will is analogous to the human will. The four presentations of creation cover the entire range of biblical revelation, and, because of the contrasting nature of the stories themselves, they give a vivid portrayal of the will of God as it was apprehended by the people of the Bible.

a. The natural world. The most primitive idea of the creation of the natural world is contained in a few allusions to an almost forgotten epic of the slaughter of RAHAB, the dragon of the sea, by Yahweh. It appears in the great poetry of Job 9:13; 26: 12; Ps. 89:9-10; Isa. 51:9-10. These faint echoes out of the past remind us of the Babylonian myth of the slaughter of Tiamat by Marduk; the Rig-Vedic combat between Indra and Vritra; and, among others, the Shinto myth of Susanowo and the dragon. In this primeval Hebrew story we catch a glimpse of creation as Yahweh begins to impose his will upon chaos in a violent combat. He slays the dragon of the sea. God is the cosmic warrior. He wins the contest by the skill of his mighty arm.

The J story of Gen. 2:4-24 (*see* PENTATEUCH § A3) in its fascinating way relates how Yahweh created man, animals, birds, and woman. He forms the bodies of man and the animals and birds out of the formless earth, but makes woman out of one of man's ribs, which he takes from man's side after he has put him to sleep. Morever, he plants a garden in Eden as their home. This story presents God, first of all, as a potter shaping forms out of clay; second, as a gardener selecting and planting appropriate seeds for his paradise; and third, as a surgeon, who puts man to sleep and deftly removes a rib and builds it into a woman. No greater contrast can be imagined between conceptions of will than that between the ferocious conqueror of Rahab and the gentle Yahweh who presides over the pastoral scene of Eden.

The most complete and advanced account of the creation of the natural world is given by P in Gen. 1:1-2:3. It begins with a picture of chaos. What is to become the earth is still formless substance floating in a primeval sea, which is shrouded in darkness, but the Spirit of God is moving over it. Creation takes place as God brings his omnipotent will to bear upon this orderless mass in a series of seven decisive actions, each of which in turn is one day of time. The seven days are the world's first week. Creation begins on Sunday. On that first day God creates light, and then divides it into day and night. On the second day he creates the sky, which is a solid dome. It separates the waters which are above it from those which are below it. This firmament of sky God calls the heavens. On the third day God divides the waters below the heavens into the dry land and the seas. Then he causes the dry land to produce vegetation. On the fourth day the sun, moon, and stars are created and set in the sky to be signs of day and night and the seasons. On the fifth day God creates living creatures of the sea and birds. On the sixth day he makes land creatures of all kinds, including man. With his labors finished, on the seventh day God rests from all that he has done. He blesses this seventh day and sets it apart. This is the origin of the Hebrew sabbath.

The unique element in this story is the omnipotence of God's will. Unlike the primordial struggle with chaos, in which Yahweh slaughters the dragon in fierce combat, in this majestic conception there is no exertion of physical energy whatever; nor is there the experimental hesitation of Yahweh in Eden as he makes one animal after another in search of a suitable companion for man. Here God has omniscience, omnipotence, certainty, precision, complete mastery. The strength of his will is absolute. He creates by merely uttering a word. His role has no complete human analogue. Remote similarities are suggested by persons occupying positions of great power, such as rulers, military leaders, presidents of corporations, architects, engineers, or surgeons, whose simple commands are enough to inaugurate and carry to their consummation gigantic enterprises or operations. Perhaps the nearest analogy is the shaman, thaumaturge, or magician of primitive life, the mana of whose incantations is supposed to be automatic and instantaneous. But this primitive concept also falls short. God uses no magical device; he utters no incantation; omnipotence is within himself; his word is self-sufficient. There is no uncertainty, no struggle, as he transforms chaos into the natural world, which in his sight is good.

b. The creation of man. As was noted above, the creation of man, on the biological level, belongs to the natural order. The structure of his body and his cycle of life are in essential ways like those of the animals. Yet this is only one aspect of man. Far more important is that which differentiates man from the animals and gives him a unique position in the world. That which distinguishes man from all the animals is the high quality of his intelligence and his freedom of will. This is what P means in Gen. 1:26-27 when he says that man is created in the image of God. In other words, he means that to be in the image of God is to have intelligence and freedom of will. In this respect man is like God; this is something which cannot be said of any of the animals, to which man is biologically related. It could not be said that the animals are created in God's image. They lack both his kind of intelligence and his freedom of will. It is in this way that we are to understand how P could say that God gave man dominion over every other form of life on the earth.

This conception of man is assumed as the presupposition of biblical religion. One cannot understand the Bible unless he keeps this high conception in mind. But even biblical writers at times express amazement at man's position on the earth. The author of the eighth psalm, e.g., as he contemplates the beauties of the natural world, feels a sense of humility and wonder when he ponders the dignity of man.

The unique nature of man allows us a deeper insight into the will of God. Man's intelligence and freedom of will constitute him a moral being. He may choose evil as well as good, but he cannot avoid the issue of morality. As God has chosen to give man this moral capacity, it is evident that to this extent he must refrain from the exercise of his own omnipotent will and deal with man on a moral level. The creation of man's moral nature introduces a vastly complicated factor into the drama of the divine will.

Whereas P has consolidated his view of the moral nature of man into the remarkable concept of the image of God, J has dealt with this mystery of man's character in the wonderful story of Gen. 3. This allegory portrays man's moral life at the same time that it delineates the will of God. At the moral level the will of man and the will of God impinge upon one another, and light on one clarifies the other. The four characters in the short story are God, Adam, Eve, and the serpent. Submotifs are physical death, fear of serpents and their habits, suffering and subjection of woman, and the custom of wearing clothing. But man's moral nature is the real theme. Four elements which enter into the moral act are the standard of right, which God himself defines, and desire, freedom of will, and intelligence, which are characteristic of human nature. Reason enters in the cynical role of the serpent, who casts doubt on the wisdom of God and then rationalizes the uninhibited satisfaction of desire. This is the eternal picture of man's moral life. God tells him what is right, but then allows him freedom to see what he will do. Man's desire causes him to become a cynic and indulge in self-expression. The same divine act which creates the possibility of moral character in man opens the door to sin, with all the tragedies which follow upon it. The cause of man's plight is not ignorance of the right, but his own desire, which leads him to substitute his will for the will of God. According to the story of Eden, rebellion against God is the dominant tendency of the human will. By deliberate choice man separates himself from God, who creates him and gives him freedom. It is characteristic of the natural state of man, therefore, to be in need of reconciliation and redemption.

c. The kingdom of God. The third stage in the expression of the divine will, as it is revealed in the Bible, is the creation of the KINGDOM OF GOD. It presupposes, absorbs, and transcends the creation of the natural world and man. In fact, both the earlier processes continue. New forms of energy, life, and morality reveal the continuous action of God's will.

God's kingdom begins in the natural world with one man, but its basic concept is the society in which man lives. It is a social order in harmony with God's will. The biblical story begins with Abraham (Gen. 12:1), and unfolds with the growth of his family and descendants into the Hebrew nation. God prospers his people so long as they keep faith with him. Like Adam, they have to deal with God on a moral basis. The concept of morality is broadened and deepened with the centuries.

In time it was revealed to prophets like Amos (9:7-8) that the Hebrew nationalistic view of God's kingdom was parochial; that God's will included all nations; that God was leading other peoples too; that God's revelation, grace, and redemption were available to all the world. This expanding concept of the kingdom of God was grasped by all the great successors of Amos. The author of Jonah put it into his powerful story as the high point of OT revelation.

But Hebrews found it impossible to give up their nationalistic idea of God's kingdom. This is the basic reason why as a people they rejected Jesus and the Christian gospel of the divine will, in which all forms of nationalism and racialism are repudiated. Building on the broad foundation of the prophets, the NT reveals the will of God to extend his kingdom to every frontier of human habitation. Yet his means of conquest is moral and spiritual. The divine will never coerces man's will, but whoever responds to the overture in Christ finds redemption.

d. Satan overcome. The victory over Satan is the supreme revelation of the will of God in the Bible. Satan finds no place in the early religion of the OT. He appears first in Job 1:1–2:7, where he is the cynical scoffer at moral integrity. Zech. 3:1 gives a glimpse of Satan accusing the high priest before the angel of the Lord. I Chr. 21:1-6 tells how he incited David to introduce military registration. But after these allusions in the late OT writings, Satan achieved full stature as the archrebel against God's will, and the tempter of man. But he also seeks to disorganize, defeat, and destroy man through dangerous creatures of nature (Luke 10:17-19) and diseases, especially mental illness, which the Bible calls demon possession (Luke 11:20; *see* DEMON; DEMONIAC). Satan is also the prince of this world (Matt. 4:8-10), who permits human kings to serve only as his vassals.

In the concept of Satan the struggle of the will of God to establish the kingdom takes place on a transcendental plane. What we have already seen in the creation of nature, man, and the kingdom of God is now absorbed into a struggle between God and Satan, in which no quarter is given. Satan is supported by the demons, while God works through his Son and the angels.

In this last act of the biblical drama we are reminded of the first. Rahab, who was slain by Yahweh, and the serpent, who led Eve astray, are still carrying on their demonic work. The ancient myth related that the dragon was slain, but now we discover that his death was only apparent. The dragon reappears in later Hebrew and Christian thought. From such passages as Rev. 12:7; 20:1-3 we learn that the combat with Satan in the form of the serpent and the dragon goes on till the end of time. The process of creation, therefore, in which Yahweh is imposing his will upon chaos, continues so long as the world stands. This conception of creation pictures God in the agony of an agelong struggle with the hostile, rebellious, recalcitrant spirit of the world, expressed first in nature, second in man, and third in human society. Christian faith affirms that in the cross of Christ, God makes atonement for man, whom Satan has led astray; and that the final encounter comes to its close with the will of God in triumph. *See* RAHAB (DRAGON); SATAN.

3. The humanity of God. In the long course of biblical revelation God is presented in many ways, but usually he has the attributes of a man. The myth of Rahab, as we have seen, presents God as a cosmic warrior. Like a giant with good armor and weapons, he grapples with the foe. Hab. 3:1-16 presents a similar picture, where with his glory filling the heavens God mounts his war chariot, draws his bow from its sheath, fires arrows like bolts of lightning, and casts a spear at the enemy. Judg. 5:4-5 relates how Yahweh came by a swift march from Sinai to rescue the Hebrews from the Canaanites. Isa. 63:1-6 describes God as he returns from the slaughter of Edom covered with blood. It is common in the OT to refer to Yahweh as the God of hosts— i.e., of armies.

Vindictive cruelty is sometimes ascribed to the will of God. Exod. 20:5 represents God as saying that he visits sins of fathers upon their children to the third or fourth generation. According to Josh. 7:24-26, God required the Hebrews to punish Achan for his sin by stoning, not only him, but his sons, daughters, and animals to death, burning them, and raising a heap of stones over them. The same vindictiveness is reflected in II Kings 5:27, where Elisha punishes Gehazi for his avarice by afflicting him with leprosy and saying that the disease would cleave to his descendants forever. From our point of view, this is irrational cruelty, but the idea involved is a logical interpretation of a fact of nature. It is still true with us as it was with them that the sins of a father are visited upon his children. Our courts would not punish a child for his father's crime, but children nevertheless suffer from a father's evil reputation. The saying of Elisha about Gehazi's leprosy was a natural inference the Hebrews drew, lacking scientific medicine as they did, from what we know as natural facts of heredity, infection, or contagion. And if we agree that nature is created by God, we too must still grapple with this same cruel fact.

An arbitrary will is sometimes attributed to God. In the story of Exodus about the escape of the Hebrews from Egypt, it is stated several times that after Pharaoh had made up his mind to let the slaves go, God hardened his heart, so that he broke his promise. Probably the explanation of this strange phenomenon is that the Hebrews made the mistake of ascribing to God the conscienceless immorality of the king, who possessed freedom of will but felt himself bound by no moral law. A somewhat similar episode is the passage from II Sam. 24, where God first incites David to take the registration and then sends a pestilence upon the land because he has done it. But the author of I Chr. 21:1-29, who wrote a revision of this story many years later after ideas of God had changed, says that Satan was the one who incited David to make the registration, but that God punished him for doing it. As a matter of fact,

granting their theological presuppositions, both these writers, unaware of bacteria and contagion, drew logical conclusions from the data.

On the other hand, it is a commonplace in the Bible to assign a tender, flexible, responsive will to God. Gen. 18:22-23 relates that Abraham, in order to save Lot from destruction in Sodom, bargained with God as if he were a merchant in a market place. Jesus reflects the same idea by encouraging his disciples to keep on asking God for what they want. He tells about a widow (Luke 18:1-8) who finally got justice from a harsh judge as a result of her continued pleading. Luke 11:5-8 portrays a man who by persistence was able to arouse his neighbor from sleep and borrow a loaf of bread.

Biblical writers also give prominence to the idea that God's will is controlled by love. A notable example in the OT is Hosea, who presents God first as the faithful husband of Israel the faithless wife, and then as the sad father of Israel the obstinate son. This view is central in the teachings of Jesus and early Christians. Luke 15 tells three great stories —the lost sheep, the lost coin, and the lost son—to illustrate how the divine will is guided by an unfailing love.

One of the most extraordinary concepts of the Bible is that God himself must suffer in order to implement his will. God's love for man chains his omnipotent will as he beholds his own Son die. Because of the identity of Father and Son, Christian faith affirms and contemplates a God who himself dies as the ultimate revelation of his will. *See* GOD, OT VIEW OF; GOD, NT; ATONEMENT; INCARNATION.

4. Will of God and will of man. The question here is the tension between the will of God and the will of man. Does the freedom of man's will condition and set limits to the will of God? When God creates man with freedom, does this inevitably mean that God himself accepts a finite status? The general trend of biblical teaching is that God by an act of his own free will limits himself to the extent of allowing freedom to the will of man. Voluntary self-limitation, however, is far different from saying that God is finite. On the other hand, the Bible teaches that conflict arises between man and God only when man attempts to substitute his own will for the will of God; when man fails to realize that the universe in which he lives—physical, moral, and spiritual— embodies the will of God in its structure; and that a full recognition of this fact is the first presupposition of his own freedom. The freedom of God and the freedom of man do indeed constitute a paradox —not a contradiction—the resolution of which is not futile rebellion of the finite against the infinite, but the insight that it is only in the service of God that man can find freedom. *See* LIBERTY.

5. Will of God and moral law. It is accepted in the Bible that the will of God established the moral law for man. Far more difficult is the question whether God himself obeys the moral law which he prescribes. The question receives various answers. The view of Exod. 20:5 that children suffer for sins of their fathers is repudiated in Deut. 24:16; Jer. 31:29-30; Ezek. 18:2-4. In its place the prophets taught that every man suffers only for his own sin, and its corollary that man gets a just recompense in this life. This is a sound principle as it is applied in courts of law, but when it is used as a theological concept to explain everything that happens in life, whether good or evil, it is dangerous. The idea is challenged and repudiated by the author of Job, who searches in agony for an answer to the question why innocent persons suffer. If the world is controlled by God, how are we to explain irrational tragedies resulting from heredity, infections, catastrophes of nature, and accidents of many kinds? If God is omnipotent, is he good? If he is good, is he omnipotent? If he were both good and all-powerful, would he permit irrational tragedies? One has to face the question whether God's own will is controlled by the moral law. Job's final approach was to recognize the mystery in God and the limitations of human understanding. We can see that the men of Job's time were handicapped by their humanistic view, which limited rewards and punishments to this life; they had not seen that revelation implies a hereafter, in which injustice can be rectified. Further, freedom of will requires the possibility of mistakes, accidents, tragedy. God opens the possibility of tragedy by creating man free. Moreover, through its challenge to intelligence and good will, the stern discipline contributes to moral character. It is one important means God uses in the creation of man.

6. Is anthropomorphism true? The roles attributed to God in the course of this discussion are anthropomorphic. They are roles which men normally take. He is a soldier, king, husband, or father. In each case his temperament is appropriate for the character he takes. Almost all the attributes of man are ascribed to God somewhere in the Bible. In what sense are we to understand these anthropomorphisms? Are they true? The answer is that in these varied symbols biblical writers have attempted to express what they apprehended of the divine revelation. The truth of the symbols is really the question of the validity of biblical faith. That God is personal is the deepest intuition of faith. Roles ascribed to God were refined, broadened, deepened, and came to their culmination in the conception of God as father in the words of Jesus. Faith still provides its own autonomous confirmation in the hearts of believers. *See* MIRACLE § 10.

Bibliography. E. S. Brightman, *A Philosophy of Religion* (1940); R. Niebuhr, *Nature and Destiny of Man*, vol. I (1941); M. Burrows, *Outline of Biblical Theology* (1946); J. A. Nicholson, *Philosophy of Religion* (1950); S. V. McCasland, *By the Finger of God* (1951); P. Tillich, *Biblical Religion and the Search for Ultimate Reality* (1955). S. V. McCasland

WILLOW TREE [צפצפה, *ṣaphṣaphâ;* Arab. *ṣafṣâf*]; **WILLOWS** [ערבים, *'arābhîm;* Arab. *gharab*]. A tree commonly found along water courses, belonging to the genus Salicaceae, which includes both the willows (*Salix* L.) and the poplars (*Populus* L.). Both trees, each with several species, are common in the Near East. The similarity of habitat and certain structural features of these trees may have been responsible for confusion in biblical usage. Many scholars prefer "willow" for צפצפה (found in Ezek. 17:5 only) and "poplar" for ערבים (Lev. 23:40; Job 40:22; Ps. 137:2; Isa. 15:7; 44:4; *cf.* FLORA § A9*t*).

It has been suggested that the latter might refer to the oleander, which grows very prominently in some spring-fed valleys today (*see* ROSE). Willows and poplars are especially prominent along the banks of the Jordan River and other water courses which have a steady supply of water.

The ease with which the willow takes root from a twig is used figuratively in Ezekiel's allegory of the two eagles (17:5; cf. Isa. 44:4). The branches were used with others for the Feast of Booths (Lev. 23:40). The Jews exiled in Babylon hung their lyres on the willows (Ps. 137:2). The "Brook of the Willows" (Isa. 15:7) in Moab may refer to the Wadi el-Hesa (*see* ZERED, BROOK), SE of the Dead Sea. *Cf.* the "willows of the brook" in Job 40:22.

See also ARABAH; POPLAR.

Bibliography. I. Löw, *Die Flora der Juden*, III (1924), 322-40; A. L. and H. N. Moldenke, *Plants of the Bible* (1952), pp. 183-84, 216-18. J. C. TREVER

WILLOWS, BROOK OF THE [נחל הערבים]. A wadi on the frontier of Moab, across which the Moabite fugitives carried their possessions (Isa. 15:7). If, as seems likely, their flight was southward, the wadi in question may be the Seil el-Qurahi, the lower course of the Wadi el-Hesa (*see* ZERED, BROOK). Here there is a small plain, in places rather swampy and suitable for willows. E. D. GROHMAN

WIMPLE. KJV archaism used to translate מטפחת (RSV CLOAK) in Isa. 3:22. A wimple was a covering for the head and neck, worn by women out of doors.

WIND [רוח; πνεῦμα]. There are several uses of the word "wind" in the Bible:

a) The horizontal movement of air, impressing men with its power (Job 21:18), speed (Ps. 18:10— H 18:11), emptiness (Jer. 5:13), immateriality (Eccl. 1:14), rushing sound (Acts 2:2), unpredictability (John 3:8), and variableness (Eph. 4:14). It is often a storm wind (סער, סופה), and a token of God's unseen power, especially in judgment (Hos. 13:15). *See* EAST WIND.

b) The storm wind of Yahweh's theophany (II Sam. 22:11; Ezek. 1:4).

c) The wind (spirit?) which is Yahweh's instrument in overcoming chaos (Gen. 1:2; 8:1), and in transporting a prophet (I Kings 18:12; II Kings 2:16; cf. 2:11; Ezek. 8:3; 11:1).

See also PALESTINE, CLIMATE OF; WHIRLWIND.

R. B. Y. SCOTT

WINDOW [שקף, outlook; Aram. כוין; θυρίς; KJV צהר, light (Gen. 6:16; RSV ROOF); שמשת, sun (Isa. 54:12; RSV PINNACLE)]. In biblical times, a rectangular opening in the wall of a house. It could be covered with latticework, which could be turned aside or through which one could look while it was closed. The movable part was called ארבה, and the opening חלון.

The "windows with recessed frames" (I Kings 6:4; Ezek. 41:16), described also as "narrowing inwards into their jambs" (Ezek. 40:16), in the temple can be illustrated from representations on ivory

By permission of the Palestine Exploration Fund

22. Ivory carving showing window with recessed frame, from Samaria

Courtesy of E. G. Howland

23. Detail of nave of the Jerusalem temple, from model by E. G. Howland, showing pilasters with "proto-Ionic" capitals after examples from Samaria and Megiddo, and windows with recessed frames

plaques from Samaria and Arslan Tash. Figs. TEM 21; WIN 22-23.

See also ARCHITECTURE; HOUSE; LATTICE.

O. R. SELLERS

WINE. From ancient times Palestine-Syria has been famous for the quality and quantity of its wine; Sinuhe reports that "it had more wine than water" (*see bibliography*). It is not surprising that the spies sent by Moses from the wilderness were impressed by the marvelous fruitfulness of the land; they were able to bring back a cluster of grapes so large that it had to be carried on a pole (Num. 13:21-27). Wine was one of the chief products of Israel throughout its history, and is naturally cited by Ben Sirach as one of the "good things . . . created for good people" (Ecclus. 39:25-26). Nor was it of less importance in NT times; wine and oil alone are to be protected from the apocalyptic famine (Rev. 6:6).

  1. Varieties

    a. Terminology

    b. Mixed wine

    c. Wine districts

  2. Preparation

    a. Wine vats

    b. Pressing of grapes

    c. Fermentation and storage

  3. Uses

    a. In everyday life

    b. In offerings

  4. Attitudes toward wine

    a. In the OT

    b. In the NT

  5. Wine in biblical imagery

    a. In the OT

    b. In the NT

  Bibliography

1. Varieties. Although wine made from dates and pomegranates was widely produced in the ancient world generally, Palestinian wine was almost exclusively fermented grape juice (cf. Song of S. 8:2, where "juice of . . . pomegranates" stands in parallel to "spiced wine"). Various methods were used for producing this wine, however, and the varieties are increased by adding spices.

a. Terminology. Some of the following terms for "wine" are synonyms or poetic expressions; in general, however, distinctions can be made between the various words.

a) יין. This Hebrew term, almost always rendered "wine" in both the KJV and the RSV, denotes wine in general. Statistically it is used far more often in the Hebrew Bible than any of its counterparts, and has cognates in other Semitic languages. The word may not be Semitic in origin, however; it is probable that it was imported from the Caucasus (*see bibliography*). The corresponding Greek term is οἶνος.

b) תירוש. Occasionally the KJV and the RSV translate "new wine," but the usual rendering is again simply "wine"; the LXX always uses οἶνος. The term can refer to freshly expressed grape juice (cf. Mic. 6:15: "You shall tread . . . תירוש, but not drink [the resulting] wine"; Isa. 65:8: "The new wine is found in the cluster" [KJV]). Thus the word is usually derived from the Hebrew root ירש, "to drive out." Nevertheless, the drink was intoxicating; it "take[s] away the understanding" (Hos. 4:11). In actual usage the word came to be an archaic term for "wine." It often appears with similar archaisms for "grain" (דגן) and "oil" (יצהר) in summaries of the products of agriculture (Gen. 27:28; Deut. 7:13; 11:14; 18:4; II Kings 18:32; Jer. 31:12; etc.). In later times it was used as a poetic expression for ritual wine; the Qumran texts thus use תירוש to the exclusion of יין (*see bibliography*). In the NT the term γλεῦκος refers to "new wine"; some of those who heard the speaking in tongues at Pentecost thought that the disciples were "filled with new wine" (Acts 2:13).

c) עסיס. Derived from the root עסס, "to press, crush," this term literally means "juice" (cf. Song of S. 8:2), and is apparently a poetic synonym of תירוש. Like the latter, it was intoxicating; Deutero-Isaiah says that Israel's oppressors "shall be drunk with their own blood as with wine" (Isa. 49:26).

d) חמר. This is the usual word in Aramaic (Ezra

6:9; 7:22; Dan. 5:1-2, 4, 23), a poetic term in Hebrew. It is probably derived from חמר I, "to foam, ferment."

Because of its color wine could also be called the "blood of the grape" (Gen. 49:11; Deut. 32:14; Ecclus. 39:26; 50:15; cf. Isa. 63:3; Rev. 14:20). A similar phrase is found in Ugaritic epics (*see bibliography*). It is possible that this terminology was in Jesus' mind when he "took a cup, and . . . gave it to them, saying, 'Drink of it, all of you; for this is my blood of the covenant' " (Matt. 26:27-28; cf. Mark 14:23-24; I Cor. 11:25).

b. Mixed wine. In the Roman period it was quite common to mix wine with water; the author of II Maccabees says that such a mixture "is sweet and delicious and enhances one's enjoyment" (II Macc. 15:39). For the most part, however, the addition of water to wine was considered to be an adulteration. Isaiah says to Jerusalem:

> Your silver has become dross,
> your wine mixed with water
> (Isa. 1:22).

On the other hand, wine was often mixed with spices, following the general usage of the ancient Near East. Such a drink was, of course, especially intoxicating. A cup of "foaming wine, well mixed," is prepared by Yahweh for the wicked of the earth (Ps. 75:8—H 75:9); conversely, mixed wine is appropriate at a banquet (Prov. 9:2, 5; cf. Song of S. 8:2). In general, however, "those who go to try mixed wine" have woe, sorrow, strife, and complaining (Prov. 23:29-30).

Wine mixed with MYRRH or gall was used as a drug; as an act of mercy the soldiers offered Jesus such a potion when he was hanging on the cross (Matt. 27:34; Mark 15:23).

c. Wine districts. In Egypt wines were often named after the districts in which they were produced, and although the Bible does not contain such names for Palestinian wines, certain areas were famous for their products. In Judah the district surrounding Hebron was especially noted; several of the place names have to do with viticulture (*see* ABEL-KERA-MIM; ANAB; BETH-HACCHEREM; ESHCOL 2). Transjordan was also a fruitful district; Isaiah speaks of the vine of Sibmah,

> which reached to Jazer
> and strayed to the desert
> (Isa. 16:8).

But the wines of Syria were world-famous. Among the merchandise sent by Damascus to Tyre were "wine of Helbon . . . and wine from Uzal" (Ezek. 27:18-19). The former is mentioned as one of the ten best brands of wine in a list found in the library of Ashurbanipal, and was preferred above all others by the Persian kings.

2. Preparation. The grapes were harvested in August and September (*see* VINE § 3*e*) and were spread out in the sun for a time before they were made into wine. The vintage took place in September; it is mentioned in connection with the Feast of Booths, which occurs at that general time (Deut. 16:13).

a. Wine vats. Even after the invention of mechanical wine presses the produce of grapes trodden in wine vats was preferred because of its quality and consistency. Such vats, used both in OT and NT times, consisted of a pair of square (occasionally circular) pits, usually hewn out of rocky ground.* The vat in which the grapes were trodden (גת; ληνός) was higher than its counterpart (יקב; ὑπολήνιον) and was connected to it by a channel; naturally the expressed juice flowed from one to the other. In area the upper vat was usually about twice as large as the lower; the latter, however, was deeper. The whole vat could be described by any one of the terms mentioned above, or by the term פורה (Isa. 63:3). There were individual variations in construction, of course; in Roman times three or four vats were connected by channels. Fig. GIB 31.

b. Pressing of grapes. Although heavy stones were sometimes used to hasten the production of juice, the chief method of pressing grapes was simply to

Courtesy of the Oriental Institute, the University of Chicago

24. Men pressing out wine; from tomb of Mereru-ka, Saqqarah; Sixth Dynasty (*ca.* 2350-2200 B.C.)

tread them by foot.* The Hebrew term used is the ordinary word for "walk" (דרך; Neh. 13:15; Job 24:11; Isa. 16:10; etc.). It was customary for several men to tread out the grapes together; this is the point of Trito-Isaiah's reference to treading the wine press alone (Isa. 63:3). Naturally the vintage season was a joyous time. The men shouted as they worked (Isa. 16:10; Jer. 25:30; 48:33), and songs were sung. Three of the psalms (8; 81; 84) have the superscription "according to The Gittith" (על-הגתית); the root is the same as that of one of the terms for "wine vat," and it is possible that these particular psalms were vintage songs. *See bibliography.* Fig. WIN 24.

Since the harvest of olives is later than that of grapes, it is probable that wine vats were also used for making olive OIL. Furthermore, Gideon used his wine vat to beat out wheat (Judg. 6:11).

c. Fermentation and storage. The first stage of fermentation, which began as soon as six hours after the pressing, took place in the lower vat itself. Then the wine was transferred to jars (Jer. 13:12; 48:11) or skins for further fermentation and storage. These skins were usually made from whole goat hides, the neck and the feet being tied. Naturally an opening was left to allow for the escape of gases formed by fermentation. Elihu, "full of words," says:

> Behold, my heart is like wine that has no vent;
> like new wineskins, it is ready to burst
> (Job 32:18-19).

Of course, freshly made wine was put into new wineskins; old skins would burst under the pressure (Matt. 9:17; Mark 2:22; Luke 5:37-38). *See* BOTTLE.

3. Uses. Because WATER was relatively scarce and often polluted in biblical times, wine was used much more extensively than it is today.

a. In everyday life. In addition to its use in everyday meals, wine was liberally provided at banquets (*see* BANQUET); indeed, the Hebrew word for "banquet" or "feast" is משתה, "drinking." Naturally wine was included in gifts to a superior; both Abigail and Ziba brought skins of wine to David (I Sam. 25:18; II Sam. 16:1). Correspondingly wine was an article of trade; Solomon gave the servants of Hiram, king of Tyre, twenty thousand baths of wine (among other things) in return for the timber required in the building of the temple (II Chr. 2:8-10, 15).

At the meal itself wine was strained through a cloth before it was drunk. This purified it from the LEES and foreign matter, such as insects (Matt. 23: 24). Naturally, old wine was preferred to new (Ecclus. 9:10; Luke 5:39) because it was both sweeter and stronger.

Wine was used as a medicine as well as a drink. It revives those who are fainting (II Sam. 16:2), and is generally prescribed "for the sake of your stomach and your frequent ailments" (I Tim. 5:23). Furthermore, it was commonly used in dressing wounds; the Samaritan bound up the traveler's wounds and poured in wine and OIL (§ 2*e;* Luke 10:34).

b. In offerings. Wherever wine is produced, it is used in sacrifices and offerings. Libations were made to false gods (Deut. 32:37-38; Isa. 57:6; 65:11; Jer. 7:18; 19:13; etc.), but this did not prevent the use of wine in the orthodox cult. The worshiper naturally brought a skin of wine whenever he made a pilgrimage to the temple (I Sam. 1:24; 10:3). It is possible, however, that the use of wine replaced an earlier custom of offering blood; however this may be, wine was often treated as if it were blood, and was thus poured out at the base of the altar (Ecclus. 50:15; cf. Jos. Antiq. III.ix.4). But wine was never offered by itself; it was always accompanied by a lamb, fine flour, oil, or a combination of these (Exod. 29:40; Lev. 23:13; Num. 15:7, 10; 28:14; etc.). Wine was not used in the celebration of PASSOVER until Hellenistic times; it is first mentioned in Jub. 49:6. *See* DRINK OFFERING.

4. Attitudes toward wine. Wine is praised and condemned in both the OT and the NT; in this respect a sharp distinction cannot be made between the two testaments. *See* DRUNKENNESS.

a. In the OT. The earliest narratives contained in the OT seem to have a negative attitude toward wine. The J document (*see* PENTATEUCH § A3) presents Noah as the father of viticulture; he proceeds to become drunk and lies naked in his tent. The ultimate result is the curse of Canaan (Gen. 9:20-27; cf. 19:32-35). The prophets carry on this tradition. Isaiah condemns those who

> tarry late into the evening
> till wine inflames them!
> (Isa. 5:11; cf. vs. 22).

Habakkuk contends that "wine is treacherous" (Hab. 2:5; cf. Hos. 4:11), and Micah complains that the people want a preacher who will speak of wine and strong drink (Mic. 2:11). Of course, excessive use of wine by the leaders of the people was especially blameworthy. Trito-Isaiah mocks the "shepherds"

(kings) who are merely interested in procuring wine and filling themselves with strong drink (Isa. 56:11-12; cf. Hos. 7:5), and Isaiah condemns the priests and the prophets who "reel" and "stagger" because of wine (Isa. 28:7). In consequence priests were later forbidden to drink wine when engaged in their duties (Lev. 10:9; Ezek. 44:21).

The book of Proverbs is most explicit in its condemnation of immoderation. Wine is a "mocker" and strong drink a "brawler" (Prov. 20:1); those who inordinately love wine will not be rich (21:17; cf. 23:20-21). The author warns:

> Do not look at wine when it is red,
>   when it sparkles in the cup
>   and goes down smoothly
>   (23:31).

A humorous description of drunkenness follows (vss. 32-35).

As a protest against the orgiastic luxury of Canaanite civilization the Nazirites (*see* NAZIRITE) took vows never to drink wine, strong drink, or any product of the grapevine (Num. 6:3). Even the mother of a Nazirite was forbidden these (Judg. 13:4, 7, 14). A later group, the Rechabites (*see* RECHAB), not only abstained from wine but also refused to build houses (Jer. 35:6-7).

In later times, however, the opposition to wine decreased. The psalmist praises Yahweh for giving "wine to gladden the heart of man" (Ps. 104:15; cf. Judg. 9:13; Eccl. 10:19). Ben Sirach concludes:

> Wine drunk in season and temperately
>   is rejoicing of heart and gladness of soul.
> Wine drunk to excess is bitterness of soul,
>   with provocation and stumbling
>   (Ecclus. 31:28-29).

b. In the NT. Whereas John the Baptist, perhaps following a Nazirite vow, drank no wine (Luke 1:15), Jesus did not refute the charge that he was a "glutton and a drunkard" (Matt. 11:18-19; Luke 7:33-34; cf. 1:15). Thus there is no absolute condemnation of wine in the NT; the recommendation to Timothy has already been noted. Of course, the drinking of wine to excess is disapproved; such immoderation will not prepare one for the coming of the kingdom (Luke 21:34). Furthermore, those in positions of authority are to be especially careful; bishops and deacons are not to be drunkards (I Tim. 3:3, 8). Yet no Christian should become drunk with wine; rather, he should be filled with the Spirit (Eph. 5:18). Drunkenness is characteristic of Gentile culture (I Pet. 4:3); therefore, the thoughtful Christian should not drink any wine at all if it will cause his weaker brother to slip back into Gentile ways (Rom. 14:21).

5. Wine in biblical imagery. Since wine was one of the necessities of life, expressions derived from its production and consumption are commonly used in biblical imagery. *See* VINE § 5.

a. In the OT. God's judgment upon his own people or upon foreign nations is often expressed in terms of a cup of wine; he will force the wicked to drain the cup, and they will reel and stagger (Pss. 60:3—H 60:5; 75:8—H 75:9; Jer. 25:15; 51:7; etc.). Similarly this judgment is compared to the treading out of grapes. As the agents of Yahweh's wrath the nations are commanded:

Put in the sickle,
  for the harvest is ripe.
Go in, tread,
  for the wine press is full.
The vats overflow,
  for their wickedness is great
    (Joel 3:13—H 4:13).

Elsewhere Yahweh is pictured as treading the wine press in his wrath, on a day of vengeance; the peoples of the earth are his victims (Isa. 63:2-6).

Abundance of wine is an expression of God's blessing, however. Isaac asks that God give Jacob "plenty of grain and wine" (Gen. 27:28), and Joel looks forward to the time when "the vats shall overflow with wine and oil" (Joel 2:24; cf. 3:18—H 4:18; Amos 9:13; Zech. 10:7).

b. In the NT. Jesus' comparison of his blood to the cup of wine at the Last Supper (*see* LORD'S SUPPER § 3a) is, of course, the most important use of wine in NT imagery. Elsewhere, however, Jesus compares his new teaching to new wine; it cannot be contained by the old wineskins (Matt. 9:17 and parallels). This is paralleled by the miracle of the changing of water into wine (John 2:1-11); the water probably represents Judaism and the wine Christianity. Finally, the book of Revelation contains several descriptions of God's final judgment in terms of the treading of a wine press (14:19-20; 19:15) and the drinking of a cup of wrath (14:10; 16:19).

See also DRINK; STRONG DRINK.

Bibliography. F. Hommel, "Ueber das Wort Wein im Südsemitischen," *ZDMG,* XLIII (1889), 653. P. Jensen, "Das Wort Wein im Semitischen," *ZDMG,* XLIV (1890), 705. M. Jastrow, Jr., "Wine in the Pentateuchal Codes," *JAOS,* XXXIII (1913), 180-92. R. Kittel, *Die Psalmen,* in E. Sellin, ed., *KAT,* XIII (1914), under Pss. 8; 81; 84. V. Zapletal, *Der Wein in der Bibel,* Bibl. Stud., XX.1 (1920). E. Busse, *Der Wein im Kult des ATs,* Freiburger Theologische Studien, 29 (1922). H. F. Lutz, *Viticulture and Brewing in the Ancient Orient* (1922). J. Döller, "Der Wein in Bibel und Talmud," *Bibl.,* IV (1923), 143-67, 267-99. D. Barthélemy and J. T. Milik, *Qumran Cave I, Discoveries in the Judaean Desert,* I (1955), p. 118, on the use of the term תירוש. J. B. Pritchard, ed., *ANET* (2nd ed., 1955), pp. 19 (on Sinuhe), 133 (on wine as "blood of the grape" in Ugaritic epics). R. J. Forbes, *Studies in Ancient Technology,* III (1955), pp. 70-77.   J. F. ROSS

WINEPRESS. *See* WINE §§ 2, 5.

WINESKIN. *See* WINE § 2c.

WINEVAT. *See* WINE §§ 2, 5.

WING [כָּנָף; πτέρυξ]. A word used in its literal sense (e.g., Gen. 1:21; Lev. 1:17; Deut. 4:17; Job 39:13; Ps. 78:27; Ps. 68:13 may refer to an item from the spoils of war), including a wide variety of nuances (e.g., "skirt" of a garment [Ruth 3:9; cf. 2:12; I Sam. 15:27], "extremity" [Job 37:3; Isa. 11:12]); but most often used figuratively. It appears in descriptions of military attack (Jer. 48:40; 49:22), terror before the enemy (Isa. 10:14), glorious national pride and power (Ezek. 17:3, 7), the sustaining care of Yahweh for Israel (Exod. 19:4; cf. Deut. 32:11), vanishing wealth (Prov. 23:5), the talebearer (Eccl. 10:20), the storm of judgment (Hos. 4:19), the speed of daybreak (Ps. 139:9; cf. 55:6). The "land of whirring wings" (Isa. 18:1; cf. 7:18) may refer to the insect-ridden Nile

Delta, or to the "winged" boats of the Nile. For the winged mythological beasts (Exod. 25:20; Isa. 6:2; Ezek. 1; 3:14; 10; cf. Rev. 4:6 ff; 9:9), *see* CHERUB; SERAPHIM. Winged figures similar to the women of Zech. 5:9 (cf. Rev. 12:14) are found in Eastern folk tales.

Yahweh, conceived as riding through the skies on clouds or cherubim (Deut. 33:26; Pss. 18:10; 68:4; 104:3), moves "on the wings of the wind" (i.e., with dazzling speed) in Pss. 18:10; 104:3. The "wings" of Yahweh are a metaphor of his protection ("shadow" [Pss. 17:8; 36:7; 57:1; 63:7]; "shelter" [Ruth 2:12; Ps. 61:4 (cf. 91:4); Matt. 23:37]), and may refer to the temple in Jerusalem (cf. Pss. 57:1; 61:4; 63:7). Mal. 4:2—H 3:20 apparently alludes to the emblem (originally Egyptian) of the winged sun disk, which was widespread in the ancient Near East, here describing the dawn of the eschatological aeon.

For the five NT occurrences of πτέρυξ, *see also* BIRDS; FOWL; LOCUST.

Bibliography. F. Horst, *Die Zwölf Kleinen Propheten* (1954), pp. 235, 274. R. B. Y. Scott, Exegesis of Isaiah, *IB,* V (1956), 276.   J. A. WHARTON

WINNOWING [זרה; Arab. *zarâ,* scatter, cause to fly; διασκορπίζω, scatter, strew]. The process of throwing the cut stalks of grain into the air so that the kernels will fall into a pile and the refuse will be carried away by the wind. Fig. WIN 25.

Winnowing follows THRESHING (Isa. 41:15-16). At the beginning of the work a FORK is used and later a SHOVEL (Isa. 30:24). It is done on the thresh-

Courtesy of Herbert G. May
25. The winnowing of grain

ing floor in the late afternoon and evening, when the wind will be blowing (Ruth 3:2). As the stalks are tossed, the grain falls at the worker's feet, the straw is carried a short distance, and the CHAFF is often blown beyond the borders of the threshing floor (Matt. 3:12).

Winnowing is often used figuratively to represent the destruction of evil (e.g., Jer. 15:7; 51:2).

          H. N. RICHARDSON

WINTER. *See* SUMMER AND WINTER; PALESTINE, CLIMATE OF.

*WISDOM [חכמה; σοφία; *rarely, also,* φρόνησις]. A quality of mind distinguishing the wise man, by virtue of which he is skilled and able to live well and both succeed and counsel success; also a quality in itself apart from man, above and beyond man, existing ideally with God and imparting form to creation.

In what follows, the concrete manifestations of wisdom in (*a*) the wise man and (*b*) the literature of wisdom are considered before the abstraction, (*c*) Wisdom.

1. The wise man
   a. At court
   b. Royal wisdom
   c. In extrabiblical literature
   d. Prophets and the wise
   e. Wise men at large
2. The literature of wisdom
   a. The proverb
   b. The book of Proverbs
   c. Job
   d. Ecclesiastes
   e. Daniel and IV Maccabees
   f. Wisdom psalms
   g. Ecclesiasticus
   h. The Wisdom of Solomon
3. "Where shall wisdom be found?"
   a. In man
   b. With God
Bibliography

1. The wise man. The wise man is many things, from artisan to astrologer, from parent to philosopher. And he is found in the royal court as well as the academy.

a. At court. Biblical writers often refer to the wise man in a way which suggests that being wise was an occupation, and one which brought men to the attention of kings. Professional wise men were, indeed, frequently resident in the courts of kings, and not in Jerusalem alone but in other world capitals as well.

One of the latest biblical books contains one of the most detailed descriptions of such wise men of the court. A legend in Daniel lays the scene in the court of the Babylonian king Nebuchadnezzar. Troubled by a dream, this sly monarch demands of his "wise men" that they both relate and interpret his dream; and when they insist that he has required the impossible, he orders the execution of their whole corporation, Daniel and his three companions among them. But Daniel with God's help declares and explains the dream, and so saves his own life and theirs.

The general term "wise men" (Aramaic חכימיא; Dan. 2:12-14) includes the "magicians, the enchanters, the sorcerers, and the Chaldeans" (Hebrew חרטמים, אשפים, מכשפים, and כשדים; Dan. 2:2) as well as "astrologers" (Aramaic גזרין; 2:27; 4:7—Aramaic 4:4; 5:7). Daniel and his companions, who were counted among the wise, are "skilful in all wisdom [חכמה], endowed with knowledge [דעת], understanding learning [מדע], and competent to serve in the king's palace"; furthermore, they were "educated" for three years "to teach them the letters [ספר] and language of the Chaldeans," before they took up their duties (1:4-5). Daniel himself, divinely endowed (2:19-23), is especially gifted in the understanding of visions and dreams (1:17, 20), and rises to the position of "chief prefect over all the wise men of Babylon" (2:48; cf. 5:11-12). But Daniel can also

prescribe for the king the practice of righteousness (4:27—Aram. 4:24).

Though legendary and later and given an imaginary setting, this developed picture of the wise man at the royal court throws light upon the numerous less detailed descriptions of the wise scattered through the Bible. Two of the classes of wise men in this court with Daniel bear the same titles as their colleagues in the court of the Egyptian pharaohs and recall the days of Moses and Aaron. These are the "sorcerers" (מכשפים) and the "magicians" (חרטמים) of Egypt, who match their skill against the skill of the Israelites. When God, through Moses and Aaron, demanded the release of his people from Egyptian bondage, the pharaoh would not "listen" and had to be convinced. To this end Moses and Aaron performed miracles in his presence, but he "summoned the wise men and the sorcerers; and they also, the magicians of Egypt, did the same by their secret arts" (Exod. 7:11; cf. 7:22; 8:7). The success of the pharaoh's wise men was, however, limited; once "they could not," and admitted: "This is the finger of God" (8:18-19—H 8:14-15), and in the denouement "the magicians could not stand before Moses . . . , for the boils were upon the magicians" (9:11); grievous was their defeat. In the contest of magic-wisdom Moses and his brother were, like Daniel and his companions, "ten times better than all the magicians and enchanters" (Dan. 1:20)—and were so because through them God worked his wonders to show forth his power to the end that his name might "be declared throughout all the earth" (Exod. 9:15-16; cf. 7:3-5; Isa. 19:11-12). This wisdom contest is a feature of the "priestly" version of the Exodus narrative—written not too many centuries before the Daniel legends.

Another Israelite in an Egyptian court also resembled Daniel; this was Joseph, whose success as an interpreter of dreams won him advancement, and prefigured Daniel's experience. As Potiphar's slave Joseph gave evidence of superior intelligence (Gen. 39:1-6), and he did not lose his gifts when apparent misfortune sent him to prison (39:21-23). It was there also that he first gave evidence of the God-given wisdom which made him an interpreter of dreams (Gen. 40) and brought him to the attention of Pharaoh. When this pharaoh dreamed, he called "all the magicians of Egypt and all its wise men" (41:8), but it was only after they brought Joseph from the dungeon that the dreams yielded their meaning (41:9-32). Furthermore, Joseph gave sound advice and, being recognized as superior in discretion and wisdom through the spirit of God, became great in the land, second only to Pharaoh (41:33-44).

These three situations (first Joseph, then Moses and Aaron at the Egyptian court, and Daniel at the court of Babylonia) have this in common: in a contest with the wise men of the foreign court, with the help of God the Hebrews triumph. Parts of the Second Isaiah further illustrate this theme—God's agents defeat the "wise men" in Babylon's court. It is Israel's God

who frustrates the omens of liars,
    and makes fools of diviners;
who turns wise men back,
    and makes their knowledge foolish;

who confirms the word of his servant,
and performs the counsel of his messengers
(Isa. 44:25-26a).

At the approach of Cyrus the conquerer, Israel's God taunts the arrogant "daughter of Babylon" (Isa. 47) and refers with special scorn to the court astrologers. Like the magicians in Egypt, they suffer humiliation and disaster:

Let them stand forth and save you,
those who divide the heavens,
who gaze at the stars,
who at the new moons predict
what shall befall you.
Behold, they are like stubble,
the fire consumes them;
they cannot deliver themselves
from the power of the flame
(Isa. 47:13 [with a minor correction], 14a; cf. Jer. 50:35-38;
51:57).

Somewhat more may be added as concerns the "wise" at foreign courts according to biblical tradition. There were wise women in the court of Sisera (not, probably, the "general of Jabin's army," as he is called in Judg. 4:7, but by his own right king of a Canaanite city), and these too are the butt of cruel irony, in the "song of Deborah" (Judg. 5:29-30). The counselors in foreign courts seem mostly to have been futile (cf. also II Kings 6:8, 11-12), and their advice is sometimes more amusing than sound, as when the wise men about the Persian Ahashuerus advised approximately that every man should "be lord in his own house" (Esth. 1:13-22; cf. 2:2). Another Persian king, Artaxerxes, had a staff of "seven counselors" (Ezra 7:14-15); among the wise men at the courts of foreign kings, of these alone no evil is spoken. (See also I Esd. 3:1–4:41.)

It was not foreign courts alone which according to the biblical sources had their resident wise men. There were official advisers at the courts of Israelite kings as well, distinguished not so much by reason of their magical powers, powers of divination, and insight into the meaning of dreams (though such appear in Isa. 3:3), as by their political sagacity, wisdom, and judgment. No one in this capacity was more famous than David's traitorous counselor AHITHOPHEL (II Sam. 15:31-37; 16:20–17:23); "the counsel which Ahithophel gave was as if one consulted the oracle of God" (16:23). David had at least one other such aid; his uncle Jonathan "was a counselor, being a man of understanding and a scribe" (I Chr. 27:32). Two of David's sons took counsel with various persons—the rebellious Absalom with Hushai (II Sam. 17:14) as well as Ahithophel, and the lovesick Amnon with Jonadab, reputedly a wise man (II Sam. 13:3: "crafty"). The statesman Joab gained David's ear by way of a wise woman from Tekoa (II Sam. 14:1-24). Twice besides, we hear of wise women—the wise woman of Abel, who effectively appealed to this same Joab to spare her city (II Sam. 20:16-22), and the wise women in the court of Sisera (*see above*). Rehoboam, son of Solomon, forsook the sage counsel of the old men of Solomon's court (so the wise king Solomon also had his royal counselors) and acted according to the counsel of his rash contemporaries there, and to his grief (I Kings 12:3-14).

It is particularly in the days of this cluster of kings, David, Solomon, and Rehoboam, that we read of wise men at the Israelite court to match the magicians, sorcerers, diviners, and astrologers at the courts of Egypt, Babylonia, Persia, and the other nations. But it would be a mistake to assume that only in those early times the kings had their counselors. It is safe to infer from II Chr. 25:16-17 that the expression "royal counselor" was still in use some centuries later. There, silencing a prophet who dared criticize him, King Amaziah asks of the prophet: "Have we made you a royal counselor?" According to Deuteronomy, Moses, though not a king, had a staff of "wise, understanding, and experienced men" (1:9-15; cf. Exod. 18:19-22); for this description the Deuteronomist may have drawn upon his experience of royal courts.

b. Royal wisdom. As Moses towered above the wise and experienced men with whom he surrounded himself, so according to the tradition Solomon outshone his professional advisers. Solomon is renowned as the biblical exemplar of royal wisdom.

David, his father, was graced with intelligence as a youth (I Sam. 16:18) and recognized for his wisdom in old age (II Sam. 14:20). But it is Solomon who is celebrated as the wise king. David was aware of this son's potential for wisdom (I Kings 2:6, 9; cf. I Chr. 22:12). According to the account his potential was realized when God appeared in his dream and granted his request: "an understanding mind," "understanding to discern what is right," "wisdom and knowledge" (I Kings 3:5-14; II Chr. 1:7-12). According to the order of the narrative in Kings, Solomon's wisdom was immediately put to the test in a difficult case at law, and all Israel stood in awe at the divine wisdom he then displayed in rendering justice (I Kings 3:16-28; for a much later parallel cf. Sus. 44-62). But so excellent was his wisdom that his fame at once spread abroad beyond the borders of his land: "God gave Solomon wisdom and understanding beyond measure, and largeness of mind like the sand on the seashore, so that Solomon's wisdom surpassed the wisdom of all the people of the east, and all the wisdom of Egypt. For he was wiser than all other men, wiser than Ethan the Ezrahite, and Heman, Calcol, and Darda, the sons of Mahol; and his fame was in all the nations round about. He also uttered three thousand proverbs; and his songs were a thousand and five. He spoke of trees, from the cedar that is in Lebanon to the hyssop that grows out of the wall; he spoke also of beasts, and of birds, and of reptiles, and of fish. And men came from all peoples to hear the wisdom of Solomon, and from all the kings of the earth, who had heard of his wisdom" (I Kings 4:29-34—H 5:9-14; cf. 5:12a—H 5:26a). Hiram, the king of Tyre, acknowledged Solomon's wisdom (I Kings 5:7—H 5:21; II Chr. 2:11-12); and Solomon had no greater admirer than the queen of distant Sheba, who "came to test him with hard questions" and had to exclaim in breathless astonishment: "Behold, the half was not told me; your wisdom and prosperity surpass the report which I heard" (I Kings 10:1-9; II Chr. 9:1-8). But she was not alone; because "Solomon excelled all the kings of the earth . . . in wisdom," "all the kings of the earth sought the presence of Solomon to hear his wisdom, which God had put into his mind" (I Kings 10:23-24; II Chr. 9:22-23).

The biblical tales of wise men at the courts of foreign kings are tendentious and polemical, designed to glorify Israel's God and his agents and to unmask all pretenders. The stories told of Solomon have the flavor of folk tales and legend, and they too may not be used uncritically as historical records. Undoubtedly, Solomon was a great organizer and administrator, and his rule brought to the united kingdom new prosperity and prestige; but the tales that are told of him are the efforts of later generations to recover in fancy the then vanished splendor of his glorious times. The attribution to him in the passage in Kings of proverbs and songs is a part of the trend which made him also the author of Proverbs, the Song of Songs, and Ecclesiastes among the biblical books, and of the Wisdom of Solomon of the Apoc.

A passage in Ezekiel also speaks of royal wisdom, this time ironically, in a barb aimed at the king of Tyre (Ezek. 28:2-10; cf. vss. 12-19); another, in Isa. 10:12-13, mocks the presumed wisdom of the king of Assyria; and yet another satirizes the princes of Zoan, sons of ancient Egyptian kings, for their pretense of wisdom (Isa. 19:11-13; cf. also Jer. 10:7; Dan. 8:23).

In view of the biblical tendency to attribute wisdom to kings, it is perhaps not strange that parts of the literature of wisdom should be attributed to King Solomon, or that Hezekiah should be known as a patron of the art of wisdom (Prov. 25:1), together with an unknown King Lemuel, of an unknown kingdom (Prov. 31:1).

Also, it is quite natural that wisdom should be ascribed to the awaited messianic king, descended like Solomon from David, and destined to reign in equal splendor. Properly, then, his symbolic name contains as its first element "Wonderful Counselor" (Isa. 9:6—H 9:5), and he is described as one upon whom "the Spirit of the LORD shall rest,"

> the spirit of wisdom and understanding,
> the spirit of counsel and might,
> the spirit of knowledge and the fear of the LORD
> (Isa. 11:2; cf. Prov. 8:15-16).

The data suggest a tendency in biblical times to associate wisdom, both foreign and domestic, in early times and late, with kings and the courts of kings. Literature of the ancient Near East, other than the Bible, has this same characteristic.

c. In extrabiblical literature. Beyond question, the wise man in Israel was part of a general pattern of culture in the ancient Near East. The biblical sources did not invent the fact; there were wise men in the courts of Egypt, Babylonia, Persia, and other neighboring lands. There were kings and others with a reputation for superior wisdom among "all the people of the east." And, for a fact, recorded wisdom in Egypt and the Assyrian-Babylonian cultures was predominantly royal wisdom or wisdom of royal counselors. It was the concern of pharaohs and kings to educate their sons as their successors. The concern of viziers was to train their sons to serve royalty, and wisdom was the content of knowledge in the schools for the royal scribes. The address "my son" is the mode (in that literature as it is in Proverbs), and success is usually the goal of instruction. What most

frequently is taught is prudent behavior, conduct befitting kings, conduct for one who would stand before kings. This type of instruction makes up a large part of the preserved Egyptian and Akkadian wisdom literature (*see bibliography*) but not all of it. There is instruction likewise for everyone, observations too on life and man's fate, much that has a kinship with biblical wisdom in mood and matter.

The common ground occupied by biblical and other Near Eastern wisdom literature is considerable, but the discovery of this common ground has sometimes led to excessive claims. So close is the correspondence between the "thirty chapters" of Amenem-opet and Prov. 22:17-23:14 that the influence of the Egyptian source itself, or at any rate some derivative source, upon this section of Proverbs is pretty much beyond question (*see* PROVERBS, BOOK OF, § 8). More general but quite probable is the influence also of Canaanite (Ugaritic) and Akkadian sources here and there upon biblical wisdom. The dependence of Proverbs on the Aramaic sayings of Ahiqar is possible but not beyond question. It would be futile and pointless to deny that the wisdom literature of the Bible is a segment of the "wisdom of the east"—but the fact remains that much of the influence of Egypt, Phoenicia, or Babylonia upon biblical wisdom is more diffuse than specific. A considerable area of the specific contact is that in which wisdom is associated with kings and officials of the court.

d. Prophets and the wise. It is quite probable that when Isaiah, Jeremiah, and Ezekiel spoke of the wise, they too referred to advisers in the courts of Judean kings. Isaiah might very well have meant the political counselors of King Hezekiah when, in 29:14 and again in 29:15 plus 30:1-5, he spoke of the wise whose counsel was resistance with the expectation of aid from Egypt (cf. 36:4-6), although God's counsel was otherwise (cf. 31:1-2). Jeremiah and Ezekiel may have meant the same (with changes in terms to suit their times). When Jeremiah complained of those who said: "Come, let us make plots against Jeremiah, for the law shall not perish from the priest, nor counsel from the wise, nor the word from the prophet" (Jer. 18:18), and when Ezekiel threatened: "Disaster comes upon disaster . . . ; they seek a vision from the prophet, but the law perishes from the priest, and counsel from the elders" (Ezek. 7:26), both seemingly pointed to a defined group or caste, which the one called the "wise" and the other called the "elders." Both of these contemporary prophets knew of a group distinguished from priests and from prophets, a group whose function was to provide עֵצָה, "counsel." Ezekiel's elders are surely to be equated with Jeremiah's wise men (cf. Deut. 32:7; Job 12:12; 32:7; *see* AGE, OLD, § 4); their social role is the same.

Now since Jeremiah's activity must often have appeared to be political, as when he counseled submitting to Babylonia, and since he thus came into conflict with the king's official family, the wise men who were plotting against him may quite well have been the royal counselors; since also the disaster foreseen by Ezekiel would have meant egregious failure for their foreign policy, he too may have pointed the finger at the king's "brain trust," then about to be repudiated, as he thought, by the march of events. Listed along with the "mighty man" and the "rich man" in Jer. 9:23—H 9:22, the "wise man" here too, though not quite so clearly, appears to be one of a distinguishable group, not impossibly officials of the royal court.

The use of the word עצה, "counsel," in these latter passages strengthens the impression that these wise men are the king's counselors; it does so because it aligns these passages with the many which set off God's counsel against that of the strutting nations and taunt the obviously weaker. Passages cited above (§ 1a) ridicule the putative wise men of other nations whose counsel is to yield before God's (cf. also Isa. 7:5-7; 8:10; 14:24-27; 46:10; the thought is frequently expressed). Now Judah with its wise men, the royal counselors in the court at Jerusalem, takes its place among those whose counsel must yield before God's. Isaiah, Jeremiah, and Ezekiel introduce this ironical note. It sounds quite clearly through a passage like Isa. 5:19, 21, where the prophet pronounces a woe upon "those who are wise in their own eyes" and who flout "the purpose of the Holy One of Israel" (cf. Jer. 19:7; Ezek. 11:2).

e. Wise men at large. It would, however, be wrong to count all the wise, so styled in prophetic literature, among the kings and the royal counselors. A prophet can use the word "wise" and be speaking quite generally. It is still possible that Jeremiah is speaking to a group of the king's advisers—those, namely, who supported Josiah in the deuteronomic program—when in 8:8-9 he demands of them:

> How can you say, "We are wise,
> and the law of the LORD is with us"?
> But, behold, the false pen of the scribes
> has made it into a lie.
> The wise men shall be put to shame,
> they shall be dismayed and taken;
> lo, they have rejected the word of the LORD,
> and what wisdom is in them?

Jeremiah's equation here of "wise men" and "scribes" supports, rather than casts doubt upon, their being counted among the king's counselors; note the similar equation in I Chr. 27:32; Dan. 1:17. But Jeremiah is not pointing to any single professional group when he says of God's people:

> They are stupid children,
> . . . .
> skilled [wise] in doing evil,
> but how to do good they know not
> (4:22).

And it would certainly be wrong to put a narrow limitation on the sorts of persons that in biblical literature as a whole are termed wise. The varieties are many. Persons possessing certain skills are counted among those who bear the title: Bezalel and Oholiab (Exod. 31:2-6; 35:30—36:2) and many unnamed craftsmen, and skilled women as well, who worked on the wilderness tabernacle and its fittings (Exod. 28:3; 35:10, 25-26; 36:4, 8) or on Solomon's temple in Jerusalem (I Kings 7:14; I Chr. 22:15; II Chr. 2:7, 13-14—H 2:6, 12-13); these were possessed of חכמה, of "wisdom," and even a craftsman who wasted his talents fashioning an idol might be called a חכם (Isa. 40:20; Jer. 10:9). The same word was used of skilled pilots and shipbuilders in Ezek. 27:8-9, and Jeremiah referred to women as wise by virtue of their training in the art of lamentation:

> Call for the mourning women to come;
> send for the skilful women to come
> (Jer. 9:17—H 9:16).

In addition, then, to the aristocracy of the wise, the officially wise, there were in Israel the simply wise. These were not only the skilled and experienced, the workmen with technical knowledge, those learned in the ancient arts and lore; the elders, the fathers and the mothers, the teachers in the schools for wisdom, the writers of songs and fables and allegories, the makers of riddles and proverbs, the judges, the philosophers, were also among the wise. A definition too narrow would be false.

The literature, particularly those biblical and apocryphal books known as the wisdom literature, reveals the diffusion of wisdom in Israel, though it was, in fact, somewhat upper-class and not really for the masses. The most of it pertains to the leisure class (cf. Ecclus. 38:24-25). The follies, the virtues, and the attitudes illustrated in the literature have their home in upper-class society, and here too the literature has a purpose (*see* PROVERBS, BOOK OF, § 10; SIRACH, SON OF). In the book of Proverbs (but no longer in Job) there is about wisdom something of the smugness of the fortunate.

Though mostly reserved for the gentry, the appeal of wisdom was general, and its custodians were many. Parents and elders had knowledge and experience:

> Ask your father, and he will show you;
> your elders, and they will tell you
> (Deut. 32:7).

> Wisdom is with the aged
> (Job 12:12; cf. 32:7).

It seems conventional in wisdom literature to address the learner as "son," in Egyptian and Akkadian wisdom (*see* § 1c *above*) as well as in Proverbs and Ecclesiasticus; the use of the term does not, then, prove that a parent is speaking. Usually the "father" in this literature is the master of the academy or the author of the text; nevertheless, occasionally, as in Prov. 31:1; 4:3-4, the words must be taken literally—fathers and mothers share with their sons their wisdom.

Elders, teachers, and parents were custodians of a tradition, in part a literary tradition. They had at hand collections of sayings that were known as "words of the wise" (cf. Prov. 22:17; 24:23), an expression which in turn identifies the wise with poets and writers of proverbs (*see* PROVERB § 3a), and sages who sought to put in brief and vivid language and in a variety of literary forms the yield of their learning and experience. The wise also were persons versed in law and letters qualified to serve as judges in the gates (cf. I Kings 3:28; Deut. 16:18-20: "A bribe blinds the eyes of the wise") and as recorders (Isa. 36:3) and scribes (I Chr. 27:32; Jer. 8:8-9; Dan. 1: 17). Finally, among the wise are to be counted the great independent thinkers who created books like Job and Ecclesiastes and other related but less extensive compositions, some of them now lodged among the Psalms. Of such variety were the "wise men" of Israel in Bible times.

2. The literature of wisdom. What the wise men taught and wrote has been preserved in part in the biblical books of Proverbs, Job, and Ecclesiastes, in some of the Psalms, and in brief passages in other contexts. Some of their writings were not received into the canon and are counted among the apocryphal books (Ecclesiasticus, Wisdom of Solomon) and among the other literary products of early Judaism (e.g., IV Maccabees).

a. The proverb. The seed of wisdom literature, the *māshāl* or PROVERB in its primitive form, is ubiquitous, common to all cultures and times; and no doubt it always existed in Israel. Old men said: "Like mother, like daughter" (Ezek. 16:44), and that settled the matter; or they said: "Out of the wicked comes forth wickedness" (I Sam. 24:13—H 24:14), or "Physician, heal yourself" (Luke 4:23), to suit the situation, and believed they had given expression to a profound truth tested by the generations. There is no reason to suppose that the art form of the proverb developed late in biblical times. On the contrary, poetic bits occur among the earliest literary remains in the Bible, and proverbs in rhythmic form may well have circulated in Israel in premonarchic days. The supposition is strengthened by the observation that such proverbs appear in prebiblical Ugaritic sources, for which literature the Bible has many affinities, and the further observation that Egyptian wisdom, which demonstrably influenced biblical wisdom literature (*see* § 1*c above*), has the developed art form and antedates biblical literary production. Proverbs in parallelistic form surely circulated in Israel in earliest times, but to determine which, if any, of such proverbs preserved in the Bible go back to most ancient times is beyond the reach of sober scholarship. Most of those which have come down to us are probably the result of the literary activity of sages in the academies. That portion of Proverbs (22:17–23:14) which is related to Amen-em-opet is not just a translation of the Egyptian; it is a product of conscious creative literary art by a Jewish wisdom writer who was acquainted with the earlier composition in some form or other.

As well as the proverb in its primitive and its rhythmic form, other wisdom types circulated in early times. A certain skill akin to wisdom went into the propounding as well as the solving of riddles. When he solved all her riddles, the queen of Sheba was impressed by the wisdom of Solomon (I Kings 10:1-5; cf. Dan. 5:12). The RIDDLE was a form of folk wisdom from early times onward, and it could be adapted for prophetic utterance. The numbers proverb too: "Three things . . . ; four . . ." (Prov. 30:18-19), may be a descendant. Also the FABLE was a product of wisdom and served a didactic purpose. The tradition that the wise Solomon "spoke of trees" and "spoke also of beasts" (I Kings 4:33—H 5:13) may mean simply that he was a maker of fables. The PARABLE and the ALLEGORY, the byword and the taunt (*see* PROVERB § 2*d*), are forms all more or less related to the proverbial literature of wisdom, and examples of these are scattered throughout the Bible (e.g., the "discourses" of Balaam).

b. The book of Proverbs. The earliest extensive wisdom document is the book of Proverbs (*see* PROVERBS, BOOK OF). Although a section of the book is related ultimately to an Egyptian composition which took form in the second pre-Christian millen-

nium, although there are traces of Canaanite-Phoenician influence from the same millennium, although folk wisdom from dim antiquity undoubtedly left its mark upon the book, although the possibility exists that the tradition concerning Solomon's interest in proverbs has some basis in fact, and although, finally, the editor who referred to the activity of the men of the King Hezekiah in Prov. 25:1 believed he had some fairly early material before him, the probability is nevertheless very great that the actual authors of the book of Proverbs were wisdom teachers of the fifth or fourth pre-Christian centuries and that these then newly expressed in artistic forms some more ancient wisdom, but mostly created from experience and reflection new texts for the guidance of the youngest generation.

This is the nature of Proverbs, a book designed to help the youth of its day achieve success in life and avoid all snares and dangers. It is an optimistic book, in the sense that it finds an order in the world which a man can know and, knowing, conform with to his benefit. It is this naïve optimism which both characterizes its wisdom and suggests approximately when it was written. A fairly just and individual accounting and balancing is assumed, so that a person will get what he deserves of life; let him only not be a fool, let him act with prudence, and God's justice and the natural law of compensation will do the rest. This complete and unquestioning acceptance of the doctrine of retribution on the *individual* level means that the contest of Ezek. 18 was among the "battles long ago." The belief in rewards for personal merit and penalties for personal guilt has become an orthodoxy, and righteousness can be equated with wisdom and evil with folly (*see* FOOL). Even as the book of Proverbs presupposes Ezekiel (by at least a generation or two in the slow-moving East), Job and Ecclesiastes presuppose Proverbs (*see below*).

The book contains a certain variety of materials; single, balanced-line proverbs preponderate, but there are discourses as well, discourses on such subjects as the advantage of wisdom, the folly of unchastity, the worth of the good wife; and there are keen observations on human nature and fine poetic similes.

c. Job. The book of JOB is the unchallenged best of the wisdom literature. Its poetic eloquence, its majesty and profundity, are unexcelled—and not in the literature of biblical wisdom alone but in world literature. Daringly its author explores religion in its deepest depths. For his purpose he chooses dialogue as his literary medium; he sets the perplexing scene with a narrative, introduces interlocutors, and then puts in their mouths his discourses. He chooses as his central figure the pious Job of legend (cf. Ezek. 14:14) and associates with Job three friends whom he brings from the East, traditionally a home of wise men. His device converts a treatise into a living drama; in the dialogue which grows out of the narrative, although each man's thought becomes a discourse, the argument develops vividly with mounting intensity until Job rests his case and God has the last word.

The progress of the thought is marred by the confused order of the text in the third round of discourses (chs. 22–27), by the introduction of an anti-climax in the person of a fourth friend, Elihu (chs. 32–37), and by the addition of a poem glorifying wisdom (ch. 28), a great poem which, however, where it stands, blunts the point of the Job drama. Other parts may be secondary (parts of God's answer, a part of the narrative epilogue), but they do not so much disturb the exposition of the thought.

It is the thought which permits a guess at the time when the book was written. The absolute date of the book of Job is by no means apparent, but Job seems to follow on the book of Proverbs—or at least on most of the matter which makes up that book. In the age in which the argument of Job was conceived the dominant spirit was the spirit of Proverbs. It is the proverbialists' uncritical acceptance of their dogmatic position on personal retribution which compelled the author of Job to write his book. And this suggests that he wrote after Proverbs, perhaps early in the fourth century, though such a date is hardly more than an informed guess.

Job is a religious book. Its author does not deny providence—that would be leaving the orbit of religion. What he denies is the simple arithmetic of divine justice; so doing, he attacks the arrogance of the fortunate and reassures all persons (like Job) who are perplexed by adversity. The author of Job had learned that man is more complicated and God less transparent than the teachers of proverbs and their complacent clients assumed. The orthodox view of those teachers appears in the discourses of Job's three friends (and of the appended fourth); the author himself becomes articulate through Job and God, and he leaves us with his own loyal reservations. Far from denying God or the fact of his dealings with men, he ends by siding with God, with whom he feels sympathy and whose nearness he prizes above all.

The book of Job is a product of the wisdom schools; its author was among the wise, but he stands out as a man apart, a rare religious genius. He gives of his nobility to the literature of wisdom.

d. Ecclesiastes. The book of ECCLESIASTES, another of the wisdom books, is, like Job, the product of a genial, independent, philosophic spirit. Though the book was attributed to Solomon, as Proverbs was, we do not know who wrote it. Its anonymous author, writing with the pen name "Koheleth," was a cultured and cosmopolitan, probably wealthy, elderly sage in Jerusalem who lived in the latter half of the third century.

The book is a fairly unified work with a minimum of glosses, such as there are being mostly designed to correct the false doctrine that the virtuous go unrewarded and the sinful without penalty. For the book Ecclesiastes is shockingly heterodox, and it is not surprising that the authorities thought well before admitting it to the canon, noticing that it contains contradictions and that it is indeed no divine revelation but one man's opinion.

Like the author of Job, the writer of Ecclesiastes was notable in his time for his free and inquiring mind. He took the position that a person knows only what through experience and reflection he finds out for himself. To himself Koheleth said he believed nothing which he had not personally tested; this he said, but he was in fact less free than he would admit. As concerns right and wrong, he used a conventional vocabulary in a conventional sense, and his attitudes were benevolent. He only said he recognized no standards; his behavior was probably quite correct in all particulars.

Koheleth set out to discover what it is good for a man to do the few days of his life. He experimented with folly and with drink, with commerce and with the arts; he considered the nature of wisdom and the ways of human society; and he concluded that, when all is seen and done, everything is only "vanity and a striving after wind" (1:14), and the best that men can do is "to be happy and enjoy themselves as long as they live" (3:12 and often) and in all things be moderate: neither too wise and good nor yet too wicked and foolish (7:16-18a). This is the benevolently casual attitude which Koheleth achieved. And certain general considerations buttressed his conclusions: There is too much in life that we do not and cannot know (7:23-24; 8:16-17). Moreover, the fate of the righteous and the fate of the wicked are distressingly the same, and "the dead know nothing" (9:2-5).

This argument runs no straight course in Ecclesiastes; the unity is one of mood rather than order. The author's musings frequently take the form of groups of balanced-line sayings (e.g., 7:1-13) which are both reminiscent of Proverbs and characteristic of Koheleth, being tinged with his own brand of humor and irony.

e. Daniel and IV Maccabees. The book of DANIEL is apocalypse and only incidentally related to wisdom —through the person of the wise Daniel, reader of riddles and interpreter of dreams (see § 1a above). And yet, to some extent Daniel (ca. 167 B.C.) looks forward to a book like IV Maccabees (ca. A.D. 100), in which martyrs for the faith prove that reason is stronger than the human passions, even as Daniel and his companions had proved that God protects from martyrdom the faithful. Both books would educate men to loyalty and fortitude. See MACCA-BEES, BOOKS OF, § E.

f. Wisdom psalms. Among the canonical psalms are a number which share features with the other wisdom literature (see PSALMS, BOOK OF, § B3); the house of instruction was not independent of the house of prayer. Though books like Proverbs, Job, and Ecclesiastes do not give evidence of a lively interest in temple service, or ritual, or devotion, the wisdom teachers prayed. And it is natural to find wisdom within the devotional literature.

The spirit of some of the psalms is akin to the spirit of Proverbs—their authors were fully confident, like Job's friends, that rewards and punishments are dealt out in just measure (Pss. 1; 34; 37; cf. Jer. 17:5-8) and commended the way of righteousness (Pss. 92; 112; 127—128; 133) or life according to the law (Ps. 19:7-14—H 19:8-15). Similar, but related rather to the Deuteronomic histories, a psalm like 78 draws lessons from Israel's national experience and counsels obedience and faithfulness. The author of one psalm (73) struggled, as did the author of Job, with the problems which the apparent miscarriage of divine justice present, and his psalm is a record of notable achievement. Like Job, he did not take refuge in the expectation of heavenly reward (this is not the meaning of vs. 24, the Hebrew text of which is in disorder); instead, he found complete satisfaction of his earthly desires in the consciousness of his kinship with God: "It is good to be near God" (vs. 28; cf. vs. 25). The writer of another psalm (49) shared some sentiments with Koheleth, shared at least his wistful skepticism:

> Man cannot abide in his pomp,
> he is like the beasts that perish
> (vss. 12, 20—H 13, 21);

"even the wise die" (vs. 10—H 11), and man can "carry nothing away" (vs. 17—H 18). Unlike Koheleth, the writer of this psalm offered no remedy, even temporary; he only published his sad knowledge of life's vanity (vs. 15—H 16 is a gloss like those in ECCLESIASTES § 6, designed to absorb some of the shock of his unorthodox views, and it does not, at any rate, refer to life after death).

These examples do not exhaust the list of wisdom psalms; there are others which are wholly or in part didactic. The book of Psalms, which took form in the age of wisdom literature, naturally reflects not a few of wisdom's features.

g. Ecclesiasticus. A decade or two older than Daniel, though not like Daniel admitted to the canon, the book Ecclesiasticus is the foremost representative of wisdom literature in the Apoc. This book, also known as Sirach or Ben Sirach (*see* SIRACH, SON OF), can be quite confidently dated *ca.* 190 B.C. It has very much in common with the book of Proverbs, which seems to have served its author as model. But unlike the book of Proverbs, it was not ascribed to Solomon. The book was, in fact, known to be a recent product, and it could not for that reason be recognized as "holy" (*see* ECCLESIASTES § 2). Originally composed in Palestine by Jesus the son of Sirach, the book was brought to Egypt in 132 B.C. by the author's grandson, who translated it into Greek (Prologue to Ecclesiasticus and 50:27). The Greek and a large part of the Hebrew text are preserved.

Balanced-line proverbs sometimes appear singly in Ecclesiasticus, as they do characteristically in Proverbs, but more often they appear clustered according to subject or in an expanded form. As a result, the thought units are longer than in Proverbs, and discourses or brief essays are of more common occurrence. But both the smaller and the larger units in Ecclesiasticus often deal with the topics which also occupied the authors of Proverbs, and from a study of his book Ben Sirach emerges as a schoolman like them (cf. 51:23), concerned as they with the education of patrician youth in the ways of prudence and the good life; possibly Ecclus. 39:1-11 is an uninhibited self-portrait of himself as scribe (cf. 33:16-18).

The content of instruction is in large part the same as in Proverbs. But Ecclesiasticus also contains quite a lot of matter that is without parallel there. The "plus" in Ecclesiasticus includes hymns not clearly reflecting the features of wisdom (prayers like 36:1-17; praise like 42:15–43:33; thanksgiving like 51:1-12) and laudatory poems celebrating great personalities of the Bible (chs. 44–49), along with the author's older contemporary the high priest Simon (ch. 50), and not neglecting the God who gave them

(50:22). These latter poems have a more educational purpose and more obvious relevance to wisdom than do the hymns. Didactic, too, is the poem glorifying God the creator, 16:24–18:14.

When Ben Sirach treats themes touched also by Proverbs and Ecclesiastes, he sometimes goes new ways. In the canonical books of wisdom, folk traditions are notably absent, as well as all references to national figures, happenings, and expectations—the focus is not on a people but on humanity. Ecclesiasticus, to the contrary, alludes at length to great men and events of Bible times in the laudatory poems (chs. 44–49), but also elsewhere to biblical traditions (e.g., in 16:6-10; 25:24; 33:10, 12; 38:5). Significant is the thought that wisdom chose to reside in Jerusalem (24:8-12). Ben Sirach holds also with the tradition that Moses commanded the law for Jacob (24:23). For him the law, and, for that matter, the prophets and "wisdom," all are the source of all wisdom (39:1; cf. 9:15; 19:20; 45:5). Although like the biblical teachers of wisdom he has but moderate enthusiasm for the temple cult and values righteousness above sacrifices (e.g., 7:8-10), he yet speaks more warmly of the rituals, holy seasons, and priests than do any of the others (cf. 7:29-31; 24:10, 15; 33:7-9; 35:4-7; 36:13-14; 43:7; the priesthood particularly in the laudatory hymns in chs. 44–50). Even expectations for national triumph, sometimes with messianic coloring, appear—though rarely (cf. 35:17-19; 36:15-16; 47:22). He combined a concern for his people ("May it never be found in the inheritance of Jacob!" 23:12) with alarm at the current progress of Hellenization.

There is as yet no expression of a hope for personal immortality or resurrection, as, ten or twenty years later, there is in Daniel (12:2). Ben Sirach says: "The decree from of old is, 'You must surely die!' " (Ecclus. 14:17).

h. The Wisdom of Solomon. Probably composed in Alexandria in Greek during the first pre-Christian century, the Wisdom of Solomon carried on further, to the point of radically breaking with OT tradition, tendencies developing in the wisdom literature. Without calling himself Solomon, the author, speaking in the first person, so describes himself in 7:5; 8:21; 9:7-8, that one must think of Solomon (the device used also by the author of Ecclesiastes [cf. 1:12]); and the book was, according to its Greek title, indeed ascribed to him. The ascription only calls attention, however, to the distance which wisdom had traversed since the wise king's day. It had moved from prudence to an otherworldly eschatology.

There is more to the relation between the Wisdom of Solomon and Ecclesiastes than their being ascribed to the same person; in Wisd. Sol. 2 "Solomon" disputes, misrepresents, and deprecates the views which in Ecclesiastes "Solomon" announced as his convictions, the fruit of his extended search. Like Job, Koheleth had questioned the operation of the doctrine of individual retribution, which before him Ezekiel had developed and which had become unquestionable dogma for the generation of Proverbs. For this heterodoxy the author of the Wisdom of Solomon takes the like of Koheleth seriously to task, but not by reaffirming the earlier orthodoxy; he does not defend the proposition that virtue is always rewarded, evil punished, in life; he replaces it with a doctrine of the soul's recompense after the body's corruption (a doctrine which later the author of IV Maccabees exploits to the full).

In his teachings concerning the soul and its fate and those concerning the nature of wisdom (*see below*) the author of the Wisdom of Solomon draws so heavily upon concepts at home in Greek philosophy that his book has little in common with the earlier literature of wisdom. At any rate, he strikes out on new paths. *See* WISDOM OF SOLOMON.

3. "Where shall wisdom be found?" Wisdom, then, has many faces. Persons may be counted wise for sundry reasons; and the wise, in their literature, speak a varied language. Biblical wisdom is what the wise men are and what they say. The manifestations of wisdom have been reviewed in §§ 1-2 *above*. Yet to be considered is the nature of the abstraction wisdom itself. Biblical thought about wisdom brings it into relation with both man and God.

a. In man. There is some ambiguity in biblical thought as to the source of human wisdom—as to what makes a man wise. It sometimes appears that a man is wise by nature, with a kind of native talent or intelligence (I Sam. 16:18; I Kings 2:9). The thought appears oftener that the originally simple have it in their power to acquire wisdom—that, given a proper attitude, a religious attitude (Prov. 1:7; Ecclus. 1:14), and good will, the unlearned can attain wisdom by their own efforts; accordingly, the custodians of wisdom advertise their wares and urge men to partake—young men in particular (Prov. 1-9; Wisd. Sol. 6:12-20). This wisdom which is at hand to be learned appears to have a tangible form. It is a fund of racial experience which parents and teachers have received as their heritage and dutifully and lovingly transmit to new generations (cf. Proverbs; Ecclesiasticus). It is available in the schools and in the homes. Or else it is what one man in his lifetime of earnest seeking has himself learned by experience and experiment and reflection, which now he records and publishes for others to share (Job; Pss. 49; 73; Ecclesiastes).

As over against this wisdom which a man has or seeks in textbooks and schools or achieves through tortured living and meditation, there is the human wisdom which comes to a man as a gift, divinely bestowed. This is not only the revealed word of God, once recorded and now studied as the Law and the Prophets (Ecclus. 24:23; 39:1; and often), but it is also a present giving (as to Solomon in his dream in response to his prayer; cf. Wisd. Sol. 7-8; also Daniel). It is wisdom through the spirit of God (Gen. 41:38-39; Isa. 11:2, of the messianic king). This is the wisdom of which the poet in Job 28 says: "Man does not know the way to it" (vs. 13 LXX; cf. Ecclus. 3:20-21).

In the development of rabbinic Judaism the tendency to look to the Scriptures for wisdom—wisdom divinely given, revealed, and recorded—became a notable feature. Like Ben Sirach, scribe, scholar, and teacher, searching law, wisdom, and prophets, and declaring wise instruction (Ecclus. 39:1, 8), and like Ezra before him, Ezra the "scribe skilled in the law of Moses which the LORD the God of Israel had given" (Ezra 7:6), the tannaim who wrote the

Mishna and the early midrashim, concerned with both halachah and haggadah, searched the OT for meaning. So also did the community described in the Dead Sea Manual of Discipline, as well as the early Christian community—these two latter groups, however, with a predominantly eschatological interest. They carry on with this type of wisdom, wisdom which God has made available to man.

b. With God. This thought—that human wisdom comes as a gift from God (through ancient revelation, in answer to prayer, or by way of God's spirit)— derives, of course, from the thought that God is wise. This concept indeed appears (Ps. 104:24; Prov. 3:19; Isa. 31:2; Jer. 10:12; Dan. 2:20). It is expressed quite often in the literature, but more usually in a poetic form, a form which leaves room for an alternative interpretation: not that God *is* wise, but that wisdom is *with* God. The Hebrew poet was capable of the vivid personification even of abstractions, and the authors of Job 28; Prov. 8-9; Ecclus. 24; Wisd. Sol. 7-8; and other such compositions probably meant to do no more than describe God as wise when in their poetic exuberance they made of wisdom God's first creation and his delight, "rejoicing before him always" (Prov. 8:22, 30; Ecclus. 1:4, 9; 24:9), hidden in a secret place to which God alone knows the way (Job 28:23), God's breath, an emanation of his glory (Ecclus. 24:3; Wisd. Sol. 7:22-8:1), present with him, his counselor, at the creation of the world (Wisd. Sol. 9:9).

The Egyptians and the Babylonians had gods of wisdom, and mythological features might easily have found lodging in OT wisdom; the idea of wisdom as a person in a heavenly court cannot be ruled out as impossible. But such an explanation would be gratuitous, and the mythological features are probably no more than a literary device.

Jas. 3:17 undoubtedly reflects the description of wisdom in Wisd. Sol. 7:22-24, and the NT *logos* theme did not develop independently of the personification of wisdom in the wisdom literature of the OT and the Apoc. (*see* LOGOS). It was this aspect of wisdom which impressed itself upon emerging Christianity.

Without the literature of wisdom the Scriptures would be decidedly poorer. Meaningful as is the Law, powerful as is the prophetic element, wisdom yet adds a dimension. Wisdom is a deposit of reflections upon human experience, the trivial along with the ultimate, both superficial and profound. It is philosophy rooted in the soil of life: truth springs out of the earth. It is philosophy although it is not reduced to a system. It teaches rational living, which, at the same time, is good and godly living. It teaches that the life controlled by reason is the life beset by the fewest sorrows. And it teaches how when troubles come, as apparently at best they do, the wise can bear them. Righteousness and peace kiss each other.

Bibliography. W. O. E. Oesterley, *The Wisdom of Egypt and the OT* (1927); H. Ranston, *The OT Wisdom Books and Their Teaching* (1930); D. B. Macdonald, *The Hebrew Philosophical Genius* (1936); O. S. Rankin, *Israel's Wisdom Literature* (1936); J. C. Rylaarsdam, *Revelation in Jewish Wisdom Literature* (1946); W. A. Irwin, "The Wisdom Literature," *IB*, I (1952), 212-19; R. H. Pfeiffer, "The Literature and Religion of the Apoc.," and "The Religion and Literature of the Pseudep.,"

IB, I (1952), 391-419, 421-36; M. Noth and D. W. Thomas, eds., *Wisdom in Israel and in the Ancient Near East* (essays presented to H. H. Rowley), *Supplements to Vetus Testamentum,* vol. III (1955); J. B. Pritchard, ed., "Didactic and Wisdom Literature," *ANET* (2nd ed., 1955), pp. 405-52.

See also the bibliographies under PROVERB; PROVERBS, BOOK OF; JOB; ECCLESIASTES; DANIEL; PSALMS; SIRACH, SON OF; WISDOM OF SOLOMON; LOGOS. S. H. BLANK

WISDOM OF SIRACH. *See* ECCLESIASTICUS.

WISDOM OF SOLOMON sŏl'ə mən [Σοφία, Σαλ-ωμῶνος]. A book of the Greek, but not the Hebrew, Bible, placed between Job and Ecclesiasticus, called *Liber sapientiae* in the Vulg. (which reproduces the Itala); deuterocanonical in the Roman Catholic Church and apocryphal in other communions. Wisdom ranks high among the apocryphal books for its elevated thought, its artistic style, and its pioneer fusion of Greek and Hebrew elements.

1. Contents
2. Literary character
3. Greek and Hebrew elements
4. Provenience
5. Authorship
6. Date
7. Aims and doctrine
8. Influence
9. Text and editions
Bibliography

1. Contents. The unifying theme is praise of WISDOM, which is hypostatized as in Proverbs but not given so definite a personality or function as the Logos in Philo. In the first portion (chs. 1-9) the theme is righteousness and wisdom, and the second illustrates the effectiveness of righteousness in the early history of Israel. The first part itself falls into two fairly clearly defined segments, so that the book as a whole may be conveniently divided into three sections: *a* (1-5) contrasts the wicked and the pious and their respective destinies (the section as a whole is an admonition to seek God in righteousness and thereby to acquire wisdom and life; 1:16–2:24 reports the frivolous views of the godless and their refutation by the wise; and 3:1–5:23 compares the temporal and eternal doom of the righteous and the godless); *b* (6:1–9:18) describes wisdom, its significance for mankind, and the modes of attaining it (ch. 6 is Solomon's admonition to rulers to strive after wisdom; in 7:1–8:21, Solomon tells how he himself acquired and profited by wisdom; and 9:1-18 is Solomon's own prayer for wisdom); *c* (10–19) recounts the effectiveness of wisdom in history (10:1–11:1 shows wisdom's power to deliver or punish during the period from Adam to Moses; and 11:2–19:22 compares God's chastisement of the Egyptians and his benevolence to the Hebrews). The third section contains two digressions: 11:15–12:22 shows how God fits the punishment to the crime but is merciful withal, and 13:1–15:17 attacks the folly of heathenism. The later chapters are more flamboyant in style and less solid in substance than the earlier, and the tame and abrupt ending has been taken to indicate either that the author had exhausted his matter or that the conclusion of the book has been lost.

2. Literary character. Wisdom belongs to the category of wisdom literature but differs from other works in this category in form and temper. Unlike Proverbs and Ecclesiastes, it is not composed in short gnomic utterances but is fluid and varied in style. Its closest affinity is with IV Maccabees, and it is second only to that work as an example of the fusion of Greek and Hebrew elements in late Hellenistic literature. The form of both books is that of a spoken discourse in artistic Greek style employing both Hebrew and Greek modes of thought and expression. In both, the style alternates between exposition and lyrical enthusiasm and employs the various literary devices taught by the rhetoricians (assonance, alliteration, etc.; sorites, syncrisis, antithesis, etc.). Unlike IV Maccabees, which maintains the sermonic form throughout and is addressed to a cultured Jewish congregation, Wisdom recalls the more popular Cynic-Stoic diatribe, seems to envisage a Jewish, mixed, and Gentile audience at various points, and interlards the discourse with prayers, historical summaries, definitions, and the like. As in IV Maccabees, furthermore, and other apocryphal writings (and most noticeably in the apocryphal additions to canonical books), the motivation is exclusively religious; any nonreligious material that may be used is given a specifically religious application.

3. Greek and Hebrew elements. As would be expected of a cultured writer of Greek in the post-classical period, our author has obviously read Homer and the tragedians and perhaps Xenophon, and is acquainted with the doctrines of Plato, the Stoics, and perhaps Pythagoras. The enumeration of the cardinal virtues in 8:7 is clearly Stoic, and the statement that creation was *ex amorphou hyles* in 11:17 Platonic. Such expressions need not, however, imply special competence in philosophy (the author of IV Maccabees was a better philosopher) but were the common store of contemporary literacy. Some apparently purposeful departures from Hebrew thought may be inevitable extensions of meaning implicit in the use of Greek words, which give the familiar Hebrew ideas they represent new connotations—as "ambrosia" means more than "manna," and as "psyche" means more, and is more precise, than "nephesh." Other current terms to which the philosophers had given quasi-technical meaning similarly introduce new connotations and new precision to vaguer antecedent ideas; providence, conscience, virtue, are examples. Greek modes of thought are obvious in such notions as that wisdom is an emanation of God; that wisdom initiates into its secrets; that God loves humanity; that God is omniscient, omnipresent, and universally active; that wisdom has specific attributes. The definite personification of wisdom (as contrasted with the vaguer personification in Proverbs) is Greek; here wisdom possesses not only moral and religious virtue but also all the secular knowledge the Greeks had acquired. This innovation has special importance as a stage in the development of the doctrine of the Logos. The other innovation attributable to Greek influence which exerted a major influence on subsequent religious development is the explicit doctrines of immortality. *See* § 7 *below.*

However significant they may be, the Greek elements are only in the nature of a modernization and naturalization of a basically Hebraic work. The author looks to and reflects scripture at every point and even emulates the stichic parallelism characteristic of Hebrew scripture. He uses the LXX rather than the MT (at 2:12 he uses LXX Isa. 3:10, which does not agree with the MT; this is convincing proof), but this is not remarkable in the Greek Diaspora. Original compositions for liturgical use employed "translation Greek" for its religious associations; hence, for all its Hebraisms, Solomon's prayer (ch. 9) may have been composed in Greek for liturgical use in Alexandria. But the Hebraic character of Wisdom is most apparent in its use of traditional midrashic exegesis, which elaborates scriptural texts with fanciful additions (*see* § 7 *below*). It is remarkable, and perhaps significant for dating (*see* § 6 *below*), that the midrashic method, and not the allegorical method of Philo, is used. In this respect Wisdom is much more integral to Jewish tradition than is Philo.

4. Provenience. The Wisdom of Solomon was certainly composed in and for a Greek-educated Jewish community, probably at Alexandria, for it fits into the Greek-Jewish literary tradition of Alexandria and displays familiarity with the Hellenistic Egyptian environment. The author seems to have seen the cult of animal-worship, which had a revival in late Hellenistic Egypt; he knows Greek art and thought which flourished there, and is particularly concerned with the Egyptian phase of Israelite history. But Palestine (where Greek culture had wider currency even among the pious than has heretofore been suspected) is a possibility. The opening chapters, indeed, seem to fit Palestinian conditions better than any other, and the remainder Egyptian; and the two portions may reflect different sources. *See* § 5 *below*.

5. Authorship. The ascription to Solomon was early recognized as merely a literary device (in his preface to the book Jerome says: "The book called Wisdom is not Hebrew; rather, the style itself is redolent of Greek eloquence"), perhaps to give force to the apparent refutation (1:10–2:20) of Epicurean doctrine ascribed to Solomon in Ecclesiastes. All scholars are agreed that in the main the book is an original Greek composition, not a translation; and the general consistency of style, the use of favorite "theme" words which serve to mesh widely separated sections, and the striking fact that the verb μεταλλεύειν is given the same wrong sense at 4:12; 16:25 have convinced all critics that the book in its present form is the work of a single hand. But apparent inconsistencies in point of view and manner between sections of Wisdom have led some critics to question its original unity. Proposals brought forward in the eighteenth and early nineteenth century, to distribute portions of the book among disparate authors, were adequately refuted in the excellent edition of Grimm (1860), but new objections and proposals have been advanced in the twentieth century. The most plausible position (set forth most fully by Focke in 1912) is that section *a* is direct translation from Hebrew and the remainder an original continuation by the translator himself. The basis for the argument that *a* is a translation is that

it contains a smaller proportion of particles, fewer compounds, peculiarities in word order, and a more careful observance of Hebraic parallelism; and that it is Jewish in content and addressed to Jewish rulers, whereas the remainder is in a less constrained style with more rhetorical flourishes and frequent tautology, makes use of pagan teachings, and is addressed to a different audience. Some scholars have sought to prove a Hebrew original for the early chapters on the basis of assumed mistranslations in the Greek. The preponderance of modern scholarship holds to unity of authorship. Roman Catholic editors insist upon it strongly; some others accept it more tentatively.

Actually the problem is of minor importance. Whether or not our author translated directly, it is clear that he used pre-existing materials, as in the prayer of Solomon or the midrashic elaborations, and that he did not always take pains to regularize his composition; in 10:1–11:1, e.g., it is wisdom which directs events, and God does not appear, whereas from 11:3 onward wisdom disappears and God is appealed to and acts directly. In theological and ethical premises there is no significant difference between the parts, but, on the contrary, striking resemblances. If section *a* derives from a pietist group such as that at Qumran, the remainder also reflects their teaching. At 7:1 Solomon asserts:

> I also am a mortal, like all men,
> a descendant of the first-formed child of the earth.

This is very like the egalitarian ideal insisted upon in the so-called Manual of Discipline.

6. Date. The hypothesis of a Palestinian Hebrew source for the first section and an Alexandrian origin for the remainder facilitates, and receives support from, the establishment of a date. The polarization of the godless and the righteous, the exhortation to Jewish rulers to pursue righteousness, and the outspoken indictment of their worldliness fit the reign of Alexander Janneus most appropriately, when the tension was at its height and Janneus vented his wrath against the pious opposition by crucifying eight hundred of them and slaughtering their women and children before their eyes as he watched the spectacle, while he reveled with his concubines (Jos. War I.iv.6; Antiq. XIII.xiv.2). The source may well have emanated from some such pietist group as that which occupied the retreat at Qumran. This would explain the spiritual tone and warmth of the invective and give point to the attack on the Epicureanism of worldly rulers for which Ecclesiastes had made Solomon himself sponsor (cf. Wisd. Sol. 2:1 with Eccl. 2:22; 3:10; 4:1 ff; 6:12; Wisd. Sol. 2:4-6 with Eccl. 2:16; 9:5).

For fixing the lower limit the best evidence is the denunciation of idolatry, and especially Egyptian theriolatry, in 13–15. This can only have been written when the *rapprochement* with the Gentile environment which Artisteas had sought to promote, and which the Egyptian Jewish community had sought to preserve in order to maintain their social and economic position in the general community, had been destroyed by the advent of Roman rule after the Battle of Actium and had been replaced by uncompromising hostility. The Roman introduction of the poll tax (*laographia*) for noncitizens had deprived the Jews of their *de facto* privileges and sharply reduced their status. This would place Wisdom at the beginning of Roman rule in Egypt, or near 30 B.C. III Maccabees, which was written under the same pressure, exhibits the same abhorrence of any compromise with heathenism and the same impatience with Jews who had compromised with heathen ways.

An alternative dating makes Wisdom precede Philo (placing its lowest limit at *ca.* 50 B.C.), on the grounds that if it were later and in the same tradition, the author would surely have copied Philo's use of the Logos (which would be peculiarly appropriate to his approach) and would have followed Philo in interpreting scripture allegorically. He fails to do so in such tempting passages as those dealing with Aaron's vestments (18:24), Lot's wife (10:7), or the brazen serpent (16:5-6), where Josephus too had followed Philo's exegesis. But Philo appears to have stood outside the main stream of Jewish tradition even in Alexandria, and a writer whose object was to resist latitudinarianism might purposely ignore him. It is a sign of our author's adherence to the main body of Jewish tradition that he does in fact employ the midrashic, rather than the allegorical, mode of interpretation.

7. Aims and doctrine. The object of Wisdom is to hearten the pious by showing that the dominance of evil is only apparent and transitory, to admonish backsliders by showing that the secular philosophy which had relaxed their faith can in fact support it, to recover apostates and perhaps convert Gentiles by showing the folly of heathenism. God is ubiquitous and aware of the good and evil in the world; each will receive due requital, but rewards need not be temporal. Death came into the world through the envy of the devil (2:24; *Diabolos* translates the Hebrew *Satan*, who is thus first given this role in literature).

> But the souls of the righteous are in the hand of God,
> . . . .
> their hope was full of immortality.
>
> The hope of the ungodly man is like chaff carried by the wind. (3:1-4; 5:14.)

Our author would appear to be the earliest Jewish writer to make individual immortality so specific and to make righteousness a condition of eternal salvation. But 3:8; 5:16; 6:17-20 merge into the more usual concept of national immortality. Significant of the eschatological interest of our author is the allusion to Enoch (4:10-14), who is expected to be recognized without his name being mentioned. The second and more traditional part of Wisdom does not speak of messianic hopes. The sacrificial cult is never mentioned, and Moses is spoken of (11:1) as a prophet rather than a lawgiver. This would suit the premise of an origin either among a pietist group in a Palestinian retreat or in the Alexandrian diaspora. Efforts to systematize the theology and eschatology must remain futile, because our author is an ardent preacher rather than a systematic thinker. As in contemporary Stoicism, the reader feels that the communication of faith is more important than the logical theory behind it.

8. Influence. There are no direct citations of Wisdom in the NT, but a number of striking echoes have convinced many scholars that Paul and John made use of it. As in the case of echoes of IV Maccabees, however, the explanation may well be that the Christian and Jewish authors were affected by the same religious atmosphere and the same modes of discourse. Passages in the NT letters which appear to parallel Wisdom are: Rom. 1:18 ff (11; 13; 15); 2:4 (11:23; 12:10, 19); 9:21 (15:7); II Cor. 5:5, 7 (9:15); Eph. 6:11-17 (5:17 ff); Heb. 1:3 (7:25-26); 12:17 (12:10); Jas. 3:17-18 (7:22-23); I Pet. 1:6-7 (3:5-6). John's teaching of the Logos exhibits many parallels—e.g., John 1:1, 18 (8:3; 9:4); 1:3, 10 (7:21; 8:6; 9:1, 9); 5:20 (8:4; 9:9 ff). It may be that the sounding of the trumpets in Rev. 8-9 reflects the arrangement of visitations in Wisd. Sol. 11:16-19. Wisdom is frequently cited by patristic and later authors, generally as inspired; it was recognized as canonical by the Council of Trent (1546) and has been drawn upon in Roman Catholic liturgy.

9. Text and editions. The text of Wisdom is well preserved, in whole or in part, in the four great uncial MSS—B (Vaticanus), ℵ (Sinaiticus), A (Alexandrinus), and C (Codex Ephraemi Rescriptus) —and in a number of minuscules. The best text is B, which is the basis of the critical editions of Swete and of Rahlfs. For textual criticism the most useful of the versions is the Itala, which has passed into the Vulg.; this contains a number of glosses and doublets. There are also Armenian and Syrohexaplar versions.

Bibliography. Among modern translations, introductions, and commentaries the following deserve mention: C. L. W. Grimm, *Das Buch der Weisheit* (1860); W. J. Deane, *Book of Wisdom* (1881); P. Heinisch, *Das Buch der Weisheit* (1912); S. Holmes in R. H. Charles, *Apoc. and Pseudep. of the OT* (1913); F. Feldmann, *Das Buch der Weisheit* (1926); J. Fichtner, *Weisheit Salomos* (1933); J. Fischer, *Das Buch der Weisheit* (1950); E. Osty, *Le Livre de la Sagesse* (1950); J. Reider, *The Book of Wisdom* (1957).

Other works used as references in the preceding paragraphs are: F. Focke, *Die Entstehung der Weisheit Salomos* (1913); E. A. Speiser, "The Hebrew Origin of the First Part of the Book of Wisdom," *JQR,* 14 (1924), 455 ff; C. E. Purinton, "Translation Greek in the Wisdom of Solomon," *JBL,* 47 (1928), 276 ff; C. C. Torrey, *The Apocryphal Literature* (1945); R. H. Pfeiffer, *History of NT Times with an Introduction to the Apoc.* (1949); M. Hadas, *Aristeas to Philocrates* (1950); M. Hadas, *III and IV Maccabees* (1953); A. Dupont-Sommer, *The Jewish Sect of Qumran and the Essenes* (1955).
M. HADAS

WISE MEN. *See* MAGI.

WIT. *See* HUMOR.

WITCH, WITCHCRAFT. *See* SORCERY.

WITHERED HAND [ἐξηραμμένην ἔχων τὴν χεῖρα]. The cure of a man's withered hand is reported in parallel by Matt. 12:9-14; Mark 3:1-6; Luke 6:6-11. No accurate diagnosis of the diseased condition is now possible. Luke adds that it was the man's *right* hand. According to Jerome on Matt. 12:13, the Gospel of the Hebrews said that the man was a mason, who wished to earn his living again. The same Greek word is used of Jeroboam's hand in I Kings 13:4, where the condition appears to have been hysterical paralysis; and in Mark 9:18, referring to an epileptic spasm.

Bibliography. M. R. James, *The Apocryphal NT* (1924), pp. 4-5; W. Bauer, *Greek-English Lexicon of the NT* (1957), pp. 550-51.   S. V. McCASLAND

WITNESS [עֵד; μάρτυς]. A person who has firsthand knowledge of a fact or an event. Biblical law requires the testimony of at least two witnesses to establish the guilt of any offense (Deut. 19:15; and Num. 35:30; Deut. 17:6 reiterate this in connection with capital offenses); the rule is illustrated in the trial of Naboth (I Kings 21:10, 13). Nothing is said in the Bible regarding qualification. According to Jos. Antiq. IV.viii.15, the credibility of a witness was determined by his past life, but neither women nor slaves were qualified to testify (cf. M. Bek. 4.10; R.H. 1.8; Sanh. 3.3-5).

Important commercial transactions—e.g., the transference of property—were carried out in the forum (Gen. 23; Ruth 4). If a document was involved, it was signed by the witnesses (Jer. 32:12).

Witnesses did not testify under oath. However, if none voluntarily presented himself, the victim of an injustice could publicly adjure all persons capable of testifying on his behalf to do so under pain of a curse (Lev. 5:1; Prov. 29:24; cf. Judg. 17:2).

A witness to a grave public offense was obligated to prosecute the offender (Lev. 24:11 [cf. I Kings 21:10]; Num. 15:33; Deut. 13:8—H 13:9; Jer. 26:8). When the crime was punished with stoning, the witnesses flung the first stone (Deut. 13:9—H 13:10; 17:7; cf. Acts 7:58).

Bearing false witness is banned in the laws (Exod. 20:16; 23:1; Deut. 5:20—H 5:17) and condemned in the wisdom literature (Prov. 6:19; 14:25; 19:5, 9; 21:28; 25:18). One who, upon examination, proves to have been a false witness is subjected to the penalty that he had schemed to inflict upon the accused (Deut. 19:16-21; cf. Code of Hammurabi 1-4). By later interpretation this form of talion was applied only when the false testimony had been accepted and a verdict delivered on its basis (Jos. Antiq. IV.viii.15; M. Mak. 1.6; cf. Sus. 36 ff). Contradictory testimony was thrown out of court (M. Sanh. 5.2; cf. Mark 14:56-57).

God is called upon as a witness—a prosecuting witness and judge (cf. Mal. 3:5)—to solemn undertakings or prophetic warnings (Gen. 31:50; I Sam. 12:5; Jer. 29:23; 42:5; Mic. 1:2; Mal. 2:14). Enduring inanimate objects are invoked as witnesses as well (Gen. 31:48 [stones]; Deut. 31:19, 21, 26 [a traditional poem]; Josh. 22:27-28, 34 [an altar]; Ps. 89:37—H 89:38 [the moon]). The Second Isaiah considers Israel a witness to Yahweh: by its very presence, and as a repository of prophetic predictions which have come true, it attests the power of God as Deliverer and Lord of history (Isa. 43:9-10; 44:8-9).

In the NT the procedural rule of two witnesses is made applicable to the Christian community by Matt. 18:15 ff; I Tim. 5:19. Those who attest truths about God are called witnesses (John 3:11, 32; 8:18; Rev. 1:5; 11:3), as are those who testified what they saw or heard concerning Jesus (Luke 24:48; Acts

1:8; 10:41; 22:20). The violent end that many such faithful met gave the Greek word MARTYR its present meaning (Rev. 2:13; 17:6).   M. GREENBERG

WITNESS, ALTAR OF [עֵד, *'ēdh*]; KJV transliterates ED ĕd. An altar erected by the Transjordan tribes on the W side of the Jordan River, that they might have a "witness" that they, as well as the W Jordan tribes, had a portion in the Lord (Josh. 22:27-34). The altar was given the name "Witness," although the name has been dropped by a scribe from the text of Josh. 22:34 and has to be supplied. This passage may have influenced Isa. 19:19-20.

H. G. MAY

WIZARD [יִדְּעֹנִי, necromancer]. *See* FAMILIAR SPIRIT.

WOLF [זְאֵב, *cf.* Akkad. *zību*, Arab. *dhi'b; λύκος*]. With the exception of some breeds of domestic dogs, the wolf (*canis lupus*) is the largest living member of the family of carnivorous mammals known as Canidae (which includes wolves, jackals, foxes, and dogs). It hunts singly or in pairs, and also in packs. It is known for its boldness, fierceness, and voracity; it will commonly kill much more than it can eat or take away, being a special enemy of sheep.

The wolf was well known in ancient Palestine, though curiously all the biblical references to wolves, with the exception of Isa. 11:6; 65:25; John 10:12, are figurative (cf., however, M. Ta'an. 3.6; B.K. 1.4; B.M. 7.9; Hullin 3.1). In Gen. 49:27 Benjamin is described as a ravenous wolf; in Jer. 5:6 Judah's enemy is represented as a wolf from the desert; and in Ezek. 22:27 Judah's princes are compared to rapacious wolves. The nocturnal depredations of wolves supply the figures applied to the Chaldean horses in Hab. 1:8 and to Jerusalem's judges in Zeph. 3:3. In Matt. 7:15 false prophets are designated as wolves, as are false teachers in Acts 20:29. In Matt. 10:16; Luke 10:3 the same term is applied to the critics and opponents of the early apostles. The traditional enmity between wolves and sheep (cf. Ecclus. 13:17), and the former's predilection for the flesh of the latter, gives point to the hope that in the universal peacefulness of the messianic age, even the wolf and the lamb shall dwell together (Isa. 11:6; 65:25).   W. S. McCULLOUGH

*WOMAN [אִשָּׁה; γυνή]. The function and status of woman in the Bible are strongly influenced by the patriarchal form of family life which prevailed. Woman's principal function is performed in her role as wife and mother. In this connection she makes her sexuality available to her husband for his pleasure and for reproductive purposes. As a mother she sustains a relationship to children which involves their care and nurture. In her wider relationships which extend beyond the family, she takes part in the economic and social life of the community and in its political and even military affairs. She shares also in the religious life of her contemporaries, both in the home and in the tribe, city, or national community of worship.

The position of woman in the NT, especially as this is reflected in the activities of those who were connected with the life of Jesus and with the early church, was of considerable importance.

1. The subjection of woman
   a. Her status and role as a wife
   b. Her status and role as a mother
2. Woman in social-economic life
3. Woman in political and military life
4. Woman and the arts
5. Woman in religious life
6. The ideal woman
7. Negative attitude toward woman
8. Woman's beauty
9. Woman's legal rights and disabilities
10. Figurative use of "woman"
11. Woman's role in the NT
    a. In the life of Jesus
    b. In the life of the early church
Bibliography

1. The subjection of woman. Woman's position in the Bible is largely that of subordination to her father or her husband. In several instances the word for "wife" signifies "woman belonging to a man" (Gen. 2:24-25; 3:8, 17; 4:1, 17). This inferior status is doubtless reflected in the false but popular etymology of the Hebrew words for "man" and "woman" (*see* SEX). Her father gave a woman to be the wife of another man; her husband could freely divorce her (*see* DIVORCE); either could decide whether an oath she had taken was valid; her husband ruled over her (3:16), yet she had considerable freedom to act (19:31-35).

a. Her status and role as a wife. Although a woman did not usually choose her own husband, her desires were not always ignored (Num. 36:6). The father received a bride price for his daughter and thus engaged in a contract with the prospective husband to make her sexuality available to him. This transaction, however, was not a transfer of chattel property. Rather it was the surrender of authority over a woman by one man to another. She remained a person and could also have personal relations with her husband, by whose name she was called. She evidently kept her own name and individuality also, as may be seen below. She was sometimes the stronger character. We may note the initiative of Sarai in directing her husband to take her maid in order to have children by her (Gen. 16:2; cf. I Sam. 25; II Kings 4:8-10). In spite of her inferior status in the patriarchal family, woman found it possible to experience love in marriage (Gen. 24:67; 29:20; 34:3 ff; I Sam. 1:8). *See* MARRIAGE; SEX; FAMILY.

b. Her status and role as a mother. Respect toward one's mother was demanded in biblical society, and disrespect was severely punished (Lev. 20:9; Deut. 27:16). Her influence was considerable. Perhaps the alleged etymology of the name Eve (חוה), "mother of all living," is motivated by the prominence of woman's role as mother in the Bible. As mother, woman was more than the bearer of children. She also had the responsibility of caring for them. She was busy in the various tasks that the family required, making clothing, carrying water, making bread, and generally providing for her husband and children (Gen. 24:11, 13-16, 19-20; 27:9, 14; Matt.

13:33; 24:41; Tit. 2:4-5 ["domestic" virtues stressed]). *See* FAMILY.

2. Woman in social-economic life. Women's participation in the social life of the community was considerable. Their presence at weddings and funeral obsequies, as well as on other occasions of a social nature, is reported. Mourning for the dead was done by women when Saul and Jonathan were killed (II Sam. 1:24; conversely here there is fear that the women of the Philistines will exult if they hear the news, perhaps by publicly singing and dancing [vs. 20]; see also Song of S. 2:7; 3:10; Jer. 9:17; 31:15; etc.; *see* MARRIAGE). Women shared in the festivals of the harvest, no doubt, such as the treading out of the grapes (Joel 3:13), although this is not specifically stated.

Woman's economic activities receive attention in Prov. 31, where her real-estate ventures (vs. 16), her manufacture and sale of linen garments (vs. 24), are pointed out with approval. Such business enterprise on the part of biblical women was rare, however, doubtless because of their sexual-social function in Israelite life and also because of the relatively undeveloped economy peculiar to their culture. Yet both Ananias and his wife, Sapphira, sold property (Acts 5:1); one Lydia of Thyatira was a seller of purple goods (16:14); Aquila and his wife Priscilla were both tentmakers (18:2-3).

3. Woman in political and military life. It is true that the list of the nation's heroes, "distinguished men," compiled by a second-century writer contains only the names of men (Ecclus. 44:1–50:29). But this hardly does justice to the actual facts. The influence of women as related to affairs of state is seen in the biblical accounts of Deborah (Judg. 5); Bathsheba (I Kings 1:11 ff); Jezebel (19:1 ff); and perhaps the women who are with one exception only named, but who were mothers of kings (II Kings 8: 26—the exception [see 11:1]; 12:1; 14:2; 15:2, 33; 18:2; 21:1, 19; 22:1; 23:36; 24:8, 18).

4. Woman and the arts. Women more than men engaged in the arts of dancing and singing, preserving their ancient forms and exhibiting these on social and religious occasions. Cultic dancing was practiced by the prophetic bands which roamed the countryside (I Sam. 10:5; I Kings 18:26). This was, of course, done by men; although ritual dancing by women was not unknown (*see* DANCING). Miriam and other Hebrew women played upon timbrels and danced to celebrate their people's escape from Egypt (Exod. 15:20). The "singing women" who sang laments over the fate of Josiah are named along with the "singing men" (II Chr. 35:25). The whole assembly of Israelites, according to another writer, included 245 singers, "male and female" (Neh. 7:67). Some women practiced magic and literally wove magical spells by sewing wrist bands and veils for the purpose of "hunting souls" (Ezek. 13:18; *see* MAGIC). Although there are allusions to the art of weaving in the Bible (Exod. 35:35; Ps. 45:13; Prov. 31:19), only the last of these relates it to women as the weavers (cf. Exod. 35:25). There is no indication that this special skill was associated with women.

5. Woman in religious life. Women participated fully in the religious activities revolving around the great festivals of the Passover, Pentecost, and the Feast of Tabernacles. They are undoubtedly included in the words "all the congregation of Israel" (Exod. 12:3). In prescribing the manner of keeping the Feast of Booths (Tabernacles) a man's daughter, maidservant, and widows are specifically named (Deut. 16:14). In the Qumran community described in some of the Dead Sea Scrolls, the whole group, including women, must observe the rules of the order (1QS 1.1). Women attended religious gatherings and shared in sacrificial meals. At the yearly feast of the Lord in Shiloh, the daughters of that place came out to dance (Judg. 21:19-21). A woman might be expected to go to the shrine to engage in the Festival of the New Moon or the sabbaths (II Kings 4:23). She could not serve as a priest. Both her ritual uncleanness and her sexual nature as a woman barred her from serving in this capacity.

Huldah the prophetess was consulted regarding the newly found Book of the Law (II Kings 22:14). The term "prophetess" is used also in connection with Miriam and Deborah (Exod. 15:20; Judg. 4:4). The wife of Isaiah is called a prophetess, probably just because she is a prophet's wife (Isa. 8:3); and a false prophetess, Noadiah, appears in Neh. 6:14 (cf. Joel 2:28; Acts 2:17; 21:9). The religious influence of women, including the unnamed multitudes of mothers of biblical homes and those whose names have survived in the Bible, was undoubtedly great. The bitter feud between Jezebel, Israel's queen from Tyre, and Elijah the prophet was based largely upon the former's effort to establish the Tyrian cult in Israel (I Kings 21).

6. The ideal woman. From several observations we may construct a concept of the ideal woman, especially from the later writings. She is gracious, restrained in speech, discreet, peaceful (Prov. 9:13; 11:16, 22; 21:9). She is also trustworthy, efficient in the conduct of business, industrious, unafraid of the future, provident, wise, kind, and reverent (31:10-31). In the book of Judith the ideal woman is reverent, beautiful, intelligent, loyal (8:28-31, etc.). She forgets her modesty only to use her charms for the purpose of overcoming her people's enemy, Holofernes. Another writer names woman's grace, knowledge, silence, self-control, modesty, beauty, domestic efficiency, good figure, "beautiful feet with a steadfast heart" (Ecclus. 26:13-18). Susanna was a pious, chaste, and beautiful woman; and the piety of the mother of seven martyred sons is told in another story (II Macc. 7:20 ff). Young women should be trained to love their husbands and children, to be sensible, chaste, domestic, kind, and submissive to their husbands (Tit. 2:4). The ideal of patriotism, loyalty to the Jewish community, is strongly revealed in the book of Esther. The power of woman, idealized and rationalized, is brought out in the words of a young Persian attached to the court of Darius. He answered the question, What one thing is strongest? with the words: "Women are strongest." He explained that women bear men, nurture them, clothe them. Men give up a fortune looking for a woman, losing their heads for her (I Esd. 3:12).

7. Negative attitude toward woman. Disparagement of woman's character and nature is at times forthrightly asserted. The most radical relates to the origin of sin:

> From a woman sin had its beginning,
> and because of her we all die
> (Ecclus. 25:24).

Disagreeable characteristics are enumerated also. Woman is, or may be, contentious, noisy, indiscreet (Prov. 9:13; 11:22; 25:24). Even though woman sinned in the garden, she will be saved through childbearing (I Tim. 2:14-15). A late editor of the prophecies of Micah cannot avoid inserting a proverb reflecting a negative attitude toward woman:

> Guard the doors of your mouth
> from her who lies in your bosom
> (Mic. 7:5).

Taking hold of a wicked woman is like grasping a scorpion (Ecclus. 26:7; cf. 42:12-14), affirms another writer.

8. Woman's beauty. A woman's beauty is extravagantly depicted in an anthology of love songs. Her eyes are like doves, her hair like a flock of goats, teeth like shorn ewes, lips like a scarlet thread (Song of S. 4:1a, 1e, 2a, 3). Her cheeks are like a pomegranate, and her breasts are like two fawns that feed among the lilies (4:3-5). The process of beautification involves the use of gold ornaments, scarlet dresses, and the enlargement of the eyes with special paint (Jer. 4:30). "Delicate" women wear veils and robes (Isa. 47:2). In outlining the physical development of a woman from birth to sexual maturity, her beauty is not unnoticed by the prophet Ezekiel, even though he is telling a parable. He writes: "You grew up and became tall . . . ; your breasts were formed, and your hair had grown" (Ezek. 16:7). A woman's hair ought not to be exposed; it should be either covered or cut, because of the temptation it might afford to the angels (I Cor. 11:6-10; cf. Gen. 6:4).

9. Woman's legal rights and disabilities. Many Hebrew laws treat men and women as equals: Both the adulterer and the adulteress are to be put to death (Lev. 20:10); both the father and the mother must receive reverence as parents (Lev. 19:3; Deut. 5:16); food taboos are mandatory upon both sexes (Lev. 11); death is demanded for both in cases of incest (20:11, 17-18). Woman's inferior status, however, is reflected in laws which show discrimination: A daughter is less desirable than a son (Lev. 12:1-5); she could be sold for debt by her father (Exod. 21:7; cf. Neh. 5:5); she could not be freed at the end of six years, as could a man (Lev. 25:40). She could be made a prostitute by her father (Judg. 19:24; but cf. Lev. 19:29). The man had the right of DIVORCE. The valuation of a man differs from that of a woman when a special vow is made (Lev. 27:1-7). *See* SEX; MARRIAGE; FAMILY.

10. Figurative use of "woman." Traits of feminine character are applied to men or nations considered collectively, by some biblical writers. Feminine characteristics are applied to the Egyptians, who "like women" will tremble with fear (Isa. 19:16). The concept of woman occurs to represent wickedness, sitting in an ephah measure. Two winged women carry the basket and its occupant to the land of Shinar (Zech. 5:7-11). In the book of Revelation appears the form of a woman clothed with the sun, with the moon under her feet. She is pregnant and cries out in anguish for delivery (Rev. 12:1-2, 5-6, 13-17). The use of this figure to personify wisdom occurs frequently (e.g., Prov. 1:20-21; 8:1-3; etc.; Wisd. Sol. 7:12-22; Ecclus. 1:6-20; etc.).

11. Woman's role in the NT. While not differing radically from the concept which the OT presents, the view of woman in the NT reflects the influence of the Christian as well as the Jewish community.

a. In the life of Jesus. Many anonymous women appear in the gospel accounts of Jesus' life and ministry (Matt. 9:20-22; 14:21; 15:22; 26:7-13; Mark 1:31; Luke 13:11-13; John 4:7-26). Women who are called by name include Mary Magdalene, Mary the mother of James and Joseph, and the mother of the sons of Zebedee, as well as the "other Mary" (Matt. 27:55, 61; 28:1). There were also Mary and Martha (Luke 10:38-42; John 11:1 ff) and Mary the mother of Jesus "with the women" (Acts 1:14). The women who are explicitly named or generally alluded to fall principally into two classes—those who were healed by him and those who followed and watched over him. Jesus occasionally taught through allusions to woman's activities in the home: A woman loses a coin and searches for it (Luke 15:8); two women will be grinding grain at a mill (17:35), to show the suddenness of the coming of the end.

b. In the life of the early church. The gospel was available to all men without regard to sex. Women received it and helped to promote it in the NT church. Men and women were dragged to prison for their faith (Acts 8:3; 9:2). On the other hand, the Jews incited "devout women of high standing" against Paul and Barnabas (13:50), but "not a few" joined them (17:4). Both Aquila and his wife Priscilla instructed Apollos in the faith (18:26); women served as deaconesses in the early church (Rom. 16:1). As examples of faith Timothy's mother, Eunice, and his grandmother, Lois, are held up (II Tim. 1:5). Against the power of pagan cults and customs, the Christian community erected a wall of protection in the form of rules of conduct for women. Accepting the biblical view of woman's subordination to man, the writers of the NT stressed the duty of modesty, submission, and piety. Women were not to speak in church (I Cor. 14:34-36), because God had created them from man and *for* him as well. They should not teach or in any other way usurp man's position in the church (I Tim. 2:12). Women should be known for their works and their faith rather than for their words (vss. 14-15). Older women are to be treated like mothers and younger ones like sisters (5:2). The above evidence shows that, in theory at least, woman was expected to exhibit chiefly the domestic virtues as a demonstration of her piety and faith. In actual practice, her leadership and influence extended into the life of the entire Christian community, as the NT itself reveals.

See also FAMILY; MARRIAGE; SEX.

Bibliography. H. Zschokke, *Das Weib im AT* (1883). I. J. Peritz, "Woman in the Ancient Hebrew Cult," *JBL*, XVII (1898), 111-48. M. Löhr, *Die Stellung des Weibes zu Jahwe Religion und Kult* (1908). C. M. Breyfolge, "The Religious Status of Woman in the OT," *BW*, XXXV (1910), 405-19;

"The Social Status of Woman in the OT," *BW*, XXXV (1910), 107-16. G. Beer, *Die soziale und religiöse Stellung der Frau im israelitischen Altertums* (1919). E. McDonald, *The Position of Woman as Reflected in Semitic Codes of Law* (1931). F. J. Leenhardt, *La place de la femme dans l'église d'après le NT* (1948).

See also the bibliographies under MARRIAGE; SEX; FAMILY.

O. J. BAAB

WONDER, WONDERS. See SIGNS AND WONDERS.

WOOD [יַעַר (*alternately* FOREST); עֵץ; KJV חֹרֶשׁ, *see below;* Aram. אָע; ξύλον, ξύλινος]. The material provided by various trees for construction of boats, public buildings, houses, furniture, idols, utensils, and musical instruments, as well as for use as fuel. Wood is at a premium in Palestine today, but the evidence from the Bible supports the belief that in ancient times it was much more abundant. Frequent wars and liberal use of wood for fuel, without concern for reforestation, during many centuries, can easily account for the barrenness in modern times. Frequent references to יַעַר (more often "forest" in the RSV than in the KJV, where "wood" is frequently the translation) in the OT hardly fit the modern scene (Deut. 19:5; I Sam. 14:25-26; II Sam. 18:6; etc.; cf. Ezek. 34:25: "woods"). The implication of Josh. 17:15, 18, is that the Hebrews found the central highlands heavily forested. Jotham built "forts and towers on the wooded hills" of Judea (II Chr. 27:4). Hag. 1:8 implies that the hills would produce enough wood for construction of the new temple *ca.* 520 B.C. According to legend, as Elisha was going from Jericho to Bethel, "she-bears came out of the woods," in an area that is a barren wilderness today (II Kings 2:24).

Wood was used freely for burnt offerings on ancient Canaanite and Hebrew altars (Gen. 22:3-9; Lev. 1:7-17; 4:12; Neh. 10:34; cf. Jub. 21:12-13). The temple cultus called for a wood fire that burned continuously (Lev. 6:12-13). "Hewers of wood" were necessary to provide for daily fuel needs (Deut. 29:11; Josh. 9:21-27), though dried thorns were often used for cooking fires. *See* THISTLE.

Several different kinds of wood are specifically mentioned: GOPHER WOOD was used for Noah's ark (Gen. 6:14; *see* CYPRESS); ACACIA (KJV "shittim wood") was used for the tabernacle, its ark, poles, altars, and other equipment (Exod. 25-27; 35-37); CEDAR and PINE (or cypress) from Lebanon were used in great quantities in Solomon's temple and other buildings in Jerusalem for paneling the walls and covering the floors (I Kings 6:15), for the main doors (vs. 36), and for the ceiling beams and pillars (6:36; 7:2-3); carved olivewood (*see* OLIVE TREE) was used for the doors and posts of the temple's inner sanctuary (6:32-33) and the cherubim (6:23; cf. II Chr. 3:10). Some special woods were imported: ALMUG wood (perhaps sandalwood) for musical instruments (I Kings 10:12) and SCENTED WOOD (Rev. 18:12).

In addition to its use in buildings and for fuel, wood was used for making ships (I Kings 9:26), wagons (I Sam. 6:14), threshing sledges (I Chr. 21:23), yokes (Jer. 27:2; 28:13), furniture (Exod. 25:9-28), vessels (Exod. 7:19; Lev. 15:12; II Tim. 2:20), and musical instruments (I Kings 10:12), and for carving (Exod. 31:5; 35:33). Idols were often made of wood and are frequently mentioned as a concern of the prophets (Deut. 4:28; 28:36; Isa. 40:20; 44:9-20; 45:20; Dan. 5:4, 23; Rev. 9:20; etc.). Wood also appears in figures of speech (Isa. 60:17; Jer. 5:14; Lam. 4:8; Ezek. 15:2-6; 39:10; II Tim. 2:20-21).

The difficult "instruments made of fir wood" (II Sam. 6:5 KJV) is probably an error (*see* PINE; cf. I Chr. 13:8). The puzzling מסכן (*mᵉsukkān;* Akkadian *musukkānu*) in Isa. 40:20 may refer to a type of hardwood used for making idols in Mesopotamia; a good case has been made for the East Indian "sissoo" tree (*Dalbergia sissoo* L.) as the reference here. *See bibliography.*

חרש, translated "wood" in the KJV (I Sam. 23:15-19), is now thought to be a place. *See* HORESH.

See also EBONY; FIR; FLORA §§ A8-9; JUNIPER; OAK; OIL TREE; PALM TREE; PLANE TREE.

J. C. TREVER

WOOL [צמר, עמר; ἔριον]. Prominently a product of Palestine, wool constituted the tribute which King Mesha of Moab paid to King Ahab of Israel (II Kings 3:4). The frequency of the verbal/literary figure of the SHEEP and the shepherd in both the OT and the NT testifies to the significant place of wool in the common economic life of Palestine.

For reasons not now altogether clear, the Israelite law forbade (Deut. 22:11; cf. Lev. 19:19) the wearing of material combining wool and linen, possibly, as the first-century Jewish historian Josephus understood it (Antiq. IV.viii.11), because cloth of mixed wool and linen was the special material of priestly garments.

In a country where snow was seldom seen, wool became the common metaphor of whiteness and purity (Ps. 147:16; Isa. 1:18, which also employs snow as a parallel simile; Dan. 7:9; Rev. 1:14).

B. D. NAPIER

WORD, THE. In the OT, the characteristic means whereby God makes his will known to men in law and prophecy, and achieves his purposes in the providential guidance of the world. By it, indeed, he created the heavens and the earth. In the NT, the Word is also important; in some places it still has its OT connotation, but in others shows a development from it. The Word of the Lord is frequently, in fact, the Word of Christ, the gospel which he first preached, and of which later he became the principal theme. A further development appears in John and Revelation, where the Word or the Word of God is a title of Christ, proclaiming him God's agent both in creation and in revelation.

1. Terminology of "Word" in the Bible
2. In the OT
3. In nonbiblical Greek
4. In the Greek OT and Philo
5. In the NT
   a. When not used as a title of Christ
   b. When used as a title of Christ
Bibliography

1. Terminology of "Word" in the Bible. The most important equivalent of "word" in Hebrew is דבר; there are others, such as אמר and אמרה, derived from the root אמר, "say," and מלה, but these are used much less frequently than דבר, and then chiefly in poetry. דבר, on the other hand, occurs in all periods and styles of Hebrew.

The etymology of דבר is a matter of dispute. The same root consonants appear in the words דביר, the inner sanctuary of Solomon's temple; and מדבר, "wilderness"; and the attempt has been made to find a root meaning to cover all three terms and those allied to them in other Semitic languages. It has been suggested, e.g., that "back" is the root meaning, and that דביר means "back room," מדבר "hinterland," and דבר what is "behind" a thing, its "sense" or "meaning." But it is doubtful if the etymology of דבר, even if it could be established, would contribute anything very material to the understanding of the term beyond what can already be discovered from its uses in the Hebrew OT. These can all be explained on the simple assumption of a root meaning "to speak." דבר is primarily "word" in the sense of articulate and intelligible utterance. The meaning "matter, affair, thing," is derived from this, as "matter about which one speaks."

In biblical Greek the principal equivalents of "word" are λόγος and ῥῆμα. Both are used in the LXX to render דבר, and are treated as synonymous. There is a marked preference for ῥῆμα in the Pentateuch, and an even more marked preference for λόγος in the Prophets. In the NT also, λόγος is used much more frequently than ῥῆμα. The Homeric term ἔπος, though it continues in use beyond the classical period, occurs in the NT only in Heb. 7:9 in the stereotyped phrase ὡς ἔπος εἰπεῖν, where it stands as evidence of the more literary character of this letter. Λόγιον, a derivative either of λόγος or of its kindred adjective λόγιος, occurs occasionally in the LXX; in the NT it is found four times only (Acts 7:38; Rom. 3:2; Heb. 5:12; I Pet. 4:11), in each case in the plural and with the meaning "oracles."

Λόγος has a great range of meanings in classical Greek, which reflect those of the verb λέγω, from which it is derived. The root meaning of λέγω appears to be "pick up"; from this come its secondary senses: (*a*) "count, tell, recount," and (*b*) "say, speak" (cf. in English the similar double meaning of "tell," "tale," and "account"). Λόγος acquires from the former sense the meanings "account," "explanation," "rule," "ratio," "reason" (both in the sense of "grounds" and in that of the faculty of reasoning), and from the latter sense "narrative," "saying," "talk," "subject matter about which one talks."

'Ρῆμα, derived from an old root meaning "speak," is primarily "that which is spoken." Occasionally in the LXX and in the NT (e.g., Luke 1:37; 2:15) ῥῆμα has the meaning "matter," but this is a Hebraism, due to the use of the word to translate דבר, and not natural to Greek, as is the corresponding use of λόγος. In grammar ῥῆμα is the technical term for "verb," "noun" being ὄνομα ("name").

2. In the OT. The "word of the Lord" is the phrase used most frequently in the OT to describe the medium of revelation. God speaks, and his prophet hears. Thus the books of Jeremiah, Hosea, Joel, Jonah, Zephaniah, Haggai, and Zechariah all have at, or very near, the beginning the formula:

"The word of the LORD that came to . . ." or some slight variation of it, and the formula is frequently repeated in the course of the books. "Thus says the LORD" and "Hear the word of the LORD" also occur very often in the Prophets. Malachi begins: "The oracle of the word of the LORD to Israel by Malachi."

Other prophets, however, describe the content of their prophecies as "visions" (cf. Ezek. 1:1: "I saw visions of God"; Nah. 1:1: "The book of the vision of Nahum of Elkosh"; Hab. 1:1: "The oracle of God which Habakkuk the prophet saw"). Amos, Obadiah, and Micah have opening formulas which combine the two: "The words of Amos . . . which he saw . . ."; "The vision of Obadiah. Thus says the Lord GOD . . ."; "The word of the LORD that came to Micah . . . which he saw . . ." (cf. Isa. 2:1: "The word which Isaiah the son of Amoz saw"; Jer. 38:21 KJV: "This is the word that the LORD hath showed me"). Visions are described, as in Isa. 6 and elsewhere, but generally words are heard during the vision, which are at least as important as, or even more important than, the vision itself as a medium of revelation.

Thus, while other religions stress vision as the principal means for attaining to the knowledge of God, the religion of the OT tends to regard it as subsidiary, and hearing as primary. It is possible that at an earlier stage vision had been more important than it afterward became. Anciently a prophet was called a "seer" (I Sam. 9:9). The emphasis on word rather than vision may be connected with the Hebrew rejection of idolatry and, indeed, mistrust of any visual aids to religious faith such as are found in most religions, including Christianity itself.

Revelation by word, and, indeed, also by vision, may also be contrasted with that by inspiration or possession, which was typical of primitive Hebrew prophecy. It is not compulsive in the same way. It is true that there is an element of compulsion in the word of God:

> The lion has roared;
>   who will not fear:
> The Lord GOD has spoken;
>   who can but prophesy?
>   (Amos 3:8).

But the man to whom the word comes remains in possession of his normal faculties; he is not "turned into another man" like the subject of possession (cf. I Sam. 10:6). When Jeremiah says:

> If I say, "I will not mention him,
>   or speak any more in his name,"
> there is in my heart as it were a burning fire
>   shut up in my bones,
> and I am weary with holding it in,
>   and I cannot (20:9),

he at least contemplates the possibility of silence, unthinkable for the prophet inspired by possession. Thus, while the initiative remains with God, the freedom of the prophet is also respected. God communicates with man in a way which men can understand, since it is analogous to the way in which they communicate with one another.

By his word spoken to the prophets, God makes known, not the elaborate information about the supernatural order which, e.g., the Gnostics claimed to possess, but his righteous will, concerned with man's conduct in this world, which was, indeed, the limit of the Hebrews' hopes and fears. Such information as is incidentally imparted about the supernatural order in visions such as those of Isaiah (ch. 6) and Ezekiel (ch. 1) is subordinate to the message given at the same time as the vision. The sum total of the revelation of God's will is his law; and Ps. 119, e.g., uses "word," "law," "statutes," as if they were virtually synonymous and interchangeable. God's word is a word of command; its characteristic mood, it may be said, is the imperative.

As a word of command it comes not only to man, but also to the whole universe. Indeed, God called all things into being by his word. Men have to labor and contrive, in order to "create," but their "creation" is only the refashioning of already existing material. The creator-gods in ancient mythologies do the same, but in the OT all God had to do was to speak, and his purpose was thereby accomplished. "God said, 'Let there be light'; and there was light" (Gen. 1:3). "By the word of the LORD the heavens were made" (Ps. 33:6). The forces of nature continue to obey the word which called them into being; thus Ps. 148:8 speaks of

> fire and hail, snow and frost,
>   stormy wind fulfilling his command
> [lit., "word," דבר].

The power of God's word is illustrated in a vivid simile in Isa. 55:10-11.

That power should be attributed to God's word is not surprising, but it is also attributed to the words of men, particularly to blessings and curses. Words still possess, in Hebrew thought, the quality of a magic spell. A word once uttered takes on a life of its own beyond the control of the speaker and achieves its effect by a kind of innate power. When Isaac had been tricked into blessing Jacob instead of Esau, he could not cancel the blessing (Gen. 27: 32-38). Blessings, curses, and words of good and bad omen thus had a power which was something more than that of producing a psychological effect on those who heard them. They were believed to influence the course of events. This comes out, e.g., in the stories of Balaam and Balak (Num. 22–24) and of Ahab, Jehoshaphat, and the prophet Micaiah (I Kings 22:5-38). The "false" prophet was one who was willing to speak favorable words and so produce the result which his patron desired, while the "true" prophet's rule was to say only what God commanded him (Num. 22:38; I Kings 22:14). The false prophets' word must have been regarded as effective, or there would have been no point in employing them.

This belief in the quasi independence of the word, once it had been spoken, must have facilitated the later personification of the word.

3. In nonbiblical Greek. The earliest use of λόγος which has been thought to throw light on its distinctive use in the Prologue of John is that made of it by Heraclitus of Ephesus, born before 500 B.C. He was understood by the Stoics to have anticipated their doctrine that the universe is controlled by λόγος in the sense of "reason" or "law," and accordingly he was regarded by early Christian writers as a kind of prophet of the Gentiles. But Plato, who certainly knew Heraclitus' teaching, did not interpret him in this way, and it seems more likely that the Stoics were simply reading back their own ideas into the admittedly enigmatic words of Heraclitus.

Stoicism (*see* STOICS), as taught by its founder, Zeno, and his immediate successors, was a form of pantheistic materialism, or rather hylozoism, in which the universe was identified with God and was regarded as permeated and controlled by a fiery vapor, very subtle but nevertheless definitely material in substance, which was also λόγος. Early Stoicism was uncompromising in its opposition both to Platonic idealism and to popular religion, but later Stoics came to terms with both. Then λόγος was no longer spoken of in material terms, but became the divine Reason governing the world. Moreover, by means of the technique of allegorical exegesis which they elaborated, the later Stoics interpreted popular mythology in terms of their own beliefs. Then the gods of the popular religion were allegorized as personifications of abstract ideas. Hermes in particular was interpreted as λόγος. It was this later Stoicism which was so influential in Hellenistic religion, and which Philo found so convenient for his purposes. Allegory was invaluable to him. But, if it was possible to allegorize gods into abstract ideas, the reverse process, that of personifying abstractions, was also possible. And in the period when Judaism was open to the influence of Stoic ideas, an impetus appears to have been given to the personification of such divine attributes as Wisdom and the Word. The Word of the Lord was assimilated to the Stoic λόγος, though its original connotation had been very different. A similar influence was exercised by Stoicism on other Eastern religions, producing, e.g., the philosophical and religious doctrine taught in the Corpus Hermeticum (*see* JOHN, GOSPEL OF, § D2*d*). In *Poimandres,* the first treatise in the Corpus, a creation myth similar to that found in Genesis, if not actually borrowed from it, is reinterpreted with the Stoic λόγος taking the part of the creative divine word.

Thus the way was prepared, if not for the actual teaching of John about the λόγος, at least for its acceptance by the Hellenistic world.

4. In the Greek OT and Philo. In the LXX the use of λόγος to translate דבר understandably enough led readers who had its Stoic associations in mind to interpret the Genesis creation myth in terms of creation by the divine reason, in a manner similar to that found some time later in *Poimandres.* Now it was already taught in the OT that God created the world "by his wisdom" (cf. Ps. 104:24; Jer. 10:12, repeated in Jer. 51:15), and so the "Word" tended, through the Stoic associations of λόγος, to be equated with the originally distinct concept of WISDOM. Moreover, there was in the early Hellenistic period a tendency to put a fresh emphasis on the transcendence of God, so as to remove him from direct contact with the world by interposing angelic intermediaries of various kinds between him and it. The next step then was to personify both "Wisdom" and "Word" and to regard them as divine agents in creation. Wisdom appears already fully personified

in Prov. 8:22-31, and again later in Wisd. Sol. 9:9; Ecclus. 24:9. The Word does not appear until Wisd. Sol. 9:1-2, where it is mentioned along with Wisdom:

> O God of my fathers and Lord of mercy,
> who hast made all things by thy word,
> and by thy wisdom hast formed man.

This does not go any further than Ps. 33:6, but later in the book the Word is clearly personified; cf. Wisd. Sol. 18:15:

> Thy all-powerful word leaped from heaven, from
> the royal throne,
> into the midst of the land that was doomed,
> a stern warrior carrying the sharp sword of thy
> authentic command.

The next step, taken by Philo (*see* JOHN, GOSPEL OF, § D2*c*), was to make the Word or Logos the intermediary between the transcendent God and the created order. In this Philo carried to its logical conclusion the identification of the OT "Word" with the Stoic λόγος. For him God is absolutely transcendent, and it is unthinkable that he should have any direct contact with the universe. He conceived the ideal universe, corresponding to the Platonic world of ideas, as the pattern to be followed by his Logos in the creation of the actual world. Exploiting the two senses of λόγος, Philo calls this ideal universe also λόγος. Thus the Logos is both "pattern" and "instrument" of God in creation (παράδειγμα and ὄργανον). A great variety of titles describe his functions as mediator between God and the world. Thus he is God's "first-born son" (πρωτόγονος υἱός), second only to God himself, his "image" (εἰκών) and "shadow" (σκιά), and can, indeed, be described as θεός (without the article, to distinguish him from God, ὁ θεός). The Logos is also God's "ambassador" (πρεσβευτής) to men, and man's "suppliant" (ἱκετῆς) and "advocate" (παράκλητος) to God, and so "high priest" (ἀρχιερεύς). He is sometimes identified with Wisdom; sometimes Wisdom is the mother of Logos. In all this there is much that recalls John (and also Hebrews), but it is questionable whether Philo is really an intermediary between the wisdom literature and John. John could have developed his doctrine independently. He had available all the material which Philo had, and, in addition to that, the conviction that in Jesus Christ God had spoken, and acted, and revealed himself in a new way. So John goes beyond Philo, whose Logos is never more than a personification, to affirm that in Jesus Christ the "Word" became flesh—a conception which Philo could not have formed, and would certainly have rejected if he could have heard of it.

5. In the NT. The meaning of "word" in the NT, both generally and specifically as a title for Christ, is colored rather by the OT associations of דבר than by the use of λόγος in classical Greek.

a. When not used as a title of Christ. The following special uses of λόγος in the NT, all of which fall within the range of meanings common to λόγος and דבר, may be noted.

"The word of God" (ὁ λόγος τοῦ θεοῦ) is used of: (*a*) the OT law (cf. Mark 7:13 = Matt. 15:6, where it is contrasted with the tradition of the Jews); (*b*) a particular OT passage (cf. John 10:35, referring to Ps. 82:6); (c) in a more general sense, God's revealed will, or his whole plan and purpose for mankind (cf. Luke 11:28; Rom. 9:6; Col. 1:25-27, where it is defined as the "mystery hidden for ages and generations but now made manifest to his saints . . . , which is Christ in you"; Heb. 4:12); (d) the word preached by Jesus (cf. Luke 5:1; perhaps also 11:28, cited in c above); and the references made by Jesus to the word of God which he has preached (described as "his word" or "thy word," according to the context) in John 5:38; 8:55; 17:6; etc.; (e) following naturally, and not always clearly distinguishable, from a, the Christian message (cf. Luke 8:11; Acts 4:31; I Cor. 14:36; and many instances in Acts and Paul; Rev. 1:2, etc.).

The "word of the Lord" (ὁ λόγος τοῦ κυρίου) is also used in the sense of d above, as in I Thess. 4:15 (presumably a word revealed to Paul in prophecy), and e above, as in Acts 8:25, etc. (the MSS often giving θεοῦ and κυρίου as variants); I Thess. 1:8; II Thess. 3:1; etc.

The Christian message is also described as the "word of Christ" (Col. 3:16; Heb. 6:1, where the "elementary doctrines of Christ" is a paraphrase of τὸν τῆς ἀρχῆς τοῦ Χριστοῦ λόγον). In Acts 20:35 the "words of the Lord Jesus" introduce an actual saying of Jesus not otherwise recorded. In I Tim. 6:3, the "sound words of our Lord Jesus Christ" may refer either to the preaching of Christ or to that about him, or more probably to both, no clear distinction being made.

"Word" without further qualification is also found in all the senses listed under the "word of God" above. Cf. the following: (a) Heb. 2:2 ("message"); (b) John 15:25 (Ps. 35:19); Rom. 13:9 (Lev. 19:18: "sentence"); I Cor. 15:54 (Isa. 25:8: "saying"); (c) Jas. 1:21-23 (unless this should be classified under e below); (d) Mark 2:2; Luke 4:32; John 2:22; etc. (cf. also the many uses of "my word" and "my words" in the gospels); (e) Mark 4:14-20 = Matt. 13:19-23 = Luke 8:12-15 (Luke 8:11 has "the word of God"); Luke 1:2; Acts 8:4, etc.; Gal. 6:6; I Thess. 1:6.

Λόγος as the Christian message can also be described as, e.g., the "word of truth" (Eph. 1:13; Col. 1:5; II Tim. 2:15); the "word of life" (Phil. 2:16; I John 1:1 [but see § 5b below]; cf. Acts 5:20: the "words [ῥήματα] of this Life").

'Ρῆμα is also used in some of these senses of λόγος (cf. Acts 11:16, where the "ῥῆμα of the Lord" introduces a saying of Jesus; and Rom. 10:8, where the ῥῆμα mentioned in Deut. 30:14 is interpreted as the "ῥῆμα of faith which we preach"); similarly I Pet. 1:25 interprets ῥῆμα in Isa. 40:8 as the "good news which was preached to you." Two passages in which ῥῆμα is used where there is no parallel in the NT uses of λόγος (though both are parallel to OT uses of דבר) are Luke 3:2: "The word of God came to John," and Heb. 11:3: "The world was created by the word of God."

There is an intimate connection between Christ and the word of which he was first the author and then the theme (cf. Heb. 2:3). This is shown by the way in which the verb "preach" (κηρύσσειν) can have as object "the word" (Rom. 10:8; II Tim. 4:2); "the gospel" (Gal. 2:2; Col. 1:23; I Thess. 2:9);

"Jesus" (II Cor. 11:4); "Christ" (I Cor. 1:23; 15:12; Phil. 1:15); "Jesus Christ" (II Cor. 1:19). Moreover, the word is not a formula, but something living and dynamic (cf. Heb. 4:12); it was accompanied by manifestations of divine power (cf. Heb. 2:4), both in the case of Christ and in that of his apostles. It is the "power of God" (I Cor. 1:18; cf. I Cor. 2:4: "My speech [λόγος] and my message [κήρυγμα] were not in plausible words of wisdom, but in demonstration of the Spirit and power"); and a little further on, Paul describes *Christ* as the "power of God" (I Cor. 1:24). This intimate connection of Christ and the word makes less surprising their eventual identification.

b. When used as a title of Christ. Three passages are in question here: I John 1:1; Rev. 19:13; John 1:1-14. I John 5:7 in the KJV reads: "There are three that bear record in heaven, the Father, the Word, and the Holy Ghost: and these three are one," but this is an interpolation, of which there is no trace before the late fourth century.

In I John 1:1, the KJV has the "Word of life," and the RSV the "word of life." The MSS, which do not use capitals in the modern fashion, give no help in deciding between them. The passage gives a perfectly good sense if it is taken as a reference to the gospel (as in Phil. 2:16), with which, in fact, the author is concerned here rather than with cosmology. In favor of the opposite view is the close relationship which exists between the Letters and the Gospel of John. It can hardly be maintained, however, that the usage in I John 1:1 is as explicit as it is in John 1:1-14. Nevertheless, it is on the line of development that leads to it, and a stage further along this line than Col. 1:25-27.

In Rev. 19:13, the rider on the white horse, leader of the armies of heaven, whose name is "The Word of God," is clearly meant to represent the Christ, as may be seen from a comparison of Rev. 19:11-16 with the vision of the "one like a son of man" in Rev. 1:13-16. The imagery of this vision of the Warrior Word is clearly drawn from Wisd. Sol. 18:15-16 (*see* § 4 *above*). The precise relationship of this passage to John 1:1-14 is difficult to determine. Revelation offers us a symbol, John a description. For Revelation the exalted Christ is the Word of God; for John the Christ is equally such while still on earth. The writer of one passage may well have known of the other, but which came first is hard to decide. On the whole, it seems more likely that the author of Revelation knew John and was led by the use of "Logos" in the gospel to find in Wisd. Sol. 18: 15-16 the convenient imagery for his vision of the exalted Christ.

In John 1:1-14 (*see* JOHN, GOSPEL OF, § D1), John's assertion that in Jesus of Nazareth the Word became flesh (John 1:14)—i.e., an actual human being (*see* FLESH IN THE NT)—was an attempt—apparently successful, if the subsequent influence of the gospel is any criterion—to put into language intelligible and acceptable to his contemporaries, pagan as well as Jewish and Christian, the basic Christian conviction that through the life, teaching, actions, and death of the man Jesus a new revelation of God had been given, different in kind from that made through the prophets (cf. Heb. 1:1).

The developments in the use and meaning of λόγος which have already been described may help to explain how John came to choose this term as a description of the status and function of Christ sufficiently intelligible in itself to be introduced without explanation at the very beginning of his gospel. In order to complete the account of the background to John's use of "Logos," it is necessary to consider other attempts made in the NT to find an acceptable terminology for Christ's status and function.

The eschatological terminology of the Jewish messianic hope which had been used by Jesus himself and the first apostles proved inadequate as soon as the gospel came to be preached beyond the confines of Judaism. But there were two titles belonging to the original Christian terminology which it was possible to adapt to a new use—"Son of God" and "Son of man." They had originally described Christ's eschatological function; they were made to express his ontological status.

"Son of God" was seen to imply Christ's preexistence (cf. Gal. 4:4; Phil. 2:6; Col. 1:15, 17), which is affirmed of the Logos in John 1:1. From his pre-existence, and his function of God's agent in redemption (the new creation), it was inferred that he was also God's agent in creation (cf. John 1:3; I Cor. 8:6; Col. 1:16; Heb. 1:2).

"Son of man" is, of course, not used outside the gospels and Acts 7:56, but it is probable that it underlies Paul's use of the "man from heaven" and the "second Adam" as descriptions of Christ, for "man" (ἄνθρωπος) is the idiomatic Greek rendering of the Aramaic translated literally—and barbarously—as "the son of man" (ὁ υἱὸς τοῦ ἀνθρώπου). Christ is the archetypal, true man, the man "made in God's image" (Gen. 1:27); that Christ is the image of God is affirmed in II Cor. 4:4; Col. 1:15; Heb. 1:3; and implied in John 1:14. Now Wisdom, already personified, and regarded as God's agent in creation, is also described as

a reflection of eternal light,
a spotless mirror of the working of God,
and an image of his goodness
(Wisd. Sol. 7:26).

It is not surprising, therefore, that there are traces in the NT of a tentative identification of Christ with Wisdom (cf. I Cor. 1:24, 30; Col. 2:3). In the wisdom literature (see § 4 above) "wisdom" and "word" are very close to each other in meaning, and, since "wisdom," as a feminine noun in Greek, is not very suitable as a masculine title, it may fairly be said that the adoption of "Logos" in its place was almost inevitable. Paul has very nearly reached it in Col. 1:25-27. So also has Heb. 1:1-3, in which all the christological themes under discussion appear together—the pre-existent Son of God, who is his Father's agent in creation and "bears the very stamp of his nature" (Heb. 1:3), through whom God has spoken to man.

It is this conviction of the author of Hebrews, that in Christ God has spoken to man, and that his whole plan and purpose for mankind has thereby been made apparent, that is the real ground for John's affirmation that Jesus is the Word made flesh. See also CHRIST.

Bibliography. The commentaries listed under JOHN, GOSPEL OF, may be consulted. See also: J. R. Harris, *The Origin of the Prologue to St. John's Gospel* (1917); R. Bultmann, *Der Begriff des Wortes Gottes im NT, Glauben und Verstehen* (1933), pp. 268-93; R. G. Bury, *The Fourth Gospel and the Logos-Doctrine* (1940); λέγω, λόγος, in *TWNT;* C. H. Dodd, *The Interpretation of the Fourth Gospel* (1953), pp. 263-85; O. Cullmann, "Jesus der Logos," in *Die Christologie des NTs* (1957), pt. 4, pp. 255-75.   J. N. SANDERS

WORKS OF GOD, THE. An expression denoting either (*a*) "deeds done by God," especially of deliverance or judgment, or (*b*) "things made by God." In Ps. 145:4, 9-10, 17, both kinds of works are in mind: "that he has made" (vs. 9) and "his doings" (vs. 17) are both for מעשיו, "his works"; and "thy works" is used in the one sense in vs. 4 and in the other in vs. 10.

More often than not, the expression is in the singular, "the work of God," especially when used in sense *a*. Yahweh's "deed," even when it is manifest in a succession of "mighty acts" (גבורות) or "wonders" (נפלאות; *see* SIGNS AND WONDERS), is one whole. Sometimes where the MT has the construct plural מעשי, there are MSS which have the singular מעשה, and this is probably the original reading (so in Pss. 8:3—H 8:4; 92:4*b*—H 92:5*b;* 107:24*a;* 118: 17; 138:8). The forms מעשיך, מעשיו "thy (his) work(s)," can be construed as singular, the *yodh* being the original *yodh* of the stem עשה=עשי. Very much as in the OT the usual expression is "the word" (דבר), not "the words" (דברי), of Yahweh, "the work of God" is indivisible, though its manifestations may vary in time and manner.

1. In the OT. A typical passage is Judg. 2:7, 10: "The people served the LORD all the days of Joshua, and all the days of the elders who outlived Joshua, who had seen all the great work which the LORD had done for Israel. . . . And there arose another generation after them, who did not know the LORD or the work which he had done for Israel" (similarly Josh. 24:31). Here the Hebrew is מעשה, and the reference is to the historical deliverance at the Exodus. In Isa. 5:12:

They do not regard the deed [פעל, singular;
RSV "deeds"] of the LORD,
or see the work [מעשה] of his hands,

the stress is upon Yahweh's "work" in judgment (similarly Ps. 28:5; Isa. 5:19). Note the anthropomorphisms "the work of his (thy) hands" (Job 14:15; 34:19; Pss. 8:6—H 8:7; 19:1—H 19:2; 28:5; 102:25—H 102:26; Isa. 5:12) and "the work of thy fingers" (Ps. 8:3—H 8:4), usually with reference to God's work in creation.

The work of God is described as "terrible" (נורא, "to be feared"; Ps. 66:3), "great" (92:5—H 92:6), "wonderful" (139:14). No works are like his (86:8). Idol-gods are but the "work of men's hands" (115:4; 135:15). God's work is "done in faithfulness" (33:4; 111:7), and all that he has made has been made "in wisdom" (104:24). "His compassion is over all that he has made" (145:9). Godly men are to "meditate" and "muse" on all God's works (77:12—H 77:13; 143:5), "call to mind" and "remember" them (77:11 —H 77:12; 105:5), "have pleasure" in them (111:2), be thankful for them (107:15, 21, 31), and bless and praise the God who has done them (72:18; 105:1-2).

Other words besides מעשה are used of God's work. Most frequent is פעל (pô'al), a poetical synonym of מעשה, with which it is sometimes parallel (Deut. 32:4; Job 36:24; Pss. 44:1—H 44:2; 64:9—H 64:10; some ten times in all). The RSV also retains the KJV "work(s)" for יגיע (lit., "toil") in Job 10:3; for יד (lit., "hand," in sense of "power") in Exod. 14:31; for מלאכה (lit., "occupation") in Gen. 2:2-3; Ps. 73: 28; Jer. 50:25; for מעבד in Dan. 4:37—A 4:34; for מעלל ("deed") in Ps. 78:7; and for three other nouns from the stem פעל in Pss. 28:5; 46:8—H 46:9; 66:5. It should be added that a full concordance of the "work(s) of God" should take account of the verbs עשה and פעל with God as subject.

The relation between the "work" of God and the "word" of God is closer than the very few passages in which they are mentioned together might seem to indicate.

> By the word of the LORD the heavens were made,
> and all their host by the breath of his mouth
> (Ps. 33:6).

In vs. 4 of the same psalm "word" and "work" are in parallelism. This summarizes the account of Creation in Gen. 1, with its "and God said" followed by "and God made" (vss. 6-7, 14-16, 20-21, 24-25, 26-27). The Hebrew דבר, "word," can have the sense of "task," "act," "occupation," as in "the acts of" (lit., "the words of the days of"; I Kings 14:29 and frequently), or "they had no dealings [lit., 'word'] with any one" (Judg. 18:7, 28). Action originates in thought, and the formulated thought or "word" is the middle term between thought and deed. The same applies to WISDOM, which in Prov. 8 is hypostatized and becomes the agent in creation.

2. In the NT. The conclusion of the preceding paragraph is amplified in the Prologue to the Fourth Gospel, in which the Logos, the divine thought or reason, is the creative ground of all existence. "In the beginning was the Word, and the Word was with God, and the Word was God. He was in the beginning with God; all things were made through him" (πάντα δι' αὐτοῦ ἐγένετο; John 1:1-3).

The Greek word for "work" in the NT is usually ἔργον, but μεγαλεῖα ("mighty works"; Acts 2:11), μεγάλα ("great things"; Luke 1:49), ποίημα ("workmanship"; Eph. 2:10), and ἐνέργεια ("working"; Eph. 1:19; 3:7; "power" in Phil. 3:21) are found. See also δύναμις, τέρας, and σημεῖον—the three words occur together in the "mighty works and wonders and signs" which God did through Christ (Acts 2:22).

The most distinctive teaching about "the work of God" is to be found in the Fourth Gospel. The works (ἔργα) of Jesus are such as no one else has done (John 15:24), the works which the Father has granted him to accomplish (5:36; 10:32; 17:4), works done in the Father's name (10:25), and in this sense done by the Father himself (14:10-11). Those who believe in Jesus will do even greater works than he has done (14:12). In answer to the question: "What must we do, to be doing the work of God?" Jesus replies: "This is the work of God, that you believe in him whom he has sent" (6:28-29). When the disciples besought him to eat, he said to them: "My food is to do the will of him who sent me, and to

accomplish his work" (4:34; see also 5:20; 7:3, 21; 9:3-4; 10:37-38).

In Rom. 14:20; I Cor. 15:58; 16:10; Phil. 2:30, "the work of God/the Lord/Christ" is used of the spread of the Christian evangel.

See also GOD; CREATION; WORD.

Bibliography. O. Linton, "Gärningar," *Svenskt Bibliskt Uppslagsverk,* vol. I (1948), cols. 761-64.

C. R. NORTH

WORLD, THE. A term which, in English Bibles, as also in modern English usage, has a wide variety of meanings. In the RSV four Hebrew and two Greek words denoting a spatial entity are translated "world." One of the Greek words, κόσμος, has many nuances: it is used of the universe as a whole, of the planet Earth, of "people" generally, of "the world" as being at enmity with God, and of the world as the scene and object of God's redemptive purpose. There are also words and phrases which have a time, rather than a space, reference (cf. "world without end"), in which the rendering "world" is occasionally retained even in the RSV —e.g., αἰών (Matt. 13:22) and ἐκ τοῦ αἰῶνος (John 9:32). This may seem confusing but is not surprising, since the world is an entity both in space and in time.

The purpose of this article is theological, to deal with the biblical concept of "the world" as the cosmos, the ordered system of nature, in its relation to God. (For this sense of κόσμος we should say "the universe," but the universe is on a vastly bigger scale than anything the ancient Hebrews or Greeks envisaged.) But since the world is not devoid of life but is the home of sentient and intelligent creatures (cf. Isa. 45:18), and since "the world" sometimes denotes the human race, as indeed it frequently does in contemporary English usage, the final emphasis will be more on God's providential and redemptive purpose for the world than on cosmology. For biblical cosmology, *see* COSMOGONY; CREATION; HEAVEN; EARTH; etc.; and for human nature and its psychology, *see* MAN, NATURE OF.

A. In the OT
  1. ארץ
  2. תבל
  3. חלד and חדל
  4. [ה]עולם
B. The Greek concept of κόσμος
C. In the LXX and the Apoc.
D. In the NT
  1. Οἰκουμένη
  2. Κιῶν
  3. Κόσμος
    a. The universe
    b. The earth and/or its inhabitants
    c. The scene of human activity
    d. The world at enmity with God
    e. The world Christ came to save
Bibliography

A. *IN THE OT*. Several Hebrew words are translated "world" in both the KJV and the RSV. They are:

1. ארץ. This word occurs 2,407 times, and the corresponding Aramaic ארקא ארעא (Jer. 10:11), 21 times. The most frequent translations of it are "earth," "land" ("the land of Egypt" [Num. 1:1]), "country" (KJV 140; less often RSV; but cf. Gen. 12:1, etc.), "ground" (KJV 96; less often RSV; but cf. Deut. 15:23). Of the 4 places in which the KJV has "world," the RSV retains "world" in Isa. 23:17; Jer. 25:26; this is because it is followed by "the face of the earth" (אדמה, which properly means "ground"). The reason why ארץ is seldom rendered "world" is that it occurs so often in conjunction with תבל (see § A2 below). Otherwise the natural rendering would sometimes be "world"; e.g., for KJV "in the earth," RSV "on the earth" (Gen. 6:4), we should say "in the world." But ארץ is nowhere the universe. In Gen. 1:10 it even appears to be restricted to the "dry land" (יבשה), as distinct from "seas" (ימים; cf. Jonah 1:9). It is a word common to the Semitic languages, but its etymology is unknown. Its wide latitude of meanings, from "land"-"territory" to "earth"-"world," can be accounted for by supposing that the early Semite gave the name ארץ to the territory with which he was familiar, and continued to use the word for "earth"-"world" as his geographical horizons widened.

2. תבל. This word occurs 36 times in the OT and twice in the Apoc. (Ecclus. 10:4; 37:3). The RSV throughout retains the "world" of the KJV. תבל is used only in poetry, never takes the article, and in 22 instances is parallel with ארץ, with which it is practically synonymous. Its etymology is obscure, but there are indications that, like ארץ, it originally denoted dry land: it is parallel with "sea" in II Sam. 22:16; Pss. 18:15—H 18:16; 98:7 (parallels can be complementary as well as synonymous); and in Akkadian êli tabali ("by land") is parallel with êli nâru ("by water"). A few passages (I Sam. 2:8; Ps. 90:2; Prov. 8:31; Job 37:12—the last two lit. "the world of his earth") suggest that תבל should be distinguished from ארץ; but it would be hazardous to try to form a clear picture of these poetical figures, and in Ps. 90:2 the expression "the earth and the world" is probably a hendiadys. Expressions such as "תבל and its inhabitants" occur in Pss. 24:1; 33:8; 98:7; Isa. 26:9, 18; Lam. 4:12; Nah. 1:5. In Ps. 9:8—H 9:9, תבל is parallel with לאמים ("peoples"), and in Pss. 96:13; 98:9 with עמים ("peoples"); and in Isa. 13:11 we have "world" parallel with "wicked," as if to anticipate the pejorative sense of κόσμος in the NT. In these passages Yahweh is coming to "judge" the earth/world. This is nowhere expressed more strongly than in Isa. 34:1-2, where we find the elaborate parallelism of "nations"/"peoples" with "earth"/"world." It is clear that תבל is no more the universe than is ארץ. In Ps. 89:11; Jer. 10:12; 51:15 the heavens, the earth, and the world appear to make up a totality (cf. "the heavens and the earth" of Gen. 1:1).

3. חדל and חלד. Of the five passages in which חלד is found, the KJV and RSV twice use "world" (Pss. 17:14; 49:1—H 49:2). The word is related to Arabic ḥalada ("abide," "continue"), ḥuldⁿ ("eternity"), and is therefore equivalent to αἰών, not κόσμος. The hapax legomenon חדל (Isa. 38:11) properly means "cessation" (cf. ERV-ASV mg.: "among them that have ceased to be"). The RSV retains the KJV "inhabitants of the world," which is probably for "inhabitants of (the world of) cessation."

Some few Hebrew MSS read חלד, and this is favored by most scholars.

4. העולם. It should be said that the KJV twice (Ps. 73:12; Eccl. 3:11) has "world" for ה[עולם], but this rendering is not retained in the RSV. The general sense of עולם is "long duration." It is not in doubt that the word came in postbiblical Hebrew, Aramaic-Syriac, and Arabic to mean the spatial world, much as αἰών=κόσμος occasionally in the NT (see § D2 below). But even though Eccl. 3:11 is late, the RSV and the ERV mg. rightly substitute "eternity" for "the world." The immediate context, "from the beginning to the end," amply justifies this.

The Hebrews had no one word for the "universe." They had to resort to periphrases like "the heavens and the earth" (Gen. 1:1), or, to be all-inclusive, "heaven and earth, the sea, and all that is in them" (Exod. 20:11), or "heaven, the heaven of heavens, with all their host, the earth and all that is on it, the seas and all that is in them" (Neh. 9:6). Or they could express the totality of things by a simple כל ("all"; Isa. 44:24) or הכל ("the all"; Jer. 10:16; 51: 19). The skeptical Ecclesiastes might conclude that "the totality of things [הכל] is vanity" (Eccl. 1:2), but even he (cf. Eccl. 12:1) would hardly have denied the unanimous testimony of the OT, that heaven and earth were created by God, that Yahweh's "kingdom rules over all" (Ps. 103:19), and that his "compassion is over all that he has made" (Ps. 145:9).

The OT is fully committed to the doctrine of creation, which finds its highest expression in Gen. 1:1-2:3; in Second Isaiah;.in certain psalms (e.g., 104); and in Job 38 ff. The primary meaning of the Hebrew verb "create" (ברא) was probably "to build," but in the OT (some fifty times) it has become a theological term, always with God as subject. It does not in itself imply creation *ex nihilo.* Indeed, Gen. 1 was written against a background of Babylonian mythology, in which heaven and earth were fashioned from the body of Tiamat the chaos monster (תהום, "[the] deep," of Gen. 1:2; *see* CREATION; COSMOGONY). A literal translation of Gen. 1:1-2 would be: "When God began to create the heavens and the earth, the earth was formless and void . . ." (cf. RSV mg.). This is perhaps the reason why the author of the Wisdom of Solomon (11:17) still wrote of God's "all-powerful hand, which created the world out of formless matter" (κτίσασα τὸν κόσμον ἐξ ἀμόρφου ὕλης). The contrast between creation and emanation (*see* § B *below*) is more significant and important than that between the OT concept of creation and the *ex nihilo* doctrine of the NT (probably) and the early Christian fathers.

B. THE GREEK CONCEPT OF ΚΟΣΜΟΣ. Any treatment of "the world" in the NT must be prefaced by a summary of the Greek concept of κόσμος. The word primarily denoted what is well built or artistically arranged. The Greek could speak of the κόσμος of a horse, or of well-chosen words. He had a lively awareness of the beauty of any such κόσμος, and his appreciation of feminine beauty (γυναικεῖος κόσμος) is still echoed in the NT (cf. I Pet. 3:3, where women are warned against "outward adorning" and "wearing of robes" [ἐνδύσεως ἱματίων κόσμος]). From denoting what is well ordered, κόσμος came, in the sixth century B.C., to be used of the world system, the universe as a whole. In this sense it could be synonymous with οὐρανός ("heaven"). Alike for Plato and the Stoics, it is τὸ ὅλον ("the whole") or τὸ πᾶν ("the all"). There is nothing outside the κόσμος, which is without beginning or end.

The relation between God and the world was somewhat differently conceived as between Platonist and Stoic. Platonists distinguished between the world perceptible by the senses (κόσμος αἰσθητός) and the world intelligible to the mind (κόσμος νοητός). God —or whatever name was given to the supreme principle—was either the highest Idea or Essence in the κόσμος νοητός, or the latter's cause and ground. In the *Republic* the idea of the Good so far transcends the other ideas that it is said to be altogether "beyond being" (ἐπέκεινα τῆς οὐσίας). The ultimate logic of this strain in Plato was that no quality, not even the category of being, can be ascribed to God. For the Stoics, God was the principle of reason (λόγος) that pervaded and governed the universe. This λόγος did not transcend the world but was entirely confined within it. Man was a "part" of God, a fragment of the world-soul.

No Greek ever posited the relationship between God and the world as that between Creator and creature. Even though the Platonists were sometimes prepared to place God beyond the κόσμος νοητός, God did not create the world. Creation in the proper sense (κτίζω) was unknown to the Greeks. According to the myth in Plato's *Timaeus*, the Demiurge (called ποιητὰς καὶ πατήρ τοῦδε τοῦ παντός) "begat" the world, but he did so by imposing form on prior-existing matter. Therefore, neither was the Demiurge in the full sense God, nor was the κόσμος properly a creature. The difference between God and every other existent is one of degree, not of kind.

Whether the world is an emanation from the divine being (Platonism) or animated by the divine Logos (Stoicism), there is a sense in which it must itself be divine. Nevertheless, a strain of pessimism was always latent in the Greek attitude toward the world. Each successive emanation meant one farther remove or declension from the source of being. Thus there emerged a kind of dualism: the material world, if not actually evil, was an obstruction to the soul (ψυχή) or mind (νοῦς) by which man was related to the divine. Redemption came to be conceived as a release from matter (ὕλη) or the body (σῶμα). Disparagement of the world was deepened by the independent growth of astrology as Greek thought came into contact with the Orient: the stars, which were so many embodiments of the divine, and which controlled a man's destiny, were obviously capable of exercising bad as well as good influences. This pessimism, and its consequent attitude of world-negation, was deepened with the decline of the polis and the political insecurities of the Hellenistic period.

It should be added that, much as κόσμος came early to signify "heaven," it also came to be used of the earth, as an integral part of the world-whole. In Koine Greek it is found in the sense of the inhabited world (οἰκουμένη), the earth and its inhabitants, and even mankind, "people" generally, much as "the world" can have these meanings in English today. Nero is called on a Greek inscription on Samos the "lord of the whole world" (ὁ τοῦ παντὸς κόσμου κύριος). Similarly, Nerva is even called σωτήρ τοῦ πάντος κόσμου.

C. IN THE LXX AND THE APOC. All Greek philosophies found a home in Alexandria, where there was a considerable and influential Jewish population. Greek-speaking Jews readily took the word κόσμος into their vocabulary, and for them it came to have a definitely religious connotation.

In the LXX, κόσμος is employed as a rendering of צבא, "the host [of heaven]," in Gen. 2:1; Deut. 4:19; 17:3 (ὁ κόσμος τοῦ οὐρανοῦ); Isa. 40:26; etc. It is also used in the old sense of "adornment," "beauty," for a number of Hebrew words—e.g., עֲדִי ("ornaments") in Exod. 33:5-6; II Sam. 1:24; etc.; תפארת ("glory") in Prov. 20:29; מעדנים ("delight") in Prov. 29:17. This sense is also found in the originally Greek apocrypha, which, of course, were part of the LXX Bible. Especially noteworthy is the παντὶ τῷ κόσμῳ τῷ γυναικείῳ of Jth. 12:15 (*cf.* § B *above*).

The translators from Hebrew had no occasion to render "heaven" and "earth" otherwise than by οὐρανός and γῆ (so in Gen. 1:1; Γένεσις κόσμου occurs as the title of Genesis only in Aq.). ארץ is generally γῆ, and תבל is οἰκουμένη. But in the originally Greek compositions κόσμος is frequently used for the world-universe (Wisdom of Solomon nineteen, II Maccabees five, IV Maccabees four times), and God is described as "Creator" (κτίστης; II Macc. 7:23; 13:14), "Sovereign" (δυνάστης; II Macc. 12:15), and "King" (βασιλεύς; II Macc. 7:9) of the world. Wisd. Sol. 11:22 has it that "the whole world [ὅλος ὁ κόσμος] before thee is like a speck that tips the scales" (cf. Isa. 40:15). In Wisd. Sol. 7:17 the author speaks of knowing the "structure of the world" (σύστασιν κόσμου) and the "activity of the elements" (στοιχεία)—both words were used by Plato and were taken up by Philo. In 16:17 (cf. 5:20) the κόσμος— i.e., the whole order of nature—is said to be the defender of the righteous.

As in Hellenistic Greek generally, κόσμος came to be used of the earth-world, as in Wisd. Sol. 9:3, which says that man was formed to "rule the world in holiness and righteousness." For a man to be born is "to come into the world" (εἰς τὸν κόσμον; Wisd. Sol. 7:6; cf. Heb. 10:5). When Adam is called the "first-formed father of the world" (Wisd. Sol. 10:1), "the world" presumably means "mankind" (cf. 6:24; 14:6). Finally, not all is well with the world: by the vaingloriousness of men, idols have entered into it (14:14). In 2:24 death is said to have entered the world (cf. Rom. 5:21) "through the devil's envy."

D. IN THE NT. Three Greek words, οἰκουμένη, αἰών, and κόσμος, are translated "world" in the English NT. (The translation of γῆ by "world" in Rev. 13:3 KJV may be left out of account, even though "world" would better accord with present-day idiom than the RSV "earth"; *see* § A1 *above*.) The three words are in some of their meanings near-synonyms and can occasionally, as will appear, be interchanged with one another.

1. **Οἰκουμένη.** This is an abbreviation of (ἡ) οἰκουμένη (γῆ), "(the) inhabited (earth)." It occurs fifteen times. The KJV translates "earth" in Luke 21:26, otherwise "world." The ERV and the RSV always have "world," but the ERV mg. everywhere

has the note "Gr. *the inhabited earth.*" This note does not appear in the RSV, and, without an annotated concordance, the word is lost to the non-Greek-reading student. Οἰκουμένη was originally a designation of the Greek world as opposed to "barbarian" lands. By NT times it had come to be used of the Roman world (so Acts 24:5). "All the world" in Luke 2:1 may be either a "pleasant hyperbole" or a reference to the Roman claim to world-wide empire. In modern missionary thinking, and sometimes even in its contexts, οἰκουμένη is capable of expansion to include the whole world of men, as in Matt. 24:14 (cf. Matt. 26:13 = Mark 14:9; Mark 16:15, where the word is κόσμος). Similarly in Rom. 10:18, a quotation from Ps. 19:4—H 19:5, οἰκουμένη has as wide a connotation as תבל. A world-wide sense probably attaches to the word in Luke 4:5 (cf. Heb. 1:6), for which the parallel Matt. 4:8 has κόσμος. Heb. 2:5, where the dutifully consistent ERV mg. would sound pedantic, speaks of the "οἰκουμένη to come" (τὴν οἰκουμένην τὴν μέλλουσαν). Here οἰκουμένη clearly has much the same meaning as αἰών = עולם (cf. Matt. 12:32; Eph. 1:21; Heb. 6:5 [ὁ μέλλων αἰών]). It thus passes over to the sense of αἰών = κόσμος (*see* § D2 *below*).

2. Αἰών. This word, like עולם, has the general sense of "long duration." It appears in the KJV (rather more than thirty times) as "world"; similarly in the ERV, except in I Cor. 10:11 ("ages"); Heb. 6:5 ("age"). The ERV mg. always has "age," except in I Cor. 2:7-8. The RSV has "age," except that "world" is preferred in Matt. 13:22 = Mark 4:19; Luke 16:8 (mg. "Greek *age*"); Rom. 12:2 (mg. ("Greek *age*"); II Cor. 4:4; I Tim. 6:17; II Tim. 4:10; Heb. 1:2; 11:3. The translation "world" rather than "age" is justified in some, at least, of these passages. Thus, the "cares of the world" (αἱ μέριμναι τοῦ αἰῶνος) of Mark 4:19 = Matt. 13:22 are nowise different from the "worldly affairs" (τὰ τοῦ κόσμου) about which the married man "is anxious" (μεριμνᾷ) in I Cor. 7:33. And "this present world," with which Demas is "in love" (II Tim. 4:10), is material enough. The created αἰῶνας of Heb. 1:2; 11:3 must be spatial entities rather than aeons of time. The worlds of space and time cannot be separated from one another, and there are not wanting examples in nonbiblical Greek of αἰών = κόσμος, much as עולם came (*see* § A4 *above*) in rabbinical Hebrew to be used of the sensible world.

3. Κόσμος. This word is found 188 times in the NT. More than half (104) the examples are in the Johannine writings, and, of the remainder, 46 are in the Pauline (including the Pastoral) letters. Except in I Pet. 3:3 (*see* § B *above*) all the standard English versions translate it "world." Most of the senses which κόσμος acquired in native Greek authors are represented in the NT, but the word came to have other meanings which have no parallels outside the NT and literature directly influenced by it.

a. The universe. The fullest definition of the word in this sense is in Acts 17:24: "The God who made the world and everything in it [καὶ πάντα τὰ ἐν αὐτῷ], being Lord of heaven and earth . . . ." The expression "heaven and earth" derives from the OT. Further expansions of it are "the heaven and the earth and the sea and everything in them" (Acts 4:24), and "heaven and what is in it, the earth and

what is in it, and the sea and what is in it" (Rev. 10:6; cf. Neh. 9:6). The words "heaven and earth" would come naturally to Jesus, steeped as he was in the OT (Matt. 5:18; 24:35 and parallels), and he addressed God as "Father, Lord of heaven and earth" (Matt. 11:25 = Luke 10:21). But it is probably not without significance (*see below*) that God is never in the NT called κύριος τοῦ κόσμου, after the manner of the Apoc.

A number of passages speak of the "foundation of the world": Matt. 25:34; Luke 11:50; John 17:24; Eph. 1:4; Heb. 4:3; 9:26; I Pet. 1:20 (πρὸ καταβολῆς κόσμου); Rev. 13:8; 17:8 (ἀπὸ καταβολῆς κόσμου). Matt. 24:21 has "from the beginning of the world" (ἀπ' ἀρχῆς κόσμου); Rom. 1:20 "since the creation of the world" (ἀπὸ κτίσεως κόσμου); and John 17:5 "before the world was made" (πρὸ τοῦ τὸν κόσμον εἶναι). In some of these passages the κόσμος in mind in the first instance may have been the Hebrew ארץ or תבל; but in the context of the NT it must have acquired the wider meaning of the "universe." In Phil. 2:15: "You shine as lights in the world" (ὡς φωστῆρες ἐν κόσμῳ), the figure suggests luminaries in heaven (but cf. Matt. 5:14-15). In John 21:25 "the world itself" may be hyperbolical for the whole universe.

Synonyms of κόσμος are: (*a*) κτίσις, "creation," in its meaning of the whole created order (Mark 10:6; 13:19; Rom. 1:20, 25; II Pet. 3:4; Rev. 3:14); (*b*) (τὰ) πάντα, "all things" (John 1:3 [cf. 1:10: ὁ κόσμος]; I Cor. 8:6; 15:27-28; Eph. 1:10; Phil. 3:21; Col. 1:16-17, 20; Heb. 1:2-3 [RSV "the universe"]; 2:8, 10; I Pet. 4:7). Anything, therefore, that is said of the κτίσις and τὰ πάντα, applies equally to κόσμος in its universal meaning.

That God created the universe is sometimes said (Mark 13:19; Acts 17:24) and is always assumed, following upon the OT; but the doctrine of creation was not prominent in the Christian kerygma. Christianity was concerned with redemption, rather than with the creation of the world. Yet there are two points in which the NT conception of creation is an advance upon that of the OT: (*a*) The NT shows no trace of the idea of pre-existent matter. A doctrine of creation *ex nihilo* appears to be implicit in Col. 1:15-17 and the Prologue to the Fourth Gospel, though it is not explicitly formulated. (*b*) Paul, the Letter to the Hebrews, and the Prologue to the Fourth Gospel, all speak of Christ as the agent of creation. In Col. 1:16-17 all things were created in, through, and for Christ, the Son (ἐν αὐτῷ ἐκτίσθη τὰ πάντα . . . . τὰ πάντα δι' αὐτοῦ ἔκτισται; cf. I Cor. 8:6). According to Heb. 1:2, it was through a Son— i.e., Christ—that God made the worlds (δι' οὗ καὶ ἐποίησεν τοὺς αἰῶνας). In the Prologue to the Fourth Gospel "the Word [Λόγος] . . . was in the beginning with God; all things were made through him [πάντα δι' αὐτοῦ ἐγένετο], and without him was not anything made that was made. . . . And the world was made through him [ὁ κόσμος δι' αὐτοῦ ἐγένετο] . . . . And the Word became flesh" (John 1:2-3, 10, 14). This is not the place to elaborate these statements or to discuss their alleged "mythological" implications, but only to note that they are made in the NT. *See* CHRIST.

Two aspects of Paul's thought about the universe

offer a challenge to theologians today. Neither is fully worked out, nor is it clear how, or even whether, they are related to one another. The first is almost prophetic of modern attitudes toward the enigma of the universe. The second appears to have a "mythological" background and received little attention from "liberal" theologians; more recently it has compelled attention, even though there may be no agreement as to how its "mythological" elements should be interpreted.

a) In Rom. 8:19-25, Paul writes that "the creation [ἡ κτίσις] was subjected to futility [ματαιότης; *see* VANITY], not of its own will but by the will of him who subjected it in hope; because the creation itself [αὐτὴ ἡ κτίσις] will be set free from its bondage to decay [φθορά; cf. II Pet. 1:4: ἡ ἐν τῷ κόσμῳ ἐν ἐπιθυμίᾳ φθορά; *see* CORRUPTION] and obtain the glorious liberty of the children of God. We know that the whole creation [πᾶσα ἡ κτίσις] has been groaning in travail together until now." This seems to say that ματαιότης and its consequent φθορά were part of the initial purpose of God in creation and that the ultimate purpose it was to serve was the "revealing of the sons of God" (vs. 19), in which the whole creation will share.

b) Paul evidently shared the current and widespread belief that the world was in some way in the grip of a "lowerarchy" of demonic powers. These are variously described as the "prince of the power of the air" (ὁ ἄρχων τῆς ἐξουσίας τοῦ ἀέρος; Eph. 2:2); the "rulers of this age" (οἱ ἄρχοντες τοῦ αἰῶνος τούτου; I Cor. 2:6); the "god of this world" (ὁ θεὸς τοῦ αἰῶνος τούτου), who "has blinded the minds of the unbelievers" (II Cor. 4:4); the "principalities, . . . the powers [αἱ ἀρχαὶ καὶ αἱ ἐξουσίαι; cf. Col. 2:15], . . . the world rulers of this present darkness [οἱ κοσμοκράτορες τοῦ σκότους τούτου], . . . the spiritual hosts of wickedness in the heavenly places" (τὰ πνευματικὰ τῆς πονηρίας ἐν τοῖς ἐπονραίοις; Eph. 6:12). Over all these powers Christ triumphed on the cross (Col. 2:15); they were created "in" (ἐν), "through" (διά), and "for" (εἰς) Christ (Col. 1:16), and it was God's purpose that they should all (τὰ πάντα) be reconciled to him "by the blood of his cross" (Col. 1:20). *See* DEMON.

b. The earth and/or its inhabitants. When ὁ κόσμος is used of the planet Earth, it can have the same ambiguity—or, rather, double meaning—that "the world" has in English. In passages which speak of "coming into" (John 1:9 and several other times in the Fourth Gospel; I Tim. 1:15; 6:7), "being in" (John 1:10; 9:5; 17:11), "being born into" (John 16:21), and "departing out of" (John 13:1; I Cor. 5:10), "the world," ὁ κόσμος = ἡ γῆ. But in "Show yourself to the world" (John 7:4), and "The world has gone after him" (John 12:19), "the world" means "people generally." In Rom. 1:8: "Your faith is proclaimed in all the world" (similarly Matt. 5:14; 13:38; 26:13; I Cor. 4:9), the word may have either meaning. In "all the kingdoms of the world" (Matt. 4:8) and similar expressions, "the world" is ἡ γῆ, but the emphasis of the whole is on its human inhabitants. In Rom. 11:12, 15, "the world" is the Gentile world. The distinction between the geophysical earth and its human inhabitants in these passages has no theological significance.

c. **The scene of human activity.** This is the world in which man pursues riches and pleasure, or suffers hardship and grief (λύπη; II Cor. 7:10). It profits a man nothing if he "gains the whole world and forfeits his life" (Matt. 16:26 and parallels). "Worldly affairs" (I Cor. 7:33-34) are an anxiety, and Paul exhorts "those who deal with the world" to be "as though they had no dealings with it. For the form of this world is passing away" (παράγει γὰρ τὸ σχῆμα τοῦ κόσμου τούτου; I Cor. 7:31). Still more emphatic is I John 2:15-17: "Do not love the world or the things in the world [τὰ ἐν τῷ κόσμῳ]. If any one loves the world, love for the Father is not in him. For all that is in the world, the lust of the flesh and the lust of the eyes and the pride of life, is not of the Father but is of the world. And the world passes away, and the lust of it." From this it is but a short stage to the idea of § D3*d below.*

d. **The world at enmity with God.** This is the fallen race of mankind. Something of this pejorative sense of κόσμος may be seen in Heb. 11:7: "He [Noah] condemned the world," and 11:38: the martyrs "of whom the world was not worthy." It appears also in Jas. 1:27, in which "religion that is pure and undefiled before God" is defined as "to keep oneself unstained from the world," and 4:4: "Do you not know that friendship with the world is enmity with God? Therefore whoever wishes to be a friend of the world makes himself an enemy of God." II Pet. 1:4 speaks of "the corruption [φθορά] that is in the world"; cf. 2:20: "the defilements [τὰ μιάσματα] of the world."

Condemnation of "the world" comes to its fullest expression in the Pauline and Johannine writings.

For Paul "the wisdom of this world [ἡ σοφία τοῦ κόσμου τούτου] is folly with God" (I Cor. 3:19; cf. 1:20-21, 26-28). "None of the rulers of this age" (τοῦ αἰῶνος τούτου) understands the hidden wisdom of God (I Cor. 2:7-8). Christians have received "not the spirit of the world [τὰ πνεῦμα τοῦ κόσμου] but the spirit which is from God" (I Cor. 2:12). For his part, Paul testifies: "Far be it from me to glory except in the cross of our Lord Jesus Christ, by which the world has been crucified to me, and I to the world" (Gal. 6:14). This attitude toward the world is entirely unrelated to the strain of pessimism latent in the Greek attitude toward the world, with its conception of redemption as a release from matter or the body (*see* § B *above*). Paul would not have denied that "God saw everything that he had made, and behold, it was very good" (Gen. 1:31). But he doubtless took quite literally the story of Adam's transgression, as a consequence of which sin and death had entered the world (Rom. 5:12-14; I Cor. 15:21-22). What he accepted as doctrine was confirmed by what he observed of the corruption of the world in which he lived (Rom. 1:18-32). The true state of the world was revealed to him by the cross as it could never previously have been perceived.

In the Johannine literature condemnation of "the world" is more frequent, and in even stronger terms, than in Paul. This may be because of intensified opposition from "the Jews" (John 7:1 and frequently; cf. 16:2), of Roman persecution (cf. Rev. 18), and, possibly, of dualism of a Gnostic type. It may be noted that the word αἰών is never used in the Johannine writings except in εἰς τὸν αἰῶνα, "for ever"

(John 6:51 and five other times), and in John 9:32, where ἐκ τοῦ αἰῶνος οὐκ has only the sense of "never." Sometimes "the world," and especially "this world" (John 12:31), seem to denote what elsewhere in the NT is called "this present age/world" (ὁ νῦν αἰών; Tit. 2:12). Presumably κόσμος is preferred to αἰών as being more intelligible to Gentile readers. The sum of the matter is that "the whole world is in the power of the evil one" (ἐν τῷ πονηρῷ; I John 5:19). "This world," in contrast with the world to come (John 8:23; 12:25; 13:1; 18:36; I John 4:17), lies under the dominion of the "ruler of this world" (John 12:31; 14:30; 16:11)—i.e., the devil (I John 3:8, 10). Christians must expect the hatred of the world, which has already hated their Master (John 7:7; 15:18-19; 17:14; I John 3:13). See further John 1:10; 3:19; 14:17, 27; 16:8, 20, 33; 17:9, 25; I John 2:15-17; 3:1; 4:5; 5:4-5.

In accordance with the foregoing, the adjective κοσμικός is used (Tit. 2:12) of "worldly" passions; this is a sense it never has in classical Greek.

e. The world Christ came to save. The world at enmity with God is the very world which God "so loved . . . that he gave his only Son, that whoever believes in him should not perish but have eternal life" (John 3:16; cf. I John 4:9). Christ is the "Savior of the world" (John 4:42; 12:47; I John 4:14; *contrast* § B *above*), the "light of the world" (John 8:12; 9:5; 12:46), the "expiation for . . . the sins of the whole world" (I John 2:2). The word "world" is less frequently used in this sense by Paul, but his whole doctrine of salvation is summed up in the statement: "God was in Christ reconciling the world to himself" (II Cor. 5:19); cf. I Tim. 1:15: "Christ Jesus came into the world to save sinners." *See* § D3a *above.*

Insofar as the world is redeemed, it ceases to be κόσμος or αἰών οὗτος, and becomes instead the "kingdom of God," the "world/age [αἰών] to come" (Mark 10:30), or, going back to Hebraic idiom, a "new heaven and a new earth" (Rev. 21:1). "The kingdom of the world has become the kingdom of our Lord and of his Christ" (Rev. 11:15).

See also ESCHATOLOGY; TIME.

Bibliography. H. Sasse, κόσμος, *TWNT*, III (1938), 867-96, is masterly. C. H. Dodd, *The Interpretation of the Fourth Gospel* (1953), *passim.* R. Bultmann, *Theology of the NT* (English trans.; vol. I, 1951; vol. II, 1955). For the problem of Christ and creation, with references to current literature, see G. V. Jones, *Christology and Myth in the NT* (1956), pp. 148-201. For the Pauline concept of world powers, see G. B. Caird, *Principalities and Powers: A Study in Pauline Theology* (1956).　　　　C. R. NORTH

WORM [סס; תּוֹלֵעָה; תּוֹלַעַת; תּוֹלָע; רִמָּה; σκώληξ; σκωληκόβρωτος; *see below*]. A small, slender, creeping animal, usually limbless and soft-bodied. The most typical are the *Annelida,* of which the earthworms (*Lumbricidae*) are the most familiar. The term "worm" can, however, be applied to the larva of various insects, as of beetles, moths, etc. Most of the biblical references appear to be to insect larvae.

Several Hebrew words are translated "worm" in the OT. סס, *sās* (cf. Akkadian *sāsu, ṣāṣu,* "moth"; Arabic *sūs,* "moth-worm"; Jewish Aramaic ססא and Syriac *sosā,* "moth, worm"), is used in Isa. 51:8 and

probably refers to the larva of one of the various clothes moths (*Tineidae*). *See* MOTH.

תּוֹלֵעָה (Deut. 28:39; Jonah 4:7) perhaps means "biter" (cf. מַתְלְעוֹת, "teeth," in Job 29:17, etc.; cf. also Akkadian *tultu,* "worm," and Syriac *tawl'ā,* "worm, grub"). The word presumably refers to the larvae of some leaf-eating insect, as of moths (*Lepidoptera*) or beetles (*Coleoptera*).

The "worms" of Exod. 16:20 (תּוֹלָע) and of 16:24 (רִמָּה) are probably ants (of the family *Formicidae*), feeding upon the honeydew excretions of various plant lice and scale insects. *See* MANNA.

Both רִמָּה (*rimmâ;* cf. Arabic *ramma,* "to be decayed" [of bone]) and תּוֹלֵעָה are used of the wormlike creatures which feed upon corpses (רִמָּה is translated "maggot" in Job 25:6; Isa. 14:11). These are mostly larvae of various beetles (e.g., the Churchyard beetle, *Blaps mortisaga,* of the family *Heteromera;* the *Silphidae* of the superfamily *Staphylinoidea*). Worms thus come to form part of the Hebrew picture of the grave or of the land of the dead (Job 17:14; 21:26; Isa. 14:11; Enoch 46:6; M. Ab. IV.4). As Israel's eschatology developed, worms and fire were envisaged as the lot of the ungodly after death (Jth. 16:17; Ecclus. 7:17)—in Isa. 66:24; Mark 9:48 this is represented as an eternal condition.

In the NT, the word σκώληξ is used in Mark 9:48 to refer to larvae. Σκωληκόβρωτος (Acts 12:23), possibly used metaphorically, describes the sickness or disease, presumably abdominal (the rupture of an infected appendix, of a hydatid cyst, etc.), which brought about the death of Herod Agrippa in A.D. 44 (cf. Jos. Antiq. XIX.viii). On the association of worms with a fatal illness, see Herodotus IV.205 (Pheretime); II Macc. 9:9 (Antiochus IV); Jos. Antiq. XVII.vi (Herod the Great).

"Worm" serves as a figure to denote the lowliness and insignificance of the speaker (Ps. 22:6—H 22:7) or of man in general (Job 25:6; 24:20 is a doubtful text [cf. RSV "their name"]). In Isa. 41:14 the word "worm" is applied by the Lord to Israel.

The meaning of "My flesh is clothed with worms [רִמָּה]" (Job 7:5) is not clear. The context appears to exclude the view that the phrase reflects Job's awareness of his mortal nature. It is difficult to believe that the words are to be taken literally, unless we interpret "worms" as "flies." Possibly the expression is a hyperbolic figure for an ulcerous condition.

See also CRAWLING THINGS.　　　W. S. MCCULLOUGH

WORMWOOD [לַעֲנָה, *la'anâ;* ἄψινθος]. A plant with a bitter taste, probably referring to several species of the genus Artemisia, of which the *Artemisia herba-alba* Asso is most common. The Hebrew word is often used with "GALL" (Deut. 29:18 KJV—H 29:17; Jer. 9:15 KJV; 23:15 KJV; Lam. 3:19; Amos 6:12 KJV), and is always used metaphorically of bitterness and sorrow. The LXX never translates as "wormwood," but uses various words meaning "bitterness."

Youth is warned against the "loose woman," whose honeyed words lead to bitter experiences (Prov. 5:4). The prophets describe the judgment of God in terms of being fed with wormwood (Jer. 9:15; 23:15), condemn those who "turn justice to wormwood" (Amos 5:7; cf. 6:12), and compare the destruction of Jeru-

From Crowfoot and Baldensperger, *From Cedar to Hyssop*

26. Wormwood

salem in 586 B.C. to the bitterness of wormwood and gall (Lam. 3:15, 19).

Rev. 8:10-11 describes the blazing star called "Wormwood" as falling from heaven and turning the waters bitter with wormwood until "many men died of the water" (wormwood is not poisonous). *Artemisia absinthium* L. is the sage known to the Greeks and thus could be the wormwood of John of Patmos. Cf. Heb. 12:15, where the LXX of Deut. 29:18—G 29: 17, "root of bitterness," is quoted.

Fig. WOR 26. *See also* FLORA § A14b; POISON.

Bibliography. I. Löw, *Die Flora der Juden,* I (1926), 379-90; H. N. and A. L. Moldenke, *Plants of the Bible* (1952), pp. 48-50.   J. C. TREVER

WORSHIP IN THE OT. Worship (from Saxon *weorthscipe,* "worthship") is homage—the attitude and activity designed to recognize and describe the worth of the person or thing to which the homage is addressed. Worship is thus synonymous with the whole of a reverent life, embracing piety as well as liturgy. The range of meaning is therefore very great. Here "worship" is used to describe the activities and attitudes, the behavior, proper to the sanctuary; in Christian parlance, divine worship.

1. Terminology
2. In the patriarchal age
3. Mosaic worship
4. The early monarchy
5. Temple and cultus
6. Josiah's reform
7. In the postexilic period
8. Personal worship
9. Characteristics
Bibliography

1. Terminology. A very rich vocabulary illustrates and defines the activity of worship in the OT. The verbs עָבַד, "to serve" (cf. עֲבוֹדָה, "service, adoration" =λατρεία), and הִשְׁתַּחֲוָה, "to prostrate oneself" (προσκυνεῖν), are basic terms within such generally descriptive terms as "to draw near," "to seek the face of Yahweh," etc.

2. In the patriarchal age. It is no longer possible to state that worship in the days of the founding fathers of Israel can be described in terms of animism and the like. The religious background of Canaan revealed by archaeology, and the corresponding account of El religion in Genesis, show that patriarchal religion was at least polytheistic. This in turn permits of a henotheistic possibility as in the case of Abraham. But the patriarchal legends reflect nomadic and eventful tradition in distinction from the agricultural and fertility interests of their contemporaries. There are accordingly theophanies to the individual patriarchs and resultant places of worship, altars for sacrifice and for gifts. Beyond these it is difficult to go for certain, though Genesis provides evidence of various ritual actions (cf. the beginnings of sacrifice in 4:3-4; of worship in 4:26; Noah's altar and worship in 8:20-22). Again in Gen. 14 Abraham is said to have met Melchizedek the king-priest of El Elyon, and to have committed himself to El Elyon (vss. 18-23). The promise of the land in 15:7 is linked with and expressed in various theophanic and ritual actions (vss. 8-21). In Gen. 22 worship is seen to consist in sacrifice, though later interests are, of course, at work in the condemnation of human sacrifice. In 28:17 the sacred Bethel is described in terms reminiscent of cosmic symbolism. Other ritual actions such as purifications, changes of garments, offerings of drink and oil, occur in ch. 35, and blessings also are often given. Israelite worship in Genesis is, however rudimentary, personal and family.

3. Mosaic worship. At the bush Moses is bidden to remove his sandals, and he also veils his face. Moses requests Pharaoh to permit Israel to make a pilgrimage feast of three days' journey into the wilderness for sacrifice (Exod. 5:1-3, etc.). Behind the legislative narratives and traditions of the Passover in Exod. 12–13 lies doubtless an old nomadic feast of firstlings, and it is a question if Moses did not use this feast and adapt it as a vehicle of his own faith and message. Certainly Miriam had used her timbrel, and the women had danced and sung before, even if now they did all these things with a new song in honor of a new or revived deity. Jethro led Israel's worship in confession, sacrifice, and sacred meal (18: 10-12). Various ritual actions following the theophany are prescribed in ch. 19, and there is no reason to doubt that 24:3-8 gives the details of the covenant acts of worship. Perhaps vision and meal details of 24:11 preserve details of Kenite worship (cf. 3:2; 18: 12). These stories show how faith is enshrined in and expressed by ritual action. The place and the acts of worship are part of the covenant religion in the Sinai stories. Ancient religious customs are being pressed into the service of the new faith.

How much religious observance was maintained in the desert cannot be known at present, but the departure from Sinai is accompanied by ritual action (Exod. 33:4-6); and, in the institution of the tent, if not in the ark, provision is made for religious occasions during the wanderings (vs. 6). Elements of early (false) worship (32:1-6) and late (true) worship (vss. 30-34) are combined in that black chapter of Exodus.

While it is difficult to accept the view that conceptions and events in Exodus and Numbers really reflect the practices of the Jerusalem temple, Israel's crossing into Canaan and the capture of Jericho are as much religious processions as military movements. Doubtless, too, Josh. 4 contains the sanctuary legend for Gilgal, and it is extremely likely that it was this Gilgal which saw Israel's first acts of worship in the new land. The Gilgal sanctuary became a famous one. Saul was crowned there. Amos attacks the place. Perhaps there was an annual celebration at Gilgal of Israel's crossing into Canaan.

In the confused periods of the settlement and the judges, private practices and observance would be maintained, at least for a time. There are various references in Joshua–II Samuel to religious practices and in particular to those associated with the holy war. Inevitably there are periods of change and confusion. This is best described as syncretism, the mingling of two ways of life and worship. The fact of this syncretism is no longer in question, but only its extent and duration. As Israel took over the land, they inevitably took over the sanctuaries. Dan, Gilgal, perhaps Bethel, Beer-sheba, Shechem, and Shiloh are the foremost sanctuaries of the period. Josh. 24 probably relates how Joshua's invading Israel covenanted with the pre-Israelite Hebrew amphictyony centered in Shechem. But numerous were the shrines and altars in the land. Every city and large village would have its own high place, for the practices of worship would be widespread through the land. From this union perhaps Deut. 27 and more likely the Book of the Covenant—i.e., probably Shechem's law code—entered Israel's life. Thus Israel soon adopted the festal calendar of the three feasts as provided for in Exod. 23:14-19. The account of Ephraim's sanctuary at Shiloh, shrine, ark, tent and sacred fire, rooms, altars, festal chamber, elaborate cultus and organized priesthood, shows Israelites participating in Canaanite religious practices (I Sam. 1-3; 9-10). To all intents and purposes Yahweh the God of Israel was becoming a Baal. Rechabites maintained a pristine worship, whatever that was; many Israelite farmers simply turned Yahweh into a Baal; yet others continued to worship Yahweh but did so as though he were a Baal. Hannah's praying and vow (I Sam. 1) are genuine acts of worship; but the corrupt acts of the priests (vss. 12-17), the fetish value of the ark (4:3), reveal other aspects. No doubt, Israel's worship at the high places was being increasingly fused with Canaanite forms motivated by sympathetic magic and directed to the success of the fertility system.

4. The early monarchy. The decline of Israel before the Philistine menace, the loss of Shiloh, the virtual disappearance of the ark from Israel's life, the pathetic but ineffective Yahwism of Saul, must have been reflected in a Yahwism at a low ebb, until David arrived to initiate a revival of Yahwism in a new Israel. It is probable that the religious achievements of David reflect a further and most important installment of syncretism, even though this syncretism exhibits also a synthesizing tendency. On the one side there is David's own personal loyalty to Yahweh,

which is reflected throughout I and II Samuel; there is the revival connected with the purchase of Araunah's threshing floor for a sacred site, and with the bringing of the ark to Jerusalem. There is also the person and the activity of the priest Abiathar. On the other side there is the sudden appearance of Zadok and Nehushtan, and there is the god El Elyon—the ancient deity of Jerusalem. The suggestion that David achieved a synthesizing syncretism of El Elyon with Yahweh, with their respective priesthoods and religious customs, is commanding ever widening support. Out of the syncretism there grows the royal ideology and covenant of the Davidic dynasty. Thus David was probably the architect of the cult and music practiced later in the temple of his son.

5. Temple and cultus. Solomon's erection of the temple, royal sanctuary though it was, was another major event in the syncretism. As David worked out the principles, the spirit, and some of the forms, so Solomon erected the shrine for the Davidic synthesis. The plan, furnishings, cosmic symbolism, and patterns of worship testify to Canaanite (Shechem), Phoenician, and Egyptian influences. It has accordingly been claimed that the erection of Solomon's royal chapel was an idea alien to Israel's Yahwism. From some points of view this is true, but it cannot be claimed that the idea of the sanctuary is anything new in Israel. The idea of the sacred place, whether it be a mountain, a portable shrine like the ark or tent, or a provincial sanctuary like Shechem or Shiloh, is constant and prominent in Israel's religion. Even if certain aspects of Solomon's temple are alien to Yahwism, this is not to say that Yahwism did not benefit from it and, indeed, all church architecture ever since. Thus experience shows that the dimensions of Solomon's chapel are, numinously speaking, sound. This is true of the axis of approach—courts, holy place, holy of holies (cf. the parallel in Exodus: people, 19:17 [cf. 20:21]; priests and elders, 24:1-2, 9-11; Moses, 20:21; 24:2, 18). Similarly cedar wood is most suitable for sanctuaries. Certainly the decorating motifs on the altar, pillars, and walls, and the symbolism of the lights, the bread of the presence, the lavers, and the brazen sea were parts of Israelite worship.

The cultus comprised basically three agricultural FEASTS celebrated throughout the land. There was Unleavened Bread with its eating of unleavened cakes, offering of first fruits, and waving of a sheaf of first fruits, preceded by Passover with its slain lamb, blood-besprinkled doorposts and lintels, and possibly a "limping" dance (*see* PASSOVER AND FEAST OF UNLEAVENED BREAD). The second feast was WEEKS (Pentecost), a midsummer—between barley and wheat harvests—feast with waving of two leavened loaves before God. The third feast, Asiph, Ingathering (*see* BOOTHS, FEAST OF), was the greatest. It was harvest thanksgiving marked by first-night illuminations and dancing (Isa. 30:29), when Israel lived seven days in booths and also celebrated the New Year, poured water and offered prayer for the coming of the former rains (cf. Zech. 14:16-17).

Rites and festivals long familiar to Israel were to be seen in Solomon's temple, but how much non-Israelite also appeared? There were undoubtedly elements of sun worship (cf. II Kings 23:11; Ezek. 8: 14-16; Suk. V.4), though the cultus was scarcely devoted to sun worship. Did the "myth-and-ritual" pattern, with its myth of creation, the deity's death and resurrection, combat, marriage and procession, and other features find celebration at Jerusalem? Did the New Year Feast also serve as a coronation feast for Yahweh? None of these claims may be said to be fully substantiated, though there is abundant evidence for a more cultic interpretation of many of the Psalms. Even if it is necessary to reject Mowinckel's theory of this New Year Festival, yet his suggestion that the Psalms are to be understood in terms of "cultic reality," rather than "poetic fiction," affords an abiding principle of interpretation. It is this quest for "cultic reality" and the cultic nucleus which now dominates contemporary study of the Psalms, an increasing number of which may be safely regarded as pre-exilic. The Psalter is the prayer book of the first, as well as of the second, temple.

At Jerusalem, as at other sanctuaries through the land, worshipers came to rejoice before their God. With their tithes, first fruits, and their sacrificial offerings in general, they came to sanctuary: music, solos, anthems, shoutings, dancing, processions with all manner of instruments; with incense, rings and jewelry, elementary preaching in the form of all kinds of oracles, oracles of peace and reassurance, sacred recitings of the stories of the shrine and of old Israel, its fathers, heroes, saints, and soldiers, petitions, prayers, vows, vigils, promises, saying of creeds and confessions, sacred meals and washings—fires of altar and illuminations from Boaz and Jachin, and people, people, people everywhere, where God had recorded his name (Exod. 20:24) and had stored up his holiness, his presence, and his blessing for those who sought him out. There is silence, too, in Israelite worship (Pss. 4:4; 46:10; 76:8 [cf. 83:1 of God]). There is also the ministry of memory and remembrance, whereby men in difficulty find the way of spiritual revival as they remember God and all his grace, his covenant mercies, and his mighty deeds of former days. Thus Israel rejoiced before God, seeing God and eating and drinking. The psalmist succinctly defines the character and the purpose of worship by desiring to dwell in the house of the Lord all his life

> to behold the beauty of the LORD,
> and to inquire in his temple
> (27:4).

Perhaps it was the unveiling of the ark that revealed the beauty, as it was certainly the oracles of the sanctuary which answered the inquiries. In this context sacrifices of joy are spontaneous offerings, for God himself says:

> "Seek ye my face."
> My heart says to thee,
> "Thy face, LORD, do I seek"
> (27:8).

To how much then does this cultic activity of the Psalms add up? There is no evidence that the Ras Shamra cult was ever paralleled at any Israelite sanctuary. Certainly it is well-nigh impossible that the myths of the death and resurrection of a god could ever be related of Yahweh. Even his marriage is difficult, though the appearance of Anath-Yahu

and other goddesses, at Elephantine, suggests a consort for Yahweh. There was ritual prostitution in Israel. On the other hand, so gifted is Israel in ritual behavior, that there is more to be said for, and ever growing acceptance of, the view that there was for some centuries an annual royal festival which represented a Davidic synthesis. On the one hand there are ancient Jerusalem motifs, El Elyon, NEHUSTAN, righteousness, and welfare, and perhaps a priest-king ideology; on the other, Yahwistic features like ARK OF THE COVENANT; COVENANT; tabernacling PRESENCE; and the GLORY of Yahweh. The ritual center of this thesis is, of course, II Samuel with Ps. 132. With these passages must also be associated such psalms as 2; 18; 23–24; 29; 46–48; 68; 72; 81; 84; 89; 93; 95–101; 110; 113–18; 120–34; 149; etc. These psalms, together with such cultic remains buried in, e.g., Isa. 40–55 and P, are probably the cultic nucleus of the Psalter and of the Davidic festival at Jerusalem.

Whatever the range of cultic activity at Jerusalem, it is clear that Israel rejoiced before God in the ancient sanctuaries. Such joyous attitudes before God no prophet, not even Amos or Isaiah or Jeremiah, could denounce. (Hos. 3:4 shows how the loss of sacrifice and pillar, of ephod and teraphim, are punishment for Israel's sins.) Indeed, they had doubtless shared in it, for Amos is by no means reluctant to express himself in participial hymns of praise. Isaiah was called when at worship, and Jeremiah continually resorted to the temple to preach.

Yet the prophets had much to condemn, and their condemnation is so far reaching as to appear as a total condemnation of sacrifice and worship. There were also the evils attendant upon the division of the kingdom and the practices of the N shrines. Amos denounces ritual lawbreaking (2:8), as well as ritual prostitution (vs. 4), acts of worship not accompanied by repentance (4:4-6), and he announces God's detestation of Israel's feasts (5:21-24). Likewise Hosea promises that God will punish Israel by ending her festive occasions, feasts, New Moons, and sabbaths, for God desired mercy rather than sacrifice. Isaiah complains that his people's whole head and whole heart are sick and faint (1:5), and consequently the entire worship is wrong. Even so, the condemnation of worship and the cult does not bulk so largely in their pages as is commonly supposed. These prophets also testify to the presence of idolatrous emblems in contemporary worship (II Kings 18:4; Isa. 2:8, 20; Hos. 8:4-6; 13:1-2). In their denunciations the prophets had had forerunners, as Deut. 18:9-15 shows. All magical, divinatory, spiritualist, and necromantic forms of religious activity are absolutely alien to Israel's faith and are now denounced and prohibited in laws and prophecy alike.

6. Josiah's reform. The eighth-century prophets had protested in vain. Indeed, Ahaz had set up an Assyrian altar in Jerusalem (II Kings 16:10-16). There had long been a serpent cult in the temple— probably a cult image of the El Elyon god. This Hezekiah had removed from the temple as part of his reform (II Kings 18:4). But his son, Manasseh, in dependence upon Assyria, introduced a new age of syncretism, so that Israel was more wicked than its neighbors. Josiah, following the discovery of the law book (probably Deut. 5–28), set about the reform of the religious worship of his day. He centralized personal and all other kinds of sacrifice at Jerusalem; he abolished local shrines and disestablished local priestly families. He suppressed local cults and all idolatrous rites, and so sought a purification of worship in Jerusalem and throughout his kingdom (II Kings 23:4-25). But after Josiah's death there was a further relapse (23:32, 37; 24:9, 19; Jer. 44:17 ff). It is clear that in the long history of Solomon's temple the degree of syncretism varied according to the sympathies of the reigning monarch.

7. In the postexilic period. The work of Josiah, Deuteronomy, and Ezekiel eventually brought about a reformed cultus. The main feasts were continued; the relationships of priests, Levites, and other priestly groups were defined. Those who had been cult prophets were probably consolidated into the postexilic choirs of temple singers, each choir aiming to possess its own book of psalms. Various changes in sacrifices also took place, and the *chaṭṭath* (sin offering) and the *'asham* (guilt offering) appear prominently.

In the second temple there was a morning sacrifice and another between the two evenings, with additions for sabbaths and all special feasts (Exod. 29:38-41; Num. 28:9). There is information in the Mishna and other rabbinical writings of the distribution of psalms in the festivals and holy days of the Jewish year. Songs of ascents (Pss. 120–34) were used at tabernacles and the Hallel psalms (113–18; 136) at all the great festivals, and so on.

The postexilic period also saw great changes in the pre-exilic feast of 'Asiph. This was now divided into three separate festivals. On the first day of Tishri, New Year's Day (*see* NEW YEAR), Rosh Hashanah was celebrated; the tenth day was the most solemn day of all—the Day of Atonement, when the high priest was especially involved in a number of archaic ceremonies; and thirdly, the Feast of Tabernacles, Sukkoth, continued for eight days from the fifteenth of the month. On the Day of Atonement (Lev. 16; *see* ATONEMENT, DAY OF) an annual purification was made for temple, priests, and people. It is not possible to go into the different items of this chapter, or the form, meaning, and sequence of the different portions of the ritual. Some portions of the ritual are archaic—but both the need for the occasion and the central figure and activity of the high priest are new. It remains a speculation whether Lev. 16 does not now embalm ideas and ritual which, in pre-exilic days, belonged to the king and were performed by him. This speculation offers a plausible approach to the problems of Lev. 16.

8. Personal worship. The rich themes of the community celebrations of Israel's covenant faith must not blind us to the equally rich strains of personal religion and worship present in the OT. Many personal acts of worship are told of the patriarchs, of Moses and Joshua. The story of Hannah at prayer (I Sam. 1) could not have been unique in ancient Israel. Many brought their needs and vows to the sanctuary. Indeed, many of the laws control personal acts of offering and worship. Apart from the possibility that David may have been the author of such psalms as 23; 51, there is a personal side to his re-

ligion. David is portrayed as one of the most gifted individuals in God's presence (II Sam. 7:18-29), and his ritual behavior sometimes causes surprise (II Sam. 6:20-23; 12:16-23). The royal cult must have meant, for good kings at least, acts of personal consecration, as well as the outward fulfilment of the ritual appropriate to the monarchy (e.g., I Kings 8:1–9:9). Further, the Psalter is known to contain personal hymns of thanksgiving, psalms of trust, and individual laments. The "I" of the psalm is rarely a singular collective for Israel; and even if often used by the king, nevertheless the democratization of the royal cult and of the royal "I" made the Psalms available for all and sundry in Israel. The Psalms contain many individual acts of prayer and devotion. It has long been recognized that in the concentration on the law and testimony among Isaiah's disciples (Isa. 8: 16-20) there are new insights into a personal religion of faith dependent on God's Word alone. The so-called confessions of Jeremiah, the prophet Habakkuk, the author of Ps. 73, the lyrical outpourings in Isa. 40–55, the personal concentration on law (Pss. 1; 19; 119), and such an appeal as Isa. 55:6-9 disclose vistas of personal religion. Then, too, there are those postures which are appropriate to adoration and to prayer: standing, sitting, prostration, kneeling, bowing; hands folded, outstretched, uplifted, clasped; eyes cast down and lifted up; removal of sandals, the stroking of sacred images or places like altars; the hand to lips (Job 31:27)—perhaps the physical basis of adoration (lit., *adoro,* "I lift my hand to my mouth").

The fall of Jerusalem and of the first temple, the long sojourn in exile away from the shrine, the abandonment of local sacrificial shrines after the building of the second temple, the growth of the idea of scripture, and the decline of the prophetic ministry inevitably gave rise to new modes of worship— meetings for praise, prayer, preaching, teaching, and explanation. At some time or other new centers arose, though it is unlikely that the SYNAGOGUE is mentioned in OT times (cf. Ps. 74:8). The synagogue is vouched for from the third century B.C., at least.

9. Characteristics. Mowinckel may not have gained universal acceptance for his theory of the New Year Festival, but there is no doubt that in his category of "cultic reality" he has established a permanent mode of interpretation for certain psalms in particular and for Hebrew worship in general. As prophetic oracles are sometimes enshrined in prophetic symbolism, so much of Hebrew religion finds ritual expression. Revelation is given ritual expression. Thus the strange ritual of Gen. 15:9-21 carries or embodies a revealed promise (cf. vss. 7-8). In Exod. 24 the divine side of the covenant, as well as the human, is conveyed in ritual. Religion achieves a quasi-sacramental expression in ritual. On the human side, the varied approach to God even achieves appropriate ritual and dramatic expression.

This ritual religion nevertheless is dominated by what has been called holy history. The worship is carried on within a tradition of sacred history. Agricultural feasts have been related to the divine acts within Israel's history. The Psalter contains psalms which recapitulate that sacred story, and many illustrations of sacred recital or the making known of

Yahweh's works. The worshiper remembers and thus makes present to himself the sacred history to which he belongs. The particular form of the historical implications of Israel's worship is the covenant. That is the presupposition of the worship, and very often the substance of the short creedal statements which characterize so many of the Psalms. The aspect of covenant also plays its part in the role of the king and of the Davidic house in Israel's worship. Akin to the sacred history is the Lord's control of and gifts in harvest. Thus harvest thanksgiving and joy are prominent in Israel's festal calendar, and largely control the timing.

Since the system of worship is revealed, then the fulfilment of worship is obedience to God. The Western tendency to distinguish between ethical obedience and ritual obedience divides the life of the worshiper. There are accordingly Torah liturgies in Pss. 15; 24 which lay down ethical requirements for worship, as does Mic. 6:6-8. Without the requirements, experiences, and exhibitions of such ethical behavior in worship, there would be no possibility of the idealizing tendencies which properly belong to worship and which issue in present well-being and eschatological hope.

Israelite worship centers on Israel's God. He is the author of sacrifice (Lev. 17:11) and of Israel's system of worship. He both gives grace and glory and receives worship and glory. True Israelite worship is dominated by enthusiasm for God. Thus Israel's worship is performed, not merely that she may thereby set an example to other nations, and not merely that she may derive blessing or welfare from this worship, but that she may glorify God. Israelite worship centers on the cultic presence of Israel's tabernacling God. The heart of this presence is a divine "I am" sentence—an "autokerygmatic" sentence—"I am Yahweh." This sentence is doubtless the heart of scripture, of revelation, and of Israel's faith as recapitulated in her worship. Correspondingly, to call upon the NAME of Yahweh or to bless in his name is the supreme act of worship. But "call on the name" is not a synonym for prayer and invocation. The phrase means to "call with the name"—i.e., give utterance to the name itself. Similarly, in blessing, Yahweh's name is put upon the people of Israel (Num. 6:17).

Concerning emphasis on the sanctuary, *see* HIGH PLACE.

Bibliography. W. R. Harper, *The Priestly Element in the OT* (1909), pp. 1-57, 273-80. G. B. Gray, *Sacrifice in the OT* (1925). W. O. E. Oesterley, *The Jewish Background of the Christian Liturgy* (1925), "Worship and Ritual," in A. S. Peake, ed., *The People and the Book* (1925), pp. 323-51. S. H. Hooke, *The Origins of Early Semitic Ritual* (1935); *The Labyrinth* (1935). N. H. Snaith, "The Religion of Israel: Worship," in H. W. Robinson, ed., *Record and Revelation* (1938), pp. 250-74. H. J. Kraus, *Die Königsherrschaft Gottes im AT* (1951); "Gilgal; ein Beitrag zur Kultusgeschichte Israels," *Vetus Testamentum*, vol. I (1951). G. Delling, *Der Gottesdienst im NT* (1952). S. Mowinckel, *Religion und Kultus* (1953). O. R. Sellers, "Seeking God in the OT," *JBR*, XXI (1953), 234-37. H. J. Kraus, *Gottesdienst in Israel* (1954). A. R. Johnson, *Sacral Kingship in Ancient Israel* (1955). D. R. Ap-Thomas, "Notes on Some Terms Relating to Prayer," *Vetus Testamentum*, VI (1956), 225-41. E. Jacob, *Theology of the OT* (1958), pp. 262-70. S. H. Hooke, *Myth, Ritual and Kingship* (1958). T. C. Vriezen, *An Outline of OT Theology* (1958), pp. 276-314. A. S. Herbert, *Worship in Ancient Israel* (1959).

See also bibliographies under PRAISE; HYMNS; TEMPLE; JERUSALEM; PRAYER.   G. HENTON DAVIES

WORSHIP IN NT TIMES, CHRISTIAN. Until the middle of the second century, when Justin Martyr provided his pagan opponents with a fairly adequate account of a Christian service, our knowledge of early Christian worship is very sketchy. The NT contains only one record (and that not altogether clear) of the celebration of the Lord's Supper, and none of baptism. We have a curious set of eucharistic prayers, coming perhaps from the late first century, in the Didache; and a few years later a pagan governor, Pliny, wrote his emperor a confused account of a Christian service. For the rest we are dependent upon conjectures made from casual references in the NT, and we have to eke out our knowledge by inferences from current Jewish and Hellenistic worship, and from occasional notices in the early fathers.

Nevertheless, it is possible to trace the main lines of the development and to infer much that is not apparent on the surface. In general we may say that Christian worship in NT times found its focus in baptism, in preaching, and in the Lord's Supper, and was dominated by its faith in Jesus as the risen Messiah and the living Lord. It took over much from its Jewish background, both remolding and reinterpreting it; to a lesser extent it was influenced by Gentile practices; and beyond the central elements we have noted, it enjoyed a quite rich liturgical life of public prayer, psalmody, scripture reading, instruction, and private devotions. There were, too, many special observances such as ordinations, ministry to the sick (with prayer, anointing, and exorcism), benedictions at marriage, funeral banquets, and weekly and annual days of fasting and of celebration.

1. The inheritance from Judaism
2. The Gentile inheritance
3. The Lord's Supper
4. The service of word and sacrament
5. Baptism and confirmation
6. The ministry to the sick
7. Ordinations
8. Discipline and excommunication
9. Marriages and funerals
10. Private devotions, vows, and fasts
11. The church week and year
Bibliography

1. The inheritance from Judaism. Born within Judaism, Christianity naturally developed its liturgical life within the context of its Jewish heritage. The earliest Christians, according to Acts 2:46, "day by day, attending the temple together and breaking bread in their homes, . . . partook of food with glad and generous hearts." From this we are to assume that what was distinctive to Christianity was its communal meal, while for the rest it continued to observe the Jewish modes of public and private worship (Acts 5:42). Soon, however, the cleavage between Judaism and Christianity became complete; and, forbidden access to temple and synagogue, the

Christians developed their independent services. Central to these were baptism and the Lord's Supper, with many other acts of worship clustered around.

The break with Judaism was perhaps not so abrupt as we sometimes think, nor did it occur at the same time in all places. Paul, e.g., seems to have begun his missionary labors, as a rule, by preaching in the synagogue, and to have continued worshiping there until, on each specific occasion, he was forced to withdraw, and either to hire a lecture hall, as he did at Ephesus (Acts 19:9; the lecture hall of Tyrannus), or to continue his work from some private house (e.g., that of Stephanas in Corinth; I Cor. 16:15). The earliest Christians thus worshiped in temple and synagogue, supplementing this worship by their distinctive common meal.

When, however, the primitive Christians were forced to make their own provisions for worship, they naturally relied on the familiar forms they had inherited from Judaism. But these forms underwent a radical transformation in the light of the Christian message. So far as the sacrificial system of the temple was concerned, the Christians abandoned this altogether, regarding it as having been fulfilled in the death of Christ (see especially the leading argument of the Letter to the Hebrews); and, indeed, with the destruction of the temple by the Romans in A.D. 70, it ceased even for Judaism. From temple worship Christianity inherited, not a cultus, but an idea, a way of expressing the meaning of Christ's passion, rather than an actual form of worship. This understanding of the Cross became of fundamental importance for the development of the Lord's Supper, whose sacrificial character lay in the "recalling" or solemnly "proclaiming" before God the sacrifice once offered (I Cor. 11:26). The only other aspect of temple worship which affected Christianity was the psalmody; but this probably entered Christian liturgy not so much directly from the temple as indirectly through the synagogue.

From the synagogue, the local center of worship in postexilic Judaism (see WORSHIP IN NT TIMES, JEWISH), Christianity came to inherit most of what we think of as the service of the word. Scripture reading (especially of the Law and the Prophets), preaching, psalmody, and public prayer had by the second century become the first part of the regular weekly service of the Christians. How early the service assumed this form, we must discuss later. Here we need only remark on the similarity and contrast with Judaism. There was similarity in most of the items, but dissimilarity both in their content and in the order in which they came.

While we do not know precisely how the Jewish service was constructed in the first century (and it doubtless displayed local differences), we may reasonably assume that it went something like this:

I. Antiphonal recitation of the Decalogue (only in some places)
II. The Shema (antiphonal recitation of the creed of Israel, Deut. 6:4-9, etc.)
III. The Shemone Esreh (a series of blessings of God, now nineteen, at that time perhaps six)
IV. Pentateuch lesson (with translation verse by verse into Aramaic or Greek)

V. Psalmody (perhaps between the lections, and in the responsorial method, the cantor singing the verses, the congregation replying with a constant refrain)
VI. Sermon (only occasionally)

Three further points may be noted. At the conclusion of prayers the congregation recited vigorously the *Amen*—the word expressing God's fixed and constant nature, whereby he would bring the petition to effect. Second, form and freedom seem to have been united in the liturgy. There was a fixed structure, but the leader of the congregation who recited the benedictions was not bound by the actual words, only by the content. Finally, the liturgy was a lay liturgy. The "ruler" of the synagogue would choose different members of the congregation to lead in the Shema and benedictions, to read the lessons, and, on occasion, to preach.

The Christian service will be discussed in § 4. There it will be noted that most of these items of synagogue worship were retained, but the demands of the Christian message altered them considerably.

Another area of Jewish worship which profoundly affected the Christian liturgy was the home ritual of the Passover meal (see PASSOVER AND FEAST OF UNLEAVENED BREAD). This forms the background for the Lord's Supper and raises some of the most insoluble problems of NT study (see LAST SUPPER). It is not clear whether the Last Supper (from which the Lord's Supper is derived) was the actual Passover meal or occurred some twenty-four hours before it. The first three gospels take the former view, while John's Gospel dates the Passion at the time of the slaying of the Passover lambs, and hence a day earlier. It is not possible to tell decisively which is correct; the arguments and objections on both sides tend to cancel each other out. But in either case, what is important is that the traditions of the Passover have vitally affected the development of the Lord's Supper. The essence of Passover (whose remote origins go back to two Canaanite spring festivals) lay in the recalling of Israel's redemption, by a symbolic feast which re-enacted the last dramatic night before the crossing of the Red Sea. A haggadah (tradition) was recited by the master of the house, who in answer to questions posed by the youngest present, retold the slaughter of the first-born, the flight from Egypt, and the delivery from slavery under the Pharaohs. The meal looked backward to God's saving act in Israel's redemption, but it also looked forward to the culmination of his promises in the kingdom. Thus, e.g., of the unleavened bread which was eaten, it was said: "This is the bread of affliction which our fathers ate in the land of Egypt . . . . Now we are here, but next year may we be in the land of Israel! Now we are slaves, but next year may we be free men!" This ancient verse, which comes perhaps from the later Babylonian captivity, voices the twofold theme of Passover: it recalls the redemption from Egypt and looks toward the final triumph of God's kingdom.

It is precisely this dual concern which is characteristic of the Last Supper and the LORD'S SUPPER. The redemption wrought by Jesus is "shewn forth" in the bread and wine; while the hope of the future kingdom also finds expression, in the words both of Jesus (Mark 14:25; Luke 22:16) and of Paul (I Cor. 11:26: "until he comes").

The actual details of a Jewish meal have also provided both the framework for Jesus' act and the structure of the earliest Christian prayers at the Lord's Supper. This applies whether or not the Last Supper was an actual Passover, because in either case the beginning and the end of the meal would be similar, though the Passover forms would be more elaborate. The dinner would open with a grace before meals, which involved both a blessing of God for the bread, and the distribution of small pieces of the loaf to each of the guests. This was (and is still) the normal way for a Jew to say grace. Evidently Jesus took this occasion to relate the bread to the sacrifice of his body; and the memory of this determined the opening of the Lord's Supper, even in a community like Corinth, which was largely Gentile (I Cor. 11:23-24). The meal would conclude, on festive occasions, with the grace after meals said in connection with a cup of wine shared by all (at Passover there would be individual cups, but the evidence for this in the first century is disputed). There would be a preliminary dialogue, depending on the number of guests present, and opening: "Let us bless our God." This would be followed by a blessing of God for the wine and a longer blessing, in three parts, for the food, the land, and the people. There was some dispute in Jewish circles as to which of these two blessings should come first (Ber. 8.9). Apparently Jesus took the occasion of this celebration to relate the wine to his forthcoming passion; and it is clear that the blessing over the cup terminates the meal in Paul's account (I Cor. 11:25).

We must remember that the Lord's Supper was a long period, and perhaps as late as the end of the first century, an actual meal. Thus it retained its distinctively Jewish structure of grace before and after meals said in connection with bread and wine; and, as we see later, the earliest Christian prayers we have reflect the structure of the Jewish graces.

The importance of sacred meals involving bread and wine has been brought home to us in another relation with the recent discovery of the Qumran material. In a fragment probably forming part of the Manual of Discipline we have an account of a communal meal at which the high priest of the community presides, and at which "he utters a blessing over the first portion of the bread and wine, and [stretches out] his hand over the bread first of all." The "Messiah of Israel" then "stretches out his hands upon the bread." The nature of this meal of the Qumran community is admittedly obscure; but it clearly has a messianic reference, though it is not made plain whether the awaited Messiah is actually represented by someone at the recurring meal. What, however, is important is that the Qumran material witnesses to the existence of a type of sacred meal which bears a striking resemblance to the later Lord's Supper, the messianic character of which is discussed in § 3 *below*.

Judaism provided the background for many other acts of Christian worship besides its central service of word and sacrament. Jewish proselyte baptism, e.g., is a source both for John's rite and for the Christian one. Similarly in unction, exorcism, ordination, fasting, etc., the Jewish forms affected the Christian. It will, however, be more convenient to discuss these under the separate sections which follow the treatment of the main weekly liturgy.

2. The Gentile inheritance. It is much more difficult to assess the Gentile influences on Christian worship than the Jewish. This is so because the latter are more obvious, and because, with the exception of peripheral items such as the funeral feast and some marriage customs, no specific elements of the early Christian liturgy can be directly traced to Hellenistic sources. Until the fourth century, almost everything important can be explained by Christian remolding of Jewish forms. Yet the question cannot be left there; for while so much of Christian worship stood in marked contrast to pagan (its lack of temples, sacrifices, idols, and augury), there were subtle similarities which have led some scholars to view Christianity as one more example of a prevalent type of pagan worship in the first century—viz., that of the mystery religions.

Fundamental to these mystery religions was the ritual associated with the dying and rising god. Also fundamental were the sacred meals at which the god was believed to be present, and in the course of which holy food was taken, believed to have some relationship with divine life (e.g., the initiation ritual of the cult of Attis, and the communal meal of bread and wine in Mithraism). Obvious connections between these religions and the Christian belief in the death and resurrection of Christ and in the communion of his body and blood in the Lord's Supper, can be made. While the structure of Christian worship is sufficiently accounted for by its Jewish heritage and by the symbolic act of Jesus at the Last Supper, the relation with the mystery religions in these themes is apparent. For the converted Gentile, moreover, the Christian cultus must not have seemed altogether unlike the cult libations and initiations with which he was familiar. (Paul himself seems to have in mind cult libations in I Cor. 10:16-21, which explains why here the cup precedes the bread.) The Gentile convert would read into religious forms which had a Jewish origin, ideas and associations from his pagan background. Christianity, for him, was doubtless some kind of mystery religion, however much it might differ in detail from his previous allegiances.

The main points of difference were clear: the cults were syncretic, while Christianity was exclusive; the cults closely guarded their "mystery" in secret, while early Christianity proclaimed the mystery of God's action in Christ from the housetops (cf. Rom. 16:25); initiation in the cults was, on the whole, costly, while Christianity recruited a large part of its congregation from the underprivileged; the cults were concerned first with the triumph over death, while Christianity related this to the triumph over moral evil; the cult gods were personifications of the fertility myth of dying and rising, while Christianity was rooted in the historic acts of an actual person. But the deepest difference lay in the conception of the divine suffering. The cult gods died unwillingly, smitten by the forces of fate, while Christianity preached a God who willingly took upon himself the suffering involved in the redemption of man.

There was thus similarity and dissimilarity between Christian worship and pagan cultus. Of the items which most clearly relate to the pagan background, we may mention, first, language and metaphor. "Dying and rising," "regeneration" (Tit. 3:5), and similar expressions have a Hellenistic overtone, whatever their origin; and the privative attributes of God in Christian prayers come from the traditions of Greek philosophy (cf. I Tim. 6:16). When, furthermore, the Gentile Christian addressed Christ as *Kyrios* (Lord), while the term came into Christianity through Aramaic, it must have had for him associations derived from the savior "lords" and "gods" of paganism. Later on, in Clement of Alexandria, the new faith can be directly and consciously spoken of in terms taken from the mystery religions (Protrep. 12).

A second factor concerns the blessing of *things*. Jewish prayer is marked by benedictions which bless God *for* things; Gentile practice is seen in prayers which ask God's blessing *on* things. The blessing of the bread and wine of the Lord's Supper, e.g. (implicit in the later consecration prayers), betrays Hellenistic usage. It has its origin in the conception of the divine being present *in* things; whereas the prophetic strain of Jewish religion lays the emphasis on blessing God *for* things. Similarly, it is possible to view the stark language in John 6:56 on "eating the flesh" of Christ as reminiscent of the Dionysiac orgies in which the raw flesh of a bull was devoured in the belief that it contained divine power. That there is a trace of pagan language here is likely; but the author's concern to interpret the rite spiritually is also evident (see vs. 63). If he speaks in language familiar to his hearers, it is with a vastly different message.

3. The Lord's Supper. The distinctive communal meal of the Christians, known by the technical term of the "breaking of bread" (Acts 20:7, 11; an expression in Judaism for that ritual act of grace before meals which had special significance for the Christian), was at first supplemental to the temple and synagogue services (Acts 2:46), and was celebrated daily, or at any rate with great frequency. Naturally it was held in the homes of Christians, as it was an actual meal; and to judge by Jewish customs as well as by Paul's reference in I Cor. 11:21, each guest provided either his own supper or a contribution to the common table. It was characterized by "great joy" (the Greek expression in Acts 2:46 is emphatic), because it celebrated the messianic banquet and bore witness to the presence of the risen Christ. The Emmaus story (Luke 24:13 ff) is probably intended as a type of the Christian Eucharist: "He was known to them in the breaking of the bread." This means that the Christian meal was a continuation of the Easter meals of the Resurrection (Mark 16:14; John 21; Acts 10:41), and fulfilled the Jewish expectations of the coming of the Messiah and the kingdom. These expectations had often been clothed in language suggesting a banquet at the end of the ages, when the Messiah would come bringing with him the manna ground in the mills of heaven (cf. Zech. 8:19; Enoch 10:17 ff; 62:14; Luke 14:15; John 6:49 ff). For the Christian this was fulfilled in the Lord's Supper, which both celebrated the presence of the Messiah and looked toward the final climax when he would appear in glory (I Cor. 11:26).

The meal followed the pattern already explained. There was a grace before meals with the distribution of the bread, a ritual given new meaning by the act of Christ at the Last Supper; and, after the supper, a concluding grace over a cup of wine, again a ritual given a new interpretation in the light of Christ's action. The NT does not preserve for us the form of these graces, to which the sacramental words recorded by Paul were doubtless attached (I Cor. 11:23 ff). The antiquity, however, of the present Jewish forms helps us here; and reconstructions by Jewish scholars lead us to suppose that Jews said grace something like this in the first century: over the bread, "Blessed art thou, O Lord our God, King of the universe, who bringest forth bread from the earth"; after the meal and over the cup, a dialogue:

V. "Blessed be He."

R̥. "Blessed be the Lord our God, the God of Israel, the God of hosts, dwelling between the cherubim, for the meal that we have eaten."

Then follows the blessing: "Blessed art thou, O Lord our God, who hast made the fruit of the vine.

"Blessed art thou, O Lord our God, King of the universe, who sustaineth the whole world with goodness, with kindness, and with mercy.

"We thank thee O Lord our God, that thou hast caused us to inherit a pleasant, good, and wide land.

"Have mercy, O Lord our God, on Israel, thy people, and on Jerusalem, thy city, and on Zion, the abiding place of thy glory, on thy altar and thy temple. Blessed art thou, O God, who buildest Jerusalem."

The Christian forms would doubtless have been reworded in the light of the new faith; and the prayers which have survived in the Didache preserve just such a remodeling of the ancient blessings. Although the Didache itself is a second-century compilation, its eucharistic prayers (chs. 9–10) go back to A.D. 90 or earlier, and come perhaps originally from Judea. They have suffered some displacement, and for some curious reason the wine benediction is given first. But this is probably a scribal error, for we have no evidence that the cup ever preceded the bread. Here are the prayers:

"We thank thee, our Father, for the holy vine of David, thy child, which thou hast revealed through Jesus, thy child. To thee be glory forever.

"Then in connection with the piece [broken off the loaf]: We thank thee, our Father, for the life and knowledge which thou hast revealed through Jesus, thy child. To thee be glory forever.

"As this piece [of bread] was scattered over the hills and then was brought together and made one, so let thy Church be brought together from the ends of the earth into thy Kingdom. For thine is the glory and the power through Jesus Christ forever.

"After you have finished your meal, say grace in this way: We thank thee, holy Father, for thy sacred name which thou hast lodged in our hearts, and for the knowledge and faith and immortality which thou hast revealed through Jesus, thy child. To thee be glory forever.

"Almighty Master, thou hast created everything

for the sake of thy name, and hast given men food and drink to enjoy that they may thank thee. But to us thou hast given spiritual food and drink and eternal life through Jesus, thy child.

"Above all, we thank thee that thou art mighty. To thee be glory forever.

"Remember, Lord, thy Church, to save it from all evil and to make it perfect by thy love. Make it holy, and gather it together from the four winds into thy kingdom which thou hast made ready for it. For thine is the power and the glory forever.

"Let Grace come and let this world pass away.

"Hosanna to the God of David!

"If anyone is holy, let him come. If not, let him repent.

"Our Lord, come!

"Amen."

The reader who compares these prayers with the Jewish ones will note the striking similarity, particularly in the form "We thank thee" (which is synonymous with "We bless thee," or "Blessed art thou"), and in the content of the long thanksgiving at the end which substitutes the themes of Christ, creation, and redemption, for the Jewish ones of the food, the land, and the people. It may be noted that the liturgy in the Didache clearly envisions an actual meal (10.1).

The earliest Eucharists seem to have concluded with (or contained at some point) psalm singing, exhortation, prophecy, and speaking with tongues (I Cor. 14:26). Perhaps a vestige of this is to be seen in the ecstatic cries, "Let grace come, let this world pass away," etc., which end the Didache service (10.6).

It will be noted that the Didache prayers do not directly refer to Christ's words of institution, and while the whole gospel of redemption in Christ is implicit in them, they do not make overt reference to the Passion. Some have contended, therefore, that there were originally two types of early Eucharist—a joyful type centered in the Resurrection, like the Didache's, and a more solemn one like that of Paul in I Cor. 11, centered in the Cross. Such a theory is unnecessary to explain the differences. The early Lord's Supper was doubtless a most joyful occasion, and the accent fell upon the themes of Resurrection and messianic banquet. But underlying these were the motifs of the New Covenant and the Cross. The peculiar solemnity of Paul's account may partly be explained by the prominence of the Cross in his theology; but it was the excesses to which the Corinthian feasting and the unsocial behavior of the well-to-do (who refused to share their "picnic" baskets with their less privileged fellows) which led him to stress the more somber note of the celebration (I Cor. 11:20 ff). We do not need to posit two different types of Eucharist. Rather is there a difference of emphasis because of circumstances.

When the break between Christianity and Judaism forced the new community to provide for its total needs of worship, changes in the supper doubtless occurred. For one thing, preaching would be added to it, and the story in Acts 20:7-12 indicates this. Then again, the Christian liturgy became regularized as weekly worship, and Sunday (see LORD'S DAY) was celebrated as the Christian day, the Lord's

Supper coming in the evening, as the same passage from Acts indicates. We have no evidence that a Christian service in the morning parallel to that of the synagogue immediately developed. The first we hear of it is around the turn of the century in Pliny's letter to Trajan, and while it is doubtless considerably older than that, we cannot date its appearance. Nor can we be sure whether the general prayers mentioned in I Tim. 2:1-2, 8, belong to the Lord's Supper or to a separate service. It is possible that some of the items of the synagogue service came to precede the Lord's Supper, as preaching did. Perhaps scripture reading was included, as well as the reading of Christian letters which Paul assumes in Col. 4:16 (though the reference here is not specifically to the Lord's Supper). Many of the fragmentary liturgical echoes which we find in the NT, such as benedictions (e.g., Gal. 6:18; Phil. 4:23), doxologies (e.g., Rom. 1:25; 9:5; II Cor. 11:31; Eph. 1:3; II Tim. 4:18), and new Christian hymns (e.g., Eph. 5:14; Phil. 2:6 ff; Col. 1:12-14; I Tim. 3:16; Rev. 5:9, 12-13; 12:10-12; 19:1-2, 6), probably came to form a part of the meal. What, however, forced the Christians to undertake a thorough revision of the liturgy was the imperial edict (based on the old *lex Julia*) forbidding unlicensed clubs to hold meals. This was enforced in Trajan's time, and from that period there developed a service of word and sacrament distinct from the actual supper, though incorporating its most important features.

4. The service of word and sacrament. The imagery of Revelation gives us our only indication in the NT of the Christian liturgy as it developed at the end of the first century. Because of the nature of these visions it is extremely hard to be sure of the details; but chs. 4–6 suggest that the author has cast his vision in forms derived from the liturgy. The throne would be the bishop's chair; the seats of the elders would be those of the presbyters on either side of the bishop; the lamb would be the consecrated bread and wine; the book would be the gospel MS; some of the refrains might reflect Christian hymns (the Sanctus, e.g., appears in 4:8); and the Amen (5:14) certainly played a significant role in Christian worship, being the congregation's response to all prayers. If we are to read these chapters of Revelation in this way, it would appear that the type of service known to us in the second century by Justin's account (*see below*), was already established by the 90's in some parts of Asia Minor.

We are on somewhat more certain ground when we take into account Pliny's evidence. This governor of Bithynia, in his letter to Trajan on the Christians (10.96; *ca.* A.D. 113), records the description of their worship given him by some who later apostatized: "They contended that the sum of their guilt or error had lain in this, that they were accustomed on a special day to assemble before daylight and to sing antiphonally a hymn to Christ as if he were a god, and to bind themselves by an oath not for any wrong purpose, but not to commit theft or robbery or adultery, not to break their word or to deny a deposit when asked for. After this it was their custom to depart, and to meet together again to take food, but ordinary and harmless food. Even this they gave up after my edict, by which I had forbidden the existence of unlicensed clubs in accordance with your orders."

While this text involves some difficulties of interpretation, it would seem that the Christians of Bithynia observed two separate services. They met before dawn for a liturgy which included antiphonal hymnody (perhaps the singing of the messianic psalms in reference to Christ, or of new Christian hymns, fragments of which have survived in the NT), and a recitation of the Decalogue. (The latter is clear, as the last three commandments are specifically mentioned. The tenth is interestingly interpreted by the situation where covetousness was a major temptation—viz., in refusing to give back money or precious goods entrusted by some traveler at a time when there were no banks and safe-deposit boxes.)

Later that same day (the "special day" is doubtless Sunday), they held a communal meal, which they had to abandon when the *lex Julia* was enforced. It is unclear whether this meal was the actual Lord's Supper, or whether the sacramental part of the meal had already been transferred to the dawn liturgy (as we find later in Justin), leaving only an ordinary "church supper" or AGAPE, as it was called. Some have contended that the latter is the case, because Christians would never have given up their most solemn act of worship. Yet it may well be precisely this situation of the enforcement of the *lex Julia* that led to the separation of the actual supper from its sacramental actions. However this may be, what is clear is that a service of the word with features from the synagogue liturgy had now developed and was held very early in the morning. The reason for the choice of this time was partly the desire to accommodate slaves, who formed a large part of an early Christian congregation and were not free at other hours, and partly the necessity that a persecuted group hold its meetings in secret.

With the account of the Christian liturgy in Justin Martyr, who reflects the Roman practice (I Apol. 65-67; *ca.* A.D. 150), we reach clear daylight. We find the form of service with which we are familiar and which provided the framework for the whole later development. The service was held on Sunday and opened abruptly with the reading of scripture, which by Justin's time included both the LXX and the gospels (there is no evidence of a lectionary system, but as one was probably in vogue in the synagogue, some order may have been adopted in early Christianity). There followed the sermon, with the bishop (Justin calls him the "president"—a term his pagan readers would better understand) seated in his chair in the customary way of teaching in the ancient world (cf. Luke 4:20). Then came the common prayers, for which the congregation rose. They prayed with arms outstretched, in the usual way for Jews and Romans to plead with God, though the Christian saw in this gesture the form of the cross (Tert. *On Prayer* 14). The structure of the prayers is not clear. It is possible that a long intercession of the type preserved in I Clem. 59 ff was in vogue; but it is more likely that a litany form, similar to that in the oldest parts of the Roman liturgy, was in use. A subject of prayer would be proposed by the deacon: "Let us pray for . . . ." There would follow

an interval of silence, during which each would offer his individual prayers; and finally the bishop would intone a brief concluding "collect" summing up (as the word suggests) the united prayers of the congregation. The prayers would be intoned in a manner between our speaking and singing, something like the "recitative" of an opera. Such musical speech was the customary mode of Jewish prayer as well as of pagan. It was used for acoustical reasons as well as because of the advantages of musical rhythm. (Spoken public prayer is medieval in origin, and connected with the rise of Low Masses.) The prayers would be extemporaneous. There were no set forms until the fourth century, though there were model prayers and a fixed structure of the service (Hippolytus *Apostolic Tradition* 10.4).

The prayers concluded with a vigorous Amen by the congregation. Justin uses an emphatic word, ἐπευφημεῖ ("shout in applause"). By his time "Amen" was understood to mean merely "so be it," but in the NT there is evidence that the Christian read into the original Hebrew word a good deal more. Instead of the reference being future—the expectation that God *would* bring the petition to pass—the word was connected with the fulfilment already present in Christ. All the promises of God, says Paul, are "Yes" in Christ, and that is why we say "Amen" through him to God's glory (II Cor. 1:20). Behind this lies the conviction that the kingdom is already begun in the work of Christ, though it has not yet reached its climax.

When the common prayers were ended, the kiss of peace was given. This oriental salutation, the equivalent of our shaking of hands (Luke 7:45), had passed into Gentile worship from the natural greetings of Jewish Christians as they assembled for the primitive Lord's Supper, and had become a liturgical action to seal the supernatural fellowship of the church.

The offertory followed. This was not of money (the collection was deposited with the bishop after the service), but of bread and wine. Each Christian had brought his own offering of these (the relics of the time when the Lord's Supper had been a "picnic" meal at which each guest provided something for the common feast). The deacons now arranged these on a table before the bishop, who proceeded to the consecration prayer. This was opened by a dialogue which was a Christian remodeling of the Jewish dialogue before grace after meals. It had assumed the form of the *sursum corda* by the time of Hippolytus (*Apostolic Tradition* 6.3), but it is doubtless considerably older than his time, the late second century, and may well have been known to Justin. The consecration prayer itself is not given by Justin, but we can infer from another work of his (*Trypho* 41) and from Hippolytus that it was composed of a series of thanksgivings to God for creation and deliverance from evil and its powers, and contained some reference to the words of institution at the Last Supper (66). The prayer was extemporaneous (the bishop prayed "to the best of his ability"; 67) and extended (ἐπὶ πολύ). It concluded with the congregational Amen, whereupon the deacons served the Communion (the people probably standing before the table), and took portions of it away to those who had been absent through sickness or for other reasons.

With the Communion the service ended. There was no benediction or other post-Communion devotion. The Communion was the climax, as it is in Hippolytus. What it meant is reasonably clear in Justin (66). The bread and wine were in some way the flesh and blood of Jesus; and the sacramental action thus followed the lines of the Incarnation. As the Word was once made flesh, so he was here made bread and wine. Justin offers no further theory of consecration, but his thought clearly moves along lines suggested by John's Gospel. Where Paul, as a Jew, specifically avoids reference to eating the flesh and drinking the blood of Jesus (he prefers vaguer language, like "participation in the blood . . . [and] body" in I Cor. 10:16, the body perhaps being the church and the blood Christ's sacrifice), this is not true where Gentile influences are at work. The Jewish abhorrence of drinking blood as something taboo was not shared by Gentiles; and the prophetic nature of Jesus' action at the Last Supper (reminiscent of the enacted parables of the ancient prophets—e.g., Jer. 13; 19) was inevitably interpreted in a more realistic way in Hellenistic circles.

The officiant at Justin's service was the bishop. By his time the monepiscopacy was the settled form of church government. Earlier the presbyter-bishop (as in I Clem. 44.4) would be the officiant. Earlier still, it is possible that Christians were chosen for this duty according to their special gifts, in the same way that the synagogue liturgy was a *lay* liturgy, and any qualified Jew might be chosen to read the lessons or preach, as Jesus was, on one occasion, in Nazareth (Luke 4:16-30). The picture Paul leaves in our minds when we read I Cor. 14 is of a congregation, each member of which prayed, prophesied, exhorted, spoke with tongues, and even consecrated the Lord's Supper (vs. 16), according as he was called by the Spirit and given the appropriate charisma. But of this we cannot be sure, though a relic of it may survive in the regulation in the Didache (10.7) that the prophets may celebrate the Eucharist in their own way.

To summarize: from the home ritual of Judaism and the act of Jesus at the Last Supper, there developed the distinctively Christian Lord's Supper. Around the turn of the first century the sacramental aspect of this meal was transferred to a service very early in the morning. Much of the first part of this liturgy was a Christian form of the synagogue worship, with its prayers, lections, and sermon. Because of these Jewish features it is unlikely that this service of the word was a late development in Christianity. Rather must we assume that, to meet the needs of the primitive Christians when they were banned from the synagogue, *either* (and this is the more probable) some service of the word came to precede the meal of the Lord's Supper, *or* a separate morning service was constructed and to this was later added the sacramental part.

When the sacramental aspect of the Lord's Supper was divorced from the actual meal, the latter lost its original significance and dwindled in importance. It was known as the *agape* (the "love," a word originally used for the Lord's Supper itself; Jude 12; Ign.

Smyr. 8.2), and could only be held intermittently when the *lex Julia* was not strictly enforced. It did, however, retain some of its religious character, and we hear of it from time to time, especially in connection with entertaining the poor (Tert. Apol. 39; Hippolytus *Apostolic Tradition* 26; Chrysostom *Homily* 27 on I Corinthians). Eventually it was suppressed, as it became associated with the cult of the dead and subject to the undue excesses of pagan feasting and debauchery which often characterized such memorials (Augustine *Epistles* 22.6; 29.11; Council of Laodicea, Canon 28).

The Christian services doubtless differed somewhat from place to place. In Bithynia, e.g., the Decalogue was retained, while in Rome it was not. The general structure of the liturgy, however, must have been fairly uniform; and while one author may mention one item and another omit it, we should not take these omissions too seriously. Justin does not happen to mention hymn singing, but it would be extremely unlikely that responsorial psalmody between the lections was lacking in Rome at his time.

For further discussion of this topic, *see* LORD'S SUPPER; HYMNS; PREACHING; MUSIC; AGAPE, THE.

5. Baptism and confirmation. Owing to the widespread use of lustral purifications in Judaism and in the ancient world in general, it is no matter of surprise that Christianity should have adopted water baptism as its rite of initiation. We do not have to look far, furthermore, to discover the immediate background of Christian baptism. The Jewish custom of proselyte baptism, the lustrations of the Qumran community, and the rite of John the Baptist—all indicate an environment to which Christianity owed much in the development of its ceremony.

Gentile sources play little or no role in the very early period, though at a later date they may have exerted some influence. Reference may be made to the purification ceremonies in Mithra (Tert. Presc. Her. 40); to those undergone by Apuleius previous to his initiation into the cult of Isis (Metam. 11.22); to the significance of "sacred drowning" in the cult of Osiris (Herodotus *History* 2.90); and to the blood bath (*taurobolium*) in Magna Mater and Attis (Corpus Inser. Lat. 12.1569; 9.3014). The Gentile convert familiar with these and similar rites, doubtless brought over pagan associations to the Christian ceremony, and there are striking similarities between the Christian and pagan language on initiation (see Clement Protrep. 12). But these concern the later development, rather than the origins, of the Christian rite.

The Gentile converted to Judaism was required first to be circumcised, then to undergo a bath of immersion to purify him from his former paganism (a bath from which he emerged as a "newborn child"), and finally to offer sacrifice in the temple. The last requirement was, of course, impossible to fulfil outside Jerusalem, and there is some slim evidence that even the first was on rare occasions dispensed with (see Jos. Antiq. XX.ii.4). In consequence, the initiatory bath was heightened in significance. It was performed by self-immersion in the presence of two witnesses, men learned in the law, who stood near the candidate as he dipped himself, and instructed him in the "lighter" and "weightier" commandments (Yeb. 47a; Gerim. 1). Whether the rite should be understood to involve the forgiveness of sins is a matter which was in dispute within Jewish circles themselves (Yeb. 48a; Gerim. 1). Its fundamental meaning was separation from a pagan past and entrance into a new and acceptable relation with God. This is why the convert was like a newborn child.

There can be little question that John's baptism owed something to this proselyte ceremony. What was original, however, in John's rite was its application to Jews (the idea being that even one of the chosen race needs purification), and its strong eschatological reference. For John the end of the age was rapidly approaching, and God was about to purge and re-create the world. The transcendent Messiah would soon appear to destroy with his fiery spirit (breath) the ungodly. Hence an act of repentance was essential, even for Israel; and the baptism of John meant a pre-enacting of the divine judgment. The River Jordan was a symbol of the river of fire flowing from the throne of the Ancient of Days (cf. Dan. 7:10; II Esd. 13:10-11), and the repentant convert showed his willingness to submit to God's judgment by undergoing the baptism of repentance (Luke 3:16-17).

From the recently discovered Qumran material we have further evidence of the importance of lustral rites in first-century Judaism. The Manual of Discipline has several references to these ceremonies, and associates the sprinkling of water with washing from impurity and the reception of the Spirit of Truth. "God will sprinkle upon him the Spirit of Truth like water for impurity . . . to make the upright perceive the knowledge of the Most High." Perhaps these baptisms are to be associated with the daily lustrations of the Essenes, attested to by Josephus (War II.viii.5).

From these sources, then, the Christian rite of baptism developed; but it owed its distinctive character to the experience and mission of Jesus, and to the understanding of his work and person by the church.

Jesus' ministry began with his association with John's movement, and a number of his first disciples were recruited from John's followers (John 1:37). But a break between Jesus and John became inevitable. For one thing, the experience of his baptism led Jesus to the conviction that in some way the powers of the kingdom were already present in him, being manifested above all in his healings. While the accounts of his baptism in the NT are colored by the church's later reflection upon this event, they surely indicate that at this moment Jesus underwent a decisive experience, both in understanding his unique relation to God and in grasping the sacrificial nature of his mission. The vision of the descent of the dove (Mark 1:10) is important as indicating that for Jesus the breath of God's power, his Spirit, is to be seen in a sacrificial symbol rather than in one of destroying fire. Certainly the latter element is not lacking in Jesus' thought, and the divisive and perturbing consequences of his sacrificial mission are seen in the way he later connects his baptism with fire (Luke 12:49-50). But the central point is that the sacrificial dove has taken the place of John's sterner proclamation.

A second reason for the separation of Jesus from John is to be found in their differing views of ceremonial purification. The "Jew" with whom John's disciples disputed in John 3:25 is probably a reference to Jesus from some Baptist source, and reflects Jesus' freer attitude toward purifying customs.

The break between Jesus and John had as a consequence that the rite of baptism was not continued by Jesus during his mission. In this the proclamation of the coming kingdom and its manifestation in the healings were central. The reference to Jesus' baptizing in John 3:22 must refer to the period before the break with John; and in 4:1 a gloss is added to the effect that not Jesus, but his disciples, did the baptizing.

How then did the church come to adopt baptism, if it ceased to figure in Jesus' mission? The answer lies in several considerations. For one thing, if a significant number of early Christian converts had originally been members of John's movement (see Acts 19:3), the transformation of John's baptism into a Christian type would have been likely in any case. But a more important reason for the emergence of Christian baptism lies in the church's reflection upon Jesus' own baptism. For them this was the first manifestation of Jesus as Messiah, when he was anointed with the Holy Spirit (Acts 10:37-38); and the connection between the Spirit and a water rite was thus firmly established in their minds. For the Christian convert, therefore, to enter the Spirit community of Pentecost, meant to undergo a rite similar to John's but with a new Christian meaning. It meant to wash away sin and to receive the Spirit in the same way Jesus had received the Spirit (Acts 2:38). Baptism in the *name* of Jesus made all the difference. It meant baptism as associated with him, and initiation into the messianic community of his person.

We have no adequate description of the baptismal rite in the NT. From fragmentary references, however, we can gather a few impressions:

The supreme importance of the rite of baptism emerges from the large number of allusions to it as well as from such a verse as Eph. 4:5: "one Lord, one faith, one baptism." It is already a firmly established custom, to be taken for granted, by the time of Paul's ministry, and there is no indication in the NT that it was ever a cause of controversy.

The story of the baptism of the eunuch by Philip (Acts 8:36-39), taken in connection with a number of other references (Matt. 3:13-15; Acts 10:47; 11:17; Gospel of the Ebionites in Epiphanius *Panarion* 30. 13), leads us to suppose it was not self-baptism (as the proselyte rite), but administered by an officiant in connection with a liturgical question and a confession of faith. (That it was not self-baptism is very clear from I Cor. 1:14; though in an emergency it might be, as in Acts of Paul 2:34.) It rather seems, furthermore, that a liturgical question was posed by the candidate: "What prevents my being baptized?" This was followed by the minister's reply: "If you believe with all your heart you may"; and by the candidate's brief confession of the lordship of Christ: "I believe that Jesus Christ is the Son of God." (While the last two items are attested by the Western text, they indicate a very early formula.) These forms might vary. The confession given by Paul in I Cor.

12:3: "Jesus is Lord," is perhaps the earliest, and corresponds to the typical pagan affirmation: "Caesar is Lord" (Mart. Polyc. 8.2). The NT has preserved a number of further confessions, some of which may have a baptismal origin (e.g., John 2:22; Rom. 1:3-6; 8:34; I Cor. 15:3 ff; I Tim. 3:16; 6:13-14; II Tim. 2:8; I Pet. 3:18-22), though there were many other circumstances than baptism, which led the church to develop such formulas (e.g., preaching, instruction, exorcism). It is out of these confessions that the later creeds developed as formulas of faith at baptism. The characteristic of these primitive creeds is the central place given to the confession of Jesus as Lord, Messiah, or Son of God. Later on, the baptismal formula was divided into three distinct parts, as we find it in Hippolytus (*Apostolic Tradition* 21.12 ff). Another point to note is the interrogatory nature of early baptismal creeds. In Hippolytus' time, e.g., the confession is posed in the form of three questions to which the candidate responds: "I believe"; and while very brief declarations may have been in vogue in primitive baptism, the interrogatory form is the one that became current in the early liturgies.

We may note that there was probably no formula of baptism in the early church, such as we are familiar with. Such phrases as that in Matt. 28:19: "baptizing them in the name of the Father and of the Son and of the Holy Spirit," and the briefer ones in Acts 2:38; 8:16, etc.: "in the name of Jesus Christ," do not imply a formula: "I baptize you in the name of. . . ." They mean rather that the Christian baptismal act is one "under the auspices of," "in reference to," Jesus Christ. The formula was the confession, either interrogatory or declaratory, of which we have spoken. When such confessions were no longer rendered in the water, because of the widespread use of infant baptism, the new type of formula came into vogue. It is attested in the East by the fourth century (*Apostolic Constitution* 3.16; 7.22), but is considerably later in the West.

In NT times baptism was by a single immersion, preferably in running water. (Triple immersion first appears in Did. 7.) However, in cases of sickness or lack of water, affusion soon came into vogue (Did. 7.3; Cyprian *Epistle* 75.12-16), though it was regarded as exceptional.

There was baptism for the dead. Exactly what the curious reference in I Cor. 15:29 means has never been fully explained. Yet there can be little doubt that Paul knew (at least in Corinth) of cases where vicarious baptism had been undertaken.

Whether or not infant baptism was practiced in NT times is a much disputed question. The first clear evidence of it comes from the late second century (Tert. *On Baptism* 18); and we cannot be sure whether or not children were included in the "households" baptized by Paul (Acts 16:15, 33; I Cor. 1: 16). It has been argued that Paul's analogy between baptism and circumcision in Col. 2:11-12 implies that the Christian custom, like the Jewish, was applicable to children. But if we are to press such analogies, we should take account of I Cor. 7:14. There the implication is that, just as in proselyte baptism the children born after the parents' conversion do not need to undergo such a rite, since they already belong to the people of promise by their birth, so children born of Christian families do not *ever* need to be baptized! On the other hand, those born before the parents' conversion would have been baptized, on the proselyte analogy. In point of fact, the NT evidence is insufficient to solve the problem of infant baptism one way or the other. The most that can be said is that the way the story of Jesus' blessing the children is told (Mark 10:13-16) seems to reflect the church's desire to defend the practice.

Even more difficult is the question of confirmation. Was there a primitive rite of laying on of hands in addition to baptism? The author of Acts recounts two stories which suggest that water baptism, by itself, was an incomplete rite, and needed to be supplemented with the apostolic laying on of hands. In Acts 8:14-17 Peter and John are sent to Samaria to lay hands on the new converts, who, while already baptized, have not yet received the gift of the Holy Spirit, which the apostles thereupon confer on them. Similarly in Acts 19:1-6, after granting Christian baptism to some converts from John's movement, Paul lays his hands on the neophytes, and they thus receive the Spirit and proceed to speak with tongues.

On the other hand, there are NT passages which just as clearly associate the descent of the Spirit with the water rite. This is patent in John 3:5; Acts 2:38; I Cor. 6:11; 12:13; Tit. 3:5; and the discussion in Rom. 6. It is true that some of these passages are ambiguous and that "baptism" for their authors *may* include more than the water rite. Yet it is extremely difficult to imagine that, if the laying on of apostolic hands *alone* guaranteed the gift of the Spirit, such passages could ever have been written in that way. One is always faced with the question, How defective was the initiation which the eunuch received at Philip's hands (Acts 8:38)?

The problem is further complicated by the fact that not only the laying on of hands, but the use of oil in baptism also enters in. In II Cor. 1:21-22; I John 2:20 the gift of the Spirit is spoken of as an anointing, and it has been argued that anointing with oil was a part of primitive baptism and connected with the Spirit's descent.

With the sources available to us it is impossible to solve these problems. It rather looks as if the administration of baptism differed in various localities and was variously interpreted. The water rite certainly included more than mere water. There was an officiant who doubtless laid his hand on the convert as he was dipped in the water. (This is clear from catacomb art, and derives from Judaism. In the latter case a master had to keep his hand on his slave's head during the baptism [Yeb. 46a]. Can the Christian connection be that the convert is the "slave" of Christ?) There was also the process of taking off the clothes and putting them on. There was finally the anointing, since this was a feature of all bathing in the ancient world (cf. Ezek. 16:9; Sus. 17). It was only natural that these various practices should have played a part in the development of the symbolism of baptism. The clothing and unclothing suggests to Paul the putting off of the old man and the putting on of Christ, or the new man (Gal. 3:27; Col. 3:9-11); and eventually the neophytes came to wear white robes to signalize their new estate (Cyril of Jerusalem *Catechetical Lecture* 4.8).

More important for our purposes, however, are the connections made between the gift of the Spirit on the one hand and the anointing and laying on of hands on the other. In the first case the associations go back to the anointing of the OT kings (I Sam. 16:13; Isa. 61:1); in the latter case to the transfer of the Spirit to elders and rabbis (Num. 11:16-17). The reason why these elements in the baptismal rite should have assumed such importance over against the water, has to do with the fact that they more obviously symbolized the descent, the downward motion of the Spirit, than did the process of being dipped in the water. There is a notable absence in the NT of a symbolism of being dipped in the Spirit or drenched with Spirit, which the water rite might have suggested.

Eventually the separate parts of what had been a single rite became distinguished, and the gift of the Spirit was detached from the actual water ceremony, which was viewed as a cleansing preparation for it (cf. Heb. 6:2). The process was long and complicated and issued in different solutions; but it had its roots in the NT association of the descent of the Spirit with anointing and the laying on of hands.

One further factor played a role. In the primitive church the gifts of the Spirit were viewed rather realistically, manifesting themselves in ecstatic utterances, miracles, etc. It was doubtless the lack of such phenomena in Samaria that occasioned the visit of Peter and John in Acts 8:14-25; and it is precisely these charismatic outbursts which the author of Acts notes to be the result of Paul's laying on of hands in 19:6.

From these considerations we cannot say that there were two distinct rites of baptism and confirmation in the earliest NT times. It is more likely that there was originally a single water rite which was viewed as the occasion of the gift of the Spirit; but because of the difficulty of symbolizing the descent of the Spirit adequately, especially in view of the very realistic way his manifestations were thought of, the early Christians tended to give to other, more accidental, parts of the rite a prominence they originally lacked.

It is not made clear in the NT who is the normal officiant at baptism. Certainly the apostles baptized, though Paul does not regard this as his primary duty (I Cor. 1:17); and it was doubtless left to the local ministry of the presbyter-bishops. Philip, one of the Seven (who were probably the first presbyter-bishops, not deacons), baptized in the story in Acts 8:26-38. When the monepiscopacy arose, the bishop normally officiated, though the authority to do so could be delegated (Ign. Smyr. 8.1). Lay baptisms in emergency (but not by women) are attested by the time of Tertullian, who argues that one can give as much as one has received (*On Baptism* 17). This, however, probably applies only to the water rite, not to the laying on of hands, reserved to the bishop.

The meaning of baptism is variously interpreted in the NT, but these variations are on a single theme. It is the washing away of sin (Acts 2:38; 22:16); the appeal to God of a clear conscience as a result of this (I Pet. 3:21); it is putting on Christ (Gal. 3:27), and putting off the old man (Col. 3:9-11); it is rebirth (John 3:7; Tit. 3:5); it is burial with Christ in its

simulated drowning (Rom. 6:4), as it is also rising with Christ as one emerges from the water (Col. 2:12). All these are ways of expressing the basic Christian conviction that by baptism a new life begins in the messianic community of the risen Lord. In the symbolism of dying and rising and of rebirth we perhaps have echoes of Hellenistic language; whereas the emphasis on washing away sin and receiving the Spirit are more characteristic of a Jewish milieu. Yet it is the same gospel which lies behind the differing modes of expression.

For further discussion of this topic, *see* BAPTISM; CONFIRMATION.

6. The ministry to the sick. From its origins Christianity was a healing cult, and salvation was understood to involve the body as well as the soul. The healings of Jesus were signs of the presence of the kingdom (Luke 11:20; John 9:3); and it was not only to preach the gospel but also to heal the sick that Jesus sent forth the disciples on their mission (Mark 6:7; Luke 9:1-2).

Of the modes of healing in the NT, exorcism is the most prominent. Jesus commands the unclean spirits to come out of those possessed (Mark 1:25; 5:8; etc.), and they respond to his word, recognizing in him the Messiah. Exorcism was a familiar feature of Judaism (Jos. Antiq. VIII.ii.5; Juvenal *Satires* 6.542 ff), especially in Galilee; and we hear of "itinerant Jewish exorcists" in Acts 19:13. The primitive church continued this ministry, as many passages of Acts attest (e.g., 8:7 of Philip; 19:12 of Paul). The formula used was one that specifically included the name of Jesus, as is clear from the attempt of the priest Sceva to imitate the Christian practice (Acts 19:13 ff; cf. 16:18). The ability to exorcise was viewed as a special charisma (I Cor. 12:4 ff; Heb. 2:4); and in the early church there developed an order of exorcists and healers who were not ordained, as their gift was personal, not sacramental (Hippolytus *Apostolic Tradition* 15).

Along with exorcism were current other modes of healing. Some, perhaps, had a semimagical character, such as the use of handkerchiefs and aprons which had touched Paul's body, and the power associated with Peter's shadow (Acts 5:15; 19:11-12). More usual, however, was the use of prayer (Mark 10:29), anointing (Mark 6:13; Jas. 5:14), and laying on of hands (Mark 16:18; Acts 9:17). The passage in Jas. 5:14 ff is important as indicating a regular ministry in which the elders of the church visited the sick and anointed them. (A similar use of oil by Jewish healers is attested by the Babylonian Talmud, Yom. 77*b*.) Confession of sins seems also to have played a role in this ministry.

For further discussion of this subject, *see* HEALING; HEALING, GIFTS OF.

7. Ordinations. The use of the laying on of hands in connection with appointment to an office goes back to Judaism, whose elders and rabbis were so ordained. The practice was viewed as a continuation of the act of Moses whereby, in Num. 11:24-25, he imparted his spirit to the Seventy. It is probable that the choosing of the Seven in Acts 6:1-6 represents the effort of the church to organize itself in a way not dissimilar to Judaism, where every village had its seven ruling elders. If this is so, the founding, not of the diaconate, but of the presbyterate, is reflected in this passage; and we may reasonably assume that the ordination prayer for presbyters in Hippolytus (*Apostolic Tradition* 8.2 ff) has preserved a very ancient tradition. There it is prayed: "As thou didst look upon the people of thy choice and didst command Moses to choose elders whom thou didst fill with the Spirit which thou hadst granted to thy servant, so now, O Lord, grant that there may be preserved among us unceasingly the spirit of thy grace." We should perhaps imagine that some such prayer was in vogue in very early times, and used on such occasions as Acts 6:6; I Tim. 4:14; II Tim. 1:6 record. From the second of these passages, furthermore, we gather that ordinations were preceded by prophetic utterances whereby the candidate was chosen for the office. Fasting, moreover, seems to have been observed before ordinations (Acts 14:23).

For further discussion of this subject, *see* MINISTRY; LAYING ON OF HANDS.

8. Discipline and excommunication. That cases of discipline were handled at gatherings for worship is clear from both Matt. 18:17 and I Cor. 5:3-6. In the latter instance a solemn excommunication "in the name of the Lord Jesus Christ" is to be visited upon the incestuous man; while the other passage suggests that differences between Christians are brought before the assembled church. Appropriate rebukes were given, and in the event an offender proved recalcitrant, he was excluded from the community. From these beginnings then developed the liturgical aspects of the penitential system reflected in Tert. *On Penance* 9 and in the Didascalia, chs. 6 ff.

For further discussion of this subject, *see* EXCOMMUNICATION.

9. Marriages and funerals. The NT provides us with no information on the Christian form of these rites, and we have to assume that customs familiar to Jews or Gentiles were continued depending on the cultural background of the Christian convert. In Jewish circles marriage involved a ceremony of betrothal, which included the giving of a ring (or sometimes a coin) as part of the earnest money for the bride, and was accompanied by crowning with garlands. The night procession was the principal feature of the wedding—the bridegroom would go to fetch the bride to his house at midnight (Matt. 25:1 ff). A benediction was pronounced on the marriage, and the wedding feast followed. Among Christians the benediction doubtless included some reference to Christ; and it is not impossible that at times the marriage feast was associated with the Lord's Supper.

In Roman circles the betrothal was less ceremonious and involved little more than an initial business arrangement followed by a family party at which the future bride and bridegroom exchanged gifts, to be forfeited if the contract were later broken. In the evening of the wedding the bride was escorted in a torchlight procession to her new home. In the more formal marriage of patricians (*confarreatio*) the bride and bridegroom sat on chairs covered by a sheepskin and ate a special cake (*far*, hence *confarreatio*) together and joined hands. Nuts, sweets, and cakes were then showered among the guests to signify the plenty to attend the union. All this, with the nuptial banquet which followed, took place in the bride's house. Finally she was brought in an elaborate procession to her future home.

Just how these ceremonies were Christianized in the early period is not clear. A marriage benediction is perhaps implied by Ignatius (Polyc. 5), who requires the bishops' consent for a Christian marriage. The ring is mentioned by Tertullian (Apol. 6), as are also nuptial eucharists (*To His Wife* 2.8).

With regard to funerals we have even less information. No religious ceremonies attended them in Judaism, perhaps because the customs originated before belief in resurrection. There were paid mourners; and the body was buried after anointing and shrouding (Mark 5:38; 15:46; 16:1). Pagan funeral processions were more elaborate, being preceded by actors wearing the wax death masks of the family. The funeral banquet played a large role, and is constantly depicted on sarcophagi and tombs. This was transformed by Christianity into the funeral *agape*, so many pictures of which survive in the catacombs, and which was originally a celebration of the Lord's Supper before the sacrament had been separated from the actual meal.

The two points at which Christian funerals must have stood in marked contrast to Jewish and pagan ones are: (*a*) the joyful note of resurrection was present. Later this was symbolized in the avoiding of black robes of mourning (Cyprian *On Death* 20.20), by the carrying of palm branches (symbols of triumph), and by the chanting of "Alleluia" (Jerome *Epistle* 77.11; Chrysostom *Homily* 4 on Heb. 7). While none of these customs is early, the spirit which informed them is that of the NT. (*b*) The celebration of the Lord's Supper at funerals (and later at the anniversaries of martyrs and of the Christian dead; Mart. Polyc. 18), was characterized by the offering of a sacrifice *for* them, instead of *to* them. Such oblations for the dead are to be found in Tertullian (*On the Chaplet* 3; *On Monogamy* 10) and in Cyprian (*Epistle* 33.3).

For further discussion of this subject, *see* MARRIAGE; BURIAL.

10. Private devotions. The Christian times of private prayer are an adaptation of the Jewish practice. The devout Jew prayed three times daily—in the early morning at the time of the temple sacrifices, at 3:00 P.M. when the evening sacrifices were offered, and at dusk when the lamps were lit. Threefold daily prayer is mentioned by the Didache (8); at each of the three times the Christian is to recite the Lord's Prayer. (It is curious that this model prayer seems to have played no part at first in the liturgy, but to have characterized private devotions. It does not appear in the Eucharist until the fourth century, in Cyril of Jerusalem *Catechetical Lecture* 23.) Further hours of prayer were gradually added until a daily round of six periods of private devotion was established by the time of Hippolytus (*Apostolic Tradition* 36). It is from these hours that the daily offices later developed.

In addition to daily prayer, the primitive Christian undertook vows (Acts 18:18; 21:24) and periods of fasting. The former custom was a familiar feature of Judaism, and Christian vows (such as those of celibacy; Ign. Polyc. 5), owe something to such practices. Fasting also was taken over from Judaism.

The earliest Christians probably observed the one obligatory fast in the Law, the Day of Atonement (see Acts 27:9), and Paul stresses his constant fasts in II Cor. 6:5; 11:27. Christians seemed to have fasted before ordinations (Acts 14:23) and other solemn assemblies (Acts 13:3), as well as before baptisms (Did. 7; Just. Apol. 61). Wednesday and Friday, furthermore, are noted by the Didache (8.1) as the Christian fast days in contrast to the fasts of strict Pharisees on Monday and Thursday. It is possible, too, that the paschal fast is reflected in the saying in Mark 2:20.

For further discussion of this subject, see LORD'S PRAYER; VOWS; FASTING.

11. The church week and year. The development of the church calendar was a remarkably slow process in Christianity, and equally striking is the fact that so little of the Jewish year finally found a place in Christian celebrations. Where we should have expected a Christian transformation of Rosh Hashanah, Yom Kippur, Succoth, Chanukah Purim, etc., we find only the retention of the paschal festival. This is due to the fact that the church year was largely the creation of the Gentile church, and the background of such notable days as Christmas, Epiphany, Ember, etc., is pagan, not Jewish.

We must, however, suppose that the earliest Christians continued to observe the Jewish year and week, until the break with the synagogue was complete. Of definitely Christian days, distinct from those of Judaism, the NT affords us only one certain example, that of Sunday. This was observed as the day of the Lord's resurrection and is well attested in the NT (John 20:19, 26; Acts 20:7; I Cor. 16:2; Rev. 1:10). The day was kept by the celebration of the Lord's Supper in the evening (Acts 20:7). As it was a regular working day for Jew and Gentile alike, it could not be observed as a holiday or day of rest. This use of Sunday belongs to the fourth century, when Constantine legislated the public holiday, though by the late third century some Christians had already begun to defer their business in honor of the day (Tert. On Prayer 23). However, there was never any confusion in the mind of the early church between sabbath and Sunday. The days were clearly contrasted; and the early Christians never applied the sabbath legislation to Sunday. The sabbath was viewed by them as part of the ceremonial law now abrogated in Christ, and symbolic of the future rest of the kingdom (Barn. 15.8). While Jewish Christians doubtless continued to observe the sabbath, it was never made binding on Gentile converts (Col. 2:16). Indeed, by the second century its celebration was viewed as a feature of "Judaizing" (Ign. Magn. 9.1).

Within NT times—i.e., up to the middle of the second century—three other Christian observances can be traced. There were, in some localities, the Station Days (or "fixed days")—the fast days of Wednesday and Friday, adopted in contrast to the Pharisaic fasts of Monday and Thursday, and mentioned in the Didache (8.1). It is possible that Wednesday and Friday were chosen as the days of Christ's betrayal and passion; but this explanation is no earlier than the fourth century (Peter of Alexandria Canonical Epistle 15). There were also martyr's days, celebrating the passion or "birthday" of the martyr. They are first recorded in the Martyrdom of Polycarp (18), but doubtless antedate that letter of A.D. 155 or 167.

Finally, there was the observance of Easter, which is more ancient than the others and goes back to the Jewish Christian church. (Perhaps there is an echo of it in I Cor. 5:6-8.) It was a Christian form of the annual Passover festival, held like the Jewish feast on Nisan 14, and celebrating the death and resurrection of Christ at an evening Lord's Supper. When it became usual to have the sacrament in the early morning instead of in conjunction with an evening meal, the Easter rite underwent change. The West transferred the celebration to the Sunday morning next after Nisan 14 (Euseb. Hist. 5.24; the custom goes back to A.D. 120), while the East continued to keep Nisan 14, but observed the night in a vigil and held the Eucharist at cockcrow (Epistle of the Apostles 7-9). In both instances only one day was kept as Easter (there was no Holy Week), though there was a fast leading up to it. This differed in length in various localities (Irenaeus in Euseb. Hist. 5.24), and is perhaps reflected in Mark 2:20. Attempts have been made to read I Peter as a paschal homily and to see in the farewell discourses of John's Gospel reflections of an Easter rite. While these views are far from conclusive, they may have some substance to them.

For further discussion of this subject, see LORD'S DAY; FEASTS.

Bibliography. Only the most important works and those of a general nature are listed here. For further material, see the bibliographies under AGAPE, THE; BAPTISM; BURIAL; FASTING; FEASTS; HYMNS; LAST SUPPER; LORD'S DAY; LORD'S SUPPER; MARRIAGE; MUSIC; ORDINATION; PRAYER; PREACHING; WORSHIP IN NT TIMES (JEWISH).

J. Keating, Agape and Eucharist (1901). J. Dowden, The Church Year and Calendar (1910). T. Thompson, The Offices of Baptism and Confirmation (1914). W. O. E. Oesterley, The Jewish Background of the Christian Liturgy (1925). F. Gavin, The Jewish Antecedents of the Christian Sacraments (1928). Y. Brilioth, Eucharistic Faith and Practice (1930). F. Cabrol, The Prayer of the Early Christians (1930). L. Duchesne, Christian Worship, Its Origin and Development (1931). W. K. L. Clarke and C. Harris, eds., Liturgy and Worship (1932). R. M. Wooley, Exorcism and the Healing of the Sick (1932). L. Eisenhofer, Handbuch der katholischen Liturgik (2 vols.; 1932-33). A. Macdonald, Christian Worship in the Primitive Church (1934). N. Micklem, ed., Christian Worship (1936). G. Dix, The Shape of the Liturgy (1944). J. H. Smawley, The Early History of the Liturgy (2nd ed., 1947). O. Cullmann, Baptism in the NT (1950). G. W. H. Lampe, The Seal of the Spirit (1951): on the relation of baptism to confirmation. O. Cullmann, Early Christian Worship (1953). J. A. McArthur, The Evolution of the Christian Year (1953). B. Stewart, The Development of Christian Worship (1953). J. A. Jungmann, The Mass of the Western Rite (2 vols.; 1951, 1955). J. Jeremias, The Eucharistic Words of Jesus (1955).

The relevant articles in the following dictionaries should also be consulted: F. Cabrol and H. Leclercq, Dictionnaire d'archéologie chrétienne et de liturgie. J. Hastings, Dictionary of the Apostolic Church; Dictionary of the Bible; Encyclopedia of Religion and Ethics. T. Klauser, Reallexikon für Antike und Christentum. W. Smith and S. Cheetham, Dictionary of Christian Antiquities. C. C. RICHARDSON

WORSHIP IN NT TIMES, JEWISH. In accordance with present-day usage, we shall take worship to mean prayer and the ceremonial reading, quoting, or interpreting of scripture, frequently, though not always, accompanied by prayer. Burnt offerings characterized worship in the temple at Jerusalem and the temple at Leontopolis in Egypt (Jos. Antiq. XIII.iii.1; War VII.x.2-4; Men. 13.10). *See* SACRIFICES AND OFFERINGS.

Our chief source of information for Jewish worship in the NT period is the Mishna (*see* TALMUD), a codification of Jewish laws, rules, and regulations compiled *ca.* the year 200 of the Christian era. Though produced two generations later than NT times, the Mishna contains fairly reliable accounts of Jewish practices that prevailed during NT times. Like any compilation, the Mishna is a compilation of older material. The authorities quoted in the Mishna were mostly persons who lived during the first 130 years of the Christian era.

1. Places of worship
  a. Congregate worship
  b. Noncongregate worship
2. Times of worship
  a. Times not fixed
  b. Times fixed
3. Texts of worship
  a. Wording prescribed
  b. Wording not prescribed
  c. Spontaneous and original prayer
4. The use of scripture in worship
  a. Scriptural recitations
  b. Scriptural readings
  c. The use of the Psalms
  d. The "Hear, O Israel"
5. Accessories of worship
  a. Singing
  b. Appurtenances
  c. Postures of worship
  d. Processions
  e. Fasting
  f. Language of worship
  g. Numbers in attendance
  h. Leaders of worship
  i. Assistance at worship
  j. Exemptions and exclusions
  k. Disturbing heresies
  l. Frame of mind
  m. Repetitions
6. The spirit of worship
Bibliography

1. Places of worship. Places of worship varied according to circumstances. One of the determining factors was the difference between congregate worship and noncongregate worship.

a. Congregate worship. Among the places of congregate worship, we find the temple at Jerusalem (*see* TEMPLE, JERUSALEM; TEMPLES). Acts of worship in addition to those of burnt offerings had developed at the temple by NT times. Before the priests began their morning sacrifices, they would assemble and recite certain passages from scripture and certain prayers (Tam. 5.1). After the burnt offerings had been rendered, the priests would step to the temple porch and there, facing the multitude gathered in the courtyard, would invoke the Aaronic benediction (Num. 6:24-27; Tam. 7.2). On the Day of Atonement, the ritual of prayer and of reading from scrip-

ture, both inside the temple edifice and in the temple court, was striking (Yom. 6.2).

For congregate worship the chief place was, of course, the SYNAGOGUE. In the NT period synagogues existed, not only in Palestine, but throughout the Greco-Roman world. But there were places of congregate worship other than temple or synagogue. Grace was recited before and after each meal, wherever eaten (Ber. 6.6; 7.1, 3, 4-5; Jos. War II.viii.5; Sibylline Oracles IV.25.26). The same applies to the dinner-table devotions on the evening which marked the beginning of Passover (Pes. 10.1-9). The NT contains frequent reference to the words of thanksgiving spoken at the "breaking of bread" (Matt. 14:19; 15:36; 26:26; Mark 6:41; 8:6; 14:22; John 6:11; Rom. 14:6; I Cor. 10:30), while the dinner-table prayers at the outset of Passover are mentioned in Matt. 26; Mark 14; Luke 22; John 13. Nor was the priestly benediction confined to the temple. Persons of priestly lineage, residing in various parts of Palestine, would invoke the benediction at local religious services (Tam. 4.1).

b. Noncongregate worship. Certain prayers were offered by the individual in the home (Ber. 1.1-3). Matt. 6:5 mentions with disapproval those who pray while standing in the street. Another act of worship that could take place privately was the ritualistic reading of the book of Esther (Meg. 2.3). There were, in addition, the blessings to be recited before partaking of wine or of certain kinds of food (Ber. 6.1-3); a prayer to be uttered when entering and one to be uttered when leaving a fortified city (Ber. 9.4); a prayer when beginning the use of a newly built house or of new furnishings (Ber. 9.3); prayers to be spoken when beholding comets, meteors, lightning, mountains, hills, seas, rivers, or deserts, and when hearing thunder or encountering windstorms or earthquakes (Ber. 9.2); prayers to be said in places of danger (Ber. 4.4), or at the supposed scenes of miracles or in places which had witnessed the uprooting of idolatry (Ber. 9.1). One might perform certain devotions when riding on a beast or on a raft (Ber. 4.5-6), or when working high up in a tree or upon a wall (Ber. 2.4). There was a blessing to be pronounced upon receiving good news and one to be pronounced upon receiving bad news, regardless of one's location (Ber. 9.2).

Wherever he might chance to be, a certain Hanina, who lived in the first Christian century, would pray for the recovery of the sick (Ber. 5.5). There was only one kind of place from which prayer was debarred: when praying, one had to be removed at least four cubits from any filth (Ber. 3.5).

2. Times of worship. Some acts of worship took place as the occasion arose, regardless of date or hour. For other acts of worship the dates or hours or both were fixed.

a. Times not fixed. There could obviously be no fixed date or hour for various of the benedictions previously mentioned. The same would apply to the formalities of marriage and to eulogies for the dead (Meg. 4.3). These acts of worship would occur as occasion demanded.

b. Times fixed. But there were many acts of worship for which the time was fixed. Certain prayers were recited three times a day—morning, afternoon, and evening (Ber. 4.1). Such may be the prayers to which there is allusion in Wisd. Sol. 16:28; Acts 3:1; 10:30. Other acts of worship occurred twice a day—in the morning any time after there was light enough to distinguish between blue and white or between blue and leek green (Ber. 1.2), and in the evening any time after one could perceive the stars (Ber. 1.1). Grace was pronounced at every meal (Ber. 8.7). The public reading from scripture took place every sabbath (Saturday; Jos. Apion II.xvii; Luke 4:16; Acts 13:14-15; 15:21), every Monday, and every Thursday (Meg. 1.3; 3.6; 4.1). Then there were the forms of worship scheduled for once a week, such as the special prayers for the sabbath (Tosef. Ber. 3.12; Ber. 29a; Palestinian Ber. IV.3). At the temple the contingent of priests beginning duty on a given sabbath would invoke a blessing upon the contingent whose week of duty had just terminated (Tam. 5.1). Another once-a-week act of worship, also at the temple, was the Psalm singing of the Levitical choir: Sunday, Ps. 24; Monday, Ps. 145; Tuesday, Ps. 82; Wednesday, Ps. 94; Thursday, Ps. 81; Friday, Ps. 93; Saturday, Ps. 92 (Tam. 7.4).

The priestly benediction (Num. 6:24-27) would, on certain occasions, be invoked four times a day, twice in the morning and twice in the afternoon. These occasions came three times a year (Ta'an. 4.1). While certain prayers were recited three times a day, certain insertions into these prayers were made only during the months of fall and winter (Ber. 5.2; Ta'an. 1.1-2). Among the DEAD SEA SCROLLS, the Manual of Discipline prescribes that "the general members of the community are to keep awake for a third of all nights of the year, reading the Book (of the Law) and studying the Law and worshiping together."

Somewhat less frequent were the devotions of the "stand-by" (Ta'an. 4.2). For ministering at the temple in Jerusalem, there were twenty-four teams, serving in rotation, each a week at a time, twice a year. Every team consisted not only of priests and Levites but also of laymen who, though not active at the altar, *stood by* as representatives of the nation. Some, possibly all, of these teams had members who resided in Palestinian localities outside Jerusalem. The priests and Levites who lived outside Jerusalem would go there when the week arrived in which their team was to function. Lay members residing outside Jerusalem did not go there but remained at home, where, during the week of their team's ministry, they gathered every day for religious observance. Such a contingent was called a *Ma'amad.* To translate the word *Ma'amad,* the English "stand-by" seems to be as near as we can get. It is reported (Ta'an. 4.3-4) that during the week of their team's participation those home-town groups would, barring certain special conditions, meet for worship four times a day. There is a reference to these contingents in Jos. Life I.i.

The annual days of observance were PURIM, which fell in February-March (the Feast of Lots), associated with the story of Esther; PASSOVER, which fell in March-April; PENTECOST, the Feast of the FIRST FRUITS, which fell in May-June; NEW YEAR, the day of the hornblowing, which fell in September-October; the Day of Atonement (*see* ATONEMENT,

DAY OF), which fell in September-October; the Feast of Tabernacles (*see* BOOTHS, FEAST OF), which fell in September-October; and the Feast of Dedication (*see* DEDICATION, FEAST OF)—Josephus calls it the Feast of Lights (Antiq. XII.vii.7)—which fell in November-December. The Feast of Dedication (I Macc. 4:56, 59; II Macc. 10:8) commemorated the dedication of the new altar after the Syrian monarch Antiochus had, in the course of his persecutions, brought about the defilement of the previous altar. Passover is mentioned in Matt. 26; Mark 14; Luke 22; John 13. Pentecost is mentioned in Acts 2:1; I Cor. 16:8; as well as in II Macc. 12:32; Jos. Antiq. III.x.6; XVII.x.2; Jos. War II.iii.1; and in Philo's *Concerning Seven* 20. The Feast of Tabernacles is mentioned in John 7:2, and the Feast of Dedication in John 10:22. Each of these anniversaries had its unique elements of ceremonial, prayer, and reading from scripture (Tosef. Meg. IV).

It is reported (Soṭ. 7.8) that the ordinance in Deut. 31:10-11 was fulfilled by having the king read in public certain passages from Deuteronomy. This occurred once every seven years. A moving incident is related in connection with the reading performed once by King Agrippa (Soṭ. 7.8). Inasmuch as the last of the kings by this name died in the year 100, the practice must still have prevailed in NT times. An Agrippa is mentioned several times in Acts.

3. Texts of worship. For various prayers of NT times the Mishna proffers the wording. In other instances the Mishna refers to the prayers by title only; the wording has to be sought in later sources.

a. Wording prescribed. These are some samples of prescribed phraseology (Ber. 9.2-3): "Blessed be He whose power and whose might fill the universe"—recited upon beholding meteors, comets, earthquakes, lightning, thunder, and windstorms; "Blessed be He who hath created the world"—upon seeing mountains, hills, oceans, rivers, deserts. Other benedictions read: "Blessed be He who is good and who doth good"—to be spoken upon receiving good news; "Blessed be the truthful Judge"—upon receiving doleful news. Upon beginning the use of a new house or of new furnishings, one was to pray: "Blessed art thou, O Lord our God, King of the universe, who hast permitted us to live, hast enabled us to endure, and hast brought us to this time" (Ber. 9.3).

A certain teacher who lived in NT times proposed a prayer to be recited in places of danger: "Lord, save Thy people, Israel. At every parting of the ways let their needs stand before Thee. Blessed art Thou, O Lord, Who hearest prayer" (Ber. 4.4). Then there were the benedictions to be pronounced before drinking wine, before eating bread, fruit, or vegetables, or before eating any combination of such. These were respectively (Ber. 6.1-3): "Blessed art Thou, O Lord, our God, King of the universe, who createst the fruit of the vine"; "Blessed art Thou, O Lord, our God, King of the universe, who bringest forth bread from the earth"; "Blessed art Thou, O Lord, Our God, King of the universe, who createst the fruit of the tree"; "Blessed art Thou, O Lord, our God, King of the universe, who createst the fruit of the earth"; "Blessed art Thou, O Lord, our God, King of the universe, at whose word all things come into being." There was a benediction to be uttered upon arriving at a place where miracles had supposedly been performed, and one to be uttered upon reaching a place at which had occurred the eradication of idolatry: "Blessed be He who hath performed miracles in this place"; "Blessed be He who hath uprooted idolatry from our land" (Ber. 9.1). There was even a benediction to be spoken before taking a drink of water (Ber. 6.8). *See* BLESSINGS AND CURSINGS.

The ritual at the fast-day service in time of drought (Ta'an. 2.1) was impressive. An elder would address the multitude: "Brethren, it is not said of the Ninevites 'God saw their sackcloth and their fast,' but it is said: 'God saw their works, that they turned from their evil way' [Jonah 3:10]. Also it is said 'Rend your hearts and not your garments' [Joel 2:13]." Among the prayers offered at such drought-time devotions was one which read: "May He who heeded Abraham at Mount Moriah answer you and this day hear your cry. May He who answered our fathers at the Red Sea answer you and this day hear your cry"; and similarly, "He who answered Samuel at Mizpah," "He who answered Elijah at Carmel," "He who answered Jonah from the entrails of the fish," "He who answered David and his son Solomon at Jerusalem"—"may He answer you and this day hear your cry" (Ta'an. 2.4).

A striking feature of Passover was the solemnities in the home, around the dinner table, on the evening which marked the beginning of the festival (Matt. 26:17; Mark 14:12; Luke 22:8). A child of the family was primed to ask: "Wherein does this night differ from all other nights? On all other nights, we eat both leavened food and unleavened food; to-night it is only unleavened food; on all other nights, we partake of herbs other than bitter herbs; to-night it is bitter herbs. On all other nights, we consume meat that is either roasted or seethed or boiled; to-night all of the meat served is roasted. On all other nights, we dip our morsel into the sauce once; to-night we dip twice" (Pes. 10.4). The father would respond by quoting Deut. 26:5-11, the reference to the Egyptian bondage and the deliverance.

There have been preserved for us the wordings of some of the prayers offered on the Day of Atonement. At a certain moment in the day's sacrificial routine, the high priest would supplicate: "O Lord, I have acted perversely, I have transgressed, I have sinned before Thee. O Lord, pardon the iniquities, the transgressions, and the sins wherein I have acted perversely, transgressed and sinned before Thee, I and my house and the sons of Aaron, Thy holy people, as it is written in the Law of Moses, Thy servant, 'For on this day shall atonement be made for you, to cleanse you; from all your sins shall ye be clean before the Lord' " (Lev. 16:30). Upon hearing the divine name, the multitude, crowding the temple court, would prostrate themselves and exclaim: "Blessed be the name of the glory of His kingdom forever and ever" (Yom. 3.8; 4.2). Later, the high priest, having confessed his own sins and those of his family and of his associates, would speak confession in behalf of the people: "Pardon the iniquities, the transgressions, and the sins wherein Thy people, the house of Israel, have acted perversely, have transgressed, have sinned before Thee, as it is written,"

etc. Again, upon hearing the divine name, the multitude would prostrate themselves and proclaim: "Blessed be the name of the glory of His kingdom forever and ever" (Yom. 6.2).

The following is a passage from the ritual for the Feast of Tabernacles. On the second day of the feast there would occur, within the temple area, a torchlight procession before sunrise. When the marchers reached the E gate, veering around, they would face the W and chant: "Our fathers, in this place, turned their faces east. With their backs toward the shrine, they made obeisance toward the sun. But we turn our eyes toward God" (Suk. 5.4).

In the repertoire of devotional texts, we may now include the hymns preserved in the Dead Sea Scrolls. These hymns are couched in the style of the biblical Psalms and of the pseudepigraphic Psalms of Solomon. The hymns of Qumran dwell upon God's concern for the worshiper; upon the worshiper's sins, repentance, and forgiveness; upon the banefulness of the worshiper's opponents; and upon the divine retribution in store for those opponents.

b. Wording not prescribed. We often come upon references to acts of worship in which, while the prayer is prescribed, the wording of the prayer is not given. The wording appears to have been fluid or optional. An example would be the prayers to be spoken when entering or leaving a fortified city (Ber. 9.4). The Mishna ordains the prayers but does not quote them. For the wording we must go to later sources. This wording may or may not have prevailed in NT times, but the sense indicated by the wording did, in all probability, prevail. The wordings run as follows: "May it be Thy will to bring me to this city in peace"; "I thank Thee that Thou hast brought me to this city in peace"; "May it be Thy will to bring me forth from this city in peace"; "I thank Thee that Thou hast brought me forth from this city in peace" (Tosef. Ber. 7.16; Ber. 60a; Palestinian Ber. 14b).

We are provided with a similar surmise as to the benediction bestowed, every sabbath, upon the withdrawing contingent of priests by the contingent beginning its duties (Tam. 5.1): "He Who hath made this house a dwelling place for His name, may He cause to dwell, among you, love and brotherhood, friendship and peace" (Ber. 12a).

The Day of Atonement was the only day in the year upon which entrance was permitted into the holy of holies, and the only person permitted to enter was the high priest. We are apprised that, immediately upon emerging from the holy of holies, the high priest would offer a prayer, a brief prayer, lest the waiting multitude in the courtyard become anxious over his delay (Yom. 5.1). The Mishna mentions the prayer but does not quote it. The prayer is quoted elsewhere (Yom. 53b; Palestinian Yom. V. 42c). As quoted, the prayer reads: "O Lord, my God, may it be Thy will that, if the year is to be one tending toward drought, the rainfall may nonetheless be sufficient. Let not him who reigns pass from the house of Israel; let not the wielder of rule pass from the house of Judah. May Thy people Israel need alms neither from one another nor from outsiders. Let there not reach Thee the prayers of the wayfarers" (wayfarers prayed for the withholding of rain). It is a fair guess that such were the high priest's thoughts and possibly his actual words.

Another example is furnished by the praises sung at the torchlight procession on the Feast of Tabernacles (Suk. 5.4). We are apprised that the men of piety and prestige would use the words: "Happy our youth, since our old age is free of shame!" Penitents would say: "Happy our old age that atones for our youth!" All would say: "Happy the sinless and happy the forgiven!" Such may or may not have been the words used in NT times; but the thought is, in all likelihood, correctly reproduced (Suk. 53a).

By all odds the most important of the Jewish prayers was the one known as the "Eighteen Benedictions." Every Jewish person was expected to recite the Eighteen Benedictions every morning, every afternoon, and every evening (Ber. 3.3; 4.1). Here again, though the prayer was prescribed, its wording was not fixed. In the NT period the wording varied from locality to locality, from group to group, and even from individual to individual. We infer the substance from the wording which was committed to writing in later centuries.

The first of these Eighteen Benedictions was eventually formulated to read: "Blessed art Thou, O Lord, our God and God of our fathers, God of Abraham, God of Isaac, and God of Jacob, the great, mighty, and revered God, the most high God, who bestowest lovingkindnesses, and possessest all things; who rememberest the pious deeds of the patriarchs, and in love wilt bring a redeemer to their children's children for Thy name's sake, O King, Helper, Saviour, Shield. Blessed art Thou, O Lord, shield of Abraham."

The second of the Eighteen Benedictions speaks of divine help for the falling, the sick, and the imprisoned, and of the resurrection of the dead. It ends with the words: "Blessed art Thou, O Lord, Who quickenest the dead."

The theme of the third paragraph is the divine holiness. Its terminal words are: "Blessed art Thou, O Lord, the holy God." All the paragraphs follow the same pattern, a pattern which must have existed already in NT times (R.H. 4.5); the terminal sentence usually indicates the paragraph's content. Thus the fourth of the eighteen paragraphs concludes: "Blessed art Thou, O Lord, the gracious giver of knowledge." The fifth concludes: "Blessed art Thou, O Lord, who delightest in repentance." The terminals of the remaining paragraphs are: "who redeemest Israel"; "who healest the sick"; "who blessest the year"; "who gatherest the banished ones of Thy people Israel"; "who rebuildest Jerusalem"; "who causest the horn of salvation to flourish"; "who hearkenest unto prayer"; "who restorest Thy divine presence to Zion"; "unto whom it is becoming to give thanks"; "who makest peace."

The written paragraphs of later generations are not at all hard to identify with the paragraphs mentioned in the Mishna by title only (Yom. 7.1; Tosef. Yom. 3.18; Soṭ. 7.7; Tam. 5.1). The paragraphs committed to writing give us a significant glimpse into the prayer life of the Jews in NT times.

Between the eleventh and the twelfth paragraphs of the Eighteen Benedictions, there came to be inserted a nineteenth paragraph. It reads: "For slan-

derers let there be no hope, and let all wickedness perish in a moment; let all thine enemies be speedily cut off, and the dominion of arrogance do thou uproot and crush, cast down and humble speedily in our days. Blessed art thou, O Lord, who breakest the enemies and humblest the arrogant." These restive words reflect the conflicts of that day between Israel and Rome. Variant readings of the paragraph indicate that originally it could also have referred to Sadducees, Samaritans, Christians, or Gnostics.

But this paragraph about the "slanderers" was not the only insertion. During the months of fall and winter there would be inserted into one of the paragraphs the sentence: "Thou causest the wind to blow and the rain to fall" (Ta'an. 1.1). On the sabbath, the festivals, and Atonement Day, a special paragraph, differing from the others, was substituted for paragraphs 4-15 (Tosef. Ber. 3.12; Palestinian Ber. IV.3; Tosef. R.H. 4.11). Still other appropriate insertions would take place on the New Year (R.H. 4.5), on the Day of Atonement (Yom. 7.1; Sot. 7.7; Tosef. Ber. 3.12), and doubtless on some of the other sacred dates (Ta'an. 1.2; Tosef. Ber. 3.10; Tosef. Suk. 4.5). Vestiges of the Eighteen Benedictions have been traced in the Lord's Prayer of Matt. 6:9-13.

c. Spontaneous and original prayer. Meanwhile, there was abundant scope for prayers that were spontaneous and original. This can be seen from the pseudepigraphic writings, as well as from the NT itself (Luke 1:13; Acts 6:4, 6). Spontaneous prayers can be discerned also in the Mishna. No fixed wording is reported of Hanina's prayers for healing the sick (Ber. 5.5). A Rabbi Nehunya, of the first–second Christian centuries, would offer prayer as he entered and as he left his schoolhouse (Ber. 4.2). When he entered, he would pray that, through him, there might occur no stumbling; upon leaving he would express thanks for his lot as a man of study. But these acts of worship were original and spontaneous. The Rabbi was bound to no fixed forms. An ancient source (Tosef. Ber. 3.6) mentions the practice of adding to the prescribed prayers confession of one's own sins and petitions of one's own composing. In the noncanonical literature reflecting NT times, references to spontaneous and original prayer abound.

4. The use of scripture in worship. Passages from scripture constituted a large part of Jewish worship in NT times (see SCRIPTURE, AUTHORITY OF). But we have to distinguish between scriptural recitations and scriptural readings.

a. Scriptural recitations. Scriptural passages were extensively incorporated into the liturgy. The morning devotions conducted by the priests in the temple at Jerusalem (Tam. 5.1; 7.2; Soṭ. 7.6) would include the Decalogue and the Aaronic benediction. The psalms sung daily in rotation by the Levites have already been noted. The drought-time service utilized the sequence: Pss. 120; 121; 130; 102; I Kings 8:37 ff, Solomon's prayer that there might never be any lack of rain, or Jer. 14:1 ff, the vivid description of a drought and its sufferings (Ta'an. 2.3). At the Passover dinner, as we have seen, the father, answering the child, quoted Deut. 26:5-11, synopsizing the Egyptian bondage and the deliverance (Pes.

10.4). Likewise quoted at the Passover dinner were Pss. 113; 114; 115–18 (Pes. 10.7). A further use of Deut. 26:5-11 was made at the offering of the first fruits (Bik. 3.6). On New Year Day, certain biblical verses were recited before each blowing of the ram's horn (R.H. 4.6). Characteristic of the Feast of Tabernacles was the chanting of Ps. 118 (Suk. 4.1, 5, 8).

b. Scriptural readings. But, in addition to this and outside of this, there existed an elaborate reading schedule. For the New Moon, the reading was from Num. 28:11-15, which lists the offerings to be brought on New Moon Day to the tabernacle in the wilderness (Meg. 3.6). The readings at the local "stand-by" solemnities were taken from the story of creation in the first chapter of Genesis (Meg. 3.6); vss. 1-8 on Sunday, 6-12 on Monday, 9-18 on Tuesday, 14-22 on Wednesday, 20-26 on Thursday, and 1:24–2:3 on Friday (Ta'an. 4.3). For certain fast days, the reading was Lev. 26:3-46, which sets forth the divine rewards for compliance with the divine commands, and the punishments for noncompliance (Meg. 3.6). Once a year, on a certain sabbath, there was to be a public reading about the poll tax in Exod. 30:11-16. To be read on another sabbath was the exhortation in Deut. 25:17-19 to wage war against the Amalekites. On yet another sabbath, the passage was Exod. 12:1-20, with its instructions about the preparation of the paschal lamb (Meg. 3.4).

On the Feast of Lots, in February-March, the reading was the entire of the book of Esther (Meg. 1.1). For the Feast of Lots there was also a public reading of Exod. 17:8-16, which deals with the attack of the Amalekites upon the Hebrews in the wilderness; Haman, the villain of the book of Esther, was on the basis of Esth. 3:1 understood to be a descendant of the Amalekite king Agag, who, according to I Sam. 15:33, was captured by King Saul and slain by the prophet Samuel. The public reading for Passover was the schedule of sacrifices in Num. 28:16-25 (Meg. 3.5).

For Pentecost the reading was Deut. 16:9-12, relating to the observance of the Feast of Weeks (Meg. 3.5). The reading for the New Year included Lev. 23:24-25, in which the observance of the New Year is instituted (Meg. 3.5). On Atonement Day, before the destruction of the temple, the high priest himself would read in public the pertinent passages, Lev. 16:1-28; 23:26-32; Num. 29:7-11 (Yom. 7.1; Soṭ. 7.7). Outside the temple also, Lev. 16 was read on Atonement Day at various places of gathering (Meg. 3.5). The reading for the first day of the Feast of Tabernacles was Num. 29:1-39, which sets forth the sacrificial program for the eight days of the observance. On each of the succeeding days there would be read, from this chapter, the verses pertinent to that particular day (Meg. 3.5). Every seven years, on the eighth day of the feast, the king, compliant with Deut. 31:10-11, would read in public Deut. 17:14; 1:1–6:9; 14:22-27; 28 (Soṭ. 7.8). For the Feast of Dedication in November-December, the section to be read was Num. 7, which lists the offerings donated by the princes of Israel to the newly constructed tabernacle in the wilderness (Meg. 3.6).

Of course, every sabbath there was the reading of some selection from the Pentateuch and one from the Prophets (Meg. 4.1-5; Luke 4:17; Acts 13:15), except that the public reading of the Aaronic benediction (Num. 6:24-27), also of Ezek. 1, according to some, and of Ezek. 16, was forbidden (Meg. 4.10). Included likewise were readings from the Hagiographa, such as the book of Esther, on the Feast of Lots (Meg. 1.1). But the reading of II Sam. 11, the story of David and Bathsheba, is reported to have been prohibited (Tosef. Meg. 4.38).

c. The use of the Psalms. We have already noted some of the uses of the Psalms, daily and for special occasions. The NT mentions the quoting of Ps. 118:26 by the multitude that greeted Jesus (Matt. 21:9; John 12:13).

The Mishna relates that a part of the temple service once consisted of Ps. 44 but that this was discontinued (Ma'as Sh. 5.15). Later sources allege the reason for the discontinuation to have been the objectionability of vs. 23: "Awake, why sleepest thou, O Lord?" (Soṭ. 48*a*). Later accounts also maintain— with how much anachronism we can only guess— that, in the ancient temple (according to Masseket Soferim 18.2-3), the Levites sang Ps. 7 on the Feast of Lots, Ps. 83 or Ps. 148 on the First Day of Passover, Ps. 136 on the Last Day of Passover, and Pss. 72 and 104 on the intervening days; Ps. 29 on the Feast of Weeks; Ps. 145 on the Feast of Dedication; and (according to Suk. 55*a*) Ps. 29 on the first intervening day of the Feast of Tabernacles, Ps. 50:16 on the second, Ps. 94:16 on the third, Ps. 94:8 on the fourth, Ps. 81:17 on the fifth, Ps. 82:5 on the sixth. Such being the synagogal usage of those later centuries, the reports seek to convey that synagogal usage merely copied temple usage. The Mishna further enumerates the formalities observed when extending the areas of Jerusalem and of the temple court (Shebu. 2.2). A later source tells us that those formalities included a sacred procession and that the marchers in such procession would sing Pss. 30; 91:3 (Shebu. 15*b*). *See* PSALMS, BOOK OF.

d. The "Hear, O Israel." A liturgical unit, in which biblical material and nonbiblical material are combined, constituted one of the foremost acts of Jewish worship, surely prevalent as early as NT times. This is the set of paragraphs known as the "Hear, O Israel," the name deriving from the initial word of Deut. 6:4. The recitation of the "Hear, O Israel" occurred every morning and every evening. It immediately preceded the recitation of the Eighteen Benedictions.

The biblical passages embraced in the "Hear, O Israel," are Deut. 6:4-9; 11:13-21; Num. 15:37-41; the first dealing with the duty of keeping in mind the divine commands; the second announcing the rewards for obedience, the punishments for disobedience, and the duty of remembering the divine commands and teaching them to the young; the third prescribing that fringes be attached to the garments. Such fringes are mentioned in Matt. 23:5. Deut. 6:8 was construed as bidding, not figuratively but literally, that the sacred words be bound as a sign upon the hand and worn as frontlets between the eyes. Hence the phylacteries mentioned in Matt. 23:5.

This trio of biblical passages was preceded and followed by some paragraphs of supplication. The supplications voiced in the morning differed from those of the evening. While the Mishna alludes to these supplications by name, it does not supply the wording. To gauge the sense of these supplications as spoken in NT times, we have to look at the wordings written down in later centuries. The following selections come from the two supplicatory paragraphs which open the "Hear, O Israel," in the morning: "Blessed art thou, O Lord, our God, King of the universe, who formest light and createst darkness, and who makest peace and createst all things, who in mercy givest light to the earth and to them that dwell thereon, and in thy goodness, renewest the creation every day continually.

"With abounding love hast thou loved us, O Lord, our God, with great and exceeding pity hast thou pitied us. . . . O our Father, merciful Father, ever compassionate, have mercy upon us; O put into our hearts to understand and to discern, to mark, learn, and teach, to heed, to do and to fulfil in love all the words of instruction in thy Law."

The following is taken from the one paragraph which concludes the "Hear, O Israel," in the morning (Ber. 1.4): "True and firm, established and enduring, right and faithful, beloved and precious, desirable and pleasant, well-ordered and acceptable, good and beautiful is thy word unto us forever and ever. . . . King and God, who liveth and endureth, who is high and exalted, great and revered, who bringeth low the haughty, and raiseth up the lowly, leadeth forth the prisoners, delivereth the meek, helpeth the poor, and answereth his people when they cry unto Him."

The following selections intimate the content of the introductory paragraphs recited in the evening: "Blessed art thou, O Lord, our God, King of the universe, who at thy word bringest on the evening twilight. . . . Thou createst day and night; thou rollest away the light from before the darkness, and the darkness from before the light; thou makest the day to pass and the night to approach, and dividest the day from the night, the Lord of hosts is thy name.

"With everlasting love hast thou loved the house of Israel, thy people . . . and mayest thou never take away thy love from us. Blessed art thou, O Lord, who lovest thy people Israel."

Finally, one of the two supplications with which the "Hear, O Israel," concludes in the evening is: "Cause us, O Lord, our God, to lie down in peace, and raise us up, O our King, unto life. Spread over us the tabernacle of thy peace; direct us aright through thine own good counsel; save us for thy name's sake; be thou a shield about us; remove from us every enemy, pestilence, sword, famine, and sorrow; remove also the adversary from before us and from behind us."

The Mishna, it must be repeated, while it recurrently mentions these liturgical pieces and refers to them in unmistakable terms, does not anywhere supply us with the wording (Ber. 1.4-5; Pes. 10.6; Tam. 5.1). In NT times and for centuries thereafter, the wording was carried in memory. It is nonetheless probable that those pieces as quoted here did not differ greatly in their content, even if they differed in wording, from the supplications with which NT times were conversant.

5. Accessories of worship. The accessory features of Jewish worship in NT times were many. These include such items as appurtenances, postures, processions, fasts, translations, numbers in attendance, leaders, assistance for the unlettered, exclusions, precautions against heresy, frame of mind, and repetitions.

a. Singing. The NT mentions singing in connection with the dinner-table devotions at the outset of Passover (Matt. 26:30; Mark 14:26). That the hymn consisted of Pss. 113–18 is fairly certain. While Jewish sources do not state explicitly that such singing, outside the sanctuary, was the usage at that period, intimations to this effect are not lacking (Pes. 10.7; Tosef. Pes. 8.22; 10.6-9). Otherwise, Jewish accounts mention singing only in connection with the temple (i.e., Ecclus. 50:18). As a rule, the singers were Levites (Jos. Antiq. XX.ix.6; Tam. 7.4; Bik. 3.4). However, among the singers in the torchlight procession within the temple precincts on the Feast of Tabernacles, layfolk of piety and prestige were apparently included (Suk. 5.4). The same seems to have characterized the procession which took place at the official extension of sacred areas (Shebu. 15*b*). In the course of time, all Jewish worship was sung or chanted. Our sources, nevertheless, fail to indicate that, as early as the NT period, sacred singing was a practice outside the temple, except at the Passover dinner. *See* SINGERS, SINGING.

b. Appurtenances. An invariable appurtenance of the synagogue was the ark of the Law, in which were preserved the scrolls of the Pentateuch. At the drought-time service, the ark would be placed in the open. Upon it would be strewn ashes (Ta'an. 2.1). The service would be attended by the highest dignitaries of the community, and these could be seen putting ashes upon their heads.

At the table devotions on the evening which marked the beginning of Passover, there occurred the ceremonial drinking of four cups of wine (Pes. 10.7). Another ceremony was the conveying of the first fruits to the temple in baskets, as ordained in Deut. 26:1-11. The poor may have carried baskets made of stripped twigs of willow, but the rich carried baskets of gold or silver (Bik. 3.8).

The ritual for New Year Day required several blowings of the ram's horn (R.H. 4.1, 5-7). The ram's horn was sounded also in the fast-day service at drought time (Ta'an. 2.5; 3.1, 9) and on other occasions of calamity (Ta'an. 3.4-7). Trumpets, as distinguished from rams' horns, would be blown during the torchlight procession on the Feast of Tabernacles, when there also figured harps, psalteries, and cymbals (Suk. 5.4). The horns and the trumpets were blown by priests, and the musical instruments were played by priests (Ta'an. 2.5). Into the observance of the Feast of Tabernacles entered also the palm branch (Suk. 3.1, 9, 13), the citron (Suk. 3.5-7), and the sprigs of myrtle and of willow (Suk. 3.3-4) held in the hands of every worshiper. The palm branch would be waved when, in the course of the solemnities, the recitation of Ps. 118 would reach vs. 1 and vs. 25 (Suk. 3.9).

Also to be noted apropos of appurtenances, is the report that, when pronouncing the benediction every morning in the courtyard of the temple, some of the priests would still be holding their sacrificial implements in their hands (Tam. 7.2).

c. Postures of worship. Prostration would, on occasion, be the prayer posture. This applied particularly, though not exclusively, to the ministrations of the priests (Tosef. Ber. 3.5; Sheķ. 6.13; Tam. 7.1). On the Day of Atonement there were moments when the entire assembled multitude fell upon their faces.

> Then all the people together made haste
>   and fell to the ground upon their faces
> to worship their Lord,
>   the Almighty, God Most High,

says Ecclus. 50:17. And though Ecclesiasticus may date from a period earlier than NT times, the ritual of mass prostration did undoubtedly prevail in NT times (Yom. 6.2; Ab. 5.8). At table, people sometimes sat, but sometimes they reclined on couches. In the former case, each would recite for himself the grace before eating; in the latter case, one would recite for the entire company (Ber. 6.6). It was the practice of some to assume a reclining position for the evening "Hear, O Israel," literally carrying out the directive in Deut. 6:7 about pondering the sacred words not only "when thou risest up" but also "when thou liest down" (Ber. 1.3). The priests were required to hold their hands at a specified height when pronouncing the Aaronic benediction (Tam. 7.2). And when, on Atonement Day, the high priest would speak the formula of confession first for himself, his family, and his associates (Yom. 3.8; 4.2), and then for the entire community (Yom. 6.2), he would have his hands on the head of a bullock to be sacrificed.

d. Processions. There were rituals that involved marching in procession, such as the ceremony of the water drawing, with its hymns and praises, on the Feast of Tabernacles (Suk. 4.1, 5; 5.4). The torchlight procession begun before cockcrow on the morning after the first day of the feast (Suk. 5.4) has already been mentioned. Carrying torches, men of piety and prestige would leap and dance as they marched (Suk. 5.4). Every courtyard in Jerusalem is said to have caught the glow of the illumination (Suk. 5.3). On each of the eight days of the Feast of Tabernacles there would be a circling of the altar; seven times on the last day, once on each of the preceding days (Suk. 4.5). There would also be a procession at the bringing of the first fruits, as ordained in Deut. 26:1-11 (Bik. 3.2-4). Pilgrims would assemble with their offerings at the nearest town. From there they would march to Jerusalem; the procession would be headed by an ox with gilded horns and a wreath of olive on its head. At the outskirts of Jerusalem, dignitaries of the city would come forth to meet the marchers. As the marchers passed through the city, workingmen on the streets would salute them: "Our brethren of such-and-such a place, ye have come in peace." Led by a flute player, the visitors would arrive at the temple mount. On such occasions, King Agrippa himself would place a basket on his shoulder and enter the temple court. At the temple the Levites would sing Ps. 30:1:

> I will extol thee, O Lord, for thou hast drawn me up,
>   and hast not let my foes rejoice over me.

e. Fasting. Fasting attended not only the observance of Atonement Day but also the supplications of drought time (Ta'an. 1.4-7). There would be increasing degrees of austerity as the drought grew worse (Ta'an. 1.4-7; 4.7). During the week of the local "stand-by" services, there would be fasting by the participants (Ta'an. 4.3). *See* FEASTS AND FASTS.

f. Language of worship. While certain devotional pieces might be recited in any language, there were others that required Hebrew (Soṭ. 7.1). Any language might be used for the Eighteen Benedictions or for grace at meals or for the "Hear, O Israel" (Soṭ. 7.1). But Hebrew was mandatory for the words in Deut. 26:5-10, to be spoken at the depositing of the first fruits in the temple; for the blessings and the curses listed in Deut. 27:15-28:69; for the Aaronic benediction (Num. 6:24-27); and for the rules pertaining to the kingship in Deut. 17:14-30; similarly for the eight benedictions—selected from the Eighteen Benedictions—which the high priest would recite in connection with his public readings on the Day of Atonement (Soṭ. 7.7). Ancient sources indicate that the language of Jewish worship was Greek in Greek-speaking communities.

Only in the temple and not elsewhere, and by the priests but by no others, could there be the pronunciation of the actual name of God (Soṭ. 7.6; Tam. 7.2). The divine name was otherwise not uttered. In its place "Adonai" ("My Lord") was always substituted.

Among those who functioned at the reading of scripture was the translator (Meg. 4.6, 10). Certain readings were occasionally rendered in translation only (Meg. 2.1; Tosef. Meg. 4.13). Of some passages, however, translation was forbidden—e.g., the story of Reuben and Bilhah in Gen. 35:22 or the passage in Exod. 32:21-25 about the golden calf (Meg. 4.10; Tosef. Meg. 4.35). *See* LANGUAGES OF THE BIBLE.

g. Numbers in attendance. The number participating in an act of worship was also a factor. The presence of ten adult males was required for congregate worship as well as for certain rituals connected with marriages and with obsequies (Meg. 4.3). The wording of the grace after meals depended upon the number of those dining (Ber. 7.1, 3). When three dined together, one of them would open the saying of grace with the words, "Let us bless the Lord" (Ber. 7.1, 3). A different introductory would be used if four dined together, still different if there were nine, still different if the number was ten or a hundred, and so on. There would be corresponding variations in the response formulas of those addressed.

h. Leaders of worship. At congregate worship, leaders performed a variety of functions. There was the person who led at the reciting of the Eighteen Benedictions and the one who led in the "Hear, O Israel" (Meg. 4.5). The admonition is expressed that if, because of some circumstance, the regularly functioning leader becomes disqualified, one should not, out of modesty, decline to step in as a substitute; one should not have to be coaxed (Ber. 5.3; Meg. 4.8). A priest, if present at the service, would pronounce the Aaronic benediction (Meg. 4.5; Ta'an. 4.1; Soṭ. 7.6). According to some, a priest might not raise his hands in benediction if they were stained or blemished (Meg. 4.7). The question is debated whether, on certain occasions, one and the same person might function as priest and also as leader of prayer (Ber. 5.4). It was held that such a combination of functions was permissible if the person functioning could change from one role to another without committing blunders (Meg. 4.5). At the drought-time service, the officiant had to be not only conversant with the prayers but also old and poor and the father of children (Ta'an. 2.2).

Another function at congregate worship was that of reading from scripture (Meg. 4.5). There was a fairly elaborate system of assigning readers for various passages and occasions. On an ordinary sabbath, the Pentateuchal portion was divided among seven persons (Meg. 4.2). Six would read the section assigned for the Day of Atonement; on certain other sacred days the number would be five. Four would read on New Moon days and on the days between the first day and the last day of Passover and of the Feast of Tabernacles. No one was to read fewer than three verses (Meg. 4.4). Among the several readers, a priest, if present, would read first, a Levite would come second, and then would come the lay folk (Giṭ. 5.8). *See* PRIESTS AND LEVITES.

According to Luke 4:16-20, Jesus read in the synagogue from Isa. 61. At Antioch, Paul and his associates listened to the readings from the Law and the Prophets (Acts 13:15). We have noticed that there was an occasion when the high priest (Yom. 7.1; Soṭ. 7.7), and also an occasion when the king (Soṭ. 7.8), would read in public. On the Day of Atonement the high priest, after reading before the multitude Lev. 16; 23:27-32, would roll up the scroll and place it in his bosom. Then he would announce: "More than what I have read before you is here written." He would thereupon recite from memory Num. 29:7-11, detailing the sacrificial program for the occasion (Yom. 7.1; Soṭ. 7.7). The robe worn by the high priest was white; if he wished, it would be of linen (Yom. 7.1).

Also in synagogues everywhere, Num. 29:7-11 was, on the Day of Atonement, recited from memory (Tosef. Meg. 4.7). Recitation from memory, in lieu of reading, took place likewise at the afternoon worship of the "stand-by" (Ta'an. 4.3).

Approximating the routine laid down in the Mishna (Yom. 7.1; Soṭ. 7.7-8) was the usage described when Luke 4:16-20 pictures Jesus receiving the scroll from, and returning it to, the attendant. The readings, moreover, would be preceded and followed by suitable benedictions (Yom. 7.1; Meg. 4.1-2).

Another function was that of the translator (Meg. 4.5). A minor might read from the Pentateuch and might translate, but was not qualified to lead at the Eighteen Benedictions or at the "Hear, O Israel" (Meg. 4.6). A poorly clad person was permitted to lead at the "Hear, O Israel," and to act as translator, but was not qualified to read from the Pentateuch (Meg. 4.6). There was difference of opinion whether a blind person might lead at the "Hear, O Israel," or might act as translator (Meg. 4.6). Then there was the one who, on New Year Day, called the several blowings of the ram's horn (R.H. 4.7). There was also the one who led the saying of grace when a number of persons dined together (Ber. 6.6).

i. Assistance at worship. If a person was not conversant with the psalms recited at the Feast of Tabernacles, someone else might speak them for him. The person thus helped would, under some circumstances, repeat what he had heard; under other circumstances, he would merely respond, "Hallelujah," presumably after each verse (Suk. 3.10). At the offering of the first fruits, there would be available, at the temple, expert assistance for the reading of Deut. 26:3-11 (Bik. 3.7). Originally such assistance was provided only for the illiterate; later, to avert embarrassment, this aid was accorded everyone. Some held that every individual was obligated to recite the prayers, and that the leader could represent only those not versed in the prayers (R.H. 4.9). Others held that the leader spoke for all. Of course, "Amen," as well as other frequent responses, devolved upon everyone (Soṭ. 7.6; Tam. 7.2).

j. Exemptions and exclusions. Women, slaves, and minors (Ber. 3.3), as well as bridegrooms on the wedding night (Ber. 2.5), were exempt from the obligation to recite the "Hear, O Israel." Mourners, before the burial, were exempt from the obligation to recite the "Hear, O Israel," and to recite the Eighteen Benedictions; similarly pallbearers (Ber. 3.1). From certain acts of worship, ritually defiled persons were barred (Ber. 3.4-5); while women, slaves, and minors were not included among those meant by the summons to grace after meals (Ber. 7.2).

k. Disturbing heresies. Jewish worship in NT times entailed unrest over various heresies, among which, no doubt, was that of nascent Christianity. Daily worship outside the temple, as well as in the temple, at one time included the recitation of the Decalogue (Tam. 5.1). Outside the temple the practice was discontinued, because, as later tradition words it, of "the contentions of the heretics" who maintained that the Decalogue only was of Sinaic origin (Ber. 12a; Palestinian Ber. I.3c). There is mention of certain objectionable insertions made by some when reciting the Eighteen Benedictions, insertions such as: "The good shall praise Thee," "Thy compassion extendeth over the bird's nest," "By virtue of good be Thy name remembered" (Ber. 5.3; Meg. 4.9). The same applied to various metaphorical interpretations of the laws against incest in Lev. 18; 20, or to the passage in Lev. 18:21 about giving one's seed to Molech (Meg. 4.9). We are apprised that a certain prayer, offered at the temple, once contained the phrase "from everlasting." When the sect arose which denied a hereafter, the phrase was extended to read: "from everlasting to everlasting," thus affirming the existence not of one world but of two (Ber. 9.5). It was forbidden to pronounce benedictions over lights or spices prepared by idolaters (Ber. 8.6). To a benediction spoken by any sectarian, "Amen" was not to be appended until the benediction had been heard *in toto;* one might inadvertently be saying "Amen" to something heretical (Ber. 8.8). We have noted that an entire paragraph alluding to such troublemakers was inserted into the Eighteen Benedictions.

l. Frame of mind. Other factors considered in connection with Jewish worship in NT times were such as attentiveness, interruptions, errors, audibility, and fluency. The question is raised whether it is permissible to recite the "Hear, O Israel," mechanically and inattentively (Ber. 2.3). Some assert, and some deny, that the reciter has to be conscious of each letter (Ber. 2.3). There is a similar division of opinion as to the permissibility of altering the sequence to the various parts of the "Hear, O Israel." Whether or not the recitation of the "Hear, O Israel," had to be audible was also a matter of debate (Ber. 2.3). To read the book of Esther in a desultory manner was expressly forbidden (Meg. 2.1), although there was no objection to reading the book of Esther interruptedly, even if the reader slept in the intervals (Meg. 2.2).

One was not allowed to interrupt one's recitation of the "Hear, O Israel," except at the breaks between the paragraphs. At these points one might pause to return a salute or, out of respect for someone, even accord a salute (Ber. 2.1). In the midst of a paragraph, such saluting was prohibited except when failure to do so might bring upon the worshiper someone's dangerous enmity.

In the recitation of the Eighteen Benedictions, certain abridgments were permitted to one whose recitation of the prayer lacked fluency (Ber. 4.3). Rabbi Hanina, who lived in the first Christian century, believed that his prayers for the recovery of the sick were efficacious when they proceeded fluently from his lips, but inefficacious otherwise (Ber. 5.5).

If one forgets the requisite benediction before one eats, the benediction continues nonetheless pertinent until the end of digestion (Ber. 8.7). An error in the reciting of a prayer was regarded as an ill omen for the worshiper, and if the error was committed by someone officiating for an assembly, it was an ill omen for the congregation (Ber. 5.5). The Eighteen Benedictions were not to be recited by one who was in a state of sexual defilement, until he had performed certain ablutions (Ber. 3.5-6).

m. Repetitions. On certain occasions, at congregate worship, certain liturgic passages would be repeated at one and the same service. E.g., on sabbaths and on holidays the Eighteen Benedictions, recited in the morning, were, with certain modifications, again recited later in the morning (Ber. 4.1, 7; Tosef. Ber. 3.3; Ta'an. 4.1, 4). On the Feast of Tabernacles, in some localities, when Ps. 118 was read, vs. 21 and each subsequent verse would be read twice (Suk. 3.11). We have already noted the repetition of certain phrases in the supplication for the relief of drought (Ta'an. 2.4). It may be that the reproof in Matt. 6:7 alludes to such repetitions.

6. The spirit of worship. There were Jewish teachers in NT times who cautioned against prayer of the routine mechanical type (Ber. 4.4; Ab. 2.18). Prayer was to be an "appeal for mercy and grace before the All-Present" (Ab. 2.18). Greater devoutness, in fact, was expected for the recitation of the Eighteen Benedictions, which consisted entirely of prayer, than of the "Hear, O Israel," which consisted of prayer only in part (Ber. 2.4). Men might, as we saw, recite the "Hear, O Israel," while working in a tree or on top of a wall, but this was not permitted for the Eighteen Benedictions (Ber. 2.4). For prayer, a reverent mood was indispensable (Ber. 5.1). The Mishna reports that certain of the old-time saints would, before praying, spend an entire hour in silent meditation, "directing their heart

toward the Infinite" (Ber. 5.1). Not even if one were saluted by the king—yes, not even if one's heel became entwined by a serpent—was one's prayer to be interrupted (Ber. 5.1). Ex post facto prayers, however, were deprecated (Ber. 9.3). If one's wife were pregnant, one was not to pray: "God grant that the child be a male"; if, upon returning from a journey, one were to hear a wailing in one's town, one should forbear to pray: "God grant that the house thus afflicted be not my house." Such prayer is "vain prayer" (Ber. 9.3).

Gamaliel, the grandson of the Gamaliel mentioned in Acts 5:34; 22:3, speaking of the ritual for Passover, urged that "in every generation one should feel as if he had himself personally come forth out of Egypt" (Pes. 10.5). And though the book of Ecclesiasticus somewhat antedates the NT period, there can be little doubt that the words of Ecclus. 50 were still applicable to the first decades of the NT period in describing the fervor and the impressiveness of the worship in the ancient temple.

Bibliography. E. Schürer, *Lehrbuch der neutestamentlichen Zeitgeschichte* (1874); *Geschichte des jüdischen Volkes im Zeitalter Jesu Christi* (1898). W. Bousset, *Die Religion des Judentums im neutestamentlichen Zeitalter* (1903). S. Singer, *Authorized Daily Prayer Book with a New Translation* (1904). "Shemoneh 'Esreh," in *Jewish Encyclopedia*, XI (1905), 270-83. I. Elbogen, *Der jüdische Gottesdienst in seiner geschichtlichen Entwicklung* (1924). W. Bousset, *Die Religion des Judentums im späthellenistischen Zeitalter* (1926). H. Danby, *The Mishnah Translated from the Hebrew* (1933). T. H. Gaster, *The Dead Sea Scriptures in English Translation* (1956).   Abraham Cronbach

WRATH OF GOD. The biblical conception of the Deity's threatening with annihilation the existence of whatever opposes his will and purpose or violates his holiness and love (*see* HOLINESS; LOVE; SALVATION). Throughout the OT and the NT the divine wrath is regarded, along with the other aspects of God's self-revelation, as a manifestation of the very will of God himself. Its operation is seen, not only as part of a final judgment in the end time, but also in particular historical and natural catastrophes, as well as in private and personal disasters, while not all such events are interpreted in this way necessarily. The biblical writers can draw analogies from the human affect in order to describe the wrath of God, yet ANGER in man is sharply distinguished from God's wrath.

1. Terminology of the wrath of God in the Bible
   a. In biblical Hebrew
   b. In LXX Greek
   c. In NT Greek
2. The wrath of God in the OT
   a. Irrational wrath
   b. Wrath and sin
   c. Instruments of the divine wrath
   d. The Day of Wrath
   e. Salvation from the wrath of God
   f. The wrath of God and his love
3. The wrath of God in the Apoc. and the Pseudep.
4. The wrath of God in the Dead Sea Scrolls
5. The wrath of God in the NT
   a. The wrath of God and the ministry of Christ
   b. Wrath and the Atonement
   c. Wrath and sanctification

d. The Day of Wrath and the lordship of Christ
e. The termination of the wrath of God
Bibliography

1. Terminology of the wrath of God in the Bible. There are several hundred references to the divine wrath in the OT, and in the shorter NT the frequency is proportionately little less. Here, as with other aspects of the divine activity, the language of scripture is as concrete as the subject with which it has to do.

a. In biblical Hebrew. The expression most often used to represent anger—and in particular the anger of God—is the noun אַף (Ps. 96:7), derived from the verb אָנַף, "to be angry" (Isa. 12:1), probably once having meant "to snort." The noun is also the common Hebrew word for "nose" (Amos 4:10), which organ was for ancient Hebrew psychology the seat of anger. Thus in God's wrath "smoke went up from his nostrils" (Ps. 18:8). Fire and heat are characteristically associated with the rage and fury of wrath, and the verb חרה, "to burn," is in the *qal* voice used only to refer to the "kindling" of anger (Hos. 8:5). The derived noun חרון by itself (Ezek. 7:12) or in the more usual combination חרון אף (used in the OT only of God, as it happens—e.g., Exod. 32:12) connotes the fierceness of anger (lit., the "burning of anger"). Similarly, another common synonym for אַף is חמה, "rage," "heat" (Jer. 4:4), used also to denote the intoxication of wine (Hos. 7:5), the sun's fierce heat (Ps. 19:6), and the venom of serpents (Deut. 32:24). Other frequently used expressions for wrath or anger are עברה, "overflowing rage" (Hos. 5:10; cf. the verb עבר in the *hithpa'el*, "to vent one's wrath" [Ps. 78:62]); the verb קצף, "to be angered" (Deut. 1:34), with its noun form קצף, "wrath," "ill humor" (Ps. 38:1); זעם, the verb and noun forms denoting "angry indignation" (Nah. 1:6; Mal. 1:4; used only of God in the OT); and כעס (in Job כעש [e.g., 5:2]), the verb and noun forms signifying "vexation," especially "provocation to anger" (I Kings 15:30; Neh. 4:5). God's wrath is otherwise often suggested through expressions and metaphors drawn from the vocabulary of flood, famine, and conflagration, or from the language of cursing, devouring, reaping, demolishing, slaughtering, smelting or refining, and the like, and of military siege and battle (*see* BLESSINGS AND CURSINGS). Such imagery is to be distinguished (but not dissociated) from those concrete natural and historical occurrences which are themselves considered to be directly the operation and manifestation of the divine wrath itself. *See* § 2c below.

b. In LXX Greek. The Greek translation of the OT renders the various Hebrew expressions for God's anger or wrath by either of two nouns, ὀργή and θυμός, together with their cognate verbs (ὀργίζω, παροργίζω, θυμόω, etc.). Originally θυμός stood in the older Greek for the inner affect or emotion of anger; ὀργή, for the outward effect or manifestation. But in the LXX the two words appear to be interchangeable, and either, or both together, appear to be used indifferently for any of the Hebrew terms.

c. In NT Greek. The references to divine anger in the NT seem to follow the LXX terminology, using either ὀργή (Rom. 1:18) or θυμός (Rev. 15:1, 7), each

signifying "anger," "wrath." The two appear also in combination with each other: "fury of wrath" (θυμὸς τῆς ὀργῆς; Rev. 16:19). It is difficult to distinguish any clear difference of meaning between the two words, although when the subject is divine as distinguished from human anger, Revelation prefers θυμός, the other NT literature ὀργή.

2. The wrath of God in the OT. In the OT the wrath of God may be provoked against Israel (Exod. 32:11; Deut. 9:8; Ps. 74:1; Isa. 47:6; Lam. 2:1; Ezek. 5:15; Dan. 9:16; etc.) or against individuals and groups within Israel (Lev. 10:2; Deut. 1:34, 37; Ps. 6:1; Jer. 21:5). Nations and their rulers become objects of the divine anger (Gen. 19:24-25; Ps. 110:5; Isa. 10:12-19; Jonah 3:9; Mal. 1:4) as well as mankind in general (Gen. 4:14; 6:7; 11:8; Job 14; 40:11; Ps. 90:9; Eccl. 5:6; 12:14). It affects the world of nature (Gen. 3:14, 17; Deut. 32:22; Isa. 13:9; 50:2; Jer. 10:10; Mal. 3:11), where even the mythical creatures are overcome by it (Job 9:13; 26:12; Ps. 89:10; Isa. 51:9). In many of these examples the wrath of God is clearly the subject, although the express terminology of anger (*see* § 1a above) may be absent; cf. God's "strange work" (Isa. 28:21).

a. Irrational wrath. On occasion the OT picture of God contains an undeniable element of irrationality bordering on cruel caprice. "At a lodging place on the way" the Lord met Moses "and sought to kill him" (Exod. 4:24). Israel at Sinai must beware "lest they break through to the LORD to gaze and many of them perish" (Exod. 19:21; cf. Gen. 16:13; Judg. 13:22). The good intentions of Uzzah, steadying the ark of the Lord, do not save him from annihilation (II Sam. 6:7; cf. I Sam. 6:19). One might be inclined to trace such elements to primitive superstitions alien to biblical faith, but the explanation need hardly be sought outside the character of Yahweh himself. In the biblical view, this mysterious and dangerous element is not inconsonant with that aspect of his holiness which is marked by its transcendence, inscrutability, and radical separation from the creatures, and which contains inherently a menace of death for whoever stumbles upon it carelessly. *See bibliography; see also* FEAR; GOD, OT; HOLINESS.

b. Wrath and sin. Normally, however, the OT traces the provocation of God's wrath to deliberate human attempts to thwart his will and purpose for man's salvation. Israel herself most often becomes the object of God's displeasure, whether collectively or through some individual in the community (*see* SIN).

> Sons have I reared and brought up,
> but they have rebelled against me.
> (Isa. 1:2.)

In the wilderness the Israelites murmur against him, bringing down the divine fury upon themselves (Num. 11:1; Deut. 1:26-36; Ps. 78:21-22). God's anger is kindled at disobedience of his express command (Josh. 7:1), while the Chronicler summarizes Israel's career until the Exile as a history of scorn for God's word, which brings destruction and sorrow upon her (II Chr. 36:15-16; cf. Lam. 2:1, 22; Ezek. 22:23-31; etc.). Social injustice within the community of God's chosen people causes him to pour out his wrath upon them (Ps. 50:21-22; Isa. 1:23-24; 42:24-

25; Amos 8:4-10; Mic. 6). Neither prophet, priest, nor king is exempt from responsibility and divine judgment (II Sam. 12:10-14; Jer. 14:15; 22:15-16; Mal. 2:1-9).

A recurring and major theme is that of Israel's repeated apostasy—the abandonment of Yahweh to "go after other gods" (Deut. 13:2, 6, 13), or to introduce alien cults into Israel to occupy a place alongside that of Yahweh. Thus his anger burns when the people erect the golden calf (Exod. 32:1-10); again when they sacrifice to the Baal of Peor (Num. 25:1-5). The threat of annihilation stands behind the Deuteronomic exhortations to cultic purity (Deut. 11:16-17; 13; 29:16-28; cf. Judg. 2:11-15; II Kings 22:16-17; etc.), and the theme prevails into the latest OT literature (II Chr. 25:14-15; Isa. 65:1-7; Ezek. 7:1-23; Dan. 9:11-16; see JEALOUSY).

When God vents his wrath against the nations, this too is seen by the OT writers as a consequence of the opposition of these powers to the divine purpose in history—usually in terms of their oppression of God's people Israel (I Sam. 15:2-3; cf. I Sam. 28:18; Ps. 2:1-6). At the same time, the nations' idolatry and immorality are seen in their own right as sin against God (Deut. 7:5; Dan. 5:23-28; Amos 1:3–2:3; Jonah 1:2; 3:7-9; Nah. 1–3; etc.). Such passages contain elements of chauvinism on the part of those who speak or write them, yet the fact that they lie everywhere in a context of the divine wrath proclaimed even more strongly against Israel herself prevents the interpreter from reading them merely as unbridled patriotism. The point of view is basically one which sees all history subject to the divine providence, and the object of God's wrath ultimately as man the sinner in rebellion against his Creator (Gen. 4:14; 6:7; cf. Gen. 11:8 with Zeph. 3:8-9; Gen. 19: 24-25; Job 14; 40:11; Ps. 90:9; Eccl. 5:6; 12:14). See HISTORY.

c. Instruments of the divine wrath. While the OT does not necessarily see human trouble in every time and place as a manifestation of the divine anger, it nevertheless finds the wrath of God directly revealed in a variety of particular, concrete, natural and historical catastrophes, consonant with its belief in a God who makes his will known through the events of human history. Thus the natural elements may be agents of his fury (Gen. 6:17; 19:24; Ps. 104:4; Isa. 30:30; Jer. 21:14; Joel 1), and his displeasure makes itself felt in sickness, famine, and pestilence (Num. 11:33; Deut. 28:20-24, 58-61; II Sam. 24:15; Ps. 78: 50; Ezek. 5:13-17; 7:15). Personal affliction may also be the outworking of his anger (II Sam. 12:15-18; I Kings 17:18; Job 14; 30:23; Pss. 88:16; 90:5-8; 102:9-11).

The mightiest agents of the divine wrath in the OT prove to be the historical powers—the nations. Thus Assyria, threatening Ephraim and Judah, is used:

> Ah, Assyria, the rod of my anger,
>   the staff of my fury!
>
> . . . .
>
> Against the people of my wrath I command him
>   (Isa. 10:5-6; cf. 7:17-20; 13:5).

Aggression by neighboring political powers is Yahweh's punishment of Israel for apostasy (Judg. 2:11-15; 4:1-2; 6:1-2; cf. Deut. 28:25-27; II Kings 13:3;

etc.). The great and sobering example for the Jewish people of the later OT period was the fall of Jerusalem and the Babylonian exile (II Chr. 36:17-21; Ps. 106:40-41; Lam. 2, etc.; Zech. 7:11-14).

On the other hand, God's wrath against Israel's enemies, who may thus be enemies of Yahweh, makes itself known in disasters suffered by those nations (Jer. 50:25; Ezek. 20:33; Mal. 1:2-5). Here, in part, is to be found the rationale of such institutions as the ḥērem and holy war, where Israel herself is Yahweh's instrument of wrath against his adversaries (see DEVOTED; WAR, IDEAS OF; cf. Deut. 7:1-5; Josh. 6:17; 7:1; I Sam. 15:3, 20-21, 33).

In this regard, also, a few stylized representations of the divine wrath in the OT show possible literary affinities with some of the literature of NW Semitic cults outside Israel. See bibliography.

d. The Day of Wrath. More and more the OT prophetic preaching and finally the apocalyptic writings look for a climactic display of Yahweh's wrath on the day when his saving purpose is accomplished. "The LORD of hosts has a day against all that is proud and lofty, against all that is lifted up and high" (Isa. 2; cf. 13:11; 27:1; Ps. 110:5; Amos 5:18-20; etc.; see DAY OF THE LORD; ESCHATOLOGY OF THE OT). The later psalmists invoke this eschatological wrath upon the heathen as well as upon apostates within the community, while they expect that their own piety will shield themselves from it in that day (Pss. 7:6-8; 11:5-7; 56:7, 9; 79:5-13; 94:1-2, 12-15). However, this faith is scarcely something glib. Whether by prayers seeking this assurance or else boasting of it to the point of exaggeration, the righteous worshiper betrays that he is not without anxiety as he anticipates God's judgment (Pss. 22:1-21; 30: 8-10; 139:1-12, 19-24; cf. Lam. 5:22; Dan. 9:3-19; 12:8; Mal. 4:5-6).

e. Salvation from the wrath of God. While God's wrath may operate as his instrument of salvation on behalf of his people, delivering them from their oppressors (I Sam. 15:2; Amos 1:3-15; Nah. 1:2-15), the truly serious concern for Israel is her deliverance from the divine anger itself (Exod. 32:12; Job 7:21; Ps. 79:8; Isa. 6:11; Dan. 9:16; Amos 7:2). There is a fundamental difference at this point between Israel and her neighbors; unlike them, she is denied recourse to magical practices whose purpose is to forfend hostile deities. Rather, she is dependent on Yahweh himself for this (Num. 14:17-19; II Sam. 12:13; Joel 2:18; etc.). Even where magic seems formally to be used, it will be noted that the procedure does not constrain Yahweh, but rather depends on his will for its efficaciousness (Num. 21:7-9; cf. Wisd. Sol. 16:7). The circumcision of Moses' son by Zipporah is not an exception to this generalization (Exod. 4:24-26).

OT prophetic preaching sought to avert Yahweh's wrath through the people's repentance—a complete turning about and return to the obedient service of Yahweh—which would lead him to turn his wrath away (Jer. 4:4; 36:7; Amos 5:15; Mal. 3:7, 16; see REPENT). Later tradition saw the priests and the cultic ritual protecting the community: "The Levites shall encamp around the tabernacle of the testimony, that there may be no wrath upon the congregation of the people of Israel" (Num. 1:53). In the older stories there are times when the divine anger is lifted only by the death of the guilty (Num. 25:1-5; Josh. 7:22-26), while in the later period, again, the Exile could be seen as the great expiation for Israel's sin, moving God to pour out his compassion (Isa. 40:2; 51:22; Lam. 4:22).

The radical seriousness of Israel's situation is set forth, however, where the requirements for her deliverance are found to lie beyond human accomplishment, so that either hope is abandoned (Amos 3:12; cf. 5:18-20), or else the fulfilment of the necessary condition is carried through by Yahweh himself—by his establishing a new covenant with Israel (Deut. 30:6; Jer. 31:31-34; 32:39-40; cf. Ezek. 36:26-27), or by the sending of his emissary to effect the necessary change of heart (Mal. 4:5-6).

f. The wrath of God and his love. It is theologically significant that where a term for wrath is connected with a name for the Deity in the OT, the divine name is almost always that of Yahweh, the covenant God (Exod. 32:1-10; Deut. 11:16-17; 29:16-28; II Kings 24:20; etc.; *see bibliography; see also* GOD, OT; COVENANT). There is thus an intimate association between the wrath of God and the historical election-covenant faith of Israel, a relation given classical utterance through the prophet Amos:

> You only have I known
> of all the families of the earth;
> therefore I will punish you
> for all your iniquities
> (Amos 3:2).

According to the OT scheme, when collective or individual life in Israel did not comport in terms of reverence, justice, and grace with those unmerited acts of Yahweh's love which called her into being as a people and guided now her destiny in world history, that love had inevitably to display its wrath (II Chr. 36:15-16; Ps. 78:21-22, 56-66; Isa. 63:9-10; Jer. 5:7-9). Israel's deviations from this norm were a denial of the very ground of her historical existence (*see* ELECTION).

> I am Yahweh your God
> from the land of Egypt;
> you know no God but me,
> and besides me there is no savior.
> (Hos. 13:4.)

Yet, because Israel had presumed upon this love, says Yahweh: "I will fall upon them like a bear robbed of her cubs" (Hos. 13:8). The theriomorphism is aptly chosen for its fierce imagery of the inherent wrath in wounded love.

If Israel's betrayal of the covenant relationship provokes the divine fury, the faithfulness of God to it in love also constrains his anger:

> How can I give you up, O Ephraim!
> How can I hand you over, O Israel!
> (Hos. 11:8; cf. Exod. 32:10,
> 12-14; Ps. 103:8; Isa. 54:7-8,
> 10; Mic. 7:18).

This conflict, which the OT finds in Yahweh himself, is scarcely resolved in the OT, unless it should be in the profound perception of divine grace shown by Deutero-Isaiah in the figure of the Suffering Servant, who was "wounded for our transgressions" and "bruised for our iniquities," and upon whom was

the "chastisement that made us whole" (Isa. 53:5). But even here there is no lasting assurance that wrath has been stayed. The prophetic canon and the Writings both still dwell on it in their closing lines (II Chr. 36:16; Mal. 4:1), as does the Pentateuch in the later chapters of Deuteronomy (e.g., 31:29).

3. The wrath of God in the Apoc. and the Pseudep. With the exception of Aristeas, for whom "God rules the whole world in the spirit of kindness and without wrath at all" (μετ' εὐμενείας καὶ χωρὶς ὀργῆς ἁπάσης; Aristeas 254), the picture of God in the Apoc. and the Pseudep. displays his wrath as both a historical and an eschatological force to be reckoned with. It may operate as a function of his righteousness, punishing the wicked (Prayer Man. 10; Jub. 36:10; IV Macc. 4:21), or of his mercy, disciplining the faithful (Wisd. Sol. 11:9-10). Times of national distress are seen as the divine judgment in wrath (Bar. 4:6, 25; I Macc. 1:64; Asmp. Moses 8:1). The visions of Enoch behold the entire race of man subject to God's anger (Enoch 84:4). Even the moon and the stars have incurred God's wrath (III Bar. 9:7; Enoch 18:16).

The averting of God's wrath is sought variously through prayer (Test. Reuben 1:8; Enoch 84:5); a life of righteousness (Ecclus. 44:17); repentance (Prayer Man. 8, 13; Ecclus. 17:24; Test. Judah 23: 5); a new priesthood (Test. Levi 18:1-14); intervention of Moses or of Elijah (Wisd. Sol. 18:21; Ecclus. 48:10; cf. Mal. 4:5-6); or by God's own intercession directly:

> He who turned toward it was saved, not by what he saw,
> but by thee, the Savior of all
> (Wisd. Sol. 16:7; cf. Num. 21:5-6).

The full OT notion of God's wrath is taken up in the Talmudic literature, continuing as a significant feature in the theology of the rabbinical exposition of scripture. *See bibliography.*

4. The wrath of God in the Dead Sea Scrolls. The noncanonical writings among the Qumran scrolls seem to dwell mainly on the effects of God's wrath more than on the "affect" in the Deity himself—a distinction applicable to the NT also. A sharp line is drawn in these writings between those who can expect divine blessing, on the one hand, and those who can expect annihilation at the hand of God, on the other. The "period of wrath" (קץ חרון) is a time of punishment from God in suffering and trouble for the community (CDC 1.5; 1QH 3.28), and the author of the Damascus Document reads Israel's history as a repeated kindling of God's wrath (1.17; 2.4; 3.7; 4.7; 7.17; 9.13, 22, 26, 40). The Manual of Discipline promises "eternal perdition in the fury of the God of vengeance" to those who walk by the "spirit of error" (*see bibliography;* 1QS 4.12), and among the legends inscribed on the trumpets and standards appearing in the War of the Sons of Light are several that display wrath termini. Prominent in the imagery of divine wrath is the metaphor of refining or the refiner's crucible, denoting an experience through which the saints must persevere (זקק [1QS 4.20]; מצרף [1QS 1.16; 8.4; CDC 20.27; 1QM 17.9; cf. Mal. 3:2-3]).

5. The wrath of God in the NT. The view advocated by Marcion in the second century, and by others since, that the righteous anger of the OT deity is alien to the loving God who is the Father of Jesus Christ, does not gain support from the NT itself (*see* MARCION, GOSPEL OF). Here, as in the OT (*see* § 2*f above*), the dimension of God's love measures the severity of his wrath (cf. John 3:16, 36). Here, as there, the idea draws its seriousness from historical memories and expectations within the believing community. It describes a part of the concrete experience of faith rather than an abstract speculation on the nature of God.

a. The wrath of God and the ministry of Christ. Only on a single occasion do the gospels attribute anger to Jesus by using an explicit word for it (ὀργή; Mark 3:5), and only once does Jesus himself refer thus explicitly to divine anger (Luke 21:23). But while these passages are important by themselves, there is a large number of others also in which wrath proves to be a significant aspect of God's revelation in the ministry of Jesus.

Certain parables and sayings, considered together, scarcely allow another interpretation when one observes such characters and symbols as the angry householder (Luke 14:21); the angry king (Matt. 18:34; cf. vs. 35!); the house ruined by storm (Matt. 7:27); the punishable stewards (Luke 12:47-48); the vindication of the elect (Luke 18:7); exclusion from the kingdom of God (Mark 10:15); the shut door (Matt. 25:10); outer darkness (Matt. 8:12, etc.); the great tribulation (Mark 13:19); fire (Matt. 7:19; John 15:6); hell (γέεννα; Mark 9:43-48; cf. Luke 12:5 and "eternal fire" in Matt. 18:8-9; etc.); and the rejection at judgment (Matt. 7:23; Mark 8:38; etc.).

The divine anger is clearly the presupposition whenever Jesus denounces those who flout what they know to be the will and purpose of God, or who scorn repentance (cf. Mark 9:42). The "woes" of Matt. 23 condemn the sinfully arrogant and proud, while according to Luke 13:4-5, except each of us repent, he will perish as "those eighteen upon whom the tower of Siloam fell and killed them" (cf. 13:1-3 also), and Jesus finds it possible to speak of him who "never has forgiveness" (Mark 3:29; *see* UNFORGIVABLE SIN). The compassion and mercy of Jesus find an element of their strength in his very capacity for anger (as much as for sorrow) whenever he finds the gracious will and purpose of God met with human hardness of heart (cf. Mark 3:5). He reacts with angry irritation (ἀγανάκτησις) to the disciples' arrogance toward the children (Mark 10:14). Evident behind his actions at the cleansing of the temple (Mark 11:15; cf. John 2:15) and beneath his stout words against an unbelieving audience (John 8:44; cf. Matt. 12:34; 15:7) is a deep indignation at hypocrisy and at profanation of the holy. These and the many other examples of the deep disturbance within Jesus at human trespass against the divine love point to the reaction in holy wrath of that love itself; indeed, the divine wrath is here operative.

b. Wrath and the Atonement. Jesus treats the divine wrath with full seriousness, but never as if he felt at ease with it; far less, as if he gained satisfaction from its outworking (cf. Matt. 23:37-39!). Rather, he arouses men to its reality as a part of his total work of bringing them to accept with him the regenerat-

ing love of the God under whose wrath the whole race stands. To this end he requests baptism from John, thereby casting his lot with the sinner (Matt. 3:15). He becomes obedient to his Father's will "even [to] death on a cross" (Phil. 2:8). He alludes to his death as the cup that he must drink (Mark 10:38) which the Father has given him (John 18:11); and of this "cup" he prays that, if possible, it pass from him (Luke 22:42-44; cf. John 12:27), before he accepts it in the Cross. Whoever recalls other contexts of crisis in the Bible where the cup is the symbol of divine wrath (e.g., Pss. 60:3; 75:8; Isa. 51:17; Jer. 25:15; 49:12; etc.), and takes with full seriousness the cry of Jesus on the cross: "My God, my God, why hast thou forsaken me?" (Matt. 27:46; Mark 15:34; cf. Ps. 22:1), can scarcely escape the conclusion that as Jesus approached his death, he knew the full weight—without himself being its provocation—of the wrath of God.

It is clear in any case that the NT writers saw in the crucifixion and resurrection of Christ the lifting of God's wrath from all who so accepted it in faith (*see* JUSTIFICATION). For Paul he is "Jesus who delivers us from the wrath to come" (I Thess. 1:10; 5:9-10; cf. Rom. 5:9), so that "there is therefore now no condemnation for those who are in Christ Jesus" (Rom. 8:1). "For our sake he made him to be sin who knew no sin, so that in him we might become the righteousness of God" (II Cor. 5:21). Nearly all the NT writers proclaim their like conviction on this matter in one fashion or another (cf. Gal. 3:13; Eph. 2:3-7; II Tim. 1:10; Tit. 3:3-5; Heb. 9:15, 26; I Pet. 1:18-19; etc.). *See* ATONEMENT.

c. Wrath and sanctification. Against those Christians who "outraged the Spirit of grace" (Heb. 10: 29) by supposing that they now rested in complacent security apart from moral issues and the serious questions of faith and practice—as if one might "continue in sin that grace may abound" (Rom. 6:1; cf. vs. 15; 3:8)—the NT writers warn that conversion into the New Covenant brings, not less concern with obedience to the divine will, but, for the first time, a true appreciation of its demands on the believer and of his utter and continuing dependence on the grace of God as revealed in Jesus Christ (Rom. 7:15-25; Eph. 4:1, 17; 5:1-2; Col. 3:5-17; I Pet. 1:14-16; 4:17; *see* SANCTIFICATION)—and, by the same token, a graver consequence if the new responsibility is scorned.

"These things are warnings for us"—thus do Paul and others draw a lesson from the loosing of God's wrath against his chosen people as told in the OT (I Cor. 10:6; cf. vss. 1-12; Heb. 3:7-19; Jude 3-16 [cf. Exod. 32; Num. 25]; etc.). And addressing the church, the author of Hebrews ponders in all soberness: "How shall we escape if we neglect such a great salvation?" (Heb. 2:3).

d. The Day of Wrath and the lordship of Christ. The "Day of the LORD" proclaimed by the OT prophets was for them already a "day of wrath" for all who stood opposed to the divine plan of salvation (*see* § 2*d above*). For the NT likewise, the drama of salvation is to play itself out in one final "judgment of the great day" (Jude 6), bringing therewith the conclusion of history. On the presupposition that anyone's rejection of God's redemptive work in

Christ is his own considered choice in that time, far from its being an occasion of general indulgence, the NT anticipates it as the "day of wrath when God's righteous judgment will be revealed" (Rom. 2:5; cf. Rev. 6:15; *see* DAY OF JUDGMENT; ESCHATOLOGY OF THE NT). The NT both ends and begins with warnings about the "wrath to come" (Matt. 3:7; Rev. 19:15; 22:12, 18), and the theme recurs in the gospels (*see* § 5*a above*) and letters (Rom. 5:9; I Cor. 5:5; Eph. 5:6; I Thess. 1:10; II Thess. 2:8; II Tim. 1:12, 18; 3:1; etc.).

One of the most striking images of the unfolding Day of Wrath, and certainly one of the most significant for the understanding of NT thought, is that of the flight of men to hide "in the caves and among the rocks of the mountains" from the "face of him who is seated on the throne, and from the wrath of the Lamb" (Rev. 6:15-16; *see* PAROUSIA). Under the figure of the Lamb, who is at once the "Lion of the tribe of Judah," Jesus Christ is himself the agent of the divine wrath (Rev. 5:5, 6-14; etc.). Here, indeed, "Jesus Christ is Lord" (Phil. 2:11), and "the Father . . . has given all judgment to the Son" (John 5:22; cf. Matt. 28:18). This aspect of the Lordship of Christ has already been anticipated by Paul, e.g., who sees in him the revelation not only of the righteousness but also of the wrath of God (Rom. 1:17-18), and by the author of the Fourth Gospel, who finds that "he who does not obey the Son shall not see life, but the wrath of God rests upon him" (John 3:36; cf. vs. 18). In fact, it is not impossible to trace the full idea to Jesus himself, saying with regard to his own ministry: "I came to cast fire upon the earth; and would that it were already kindled!" (Luke 12:49; cf. vss. 51-53).

e. The termination of the wrath of God. One may conclude, therefore, that the NT differs on two counts at this point from the OT. On the one hand, it takes a graver view of the wrath of God than do even the OT prophets; on the other, it has discovered a hope of reconciliation with God unknown to the OT. "God has not destined us for wrath, but to obtain salvation through our Lord Jesus Christ" (I Thess. 5:9).

While the concluding chapters of the NT find that "the devil," "the beast," and "the false prophet" will be "tormented day and night for ever and ever" (Rev. 20:10), God's wrath shall not burn in eternity, since whatever opposes his love has ceased to be; for them creation is undone (Rev. 20:14-15). But in the "new heaven" and the "new earth," "death shall be no more, neither shall there be mourning nor crying nor pain anymore"—there is no wrath—"for the former things have passed away" (Rev. 21:1, 4; note Isa. 25:8; 35:10).

Bibliography. Lactantius *On the Anger of God* (*ca.* A.D. 312), in *Ante-Nicene Fathers* (trans. Fletcher; 1886). P. Volz, *Das Dämonische in Jahweh* (1924). G. Aulén, *Christus Victor* (1931), pp. 113-16, on wrath and the Atonement. R. P. C. Hanson, "The Wrath of God," *ET*, 58 (1946-47), 216-18. J. Gray, "The Wrath of God in Canaanite and Hebrew Literature," *Journal of Manchester University Egyptian and Oriental Society*, no. XXV (1947-53; reprint 1954), pp. 9-19, compares, e.g., Isa. 63:1-2 with possible Canaanite parallels; cf. Ginsberg, trans., "Baal and Anath," in J. B. Pritchard, ed., *ANET* (1955), p. 136*b*. R. V. G. Tasker, *The Biblical Doctrine of the Wrath of God* (1951): an important study of the relevant

biblical texts. J. Fichtner *et al.,* "ὀργή," in Kittel-Friedrich, eds., *TWNT*, V (1954), pp. 382-448: a valuable study in the biblical, apocryphal, rabbinical, and classical Greek and Roman literature. M. Burrows, *The Dead Sea Scrolls* (1955), p. 375. A. T. Hanson, *The Wrath of the Lamb* (1957): on wrath in the NT.   B. T. DAHLBERG

WREATH. The translation of the following words, all of which refer to some type of circular adornment:

a) גדלים (I Kings 7:17). A circle of chain work adorning the capitals of the pillars JACHIN AND BOAZ in Solomon's temple.

b) ליה (I Kings 7:29-30, 36; KJV ADDITION; cf. לויה, "garland"). A decoration of bronze on the stands for the lavers before Solomon's temple. The wreaths surrounded the representations of lions, oxen, cherubim, and palm trees on the stand and were also at the sides of the supports for the lavers. *See* LAVER.

c) Στέφανος (I Cor. 9:25; KJV CROWN). The prize for winning an athletic contest.

In addition to these words translated "wreath," the KJV uses "wreathen work" to render שבכה (II Kings 25:17; II Chr. 4:12-13; RSV NETWORK) and עבת (Exod. 28:14, 22, 24-25; 39:15, 17-18; RSV "cords"; *see* CORD; BREASTPIECE OF THE HIGH PRIEST).

E. M. GOOD

WRESTLING. In OT times, when warfare had already achieved a series of tactical and strategic levels, with steadily advancing systems of weapons, mankind looked back to a simpler and more romantic past, when heroes triumphed or fell in hand-to-hand combat. This combat is usually reflected in terms of wrestling. The best-known illustration is Gen. 32:25-33, where Jacob "wrestled" (Hebrew root אבק) with a divine being and emerged as the victor.

The distinctive form of wrestling in the Bible world is belt-wrestling, whereby the combatants wear special belts upon which the holds are made.* This belt, called by various names in Hebrew, became an important possession of every man of consequence. Thus Judah's three personal articles of identification are his seal, staff, and wrestling belt ([פתיל]ים) in Gen. 38:18, 25. The same root (פתל) describes poetically the strugglings of Rachel with her sister (Gen. 30:8) in explanation of the name Naphtali. Fig. WRE 27.

Courtesy of the University Museum of the University of Pennsylvania

27. Belt wrestlers, in bronze, from Khafajah; Early Dynastic (first part of third millennium)

An awareness of belt-wrestling is necessary for perceiving the imagery in certain passages. E.g., Isa. 11:5 describes the Davidic king in the golden age thus:

> Righteousness shall be the belt [אֵזוֹר;
>   RSV "girdle"] of his waist,
>   and faithfulness the belt [אֵזוֹר; RSV "girdle"]
>   of his loins.

The undertones might be paraphrased as follows: The Messiah will be a hero, not of physical violence, but of virtue. Indeed, in the Hebrew expression "gird your loins" (in the sense of "get ready for action," which has become part of the English language also), an echo of ancient belt-wrestling continues to reverberate.

Bibliography. C. H. Gordon, "Belt-wrestling in the Bible World," *HUCA*, XXIII (1950-51), 131-36, pls. I-V.
C. H. GORDON

WRITING AND WRITING MATERIALS. Writing was known and practiced in the ancient Near East long before the Hebrews took possession of Palestine. As we shall see, the early claims that writing was unknown in Palestine in patriarchal times are quite unfounded. We shall first discuss the development of the writing systems indigenous to the various areas of the Mediterranean world, then describe the materials employed, and finally trace the evolution of the book from scroll to codex.

A. *DEVELOPMENT OF WRITING.* 1. Mesopotamia. The first system of writing for which we have evidence is probably that invented in Mesopotamia sometime after the middle of the fourth millennium B.C. This was most likely the creation of the Sumerians (*see* SUMER) to meet their administrative and economic needs. It developed, as did all the earliest scripts, from a pictographic stage—i.e., the use of pictures to tell a story.* These pictures were then employed to designate both the objects depicted and the ideas associated with them. Thus a picture of the sun represented, not only the sun itself, but also the concepts "day," "bright," etc.; that of a foot

From Driver, *Semitic Writing* (The British Academy, Schweich Lectures, 1944)
   28. Archaic pictographic tablet, from Kish

meant also "stand," "walk," or "carry." This stage may be called the logographic, in which logograms —also called ideograms—or "word signs" are employed. Fig. WRI 28.

The limitations of such a system are apparent when it becomes necessary to record an abstract concept or a proper name. An ingenious solution was devised on the "rebus" principle, whereby the logogram for an object might be used to represent a homophone—i.e., another word having the same sound; cf. our use in children's books of the picture of an eye to represent the pronoun "I," or the drawing of a tin can to express the verb "to be able." At this stage the system becomes phonetic, and since Sumerian—an agglutinative language—is composed of elements which are usually of one syllable (rarely two), the phonetic value of the signs tends to be syllabic.

It now becomes possible to indicate grammatical elements by the use of signs with such syllabic values—e.g., *gar,* "make"; *e-gar,* "he made"; *e-gar-re-éš,* "they made"; *é,* "house"; *é-ta,* "from the house." Moreover, the various possible readings of a logogram may be distinguished by the use of "phonetic complements," which indicate the final syllable of the word. Finally, certain signs known as "determinatives" were used as classifiers, to indicate the range of meaning of certain words written by means of logograms, such as objects of wood or stone, proper names, fish, etc. Such means of reducing ambiguity were offset, however, by the system's inherent polyphony, for many signs representing homophones had the same sound, and one sign might likewise possess more than one phonetic value.

These signs were incised on tablets of soft clay with a stylus (*see* §§ B1*c*, 2*a*, *below*). At first they were written in vertical columns like Chinese, beginning at the upper right-hand corner of the tablet. Later, the manner of holding the tablet was altered, so that the signs were turned ninety degrees, resulting in horizontal lines of writing running from left to right. Since the use of clay as a writing material favored straight lines rather than curved, the pictures gradually became stylized and simplified, and use of the stylus led to the wedge-shaped lines from which comes the name CUNEIFORM. Fig. WRI 29.

During the first half of the third millennium the system was adopted by the Akkadians (*see* ASSYRIA AND BABYLONIA) to write their Semitic tongue. Logograms, phonetic complements, determinatives, and syllabic signs were all employed, and many addi-

	A Original pictograph	B Pictograph in position of later cuneiform	C Early Babylonian	D Assyrian	E Original or derived meaning
1					bird
2					fish
3					donkey
4					ox
5					sun / day
6					grain
7					orchard
8					to plow / to till
9					boomerang to throw / to throw down
10					to stand / to go

From Henri Frankfort, *The Birth of Civilization in the Near East* (Indiana University Press)

29. Table showing the development of cuneiform signs

tional values were given to signs to express the sounds peculiar to Semitic speech, so that the system became a very cumbersome one, requiring in its classical form some six hundred signs. So effective was it, however, that it was very soon appropriated by the Elamites (*see* ELAM), in a simplified form, to replace their earlier pictographic script. In the second millennium it was adopted by the Hurrians (*see* HORITES) and HITTITES, and finally by the Urartians of Armenia in the first half of the first millennium. Thus the system was eventually employed to write at least six unrelated languages. It also influenced the development of two other cuneiform scripts: the alphabetic script of Ugarit (*see* § A4 *below*) and the syllabic system of Old Persian, composed of fifty-one signs.

The Aramaic language, written in a cursive alphabetic script (*see* § A4 *below*), was also used in Mesopotamia during the Neo-Assyrian period, as is attested by Aramaic notations on some cuneiform tablets. Since papyrus or leather would be the usual writing materials in this case, they have long since perished in the damp Mesopotamian soil. However, Assyrian reliefs of the eighth and seventh centuries B.C. portray scribes writing on a flexible material with pens beside other scribes who use a stylus to incise cuneiform signs on clay tablets.

2. Egypt. Archaeological evidence from Egypt points clearly to a period of fertile Mesopotamian influence at the end of the fourth millennium. Since the hieroglyphic system of writing makes its appearance at this point, and springs forth full-blown with no indications of development such as are present in Mesopotamia, it may be assumed that Asiatic influ-

ence was at work here too. This is not to say that the Egyptians took over the Sumerian writing system, but rather that they adopted its principles, including such features as logograms, phonetic complements, and determinatives. *See* § A1 *above*.

With this initial impetus, the Egyptians soon developed along independent lines. The forms of the individual hieroglyphs changed but little during their long history,* and were at all times clearly recognizable, unlike the highly stylized cuneiform signs. This was because they were carved in stone, and regarded as a form of art complementary to the finely carved reliefs. A second major difference was the fact that the phonetic symbols were not syllabic, as in cuneiform, but consonantal only. Thus the plan of a house, for which the Egyptian word was *pāru, could be used for any word which required the consonants *pr* in that order, such as *pīre, "to go out." Similarly, the representation of a mouth, Egyptian *ra, could be employed to render the consonant *r*. The picture of a rib, the word for which contained the consonants *spr*, provided a means of writing the word *sāpĕr, "to approach." The total disregard of vowels in the hieroglyphic script, a feature of most Semitic alphabetic scripts also, means that we are ignorant of the pronunciation of ancient Egyptian, except insofar as we can reconstruct its vowels from contemporary transcriptions of Egyptian words into syllabic cuneiform or from Coptic, the latest stage of Egyptian, which was written with Greek letters. Fig. WRI 30.

Hieroglyphic					Hieroglyphic Book Hand	Hieratic			Demotic
2700-2600 B.C.	2500-2400 B.C.	2000-1800 B.C.	ca. 1500 B.C.	500-100 B.C.	ca. 1500 B.C.	ca. 1900 B.C.	ca. 1300 B.C.	ca. 200 B.C.	400-100 B.C.

From *When Egypt Ruled the East* (The University of Chicago Press)

30. Egyptian hieroglyphs and their cursive equivalents

These logograms which became phonetic signs contain from one to three consonants. The fact that there were sufficient uniconsonantal signs to express all twenty-four of the consonantal phonemes in the Egyptian language made it possible for hieroglyphic to become an alphabetic system. This revolutionary step was never taken, however, and it remained for the Semites in Syria-Palestine to devise such an alphabet. *See* § A4 *below*.

Although hieroglyphic was normally reserved for stone inscriptions, it was occasionally written with a pen in a somewhat cursive fashion. For more rapid writing with pen and ink on papyrus, however, a still more cursive form was developed at the very beginning, known to us as hieratic. In this form of script the signs were much simplified, and ligatures were frequent. At the end of the eighth century B.C. a still more abbreviated form of the script was introduced for letters and business documents, which we call demotic. By this time the original forms of the signs were but rarely recognizable. All three methods of writing were employed side by side for some centuries: hieratic until the third century A.D.; demotic until the end of the fifth century A.D.; and hieroglyphic, in a debased form, till as late as the fourth or fifth century A.D. Finally, *ca.* the third century A.D., the Greek alphabet was adopted for the writing of the Egyptian language. This phase, which is known as Coptic, lasted as a living language until the sixteenth century. Egyptian is thus unique in affording us written evidence of a single language over a period of some four and a half millenniums.

Hieroglyphic was written normally from right to left, but occasionally from left to right, and though at first only in vertical columns, later also in horizontal lines. Hieratic was written only from right to left, until the nineteenth century B.C. in vertical columns, and thereafter in horizontal lines. Demotic is found only in horizontal lines, from right to left.

During the fourteenth century B.C., Akkadian was the international language, and consequently cuneiform writing on clay tablets was also employed by the Egyptian royal scribes in their correspondence with Western Asiatic states. A notable example is the letters discovered at TELL EL-AMARNA* (*see also* INSCRIPTIONS § 2). In the Persian period, Aramaic was in common use, and in a later period, Greek (*see* INSCRIPTIONS §§ 4-5). Figs. CLA 35; TEL 10.

3. Anatolia. At some time during the first half of the second millennium B.C., the inhabitants of E Asia Minor whom we know as the HITTITES adopted the cuneiform syllabary of Mesopotamia (*see* § A1 *above*) to write their Indo-European language on clay tablets. The script was ingeniously adapted to express such characteristics of the language as consonantal clusters unknown to Sumerian or Akkadian. An interesting feature of Hittite cuneiform is "allography"—i.e., the use of Sumerian logograms or syllabically spelled Akkadian words intended to be read with their Hittite equivalents. A few texts contain passages in another language closely related to Hittite, known as Luwian, and written in the same script.

Between 1500 and 700 B.C. another script, indigenous to Anatolia, was in use for inscriptions on stone found at various sites throughout S Anatolia and N Syria. This is a hieroglyphic system, unrelated to that of Egypt, although perhaps stimulated by it. It appears to have been especially in vogue for royal inscriptions of the Neo-Hittite petty kingdoms at such places as Carchemish, Zenjirli, and Hamath. It is the rulers of these states who are described in the OT as the "kings of the Hittites" (II Kings 7:6; II Chr. 1:17).

The hieroglyphic signs, unlike those of Egypt, express syllabic values. They are composed of consonant plus vowel only, unlike the cuneiform system, which also has signs for vowel plus consonant and for consonant plus vowel plus consonant. The texts are written boustrophedon—i.e., in horizontal lines reading from right to left and left to right alternately. The language of these inscriptions, but recently deciphered, is called, for want of a better name, Hieroglyphic Hittite. Although related to cuneiform Hittite and Luwian, it is not the same. The great bilingual inscription from Karatepe (*see* INSCRIPTIONS § 3), containing versions in Phoenician and Hieroglyphic Hittite, confirms in a remarkable fashion the pioneer efforts to read and understand the language. It is likely that the hieroglyphic script was also written on wood or other perishable materials, but these have long since disappeared.

The Akkadian language was also well known in Anatolia. At Kültepe in E Asia Minor, a colony of Assyrian merchants of *ca.* 1900 B.C. has left a great horde of clay tablets written in Old Assyrian. Some five centuries later, Akkadian was the language of international trade and diplomacy throughout the ancient Near East, and was employed by the Hittite rulers for their treaties with Egypt and their correspondence with the Egyptian pharaoh. Excavations at Hittite sites have also yielded some cuneiform texts in Hurrian, the language of the HORITES.

4. Syria-Palestine. The unique position of this area as a bridge between Egypt and Western Asia, subject to the cross-currents flowing from these culturally productive centers, produced a remarkably complicated development in the history of writing. As a result, many experiments were made, and it was here that the revolutionary step was taken of creating the first true alphabet.

As might be expected, the writing systems of the neighboring empires are to be found in use in Syria-Palestine. Egyptian hieroglyphic inscriptions on a multitude of scarabs* and many stelae and statues (*see* INSCRIPTIONS § 1) testify to Egyptian influence from early times. This should occasion no surprise, as the region formed part of the Egyptian Empire during the Eighteenth to Twentieth Dynasties, and long before this time was in close contact through trade relations. Fig. SEA 35.

The same situation holds true for Akkadian cuneiform. Although the use of clay as a writing material was not native to Palestine, about a score of tablets in the form of letters, business documents, and lists have been found at Taanach, Tell el-Hesi, Gezer, Jericho, Megiddo, and Shechem. As elsewhere dur-

From Driver, *Semitic Writing* (The British Academy, Schweich Lectures, 1944)

31. A pseudo-hieroglyphic inscription, from Gebal

ing the fourteenth century, Imperial Akkadian was the lingua franca, so that the local governors of Syria-Palestine reported to the Egyptian court in that language, as the Tell el-Amarna Tablets bear witness (*see* INSCRIPTIONS § 2). In such cosmopolitan centers in Syria as Ugarit, cuneiform tablets in Hurrian and Sumerian were also found.

A stela from Balu'ah in ancient Moab bears an inscription in a linear script dated by some scholars to the late third millennium. So badly weathered is it that the writing is not sufficiently legible for certainty with regard to the signs. It may be that this is an example of the first indigenous script in the area. It is also possible that the script of the Balu'ah

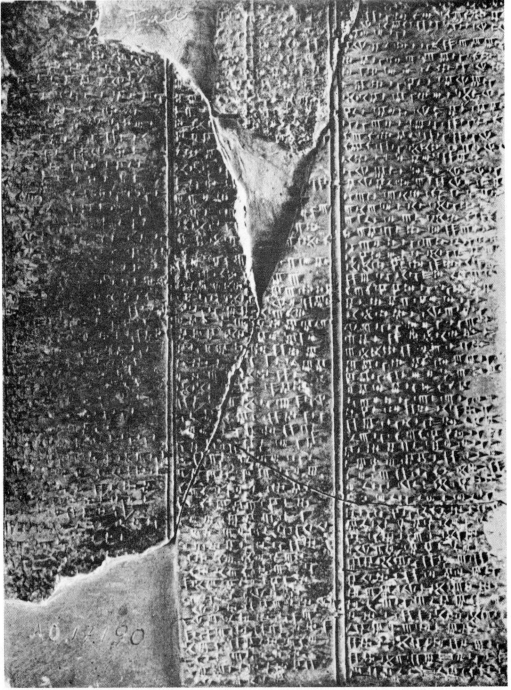

Courtesy of the American Schools of Oriental Research

32. Alphabetic clay tablet, from Ugarit (fourteenth century B.C.), with legend of Keret, king of the Sidonians

stela is the same as that of a small group of inscriptions on stone and bronze tablets unearthed at Byblos, the biblical Gebal (*see* GEBAL 1).* These "pseudo-hieroglyphic" inscriptions, as they have been called, date perhaps from the period between the eighteenth and fifteenth centuries. Since there are 140 or more signs, the system cannot be alphabetic, but must be syllabic. Whether there was any influence from Egyptian hieroglyphic is doubtful. The writing appears to run from right to left. Although several attempts at decipherment have been made, the inscriptions cannot yet be said to have been satisfactorily read. Fig. WRI 31.

An archaeological event of unusual importance was the discovery in 1929 of hundreds of clay tablets at the site of ancient UGARIT in N Syria.* Dating from the early fourteenth century, these tablets were inscribed in a hitherto unknown cuneiform script. Since there were only twenty-nine signs (some with variant forms), it was evident that this script must be alphabetic. When deciphered, the language proved to be an early form of Canaanite. Like the other cuneiform systems, Ugaritic reads from left to right, although three texts are written in the reverse direction! The alphabet is purely consonantal, but is unusual in that there are three signs for '*āleph* (the glottal stop), depending upon whether the accompanying vowel is "a," "i," or "u." The reason for this may be the fact that the Ugaritic script was also employed to write the unrelated Hurrian language, in which, unlike Ugaritic, words might begin with vowels. One of the alphabetic signs, indeed, was specially devised to represent a non-Semitic phoneme peculiar to Hurrian. Figs. WRI 32; UGA 3, 11.

One helpful feature of the script is the use of wedges to indicate the word division. In the development of this script, one may suspect the influence of the cuneiform system of Mesopotamia on the one hand, and that of the Palestinian linear alphabet, to be discussed in a moment, on the other. Two short inscriptions in this script have turned up in Palestine: one on a tablet from Beth-shemesh, and another on a copper knife from the vicinity of Mount Tabor.

As has been suggested, the Ugaritic script was not the first alphabet. This honor belongs to a linear script developed in the S, represented by about twenty-five inscriptions from the Egyptian turquoise

Courtesy of the Cairo Museum

33. Inscription in alphabetic script, from a statue at Serabit el-Khadem in Sinai

mines in the Sinai Peninsula.* To be dated *ca.* 1500 B.C., these proto-Sinaitic inscriptions are written in a consonantal ALPHABET which was clearly derived from Egyptian hieroglyphic on the acrophonic principle, to be read in vertical columns or in lines from right to left. The same alphabet is employed in three short inscriptions from Gezer, Lachish, and Shechem, probably of a somewhat earlier date. Far from being illiterate, therefore, the inhabitants of Syria-Palestine were making use of at least five systems of writing during the Late Bronze Age (nineteenth to fifteenth centuries). Fig. WRI 33.

A later stage of this script is represented by a number of inscriptions from such sites as Beth-shemesh, Byblos, and Lachish. These proto-Canaanite texts, as they are termed, dating from the thirteenth and twelfth centuries, form the link between the proto-Sinaitic inscriptions and the tenth-century Phoenician inscriptions from Byblos (*see* EPIGRAPHY). The script was adopted by the Arameans between the eleventh and tenth centuries. It was they who introduced the practice of using the letters for *w, y,* and *h* to indicate the presence of final long vowels (*matres lectionis*), a feature which appears in Moabite and Hebrew texts from the ninth century on. In the eighth-century Aramaic inscriptions this device was further extended to represent medial long vowels, and eventually '*āleph* was also employed as a vowel letter. Word dividers were frequently used in the Aramaic, Moabite, and Hebrew inscriptions.

The script, both lapidary and cursive, in which Hebrew was written from the beginning of the tenth century B.C. to the second century A.D., was a form of the Phoenician script.* However, sometime between the third and second centuries B.C., modified forms of the Aramaic characters, which had by this time deviated considerably from the contemporary "Phoenician" forms, were adopted by the Jews. This script was to be known later as the "square" character, and is that of our modern printed Hebrew Bibles. Jesus' reference to the "jot" (RSV "iota")—i.e., *yōdh*—as the smallest of letters (Matt. 5:18) was true only for the square script. The "Phoenician" forms still continued to be used for some time, appearing on Hebrew coins from the second century B.C. to the second century A.D. and, most surprising of all, in some of the DEAD SEA SCROLLS. They also survived in a somewhat ornate form in the Samaritan script. Fig. WRI 34.

An innovation in the Aramaic or square script was the use of special final forms of certain letters. These begin to appear first in papyri of *ca.* 300 B.C. from Egypt, but did not come into general use until later. The employment of word dividers in earlier inscriptions has already been noted. Such dividers are also used in Dead Sea MSS written in the archaic script. The separation of words by spaces is also a feature of some of these scrolls written in the square characters. Apart from the use of *matres lectionis*, there was no attempt to indicate the vocalization of the consonantal script until the development of vowel signs between the fifth and seventh centuries A.D. At first two supralinear systems were devised, one Palestinian and the other Babylonian. A third system, known as the Tiberian and introduced at the end of the eighth century, was sublinear. This latter is the method still in use in our Hebrew Bibles.

There is clear evidence, then, for the use of writing in Syria-Palestine from the earliest times. The report of Wen-amon, an Egyptian official who was sent to Byblos *ca.* 1100 B.C., mentions that five hundred papyrus rolls were delivered to the Syrian ruler in partial payment for a load of timber. This gives some indication of the extent to which writing was

practiced there. The OT references to writing in the time of Moses (Exod. 17:14; 24:4; 39:14, 30; Deut. 27:3; 31:24; cf. Josh. 18:4-9) are thus not to be regarded as anachronisms. An episode from the time of Gideon, in the twelfth or eleventh century, bears witness to the knowledge of writing on the part of a young man from a small town who was captured at random (Judg. 8:14). As in Egypt and Mesopotamia, those who were able to write were usually govern-

Courtesy of Princeton University Press

34. Examples of alphabetic writing as found on a variety of documents: (1) Ahiram Inscription; (2) Yehimilk Inscription; (3) Samaria Ivories; (4) Gezer Calendar; (5) Moabite Stone; (6) Kilamuwa Inscription; (7) Samaria Ostraca; (8) Shema Seal; (9) Bar Rakab Inscription; (10) Siloam Inscription; (11) Nerab Stelae; (12) Pharaoh Letter; (13) Lachish Ostraca; (14) Jewish Seals; (15) Meissner Papyrus; (16) Leviticus Fragments; (17) Elephantine Papyri; (18) Eshmunazar Sarcophagus

ment officials, as in the case of David's "scribe" (RSV "secretary") Seraiah (II Sam. 8:17). We must assume the existence of scribal schools as in the neighboring nations. The products of such schools would be known as "ready scribes" (Ps. 45:1). Isaiah could read and write (Isa. 8:2) in the eighth century, although this was not true of all (Isa. 29:12). By the late seventh century, however, a certain degree of literacy was presupposed (Deut. 6:9; 24:1).

5. Crete, Cyprus, and Greece. The Minoan civilization which flourished on the island of Crete developed a form of writing *ca.* 2000 B.C. Inscribed on stone or clay tablets, this is a hieroglyphic system as yet undeciphered. It reads from left to right or boustrophedon—i.e., alternately from left to right and the reverse. Between the seventeenth and sixteenth centuries a cursive script known to scholars as Linear A replaced the earlier system. It has been found incised on tablets of stone, metal, or clay, as well as written with ink on potsherds. Unfortunately this too has not yet been satisfactorily deciphered.

Ca. 1400 B.C., Crete came under the domination of the Mycenaean civilization, which had made its appearance on the Greek mainland. Coincident with this a new form of writing known as Linear B came into use which continued to be employed until the overthrow of the civilization *ca.* 1200. Many clay

From *Mycenae Tablets* (Philadelphia: The American Philosophical Society, 1953)

35. Clay tablet from the House of the Oil Merchant, Mycenae, in Linear B script (*ca.* 1200 B.C.)

tablets from the beginning of this period have been unearthed at Knossos, while hundreds of others, dating to the end of the period, have been excavated on the Greek mainland at Pylos and Mycenae.* In 1953 this script was deciphered, and proved to be a syllabary—composed of consonant plus vowel or vowel alone—written from left to right and representing an early form of Greek. Fig. WRI 35.

From these Minoan-Mycenean linear scripts the inhabitants of the island of Cyprus derived *ca.* 1400 a form of writing, still undeciphered, known as Cypro-Mycenean. Introduced probably by Mycenean settlers, it remained in use at least until the middle of the eleventh century. By the seventh century we encounter still another script, which seems to be a further development of the preceding, and was destined to remain until the first century B.C. This Cypriote script is likewise a syllabary of fifty-four signs expressing a simple vowel or consonant plus vowel, and written either from right to left—occasionally left to right—or boustrophedon. It was designed for an undeciphered non-Greek language, but the majority of texts found so far are in Greek.

The most significant development, however, was the adoption of the linear alphabetic system devised in Syria-Palestine (*see* § A4 *above; see also* ALPHABET). This purely consonantal Phoenician script was employed for the writing of Greek *ca.* 800 B.C. A major advance was made when certain signs which represented consonants not phonemic to Greek were used to indicate vowel sounds—viz., ' for *a*, *h* for *e*, *ḥ* for *ē*, *y* for *i*, and ' for *o*. To this were later added further symbols. This was the alphabet which was passed on to Italy for the writing of Etruscan and Latin, and which is the ancestor of our own.

First written from right to left as in Syria-Palestine, it was soon written boustrophedon and finally exclusively from left to right. No attempt was made to indicate the division of words. Cursive forms of the letters soon developed for use in business texts. For literary use, however, uncials—i.e., what we call capitals—were used until the tenth century A.D. In the preceding century a literary cursive hand was developed known as minuscule.

B. WRITING MATERIALS. 1. Writing surfaces. a. Stone. In all ages stone has been used for inscriptions when a high degree of permanence was desired. In Egypt, where stone is plentiful, the walls of countless temples and tombs which were built for eternity were covered with carved hieroglyphic texts. Stelae and rock inscriptions are also common.* Discarded flakes of limestone were sometimes used as a cheap writing material, and were inscribed in ink with hieratic, demotic, or Coptic texts. Figs. BET 33, 36; MER 40.

Stone is relatively scarce in Mesopotamia, however, so that cuneiform inscriptions on this material are confined almost exclusively to royal texts or public stelae like that which bears the Code of Hammurabi.* The same situation holds true for inscriptions in Elamite, Hieroglyphic Hittite, and Old Persian. Fig. WRI 36.

In Syria-Palestine stone was likewise used for inscriptions in Aramaic or Canaanite intended for public display, such as the Moabite Stone,* Siloam Inscription,* etc. (*see* INSCRIPTIONS §§ 3-4). The He-

From *They Wrote in Clay* (The University of Chicago Press)

36. Weight-stone inscribed in three languages: Old Persian, Elamite, and Babylonian

brew Gezer Calendar, incised on limestone, is an example of the use of this cheaper material for less important purposes, since this may well be a school text. There are several references to the use of stone in the OT, beginning with Moses' tables of stone (Exod. 24:12; 34:1; Deut. 4:13). The stone might be prepared to receive the writing by a layer of plaster (Deut. 27:2-3). Joshua is said to have written on stone (Josh. 8:32), and Job cried out that his words might be so inscribed indelibly (Job 19:24). Figs. MOA 66; INS 14.

b. Metal. As a writing material, metal is much less common than stone. Cuneiform inscriptions in Sumerian, Akkadian, and Old Persian were incised on objects made of gold, silver, copper, and bronze, and occasionally on tablets or plaques of such metals. Hittite cuneiform texts also occur on bronze tablets. Some of the pseudo-hieroglyphic inscriptions from Byblos are written on bronze tablets, and inscribed copper arrow or lance heads have been found in Palestine. That bronze plaques were used there is clear from I Macc. 8:22; 14:18, 27, 48. To this must be added the copper scroll discovered at Qumran (*see* DEAD SEA SCROLLS) purporting to contain a description of the hiding places of the treasures of the sectarian community. It has been plausibly suggested that the word ספר, translated "book" in Job 19:23; Isa. 30:8, may represent the Akkadian *sipparu*, "bronze," since the accompanying verb in both cases is חקק, "to carve, engrave." Gold is mentioned in Exod. 28:36 as a writing surface.

Lead was extensively used in Greece and Italy for magical charms, and occasionally for literary works such as those of Hesiod. A lead roll inscribed with Ps. 80 in Greek was found at Rhodes. Inscriptions on the same material from Carthage bear Punic texts. From a much earlier period is the use of lead

for some Hittite texts. It may be that the enigmatic passage in Job 19:24 refers to this practice, if בעט ברזל ועפרת can mean "with an iron stylus *on* lead." However, perhaps the last word should be read וצפרן—i.e., "with an iron pen and point" (cf. Jer. 17:1). *See* PEN.

c. Clay. The alluvial soil of the Tigris-Euphrates Valley made clay the most readily available and thus the cheapest material for writing purposes in Mesopotamia. It was this fact that led to the development of the Sumero-Akkadian pictographic signs into the peculiar cuneiform shapes. The later spread of this script to such peoples as the Hittites, Hurrians, and Elamites was likewise accompanied by the use of CLAY TABLETS. The moist clay was first kneaded into shape, and the surface smoothed with one end of the stylus. Normally the tablets were flat on one side and convex on the other. The signs were then impressed on the clay with the stylus, first on the flat side and then, if necessary, continuing on the convex side. The clay tablets would soon harden, but to increase their strength they were often baked in the sun. If greater durability was desired, they might be baked in a fire.

Legal documents were usually signed by means of cylinder seal impressions. For the greater protection of such documents they might be encased in an envelope of clay,* on which a copy or merely a summary of the contents would be written. For longer

From *They Wrote in Clay* (The University of Chicago Press)

37. A clay tablet in its envelope

literary works a series of tablets, each carefully labeled and numbered, might be employed, or larger tablets containing several columns could be used. Royal annals were usually recorded on clay cylinders or prisms of from six to ten sides. Fig. WRI 37.

The use of clay tablets was not confined to Mesopotamia and Anatolia, but spread to Syria-Palestine and Egypt when Akkadian became the language of international diplomacy. The best evidence of this is the correspondence between the Egyptian pharaoh and the Babylonian, Mitannian, Hittite, and Arzawan rulers, as well as the local governors of the dependent states in Syria-Palestine between the fifteenth and thirteenth centuries which have come to light at TELL EL-AMARNA in Egypt and several sites in Syria-Palestine.

Probably under Mesopotamian influence, the use of clay tablets with a cuneiform alphabetic system during the early fourteenth century is found at UGARIT in N Syria. The hieroglyphic and linear syllabaries in use on the island of Crete were also written on clay tablets. There is no reference to the use of clay for writing purposes in the OT.

d. Potsherds. The use of pieces of broken and discarded pottery as a writing material was widespread throughout the ancient world. These OSTRACA were always in plentiful supply, and took the place of papyrus (see § B1g below), which was relatively expensive. With no preparation, they could easily be written on with pen and ink and even, if necessary, reused if the previous text were washed off. We find them in common use in Egypt from the Old Kingdom (ca. 2664-2155 B.C.) on, especially for school exercises containing both literary and nonliterary texts and for the needs of daily life such as letters, receipts, accounts, etc. Such texts have been found in Egyptian (hieratic, demotic, and Coptic), Aramaic, and Greek.

The use of ostraca in Mesopotamia was far more limited, since they could be used only for a script like Aramaic, which was written with pen and ink. In classical times the Athenians used them for recording the names of persons to be banished, hence the term "ostracize." A number of ostraca have been unearthed in Palestine, especially at Samaria and Lachish (see INSCRIPTIONS § 3). Although potsherds are mentioned in the OT (Job 2:8; Ps. 22:15; Isa. 30:14), there is no reference to their use for writing purposes.

e. Linen. From the third millennium on, linen is found as a writing material in Egypt, although it is not common. Because of its perishable nature, no trace of its use has survived in Western Asia, if indeed it was used. At a very much later time it was employed in Italy by the Romans and especially by the Etruscans. There is no indication of its use in biblical literature.

f. Wood and bark. Apart from the carving of hieroglyphic inscriptions on wooden statues and reliefs in ancient Egypt,* wooden tablets coated with stucco were frequently used, especially for schoolboy exercises. In Mesopotamia, despite the fact that such wooden tablets must all have perished in the damp soil, there are clear indications of their use, since the Akkadian word lē'u (Hebrew לוח), "tablet," is often preceded by the determinative for "wood." A Neo-Babylonian letter instructs the reader to "open the tablet of Shamash," so we may conclude that this was a hinged tablet or diptych. Confirmation of this is to be found in the depiction of scribes with just such wooden diptychs on Assyrian reliefs of ca. 700 B.C. Unless these were used for writing with pen and ink, they must have been coated with clay or wax. An eighth-century relief from Zenjirli in N Syria

Courtesy of the Cairo Museum

38. A functionary with his scepter, staff, and writing materials; on a wood panel, from the tomb of Hesi-Re at Saqqarah; Fourth Dynasty (ca. 2650-2500 B.C.)

shows a similar scene. The sole reference to writing in the Homeric epics speaks of King Proetus inscribing signs ἐν πίνακι πτυκτῷ, "on a folding tablet" (Iliad VI.169). In Greece of the early sixth century, Solon's laws were inscribed on triangular tablets of wood, according to Plutarch. Fig. WRI 38.

When we turn to the OT, we find clear evidence of the use of wood for writing—e.g., the wooden rods or staves in Num. 17:2-3—H 17:16-17, and the "sticks" (עץ) in Ezek. 37:16-17. The fact that the two "sticks" in the latter passage are to be joined together may suggest that a diptych is meant. The suggestion of some scholars that the letter in Isa. 37:14 was also a diptych is unlikely, since the same verb, פרש, "to spread out," is elsewhere used of a scroll (Ezek. 2:10). The use of the term דלת, "door," to describe a column of writing probably derives from the hinged "doors" of the diptych.

The word לוח in Isa. 30:8; Hab. 2:2 most likely means a wooden tablet, although in the former case it may be of metal (cf. § B1b above). The term גליון, translated "roll" in Isa. 8:1 KJV, although thought by some to be a blank sheet of papyrus because of its use in Late Hebrew to mean the margin of a scroll, almost certainly designates a wooden tablet, since it is to be inscribed with a חרט, used for carving in Exod. 32:4 (see PEN). In Greece and Italy wooden tablets were usually coated with wax, and such a tablet is referred to as a πινακίδιον in Luke 1:63.

Bark was in common use as a writing material at Rome until it was replaced by papyrus late in the second century B.C. However, it continued in use to some degree until the fifth century A.D. Indeed, the Latin word for "bark," *liber,* acquired the meaning "book."

g. Papyrus. The ancient Egyptians employed papyrus plants, which grew in profusion throughout the land, for many purposes. By far the most important of these was the manufacture of an excellent writing material which the Greeks called PAPYRUS, from which is derived our word "paper." Strips were cut from the stalk of the plant and laid side by side, then a second layer superimposed at right angles. When beaten and smoothed, it formed a light but sturdy material. The sheets might then be joined together to form a long strip which could be rolled up. *See* § C *below.* Fig. EGY 20.

When papyrus was first made in Egypt we do not know, but a blank roll has been recovered from the tomb of Hemaka, chancellor of King Wedimu of the First Dynasty (*ca.* 3000 B.C.). The earliest extant inscribed roll comes from the reign of Neferirkare of the Fifth Dynasty (*ca.* 2470). It became the commonest writing material in the ancient world, and remained in use until it was replaced by true paper *ca.* the tenth century A.D. The latter, invented in China, did not reach the Near East until the seventh or eighth century.

Papyrus was used in Egypt for both literary and nonliterary texts. These were written with pen and ink in hieratic—rarely in cursive hieroglyphs—demotic, and Coptic, as well as in Aramaic and Greek. The use spread to other regions, and the production and export of papyrus became a major industry in Egypt. The receipt of five hundred rolls of "fine quality papyrus" by the Syrian ruler of Byblos in return for a consignment of timber is recorded *ca.* 1100 B.C. in the report of the Egyptian Wen-amon.

We may assume that the scribes who wrote Aramaic made use of papyrus in Mesopotamia, but the nature of the soil has preserved no remnants of it. The Assyrian reliefs of scribes writing with pens on sheets or rolls of a pliable material probably have to do with leather (*see* § B1*h below*). Papyrus was introduced to Greece at least as early as the fifth century B.C., and to Italy by the second century. We have seen that it was extensively used in Syria by the beginning of the eleventh century. That it was also in use in Palestine by the sixth century is proved by the impressions made by the fibers of the now decayed papyrus document visible in the clay seal of Gedaliah excavated at Lachish, although we may be sure that it was already well established by then.

Despite the fact that the OT several times refers to the papyrus plant (גּמֶא; Exod. 2:3 ["bulrushes"]; Job 8:11; Isa. 18:2; 35:7 ["rushes"]), there is no clear indication of its use in writing. However, the deed of purchase signed by Jeremiah (Jer. 32:10-14) was undoubtedly a papyrus document, folded and sealed like those found at Elephantine. It is also most likely that the scroll written by Baruch at Jeremiah's dictation was of papyrus rather than leather, since the odor of burning leather (Jer. 36:23) would have been quite unbearable. Moreover, the LXX version of this chapter renders the Hebrew מְגִלָּה, "scroll," by χαρτίον (36:2, 4, 6, 14—G 43:2, 4, 6, 14) or χάρτης (36:23—G 43:23), both words denoting a sheet of papyrus. Some of the MSS recovered from the caves

in the Wadi Qumran* and the Wadi Murabba'at were on papyrus, and so was the famous NASH PAPYRUS. Papyrus was the material on which the Pauline letters and other early NT documents were written. This is clearly indicated by the word χάρτης in II John 12. Fig. DEA 10.

h. Leather and parchment. The use of tanned skins for writing purposes goes back to the early third millennium in Egypt. The earliest mention of leather documents is found in a text of the Fourth Dynasty (*ca.* 2550 B.C.), and the oldest extant example dates from the Twelfth Dynasty (*ca.* 2000). It remained in use in Egypt until the Arab conquest in the seventh century A.D. A collection of Aramaic letters to Persian officials in Egypt dating from the fifth century B.C. is all on leather.

Leather, like papyrus, could not survive the climate of Mesopotamia, so that no examples survive. However, Assyrian reliefs of the eighth and seventh centuries depict scribes writing, not only on clay tablets, but also on a flexible material which could be papyrus or leather. The probabilities favor the latter. In the Neo-Babylonian period cuneiform texts mention the use of leather for writing, and by the Persian period the Akkadian words for "deed" and "missive" are sometimes preceded by the determinative for leather objects. Diodorus Siculus preserves a statement of Ctesias to the effect that the Persians used διφθέραι, "skins," for their historical records, and Herodotus tells how the Ionian Greeks employed them also.

Though hides were tanned by the Hebrews (cf. Num. 31:20; II Kings 1:8), the OT makes no reference to writing on leather. As seen above, the scroll described in Jer. 36:23 was probably of papyrus rather than leather. Yet most of the DEAD SEA SCROLLS were of leather, and Talmudic law required copies of the Hebrew Torah which were intended for public worship to be inscribed on leather rolls (cf. Aristeas 176).

PARCHMENT began to replace leather *ca.* the third century B.C. Instead of tanning the hides of sheep or goats, they were now prepared by removing the hair and rubbing them smooth. Pliny mentions the belief that Eumenes II (197-158 B.C.) of Pergamum was the inventor of parchment. But a Greek document on this material dating *ca.* 195 B.C. has been found at Dura-Europos, which shows that this could not have been so. The story more likely reflects the fact that it was at this time, early in the second century, that parchment became a popular writing material.

The term "vellum" is usually reserved for parchment of an especially fine quality prepared from the skins of calves or kids. It superseded ordinary parchment for the best books in the first half of the fourth century A.D.

2. Writing instruments. a. Stylus. For inscriptions on stone or metal, of course, a chisel would be required. But for the incising of texts on softer materials such as clay or wax, a stylus would suffice. In Mesopotamia this was of reed, hardwood, and perhaps bone or metal. The tip of those employed to write cuneiform was either square or triangular. The representations on Assyrian monuments of the stylus wielded by scribes are unfortunately too vague for certainty on this point. Fig. WRI 39.

Courtesy of the Librairie Orientaliste Paul Geuthner, Paris

39. The Assyrian bearded scribe on the right writes on a clay tablet with a stylus; the scribe on the left is writing with a brush on either skin or papyrus; from a wall painting at Tell Ahmar (perhaps early eighth century B.C.)

The OT speaks of an iron stylus or chisel (עֵט; Job 19:24; Jer. 17:1) for use on stone. In Jer. 17:1 it is associated with a צִפֹּרֶן שָׁמִיר—i.e., a point, or perhaps stylus, of DIAMOND or flint; the term צִפֹּרֶן may also have been present in the original text of Job 19:24 (see PEN). The חֶרֶט of Isa. 8:1, which was a tool for carving (Exod. 32:4), must surely have been a stylus for use on a wooden tablet. See § B1f above.

b. Pen. For writing with ink on papyrus, leather, parchment, wooden tablets, or ostraca, the Egyptians used a rush cut obliquely and then frayed at the end to form a brush. The same kind of instrument was used by the Hebrews to write on the ostraca from Samaria and Lachish, and we may be sure that this is what is meant by the term עֵט—which also means "stylus"—in Ps. 45:1—H 45:2; Jer. 8:8, and hence that Baruch used such a brush to write the scroll mentioned in Jer. 36.

At the end of the third century B.C., about the time when parchment made its appearance, Greek writers in Egypt devised a new type of pen by pointing the end of a reed and splitting it to form a nib. This was adopted by the Egyptians for the writing of their own language at the beginning of the Christian era. This true pen was called κάλαμος, "reed," in Greek, and is thus named in III John 13.

c. Ink. The Egyptians, because of the nature of their script, used ink from the earliest times. Black ink was made from carbon in the form of soot mixed with a thin solution of gum. This was dried into cakes, and then moistened with water for use. Red ink was also used, especially for headings—hence our use of the term "rubric." For carbon, red ocher or red iron oxide was substituted.

The Hebrews probably used the same kind of black ink, although that of the Lachish Letters apparently contained some iron. This ink, which was called דְּיוֹ (Jer. 36:18), could be washed off (Exod. 32:33; Num. 5:23; Ps. 69:28—H 69:29), as was the case in Egypt. The NT term for "ink" is μέλαν, "black" (II Cor. 3:3; II John 12; III John 13).

d. Scribal equipment. In Mesopotamia scribes carried their styluses in a case, probably made of leather, which was worn in the waistband. In early times Egyptian scribes made use of a hollow reed

Courtesy of the Oriental Institute, the University of Chicago

40. Egyptian scribal outfit consisting of a slate palette with restored water jug and a brush case with a rush pen

case for their brushes. To this they added a wooden palette containing two cavities for the cakes of black and red ink, which was joined by a cord to a small pot designed to hold water for the moistening of the ink.* From this combination came the hieroglyph for "writing" and "scribe." Fig. WRI 40.

Figs. WRI 41-42.

At a later period, the case and palette were combined. These wooden or ivory palettes had receptacles for the ink as well as a slot for the brushes, and could be tucked in the belt. In this form they became common throughout the Near East and were used by the Hebrews (Ezek. 9:2-3, 11; RSV "writing case"; KJV "inkhorn"). Even the Hebrew word קֶסֶת, denoting the scribal kit, was borrowed from the Egyptian name *gsti.*

A straight edge for ruling lines, pumice stone for smoothing the papyrus, a cloth or sometimes a sponge for washing off the ink when an erasure was required, and a knife for cutting leather or papyrus and sharpening pens (Jer. 36:23; see PENKNIFE) completed the equipment required by a scribe.

C. *DEVELOPMENT OF THE BOOK.* The use of clay tablets in Mesopotamia meant that long literary works posed a problem, for either large tablets of many columns were required, or else the text had to be distributed over several separate tablets. In the latter case a series of tablets—e.g., seven for the

Creation Epic, twelve for the Epic of Gilgamesh—
were inscribed with portions of the text, each ending
in a colophon giving the name of the work, the number of the tablet, and a "catchword"—i.e., the opening words of the following tablet.

Egypt was fortunate in that papyrus and leather
were much more suitable—or at least manageable—
for the production of lengthy works. Sheets of papyrus were pasted together to form long strips which,
like leather, could be rolled up into a convenient
size. Such papyrus scrolls were usually between nine
and eleven inches in height and rarely exceeded
thirty feet in length, since longer scrolls would prove
unwieldy. There were exceptions, the most outstanding being the Harris Papyrus, which measured 133

42. A diorite statue of Amen-em-het, a scribe of the
Eighteenth Dynasty in Egypt (*ca.* 1570-1310 B.C.)

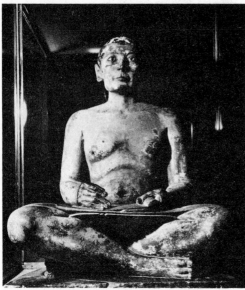

41. An Egyptian scribe holding a papyrus roll in his
hands; his eyes are inlaid with quartz, ebony wood,
and crystal; of the Fifth Dynasty (*ca.* 2500-2350 B.C.),
from Saqqara

feet by 17 inches, and a copy of the Book of the
Dead, which was 123 feet by 19 inches. Our word
"volume" is derived from the Latin *volumen*, "something rolled up," hence "book roll." Egyptian papyrus rolls were but rarely inscribed on both sides. The
text was written in columns of a convenient width,
with spaces between them.

The Hebrews also rolled up their documents of
papyrus or leather (Isa. 34:4; cf. Rev. 6:14), and
hence called them by the term מגלה, "roll," or
מגלת ספר, "book roll." This latter expression is rendered in the NT by κεφαλὶς βιβλίου (Heb. 10:7) in
a passage which quotes from Ps. 40:7—H 40:8. Occasionally they would write on both sides of a scroll
(Ezek. 2:10; cf. Rev. 5:1). The text was likewise
written in columns (דלת; Jer. 36:23), leaving ample
margins. Since *ca.* thirty feet was the normal length
of a scroll, it was just sufficient for a book like Isaiah,
but necessitated the division of the Pentateuch into
five sections. Samuel, Kings, and Chronicles would
each fill one scroll in the unvocalized Hebrew

script; but when these were rendered into Greek,
each book required two scrolls, because the use of
vowels in the Greek script doubled the length of
the text—hence our present division into I and II
Samuel, etc. Scrolls were often stored in pottery jars
(Jer. 32:14), as were cuneiform tablets in Mesopotamia, Egyptian and Aramaic papyri in Egypt, and
the scrolls from the Dead Sea region.

For legal or business documents the Greeks and
Romans had used tablets of wood or lead, the former
coated with wax. These were often laid on each other
and joined together by boring holes near the edges
and securing them by thongs like the earlier diptychs
(*see* § B1*f above*). The Latin word *caudex* or *codex*,
which denoted a tree trunk or block of wood, was
used to describe these.

After a time the advantage of this arrangement
over the scroll, which was inconvenient, since it
required two hands to unroll and roll it for reading
or writing, led someone to experiment with a
"codex" of papyrus sheets. Four or five sheets of
papyrus were folded over and stitched together to
make a quire of eight or ten leaves. Parchment was
also treated in the same way; but since there was
a slight difference in appearance between the flesh
side and the hair side, the quires were so folded
that the hair sides faced each other, and the flesh
sides likewise. A number of such quires produced a
codex similar to our modern book.

Influenced still by the practice followed in writing
on scrolls, the columns of writing were still narrow.
Thus the famous biblical codices SINAITICUS;

VATICANUS; ALEXANDRINUS were written with four, three, and two columns respectively to a page.* Eventually only one or two columns became usual. Figs. SIN 65; VAT 1; ALE 15.

The codex form gradually displaced the scroll for non-Christian literature at least as early as the first century A.D. By the second and third centuries, however, the codex was in most common use in Christian circles. During the first half of the fourth century parchment gave way to vellum for the finest books.

Bibliography. J. H. Breasted, "The Physical Processes of Writing in the Early Orient and Their Relation to the Origin of the Alphabet," *AJSL,* XXXII (1915-16), 230-49; F. G. Kenyon, *Ancient Books and Modern Discoveries* (1927); R. P. Dougherty, "Writing upon Parchment and Papyrus Among the Babylonians and the Assyrians," *JAOS,* XLVIII (1928), 109-35; C. C. McCown, "Codex and Roll in the NT," *HTR,* XXXIV (1941), 219-50; J. P. Hyatt, "The Writing of an OT Book," *BA,* VI (1943), 71-80; F. W. Beare, "Books and Publication in the Ancient World," *University of Toronto Quarterly,* XIV (1945), 150-67; D. Diringer, *The Alphabet* (1947); J. Černý, *Paper and Books in Ancient Egypt* (1952); I. J. Gelb, *A Study of Writing* (1952); G. R. Driver, *Semitic Writing from Pictograph to Alphabet* (2nd ed., 1954).   R. J. WILLIAMS

WRITING CASE [קֶסֶת הַסֹּפֵר, kit of the scribe, *from* Egyp. *gst*] (Ezek. 9:2-3, 11); KJV WRITER'S INK-HORN. The scribe's kit, consisting of a wooden palette for mixing ink and a case for pens, carried in the belt. *See* WRITING AND WRITING MATERIALS.

WYCLIF'S VERSION wĭk′lĭf. The first translation (1380-82) of the complete Bible into English, by John Wyclif, with assistance from Nicholas of Hereford.

43. Leaf from Wyclif's Bible (A.D. 1382)

The NT was published in 1380, the whole Bible in 1382. Originally based on the Latin Vulg., the version was revised *ca.* 1400 by John Purvey on the basis of a corrected Latin text.

See also VERSIONS, ENGLISH, § 2.

Fig. WYC 43.   J. R. BRANTON

Courtesy of the Oriental Institute, the University of Chicago

XANTHICUS zăn'thĭ kəs [Ξανθικός]. A month in the Seleucid or Macedonian calendar, corresponding to the Jewish month Nisan (April), mentioned in the letters of Antiochus V and the Romans to the Jews in II Macc. 11:27-38.

XERXES zûrk'sēz [Old Pers. *xšayāršan;* Elam. *ik-še-ir-iš-ša;* Akkad. *ḫi-ši-'-ar-ša;* Ξέρξης; Aram.-Heb. חשיארש, חשירש (Papyri)]. **1.** Xerxes I, a Persian king of the Achaemenian Dynasty (486-465 B.C.).

Xerxes was a son of Darius the Great (*see* DARIUS 1)* and Atossa, daughter of Cyrus the Great (*see* CYRUS); also, the husband of Amestris. Xerxes succeeded his father in 486, after having been designated as his heir apparent, according to his own statement: "Other sons of Darius there were, (but) . . . Darius my father made me the greatest after himself. When my father Darius went away from the throne [died], by the will of Ahuramazdā I became king on my father's throne";[1] this account agrees with the fuller story given by Herodotus (VII.1-4). Figs. XER 1; DAR 4; AHU 6.

The memory of the difficulties, such as revolts in Egypt, Babylonia, and elsewhere, which Xerxes had to meet in the beginning of his reign, is preserved in one of his own inscriptions as follows: "When that I became king, there was rebellion among these countries which are inscribed above [referring to the preceding list of satrapies]. Then Ahuramazdā bore me aid; by the favor of Ahuramazdā I smote that country and put it down in its place." His attitude in matters of religion is illustrated by the following passage from the same inscription: "And among these countries there was (a place) where previously false gods [*daiva*] were worshipped. Afterwards, by the favor of Ahuramazdā, I destroyed that sanctuary of the false gods [*daivadāna*], and I made proclamation, 'The false gods shall not be worshipped!' Where previously the false gods were worshipped, there I worshipped Ahuramazdā."[1]

Simultaneously, large-scale preparations for a major war against continental Greece were under way. At first the expedition met with success. Four months after the spectacular crossing of the Helles-

[1] R. G. Kent, *Old Persian* (New Haven, Conn.: American Oriental Society).

1. Darius (522-486 B.C.) on the throne, with Xerxes (486-465) behind him and the symbol of Ahura-mazda above him; from the Council Hall at Persepolis

pont (480), Xerxes had succeeded in occupying Attica and maneuvering the enemy fleet into a position of virtual blockade in the Bay of Salamis. The ensuing naval battle ended, however, in disaster (480), and after an indecisive land battle at Plataeae (479) the Persian armies withdrew from Greece, while the Persian fleet suffered a surprise defeat at Mycale in Ionia (479). Internal troubles which kept him occupied until the time of his death (465) provide a partial explanation for the little interest taken by Xerxes in the subsequent struggle for the liberation of the Greek cities of Cyprus and the coast of Asia Minor, which was stubbornly fought by Cimon and others in an atmosphere of political tension in favor of continued warfare kept alive by the performance of such dramas as Phrynichus' *Phoenissae* and *Capture of Miletus* and Aeschylus' *Persae.*

The king AHASUÉRUS of the book of Esther has been identified with King Xerxes. *See* ESTHER, BOOK OF.

2. Xerxes II (424), who reigned forty-five days.

Bibliography. The events of the years 480-479 B.C. form the subject matter of Herodotus, bks. VII-IX. The quotations from the Old Persian inscription *above* are from R. G. Kent, *Old Persian* (1950), pp. 150-51; the Akkadian version of this inscription is in J. B. Pritchard, ed., *ANET* (1955), pp. 316-17. *See also* the bibliography under PERSIA, HISTORY AND RELIGION OF. M. J. DRESDEN

YAHWEH yä′wə [יהוה]. The vocalization of the four consonants of the Israelite name for God which scholars believe to approximate the original pronunciation. *See* GOD, NAMES OF, § B.

YARD. 1. The translation of גזרה (related to the verb גזר, "separate") in Ezek. 41:12–42:13 (KJV "separate place"). The yard, containing a building, was behind the temple and was a hundred cubits long (41:13*b*). In its only other occurrence (Lam. 4:7) the meaning of גזרה ("form") is uncertain.

2. The unit of measure used in translating the Greek "two hundred cubits" ("a hundred yards") in John 21:8. *See* WEIGHTS AND MEASURES § D4*a*.

O. R. SELLERS

YARN. KJV translation of מקוה in I Kings 10:28; II Chr. 1:16. *See* KUE.

YEAR [שׁנה]. In the course of its political, economic, social, and religious evolution during the biblical period the Israelite people employed several different calendars (*see* CALENDAR), in each of which the year was reckoned in varying manner.

The oldest calendar, aptly termed the pentecontad calendar (*see* SABBATH), borrowed from their Canaanite predecessors in Palestine and employed by Israel uninterruptedly until the time of Solomon, was of distinctly agricultural character in that it reckoned time primarily by the state of the annual crop. The day of cutting the first sheaf of the new crop constituted its New Year's Day (*see* NEW YEAR). Such a year was naturally of practically the same duration as a solar year. This calendar divided its year into seven pentecontads, periods of fifty days each—i.e., seven weeks plus one day, a day of sacred character at the close of the pentecontad, which stood outside the week and bore the distinctive title עצרה "(Festival of) Conclusion." These seven pentecontads plus two especial, festival periods, each of seven days, one following immediately upon the fourth pentecontad (*see* BOOTHS, FEAST OF) and the other immediately upon the seventh pentecontad—i.e., during the final seven days of the year (*see* PASSOVER AND FEAST OF UNLEAVENED BREAD)—plus the New Year's Day, a day naturally of supreme

sanctity, which likewise stood outside the week and followed immediately upon the second seven-day festival, constituted the year of this early calendar, 365 days in all.

Apparently this calendar took no cognizance whatever of the moon and did not in any way reckon time by months. Inasmuch as crop conditions varied considerably even in closely neighboring districts, it follows that this calendar was entirely local in character, and that accordingly there could have been as yet no single, uniform calendar for the entire land or people. However, during the pre-Israelite, Canaanite period, when the city-state, with limited territorial range, was the normal political unit, and likewise during the initial period of Israelite sojourn in the land, when the clan or the tribe was the normal unit of folk organization, during both of which periods agriculture was the dominant occupation, this pentecontad calendar, despite its distinctly localized character, plainly sufficed as an instrument of time-reckoning.

However, with the gradual fusion of the various Israelite tribes into a single nation and the establishment by David of an Israelite empire, the attendant development of international political relations and the inauguration of international commerce, the inadequacy of the localized pentecontad calendar became increasingly apparent. A calendar which would be uniform, not only for the entire Israelite nation itself, but also for its neighbors, was indispensable—in other words, a calendar of international, and even of universal, character. By the first quarter of the tenth century B.C. the Tyrians, then the world's foremost colonizing and internationally commercial people, had evolved such a calendar, one distinctly solar in character. Solomon borrowed this calendar from his Tyrian allies and made it official for Israel. The year of this calendar was, of course, specifically solar. Solomon set its New Year's Day upon the day of the autumnal equinox. This day, and with this, of course, the precise duration of the year, could be determined quite accurately (*see* NEW YEAR). This solar year consisted normally of 365 days, but, whenever necessary, a leap year was celebrated. This solar year was divided into 12 months, of 30 days each, with a 5- or, in leap years, 6-day supplementary period inserted, most probably at the end of the year, where it was co-ordinated in some meaningful manner with the 7-day Festival of Ingathering, a festival of the earlier, pentecontad calendar, which Solomon incorporated into this new calendar and transferred from its original time of celebration, immediately after the fourth pentecontad—i.e., normally late in October—to a time about a month earlier, the 7 final days of the new solar year, the week immediately preceding the autumnal equinox. The 12 months of this solar year were known in Israel at first by their borrowed Tyrian names. Of these three are cited in the Bible: Ziv (I Kings 6:1, 37), Ethanim (I Kings 8:2), and Bul (I Kings 6:38), and perhaps also a fourth, Abib (Exod. 13:4; 23:15; 34:18; Deut. 16:1). Later, apparently under Assyrian cultural influence, the months came to be designated by number, reckoned, following Assyrian practice, from the vernal equinox. Accordingly the New Year's Day of this solar calendar was celebrated, under this system of month-designation, upon VII/10.

However, even though this solar calendar continued as the official calendar of Judah as long as the temple stood, it never completely supplanted in popular usage the earlier, pentecontad calendar. Farmers and shepherds tend to cherish ancient beliefs, institutions, and customs indefinitely. And when, after the Babylonian overthrow of the Judean kingdom in 586 B.C., agriculture became again the dominant occupation of the people remaining in the land (II Kings 25:12), not at all surprisingly the pentecontad calendar came once again into general use. However, with the dedication of the second temple in 516 B.C., the solar calendar was revived and functioned as the official calendar of the Jewish community of Palestine until the destruction of this second temple in 485 B.C. Even during this period the pentecontad calendar continued to flourish in rural circles. Following the destruction of the second temple, it persisted as the calendar in general use by the Jewish people of Palestine, but in a modified form, because it had borrowed certain elements of the solar calendar, particularly the reckoning of the year by months. In this modified pentecontad calendar the year consisted of 52 weeks or 364 days, divided still further into 12 months, of 30 days each, with 4 additional days inserted, one each at the ends of the third, sixth, ninth, and twelfth months. This calendar, with this distinctive reckoning of the year, came eventually to be employed by various Jewish sects, composed largely of rural groups, for their own inner affairs and religious practice, from the fifth century B.C. onward, and found concrete record in such sectarian writings as Jubilees, Enoch, and the newly discovered Qumran documents, and likewise in some measure in the NT.

At *ca.* 450 B.C. an altogether new calendar, distinctly lunar in character, was instituted. Of the details of time-reckoning according to this calendar, particularly in the biblical period, we know little, because of paucity of reference thereto in biblical writings. Our main biblical source of information with regard to it is the Priestly Code, particularly its secondary strata. It reckoned the normal lunar year as of 354 days, divided into 12 months of alternately 30 and 29 days each, with a thirteenth, intercalary month, consisting of either 29 or 30 days, inserted, usually following the twelfth month, whenever lunar observation, coupled with solar time-reckoning, indicated a need for this.

As long as the third temple stood, this procedure was undoubtedly regulated by the priests. The practice of designating the months of this new lunar calendar by number persisted for some time; but eventually, apparently in the fourth century B.C., the Babylonian month names came to be employed regularly in connection with this calendar. Probably at this time and as a phase of this same trend, the system of reckoning the day from sunset to sunset superseded the older system of reckoning from sunrise to sunrise. And undoubtedly in connection with this change the two ancient, seven-day festivals, Passover and Booths, were set to begin at sunset of the full-moon days of the first and the seventh months respectively. Such was the lunar calendar

and year in Jewish practice until the close of the biblical period.

Following the downfall of the Jewish state and the destruction of the Herodian temple by the Romans in A.D. 70, and with the consequent speedy termination of priestly authority, supervision of the calendar passed into the hands of the Rabbis. By them during the ensuing three centuries this lunar calendar was developed with regard to precise determination of new-moon days and also coordination with the solar year and its seasons, and thus gradually evolved into the calendar employed for Jewish religious time-reckoning still today.

Bibliography. J. Benzinger, *Hebräische Archäologie* (1894), pp. 198-203. E. König, "Kalenderfragen im althebräischen Schrifttum," *ZDMG*, LX (1906), 605-44. J. Morgenstern, "The Three Calendars of Ancient Israel," *HUCA*, I (1924), 13-78; "Additional Notes on the Three Calendars of Ancient Israel," *HUCA*, III (1926), 77-107; "The Gates of Righteousness," *HUCA*, VI (1929), 1-37; "Supplementary Studies in the Calendars of Ancient Israel," *HUCA*, X (1935), 1-148; "The Chanukkah Festival and the Calendars of Ancient Israel," *HUCA*, XX (1947), 1-36; XXI (1948), 365-496; "The Reckoning of the Day in the Gospels and Acts," *Crozer Quarterly*, XXVI (1949), 232-40. A. Jaubert, "Le calendrier des Jubilés et de la secte de Qumrân," *Vetus Testamentum*, III (1953), 250-64. J. Morgenstern, "The Calendar of the Book of Jubilees, Its Origin and Its Character," *Vetus Testamentum*, V (1955), 34-76; "Jerusalem—485 B.C.," *HUCA*, XXVII (1956), 101-79; XXVIII (1958), 15-47.

J. MORGENSTERN

YEAST. The translation of ζύμη (KJV LEAVEN, as elsewhere) in Gal. 5:9.

YELLOW. A color noted in medical diagnosis and the description of gold in the OT. The Hebrew word צהב (LXX ξανθίζουσα) translated "yellow" in Lev. 13:30, 32, 36, refers to the color of hair indicating the presence of leprous disease. The two final consonants of צהב, a root suggesting the gleam of bronze, are identical with those of זהב, "gold." While the similarity is striking, no etymological relationship between these two words has been established.

Gold plating, on the wings of a dove, represented as "yellow" (KJV) or "green" (RSV) in Ps. 68:13, is a rendering of ירקרק. This word is derived from the root ירק, meaning "to grow green or pale," and elsewhere is translated "greenish."

See also GREEN; COLORS.   C. L. WICKWIRE

YIRON yĭr'ɔn [יראון] (Josh. 19:38); KJV IRON ī'rŏn. A fortified town in Naphtali. It is probably to be located at modern Yarun, in N Galilee.

YOKE [מוטה, צמד (*alternately* COUPLE, PAIR); ζυγός]. Basically, a wooden frame placed over their necks to join two oxen or other draft animals. The pull of the plow, sled, or cart was against the broad shoulders of the draft animal. For horses, a different harness was developed. Construction of the yoke varied. The single yoke-bar (Jer. 28:10) with two loops of rope or nooses for the necks is the most simple form. A rod with two pairs of smaller rods at right angles to the yoke-bar like teeth, fitting over the necks and shoulders, was also used for pulling (Num. 19:2; Deut. 21:3). To the middle of the yoke-bar was connected a single shaft, which pulled the plow or cart. This was usually lashed to the yoke-bar (עֹל; I Sam. 6:7). The carpenter probably made both yokes and plows. Joseph and Jesus undoubtedly had experience in making yokes.

The yoke was used on human beings when they were taken captive (Jer. 28:10; cf. I Kings 12:9; II Chr. 10:4). Slaves were sometimes kept under such a real yoke of wood or iron (I Tim. 6:1). It is a small step from this use to the figurative use of the yoke as a symbol of subjection and servitude. It was predicted that Jacob would put a yoke on Esau (Gen. 27:40). Under Jeroboam the people complained of the forced labor as an unjust yoke (I Kings 11:28; 12: 11, 14). Slavery is like a yoke (Ecclus. 33:27); so is any hardship (Lam. 3:27; Ecclus. 40:1). The humiliation and oppression of one nation by another is expressed by the yoke of bondage (Jer. 27:8; 28:4; Hos. 11:7; cf. Deut. 28:48; Isa. 47:6). To break out of slavery or subjugation was expressed as "breaking the yoke" (Jer. 28:2; cf. Isa. 9:4; 14:25). God promises to break the "dominion" (KJV "yokes") of Egypt (Ezek. 30:18). To break away from God and to disobey as a sinner or rebel is to break his yoke (Jer. 2:20; 5:5; Ecclus. 51:39). The yoke of obedience to Christ is easy, compared with the subjugation of a person by the law, sin, and evil (Matt. 11:29). Sin is a yoke (Lam. 1:14). The law legalistically applied is a yoke (Acts 15:10; Gal. 5:1).

A team or pair of oxen tied together with a yoke is called a "yoke" (צֶמֶד; ζυγός; I Sam. 11:7; I Kings 19:21; Luke 14:19; when used of other than oxen, these terms are not translated "yoke"). Oxen usually work in pairs, but occasionally four are used for more pull. To be yoked with Baal is a sin (Num. 25:3, 5). Paul uses the term "yokefellow" to refer to his helpers (Phil. 4:3). This may mean they are a team, but it is probably better to interpret that they are all under the yoke of Christ.

A measure of land translated "acre" was called a צֶמֶד because it was the amount of land a pair of oxen could plow in a single day (I Sam. 14:14; Isa. 5:10).

                                             C. U. WOLF

YOKEFELLOW. *See* EUODIA.

YOM KIPPUR yŏm kĭp'ər. *See* ATONEMENT, DAY OF.

YOUTH. The time, with no fixed limit, beyond infancy and before a person's prime; a time of vigor and opportunity, though not of judgment and maturity.

The commonest Hebrew terms are נַעַר (feminine נַעֲרָה), עֶלֶם (feminine עַלְמָה), and בָּחוּר, "a youth"; and נְעוּרִים and בְּחוּרוֹת, "youth" (abstract noun). The first of these terms often means "manservant" or "maid," but basically all the terms mean "the young" or "youth." The one word בָּחוּר is so often paired with the term for "virgin" that it seems to be reserved for young men before marriage. But a girl may still after marriage be called a נַעֲרָה (e.g., Judg. 19:3) or an עַלְמָה. *See* VIRGIN.

The numerical age intended is by no means clear. The word נַעַר is used at times even for infants or the very young (Exod. 2:6; Judg. 13:8; I Sam. 1:22; 4:21), for whom there are also other words (*see* CHILD), but it is used for the fully grown as well (cf. Gen. 34:19; II Sam. 18:5). Lev. 27:1-8 might suggest the age of twenty as the time when one passed from youth to maturity. There, for the purpose of fixing a scale of values, persons are divided into groups according to age, and twenty appears as the lower age limit of the group most highly valued, therefore presumably in the prime of life. The census taker counted the population from twenty years old upward (Exod. 30:14). These were subject to the poll tax, and the males at this age were "able to go forth to war" (Num. 1:3). From Num. 14:29 we may also infer that moral responsibility arrived with the age of twenty. But Levites were not admitted to service in the tent of meeting until they were twenty-five (Num. 8:24). Yet despite the limit suggested by Num. 1:3, the soldier is often called נַעַר, and the upper age limit of "youth" is not a fixed number.

It is probable that the term "youth" was sometimes used merely to denote immaturity. Several biblical personalities refer to themselves disparagingly as "young." Thus Jeremiah says nothing clearly about his numerical age when he protests: "Ah, Lord GOD! Behold, I do not know how to speak, for I am only a youth" (Jer. 1:6), nor does King Solomon when he prays: "O LORD my God, thou hast made thy servant king . . . , although I am but a little child" (I Kings 3:7); they only display a becoming modesty. Cf. Judg. 6:15.

As "the beauty of old men is their gray hair," so "the glory of young men is their strength" (Prov. 20:29), and when "fair virgins" and "young men . . . faint for thirst" (Amos 8:13), the ultimate in tragedy is at hand.

The young, of course, lack the experience and the wisdom of their elders; therefore the repeated admonitions in such a book as Proverbs, where the "sons" addressed are everyman's sons (e.g., Prov. 7:24). These youth are invited to find wisdom and gain understanding (Prov. 8:32-36 and often), and they are warned to shun the "loose woman" who lies in wait for youthful victims (Prov. 7:4-12).

But Koheleth, aware of the infirmities of old age (*see* AGE, OLD, § 2), begs youth to have its fling "before the evil days come": "Rejoice, O young man, in your youth, and let your heart cheer you in the days of your youth" (Eccl. 11:9; 12:1).

Not infrequently Israel's early history is poetically termed its "youth" and either regretted as the time of national perversity (Ezek. 23:19), or fondly remembered as a time of good faith between God and people (Hos. 2:15—H 2:17), according to the writer's mood or purpose.   S. H. BLANK

ZAANAIM. KJV alternate form of ZAANANNIM.

ZAANAN zā'ə năn [צָאֲנָן]. An unidentified town in W Judah (Mic. 1:11). Often considered same as Zenan (Josh. 15:37). Both names are mentioned in context with Lachish.

ZAANANNIM zā'ə năn'ĭm [צַעֲנַנִּים]; KJV BEZA-ANANNIM bĭ zā'ə năn'ĭm [בְצַעֲנַנִּים] (Josh. 19:33); KJV ZAANAIM zā'ə nā'əm [צַעֲנַיִם] (Judg. 4:11). A border point in the territory of Naphtali (Josh. 19:33); the site of the encampment of Heber the Kenite, where Sisera was slain (Judg. 4:11).

Textual problems preclude certainty in the reading of the place name. Whether אֵלוֹן should be read "oak" (so RSV), or as the first element of a compound name "Elon-bezaanannim," is not clear; however, the absence of the article before אֵלוֹן supports the latter view. Arguments can also be advanced in favor of reading "Zaanaim" or "Bezaanannim" for "Zaanannim," although the latter has the weight of tradition on its side.

Its location is unknown, owing largely to the textual disorder of Judg. 4. It has been suggested that the site mentioned in Josh. 19:33 is to be identified with Khan et-Tujjar, a caravan station on the road from Beth-shan to Damascus *ca.* four miles SE of ADAMI, while that of Judg. 4:11 is located at Lejjun between Megiddo and Tell Abu Qedeis, possibly the Kedesh of this reference. It is also possible that the same site—the one in Naphtali—is referred to in both passages.

Bibliography. G. F. Moore, *Judges,* ICC (1895), pp. 119, 121; F.-M. Abel, *Géographie de la Palestine,* II (1938), 64, 439.
G. W. VAN BEEK

ZAAVAN zā'ə văn [זַעֲוָן, *perhaps from* זוּעַ, tremble, quake; Samar. *and* LXX *point to* זַעֲוָן] (Gen. 36:27; I Chr. 1:42); KJV ZAVAN zā'văn in I Chr. 1:42. The second son of clan chief Ezer; ancestor of a native Horite subclan in Edom.

ZABAD zā'băd [זָבָד, he (God) has given, *or* gift; *shortened form, of* Proto-Aram. *origin; cf.* Palmyrene, S Arab., Elephantine, *and* Babylonian *parallels;* Apoc. Σαβανναιοῦς, Σαβαθος, Σαβαδαίας]; KJV Apoc.

BANNAIA bə nā'yə (I Esd. 9:33); SABATUS săb'ə təs (I Esd. 9:28); ZABADAIAS zăb'ə dā'yəs (I Esd. 9:35). **1.** A name in a list tracing the descent of Elishama (I Chr. 2:36-37; cf. vs. 41). The list identifies Elishama's ancestor Sheshan (vss. 34-35) with Sheshan the Jerahmeelite (vs. 31), thus placing Elishama in the line of Judah.

2. A link in a postexilic Ephraimite genealogy which traces the genealogical tree of Joshua (I Chr. 7:21), if vss. 25-27 are to be read as the continuation of "Zabad his son" in vs. 21*a*. Comparison with Num. 26:35-36 suggests that here Ephraimite names have been realigned and several genealogical trees combined in replete presentation of the ancestry of Joshua.

3. Son of Ahlai; one of David's Mighty Men (I Chr. 11:41), in a list of names (vss. 41*b*-47) which the Chronicler attaches to a list (vss. 26-41*a*) comparable to the list of David's select fighting order of the Thirty (II Sam. 23:24-39*a*).

4. One of two servants of King Joash who assassinated him for ordering Zechariah the son of Jehoiada stoned to death (II Chr. 24:26; cf. vss. 20-22). He is called Jozacar in II Kings 12:21, where BH[3] and some MSS read "Jozabad" (the differences in the last two consonants may be due to their resemblance in Hebrew). Perhaps in Chronicles somehow "Jozabad" was read and abbreviated to "Zabad." He was the son of Shimeath the Ammonitess (his father in II Kings 12:21).

5. A layman among those who put away their foreign wives and their children according to Ezra's reform banning foreign marriage (Ezra 10:27; I Esd. 9:28).

6. Another layman in the list with 5 *above* (Ezra 10:33; I Esd. 9:33).

7. A third layman in the list with 5-6 *above* (Ezra 10:43; I Esd. 9:35).

Bibliography. G. B. Gray, *Studies in Hebrew Proper Names* (1896), pp. 222-24; M. Noth, *Die israelitischen Personennamen* (1928), pp. 22, 46-47.
T. M. MAUCH

ZABADEANS zăb'ə dē'ənz [Ζαβαδαιοι] (I Macc. 12:31). Arab inhabitants of a town called Zabad.

Jonathan Maccabeus pursued his enemies, who retired to the other side of the river Eleutherus (modern Nahr el-Litany in the Biq'a), turned against the Arab Zabadeans, and defeated them and carried off their property.

The name of Zabad is found in several other connections and probably refers to different places. In *Corpus inscriptionum graecarum* No. 9893 a town called Zabad is said to have been situated in the region of Apamea, NW of Hamath. Curiously enough, the Greek text has "Kaprozabadeans," a Greek word form from *kepher Zabad,* "the town of Zabad." Since this Zabad is situated not far from the Orontes, it does not seem to be the same as that which is referred to in I Maccabees. But since it is mentioned in connection with the river Eleutherus, the last-mentioned town may have been situated E of that river, for it is said that Jonathan marched to Damascus after his capture of Zabad. Or that town may possibly be modern Zebedani, NW of Damascus. Zebedani is situated in a valley which is a natural line of communication from the Biq'a to Damascus.

Bibliography. E. Honigmann, "Historische Topographie v. Nordsyrien im Altertum," *Zeitschrift des Deutschen Palästina-Vereins*, 46-47 (1923-24).   A. HALDAR

ZABBAI zăb'ī [זבי, *perhaps hypocoristic for* זבד, (God) has given; Apoc. 'Ωζάβαδος (A)]; KJV Apoc. JOS-ABAD jō'zə băd. One of the Jews contemporary with Ezra who were listed as having married foreign wives (Ezra 10:28; I Esd. 9:29). He is perhaps the same individual who is mentioned as the father of a certain Baruch who worked on the Jerusalem wall in the time of Nehemiah (Neh. 3:20), unless with the *Qere* one reads "Zaccai" (זכי).

Bibliography. M. Noth, *Die israelitischen Personennamen* (1928), pp. 39, 47.   B. T. DAHLBERG

ZABBUD. KJV form of ZACCUR.

ZABDEUS. KJV Apoc. form of ZEBADIAH.

ZABDI zăb'dī [זבדי, (Y *or* God) has given(?), gift (of Y *or* God)(?), my gift(?); *a shortened form; cf.* ZABAD]. Alternately: ZIMRI zĭm'rī [זמרי] (I Chr. 2:6). **1.** A descendant of Judah, of the family of Zerah; the father of Carmi. He founded a house one of whose members was Achan (Josh. 7:1, 17-18). He is called Zimri in I Chr. 2:6 (perhaps because of confusion in transmission: the last two consonants in these two names are similar in Hebrew; *see* ALPHABET).

2. A family of the tribe of Benjamin (I Chr. 8:19).

3. A Shiphmite; one of David's officials over the royal possessions. He was in charge of the "produce of the vineyards for the wine cellars"—probably the king's wine steward (I Chr. 27:27).

4. A Levite individual or family descended from Asaph (Neh. 11:17); probably to be identified with Zichri in I Chr. 9:15 (the last two consonants in these two names are similar in Hebrew).

Bibliography. M. Noth, *Die israelitischen Personennamen* (1928), pp. 38, 46-47.   T. M. MAUCH

ZABDIEL zăb'dĭ əl [זבדיאל, El (God) has given(?), gift of God(?), my gift is God(?); *see* ZABAD; *cf.* Palmyrene *Zabd-ila*, Akkad. *Zab-di-ilu*, present of the god; Apoc. Σαβδιήλ]. **1.** A descendant of Perez of the tribe of Judah, from whom David also was descended. Zabdiel was the father of Jashobeam (I Chr. 27:2).

2. Overseer of a group of priests. He is called the son of Haggedolim (Neh. 11:14).

3. An Arabian who decapitated Alexander Balas when he fled to Arabia for shelter, and sent the head to Ptolemy Philometer (I Macc. 11:17). Josephus calls him a prince (Antiq. XIII.iv.8).

Bibliography. G. A. Cooke, *A Text-Book of North-Semitic Inscriptions* (1903), p. 272; K. Tallqvist, *Assyrian Personal Names* (1914), p. 245; M. Noth, *Die israelitischen Personennamen* (1928), pp. 33-35, 46-47.   T. M. MAUCH

ZABUD zā'bŭd [זבוד, given; זבור *in some MSS;* G^L Ζαχουρ] (I Kings 4:5). A son of Nathan. He served in the capacity of priest and royal friend to Solomon.

ZABULON zăb'yə lən [Ζαβουλών]. The Greek (NT) spelling for ZEBULUN.

ZACCAI zăk'ī [זכי, (Y has) remembered, *or* (Y) remember(?); *a shortened form; cf.* ZECHARIAH] (Ezra 2:9; Neh. 7:14). Eponym or head of one of the families members of which returned from exile.

Bibliography. M. Noth, *Die israelitischen Personennamen* (1928), pp. 38, 186-87.   T. M. MAUCH

ZACCHAEUS ză kē'əs [Ζακχαῖος=זכי, the righteous *or* pure one]; KJV ZACCHEUS.

1. An officer of Judas Maccabeus' army (II Macc. 10:19).

2. A tax collector of Jericho, whose life was transformed through contact with Jesus (Luke 19:1-10).

A name with this meaning, borne, e.g., by the famous rabbi Johanan ben Zakkai in the latter half of the first century A.D., must have seemed to pious Jews ill carried by a tax collector, a collaborator with the hated Romans.

As "chief tax collector" (Luke 19:2), Zacchaeus appears as an official with general responsibility for the tax collectors of a district. Jericho, the gateway for Judea's E trade and the center of a remarkably fertile agricultural area, noted especially for its palm and balsam groves (Jos. Antiq. XV.iv.2; War IV. viii.2-3), would provide abundant opportunities for a commissioner of taxes to enrich himself.

The Jericho where Zacchaeus lived lay *ca.* two miles S of old Jericho. It was enlarged and beautified by Herod the Great, who made it his winter capital. In 1950-51 it was partly excavated by the American Schools of Oriental Research.

Jesus' encounter with Zacchaeus at the sycamore tree and subsequently in his home reveals the depth of Jesus' concern for outcasts, the radical character of his unconventionality, and the redemptive power of his spirit. It discloses Zacchaeus' resourcefulness in the presence of handicaps, his religious hunger, his decisiveness, and his capacity for radical repentance and restitution.

According to late, untrustworthy tradition, Zacchaeus became bishop of Caesarea (Clem. *Homilies* III.63; *Recog.* III.66).

Bibliography. H. L. Strack and P. Billerbeck, *Kommentar zum NT aus Talmud und Midrasch*, II (1924), 249-51; E. Klostermann, *Das Lukasevangelium* (2 Aufl., 1929), pp. 184-85; J. B. Pritchard, "The 1951 Campaign at Herodian Jericho," *BASOR*, 123 (Oct., 1951), 8-17; J. L. Kelso, *Excavations at NT Jericho and Khirbet En-Nitla* (1955).   E. P. BLAIR

ZACCUR zăk'ər [זכור, remembered, *or* mindful, *a shortened form*]; KJV ZACCHUR in I Chr. 4:26; ZABBUD zăb'ŭd [*Kethibh*, זבור] in Ezra 8:14; BACCHURUS bă kyŏor'əs [Βακχοῦρος] in I Esd. 9:24. **1.** An individual or family of the tribe of Reuben (Num. 13:4).

2. A family or clan of Simeon (I Chr. 4:26), descended from Mishma, which in Gen. 25:14; I Chr. 1:30 is an Ishmaelite name. Perhaps this family was a commingling of Simeonites and nomads of N Arabia.

3. A Levite, descendant of Merari; son of Jaaziah (I Chr. 24:27).

4. A postexilic family of singers of the Asaph group (I Chr. 25:2, 10; Neh. 12:35).

5. A descendant of Bigvai named with Uthai as

accompanying Ezra on the return from Babylon (Ezra 8:14); or, emending on the basis of "Uthai the son of Istalcurus" in the parallel (I Esd. 8:40), the father or other ancestor of Uthai. *See* ISTALCURUS.

6. A postexilic temple singer among those forced to put away foreign wives and children (I Esd. 9:24). The name is omitted from the parallel in Ezra 10:24.

7. Son of Imri; one of those who helped to rebuild the walls of Jerusalem (Neh. 3:2).

8. A postexilic Levite among those who signed the pledge of reform (Neh. 10:12).

9. A name tracing the descent of Hanan, appointed assistant treasurer by Nehemiah (Neh. 13:13).

Bibliography. M. Noth, *Die israelitischen Personennamen* (1928), pp. 38, 186-87; D. Diringer, *Le iscrizioni antico-ebraiche palestinesi* (1934), pp. 204-5.   T. M. MAUCH

ZACHARIAH, ZACHARIAS, ZACHARY, ZACHER. KJV alternate forms of ZECHARIAH.

ZADOK zā'dŏk [צָדֹק [ק(ו)], righteous; NT Σαδώκ]; KJV Apoc. SADDUC săd'ək; KJV NT SADOC sā'dŏk. **1.** Leader of one of the divisions of armed troops which came to Hebron to turn the kingdom of Saul over to David (I Chr. 12:28). Josephus (Antiq. VII.ii.2) equates him with Zadok the priest, but it is not certain that this is the Chronicler's intention.

2. *See* ZADOK THE PRIEST.

3. Grandfather of Jotham king of Judah (II Kings 15:33; II Chr. 27:1); possibly the same as 4 *below*.

4. A descendant of Zadok the priest (I Chr. 6:12—H 5:38; 9:11; Neh. 11:11). But the similarities between these genealogies and those of the earlier Zadok cast doubt on their trustworthiness.

5. A descendant of Baana who repaired a section of the Jerusalem wall at the time of Nehemiah (Neh. 3:4; cf. Ezra 2:2).

6. A descendant of Immer who worked on the Jerusalem wall (Neh. 3:29; cf. Ezra 2:37).

7. A signer of the covenant of Ezra (Neh. 10:21). Probably the name has been added here from the list of builders in ch. 3.

8. A scribe appointed treasurer by Nehemiah (Neh. 13:13; cf. the list in Neh. 3:29, where three of the names which appear here, including Zadok, are found in the same order).

9. An ancestor of Jesus (Matt. 1:14).
          R. W. CORNEY

*ZADOK THE PRIEST. Priest of David. His descendants gained control of the priesthood of the Jerusalem temple. Zadok first appears, together with Abiathar, as priest in charge of the ark at the time of Absalom's revolt (II Sam. 15:24-37). We next hear of him as a supporter of Solomon in the dynastic struggle of David's last days (I Kings 1:22-39). After the exile of Abiathar, Zadok became the chief priest of the Jerusalem sanctuary (2:35).

1. Origin. Nowhere does the OT provide us with a clear and accurate picture of the background of Zadok. The genealogy of II Sam. 8:17, which makes Zadok a son of Ahitub and hence a descendant of ELI, is clearly the result of a textual corruption. Indeed, the prophecy *post eventum* of I Sam. 2:27-36 (cf. I Kings 2:27) makes it clear that the house of

Zadok was considered to have supplanted the house of Eli. Nor are the genealogies in Chronicles and Ezra (I Chr. 6:1-8—H 5:27-34; 6:50-53—H 6:35-38; Ezra 7:2), which treat Zadok as a descendant of the Aaronide house of Eleazar, any more reliable, for they repeat the error of II Sam. 8:17. *See below.*

However, it seems likely that David had a strong reason for making Zadok the equal of Abiathar, who had served his king loyally from the time of his break with Saul. This reason is doubtless related to the position occupied by Zadok before he entered the service of David.

a. Gibeon. According to I Chr. 16:37-41 there were two important sanctuaries at the time of David—one at Jerusalem, to which David moved the ark, and a second at Gibeon, where the tabernacle was to be found. It was at the latter that Zadok is said to have officiated. Though the historicity of the passage is debatable, it may be argued that it preserves a genuine memory of a connection between the Gibeon shrine and Zadok. Perhaps as part of David's program for making Jerusalem the focal point for the loyalty of the twelve tribes he installed the Gibeonite priest Zadok as one of the chief priests at Jerusalem, even as he brought the ark up from Kiriath-jearim. In support of this theory it is pointed out that after the exile of Abiathar not only was Zadok made the sole chief priest, but also Solomon went to Gibeon to sacrifice (I Kings 3:4).

b. Kiriath-jearim. To account for the connection between Zadok and the ark, it has been suggested that Zadok was a priest with the ark at Kiriath-jearim. He is identified as the brother of Uzzah, the son of Abinadab, who helped bring the ark to Jerusalem (II Sam. 6:3, reading "his brother" for "Ahio"). This theory can be combined with that of Zadok's Gibeonite origin by assuming that the house of Abinadab had moved from Gibeon to Kiriath-jearim after the ark had been returned by the Philistines.

c. Jerusalem. The most probable theory is that Zadok was the priest of the Jebusite sanctuary at Jerusalem when the town was captured by David, and that David permitted him to retain his priestly function in order to help reconcile the old inhabitants to their new master. The name Zadok seems to have had a special association with pre-Israelite Jerusalem. Adoni-zedek was the king of Jerusalem at the time of Joshua (Josh. 10:1, 3), and Melchizedek was its priest-king to whom Abraham gave a tithe of all he possessed (Gen. 14:17-20). The latter story may well be an etiological legend to justify the retention of the Jebusite Zadok by David; David was doing no more than Abraham had done before him. Melchizedek also appears in Ps. 110:4, where reference is made to an everlasting priesthood "after the order of Melchizedek" (cf. I Sam. 2:35, where the "faithful priest" who is to replace Abiathar is to be priest "for ever").

If Zadok was a Jebusite, it might explain why he supported Solomon instead of Adonijah for successor to David. Those who followed Adonijah had been companions of David in the early struggles of his career; the backers of Solomon appear for the first time in connection with the court at Jerusalem. Perhaps the former desired a king who would rule in accord with the old Israelite tribal ideals, while the latter desired a more powerful, centralized monarchy based on the common oriental pattern—a desire probably shared by the non-Israelite Zadok.

2. The descendants of Zadok. The triumph of Solomon meant the triumph of Zadok; his descendants became the dominant priestly family in Jerusalem. Solomon appointed one of his sons priest (I Kings 4:2); Hezekiah's chief priest Azariah was "of the house of Zadok" (II Chr. 31:10). The more Jerusalem became the center of national life, the greater was the prestige of the Zadokites.

The fortunes of the Zadokites after the Exile are reflected in the position given to Zadok in Ezekiel and Chronicles. In the plan for the restoration of the temple and its worship given in Ezek. 40–48, the exiled Zadokites expect as the reward for their faithfulness to Yahweh that they alone shall perform the priestly functions in the new temple; the rest of the Levites are to be reduced to the status of servants (Ezek. 40:46; 43:19; 44:15; 48:11). Chronicles shows that after the Return this program was not put into practice, for we find Zadok enrolled in the larger priestly family of Aaron. But the Chronicler reserves for the family of Zadok the position of chief or "anointed" priest by placing him in the family of Eleazar, Aaron's eldest son (I Chr. 6:1-8—H 5:27-34; 6:50-53—H 6:35-38; 24:3; Ezra 7:2; I Esd. 8:2; cf. I Chr. 29:22, where it is stated that when Solomon was anointed king, Zadok was anointed priest).

See also PRIESTS AND LEVITES.

Bibliography. W. R. Arnold, *Ephod and Ark* (1917), pp. 61-62; R. H. Kennett, *OT Essays* (1928), pp. 82-90; E. Auerbach, "Die Herkunft der Saḏokiden," *ZAW*, VIII (1931), 327-28; H. H. Rowley, "Zadok and Nehushtan," *JBL*, LVIII (1939), 113-41; R. H. Pfeiffer, *Introduction to the OT* (1948), pp. 263, 555-57; H. H. Rowley, "Melchizedek and Zadok," *Festschrift Alfred Bertholet* (1950), pp. 461-72.   R. W. CORNEY

ZADOKITE FRAGMENTS ză′də kīt. The remains from two medieval copies of a sectarian manual in Hebrew, which were found in 1896-97 and are now in the possession of the Cambridge University Library, England. They were related to different Jewish groups like the Pharisees, the Sadducees, or the Dositheans. However, the famous MS finds in the caves near the Dead Sea (*see* DEAD SEA SCROLLS) have proved that the original Zadokite work was composed and used in an Essene community. Along with the other Essene writings, the Zadokite Fragments are very important for a better understanding of the main trends in Jewish piety at the time of Jesus and of early Christianity itself. Fig. ZAD 1.

A. Name
B. Condition
C. Author
D. Contents
  1. The admonition
    a. The course of history
    b. The goal of history
    c. The preparation for this goal
  2. The law
E. The Community
  1. Organization
  2. Life

F. Historical conclusions
Bibliography

A. *NAME.* "Zadokite Fragments" is one of the titles for an old Jewish writing whose original name is unknown. It was discovered in 1896-97 in the Genizahi—a repository for sacred MSS which were no longer suitable for use—of the Ibn-Ezra Synagogue at Old Cairo, along with other MSS written by the Karaites. The Karaites ("readers" [of the law]) were a Jewish sect flourishing in the Middle Ages, which rejected the rabbinic tradition of the Talmud, restricted itself to the study of the Scriptures alone, and therefore held old, prerabbinical writings in a high esteem.

From S. Zeitlin, *Jewish Quarterly Review;* by permission of Dropsie College for Hebrew and Cognate Learning

1. A page from the Zadokite Fragments, from the Cairo Genizah collection in the library at Cambridge University

S. Schechter, who edited these fragments in 1910, called them "Fragments of a Zadokite Work," because he believed that "their text is constituted of fragments forming extracts of a Zadok book," and he related them to the Dositheans, a sectarian offshoot of the Sadducees. This theory, however, is erroneous.

Since the community of this script called itself the "New Covenant in the Land of Damascus" (6.19; 8.21; cf. 20.12), in Germany its writing is usually called *Damaskusschrift,* in France *Écrit de Damas* or *Document de Damas.* The abbreviation for quotations is "CD"; sometimes "CDC" or "Dam" is still found.

The name Zadokite Fragments, however, is right insofar as the name Zadok is mentioned there. Zadok is said to have revealed the Law, which was hidden in the ark of the covenant after the death of Eleazar, Joshua, and the elders, and therefore unknown even to King David (5.2-5). This statement certainly refers to the report in II Kings 22, according to which the priest Hilkiah discovered the Law in the temple and gave rise to the religious reform under King Josiah in 622 B.C. The sect, however, seems to have ascribed this important deed to Zadok, the chief priest under Solomon and ancestor of the priests of the sect. These priests emphasized their Zadokite origin by reference to Ezekiel, according to whom only the Zadokites are the legitimate priests for the perfect and final worship at the temple (cf. the explanation of Ezek. 44:15 in CD 3.21–4.5). They also claimed to live in a new era of rediscovering the Law. They shared this conviction with the community of the DEAD SEA SCROLLS. Although the name Damascus is not mentioned in these scrolls, the "Sons of Zadok" occur in the Manual of Discipline as the priests of the sect (1QS 5.2, 9; cf. 9.14 and 1QSa 1.2, 24; 2.3; 1QSb 3.22). The use of this name may have been extended also to the lay members of the community, since they all, the "elect of Israel," as those who participated in the holy service of God, were "Sons of Zadok" (5.3). This gave rise to a purposeful play on the words "Zadok" and *zedek* ("righteousness"): the "Sons of Zadok" were the "Sons of Zedek"—i.e., the true worshipers of God (cf. 1QS 9.14).

B. CONDITION. The fragments consist of two parts. To the first (text A) belong eight leaves of parchment measuring 8½ by 7½ inches and written on both sides. These sixteen pages of twenty-one to twenty-three lines each were written in the tenth century A.D., while the second part (text B), consisting of one great leaf with two pages of thirty-five lines each, is of a later date, perhaps the eleventh or twelfth century. Text A presents on its first eight pages a long admonition revealing the eschatological mission of the sect, and on the last eight pages a collection of laws ruling its life. The admonition is better preserved than the laws, for pp. 13-16 are badly mutilated, and sometimes the scribe gave only the headings of a new law collection (12, 19-22; 13, 20). But text A also is incomplete. This is proved in that text B presents on its first page (B 19) a text parallel to the last part of the admonition in text A (7.15-8. 21), while the content of the second page (B 20) is not given in text A. On the other hand, A 7.10-20 is omitted in text B. Also, the beginning and the end of both parts, admonition and laws, seem to have been lost. They can probably be partially reconstructed with the aid of some fragments found in the Qumran caves IV and VI. The largest of these fragments offers a text corresponding to A 5.18–6.2. In cave IV have been found fragments of seven copies of the Zadokite work, some of them containing passages hitherto unknown. The number of copies used in Qumran reveals the importance of this work for the sectarians who lived there.

C. AUTHOR. The traces of authorship are scarce. The preacher in the admonition claims to impart a new revelation to his hearers, whom he addresses as "sons" (2.14). This term indicates the intimate and esoteric character of his message and points to the position of the speaker. He is a teacher who in the Thanksgiving Psalms compares his disciples to his sons or to children at the breasts of a nurse (1QH 7.2), and more precisely he can be the "overseer of the camp," who has to love its members as a father loves his sons (13.7-9). The overseer is the primary authority in explaining the exact meaning of the

Torah (13.5). He also gives insight into the mighty deeds of God and even foretells future events in detail (13.8). This task precisely is fulfilled in the two parts of our writing. The admonition illuminates both the present and the imminent future, by drawing a lesson from God's mighty deeds in the past, and the laws of the sect represent the exact meaning of the Torah. Thus the Zadokite Fragments have their setting in the catechetical practice of the sect. They were used as a manual to teach applicants and members the aims and customs of this community.

D. CONTENTS. 1. The admonition. a. The course of history. At the beginning of his revelation the teacher calls attention to an important statement. He says:

> And now, hearken all ye that know righteousness
> and consider the works of God,
> for He hath a controversy with all flesh
> and He executes judgment upon all that despise Him.
> Whenever Israel sinned in that they forsook Him,
> He hid His face both from them and from His sanctuary
> and gave them to the sword.
> But when He remembered the covenant
> which He had made with their forefathers,
> He caused a remnant to remain for Israel
> and did not consign them to utter extinction (1.1-5).

His summons strongly recalls the law of history which was recognized by the Deuteronomist and used in his work (cf. Judg. 2:13-23). But this law undergoes change at his hand: For the Deuteronomist, Israel as a whole is punished for its disloyalty and saved by its conversion; but the preacher of the sect knows salvation for only a small part of it, the remnant. This reveals his sectarian standpoint, according to which faithfulness belongs to the few, while the many always forsake God.

The teacher expounds this point of view by going through the Scriptures "from old times until now" (2.17). His arguments, however, are not well ordered or easily understood. The introduction, in which he speaks of a "right-teacher," his followers, and his foes, is rather veiled. It probably refers to the origin of the sect. In 2.2 ff, however, he goes into the remote past. The history of sin and punishment starts with the fall of the angels, who "walked in the stubbornness of their hearts" and therefore did not keep the commandments of God (2.17-18). The sin of the angels penetrated all mankind. It led astray the sons of Noah (3.1), the sons of Jacob and their descendants in Egypt (3.4-5), the generation of Moses in the desert (3.7-8), and the people in the promised land (3.9-10).

On the other hand, there always existed an unbroken line of pious ones. Piety and sin are related to the covenant: piety means faithfulness to the covenant and keeping its orders; sin is leaving it and transgressing the boundaries of the law. God's covenant is an eternal one (3.13), but the way of keeping it differs in the subsequent periods of time. This is because God reveals his will to the elect—i.e., the true meaning of the Torah in their own time. Every successive stage of revelation opens up a new era of the covenant, which can then be called a new one. It is characterized by outstanding men who are called by God to receive and preach his revelation. One can reconstruct seven eras connected with these names:

(a) Noah (3.1); (b) the patriarchs (3.2-3); (c) Moses and Aaron (5.17-18); (d) Eleazar, Joshua, and the elders (5.3-4); (e) Zadok (5.5); (f) the right-teacher of the sect (1.11); (g) the right-teacher of the messianic age (6.11). The seventh stage is a sabbatical one which corresponds to the time before the Fall when Abraham and Enoch lived close to God and were taught by the angels.

b. The goal of history. The sect does not think merely in cycles but knows a development of history toward the end which God has determined for it. God's will and knowledge comprehend all ages, working secretly "from the day of eternity" (2.7) and appearing triumphantly at the end of days. Nothing happens in heaven and on earth which is not ordered and predetermined by God. Before man comes into existence, God has chosen him, or knows his wicked deeds in the future (2.7-8). Both the elect and the sinners are separated into two large groups, the "lots," which are headed by Belial and the "Prince of Light," and these two supreme angels are the acting forces in history (5.17-19). This theory of predestination, though leaving God's sovereignty, does not exclude the responsibility of man. Even a member of the sect can fail and transgress the limits of the law (20.25), which alone can protect him against the aggressive force of evil (16.5). This struggle against temptation will end in the messianic age. The sect is waiting for two messiahs, one of Aaron and one of Israel (19.10-11; 20.1; 12.23; cf. 1QS 9.11; the singular in the CD passages is due to a change by the Karaite copyist). The messiah of Judah is the victorious fighter against the enemies of God (7.20; cf. Num. 24.17), and the messiah of Aaron probably is identical with the last right-teacher at the end of days (6.11). While the wicked will be punished, the elect will live "in the House of the Law" (20.10, 13)—i.e., in an order where the law is fully revealed and perfectly done.

c. The preparation for this goal. Until this messianic age the law has to be studied in order to be understood, for many things are hidden in it (3.14; cf. 1QS 5.11-12; Deut. 29:28). The teacher of the sect compares the law to a well of living water for which man has to dig (6.3-4; cf. 3.16-17)—i.e., he has to study and find out the exact meaning of God's will. Both human effort and divine illumination are needed for revelation. Thus the faithful of the Mosaic age "digged a well for many waters" (3.16), and God revealed "hidden things concerning which all Israel had gone astray" (3.14). Here the expositor of the sect refers to the song of the well (Num. 21:18), as he shows (6.3-11), where he quotes and explains it allegorically. He shows the members of the sect digging the well of the Law. Among them especially the "Staff" (*Meḥôqēq*) performs this task. He is not only the "Searcher of the Law," but also the "Lawgiver"—a play on the word *meḥôqēq*="staff" is made) —for precisely by searching in the Book of the Law he finds out new commandments, which form the halachah for this era (6.10). The time of Moses represents the great ideal for the sect: Its teacher is a second Moses, and with his followers he even performs a kind of exodus like Moses and his people. But this exodus leads into the opposite direction, since the members of the sect "went out from the

Land of Judah and sojourned in the Land of Damascus" (6.5). It is justified by the passage in Amos 5:26-27, where the prophet announces the terrible way into the exile "beyond Damascus." This dark oracle is explained allegorically as a word of salvation for the sect and is a fine example of the way it digs in the Law. Very often the sect uses the Hebrew words in a double sense, a spiritual and a real one. The exodus too has its real and spiritual aspect, for going away from Judah means turning away from impiety (6.5) and returning to the law (15.9; 16.1-2; cf. 1QS 5.8-9). Together with the members of the sect, God leads the law into exile (7.14-15), but exiling (*gālâ*) the law also means to reveal and establish it anew for the new covenant in the "Land of Damascus" where the "Searcher of the Law" does his work (7.18-19).

2. The law. The divine law is the very heart of the sect's life and teaching. The oath by which every member binds himself to the covenant and which resembles the Shema, obliges one "to return to the Law of Moses with all one's heart and with all one's soul" (15.9-10; 16.1-2; cf. 1QS 5.8-9). Every Jew outside the sect is considered to live outside the law. "He goes astray," because he does not know the "exact meaning of the Law" (6.14), which can be found only by the research in the sect (cf. the parallelism of "exact meaning" and "finding" [6.18-19]). The sect is aware of the interim validity of its interpretation when compared with the eventual knowledge in the messianic age, but still contends strongly for it. It inveighs against false teachers, calling them in biblical terms "removers of the boundary" (5.20) or "removers of the landmark" (1.16) and "searchers of smooth things" (1.18; cf. 1QH 2.32). This offense refers to a lax interpretation of the law, and one may think of the Pharisees who tried to accommodate the Mosaic law to actual conditions of the moment. But the main enemies of the sect are the official priests at Jerusalem. They belong to the lot of the wicked, for they are caught in "three nets of Belial" (4.15)—i.e., three main sins: whoredom, wealth, and conveying uncleanness to the sanctuary (4.17-18). They all originate in a wrong interpretation of the law, whereby "whoredom" means allowing divorce or marrying a niece (4.20–5.6), "wealth" an unjust handling of the vows to the sanctuary (6.15-17), and uncleanness a wrong teaching of CLEAN AND UNCLEAN (6.17) and especially the profanation of the holy times by use of a false calendar (6.18-19). The last point is very important. The sect had its own calendar (cf. 3.13-15; 16.2-4), and it was certainly the solar calendar which is found in the Dead Sea Scrolls (1QS 10.1-8; 1QH 11.6-8; 1QM 2.2), in the book of Jubilees (6:23-32), and in the book of Henoch (72-82). Of course, it was impossible for the sect to live together with the Jews in general, who used a calendar based upon the phases of the moon; and this fact necessarily leads to the supposition that all these writings belong to the same religious group.

The laws listed in the legal code do not differ much from the Pharisaic halachah of that time, but many of them reveal the sect's tendency to rigorism. There are regulations regarding the oath (9.9-10; 16.10-12) and vows (16.13-19), the ritual purification with water (10.10-13), and especially the sabbath

(10.14–11.18). These sections all carry headings, while other prescriptions for the holy life of the sect are offered in a rather loose order (11.19–12.22).

E. *THE COMMUNITY*. 1. Organization. More revealing for the character of the sect are the orders pertaining to its administration, given largely in cols. 13–16.

The members of the community lived in "camps" (12.23; 13.7, 13; 14.3), following the example of Israel in the wilderness (cf. Num. 2) and expecting the holy war at the end of times which is prescribed in the War Scroll of Qumran. They are grouped together in military units of ten, fifty, a hundred, and a thousand, like Israel's army (12.22–13.2; cf. 1QS 2.21-2), and they call themselves "men of war" (20.14). Each camp is headed by an overseer (*məbaqqēr*) who has to examine the applicants (13.11-13; 15.11) and novitiates (15.14), to teach the members (13.7-8), and to decide in difficult cases of various kinds (9.22; 13.5-6; 13.15-17). There also exists an "overseer of all the camps" (14.9-11). The institution of overseers seems to have been derived from the administration of Israel ordered by Jethro and Moses at Mount Sinai (Exod. 18). It also foreshadows the task of the bishop (*episkopos*=overseer) in the early Christian church.

For juridical cases the community has its own court, to which belong four priests and six laymen (10.5-6). They have to be instructed in the "Book of Meditation" (10.6), which seems to be a collection of basic rules, won by meditation of the Torah, and used as a kind of Mishna beside the Law itself (14.7-8).

Along with the court there is the general assembly of the full members (the "Many" [13.7]) of the sect (12.19), who live dispersed among the cities of Israel under the guidance of a priest (14.6-7).

The sect has four different classes: the priests, the Levites, the children of Israel, and the proselytes (14.3-6; cf. 4.2-4). This corresponds to the order of Israel in general and of the community (*yaḥadh*) in the Manual of Discipline (1QS 2.19-21). The priests, having taken the initiative at the exodus (4.2-3), are the leading element in the sect, and even the smallest unit of it is guided by a priest (13.2-3; cf. 1QS 6.3-8). A Levite might replace him (13.3-4), but otherwise the role of the Levites is unimportant.

2. Life. The priestly element pervades the whole sect. All its members, expecting the adventure of God, strive to perform a permanent holy service. In addition to the Levitical duties prescribed in the Priestly Code of the Pentateuch, the holy service of the sect is characterized by the eschatological order of worship given in the last chapters of Ezekiel. Its laws are sometimes modified and spiritualized. But the sect does not participate in the temple worship at Jerusalem, because it believes that this sanctuary is polluted by the unclean priesthood functioning there. Therefore, it entered upon the exodus to build up a brotherhood of holy worshipers for God. The significant features of the community must be derived from its holy service. Hence the strong tendency to chastity—the order for the camps mentions wives (7.6-7), but sexual intercourse seems to be allowed only for begetting children, and is forbidden "in the

city of the sanctuary" (12.1-2). The brotherhood also becomes defiled by striving for money or by hate and envy of the brother (cf. 6.11-7.6; 8.5-7). Thus it realizes a strong fellowship of love (6.20-21; 9.2-8, interpreting Lev. 19:17-18), of special care for orphans and lonely ones (14.14-17), and of large contributions to the welfare fund (14.14). However, a strict and moneyless economy, as is told of the ESSENES, does not exist here.

F. *HISTORICAL CONCLUSIONS*. The Zadokite Fragments are closely related to the Dead Sea Scrolls, especially to the Manual of Discipline and its attached rule (1QSa). These writings belong to the same sect which had its center at Qumran and was called from outside "the Essenes"—i.e., the pious ones. The differences between these writings are due mainly to the fact that the Manual is written for the closed Essene community at Qumran (the *yaḥadh*), while the Zadokite Fragments are concerned with those Essenes who settled in different camps and cities of Palestine. They, representing the second order mentioned by Josephus (War II.viii.13), were usually married and lived a less monastic life than was possible at Qumran.

From this we can try to approach the difficult problem of the history of the sect. It is bound up with the person of the "right-teacher" and with the term "Land of Damascus."

The founder of the sect is called the "right-teacher," just as the key figure in the *pesharim* of the Qumran sect. In the Zadokite Fragments this title seems to be used for the principal true teacher in each period of revelation. Thus the founder of the sect is the right-teacher in the present period of wickedness, and there will appear a right-teacher at the end of the days (6.11). The right-teacher of the sect is certainly identical with the "Searcher of the Law" who came to Damascus (7.19) and gave there the rules for fulfilling the law in the present age (6.9-11). According to MS B, this teacher, whose title is slightly different (cf. the terms in 20.1 and 20.14), is dead already (19.35; 20.14).

This man probably is the same as the right-teacher of the *pesharim*. The Zadokite Fragments tell nothing about his controversy with the "wicked priest," mentioning only the "man of lie" (20.15; cf. 1Qp Hab. 2.1-2; 5.11), who must have been a very serious opponent, since Fragment B admits that a part of the members of the sect "have returned with him" (20.14-15)—i.e., have forsaken the sect.

The Fragments offer some dates which seem to give a key to the historical problems. According to 1.5-8, 390 years after the fall of Jerusalem by Nebuchadnezzar, God "has caused to grow forth a root of cultivation, to possess the land." This refers to a group of penitents for whom God 20 years later raised the right-teacher (1.10-11). From the death of the teacher until the final judgment, forty years will elapse (20.14-15). These numbers are probably all derived from the Scriptures—the 390 years from Ezek. 4:5, the 20 years from Neh. 1:1, while the 40 years are the period of one generation and the time of Israel's sojourn in the wilderness. If we reckon another 40 years for the active life of the teacher, we get 490 years altogether, and this is exactly the time given in Dan. 9:2, 24 (cf. Test. Levi 16:1) as the period between the catastrophe under Nebuchadnezzar and the final judgment. Thus all these figures certainly have a symbolic meaning. But besides this they may also indicate roughly the history of the sect, pointing into the second or first century B.C.

The term "Damascus" too has to be understood in its real, geographical sense. It has sometimes been suggested that Damascus is merely a veiled designation of Qumran. But since Qumran is situated in the area which is called "wilderness of Judah," it would be unlikely to speak of the sect as having left the land of Judah for sojourn in the land of Damascus (= Qumran; cf. 6.5). Moreover, in the exegesis of Amos 5:26-27 in 7.15-18, almost every word of the quotation is explained allegorically except the term "Damascus," which means that it has to be understood literally. Probably the exodus to the land of Damascus took place in the time of King Alexander Janneus (103-78 B.C.; see JANNEUS, ALEXANDER), when the Seleucid Demetrius III, reigning at Damascus, after unsuccessfully assisting the pious Jews to revolt against their despotic king, left them to the king's cruelty. According to Josephus (Antiq. XIII; XIV.2), eight thousand Jews left Judea suddenly, and many of them could have gone to the "Land of Damascus" under Demetrius' protection. After the king's death they returned, and some of the Essenes among them may have gone to Qumran and vicinity, where others already lived. There the term "Damascus" probably had an allegorical meaning also. Unfortunately, it is not known. It may have been connected with the number of the word *dmsk*, which is 444, or the term *maskeh* ("drink"), being the most solemn ceremony of the sect (1QS 6.23) and besides this used for teaching and revelation (cf. the "drink of knowledge" [1QH 4.11]). The "Land of Damascus" would have been then a figure for the "land of the drink"—i.e., of teaching God's revealed truth—whereby "d" is taken as Aramaic "of" and "s" replaced by "š." Another historical conclusion might be drawn from 8.11, where it is mentioned that the "head of the kings of Javan" will take vengeance upon the enemies of the sect. This probably refers to the intervention of Pompey, who started from Damascus to Jerusalem and took it in 63 B.C. This year would then be the *terminus a quo* for the composition of this writing, and the *terminus ad quem* is A.D. 68, when the scrolls were hidden in the caves. As the author was still awaiting the final judgment, which was expected forty years after the death of the teacher, his writing must have occurred in the second half of the first century B.C.

Bibliography. S. Schechter, *Documents of Jewish Sectaries,* I: *Fragments of a Zadokite Work* (1910); L. Rost, *Die Damaskusschrift* (1933); H. H. Rowley, *The Zadokite Fragments and the Dead Sea Scrolls* (1952); S. Zeitlin, *The Zadokite Fragments* (Facsimile of the MSS; 1952); C. Rabin, *The Zadokite Documents* (1954). *See also* the bibliography under DEAD SEA SCROLLS.
O. BETZ

ZAHAM zā'hăm [זהם, loathing] (II Chr. 11:19). A son of King Rehoboam.

ZAIN zā'ən (Heb. zä'yĭn) [ז, z (*zayin*)]. The seventh letter of the Hebrew ALPHABET as it is placed in the KJV at the head of the seventh section of the acrostic psalm, Ps. 119, where each verse of this section of the psalm begins with this letter.

ZAIR zā'ər [צעיר, smallness; a narrow pass(?)]. A place the location of which is unknown, unless it is identical with ZIOR, which may be Si'ir, *ca.* five miles N-NE of Hebron, as is sometimes suggested (the LXX B reads Σειώρ, Seior). On the basis of the implications of the text, it is more likely that one should look for Zair closer to Edom, perhaps S of the Dead Sea.

It was at Zair that Jehoram (or Joram) of Judah (*ca.* 849-842) met the Edomites in a night raid. Though his chariotry launched a successful initial attack, his army did not press the attack but deserted, so the Edomite revolution succeeded (II Kings 8: 20 ff). In the parallel passage (II Chr. 21:8-10) no place is mentioned.   V. R. GOLD

ZAKKUR zăk'ər. The spelling of ZACCUR 5 in early editions of the RSV.

ZALAPH zā'lăf [צלף, caper-plant (*cf.* New Heb. צלף)] (Neh. 3:30). The father of Hanun, who helped repair the wall of Jerusalem in the time of Nehemiah.

Bibliography. M. Noth, *Die israelitischen Personennamen* (1928), p. 231.

ZALMON zăl'mən [צלמון]. 1. An Ahohite who was among the Mighty Men of David known as the "Thirty" (II Sam. 23:28). In I Chr. 11:29 he is called Ilai (עילי), which perhaps should be read "Zilai" (צילי) and construed as a hypocoristic form of "Zalmon."   E. R. DALGLISH

2. Mount Zalmon (הר צלמון), a mountain in the vicinity of Shechem. It was the source of brushwood which was cut by Abimelech and his men for the purpose of burning the Tower of Shechem (Judg. 9: 48; *see* SHECHEM, TOWER OF). Because of the proximity of Mount Gerizim to Shechem, it has usually been assumed that Zalmon was a peak of Gerizim. It is more probable that Mount Zalmon referred to another hill near Shechem, but far enough away so the Shechemites were unaware of the preparation being made to destroy them.

3. A region or mountain in Bashan(?) (Ps. 68:14 —H 68:15; KJV SALMON). Some scholars have proposed that צלמון here means "dark" or "dark place" and is not a proper name. However, the mention of the mountain of Bashan in the following verse is usually understood as referring to Zalmon. Because there is often snow on Mount Hermon, it is possible that the psalmist has reference to an unusually heavy snowfall which occurred at a time when the enemies of the Hebrews were being defeated in battle. It is also possible that the snow may be a figure of speech alluding to a mountain in Bashan which was covered with the bleached bones of the slain.   W. L. REED

ZALMONAH zăl mō'nə [צלמנה, dark, shady] (Num. 33:41-42). The first stopping place of the Israelites after they left Mount Hor and before they reached Punon. The place cannot be identified. It may be the name of a wooded mountain, as is Zalmon in Judg. 9:48; Ps. 68:14.   J. L. MIHELIC

ZALMUNNA. *See* ZEBAH AND ZALMUNNA.

ZAMBIS zăm'bĭs. KJV Apoc. form of AMARIAH 8.

ZAMBRI. KJV Apoc. form of ZIMRI 2.

ZAMOTH. KJV Apoc. alternate form of ZATTU.

ZAMZUMMIM zăm zŭm'ĭm [זַמְזֻמִּים; *cf.* Arab *zamzamah, a distant sound, confused and continued, or inarticulate speech uttered while eating*]. The apparently contemptuous name which the Ammonites employed for their precursors in the Transjordan territory they came to occupy. Hitherto suggested etymologies are not completely satisfying, and we have no parallels for the name in the onomastic data for the second millennium B.C. The frequent identification with the ZUZIM in Gen. 14:5 cannot be demonstrated.

According to the Deuteronomic historian (Deut. 2:20), the Zamzummim belonged to a larger group known as the REPHAIM, who early in the second millennium suffered a severe blow at the hands of the "kings of the east" (Gen. 14:5). As descendants of the Rephaim, the Zamzummim continued to live in Transjordan following this cataclysm, and the Ammonites had to dispossess them in order to settle in the land of their choice. It would appear that the Ammonites held their precursors in high esteem, as in no other way can we explain the curious observation in Deut. 3:11 that the bed of King Og of Bashan, who is described as the only one left of the remnant of the Rephaim, could be found in Rabbah, the capital of Ammon. The bed may have been brought to Rabbah because certain Zamzummim were still living among the Ammonites in the thirteenth-twelfth centuries. It suggests a desire to venerate the memory of Og, who was beginning to assume something of the nature of a legendary hero among the Ammonites (*see* AMMON § 2*b*). Thus, it is not unlikely that the Zamzummim were responsible for a very early Ammonite tradition.

Bibliography. P. Karge, *Rephaim: Die vorgeschichtliche Kultur Palästinas und Phoniziens* (1918), pp. 148, 627, 645, 696.
G. M. LANDES

ZANOAH zə nō'ə [זָנוֹחַ]. **1.** A village of Judah in the Shephelah district of Zorah-Azekah (Josh. 15:34). In the parallel list in Nehemiah (11:30), it is noted that Zanoah was one of the cities reoccupied by Jews returning from the Exile. Hanun and the inhabitants of Zanoah were assigned the repairs of the Valley Gate in the program of reconstructing the wall of Jerusalem (Neh. 3:13).

Zanoah is identified with Khirbet Zanu' (or Zanuh), *ca.* three miles S-SE of Beth-shemesh. It is located on a hill, difficult to approach on the E, W, and N. Remains of a city wall and pottery from the period of the monarchy, as well as Byzantine and Arabic ware, have been found.

2. A town of Judah in the hill country district of Maon (Josh. 15:56; *cf.* I Chr. 4:18). The identification of Zanoah with Khirbet Zanuta, ten miles SW of Hebron, is difficult, since the site seems to date only from the Roman period and it is somewhat out of the provincial territory. Another alternative is Khirbet Beit Amra in the Wadi Abu Zenah, part of the Wadi el-Khalil, *ca.* 1¼ miles NW of Yattā

(Jutah; Josh. 15:55), a much more satisfactory location. The present Byzantine ruins on the strategically located position may cover remains of earlier occupations (as in the case of Tekoa).

Bibliography. W. F. Albright, "Topographical Researches in Judaea," *BASOR*, 18 (1925), 10-11.
V. R. GOLD

ZAPHENATH-PANEAH zăf'ə năth pə nē'ə [צָפְנַת פַּעְנֵחַ, *properly the transcription of* Egyp. *ḏd-pʾ-ntr-w.f-'nh, the god speaks and he* (the one who bears the name) *lives*] (Gen. 41:45). The name that was given to Joseph by the Pharaoh when he set Joseph in a position of high authority. The changing of names is a common feature among the biblical stories. Such a change of name was not, however, essential on the part of the Egyptian high officials. We have a number of good Semitic names among the official documents of Egypt (cf. Baal-mahar, Yanhamu, and even the Hyksos ruler Jacob-Har). There was, however, some tendency among the Hyksos to adopt Egyptian names, especially in the case of royal throne names.

There has been much discussion about the meaning of this name. The interpretation given above was first offered by Georg Steindorff in 1889 and offers a grammatically sound correspondence. The vocalization of the Hebrew form is, however, not what we would expect, but we must remember the late date of the Masoretic vocalization. Names which have this particular form do not appear in Egypt before the twelfth century at the earliest, so that this name is a good example of anachronism in the biblical account.

The LXX writing (ψονθομφανηχ) apparently reflects some other name, but so far no Egyptian prototype has been convincingly presented.
O. S. WINTERMUTE

ZAPHON zā'fŏn [צָפוֹן]. A city of Gad, situated N of Succoth (Josh. 13:27). The name probably indicates that it was a shrine of Baal-zephon, one of the chief Canaanite deities. It appears in Egyptian records of the Nineteenth Dynasty as *dapuna;* it is mentioned in one of the Amarna letters as *Sapuna,* and as the residence of a princess known as the "lady of the lions," who appeals to the Pharaoh of Egypt for help. After Jephthah had defeated the Ammonites, the Ephraimites crossed the Jordan and encamped near Zaphon, where they assailed Jephthah for not having called them to participate in his campaign; a battle ensued, probably near the place, and the Ephraimites were trounced (Judg. 12:1-6). A clan of Gad, the Zephonites (Num. 26:15) or Ziphionites (cf. Gen. 46:16), seems to have taken its name from the city.

The site of Zaphon has been identified as Tell el-Qos on the N side of the Wadi Rajeb, which commands a rich sweep of valley lands and is close to the N-S road along the valley. It is also sufficiently far from the fords of the Jordan to fit the narrative in Judg. 12.

Bibliography. N. Glueck, "Explorations in Eastern Palestine IV," *AASOR*, XXV–XXVIII (1951), pt. I, 297-300, 334-55.
S. COHEN

ZARA, ZARAH zâr'ə. KJV alternate forms of ZERAH 2.

ZARACES. KJV Apoc. form of ZARIUS.

ZARAIAS zə rā′yəs [Ζαραιας (A), B *omits*]. KJV
Apoc. form of ZERAHIAH; ZERAIAH. In I Esd. 8:2 the
name appears in the KJV but not in the RSV; it
corresponds, however, to Zerahiah in the parallel
Ezra 7:4.   C. T. FRITSCH

ZARATHUSTRA zăr′ə thōōs′trə; more accurately
ZARATHUSHTRA. The prophet of ancient Iran,
founder in the sixth century B.C. of the religion
known as Zoroastrianism (*see* PERSIA, HISTORY AND
RELIGION OF, § E) from the Greek form of his name
(Ζωροάστρης; Latin *Zoroaster*).

The exact dates of his life are controversial. According to the Zoroastrian tradition King Vishtāspa,
Zarathushtra's royal protector and patron, was converted 258 years before Alexander (the Great). If by
"Alexander" is meant the beginning of Alexander's
rule over Iran in 330 B.C., if Zarathushtra was forty-
two years old at the time of Vishtāspa's conversion
and if he lived to the age of seventy-seven, his dates
may have been 630-553. Other arguments leading to
somewhat different results can, however, be given.

Many attempts have been made to explain the
prophet's name. In recent years later forms such as
(*zrdrwšt* (*zar(a)društ;* cf. Ζαραθρούστης), *zrhwšt*
(*zar(a)hušt*), and *zr′wšt* (*zrušt<*zar(a)huštr*) have become known. These and other factors have led to the
theory that it means "he who drives camels" or "he
who can manage camels." *See bibliography.*

As to Zarathushtra's homeland and the scene of
his activities, many and diverse opinions have been
held. Certain indications seem to point to E Iran
rather than W Iran. The later commentators may
have preferred W Iran and the region of Ray(y), near
the modern capital Teheran, for reasons of prestige
rather than of historical accuracy.

Zarathushtra's meditations and teachings are contained in the Gāthās (*see* AVESTA), of which he is traditionally the author. In them he admonishes man
to side with the Good against the Evil by means of
an appeal to the individual's free decision to make
the right choice. Next the Gāthās reflect the social
and economic conditions of the people among whom
Zarathushtra lived. Insistent emphasis is put on the
merits and benefits of husbandry and cattle breeding,
and the beliefs of their practitioners and nonprac-
titioners are sharply opposed. Local areas were ruled
by chiefs who are referred to by the generic title *kavi,*
and one of them, Kavi Vishtāspa, was the first to
lend Zarathushtra official recognition and support.
The Gāthās, finally, contain such biographical data
to which the later tradition added many an em-
bellishing feature as Zarathushtra's family name
(*Spitāma*), the name of his daughter (*Pourucištā*) and
the names of *Frašaoštra* and *Jāmāspa*—according to
the tradition his father-in-law and son-in-law
respectively.

Bibliography. A. V. Williams Jackson, *Zoroaster, the Prophet
of Ancient Iran* (1899), pp. 12 ff, 147 ff, discusses the older explanations of the name. H. Lommel, *Die Religion Zarathustras*
(1930). E. Herzfeld, *Zoroaster and His World* (2 vols.; 1947).
J. Duchesne-Guillemin, *Zoroastre, étude critique avec une
traduction nouvelle des Gâthâ* (1948). W. B. Henning, *Zoroaster,
Politician or Witch-Doctor* (1949). A. D. Nock, "The Problem
of Zoroaster," *AJA,* LIII (1949), 272-85. H. W. Bailey, *Trans-*

actions of the Philological Society (1953), pp. 40-41, discusses the
meaning of the name.

The many problems connected with the general topic of
Zarathushtra and the outside world (Judaism, Greece, etc.)
are discussed by: J. Bidez and F. Cumont, *Les mages hellénisés,
Zoroastre, Ostanès et Hystaspe d'après la tradition grecque* (2 vols.;
1938). J. Bidez, *Éos ou Platon et l'Orient* (1945). W. J. W.
Koster, *Le mythe de Platon, de Zarathoustra et des Chaldéens,
étude critique sur les relations intellectuelles entre Platon et l'Orient*
(1951). J. Duchesne-Guillemin, *Ormazd et Ahriman, l'aventure
dualiste dans l'antiquité* (1953); *The Western Response to Zoroaster*
(1958).

In his *Also sprach Zarathustra,* Friedrich Nietzsche (1844-
1900) used Zarathushtra's personality, or rather his own peculiar concept of it, only as a peg on which to hang his own
philosophical speculations and his glorification of the
"*Uebermensch.*"   M. J. DRESDEN

ZAREAH. KJV form of ZORAH in Neh. 11:29.

ZAREATHITES. KJV form of ZORATHITES in I
Chr. 2:53.

ZARED. KJV form of Zered in Num. 21:12. *See*
ZERED, BROOK.

*****ZAREPHATH** zăr′ə făth [צרפת; Akkad. *Ṣariptu,*
from the verb *ṣarapu,* to dye; Gr. Σαρέπτα]; KJV
SAREPTA sə rĕp′tə in the NT. A Phoenician town
between Sidon and Tyre.

Zarephath was situated on the coast of the Mediterranean, *ca.* six miles S of Sidon. It is mentioned
in a papyrus from the fourteenth century B.C. The
town was famous for its production of excellent glassware, made from the same kind of sand which was
found near Sidon. The Akkadian name of the town
indicates that Zarephath, like Sidon and Tyre, produced dye, for which Phoenicia was famous.

The narrative in I Kings 17:8-24 tells how the
prophet Elijah was ordered by God to go to Zarephath, which belonged to the city-state of Sidon, and
dwell there for some time. He met a poor widow
whom he helped, so that her jar and her cruse were
filled till the rains came. The story is also mentioned
in Luke 4:26. In Obad. 20 Zarephath is mentioned
as part of Phoenicia. It is now called Sarafand.

A. S. KAPELRUD

*****ZARETHAN** zăr′ə thăn [צרתן]; KJV ZARETAN
zăr′ə tăn (Josh. 3:16); ZARTANAH zär′tə nə (I
Kings 4:12); ZARTHAN zär′thăn (I Kings 7:46).
A city located on the E side of the Jordan Valley.

1. History. The first reference to Zarethan occurs
in Josh. 3, where there is a description of the
stoppage of the Jordan River which enabled the
Israelites under Joshua to cross and attack the city
of Jericho. Vs. 16, which describes the extent of the
lake which was formed by the backing up of the
waters of the river, has a text that is somewhat corrupt, but it must have meant that the waters extended from the city of Adam (Tell ed-Damiyeh),
which is almost opposite Jericho, as far N as the side
(Glueck suggests "fortress") of Zarethan. It cannot
mean, as has been supposed, that Zarethan was
across the river from Adam, as obviously the waters
extended the width of the valley, and the striking
feature of the event was the distance which they
backed up.

Zarethan is again mentioned in the time of Solomon. It is described as being part of the fourth district of Solomon, which embraced areas on both sides of the Jordan, and the description shows it was not far from Beth-shan (I Kings 4:12). It was in the area between Succoth and Zarethan that Hiram, the artificer of Solomon, cast the bronze vessels for the temple (I Kings 7:46). It is generally agreed that in the parallel passage in II Chr. 4:17 "Zarethan" should be read instead of "ZEREDAH," unless the change was made to locate the casting in Cisjordan.

2. Location. From the passages given above it can be seen that Zarethan must have been a very conspicuous point, located not far from the Jordan, between Adam and Succoth. There is also a statement in the Jerusalem Talmud (Soṭ. 7.5) that it was twelve miles from Adam. The site that fits these conditions is the outstanding double site of Tell es-Sa'idiyah, *ca.* fourteen miles N of Tell ed-Damiyeh, situated in a strategic position overlooking the Wadi Kufrinjeh, and with a long history of sedentary occupation from the Chalcolithic period all the way through the time of the Israelite settlement. *See also* ZERERAH.

Bibliography. N. Glueck, "Explorations in Eastern Palestine IV," *AASOR,* XXV-XXVIII (1951), pt. I, 334-47.

S. COHEN

ZARETH-SHÀHAR. KJV form of ZERETH-SHAHAR.

ZARHITES. KJV form of ZERAHITES. *See also* ZERAH 2.

ZARIUS zâr'ĭ əs [Ζάριος] (I Esd. 1:38); KJV ZARACES zâr'ə cēs. Brother of King Jehoiakim. When the King of Egypt placed Jehoiakim upon the Judean throne, Jehoiakim rescued Zarius from Egypt (but cf. II Chr. 36:4). J. C. SWAIM

ZARTANAH. KJV alternate form of ZARETHAN.

ZARTHAN. KJV alternate form of ZARETHAN.

ZATTU zăt'ōō [זתוא; Apoc. Ζαμόθ, Ζαθοής, Ζαθθουί]; KJV ZATTHU zăth'ōō in Neh. 10:14; KJV Apoc. ZAMOTH zā'mŏth (I Esd. 9:28); ZATHOE zăth'ō ĭ (I Esd. 8:32); ZATHUI zăth'ōō ī (I Esd. 5: 12). Eponym or head of one of the lay families of which some members returned from exile (Ezra 2:8; 8:5; Neh. 7:13; I Esd. 5:12; 8:32). Some members of this family were among those who put away foreign wives and their children according to Ezra's reform banning foreign marriage (Ezra 10:27; I Esd. 9:28). The then head of this family was one of the laymen who signed the pledge of reform (Neh. 10:14).

T. M. MAUCH

ZAVAN. KJV form of ZAAVAN in I Chr. 1:42.

ZAZA zā'zə [זזא, *a short form fashioned by duplicating one sound from a full word; formed in childhood as a name of endearment*] (I Chr. 2:33). Part of the postexilic clan of Jerahmeel.

Bibliography. M. Lidzbarski, *Ephemeris für semitische Epigraphik,* II (1908), 20; M. Noth, *Die israelitischen Personennamen* (1928), pp. 40-41. T. M. MAUCH

ZEAL [קנאה, zeal, jealousy; ζῆλος, zeal, jealousy]; **ZEALOUS** [קנא, to be jealous, zealous; ζηλόω, to be zealous, jealous; ζηλεύω, to be zealous, jealous; παραζηλόω, to be overwhelmingly zealous]. The attitude of single-minded devotion to another. The difference between "zeal" and "jealousy" in the Bible is very slight, the context alone determining which is the meaning of any particular occurrence of the Greek or Hebrew expressions.

See also JEALOUSY; ZEALOT. E. M. GOOD

*ZEALOT [ζηλωτής; Aram. קנאנא, *see below*]. A term currently and particularly used to designate the more radical and warlike Jewish rebels against foreign, especially Roman, rule; but actually a term of much broader meaning. The word occurs in Luke 6:15; Acts 1:13 as a designation of one of the disciples of Jesus, called Simon the Zealot to distinguish him from Simon Peter. The Aramaic form of the name, *qan'ana,* has been preserved in "Simon the Cananaean," found in Matt. 10:4; Mark 3:18. The Hebrew root קנא, lying behind the Aramaic, means "to be jealous." The Zealot gave himself over to God to be an agent of God's righteous wrath and judgment against idolatry, apostasy, and any transgression of the law which excited God's jealousy ("jealousy" and "zeal" both having the same Hebrew root). With reference to the man who calls upon the name of God in vain, Philo writes: "He will never escape [the chastisements of men]; for there are thousands of men keeping watch, zealots of the laws [ζηλωταὶ νόμων], strictest guardians of the institutions of their fathers [τῶν πατρίων], merciless to those who would do anything to subvert these" (*On the Special Laws* 2.253). Jesus was remembered by his disciples to have acted like a "zealot" when he drove the money changers out of the temple: "Zeal [ὁ ζῆλος] for thy house will consume me" (John 2:17; cf. Ps. 69:9—H 69:10). Paul's persecution of the church was rooted in zeal for the law.

1. In postexilic Judaism
   a. Simeon and Levi
   b. Phinehas
   c. Elijah
2. Simon the Zealot
3. Paul
4. Conclusions
Bibliography

1. In postexilic Judaism. In postexilic Jewish tradition the prototypes of "zeal" were Simeon and Levi, Phinehas, and Elijah. This is essentially a priestly tradition. Phinehas, a priest, was a descendant of Levi; and Elijah, a priest, was identified in rabbinic tradition as Phinehas redivivus.

a. Simeon and Levi. Simeon and Levi were the sons of Jacob who slew the men of Shechem out of vengeance for the rape of their sister Dinah (Gen. 34:4 ff). *Ca.* the middle of the second century B.C. the story of Simeon and Levi was appealed to in efforts to stop intermarriage with Gentiles: "And thus let it not be done from henceforth that a daughter of Israel be defiled; for judgment is ordained in heaven against them that they should destroy with the sword all the men of the Shechemites because they had wrought shame in Israel. And the Lord delivered them into the hands of the sons of Jacob that they might exterminate them with the sword and execute judgment upon them, and that it might not thus again be done in Israel that a virgin of Israel should be defiled. And if there is any man who wishes in Israel to give his daughter or his sister to any man who is of the seed of the Gentiles he shall surely die, and they shall stone him with stones; for he hath wrought shame in Israel; and they shall burn the woman with fire, because she has dishonoured the name of the house of her father, and she shall be rooted out of Israel. And let not an adulteress and no uncleanness be found in Israel throughout all the days of the generations of the earth; for Israel is holy unto the Lord, and every man who has defiled (it) shall surely die: they shall stone him with stones . . . , because he has given his seed to Moloch . . . . 'See how the Shechemites . . . were delivered into the hands of two sons of Jacob, and they slew them under tortures, and it was (reckoned) unto them for righteousness. . . . And the seed of Levi was chosen for the priesthood, . . . for he was zealous [Ethiopic *kāně°ā*] to execute righteousness and judgment and vengeance on all those who arose against Israel. . . . And we remember the righteousness which the man fulfilled during his life, at all periods of the year; until a thousand generations they will record it, and it will come to him and to his descendants after him' " (Jub. 30:5-20).[1]

In other circles in the same period it was not Levi but Simeon who was given priority. The pious widow Judith prays: "O Lord God of my father Simeon, to whom thou gavest a sword to take revenge on the strangers who had loosed the girdle of a virgin to defile her, and uncovered her thigh to put her to shame, and polluted her womb to disgrace her; for thou hast said, 'It shall not be done'—yet they did it. So thou gavest up their rulers to be slain, and their bed, which was ashamed of the deceit they had practiced, to be stained with blood, and thou didst strike down . . . princes on their thrones; and thou gavest their wives for a prey and their daughters to captivity, and all their booty to be divided among thy beloved sons, who were zealous for thee [ἐζήλωσαν τὸν ζῆλόν σου], and abhorred the pollution of their blood, and called on thee for help—O God, my God, hear me also" (Jth. 9:2-4).

b. Phinehas. "While Israel dwelt in Shittim the people began to play the harlot with the daughters of Moab . . . . And behold, one of the people of Israel came and brought a Midianite woman to his family, in the sight of Moses and in the sight of the whole congregation of the people of Israel . . . . When Phinehas the son of Eleazar, son of Aaron the priest, saw it, he rose and left the congregation, and took a spear in his hand and went after the man of Israel into the inner room, and pierced both of them, the man of Israel and the woman, through her body. Thus the plague was stayed from the people of Israel" (Num. 25:1-8). Perhaps the most important single passage for understanding the theology of zeal follows immediately: "And the LORD said to Moses,

[1] R. H. Charles, ed., *The Apocrypha and Pseudepigrapha of the Old Testament* (Oxford: The Clarendon Press).

'Phinehas . . . has turned back my wrath from the people of Israel, in that he was jealous with my jealousy [בקנאו את‑קנאתי] among them, so that I did not consume the people of Israel in my jealousy [בקנאתי]. Therefore say, 'Behold, I give to him my covenant of peace; and it shall be to him, and to his descendants after him, the covenant of a perpetual priesthood, because he was jealous [קנא] for his God, and made atonement for the people of Israel' " (vss. 10-13). The idea that "zeal" for God is propitiatory, and atones for sin, explains the otherwise inexplicable fanaticism and cruelty of the "zealot." Phinehas became the "zealot" prototype par excellence. In the pre-Maccabean period, Ben Sirach in his praise to the fathers, after mentioning the glory of Moses and Aaron, writes:

> Phinehas the son of Eleazar is the third in glory,
>   for he was zealous [ζηλῶσαι] in the fear of the Lord,
> and stood fast, when the people turned away,
>   in the ready goodness of his soul,
>   and made atonement for Israel.
> Therefore a covenant of peace was established with him,
>   that he should be leader of the sanctuary and of his people,
> that he and his descendants should have
>   the dignity of the priesthood for ever (Ecclus. 45:23-24).

In I Maccabees, Phinehas, "because he was deeply zealous [ἐν τῷ ζηλῶσαι ζῆλον]," was singled out as forefather of Mattathias and his sons (2:54). In Ps. 106, the tradition about Phinehas orients his zealous act around Israel's apostasy in eating sacrifices offered to the gods of the Moabites:

> Then Phinehas stood up and interposed,
>   and the plague was stayed.
> And that has been reckoned to him as righteousness
>   from generation to generation for ever
>   (vss. 30-31).

The author of I Maccabees interprets the outbreak of the national resistance to the Seleucids as motivated by the theology of "zeal" as it is expressed in the tradition of Phinehas. "Then the king's officers who were enforcing the apostasy came to the city of Modein to make them offer sacrifices . . . . But Mattathias answered and said . . . : 'Far be it from us to desert the law and the ordinances . . . .' When he had finished . . . , a Jew came forward in the sight of all to offer sacrifice upon the altar in Modein, according to the king's command. When Mattathias saw it, he burned with zeal [ἐζήλωσε] and his heart was stirred. He gave vent to righteous anger; he ran and killed him upon the altar. At the same time he killed the king's officer who was forcing them to sacrifice, and he tore down the altar. Thus he burned with zeal for the law [ἐζήλωσε τῷ νόμῳ], as Phinehas did . . . . Then Mattathias cried out . . . : 'Let every one who is zealous for the law [πᾶς ὁ ζηλῶν τῷ νόμῳ] and supports the covenant come out with me!' And he and his sons fled to the hills and left all that they had in the city" (2:15-28). Thereafter they lived outside the law of the Seleucid authorities, and supported themselves in their resistance against the Gentiles by brigandage. Thus they set the pattern for all the later "zealot-like" groups which resisted the authority of Rome, by refusing to pay taxes and living as brigands. We know of one such group of brigands who were actually known by the name "zealots" (War II.xxii.1; IV.iii.9). We do not know the history of this group, except for the part they played in the war of A.D. 66-70.

c. Elijah. Elijah had ordered all the prophets of Baal slain (I Kings 18:40; 19:10-14). This was interpreted as an act of "zeal" in later Jewish tradition; "by his zeal [τῷ ζήλῳ αὐτοῦ] he made them few in number" (Ecclus. 48:2). "Elijah because of great zeal for the law [ἐν τῷ ζηλῶσαι ζῆλον νόμου] was taken up into heaven" (I Macc. 2:58). In this tradition about Elijah the propitiatory power of "zeal" was brought into relationship with the messianic role of Elijah as expressed in Mal. 4:5-6—H 3:23-24.

How glorious you were, O Elijah, in your wondrous deeds!
. . . .
You who were taken up by a whirlwind of fire,
  in a chariot with horses of fire;
you who are ready at the appointed time, it is written,
  to calm the wrath of God before it breaks out in fury,
to turn the heart of the father to the son,
  and to restore the tribes of Jacob (Ecclus. 48:4, 9-10).

2. Simon the Zealot. In addition to Simon the Zealot, the only other instance in pre-rabbinic Judaism where the cognomen "zealot" is applied to an individual is found in IV Maccabees, where Phinehas is referred to as "the Zealot Phinehas" (τὸν ζηλωτὴν Φινεές; 18:12). Simon the Zealot, before becoming a disciple of Jesus, had probably been a member of some "zealotlike" group in the Phinehas-Maccabean tradition of zeal for the law. There are indications that a multiplicity of such groups were active in Palestine during the first century A.D. and that these groups constituted an important part of the hard core of national resistance to Rome from the time of Pompey onward.

3. Paul. Before he became a Christian, Paul was chiefly motivated by a theology of zeal for the law. We gain important insights into "zealotism" by a study of Paul's relationship to and statements about this aspect of Judaism. Paul wrote to the Galatians: "You have heard of my former life in Judaism, how I persecuted the church of God violently and tried to destroy it; and I advanced in Judaism beyond many of my own age among my people, so extremely zealous [or 'so strict a zealot'; ζηλωτής] was I for the tradition of my fathers" (Gal. 1:13-14). In another passage Paul directly connects his activity as a persecutor of the church with zeal: "as to zeal [ζῆλος] a persecutor of the church" (Phil. 3:6). Paul had been a Pharisee (vs. 5). But he had gone beyond the requirements of this party in taking on the responsibilities of being a "zealot." This interpretation of the above autobiographical statements of Paul is corroborated by the account in Acts. According to it, Paul on his last visit to Jerusalem was warned about the thousands of Jews who were "zealots" of the law (ζηλωταὶ τοῦ νόμου) and who threatened his life because they had heard that he encouraged transgression of the laws of Moses among the Jews of the Diaspora (21:20-21). Later Paul was seized in the temple by a violent crowd, dragged outside, and beaten. The crowd wanted to kill him, without waiting for a trial to weigh the charges against him, but the Roman soldiers intervened (vss. 27-36). There-

upon Paul made a speech to the crowd in which he said: "I am a Jew, . . . educated according to the strict manner of the law of our fathers [τοῦ πατρῴου νόμου], being zealous for God [ζηλωτῆς ὑπάρχων τοῦ θεοῦ] as you all are today" (22:3). In recounting his confession to God following his conversion, Paul says: "In every synagogue I imprisoned and beat those who believed in thee" (vs. 19).

The day following the unsuccessful attempt on the part of those who were "zealous for the law," to kill Paul, forty of them bound themselves by an oath to continue the effort to kill him (Acts 23:12-14). This leads to a consideration of the Sicarii, or ASSASSINS, with whom the tribune in Acts 21:38 confused Paul.

Paul's judgment upon the theology of zeal for the law is given in his discussion concerning Israel's pursuit of the righteousness which is based on law. "Brethren, my heart's desire and prayer to God for them is that they may be saved. I bear them witness that they have a zeal [ζῆλον] for God, but it is not enlightened. For, being ignorant of the righteousness that comes from God, and seeking to establish their own, they did not submit to God's righteousness. For Christ is the end of the law, that every one who has faith may be justified" (Rom. 10:1-4). In order to understand Paul, it is necessary to recognize that he came into the church out of a background in Judaism in which the current of zeal for the law ran strong. His doctrine of justification should be studied against the background of a theology in which zeal for the law was regarded as redemptive.

4. Conclusions. The theology of zeal which motivated the Zealot originated in the exclusivistic worship of the one true God of Israel: "I the LORD your God am a jealous God," and "you shall have no other gods before me." Israel was a holy people, and the law had been given to keep Israel holy unto God. Thus when Israel excited God's jealousy by her apostasy, his wrath was poured upon his people. The propitiatory act of the Zealot therefore was in a sense prophylactic. Like a surgeon excising a cancerous tissue, the Zealot extirpated the apostates from Israel with the sharp edge of the sword. Once zeal for the covenantal God of Israel was transferred to his law, which certainly happened by the Maccabean period, then the basis was laid for Zealotism as we know it in the Greco-Roman period. The Zealot was the strict interpreter of the law, who was willing to follow the way of "zeal for the law of the God of Israel" unto death (cf. Acts 22:4)—i.e., the Zealot was willing, not only to kill a Gentile, or to lay down his own life rather than transgress the law, but he was quite prepared to take the life of a fellow Israelite, if necessary, out of his zeal for the law.

The theology of zeal was gradually circumscribed by the Jewish spiritual leaders after the crushing national defeats of 70 and 135. In rabbinic Judaism zeal was replaced by "shalom" as the dominant theological motif governing Israel's relations with the Gentiles.

In Christianity zeal was redirected in terms consonant with the new theology (cf. I Cor. 14:12; Tit. 2:14; I Pet. 3:13; Rev. 3:19).

Bibliography. See the important article on "Zealots" by K. Kohler in the *Jewish Encyclopedia* (1905), where an attempt is made to trace the historical development of the Zealots from the time of Herod onward. The evidence indicating that the Maccabees were historical counterparts of the politically orientated Zealot groups in the Roman period, and the argument that these Zealot groups were inspired and motivated by the example and teaching of the Maccabees, may be found in W. R. Farmer, *Maccabees, Zealots and Josephus* (1956).

W. R. FARMER

ZEBADIAH zĕb′ə dī′ə [זבדיה, זבדיהו, Y has given; *see* ZABAD; Apoc. Ζαβδαῖος]; KJV Apoc. ZABDEUS zăb′dī əs (I Esd. 9:21). Alternately: ZERAIAH zə rā′yə [Ζαραίας] (I Esd. 8:34); KJV ZARAIAS —yəs. **1.** A Benjaminite family, descended from Beriah (I Chr. 8:15).

2. A Benjaminite family, descended from Elpaal (I Chr. 8:17).

3. One of the two sons of Jeroham who joined David at Ziklag (I Chr. 12:7).

4. A gatekeeper, of the Levitical family of Korah (I Chr. 26:2). The name occurs in an organization of gatekeepers presented as one of David's preparatory arrangements for the future temple (chs. 23-26).

5. One of David's officers in charge of one of the twelve divisions of the army which alternated service each month. He was a son of Asahel the brother of Joab (I Chr. 27:7).

6. One of nine Levites (*see* PRIESTS AND LEVITES; cf. Deut. 6:6-9; 27:11-26; 31:9-13) in a commission of sixteen men (of which only two were priests) sent by Jehoshaphat to teach the law in the towns of Judah (II Chr. 17:8). The story appears only in Chronicles.

7. The eldest of the tribe of Judah (not a royal official, as "the governor of the house of Judah" might suggest) who was the chief judicial functionary for civil cases in a similar and also higher court at Jerusalem which headed a system of local courts established by Jehoshaphat (II Chr. 19:11). Vss. 4-11 are rich in judicial data and perspectives. *See also* LAW IN THE OT § C; COURT OF LAW; JUDGE.

8. Head of a lay family who returned from Babylonia with Ezra (Ezra 8:8; I Esd. 8:34).

9. A priest in lists of those who put away foreign wives and their children according to Ezra's reform banning foreign marriage (Ezra 10:20; I Esd. 9:21).

Bibliography. M. Noth, *Die israelitischen Personennamen* (1928), pp. 21, 46-47; A. C. Welch, *The Work of the Chronicler* (1939), pp. 81-96, 129-31; W. Rudolf, *Chronikbücher*, HAT (1955), p. 257.

T. M. MAUCH

ZEBAH AND ZALMUNNA zē′bə, zăl mŭn′ə [זבח, sacrifice; צלמנע, protection withheld; *see below*]. Two Midianite kings slain by Gideon in blood revenge for their murder of his brothers (Judg. 8:4-21; Ps. 83:11—H 83:12).

The names of both these kings were probably originally Old S Arabic or Midianite names which have been distorted into their present Hebrew forms suggestive of their fate. זבח (verb, "to slaughter"; noun, "sacrifice") obviously is taken as a proper name meaning "victim which is sacrificed." צלמנע is taken as being from צל, "shadow," meaning "protection," as in Num. 14:9; Ps. 91:1; Eccl. 7:12; Jer. 48:45; Lam. 4:20, and from מנע, "to withhold" or "to deny." Thus the protection of Zalmunna's deity was fore-

gone when he fell into the hands of Gideon and his God.

The original forms of these names are not now recoverable. In Old S Arabic the root meaning of זבח is "born at the day of sacrifice." "Zalmunna" has been properly compared with the name of the priest צלמשזב, "*Ṣalm-shezeb*," "(the god) Ṣalm has been delivered," in a probably fifth-century-B.C. N Arabian Aramaic inscription from Teima. The god name "Ṣalm" may be the proper reading in Num. 14:9: not "their shadow has departed from them" (RSV "their protection is removed from them"), but "Ṣalm has departed . . . ." With צלם, "image," in Hebrew may be compared Akkadian *ṣalmu*, "image (of the god)," regarded by some as identical with the Arabic divinity Ṣalm. Thus the name Zalmunna probably comes from an originally genuine Midianite word meaning "(the god) Ṣalm is king," as though it were צלממלך.

The story of Zebah and Zalmunna is told in the early narrative of Gideon's pursuit of fleeing Midianites (Judg. 8:4-21). There seems to be an obvious parallel intended between the names of these two Midianite kings and that of the princes Oreb and Zeeb (7:24–8:3) in the later narrative, Zebah corresponding to Zeeb and Zalmunna to Oreb. Thus it has been conjectured that in Hebrew etymology both "Zebah" and "Zeeb" were from "Zebib," "the long-haired," and that Zalmunna was originally Ishmael and Oreb originally Arab.

There are both barbaric primitivity and haughty, kingly dignity in the story of Gideon and these two Midianites. Presumably Zebah and Zalmunna were leaders of the annual camel-riding raids into Israelite farming territory (Judg. 6:2-6). According to the late tradition of the psalmist these raids were for taking possession of the "pastures of God" (Ps. 83:11-12— H 83:12-13), but actually they were simply nomadic forays at harvesttime to steal the settled farmers' crops. Zebah and Zalmunna first appear in the story when Gideon was pursuing the fugitives from his surprise defeat of the Midianite camp at the foot of Mount Gilboa (Judg. 8:4). Gideon's request for help from the E Manasseh communities of Succoth and Penuel on the Jabbok River was refused. The citizens of Succoth, derisive of Gideon's possibly being victorious with only his little band of three hundred Abiezrite clansmen, inquired: "Do you already have the amputated palms of Zebah and Zalmunna in your hands as tokens of victory, that we should feed your army?" (orig. tr.). With a vow of vengeance, Gideon pressed on relentlessly.

According to the exaggerated figures, a mere 15,000 of the original 135,000 Midianites under Zebah and Zalmunna's leadership had been able to escape across the Jordan and then S to Karkor in the Valley of Sirhan E of the Dead Sea. There, more than a hundred miles from the scene of their defeat, they let their guard down. Gideon meanwhile was pushing forward up the Jabbok and S via the "caravan route east of Nobah [site unknown] and Jogbehah" (perhaps modern Jubeihat, fifteen miles SE of Penuel) to their camp.

With victory achieved and his two kingly prisoners taken, Gideon returned "by the ascent of Heres" (site unknown). After learning the names of the leading citizens of Succoth from a captured youth who could write, Gideon wreaked his primitive vengeance, as he "taught" (the verb in the MT of vs. 16 needs no emendation to "threshed") them by the torture of threshing them with thorns and briers. He later slew citizens of Penuel and broke down the tower of their evidently unwalled city.

It is at this point in the story that the personal motivation for Gideon's relentless pursuit is made clear. It was the solemn duty of blood revenge. Zebah and Zalmunna were answerable not only for raids on the countryside. They had slain Gideon's own brothers at Tabor. This reference to Tabor, not Ophrah, as apparently Gideon's home is one reason for varying interpretations as to the identity and roles of Gideon and Jerubbaal (for discussion, *see* GIDEON).

Gideon's question (Judg. 8:18), while it may be emended to: "What of the men . . . ?" contains sharp irony as it stands: "Where are the men . . . ?" The reply was that of hardy and haughty desert kings ready for their fate. As in more recent Arabian custom, the high privilege of executing blood revenge was offered to Gideon's youthful son, but he could not bring himself to raise his hand against such sacred personages as kings. Therefore Zebah and Zalmunna properly met their death at the hands of a brave, kingly person like themselves. Then Gideon relieved them of their crescents worn both by camels and by their jewelry-loving Bedouin masters (*see* CRESCENT; Isa. 3:18).

Bibliography. G. A. Cooke, *A Text-Book of North Semitic Inscriptions* (1903), pp. 195-99; K. Tallqvist, *Assyrian Personal Names* (1914), pp. 205, 260; H. Bauer, "Die israelitischen Personennamen im Rahmen der gemeinsemitischen Namengebung," *OLZ,* XXXIII (1930), 588-90. C. F. KRAFT

ZEBAIM zĭ bā′əm. KJV translation of הצבים in Ezra 2:57; Neh. 7:59. *See* POCHERETH-HAZZEBAIM.

ZEBEDEE zĕb′ə dē [Ζεβεδαῖος, *from* Aram. זבדי = Heb. זבדיה, gift of Y]. The father of the apostles James and John (Mark 1:19-20) by Salome (Mark 15:40; Matt. 27:56).

Zebedee and his sons were associated with Simon and Andrew in a fishing business at Capernaum (Mark 1:16-20; Luke 5:10). The fact that he had servants (Mark 1:20) and that his wife seems to have contributed toward Jesus' support (Mark 15:40-41; cf. Luke 8:2-3) makes it appear that he was a man of some means. The gospels offer no evidence that he actively followed Jesus, though he seems not to have hindered the activities of his wife and sons.

It is interesting that a column of the Capernaum synagogue (built *ca.* A.D. 200) bore an Aramaic inscription naming a certain son of Zebida (בר זבידה) as the maker of the column.

Bibliography. G. Dalman, *The Words of Jesus* (1902), pp. 49-50; H. L. Strack and P. Billerbeck, *Kommentar zum NT aus Talmud und Midrasch,* I (1922), 188; E. L. Sukenik, *Ancient Synagogues in Palestine and Greece* (1934), p. 72. E. P. BLAIR

ZEBIDAH zĭ bī′də [זבידה (*Kethibh*), gift] (II Kings 23:36); KJV ZEBUDAH —bū′—[זבודה]. The mother of Jehoiakim.

ZEBINA zĭ bī′nə [Aram. זבינא, purchased (*e.g., a child bought from parents*)] (Ezra 10:43). One of the Jews contemporary with Ezra who were listed as having married foreign wives. The name does not appear in the parallel I Esd. 9:35.

Bibliography. M. Noth, *Die israelitischen Personennamen* (1928), p. 231; R. A. Bowman, Exegesis of Ezra, *IB,* III (1954), 661. B. T. DAHLBERG

ZEBOIIM zĭ boi′əm [צבאים, צבים, צבוים]. One of the "cities of the valley," which were destroyed by the Lord because of their wickedness (Gen. 19:24-29). Zeboiim is mentioned in connection with the boundary of the territory of the Canaanites (10:19) and was one of the five cities attacked by Chedorlaomer and the other three Eastern kings. Shemeber king of Zeboiim, with his four allies, joined battle with these invaders in the Valley of SIDDIM and met defeat (14:2, 8, 10).

The destruction of Zeboiim is implied in the account of the overthrow of the cities of the valley (Gen. 19:24-29), and Moses recalls the overthrow of Zeboiim and the other three cities by the wrath of the Lord (Deut. 29:23). Hosea presents the fate of Zeboiim as an example (Hos. 11:8).

Zeboiim is specifically linked with Admah twice (Deut. 29:23; Hos. 11:8), and was probably situated near it, in the area now under the waters of the S part of the Dead Sea. *See* map under SODOM.

For *bibliography*, *see* CITIES OF THE VALLEY. J. P. HARLAND

ZEBOIM zĭ bō′əm [צבעים, hyenas]. **1.** One of the towns occupied by Benjaminites following the return from Babylonian captivity (Neh. 11:34). Though its location is at present uncertain, it is listed in company with Hadid, Neballat, Lod, and Ono. It should probably be sought, therefore, to the N of Lydda, possibly at Khirbet Sabieh. **2.** A valley in Benjamin, located SE of Michmash and between that city and the wilderness overlooking the Jordan (I Sam. 13:17-18). Both the ancient name and the vicinity are preserved by the modern Wadi Abu Daba' ("Valley of the Father of Hyenas" or "Hyena Valley"), a tributary of the Wadi el-Kelt. W. H. MORTON

ZEBUDAH. KJV form of ZEBIDAH.

ZEBUL zē′bəl [זבל]. A resident prefect (פקיד in Judg. 9:28; שר העיר in vs. 30) of Shechem whose prompt advice to his royal master, Abimelech son of Jerubbaal (Gideon), defeated the rebellious plot of Gaal and his adherents (Judg. 9:30-41).

Political unrest began to develop as soon as Gaal and his clan moved into the city of Shechem, and reached its climax in an incendiary speech by Gaal at a vintage festival, when he clamored that Abimelech be deposed in favor of a full-blooded Canaanite ruler and offered himself as liberator. When Zebul learned of this sedition, he informed the nonresident king immediately and advised him what action appeared best in the circumstances. Speedily Abimelech arrived at Shechem with his forces and stationed them in ambuscades about the city. In the morning, while standing in the entrance of the gate of the city, Gaal espied the troops, which were advancing from all directions, and directed the attention of Zebul to their movement. Identifying these forces as Abimelech's, Zebul twitted Gaal to make good his boasts now. When Abimelech completely routed the rebels in the ensuing battle, the cause of Gaal was lost, and Zebul expelled him and his clan from Shechem.   E. R. DALGLISH

ZEBULUN zĕb′yə lən [זְבוּלֻן, *an abbreviated form with the ending -ûn; the meaning of the element zᵉbûl is uncertain; the name of a god or an appellative for a dwelling place*]; **ZEBULUNITE** —lə nīt [זְבוּלֹנִי]. The tenth son of Jacob, and the *heros eponymos* of the tribe of Zebulun. He was a younger child of Leah (Gen. 30: 20; hence the derivation of the name from זבד, "to present," as well as from זבל, "to dwell"). In the lists of the sons he is always the last of Leah's group of six, after Issachar, with whom he belongs especially as a younger child (Gen. 35:23; 46:14; Exod. 1:3; I Chr. 2:1).

The tribe of Zebulun is closely connected in its origins with the tribe of Issachar. This is indicated, not only by its position in the scheme of Gen. 29–30 and the fact that they were neighbors geographically in S Galilee (cf. Josh. 19:10-16, 17-23), but also by the text of the Blessing of Moses, which still refers to Zebulun and Issachar together. It speaks of their economic wealth, which they drew from the sea (probably the Sea of Chinnereth) and "sand" and, in addition, of their common sanctuary, Mount Tabor, at the edge of the territory they had settled, and to which they invited the related tribes of the amphictyony for sacrificial feasts (Deut. 33:18-19).

Zebulun had, in the meantime, begun its own separate development, which enabled it to become an independent tribe, like Ephraim in relation to Manasseh. The parallel with Ephraim forces itself upon one in other respects as well; not only did Zebulun also probably take its name from a geographical factor in the territory in which it settled (a mountain? a village?), but Zebulun also had less to do there with the Canaanites than its brother tribe Issachar, so that its fate was not so negatively destined in that way as was Issachar's—for a time, at least. The territory of Zebulun lay farther off in the country than that of Issachar, which was definitely a thoroughfare. There were no older cities there, and even today it is relatively rich in forest. According to the item in the "negative inventory of possessions" (Judg. 1:30), Zebulun laid claim to the Plain of Acco, but the claim could not be realized and presumably also should not have been made to begin with. Even the old description of the boundaries in Josh. 19:10-16 knows nothing of such territorial expansion. The dwelling on the seashore of which the Zebulun passage in the Blessing of Jacob speaks (Gen. 49:13) refers, then, either to an early period in which Zebulun was still trying, along with Issachar, to become established on the Sea of Chinnereth or else to a very late period, if the reference is not just to the sojourn of a few oarsmen on the coast of the Mediterranean. The mention of the vicinity of Sidon does not argue against the first interpretation, which is the more

probable; "His border [flank] at Sidon" is to be explained without difficulty by the circumstance that the W flank of the S Galilee highland, settled by the Zebulunites, actually borders on Phoenician territory in the Plain of Acco. Zebulun lived its life apart; for this reason there were no complications in the history of its occupation of the land. For the same reason Zebulun, like Asher, had no great importance. Nevertheless, as a fully qualified member of the amphictyony, Zebulun furnished the judge Elon (Judg. 12:11-12). In the Battle of Deborah, Zebulun distinguished itself, so that it is deemed worthy of special praise by the poet and is the only tribe mentioned twice (5:14, 18; cf. also 4:6, 10). Also in the battle which Gideon fought against the Midianites in the Plain of Jezreel, Zebulun performed its duty faithfully (6:35).

Zebulun does not appear in Solomon's list of districts (I Kings 4:7 ff); the territory was added to one of the three other Galilean districts, presumably because of its inferior economic strength. Isaiah mentions the land of Zebulun along with the land of Naphtali at the time when the Assyrians made Galilee their province (Isa. 9:1—H 8:23). The naming of only the princes of Zebulun and Naphtali along with those of Judah and with Benjamin in Ps. 68: 27—H 68:28 is strange and yet probably influenced by Isa. 9:1. The later literature knows Zebulun almost exclusively in lists and similar material. It is enumerated regularly after Issachar in the Priestly Code (Num. 1:9, 30-31; 2:7; 7:24; 10:16; 26:26-27). Only in the commission for the division of the land (34:25) does Zebulun precede Issachar, and the list of the scouts puts it in an entirely different position (13:10). In Deut. 27:13, Zebulun belongs to the speakers of the curse. In the list of the cities of the Levites it is ranked in the fourth group, also separated from Issachar, once at the end (Josh. 21:7; I Chr. 6:63—H 6:48), once at the beginning (Josh. 21:34; I Chr. 6:67—H 6:62). In Ezek. 48:26, 33, it follows Issachar as usual. It is the same in the lists of Chronicles: I Chr. 12:33—H 12:34; 27:19. In the genealogies in I Chr. 4–7, Zebulun is missing, probably only because of textual deficiency (cf. Dan, also Naphtali). Otherwise the Chronicler occasionally uses "Zebulun" in paraphrases for N Israel (I Chr. 12:40—H 12:41; II Chr. 30:10 ff, 18).

In the NT, with the exception of the quotation in Matt. 4:13, 15, Zebulun appears only in the list in Rev. 7:8, after Issachar.

For the territory of Zebulun, *see* TRIBES, TERRITORIES OF, § D6. *See* the bibliography under ASHER.
K. ELLIGER

ZECHARIAH zĕk′ ə rī′ə [זְכַרְיָה, זְכַרְיָהוּ, Y has remembered; Ζαχαρίας]; KJV **ZACHARIAH** zăk′— (II Kings 14:29; 15:8, 11; 18:2); **ZACHARIAS** zăk′ə rī′əs (I Esd. 1:8, 15; 6:1; 7:3; 8:30, 37, 44; 9:27; I Macc. 5:18, 56; Matt. 23:35; Luke 1:5-67; 3:2; 11: 51). **ZACHARY** —rĭ (II Esd. 1:40). Alternately: **ZECHER** zē′kər [זֶכֶר] (I Chr. 8:31); KJV **ZACHER** ză′—. **1.** A person or family of Benjamin (I Chr. 9: 37). In the parallel list he is called Zecher, probably an abbreviation (I Chr. 8:31).

2. Head of a family of Reubenites (I Chr. 5:7).

3. A Levite gatekeeper; son of Meshelemiah (Shelemiah in vs. 14); descendant of Korah. He is presented as a keeper of the N gate in the ascription to David of arrangements for the future temple (I Chr. 26:2, 14) and as the "gatekeeper at the entrance of the tent of meeting" (9:21) in a passage which glorifies the gatekeepers (vss. 18b-26a). The latter ascription places him at the E entrance of either: the tabernacle at Gibeon, or the tent for the ark during the time of David, or the Mosaic tent (where this focal location was occupied by Moses and the priests; Num. 3:38).

4. A Levite harpist among those whom David charged to provide music during the transportation of the ark from the house of Obed-Edom to Zion (I Chr. 15:18, 20) and to maintain musical worship before the ark thereafter (16:5). *See* MUSIC.

5. One of the priests cited as blowing trumpets before the ark when David brought it to Zion (I Chr. 15:24).

6. A Levite; a descendant of Uzziel (I Chr. 24:25).

7. A gatekeeper, of the Levitical family of Merari (I Chr. 26:11).

8. A Manassite; the father of Iddo (I Chr. 27:21).

9. One of five lay officials in a commission of sixteen men sent by King Jehoshaphat to teach the law in the towns of Judah (II Chr. 17:7). Only two were priests; the majority were Levites. The story appears only in Chronicles, and it may be an ascription to Jehoshaphat of a postexilic practice.

10. A Levite; a descendant of Asaph; the father of Jahaziel (II Chr. 20:14).

11. A son of King Jehoshaphat, who gave him and his brothers great treasures and fortified cities (II Chr. 21:2). He and his brothers were slain by the first-born, Jehoram, when he became king.

12. Son of the priest Jehoiada. During the reign of Joash the Spirit of God took possession of (lit., "clothed itself with") him, and he called the people to account for their apostasy and announced the judgment of Yahweh. The people conspired against him and by the command of Joash stoned him "in the court of the house of the LORD" (II Chr. 24:20-21). Joash forgot that Zechariah's father, Jehoiada, had helped to save his life and had made him king (24:22; cf. 22:10-24:19), and two of his own servants slew Joash to avenge the death of Zechariah (24:22, 25-26). The martyrdom of Zechariah was cited by Jesus when he declared that judgment would come upon his contemporaries for the whole sequence of rejection of those sent by God (Matt. 23:35, where "son of Barachiah," the well-known prophet after the Exile [*see* 21 *below*], probably is a mistaken marginal note incorporated into the text; Luke 11:51).

13. A man of God who counseled King Uzziah in the early years of his reign (II Chr. 26:5). *See* FEAR § 2e.

14. A king of Israel; son of Jeroboam II, of the dynasty of Jehu. He became king in the thirty-eighth year of Uzziah (Azariah) king of Judah, and after a reign of only six months was murdered by Shallum, who succeeded him (II Kings 14:29; 15:8, 11). Thus the dynasty of Jehu numbered five kings, according to prophecy (15:12; cf. 10:30). The customary Deuteronomic judgment of the kings of N Israel (15:

9) is the only statement in the book of Kings concerning his rule. The rapid replacement of kings in 747-746 B.C. (*see* CHRONOLOGY OF THE OT § 3c) and the words of the prophet Hosea indicate the decay and confusion in the face of resurgent Assyria.

15. Son of Jeberechiah; one of two reliable men, evidently prominent and trusted citizens, whom Isaiah got as witnesses to a prophetic oracle written on a tablet (Isa. 8:2). Either their action added to the oracle the weight of legal formality; or, especially when it was fulfilled, they could support the evidence showing that Isaiah had indeed delivered a sign from God (cf. Deut. 18:22).

16. The father of Abijah (Abi), the mother of King Hezekiah (II Kings 18:2; II Chr. 29:1).

17. A descendant of Asaph, in a list of Levites with which the Chronicler sets forth the cleansing of the temple by Hezekiah (II Chr. 29:13).

18. A Kohathite Levite; one of four Levites who were overseers of the workmen repairing the temple in the reign of Josiah (II Chr. 34:12).

19. One of three high-ranking priests (Hilkiah is named first) who liberally donated animals to the priests for the celebration of the Passover held by Josiah (II Chr. 35:8; I Esd. 1:8).

20. The name occurring in I Esd. 1:15 instead of the Heman of II Chr. 35:15, where the names of the three chief groups of Levitical singers appear: Asaph, Heman, and Jeduthun (cf. I Chr. 25:1; II Chr. 5:12).

21. A prophet (Zech. 1:1, 7; 7:1, 8), one of the twelve Minor Prophets (cf. II Esd. 1:40). He was either a son or a descendant of Iddo. He is called the son of Iddo in Ezra 5:1; 6:14; I Esd. 6:1; and in Zech. 1:1 if "Berechiah" is a corruption of "Jeberechiah" and an insertion to identify this Zechariah with the Zechariah in Isa. 8:2 (*see* 15 *above*). "Son" may also mean "descendant"; he appears as the descendant of Iddo in Neh. 12:16 (where Iddo is a remote ancestor of Zechariah the contemporary representative of the line), and in Zech. 1:1 if Iddo is understood as a distinguished ancestor. He is not called the son of Iddo in I Esd. 7:3 (cf. Ezra 6:14). The Iddo named may be the head of a family of priests who returned with Zerubbabel (Neh. 12:4), in which case Zechariah was a priest as well as a prophet, or Iddo the seer or prophet in the early period of the Divided Monarchy (II Chr. 9:29; 12:15; 13:22). Zechariah's recorded prophetic activity extended from 520 to 518 B.C. during the reign of Darius I Hystaspis (Zech. 1:1; 7:1). He was a contemporary of Zerubbabel, and his early career coincided with the final activity of Haggai. He rekindled the people's hope and urged them to rebuild the house of God (Ezra 5:1; 6:14).

See also ZECHARIAH, BOOK OF.

22. A descendant of Parosh; head of a lay family who returned from Babylonia with Ezra (Ezra 8:3; I Esd. 8:30).

23. A descendant of Bebai; head of a lay family who returned from exile with Ezra (Ezra 8:11; I Esd. 8:37).

24. One of a delegation sent by Ezra to Iddo at Casiphia to obtain Levites, when it was discovered en route that they were lacking in the group returning from Babylonia (Ezra 8:16; I Esd. 8:44).

25. A descendant of Elam in a list of those who put away foreign wives and their children according to Ezra's reform banning foreign marriage (Ezra 10: 26; I Esd. 9:27).

26. One of the men, named without title or paternity and thus probably laymen, who stood with Ezra at the public reading of the law (Neh. 8:4; I Esd. 9:44).

27. A man of Judah, of the family of Perez (Neh. 11:4).

28. A man of Judah, called the son of the Shilonite (Neh. 11:5).

29. A priest of the family of Pashhur, house of Malchijah (Neh. 11:12).

30. A descendant of Asaph; leader of the Levites in the counterclockwise procession on the walls of Jerusalem during their dedication (Neh. 12:35).

31. A priest, listed as one of the trumpeters at the dedication of the walls of Jerusalem, probably in the clockwise procession (Neh. 12:41).

32. The father of Joseph, a Maccabean captain (I Macc. 5:18, 56).

33. The father of John the Baptist (Luke 1:5-67; 3:2). He was a righteous priest of the division of Abijah (cf. I Chr. 24:7-19). At one time, when this division assembled for duty in the temple, the lot fell to him to burn incense. While he was performing this service, an angel of the Lord appeared to him and announced that his old supplication for a son would be answered. The son, to be called John, would be filled with the Holy Spirit and would prepare the people for God's rule. Since Zechariah and his wife, Elizabeth, were aged, Zechariah asked for a sign, and Gabriel declared it: dumbness for unbelief, until the promise was fulfilled. As he was unable to pray for and to bless worshipers when he finally came out of the temple, they knew he had seen a vision (Luke 1:8-23). When the child was circumcised, Zechariah, a deaf-mute, amazed the gathering of neighbors and kinsfolk by confirming his wife's unusual choice of a name, writing on a tablet: "His name is John." Whereupon, able again to speak, he blessed God and, filled with the Holy Spirit, prophesied the fulfilment of Israel's messianic hope (vss. 57-79).

Bibliography. M. Noth, *Die israelitischen Personennamen* (1928), pp. 21, 186-87; A. C. Welch, *The Work of the Chronicler* (1939), pp. 73-75, 81-96, 129; W. Rudolf, *Chronikbücher,* HAT (1955), pp. 87-89.   T. M. Mauch

*ZECHARIAH, BOOK OF. The eleventh in the series of twelve short prophetic books which forms the concluding section of the OT. Together with Haggai and Malachi, it belongs to a group of prophecies delivered after the Exile and sheds valuable light on the thought and conditions of that period. The prophet Zechariah was a contemporary of the prophet Haggai and like him was concerned with the rebuilding of the Temple at Jerusalem in 520. Unlike the book of Haggai, however, the prophecies of Zechariah spread over a wider range than this one topic and contribute considerably to our understanding of the later stages of OT theology. Angelology, messianism, and apocalyptic feature largely in this book, which in parts is more obscure than any other OT writing.

It is generally considered that the prophecies are not homogeneous. The first section, containing the prophecies of Zechariah (chs. 1-8), is approximately contemporary, consisting of oracles and visions recorded by the prophet or a disciple before the end of the sixth century B.C. The second section (chs. 9-14), consisting largely of apocalyptic material, is of later date. Various indications appear to point to the

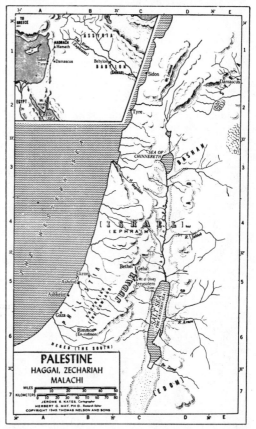

PALESTINE
HAGGAI, ZECHARIAH
MALACHI

third century B.C. as the date of this second part of Zechariah, although some commentators detect preexilic material in these chapters, while others suggest dates as late as the second century. It is possible that these chapters, together with the book of Malachi, originally formed an appendix to the prophetic corpus, but that the prophecies now contained in Malachi were detached from the rest because of their distinct character and in order to make up the sacred number of twelve prophets. Significant use is made of the book of Zechariah in the NT, notably in the messianic entry into Jerusalem (Matt. 21:1-11; cf. Zech. 9:9-10) and the betrayal (Matt. 26:14-16; cf. Zech. 11:12). It will be most convenient to deal with the two sections separately.

   1. Chs. 1-8
     a. The prophet
     b. Historical background
     c. The prophecies
     d. The significance of chs. 1-8
   2. Chs. 9-14
     a. First collection (chs. 9-11)

    b. Second collection (chs. 12–14)
    c. The significance of chs. 9–14
Bibliography

1. Chs. 1–8. *a. The prophet.* Little is known of Zechariah. The name means "Yahweh remembers." He is described (1:1) as the "son of Berechiah, son of Iddo." In Ezra 5:1; 6:14; Neh. 12:16, however, he is referred to as the son, not the grandson, of Iddo. The discrepancy has been accounted for by supposing that a copyist confused the "Zechariah the son of Jeberechiah" of Isa. 8:2 with this prophet, and that the words "the son of Berechiah" are an intrusion. Zechariah would thus be the son of Iddo. Alternatively the discrepancy is held to be only apparent, since in Hebrew *ben* may mean either "son of" or "grandson of."

Iddo, father or grandfather of Zechariah, is included among the heads of the priestly families who returned from exile to Jerusalem (Neh. 12:4). Zechariah himself is numbered among the priests (vs. 16); this would suggest that he may have been a cultic prophet. Whatever his relationship with Iddo, Zechariah is generally assumed to have been still a young man when he was associated with Haggai as an advocate of the immediate rebuilding of the temple (Ezra 5:1-2; 6:14). The oracles of Haggai in this connection are dated within the four months August-September to November-December, 520 B.C. (i.e., the second year of Darius I Hystaspis; Hag. 1:1). Those of Zechariah cover a longer period of two years from October-November, 520 (1:1), to November-December, 518 (7:1). The oracular activity of the two prophets thus overlapped by one month.

b. Historical background. The historical background of Zechariah is therefore largely the same as that of HAGGAI. The temple has lain in ruins since its destruction at the hands of the Babylonians in 586. Enemies without and apathy within the city have contributed to this sorry state. The picture which the book of Haggai gives of a poverty-stricken and dispirited community is supported by the evidence of Zechariah (8:10; 1:17). Moved, however, by the twin portents, as he believed them to be, of the general upheaval in the Persian Empire on the accession of Darius in 522, and the presence of a Davidic prince, in the person of Zerubbabel, as governor of Judah, Haggai had been led to rouse the despondent inhabitants of Jerusalem to embark upon the rebuilding of the temple. In his eyes these factors were the certain precursors of the messianic age. Yahweh was about to establish his kingdom. His ancient dwelling place in Zion must be restored to its former glory, so that he might once again be enthroned among his people and from there achieve his purposes.

Fired by the prophet's zeal, the people had begun the work of restoration (Hag. 1:14-15), but it seems that before long the enthusiasm of the builders waned. A month after operations had commenced, the prophet had to rally the people once again (2:3), and it would appear that shortly after this (Zech. 1:1), Zechariah added his plea in prophetic exhortation. When Haggai's voice was no longer heard, Zechariah continued for two years (520-518) to proclaim the coming of the messianic kingdom and to

urge the rebuilding of the temple as the necessary prelude. As a result of the combined vigor of the two prophets, the restoration was completed in 516 (Ezra 6:15).

The emphasis of Haggai had been more upon the material prosperity which would return to Judah when the people recognized their obligation to restore the house of the Lord. Zechariah fixes his eyes rather upon the subsequent glories of the messianic kingdom and ZERUBBABEL its ruler (3:8; 6:12). It would appear from the rather obscure reference in 6:9-14 that Zechariah proposed to crown Zerubbabel king. Whether for this reason (cf. Neh. 6:7) or because Zerubbabel contemplated rebuilding the walls of the city as well as the temple (Zech. 2:1-5), it seems likely that the Persian government relieved him of his governorship. At all events, he mysteriously disappears from the scene, and the text of 7:1-2 may imply that a new governor, Bethel-Sharezer, had been appointed in his place by 518.

c. The prophecies. The text of chs. 1–8 has not, on the whole, suffered more in transmission than the prophetic books generally. There is every reason to believe that basically these are the authentic words of the prophet, possibly arranged in their present order by Zechariah himself, but more probably collected and edited shortly after his day. As in the case of Haggai, Zechariah is spoken of impersonally as "the prophet" (1:1, 7), but, unlike the book of Haggai, there is a large element of personal reporting (1:8, etc.). Such redundancy and corruption as exist may be attributed to copyists, and here the text of the LXX is often helpful, but some of the difficulties are inherent in the nature of the writings. These chapters consist of a mixture of oracles in the normal prophetic style, and night visions, which constitute a distinctive feature of Zechariah. These eight visions, which are represented as having taken place in a single night in February-March, 519, have the general theme of reassuring the people that, despite all appearances to the contrary, the messianic age is about to begin.

The striking difference in style and the difficulty of completely harmonizing the contents of the oracles with those of the visions has led to the view that there may have been, even within these eight chapters, two distinct authors: (*a*) an earlier writer whose oracles echo, albeit faintly, the themes of the classical Hebrew prophets, and whose eschatological hopes centered on Zerubbabel as the coming messianic king; and (*b*) a later writer, in the tradition of Ezekiel, who, after Zerubbabel's fall from power, transferred his hopes to a supernatural intervention of Yahweh, which he expresses in apocalyptic visions of the new age, involving the destruction of the Gentiles and the subsequent centrality of the priesthood and the cultus of the temple. The majority of scholars take the view, however, that the oracles and the visions follow each other in a more or less logical sequence, and should be regarded as the work of the same prophet.

In the first oracle (1:1-6) Zechariah calls the whole people to repentance. Then come three visions. These appear to convey the message: (*a*) that although the widespread revolts in the Persian Empire in 522 had been quelled and the world was now at peace,

Haggai had not been wrong in seeing the "shaking of the nations" (Hag. 2:6-7) as a sign of the impending messianic age. Yahweh's love for his people will ensure his return to his own city and to his own temple (Zech. 1:7-17). (*b*) The proud and aggressive Gentiles will be laid low (vss. 18-21). (*c*) Jerusalem's walls will not be able to contain its future population, nor, indeed, will it need walls, since Yahweh himself will protect it (2:1-5).

In the second oracle (2:6-13) the prophet summons to a greater Jerusalem those of Yahweh's people who are still in Babylon. Then come two further visions. In the fourth vision (ch. 3) the prophet sees Joshua, the high priest, symbolically accepted as worthy of his great office. As representative of the people he is declared to be cleansed and forgiven. Charged with the oversight of the civil and religious life of the community, he is promised access to God on terms of equality with the angelic host. The fifth vision (4:1-6*a*, 10*b*-14) is notoriously difficult. The "two anointed" (vs. 14) may be the high priest and his deputy, or, more probably, Zerubbabel and Joshua, the civil and religious heads of the community. The vision guarantees their divine authority and the watchful care of Yahweh for his people.

In the third oracle (4:6*b*-10*a*) Zerubbabel's restoration of the temple is to be brought to completion as the prelude to the messianic kingdom. Three more visions follow. The sixth and seventh visions are both concerned with the moral standards of the new community. There will be no place in it for thieves and perjurers; the curse of Yahweh will fall upon them (5:1-4). Sin itself will be rooted out and banished (5:5-11). The eighth and final vision (6:1-8) sees the whole world once again at peace (cf. 1:7-17), but this time under the control of Yahweh.

The remaining chapters (6:9-8:23) consist of a series of oracles which play upon the theme of the glory of the messianic age. Zerubbabel will be crowned as the Davidic messianic king, and the rebuilding of the temple will be completed (6:9-15; cf. 3:8). (It seems probable that after this messianic hope had not materialized, the name of Joshua was substituted for that of Zerubbabel in 6:11 by a later editor.) Unlike their forefathers, the Jews of the new community will live in obedience to Yahweh and in unity with one another (ch. 7). The new Jerusalem will mean peace and prosperity for old and young. Joy and gladness will drive out the memory of past distresses (cf. 3:10). Yahweh's people, gathered from afar, will be joined in his holy city by the Gentiles, who have been led to know the truth by the faithful witness of the Jews, and together they will share in the blessings of the golden age (ch. 8).

d. The significance of chs. 1-8. The work of Zechariah is often dismissed as a blend of unoriginal prophecy, barren formalism, and obscure apocalypticism. It is true that he has nothing to add to the ethical insights of the earlier masters. In his insistence on the moral obligations of the community, he draws on the thought of classical prophecy. But that he emphasizes the inwardness of the religious life so strongly (e.g., 4:6; 5:5-11) is sufficiently remarkable at a time when the ancient fires of prophetic utterance were giving place to insistence on the cor-

rectness of the cultus. Like Haggai, he saw the temple as the focus of the right relationship between Yahweh and his people, but Zechariah has at the same time a far deeper conception of the danger of formalism and of the individual's need for personal commitment and obedience.

While Zechariah is enough of a child of his time to share its nationalist aspirations and its hope in the triumph of Jewry and the destruction of the Gentiles, it would almost seem as if it is with reluctance and hesitation that he does so. His basic thought is the Utopian dream of a world at peace, with Jew and Gentile gathered together in a worshiping community centered on the temple. The downfall of the Gentile oppressors and the material prosperity of the Jews, so strongly emphasized in Haggai, are in Zechariah almost glossed over as incidental. His visions (*see* VISION)—or, more properly, visual allegories—although clearly of an apocalyptic character, have more kinship with the traditional eschatological hopes of the great prophets than with the bizarre fantasies of the intertestamental period.

Zechariah marks a significant stage in the increasing sense of the remoteness of God which Ezekiel had fathered. Not only do angels (*see* ANGEL) feature frequently in the visions as intermediaries between God and man, but the word of God itself, which the great prophets recognized as coming directly to them, is now communicated even to one who is himself a prophet by an interpreting angel. It is in keeping with this development of angelology that the beginnings of a thoroughgoing demonology can also be detected. "The SATAN," not yet the powerful personage of the Prologue of the book of Job, far less the independent demonic power of I Chr. 21:1, paves the way for the NT conception of the ruler of the kingdom of Satan, who wages deadly warfare upon the kingdom of God. It is significant also for future developments in the doctrine of evil that in the seventh vision there is the suggestion that sin is a demonic force, rather than the product of man's disobedience, and that it finds its true home among the Gentiles, the enemies of the people of God.

2. Chs. 9-14. The latter part of the book of Zechariah presents vast and, in part, insoluble problems in respect of authorship, date, and interpretation. While it is not possible to establish beyond dispute whether one, two, three, or a variety of authors were responsible for chs. 9-14, it is almost universally agreed that on linguistic and stylistic grounds, as well as in theological ideas and historical background, the author of these chapters cannot be the prophet Zechariah.

Zech. 9:1; 12:1; Mal. 1:1, each of which introduces the subsequent section as an "oracle, the word of the Lord," suggest that Zech. 9:1-Mal. 4:6 constitutes an anonymous collection of prophecies, which editors of the Book of the Twelve have divided into three parts. Two of these have been added to the last identifiable prophetic work, that of Zechariah; while the final section, being different in character, has been given an independent existence under the name of Malachi to make up the numerically significant total of twelve prophets. The two earlier sections which fall within the present compass of the book of

Zechariah consist therefore of chs. 9–11; 12–14, and may be dealt with separately.

a. First collection (chs. 9–11). The first collection of prophecies opens with an oracle (9:1-12) of the impending judgment of Yahweh upon the cities of Syria, Phoenicia, and Philistia. What then remains of the Philistines will be incorporated in Judah. They will become Jewish by adoption, forswearing their heathen disregard of the Levitical food laws. Yahweh will then encircle his temple with his protecting presence, and the messianic king will enter Jerusalem in triumph to inaugurate a reign of peace. The scattered remnants of Israel will be brought back to the homeland to share in the golden age.

This oracle is generally considered to refer to the victorious campaigns of Alexander the Great, who defeated Darius, king of Persia, at the battle of Issus in 333, and thereafter proceeded southward through Syria and Palestine to the conquest of Egypt. If this is so, the prophecy sees this march of the irresistible world-conqueror as the hand of Yahweh preparing the way for the establishment of the messianic kingdom.

The following verses (9:13-17) may be taken either as an independent oracle or as an integral part of vss. 1-17. In the latter case they would have to precede vs. 8, since they present a picture of the victorious Greeks being laid low by the combined forces of the Jews, which presumably would be the prelude to the arrival of the messianic reign of peace. If, on the other hand, this is a separate utterance, it reflects a historical situation quite different from that of 9:1-12. The Greeks are no longer Yahweh's instrument but enemies who must be exterminated. This is depicted in particularly ferocious terms as a veritable blood bath, after which comes peace.

There is considerable textual corruption in this chapter which is difficult to resolve. Equally difficult is the question of how the chapter should be subdivided. Some authorities detect as many as four independent oracles (vss. 1-8, 9-10, 11-13, 14-17). The main difficulty, however, is to reconcile the ruthlessness of vs. 15 with the idyllic vision of vss. 10, 17.

10:1-2 contains a fragment on divination which appears to have no more than a verbal connection with what precedes and what follows. 10:3-12, on the other hand, bears a marked resemblance to 9:11-17 in that it is an oracle denouncing the foreign rulers of Judah ("shepherds") and predicting their downfall at the hands of the Jews, who are to be restored to their own land from the countries of their dispersion.

The problem here is to identify the "shepherds." They may be the Ptolemies and the Seleucids ("Egypt" and "Syria" [vss. 10-11]). It has, however, been held that the "Cornerstone," "Tent peg," and "Battle bow" in vs. 4 represent Simon, Jonathan, and Judas, thus indicating the Maccabean period as the date of the oracle. On the other hand, these curious allusions may be a triple designation of the Messiah, and the oracle might well refer to a situation a century earlier or more. This prophecy is followed by a fragment (11:1-3) in which the annihilation of the Gentile "shepherds" is hailed with exultation.

The next oracle (11:4-14) is by common consent one of the most enigmatic passages in the OT. The most convincing interpretation would seem to be that the prophet, in an allegorical vision, sees himself in the role of Yahweh as shepherd of Judah. He tends his flock, knowing full well both that they are themselves worthless, and that they are doomed to slaughter at the hands of their foreign owners. One by one he breaks the two pastoral rods, "Graciousness" and "Bond of Union," with which he controls his sheep, and by this symbolic act signifies the end of the relationship between Yahweh and Judah and also the end of national unity.

In a short allegory which follows (11:15-17), the prophet is charged to assume the role of a worthless shepherd, as an indication to the people of what they may expect if they are unfaithful to Yahweh. This passage is doubtless replete with allusions to a historical situation which must have been crystal clear to the readers, but it is impossible now to do more than speculate on the identity of the "three shepherds" (vs. 8) or the "worthless shepherd" (vs. 17). The oracle has been dated variously from the fall of Samaria to the Maccabean period.

b. Second collection (chs. 12–14). The second collection consists of two main oracles of an apocalyptic character (chs. 12–13; ch. 14) dealing with the final assault upon Jerusalem by the heathen powers, followed by its deliverance and the triumph of Yahweh as Lord of all nations, with Jerusalem as his dwelling place and as the center of the religious life of the world.

In the first oracle the prophet sees the ultimate climax of history. Jerusalem is attacked by the massed array of the Gentiles (cf. Ezek. 38–39). Even the hinterland of Judah joins in the rebellion, until its people see the hand of Yahweh routing the invaders, and they too join in the defense of the holy city (12:1-9). When victory has been won, there takes place a national act of mourning for some notable figure who has died a martyr's death (12:10-14), followed by a purification of the life of the nation from sin, idolatry, and prophecy (13:1-6). The short oracle in 13:7-9 is frequently regarded as misplaced, and is held to belong properly to the "worthless shepherd" allegory of 11:15-17. There is, however, more reason to suppose that it finds its proper place here as a picture of the messianic woes which precede the end.

Once more, historical allusions are rife but puzzling. The antagonism between the city and the country districts (12:2-5) suggests the Hellenizing period before the blundering policy of Antiochus Epiphanes made revolt inevitable. If the assassination referred to in 12:10-14 is that of the high priest Onias III, this date would be confirmed. On the other hand the "shepherd" of 13:7 may be an unspecified messianic figure, identifiable with or distinct from an equally imprecise presentation of the Suffering Servant idea in 12:10. The early church regarded the whole passage as christological.

The final oracle (ch. 14) consists likewise of a description of the end event, with an even stronger apocalyptic emphasis. In the great final assault of the heathen powers upon Jerusalem, the plight of Yahweh's people will be so desperate that half of them will be carried off to exile, but the other half will escape through a miraculous gorge in the Mount of Olives. When all seems lost, Yahweh intervenes with his heavenly host. The earth is transformed, and Yahweh reigns as king over all the world from the heights of Mount Zion. The heathen warriors perish miserably, but the Gentiles learn by their fate to acknowledge Yahweh's sovereignty. Year by year they come to Jerusalem on pilgrimage to attend his enthronement at the Feast of Tabernacles. Even the former war horses bear the emblem of holiness, and so great will be the throng to perform the Levitical rites that the household pots and pans of Jerusalem must be utilized for the sacred ceremonial, and may be used with impunity, since everything will be consecrated to the service of Yahweh.

c. The significance of chs. 9-14. It is clear from the foregoing brief examination of these chapters that we can say little with certainty about their contents. Possibly the most that can be said is that they constitute a collection of anonymous and mainly apocalyptic utterances, having their origin within a range of time between the fourth and second centuries B.C. Even the apparently cogent argument against a Maccabean date, that it would be impossible to add extra material after the canon of the Twelve had been fixed (cf. Ecclus. 49:10; *ca.* 200 B.C.), is not accepted by some authorities.

Nevertheless, these chapters provide us with valuable insights into the theological trends of this Hellenistic period about which relatively little is known. They reflect the various levels of thought which characterized a people who saw little outward evidence of the fulfilment of prophetic promises, yet who never relinquished their invincible hope in the vindication of Yahweh and his people. The strong apocalyptic note, born of despair, looks more and more toward supernatural intervention as the only salvation of the tiny community of God from the world-wide supremacy of paganism.

It is in this light that we must evaluate the bloodthirsty treatment of the Gentiles in 9:15; 14:12. In apocalyptic thinking the Gentiles have almost ceased to be regarded as human beings and have become synonymous with the power of evil that violates every law of God. Yet despite this, there is the emergent realization that the consummation of God's purpose cannot consist merely in the destruction of evil but must include the conversion of evil to good. In the end the Gentiles must be won for God, and Jerusalem must become the spiritual center of the world, even if this is seen within the limited conception of worship as consisting of Levitical correctness (cf. 9: 7; 14:16-21). It is not surprising that this restricted view of worship and holiness should exist at a time when prophecy had sunk to such a low ebb, that there was more honor in bearing the scars of a tavern brawl than the marks of a spokesman of Yahweh (cf. 13:4-6). *See* WORSHIP IN THE OT.

For many, however, the supreme significance of these chapters will be felt to lie in the two passages which find their fulfilment in the gospel. On Palm Sunday, Jesus' entry into Jerusalem (Matt. 21:1-11) is a deliberate adoption of the profound messianic symbolism of 9:9; while the paltry thirty pieces of silver in 11:12, which Yahweh receives as the price

of his service from his faithless people, point to a more than mechanical fulfilment in the traitor's price for the body of Christ (Matt. 26:14-16).

See also APOCALYPTICISM; ESCHATOLOGY OF THE OT.

Bibliography. Commentaries: S. R. Driver, Century Bible (1906); H. G. Mitchell, ICC (1912); W. E. Barnes, CB (1917); G. A. Smith, EB (1928); E. Sellin, *KAT* (1929); F. Horst, *HAT* (1954); T. Winton Thomas, *IB,* VI (1956), 1053-88; R. C. Dentan, *IB,* VI (1956), 1089-1114. See also introductions to literature of the OT by Driver, Pfeiffer, Bentzen, etc.

For background on chs. 1-8, see: L. E. Browne, *Early Judaism* (1920).

Special studies on chs. 1-8: J. W. Rothstein, *BWAT,* VIII (1910); L. G. Rignell, *Die Nachtgesichte des Sacharja* (1950).

For background on chs. 9-14, see: H. H. Rowley, *The Relevance of Apocalyptic* (1944); S. B. Frost, *OT Apocalyptic* (1952).

Special studies on chs. 9-14: E. G. Kraeling, "The Historical Situation in Zech. 9:1-10," *AJSL,* XLI (1924-25), 24-33; W. W. Cannon, "Some Notes on Zech. ch. 11," *AFO,* IV (1927), 139-46; B. Heller, "Die letzten Kapitel des Buches Sacharja im Lichte des späteren Judentums," *ZAW-NF,* IV (1927), 151-55; J. Kremer, "Die Hirten-Allegorie im Buche Zacharias," *AA,* XI (1930), 2.   W. NEIL

ZECHER; KJV ZACHER. Alternate form of ZECHARIAH 1.

ZEDAD zē'dăd [צדד]. A place in the N borderland of Canaan (Num. 34:8; Ezek. 47:15). It is identical with Sadad, which is situated N of the road between Palmyra and Riblah.

Bibliography. R. Dussaud, *Topographie historique de la Syrie* (1927), pp. 282-83; A. Alt, *Festschrift Otto Eissfeldt* (1947), p. 15.   A. S. KAPELRUD

ZEDEKIAH zĕd'ə ki'ə [(ו)צדקיה, Yahu is (my) righteousness; Σεδεκιας]; KJV ZIDKIJAH zĭd kī'jə in Neh. 10:1; KJV Apoc. ZEDECHIAS zĕd'ə kī'əs. **1.** Son of Chenaanah; a prophet who promised Ahab victory against the Arameans at Ramoth-gilead (I Kings 22:1-28; II Chr. 18:1-27). At the urging of his Judean ally Jehoshaphat, Ahab consulted the four hundred cultic prophets of Samaria about the chances of the proposed expedition against Ramoth-gilead. The ensuing account provides one of the best pictures of the activity of the group prophet in the OT.

The prophesying took place outside the city on a threshing floor, since a large area was, no doubt, required for the type of activity in which the prophets engaged (cf. I Sam. 10:5-6, 10-11). At first the prophets acted as one man, chanting a prophecy of victory. Then, as the ecstatic activity of the group intensified, Zedekiah stood out from his companions. He placed horns of iron on his head, a symbol of great power (cf. Deut. 33:17), signifying that Ahab would defeat the Arameans. By creating victory before the battle, the prophet ensured the success of his sovereign's mission.

Zedekiah's assurance conflicted with the prophecy of defeat from Micaiah. Yet there was no doubt in the minds of the participants that both prophecies were inspired by Yahweh. The false prophecy was the result of a "lying spirit" sent by Yahweh to tempt Ahab to his destruction (cf. Ezek. 14:9).

Bibliography. T. H. Robinson, *Prophecy and the Prophets in Ancient Israel* (1953), pp. 30-32; J. Pedersen, *Israel*, I-II (1954), 141.   R. W. CORNEY

2. A contemporary of Jeremiah the prophet, and son of Maaseiah. Jeremiah charged Zedekiah with immoral conduct and with prophesying falsely, and predicted his death at the hands of Nebuchadnezzar king of Babylon (Jer. 29:21-23).   B. T. DAHLBERG

3. Son of Hananiah; one of the princes of Judah under King Jehoiakim. He heard Baruch read the scroll of Jeremiah's oracles (Jer. 36:12).

J. M. WARD

4. The last king of Judah (*ca.* 597-587 B.C.); uncle and successor of Jehoiachin; put to death by Nebuchadrezzar.

His given name was Mattaniah (II Kings 24:17; see also the name מתניהו in Lachish Letter No. 1).

Zedekiah was twenty-one years old when he became king, and he reigned eleven years in Jerusalem (II Kings 24:18; II Chr. 36:11). His mother was Hamutal (or Hamital), daughter of Jeremiah of Libnah (II Kings 24:18). He would thus be Jehoiachin's uncle, as II Kings 24:17 states, and a younger brother of Jehoahaz and Jehoiakim. The genealogical list in I Chr. 3:15 makes him the third son of Josiah. II Chr. 36:10, however, calls him the "brother" of Jehoiachin. This is probably an error (cf. Jer. 27:1, where "Zedekiah" is to be read for "Jehoiakim").

Zedekiah came to the throne at a time when Judah's days were numbered. It would appear that in 597 Nebuchadrezzar had deported most of the nobility to Babylon along with King Jehoiachin. This move brought disastrous results, for it meant that the policy of Judah was framed by men with little or no experience of statecraft. Jeremiah used a striking image to describe those left behind in Judah (ch. 24). They were like rotten figs, unfit to be eaten. As he saw it, the future lay with ·the exiles, whom he likened to good figs. In the circumstances Zedekiah was not the best choice as king. The picture Jeremiah gives is of a man who was continually torn by conflicting emotions. He recognized that the prophet's advice was sound, but he was unable to combat the strong pro-Egyptian feelings of the people, who were sharply divided into pro-Egyptian and pro-Babylonian factions. It is noteworthy that Jeremiah nowhere condemned the king, but he bitterly denounced his advisers. Torn asunder by rival parties, Judah went to her doom.

Both Kings and Chronicles pass quickly over the events of Zedekiah's reign until the final siege of Jerusalem. The Babylonian Chronicle, however, supplies us with a few details of the intervening years. These indicate that Nebuchadrezzar had difficulties both at home and among the conquered peoples. In particular, a revolt broke out in Babylonia in 595-594. This was put down only after the rebel leader had been captured and many of his troops killed. Frequent disturbances seem to have taken place, probably as the result of constant campaigns, but actual details of these are missing. The Chronicle ends with the notice that Nebuchadrezzar gathered his army to march to Syria in December, 594.

Jeremiah, too, has preserved factual material which deals with these years (*see* ISRAEL, HISTORY OF). The insurrection which occurred in Babylon in 595-594 may have given rise to hopes of an early collapse of Babylonian power. It is against this background that Hananiah's speech (Jer. 28:1 ff), dated in the fourth year of Zedekiah (594-593), is to be understood. Hananiah announced that God had broken the yoke of the king of Babylon and that the exiles would return and Jehoiachin be reinstated as king of Judah within two years. It is certain that much intrigue was being carried on, both in Judah and among the exiles, roused by the patriotic zeal of the false prophets (ch. 29). At the same time Egypt continued to foment trouble. In Judah itself there was a sharp division of opinion between following a pro-Babylonian or a pro-Egyptian policy. In such a situation the proximity of Egypt was a factor to be taken into account. Jer. 27:2 ff gives a picture of an attempt by the smaller nations of the West to band together against Nebuchadrezzar.

Envoys came to Jerusalem from Edom, Moab, Ammon, Tyre, and Sidon to persuade Zedekiah to join in a revolt against Babylon. But they were unsuccessful in their mission, perhaps because of the firm attitude taken by Jeremiah. This incident may be related to the death of Neco and the accession of Psammetichus II, *ca.* 594. In this connection the reference to the visit of Zedekiah to Babylon in the fourth year of his reign is to be considered (Jer. 51:59). A reliable tradition may be preserved here. If it is historical, it appears that news of the impending revolt had reached Nebuchadrezzar, who summoned Zedekiah to Babylon. This would serve in part to explain his refusal to join the anti-Babylon alliance. Judah was in a very difficult position, caught between the two powerful opposing forces of Babylonia and Egypt. The prophecies of Jeremiah and Ezekiel indicate how strong was the opposition to submission to Babylonia as God's appointed instrument. Zedekiah vacillated between the two points of view. He respected Jeremiah, sought him out, and requested his advice. But finally the pressure upon him became too great, and he rebelled against the king of Babylon (II Kings 24:20).

The immediate cause of his rebellion seems to have been the sea attack on Philistia made by the Pharaoh Hophra of Egypt (Jer. 44:30), who had succeeded to the throne on the death of Psammetichus II, and is known otherwise as Apries. Nebuchadrezzar marched to the W and set up his headquarters at Riblah on the Orontes (II Kings 25:6, 20 ff). Zedekiah was forced to make a decision, and he threw in his lot with the pro-Egyptian party. Ammon also joined in the revolt. Ezekiel has preserved a tradition of Nebuchadrezzar's indecision regarding his plan of campaign (Ezek. 21:18 ff). After consulting his oracles he sent his army to attack Jerusalem. It is clear that he himself did not take part in the siege. He remained at Riblah, as II Kings 25:6, 20 ff, indicates. This is also in agreement with Jer. 38:17 ff, where it is said that "if you will surrender to the princes of the king of Babylon, then your life shall be spared."

The account of the siege and fall of Jerusalem in II Kings 25:1-21 is paralleled in Jer. 39:1-10; 52:1-30. The former is an insertion in the book of Jeremiah, based on II Kings 25:1-12. The siege began in the ninth year of Zedekiah's reign (589), in the tenth month on the tenth of the month (II Kings 25:1; Jer. 39:1; 52:4). In the fourth month on the ninth of the month a breach was made in the city walls (II Kings 25:4; Jer. 39:2; 52:7). Zech. 8:19 mentions that the "fast of the fourth month" and the "fast of the tenth," along with two other fasts, were kept in later times, presumably in memory of these two occasions. But now they would be "seasons of joy and gladness, and cheerful feasts," instead of mourning. The Babylonians thus began the siege of Jerusalem in December, 589. The siege was lifted for a time when word reached them that the Egyptians were advancing (Jer. 37:5). The Babylonian army marched to meet this new threat. No details have been preserved of what happened. It is possible that the Egyptians withdrew. If a battle took place, the Babylonians were victorious, and they immediately resumed the siege of Jerusalem. It is against this background that the oracle of Jeremiah is to be understood, in which he accuses the rulers and people of a breach of faith (34:8 ff). King Zedekiah had made a covenant with all the people in Jerusalem that everyone should set free his Hebrew slaves, male and female. When the Babylonians withdrew from the city to meet the Egyptian army, those who had been set free were enslaved again.

A breach was made in the walls of the city in July, 587. By this time famine had reduced the beleaguered city to desperate straits (Jer. 37:21). Cf. Lam. 2; 4 for what is perhaps an eyewitness account of the horrors of the siege. Zedekiah, seeing that all was lost, tried to escape by fleeing in the direction of the Arabah. But he was overtaken and captured by the Chaldean army. His men of war may have tried to escape along with him, but they became separated from one another. Ezekiel has an acted picture of the king's flight in 12:1-4. Apparently the Edomites gave assistance to the Babylonians at this time, cutting off the stragglers and handing over the survivors. If the oracle in Obadiah (vss. 11-14) is correctly dated *ca.* 460, as seems probable, the part played by the Edomites more than a century after the sack of Jerusalem was remembered by the prophet, who lashes them with withering invective. Zedekiah was brought before the king of Babylon at Riblah, where sentence was passed upon him. His sons were slain before his eyes. Then he himself was blinded, bound in fetters, and brought to Babylon. The prophecies of Jeremiah (34:2 ff) and Ezekiel (12:13) had been fulfilled.

There is some discrepancy in the biblical records regarding the actual dates of these events. According to Jer. 52:28-29, the first capture of Jerusalem took place in the seventh year of Nebuchadrezzar, the second capture and the destruction in the eighteenth year of Nebuchadrezzar. II Kings 24:12, however, dates the first captivity in the eighth year of Nebuchadrezzar, and 25:8 the second in the nineteenth year of Nebuchadrezzar. The solution to these discrepancies is perhaps to be found in the suggestion that the writer of Kings dated Nebuchadrezzar's reign from 605 because he was in sole command of the Babylonian armies at Carchemish. Actually, he did not become king till the following year.

Zedekiah occupied a somewhat anomalous position as king of Judah, the appointee of Nebuchadrezzar. Although Jehoiachin had been exiled to Babylon, there were many who clearly believed that he would soon return to take his rightful place as king of Judah. This is evidenced in the speech of Hananiah (Jer. 28:3-4, 11). Jehoiachin himself may have had hopes of being restored to his native country (22:24-30). But Jeremiah clearly believed that this would not happen. It is interesting to note that Ezekiel dated his prophecies according to the exile of Jehoiachin (8:1; 20:1; etc.), and not to the reign of Zedekiah. The Babylonians themselves may deliberately have kept Jehoiachin in Babylon against the day of his possible return, should the circumstances be favorable, for Jehoiachin still retained the title of king of Judah. The three stamped jar handles from Kiriath-sepher and Beth-shemesh, with the inscription "Belonging to Eliakim, steward of Yau-qîn," may point in the same direction.

Bibliography. W. F. Albright, "The Seal of Eliakim," *JBL,* LI (1932), 77-106. W. O. E. Oesterley and T. H. Robinson, *A History of Israel* (2nd ed., 1934), pp. 435 ff. W. F. Albright, "The Excavation of Tell Beit Mirsim III," *AASOR,* XXI-XXII (1943), 68. A. M. Honeyman, "The Evidence for Regnal Names Among the Hebrews," *JBL,* LXVII (1948), 13-25. W. F. Albright, *The Archaeology of Palestine* (Pelican Books A 199; 2nd ed., 1951), pp. 128 ff. J. Simons, *Jerusalem in the OT* (1952), p. 127. W. F. Albright, Review of Lachish III: The Iron Age, *BASOR,* 132 (1953), 46; *The Biblical Period* (reprinted from *The Jews: Their History, Culture and Religion;* 1955), pp. 45-48. J. B. Pritchard, ed., *ANET* (2nd ed., 1955), pp. 321-22. D. N. Freedman, "The Babylonian Chronicle," *BA,* XIX (1956), 50-60. J. P. Hyatt, "New Light on Nebuchadrezzar and Judean History," *JBL,* LXXV (1956), 277-84. M. Noth, *Geschichte Israels* (3rd ed., 1956), pp. 256 ff. D. J. Wiseman, *Chronicles of Chaldaean Kings* (1956), pp. 31-37, 73. G. E. Wright, *Biblical Archaeology* (1957), pp. 175 ff.

H. B. MacLean

5. A prominent Jewish official signatory to the covenant of Ezra (Neh. 10:1).

Bibliography. For a summary of theories regarding the identity of this individual, see R. A. Bowman, Exegesis of Nehemiah, *IB,* III (1954), 759.   B. T. Dahlberg

ZEEB. *See* Oreb and Zeeb.

ZELA zē'lə [צֵלַע, rib, side, slope]; KJV ZELAH. One of the cities allotted to Benjamin (Josh. 18:28); significant as the site of the tomb of Kish—the final repository for the bones of Saul and Jonathan (II Sam. 21:14). The presence of the family sepulchre suggests that the town was Saul's native home. A possible long form of the name would include the word which follows in the Hebrew text of Josh. 18:28 and read "Zela ha-eleph." In either case, however, its location is uncertain, except that it is included in a list of fourteen cities which are generally to be located in the hill country N and W of Jerusalem. Khirbet Salah, between Jerusalem and Gibeon, is a possible identification of the site.   W. H. Morton

ZELEK zē'lĕk [צֶלֶק] (II Sam. 23:37; I Chr. 11:39). An Ammonite who was a member of the Mighty Men of David known as the "Thirty."

ZELOPHEHAD zĭ lō'fə hăd [צלפחד; LXX Σαλπααδ, shadow (*i.e.*, protection) from terror(?)]. A descendant of Manasseh. He died in the wilderness without a male heir (Num. 26:33; 27:1, 7; 36:2, 6, 10-11; Josh. 17:3; I Chr. 7:15). Upon Zelophehad's death his five daughters, Mahlah, Noah, Hoglah, Milcah, and Tirzah (perhaps clan names), appeared before Moses to request the recognition of female heirs. This alteration in inheritance laws was sought in order that the father's name might be kept alive. The request was granted, and the line of inheritance was traced for this and other eventualities. No mention is made of the levirate law (*see* MARRIAGE).

The inadequacy of female inheritance as an arrangement to continue the father's name and retain family possession of his property is demonstrated by the additional regulation in Num. 36 that heiresses must marry within the father's tribe. It is the male, then, who is the central figure in preserving family continuity in name and in property, which are intimately related.

Bibliography. J. Pedersen, *Israel*, I (1926), 94-96; M. Noth, *Die israelitischen Personennamen* (1928), p. 256.

R. F. JOHNSON

ZELOTES zĭ lō'tēz. KJV translation of Ζηλωτής in Luke 6:15; Acts 1:13. *See* ZEALOT; SIMON 8.

ZELZAH zĕl'zə [צלצח]. A site near Rachel's tomb in the territory of Benjamin, significant as the scene of the first of three promised signs confirming to Saul his anointment by the Lord to be prince of Israel (I Sam. 10:1-2).

Though a late and erroneous gloss on Gen. 35:19 would locate Rachel's tomb near EPHRATH, which is there identified with Bethlehem, I Sam. 10:2; Jer. 31: 15 suggest that Rachel was buried in the vicinity of Ramah. The name Zelzah, however, is completely unknown and is quite possibly the result of a textual corruption, for the LXX, which reads "leaping mightily" at this point, clearly has behind it a different textual tradition.

Bibliography. E. G. Kraeling, *Bible Atlas* (1956), pp. 177-78.

W. H. MORTON

ZEMARAIM zĕm'ə rā'əm [צמרים, double peak(?)]. 1. A site near the N border of Benjamin, listed in the E division of cities allotted to that tribe (Josh. 18:22). The most probable location is Ras ez-Zeimara, *ca.* five miles NE of Bethel and in the hill country between et-Taiyibeh and Rammun. W. H. MORTON

2. A mountain in the hill country of Ephraim (I Chr. 13:4); the scene of Abijah's speech of rebuke against Jeroboam and the Israelites. I Kings 15:7, where Abijah is called Abijam, does not refer to the place or the speech but does mention a war between Abijam and Jeroboam. The mountain has not been located; it is only a conjecture which would link its name with 1 *above*. W. L. REED

ZEMARITES zĕm'ə rīts [צמרי; Akkad. *Şimirra;* Amarna *Şumur*]. Canaanites from Syria, N of Lebanon. The Zemarites are mentioned in Gen. 10:18; I Chr. 1:16, in both cases as sons of Canaan and brothers of the Arvadites (*see* ARVAD) and the

Hamathites (*see* HAMATH). They lived N of Lebanon, between Arvad and Tripolis, where there is today a little town called Sumra. A. S. KAPELRUD

ZEMER zē'mər [צמר] (Ezek. 27:8). The native city of the ZEMARITES. According to a widely accepted emendation, which has been followed by the RSV, the words צור חכמיך (KJV "thy wise men, O Tyrus") should be read as חכמי צמר, "the skilled men of Zemer." The city is mentioned as *Şumur* in the Tell Amarna Letters and as *Şimirra* in Assyrian texts; the name and location survive in the town of Sumra, between Ruad and Tripoli. S. COHEN

ZEMIRAH zĭ mī'rə [זמירה; *because of the feminine ending,* Noth *suggests* זמריה, Zemariah (*following* LXX AL), *according to* S Arab. *names derived from an original root* דמר *and meaning* Y has helped; *cf.* ZIMRI] (I Chr. 7:8); KJV ZEMIRA. A name in what may be a tripartite grouping of postexilic Benjaminite families, or a list of families of Zebulun otherwise lacking in the lists of the tribes in Chronicles.

Bibliography. M. Lidzbarski, *Ephemeris für semitische Epigraphik*, I (1902), 11. M. Noth, *Die israelitischen Personennamen* (1928), pp. 175-76, 242. T. M. MAUCH

ZENAN zē'nən [צנן, place of flocks]. A village of Judah in the Shephelah district of Lachish (Josh. 15: 37). Probably it is the same as Zaanan (Mic. 1:11) and to be identified with 'Araq el-Kharba.

ZENAS zē'nəs [Ζηνᾶς, *contraction of* Ζηνόδωρος, gift of Zeus] (Tit. 3:13). Someone whom, with Apollos, "Paul" asked Titus to send to him quickly and lacking nothing. Zenas was apparently a Christian who lived in Crete. He is also described as a lawyer, perhaps to differentiate him from others of the same name. Whether he professed Greek, Roman, or Jewish law is not known.

According to late tradition Zenas was the first bishop of Diospolis (Lydda) in Palestine and was the author of a Life of Titus—the association, no doubt, stemming from the reference to Zenas in Titus. B. H. THROCKMORTON, JR.

ZEPHANIAH zĕf'ə nī'ə [צפניהו, צפניה, Y has sheltered, *or* Y has treasured; *cf.* Punic צפנבעל; Apoc. *Sophoniae*]; KJV Apoc. SOPHONIAS sŏf'ə nī'əs (II Esd. 1:40). 1. A prophet during the reign of Josiah (Zeph. 1:1); one of the twelve Minor Prophets (cf. II Esd. 1:40). In addition to the usual citation of the prophet's father (Cushi), his ancestry is traced back four generations: his fourth ancestor, Hezekiah, must have been the king of this name. Thus he was a distant relative of Josiah. He lived in Jerusalem (cf. Zeph. 1:4) and prophesied there.

See also ZEPHANIAH, BOOK OF.

2. A priest; son of Maaseiah. He was one of two men in a deputation sent by Zedekiah to Jeremiah; they took back to the king an oracle of the prophet denouncing dependence upon Egypt and resistance against the Chaldeans (Jer. 21:1; 37:3). When Shemaiah wrote from Babylon to Zephaniah as overseer of the temple, rebuking him for not imprisoning Jeremiah for his message to the exiles, even though

Zephaniah belonged to the anti-Babylon party, he read the letter to Jeremiah and did not imprison him (29:25, 29). After the final siege and fall of Jerusalem, "Seraiah the chief priest, and Zephaniah the second priest" were among those taken to the king of Babylon at Riblah and put to death (II Kings 25:18; Jer. 52:24).

3. The father of Josiah, an exile who returned from Babylon (Zech. 6:10, 14).

4. A name in a postexilic list which traces both the Levitical descent of Heman and the Levitical line from Kohath (I Chr. 6:36).

Bibliography. M. Lidzbarski, *Ephemeris für semitische Epigraphik,* I (1902), 25; II (1908), 172. M. Noth, *Die israelitischen Personennamen* (1928), pp. 21, 178.   T. M. MAUCH

ZEPHANIAH, APOCALYPSE OF. A lost Jewish pseudepigraphic work, known through a citation by Clement of Alexandria (end of second century A.D.) in his *Stromata* (V.11). The quotation states that Zephaniah was taken by the Spirit to the fifth heaven, where he saw and heard glorious angels on their thrones singing hymns of praise to the ineffable Most High God. This scene resembles several observed by the prophet Isaiah according to the Ascension of Isaiah 7-9 (*see* ISAIAH, ASCENSION OF). A short fragment of a Christian Apocalypse of Sophoniah (i.e., Zephaniah) is preserved on two pages of an early-fifth-century Coptic (Sahidic dialect) papyrus MS. Sophoniah saw a human soul in the lower world being terribly flogged by angels for sins which had gone unrepented. He then was taken to another place, where he saw myriads of angels of horrendous appearance. From this point on, the text is illegible. The relation of this Sophoniah fragment to the Zephaniah fragment cited by Clement is uncertain. Another Coptic (Akhmim dialect) papyrus MS of the fourth century contains a much larger fragment (eighteen pages) of a work similar to the Sophoniah fragment. Its title has not been preserved; hence it is called the Anonymous Apocalypse, though some believe that it, too, is from an Apocalypse of Sophoniah. Much of it describes the terrible punishments of the wicked in hell similar to punishments described in the second-century Apocalypse of Peter (*see* PETER, APOCALYPSE OF). There is also a description of the mighty angel who records the good deeds of the living in the Book of Life.

See also PSEUDEPIGRAPHA.

Bibliography. G. Steindorff, *Die Apokalypse des Elias, Eine unbekannte Apokalypse, und Bruchstücke der Sophonias-Apokalypse* (1899), contains introduction, Coptic texts, German translation.   M. RIST

*ZEPHANIAH, BOOK OF. The work of a Judean prophet whose activity is dated by the Scythian invasion (630-625 B.C.; *see bibliography*); ninth, among the minor prophets in the OT canon.

Zephaniah was born probably not earlier than 660 B.C. His great-great-grandfather was Hezekiah king of Judah (715-697 B.C.).

1. Political and religious situation
2. Contents
   a. Indictment of Judah
   b. Indictment of the nations

   c. Jerusalem refuses correction
   d. A remnant to be saved
3. Composition of the book
4. Zephaniah's teaching
Bibliography

1. Political and religious situation. Zephaniah lived in a period when the power of Assyria in the West was rapidly expanding. The trend toward things Assyrian became increasingly conspicuous. Official protection was given in Judah to the magical arts of diviners and enchanters. Astral religion became so popular that MANASSEH erected on the roof of the upper chamber of King Ahaz altars and chariots for the worship of the sun, the moon, the signs of the zodiac, and all the host of heaven (II Kings 23:11 ff). New impetus was now given to the worship of the Queen of Heaven, the mother-goddess of Assyrian-Babylonian religion.

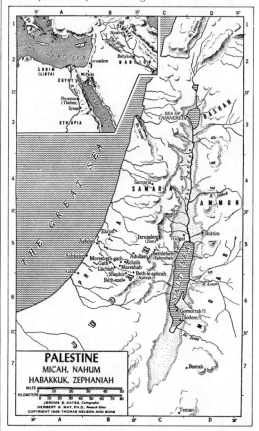

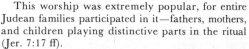

PALESTINE
MICAH, NAHUM
HABAKKUK, ZEPHANIAH

This worship was extremely popular, for entire Judean families participated in it—fathers, mothers, and children playing distinctive parts in the ritual (Jer. 7:17 ff).

It was the invasion of Palestine by the Scythians that awakened Zephaniah to Yahweh's call to be a prophet. The Scythians were barbarian hordes who poured down through Asia Minor into Palestine and down to the borders of Egypt in terrorist raids, leaving calamity in their track. At the bribe of Psammetichus I of Egypt (Herodotus I.103-106) they retreated from his borders, pillaged Ashkelon, and mastered Beth-shean.

2. Contents. *a. Indictment of Judah (1:1-2:3).* Zephaniah came to feel that the Scythians were harbingers of a judgment which Yahweh was bringing not only upon Judah but also upon all men and animals, birds and fish—indeed, upon the face of the whole earth (1:2-3).

Pagan worship which had infiltrated into Judah led him to condemn the whole nation and the inhabitants of Jerusalem (1:4-6). The businessmen and city leaders thought that demonic spirits dwelt both above and under the thresholds of houses, alien spirits other than Yahweh, and by leaping over the threshold the Judeans avoided perilous contact with them (1:8-9).

Zephaniah's words are source material of firsthand importance for the Jerusalem of his day. Merchants carried on their business at the "Fish Gate," located in the N section, and in the "Makhtesh," which was the trough of the cheese makers in the "Tyropoeon" Valley to the S, the center of trade. In such areas, Zephaniah uttered Yahweh's condemnation. As the prophet contemplated the judgment that awaited the people, in solemn imagination he heard their wailing cries (1:10-11). He also portrayed Yahweh with a search lamp hunting down for destruction the property and homes of those who lived in Jerusalem and whose lives were utterly untouched by concern for ethical conduct in daily business transactions (1:12-13*a*).

For this prophet more than for any other, the major theme was the DAY OF THE LORD. It was to be a day of wrath, of trouble and distress, of crashing ruin and devastation, of darkness and calamity, of clouds and gloom (1:15), which would mark the destruction of all the inhabitants of the earth (1:18). Would a like fate come to Judah? To Zephaniah there was to this inevitable question but one answer: Yahweh, the master of heaven and earth, shows no favorites. But if Judah would escape a similar judgment, a new spirit must characterize her life. Judah is still a nation. It is with eagerness of spirit and tenderness of appeal that the prophet pleads with his people. These are among his greatest utterances. Influence both of Amos and of Hosea may be seen in the tender and mighty words (2:1-3).

b. Indictment of the nations (2:4-15). Zephaniah, with considerable detail and geographical definiteness, shows how the judgment of God would affect the nations with which Judah is most vitally concerned. First he deals with the four vigorous and prosperous cities of Philistia, Judah's neighbor to the W—Gaza, Ashkelon, Ashdod, and Ekron. Philistia, now populous and wealthy, will be reduced to pastoral solitudes. He then turns to the fate of Egypt. Egypt had begun to reach out its arm of conquest toward Palestine and Syria; but the Ethiopians, who had themselves once ruled Egypt, would themselves fall by the sword (2:12).

Next he deals with Assyria. Yahweh's outstretched hand will make of proud Nineveh a desolation (2:13-14*a*). What once were beautiful capitals, windows, and thresholds will be but haunts of screech owls, porcupines, and ravens! (2:14*b-c.*) The prophet, in anticipation, pictures the ultimate and irrevocable collapse of that arrogant, haughty metropolis.

It was with solemnity and awe, and in the deep consciousness of being the spokesman of divine judgment that he contemplated the irrevocable fall of Nineveh. Already the barbarous Medes, percursors of the yet more barbarous Scythians, had attacked Assyria on the E. Now the prophet taunted Nineveh with a mock lament (2:15).

c. Jerusalem refuses correction (3:1-8). The prophet now pronounces impending judgment upon the capital, because Jerusalem has not listened to the prophetic voice, has refused to accept prophetic correction, and has not trusted or drawn near to God (vss. 1-2). Jerusalem's officials, judges, prophets, and priests come under the divine condemnation because they are licentious and profane (vss. 3-4). Yahweh, who remains righteous and blameless, will deal justly with his people (vs. 5). Although he has striven to correct them by showing them the nations' fate, they are unresponsive to his counsel and refuse to change their conduct (vss. 6-7). Yahweh will pour out upon all nations and kingdoms his indignation and judgment (vs. 8).

d. A remnant to be saved (3:9-20). Destruction is not God's last word. There are many evil people in Judah; but Judah is still in the hands of Yahweh, who is at work in the hearts and minds of a righteous minority. In Judah there are those who are not rebellious and proud, but who are humble and lowly, blameless in character and truthful in speech, and who have made God their refuge (vss. 9-13). To this creative nucleus of the future Judah, Yahweh will give spiritual renewal (vs. 17*b*), and he will find joy in them (vss. 14-17). They will not endure disaster any more. Yahweh will save the lame, gather the outcast, and, having brought home the scattered people, he will cause them to be honored among all the nations of the earth (vss. 18-20).

3. Composition of the book. If one admits with the superscription (1:1) that Zephaniah preached only during the reign of Josiah (640-609 B.C.), some elements of the book raise literary and historical problems. A number of scholars consider that chs. 2–3 contain later poems and that even the authentic oracles of Zephaniah have been somewhat amplified in the postexilic period. It is not necessary, however, to maintain that the picture of universal destruction (1:18*c;* 3:8*d*) represents the pattern of later apocalyptics. Nevertheless, the oracle of Moab and Ammon (2:8-9) may reflect the attitude of later Jewish nationalism (see especially vs. 9*d;* cf. 2:7*a, c*). Likewise, the international situation implied by 3:1-7 is characteristically different from that of Zephaniah during the Scythian invasion (chs. 1–2). Then, the nations were not yet destroyed; now, the picture of the international desolation is used as an object lesson destined to bring about the repentance of Jerusalem (3:6-7). Again, the conversion of all peoples to the worship of Yahweh (3:9) and the gathering of the Diaspora (3:10) constitute typically postexilic themes, bearing the influence of Deutero-Isaianic theology. The final poem (3:16-20) belongs to the eschatological pattern in which Yahweh himself, the "king of Israel," is "in the midst of his people," and the NATIONS become witnesses of the restored fortunes of Judah.

4. Zephaniah's teaching. While Zephaniah does not offer the same originality as his predecessors, Amos and Isaiah, or of his younger contemporary, Jeremiah, he contributes a note of his own. He knows the corrupting character of magical practices, and he declares that they have no place in the religion of Yahweh. Unless renewed by God, human nature is dishonest and deceitful. Foreign nations are used by the master of history to discipline the chosen people. Zephaniah's oracle on the Day of Yahweh has become classic through the medieval hymn *"Dies irae, dies illa."*

Bibliography. Commentaries: S. R. Driver, ed., *The Minor Prophets*, New Century Bible, vol. II (1906); J. M. P. Smith et al., *A Critical and Exegetical Commentary on Micah, Zephaniah, Nahum, Habakkuk, Obadiah, and Joel*, ICC (1911); A. B. Davidson, *The Books of Nahum, Habakkuk and Zephaniah*, Cambridge Bible (1920); E. Sellin, *Das Zwölfprophetenbuch* (1922); W. Nowack, *Die kleinen Propheten* (1922); C. V. Pilcher, *Three Hebrew Prophets* (1928); G. A. Smith, *The Book of the Twelve Prophets* (1929), vol. II; G. G. Stonehouse, *Zephaniah*, WC (1929); H. O. Kuhner, *Zephanjah* (1943); J. Coppens, *Les douze petits prophètes: Bréviaire du Prophétisme* (1950); K. Elliger, *Das Buch der zwölf kleinen Propheten*, Das Alte Testament Deutsch, vol. II (1950); A. George, *Michée, Sophonie, Nahum* (1952); F. Horst, *Die zwölf kleinen Propheten*, vol. II (1954); C. L. Taylor, Introduction and Exegesis of Zephaniah, IB, VI (1956), 1107-34.

Special studies: H. Ferguson, "The Historical Testimony of the Prophet Zephaniah," *JBL* (1883), pp. 42-59; C. P. Fagnani, "The Structure of the Text of the Book of Zephaniah," *OT and Semitic Studies in Memory of W. R. Harper*, II (1908), 260-75; A. F. Kirkpatrick, *The Doctrine of the Prophets* (1912); A. R. Gordon, *The Prophets of the OT* (1916); R. E. Wolfe, *The Editing of the Book of the Twelve* (1935); E. A. Leslie, *The Prophets Tell Their Own Story* (1939); G. Gerleman, *Zephanja textkritisch und literarisch untersucht* (1942); P. Hyatt, "The Date and Background of Zephaniah," *Journal of Near Eastern Studies*, VII (1948), 125-33; L. P. Smith and E. R. Lacheman, "The Authorship of Zephaniah," *Journal of Near Eastern Studies*, IX (1950), 137-42; A. Edens, *A Study of the Book of Zephaniah* (1953); G. Edwards, *The Editing of the OT Prophetic Books* (1955); T. T. Rice, *The Scythians* (1957); K. Sullivan, "The Book of Sophonias," *Worship*, XXXI (1957), 130-39; E. Balla, *Die Botschaft der Propheten* (1958).

E. A. LESLIE

ZEPHATH zē'fäth [צְפַת, watchtower]. A city in the SW part of Judah, in the neighborhood of Arad. According to Judg. 1:17, the tribes of Judah and Simeon attacked the city and utterly destroyed it, changing its name to HORMAH.

There is another possible reference to Zephath in II Chr. 14:10—H 14:9, when Asa went out to battle with Zerah the Ethiopian king, and a conflict took place "in the valley of Zephathah at Mareshah." But the Hebrew construction in this verse is awkward, so it is better to follow the LXX and read *miṣṣephôn lᵉmārēshâ*, "north of Mareshah."

S. COHEN

ZEPHATHAH zĕf'ə thə [צְפָתָה, watchtower] (II Chr. 14:10—H 14:9). A valley near Mareshah (Tell Sandahannah) in which Asa (*ca.* 913-873) met and defeated the Ethiopian raiding party under Zerah, commandant of the Egyptian garrison in Gerar. The LXX says the battle occurred N of Mareshah. Zephathah might be Safiyeh *ca.* 1⅔ miles NE of Beit Jibrin (Eleutheropolis). Wadi Safiyeh begins *ca.* a

mile NE of Beit Jibrin and continues for a short distance toward the NE.

V. R. GOLD

ZEPHI zē'fī [צְפִי; *cf.* Akkad. *personal name* Ṣupū; LXX Σωφαρ (*cf.* Job 2:11)] (I Chr. 1:36). Alternately: ZEPHO —fō [צְפוֹ] (Gen. 36:11, 15). The third son of Eliphaz the Edomite. The two forms of the name vary only by the slight consonantal confusion observed in Shephi/Shepho.

L. HICKS

ZEPHON zē'fŏn [צְפוֹן, *perhaps from* צפה, look out; *cf. personal names* צְפוֹ, צְפִי, צְפִיוֹן; *place names* צָפוֹן, מִצְפֶּה] (Num. 26:15); **ZEPHONITES** —fə nīts. The eldest son of Gad. The Samar. and the LXX support identification with ZIPHION.

ZER zûr [צֵר] (Josh. 19:35). A fortified town in the territory of Naphtali. It has been suggested that Zer is perhaps to be identified with MADON, which is not listed in Josh. 19, and that it is possibly the Israelite name of this town. This suggestion, however, must be regarded as uncertain. The LXX B, following the CT, but with a different vowel, reads "Tyre," which is topographically and textually impossible.

Bibliography. F.-M. Abel, *Géographie de la Palestine*, II (1938), 65, 457.

G. W. VAN BEEK

ZERAH zĭr'ə [זֶרַח, scarlet(?), *or* dawning, *or* shining forth; *perhaps a shortened form:* he (God) has shone forth (*cf.* ZERAHIAH, S Arab. דרחאﺍ, Akkad. *Za-ar-ḫi-ilu*); NT Ζάρα]; KJV ZARAH zâr'ə in Gen. 38:30; 46:12]; ZARA in Matt. 1:3; ZERAHITES zĭr'ə hīts; KJV ZARHITES zär'—. Alternately: ZOHAR zō'här [צֹחַר] (46:10; Exod. 6:15]. **1.** A chief of Edom; descended from both Esau and Ishmael, since he was a son of Reuel, who was the son of Esau by Basemath the daughter of Ishmael (Gen. 36:13, 17 [*cf.* vss. 2-4]; I Chr. 1:37). The name appears again as that of the father of an early Edomite king Jobab (Gen. 36:33; I Chr. 1:44).

2. One of the twins born to Judah by Tamar, his daughter-in-law (Gen. 38:30; 46:12; I Chr. 2:4). His name is ascribed to what happened as he and his brother were born: a scarlet thread was tied on his hand before his brother (*see* PEREZ) came out first (Gen. 38:27-30). He was the founder of a family of the tribe of Judah called Zerahites (Num. 26:20) and also called the "sons of Zerah" (I Chr. 9:6; Neh. 11:24). His descendants are named (I Chr. 2:6). He was the ancestor of Achan (Josh. 7:1, 18, 24; 22:20) and of Pethahiah (Neh. 11:24). Alongside Perez, his twin brother, his name appears in a genealogy of Jesus (Matt. 1:3).

3. A son of Simeon (Num. 26:13; I Chr. 4:24). He was the founder of a family of the tribe of Simeon called Zerahites (Num. 26:13). In Gen. 46:10; Exod. 6:15 he is named Zohar.

4. A Levite, of the family of Gershom (I Chr. 6: 21, 41).

5. An Ethiopian (RSV-KJV), or a Cushite (Hebrew). Sabean דרח (Hebrew זרח; *see above*) is a princely title (*see* SABEANS). He was the leader of an attacking force vanquished by Asa king of Judah at Mareshah and pursued to obliteration at Gerar (II Chr. 14:9-15). He was probably the leader of raiding Arabian Bedouin tribes: tents and camels are mentioned in the plundering, which took place in Gerar and its environs (vss. 12-15). The Chronicler or a later redactor in 16:8 evidently mistook Zerah as the leader of an Egyptian host. Zerah is not to be identified with Pharaoh Osorkon I or Osorkon II, as some have held.

Bibliography. F. Hommel, "Zerah the Cushite," *ET*, VIII (1896-97), 378-79; K. Tallqvist, *Assyrian Personal Names* (1914), p. 247; M. Noth, *Die israelitischen Personennamen* (1928), p. 184; W. Rudolf, *Chronikbücher*, HAT (1955), p. 243; W. Albright, *From the Stone Age to Christianity* (1957), pp. 46-47. T. M. Mauch

ZERAHIAH zĕr' ə hī'ə [זרחיה, Y has shone forth; *cf.* S Arab. דרחאל, Akkad. *Za-ar-ḫi-ilu;* Apoc. Ζαραιά]; KJV Apoc. ZARAIAS zə rā'yəs. **1.** A priest; son of Uzzi and descendant of Eleazar; an ancestor of Ezra (I Chr. 6:6, 51; Ezra 7:4; I Esd. 8:2 KJV, omitted by RSV with B; *cf.* Arna in II Esd. 1:2).
2. A layman; the father of Eliehoenai, who returned to Judah from the Exile with Ezra (Ezra 8:4; I Esd. 8:31).

Bibliography. K. Tallqvist, *Assyrian Personal Names* (1914), p. 247; M. Noth, *Die israelitischen Personennamen* (1928), p. 184. T. M. Mauch

ZERAHITES zĭr'ə hīts [זרחי]; KJV ZARHITES zär'—. A name for a family descended from Zerah. There was a family of this name in the tribe of Simeon (Num. 26:13; *see* Zerah 3), and another in the tribe of Judah (Num. 26:20; Josh. 7:17; *see* Zerah 2). Two of David's Mighty Men belonged to this family: Sibbecai the Hushathite and Maharai the Netophathite (I Chr. 27:11, 13).

T. M. Mauch

ZERAIAH; KJV ZARAIAS. Apoc. form of Zebadiah 8.

ZERDAIAH; KJV SARDEUS. Apoc. form of Aziza.

ZERED, BROOK zĭr'ĭd [נחל זרד]. Alternately: VALLEY OF ZERED (Num. 21:12); KJV VALLEY OF ZARED zâr'ĭd. The stream which the Israelites crossed marking an end to their thirty-eight years of wandering in the wilderness (Num. 21:12; Deut. 2:13-14). It is identified with the Wadi el-Hesa, which flows into the SE end of the Dead Sea. For a short distance before entering the Dead Sea after it has emerged into the plain, it is called the Seil el-Qerahi. The Zered is *ca.* 35 miles long and has a fall of *ca.* 3,900 feet. Through its tributaries it drains the entire N section of the Jebel esh-Shera' (Jebal). The valley itself is 3½-4 miles across at the top.

Trajan's road crosses the Zered at el-'Ainab, following the route dating from the Early Bronze age. A series of Edomite fortresses guarded the approaches to the plateau S of the Zered. The Zered constituted the N boundary of the kingdom of Edom and the S boundary of the kingdom of Moab.

The "Brook of Willows" in Isaiah's oracle against Moab is usually identified with the Brook Zered (Isa. 15:7).

Bibliography. N. Glueck, *Explorations in Eastern Palestine*, II, *AASOR,* XV (1934-35), *passim;* III, *AASOR,* XVIII-XIX (1937-39), *passim.* V. R. Gold

ZEREDAH zĕr'ə də [צרדה, *locative* צרותה]; KJV ZEREDA (I Kings 11:26); ZEREDATHAH zĕr'ə dā'thə (II Chr. 4:17). **1.** The home of Jeroboam; his place of residence prior to his working for, and revolt against, Solomon. The only clue to the location of the town is the reference to "Ephraimite," which can be understood as indicating the territory of Ephraim. It has been suggested that Zeredah was not in a central location and that for this reason Jeroboam moved to, and fortified, Shechem rather than his native town. A possible location for Zeredah at the spring 'Ain Seridah in the Wadi Deir Ballut in W Samaria has been suggested. Some commentators have identified it with modern Deir Ghassaneh, located *ca.* fifteen miles SW of Shechem.

Bibliography. W. F. Albright, "The Administrative Divisions of Israel and Judah," *JPOS*, V (1925), 33, 37.
2. A city in the Jordan Valley (II Chr. 4:17); it probably should be read "Zarethan" (צרתן), as in I Kings 7:46. Most commentators suggest this should also be the reading in Judg. 7:22, instead of "Zererah" (RSV mg. "Zeredah," with some Hebrew MSS; *cf.* Josh. 3:16; I Kings 4:12; 7:46).

W. L. Reed

ZERERAH zĕr'ə rə [צררה]; KJV ZERERATH —räth. A place along the route by which the Midianite host fled after its first defeat by Gideon (Judg. 7:22). The exact form of the name is uncertain; if it is merely a variant of Zarethan, the KJV form would be correct. Other scholars, supposing a confusion between the Hebrew letters *r* and *d* (ר and ד), have proposed a reading "Zeredah" (cf. II Chr. 4:17), which is also probably a variant of Zarethan.

S. Cohen

ZERESH zĭr'ĭsh [זרש] (Esth. 5:14; 6:13). The wife of Haman, and apparently his chief counselor, first in his plans for vengeance and later in warning him of defeat. The name may be Persian (possibly "gold" or "mophead"; *see bibliography*), or it may represent the Elamite goddess Kirisha.

See also Vashti; Esther.

Bibliography. H. S. Gehman, *JBL*, XLIII (1924), 326.
D. Harvey

ZERETH zĭr'ĭth [צרת] (I Chr. 4:7). A descendant of Judah; the first son of Helah, the wife of Ashhur.

ZERETH-SHAHAR zĭr'ĭth shā'här [צרת השחר]; KJV ZARETH-SHAHAR zâr'—. A city of the tableland of Moab, assigned by Moses to the tribe of Reuben (Josh. 13:19). It was located "on the hill of the valley" (בהר העמק), presumably a hill overlooking the basin of the Dead Sea (cf. vs. 27). Many identify Zereth-shahar with modern Zarat, at the hot springs of Callirhoe, on the E shore of the Dead Sea not far from Machaerus. E. D. Grohman

ZERI zĭr'ī [צרי, balsam] (I Chr. 25:3). Head of a possibly Davidic, and postexilic, family of singers of the Jeduthun group. An initial letter may have been lost (*cf.* Izri, יצרי, in vs. 11). *See* Jeduthun; Music.

ZEROR zĭr'ôr [צְרוֹר] (I Sam. 9:1). An ancestor of Saul; a son of Becorath, and the father of Abiel.

ZERUAH zĭ rōō'ə [צְרוּעָה, having a skin disease] (I Kings 11:26). The mother of Jeroboam.

ZERUBBABEL zĭ rŭb'ə bəl [זְרֻבָּבֶל, Akkad. *zēr-bābili*, scion of Babylon; Ζοροβαβέλ]; KJV Apoc. and KJV NT **ZOROBABEL** zō rŏb'—. A Babylonian Jew who returned to Palestine (Ezra 2:2) to become governor (*peḥâ*) in postexilic Jerusalem under the Persian king Darius I (Hystaspis; 522-486 B.C.). Zerubbabel is probably not to be identified with Sheshbazzar (1:8, etc.). Although such an identification has often been defended, the latter must rather be Zerubbabel's uncle (on this problem, *see bibliography and* SHESHBAZZAR).

Aroused and spurred on by the prophetic preaching of Haggai and Zechariah, Zerubbabel, with Joshua the high priest, resumed the work of rebuilding the temple at Jerusalem in the second year of Darius (520; cf. Ezra 3:2-13; 5:1-2; Hag. 1:1-2:9; Zech. 4:9)—a work which had been started under Sheshbazzar (Ezra 5:16) but which was only now to be completed (*ca.* 515; cf. Ezra 6:15), some twenty-three years after the edict of Cyrus (538) permitting the Jews to return to Palestine. The work was accomplished despite the opposition and hostile legal maneuvering of the "adversaries of Benjamin and Judah" in adjacent provinces (ch. 4; 5:3–6:15).

It would seem at first glance that Ezra 3-4 places the beginning of Zerubbabel's work in the reign of Cyrus, but the chronological references in these passages are clearly ambiguous and contradictory. The greater historical trustworthiness of Haggai and Zechariah suggests that the Ezra passages describe events during the reign of Darius, not of the earlier Cyrus. *See* EZRA AND NEHEMIAH, BOOKS OF; and *see bibliography.*

In every genealogical reference except one, Zerubbabel is the "son of Shealtiel" (Ezra 3:2, 8; 5:2; Neh. 12:1; Hag. 1:1, 12, 14; 2:2, 23; Matt. 1:12; Luke 3:27). In I Chr. 3:19 he appears as the son of Pedaiah. It has been conjectured that Shealtiel may have died childless but that Zerubbabel was born to his widow by the deceased man's brother in a levirate marriage, so that the offspring of Pedaiah the brother would be legally the son of Shealtiel. But if this were the case, it is difficult to understand why Zerubbabel is not listed as Shealtiel's son in this passage also, or such an explanation given. More probably either the Chronicler is in error here, or possibly the reference is to another person, who would then be a cousin of Zerubbabel his namesake. The name is shown by actual inscriptions from the time of Darius to have been a common one in Babylon. In either case Zerubbabel stands in the Davidic line, being a grandson of the exiled king of Judah, Jehoiachin (cf. I Chr. 3:17-19). Matt. 1:12; Luke 3:27 place him in the ancestral line of Jesus Christ.

The prophets Haggai and Zechariah, doubtless prompted by the disturbances in the Persian Empire which followed the death of Cyrus' successor, Cambyses, and the consequent accession to the throne of Darius I in 522 B.C., anticipate as a providential consequence of the international upheavals Judah's restoration to national power under Zerubbabel, who represents for them now the ideal of the Davidic kingship (Hag. 2:21-22; Zech. 4:6-7). For Haggai he is Yahweh's "servant" and his "chosen one," his "signet ring" (Hag. 2:23; cf. Jer. 22:24), and Zechariah's references to "the Branch" (3:8; 6:12) must be taken to mean Zerubbabel as David's descendant (cf. Isa. 11:1; Jer. 23:5-6; 33:14-16). Zech. 6:12 seems certainly to have referred originally to Zerubbabel, not Joshua (*see bibliography*). Thus a messianic hope focuses on the figure of Zerubbabel. However, a restoration of the Davidic kingdom was consummated neither under him nor afterward, and the Persian rulers evidently did not continue to appoint governors of Judah from the house of David.

The circumstances of the end of Zerubbabel's service as governor are unknown, as are those of his death. Because no known Davidic ruler appears to have followed Zerubbabel in the governorship, and because Ezra 6:14 omits his name from among those mentioned who participated in the completion of the temple construction, it has been conjectured that he was removed from office by the Persian throne for rebelling or threatening to rebel against it. Biblical sources are silent about this, however, unless Zech. 6:11 suggests such an attempt. But probably the coronation here referred to is a symbolic act, particularly in view of 4:6, which is addressed to Zerubbabel: "Not by might, nor by power, but by my Spirit, says the LORD of hosts." In this general connection, an attempt to see the "suffering servant" of Isa. 53 as referring to a martyrdom of Zerubbabel has not received support among most biblical scholars. *See bibliography.*

An anonymous Jewish chronicle of the sixth century A.D., *Seder ʿOlam Zuṭa,* asserts that Zerubbabel returned to Babylon after the temple was completed and there succeeded his father, Shealtiel, as an exilarch, or prince of the Exile. But the reference appears in a context where much else is known to be historically erroneous, and this late tradition is unreliable—its primary purpose being an attempt to demonstrate the Davidic lineage of the later Babylonian exilarchs. *See bibliography.*

But it is evident in any case that Zerubbabel received a place of honor in Jewish tradition. Ecclus. 49:11 celebrates him as one of Israel's renowned men, and a midrash in a thirteenth-century A.D. haggadic compilation, *Yalqûṭ Shimʿônî* (II.296) represents Zerubbabel as God's herald in the messianic Garden of Eden. Most striking is a passage in the Hanukkah hymn, "Moʿoz ṭzur," also from the thirteenth century (attributed to Mordecai ben Isaac), which recounts God's redemptive acts toward Israel in part with these words (*see bibliography*):

> Torn from all I cherished, almost had I perished;
> Babylon fell;
> Zerubbabel
> Bad'st thou to restore me![1]

Doubtlessly more familiar is the legend associated in the Apoc. with Zerubbabel which recounts a forensic contest between three young bodyguards of

[1] J. H. Hertz, *The Authorized Daily Prayer Book* (New York: Bloch Publishing Co., Inc.).

Darius the Persian king (I Esd. 3:1-5:6), and which is followed by the historian Josephus (*ca.* A.D. 100), who represents Zerubbabel as already having been governor in Jerusalem and an "old friend" of Darius. (Antiq. XI.iii.) One of the young contestants is Zerubbabel, whose display of wisdom gains the admiration of the king, who thereupon provides the enabling decrees and the material support for Zerubbabel's return to rebuild Jerusalem and the temple. Clearly the story is a legendary embellishment of the tradition where historical details were lacking, but it may reflect some valid memory of Zerubbabel's early training in the Persian court, after the analogy of Daniel and his three friends (Dan. 1:1-21).

Bibliography. A detailed and important study of the sources for Zerubbabel's life and work, including an attempted defense of his identification with Sheshbazzar, as well as the quotation from *Yalqûṭ Shim'ônî*, is given in J. Gabriel, *Zorobabel* (in German; 1927).

A valuable discussion of Zerubbabel as a messianic figure is given in S. Mowinckel, *He That Cometh* (trans. G. W. Anderson; 1955), pp. 119-22, 155-62.

For an attempt to see references to Zerubbabel in Isa. 53, see E. Sellin, *Serubbabel* (1898), pp. 148 ff.

On the story of the three youths (I Esd. 3:1 ff), see C. C. Torrey, *Ezra Studies* (1910), pp. 37-61.

See also: Josephus Antiq. XI.i-iv; M. Seligsohn, "Seder 'Olam Zuṭa," *JE*, XI (1905), 150; H. G. Mitchell, *Haggai and Zechariah*, ICC (1912), pp. 42-43, 53-56, 76-79, 190-93; L. W. Batten, *Ezra and Nehemiah*, ICC (1913), pp. 71-74, 112-82; R. H. Charles, "Introduction to I Esdras," *The Apoc. and Pseudep. of the OT* (1913), I, 15-17; M. Noth, *Die israelitischen Personennamen* (1928), p. 63; W. O. E. Oesterley and T. H. Robinson, *A History of Israel*, II (1932), 74-94; S. Solis-Cohen, trans., *"Mo'oz tzur,"* in J. H. Hertz, ed., *The Authorized Daily Prayer Book* (1948), p. 951; W. F. Albright, *The Biblical Period* (1950), p. 49.   B. T. DAHLBERG

ZERUIAH zĭ rōō'yə [צרויה] *or (three times)* צריה, *from* צרי, perfumed with mastix]. The mother of Joab, Abishai, and Asahel, three loyal followers of David and commanders of his army (II Sam. 2:18; etc.). These men are identified always as sons of Zeruiah, and not by the name of their father. It may be that Zeruiah was an outstanding woman, or possibly that the ancient custom of tracing descent by the female line has been preserved in this case. According to I Chr. 2:16, Zeruiah and Abigail were sisters of the sons of Jesse. In II Sam. 17:25, however, Abigail is called the daughter of Nahash. It may be that Jesse's wife was once married to Nahash; that the name Nahash has been introduced into vs. 25 from vs. 27, where it belongs; or possibly that a matriarchal reckoning is involved. In any case, Zeruiah and Abigail seem to have been sisters or half sisters of David.

D. HARVEY

ZETHAM zē'thəm [זתם, olive tree] (I Chr. 23:8; 26:22). A Gershonite Levite.

ZETHAN zē'thən [זיתן, olive tree, *or* one who deals with olives] (I Chr. 7:10). Listed as a Benjaminite family in what is probably a list of families of Zebulun.

ZETHAR zē'thär [זתר, *possibly* slayer *or* victor; *see bibliography*] (Esth. 1:10). One of the seven eunuchs who served King Ahasuerus as chamberlains.

Bibliography. On etymology, see L. B. Paton, *Esther*, ICC (1908), pp. 68, 148; J. D. Davis and H. S. Gehman, *The Westminster Dictionary of the Bible* (1944), p. 656.

B. T. DAHLBERG

ZEUS zōōs [Ζεύς, *genitive* Διός, *probably from* to shine, be bright]. The Greek form of the great Indo-European sky-god, sometimes the divine Sky itself; cf. Sanskrit Dyaus and Latin Jovis or Juppiter (Jovispater). Zeus "rains" or sends the rain; he hurls the dreadful thunderbolt; he releases the winds; all aspects of the weather are under his control. But he is also the supreme governor of the universe, lord over gods and men, and none can resist his will. He is the guardian of hospitality, and avenges wrongs done to guest or host. In the representations of sculpture, he sits enthroned in majesty, grave but kindly; this form is subsequently adapted in Christian art for the representation of Christ enthroned and of God the Father. Always the greatest of the Greek gods, the undisputed master of Olympus—"King of kings, most blessed of the blessed ones, most perfect Might of the Perfect" (Aeschylus)—he becomes in later Greek religion a symbol of divinity itself. The Stoics use his name as a personal symbol for the Power that governs all things, which may also be called Fate or Providence or Right Reason or the General Law. In the Hellenistic syncretism, he is identified with the high gods of all the nations.

Courtesy of Theresa Goell

2. Altar of Zeus at Pergamum

When the people of Lystra called Barnabas Zeus (Acts 14:12), they clearly took him for the manifest form of the high god, who allowed Paul to be his spokesman. It is often suggested that the names Zeus and Hermes have been substituted for some pair of native (non-Greek) divinities, since the people were clamoring in Lycaonian. No such distinction was in the mind of the author of Acts; for the "oxen and garlands" (vs. 13) were the sacrifices appropriate to Zeus, and it was the eloquence of Paul which caused him to be taken for Hermes, the god of oratory. In vs. 13, there can be little doubt that the reading of D should be adopted: τοῦ ὄντος Διὸς Προπόλεως, "the local Zeus-before-the-city"; an inscription "to Zeus before-the-city" (Διῒ Προαστίῳ) has actually been found in a town near Lystra. There is no suggestion of a temple in the Greek text, and it is probable that there would have been only an altar, perhaps with an image, at the city gates.

Fig. ZEU 2.   F. W. BEARE

ZIA zī'ə [יִיעַ, the trembler(?)] (I Chr. 5:13). A head of a father's house in the tribe of Gad.

ZIBA zī'bə [צִבָא, צְבָא (II Sam. 16:4)]. A servant of the house of Saul whose artfulness ultimately gained for him half of his master's possessions. When David sought to locate the surviving members of the house of Saul, Ziba informed the king that Mephibosheth, the lame son of Jonathan, was living in the home of Machir the son of Ammiel, in Lo-debar (II Sam. 9: 1-4). The king invited Mephibosheth to become a member of the royal board and bestowed upon him all the lands of the house of Saul. Ziba, who appears to have seized control of the lands of his master, was then appointed administrator of the lands, while his household, consisting of fifteen sons and twenty servants, also became servants of Mephibosheth.

The rebellion of Absalom gave Ziba an opportunity to rid himself of this onerous connection with his new master. David fled the capital so hurriedly that he was without provisions for his entourage. Ziba met the king in his flight with timely supplies and did not find it difficult to convince him that Mephibosheth had remained in Jerusalem because he sought to regain the crown for the house of Saul. Persuaded by this treacherous ruse, David forthwith transferred to Ziba all the possessions of Mephibosheth (II Sam. 16:1-4). After the suppression of the rebellion of Absalom, Ziba and his household rushed to greet the returning king and to be of service (19:17). However, Mephibosheth also met the king at the Jordan and exposed the duplicity of his servant by explaining that when he had commanded Ziba to saddle his ass so that he could join the king in his flight, Ziba had made off with the asses and left him, in his lameness, behind. Convinced, no doubt, of the general integrity of Mephibosheth, but nevertheless grateful for the indispensable aid of Ziba, David ruled that the lands of the house of Saul should be divided between Mephibosheth and Ziba (19:24-29).　　　　　　　　　　E. R. DALGLISH

ZIBEON zĭb'ĭ ən [צִבְעוֹן, hyena; cf. ZEBOIM]. The third son of Seir, and a clan chief (אַלּוּף צִבְעוֹן; perhaps better "clan chief of Zibeon") of the native Horite inhabitants of Edom (Gen. 36:20, 24, 29; I Chr. 1:38, 40). In Gen. 36:2, 14, the KJV "daughter of Zibeon" should be read "son . . ." with the RSV; the writer possibly understood "Anah" to have feminine gender.　　　　　　　　　　L. HICKS

ZIBIA zĭb'ĭ ə [צִבְיָה, gazelle] (I Chr. 8:9). A head of a father's house in the tribe of Benjamin; listed among others (one of them a Mesha) as sons of Shaharaim which he had in the country of Moab by his wife Hodesh.

ZIBIAH zĭb'ĭ ə [צִבְיָה, gazelle] (II Kings 12:1—H 12: 2; II Chr. 24:1). The mother of Joash king of Judah.

ZICHRI zĭk'rī [זִכְרִי, remembrance, or mindful(?); *perhaps a shortened form; cf.* ZECHARIAH]. **1.** A person or subdivision of the Levitical family of Izhar (Exod. 6:21).

2. A family of the tribe of Benjamin, descended from Shimei (I Chr. 8:19).

3. A family of the tribe of Benjamin, descended from Shashak (I Chr. 8:23).

4. A family of the tribe of Benjamin, descended from Jeroham (I Chr. 8:27).

5. A Levite individual or family (*see* PRIESTS AND LEVITES) descended from Asaph (I Chr. 9:15). Probably he was the same person called Zaccur (same root) in I Chr. 25:2, 10; Neh. 12:35, and called Zabdi in Neh. 11:17 (the consonants in these three names are identical or similar in Hebrew; *see* ALPHABET).

6. A Levite; the father of Shelomoth (I Chr. 26:25).

7. A Reubenite; the father of Eliezer (I Chr. 27:16).

8. A man of Judah; the father of Amasiah (II Chr. 17:16).

9. The father of Elishaphat (II Chr. 23:1).

10. An Ephraimite; a mighty fighter in the army of Pekah. The Chronicler attributes to him the slaying of several high personages in the court of Ahaz, in a presentation of the Syrian and Israelite invasions as punishment for Ahaz' idolatry (II Chr. 28:7).

11. A Benjaminite, the father of Joel (Neh. 11:9).

12. A postexilic priest (Neh. 12:17).

　　　　　　　　　　T. M. MAUCH

ZIDDIM zĭd'ĭm [צִדִּים, flanks *or* sides]. A fortified town in the territory allotted to Naphtali (Josh. 19: 35). The exact location of the site is unknown. The Talmud identified Ziddim with Caphar Hittaia, modern Hattin el-Qadim, which is located approximately eight miles W-NW of Tiberias, near MADON; but this is not certain.

Bibliography. C. R. Conder and H. H. Kitchener, *SWP*, I (1881), 360, 365; F.-M. Abel, *Géographie de la Palestine*, II (1938), 65, 460-61.　　　　　　　　　　G. W. VAN BEEK

ZIDKIJAH. KJV form of ZEDEKIAH 5.

ZIDON, ZIDONIANS. KJV forms. *See* SIDON.

ZIF. KJV form of ZIV.

ZIHA zī'ə [צִיחָא, צָחָא (Neh. 7:46), *a foreign name; cf.* Egyp.-Aram. צָחָא, Akkad. Ṣi-ḥa-a]; KJV Apoc. ESAU ē'sô. Eponym of a family of NETHINIM (temple servants), which returned from the Exile (Ezra 2:43; Neh. 7:46; I Esd. 5:29). An individual of this name is cited as an overseer of the temple servants in a supplementary verse (Neh. 11:21).

Bibliography. K. Tallqvist, *Assyrian Personal Names* (1914), p. 205. M. Noth, *Die israelitischen Personennamen* (1928), pp. 63-64.　　　　　　　　　　T. M. MAUCH

＊ZIKLAG zĭk'lăg [צִיקְלַג, צִקְלַג]. A city, probably modern Tell el-Khuweilfeh, *ca.* ten miles E of Tell esh-Sheri'a, and *ca.* five miles S-SW of Tell Beit Mirsim (Debir).

Ziklag first belonged to the Simeonites (Josh. 19:5; I Chr. 4:30) and later, in the royal administrative division of Judah, became a part of the Negeb province (Josh. 15:31). After the Philistine invasion in the early twelfth century, it was under Philistine control until the time of David.

During Saul's reign, David was given Ziklag by Achish king of Gath, and used it as a base for raids against the Amalekites and others (I Sam. 27:6, etc.). When the Philistines went up to Jezreel to do battle against Saul and his army, David, at their request, returned to Ziklag and discovered that it had been sacked by the Amalekites and its populace, including David's two wives, carried off by the raiders. He pursued the Amalekites, defeated them, and rescued the booty and citizens of Ziklag. Returning to Ziklag, he sent gifts of appreciation from the booty to the cities in the Negeb and S Judean hill country for kindnesses shown him and his men during their movements among them (I Sam. 30; I Chr. 12:1-20).

It was at Ziklag, a couple of days later, that an Amalekite told David of Saul's defeat and death in the Battle of Gilboa (II Sam. 1:1; 4:10). David's connection with Ziklag and later defeat of the Philistines resulted in the permanent return of Ziklag to Israelite control. After the Exile, Ziklag was among those cities reoccupied by the returning Jews (Neh. 11:28).

V. R. GOLD

ZILLAH zĭl´ə [צלה, shadow; *cf. masculine names* בצלאל *and* צלתי (Gen. 4:19-23). The second wife of Lamech; the mother of Tubal-cain and his sister Naamah.

Bibliography. M. Noth, *Die israelitischen Personennamen* (1928), p. 152.   L. HICKS

ZILLETHAI zĭl´ə thī [צלתי, (Y is) a shadow, protection; *a shortened form*]; KJV ZILTHAI zĭl´thī. 1. A family of the tribe of Benjamin (I Chr. 8:20).
2. A Manassite who joined David at Ziklag (I Chr. 12:20).

Bibliography. M. Noth, *Die israelitischen Personennamen* (1928), pp. 39, 152.   T. M. MAUCH

ZILPAH zĭl´pə [זלפה, *perhaps* short-nosed]. The mother of Gad and Asher. She was given by Laban to Leah as her maid (Gen. 29:24; 46:18), and by Leah to Jacob as his "wife" (30:9; 37:2), and bore his sons Gad and Asher (30:10, 12; 35:26).

See also TRIBES, TERRITORIES OF.

Bibliography. On etymology, see H. Bauer, *ZAW,* XLVIII (1930), 78.   S. J. DE VRIES

ZILTHAI. KJV form of ZILLETHAI.

ZIMMAH zĭm´ə [זמה, *a shortened form, the second consonant of the original root doubled:* (Y has) considered, purposed] (I Chr. 6:20, 42; II Chr. 29:12). A Levite descended from Gershom.

Bibliography. M. Noth, *Die israelitischen Personennamen* (1928), pp. 39, 176.   T. M. MAUCH

ZIMRAN zĭm´răn [זמרן]. A son of Abraham and Keturah and hence the name of an Arabian locality (Gen. 25:2; I Chr. 1:32). It is apparently the same as the ZIMRI of Jer. 25:25. Its location is uncertain, but it is probably somewhere along the shore of the Red Sea, where Ptolemy mentions a Zabram to the W of Mecca.   S. COHEN

ZIMRI zĭm´rī [זמרי, awe of Yahy(?); Apoc. Ζαμβρι]; KJV Apoc. ZAMBRI zăm´brī. Alternately: ZABDI

zăb´dī [זבדי] (Josh. 7:1, 17-18). 1. One of the five sons of Zerah; grandson of Judah and Tamar (I Chr. 2:6). In Josh. 7:1, 17-18, he is called Zabdi, doubtless through confusion between ב ("b") and מ ("m"), as happened frequently.
2. Son of Salu, prince of Simeon (Num. 25:6-18; cf. I Macc. 2:26).

This story comes from the P source and refers to Israel's intercourse with foreign women and the resultant idolatry. A plague had come upon Israel, and the people were weeping at the door of the tent of meeting. Just at this time an Israelite brought a Midianite woman into his family. Both of them were killed by Phinehas son of Eleazar son of Aaron the priest—an action which stayed the plague, but only after twenty-four thousand had died. The guilty man was Zimri, a prince of Simeon. The woman was Cozbi ("deceiver"), a princess of Midian.
3. King of Israel *ca.* 876 B.C.; successor to Elah, whom he murdered.

The root of the name is perhaps the Syriac *dmr,* "wonder" or "awe," but it is very old, appearing on Akkadian tablets from Mari. The word itself may be a contraction of זמריה—i.e., Ζαμαρίας, or זמריהו, "strength of Yahu"(?). The name occurs in the LXX and Josephus as Ζαμβρ(ε)ι, which is the older vocalization.

Zimri reigned for seven days in Tirzah (I Kings 16:15). No mention is made of his father. The dynasty which Baasha attempted to establish was overthrown with the murder of Baasha's son Elah and the extermination of his whole house by Zimri (vss. 11-13). The reason alleged for the complete destruction of Baasha's house is remarkable in that elsewhere Jeroboam is blamed for causing Israel to sin. No details of the sins of Baasha and Elah are given.

Zimri, an army commander, seized his chance when the army was again occupied with the siege of Gibbethon (cf. I Kings 15:27). King Elah had remained in Tirzah, where he was engaging in a drunken orgy in the house of Arza, the royal chamberlain, when Zimri murdered him, presumably with the aid of his half-squadron of chariots.

When news of Zimri's coup reached the army in the field, they made Omri, the commander-in-chief, king. This was clearly an act of the army, not of "all Israel" (I Kings 16:16-17). The siege of Gibbethon was raised immediately, and Omri marched to Tirzah, which he captured. Zimri had taken refuge in the citadel of the palace, which he burned down, thus causing his own death.

The name occurs again in II Kings 9:31, where Jezebel greeted Jehu as he entered the gate of the city of Jezreel with the words: "Is it peace, you Zimri, murderer of your master?"

Bibliography. J. A. Montgomery, *The Book of Kings,* ICC (1951), p. 289.
4. A Benjaminite; a descendant of Jonathan, Saul's son. His father's name was Jehoaddah (I Chr. 8:36; cf. 9:42, where the father's name is given as Jarah).

H. B. MACLEAN

ZIN, WILDERNESS OF zĭn [מדבר צן]. A wilderness through which the Israelites passed on their journey to Canaan (Num. 13:21; 20:1; 27:14; 33:36; 34:3-4; Deut. 32:51; Josh. 15:1, 3). Its location can be ascertained from the description of the future Israelite (Judean) territory in Canaan as given, with slight variations, by both Num. 34:3-4; Josh. 15:1, 3: "Your south side shall be from the wilderness of Zin along the side of Edom, and your southern boundary shall be from the end of the Salt Sea on the east; and your boundary shall turn south of the ascent of Akrabbim, and cross to Zin, and its end shall be south of Kadesh-barnea." The expression "south of the ascent of Akrabbim, and cross to Zin," is identical in both accounts. The word "Zin" occurs by itself only in these two passages, and may refer to an area or a place which gave the surrounding territory its name, "the wilderness of Zin."

Num. 13:21 states that the spies sent out by Moses "spied out the land from the wilderness of Zin to Rehob" (cf. Deut. 1:19-20). Num. 20:1 simply records that "the people of Israel . . . came into the wilderness of Zin in the first month [the year is omitted], and the people stayed at Kadesh; and Miriam died there, and was buried there." In vss. 2-13 the account narrates the events which took place at the "waters of Meribah" (see MASSAH AND MERIBAH). According to these two accounts the Wilderness of Zin lay N of PARAN and included Kadesh. Num. 27:12-14; Deut. 32:49-52 (duplicate accounts) relate the punishment which Moses received from Yahweh for his failure to glorify him "at the waters of Meribah of Kadesh in the wilderness of Zin." And in Num. 33:36 the Wilderness of Zin is referred to as the first stopping place of the Israelites after they left Ezion-geber.

From the above references a number of conclusions may be drawn: (a) The Wilderness of Zin is not identical with the "Wilderness of Sin," even though both the LXX and the Vulg. spell both names the same in all places, except in Num. 34:3-4; Josh. 15:1, 3. The Wilderness of Sin was probably located at Debbet er-Ramleh, on the W fringe of Sinai Plateau (see SIN, WILDERNESS OF). (b) The Wilderness of Zin was adjacent to and N of the Wilderness of Paran, with Kadesh regarded as being in either region. (c) It was a part of the SE border of Judah toward the Dead Sea.

According to archaeological researches the Wilderness of Zin and Kadesh-barnea must have comprised the territory of the modern 'Ain el-Qudeirât, Kossaima, Muweilleh, and 'Ain Qadeis.

Bibliography. A. Musil, *Arabia Petra* (1907), vol. II, pt. 1, p. 211; C. L. Woolley and T. E. Lawrence, *The Wilderness of Zin* (new ed., 1936).   J. L. MIHELIC

ZINA. Alternate form of ZIZAH.

ZION zī'ən [ציון; Σιών]; KJV SION sī'ən. Originally the fortified hill of pre-Israelite Jerusalem. The etymology of the name is uncertain. It may be related to the Hebrew ציון (ṣāyōn), "dry place," "parched ground" (Isa. 25:5; 32:2), or to the Arabic ṣahweh, interpreted as "hillcrest," "mountainous ridge," from which the Arabic name for Zion—viz., Ṣahyūn or Ṣihyūn—obviously derives (cf. the Syriac Ṣēhyûn). According to a recent hypothesis, mentioned here for the record only, Zion ought to be interpreted by the

Hurrian ṣeya, "river," "brook," and the expression "stronghold of Zion" (II Sam. 5:7) would apply to the Jebusite fortress (see JEBUS), located directly above the spring (and the brook) of GIHON.

The name Zion appears for the first time in the narrative of the conquest of Jerusalem by David (II Sam. 5:6-10; I Chr. 11:4-9) in the expression מצדת ציון, "stronghold of Zion," which need not be interpreted restrictively as a single building or detached fortress, but rather as the fortified crest of the hill wedged between the valleys of the Tyropoeon and the Kidron, S of the temple area or Haram esh-Sherif, whereas the name of Urusalim (the ancient form of Jerusalem) was that of the city-state as a whole, including miscellaneous hamlets and isolated houses outside the fortifications. The same passage explains how the expression "City of David" (see DAVID, CITY OF) was substituted for the name Zion, to apply to the area within the fortified perimeter restored and eventually modified or extended by David. Conversely, the term "City of David" is explained by means of the gloss, "which is Zion" (I Kings 8:1; II Chr. 5:2). These two passages record the transfer of the ark of the covenant from the city of David to the temple recently built by Solomon.

The transfer of the ark from the city to the temple may explain why the name Zion was subsequently extended to the temple area itself, as evidenced by numerous passages of the Psalms. Yahweh is said to dwell on the mountain of Zion. Some texts associate the King with God, perhaps in view of the architectural unity of the compound palace-temple (Pss. 2:6; 132:13). More frequently, Yahweh alone is mentioned (Pss. 48:2; 74:2; 84:7; Isa. 18:7). Throngs of pilgrims long to mount to Zion and present themselves before God (Ps. 84:5). The topographical equivalence Zion-temple occurs repeatedly in the Maccabean period, when the Jews had fortified the sanctuary to resist the attacks directed by the Syrians from their fortress on the Acra (see JERUSALEM § 9; I Macc. 4:37, 60; 5:54; 6:48, 62; 7:33; 10:11; 14:27—G 14:26). The book of Jubilees also refers to the hill on which the temple stood as "Mount Zion" (Jub. 4:26; 8:19; 18:13).

In the poetic books and the prophetic writings, Zion becomes an equivalent of Jerusalem considered as the religious capital, or as being the object of God's favor or punishment (Isa. 28:16; cf. Rom. 9:33; I Pet. 2:6). In many cases, there is scarcely anything more than mere poetic parallelism (Ps. 51:18; Isa. 10:12; 24:23; 31:4; 40:9; Joel 3:16; Mic. 3:10, 12). In some passages, however, the local sense is clear: The inhabitants of Zion compare with those of Samaria for their self-complacency (Amos 6:1); God encourages his people who "dwell in Zion" (Isa. 10:24); the exiles shall be brought back to Zion (Jer. 3:14).

In similar texts of religious import, "Zion" is often used as a synonym for the people of Jerusalem as a community, or a moral person whose destiny lies in God's hand (Ps. 97:8; Isa. 1:27; 33:5). Such expressions as "sons of Zion" (Ps. 149:2; Lam. 4:2; Joel 2:23), or "daughters of Zion" (Isa. 3:16; 4:4; Jer. 4:31; 6:2; Zech. 9:9; cf. Matt. 21:5; John 12:15), refer to the men and women of Jerusalem as beneficiaries of God's mercy, or the victims visited in his wrath. In some instances, however, the expression "daughters of Zion" means simply the women of Jerusalem, without special reference to their religious condition (Song of S. 3:11; Isa. 10:32; 16:1).

Eschatological and apocalyptic writings commonly use the name of Zion with the same religious overtones as above: the glorification of the messianic community shall take place on Zion's holy mountain, where the Messiah shall appear, at the end of time, or even beyond the consummation of time; in this last instance, Zion becomes the equivalent of the heavenly Jerusalem (Isa. 60:14; Heb. 12:22; Rev. 14:1). A similar usage occurs in the Pseudep., as, e.g., in IV Esd. 13:35-36. The (rare) references to Zion in the sectarian writings of Khirbet Qumran (*see* DEAD SEA SCROLLS) are not particularly characteristic.

The religious significance attached to the name of Zion toward the beginning of the Christian era is manifested by the relative popularity of the feminine name Σαλαμψιώ, a Hellenized form of שלם ציון, the "peace [or salvation] of Zion." It was the name of a daughter of Herod, as well as of several private persons, as evidenced by inscriptions found on ossuaries. The historical objectivity intended by Josephus in his writings may explain his abstention of the use of Zion as a toponym.

In Christian usage, the name of Zion became attached to the SW hill of Jerusalem as early as the fourth century. The reason for this transfer is probably the common belief that the house in which the apostles were gathered together on the day of Pentecost was located in these parts of the city (*see* UPPER ROOM). Thus the Christian Zion, where the preaching of the gospel had begun, was contrasted with the Mountain of Zion, the center of OT worship.

Epiphanius mentions the existence of a small church which would have outlasted the destruction of the city in the sieges by Titus (A.D. 70) and Hadrian (A.D. 134). Toward the end of the fourth century, it was replaced by a monumental basilica named the "Holy Zion, Mother of All Churches." The Upper Room of the Lord's Supper was identified with the Upper Room of Pentecost prior to the sixth century, and consequently the Eucharistic institution became the object of a special commemoration in the basilica, near which a tradition of the seventh century pointed to the place where Mary died. The basilica lay in ruins when the Crusaders conquered Jerusalem. Part of the medieval chapel which was built as a substitute still exists today, SE of the modern Abbey of the Dormitio (the "sleeping-in" of Mary). The Chapel of the Upper Room became a mosque in 1524, where Muslims visit an apocryphal tomb of David, following a twelfth-century folklore. *See* TOMBS OF THE KINGS.

The confusion between Davidic Zion and Christian Zion prevailed until the first decade of the twentieth century, when the location of the city of David was established beyond reasonable doubt on the crest of the E hill. Unfortunately the topography of the guides has not generally caught up with the scientific development.

Fig. NEH 13.

Bibliography. G. A. Smith, *Jerusalem,* I (1907), 134-69; H. Vincent, *Jérusalem Antique* (1912), pp. 142-46; G. Dalman,

Jerusalem und sein Gelände (1930), pp. 126-30; J. Simons, *Jerusalem in the OT* (1952), pp. 60-64. On the Christian traditions concerning Mount Zion, see H. Vincent and F.-M. Abel, *Jérusalem Nouvelle,* III (1922), 421-81.   G. A. BARROIS

*ZION, DAUGHTER OF [בת ציון]. A phrase frequently used in the OT as a poetic synonym for Jerusalem and its inhabitants. The usage is derived from the common Hebrew practice of describing the characteristics of a person in terms of family relationships. Thus "sons of strangers"="strangers" (Isa. 60:10 KJV), and "children of iniquity"="iniquitous people" (Hos. 10:9 KJV). The idea behind the idiom is that the children belong to or are identifiable with the parents. Hence while on occasion "daughters" imply specifically women (e.g., "daughters of Shiloh" [Judah. 21:21]; "daughters of Zion" [Isa. 3:16]), the term can also be used to cover the whole community.

Cities, towns, and villages are regarded as "daughters" of the country or of the metropolis (e.g., "daughters [=cities] of Judah" [Ps. 97:8]; "daughters [=cities] of the Philistines" [Ezek. 16:27]; "in Heshbon, and in all its villages" [lit., in all her daughters; Num. 21:25]; "Beth-shean and its villages" [lit., her daughters; Josh. 17:11]). "Daughter of Zion," which occurs frequently, is likewise a personification of the city of Jerusalem, which was built on Mount Zion (cf. "daughter of Tarshish"= Tarshish [Isa. 23:10]; "daughter of Sidon"=Sidon [vs. 12]). It is used in this sense generally in the OT (e.g., II Kings 19:21; Ps. 9:14; Isa. 1:8; 10:32; 16:1; 37:22; 52:2; 62:11; Jer. 4:31; 6:2, 23; Lam. 1:6; 2:1, 4, 8, 10, 13, 18; 4:22; Mic. 1:13; 4:8, 10, 13; Zech. 2:10; 9:9). In the gospels it occurs in Matt. 21:5; John 12:15, where the words of Zech. 9:9 are quoted in connection with the messianic entry of Jesus into Jerusalem.

See also DAUGHTER; FAMILY; ZION.   W. NEIL

ZIOR zī'ôr [ציער, smallness]. A village of Judah in the hill-country province of Hebron (Josh. 15:54). Though archaeological exploration would indicate its improbability, Si'ir (or Sa'ir), in a valley *ca.* five miles N-NE of Hebron, has been proposed for Zior. Nearby tombs hewn in the rock testify to an ancient occupation, but probably no earlier than the Byzantine period. Local tradition reveres one tomb as the tomb of Esau. It would appear that the ancient site of Zior remains to be identified. *See* ZAIR.

Bibliography. W. F. Albright, "Topographical Researches in Judaea," *BASOR,* 18 (1925), 6-9.   V. R. GOLD

ZIPH zĭf [זיף]; **ZIPHITE** — īt [זיפי]; KJV once **ZIPHIMS** —īmz. 1. A family or clan of the tribe of JUDAH (I Chr. 4:16).   T. M. MAUCH

2. A town of Judah in the hill country province of Maon (Josh. 15:55).

Eusebius mentions a village of Ziph *ca.* nine (Roman) miles E (correctly, SE) of Hebron. It is really *ca.* five (Roman) miles SE of Hebron to Tell Zif, an excellent location dominating the desert of Judah at about the same latitude as En-gedi.

In the wilderness near Ziph, David hid from Saul (I Sam. 23:14-15; cf. superscription to Ps. 54—H 54: 1-2, by which this psalm was associated by tradition with the events of I Sam. 23:19; 26:1 ff) and in the same area later showed Saul his good will by taking his spear and water jug rather than his life (I Sam. 26:1 ff).

After the revolt of the N kingdom, Rehoboam (ca. 922-915) strengthened the fortifications of Ziph (II Chr. 11:8).

3. A town of Judah in the Negeb province (Josh. 15:24; cf. I Chr. 2:42; 4:16); probably modern Khirbet ez-Zeifeh, SW of Kurnub, about parallel to the S end of the Dead Sea.　　　　　V. R. Gold

ZIPHAH zī′fə [זיפה] (I Chr. 4:16). A family or clan of the tribe of Judah.

ZIPHIMS. KJV form of Ziphites in the superscription of Ps. 54.

ZIPHION zĭf′ĭ ən [צפיון] (Gen. 46:16). The eldest son of Gad. The Samar. and the LXX support identification with Zephon.

ZIPHRON zĭf′rŏn [זפרון]. A place in the N borderland of Canaan, near Hazar-enan (Num. 34:9). The exact location is not known.

ZIPPOR zĭp′ôr [צפור, צפר, bird]. The father of Balak, the king of Moab who summoned Balaam to curse the Israelites (Num. 22:2, 4, 10, 16; 23:18; Josh. 24:9; Judg. 11:25). For the significance of the application of animal names to persons, see Name; Totemism.

Bibliography. M. Noth, *Die israelitischen Personennamen* (1928), pp. 229-30.　　　　　R. F. Johnson

ZIPPORAH zĭp′ə rə [צפרה, see below]. One of the seven daughters of Reuel (another name for Jethro); the first wife of Moses; and the mother of Gershom and Eliezer (Exod. 2:16, 21-22). A brief narrative preserved in the J document says that Yahweh sought to kill Moses when he and his family were on their way from Midian to Egypt, but Zipporah circumcised her son and averted the catastrophe (4:24-26; see Circumcision). She and her sons were later taken back by Jethro (18:2-4). Her name means "swallow" (see Zippor), and similar names are found in Ugaritic, Palmyrene, and Arabic sources.　　　J. F. Ross

ZITHRI. KJV form of Sithri.

ZIV zĭv [זו, brightness(?)] (I Kings 6:1, 37); KJV **ZIF** zĭf. The early (probably Canaanite) name for the second Hebrew month, later known as Iyyar. See Calendar.

ZIZ, ASCENT OF zĭz [מעלה הציץ, *ma'ălê haṣṣîṣ*]. A mountain pass in the SE part of Judah, not far from En-gedi (II Chr. 20:16), by which the invading Moabites, Ammonites, and Meunites were advancing in the time of Jehoshaphat. It led into a valley near the wilderness of Jeruel, a part of Judah which has not been identified, but was, from the context, not far from Tekoa. This ascent seems to be the same as the Wadi Hasasa, SE of Tekoa and along the road which runs from En-gedi to Bethlehem; in accord with this

the text may originally have read *ḥ* instead of *h*— i.e., מעלה חציץ (*ma'ălê ḥāṣîṣ*), "the ascent of Haziz."
　　　　　　S. Cohen

ZIZA zī′zə [זיזא, *a short form fashioned by duplicating, with slight variation, one sound from a full word now unidentifiable; formed out of childhood as a name of endearment*]. 1. A chief of Simeon whose ancestry is traced back five generations. His family participated in a Simeonite expansion toward Gedor (I Chr. 4:37).

2. A son of Rehoboam, by Maacah (II Chr. 11: 20).

Bibliography. M. Lidzbarski, *Ephemeris für semitische Epigraphik,* II (1908), 20; M. Noth, *Die israelitischen Personennamen* (1928), pp. 40-41.　　　　　T. M. Mauch

ZIZAH zī′zə [זיזה, *see* Ziza] (I Chr. 23:11). Alternately: **ZINA** zī′nə [זינא] (I Chr. 23:10). Head of a father's house of Levites, of the family of Shimei. In vs. 10 he is called Zina probably by transcriptional error: (*a*) the middle consonants are similar in Hebrew (*see* Alphabet), and the final consonants are similar phonetically; (*b*) the LXX and one Hebrew MS support the identification.　　　　　T. M. Mauch

ZOAN zō′ən [צען; LXX Τανις]. A city in NE Egypt, known also as Avaris, the capital of the Hyksos; as Per-Ramses, the capital and residence of Ramses II; and later as Tanis.

"Zoan" is the Hebrew version of the Egyptian name *D'n.t,* which survives in Coptic as *Ğa'ne* and in Greek as Τανις. The site of the city, known in modern times as San el-Hajar, is strategically located in the E section of the Delta and served as the capital of the Hyksos Empire until it was recaptured by Amosis I *ca.* 1560 B.C. The importance of the city for biblical studies is due to the prominence it achieved during the rule of Ramses II (*ca.* 1290-1224), who is presumably the Pharaoh of the Exodus. This king established his capital at Tanis, which was renamed Per-Ramses in his honor, and made the city his official residence.

Although there is still room for doubt, the majority of scholars who have studied the problem see Avaris, Per-Ramses, and Tanis as successive names of the same site. It is thus to be identified with the Rameses of the OT (*see also* Pithom), from the region of which the Exodus was begun. The name Tanis (Zoan), which is found only in post-Ramesside Egyptian texts, occurs in Isa. 19:11, 13; 30:4; Ezek. 30:14. The "fields of Zoan" mentioned in Ps. 78:12, 43, is a faithful rendition of the Egyptian phrase *sḫt D'n.t,* which is found associated with the region of Tanis.

Bibliography. W. F. Petrie, *Tanis* (1885). A. H. Gardiner, "Tanis and Pi-Ra'messe," *JEA,* 19 (1933), 122-28. P. Montet, *Tanis* (1942); *Fouilles de Tanis,* vol. I (1942); vol. II (1951). J. von Beckerath, *Tanis und Theben* (1951).
　　　　　　T. O. Lambdin

ZOAR zō′ər [צער, צוער, little]. One of the "cities of the valley" (Gen. 13:12; 19:29), which, along with the other four, was attacked by the four Eastern kings in the Valley of Siddim and subjugated (14:1-12).

Though the names of the kings of Sodom, Gomorrah, Admah, and Zeboiim are mentioned (Gen. 14:

2), that of the king of Zoar is seemingly omitted. The text reads: "the king of Bela (that is, Zoar)" (vss. 2, 8). Bela may be the name of the king of Zoar but, by an error of a copyist, given as a variant of Zoar. Or Bela may be an older name of Zoar.

When the Lord decided to destroy the wicked cities of the valley, Lot and his family were to be spared (Gen. 18:20–19:17). Fearing that he could not reach the hills, Lot was allowed to escape to a city, a "little one" (19:18-21). "Therefore the name of the city was called Zoar" (vs. 22)—meaning "little," according to popular etymology.

However, afraid to remain in Zoar, Lot and his two daughters—his wife had already been transformed into a pillar of salt (Gen. 19:26)—"went up out of Zoar, and dwelt in the hills" (vs. 30). Here was born to Lot's older daughter a son, Moab, who became the father of the Moabites (vs. 37).

It would seem that Zoar was not destroyed by the "brimstone and fire from the LORD out of heaven," as were the other cities of the valley, for the Lord allowed Lot to escape from Sodom to Zoar and promised that he would not overthrow that city (Gen. 19:21). In that case, the site of Zoar is not really to be located in the valley, for the Lord destroyed the cities of the valley, "and all the inhabitants of the cities, and what grew on the ground" (vss. 25, 29).

A late tradition—*ca.* 100 B.C.—indicates that the fire was thought to have descended upon all the Five Cities, or Pentapolis (Wisd. Sol. 10:6), and that Lot was afraid to dwell in Zoar. But his leaving may have been due to the site's proximity to the destruction which was taking place.

However, a Zoar, whether the original one or a nearby, rebuilt Zoar, existed in later times. To Moses on Mount Nebo, the Lord showed the land, extending southward, as far as Zoar (Deut. 34:3). And in the times of Isaiah and Jeremiah—*ca.* 700 and 600 B.C., respectively—a Zoar existed: Fugitives from Moab fled to Zoar, and a cry over Moab's destruction was heard as far as Zoar, and from Zoar the cry went to other sites (Isa. 15:5; Jer. 48:4, 34).

Josephus (A.D. 37-93) mentions a Zoara of Arabia (Jos. War IV.viii.4), and refers to a place "still called Zoor, that being the Hebrew for 'little' " (Jos. Antiq. I.xi.4). It had submitted to the Maccabean Alexander Janneus (A.D. 104-78), with other towns of Moab, and later was ceded to Aretas IV, the Nabatean king, between 9 B.C. and A.D. 40 (Jos. Antiq. XIII.xv.4; XIV.i.4). There is mention of a bishop of Zoara in the year 381.

Sir John Mandeville writes that Segor (i.e., Zoar) was set upon a hill and that its walls could be seen in his day (1322-56). He was, of course, referring to the medieval site.

A site for Zoar in the S part of the Dead Sea Basin and on the E or Moabite side best meets the requirements of the biblical narratives (*see above* and Gen. 19:37; 21; 25; 29). A proposed location in the center of the peninsula el-Lisan seems too far to the N.

If any weight is to be attached to the tradition that Lot escaped from SODOM to Zoar, then Zoar should have been to the E of Sodom and toward Moab. Now Sodom was probably near Jebel Usdum, and so a site on the stream Seil el-Qurahi, around es-Safi,

seems a logical location for the Zoar of the Genesis legend. *See* map under SODOM.

Es-Safi is in a fertile region near the present mouth of the Seil el-Qurahi, as the lower end of the Wadi el-Hesa is called. This stream flows into the S end of the E shore of the Dead Sea. Here are remains of Roman and Nabatean settlements. Here also the evidence of sugar and indigo plantations and the ruins of sugar mills amply attest the occupation of this area in Byzantine and Arabic times. In the Middle Ages the Dead Sea was called the Sea of Zugar, a name doubtless derived from Zogara, the Roman and Byzantine name of the town.

Graves, with pottery of the end of the Early Bronze and of the beginning of the Middle Bronze ages—i.e., *ca.* 2000-1900 B.C.—indicate that this site was inhabited during the time of the cities of the valley. Furthermore, ruins of smelting furnaces have been discovered around es-Safi, which may have been in operation as far back as the Early Bronze Age, when the cities were flourishing. Future excavations around es-Safi may reveal that the Roman-Byzantine-Arabic Zoar may also have been the site of Israelite Zoar and possibly of the more ancient Canaanite city.

If the original Zoar of Genesis was destroyed along with Sodom and Gomorrah in the Valley of Siddim, then its site may be under the waters of the S end of the Dead Sea, possibly on the westward prolongation of the Seil el-Qurahi. Then the Israelite Zoar may have been built eastward up this stream near es-Safi.

But even at es-Safi there seems to have been habitation at the time of the cities of the valley. So the site of the Zoar of Lot's time—if it did escape destruction—may have been situated around the present site of es-Safi by the Seil el-Qurahi.

Bibliography. In addition to the bibliography under CITIES OF THE VALLEY, see: J. Mandeville, *Early Travels in Palestine* (1866 ed.), p. 179. M. G. Kyle, *Explorations in Sodom* (1924). W. F. Albright, *BASOR*, 14 (1924), 2-12; *AASOR*, VI (1924-25), 13-74. F. Frank, "Aus der Arabah II," *ZDPV*, 57 (1934), 191-280. N. Glueck, *Explorations in Eastern Palestine*, II, *AASOR*, XV (1934-35), 7-9; *BASOR*, 67 (1937), 20-21. F.-M. Abel, *Géographie de la Palestine*, II (1938), 466-68. J. P. Harland, "The Location and Destruction of the Cities of the Plain," *BA*, V (1942), 17-32; VI (1943), 41-54.

J. P. HARLAND

ZOBAH zō'bə [אֲרַם צוֹבָה, צוֹבָא, צוֹבָה; Akkad. *probably Ṣubiti (mentioned by* Ashurbanipal)]. An Amorite, later Aramaic, town and kingdom, presumably situated in the Biqa'—i.e., the valley between Lebanon and Anti-lebanon. In I Sam. 14:47 we are told that Saul, the first king of Israel, made war against the kings of Zobah. Also David had to fight against Zobah, where at that time Hadadezer was the king (II Sam. 8:3, 5, 9; cf. I Chr. 18:3, 5, 9). In II Sam. 8:8, David brought much copper from Hadadezer's towns Betah and Berothai. Betah has been assumed to be identical with Tubiḫi, occurring in an Amarna letter (*VAB* 2:1, pp. 690-91; 2:2, p. 1279); and according to the text mentioned, Tubiḫi was situated in the country of Amurru. This is no very concise information about the localization; but if Berothai is identical with Bereitan in the Biqa', Tubiḫi was probably also situated in this region. Since the two towns belonged to Hadadezer's kingdom, Zobah was probably situated not far from the region mentioned. Other views on the situation of Zobah have been set forth, but they do not seem plausible.

After the events referred to in II Sam. 8, Zobah was in alliance with the Ammonites, who, according to II Sam. 10:6 (cf. I Chr. 19:6), hired a large number of soldiers from Aram-beth-rehob, Aram-zobah, and Maacah; but all the allied were defeated by Joab, David's famous general. According to vs. 2, Ps. 60 refers to these events. In the reign of Solomon a certain Rezon, son of Eliada, a vassal of Hadadezer, the above-mentioned king of Zobah, was one of the king's enemies (I Kings 11:23).

On Hamath-zobah, see HAMATH.   A. HALDAR

ZOBEBAH zō bē′bə [צֹבֵבָה] (I Chr. 4:8). Listed as a family of the tribe of Judah in a difficult sequence of names.

ZOHAR zō′här [צֹחַר, *from* yellowish-red *or* tawny; LXX Σααρ]. **1.** The father of Ephron the Hittite (Gen. 23:8; 25:9).

2. Alternate form of ZERAH 3.

ZOHELETH, STONE OF zō′ə lĕth. KJV translation of זֹחֶלֶת. See SERPENT'S STONE.

ZOHETH zō′hĕth [זוֹחֵת, proud] (I Chr. 4:20). A family or clan of the tribe of Judah.

Bibliography. M. Noth, *Die israelitischen Personennamen* (1928), p. 229.

ZOPHAH zō′fə [צוֹפָח, bellied jug] (I Chr. 7:35-36). Eponym of a clan of the tribe of Asher.

ZOPHAI. Alternate form of ZUPH 1.

ZOPHAR zō′fär [צֹפַר, צוֹפַר, *perhaps* twittering bird (*cf.* צִפּוֹר, צִפֹּר, bird; *see* ZIPPOR *in* Num. 22:2, 10, etc.), *or perhaps* sharp nail *or* goatlike jumper (*see bibliography*)]. One of the three friends of Job, called "the Naamathite" (Job 2:11; 11:1; 20:1; 42:9; *see* NAAMAH).

Bibliography. S. R. Driver and G. B. Gray, *Job,* ICC (1921), pp. xxviii-xix; S. L. Terrien, Exegesis of Job, *IB,* III (1954), 923.   B. T. DAHLBERG

ZOPHIM zō′fîm [צֹפִים, watchers]. A high place near the NE end of the Dead Sea to which Balak took Balaam for his second view of the Israelites. They went "to the field of Zophim, to the top of PISGAH" (Num. 23:14). Zophim may possibly not be a proper name, so that we would simply read "field of watchers." The various places named MIZPAH have the same Hebrew root. Possibly the name survives in modern Tela'at es-Safa.

For the compound name Ramathaim-zophim (I Sam. 1:1), *see* RAMAH 4.   E. D. GROHMAN

ZORAH zôr′ə [צָרְעָה]; KJV ZOREAH zôr′ĭ ə (Josh. 15:33), ZAREAH zâr′ĭ ə (Neh. 11:29); ZOR-ATHITES zôr′ə thīts [צָרְעָתִי] (I Chr. 2:53; 4:2); ZORITES zôr′īts [צָרְעִי] (I Chr. 2:54); KJV once ZAREATHITES zâr′ĭ ə thīts (I Chr. 2:53). A city (modern Sar'ah) situated on the N side of the Wadi

es-Sarar (*see* SOREK, VALLEY OF), on a summit dominating the wadi. Although Eusebius says that Saraa (Σαραά=Zorah) was ten (Roman) miles N of Eleutheropolis (Beit Jibrin), it was actually *ca.* fifteen.

Zorah apparently first belonged to Dan (Josh. 19: 41; cf. Judg. 13:2; 18:2), and then, in the royal administrative division of Judah, became a part of the Shephelah district of Zorah-Azekah (Josh. 15:33).

Zorah was the home of Manoah, Samson's father (Judg. 13:2). At Mahaneh-Dan, between Zorah and Eshtaol, Samson first felt moved by the Spirit of the Lord (vs. 25); he was buried in the tomb of his father between Zorah and Eshtaol (16:31).

In the account of their northward migration, Danite spies from Zorah and Eshtaol reconnoitered at Laish (Dan) and then led their countrymen from the same two places to Laish. En route through Ephraim, they kidnapped the Levite whom Micah had installed as his priest. After their successful attack against Laish, they set up Micah's golden image in the shrine at Dan (Judg. 18 *passim*).

In the list of the descendants of Judah, the Zorathites are mentioned as descendants of Kiriath-jearim (I Chr. 2:53-54; 4:2; cf. Judg. 18:12). The Zorites of I Chr. 2:54 may be the S part of the clan of the Manahathites (reading "Menuhoth" of vs. 52 as "Manahathites"). They are probably not the same as the Zorathites of vs. 53. The center of the Zorites is therefore unknown at present.

After the division of the monarchy, Rehoboam (*ca.* 922-915) strengthened its fortifications (II Chr. 11: 10). Returnees from the Exile reoccupied it (Neh. 11:29).   V. R. GOLD

ZORATHITES zôr′ə thīts [צָרְעָתִי] (I Chr. 2:53; 4:2); KJV ZAREATHITES zâr′ĭ ə— in I Chr. 2:53. Descendants of Shobal; inhabitants of ZORAH.

ZORITES zôr′īts [צָרְעִי] (I Chr. 2:54). Descendants of Salma, of the line of Judah. Apparently they are to be distinguished from the Zorathites (צָרְעָתִי) of the preceding verse. See ZORAH.

ZOROASTRIANISM zō′rō ăs′trĭ ən ĭzm. As a general term, the religion founded by Zarathushtra. In a more restricted sense, the form of this religion as developed by the later Zoroastrian theologians, who aimed at harmonizing the original teachings of Zarathushtra as exposed in the *Gāthās* (*see* AVESTA) and the ancient Iranian polytheism. Its literary sources are the Avesta and an extensive literature in Pahlavi. For a detailed discussion, *see* PERSIA, HISTORY AND RELIGION OF, § E.

A tendency toward emphasizing monotheism is noticeable in Parsiism, the form of Zoroastrianism current among the Parsis in India today. The ancient customs, such as the exposure of the dead on "towers of silence" (*dakhma*), and the ancient rites (maintenance of an eternal fire in the temples, keeping pure of the domestic fire, etc.) are still observed. Generosity, formerly restricted to Parsis, is nowadays extended to members of other castes, races, and religions. Religious propaganda is foreign to Parsiism.

Bibliography. In addition to the bibliography under PERSIA, HISTORY AND RELIGION OF, see J. J. Modi, *Religious Ceremonies and Customs of the Parsees* (2nd ed., 1937).

M. J. DRESDEN

ZOROBABEL. KJV Apoc. and NT form of ZERUBBABEL.

ZOSTRIANUS, APOCALYPSE OF zŏs'trĭ ā'nəs. A Gnostic work in Coptic, found at Chenoboskion in Upper Egypt in 1945 (*see* APOCRYPHA, NT). It appears to have been one of the five writings which Plotinus is reported by Porphyry to have attacked. It has been hazarded that another of these five, the Apocalypse of Zoroaster, is actually a part of Zostrianus; but this is, at best, uncertain. M. S. ENSLIN

ZUAR zōō'ər [צוּעָר, small *or* young]. The father of Nethanel, who was the leader of Issachar in the wilderness (Num. 1:8; 2:5; 7:18, 23; 10:15).

Bibliography. M. Noth, *Die israelitischen Personennamen* (1928), p. 225.

ZUPH zŭf [צוּף, honeycomb(?); *Kethibh* צִיף (I Chr. 6:35)]. Alternately: ZOPHAI zō'fī [צוֹפַי] (I Chr. 6: 26). **1.** An ancestor of ELKANAH and of SAMUEL (I Sam. 1:1; I Chr. 6:26, 35). In I Samuel he is an Ephraimite (*see* EPHRAIM) and in I Chronicles a Levite (*see* PRIESTS AND LEVITES) descended from KOHATH. Possibly he was both, if "Levite" originally was a professional and not a tribal designation (*see* 2 *below*). T. M. MAUCH

2. A district mentioned only in I Sam. 9:5, the "land of Zuph," a region visited by Saul and his servant in search of the lost asses. Elkanah, the father of Samuel, came from Ramathaim-zophim (רָמָתַיִם צוֹפִים) in the hill country of Ephraim, and was a descendant of Zuph, an Ephraimite. The district probably received its name from the family of Zuph, which may have settled there, and the name of the city of Elkanah identified with this district. On the strength of a connection with this city, the region is usually located *ca.* twenty-five miles SW of Shechem, although the exact area is unknown. W. L. REED

ZUR zûr [צוּר, rock]. **1.** A Midianite leader; the father of Cozbi, who was slain with her Israelite husband after their marriage (Num. 25:15; 31:8; Josh. 13:21). This marriage is connected with accounts of religious apostasy, and it was followed by war against Midian during which Zur, one of five Midianite kings, was slain. However, according to the account in Josh. 13:21, Zur fell in the battle in which Moses defeated Sihon the Amorite king.

2. A Benjaminite; son of Jeiel, and brother of Kish, Saul's father (I Chr. 8:30; 9:36).

Bibliography. M. Noth, *Die israelitischen Personennamen* (1928), pp. 37, 156. R. F. JOHNSON

3. An ancient synonym for "God" used frequently in the OT and translated "Rock" (e.g., Deut. 32:4; II Sam. 22:2-3; Ps. 18:31, 46—H 18:32, 47; Isa. 17: 10). Having its background in the mountain imagery inherited by the patriarchs from NW Mesopotamia, it came to designate the traits of God as known within the covenant: strength, constancy, trustworthiness, never-failing mercy. In this sense, Yahweh was known as the "Rock of Israel."

See also GOD, NAMES OF, § D1. B. W. ANDERSON

ZURIEL zōōr'ĭ əl [צוּרִיאֵל, God is a rock(?), my rock is God(?), rock is God(?)] (Num. 3:35). A Levite of the family of Merari; son of Abihail. In the wilderness he was head of the Merarites, who encamped to the N of the tabernacle and were the carpenters of its framework.

Bibliography. M. Noth, *Die israelitischen Personennamen* (1928), pp. 17-18, 129-30, 140. T. M. MAUCH

ZURISHADDAI zōōr'ĭ shăd'ī [צוּרִישַׁדַּי, Shaddai is a rock]. The father of Shelumiel, who was the leader of Simeon in the wilderness (Num. 1:6; 2:12; 7:36, 41; 10:19). The use of "rock" with reference to the deity, as in Zurishaddai and other names, is to be understood as a figurative description of God, the source of security, the "Rock of my salvation" (Ps. 89:26—H 89:27). For the meaning of "Shaddai," *see* GOD, NAMES OF.

Bibliography. M. Noth, *Die israelitischen Personennamen* (1928), 129-30, 156. R. F. JOHNSON

ZUZIM zōō'zĭm [הַזּוּזִים; LXX ἔθνη ἰσχυρά; *possibly confused with* הָעַזִּים *or* עַזּוּזִים; *cf.* Arab. *zîzîm, a word imitative of the low or faint sound of the jinn or genii that is heard by night in the deserts*] (Gen. 14:5). The name of a people who lived in HAM, whom CHEDORLAOMER and his allies subdued in the course of their advance through Transjordan against the coalition of kings in the Valley of Siddim. The exact meaning of the name is uncertain, and nothing else is known about the Zuzim. Many scholars identify them with the ZAMZUMMIM in Deut. 2:20. In the Aramaic Dead Sea Scroll (*see* DEAD SEA SCROLLS), the so-called "Genesis Apocryphon," which preserves a passage elaborating Gen. 14, the Zuzim are represented by what the scribe intended for "Zamzummim" (זמזומיא; column XXI, line 29). This represents Jewish opinion in the first century B.C., and should not be considered a decisive criterion for identifying the two names. Moreover, the localization of the Zuzim in Ham places them N of the territory where the Zamzummim are found at the beginning of the Iron Age.

Bibliography. P. Karge, *Rephaim: Die vorgeschichtliche Kultur Palästinas und Phoniziens* (1918), pp. 148, 627, 645; N. Glueck, *Explorations in Eastern Palestine*, III, *AASOR*, 18-19 (1939), 91-92; N. Avigad and Y. Yadin, *A Genesis Apocryphon* (1956), column XXI (see also p. 35). G. M. LANDES

THE OLD TESTAMENT

Genesis	Song of Solomon
Exodus	Isaiah
Leviticus	Jeremiah
Numbers	Lamentations
Deuteronomy	Ezekiel
Joshua	Daniel
Judges	Hosea
Ruth	Joel
I and II Samuel	Amos
I and II Kings	Obadiah
I and II Chronicles	Jonah
Ezra	Micah
Nehemiah	Nahum
Esther	Habakkuk
Job	Zephaniah
Psalms	Haggai
Proverbs	Zechariah
Ecclesiastes	Malachi

THE APOCRYPHA

I and II Esdras
Tobit
Judith
Additions to Esther
Wisdom of Solomon
Ecclesiasticus (Wisdom of Jesus
    the Son of Sirach)
Baruch
Letter of Jeremiah
Prayer of Azariah
Song of the Three Young Men
Susanna
Bel and the Dragon
Prayer of Manasseh
I and II Maccabees